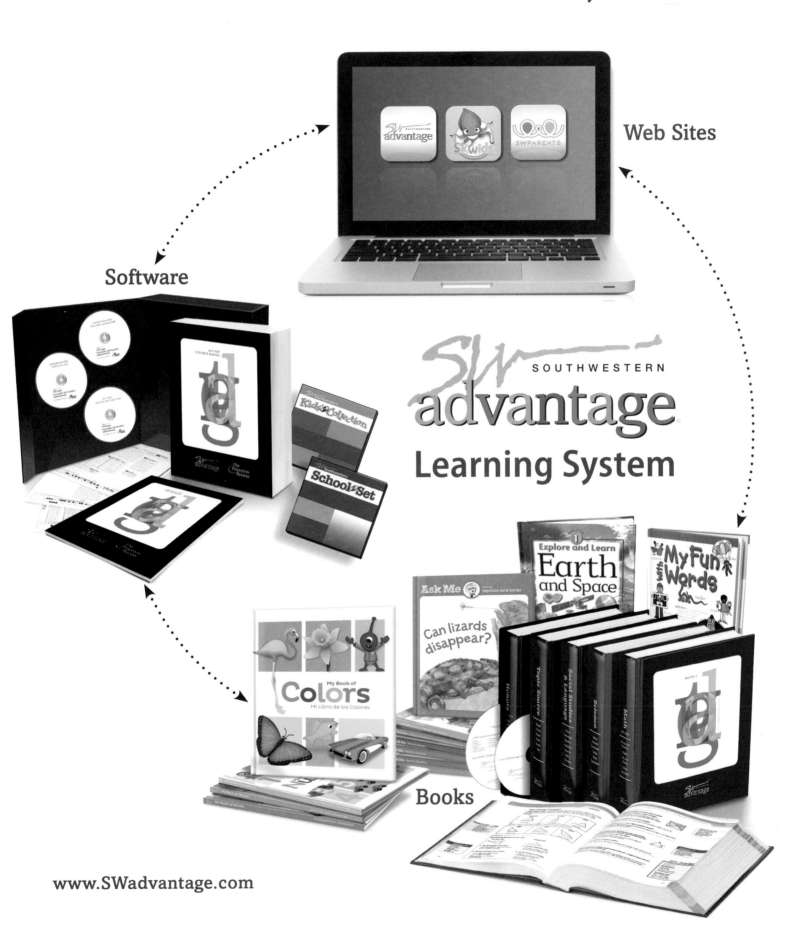

Web Sites

Software

SW SOUTHWESTERN
advantage
Learning System

Books

www.SWadvantage.com

Sharing the Advantage

Southwestern Advantage is an effective learning system and an important key to a better education and achieving success in life. Our mission is to share education and learning skills with every child and every family, regardless of their circumstances, through qualified nonprofit partnerships and local community involvement with organizations focused on helping young people. Southwestern Advantage will also donate one SWadvantage.com membership for each one purchased.

Thank you for helping us Share the Advantage!

TOPIC SOURCE

SOUTHWESTERN
advantage

www.SWadvantage.com

Printed on Recycled Paper

TOPIC SOURCE

www.SWadvantage.com

SOUTHWESTERN
advantage

Reissued as *Southwestern Advantage Topic Source* © 2011 Southwestern
© 2013 Southwestern Advantage, Inc.
Nashville, Tennessee
ISBN 978-0-87197-556-0

Originally published as *Student Handbook* (Book 4)
Southwestern/Great American, Inc., dba The Southwestern Company
© 2008 The Southwestern Company
Nashville, Tennessee
ISBN 978-0-87197-544-7

Henry Bedford
Chief Executive Officer, Southwestern/Great American, Inc.

Dan Moore
President, Southwestern Advantage

Printed in the United States of America by R.R. Donnelley

Article text, with the exception of Search Strings, compiled by and used with permission of
World Book. The maps on the following pages are used with permission of World Book:

Book: 143, 233, 238, 239, 271, 272, 284, 286, 287, 312, 314, 317, 338, 356, 361, 368, 410, 428,
440, 445, 455, 498, 508, 524, 527, 536, 580, 640, 648, 670, 672, 678, 696, 698, 716, 750, 770, 775,
778, 806, 809, 830, 831, 856, 880, 922, 927, 928, 932, 971, 975, 976, 978, 980, 982, 992, 996, 1002,
1006, 1009, 1012, 1352

DVD: 94, 96, 105, 112, 115, 116, 140, 142, 151, 186, 189,194, 216, 234, 236, 240, 256, 290, 306,
326, 328, 334, 337, 340, 341, 354, 356, 363, 380, 382, 387, 395, 397, 414, 416, 419, 432, 435, 440,
470, 472, 476, 500, 504, 506, 578, 581, 585, 587, 588, 590, 603, 688, 697, 700, 748, 960, 961

PREFACE

Although vast amounts of material exist on the Internet and elsewhere, much of it is unsubstantiated, unreliable, and/or unverifiable. This volume has been created expressly to serve as a primary filter for students looking for topics and credible information for their report writing.

This book and its accompanying DVD contain articles on ninety-five separate research topics, which in many cases will include sufficient material for an entire paper. Each article also includes several Hot Topics, suggesting additional ideas and directions you might like to pursue.

The Search Strings give strings of search terms one researcher used for most of the Hot Topics and the number of hits those terms returned in a search engine. We've reproduced them exactly as the researcher used them—complete with inconsistencies in capitalization and other things. They aren't intended to be all-inclusive, but they can give you some ideas for how to refine and narrow your search.

The DVD also includes a section on developing your research skills and on writing research papers and reports.

Even if the particular country or state or animal you're researching isn't contained here, the ones that are can serve as a good template, or model, for the types of information you will probably want to include in your report.

Every effort has been made to ensure that these books are as accurate as possible. If errors or omissions should be discovered, however, we would appreciate hearing from you. Please send comments or suggestions to editor@southwestern.com, or to Editor, The Southwestern Company, P.O. Box 305142, Nashville, Tennessee 37230.

—*The Editors*

Southwestern Advantage Topic Source

Book Contents

PLACES

WARS

ANIMALS

HISTORY

SCIENCE

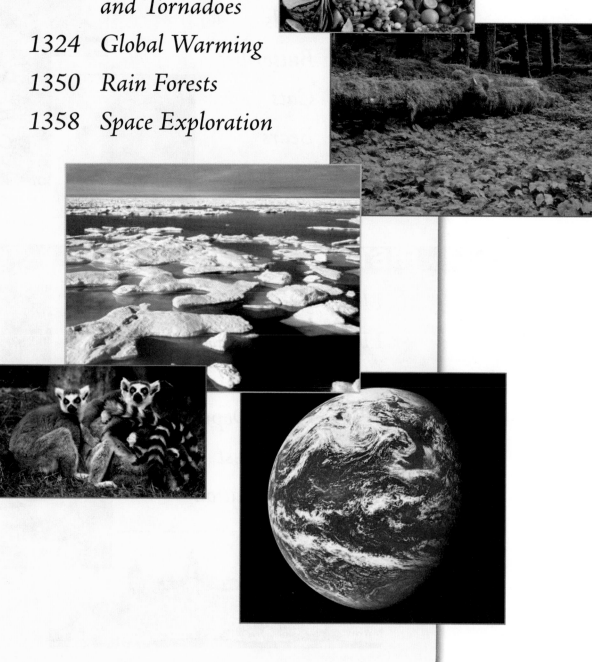

DVD
Contents

PLACES

HISTORY

SCIENCE

Articles

 denotes Hot Topics

Christopher Columbus

Christopher Columbus was an outstanding navigator and organizer of expeditions. He achieved fame by sailing west across the Atlantic Ocean from Europe in search of a western sea route to Asia.

HOT topics

Sailing West/Dead Reckoning. Columbus had few navigational instruments. He knew enough about celestial navigation to measure latitude by using the North Star. However, he had no instruments for determining the ship's position from the stars except a crude quadrant that was not accurate when the ship rolled. He used a compass to plot his course, estimated distances on a chart, relied on a half-hour glass to measure time, and guessed his speed. Together, these activities make up a method of navigation known as *dead reckoning*.

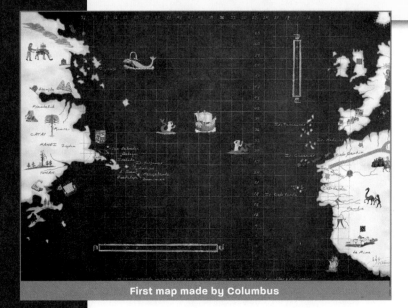

First map made by Columbus

HOT topics

Trouble, Exploration, and Disease.

A tragic consequence of the first transatlantic voyages was that Europeans unintentionally brought many deadly diseases to America. The previous separation of the Native American peoples from those of Europe and Asia meant that the Native Americans had no natural immunity to these diseases. As a result, measles, smallpox, typhus, and other infectious diseases swept through the newly exposed populations, killing vast numbers of people. In turn, some Europeans became infected by a form of syphilis unknown in Europe.

Young Columbus.

While a young man, Columbus worked as an agent for the Spinolas, Di Negros, and Centuriones—powerful Genoese commercial families. In the mid-1470s, in his first documented voyage, Columbus took part in a trading expedition to the island of Chios, a Genoese possession in the Aegean Sea. A few years later he settled in a Genoese colony in Lisbon, Portugal. According to legend, he reached Portugal by swimming ashore clinging to an oar after being attacked by pirates. He next voyaged to the Canary Islands and the Azores, island groups in the Atlantic Ocean west of Africa. Some historians believe he also sailed to England and Ireland, even to Iceland, where he may have learned of early Norse explorations.

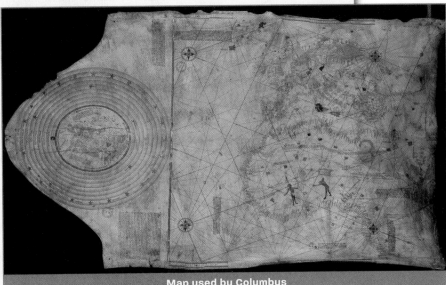

Map used by Columbus

Ships and Crews/Life at Sea.

About 90 crew members sailed aboard Columbus's three ships. In addition to the officers and sailors, the expedition included a translator, three physicians, servants for each captain, a secretary, and an accountant. Aboard ship, there was endless work to be done handling the sails and ropes and pumping out water that seeped or washed aboard. Cleaning and repair work filled the remaining hours. The crews cooked on portable wood-burning stoves. Their main meal consisted of a stew of salted meat or fish, hard biscuits, and watered wine. The sailors had no sleeping quarters, so they huddled on deck in good weather or found a spot below deck during storms. Only a few officers had bunks.

TRUE or FALSE?

In formulating the plan for his historic voyage, Columbus underestimated the circumference of the world by about 5 percent.

THE BASICS

Christopher Columbus (1451–1506) was an outstanding navigator and organizer of expeditions. He achieved fame by sailing west across the Atlantic Ocean from Europe in search of a western sea route to Asia. However, he never accomplished this goal. Instead, in 1492, he encountered islands in the Caribbean Sea. Until that time, Europeans and Native Americans had not been aware of each other's existence. During his four voyages westward—between 1492 and 1504—Columbus explored the Caribbean region and parts of Central and South America.

Columbus was not the first European to reach the Western Hemisphere. The Norse (also called the Vikings) had settled for a time on the coast of North America about A.D. 1000. But that contact did not last, and most Europeans of the 1400s did not know it had taken place. Columbus's voyages led to enduring links between the Eastern and Western hemispheres.

The World of Columbus

The Europe into which Columbus was born in 1451 was struggling against the growing power of the Ottoman Empire, which had conquered much of southeastern Europe. In 1453, the Ottomans took control of Constantinople (now Istanbul, Turkey), a major center of trade between Europe and Asia. They made Constantinople the capital of their empire, cutting off easy European access to highly valued Asian goods. The only alternative to a difficult, dangerous, and expensive land journey was a sea route—either around Africa or westward across the Atlantic. This desire to establish a sea route to Asia launched a remarkable wave of European exploration.

Christopher Columbus

Early Years

Boyhood. The exact date of Columbus's birth is not known. He was born sometime between August 25 and October 31, 1451, in Genoa, then capital of a self-governing area on the northwest coast of Italy. Genoa was an important seaport with a long seafaring tradition, and its ships traded throughout the Mediterranean region.

Christopher's given and family name was *Cristoforo Colombo*. In English, he is known as *Christopher Columbus*, the Latinized form of the name. He called himself *Cristóbal Colón* after he settled in Spain. His father, Domenico Colombo, was a wool weaver. To increase his modest income, Domenico also worked as a gatekeeper and wine merchant. Christopher's mother, Susanna Fontanarossa, was the daughter of a wool weaver.

Christopher was the oldest of five children. His brothers, Bartholomew and Diego, worked closely with him on many of his enterprises. Christopher and his brothers may have been tutored or sent to a monastery school to learn basic Latin and mathematics, though Christopher's formal education apparently ended at about age 14.

Young adulthood. Christopher's ambitious father pushed the boy into a business career, and Christopher began to sail on trading trips. He worked as an agent for the Spinolas, Di Negros, and Centuriones—powerful Genoese commercial fam-

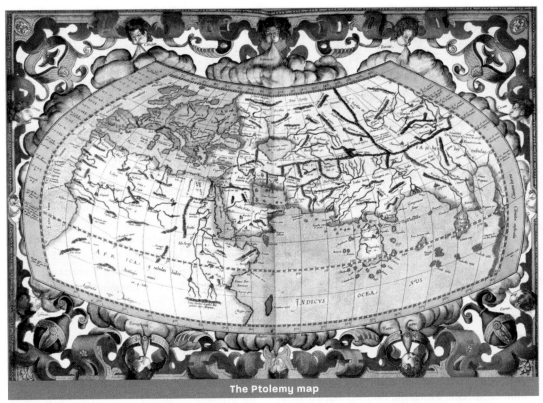

The Ptolemy map

ilies. In the mid-1470s, in his first documented voyage, Columbus took part in a trading expedition to the island of Chios, a Genoese possession in the Aegean Sea. In 1476, he settled in a Genoese colony in Lisbon, Portugal. There is a legend that he reached Portugal by swimming ashore clinging to an oar after being attacked by pirates. In Lisbon, Columbus joined with his brother Bartholomew to draw and sell maps.

Columbus often attended Mass at a chapel at the Convento dos Santos, a school for aristocratic young women. There, he met Felipa Perestrello Moniz, whom he married in 1479. Felipa's father was the first governor of Porto Santo, a Portuguese island in the Madeira group off northern Africa's Atlantic coast. The couple moved to Porto Santo, then to the nearby island of Madeira. Their only child, Diego, was born in 1480. Felipa died in 1484 or 1485.

Between 1480 and 1482, Columbus made several voyages to the Canary Islands and the Azores, island groups in the Atlantic Ocean west of Africa. Columbus also visited Portugal's fortified trading posts in western Africa, where he observed the trade in gold and slaves. Some historians believe Columbus also went to England and

Ireland, and even to Iceland, where he may have learned of early Norse explorations. On the voyages, Columbus gained experience of Atlantic wind systems.

The Plan to Sail Westward

The basis of the plan. By the 1480s, the Portuguese had invented the *caravel*, a fast sturdy ship that was better at sailing against the wind than traditional vessels were. They were trying to reach the Indies—what are now India, China, the East Indies, and Japan—by sailing around Africa. By doing this, they hoped to gain direct access to gold, silk, gems, and spices. The cloves, nutmeg, and mace of the Spice Islands (now the Moluccas of Indonesia) served as medicines as well as seasonings. These valuable items had been transported to Europe by means of dangerous and costly overland caravans that were often hindered by Ottoman officials. While Portuguese sailors were trying to reach Asia by sailing around Africa, Columbus proposed what he believed to be an easier route—sailing due west.

A map of the world made by Ptolemy, an astronomer and geographer in Alexandria, Egypt, in the A.D. 100s, might have been the basis for

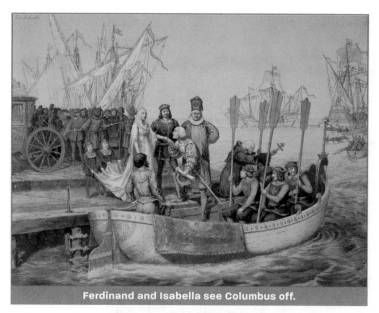

Ferdinand and Isabella see Columbus off.

Columbus's notions of geogaphy. Ptolemy's map showed most of the world as covered by land. However, Columbus found confirmation for his idea of sailing west to Asia in the letters and charts of Paolo Toscanelli, an influential scholar from Florence, Italy. Toscanelli believed that Japan lay only 3,000 nautical miles (5,560 kilometers) west of the Canary Islands. Columbus planned to sail 2,400 nautical miles (4,500 kilometers) west along the *latitude* (distance from the equator) of the Canaries until he reached islands that supposedly lay east of Japan. There, he hoped to establish a trading town and base for further exploration.

Columbus's plan was based in part on two major miscalculations. First, he underestimated the circumference of the world by about 25 percent. Columbus also mistakenly believed that most of the world consisted of land rather than water. This mistake led him to conclude that Asia extended much farther east than it actually did.

Presentation of the plan to Portugal.

About 1483, Columbus gained audiences with King John II of Portugal. The king placed Columbus's proposal before his council, which rejected it. Columbus did not have to prove to the council that the world was round because educated people at that time knew it was. The council turned down his plan on the correct belief that he had greatly underestimated the length of the journey. The king's advisers concluded that Portugal's resources should be invested in finding a route around Africa to Asia.

Years of waiting. In 1485, Columbus and his son went to Spain, a bitter rival of Portugal. At that time, Spain consisted of the united kingdoms of Castile and Aragon. Columbus arrived during Spain's war to drive the Muslims out of Granada, the only remaining Islamic kingdom on Spanish soil. Two wealthy Spanish aristocrats offered to give Columbus some ships. But to do so, they needed the permission of Spain's King Ferdinand and Queen Isabella. In 1486, Columbus gained an interview with the monarchs, but they were in no position to finance an expedition at that time. They were also cautious about reopening conflict with Portugal. Spain and Portugal had recently settled their disputes over various islands off Africa. The Treaty of Alcaçovas, signed in 1479, had conceded the Canary Islands to Spain and the Madeira and Cape Verde islands and the Azores to Portugal.

Although they were cautious, the Spanish monarchs were nevertheless willing to consider a plan that could give them an advantage over Portugal in the race for Asia. Columbus also appealed to the intensely religious monarchs by vowing to use the proceeds from his expedition in the recapture of Jerusalem from the Muslims. There, he said, he would rebuild the Jews' holy Temple and bring on a new "Age of the Holy Spirit."

Queen Isabella was about the same age as Columbus, and she admired men of conviction. At her insistence, Columbus's plan was put before a commission of experts. They met in the Spanish cities of Salamanca and Córdoba during 1486 and 1487 under the leadership of Isabella's spiritual adviser, Hernando de Talavera. Although the committee's first report rejected Columbus's plan, Isabella granted him a small salary to keep him at the royal court. During this period, Columbus lived with a woman named Beatriz Enriquez de Harana. She gave birth to his second son, Ferdinand, in 1488.

For the next several years, Columbus followed the Spanish court as it traveled through the country. In 1490, the experts issued a final report. They scoffed at his plan—not because they thought that the world was flat or sea monsters would devour the ships, but because they still believed his estimates were wrong. The committee favored the belief that the world was large and covered mostly by water rather than small and composed mostly of land. In addition, Columbus's demands had increased. He wanted to become a titled aristocrat, to rule the lands he discovered, and to be able to pass these privileges on to his sons. Columbus also wanted to be given a percentage of the wealth he brought back to Spain.

Success in Spain. Columbus refused to give up. He sent his brother Bartholomew to seek support from the English and French courts, but the attempts were unsuccessful. Columbus's chance finally came when Spain conquered Granada in January 1492. In the aftermath of this victory, Luis de Santangel, a royal treasurer, played a decisive role in convincing Isabella that she was missing a great opportunity. Thus, in April 1492, Columbus's plan suddenly received royal approval. There is no truth to the story that Isabella offered to pawn her jewels to pay for the voyage. Santangel advanced the funds for the relatively low costs of the expedition.

First Voyage Westward

Ships and crews. Palos, a small port in southwestern Spain, was home to the Pinzón and Nino families. In payment of a fine they owed the monarchy, they provided two of the ships and selected the crews for Columbus's first voyage. Martín Alonso Pinzón, an experienced seafarer, captained the *Pinta*, a caravel with square-rigged sails that could carry about 53 long tons. (A long ton is equal to 2,240 pounds or 1.016 metric tons.) His brother Vicente Yañez Pinzón captained the slightly smaller *Nina*. Columbus captained the third vessel, the *Santa Maria*. It was chartered from Juan de la Cosa, who came along as sailing master. It was slightly bigger than the other two ships but provided few comforts.

A total of about 90 crew members sailed aboard the three ships. In addition to the officers and sailors, the expedition included a translator, three physicians, servants for each captain, a secretary, and an accountant.

Aboard ship, there was endless work to be done handling the sails and ropes and pumping out water that seeped or washed aboard. Cleaning and repair work filled the remaining hours. The crews cooked on portable wood-burning stoves. Their main meal consisted of a stew of salted meat or fish, hard biscuits, and watered wine. The sailors had no sleeping quarters, so they huddled on deck in good weather or found a spot below deck during storms. Only a few officers had bunks.

Sailing west. The fleet set out from Palos on August 3, 1492, and sailed to the Canary Islands, a Spanish possession off Africa's coast. Repairs were made on the island of Gran Canaria, and the crews loaded provisions on the island of Gomera. The ships left Gomera on September 6. Columbus journeyed south before sailing west in order to take advantage of the trade winds. At that latitude, these winds always blow from the northeast.

Columbus had few navigational instruments. He knew enough about celestial navigation to measure latitude by using the North Star. However, he had no instruments for determining the ship's position from the stars except a crude quadrant that was not accurate when the ship rolled. He used a compass to plot his course, estimated distances on a chart, relied on a half-hour glass to measure time, and guessed his speed. Together, these activities make up a method of navigation known as *dead reckoning*.

After a month of smooth sailing, the crews became anxious that they had not yet reached the islands Columbus had led them to expect. They had not sighted land for longer than any other crew of that time. Only the authority of the Pinzón brothers enabled Columbus to quiet the crews' loudly expressed doubts. Then, signs of approaching land began to appear, such as coastal

The fleet sets sail.

seaweed on the surface of the water and land-based birds flying overhead.

Between the evening of October 11 and the morning of October 12, a sailor on the *Pinta* named Juan Rodriguez Bermejo called out, "Land, land!" Isabella had offered a reward to the first person to sight land. However, Columbus said that he had seen a flickering light hours earlier, and he claimed the reward.

The first landing. Before noon on October 12, the ships landed on an island in the Caribbean Sea. Columbus named the island *San Salvador* (Spanish for *Holy Savior*). He later learned that inhabitants of the area called the island Guanahani. However, historians are not sure which island this is. In 1926, Watling Island in the Bahamas was officially renamed San Salvador Island because Columbus scholars considered it the most likely landing site. Other islands where he might have landed include Samana Cay and Conception in the Bahamas, and Grand Turk in the Turks Islands.

Columbus believed he had arrived at an island of the East Indies, near Japan or China. Because of this belief, he called the islanders *Indians*. People realized within a few years that Columbus had not reached the Indies, but the name *Indian* continued to be used.

The islanders were probably the Taíno, a subgroup of the Arawak people. They were skilled

Ferdinand and Isabella welcome Columbus home.

farmers who made cotton cloth, grouped their dwellings into villages, and had well-developed social and governmental systems. Columbus described them as gentle, "primitive" natives living in an island paradise. However, his attitude toward them held contradictions. The islanders' apparent innocence and simplicity made them seem like ideal candidates for conversion to Christianity. But these qualities also made them targets for mistreatment, and Columbus did not hesitate in kidnapping several islanders to present to his patrons in Spain. Columbus's conflicting feelings about the Native Americans would be echoed throughout the development of Spain's American empire.

On October 28, the fleet entered the Bay of Bariay off Cuba. Thinking they were near the Asian mainland, the captains explored harbor after harbor. They then sailed along the northern coast of the island of Hispaniola, now divided between the Dominican Republic and Haiti. Columbus called it *La Isla Espanola* (the Spanish Island).

The night of December 24, an exhausted Columbus gave the wheel of the *Santa Maria* to a sailor, who passed it to a cabin boy. The ship crashed and split apart on a reef near Cap-Haïtien, in present-day Haiti. Aided by a local chief, the crew built a makeshift fort. Columbus left about 40 men there to hunt for gold. He then started home on the *Nina*, sailing from Samana Bay on the northeast coast of Hispaniola on January 16, 1493. He brought several captured Taíno with him. Martín Pinzón captained the *Pinta*.

Return to Spain. The homeward voyage was rough and difficult. Some of the Taíno died. After about a month of travel, the *Nina* and the *Pinta* became separated during a storm. The *Nina* came ashore on the Portuguese island of Santa Maria in the Azores. Columbus and his crew were almost arrested by the governor, who assumed they had been trading illegally in Africa. Columbus was permitted to set out again, but storms forced him to seek shelter in Lisbon. The *Nina* finally reached Palos on March 15, 1493.

Columbus had been concerned that Martín Pinzón, with whom he had quarreled at times, would reach Spain first and claim the glory. Indeed, Pinzón had reached a small village in Spain a few days earlier and had notified the monarchs of his arrival. However, they refused to see him until they had heard from Columbus, and

Pinzón died before he could tell his story. The *Pinta* arrived at Palos a few hours after the *Nina*.

Columbus reported to Ferdinand and Isabella at Barcelona, Spain, where they gave him a grand reception. Columbus had little to show except some gold trinkets, parrots, and the few Taíno, but the monarchs determined to exploit his find. They quickly asked Pope Alexander VI to recognize their control over Columbus's current and future discoveries. The pope granted Ferdinand and Isabella the right to preach the Christian faith in the islands, and they used this right as the basis for sweeping claims over the lands. To avoid conflicts, the pope also established a Line of Demarcation. He gave Spain the right to explore and to claim new lands west of the line and gave Portugal the same rights east of the line. However, Portugal complained that these terms violated an earlier treaty and that the line was too close to its discoveries.

In 1494, negotiations opened in the town of Tordesillas in Spain. Spain and Portugal eventually agreed to move the imaginary line farther west. At the time, they thought their new line was about midway between Portugal's claims on the Cape Verde Islands and Columbus's new discoveries. This treaty set the foundation for Spanish land claims in the Americas and later enabled Portugal to claim Brazil and the Newfoundland Banks.

Second Voyage Westward

Return to the islands. Columbus's first expedition caused such excitement that he was put in charge of 17 ships for a second voyage. The crew of about 1,200 to 1,500 men included colonists and private investors who intended to settle in the islands. Most dreamed of quick wealth and a rapid return home. Friars went along to try to convert the Indians to Christianity.

The fleet sailed from Cadiz, Spain, on September 25, 1493. It took on supplies in the Canaries and completed the ocean crossing in a speedy 21 days. In another three weeks, the ships reached Hispaniola. They passed many islands. Columbus named one of them—present-day Marie-Galante in the eastern Caribbean—after his flagship. Columbus also landed briefly at Puerto Rico.

Trouble, settlement, and exploration.

In Hispaniola, Columbus searched in vain for the sailors he had left at the fort. No one discovered

exactly what had happened, but apparently the crew had fought among themselves possibly over local women. The survivors probably had been killed by the Taíno, whom they had mistreated.

Columbus moved eastward along the north coast of Hispaniola and established Isabela and other fortified posts. There, the Spanish colonists quickly saw that the riches promised by Columbus would not materialize. They resented being given orders by a Genoan rather than a Spaniard, and some fell ill from tropical fevers. Shortly after their arrival, 12 of the 17 ships returned to Spain with orders to bring more supplies to Isabela. The ships also carried discontented colonists back to Spain. To prevent rebellion, and also to make the voyage produce a quick profit to impress his backers, Columbus sent some men into Hispaniola's interior to search for gold.

Leaving his brother Diego in charge, Columbus left Isabela during the spring of 1494 to explore the southern coast of Cuba (which he called *Juana*). After traveling down its long coastline, Columbus declared that it was the Asian main-

Columbus at Hispaniola

land. Although this was not so, he forced the crews to sign an affidavit saying they agreed with him. Columbus did this because it was crucial to his contract with the Spanish monarchs to have discovered Asia. Otherwise, they could deny him the desired titles for which he had negotiated. Columbus also landed at Jamaica.

When Columbus returned to Hispaniola, he found his brothers Bartholomew and Diego waiting for him. Columbus immediately appointed Bartholomew provincial governor of Hispaniola. This appointment angered many of the Spanish settlers. In addition, they complained about having only *cassava* (tapioca), corn, fish, and yams to eat.

The brothers sought to punish the Taíno, who were no longer peaceful after the Europeans had treated them harshly. In addition, the Taíno had begun to suffer and die from infectious diseases brought over unintentionally by the Europeans, and food had become scarce. Such was his need for profits that Columbus tried to force all the male Taíno over age 14 to pan rivers for gold. Those who failed to collect an assigned quota of gold were punished, sometimes by having their hands cut off. But the quotas could not be met. When the Taíno threatened to rebel, Columbus used their rebellion to justify enslaving them.

In Spain, the friars and Spanish colonists who had left Hispaniola in early 1494 complained to Ferdinand and Isabella about conditions in Hispaniola. The friars criticized the maltreatment of the Taíno, and the colonists charged Columbus with misgovernment in the colony. Columbus decided to return to Spain to defend himself, arriving in June 1496. Again, Columbus's powerful oratory and impressive presence succeeded. The king and queen reconfirmed his titles and privileges, and they granted his request for additional men, supplies, and ships. But few men wanted to sail with him this time because the islands had failed to yield the expected profit. To assemble crews, Ferdinand and Isabella had to pardon prisoners. So low had Columbus's reputation sunk that his sons, who served as pages at court, were mocked by other boys. They jeered, "There go the sons of the Admiral of the Mosquitoes."

Third Voyage Westward

Third journey to the west. On May 30, 1498, Columbus departed from Sanlúcar, Spain, with six ships. He charted a southerly course. Ferdinand and Isabella wanted Columbus to investigate the possibility that the Asian mainland lay south or southwest of the lands he had already

Columbus in chains

explored. The possibility that such a mainland existed had been accepted by the king of Portugal, and Spain wanted to stake its claim.

The fleet ran into a windless region of the ocean and was becalmed in intense heat for eight days. It reached an island Columbus called *Trinidad* (meaning *Trinity*) on July 31 and then crossed the Gulf of Paria to the coast of Venezuela. Columbus observed an enormous outflow of freshwater—later found to come from the Orinoco River—that made him realize this land could not be an island. He wrote in his journal: "I believe that this is a very great continent which until today has been unknown." Columbus imagined that the great rush of freshwater must be a river flowing from the Garden of Eden.

Some scholars believe that while in Spain, Columbus had heard of an English-sponsored landing in 1497 along North America's northeastern coast by Italian explorer John Cabot. The news may have made Columbus doubt whether he himself really had reached Asia. Columbus did not mention his doubts, preferring to first explore and claim the area where he had landed for Spain. Columbus's failure to acknowledge that he had landed on a new continent had the effect that instead of being named for Columbus, America came to be named after Amerigo Vespucci, a later Italian navigator. A few years later, a document backdated to 1497 erroneously claimed that Vespucci had been the first to explore the mainland of a "New World."

Problems in Hispaniola.
Columbus found the Hispaniola colony seething with discontent. He tried to quiet the settlers by giving them land and letting them enslave the Taíno to work it, but that failed to satisfy many. A rebellion had been led by the chief justice, Francisco Roldán. For a time, Roldán and the Taíno—with whom he had established an alliance—held part of the island. Columbus managed to subdue the rebellion through negotiation and a show of force.

Columbus in disgrace.
By 1500, many complaints about Columbus had reached the Spanish court. Ferdinand and Isabella sent a commissioner named Francisco de Bobadilla to investigate. Upon arrival in Santo Domingo—the capital of Hispaniola—in August 1500, Bobadilla was shocked by the sight of several Spanish rebels swinging from gallows. He freed the remaining prisoners, arrested Columbus and his brothers, put them in chains, and sent them to Spain for trial. Once at sea, the captain of Columbus's ship offered to unchain him. But Columbus refused, saying he would only allow the chains to be removed by royal command.

In Spain, Columbus and his brothers were released by order of the king and queen. The rulers forgave Columbus, but with conditions. Columbus was allowed to keep his titles, but he would no longer be permitted to govern Hispaniola. The king and queen sent Nicolás de Ovando, with about 30 ships carrying 2,500 colonists, to govern the island.

Fourth Voyage Westward

The final voyage.
Columbus planned still another journey, which he called the "High Voyage." He saw it as his last chance to fulfill the promise of his earlier expeditions. His goal was to find a passage to the mainland of Asia. Columbus still believed that China lay close by. Ferdinand and Isabella granted his request for ships because they, too, believed he had come close to his goal, and they did not want to lose his services to another country. But they instructed him not to stop at Hispaniola unless absolutely necessary to get supplies, and then only in preparation for his return to Spain.

On May 9, 1502, Columbus set sail from Cadiz, Spain, with four ships. Columbus's son Ferdinand, about 14 years old, sailed with his father. Ferdinand's account of the trip, though written many years later, remains the best record of the voyage. The fleet stopped briefly at the Canary Islands, then sailed to Martinique in the eastern Caribbean in just 21 days. It then headed toward Hispaniola.

A dangerous hurricane.
Governor Ovando was sending 21 ships to Spain when he received a message from Columbus warning of an impending storm and asking permission to land. Feeling contempt for Columbus, and reminding him that he was forbidden to land at Hispaniola, Ovando ignored the warning and sent his ships to sea. Columbus's fleet weathered the storm. However, all but one of Ovando's ships sank in a hurricane. Columbus's enemies Bobadilla and Roldán drowned. The ship that reached Spain was the one carrying Columbus's share of the gold collected in Hispaniola, and the personal possessions he had left there.

Further explorations.
At the end of July, Columbus and his fleet reached the coast of Honduras. For the rest of the year, they sailed east and

south along the coasts of what are now Honduras, Nicaragua, Costa Rica, and Panama. The ships were battered by rough winds and driving rains, and the voyage demonstrated Columbus's considerable navigational skill.

At the narrowest part of the Isthmus of Panama, Columbus heard tales that a large body of water lay a few days' march across the mountains. But he did not follow up on this information, so he missed a chance to become the first European to see the Pacific Ocean. He also narrowly missed establishing contact with the rich, advanced Maya culture. Columbus abandoned his search for a passage to Asia on April 16, 1503. He was exhausted and probably suffering from malaria, which made him delirious.

The hard journey home. Columbus's fleet had to move slowly, because his ships were leaking badly from holes eaten in the planking by shellfish. On June 25, the two remaining ships had to be beached at St. Ann's Bay, which Columbus had called Santa Gloria, on the northern coast of Jamaica.

Columbus realized that the chances were slim that another expedition would arrive to rescue him and his crew. Captain Diego Mendez paddled to Hispaniola in a dugout canoe for help. Mendez reached Hispaniola, but Governor Ovando refused to provide a ship until more vessels arrived from Spain.

The crews had no tools to repair the ships or to build new ones, and they made no effort to feed themselves. Instead, they relied on the islanders to provide food. The Jamaicans started avoiding them. Columbus later claimed that he used information from an almanac to predict a total eclipse

of the moon, which so impressed the islanders that they resumed providing food.

At last, at the end of June in 1504—after being marooned for a year—Columbus and the 100 surviving crew members sailed from Jamaica on a ship chartered by Mendez. They reached Sanlúcar, Spain, on November 7, 1504.

Final Days

Queen Isabella died just a few weeks after Columbus returned to Spain. King Ferdinand granted Columbus an audience and listened to his requests. Ferdinand tried to persuade Columbus to trade in the rewards and privileges due him in exchange for an estate in north-central Spain. Columbus, in turn, tried to persuade Ferdinand to restore his authority and increase his income, but these requests were not granted.

Columbus spent his last days in a modest house in Valladolid, Spain, suffering from a disease that may have been Reiter's syndrome, a form of joint inflammation. On May 20, 1506, Columbus died. Many people believed Columbus was poor at the time of his death, but he actually died wealthy.

Columbus's remains were transported to Seville, Spain, and later to Santo Domingo, in what is now the Dominican Republic. Some people believe that his bones were moved to Havana, Cuba, in 1795, and, finally, back to Seville in 1899. Others believe that the bones of one of Columbus's brothers or of his son Diego were removed from Santo Domingo instead. In 2006, Spanish researchers found DNA evidence that at least some of Columbus's remains are in Seville.

Columbus's Impact on History

Christopher Columbus had a strong will and stuck with his beliefs. His single-minded search for a westward route to Asia unintentionally changed Europeans' commonly accepted views of the world and led to the establishment of contact between Europe and the Americas.

Many exchanges took place between the Eastern and Western hemispheres as a result of Columbus's voyages. The Europeans grew important cash crops—cotton, rubber, and sugarcane—in the Americas. They established vast plantations worked by Native Americans and by imported African slaves. They also obtained such precious metals as gold and silver in vast quantities. These

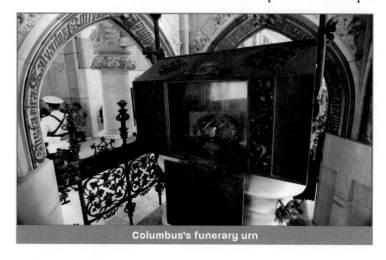

Columbus's funerary urn

valuable resources created fortunes for the Dutch, English, French, Portuguese, Russians, and Spanish. The wealth and human resources of the Western Hemisphere gave these countries a huge advantage over the rest of the world in later centuries.

The Americas also provided many foods that became popular throughout the world, including *maize* (corn), cassava, cayenne, chocolate, hot peppers, peanuts, potatoes, and tomatoes. Europe and Asia, in exchange, supplied the Americas with cattle, goats, honey bees, horses, pigs, rice, sheep, and wheat, as well as many trees and various other plants. This agricultural exchange revolutionized the economies and styles of cooking of both hemispheres.

Europeans unintentionally brought many deadly diseases to America. The previous separation of the Native American peoples from those of Europe and Asia meant that the Native Americans had no natural immunity to these diseases. As a result, measles, smallpox, typhus, and other infectious diseases swept through the newly exposed populations, killing vast numbers of people. In turn, some Europeans became infected by a form of syphilis unknown in Europe.

Research in the late 1900s and early 2000s into the life and times of Christopher Columbus has somewhat diminished his heroic image as an isolated visionary by placing him in the context of a broad wave of exploration. Historians continue to praise his persistence, courage, and maritime ability. Critics point to his cruelty to the Native Americans, his poor administration of Hispaniola, and his role in beginning the heedless exploitation of the natural resources of the Americas. Nevertheless, Columbus's explorations ended centuries of mutual ignorance about what lay on either side of the Atlantic Ocean. To him belong both the glory of the encounter and a share of the blame for what followed.

Columbus Day honors Christopher Columbus's first voyage to America in 1492. Columbus Day became a legal federal holiday in the United States in 1971. It is celebrated on the second Monday in October. Before 1971, a number of states celebrated Columbus Day on October 12. Cities and organizations sponsor parades and banquets on Columbus Day.

The first Columbus Day celebration was held in 1792, when New York City celebrated the 300th

Statue of Columbus, Lisbon, Portugal

anniversary of the landing. In 1892, President Benjamin Harrison called upon the people of the United States to celebrate Columbus Day on the 400th anniversary of the event. Columbus Day has been celebrated annually since 1920.

Although the land Columbus reached was not named after him, many monuments honor him. The Republic of Colombia in South America and the District of Columbia in the United States bear his name. So do towns, rivers, streets, and public buildings. The name *Columbia* has also been used as a poetic personification of the United States. The Columbus Memorial Library in Washington, D.C., contains about 350,000 volumes on the American republics.

Many Latin-American countries celebrate October 12 as the *Dia de la Raza* (Day of the Race). It honors the Spanish heritage of the peoples of Latin America. Celebration ceremonies feature speeches, parades, and colorful fiestas.

Columbia is a name sometimes used in referring to the United States. Long before the Revolutionary War in America (1775–1783), many people felt that America should have been named Columbia after the explorer Christopher Columbus. During the war, colonial poets used the name to describe the new nation that was to become the United States. Phillis Wheatley, for

A modern replica of the *Pinta*

example, a black slave poet in Massachusetts, used the term in a poem honoring George Washington. Philip Freneau, a poet and journalist, popularized the term in several poems during and after the Revolutionary War. In 1784, King's College in New York City became Columbia College. Towns, counties, and institutions throughout the United States have since adopted the name.

Many artists have symbolically pictured Columbia as a tall, stately woman dressed in flowing garments and holding an American flag. A blue drape with white stars is usually part of her costume. The earliest image of Columbia showed her as a Native American woman. In the 1800s, she appeared on the prows of ships, in patriotic paintings, and in pageants representing the Revolutionary War. The *Statue of Freedom*, on top of the U.S. Capitol in Washington, D.C., is often incorrectly identified as a statue of Columbia.

MLA Citation

"Christopher Columbus."
*The Southwestern
Advantage Topic Source.*
Nashville: Southwestern. 2013.

ADDITIONAL RESOURCES

Books to Read

Level I

Landau, Elaine. *Columbus Day*. Enslow, 2001.
Osborne, Mary P. *The Story of Christopher Columbus*. 1987. Reprint. Gareth Stevens, 1997.
Roop, Peter and Connie. *Christopher Columbus*. Scholastic, 2000.
Twist, Clint. *Christopher Columbus*. Raintree Steck-Vaughn, 1994.

Level II

Davidson, Miles H. *Columbus Then and Now*. University of Oklahoma Press, 1997.
Phillips, William D., Jr., and Carla R. *The Worlds of Christopher Columbus*. Cambridge, 1992.
Schnaubelt, Joseph C., and Van Fleteren, Frederick, eds. *Columbus and the New World*. Peter Lang, 1998.
Zamora, Margarita. *Reading Columbus*. University of California Press, 1993.

Web Sites

Christopher Columbus

http://www.rmg.co.uk/explore/sea-and-ships/facts/explorers-and-leaders/christopher-columbus
A fact sheet from the UK's National Maritime Museum in Greenwich, London.

Christopher Columbus—Man and Myth
http://lcweb.loc.gov/exhibits/1492/columbus.html
Information about the first voyage of Columbus to the New World.

Columbus Letter to the King and Queen of Spain
http://www.law.ou.edu/hist/columlet.html
Contains a letter Columbus wrote to the king and queen of Spain regarding the colonization of the lands he discovered for Spain.

Introduction to 1492: An Ongoing Voyage
http://lcweb.loc.gov/exhibits/1492/intro.html
The story of how America was discovered by Europeans.

Ships of Discovery
http://www.shipsofdiscovery.org/columbus.htm
Information about the ships Columbus lost during his explorations in the Caribbean Sea.

The Columbus Letter
http://www.usm.maine.edu/~maps/columbus/
Digital version of the 1494 Basel edition of Columbus's letter announcing the success of his voyage to the "islands of the India sea." Maintained by the University of Southern Maine.

Search Strings

Dead Reckoning

Christopher Columbus navigation dead reckoning (3,570)

Christopher Columbus navigation "dead reckoning" (2,260)

Christopher Columbus navigation "dead reckoning" North Star quadrant compass (164)

Exploration and Disease

exploration disease transatlantic voyages Europeans "Native Americans" (1,360)

exploration disease transatlantic voyages (4,770)

Young Columbus

Christopher Columbus youth early voyages (19,600)

Christopher Columbus youth early voyages Genoa Portugal (1,830)

Life at Sea

Christopher Columbus life at sea crew tasks (147,000)

Christopher Columbus life at sea "crew members" jobs (21,200)

life at sea with Christopher Columbus (951,000)

Leonardo da Vinci

A key figure of the Renaissance, Leonardo da Vinci was one of the greatest painters and most versatile geniuses in history.

HOT topics

Mona Lisa. Leonardo's most famous portrait, and probably the most famous portrait ever painted, the *Mona Lisa* likely depicts the young wife of a rich Florentine silk merchant, Francesco del Giocondo. *Mona Lisa* is a shortened form of *Madonna Lisa* (my lady, Lisa). The woman is also often called *La Gioconda*, which is the feminine form of her husband's last name. The painting is known for the simple geometry of its composition, but the landscape in its background, which reflects Leonardo's studies of geology, is also of interest. He was one of the first people to grasp that geological time is revealed in rock layers and to understand such processes as erosion.

Life Sciences. Leonardo studied anatomy by dissecting human corpses and the bodies of animals. He made scientific drawings that clarify not only the appearance of bones, tendons, and other body parts, but also their function. These drawings are considered the first accurate portrayals of human anatomy. He also tried to understand the human body as a mechanism. As his studies progressed, he also tried to understand the forces of life that animated the body. His drawings, for example, extended to investigations of human reproduction and

HOT topics

embryology and the circulation of the blood. His famous study of human proportions, *Vitruvian Man*, done about 1487, is one of the most famous images in European art. The mystery of life was the unifying theme of his work.

Physical Sciences.
Leonardo was interested in mechanics (the science of motion and force), and many of his ideas and designs were far ahead of their time. For example, he drew plans for aircraft, including a helicopter, and for a parachute. Like many Renaissance artists, Leonardo sometimes worked as an engineer or military architect. He produced designs for a variety of war machines, among them tanks, machine guns, and movable bridges.

The Last Supper.
When painting *The Last Supper*, Leonardo rejected the fresco technique normally used for wall paintings. The technique requires an artist to mix dry pigments with water and brush them onto damp, freshly laid plaster. An artist who uses the fresco method must work quickly. But Leonardo wanted to paint slowly, to revise his work, and to use shadows—all of which would have been impossible in fresco painting. He developed a new technique that involved coating the wall with a compound he had created. But the compound, which was supposed to hold the paint in place and protect it from moisture, did not work. Soon after Leonardo completed the picture, the paint began to flake away. The Last Supper still exists, but in poor condition, despite many attempts to restore it.

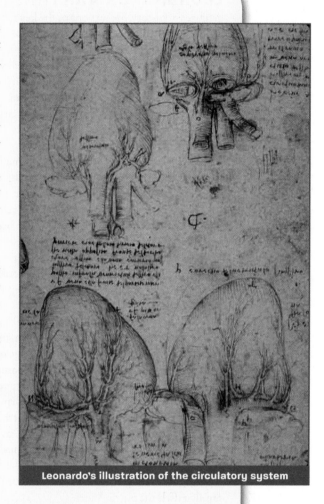

Leonardo's illustration of the circulatory system

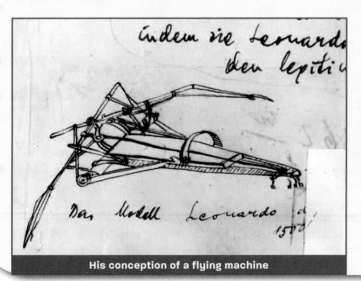

His conception of a flying machine

TRUE or FALSE?
Leonardo built and flew the world's first flying machine.

THE BASICS

Leonardo da Vinci (1452–1519) was one of the greatest painters and most versatile geniuses in history. He was one of the key figures of the Renaissance, a great cultural movement that had begun in Italy in the 1300s. His portrait *Mona Lisa* and his religious scene *The Last Supper* rank among the most famous pictures ever painted.

Leonardo, as he is almost always called, was trained to be a painter. But his interests and achievements spread into an astonishing variety of fields that are now considered scientific specialties. Leonardo studied anatomy, astronomy, botany, geology, geometry, and optics, and he designed machines and drew plans for hundreds of inventions.

Because Leonardo excelled in such an amazing number of areas of human knowledge, he is often called a universal genius. However, he had little interest in literature, history, or religion. He formulated a few scientific laws, but he never developed his ideas systematically. Leonardo was most of all an excellent observer. He concerned himself with what the eye could see, rather than with purely abstract concepts.

Leonardo's Life

Early career. Leonardo was born on April 15, 1452, probably outside the village of Vinci, near Florence in central Italy. The name *da Vinci* simply means *from Vinci*. At that time, Florence and its surrounding villages and farms made up a nearly independent area called a city-state. Florence was also a commercial and cultural center. Leonardo was the illegitimate son of Ser Piero da Vinci, a legal specialist, and a peasant woman named Caterina. Ser Piero's family raised the boy in Vinci.

During the late 1460s, Leonardo became an apprentice to Andrea del Verrocchio, a leading painter and sculptor in Florence. He remained with Verrocchio as an assistant for several years after completing his apprenticeship. Verrocchio and Leonardo collaborated on the painting *The Baptism of Christ* about 1472.

Self-portrait

From about 1478 to 1482, Leonardo had his own studio in Florence. During this period, he received an important commission to paint a church altarpiece now known as the *Adoration of the Kings*.

Years in Milan. Leonardo never finished the *Adoration of the Kings* because he left Florence about 1482 to become court artist for Ludovico Sforza, the Duke of Milan. Leonardo lived in Milan until 1499. He had a variety of duties in the duke's court. As a military engineer, he designed artillery and fortresses. As a civil engineer, he devised a system of locks for Milan's canals and designed revolving stages for pageants. As a sculptor, he planned a huge monument of the duke's father mounted on a horse.

About 1483, Leonardo painted the *Madonna of the Rocks*. This painting is his earliest major work that survives in complete form. During his years in Milan, he also created his famous wall painting *The Last Supper*.

Return to Florence. In 1499, the French overthrew Ludovico Sforza and forced him to flee Milan. Leonardo also left the city. He visited Mantua, where he made a famous drawing of Isabella d'Este, the wife of the Duke of Mantua. He also visited Venice briefly before returning to Florence.

Leonardo's paintings during his stay in Milan had made him famous, and the people of Florence received him with great respect. The early work Leonardo had done in Florence before he left for Milan had strongly influenced a number of young artists, including Sandro Botticelli and Piero di Cosimo. These artists had become the leaders of the next generation of Florentine painters. The work Leonardo was to create after his return to Florence would inspire yet another generation of artists. This generation included Andrea del Sarto, Michelangelo, and Raphael.

When Leonardo returned, Florence was building a new hall for the city council. The Florentine government hired Leonardo and Michelangelo to decorate the walls of the hall with scenes of the city's military victories. Leonardo chose the *Battle of Anghiari*, in which Florence had defeated Milan in 1440. His painting showed a cavalry battle, with tense soldiers, leaping horses, and clouds of dust.

In painting the *Battle of Anghiari*, Leonardo tried an experimental technique that did not work. The paint began to run, and he never finished the project. The painting no longer exists. Its general appearance is known from Leonardo's sketches and from copies made by other artists. About 1503, while working on the *Battle of Anghiari*, Leonardo began painting the *Mona Lisa*, probably the most famous portrait ever painted. He completed it three or four years later.

Last years. In 1513, Pope Leo X gave Leonardo rooms for his use in the Vatican Palace. Leonardo did little painting during his later years. However, about 1515, he completed *The Deluge*, a series of drawings in which he portrayed the destruction of the world in a tremendous flood. These drawings are the climax of Leonardo's attempts to visualize the forces of life and nature.

Renaissance rulers competed to surround themselves with great artists and scholars. In 1516, Francis I, the king of France, invited Leonardo to become "first painter and engineer and architect of the king." He provided Leonardo a residence connected to the Palace of Cloux at Amboise, near Tours. Leonardo devoted his time to doing anatomical drawings,

Isabella d'Este

drafting architectural plans, and designing sets for court entertainments. He died on May 2, 1519.

Leonardo's Works

Drawings and scientific studies. Leonardo used drawings both as a tool of scientific investigation and as an expression of artistic imagination. He changed forever the art of drawing. He made drawings in much greater numbers than any artist before him, and he was one of the first artists to use sketches to work out his artistic and architectural compositions. Drawing was indispensable to Leonardo's processes of observation, creation, and invention.

Physical sciences. Leonardo was interested in mechanics (the science of motion and force), and many of his ideas and designs were far ahead of their time. For example, he drew plans for aircraft, including a helicopter, and for a parachute. Like many Renaissance artists, Leonardo sometimes worked as an engineer or military architect. He produced designs for a variety of war machines, among them tanks, machine guns, and movable bridges.

Life sciences. Leonardo studied anatomy by dissecting human corpses and the bodies of animals. He made scientific drawings that clarify not only the appearance of bones, tendons, and other body parts, but also their function. These drawings are considered the first accurate portrayals of human anatomy.

Leonardo tried to understand the human body as a mechanism. As his studies progressed, he also tried to understand the forces of life that animated the body. His drawings of anatomy, for example, extended to investigations of human reproduction and embryology and the circulation of the blood. None of these things were understood at the time. His anatomical drawing of a female, which he made about 1508, is his attempt, partly erroneous in detail, to illustrate the body's circulatory and other systems in a single image.

Like other artists, Leonardo was interested in the proportions of the human body. He drew a famous study of human proportions based on the statement of the Roman architect Vitruvius that the "well-shaped man" fits into the perfect shapes of the square and circle. According to Vitruvius, the parts of the body are related to one another in ratios of whole numbers, and these ratios should be used in the design of architecture. Leonardo's drawing of the *Vitruvian man*, done about 1487, is one of the most famous images in European art.

Leonardo also worked to understand the relation between the life of the human body and that of the larger world. For Leonardo, principles of proportion similar to those that shaped the human body also governed the growth of trees, the flight of birds, and the flow of water. When Leonardo drew the leaves of a plant, he intended the lines to show living energy responding to light, water, and soil. The mystery of life was the unifying theme of his work.

Leonardo's notebooks. Leonardo planned to write books on many subjects, including painting, human movement, and the flight of birds, but he never completed any of them. The writings exist in partial drafts and fragments in notebooks. Leonardo's notebooks also include his scientific observations and ideas for inventions, as well as detailed drawings. Most of the notebooks were not published until nearly 400 years after Leonardo's death. By the time his scientific and technical investigations became widely known, other people had come up with the same ideas.

Paintings. For much of his life, Leonardo was interested in optics, which is concerned with the properties of light. Leonardo carefully analyzed such things as the pattern of light and shadow on a sphere before a window. The understanding he gained from such study is evident in the rich effects of light, dark, and color in such paintings as the *Mona Lisa* and *The Virgin and Child with Saint Anne* (early 1500s).

Leonardo also explored the techniques of perspective, which painters use to create an illusion of depth on a flat surface. Florentine artists began to use these techniques in the early 1400s. *Linear perspective* is based on the optical illusion that parallel lines seem to converge as they recede toward one point, called a *vanishing point. Aerial perspective* is based on the fact that light, shade, and color change with an object's distance from the viewer.

Early paintings. Verrocchio and Leonardo shared the work of painting *The Baptism of Christ*. Leonardo painted the left angel, the distant landscape, and possibly the skin of Christ. Leonardo's parts of the painting, with their soft shadings and shadows concealing the edges, are an early example of the *sfumato* (smoky) quality of his paintings. Verrocchio's figures, on the other hand,

Human movement

are defined by hard lines typical of early Renaissance painting. Leonardo's more graceful approach marked the beginning of the High Renaissance style, which did not become popular in Italy until about 25 years later.

Leonardo's *Adoration of the Kings* exists today in an unfinished form, with the figures visible only as outlines of contrasting light and dark areas. This kind of composition is called *chiaroscuro*, a word which combines the Italian words for *light* and *dark*. Chiaroscuro is characteristic of the High Renaissance style.

The *Adoration of the Kings* shows three kings worshiping the newborn Christ child. Leonardo abandoned the traditional treatment of this popular subject. Earlier versions showed the figures in profile, with the Virgin Mary and Jesus on one side of the painting and the kings on the other. To give the Holy Family more emphasis, Leonardo placed them in the center, facing the viewer. The kings and other figures form a semicircle around Mary and Jesus. Leonardo sharply contrasted foreground and background. Strong light-dark contrasts and simple geometric forms were basic features of Leonardo's mature style as a painter.

In the *Adoration of the Kings*, Mary and the Christ child are arranged in a pyramid shape. Leonardo also used this arrangement in other paintings, including the *Madonna of the Rocks* and *The Virgin and Child with Saint Anne*. In *The Virgin and Child with Saint Anne*, the gazes of all the figures are concentrated on one side of the pyramid, giving it a new psychological and dramatic unity.

The Last Supper. Leonardo finished painting *The Last Supper* about 1497. He created the famous scene on a wall of the dining hall in the monastery of Santa Maria delle Grazie. The painting shows the final meal of Jesus Christ and His 12 apostles. Jesus has just announced that one of them will betray him.

When painting *The Last Supper*, Leonardo rejected the *fresco* technique normally used for wall paintings. The technique requires an artist to mix dry pigments with water and brush them onto damp, freshly laid plaster. An artist who uses the fresco method must work quickly. But Leonardo wanted to paint slowly, to revise his work, and to use shadows—all of which would have been impossible in fresco painting. He developed a new technique that involved coating the wall with a compound he had created. But the compound, which was sup-

The Last Supper

posed to hold the paint in place and protect it from moisture, did not work. Soon after Leonardo completed the picture, the paint began to flake away. *The Last Supper* still exists, but in poor condition, though many attempts have been made to restore it.

Leonardo also changed the traditional arrangement of the figures. Christ and His apostles are usually shown in a line, with Judas, the betrayer, set apart in some way. Leonardo painted the apostles in several small groups. Each apostle responds in a different way to Christ's announcement that one of them will betray Him. Jesus sits in the center of the scene, apart from the other figures. Leonardo's composition creates a more active and centralized design than earlier artists had achieved. The composition, in which the space recedes to a point behind the head of Christ, is one of the great examples of one-point perspective in Italian Renaissance painting. Leonardo used linear perspective to focus attention on the painting's religious and dramatic center, the face of Jesus Christ.

Mona Lisa is probably a portrait of the young wife of a rich Florentine silk merchant, Francesco del Giocondo. *Mona Lisa* is a shortened form of *Madonna Lisa* (my lady, Lisa). The woman is also often called *La Gioconda*, which is the feminine form of her husband's last name.

The portrait shows a young woman seated on a balcony high above a landscape. Leonardo used a pyramid design to place the woman simply and calmly in the space of the painting. Her folded hands form the front corner of the pyramid.

Her breast, neck, and face glow in the same light that softly models her hands. The light softens the painting's underlying geometry of spheres and circles, which includes the arc of her famous smile, and gives the texture of living surfaces to the geometric shapes. Behind the figure, a vast landscape recedes to icy mountains. Winding paths and a distant bridge give only the slightest indications of human presence. The landscape reflects Leonardo's studies of geology. He was one of the first people to grasp that geological time is revealed in rock layers and to understand such processes as erosion.

Leonardo's Importance

Leonardo had one of the greatest scientific minds of the Italian Renaissance. He wanted to know the workings of what he saw in nature. Many of his inventions and scientific ideas were centuries ahead of his time. For example, he was the first person to study the flight of birds scientifically. Leonardo's importance to art was even greater than his impor-

tance to science. He had a strong influence on many leading artists, including Raphael and Michelangelo. Leonardo's balanced compositions and idealized figures became standard features of later Renaissance art. Painters also tried to imitate Leonardo's knowledge of perspective and anatomy, and his accurate observations of nature.

What most impresses people today is the wide range of Leonardo's talent and achievements. He turned his attention to many subjects and mastered nearly all. His inventiveness, versatility, and wide-ranging intellectual curiosity have made Leonardo a symbol of the Renaissance spirit.

MLA Citation

"Leonardo da Vinci."
*The Southwestern
Advantage Topic Source.*
Nashville: Southwestern. 2013.

ADDITIONAL RESOURCES

Books to Read

Anderson, Maxine. *Amazing Leonardo da Vinci Inventions You Can Build Yourself.* Nomad Press, 2006.
Kemp, Martin. *Leonardo da Vinci.* Viking Penguin, 2004.
Nicholl, Charles. *Leonardo da Vinci.* Viking Penguin, 2004.
Reed, Jennifer. *Leonardo da Vinci.* Enslow, 2005.

Web Sites

Artist: Leonardo da Vinci

http://www.nga.gov/cgi-bin/psearch?Request=S&imageset=1&Person=18300
The National Gallery of Art in Washington, D.C., displays art by Leonardo da Vinci.

Bear Walking

http://www.metmuseum.org/Collections/search-the-collections/150000235
A drawing by Leonardo da Vinci displayed by the Metropolitan Museum of Art in New York City.

Exploring Leonardo

http://www.mos.org/sln/Leonardo/LeoHomePage.html
A resource for students and teachers developed by the Museum of Science in Boston. This site
    includes biographical information, highlights some of Leonardo's futuristic inventions, and
    introduces Renaissance techniques for representing the 3-D world.

Head of the Virgin

http://www.metmuseum.org/Collections/search-the-collections/90004537
Leonardo da Vinci's sketch, displayed by the Metropolitan Museum of Art in New York City.

Leonardo's Horse

http://www.pbs.org/newshour/bb/entertainment/july-dec99/leonardo_9-10.html
PBS presents the transcript of an episode of The News Hour that focused on the art of
    Leonardo da Vinci.

Studies for the Nativity

http://metmuseum.org/Collections/search-the-collections/90004535

The Metropolitan Museum of Art in New York City presents diagrams by Leonardo da Vinci.

The Mona Lisa

http://www.louvre.fr/en/oeuvre-notices/mona-lisa-%E2%80%93-portrait-lisa-gherardini-wife-francesco-del-giocondo

Leonardo da Vinci's famous painting, displayed by the Louvre in Paris.

The Virgin and Child with St. Anne

http://www.louvre.fr/en/oeuvre-notices/virgin-and-child-saint-anne

A painting by Leonardo da Vinci exhibited by the Louvre in Paris.

Virgin of the Rocks

http://www.louvre.fr/en/oeuvre-notices/virgin-rocks

The Louvre in Paris presents a painting by Leonardo da Vinci.

Search Strings

Mona Lisa

"Mona Lisa" portrait painting famous (154,000)

"Mona Lisa" portrait painting famous Leonardo da Vinci (73,800)

"Mona Lisa" portrait painting famous Leonardo da Vinci Giocondo background (436)

Life Sciences

Leonardo da Vinci anatomy study scientific drawings life science (7,100)

Leonardo da Vinci anatomy study scientific drawings life science Vitruvian Man (663)

Physical Sciences

Leonardo da Vinci physical sciences mechanics motion force (63,700)

"Leonardo da Vinci""physical sciences" mechanics motion force (649)

"Leonardo da Vinci" physical sciences mechanics motion force engineer military architect (2,550)

The Last Supper

Leonardo da Vinci "The Last Supper" painting technique fresco (11,500)

Leonardo da Vinci "The Last Supper" painting technique fresco condition (580)

William *William* Shakespeare

William Shakespeare (1564–1616) was an English playwright and poet. He is generally considered the greatest dramatist the world has ever known and the finest poet who has written in the English language.

HOT topics

Who Wrote Shakespeare's Plays?

Some people so admired Shakespeare's plays that they refused to believe an actor from Stratford-upon-Avon could have written them. They believed that only an educated, sophisticated man of high social standing could have written the plays. Sir Francis Bacon was the first and, for many years, the most popular candidate proposed as the real author of Shakespeare's plays. Bacon's followers still remain convinced, but Edward de Vere, the 17th Earl of Oxford, is now a more popular candidate. Some anti-Stratfordians have also claimed that the writer Christopher Marlowe was the actual author. In spite of the claims made for these men, no important Shakespearean scholar doubts that Shakespeare wrote the plays and poems.

HOT topics

Dramatic Conventions.
The writing and staging of Elizabethan plays were strongly influenced by various dramatic conventions (customs) of that time. The most widespread convention was the use of poetic dialogue. Although Shakespeare's plays contain prose and rhymed verse, he chiefly used an unrhymed, rhythmical form of poetry called blank verse. Two common conventions that audiences expected were soliloquies and asides. In a soliloquy, an actor, who is alone on the stage, recites a speech directly to the audience. Or he speaks aloud to himself his thoughts and feelings. In an aside, a character speaks words that the other characters onstage are not supposed to hear. Audiences also liked and expected long lyrical speeches.

Vocabulary.
Shakespeare changed words, invented words, and borrowed words from other languages. He even used nouns as verbs for dramatic effect. In *Measure for Measure*, for example, a character remarks that Angelo "dukes it well," referring to the forceful way in which Angelo handles the duties of the absent Duke of Vienna. Shakespeare also used verbs in both their modern form—for example, has— and in their older form—hath. In the same way, Shakespeare used both modern pronouns, such as you, and older pronouns, such as thee or thou. Some of Shakespeare's words may be unfamiliar or confusing to modern readers and theatergoers. His vocabulary basically resembles modern English, but he employed many words that are no longer used.

Shakespeare's works have been published many times over.

TRUE or FALSE?
Despite Shakespeare's widespread and enduring appeal, Hollywood has produced no film versions of his plays.

THE BASICS

William Shakespeare (1564–1616), was an English playwright, poet, and actor. Many people regard him as the world's greatest dramatist and the finest poet England has ever produced.

Shakespeare wrote at least 38 plays, two major narrative poems, a sequence of sonnets, and several short poems. His works have been translated into a remarkable number of languages, and his plays are performed throughout the world. His plays have been a vital part of the theater in the Western world since they were written about 400 years ago. Through the years, most serious actors and actresses have considered the major roles of Shakespeare to be the supreme test of their art.

Shakespeare's plays have attracted large audiences in big, sophisticated cities and in small, rural towns. His works have been performed on the frontiers of Australia and New Zealand. They were part of the cultural life of the American Colonies and provided entertainment in the mining camps of the Old West. Today, there are theaters in many nations dedicated to staging Shakespeare's works.

Shakespeare used language of startling originality to portray many-sided characters and tell fascinating stories. Critics and readers celebrate him as a great student of human nature. A remarkable group of vivid characters populate his plays. They include rogues and aristocrats, housewives and stuffy teachers, soldiers and generals, shepherds and philosophers. The most successful of these characters create an impression of psychological depth never before seen in English literature.

Shakespeare has had enormous influence on culture throughout the world. His works have helped shape the literature of all English-speaking countries. His work has also had an important effect on the literary cultures of such

Shakespeare helped shape all of English literature.

countries as Germany and Russia. In addition, his widespread presence in popular culture extends to motion pictures, television, cartoons, and even songs.

Shakespeare's characters, language, and stories are a source of inspiration, quotation, and imitation. Many words and phrases that first appeared in his plays and poems have become part of our everyday speech. Examples include such common words as *assassination, bump, eventful, go-between, gloomy*, and *lonely*, as well as such familiar phrases as *fair play, a forgone conclusion*, and *salad days*.

Shakespeare has so saturated modern culture that many people who have never read a line of his work or seen one of his plays performed can identify lines and passages as his. Examples include "To be, or not to be," "Friends, Romans, countrymen, lend me your ears," "Parting is such sweet sorrow," "A rose by any other name would smell as sweet," and "A horse! A horse! My kingdom for a horse!"

Shakespeare's poetry is full of vivid metaphors and brilliant images. His verbal skill also reveals itself in a tendency for word play and puns. Critics and readers acknowledge his superb way with words even when the richness of his language blurs the sense of what his text means.

Besides influencing language and literature, Shakespeare has affected other aspects of our culture. His plays and poems have long been a required part of a liberal education. Generations of people have absorbed his ideas concerning heroism, romantic love, loyalty, and the nature of tragedy as well as his portraits of particular historical characters. To this day, most people imagine Julius Caesar, Marc Antony, Cleopatra, and Richard III as Shakespeare portrayed them.

Shakespeare's plays appeal to readers as well as to theatergoers. His plays—and his poems—have been reprinted and translated countless times. Indeed, a publishing industry flourishes around Shakespeare, as critics and scholars examine every aspect of the man, his writings, and his influence. Each year, hundreds of books and articles appear on Shakespearean subjects. Thousands of scholars from all over the world gather in dozens of meetings annually to discuss topics related to Shakespeare. Special libraries and library collections focus upon Shakespeare. Numerous motion pictures have been made of his plays. Composers have written operas, musical comedies, and instrumental works based on his stories and characters.

The world has admired and respected many great writers. But only Shakespeare has generated such varied and continuing interest—and such constant affection. The extent and durability of Shakespeare's reputation is without equal.

Shakespeare's Life

During Shakespeare's time, the English cared little about keeping biographical information unrelated to affairs of the church or state. In addition, playwriting was not a highly regarded occupation, and so people saw little point in recording the lives of mere dramatists. However, a number of records exist that deal with Shakespeare's life. They include church registers and accounts of business dealings. Although these records are few and incomplete by modern standards, they provide much information. By relating these records to various aspects of English history and society, scholars have constructed a believable and largely comprehensive account of Shakespeare's life. However, gaps remain. Perhaps the most frustrating gap is the general absence of personal papers that might provide access to the playwright's thoughts and feelings. As a result, biographers almost always examine the plays and poems for autobiographical clues.

His Life in Stratford

Shakespeare's parents belonged to what today would be called the middle class. John Shake-

speare, William's father, was a glove maker who owned a shop in the town of Stratford-upon-Avon. Stratford is about 75 miles (120 kilometers) northwest of London in the county of Warwickshire. John Shakespeare was a respected man in the town and held several important positions in the local government.

William Shakespeare's mother was born Mary Arden. She was the daughter of a farmer but related to a family of considerable social standing in the county. John Shakespeare married Mary Arden about 1557. The Ardens were Roman Catholics. Mary may also have been a Catholic, but the Shakespeares publicly belonged to the Church of England, the state church.

Early years. William Shakespeare was born in the small market town of Stratford-upon-Avon in 1564, the third of eight children. The register of Holy Trinity, the parish church in Stratford, records his baptism on April 26. According to the custom at that time, infants were baptized about three days after their birth. Therefore, the generally accepted date for Shakespeare's birth is April 23.

The Shakespeares were a family of considerable local prominence. In 1565, John Shakespeare became an alderman. Three years later, he was elected *bailiff* (mayor), the highest civic honor that a Stratford resident could receive. Later, he held several other civic posts. But toward the end of his life, John Shakespeare had financial problems.

Beginning at about the age of 7, William probably attended the Stratford grammar school with other boys of his social class. The school's highly qualified teachers were graduates of Oxford University. Students spent about nine hours a day in school. They attended classes the year around, except for three brief holiday periods. The teachers enforced strict discipline and physically punished students who broke the rules. The students chiefly studied Latin, the language of ancient Rome. Knowledge of Latin was necessary for a career in medicine, law, or the church. In addition, the ability to read Latin was considered a sign of an educated person. Young Shakespeare may have read such outstanding ancient Roman authors as Cicero, Ovid, Plautus, Seneca, Terence, and Virgil.

In spite of the long hours he spent in school, Shakespeare's boyhood was probably not all boring study. As a market center, Stratford was a lively town. In addition, holidays provided popular pageants and shows, including plays about the legendary outlaw Robin Hood and his merry men. By 1569, traveling companies of professional actors were performing in Stratford. Stratford also held two large fairs each year, which attracted numerous visitors from other counties. For young Shakespeare, Stratford could thus have been an exciting place to live.

Stratford also offered other pleasures. The fields and woods surrounding the town provided opportunities to hunt and trap small game. The River Avon, which ran through the town, had fish to catch. Shakespeare's poems and plays show a love of nature and rural life. This display undoubtedly reflects his childhood experiences and his love of the Stratford countryside.

Marriage. On November 27, 1582, Shakespeare received a license to marry Anne Hathaway, the daughter of a local farmer. The two families knew each other, but the details of the relationship between William and Anne have been a source of speculation. At the age of 18, William was young to marry, while Anne at 26 was of normal marrying age. The marriage appears to have been hurried, and the birth of their first child, Susanna, in May 1583 came only six months after marriage.

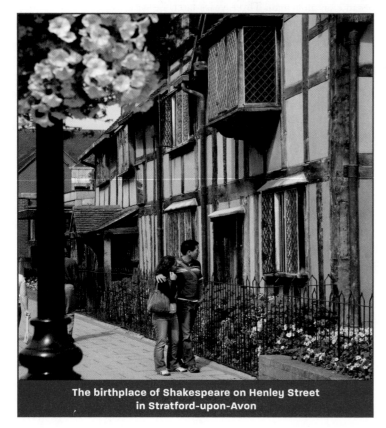

The birthplace of Shakespeare on Henley Street in Stratford-upon-Avon

Some scholars have suggested that William may have been forced to marry Anne because she was pregnant. However, birth and marriage records indicate that many women in England at that time were already pregnant before they married, and so Shakespeare's marriage was not unusual. Early in 1585, Anne gave birth to twins, Judith and Hamnet. The record of baptism marks the start of an important gap in the documentary evidence of Shakespeare's life.

The lost years. Scholars have referred to the period between 1585 and 1592, when Shakespeare was called an "upstart" by a London writer, as the "lost years." Scholars have proposed a number of theories about his activities during that time. But what is certain is that some time before 1592 Shakespeare arrived in London and began to work in the theater.

Early Career in London

By 1592, Shakespeare apparently attracted the hostile attention of a jealous rival. Robert Greene was a university-trained writer who was among the first to attempt to make a career of writing for the stage and the commercial press. *Greene's Groats-Worth of Wit Bought with a Million of Repentance*, a pamphlet published after Greene's death in 1592, contains a harsh reference to Shakespeare. The English playwright Henry Chettle prepared the pamphlet for publication and may have been the true author. A passage in the pamphlet addressed to playwrights says:

… an upstart Crow, beautified with our feathers, that with his *Tiger's heart wrapped in a Player's hide*, supposes he is as well able to bombast out a blank verse as the best of you: and being an absolute *Johannes fac totum* [Jack of all trades], is in his own conceit the only Shake-scene in a country.

The line "Tiger's heart wrapped in a Player's hide" echoes a line spoken by the Duke of York in Shakespeare's *Henry VI*, Part III. The line is "O tiger's heart wrapped in a woman's hide." The pun on Shakespeare's name makes the object of attack clear. Whether written by Greene or Chettle, this passage indicates that Shakespeare was in 1592 an actor who also wrote plays. He was successful enough to provoke the scorn and jealousy of competitors who considered themselves socially and culturally superior.

His work in theater companies. After arriving in London, Shakespeare began an association with one of the city's *repertory* theater companies. These companies consisted of a permanent cast of actors who presented a variety of plays week after week. The companies had aristocratic patrons, and the players were technically servants of the nobles who sponsored them. But the companies were commercial operations that depended on selling tickets to the general public for their income.

Scholars do not know which of the various companies first employed Shakespeare. Scholars have noted connections between Shakespeare's early plays and a number of plays that were performed by the Queen's Men, a company that played in Stratford in 1587. What is certain is that by 1594 Shakespeare was a *sharer* in the Lord Chamberlain's Men. As a sharer, Shakespeare was a stockholder in the company and entitled to a share in the company's profits.

The Lord Chamberlain's Men were one of the most popular companies in London. In large part because of Shakespeare's talents, they would go on to become the dominant company in England during the late 1500s and early 1600s. Shakespeare's position as sharer allowed him to achieve a level of financial success unmatched by other dramatists of the age, many of whom lived in poverty. Most playwrights were freelancers who were paid a one-time fee for their plays and usually worked for several companies. After 1594, Shakespeare maintained a relationship with a single company.

His first poems. From mid-1592 to 1594, London authorities frequently closed the theaters because of repeated outbreaks of plague. Without the income provided by acting and playwriting, Shakespeare turned to poetry. In 1593, *Venus and Adonis* became the first of Shakespeare's works to be published. The publisher was Richard Field, a native of Stratford who may have known Shakespeare in childhood. As was customary at the time, Shakespeare dedicated his volume to a noble patron, in this case Henry Wriothesley, the Earl of Southampton. *Venus and Adonis* proved to be extremely popular and was reprinted at least 15 times in Shakespeare's lifetime.

In 1594, Field printed Shakespeare's *The Rape of Lucrece*. The book's dedication to Southampton suggests a closer acquaintance between the writer

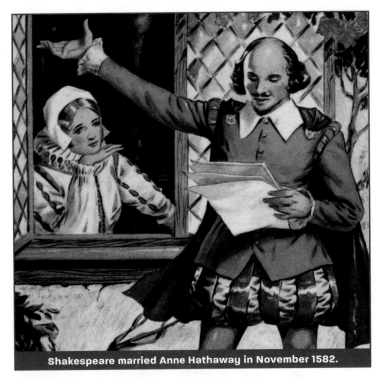

Shakespeare married Anne Hathaway in November 1582.

and the aristocrat. The volume was not as popular as *Venus and Adonis*, but it still sold well. Seven editions had been published by 1632. Despite the commercial success of these early publications, Shakespeare made no effort to make a career of poetry. When the theaters reopened, he returned to acting and playwriting.

The Years of Fame

Throughout the 1590s, Shakespeare's reputation continued to grow. From 1594 to 1608, he was fully involved in the London theater world. In addition to his duties as a sharer and actor in the Lord Chamberlain's Men, he wrote an average of almost two plays a year for his company. During much of this period, Shakespeare ranked as London's most popular playwright, based on the number of times his plays were performed and published. But his reputation was largely that of a popular playwright, not of a writer of unequaled genius.

Few people gave Shakespeare the praise that later generations heaped on him. An exception was the English clergyman and schoolmaster Francis Meres. In 1598, Meres wrote *Palladis Tamia: Wit's Treasury*, a book that has become an important source of information about Shakespeare's career. In this book, Meres said of Shakespeare: "As

Plautus and Seneca are accounted the best for Comedy and Tragedy among the Latins: so *Shakespeare* among the English is the most excellent in both kinds for the stage." Although Meres's praise did not represent everyone's opinion, it indicates that Shakespeare had become an established writer by at least the late 1590s.

The First Globe Theatre

Shakespeare's name did not appear on his earliest published plays, but the 1598 edition of *Love's Labour's Lost* includes his name on the title page. Later editions prominently advertise his authorship, in some cases falsely. In 1599, a printer named William Jaggard published *The Passionate Pilgrim*, a collection of 20 poems supposedly written by Shakespeare. However, the volume offered only five sonnets by Shakespeare, three taken from *Love's Labour's Lost*. By the end of the 1590s, Shakespeare's reputation was being used to sell books. And he had not yet written most of his great tragedies, such as *Hamlet, Othello, King Lear,* and *Macbeth.*

By the late 1590s, Shakespeare not only had become an established writer but also had become prosperous. In October 1596, John Shakespeare was granted a coat of arms, an emblem symbolic of family history, about 25 years after his initial application. Most scholars have suggested that William Shakespeare renewed the application on his father's behalf and paid the necessary fees. To have a coat of arms was an important mark of social standing in England at that time. Certainly Shakespeare was eager to establish himself in Stratford. In May 1597, he purchased New Place, one of the town's two largest houses. Shakespeare obviously remained a Stratford man at heart in spite of his busy, successful life in London. Records

of business dealings and of minor lawsuits reveal that he preferred to invest most of his money in Stratford rather than in London.

The Globe Theatre. As was customary, Shakespeare's company, the Lord Chamberlain's Men, rented performance space. For most of the 1590s, the Lord Chamberlain's Men performed in a building called The Theatre. The English actor and theatrical manager James Burbage had built the structure on leased land. Burbage was the father of the famous actor Richard Burbage, star of the Chamberlain's Men. After a disagreement with the landlord, the company was forced to find new accommodations. Richard Burbage and the Lord Chamberlain's Men dismantled The Theatre and moved it across the River Thames to a new site in Southwark. There they used the old timbers to erect a new theater called the Globe Theatre. The Globe could accommodate 3,000 spectators.

Shakespeare was one of six shareholders who signed the lease for the new site in 1599. He thus became part of the first group of actor-sharers to also be theater owners. Although this arrangement meant considerable financial risk, it also promised to be profitable if the new theater was a success. The Globe proved to be a wise investment, and it remained a home to Shakespeare's acting company until the religious reformers known as Puritans closed the theaters in 1642, during the English Civil War.

The King's Men. In 1603, Queen Elizabeth I died and was succeeded by her cousin James VI of Scotland. As king of England, he became James I. James enjoyed and actively supported the theater. He issued a royal license to Shakespeare and his fellow players, which allowed the company to call itself the King's Men. In return for the license, the actors entertained the king at court on a more or less regular basis.

James's support came at a convenient time. An outbreak of plague in 1603 had closed the theaters for long periods, making theatrical life uncertain. In fact, James's entry into London as king had to be postponed until 1604 because of the plague.

When James finally made his royal entry into London, the King's Men accompanied him. The members of the company were officially known as *grooms of the chamber.* In spite of this title and the name King's Men, the actors were not actually friends of the king. Their relationship to the royal court was simply that of professional entertainers.

The King's Men achieved unequaled success and became London's leading theatrical group. In 1608, the company leased the Blackfriars Theatre for 21 years. The theater stood in a heavily populated London district called Blackfriars. The Blackfriars Theatre had artificial lighting, mainly candles. The theater was probably heated and served as the company's winter playhouse. The King's Men performed at the Globe during the summer.

The period from 1599 to 1608 was a time of extraordinary literary activity for Shakespeare. During these years, he wrote several comedies and almost all the tragedies that have made him famous. Shakespeare's masterpieces during this period include the comedies *Much Ado About Nothing* and *Twelfth Night*; the history *Henry V*; and the tragedies *Antony and Cleopatra*, *Hamlet*, *Julius Caesar*, *King Lear*, *Macbeth*, and *Othello*.

The sonnets. In 1609, a London publisher named Thomas Thorpe published a book called *Shakespeare's Sonnets*. The volume contained more than 150 sonnets that Shakespeare had written over the years. Scholars have long been curious about the book's puzzling dedication. It reads, in modernized spelling: "To the only begetter of these ensuing sonnets Mr. W. H." We do not know whether these are Shakespeare's or Thorpe's words, nor do we know the identity of the mysterious W. H. For additional information on the sonnets, see the section *Shakespeare's poems*.

His Last Years

During his last eight years, Shakespeare was the sole author of only three plays—*Cymbeline*, *The Tempest*, and *The Winter's Tale*. He collaborated with John Fletcher, another English dramatist, in writing three more plays. In the past, some scholars argued that *The Tempest*, written about 1610, was Shakespeare's last play. Such a theory was encouraged by the presence in the play of passages that sound like a farewell to the stage. However, in 1612 and 1613, Shakespeare worked closely with Fletcher, who replaced him as the chief dramatist for the King's Men, on *Cardenio* (now lost), *King Henry VIII*, and *The Two Noble Kinsmen*. In addition, Shakespeare purchased a house in the Blackfriars district of London in 1613. The evidence thus suggests that Shakespeare gradually reduced his activity in London rather than ending it abruptly.

By 1612, Shakespeare had become England's most successful playwright. He apparently divided his time between Stratford and London. He had lodgings in London at least until 1604 and probably until 1611. Such family events as his daughter Susanna's marriage in 1607 and his mother's death in 1608 would likely have called him back to Stratford. By 1612, he may have spent much of his time in the comforts of New Place in Stratford.

On February 10, 1616, Shakespeare's younger daughter, Judith, married Thomas Quiney, the son of his Stratford neighbor Richard Quiney. Six weeks later, Shakespeare revised his will. Within a month, he died. He was buried inside the Stratford parish church. His monument records the day of death as April 23, the generally accepted date of his birth.

The Genius of Shakespeare, published by W. Hobbs & Sons

Shakespeare's son, Hamnet, died in 1596 at the age of 11. The playwright's daughter Susanna had one child, Elizabeth, who bore no children. Shakespeare's daughter Judith gave birth to three boys, but they died before she did. Shakespeare's last direct descendant, his granddaughter Elizabeth, died in 1670.

England of Shakespeare's Day

During most of Shakespeare's lifetime, England was ruled by Queen Elizabeth I. Her reign is often called the Elizabethan Age. Shakespeare's works reflect the cultural, social, and political conditions of the Elizabethan Age. Knowledge of these conditions can provide greater understanding of Shakespeare's plays and poems. For example, most Elizabethans believed in ghosts, witches, and magicians. No biographical evidence exists that Shakespeare held such beliefs, but he used them effectively in his works. Ghosts play an important part in *Hamlet, Julius Caesar, Macbeth,* and *Richard III.* Witches are major characters in *Macbeth.* Prospero, the hero of *The Tempest,* is a magician.

Shakespeare's London had grown from 120,000 inhabitants in 1550 to 200,000 by 1600. By 1650, London contained 375,000 people. This exceptional population growth is remarkable considering London's high mortality rate. The crowded and unsanitary city often experienced outbreaks of plague that regularly reduced the population. Sewage flowed in open ditches that drained into the Thames, and overbuilding led to slum conditions in many parts of the city. However, London continued to grow as the result of a massive flow of migrants, like Shakespeare himself, from the English countryside.

The crowded streets helped give London an air of bustling activity. But other factors also made London an exciting city. It was the commercial and banking center of England and one of the world's chief trading centers. London was also the capital of England. The queen and her court lived there for much of each year, adding to the color and excitement. The city's importance attracted people from throughout England and from other countries. Artists, teachers, musicians, students, and writers all flocked to London to seek advancement.

Although large for its day, London was still small enough so that a person could be close to its cultural and political life. The wide range of knowledge that Shakespeare showed in his plays has amazed many of his admirers. Yet much of this knowledge was the kind that could be absorbed by being in the company of informed people. The range of Shakespeare's learning and the variety of his characters owe something to his involvement in London life.

Elizabethan society. It was once common to claim that in the late 1500s, when Shakespeare first began to write his plays, the English people were experiencing a period of great optimism and patriotism. Under Elizabeth I, they enjoyed a long period of relative peace while continental Europe was burdened by war. In 1588, the English Navy defeated the Spanish Armada, an invasion fleet designed to return Protestant England to Catholicism. After this victory, many English writers declared that God had chosen England to play a special role in world history.

However, there were tensions beneath the surface in English life. England was still a Protestant country on the margins of a Europe dominated by Catholic forces. As the 1500s drew to a close, the aged and childless Elizabeth refused to name a successor, leading to uncertainty about what would follow her death. The possibility of a succession crisis leading to a foreign invasion or civil war disturbed both the political powers and the common people.

The peaceful accession of James I in 1603 eased these anxieties, but the enormous expectations put upon the new king soon led to disappointment. Although initially met with enthusiasm, James quickly made enemies of a number of important parts of English society. The early 1600s saw an increase in dramas portraying corrupt courts, though they were always represented as Italian. To many English people, the world appeared to be deteriorating and becoming, in Hamlet's words, "an unweeded garden/That grows to seed."

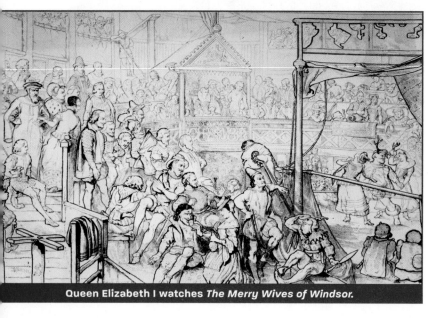

Queen Elizabeth I watches *The Merry Wives of Windsor.*

Certainly Shakespeare's plays reveal a shift from optimism to pessimism. All his early plays, even the histories and the tragedy *Romeo and Juliet*, have an exuberance that sets them apart from the later works. After 1600, Shakespeare's dramas show the confused, gloomy, and often bitter social attitudes of the time. During this period, he wrote his greatest tragedies. Even the comedies *Measure for Measure* and *All's Well That Ends Well* have a bitter quality not found in his earlier comedies. A character in the tragedy *King Lear* cries out in despair, "As flies to wanton boys are we to the gods./ They kill us for their sport." These lines reflect the uncertainties of the time.

Elizabethans were keenly aware of death and the brevity of life. They lived in constant fear of plague. When an epidemic struck, they saw victims carted off to common graves. Yet death and violence also fascinated many Elizabethans. Londoners flocked to public beheadings of traitors, whose heads were exhibited on poles. They also watched as criminals were hanged, and they saw the corpses dangle from the gallows for days. Crowds also flocked to such bloodthirsty sports as bearbaiting and bullbaiting, in which dogs attacked a bear or bull tied to a post.

Elizabethan literature mirrored the violence and death so characteristic of English life. Shakespeare's tragedies, like other Elizabethan tragedies, involve the murder or suicide of many of the leading characters.

In spite of their tolerance of cruelty, Elizabethans were extremely sensitive to beauty and grace. They loved many forms of literature, including poetic drama, narrative and lyric poetry, prose fiction, and essays. People of all classes enjoyed music, and English composers rivaled the finest composers in all Europe.

Instrumental music, singing, and dancing are important in Elizabethan drama. Some of Shakespeare's romantic comedies might almost be called "musical comedies." *Twelfth Night*, for example, includes instrumental serenades and rousing drinking songs as well as other songs ranging from sad to comic. Dances form part of the action in *The Tempest*, *The Winter's Tale*, and *Romeo and Juliet*.

The English ruler. Shakespeare's 10 history plays deal with English kings and nobility. Nine of the plays concern events from 1398 to the 1540s. A knowledge of these events and of the

Queen Elizabeth I

Elizabethans' attitude toward their own ruler can help a playgoer or reader understand Shakespeare's histories.

During the 100 years before Elizabeth I became queen, violent political and religious conflicts had weakened the throne. From 1455 to the 1480s, a series of particularly bitter civil wars tore England apart. The wars centered on the efforts of two rival families—the House of Lancaster and the House of York—to control the throne. The wars are called the Wars of the Roses because Lancaster's emblem was said to be a red rose and York's a white rose. Four of Shakespeare's historical plays deal with the Wars of the Roses. These plays, in historical order, are *Henry VI*, Parts I, II, and III; and *Richard III*. A second sequence of plays, *Richard II*, *Henry IV*, Parts I and II, and *Henry V*, deal with earlier events that led up to the Wars of the Roses. These eight plays together describe events leading up to the establishment of the Tudor *dynasty* (line of rulers) and form an extended and sophisticated meditation on a long and turbulent period in English history.

Religion. The two history plays that are not part of the major sequence running from *Richard II* to *Richard III* are *King John* and *Henry VIII*. Both deal largely with the problem of religious conflict. King Henry VIII broke with the Roman Catholic Church and tentatively moved the English church toward Protestantism. His son, Edward IV, was fully committed to the Protestant cause and instituted sweeping reforms after he came to the throne in 1547. After Edward's early death, his sister Mary succeeded in 1553 and returned England to the Catholic faith. Mary's short reign was followed by the accession of Elizabeth, who reestablished Protestantism in 1558. Thus, from 1534, when Henry first declared independence from Rome, to 1558, when Elizabeth took the throne, every change in monarch was accompanied by a change in the official religion. A change in religion was always accompanied by attempts to suppress, often violently, those who remained loyal to the other faith.

Inside the modern Globe Theatre

As a result of the dynastic struggles of the 1400s and the religious conflicts of the 1500s, many Elizabethans came to believe that a strong but just ruler was necessary to keep social order. In seeing Shakespeare's history plays, they would have understood his treatment of royal responsibilities as well as royal privileges. Elizabethans would have been aware of the dangers of a weak king—dangers that Shakespeare described in *Richard II*. They would also have been alert to the dangers of a cruel and unjust ruler, which Shakespeare portrayed in *Richard III*.

The Elizabethan Theater

Shakespeare wrote his plays to suit the abilities of particular actors and the tastes of specific audiences. The physical structure of the theaters in which his works were presented also influenced his playwriting. He used many dramatic devices that

were popular in the Elizabethan theater but are no longer widely used. Modern readers and theatergoers can enjoy Shakespeare's plays more fully if they know about the various theatrical influences that helped shape them.

Theater buildings. By the late 1500s, Elizabethan plays were being performed in two kinds of theater buildings—later called *public* and *private* theaters. Public theaters were larger than private ones and held at least 2,500 people. They were built around a courtyard that had no roof. Public theaters gave performances only during daylight hours because they had no artificial lights. Private theaters were smaller, roofed structures. They had candlelight for evening performances. Private theaters charged higher prices and were designed to attract a higher-class audience. The King's Men only acquired an indoor theater, the Blackfriars, in 1608 and began to perform there in 1609.

Most of Shakespeare's plays were written for the public theater. However, *The Winter's Tale*, *Cymbeline*, and *The Tempest* all take advantage of the different kinds of staging made possible by the Blackfriars. For example, these later plays used the more sophisticated stage machinery to represent flight. The more intimate space also allowed the inclusion of more musical interludes, both during the plays and during intermissions. Although the Blackfriars had an important impact on these later plays, what follows will focus chiefly on the design and structure of public theaters.

In 1576, James Burbage built England's first successful public theater, called simply The Theatre. It stood in a suburb north of London, outside the strict supervision of London government authorities. Soon other public theaters were built in the London suburbs. These theaters included the Curtain, the Rose, and the Swan. In 1599, Shakespeare and his associates built the Globe Theatre. Detailed evidence of how the Elizabethan public theaters looked is limited. But scholars have been able to reconstruct the general characteristics of a typical public theater.

The structure that enclosed the courtyard of a public theater was round, square, or many-sided. In most theaters, it probably consisted of three levels of galleries and stood about 32 feet (10 meters) high. The courtyard, called the pit, measured about 55 feet (17 meters) in diameter. The stage occupied one end of the pit. For the price of admission, the poorer spectators, called *groundlings*, could stand in the pit and watch the show. For an extra fee, wealthier patrons could sit on benches in the galleries.

The stage of a public theater was a large platform that projected into the pit. This arrangement allowed the audience to watch from the front and sides. The performers, nearly surrounded by spectators, thus had close contact with most of their audience.

Actors entered and left the stage through two or more doorways at the back of the stage. Behind the doorways were *tiring* (dressing) rooms. At the rear of the stage, there was a curtained *discovery* space. Scholars disagree about the details of this feature. But the space could be used to "discover"—that is, reveal—one or two characters by opening the curtains. Characters could also hide there or eavesdrop on conversations among characters up front on the main stage. The gallery that hung over the back of the main stage served as an upper stage. It could be used as a balcony or the top of a castle wall. The upper stage allowed Elizabethan dramatists to give their plays vertical action in addition to the usual horizontal movement. Some theaters may have had a small third-level room for musicians.

A half roof projected over the upper stage and the back part of the main stage. Atop the roof was a hut that contained machinery to produce sound effects and various special effects, such as the lowering of an actor playing a god. The underside of the hut was sometimes called the *heavens*. Two pillars supported the structure. The underside of the heavens was richly painted, and the interior of the theater undoubtedly had a number of other decorative features.

The main stage had a large trap door. Actors playing the parts of ghosts and spirits could rise and disappear through the door. The trap door, when opened, could also serve as a grave.

Scenic effects. Unlike most modern dramas, Elizabethan plays did not depend on scenery to indicate the *setting* (place) of the action. Generally, the setting was unknown to the audience until the characters identified it with a few lines of dialogue. In addition, the main stage had no curtain. One scene could follow another quickly because there was no curtain to close and open and no scenery to change. The lack of scenery also allowed the action to flow freely from place to place, as in modern motion pictures. The action of Shakespeare's *Antony and Cleopatra*, for example, shifts smoothly and easily back and forth between ancient Egypt and Rome.

Although the stage lacked scenery, the actors employed various *props* (objects used on stage), such as thrones, swords, banners, rocks, trees, tables, and beds. *Richard III* calls for two tents, one at each end of the stage.

Costumes and sound effects. The absence of scenery did not result in dull or drab productions. Acting companies spent much money on colorful costumes, largely to produce visual splendor. Flashing swords and swirling banners also added color and excitement.

Sound effects had an important part in Elizabethan drama. Trumpet blasts and drum rolls were common. Sometimes unusual sounds were created, such as "the noise of a sea-fight" called for in *Antony and Cleopatra*. Music also played a vital role. Shakespeare filled *Twelfth Night* with songs. In *Antony and Cleopatra*, the playwright included mysterious-sounding chords to set the mood before a fatal battle.

Acting companies consisted of only men and boys because women did not perform on the Elizabethan stage. A typical acting company had 8 to 12 sharers, a number of salaried workers, and apprentices. The sharers were the company's lead-

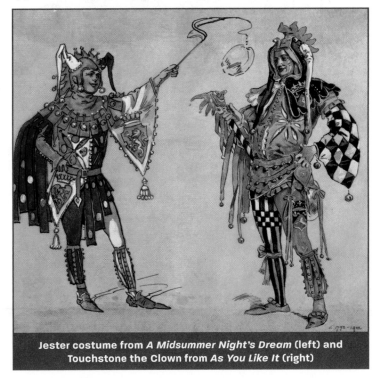

Jester costume from *A Midsummer Night's Dream* (left) and Touchstone the Clown from *As You Like It* (right)

ing actors as well as its stockholders. They had charge of the company's business activities. They bought plays and costumes, rented theaters, paid fees, and split the profits. The salaried workers, who were called *hirelings*, took minor roles in the plays, performed the music, served as prompters, and did various odd jobs. The apprentices were boys who played the roles of women and children.

The acting companies operated under the sponsorship either of a member of the royal family or of an important noble. Most sponsorships were in name only and did not include financial support. From 1594 to 1603, Shakespeare's company was sponsored, in turn, by the first and second Lord Hunsdon, a father and son. The first Lord Hunsdon held the important court position of lord chamberlain until he died in 1596. In 1597, his son became lord chamberlain. Thus from 1594 to 1603, Shakespeare's company was mostly known as the Lord Chamberlain's Men. After James I became king of England in 1603, he singled out the company for royal favor. It was then known as the King's Men.

Woodcut of William Kempe dancing a jig

Shakespeare was unusual among Elizabethan playwrights. He not only wrote exclusively for his own company but also served as an actor and sharer in it. The close association between Shakespeare, his fellow actors, and the conditions of production had enormous influence on his dramas. Shakespeare wrote most of his plays with a particular theater building in mind and for performers whom he knew well. Each major actor in the company specialized in a certain type of role. For example, one played the leading tragic characters, and

another the main comic characters. Still another actor played old men. Shakespeare wrote his plays to suit the talents of specific performers. He knew when he created a Hamlet, Othello, or King Lear that the character would be interpreted by Richard Burbage, the company's leading tragic actor.

Shakespeare's comedies reveal the influence that specific actors had on the creation of his plays. From 1594 to 1599, the company's leading comic actor was Will Kempe. During this time, many of the comedies seem designed to take advantage of Kempe's talents as a physical comedian who specialized in playing rustic characters. He was especially known for performing *jigs*, short pieces of song and dance with simple plots that were performed at the end of the main play. After Kempe left the company, Robert Armin took his place, and the style of Shakespeare's comedy shifted noticeably. The playwright skillfully used Armin's more sophisticated and intellectual comic talents in such lively but thoughtful comedies as *Twelfth Night* and *As You Like It*.

Elizabethan acting companies were eager to stage plays that had roles for all their major performers. This, in part, explains the appearance of comic characters—such as the first gravedigger in *Hamlet*, the porter in *Macbeth*, and the fool in *King Lear*—in even the most violent and severe of Shakespeare's tragedies.

The exact nature of Elizabethan acting style remains a puzzle. Parodies of acting—such as the "Pyramus and Thisbe" play in *A Midsummer Night's Dream* or the "Mousetrap" in *Hamlet*—provide some clues about what was considered good acting. Occasional comments on performance, such as Hamlet's famous advice to the players, provide another way in which scholars can reconstruct standards of performance. In addition, a consideration of the physical conditions of the theater allows for some conclusions. Most scholars agree that Elizabethan actors spoke their lines more rapidly than modern performers do. In addition, Elizabethan actors had an especially clear and musical speaking style. This method of speaking developed from years of acting experience and from the Elizabethan love for the musical possibilities of the English language.

Dramatic conventions. The writing and staging of Elizabethan plays were strongly influenced by various dramatic *conventions* of that time—customs that the audience accepted and did not take literally. The most widespread convention was the use of poetic dialogue. Although Shakespeare's plays contain prose and rhymed verse, he chiefly used an unrhymed, rhythmical form of poetry called *blank verse*.

Two common conventions that audiences expected were *soliloquies* and *asides*. In a soliloquy, an actor, who is alone on the stage, recites a speech directly to the audience. Or he speaks aloud to himself his thoughts and feelings. In an aside, a character speaks words that the other characters onstage are not supposed to hear. Audiences also liked and expected long lyrical speeches. Many of these speeches had little direct relation to the play's action. Mercutio's "Queen Mab" speech in *Romeo and Juliet* is a famous example.

The boy actors were thoroughly trained and highly skilled, but Shakespeare was always aware of the artificial nature of boys playing female roles. Frequently, the audience was reminded of this fact, as when Cleopatra worries that the victorious Romans will make her watch "Some squeaking Cleopatra boy my greatness." This forces the audience to recognize that the actor voicing this concern is himself a boy. At the same time, the fiction of Cleopatra's remarkable attractiveness succeeds largely on the strength of Shakespeare's poetry. The same is true of other beautiful women in the plays. "The Beauty too rich for use, for earth too dear" of Juliet lies more in Shakespeare's language than in the physical attractions of the performer.

Disguise played an important part in Elizabethan drama. Audiences enjoyed comic situations in which a boy played a girl character who disguised herself as a boy. Female characters masquerade as men in several of Shakespeare's plays, including *As You Like It*, *The Merchant of Venice*, and *Twelfth Night*. Social conditions also made disguise an effective theatrical device in Elizabethan times. The Elizabethans recognized sharp distinctions between social classes and between occupations. These distinctions were emphasized by striking differences in dress. Nobles were immediately recognized by their clothing, as were doctors, lawyers, merchants, or pages. Characters could thus easily disguise themselves by wearing the garments of a certain social class or occupation.

Another convention found in Shakespeare's plays is called the "bed trick" and is used in *All's Well That Ends Well* and *Measure for Measure*. In this convention, a male character is tricked into believing that he has had sexual relations with one woman when another has secretly substituted herself for the object of his desire.

Shakespeare's audiences. Shakespeare wrote most of his plays for audiences with a broad social background. To the Globe Theatre came a cross section of London society, ranging from apprentices skipping work to members of the nobility passing the time. But most of the Globe's audience consisted of prosperous citizens, such as merchants, craftworkers, and their wives, and members of the upper class. The theaters of London were an attraction, and visitors to the city were often part of the audience.

Shakespeare's plays were also produced at the royal court, in the houses of noble families, and sometimes in universities and law schools. For most of his career, he thus wrote plays that had to appeal to people of many backgrounds and tastes.

Shakespeare's Plays

Scholars do not know exactly what Shakespeare wrote. With the possible exception of a short passage from *Sir Thomas More*, no manuscripts in Shakespeare's handwriting exist. Thus, editors have had to sort through the early printed documents to determine what was written by Shakespeare. Their labors have been greatly assisted by Shakespeare's *Comedies, Histories & Tragedies*, published in 1623. This volume, called the First Folio, was published by a group of publishers led by Isaac Jaggard and Edward Blount. The publishers were assisted by two leading members of the King's Men, John Heminge and Henry Condell, who were able to provide copies of the 18 plays that had not appeared before in print. Along with these 18 plays, the First Folio republished an additional 18 plays, making a total of 36.

The 36 plays in the First Folio form the basis of what has become known as Shakespeare's *canon* (accepted complete works). Although *attributed* (credited) to Shakespeare in versions published in 1609 and 1611, *Pericles* was not included in the First Folio. Most scholars accept the play as Shakespeare's, though many argue that it is a collaboration with the English dramatist George Wilkins.

More open to dispute is *The Two Noble Kinsmen*, thought to be a collaboration between Shakespeare and John Fletcher. Past scholars regularly excluded this play from the canon. Since the mid-1900s, however, most collections of Shakespeare's works have included it, bringing the total number of plays to 38. Collaboration, which was common among playwrights of the period, is one of the complicating factors in determining what Shakespeare wrote. It is now generally accepted that several plays in the First Folio are not solely his work.

Further complicating the establishment of the canon is the existence of various *apocryphal plays*—that is, plays not now considered Shakespearean texts. However, *Edward III*, long considered an apocryphal play, has been included in a number of prestigious editions. There are also two lost plays, *Love's Labour's Won* and *Cardenio*, credited to Shakespeare in records of his day.

The Shakespeare canon is not permanently fixed. New attributions remain possible. But when considered as a whole, the body of work accepted as Shakespearean has remained remarkably stable over the last 300 years.

Much Shakespearean research has been devoted to determining the order in which Shakespeare's plays were written and first performed. The Elizabethans kept no records of premieres of plays, and no newspapers existed to provide opening-night reviews. The publication dates of the individual plays provide some help because plays were almost always performed before they were published. But because there was often a considerable delay between performance and publication, the publication dates do not indicate exactly when a play was performed.

To establish the order in which Shakespeare's plays were probably written and first performed, scholars have relied on a variety of literary and historical evidence. This evidence includes records of performances, mention of Shakespeare's works by other Elizabethan writers, and references in Shakespeare's plays to events of the day. Scholars can also roughly date a play by Shakespeare's literary style. But for many of the plays, precise dates remain uncertain.

The First Folio divided the plays into three categories—comedies, histories, and tragedies. Modern scholars have added a fourth category, romance. At each stage of his career, Shakespeare tended to concentrate on a certain kind of drama, depending on the tastes of his audience at that time. For example, he wrote 9 of his 10 histories during a period when such plays were especially popular.

Shakespeare generally followed the Elizabethan custom of basing his plots on published historical and literary works. But he differed from most other dramatists in one important way. In retelling a story, Shakespeare shaped the borrowed material with such genius that he produced a work of art that was uniquely different from its source.

This section describes the plots and notable characteristics of the 38 existing plays that make up the generally accepted canon of Shakespeare's dramatic work. The plays have been divided into four periods, each of which reflects a general phase of Shakespeare's artistic development. Within each period, the plays are discussed in the order in which they were probably first performed.

For readers interested in a specific play, the *Shakespeare's plays* table with this article lists the plays alphabetically and gives the period in which a description of each play may be found.

The First Period (1590–1594)

The plays of Shakespeare's first period have much in common, though they consist of comedies, histories, and a tragedy. The plots of these plays tend to follow their sources more closely than do the plots of Shakespeare's later works. The plots also tend to consist of a series of loosely related episodes, rather than a tightly integrated dramatic structure. In addition, the plays generally emphasize events more than the portrayal of character.

In his first period, Shakespeare's use of language indicates that he was still struggling to develop his own flexible poetic style. For example, Shakespeare's descriptive poetry in this period is apt to be flowery, rather than directly related to the development of the characters or the story. Speeches often use highly patterned schemes that involve word and sound repetitions.

The Comedy of Errors is a comedy chiefly based on the play *Menaechmi* by the Roman playwright Plautus. The play was first performed during the period from 1589 to 1594 and first published in 1623.

The action in *The Comedy of Errors* takes place in the ancient Greek city of Ephesus. The plot deals with identical twin brothers, both named Antipholus. Each brother has a servant named Dromio, who also happen to be twin brothers. The twins of each set were separated as children, and neither twin knows where his brother is living. One twin and his servant live in Ephesus. Their brothers live in Syracuse. After Antipholus and

Dromio of Syracuse arrive in Ephesus, a series of mistaken identities and comical mix-ups develops before the twin brothers are reunited.

The Comedy of Errors has little character portrayal or fine poetry. But the play is filled with intrigue, broad humor, and physical comedy, which makes it highly effective theater.

Henry VI, Parts I, II, and III, are three related histories partly based on *The Union of the Two Noble and Illustrious Families of Lancaster and York* (1548) by the English historian Edward Hall and on the *Chronicles of England, Scotland, and Ireland* (1577) by the English historian Raphael Holinshed, often called *Holinshed's Chronicles*. Each part was probably first performed during the period from 1589 to 1592. Part I was published in 1623, Part II in 1594, and Part III in 1595.

The three parts of *Henry VI* present a panoramic view of English history in the 1400s. The action begins with the death of King Henry V in 1422. It ends with the Battle of Tewkesbury in 1471. The plays vividly mirror the Wars of the Roses—the series of bloody conflicts between the houses of York and Lancaster for control of the English throne. Part I deals largely with wars between England and France. But all three plays dramatize the plots and counterplots that marked the struggle between the two royal houses.

The *Henry VI* plays are confusing to read because of their large and shifting casts of characters. The plays are more successful on the stage. In performance, the constant action, exaggerated language, and flashes of brilliant characterization result in lively historical drama.

Richard III is a history partly based on Hall's 1548 *The Union of the Two Noble and Illustrious Families of Lancaster and York* and on Holinshed's *Chronicles* of 1577. The play was probably first performed from 1592 to 1594 and was first published in 1597.

The play deals with the end of the Wars of the Roses. It opens with the hunchbacked Richard, Duke of Gloucester, confiding his villainous plans to the audience. He addresses the audience in a famous soliloquy that begins, "Now is the winter of our discontent/ Made glorious summer by this sun of York." Richard refers to the success of his brother Edward, Duke of York. Edward has overthrown Henry VI of the House of Lancaster and taken the English throne. Now weak and ill, he rules England as Edward IV. Richard wants to

Act II, Scene V, from *Henry VI*, Part I

gain the crown for himself. He has his other brother, the Duke of Clarence, murdered. After King Edward dies, Richard sends the Prince of Wales, the dead king's son, and the prince's younger brother to the Tower of London. After seizing the throne as Richard III, he has the two boys murdered.

Before long, Richard's allies turn against him and join forces with the Earl of Richmond, a member of the House of Lancaster. Richmond's forces defeat Richard's army at the Battle of Bosworth Field. Richard utters the famous cry "A horse! a horse! my kingdom for a horse!" after his mount is slain during the battle. Richmond finally kills Richard and takes the throne as King Henry VII.

Richard is a superb theatrical portrait of evil. Although Richard is thoroughly wicked, his soliloquies give his character depth, and his frequent asides engage the audience. He pursues his schemes with such energy and resourcefulness that he wins the grudging admiration of the audience.

The Taming of the Shrew is a comedy possibly based on *The Taming of a Shrew* by an unknown English playwright and on *Supposes*

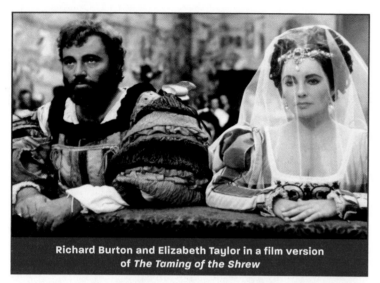

Richard Burton and Elizabeth Taylor in a film version of *The Taming of the Shrew*

(1566), a comedy by the English author George Gascoigne. Shakespeare's version was probably first performed in 1593 and was first published in 1623.

This play dramatizes how Petruchio, an Italian gentleman, woos the beautiful but *shrewish* (bad-tempered) Katherine, whose biting tongue has discouraged other suitors. Petruchio marries her. But before and after the wedding, he systematically humiliates Katherine to cure her of her temper. After many comical clashes between the two, Petruchio's strategy succeeds and Katherine becomes an obedient wife. At this point, Petruchio reveals himself to be genuinely fond of Katherine.

The Taming of the Shrew is a broad and vigorous comedy that provides two outstanding roles in the characters of the battling lovers. The parts of Petruchio and Katherine have been a showcase for generations of gifted actors.

Titus Andronicus is a tragedy possibly based in part on *The History of Titus Andronicus*, a story by an unknown English author. The play was probably first performed about 1594 and was first published in 1594. Some scholars believe the English dramatist George Peele wrote part of the play.

This play is a revenge tragedy, which was popular in the Elizabethan theater. The action takes place in and around ancient Rome and involves a succession of violent acts. The central conflict is between Tamora, the captured queen of the Goths, and Titus Andronicus, a Roman general. The exchange of insults and injuries reaches its climax at a feast in which Titus serves Tamora a pie containing the remains of two of her sons.

In spite of the play's emphasis on spectacular violence, it does have moments of highly charged and effective poetry. The most complex character is Aaron the Moor, Tamora's lover and a self-declared villain in the mold of Richard III. Aaron's plotting drives much of the action, but when the child he has fathered with Tamora is threatened with death, he displays an unexpected warmth and humanity.

The Two Gentlemen of Verona is a comedy partly based on *Diana* (about 1559), a story by the Spanish author Jorge de Montemayor, and on *The Book of the Governor* (1531), an educational work by the English author Sir Thomas Elyot. The play was probably first performed in 1594 and was first published in 1623.

The play is a witty comedy of love and friendship set in Italy. Two friends from Verona, Valentine and Proteus, meet in Milan. They soon become rivals for the love of Silvia, the daughter of the Duke of Milan. Valentine discovers Proteus as his friend is about to force his attentions on Silvia. Proteus repents his action, and Valentine forgives him. Valentine then tells his friend that he can have Silvia. But Valentine's generosity becomes unnecessary. Proteus learns that Julia, his former mistress, has followed him to Milan disguised as a page. Proteus realizes that he really loves Julia. He marries her at the end of the play, and Valentine marries Silvia.

In *The Two Gentlemen of Verona*, Shakespeare introduced several features and devices that he later used so effectively in the great romantic comedies of his second period. For example, he included beautiful songs, such as "Who Is Silvia?"; scenes in a peaceful, idealized forest; and a young woman, disguised as a page, braving the dangers of the world.

King John is a history primarily based on *The Troublesome Reign of John, King of England* (1591), a play by an unknown English author. *King John* also uses *Holinshed's Chronicles* and may draw on other historical sources as well. Shakespeare's play was probably first performed about 1594 and was first published in 1623.

The story concerns the efforts of England's King John to defend his throne against the claims of his older brother's son, Arthur, the young Duke of Brittany. John defeats and captures Arthur, who is supported by the king of France. When the young prince dies under suspicious circumstances, many of John's nobles abandon him and join an invading French force. The rebellious English lords only return to John when they learn that the French, if victorious, will execute their English supporters. A long war is avoided by the intervention of Pandulph, the papal representative, just as King John dies either from poison or illness.

Although King John is on morally questionable ground, he is supported by Philip Faulconbridge, the illegitimate son of Richard I. Faulconbridge is arguably the moral center of the play. His sarcastic and witty comments on the action orient the audience's response to the play, which is deeply concerned with loyalty, allegiance, and legitimacy.

The Second Period (1595–1600)

During his second period, Shakespeare brought historical drama and Elizabethan romantic comedy to near perfection. Particularly in his histories and comedies of this period, Shakespeare demonstrated his genius for weaving various dramatic actions into a unified plot, rather than writing a series of loosely connected episodes. Throughout the second period, Shakespeare steadily developed the matchless gift for characterization that marks the great tragedies he produced in the early 1600s.

A Midsummer Night's Dream is a comedy probably based on several sources, none of which was a chief source. The play was probably first performed in 1595 and was first published in 1600.

The play begins in Athens, Greece, with preparations for a wedding between Theseus, Duke of Athens, and Hippolyta, queen of the Amazons. But most of the action takes place in an enchanted forest outside Athens. In the forest, two young men, Lysander and Demetrius, and two young women, Hermia and Helena, wander about together after they become lost. Lysander and Demetrius both love Hermia and ignore Helena, who loves Demetrius. Oberon, king of the fairies, orders the mischievous elf Puck to anoint Demetrius's eyes with magic drops that will make him love Helena. However, Puck mistakenly anoints Lysander's eyes, creating much comic confusion. Puck finally straightens out the mix-up.

In a subplot, Oberon quarrels with Titania, his queen. He then anoints Titania's eyes with the magic drops while she sleeps so that when she awakens, she will love the first living thing she sees.

At this time, Nick Bottom, a weaver, and his comical friends are rehearsing a play they plan to present at the duke's wedding. When Titania awakens, she sees Bottom and falls in love with him. To increase Titania's humiliation, Puck gives Bottom the head of a donkey. Aided by her fairy attendants, Titania woos Bottom until Oberon takes pity on her and has Puck remove the spell. The play ends with the duke's wedding. The two young couples—Lysander and Hermia and Demetrius and Helena—also marry during this ceremony. Bottom and his friends perform their hilariously silly play at the wedding celebration.

For *A Midsummer Night's Dream*, Shakespeare wrote some of his most richly lyrical poetry. Oberon tells Puck, "I know a bank where the wild thyme blows / Where oxlips and the nodding violet grows." The passage transports the audience in imagination to a magic wood where flowers bloom and fairies play. Shakespeare balanced this romantic fantasy with the rough humor of Bottom and his friends. The self-absorbed Bottom ranks as one of Shakespeare's finest comic figures. The comedy also has a serious side. Gaily but firmly, it makes fun of romantic love. As Puck comments, "Lord, what fools these mortals be!"

Richard II is a history partly based on *Holinshed's Chronicles*. The play was probably first performed in 1595 and was first published in 1597.

As the play begins, King Richard exiles his cousin Bolingbroke from England. Later, Richard seizes Bolingbroke's property. While Richard fights rebels in Ireland, Bolingbroke returns to England and demands his property. After Richard learns of Bolingbroke's return, he hurries back to England to find his cousin leading a force of nobles who are discontented with Richard's rule. Instead of preparing the royal army to fight Bolingbroke, Richard wastes his time in outbursts of self-pity. He finally gives up his crown to Bolingbroke without a fight. Bolingbroke then orders that Richard be put in prison.

After Bolingbroke is crowned Henry IV, the imprisoned Richard is killed by a knight who mistakenly believed that the new king wanted Richard murdered. At the end of the play, Henry vows to make a journey to the Holy Land to pay for Richard's death.

In *Richard II*, Shakespeare seriously explored for the first time the idea that a person's character determines his fate. The play is a study of a weak,

Balcony scene from *Romeo and Juliet*

end, the men propose to their visitors, who promise to give their answer in a year and a day.

This witty comedy has more references to events of the day than do any of Shakespeare's other plays. Many of these references have lost their meaning for modern audiences, which makes numerous passages difficult to understand. In addition, much of the language is elaborate and artificial. But Shakespeare included two simple and lovely songs—"When Daisies Pied and Violets Blue" and "When Icicles Hang by the Wall." *Love's Labour's Lost* also has handsome scenes of spectacle and several entertaining comic characters.

Romeo and Juliet is a tragedy based on *The Tragicall Historye of Romeus and Juliet* (1562), a poem by the English author Arthur Brooke. The play was probably first performed in 1596 and was first published in 1597.

Romeo and Juliet deals with two teenage lovers in Verona, Italy, who are caught in a bitter feud between their families, the Montagues and the Capulets. Romeo, a Montague, and his friends come uninvited to a masked ball given by the Capulets. At the ball, Romeo meets Juliet, a Capulet, and they fall in love. The next day, the couple are secretly married by Friar Laurence. Returning from the wedding, Romeo meets Juliet's cousin Tybalt, who tries to pick a fight with him. But Romeo refuses to fight his new relative. To defend the Montague honor, Romeo's friend Mercutio accepts Tybalt's challenge. As Romeo attempts to part the young men, Tybalt stabs and kills Mercutio. In revenge, Romeo kills Tybalt. As a result, Romeo is exiled from Verona.

Juliet's father, unaware that she is already married, tries to force her to marry a kinsman named Paris. To allow Juliet to escape from her father's demand, Friar Laurence gives Juliet a drug that puts her into a deathlike sleep for 42 hours. The friar sends a messenger to the exiled Romeo to tell him of the drug, but the messenger is delayed. Romeo hears that Juliet is dead and hurries to the tomb where she has been placed. There, he takes poison and dies by Juliet's side. Juliet awakens to find her husband dead and stabs herself. The discovery of the dead lovers convinces the two families that they must end their feud.

The popularity of *Romeo and Juliet* owes much to Shakespeare's sympathy for the young people in the play. Although the play does suggest that the boldness of young love is dangerous, Shakespeare

self-centered man. Richard becomes so out of touch with reality that his only defense of his kingdom is the hope that his "master, God omnipotent, / Is mustering in his clouds on our behalf / Armies of pestilence." When he faces the certain loss of his crown, Richard compares himself to Christ, who "in twelve, / Found truth in all but one; I, in twelve thousand none."

Love's Labour's Lost is a comedy probably based on several sources, none of which was a chief source. The play was probably first performed in 1596 and was first published in 1598.

King Ferdinand of Navarre and his friends Berowne, Longaville, and Dumain vow to live in seclusion without the company of women for three years to pursue philosophical study. But the princess of France unexpectedly arrives at the king's court with three female companions. The comedy centers on the efforts of the men to woo the women while pretending to keep their vow. At the play's

does not present Romeo and Juliet as responsible for their fate. Instead, the play draws attention to the violence and aggressiveness that shapes the adult world. The success of the play also comes from effective characterizations and intensely lyrical poetry. Shakespeare's language shows signs of the simpler, more direct style he would use in his later tragedies.

The Merchant of Venice is a comedy partly based on a story in *Il Pecorone*, a collection of tales written about 1378 by the Italian author Giovanni Fiorentino. The play was probably first performed in 1597 and was first published in 1600.

Antonio, a merchant in Venice, Italy, borrows money from the Jewish moneylender Shylock to help his friend Bassanio. Antonio has promised Shylock a pound of his flesh if he does not repay the loan in three months. The three months pass, and Shylock demands his money. But Antonio cannot pay. Shylock then demands the pound of flesh.

Meanwhile, Bassanio has courted and married the beautiful and gifted heiress Portia. She has a plan to save Antonio from Shylock. Shylock goes to court to demand the flesh. Portia, disguised as a learned lawyer, asks him to reconsider in a famous speech that begins, "The quality of mercy is not strained." Shylock remains firm. Portia then explains that he can, according to the contract, take one pound of flesh but not a drop of blood. If Shylock spills any blood, he will not only forfeit his own property but his life as well. Shylock drops his demand, and Antonio is saved.

In *The Merchant of Venice*, Shakespeare combined comic intrigue with a vivid portrait of hatred and greed. Although the play ends happily for everyone except Shylock and the melancholy Bassanio, it is not a light-hearted comedy. In Shakespeare's time, both the church and the state considered moneylending at high interest a crime. Shylock was thus a natural object of scorn. On the surface, Shakespeare's view of him reflected the attitudes of the day. But the dramatist treated the moneylender as a human and even sympathetic person. For example, Shakespeare provided Shylock with an eloquent statement of how it feels to be part of a harshly treated minority: "If you prick us, do we not bleed? If you tickle us, do we not laugh? If you poison us, do we not die? And if you wrong us, shall we not revenge?"

Henry IV, Parts I and II, are two related histories based on *Holinshed's Chronicles* and on *The Famous Victories of Henry the Fifth*, a play by an unknown English author. Part I was likely first performed in 1597 and was first published in 1598. Part II was probably first performed in 1598 and was first published in 1600.

The two parts of *Henry IV* dramatize events that follow the murder of England's King Richard II. In Part I, the guilt-ridden Henry IV wants to go to the Holy Land in repentance for Richard's death. But political unrest in England prevents him. At the same time, Prince Hal, his son, leads an apparently irresponsible life with his brawling friends, led by the fat, jolly knight Sir John Falstaff. Falstaff's clowning provides most of the play's humor. The king quarrels with Henry Percy, known as Hotspur, the fiery young son of the powerful Earl of Northumberland. As a result of the quarrel, the Percy family revolts. At the Battle of Shrewsbury, Hal reveals himself to be a brave warrior and kills Hotspur.

Part II of *Henry IV* also has many scenes of Falstaff's clowning. These scenes are set against the background of the continuing Percy rebellion and the approaching death of Henry IV, who is ill. Hal's brother, Prince John, finally defeats the rebels. The king dies, and Hal takes the throne as Henry V. He quickly reveals his royal qualities and rejects Falstaff and his friends, telling them to stay away until they have abandoned their wild living.

Of the two plays, Part I is more memorable. It introduces Falstaff, best characterized by his comment in Part II that "I am not only witty in myself, but the cause that wit is in other men." Falstaff is a bragging, lying, and thievish drunkard. But his faults are balanced by his clever sense of humor, his contagious love of life, and his refusal to take either himself or the world seriously. Falstaff is one of the great comic roles in the theater.

As You Like It is a comedy partly based on *Rosalynde* (1590), a novel by the English author Thomas Lodge. The play was probably first performed in 1599 and was first published in 1623.

Rosalind and her cousin Celia leave the court of Celia's father, Duke Frederick, after he unjustly banishes Rosalind. Accompanied by Touchstone, the court jester, the two young women take refuge in the Forest of Arden. Also in the forest are Orlando, who loves Rosalind; Jaques, a melancholy philosopher; Audrey, a goatherd; Silvius, a shepherd; and Phebe, a shepherdess. Duke Frederick's brother, who is Rosalind's father and the rightful ruler of the land, also lives in the forest with a band of merry outlaws.

Rosalind, disguised as a young shepherd named Ganymede, meets Orlando in the forest. Not recognizing the young woman in disguise, Orlando agrees to pretend that Ganymede is Rosalind so he can practice his declarations of love. Rosalind finally reveals her identity and marries Orlando. Oliver, Orlando's formerly wicked brother, marries Celia, Touchstone marries Audrey, and Silvius marries Phebe. The news that Rosalind's father has been restored to his dukedom completes the comedy's happy ending.

Like many other Elizabethan romantic comedies, *As You Like It* concerns young lovers who pursue their happy destiny in a world seemingly far removed from reality. Although evil threatens, it never harms. Shakespeare enriched the play with beautiful poetry as well as several charming songs.

Shakespeare consistently balanced the merry laughter of *As You Like It* with notes of seriousness and even sadness. Touchstone's wit and Jaques's remarks question the nature of love and the values of society. The play discusses the advantages and disadvantages of city and country life.

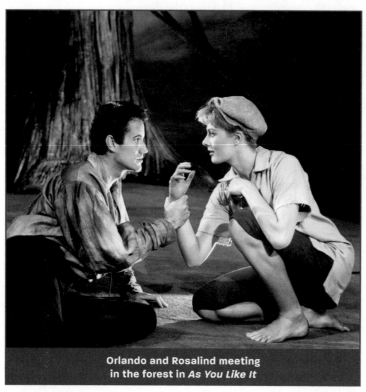

**Orlando and Rosalind meeting
in the forest in *As You Like It***

Jaques adds a strong note of melancholy to the play with his famous description of the seven ages of man. At the end of the description, he claims that man's final fate is "second childishness and mere oblivion, / Sans [without] teeth, sans eyes, sans taste, sans everything."

Henry V is a history partly based on *Holinshed's Chronicles* and on *The Famous Victories of Henry the Fifth*, a play by an unknown English author. *Henry V* was probably first performed in 1599 and was first published in 1600.

The play continues the action of *Henry IV*, Part II, and presents an idealized portrait of England's King Henry V. The king decides to press a claim he believes he has to the French throne. He heads an army that lands in France. Inspired by Henry's leadership, the outnumbered English troops defeat the French at the town of Harfleur. The two armies then meet in battle near the village of Agincourt. Against overwhelming odds, the English win a great victory. The triumphant Henry is received at the French court. There he is promised the throne and the hand of Katherine, the French princess.

The play consists of loosely related episodes unified by the character of the brave but modest king. Shakespeare filled *Henry V* with patriotic passages, especially the king's famous address to his troops at Harfleur. It begins, "Once more unto the breach, dear friends, once more." The speech concludes, "The game's afoot! / Follow your spirit; and upon this charge / Cry 'God for Harry! England and Saint George!'"

Henry claims to hate war in general. Yet he finds himself carried away by the glamour and glory of the French campaign. Although the play occasionally seems to glorify war, Shakespeare sets the heroics against a background of political treachery and empty honor. Comic scenes mock the vanity of the royal court. These scenes remind audiences that monarchs and their councils plan wars, but ordinary people must fight and die in them.

Julius Caesar is a tragedy partly based on *Lives* by the ancient Greek biographer Plutarch, as translated by the English writer Sir Thomas North. The play was probably first performed in 1599 and was first published in 1623.

The play takes place in ancient Rome and concerns events before and after the assassination of the Roman ruler Julius Caesar. In spite of its title, the play's central character is Brutus, a Roman senator and Caesar's best friend. Brutus reluctantly joins a plot to murder Caesar because he believes Rome's preservation requires Caesar's death. The conspirators attack Caesar in the Roman Capitol, and his final words are "Et tu, Brute? [You too, Brutus?] Then fall, Caesar!"

Brutus defends the assassination to a crowd of Romans. But he unwisely allows the clever and eloquent Marc Antony to deliver a funeral speech over Caesar's body. Antony tells the people, "I come to bury Caesar, not to praise him." He then describes the plotters with heavy sarcasm as "honorable men." At the same time, Antony points out Caesar's virtues and thus gradually turns the crowd into a mob ready to avenge Caesar's death. The conspirators are forced to flee Rome.

Marc Antony leads an army that defeats the conspirators at the Battle of Philippi. At the end of the battle, Brutus commits suicide. Over his corpse, Antony states, "This was the noblest Roman of them all." Antony says that the other plotters killed Caesar out of envy but only Brutus acted with "honest thought / And common good to all."

Julius Caesar has become a popular play because of its magnificent language and sharp character portraits. For example, Caesar describes the plotter Cassius as having a "lean and hungry look." But the real interest in Julius Caesar centers on the character of Brutus. A thoughtful, withdrawn man, he is torn between his affection for Caesar and his strong sense of duty to the Roman republic.

Much Ado About Nothing is a comedy partly based on *Orlando Furioso* (published in 1516, revised in 1521 and 1532), an epic poem by the Italian author Ludovico Ariosto, and on a story in *Novelle* (1554–1573), a collection of tales by the Italian author Matteo Bandello. The play was probably first performed in 1599 and was first published in 1600.

This romantic comedy concerns the attempts by the villainous Don John to slander the virtue of Hero, the daughter of the governor of Messina, Italy. Hero is about to be married to Claudio, a young lord from Venice. Don John manufactures an accusation of infidelity that causes Claudio to jilt Hero at the altar. After much intrigue, Don John's plot is exposed and the couple happily marry. Much of the interest in the play centers on the relationships between Beatrice, Hero's cousin, and Benedick, a lord of Padua. These two witty

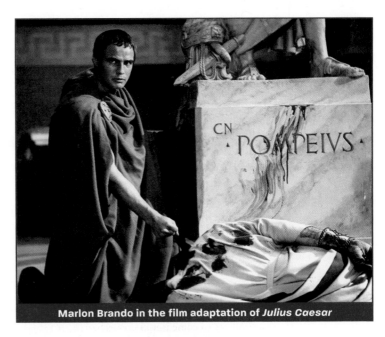

Marlon Brando in the film adaptation of *Julius Caesar*

characters trade insults for much of the play, but they come together in an attempt to restore Hero's damaged honor and soon realize that they are themselves in love. This combination of sharp intelligence and lack of self-knowledge produces rich comedy. Broad humor is supplied by the talkative village constable, Dogberry, and his assistant, Verges.

Twelfth Night is a comedy partly based on a story in *Barnabe Riche: His Farewell to Military Profession* (1581), a collection of tales by the English author Barnabe Riche. Shakespeare's *Twelfth Night* was probably first performed in 1600 and was first published in 1623.

Viola and Sebastian, who are twins, become separated during a shipwreck. Viola finds herself stranded in the country of Illyria. She disguises herself as Cesario, a page, and enters the service of Duke Orsino. The duke sends the page to woo Countess Olivia for him. But the countess falls in love with Cesario. Meanwhile, Viola only complicates matters further by falling in love with the duke.

The romantic action alternates with scenes of realistic comedy involving the fat knight Sir Toby Belch and his friends. One friend, Sir Andrew Aguecheek, fights Cesario in a comic duel. Maria, Countess Olivia's lady-in-waiting, tricks the countess's steward, Malvolio, into thinking that Olivia loves him. The plot becomes increasingly tangled when Sebastian, Viola's twin brother, appears and readily agrees to marry Olivia. In the final scene, Viola, still disguised, is confronted by Olivia, who is confused by the youth's refusal to acknowledge their recent marriage. Duke Orsino is enraged by the treachery of "Cesario" and threatens violence. But all is resolved when Sebastian reappears and Viola reveals her identity. Viola and Orsino then declare their mutual love, and the play concludes anticipating their marriage. Only Malvolio is left unhappy.

In *Twelfth Night*, Shakespeare created a perfect blend of sentiment and humor. In addition, he provided Feste, Olivia's clown, with witty comments on the foolish ways of people. Feste's songs contribute both gaiety and sadness to the mood of the play. In one famous song, he reminds the audience that they should enjoy the present because nobody can know what the future will bring:

> What is love? 'Tis not hereafter;
> Present mirth hath present laughter;
> What's to come is still unsure:
> In delay there lies no plenty;
> Then come kiss me, sweet and twenty!
> Youth's a stuff will not endure.

Only Malvolio, who thinks he is more moral than other people, spoils the gentle mood of the play. Sir Toby Belch angrily asks him, "Dost thou think, because thou art virtuous, there shall be no more cakes and ale?"

The Merry Wives of Windsor is a comedy possibly based on an unknown source or sources. The play was probably first performed in 1600 and was first published in 1602.

According to a popular though unproven story, Queen Elizabeth requested the play. She so enjoyed the comic character Sir John Falstaff in the *Henry IV* plays that she asked Shakespeare to write a comedy portraying Falstaff in love. The comedy dramatizes Falstaff's efforts to make love to Mistress Ford and Mistress Page, two honest housewives in the town of Windsor. Instead of winning their love, Falstaff ends up the victim of a number of comical tricks invented by the women.

Although *The Merry Wives of Windsor* lacks the romantic poetry of most Shakespearean comedies, the play is highly entertaining. The Falstaff in this work has less imagination and wit than the Falstaff in the *Henry IV* plays. But the character remains theatrically effective, even though the audience laughs at him rather than with him, as in the earlier plays.

The Third Period (1601–1608)

Shakespeare wrote his great tragedies during the third period of his artistic development. Except possibly for *Pericles*, every play of this period shows Shakespeare's awareness of the tragic side of life. Even the period's two comedies—*All's Well That Ends Well* and *Measure for Measure*—are more disturbing than amusing. For this reason, they are often called "problem" comedies or "bitter" comedies. *Pericles* represents Shakespeare's first romance—a drama that is generally serious in tone but with a happy ending.

During this period, Shakespeare's language shows remarkable variety and flexibility, moving easily back and forth between verse and prose. The verse shows an increasing tendency to allow sentences to extend past the end of the verse line. Shakespeare used a rhythmic pattern called *iambic pentameter* in most of his writing. This pattern, or meter, consists of 10 syllables alternately unaccented and accented in each line. In the third period, he shows a marked tendency to vary the standard iambic pentameter line, creating an overall effect of increased verbal fluidity. The writing of this period also is marked by especially dense descriptive language. Shakespeare's language

Laurence Olivier as Hamlet

becomes a flexible dramatic tool that makes possible the skillful psychological portraits that mark this period.

Hamlet is a tragedy partly based on *Hamlet*, a lost play by an unknown English author, and on a story in *Histoires Tragiques* (1559–1580), a collection of tales by the French author François de Belleforest. Shakespeare's *Hamlet* was probably first performed in 1601 and was first published in 1603.

Prince Hamlet of Denmark deeply mourns the recent death of his father. He also resents his mother's remarriage to his uncle Claudius, who has become king. The ghost of Hamlet's father appears to the prince and tells him he was murdered by Claudius. The ghost demands that Hamlet take revenge on the king.

Hamlet broods about whether he should believe the ghost. In his soliloquies, he criticizes himself for not acting against his uncle. He also considers suicide. Hamlet decides to have a band of traveling actors perform "something like the murder of my father" before the king to see if Claudius will show any guilt. The king's violent reaction convinces Hamlet that the ghost has told the truth. But Hamlet rejects a chance to kill Claudius while the king is on his knees in prayer.

Polonius, the king's adviser, decides to eavesdrop on Hamlet while the prince is visiting his mother in her sitting room. He hides behind a curtain, but Hamlet becomes aware that someone is there. Hamlet stabs Polonius through the curtain and kills him.

Claudius exiles Hamlet to England for killing Polonius. He also sends secret orders that the prince be executed after he arrives in England. But Hamlet intercepts the orders and returns to Denmark. He arrives in time to see the burial of Ophelia, the daughter of Polonius. The young woman, whom Hamlet had loved, had gone insane following her father's death and drowned after falling into a river.

Laertes, Ophelia's brother, blames Hamlet for the deaths of his sister and father. He agrees to a plot suggested by Claudius to kill Hamlet with a poisoned sword in a fencing match. Laertes wounds Hamlet during the duel and, in turn, is wounded himself by the poisoned weapon. While watching the match, Hamlet's mother accidentally drinks from a cup of poisoned wine Claudius had prepared for Hamlet. Although dying from his wound, Hamlet kills Claudius. At the end of the play, Hamlet, his mother, Claudius, and Laertes all lie dead.

Shakespeare handled the complicated plot of *Hamlet* brilliantly. In this play, he also created perhaps his greatest gallery of characters. The role of Hamlet in particular is considered one of the theater's greatest acting challenges. Shakespeare focused the play on the deep conflict within the thoughtful and idealistic Hamlet as he is torn between the demands of his emotions and the hesitant skepticism of his mind. Hamlet reveals this conflict in several famous and eloquent soliloquies. The best known is the soliloquy that begins, "To be, or not to be."

Troilus and Cressida is a dark comedy based on several sources, none of which was a chief source. The play was probably first performed in 1602 and was first published in 1609.

The story takes place during the Trojan War, fought between ancient Greece and the city of Troy. It dramatizes the disastrous love affair between two Trojans—Troilus, one of the king's sons, and Cressida, a woman whose father has joined the Greeks. Cressida is suddenly sent to the Greek camp in exchange for a Trojan prisoner. Despite her promise to be faithful to Troilus, she accepts the love and protection of the Greek warrior Diomedes in the enemy camp. The play ends with the death of Troilus's brother, the great Trojan hero Hector.

In spite of its heroic setting, *Troilus and Cressida* is neither noble nor stirring. The play's satirical account of the heroic virtue associated with the epic tradition results in dark cynicism. Although the play has some splendid language, no single character provides an authoritative vision of the events shown. This atmosphere of moral confusion, along with the play's extreme shifts between sexual humor and psychological realism, have led many critics to classify it as one of Shakespeare's "problem plays" because it does not seem to fit neatly into any recognized dramatic category.

All's Well That Ends Well is a comedy partly based on a story in *The Palace of Pleasure* (1567, revised in 1575), a collection of tales by various European authors, translated by William Painter, an English author. The play was probably first performed in 1603 and was first published in 1623.

This play takes place in France and Italy. Helena, the beautiful orphaned daughter of a physician,

Scene from *All's Well That Ends Well*

loves Bertram, a nobleman. In Paris, Helena cures the French king of an illness and wins Bertram as her husband in reward. But Bertram considers Helena beneath him socially and deserts her immediately after the wedding. He tells her in a letter that she can never call him husband unless she gets a ring from his finger and becomes pregnant by him. In Florence, Bertram attempts to seduce the young Diana. But Helena, having followed her husband, intervenes. She has Diana demand Bertram's ring in exchange for meeting him. Using the bed trick, Helena substitutes herself for Diana and makes love to Bertram. When Bertram finds that Helena has fulfilled both conditions, he is forced to accept her as his wife.

On the surface, *All's Well That Ends Well* resembles other Elizabethan comedies of romantic intrigue. But unlike Shakespeare's earlier comedies, it has little gaiety and romance. Helena has many of the virtuous traits found in other Shakespearean heroines, but her dogged pursuit of the unworthy Bertram puzzles some critics. Although the play does not emphasize character development, Helena's struggle to save Bertram from his own worst inclinations does present a complex vision of human nature. The play anticipates elements of the late romances in its use of such fairy-tale elements as miraculous cures, and its emphasis on reconciliation.

Measure for Measure is a comedy partly based on *Promos and Cassandra* (1578), a play by the English author George Whetstone. Shakespeare's play was probably first performed in 1604 and was first published in 1623.

Vincentio, Duke of Vienna, turns over the affairs of the city to Angelo, his stern deputy. The duke hopes Angelo will introduce needed moral reforms in Vienna. In one of his first acts, Angelo sentences Claudio to death for making Juliet, his fiancée, pregnant. Claudio's sister, Isabella, pleads with Angelo for Claudio's life. Overcome by her beauty, Angelo agrees to save Claudio if she will allow him to make love to her. Isabella refuses, preferring to let her brother die rather than yield her honor. After much intrigue and plotting, including a bed trick like the one that appears in *All's Well*, Claudio is saved, Isabella keeps her virtue, and Angelo's wicked deeds are exposed.

Many critics have objected to the happy ending of *Measure for Measure*. They consider it false to the spirit of the play. The first part of the play is serious, almost tragic. The latter part becomes a typical romantic intrigue. This lack of artistic unity creates problems. The first part of the play, for example, raises serious questions about the nature of justice that remain unanswered at the play's end. Because of these perplexing moral entanglements, *Measure for Measure* is another play that critics have classed as a "problem play" that cannot easily be categorized.

In spite of its flaws, *Measure for Measure* has many excellent features. Shakespeare drew the characters of Angelo and Isabella with keen understanding. He also included much broad comedy that is highly effective. In addition, his dramatic poetry at times equals that of the best in his tragedies.

Othello is a tragedy partly based on a story in *Hecatommithi* (about 1565), a collection of tales by the Italian author Giambattista Giraldi, who wrote under the name Cinthio. The play was probably first performed in 1604 and was first published in 1622.

Othello, a noble black *Moor* (North African), has spent his life as a soldier and become a general in the army of Venice, then a self-governing area called a *city-state*, ruled by nobles. Othello elopes with Desdemona, the beautiful daughter of a Venetian senator. Immediately after the marriage, Othello is ordered to Cyprus to defend against an expected attack from the Turks. Desdemona insists on accompanying her new husband. Iago, Othello's aide, declares his hatred of the Moor and begins to plot his downfall. The play's dramatic core consists of scenes in which Iago convinces Othello that Desdemona has been unfaithful to him with Michael Cassio, Othello's lieutenant. A master of psychological manipulation, Iago prefers insinuation to outright lying. He successfully exploits Othello's insecurity over his race, age, and lack of sophistication. Tormented by thoughts of Desdemona's infidelity, Othello murders her. After the Moor learns he has been tricked, he stabs himself and dies, describing himself as "one that loved not wisely, but too well."

Othello is one of Shakespeare's most powerful tragedies. The action moves rapidly without any unimportant plot developments. The language is also direct and forceful. Both Othello and Iago use especially vivid images, but when Othello is enraged, his language becomes fractured and incoherent. The play is centered on the impossibility of truly knowing the mind of another and insists on the fragility of human goodness and love.

King Lear is a tragedy partly based on *Holinshed's Chronicles*; on *The True Chronicle History of King Leir*, a play by an unknown English author; and on *Arcadia* (1590), a romance in prose and verse by the English author Sir Philip Sidney. *King Lear* was probably first performed in 1605 and was first published in 1608.

The main plot concerns Lear, an aged king of ancient Britain. He prepares to divide his kingdom among his three daughters—Regan, Goneril, and Cordelia. Lear becomes angry when Cordelia, his youngest daughter, refuses to flatter him to gain her portion of the kingdom. Lear rashly disinherits her, but the king of France agrees to marry her even though she has no dowry. Lear also exiles his trusted adviser, Kent, for supporting Cordelia.

Regan and Goneril soon show their ingratitude. They deprive Lear of his servants and finally force him to spend a night outdoors during a storm accompanied only by his jester, called the Fool. Lear's mind begins to snap under the strain. But as he descends into madness, he finally sees his errors and selfishness. Cordelia returns from France leading an army and finds the king insane. Lear recovers his sanity and recognizes her. Armies raised by the wicked sisters capture Lear and Cordelia, who is put to death. Meanwhile, Goneril has poisoned Regan in a bitter quarrel over a man they both love and then killed herself. Order is finally restored in the kingdom. But Lear dies of a broken heart as he kneels over the body of Cordelia.

Othello and Desdemona, from *Othello*

Shakespeare skillfully wove a subplot into the main story of Lear and his daughters. Gloucester, a nobleman in Lear's court, makes the mistake of banishing his faithful son, Edgar, and trusting his wicked son, Edmund. Edmund soon betrays his father, who is blinded by Regan's husband. Edgar, disguised as a beggar, discovers his blind father and comforts him. Having realized his error in rejecting Edgar, Gloucester wants only to commit suicide. Edgar remains in disguise and attempts to teach his father the importance of patience and optimism. But after the battle between Cordelia's forces and those of her sisters, Edgar reveals himself to his father, who dies overwhelmed by joy and grief.

In *King Lear*, Shakespeare created the brilliant characterizations that mark his dramas at their best. The characters realize their mistakes, which reflects Shakespeare's basic optimism. But they do so too late to prevent their destruction and that of the people around them. *Lear* is widely regarded as the bleakest of Shakespeare's tragedies.

Macbeth is a tragedy partly based on *Holinshed's Chronicles*. *Macbeth* was probably first performed in 1606 and was first published in 1623.

This play is set in Scotland. Returning from battle with his companion Banquo, the nobleman Macbeth meets some witches. They predict that Macbeth will first become *thane* (baron) of Cawdor and then king of Scotland. After the first part of the witches' prophecy comes true, he begins to think the second part may also come true. King Duncan visits the Macbeths. Encouraged by Lady Macbeth, Macbeth murders Duncan and throws suspicion on the king's two sons, Malcolm and Donalbain. The princes, fearing for their lives, flee, and Macbeth is crowned king of Scotland.

But Macbeth has no peace. Malcolm has escaped to England, where he seeks support against Macbeth. In addition, the witches had also predicted that Banquo's descendants would be kings of Scotland. Macbeth therefore orders the murder of Banquo and his son, Fleance. Macbeth's men kill Banquo, but Fleance escapes. Macbeth is now hardened to killing. He orders the murder of the wife and children of his enemy Macduff, who has fled to England. Macduff joins Malcolm, who leads an army against Macbeth. By this time, Lady Macbeth, burdened with guilt over the murders, has become a sleepwalker. She finally dies. At the end of the play, Macduff kills Macbeth in battle. Duncan's son Malcolm is then proclaimed king of Scotland.

In *Macbeth*, Shakespeare wrote a tragedy of a man's conscience. During the course of the play,

Peter O' Toole as the Scottish king, Macbeth

Macbeth changes from a person of strong but imperfect moral sense to a man who will stop at nothing to get and keep what he wants. By the play's end, he has lost all emotion. He cannot even react to his wife's death, except to conclude that life is only "a tale / Told by an idiot, full of sound and fury, / Signifying nothing." On the other hand, Lady Macbeth encourages murder in the beginning. But her conscience grows as her husband's lessens. In addition to its psychological insights, *Macbeth* has many passages of great poetry. The play is also noted for its bitter humor, which reinforces the tragic action.

Timon of Athens is a tragedy partly based on Plutarch's *Lives* as translated by Sir Thomas North. The play was probably first performed in 1607 and was first published in 1623. Some scholars believe that Thomas Middleton wrote part of the play.

Timon is a nobleman in ancient Athens. Surrounded by flatterers, he spends his money extravagantly. But after he becomes penniless, his friends desert him. Their ingratitude turns Timon into a bitter person who hates humanity. Timon leaves Athens and goes to live in a cave near the sea, where he finds a buried treasure. But his newfound wealth brings him no happiness. He dies, still bitter, in his cave.

Although *Timon of Athens* has flaws, it also has passages of great eloquence. Several such passages occur when Timon pours out his scorn for humanity. Throughout the play, Shakespeare portrays people at their worst, with few of the noble qualities that lighten the gloom in his great tragedies.

Pericles is a romance partly based on a story in *Confessio Amantis* (1390), a collection of European tales retold by the English poet John Gower. *Pericles* was probably first performed in 1607 and was first published in 1609. Some scholars believe that George Wilkins wrote part of the play.

This play consists of many loosely related episodes and is uneven in quality. The action in *Pericles* covers many years and ranges over much of the ancient Mediterranean world. The plot deals with the adventures of Prince Pericles of Tyre. Upon discovering that the beautiful woman he has been courting is corrupt and vicious, Pericles flees, only to become shipwrecked. Poor and unknown, he comes ashore at Pentapolis. Despite his tattered appearance, the king's daughter, the virtuous Thaisa, recognizes his basic nobility, and they marry. They have a daughter, Marina, but soon the three family members are separated. The loss of his wife and daughter causes Pericles to fall into a deep melancholy from which he recovers only when reunited first with his daughter and then with his wife.

Pericles shares a number of qualities with the later romances *Cymbeline, The Winter's Tale,* and *The Tempest.* Character development is less important than a complex plot that threatens to end in tragedy only to come to an almost miraculous happy conclusion. Along the way, there is real suffering and even death, but all difficulties are redeemed by the joy of recovery and reunion. The two characters who are most fully portrayed are Pericles and Marina, whose radiant and saintly virtue protects her from the evils of the world.

Antony and Cleopatra is a tragedy partly based on Plutarch's *Lives* as translated by Sir Thomas North. The play was probably first performed in 1607 and was first published in 1623.

Marc Antony shares the rule of the Roman Empire with Octavius Caesar and Lepidus. Antony lives in Roman-conquered Egypt, where he pursues a love affair with Cleopatra. Political problems in Rome and the death of his wife force Antony to leave his life of pleasure and return home. In Rome, he marries Octavius's sister Octavia for political reasons. But Antony soon returns to "his Egyptian dish." Octavius then prepares for war against him.

Antony decides unwisely to fight Octavius at sea. During the battle, Cleopatra's fleet deserts him, and Antony flees with the queen. After Cleopatra's ships desert him in a second battle, Antony finally realizes that he has lost everything. Cleopatra deceives him into thinking that she is dead, and Antony attempts suicide. But before he dies, he learns that Cleopatra is still alive. Antony returns to her and dies in her arms. Cleopatra is captured by Octavius, who plans to lead her in triumph through Rome. Although under guard, Cleopatra obtains poisonous snakes and uses them to commit suicide. She dies anticipating her reunion with Antony in the afterlife.

The dazzling poetry of *Antony and Cleopatra* is one of the play's most notable features. Early in the play, Enobarbus, one of Antony's officers, gives a famous description of Cleopatra that begins, "The barge she sat in, like a burnished throne, / Burned on the water." Cleopatra is a wonderfully complex

***Antony and Cleopatra* is noted for its dazzling poetry.**

character. She goes from playfulness to irritation, from sweet intimacy to fierce anger, all in an instant. At the same time, she shows courage and determination. As Enobarbus says, "Age cannot wither her, nor custom stale / Her infinite variety."

When Enobarbus becomes convinced that Antony has abandoned reason, he deserts him to join the realist Octavius. In a grand gesture, Antony sends Enobarbus the treasure he has left behind. Enobarbus, overwhelmed by his own disloyalty, dies of a broken heart.

Shakespeare's dramatic use of poetry creates portraits of the play's two main characters that are filled with ambiguity. From the perspective of the Romans especially, they appear to be nothing more than aging pleasure seekers. But the lovers describe themselves in lofty poetic language. The play suggests that there is something noble about them.

Coriolanus is a tragedy partly based on Plutarch's *Lives* as translated by Sir Thomas North. The play was probably first performed in 1608 and was first published in 1623.

Caius Marcius, a general in ancient Rome, wins the name Coriolanus after he captures Corioli, the capital city of a people known as the Volscians. Coriolanus returns to Rome in triumph and is nominated for the important office of consul. But he cannot hide his scorn for the common people, whose support he needs to become consul. Coriolanus's superior attitude leads to his exile. He joins forces with his old enemy, the Volscian general Tullus Aufidius, and heads an army against Rome. Coriolanus's mother, wife, and young son meet him outside the city and beg him to spare it. Moved by their pleas, Coriolanus withdraws his troops. Aufidius denounces him as a traitor and has him murdered.

In *Coriolanus*, Shakespeare raised issues that remain particularly important today. The tragedy questions the values of personal popularity and political success. It also debates the conflicting interests of public and private life. Shakespeare's direct and dramatic verse contributes to the play's power.

The Fourth Period (1609–1614)

During his final period, Shakespeare wrote five plays—four romances and a history. Scholars believe Shakespeare collaborated with John Fletcher, who took over for Shakespeare as the lead dramatist for the King's Men, on two of these plays—*Henry VIII* and *The Two Noble Kinsmen*.

The four romances are beautifully constructed, and their poetry ranks among Shakespeare's finest writing. But unlike his masterpieces of the third period, the romances seem detached from reality. Scholars disagree on the reason for this change in Shakespeare's works. Some claim he was calmly looking back on his life and philosophically summing up his career. Other scholars believe that the romances are a response to the growing popularity of plays that mixed comic and serious elements and that in writing them Shakespeare was adapting his work to the changing tastes of his audience. These claims are not, however, mutually exclusive. Throughout his career, Shakespeare was attentive to the desires of his audience. At the same time, his work never appears merely commercial.

Cymbeline is a romance partly based on several sources, none of which was a chief source. *Cymbeline* was probably first performed in 1609 and was first published in 1623.

Cymbeline, king of Britain, angrily exiles the poor but honorable Posthumous after the young man marries Imogen, the king's daughter. The treacherous Iachimo bets Posthumous that Imogen is not virtuous. Iachimo then tries to seduce her. He fails but tricks Posthumous into believing that he has succeeded. Posthumous orders his wife killed, but she escapes disguised as a court page. After many adventures, Imogen and her husband are happily reunited. Iachimo, filled with regret, confesses his wickedness.

Cymbeline is a lively mix of historical elements. It includes portrayals of ancient Britons, classical Romans, and, in Iachimo, an Italian plotter who appears modern. Cymbeline's queen is the sort of wicked stepmother found in fairy tales. Her son, Cloten, is a cowardly clown. Although Posthumous is brave and virtuous, the play's most appealing character is the loyal and resourceful Imogen.

The play includes a subplot that involves the recovery of Imogen's two brothers, who had been stolen in infancy. These elements unfold against the background of an international conflict between Britain and the Roman Empire. The resolution of all these conflicts allows the play to end in a celebration of global peace.

The Winter's Tale is a romance partly based on *Pandosto* (1588), a prose romance by the English author Robert Greene. The play was probably first performed in 1611 and was first published in 1623.

Leontes, king of Sicilia, becomes uncontrollably jealous of his faithful wife, Hermione, and suspects her of sleeping with his boyhood friend Polixenes. Polixenes is now the king of Bohemia, and he has been visiting Sicilia for the past nine months. Leontes tries to have Polixenes murdered, but he escapes and returns to Bohemia. Leontes then orders his wife to prison, where she gives birth to their daughter, Perdita. Leontes declares the child illegitimate and orders that she be abandoned in a deserted place. Leontes sends agents to consult the oracle of Apollo and puts Hermione on trial for adultery. As the trial begins, a report arrives from the oracle declaring Hermione's innocence. But Leontes rejects the oracle and immediately learns that his young son has died of grief. At this news, Hermione falls into a deathlike faint. Suddenly convinced of his error, Leontes is left to mourn the loss of his wife, daughter, and son.

Meanwhile, Perdita has been saved by an old shepherd. She grows into a lovely young woman and wins the love of Florizel, prince of Bohemia. But Florizel's father, Polixenes, angrily disapproves of their romance, and the couple flee to Leontes's court for protection. There, Leontes discovers that

Perdita is his daughter. The king's happiness is complete when he is also reunited with his wife, who was thought to be dead. Instead, with the help of a lady-in-waiting, she had been living in seclusion, hoping for Perdita's return.

Like *Cymbeline*, *The Winter's Tale* concerns exile, women suffering from male jealousy, and the reuniting of loved ones. Also like the earlier play, *The Winter's Tale* takes a potentially tragic situation and uses it to stress recovery rather than destruction. Still, there is loss. The young prince and the lord sent to dispose of Perdita are both dead. The play's conclusion includes a wonderful piece of theater in which a supposed statue of Hermione comes to life. The conclusion is finely balanced between the joy of reconciliation and the painful knowledge of loss.

The Tempest is a romance partly based on several sources, none of which was a chief source. *The Tempest* was probably first performed in 1611 and was first published in 1623.

Prospero, the wrongfully deposed Duke of Milan, Italy, lives on an enchanted island with his beautiful daughter, Miranda. The mischievous spirit Ariel and the monster Caliban serve Prospero, who is a skilled magician. Using magic, Prospero creates a *tempest* (storm) that causes a ship carrying his enemies to be wrecked on the island.

Ralph Richardson as Prospero

The ship also carries the young prince Ferdinand. Miranda loves him at first sight and cries out, "O brave new world that hath such creatures in it." With his magic, Prospero brings Miranda and Ferdinand together and upsets plots laid against him by his shipwrecked enemies. Prospero appears before his enemies and forgives them. He decides to give up his magic and return to Italy, where Ferdinand and Miranda can marry.

Like *Cymbeline* and *The Winter's Tale*, *The Tempest* tells a story in which old injuries are forgiven and the characters begin a new and happier life. In *The Tempest*, Shakespeare blended spectacle, song, and dance with a romantic love story, beautiful poetry, and broad comedy. The result of this blending is a brilliant dramatic fantasy. In one of Shakespeare's most famous speeches, Prospero tells the audience:

> Our revels now are ended. These our actors,
> As I foretold you, were all spirits and
> Are melted into air, into thin air;
> And, like the baseless fabric of this vision,
> The cloud-capped tow'rs, the gorgeous palaces,
> The solemn temples, the great globe itself,
> Yea all which it inherit, shall dissolve,
> And, like this insubstantial pageant faded,
> Leave not a rack behind.

Many scholars have taken these lines to be Shakespeare's farewell to his profession. But no one knows if he intended the speech to be autobiographical.

Henry VIII is a history partly based on *Holinshed's Chronicles* and on *The Book of Martyrs* (1563), a religious work by the English author John Foxe. The play was probably first performed in 1613 and was first published in 1623. Many scholars believe that John Fletcher wrote part of the play.

The play dramatizes the events that led to England's break with the Roman Catholic Church. It deals with King Henry VIII's *annulment* (cancellation) of his marriage to Catherine of Aragon (spelled Katherine in the play) and his marriage to Anne Boleyn. The play also covers the fall of Cardinal Thomas Wolsey as the king's adviser and the rise of Archbishop Thomas Cranmer as Wolsey's replacement. *Henry VIII* is a loosely constructed drama and better known for its pageantry than for its characterization. But the play attempts to move

Henry VIII **is better known for its pageantry than its creative verse.**

the condition that they return in a month to fight each other. The winner will marry Emilia, and the loser will be executed.

In preparation for the fight, Arcite prays to Mars, the god of war. Palamon prays to Venus, the goddess of love, and Emilia prays to Diana, the goddess of virginity. Arcite wins the fight but afterward is thrown from his horse and fatally injured. Palamon, on the verge of execution, is permitted a final interview with his dying friend, who confesses that he has wronged Palamon and urges him to take Emilia. Theseus spares Palamon and agrees to his marriage to Emilia.

The Two Noble Kinsmen, like other late romances, has an artificial quality and an improbable plot designed to highlight the guiding role of Providence in human affairs. Like *Henry VIII*, the play emphasizes courtly ceremony and pageantry. However, the play's central focus is on a friendship between two men that is jeopardized by their rivalry for the same woman. Some of the play's best dialogue concerns the qualities and claims of friendship.

Shakespeare's Poems

Shakespeare wrote two long poems, *Venus and Adonis* and *The Rape of Lucrece*. Both are *narrative* poems—that is, they tell a story. Shakespeare also composed a sequence of 154 sonnets, which concludes with a short poem called "A Lover's Complaint." He contributed another short lyric, "The Phoenix and the Turtle," to an anthology of poetry titled *Love's Martyr* (1601).

The Narrative Poems

Venus and Adonis (1593) draws on the *Metamorphoses*, a collection of tales in verse by the ancient Roman poet Ovid. The poem tells how Venus, the goddess of love, tries to win the love of the handsome young mortal Adonis. He resists her and is finally killed by a wild boar while hunting.

Shakespeare wrote *Venus and Adonis* in six-line stanzas. Most of the lines are iambic pentameter. The lines of *Venus and Adonis* rhyme *ababcc*, which means the first and third lines rhyme, as do the second and fourth, and the fifth and sixth.

The poem is witty and filled with sexual references. But the work is most notable for its vivid settings and its formal and elaborate speeches. *Venus and Adonis* represents Shakespeare's successful attempt to write the kind of love poetry

beyond the anger found in almost all the historical accounts of England's split from Catholicism available during Shakespeare's lifetime. The play's alternate title, *All Is True*, suggests a mildly ironic attempt to create an account of the country's recent past that covers all the major events and invites agreement among the various sides.

The Two Noble Kinsmen is a romance chiefly based on "The Knight's Tale" from Geoffrey Chaucer's *Canterbury Tales*. The play was probably first performed in 1613 or 1614 and was first published in 1634. Most scholars believe Shakespeare wrote it with John Fletcher.

The play tells the story of two young aristocrats from Thebes—Palamon and Arcite. Although Thebes is ruled by the tyrant Creon, the two friends decide that loyalty requires them to help defend their city against the attack of Theseus, king of Athens. The two are captured in battle and taken to Athens. In prison, Palamon sees and falls in love with Emilia, the sister of Hippolyta, the wife of Theseus. Arcite, too, falls in love with Emilia.

The two friends argue bitterly over their claims to Emilia. Arcite is released from prison and exiled, but he remains in Athens in disguise. Palamon manages to escape from prison and encounters the disguised Arcite in the woods. The two are about to fight a duel over Emilia when they are discovered by Theseus, who condemns them both to death. The king is talked into sparing the two on

that was fashionable in court circles and enormously popular.

The Rape of Lucrece (1594) is also partly based on the works of Ovid, as well as on writings by other authors. The poem tells of Lucrece, the virtuous wife of a Roman nobleman. Raped by Sextus Tarquinius, son of the tyrant Roman king Lucius Tarquinius, Lucrece demands that her husband and his friends swear to revenge her ruined honor. She then kills herself. Her supporters publicize the deed, and the people expel the Tarquins and establish the Roman Republic.

Shakespeare wrote *The Rape of Lucrece* in rime royal, which uses seven-line stanzas of iambic pentameter that are rhymed *ababbcc*. The poem is more serious in tone than *Venus and Adonis*. Although the poem describes a violent event that has enormous consequences, it mostly consists of elaborate speeches.

The Sonnets

In the late 1500s, it was fashionable for English gentlemen authors to write sequences of sonnets. Some sonnet sequences followed a narrative pattern that was autobiographical in varying degrees. For this reason, scholars have tried to learn about Shakespeare's life from his sonnets. But they have reached no general agreement on autobiographical information that the poems might contain.

Scholars generally do agree, however, that Shakespeare addressed the first 126 sonnets to a young nobleman and that the next 26 concentrate on a woman. But they have not been able to identify either person. They have long debated over the nature of Shakespeare's relationship with the young man and have come to no general conclusion. A similar uncertainty surrounds the woman known as the "dark lady." The sexually charged sonnets concerning this figure reveal a mixture of desire and disgust. Attempts to identify the "dark lady" have been unconvincing.

In several of the first 126 sonnets, the speaker refers to another poet he considers a rival for his young friend's affection and support. Scholars have proposed many candidates for the role of the "rival poet," but no general agreement has emerged. Sonnets 153 and 154 are a notable departure from the preceding poems. Ultimately inspired by an epigram in Greek, both sonnets treat Cupid, the Roman god of love. This shift in subject matter has caused some scholars to question the authenticity of these last two sonnets. The volume concludes with "A Lover's Complaint," which tells the story of a jilted woman in 47 stanzas of rime royal.

Composition and publication. Shakespeare probably wrote the sonnets over several years, though their dates are not clear. He wrote the poems in three units of four lines each with a concluding *couplet* (two-line unit). Shakespeare's sonnets rhyme *abab cdcd efef gg*.

Two of the sonnets originally appeared in a book of poetry called *The Passionate Pilgrim* (1599). Thomas Thorpe published the sonnets as a collection in 1609. Thorpe dedicated the book to Mr. W. H., whom he called "the only begetter of these ensuing sonnets." Scholars do not know who Mr. W. H. was or even if he inspired the poems or merely collected them for the publisher. The individual poems have no titles. Scholars refer to them either by their first line or by the number Thorpe assigned to them. Because the volume was not clearly authorized by Shakespeare, scholars have raised questions about the order in which the poems appear.

Themes. In the sonnets addressed to his aristocratic friend, Shakespeare treated a variety of subjects. "Shall I compare thee to a summer's day?" (sonnet 18) praises physical beauty. "When, in

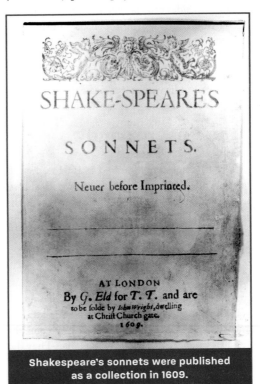

Shakespeare's sonnets were published as a collection in 1609.

disgrace with Fortune and men's eyes" (sonnet 29) describes the power of friendship to cheer the poet. "Devouring time, blunt thou the lion's paws" (sonnet 19) tells of poetry's power to confer immortality.

The sonnets' most common themes concern the destructive effects of time, the quickness of physical decay, and the loss of beauty, vigor, and love. Although the poems celebrate life, it is always with a keen awareness of death. This awareness of death is perhaps best expressed in "Poor soul, the center of my sinful earth" (sonnet 146).

A distrust of love and human nature runs through the "dark lady" sonnets. Sonnet 138, which appears below, reflects this attitude. In addition, the poem is representative of the entire sequence in two ways. The sonnet tells of the poet's concern over the passing of time, and it shows his strong emotion controlled by his highly intellectual wit.

When my love swears that she is made of truth
I do believe her, though I know she lies,
That she might think me some untutored youth,
Unlearned in the world's false subtleties.
Thus vainly thinking that she thinks me young,
Although she knows my days are past the best,
Simply I credit her false-speaking tongue:
On both sides thus is simple truth suppressed.
But wherefore says she not she is unjust?
And wherefore say not I that I am old?
O, love's best habit is in seeming trust,
And age in love loves not to have years told.
Therefore I lie with her and she with me,
And in our faults by lies we flattered be.

"The Phoenix and the Turtle"

This 67-line poem appeared in 1601 in the collection called *Love's Martyr*. It praises ideal love, using as symbols two birds, the phoenix and the turtledove. The poem has philosophical and symbolic qualities that have led to various biographical, political, and religious interpretations by critics.

Shakespeare's Style

Writing at a time when early modern English was assuming its fully modern form, Shakespeare and other Elizabethan writers looked upon the English language as alive and changing. They did not consider it fixed for all time in a set of correct and unbreakable rules. Shakespeare, for example,

used both *has* and its earlier form *hath*. In the same way, he used the pronouns *thee* and *thou* as well as their modern equivalent, *you*. Shakespeare experimented freely with sentence structure and vocabulary to create special effects. He also used various literary devices to present information and ideas in a dramatic and appealing way. But Shakespeare's style is perhaps best known for its brilliant use of language to create vivid pictures in the mind.

Shakespeare's style has helped shape the language of all English-speaking countries. This influence has chiefly been felt directly through his writings. But it has also been felt through the interest his work has aroused in the literature of the Elizabethan period in general. Many later writers in English have accepted the Elizabethan style as their model. As a result, much English and American literature reflects the highly individualized enthusiasm of most Elizabethan writing.

To the Reader.

This Figure, that thou here seest put,
It was for gentle Shakespeare cut;
Wherein the Graver had a strife
With Nature, to out-doo the life:
O, could he but have drawne his Wit
As well in Brasse, as he hath hit
His Face; the Print would then surpasse
All, that was ever writ in Brasse.
But, since he cannot, Reader, looke
Not on his Picture, but his Booke.

B. I.

**Ben Jonson's dedication to Shakespeare
in the *First Folio* edition**

Vocabulary. Shakespeare's vocabulary of about 29,000 words is remarkably rich. Like his fellow writers, he put old words to new uses, borrowed from other languages, and invented new terms. What sets apart Shakespeare's verbal creativity is that so many of his innovations were adopted by English speakers. Thomas Nashe, a contemporary of Shakespeare's, also freely invented words, but most of them are now forgotten.

However, the richness of Shakespeare's vocabulary sometimes raises difficulties for modern readers. Not all the words and meanings used by Shakespeare remain current. Perhaps the trickiest are the class of words that look familiar and modern but carry changed meanings and associations. The adjective *silly* was beginning to carry the modern meaning of *foolish* or *stupid*, and Shakespeare uses it in this sense in *Love's Labours Lost* and *A Midsummer Night's Dream*. But the word was used in its earlier meaning of helpless when Queen Margaret describes herself as a "silly Woman" in *Henry VI*, Part III. Most editions of Shakespeare's plays include notes that define such words.

Rhetoric. Shakespeare and other Elizabethan writers were trained in *rhetoric*—the art of using language to persuade. Based on classical and medieval models, Renaissance rhetoric was an established discipline offering a body of rules and techniques that could be studied, practiced, and absorbed. Rhetorical training was so central to Elizabethan culture that some critics, such as Sir Francis Bacon, began to worry that it promoted an interest in words at the expense of a knowledge of things. Traditionally, the discipline of rhetoric is divided into (1) invention, (2) arrangement, (3) style, (4) memory, and (5) delivery. Although Shakespeare was familiar with each of these parts, style is the most important category for the study of his work. Style includes *rhetorical figures*—devices or patterns in language that change or embellish meaning. These figures are conventionally divided into *tropes* and *schemes*. Tropes involve a change in a word's usual meaning. Schemes are verbal patterns that do not change the meaning of the words.

Classical rhetoric has an extensive classification of schemes, most of which involve word or sound repetition. For example, Shakespeare made frequent use of *anaphora*, the repetition of the same word or words at the beginning of successive clauses or lines of verse. In the opening of *Richard III*, the Duke of Gloucester says:

> Now are our brows bound with victorious
> wreaths,
> Our bruised arms hung up for monuments,
> Our stern alarums changed to merry meetings
> Our dreadful marches to delightful measures.

In addition, this passage uses *antithesis*, the joining of opposite ideas, to emphasize the contrast between past and present. When the anguished King Lear realizes he will never see his dear, dead daughter again, he laments "Never, never, never, never, never." This is an example of *epizeuxis*, the emphatic repetition of a word, and a perfect example of iambic pentameter. The line is also a powerful and entirely natural expression of loss.

The most important trope is *metaphor*—a figure of speech in which one thing is identified as another. For example, when Ophelia calls Hamlet "The expectancy and rose of the fair state," she is identifying him as a perfect example of young manhood. In *As You Like It*, for example, Jaques begins a famous soliloquy with a metaphor:

> All the world's a stage,
> And all the men and women merely players.
> They have their exits and their entrances,
> And one man in his time plays many parts,
> His acts being seven ages.

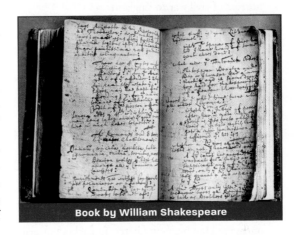

Book by William Shakespeare

Shakespeare enjoyed using puns. When Claudius, who is both uncle and stepfather to Hamlet, addresses the prince as "son," Hamlet bitterly remarks "A little more than kin, and less than kind." This pun plays on the sense of *kind* as benevolent and as belonging to the natural order. Hamlet is suggesting that Claudius's marriage to Gertrude is both unnatural and malicious. Claudius then asks, "How is it that the clouds still hang upon you?" Hamlet replies, "Not so, my lord. I am too much in the sun." The *sun/son* pun refers back to Claudius's initial form of address. Such serious punning is an essential part of Hamlet's character. Elsewhere, Shakespeare's characters pun for the sheer fun of it.

Imagery. Shakespeare used rhetorical techniques to create rich imagery that gives his writing its unique style. A famous example of his brilliant imagery comes from *Macbeth*. Horrified by his murder of King Duncan, Macbeth looks at his bloodstained hands and says:

> What hands are here? Ha! They pluck out
>   mine eyes!
> Will all great Neptune's ocean wash this blood
> Clean from my hand? No. This my hand
>   will rather
> The multitudinous seas incarnadine,
> Making the green one red.

The image of Duncan's blood turning all the oceans *incarnadine* (blood-red) reveals the terrifying guilt Macbeth feels over committing the murder.

Another vivid example of Shakespeare's imagery appears in *Richard II*. Richard warns Bolingbroke that his rebellion against the king will bring the horrors of civil war to England:

> He is come to open
> The purple testament of bleeding war.
> But ere the crown he looks for live in peace,
> Ten thousand bloody crowns of mothers' sons
> Shall ill become the flower of England's face,
> Change the complexion of her maid-pale peace
> To scarlet indignation, and bedew
> Her pastures' grass with faithful English blood.

Verse form. Shakespeare reinforced his imagery with the rhythm of his verse. He composed his plays largely in blank verse—that is, in lines of unrhymed iambic pentameter. In such a pattern, each line is divided into five units called *feet*, with the accent falling on every second syllable. Of all English metrical patterns, blank verse—particularly when occasionally varied—comes closest to the rhythms of everyday speech. In his earliest plays, much of Shakespeare's blank verse was highly regular and stopped or paused at the end of each line. In addition, plays from his first decade of work display a high percentage of rhymed lines, which make the verse more forced. But as his writing developed, Shakespeare's verse became increasingly flexible and natural sounding. Perhaps most significantly, verse dialogue in Shakespeare's later work increasingly tends to have a speaker end at midline with the next speaker completing the verse line.

While Shakespeare's verse becomes increasingly accomplished, his plays also employ prose in a sophisticated way. A number of early plays do not use prose, but most of the plays beginning with Shakespeare's second period exhibit some mixture of prose and verse. The two plays with the highest percentage of prose are *The Merry Wives of Windsor* and *Much Ado About Nothing*. In addition, most of the characters associated with prose, such as Falstaff, are notably comic and witty. Whether comic or serious, prose usually serves to mark a shift in tone.

Publishing History

No manuscripts of Shakespeare's plays exist. As a result, modern editions of the plays must be based on early published texts. There are two kinds of these texts—*quartos* and *folios*. A quarto is a small volume containing one Shakespeare play. A folio is a large volume of his collected plays. Twenty of Shakespeare's plays first appeared in quarto form. For his remaining 18 plays, the First Folio of 1623 is the only source.

The publishing history of Shakespeare's plays has been a story of constant attempts by editors to correct errors and deficiencies in the quartos and folios. Editors have also worked to make Shakespeare's text accessible to their readers by marking scene and act divisions, commenting on stage directions, and explaining difficult words and phrases.

Quartos have traditionally been classified as *good* or *bad*. The good quartos are thought to have been printed either from Shakespeare's own manuscripts or from accurate handwritten copies. Generally, the good quartos provide a clear and readable text, but they are not free from error. The bad quartos, in contrast, have some notable deficiencies, including textual errors and a tendency toward compression or abbreviation. Initially, five plays were identified as bad quartos, but soon an additional three plays were added. For a long time, scholars believed that the bad quartos were illegally produced by *memorial reconstruction*—a process in which an actor or actors who appeared in a play would recall the play's language for transcription and publication. Scholars are increasingly skeptical of whether the entire set of bad quartos can be explained as memorial reconstructions. Scholars now agree generally that the bad quartos contain valuable textual information.

Folios. Shakespeare did not live to supervise the publication of his own work. The first edition of his collected plays, known as the First Folio, was published in 1623, seven years after Shakespeare's death. It included 36 plays (*Pericles* and *The Two Noble Kinsmen* were excluded) arranged in three categories: comedies, histories, and tragedies. The two principal publishers, Isaac Jaggard and Edward Blount, formed a group that included William Jaggard (Isaac's father), John Smethwick, and William Aspley to share the costs of production and split the profits.

The initiative behind the First Folio probably came from John Heminge and Henry Condell, who had been shareholders with Shakespeare in the Lord Chamberlain's Men and later the King's Men. As long-time members of Shakespeare's company, Heminge and Condell presumably had access to unpublished manuscripts, and they gathered the texts that appeared in the First Folio. In their introduction, they boast, "As where (before) you were abused with diverse stolen, and surreptitious copies, maimed, and deformed by the frauds and stealths of injurious imposters, that exposed them: even those, are now offered to your view cured, and perfect in their limbs; and all the rest, absolute in their numbers, as he conceived them." Although the First Folio does not quite live up to this statement, it remains an outstanding publishing achievement for its time.

Heminge and Condell obtained the texts of the plays from various sources, including quartos and playhouse *promptbooks*. A promptbook was a copy of the script with detailed directions for performing the play. The First Folio was followed by the Second Folio (1632); the Third Folio (1663-1664), which added seven plays (*Pericles* and another six now referred to as the Shakespeare Apocrypha and not considered authentic); and the Fourth Folio (1685). The final three folios show attempts at editorial corrections, but since each successive folio is based on the preceding one, these corrections are not considered authoritative.

Editions of the 1700s and 1800s.
During the 1700s, the business of editing Shakespeare began seriously. In 1709, Nicholas Rowe produced an innovative multivolume edition that represented a profound departure from the earlier folios. Among Rowe's innovations were adding a short biography of Shakespeare, carefully observed scene and act divisions, elaborate stage directions that identify locations as well as actions, and illustrations showing dramatic moments in the plays.

Other notable editors of the 1700s, with the year in which their edition appeared, included Alexander Pope (1725), Lewis Theobald (1733), Samuel Johnson (1765), Edward Capell (1768), and Edmund Malone (1790). Theobald's edition is particularly important for its many corrections that try to restore the text to its original meaning. Johnson's edition is significant for its scholarly comments on the plays themselves. Malone's edition is notable for its commitment to authenticity. It is the first edition to include a scholarly description of the language and poetry of the Elizabethan Age, a rigorous examination of the many unverified facts included in Rowe's biography, a full chronology of the plays, and Shakespeare's sonnets.

The first *variorum* editions of the plays appeared in the 1800s. Variorum editions include notes by previous editors as well as alternate versions of disputed passages. The most elaborate is the *New Variorum* edited by H. H. Furness and others. The first volume was published in 1871. The project was later taken over by the Modern Language Association, a professional association for scholars of language and literature.

In the 1800s, the most important edition of the plays probably was the nine-volume *Cambridge Shakespeare* (1863–1866) edited by W. G. Clark, J. Glover, and W. Aldis Wright. In 1864, the edition was published in a single volume. Known as *The Globe Shakespeare*, it became the standard work for scholarly reference.

Modern Shakespeare editions reveal an increasing tendency toward specialized marketing. Editors and publishers concentrate on producing editions for a particular target audience. For example, the Folger Shakespeare Library and Barnes & Noble publish editions designed to make Shakespeare accessible to high school readers. Bantam Classics Shakespeare and the Penguin Group's Pelican Shakespeare and Signet Classics Shakespeare all offer paperbacks with light annotations intended to appeal to both the college market and general readers. Oxford University Press, Cambridge University Press, and the Arden Shakespeare publish series of single volumes for the scholarly market. Editions of the complete works, with texts and reliable commentary, include *The Riverside Shakespeare* and *The Complete Works of Shakespeare* edited by David Bevington.

Shakespearean Criticism
Shakespearean criticism—that is, serious analysis of Shakespeare and his works—did not begin

until the late 1600s. During Shakespeare's lifetime, Robert Greene apparently attacked Shakespeare for thinking he could write as well as university-educated playwrights. Francis Meres considered Shakespeare the best English stage dramatist for comedy and tragedy. The First Folio, which appeared in 1623 after Shakespeare's death, contained a number of poems praising Shakespeare. The poems included a famous tribute by the playwright Ben Jonson. Jonson said of Shakespeare, "He was not of an age, but for all time!" The poet John Milton's first published poem was a tribute to Shakespeare that appeared in the Second Folio of 1632. In another poem of the same period, Milton described Shakespeare as "fancy's child" singing "native wood-notes wild." These writings contain the seeds of future Shakespearean criticism, but they are too brief to be considered formal criticism.

Neoclassical criticism. Scholars have traditionally called the period of English literature from 1660 to 1798 the Neoclassical period because of its interest in the classical writers of ancient Greece and Rome. During this period, drama criticism was heavily influenced by the theories of the ancient Greek philosopher Aristotle. Neoclassical critics believed that Aristotle had established certain rules for writing drama. Among these were the three *unities* of action, place, and time. According to these unities, a play should depict a single action without the distraction of subplots and that action should be confined to a single place and a single day. *The Tempest* is the only Shakespeare play to observe the three unities. Shakespeare's refusal to observe the unities as well as his tendency to mix comedy with tragedy provoked the scorn of critics who worshiped the classical past. However, many Neoclassical critics were willing to attribute Shakespeare's violation of classical rules to ignorance. Such critics identified Shakespeare as a natural genius who did not need the resources of classical culture.

A landmark of Neoclassical criticism of Shakespeare appeared in John Dryden's *An Essay of Dramatic Poesy* (1668). This work is usually considered the first major critical engagement with Shakespeare's work. In the essay, Dryden contrasted the "irregular" Shakespeare with the "regular" Ben Jonson. Dryden wrote that he admired Jonson for being "the more correct poet." However, he loved Shakespeare, who "needed not the spectacles of books to read Nature" but "looked inwards, and found her there."

The most sensitive Neoclassical criticism came from the writer Samuel Johnson. He praised Shakespeare for holding up a "faithful mirror of manners and of life." He also recognized the universal appeal of Shakespeare's plays. At the same time, Johnson criticized what he considered to be Shakespeare's weaknesses. For example, Johnson objected to many comic sexual passages, which he considered vulgar, and thought that Shakespeare was often distracted by punning and wordplay. Perhaps more seriously, Johnson accused Shakespeare of frequently failing to observe *poetic justice*, in which the good should be rewarded and the wicked punished.

Romantic criticism. A movement called Romanticism, which stressed imagination, emotions, and love of nature, began to influence English literature in the 1790s. Its influence lasted through most of the 1800s. The Romantic critics tended to glorify Shakespeare almost as a god who could do no wrong. They celebrated Shakespeare's failure to observe the rules of classical literature—which the Neoclassical critics had seen as a flaw—as evidence of Shakespeare's genius. Some Romantic critics argued that Shakespeare's plays should properly be read as magnificent poetry. According to this view, staging diminishes plays that only operate at their full potential in the reader's imagination.

The Romantics produced many outstanding works of criticism. These works included Charles Lamb's *On the Tragedies of Shakespeare* (1811) and William Hazlitt's *Characters of Shakespeare's Plays* (1817). The lectures and essays of Samuel Taylor Coleridge also rank as landmarks of Shakespearean criticism.

Romantic criticism reached its peak in Edward Dowden's influential *Shakspere: A Critical Study of His Mind and Art* (1875). Dowden has perceptive things to say about the individual characters, but he always pursues his ultimate goal, "a real apprehension of Shakespeare's character and genius."

The anti-Stratfordians. During the 1800s, admiration for Shakespeare grew so intense that it resulted in a totally uncritical attitude toward the man and his works. Some people so admired Shakespeare's plays that they refused to believe an actor from Stratford-upon-Avon could have written them. Shakespeare's commonplace country background did not fit their image of the genius who wrote the plays. These people, called *anti-Stratfordians*, proposed several other writers as the author of Shakespeare's works. The writers they suggest are sometimes called *claimants*. Almost all the claimants were members of the nobility or the *gentry*, the class just below the nobility. The anti-Stratfordians believed that only an educated, sophisticated man of high social standing could have written the plays.

Sir Francis Bacon was the first and, for many years, the most popular candidate proposed as the real author of Shakespeare's plays. Bacon's followers remain active today. However, other anti-Stratfordians have had their own favorites. Edward de Vere, the 17th Earl of Oxford, is now more popular than Bacon. Other people to whom authorship has been credited include Roger Manners, the 5th Earl of Rutland; William Stanley, the 6th Earl of Derby; and Sir Walter Raleigh. Some anti-Stratfordians have also claimed that the writer Christopher Marlowe was the actual author. Despite the claims made for these men, no important Shakespearean scholar doubts that Shakespeare wrote the plays and poems.

The early and middle 1900s. The first important work of Shakespearean criticism of the 1900s was *Shakespearean Tragedy* (1904) by the English scholar A. C. Bradley. Bradley's work represents the peak of character criticism, an approach to the plays that gives priority to the psychological complexity and realism of the characters. Bradley's achievement provoked a number of criticisms and reactions. Other scholars accused him of treating literary characters as though they were real people. In *The Wheel of Fire* (1930), G. Wilson Knight explored how metaphors and other figurative language conveyed Shakespearean themes. In *Shakespeare's Imagery* (1935), Caroline Spurgeon approached the plays by studying the clusters of images they used.

The British playwright Harley Granville-Barker wrote an influential series called *The Prefaces to Shakespeare* (1927–1945) that approached the plays scene by scene from the practical standpoint of the actor. Psychoanalytic approaches tried to understand the unconscious motives of Shakespeare's characters. The British psychoanalyst Ernest Jones wrote *Hamlet and Oedipus* (1949), an influential psychoanalytic account of *Hamlet*. E. M. W. Tillyard of the United Kingdom and Hardin Craig of the United States used intellectual history to chart the Elizabethan world of ideas

that produced Shakespeare and his plays. The American scholar Lily B. Campbell emphasized the ways in which the plays offered commentary on Elizabethan political events.

Modern criticism uses a variety of approaches to the study of Shakespeare. One major development in Shakespeare scholarship during the late 1900s was feminist criticism. In its initial phase, feminist criticism focused on recovering female voices and experience, often by paying particular attention to female characters in the plays. Later work turned to questions of gender and sexuality and has studied the way in which Shakespeare's plays and poems contribute to the formation of culturally specific forms of femininity and masculinity.

Another dominant form of Shakespeare criticism is called New Historicism. New Historicism tries to understand Shakespeare's plays as products of the time and place in which they were written. It examines how they relate to the economic and political system of Elizabethan England. Unlike earlier historical forms that understood literature as a simple reflection of historical circumstances, New Historicism emphasizes the way in which the plays actually contributed to the shaping of early modern English culture.

A branch of criticism called *performance studies* focuses on acting, stage design, and the theoretical implications of performance. Such work is unified by a desire to treat the plays as plays—drama performed under particular, concrete circumstances. Still another major development in Shakespeare criticism focuses on the early printed texts. Such work has deepened our understanding of the way in which Shakespeare's texts circulated well beyond the playhouses of London and have contributed to a sense that there are multiple versions of many of Shakespeare's plays.

MLA Citation

"William Shakespeare."
*The Southwestern Advantage
Topic Source.*
Nashville: Southwestern. 2013.

DATA
Shakespeare's Plays

Play	Period	Probably first performed	First published
All's Well That Ends Well	Third	1603	1623
Antony and Cleopatra	Third	1607	1623
As You Like It	Second	1599	1623
Comedy of Errors, The	First	1590–1594	1623
Coriolanus	Third	1608	1623
Cymbeline	Fourth	1609	1623
Hamlet	Third	1601	1603
Henry IV, Parts I and II	Second	1597; 1598	1598; 1600
Henry V	Second	1599	1600
Henry VI, Parts I, II, and III	First	1590–1592	1623; 1594; 1595
Henry VIII	Fourth	1613	1623
Julius Caesar	Second	1599	1623
King John	First	1594	1623
King Lear	Third	1605	1608
Love's Labour's Lost	Second	1596	1598
Macbeth	Third	1606	1623
Measure for Measure	Third	1604	1623
Merchant of Venice, The	Second	1597	1600
Merry Wives of Windsor, The	Second	1600	1602
Midsummer Night's Dream, A	Second	1595	1600
Much Ado About Nothing	Second	1599	1600
Othello	Third	1604	1622
Pericles	Third	1607	1609
Richard II	Second	1595	1597
Richard III	First	1593	1597
Romeo and Juliet	Second	1596	1597
Taming of the Shrew, The	First	1593	1623
Tempest, The	Fourth	1611	1623
Timon of Athens	Third	1607	1623
Titus Andronicus	First	1594	1594
Troilus and Cressida	Third	1602	1609
Twelfth Night	Second	1600	1623
Two Gentlemen of Verona, The	First	1594	1623
Two Noble Kinsmen, The	Fourth	1613	1624
Winter's Tale, The	Fourth	1610	1623

ADDITIONAL RESOURCES

Books to Read

General

Andrews, John, F., ed. *Shakespeare's World and Work: An Encyclopedia for Students*. 3 vols. Scribner, 2001.

Dobson, Michael, and Wells, S. W., eds. *The Oxford Companion to Shakespeare*. Norton, 1997.

Greenblatt, Stephen, and others, eds. *The Norton Shakespeare: Based on the Oxford Edition*. 2 vols. Oxford, 1988. First published in 1930.

Kastan, David S., ed. *A Companion to Shakespeare*. Blackwell, 1999.

Shakespeare's life and times

Burgess, Anthony. *Shakespeare*. 1970. Reprint. Carroll & Graf, 2002.

Chrisp, Peter. *Shakespeare*. DK Publishing, 2002. Younger readers.

Honan, Park. *Shakespeare: A Life*. 1998. Reprint. Oxford, 2000.

Southworth, John. *Shakespeare, the Player: A Life in the Theatre*. Sutton, 2000.

Shakespeare's theater

Aliki. *William Shakespeare & the Globe*. HarperTrophy, 1999. Younger readers.

Barton, John. *Playing Shakespeare: An Actor's Guide*. Anchor Books, 2001.

Fallon, Robert T. *A Theatergoer's Guide to Shakespeare*. Ivan R. Dee, 2001.

Meagher, John C. *Shakespeare's Shakespeare: How the Plays Were Made*. Continuum, 1997.

Web Sites

Selected Poetry of William Shakespeare

http://rpo.library.utoronto.ca/poet/295.html

This page is part of Poetry On-Line, a site from the Department of English at the University of Toronto that features poetry, biographical information, and literary criticism.

Shakespeare for Kids

http://www.folger.edu/template.cfm?cid=588

The Folger Shakespeare Library presents this Web site for children and parents with interactive games and facts about William Shakespeare's life and plays.

Shakespeare Oxford Society Home Page

http://www.shakespeare-oxford.com/

Official site of the Shakespeare Oxford Society.

Shakespeare's Globe Research Database

http://www.Shakespearesglobe.com/about-us/history-of-the-globe

The University of Reading (UK), provides background information on Shakespeaere's Globe Theatre. Site includes pages devoted to the original Globe and other playhouses in Early Modern London as well as reports on reconstruction and performances

Shakespeare's Life and Times

http://web.uvic.ca/shakespeare/Library/SLTnoframes/intro/introsubj.html

Information about William Shakespeare's life and work and the Elizabethan times

The Complete Works of William Shakespeare

http://Shakespeare.mit.edu//works.html

The Tech, MIT's on-line newspaper, site of the complete works of William Shakespeare.

The Folger Shakespeare Library

http://www.folger.edu/index.cfm

Information about the Folger Shakespeare Library in Washington, D.C., which contains one of the world's most complete collections of Shakespeare's work and some work of other British authors.

Benjamin Franklin

Many historians consider Benjamin Franklin to have been the ablest and most successful diplomat in American history. He was also a printer, a scientist, and an inventor unequaled in the United States until the time of Thomas Edison.

HOT topics

Experiments with Electricity. Franklin was one of the first persons in the world to experiment with electricity. In 1752, he described how he flew a homemade kite during a thunderstorm to prove that lightning is electricity. According to Franklin, a bolt of lightning struck a pointed wire fastened to the kite and traveled down the kite string to a key fastened at the end, where it caused a spark. Franklin also tamed lightning by inventing the lightning rod. Authorities generally agree that Franklin created such electrical terms as *armature*, *condenser*, and *battery*.

Portrait of Benjamin Franklin

HOT topics 🔥

Franklin the inventor. The Franklin stove proved his most useful invention to the people of his day. By arranging the flues in his own stove in an efficient way, Franklin could make his sitting room twice as warm with one-fourth as much fuel as he had been using. People everywhere appreciate his invention of bifocal eyeglasses. This invention allowed both reading and distant lenses to be set in a single frame. He refused to patent any of his inventions or to use them for profit. He preferred to have them used freely as his contribution to the comfort and convenience of everyone.

Franklin and the Stamp Act. The opposition of the American Colonies to Britain's proposed Stamp Act led to one of the high points of his career. Franklin appeared before the House of Commons to answer a series of 174 questions dealing with "taxation without representation." Members of the House threw questions at him for nearly two hours. He answered briefly and clearly. His knowledge of taxation problems impressed everyone, and his reputation grew throughout Europe. The Stamp Act was repealed a short time later, and he received much of the credit.

Statesman for a New Nation. The people of Philadelphia chose Franklin to serve in the Second Continental Congress. He submitted a proposed Plan of Union that laid the groundwork for the Articles of Confederation. He later helped draft the Declaration of Independence, and was one of the document's signers. Shortly after the Declaration was adopted in July 1776, Congress appointed Franklin as one of three commissioners to represent the United States in France. Franklin was admired and embraced by the French people and eventually won French support during the Revolutionary War. He helped draft the Treaty of Paris, which ended the Revolutionary War, and was a signer of that document as well.

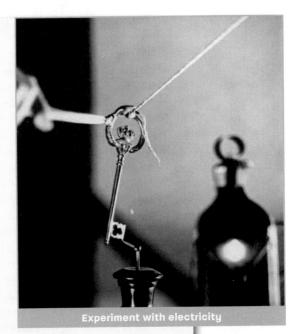

Experiment with electricity

QUOTATIONS

Franklin wrote the almanac *Poor Richard*. In each edition, Richard offered his readers a number of proverbs about thrift, duty, hard work, and simplicity. Many of these sayings became famous, including:

"A penny saved is a penny earned."

"God helps them that help themselves."

"Early to bed and early to rise,
Makes a man healthy, wealthy, and wise."

TRUE or FALSE?

Franklin's last public act was to sign an appeal to Congress calling for the speedy abolition of slavery.

hot topics hot topics hot topics hot topics

THE BASICS

Benjamin Franklin (1706–1790) was a jack-of-all-trades and master of many. No other American, except possibly Thomas Jefferson, has done so many things so well. During his long and useful life, Franklin concerned himself with such different matters as statesmanship and soap making, book printing and cabbage growing, and the rise of tides and the fall of empires. He also invented an efficient heating stove and proved that lightning is electricity.

As a statesman, Franklin stood in the front rank of the people who built the United States. He was the only person who signed all four of these key documents in American history: the Declaration of Independence, the Treaty of Alliance with France, the Treaty of Paris making peace with Britain (now the United Kingdom), and the Constitution of the United States. Franklin's services as a diplomat in France helped greatly in winning the Revolutionary War. Many historians consider him the ablest and most successful diplomat that America has ever sent abroad.

Franklin was the leader of his day in the study of electricity. As an inventor, he was unequaled in the United States until the time of Thomas A. Edison. People still quote from Franklin's *Sayings of Poor Richard* and read his *Autobiography*. Franklin helped establish Pennsylvania's first university and America's first city hospital.

Franklin's fame extended to Europe as well as America. Thomas Jefferson hailed him as "the greatest man and ornament of the age and country in which he lived." A French statesman, Comte de Mirabeau, referred to Franklin as "the sage whom two worlds claimed as their own."

Early Life

Benjamin Franklin was born in Boston, Massachusetts, on January 17, 1706. He was the 15th child and youngest son in a family of 17 children. His parents, Josiah and Abiah Franklin, were hardworking, God-fearing folk. His father made soap and candles in his shop "at the sign of the Blue Ball" on Milk Street.

Student and apprentice. Benjamin attended school in Boston for only two years. He proved himself excellent in reading, fair in writing, and poor in arithmetic. Josiah Franklin decided that he could not afford further education for his youngest son. He kept Benjamin home after the age of 10 to help cut wicks and melt tallow in the candle and soap shop.

Franklin's schooling ended, but his education did not. He believed that "the doors of wisdom are never shut," and continued to read every book that he could get. He worked on his own writing style, using a volume of the British journal *The Spectator* as a model. His prose became clear, simple, and effective. The boy also taught himself the basic principles of algebra and geometry, navigation, grammar, logic, and the natural and physical sciences. He studied and partially mastered French, German, Italian, Spanish, and Latin. He eagerly read such books as *Pilgrim's Progress*, Plutarch's *Lives*, Cotton Mather's *Essays to Do Good*, and Daniel Defoe's *Robinson Crusoe*. Franklin made himself one of the best-educated persons of his time.

Franklin did not care much for the trade of candle making. When the boy was 12, his father persuaded him to become an apprentice to his older brother James, a printer. James proved to be a good teacher, and Benjamin a good pupil. He soon became a skilled printer. He wrote several newspaper articles, signed them "Mrs. Silence Dogood," and slipped them under the print shop door. James admired the articles, and printed several of them. But he refused to print any more when he discovered that Benjamin had written them. The brothers quarreled frequently, and Benjamin longed to become his own master. At 17,

Engraving titled "Franklin's First Visit to Philadelphia"

Franklin ran away to Philadelphia, which was then the largest city in the American Colonies. The story of his arrival there has become a classic of American folklore. Many tales describe the runaway apprentice trudging bravely up Market Street with a Dutch dollar in his pocket, carrying one loaf of bread under each arm and eating a third.

Printer. From 1723 to 1730, Franklin worked for various printers in Philadelphia and in London, England, where he was sent to buy printing presses. He became part owner of a print shop in 1728, when he was 22. Two years later, he became sole owner of the business. He began publishing *The Pennsylvania Gazette*, writing much of the material for this newspaper himself. His name gradually became known throughout the colonies. Franklin had a simple formula for business success. He believed that successful people had to work just a little harder than any of their competitors. As one of his neighbors said: "The industry of that Franklin is superior to anything I ever saw . . . I see him still at work when I go home from the club, and he is at work again before his neighbors are out of bed."

Later in 1730, Franklin married Deborah Read, the daughter of his first Philadelphia landlady. Deborah was not nearly so well educated as her husband. Her letters to him have many misspelled words. The Franklins were a devoted couple. He addressed his letters to "my dear Debby," and she signed her replies, "your afeckshonet wife."

Franklin had three children, two boys and a girl. One of the boys, William, became governor of New Jersey.

The First Citizen of Philadelphia

Publisher. Franklin's printing business prospered from the start. He developed *The Pennsylvania Gazette* into one of the most successful newspapers in the colonies. He always watched carefully for new ideas. Historians credit him as the first editor in America to publish a newspaper cartoon, and to illustrate a news story with a map. He laid many of his projects for civic reform before the public in his newspaper. Franklin published *The Pennsylvania Gazette* from 1729 until 1766.

But Franklin achieved even greater success with *Poor Richard's Almanac* than with his newspaper. He wrote and published the almanac for every year from 1733 to 1758. The fame of the almanac rests mainly on the wise and witty sayings that Franklin

Poor Richard, 1733.

AN
Almanack

For the Year of Chrift

1733,

Being the Firft after LEAP YEAR:

And makes fince the Creation	Years
By the Account of the Eastern *Greeks*	7241
By the Latin Church, when ☉ ent. ♈	6932
By the Computation of *W. W.*	5742
By the *Roman* Chronology	5682
By the *Jewiſh* Rabbies	5494

Wherein is contained

The Lunations, Eclipfes, Judgment of the Weather, Spring Tides, Planets Motions & mutual Afpects, Sun and Moon's Rifing and Setting, Length of Days, Time of High Water, Fairs, Courts, and obſervable Days.

Fitted to the Latitude of Forty Degrees, and a Meridian of Five Hours Weft from *London*, but may without fenfible Error, ferve all the adjacent Places, even from *Newfoundland* to *South-Carolina*.

By *RICHARD SAUNDERS*, Philom.

PHILADELPHIA:
Printed and fold by *B. FRANKLIN*, at the New Printing-Office near the Market.

Poor Richard's Almanac

scattered through each issue. Many of these sayings preach the virtues of industry, frugality, and thrift. "Early to bed and early to rise, makes a man healthy, wealthy, and wise." "God helps them that help themselves." "Little strokes fell great oaks." Other sayings reflect a shrewd understanding of human nature. "He's a fool that makes his doctor his heir." "He that falls in love with himself will have no rivals."

Civic leader. Franklin never actively sought public office, although he was interested in public affairs. In 1736, he became clerk of the Pennsylvania Assembly. The poor service of the colonial postal service disturbed him greatly. Hoping to improve matters, he agreed to become Philadelphia's postmaster in 1737. He impressed the British government with his efficiency in this position, and in 1753 he became a deputy postmaster general for all the colonies. Franklin worked hard at this job, and introduced many needed reforms. He set up the first city delivery system and the first Dead-Mail Office. He speeded foreign mail deliveries by using the fastest packet ships available across the Atlantic Ocean. To speed domestic mail service, he hired more post riders, and required his couriers to ride both night and day. Franklin also helped Canada establish its first regular postal service. He opened post offices at Quebec, Montreal, and Trois Rivieres in 1763. He also established messenger service between Montreal and New York.

Franklin was public-spirited, and worked constantly to make Philadelphia a better city. He helped establish the first subscription library in the American Colonies. The members of this library contributed money to buy books, and then used them free of charge. The original collection still exists. Fire losses in Philadelphia were alarmingly high, and Franklin organized a fire department. He reformed the city police when he saw that criminals were getting away without punishment. City streets were unpaved, dirty, and dark, so he started a program to pave, clean, and light them. Philadelphia shamefully neglected the sick and insane during Franklin's time. He raised money to help build a city hospital, the Pennsylvania Hospital, for these unfortunates. Scholars in the American Colonies had no professional organization, so Franklin helped establish the American Philosophical Society, with headquarters in Philadelphia. The city had no school for higher education, so Franklin helped found the academy that grew into the University of Pennsylvania. As a result of

Currier and Ives lithograph

projects such as these, Philadelphia became the most advanced city in the 13 colonies.

The Scientist

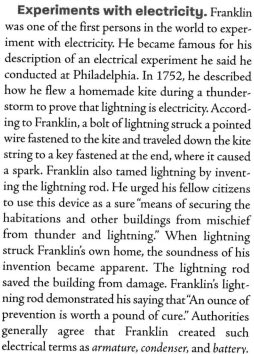

Experiments with electricity. Franklin was one of the first persons in the world to experiment with electricity. He became famous for his description of an electrical experiment he said he conducted at Philadelphia. In 1752, he described how he flew a homemade kite during a thunderstorm to prove that lightning is electricity. According to Franklin, a bolt of lightning struck a pointed wire fastened to the kite and traveled down the kite string to a key fastened at the end, where it caused a spark. Franklin also tamed lightning by inventing the lightning rod. He urged his fellow citizens to use this device as a sure "means of securing the habitations and other buildings from mischief from thunder and lightning." When lightning struck Franklin's own home, the soundness of his invention became apparent. The lightning rod saved the building from damage. Franklin's lightning rod demonstrated his saying that "An ounce of prevention is worth a pound of cure." Authorities generally agree that Franklin created such electrical terms as *armature*, *condenser*, and *battery*.

Franklin's experiments with electricity involved some personal risk. He knocked himself unconscious at least once. He had been trying to kill a turkey with an electric shock, but something went wrong and Franklin, not the bird, was stunned. Franklin later said: "I meant to kill a turkey, and instead, I nearly killed a goose."

Other studies. Franklin's scientific interests ranged far beyond electricity. He became the first scientist to study the movement of the Gulf Stream in the Atlantic Ocean. He spent much time charting its course and recording its temperature, speed, and depth. Franklin was the first to show scientists and naval officers that sailors could calm a rough sea by pouring oil on it. He favored daylight saving time in summer. It struck him as silly and wasteful that people should "live much by candle-light and sleep by sunshine."

Franklin gave the world several other valuable inventions in addition to the lightning rod. The Franklin stove proved most useful to the people of his day. By arranging the flues in his own stove in an efficient way, he could make his sitting room twice as warm with one fourth as much fuel as he had been using. People everywhere appreciate his invention of bifocal eyeglasses most of all. This invention allowed both reading and distant lenses to be set in a single frame. Franklin discovered that disease flourishes in poorly ventilated rooms. Franklin also showed Americans how to improve acid soil by using lime. He refused to patent any of his inventions, or to use them for profit. He preferred to have them used freely as his contribution to the comfort and convenience of everyone.

Franklin quickly appreciated the inventive efforts of other people. He once said that he would like to return to earth a hundred years later to see what progress humanity had made. The first successful balloon flight took place in 1783, during Franklin's stay in Paris. Many bystanders scoffed at the new device and asked, "What good is it?" Franklin retorted, "What good is a newborn baby?"

Franklin's scientific work won him many high honors. The Royal Society of London elected him to membership, a rare honor for a person living in the colonies. Publishers translated his writings on electricity into French, German, and Italian. The great English statesman William Pitt told the House of Lords that Franklin ranked with Isaac Newton as a scientist. He called Franklin "an honor not to the English nation only but to human nature."

The Public Servant

The Plan of Union. In the spring of 1754, war broke out between the British and French in America. Franklin felt that the colonies had to unite for self-defense against the French and Indians. He printed the famous "Join or Die" cartoon in his newspaper. This cartoon showed a snake cut up into pieces that represented the colonies.

Franklin presented his Plan of Union at a conference of seven colonies at Albany, New York. This plan tried to bring the 13 colonies together in "one general government." The Plan of Union contained some of the ideas that were later included in the Constitution of the United States. The delegates at the Albany Congress approved Franklin's plan, but the colonies failed to ratify it. Said Franklin: "Everyone cries a union is absolutely necessary, but when it comes to the manner and form of the union, their weak noddles are perfectly distracted."

The war forced Franklin to turn his attention to the unfamiliar field of military matters. Early in 1755, General Edward Braddock and two British regiments arrived in America with orders to capture the French stronghold of Fort Duquesne, at

the point where the Allegheny and Monongahela rivers met. The British had trouble finding horses and wagons for the expedition, and Franklin helped provide the necessary equipment. However, the French and Indians ambushed the British on the banks of the Monongahela River. Braddock was killed, and the British army was almost destroyed. In the meantime, Franklin raised volunteer colonial armies to defend frontier towns, and supervised construction of a fort at Weissport in Carbon County, Pennsylvania.

A delegate in London. In 1757, the Pennsylvania legislature sent Franklin to London to speak for the colony in a tax dispute with the *proprietors* (descendants of William Penn living in Britain). The proprietors controlled the governor of the colony, and would not allow it to pass any tax

The Franklin printing press

bill for defense unless their own estates were left tax-free. In 1760, Franklin finally succeeded in getting the British Parliament to adopt a measure that permitted the taxation of both the colonists and the proprietors. Franklin remained in Britain during most of the next 15 years as a sort of unofficial ambassador and spokesman for the American point of view.

A serious debate developed in Britain in the early 1760s at the end of the French and Indian War. The French, who lost the war, agreed to give the British either the French province of Canada or the French island of Guadeloupe in the West Indies. At the height of the argument, Franklin published a pamphlet that shrewdly compared the boundless future of Canada with the relative unimportance of Guadeloupe. Europeans and Americans read it carefully. Some historians believe that it influenced the British to choose Canada.

Franklin also took part in the fight over the Stamp Act. He seems to have been rather slow to recognize that the proposed measure threatened the American Colonies. But once he realized its dangers, he joined the struggle for repeal of the act. This fight led to one of the high points of his career. On February 13, 1766, Franklin appeared before the House of Commons to answer a series of 174 questions dealing with "taxation without representation." Members of the House threw questions at him for nearly two hours. He answered briefly and clearly. His knowledge of taxation problems impressed everyone, and his reputation grew throughout Europe. The Stamp Act was repealed a short time later, and he received much of the credit.

Political relations between Britain and the colonies grew steadily worse. Franklin wanted America to remain in the British Empire, but only if the rights of the colonists could be recognized and protected. He pledged his entire fortune to pay for the tea destroyed in the Boston Tea Party if the British government would agree to repeal its unjust tax on tea. The British ignored his proposal. Franklin realized that his usefulness in Britain had ended, and sadly sailed for home on March 21, 1775. Franklin had done everything possible to keep the American Colonies in the empire on the basis of mutual respect and good will.

The Statesman

Organizing the new nation. Franklin arrived in Philadelphia on May 5, 1775, about two weeks after the Revolutionary War began. The next day, the people of Philadelphia chose him to serve in the Second Continental Congress. Franklin seldom spoke at the Congress, but became one of its most active and influential members. He submitted a proposed Plan of Union that contained ideas from his earlier Albany Plan of Union. This plan laid the groundwork for the Articles of Confederation. Franklin served on a commission that went to Canada in an unsuccessful attempt to persuade the French Canadians to join the Revolutionary War. He worked on committees dealing with such varied matters as printing paper money, reorganizing the Continental Army, and finding supplies of powder and lead.

The Continental Congress chose Franklin as postmaster general in 1775 because of his experience as a colonial postmaster. The government directed him to organize a postal system quickly. He soon had mail service from Portland, Maine, to Savannah, Georgia. He gave his salary to the relief of wounded soldiers.

**Drafting the Declaration of Independence (left to right):
Franklin, Thomas Jefferson, John Adams,
Robert Livingston, and Roger Sherman**

Franklin helped draft the Declaration of Independence, and was one of the document's signers. During the signing ceremonies, according to tradition, John Hancock warned his fellow delegates, "We must be unanimous; there must be no pulling different ways; we must all hang together." "Yes," Franklin replied, "we must indeed all hang together, or assuredly we shall all hang separately."

Serving in France. Shortly after the Declaration of Independence was adopted in July 1776, Congress appointed Franklin as one of three commissioners sent to represent the United States in France. The war was not going well, and Congress realized an alliance with France might mean the difference between victory and defeat. Late in 1776, at the age of 70, Franklin set forth on the most important task of his life.

Franklin received a tremendous welcome in Paris. The French people were charmed by his kindness, his simple dress and manner, his wise and witty sayings, and his tact and courtesy in greeting the nobility and common people alike. Crowds ran after him in the streets. Poets wrote glowing verses in his honor. Portraits and busts of him appeared everywhere.

In spite of Franklin's popularity, the French government hesitated to make a treaty of alliance with the American Colonies. Such a treaty would surely mean war between France and Britain. So with tact, patience, and courtesy, Franklin set out to win the French government to the American cause. His chance came after British General John Burgoyne's army surrendered at Saratoga. The French were impressed by this American victory, and agreed to a treaty of alliance. The pact was signed on February 6, 1778. Franklin then arranged transportation to America for French officers, soldiers, and guns. He managed to keep loans and gifts of money flowing to the United States. Many historians believe that without this aid the Americans could not have won their independence.

In 1778, Franklin was appointed minister to France. He helped draft the Treaty of Paris, which ended the Revolutionary War. France, Britain, and Spain all had interests in the American Colonies, and Franklin found it difficult to arrange a treaty that satisfied them all. The treaty gave the new nation everything it could reasonably expect. Franklin was one of the signers of the Treaty of Paris in 1783.

Franklin's return from France

The Twilight Years

Franklin returned to Philadelphia in 1785. For the next two years, he served as president of the executive council of Pennsylvania. This office resembled that of a governor today. In 1787, Pennsylvania sent the 81-year-old Franklin to the Constitutional Convention. The delegates met in Independence Hall and drafted the Constitution of the United States. Age and illness kept Franklin from taking an active part. But his wisdom helped keep the convention from breaking up in failure. Franklin was the oldest delegate at the convention.

Franklin also helped the convention settle the bitter dispute between large and small states over representation in Congress. He did this by supporting the so-called Great Compromise. The compromise sought to satisfy both groups by setting up a two-house Congress. In his last formal speech to the convention, Franklin appealed to his fellow delegates for unanimous support of the Constitution.

Franklin's attendance at the Constitutional Convention was his last major public service. However, his interest in public affairs continued to the end of his life. He rejoiced in Washington's inauguration as the first president of the United States. He hoped that the example of the new nation would lead to a United States of Europe. In 1787, he was elected president of the first antislavery society in America. Franklin's last public act was to sign an appeal to Congress calling for the speedy abolition of slavery.

Franklin died on the night of April 17, 1790, at the age of 84. About 20,000 people honored him at his funeral. He was buried in the cemetery of Christ Church in Philadelphia beside his wife, who had died in 1774. Franklin accomplished much in many fields, but he began his will with the simple words: "I, Benjamin Franklin, printer ..." Franklin left $5,000 each to Boston and Philadelphia, part to be used for public works after 100 years, and the rest after 200 years. Part of this money has been used to establish the Franklin Technical Institute, a trade school in Boston, and the Franklin Institute Science Museum in Philadelphia.

His Place in History

Franklin led all the people of his time in his life-long concern for the happiness, well-being, and dignity of humanity. George Washington spoke for a whole generation of Americans in a letter to Franklin in 1789: "If to be venerated for benevolence, if to be admired for talents, if to be esteemed for patriotism, if to be beloved for philanthropy, can gratify the human mind, you must have the pleasing consolation to know that you have not lived in vain."

Franklin's name would almost certainly be on any list of the half-dozen greatest Americans. His face has appeared on postage stamps, and on the coins and paper money of the United States. Two presidents of the United States proudly bore his name: Franklin Pierce and Franklin D. Roosevelt.

Philadelphia has also revered the memory of its most famous citizen. The University of Pennsylvania named its athletic field in his honor. One of the showplaces of the city is the spacious Benjamin Franklin Parkway. Midway along the parkway stands the Franklin Institute Science Museum, dedicated to popularizing the sciences that Franklin loved so well. This building contains the Benjamin Franklin National Memorial, with its great statue of the seated philosopher by James Earle Fraser. The museum has also set up a reconstruction of Franklin's printing shop, with his own printing presses.

MLA Citation

"Benjamin Franklin."
*The Southwestern
Advantage Topic Source.*
Nashville: Southwestern. 2013.

ADDITIONAL RESOURCES

Books to Read

Adler, David A. *B. Franklin, Printer.* Holiday House, 2001. Younger readers.

Brands, H. W. *The First American: The Life and Times of Benjamin Franklin.* Doubleday, 2000.

Fleming, Candace. *Ben Franklin's Almanac.* Atheneum, 2003. Younger readers.

Giblin, James. *The Amazing Life of Benjamin Franklin.* Scholastic, 2000. Younger readers.

Isaacson, Walter. *Benjamin Franklin.* Simon & Schuster, 2004.

Morgan, Edmund S. *Benjamin Franklin.* Yale, 2002.

Schiff, Stacy. *A Great Improvisation: Franklin, France, and the Birth of America.* Henry Holt, 2005.

Wood, Gordon S. *The Americanization of Benjamin Franklin.* Penguin, 2004.

Web Sites

Benjamin Franklin

http://www.npg.si.edu/col/age/frank.htm

A portrait by Jean-Antoine Houdon from the National Portrait Gallery in Washington, D.C.

The Electric Ben Franklin

http://www.ushistory.org/franklin/

Includes biographical information about Franklin as well as quotations from his works and virtual tours of Franklin-related sites.

Theater of Electricity

http://www.mos.org/sln/toe/

An on-line exhibit about electricity and the forms it takes, from the Museum of Science in Boston.

Search Strings

Experiments with Electricity

Benjamin Franklin experiments electricity lightning (32,100)

Benjamin Franklin experiments electricity lightning rod (146,000)

Benjamin Franklin experiments electricity lightning kite spark (5,550)

Franklin the Inventor

Benjamin Franklin inventor "Franklin stove" bifocals (873)

Benjamin Franklin inventor patent "Franklin stove" bifocals (937)

Franklin and the Stamp Act

Benjamin Franklin "Stamp Act" (79,000)

Benjamin Franklin "Stamp Act" "taxation without representation" (5,280)

Benjamin Franklin "Stamp Act" House of Commons "taxation without representation" (845)

Statesman for a New Nation

Benjamin Franklin Second Continental Congress Plan of Union Declaration of Independence Treaty of Paris (54,300)

Benjamin Franklin "Second Continental Congress" "Plan of Union" "Declaration of Independence" "Treaty of Paris" (614)

Benjamin Franklin statesman "Second Continental Congress" "Plan of Union" "Declaration of Independence" "Treaty of Paris" (343)

George Washington

Called the Father of Our Country, George Washington commanded the Continental Army that won American independence from Britain in the Revolutionary War, and he was elected first president of the United States.

HOT topics

Early Military Career. At the young age of 22, George Washington was promoted to lieutenant colonel and told to enlist colonists to fight for the British against the French. In 1754 he led 100 poorly paid and poorly trained soldiers against French forces that had captured a British fort. He surprised the French, killed 10, wounded 1, and took 21 prisoners. Only one of Washington's men was killed. But Washington would suffer numerous defeats as a young officer, often receiving little support and fighting with men who were hungry and sick. He soon became the most famous American-born soldier. His early experiences taught him how to train other soldiers and to run an army.

Revolutionary War ships

HOT topics

The Young Legislator.
At the age of 26, Washington turned to seeking happiness as a country gentleman and to building a fortune. During the next 16 years, he became known as a skilled farmer, an intelligent businessman, a popular legislator, a conscientious warden of the Church of England, and a wise county court judge. He had been elected to the House of Burgesses in 1758, while still on the frontier. He was reelected time after time to the legislature, where he learned the process of representative government. The experience gave him patience in later years when he had to deal with Congress during the Revolutionary War and as president. He also became acquainted at this time with Thomas Jefferson, Patrick Henry, and other Virginia leaders.

Winning the War/Strategy in the War of Independence.
From the beginning of the war, Washington knew the powerful British navy gave the enemy a great advantage. The ships of the British could carry their army anywhere along the American coast. Washington's tiny, ragged army could not possibly defend every American port. On the other hand, Washington knew from his experience in the French and Indian War that the British army moved slowly on land and that it could be beaten. He proved that he could stay one jump ahead of the British by quick retreats. Meanwhile, Washington waited and prayed for the French to send a large fleet of warships to America. He hoped that he could then trap the British while the French navy prevented them from escaping.

Portrait of George Washington

Elected President.
By the summer of 1788, enough states had approved the Constitution to allow for the reorganization of the government. Throughout the country, people linked Washington's name directly to the new Constitution. They took it for granted that he would be chosen as the first president. Despite Washington's doubts as to whether he should accept the position, he was elected president with the largest number of votes possible. John Adams was elected vice president.

TRUE or FALSE?
George Washington held the office of President of the United States for a total of three terms.

THE BASICS

George Washington (1732–1799) won a lasting place in American history as the "Father of the Country." For nearly 20 years, he guided his country much as a father cares for a growing child.

In three important ways, Washington helped shape the beginning of the United States. First, he commanded the Continental Army that won American independence from Britain in the Revolutionary War. Second, Washington served as president of the convention that wrote the United States Constitution. Third, he was elected the first president of the United States.

Most Americans of his day loved Washington. His army officers would have tried to make him king if he had let them. From the Revolutionary War on, his birthday was celebrated each year throughout the country.

Washington lived an exciting life in exciting times. As a boy, he explored the wilderness. When he grew older, he helped the British fight the French and Indians. Several times he was nearly killed. As a general, he suffered hardships with his troops in the cold winters at Valley Forge, Pennsylvania, and Morristown, New Jersey. He lost many battles, but led the American army to final victory at Yorktown, Virginia. After he became president, he successfully solved many problems in turning the plans of the Constitution into a working government.

Washington went to school only until he was about 14 or 15. But he learned to make the most of all his abilities and opportunities. Washington's remarkable patience and his understanding of others helped him win people to his side in times of hardship and discouragement.

There are great differences between the United States of Washington's day and that of today. The new nation was small and weak. It stretched west only to the Mississippi River and had fewer than 4,000,000 people. Most people made their living by farming. Few children went to school. Many men and women could not read or write. Transportation and communication were slow. It took Washington 3 days to travel about 90 miles (140 kilometers) from New York City to Philadelphia, longer than it now takes to fly around the world. There were only 11 states in the Union when Washington became president and 16 when he left office.

Portrait of President Washington

Many stories have been told about Washington. Most are probably not true. So far as we know, he did not chop down his father's cherry tree, and then confess by saying: "I cannot tell a lie, Pa." He probably never threw a stone across the Rappahannock River. But such stories show that people were willing to believe almost anything about his honesty and his great strength. One of Washington's officers, Henry "Light Horse Harry" Lee, summed up the way Americans felt and still feel about Washington: "First in war, first in peace, and first in the hearts of his countrymen."

Washington the Man

Washington's appearance caused admiration and respect. He was tall, strong, and broad-shouldered. As he grew older, cares lined his face and gave him a somewhat stern appearance. Perhaps the best description of Washington was written by a friend, George Mercer, in 1760:

"He may be described as being straight as an Indian, measuring 6 feet 2 inches in his stockings, and weighing 175 pounds . . . A large and straight rather than a prominent nose; blue-gray penetrating eyes . . . He has a clear though rather colorless pale skin which burns with the sun . . . dark brown hair which he wears in a queue . . .

His mouth is large and generally firmly closed, but which from time to time discloses some defective teeth ... His movements and gestures are graceful, his walk majestic, and he is a splendid horseman."

Washington set his own strict rules of conduct, but he also enjoyed having a good time. He laughed at jokes, though he seldom told any.

One of the best descriptions of Washington's character was written after his death by Washington's fellow Virginian Thomas Jefferson:

"His mind was great and powerful . . . as far as he saw, no judgment was ever sounder. It was slow in operation, being little aided by invention or imagination, but sure in conclusion. ...

"Perhaps the strongest feature in his character was prudence, never acting until every circumstance, every consideration, was maturely weighed; refraining if he saw a doubt, but, when once decided, going through with his purpose, whatever obstacles opposed.

"His integrity was most pure, his justice the most inflexible I have ever known . . .

"He was, indeed, in every sense of the words, a wise, a good and a great man . . . On the whole, his character was, in its mass, perfect . . . it may truly be said, that never did nature and fortune combine more perfectly to make a man great . . ."

Family background.
George Washington inherited much more than a good mind and a strong body. Washington belonged to an old colonial family that believed in hard work, in public service, and in worshiping God. The Washington family has been traced back to 1260 in England. The name at that time was de Wessington. It was later spelled Washington. Sulgrave Manor in England is regarded as the home of George Washington's ancestors.

George's great-grandfather, John Washington (1632–1677), came to live in America by accident. He was mate on a small English ship that went aground in the Potomac River in 1656 or 1657. By the time the ship was repaired, he had decided to marry and settle in Virginia. He started with little money. Within 20 years he owned more than 5,000 acres (2,000 hectares), including the land that later became Mount Vernon. Lawrence Washington (1659–1698), the eldest son of John, was the grandfather of George.

Washington's birthplace

Washington's parents.
George's father, Augustine Washington (1694–1743), was Lawrence's youngest son. After iron ore was discovered on some of his land, he spent most of his time developing an ironworks. He had four children by his first wife, Jane Butler. She died in 1729. In March 1731, he married Mary Ball (1709?–1789), who became George's mother.

Mary Ball did not have a very happy childhood. Her father and mother both died before she was 13. Although she had inherited property from her mother, she spent all her life worrying about money. After her son George became a man, she wrote him many letters asking for money even though she did not always need it.

Augustine and Mary Ball Washington had six children. Besides George, there were: Betty (1733–1797), Samuel (1734–1781), John Augustine (1736–1787), Charles (1738–1799), and Mildred (1739–1740).

Boyhood.
George Washington was born on Pope's Creek Plantation in Westmoreland County, Virginia, on February 22, 1732 (February 11, on the Old Style Calendar then in use). When George was about 3 years old, his family moved to the large, undeveloped plantation that was later called Mount Vernon. It lay about 50 miles (80 kilometers) up the Potomac River in Virginia and was then called Little Hunting Creek Farm. George's only playmates at the plantation were his younger sister and brothers. No neighbors lived close by. But George probably had fun exploring the nearby woods and helping out in farm work. He saw little of his father, who made many trips to his ironworks, about 30 miles (48 kilometers) away.

In 1738, when George was nearly 7, his father decided to move closer to the ironworks. He bought the 260-acre (105-hectare) Ferry Farm which lay on the Rappahannock River across from Fredericksburg, Virginia.

Education. George probably began going to school in Fredericksburg soon after the family moved to Ferry Farm. No accurate records have been found that tell who his teachers were. Altogether, he had no more than seven or eight years of school. His best subject was arithmetic. He wrote his lessons in ink on heavy paper. His mother or a teacher then sewed the paper into notebooks.

George studied enough history and geography to know something of the outside world. But he never learned as much about literature, foreign languages, and history as did Thomas Jefferson or James Madison. They had the advantage of much more formal education.

By the time he ended his schoolwork at the age of 14 or 15, George could keep business accounts, write clear letters, and do simple figuring. During the rest of his life he kept diaries and careful accounts of his expenses.

George's father had probably planned to send him to school in England because there were few schools in Virginia. But Augustine Washington died when George was only 11, and the plans came to nothing. After his father's death, George's mother did not like to have him away from home for long. George was to inherit Ferry Farm when he reached 21. Meanwhile, he, his younger sister and brothers, and the farm were left in the care of his mother.

Plantation life. Growing up at Ferry Farm, young George helped manage a plantation worked by 20 black slaves. He was observant and hardworking. He learned how to plant and produce tobacco, fruit, grains, and vegetables. He saw how many things a plantation needed to keep operating, such as cloth and iron tools. He also developed his lifelong love for horses. At the same time, Washington enjoyed the life of a young Virginia country gentleman. He had boyhood romances and wrote love poems. He became a good dancer. And he enjoyed hunting, fishing, and boating on the river.

Development of character. As a youth, Washington was sober, quiet, attentive, and dignified. His respect for his elders and his dependability made him admired. He experienced the hardships of colonial life on the edge of the wilderness. He learned that life was difficult. This helped make him become strong and patient.

As a schoolboy, Washington copied rules of behavior in an exercise book, perhaps at the suggestion of his mother or a teacher. Following are some of these rules in his own spelling, capitalization, and punctuation:

Turn not your Back to others especially in Speaking, Jog not the Table or Desk on which Another reads or writes, lean not upon any one.

Use no Reproachfull Language against any one neither Curse nor Revile.

Play not the Peacock, looking every where about you, to See if you be well Deck't, if your Shoes fit well, if your Skokings Sit neatly, and Cloths handsomely.

While you are talking, Point not with your Finger at him of Whom you Discourse nor Approach too near him to whom you talk especially to his face.

Be not Curious to Know the Affairs of Others neither approach those that Speak in Private.

It's unbecoming to Stoop much to ones Meat Keep your Fingers clean & when foul wipe them on a Corner of your Table Napkin.

George Washington's admiration for his half brother Lawrence (1718–1752) also influenced his development. Lawrence had been educated in England. He had the polish of a young English gentleman. From 1740 to 1742, Lawrence had gone to South America as a Virginia volunteer captain in a brief war between Britain and Spain. Lawrence took no part in the actual fighting. But he returned to Virginia with many war stories. These tales excited George's imagination. George

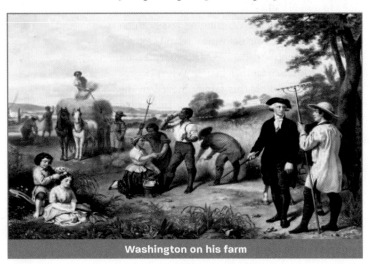

Washington on his farm

became a frequent visitor to the fashionable new house that Lawrence had built at Mount Vernon.

Lawrence decided that 14-year-old George should join the British Royal Navy. George wanted to go, but he needed his mother's permission. No matter how much he argued, she would not let him go. She asked advice of her half brother, Joseph Ball. He suggested somewhat jokingly that rather than let George become a sailor, it would be better to apprentice him to a *tinker*, a mender of pots and pans.

Washington the Surveyor (1747–1752)

After teenaged George Washington gave up hopes of becoming a sailor, he became interested in exploring the frontier. Becoming a surveyor and marking out new farms in the wilderness would give him a chance to seek adventure and earn money. He enjoyed mathematics, and he easily picked up an understanding of fractions and geometry. Then he took his father's old set of surveying instruments out of storage. At 15, he began studying to be a surveyor.

On one of his frequent visits to Mount Vernon, George met Lord Fairfax, the largest property owner in Virginia. Fairfax was a cousin of Lawrence Washington's wife. He owned more than 5 million acres (2 million hectares) of land in northern Virginia. These lands extended to the Allegheny Mountains and included much of the Shenandoah Valley.

First expedition. Lord Fairfax began planning an expedition to survey his western lands. James Genn, an expert surveyor, was put in charge of the expedition. Sixteen-year-old George Washington was invited to go along. The boy persuaded his mother to let him make his first long trip away from home.

The month-long expedition set out on horseback in March 1748. Washington learned to sleep in the open and hunt for food. By the time he returned to Mount Vernon, he felt he had grown into a man.

Professional surveyor. In July 1749, Washington was appointed official surveyor for Culpeper County. In November, Lord Fairfax allowed him to make a short surveying trip on his own to the Allegheny Mountains.

Washington lived at Mount Vernon for part of that winter. His surveying work paid him well. It

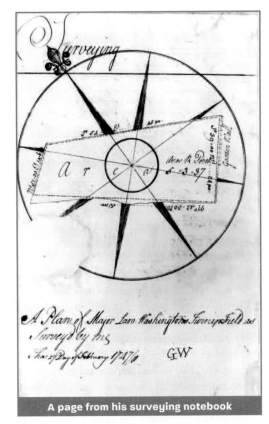

A page from his surveying notebook

was one of the few occupations in which a person could expect to be paid in cash. Most other business in Virginia was carried on with payments in tobacco. Washington kept track in his account book of small loans he made to his relatives and friends. He also wrote down winnings and losses at playing cards and billiards.

During the next three years, Washington made more and more surveys as settlers moved into the Shenandoah Valley. He carefully saved his money. When he saw a particularly good piece of land, he bought it. By 1752, he owned about 2,300 acres (930 hectares).

Only foreign trip. In 1751, George Washington made his only trip away from the shores of America. Lawrence Washington had become seriously ill. He decided to sail to the warm climate of Barbados Island in the British West Indies for his health. He asked George to go along.

The brothers arrived at the island in November. George's diary shows he was interested in comparing farming methods on the island with those of Virginia. Two weeks after arriving, George became ill with smallpox. He carried a few pox scars on his face the rest of his life. A week after recovering,

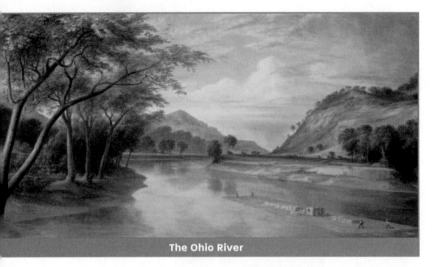

The Ohio River

George decided to return to Virginia while Lawrence remained in the tropics.

George was now 20. He fell in love with 16-year-old Betsy Fauntleroy, the daughter of a Richmond County planter and shipowner. George proposed to her at least twice. Each time he was refused. He sadly wrote that she had given him a "cruel sentence."

In early June 1752, Lawrence Washington suddenly returned home. He died of tuberculosis before the end of the month. Lawrence left Mount Vernon to his wife for as long as she lived, then to his daughter. He provided that the estate should go to George if his daughter died with no children of her own. He also left George an equal share of his land in the Shenandoah Valley with his other three brothers.

Early Military Career (1753–1758)

At the age of 20, George Washington had no experience or training as a soldier. But Lawrence's war stories had interested him in military affairs. He applied to the governor for a commission in the militia. In December 1752, he was commissioned as a major and put in charge of training militia in southern Virginia. Washington probably prepared for his new duties by reading books on military drills and tactics.

Messenger to the French. In October 1753, Washington learned that Robert Dinwiddie, the acting governor of Virginia, planned to send a message to the French military commander in the Ohio River Valley. Dinwiddie intended to warn the French that they must withdraw their troops from the region. Both the French and the British wanted the Ohio River Valley for fur trading, and British speculators wanted to invest in land there. Washington volunteered to carry the message. Dinwiddie gave him the task.

In mid-November, Washington set out on the dangerous trip. With him went Christopher Gist, a frontier guide; an interpreter; and four frontiersmen. Washington's party traveled north into western Pennsylvania. Sometimes the men covered as much as 20 miles (32 kilometers) in a day. They stopped at an Indian village near the site of present-day Pittsburgh, Pennsylvania. There, three Indian chiefs agreed to accompany the party to visit the French. The Indians gave George the name *Conotocarious*, which meant Towntaker.

Early in December, Washington reached French headquarters at Fort Le Boeuf, just south of present-day Erie, Pennsylvania. The French commander rejected Dinwiddie's warning. He said that his orders were to take and hold the Ohio River Valley. He gave Washington a letter to carry back to the British. Washington experienced many hardships and dangers on the return trip to Virginia. It was late December and bitterly cold. Snow lay deep on the ground. Once, Washington nearly drowned trying to cross the Allegheny River on a raft.

On January 16, 1754, Washington reached Williamsburg, Virginia, and delivered the French reply to Dinwiddie. Washington urged Dinwiddie to build a fort where the Ohio and Allegheny rivers joined (the site of present-day Pittsburgh). He also drew a detailed map of the region. Before the end of the month, Dinwiddie ordered a force of frontiersmen to build the fort. The governor had unknowingly taken the first step toward the French and Indian War, which was to spread to many other countries. This war was known in Canada and Europe as the Seven Years' War.

First military action. The 22-year-old Washington was promoted to lieutenant colonel. He received orders to enlist troops to man the new fort. He found Americans resentful because the Virginia government refused to pay them as much as regular British soldiers. Washington himself angrily threatened to resign because his pay was lower than that of a lieutenant colonel in the regular British army. Perhaps for the first time he realized that American colonists were treated unfairly. It also may have been the first time he thought of himself as an American rather than as an Englishman.

"Discipline is the soul of an army. It makes small numbers formidable; procures success to the weak, and esteem to all."
—Source: Letter of instructions to the captains of the Virginia Regiments, July 29, 1757.

Washington set out with about 160 poorly trained soldiers in April 1754. He was still 100 miles (160 kilometers) from the fort when he learned the French had captured it. Washington decided to move on toward the fort, which the French had named Fort Duquesne.

On May 28, 1754, Washington's men fired the first shots of the war. He surprised a group of French troops, killed 10, wounded 1, and took 21 prisoners. Only one of Washington's men was killed. Washington described his feelings in the short fight: "I heard bullets whistle and believe me there is something charming in the sound."

Surrender of Fort Necessity. Washington's men built a fort about 60 miles (97 kilometers) south of Fort Duquesne. They completed it in June and named it Fort Necessity. Meanwhile, Washington had been promoted to the rank of colonel.

Early in June, about 180 Virginia soldiers arrived to reinforce Fort Necessity. Some friendly Indians also joined Washington's forces. But no food arrived. On June 14, just as the last food was being eaten, a company of about 100 British regular army troops arrived. They brought with them some vitally needed supplies.

On July 3, the French attacked Fort Necessity. Washington had fewer than 400 men. Many of the troops were sick, and all of them were hungry. The French fired from behind trees and rocks. About 30 of Fort Necessity's defenders were killed and 70 wounded. A rainstorm turned the battlefield into a sea of mud. As night fell, the young colonel had few men, little food, and no dry gunpowder. His position was hopeless. About midnight, Washington agreed to surrender Fort Necessity. The French let him march out of the fort and return to Virginia with his men and guns.

A discouraged Washington returned to Williamsburg two weeks later. The colonists did not blame the young colonel for losing the fort. They praised Washington and his men for their bravery.

In October, Washington again visited Williamsburg. He was shocked when Dinwiddie told him he had orders from London not to allow colonial officers to have ranks above captain. Washington wanted a military career, but he angrily resigned, rather than be lowered from the rank of colonel to captain.

Washington had inherited Ferry Farm from his father, but he did not wish to go there to live with his mother. Instead, he rented Mount Vernon from the widow of his half brother Lawrence. He agreed to pay a rent of 15,000 pounds (6,800 kilograms) of tobacco a year.

Braddock's defeat. In March 1755, Washington received a message from Major General Edward Braddock. The British general invited Washington to help him in a new campaign against the French at Fort Duquesne. Washington agreed to serve without pay as one of Braddock's aides. He believed this was an excellent opportunity to learn from an experienced general.

Braddock assembled his forces at Fort Cumberland, Maryland, about 90 miles (140 kilometers) southeast of Fort Duquesne. On June 7, the troops started across the rough country. Washington was upset by the slow march. He wrote in a letter: "They were halting to level every mole hill, and to erect bridges over every brook; by which means we were 4 days getting 12 miles."

During the second week of the march, Washington became seriously ill with a high fever. He was forced to remain behind in camp for two weeks. He warned Braddock to be careful of "the mode of attack, which more than probably, he would experience from the Canadian French, and their Indians."

On July 9, the British had nearly reached Fort Duquesne. After making two dangerous crossings of the Monongahela River, Braddock ordered his long column to march forward. Wearing bright red uniforms, the British soldiers looked as though they were parading before the king. Washington was not yet well, but he had rejoined the army and rode his horse with pillows tied to the saddle. Braddock was confident that the French now would wait at their fort for his attack. What happened next was later described by Washington:

At Fort Necessity

"We were attacked (very unexpectedly I must own) by about 300 French and Indians; our numbers consisted of about 1300 well-armed men, chiefly regulars, who were immediately struck with such a deadly panic, that nothing but confusion and disobedience of orders prevailed amongst them.

"... the English soldiers ... broke and ran as sheep before the hounds ... The general (Braddock) was wounded behind the shoulder, and into the breast; of which he died three days after ...

"I luckily escaped without a wound, though I had four bullets through my coat and two horses shot under me ..."

With Braddock's defeat and death, Washington was released from service. He rode home to Mount Vernon. Shortly after, in a letter to one of his brothers, he summed up his military career thus far:

"I was employed to go a journey in the winter (when I believe few or none would have undertaken it) and what did I get by it? My expenses borne! I then was appointed with trifling pay to conduct a handful of men to the Ohio. What did I get by this? Why, after putting myself to a considerable expense in equipping and providing necessaries for the campaign—I went out, was soundly beaten, lost them all—came in, and had my commission taken from me, or in other words, my command reduced, under pretense of an order from home ... I have been on the losing order ever since I entered the service ..."

Frontier commander. The French encouraged the Indians to attack English settlers. In August 1755, Dinwiddie persuaded Washington to accept a new commission as colonel. Washington would take command of Virginia's colonial

Marriage to Martha Dandridge Custis

troops to defend the colony's 350-mile (563-kilometer) western frontier.

Many of the Virginians recruited by Washington and his officers were homeless men. Sometimes Washington had less than 400 of the 1,500 men that he was supposed to have. Often he had to call the militia to help him. But the militia would not stay with him very long, and many of the militiamen did not even have weapons.

Washington constantly urged that a new attack be made on Fort Duquesne. The British finally decided in 1758 to attack Fort Duquesne again. An advance British force of 800 men again was ambushed by the French and Indians. More than 300 British soldiers were killed. When the main army, including Washington, finally reached the fort in late November, the French had burned it and retreated toward Canada.

Washington returned to Virginia to hang up his sword. He was now the most famous American-born soldier. He knew how to train other soldiers and how to run an army. More important, he had shown courage and patience in leading his men.

The Peaceful Years (1759–1773)

At the age of 26, Washington turned to seeking happiness as a country gentleman and to building a fortune. During the next 16 years, he became known as a skilled farmer, an intelligent businessman, a popular legislator, a conscientious warden of the Church of England, and a wise county court judge.

Marriage. On January 6, 1759, Washington married Mrs. Martha Dandridge Custis. She was a widow, eight months older than George. The marriage probably took place in New Kent County, Virginia, at the bride's plantation home, which was called the *White House.* Her first husband had left a fortune of about 18,000 acres (7,300 hectares) of land and 30,000 pounds. This was divided equally among the widow and her two children, John "Jackie" Parke Custis (1754–1781) and Martha "Patsy" Parke Custis (1756–1773). Washington became a loving stepfather to the children. He and Martha had no children of their own.

Legislator. After a six-week honeymoon at the White House, Washington took his new family to Williamsburg. There he served for the first time in the colonial legislature. He had been elected to the House of Burgesses in 1758, while still on the frontier. Although he had not personally campaigned, he had paid bills for his friends to entertain voters during the campaign.

During the next 15 years, Washington was reelected time after time to the legislature. He seldom made speeches and did not put any important bills before the legislature. More important, he learned the process of representative government. He saw the difficulties in getting a law passed. The experience gave him patience in later years when he had to deal with Congress during the Revolutionary War and as president. He also became acquainted with Thomas Jefferson, Patrick Henry, and other Virginia leaders.

Farmer and landowner. Washington brought his wife and children to Mount Vernon in April 1759. He found it badly run down by the neglect of his overseers.

In 1761, Washington inherited Mount Vernon because his half brother Lawrence's widow and daughter had both died. He began to buy farms that lay around the estate. He also bought western lands for future development. In 1770, Washington made a trip west as far as the present town of Gallipolis, Ohio, searching for good land to buy. By 1773, he owned about 40,000 acres (16,000 hectares). Washington also controlled the large Custis estate of his wife and her children. He rented much of his land to tenant farmers.

Washington was a careful businessman. He did his own bookkeeping and recorded every penny of expense or profit. His ledgers tell us when he bought gifts for his family, and what prices he received for his crops.

As a large landowner, Washington had to supervise many different activities. He wanted to learn more about farming, so he bought the latest books on the subject. When he discovered he could not grow the best grade of tobacco at Mount Vernon, he switched to raising wheat. He saw the profit in making flour, so he built his own flour mill. Large schools of fish swam in the Potomac River, and Mount Vernon became known for the barrels of salted fish it produced. Washington experimented with tree grafting to improve his fruit orchards.

Social life at Mount Vernon revolved around receiving visitors. Many people came there for pleasure as well as for business. The men often joined Washington in his favorite sport, fox hunting. Both men and women enjoyed dining and playing cards in the beautiful rooms of the mansion. Washington often visited other plantations.

Mount Vernon, lithograph by Currier and Ives

Several times a year, he went to such towns as Williamsburg and Alexandria, Virginia, and Annapolis, Maryland, to attend plays and dances, watch horse races, and shop.

The Coming Revolution (1774–1775)

The American colonists in the late 1760s and early 1770s grew angrier and angrier at the taxes placed on them by Britain. As a legislator and as a leading landowner, Washington was deeply concerned as relations with Britain worsened. During this time his knowledge of colonial affairs increased. He read many newspapers and political pamphlets and often discussed the growing crisis with his neighbor, George Mason, a leading statesman of the time.

Lord Botetourt, the British governor, dismissed the Virginia legislature in 1769 because the representatives had protested the taxation imposed by the British Townshend Acts. Washington met with other legislators in a Williamsburg tavern. He presented a plan that he and Mason had discussed for forming an association to boycott imports of British goods. The plan was quickly adopted.

Washington became one of the first American leaders to consider using force to "maintain the liberty of the colonies." He wrote Mason in April 1769: ". . . That no man should scruple, or hesitate a moment to use arms in defense of so valuable a blessing, on which all the good and evil of life depends, is clearly my opinion; yet Arms I would beg leave to add, should be the last . . . resort."

In 1774, the British closed the port of Boston as punishment for the Boston Tea Party. Virginia leg-

"I am embarked on a wide ocean, boundless in its prospect and from whence, perhaps, no safe harbor is to be found."

—Source: Written in 1775, a few days before going to Boston as commander in chief of the Revolutionary forces.

islators who protested were dismissed by Governor Lord Dunmore. Again the representatives met as private citizens. They elected seven delegates, including Washington, to attend the First Continental Congress in Philadelphia. Washington wrote: "...shall we supinely sit and see one province after another fall a prey to despotism?"

First Continental Congress. The Continental Congress met in September 1774. There, Washington had his first chance to meet and talk with leaders of other colonies. The members were impressed with his judgment and military knowledge. Washington made no speeches and he was not appointed to any committees. But he worked to have trade with Britain stopped by all the colonies. The trade boycott was approved by the Congress. Then Congress adjourned.

In March 1775, representatives from each Virginia county met in a church in Richmond, Virginia. Washington and the others heard Patrick Henry's famous speech in which he said: "Give me liberty or give me death!" But Washington's quiet common sense impressed people as much as Henry's dramatic words did. The representatives again elected Washington to attend the Second Continental Congress in Philadelphia.

Elected commander in chief. By the time Washington left Mount Vernon to attend the Second Continental Congress, the Battles of Lexington and Concord already had been fought in Massachusetts. The Congress opened on May 10, 1775. For six weeks the delegates to the Congress debated and studied the problems facing the colonies. The majority, including Washington, wanted to avoid war. At the same time, they feared they could not avoid it.

To express his desire for action, Washington began wearing his red and blue uniform of the French and Indian War. He was appointed to one military committee after another. He was asked to prepare a defense of New York City, to study ways to obtain gunpowder, to make plans for an army, and to write army regulations.

Then, on June 14, Congress called on Pennsylvania, Maryland, and Virginia to send troops to aid Boston, which had been placed under British military rule. John Adams, who in later years would be Washington's vice president and successor as president, rose to discuss the need of electing a commander in chief. Adams praised Washington highly and said his popularity would help unite the colonies. Many New England delegates believed a northerner should be made commander in chief. But the following day Washington was elected unanimously.

Washington had not sought the position. He particularly wanted to make everyone understand he did not want the $500 monthly pay that had been voted. He said he would keep track of his expenses, and would accept nothing else for his services. His acceptance speech, on June 16, was presented with modesty.

"I beg it may be remembered by every gentleman in the room," Washington said, "that I this day declare with the utmost sincerity, I do not think myself equal to the command I am honored with."

"First in War" (1775–1783)

"These are the times that try men's souls," Thomas Paine wrote during the Revolutionary War. "The summer soldier and the sunshine patriot, will in this crisis, shrink from the service of their country ..."

During the eight years of war, Washington's soul was tried many times both by "summer soldiers," who did not care to fight in winter, and by "sunshine patriots," who were friendly to the American cause only when things went well. Only his strong will to win made it possible for Washington to overcome his many discouragements.

The following sections describe the most important problems that Washington overcame to win the Revolutionary War.

Symbol of independence. To most Americans of his time, Washington became the chief symbol of what they were fighting for. The colonists had been brought up to respect the

Taking command of the Army at Cambridge

British king. They did not easily accept the idea of independence. The Congress that approved the Declaration of Independence on July 4, 1776, was not elected by the people, but by the legislatures of the states. And the legislatures were elected only by property owners. As a result, some people who did not own property and had no vote viewed independence with suspicion. Thousands of *Loyalists*, as British sympathizers were called, refused to help the fight for independence in any way.

Although many people did not especially wish for independence and did not trust Congress, they came to believe in Washington. They sympathized with him for the misery he shared with his soldiers. They cheered his courage in carrying on the fight.

"Washington retreats like a General and acts like a hero," the *Pennsylvania Journal* said in 1777. "Had he lived in the days of idolatry, he had been worshiped as a god." That same year, the Marquis de Lafayette wrote to Washington: "... if you were lost for America, there is nobody who could keep the army and the Revolution for six months."

Discouragement. Praise did not keep Washington from feeling discouraged. Often he believed he could not hold out long enough to win. Following are several comments he wrote throughout the war.

1776—"Such is my situation that if I were to wish the bitterest curse to an enemy on this side of the grave, I should put him in my stead with my feelings..."

1779—"... there is every appearance that the Army will infallibly disband in a fortnight."

1781—"... it is vain to think that an Army can be kept together much longer, under such a variety of sufferings as ours has experienced."

The army. Throughout the war, Washington seldom commanded more than 15,000 troops at any one time. He described his soldiers as "raw militia, badly officered, and with no government." There were two kinds of troops: (1) soldiers of the Continental Army, organized by Congress, and (2) militia, organized by the states.

Washington had trouble keeping soldiers in the Continental Army. At the beginning of the war, Congress let soldiers enlist for only a few months. Toward the end of the war, Washington convinced Congress that enlistments had to be longer. When their enlistments were up, the soldiers of the Continental Army went home. Sometimes a thousand men marched off at once.

Washington often had to plan battles for certain dates, because if he waited longer the soldiers' enlistments would be up. For example, Washing-

"The time is now near at hand which must probably determine, whether Americans are to be freemen or slaves... The fate of unborn millions will now depend, under God, on the courage and conduct of this army— our cruel and unrelenting enemy leaves us no choice but a brave resistance, or the most abject submission... We have therefore to resolve to conquer or die."

—Source: General orders to the Continental Army, July 2, 1776.

Crossing the Delaware

ton attacked the Hessian (German) troops at Trenton, New Jersey, on December 26, 1776, for this reason. His army had shrunk to only about 5,000 men and the enlistments of most of his soldiers would be up at the end of December. The victory at Trenton inspired many of his soldiers to reenlist.

From time to time, Washington asked the states to call out their militia to help in a particular battle. The militia included storekeepers, farmers, and other private citizens. They were poorly trained and did not like being called from their homes to fight. The militia complained so much that troops of the Continental Army called them "long faces." Washington's army was defeated many times because the militia turned and ran when they saw red-coated British soldiers.

Desertion by his soldiers was another one of Washington's major problems. Many soldiers enlisted only to collect bonuses offered by Congress. At some times, as many men deserted each day as were enlisted. Washington authorized harsh punishment for deserters. He had some hanged. Dangerous mutinies also occurred.

"We are, during the winter, dreaming of independence and peace, without using the means to become so," a concerned Washington wrote in 1780. "In the spring, when our recruits should be with the Army and in training, we have just discovered the necessity of calling for them, and by the fall, after a distressed, and inglorious campaign for want of them, we begin to get a few men, which come in just in time enough to eat our provisions. . ."

From the time Washington took command to the end of the war, he had to put up with many incompetent officers. Congress sometimes appointed the generals without asking Washington's advice. The states appointed the lower-ranking officers in the Continental Army and all of the militia officers. Most officers were chosen for political reasons. Some generals, such as Charles Lee and Horatio Gates, believed they should have been chosen commander in chief. They sometimes ignored Washington's orders. In the winter of 1777–1778, a few army officers and members of Congress hoped that Washington might be replaced by Gates. This group became known as the *Conway cabal.* It was named for the foreign-born general Thomas Conway, who had criticized Washington sharply. But there was no organized movement against Washington. Congress continued to support him.

Shortage of supplies. Washington's troops lacked food, clothing, ammunition, and other supplies throughout the war. If the British had attacked the Americans around Boston in 1775, Washington could have issued only enough gunpowder for nine shots to each soldier. He had to give up Philadelphia to the British in 1777 because he could not risk losing the few supplies he had. The army repeatedly ran out of meat and bread. Sometimes hundreds of troops had to march barefoot in the snow because they had no shoes.

"The want of clothing, added to the misery of the season," Washington wrote in the winter of 1777–1778 at Valley Forge, Pennsylvania, "has occasioned (the soldiers) to suffer such hardships as will not be credited but by those who have been spectators."

In the winter of 1779–1780 at Morristown, New Jersey, Major General Nathanael Greene described Washington's army: "Poor fellows! They exhibit a picture truly distressing—more than half naked and two thirds starved. A country overflowing with plenty are now suffering an Army, employed for the defense of everything that is dear and valuable, to perish for want of food."

Winning the war. From the beginning of the war, Washington knew the powerful British navy gave the enemy a great advantage. The ships of the British could carry their army anywhere along

At Yorktown

the American coast. Washington's tiny, ragged army could not possibly defend every American port.

On the other hand, Washington knew from his experience in the French and Indian War that the British army moved slowly on land. He also knew it could be beaten. He proved that he could stay one jump ahead of the British by quick retreats. Meanwhile, Washington waited and prayed for the French to send a large fleet of warships to America. He hoped then to trap the British while the French navy prevented them from escaping.

Washington's prayers came true at Yorktown, Virginia. There, on September 28, 1781, he surrounded Lord Cornwallis's army. The French fleet prevented the British from escaping by ship. Washington began attacking on October 6. On October 19, Cornwallis and 8,000 men surrendered.

Turning down a crown. After Cornwallis surrendered, the British lost interest in continuing the war. Peace talks dragged on in Paris for many months.

In May 1782, Colonel Lewis Nicola sent a document to Washington on behalf of his officers. It complained of injustices the army had suffered from Congress. It suggested that the army set up a monarchy with Washington as king. Washington replied that he read the idea "with abhorrence." He ordered Nicola to "banish these thoughts from your mind."

In November 1783, word finally arrived that the Treaty of Paris had been signed two months earlier. The last British soldiers went aboard ships at New York City on November 25. That same day Washington led his troops into the city. About a week later, on December 4, he said goodbye to his officers at Fraunces Tavern. On his way home to Virginia, he stopped at Annapolis, Maryland, where Congress was meeting. He returned his commission as commander in chief, saying ". . . I resign with satisfaction the appointment I accepted with diffidence."

"First in Peace" (1784–1789)

Washington, now 51 years old, reached Mount Vernon in time to spend Christmas 1783 with Martha. The war had aged him. He now wore glasses. As he had told his officers: "I have grown gray in your service and now find myself growing blind."

For the next five years, Washington lived the life of a Virginia planter. Many guests and visitors dropped in at Mount Vernon. His entertainment expenses were large. In 1787, he wrote: "My estate for the last eleven years has not been able to make both ends meet."

Washington believed strongly in the future development of the West. This made him search for more land to buy. In 1784, he made a 680-mile (1,090-kilometer) trip on horseback through the wilderness to visit his land holdings southwest of Pittsburgh. He helped promote two companies interested in building canals along the Potomac and James rivers. He took part in plans to drain the Dismal Swamp in southern Virginia.

Washington also widened his interest in farming. In many ways his farm methods were ahead of the times. He began breeding mules. He introduced rotation of crops to his farms. He began using waste materials from his fishing industry as fertilizer. He also took steps to prevent soil erosion.

Constitutional Convention. In 1786, Washington wrote: "We are fast verging to anarchy and confusion." In Massachusetts, open revolt broke out. Finally, the states agreed to call a meeting in 1787 to consider revising the weak Articles of Confederation. Washington was elected unanimously to head the Virginia delegates. A huge welcome

> "Liberty, when it begins to take root, is a plant of rapid growth."
> —*Source: Letter to James Madison, March 2, 1788.*

Inauguration, April 30, 1789

greeted him when he arrived in Philadelphia in May. All the bells in the city were rung. The Constitutional Convention opened on May 25. The delegates elected Washington president of the convention.

Debate on the proposed constitution went on throughout the hot summer. Washington wrote: "I see no end to my staying here. To please all is impossible. . ." As president, Washington took little part in the debates, but helped hold the convention together. The convention finally reached agreement in September.

Elected president. By the summer of 1788, enough states had approved the Constitution to allow for the reorganization of the government. Throughout the country, people linked Washington's name directly to the new Constitution. They took it for granted that he would be chosen as the first president. But Washington had many doubts as to whether he should accept the position. He wrote: ". . . If I should receive the appointment, and if I should be prevailed upon to accept it, the acceptance would be attended with more diffidence and reluctance than I ever experienced before in my life."

In February 1789, members of the first Electoral College met in their own states and voted.

Martha Washington

Each elector voted for two candidates. The candidate who received the most votes became president, and the runner-up became vice president. Washington was elected president with a total of 69 votes—the largest number possible—from the 69 electors. John Adams was elected vice president with 34 votes.

First Administration (1789–1793)

Washington's journey from Mount Vernon to New York City was the parade of a national hero. Every town and city along the way held a celebration.

Inauguration Day was April 30, 1789. The 57-year-old Washington rode in a cream-colored coach to Federal Hall at Broad and Wall streets. Washington walked upstairs to the Senate Chamber, then out onto a balcony. Thousands watched as Washington raised his right hand and placed his left hand on an open Bible. Solemnly he repeated the presidential oath of office given by Robert R. Livingston of New York. Washington added the words, "So help me God!" and kissed the Bible. Cannons fired a 13-gun salute. Then President Washington walked back to the Senate Chamber and delivered his inaugural address.

Life in the Executive Mansion. The house of Samuel Osgood on Cherry Street in New York City was the first Executive Mansion. In February 1790, Washington moved to a larger house on Broadway. When Congress later made Philadelphia the capital, the Washingtons moved into the home there of financier Robert Morris. It was the finest house in the city.

The Washingtons entertained a great deal. They had a large staff of servants and slaves. The president held two afternoon receptions each week so he could meet the hundreds of people who wanted to see him. Every Friday night, Mrs. Washington held a formal reception. These affairs ended at 9 p.m. because, she said, the president "always retires at 9 in the evening." Each year on his birthday, Washington gave a ball at which dancing lasted until well after midnight.

Martha Washington's two young grandchildren, Eleanor Parke Custis and George Washington Parke Custis, came to live with the Washingtons in the early 1780s. Their father, John Custis, had died during the Revolutionary War and their mother had remarried.

Martha Washington was described in a letter by Abigail Adams, wife of the vice president: "She is plain in her dress, but that plainness is the best of every article . . . Her hair is white, her teeth beautiful, her person rather short . . . Her manners are modest and unassuming, dignified and feminine. . ."

The Washingtons made many trips home to Mount Vernon during the next eight years. The president sometimes stayed there as long as three months when Congress was not in session.

New precedents of government. "I walk on untrodden ground," Washington said as he began the new responsibilities of his office. "There is scarcely any part of my conduct that may not hereafter be drawn into precedent."

Washington believed strongly in the constitutional provision that the executive, legislative, and judicial branches of the government should be kept as separate as possible. He thought the president should not try to influence the kinds of laws that Congress passed. However, he believed that if he disapproved of a bill, he should let Congress know by vetoing it. Washington regarded the duties of his office largely as administering the laws of Congress and supervising relations with other countries.

In 1789, at the beginning of Washington's presidency, 11 of the original 13 colonies had ratified the Constitution. North Carolina accepted the Constitution in November 1789, and Rhode Island in 1790. Three other states joined the Union while Washington was in office—Vermont in 1791, Kentucky in 1792, and Tennessee in 1796.

On July 4, 1789, Washington received the first important bill passed by the new Congress. It provided income to run the government by setting taxes on imports. He signed it with no comment.

By September, Congress had established three executive departments to help run the government: the Department of Foreign Affairs (now Department of State), the Department of War, and the Department of the Treasury. Congress provided for an Attorney General and a continuation of the Post Office. Congress also adopted the Bill of Rights and established a system of federal courts.

Cabinet. In September, Washington began making important appointments. He chose men whom he knew and could trust:

Chief justice of the United States—John Jay, who had been secretary of foreign affairs under the Articles of Confederation.

Secretary of state—Thomas Jefferson, who had served with Washington in Virginia's legislature.

Secretary of war—Henry Knox, Washington's chief of artillery during the Revolutionary War.

Secretary of the treasury—Alexander Hamilton,

"To be prepared for war is one of the most effectual means of preserving peace."
—Source: First Annual Address, presented to both houses of Congress, January 8, 1790.

Laying the cornerstone of the U.S. Capitol

who had been one of Washington's military aides.

Attorney general—Edmund Randolph, former governor of Virginia and a member of the Constitutional Convention. He had been Washington's friend for many years.

During his first administration, Washington relied heavily on the advice of Hamilton and James Madison, a congressman from Virginia. At first, Washington did not call his department heads together as a group. Instead, he asked them to give him written opinions or to talk with him individually. Washington allowed his department heads to act independently. He did not try to prevent Hamilton, Jefferson, or the others from influencing Congress. Toward the end of his first administration, he began calling the group together for meetings. In 1793, Madison first used the term *cabinet* to refer to the group.

Finances. Washington's new government had millions of dollars in debts which the Congress of the Articles of Confederation had been unable to pay. Hamilton drew up a plan to straighten out the finances. There was much argument, but finally the plan passed in July 1790. The law provided that the national government would assume the wartime debts of the states. It also called for borrowing $12 million from other countries and for paying interest on the public debts.

New national capital. Congress approved a bill in July to transfer the government to Philadelphia until 1800. After that, the capital would be moved to a federal district to be located on the Potomac River. The president took up residence in Philadelphia in November 1790. During the next several years, Washington devoted much time to the plans for the new national capital, which came to bear his name.

Constitutional debate. Hamilton obtained passage in 1791 of a bill setting up the First Bank of the United States. Washington had to decide whether the government had powers under the Constitution to charter such a corporation. Jefferson and Randolph believed that the bill was unconstitutional. They said such powers were not mentioned in the Constitution. Hamilton argued that the government could use all powers except those denied by the Constitution. Washington, who believed in a strong national government, took the side of Hamilton and signed the law.

First veto by Washington of congressional legislation was made in April 1792. The first census of the United States had shown that the population was 3,929,214, including 697,000 slaves. Congress then passed a bill in March to raise the number of U.S. representatives from 67 to 120. Washington believed the bill was unconstitutional because some states would have greater representation in proportion to population than other states. Many people thought the bill favored Northern States over Southern States. Congress failed to override Washington's veto, and then revised the bill to provide for a House of 103 members.

Rise of political parties. Washington was disturbed as he saw that Jefferson and Hamilton were disagreeing more and more with each other. Men and newspapers who supported Hamilton's views of a stronger and stronger national government called themselves *Federalists*. The Federalists became the party of the Northern States and of banking and manufacturing interests. Those who favored Jefferson's ideas of a strict interpretation of the

The Whiskey Rebellion

Constitution in defending states' rights became known as *Anti-Federalists*, or *Democratic-Republicans*. The Democratic-Republicans mainly represented the Southern States and the farmers.

Washington attempted to favor neither party. He tried to bring Hamilton and Jefferson into agreement and tried to discourage the growth of political parties.

Reelection. In 1792, Washington began to make plans for retirement. In May, he asked Madison to help him prepare a farewell address. Madison did so, but he urged Washington to accept reelection as president. Hamilton, Knox, Jefferson, and Randolph each asked Washington to continue as president. Perhaps one of the strongest arguments came from Jefferson, who wrote: "Your being at the helm will be more than an answer to every argument which can be used to alarm and lead the people in any quarter into violence or secession. North and South will hang together if they have you to hang on."

Members of the Electoral College cast their votes in December 1792. Their ballots were counted on February 13, 1793, and Washington again was elected president with the largest number of votes possible—132. Adams received 77 votes and was again the runner-up and vice president.

Second Administration (1793–1797)

Washington's second inauguration took place in Congress Hall in Philadelphia on March 4, 1793. The 61-year-old Washington faced greater problems during his second administration than during his first.

Neutrality proclamation. Word came in April 1793 that a general war had begun in Europe. Britain, Spain, Austria, and Prussia were all fighting against the new French republic. Although the United States had signed an alliance with the French king in 1778, Washington wanted to "maintain a strict neutrality." Jefferson, who favored the recent French Revolution, did not want to issue a neutrality statement. Hamilton believed neutrality was necessary.

Washington ordered Attorney General Randolph to write up a statement. On April 22, the president signed the Neutrality Proclamation which called for "conduct friendly and impartial" to all the warring nations. It also forbade American ships from carrying war supplies to the fighting countries.

Relations with France. The United States decision to stay out of the European war pleased the British, but it angered the French. Leaders of the French Revolution believed the United States should stand by its alliance of 1778 with King Louis XVI. But the revolutionaries had beheaded the king who made the alliance. This posed a delicate point in international law, and Washington had no precedents to guide him. He finally decided to be cool and formal in receiving Edmond Genet, the new minister appointed by the French republic.

Genet seemed determined to draw Americans into the war on the side of France. He tried secretly to win Democratic-Republicans to the French cause during the spring and summer of 1793. This upset Washington. The president's patience gave out when Genet tried to outfit warships in American ports and send them to sea against the British.

After a stormy Cabinet meeting in July 1793, Washington asked France to recall Genet because he endangered American neutrality. Genet was stripped of his power, but was allowed to stay in the United States. The neutrality crisis of 1793 passed, and the United States remained at peace.

"If the laws are to be so trampled upon, with impunity, and a minority . . . is to dictate to the majority there is an end put, at one stroke, to republican government."
—Source: Response to the Whiskey Rebellion, 1794.

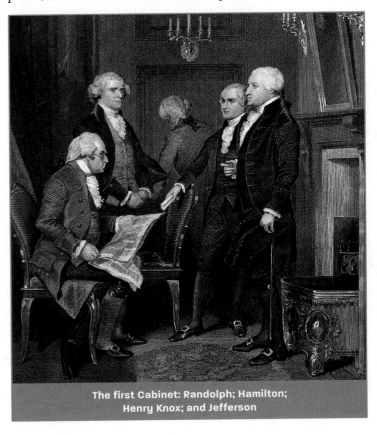

The first Cabinet: Randolph; Hamilton; Henry Knox; and Jefferson

Whiskey Rebellion. In 1794, Washington proved that the government could enforce federal laws in the states. Farmers in four counties in western Pennsylvania had refused to pay federal taxes on manufacturing whiskey. They armed themselves and attacked federal officials. Washington raised nearly 13,000 troops and sent them to western Pennsylvania. By November 1794, the rebellion had been crushed and the ringleaders arrested.

Relations with Britain. Washington worried as relations with Britain grew worse. British warships stopped American ships carrying food supplies to France and seized their cargoes. They sometimes took seamen off the American ships and forced them into the British navy. British troops refused to give up western frontier forts they were supposed to have surrendered under terms of the treaty of 1783. The British also were stirring up Indian fighting on the western frontier. In an effort to settle problems with Britain, Washington sent Chief Justice John Jay to London in 1794.

In March 1795, Washington received a copy of a treaty Jay had signed on November 19, 1794. Earlier copies had been lost in the mail. Most of the treaty had to do with regulation of trade between America and Britain. It also called for British troops to give up the frontier forts in 1796. But it contained no agreement that British ships would stop waylaying American ships and taking seamen.

Washington called a special session of the Senate in June to study the treaty. Federalists supported the Jay Treaty because it insured continuing trade with Britain. The Democratic-Republicans violently opposed the treaty because they believed it would harm France. The Federalists controlled the Senate, so the treaty was ratified by a vote of 20 to 10, except for one section. This section opened trade with the British West Indies to United States ships, but it also severely restricted this trade. Washington could not make up his mind whether or not to sign the treaty. He went home to Mount Vernon to think about it.

At Mount Vernon, the president received word of riots in many cities protesting the Jay Treaty. A mob in New York City stoned Hamilton. A Philadelphia mob broke windows at the British embassy.

Cabinet scandal. Washington returned to Philadelphia on August 11, 1795. He learned that the British had captured a French diplomatic message which seemed to indicate that Edmund Randolph, who was now secretary of state, was a traitor. Washington read a translation of the French message. He believed that Randolph might have sold secrets to the French.

Without saying anything to Randolph about his suspicions, Washington called a cabinet meeting to discuss the Jay Treaty. At the meeting, Randolph argued against signing the treaty as long as Britain continued to seize American ships. Washington became convinced Randolph was in the pay of France, so he signed the treaty.

As soon as the Jay Treaty had been delivered to the British embassy, Washington called in Randolph and showed him the French message. Randolph denied his guilt, but resigned. He swore he would prove his innocence. Randolph later published a book in which he declared that he had never betrayed his country.

Washington now suffered the bitterest criticism of his career. He was accused by Democratic-Republican newspapers of falling victim to a Federalist plot in signing the Jay Treaty. It was even suggested that he should be impeached because he had overdrawn his $25,000 salary. Washington's feelings were badly hurt.

Plan for Washington, D.C., as originally laid out

Public opinion of Washington began to improve when he was able to announce a few months later that a treaty had been negotiated with Spain opening up the Mississippi River to trade. Agreement also had been reached with the Barbary States to release American prisoners and to let American ships alone for a payment of $800,000 ransom, plus $24,000 tribute each year. Sea raiders licensed by these states were attacking U.S. and other ships in the Mediterranean Sea. Peace treaties also had been signed with Indian tribes on the frontier.

Farewell Address. Washington, who believed the office of president should be above political attack, had become tired of public office. The new House of Representatives had a large Democratic-Republican majority and was unfriendly to Washington. He also felt himself growing old.

In May 1796, Washington dusted off the draft of his *Farewell Address* that he and James Madison had worked on four years earlier. He sent it to Jay and to Hamilton for their suggestions. Finally, in September, the much-edited address, all in Washington's handwriting, was ready. He gave it to the editor of the *American Daily Advertiser*, a Philadelphia newspaper, which published it on September 19.

In the election campaign that followed, Washington favored John Adams, the Federalist candidate for president. But Washington did not take an active part in the campaigning. The Democratic-Republican candidate was Thomas Jefferson. When the Electoral College met, it gave 71 votes to Adams and 68 to Jefferson. Under the existing constitutional provision, Adams became president and Jefferson vice president.

At the inauguration in March 1797, Adams sensed Washington's relief at retirement. Adams wrote to his wife: "He seemed to me to enjoy a triumph over me. Methought I heard him say, 'Ay! I am fairly out and you fairly in! See which of us will be the happiest!'"

"First in the Hearts of His Countrymen" (1797–1799)

Washington was 65. He happily went home to Mount Vernon. Friends said he looked even older. But he did not lose touch with public affairs. Almost every day visitors dropped in to see him. On July 31, 1797, he wrote: "Unless someone pops in unexpectedly—Mrs. Washington and myself will do what has not been done within the last twenty years by us—that is to set down to dinner by ourselves." He described his daily routine in a letter:

"I begin . . . with the sun . . . if my hirelings are not in their places at that time I send them messages expressive of my sorrow for their indisposition . . . breakfast (a little after seven o'clock) . . . This over, I mount my horse and ride round the farms . . . The usual time of sitting at table; a walk, and tea, brings me within the dawn of candlelight . . . I resolve that . . . I will retire to my writing table and acknowledge the letters I have received; but when the lights are brought, I feel tired, and disinclined to engage in this work."

Managing the several farms which made up the more than 7,600 acres (3,075 hectares) of Mount

---

. . . The basis of our political systems is the right of the people to make and to alter their constitutions of government. But the constitution which at any time exists, 'till changed by an explicit and authentic act of the whole People, is sacredly obligatory upon all . . .

. . . Let me now . . . warn you in the most solemn manner against the baneful effects of the spirit of party . . . It agitates the Community with ill founded jealousies and false alarms, kindles the animosity of one part against another, foments occasionally riot and insurrection.

. . . Of all the dispositions and habits which lead to political prosperity, religion and morality are indispensable supports.

. . . Promote . . . institutions for the general diffusion of knowledge . . . it is essential that public opinion should be enlightened.

. . . Observe good faith and justice towards all Nations. Cultivate peace and harmony with all . . . nothing is more essential than that permanent, inveterate antipathies against particular Nations and passionate attachments for others should be excluded . . . The nation, which indulges toward another an habitual hatred, or an habitual fondness, is in some degree a slave. It is a slave to its animosity or to its affection, either of which is sufficient to lead it astray from its duty and its interest.

. . . 'Tis our true policy to steer clear of permanent Alliances, with any portion of the foreign world . . . Taking care always to keep ourselves, by suitable establishments, on a respectably defensive posture, we may safely trust to temporary alliances for extraordinary emergencies . . . There can be no greater error than to expect, or calculate upon real favors from nation to nation.

—Source: *Farewell Address*, published in the *American Daily Advertiser*, a Philadelphia newspaper, September 19, 1796.

Vernon took much of his time. He made frequent trips to watch construction in the new city of Washington, D.C., which then was called the Federal City.

Recall to duty. While Washington enjoyed his retirement, relations between the United States and France grew worse. The government decided to raise an army for defense. President Adams asked Washington's help. On July 4, 1798, Washington was commissioned as "Lieutenant General and Commander in Chief of the armies raised or to be raised."

He went to Philadelphia for a few weeks in November to help plan the new army. He had dinner one night in debtors' prison with financier Robert Morris, in whose Philadelphia home he had lived while president. Morris had gone to prison because he could not pay his debts.

During his last year of life, Washington wrote many letters to the various men he chose as generals for the new army. Federalist leaders asked if he would consider running for a third term as president. He said no. Washington also was saddened by the deaths of friends and relatives. Patrick Henry died on June 6, 1799, and Washington's last living brother, Charles Washington, died on September 20, 1799.

Death. On December 12, Washington wrote his last letter. It was to Alexander Hamilton. In it he discussed the importance of establishing a national military academy. After finishing the letter, Washington went for his daily horseback

The Washington Monument

ride around Mount Vernon. The day was cold, with snow turning into rain and sleet. Washington returned after about five hours and sat down to dinner without changing his damp clothes. The next day, he awoke with a sore throat. He went for a walk. Then he made his last entry in his diary, noting down the weather: "Morning Snowing & abt. 3 Inches deep ... Mer. 28 at Night." These were his last written words.

Between 2 and 3 a.m. on December 14, 1799, Washington awakened Martha. He had difficulty speaking and was quite ill. But he would not let her send for a doctor until dawn. James Craik, who had been his friend and doctor since he was a young man, hurried to Mount Vernon. By the time he arrived, Washington already had called in an overseer and had about a cup of blood drained from his veins. Craik examined Washington and said the illness was "inflammatory quinsy." Craik bled Washington again. Present-day doctors believe the illness was a streptococcal infection of the throat.

Two more doctors arrived in the afternoon. Again Washington was bled. Late in the afternoon he could hardly speak, but told the doctors: "You had better not take any more trouble about me; but let me go off quietly; I cannot last long."

About 10 p.m. on December 14, Washington whispered: "I am just going. Have me decently buried, and do not let my body be put in the vault in less than two days after I am dead. Do you understand me?" His secretary answered: "Yes, sir." Washington said: "'Tis well." He felt for his own pulse. Then he died.

On December 18, Washington was given a military funeral. His body was laid to rest in the family tomb at Mount Vernon. Throughout the world, people were saddened by his death. In the United States, thousands of people wore mourning clothes for months.

No other American has been honored more than Washington. The nation's capital, Washington, D.C., was named for him. There, the giant Washington Monument stands. The state of Washington is the only state named after a president. Many counties, cities, towns, streets, bridges, lakes, parks, and schools bear his name. Washington's portrait appears on postage stamps, on the $1 bill, and on the quarter.

After the siege of Boston in 1776, the Massachusetts legislature in a resolution had said: "... may future generations, in the peaceful enjoyment of that freedom, the exercise of which your sword shall have established, raise the richest and most lasting monuments to the name of Washington." The legislators foresaw the place he would hold forever in the hearts of Americans.

At his death, Washington held the title of lieutenant general, then the highest U.S. military rank. But through the years, he was outranked by many U.S. Army officers. In 1976, Congress granted Washington the nation's highest military title, General of the Armies of the United States. This action confirmed him as the senior general officer on the Army rolls.

MLA Citation

"George Washington."
The Southwestern Advantage Topic Source.
Nashville: Southwestern. 2013.

DATA

The World of George Washington

The French Revolution began in 1789. In one of the first major acts of rebellion, French citizens captured the Bastille, a royal fortress and hated symbol of oppression.

The first U.S. census was begun in August 1790 and took 18 months to complete. It counted 3,929,214 people.

The Industrial Revolution in the United States made a big advance in 1790, when Samuel Slater established the nation's first water-powered cotton mill in Pawtucket, Rhode Island.

Plans for a permanent national capital moved forward when President Washington selected a site on the Potomac River in 1791. Construction of the White House began the next year.

The Bill of Rights became law in 1791. These first 10 amendments to the U.S. Constitution guaranteed basic liberties.

The New York Stock Exchange was established in 1792.

Eli Whitney's cotton gin, patented in 1794, revolutionized the economy of the South. The device led to mass production of cotton and increased the demand for slave labor.

General Anthony Wayne defeated the Indians in 1794 in the Battle of Fallen Timbers. A treaty signed the following year opened a huge tract of land in Ohio to white settlers.

The first important turnpike in the United States was completed in 1795 between Philadelphia and Lancaster, Pennsylvania. Other toll roads built in the 1790s encouraged development in New England and the Middle Atlantic region.

The first smallpox vaccination was given by English physician Edward Jenner in 1796. It represented a major advance in the battle against this dreaded disease.

DATA

Washington's Life in Brief

1732	(February 22) Born in Westmoreland County, Virginia.
1749	Became official surveyor for Culpeper County, Virginia.
1751	Went to Barbados Island, British West Indies.
1753	Carried British ultimatum to French in Ohio River Valley, as a major.
1754	Surrendered Fort Necessity in the French and Indian War, as a colonel.
1755	(July 9) With General Edward Braddock when defeated by French and Indians.
1755–1758	Commanded Virginia's frontier troops, as a colonel.
1759	(January 6) Married Mrs. Martha Dandridge Custis.
1774	Elected delegate to First Continental Congress.
1775	Elected delegate to Second Continental Congress.
1775	(June 15) Elected commander in chief of Continental Army.
1781	(October 19) Victory at Yorktown.
1787	(May 25) Elected president of the Constitutional Convention.
1789	Elected first President of the United States.
1792	Reelected President of the United States.
1796	(September 19) Published *Farewell Address*, refusing a third term.
1798	(July 4) Commissioned lieutenant general and commander in chief of new United States Army.
1799	(December 14) Died at Mount Vernon at age 67.

ADDITIONAL RESOURCES

Books to Read

Ellis, Joseph J. *His Excellency: George Washington*. Knopf, 2004.

Johnson, Paul. *George Washington*. HarperCollins, 2005.

Lengel, Edward G. *General George Washington: A Military Life*. Random House, 2005.

Lengel, Edward G. *Inventing George Washington: America's Founder, in Myth and Memory*. Harper, 2011.

Murphy, Jim. *The Crossing: How George Washington Saved the American Revolution*. Scholastic, 2010.

Schecter, Barnet. *George Washington's America: A Biography Through His Maps*. Walker, 2010.

Web Sites

George Washington

http://www.whitehouse.gov/history/presidents/gw1.html

Official White House biography of George Washington. Includes a link to Washington's papers at the University of Virginia and a link to the biography of Martha Washington.

George Washington Birthplace National Monument Home Page

http://www.nps.gov/gewa/

National Park Service site on the George Washington Birthplace National Monument.

Martha Dandridge Custis Washington

http://www.whitehouse.gov/about/liveproduction/martha-dandridge-custis-washington

The White House site on America's first First Lady, Martha Washington.

President George Washington's Inaugural Address

http://www.law.ou.edu/hist/wash1.html

An exhibit from the University of Oklahoma Law Center that features the full text of Washington's first inaugural address.

Sulgrave Manor—Ancestral home of George Washington

http://www.sulgravemanor.org.uk/

A visitor's guide and information about the Washington family home in Sulgrave, England.

The Papers of George Washington

http://www.virginia.edu/gwpapers/

The Papers of George Washington was established in 1969 at the University of Virginia to publish a complete edition of Washington's correspondence. This Web site includes letters written to Washington and letters and documents that he wrote.

Washington Monument Home Page

http://www.nps.gov/wamo/

Official home page of the Washington Monument from the National Park Service.

Search Strings

Early Military Career

"George Washington" early military career battles (91,700)

"George Washington" "early military career" battles French British (90)

early military career of "General George Washington" (5,000)

The Young Legislator

"George Washington" legislator "House of Burgesses" Congress President (20,200)

"George Washington" legislator "House of Burgesses" Congress President "Revolutionary War" (9,660)

Strategy in the War of Independence

"War of Independence" strategy "George Washington" (15,700)

"War of Independence" strategy "George Washington" "Revolutionary War" British (10,600)

strategy of George Washington in the War of Independence (147,000)

Elected President

George Washington constitution elected president (221,000)

"George Washington" Constitution president election (67,500)

"George Washington" Constitution president election "John Adams" (123,000)

Thomas Jefferson

The third President of the United States, Thomas Jefferson (1743–1826), is known primarily for authoring the United States' Declaration of Independence (1776) and spearheading the Louisiana Purchase (1803). A founding member of the Democratic-Republican party, he argued for preferring states' rights to a centralized, federal power.

HOT topics

The Sally Hemings Affair. Jefferson was rumored to have fathered out-of-wedlock children by Sally Hemings, one of his slaves. After DNA tests of their respective descendents supported the possibility, an examination of scientific and historical documents has led most historians to acknowledge a probable relationship between the two. The matter, however, remains deeply controversial.

The Declaration of Independence and the Committee of Five. The Second Continental Congress designated five men—John Adams, Benjamin Franklin, Thomas Jefferson, Robert Livingston, and Roger Sherman—to assert the colonies' autonomy. Jefferson drafted the Declaration of Independence himself in June of 1776. The document was revised and signed on July 4, 1776.

Democratic-Republicanism. In the aftermath of the colonies' declaration, Jefferson returned to Virginia to hold office, first as a delegate (1776–1778) and then, succeeding Patrick Henry, as governor (1779–1781). The abolition of primogeniture and the improvement of education by means of the first student honor codes became tenets of Democratic-Republicanism, the political philosophy Jefferson cofounded with James Madison in order to counteract the Federalist ideology espoused by Adams and Alexander Hamilton.

Dueling Vice President. After losing the 1796 presidential campaign, in which he finished second to Adams, Jefferson, as vice president, ran against Aaron Burr in the election of 1800. The two

HOT topics

candidates, both Democratic-Republicans, received an equal number of electoral votes, forcing the Federalist-controlled House to choose a winner. Alexander Hamilton detested both men, but decided that Jefferson was the lesser evil and lobbied for him. Jefferson became president and Burr vice president. But Burr refused to concede defeat, producing lasting tension between him and Hamilton. Eventually Burr dueled with Hamilton, after which he was unable to mend bridges with Jefferson. He was therefore not vice president during Jefferson's second term in office.

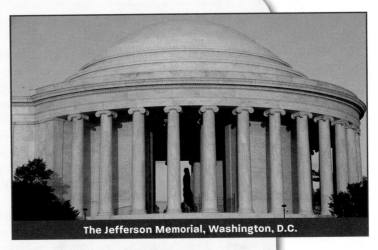

The Jefferson Memorial, Washington, D.C.

The Louisiana Purchase.
Eyeing New Orleans, situated at the mouth of the Mississippi River, as a lucrative port, Jefferson looked into buying it from France. After Jefferson dispatched Madison and Livingston for two years of negotiation in Paris, Napoleon Bonaparte offered Jefferson the entire Louisiana Territory for about $15 million. Jefferson was unsure that such a transaction was constitutional, but he submitted the treaty to the Senate, and it was ratified in 1803. In 1804, Jefferson sent Meriwether Lewis and William Clark to explore the United States' newest acquisition.

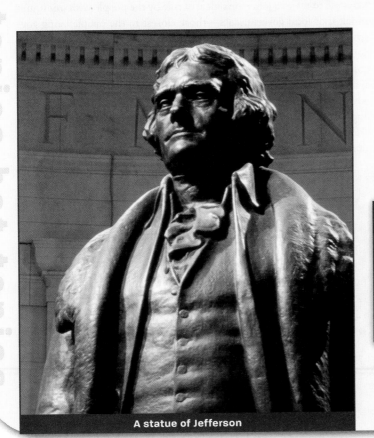

A statue of Jefferson

TRUE or FALSE?
Jefferson regarded such accomplishments as being "Father of the University of Virginia" as more important than serving as president of the United States.

THE BASICS

Thomas Jefferson (1743–1826), was the third president of the United States. He was also a leading figure in America's movement toward independence and development as a nation. Jefferson was a tall man with red hair. He was a native of central Virginia, where he became a leading lawyer and plantation owner. During the American Revolution (1775–1783), he rose to a position of leadership in both his state and the nation, most famously as the author of the Declaration of Independence. After the Americans won independence from Great Britain (later also called the United Kingdom), Jefferson held political office almost continuously until his retirement in 1809. He was president of the United States from 1801 to 1809. His presidency was a period of tremendous growth for the nation.

In addition to his two terms as president, Jefferson served in many other offices. He was a member of the Virginia legislature, a delegate to the Continental Congress, governor of Virginia, U.S. minister to France, U.S. secretary of state, and vice president of the United States. He also was a lifelong supporter of the arts, sciences, and education.

Jefferson was a transitional figure between the age of monarchy and the age of democracy. His political ideology was firmly within the tradition of the English Whigs. The Whigs believed the power of rulers, including monarchs, came from the people and should be limited. Jefferson embraced many of the ideas of the Enlightenment, a period from the 1600s to 1700s. During the Enlightenment, philosophers emphasized the use of reason and science. Jefferson was greatly influenced by the ideas of the English philosopher John Locke. Locke emphasized basic human rights and believed that people should revolt against governments that violated those rights. Jefferson also was influenced by such political writers as James Harrington and Algernon Sidney of England and Montesquieu of France. Historians often disagree over which thinkers affected Jefferson the most.

Jefferson's defenses of individual liberty and representative government continue to inspire people today. The term *Jeffersonian democracy* has come to refer to Jefferson's ideal of rule by the people with minimum government interference. Jefferson felt that local governments—those closest to the people being governed—should be the most powerful. He felt that distant general governments should have only limited powers. Jefferson argued for freedom of speech, of the press, and of religion. He pressed for the addition of a bill of rights to the Constitution of the United States. However, many modern critics point out that, despite his public support for civil liberties, Jefferson held slaves throughout his adult life.

Beyond politics, Jefferson's interests and talents were wide-ranging. He was one of the leading American architects of his time, designing the Virginia Capitol, the University of Virginia, and his own home, Monticello. He greatly appreciated art and music and encouraged their advancement in the United States. Jefferson also served as president of the American Philosophical Society, an organization that encouraged a wide range of scientific and intellectual research.

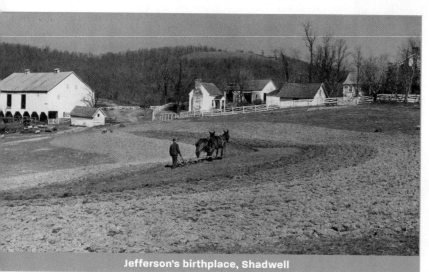

Jefferson's birthplace, Shadwell

Early Life and Family

Boyhood. Thomas Jefferson was born on April 13, 1743, at Shadwell, the family farm in Goochland (now Albemarle) County, Virginia. (The date was April 2 by the calendar then in use.) Thomas was the third child in the family and grew up with six sisters and one brother. Two other brothers died in infancy. His father, Peter Jefferson, had served as a surveyor, sheriff, colonel of militia, and member of Virginia's House of Burgesses, a colonial legislative body. Thomas's mother, Jane Randolph Jefferson, came from one of the oldest families in Virginia.

Thomas was 14 years old when his father died. As the oldest son, he became head of the family.

He inherited more than 2,500 acres (1,010 hectares) of land and at least 20 enslaved African Americans. Thomas's guardian, John Harvie, managed the estate until Jefferson was 21.

Education. The colony of Virginia had no public schools, so Thomas began his studies under a tutor. At age 9, he went to live with a Scottish clergyman who taught him Latin, Greek, and French. After his father died, Thomas entered the school of James Maury, an Anglican clergyman, near Charlottesville.

In 1760, when he was 16, Jefferson entered the College of William and Mary at Williamsburg. The town had a population of only about 1,000. But as the provincial capital, it had a lively social life. There, young Jefferson met two men, William Small and Judge George Wythe, who would have a great influence on him.

Small, a Scot who had been educated in Aberdeen, was a professor at the college. It was through Small that Jefferson was exposed to Enlightenment thinkers from Europe. A number of writers from England and Scotland—such as John Locke, Algernon Sidney, Francis Hutcheson, and Henry Home, Lord Kames—would prove enormously influential to Jefferson's political philosophy. In addition, the writings of the English statesman Viscount Bolingbroke had a significant impact on Jefferson's religious beliefs. Jefferson had been raised in the Anglican Church, but he soon developed a distrust of organized religion. He continued to attend Anglican services, but his religious views came to resemble those of the Unitari-

ans, who emphasize the unity of God rather than the doctrine of the Trinity.

Small introduced Jefferson to Wythe, one of the most learned lawyers in the province. Through Small and Wythe, Jefferson became friendly with Governor Francis Fauquier. It was during these years as a student that Jefferson also met Patrick Henry, who would later become a distinguished lawyer, statesman, and orator. Jefferson spent 2 years at William and Mary. Like most college students at the time, he did not earn a degree.

Lawyer. After leaving college in 1762, Jefferson studied law with George Wythe. Because there were no formal law schools in the colonies at that time, Jefferson's studies involved reading law books under Wythe's supervision and watching Wythe practice law in court.

Jefferson was admitted to the *bar* (legal profession) in 1767. He practiced law with great success until public service began taking all his time. He divided his time between Williamsburg and Shadwell. At Shadwell, he designed and supervised the building of his new home, Monticello, on a nearby hill. Jefferson's estate, like that of his father, lay in the rolling hills of Virginia's Piedmont region, in what is now Albemarle County.

Jefferson's family. In 1772, Jefferson married Martha Wayles Skelton (October 19, 1748–September 6, 1782), a widow. The couple, who shared a love of music and literature, settled at Monticello while it was still under construction. The Jeffersons had one son and five daughters, but only two chil-

Jefferson's daughter, Martha Jefferson Randolph

dren lived to maturity—Martha (1772–1836) and Mary (1778–1804). Mrs. Jefferson died in 1782, after complications arising from childbirth. Thomas Jefferson never remarried.

Mrs. Jefferson's father was John Wayles, a prominent lawyer who lived near Williamsburg. After Wayles died in 1774, he left a large inheritance to the couple. The inheritance included about 11,000 acres (4,450 hectares) of land, including the Poplar Forest plantation in Bedford County, and 135 enslaved African Americans. One of the slaves was Elizabeth (Betty) Hemings, with whom Wayles had fathered several children.

In addition to land and slaves, the Wayles inheritance left Jefferson with the debts that Wayles had owed. Jefferson immediately sold much of the land to pay off some of the

"Determine never to be idle. No person will have occasion to complain of the want of time who never loses any. It is wonderful how much may be done if we are always doing."

—Letter to his daughter Martha, May 5, 1787

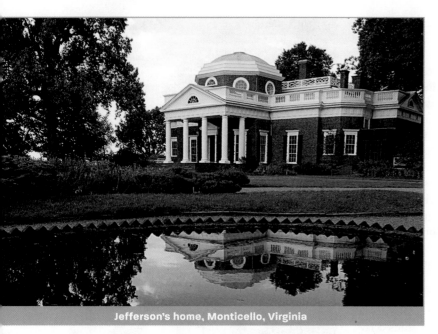

Jefferson's home, Monticello, Virginia

for evidence of a relationship. The scientists examined the descendants' DNA, in particular the Y chromosome, which is almost always passed unchanged from father to son. The study compared the DNA from male-line descendants of Jefferson's uncle with DNA from male-line descendants of two of Sally Hemings's sons. The study could not include male-line descendants of Jefferson and his wife because they had no sons who lived to adulthood. The authors concluded that Jefferson could have fathered at least one of Hemings's children, Eston Hemings.

However, the scientists acknowledged that their study did not include the descendants of other male Jeffersons, particularly of Jefferson's brother Randolph, who had five sons. These relatives carried the same Y-chromosome characteristics as Thomas. The authors of the study later conceded that these relatives could have fathered one or more of Hemings's children.

After the *Nature* study was published, the Thomas Jefferson Foundation, which owns and operates Monticello, appointed a committee to review the controversy. Committee members examined historical and scientific documents and interviewed descendants of Monticello slaves and others. In early 2000, the foundation announced that the likelihood is strong that Jefferson and Sally Hemings had a long-term relationship and that Jefferson was the father of at least one, if not all six, of Hemings's children. Although most professional historians acknowledge a relationship between Jefferson and Hemings, some people do not, and the matter remains deeply controversial.

Colonial Statesman

Revolutionary leader. Jefferson was elected to Virginia's House of Burgesses (later the Virginia House of Delegates) in 1769 and served there until 1775. He was not a great public speaker but proved himself to be an able writer of laws and resolutions.

Jefferson became a member of a group of statesmen that included Patrick Henry, Richard Henry Lee, and Francis Lightfoot Lee. These men challenged the control that political elites known as *Tidewater aristocrats* held over Virginia's government. They also took an active part in the ongoing disputes between colonial leaders and the British Parliament. In 1769, the men organized a *nonimportation association* to protest the import duties

debts. But the remainder of the Wayles debt would trouble him for decades to come.

Slave ownership. Enslaved African Americans were a vital part of the plantation community at Monticello and other farms that Jefferson owned. Jefferson hired some white laborers, but slaves performed the vast majority of the work. Slaves planted and harvested wheat, tobacco, and other crops; constructed buildings and furniture; and were responsible for cooking, cleaning, and other household chores. Jefferson freed a few of his slaves during his life, but he did not attempt to free all, or even most, of his slaves in his will.

Jefferson and Sally Hemings. In the early 1800s, rumors began circulating that Jefferson had engaged in a sexual relationship and fathered children with one of his slaves, Elizabeth Hemings's daughter Sally Hemings (1773–1835). Some historians believe it is likely that John Wayles was Sally's father, and that Jefferson's wife and Sally Hemings were half-sisters. One of Sally Hemings's sons, Madison Hemings, later claimed that he was Jefferson's son and that the relationship between his mother and Jefferson began during Jefferson's mission to France in the 1780s. The rumors caused a great deal of controversy during Jefferson's life, and they remained a topic of debate among historians for many years.

In 1998, the science journal *Nature* published a study in which scientists analyzed genetic material from Jefferson and Hemings descendants, looking

created by the British government's Townshend Acts. The Virginians resolved to not buy any British goods until Parliament repealed the duties.

In 1774, the British government passed a series of laws to strengthen British authority in Massachusetts. These laws became known in America as the Intolerable Acts or the Coercive Acts. After their passage, Jefferson took the lead in organizing another nonimportation agreement. He also called for a meeting of all the colonies to consider their grievances.

Jefferson was chosen to represent Albemarle County at the First Virginia Convention, which in turn was to elect Virginia's delegates to the First Continental Congress. He became ill and could not attend the meeting, but he forwarded a paper that presented his views of the crisis. The paper was soon published as *A Summary View of the Rights of British America* (1774). Jefferson argued that the British Parliament had no control over the American Colonies, and that Parliament's efforts to limit their economic and political liberties were illegal and unjust.

Jefferson attended the Second Virginia Convention in the spring of 1775. The members of this convention chose Jefferson as one of the delegates to the Second Continental Congress.

The Declaration of Independence. Jefferson took a leading role in the Continental Congress. After the first major battles of the Revolutionary War, he was asked to draft a "Declaration of the Causes and Necessity of Taking up Arms." However, the Congress found Jefferson's declaration "too strong." The more moderate John Dickinson drafted a substitute, which included much of Jefferson's original version.

During the spring of 1776, sentiment rapidly grew stronger in favor of seeking independence from Britain. On June 7, Richard Henry Lee of Virginia introduced a resolution stating that "these United Colonies are, and of right ought to be, free and independent States." The Congress appointed a committee to draw up a declaration of independence. On the committee were Jefferson, John Adams, Benjamin Franklin, Roger Sherman, and Robert Livingston. The committee unanimously asked Jefferson to prepare the draft and approved it with few changes. On July 2, Congress as a whole approved Lee's resolution and began reviewing the draft declaration. The lawmakers made certain changes. For instance, a clause blaming the British government for slavery in America—because the king had not closed off the slave trade—was deleted. The Congress adopted the Declaration on July 4.

The Declaration of Independence remains Jefferson's best-known work. It set forth with eloquence, supported by legal argument, the position of the American revolutionaries. It affirmed belief in the natural rights of all people. Few of the ideas were new. Jefferson said his object was "to place before mankind the common sense of the subject, in terms so plain and firm as to command their assent ... Neither aiming at originality of principle or sentiment, nor yet copied from any particular and previous writing, it was intended to be an expression of the American mind ..."

Signing the Declaration of Independence

Before Jefferson began writing the Declaration, he had spent part of his time outside Congress meetings preparing a draft constitution for Virginia. Jefferson sent his draft to Virginia in mid-June, but lawmakers there were already revising another draft constitution. They added Jefferson's preamble and several other points from his draft to the final text of the state constitution.

Virginia lawmaker. In September 1776, Jefferson resigned from the Congress and returned to the Virginia House of Delegates. He had no interest in military life and did not fight in the Revolutionary War. He felt that he could be more useful in Virginia as a lawmaker.

Jefferson's early legislative efforts in Virginia involved land distribution and social reform. He sponsored a bill abolishing *entail*, which requires property owners to leave their land to specified descendants, rather than disposing of it as they wish. Jefferson then succeeded in outlawing *primogeniture*, whereby all land passes to the eldest son. Without entail and primogeniture, great estates could be broken up. Jefferson described the purposes of land reform when he wrote: "instead of an aristocracy of wealth ... to make an opening for the aristocracy of virtue and talent." At this time in Virginia, only white men who owned land could vote. After large estates were broken up, more white men owned property, and the number who could vote increased. Another bill introduced by Jefferson provided that immigrants could become naturalized after living in Virginia for 2 years.

Even more important were Jefferson's bills designed to assure religious toleration. Jefferson sought to abolish the special privileges of the Anglican Church, which had remained Virginia's established church even after the colonies had declared independence. He believed that public funds should not be used to favor an established church over others. He thought that the best way to ensure that people were not forced to support religious institutions they did not believe in was to forbid the use of tax money to pay clergymen or

support any churches. Jefferson's proposals aroused hostility not only among Anglicans, but also among some members of other denominations, who feared that a separation of church and state would loosen all religious ties. Nonetheless, Jefferson's proposals were eventually enacted. Virginia ended the Anglican Church's position as a state church in 1779. It took the church's clergy off the public payroll and exempted Virginians from paying taxes to support the church. In 1786, when Jefferson was in France, lawmakers passed his Statute of Religious Freedom, which guaranteed religious liberty in Virginia.

Jefferson also worked to revise Virginia's legal system. He pushed through numerous reforms, especially in the areas of land law and criminal law. The legislature defeated his plan for a system of free public education with a state-supported university, but parts of the plan later became law.

Governor. The Virginia Assembly elected Jefferson governor for 1-year terms in 1779 and 1780. During his administration, the state suffered severely from the effects of the Revolutionary War. At the request of General George Washington, Jefferson had *redeployed* (changed the position of) Virginia's defenses to aid the Continental Army. Among those who recruited Virginians for military service was James Monroe, who at that time was a lieutenant colonel in the Army. Jefferson and Monroe formed a lasting friendship.

British troops under Benedict Arnold and Lord Cornwallis invaded Virginia in 1781. Because almost all of Virginia's troops had been redeployed the previous year, the state could put up little resistance. Jefferson himself barely escaped capture on June 4 when troops led by Lieutenant Colonel Banastre Tarleton swept down on Monticello.

Jefferson's term had ended on June 2. The Virginia legislature chose Thomas Nelson, Jr., the top officer of the state militia, to succeed Jefferson as governor. Jefferson was criticized for the state's lack of resistance against the British invasion. An official investigation later cleared him of blame, but many years passed before Jefferson regained prestige in his home state. The criticism wounded him deeply, and he left public office with genuine relief.

Delegate to the Congress. Jefferson returned to Monticello embittered and determined to give up public life forever. In response to questions he had received from a French diplomat, Jefferson began writing what would become his only

> "Ignorance is preferable to error: and he is less remote from the truth who believes nothing, than he who believes what is wrong."
> —*Notes on the State of Virginia (1784–1785)*

An engraving of Jefferson

published book, *Notes on the State of Virginia* (1784–1785). The book included much information on Virginia's geography, history, legal system, and population, in addition to statements by Jefferson about politics, science, and race. It was in *Notes on the State of Virginia* that Jefferson called for an end to the institution of slavery. However, he also argued that blacks were biologically inferior to whites.

The death of Jefferson's wife, Martha, in September 1782 left him stunned and distraught. For several months, he spoke to few people and wrote to none. In 1783, Jefferson was selected to serve, once again, as one of Virginia's delegates to the Continental Congress. He accepted the office because he felt it would take his mind off his personal sorrows. During his year in the Congress, he served as chairman of several committees and devised a decimal system of currency. Most important was Jefferson's work on the Ordinance of 1784 and the Land Ordinance of 1785. These measures formed the basis for later American land policies.

The problem of western lands had troubled the colonies from the beginning of the American Revolution. Several colonies claimed land west of the Appalachian Mountains. Virginia, under Jefferson's leadership, gave up its claims to the area in 1784. Other states followed, and the region north of the Ohio River and west of Pennsylvania became the first American territory, the Northwest Territory. Problems of how to govern the area and how to use its land then arose. The Congress appointed two committees to consider the issues and made Jefferson chairman of both. In 1784, Jefferson submitted a draft of an ordinance for the political organization of the western lands. It would have divided the entire region into several states. Each state would eventually be admitted to the Union on a basis of complete equality with the original 13 states. Jefferson's provision forbidding slavery west of the Appalachians lost by a single vote. The Ordinance of 1784 never went into effect, but it furnished the basis for the Northwest Ordinance of 1787, which provided for the government of the Northwest Territory.

Minister to France. In May 1784, the Congress sent Jefferson to France to join John Adams and Benjamin Franklin in negotiating European treaties of commerce. The next year, Franklin resigned as minister to France, and Jefferson succeeded him. The United States was suf-

Depiction of George Washington, Alexander Hamilton, and Jefferson

fering from a weak central authority under the Articles of Confederation, which served as the basic charter of the early U.S. government. Jefferson found himself troubled by what he described as "the nonpayment of our debts and the want of energy in our government." Nonetheless, he did work out several important commercial agreements. Such agreements enabled American farmers to sell crops to foreign markets.

In 1789, the French Revolution began. French reformers regarded Jefferson as a champion of liberty because of his political writings and his legal reforms in Virginia. The Marquis de Lafayette, who had fought for American independence, and other moderates often sought Jefferson's advice. Jefferson tried to keep out of French politics, but he did draft a proposed Charter of Rights to be presented to the king. This document and his other suggestions urged moderation because Jefferson felt that the French were not yet ready for a representative government of the American type. Jefferson hoped that the French would move from an absolute monarchy to a constitutional monarchy. Overall, he sympathized with the French Revolution, feeling it was similar in purpose to the American Revolution.

Jefferson had taken his daughter Martha to France with him, and Mary joined them in 1787. Both girls attended a convent school in Paris. Jefferson traveled widely in Europe. He broadened his knowledge of many subjects, especially archi-

"... were it left to me to decide whether we should have a government without newspapers, or newspapers without a government, I should not hesitate a moment to prefer the latter."
—*Letter to Colonel Edward Carrington, an American statesman, January 16, 1787*

"I hold it that a little rebellion now and then is a good thing, and as necessary in the political world as storms in the physical."
—*Letter to the American statesman James Madison, January 30, 1787*

"The tree of liberty must
be refreshed from time
to time with the blood of
patriots and tyrants. It
is its natural manure."
—*Letter to Colonel
William Stephens Smith,
American diplomat,
November 13, 1787*

"... delay is preferable
to error."
—*Letter to President
George Washington,
May 16, 1792*

"... unmerited abuse
wounds, while
unmerited praise has not
the power to heal."
—*Letter to Edward
Rutledge, American
political leader,
December 27, 1796*

tecture and farming. He applied for a leave in 1789 and sailed for home in October. He wanted to settle his affairs in America and take his daughters back home. Jefferson expected to return to represent the United States in France.

National Statesman

During Jefferson's stay in France, Americans at home had begun reorganizing the government. In 1787, statesmen assembled at the Constitutional Convention in Philadelphia and drew up the document that became the Constitution of the United States. Jefferson's friend James Madison sent him a draft, which he approved. But Jefferson objected strongly to the lack of a bill of rights and wrote letters urging one. Soon after the Constitution went into effect, Madison introduced the 10 amendments that became the Bill of Rights.

Secretary of state. Jefferson arrived in the United States in November 1789. A letter from President George Washington awaited him, asking Jefferson to be secretary of state in the new government. Jefferson received this invitation "with real regret," but he finally yielded to Washington's urging.

Jefferson and Hamilton. Sharp differences of opinion soon arose between Jefferson and the secretary of the treasury, Alexander Hamilton. Hamilton, though younger than Jefferson, had gained prominence as an associate of George Washington and a spokesman for the Constitution. Hamilton believed that the Constitution gave the majority of power to the central, or *federal*, government. Jefferson, however, interpreted the Constitution differently. He believed that, although the Constitution had granted many responsibilities to the federal government, the bulk of the decision-making authority belonged at the state level. Hamilton's financial program brought these differences into the open.

Jefferson supported Hamilton's plan for funding the debts of the previous American governments. He also agreed, reluctantly, that the new Congress should accept responsibility for the debts taken on by the states during the Revolutionary War. This proposal aroused considerable opposition, especially in Virginia and other Southern states that had already paid off much of their own debt. Such states did not want to pay the debts of other states. Some Southern members of Congress agreed to vote for paying the state debts in return for having

the national capital in the South. Jefferson helped arrange this compromise, which led to the movement of the capital to its present location at Washington, D.C., on the Potomac River between Maryland and Virginia.

Key disagreements between Jefferson and Hamilton involved Hamilton's plans to encourage commerce and manufacturing and to establish a national bank. Jefferson wanted the United States to remain chiefly committed to agriculture. He feared that a national bank would encourage financial speculation and hurt farming interests. Jefferson also thought it would give the government too much power. President Washington asked his Cabinet to submit opinions on the constitutionality of a national bank. Jefferson argued that the federal government should assume only the powers expressly given it by the Constitution, a theory later called "strict construction." Hamilton responded with the notion of "loose construction," claiming that the federal government could assume all powers not expressly denied it in the Constitution. Washington, who generally favored Hamilton in domestic affairs, approved the bank.

The differences between Jefferson and Hamilton grew into a bitter personal feud. Their conflicting points of view also led to the development of the first American political parties. The Federalists adopted Hamilton's principles. Jefferson led the party that historians label the Democratic-Republicans. The Democratic-Republicans generally called themselves Republicans during Jefferson's time, but the group was not connected to the modern Republican Party. In fact, historians regard the Democratic-Republicans as the early form of the group that became the Democratic Party in the late 1820s and the 1830s.

International relations. Jefferson wanted the United States to build commercial and political relationships with as many European nations as possible. This, too, led to disagreements with Hamilton, who favored a close relationship with Britain. Jefferson urged recognition of the revolutionary government of France. But as the French Revolution grew more radical, he reluctantly supported Washington's Neutrality Proclamation, which called for "conduct friendly and impartial" to France and other European nations. Jefferson agreed on demanding the recall of Edmond Genet, a controversial minister from France.

Jefferson supported Washington's policy of acquiring American Indian lands through treaty. He also tried to persuade the British to abandon their forts in the Northwest Territory and worked for free navigation of the Mississippi River.

Vice president. Jefferson joined his fellow cabinet members in urging Washington to accept a second term as president, which began in 1793. But Jefferson, frustrated over losing cabinet disputes to Hamilton, resigned as secretary of state at the end of that year. Jefferson spoke publicly about remaining retired from politics, but this talk did not last long.

In 1796, Jefferson's Democratic-Republican supporters nominated him as a candidate for president. He ran against John Adams, the Federalist candidate, in the first party contest for the American presidency. Adams received 71 electoral votes and was elected president. Jefferson received 68 electoral votes, the second largest number. By the law of the time, he became vice president.

Jefferson took no active part in the new administration because it was largely Federalist. Because the vice president also serves as president of the Senate, Jefferson observed legislative debates but could not participate in them. He compiled *A Manual of Parliamentary Practice* (1801), a document of Senate procedures that still forms part of the basis for rules of procedure in both houses of Congress. During his time as vice president, Jefferson worked behind the scenes to strengthen the Democratic-Republican Party. He found strong support among small farmers, frontier settlers, and Northern laborers. Also during this time, he served as president of the American Philosophical Society.

In 1798, a diplomatic dispute known as the XYZ Affair aroused great hostility to France. Concerns of a possible war with France led the Federalists to pass the Alien and Sedition Acts. These laws made it a crime for anyone to criticize the president or Congress. In effect, they deprived the Democratic-Republicans of freedom of speech and of the press. The laws aroused much opposition, and Jefferson led the attack against them.

Jefferson prepared a series of resolutions that were passed by the Kentucky legislature, and his friend James Madison prepared similar resolutions for Virginia. These Kentucky and Virginia Resolutions set forth the "compact" theory of the Union—the idea that the Union was a *compact* (agreement) among the states—and asserted the right of the states to judge when the compact had been broken. The resolutions were later used by advocates of *nullification*, who claimed that each U.S. state had a right to *nullify* (reject) national laws.

Election of 1800. The Democratic-Republicans again nominated Jefferson for president in 1800, and they named former Senator Aaron Burr of New York for vice president. The Federalist Party renominated President Adams and chose diplomat Charles C. Pinckney of South Carolina as his running mate.

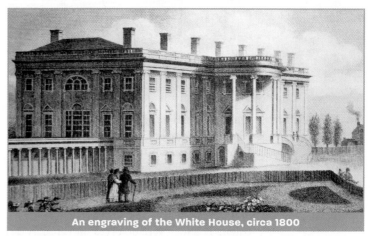

An engraving of the White House, circa 1800

The Federalists claimed that Jefferson was a revolutionary, an anarchist, and an atheist. However, the Federalists were divided among themselves, because a quarrel between Adams and Hamilton had divided Federalist voting *blocs* (groups with common interests). In addition, the unpopular Alien and Sedition Acts persuaded many voters to switch party allegiances, bringing about Democratic-Republican gains at the state and national levels.

Between the presidential candidates, Jefferson received 73 electoral votes to 65 for Adams. At the time, however, electors did not distinguish between votes for president and vice president, and each Democratic-Republican elector had cast one vote for Jefferson and the other for Burr. As a result, Jefferson and Burr tied, and the decision moved to the House of Representatives.

The House at that time was still controlled by the Federalists, because the newly elected Democratic-Republican Congress had not yet taken office. Many Federalists did not want to give the presidency to Jefferson. Some considered schemes that would have kept a Federalist as president or

"The second office of the government is honorable and easy, the first is but a splendid misery."
—*Letter to the American statesman Elbridge Gerry comparing the vice presidency with the presidency, May 13, 1797*

"... I have sworn upon the altar of God, eternal hostility against every form of tyranny over the mind of man."
—*Letter to Benjamin Rush, American physician and political leader, September 23, 1800*

A statue of Jefferson on the Columbia University campus

that would have made Burr president. However, when it became obvious that the selection of a Federalist president would not stand, many saw Jefferson as the more reasonable alternative. Hamilton—who trusted Burr even less than he did Jefferson—threw his influence to the support of Jefferson, and Jefferson won election on the 36th ballot. The final vote occurred on February 17, 1801. Burr became vice president.

The election of 1800 led to an amendment to the Constitution. Under Amendment 12, electors in the Electoral College vote for one person as president and for another as vice president.

Jefferson's First Administration (1801–1805)

The first term of Jefferson's presidency was a time of growth and prosperity. The United States was at peace with the United Kingdom, France, and Spain, as well as with American Indian groups. The United States increased greatly in size, and its economy expanded.

Life in the White House. The so-called "President's House" was only partly built when Jefferson moved in. He felt somewhat lonely in what he described as "a great stone house, big enough for two emperors, one pope and the grand lama." Jefferson's wife had been dead 18½ years when he became president. The White House's most popular hostess at this time was Dolley Madison, the wife of James Madison, who had become secretary of state. Jefferson's daughter Martha Randolph

also served as hostess from time to time. Jefferson's grandson, James Randolph, was the first child born in the White House.

Jefferson kept a French steward and chef, but he tried to eliminate some of the formality in White House protocol. He began the practice of having guests shake hands with the president instead of bowing. He also placed dinner guests at a round table so that everyone would feel equally important. Always interested in architecture, Jefferson developed some ideas for the addition of east and west terraces and a north portico to the White House. He employed the English-born architect Benjamin H. Latrobe to carry out these ideas.

New policies. Jefferson believed that the federal government should play a limited role in citizen's lives. With the help of his secretary of the treasury, Albert Gallatin, he strictly managed government programs and spending. Under Jefferson's leadership, the federal government sharply cut expenditures for the Army and Navy. At the same time, however, Jefferson oversaw the founding of the United States Military Academy at West Point, New York. The federal government under Jefferson also made substantial payments on the national debt and repealed *excise taxes* (taxes on specific products or services). Excise taxes had aroused opposition under the Federalists.

Jefferson's administration also reversed other Federalist policies, particularly the laws that made up the Alien and Sedition Acts. The government repealed the Naturalization Act, and the Alien Friends Act and the Sedition Act were not renewed. The Alien Enemies Act was greatly amended.

Jefferson believed that appointments to federal government jobs should be based on merit. But Federalists held all the offices, and he quickly discovered that vacancies "by death are few; by resignation none." He removed some Federalists, and generally appointed Democratic-Republicans to fill the vacancies. By the end of Jefferson's second term, his party held most federal offices. Jefferson's actions foreshadowed the *spoils system*, the practice of giving appointments to public office as political rewards for party service.

The courts. Jefferson's administration asked Congress to repeal the Judiciary Act of 1801. This act had allowed President Adams to make more than 200 "midnight appointments" of judges and other court officials just before he left office. Some of these judges had no commissions, no duties, and no salaries. Jefferson told the judges to consider their appointments as never having been made.

William Marbury was a justice of the peace whom Adams had appointed to a five-year term in the District of Columbia. When Secretary of State James Madison withheld his appointment, Marbury asked the Supreme Court, under Section 13 of the Judiciary Act of 1789, to force Madison to grant the appointment. Marbury's action led to *Marbury v. Madison* (1803), one of the most important Supreme Court decisions in U.S. history. In its decision, the court declared that Section 13 gave the Supreme Court powers not provided by the Constitution and was therefore unconstitutional. The court's decision, written by Chief Justice John Marshall, thus established the power of *judicial review*—the court's authority to declare laws unconstitutional. The court refused to force Madison to deliver Marbury's commission.

On the surface, the decision was a victory for Jefferson and his Democratic-Republicans, because the administration did not have to deliver commissions to the "midnight judges" appointed by Adams. However, the Democratic-Republicans were disturbed by the idea that the Supreme Court could declare unconstitutional a law passed by Congress. This principle placed a powerful tool in the hands of the courts, which the Federalists still controlled. Many Democratic-Republicans feared that the Supreme Court would use its power to help the Federalists.

The Democratic-Republicans used the *impeachment* (removal) of judges as one way of checking the federal courts. First they impeached John Pickering, a New Hampshire judge who had reportedly become insane. After the Senate removed Pickering from office, the House brought impeachment charges against Justice Samuel Chase of the Supreme Court. The House charged that Chase had criticized the Jefferson administration unfairly. The Senate acquitted him, much to Jefferson's disappointment. This series of events helped establish that political changes do not affect the tenure of judges.

War with Tripoli. Ever since Jefferson had been minister to France, he had urged the United States to act against the *corsairs* (pirates) that were linked to North Africa's Barbary States (now part of Algeria, Libya, Morocco, and Tunisia). The four Barbary States—Algiers, Morocco, Tunis, and Tripoli—had authorized corsairs to attack ships from other countries unless those countries gave an annual *tribute* (payment of money) to the states. The United States had negotiated treaties with all four of the Barbary States. However, in 1801, Tripoli opened war on American shipping because it wanted a greater amount of tribute money. The United States Navy blockaded Tripoli's ports, bombarded fortresses, and eventually forced a resolution to the conflict. The war with Tripoli caused Jefferson to abandon his plan to put U.S. Navy ships in dry dock and to rely only on short-range gunboats for coastal defense.

The Louisiana Purchase. The Louisiana Territory, a vast region between the Mississippi River and the Rocky Mountains, had been transferred from France to Spain in 1762. In 1801, Jefferson learned that Spain planned to *cede* (hand over) the area back to France. Spanish control of Louisiana had posed no threat to the United States. However, Jefferson had concerns about France gaining the territory. He feared that the French government, under Napoleon I, might restrict commerce through New Orleans or try to establish new French colonies on the Mississippi.

In January 1803, Jefferson obtained $2 million from Congress for "extraordinary expenses." He sent James Monroe to Paris to help the American minister, Robert Livingston, negotiate with France. Jefferson hoped to buy New Orleans and the Flori-

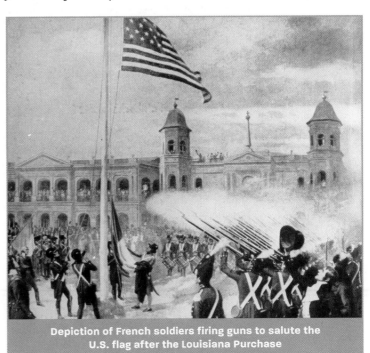

Depiction of French soldiers firing guns to salute the U.S. flag after the Louisiana Purchase

das (with West Florida at the time extending to the Mississippi). He at least wanted to get a guarantee of free navigation of the Mississippi and various commercial privileges at New Orleans.

Before Monroe reached Paris in April, Livingston proposed a modest purchase of New Orleans. Talleyrand, the French foreign minister, astounded Livingston by asking what the United States would give for the whole of Louisiana. After Monroe arrived, he and Livingston quickly struck a bargain. They agreed to pay 60 million francs and give up American claims against France—making a total price of about $15 million. The deal enabled the government to gain control of the Mississippi River and almost double the nation's size.

Jefferson was uncertain whether the government had a right under the Constitution to add this vast new territory to the Union. But his doubts did not keep him from submitting the treaty to the Senate, which ratified it by a vote of 24 to 7 in October 1803.

Exploration and expansion. In January 1803, Jefferson secretly petitioned Congress to authorize an exploration through the Louisiana Territory and the Oregon region. He hoped that the expedition would find a route to the Pacific Ocean along the Missouri and Columbia rivers. Congress authorized the expedition, and Jefferson chose Meriwether Lewis, a U.S. Army captain and Jefferson's private secretary, to lead it. Lewis selected William Clark, a former Army officer, to join him. Between 1804 and 1806, Lewis, Clark, and their companions traveled from a camp near St. Louis to the headwaters of the Missouri River, across the Rockies to the Pacific, and finally back to St. Louis. They returned with maps of their route and the surrounding areas, descriptions of plant and animal life and natural resources, and information about American Indian cultures.

The population of the Northwest Territory grew rapidly during Jefferson's first administration. Ohio joined the Union in 1803 as the 17th state. In 1804, the government encouraged western settlement by cutting in half—from 320 to 160 acres (130 to 65 hectares)—the minimum number of acres of western land that could be bought. Anyone with $80 in cash could make the first payment on a frontier farm.

Policies toward American Indians. Jefferson studied accounts of American Indian cultures in great detail and collected information about Indian languages. As president, he continued the policies toward Indians that George Washington and John Adams had pursued. Jefferson's agents were instructed to encourage trade with Indian leaders and communities. The administration hoped that commerce would make Indian ways of life more similar to those of European Americans. If Indians became more "civilized," Jefferson reasoned, they would be more likely to become settled farmers and sell extra traditional hunting lands to the government. Jefferson also proposed the idea that Indians could be relocated to the area west of the Mississippi River.

Indian groups differed in their reactions to such "civilization" plans. Some members of groups like the Cherokee and Creek adopted European ways, including plantation agriculture and slavery. Other groups, such as the Shawnee, resisted. The Shawnee leader Tecumseh defended Indian culture and organized resistance to the white settlers.

Election of 1804. Jefferson ran for reelection in 1804. But Vice President Aaron Burr was left off the ballot because he had become a notorious figure after killing Alexander Hamilton in a duel in July 1804. The Democratic-Republicans nominated Governor George Clinton of New York for vice president. The final electoral count gave 162 votes to Jefferson and only 14 to the Federalist candidate, Charles C. Pinckney.

Jefferson's Second Administration (1805–1809)

Jefferson's second term as president began, as he later put it, "without a cloud on the horizon." However, his second term became more troubled than his first, as conflict overseas nearly pushed the nation into war.

The Burr conspiracy. After leaving the office of vice president, Aaron Burr became involved in a scheme to create a new independent state in the lower Mississippi Valley. Historians believe that he planned to create the state by breaking Western lands away from the United States, invading Spanish territory, or both. The details of the scheme remain unclear and have been debated by historians.

Burr was unable to gain support from the British, French, or Spanish, but he did raise a small military force of his own. In 1806, Burr set off down the Ohio River for New Orleans, hoping to

Depiction of Jefferson
drafting the Declaration of Independence

gather recruits along the way. General James Wilkinson, the governor of the Louisiana Territory, had encouraged Burr to expect his support. However, Wilkinson exposed Burr's plot and wrote to Jefferson about a "deep, dark, wicked, and widespread conspiracy."

Jefferson had Burr captured and taken to Richmond, Virginia, where he was tried for treason. However, Chief Justice John Marshall presided over the trial and interpreted the charge of treason so narrowly that the jury had to acquit Burr.

The struggle for neutrality. War had broken out between the United Kingdom and Napoleon's France in May 1803. As fighting continued, Jefferson found that his chief tasks were to keep the United States out of the war and to uphold the country's rights as a neutral.

The United Kingdom and France were destroying each other's merchant shipping. As a result, a large part of the trade between Europe and the Caribbean fell into American hands. American shipbuilding and commerce grew rapidly, and thousands of sailors were needed. Most of these sailors came from New England, but many had deserted from British ships. The United Kingdom, desperately needing seamen, began stopping American ships on the high seas and removing sailors suspected of being British. But because it

was hard to tell British and Americans apart, thousands of Americans were seized and forced into the British Navy.

The struggle in Europe soon became so intense that both sides ignored the rights of neutral nations. In the Berlin and Milan decrees of 1806 and 1807, Napoleon announced his intention to seize all neutral ships bound to or from a British port. The British issued a series of *Orders in Council* (government decrees) that blockaded all ports in the possession of France or its allies. In practice, this meant that the British would try to seize any ship bound for the European continent, while the French would attempt to seize ships sailing almost anywhere else.

In June 1807, the British warship *Leopard* launched an unprovoked attack on the American ship *Chesapeake*. The *Leopard* fired on the *Chesapeake* after the captain of the American vessel refused to let the British search his ship for deserters. The incident threatened to bring the two nations to war.

The embargo. Jefferson felt that he could bring the United Kingdom and France to reason by closing American markets to them and not selling them any American supplies. In 1807, he sent the Embargo Act to Congress, and it quickly passed. The law prohibited exports from the United States and barred American ships from sailing into foreign ports.

In practice, however, the embargo affected the United States far more than it did either the United Kingdom or France. Ships lay idle, sailors and shipbuilders lost their jobs, and exports piled up in warehouses. Many Americans evaded the law, and smuggling flourished.

The government had to pass additional laws to increase the nation's coastal defenses and to enforce the embargo. After 14 months, it became clear that the embargo would force no concessions from either the United Kingdom or France. Public clamor against the measure grew overwhelming, and Congress repealed it in March 1809 by passing the milder Non-Intercourse Act.

Many people urged Jefferson to run for reelection again in 1808. Jefferson, however, chose to follow George Washington's example and retired at the conclusion of his second term. After James Madison became the fourth president of the United States in March 1809, Jefferson returned to Monticello.

"1. Never put off till tomorrow what you can do to-day.

2. Never trouble another for what you can do yourself.

3. Never spend your money before you have it.

4. Never buy what you do not want, because it is cheap; it will be dear to you.

5. Pride costs us more than hunger, thirst and cold.

6. We never repent of having eaten too little.

7. Nothing is troublesome that we do willingly.

8. How much pain have cost us the evils which have never happened.

9. Take things always by their smooth handle.

10. When angry, count ten, before you speak; if very angry, an hundred."

—*Letter to his namesake Thomas Jefferson Smith, February 21, 1825*

Later Years

Jefferson was 65 when he retired from the presidency. In his later years, he divided his time between his plantations at Monticello and Poplar Forest. His major public activity during his retirement was guiding the creation of the University of Virginia.

The sage of Monticello. In retirement, Jefferson turned to music, architecture, chemical experiments, and the study of religion, philosophy, law, and education. He also improved his flower and herb gardens and experimented with new crops and farming techniques.

Jefferson carried on correspondence with people in all parts of the world. He improved a copying device called the *polygraph*, which made file copies of the many letters he wrote. He entertained numerous guests who came to pay their respects. In 1811, Jefferson was reconciled with his political rival John Adams, and the two men renewed their old friendship. Their letters ranged widely over the fields of history, philosophy, politics, religion, and science. In 1815, Jefferson sold his personal library to Congress to replace books that had been destroyed when the British burned the U.S. Capitol during the War of 1812 (1812–1815).

Jefferson had withdrawn from politics, but he was often consulted on public affairs. Presidents Madison and Monroe, his successors in the White House, frequently sought his advice. Many of Jefferson's friends urged him to speak out against slavery, but Jefferson claimed his views on the subject were well known. He never spoke publicly on slavery during his retirement.

Jefferson never recovered from the debt he inherited from his father-in-law. Though he sought to make his plantations as profitable as possible, he also spent a great deal of money. He made additions to Monticello, entertained lavishly, and supported members of his family. Public contributions aided Jefferson in his later years, but they did not solve his financial problems. After Jefferson's death, much of his property, most of his slaves, and Monticello itself were sold by Jefferson's heirs to pay his creditors.

University founder. Jefferson's most important contributions in his later years were in the field of education. As a young legislator, he had worked for the reform of Virginia's system of public education. Later, he had tried to improve William and Mary College. In time, he became convinced that the state needed an entirely new university.

After he retired from politics, Jefferson worked to create the University of Virginia. He projected his character, interests, and talents into the planning of a university "based on the illimitable freedom of the human mind to explore and to expose every subject susceptible of its contemplation." Jefferson organized the curriculum, hired the faculty, and selected the library books. He also drew the plans for the buildings and supervised their construction. As a result of his efforts, scholars from other countries came to teach at the university. In March 1825, Jefferson saw the University of Virginia open with 40 students.

On July 4, 1826, 50 years after the adoption of the Declaration of Independence, Jefferson died. He was buried at Monticello, where an *obelisk* (stone monument) marked his grave. The inscription that Jefferson wrote for the obelisk reads: "Here was buried Thomas Jefferson, Author of the Declaration of American Independence, of the Statute of Virginia for religious freedom, & Father of the University of Virginia." In 1883, descendants of Jefferson's gave the original obelisk to the University of Missouri at Columbia in honor of the first state university to be founded within what had been the Louisiana Territory. A replica sits atop Jefferson's grave at Monticello today.

Jefferson is one of four U.S. presidents honored at Mount Rushmore National Memorial, in the Black Hills of South Dakota. Mount Rushmore features the faces of Jefferson, George Washington, Theodore Roosevelt, and Abraham Lincoln carved into a granite cliff. Work on the memorial began in 1927 and continued for more than 14 years. Jefferson is also honored on the U.S. nickel. Pictures of Jefferson and Monticello first appeared on the coin in 1938. The Jefferson Memorial stands at the edge of the Tidal Basin, near the National Mall, in Washington, D.C. The memorial, which was dedicated in 1943, contains a statue of Jefferson and quotations from his writings.

MLA Citation

"Thomas Jefferson."
*The Southwestern
Advantage Topic Source.*
Nashville: Southwestern. 2013.

DATA

1801	(June 10) Tripoli declared war on America.
1802	(July 4) The U.S. Military Academy opened.
1803	(February 24) The Supreme Court decided the case of *Marbury versus Madison*.
1803	(March 3) John Pickering became the first federal judge to be impeached.
1803	(May 2) The Louisiana Territory was purchased from France, by a treaty predated April 30.
1804	(May 14) The Lewis and Clark Expedition set out for the Northwest.
1804	(September 25) Amendment 12 to the Constitution was adopted.
1805	(June 4) The United States and Tripoli signed a peace treaty.
1807	(December 22) Congress passed the Embargo Act against international commerce.
1808	(January 1) The act prohibiting the importation of black slaves became law.
1809	(March 1) The Non-Intercourse Act was passed, banning trade with France and Britain.

The World of President Jefferson

War with Tripoli, a Barbary State of northern Africa, broke out in 1801 after Barbary sea raiders attacked American shipping. The United States won the war in 1805.

The Louisiana Purchase, a territorial agreement with France, doubled the size of the United States in 1803.

Dalton's Theory of the Atom, one of the foundations of chemistry, was developed in 1803. English chemist John Dalton proposed that all matter was made up of atoms.

Marbury versus Madison, a landmark Supreme Court ruling, established the Court's right to declare laws unconstitutional.

The Lewis and Clark Expedition crossed the Rocky Mountains to the Pacific Ocean and mapped much of the vast northwestern wilderness. The explorers left in 1804 and returned in 1806.

Napoleon crowned himself emperor of the French in 1804.

The Steam Age revolutionized transportation. Richard Trevithick, an English engineer, invented the steam-powered locomotive in 1804. American inventor Robert Fulton began the first commercially successful steamboat service in 1807.

The Romantic Movement dominated literature. Sir Walter Scott's *The Lay of the Last Minstrel* (1805) and William Wordsworth's *Poems in Two Volumes* (1807) stressed imagination, passionate feeling, and unusual experiences.

The Embargo Act of 1807 prohibited ships from entering or leaving U.S. harbors. It sought to end interference with U.S. shipping by Britain and France, who were at war.

The importation of slaves was prohibited by Congress in 1808.

The United States doubled its area in 1803 with the Louisiana Purchase. Ohio became the seventhth state in 1803. Congress extended the Mississippi Territory and created the Michigan and Illinois territories.

DATA

Vice Presidents and Cabinet

Vice president	Aaron Burr George Clinton (1805)
Secretary of state	James Madison
Secretary of the treasury	Samuel Dexter Albert Gallatin (1801)
Secretary of war	Henry Dearborn
Attorney general	Levi Lincoln John Breckinridge (1805) Caesar A. Rodney (1807)
Secretary of the Navy	Robert Smith

Jefferson's Life in Brief

1743	(April 13) Born in Goochland (now Albemarle) County, Virginia.
1772	(January 1) Married Martha Wayles Skelton.
1776	Wrote the Declaration of Independence.
1779	Elected governor of Virginia.
1782	Mrs. Martha Jefferson died.
1785	Appointed minister to France.
1789	Became United States secretary of state.
1796	Elected vice president of the United States.
1801	(February 17) Elected president of the United States.
1804	Reelected president.
1819	Founded the University of Virginia.
1826	(July 4) Died at Monticello, his Virginia home.

ADDITIONAL RESOURCES

Books to Read

Appleby, Joyce O. *Thomas Jefferson*. Henry Holt, 2003.

Bernstein, Richard B. *Thomas Jefferson*. Oxford, 2003.

Brown, David S. *Thomas Jefferson: A Biographical Companion*. ABC-CLIO, 1998.

Ellis, Joseph J. *American Sphinx: The Character of Thomas Jefferson*. Knopf, 1996.

Ferling, John E. *Adams vs. Jefferson: The Tumultuous Election of 1800.*Oxford, 2004.

Gilreath, James, ed. *Thomas Jefferson and the Education of a Citizen*. U.S. Government Printing Office, 1999.

Web Sites

Jefferson National Expansion Memorial

http://www.nps.gov/jeff/index.htm

National Park Service site on the Jefferson National Expansion Memorial and the Gateway Arch in St. Louis, Missouri.

Jefferson's Blood

http://www.pbs.org/wgbh/pages/frontline/shows/jefferson/

This special feature from PBS focuses on the relationship between Thomas Jefferson and Sally Hemings, a slave who may have borne him children.

Monticello, Home of Thomas Jefferson

http://www.monticello.org/

The official Web site of the Thomas Jefferson Memorial Foundation provides information about Thomas Jefferson's home at Monticello.

Notes on the State of Virginia

http://xroads.virginia.edu/~HYPER/JEFFERSON/cover.html

The full text of Notes on the State of Virginia, by Thomas Jefferson, from the University of Virginia Department of American Studies.

Thomas Jefferson

http://www.whitehouse.gov/history/presidents/thomasjefferson

Official White House biography of Thomas Jefferson. Includes a link to a biography of Martha Wayles Skelton Jefferson.

Thomas Jefferson Online Resources

http://etext.lib.virginia.edu/jefferson/

The University of Virginia presents a collection of Jefferson resources, including quotes from the president and electronic texts of his writings.

Search Strings

The Sally Hemings affair

"Thomas Jefferson" "Sally Hemings" affair slave (17,300)

"Thomas Jefferson" "Sally Hemings" affair slave DNA descendants (549)

The Declaration of Independence and the Committee of Five

Thomas Jefferson Declaration of Independence "Committee of Five" Second Continental Congress (3,190)

Thomas Jefferson Declaration of Independence "Committee of Five" Second Continental Congress colonies autonomy (328)

Democratic-Republicanism

Thomas Jefferson Democratic-Republicanism political philosophy (323)

Thomas Jefferson Democratic-Republicanism political philosophy tenets (47)

Louisiana Purchase

"Louisiana Purchase" Thomas Jefferson New Orleans Mississippi River France (35,000)

"Louisiana Purchase" Thomas Jefferson New Orleans Mississippi River France Meriwether Lewis

Abraham Lincoln

The sixteenth president of the United States, Abraham Lincoln (1809–1865), is known best for his presidential efforts during the most devastating era in American history, the American Civil War (1861–1865), ending slavery in the United States, and being the first president of the United States to be assassinated.

HOT topics

Greatest Speeches
Emancipation Proclamation
Critical Involvements in War Effort
Highlights of Lincoln's Administration
Assassination

HOT topics

Greatest Speeches. Lincoln's Gettysburg Address, given during the dedication ceremonies at a cemetery on the Gettysburg battlefield on November 19, 1863, is well-remembered and often quoted. Also of historical significance is Lincoln's Second Inaugural Address. Both speeches are etched in stone on the Lincoln Memorial in Washington, D.C.

Emancipation Proclamation. On January 1, 1863, President Lincoln issued the Emancipation Proclamation, declaring freedom for slaves within the Confederacy. The proclamation also

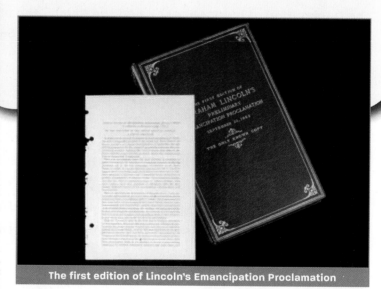

The first edition of Lincoln's Emancipation Proclamation

HOT topics

allowed blacks to serve in the Union Army and Navy, which greatly affected the outcome of the war. Although the Emancipation Proclamation did not free all slaves, it led to the Thirteenth Amendment to the Constitution, which became law in 1865 and officially ended slavery in all of the United States.

Critical Involvements in War Effort.
Some historians believe Lincoln was the chief architect of military strategy for the Union. He chose which officers would lead specific military campaigns. He blocked the Southern ports, called for 75,000 men for the army, and ordered spending of federal funds. He also suspended *habeas corpus*, thus allowing Southern sympathizers to be detained or imprisoned. He strengthened relations with border states as well as foreign nations (notably during the "Trent Affair").

Highlights of Lincoln's Administration.
Besides conducting the war effort and issuing the Emancipation Proclamation, Lincoln's administration also approved the Homestead Act of 1862, which encouraged farm ownership; signed the Pacific Railroad Act in 1862, starting the transcontinental railroad; signed the Land Grant Act, which set aside land for state colleges; and approved the Nation Bank Act of 1863, which established the current American system of national banks.

Assassination.
Abraham Lincoln was the first president of the United States to be assassinated. On April 14, 1865, less than a week after the war ended, John Wilkes Booth shot President Lincoln in the head while Lincoln was attending a performance at Ford's Theatre in Washington. Booth escaped but was killed later by federal troops in an attempt to capture him. Several people were tried as conspirators with Booth in Lincoln's assassination and in a plot to kill other government officials.

Lincoln on his deathbed

TRUE or FALSE?
Lincoln regarded the fate of world democracy, not abolition of slavery, as the central issue of the Civil War.

THE BASICS

Abraham Lincoln (1809–1865) was one of the truly great men of all time. He led the United States during the American Civil War (1861–1865), which was the greatest crisis in U.S. history. Lincoln helped end slavery in the nation and helped keep the American Union from splitting apart during the war. Lincoln thus believed that he proved to the world that democracy can be a lasting form of government. Lincoln's Gettysburg Address, Second Inaugural Address, and many of his other speeches and writings are classic statements of democratic beliefs and goals. In conducting a bitter war, Lincoln never became bitter himself. He showed a nobility of character that has worldwide appeal. Lincoln, a Republican, was the first member of his party to become president. He was assassinated near the end of the Civil War and was succeeded by Vice President Andrew Johnson. Lincoln was the first U.S. president to be assassinated.

The American people knew little about Lincoln when he became president. Little in his past experience indicated that he could successfully deal with the deep differences between Northerners and Southerners over slavery. Lincoln received less than 40 percent of the popular vote in winning the presidential election of 1860. But by 1865, he had become in the eyes of the world equal in importance to George Washington. Through the years, many people have regarded Lincoln as the greatest person in United States history.

During the Civil War, Lincoln's first task was to win the war. He had to view nearly all other matters in relation to the war. It was "the progress of our arms," he once said, "upon which all else depends." But Lincoln was a peace-loving man who had earlier described military glory as "that attractive rainbow, that rises in showers of blood—that serpent's eye that charms to destroy." The Civil War was by far the bloodiest war in U.S. history. In the Battle of Gettysburg, for example, the more than 45,000 total casualties (people killed, wounded, captured, or missing) exceeded the number of casualties in all previous American wars put together.

Portrait of Abraham Lincoln

Lincoln became a remarkable war leader. Some historians believe he was the chief architect of the Union's victorious military strategy. This strategy called for Union armies to advance against the enemy on all fronts at the same time. Lincoln also insisted that the objective of the Union armies should be the destruction of opposing forces, not the conquest of territory. Lincoln changed generals several times because he could not find one who would fight the war agressively. When he finally found such a general, Ulysses S. Grant, Lincoln stood firmly behind him.

Lincoln's second great task was to keep up Northern morale throughout the horrible war in which many relatives in the North and South fought against one another and hundreds of thousands died. He understood that the Union's resources vastly exceeded those of the Confederacy, and that the Union would eventually triumph if it remained dedicated to victory. For this reason, Lincoln used his great writing and speechmaking abilities to spur on his people.

If the Union had been destroyed, the United States could have become two, or possibly more, nations. These nations separately could not have become as prosperous and important as the United States is today. By preserving the Union, Lincoln influenced the course of world history. By ending slavery, he helped assure the moral strength of the United States. His own life story, too, has been important. He rose from humble origins to the nation's highest office. Millions of people regard Lincoln's career as proof that democracy offers all people the best hope of a full and free life.

Life in the United States during Lincoln's administration revolved around the war. But almost miraculously, the nation also laid out a blueprint for modern America during the war years. Economic development played an important role in Lincoln's vision of America's future, in which all people would have the right to rise in life. National banking legislation provided for paper money as we know it today—and for federal controls to assure sound banking and credit. U.S. tariffs on European manufactured goods helped limit foreign competition and encouraged the growth of American industry. The administration encouraged labor unions. The government's homestead laws gave free land to settlers. Immigration was encouraged, as was the settlement of the West. Land was also granted for colleges that later became great state universities and for the construction of the nation's first transcontinental railroad. In addition, the nation's first income tax was levied to provide funds for the war.

Soldiers and civilians alike sang "The Battle Hymn of the Republic" or "Dixie." Winslow Homer's painting *Prisoners from the Front* brought him his first fame. Patriotic literature of the time included John Greenleaf Whittier's poem "Barbara Frietchie" and Edward Everett Hale's story "The Man Without a Country." Lincoln and numerous other Americans chuckled at the humorous writings of Artemus Ward and admired the patriotic prints of Currier and Ives.

Early Life

Family background. Soon after Lincoln was nominated for the presidency, he wrote an autobiography. It began: "Abraham Lincoln was born February 12, 1809, then in Hardin, now in the more recently formed county of Larue, Kentucky. His father, Thomas, and grandfather, Abra-

Statue of Lincoln at the Lincoln Memorial, Washington, D.C.

ham, were born in Rockingham County, Virginia, whither their ancestors had come from Berks County, Pennsylvania. His lineage has been traced no farther back than this."

Since Lincoln's time, his ancestry has been traced to a weaver named Samuel Lincoln, who emigrated from Hingham, England, to Hingham, Massachusetts, in 1637. Samuel Lincoln founded the Lincoln family in America. The families of several of his children played important parts in Massachusetts history.

Descendants of Mordecai Lincoln, a son of Samuel, moved to New Jersey, Pennsylvania, and Virginia. One was a great-great-grandson named Abraham. This Abraham Lincoln was the grandfather of the future president. He owned a farm in the Shenandoah Valley of Virginia during the Revolutionary War. In 1782, he and his wife and five small children traveled to the wilderness of Kentucky. An Indian killed him there in 1786.

One of his sons, Thomas Lincoln, became the father of the future president. In later years, the president said his father was "a wandering laboring boy, and grew up literally without education." Thomas Lincoln worked as a frontier farm hand during most of his youth. But he learned enough skill at woodworking to earn a living as a carpenter. In 1806, when he was twenty-eight years old, he married Nancy Hanks. Nancy came from what her son described as an "undistinguished" Virginia family of humble, ordinary people. Historians know only that she was the daughter of a Lucy Hanks.

Thomas and Nancy Lincoln lived in Elizabethtown, Kentucky, for the first eighteen months of their marriage. Their first child, Sarah, was born there in 1807. The next year, Thomas Lincoln bought a farm on the South Fork of the Nolin River, about 5 miles (8 kilometers) south of Elizabethtown. Abraham Lincoln was born on this farm.

Boyhood. The Lincolns lived for two years on the farm where Abraham was born. Then they moved to a farm on Knob Creek, 10 miles (16 kilometers) away. When Sarah and Abraham could be spared from their chores, they went to a log schoolhouse. There the children learned reading, writing, and arithmetic.

Many people believe that because Lincoln began his life in a log cabin, he was born in poverty. But many people then lived in log cabins. The Lincolns were as comfortable as most of their neighbors, and Abraham and Sarah were well fed and well clothed for the times. A third child, Thomas, died in infancy.

Thomas Lincoln had trouble over property rights throughout his years in Kentucky. In 1816, he decided to move to Indiana, where people could buy land directly from the government. Besides, Thomas Lincoln did not believe in slavery, and Indiana had no slavery.

The Lincolns loaded their possessions into a wagon. They traveled northward to the Ohio River and were ferried across. Then they traveled through the thick forests to Spencer County, in southwestern Indiana. There, Thomas Lincoln began the task of changing 160 acres (65 hectares) of forest land into a farm.

The Lincolns found life harder in Indiana than in Kentucky. They arrived early in winter and needed shelter at once. Thomas and his son built a three-sided structure made of logs, called a "half-faced camp." A fire on the fourth side burned night and day. Soon after finishing this shelter, the boy and his father began to build a log cabin. The family moved into it in February 1817.

Bears and other wild animals roamed the forests of this remote region. Trees had to be cut and fields cleared so that a crop could be planted. Although Abraham was only eight years old, he was large for his age and had enough strength to swing an ax. For as long as he lived in Indiana, he was seldom without his ax. He later called it "that most useful instrument."

Slowly, life became happier on the farm. But in October 1818, Nancy Lincoln died of what the pioneers called "milk sickness." This illness was probably caused by poison in the milk of cows that had eaten snakeroot. Thomas buried his wife among the trees on a hill near the cabin.

Life on the farm became dull and cheerless after the death of Nancy Lincoln. Sarah, now twelve, kept house as well as she could for more than a year. Then Thomas Lincoln returned to Kentucky for a visit. While there, on December 2, 1819, he married Sarah Bush Johnston, a widow. He had known her before her first marriage. The new Mrs. Lincoln brought along her three children, aged twelve, eight, and five. Her arrival at the cabin in Indiana ended the long months of loneliness.

Education. Abraham Lincoln grew from a boy of seven to a man of twenty-one on the wild Indiana frontier. His education can best be described in his own words:

"There were some schools, so called; but no qualification was ever required of a teacher, beyond 'readin, writin, and cipherin,' to the Rule of Three. If a straggler supposed to understand latin, happened to sojourn in the neighborhood, he was looked upon as a wizzard. There was absolutely nothing to excite

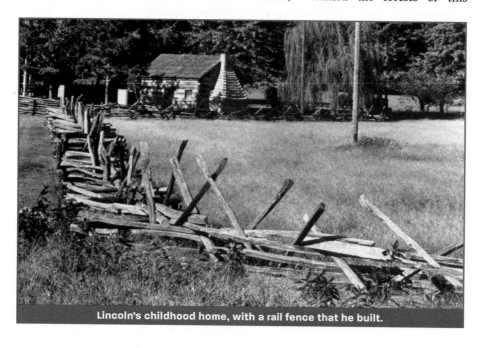
Lincoln's childhood home, with a rail fence that he built.

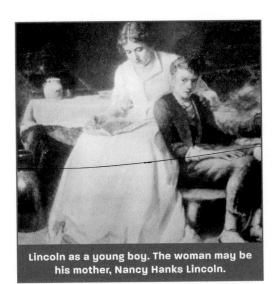

Lincoln as a young boy. The woman may be his mother, Nancy Hanks Lincoln.

days of my being able to read, I got hold of a small book, such a one as few of the younger members have ever seen, Weems's *Life of Washington*. I remember all the accounts there given of the battle fields and struggles for the liberties of the country...and you all know, for you have all been boys, how these early impressions last longer than any others. I recollect thinking then, boy even though I was, that there must have been something more than common that those men struggled for."

Youth on the frontier. Abraham reached his full height of 6 feet 4 inches (193 centimeters) long before he was twenty. He was thin and awkward, big-boned and strong. The young man developed great strength in his chest and legs, and especially in his arms. He had a homely face and dark skin. His hair was black and coarse and stood on end.

Even as a boy, Lincoln showed ability as a speaker. He often amused himself and others by imitating some preacher or politician who had spoken in the area. People liked to gather at the general store in the crossroads village of Gentryville. Lincoln's gift for telling stories made him a favorite with the people there. In spite of his youth, he was well known in his neighborhood.

A boy of Lincoln's size and strength had no trouble finding hard work. People always needed great piles of cut wood for cooking and for warmth. He could split logs for fence rails. He could plow fields, cut and husk corn, and thresh wheat with a flail. Lincoln worked for a neighbor when his father could spare him.

The Ohio River, 15 miles (24 kilometers) away, attracted Lincoln strongly. The first money he earned was for rowing passengers to a steamboat in midstream. In 1828, he helped take a flatboat loaded with farm produce to New Orleans. The trip gave him his first view of the world beyond his own community. That same year, his sister died in childbirth.

In 1830, Thomas Lincoln decided to move again. The years in Indiana had not been successful. The dreaded milk sickness was again striking down settlers. Relatives in Illinois sent word of deep, rich, black soil on the treeless prairies. The Lincolns and several other families started west. They reached their destination two weeks later, and settled 10 miles (16 kilometers) west of Decatur, on the north bank of the Sangamon River.

Lincoln was now twenty-one and free to strike out for himself. But he remained with his father

ambition for education. Of course when I came of age I did not know much. Still somehow, I could read, write, and cipher to the Rule of Three; but that was all."

Lincoln's formal schooling totaled less than a year. Books and paper were scarce on the frontier. Like other boys and girls of his time, Lincoln made his own arithmetic textbook. Several of its pages still exist. Abraham often worked his arithmetic problems on boards, then shaved the boards clean with a drawknife, and used them again and again. He would walk a great distance for a book. The few he could borrow were good ones. They included *Robinson Crusoe*, *Pilgrim's Progress*, and Aesop's fables. Lincoln also borrowed a history of the United States and a schoolbook or two.

In 1823, when Abraham was fourteen, his parents joined the Pigeon Creek Baptist Church. There was bitter rivalry among Baptists, Methodists, Presbyterians, and other denominations. This may help explain why Lincoln never joined any church and why he never attended church regularly. Yet he became a man of deep religious feelings. He came to know the Bible thoroughly. Biblical references and quotations enriched his later writings and speeches. As president, he kept a Bible on his desk and often opened it for comfort and guidance.

Another book also impressed young Lincoln deeply—a biography of George Washington. He told about it years later in a speech before the New Jersey Senate:

"May I be pardoned if, on this occasion, I mention that away back in my childhood, the earliest

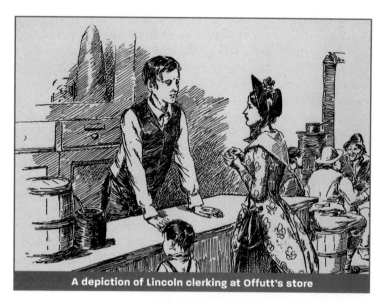

A depiction of Lincoln clerking at Offutt's store

The Black Hawk War. By late 1831, the federal government had moved most of the Sauk and Fox Indians from Illinois to Iowa. In the spring of 1832, Chief Black Hawk led a band of several hundred Indians back across the Mississippi River to try to regain their lands near Rock Island. The governor called out the militia, and Lincoln volunteered for service.

Lincoln's company consisted of men from the New Salem area. The men promptly elected him captain. This was only nine months after he had settled in the village. Even after he had been nominated for president, Lincoln said this honor "gave me more pleasure than any I have had since." It provided the first significant indication of his gift for leadership. Lincoln's comrades liked his friendliness, his honesty, and his skill at storytelling. They also admired his great strength and his sportsmanship in wrestling matches and other contests.

Lincoln's term of service ended after thirty days, but he reenlisted, this time as a private. A month later, he enlisted again. He served a total of ninety days, but saw no fighting. He later described his militia experiences as "bloody struggles with the musquetoes" and "charges upon the wild onions."

Search for a career. Before his military service, many of Lincoln's friends had encouraged him to become a candidate for the state legislature. Spurred by their faith, he announced his candidacy in March 1832. The Black Hawk War prevented him from making much of a campaign. He arrived home in July, only two weeks before the election. Lincoln was defeated in the election, but the people in his own precinct gave him 277 of their 300 votes.

Lincoln faced the problem of making a living. He thought of studying law, but decided he could not succeed without a better education. Just then, he had a chance to buy a New Salem store on credit, in partnership with William F. Berry. Lincoln later recalled that the partnership "did nothing but get deeper and deeper in debt." The store failed after a few months.

In May 1833, Lincoln was appointed postmaster of New Salem. Soon afterward, the county surveyor offered to make him a deputy. Lincoln knew nothing about surveying, but he prepared for the work by hard study. Odd jobs and fees from his two public offices earned him a living.

Berry died in 1835, leaving Lincoln liable for the debts of the partnership, about $1,100. It took Lincoln several years to pay these debts, but he

one more year. He helped plant the first crop, and he split rails for a cabin and fences. He worked for neighboring settlers during the winter. In the spring of 1831, a trader named Denton Offutt hired Lincoln and two other young men to take a flatboat to New Orleans. This trip gave Offutt a good impression of his lanky boat hand. He hired Lincoln as a clerk in his new store in the village of New Salem, Illinois, 20 miles (32 kilometers) northwest of Springfield. While Lincoln was away, his parents moved to Coles County, where they lived for the rest of their lives.

New Salem Years

Life on his own began for Lincoln when he settled in New Salem. He lived there almost six years, from July 1831 until the spring of 1837. The village consisted of log cabins clustered around a mill, a barrel-maker's shop, a wool-carding machine, and a few general stores.

The villagers helped Lincoln in many ways. The older women mended his clothes and often gave him meals. Jack Kelso, the village philosopher, introduced him to the writings of the English dramatist William Shakespeare and the Scottish poet Robert Burns. These works, and the Bible, became his favorite reading.

Lincoln arrived in New Salem, as he said, "a piece of floating driftwood." He earned little and slept in a room at the rear of Offutt's store. Within a few months the business failed. Lincoln would have been out of a job if the Black Hawk War had not begun in 1832.

finally did it. His integrity helped him earn the nickname "Honest Abe."

In New Salem, Lincoln grew close to a girl named Ann Rutledge. When she died in the summer of 1835, he grieved deeply. Scholars have debated their relationship for years. Although Ann was engaged to another man, it seems likely that she and Lincoln did fall in love. But, within 18 months, Lincoln recovered from his loss and proposed marriage to a Kentucky girl, Mary Owens. He met her while she was visiting her sister in New Salem. Their affection for each other was not especially deep, however, and Owens rejected him.

Lincoln as a lawyer, before becoming president

Success in politics. In 1834, Lincoln again ran for the legislature. He had become better known by this time and won election as a Whig. He served four successive two-year terms in the lower house of the Illinois General Assembly. During his first term, he met a young Democratic legislator, Stephen A. Douglas.

Lincoln quickly came to the front in the legislature. He was witty and ready in debate. His skill in party management enabled him to become the Whig floor leader at the beginning of his second term. He took leading parts in the establishment of the Bank of Illinois and in the adoption of a plan for a system of railroads and canals. This plan broke down after the Panic of 1837. Lincoln also led a successful campaign for moving the state capital from Vandalia to Springfield.

While in the legislature, Lincoln made his first public statement on slavery. In 1837, the legislature passed, by an overwhelming majority, resolutions condemning abolition societies. These societies urged freedom for slaves. Lincoln and another legislator, Dan Stone, filed a protest. They admitted that Congress had no power to interfere with slavery in the states where it existed. They believed "the promulgation of abolition doctrines tend rather to increase than abate its evils." Their protest arose from the legislature's failure to call slavery an evil practice. Lincoln and Stone declared that "the institution of slavery is founded on both injustice and bad policy." Slavery had become a much greater issue twenty-three years later, when Lincoln was nominated for president. He said then that his protest in the Illinois legislature still expressed his position on slavery.

Lincoln the Lawyer

Study. In 1834, during Lincoln's second campaign for the legislature, John T. Stuart had urged him to study law. Stuart was an attorney in Springfield and a leading member of the legislature. Lincoln overcame his doubts about his education. He borrowed law books from Stuart and studied them. He sometimes walked 20 miles (32 kilometers) from New Salem to Springfield for books. Henry E. Dummer, Stuart's law partner, recalled:

"Sometimes he walked, but generally rode. He was the most uncouth looking young man I ever saw. He seemed to have but little to say; seemed to feel timid, with a tinge of sadness visible in the countenance, but when he did talk all this disappeared for the time and he demonstrated that he was both strong and acute. He surprised us more and more at every visit."

On September 9, 1836, Lincoln received his license to practice law, although his name was not entered on the roll of attorneys until March 1, 1837. The population of New Salem had dropped by that time, and Lincoln decided to move to the new state capital. Carrying all he owned in his saddlebags, he rode into Springfield on April 15, 1837. There he became the junior partner in the law firm of Stuart and Lincoln.

In Lincoln's time, there were few law schools. Most lawyers simply "read law" in the office of an attorney. Years later, in giving advice to a law student, Lincoln explained his method of study:

"If you are resolutely determined to make a lawyer of yourself, the thing is more than half done already.

"I go for all sharing the privileges of the government who assist in bearing its burdens."
—*Letter to the editor of the* Sangamon Journal, *New Salem, Illinois, June 13, 1836*

It is but a small matter whether you read with anybody or not. I did not read with anyone. Get the books, and read and study them till you understand them in their principal features; and that is the main thing. It is of no consequence to be in a large town while you are reading. I read at New Salem, which never had three hundred people living in it. The books, and your capacity for understanding them, are just the same in all places...Always bear in mind that your own resolution to succeed is more important than any other one thing."

Early practice. Lincoln's partnership with Stuart lasted until the spring of 1841. Then he became the junior partner of Stephen T. Logan, one of the greatest lawyers who ever practiced in Illinois. This partnership ended in the fall of 1844.

Lincoln then asked William H. Herndon to become his partner. Herndon, nine years younger than Lincoln, had just received his license to practice law. Lincoln called him "Billy," but Herndon always called his partner "Mr. Lincoln." The two men never formally dissolved their law firm. More than sixteen years later, Lincoln visited his old office on his last day in Springfield before leaving for Washington to be inaugurated as president. He noticed the firm's signboard at the foot of the steps and said: "Let it hang there undisturbed. Give our clients to understand that the election of a president makes no change in the firm of Lincoln and Herndon."

The practice of law in Illinois was not specialized in Lincoln's time. He tried his first case in the circuit court of Sangamon County. He practiced in the Illinois federal courts within two years after his admission to the bar. A year later, he tried the first of many cases in the state supreme court. But all the while, he also handled cases before justices of the peace. He also gave advice and opinions on many matters for small fees.

Lincoln's family. Soon after Lincoln moved to Springfield, he met Mary Todd (December 13, 1818–July 16, 1882), a woman from Kentucky who lived there with a married sister. They had a stormy courtship and at one time broke their engagement. They were married on November 4, 1842, when Lincoln was thirty-three and his bride was twenty-three.

Mary Todd Lincoln was high-strung and socially ambitious. Lincoln tended to be moody and absentminded. Their contrasting personalities sometimes caused friction. But they had a loving marriage that lasted until Abraham's death.

Lincoln and his bride first lived in a Springfield boardinghouse, where they paid $4 a week. Eighteen months after his marriage, Lincoln bought the plain but comfortable frame house in which the family lived until he became president. By the time he bought the house, his first son, Robert Todd, was nine months old. The Lincolns' second son, Edward Baker, was born in 1846, but died four years later. William Wallace, born in 1850, died in the White House at the age of eleven. Their fourth son, Thomas, usually called Tad, became ill and died in 1871 at age eighteen.

The family lived comfortably. Lincoln became a highly successful lawyer and politician, and was not the poverty-stricken failure sometimes portrayed in legend. He often cared for his own horse and milked the family cow, but so did most of his neighbors. The Lincoln family usually employed a servant to help with the housework.

Riding the circuit. The state of Illinois was, and still is, divided into circuits for judicial purposes. Each circuit consisted of several counties where court was held in turn. The judge and many lawyers traveled from county to county. They tried such cases as came their way during each term.

Lincoln "traveled the circuit" for six months each year. He loved this kind of life. The small inns where the lawyers stayed had few comforts, but they offered many opportunities for meeting people.

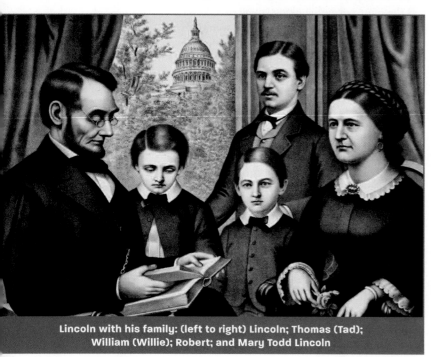

Lincoln with his family: (left to right) Lincoln; Thomas (Tad); William (Willie); Robert; and Mary Todd Lincoln

Lively talk and storytelling appealed to Lincoln. He also liked the long rides across the prairies. Lincoln's circuit at its largest included fifteen counties and covered about 8,000 square miles (21,000 square kilometers).

Lincoln developed traits as a lawyer that made him well known throughout Illinois. He could argue a case strongly. He sometimes persuaded clients to settle their differences out of court, which meant a smaller fee, or no fee at all, for him. In court, Lincoln could present a case so that twelve jurors, often poorly educated, could not fail to understand it. He could also argue a complicated case before a well-informed judge. He prepared his cases thoroughly and was unfailingly honest.

National Politics

Search for advancement. After four terms in the Illinois legislature, Lincoln wanted an office with greater prestige. He had served the Whig Party well, and election to Congress became his goal.

In 1840, Lincoln made a speaking tour of the state for William Henry Harrison, the Whig candidate for president. He campaigned on the issue of a sound central banking system, speaking out in favor of rechartering the Bank of the United States. Lincoln believed his service had earned him the nomination for Congress from his district. In 1843, and again in 1844, the nomination went to other candidates.

Disappointed, but not bitter, Lincoln worked for the election of Henry Clay, the Whig presidential candidate in 1844. During this campaign, Lincoln focused on the need for a tariff, which would raise the cost of imports and aid American industrial growth. Two years later, Lincoln received his reward and won the Whig nomination for the U.S. House of Representatives. His opponent in the election was Peter Cartwright, a well-known Methodist circuit rider. The Whigs firmly controlled Lincoln's district, and he got 6,340 of the 11,418 votes cast.

Congressman. Lincoln took his seat in Congress on December 6, 1847. By that time, the United States had won the Mexican War, although a peace treaty between Mexico and the United States had not yet been signed. Lincoln joined his fellow Whigs in blaming President James K. Polk for the war. He said of Polk, "The blood of this war, like the blood of Abel, is crying to heaven against him." He warned that "military glory" was

An 1860 campaign poster

an "attractive rainbow" that could result in "showers of blood." But he would not abandon U.S. troops on the battlefield and voted to supply them with equipment.

Lincoln failed to make the reputation he had hoped for in Congress. He gave notice that he intended to introduce a bill to free the slaves in the District of Columbia, but he never did. He emphasized his position on slavery by supporting the Wilmot Proviso, which would have banned slavery in any territory acquired from Mexico.

Throughout his term, Lincoln supported the Whig policy of having the federal government pay for internal improvements. He made several speeches in support of this policy, and once reproved President Polk for vetoing funds to make rivers and harbors more navigable and thus increase commerce. Lincoln worked for the nomination and election of Zachary Taylor, the Whig candidate for president in 1848.

Return to law. Lincoln's term ended on March 4, 1849. He tried unsuccessfully to get an appointment as Commissioner of the General Land Office. The administration offered to appoint him secretary, then governor, of Oregon Territory. Lincoln refused both offers.

Lincoln returned to Springfield. He practiced law more earnestly than ever before. He continued to travel the circuit, but appeared more often in the higher courts. He also handled more important cases. Corporations and big businesses were becoming increasingly important in Illinois and neighboring states. Lincoln represented them frequently in lawsuits, and he soon prospered. The

A depiction of a Lincoln-Douglas debate

largest fee he ever received, $5,000, was for his successful defense of the Illinois Central Railroad in an important tax case. After 1849, Lincoln's reputation grew steadily. In the 1850s, he was known as one of the leading lawyers of Illinois.

Reentry into politics.
A sudden change in national policy toward slavery brought Lincoln back into the center of political activity in Illinois. The Missouri Compromise of 1820 had prohibited slavery in new territories north of an east-west line that was an extension of Missouri's southern boundary. Early in 1854, Senator Stephen A. Douglas of Illinois introduced a bill to organize the territories of Kansas and Nebraska. As approved by Congress, this Kansas-Nebraska Act repealed the Missouri Compromise. It provided that the settlers of new territories should decide for themselves whether they wanted slavery.

Lincoln and many others had believed that slavery had been permanently limited and would in time die. Lincoln believed that the new policy gave new life to slavery, and it outraged him.

Lincoln revered the Founding Fathers. He believed they had written a promise of freedom and equality into the Declaration of Independence. He once said: "I have never had a feeling politically which did not spring from the sentiments embodied in the Declaration of Independence." During his early years in politics, Lincoln had looked up to Henry Clay as an ideal politician. But he looked to Thomas Jefferson for his democratic political principles and to Alexander Hamilton for his economic principles.

Lincoln always opposed slavery, but he never became an abolitionist. He believed that the bonds holding the nation together would be strained if Americans made a rapid break with the past. He also knew that abolitionists could never aim for national office. Lincoln granted that slavery should have the protection that the Constitution

gave it. But he wanted the people to realize that slavery was evil and that it should be put on "the road to ultimate extinction."

Douglas refused to admit that slavery was wrong. He said he did not care whether the people of new territories voted for or against slavery. Lincoln believed that the nation stood for freedom and equality. He felt it must not be indifferent to the unjust treatment of any person. To ignore moral values, he said, "deprives our republican example of its just influence in the world." It enabled the enemies of free institutions "to taunt us as hypocrites." Lincoln resolved to do what he could to reverse the Kansas-Nebraska Act.

A turning point in Lincoln's life came with the rise of the slavery controversy. Fighting against what he termed the "cancer" of bondage, he rose to the presidency and directed a bloody civil war that would put an end to what he saw as an evil institution. But first, many political battles had to be fought.

Lincoln entered the congressional election campaign of 1854 to help a candidate who opposed the Kansas-Nebraska Act. But when Senator Douglas returned to Illinois to justify the new law, Lincoln opposed him wherever he could. At Springfield, Peoria, and Chicago, Lincoln delivered such powerful speeches that he became known as the leader of the Illinois forces opposing the Kansas-Nebraska Act. He was again elected to the Illinois legislature, but resigned in order to run for the United States Senate.

At that time, the legislature elected senators. On the first ballot, Lincoln received forty-five votes, which was five short of a majority. On each succeeding ballot, his vote dwindled. Finally, to keep a Douglas supporter from being elected, Lincoln persuaded his followers to vote for Lyman Trumbull, who had started with only five votes. Trumbull was elected.

The Whig Party began falling apart during the 1850s, largely because party members in various parts of the country could not agree on a solution to the slavery problem. In 1856, Lincoln joined the antislavery Republican Party, then only two years old. During the presidential election campaign that year, he made more than a hundred speeches in behalf of John C. Fremont, the Republican candidate. Fremont lost the election to Democrat James Buchanan. But Lincoln had strengthened his own position in the party through his unselfish work.

The debates with Douglas. In 1858, Lincoln was nominated to run against Douglas for the U.S. Senate. He accepted the honor with a speech that aroused much controversy. Many people thought his remarks stirred up conflict between the North and South. Lincoln said:

"A house divided against itself cannot stand. I believe this government cannot endure, permanently half slave and half free. I do not expect the Union to be dissolved—I do not expect the house to fall—but I do expect it will cease to be divided. It will become all one thing, or all the other. Either the opponents of slavery will arrest the further spread of it, and place it where the public mind shall rest in the belief that it is in the course of ultimate extinction; or its advocates will push it forward till it shall become alike lawful in all the States—old as well as new, North as well as South."

After a few speeches, Lincoln challenged Douglas to a series of debates. Douglas accepted and named seven towns for the meetings. The first debate was held at Ottawa, Illinois, on August 21, 1858. The last was at Alton, Illinois, on October 15. Each candidate spoke for an hour and a half. Large crowds attended each debate except the one at Jonesboro, in the southernmost part of the state. Newspapers from around the country reported the debates, and the two men drew national attention.

The debates centered on the extension of slavery into free territory. Douglas defended the policy of the Kansas-Nebraska Act. He called this policy *popular sovereignty.* His opponents ridiculed it as *squatter sovereignty* and warned that it would make slavery national and permanent. Lincoln argued that the Supreme Court of the United States, in the *Dred Scott* decision, had opened the way for slavery to enter all the territories. In the debate held at Freeport, Illinois, Douglas denied this argument. He contended that the people of any territory could keep slavery out of that territory simply by refusing to pass local laws protecting it. This position became known as the *Freeport Doctrine.* Lincoln insisted that there was a fundamental difference between Douglas and himself. Douglas ignored the moral question of slavery, but Lincoln regarded slavery "as a moral, social, and political evil." Douglas, in turn, tried to depict Lincoln as a dangerous radical who favored racial equality.

In addition to the debates, both men spoke almost daily to rallies of their own. Each traveled throughout the state. Before the exhausting campaign ended, Douglas' deep bass voice had become so husky that it was hard to understand him. Lincoln's high, penetrating voice still reached the limits of a large audience.

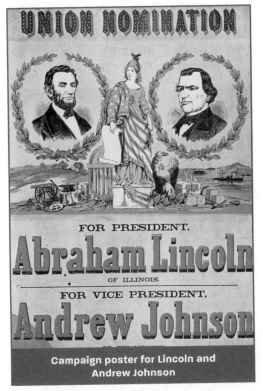

Campaign poster for Lincoln and
Andrew Johnson

In the election, Lincoln candidates for the legislature received more votes than their opponents. But the state was divided into districts in such a way that Douglas candidates won a majority of the seats. As a result, Douglas was reelected by a vote of fifty-four to forty-six.

"What constitutes the bulwark of our own liberty and independence? It is not our frowning battlements, our bristling sea coasts, our army and our navy. . . Our reliance is in the love of liberty which God has planted in us. Our defense is in the spirit which prized liberty as the heritage of all men, in all lands everywhere. Destroy this spirit and you have planted the seeds of despotism at your own doors. Familiarize yourselves with the chains of bondage and you prepare your own limbs to wear them. Accustomed to trample on the rights of others, you have lost the genius of your own independence and become the the fit subjects of the first cunning tyrant who rises among you."
—*Speech at Edwardsville, Illinois, September 11, 1858*

The debates made Lincoln a national figure. Early in 1860, he delivered an address at Cooper Union in New York City. The speech ended with the famous plea: "Let us have faith that right makes might, and in that faith let us to the end dare to do our duty as we understand it." This address and others delivered later in New England made a strong impression on many influential eastern Republicans.

Election of 1860. The Republican National Convention met in Chicago on May 16, 1860. Lincoln was by no means unknown to the delegates. The week before, at the Illinois state Republican convention, his supporters had nicknamed him "the Railsplitter." This nickname, recalling the days when Lincoln had split rails for fences, helped make him even better known to the delegates. But other party leaders had larger followings. Senator William H. Seward of New York had the strongest support, but he also had many enemies. Senator Salmon P. Chase of Ohio lacked the united support of even his own state. Lincoln had never held a prominent national office and had no bitter enemies. He held moderate views on the slavery question. His humble background could be counted on to arouse great enthusiasm among the voters.

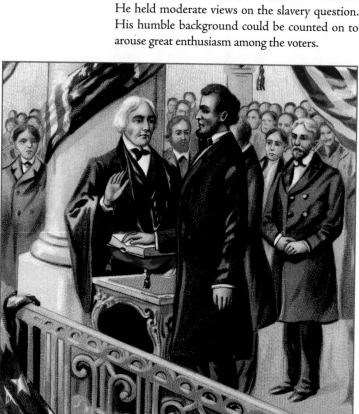

A depiction of Lincoln's inauguration

On the first ballot, Seward received 173½ votes, Lincoln 102, and Chase 49. Lincoln gained the support of Pennsylvania and Indiana on the second ballot and received 181 votes to 184½ for Seward. During the third ballot, Lincoln continued to gain strength. Before the result was announced, Ohio switched four votes from Chase to Lincoln. This gave Lincoln more than the 233 votes needed to win the nomination. The delegates nominated Senator Hannibal Hamlin of Maine for vice president.

Like other presidential candidates of his period, Lincoln felt it was undignified to campaign actively. He stayed quietly in Springfield during the election campaign. His followers more than made up for his inactivity. The opposing Democratic Party broke into two factions, which helped Lincoln immensely. Senator Douglas, the nation's leading Democrat, had angered the proslavery wing of his party. Northern Democrats nominated him for president. The Southern faction of the Democratic Party chose Vice President John C. Breckinridge. A fourth party, calling itself the Constitutional Union Party, nominated former Senator John Bell of Tennessee.

Lincoln won election easily, receiving 180 electoral votes to 72 for Breckinridge, 39 for Bell, and 12 for Douglas. But more Americans voted against Lincoln than for him. The people gave him 1,865,908 votes, compared to a combined total of 2,819,122 for his opponents. All Lincoln's electoral votes, and nearly all his popular votes, came from the North. Never before had a president been elected by one region alone.

Lincoln's Administration (1861—1865)

The South secedes. During the months before Lincoln's inauguration, many Southern leaders threatened to withdraw their states from the Union if Lincoln should win the election. On December 20, 1860, South Carolina passed an Ordinance of Secession that declared the Union dissolved as far as that state was concerned. By the time Lincoln became president, six other Southern states had withdrawn from the Union. Four more states followed later. The seceded states organized themselves into the Confederate States of America.

First inauguration. Lincoln said farewell to his Springfield neighbors on February 11, 1861. He parted with these words: "Here I have lived a quarter of a century, and have passed from a young to an old man. Here my children have been born,

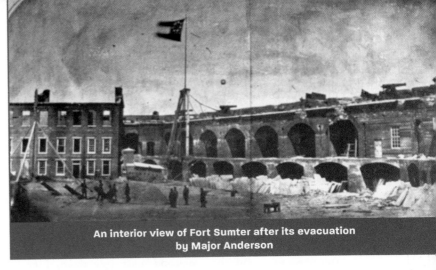

An interior view of Fort Sumter after its evacuation by Major Anderson

and one is buried. I now leave, not knowing when, or whether ever, I may return, with a task before me greater than that which rested upon Washington. Without the assistance of that Divine Being who ever attended him, I cannot succeed. With that assistance I cannot fail. Trusting in Him, who can go with me, and remain with you and be everywhere for good, let us confidently hope that all will yet be well. To His care commending you, as I hope in your prayers you will commend me, I bid you an affectionate farewell."

The long train trip to Washington, D.C., had been carefully planned to include stops at most large Eastern cities. This allowed many thousands of people to see the man who would be their next president. Lincoln had grown a beard that gave him a more dignified appearance. While in Philadelphia, Lincoln heard a report of an assassination plot in Baltimore, the only Southern stop along his route. His advisers persuaded him to cut short his trip. Lincoln continued in secret to Washington, arriving early on the morning of February 23.

On March 4, 1861, Lincoln took the oath of office and became the sixteenth president of the United States. In his inaugural address, Lincoln denied that he had any intention of interfering with slavery in states where the Constitution protected it. He urged the preservation of the Union. Lincoln warned that he would use the full power of the nation to "hold, occupy, and possess" the "property and places" belonging to the federal government. By "property and places," he meant forts, arsenals, and custom houses. Lincoln's closing passage had great beauty and literary power. He appealed to "the mystic chords of memory, stretching from every battlefield and patriot grave to every living heart and hearthstone all over this broad land."

Lincoln announced his Cabinet the day after his inauguration. Four members—William H. Seward, Salmon P. Chase, Simon Cameron, and Edward Bates—had been his rivals for the presidential nomination. The Cabinet members represented many shades of opinion within the Republican Party and included a Democrat for balance. On the whole, they were an exceptionally able group.

Fort Sumter and war. As the Southern states seceded, they seized most of the federal forts within their boundaries. Lincoln had to decide whether the remaining forts should be strengthened and whether to try to retake the forts already in Southern hands.

Fort Sumter, in Charleston Harbor, became a symbol of an indivisible Union. Major Robert Anderson commanded the Union garrison there. If Lincoln withdrew the troops, a storm of protest would rise in the North. If he reinforced Fort Sumter, the South would consider it an act of war.

As a compromise, Lincoln decided to send only provisions to Anderson, whose supplies were running low. He informed South Carolina of his intention. Leaders of the state regarded the relief expedition as a hostile act and demanded Anderson's surrender. Anderson refused, and on April 12, General Pierre G. T. Beauregard ordered Confederate artillery to fire on the fort. Anderson surrendered the next day. The attack on Fort Sumter marked the start of the Civil War.

Lincoln met the crisis with energetic action. He called out the militia to suppress the "insurrection." He proclaimed a blockade of Southern ports and expanded the army beyond the limit set by law. However, Southern sympathizers living in the North objected to and obstructed the war effort. As a result, Lincoln suspended the privilege of *habeas corpus* in areas where these Southern sympathizers were active. The action meant that antiwar Northerners could be arrested and held without formal charges. In addition, Lincoln ordered the spending of federal funds without waiting for congressional appropriations.

Lincoln believed all these actions to be within the war powers granted the president by the Constitution. He justified his acts when Congress met for the first time in his administration in July 1861. The message Lincoln delivered to Congress ranks as one of his greatest state papers. Chief Justice Roger B. Taney had attacked Lincoln bitterly for suspending habeas corpus. In his message, Lincoln posed a question that even today is difficult to answer: "Are all the laws but one to go unexecuted, and the government itself go to pieces lest

"Work, work, work, is the main thing."
—Letter to
John M. Brockman,
September 25, 1860

"Ballots are the rightful and peaceful successors to bullets."
—Message to Congress,
July 1861

"Fair play is a jewel."
—Letter to
Simon Cameron,
August 10, 1861

that one be violated?" Lincoln called the historic choice a "people's contest."

Lincoln felt that the breakup of the American nation would be a tragedy. Not only Americans, but ultimately all people, would suffer. To him, the United States represented an experiment in the people's ability to govern themselves. If it failed, monarchs, dictators, and their supporters could say that people were not capable of ruling themselves and that someone must rule them. Lincoln regarded the fate of world democracy as the central issue of the Civil War.

Building the army. Two days after Fort Sumter fell, Lincoln called for 75,000 men for the army. The North offered far more volunteers than the government could equip. By July 1861, an army had been assembled near Washington. An equal force of Confederates had taken position across the Potomac River in Virginia.

Many Northerners clamored for action. They believed the Union forces could end the war by defeating the Confederates in one battle. Newspaper headlines blazed with the cry "On to Richmond!" The administration yielded to these pressures. Lincoln ordered the Northern army forward under General Irvin McDowell. The result was the first Battle of Bull Run (known in the South as the first Battle of Manassas) on July 21, in which Confederate forces defeated the Union troops. People in the North now realized the war would be a long one.

As commander in chief of the army, Lincoln had to select an officer capable of organizing untrained volunteers into armies and leading them to victory. General George B. McClellan turned out to be a fine organizer. But his Peninsular Campaign of 1862 ended in failure. This campaign had been aimed at capturing Richmond, Virginia, the Confederate capital. Lincoln relieved McClellan of much of his command. General John Pope was made commander of troops in Virginia. He was defeated in the second Battle of Bull Run (also called Manassas) on August 29–30, 1862, and Lincoln called on McClellan to defend Washington. On September 17, "Little Mac" turned back the army of General Robert E. Lee in the Battle of Antietam. Then McClellan refused to move. In early November, Lincoln removed him for the second time and put General Ambrose E. Burnside in command. Burnside met defeat in the Battle of Fredericksburg on December 13. His successor, General Joseph Hooker, lost the Battle of Chancellorsville on May 1–4, 1863.

Union forces made some progress only in the West, in the valley of the Mississippi River. There, General Ulysses S. Grant in 1862 took Fort Henry on February 6 and Fort Donelson on February 16. In early April, Grant's troops forced a Confederate army to retreat in the Battle of Shiloh, but only after the Union army had suffered enormous losses.

A depiction of the Battle of Shiloh

Strengthening the home front. Organization for military success was only one of Lincoln's tasks. He also had to arouse popular support for the Union armies. Different opinions among the people became plain after their first enthusiasm wore off. Many Northerners were willing to fight to preserve the Union, but not to destroy slavery. Other Northerners demanded that the destruction of slavery should be the main goal.

Lincoln realized that the border states would secede if the antislavery extremists had their way. This would mean the secession of Kentucky, Missouri, Delaware, and Maryland. The task of defeating the South would probably be impossible without the support of these states. Besides, the Constitution protected slavery in the states where it existed. Impulsive generals sometimes issued proclamations freeing slaves, but Lincoln overruled them. Lincoln's moderate position helped keep the border states in the Union. Lincoln also managed to keep the support of the majority of Northerners, who favored fighting to preserve the Union over fighting to free the slaves.

Foreign relations. While meeting his other challenges, Lincoln managed to keep a check on foreign policy. In 1861, Secretary of State Seward suggested that the United States could be unified by provoking several European nations to war. The president quietly ignored this proposal.

In November 1861, Captain Charles Wilkes of the U.S. Navy stopped the British ship *Trent* and removed two Confederate commissioners, James M. Mason and John Slidell. The British angrily demanded the release of the two men and prepared for war to support their demand. However, the United States later freed Mason and Slidell. Thus, Lincoln avoided a war that would have been disastrous to the United States.

Life in the White House. To Lincoln, the presidency meant fulfillment of the highest ambition that an American citizen could have. The Civil War destroyed any hope he may have had for happiness in the White House. Aside from directing military affairs and stiffening the will of the North, he carried an enormous burden of administrative routine. His office staff was small. He wrote most of his own letters and all his speeches. He made decisions on thousands of political and military appointments. For several hours each week, he saw everyone who chose to call. During all his years in office, Lincoln was away from the capital less than a month.

A depiction of Lincoln drafting the Emancipation Proclamation

Lincoln found some relaxation in taking carriage drives, and he enjoyed the theater. He regarded White House receptions and dinners more as duties than as pleasures. Lincoln's frequent visits to army hospitals saddened him. Late at night, he sometimes found solace by reading works of Shakespeare or the Bible. But his official duties left little time for diversion.

To Mrs. Lincoln, life in the White House was a tragic disappointment. Her youngest brother, three half brothers, and the husbands of two half sisters were serving in the Confederate Army, and she faced constant suspicion of disloyalty. The pressures of everyday life weighed heavily on her high-strung nature. Jealousy and outbursts of temper cost her many friendships.

Two of Lincoln's sons, William Wallace and Thomas, lived in the White House. For nearly a year, "Willie" and "Tad" enlivened the mansion with their laughter and pranks. Willie's death on February 20, 1862, grieved Lincoln deeply. Mrs. Lincoln could not be consoled. Robert Lincoln had been a student at Harvard when his father was elected. He remained there until February 1865, when he was appointed to General Grant's staff as a captain.

The Emancipation Proclamation. By late summer of 1862, Lincoln was convinced that the time had come for a change in policy toward slavery. Several foreign governments sympathized with the South. But they condemned slavery as evil and thus did not dare support the Confederacy. Emancipation would ensure these governments' neutrality in America's war.

At home, thousands of slaves had already begun fleeing their masters. Known as "contrabands," these people had no legal status and presented Lincoln with a difficult situation. Lincoln believed that freed slaves could serve as Union soldiers. At the same time, a growing number of Northerners who had been indifferent to slavery now believed that it had to be stamped out. Lincoln finally decided to issue a proclamation freeing the slaves. He did not ask the advice of his Cabinet, but he did tell the members what he intended to do. On Seward's advice, he withheld the proclamation until a Northern victory created favorable circumstances.

The Battle of Antietam, fought on September 17, 1862, triggered the announcement. Lincoln issued a preliminary proclamation five days later. It declared that all slaves in states, or parts of states, that remained in rebellion on January 1, 1863, would be free. He issued the final proclamation on January 1. Lincoln named the states and parts of states in rebellion, and declared that the slaves held there "are, and henceforward shall be, free."

Actually, the proclamation freed no slaves on the day it was issued. It applied only to Confederate territory, where federal officers could not enforce it. The proclamation did not affect slavery in the loyal border states. But Lincoln repeatedly urged those states to free their slaves and to pay the owners for their loss. He promised financial help from the federal government for this purpose. The failure of the states to follow his advice was one of his great disappointments.

Maryland, however, did later move on its own to abolish slavery.

The Emancipation Proclamation eventually freed hundreds of thousands of slaves. Whenever Union troops took control of Southern territory, they liberated slaves in their path. The proclamation had a major long-range impact. In the eyes of other nations, it gave a new character to the war. In the North, it gave a high moral purpose to the struggle and paved the way for the Thirteenth Amendment to the Constitution. This amendment, adopted in December 1865, ended slavery in all parts of the United States.

The Gettysburg Address. Union armies won two great victories in 1863. General George G. Meade's Union forces defeated the Confederates under Lee at Gettysburg, Pennsylvania, during the first three days of July. On July 4, Vicksburg, Mississippi, fell to Grant's troops. This city had been the last Confederate stronghold on the Mississippi River. "The Father of Waters again goes unvexed to the sea," Lincoln declared.

On November 19, 1863, ceremonies were held to dedicate a cemetery on the Gettysburg battlefield. The principal speaker was Edward Everett, one of the greatest orators of his day. He spoke for two hours. Lincoln was asked to say a "few appropriate remarks" and spoke for about two minutes.

Many writers have said that Lincoln scribbled his speech while traveling on the train to Gettysburg. This is not true. He prepared the address carefully, in advance of the ceremonies, although he revised the text in Gettysburg. Everett and many others knew at once that Lincoln's ringing declaration that "government of the people, by the people, for the people, shall not perish from the earth" would live as long as democracy itself.

The victories at Gettysburg and Vicksburg seemed to promise an early peace. But the war went on. In March 1864, Lincoln put Grant in command of all the Union armies. The Army of the Potomac started to march toward Richmond two months later. At the same time, General William T. Sherman began his famous march from Tennessee to Atlanta and then to the sea.

Election of 1864. Grant met skillful resistance in the South and suffered thousands of casualties. Many people called him "the butcher" and condemned Lincoln for supporting him. In 1864, Lincoln skillfully turned back efforts by some fellow Republicans to replace him in the White House.

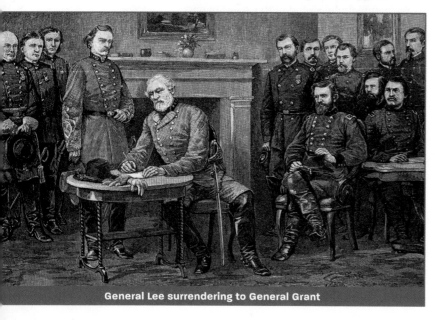

General Lee surrendering to General Grant

Republicans and War Democrats—Democrats who supported Lincoln's military policies—formed the Union Party. In June that year, the party nominated Lincoln for president. It selected former Senator Andrew Johnson of Tennessee, a leading War Democrat, for vice president. The Democrats chose General George B. McClellan as their candidate for president and Representative George H. Pendleton of Ohio for vice president.

Lincoln became less popular as the summer wore on. Late in August, he confessed privately that "it seems exceedingly probable that this administration will not be reelected." Then the military trend changed. Rear Admiral David G. Farragut had won the Battle of Mobile Bay on August 5, and Sherman's troops captured Atlanta on September 2. A series of Union victories cleared Confederate forces from the Shenandoah Valley of Virginia. In a famous duel off the coast of France, the USS *Kearsarge* sank the Confederate cruiser *Alabama*, which had preyed on Union merchant ships. Many discouraged Northerners took heart again.

The Union victories helped Lincoln win reelection. He defeated McClellan by an electoral vote of 212 to 21, and a popular majority of more than 400,000 votes.

Second inauguration. The end of the war was clearly in sight when Lincoln took the oath of office a second time, on March 4, 1865. Grant had besieged Lee's weary troops at Petersburg, Virginia. The Southern armies were wasting away in Grant's bulldog grip. Sherman left a wide track of destruction as he marched through Georgia and the Carolinas.

As a result, Lincoln could concentrate on reuniting the nation. In his Second Inaugural Address, he explained that the Civil War had to be fought to abolish slavery. It was God's will, he declared, that the North and South together pay the price for slavery. He urged the people to maintain their faith in God's goodness and justice even if the war should continue "until all the wealth piled by the bondsman's two hundred and fifty years of unrequited toil shall be sunk, and until every drop of blood drawn with the lash shall be paid by another drawn with the sword...." He closed with a moving plea for "malice toward none" and "charity for all," North and South alike.

Photographs taken of Lincoln shortly after his second inauguration show the effect of four years of war. His face had become gaunt and deeply lined. He slept little during crises in the fighting, and his eyes were ringed with black. Lincoln ate his meals irregularly and had almost no relaxation.

In spite of his exhaustion, Lincoln continued to see widows and soldiers who called at the White House. His delight in rough humor never deserted him. More than once, he shocked members of his Cabinet by reading to them from such humorists as Artemus Ward and Orpheus C. Kerr. Even so, the strain of melancholy that had appeared in him as a young man deepened.

Lincoln came to have a quiet confidence in his own judgment as he met the trials of war. Yet he had no false pride. He was a man of genuine humility. The war brought out his best qualities. He could rise to each new challenge. He was a master politician, and he timed his actions to the people's moods. He led men by persuasion. Horace Greeley said: "He slowly won his way to eminence and fame by doing the work that lay next to him—doing it with all his growing might—doing it as well as he could, and learning by his failure, when failure was encountered, how to do it better."

End of the war. On April 9, 1865, Lee surrendered to Grant at Appomattox Court House in Virginia. Under authority from Lincoln, Grant extended generous terms to Lee and his army. A great wave of joy swept the North when the fighting ended.

A few days before, Lincoln had quietly entered Richmond, accompanied by his son Tad. There he was greeted as a savior by the city's once-enslaved African Americans.

Lincoln spoke soberly of the future to a crowd that serenaded him on the night of April 11. Louisiana had applied for readmission to the Union under Lincoln's plan of reconstruction. Many Northerners wanted to impose harsher terms on the state. Some complained that blacks would not receive the right to vote under Louisiana's new government. "I would myself prefer," said Lincoln, "that it [the vote] were now conferred on the very intelligent, and on those who serve our cause as soldiers." The speech marked the first time an American president had spoken of extending the vote to blacks. An outraged member of the audience that night, infuriated by Lincoln's speech, vowed to kill him. That man was John Wilkes Booth.

Many people insisted that Lincoln decide if "the seceded states, so called, are in the Union or out of it." No matter, said the president in his last public

"Property is the fruit of labor—property is desirable—is a positive good in the world. That some should be rich, shows that others may become rich, and hence is just encouragement to industry and enterprise. Let not him who is houseless pull down the house of another, but let him work diligently and build one for himself, thus by example assuring that his own shall be safe from violence when built."

—Reply to Workingmen's Association, March 21, 1864

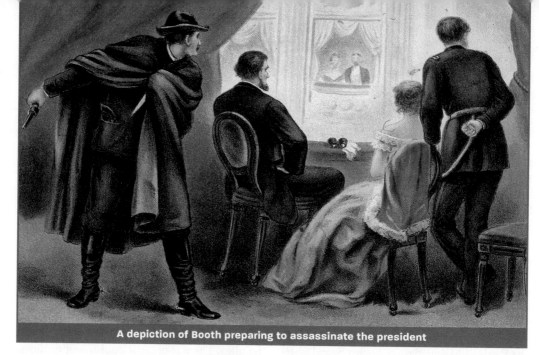

A depiction of Booth preparing to assassinate the president

address on April 11, 1865, "finding themselves safely at home, it would be utterly immaterial whether they had ever been abroad." Lincoln admitted that the new government of Louisiana was imperfect. But, he asked, "Will it be wiser to take it as it is and help improve it, or to reject and disperse it?"

Assassination. On the evening of April 14, 1865, Lincoln attended a performance of *Our American Cousin* at Ford's Theatre in Washington. At 10:22 p.m., a shot rang through the crowded house. Booth, one of the best-known actors of the day, had shot the president in the head from the rear of the presidential box. In leaping to the stage, Booth caught his spur in a flag draped in front of the box. He fell and broke his leg. But he limped across the stage brandishing a dagger and crying: "Sic semper tyrannis" (Thus always to tyrants), the motto of Virginia.

Lincoln was carried unconscious to a boardinghouse across the street. Lincoln's family and a number of high government officials surrounded him. Lincoln died at 7:22 a.m. on April 15.

As president, Lincoln had been bitterly criticized. After his death, even his enemies praised his kindly spirit and selflessness. Millions of people had called him "Father Abraham." They grieved as they would have grieved at the loss of a father. The train carrying Lincoln's body started north from Washington, to Baltimore, before heading west. Mourners lined the tracks as it moved across the country. Thousands wept as they looked upon him for the last time. On May 4, Lincoln was buried in Oak Ridge Cemetery in Springfield, Illinois. The monument over his grave is a place of universal pilgrimage, as are other spots that his life had touched in Kentucky, Indiana, Illinois, and, above all, in Gettysburg, Pennsylvania.

The trial of the conspirators. After shooting Lincoln, Booth fled to Maryland on horseback. A friend, David E. Herold, a former druggist's clerk, joined Booth there and helped him escape to Virginia. On April 26, 1865, federal troops searching for Booth trapped the two men in a barn near Port Royal, Virginia. Herold surrendered, but Booth was shot and killed.

Several people were believed to have been involved with Booth in both Lincoln's assassination and a plot to kill other government officials. Secretary of War Edwin M. Stanton ordered agents of his department to arrest them. Besides Herold, the accused conspirators included George Atzerodt, a carriage maker, for planning the murder of Vice President Andrew Johnson; Lewis Paine, a former Confederate soldier, for attempting to kill Secretary of State William H. Seward; and Mary E. Surratt, the owner of a Washington boardinghouse, for helping the plotters. Booth and the others supposedly planned the crimes in Surratt's house.

The Department of War also accused Samuel Arnold and Michael O'Laughlin, boyhood friends of Booth's, of helping him plan the crimes. Samuel A. Mudd, a Maryland physician who had set Booth's broken leg after the assassination of Lincoln, was charged with aiding the plotters. Edward Spangler, a stagehand at Ford's Theatre, was charged with helping Booth escape. Some people accused Confederate President Jefferson Davis and his secret service of approving and funding the plot, but the charges were never proved.

A nine-man military commission tried the accused conspirators in Washington. The trial began on May 10, 1865, and lasted until June 30. The commission convicted all eight defendants and sentenced Atzerodt, Herold, Paine, and Surratt to death. They were hanged on July 7. Arnold, Mudd, and O'Laughlin received sentences of life imprisonment, and Spangler received a six-year sentence. O'Laughlin died in prison of yellow fever in 1867. President Johnson pardoned Arnold, Mudd, and Spangler in 1869.

Presidential library. The library portion of the Abraham Lincoln Presidential Library and Museum opened in Springfield, Illinois, in 2004. The library serves as a center for research and study about Lincoln. The museum, which opened in 2005, offers interactive exhibits and dramatic presentations about Lincoln's life and times.

 THE GETTYSBURG ADDRESS is a short speech that United States President Abraham Lincoln delivered during the American Civil War at the site of the Battle of Gettysburg in Pennsylvania. He delivered the address on November 19, 1863, at ceremonies to dedicate a part of the battlefield as a cemetery for those who had lost their lives in the battle. Lincoln wrote the address to help ensure that the battle would be seen as a great Union triumph and to define for the people of the Northern states the purpose in fighting the war. Some historians think his simple and inspired words, which are among the best remembered in American history, reshaped the nation by defining it as one people dedicated to one principle—that of equality.

Lincoln wrote five different versions of the speech. He wrote most of the first version in Washington, D.C., and probably completed it at Gettysburg. He probably wrote the second version at Gettysburg on the evening before he delivered his address. He held this second version in his hand during the address. But he made several changes as he spoke. The most important change was to add the phrase "under God" after the word "nation" in the last sentence. Lincoln also added that phrase to the three versions of the address that he wrote after the ceremonies at Gettysburg.

Lincoln wrote the final version of the address—the fifth written version—in 1864. This version also differed somewhat from the speech he actually gave, but it was the only copy he signed. It is carved on a stone plaque in the Lincoln Memorial.

Many false stories have grown up about this famous speech. One story says that the people of Lincoln's time did not appreciate the speech. But the reaction of the nation's newspapers largely followed party lines. Most of the newspapers that backed the Republican Party, the party to which Lincoln belonged, liked the speech. A majority of the newspapers that supported the Democratic Party did not. Edward Everett, the principal speaker at the dedication, wrote to Lincoln: "I should be glad if I could flatter myself that I came as near to the central idea of the occasion in two hours as you did in two minutes."

Fifth written version. Four score and seven years ago our fathers brought forth on this continent, a new nation, conceived in Liberty, and dedicated to the proposition that all men are created equal.

Depiction of Lincoln giving the Gettysburg Address

Now we are engaged in a great civil war, testing whether that nation, or any nation so conceived and so dedicated, can long endure. We are met on a great battlefield of that war. We have come to dedicate a portion of that field, as a final resting place for those who here gave their lives that that nation might live. It is altogether fitting and proper that we should do this.

But, in a larger sense, we can not dedicate—we can not consecrate—we can not hallow—this ground. The brave men, living and dead, who struggled here, have consecrated it, far above our poor power to add or detract. The world will little note, nor long remember what we say here, but it can never forget what they did here. It is for us the living, rather, to be dedicated here to the unfin-

Portrait of John Wilkes Booth

ished work which they who fought here have thus far so nobly advanced. It is rather for us to be here dedicated to the great task remaining before us—that from these honored dead we take increased devotion to that cause for which they gave the last full measure of devotion—that we here highly resolve that these dead shall not have died in vain—that this nation, under God, shall have a new birth of freedom—and that government of the people, by the people, for the people, shall not perish from the earth.

Reporter's shorthand version. Four score and seven years ago our fathers brought forth upon this continent a new nation, conceived in Liberty, and dedicated to the proposition that all men are created equal.

Now we are engaged in a great civil war, testing whether that nation or any nation so conceived and so dedicated can long endure. We are met on a great battlefield of that war. We are met to dedicate a portion of it as the final resting place of those who here gave their lives that that nation might live. It is altogether fitting and proper that we should do this.

But in a larger sense we cannot dedicate—we cannot consecrate—we cannot hallow this ground. The brave men living and dead who struggled here have consecrated it far above our poor power to add or detract. The world will little note nor long remember what we say here, but it can never forget what they did here. It is for us, the living, rather to be dedicated here to the unfinished work that they have thus far so nobly carried on. It is rather for us to be here dedicated to the great task remaining before us—that from these honored dead we take increased devotion to that cause for which they here gave the last full measure of devotion—that we here highly resolve that the dead shall not have died in vain—that the nation shall, under God, have a new birth of freedom—and that governments of the people, by the people, and for the people, shall not perish from the earth.

JOHN WILKES BOOTH (1838–1865) assassinated President Abraham Lincoln at Ford's Theatre in Washington, D.C., on April 14, 1865. He entered Lincoln's private box and shot him in the head during the play *Our American Cousin.* Booth approved of slavery and sympathized with the South in the American Civil War (1861–1865). He believed that Lincoln was responsible for the war.

Booth was born on May 12, 1838, near Bel Air, Maryland. His father, Junius Brutus Booth, and his brother Edwin Booth were famous actors, and John himself was one of the most promising performers of the time. At first, Booth organized a group that planned to kidnap Lincoln and exchange him for captured Confederate soldiers. Booth changed the plot to murder after the main Confederate army surrendered on April 9, 1865. The group then planned to kill Lincoln, Vice President Andrew Johnson, General Ulysses S. Grant, and Secretary of State William H. Seward. They managed to kill only Lincoln.

After shooting Lincoln, Booth leaped to the theater stage shouting what some understood as *sic semper tyrannis* (Thus always to tyrants), the Virginia state motto. Booth broke his leg in the jump but escaped on horseback to Virginia. Federal troops trapped him in a barn near Port Royal, Virginia. There, on April 26, 1865, Booth was shot to death.

THE EMANCIPATION PROCLAMATION was a historic document that led to the end of slavery in the United States. President Abraham Lincoln issued the proclamation on January 1, 1863, during the American Civil War. It declared freedom for slaves in all areas of the Confederacy that were still in rebellion against the Union. The proclamation also provided for the use of blacks in the Union Army and Navy. As a result, it greatly influenced the North's victory in the war.

Events Leading to the Proclamation

Early views on emancipation. The eleven states of the Confederacy seceded (withdrew) from the Union in 1860 and 1861. They seceded primarily because they feared Lincoln would restrict their right to do as they chose about the question of black slavery. The North entered the Civil War only to reunite the nation, not to end slavery.

During the first half of the war, abolitionists and some Union military leaders urged Lincoln to issue a proclamation freeing the slaves. They argued that such a policy would help the North because slaves were contributing greatly to the Confederate war effort. By doing most of the South's farming and factory work, slaves made white men available for the Confederate Army.

Lincoln agreed with the abolitionists' view of slavery. He once declared that "if slavery is not wrong, nothing is wrong." But early in the war, Lincoln believed that if he freed the slaves, he would divide the North. Lincoln feared that four slave-owning border states—Delaware, Kentucky, Maryland, and Missouri—would secede if he adopted such a policy.

Lincoln's change of policy. In July 1862, with the war going badly for the North, Congress passed a law freeing all Confederate slaves who came into Union lines. At about that same time, Lincoln decided to change his stand on slavery. But he waited for a Union military victory, so that his decision would not appear to be a desperate act.

On September 22, 1862, five days after Union forces won the Battle of Antietam, Lincoln issued a preliminary proclamation. It stated that if the rebelling states did not return to the Union by January 1, 1863, he would declare their slaves to be "forever free." The South rejected Lincoln's policy, and so he issued the Emancipation Proclamation on January 1, 1863. Lincoln took this action as commander in chief of the Army and Navy of the United States. He called it "a fit and necessary war measure."

Effects of the proclamation. The Emancipation Proclamation did not actually free a single slave, because it affected only areas under Confederate control. It excluded slaves in the border states and in such Southern areas under Union control as Tennessee and parts of Louisiana and Virginia. But it did lead to the Thirteenth Amendment to the Constitution. This amendment, which became law on December 18, 1865, ended slavery in all parts of the United States.

As Lincoln had hoped, the Emancipation Proclamation strengthened the North's war effort and weakened the South's. By the end of the war, more than 500,000 slaves had fled to freedom behind Northern lines. Many of them joined the Union Army or Navy or worked for the armed forces as laborers. By allowing blacks to serve in the Army and Navy, the Emancipation Proclamation helped solve the North's problem of declining enlistments. About 200,000 black soldiers and sailors, many of them former slaves, served in the armed forces. They helped the North win the war.

The Emancipation Proclamation also hurt the South by discouraging the United Kingdom and France from entering the war. Both of those nations depended on the South to supply them with cotton, and the Confederacy hoped that they would fight on its side. But the proclamation made the war a fight against slavery. The United Kingdom and France had already abolished slavery, and so they gave their support to the Union.

FORT SUMTER was the site of the first shot fired in the American Civil War (1861–1865). On April 12, 1861, Confederate forces fired on the fort, which stood on an island in the harbor of Charleston, South Carolina. The following day, after heavy bombardment, United States troops

Poster offering financial inducement for black men to join the Union army

Portrait of Andrew Johnson

under Major Robert Anderson surrendered to Confederate forces led by General Pierre G. T. Beauregard. On April 14, the U.S. troops withdrew from the fort. Not a single person was killed in the battle, the first in what would become the country's bloodiest war.

Fort Sumter had been a symbol of *sovereignty* (supreme authority) for both the North and the South since December 1860, when South Carolina became the first Southern state to secede (withdraw) from the Union. After South Carolina's secession, the two sides turned their guns toward each other. The crisis reached its peak when President Abraham Lincoln ordered that supplies be sent to the fort. The Confederacy chose to fire on the fort rather than allow it to be resupplied. The Union sought to retake the fort several times. But the Stars and Stripes did not fly over Fort Sumter again until February 1865.

MARY TODD LINCOLN (1818–

1882), the wife of President Abraham Lincoln, was the daughter of Robert S. Todd, a banker of Lexington, Kentucky, and his wife, Eliza Parker Todd. In 1839, at the age of twenty-one, she moved to Springfield, Illinois, to live with a married sister. There she met Abraham Lincoln, a young lawyer. They were married on November 4, 1842.

Mary Lincoln achieved her greatest ambition when her husband was elected president. But her four years as first lady brought sorrow rather than happiness. Many people unjustly suspected her of disloyalty to the Union because she came from the

South. In addition, Mrs. Lincoln's haughty manner made her unpopular among the wives of government officials. The death of the Lincolns' third son, William Wallace, in 1862 caused her deep grief. In 1865, the shock of the assassination of Lincoln left her both a mental and a physical wreck.

Years of travel failed to restore Mrs. Lincoln's health, which was further weakened in 1871 by the death of another son, Thomas. Her mental depression deepened until her oldest son, Robert, committed her to a private sanitarium in 1875. She was released later that year. Mrs. Lincoln died on July 16, 1882, in the Springfield home of her sister. She was buried in the Lincoln Tomb in Springfield.

ANDREW JOHNSON (1808–

1875), the first president to be impeached, became chief executive upon the assassination of Abraham Lincoln. The Civil War had just ended. Johnson, a Democrat from Tennessee, inherited the wartime dispute between Lincoln and Congress over how to treat the South after the war. This disagreement soon intensified, as more and more Republicans in Congress came to oppose Johnson's views. Congress enacted its policies in spite of his repeated vetoes. The division became so wide that the United States House of Representatives voted to impeach him. But the Senate failed by one vote to remove Johnson from office.

Throughout his life, and especially his presidency, Johnson aroused either strong support or fierce dislike. Historians have also been divided in their estimation of him. Some view him as an unfit leader who was too generous to the Southerners after the war. Others have portrayed him as a leader of unusual vision who accurately saw that harsh treatment of the Southern states would increase divisions in the Union. Some scholars believe Johnson's acquittal in the impeachment trial preserved the independence of the presidency.

The stocky Johnson was a typical man of the frontier. A tailor by profession, he lacked formal schooling and educated himself with the help of his wife. She taught him how to write and do arithmetic. Johnson had the touchy pride of a self-made man.

A serious man, Johnson had limited tact and patience. He reserved humor for family and friends. Johnson lacked Lincoln's skill in getting people to work together. But he was honest, brave, and intelligent. An unshakable faith in the Constitution guided his actions during his twenty years as a U.S. representative, a governor, and a U.S. senator. One of his lawyers at the impeachment trial wrote: "He is a man of few ideas, but they are right and true, and he could suffer death sooner than yield up or violate one of them."

During Johnson's term, the United States purchased Alaska, and Nebraska became a state. Southerners worked to repair their ruined towns and farms and to reorganize their economy without slavery. Important "firsts" during this time included the first oil pipeline, practical typewriter, and railroad refrigerator car.

THE ABOLITION MOVEMENT

was activity that took place in the 1800s to end slavery. Most abolitionist activity occurred in the United States and the United Kingdom, but antislavery movements operated in other countries as well.

In the United States, antislavery activity began in colonial days. During the 1680s, Quakers in Pennsylvania condemned slavery on moral grounds. In the late 1700s, several leaders of the American revolutionary movement, including Thomas Jefferson and Patrick Henry, spoke out against slavery.

The American Colonization Society, founded in 1816, led antislavery protests during the early 1800s. It tried to send freed slaves to Liberia in Africa. The abolitionist Elihu Embree published the first periodicals devoted wholly to the abolition of slavery. He established a weekly newspaper in Jonesborough, Tennessee, in 1819 and a monthly publication, *The Emancipator*, which appeared in 1820. In 1831, the abolitionist William Lloyd Garrison began publication of his newspaper, *The Liberator*. Garrison demanded immediate freedom for slaves. The American Anti-Slavery Society, founded in 1833, supported Garrison's crusade. The abolition movement gradually spread throughout the Northern states despite bitter and violent opposition by Southern slaveholders and Northerners who favored slavery. In 1837, a mob murdered Elijah P. Lovejoy, a newspaper editor of Alton, Illinois, who had published antislavery editorials.

Many famous abolitionists came from New England. They included Garrison, poets James Russell Lowell and John Greenleaf Whittier, and reformer Wendell Phillips. Others, such as the merchant brothers Arthur and Lewis Tappan and the reformer Theodore Weld, came from Middle Atlantic or Midwestern states.

Women also played an important role in the abolition movement. Lucretia Mott and the sisters Sarah and Angelina Grimke organized groups and made speeches. Many free blacks also joined the abolitionists. They included James Forten and Robert Purvis, wealthy Philadelphia merchants; Frederick Douglass, a former fugitive slave from Maryland; and Sojourner Truth, a freed slave from New York.

The movement entered a new phase in 1840, when some of its leaders entered politics and founded the Liberty Party. James G. Birney, a former slaveholder born in Kentucky, ran as the party's candidate for president in 1840 and 1844. In 1848, abolitionists became an important element in the Free Soil Party. After 1854, most abolitionists supported the Republican Party.

Even after abolitionists entered politics, they remained more interested in their cause than in political offices. They combined political protest with direct action. Their homes often became stations on the *underground railroad*, which helped slaves fleeing to the free states or to Canada.

After the Civil War began in 1861, abolitionists rallied to the Union cause. They rejoiced when President Abraham Lincoln issued the Emancipation Proclamation on January 1, 1863, declaring the slaves free in many parts of the South. In 1865, the Thirteenth Amendment to the United States Constitution abolished slavery in the country. Large numbers of abolitionists then joined the fight to win social and political equality for blacks.

In the United Kingdom, abolitionists worked to end the international slave trade and to free slaves in the British colonies. Slavery had never flourished in England itself. On the other hand, many English people had become wealthy through the slave trade.

William Wilberforce, a statesman and orator, headed the antislavery movement in England. In 1807, he helped persuade Parliament to pass a bill outlawing the slave trade. In 1833, another bill abolished slavery throughout the British Empire.

MLA Citation

"Abraham Lincoln."
*The Southwestern
Advantage Topic Source.*
Nashville: Southwestern. 2013.

ADDITIONAL RESOURCES

Books to Read

Burlingame, Michael. *Abraham Lincoln*. 2 vols. Johns Hopkins, 2008

Burton, Orville V. *The Age of Lincoln*. Hill & Wang, 2007.

Herbert, Janis. *Abraham Lincoln for Kids*. Chicago Review Press, 2007.

Kunhardt, Philip B., III, and others. *Lincoln, Life-Size*. Knopf, 2009.

McGovern, George S. *Abraham Lincoln*. Times Books, 2009.

McPherson, James M. *Tried by War: Abraham Lincoln as Commander in Chief*. Penguin Press, 2008.

Miller, William L. *President Lincoln*. Knopf, 2008.

Roberts, Jeremy. *Abraham Lincoln*. Lerner, 2004.

Waryncia, Lou, and Hale, Sarah E. *Abraham Lincoln*. Cobblestone Publishing Co., 2005.

White, Ronald C., Jr. *Lincoln*. Random House, 2009.

Web Sites

Abraham Lincoln

http://www.whitehouse.gov/about/presidents/abrahamlincoln/

Official White House biography of Abraham Lincoln. Includes a link to a biography of Mary Todd Lincoln.

Abraham Lincoln Birthplace National Historic Site

http://www.nps.gov/abli/

The National Park Service presents information about Lincoln and the site of his birth.

Abraham Lincoln On Line

http://showcase.netins.net/web/creative/lincoln.html

Information about Abraham Lincoln, including quizzes, writings, and recommended reading.

Civil War Soldiers and Sailors System

http://www.itd.nps.gov/cwss/

A computerized database containing basic facts about soldiers who served on both sides during the Civil War. From the National Park Service.

Ford's Theatre National Historic Site

http://www.nps.gov/foth/

Information about the theater where President Abraham Lincoln was assassinated.

Lincoln Home National Historic Site

http://www.nps.gov/liho/

The National Park Service provides historical information about Abraham Lincoln, his family, and his home.

Lincoln, Abraham (1809–1865) Biographical Information

http://bioguide.congress.gov/scripts/biodisplay.pl?index=L000313

The Biographical Directory of the United States Congress site on Abraham Lincoln.

Mary Todd Lincoln

http://www.whitehouse.gov/about/first-ladies/marylincoln

Official White House biography of first lady Mary Todd Lincoln.

The Emancipation Proclamation

http://www.nps.gov/ncro/anti/emancipation.html

Text of the Emancipation Proclamation, President Abraham Lincoln's order to free the slaves in rebel states in 1863.

Search Strings

Greatest Speaches

speech abraham lincoln important gettysburg address second inaugural address (returned 47,000)

abraham lincoln greatest speeches gettysburg address second inaugural address (47,900)

abraham lincoln quoted speeches second inaugural address gettysburg address (3,360)

Emancipation Proclamation

Abraham Lincoln emancipation proclamation thirteenth amendment slavery end (24,000)

slavery end thirteenth amendment emancipation proclamation (20,500)

Civil War emancipation proclamation effects thirteenth amendment freedom end slavery (24,400)

Critical Involvements in War Effort

Civil War Abraham Lincoln involvement military strategy Union (22,400)

Abraham Lincoln chief architect military strategy civil war Union (9,860)

Abraham Lincoln critical involvement civil war military strategy union (18,300)

Highlights of Lincoln's Administration

Abraham Lincoln highlights administration accomplishments important (13,800)

abraham lincoln emancipation proclamation homestead act pacific railroad act land grant act nation bank act (1,210)

Assassination

john wilkes booth death assassination president abraham Lincoln (65,400)

assassinators john wilkes booth (45,500)

first assassination united states president abraham lincoln john wilkes booth (17,000)

Harriet Tubman

Harriet Tubman was an African American whose daring rescues in the 1850s helped hundreds of slaves escape to freedom.

HOT topics

The Underground Railroad. Tubman was the most famous leader of the Underground Railroad, a system which aided slaves in fleeing from the southern United States to the northern United States, Canada, and other places that prohibited slavery in the mid-1800s. The system was neither underground nor a railroad. It was called the Underground Railroad because of the swift, secret way in which the slaves escaped. The slaves traveled by whatever means they could.

Harriet Tubman

HOT topics

Childhood. Harriet Tubman's father taught her a knowledge of the woods that later helped her in her rescue missions. When she was a child, she tried to stop a supervisor from punishing another slave. The supervisor fractured Harriet's skull with a metal weight. Because of the injury, Harriet suffered blackouts which she interpreted as messages from God. Her actions as a child foretold the bravery that would distinguish Tubman in adulthood.

Daring Escapes. Tubman, acting alone, escaped from slavery in 1849 and went to Philadelphia. She made her first trip back south shortly after Congress passed the Fugitive Slave Act of 1850, which made it a crime to help a runaway slave. Tubman returned 18 more times during the 1850s. On one rescue mission, she sensed that pursuers were close behind, and so she and the fugitives got on a southbound train to avoid suspicion. On another mission, Tubman had just bought some live chickens when she saw her former master walking toward her. She quickly let the chickens go and chased after them before he could recognize her. In 1857, Tubman led her parents to freedom in Auburn, New York. Tubman never was captured nor were any of the 300 slaves she helped liberate. Slave owners offered thousands of dollars for her arrest.

John Brown. In the late 1850s, Tubman met the radical abolitionist John Brown, who told her of his plan to end slavery by launching a massive slave revolt. Tubman approved of his plan. From his youth, Brown hated slavery and helped fugitive slaves to escape to Canada. While in the Northeast, he organized a league among blacks for their protection against slave catchers. In New York, he lived in an area that was settled by blacks, where he was later buried. After moving to Kansas, Brown and his followers clashed violently with proslavery groups. He was captured and hanged for treason after storming an arsenal at Harper's Ferry in a bid to seize weapons. His execution helped propel the United States into Civil War.

TRUE or FALSE?

Blacks called Tubman Moses, after the Biblical figure who led the Jews from Egypt.

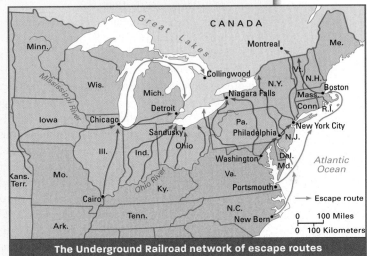

The Underground Railroad network of escape routes

hot topics hot topics hot topics hot topics

THE BASICS

Harriet Tubman (1820?-1913), was an African American who helped hundreds of slaves in the southern United States escape to freedom. She became a famous leader of the *Underground Railroad.* The Underground Railroad was a secret system that helped slaves escape to the northern United States or to Canada. Admirers called her Moses. The name referred to the Biblical figure who led the Jews out of slavery in Egypt.

Tubman was born into slavery on Maryland's Eastern Shore. Her name was Araminta Ross, but she came to be known by her mother's name, Harriet. Her father taught her a knowledge of the outdoors that later helped her in her rescue missions. When Harriet was a child, she tried to stop a supervisor from punishing another slave. The supervisor fractured Harriet's skull with a metal weight. Because of the injury, Harriet suffered blackouts which she interpreted as messages from God. She married John Tubman, a free black man, in 1844.

Harriet Tubman, acting alone, escaped from slavery in 1849. After arriving in Philadelphia, she vowed to return to Maryland and help liberate other slaves. Tubman made her first of 19 trips back shortly after Congress passed the Fugitive Slave Act of 1850. This law made it a crime to help runaway slaves.

Tubman became a conductor on the Underground Railroad. She carried a gun and promised to use it on anyone who threatened the success of her operation. She was assisted by white and free black abolitionists. She also got help from members of a religious sect known as the Quakers. On one rescue mission, she and a group of fugitives boarded a southbound train to avoid suspicion. On another mission, Tubman noticed her former master walking toward her. She quickly released a group of chickens and chased after them to avoid being recognized. In 1857, Tubman led her parents to freedom in Auburn, New York. Slave owners offered thousands of dollars for Tubman's arrest. But they never captured her or any of the 300 slaves she helped liberate before the American Civil War (1861–1865).

In the late 1850s, Tubman met the radical white abolitionist John Brown. He told her of his plan to end slavery by launching a massive slave revolt. Tubman approved of his plan. She remained one of Brown's greatest defenders after his arrest and execution in 1859.

Tubman continued her courageous actions during the Civil War. She served as a nurse, scout, and spy for the Union Army. During one military campaign along the Combahee River in South Carolina, she helped free more than 750 slaves. After the war, Tubman became the subject of numerous biographies. Upon returning to Auburn, she spoke in support of women's rights. She established the Harriet Tubman Home for elderly and needy African Americans. She died on March 10, 1913. The people of Auburn erected a plaque in her honor. The U.S. Postal Service issued a postage stamp bearing her portrait in 1978.

Underground Railroad

The Underground Railroad was an informal system that helped slaves in the southern United States escape to the northern United States, Canada, and other places that prohibited slavery during the mid-1800s. The system was neither underground nor a railroad. Americans called it the Underground Railroad because of the swift, secret way in which the slaves escaped. Several thousand people who walked, ran, swam, and sailed to freedom successfully reached their destinations. Many others did not.

The Underground Railroad had no formal organization. Some whites and free blacks provided runaways with food, clothing, directions, and places to hide. Some enslaved people in the South also helped fugitives escape. In the North, abolitionists furnished hiding places and helped slaves move from one refuge to the next.

Americans first coined the term *Underground Railroad* around 1830. From then until 1860, the system helped escaped slaves reach the North. There, however, they could still be captured and returned to slavery. Therefore, many fled to Canada and other regions outside the United States, especially after 1850. That year, Congress passed a strict fugitive slave law. Major havens for runaways included Boston, Detroit, and southern Ontario, Canada.

The most heavily traveled routes of the Underground Railroad ran through Maryland, Delaware, and Kentucky in the South, and Ohio, Indiana, and Pennsylvania in the North. Such mid-Atlantic cities as

Washington, D.C.; Baltimore; Philadelphia; and New York City were major hubs on the Underground Railroad. Escaped slaves in the Deep South sought their freedom by stowing away on vessels sailing from New Orleans; Mobile, Alabama; Pensacola, Florida; and Charleston, South Carolina.

A few people became famous for their contributions to the Underground Railroad. Levi Coffin and Thomas Garrett, who were members of the Society of Friends, a religious sect also known as the Quakers, helped at least 5,000 slaves escape. William Still was known as the "father of the underground railroad." He sheltered hundreds of fugitives in his Philadelphia home. He published the Underground Railroad's first history in 1872. The most fearless conductor of the Underground Railroad was Harriet Tubman. A runaway slave herself, Tubman returned to the South 19 times and helped about 300 enslaved people escape to freedom.

The Underground Railroad showed the determination of a small group of Americans to end slavery. Its success angered many people. It also contributed to the hostility between North and South that led to the American Civil War (1861–1865).

MLA Citation

"Harriet Tubman." *The Southwestern Advantage Topic Source.* Nashville: Southwestern. 2013.

ADDITIONAL RESOURCES

Books to Read

Clinton, Catherine. *Harriet Tubman: The Road to Freedom.* Little, Brown, 2004.

Larson, Kate C. *Bound for the Promised Land: Harriet Tubman, Portrait of an American Hero.* 2003. Reprint. One World/Ballantine, 2004.

Sawyer, Kem K. *Harriet Tubman.* DK Publishing, 2010.

Stein, R. Conrad. *Harriet Tubman.* Enslow, 2010.

Web Sites

Harriet Tubman

www.pbs.org/wgbh/aia/part4/4p1535.html

Short biography based on the PBS series *Africans in America.*

Harriet Tubman

www.americaslibrary.gov/aa/tubman/aa_tubman_subj.html

Harriet Tubman was a runaway slave from Maryland who became known as the "Moses of her people."

Search Strings

The Underground Railroad

"Harriet Tubman" "underground railroad" slaves secret escape (26,800)

"Harriet Tubman" "underground railroad" slaves escape (8,400)

Daring Escapes

Harriet Tubman daring escapes slavery runaway (13,600)

Harriet Tubman slavery runaway adventure (3,260)

John Brown

Harriet Tubman John Brown free slaves (85,400)

John Brown slaves free abolitionist Harriet Tubman (40,300)

"John Brown" slaves free radical abolitionist Harriet Tubman (9,410)

Thomas Alva Edison

Thomas Alva Edison (1847–1931) was one of history's greatest inventors and technological innovators. Among others, his most famous inventions include practical electric lighting, the world's first electric power system, and the phonograph, as well as improvements to the telegraph, telephone, and motion pictures. Some scientists regard Edison's creation of one of the first modern research laboratories, his laboratory for inventing, as his greatest achievement.

HOT topics

Young Hero and the Telegraph. As a child, Edison continually read science books, experimented with chemicals, and constructed elaborate models. When he was 15, a telegraph operator gave Thomas telegraph lessons as a reward for saving his son from an oncoming railroad car. Soon Edison began working as a telegraph operator for the Western Union Telegraph Company. He made improvements on printing telegraphs for stockbrokers, on a device to transmit images over telegraph lines, and on stock tickers. This led to Edison starting a stock ticker manufacturing company where he continually improved the devices that he manufactured. He also created the quadruplex, a faster, more efficient telegraph that could send four messages at a time on one wire.

HOT topics

Menlo Park Laboratory. In 1876, Edison built his Menlo Park laboratory. There, he and his assistants began their research. Inventions created at Menlo Park that transformed the world include the telephone transmitter, the phonograph, and the electric light.

Bright Idea/The Electric Light. In the late 1870s, Edison invented the incandescent electric lamp. In order to make this invention practical for everyday use, electricity had to be readily available to customers. Edison began promoting the idea of producing electricity in central power plants and distributing it over wires to homes and businesses. He and his associates built a steam electric power plant on Pearl Street in New York City. Within 10 years, hundreds of communities throughout the world had Edison power stations. In order to make his system commercially successful, Edison and his associates also invested in companies that manufactured power cables, generators, electric lamps, and lighting fixtures. In 1892, these companies and others combined to become the General Electric Company.

West Orange Laboratory. In 1886, Edison built a laboratory 10 times larger than the one in Menlo Park. This laboratory housed thousands of books and journals, space for chemical, mechanical, and electrical experiments, and, eventually, manufacturing facilities for Edison's devices. There, he and his assistants created the peephole kinetoscope (motion-picture device), batteries, and the Ediphone (a dictating machine). Edison also designed ore milling equipment, mass-produced portland cement used to make concrete, and sought a natural source of latex.

Thomas Edison in his lab, 1906

TRUE or FALSE?

Edison was a major contributing factor to the United States becoming an industrial world power.

THE BASICS

Thomas Alva Edison (1847–1931), was one of the greatest inventors and technological innovators in history. His most famous contributions include useful electric lighting and the world's first electric power system. He invented the first practical machine that could record and play back sound. He called this device the *phonograph*. Edison also made improvements to telegraphs, telephones, and motion pictures.

Edison looked for many different solutions when attempting to solve problems. When he created new or improved devices, he made a variety of designs. Sometimes, he borrowed features from one technology and adapted them to another. Edison obtained 1,093 U.S. patents, the most the U.S. Patent Office (now the U.S. Patent and Trademark Office) has ever issued to one person. Altogether, he received thousands of patents from some two dozen nations.

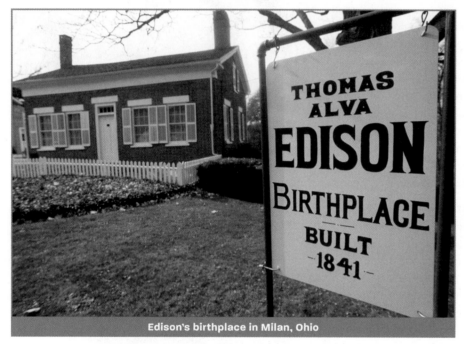

Edison's birthplace in Milan, Ohio

Edison also created one of the first modern research laboratories. Some scientists and historians regard this development as Edison's greatest achievement. Edison's research laboratory grew out of the way he worked. He often worked alongside his assistants. He observed how others solved mechanical, electrical, and chemical problems. Then he tried to improve upon their ideas. By the early 1900s, many industrial corporations had seen the success of research labs and established their own.

Edison was an active businessman. He created new companies to manufacture and sell his products. Income from selling his products helped support his research laboratory and the development of more devices. As a result, Edison and other manufacturing pioneers in the late 1800s helped make the United States an industrial world power.

Armed with self-confidence and determination, Edison overcame a number of technical and commercial failures. He became world famous by his mid-30s and a millionaire by his mid-40s. His name—and the electric light bulb that he designed—became worldwide symbols of bright ideas and technical creativity.

Early Life

Boyhood. Edison was born on February 11, 1847, in Milan, Ohio. He was the seventh and youngest child of Samuel and Nancy Elliott Edison. Edison's father fled from Canada during the rebellions of 1837, in which Canadian rebels unsuccessfully revolted against British rule. Samuel Edison worked as a shingle maker and land investor. When Al—as the family called young Edison—was 7 years old, the Edisons moved to Port Huron, Michigan. There his father ran businesses in lumbering and land investing.

Early interests. Edison received limited formal education. His mother, a former teacher, guided his learning. Edison was mischievous and inquisitive. He loved to pull pranks and practical jokes. He was also eager to read, particularly science books. His reading led him to experiment with chemicals and to construct elaborate models. He built models of a working sawmill and a railroad engine, both powered by steam.

Even as a child, Edison was interested in business. He grew vegetables on his father's farm and sold them in town. At age 12, Edison began to sell newspapers, candy, and sandwiches on passenger trains between Port Huron and Detroit. When he was 15, he published and sold a newspaper called the *Weekly Herald*.

By this time, Edison had developed hearing problems. His hearing worsened as he grew older. Late in life, he could only hear people shouting directly into his ear.

The young telegrapher. At age 15, Edison rescued the son of a telegraph operator from the path of a railroad car. As a reward, the operator gave Edison telegraph lessons. In 1863, Edison began work as a telegraph operator for the Western Union Telegraph Company. During the following 4 years, he worked as a telegrapher in a number of Midwestern cities. Edison learned much about the scientific aspects of telegraphic communication. He experimented with telegraph equipment. He also read newspapers, scientific journals, and books.

Inventor and Businessman

In 1868, Edison moved to Boston as a telegraph operator. He soon made improvements to the process used to print telegraphs and to a device that transmitted images over telegraph lines. Edison also applied for his first patent. But the invention—an electric vote-recorder for legislatures—was never used.

In 1869, Edison moved to New York City. There he met

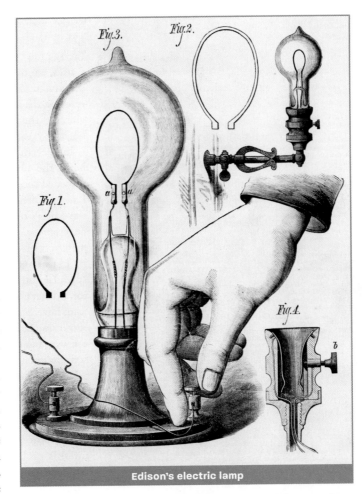

Edison's electric lamp

leaders in the business community, who appreciated his work as an inventor. At the time, Edison's inventions included improved *stock tickers*, telegraph devices used to report the purchase and sale of stocks. In 1870, Edison moved to Newark, New Jersey, and started a stock ticker manufacturing company.

Edison hired associates with mechanical talent to help develop a steady stream of inventions. He continually tried to improve the devices he sold. He also kept systematic notes of his activities. He used these notes to organize research and to defend his patents.

In 1874, Edison completed the design of the *quadruplex*, a device that made telegraphs faster and more efficient. Edison called it the *quadruplex* because it could send four messages at the same time over a single wire. In 1875, Edison and his staff developed an electric pen that cut stencils out of paper for copying documents.

The Wizard of Menlo Park. In the spring of 1876, Edison built his first research laboratory in the rural community of Menlo Park, New Jersey. The work done by Edison and his assistants at Menlo Park would make him famous throughout the world. Three of his greatest inventions originated there: (1) an improved telephone transmitter, (2) the phonograph, and (3) the electric

Edison with his just-invented phonograph

rested against a rotating cylinder wrapped with tinfoil. When the disk vibrated, the needle made varying impressions in the foil. To reproduce the sound, another needle was attached to a diaphragm and funnel-like horn. This needle retraced the impressions or grooves in the foil. It vibrated the diaphragm and thus the air in the horn, re-creating the original sound waves.

In December 1877, Edison had a machinist build the phonograph. When it was done, he recorded the nursery rhyme "Mary Had A Little Lamb." Then Edison showed his phonograph to the editors of *Scientific American* magazine. The next spring, he demonstrated it for scientists, members of Congress, and President Rutherford B. Hayes. Newspapers and magazines helped spread enthusiasm for the invention and its inventor. Edison became one of the most famous Americans alive. Stories of his childhood, pictures of his "invention factory," and interviews with the inventor went out to the whole world. As a result, Edison became known around the world as the "Wizard of Menlo Park."

The electric light. In 1878, Edison began his most ambitious project. He developed a system of electric lighting to be used in homes, stores, offices, and factories. He found support for this project from J. P. Morgan, a powerful banker. Many inventors at the time were investigating electric lighting. They thought electric lighting would be cheaper, safer, and more reliable than the gas lighting that was popular in cities and suburbs.

Edison threw himself and his assistants into the complex work of developing a variety of electric light and power devices. This work required a system of generators, wires and cables, switches, motors, meters, and *lamps* (light bulbs). The lamps were probably the most famous component of the system.

An *incandescent lamp* produces light by passing an electric current through a *filament* (fine thread or wire). The electric current heats the filament so that it glows. Edison had to figure out how to make practical, long-lasting incandescent lamps.

Edison and his associates placed the filament inside a glass vacuum bulb. They spent months searching for an affordable filament material that would produce the best light. In October 1879, they tested a carbon filament made from burned sewing thread, resulting in their first practical

light. Menlo Park is now part of a township known as Edison.

Telephone transmitter. Edison was one of many inventors who improved the "speaking telegraph," as the telephone was then called. Alexander Graham Bell, a Scottish-born inventor, patented the telephone in 1876. In 1877, Edison designed a carbon-based transmitter. It made the voice of a speaker louder and clearer over the telephone. Before his invention, people had difficulty hearing anything said over the telephone. Until the 1980's, most phones used transmitters based on Edison's improvement.

The phonograph. In 1876 and 1877, Edison experimented with ways to record and replay messages. These experiments led to the invention of his phonograph. To record messages, Edison attached a needle to a *diaphragm*, a metal disk that vibrated in response to sound waves. The needle

incandescent light bulb. In 1880, they began using bamboo filaments, which lasted longer.

Electric utilities and manufacturing. In 1881, Edison moved back to New York City. He personally supervised the construction of his first central power station in the United States. It opened in 1882 on Pearl Street and served the business community in lower Manhattan. By 1884, this station delivered electric lighting to more than 500 customers and more than 10,000 lamps.

Edison's agents introduced his lighting system in other countries. They established companies to install Edison's system abroad. In 1882, small central stations opened in London and in Santiago, Chile. In 1883, an Edison central station began operating in Milan, Italy. In 1885, a major station opened in Berlin, Germany. By the 1890s, hundreds of communities throughout the world had Edison power stations. Edison also developed and sold small generating plants. They could be used in individual houses, businesses, or ships.

Edison started companies that manufactured his inventions. The products of these companies included power stations, light bulbs, and underground conductors. In 1892, the American businesses that manufactured Edison's electric lighting components became part of the General Electric Company.

Edison in West Orange. In 1886, Edison moved to Llewellyn Park, a residential area of West Orange, New Jersey, near New York City. Just blocks away, he built a laboratory 10 times the size of the one in Menlo Park. Edison envisioned the lab as a large-scale research facility for the industrial development of inventions.

The West Orange lab carried out chemical, mechanical, and electrical experiments. Edison added a staff of more than 50 experimenters, machinists, and draftsmen. The new lab also included a library with thousands of journals and books. Eventually, Edison's research and development center included manufacturing plants.

Motion pictures. Edison helped found the motion-picture industry. His interest seemed to take shape after he met Eadweard Muybridge, an English photographer. Like many people at the time, Muybridge was experimenting with photographing motion. In 1888, Edison envisioned a motion-picture device that "does for the Eye what the phonograph does for the Ear." His assistant, W. K. L. Dickson, began to record a series of images on celluloid film. Showing the images in rapid succession made them look like continuous action.

Edison's staff developed a camera and built the first film studio. In 1894, Edison's company introduced a commercial device for viewing motion pictures, called the *kinetoscope*. It consisted of a cabinet with a peephole or eyepiece on top. A customer put a coin in the machine to watch a short motion picture through the hole. In 1896, Edison's company introduced projectors designed by other inventors. *The Great Train Robbery* (1903), directed by Edwin S. Porter, ranks among the most notable films in the Edison catalog.

In the late 1800s, Edison also began working on motion pictures that included sound. Dickson had experimented in this area, and other inventors were working on it. One problem was that the sound was not loud enough for large audiences to hear. In addition, getting the sound to match the images was difficult. Edison's new version of the *kinetophone*—a combination kinetoscope and phonograph—debuted in 1913. It solved the problem of *synchronizing* (matching) the sound and images. The device used a pulley to attach a phonograph to a projector.

Edison and other inventors tried to control the motion-picture industry. In 1908, they formed the Motion Picture Patents Company. The company largely controlled the production, distribution, and exhibition of motion pictures in the United States.

Edison's home cinema

But in 1915, a federal court declared the company to be an illegal *monopoly*—that is, a business that unfairly controls the market for a product. Afterward, Edison and most other members of the Motion Picture Patents Company lost much of their influence in filmmaking.

Phonograph with cylindrical records

Phonograph developments. Edison exercised more direct control over his phonograph business than over his motion-picture business. He kept a close interest in the commercial and technical development of phonographs and recordings, especially when new competition emerged. Edison also set the general policies and strategies for his phonograph business. His guidelines determined which artists and tunes his company should record and release. The phonograph remained Edison's favorite invention.

In the early 1900s, the preferred format for sound recordings shifted from cylinders to flat discs. Discs were easier to mass produce and store than cylinders. Edison adopted the disc format in 1913. However, he continued to offer cylinder machines and recordings until 1929. The Ediphone, Edison's dictating machine, was based on his cylinder phonograph.

Ore milling and cement. In the late 1800s, Edison planned a complete system for min-

ing and refining iron ores. Steel mills in the eastern United States needed high-grade ore. Edison would crush low-grade ore and use electromagnets to separate the iron, thus making a concentrated ore for the mills. For this enterprise, Edison designed huge equipment and built a plant in New Jersey. At the plant, raw ore moved continuously on conveyor belts. The system resembled the assembly line later perfected by the American automaker Henry Ford.

Edison invested more than $1 million in ore milling. But the project ended in failure. Rich iron ore discovered in Minnesota proved cheaper to mine and process.

In the early 1900s, Edison manufactured *portland cement*, a gray powder used to make concrete. The manufacturing plant made use of his iron ore project's crushing and grinding technology and its large-scale mass-production techniques. Edison's portland cement went into new bridges, highways, and buildings. More than 45,000 barrels of the cement were used to build the original Yankee Stadium in New York City. Edison also devised a way to build concrete houses quickly.

Batteries. Edison had worked with batteries since his earliest days as a telegrapher. During the 1880s and 1890s, he experimented with lighter, more durable, and more powerful batteries. In the early 1900s, Edison began to manufacture rechargeable storage batteries of a nickel-iron-alkaline design. He also set up a chemical plant to provide the materials. Edison batteries were used in electric trucks and automobiles and for electric starters in gasoline-powered cars. They were also used in railway cars, submarines, and mining lamps.

Final work. During World War I (1914–1918), Edison headed the Naval Consulting Board, a group of inventors and business people who aided the war effort. He also faced manufacturing problems. They were caused by shortages of *phenol*, a chemical used in the production of phonograph records. During the 1920s, Edison turned most of his businesses over to his son Charles. Edison continued to work and experiment while suffering from several illnesses in his later years. From the late 1920s until the end of his life, Edison sought a natural substitute for rubber plants as a source of latex. He died at his home in Llewellyn Park on October 18, 1931.

Edison the Man

Edison valued long, hard work. He believed that inventors should focus on practical projects that businesses or consumers would buy. "Genius is 1 percent inspiration and 99 percent perspiration" is a quotation often associated with Edison—although Edison once wrote that he could not remember ever saying it.

Edison tried to learn from mistakes, but he was selective in admitting his errors. It was easy for him to learn something from a series of failed chemical tests. But he had difficulty admitting more serious mistakes. For example, Edison failed to appreciate the advantages of the Serbian engineer Nikola Tesla's *alternating current* (AC) electric power system over his own *direct current* (DC) system. Direct current is an electric current that flows in only one direction. Alternating current, on the other hand, changes direction many times each second.

Family and friends. On December 25, 1871, Edison married Mary Stilwell, who had worked in one of his companies. The couple had three children—Marion; Thomas Alva, Jr.; and William. Edison nicknamed Marion and Tom "Dot" and "Dash" after the telegraph code. Mary died in 1884.

In 1885, Edison met Mina Miller, the daughter of a wealthy Ohio industrialist. They married in 1886 and had three children—Madeleine, Charles, and Theodore. Of Edison's six children, Charles became the most famous. He served as secretary of the U.S. Navy in 1940 and as governor of New Jersey from 1941 to 1944.

One of Edison's most famous friends was Henry Ford. The industrial leaders became friends after Edison encouraged Ford to use gasoline engines in automobiles. The two friends later took automobile camping trips with the industrialist Harvey Firestone and the naturalist John Burroughs. The Edisons and the Fords also kept adjoining winter homes in Fort Myers, Florida.

Philosophy. Always a man of many ideas, Edison stayed informed about technology, business, and current affairs. He had a down-to-earth manner and a frank opinion on most matters. Edison often expressed faith in progress and industry. He believed that mass production would bring a higher standard of living. He also believed that technology could solve social problems.

Edison's West Orange home

Honors. Edison received honors from throughout the world. France appointed him to the Legion of Honor, its highest civilian award, in 1878. The U.S. Congress presented him with the Congressional Gold Medal, the highest honor it can give, in 1928. Henry Ford brought Edison much attention with an international celebration called "Light's Golden Jubilee" in 1929. It honored Edison and the 50th anniversary of his incandescent lamp.

A number of major historical sites and museums in the United States honor Edison. They include his birthplace in Milan, Ohio, and his winter home in Fort Myers, Florida. There is also the restored Menlo Park laboratory in Dearborn, Michigan. The Thomas Edison National Historical Park at West Orange, New Jersey, includes Edison's laboratory and home.

MLA Citation

"Thomas Alva Edison."
*The Southwestern
Advantage Topic Source.*
Nashville: Southwestern. 2013.

ADDITIONAL RESOURCES

Books to Read

Baldwin, Neil. *Edison: Inventing the Century*. 1995. Reprint. University of Chicago Press, 2001.

Collins, Theresa M., and others. *Thomas Edison and Modern America*. Bedford/St. Martin's, 2002.

Delano, Marfe F. *Inventing the Future: A Photobiography of Thomas Alva Edison*. National Geographic Society, 2002. Younger readers.

Edison, Thomas A. *The Papers of Thomas A. Edison*. Johns Hopkins, 1989. Multivolume work.

Israel, Paul. *Edison: A Life of Invention*. Wiley, 1998.

Sproule, Anna. *Thomas A. Edison*. Blackbirch Press, 2000. Younger readers.

Web Sites

Edison Birthplace Museum

http://www.tomedison.org/index.html

Highlights of Thomas Edison's life and career from the museum in Milan, Ohio.

Edison National Historic Site

http://www.nps.gov/edis/

National Park Service site on Edison National Historic Site in West Orange, New Jersey.

Super Scientists: A Gallery of Energy Pioneers

http://www.energyquest.ca.gov/scientists

Biographies of scientists who made important contributions to areas of science concerning energy production.

Thomas A. Edison Papers

http://edison.rutgers.edu/

An exhibit by Rutgers, the State University of New Jersey, documents Edison's career.

Thomas Alva Edison

http://www.invent.org/hall_of_fame/50.html

A Web site with biographical information on Thomas Edison.

Search Strings

Young Hero and the Telegraph

"Thomas Edison" telegraph "stock tickers" (685)

"Thomas Edison" telegraph (77,500)

"Thomas Edison" telegraph improvements (4,540)

Menlo Park Laboratory

"Thomas Edison" "Menlo Park" laboratory (33,400)

"Thomas Edison" "Menlo Park" laboratory research inventions (15,900)

"Thomas Edison" "Menlo Park" laboratory research inventions "Western Union" (297)

Bright Idea

"Thomas Edison" electricity (98,900)

"Thomas Edison" electricity central power plants wires (53,200)

"Thomas Edison" electricity central power plants wires "General Electric" (12,000)

West Orange Laboratory

"Thomas Edison" "West Orange Laboratory" (1,460)

"Thomas Edison" "West Orange Laboratory" inventions (795)

Albert Einstein

Albert Einstein was the most important physicist of the 1900s and one of the greatest and most famous scientists of all time.

HOT topics

The Special Theory of Relativity.
Einstein said that constant motion does not affect the velocity (speed in a particular direction) of light. That is, light does not obey the same laws that govern the velocities of material objects. For example, a ball thrown forward inside a railroad car would have a velocity equal to the velocity of the car plus the velocity of the ball as measured in the car. This is not true of the speed of light, which Einstein described as a universal "speed limit." Nothing can move through space faster than the speed of light.

E = mc².
Einstein's famous equation, $E = mc^2$, resulted from his special theory of relativity, which says that a body's energy, *E*, equals the body's mass, *m*, times the speed of light, *c*, squared (multiplied by itself).

DEFINITIONS

inertia: the tendency of all objects and matter in the universe to stay still if still, or, if moving, to go on moving in the same direction, unless acted on by some outside force

physics: the science that deals with matter and energy, and the action of different forms of energy, excluding chemical and biological change. Physics studies force, motion, heat, light, sound, electricity, magnetism, radiation, and atomic structure.

relativity: a theory dealing with the physical laws that govern time, space, mass, motion, and gravitation, expressed in certain equations by Albert Einstein; special theory of relativity. According to it, the only velocity we can measure is velocity relative to some body, for if two systems are moving uniformly in relation to each other, it is impossible to determine anything about their motion except that it is relative, and the velocity of light is constant, independent of either the velocity of its source or an observer. Thus it can be mathematically derived that mass and energy are interchangeable, as expressed in the equation $E = mc^2$, where c = the velocity of light; that a moving object appears to be shortened in the direction of the motion to an observer at rest; that a clock in motion appears to run slower than a stationary clock to an observer at rest; and that the mass of an object increases with its velocity.

HOT topics

The speed of light is so high that the conversion of a tiny quantity of mass releases a tremendous amount of energy. The conversion of mass creates energy in the sun and other stars and produces the heat energy that is converted to electric energy in nuclear power plants. It also creates the tremendous destructive force of nuclear weapons.

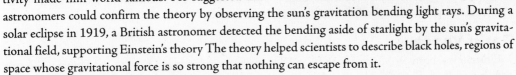

General Theory of Relativity.

Einstein's 1916 paper on the general theory of relativity made him world-famous. He suggested that astronomers could confirm the theory by observing the sun's gravitation bending light rays. During a solar eclipse in 1919, a British astronomer detected the bending aside of starlight by the sun's gravitational field, supporting Einstein's theory The theory helped scientists to describe black holes, regions of space whose gravitational force is so strong that nothing can escape from it.

Einstein and Atomic Energy.
In the summer of 1939, Einstein and the Hungarian refugee physicist Leo Szilard wrote a letter to President Franklin D. Roosevelt, warning that German scientists might be working on an atomic bomb. The letter led to the establishment of the Manhattan Project, which produced the first atomic bomb in 1945. After World War II, Einstein worked tirelessly for international controls on atomic energy.

Political and Social Causes.
Einstein was known for his support of political and social causes. Those included pacifism, a general opposition to warfare; Zionism, a movement to establish a Jewish homeland in Palestine; and socialism, a political system in which the means of production would be owned by society and production would be planned to match the needs of the community.

Albert Einstein, circa 1950

TRUE or FALSE?
Albert Einstein was a high-school dropout.

THE BASICS

Albert Einstein (1879–1955) was the most important physicist of the 1900s and one of the greatest and most famous scientists of all time. He was a *theoretical physicist,* a scientist who creates and develops theories of matter and energy. Einstein's greatness arose from the fact that his theories solved fundamental problems and presented new ideas. Much of his fame came from the fact that several of those ideas were strange and hard to understand—but proved true.

Some of Einstein's most famous ideas make up parts of his *special theory of relativity* and his *general theory of relativity.* For example, the special theory describes an entity known as *space-time.* This entity is a combination of the dimension of time and the three dimensions of space—length, width, and height. Thus, space-time is four-dimensional. In the general theory, matter and energy *distort* (change the shape of) space-time; the distortion is experienced as gravity.

Einstein also became known for his support of political and social causes. Those included *pacifism,* a general opposition to warfare; *Zionism,* a movement to establish a Jewish homeland in Palestine; and *socialism,* a political system in which the means of production would be owned by society and production would be planned to match the needs of the community.

Early Years

Einstein was born on March 14, 1879, in Ulm, in southern Germany, the son of Hermann Einstein and Pauline Koch Einstein. The next year, Hermann moved the family about 70 miles (110 kilometers) to Munich.

Albert Einstein's younger sister, Maria—whom he called Maja (pronounced *MAH yah*)—recalled that Einstein was slow to learn to speak. But even as a young child, he displayed the powers of concentration for which he became famous.

Einstein recalled seeing the seemingly miraculous behavior of a magnetic compass when he was about five years old. The fact that invisible forces acted on the compass needle made a deep impression on the boy.

A booklet on Euclidean geometry made a comparable impression on Einstein when he was around twelve years old. Euclidean geometry is based on a small number of simple, *self-evident* (obviously true) statements about geometric figures. Mathematicians use those statements to *deduce* (develop by reasoning) other statements, many of which are complex and far from self-evident. Einstein was impressed that geometric statements that are not self-evident could be proved clearly and with certainty.

Einstein and his sister, Maria

Education. Einstein began to take violin lessons when he was six years old. He eventually became an accomplished violinist, and he played the instrument throughout his life.

At the age of nine, Einstein entered the Luitpold Gymnasium, a distinguished secondary school in Munich. He enjoyed some of his classes and performed well, but he disliked the strict discipline. As a result, he dropped out at the age of fifteen to follow his parents to Pavia, Italy, near Milan.

Einstein finished high school in 1896, in Aarau, Switzerland. He then entered a school in Zurich, Switzerland, that ranked as one of Europe's finest institutions of higher learning in science. The school is known as the Swiss Federal Institute of Technology Zurich, or the ETH Zurich, from the initials for *Federal Institute of Technology* in German. While at the ETH, Einstein met and fell in love with Mileva Maric. Mileva was a physics student from Novi Sad, in what is now Serbia.

Einstein often skipped class, relying on the notes of others. He spent his free time in the library reading the latest books and physics journals. Einstein's behavior annoyed Heinrich F. Weber, the professor who supervised his course work. Although professors customarily helped their students obtain university positions, when Einstein neared graduation, Weber did not help him get a university post. Instead, a friend helped him find a job as a clerk in the Swiss Federal Patent Office in Bern. He became a Swiss citizen in 1901.

First marriage. Meanwhile, Mileva had become pregnant. Albert and Mileva's child, a daughter they named Lieserl, was born in January 1902 at the home of Mileva's parents. In January 1903, Albert and Mileva married. They had two more children, Hans Albert in 1904 and Eduard in 1910. However, Lieserl never joined them in Bern, and her fate remains a mystery.

Famous theories. Einstein worked at the patent office from 1902 to 1909. Those years were among Einstein's most productive. The job of reviewing patent applications left him with much time for physics. In 1905, he obtained a Ph.D. degree in physics by submitting a *dissertation* (a long, formal paper) to the University of Zurich. He had already completed all the necessary classwork at the ETH.

The year 1905 is known as Einstein's *annus mirabilis*—Latin for *year of marvels*. In that year, the German scientific periodical the *Annalen der Physik (Annals of Physics)* published three of his papers that were among the most revolutionary in the history of science.

The photoelectric effect. The first paper, published in March 1905, deals with the *photoelectric effect*. By means of that effect, a beam of light can cause metal atoms to release subatomic particles called *electrons*. In a photoelectric device, these freed electrons flow as electric current, so the device produces a current when light shines on it.

Einstein explained that the photoelectric effect occurs because light comes in "chunks" of energy called *quanta*. The singular of *quanta* is *quantum*. A quantum of light is now known as a *photon*. An atom can absorb a photon. If the photon has enough energy, an electron will leave its atom. Einstein received the 1921 Nobel Prize in physics for his paper on the photoelectric effect.

The principle that light comes in quanta is a part of an area of physics known as *quantum mechanics*.

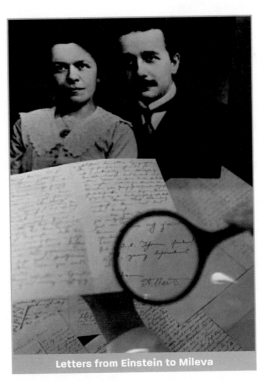
Letters from Einstein to Mileva

Quantum mechanics is one of the "foundation blocks" of modern physics; Einstein's relativity theories are two others.

Brownian motion. In the second paper, published in May 1905, Einstein explained *Brownian motion*, an irregular movement of microscopic particles suspended in a liquid or a gas. Such motion was named for the Scottish botanist Robert Brown, who first observed it in 1827. Einstein's analysis stimulated research on Brownian motion that produced the first experimental proof that atoms exist.

The special theory of relativity. The third paper, published in June, presented the special theory of relativity. In that paper, titled "On the Electrodynamics of Moving Bodies," Einstein made a remarkable statement about light. He said that constant motion does not affect the *velocity* (speed in a particular direction) of light.

Imagine, for example, that you are on a railroad car traveling on a straight track at a constant speed of one-third the speed of light. You flash a light from the back of the car to the front of the car. You precisely measure the speed of the light. You find that the speed is 186,282 miles (299,792 kilometers) per second—represented by the letter c in scientific equations. A friend standing on the ground also measures the speed of the light.

You might expect your friend's result to be $c + \frac{1}{3}c$. That would be a "common-sense" result consistent with ordinary experience with the velocities of material objects. For example, a ball thrown forward inside a railroad car would have a velocity—as measured by an observer on the ground—equal to the velocity of the car plus the velocity of the ball as measured in the car. But, strangely, in the case of the light beam, your friend's answer turns out to be the same as yours: c.

The strange fact that the velocity of light is constant has even stranger results. For example, a clock can appear to one observer to be running at a given rate, yet seem to another observer to run at a different rate. Two observers can measure the length of the same rod correctly but obtain different results.

Einstein also said that c is a universal "speed limit." No physical process can spread through space at a velocity higher than c. No material body can reach a velocity of c.

Interchangeability of mass and energy. In a fourth paper, published in September 1905, Einstein discussed a result of the special theory of relativity—that energy and mass are interchangeable.

Mass is a measure of an object's *inertia*, its resistance to a change in its motion. An object at rest tends to remain at rest due to inertia. A moving object tends to maintain its velocity. In addition, an object's weight is proportional to its mass; more massive objects weigh more.

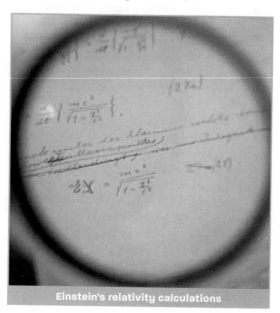

Einstein's relativity calculations

The paper introduced Einstein's famous equation $E = mc$-squared ($E = mc^2$). The equation says that a body's energy, E, equals the body's mass, m, times the speed of light, c, *squared* (multiplied by itself). The speed of light is so high that the conversion of a tiny quantity of mass releases a tremendous amount of energy.

The conversion of mass creates energy in the sun and other stars. It also produces the heat energy that is converted to electric energy in nuclear power plants. In addition, mass-to-energy conversion is responsible for the tremendous destructive force of nuclear weapons.

Middle Years

Academic appointments. By 1909, Einstein was famous within the physics community. That year, he accepted his first regular academic appointment, as an associate professor of theoretical physics at the University of Zurich. In 1911, he became a professor at the German University in Prague, Austria-Hungary (now Charles University in the Czech Republic). In 1912, he returned to the ETH as a professor.

Einstein moved to Berlin in 1914 to become a member of the Prussian Academy of Sciences, a professor at the University of Berlin, and the director of the Kaiser Wilhelm Institute for Physics, a research center then in the planning stage. He headed the institute until 1933. After World War II (1939–1945), the institute was renamed the Max Planck Institute (MPI) for Physics. Several other MPIs for various branches of physics and for other fields of study were later founded.

Second marriage. Mileva went with Albert to Berlin in March 1914 but returned to Zurich in June. Their marriage had become unhappy; and, in 1919, Albert divorced Mileva and married his cousin Elsa Einstein Lowenthal. Einstein's sons stayed in Zurich with Mileva, and Albert adopted Elsa's daughters, Ilse and Margot.

The general theory of relativity. In 1916, the *Annalen der Physik* published Einstein's paper on the general theory of relativity. This paper soon made Einstein world-famous. He suggested that astronomers could confirm the theory by observing the sun's gravitation bending light rays. During a solar eclipse in 1919, the British astronomer Arthur S. Eddington detected the bending aside of starlight by the sun's gravitational field. His observation supported Einstein's theory.

In his theory, Einstein also showed that gravity affects time—the presence of a strong gravitational field makes clocks run more slowly than normal. In addition, equations in the general theory are the basis of descriptions of *black holes*. A black hole is a region of space whose gravitational force is so strong that nothing can escape from it. A black hole is invisible because it traps even light.

Attacks on Einstein. Einstein's world fame came at a price. Einstein was of Jewish descent, and *anti-Semitism* (prejudice against Jews) was increasing in Germany. The physicist and his theories became targets of anti-Semitic verbal attacks. Following the 1922 murder of German foreign minister Walther Rathenau, who was Jewish, Einstein temporarily left Germany. He visited Palestine and a number of other Asian countries, Spain, and South America.

World travel. Threats of danger did not prevent Einstein from using his fame to promote causes dear to his heart. He took his first trip to the United States in 1921. The main purpose of the trip was not to lecture on physics but to raise money for a planned Hebrew University of Jerusalem. In July 1923, he traveled to Sweden to accept the Nobel Prize in physics that had been awarded to him in 1921.

Further scientific work. After creating the general theory of relativity, Einstein worked on a *unified field theory* that was to include all electric, magnetic, and gravitational phenomena. Such a theory would provide a single description of the physical universe, rather than separate descriptions for gravitation and other phenomena. Einstein worked on the theory for the rest of his life but never finished it; to this day, no one has developed a fully successful unified field theory.

Through the mid-1920s, Einstein was a major contributor to the development of quantum mechanics. By the late 1920s, however, he had begun to doubt the theory.

One reason for Einstein's doubt was that parts of quantum mechanics did not seem to be *deterministic*. Determinism states that strict laws involving causes and effects govern all events. As an example of apparent nondeterminism in quantum mechanics, consider an atom that absorbs a photon, thereby becoming more energetic. At a later moment, the atom reduces its energy level by releasing a photon. But a physicist cannot use quantum mechanics to predict the moment of release.

In 1926, Einstein wrote a famous letter to the German physicist Max Born expressing his doubts about quantum mechanics. Einstein wrote, "The theory produces a good deal but hardly brings us closer to the secret of the Old One [by which Einstein meant God]. I am at all events convinced that *He* does not play dice."

In 1936, Einstein and the German physicists Boris Podolsky and Nathan Rosen published an article, which became known as the "EPR paper," arguing that quantum mechanics is not a complete theory. The EPR paper and a reply from the Danish physicist Neils Bohr became the basis for a scientific debate that continues to this day.

Einstein; his secretary, Helen Dukas (left); and his daughter, Margaret, becoming American citizens

Later Years

Einstein in the United States. In December 1930, Einstein traveled to the United States. His trip was the first of what were meant to be annual visits to lecture at the California Institute of Technology. But in January 1933, during Einstein's third trip, the Nazi Party seized power in Germany. The Nazis had an official policy of anti-Semitism, and so Einstein never set foot in Germany again. He returned to Europe in March 1933, staying in Belgium under the protection of that country's royal family. He then went to England.

In September 1933, Einstein sailed to the United States to work at the Institute for Advanced Study, an independent community of scholars and scientists doing advanced research and study. The institute had recently been established in Princeton, New Jersey, and now consists of schools of Historical Studies, Mathematics, Natural Sciences, and Social Science. Princeton would be Einstein's home for the rest of his life. Einstein became a United States citizen in October 1940.

Letter to President Roosevelt. Einstein undertook one of his most important acts in the summer of 1939, shortly before the outbreak of World War II. At the urging, and with the help, of the Hungarian refugee physicist Leo Szilard, Einstein wrote a letter to President Franklin D. Roosevelt. The letter warned that German scientists might be working on an atomic bomb. The letter led to the establishment of the Manhattan Project, which produced the first atomic bomb in 1945.

Continuing fame. After World War II, Einstein worked tirelessly for international controls on atomic energy. He had a wide circle of professional acquaintances and friends, and he was still a world figure. In 1952, he was offered the presidency of Israel—the modern state of Israel had existed only since 1948—but he declined.

Final days. By the early 1950s, Einstein's immediate family had dwindled. His son Eduard had been confined to a mental institution in Zurich for years, suffering from schizophrenia. Einstein's first and second wives, his stepdaughter Ilse, and his sister Maja, to whom he had been especially close, had died. Einstein's son Hans Albert was a professor of civil engineering at the University of California in Berkeley. Of the people who were emotionally close to Albert Einstein,

only his stepdaughter Margot and Helen Dukas, his secretary since 1928, remained with him in Princeton.

Einstein signed his last letter one week before his death. In the letter, to the British philosopher and mathematician Bertrand Russell, Einstein agreed to include his name on a document urging all nations to give up nuclear weapons. Einstein died in Princeton on April 18, 1955.

Einstein's theories of relativity. In the early 1900s, the German-born physicist Albert Einstein noted that the laws of physics seemed to show that nothing could travel faster than the speed of light. This appeared to contradict Galileo's relativity principle. Imagine, for example, that an airplane passenger shines a flashlight toward the front of the plane. To the passenger, the light appears to travel at the speed of light. Using Galilean relativity, we might expect an observer on the ground to see the light moving 500 miles per hour faster than the speed of light.

Einstein proposed that the speed of light appeared the same to all observers, regardless of their relative motion. He replaced Galileo's principle with a principle called *special relativity*. In special relativity, both time and space are different in frames of reference that are moving in relation to one another. Experiments soon confirmed many predictions of special relativity. However, Galilean relativity remains useful because it provides an accurate description of motion at speeds well below the speed of light.

In 1916, Einstein realized that Newton's laws of motion could not be exactly correct for objects moving under the influence of gravity. He developed a theory called *general relativity* to explain the effects of gravity on motion. General relativity holds that mass and energy distort the structure of space and time, affecting the motion of objects. Scientists still use Newton's laws for many things because, in most cases, the predictions of Newton's laws agree closely with general relativity.

E = mc-squared is a formula developed by the physicist Albert Einstein that relates *mass* (amount of matter) and energy. In the formula, *E* stands for energy, *m* stands for mass, and *c-squared* is a constant factor equal to the speed of light squared. The equation shows that mass is a form of energy and that a tiny amount of mass can be changed into large quantities of other kinds of energy. For example, a mass of one gram could pro-

Einstein in his study

duce about twenty-five million kilowatt-hours of energy for use as electric power. This energy could power a home for several thousand years.

The formula laid the basis for the application of nuclear energy. When Einstein announced it in 1905, scientists knew of no way to change mass into energy or energy into mass. But scientists now know of two ways to release this energy. *Fission* involves splitting certain heavy atoms into lighter ones. This process powers nuclear reactors and simple nuclear weapons. *Fusion* involves combining certain light atoms into heavier ones. This process keeps the sun and stars hot and bright and powers advanced nuclear weapons. In both fission and fusion, the atoms at the end of each process have less total mass than did the atoms at the beginning of each process. This missing mass, or *mass defect*, is converted to energy according to Einstein's equation.

Relativity is either of two theories of physics developed by the German-born American physicist Albert Einstein. Those theories are (1) the special theory of relativity, which was published in 1905; and (2) the general theory of relativity, announced in 1915. Einstein's theories explain the behavior of matter, energy, and even time and space. They are two of the "foundation blocks" upon which modern physics is built.

The theories of relativity describe events so strange that people find it difficult to understand how they could possibly occur. For example, one person can observe that two events happen at the same time, while another person observes that they occur at different times. A clock can appear to one observer to be running at a given rate, yet seem to another observer to run at a different rate. Two observers can measure the length of the same rod correctly but obtain different results. Matter can turn into energy, and energy can turn into matter.

Galilean Relativity

In developing his theories, Einstein used ideas from a principle of relativity developed by the Italian astronomer and physicist Galileo. That principle is now known as *Galilean relativity*.

Undetectable motion. Galileo presented the main idea behind Galilean relativity in the *Dialogue Concerning the Two Chief World Systems* (1632). In this work, a character named Salvatius describes two scenarios involving a ship's cabin. In both scenarios, two friends are in the cabin, along

Galileo Galilei

with butterflies and other small flying animals, fish swimming in a bowl, a bottle from which drops of water fall into another container, and a ball. The cabin is below deck, so neither person can see outside.

In the first scenario, the ship is at rest. The animals move about naturally, and the two friends throw the ball to each other and jump about. The friends observe that the flying animals fly with equal speed to all sides of the cabin, the fish swim in all directions, and the drops of water fall straight downward. When one friend throws the ball to the other, the effort required for the throw does not depend on the direction of the throw. When either person jumps forward, the effort required for the jump does not depend on the direction of the jump.

In the second scenario, the ship is traveling at a *constant velocity*. That is, both the speed and direction of the ship are unchanging. All the events that occurred in the first scenario happen again: The small creatures fly and swim, the water drips, and the two friends throw the ball and jump. The motion of the ship has no effect on any of these events. Salvatius explains why this is so: All the objects in the cabin, including the living things, share in the motion of the ship.

Because the ship's motion has no effect on the events in the cabin, neither friend can tell by observing those events whether the ship is at rest or moving. This is the main idea behind Galilean relativity.

Strictly speaking, an actual ship would not travel at a constant velocity. For example, the ship would travel in a curve because Earth's surface—including the surface of the water—is curved. The ship would also curve due to Earth's rotation on its axis and its revolution around the sun. During periods of a few seconds, however, the ship's velocity could be almost perfectly constant.

Inertial frames. Physicists would refer to the cabin as an *inertial frame*. This term comes from the fact that, in the cabin, the *principle of inertia* would apply relative to the cabin. Inertia is a body's resistance to a change in its motion. A body that is at rest tends to remain at rest due to inertia. A moving body tends to maintain its velocity. For example, the fishbowl would be at rest relative to the cabin. Due to inertia, the bowl would tend to remain at rest relative to the cabin.

But suppose the ship suddenly gained speed, causing the bowl to slide. The friends in the cabin would observe that the principle of inertia no longer applied relative to the cabin. The cabin would no longer be moving at a constant velocity, so it would no longer be an inertial frame. Because the cabin was *accelerating* (gaining speed), it would be an *accelerating frame of reference*.

The principle of inertia is also known as *Newton's first law of motion*. It is one of three laws of motion discovered by the English scientist Isaac Newton. Those laws were published in 1687 in *Philosophiae naturalis principia mathematica (Mathematical Principles of Natural Philosophy)*, a work usually called simply *Principia* or *Principia mathematica*.

Until the late 1800s, most scientists thought that all natural events could be explained by Newton's laws. So the principle of Galilean relativity could be stated as: "The laws of nature are the same in all inertial frames," where the laws of nature were understood to be Newton's laws of motion and any laws based on them.

Galilean transformations. Certain kinds of calculations involving Galilean relativity are an important part of the background of Einstein's theories. Such calculations are known as *Galilean transformations*. They show how an event occurring in one inertial frame would appear to an observer in another inertial frame.

Galilean transformations apply a principle that is based on Newton's first law: Any frame of reference that is moving at a constant velocity relative to an inertial frame is also an inertial frame.

Suppose, for example, two jet aircraft, Jet A and Jet B, are flying in the same direction. Jet A is traveling 30 kilometers per hour (kph) faster than Jet B. A flight attendant in Jet A is walking at a speed of 5 kph in Jet A's direction of flight. A Galilean transformation will give the speed of the flight attendant relative to Jet B. The transformation will be an addition: 30 kph + 5 kph = 35 kph.

Now, suppose the attendant turns around and walks at a speed of 5 kph in the opposite direction. The Galilean transformation will be a subtraction: 30 kph − 5 kph = 25 kph.

The Michelson-Morley experiment. In 1887, an experiment conducted by two American physicists showed that there was something incorrect about Galileo's principle of relativity. The physicists, Albert A. Michelson and Edward W. Morley, performed their experiment on light rays.

The Michelson-Morley experiment can be traced back to a theory produced in 1864 by the Scottish scientist James Clerk Maxwell. Part of this theory describes the relationship between electric and magnetic *fields*. An electric field is an influence that an electrically charged object creates in the region around it. Electrically charged objects can act through their electric fields to attract or repel one another. Similarly, a magnetic field is an influence that a magnet or an electric current creates in the region around it. And similarly, magnets and objects that carry current can act through their magnetic fields to attract or repel one another.

Maxwell developed equations showing that electric and magnetic fields can combine in ways that create waves. The equations also indicate that these *electromagnetic waves* travel at the speed of light. Maxwell said that light itself consists of electromagnetic waves—a statement later proved to be true. He also said that other kinds of electromagnetic waves exist. The German physicist Heinrich Hertz discovered such waves—now known as radio waves—between 1886 and 1888.

Physicists reasoned that, if light consisted of waves, the waves had to travel through some substance, just as water waves travel through water. They called the substance *ether*, and they imagined that it filled all space. Although the ether could transmit waves, they said, it could not move from place to place. The ether's immovability made it a special inertial frame.

Maxwell's equations indicate that light moves at a particular speed, represented by the letter c. The value of c is now known to be 186,282 miles (299,792 kilometers) per second. Maxwell assumed that c was the speed of light relative to the ether. According to this assumption, light would travel faster or slower than c in an inertial frame moving relative to the ether.

Physicists also reasoned that Earth moved through the ether as the planet spun on its axis and circled the sun. Thus, any object on Earth's surface—including Michelson and Morley's laboratory—moved relative to the ether. The speed of light relative to the lab would therefore be different for light rays moving in different directions relative to the lab. And one could use Galilean transformations to calculate the speed of various rays relative to the lab.

For example, suppose the lab moved through the ether at a speed of 150 kilometers per second (kps). Imagine that a ray of light was emitted in the direction of the lab's movement. A Galilean transformation would show that the expected speed of the light relative to the lab would be $c - 150$ kps.

Now, imagine that a light ray was emitted in the opposite direction. The expected speed of the light relative to the lab would be $c + 150$ kps.

Michelson and Morley conducted their experiment to measure expected differences in the speed of light relative to their laboratory. Although light travels extremely rapidly, their experiment could measure tiny differences in speed. Surprisingly, Michelson and Morley found no difference at all. This result was a great puzzle. Physicists tried without success to determine how light could act in a manner consistent with both Galilean relativity and the Michelson-Morley experiment.

Special Relativity

Einstein noted that there was no evidence for the existence of the ether. He therefore eliminated the ether from consideration. He argued that Maxwell's equations mean that the speed of light must be the same in all inertial frames. Therefore, Galileo's principle cannot be absolutely correct.

Accordingly, Einstein introduced a new principle, the special principle of relativity. This principle has two parts: (1) There is no ether, and the speed of light is the same for all observers, whatever their relative motion. (2) The laws of nature are the same in all inertial frames, where the laws are understood to include those described by Maxwell.

Einstein based his special theory of relativity on this principle. The theory solved the puzzle of the Michelson-Morley experiment. It also made dramatic new predictions that were verified by later experiments.

Lorentz transformations. Special relativity uses equations known as *Lorentz transformations* to describe how an event occurring in one inertial frame would appear to an observer in another inertial frame. The equations are named for the Dutch physicist Hendrik A. Lorentz, who first wrote them down in 1895. Lorentz developed the equations in an attempt to understand the Michelson-Morley experiment.

In the complex mathematics of special relativity, time and space are not absolutely separate. Instead, physicists refer to a single entity, *space-time*. This entity is a combination of the dimension of time and the three dimensions of space—length, width, and height. Thus, space-time is four-dimensional.

Time dilation. The Lorentz transformations show that a number of strange effects can occur. One of these is known as *time dilation* (*dilation* means *widening*).

For an example of this effect, consider two spaceships, A and B. The ships are moving relative to each other at a speed close to c. There is a clock in each ship. Both clocks keep time accurately, and people in both ships can see both clocks. Strangely, the people in the two ships will read the clocks differently. The people in Spaceship A will observe that the clock in Spaceship B is running more slowly than the clock in Spaceship A. But the people in Spaceship B will observe that the clock in Spaceship A is running more slowly than the clock in Spaceship B.

Time dilation actually occurs at all relative velocities. But at everyday velocities, even the most sensitive instruments cannot detect it. Thus, people are not aware of time dilation as they go about their normal activities.

However, time dilation is important in the study of *cosmic rays*, high-energy particles that travel through space. Some cosmic rays that originate in outer space collide with atoms at the top of Earth's atmosphere. The collisions create a variety of particles, including *muons*. The muons travel at almost the speed of light. In addition, they are *radioactive*—that is, they break apart as they travel.

Each muon can be considered to be its own reference frame. Physicists have measured how quickly muons break apart in terms of the passage of time in their reference frames. They break apart so rapidly that one might conclude that hardly any of them could ever reach Earth's surface. However, due to time dilation, the muons break apart much more slowly relative to the reference frame of Earth. As a result, many of them reach the surface.

Lorentz-Fitzgerald contraction. Another strange effect of special relativity is the *Lorentz-Fitzgerald contraction*, or simply the *Fitzgerald contraction*. Lorentz proposed that contraction occurred as an effect of the Lorentz transformations. In 1889, the Irish physicist George F. Fitzgerald had made a similar proposal.

For an example of the Lorentz-Fitzgerald contraction, again consider the two spaceships. The people in Spaceship A will observe that Spaceship B and all the objects in it have become shorter in the direction of Spaceship B's motion relative to Spaceship A. But they will observe no change in the size of Spaceship B or any of the objects as measured from top to bottom or from side to side.

This effect, like time dilation, also occurs in reverse: The people in Spaceship B will observe that Spaceship A and all the objects in it have shrunk in the direction of Spaceship A's motion relative to Spaceship B. The Lorentz-Fitzgerald contraction also occurs at all relative velocities.

Mass-energy relationship. One of the most famous effects of special relativity is the relation between mass and energy: $E = mc\text{-}squared$ ($E = mc^2$). Mass can be thought of as the amount of matter in an object. The equation says that an object at rest has an energy E equal to its mass m times the speed of light c multiplied by itself, or *squared*.

The speed of light is so high that the conversion of a tiny quantity of mass releases a tremendous amount of energy. For example, the complete conversion of an object with a mass of 1 gram would

U.S. Navy nuclear test, Bikini Atoll

release 90 trillion joules of energy. This quantity is roughly equal to the energy released in the explosion of 22,000 tons (20,000 metric tons) of TNT.

The conversion of mass creates energy in the sun and other stars. It also produces the heat energy that is converted to electric energy in nuclear power plants. In addition, mass-to-energy conversion is responsible for the tremendous destructive force of nuclear weapons.

General Relativity

Einstein developed the general theory of relativity to modify Newton's law of gravitation so that it would agree with special relativity. The key disagreement lay in descriptions of how objects exert forces on one another.

In special relativity, nothing can travel between two points faster than the speed of light. This principle applies to forces as well as rays of light.

Consider, for example, an atom of the simplest form of hydrogen. This atom consists of a single electron in orbit around a single proton. The electron carries a negative electric charge, while the proton is positively charged. The position of the proton determines the motion of the electron. It does so by exerting a force of attraction on the electron—an application of the familiar principle "opposite charges attract."

The proton exerts the force by means of electromagnetic waves that can be thought of as light rays. The proton *emits* (sends out) a ray, which the electron then absorbs. Thus, the electron's motion depends on what the position of the proton was when the proton emitted the ray.

In the *Principia*, Newton had given the law of gravity as $F = m_1 m_2 \div d^2$, where F is the gravitational force between two objects, m_1 and m_2 are the masses of the objects, and d^2 is the distance between them squared. This law explained the motion of the planets. According to the law, a planet's motion depends on the position of the sun and the other planets. All these objects influence one another by means of gravitational force.

But Newton's law says that the force between two objects is transmitted instantaneously, no matter how far apart the objects are. That is, the law describes a gravitational *action at a distance*. This description disagrees with special relativity, which says that there is no action at a distance.

Principle of equivalence. To eliminate action at a distance from Newton's laws, Einstein

began with an observation that he called the *principle of equivalence*. According to this principle, an object's *gravitational mass* equals its *inertial mass*.

Gravitational mass helps determine the force of gravity on an object. The masses m_1 and m_2 in Newton's law of gravity are gravitational masses.

Inertial mass is a measure of an object's inertia. Inertial mass is given in the equation for Newton's second law of motion: $F = ma$, where F is the force exerted on an object, m is the inertial mass of the object, and a is the acceleration of the object. This equation applies, for example, when you push an object across the floor. If your force is greater than the force of friction between the object and the floor and any other force that is working against you, the object will go faster and faster. The amount of acceleration will depend on the mass of the object and on your force minus the opposing forces.

The Hungarian physicist Lorand Eotvos had verified the principle of equivalence experimentally in 1889. Einstein saw that the principle reveals a close connection between the way an object moves through space-time and the gravitational force that acts on the object. He recognized that gravity is therefore related to the structure of space-time.

A "thought experiment." To describe how he would work to eliminate action at a distance, Einstein offered an example called a "thought experiment": First, consider an elevator that is falling freely toward Earth's surface. Suppose a person in the elevator drops a rock. The rock will fall with the person, and so it will merely hover in the air beside the person.

Now, imagine that the elevator is in outer space—so far from any planet or star that almost no gravitational force is present. The person drops the rock and, again, the rock hovers beside the person.

Einstein said that the "thought experiment" reveals a general truth: A person in free fall cannot determine by observation within his or her reference frame that gravitation is present. Thus, gravitation must be a characteristic of the space-time in which the observer is falling.

Nowadays, the principle that underlies Einstein's example is familiar in the phenomenon of *weightlessness*. Astronauts in the space shuttle are so close to Earth that the planet's gravity acts on them. But, like the rock in the elevator, the shuttle and its passengers are in free fall. Therefore, their

Group of four galaxies (photographed by the Hubble Space Telescope)

experience is the same as it would be if there were no gravity at all.

Distortions in space-time. Einstein translated this principle into mathematical terms in his general theory of relativity. In this theory, matter and energy *distort* (change the shape of) space-time, and the distortion is experienced as gravity. A more common—but less precise—way of explaining the distortion is "Mass curves space."

Einstein suggested that astronomers could make certain observations to test the general theory of relativity. The most dramatic of these would be a bending of light rays by the sun's gravitation. In relativity, mass and energy are equivalent; and, because light carries energy, it also is affected by gravity. The light-bending effect is small, but Einstein calculated that it could be observed during a solar eclipse. In 1919, the British astronomer Arthur S. Eddington observed it, thereby making Einstein world-famous.

Gravitational waves. General relativity indicates that *gravitational waves* transmit gravitational force, just as electromagnetic waves transmit electric and magnetic forces. Scientists have observed gravitational waves indirectly in a pair of *neutron stars* that orbit each other. Neutron stars are the smallest and densest stars known. A neutron star measures only about 12 miles (20 kilometers) across, but has more mass than the sun.

By observing the pair of stars for several years, the scientists determined that the stars' orbit is becoming smaller. Calculations involving equations of general relativity show that the orbit is shrinking because the stars are emitting gravitational waves.

Most gravitational waves produce such small distortions of space-time that they are impossible to detect directly. However, collisions between neutron stars and even more compact objects called *black holes* create tremendous distortions. Physicists are building observatories to detect the resulting waves directly.

An observatory known as the Laser Interferometer Gravitational-Wave Observatory (LIGO) has three facilities—two in Hanford, Washington, and one in Livingston, Louisiana. Each facility is designed to detect gravitational waves by sensing their effect on two metal tubes that are 2 1/2 miles (4 kilometers) long. The tubes are built along the ground, and they are connected to each other in the shape of an L. When a gravitational wave passes through them, it changes their lengths by an amount much smaller than an atomic nucleus. A laser system detects changes in the lengths.

MLA Citation

"Albert Einstein." *The Southwestern Advantage Topic Source.* Nashville: Southwestern. 2013.

ADDITIONAL RESOURCES

Books to Read

Bodanis, David. *E=mc² : A Biography of the World's Most Famous Equation*. Walker, 2000.

Pirotta, Saviour. *Albert Einstein*. Raintree Steck-Vaughn, 2002.

Severance, John B. *Einstein: Visionary Scientist*. Houghton, 1999.

Strathern, Paul. *Einstein and Relativity*. 1997. Reprint. Doubleday, 1999.

Web Sites

Einstein—Image and Impact

http://www.aip.org/history/einstein/

This on-line guide to the life and work of Albert Einstein features more than 100 pages of text and pictures. Presented by The Center for History of Physics, a division of the American Institute of Physics.

Einstein Revealed

http://www.pbs.org/wgbh/nova/physics/einstein-revealed.html

This PBS program traces the history of Albert Eistein and the journey of his mind and groundbreaking ideas.

Super Scientists: A Gallery of Energy Pioneers

http://www.energyquest.ca.gov/scientists

Biographies of scientists who made important contributions concerning energy production.

Search Strings

Special Theory of Relativity

albert einstein special theory of relativity speed of light constant motion velocity (82,100)

speed of light velocity special theory of relativity albert einstein (104,000)

special theory of relativity einstein constant motion does not affect the velocity speed in a particular direction of light does not obey same laws that govern velocities of material objects (809)

albert einstein special theory of relativity body's energy equals body's mass times speed of light squared (17,200)

Equation

albert einstein famous equation conversion of mass creates energy produces heat energy (90,200)

body's energy equals body's mass times speed of light squared conversion creates energy albert Einstein (80,300)

General Theory of Relativity

general theory of relativity albert einstein confirm sun's gravitation bending light rays (14,800)

general theory of relativity albert einstein black holes gravity (148,000)

Atomic Energy

albert einstein atomic energy leo szilard manhattan project (15,900)

albert einstein leo szilard franklin roosevelt atomic energy (10,900)

atomic energy szilard einstein roosevelt manhattan project (14,100)

Political and Social

albert einstein political social causes pacifism zionism socialism (10,700)

albert einstein beliefs causes political social (33,500)

Adolf Hitler

Adolf Hitler, a dictator who ruled Germany from 1933 to 1945, turned Germany into a powerful war machine and provoked World War II in 1939.

HOT topics

Persecution of the Jews. In 1935, Jews were declared citizens of lesser rights. In Germany, Hitler forced them out of the civil service, universities and other schools, and professional and managerial positions. Thousands left the country. Many who stayed were sent to concentration camps, along with hundreds of thousands of political suspects. Hitler also ordered Jews removed and killed in other countries he controlled. Altogether, Hitler's forces killed about six million European Jews and about five million other people that he regarded as racially inferior or politically dangerous.

Hitler's Leadership/Birth of the Nazi Party.
Hitler began his rise to political power the year after World War I ended. Germany had been defeated, and the nation's economy lay in ruins. Hitler joined a small group of men who became known as Nazis. A skillful politician and organizer, he became leader of the Nazis and quickly built party membership—partly by his ability to stir crowds with his speeches. His fiery words and brilliant blue eyes seemed to hypnotize those who listened to him. Hitler convinced many Germans that the Nazi Party could restore the economy and lead Germany to greatness again. Hitler had a clear vision and the daring to pursue it. But his aims had no limits, and he overestimated the resources and abilities of Germany.

Adolf Hitler

HOT topics 🔥

Mein Kampf. Hitler began writing his book *Mein Kampf* (My Struggle) while imprisoned for a failed attempt to overthrow the German government in 1923. In the book, he stated his beliefs and his ideas for Germany's future, including his plan to conquer much of Europe. Hitler also wrote that Germans represented a superior form of humanity. They must stay "pure," he said, by avoiding marriage to Jews and Slavs. Hitler blamed the Jews for the evils of the world. He accused them of corrupting everything of ethical and national value. Democracy, said Hitler, could lead only to Communism. A dictatorship was the only way to save Germany from the threats of Communism and Jewish treason.

Hitler's New Order. The *New Order* was Hitler's name for his reordering of German society and for his plans to reorder the rest of Europe. The Nazi regime applauded military training, rearmament, national pride, and industry. They used the press, radio, and films to flood Germany with propaganda praising the New Order. Within the New Order, citizens needed official permission to accept or change jobs, move, or travel abroad. The government regulated wages, housing, and production of goods. All German children were required to join Nazi youth groups from the age of ten. They wore uniforms, marched, and learned Nazi beliefs. The Nazis taught children to spy on their own families and report any anti-Nazi criticism they might hear.

TRUE or FALSE?

Adolf Hitler and Eva Braun, his mistress since the 1930s, were married in a bomb shelter in 1945 and then fled Germany to live in Argentina.

DEFINITIONS

chancellor: the prime minister or other very high official in Austria and in Germany, and many other European countries.

fascism: the form of government in Italy from 1922 to 1943, under the leadership of Benito Mussolini. It was ruled by a dictator, with strong control of industry and labor by the central government, great restrictions upon the freedom of individuals, and extreme nationalism and militarism. It was opposed to radical socialism and Communism.

genocide: the systematic extermination of a cultural or racial group.

the Holocaust: the mass destruction or extermination of European Jews by the Nazis during World War II.

Nazi: a member or supporter of the National Socialist Party, a fascist political party in Germany, led by Adolf Hitler; advocate of Nazism. It came to power in Germany in 1933 and believed in state control of industry, denunciation of Communism and Judaism, and the dominance of Germany as a world power.

propaganda: systematic efforts to spread opinions or beliefs; any plan or method for spreading opinions or beliefs.

Reichstag: the former elective legislative assembly of Germany, now called the Bundestag.

Schutzstaffel: the SS Troops, especially those of the German army during World War II.

Third Reich: the totalitarian state in Germany (from 1933 to 1945) under Adolf Hitler.

THE BASICS

Adolf Hitler (1889–1945) ruled Germany as dictator from 1933 to 1945. He turned Germany into a powerful war machine and provoked World War II in 1939. Hitler's forces conquered most of Europe before they were defeated in 1945.

Hitler spread death as no person has done in modern history. "Have no pity! Act brutally!" he told his soldiers. He ordered tens of thousands of those who opposed him to be executed, and hundreds of thousands to be thrown into prison.

Hitler particularly persecuted Jews. He ordered them removed and killed in countries he controlled. Hitler set up concentration camps where about four million Jews were murdered. Altogether, Hitler's forces killed about six million European Jews as well as about five million other people that Hitler regarded as racially inferior or politically dangerous.

Adolf Hitler began his rise to political power in 1919, the year after World War I had ended. The German Empire had been defeated, and the nation's economy lay in ruins. Hitler joined a small group of men who became known as Nazis. He soon became their leader. Hitler and his followers believed he could win back Germany's past glory. He promised to rebuild Germany into a mighty empire that would last a thousand years.

Many people did not take Hitler seriously. But his fiery words and brilliant blue eyes seemed to hypnotize those who listened to him. Many Germans believed he was their protector and friend. His emotional speeches made crowds cheer "Heil, Hitler!" ("Hail, Hitler!").

Hitler became dictator of Germany in 1933 and quickly succeeded in regaining some territories taken from Germany as a result of World War I. He threatened war against Czechoslovakia in 1938 but was stopped by a combination of counter-threats and concessions. His forces invaded Poland in 1939. Then Britain, France, Australia, New Zealand, South Africa, and Canada declared war on Germany, and World War II began.

Hitler had a clear vision of what he wanted, and he had the daring to pursue it. But his aims had no limits, and he overestimated the resources and abilities of Germany. Hitler had little regard for experts in any field. He regularly ignored the advice of his generals and followed his own judgment, even while Germany was being defeated in the last years of the war. Finally, as United States, British, and Soviet troops closed in on the heart of Germany, Hitler killed himself.

Hitler's baby picture, circa 1890

Early Life

Boyhood. Adolf Hitler was born on April 20, 1889, in Braunau, Austria, a small town across the Inn River from Germany. He was the fourth child of the third marriage of Alois Hitler, a customs official. Alois Hitler was fifty-one years old when Adolf was born. Adolf's mother, Klara Polzl, was twenty-eight years old. She was a farmer's daughter.

Alois Hitler was born to an unmarried woman named Anna Maria Schicklgruber. A wandering miller named Johann Georg Hiedler married her about five years later. Hiedler died in 1856, when Alois was twenty years old, having never recognized Alois as his child. In 1876, Hiedler's brother arranged for Alois to be registered as the legitimate son of Johann Georg and Maria Hiedler. The priest who made the entry spelled the name "Hitler." Years later, before he came to power, some of Hitler's political opponents called him Schicklgruber as an insult. Only four of Alois Hitler's eight children lived to adulthood. Adolf had a sister, Paula; a half brother, Alois; and a half sister, Angela.

About six years after Adolf's birth, his father retired and moved near Linz, Austria. Adolf received good marks in elementary school, but he was a poor student in high school. His low marks angered his harsh, ill-tempered father. Alois wanted his son to have a career as a civil servant. But the boy wanted to be an artist.

Alois Hitler died in 1903, and Adolf left high school two and a half years later at the age of sixteen. His mother drew a widow's pension and owned some property. Adolf did not have to go to work. He spent his time daydreaming, drawing pictures, and reading books.

Years in Vienna. In 1907, Hitler went to Vienna, the capital of Austria-Hungary. He wanted to be an art student, but he twice failed the entrance examination of the Academy of Fine Arts. His mother died in 1907. Adolf had an income from the money his mother left her children and inherited some money from his aunt. He also claimed an orphan's pension. Sometimes he sold his drawings and paintings. He lived comfortably and idly during most of his stay in Vienna, considering himself an artist.

Hitler also concerned himself with political observations, admiring the effective leadership and organization of the Social Democratic Workers' Party in Vienna. He developed a growing hatred for Jews and Slavs. Like many German-speaking Austrians, Hitler became fiercely nationalistic. He thought no form of government could last if it treated people of different nationalities equally.

Corporal Hitler. In 1913, Hitler moved to Munich, Germany. The Austrian Army called him for a physical examination, but he was found unfit for service.

World War I began in August 1914. Hitler volunteered immediately for service in the German Army and was accepted. He served valiantly as a messenger on the Western Front for most of the war, taking part in some of the bloodiest battles. He was wounded and twice decorated for bravery. But Hitler rose only to the rank of corporal. When Germany surrendered in November 1918, he was in a military hospital recovering from temporary blindness that resulted from his exposure in battle to mustard gas. He was deeply shaken by news of the armistice. He believed that the unity of the German nation was threatened and that he must attempt to save Germany.

Rise to Power

Defeat in World War I shocked the German people. Despair and turmoil increased as the army returned to a bankrupt country. Millions of Ger-

Hitler in his field uniform during World War I

mans could not find work. A socialist-liberal republic replaced the defeated empire.

After World War I, Germany was forced to sign the Treaty of Versailles. The treaty held Germany responsible for the war. It stripped the nation of much territory and restricted the German Army to 100,000 men. It also provided for a fifteen-year foreign occupation of an area of western Germany called the Rhineland. But the harshest part was the demand that Germany pay huge *reparations* (payments for war damages). The sums demanded by the treaty were so great that they made peace difficult. Nationalists, Communists, and others attacked the new government. The nationalists demanded punishment for the "criminals" who had signed the treaty.

Birth of the Nazi Party. After Hitler recovered from the mustard gas, he returned to Munich and remained in the army until March 1920. In the autumn of 1919, he began to attend meetings of a small nationalist group called the German Workers' Party. He joined the party and changed its name to the National Socialist German Workers' Party. The group became known as the Nazi Party. The Nazis called for the union into one nation of all Germans, including the Austrians and German minorities in Czechoslovakia and other countries. They demanded that citizens of non-German or Jewish origin be deprived of German citizenship, and they called for the cancellation of the Treaty of Versailles.

Hitler was a skillful politician and organizer. He became leader of the Nazis and quickly built up party membership—partly by his ability to stir crowds with his speeches. Hitler attacked the government and declared that the Nazi Party could restore the economy, assure work for all, and lead Germany to greatness again.

Hitler also organized a private army he called storm troopers. He used brown-shirted uniforms and the swastika emblem to give his party and the *storm troopers*—known as the SA—a sense of unity and power. The troopers fought the armies of the Communist, Social Democratic, and other parties who opposed Nazi ideas or tried to break up Nazi Party rallies. By October 1923, the storm troopers numbered 15,000 members. They had a considerable number of machine guns and rifles.

The Beer Hall Putsch. In 1923, Germany was in deep trouble. France and Belgium had sent troops to occupy the Ruhr District, the chief industrial region. German workers there responded by going on strike. The strike aggravated a crisis in Germany's economy, which had already been weakened by the reparations payments, and German money lost almost all value. Communist and

nationalist revolts flared up throughout Germany, and the state of Bavaria was in open conflict with the central government in Berlin. Hitler saw an opportunity amid these troubles to overthrow both the Bavarian and national German governments.

On November 8, 1923, at a rally in a Munich beer hall, Hitler proclaimed a Nazi revolution, or *putsch*. The next day, he tried to seize the Bavarian government in what became known as the Beer Hall Putsch. Hitler, supported by the German General Erich F. W. Ludendorff, led over 2,000 storm troopers on a march against the Bavarian government. But state police opened fire and stopped the procession, killing sixteen marchers. The plot failed. Hitler was arrested and sentenced to five years in prison.

Mein Kampf. While he was imprisoned, Hitler began writing his book *Mein Kampf* (My Struggle). In the book, he stated his beliefs and his ideas for Germany's future, including his plan to conquer much of Europe. Territories lost in World War I would be recovered. Austria and parts of Czechoslovakia where Germans lived would be added to Germany. The growing German nation would seize *lebensraum* (living space) from Poland, the Soviet Union, and other countries to the east.

Hitler also wrote that Germans represented a superior form of humanity. They must stay "pure," he said, by avoiding marriage to Jews and Slavs. Hitler blamed the Jews for the evils of the world. He accused them of corrupting everything of ethical and national value. He said: "By defending myself against the Jews, I am doing the Lord's work." Democracy, said Hitler, could lead only to Communism. A dictatorship was the only way to save Germany from the threats of Communism and Jewish treason.

Rise of the Nazis. Hitler was freed about nine months after his trial. He left prison in December 1924.

Great changes had taken place in Germany during 1924. A schedule for Germany's reparations payments helped stabilize the German currency, and the nation showed signs of recovering from the war. Most people had work, homes, food, and hope for the future.

The government had outlawed the Nazis after the Beer Hall Putsch. Many party members had drifted into other political groups. After Hitler was released from prison, he began to rebuild his party. He gradually convinced the government that the

Hitler reading a newspaper during his imprisonment in Landsberg

party would act legally, and the government lifted its ban on the Nazis. Hitler won friends in small towns, in labor unions, and among farmers and a few business people and industrialists. He also set up an elite party guard, the *Schutzstaffel*, known as the SS. By 1929, though the Nazis had not yet gained substantial voter support, their organization and discipline had made them an important minority party.

By this time, Hitler had assembled some of the people who would help him rise to power. They included Joseph Goebbels, the chief Nazi propagandist; Hermann Goring, who became second in command to Hitler; Rudolf Hess, Hitler's faithful private secretary; Heinrich Himmler, the leader of the SS; Ernst Rohm, the chief of the SA; and Alfred Rosenberg, the party philosopher.

In 1930, the worldwide Great Depression hit Germany. Workers again faced unemployment and hunger. That same year, Germany agreed to the Young Plan of 1929 to reschedule reparations payments. In 1929, Hitler had launched a nationwide campaign to defeat the plan. This campaign helped him become a major political force throughout the country. He led protest marches, organized mass meetings, and delivered speeches all over Germany.

Hitler used his old arguments in the campaign against the Young Plan and in a national election campaign that took place in 1930. But he toned down his violent speeches against Jews, which failed to attract many votes. Hitler promised to rid Germany of Communists and other "enemies" and to reunite Germany and all the other parts of Europe in which German was spoken.

In 1932, five major elections were held in Germany as its leaders struggled to give the nation political stability. In the July elections for the *Reichstag* (parliament), the Nazis became Germany's strongest party, receiving nearly 38 percent of the vote. Leaders of the other parties offered Hitler Cabinet posts in exchange for Nazi support. But as leader of the strongest party, he refused to accept any arrangement that did not make him *chancellor* (prime minister) of Germany.

The majority of the German people and the leading politicians did not want Hitler to become chancellor. They understood that he would make himself dictator and set up a reign of terror. Germany's president, Paul von Hindenburg, also had serious misgivings about Hitler. But the 85-year-old Hindenburg, persuaded by his friends

and his son Oskar, accepted Hitler's promise to act lawfully if he were named to form a government. On January 30, 1933, Hindenburg named Hitler chancellor.

Dictator of Germany

There were only two Nazis in the Cabinet besides Hitler—Goring and Wilhelm Frick. The rest of the eleven-member Cabinet was made up of politicians who were more moderate than the Nazis. The vice chancellor, Franz von Papen, and his political allies thought this arrangement would limit Hitler's power. But Hitler had never settled for anything less than full control. He moved steadily toward dictatorship. There was no place for freedom under his government, which Hitler called the *Third Reich*.

The New Order. The Nazis, through Frick's key position as minister of the interior, controlled all national police authority. Goring controlled the Prussian police. An emergency decree signed by Hindenburg on February 4, 1933, gave the Nazis legal authority to prohibit assemblies, to outlaw newspapers and other publications, and to arrest people on suspicion of treason. The Nazis were thus able to put down much of their political opposition. Goring created an auxiliary police force made up of thousands of storm troopers and ordered them to shoot in encounters with "enemies."

Hitler shaking hands with Hindenburg

On February 27, 1933, a fire began that destroyed the Reichstag building. Many historians believe that it was planned by the Nazis. A pro-Communist Dutch anarchist was found at the site of the fire and admitted that he had set it. The Nazis quickly blamed the Communists. Hindenburg signed another emergency decree that gave the government almost unlimited powers.

Elections for a new Reichstag were held on March 5, 1933. Hitler hoped to win more than 50 percent of the vote for the Nazi Party. But the party received only 43.9 percent despite using terror to influence voters.

After the election, the Communist deputies were arrested or not admitted to the Reichstag. This gave the Nazis a majority of the seats. On March 23, 1933, the Nazi-dominated Reichstag passed a law "for the removal of distress from the people and the state." This law, known as the Enabling Act, gave the government full dictatorial powers and, in effect, suspended basic civil and human rights for four years. When the president had signed it, Hitler had a firm "legal" basis on which to govern as he pleased. He had also destroyed the constitution through outwardly legal means.

By mid-July 1933, the government had outlawed freedom of the press, all labor unions, and all political parties except the Nazis. The *Gestapo* (secret state police) hunted down the enemies and opponents of the government. People were jailed or shot on suspicion alone. By the time Hindenburg died in August 1934, Hitler ruled Germany completely. He assumed the title *Fuhrer und Reichskanzler* (leader and reich chancellor).

The Nazis used the press, radio, and films to flood Germany with propaganda praising the *New Order*, Hitler's term for his reordering of German society and for his plans to reorder the rest of Europe. The regime applauded military training, rearmament, national pride, and industry. Jews were forced out of the civil service, universities and other schools, and the professions and managerial positions. In 1935, German Jews were declared citizens of lesser rights. Thousands left the country. Many who stayed were sent to concentration camps, along with hundreds of thousands of political suspects. A person needed official permission to accept work, change jobs, move, or travel abroad. The government regulated wages, housing, and production of goods. All workers and employers were supposed to belong to the German Labor Front, which was intended to replace Germany's labor unions. Through the Labor Front, the government regulated production, wages, working hours, and leisure activities.

Hitler also set up organizations for young people between the ages of six and eighteen. These groups included the *Hitler Youth* for boys fourteen years and older and the *Society of German Maidens* for girls fourteen years and older. The organizations were designed to condition German children to military discipline and to win their loyalty to the Nazi government. All German children were required to join such groups from the age of ten. They wore uniforms, marched, exercised, and learned Nazi beliefs. The Nazis taught children to spy on their own families and report anti-Nazi criticism they might hear.

A network of spies kept watch on the German people and maintained an atmosphere of terror. The Reichstag met only to listen to Hitler's public speeches. Judges and courts continued to function, but Hitler or his lieutenants reversed any decision they did not agree with.

The road to war. From 1933 onward, Hitler prepared Germany for war. He rearmed the nation, first secretly, then in open violation of the Treaty of Versailles. No nation acted to stop him, and so Hitler's steps became bolder. Hitler planned to establish Germany as the world's leading power and to destroy the Jewish people.

In 1936, Hitler sent troops into the Rhineland, again violating the Treaty of Versailles. His generals had opposed this dangerous challenge to France. But Hitler guessed correctly that France would not stop him. The stationing of German troops in the Rhineland was the first of the Nazi dictator's victories without war.

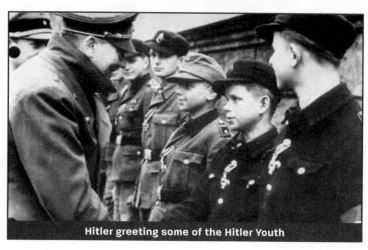

Hitler greeting some of the Hitler Youth

In March 1938, Hitler's troops invaded Austria. Austria then became part of Germany. In September, France and Britain consented to Hitler's occupation of the German-speaking areas of Czechoslovakia that had belonged to Austria-Hungary before World War I ended. After this move, Hitler said he wanted no more territory. But after each success, he planned a new takeover. He took control of the rest of Czechoslovakia in March 1939.

Poland came next on Hitler's list. But Britain and France took action to try to stop any further German expansion. They guaranteed Poland's independence, saying that they would go to war against Germany if Hitler attacked Poland. Hitler doubted that they would do so. In August 1939, Germany and the Soviet Union signed treaties of friendship. They promised mutual cooperation, trade privileges, and neutrality in case of war with other countries. In a secret part of the treaties, the two nations planned to work to divide Poland and much of the rest of eastern Europe between themselves. On September 1, 1939, Germany invaded Poland. Britain and France declared war on Germany two days later.

World War II. Hitler's armies overran Poland in just a few weeks. In the spring of 1940, they easily conquered Denmark, Norway, the Netherlands, Belgium, Luxembourg, and France. Benito Mussolini, Italy's dictator, declared war on France and Britain on June 10, 1940, when the defeat of France seemed certain. On June 22, 1940, France signed an armistice with Germany.

Britain fought on alone. A major German air offensive failed to weaken British resistance. Hitler kept delaying an invasion of Britain. Instead, he considered invading the Soviet Union. He explained to his generals that Britain would not surrender until its last potential ally on the European continent had been defeated.

In June 1941, the attack on the Soviet Union began. At first, the German forces made rapid progress. But their advance began to slow in November. By December, it was halted outside Moscow. An unusually bitter winter, Soviet reinforcements, and supplies sent by the United States helped the Soviet forces stop the Germans and begin to push them back during the winter. Renewed German attacks in 1942 and 1943 could not break through. During the Battle of Stalingrad, which lasted for five months during 1942 and 1943, the Soviets wiped out an entire German

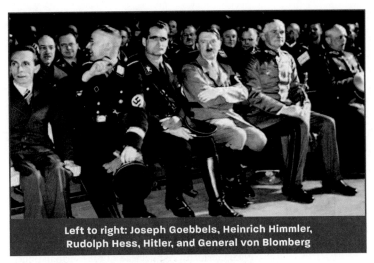

Left to right: Joseph Goebbels, Heinrich Himmler, Rudolph Hess, Hitler, and General von Blomberg

army of 300,000 men. This German defeat was a major turning point in the war.

While his empire lasted, Hitler directed the storm troopers, Nazi officials, and members of the army and the civil service in a campaign of mass slaughter. About six million Jews—more than two-thirds of the Jews of Europe—were murdered. More than three million Soviet prisoners of war were starved and worked to death. Hitler's victims also included large numbers of Roma (sometimes called Gypsies), Poles, Slavs, Jehovah's Witnesses, priests and ministers, mental patients, and Communists and other political opponents.

The German resistance had tried since 1938 to kill Hitler and overthrow the Nazis. But repeated plots failed. On July 20, 1944, Hitler narrowly escaped death when a German Army officer placed a bomb in Hitler's briefing room.

Early in 1945, the Allies marched into the heart of Germany against rapidly dwindling opposition.

Death. By April 1945, Hitler had become a broken man. His head, hands, and feet trembled, and he was tortured by stomach cramps. Eva Braun, Hitler's mistress since the 1930s, joined him at his headquarters in a bomb shelter under the Reich Chancellery in Berlin. She and Hitler were married there on April 29. The next day, they killed themselves. Aides burned their bodies. Seven days later, Germany surrendered.

EVA BRAUN (1912–1945) was the mistress of Adolf Hitler, dictator of Germany from 1933 to 1945. Braun met Hitler in Munich in 1929 while working as an assistant to Heinrich Hoffmann, Hitler's personal photographer. Hitler gave her a suite of rooms in his personal residence. Braun had no influential or political role in government, and she never sought to interfere in Hitler's work or official activities. She made few demands on Hitler and was totally devoted to him. Hitler made her wealthy and kept her out of public view.

Eva Braun was born in Munich, Germany, to a middle-class Bavarian couple. She married Hitler near the end of World War II, on April 29, 1945, in a bomb shelter in Berlin. The next day, as Soviet troops closed in on the place where they were hiding, both Braun and Hitler committed suicide.

HEINRICH HIMMLER (1900–1945) was one of the most powerful leaders of Nazi Germany. As the head of the German police, including the *Gestapo*, Himmler ordered the deaths of millions of people. These killings began with the "blood purge" of 1934 and ended with systematic killings in concentration camps that were operated by Himmler's *Schutzstaffel* troops, also referred to as the SS. Himmler was born on October 7, 1900, in Munich. He was a follower of Adolf Hitler from the days of Hitler's unsuccessful attempt to gain power in 1923. Himmler became chief of police for all Germany in 1936, minister of the interior in 1943, and minister of home defense in 1944. He committed suicide on May 23, 1945, after Allied troops captured him.

THE HOLOCAUST was the systematic, state-sponsored murder of Jews and others by the Nazis during World War II (1939–1945). The Nazi dictator Adolf Hitler wanted to eliminate all Jews as part of his aim to conquer the world. By the end of the war, the Nazis had killed about six million Jewish men, women, and children—more than two-thirds of the Jews in Europe.

In addition to Jews, the Nazis systematically killed millions of other people whom Hitler regarded as racially inferior or politically dangerous. The largest groups included (1) Germans with physical handicaps or mental retardation, (2) Roma (sometimes called Gypsies), and (3) Slavs, particularly Poles and Soviet prisoners of war. Nazi victims also included many homosexuals, Jehovah's Witnesses, priests and ministers, members of labor unions, and Communists and other political opponents. Historians estimate that perhaps as many as eleven million people were killed, including the Jews. Many of the Holocaust victims were killed in specially constructed gas chambers, and their bodies were then burned. The word *holocaust* means *a sacrificial offering that is completely burned.*

THE NUREMBERG TRIALS were thirteen trials held to judge leaders of Germany for their actions during World War II (1939–1945). The trials took place from 1945 to 1949 in Nuremberg (also spelled Nuremburg), Germany, where the Nazi Party had staged huge rallies. This party, led by dictator Adolf Hitler, ruled Germany during World War II.

In the trials, Nazi leaders faced charges of committing aggressive acts and war crimes. These crimes included the murder of about six million Jews, known as the *Holocaust*, and about five million other Europeans.

The Nuremberg Trials were the first war crimes trials conducted by the victors of a war in modern times. They were organized by the United States, the Soviet Union, the United Kingdom, and France.

The trials. The Nazi leaders were charged with crimes in four major areas—conspiracy to commit crimes against peace, crimes against peace, war crimes, and crimes against humanity. Conspiracy to commit crimes against peace included the planning of a war of aggression. The crimes against peace included carrying out a war of aggression. War crimes covered such acts as the murder of prisoners of war and of civilians, and the excessive destruction of land and cities. Crimes against humanity referred to three main offenses: (1) deporting civilians and using them for slave labor, (2) conducting inhumane medical experiments, and (3) persecuting and murdering

Nuremberg Trials

people because of political beliefs, race, or religion.

A group called the International Military Tribunal conducted the first trial. This trial ran from November 1945 to October 1946. It had eight judges, two each from the United States, the United Kingdom, France, and the Soviet Union. Twenty-two people were tried. They included such chief Nazi Party advisers and diplomats as Hermann Goring, Albert Speer, Rudolf Hess, Joachim von Ribbentrop, and Martin Bormann. Military leaders who were charged included Grand Admiral Karl Donitz and Colonel General Alfred Jodl. Hitler and two of his chief aides, Joseph Goebbels and Heinrich Himmler, committed suicide or had themselves killed before the trials.

The judges convicted nineteen defendants. Twelve of them, including Bormann, Goring, von Ribbentrop, and Jodl, received death sentences. Ten were hanged on October 16, 1946. Goring committed suicide a few hours before. Bormann's whereabouts were unknown at the time, and he was tried *in absentia* (while absent). Hess, Donitz, and five others received prison sentences ranging from ten years to life in Spandau Prison in Berlin.

Twelve more trials took place at Nuremberg from 1946 to 1949. They were conducted by U.S. judges. They involved 185 defendants, including Nazi Party officials, judges, business executives, and doctors. More than half were sentenced to prison, some received death sentences, and others were found not guilty.

Reaction. The Nuremberg Trials aroused considerable controversy. Some observers considered a number of the sentences too harsh. Other critics have pointed out that the victorious nations committed some of the same types of acts for which the Nazis were tried. Also, the Nazis on trial were not allowed to use this argument in their defense.

Nevertheless, the Nuremberg Trials have had far-reaching effects. They carefully documented the Holocaust and other Nazi crimes. The trials also rejected the argument that orders from superiors relieve people from responsibility for war crimes. Thus, the Nuremberg Trials emphasized the idea that soldiers and citizens have a moral duty to disobey inhumane orders or laws.

BENITO MUSSOLINI (1883–1945)
founded fascism and ruled Italy for almost twenty-one years, most of that time as dictator. He dreamed of building Italy into a great empire, but he led his nation to defeat in World War II (1939–1945) and was executed by his own people.

Early life. Mussolini was born on July 29, 1883, in Dovia, near Forli, in northeastern Italy. He earned a teaching certificate and briefly taught in an elementary school. From 1902 to 1904, he lived in Switzerland, where he increased his knowledge of socialism. Mussolini served in the Italian military in 1905 and 1906, and then taught school again and became a local socialist leader. In 1909, he went to Trent, Austria (now Trento, Italy), and worked for a socialist newspaper. But Austrian authorities expelled him from Austria for revolutionary activities.

In 1912, Mussolini became editor of the Italian Socialist Party's official newspaper. In this paper, he supported Italian involvement in World War I (1914–1918). Many socialists criticized this position. He then resigned as editor and, in November 1914, founded his own newspaper, *Il Popolo d'Italia*, in which he urged Italy to enter the war against Germany and Austria-Hungary. Later that month, the Socialist Party expelled Mussolini. Italy entered the war in 1915, and Mussolini served in the army until he was wounded in 1917.

Fascist dictator. In 1919, Mussolini founded the *Fasci di Combattimento* (Combat Groups). This movement appealed to war veterans with a program that supported government ownership of national resources and that put the interests of Italy above all others. In 1921, he transformed the Fasci into the National Fascist Party, adopting a more conservative program to gain the support of property-owning Italians. The Black Shirts, armed squads who supported Mussolini, used violence to combat anti-Fascist groups. In 1922, the Black Shirts staged a march on Rome and forced King Victor Emmanuel III to appoint Mussolini prime minister.

In 1925, Mussolini declared a dictatorship. He abolished other political parties and imposed government control on industry, schools, and the press and police. In 1929, he signed agreements that settled long-standing disputes between the government

Benito Mussolini

Left to right: Rudolf Hess, Hermann Goring, Julius Streicher, and Joseph Goebbels

and the Roman Catholic Church. He also sought to make Italy a corporate state, in which the government would help resolve disputes between employers and workers. The powerful Mussolini was called *Il Duce* (The Leader).

Foreign policy. Mussolini sought to make Italy a major power and to create an Italian colonial empire. He invaded and conquered Ethiopia in 1935 and 1936. But this action was condemned by Britain, France, and other countries and drove Mussolini toward an alliance with the German dictator, Adolf Hitler. In 1936, he joined Hitler in sending troops to fight in the Spanish Civil War in support of the rebel leader General Francisco Franco. In 1939, Italy conquered and annexed Albania.

World War II began in 1939, and France and Britain declared war on Germany. After Germany had almost conquered France in 1940, Mussolini entered the war and invaded France. A few days later, France surrendered. But Mussolini's troops soon suffered serious setbacks in North Africa and Greece. They met even stronger opposition after the Soviet Union, and later the United States, joined the war against Italy and Germany.

In July 1943, members of the Italian government deposed Mussolini and restored authority to the king, who then had Mussolini arrested. Mussolini was rescued by German commandos and became the head of a puppet government in northern Italy. In the spring of 1945, the German forces in northern Italy collapsed. On April 27, 1945, Italians opposed to fascism captured Mussolini as he attempted to escape to Switzerland. The next day, he was shot to death.

AUSCHWITZ was a forced-labor and extermination center run by the German Nazis during World War II (1939–1945). About 1.25 million people died at Auschwitz from September 1941 to January 1945. The Nazis used gas chambers and other methods to murder most of these people. Other victims died of starvation or disease, and some were worked to death in nearby factories. Most of the victims at Auschwitz were Jewish. The Nazis killed them as part of a plan to murder all the Jews in Europe.

Auschwitz was located in Poland, near what is now Oswiecim. It consisted of three concentration camps—Auschwitz I, built in 1940; Auschwitz II, or Birkenau, built in 1941; and Auschwitz III, or Monowitz, built in 1942. Today, Auschwitz is a museum and archive that is preserved by the Polish government.

Bergen-Belsen was a concentration camp near Hanover in north-central Germany, during World War II. The Nazis built the facility in 1943 as a detention camp for Jews. In the winter of 1944–1945, the camp's population soared. At that time, German forces were in retreat from Allied forces. The Nazis evacuated concentration camps outside Germany and moved many of the prisoners to Bergen-Belsen, which became dangerously overcrowded. From January to mid-April 1945, almost 50,000 people died there of starvation, disease, or exhaustion, or were murdered by the guards. British troops liberated the camp on April 15, 1945. The soldiers found about 60,000 starving prisoners and more than 10,000 unburied corpses.

BUCHENWALD was a concentration camp in Nazi Germany. The Nazis built the camp between 1935 and 1937 near the city of Weimar. People held at Buchenwald included political prisoners and such ethnic prisoners as Jews and Poles. About 57,000 of the prisoners were murdered by the Nazis or died from such causes as starvation and disease. Many of those who died were worked to death in Nazi-controlled factories surrounding the camp. The United States Army freed the surviving prisoners in April 1945.

DACHAU was the first permanent concentration camp set up in Germany by the Nazis. It became the model for all other Nazi concentration camps. The facility stood at the edge of the town of Dachau, near Munich, in southeastern Germany.

Dachau was built in 1933 to hold Jews and political prisoners. After 1942, many of the prisoners were used as slave labor on farms or in weapons factories near the camp.

At Dachau, the Nazis performed brutal medical experiments on more than 3,500 prisoners, most of whom died. About 28,500 other prisoners were murdered or died of starvation and disease. United States forces found about 10,000 dead bodies and more than 32,000 starving prisoners when they liberated the camp on April 29, 1945.

JOSEPH GOEBBELS (1897–1945)

was the official propagandist of Nazi Germany. As minister of popular enlightenment and propaganda, he tried to persuade both the Germans and the outside world to believe what the Nazis wanted them to believe. Goebbels controlled publications, radio programs, motion pictures, and the arts in Germany, and in German-dominated Europe.

Paul Joseph Goebbels was born in Rheydt into a working-class family. Appointed propaganda leader of the Nazi Party in 1929, Goebbels helped Hitler bring the Nazis to power in 1933. During Nazi rule, Goebbels worked at persuading the German public to support the Hitler regime. When Germany fell, Goebbels and his wife, Magda, poisoned their six children. Then, at Goebbels' request, a Nazi attendant shot Goebbels and his wife to death.

HERMANN WILHELM GORING (1893–1946) was second to Adolf Hitler

as a leader of Nazi Germany. He became reich marshal and commanded the German air force. He also directed the buildup of Germany's war industry before the outbreak of World War II in 1939. Goring, also spelled Goering, had earned a distinguished record in World War I (1914–1918). In that war, he served as the last commander of the famous squadron of fighter aircraft previously led by Baron Manfred von Richthofen.

Goring was born at Rosenheim on January 12, 1893, and became one of Hitler's followers in the early 1920s. Elected to the Reichstag (German legislature) in 1928, he became its president. This enabled him to frustrate democratic procedures and help Hitler gain unlimited power in 1933. At the start of World War II, Hitler chose Goring as his chief aide. But Goring's influence declined when the air force failed to subdue England or stop the invasion of the European continent or the bombing of Germany.

Goring loved extravagant entertainment, lavish uniforms, and unusual military decorations. But although he was jovial, he was ruthless with opponents and rivals. Goring was judged guilty of war crimes at Nuremberg. He committed suicide by taking poison on October 15, 1946, just before he was to be hanged.

RUDOLF HESS (1894–1987) served as

deputy leader of the Nazi Party in Germany during the 1930s. In addition, he was German dictator Adolf Hitler's private secretary and one of his most loyal followers. In May 1941, during World War II, Hess piloted a plane to Scotland to persuade Britain to get out of the war and leave Europe to the Germans. Hess said that Hitler had no knowledge of Hess's plan. Hess was imprisoned in Britain until after the war ended in 1945. Later, at Nuremberg, Germany, Hess was tried and sentenced to life imprisonment for war crimes. He died in Spandau Prison in Berlin on August 17, 1987, at the age of ninety-three. Prison officials reported that Hess had hanged himself in his cell.

Hess was born on April 26, 1894, in Alexandria, Egypt. He served in the German Army in World War I (1914–1918). He became a Nazi in 1920, while a student at the University of Munich. He joined the Nazi Party after hearing its leader, Adolf Hitler, speak. Hitler was imprisoned in 1923 after a failed attempt to overthrow the German government. Hess began serving as Hitler's secretary while the imprisoned Hitler was writing *Mein Kampf* (1925), a book about his life and political ideas. In 1933, after Hitler became head of Germany, he appointed Hess deputy leader of the Nazi Party.

MLA Citation

"Adolf Hitler." *The Southwestern Advantage Topic Source.* Nashville: Southwestern. 2013.

ADDITIONAL RESOURCES

Books to Read

Baynes, Norman, H., ed. *Speeches of Adolf Hitler*. Howard Fertig, 2006.

Kershaw, Ian. *Hitler: A Biography*. Norton, 2010.

Price, Sean S. *Adolf Hitler*. Franklin Watts, 2010.

Schroeder, Christa. *He Was My Chief: The Memoirs of Adolf Hitler's Secretary*. Frontline, 2009.

Weber, Thomas. *Hitler's First War: Adolf Hitler, the Men of the List Regiment, and the First World War*. Oxford, 2010.

Web Sites

Hitler Comes to Power

http://www.ushmm.org/education/forstudents

This is the first Web page in an on-line overview of the Holocaust for students presented by the United States Holocaust Museum.

Holocaust Denial

http://www.adl.org/hate-patrol/holocaust.asp

The Anti-Defamation League provides information about an anti-Semitic propaganda movement that seeks to deny the reality of the Holocaust.

Teacher's Guide to the Holocaust

http://fcit.coedu.usf.edu/Holocaust/

From the Florida Center for Instructional Technology, College of Education, University of South Florida, an overview of the people and events of the Holocaust presented through text, documents, photographs, art, and literature.

The First Steps Leading to the Final Solution

http://remember.org/Facts.root.solution.html

Information about events leading to the Holocaust, the destruction of the Jews in Europe by Hitler's Third Reich.

The Holocaust: A Guide for Teachers

http://remember.org/guide/index.html

Linda Hurwitz, director of The Holocaust Center of Greater Pittsburgh, prepared this teacher guide, which includes 11 units. Presented by the Cybrary of the Holocaust.

Search Strings

Persecution of the Jews

nazi concentration camps jewish persecution (59,600)

jews world war+II persecution refugees (48,200)

jews world war+II genocide adolf Hitler (25,000)

Hitler's Leadership

nazi leadership restore economy germany adolf Hitler (14,000)

hitler politician organizer leadership (10,300)

Mein Kampf

mein kampf hitler beliefs theories ethics (3,960)

mein kampf hitler author beliefs ideas democracy communism dictatorship (3,300)

Hitler's New Order

Hitler's New Order reordering German society (31,700)

New Order society rules regulations activities germany Hitler (37,400)

BACKGROUND INFORMATION

The World Remembers D-Day (1994)

Fifty years after the historic World War II invasion that liberated France from the Germans, the Allies gather once again on the beaches of Normandy.

By James L. Stokesbury

D-Day—June 6, 1944—the invasion of Nazi-occupied Europe, was the dramatic high point of World War II (1939–1945) and the beginning of the end for Germany's Adolf Hitler and his Third Reich. The epic assault, across the English Channel and onto the heavily defended beaches of Normandy, on the northern coast of France, was the largest seaborne invasion in history. For the millions of men and women who planned and carried out the operation—soldiers, sailors, airmen, and civilians—it was the single most important public event of their lives.

On June 6, 1994, thousands of D-Day veterans gathered in France to commemorate the fiftieth anniversary of D-Day. The ceremonies were an emotional celebration of sacrifice and survival and eventual triumph. The visiting celebrants were from the United States, the senior partner in the Allied forces on D-Day; the two other nations playing leading roles in the invasion, Canada and the United Kingdom; and veterans of the French and Polish armies who also confronted the Germans on D-Day. In addition, France played host to all the official and private visitors to the battlegrounds and towns of Normandy.

Germany excluded from D-Day celebrations

Germany, to the dismay of many Germans, was excluded from the ceremonies. Several arguments were put forth in favor of German participation: that the hatreds of World War II are long past, that thousands of German soldiers killed during the D-Day assault are buried in Normandy, and that many Germans who lived during the Nazi era feel that they, too, were victims of Hitler's tyranny. Nonetheless, the French government decided to invite only the Allied nations that were involved in the invasion.

Using that criterion, France also declined to invite representatives from Russia, part of the former Soviet Union. Although the Soviet Union was one of the Allies in 1944, it did not take part in D-Day. It was, however, an important factor in the success of the invasion. At the time, the Soviet army was fighting a huge German force that had invaded Russia in 1941. If the hundreds of thousands of German soldiers in Russia had been available for the defense of Normandy, the D-Day invasion would have been much harder for the Western Allies.

But controversies over who was included in the ceremonies and who was excluded paled before the sheer emotional power of the thousands of men and women who gathered to remember D-Day. Some had returned to Normandy for the first time since the war.

We are the children of your sacrifice

The commemoration, spread over several days and culminating on June 6, included a series of reenactments of D-Day events. The main ceremonies were held on June 6 at the invasion beaches. The American cemetery overlooking Omaha Beach, the most storied of those battlegrounds, was the site of the day's largest gathering. French President François Mitterrand presided over the program, and speakers included U.S. President Bill Clinton. Standing in sunlight that broke through overcast skies and illuminated the many rows of white headstones, Clinton said, "When they were young, these men saved the world....We are the children of your sacrifice."

Fifty years before, when the battle of D-Day had yet to be decided, those men had jumped out of airplanes in the dark, hurtled into the night-shrouded French countryside in rickety gliders, or staggered onto beaches under heavy enemy fire. Despite the many medals that were awarded after the battle, almost every veteran attending the ceremonies denied having exhibited any special heroism, insisting that they were just doing a job that needed to be done. But it was a monumental job. The liberation of "Fortress Europe" from Nazi domination was one of the greatest military achievements of this century.

Germany's iron grip on Western Europe from June 1940

Nazi Germany had ruled nearly all of Western Europe since June 1940, when its forces conquered France and drove the British army into the sea. The Germans anticipated that the Western Allies would eventually strike back from their stronghold in Britain. But even after the United States entered the war in December 1941, the Allies were too weak to challenge German power directly in a cross-channel invasion. Instead, they were forced to fight a long diversionary campaign against German forces in North Africa and then, from 1943 on, in Italy. Meanwhile, the Soviet Union grappled with the Germans on the huge Eastern Front, dealing several crushing defeats to Hitler's armies.

Buildup and anticipation—on both sides

For all that time, the Western Allies sought to assemble an invasion force in England that would be strong enough to land in France—and to stay there. In January 1944, American General Dwight D. Eisenhower, who had been named supreme commander of the Allied Expeditionary Force in Europe, arrived in London to head the immense undertaking. The Normandy invasion would be the largest and probably the most dangerous operation of the entire war.

The buildup had begun in 1942, and by the spring of 1944 people joked that if the invasion did not come soon, southern England would tilt and sink under the weight of personnel and war material. Altogether there were more than 2.5 million men in uniform, tens of thousands of trucks and tanks, more than 10,000 planes, and 5,300 vessels, ranging from battleships and cruisers to landing craft.

On the far side of the channel, some 50,000 German troops, under the command of Field Marshal Erwin Rommel, manned the beach defenses and waited. Under Rommel's direction, the Germans had spent much of the year fortifying the defenses of the so-called Atlantic Wall. The French coastline bristled with landing-craft obstacles, concrete bunkers, guns of every caliber, and six million explosive mines. Rommel's plan for defeating the expected invasion force was to pin the Allies down on the beaches and then drive them into the sea with his armored divisions. But the Germans were kept guessing about where the invasion would come. An elaborate Allied deception plan, complete with dummy tanks and imaginary armies sending out radio messages, convinced the Germans that the landings would be farther to the north, near Calais, where the channel is narrowest.

A plan to strike at Normandy

But the Allies had decided to strike at Normandy. Eisenhower's invasion plan, dubbed Operation Overlord, called for a force of more than 176,000 men in nine divisions to land in France on the first day. During the night prior to D-Day, British and American paratroopers and glider-borne soldiers would land behind German lines to protect the flanks of the invasion force from German counterattacks and to capture bridges and other important targets. In the morning, after a heavy shore bombardment by planes and ships to soften German defenses, the landing forces would come ashore at five beaches, code-named Gold, Sword, Juno, Omaha, and Utah. Gold and Sword were British; Juno, Canadian; and Omaha and Utah, American.

By early June, all the pieces of Operation Overlord were in place, and Eisenhower was faced with the decision of when to launch the invasion. The schedule of tides in the English Channel indicated that June 5, 6, and 7 would be the best days for the landings. On those days, there would be a low tide near dawn on the French coast and bright moonlight. On June 5, the channel was whipped up by a storm, but weather forecasters issued a cautious prediction for calm seas on June 6. Rather than

General Eisenhower in England

delay the invasion for two weeks until the desired conditions recurred and risk losing the element of surprise, Eisenhower gave the order for the invasion to proceed. By nightfall, the great armada was on its way.

June 6, 1944: first forces land and the Germans wonder

During the night, the glider and parachute forces landed at a number of sites in Normandy. These advance troops suffered high casualties, particularly the American paratroopers, who came down in widely scattered groups and had difficulty regrouping. Some paratroopers ran into heavy enemy resistance, while others drowned in areas that the Germans had flooded. Nonetheless, the airborne troops managed to carry out most of their objectives.

In the predawn hours of D-Day, Allied ships and planes pounded German positions along the coast. Then, as the sky turned light, the bombardment was lifted and swarms of landing craft headed for shore. Now, for the first time, the German defenders could see the immensity of what was bearing down on them from the sea. But even then, the German high command in Berlin was still so convinced that Calais was the Allied target that they dismissed the Normandy landings as a diversionary action. For hours, the Germans held back their armored divisions as they waited in vain for the "real" invasion.

Onto the beaches and into France

While the Germans delayed, the Allies were gaining a foothold on the beaches. The British and Canadian landings went more or less as planned, though resistance was heavy. At Utah Beach, where thin German defenses had been torn up by naval guns, American troops landed with no difficulty. But the landing at Omaha Beach was nearly a disaster. The first wave of troops, wading through neck-deep water full of mines and obstacles and swept by intense German fire, was almost wiped out. Many of the men who were not shot, drowned. But those who made it to shore finally took control of the beach. They were helped by Army Rangers, who destroyed a major gun emplacement at a coastal overlook called Pointe du Hoc, and by U.S. Navy destroyers that came in close to shore to blast German positions.

By the end of the day, more than 155,000 Allied troops were securely ashore at the five landing sites and were moving inland. Allied dead, wounded, and missing amounted to nearly 5,000. German casualties, though hard to determine, were apparently slightly lower.

After June 6—breakout from Normandy and liberation of France

After June 6, the Allies built up their forces rapidly—by the end of the month, they had more than one million troops in France. In the weeks after the invasion, Allied divisions waged a series of fierce battles with the Germans, and British and American planes by the thousands bombed and strafed German positions at every opportunity. But the Germans fought back stubbornly, stalling the Allied advance. Finally, beginning in August, the Allies broke out of Normandy, liberated all of France, and pressed on toward the German frontier.

Although much bitter combat was still to come—most notably a desperate December 1944 German counterattack remembered as the Battle of the Bulge—the outcome of the war was no longer in doubt. Pummeled on the west by the Allies and on the east by the advancing Soviet army, Germany's fate was sealed. On April 30, 1945, with his "Thousand-Year Reich" in ruins, Hitler committed suicide in his underground bunker in Berlin. On May 7, Germany surrendered.

Hitler had clung to impossible visions of victory almost to the last, but a prediction by Rommel as he prepared for the cross-channel invasion—"The war will be won or lost on the beaches"—had proved correct. Once they had overrun the coastal defenses, the Allies could be bloodied but not beaten. D-Day thus signaled the ultimate end of Nazi Germany.

American soldiers landing on the coast of France

Rosa Louise Parks

Rosa Louise Parks (1913–2005) was an African American woman who refused to give up her seat to a white passenger on a bus in Montgomery, Alabama, on December 1, 1955. She was arrested for violating the city laws that required racial segregation on the city buses. Montgomery's black leaders chose Martin Luther King, Jr. to lead the organization that would use Parks's arrest to trigger a boycott of the bus system. This event initiated the civil rights movement in the United States.

HOT topics

- Montgomery Bus Boycott
- Events That Led to Parks's Decision Not to Give Up Her Seat
- After the Fact

HOT topics

Montgomery Bus Boycott. Rosa Parks' arrest for refusing to give up her seat to a white person was used to initiate a boycott of Montgomery's bus system. Because about three quarters of the bus patrons were African American, boycotting the bus system made a strong statement. African Americans refused to ride the buses in Montgomery from December 5, 1955, until December 20, 1956, when the U.S. Supreme Court ordered Montgomery to desegregate their buses. The Montgomery Improvement Association, under the leadership of Martin Luther King, Jr., organized carpools and weekly meetings in order to keep the African Americans rallied behind the cause. Although King's home was bombed during this time, he continued to insist that African Americans use nonviolent protests to gain civil rights.

HOT topics

Events That Led to Parks's Decision Not to Give Up Her Seat. In 1932, Rosa married Raymond Parks, a member of the National Association for the Advancement of Colored People (NAACP). In 1943, she became secretary of the Montgomery chapter and was secretary for 14 years. In 1944, she worked at Maxwell Air Force Base where she saw life without racial segregation. She also worked for a white couple who, in the summer of 1955, encouraged and sponsored her to attend the Highlander Folk School, an education center for workers' rights and racial equality. The horrendous murder of fourteen-year-old African American Emmett Till, the murders of civil rights activists Lamar Smith and George W. Lee, and the arrest of pregnant 15-year-old Claudette Colvin for refusing to give up her seat to a white person on a Montgomery bus earlier that year were some of the other events that led up to Rosa's decision.

Rosa Parks, about to receive the Congressional Gold Medal

After the Fact. After Rosa Parks was arrested, she was fined $10 plus $4 court costs, she lost her job, and her husband quit his. They eventually moved to Detroit where, in 1965, she began working on the staff of Democrat John Conyers, Jr. as a secretary and receptionist until she retired in 1988. Rosa was awarded the Spingarn Medal, the Presidential Medal of Freedom, and the Congressional Gold Medal. She also wrote an autobiography. She died on October 24, 2005.

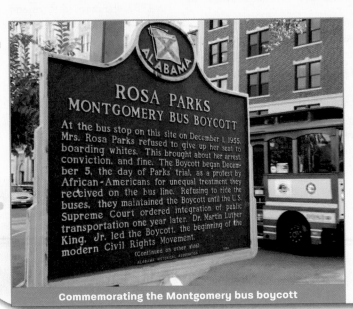

Commemorating the Montgomery bus boycott

TRUE or FALSE?

With her refusal to give up her seat, quiet and dignified Rosa Parks made a loud statement.

THE BASICS

Rosa Louise Parks (1913–2005), an African American civil rights activist, became best known for her role in a 1955 boycott of the Montgomery, Alabama, bus system. Parks triggered the boycott when she refused to give up her seat to a white passenger on a bus. Her action helped bring about the civil rights movement in the United States.

Parks was arrested for violating a city law requiring that whites and blacks sit in separate rows on buses. She refused to give up her seat in the middle of the bus when a white man wished to sit in her row. The front rows were for whites only. The law required blacks to leave their seats in the next rows when all seats in the front rows were taken and other whites still wanted seats.

Even before Parks's arrest, Montgomery's black leaders had been discussing a protest against racial segregation on the city's buses. Parks allowed the leaders to use her arrest to spark a boycott of the bus system.

Rosa Parks (center) riding a newly integrated bus

The leaders formed an organization to run the boycott. Martin Luther King, Jr.—then a Baptist minister in Montgomery—was chosen as president.

For 382 days, from December 5, 1955, to December 20, 1956, thousands of blacks refused to ride Montgomery's buses. Their boycott ended when the U.S. Supreme Court declared segregated seating on the city's buses unconstitutional. The boycott's success encouraged other mass protests demanding civil rights for blacks.

Rosa Louise McCauley was born on February 4, 1913, in Tuskegee, Alabama. She attended Alabama State Teachers College. In 1932, she married Raymond Parks, a barber. She held a variety of jobs and, in 1943, became one of the first women to join the Montgomery Chapter of the National Association for the Advancement of Colored People (NAACP). She served as the organization's secretary from 1943 to 1956.

Parks lost her job as a seamstress as a result of the Montgomery boycott. She moved to Detroit in 1957. From 1967 to 1988, she worked on the Detroit staff of John Conyers, Jr., a Democratic member of the U.S. House of Representatives. In 1979, she won the Spingarn Medal for her work in civil rights. She wrote an autobiography, *Rosa Parks: My Story* (1992). In 1996, she was awarded the Presidential Medal of Freedom. In 1999, she was awarded a Congressional Gold Medal. Parks died on October 24, 2005. Legislation was enacted later that year to add a likeness of Parks to Statuary Hall in the U.S. Capitol.

MLA Citation

"Rosa Louise Parks."
*The Southwestern
Advantage Topic Source.*
Nashville: Southwestern. 2013.

ADDITIONAL RESOURCES

Books to Read

Parks, Rosa, and Haskins, Jim. *Rosa Parks: My Story*. Puffin, 1992.

Siegel, Beatrice. *The Year They Walked: Rosa Parks and the Montgomery Bus Boycott*. MacMillan, 1992.

Web Sites

Rosa Parks Biography

www.achievement.org/autodoc/page/par0bio-1

Biography of the civil rights pioneer.

Rosa Parks: The Woman Who Changed a Nation

http://www.grandtimes.com/rosa.html

Rosa Parks interview and personal biography.

Search Strings

Montgomery Bus Boycott

"Montgomery Bus Boycott" Rosa Parks bus system (5,860)

"Montgomery Bus Boycott" Rosa Parks bus system segregation (24,200)

"Montgomery Bus Boycott""Rosa Parks" bus system desegregation "Supreme Court" Martin Luther King "Montgomery Improvement Association" (512)

Events That Led to Parks's Decision Not to Give Up Her Seat

"Rosa Parks" NAACP "Highlander Folk School""Emmett Till""Lamar Smith" murder "George W. Lee" arrest "Claudette Colvin" (4)

"Rosa Parks" events leading to her decision not to give up her seat on the Montgomery bus (25,200)

"Rosa Parks" events leading to her decision not to give up her seat on the Montgomery bus timeline (968)

After the Fact

"Rosa Parks" timeline after "Montgomery Bus Boycott" (7,320)

"Rosa Parks" arrest monetary fine job loss move to Detroit Spingarn Medal Presidential Medal of Freedom Congressional Gold Medal (20)

"Rosa Parks" arrest monetary fine job loss move to Detroit life events (23,000)

John Fitzgerald Kennedy

John Fitzgerald Kennedy (1917–1963) was the 35th president of the United States and the youngest man ever elected as president. He was also the youngest president to be assassinated. On November 22, 1963, after only two years and 10 months in office, he was shot to death by Lee Harvey Oswald. Kennedy's administration reduced the threat of atomic war with the Soviet Union and promoted the possibility of sending U.S. astronauts to the moon.

HOT topics

Controversy Surrounding His Assassination.

Controversy surrounding JFK's assassination still abounds today. Although Lee Harvey Oswald was arrested for shooting the president, he was in turn assassinated by a man named Jack Ruby just two days after the president's assassination. Because that made it impossible for a trial to take place, the Warren Commission investigated the assassination. It concluded that Oswald had acted alone. Critics disputed the findings, however, believing that Oswald was part of a conspiracy group. During the 1970s, a special committee of the House of Representatives reexamined the evidence surrounding the assassination and concluded that Kennedy "was probably assassinated as a result of a conspiracy." Other authorities, including the National Research Council, disputed the House committee's conclusion.

HOT topics

Issues Faced by Kennedy as President.

Increased racial tensions, a sluggish economy, and unemployment were the major issues that President Kennedy faced within the country. The major concerns he faced in foreign affairs were the threat of nuclear war and the spread of Communist influence. Kennedy was instrumental in averting war during the Cuban missile crisis.

Promotion of Moon Landing.

The first manned space flights occurred during Kennedy's administration. He was enthusiastic about sending the first spacecraft to the moon, and did everything in his power to support that effort. To honor that endeavor, when President Johnson succeeded Kennedy after his assassination, he named the National Aeronautics and Space Administration installation in Florida the John F. Kennedy Space Center.

MEDIUM RANGE BALLISTIC MISSILE BASE IN CUBA
SAN CRISTOBAL

LAUNCH POSITION

MISSILE-READY TENTS

MISSILE ERECTORS

LATE OCTOBER

Aerial photo of Cuban missile base

Famous Speeches and Quotes.

JFK spoke many memorable lines during his lifetime. The following are just two examples still remembered and quoted today. "And so, my fellow Americans: ask not what your country can do for you—ask what you can do for your country."—Source: Inaugural Address, January 20, 1961. "We choose to go to the moon in this decade and do the other things, not because they are easy, but because they are hard."—Source: Address at Rice University in 1962.

President Kennedy greeting Peace Corps volunteers at the White House

TRUE or FALSE?

One of the most successful of Kennedy's programs was the U.S. Peace Corps.

THE BASICS

John Fitzgerald Kennedy (1917–1963) was the youngest man ever elected president of the United States, and he was the youngest ever to die in office. He was shot to death on November 22, 1963, after two years and 10 months as chief executive. The world mourned Kennedy's death, and presidents, premiers, and members of royalty walked behind the casket at his funeral. Kennedy was succeeded as president by Vice President Lyndon B. Johnson.

Kennedy, a Democrat, won the presidency with his "New Frontier" program, after a series of television debates with his Republican opponent, Vice President Richard M. Nixon. At 43, Kennedy was the youngest man ever elected president. (Theodore Roosevelt was 42 when he became president upon the death of William McKinley. He was 46 when he was elected president.) Kennedy was the first president of the Roman Catholic faith. He also was the first president born in the 1900s.

President-elect John F. Kennedy and his wife, Jacqueline

In his inaugural address, President Kennedy declared that "a new generation of Americans" had taken over leadership of the country. He said Americans would "...pay any price, bear any burden, meet any hardship, support any friend, oppose any foe to assure the survival and the success of liberty." He told Americans: "Ask not what your country can do for you— ask what you can do for your country."

Kennedy became widely known by his initials, JFK. He won world respect as the leader of the Free World. He greatly increased U.S. prestige in 1962 when he turned aside the threat of an atomic war with the Soviet Union while carrying out negotiations that resulted in the Soviets withdrawing missiles from Communist Cuba. The Kennedy action marked the start of a period of "thaw" in the Cold War as relations grew friendlier with the Soviet Union. In 1963, the United States, the Soviet Union, and more than 100 other countries signed a treaty outlawing the testing of atomic bombs under water and on or above ground. On the home front, the United States enjoyed its greatest prosperity in history. African Americans' demands for civil rights caused serious domestic problems, but African Americans made greater progress in their quest for equal rights than at any time since the Civil War. During Kennedy's administration, the United States made its first piloted space flights and prepared to send astronauts to the moon.

Early Life

Family background. John Fitzgerald Kennedy was the second son of Joseph Patrick Kennedy (1888–1969) and Rose Fitzgerald Kennedy (1890–1995). The president's ancestors were Irish farmers of Wexford County in southeastern Ireland. His great-grandfather, Patrick Kennedy, left Ireland during the great potato famine of the 1840s and settled in Boston. The president's grandfather, Patrick J. Kennedy, became a state senator and the political "boss" of a ward in Boston.

The president's mother also came from a political family. Her father was John F. ("Honey Fitz") Fitzgerald, a colorful politician. Fitzgerald served in the state senate and the United States House of Representatives. He also served as mayor of Boston for two terms.

Joseph P. Kennedy, the president's father, was a self-made millionaire. During the administration of President Franklin D. Roosevelt, he served as the first chairman of the Securities and Exchange Commission, and as U.S. ambassador to the United Kingdom.

Boyhood. Kennedy was born on May 29, 1917, in Brookline, Massachusetts, a Boston suburb. The other eight Kennedy children were Joseph, Jr. (1915–1944), who was killed in World War II; Rosemary (1918–2005); Kathleen (1920–1948); Eunice (1921–2009); Patricia (1924–2006); Robert F. (1925–1968), who became attorney general under his brother and then served as U.S. senator from New York from 1965 until his assassination; Jean (1928–); and Edward M. "Ted" (1932–2009), who served as a U.S. senator from Massachusetts for 47 years.

The Kennedys moved often, to bigger homes and better neighborhoods, as the family grew and as Joseph Kennedy became wealthier. From Brookline, they moved to Riverdale, New York, then Bronxville, New York, both New York City suburbs.

As the Kennedy children grew up, their parents encouraged them to develop their own talents and interests. Loyalty to each other was important to the Kennedys. But the children also developed a strong competitive spirit. Jack, as his family called him, and Joe, his older brother, were especially strong rivals. Jack was quiet and often shy, but he held his own in fights with Joe. The boys enjoyed playing touch football.

Education. John Kennedy attended elementary schools in Brookline and Riverdale. In 1930, when he was 13 years old, his father sent him to the Canterbury School in New Milford, Connecticut. The next year, he transferred to Choate Academy in Wallingford, Connecticut. Kennedy was graduated from Choate in 1935 at the age of 18. His classmates voted him "most likely to succeed."

Kennedy spent the summer of 1935 in England. He enrolled at Princeton University that fall, but he developed jaundice and left school after Christmas. He entered Harvard University in 1936. There he majored in government and international relations.

In 1939, Kennedy spent the spring and summer in Europe. Traveling from country to country, he interviewed politicians and statesmen. He sent his father detailed reports on their views of the crisis that soon led to World War II in September 1939. Back at Harvard, Kennedy tried to explain in his senior thesis why the United Kingdom had not been ready for war. His thesis, published as *Why England Slept*, became a best-selling book.

Kennedy was graduated *cum laude* in 1940. He then enrolled in the Stanford University graduate business school, but dropped out six months later.

The Kennedy family, 1931

After taking a trip through South America, Kennedy enlisted as a seaman in the U.S. Navy.

War hero. For a few months, Kennedy was stationed in Washington, D.C. He applied for sea duty following the Japanese attack on Pearl Harbor on December 7, 1941. Kennedy was assigned to a PT boat squadron late in 1942. After learning to command one of the small craft, he was commissioned as an ensign.

Kennedy's PT boat was assigned to patrol duty off the Solomon Islands in the South Pacific. Shortly after midnight on August 2, 1943, a Japanese destroyer cut his boat in two. Two of the crewmen were killed. Kennedy and the other 10 men clung all night to the wreckage of their boat. The next morning, Kennedy ordered his men to swim to a nearby island. Despite an injured back, he spent five hours towing one of the disabled crewmen to shore. Kennedy spent most of the next four days in the water, searching for help. On the fifth day, he persuaded friendly islanders on Cross Island to go for help. Kennedy's crew was rescued on August 7. For his heroism and leadership, Kennedy received the Navy and Marine Corps Medal. For being wounded in combat, he was awarded the Purple Heart.

In December 1943, the Navy returned Lieutenant Kennedy to the United States. He was suffering from malaria and his injured back gave him great pain. After recovering, Kennedy spent the rest of his naval service as an instructor and in various military hospitals. He then had a short career as a newspaper reporter.

Career in Congress

The Kennedys had thought Jack would become a writer or a teacher. His brother Joe was going to be the family politician. But Joe's death in 1944 changed Jack's future. Later, as a U.S. Senator, Kennedy said: "Just as I went into politics because Joe died, if anything happens to me tomorrow, my brother Bobby would run for my seat in the Senate. And if Bobby died, Teddy would take over for him."

U.S. representative. Kennedy began his political career in 1946. He ran for the U.S. House of Representatives. He opposed nine others for nomination in the solidly Democratic 11th Congressional District of Massachusetts. He won the nomination and went on to easily defeat his Republican opponent.

The 1946 campaign set a pattern that played a major part in Kennedy's political success. His brothers and sisters helped him win the nomination. So did his mother. The women organized teas in the homes of voters. But his father was not active in Kennedy's campaigns. His isolationism before World War II, his conservatism, and his wealth made him a controversial figure.

In January 1947, Kennedy took his seat in Congress. Later that year, he became seriously ill, and doctors discovered that he was suffering from a malfunction of the adrenal glands. To control the ailment, he had to take medicine daily for the rest of his life. But he kept that fact from public view. In

On a sailboat in Cape Cod, shortly before their marriage

Congress, Kennedy voted for most of the social welfare programs of President Harry S. Truman. He was reelected to the House in 1948 and 1950.

Campaign for the Senate. In April 1952, Kennedy announced that he would oppose Republican Senator Henry Cabot Lodge, Jr. Lodge, a popular and experienced legislator, seemed certain to win reelection.

Kennedy's mother and his brothers and sisters and their spouses joined him in the campaign. Dwight D. Eisenhower, the Republican presidential candidate, carried Massachusetts in the 1952 election. But Kennedy upset Lodge by 70,637 votes.

Kennedy's family. In 1951, Kennedy met his future wife at a dinner party in Washington, D.C. Jacqueline "Jackie" Lee Bouvier (July 28, 1929–May 19, 1994) was the daughter of a wealthy Wall Street broker, John V. Bouvier III. She had attended Vassar College and the Sorbonne in Paris. When she met Kennedy, she was a student at George Washington University in Washington. Later, she worked as an inquiring photographer for the *Washington Times-Herald*. She and Kennedy were married on September 12, 1953. A daughter was stillborn on August 23, 1956, and was unnamed. Their daughter Caroline was born on November 27, 1957. Their son John F., Jr., was born on November 25, 1960. He was killed in an airplane crash in 1999. Another son, Patrick Bouvier, was born prematurely on August 7, 1963. He died on August 9, 1963. Five years after Kennedy's death, Mrs. Kennedy married Aristotle Onassis, a Greek millionaire.

Senator Kennedy focused at first on helping industries in Massachusetts and New England. He sponsored bills to help such industries as fishing, textile manufacturing, and watch-making. Kennedy served on the Senate Labor Committee, and the Government Operations Committee, chaired by Senator Joseph R. McCarthy. Robert Kennedy, his brother, served on the Government Operations Committee staff as an assistant counsel.

At the time, McCarthy was the most controversial figure in American politics. Many persons praised him for his attacks on Communist influence in government. Others criticized McCarthy because they felt he had violated the civil liberties of persons investigated by his committee. Kennedy felt that McCarthy often abused his power and was endangering the honor of the Senate. Kennedy was ill when the Senate condemned McCarthy in

1954. But he said later that if he had been present, he would have voted for the condemnation.

During his first Senate term, Kennedy's back caused him severe pain. In October 1954, and in February 1955, he underwent corrective surgery. While recovering, he wrote a book about some of the brave deeds of U.S. senators. For the book, *Profiles in Courage*, Kennedy was awarded the Pulitzer Prize for biography in 1957.

In 1957, Kennedy was appointed to the Senate Foreign Relations Committee, a key assignment in Congress. He criticized the foreign policy of the Republican administration, and supported a program of increased aid to underdeveloped countries.

Kennedy also worked for moderate legislation to end alleged corruption in labor unions. He was a member of a Senate committee investigating racketeering in labor-management relations. Kennedy's brother Robert was counsel for the committee. The Kennedys and other committee members engaged in dramatic arguments with controversial labor leaders, including James R. "Jimmy" Hoffa, of the Teamsters Union.

Bid for the vice presidency. In June 1956, a movement to nominate Kennedy for vice president had gained strength among Democratic leaders. At the party's national convention in Chicago, Kennedy made the presidential nominating speech for former Governor Adlai E. Stevenson of Illinois. The delegates chose Stevenson to oppose Eisenhower for the second time. Kennedy worked furiously for the vice presidential nomination. But he lost to Senator Estes Kefauver of Tennessee after a nip-and-tuck battle.

Election as President

Steps to the White House. Kennedy began working for the 1960 presidential nomination right after the 1956 convention. He spent nearly every weekend campaigning. In 1958, Kennedy won reelection to the Senate by a majority of 874,608 votes.

Many Democratic leaders thought Kennedy had several disadvantages as a presidential candidate. His main drawback was his religion. Alfred E. Smith, the only Roman Catholic ever nominated for president by a major political party, had been badly defeated in 1928. Other possible shortcomings included Kennedy's youth, his family wealth, and his relative inexperience in international affairs. Some Democrats opposed Kennedy because they

During the presidential campaign

thought he was too conservative and because he never actively opposed Senator McCarthy.

Kennedy decided that the key to the presidential nomination would be to win as many state primary elections as he could. He believed that victories in the primaries would prove he could win the presidency. Kennedy entered and won primaries in seven states.

At the Democratic national convention, Kennedy's chief opponents for the presidential nomination were Senator Lyndon B. Johnson of Texas, Senator Stuart Symington of Missouri, and Stevenson. Kennedy won on the first ballot. The delegates, at the request of Kennedy, nominated Johnson for vice president.

The Republicans chose Vice President Richard M. Nixon to oppose Kennedy for the presidency. Kennedy's old opponent, Henry Cabot Lodge, Jr., then-U.S. delegate to the United Nations (UN), was Nixon's running mate.

The 1960 campaign was a hard-fought race. Both candidates were young, vigorous campaigners. At first, most experts believed Nixon would win. He had the advantage of being vice president under Eisenhower, an unusually popular president.

But Kennedy was not as unknown as some people believed. His good looks, wealth, and attractive wife had made him a popular subject for articles in newspapers and magazines. Television also helped Kennedy greatly during his four televised debates with Nixon. His poise helped answer criticism that he lacked the maturity needed for the presidency. The debates marked the first time that presidential candidates argued campaign issues face-to-face.

Nixon ran chiefly on the record of the Eisenhower administration. Kennedy promised to lead Americans to a "New Frontier." He charged that, under the Republicans, the United States had lost ground to the Soviet Union in the Cold War.

Kennedy defeated Nixon by fewer than 115,000 popular votes. But he won a clear majority of votes in the Electoral College. Kennedy received 303 electoral votes to 219 for Nixon. Senator Harry F. Byrd of Virginia received 15 electoral votes.

Kennedy was inaugurated president on January 20, 1961. As he took charge of the federal government, he faced such internal problems as increased racial tensions, unemployment, and a sluggish economy. In foreign affairs, he faced the continuing spread of Communist influence, and the threat of nuclear war.

The National Scene

The New Frontier, the name Kennedy gave to his program, got off to a slow start. But the 87th Congress finally began passing measures sponsored by the administration. In April 1961, the legislators approved aid to economically depressed areas. In May, Congress approved an increase in the minimum hourly wage from $1 to $1.25. In September 1962, Congress passed Kennedy's Trade Expansion Act. The act gave the president wide powers to cut tariffs so the United States could trade freely with the European Economic Community (now part of the European Union).

One of the most successful of Kennedy's programs was the U.S. Peace Corps. It was launched by executive order in March 1961, and was later authorized by Congress. The corps sent thousands of Americans abroad to help people in developing nations raise their standards of living. The Peace Corps seemed to carry the enthusiasm of the president to the people of other countries, who often called it "Kennedy's Corps."

Kennedy also met major legislative defeats. Congress rejected a cabinet-level Department of Urban Affairs and Kennedy's plan for medical care for the aged. Both measures later passed during Johnson's presidency. Kennedy's farm program also suffered defeats.

Kennedy reorganized the nation's defense policies by increasing conventional weapons. He wanted to be prepared for nonnuclear wars and to make every effort to avoid using nuclear weapons.

Business and labor. In March 1962, the major steel producers signed a contract with the steelworkers union that increased workers' benefits, but not their wages. Kennedy praised the contract, which he said would help prevent inflation. On April 10, the United States Steel Corporation led a move to raise steel prices $6 a ton. Kennedy angrily denounced the move as causing needless inflation, and the companies canceled it.

In May, prices on the New York Stock Exchange made their sharpest drop since 1929. Many people blamed the Kennedy administration. They felt the president's action toward the steel companies reflected an anti-business attitude. The president tried to answer these charges in a speech. He said there are three great ideas, or "myths," in our domestic affairs that may prevent effective action: (1) that the federal debt is too large; (2) that the

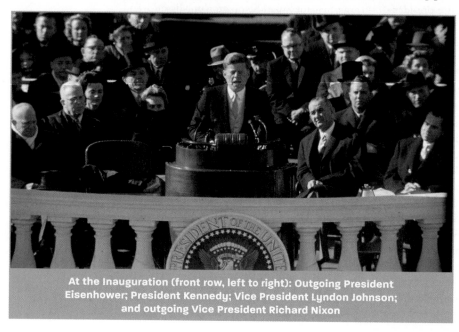

At the Inauguration (front row, left to right): Outgoing President Eisenhower; President Kennedy; Vice President Lyndon Johnson; and outgoing Vice President Richard Nixon

federal government is too big; and (3) that business cannot place its confidence in his administration.

Kennedy aided business by increasing tax benefits for companies investing in new equipment. In 1963, he proposed a $10 billion tax cut, which included lowering corporate taxes. He thought that the public would be able to spend more if taxes were cut. The increased spending would generate new business, and the taxes received from an expanded economy would more than offset the revenue lost in the tax cut.

Civil rights. Demands for equal rights for African Americans became the major domestic issue during the Kennedy administration. In 1961, a group of nonviolent *freedom riders*, made up of blacks and whites, entered Montgomery, Alabama, by bus to test local segregation laws. White rioters attacked them, and Attorney General Robert F. Kennedy sent U.S. marshals to the city to help restore order. In 1962, James Meredith became the first black to enroll at the University of Mississippi, despite much opposition. Two people were killed in the rioting that followed on the university campus at Oxford. The president ordered 3,000 federal troops to the area to restore order.

In 1963, demands by African Americans for equal civil and economic rights increased. Racial protests and demonstrations took place across the United States. In May 1963, rioting broke out in Birmingham, Alabama. In June, Kennedy federalized the Alabama National Guard to enforce the integration of the University of Alabama. Kennedy federalized the Guard again in September to ensure the integration of public schools in three Alabama cities. On August 28, 1963, more than 200,000 persons staged a *Freedom March* in Washington, D.C., to demonstrate their demands for equal rights for blacks.

To meet growing demands of African Americans, Kennedy asked Congress to pass legislation requiring hotels, motels, and restaurants to admit customers regardless of race. He also asked Congress to grant the attorney general authority to begin court suits to desegregate schools on behalf of private citizens unable to start legal action themselves. In requesting the sweeping civil rights legislation, the president said, "The time has come for the Congress of the United States to join with the executive and judicial branches in making it clear to all, that race has no place in American life or law."

Daughter Caroline Kennedy

Other developments. Kennedy's Democratic Party gained four seats in the Senate and lost only two seats in the House in the 1962 elections. This was only the third time in the 1900s that the party in power increased its representation in Congress in a midterm election. In his second year in office, Kennedy appointed two justices of the Supreme Court. The first was Byron R. White, then Deputy Attorney General. The second was Secretary of Labor Arthur J. Goldberg.

Life in the White House. The Kennedys brought youth and informality to the White House. Caroline and John, Jr., were the youngest children of a president to live in the White House in more than 60 years. Caroline's antics and bright comments amused the nation.

Women in many countries copied Jacqueline Kennedy's stylish clothes and hairstyle. In 1961, Mrs. Kennedy flew to Europe with her husband. Wherever she went, huge crowds gathered. President Kennedy presented himself to a Paris luncheon by saying, "I am the man who accompanied Jacqueline Kennedy to Paris. . ." In March 1962, Mrs. Kennedy toured Pakistan and India without the president. Mrs. Kennedy won praise for her redecoration of the White House. She gathered furnishings of past presidents and made the mansion a historic showplace and a tourist attraction.

The president gave recognition to the creative arts by appointing a special adviser on the arts. Many artists were invited to the White House.

Foreign Affairs

Cuba. On April 17, 1961, Cuban rebels invaded their homeland to overthrow Fidel Castro, the Communist-supported dictator. The assault ended in disaster. President Kennedy accepted blame for the ill-fated invasion, which had been planned by the United States.

Another Cuban crisis erupted in October 1962, when the United States learned that the Soviet Union had installed missiles in Cuba capable of striking U.S. cities. Kennedy ordered the U.S. Navy to *quarantine* (blockade) Cuba. Navy ships were ordered to turn back ships delivering Soviet missiles to Cuba. Kennedy also called about 14,000 Air Force reservists to active duty.

For a week, war seemed likely. Then, Soviet Premier Nikita S. Khrushchev ordered all Soviet offensive missiles removed. Kennedy then lifted the quarantine. For more details, see Cuban missile crisis section.

Berlin. In 1961, the Soviet Union threatened to give Communist East Germany control over the West's air and land supply routes to Berlin. The threat was part of a Soviet effort to end the combined American, British, French, and Soviet control of Berlin, begun in 1945, when World War II ended. The Western nations opposed any threat to the freedom of West Berlin.

In June 1961, Kennedy discussed Berlin with Khrushchev at a two-day meeting in Vienna, Austria. Nothing was settled, and the crisis deepened. Both countries increased their military strength. In August, the East Germans built a wall between East and West Berlin to prevent persons from fleeing to the West. Kennedy called up about 145,000 members of the National Guard and reservists to strengthen U.S. military defense. They were released about 10 months later.

With Nikita Khruschev at their summit meeting in Vienna

Other developments. In 1961, the United States established the Alliance for Progress, a 10-year program of aid for Latin American countries that agreed to begin democratic reforms. Kennedy hoped this program would bring social and political reform as well as fight poverty.

In 1961, Kennedy was interviewed by Khrushchev's son-in-law, then editor of *Izvestia*, the Soviet government newspaper. *Izvestia* printed the entire interview.

In 1962, Congress approved a plan to purchase up to $100 million worth of bonds to help finance the UN.

The western Atlantic alliance remained strong, but Kennedy had trouble establishing a united NATO nuclear force. President Charles de Gaulle refused to commit France to the NATO nuclear force. He preferred an independent role for his country. Kennedy made a 10-day tour of Europe in the summer of 1963. He visited West Germany, Italy, Ireland, and the United Kingdom.

Southeast Asia continued to be a trouble spot. Kennedy ordered U.S. military advisers to the area in 1961 and 1962 when the Communists threatened South Vietnam and Thailand. Kennedy also sent advisers to Laos. In the summer and autumn of 1963, the United States severely criticized the South Vietnamese government headed by Ngo Dinh Diem for its repressive policies against the country's Buddhists. The government imprisoned many Buddhist leaders and students who were leading demonstrations against the Diem government. Kennedy sent former Republican senator and vice presidential candidate Henry Cabot Lodge, Jr., to South Vietnam as ambassador in 1963.

Arms control. In September 1961, the Soviets resumed testing atomic weapons. The tests broke an unofficial test ban that had lasted nearly three years. The United States began testing shortly after the Soviets resumed their tests, but the United States conducted its tests underground, which created no dangerous fallout. But in April 1962, the United States resumed testing in the atmosphere over the Pacific Ocean.

In July 1963, the Soviet Union, the United States, and the United Kingdom signed a treaty banning atomic testing in the atmosphere, outer space, and underwater. Testing was permitted underground. Many countries that had no atomic weapons also signed the treaty.

Kennedy's Assassination

John F. Kennedy was shot to death by an assassin on November 22, 1963, as he rode through the streets of Dallas. His death continued the unhappy coincidence that, until that time, every American president since William H. Harrison who was elected in a year that ended in "0" had died while in office. These presidents and the years of election were Harrison, who was elected in 1840; Abraham Lincoln, elected in 1860; James A. Garfield, 1880; William McKinley, 1900; Warren G. Harding, 1920; and Franklin D. Roosevelt, 1940.

Kennedy was succeeded by his vice president, Lyndon B. Johnson. Johnson was the first Southerner to become president since Andrew Johnson succeeded Lincoln when Lincoln was assassinated in 1865.

The death of the president. Kennedy came to Texas accompanied by his wife and Vice President and Mrs. Lyndon B. Johnson. The chief purpose of his trip was to heal a split in the Texas Democratic Party before the 1964 presidential campaign in which Kennedy planned to run for a second term. The Kennedy party left Washington, D.C., on Thursday, November 21, and flew to San Antonio, Houston, and Fort Worth. At 11:37 a.m. the next day, the president's plane arrived in Dallas after a short trip from Fort Worth.

Plans called for the president, Mrs. Kennedy, Johnson, and others to travel in a motorcade through the streets of Dallas to the Dallas Trade Mart. Kennedy was scheduled to speak there at a luncheon. After leaving the plane, Kennedy entered an open limousine for the trip to the Trade Mart. The president sat in the rear seat on the right side of the car. His wife, Jacqueline, sat on his left. Texas Governor John B. Connally sat in a "jump" seat in front of the president, and Mrs. Connally sat to her husband's left.

Behind the president's car was a limousine filled with Secret Service agents. Vice President and Mrs. Johnson rode in the third car, also accompanied by Secret Service men. Many other special security precautions had been taken. Dallas had a reputation as a center for people who strongly opposed Kennedy. But friendly, cheering crowds lined the streets.

At 12:30 p.m., the cars approached an expressway for the last leg of the trip. Suddenly, three shots rang out and the president slumped down, hit in the neck and head. Connally received a bullet in the back. Mrs. Kennedy held her stricken

The Dallas motorcade, just before the assassination

husband's head in her lap as the limousine raced to nearby Parkland Hospital.

Doctors worked desperately to save the president, but he died at 1:00 p.m. without regaining consciousness. Doctors said that Kennedy had no chance to survive when brought into the hospital. Governor Connally, although seriously wounded, later recovered.

The new president. Television and radio flashed the news of the shooting to a shocked world. Vice President Johnson raced to the hospital and remained until Kennedy died. Then, he went to the airport where the presidential plane waited. Mrs. Kennedy and the coffin holding her husband's body arrived later. At 2:39 p.m., U.S. District Judge Sarah T. Hughes administered the oath of office to Johnson, who became the 36th president of the United States. As Johnson took the oath in the airplane, he was flanked by his wife and by Mrs. Kennedy.

Then the plane carrying the new chief executive and his wife, the body of the dead president, and the late president's widow returned to Washington. When the plane arrived, Johnson told the nation: "This is a sad time for all people. We have suffered a loss that cannot be weighed. . ."

The death of Oswald. Witnesses said the shots that killed the president came from a sixth-floor window of the Texas School Book Depository, a building along the route of the motorcade. Police raced into the building but could not find the killer. Then they began a search for a building employee who had left the scene a few minutes after the shooting. About 1:15 p.m., the employee, Lee Harvey Oswald, is said to have shot and killed a Dallas policeman, J. D. Tippit, while resisting arrest.

Oswald was finally arrested in a theater a short while later, and was charged with the murders of President Kennedy and Tippit. Oswald had been given a hardship discharge from the U.S. Marines and had once tried to become a Soviet citizen. An admitted Marxist, Oswald had a Soviet wife. He also had been active in the Fair Play for Cuba Committee, a group that supported Cuba's Communist dictator Fidel Castro.

The police questioned Oswald for two days, but he denied both murders. Dallas police claimed that the evidence against Oswald was overwhelming. The murder weapon, an Italian rifle with a telescopic sight, was found hidden in the School Book Depository. The rifle had been purchased by Oswald from a mail-order firm for $12.78. Oswald's palm prints were found on the weapon.

At President Kennedy's funeral (front, left to right): Edward (Ted) Kennedy; daughter Caroline; wife, Jacqueline; Robert Kennedy; and John Jr.

On Sunday, November 24, two days after the assassination, Oswald was scheduled to be taken from the Dallas city jail to the county jail. As he was being led to an armored car for the trip, a Dallas nightclub owner, Jack Ruby (or Rubinstein), stepped out of the crowd and shot Oswald to death. A nationwide television audience witnessed the shooting. Oswald was taken to the same hospital where the president died. He died at 1:07 p.m., 48 hours after Kennedy's death. Jack Ruby was convicted of Oswald's murder in 1964, but the conviction was overturned in 1966. Ruby died in 1967, awaiting a new trial.

The world mourns. The sudden death of the young and vigorous American president shocked the world. Kennedy's body was brought back to the White House and placed in the East Room for 24 hours. On the Sunday after the assassination, the president's flag-draped coffin was carried to the Capitol Rotunda to lie in state. Throughout the day and night, hundreds of thousands of people filed past the guarded casket.

Representatives from more than 90 countries attended the funeral on November 25. Among them were Irish president Eamon de Valera, French president Charles de Gaulle, Belgian King Baudouin, Ethiopian Emperor Haile Selassie, Philippine president Diosdado Macapagal, and West German president Heinrich Luebke.

Kennedy was buried with full military honors at Arlington National Cemetery across the Potomac River from Washington, D.C. At the close of the funeral service, Mrs. Kennedy lighted an "eternal flame" to burn over the president's grave. When Mrs. Kennedy died in 1994, she was buried next to her late husband.

In one of his first acts, President Johnson named the National Aeronautics and Space Administration installation in Florida the John F. Kennedy Space Center. Other public buildings and geographical sites throughout the world were named for Kennedy. Congress voted funds for the John F. Kennedy Center for the Performing Arts in Washington, D.C. The United Kingdom made 1 acre (0.4 hectare) of ground permanent United States territory as part of a Kennedy memorial at Runnymede. In 1979, the John F. Kennedy Library opened in Boston.

The assassination controversy. The Warren Commission, headed by Chief Justice Earl Warren, investigated the assassination. In 1964, the commission reported that Oswald had acted alone. But critics disputed the findings. Many believed Oswald was part of a group that had planned to murder Kennedy.

During the 1970s, a special committee of the United States House of Representatives reexamined the evidence surrounding the assassination. The committee accepted the testimony of *acoustical* (sound) experts who claimed that shots were fired from two locations along the motorcade at almost the same time. In 1978, the committee concluded that Kennedy "was probably assassinated as a result of a conspiracy." But other authorities strongly disputed the committee's conclusion. In 1982, the National Research Council, a scientific research

Jackie Kennedy and John Jr.

organization, also disagreed with the House committee's finding.

JACQUELINE KENNEDY ONASSIS

(1929–1994), the wife of President John F. Kennedy, was one of the most popular first ladies in United States history. President Kennedy was assassinated in 1963. Five years later, Mrs. Kennedy married Aristotle Onassis, a wealthy Greek businessman.

Jacqueline Kennedy Onassis was born in Southampton, New York. Her maiden name was Jacqueline Lee Bouvier. She graduated from George Washington University in 1951. From 1951 to 1953, she worked for the *Washington Times-Herald*, where she produced a daily column as an inquiring photographer. She asked people human-interest questions, such as whether they had done their Christmas shopping, and wrote up the replies. She took pictures of the people, which accompanied the column.

In 1953, Jacqueline Bouvier married Kennedy, who was then a U.S. senator. The couple had two children who survived infancy: Caroline, born in 1957; and John F., Jr., 1960. A daughter was stillborn in 1956, and a son born prematurely in 1963 lived only two days. Kennedy became president in 1961. As first lady, Jacqueline—who was often called "Jackie"—became known for her elegance in hairstyle, clothing, and other elements of fashion. She also won admiration for her composure and dignity following the assassination of her husband on November 22, 1963.

Jacqueline Kennedy married Onassis in 1968. He died in 1975. From 1975 until her death, Jacqueline worked as an editor for book publishers.

THE CUBAN MISSILE CRISIS

occurred in October 1962 when the United States learned that the Soviet Union had secretly installed missiles in Cuba, about 90 miles (140 kilometers) from Florida. The missiles could have been used to launch nuclear attacks on American cities. The crisis was one of the most serious incidents of the Cold War, a period of intense U.S.-Soviet rivalry that had begun after World War II ended in 1945. Most experts believe that the missile crisis brought the United States and the Soviet Union to the brink of nuclear war.

The Soviet Union had placed the missiles in Cuba earlier in 1962, after Cuban leaders became convinced that the United States was planning to attack Cuba. During the Cold War, Cuba was an ally of the Soviet Union. President John F. Kennedy of the United States learned of the missiles' presence on October 16 and demanded that the Soviet Union remove them. On October 22, he ordered a naval *quarantine* (blockade) of Cuba to stop further shipment of arms.

At first, the United States expected to invade Cuba to destroy the missiles. At one point, an invasion was scheduled for October 29 or October 30. Nearly all of Kennedy's advisers agreed that a landing of U.S. forces in Cuba would probably mean war—most likely nuclear war—with the Soviet Union.

The Soviet Union offered to remove the missiles if the United States would promise not to invade Cuba. It later said that it would not remove the missiles unless the United States would dismantle its military bases in Turkey. Turkey was a U.S. ally that bordered the Soviet Union. Kennedy agreed publicly to dismantle all U.S. missile bases in Turkey. However, to complete the deal, Kennedy and Soviet leader Nikita S. Khrushchev also made a private agreement in which Khrushchev promised to remove all Soviet missiles in Cuba in exchange for Kennedy's promise that the United States would not invade the island. On October 28, the two leaders completed the agreement, ending the crisis.

The agreement between Kennedy and Khrushchev was kept secret because many Americans opposed such a deal. Almost all Americans thus thought that Kennedy had forced the Soviet Union to remove the missiles simply by threatening war. Some experts believe that, as a result, U.S. foreign policy used greater toughness and more threats of force after the crisis.

ADDITIONAL RESOURCES

Books to Read

Level I

Cooper, Ilene. *Jack: The Early Years of John F. Kennedy*. Dutton, 2003.

Spies, Karen B. *John F. Kennedy*. Enslow, 1999.

Uschan, Michael V. *John F. Kennedy*. Lucent Books, 1999.

Level II

Dallek, Robert. *An Unfinished Life: John F. Kennedy, 1917–1963*. Little, Brown, 2003.

Kenney, Charles C. *John Fitzgerald Kennedy*. Public Affairs, 2000.

Swisher, Clarice, ed. *John F. Kennedy*. Greenhaven, 2000.

Web Sites

Cuban Missile Crisis

http://www.wyzant.com/HELP/History/HPOL/JFK/Cuban

Cuban Missile Crisis background and time line.

Jacqueline Bouvier Kennedy Onassis

http://www.whitehouse.gov/about/first-ladies/jacquelinekennedy

Official White House biography of first lady Jacqueline Bouvier Kennedy Onassis.

John F. Kennedy

http://www.whitehouse.gov/history/presidents/jk35.html

Official White House biography of John F. Kennedy. Includes a link to the John F. Kennedy Presidential Library and a link to a biography of Jacqueline Kennedy Onassis.

John Fitzgerald Kennedy (1917–1963) Biographical Information

http://bioguide.congress.gov/scripts/biodisplay.pl?index=K000107

The Biographical Directory of the United States Congress site on John F. Kennedy.

Lunar Exploration

http://nssdc.gsfc.nasa.gov/planetary/lunar/apollo_25th.html

The history of America's moon space program, culminating in the Apollo 11 moon landing of July 1969.

The History Place: John Fitzgerald Kennedy Photo Gallery

http://www.historyplace.com/kennedy/gallery.htm

An extensive gallery of captioned photos of John F. Kennedy, 35th President of the United States.

Search Strings

Controversy Surrounding His Assassination

John Fitzgerald Kennedy assassination controversy Lee Harvey Oswald Jack Ruby (15,100)

John Fitzgerald Kennedy assassination controversy Lee Harvey Oswald Jack Ruby Warren Commission conspiracy (9,300)

John Fitzgerald Kennedy assassination controversy Lee Harvey Oswald "Jack Ruby" "Warren Commission" conspiracy (562)

Issues Faced by Kennedy as President

John Kennedy president issues racial tensions economy unemployment (193,000)

John Kennedy president issues racial tensions economy unemployment Cuban missile crisis nuclear war Communist influences (3,130)

Promotion of Moon Landing

manned space flights moon landing Kennedy (140,000)

promotion of manned space flights moon landing President Kennedy (23,200)

promotion of manned space flights moon landing President Kennedy NASA (15,400)

Famous Speeches and Quotes

John Fitzgerald Kennedy speeches quotes memorable (23,900)

John Fitzgerald Kennedy speeches quotes memorable inaugural address (40,200)

BACKGROUND INFORMATION

The following article was written during the year in which the events took place and reflects the style and thinking of that time.

The Assassination of the President (1964)

It was hot; the sun was blinding; and he had just turned easily, but with grace and precision, as was his style, to wave at the Texans who lined the streets of Dallas—when the sound rapped above the noise. It was a blunt crack, like that of a motorcycle backfiring (which is what his wife thought it was); followed in 6.8 seconds by two more; then suddenly, John Fitzgerald Kennedy lay fallen, his head in his wife's lap. The sniper's bullets had found their mark. Life had left the 35th President of the United States.

The time was approximately 1:30 P.M., E.S.T. (12:30 Dallas time), Friday, November 22, 1963.

He had come to Texas the day before on the kind of mission that only a President can set for himself. The purpose stretched from the endlessly distant reaches of outer space down to the grubbiest roots of American politics. America was changing in a universe that changed; and Texas was changing within this America that changed; so the President was concerned with both changes.

The newest space center in the nation had been placed in Texas. Thus the President had come here to tell the nation how we hoped to loft the most powerful rocket ever built, the new Saturn, into outer space and thereby give America the lead in man's race for the moon. But his visit reflected another, quite different kind of change, too. As new industry swelled Texas' new cities with new kinds of people, Texas' old ways and customs were buckling under the strain. These social changes had created two rival Democratic power groups in the Lone Star State, so bitterly hateful of each other that they threatened to tear the party apart and give the state in 1964 to the Republicans. Both the reach for outer space and the turmoil within his party were presidential responsibilities; and John Fitzgerald Kennedy, who savored every aspect of his presidency, was enjoying his visit, thoroughly pleased by the unexpected size and enthusiasm of the cheering crowds, in a city considered hostile to him.

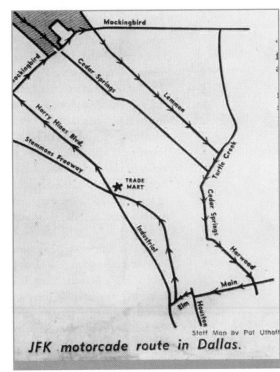

JFK motorcade route in Dallas.

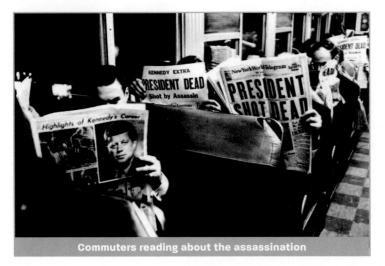

Commuters reading about the assassination

There were three shots; all apparently fired by Lee Harvey Oswald from the sixth floor of the Texas School Book Depository. He had waited there for how many hours no one knows; rested his 6.5 mail-order Italian carbine on a packing case; and aimed long and carefully through his telescopic sight as the cavalcade turned left around the bend from Houston Street, slowing as it descended Elm Street toward the Triple Underpass. He must have tracked the lead car of the procession in his cross hairs for seconds, unerringly.

There is a film, taken by an amateur, which catches alive the moment of death. The film is soundless, but in color. Three motorcycle outsiders come round the bend leading the black presidential limousine. Behind them is a gay green background—mint-green grasses, yellow-green foliage. The President, in the back seat, turns gracefully, all the way around to his right. His hand is flung out in greeting. Then it bends quickly up to touch his throat as if something hurt. His wife at this moment is also leaning forward, turning to the right. Slowly he leans back to her, as if to rest his head on her shoulder. She quickly puts her arm around him, and leans even further forward to look at him. Then, brutally, unbelievably, the head of the President is jolted by some invisible and terrible impact. It is flung up, jerked up. Had her face not been so far forward to look at him, the same bullet would have pierced both. It is terrible to see the impact of this invisible thing and the amber burst that momentarily appears as it hits. One notices the beautiful red roses spill from Mrs. Kennedy's lap as first she hugs her husband, then turns with the striking speed of an athlete to summon him

help, to scramble back across the rear deck of the car, and reach to assist the convulsive leap of Secret Service Agent Clinton Hill who bounds to the rescue. She helps Hill aboard; then the film ends as the car, with a dizzying spurt forward, disappears in the darkness of the underpass.

Limousine speeds to the hospital. With a howl and a keening of sirens, the limousine sped to Parkland Memorial Hospital, three and a half miles away. But one who has seen the filmed action knows that though, technically, the pulse continued to beat for another few minutes and some flow of blood continued, President Kennedy had ceased to be from the moment the bullet penetrated and ravaged his brain.

At Parkland, in Emergency Room Number One, whatever medical skill could be summoned converged swiftly on the operating table. The medical term later used for the President's condition on arrival was "moribund," which means that all the ingenuity the doctors showed was only an exercise in medical technology. The bullet that had torn out the brilliant mind of the 35th President of the United States had taken his life, too.

So he was dead in full prime of manhood, at 12:30 P.M. Dallas time, entering the Triple Underpass—dead without meaning, dead by the bullet of a madman, who was himself soon to die, dead by the thinking that had gone on in the grotesque mind of Lee Harvey Oswald, 24 years old. That mind, disturbed since adolescence, had carried that miserable neurotic from cause to cause, from America to Russia to betrayal of both countries. At the moment of shooting, Lee Harvey Oswald's mind was apparently committed to the cause of another fanatic, Fidel Castro of Cuba. But we will never know exactly what made him do this deed.

News shakes the country. Almost with the crack of the shot, the news was being transmitted all across America—the dash to the hospital; the administering of extreme unction by a priest; the medical pronouncement (at 1 P.M.) that the President, was, indeed, dead. The news struck the East Coast at mid-lunch, the Pacific Coast in mid-morning; it stopped all newspaper presses in their run; interrupted all TV cameras, all radios; stabbed with its pain men and women on the streets; knotted them in bunches about TV stores and paralyzed them in postures pale, stricken, or simply unbelieving. Not until he was dead, did Americans know how much sparkle the young

President had given their own lives—and how much they counted on him.

For those who did, indeed, count with numbers, there was a precise measure: the first news had reached the floor of the New York Stock Exchange at 18 minutes of 2, New York time. Ten minutes later panic was in full sweep. By 2 o'clock the ticker was hopelessly behind; in the last seven minutes of trading alone 2,200,000 shares were dumped. By the time trading was choked off at 2:07, in an emergency closing an hour and 23 minutes earlier than normal, the market had registered a loss of $15,000,000,000.

John F. Kennedy would have despised that kind of panic, or such a reaction to his passing. He would have liked better the reaction he might have seen on the road leading out of Washington toward Andrews Air Force base in Maryland that late afternoon. For, with the news of his death, every frequency and modulation of sound and transmission was telling every American of the last movements of their President, instant by instant. His body was being wheeled out of Parkland Hospital. A bronze coffin was being brought. The body was being taken to Love Field in Dallas in a white hearse; then hoisted into his airplane, Air Force One. It was due in Washington by 6:00 P.M., E.S.T.

Reception at Andrews Air Force Base. Men, women, and children across the country reacted as they could; but in the capital every man whose sense of duty or of love called was speeding to Andrews Air Force Base, where the plane was expected. Through the gathering dusk—a moist and balmy Washington evening— the huge black government limousines, the private cars, the taxis converged on Andrews Air Force Base. Yet what this writer remembers best are the people along the road. There had been no announcement of the route the President's body might take from the field. Yet all along the way, on every autumn hill, sitting in the brown fall grass were the youngsters—the teen-agers and adolescents—waiting for him to pass by, and their white shirts in the gathering dusk fleck the memory. For the next three days, it was to be this visible outwelling of emotion of the young that made the event so different from other ceremonies.

Guards patrolled the gates to the base, other guards patrolled the approaches to the field; wives and children as well as the servicemen stationed at Andrews rimmed the wire fence in front of the operations shack; and from its roof and windows, from every cranny and vantage point they watched the gathering of the great. TV had already rushed up its mobile troops, commentators, and trucks; now their glaring arcs flooded a pool of light in the darkness, as television prepared to illuminate the spectacular drama of the next three days.

In the lights one could see the masterless masters of Washington assemble. There they were from the Cabinet departments: Robert Strange McNamara, the great Secretary of Defense; W. Averell Harriman of State, tall, grim, and gaunt, last man in Washington to carry his importance vigorously on from Franklin Roosevelt's New Deal through the wars to John F. Kennedy's New Frontier; George W. Ball of State, John S. Gronouski, Anthony J. Celebrezze, Franklin D. Roosevelt, Jr. High over the Pacific Ocean another plane had been turned back and was racing home bearing the rest of the Cabinet: Rusk, Dillon, Hodges, Freeman, Udall. Here at the airport, too, were leaders of Congress—Senator Hubert Humphrey, his eyes red-rimmed with weeping, Senators Mike Mansfield and Everett Dirksen, pale, faded, and worn with their years; John W. McCormack, Speaker of the House, now first in line of succession; he, too, very old.

And then, apart from them on the apron, the younger men of the President's inner, personal staff: Theodore Sorensen, white of face, unapproachably solitary; Ralph Dungan and Arthur Schlesinger, Jr., bleak and somber; McGeorge Bundy, ice-white but contained in some unspeaking remoteness of his own.

The two groups sifted in and out of each other, the young men and older ones; together these two groups had formed the government of the United States. Normally, when together, they bubbled and simmered, laughed and babbled. He had made these two groups one team, one government. Now, dissolved by his death, they shuffled about uncomfortably. No bugle sounded taps, no drum beat its ruffle, no band pealed "Hail to the Chief" as John F. Kennedy returned for the last time to Washington, the city where he had practiced the magic art of leadership.

Air Force One arrives with Kennedy's body. It was 17 years before that he had arrived here from Boston. In the years since, his arrivals and departures had come to punctuate American history. When he arrived, the door would open and the lithe figure would come out to give that graceful wave of the arm which had become the most familiar flourish in American politics. There would follow then the burst of applause, the shouts and yells, the oohs and ahs as he tripped down the stairs with that light, graceful step which was his style.

But he came this time in silence. The faint shrill of distant jets, the sputter and cough of helicopters, the grounding and grinding of trucks on the base, the subdued conversations—all made the silence even larger. A quarter moon, hung with mists, had just made its appearance in the sky when Air Force One silently moved up the runway and soundlessly came to a stop.

One wished for a cry, a sob, a wail, any human sound. But the plane, white with long blue flashings, rested under the punishment of television lights—sealed and silent. A great glistening yellow cargo lift whose interior gleamed with dazzling white light rolled as far as the plane, and paused.

A door opened in the rear of the plane. The coffin was set down gently on the floor of the room-sized lift. It jounced, then steadied, then began to settle quietly to the ground with its burden. An honor guard of six reached out their hands to receive the coffin. There was still no noise audible except that of the broadcasters pattering as quietly as possible into their microphones. The silhouettes at the edge of the lift parted; and a slender woman in a raspberry-colored suit appeared, and then hovered at the lip of the low platform. Robert Kennedy, the President's brother was there first to aid her, as he was to be always, there, first, for the next three days.

Lyndon Johnson taking the oath of office, flanked by his wife, Lady Bird, and by Jackie Kennedy

He offered an arm to help her down; then guided her into the gray service ambulance with the red dome light—steady, not winking. Mrs. Kennedy's hand tried to open the ambulance door and fell limply; Bobby leaned forward, opened the door, guided her in. Then, silently, the ambulance rolled on to the north—followed by several limousines.

One watched and knew the nation was watching. One felt this group of men, who governed America, to sway imperceptibly after the ambulance; so many of these people for so long had been in the unquestioning habit of following immediately behind him on any tour, journey, or expedition; his dead body and physical presence drew them after, by an invisible tugging or obedience, fascination—and love. Yet now they only swayed. Held to the ground on the apron of the strip, these individuals were no longer a government—only men, leaderless. They waited immobile as they must. For the Constitution of the United States ordains that this country and its government must never for a moment remain leaderless. On the last heartbeat of John F. Kennedy, Lyndon Baines Johnson had become President of the United States, its 36th. For this new leader these people now waited. After the passage of a few minutes for decency, the door of the great plane opened a second time, and President Johnson appeared.

He had been riding in the second car back from the President when the shots came; he had been ordered almost immediately to the floor of the car by his accompanying Secret Service agent, Rufus Youngblood; and then, as the vice-presidential car spurted forward in the howling horror-bound lead echelon of presidential vehicles to the hospital, Youngblood had thrown his body over Johnson's to protect him as they raced over the road. It had been immediately certain at the hospital that President Kennedy was dying. Thus Lyndon Baines Johnson was about to become President of the United States in a city which, at that moment, seemed hostile, where perhaps some unknown conspiracy had triggered the assassin's rifle and even now sought to kill the Vice-President, too.

The Secret Service had, therefore, quickly whisked Mr. Johnson to the safety of Love Field, where guards might protect him from whatever unknown threats might develop. And it was there, at the field, in the gold-carpeted midsection cabin of the presidential plane that, after waiting for Mrs. Kennedy and the body to arrive from downtown

Dallas, he had taken the oath of office. The plane quivered under the strain of the engines which shrilled beyond the muffling of the cabin. Lyndon Johnson stood flanked on one side by his wife, on the other side by Mrs. Kennedy, his grave, thin face cocked forward as he listened to an old friend—Judge Sarah T. Hughes of Dallas—read him the oath of office. He said, "I do"; and then, turning, is reported to have said curtly, "Now let's get airborne."

He had been sworn in as President of the United States at about 20 minutes of 4 E.S.T., on November 22, 1963; and now, a little more than two hours later, his plane, having hurtled over the land he must govern at 635 miles an hour, was arriving in Washington, D.C., where he must begin immediately to lead.

He stood there, now, in the lights at the top of the ramp, in a dark suit; Mrs. Johnson behind him, neither expecting nor receiving the cheers that would in a few days greet all his comings; cheers would have profaned this moment.

He walked very slowly down the ramp, was led to the waiting microphones, spoke slowly the minimum number of words required by the occasion. He paused for a moment among the Senators and the foreign dignitaries and then he pulled away. Of those present he asked that the Secretary of Defense, McNamara, that the Under Secretary of State, George Ball, that the presidential security aide, McGeorge Bundy, join him and Mrs. Johnson for the helicopter trip to Washington.

Johnson orders an investigation. By choice of these men, and with this act, he had taken responsibility for the United States of America in a dangerously turbulent world. The waiting helicopter lifted them all from the field, its red lights blinking as it lurched through the skies toward the White House. There was little more than time in the seven-minute flight for the new President to ask each in turn whether any immediate crisis faced the United States that evening from the outer world. Each, in turn, said no. John F. Kennedy had left America strong and secure in the world the day he died.

President Johnson arrived at the White House south lawn at about 20 minutes past 6, reassured; went, via the White House, to his chambers on the second floor of the Executive Office Building (which is known better to history as the Old State Building); began to telephone; began to reach for the levers that were his to move. He spoke to J. Edgar Hoover of the FBI, and ordered the most

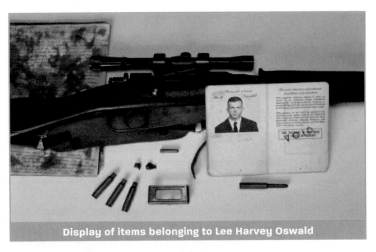

Display of items belonging to Lee Harvey Oswald

complete possible investigation of the assassination. He received numerous visitors for periods of from 10 to 15 minutes. To one, he said, "It's been a whole year since this morning." At about 25 minutes after 9, he left the building to drive to his home in the Spring Valley district of Washington.

The nation, now transfixed by television, watched an almost empty White House on Friday night. Lights played on the fountain on the north lawn. The chandelier over the great front entrance was dim—but obviously lit. Upstairs, the blinds were drawn, but one could see that there, where the President and his Lady had lived, and where his children now slept, men stirred in sorrow and the lights were on. In the East Room where old friends prepared the reception of his body, the shades were also drawn over a dim-lit room.

On the front walk, along Pennsylvania Avenue, a reinforced police guard patrolled the iron palisade that fences the grounds. But they had no need to act. All evening, until long after midnight in twos and fours and individually, a subdued float of Americans paced back and forth before the White House. They could not see anything, nor did they speak or cackle as most crowds do. They were, overwhelmingly, young—people in their 20s, or 30s; many of the young couples had brought their children. Some paced back and forth for hours.

Late that night, the wind brought rain. At 4:22 A.M., the familiar gray navy ambulance brought the body of John F. Kennedy accompanied by his wife, his brother, Robert, Secretary McNamara, and a few other friends, from the Bethesda Naval Hospital back to the White House—and then the rain let go. It was to drench the unhappy city all the next day, Saturday.

The nation begins to mourn. Saturday was the day men cried in Washington.

Friday, the wound had been so sharp and new that most emotions were numb. Now, Saturday, feeling their hurt, and the nerve ends beginning to ache, men broke. Men who had, dry-eyed, performed their duties on Friday afternoon and evening now sobbed uncontrollably.

A private mass had been celebrated for John Fitzgerald Kennedy at 10:30 in the morning in the somber East Room. Thereafter, the room was opened to an endless procession of men, great and small, who had, somehow, earned the attention or affection or respect of the late President. The great room, its polished floors gleaming, was hung with black drapes; its huge chandeliers were dimmed; in the center rested a huge dais upon which, draped with the American flag, bulked the enormous coffin.

All that afternoon, as the rain came down, soaking the city, the huge lobby smelled of dampness and of people. The White House guards, whether through gentility, or sadness, or kindness to men they recognized as old friends of the President, let them wander oddly through previously private places.

Apparent confusion was the tone of the mansion; yet under the shock, a few had already begun to pull themselves together. Some time previously, President Kennedy had gone with his good friend Robert McNamara to visit the Arlington National

President Johnson, shortly after returning to the White House

Cemetery in Virginia, and they had lingered on a slope just under the Lee mansion overlooking the capital. Kennedy had been enchanted with the unfamiliar panorama of Washington as seen from that particular spot. McNamara had remembered this visit, and now, with Robert Kennedy, on Saturday afternoon, they trudged through the downpour to inspect the site. The Attorney General felt this was the place for his brother to rest. So, returning to Washington, he and Mrs. Kennedy persuaded the rest of the grieving family that there, in Arlington National Cemetery, rather than in the family plot in Brookline, Massachusetts, should be the grave of the 35th President. With this decision the elaborate preparations for the pomp and ceremony of the next two days could proceed.

Johnson attends to business. Lyndon Johnson moved through an intense and busy Saturday. Avoiding attention as much as any President of the United States can hope to do he had, from the moment he left his Spring Valley home at 8:45 in the morning, been in constant action.

The new President arrived at the White House at 5 minutes of 9; attended his first national security briefing (delivered by White House security aide McGeorge Bundy, and Central Intelligence Agency chief John McCone) in the secret basement Situation Room at the White House; then walked back across the intervening road between the White House and his chambers in the Executive Office Building and proceeded to be President. Secretary of State Rusk came at 9:20; then Secretary of Defense McNamara at 10:12; then a delegation of congressional leaders. Then a visit to the White House to Mrs. Kennedy and a long, mourning visit to the coffin, in the East Room, where he met Dwight D. Eisenhower, also come to pay his respects. He invited Eisenhower to come back with him to his office chambers and, after visiting church, President Johnson lunched with Eisenhower.

A Cabinet meeting followed at 2:30—a brief, half-hour session. The President pleaded with those present to stay; he could not govern this country without their help, he said. Dean Rusk answered for the Cabinet in what is remembered as an eloquent pledge of full support. Adlai E. Stevenson spoke next, remarking that two-and-a-half years before all had sat in this room and given John Kennedy their hearts, their minds, their loyalties. These, he said, they now freely gave Lyndon Johnson.

President Johnson's personal staff of three—William Moyers, George Reedy, Walter Jenkins—had moved instantly the previous evening to serve their chief, the new President, moving with him, doing his errands, bearing his commands to government. Now, Saturday, men began to wonder how he would mesh these newcomers with the older presidential staff. But soon, and then insistently, it became obvious that Lyndon Johnson sought at this moment to offer to government and people, above all, a sense of unbroken continuity. He had won the Cabinet at the first meeting. Thereafter, and for the next 35 hours, he proceeded to buttonhole the private personal staff that John Kennedy had brought with him, and plead for their loyalty, their continuation, their help, too. He would govern, at least for the present, with Kennedy's crew.

Later that afternoon, it became obvious that he proposed to govern in Kennedy's direction, too. Word passed that he had asked the brilliant chief counsel of President Kennedy, Theodore Sorensen, to prepare the speech with which the new President would address Congress and the nation for the first time on Wednesday. No man knew better the heart, instinct, and political thinking of Kennedy. By nightfall it was clear that President Johnson had done a superlative job of calming the shock tremors that ran all through the disturbed capital. It was apparent that what faced the nation was tragedy—not crisis.

Radio and television reports draw the country together. Sunday was clear—cloudlessly, flawlessly, brilliantly clear. In the purest shade of its many blues, the sky looked down on the ceremonies and pageantry with which a great government proposed to do honor to a fallen President. It was a brisk November day, the wind chilly, but not uncomfortably so, and the breeze was fresh as the cortege prepared to march.

By now, Sunday, the mourning had become national. All across the nation, from Friday on, festivities had been extinguished; dances canceled; parties postponed; sports events (including the Harvard-Yale football game) wiped out; Times Square blackened; night clubs closed as the nation, mesmerized by radio and television, gave itself over to grief and wonder. Now the television networks of the nation, pooling all their facilities, were about to deliver, with exquisite good taste and sensitive understanding, such a visual unrolling of pomp and events as had never been reached anywhere before.

Jack Ruby shoots Lee Harvey Oswald.

Ruby kills Oswald; Kennedy's body lies in state. But first, a blot—a bloody, obscene, incredible blot. While waiting for the funeral cortege from White House to Capitol to start, as scheduled, at 12:30 on the dot, the television cameras of the nation had been roving the national scene with remote pickups. All three networks were, visually, in touch with the Dallas police headquarters, where authorities were holding Lee Harvey Oswald. Then, as the nation watched Oswald being taken from jail, it witnessed, to its horror, the first live murder ever televised in the land. Jack Ruby, a pudgy, boisterous, and unbalanced night club operator, the incredible crony and habitué of Dallas' police headquarters staff, pulled a pistol and shot Oswald dead. Men and women preparing in all solemnity to grieve at a funeral procession at 12:30 thus witnessed, first, murder at 12:20.

The blot was quickly left to be absorbed by the mind of the nation as best it could. The TV directors of the spectacle in Washington brought the attention of the nation back to the White House.

The scenes that followed, so indelibly visual, witnessed by more than 100,000,000 people, invite little repetition in this account by word. They will be seen and heard for generations—as long as film lasts, and as long as men are interested in the story of America:

First, at the head of the cortege, the flag-covered coffin, its six matched grays pulling and tugging and tossing their manes as if unwillingly dragging a burden in a direction they would not take; then the riderless black horse, its silver stirrups reversed, prancing and willful, turning and twisting, yet held to its course by the handler; the sound of muffled drums, at 100 steps the minute; the dome of the Capitol rising in the distance; the arrival of the cortege at the Capitol 45 minutes later; the late President's beautiful Lady in black, the haze of her black veil sheltering her face; her children; the drawn faces of other members of his family behind her; and the last gesture of Jacqueline Kennedy—to kiss the flag that draped the coffin, repeated in imitation a moment later by his daughter, stooping, touching the flag to her lips in reverence and love of father.

Thereafter, the Rotunda of the Capitol where President Kennedy lay was thrown open to all other Americans who wished to pay respects. All through the night the serpentine wound over

Dignitaries at Kennedy's funeral procession

Capitol plaza, under the floodlights and up the stairs until at 9:30 Monday it was time to take him elsewhere. So swiftly had they come, in such numbers, that when the file was suspended, a quarter of a million had passed in respect by the bier.

Johnson takes charge. Lyndon Johnson still avoided national attention on Sunday. He had attended an early morning intelligence briefing, gone to church, then accompanied Mrs. Kennedy in the limousine that carried her in the cortege. He had appeared rapt in moody thought standing behind the family at the Rotunda ceremonies, and then sped back to the Executive Offices, by a roundabout route to avoid crowds, to hold his first true meeting of state.

The first major problem of diplomacy presented to John F. Kennedy in December 1960, three years before, had been a crisis in Southeast Asia—Laos. The first major problem now presented to Lyndon B. Johnson was also in Southeast Asia—the problem of South Vietnam. The U.S. ambassador to Vietnam, Henry Cabot Lodge, had flown in from Saigon for a conference originally set by President Kennedy. Henry Cabot Lodge had been Lyndon B. Johnson's Republican rival for the vice-presidency in 1960. Now Johnson insisted on greeting Lodge as his own emissary and going through with the conference as planned. Present were McNamara, Rusk, McCone, Ball, Bundy, and others.

They conferred for a full hour. At 5:30, White House Press Secretary Salinger announced that the President had directed that all possible measures be taken to assist the new government in Vietnam. It was obvious from Salinger's manner, as he stood on a table in the crowded lobby, that Salinger spoke for a recognizable leader; and government was moving again. It was further obvious that President Johnson meant the world to know he had taken over.

Dignitaries arrive to pay their respects. The opportunity, somber and dark as it was, was proper for such a decision, because now, in Sunday's dusk, Washington's twin airports were a-buzz with the dignitaries of the world arriving for tomorrow's ceremonies. Princes and presidents, kings and chiefs of state were arriving by speed of jet from every corner of the world, at a flow so fast that the entire staff of the State Department— from secretary, through under secretaries, to junior assistant secretaries—were all committed to a frantic ceremonial shuttling between the State Department and Washington's airports. For the men who came to give dignity to John F. Kennedy, were such men as required that maximum dignity be paid them on arrival: the towering Charles de Gaulle of France and the tiny Emperor Haile Selassie of Ethiopia; Queen Frederika of Greece and King Baudouin of Belgium; from Great Britain, the Prince Consort, Philip, Duke of Edinburgh and the Queen's Prime Minister Sir Alex Douglas-Home; from West Germany, its President Heinrich Luebke, and portly Chancellor, Ludwig Erhard. On and on they came, friendly and distant, until with the arrival at 5 A.M. Monday of Nikita Khrushchev's emissary, A. I. Mikoyan, the visiting dignitaries would represent 92 different sovereignties—including the new Common Market of Europe, which sent its benign architect, Jean Monnet. By tomorrow, there would be assembled the most imposing gathering of captains of state since the crowned heads of Europe had massed to follow the cortege of Edward VII of Great Britain in 1910. To all these, Lyndon Johnson meant to show that American purpose and policy were unchanged. Thus he decided that after tomorrow's ceremonies, he would himself receive these men in the State Department's John Quincy Adams Room and televise the reception for all the world to see.

In Washington that evening, the young people, the young couples, the boys and girls, were already gathering on curbstones, wrapping themselves in blankets against the cold to sit in all night vigil and wait the passage, tomorrow, of John F. Kennedy's funeral procession.

The funeral begins. Monday was for farewell—for the final departure of John F. Kennedy. The skies still held clear and blue, with a nip of frost in the air, and one million citizens sat or stood to line the long route from the Capitol to the White House to St. Matthew's Cathedral to the Arlington Cemetery. It is estimated that more than 100,000,000 others in a nation that had all but stopped work joined with them in watching the ceremonies of burial on television.

Perhaps it was best to watch the ceremonies on television. So diffuse, so vast, so many-splendored was this great ceremony that no eyewitness could grasp it all. The television networks had pooled their lines, cameramen, commentators, mobile units; they had brought equipment from Philadelphia, from New York, from Chicago, and special lenses from as far away as Japan. It was as if the nation, watching through the 44 camera units deployed to cover the event, had 44 pairs of eyes and ears and so could be everywhere at once.

Kennedy family members pay their final respects. At 10:41 the Kennedy family, led by Jacqueline Kennedy, arrived at the Capitol to pay its last respects to the coffin in the Rotunda and bear it away. Nine pallbearers of the honor guard carried the flag-draped coffin down the steps of the Rotunda to the caisson where the six matched grays waited to carry it to the White House. Down Pennsylvania Avenue it moved. And now began the sound that echoed not only through every home in Washington, but in every parlor and listening place across the land; the

sound of the klop, klop, klop of horses' hooves, the sound of the muffled drums' cadence, 100 to the minute, the sound of somber music, slow, sad,

The casket and honor guard in the Capitol Rotunda

occasionally broken by the skirling bagpipes. This was the sound of Washington and the nation all day long while the screens showed the procession as it moved, then repeated the sight over and over again into the night.

At the White House, the cortege paused; and there began the most moving passage of the day. At the White House, Mrs. Kennedy, President Johnson, the other members of the Kennedy family climbed out of the limousines that had brought them from the Capitol. Now, on foot, behind the coffin they proposed to walk the eight blocks to St. Matthew's Cathedral, where requiem would be sung and the church murmur blessings over the body before returning its soul to God. Behind the family as they trudged, trudged the great of the world—and also the small and forlorn, unknown to fame, who had been his personal friends. Long and short, robust and frail, stooped and erect they walked, kings and princes, queens, and foreign ministers, and generals. In the endless spanking-smart, military precision of banners, troops, guards, pomp, formation, step and parade-timing of the long day, these walkers—ambling with neither pace or order—reduced all the glories and glitter they embodied to the stumbling pace of common grievers, who must be shepherded in the way they go. All this could be seen only by those who watched at a distance through the electronic eye of television.

The ceremony at St. Matthew's Cathedral. At the center of the ceremonies in St. Matthew's Cathedral of Washington, those who had come by invitation to be present at the requiem could only sit silently in their pews, rustling and shifting until far off in the distance came the sound of muffled drums; and above that the first faint strains of the dirge.

The cathedral hushes, listening; the distant band falls quiet, and from high in a corner of the cathedral begin the choristers, their pure voices singing ancient Latin airs centuries old. When they pause, the muffled tattoo is louder coming nearer; over the drums come the bagpipes, distinctly closer than the band before. After the bagpipes, those in the cathedral sing again but the tattoo is closer, always closer, ever closer, intolerably, relentlessly approaching from outside the body. There is the fragrance of incense in the cathedral; Richard Cardinal Cushing leads a file of prelates to the door to await the procession; now the band blares on the threshold—loud, immediate, insistent, there. It is playing "Hail to the Chief," but playing it so slowly, with such a dirge-like beat that it takes seconds to recognize the tune. Now the choir inside the cathedral, soft and gentle, carrying the comfort of ages, contends with the brass of the band outside, one layer of music folding over another. The voices of song die away; the band is hushed.

Then she comes—black-veiled, erect as a young wand, holding one by each hand her two children, Caroline and John-John. Both children are dressed in powder-blue shades, both wear red shoes. She is followed by her family; by the new President; the church weeps softly as they pass. An interminable five minutes is needed to seat the dignitaries of the great world; then comes the coffin itself; mass is

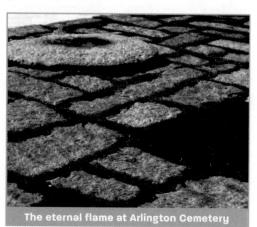

The eternal flame at Arlington Cemetery

said by the tall, gnarled figure of Cardinal Cushing, family friend from time of childhood, in his harsh, dry, Boston-Irish inflection. For those who watched on the screen, following the camera as it pointed and probed at the great and near-great crowding the benches, as it touched delicately and fleetingly the faces of the family, as it rested on the coffin, as it underlined the sequence of ceremonies that make the drama of the mass—for those who watched the art of the camera this was a moment of high drama.

But for those who sat in the cathedral, it was otherwise. This was the quiet moment of passing. Century upon century of liturgy and tradition had graven these Latin words in this form, had taught this high priest the melancholy drone that now filled the air, had instructed the singers in the sad, ageless melodies that now and then broke the service. It was a ritual, a poultice on the memory and on the hurt. When prayer had implored God to take back the spirit of this man, John F. Kennedy, it was left to those present only to take his body back to its earth.

The journey to Arlington National Cemetery. It was a splendid thing, the last cortege from the cathedral to Arlington National Cemetery. First the caisson; then again the riderless black horse, still pawing and yawing and tossing; then the limousine bearing the family and new President; then endlessly, it seemed, miles of glistening limousines, bearing statesmen in their morning coats, Arab and African chieftains in their robes of state, generals and admirals in their braid. They rolled down Connecticut Avenue, turned right on Constitution Avenue, moved slowly through the crowds past Lincoln Memorial. Then they crossed the bridge into Virginia, and entered the cemetery itself, winding up by Sherman Road to the slope before the Custis Lee mansion.

Irish Guards and Black Watch, Third Infantry troops, and green-bereted Special Forces lined the plot to do the late President honor. At 10 minutes of 3, the air force flung 50 jets in perfect formation, one for each state of the union, in a burst of sound and parallel contrails in the sky over the slope. His presidential jet followed in an instant. And then it was quick, all procedures timed meticulously: the casket, still flag-covered, was lowered to the ground. For three minutes the Cardinal prayed; the 21-gun salute thudded. As Mrs. Kennedy and his two brothers moved to the head of the casket a series of rifle volleys cracked the air. Then taps. Then the Navy Hymn. Then the flag of the coffin was snapped into its ceremonial triangle folds; and handed to Jacqueline Kennedy.

She stood there a moment and someone gave her what appeared to be a rod; she touched it to the ground; the flare of the eternal flame rose. She handed the rod to each of the brothers, and each in turn touched the rod to the flame that rose from the mound. For an instant, the three of them grouped together—she veiled in black, and they slim and gaunt beside her. They made a primitive picture, something altogether atavistic, calling to the blood and echoes of tribal life forgotten—the brothers and the widow peering into the orange tongues of flame, the wisped fringes of black smoke, trying to postpone the moment of the loss of the chief. But they must accept it. And with great dignity, after one brief turning to McNamara, she gave her hand to Robert Kennedy who led her gently down the slope away from the casket.

Portrait of John F. Kennedy

It was a quarter of an hour later, after she had departed, that they lowered the coffin holding John Fitzgerald Kennedy into the earth and that was the end.

Kennedy's legacy. Or perhaps not.

For no man there on that hillside but bore the mark of John Fitzgerald Kennedy—and would, until the day he died. Here were all the rivals he had defeated in his race for the presidency—from President Lyndon Johnson and Adlai Stevenson (who hurried quickly away from the slope because they must confer together, immediately, about problems of space), to all the other rivals of 1960 who left more slowly: Hubert Humphrey who held him ever close in heart; Stuart Symington; Richard Nixon with thoughts apparently sad, yet inscrutable. His mark rested even on those who had been Presidents of the United States—Harry Truman and Dwight Eisenhower—who now at this place made friends after their separation and drove away together to have a snack at evening as old companions. As well as on those who aspired to be President of the United States in his place—Nelson A. Rockefeller, this smiling person somber and unhappy, pausing to talk to Averell Harriman,

his predecessor as governor of New York; the pale and tense young William Scranton, governor of Pennsylvania; Barry Goldwater, a perplexing man whom the late President found personally delightful but whose philosophy he found abhorrent.

Past presidents, future presidents, might-have-been-presidents, also-ran presidents, president-makers—all were here on the slope. But it was time to go, as the sun set behind the white columns of the Lee mansion, gliding the strange view of Washington one might see from this knoll—a Washington whose row-upon-row of government buildings seemed like a frightening walled town in the distance; behind whose tawny parapets, like a mysterious city with distant towers, rose the Lincoln Memorial and the Washington Monument, and the dominant Capitol. All as it had been before he came, unchanged.

This was good. For the memory of John Fitzgerald Kennedy was not to be written in new buildings, new monuments, not even in giant new rockets scouring a blaze through black space. His memory would be that he made Americans realize that they were a young people—and youth is hope. At every turn and twist of all the ceremonies, whenever one moved in Washington to participate in the grieving, one met young people—in their teens, in their 20s, in their 30s. These, with their children, were his chief mourners. Men say that at the funeral of President Franklin D. Roosevelt, the mourners had been chiefly middle-aged men and women. But the mourners of John F. Kennedy were startlingly, spectacularly young. He had removed from them the slander of cynicism; he had believed in the future of America; and they had believed in him. In his brief moment, he had given America belief, as well as hope.

The author: Theodore H. White is the author of the Pulitzer Prize–winning book, *The Making of the President, 1960.*

Martin Luther King, Jr.

Martin Luther King, Jr. (1929–1968), a black Baptist minister, was the main leader of the civil rights movement in the United States during the 1950s and 1960s.

HOT topics

Martin Luther King, Jr. Day. Martin Luther King, Jr. Day is a United States national holiday honoring the birthday of civil rights leader Martin Luther King, Jr. The holiday is observed each year on the third Monday in January. King's actual birthday was January 15, 1929. On Martin Luther King, Jr., Day, most government offices and schools close for the day, but many private businesses remain open. Some schools hold teach-ins that focus on themes of nonviolence, racial justice, and equality.

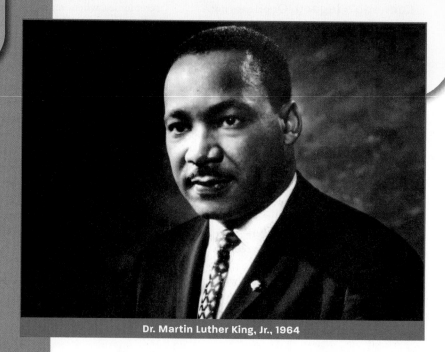

Dr. Martin Luther King, Jr., 1964

HOT topics

hot topics hot topics hot topics hot topics

The Montgomery Bus Boycott.
King's civil rights activities began with a protest of Montgomery's segregated bus system in 1955. That year, a black passenger named Rosa Parks was arrested for disobeying a city law requiring that blacks give up their seats on buses when white people wanted to sit in them or even in the same row. Black leaders in Montgomery urged blacks to boycott the city's buses. King was appointed to serve as president of the organization formed to organize the protest. Terrorists bombed King's home, but he continued to insist on nonviolent protests. Thousands of blacks boycotted the buses for over a year. In 1956, the United States Supreme Court ordered Montgomery to provide equal, integrated seating on public buses.

The March on Washington.
In 1963 King and other civil rights leaders organized a massive march in Washington, D.C. The March on Washington was intended to highlight African-American unemployment and to urge Congress to pass President John F. Kennedy's civil rights bill. More than 200,000 Americans, including many whites, gathered at the Lincoln Memorial in the capital. The high point of the rally was King's stirring "I Have a Dream" speech, which eloquently defined the moral basis of the civil rights movement. The movement won a major victory in 1964, when Congress passed the Civil Rights Act of 1964, which prohibited racial discrimination in public places and called for equal opportunity in employment and education. King later received the 1964 Nobel Peace Prize.

The Montgomery bus boycott begins with A Day of Pilgrimage, as black citizens walk to work.

King's Death.
While organizing the Poor People's Campaign, King went to Memphis to support a strike of black garbage workers. There, on April 4, 1968, King was shot and killed. James Earl Ray, a white drifter and escaped convict, pleaded guilty to the crime in March 1969 and was sentenced to 99 years in prison. King's assassination produced immediate shock, grief, and anger. Blacks rioted in more than 100 cities. A few months later, Congress passed the Civil Rights Act of 1968, which prohibited racial discrimination in the sale and rental of most housing in the nation. Many suspected a conspiracy behind King's murder, but investigations produced no evidence.

TRUE or FALSE?
King is one of only two Americans whose birthdays are observed as national holidays.

THE BASICS

Martin Luther King, Jr. (1929–1968), an African American Baptist minister, was the main leader of the civil rights movement in the United States during the 1950s and 1960s. He had a magnificent speaking ability, which enabled him to effectively express the demands of African Americans for social justice. King's eloquent pleas won the support of millions of people—blacks and whites—and made him internationally famous. He won the 1964 Nobel Peace Prize for leading nonviolent civil rights demonstrations.

In spite of King's stress on nonviolence, he often became the target of violence. White racists threw rocks at him in Chicago and bombed his home in Montgomery, Alabama. Finally, violence ended King's life at the age of 39, when an assassin shot and killed him.

Some historians view King's death as the end of the civil rights era that began in the mid-1950s. Under his leadership, the civil rights movement won wide support among whites, and laws that had barred integration in the Southern States were abolished. King became only the second American whose birthday is observed as a national holiday. The first was George Washington, the nation's first president.

King based his program of nonviolence on Christian teachings. He wrote five books: *Stride Toward Freedom* (1958), *Strength to Love* (1963), *Why We Can't Wait* (1964), *Where Do We Go from Here: Chaos or Community?* (1967), and *The Trumpet of Conscience* (1968).

Early life. King was born on January 15, 1929, in Atlanta, Georgia. His name at birth was Michael King, Jr., after his father, Michael King. But his father changed their names to Martin Luther King, Sr. and Jr., when the boy was about 5.

Martin was the second oldest child of Alberta Williams King and Michael King. He had an older sister, Christine, and a younger

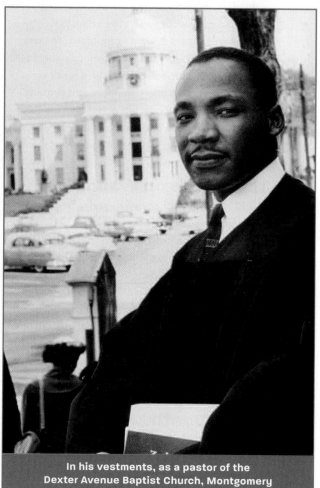

In his vestments, as a pastor of the
Dexter Avenue Baptist Church, Montgomery

brother, A. D. The young Martin was usually called M. L. His father was pastor of the Ebenezer Baptist Church in Atlanta. One of Martin's grandfathers, A. D. Williams, also had been pastor there.

In high school, Martin did so well that he skipped both the 9th and 12th grades. At the age of 15, he entered Morehouse College in Atlanta. King became an admirer of Benjamin E. Mays, Morehouse's president and a well-known scholar of black religion. Under Mays's influence, King decided to become a minister.

King was ordained just before he graduated from Morehouse in 1948. He entered Crozer Theological Seminary in Chester, Pennsylvania, to earn a divinity degree. King then went to graduate school at Boston University, where he got a Ph.D. degree in theology in 1955. In Boston, he met Coretta Scott of Marion, Alabama, a music student. They were married in 1953. The Kings had four children—Yolanda, Dexter, Martin, and Bernice. In 1954, King became pastor of the Dexter Avenue Baptist Church in Montgomery, Alabama.

The early civil rights movement. King's civil rights activities began with a protest of Montgomery's segregated bus system in 1955. That year, a black passenger named Rosa Parks was arrested for disobeying a city law requiring that blacks give up their seats on buses when white people wanted to sit in their seats or in the same row. Black leaders in Montgomery urged blacks to *boycott* (refuse to use) the city's buses. The leaders formed an organization to run the boycott, and asked King to serve as president. In his first speech as leader of the boycott, King told his black colleagues: "First and foremost, we are American citizens ... We are not here advocating violence ... The only weapon that we have ... is the weapon of protest ... The great glory of American democracy is the right to protest for right."

Terrorists bombed King's home, but King continued to insist on nonviolent protests. Thousands of blacks boycotted the buses for over a year. In 1956, the United States Supreme Court ordered Montgomery to provide equal, integrated seating on public buses. The boycott's success won King national fame and identified him as a symbol of Southern blacks' new efforts to fight racial injustice.

With other black ministers, King founded the Southern Christian Leadership Conference (SCLC) in 1957 to expand the nonviolent struggle against racism and discrimination. At the time, widespread segregation existed throughout the South in public schools, and in transportation, recreation, and such public facilities as hotels and restaurants. Many states also used various methods to deprive blacks of their voting rights. In 1960, King moved from Montgomery to Atlanta to devote more effort to SCLC's work. He became co-pastor of Ebenezer Baptist Church with his father.

The growing movement. In 1960, black college students across the South began sitting at lunch counters and entering other facilities that refused to serve blacks. Civil rights protests expanded further, including major demonstrations in Albany, Georgia. Also in the early 1960s, King

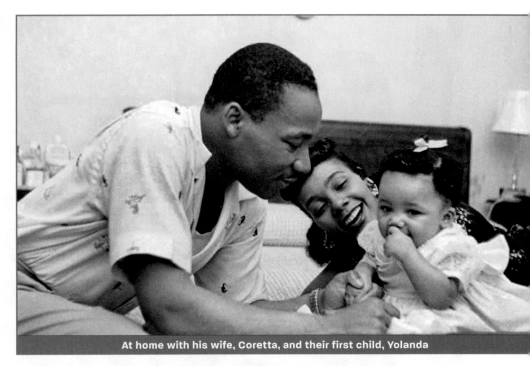
At home with his wife, Coretta, and their first child, Yolanda

became increasingly unhappy that President John F. Kennedy was doing little to advance civil rights. Early in 1963, King and his SCLC associates launched massive demonstrations to protest racial discrimination in Birmingham, Alabama, one of the South's most segregated cities. Police used dogs and fire hoses to drive back peaceful protesters, including children. Heavy news coverage of the violence produced a national outcry against segregation. Soon afterward, Kennedy proposed a wide-ranging civil rights bill to Congress.

King and other civil rights leaders then organized a massive march in Washington, D.C. The event, called the March on Washington, was intended to highlight African-American unemployment and to urge Congress to pass Kennedy's bill. On August 28, 1963, more than 200,000 Americans, including many whites, gathered at the Lincoln Memorial in the capital. The high point of the rally, King's stirring "I Have a Dream" speech, eloquently defined the moral basis of the civil rights movement.

The movement won a major victory in 1964, when Congress passed the civil rights bill that Kennedy and his successor, President Lyndon B. Johnson, had recommended. The Civil Rights Act of 1964 prohibited racial discrimination in public places and called for equal opportunity in employment and education. King later received the 1964 Nobel Peace Prize.

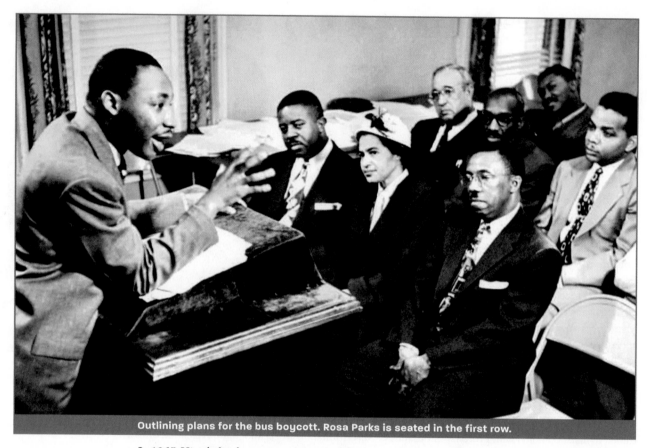

Outlining plans for the bus boycott. Rosa Parks is seated in the first row.

In 1965, King helped organize protests in Selma, Alabama. The demonstrators protested against the efforts of white officials there to deny most black citizens the chance to register and vote. Several hundred protesters attempted to march from Selma to Montgomery, the state capital, but police officers used tear gas and clubs to break up the group. The bloody attack, broadcast nationwide on television news shows, shocked the public. King immediately announced another attempt to march from Selma to Montgomery. Johnson went before Congress to request a bill that would eliminate all barriers to Southern blacks' right to vote. Within a few months, Congress approved the Voting Rights Act of 1965.

The Chicago campaign. By 1965, King had come to believe that civil rights leaders should pay more attention to the economic problems of blacks. In 1966, he helped begin a major civil rights campaign in Chicago, his first big effort outside the South. Leaders of the campaign tried to organize black inner-city residents who suffered from unemployment, bad housing, and poor schools. The leaders also protested against real estate practices that kept blacks from living in many neighborhoods and

suburbs. King believed such practices played a major role in trapping poor blacks in urban ghettos.

King and the local leaders also organized marches through white neighborhoods. But angry white people in these segregated communities threw bottles and rocks at the demonstrators. Soon afterward, Chicago officials promised to encourage fair housing practices in the city if King would stop the protests. King accepted the offer, and the Chicago campaign ended.

Later years. Continued violence against civil rights workers in the South frustrated many blacks, including members of the Student Non-violent Coordinating Committee (SNCC). In 1966, SNCC leaders urged a more aggressive response to the violence and began to use the slogan "Black Power." That phrase troubled King and many white supporters of racial equality. Many people thought the religious, nonviolent emphasis of the civil rights movement was changing. King repeated his commitment to nonviolence, but disputes among civil rights groups over "Black Power" suggested that King no longer spoke for the whole movement.

In 1967, King became more critical of American society than ever before. He believed poverty was as great an evil as racism. He said that true social justice would require a redistribution of wealth from the rich to the poor. Thus, King began to plan a Poor People's Campaign that would unite poor people of all races in a struggle for economic opportunity. The campaign would demand a federal guaranteed annual income for poor people and other major antipoverty laws.

Also in 1967, King attacked U.S. support of South Vietnam in the Vietnam War (1957–1975). He regarded the South Vietnamese government as corrupt and undemocratic. Many supporters of the war denounced King's criticisms, but the growing antiwar movement welcomed his comments.

King's death. While organizing the Poor People's Campaign, King went to Memphis to support a strike of black garbage workers. There, on April 4, 1968, at the Lorraine Motel, King was shot and killed. James Earl Ray, a white drifter and escaped convict, pleaded guilty to the crime in March 1969 and was sentenced to 99 years in prison. Ray later tried to withdraw his plea, but his conviction was upheld. Ray died in 1998.

People throughout the world mourned King's death. King was buried in South View Cemetery in Atlanta. His body was later moved near Ebenezer Baptist Church. On King's tombstone are the words: "Free at last, free at last, thank God Almighty, I'm free at last."

King's assassination produced immediate shock, grief, and anger. Blacks rioted in more than 100 cities. A few months later, Congress passed the Civil Rights Act of 1968, which prohibited racial discrimination in the sale and rental of most housing in the nation.

Years after King's death, some people still doubted that Ray had acted alone. In 1978, a special committee of the U.S. House of Representatives reported the "likelihood" that Ray was aided by others. In 2000, however, the U.S. Justice Department announced that an 18-month investigation turned up no evidence of a conspiracy.

In 1974, King's mother was shot and killed while playing the organ at Ebenezer Baptist Church. The gunman, Marcus Wayne Chenault, opposed black Christian ministers. He received the death penalty, but in 1995 was resentenced to life in prison without parole.

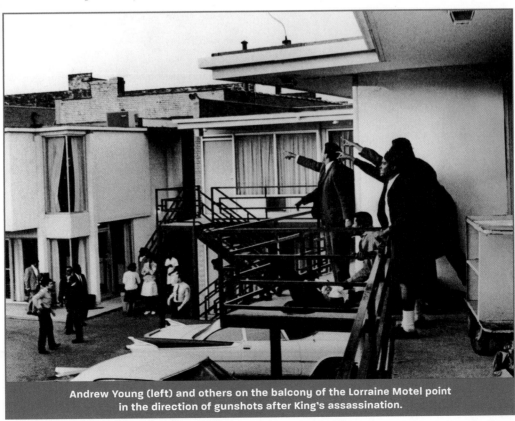

Andrew Young (left) and others on the balcony of the Lorraine Motel point in the direction of gunshots after King's assassination.

In 1980, an area including King's birthplace, church, and burial place became the Martin Luther King, Jr., National Historic Site. In 1983, Congress passed a federal holiday honoring King. The day is celebrated on the third Monday in January. In 1991, the National Civil Rights Museum opened at the site of King's assassination in Memphis. The museum's exhibits cover the history of the civil rights movement. In 2009, construction began on the Martin Luther King, Jr., National Memorial on the National Mall in Washington, D.C. The memorial opened in 2011. King's son Martin Luther King III served as president of the Southern Christian Leadership Conference from 1997 to 2004. King's widow, Coretta Scott King, died in 2006.

MLA Citation

"Martin Luther King, Jr."
The Southwestern Advantage Topic Source.
Nashville: Southwestern. 2013.

ADDITIONAL RESOURCES

Books to Read

Bolden, Tonya. *M.L.K.* Abrams Books for Young Readers, 2007.

Bruns, Roger. *Martin Luther King, Jr.: A Biography.* Greenwood, 2006.

Burns, Stewart. *To the Mountaintop: Martin Luther King, Jr.'s Mission to Save America, 1955–1968.* HarperSanFrancisco, 2004.

Carson, Clayborne, and others. *The Martin Luther King, Jr. Encyclopedia.* Greenwood, 2007.

Frady, Marshall. *Martin Luther King, Jr.* 2002. Reprint. Penguin, 2006.

Sides, Hampton. *Hellhound on His Trail: The Stalking of Martin Luther King, Jr., and the International Hunt for His Assassin.* Doubleday, 2010.

Web Sites

Selma to Montgomery

http://www.nps.gov/semo/index.htm

The National Park Service site provides the history, purpose, and mission of the Selma to Montgomery national historic trail.

Martin Luther King, Jr. National Historic Site

http://www.nps.gov/malu/

Home page of the civil rights leader's birthplace in Atlanta, Georgia.

Martin Luther King, Jr. Papers Project at Stanford University

http://mlk-kpp0l.Stanford.edu/

This site includes a biography, secondary documents written about Martin Luther King, Jr., primary documents written by King himself, and links to other resources.

March on Washington

http://www.kingian.net/march-on-washington.html

This site includes background information on the 1963 march as well as the full text of Martin Luther King's "I Have a Dream" speech.

Unanswered Questions

http://www.pbs.org/newshour/bb/race_relations/jan-june98/ray_4-23.html

PBS presents the dialogue from a *News Hour* program that aired in 1998 following the death of James Earl Ray, the man who was convicted of killing Martin Luther King, Jr.

Search Strings

Martin Luther King, Jr. Day

"Martin Luther King, Jr. Day" national holiday date (566,000)

"Martin Luther King, Jr. Day" national holiday date activities (49,900)

"Martin Luther King, Jr. Day" national holiday date activities closings (39,400)

The Montgomery Bus Boycott

Montgomery Alabama bus boycott (28,800)

"Montgomery bus boycott" segregation "Rosa Parks" Martin Luther King (34,600)

"Montgomery bus boycott" segregation "Rosa Parks" Martin Luther King "Supreme Court" (22,200)

The March on Washington

"March on Washington" civil rights bill "Martin Luther King" speech Lincoln Memorial (30,100)

"March on Washington" civil rights bill "Martin Luther King" speech Lincoln Memorial jobs unemployment (693)

King's Death

Martin Luther King death Memphis assassination (62,500)

Martin Luther King death Memphis assassination "James Earl Ray" conspiracy (11,200)

BACKGROUND INFORMATION

The following articles and features were written during the year in which the events took place and reflect the style and thinking of that time.

Civil rights (1964)

Overshadowing all other events anywhere in the field of civil rights in 1964 was the action of the Congress of the United States in passing the Civil Rights Act, designed to protect the constitutional rights of Negro citizens. This legislation, although controversial, was in keeping with the American tradition of equality under law for all citizens and of respect for the dignity of mankind. Before taking up this subject in detail, let us look at civil liberties across the world.

In Africa, several new constitutions contained elaborate provisions regarding civil liberties. In the United Arab Republic (UAR), President Gamal Abodel Nasser proclaimed, in March, a provisional constitution, which included guarantees of freedom of religion, speech, and press; free education of all citizens; and the right of labor to organize. The guarantee of free speech and press, however, was limited by the proviso reading: "within the limits of the law," which meant that restrictions on free speech and press were in the hands of the president and the national assembly rather than within the jurisdiction of the courts.

Malawi (formerly Nyasaland), the 37th African state to gain independence, was recognized by Great Britain on July 8, with a constitution containing guarantees of religious liberty and freedom of speech and press. Likewise, the independence of the Republic of Zambia (formerly Northern Rhodesia), the 38th African state, was recognized by Great Britain on October 24, with a constitution containing safeguards for the rights of individuals. But it remained to be seen how effective these paper provisions would prove.

The inadequacy of some constitutional guarantees was proved by events in Ghana. Its constitution provided for full democratic liberty. Nevertheless, under President Kwame Nkrumah, persecution of opponents of the governing political party began early. Finally, on January 27, 1964, an election by the voters gave Nkrumah power to turn Ghana into a one-party state, and also power to dismiss the judges of the supreme and high courts. According to a governmental announcement, 99.9 percent of the voters were in favor of this grant of authority. But, prior to the election, the citizens were repeatedly warned by the government-controlled press and radio that anyone failing to vote, or who voted "no," would be punished as "counter-revolutionaries." To ensure compliance, ballots were marked with the voter's serial numbers.

In the Soviet Union, the new "collective leadership" relaxed a few of the restrictions on Soviet citizens after the deposition of First Secretary Nikita S. Khrushchev. It was not certain that these new liberties would be permanent. At any rate, the new dictatorship allowed, among other things, peasants to keep gardens for their own food supply, and also to sell their produce in the market. On the other hand, the trend toward anti-Semitism was continued when the official newspaper Lzvestia published an attack on the Jews.

The United Nations. On February 4, 1964, U Thant, Secretary-General of the United Nations (UN), made a remarkable address before the Algerian national assembly. He declared that racial discrimination was a "most dangerous form of sickness," that it should be treated with "restraint and care." Otherwise there would be a disastrous "vicious circle" of hate and violence. The UN continued its concern with apartheid (separation of races) in the Republic of South Africa. On June 9, the Security Council condemned trials of violators of apartheid in South Africa. The consequences of the "vicious

circle" of hate of which Thant warned, was seen in November when Congolese rebels murdered nearly a hundred white persons held as hostages.

The Roman Catholic Church took important action against discrimination, when the bishops in the third session of Vatican Council II adopted, and sent to Pope Paul VI, a declaration that all humanity, and not simply the Jews, was responsible for the crucifixion of Christ. A proposed declaration on religious liberty, however, was postponed to the fourth session of the Vatican Council.

In the United States, the Department of Justice continued its program of protecting the voting rights of Negroes under federal laws which had been passed in 1957 and 1960. Title I (Voting Rights) of the Civil Rights Act of 1964 strengthened these acts by barring unequal application of registration procedures. Progress was also made in desegregation of public schools under federal court orders. The Supreme Court of the United States, for example, ordered the reopening of public schools in Prince Edward County, Virginia, after the school had been closed to avoid integration.

The Department of Justice used the Federal Bureau of Investigation (FBI) to apprehend persons who committed crimes against Negroes and civil rights workers. FBI agents, after weeks of investigation, found the bodies of three civil rights workers who had been murdered in Mississippi. On December 4, the FBI arrested 21 white men in connection with the crime. On December 10, in an unprecedented move, a local U.S. commissioner dismissed 19 of the men. The government served notice, however, that it would continue to prosecute the case.

Again, the FBI, after diligent search, apprehended and arrested four Ku Klux Klansmen in Georgia, charged with the sniper murder of Lemuel Penn, a Negro educator from Washington, D.C. The state of Georgia cooperated and indicted three of the men. A white jury, however, failed to convict them. In these cases, the efforts of the federal government were handicapped by the fact that criminal jurisdiction was in the hands of local authorities.

The Civil Rights Act of 1964. An entirely new authority was conferred upon the President of the United States and the Department of Justice by the Civil Rights Act, which Congress passed on July 2, 1964. This power was given in Title II.

President Johnson signing the Civil Rights Act of 1964

Under the new law, any Negro who is denied service in a segregated place may file a suit in a federal court. In such a case, the judge may name an attorney for the complainant and authorize the suit without cost to the complainant. If the judge believes that there is a chance of obtaining voluntary compliance, he may refer the case to the Community Relations Service, which was created by the law. If the service cannot settle the Negro's grievance, the suit goes to court. The first official act of the president under the new law was to appoint LeRoy Collins, former governor of Florida, as director of the service.

In each case, the Community Relations Service has 120 days to try to settle the grievance by persuasion. If its attempt fails, the Negro's suit goes to court, and the judge may issue an injunction or restraining order directing the accused restaurant owner or innkeeper to refrain from barring Negroes. If the accused defies the court order, he may be arrested and jailed for 45 days, until he agrees to obey the court, or be fined for each day that he refuses. All of this can be done by the judge alone, without a jury. Afterward, if a criminal contempt of court is filed against the accused, a jury trial is permitted.

The Civil Rights Act was passed with bipartisan support. In the Senate, 46 Democrats and 27 Republicans voted for the bill, while 21 Democrats and 6 Republicans voted against it. After the enactment of the measure, both major parties declared for loyal enforcement of the Civil Rights Act. In signing the bill, President Johnson said, "We must not approach the observance and enforcement of this law in a vengeful spirit. Its purpose is not to punish. Its purpose is not to divide, but to end divisions—divisions which have lasted too long."

In December, the Supreme Court of the United States upheld the controversial Title II of the act. It also quashed sit-in proceedings that occurred in the types of places named in the act.

Mass demonstrations and picketing preceded enactment of the act, contributed toward an atmosphere of tension that flared into mob violence in the South and in several cities in the North during the so-called "long, hot summer" of 1964. Riots occurred in New York City's Harlem; Rochester, New York; Jersey City, New Jersey; and Philadelphia, Pennsylvania.

An FBI investigation, ordered by President Johnson, reported on September 26 that there was

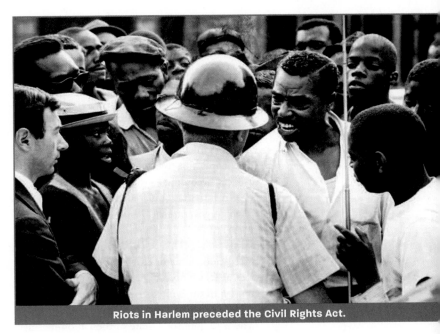

Riots in Harlem preceded the Civil Rights Act.

"no systematic planning or organization" behind the riots, that they were basically "senseless attacks on all constituted authority."

As the elections neared, it became clear that if the riots continued, their effect would rebound against the civil rights cause. Hence, rights leaders pleaded with the Negroes to cease rioting, and to halt their demonstrations until after the elections. They were successful in their pleas.

Police brutality. But still lingering after the riots were charges of police brutality against Negroes occasioned by the attempt to prevent demonstrations prohibited by local law in Southern states, and to curb mob violence in Northern states. On numerous occasions, the police used dogs, fire hose, and tear gas, and wielded billy clubs when demonstrators refused to obey orders to disperse. To preserve order, such tactics were employed not only against Negro demonstrators, but also against white violators.

In particular, Negro leaders condemned the New York Police Department for not punishing a policeman for shooting on July 16 a Negro youth who attacked him with a knife during a fracas on the street. New York's Mayor Robert Wagner resisted attempts to weaken the authority of the police department by the appointment of a civilian board to review charges of police brutality.

"One Man, One Vote." In recent years, legislatures and courts have tended to treat political rights, such as voting, as civil rights. In June, the

Supreme Court of the United States handed down a decision stating that the election districts of both houses of the state legislatures must be "substantially equal" in population. In all, the decision directly affects 15 states with cases before the Court. But the order was applicable to all of the 50 states of the Union. The 6-to-3 opinion was based on the principle of "one man, one vote." In the words of Chief Justice Warren: "Legislators represent people, not trees or acres." Unequal election districts, according to this opinion, deprived citizens in heavily populated districts of their due weight in government.

Civil rights (1966)

Racial riots in major cities across the nation and cries of "black power" made civil rights a leading concern in the United States in 1966. An agenda for new national policy was offered in President Lyndon B. Johnson's State of the Union message, calling for strict federal laws against those who "murder, attack, or intimidate" civil rights workers and for laws establishing "unavoidable requirements for nondiscriminatory jury selection" in the South. The most controversial feature of the message was the president's request that discrimination in housing sales and rentals be prohibited.

Legislation introduced in the Congress of the United States, based upon the president's proposals, prohibited discrimination on racial or religious grounds in the "purchase, rental, lease, financing, use, and occupancy of all housing." The bill promised to affect the North more than any previous civil rights measure. Public opinion, tolerant of other civil rights legislation in recent years, failed to rally behind the bill. Although it passed the House, it never came to a vote in the Senate. This proved to be the first failure of a civil rights measure in Congress in nine years.

Kentucky's plan. The year's most impressive civil rights legislation was adopted by the state of Kentucky. The first state south of the Ohio River to enact such a law, Kentucky went farther toward barring discrimination in public accommodations and hiring practices than the Civil Rights Act of 1964. The Kentucky statute opened to Negroes all businesses serving the public except barbershops, beauty shops, and small boarding houses. It guaranteed fair employment standards to the 90 percent of the labor force that works for businesses employing eight or more persons. (The federal civil rights act, even when fully extended in 1967, will cover only businesses employing 25 or more persons.)

Court battles. The courts continued to be a principal arena of the civil rights struggle. In South Carolina vs. Nicholas de B. Katzenbach, the Supreme Court of the United States upheld the Voting Rights Act of 1965, which outlawed literacy tests and other registration practices used in Southern states to keep Negroes from voting, and authorized the entry of federal registrars to enroll new voters. The Court ruled in March that these "stringent remedies" were a valid means for carrying out the commands of Section 2 of Amendment 15, which empowers Congress to take "appropriate" measures to bar voting discrimination.

The Court continued to throw out Southern convictions of persons seized in nearly every kind of civil rights demonstration. In Brown vs. Louisiana, Congress of Racial Equality (CORE) demonstrators, who staged a "stand-up" in a Clinton, Louisiana, public library, had been convicted for disturbing the peace. Yet the closeness of the vote, 5 to 4, suggested some disenchantment by the Court with ever-bolder civil rights demonstrations. Justice Hugo Black, an ardent supporter of civil rights, wrote in dissent: "It has become automatic for people to be turned loose as long as whatever they do has something to do with race. This is not the way I read the Constitution."

Early in 1966, the United States Civil Rights Commission noted that after more than a decade following the Court's school desegregation decisions only one of every 13 Negro children in the 11 states of the Old Confederacy was attending schools with white students. This was the case despite the 1964 Civil Rights Act, which empowered the U.S. Office of Education to withhold federal funds from segregated school districts. The commission attributed the poor record to the Office of Education's faulty guidelines, which permitted Negroes to attend any schools that had vacant space. This placed the burden of integration upon the Negro, who usually did not seek to integrate for fear of retaliation.

Controversial guidelines. Thus, the Office of Education quickly issued new and tighter guidelines in March suggesting: (1) that Southern school officials step-up the pace of integration of selected school faculties within a district, or risk losing federal aid; (2) that the one- and two-room

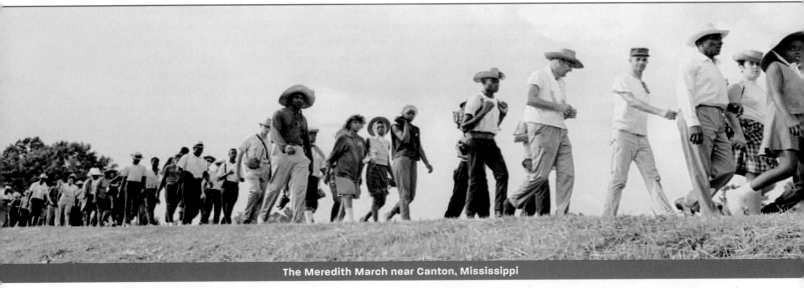

The Meredith March near Canton, Mississippi

shacks typifying many all-Negro schools in the South be closed and their students transferred to other schools; and (3) that Negroes must not be intimidated in the development of local desegregation plans. The efficacy of the new guidelines was evidenced by the outcry from Southern legislators in Congress.

Hospital's role. In a parallel development, the U.S. Public Health Service sent "a medical facilities compliance report" to some 7,600 hospitals throughout the nation, and announced that those practicing segregation will be denied federal funds. Billions of dollars of newly available Medicare benefits gave extra effect to the threat.

White House Conference on Civil Rights, headed by a 35-man council of civil rights leaders, businessmen, educators, labor union representatives, and public officials, declared in May that the federal government's civil rights progress had not been matched "by state and local government, by business and labor, the housing industry, educational institutions, and the wide spectrum of voluntary organizations that, through united effort, have the power to improve our society."

The civil rights scene provided ready illustration for the conference's contention. During the year, many Southern restaurants were turned into "clubs" to avoid compliance with the 1964 Civil Rights Act barring discrimination in public accommodations. The U.S. Department of Justice filed suits against restaurant owners following this practice.

Grenada violence. In the civil rights field, 1966 was above all a year of violence. Atlanta, Chicago, Cleveland, Dayton, San Francisco, and St. Louis erupted with racial violence. And the nation and the world was shocked to see grown men kick and strike Negro children with pipes and clubs when they entered a former all-white school in Grenada, Mississippi, under a court order. One youngster suffered a broken leg.

The Meredith March. James H. Meredith, 32, first Negro to study at the University of Mississippi, was shot from ambush near Hernando, Mississippi, during a march he undertook in June to encourage Negroes to register to vote. Meredith's march was taken up by other Negro leaders, and he was able to complete the march himself. His assailant, Aubrey James Norvell, 40, of Memphis, Tennessee, was sentenced in November to five years in prison for the highway shooting.

Black power. A schism in the Negro civil rights movement over the issue of "black power" developed in 1966. Leaders of the more radical organizations, such as Floyd McKissick, 44, of CORE, and Stokely Carmichael, 25, of the Student Nonviolent Coordinating Committee (SNCC), pleaded for black power, or for Negroes to build their own bases of power. West-Indian-born Carmichael declared that black power was intended to end the Negro's sense of inferiority in predominantly white America. In political terms, it meant seeking to take over government wherever Negroes were a majority, organizing economic boycotts, and the creation of all-Negro financial institutions.

Moderate organizations rejected the black power theme. Roy Wilkins, executive director of the National Association for the Advancement of Colored People (NAACP), said that black power "can mean in the end only black death." Martin Luther King, Jr., warned that the black power issue might split the civil rights movement permanently.

A. Philip Randolph, president of the Brotherhood of Sleeping Car Porters, urged Negro leaders to "take great care against overheating the ghettos," lest they precipitate "a race war in this nation which could become a catastrophe."

Public opinion seemed to weaken in its tolerance of Negro civil rights. Reports from university campuses indicated a decline of student interest in the subject. A backlash vote developed in several urban areas in the November elections. Primaries for the congressional elections provided scant comfort. In Louisiana, 12-term congressman James Morrison paid for his moderate racial record by losing the Democratic primary to segregationist John Rarick. In Georgia, a strident racist, Lester Maddox, was locked in a gubernatorial race that would have to be decided by the courts or the state legislature.

Elsewhere in the world, civil rights seemed healthiest in traditionally democratic countries. Generally, the new governments of Africa compiled a grim record. In South Africa and Rhodesia, white dominance tightened its grip. In Russia, the persecution of Jews continued. Communist China underwent a vast purge of dissident opinion.

But there were favorable developments, too. A severe test of civil rights is a general election, with its enormous stakes of power. One of the better elections of the year was brought off in the Dominican Republic. Tensions ran high, and to keep the proceedings honest, numerous foreign and diplomatic "observers" were on hand. The election was deemed an honest one and was widely hailed as the country's second free election since 1924.

In Spain, the Franco dictatorship took an encouraging turn when the Cortes (legislature) enacted a new press law under which publications no longer

Part of the crowds gathered for the Poor People's March

need to secure clearance prior to their appearance in print. Although the Ministry of Information can still seize an entire press run, it now must take its case promptly to the courts.

Civil rights (1968)

The assassin's bullet was the most oppressive force in the civil rights arena in 1968. Two leaders deeply involved in the civil rights movement, Martin Luther King, Jr., and Robert F. Kennedy, were murdered. King was felled in Memphis, on April 4, as he lingered on his motel balcony before supper. He was in Memphis to support a local strike of Negro garbage workers and was seeking to forestall a takeover of their cause by black militants.

In stressing brotherhood and nonviolence, King was the bridge between black and white America. But, in recent years, the violence of the cities was sweeping aside his doctrines. His murder was viewed by many as a final refutation of his nonviolent philosophy. Violence and riots erupted in 126 cities following his assassination.

An assassin again achieved momentary triumph, on June 5, when Senator Robert F. Kennedy was struck down in Los Angeles after an important election victory in California's presidential primary. As much as any other national politician, Kennedy had been involved in the civil rights movement. During his brother John F. Kennedy's presidential administration, Robert was Attorney General, and in that post was at the center of several civil rights crises. His own campaign for the presidency in 1968 stressed civil rights themes. The murders of John Kennedy, King, and Robert Kennedy seemed, to many persons, to be of a kind. "You notice," one Negro said, "that every time we get somebody willing to speak out for the black man, they cut him down." President Lyndon B. Johnson appointed a Commission on Violence, on June 10, headed by Milton Eisenhower, to study the phenomenon of violence in American life. The commission held hearings, but it was not expected to issue its report until the late spring of 1969.

The Poor People's March, one of several unfinished projects conceived by King, was a convergence of the poor of all races in Washington, D.C. Some 3,000 people came in May by rail, bus, mule train, and on foot to live in plywood and plastic shanties constructed in a glade beside the Lincoln Memorial's reflecting pool and designated

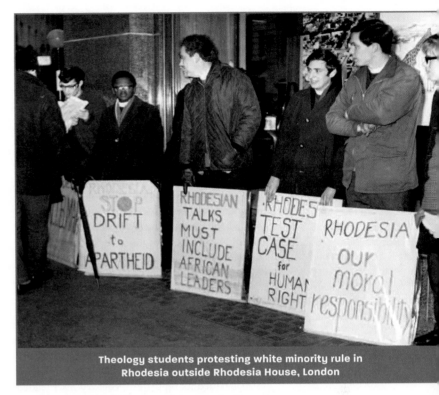

Theology students protesting white minority rule in
Rhodesia outside Rhodesia House, London

"Resurrection City." The aim of the march was to call the nation's attention to problems of poverty, and to influence the Congress of the United States to act on behalf of the poor. Little emphasis was placed on specific measures.

Despite marches to the Capitol and meetings with legislators, the Poor People's March failed to produce any new laws or make other evident gains in a Congress that was economy-minded and engrossed in the war in Vietnam. Resurrection City was also handicapped by dissidence among its leaders, by infiltrators whose creed was violence, by the toll of time and insufficient funds on its ranks, and by the vagueness of its conception. After its six-week license expired, federal and District of Columbia officials moved in to dismantle the city. King's successor, Ralph D. Abernathy, a Baptist minister, led a final march on Congress, and then submitted, with a group of followers, to peaceable arrest.

Elections. In Mississippi, a stronghold of segregation, Robert Clark, schoolteacher and grandson of a slave, was elected and seated as Mississippi's first black legislator in the 20th century. In another election contest, Charles Evers, head of Mississippi's National Association for the Advancement of Colored People (NAACP), topped six white rival candidates in a Democratic congressional primary. In a run-off, Evers was defeated, but he pledged full support to the nominee, Charles H. Griffin.

The Civil Rights Act of 1968, passed on April 10 and signed into law the following day, imposes fair housing standards on the sale and rental of 80 percent of the nation's private housing market. The law will not become operative, however, until 1970.

More indicative of the mood in Congress was its steady cutting of appropriations for poverty, housing, and other civil rights programs. The Office of Economic Opportunity, which administers the Job Corps, the Community Action Program, Upward Bound, and other programs for the urban poor, suffered severe cutbacks in funds and the reassignment of some of its functions to other agencies. Faced with congressional disinterest, President Johnson devoted only a single sentence to civil rights in his State of the Union message, delivered to Congress on January 17.

Kerner report. The National Advisory Commission on Civil Disorders, appointed in 1967, issued its report on February 29. Headed by Otto Kerner, then governor of Illinois, the commission warned that "Our nation is moving toward two societies, one black, one white—separate and unequal." The commission proposed strategies and programs far beyond anything yet undertaken in the United States. These included the creation of 2 million new jobs in the public and private sectors in the next three years, the provision of a "basic allowance" to families and individuals, and bringing 6 million new and existing dwelling units within reach of low- and moderate-income families. In these and other recommendations, the commission called for outlays whose costs it did not venture to estimate.

Black power. Changes in attitude and programs stemming from the concept of black power were noted in most organizations representing the Negro civil rights movement. The Congress of Racial Equality (CORE) took a position beyond black power, a position of black nationalism, or a commitment to convert black ghetto communities into a separate nation within a nation. Whitney Young, head of the moderate Urban League, who previously rejected the black power concept, assumed a new militancy in urging blacks to develop "the power that America respects." Also prominent in 1968 were the Black Panthers, a mil-

itant extremist group who modeled themselves and their movement on the teachings of Malcolm X.

The Negro's severest deprivation continued to be jobs. Negro unemployment was twice that of whites, and among youth unemployment was a massive 24.7 percent. Elsewhere, in society, there were some gains for the Negro. He achieved markedly stronger representation in television commercials and in the advertising agencies that produce them. Negro history, long neglected in the schoolroom, began to be represented in textbooks. One of the best received Broadway plays was The Great White Hope, relating the career of Jack Johnson, the first Negro heavyweight champion boxer.

The war in Vietnam provided several civil liberties issues. Dr. Benjamin Spock, a noted pediatrician, and other defendants were convicted, on July 11, of conspiring to encourage draft evasion. The Spock case was part of a large draft-resistance movement, which included rallies, marches, and speeches in cities and on campuses across the country.

The Supreme Court of the United States ruled on the case of one draft-card burner, David O'Brien, who contended that his act was "symbolic" of free speech under the U.S. Constitution and was therefore unpunishable. The Court held, however, on May 27, that O'Brien violated a 1965 act prohibiting draft card burning, which Congress had a right to pass under its powers to "raise and support armies." Protesters against the war in Vietnam also demonstrated against appearances by President Johnson and in the presidential campaign of 1968.

In other rulings, the Court held, on November 19, that it is unconstitutional for lower courts to delay public meetings, even when violence is threatened, without hearing testimony from those who wish to meet. The decision set up an important exception to the long-established practice by which judges frequently issue temporary restraining orders solely on the testimony of the complaining parties.

The Court also continued to grapple with the problem of electronic eavesdropping. In a case involving a gambler trapped by federal agents who bugged his favorite telephone booth, the Court held that "Wherever a man may be, he is entitled to know that he will remain free from unreasonable searches and seizures." The Court added, however, that eavesdropping is permissible if policemen and federal agents secure search warrants naming the suspect and the place where the eavesdropping device will be used.

Those who believed that recent Court decisions were eroding the power of the police found comfort in a Court ruling that the police may stop and search a suspicious citizen without violating the provision of Amendment 4 of the U.S. Constitution prohibiting law enforcement officials from unreasonable search and seizure.

Abroad, Great Britain, among other countries, struggled with problems of race. Under the terms by which it granted Kenya independence, Asiatic residents could choose between becoming citizens of Kenya or of Great Britain. Many of these "coloureds" chose Britain and migrated to the United Kingdom. Parliament then enacted a law barring automatic entry except to those who could prove that the father or paternal grandfather was born, naturalized, or otherwise registered as a British citizen. The coloureds were thus subjected to immigration quotas, and, in effect, relegated to "second-class" citizenship.

Racial conflict flared in civil war in Rhodesia. There, a quarter of a million whites, who unilaterally declared their independence from Britain three years ago, argued whether or not to institute an out-and-out white-supremicist constitution over Rhodesia's 4.3 million blacks. There was renewed fighting on the northern border, where black Rhodesians with modern weapons tried to fight their way through the hot, rocky gorges at both ends of Lake Kariba. Another band of guerrillas was active on the Rhodesia-Mozambique border.

The Republic of South Africa enacted legislation that made apartheid, or racial separation, in politics complete. It prepared for the abolition of coloured representation in the national house of assembly, and increased the authority and responsibility of the Coloured Representative Council, which will, in effect, become a parliament for the coloured people. The country was barred from the 1968 Olympics because of its apartheid policies.

Elsewhere, Belgium and Canada struggled with relations between the several nationalities within their borders. In Belgium, a dispute between Dutch-speaking Flemings and the French-speaking Walloons toppled the government. The Canadian government took steps to assure French Canadians the same rights enjoyed by English-speaking Canadians.

Earth

Earth is a planet in the Milky Way Galaxy that provides just the right amount of sunlight, water, and oxygen to support life. It has a total surface area of 196,900,000 square miles (510,000,000 square kilometers) of which 29 percent is land and 71 percent is water.

HOT topics

History of Earth. The Earth is at least $4^1/_2$ billion years old. Geologists study the strata of the Earth to find clues as to the history of the Earth. Studying space has also helped scientists to develop theories about the formation of the Earth. The history of the Earth is divided into four eons: Hadean, Archean, Proterozoic, and Phanerozoic. The Phanerozoic eon is divided into three eras: Paleozoic, Mesozoic, and Cenozoic. Fossils in rock give clues as to the development of life on Earth.

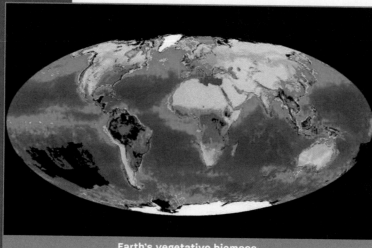

Earth's vegetative biomass

HOT topics

Earth in the Solar System.
Earth is the third planet from the sun and the fifth largest planet orbiting the sun. It has one moon. Earth completes a rotation on a tilted North-South axis about every twenty-four hours, travels around the sun about every 365 days, and revolves around the center of the Milky Way Galaxy every 240 million years. Gravity is the underlying unifying force.

Earth's Spheres.
The Earth is composed of a core and a *lithosphere*, which consists of the mantle and the crust. The layer of water and ice covering the Earth is called the *hydrosphere*, which contains a region of permanent ice called the *cryosphere*. The layer of air surrounding the Earth is called the *atmosphere*, with a constantly moving lower layer called the *troposphere* and a higher layer called the *stratosphere*. The *biosphere* consists of those sections of the hydrosphere, solid land, and atmosphere where life exists. All of these layers, or "spheres," create the planet Earth.

The world

Cycles on and in Earth.
Cycles on and in the Earth continually affect everything on the planet. Atmospheric circulation and the movement of moisture and heat around the Earth constantly create wind and weather patterns. These patterns influence ocean currents forming gyres or loops in the currents. The ocean currents cycle the ocean's heat around the Earth; this is called the global heat conveyor. Evaporation of the water from the oceans and then the snow or rainfall back to the land and waters create the hydrologic cycle. The formation of rock from the flow and cooling of lava to the breakdown of rock from weathering create the rock cycle.

Earth's Climate Changes.
Earth has experienced many ice ages which have changed the face of the Earth, creating great lakes and changing the courses of major rivers. Greenhouse gases and the depletion of the ozone layer cause a greenhouse effect warming the Earth.

TRUE or FALSE?
Two hundred million years ago Earth contained one supercontinent called Pangaea.

THE BASICS

Earth is a small planet in the vastness of space. It is one of several planets that travel through space around the sun. The sun is a star—one of hundreds of billions of stars that make up a galaxy called the Milky Way. The Milky Way and trillions of other galaxies make up the universe.

The planet Earth is only a tiny part of the universe, but it is the home of human beings and, in fact, all known life in the universe. Animals, plants, and other organisms live almost everywhere on Earth's surface. They can live on Earth because it is just the right distance from the sun. Most living things need the sun's warmth and light for life. If Earth were too close to the sun, it would be too hot for living things. If Earth were too far from the sun, it would be too cold for anything to live. Living things also must have water to live. Earth has plenty. Water covers most of Earth's surface.

The study of Earth is called geology, and scientists who study Earth are geologists. Geologists study different physical features of Earth to understand how they were formed and how they may have changed over time. Much of Earth, such as the deep interior, cannot be studied directly. Geologists must often study samples of rock and use indirect methods to learn about the planet. Today, geologists can also view and study the entire Earth from space.

DEFINITIONS

earth 1. Also, **Earth.** the planet on which we live; the globe. The earth is the fifth largest planet in the solar system, and the third in distance from the sun. *China is on the other side of the earth. The earth is a large ball or sphere of mineral matter, some 8,000 miles in diameter, the depressions on which are filled with water* (White and Renner).

2. all the people who live on this planet: *And the whole earth was of one language* (Genesis 11:1).

3. this world as the place where man lives (often in contrast to heaven and hell): *Earth's crammed with heaven, And every common bush afire with God* (Elizabeth Barrett Browning).

4. dry land; ground: *the earth, the sea, and the sky. God called the dry land earth* (Genesis 1:10).

5. soil; dirt: *The earth in the garden is good, soft soil.*

6. the hole of a fox or other burrowing animal.

7. worldly matters:...*all the fuming vanities of earth* (Wordsworth).

8. a metallic oxide from which it is hard to remove the oxygen, such as alumina: *the alkaline earths, the rare earths.*

9. *British.* the connection of an electrical conductor with the earth; ground.

10. *Obsolete.* a land or country: *this blessed plot, this earth, this realm, this England* (Shakespeare).

world 1. the earth: *Ships can sail around the world.*

2. all of certain parts, people, or things of the earth: *the world of ideas. The New World is North America and South America. Ants are parts of the insect world. With no aspirations beyond the little world in which she moved* (Benjamin Disraeli).

3. all people; the human race; the public: *The whole world knows it.*

4. the things of this life and the people devoted to them: *Monks and nuns live apart from the world.*

5. any planet, especially when considered as inhabited: The War of the Worlds *is a book about creatures from Mars who wanted to conquer Earth.*

6. any time, condition, or place of life: *Heaven is in the world to come.*

7. all things; everything; the universe; cosmos.

8. a great deal; very much; large amount: *"I...think the world of you, pal, even with all your faults"* (Saul Bellow).

Earth ranks fifth in size among the sun's planets. It has a diameter of about 8,000 miles (13,000 kilometers). Jupiter, the largest planet, is about eleven times larger in diameter than Earth. Mercury, on the other hand, has a diameter of about two-fifths that of Earth.

Earth, like all the planets in our solar system, travels around the sun in a path called an *orbit*. Earth is about 93 million miles (150 million kilometers) from the sun. It takes one year for Earth to complete one orbit around the sun. The innermost planet, Mercury, is only about one-third as far from the sun as Earth and circles the sun in only eighty-eight days. Neptune, the outermost planet, is thirty times as far from the sun as Earth and takes 165 Earth years to circle the sun.

How Earth moves. Earth has three motions. It (1) spins like a top around an imaginary line called an axis that runs from the North Pole to the South Pole, (2) it travels around the sun, and (3) it moves through the Milky Way along with the sun and the rest of the solar system.

Earth takes 24 hours to spin completely around on its axis so that the sun is in the same place in the sky. This period is called a *solar day*. During a solar day, Earth moves a little around its orbit so that it faces the stars a little differently each night. Thus, it only takes 23 hours 56 minutes 4.09 seconds for Earth to spin once so that the stars appear to be in the same place in the sky. This period is called a *sidereal day*. A sidereal day is shorter than a solar day, so the stars appear to rise about four minutes earlier each day.

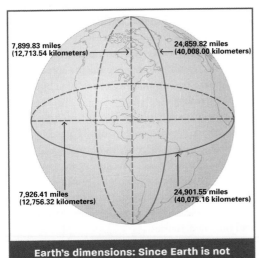

7,899.83 miles
(12,713.54 kilometers)

24,859.82 miles
(40,008.00 kilometers)

7,926.41 miles
(12,756.32 kilometers)

24,901.55 miles
(40,075.16 kilometers)

Earth's dimensions: Since Earth is not perfectly round, distances measured through the poles are shorter than those at the equator.

Earth takes 365 days 6 hours 9 minutes 9.54 seconds to circle the sun. This length of time is called a *sidereal year*. Because Earth does not spin a whole number of times as it goes around the sun, the calendar gets out of step with the seasons by about six hours each year. Every four years, a day is added to bring the calendar back into line with the seasons. These years, called *leap years*, have 366 days. The extra day is added to the end of February and occurs as February 29.

The distance around Earth's orbit is 584 million miles (940 million kilometers). Earth travels in its orbit at 66,700 miles (107,000 kilometers) an hour, or 18.5 miles (30 kilometers) a second. Earth's orbit lies on an imaginary flat surface around the sun called the *orbital plane*.

Earth's axis is not straight up and down, but is tilted by about 23$\frac{1}{2}$ degrees compared to the orbital plane. This tilt and Earth's motion around the sun cause the change of the seasons. In January, the northern half of Earth tilts away from the sun. Sunlight is spread thinly over the northern half of Earth, and the north experiences winter. At the same time, the sunlight falls intensely on the southern half of Earth, which has summer. By July, Earth has moved to the opposite side of the sun. Now the northern half of Earth tilts toward the sun. Sunlight falls intensely over the northern half of Earth, and the north experiences summer. At the same time, the sunlight falls less intensely on the southern half of Earth, which has winter.

Earth's orbit is not a perfect circle. Earth is slightly closer to the sun in early January (winter in the Northern Hemisphere) and farther away in July. In January, Earth is 91.4 million miles (147.1 million kilometers) from the sun, and in July it is 94.5 million miles (152.1 million kilometers) from the sun. This variation has a far smaller effect than the heating and cooling caused by the tilt of Earth's axis.

Earth and the solar system are part of a vast disk of stars called the Milky Way Galaxy. Just as the moon orbits Earth and planets orbit the sun, the sun and other stars orbit the tightly packed center of the Milky Way. The solar system is about two-fifths of the way from the center of the Milky Way and revolves around the center at about 137 miles (220 kilometers) per second. The solar system makes one complete revolution around the center of the galaxy in about 240 million years.

Earth's size and shape. Most people picture Earth as a ball with the North Pole at the top and the South Pole at the bottom. Earth, other planets, large moons, and stars—in fact, most objects in space bigger than about 200 miles (320 kilometers) in diameter—are round because of their gravity. Gravity pulls matter in toward the center of objects. Tiny moons, such as the two moons of Mars, have so little gravity that they do not become round, but remain lumpy instead.

To our bodies, "down" is always the direction gravity is pulling. People everywhere on Earth feel "down" is toward the center of Earth and "up" is toward the sky. People in Spain and in New Zealand are on exactly opposite sides of Earth from each other, but both sense their surroundings as "right side up." Gravity works the same way on other planets and moons.

Earth, however, is not perfectly round. Earth's spin causes it to bulge slightly at its middle, the equator. The diameter of Earth from North Pole to South Pole is 7,899.83 miles (12,713.54 kilometers), but through the equator it is 7,926.41 miles (12,756.32 kilometers). This difference, 26.58 miles (42.78 kilometers), is only $1/298$ the diameter of Earth. The difference is too tiny to be easily seen in pictures of Earth from space, so the planet appears round.

Earth's bulge also makes the circumference of Earth larger around the equator than around the poles. The circumference around the equator is 24,901.55 miles (40,075.16 kilometers), but around the poles it is only 24,859.82 miles (40,008.00 kilometers). The circumference is actually greatest just south of the equator, so Earth is slightly pear-shaped. Earth also has mountains and valleys, but these features are tiny compared to the total size of Earth, so the planet appears smooth from space.

The moon as seen from Apollo 11

Earth and its moon. Earth has one moon. Earth's moon has a diameter of 2,159 miles (3,474 kilometers)—about one-fourth of Earth's diameter.

The sun's gravity acts on Earth and the moon as if they were a single body with its center about 1,000 miles (1,600 kilometers) below Earth's surface. This spot is the Earth-moon *barycenter*. It is the point of balance between the heavy Earth and the lighter moon. The path of the barycenter around the sun is a smooth curve. Earth and the moon circle the barycenter as they orbit the sun. The motion of Earth and moon around the barycenter makes them "wobble" in their path around the sun.

Earth's Spheres

Earth is composed of several layers, or *spheres*, somewhat like the layers of an onion. The solid Earth consists of a thin outer layer, the *crust*, with a thick rocky layer, the *mantle*, beneath it. The crust and the upper portion of the mantle are called the *lithosphere*. At the center of Earth is the *core*. The outer part of the core is liquid, while the inner part is solid. Much of Earth is covered by a layer of water or ice called the *hydrosphere*. Earth is surrounded by a thin layer of air, the *atmosphere*. The portion of the hydrosphere, atmosphere, and solid land where life exists is called the *biosphere*.

The atmosphere. Air surrounds Earth and becomes progressively thinner farther from the surface. Most people find it difficult to breathe more than 2 miles (3 kilometers) above sea level. About 100 miles (160 kilometers) above the surface, the air is so thin that satellites can travel without much resistance. Detectable traces of atmosphere, however, can be found as high as 370 miles (600 kilometers) above Earth's surface. The atmosphere has no definite outer edge but fades gradually into space.

Nitrogen makes up 78 percent of the atmosphere, while oxygen makes up 21 percent. The remaining 1 percent consists of argon and small amounts of other gases. The atmosphere also contains water vapor, carbon dioxide, water droplets, dust particles, and small amounts of many other chemicals released by volcanoes, fires, living things, and human activities.

The lowest layer of the atmosphere is called the *troposphere*. This layer is in constant motion. The sun heats Earth's surface and the air above it, causing warm air to rise. As the warm air rises, air pressure decreases and the air expands and cools. The cool air is denser than the surrounding air, so it sinks and the cycle starts again. This constant cycle of the air causes the weather.

High above the troposphere, about 30 miles (48 kilometers) above Earth's surface, is a layer of still air called the *stratosphere*. The stratosphere contains a layer where ultraviolet light from the sun strikes oxygen molecules to create a gas called *ozone*. Ozone blocks most of the harmful ultraviolet rays from reaching Earth's surface. Some ultraviolet rays get through, however. They are responsible for sunburn and can cause skin cancer in people. Tiny amounts of human-made chemicals have caused some of the natural ozone to break down. Many people are concerned that the ozone layer may become too thin, allowing ultraviolet rays to reach the surface and harm people and other living things.

Water vapor, carbon dioxide, methane, and other gases in the atmosphere trap heat from the sun, warming Earth. The heat-trapping quality of these gases causes the *greenhouse effect*. Without the greenhouse effect of the atmosphere, Earth would probably be too cold for life to exist.

The hydrosphere. Earth is the only planet in the solar system with abundant liquid water on its surface. Water has chemical and physical properties not matched by any other substance, and it is essential for life on Earth. Water has a great ability to absorb heat. The oceans store much of the heat Earth gets from the sun. The electrical charges on water molecules give water a great ability to attract atoms from other substances. This quality allows water to dissolve many things. Water's ability to dissolve materials makes it a powerful agent in breaking down rocks. Liquid water on Earth affects not just the surface but the interior as well. Water in rocks lowers the melting temperature of rock. Water dramatically weakens rocks and makes them easier to melt beneath Earth's surface.

About 71 percent of Earth's surface is covered by water, most of it in the oceans. Ocean water is too salty to drink. Only about 3 percent of Earth's water is fresh water, suitable for drinking. Much of Earth's fresh water is not readily available to people because it is frozen in the polar ice caps or beneath Earth's surface. Polar regions and high mountains stay cold enough for water to remain permanently frozen. The region of permanent ice on Earth is sometimes called the *cryosphere*.

The lithosphere. The crust and upper mantle of Earth from the surface to about 60 miles (100 kilometers) down make up the lithosphere. The thin crust is made up of natural chemicals called *minerals* composed of different combinations of elements. Oxygen is the most abundant chemical element in rocks in Earth's crust, making up about 47 percent of the weight of all rock. The second most abundant element is silicon, 27 percent, followed by aluminum (8 percent), iron (5 percent), calcium (4 percent), and sodium, potassium, and magnesium (about 2 percent each). These eight elements make up 99 percent of the weight of rocks on Earth's surface.

Two elements, silicon and oxygen, make up almost three-fourths of the crust. This combination of elements is so important that geologists have a special term for it: *silica*. Minerals that contain silica are called *silicate minerals*. The most abundant mineral on Earth's surface is quartz, made up of pure silica. Another plentiful group of silicates are the *feldspars*, which consist of silica, aluminum, calcium, sodium, and potassium. Other common silicate minerals on Earth's surface are pyroxene and amphibole, which consist of combinations of silica, iron, and magnesium.

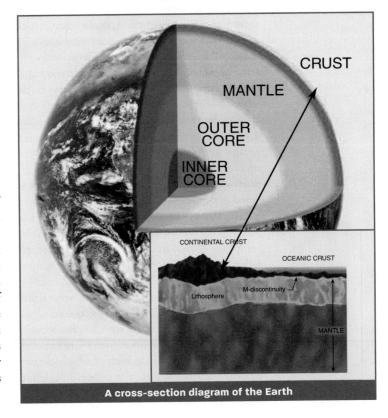

A cross-section diagram of the Earth

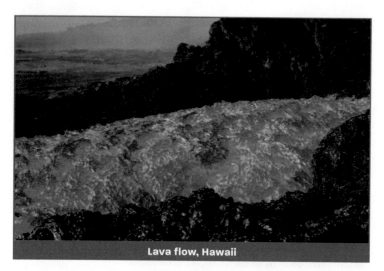

Lava flow, Hawaii

Another important group of minerals are the *carbonates*, which contain carbon and oxygen along with small amounts of other elements. The most important carbonate mineral is *calcite*, made up of calcium, carbon, and oxygen. *Limestone*, a common rock used for building, is mostly calcite. Another important carbonate is *dolomite*, composed of carbon, oxygen, calcium, and magnesium.

Earth has two kinds of crust. The dry land of the continents is made up mostly of granite and other light silicate minerals, while the ocean floors are composed mostly of a dark, dense volcanic rock called *basalt*. Continental crust averages about 25 miles (40 kilometers) thick, but it is thicker in some areas and thinner in others. Most oceanic crust is only about 5 miles (8 kilometers) thick. Water fills in the low areas over the thin basalt crust to form the world's oceans. There is more than enough water on Earth to completely fill the oceanic basins, and some of it spreads onto the edges of the continents. This portion of the continents surrounded by a band of shallow ocean is called the *continental shelf*.

The biosphere. Earth is the only planet in the universe known to have life. The region containing life extends from the bottom of the deepest ocean to a few miles or kilometers into the atmosphere. There are several million known kinds, called *species*, of living things, and scientists believe that there are far more species not yet discovered.

Life affects Earth in many ways. Life has actually made the atmosphere around us. Plants take in water and carbon dioxide, both of which contain oxygen. They use the carbon in carbon dioxide and the hydrogen in water to make chemicals of many kinds and give off oxygen as a waste product. Animals eat plants to get energy and return water and carbon dioxide back into the environment. Living things affect the surface of Earth in other ways as well. Plants create chemicals that speed the breakdown of rock. Grasslands and forests slow the erosion of soil.

Earth's Rocks

The solid part of Earth consists of rocks, which are sometimes made up of a single mineral, but more often consist of mixtures of minerals. Geologists classify rocks according to their origin. *Igneous rocks* form when molten rock cools and solidifies. *Sedimentary rocks* form when grains of rock or dissolved chemicals are deposited in layers by wind, water, or glaciers. Over time, the layers harden into solid rock. *Metamorphic rocks* develop deep in Earth's crust when heat or pressure transforms other types of rock.

Igneous rocks form from molten material called *magma*. Most of Earth's interior is solid, not molten, but it is extremely hot. At the base of Earth's crust, the temperature is about 1800 °F (1000 °C). In some portions of the crust, conditions are right for rocks to melt. Rocks can melt more easily near the crust if they contain water, which lowers their melting point.

Where conditions are right, small pockets of magma form beneath and within the crust. Some of this magma reaches the surface, where it erupts from volcanoes as lava. Igneous rocks formed this way are called *volcanic* or *extrusive*. Vast quantities of magma, however, never reach the surface. They cool slowly within the crust and may only be exposed long afterward by erosion. Such igneous rocks are called *plutonic* or *intrusive*. Plutonic rocks cool slowly. During this slow cooling, their minerals form large crystals. Plutonic rocks tend to be much coarser than volcanic rocks.

Igneous rocks that are rich in silica tend to be poor in iron and magnesium, and the opposite is also true. Volcanic rocks that are iron-rich and silica-poor are basalt. Plutonic rocks of the same makeup are called *gabbro*. Silica-rich volcanic rocks are called *rhyolite*, and plutonic rocks of the same composition are granite. Granite lies under most of the continents, while basalt lies under most of the ocean floors.

Sedimentary rocks. Rocks on Earth's surface are under constant attack by chemicals and mechanical forces. The processes that break down rocks are called *weathering*. Water is effective at dissolving minerals. When water freezes, it expands, so expanding ice helps pry apart mineral grains in rocks. In addition, living things produce chemicals that help dissolve rocks.

Once rocks break apart, the loose material is often carried away by erosion. Running water erodes rocks. Wind and glaciers also contribute to erosion. Erosion is usually a relatively slow process, but over millions of years, erosion can uncover even rocks many miles or kilometers below the surface.

Materials derived from weathering and erosion of rocks are eventually deposited to form sedimentary rocks. Rocks that are made up of small pieces of other rocks are called *clastic rocks*. Rocks containing larger pebbles are called *conglomerate*. The particles in these rocks are cemented together when minerals dissolved in the water crystallize between the grains. The most abundant sedimentary rocks, called *mudrocks*, consist of tiny particles. Some of these rocks, called *shale*, split into thin sheets when broken. Sandstone is a sedimentary rock made up of sand cemented together.

Other sedimentary rocks form when dissolved materials undergo chemical reactions and settle out as tiny solid particles. These rocks are called *chemical sedimentary rocks*. Common chemical sedimentary rocks include some types of limestone and dolomite. Some chemical sedimentary rocks form when water evaporates, leaving dissolved materials behind. Rock salt and a mineral called *gypsum* form this way.

Some sedimentary rocks, called *biogenic*, are formed by the action of living things. Coal is the remains of woody plants that have been transformed into rock by heat and pressure over time. Most limestone is formed by microscopic marine organisms that secrete protective shells of calcium carbonate. When the animals die, the shells remain and solidify into limestone.

Metamorphic rocks. When rocks are buried deeply, they become hot. Earth's crust grows hotter by about 70 °F per mile (25 °C per kilometer) of depth. Pressure also increases with depth. At a depth of 1 mile (1.6 kilometers) beneath the surface, the pressure is about 6,000 pounds per square inch (41,360 kilopascals). As rocks are heated and subjected to pressure, minerals react and the rocks become metamorphic. Shale is transformed to slate, limestone, and eventually into marble under pressure. Many metamorphic rocks contain recognizable features that tell of their origin, but others change so much that only the chemical makeup provides evidence of what they originally were.

Marble Canyon, Grand Canyon National Park

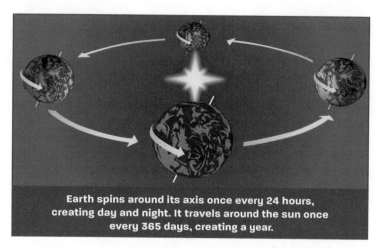

Earth spins around its axis once every 24 hours, creating day and night. It travels around the sun once every 365 days, creating a year.

 ## Cycles on and in Earth

Earth can be thought of as a huge system of interacting cycles. In each cycle, matter and energy move from place to place and may change form. Eventually, matter and energy return to their original condition and the cycle begins again. The cycles affect everything on the planet, from the weather to the shape of the landscape. There are many cycles on and within Earth. A few of the most important are (1) atmospheric circulation, (2) ocean currents, (3) the global heat conveyor, (4) the hydrologic cycle, and (5) the rock cycle.

Atmospheric circulation. Air warmed by the sun near the equator rises and flows toward Earth's poles, returning to the surface and flowing back to the equator. This motion, combined with the rotation of Earth, moves heat and moisture around the planet creating winds and weather patterns.

In some areas, the winds change directions with the seasons. These patterns are often called *monsoons*. In summer, air over Asia is heated by the sun, rises, and draws moist air from the Indian Ocean, causing daily rains over most of southern Asia. In winter, the air over Asia cools, sinks, and flows out, pushing the moist air away and creating dry weather. A similar pattern occurs in the Pacific Ocean near Mexico and brings moist air and afternoon thunderstorms to the southwestern United States in the summer.

Ocean currents are driven by the winds and follow the same general pattern. The continents block the flow of water around the globe, so ocean currents flow west near the equator, then turn toward the poles when they strike a continent, turn east, then flow back to the equator on the other side. In all the oceans, the ocean currents form great loops called *gyres*. The gyres flow clockwise north of the equator and counterclockwise south of the equator.

The global heat conveyor is an enormous cycle of ocean water that distributes the oceans' heat around Earth. Water in the polar regions is very cold, salty, and dense. It sinks and flows along the seafloor toward the equator. Eventually, the water rises along the margins of the continents and merges with the surface water flow. When it reaches the polar regions, it sinks again. This three-dimensional movement of water mixes heat throughout the oceans, warming polar waters. It also brings nutrients up from the deep ocean to the surface, where they are available for marine plants and animals.

The hydrologic cycle. Water from the oceans evaporates and is carried by the atmosphere, eventually falling as rain or snow. Water that falls on the land helps break rocks down chemically, nourishes plants, and wears down the landscape. Eventually, the water returns to the sea to start the cycle over again.

The rock cycle. Earth has many more kinds of rocks compared to other planets because there are so many processes acting to form and break down rocks. Geologists sometimes speak of the *rock cycle* to explain how different rock types are related. The cycle may begin with a flow of lava from a volcano cooling to form new igneous rocks on Earth's surface. As the rock is exposed to water, it breaks down and the resulting materials may be carried away to be deposited as sedimentary rocks. These rocks may eventually be so deeply buried that they change in form to become metamorphic rocks. They may even melt, creating the raw material for the next generation of igneous rocks.

Rocks rarely go through the entire rock cycle. Instead, some steps may be skipped or repeated. For example, igneous rocks can be subjected to heat and pressure and transformed directly to metamorphic rocks. Sedimentary rocks can be broken down by weathering and then reassembled into a new generation of sedimentary rocks. Metamorphic rocks can also be weathered to form the raw material for a new generation of sedimentary rocks. Any rock type, igneous, metamorphic, or sedimentary, can be transformed into any other type.

Geologists cannot study the interior of Earth directly. The deepest wells drilled reach less than 8 miles (13 kilometers) below the surface. Geologists know that the whole Earth differs in composition from its thin outer crust. Deep in Earth, pressures are so great that minerals can be compressed into dense forms not found on the surface.

One way geologists determine the overall composition of Earth is from chemical analysis of meteorites. Certain types of meteorites, called *chondrites*, are remains of the early solar system that persisted unchanged in space until they fell to Earth. Geologists can use chondrites to estimate the original chemical composition of the entire Earth.

Unlike chondrites, Earth is made up of layers that contain different amounts of various chemical elements. Geologists learn about Earth's interior by studying vibrations generated by earthquakes, using instruments called *seismographs*. The speed and motion of vibrations traveling through Earth depend on the composition and density of the material they travel through. Geologists can determine many properties of Earth's interior by analyzing such vibrations.

The mantle. Beneath the crust, extending down about 1,800 miles (2,900 kilometers), is a thick layer called the mantle. The mantle is not perfectly stiff but can flow slowly. Earth's crust floats on the mantle much as a board floats in water. Just as a thick board would rise above the water higher than a thin one, the thick continental crust rises higher than the thin oceanic crust. The slow motion of rock in the mantle moves the continents around and causes earthquakes, volcanoes, and the formation of mountain ranges.

The core. At the center of Earth is the core. The core is made mostly of iron and nickel and possibly smaller amounts of lighter elements, including sulfur and oxygen. The core is about 4,400 miles (7,100 kilometers) in diameter, slightly larger than half the diameter of Earth and about the size of Mars. The outermost 1,400 miles (2,250 kilometers) of the core are liquid. Currents flowing in the core are thought to generate Earth's magnetic field. Geologists believe the innermost part of the core, about 1,600 miles (2,600 kilometers) in diameter, is made of a similar material as the outer core, but it is solid. The inner core is about four-fifths as big as Earth's moon.

Earth gets hotter toward the center. At the bottom of the continental crust, the temperature is about 1800 °F (1000 °C). The temperature increases about 3 °F per mile (1 °C per kilometer) below the crust. Geologists believe the temperature of Earth's outer core is about 6700 to 7800 °F (3700 to 4300 °C). The inner core may be as hot as 12,600 °F (7000 °C)—hotter than the surface of the sun. But, because it is under great pressures, the rock in the center of Earth remains solid.

Earth's Crust

The hot rock deep in Earth's mantle flows upward slowly, while cooler rock near the surface sinks because hot materials are lighter than cool materials. The rising and sinking of materials due to differences in temperature is called *convection*. As Earth's mantle flows, it breaks the crust into a number of large slabs called *tectonic plates*, much as slabs of ice break apart on a pond. The slow flow of Earth's mantle drags the crust along, causing the continents to move, mountains to form, and volcanoes and earthquakes to occur. This constant motion of Earth's crust is called *plate tectonics*.

In some places, usually under the oceans, Earth's plates are spreading apart. New magma from the mantle rises to fill the cracks between the plates. Places where plates spread apart are called *spreading centers*. Many volcanoes occur where plates pull apart and magma wells up from within the mantle to fill the gap. The material from the mantle is made of iron and magnesium-rich silicate rocks. It hardens to form rocks and creates oceanic crust made of basalt.

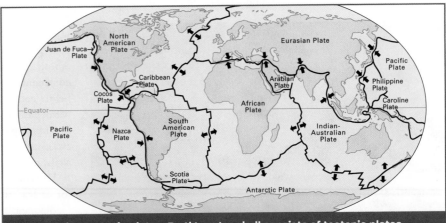

Earth's tectonic plates: Earth's outer shell consists of tectonic plates. These huge slabs slowly move in relationship to one another (see arrows).

Subduction. Earth's crust cannot spread apart everywhere. Somewhere, an equal amount of crust must be removed. When two plates push together, one of the plates sinks back into Earth's mantle, a process called *subduction*. The sinking plate eventually melts into magma in Earth's interior. Much of the magma created in subduction zones does not reach the surface and cools within the crust, forming plutonic rocks. The heat from the magma also helps create metamorphic rocks.

Because continental crust is too thick and light to sink into Earth's interior, only plates made of dense oceanic crust are subducted. The boundary where the two plates meet is marked by a deep trench on the ocean floor. The trenches are the deepest places in the oceans, up to 36,000 feet (11,000 meters) deep.

The upper plate that remains on the surface may be continental crust or oceanic crust. This plate is also changed by subduction. As the two plates move together, the edge of the upper plate is compressed. The crust becomes thicker and higher, creating a mountain range. When the rocks of the sinking plate reach a depth of about 60 to 90 miles (100 to 150 kilometers), they begin to melt and form magma. Some of the magma reaches the surface to form volcanoes. Regions with many volcanoes, such as Peru, Japan, and the northwestern United States, lie near areas where subduction is happening.

Mountain building. Occasionally, as a plate sinks into Earth's mantle, it drags along a continent or a smaller land mass. Continental crust is too thick and light to sink. Instead, it collides with the opposing plate. If the opposing plate is also a continent, neither plate will sink. This type of collision often forms a vast mountain chain in the middle of a con-

tinent. The Himalayas were formed in such a way from the collision of two plates of continental crust.

The series of events that happen during formation of a mountain range is called *orogeny*. Orogeny includes the elevation of mountains, folding and crumpling of the rocks, volcanic activity, and formation of plutonic and metamorphic rocks that occur when plates collide. Long after mountains have vanished from erosion, geologists can still see the changes orogeny produces in the rocks.

Terrane collisions. Smaller pieces of continental crust that collide with another plate are often added to the edge of the larger plate. These small added pieces of crust are called *terranes*. Most of the land in the United States west of Salt Lake City has been added to North America by terrane collisions in the last 500 million years.

Earthquakes. Earthquakes occur when rocks on opposite sides of a break in the crust, called a *fault*, slide past each other. The boundaries between plates are faults, but there are faults within plates as well. Occasionally, forces within the plates cause rocks to fracture and slip even though the rocks are not at a plate boundary. The boundaries between two plates sliding past each other are called *transform faults*. The San Andreas Fault in California is a transform fault, where a portion of crust called the Pacific Plate is carrying a small piece of California northwest past the rest of North America.

The shaping of the continents. Several times in Earth's history, collisions between continents have created a huge *supercontinent*. Although the crust of the continents is thick, it breaks more easily than oceanic crust, and supercontinents broke quickly into smaller pieces. Material from Earth's mantle filled the gaps, creating new oceanic crust. As the continents moved apart, new ocean basins formed between them. About one-third of Earth's surface is covered by continental crust, so the pieces cannot move far before colliding. As two continents collide, an old ocean basin is destroyed. The process of continents breaking apart and rejoining is called the *Wilson cycle*, after the Canadian geologist John Tuzo Wilson, who first described it.

The continents have probably been in motion for at least the past 3.8 billion years or more. Geologists, however, only have evidence from rocks to understand and reconstruct the motion over the past 800 million years. Most of the

Mt. McKinley, Alaska

oceanic crust older than that has been subducted into the mantle long ago.

Geologists have determined that, about 800 million years ago, the continents were assembled into a large supercontinent called Rodinia. What is now North America lay at the center of Rodinia. The flow of material in Earth's mantle caused Rodinia to break apart into many pieces, which collided again between 500 million and 250 million years ago. Collision between what is now North America, Europe, and Africa caused the uplift of the Appalachian Mountains in North America. Collisions between part of present-day Siberia and Europe created the Ural Mountains.

By 250 million years ago, the continents reassembled to form another supercontinent called Pangaea. A single, worldwide ocean, called Panthalassa, surrounded Pangaea. About 200 million years ago, Pangaea began to break apart. It split into two large land masses called Gondwanaland and Laurasia. Gondwanaland then broke apart, forming the continents of Africa, Antarctica, Australia, and South America, and the Indian subcontinent. Laurasia eventually split apart into Eurasia and North America. As the continental plates split and drifted apart, new oceanic crust formed between them. The movement of the continents to their present positions took place over millions of years.

Earth's Changing Climate

The ice ages. Throughout the history of Earth, the climate has changed many times. Between 800 million and 600 million years ago, during a time called the Precambrian, Earth experienced several extreme climate changes called *ice ages* or *glacial epochs*, separated by warm periods. The climate may have grown so cold that some scientists believe Earth nearly or completely froze several times. The theory that the entire Earth froze is sometimes called the *snowball Earth*. Other scientists think that the changes from a cold to a warm climate occurred too quickly for Earth to completely freeze.

Most of the time, Earth has been largely ice free. Brief ice ages occurred about 450 million years ago and again about 250 million years ago. In the last few million years, however, Earth's climate began to cool. Glaciers began forming in Antarctica about thirty-five million years ago, but the climate there was warm enough for trees to grow until about five million years ago. By about two million

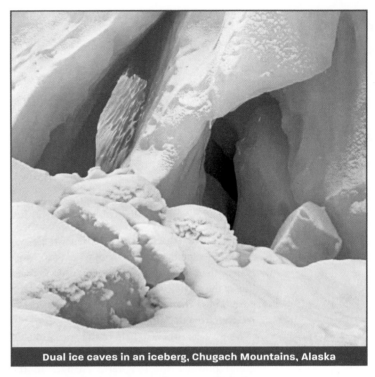

Dual ice caves in an iceberg, Chugach Mountains, Alaska

years ago, at the beginning of a time called the Pleistocene Epoch, ice had accumulated on other continents as well.

Numerous separate ice advances, periods when ice sheets covered vast areas, occurred during the Pleistocene Ice Age. The advances alternated with periods when the climate was warmer and the ice melted. Geologists analyzing sediment deposits from the North Atlantic Ocean determined that there were at least twenty advances and retreats of ice sheets in the past two million years. At least four ice advances were big enough to extend over much of Europe, cover most of Canada, and reach deep into the United States.

The most recent advance of ice began about 70,000 years ago and reached its farthest extent about 18,000 years ago. The vast glaciers and sheets of ice scoured out the basins of the Great Lakes and blocked rivers, completely changing the courses of the Mississippi, Missouri, and Ohio rivers. So much water was trapped in the form of ice that sea level around Earth dropped as much as 390 feet (120 meters), exposing parts of the present ocean floor.

The most recent ice advance ended about 11,500 years ago. Most scientists believe that Earth is currently in an *interglacial period*, and another ice advance will follow.

Rock formation and sand

Why ice ages occur. Scientists do not fully understand why Earth has ice ages. Most believe that tiny changes in Earth's orbit and axis due to the gravitational pull of other planets play a part. These changes alter the amount of energy received from the sun.

Many scientists also believe that variations in the amount of carbon dioxide in the atmosphere are responsible for long-term changes in the climate. Carbon dioxide, a "greenhouse gas," traps heat from the sun and warms Earth's atmosphere. Most of Earth's carbon dioxide is locked in carbonate rocks, such as limestone and dolomite. Earth's climate today would be much warmer if the carbon dioxide trapped in limestone were released into the atmosphere.

When mountains rich in silicate minerals wear down through weathering and erosion, calcium and magnesium erode from the rocks. These elements are carried to the sea by water. There, living organisms absorb the chemicals and use them to make protective carbonate shells. The organisms eventually die and sink to the bottom to form limestone deposits. This process, called the *carbonate-silicate cycle*, removes carbon dioxide from the atmosphere. With less carbon dioxide in the atmosphere to trap heat from the sun, Earth's climate may cool enough to cause an ice age.

Limestone and dolomite deposits exposed to weathering and erosion return carbon dioxide to the atmosphere and contribute to global warming. In addition, some limestone on the ocean floor can be carried down into Earth's mantle by subduction. Beneath the crust, the limestone breaks down into magma under heat and pressure. The carbon dioxide in the limestone can then return to the atmosphere during volcanic eruptions.

Scientists theorize that volcanoes continued to emit carbon dioxide into the atmosphere during the Precambrian ice ages. Eventually, the carbon dioxide warmed Earth through the greenhouse effect, causing the ice to melt rapidly.

History of Earth

The history of Earth is recorded in the rocks of Earth's crust. Rocks have been forming, wearing away, and reforming ever since Earth took shape. The products of weathering and erosion are called *sediment*. Sediment accumulates in layers known as *strata*. Strata contain clues that tell geologists about Earth's past. These clues include the composition of the sediment, the way the strata are deposited, and the kinds of fossils that may occur in the rock.

Space exploration has expanded our understanding of Earth's origin. The Hubble Space Telescope has observed what appear to be stars in the process of forming planets. Since the mid-1990s, scientists have found other stars that have planets surrounding them. These discoveries have helped scientists develop theories about the formation of Earth.

Age of Earth. Scientists think that Earth probably formed at about the same time as the rest of the solar system. They have determined that some chondrite meteorites, the unaltered remains from the formation of the solar system, are up to 4.6 billion years old. Scientists believe that Earth and other planets are probably that old. They can determine the ages of rocks by measuring the amounts of natural radioactive materials, such as uranium, in them. Radioactive elements *decay* (change into other elements) at a known rate. For example, uranium gives off radiation and decays into lead. Scientists know the time it takes for uranium to change to lead. They can determine the age of a rock by comparing the amount of uranium to the amount of lead.

The known history of Earth is divided into four long stretches of time called *eons*. Starting with the earliest, the eons are Hadean, Archean, Proterozoic, and Phanerozoic. The first three eons, which together lasted nearly four billion years, are grouped into a unit called the Precambrian. The Phanerozoic Eon, when life became abundant, is divided into three eras. They are, from the oldest to the youngest, the Paleozoic, Mesozoic, and Cenozoic eras. Eras are divided into *periods*, and periods are divided into *epochs*. These divisions and subdivisions are named for places where rocks of each period were studied. Periods are mostly separated by important changes in the types of fossils found in the rocks. As a result, the lengths of eras, periods, and epochs are not equal.

A chart showing an outline of Earth's history is called a *geological time scale*. On such a chart, Earth's earliest history is at the bottom, and its recent history at the top. This arrangement resembles the way rock strata are formed, with the recent over the oldest.

Formation of Earth. Most scientists believe that the solar system began as a thin cloud of gas and dust in space. The sun itself may have formed from a portion of the cloud that was thicker than the rest. The cloud's own gravity caused it to start contracting, and dust and gas were drawn in toward the center. Much of the cloud collapsed to the center to form a star, the sun, but a great ring of material remained orbiting around the star. Particles in the ring collided to make larger objects, which in turn collided to build up the planets of the solar system in a process called *accretion*. Scientists believe that many small planets formed and then collided to make larger planets.

Earth's early development. Scientists theorize that Earth began as a waterless mass of rock surrounded by a cloud of gas. Radioactive materials in the rock and increasing pressure in Earth's interior produced enough heat to melt the interior of Earth. The heavy materials, such as iron, sank. The light silicate rocks rose to Earth's surface and formed the earliest crust. The heat of the interior caused other chemicals inside Earth to rise to the surface. Some of these chemicals formed water, and others became the gases of the atmosphere.

In 2001, an international team of scientists announced the discovery of crystals of the mineral *zircon* that they determined to be 4.4 billion years old. Zircon, made up of the elements zirconium, silicon, and oxygen, is a hard, long lasting mineral that resists erosion and weathering. Through chemical analysis of the zircon, the scientists determined that liquid water probably existed on Earth's surface when the crystals were formed. They concluded that Earth's crust and oceans may have formed within about 200 million years after the planet had taken shape.

Astronomers believe that the sun was about 30 percent fainter when Earth first formed than it is today. The oldest rocks on Earth, however, provide evidence that Earth was warm enough for liquid water to exist on the surface. Scientists believe that the atmosphere must have been thicker than it is today, to trap more heat from the sun. Over millions of years, the water slowly collected in low places of the crust and formed oceans.

After the main period of planet formation, most of the remaining debris in the solar system was swept up by the newly formed planets. The collisions of the newly formed planets and debris material were explosive. The impacts created the cratered surfaces of the moon, Mars, Venus, and Mercury. Earth was also struck, but the craters produced by the impacts have all been destroyed by erosion and plate tectonics. There is evidence that plate tectonics has been active for at least 3.8 billion years.

Some scientists believe Earth's early atmosphere contained hydrogen, helium, methane, and ammonia, much like the present atmosphere of Jupiter. Others believe it may have contained a large amount of carbon dioxide, as does the atmosphere of Venus. Scientists agree that Earth's earliest atmosphere probably had little oxygen.

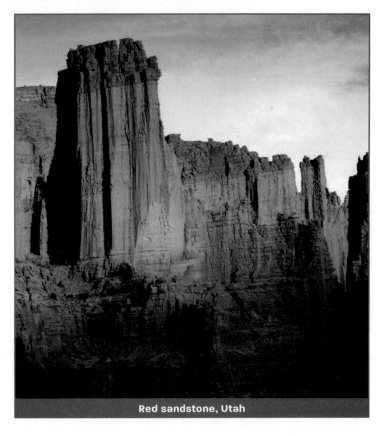

Red sandstone, Utah

Geologists have determined that, about two billion years ago, a change in Earth's atmosphere occurred. They know this because certain kinds of iron ores created in oxygen-poor environments stopped forming at that time. Instead, large deposits of red sandstone formed. The red color results from iron reacting with oxygen to form *iron oxide*, or rust. The sandstone deposits are evidence that Earth's atmosphere contained some oxygen. The air was not breathable at that time, but the atmosphere may have had about 1 percent oxygen.

The oxygen in the atmosphere today comes mainly from plants and microorganisms such as algae. These organisms use carbon dioxide and give off oxygen through the process of photosynthesis. The amount of oxygen increased in the atmosphere of the early Earth as oxygen-producing organisms developed and became more plentiful.

Life on Earth. Many rocks contain fossils that reveal the history of life on Earth. A fossil may be an animal's body, a tooth, or a piece of bone. It may simply be an impression of a plant or an animal made in a rock when the rock was soft sediment. Fossils help scientists learn which kinds of

Fossiized bones of a gigantic theropod dinosaur, found in Inner Mongolia, China

plants and animals lived at different times in Earth's history. Scientists who study prehistoric life are called *paleontologists*.

Many scientists believe that life appeared on Earth almost as soon as conditions allowed. There is evidence for chemicals created by living things in rocks from the Archean age, 3.8 billion years old. Fossil remains of microscopic living things about 3.5 billion years old have also been found at sites in Australia and Canada.

For most of Earth's history, life consisted mainly of microscopic, single-celled creatures. The earliest fossils of larger creatures with many cells are found in Precambrian rocks that are about 600 million years old. Many of these creatures differed from any living things today.

The Paleozoic Era. Fossils become abundant in Cambrian rocks that are about 543 million to 490 million years old. This apparently sudden expansion in the number of life forms in the fossil record is called the *Cambrian Explosion*, and it marks the beginning of the Paleozoic Era. The Cambrian Explosion actually occurred over tens of millions of years, but it appears sudden in the fossil record. The earliest abundant fossils consist of only a few kinds of organisms. Over the course of hundreds of millions of years, the number of species increases gradually in the fossil record.

Most fossil organisms found in Paleozoic rocks are *invertebrates* (animals without a backbone), such as corals, *mollusks* (clams and snails), and *trilobites* (flat-shelled sea animals). Fish, the earliest *vertebrates* (animals with a backbone), are first found in Ordovician rocks about 450 million years old. Silurian rocks, about 440 million years old, contain fossils of the first large land plants. Amphibians, animals capable of living on land or in the water, first appear as fossils in Devonian rocks about 380 million years old.

Fossil remains preserved in rocks show that by 300 million years ago, large forests and swamps covered the land. The carbon-rich remains of some of these forests are preserved as coal deposits in the United States, Canada, the United Kingdom, and other parts of the world. The Carboniferous Period is named for these enormous deposits of coal.

The earliest fossil remains of reptiles are found in rocks of the Carboniferous Period. Unlike amphibians, reptiles have scaly skins that keep them from drying out, and they lay eggs protected by a shell. These features enable reptiles to live their whole lives out of water. Toward the end of the Paleozoic Era, in rocks from the Permian Period, some fossil reptiles begin to show some characteristics of mammals.

Several times in Earth's history, there have been great *extinctions*, periods when many of Earth's living things die out. The greatest of these events, called the Permian extinction, happened about 250 million years ago. Almost 90 percent of the species on Earth during the Permian became extinct in a relatively short time. The cause of this event is a mystery, though many scientists suspect that huge volcanic eruptions in what is now Siberia may have disturbed the climate, causing many organisms to die out.

The Mesozoic Era. Following the Permian extinction, the fossil record shows that reptiles became the dominant animals on land. The most spectacular of these reptiles were the dinosaurs. The Mesozoic is often called the *Age of the Dinosaurs*, but mammals and birds also appear in the fossil record in rocks from 200 million to 140 million years old.

Fossil plants of the Mesozoic Era represent two main groups, *gymnosperms* and *angiosperms*. Gymnosperms have naked seeds, and most are cone-bearing. They include conifers, ginkgoes, and cycads. These gymnosperms evolved in the later part of the Paleozoic Era and were dominant into the early Cretaceous Period. Angiosperms have covered seeds and are flowering plants. They became the dominant plant group during the Cretaceous Period and continue to be so today.

The dinosaurs died out in another great extinction about 65 million years ago. Most scientists believe that the extinction was caused by the impact of a small asteroid with Earth. The impact would have thrown so much dust into the atmosphere that the surface would have been dark and cold for months, killing off plants and the animals that fed on them. Many scientists believe a large, buried crater in the Yucatán region of Mexico, called Chicxulub, is the place the asteroid struck. Debris from the collision has been found all over the world, and deposits created by large sea waves caused by the impact have been found in several places around the Gulf of Mexico.

The Cenozoic Era. The wide variety of plants and animals that we know today came into existence during the Cenozoic Era. Mammals survived the events that killed off the dinosaurs

A fossilized mammoth, displayed at the Inner Mongolia Museum

and expanded to become the dominant land animals of today. The evolutionary history of today's mammals is recorded in the fossil record of the Cenozoic Era.

During the Eocene Epoch, ancestors of the horse, rhinoceros, and camel roamed Europe and North America. By the Oligocene Epoch, dogs and cats had appeared, along with three-toed horses about as large as sheep. The mammals grew larger and developed in greater variety as prairies spread over the land during the Miocene Epoch. By the Pliocene Epoch, many kinds of mammals had grown to gigantic size. Elephant-like mammoths and mastodons and giant ground sloths roamed the prairies and forests. These animals died out at the end of the Pleistocene Epoch.

Fossils of the first humanlike creatures appeared near the beginning of the Pleistocene Epoch, about two million years ago. The first true human beings appeared later, perhaps less than 200,000 years ago. Humanity's years on Earth are only a brief moment among the billions of years during which Earth has developed.

MLA Citation

"Earth." *The Southwestern Advantage Topic Source.* Nashville: Southwestern. 2013.

DATA

Earth at a Glance

Age: At least 4½ billion years.

Mass: 6,600,000,000,000,000,000,000 (6.6 sextillion) tons (6.0 sextillion metric tons).

Motion: *Rotation* (spinning motion around an imaginary line connecting the North and South poles)—once every 23 hours 56 minutes 4.09 seconds. *Revolution* (motion around the sun)—once every 365 days 6 hours 9 minutes 9.54 seconds.

Size: *Polar diameter* (distance through the earth from North Pole to South Pole)—7,899.83 miles (12,713.54 kilometers). *Equatorial diameter* (distance through Earth at the equator)—7,926.41 miles (12,756.32 kilometers). *Polar circumference* (distance around Earth through the poles)—24,859.82 miles (40,008.00 kilometers). *Equatorial circumference* (distance around Earth along the equator)—24,901.55 miles (40,075.16 kilometers).

Area: *Total surface area*—196,900,000 square miles (510,000,000 square kilometers). *Land area*—approximately 57,100,000 square miles (148,000,000 square kilometers), 29 percent of total surface area. *Water area*—approximately 139,800,000 square miles (362,000,000 square kilometers), 71 percent of total surface area.

Surface features: *Highest land*—Mount Everest, 29,035 feet (8,850 meters) above sea level. *Lowest land*—shore of Dead Sea, 1,373 feet (419 meters) below sea level.

Ocean depths: *Deepest part of ocean*—area of the Mariana Trench in Pacific Ocean southwest of Guam, 35,840 feet (10,924 meters) below surface. *Average ocean depth*—12,200 feet (3,730 meters).

Temperature: *Highest,* 136 ºF (58 ºC) at Al Aziziyah, Libya. *Lowest,* -128.6 ºF (-89.6 ºC) at Vostok Station in Antarctica. *Average surface temperature,* 59 ºF (15 ºC).

Atmosphere: *Height*—More than 99 percent of the atmosphere is less than 50 miles (80 kilometers) above Earth's surface. The atmosphere fades into space about 600 miles (1,000 kilometers) above the surface. *Chemical makeup of atmosphere*—about 78 percent nitrogen, 21 percent oxygen, 1 percent argon with small amounts of other gases.

Chemical makeup of Earth's crust (in percent of the crust's weight): oxygen 46.6, silicon 27.7, aluminum 8.1, iron 5.0, calcium 3.6, sodium 2.8, potassium 2.6, magnesium 2.0, and other elements totaling 1.6.

ADDITIONAL RESOURCES

Books to Read

Allaby, Michael, and others. *The Encyclopedia of Earth.* University of California Press, 2008.

Huddart, David, and Stott, Tim. *Earth Environments: Past, Pesent and Future.* Wiley, 2010.

Luhr, James F., ed. *Earth.* DK Publishing, 2003.

Mathez, Edmond A., and Webster, J. D. *The Earth Machine: The Science of a Dynamic Planet.* Columbia University Press, 2004.

Zalasiewicz, Jan A. *The Planet in a Pebble: A Journey into Earth's Deep History.* Oxford, 2010.

Web Sites

American Museum of Natural History: Ology
http://ology.amnh.org/
The American Museum of Natural History features a Web site for children filled with information on various fields of science.

Destination: Earth
http://www.earth.nasa.gov/
Gateway to NASA's Earth Sciences division.

Extinctions: Cycles of Life and Death Through Time
http://hannover.park.org/Canada/Museum/extinction/tablecont.html
Information about past mass extinctions, from the Hooper Virtual Paleontological Museum.

Global Warming
http://www.ncdc.noaa.gov/ol/climate/globalwarming.html
The U.S. National Oceanic and Atmospheric Administration (NOAA) presents answers to frequently asked questions about global warming.

NASA Earth Observatory
http://www.earthobservatory.nasa.gov/
This site, sponsored by NASA, explores the causes and effects of climatic and environmental change through the use of real satellite data. Features include the NASA observation deck, library, study, newsroom, laboratory, and mission control.

The Eight Planets
http://nineplanets.org/
Information about the eight planets in our solar system.

United States Environmental Protection Agency: Ozone Depletion
http://www.epa.gov/ozone/
Information about the ozone depletion in the earth's atmosphere.

World
http://www.cia.gov/library/publications/the-world-factbook/geos/xx.html#top
Political, geographical, and sociological information about the Earth and its inhabitants, from the on-line edition of the U.S. Central Intelligence Agency's World Factbook.

Search Strings

History of Earth

Earth history age space formation (126,000)

Earth history age space formation eons fossils (4,340)

Earth in the Solar System

Earth "Solar System" moon rotation revolution (75,700)

Earth in the "Solar System" (984,000)

Earth in the "Solar System" space science "Milky Way Galaxy" gravity (51,700)

Earth's Spheres

Earth's Spheres (771,000)

Earth's Spheres core lithosphere hydrosphere cryosphere atmosphere troposphere stratosphere biosphere (147)

Earth's Spheres lithosphere hydrosphere cryosphere atmosphere troposphere stratosphere biosphere (300)

Cycles in and on Earth

Earth cycles "atmospheric circulation" "global heat conveyor" "hydrologic cycle" rock (2)

Earth cycles atmosphere ocean heat hydrologic rock (14,500)

Earth's Climate Changes

Earth climate changes greenhouse gases ozone (113,000)

Earth's climate changes "greenhouse gases" "ozone layer" warming global (28,300)

BACKGROUND INFORMATION

The following articles and features first appeared in annual publications. They were written during the year in which the events took place and reflect the style and thinking of that time.

Geology (2000)

Geologists at the Danish Center for Earth System Science reported evidence in April 2000 that low concentrations of oxygen in the Earth's atmosphere prevented animal life from diversifying until relatively late in geologic history. The atmosphere today contains about 21 percent oxygen, a gas that is vital to the survival of animal life on Earth. But when the Earth was formed, its atmosphere contained almost no oxygen. Geologists have debated for decades as to exactly when Earth's atmosphere developed enough oxygen to support complex animal life.

Geologists have found a connection between past oxygen levels and sedimentary deposits of sulfates, compounds containing sulfur and oxygen atoms. Sulfates form when certain types of bacteria process nutrients or when there is a high concentration of oxygen in the atmosphere. Scientists previously had studied sulfates in ancient sedimentary rocks but did not know whether the sulfates came from ancient bacteria or whether they indicated an oxygen-rich atmosphere. In order to better recognize properties of sulfates produced by ancient bacteria, geologists studied similar modern-day bacteria in the Gulf of California.

Donald E. Canfield, Kirsten S. Habicht, and Bo Thamdrup studied how bacteria processed sulfates in different temperatures near an active hydrothermal vent in the ocean. Canfield and his colleagues calculated that ancient sedimentary sulfates probably came from early bacteria. They then concluded that significant amounts of atmospheric oxygen did not accumulate until the late Proterozoic Era (and 700 million years ago), around the time when there was a great explosion in the diversity of animal life.

Ice ages and carbon dioxide. Geologist Nicholas J. Shackleton of Cambridge University in England reported evidence in September 2000 that atmospheric concentrations of carbon dioxide gas are closely tied to cycles of ice ages. Scientists have long been aware that Earth's Northern Hemisphere experienced cycles of ice ages, during which large ice sheets expanded and contracted across northern Asia, Europe, and North America. Throughout the past one million years, the great ice sheets waxed and waned about every 100,000 years in step with eccentricity (the shape of Earth's orbit). Geologists believed that changes in eccentricity were related to the cycle of ice ages.

Because of eccentricity, Earth would be farther from the sun at times and receive less heat. The changes in heat, however, are not great enough to directly drive the ice ages. One suggested explanation is that small changes in heat could produce small changes in the sizes of ice sheets that would, in turn, trigger even larger changes. Another hypothesis is that the ice-age cycle is driven directly by changes in the greenhouse effect (warming of the atmosphere caused by certain gases, including carbon dioxide).

Shackleton examined the composition of ancient Antarctic ice. He found that during the 100,000-year cycle, temperatures and atmospheric carbon dioxide changed together with eccentricity. However, changes in the size of the ice sheets lagged behind. Shackleton concluded that the 100,000-year cycle was not driven by ice sheet changes but rather by a greenhouse effect. His findings indicated a direct link between global climate cycles and atmospheric carbon dioxide concentrations, further strengthening concerns about global warming. However, geologists still do not understand why eccentricity variations were connected with changes in the concentration of atmospheric carbon dioxide.

Deep-sea burps. Geologists from the University of California at Santa Barbara and California State University in Long Beach reported in April the first direct evidence that linked global climate change to releases of methane from the ocean. Methane, made up of carbon and hydrogen atoms, is a greenhouse gas. Huge reserves of frozen methane are stored in sediments deep in the ocean.

James P. Kennett, Kevin G. Cannariato, Ingrid L. Hendy, and Richard J. Behl discovered that sediments in the Santa Barbara Basin in the ocean near California were layered in a pattern that coincided with changes in concentrations of methane found in ice cores. Methane from the atmosphere was trapped in the ice found in polar regions. The geologists documented brief, catastrophic episodes of methane release from sediments at the bottom of the basin. They found that the releases coincided with warming water temperatures that melted the frozen methane and "burped" large volumes of methane gas into the ocean and ultimately into the atmosphere.

Tsunami threat in the U.S. In May, geologists warned that changes in the shape of the Atlantic Ocean floor might contribute to the creation of a tsunami (a large sea wave caused by an undersea earthquake) off the East Coast of the United States—anywhere from Maryland to North Carolina. Neal W. Driscoll of the Woods Hole Oceanographic Institution in Massachusetts, Jeffrey K. Weissel of Columbia University in New York City, and John A. Goff of the University of Texas in Austin mapped a system of faults (breaks in the Earth's crust) off the shores of North Carolina and southern Virginia. They suggested that if the cracks were the precursors of a major submarine landslide, the landslide could generate a tsunami in the Atlantic Ocean.

Jupiter

Jupiter is the fifth planet from the sun. It is the largest planet in our solar system with a mass greater than the total of all the other planets' masses combined. It is a gas giant without a solid surface and consists of mainly hydrogen and helium. It is a bright object that appears as pale orange in our night sky. When viewed through a telescope or as a photograph, it appears to have many stripes of brown, white, orange, and yellow with swirling storms.

HOT topics

The Jovian System. Jupiter has a strong magnetic field surrounding the planet. Scientists call it the magnetosphere. It also has many satellites (moons) and 4 rings of dust particles encircling the planet. Together, these things form the Jovian System.

Characteristics of Jupiter. Jupiter travels around the sun in a nearly circular orbit every 12 Earth years. It rotates on a tilted axis every 9 hours and 55 minutes, faster than any other planet in our solar system. Just like Earth, it has seasons. Jupiter has a mass that

DEFINITIONS

Jupiter noun. 1. *Roman Mythology.* the ruler of the gods and men, identified with the Greek god Zeus; Jove. 2. the largest planet in the solar system. It is the fifth in distance from the sun.

HOT topics

The four Galilean moons of the planet Jupiter, photographed by the Galileo spacecraft

is about 318 times greater than that of Earth's, but its density is much lower, suggesting that it consists of light elements, mainly hydrogen and helium, instead of rock. Jupiter's effective temperature is −236°F (−149°C). Jupiter has a dipolar magnetic field.

The Great Red Spot.
Jupiter's lower atmosphere, below the tropopause, contains clouds of ammonia ice and chromophores, resulting in the colored zones and belts that we see on the planet. The planet Jupiter's Great Red Spot is a huge mass of swirling gas that travels around Jupiter at about the same latitude since its position was first recorded in 1831. The circumference of the Great Red Spot is larger than that of Earth's circumference.

Jupiter's Satellites and Rings.
So far, astronomers have discovered 63 satellites around Jupiter. They have divided those satellites into three groups: the Galilean satellites, the inner satellites, and the outer satellites. The Galilean satellites consist of Jupiter's four largest moons. This group is so named because Galileo discovered them. They include Io, Europa, Ganymede, and Callisto. Io is Jupiter's volcanic, innermost satellite. Europa also has geological activity and has fissures in an icy crust that may lie on top of deep oceans of water. Ganymede is our solar system's largest moon, and it generates its own magnetic field. Callisto is Jupiter's outermost Galilean satellite and the most heavily cratered satellite. Metis, Adrastea, Amalthea, and Thebe are the inner satellites that have orbits that are inside those of the Galilean satellites. There are many outer satellites, and 4 rings of dust particles that encircle the planet.

Planet Jupiter with its gossamer moon-formed rings, in an image taken by Voyager 2

TRUE or FALSE?
The Voyager missions revolutionized our understanding of Jupiter.

THE BASICS

Jupiter is the largest planet in our solar system. It has a *mass* (amount of matter) that is greater than the masses of all the other planets in the solar system added together. Astronomers call Jupiter a *gas giant* because the planet consists mostly of hydrogen and helium, and has no solid surface. Jupiter is named for the king of the gods in Roman mythology.

Jupiter ranks among the brightest objects in the night sky. Usually, only the moon and Venus appear brighter. When seen with the unaided eye, Jupiter has a pale orange color. Viewed through a telescope or in images taken by spacecraft, Jupiter appears as a globe covered with swirling, brightly colored clouds of brown, orange, white, and yellow.

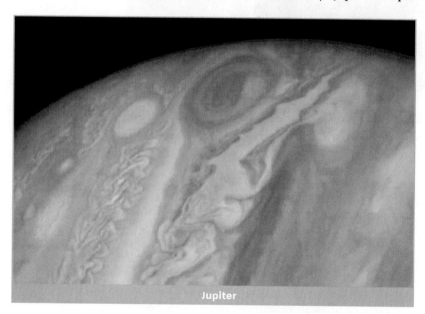
Jupiter

Jupiter lies at the center of a system of cosmic objects so vast and diverse that it resembles a miniature solar system. The planet has 16 moons that measure at least 6 miles (10 kilometers) in diameter and dozens of smaller satellites. Four faint rings of dust particles encircle the planet. Jupiter also has a strong *magnetic field*. A magnetic field is the area around a magnet in which its influence can be detected. Jupiter's magnetic field extends beyond the planet throughout a huge region of space called the *magnetosphere*. Astronomers sometimes refer to the planet together with its rings, satellites, and magnetosphere as the *Jovian system*.

Astronomers have made detailed observations of Jupiter for centuries. It was one of the first planets studied by the famous Italian astronomer Galileo in the early 1600s. Beginning in the 1970s, several spacecraft have explored the Jovian system in great detail.

 ## Characteristics of Jupiter

Astronomers determine Jupiter's characteristics using observations made through telescopes and by spacecraft. They study these characteristics to learn about the planet's structure and origin.

Orbit and rotation. Like all the planets in our solar system, Jupiter travels around the sun in an *elliptical* (oval-shaped) orbit. Jupiter's orbit is nearly circular. It lies about five times as far from the sun as Earth's orbit does. The average distance between the sun and Jupiter measures around 484 million miles (779 million kilometers). Jupiter's orbit is tilted by 1.3 degrees from the *ecliptic plane*, the imaginary plane that contains Earth's orbit. Jupiter takes nearly 12 Earth years to orbit the sun.

Jupiter rotates faster than any other planet, taking about 9 hours 55 minutes to turn completely on its axis. This is the length of a day on Jupiter. The planet's rapid spinning causes it to bulge slightly at the equator. Its diameter at the equator measures 88,846 miles (142,984 kilometers), while the distance between its *geographic poles*—the ends of its axis—measures only 83,082 miles (133,708 kilometers).

Like Earth's axis, Jupiter's axis is not perpendicular to the planet's *orbital plane*, the imaginary plane that contains its orbit. Jupiter's axis lies tilted from the perpendicular by 3.1 degrees. As a result of this tilt and its motion about the sun, Jupiter, like Earth, has seasons.

Mass and density. Jupiter's mass is about 318 times as great as the mass of Earth, but about 1,000 times smaller than that of the sun. Jupiter's average density is about 1.3 times as great as the density of water at room temperature. This density is much lower than the density of Earth. Jupiter's low density indicates that it is composed mostly of light elements rather than rock.

Chemical composition. Jupiter's elemental composition resembles that of the sun. The planet consists mostly of hydrogen (chemical symbol, H) and helium (He). It also contains small amounts of heavier elements, including oxygen (O), carbon (C), nitrogen (N), sulfur (S), and many others. In general, Jupiter has a higher concentration of heavy elements than does the sun.

Most of the elements in Jupiter's atmosphere consist of atoms linked together in molecules. Molecules that have been detected in Jupiter's atmosphere include molecular hydrogen (H_2), water (H_2O), ammonia (NH_3), methane (CH_4), and hydrogen sulfide (H_2S). Smaller amounts of other molecules form in chemical reactions in the atmosphere. These include ethane (C_2H_6), acetylene (C_2H_2), ethylene (C_2H_4), hydrogen cyanide (HCN), and other compounds. Helium exists as individual atoms in Jupiter's atmosphere.

Temperature. The actual temperature of Jupiter varies with altitude and location, but because of its great distance from the sun, Jupiter is much colder than Earth. Scientists have different ways of discussing the temperature of gaseous planets like Jupiter. One common approach gives the average temperature for an elevation that corresponds to a certain amount of pressure. At an altitude corresponding to 1 bar of pressure, Jupiter averages −162°F (−108°C). The bar is a unit of pressure in the metric system, equal to 100 kilopascals.

The amount of energy delivered in a certain period of time is called *power*. The power that Earth radiates equals the power it absorbs from the sun. Jupiter, however, radiates about twice as much power as it absorbs from the sun. This indicates that some of Jupiter's energy comes from a source other than the sun. The energy may be heat left over from Jupiter's formation. It might also come from heat created as the planet slowly contracts under the influence of gravity. Although Jupiter gives off some of its own energy, astronomers do not consider it a star because no nuclear reactions occur in its interior.

Magnetic field. Jupiter's magnetic field is mainly *dipolar*—that is, Jupiter has a magnetic north and south pole like the poles on a bar magnet. Physicists describe the overall strength of such a field using a measure called the *magnetic dipole moment*. Jupiter's magnetic dipole moment measures about 20,000 times as strong as that of Earth.

The most detailed global color map of Jupiter ever produced, from images taken by the Cassini spacecraft

Like Earth's magnetic field, Jupiter's field lies tilted by about 10 degrees from the planet's axis of rotation. Jupiter's magnetic poles are aligned opposite those of Earth. A compass needle that points north on Earth would point south on Jupiter.

Jupiter's magnetic field traps electrically charged particles, such as electrons and *ions* (charged atoms or groups of atoms). As a result, the magnetosphere contains a hot, low-density *plasma*, a form of matter made up of charged particles. The plasma is concentrated in a thin disk near the planet's equator. It comes from Jupiter's moons, especially Io. Io has active volcanoes that eject much sulfur and oxygen into the magnetosphere. The hot plasma can damage the optics and electronics of spacecraft operating in the Jovian system. The magnetosphere also deflects the *solar wind* around the Jovian system. The solar wind is a continuous flow of charged particles from the sun.

Telescopes on Earth can detect the glowing ions in Jupiter's magnetosphere. The ions also produce visible effects when they enter Jupiter's atmosphere near the poles. There, collisions between the charged particles and the atmosphere create bands and streamers of light called *auroras*. Jupiter's auroras glow brighter than those of any other planet in the solar system.

Radio emissions. Astronomers discovered Jupiter's magnetic field in 1955 when they detected radio waves *emitted* (given off) by the planet. The radio emissions result from the movement of electrons in Jupiter's magnetic field. Some electrons travel through the field in a spiral path at high speeds. Electrons that move in this way emit radio waves in a process called *synchrotron radiation*. Observations show that synchrotron radiation creates some of Jupiter's radio emissions. Other emissions result from electrons moving between Io and Jupiter and from electrons moving within the atoms of Jupiter's atmosphere.

Jupiter's radio emissions vary in strength in a pattern that repeats about every 9 hours 55 minutes. Astronomers think the planet's magnetic field takes this long to complete one rotation. They also use this value for Jupiter's rotation period because the planet lacks solid features that can be used to measure its rotation.

Structure of Jupiter

Astronomers know more about Jupiter's atmosphere than they do about the planet's interior because the atmosphere is the part of the planet that we can see. The pressure of the atmosphere grows steadily as altitude decreases until the atmosphere merges gradually into the interior. Astronomers use observations of the planet and their knowledge of chemistry and physics to determine what its interior might be like.

Atmosphere. Temperatures in the uppermost parts of Jupiter's atmosphere measure about 1500°F (800°C). Throughout the upper atmosphere, temperatures drop as altitude decreases. Temperatures reach their lowest in a region where the atmospheric pressure equals about one-fifth the pressure at the surface of Earth. This area, called the *tropopause*, separates Jupiter's upper atmosphere from its lower atmosphere. Below the tropopause, temperatures begin to increase approaching the planet's interior.

Jupiter's colorfully swirled appearance comes from clouds in its lower atmosphere. Different compounds there condense to form clouds at different altitudes, creating layers of clouds with various chemical compositions. The uppermost clouds consist primarily of ammonia ice. These clouds make up most of what we see when we look at Jupiter. Pure ammonia ice is colorless. The clouds' colors result from tiny amounts of impurities called *chromophores*. Astronomers do not know for sure what chromophores are. They may include *organic* (carbon-based) molecules, sulfur compounds, or phosphorous compounds.

Astronomers think that below the ammonia clouds there is a second cloud layer made up of ammonium hydrosulfide, which forms when ammonia and hydrogen sulfide condense together. A cloud layer composed of water ice may lie deeper still. At greater pressures, far beyond where light can penetrate, the atmosphere may contain clouds of iron or *silicates*, compounds of metals, silicon, and oxygen that form rocks on Earth.

Zones and belts. Alternating bands of light and dark clouds cover Jupiter's atmosphere. Astronomers refer to the wider, brighter bands as

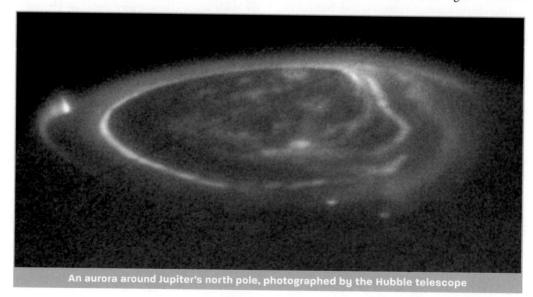

An aurora around Jupiter's north pole, photographed by the Hubble telescope

zones and to the darker, narrower bands as *belts*. The zones and belts result from wind patterns in Jupiter's lower atmosphere.

In the zones, winds blow from the west at speeds that reach up to 400 miles (650 kilometers) per hour near the equator. Winds in the belts blow from the east at slightly lower speeds. The zones appear bright because they contain high-altitude clouds that reflect much sunlight. The clouds in the belts lie at somewhat lower altitudes. Their darker appearance probably results from a higher concentration of chromophores.

Jupiter's alternating east and west winds result from *convection currents*. These currents are movements of the atmosphere created by the rising of warm gases and the falling of cooler gases. Because Jupiter's internal energy heats the atmosphere unevenly, warm gases rise in certain places and cool gases descend in others. This rise and fall creates convection currents.

Jupiter's rapid rotation bends the convection currents into patterns that stretch east and west around the entire planet. This effect of rotation, known as the *Coriolis effect*, also creates wind patterns on Earth. On Earth, the patterns vary because oceans, continents, and mountain ranges interfere with the circulation of the atmosphere. On Jupiter, which lacks a solid surface or other obstacles, the east and west winds remain remarkably stable. As a result, while individual bands continuously undergo small changes, the overall pattern of zones and belts has remained unchanged in the hundreds of years since people first observed Jupiter through telescopes.

Ovals. Jupiter's atmosphere displays many features that are oval or circular in shape. The most prominent of these is a vast, reddish oval called the Great Red Spot.

The Great Red Spot extends about 7,450 miles (12,000 kilometers) from north to south. The spot's width from east to west, which is slowly shrinking, measured about 10,500 miles (17,000 kilometers) in the early 2000s. The spot's circumference is larger than that of Earth. The spot travels around Jupiter with the wind at about 22 degrees latitude south of the equator. As with the other clouds on Jupiter, astronomers do not know exactly what causes the spot's reddish color.

The English scientist Robert Hooke first observed a large spot in Jupiter's atmosphere in 1664. Astronomers first recorded the Great Red

Jupiter's Great Red Spot, as seen by the space probe Voyager 2

Spot's precise form and position in 1831. Since then, the spot has remained near the same latitude. Images taken by the two Voyager spacecraft in 1979 revealed that the spot is a swirling cloud of gas that takes about seven days to complete one full rotation. Wind speeds at the outer edges of the spot reach up to 425 miles (685 kilometers) per hour.

Unlike the winds in hurricanes on Earth, which swirl around a low-pressure region, winds in the Great Red Spot and in other long-lived ovals in Jupiter's atmosphere swirl around areas of high pressure. Scientists call these weather systems *anticyclones.*

Other oval features in Jupiter's atmosphere include *white ovals.* White ovals are much smaller and less stable than the Great Red Spot. They tend to lie on the edges of zones but frequently move around the planet.

In the late 1990s and early 2000s, three white ovals merged to form a larger oval that later took on a reddish color. The new red spot, often called the Little Red Spot, measured roughly half the size of the Great Red Spot.

Weather. In addition to these longer-lived atmospheric patterns, such as zones, belts, and ovals, Jupiter has storms and other active weather.

Diagram of planet Jupiter shows interior layers

Astronomers first saw flashes of lightning on Jupiter's night side in images from the Voyager spacecraft. Later, the Galileo craft observed numerous lightning flashes and tracked the movement of clouds from night to day. The New Horizons spacecraft saw lightning near Jupiter's poles. Astronomers determined that the lightning flashes originate in small cloud plumes that resemble thunderheads on Earth. The lightning flashes on Jupiter are much more powerful than those on Earth.

Interior. Below the clouds, Jupiter's pressure, temperature, and density increase until the atmosphere gradually blends into the fluid interior. Eventually, the hydrogen and helium that make up most of the planet become more like a liquid than a gas.

About 6,000 miles (10,000 kilometers) below the clouds, the pressure becomes 1 million times as great as the atmospheric pressure at Earth's surface. At this depth, hydrogen atoms begin to break down, with the electrons becoming separated from their nuclei. The separated nuclei and electrons compose an unusual

form of hydrogen called *liquid metallic hydrogen* that can conduct electricity like an ordinary metal. Liquid metallic hydrogen makes up most of Jupiter's mass. Scientists believe that electric currents flowing through this hydrogen generate the planet's magnetic field.

Core. The region near Jupiter's center is difficult to probe. The pressure there equals about 70 million times the pressure at Earth's surface. Astronomers estimate the temperature of Jupiter's center to be around 45,000°F (25,000°C).

Most scientific models suggest that Jupiter has a dense core made up of substances that, under less severe conditions, would form rock and ice. They estimate the mass of the core to be about 10 to 15 times the mass of Earth. The rock-forming material in the core may include iron and silicates. The ice-forming material may include oxygen, carbon, and nitrogen. Other models indicate that Jupiter has no distinct core. Instead, they suggest that liquid metallic hydrogen merges gradually with heavier elements near the planet's center.

Satellites and Rings

Astronomers have identified at least 67 satellites of Jupiter, but the planet probably has more small moons that have yet to be discovered. Jupiter's satellites can be divided into three groups: (1) the Galilean satellites; (2) the inner satellites; and (3) the outer satellites. The inner satellites are closely related to Jupiter's system of rings.

Galilean satellites. Astronomers call Jupiter's four largest moons the *Galilean satellites* because Galileo discovered them. In order of increasing distance from the planet, they are Io, Europa, Ganymede, and Callisto.

Io, the innermost Galilean satellite, ranks as the most geologically active body in the solar system. It has many volcanoes that frequently erupt sulfur dioxide gas. Most of the gas condenses and falls back to Io as ice, but some sulfur and oxygen ions escape into Jupiter's magnetosphere. Io's eruptions result from the gravitational pulls of Jupiter, Europa, and Ganymede. These forces pull Io in different directions, squeezing the moon's interior and causing it to heat up.

Europa also shows evidence of geological activity caused by the same forces that squeeze Io. Europa's icy surface features a broken network of *fissures* (narrow cracks). The fissures may indicate that the moon's icy crust rests atop deep oceans of liquid water or slushy water ice.

Ganymede ranks as Jupiter's largest moon and the largest moon in the solar system. Ganymede is also the only moon in the solar system known to generate its own magnetic field.

Its surface features large light and dark regions. The dark regions contain more impact craters than the light regions do. The light regions typically exhibit many grooves and ridges.

Callisto, the outermost Galilean satellite, is one of the most heavily cratered bodies in the solar system. Impact craters uniformly cover its surface.

Inner satellites. The moons with orbits that lie inside those of the Galilean satellites are known as Jupiter's *inner satellites*. In order of increasing distance from the planet, they are Metis, Adrastea, Amalthea, and Thebe.

Compared to the large, round Galilean satellites, the inner satellites are small and irregular in shape. They range from 10 to 104 miles (16 to 167 kilometers) in average diameter. Amalthea is the largest, followed by Thebe, Metis, and Adrastea. Their surfaces all appear dark and red and have many craters from collisions. Astronomers have measured the average density of Amalthea, which is about the same as the density of water on Earth's surface. Amalthea must be remarkably *porous* (filled with tiny holes) to have such a low density.

Outer satellites. Jupiter also has a large number of small, irregular satellites orbiting well beyond the Galilean satellites. Astronomers have discovered dozens of these *outer satellites*, but their actual number is probably higher. Jupiter's gravitation can also trap other bodies for a time, making them *temporary satellites*.

Himalia ranks as the largest of Jupiter's outer satellites, followed by Elara, Pasiphae, Carme, Sinope, Lysithea, Ananke, and Leda. Ananke, Carme, Pasiphae, and Sinope have *retrograde orbits*—that is, they orbit in a direction opposite to that of the other satellites and the direction of Jupiter's rotation. Elara, Himalia, Leda, and Lysithea orbit in the same direction that Jupiter rotates. Unlike the orbits of the inner satellites and the Galilean satellites, the orbits of some outer satellites are tilted by many degrees from Jupiter's *equatorial plane,* the imaginary plane that contains the planet's equator.

Rings. Jupiter's four rings consist of fine dust particles, all circling the planet on individual orbits. The rings all lie close to the planet's equator and are sometimes mistaken for a single ring. Compared to Saturn's rings, Jupiter's rings are smaller and fainter, and contain much less mass. In fact, astronomers could not confirm that Jupiter's rings existed until the two Voyager spacecraft observed them close-up

in 1979. Astronomers call the brightest ring the *main ring.* Its outer edge corresponds to the orbit of Adrastea. A fainter ring called the *halo ring* lies inside the orbit of Metis. Two faint rings called the *gossamer rings* lie outside the main ring. Their outer edges correspond to the orbits of Amalthea and Thebe.

Astronomers think that the rings result from collisions between the inner satellites and tiny particles called *micrometeoroids.* These collisions eject some dust into the space around the moons. The dust particles orbit Jupiter as they fall toward the planet, forming the rings.

Formation of Jupiter

As the largest planet in our solar system, Jupiter plays a central role in our ideas about how the solar system formed. Jupiter and the sun share a similar composition. They likely formed at the same time from the *solar nebula.* The solar nebula was a giant rotating cloud of gas and dust.

The solar system began to take shape as the solar nebula collapsed under the influence of gravity. As the nebula contracted, its central region heated up while the outer regions remained cool. Around what is now Jupiter's orbit, temperatures became cold enough for water vapor to freeze into ice crystals.

According to the most widely held theory, ice and other solid material slowly gathered together to form what is now the core of Jupiter. The core grew as it attracted more material from nearby regions. As the core gained mass, its gravitational

A distant view of Jupiter's planetary system taken from Voyager spacecraft

pull became stronger. Eventually, the core's gravitational pull became strong enough to capture hydrogen and helium, which were abundant in the solar nebula. For this reason, Jupiter today consists mostly of hydrogen and helium.

Astronomers use the term *accretion* to refer to the process by which tiny particles accumulate to form giant planets. When two particles collide, they may stick together to form a larger particle. As the process continues, larger and larger bodies collide. This process happens in different locations, creating many large objects called *planetesimals*. Eventually, many of the planetesimals near what is now Jupiter's orbit combined to form the planet. Some of the other planetesimals may have formed some of Jupiter's satellites, while still others may have escaped to great distances and become comets.

History of Jupiter Study

Jupiter was known to the ancient astronomers, who tracked the planet's motion across the night sky. Astronomers first studied Jupiter through telescopes in the early 1600s. In 1610, Galileo discovered what later became known as the Galilean satellites. At the time, many people believed that every cosmic body revolved around Earth. The discovery of moons orbiting another planet helped convince Galileo and others that Earth was not at the center of the universe.

In the late 1960s, astronomers chose Jupiter as the target of the first spacecraft mission to the outer solar system. They launched the craft, called

Italian astronomer and physicist Galileo Galilei

Pioneer 10, in 1972. On December 3, 1973, Pioneer 10 became the first spacecraft to visit Jupiter when it passed within about 81,000 miles (130,000 kilometers) of the planet's cloud tops. Pioneer 11 (later renamed Pioneer-Saturn) flew by Jupiter on December 2, 1974. The two Pioneer spacecraft captured images of Jupiter and its moons. They sent back data on the planet's gravitational pull, magnetic field, radiation belts, atmosphere, and the plasma in its magnetosphere.

Astronomers used data from the Pioneer missions to design the more ambitious Voyager missions. The spacecraft Voyager 1 flew by Jupiter at a distance of about 174,000 miles (280,000 kilometers) on March 5, 1979. Voyager 2 passed within about 449,000 miles (722,000 kilometers) of the planet on July 9, 1979. The Voyager missions revolutionized our understanding of Jupiter. They discovered Jupiter's intense aurora and numerous features of the planet's atmosphere. They also confirmed the existence of Jupiter's rings. The two Voyager craft captured the first close-up views of many of the planet's moons, revealing them to be much more active and varied than astronomers had expected.

The Ulysses spacecraft, designed primarily to study the sun, passed within about 235,000 miles (378,000 kilometers) of Jupiter on February 8, 1992. Its instruments measured Jupiter's radio emissions as well as the plasma, dust, and other particles in the Jovian system. Ulysses gathered more data on Jupiter's magnetosphere when it revisited the planet from late 2003 to early 2004.

In 1993, the American astronomers Carolyn and Eugene Shoemaker and the Canadian-born astronomer David H. Levy discovered a comet passing near Jupiter. Astronomers soon realized that the comet, called Shoemaker-Levy 9, had been captured by Jupiter's gravity and broken into 21 or more fragments. Astronomers from around the world watched as most of the fragments collided with Jupiter over a period of several days in July 1994.

The Galileo spacecraft became the first craft to orbit Jupiter when it arrived at the planet on December 7, 1995. The same day, a probe Galileo had released months earlier entered Jupiter's atmosphere. The probe made the first precise measurements of the atmosphere's helium, ammonia, and many other substances. It also recorded the speed of the winds below the cloud tops. The probe surprisingly detected few clouds and little water vapor, but astronomers think that the probe entered an area that was not typical of the rest of the atmosphere.

The main Galileo spacecraft continued to orbit Jupiter for eight years, making numerous important discoveries about the Jovian system. It detected massive thunderstorms in Jupiter's atmosphere. It discovered that Ganymede has a magnetic field and found evidence that an ocean of water or soft ice lies beneath Europa's surface. Galileo also studied volcanoes on Io, determining that their eruptions were powered by hot, magnesium-rich silicates from deep in Io's interior.

The Cassini spacecraft, designed to study Saturn, flew by Jupiter at a distance of nearly 6 million miles (10 million kilometers) from the planet's cloud tops in December 2000. The Galileo spacecraft was still in orbit around Jupiter at that time, allowing astronomers to conduct coordinated observations of the planet from two different locations. The data gathered were used to study Jupiter's moons, its magnetosphere, and the weather systems in its atmosphere.

In 2007, the New Horizons spacecraft passed by Jupiter at a distance of 1.4 million miles (2.3 million kilometers) to gain speed on its voyage to Pluto and a distant region of the solar system called the *Kuiper belt*. New Horizons took images of Jupiter's Litle Red Spot, recorded a volcanic eruption on Io, and became the first craft to travel down the "tail" of Jupiter's magnetosphere.

In 2009, an Australian amateur astronomer named Anthony Wesley noticed a large discoloration on the surface of Jupiter. After astronomers examined the "spot," they determined it to be a remnant of an asteroid or comet impact, the first one observed since Shoemaker-Levy 9 in 1994.

GALILEO was a space probe launched by the United States to observe Jupiter, its moons and rings, and the radiation and magnetism in the neighboring space. The National Aeronautics and Space Administration (NASA) launched Galileo on October 18, 1989. The craft orbited Jupiter from December 7, 1995, to September 21, 2003. The spacecraft was named after the Italian astronomer and physicist Galileo, who discovered Jupiter's four largest moons in 1610.

The Galileo craft took an indirect route to Jupiter. First, it made a close approach to Venus, using energy from that planet's gravitational field

NASA's Galileo probe passing over one of Jupiter's moons

to increase its speed. It then flew past Earth twice to pick up more speed. On the way to Jupiter, it visited the asteroids Gaspra and Ida.

On the day Galileo went into orbit around Jupiter, a smaller probe that had been released by Galileo five months earlier plunged into the planet's atmosphere. The small probe encountered atmo-spheric pressures more than 20 times as great as that on Earth. The intense heat of the atmosphere shut down its instruments after 61.4 minutes. Eventually, the entire probe melted and evaporated. One of the probe's major discoveries was that Jupiter's chemical composition resembles what astronomers believe was the original composition of the sun. Jupiter has a higher proportion of heavy elements than the sun. Some of the lighter gases must have been lost during the planet's formation.

Galileo's observations of Jupiter's four largest moons produced many surprises. For example, lava from Io's volcanoes is hotter than lava on Earth. A blanket of dark, smooth material covers the surface of Callisto. Ganymede has a dense core and a *magnetic field* (a region in which magnetism can be detected). Grooves and ridges crisscross the icy surface of Europa. In places, the ice on Europa seems to have broken into blocks—suggesting that there may be an ocean of water underneath.

Voyager 2 space probe

NASA designed Galileo to orbit Jupiter for only two years, but the craft continued to provide valuable information after that period. Eventually, Galileo ran low on fuel. NASA intentionally crashed Galileo into Jupiter's atmosphere on September 21, 2003, to avoid any risk of the craft crashing into and contaminating Europa. Many scientists believe that if water exists below the surface of Europa, it may be capable of supporting life.

VOYAGER is either of two United States space probes launched in 1977 to Jupiter and beyond. The two crafts continue to provide valuable information.

Information gathered by the Voyager probes forms the basis of the modern study of Jupiter, Saturn, Uranus, Neptune, and their satellites, rings, and *magnetic fields* (regions where magnetic force can be detected). The probes discovered nearly two dozen natural satellites. They also found evidence of geologic activity on two previously known moons—volcanoes on Jupiter's moon Io and icy geysers on Neptune's moon Triton. The mission also discovered numerous craters on most of the satellites, an ancient record of intense bombardment by meteoroids and comets. Scientists used Voyager data to calculate the density of 17 satellites and to determine the composition of the atmosphere of Saturn's moon Titan.

The National Aeronautics and Space Administration (NASA) launched Voyager 1 on September 5, 1977. The probe made its closest approach to Jupiter on March 5, 1979, encountered Saturn on November 12, 1980, and then headed toward *interstellar space* (the space between the stars). Voyager 2, launched on August 20, 1977, made its closest approach to Jupiter on July 9, 1979, Saturn on August 25, 1981, Uranus on January 24, 1986, and Neptune on August 25, 1989, then traveled toward interstellar space.

The Voyagers carried identical sets of scientific instruments. One instrument measured the strength, shape, and direction of the planets' magnetic fields. Another studied waves traveling through *plasma* trapped within the fields. Plasma consists of electrically charged atoms, as well as electrons that are not parts of atoms.

Three devices measured the quantities and speeds of these charged particles. Five instruments measured ultraviolet rays, visible light, infrared rays, and radio waves given off by the planets and their satellites, rings, and plasma. Also, as the two crafts moved behind each planet, the planet's atmosphere and rings blocked the radio signals transmitted by the Voyagers in ways that revealed details of their structure.

The Voyagers' radio receivers and their particle and magnetism detectors were still operating in the early 2000s. Scientists monitored their data in hope of detecting the *heliopause*, where interstellar space begins. In late 2004, Voyager 1 crossed a shock wave called the *termination shock*, becoming the first craft to reach the region of space that lies just inside the heliopause. The crossing occurred at a distance of about 8.7 billion miles (14 billion kilometers) from the sun. By detecting the shock at different distances from the sun, the two craft confirmed scientists' belief that the solar system is not perfectly round.

MLA Citation

"Jupiter." *The Southwestern Advantage Topic Source.* Nashville: Southwestern. 2013.

ADDITIONAL RESOURCES

Books to Read

Carson, Mary K. *Far-Out Guide to Jupiter*. Bailey Books, 2011.

Fischer, Daniel. *Mission Jupiter: The Spectacular Journey of the Galileo Spacecraft*. Copernicus Books, 2001.

Landau, Elaine. *Jupiter*. Children's Press, 2008.

McAnally, John W. *Jupiter and How to Observe It*. Springer, 2008.

Web Sites

Jupiter: Mythology and Man's Early Musings

http://solarsystem.nasa.gov/scitech/display.cfm?st_id=525

Mythological stories about Jupiter and its moons.

The Eight Planets

http://nineplanets.org/

Information about the eight planets in our solar system.

Search Strings

The Jovian System

"Jovian system" Jupiter (51,300)

"Jovian system" Jupiter magnetosphere satellites moon rings dust (1,100)

"Jovian system" Jupiter magnetosphere (30,800)

Characteristics of Jupiter

Jupiter planet characteristics (51,900)

Jupiter planet characteristics orbit rotation axis seasons mass composition density (2,280)

The Great Red Spot

Jupiter "Great Red Spot" (108,000)

Jupiter "Great Red Spot" swirling gas (3,570)

Jupiter "Great Red Spot" swirling gas tropopause (314)

Jupiter's Satellites and Rings

Jupiter satellites rings Galilean inner outer moons (30,200)

Jupiter satellites rings Galilean inner outer moons rings dust particles (1,690)

BACKGROUND INFORMATION

The following articles and features were written during the year in which the events took place and reflect the style and thinking of that time.

When Worlds and Comets Collide

The spectacular comet strikes on Jupiter in 1994 showed that the solar system can be a very dangerous place.

—by Donald Goldsmith

The greatest collision between a planet and another celestial object ever witnessed by scientists happened in July 1994. For six days, Jupiter was bombarded by pieces of a disintegrated comet named Comet Shoemaker-Levy 9. One after another, more than 20 comet fragments slammed into Jupiter's dense atmosphere at speeds of about 60 kilometers (37 miles) a second, creating enormous fireballs easily visible through telescopes on Earth.

The impacts thrilled planetary scientists and amazed the world. But they also served as a reminder that the solar system can be a dangerous place. Earth, too, has been struck many times in the past by huge objects hurtling down from space. Scientists think that a mammoth collision with a large comet or asteroid about 65 million years ago may have led to the demise of the dinosaurs. And in 1908, more than 2,000 square kilometers (770 square miles) of forest near the Tunguska River in central Siberia were leveled by an immense atmospheric blast caused by an object—probably a meteor—less than 100 meters (330 feet) in diameter.

Could a comet collide with Earth? Scientists say that what has happened to Earth in the past will happen again in the future. The only question is when.

In fact, astronomers recently thought they had identified a large comet that could pose a danger to Earth a little more than a century from now. In 1992, an international organization of astronomers said the comet, named Swift-Tuttle, would come close to the Earth in August 2126. Scientists estimated the odds of a collision at 1 in 10,000. Fortunately, further calculations showed that there was no danger of an impact after all. But there are many other bodies orbiting out in space. It is possible—not likely, but possible—that Earth will be hit sometime in the next 100 years by some large object that astronomers haven't yet discovered.

Such threats seemed too remote for nonscientists to worry about until the Jupiter collisions suggested to some government leaders that catastrophic strikes from space should perhaps be taken a bit more seriously. On July 20, 1994, the day the first chunks of Comet Shoemaker-Levy plowed into Jupiter, the Science Committee of the United States House of Representatives instructed the National Aeronautics and Space Administration (NASA) to begin tracking any comets, asteroids, or meteoroids—pieces of asteroids—that might someday hit the Earth. NASA officials also named a six-member panel to study the possibility of developing an early-warning system for objects on a collision course with our planet. Meanwhile, some scientists debated how such bodies might best be destroyed or deflected into a safe orbit.

Although asteroids and large meteoroids are just as likely as comets to strike the Earth, a comet would be apt to cause more damage than a rocky body the same size, because comets, on average, travel at greater speeds. But a comet would at least give us fair warning of its coming. Even with the unaided eye, a large comet can be seen from many millions of kilometers away, its misty tail glowing in the night sky. With their telescopes, astronomers would probably be able to predict a collision with a comet at least a year in advance.

Debris from the Shoemaker-Levy 9 comet orbiting Jupiter in an irregular ellipse that eventually caused it to collide with the planet

From evil omens to dirty snowballs. People have always marveled at comets, and for most of human history they have feared them as well. Because comets appeared unpredictably in the skies, many cultures regarded these celestial visitors as omens of disaster—plagues or the overthrow of kingdoms, not the kind of devastation we now know they can bring.

In times past, no one knew what comets were. The ancient Greek philosopher Aristotle believed they were gaseous objects in Earth's atmosphere, and for centuries nobody could prove him wrong. In the late 1500s, however, the Danish astronomer Tycho Brahe made detailed observations of several comets and showed that their motions placed them well beyond the atmosphere of the Earth.

More than a century later, in the early 1700s, the British scientist Edmond Halley concluded that a comet seen in 1682 was the same one astronomers had observed in 1531 and 1607. Halley predicted the comet would return to the skies again in 1758. When the comet reappeared on schedule, it was named for Halley. In later years, astronomers determined that Halley's Comet, which returns at intervals of about 77 years, may have been the comet recorded in various historical records and works of art dating back as far as 240 B.C.

Modern observations of comets have revealed that they are essentially large, dirty snowballs. A comet consists primarily of water ice and various amounts of frozen gases, including carbon dioxide, methane, and ammonia, mixed with rocky material and dust. Most of the mass of a comet is contained in a solid core called the nucleus, typically 1 to 10 kilometers (0.6 to 6 miles) in diameter.

Huge reservoirs of comets. Astronomers think that comets were among the first objects to form in the solar system, created from the same cloud of gas and dust that gave birth to the sun and planets some 4.6 billion years ago. The outer portions of the cloud condensed into a crowded disk of icy bodies. Over the eons, gravitational interactions between these icy objects caused most of them to take up different orbits, eventually dispersing them into a huge spherical region. This vast reservoir of comet nuclei is called the Oort Cloud, named after the Dutch astronomer Jan Oort, who first deduced its existence in 1950. Astronomers think the Oort Cloud extends about halfway to the nearest star, a distance of trillions of kilometers. The objects in the Oort

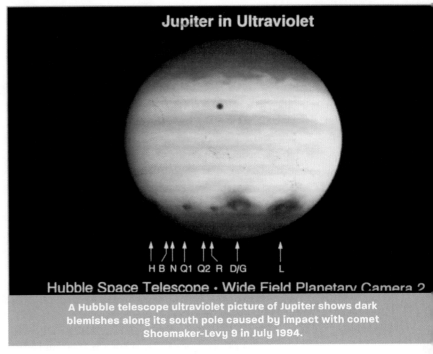

Jupiter in Ultraviolet

H B N Q1 Q2 R D/G L

Hubble Space Telescope · Wide Field Planetary Camera 2

A Hubble telescope ultraviolet picture of Jupiter shows dark blemishes along its south pole caused by impact with comet Shoemaker-Levy 9 in July 1994.

Cloud are so distant that not even our best telescopes can see them.

Also in 1950, a Dutch-born American astronomer, Gerard Kuiper (pronounced KOY per), theorized that much of the original disk of comet nuclei remains as a smaller and more densely packed reservoir of comets within the vast Oort Cloud. This region, Kuiper speculated, is still disk-shaped and begins just beyond the outermost planets. The region became known as the Kuiper Belt, but for years there was no evidence that it actually exists. Observations in the 1990s, however—including images made in 1995 by the Hubble Space Telescope—have erased most doubts about the Kuiper Belt. Several dozen icy objects orbiting beyond the planets have now been discovered.

Astronomers are certain that the number of comets visible from Earth is just a minuscule fraction of the comets in the Kuiper Belt and Oort Cloud. They think those two regions contain several trillion comet nuclei. We see only those relatively few comets whose orbits have been altered, perhaps by the gravitational influence of a nearby star or even of another comet, sending them into the inner solar system.

When a comet nears the sun. Most of the time, when a comet is orbiting far from the sun, it consists of nothing but the nucleus. But when a comet moves toward the inner parts of the solar system, it starts to assume its more familiar appearance. When the comet nears the orbit of Jupiter, the sun's heat causes the frozen gases in the outer layers of the nucleus to start evaporating, producing a large cloud of thin gas and dust called a coma. The coma, which surrounds and blocks astronomers' view of the nucleus, can be more than 100,000 kilometers (60,000 miles) across.

When the comet gets about as close to the sun as the Earth is, the pressure of sunlight and of the solar wind—a stream of fast-moving particles moving outward from the sun—pushes the gas and dust away from the coma. This effect creates a long tail that may stretch for 100 million kilometers (60 million miles), always pointing away from the sun.

After a comet circles around the sun and begins to head toward the outer reaches of the solar system, its tail shrinks and its coma dissipates. Soon, the nucleus is all that remains until its next trip into the inner solar system.

Each time the comet returns, evaporation causes its mass to decrease by about 1 percent, and eventually there will be nothing left of it. How long it takes a comet to evaporate away to nothing depends on its size and its orbit. Some comets, such as Halley's Comet, are known as short-period comets because they make return trips in less than 200 years. Astronomers think short-period comets come from the Kuiper Belt. Long-period comets, on the other hand, have orbital periods that take them out of the inner solar system for centuries, and some will not return again for thousands or even millions of years. These comets probably come from the Oort Cloud. Most long-period comets have lost only a small amount of their mass, so they tend to be larger and brighter than short-period comets.

A rare spectacle on Jupiter. Astronomers believe that the Kuiper Belt was the original home of the comet that smashed into Jupiter. The comet was discovered in March 1993 by American astronomers Eugene Shoemaker, Carolyn Shoemaker, and David Levy at the Mount Palomar Observatory in California. The astronomers were looking for new comets by comparing photographs of regions of the sky taken on different nights. If they noticed that a tiny, faint object had changed position against the background of stars, they would identify it as a comet or an asteroid. The object's speed would reveal which of the two it is, since comets move faster than asteroids.

Studying photographic images they had made of a portion of the night sky, Levy and the Shoemakers noted what appeared to be a "squashed comet." Further observations confirmed that the object was indeed a comet and that it looked squashed because it was broken into fragments. The pieces of the comet were hurtling through space one after another, lined up like pearls on a string.

By studying the path of Shoemaker-Levy 9, astronomers determined that the comet was in orbit around Jupiter and had probably been orbiting the giant planet for 60 to 100 years. But what had broken it into pieces? Physicists and planetary scientists theorized that when the comet passed close by Jupiter in July 1992, the planet's tremendous gravity had pulled the icy nucleus apart. Further calculations revealed that the comet fragments would smash into the far side of Jupiter in July 1994.

When the collisions came, they were spectacular. The largest comet fragments, which may have been more than 3 kilometers (2 miles) in diameter, created particularly stupendous displays, igniting huge atmospheric blasts, some of them thousands of kilometers across.

Because all the impacts occurred on Jupiter's far side, just over the planet's rim as seen from Earth, no telescope—not even the Hubble Space Telescope—could see the collisions as they occurred. Only the Galileo spacecraft, on its way to a rendezvous with Jupiter in December 1995, was able to photograph some of the comet strikes directly. Observers on Earth could see the impact sites about 30 minutes after each collision occurred, as Jupiter's rapid rotation (once every 10 hours) carried them into view. But several fiery plumes of gas—the tops

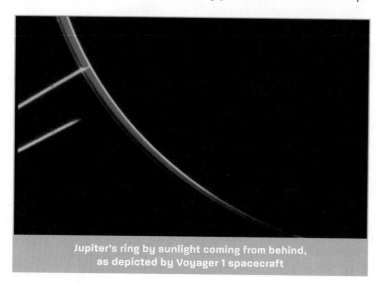

Jupiter's ring by sunlight coming from behind, as depicted by Voyager 1 spacecraft

of the largest explosions—were visible at the time of impact as they rose above the planet's rim.

Jupiter consists primarily of gases, so the impacts caused no long-term damage. The only noticeable effects were a few dark blotches in the atmosphere that persisted for several months and could still be seen as stretched-out atmospheric streaks in 1995.

Big collisons are rare. If our own planet had been the target of Comet Shoemaker-Levy 9, the outcome would have been much different. Earth, too, would have survived the bombardment, but scientists say that the collisions would have caused widespread devastation and greatly damaged the planet's complex web of life.

The extent of the destruction that would result from a comet striking the Earth at a typical speed of about 50 kilometers (30 miles) a second would depend on the size of the comet. A strike by a comet 10 kilometers (6 miles) or so in diameter would be truly catastrophic, equivalent to a billion 1-megaton hydrogen bombs exploding all at once. Besides the immediate effects of the impact, trillions of tons of pulverized debris would be thrown into the atmosphere, where it would blot out the sun for months. Much of the planet's vegetation would die, and with it much of the human and animal life that depends on it. Civilization itself might well be destroyed, and whatever scattered remnants of humanity survived—if any did—would sink into a prolonged dark age.

That is the magnitude of the collision many scientists believe occurred 65 million years ago, when the last of the dinosaurs and many other species of animals vanished forever from the Earth. Geologists think they may have identified the ancient crater produced by that event off the coast of Mexico's Yucatan Peninsula.

Fortunately, such collisions are rare. The geological record of impact craters on Earth shows that a 10-kilometer-wide object strikes our planet, on average, only once every 100 million years.

Smaller comet strikes are more common. Strikes by smaller bodies are more frequent, simply because small objects in the solar system are much more numerous than large ones. The best-preserved impact crater made within the last few tens of thousands of years—Meteor Crater in Arizona—was created by a relatively small object. About 50,000 years ago, an iron meteorite about 30 meters (100 feet) in diameter smashed

A composite image taken by the Galileo probe shows the edge of Jupiter with its Great Red Spot and the planet's four largest moons.

into the Arizona desert to produce the crater, a depression more than 1.2 kilometers (0.75 mile) across and about 175 meters (575 feet) deep. Despite the meteorite's fairly small size, it struck with the explosive force of 20 million tons of TNT.

The blast that gouged out Meteor Crater was comparable to the Tunguska explosion of 1908. Scientists estimate that a comet or meteor collision of that size occurs once every 200 to 300 years, on the average. One reason we don't have more impact craters on Earth is that many objects rapidly disintegrate in the atmosphere, just as happened in Siberia. Only very large or very hard objects make it all the way to the ground. Moreover, it is all but certain that the great majority of strikes have occurred in the ocean, because more than 70 percent of the planet is covered with water. But the scarcity of impact craters on land is due largely to erosion. As centuries pass, wind and water slowly obliterate all traces of most craters.

Contemplating catastrophe. Although a Tunguska-sized explosion over a populated area would be a calamity, the destruction would be limited to a relatively small area. Many scientists

Kitt Peak National Observatory in Tucson, Arizona

and government leaders are more concerned about the possibility of a collision with a larger body, one with a diameter of 1 kilometer (0.6 mile) or more. An object that size hits the Earth at least once every million years or so, on the average.

At a speed of 50 kilometers a second, a comet that size would hit the Earth with a kinetic energy (energy of motion) equivalent to 1 million 1-megaton hydrogen bombs, or 1 trillion tons of TNT. Experts say the destruction and loss of life resulting from such a collision would surpass anything humanity has ever experienced from a single event.

Flashing through Earth's atmosphere in about two seconds, the comet would smash into the ground with incredible force and explode in an immense fireball. The shock wave from the blast would level virtually everything for a radius of more than 100 kilometers. Within much of that area, the heat of the fireball would reduce the debris to ashes and shapeless blobs of melted stone and metal. Beyond the ring of total destruction, damage from the shock wave and heat would be severe to moderate for another 1,000 kilometers (600 miles).

The collision would produce a crater at least 20 kilometers (12 miles) across and several kilometers deep. The force of the impact would hurl molten material long distances, igniting forest fires, and eject an immense volume of dust and vaporized rock into the atmosphere. The dust and gas would spread around the planet and obscure the sun.

The atmospheric darkening would be much less severe than would result from a truly enormous impact such as the one that occurred 65 million years ago, but it would still be significant. The atmospheric effects from a 1-kilometer-comet strike might cause widespread crop failures and

starvation. So even if we had adequate warning of the collision and evacuated the areas most apt to be devastated, these secondary effects could still cause great loss of life.

If a comet plunged into the ocean. But what about the more likely possibility that a comet would hit in the ocean? Unfortunately, that too would be a disaster. Although a comet strike far out at sea might spare cities from being flattened or burned, the collision would still do plenty of damage.

After its plunge through the atmosphere, the comet would plow through several kilometers of seawater in a fraction of a second, breaking apart from the force of the impact. Still moving at immense speed, the comet would burrow into the sea floor and explode, creating a crater more than 10 kilometers in diameter and spewing material in all directions. Vast amounts of steam and vaporized rock would be thrown upward before the parted water could rush back to cover the hole in the sea floor.

The worst effect of an ocean strike might be the resulting tidal wave. The comet's sudden displacement of a huge volume of water, together with the titanic blast on the sea floor, would create a tidal wave a kilometer or more in height that would surge outward at almost 1,000 kilometers an hour. Many low-lying coastal cities would be submerged.

Watching for dangerous comets. Because a collision with a comet would have such terrible consequences, experts say it's worth considering how such a disaster might be prevented. Some astronomers have proposed the construction of a network of telescopes dedicated to searching the solar system for all near-Earth objects (NEOs), objects whose paths cross Earth's orbit and which are large enough—1 kilometer or more in diameter—to cause large-scale damage. Such a system would most likely enable scientists to identify all these threats, which astronomers think may number 2,000 or more. At present, only about 100 are known.

NASA's six-person panel was expected to recommend the development of just such a system, probably to be called Spaceguard. NASA already has a much more limited program, the Spacewatch survey, which uses a telescope at the Kitt Peak National Observatory near Tucson, Arizona, to watch for NEOs. Spacewatch observations are detecting about 30 new NEOs a year, ranging in size from about 6 meters (20 feet) to 6 kilometers

(3.7 miles) in diameter. A similar project is being carried out at Mount Palomar.

In 1995, NASA and the Air Force were also funding the development of improved electronic detectors, known as charge-coupled devices (CCDs), to increase the light-gathering ability of telescopes. The more sensitive CCDs would give small instruments the resolving power of considerably larger telescopes, making it possible to use many existing telescopes to search for NEOs. Once astronomers identify an NEO, they can chart its orbit and predict its future motions.

It may thus be possible to find and catalog every potentially dangerous asteroid, large meteoroid, and known comet. But a new short-period comet making its first trip around the sun would pose an unforeseen danger. Likewise, a long-term comet returning from a million-year circuit through the Oort Cloud might sneak up on us by surprise. Experts say we must be particularly on the lookout for these previously unknown comets.

Unfortunately, detecting a comet on a collision course with Earth will undoubtedly be easier than preventing the impact. So far, scientists and engineers have proposed several schemes, but all involve considerable risk.

Bombing a comet. One solution is to send nuclear-armed rockets into space to blow up the comet or nudge it into a new orbit. Such a mission would require extremely accurate calculations. Astronomers would have to be absolutely certain that the object was sure to strike the Earth—otherwise, the nuclear explosion might change what would have been a near-miss into a direct hit. And spaceflight engineers would have to give the rockets just the right trajectory and explode the warheads at precisely the right time to get the desired effect.

Attempting to destroy the comet outright could be a chancy proposition, however. If we were to simply blow it into large pieces, those chunks might rain down over a large region of the Earth. Calculations indicate that such an outcome could be worse than a single large collision. To be successful, engineers would have to make sure that the comet was completely pulverized. Simply altering the object's orbit might be a safer bet. That could be done by detonating warheads close enough to the object to affect its motion but not break it apart.

The farther away a comet could be intercepted, the easier it would be to push it into a safe orbit. Only a small change in the object's path would make a large difference over a distance of several billion kilometers, just as moving a rifle barrel a couple of millimeters can be the difference between hitting a far-off target dead center or missing it completely. Thus, early detection of a comet on a collision course with Earth would give engineers a tremendous advantage in diverting it.

Intercepting a comet or asteroid. With enough warning, it might even be possible to avoid explosive devices altogether. Some scientists have proposed sending astronauts to an approaching comet or asteroid to mount powerful rocket engines on it or even fit it with a huge "solar sail." The latter would be a giant reflector made of metallic foil, which would capture the pressure of sunlight the way a sloop's sails catch the wind, slowly easing the object into a new orbit. But such schemes assume a warning time measured in years. If we discovered a comet just months away from hitting the Earth, nuclear-tipped rockets might be the only feasible solution.

The odds are with us. Thankfully, astronomers say we probably have plenty of time to weigh our options. Even though comets and asteroids have crashed into our planet many times in the past, the long intervals between the largest impacts make it likely that the next big one won't arrive for thousands more years.

Still, the experts caution, we would do well to keep a close watch on the skies, especially for the smaller objects that arrive more frequently. But on the rare occasion that a major comet makes its majestic way around the sun, the odds will be good that we can simply sit back and enjoy the show.

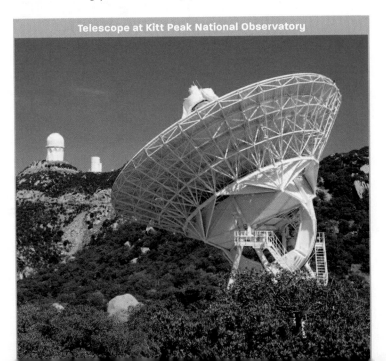

Telescope at Kitt Peak National Observatory

Africa

Africa is the second largest continent in area and in population. Only Asia covers a larger area and has more people. Africa covers about one-fifth of the world's land area and is home to one-seventh of the world's people.

HOT topics

Endangered Animals
Dance and Music
Agriculture
Deserts, Grasslands, and Forests

HOT topics

Endangered Animals. Africa once had many more wild animals than it has today, and they were more widespread. Ancient paintings on rocks show that hippopotamuses and giraffes once lived in regions that are now deserts. Gradual changes in climate partly reduced the number and range of Africa's animals. But in many regions, people have overhunted the animals and destroyed much of their natural environment to make room for farms and cities. Intensive conservation efforts are necessary to protect many African animals, including the black rhinoceros, gorilla, and elephant, which are in danger of becoming extinct.

DEFINITIONS

agriculture: the science, art, or occupation of cultivating the soil to make crops grow; the raising of crops and farm animals; farming. Synonyms include *husbandry* and *tillage*.

AIDS: acquired immune deficiency (immunodeficiency) syndrome, a viral disease that attacks and breaks down the body's immune system, leading to serious and usually fatal infections and to a form of sarcoma.

cash crop: a crop grown for sale, rather than for consumption on the farm.

colonialism: the policy of a nation that rules or seeks to rule weaker or dependent nations, often with or for economic exploitation.

continent: one of the seven great masses of land on the earth. The continents are North America, South America, Europe, Africa, Asia, Australia, and Antarctica.

epidemic: the rapid spreading of a disease so that many people have it at the same time.

malaria: a disease that causes chills, fever, and sweating. Malaria is transmitted by the bite of anopheles mosquitoes that have previously bitten infected persons. It is caused by minute parasitic animals in the red blood corpuscles.

HOT topics

Dance and Music. Music accompanies many daily events of life in Africa. Singing sustains the rhythms of manual labor in fields and villages. Traditional African music includes choral singing, music performed for entertainment, and songs and dances for religious events. In Senegal and other parts of west Africa, a professional speaker called a griot plays music while reciting history. Drums imitate the sounds of human speech and are used to relay messages from ancestors, embodied by masked dancers. African musicians use a variety of drums, string instruments, and wind instruments. Today, the influence of African music can be heard in Western popular music and jazz, West Indian calypso, and Latin American dance music.

Young bull elephants

Agriculture. African crop production is divided between staple food crops and export crops. Important staple food crops include corn, millet, rice, sorghum, wheat, cassava, potatoes, yams, peas, peanuts, beans, fruits, and vegetables. Africa's leading export crops include cacao (cocoa), coffee, cotton, kola nuts, palm oil, sugar, tea, and tobacco. Most staples are produced for local consumption by farmers working on family-owned or rented farms. There are also large plantations owned by companies, wealthy individuals, or governments. These plantations are usually used for production of export crops. Production of agricultural crops and livestock employs more workers than any other economic activity in Africa.

Deserts, Grasslands, and Forests. Deserts cover about two-fifths of Africa. The Sahara, the world's largest desert, stretches across northern Africa from the Atlantic Ocean to the Red Sea. The land is mostly bare rock and sand dunes. Grasslands, called savannas, occupy more than two-fifths of Africa. Tall grasses, bushes, and scattered trees grow in this area. Woodlands border the rain forests within the tropical region, where their swamps provide breeding sites for fish, protect the coast from damaging waves, and clean the water by filtering sediment. Thicker woodlands flourish in areas with more rainfall. Forests cover less than a fifth of Africa.

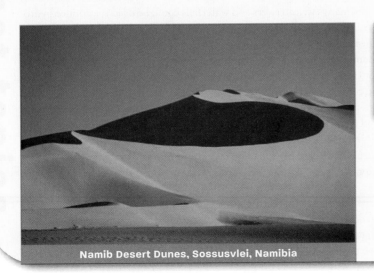
Namib Desert Dunes, Sossusvlei, Namibia

TRUE or FALSE?
The peoples of Africa speak more than 1,000 languages.

THE BASICS

Africa is the second largest continent in area and in population. Only Asia covers a larger area and has more people. Africa covers approximately 11,675,000 square miles (30,238,000 square kilometers), about a fifth of the world's land area, and has a population of more than 1 billion, about one-seventh of the world's people.

The African continent is an immense plateau, broken by a few mountain ranges and bordered in some areas by a narrow coastal plain. It is a land of striking contrasts and great natural wonders. In the tropical rain forests of western and central Africa, the towering treetops form a thick green canopy. The world's largest desert, the Sahara, stretches across northern Africa. It covers an area almost as large as the United States. Africa also has the world's longest river—the Nile. It flows more than 4,000 miles (6,400 kilometers) through northeastern Africa. Grasslands make up about a third of the continent. Elephants, giraffes, lions, zebras, and many other animals live in the vast grasslands in eastern and southern Africa.

Victoria Falls, Devil's Cataract, Zimbabwe

Africa is divided into 54 independent countries and several other political units. The largest country, Algeria, has an area of 919,595 square miles (2,381,741 square kilometers). The smallest, Seychelles, has a land area of only 176 square miles (455 square kilometers). The most heavily populated African nation, Nigeria, has about 165 million people. However, about one-third of all African countries have fewer than 5 million people each. About 905 million people—about 85 percent of Africa's total population—live south of the Sahara in the vast region called *sub-Saharan Africa*.

There are several hundred ethnic groups throughout Africa, each with its own language or dialect and way of life. The large number and various sizes of ethnic groups has made it difficult for some African countries to develop into unified, modern nations. In some African countries, national boundaries cut across traditional ethnic homelands. As a result, people may feel closer ties to neighbors in another country than to other ethnic groups within their own country. Ethnic and religious differences have led to civil wars in several countries.

Africa has great mineral wealth, including huge deposits of copper, diamonds, gold, and petroleum. It also has valuable forests. In addition, many African rivers and waterfalls could be used to produce hydroelectric power. Africa produces most of the world's cassava, cocoa beans, and yams. But Africa has the least developed economy of any continent except Antarctica.

Agriculture is the leading economic activity in Africa, but most farmers use outdated tools and methods to farm thin, poor soil. About two-thirds of all Africans live in rural areas, where they make a living growing crops or raising livestock. Since the mid-1900s, however, millions of rural Africans have flocked to cities and have adopted a more urban lifestyle. The development of manufacturing has been handicapped by a lack of money to build factories, a shortage of skilled workers, and competition from industries on other continents. Many African countries depend on only one or two farm or mineral products for more than half their export earnings. In case of crop failures or drops in world market prices, a country's economy suffers. The majority of African nations rely to some extent on aid from countries outside the continent.

One of the world's first great civilizations—ancient Egypt—arose along the banks of the Nile River more than 5,000 years ago. Later, other powerful and culturally advanced kingdoms and empires developed in Africa. Even so, for many years Westerners referred to Africa as the "Dark Continent." They used this name because they knew little about Africa's interior geography, and they mistakenly believed

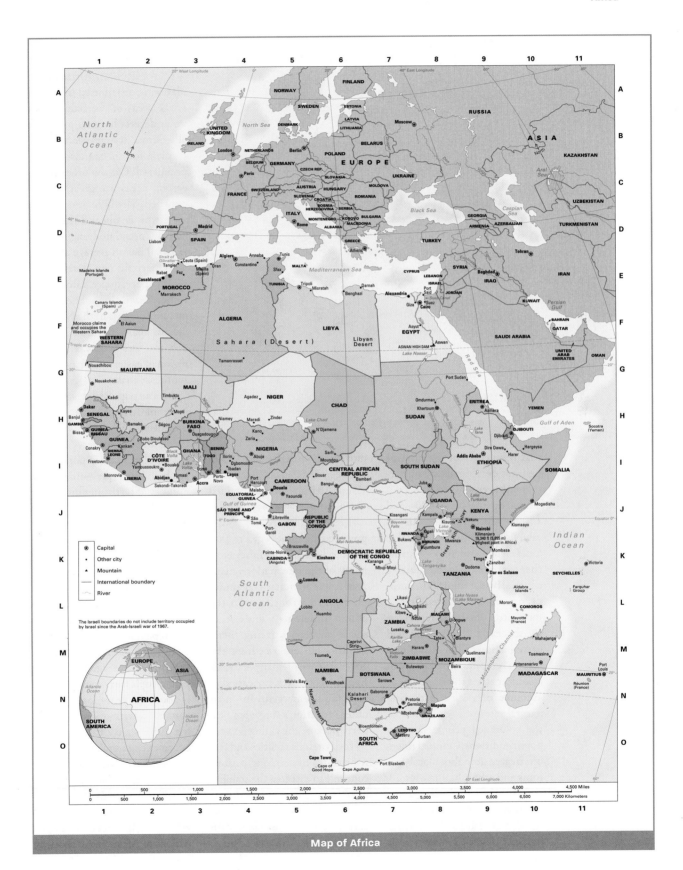

Map of Africa

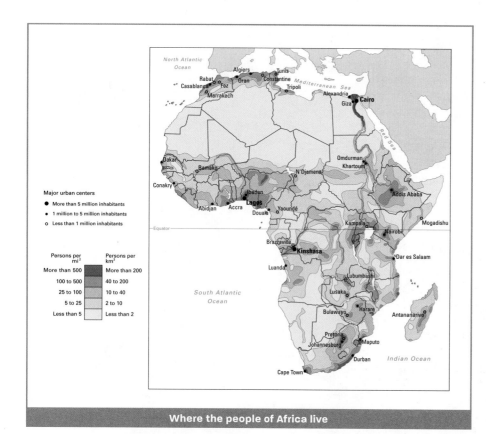

Where the people of Africa live

People

Population. Africa's population is distributed unevenly. Large areas of the Sahara and other deserts have no people at all. Some dry grasslands and tropical forests are also thinly populated. On the other hand, certain areas are greatly overcrowded. The Nile River Valley in Egypt is one of the most heavily populated regions on Earth. It has an average of about 3,500 people per square mile (1,352 per square kilometer). Other heavily populated areas include sections of the Mediterranean coast; parts of Nigeria and the west coast; the lakes region of eastern Africa; and the southeast coast.

Africa's population is increasing rapidly, partly because of improvements in medical care for children. Another reason for the rapid increase in population is a high birth rate—that is, the number of births in a given year per 1,000 people. Africa's rate of 36 births per 1,000 people is higher than the world average. But Africa's death rate—that is, the number of deaths in a given year per 1,000 people—is also higher than the world rate. The rate in Africa is 11 deaths per 1,000 people.

The average life expectancy—that is, the average number of years people can expect to live—is about 58 years for Africans, compared with about 79 years for Americans. However, life expectancy is much lower than the average in the poorer countries of Africa. For example, life expectancy in Zambia is 48 years, and in Mozambique, 52 years. In the more developed nations of Africa, life expectancy

that the people of the interior had not developed any important cultures.

During the late 1400s and 1500s, Europeans began to establish trading posts in Africa. Gold, ivory, and slaves became the continent's most valuable exports. By the late 1800s, European nations competed fiercely for control of Africa's resources. By the early 1900s, they had carved almost all of Africa into colonial empires. The European colonizers used their colonies as a source of wealth, exporting natural resources while most of the colonized people lived in poor conditions. Colonial rulers often cared little about local customs and ethnic boundaries.

Many Africans resisted colonial rule from the beginning. But the demands for independence did not become a powerful mass movement until the mid-1900s. Between 1950 and 1980, forty-seven African colonies gained independence. But years of colonial rule had left Africa poorly prepared in some ways to face the modern world. Leaders in many of the new nations managed their national economies poorly and struggled with the ethnic differences and other social challenges facing them. Military officers overthrew the governments of many nations. In a few countries, military dictatorships emerged. In most other countries, a single political party became the ruling power.

Today, ethnic rivalries and territorial disputes among nations continue to threaten the stability of Africa. Such problems as overpopulation, poverty, famine, corruption, and disease remain challenges for African leaders.

is higher than the average for the continent. For example, in both Libya and Tunisia life expectancy is about 75 years.

Several factors account for the low life expectancy in many regions of Africa. People in many parts of the continent suffer from malnutrition. Over the years, terrible famines have killed countless Africans, especially in the regions bordering the Sahara. In addition, warfare, poverty, poor sanitation, and inadequate medical services contribute to widespread disease. Serious diseases that affect life expectancy in Africa include AIDS, malaria, schistosomiasis, tuberculosis, sleeping sickness, and yellow fever.

Peoples of Africa. It is impossible to view the peoples of Africa as a single population. The African people belong to a variety of population groups and have many diverse cultural backgrounds. The terms black and black African are often used to describe people descended from the original inhabitants of the continent, whose ancestors have lived for centuries in west and sub-Saharan Africa. Today, however, many experts view such terms as inappropriate labels that apply inaccurate concepts of race to a large, ethnically diverse population. Most Africans prefer to be recognized as citizens of a particular nation or as members of a particular ethnic group rather than simply as Africans. In the north, for example, most of the people are Arabs.

Sub-Saharan Africans include the oldest, most genetically diverse human populations in the world. The peoples of sub-Saharan Africa have rich and varied cultures and ancestry. There are hundreds of ethnic groups. Some of the largest include the Igbo and Yoruba of west and central Africa, the Kikuyu of eastern Africa, and the Zulu of southern Africa. The members of various ethnic groups are linked by a shared history, culture, language, religion, artistic traditions, and way of life. However, migration, intermarriage, colonization, and other factors throughout history have complicated the patterns of physical and cultural diversity in this enormous region.

Pygmies are an African population that includes the Aka, Mbuti, Efe, Twa, and other ethnic groups who inhabit the tropical forests of the Congo River Basin in central Africa. The term Pygmy comes from an ancient Greek word and refers to the characteristic short stature of these people. Today, many people consider this name insulting. Traditionally, these people have lived by hunting animals and gathering plant foods in the forest and by trading with nearby agricultural groups.

The Khoikhoi and San are among the most ancient cultures in the world. The San and various Khoikhoi groups once lived throughout much of the southern and eastern parts of Africa. The two groups speak related languages characterized by clicking sounds. Today, the only remaining Khoikhoi populations are the Nama people who live in Namibia and a smaller population in Botswana and South Africa. The San live mainly in the Kalahari Desert of Botswana and Namibia and also in parts of South Africa and Angola.

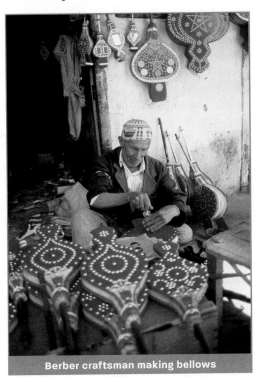

Berber craftsman making bellows

Most of Africa's millions of Arabs live in Egypt, in northern Sudan, and along the Mediterranean coast. The first Arabs settled in northern Africa during the 600s.

Berbers have lived in the northwestern part of Africa since prehistoric times. The term Berber comes from a Greek word meaning "foreigner" or "non-Greek speaker." Today, most Berbers and many experts prefer the term Amazigh instead of Berber (or the plural, Imazighen). The language they speak is called Tamazight. The Berbers live throughout much of northern Africa and the Sahara, mainly in Algeria, Libya, Morocco, Mauritania, Western Sahara, Mali, and Niger.

Europeans began to settle in Africa during the 1600s. Most of the continent's people of European ancestry are of British, Dutch, or French descent. The majority live along the Mediterranean coast, in the Republic of South Africa, in Zimbabwe, and in parts of east Africa.

Many people of Asian ancestry live in southern and eastern Africa. Most of them are descendants of people who came to Africa from India during the 1800s. Large numbers of people of Asian ancestry also live in Madagascar, an island country southeast of the African mainland. Their ancestors began to migrate to Madagascar from Indonesia about 2,000 years ago.

Languages. Most African ethnic groups have their own language or dialect. In some cases, members of different groups speak the same language. The peoples of Africa speak more than 1,000 languages. As a result, communication among Africans is difficult at times. But certain languages, such as Arabic, Swahili (also called Kiswahili), and Hausa, are widely spoken. In addition to their own language, millions of Africans speak one or more other languages, which they use when traveling or conducting business and government affairs. The languages spoken in Africa can be classified into six broad families: (1) Niger-Congo, (2) Nilo-Saharan, (3) Khoisan, (4) Afro-Asian, (5) Indo-European, and (6) Malayo-Polynesian. The first three families, known as indigenous African languages, originated in Africa and are limited to the continent.

Niger-Congo languages make up the largest of the African language families and are spoken throughout sub-Saharan Africa. This family includes about 300 Bantu languages spoken in central, eastern, and southern Africa. The term Bantu refers to both the languages and the groups of people who speak them. Swahili is the most widely spoken Bantu language. Other important Bantu languages are Ganda (Luganda), Kikuyu (Kikikuyu or Gigikuyu), Kongo (Kikongo), Rundi (Kirundi), Sesotho, and Zulu (isiZulu). The Niger-Congo family also includes many non-Bantu languages spoken mainly in western and central Africa. These languages include Akan; Igbo, or Ibo; and Yoruba.

Nilo-Saharan languages are used by people who live in parts of Chad, Kenya, Mali, Niger, Sudan, Tanzania, and Uganda. Major languages in this family include Bari, Dinka, Kalenjin, Kanuri, and Masai.

Mosque in Alexandria, Egypt

Khoisan languages are sometimes called click languages because many words are expressed with unusual click sounds. These languages are unrelated to any other African language. The San and Khoikhoi of southwestern Africa speak Khoisan languages. Two small ethnic groups in Tanzania, the Hatza (also spelled Hadza) and Sandawe, also speak these languages.

Afro-Asian languages are spoken throughout the northern half of Africa. The Afro-Asian language family includes Arabic and Berber (also called Tamazight), the two major languages of northernmost Africa. More Africans speak Arabic than any other single language. Other Afro-Asian languages include Amharic, Afaan Oromo, Hausa, and Somali.

Indo-European languages. A large number of educated Africans speak English, French, or Portuguese in addition to their local language. The use of these European languages remains as a reflection of colonial rule in many African nations. English, French, or Portuguese serves as the official language in many countries and helps unify the people. European languages are also important for communication in international business and government affairs. Two Indo-European languages—Afrikaans and English—are widely spoken in southern Africa. The Afrikaans language developed from the speech of early Dutch settlers in southern Africa. Many of the people of Asian descent who live in southern and eastern Africa speak various Indian languages. Most of them also know English.

Malayo-Polynesian languages. The people of Madagascar speak Malagasy, a language of the Malayo-Polynesian family. Their ancestors arrived in Madagascar from southeast Asia around 2,000 years ago. This language family is not found among the ethnic groups of mainland Africa.

Religions. Millions of Africans practice local traditional religions. There are hundreds of African traditional religions because each ethnic group has its own set of beliefs and practices. In general, however, local religions have many features in common. They explain how the universe was created and teach what is right and wrong. They define relationships between human beings and nature and between the young and the old. They give the reasons for human suffering and instruct people in how to live a good life and in how to avoid or lessen misfortune.

African traditional religions all recognize the existence of a supreme god. However, most of the African traditional religions emphasize that people should seek help by appealing to lesser gods or to the spirits of dead ancestors. People pray or offer sacrifices to the gods or the spirits to gain such things as good health or fertile land. Many religions conduct ceremonies to celebrate a person's passage from childhood to adulthood.

The more complex African religions include those of certain peoples of western Africa, such as the Dogon of Mali, the Yoruba of Nigeria, and the Ashanti of Ghana. The religions of these peoples include elaborate sets of beliefs about a supreme being and a pantheon of lesser gods. Women as well as men hold important religious positions in western Africa.

Millions of Africans are Muslims. Their religion, Islam, is the state religion in the countries of northern Africa. Islam is also a strong force in many neighboring nations, such as Chad and Mali. In addition, large Muslim populations have great influence in such countries as Djibouti, Somalia, Sudan, Nigeria, and Tanzania.

Millions of other Africans are Christians. Most of them belong to the Roman Catholic Church or to various Protestant churches. The Ethiopian Orthodox Church is the largest church of Ethiopia. In Egypt, a few million people belong to the Coptic Orthodox Church. A growing number of Africans belong to syncretic African churches. These churches combine Christian or Islamic beliefs with traditional African practices.

Ways of Life in Northern Africa

The six countries of northern Africa—Mauritania, Morocco, Algeria, Tunisia, Libya, and Egypt—have much in common. A large majority of the people speak the same language, Arabic; practice the same religion, Islam; and share the same history. Northern Africa lies along the Mediterranean Sea, and the region has long been in close contact with Europe and the Middle East. The Middle East has been the most important influence on the culture and history of northern Africa since the arrival of the Arab people in the 600s. Today, northern Africa is an important part of the Arab world.

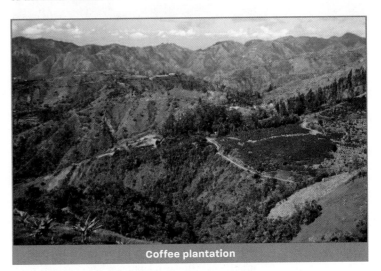

Coffee plantation

In addition to the Arab Muslim majority, northern Africa has minority groups that differ in language or religion. For example, the Berbers or Imazighen share the Islamic religion, but many maintain their own culture and language. Sub-Saharan Africans form another important minority group. Many of them speak Arabic and practice Islam. An important religious minority group in Egypt is the Copts. They are Christians who speak Arabic and follow many Arab ways of life.

The following discussion deals chiefly with the ways of life among the Arab Muslim majority in northern Africa, but even within this group there are important differences.

Rural life. About half the people in northern Africa live in rural areas. Most of them raise livestock or grow crops on small plots of land. They do much of the work by hand or with the help of animals. In some areas, farmers work on larger farms where machinery and modern agricultural practices are used. Governments or wealthy individuals own many of these large farms. Many rural

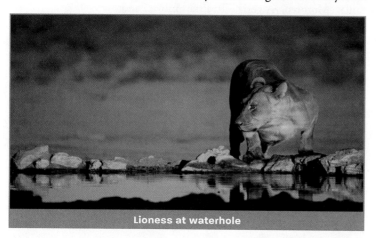

Lioness at waterhole

people lack sufficient land to support their families and must work as laborers or move to the cities or to foreign countries to find jobs. Small groups of nomads called Bedouins tend camels, goats, and sheep. Today, less than 10 percent of northern Africa's people lead a nomadic lifestyle.

In many rural parts of northern Africa, the people live in flat-roofed houses with thick adobe walls that help keep out the region's intense heat. In highland areas, houses are more often made of stucco or stone. Most rural homes are simply furnished and lack many modern conveniences. Private generators supply power in many communities, and cellular telephones have enabled rural people to maintain contact with others.

City life. Cairo, the capital of Egypt, is the largest city in Africa. About 8 million people live in the city. Other cities of northern Africa with more than a million people are Alexandria, Giza, and Shubra al Khaymah in Egypt; Tripoli, Libya; Algiers, Algeria; and Casablanca, Morocco.

The architecture of most cities in the north reflects a combination of European and Islamic styles. Many mosques (Islamic houses of worship) and suqs (outdoor markets) are typical features of the large cities. Older neighborhoods often lie within the remnants of city walls, some of them centuries old. In these quarters, houses and shops

are crowded along narrow, winding streets. Broad boulevards, parks, and modern apartment and office buildings occupy newer sections.

Most city dwellers in northern Africa have a higher standard of living than rural people. The cities offer better medical facilities and schools, and most city workers earn more than rural people. Factories and such services as banks, insurance companies, and government offices are concentrated in urban centers. Hospitals and clinics are also more common in the cities.

The attractions of urban life have led many rural people to move to the cities. Many move in with urban relatives, but others can afford to live only in slums. Such neighborhoods consist of substandard dwellings, have inadequate sanitary facilities, and lack many public services.

Marriage and the family. At one time, Islamic traditions regulated marriage practices and family life throughout northern Africa. These traditions included polygyny—the right of a man to have more than one wife. They also required a bride's family to give a dowry of household goods or money to the bridegroom. In addition, parents usually selected a husband or wife for each of their children. Today, polygamy remains legal in every northern country except Tunisia. Dowries are less common, but many people still consider at least a token dowry as essential. Arranged marriages have also decreased, though parents exert more influence on their children's choice of a spouse than do parents in Western cultures.

A typical rural household in much of northern Africa consists not only of parents and children but also of grandparents, aunts, uncles, and cousins. These extended families provide security, financial help, and social life. In the cities, the nuclear family, which consists only of parents and their children, is more common. But even in urban areas, grandparents and other relatives often share the household with the nuclear family.

The traditional role of women in northern Africa has been to remain at home to care for their families. Many older women and those who live in rural regions still follow this tradition. But a growing number of younger women have taken advantage of education and career opportunities and now work outside the home.

Food and drink. Flat breads and other grain products are the basic foods in northern Africa. Couscous, coarse grains of wheat steamed and served with a spicy stew, is a common dish in much of the region. Vegetables, often served in soups, are an important part of regional diet, as are fresh fruits. People in coastal regions often eat fish and other seafoods. Refrigerated trucks now make it possible to ship seafood to the interior, where fish consumption has increased greatly. Meat is too expensive to be part of the daily diet of most people, but chicken, goat, or lamb is enjoyed occasionally.

Tea, mint tea, and coffee are preferred hot beverages. Soft drinks and citrus and other juices are locally produced in each country, as are a wide variety of canned and processed foods.

Clothing. Many people in rural northern Africa dress in traditional clothing. The men wear long, loose robes and usually cover their heads with a turban or skullcap. In mountainous regions, where winter weather can be severe, a heavy, hooded woolen cloak called a burnoose provides additional warmth. The women wear long, simple dresses, sometimes with baggy trousers underneath. In public, rural women add a cloak or shawl, cover their heads, and often follow the Islamic tradition of covering the face with a veil.

Many city dwellers dress in clothing like that worn by Europeans and North Americans, but more traditional forms of apparel have become increasingly popular, especially among women. Women who customarily dress in European or American fashions often wear a head covering in conformity with Muslim principles.

Education. Traditionally, only religious scholars received more than an elementary school education in northern Africa. During the colonial period, European settlers established schools, but the schools served only their own children and those of a handful of important local leaders. Partly for these reasons, only about two-thirds of the people can read and write. The literacy rate (percentage of people who can read and write) is much lower in rural areas than in the cities and much lower among women than among men.

The nations of northern Africa are working to improve education, especially in rural areas. However, the population is growing faster than new schools can be built, and the costs of education are constantly increasing. Many areas have a shortage of qualified teachers, and many students must leave school to work and help support their families. Rural children often have to travel great distances

to attend school. More students, however, are going on to high school and college. A few universities in northern Africa are among the most modern in the Arab world.

Ways of Life in Sub-Saharan Africa

In general, sub-Saharan Africans follow their traditional ways and observe the customs of their ancestors. Most Africans live in rural areas and make a living by farming the land.

Mineral wealth has brought greater economic development to parts of southern Africa than to any other section of the continent. But much of the wealth from mineral production is held by people of European ancestry, who form a politically and economically powerful minority in parts of southern Africa.

This section mainly describes the ways of life among Africans living south of the Sahara.

Rural life. About 65 percent of all sub-Saharan Africans live in rural areas, chiefly in villages. Villages vary considerably in size and population. Whatever its size, each village is a closely knit community of families usually belonging to the same ethnic group and often related through either birth or marriage.

Dusk in Namibia

Among some ethnic groups, kings and chiefs command great respect, though they may have limited political power. In most cases, the position of king or chief is inherited and serves as a means to link villages of the same ethnic group. Among other ethnic groups, village elders may handle matters of local concern.

Many villages are simply a cluster of houses, surrounded by farmland. Larger settlements may have a schoolhouse, a few shops, and perhaps such facilities as a medical dispensary or a courthouse. Most villages also have a central square. The people gather in the central square for visiting, entertainment, and ceremonies.

Rural housing varies from village to village, depending on climate, lifestyle, and tradition. Many Africans live in houses built of sun-dried mud with roofs of straw, grass, or leaves. As villagers become wealthy, they may construct houses of concrete blocks with sheet-metal roofs. Almost all villages have dwellings of this type. In parts of western Africa, some houses are covered with clay and decorated with sculptured designs. The houses of African Muslims may be built around a large courtyard so that the women can go about their tasks without being seen by people outside the family. This custom follows the traditions of Islam.

In many villages, the way of life has changed little over the years. Most of the people farm the land and raise some livestock. Modern industrial methods of agriculture are used in parts of South Africa, Kenya, and Zimbabwe and in some countries of western Africa, such as Côte d'Ivoire. But the majority of farmers of sub-Saharan Africa use simple hand tools to work the land.

The soil is thin and poor in much of Africa. The people have thus traditionally practiced an agricultural technique called shifting cultivation. A farm community clears the land of trees and bushes and plants crops for several years, until the land wears out. The community then moves to a new location.

Hippopotamus, Queen Elizabeth Park, Uganda

The abandoned land eventually returns to grass or forest and can be farmed again. Shifting cultivation is still common in certain areas. But in heavily populated regions, resettlement is not possible. As a result, the farmers continue to work land that becomes poorer and poorer.

Most farm families grow food crops for their own use. In the grasslands of eastern and southern Africa, food crops include peanuts and such grains as corn, millet, and sorghum. In wetter areas, food crops include bananas, cassava, plantains, rice, and yams.

Farmers also grow various cash crops, including coffee; cacao, or cocoa beans; cotton; coconuts; and fruits. The farmers sell their cash crops for money to buy manufactured goods, canned goods, clothing, kerosene, lamps, and batteries. The farmers may also use the money from their cash crops to pay taxes as well as medical expenses and school fees.

In addition to growing crops, almost all farmers raise chickens. Many keep goats and sheep. Farmers may also sell livestock or food crops for needed money.

A typical farm family has several widely scattered plots outside the village. Each plot is planted with a different crop. Families may also rent their land or farm on land that is owned by village elders and chiefs. Some farmers also work part-time on large estates or plantations that produce cash crops. Both men and women work long hours at farming to make a living.

Rural women also spend much time doing such chores as collecting firewood, grinding grain, and obtaining water. In many villages, however, the introduction of such simple machines as water pumps and small hand- or machine-driven flour mills has given women more time to do other things. In most villages, everyone takes part in such major tasks as clearing new land and building new houses. The people work together on such tasks, while sharing food and drink and socializing.

Some African farmers—for example, those who live along the Nile River—irrigate their crops. But most farmers depend on seasonal rains. Work and other activities therefore follow a seasonal schedule. During the rainy season, farm families work long, hard days planting and tending their crops. Food may be in short supply at that time of year. During the dry season, after the crops have been harvested, food is more plentiful. The people also have more leisure time. They spend the extra hours repairing tools and houses, visiting with friends and relatives, and trading their crops for other goods. In western Africa, women have traditionally controlled trade activities. Some women have become wealthy as a result of their trading skill. In other areas of Africa, trade matters are handled either by men or women.

Community ceremonies, which are often held in the village square, are an important part of rural African life. They mark such occasions as the first rains of the growing season, the planting of crops, and harvesttime. Entire communities, as well as people from neighboring villages, may gather for ceremonies related to births, marriages, funerals, the curing of the sick, and the passage of children into adulthood. These community gatherings strengthen family ties and religious beliefs.

In many parts of rural Africa, young men leave their villages and work at least a few years as migrant laborers. They travel to cities and towns in hope of earning enough money to get married, to open a small business, or to go to school. In parts of central and southern Africa, many men work temporarily as miners. The women left behind in the villages must do much of the farm work themselves.

Nomadic herding is a way of life for people in parts of Africa, particularly in dry areas near the Sahara and in the highland regions of eastern Africa. Such nomadic peoples as the Dinka, Fulani, Masai, Toubou, Tuareg, and Turkana follow well-established routes to find grazing land for their herds of cattle, sheep, goats, or, in some cases, camels. Among some groups, including the Dinka, Masai, and Nuer, cattle herding is an ancient and proud tradition. For these people, cattle are a measure of a person's wealth and social position as well as a major source of food and other necessities.

The nomadic herders depend mainly on their livestock for food. They also trade meat and milk for grain from neighboring farming groups. The men and boys tend the herds, and the women care for the household. Some nomadic groups, such as the Masai of eastern Africa, build huge corrals for their livestock. Within the corrals, the people construct igloo-shaped houses of brush, mud, and dried manure. Other nomads live in tents made of animal skins.

City life. City dwellers make up only about 35 percent of sub-Saharan Africa's total population. But the percentage is much higher in some coun-

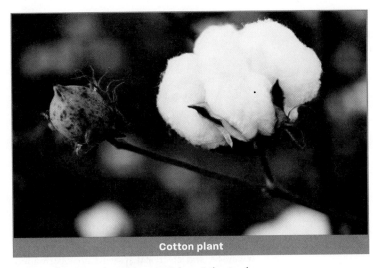
Cotton plant

tries, such as Angola, Djibouti, Gabon, Liberia, the Republic of the Congo, and South Africa. Throughout Africa, more and more rural people are moving to the cities to seek work. Cities in sub-Saharan Africa with populations of more than a million include Addis Ababa, Ethiopia; Cape Town, South Africa; Dar es Salaam, Tanzania; Johannesburg, South Africa; Kinshasa, Democratic Republic of the Congo; Lagos, Nigeria; and Nairobi, Kenya.

In most cities of sub-Saharan Africa, the architecture reflects both traditional and modern styles. The newer sections of many cities have parks, hotels, tall office and apartment buildings, and large stores. Many older neighborhoods have houses and shops crowded along narrow streets. Open-air markets, where people buy food, clothing, and a variety of other goods, are common in many cities.

Like city people in northern Africa, most city dwellers in sub-Saharan Africa have a higher standard of living than rural people. The cities provide better schools and medical facilities than the countryside. For people with skills, the cities may offer well-paying job opportunities in government, business, industry, and other fields.

City lifestyles vary widely. Some people are wealthy and live in luxury apartments or large, modern houses. Most people, however, live in unplanned neighborhoods of small, one-story houses. Many houses are built of wood or concrete blocks with corrugated iron roofs.

Like cities in the north, most cities of sub-Saharan Africa face serious problems. The sharp increase in city populations has made it difficult for governments to provide enough housing and efficient public transportation. The water supply,

Meerkats, Kalahari Desert, Botswana

sewerage, and electrical systems are overloaded. Many cities also have a large number of unemployed workers.

Marriage and the family. Strong feelings of loyalty and cooperation bind African families together. Such feelings are shared among all family members, not only parents and children but also grandparents, aunts, uncles, and cousins. The family helps its members with business concerns, employment, legal matters, and other affairs. The family also cares for members who are sick or elderly. Most Africans still seek the advice and approval of their relatives before making any important decision.

According to traditional African beliefs, marriage is more than an agreement between a man and a woman to live together. Marriage is also a way to acquire more relatives, both by gaining in-laws and by having children. In general, the families of the bride and groom must consent to a marriage before it may take place. Among most African peoples, a man or his father or uncles must provide a gift of money, livestock, or other valuables to a woman's family before the man may marry her. This gift is called the bride price or bridewealth. Africans do not regard the bride price as a payment for the bride but as a way to show her importance and the value they place upon the new ties with her relatives.

Most African ethnic groups permit polygyny (marriage to more than one woman). Many men follow this custom and so have more than one wife. The husband is expected to divide his attention and possessions equally among his various families. Each wife expects to have her own house, livestock, and other goods. Feminists, both inside and outside of Africa, and foreign missionaries have tried to end the practice of bride price and polygyny. But the traditions remain among most sub-Saharan ethnic groups.

Among some African peoples, related families form larger groups called lineages. Related lineages are organized into larger groupings called clans. All the members of a clan consider themselves to be descended from the same ancestor. Clans are usually represented by symbols called totems. Often, members of the same clan are not allowed to marry. Like the family, the clan offers protection, security, and a sense of belonging for its members.

For some sub-Saharan Africans, the strength of family ties has decreased as more and more rural people have moved to the cities. But even in the cities, relatives may live in the same neighborhood, and most city dwellers keep in close touch with relatives in the country.

Food and drink. South of the Sahara, most Africans in both the cities and the countryside eat one large meal daily, usually in the evening. They have only light snacks at other times of the day. The main meal is a time for socializing with relatives and neighbors. The men and boys generally eat separately from the women and girls. In many households, the people gather around a large bowl of food set on the ground and scoop up the food with their fingers or with pieces of bread.

A typical sub-Saharan African meal consists of a starchy food, such as rice, cassava, or corn cooked into porridge, or yams. The food is served with a sauce containing vegetables or bits of meat. A common food in tropical areas is the plantain, a large, starchy kind of banana. Plantains may be fried, boiled, baked, or grilled. They may also be dried and ground into flour.

For many African families, meat and fish are expensive and sometimes unavailable. Family members and guests expect such foods on special occasions, however. The people eat chicken, goat, lamb, or beef. Fish are important in the diet of people who live along seacoasts, rivers, and lakes. Africans who keep cattle live largely on milk, cheese, and a thick sour-milk product that resembles yogurt.

Many Africans make beer from honey or from such grains as corn and millet. They also make wine from the sap of certain kinds of palm trees.

In some parts of Africa, the people suffer from malnutrition because of periodic food shortages or the lack of a balanced diet. Long droughts, particularly in regions near the Sahara, sometimes lead to terrible famines, and thousands of people may die of starvation.

Clothing. In western Africa and regions near the Sahara, many men wear a long flowing robe or baggy trousers and a loose shirt or tunic. A small cap or turban is also customary among many African men. Many African women take a length of cloth and wrap it around themselves into a dress. They may also wrap a cloth around the head in the style of a turban or scarf. Some Muslim women follow Islamic tradition and cover the face with a veil when they go out in public. Many rural men and women tie a piece of fabric around the waist or at the shoulder to form a cloak. Some African herders wear simple garments made of leather. Colorful necklaces, bracelets, anklets, and earrings are part of the everyday clothing of some Africans. Among the Ashanti of Ghana and certain other ethnic groups, kings and their courts dress in gorgeous robes on special occasions.

Education. Centuries ago, Muslim scholars established near the edges of the Sahara some of the first schools in Africa. These schools taught Islam, the Arabic language, and science. But for most Africans, education did not involve going to school. Parents taught their children what they needed to know to get along in society and to make a living. Some young people, especially in western Africa, served as apprentices in craft associations, where they were trained in such skills as metalworking, woodcarving, pottery making, or weaving.

Christian missionaries taught some sub-Saharan Africans how to read and write as early as the 1500s. But large advances in education did not begin until the 1900s, when the European colonial powers decided they needed more Africans to fill jobs in government and industry. The United Kingdom, France, and other colonial powers established schools in Africa.

Today, many sub-Saharan African governments strive to build schools and to extend education to as many people as possible. A greater number of Africans than ever are attending elementary school and going on to high school and college.

Despite the progress in education, serious problems remain. A large number of adults in sub-Saharan Africa cannot read and write. However, the literacy rate varies greatly from country to country. In Kenya, Namibia, South Africa, and Zimbabwe, for example, the literacy rate is higher than 80 percent. But in such countries as Burkina Faso, Mali, and Niger, the literacy rate is less than 30 percent.

In many places, especially rural areas, there is a shortage of schools, educational materials, and qualified teachers. A large number of children do not attend school at all, and many others leave after only a few years to help their families earn a living.

The Arts

When one visits a museum to see African art, one often finds masks hanging on a wall or objects placed behind glass cases. Most African art, however, was initially made to be used, whether in a sacred or a secular context. Art in Africa serves an important role as a form of communication.

Ancient art. The oldest known African artworks are prehistoric engravings and paintings that have been found in southern Africa, in the Sahara, and in other areas on rocks and on the walls of caves and rock shelters. These artworks are between 2,000 and 20,000 years old and usually feature hunting scenes with men and animals.

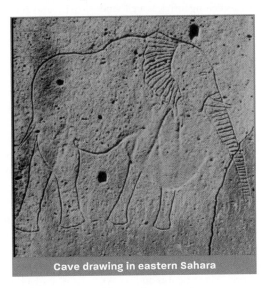
Cave drawing in eastern Sahara

Some of the oldest African sculptures come from ancient Egypt. These include small female figures made of clay and the gigantic Great Sphinx constructed about 4,500 years ago.

The oldest human sculptures from sub-Saharan Africa are terra-cotta (baked clay) figures created by the Nok culture of present-day Nigeria between 500 B.C. and A.D. 200. The Nok sculptures are human and animal figures. Most stand no more than 1 foot (30 centimeters) high, but some are

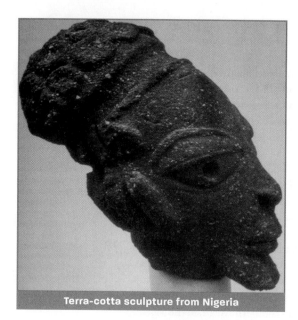
Terra-cotta sculpture from Nigeria

nearly life-sized. The Nok people were also among the earliest ironworkers in sub-Saharan Africa. The remains of their low, circular iron-smelting furnaces are found in sites in Nigeria and Benin.

During the 1100s through the 1400s, Yoruba craftworkers in west Africa created tools, weapons, and artworks of brass and iron. In the city of Ife, artists produced lifelike brass heads depicting royalty, who were regarded as gods. Sculptors in the kingdom of Benin, which flourished in western Africa from the early 1400s to the late 1800s, produced more stylized brass figures of royalty.

Fine arts. The human figure is central to many African art forms. Many figures and masks do not depict an exact likeness of a human face or body. Instead, they highlight certain features that may correspond to a particular concept of beauty or to a belief system. Ashanti carvers of Ghana, for example, favor a high, glossy forehead in the sculpting of female figures. The Mende of Sierra Leone believe that women should be reserved and not talkative. Mende masks generally depict females with a small mouth.

Throughout Africa, the human body itself often becomes a canvas on which to create art. For example, Oromo women in eastern Ethiopia use hairstyle, jewelry, and face paint to communicate their ethnic identity and family to others. Among the Nuba of Sudan, body paintings identify a man's age group or the clan to which he belongs. Among the Nuer of Sudan, patterns of scars cut into the face indicate courage and maturity in men.

Male artists traditionally work with hard materials, such as wood, stone, metals, and bone. Men also produce most ceremonial items, including masks, figures, and musical instruments. African women traditionally work with soft fibrous materials to create such useful objects as baskets, mats, beadwork, and clothing. Some art-making practices, including sewing, leatherwork, pottery, and weaving, are done by either men or women. Male weavers often use a horizontal loom for weaving cloth, while women use a vertical loom.

Materials used in African art often depend on what is available in the environment. African ethnic groups in desert or grassland areas create artworks using such available materials as stone, bone, clay, leather, and fiber. Woodcarving is most common in west and central Africa where hardwood forests are found. From these materials they make such everyday items as spoons, stools, and headrests.

In northern Africa, artists create beautiful works in a distinct style called Islamic art. The artists of northern Africa are also known for their superb textiles, metalwork, glassware, and other craftwork.

Colonialism had a profound effect on the arts of Africa. As European colonial powers introduced Christianity, many art practices associated with traditional African religions declined. Manufactured items replaced handmade objects, such as ceramic vessels, hand-dyed cloth, and woven fiber baskets. However, African artists soon began catering to a new market of middle-class urban Africans and foreigners and developed new artistic practices.

Many African artists, either self-taught or educated in art academies or mission schools, began depicting their experiences with colonialism and independence. Many contemporary African artists are also heavily influenced by traditional African art forms.

Architecture. Women are the homebuilders in many societies throughout Africa. Among north African nomadic groups, such as the Tuareg, women construct temporary tentlike homes from animal skins supported by wooden posts. The Masai of east Africa make distinctive loaf-shaped homes of mud, branches, and grass, plastered with cow manure. In southern Africa, Ndebele women build traditional homes and courtyards with a mud plaster. The Ndebele paint their buildings with geometric designs as well as symbols of modern technology, such as light bulbs and airplanes. Outstanding examples of Islamic architecture are seen in the many magnificent mosques throughout northern and western Africa.

Dance and music add to the expressiveness of many visual artworks in Africa. Dance and music often accompany the display of ceremonial art objects in public, such as at a funeral or the installation of a chief. In ceremonies and celebrations throughout Africa, dancers manipulate carved masks to the accompaniment of music. In royal festivals performed by the Kuba people of the Democratic Republic of the Congo, the beat of the drums is necessary to activate the spirit of the masks worn by dancers. Among the Yoruba, talking drums imitate the sounds of human speech and are used to relay messages from ancestors, who are embodied by masked dancers during a performance.

Music also accompanies many daily events in life in Africa. Singing often sustains the rhythms of manual labor in fields and villages. Traditional African music includes choral singing, music performed for entertainment, and songs and dances for religious events. In Senegal and other parts of west Africa, a professional speaker called a griot plays music while reciting history and praising the sponsor of the performance in song.

African musicians use a variety of drums, string instruments, and wind instruments, including harps, horns, flutes, pipes, lyres, zithers, and xylophones. Today, the influence of African music can be heard in Western popular music and jazz, West Indian calypso, and Latin American dance music.

Literature. Africa has a rich tradition of oral literature passed from one generation to the next. This oral literature includes histories of ethnic and kinship groups, legends of heroes, animal fables, proverbs, riddles, and songs in praise of chiefs and kings. Oral literature plays an important role in religious ceremonies. It also serves to record the past, to teach morals and traditions to young people, and to glorify political leaders.

Only a few areas of Africa have developed their own writing system. The ancient Egyptians developed a hieroglyphic writing system, where pictures represent ideas and sounds, nearly 5,000 years ago. Other African written literatures include Ge'ez, a religious script used in Ethiopia since the A.D. 300s. Muslim scholars in Africa have written works in Arabic since the mid-600s. They have written Swahili and Hausa works in Arabic script since the 1500s.

African writers began to produce literature in various sub-Saharan African languages in the 1800s. Most modern African literature is still written in English, French, or Portuguese, the languages of former colonial powers. The plays, novels, and poetry of modern African writers, such as Chinua Achebe and Chimamanda Adichie of Nigeria, Ama Ata Aidoo of Ghana, and Athol Fugard of South Africa, often deal with issues of modernity, colonialism, and postcolonial conditions in Africa.

The Land

Land regions. Africa can be divided into two major land regions: (1) Low Africa and (2) High Africa.

Low Africa consists of northern, western, and central Africa. Except for a few coastal plains and mountain ranges, most of the region lies from 500 to 2,000 feet (150 to 610 meters) above sea level. Low Africa can be subdivided into six smaller land regions. They are (1) the Coastal Lowlands, (2) the Northern Highlands, (3) the Saharan Plateau, (4) the Western Plateau, (5) the Nile Basin, and (6) the Congo Basin.

Kalahari Gemsbok National Park, South Africa

The Coastal Lowlands form a narrow border along most of northern Africa and the bulge of western Africa. The area has fertile farmland, forests, sandy beaches, deserts, and swamps.

The Northern Highlands are a mountainous region that stretches across parts of Algeria, Morocco, and Tunisia. The Atlas Mountains in this region have deposits of phosphate rock, iron ore, and manganese.

The Saharan Plateau covers most of northern Africa. The Sahara, in turn, occupies most of the plateau. Isolated clusters of mountains rise from the plateau in places. Valuable deposits of petroleum and other minerals lie beneath the Sahara. The desert merges with a dry grassland called the Sahel at the southern boundary of the Saharan Plateau.

The Western Plateau lies south of the Saharan Plateau. It consists of forests and grasslands. The Niger and other rivers flow through the region.

The Nile Basin is a flat region that borders the Nile River and its tributaries in northeastern Africa. In addition to fertile farmland along the Nile, the region has deserts in the north and a huge swamp called the Sudd in the south.

The Congo Basin, in west-central Africa, includes the land drained by the Congo River and its tributaries. Tropical rain forests cover much of the Congo Basin.

High Africa consists of eastern and southern Africa.

Most of the region is more than 3,000 feet (910 meters) above sea level. High Africa can be subdivided into five smaller land regions. They are (1) the Rift System, (2) the Eastern Highlands, (3) the Southern Plateau, (4) the Coastal Lowlands, and (5) Madagascar.

The Rift System extends from Eritrea to Mozambique. The region consists of the Great Rift Valley, which is a series of parallel cracks in the earth that form deep, steep-sided valleys. The three main lakes in this valley, Lake Victoria, Lake Tanganyika, and Lake Malawi, have many unique species of fish and add to the region's beauty. The region also has some of Africa's best farmland because of its rich volcanic soil.

The Eastern Highlands are grassy plains that provide grazing for livestock and many kinds of wild animals. The Rift System cuts through the Eastern Highlands.

The Southern Plateau covers most of southern Africa. Much of it is flat or rolling grassland used for crops and pasture. The region also has deserts, swamps, and forests. Rugged mountains and cliffs rim the plateau in the south and west. Deposits of diamonds and gold lie in the Southern Plateau.

The Coastal Lowlands border the high plateaus of eastern and southern Africa. The lowlands include productive farmland, sandy beaches, and swamplands.

Madagascar, the world's fourth largest island, lies about 240 miles (390 kilometers) southeast of the mainland in the Indian Ocean. The island can be divided into two chief land regions. The Coastal Lowlands form a narrow band along the east coast and broaden to a wide fertile plain on the west. The Central Highlands, which run almost the full length of the island, have some peaks over 9,000 feet (2,700 meters) above sea level.

Deserts, grasslands, and forests. Deserts cover about two-fifths of Africa. The Sahara, the world's largest desert, stretches across northern Africa from the Atlantic Ocean to the Red Sea. It covers about 3½ million square miles (9 million square kilometers). The Sahara is a region of bare rock, boulders, gravel, and sand dunes, broken only by a few oases and the fertile Nile Valley. The Namib Desert borders the Atlantic coast of southwestern Africa. The Kalahari Desert lies inland from the Namib.

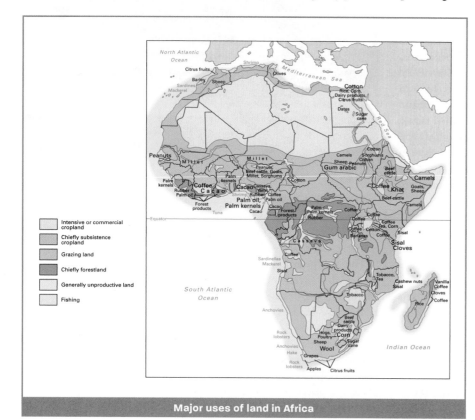

	Intensive or commercial cropland
	Chiefly subsistence cropland
	Grazing land
	Chiefly forestland
	Generally unproductive land
	Fishing

Major uses of land in Africa

Grasslands called savannas occupy more than two-fifths of Africa. They form a broad curve that extends from the Atlantic coast just south of the Sahara, across eastern Africa, and back westward to the Atlantic south of the Congo Basin. Tall grasses, thorny bushes, and scattered trees grow in this area. Thicker woodlands cover areas with more rainfall. But closer to the deserts, there are fewer trees and shorter grasses.

Forests cover less than a fifth of Africa. Most of the forests are tropical rain forests. These forests, with many kinds of broadleaf evergreen trees, grow in the Congo Basin and in parts of western Africa and Madagascar. Other forests grow in the highlands of eastern Africa, the mountains of the northwest, and parts of the south.

Woodlands border the rain forests within the tropical region. Most of these woodlands contain patches of grassland. Dense pockets of tangled mangrove swamp, where the spreading roots of mangrove trees catch and hold soil, fringe some coastal areas. These swamps provide important breeding sites for fish, protect the coast from damaging waves, and clean the water by filtering sediment.

Rivers, waterfalls, and deltas. The Nile River, the world's longest river, flows 4,160 miles (6,695 kilometers) northward from east-central Africa to the Mediterranean Sea. Most of Africa's other major rivers, including the Congo and the Niger, empty into the Atlantic. Rivers that flow into the Indian Ocean include the Limpopo and the Zambezi. All of these rivers flow through several countries and serve as major sources of hydroelectric power. They also provide flood control and water for irrigation or industry. The rivers are also major centers of wildlife biodiversity—that is, a variety of plant and animal species—and important sources of fish.

Rapids and waterfalls make navigation difficult on many African rivers. Hydroelectric power projects have been built on a number of rivers. Scientists estimate that the Congo River has the potential to generate enough hydropower for all of Africa's energy needs. Several waterfalls, including spectacular Victoria Falls on the Zambezi, are popular tourist attractions.

Large deltas where the major rivers enter the ocean along the coasts of Africa are important sites for fishing and shrimp farming, as well as critical centers of biodiversity. Major river deltas include the Congo, Niger, Nile, and Zambezi deltas. The

Okavanga Delta at sunrise, Botswana

Niger Delta in Nigeria is also an important region for its oil deposits.

Lakes. Most of Africa's large lakes lie in the east, where chains of long, deep lakes have formed in the bottoms of the rift valleys. One of these lakes, Tanganyika, is the longest freshwater lake in the world. It is 420 miles (680 kilometers) long and more than 4,700 feet (1,430 meters) deep. Other large rift lakes include Albert, Malawi, and Turkana. Africa's largest lake, Victoria, lies in a shallow basin between two chains of rift valleys. It covers 26,828 square miles (69,484 square kilometers) and is second in size only to Lake Superior in North America among the world's freshwater lakes. The rift valley lakes are centers of biodiversity and support many unique fish species.

Mountains. Volcanic activity created most of Africa's highest mountains. The two tallest peaks—19,340-foot (5,895-meter) Kilimanjaro and 17,058-foot (5,199-meter) Mount Kenya—were formed in this way. Although they rise near the equator in eastern Africa, both mountains have glaciers and are covered with snow much of the year. Volcanic activity also produced the Ethiopian Highlands; the isolated Tibesti Massif in the Sahara; and Mount Cameroon, the highest peak in western Africa. Volcanic rock covers the Drakensberg, a mountainous region where the plateau of southeastern Africa drops sharply to the sea.

Two major nonvolcanic mountain ranges of Africa are the Ruwenzori Range and the Atlas Mountains. The Ruwenzori Range rises on the border of Uganda and the Democratic Republic of the Congo. The Atlas Mountains extend from Morocco to Tunisia and form Africa's longest mountain chain. The Atlas Mountains are part of the same mountain system as the European Alps.

Climate

Most of Africa has a warm or hot climate, but the humidity and amount of rainfall vary dramatically from area to area. The maps in this section illustrate Africa's climate patterns, the average January and July temperatures, and the average yearly precipitation (rain, melted snow, and other forms of moisture).

Africa has the largest tropical area of any continent. The equator runs through the middle of Africa, and about 90 percent of the continent lies within the tropics. Temperatures are high year-round almost everywhere. The variations between summer and winter temperatures are slight. In fact, the difference between daytime and nighttime temperatures in most of the continent is greater than the difference in the average temperatures between the coldest and warmest months.

Africa's highest temperatures occur in the Sahara and in parts of Somalia. At I-n-Salah, Algeria, and along the north coast of Somalia, July temperatures soar to 115°F (46°C) or higher most days. Nighttime temperatures, however, may drop sharply. The Sahara also has the greatest seasonal range of temperatures in Africa. Winter temperatures in the Sahara average from 50 to 60°F (10 to 16°C). Near the equator, temperatures may average 75°F (24°C) or more year-round. But temperatures of more than 100°F (38°C) are rare.

The coolest regions in Africa are the northwest, the eastern highlands, and parts of the south. In Johannesburg, South Africa, for example, the average temperature in January, the warmest month, is 68°F (20°C). Frost and snowfall are common in the mountains of Africa.

Rainfall is distributed unevenly in Africa, and most areas receive either too much rain or too little. In parts of the west coast, for example, annual rainfall averages more than 100 inches (250 centimeters). In Monrovia, Liberia, an average of more than 40 inches (100 centimeters) of rain falls during the month of June alone. In contrast, more than half of Africa receives less than 20 inches (50 centimeters) of rainfall yearly. The Sahara and the Namib Desert receive an average of less than 10 inches (25 centimeters) a year.

Rain falls all year in the forests of the Congo Basin and the coastal regions of western Africa. But almost all the rest of Africa has one or two seasons of heavy rainfall separated by dry periods. In some regions, the amount of rainfall varies sharply from year to year rather than from season to season. Since the late 1960s, droughts have caused much suffering in Africa. Millions of Africans have died of starvation and related causes. The hardest-hit areas include Ethiopia, the Sahel region on the southern edge of the Sahara, and southern Africa.

Africa's climate has made agricultural improvement difficult. In areas with limited and unreliable rainfall, farmers may be uncertain of what crops to plant. Some farmers grow a number of crops with different moisture needs in the hope of having at least one successful harvest. Other farmers may grow only one or two kinds of crops and risk starvation if not

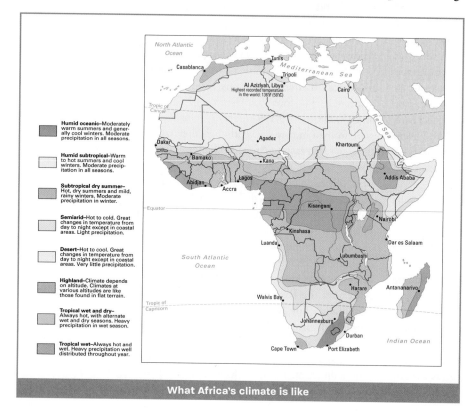

What Africa's climate is like

enough rain falls. In areas with too much rainfall, heavy downpours wash away nourishing substances in the soil. The hot, wet climate in parts of Africa encourages the spread of insects that destroy livestock and cause diseases in people.

Many scientists suspect that global warming is responsible for an increasing occurrence of extremes in the weather and changes in seasonal patterns of rainfall in Africa. Signs of global warming in Africa include the melting of glaciers on Mount Kilimanjaro, the shrinking of Lake Chad, increased droughts and flooding in different regions, and fluctuations in temperature extremes.

Technology is playing an important role in helping people deal with Africa's climate in an effort to increase agricultural output and food supply on the continent. Scientists use weather satellites to monitor climate and vegetation growth. They can then predict weather conditions and advise farmers when to plant their crops.

Animals and plants

Native animals. Africa's wild animals are world famous. The continent has thousands of species of mammals, reptiles, amphibians, fishes, birds, and insects. The kinds of animals found in any region depend largely on the climate and habitat of that region. In the east and south, huge herds of wildebeest and other species of antelope, buffaloes, giraffes, and zebras roam the grasslands. They are preyed on by such animals as cheetahs, hyenas, jackals, leopards, African wild dogs, and lions. A few remaining large herds of elephants live in the east and the southeast. Baboons and other monkeys are common in many parts of Africa. Chimpanzees and gorillas dwell in the forests of central Africa. Crocodiles and hippopotamuses live in tropical rivers and swamps. Large water birds, including flamingos, pelicans, and storks, can be found in eastern and southern Africa. Ostriches live in the south and east parts of Africa and in the western Sahara. Many bird species migrate from Europe in winter to warmer regions of Africa.

 Africa once had many more wild animals than it has today, and they were more widespread. Ancient paintings on rocks show that hippopotamuses and giraffes once lived in regions that are now deserts. Gradual changes in climate partly reduced the number and range of Africa's animals. But in many regions, people have overhunted the animals and destroyed much of their natural environment to

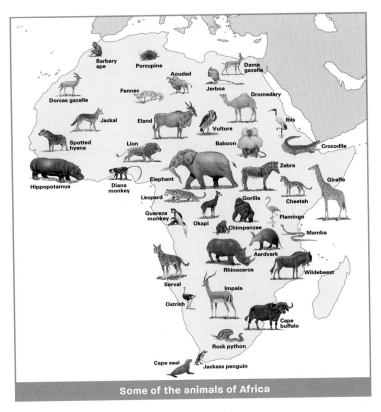

Some of the animals of Africa

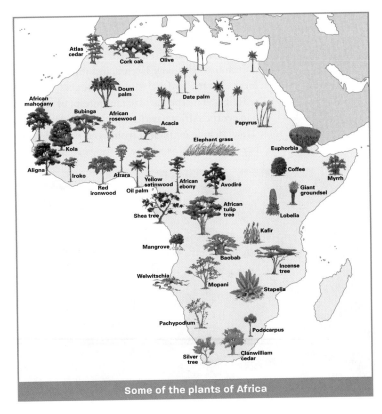

Some of the plants of Africa

make room for farms and cities. Intensive conservation efforts are necessary for many species. Some African animals, including the black rhinoceros, gorilla, and elephant, are in danger of becoming extinct and must now be protected.

African countries have taken steps to save their rich wildlife heritage. Each country has established game reserves and national parks. Hunting is forbidden in these areas, and modern methods of wildlife conservation are practiced to protect the animals. Tourists come to view wildlife in these protected areas and are an important source of income to help in conservation efforts. In some cases, hunters can go on regulated safaris (hunting expeditions). However, poaching (illegal hunting) continues to be a problem.

Some rural Africans have opposed wildlife conservation efforts. In some areas, for example, wild animals compete with farmers and herders for scarce land. Meat from hunted wild animals, called bush meat, is important in the diet of some Africans. Some rare animals, including gorillas, elephants, and rhinoceroses, are poached to sell certain body parts that are valued in some countries for supposed healing powers or other special qualities. International laws have been created to end the illegal trade in endangered animals.

Native plants. Across Africa, the overall distribution of plants is determined largely by temperature and rainfall. At local levels, plant variety is determined by many factors, including soil type, local climate, and habitat disturbances, such as wildfires. The spectacular rain forests of western and central Africa have hundreds of kinds of trees. They include oil palms; fruit trees; valuable timber trees, such as ebony, mahogany, and other hardwood trees; and softwood okoume trees, which are used to make furniture, plywood, and veneers. Mangrove trees stand on stilt-like roots in swampy areas along tropical coasts. Olive and oak trees and such evergreen bushes as myrtle grow in the northwestern parts of Africa and at the southern tip of the continent.

Plants that withstand drought and fire cover the grasslands. In addition to various grasses, grassland plants include thick-trunked baobab trees, acacia trees, and thorny euphorbia bushes. Dry grasslands near the deserts, called steppes, have shorter grasses and fewer varieties of other plants. In the desert oases and wadis (dry valleys), there are date palms, doum palms, tamarisks, and some kinds of acacias. Certain grasses and shrubs may appear briefly in the deserts after a rare rain.

In the mountainous highlands of Africa, bamboo thickets, podocarpus trees, tree ferns, and cedar trees grow on the lower slopes. On the upper slopes, meadows are covered with grasses, buttercups, and violets. Mosses and lichens grow near the mountaintops.

Land cleared for agriculture has destroyed portions of Africa's natural plant life. People use fire to clear land and to encourage grass growth for livestock. These fires suppress forest growth and maintain large areas as grasslands. Overgrazing by livestock has turned portions of the Sahel and other steppes into semidesert.

Introduced species. Some plants and animals that are common in Africa were introduced from other parts of the world by traders and colonists. These include some of Africa's most important food crops, including bananas, cassava, and corn, as well as such cash crops as cacao (cocoa) beans and tea. Eucalyptus trees, which originated in Australia, now grow in many parts of Africa and are widely used for firewood and construction. Pine trees, introduced from Mexico and other regions, are important for timber and paper. Camels, which provide food and other necessities in much of northern Africa, were domesticated in Asia.

Some introduced species have become pests. For example, eucalyptus trees use more water than native trees, reducing water available for other uses. Other species, called invasive species, have been introduced by accident and have spread quickly, destroying local habitats and species. For example, the water hyacinth was introduced from South

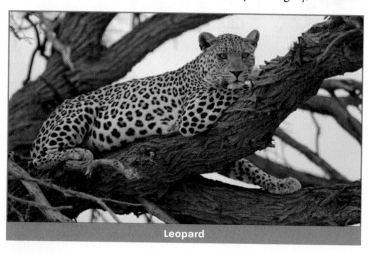

Leopard

America as a pond plant. However, it soon spread into rivers and lakes. The plant can cover entire lakes and rivers, choking out fish, limiting fishing, and making boating impossible. Nile perch were introduced into Lake Victoria to provide a new source of food fish for local people. However, this fish, which can grow to more than 200 pounds (91 kilograms), feeds on other fish. Since its introduction, the Nile perch has contributed to the loss of several fish species unique to Lake Victoria. Today, the fish are carefully monitored to prevent further destruction of native species.

Economy

African countries vary considerably in size, levels of economic development, rates of economic growth, economic development policies, and amounts of international trade. This variation is a result of unequal distribution of natural resources, variation in political and economic systems, colonialism, and various other historical factors in countries across the continent.

Economic development in Africa can be measured by the gross domestic product (GDP). GDP is the value of all goods and services produced in a country. There are different methods of measuring GDP. One method expresses the total value of a country's economic activities in terms of a foreign currency exchange rate. Another method is based on the actual cost of goods and services in a country. Using this method, Africa's total annual GDP in 2002 was about $1.75 trillion, compared to about $10.4 trillion for the United States. South Africa has Africa's largest economy, followed by Egypt, Algeria, Nigeria, and Morocco.

African countries vary considerably in annual *per capita* (per person) income. The per capita income of a country is determined by dividing the GDP by the population. In the early 2000s, the average annual per capita income in Africa was about $650. At that time, more than thirty African countries had annual per capita incomes of less than $500.

 Agriculture. Production of agricultural crops and livestock employs more workers than any other economic activity in Africa. The countries with the largest areas of land under cultivation include Egypt, Ethiopia, Nigeria, South Africa, and Sudan.

African crop production is divided between staple food crops and export crops. Staple food crops

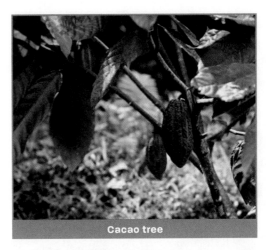
Cacao tree

produced in Africa include such grains as corn, millet, rice, sorghum, and wheat. Important root crops include cassava, potatoes, and yams. Other important staple crops include various legumes (peas, peanuts, and beans), fruits, and vegetables. Africa's leading export crops include cacao (cocoa), coffee, cotton, kola nuts, palm oil, sugar, tea, and tobacco.

Most staple crops in Africa are produced for local consumption by farmers working on family-owned or family-rented farms. There are also large plantations owned by companies, wealthy individuals, or governments. These plantations are usually used for production of export crops, such as palm oil and cocoa.

Different crops are grown in various regions of Africa depending on the environmental conditions and historical preferences. Yams and cassava are more common in the wet tropical areas of western Africa, but corn is more common in the grasslands of eastern and southern Africa. Wheat is the major staple crop in northern Africa, where irrigation is also more commonly used. In the highlands of Ethiopia and other parts of eastern Africa, a plant called khat (also spelled kat or qat) has been an important crop for centuries. The leaves of this plant contain a stimulant and they produce a mild euphoria (feeling of well-being) when chewed. Khat is grown for local use and export to the Arabian Peninsula, Europe, and North America.

In the early 2000s, many African countries experienced little growth or even declines in agricultural production. In many African countries, food production has grown more slowly than the population. This situation leads to food shortages that must be offset by food imports. However, some

Zebras

countries lack the economic resources necessary to purchase food from abroad, and hunger or famine has sometimes resulted. In these countries, foreign food contributions and aid are essential. Periodic droughts also contribute to poor agricultural production and hunger in Africa.

In Africa, most fertile lands and resources, such as fertilizer, are used for production of cash crops grown for export rather than food crops. This is partly a continuation of colonial practices, when African farmers were forced to cultivate export crops demanded in Europe. However, the production of cash crops also reflects the policies of African governments. They use export crops to obtain foreign income to purchase imported goods and materials essential for economic development.

Livestock production is an important branch of the agricultural economy, mostly in the grassland regions. The main livestock raised in Africa include camels, cattle, chickens, goats, horses, pigs, and sheep. Some regions of Africa are not suitable for livestock due to infestation with tsetse flies. Tsetse flies transmit African sleeping sickness, a disease that is fatal for many species of domestic livestock.

Mining. Africa is richly endowed with mineral resources and has a large mining industry. The continent has among the world's largest reserves of chromium, cobalt, gold, manganese, phosphates, platinum, uranium, and vanadium. Substantial quantities of other metals, including bauxite (aluminum ore), copper, iron, nickel, and zinc, are also found throughout Africa. Africa is also a major producer of oil and natural gas.

Africa's most developed mining industry is in the Republic of South Africa. Angola, Botswana, Zambia, and Zimbabwe also have large mining industries. South Africa is the world's largest gold producer, and Botswana is the leading producer of diamonds. The Democratic Republic of the Congo has a large copper industry, while Guinea and Morocco are Africa's leading producers of bauxite and phosphates. Algeria, Angola, Libya, and Nigeria are major petroleum-producing countries.

However, much of Africa has not benefited from its vast mineral resources. African countries have no control over prices of minerals on the global market, and many mining companies are foreign-owned. In addition, mining employs fewer workers than either agriculture or services, and is more expensive to operate.

In some instances, Africa's mineral wealth has contributed to environmental destruction and helped fuel political conflicts. Nigeria's large petroleum industry has contributed to pollution in the Niger River Delta. Money from illegal trade in diamonds helped finance a brutal civil war in Sierra Leone during the 1990s. Since the early 2000s, United Nations embargoes have tried to prevent trade in diamonds called conflict diamonds or blood diamonds, which are sold to fund the illegal operations of rebel, military, and terrorist groups.

Manufacturing. In much of Africa, the growth in the manufacturing industry occurred only after independence. By the 1960s, significant manufacturing industries had developed only in former colonies that had large European populations, such as Algeria, Kenya, Zimbabwe, and South Africa, or in countries that attained independence early, such as Egypt. Many African countries have since developed small manufacturing sectors mainly to produce consumer goods that they previously imported, such as beverages, processed foods, and textiles. Large-scale industrial manufacturing has proved more difficult and costly to implement. Currently, Africa produces only a small percentage of the total world manufacturing output.

Service industries in Africa include transactions conducted by the government, called the public sector, and by nongovernment businesses, the private sector. The private sector is further divided into formal and informal sectors based on their structure and size. Informal enterprises include small-scale businesses that provide goods and services but are not accurately recorded in government figures or properly taxed as are businesses in the formal sector. The informal sector is large in much of Africa, making up nearly half of the GDP in at least 23 countries.

Government spending plays a major role in all African economies. Education, health care, and other social services account for up to a third of the expenditure of many governments.

Private service industries, including financial services, retail, and tourism, have grown in Africa since the mid-1900s. Retail services range from small roadside vendors to large stores and shopping malls.

Tourism is the leading source of income in many African nations, including Egypt, Eritrea, Kenya, Mauritius, Morocco, Tanzania, and Uganda. To accommodate the tourists, these countries have constructed an extensive array of hotels and other facilities. Many foreign tourists come to visit the famous historic sites of Egypt or the game reserves of Botswana, Kenya, South Africa, Tanzania, and Uganda.

Transportation. The transportation system is poorly developed in many African countries. Only about one-quarter of Africa's roads are paved. More than a third of the total roads are in the Democratic Republic of the Congo, Nigeria, and South Africa. Automobile ownership is limited to the middle and upper classes in most nations. The vast majority of Africans depend on public transportation, such as buses, minivans, and taxis. Many people rely on bicycles or walking. In some parts of Africa, camels and donkeys are still widely used to transport goods.

Major railroads are concentrated in only a few countries, chiefly Algeria, the Democratic Republic of the Congo, Egypt, South Africa, Sudan, and Tanzania. Africa's air transportation industry is well developed mainly in Algeria, Egypt, Ethiopia, Kenya, Morocco, and South Africa, though all African countries have large airports. The African coasts have few good natural harbors, but almost every coastal country has at least one harbor, and engineers are working to equip them with modern shipping facilities. Many harbors have been constructed along Africa's extensive rivers and lakes.

Communication. Africa's communication systems, despite some rapid expansion in the late 1900s, remain underdeveloped compared to non-African countries. The number of newspapers published in Africa has increased significantly since the 1990s. However, radio remains the most popular form of mass communication. The number of public, private, and community radio stations has also grown dramatically since the 1990s. Television access is concentrated in urban areas and remains unavailable in most rural regions. Motion-picture theaters are found only in cities, and few African countries have even small motion-picture industries.

Telephone service throughout Africa has improved greatly since the 1990s. Telephone ownership remains largely concentrated in major urban centers. However, cellular telephones are increasingly common in smaller towns and villages. In the early 2000s, Africa saw the fastest growth in the cellular telephone market in the world. Computer and Internet use has also grown. However, Africa still lags behind other regions in the development of this technology. Computer and Internet access and usage is concentrated in South Africa and urban areas of western and northern Africa.

International trade. Africa's leading merchandise exporters are Algeria, Angola, Nigeria, and South Africa. Petroleum ranks as Africa's major merchandise export. Other important exports include agricultural products, minerals, and manufactured products.

Africa's merchandise imports have also grown since the 1980s. However, only three countries—Egypt, Nigeria, and South Africa—collectively account for about one-third of Africa's total imports. Food imports are increasingly important as agricultural output has failed to keep up with population growth in many countries. Other key imports include fuel and manufactured goods.

Terms of trade refers to the relationship between the prices of imports and those of exports. Declining terms of trade occur when import prices rise faster than export prices. Rising terms of trade occur when export prices grow faster. Africa's terms of trade have tended to decline since the 1970s because Africa's exports consist of mainly agricultural products and minerals that are subject to frequent price fluctuations. Many African countries are also economically vulnerable because they depend on one or two major exports. As a result, African nations have been active in international efforts to control price changes and improve trade terms. For example, the African oil-producing countries belong to the Organization of the Petroleum Exporting Countries (OPEC), a group of nations that seeks to regulate the world market for oil.

Foreign aid, debt, and investment.
Foreign aid to Africa includes grants, loans, and technical assistance in such areas as agriculture, education, and health care. The grants and loans come from a variety of international sources and are usually referred to as official development assistance (ODA). This aid is important for many African countries as they attempt to face their economic difficulties due in part to declining terms of trade.

Foreign aid has helped African countries to promote economic and social development. But it has also had some harmful effects. The loans have left many African countries with large debt and crippling interest payments. The bulk of Africa's debt is held by the larger countries, including Algeria, Egypt, Nigeria, and South Africa. But in smaller, poorer African countries, the debt load has the most severe impact. These countries must reduce investment in education, health care, and other economic development to repay debt.

In the 1980s and 1990s, international lending institutions, led by the World Bank and the International Monetary Fund, imposed strict conditions on African debtor nations. For example, they required borrowing countries to devalue (lower the value of) their currencies to promote exports and to reduce their budget deficits by cutting government funding of health care and education. Many experts believe that these strict conditions, called structural adjustment programs (SAPs), hurt a number of African economies. Today, lenders have relaxed the policy of SAPs, with the hope that African countries will return to economic growth.

History

Africa has been called the "cradle of humanity." Fossils discovered at sites in northern, eastern, and southern Africa provide the oldest evidence of humanlike creatures and people found anywhere in the world. From this evidence, most scientists have concluded that the earliest human beings lived about two million years ago in Africa. In time, human beings spread to other continents.

The development of agriculture.
Africa played an important role in the development of agriculture in the world. Previously, people obtained food by hunting, fishing, and gathering wild plant foods. The transition from food gathering to agriculture in Africa was a long process that took place over many centuries. Archaeologists and historians have identified five major centers of devel-

opment of African agriculture: the Nile Valley, Ethiopia, west Africa, central Africa, and east Africa.

In each of the regions of Africa, the domestication of native plants developed independently between about 7,000 and 2,000 years ago. In the Nile Valley, farmers domesticated sorghum. In Ethiopia, coffee, *noog* (an oil plant), ensete (a banana-like plant), millet, sorghum, and *teff* (a type of grain) were domesticated. In east Africa, farmers also grew varieties of sorghum and millet. In the savanna areas of west Africa, people cultivated varieties of African peanuts, African rice, cotton, millet, and sorghum. Crops that originated in the forest zones of central Africa include kola nuts, oil palm, and yams.

Some crops were introduced to Africa from other regions. Early farmers of western Asia probably introduced some domestic crops, such as barley and wheat, to the Nile Valley by about 7,000 years ago. Bananas were introduced to Africa from Southeast Asia more than 2,000 years ago. By the late 1400s, agricultural exchanges between Africa and the Americas became important. Corn and cassava were introduced to Africa from the Americas and have since become important food crops.

In several regions of Africa, pastoralism (raising of livestock) began before farming. Domesticated cattle, sheep, and goats were raised about 8,000 years ago in the northern Sahara region of Africa. At the time, the Sahara region was moist grassland and the center of thriving pastoral and farming communities. These communities migrated to the Nile Valley, the Mediterranean coast, and west African grasslands as the Sahara began to dry about 6,000 years ago. Pastoralism also developed before farming in east and southern Africa. Early Khoisan-speaking peoples of southern Africa were raising domestic cattle and sheep by about 2,500 years ago.

The development of agriculture had enormous consequences for Africa. Greater and more secure access to food contributed to population growth. The development and spread of agriculture was made possible and accompanied by technological developments, including the production and use of metal tools. Agriculture also led to the establishment of permanent settlements.

Early civilizations. Africa's earliest civilizations emerged in the fertile plains of the Nile Valley, where thriving agricultural communities grew into small states. These states gradually developed into larger states, the most powerful of which emerged in what later became known as Egypt and Nubia.

Several small states had emerged in various parts of Egypt by about 4000 B.C. By 3500 B.C., two kingdoms called Upper Egypt and Lower Egypt were dominant. Menes, king of Upper Egypt, unified the kingdoms about 3100 B.C. Menes was given the title pharaoh and established the first dynasty (family of rulers) of ancient Egypt. Pharaohs from 30 dynasties ruled Egypt for the next 3,000 years.

Beginning around 1085 B.C., Egypt experienced a series of revolts, invasions, and foreign rule by Assyrians, Libyans, Nubians, and Persians lasting nearly 700 years. In 332 B.C., Alexander the Great of Macedonia conquered Egypt. Ptolemy, one of Alexander's generals, later took the title of king of Egypt and founded a dynasty that ruled until 30 B.C., when the Roman Empire conquered Egypt. Roman rule lasted in Egypt until A.D. 639.

The Kush civilization arose after 1000 B.C. in Nubia, south of Egypt. The Kush maintained close relations with Egypt. Kush culture, architecture, and writing both resembled and differed from Egyptian styles. At times, Egypt extended its rule over Kush, but Kush also conquered and ruled Egypt from about 750 to 660 B.C. The civilization eventually declined due to environmental destruction, falling trade, and competition from neighbors. Around A.D. 350, Kush was invaded by Aksum, marking the end of this ancient civilization.

The kingdom of Aksum was in the Ethiopian highlands (now part of Ethiopia and Eritrea), a fertile region that was easy to defend from invasion. Aksum grew into a powerful kingdom by about A.D. 100, largely through control of trade on the Red Sea. The kingdom began to decline in the 600s due to environmental destruction and economic competition from Muslim traders.

The rise of Christianity. Egypt, Ethiopia, and Nubia were among the earliest centers of Christianity in Africa. Christianity was introduced to Egypt from western Asia sometime before A.D. 100. Over the next few hundred years, the religion spread throughout Egypt and parts of north Africa from Libya to Morocco. Historians believe Christianity was introduced in Ethiopia from Egypt in the 300s. Ezana, the king of Aksum, converted to Christianity around 333 and established it as the state religion. Christianity, however, did not spread to sub-Saharan Africa until the late 1400s, when missionaries introduced it from Europe.

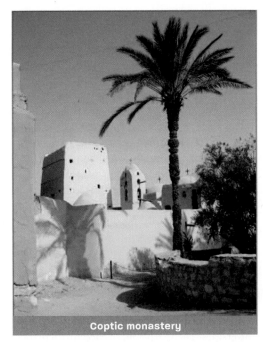
Coptic monastery

North Africa produced many of early Christianity's most influential thinkers and writers. These include Saint Augustine and the early Christian philosopher Origen. Egyptian Christians, known as Copts, emphasized the practices of solitude and monasticism. Three popes in the early church were Africans. The last African pope was Saint Gelasius I, elected in 492.

Christianity in north Africa declined sharply following the rise of Islam and Arab conquests of the region in the 600s. In Egypt, the Coptic Church declined and survived only among a minority of the population. Arab invasions between 1050 and 1056 completed the conversion of northern Africa to Islam. Only in Ethiopia did Christianity survive as the official religion of the state and the majority of the population.

The rise of Islam. The development of Islam had a profound impact on African history. Islam emerged in Arabia during the early 600s, inspired by the teaching of the Prophet Muhammad. Within years of Muhammad's death, Arab followers began a rapid campaign of conquest and conversion. By the late 700s, Arab and Arabized Muslims had built an empire that stretched from Central Asia to northern Africa to Spain.

In northern Africa, Islam spread through Arab conquests and settlement. This spread was accompanied by the conversion of the Berbers, who also adopted many other elements of Arab culture. In west Africa, Islam was introduced in the 800s. The Berbers introduced Islam by way of trade routes that crossed the Sahara. The new religion appealed to sub-Saharan rulers. Islam spread throughout Ghana, Mali, and Songhai, and farther south.

In Sudan, Islam spread from Egypt along the Nile and through trade with Arab Muslims across the Red Sea. In Somalia, Eritrea, and Ethiopia, Muslim Arabs and Persians established coastal settlements from the 700s to the 900s. In eastern Africa, the spread of Islam was aided by Arab settlement in the region during the late 700s. Intermarriage between the Arab settlers and local Africans eventually gave rise to the Swahili culture of east Africa.

Islam strengthened Africa's contacts with the outside world. Africa became a key part of the Islamic empire stretching from Spain to Indonesia. The first Islamic universities were established in northern Africa beginning around 970. These universities taught religion, science, mathematics, philosophy, geography, medicine, and history. African scholars made important contributions to Islamic thought. Similarly, Islam transformed African cultural practices, ideas, and values. In addition, it promoted long-distance trade by providing a common culture and language throughout much of Africa.

The empires of west Africa emerged in the savanna zone below the Sahara beginning somewhat before about A.D. 1000. Ghana, the first great empire to emerge, was founded by the Soninke people around A.D. 700. Soninke agricultural and iron-producing communities gradually expanded political control over neighboring regions and united

16th-century ivory bracelets from Benin

them into a single empire. Ghana traded grain and iron with gold-producing states farther south. They then traded the gold with Arab merchants for other goods, developing enormous wealth. However, Ghana went into a period of decline from about 1000 due to attacks from external enemies, internal revolts, and climate change.

Mali, founded around 1000, rose as nearby Ghana declined. By the 1200s, Mali was the largest, wealthiest empire in all of Africa. The capital city of Niani was a major center of trade. Timbuktu, Mali's largest city, had a population of about 50,000 by the 1300s. Scholars from many parts of the Islamic world came to study at the university there. Mali began to decline in the 1400s, due to political conflicts and raids from outside enemies. The empire had disappeared by the early 1600s.

Songhai formed as part of the Mali empire. Songhai first rose to prominence during the 1300s as Mali declined. Songhai's capital was Gao, a major trading city on the banks of the Niger River. At Songhai's height in the 1500s, trade and learning flourished. Invasion from Morocco in 1591, however, greatly weakened the empire. By the early 1600s, Songhai and the other great empires of west Africa had all but disappeared.

States and kingdoms. The east African coast saw the rise of several city-states, independent states that consisted of a city and the region surrounding it. The city-states arose from settlements that existed sometime after about A.D. 100. The communities prospered for centuries through trade of materials from the African interior with merchants sailing from China, India, Indonesia, the Red Sea, and the Persian Gulf. East coast ports exported gold, copper, ivory, grain, iron, timber, and other products in exchange for such goods as silk, cotton cloth, glass, and porcelain. The people came to be known as Swahili, a word that comes from an Arabic word meaning coast.

By 1000, the Swahili city-states dominated trade along the east African coast. The largest cities included Manda, Mogadishu, Mombasa, Kilwa, Pate, and Zanzibar. The city-states were all independent, but rivalries sometimes led to conflicts and war. The Portuguese, attempting to gain control of the Indian Ocean trade, attacked Zanzibar in 1503 and destroyed Kilwa in 1505. These European invasions began the decline of the Swahili civilization.

Other states and kingdoms developed in southern Africa and central Africa. Great Zimbabwe was built around the 1100s in the fertile plains of southern Africa. The region was rich in gold, iron, tin, copper, and granite. The granite was used to construct the spectacular walls and buildings of the capital and many smaller sites across the region. Great Zimbabwe declined toward the end of the 1400s due to environmental destruction, overpopulation, and a decline in trade.

The Kongo kingdom was one of a series of kingdoms that emerged in central Africa in the 1400s. It had a highly centralized government with its capital at Mbanza Kongo, in what is now the Democratic Republic of the Congo. Kongo was among the first African states in the region to have contact with European countries. During the 1400s, the Portuguese began to explore the west coast of Africa. They were interested in Africa's gold trade. By the end of the 1400s, Portugal had established trading posts at Sao Jorge da Mina (now called Elmina, in modern-day Ghana) and in the Kongo kingdom. However, Portuguese merchants, seeking to monopolize trade, increasingly turned to trading in slaves instead of gold. The effects of the slave trade, internal conflicts, and wars with neighbors weakened the Kongo kingdom and led to its eventual collapse in the early 1700s.

The Atlantic slave trade. Soon after the Portuguese arrived in western Africa, they began to ship Africans to Europe as slaves, beginning what is known as the Atlantic slave trade. Africa had sent slaves to Asia and Europe long before the Portuguese arrived, but the Atlantic slave trade was vastly larger in scale than any slave trade that preceded it. Portugal, Britain (now the United Kingdom), the Netherlands, the United States, and other countries all participated in this slave trade. Today, many scholars recognize it as the largest forced migration of people in history. They estimate that more than twelve million people were exported as slaves to the Americas between the late 1400s and mid-1800s.

African merchants and rulers were actively involved in the slave trade. The trade in gold and slaves brought wealth and power to some African kingdoms, such as Ashanti in what is now Ghana. However, it was Europeans who came to purchase the slaves, transported them in ships to the Americas, and sold them to work on plantations and mines. Europe and the Americas were the greatest beneficiaries of the slave trade.

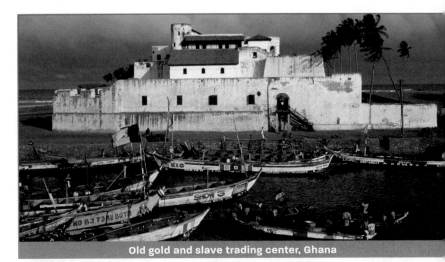
Old gold and slave trading center, Ghana

The effects of the Atlantic slave trade on Africa were disastrous. Depopulation from slave raiding and warfare disrupted economic activities and development throughout much of Africa. The slave trade also contributed to the growth of racist stereotypes against Africans, which were used to justify their enslavement and eventual colonization by European powers.

African societies in the 1800s. The 1800s were a period of revolutionary changes across Africa. In west Africa, Islamic reformist movements led to the establishment of Islamic states. In southern Africa, political upheavals generated the rise of the Zulu empire. In north Africa, there was a drive toward modernization.

In west Africa, Muslim religious reformers accused local rulers of undermining or corrupting Islam. The reformers sought to purify and spread Islam and establish a new government based on Islamic principles and law (Shariah). In 1804, Muslim reformers declared jihad (holy war) that led to the establishment of the Sokoto Caliphate, the largest state in west Africa at the time. The movement spawned other jihads in the region that led to the creation of other Islamic states in west Africa.

Societies in southern Africa also underwent revolutionary changes. A period of upheaval there between 1819 and 1838 is known to historians as the Mfecane (also called Difaqane). One center of conflict was Zululand, in what is now the South African province of KwaZulu-Natal. Competition for trade, grazing land, and water led to the emergence of several kingdoms in the region. Raids by European settlers and an increase in the trade in slaves and ivory heightened the struggle for

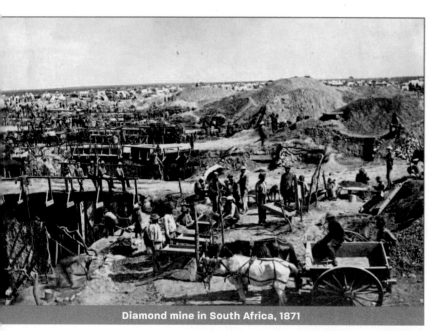

Diamond mine in South Africa, 1871

resources and forced local people to seek the protection of African military leaders ruling the kingdoms.

At the beginning of the 1800s, the Arab states of north Africa were struggling to rid themselves of foreign rule by the Ottoman Empire and to resist European intrusion. In Egypt, the government of Muhammad Ali began an ambitious program to modernize Egypt and to increase its wealth and power. This modernization program included political, military, economic, educational, and social reforms. However, heavy debt and internal disagreement over foreign involvement would eventually lead to the country's occupation by the British in 1882.

European colonization in Africa.
European interest in Africa began growing from the 1400s as European nations acquired the military and technological capacities for overseas voyages and conquest. Merchant companies were the first Europeans to come to Africa, followed by explorers and missionaries. European intervention culminated in the late 1800s in colonial invasions by European governments.

Portugal led the European expansion into Africa, capturing Ceuta in Morocco (now a Spanish city at the Strait of Gibraltar) in 1415. Early in the 1500s, Portugal established trading posts along the east and west coasts. The Portuguese destroyed Kilwa in 1505 and seized other Swahili city-states on the east African coast.

Dutch ships began visiting west Africa toward the end of the 1500s. The Netherlands soon challenged Portugal over the African trade in slaves, gold, ivory, and other goods. The Dutch East India Company was a powerful trading company that the Dutch government had granted broad governmental and military powers. In 1652, the company set up a station at the Cape of Good Hope in what is today South Africa. The station was to supply Dutch ships on their voyages to and from Asia. The station quickly expanded into the colony of Cape Town. Settlers from the Netherlands and other parts of Europe, who became known as Boers or Afrikaners, populated the town.

The United Kingdom took over the Cape from the Dutch in 1814. The discovery of diamonds in 1867 and gold in 1886 intensified the rivalries between the Afrikaners and British colonists in South Africa.

In 1787, the United Kingdom founded the colony of Sierra Leone in west Africa. In the early 1800s, the British established a presence in Zanzibar on the east coast. A profitable trade in ivory and spices attracted British merchants there. The British also wanted to halt the slave trade between east Africa and Asia. The United Kingdom had outlawed slave trading in 1807.

France established a trading post at the mouth of the Senegal River in 1638 and captured the west Africa slave depot of Goree from the Dutch in 1677. In east Africa, French colonization efforts were concentrated in the Indian Ocean islands of Mauritius and Reunion. There, the French established plantations using slave labor from east Africa. In 1830, the French colonized Algeria.

Colonial rule. As trade between Africa and Europe expanded, European merchants called upon their governments to establish political control in the regions where they were operating. By the 1880s, there were intense rivalries among the European nations as they staked claims to parts of Africa. This race to expand European colonial influence is often referred to by historians as the "scramble for Africa." In 1884, European powers convened the Berlin Conference to draw up rules among the nations establishing colonies and to prevent war over claims to African lands. No Africans were invited to attend the conference.

The Berlin Conference adopted a number of provisions. For example, it ruled that European nations had to actually occupy and administer

African lands that they claimed. It also declared that a nation already holding colonies on the African coast would have first claim on the neighboring interior. The colonial borders that were established paid little attention to previous national, ethnic, and religious boundaries. By 1914, Belgium, France, Germany, Italy, Portugal, Spain, and the United Kingdom had divided almost all Africa among themselves. Only Ethiopia and Liberia remained independent.

African societies responded to colonial conquest in a variety of ways. In some parts of Africa, colonial rule was established peacefully by treaties between the Europeans and African chiefs. But others resisted European control. For example, Africans staged violent uprisings against the British in Nigeria and what is now Ghana, against the French in western and northern Africa, and against the Germans in what are now Tanzania and Namibia. Ethiopians defeated Italian forces and retained their independence. By the mid-1920s, however, Europeans strongly controlled most of Africa.

The European colonization of Africa exacted a heavy cost in African lives. Millions were killed directly in wars of conquest and indirectly through the demands imposed upon them in colonial plantations. For example, historians estimate that the brutal regime of King Leopold II of Belgium in Congo Free State, now the Democratic Republic of the Congo, caused the death of several million Africans.

The colonial period also witnessed social transformations that included changes in the patterns of urbanization, education, and religious practice. New urban centers emerged, and many old cities expanded. In these cities, Africans created new forms of social life and leisure activities. Many Africans educated by missionaries opposed colonialism and demanded higher education or pursued it abroad. During colonial rule, both Christianity and Islam expanded.

Struggles for independence. Organized groups in some African colonies began to demand self-government in the early 1900s. But not until after World War II (1939–1945) did the demands for independence become a powerful mass movement. Some colonies achieved their independence through largely peaceful means, while for others it came after lengthy armed struggles.

In 1951, with the aid of the United Nations, Libya became the first country in Africa to gain independence. Morocco, Sudan, and Tunisia also gained their independence relatively peacefully in 1956. A revolt against the French in Algeria broke out in 1954. The bloody revolt lasted eight years and cost about one million Algerian lives before the country won independence in 1962 after 132 years of colonial rule.

In 1957, the Gold Coast became the first western African colony to gain independence. It won independence from the United Kingdom and took the name Ghana. In Kenya, a secret movement called *Mau Mau* began a revolt against British control in 1952. Although it failed, the revolt contributed to the country's eventual decolonization in 1963. By the mid-1960s, the United Kingdom, Belgium, and France had freed most of their African colonies in east and west Africa. One exception was Guinea-Bissau, where Africans waged war against the Portuguese until independence in 1974.

Kenyan police with suspected Mau Mau rebels

The most difficult wars of liberation were fought in southern Africa. Portugal fought costly wars in Angola and Mozambique before granting them freedom in 1975. In Rhodesia, blacks fought for years against white-minority rule. A government with a majority of blacks was finally elected in 1979. The following year, the United Kingdom recognized Rhodesia's independence, and the country was renamed Zimbabwe. South Africa's control over the territory of Namibia (called South West Africa until 1968) became an international issue during the mid-1900s. Most nations considered South Africa's control of Namibia to be illegal. In 1990, Namibia became an independent country. Finally, South

9TH AFRICAN UNION SUMMIT, ACCRA 2007
Heads of state at AU Summit

Africa made the transition from apartheid (strict racial segregation) to a multiracial democracy under black rule in 1994. This transition marked the end of European colonialism in Africa.

Africa since independence. African countries were confronted with many serious challenges inherited from colonialism and brought by independence. Military officers overthrew civilian governments in many countries. In a few countries, military dictatorships emerged. Civil wars broke out in Chad, the Democratic Republic of the Congo, Nigeria, and other countries. During the 1990s, struggles for democracy intensified across Africa. Today, the majority of African countries are democratic. However, the effectiveness of several African states in promoting good government and ending corruption remains an issue of concern. In some regions, ethnic or religious loyalties often clash with national loyalties.

At independence, most African economies were small and underdeveloped. In the 1960s and 1970s, various African countries pursued different development strategies. Some opted for capitalism and free enterprise, while others pursued socialist strategies of state ownership. Most countries experienced economic growth. However, this changed in the late 1970s as prices for African goods, such as coffee and cocoa, fell in world markets. National debt rose in most nations.

Other challenges to African stability include disease and warfare. In the 1990s and early 2000s, the AIDS epidemic reached disastrous levels in several parts of Africa. Internal conflicts and regional wars have devastated several countries in Africa since the 1990s. In 1994, Hutu militias massacred hundreds of thousands of Tutsi and moderate Hutu in Rwanda. Civil war in the Democratic Republic of the Congo broke out in 1998 and involved several other countries. Even after the war ended in 2003, ethnic clashes continued. Since 1998, conflict in Congo has claimed more than 5 million lives, mostly from disease and malnutrition.

Cooperation is the ideal behind the movement of *pan-Africanism*, which promotes the unity of African countries. The 1990s saw the strengthening of regional economic blocs, including the Economic Community of West African States, the Southern African Development Community, and the Arab Maghreb Union. These organizations will help determine how effectively Africa will compete in the world economy.

The drive for regional and continental integration has continued into the 2000s. The African Union (AU), an association of African states, was formed in 2002. It replaced a previous organization, the Organization of African Unity (OAU). The AU works to promote economic and political cooperation in the continent. The AU has several administrative bodies, including a Pan-African Parliament and a Peace and Security Council. These bodies are set up to promote good government, justice, and peace across Africa. These developments have given Africans hope that they can successfully overcome the challenges that face the continent.

MLA Citation
"Africa." *The Southwestern Advantage Topic Source.* Nashville: Southwestern. 2013.

DATA

Independent Countries of Africa

Name	Area in sq. mi.	Area in sq. km	Population[1]	Capital	Date of independence
Algeria	919,595	2,381,741	36,435,000	Algiers	1962
Angola	481,354	1,246,700	19,979,000	Luanda	1975
Benin	43,484	112,622	9,746,000	Porto-Novo	1960
Botswana	224,607	581,730	2,038,000	Gaborone	1966
Burkina Faso	105,869	274,200	17,268,000	Ouagadougou	1960
Burundi	10,747	27,834	9,073,000	Bujumbura	1962
Cameroon	183,569	475,442	20,717,000	Yaounde	1960
Cape Verde	1,557	4,033	523,000	Praia	1975
Central African Republic	240,535	622,984	4,994,000	Bangui	1960
Chad	495,755	1,284,000	12,110,000	N'Djamena	1960
Comoros	719	1,862	726,000	Moroni	1975
Congo, Democratic Republic of the	905,355	2,344,858	71,932,000	Kinshasa	1960
Congo, Republic of the	132,047	342,000	4,097,000	Brazzaville	1960
Côte d'Ivoire (Ivory Coast)	124,504	322,463	22,912,000	Yamoussoukro	1960
Djibouti	8,958	23,200	912,000	Djibouti	1977
Egypt (African)	363,220	940,736	81,968,000	Cairo	1922
Equatorial Guinea	10,831	28,051	730,000	Malabo	1968
Eritrea	45,406	117,600	5,511,000	Asmara	1993
Ethiopia	426,373	1,104,300	89,167,000	Addis Ababa	[2]
Gabon	103,347	267,667	1,554,000	Libreville	1960
Gambia	4,361	11,295	1,847,000	Banjul	1965
Ghana	92,098	238,533	25,192,000	Accra	1957
Guinea	94,926	245,857	10,891,000	Conakry	1958
Guinea-Bissau	13,948	36,125	1,710,000	Bissau	1974
Kenya	224,081	580,367	42,624,000	Nairobi	1963
Lesotho	11,720	30,355	2,058,000	Maseru	1966

[1] Populations are current estimates based on figures from official government and United Nations sources.

[2] Ethiopia has been independent for about 2,000 years.

[3] Date of union between Tanganyika and Zanzibar.

DATA

Independent Countries of Africa

Name	Area in sq. mi.	Area in sq. km	Population[1]	Capital	Date of independence
Liberia	43,000	111,369	4,360,000	Monrovia	1847
Libya	679,362	1,759,540	6,793,000	Tripoli	1951
Madagascar	226,658	587,041	21,146,000	Antananarivo	1960
Malawi	45,747	118,484	16,312,000	Lilongwe	1964
Mali	478,841	1,240,192	14,526,000	Bamako	1960
Mauritania	397,955	1,030,700	3,523,000	Nouakchott	1960
Mauritius	788	2,040	1,296,000	Port Louis	1968
Morocco	172,414	446,550	32,670,000	Rabat	1956
Mozambique	308,642	799,380	24,345,000	Maputo	1975
Namibia	318,261	824,292	2,286,000	Windhoek	1990
Niger	489,191	1,267,000	17,031,000	Niamey	1960
Nigeria	356,669	923,768	164,055,000	Abuja	1960
Rwanda	10,169	26,338	10,864,000	Kigali	1962
São Tomē and Principe	372	964	173,000	São Tomē	1975
Senegal	75,955	196,722	13,474,000	Dakar	1960
Seychelles	176	455	89,000	Victoria	1976
Sierra Leone	27,699	71,740	6,103,000	Freetown	1961
Somalia	246,201	637,657	9,904,000	Mogadishu	1960
South Africa	470,693	1,219,090	50,461,000	Cape Town; Pretoria; Bloemfontein	1931
Sudan	718,723	1,861,484	36,024,000	Khartoum	1956
Sudan, South	248,777	644,329	9,100,000	Juba	2011
Swaziland	6,704	17,364	1,234,000	Mbabane	1968
Tanzania	364,900	945,087	47,628,000	Dodoma	1964[3]
Togo	21,925	56,785	7,128,000	Lome	1960
Tunisia	63,170	163,610	10,711,000	Tunis	1956
Uganda	93,065	241,038	36,056,000	Kampala	1962
Zambia	290,585	752,612	13,905,000	Lusaka	1964
Zimbabwe	150,872	390,757	13,321,000	Harare	1980

[1] Populations are current estimates based on figures from official government and United Nations sources.

[2] Ethiopia has been independent for about 2,000 years.

[3] Date of union between Tanganyika and Zanzibar.

DATA

Dependencies in Africa

Name	Area in sq. mi.	Area in sq. km	Population[1]	Capital	Status
Madeira Islands	309	801	251,000	Funchal	Autonomous region of Portugal
Mayotte	144	374	213,000	Mamoudzou	French overseas region and department
Reunion	968	2,507	856,000	Saint-Denis	French overseas region and department
Saint Helena Island Group	159	412	7,000	Jamestown	British overseas territory
Western Sahara	97,344	252,120	543,000	None	Occupied by Morocco[2]

[1] Populations are current estimates based on figures from official government and United Nations sources.

[2] Claimed by Morocco and by the Polisario Front.

ADDITIONAL RESOURCES

Books to Read

Level I

Aspen-Baxter, Linda. *Africa*. Weigl Publications, 2006.

Campbell, Rusty, and others. *Atlas of Africa*. Rosen Central, 2010.

Haskins, James, and Benson, Kathleen. *Africa: A Look Back*. Benchmark Books, 2007.

Mhlophe, Gcina. *African Tales*. Barefoot Books, 2009.

Mooney, Carla. *Amazing Africa: Projects You Can Build Yourself*. Nomad Press, 2010.

Level II

Appiah, Anthony, and Gates, Henry Louis, Jr., eds. *Encyclopedia of Africa*. 2 vols. Oxford, 2010.

Gilbert, Erik, and Reynolds, J. T. *Africa in World History: From Prehistory to the Present*. 3rd ed. Pearson, 2012.

Iliffe, John. *Africans: The History of a Continent*. 2nd ed. Cambridge, 2007.

Middleton, John, and Miller, J. C., eds. *New Encyclopedia of Africa*. 5 vols. Scribner, 2008.

Visonà, Monica B., and others. *A History of Art in Africa*. 2nd ed. Prentice Hall, 2008.

Web Sites

Africa South of the Sahara
http://www-sul.stanford.edu/depts/ssrg/africa/guide.html
An index of selected Internet resources, prepared by Karen Fung for the Electronic Technology Group, African Studies Association.

African Studies Internet Resources
http://www.columbia.edu/cu/lweb/indiv/africa/cuv1/
Columbia University's collection of African Studies Internet Resources.

African Union
http://www.africa-union.org/
Official Web site of the African Union.

Art & Life in Africa
http://www.uiowa.edu/~africart/toc/index.html
The University of Iowa Obermann Center for Advanced Studies presents resources on African art and culture.

Country-Specific Pages for Africa
http://www.africa.upenn.edu/Home_Page/Country.html
University of Pennsylvania Department of African Studies site for countries in Africa.

Kids Africa
http://www.pbs.org/wonders/Kids/kids.htm
A PBS site for children on the history and geography of Africa. The site uses activities and multimedia to teach children about Africa.

Secure the Future
http://www.securethefuture.com/
The official Web site of Secure the Future, a public-private partnership that helps finance AIDS research, treatment, and prevention programs in southern Africa.

The Foundation for Democracy in Africa
http://democracy-africa.org/
A Washington, D.C.-based, nonprofit organization that promotes democracy and economic pluralism in Africa.

The Story of Africa
http://www.bbc.co.uk/worldservice/africa/features/storyofafrica/index.shtml
Information about African history from the BBC.

Wonders of the African World
http://www.pbs.org/wonders/
A companion Web site to a PBS series on archaeological finds in Africa.

Search Strings

Endangerment

causes of endangerment of animals in Africa (5,670)

conservation efforts to save african animals that are endangered (40,500)

animals in africa that are endangered and conservation efforts (65,400)

Africa Music

africa dance music traditional griot drums (9,200)

types of african music found in daily life in Africa (109,000)

africa traditional dance music drums uses daily life (88,100)

Agriculture

africa agriculture crop production staples exports (11,900)

africa effect of agriculture on economy crop production staple exports employment (18,600)

Land Types

africa deserts grasslands forests biospheres (92,300)

african topography climate biospheres (13,300)

african land types deserts grasslands rain forests Sahara woodlands (3,490)

BACKGROUND INFORMATION

The following articles were written during the year in which the events took place and reflect the style and thinking of that time.

Sudan (2006)

The continuing conflict in the Darfur region dominated news about Sudan in 2006, affecting that nation's relations with countries both inside and outside of Africa. Darfur is a western region in Sudan where fighting between government forces and rebel groups began in 2003. The fighting had led to the deaths of hundreds of thousands of people and left two million others homeless. Many international groups accused the government and government-backed militias of massive human rights abuses in Darfur.

The regional impact of the Darfur conflict was evident in January 2006, when officials in Khartoum, the Sudanese capital, hosted the African Union (AU) summit. The AU is an organization working to achieve cooperation among African states. Leaders of the nations at the summit—citing human rights violations by the Sudanese government—balked at allowing Sudan to take over the rotating chair of the AU. Sudan withdrew its bid to lead the AU in 2006 after the African leaders agreed it could chair the group in 2007.

Darfur Peace Agreement. In May 2006, the Darfur Peace Agreement was signed in Abuja, capital of Nigeria, by representatives of the Sudanese government and the Sudan Liberation Movement (SLM), the largest rebel group in Darfur. Leaders of the AU, including President Olusegun Obasanjo of Nigeria and President (and AU Chairman) Denis Sassou-Nguesso of Congo (Brazzaville), helped broker the agreement.

Khalil Ibrahim, leader of the Justice and Equality Movement, and Abdul Wahid Nur, head of a SLM faction, refused to sign the agreement. These two rebel leaders from Darfur claimed that the agreement did not recognize the political, economic, and cultural rights of the people of Darfur.

United States and United Nations.
In September, United States senators Edward M. Kennedy (D., Massachusetts) and Gordon H. Smith (R., Oregon) expressed their support for the Darfur Peace Agreement. They introduced bipartisan legislation calling for the Sudanese government to allow a United Nations (UN) peacekeeping force to enter Darfur to implement the peace treaty. The UN Security Council had approved a 17,000-member peacekeeping force for Darfur in August, but the Sudanese government refused to allow the force into the region.

The Kennedy-Smith bill also called for the North Atlantic Treaty Organization to enforce a no-fly zone over Darfur. In December, Sudan approved a phased deployment of a limited UN-AU peacekeeping force in Darfur.

Global Day for Darfur. Amnesty International and Human Rights Watch—human rights organizations based in London and New York City, respectively—were among a number of organizations that sponsored a "Global Day for Darfur" on September 17. Meetings and rallies took place in an estimated fifty cities in more than thirty countries. Speakers at the gatherings demanded that the Sudanese government allow UN peacekeepers in Darfur to protect civilians.

Conflict with Chad. In February, President Umar al-Bashir of Sudan and President Idriss Deby of Chad signed the so-called Tripoli Agreement, a peace treaty ending a border war that had devastated towns in eastern Chad and Darfur since December 2005. Muammar al-Qadhafi, the leader of Libya, was party to the agreement.

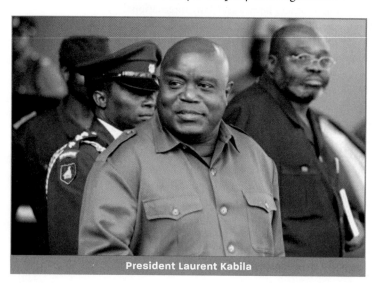

President Laurent Kabila

Just two months later, in April 2006, Chad severed diplomatic relations with Sudan. Chadian officials accused the Sudanese government of aiding rebels from the United Front for Change, a coalition of armed groups that tried to overthrow the government of Chad in April. The coup (overthrow) attempt led to the deaths of approximately 350 people, including government troops, rebels, and civilians.

Despite Sudan's denial of involvement in the coup attempt, President Deby threatened to expel some 200,000 Sudanese refugees from Chad. Many of these refugees had fled the conflict in Darfur.

The Hutu and Tutsi: A Conflict Beyond Borders

The centuries-old conflict between Hutu and Tutsi was significant far beyond the borders of Rwanda and Burundi. It also played a critical role in the revolution in Zaire.

—by Simon Baynham

On May 17, 1997, Laurent Kabila proclaimed himself president of Zaire and immediately renamed Africa's third largest country the Democratic Republic of Congo. The day before, Mobutu Sese Seko, president of Zaire for nearly thirty-two years, surrendered power and fled into exile. Mobutu's flight left the weary people of Zaire's capital, Kinshasa, waiting for the arrival of Kabila's rebel guerrillas. On May 20, Kabila entered the capital in a heavily guarded motorcade. By that time, the commander of Mobutu's elite presidential guard—the only force capable of putting up a defense—had boarded a speedboat for Brazzaville, capital of the Republic of the Congo across the Congo River.

The forcible overthrow of the Mobutu regime in Zaire was highly significant to far more people than the country's forty-five million citizens. The revolt was also a critical development in the Hutu-Tutsi ethnic conflict that has plagued Africa's Great Lakes region—Burundi, Rwanda, Tanzania, Uganda, and the Democratic Republic of Congo (Zaire)—and nearby Angola for decades.

The ethnic rivalry between Hutu and Tutsi originated when Tutsi entered the lands of the Hutu before 1400 and subjugated the Hutu. The rivalry festered from the 1890s to the mid-1900s as the reigning European colonial powers perpetuated

Tutsi rule over the Hutu, who constituted a majority in the region. The rivalry became inflamed when Rwanda and Burundi gained independence from Belgium in the early 1960s. The turmoil resulting from the rivalry spread to neighboring states, such as Zaire, when hundreds of thousands of refugees criss-crossed the region in a desperate search for peace and safety. By the mid-1990s, the Hutu-Tutsi conflict in Rwanda and Burundi had poisoned the political atmosphere of the entire Great Lakes region.

The seeds of conflict. Most historians of east and central Africa believe that the Hutu descended from a number of Bantu *clans* (a large group of African peoples made up of many individual but related tribes) that settled in the area that is now Burundi and Rwanda between A.D. 400 and 700. The *agrarian* (crop-raising) clans, who came to be referred to as Hutu, cleared much of the forest that had been home for several thousand years to the Twa, hunter-gatherer relatives of the pygmies. By approximately 1400, a group of different tribal and racial stock arrived—the *pastoralist* (cattle-herding) Tutsi. Successive waves of nomadic Tutsi herdsmen dominated the Hutu and subjected them to the authority of an expanding Tutsi kingdom.

Some historians disagree with this assessment and insist that Hutu and Tutsi are not, in fact, different ethnic groups, but rather different social classes of the same group. These historians argue that Tutsi can be identified solely by their possession of cattle, which allowed them to establish a patron relationship over the agrarian Hutu. These scholars also point out that Tutsi and Hutu share a common Bantu language.

During Burundi's and Rwanda's colonial period, Europeans calculated that 85 percent of the people of Rwanda and Burundi were Hutu, 14 percent were Tutsi, and 1 percent were Twa. The census takers used cattle ownership as a major criterion of ethnic origin. These percentages continued to be commonly accepted by demographers as accurate for the tribal composition of Rwanda and Burundi in the mid-1990s.

The creation of Ruanda-Urundi. Rwanda and Burundi are small for African states—only 10,169 square miles (26,338 square kilometers) and 10,747 square miles (27,834 square kilometers), respectively, and they were not artificially created by European conquerors. Both

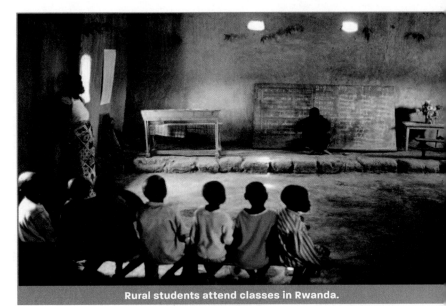

Rural students attend classes in Rwanda.

countries had existed as established feudal monarchies for several centuries before being discovered by European explorers, and both countries survived Western conquest and occupation.

Rwanda and Burundi—two remote, land-locked, mountainous kingdoms—were first explored by a European, the German Count von Gutzen, in 1894, and both countries became part of the colonial territory known as German East Africa. Following Germany's defeat in World War I (1914–1918), the area—then known as the Territory of Ruanda-Urundi—was *mandated* (given over for administration) to Belgium by the League of Nations, a now-defunct international peace association that was headquartered in Geneva, Switzerland.

Ruanda-Urundi after 1945. After World War II (1939–1945), Ruanda-Urundi became a United Nations trust territory, which Belgium continued to administer through Tutsi chiefs. The Belgians relied on the martial Tutsi to strengthen their authority—much to the resentment of the Hutu, who made up the majority of residents.

Roman Catholic and Protestant missionaries established churches and schools in Ruanda-Urundi in the late 1890s. In part, ideas about education and equality learned from the missionaries fueled *nationalism* (patriotic feelings for one's own nation) that, in turn, launched the movement for independence that spread through the territories after World War II. Tutsi traditionalists in both Ruanda and Urundi, however, were determined that independence would not mean rule under a Hutu majority. Similarly, Hutu extremists, resentful of Tutsi domination during the colonial period, decided that they would need to destroy the Tutsi hold on power before Tutsi domination could be finalized with the onset of independence. The views of Hutu moderates, who believed that Hutu and Tutsi could share power in a national government, were ignored.

Violence erupts. In 1959, Hutu farmers in the Ruandan, or northern, region of Ruanda-Urundi, organized by the Party of the Hutu Emancipation Movement, revolted against their Tutsi overlords. The Hutu greatly outnumbered the Tutsi in the fierce and brutal revolt. By the time Belgian security forces suppressed the violence, approximately 150,000 people—most of whom were Tutsi—had been killed. The Tutsi king, Kigeri V, along with thousands of his subjects, was forced into exile. A referendum in September 1961 abolished the monarchy.

Both Ruanda and Urundi gained independence in 1962. Ruanda was named Rwanda and was established as a republic, led by President Gregoire Kayibanda, a Hutu. Urundi, which changed its name to Burundi, was established as a constitutional monarchy. Burundi's elected legislature was dominated by Tutsi, and the country's ruler was Tutsi King Mwambutsa IV. Independence did not, however, settle the animosities between the two tribal groups in either country.

Hutu and Tutsi in Rwanda. Tutsi exiles, primarily from Burundi, invaded Rwanda in late 1963 in an attempt to restore a Tutsi monarchy. Their invasion unleashed mass reprisals, resulting in the death of 15,000 Tutsi at the hands of Hutu and the flight of an estimated 150,000 to 200,000 people, most of whom were Tutsi.

Civilian rule in Rwanda ended in July 1973 when a Hutu—Defense Minister Juvenal Habyarimana—staged a *coup d'etat* (an overthrow of the government) and established a one-party state. Habyarimana remained in office for the next twenty-one years.

In 1990, some 10,000 guerrillas belonging to the Tutsi-dominated Rwandan Patriotic Front, a Uganda-based group of Tutsi refugees and moderate Hutu, invaded Rwanda. Troops from Zaire assisted the small Rwandan army in halting the rebel advance on Rwanda's capital, Kigali, but intermittent fighting continued until 1993.

The plane crash that launched a bloodbath. Renewed violence followed the February 1994 assassination of government minister Felicien Gatabazi—a Hutu moderate who had advocated a peaceful settlement with the Tutsi rebels. The murder was eclipsed in April 1994 by the death of President Habyarimana, who was killed in a plane crash with Burundi President Cyprien Nta-ryamira (also a Hutu). Authorities were unable to determine who or what was responsible for the crash, but the event ushered in an orgy of violence. Hutu militants in the Rwandan armed forces slaughtered some 500,000 people, mainly Tutsi, in three months. Then-UN Secretary-General Boutros Boutros-Ghali labeled the Hutu violence against Tutsi as genocide. The Tutsi-controlled Rwandan Patriotic Front responded with another invasion and captured Kigali in July 1994.

After seizing the capital, Rwandan Patriotic Front soldiers forced the Rwandan army and huge numbers of Hutu civilians into Zaire. Before the month was out, more than two million Rwandans had fled, most into enormous refugee settlements around the Zairian city of Goma. In mid-July 1994, a new Rwandan government was established with Hutus—Pasteur Bizimungu and Faustin Twagiramungu—as president and prime minister. While the Rwandan Patriotic Front leaders emphasized national reconciliation, real power was held by the Front's militia, under the control of General Paul Kagame, a Tutsi.

Tribal tensions in Burundi. Political life in Burundi after independence was also dominated by Hutu-Tutsi tensions and recurrent ethnic violence. UN-sponsored elections in 1961 swept the National Unity and Progress Party, supported by the Hutu majority, into power. Between independence in 1962 and the end of the monarchy in 1966, King Mwambutsa's attempts to extend his constitutional authority and restrict the powers of the government forced the fall of seven consecutive governments.

In October 1965, Hutu police and military officers attacked the palace. King Mwambutsa, fearing for his life, fled the country. However, loyal troops under Michel Micombero, a Tutsi, repulsed the attack, providing a pretext for Tutsi retaliation.

Tutsi terror reigns. The army and police were purged of Hutu, and every Hutu political leader of standing was killed. In November 1966,

Micombero deposed King Ntare V, who had gained the throne by deposing his father, Mwambutsa. Micombero proclaimed a republic, with himself as head of state.

The abolition of the monarchy removed the last potentially unifying force in Burundi, opening the way for Tutsi domination. With Micombero in power, the Tutsi eliminated almost the entire educated Hutu population. As many as 200,000 people may have been killed. An additional 150,000 Hutu fled the country. In 1976, Micombero was overthrown by his cousin, Jean-Baptiste Bagaza, who was overthrown in 1987 by another Tutsi, Pierre Buyoya. A 1988 Hutu uprising led to the death of another 20,000 Hutu and the emigration of 60,000 more people to Rwanda.

A Hutu head of state in Burundi. Nevertheless, President Buyoya indicated some sympathy for the grievances of Burundi's majority Hutu by appointing a Hutu prime minister and moving cautiously toward a democratic constitution. Following the country's first multiparty elections in 1993, Melchior Ndadaye became Burundi's first Hutu head of state. He honored a campaign promise by appointing Sylvie Kinigi, a Tutsi woman, as prime minister. Kinigi was one of Africa's first women premiers.

Four months later, President Ndadaye was killed during an attempted coup staged by elements of the army. His assassination provoked a new wave of bloodletting during which more than 100,000 people died. The military embarked upon a "pacification campaign." This campaign included forcing another 700,000 Hutu to flee Burundi for Rwanda, Tanzania, and Zaire.

In 1994, Cyprien Ntaryamire, who had replaced Ndadaye as president, was killed with Rwanda's President Habyarimana when their airplane crashed. Sylvestre Ntibantunganya, another Hutu, became president of Burundi. The violence continued during Ntibantung-anya's presidency until July 1996 when Burundi's military leadership reinstalled Pierre Buyoya, a Tutsi, as head of state. Between 1993 and 1996, at least 150,000 people had died.

Refugee crisis. The migration into Zaire in 1994 of at least one million Rwandan Hutu—who left their homes in fear of reprisals for the massacre of some 500,000 Tutsi—was unprecedented in its size and long-term effects. Although governments in the Great Lakes region had grown accustomed to disorderly mass migrations since independence in the 1960s, none had been forced to deal with a migration the size of the Rwandan immigration into Zaire. In addition to the familiar housing, food, and medical problems of refugees, the Zairian government also had to contend with the presence of Hutu extremists—the Interahamwe—in the Zairian refugee camps. The Interahamwe were intent on undermining Rwanda's Tutsi-led government and used the crowded conditions of the refugee camps to hide their activities and identities. The group intimidated large numbers of Hutu moderates to work with them.

In addition to the danger the Hutu Interahamwe posed to the Rwandan government, their presence in the refugee camps of eastern Zaire helped spark the Zairian revolution. The Interahamwe came to the aid of Mobutu's Zairian security forces in their attacks on a group of Zairian ethnic Tutsi known as the Banyamulenge. While the Banyamulenge had lived in Zaire's diamond-rich eastern Kivu province for at least 200 years, Mobutu had repeatedly called the ethnic Tutsi "foreigners" and urged that they be treated as rebels and expelled. The Banyamulenge were joined by Laurent Kabila's forces—the Alliance of Democratic Forces for the Liberation of Congo-Zaire.

Neighboring countries aid the revolution. The revolution gained momentum when Rwanda and Burundi—both led by Tutsi governments that sympathized with the Banyamulenge—came to the aid of the Banyamulenge and their allies, Laurent Kabila's rebels. The governments of Rwanda and Burundi provided armed assistance in the fight against Mobutu's forces and the Interahamwe.

Uganda also lent support to the rebellion against Mobutu. Uganda was the closest ally of Rwanda's Tutsi government and, therefore, supported Rwanda's efforts to clean out the troublesome Interahamwe camps in Zaire. Observers also believe that President Museveni of Uganda aided Laurent Kabila to induce Kabila to clamp down on Uganda's own Islamic-militant rebels, who used eastern Zaire to launch attacks on Uganda. Observers credited Museveni with supporting Tutsi regimes in Rwanda and Burundi as an expedient way to impose stability in central Africa.

Angola supported Kabila's push to drive Mobutu from Zaire because Mobutu had allowed Angolan rebels—the National Union for the Total

A Tutsi family returns to Rwanda, 1994

Independence of Angola—to export diamonds and import weapons through Zaire. Angolan military support of Kabila's forces west and southeast of Kinshasa helped pave the way for Kabila's assumption of power.

Kabila's troops overrun Zaire. In a series of lightning strikes, the disciplined corps of some 15,000 predominantly Tutsi fighters under Kabila seized the provincial capitals Bukavu and Goma in eastern Zaire by early November 1996. What had begun as a Tutsi-led uprising quickly developed into a popularly supported revolution. Within seven months, the rebel forces had overrun all of Zaire, scoring victory after victory against the unpaid, ill-equipped, and demoralized army of President Mobutu, who had alienated his own people and Zaire's neighbors by threatening to deport the "alien" Banyamulenge Tutsi.

Later in November 1996, approximately 650,000 Hutu refugees left their camps in Zaire and returned to Rwanda. Their return followed a series of conciliatory statements made by the Tutsi government. This left approximately 350,000 refugees in Zaire. As many as 100,000 of the remaining refugees—believed to include many perpetrators of the 1994 massacre—were driven out of camps around Bukavu and Goma by forces under the control of Laurent Kabila. Instead of returning to Rwanda, the refugees trekked west, into Zaire's interior, walking through miles of mountainous jungle and surviving on insects and wild plants.

Between April and June 1997, another 45,000 refugees were *repatriated* (sent back) to Rwanda in what was one of the UN's biggest and most expensive airlifts. At the end of 1997, at least 200,000 refugees from the 1994 migration remained unaccounted for.

Fears of new genocide. Laurent Kabila, prior to his May 1997 entry into Kinshasa, had threatened to overrun refugee camps in eastern Zaire because of their use as havens by Hutu extremists. During late 1996 and the first few months of 1997, reports circulated that Kabila's rebels and the Banyamulenge had slaughtered Rwandan Hutu refugees, mainly in the vicinity of Kisangani, in northeastern Zaire. Some news stories reported that earthmoving equipment had been used to bury the bodies in mass graves. In other areas, refugees had simply vanished.

Throughout 1997, President Kabila repeatedly thwarted UN attempts to mount on-the-spot inquiries into the atrocities. In October, two human rights organizations, Human Rights Watch/Africa in New York City and the International Federation of Human Rights Leagues in Paris, reported that Kabila's troops continued to kill large numbers of civilian refugees. Kabila finally allowed a UN team into the Republic of Congo in mid-November to begin an investigation.

Prospects for the Republic of Congo's future. When President Kabila took office, he was surrounded by the Banyamulenge Tutsi on whose military muscle he had ridden to power. Kabila faced the daunting task of forming a truly national administration in a country with more than 250 tribes. Western powers appeared to have accepted Kabila's plan to put off elections until 1999. However, representatives of the United States, the European Union (an organization of fifteen Western European countries), the World Bank, and the International Monetary Fund, after a meeting in September 1997, set conditions for Kabila. Unless Kabila provided a plan to reconstruct the economy, granted permission for the UN team to investigate charges of atrocities, and made progress on democracy and human rights issues, no financial assistance would be provided.

Prospects for peace. Prospects for peace and democracy in Burundi remained grim in 1997, as ethnic rivals continued to see extermination as a solution to tribal conflict. President Buyoya's government had done little since resuming power in

1996 to reach meaningful political compromises with the Hutu majority. By mid-1997, many Hutu had begun to support the Hutu militias that mounted widespread attacks against an essentially Tutsi military government. Buyoya's cabinet responded by forcing 250,000 Hutu into "regroupment" camps, making it easier for the army to find and kill Hutu extremist guerrillas.

In Rwanda, Hutu rebels began filtering back into the country from Congo in May 1997 and continued their attempts to overthrow Rwanda's Tutsi-controlled government. By October, some 4,000 people had died in the fighting.

In addition, the return of Hutu refugees to Rwanda created a housing crisis, since many Hutu houses had been taken over by Tutsi who had been similarly displaced during an earlier refugee cycle. As many as 2,000 of the returning Hutu refugees were accused of planning the 1994 annihilation of Tutsi, and some 85,000 other Hutu were accused of lesser crimes. Trials under the jurisdiction of both Rwandan courts and the UN International Criminal Tribunal for Rwanda began in January 1997.

Although violence in Rwanda increased after the refugees' return, the Tutsi who controlled the country claimed that Rwanda's cycle of bloodletting could be broken. The government's commitment to national reconciliation was generally acknowledged by the international community. However, old tensions over tribal animosities could be quickly rekindled in a country with one of the most densely packed populations in Africa.

Planning a stable future. Many political analysts believe that there are basically three ways by which the Hutu and Tutsi could move toward a stable future. One possible solution would be the formation of a government that acknowledges the right of both the majority Hutu and the minority Tutsi to share governing power. Such a system was adopted in South Africa, where Nelson Mandela's Government of National Unity shared power beyond the membership of Mandela's own party, the African National Congress.

Another solution would be the election of government leaders with no regard for tribal affiliation. Ugandan President Museveni espoused such a model. Museveni refused to allow political parties to campaign in Uganda because tribal rivalries were so fierce in that country that Museveni believed multiparty politics would continue to divide people along tribal and religious lines.

Finally, some analysts have suggested that the only hope for peace between the Hutu and Tutsi would be to establish separate countries—a Hutuland and a Tutsiland—for the two tribes. Because of the current lack of consensus on these matters, it may be that an outside peace-brokering mission, such as one sponsored by the Organization of African Unity, could provide a solution. However, political analysts agree that unless the leaders and the people accept the politics of a shared humanity and mutual respect, Hutu and Tutsi—and the countries of which they are a part—will be doomed to an even bleaker future well into the twenty-first century.

About the author: Simon Baynham, Director of Research from 1989 to 1996 at Pretoria's Africa Institute of South Africa, is currently Consultant at the Research Institute for the Study of Conflict and Terrorism, in London.

Egypt

Egypt is a country in the northeastern part of Africa. Most of Egypt is a dry, windswept desert; however, the Nile River flows northward through the desert creating a vital source of life for the Egyptians. The Nile and the Suez Canal are two important waterways in Egypt. Cairo is Egypt's capital and largest city, as well as Africa's largest city.

HOT topics

Suez Canal. The Suez Canal is a 100-mile long artificial waterway that goes across the Isthmus of Suez joining the Mediterranean and Red seas. The canal was opened in 1869, but then closed during the 1967 Arab-Israeli war. It was reopened again in 1975. Although an international convention in 1888 agreed that the canal should stay open in peace and in war, ships from enemy countries are often denied access during wars.

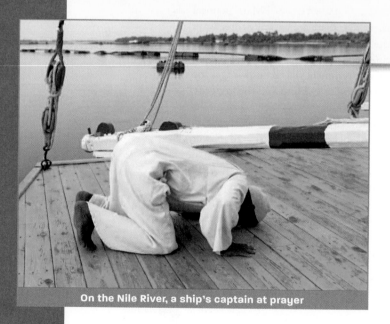

On the Nile River, a ship's captain at prayer

HOT topics 🔥

Pyramids at Giza. There are ten pyramids at Giza. The pyramids are tombs that ancient Egyptians built for their rulers, who were often mummified and then hidden inside secret chambers within the pyramids. Temples attached to the pyramids were used for funeral ceremonies. The largest pyramid, the Great Pyramid, was built for King Khufu. A huge statue of a sphinx, the Great Sphinx, also stands amongst these pyramids. These pyramids are architectural marvels which attract many tourists every year.

Egypt and Israel's Rocky History. The Jewish state of Israel officially came into existence on May 14, 1948. The next day, it was invaded by armies from Egypt and other Arab countries. After defeating the Arab forces, Israel held more territory than it had been given by the United Nations (UN) and relations continued to worsen. In the 1950s, Palestinians aided by Egypt raided Israel from the Gaza Strip; in return Israel raided the Gaza Strip. Egypt then banned Israeli ships from the Suez Canal. In response, Israel invaded Egypt. In 1967, another war erupted. The UN arranged a cease-fire, ending the war after six days. The first step towards a peace treaty between Egypt and Israel was accomplished with the Camp David Accords in 1977.

Islam Influences on Egyptian Life. The great majority of Egyptians are Muslims—they follow the religion of Islam. This affects many aspects of their lives such as stopping to pray five times a day, giving money to the poor, fasting, and making pilgrimages to the sacred city of Islam (Mecca, Saudi Arabia). The government officially controls Islam in Egypt, and it appoints major Muslim religious leaders.

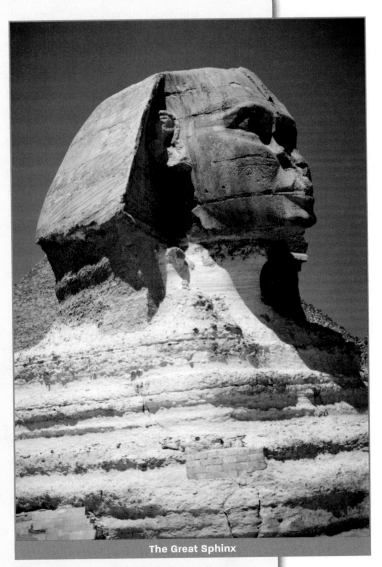

The Great Sphinx

TRUE or FALSE?
Egypt's resources are not sufficient for its large population.

THE BASICS

Egypt is a Middle Eastern country in the northeast corner of Africa. A small part of Egypt, the Sinai Peninsula, is in Asia. Little rain falls in Egypt, and dry, windswept desert covers most of the land. But the Nile River flows northward through the desert and serves as a vital source of life for most Egyptians. Almost all of Egypt's people live near the Nile or along the Suez Canal, the country's other important waterway.

Egypt is Africa's third largest country in population. Only Nigeria and Ethiopia have more people. Cairo, Egypt's capital and largest city, is also the largest city in Africa.

Egypt's population has increased tremendously since the mid-1900s. In addition, many people have moved from rural villages to cities in search of work. As a result, the cities of Egypt overflow with people.

Most Egyptians consider themselves Arabs. More than 90 percent of Egyptians are Muslims. Islam, the Muslim religion, influences family life, social relationships, business activities, and government affairs. Al-Azhar University in Cairo is the world's leading center of Islamic teaching.

For thousands of years, floodwaters from the Nile deposited rich soil on the riverbanks. As a result, the Nile Valley and Delta region of Egypt contains extraordinarily fertile farmland. Agriculture provides jobs for more than one-fourth of Egypt's workers. Cotton is one of Egypt's most valuable crops. Other crops grown in Egypt include corn, fruits, rice, sugarcane, and wheat.

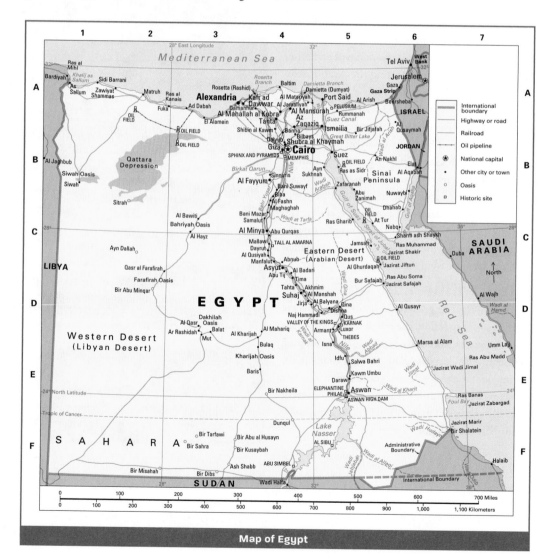

Map of Egypt

Hosni Mubarak addressing parliament

Egypt has expanded a variety of manufacturing industries since the mid-1900s. Cement, cotton textiles, and processed foods are among the chief manufactured products. Petroleum provides much energy, as does hydroelectric power from the Aswan High Dam on the Nile River.

Egypt is a birthplace of civilization. The ancient Egyptians developed a great culture about 5,000 years ago. They created the first national government, as well as early forms of mathematics and writing.

Egypt's hot, dry climate has helped preserve many products of ancient Egyptian culture. Tourists from all over the world travel to Egypt to see such wonders as the Great Sphinx, an enormous stone sculpture with the head of a human being and the body of a lion. They can also marvel at the huge pyramids that the ancient Egyptians built as tombs for their *pharaohs* (rulers).

After ancient times, Egypt was ruled by a series of foreign invaders. In 1953, Egypt became an independent republic. Since then, it has played a leading role in the Middle East, especially in Arab affairs. Egypt's official name is the Arab Republic of Egypt.

Government

Egypt is a republic with a strong national government. According to the Constitution adopted in 1971, Egypt is a democratic and socialist society, and Egyptians are part of the Arab nation. A military government took control of Egypt in 2011 and replaced the 1971 Constitution with a temporary charter. The charter would be in effect until a new constitution could be drafted and approved by a *referendum* (direct vote of the people).

National government. Egypt's national government has three branches. They are (1) an executive branch headed by a president, (2) a legislative branch to pass laws, and (3) a judicial branch, or court system.

Egyptian voters elect the president. The president appoints the vice president. The president also appoints a prime minister and Council of Ministers (cabinet). In turn, the national government selects all local administrators. Thus, the president has great influence and authority at all levels of government. The president also commands Egypt's armed forces.

Egypt's legislative body is called the People's Assembly. The Egyptian people elect most of the assembly members. Traditionally, the president appoints 10 members. The legislative branch also includes a smaller body called the Shura Council. The council's role is mainly advisory.

Local government. Egypt is divided into political units called *governorates*. A governor appointed by the president heads each governorate. The governorates are divided into districts and villages, which also are run by appointed officials. Elected councils at each level of local government assist the appointed leaders.

Politics. Egypt's political environment changed in 2011. The National Democratic Party, which had ruled for decades, was dissolved, and opposition parties were allowed to participate in general elections. All Egyptian citizens aged 18 or older are required to vote.

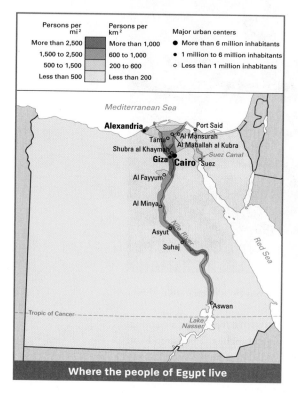

Persons per mi²	Persons per km²	Major urban centers
More than 2,500	More than 1,000	● More than 6 million inhabitants
1,500 to 2,500	600 to 1,000	• 1 million to 6 million inhabitants
500 to 1,500	200 to 600	○ Less than 1 million inhabitants
Less than 500	Less than 200	

Mediterranean Sea

Alexandria
Port Said
Tanta · Al Mansurah
Shubra al Khaymah · Al Mahallah al Kubra
Giza · Suez Canal
Cairo · Suez
Al Fayyum
Al Minya
Nile River
Asyut
Suhaj
Red Sea
Tropic of Cancer
Aswan
Lake Nasser

Where the people of Egypt live

Courts. The Supreme Constitutional Court is the highest court in Egypt. Lower courts include appeals courts, *tribunals of first instance* (regional courts), and district courts. The president appoints judges on the recommendation of the minister of justice. The courts are otherwise independent of presidential control or influence. There are no juries in Egypt's court system.

Armed forces. Egypt maintains a large military, consisting of an army, a navy, an air force, and an air defense command. About 470,000 people serve in Egypt's armed forces. In addition, the country's military reserves have about 480,000 members. Men between the ages of 18 and 30 may be drafted for three years of military service.

People

About 99 percent of all Egyptians live along the Nile River and the Suez Canal, in an area that covers only about 4 percent of Egypt's total land. The rest of the country's people live in the deserts and mountains east and west of the Nile.

Most Egyptians consider themselves Arabs. Bedouins make up a distinct cultural minority among the Arab population. Bedouins are *nomads*— that is, herders who move about to find pastures for their flock. Most former Bedouins have settled and become farmers, but some wandering tribes remain in the Egyptian deserts.

The Nubians make up the largest non-Arab minority in Egypt. These people originally lived in villages along the Nile in northern Sudan and the extreme south of Egypt, in a region called the Nubian Valley. Construction of the Aswan High Dam in the 1960s forced the Nubians to move north along the Nile.

Ancestry. Since ancient times, numerous groups of people have invaded Egypt and have intermarried with native Egyptians. As a result, present-day Egyptians can trace their ancestry not only to ancient Egyptians, but also to such groups as Arabs, Ethiopians, Persians, and Turks, as well as Greeks, Romans, and other Europeans.

Language. Arabic is the official language of Egypt. Regional Arabic dialects have different sounds and words. The dialect of Cairo is the most widely spoken dialect throughout Egypt. The Bedouin dialects differ from those spoken by the settled residents of the Nile Valley. People in some desert villages speak Berber rather than Arabic. Many educated Egyptians speak English or French as a second language.

Way of Life

Lifestyles in Egypt's cities differ greatly from those in its villages. Egyptian city dwellers cope with such typical urban problems as housing shortages and traffic congestion. Although many live in poverty, others enjoy modern conveniences and government services that the cities offer.

Rural life changed greatly during the 1900s. Many jobs in rural areas are now done with the help of machines. However, much work is still done by hand, and donkeys, water buffaloes, and camels continue to be used for some heavy tasks. For people throughout Egypt, the beliefs and traditions of Islam form a unifying bond.

City life. Cairo is Egypt's largest city and the largest city in Africa. The port city of Alexandria is Egypt's second largest city. Cities in Egypt are overcrowded. Traffic moves slowly, and public transportation is inadequate. Riders crowd onto streetcars and trains.

Great extremes of wealth and poverty characterize Egyptian cities. Attractive residential areas exist beside vast slums. Lack of sufficient housing is a serious problem. Many people crowd into small apartments. Many more build makeshift huts on land that belongs to other people, or on the roofs of apartment buildings. Some of the poorest people in Cairo take refuge in historic tombs on the outskirts of the city, in an area known as the City of the Dead.

The cities provide a variety of jobs. Educated Egyptians work in such professions as business and government. Workers with little or no education find jobs at factories or as unskilled laborers.

Rural life. Until the 1900s, the vast majority of Egyptians lived in the countryside. Today, more than half of Egypt's people still live in rural areas. Almost all of them are peasants called *fellahin*. They live in villages along the Nile River or the Suez Canal. Most of the fellahin farm small plots of land or tend animals. Many fellahin do not own land. They rent land or work as laborers in the fields of more prosperous landowners. A small minority of Egypt's rural people are Bedouins who move about the deserts with their herds of camels, goats, and sheep.

The traditional village home used to be a simple hut built of mud bricks with a straw roof. Most huts consisted of one to three rooms, with few furnishings, and a courtyard. Today, many village homes are made of fired bricks or concrete, and they are larger and more comfortable than in the past. Electric power is commonly available, as are televisions, radios, and cassette recorders. Many villages have gained wealth through the earnings of fellahin who have worked outside Egypt, especially in the rich Arab countries of the Persian Gulf. The spread of education and health services has also improved the lives of villagers. However, illiteracy, disease, and poverty remain major problems in rural areas.

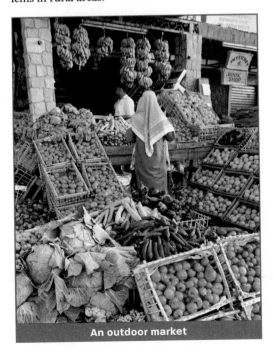

An outdoor market

Each member of a village family performs certain duties. The husband organizes the planting, weeding, and harvesting of crops. The wife cooks, carries water, and helps in the fields. Children look after the animals and help bring water to the fields.

Egyptian villages are characterized by a strong sense of community. People come together to celebrate feasts, festivals, marriages, and births. Islam, the religion of most Egyptians, provides a strong unifying bond. *Mosques* (Islamic houses of worship) serve as centers of both religious and social life.

Clothing. Styles of clothing in Egypt reflect the different ways of life. Many well-to-do city dwellers wear clothing similar to that worn in the United States and Europe. Rural villagers and many poor city dwellers wear traditional clothing. Fellahin men wear pants and a long, full shirt-like garment called a *galabiyyah*. Women wear long, flowing gowns in dark or bright colors.

Some Egyptians follow Islamic customs in their appearance. Men grow beards and wear long, light-colored gowns and skullcaps. Women wear robes and cover their hair, ears, and arms with a veil.

Food and drink. Most villagers and poor city dwellers in Egypt eat a simple diet based on bread and *ful* or *fool* (broad beans). At a typical evening meal, each person dips bread into a large bowl of hot vegetable stew.

Government-run stores in the cities distribute such food as meat, cheese, and eggs at controlled prices. However, supplies at these stores often run out. The well-to-do city people have more varied diets. They can afford to buy large quantities of meat and imported fruits and vegetables.

Sweetened coffee and tea are favorite beverages throughout Egypt. People also drink the milk of goats, sheep, and water buffaloes.

Recreation. Soccer is popular in Egypt. Many people attend matches or watch their favorite teams on television. But the main form of recreation in both cities and villages is socializing. People enjoy going to the *suq* (outdoor marketplace) to make purchases and to visit with friends. They like to sit and talk while drinking cups of coffee or tea, or relax by smoking a kind of water pipe known as a *shisha*.

Religion. Islam is the official religion of Egypt. More than 90 percent of the Egyptian people are Muslims—followers of Islam. Almost all of them follow the Sunni branch of Islam. Coptic Christians make up the largest religious minority group in Egypt.

Islam influences many aspects of life in Egypt. Religious duties include praying five times a day, *almsgiving* (giving money or goods to the poor), fasting, and, if possible, making a pilgrimage to Mecca, Saudi Arabia, the sacred city of Islam. Muslim traditions also affect government and law. For example, the government collects contributions from the wealthy and gives the money to the poor to fulfill the almsgiving requirement of Islam.

The government officially controls Islam in Egypt, and it appoints major Muslim religious leaders. In villages and city neighborhoods, some Muslims form brotherhoods and hold festivals and ceremonies outside of official control. Some of these groups use force in opposing the government and its religious leaders, whom they view as corrupted by non-Islamic values.

By law, Coptic Christians and other religious minorities may worship freely. But some radical Muslim groups have committed acts of violence against the Coptic community in Cairo and in parts of southern Egypt.

Education. About half of Egypt's adult population can read and write. Illiteracy is highest in rural areas. The government is working to improve the quality and availability of education.

According to law, all children from ages 6 up to 14 must go to school. But in some places, schools are so crowded that students go for only part of each day to make room for other students. Many teachers provide tutoring services outside school. Education at public elementary and high schools and public colleges is free. Egypt also has many private schools, and a few private universities.

Cairo University is the largest institution of higher learning in Egypt. Al-Azhar University, one of the world's oldest universities, was founded around A.D. 970. It is a center of Islamic scholarship.

Egypt's educational system has problems from the elementary through the university level because of overcrowding and lack of funds. There is a shortage of teachers and school buildings, especially in rural areas. Despite these problems, Egypt's university graduates are among the best trained in the Arab world.

The arts. Egypt has a rich artistic tradition. Ancient Egyptians created many fine paintings and statues. They also produced and enjoyed music and stories.

Today, Egypt ranks as a center of the Arab publishing and motion picture industries. The celebrated works of Egyptian writers and filmmakers have spread Egypt's culture throughout the Arab world. During the mid-1900s, the works of such writers as Tawfiq al-Hakim and Taha Hussein realistically described Egyptian and Arab society. In 1988, the Egyptian author Naguib Mahfouz became the first Arabic-language writer to win the Nobel Prize in Literature.

Egyptians enjoy traditional and classical music, as well as modern Egyptian and Western music. Egypt's most popular singer of the 1900s, Um Kulthum, blended Eastern and Western themes in her songs.

The Land

Egypt consists mostly of sparsely settled deserts. But the inhabited areas—along the Nile River and the Suez Canal—are densely populated.

Egypt has four major land regions: (1) the Nile Valley and Delta, (2) the Western Desert, (3) the Eastern Desert, and (4) the Sinai Peninsula.

The Nile Valley and Delta region extends along the course of the Nile River, which measures about 1,000 miles (1,600 kilometers) in Egypt. The Nile flows northward into Egypt from Sudan to Cairo. Just north of Cairo, the river splits

The Great Sand Sea, Libyan Desert

into two main branches and forms a delta. The Nile River delta measures about 150 miles (240 kilometers) at its base along the Mediterranean Sea, and about 100 miles (160 kilometers) from north to south.

The valley and delta region contains most of Egypt's farmland. Without the precious waters of the Nile, Egypt would be little more than a desert wasteland. For thousands of years, annual floods of the Nile deposited valuable soils upon the narrow plain on either side of the river and upon the low-lying delta. Almost all of Egypt's people live in the valley and delta region. Many of them farm its fertile soil.

In the southern part of the valley, the Aswan High Dam provides water for irrigation of the lands along the Nile. It also prevents severe damage from the Nile's annual flooding. Lake Nasser, a huge lake created behind the dam, catches and stores the floodwaters. The Aswan High Dam allows Egyptians to cultivate usable farmland more thoroughly. But the dam also collects a great deal of valuable soil. As a result, this soil is no longer deposited on the farmland that borders the Nile.

The Western Desert, also called the *Libyan Desert,* is part of the huge Sahara that stretches across northern Africa. It covers about two-thirds of Egypt's total area. The Western Desert consists almost entirely of a large, sandy plateau with some ridges and basins, and pit-shaped areas called *depressions.* The Qattara Depression, Egypt's lowest point, drops 436 feet (133 meters) below sea level. It contains salty marshes,

lakes, and *badlands* (regions of small, steep hills and deep gullies). Small villages occupy scattered oases in the desert.

The Eastern Desert, or *Arabian Desert,* is also part of the Sahara. The desert rises eastward from the Nile as a sloping, sandy plateau for about 50 to 80 miles (80 to 130 kilometers). It then turns into a series of rocky hills and deep valleys called *wadis.* The land in this region is virtually impossible to cultivate. As a result, the Eastern Desert is mostly uninhabited, except for a few villages on the coast of the Red Sea.

The Sinai Peninsula is a desert area that lies east of the Suez Canal and the Gulf of Suez. It consists of a flat, sandy coastal plain in the north, a high limestone plateau in the central area, and mountains in the south. Egypt's highest point, Jabal Katrinah, rises 8,651 feet (2,637 meters) above sea level in the southern Sinai. Though desolate, the Sinai Peninsula has valuable oil deposits. About 300,000 people live on the peninsula.

Climate

Egypt has a hot, dry climate with only two seasons—scorching summers and mild winters. Summer lasts from around May to October, and winter lasts from around November to April. January temperatures range from an average high of 65°F (18°C) in Cairo to an average high of 74°F (23°C) in Aswan. July temperatures reach an average high of 96°F (36°C) in Cairo, and 106°F (41°C) in Aswan. Daily temperatures in the deserts vary greatly. The average daytime high temperature is 104°F (40°C), while the

Major uses of land in Egypt

temperature may drop to 45°F (7°C) after sunset. North winds from the Mediterranean Sea cool the coast of Egypt during the summer, so many wealthy Egyptians spend the hot summer months of July and August in Alexandria.

Most of Egypt receives little rain. Winter rainstorms occasionally strike the Mediterranean coast, where about 8 inches (20 centimeters) of rain fall each year. Inland, rainfall decreases. Annual rainfall in Cairo averages about 1 inch (2.5 centimeters). Southern Egypt receives only a trace of rain each year.

Around the month of April, a hot windstorm called the *khamsin* sweeps through Egypt. Its driving winds blow large amounts of sand and dust at high speeds. The khamsin may raise temperatures as much as 68°F (38°C) in two hours, and it can damage crops.

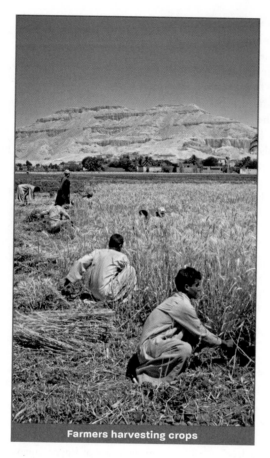

Farmers harvesting crops

Economy

Egypt is a developing country with a number of economic problems. For example, Egypt must import much of its food supply to feed its increasing population. At the same time, its petroleum exports have been reduced because of increased demand within the country. Thus, Egypt faces a foreign debt, as the cost of its imports far exceeds its income from exports.

During the 1950s and 1960s, the government of Egypt took over almost all large-scale business and industry. Farms and small businesses remained privately owned. Today, government ownership continues to dominate in most major industries, such as food processing, textiles, and steel. However, the government has tried to encourage more private investment in the production of goods and services.

Service industries are economic activities that provide services rather than produce goods. Such industries have become increasingly important to the Egyptian economy. Today, service industries account for about half of Egypt's gross domestic product (GDP) and employ nearly half of all its workers. The GDP is the total value of all goods and services produced within a country in a year.

Trade, restaurants, and hotels is the leading service industry group in terms of GDP. This group benefits from the millions of tourists who visit Egypt each year. The community, government, and personal services group employs about one fourth of Egypt's workers.

Manufacturing has expanded rapidly in Egypt since the 1950s, when the government took a leading role in promoting industrialization. Egypt has *privatized* some of the manufacturing industry, returning it to private ownership. However, the government still controls much of the country's manufacturing.

Food processing and textile production are among the most important industries. Egypt also manufactures cement, chemicals, motor vehicles, and steel. Cairo and Alexandria are the leading manufacturing centers.

Agriculture accounts for only about a sixth of Egypt's GDP. But it employs nearly a third of the country's workers. Almost all of Egypt's farmland is along the Nile River. Nearly all farmland is privately owned. Many of Egypt's farms are 1 acre (0.4 hectare) or less.

For centuries, Egyptian farmers relied on the annual floods of the Nile River to irrigate their fields and renew the topsoil. Each year, before the Nile flooded in July and August, farmers created a series of basins on surrounding farmland. When the Nile overflowed, these basins trapped the floodwaters and the *silt* (tiny particles of soil) that they carried. After the floodwaters withdrew, farmers planted their fields.

Beginning in the 1800s, Egyptians replaced the basin irrigation system with a system of year-round irrigation. They built dams, canals, and reservoirs to capture Nile water and make it available throughout the year. The changeover was completed with the building of the Aswan High Dam, which began operation in 1968. The dam has increased the amount of land irrigated all year by about 2 million acres (800,000 hectares). Today, nearly all of Egypt's farmland has continuous irrigation. As a result, farmers can plant crops year-round.

Cotton is one of Egypt's most valuable crops. Egypt produces much of the high quality *long-staple* (long-fibered) cotton. Such cotton is known for its strength and durability. Other important crops include corn, onions, potatoes, rice, sugar beets, sugarcane, tomatoes, wheat, and fruits, such as apples, bananas, grapes, oranges and other citrus fruits, and watermelons. Egypt leads the world in the production of dates, which are grown mainly in the desert oases. Egypt is also a leading producer of eggplants and figs.

Goats and sheep are raised for meat, milk, and wool. Cattle and water buffaloes, kept chiefly as work animals, also provide some milk. A large number of farmers raise chickens for meat and eggs. Some camels, ducks, and geese are also raised.

Mining. Egypt's most important minerals are petroleum and natural gas. Oil is found in the Eastern and Western deserts, the Sinai Peninsula, and offshore in the Gulf of Suez and the Red Sea. However, since the mid-1990s, Egypt's oil production has been declining. Natural gas is plentiful near Alexandria, in the Delta, and in the Western Desert. Egypt also mines gypsum, iron ore, manganese, and phosphate rock.

Tourism. Egypt's warm, dry climate and its beautiful relics from ancient times attract visitors from all over the world. Large numbers of people travel to Egypt each year to admire such wonders as the giant pyramids and the Great Sphinx at Giza. Near Luxor, ancient tombs in the Valley of the Kings and magnificent temples draw many tourists. Visitors to the city of Cairo admire its beautiful mosques, city walls and gates, and traditional Islamic architecture. Egypt's Red Sea resorts are attracting growing numbers of visitors, who come to enjoy the sunny beaches and spectacular coral reefs. But since the 1990s, Egypt's tourism industry has suffered greatly because of visitors' fears of terrorism.

Energy sources. Natural gas and petroleum provide most of Egypt's energy. The hydroelectric plant of the Aswan High Dam generates a large amount of low-cost electric power.

International trade. Egypt imports more goods than it exports. Imports include machinery, petroleum products, transportation equipment; and food products, such as corn and wheat. Egypt's major suppliers of imports are China, Germany, Italy, Kuwait, Russia, Saudi Arabia, and the United States. Egyptian exports include clothing; crude oil and petroleum products; iron and steel; and food products, such as fruits, rice, and vegetables. Major markets for exports include France, India, Italy, Spain, the United Kingdom, and the United States.

Transportation and communication. For thousands of years, the Nile River was the primary means of transportation within Egypt. Today, transportation takes many forms. Roads and railroads connect all important cities and towns. Two main highways link Alexandria and Cairo. One highway stretches across the desert and the other passes through the densely populated Nile Delta. Only a small percentage of Egypt's people own automobiles.

Cairo has Egypt's busiest international airport. Alexandria, Hurghada, Luxor, and Sharm ash Shaykh on the Sinai Peninsula also have international airports. Egypt's government-run airline, EgyptAir, provides service throughout the country and to and from foreign cities. Alexandria, on the Mediterranean Sea, ranks as Egypt's leading port. Two other major ports, Port Said and Suez, lie on the Suez Canal.

Cairo serves as the center of Egypt's communications industries. Egypt's leading daily newspapers include *Al-Ahram*, *Al-Akhbar*, and *Al-Jumhuriyah*. Although the government does not allow complete freedom of expression, a number of newspapers express political dissent. The Egyptian government owns and controls the nation's main radio and television stations. Many Egyptians can also access internationally or privately owned satellite broadcasting.

A man transporting bread on a bicycle

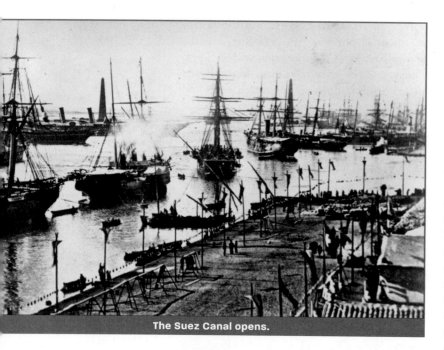

The Suez Canal opens.

History

Egypt's long, colorful history goes back more than 5,000 years to about 3100 B.C.

Muslim rule. In A.D. 639, Arab Muslims, inspired by the birth of Islam, burst out of Arabia and invaded Egypt. At the time, Egypt was a province of the Byzantine, or East Roman, Empire. The Arabs captured Alexandria, which was then the capital of Egypt, in 642. Their commander, Amr ibn al-As, established a military camp and settlement in what is now part of Cairo. The Arab conquest transformed Egypt. The Egyptian people gradually adopted the Arabic language, and many converted from the Coptic Christian religion to Islam.

Egypt became an important province of the Islamic empire, which was ruled by Arab Muslim leaders called *caliphs.* Caliphs of the Umayyad *dynasty* (family of rulers) governed Egypt from Damascus (now the capital of Syria). They were followed by the Abbasid dynasty, which ruled from Baghdad (now the capital of Iraq).

In the mid-800s, the Abbasids began to lose control over their territories. For most of the period between 868 and 969, two Turkish dynasties—the Tulunid dynasty and the Ikhshidid dynasty—ruled Egypt almost independently of the Abbasid caliphs in Baghdad.

In 969, Fatimid rulers seized Egypt. The Fatimids, who had conquered other lands in north-ern Africa, made Egypt the center of their expanding empire and broke its ties with the Abbasid state. The Fatimids claimed to be descendants of Fatimah, daughter of the Islamic prophet Muhammad. They were members of an Islamic minority group known as Shiites. The Fatimids founded the city of Al-Qahirah (modern-day Cairo), and they made it their capital in 973. They also built al-Azhar mosque, which quickly became the center of Fatimid culture and religion.

By the mid-1100s, the Fatimid empire was weakened by fighting among various factions and with the Christian Crusaders from Europe. In 1168, the Fatimid caliph asked Muslims in Syria to send an army to help defend Egypt from the Crusaders. Saladin, an officer in that army, helped drive the Crusaders out of Egypt. Then in 1171, he overthrew the Fatimid ruler, restored the Sunni form of Islam—that is, the form most Muslims follow—and created an independent state. He became the *sultan* (prince) of Egypt. Saladin was a generous and just ruler. He and his descendants formed the Ayyubid dynasty, which ruled Egypt until 1250.

A group known as the Mamluks served as the sultan's bodyguard. They were Turkish, Mongol, and Circassian slaves who were given special military training and rose to high positions in the army and government. In 1250, the Mamluks revolted against the Ayyubid sultan and seized control of Egypt. The Mamluk general Baybars, who later became sultan, saved Egypt from ruin when his forces defeated invading Mongol troops at the battle of Ayn Jalud in Palestine in 1260.

For more than 200 years, rival Mamluk groups competed for authority, with the largest, best-organized, and most ruthless group taking power. But Egypt achieved more in art, architecture, and literature under the Mamluk rulers than at any time since the beginning of the Islamic period.

Ottoman and French control. The Mamluk empire was declining by 1517. That year, Ottoman forces under Sultan Selim invaded Egypt from Syria and overthrew the Mamluks. But the Ottomans could not eliminate Mamluk influence. Mamluks became *beys* (governors) of the regions of Egypt and held the real governing power. By the mid-1700s, Egypt's government was in disarray as Ottoman and Mamluk leaders competed for power. At the same time, the economy suffered from European control of Indian Ocean trade routes that bypassed Egypt.

In 1798, Napoleon Bonaparte led French forces into Egypt. They defeated the Mamluks in the Battle of the Pyramids. Napoleon hoped to disrupt the trade routes of Britain (now the United Kingdom), France's chief enemy. He also wanted to establish a French colony in Egypt. Napoleon brought many French scholars with him to Egypt. Their scientific investigations helped revive the study of Egyptian relics, and their writings provided thorough descriptions of the country at the end of the 1700s.

Napoleon returned to France in 1799, leaving his troops behind. But military defeat, Egyptian resistance, and disease weakened them. The Ottomans, with British assistance, forced the French to withdraw in 1801.

Muhammad Ali and modernization.

Muhammad Ali was an officer in the Ottoman army that helped drive the French out of Egypt in 1801. In the disorder following the departure of the French, he gained power rapidly. By 1805, Muhammad Ali had established himself as Egypt's ruler. His killing of Mamluk rivals in 1811 made his rule secure from rebellion. From then on, he carried out a program of modernization.

Muhammad Ali was an energetic leader who ruled with absolute power. Many of his reforms came from a desire to strengthen Egypt's army. Muhammad Ali knew that his position in Egypt remained secure only as long as his army was more powerful than that of the Ottoman sultan. To achieve this goal, he brought in French military experts and patterned his army on that of France. In addition, Muhammad Ali introduced Western education into Egypt. He sent educational missions to Europe and brought European teachers to Egypt. Muhammad Ali also worked to improve agriculture. He began the transformation from basin irrigation to year-round irrigation. He also promoted the industrialization of Egypt.

Many of Muhammad Ali's reforms failed, partly because he tried to do too much too fast. His projects overtaxed the country's resources and caused hardship to much of the population. He also aroused the hostility of the United Kingdom by invading Syria and threatening the existence of the Ottoman Empire, thus upsetting the balance of power in the Middle East. In 1841, the British forced Muhammad Ali to accept a decree that limited his army to 18,000 men. At the time of his death in 1849, Muhammad Ali's industries had collapsed, his educational missions had been disbanded, and many schools had been closed.

Muhammad Ali's immediate successors did not provide strong leadership. His son Said, also called Said Pasha, ruled from 1854 to 1863. Said granted a French company a contract to build a canal through the Isthmus of Suez. The canal was designed to shorten the sailing route between Europe and eastern Asia by linking the Red Sea and the Mediterranean Sea. Construction of the Suez Canal began in 1859, and the canal opened in 1869.

Ismail, Said's nephew, ruled Egypt from 1863 to 1879 and became the *khedive* (ruler). Ismail successfully expanded the educational system; built many roads, canals, and railroads; and increased the export of cotton. But he spent large amounts of money on palaces, boulevards, and public displays. By the 1870s, Ismail's lavish spending had created a large national debt. To help pay off the debt, Ismail sold Egypt's shares of ownership in the increasingly profitable Suez Canal Company to the British government in 1875. As a result, the United Kingdom became the largest shareholder in the canal.

British control.

During the 1800s, the United Kingdom's interests in Egypt steadily increased. When Ismail tried to combat European influence in Egypt, the British helped bring about his removal in favor of his son Tawfiq. In 1881 and 1882, Egyptian army officers led by Colonel Ahmad Urabi staged uprisings in an attempt to establish a more independent and nationalist regime in Egypt. Fears that Urabi's actions would endanger foreign interests eventually led the British to invade Egypt. In September 1882, British forces defeated the Egyptian army at the battle of Tel al-Kabir and marched into Cairo. The British exiled Urabi and returned Tawfiq to power.

During the late 1800s and early 1900s, the khedive ruled Egypt in name only. A series of powerful British administrators actually directed the country's affairs. They improved some aspects of life in Egypt. They put Egypt's finances in order, constructed a series of dams to modernize its irrigation system, and provided efficient government. But educated Egyptians criticized the British for neglecting such social concerns as education and public health. Egyptian nationalism began to emerge, and some people called for independence.

World War I (1914–1918) had a powerful impact on Egypt's relationship with the United Kingdom. Egypt was still actually a part of the

Ottoman Empire when the war began. After the Ottomans allied with Germany, the British declared Egypt a *British protectorate* (territory under partial British control). The United Kingdom wanted to protect its interests in Egypt and the Suez Canal. British and Indian troops defended the canal, and British warships prevented enemy ships from using it. Egypt became an important base of Allied operations against Ottoman territory and an important source of labor and supplies. This involvement of Egypt in the war led to outpourings of anti-British sentiment.

Independence.
From 1919 to 1922, Egypt was in political turmoil. Nationalists led by Saad Zaghlul renewed demands for independence. When the British arrested and exiled Zaghlul, discontent against the British turned into revolt. For a few months in 1919, the government broke down. Negotiations produced few results.

Finally in 1922, the United Kingdom granted Egypt its independence. But the British kept many powers, including the right to station troops in Egypt. A new constitution took effect in 1923 that established Egypt as a constitutional monarchy. However, Egypt made little progress toward ridding the country of British forces or improving living standards and economic growth. The monarch struggled with the British and with various political parties for supremacy.

In 1936, Egypt and the United Kingdom agreed to a treaty that reaffirmed Egypt's independence. This treaty reduced the number of British troops stationed in Egypt and restricted them to the Suez Canal region.

Construction of the Aswan High Dam

The 1940s.
During World War II (1939–1945), Italian and German armies invaded Egypt in efforts to capture the Suez Canal. In 1942, the Allies halted the German advance into Egypt in the Battle of El Alamein. Many Egyptians blamed the British for the violence and hunger in Egypt during the war.

Egypt became a founding member of the United Nations (UN) in 1945. That same year, Egypt and other Arab countries established the Arab League.

After World War II, Egypt's parliamentary parties tried unsuccessfully to dislodge British forces from Egypt. They also had little success in dealing with such problems as poverty, illiteracy, and disease.

In 1947, the UN voted to divide Palestine into Jewish and Arab states. Israel was established in Palestine in 1948. Egypt and other Arab countries immediately went to war against Israel and were defeated. Egyptians, including army officers, blamed the government for the defeat, and support for such groups as the Muslim Brotherhood increased. The Muslim Brotherhood wanted to establish a strictly Islamic government in Egypt and to reclaim all of Palestine for the Arabs.

Republic.
In July 1952, a discontented army group known as the Free Officers seized power and sent the reigning monarch, King Faruk, into exile. Gamal Abdel Nasser led the revolt. Nasser believed that Egypt's government was corrupt and that only a change in government could bring economic progress and complete political independence to Egypt.

The Free Officers organized in a body called the Revolutionary Command Council (RCC). The RCC officially took charge of Egypt in September 1952. The army's popular commander in chief, Muhammad Naguib, became prime minister. The council banned all political parties that had participated in elections before 1952, including the Muslim Brotherhood. In June 1953, Egypt was declared a republic, with Naguib serving as both president and prime minister.

During the first two years of military rule, Naguib shared power with Nasser, the deputy prime minister. But Naguib and Nasser could not agree on policies. In April 1954, Nasser became prime minister. In October, the United Kingdom agreed to remove all its troops from Egypt by June 18, 1956. In November 1954, Naguib lost the presidency, and Nasser established unchallenged authority over Egypt.

Nasser promoted economic progress in many ways. He increased government spending on education and took over all foreign-run schools. To encourage poor Egyptians to get an education, he provided government jobs for all university graduates. He also wanted to construct a huge new dam on the Nile River to increase the supply of water for irrigation and to provide hydroelectric power.

Nasser sought financing from other countries for the Aswan High Dam project. The United States and the United Kingdom expressed support for the project, but later, in July 1956, withdrew their offers of financial assistance. In retaliation, the Egyptian government took control of the Suez Canal Company from its British and French owners later that month. Nasser announced that tolls from the canal would provide money for the Aswan High Dam project.

In the meantime, Egypt's relations with Israel worsened. During the 1950s, Egypt supported Palestinians who raided Israel from the Gaza Strip, the Egyptian-administered part of Palestine. To retaliate, Israel raided the Gaza Strip. Egypt blocked Israeli ships from the Suez Canal and the Gulf of Aqaba.

In October 1956, Israel, in cooperation with the United Kingdom and France, invaded Egypt. Israel occupied the Sinai Peninsula, and the United Kingdom and France captured Port Said. But the United States and the Soviet Union condemned the invasion and brought pressure to bear on the United Kingdom, France, and Israel. The invading troops withdrew, and the Suez Canal Company eventually was compensated for the loss of its property. A UN peacekeeping force was sent to patrol the Egyptian-Israeli border.

The United Arab Republic. Nasser emerged from the Suez incident as a powerful leader of both Egypt and the Arab world. He strongly believed in the importance of unity among the Arab countries. In 1958, a group of Syrian leaders asked Nasser to form a political union between Egypt and Syria. Nasser agreed. The two countries became the United Arab Republic (U.A.R.), and Nasser was elected president of the new nation. Syria eventually grew unhappy with Nasser's economic policies and his increasing power, and so it withdrew from the U.A.R. in 1961. But Nasser kept United Arab Republic as Egypt's official name.

In 1962, Egypt intervened in a bitter civil war in Yemen (Sanaa), now part of the country of Yemen. Egyptian soldiers could not end the conflict, but they remained in Yemen (Sanaa) until 1967.

Progress and conflict. The 1960s marked a period of economic and social change in Egypt. By 1962, Nasser's government had taken over almost all of Egypt's large-scale industries, banks, and businesses. Industry, especially textiles and food processing, expanded. Nasser turned to the Soviet Union for help in building the Aswan High Dam. Construction began in 1960, and the dam began operating in 1968. The dam improved and expanded Egypt's irrigation system and enabled Egypt to greatly increase its agricultural production.

Nasser took steps to narrow the gap between rich and poor Egyptians through land reform programs and expansion of the educational system. A law passed in 1952 made it illegal to own more than 200 *feddans* of land. (A feddan equals 1.038 acres, or 0.4201 hectare.) The government distributed any additional land to the *fellahin* (peasants). Land reform acts in the 1960s eventually limited land ownership to 50 feddans by any single landowner or to 100 feddans by a family. At the same time, the government built more schools in an attempt to improve educational opportunities. Many poor Egyptians were able to receive an education and eventually rise to professional and bureaucratic positions.

Anwar el-Sadat, Jimmy Carter, and Menachem Begin (left to right), shaking hands following the Camp David Accords

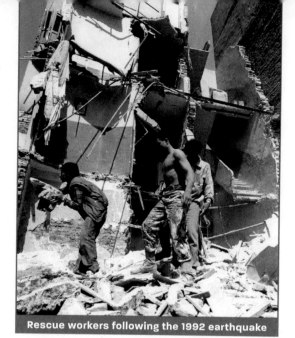

Rescue workers following the 1992 earthquake

On June 5, 1967, regional tensions erupted again in an Arab-Israeli war. This six-day conflict was brief but decisive. In the war, Israel almost completely destroyed the air forces of Egypt and other Arab countries. The Israeli army then invaded the Sinai Peninsula and positioned itself on the eastern bank of the Suez Canal. When the fighting ended on June 10, Israel also occupied the Gaza Strip, the West Bank of the Jordan River, and the Golan Heights of Syria. The UN arranged a cease-fire.

The war was a territorial and military disaster for the Arab countries. Nasser had overestimated Egypt's military preparedness. The swift Israeli assaults took the Egyptian forces by surprise.

After the 1967 war, Nasser resigned. But the Egyptian people refused to accept his resignation. Nasser remained president until his sudden death in 1970.

Renewed warfare and peace. Vice President Anwar el-Sadat won the struggle for power that followed Nasser's death. He changed Egypt's official name to the Arab Republic of Egypt in 1971.

Sadat proved to be a shrewd politician. He worked toward two goals: (1) the restoration of lands lost to Israel, and (2) economic growth. To achieve these goals, he believed that the support of the United States was vital. Thus, Sadat broke the ties with the Soviet Union that Nasser had maintained.

In October 1973, along with Syria, Sadat launched a bold and unexpected military assault across the Suez Canal against the Israelis in the Sinai Peninsula. His early success helped win support from other Arab countries. But the Israeli

army, resupplied by the United States, eventually drove Egyptian forces back across the Suez Canal. Nevertheless, Sadat drew U.S. attention to the importance of stability in the Middle East and emerged as a powerful world leader. Egypt and Israel agreed to a separation of their forces in the Sinai in 1974. In 1975, they reached an agreement in which Israel removed its troops from a part of the Sinai that it had occupied since 1967. The Suez Canal, which had been closed as a result of the 1967 war, reopened in June 1975.

Sadat sought to regain the entire Sinai Peninsula and to end the state of war readiness that existed between Egypt and Israel. In 1977, he made a historic trip to Israel and addressed the Israeli Knesset (parliament). The following year, Sadat and Israeli prime minister Menachem Begin met in the United States for discussions with U.S. president Jimmy Carter. The discussions resulted in a major agreement called the Camp David Accords. It was the first such agreement between Israel and an Arab state. The agreement guaranteed the return of the Sinai Peninsula to Egypt, and called for the creation of a peace treaty between Egypt and Israel. The treaty was signed in 1979.

At home, Sadat worked to revitalize the private sector of the economy. His economic policy, called *infitah* (opening), was designed to allow foreign investment in Egypt and greater private participation in the economy. Sadat hoped to improve relations with the United States and bring about economic growth.

Despite Sadat's vision, his policies did not meet with great success. Other Arab states rejected his treaty with Israel and criticized Sadat for negotiating independently of them. They removed Egypt from the Arab League in 1979. Many Egyptians felt Sadat had given up too much to Israel to regain the Sinai Peninsula. In addition, prosperity did not follow the signing of the Accords, as many had hoped. Discontent grew, led by radical Islamic groups. A group of extremists assassinated Sadat in October 1981 as he watched a parade.

Recent developments. Vice President Hosni Mubarak succeeded Sadat as president. He reaffirmed Sadat's peace treaty with Israel, sustained ties with the United States, and encouraged the private sector of the economy. But Mubarak was much less outspoken on many controversial issues and worked to repair Egypt's ties with other Arab countries. Egypt was readmitted to the Arab League in 1989.

Egypt's strategic importance enabled it to gain economic and military aid from the United States and the Soviet Union. But these alliances did not benefit the people greatly. Egypt's problems remain much the same as throughout the 1900s. The population is too large for Egypt's resources and continues to grow rapidly.

In 1990, Iraq invaded Kuwait. Egypt took a leading role in Arab opposition to the invasion. In early 1991, war broke out between Iraq and a coalition that was formed by the United States, Egypt, and other nations. Egyptian troops participated in the efforts to liberate Kuwait.

In October 1992, an earthquake struck Cairo and neighboring suburbs. The disaster caused more than 560 deaths and about $1 billion in property damages.

In the early 1990s, violence by radical Islamist organizations, particularly the Islamic Group, increased. These groups attacked Egyptian Christians and foreigners, especially foreign tourists. In a crackdown on the violence, Egyptian authorities raided extremist strongholds. They made mass arrests and imprisoned thousands of suspects. A number were executed. The Egyptian government also used the state-controlled media to discredit armed Islamist groups. As a result, extremist violence became less of a threat by the end of the 1990s. However, restrictive emergency regulations remained in place.

In 1997, President Mubarak launched a massive, 20-year development project to irrigate desert land and turn it into farmland. Under this project, water is to be pumped from Lake Nasser through a canal to a region of the Western Desert. The area under development is to be called the New Valley. The government expects the New Valley to provide homes and farms for Egypt's fast-growing population.

Meanwhile, Egypt's government sold some of its companies to private owners. The aim of this *privatization* was to attract domestic and foreign investment, help the country's economy, and create jobs.

In the early 2000s, Egypt saw a resumption of violence against tourist areas. Bombings in October 2004 and July 2005 killed dozens of people at resorts on the Sinai Peninsula bordering the Red Sea. Egyptian officials blamed Islamist extremists for the attacks.

In September 2005, Egypt held its first multi-candidate presidential election, and President Mubarak was reelected to a fifth term. In December 2005, Egyptians elected a new parliament. Mubarak's party retained a majority, but the Muslim Brotherhood party gained 20 percent of the seats. The Muslim Brotherhood party was banned at the time, but candidates ran as independents.

In March 2007, voters approved amendments to the Constitution in a referendum. The amendments included restrictive antiterrorism measures, increased presidential powers, and a ban on religion-based political parties and political activities. However, the Muslim Brotherhood boycotted the referendum, and opposition members claimed that it was fraudulent.

In January 2011, antigovernment protests erupted across Egypt. The protests were fueled in part by poor economic conditions and accusations of government corruption. Protesters called for an end to Mubarak's presidency. After initially refusing to resign, Mubarak stepped down on February 11. He handed power to the Egyptian military and left Cairo. The popular uprising in Egypt followed similar events in Tunisia and helped spark unrest elsewhere in the region. In August, Mubarak went on trial for the abuse of power to gain personal wealth and for ordering the killing of protesters.

Amidst steady demonstrations against military rule, Egyptians voted in parliamentary elections in 2011. Islamist parties won the vast majority of seats. In June 2012, voters elected Mohamed Morsi of the Freedom and Justice Party (FJP) as Egypt's new president. The FJP is the political arm of the Muslim Brotherhood.

In November, Morsi helped negotiate a cease-fire between Hamas and Israel in a brief Gaza Strip conflict. The same month, however, he sparked large protests in Cairo by giving himself what some Egyptians considered dictatorial powers. In December, Egyptian voters approved a new constitution, allowing for parliamentary elections in 2013.

MLA Citation

"Egypt." *The Southwestern Advantage Topic Source.* Nashville: Southwestern. 2013.

DATA

Economic Production in Egypt

Sources: Central Bank of Egypt; International Labour Organization; International Monetary Fund. Figures are for 2007.

Economic activities	% of GDP produced	Number of workers	% of all workers
Manufacturing	16	2,412,200	11
Mining	15	35,500	*
Agriculture and fishing	14	6,889,000	32
Trade, restaurants, and hotels	14	2,677,800	12
Community, government, and personal services	13	5,217,800	24
Transportation and communication	11	1,452,400	7
Finance, insurance, real estate, and business services	11	646,600	3
Construction	4	2,078,100	10
Utilities	2	282,300	1
Total	100	21,691,700	100

*Less than one-half of one percent.

ADDITIONAL RESOURCES

Books to Read

Bradley, John R. *Inside Egypt: The Land of the Pharaohs on the Brink of a Revolution.* Palgrave Macmillan, 2008.

Goldschmidt, Arthur, Jr. *Historical Dictionary of Egypt.* 3rd ed. Scarecrow, 2003.

Modern Egypt. 2nd ed. Westview, 2004.

Gutner, Howard. *Egypt.* Children's Press, 2009

Heinrichs, Ann. *Egypt.* Rev. ed. Children's Press, 2007.

Humphreys, Andrew. *The National Geographic Traveler: Egypt.* 3rd ed. National Geographic Society, 2009

Web Sites

Country Profile: Egypt

http://www.bbc.co.uk/news/world-africa-13313370

Information from the BBC.

The Institute of Egyptian Art and Archaeology

http://www.memphis.edu/egypt/

Information about art and relics from Ancient Egypt from the University of Memphis Institute of Egyptian Art and Archaeology

Search Strings

Suez Canal

Egypt Suez Canal Mediterranean Sea Red Sea (199,000)

Suez Canal Egypt war Mediterranean Sea Red Sea (94,600)

Suez Canal Egypt war "Mediterranean Sea" "Red Sea" (24,100)

Pyramids at Giza

Egypt pyramids Giza tombs mummies "Great Pyramid" "Great Sphinx" (595)

Egypt pyramids Giza tombs mummies (81,500)

Egypt pyramids Giza tombs mummies temples (59,000)

Egypt and Israel's Rocky History

Egypt Israel history Jewish state Arab Palestinians Gaza Strip (524,000)

Egypt Israel history "Jewish state" "Gaza Strip" "Camp David Accords" (1960)

Egypt Israel history "Jewish state" Palestinians "Gaza Strip" "Camp David Accords" (11,100)

Islam Influences on Egyptian Life

Egypt Islam influences Muslim culture (146,000)

Islam influences on Egyptian Life (116,000)

Islam influences on Egyptian Life Muslim culture pilgrimages government (22,700)

BACKGROUND INFORMATION

The following articles and features were written during the year in which the events took place and reflect the style and thinking of that time.

Egypt (1956)

Egypt held the center of the world stage during most of 1956 with a series of crises that threatened to start another world war. President Gamal A. Nasser bought arms from the Communist bloc, seized control of the Suez Canal, and fought a brief of war against Israel, Great Britain, and France.

National elections. Egyptians adopted a new constitution in June, providing that the country be governed by a president instead of the military council that had ruled since the ouster of King Farouk in 1952. The voters elected Nasser, the only candidate, president by more than a 9 to 1 majority. Nine out of 10 of the 5,500,000 registered voters went to the polls, and 99.87 percent approved the constitution.

British Foreign Secretary Selwyn Lloyd described Egypt's purchase of military equipment from the Soviet bloc as the greatest danger to world peace since the Communist attack on South Korea. Dag Hammarskjold, United Nations (UN) secretary-general, negotiated a truce between Egypt and Israel in April.

The Suez dispute. British forces moved out of the Suez Canal zone on June 13, turning control over to Egypt. British troops were to be allowed reoccupation of the canal zone only in case of an attack by a non-Middle East power on Egypt, the Arab countries, or Turkey. In July, the United States and Great Britain withdrew their offers of loans to help Egypt build the Aswan High Dam on the Nile River. Nasser nationalized the Suez Canal on July 26. He said he would use canal revenue to pay for the dam. This brought bitter protests and threats of military action from Great Britain and France.

Nasser rejected an 18-nation plan on August 21 that called for international control of the waterway. Then, faced with what Premier David Ben-Gurion called "imminent annihilation," Israel attacked the Sinai peninsula on October 29, thrusting within 20 miles of the Suez Canal. Two days later, Great Britain

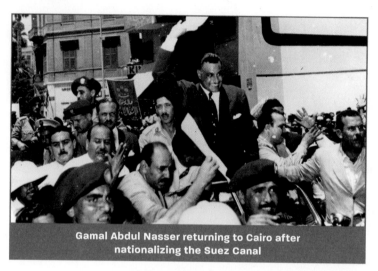

Gamal Abdul Nasser returning to Cairo after nationalizing the Suez Canal

and France launched a joint attack on Egyptian bases, with the announced intention of guarding the canal.

After days of bombing, British and French forces landed in the Port Said area. The fighting lasted only a few days, and was inconclusive. The UN General Assembly condemned the attack on Egypt, and arranged a cease-fire. The fighting stopped on November 6. A UN police force entered the fighting zone on November 15. British and French troops started leaving Egypt about December 5. The UN also started arranging for the job of clearing the canal. The waterway had been closed to all traffic after 49 ships were sunk at Port Said harbor and in the canal itself. Egypt blamed British and French bombing raids for the sinkings. Great Britain and France said Egypt deliberately sank the vessels to close the canal.

Results of the dispute. The Suez dispute strained relations between Egypt and the West. But Egypt and the Soviet Union drew more closely together. Egypt recognized Communist China in May, and severed relations with Nationalist China. British officials charged that the Soviet Union was using Egypt to penetrate Africa, but Nasser declared that Egypt never would yield to any foreign influence.

Nasser conferred with Prime Minister Jawaharlal Nehru of India and Marshal Tito of Yugoslavia in July. They endorsed "nonalignment" policies in a joint communiqué. It was after this that the United States, debating whether Egypt should be considered a "friendly neutral" or an ally of the Soviet Union, withdrew its offer to help finance the Aswan High Dam.

Everybody votes. Egypt enacted a new law in 1956, giving women and members of the armed forces the right to vote. It made voting compulsory for men over 18 years of age.

Egypt (1974)

The national euphoria released by military successes in the October 1973 war with Israel carried over into 1974. The cease-fire agreement that ended fighting between Egyptian and Israeli forces along the Suez Canal in January added more laurels to President Anwar el-Sadat's crown. As Israeli forces withdrew from parts of occupied Egyptian territory, Sadat became a greater national hero than the late president, Gamal Abdel Nasser.

With his popular mandate seemingly assured, Sadat started to liberalize and revitalize Egyptian society. An amnesty bill announced on January 28 applied to all political prisoners jailed during the Nasser and Sadat regimes. Among those released were journalist Mustafa Amin, sentenced in 1966 as a U.S. spy, and General Mahmoud Fawzi, leader of an attempt to overthrow Sadat in 1971. Amin's twin brother, Ali, subsequently returned from political exile and became editor of *al-Ahram*, Egypt's official newspaper, when editor Mohammed Heykal, a Nasser confidant, was dismissed for criticizing Sadat's policies. Press censorship ended on February 9. In November, Egyptian newspapers won the right to publish criticism of government mismanagement and corruption.

Guerrilla attack. Liberalism was not without its risks. An opposition group calling itself the Islamic Liberation Organization attacked the Cairo Military Technical Academy on April 18. Eleven persons were killed and 27 injured in the attack, and 80 guerrillas were arrested.

The group claimed it planned to kidnap Sadat and proclaim a universal Islamic community. Sadat accused Libya of financing the plot. In a Cabinet realignment on April 25, the Ministry of Libyan Affairs was abolished.

Relations with Russia cooled. Although Russia pledged a $50 million loan on October 29, it delayed promised arms deliveries. The United States gained influence, in contrast; diplomatic relations were restored in February after a seven-year break. President Richard M. Nixon received a tumultuous reception in Egypt in June and pledged $250 million in aid, including a nuclear reactor. The aid bill passed the Senate in December. The

October Arab summit conference in Rabat, Morocco, voted Egypt $1 billion in aid, and in November, Saudi Arabia approved $160 million for economic projects.

Yet Egypt's economic future remained clouded. In April, the government acknowledged that real economic growth had averaged only 4 percent a year since 1967. But a new oil field with an estimated 600 million barrels was discovered in March in the Gulf of Suez. Clearing of the Suez Canal went ahead, and the canal was expected to be open early in 1975. The government announced in May that 61 percent of the Russian loans for the Aswan High Dam had been repaid.

Rediscovering Ancient Alexandria (2001)

Explorations, including ones led by two French archaeologists, have uncovered many lost tombs, ruins, and treasures of this fabled Egyptian city.
—by Peter R. Limburg

The city of Alexandria, Egypt, was one of the glories of the ancient world. This cosmopolitan mecca, founded by Alexander the Great, was a city of broad streets, gardens, fine homes, theaters, markets, and plazas. Its library was famous, as was the lighthouse in its harbor, a towering structure that was regarded as one of the Seven Wonders of the World. With at least 400,000 residents,

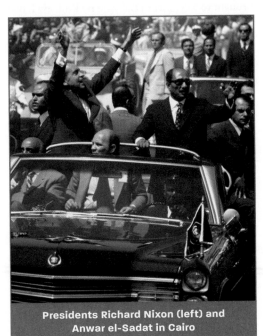

Presidents Richard Nixon (left) and Anwar el-Sadat in Cairo

Alexandria was surpassed only by Rome in population, and as a center of scholarship and scientific inquiry it had no equal.

But time was not kind to Alexandria. Unlike Athens and Rome, which retained many magnificent remnants of their glorious past, the Alexandria of old almost completely disappeared over the centuries. By the 1800s, so little was left of the ancient city that archaeologists dismissed Alexandria as an excavation site, saying it wasn't worth bothering with.

But that attitude changed. In fact, there was much to be found in Alexandria. One simply had to dig, or dive, to find it. Since the late 1800s, researchers have done just that to uncover much of Alexandria's buried past. And investigations reported in the late 1990s by two Frenchmen—archaeologist Jean-Yves Empereur and Franck Goddio, a financial consultant turned underwater explorer—have resulted in a number of new discoveries.

Much of Empereur's and Goddio's investigations have been in, and just outside, the city's harbor, where a large part of ancient Alexandria lies submerged. Their finds on the sea floor include remains that may be the ruins of royal palaces and of the famed lighthouse. These archaeological triumphs were aided by satellite technology that enabled the researchers to make detailed maps of the underwater debris. Recent discoveries have also been made on land. There, Empereur's team has assisted the Egyptian government in several excavations of ancient ruins—including of Roman houses and a vast cemetery—that were uncovered by construction crews working on building projects.

The work of both Empereur and Goddio has helped to reconstruct the Alexandria of old and to shed light on the lives of its citizens and rulers. As excavations continued, archaeologists and historians debated whether the modern city of Alexandria might be hiding the ultimate archaeological discovery: a mausoleum containing the remains of Alexander the Great.

Alexander the Great. Alexander, the Macedonian king who conquered most of the known world of his time, founded the city in 331 B.C. after taking control of Egypt from the Persian Empire. The spot he picked was on the western edge of the Nile Delta on a strip of land with the Mediterranean Sea on one side and a large freshwater lake, Lake Mareotis, on the other. A long island just offshore on the Mediterranean side, known as Pharos, shielded the site from storms and formed a partially enclosed harbor.

Tradition holds that Alexander himself traced out the perimeter for the city's fortified wall. Streets were laid out in a regular grid pattern that enabled cooling sea breezes to blow through the streets across the entire width of the city. Because the area received little rainfall, the city's builders dug a canal 20 kilometers (12 miles) to the Nile River. They also constructed the first of many cavernous cisterns—underground reservoirs—to store the water. The cisterns were artistically constructed, with graceful sculptured columns supporting high, arched ceilings. Eventually, hundreds of cisterns would be built, all fed by an underground tunnel connected to the canal.

Egypt under the Ptolemaic kings.

When Alexander died in Babylon in 323 B.C., his generals carved up the empire he had conquered. One of those officers, Ptolemy, claimed Egypt as his own and made Alexandria his capital. Ptolemy and his descendants ruled over Egypt as pharaohs for 300 years.

During his long reign, from 323 to 285 B.C., the first Ptolemy got Alexandria off to a good start. He oversaw the construction of a great "museum"—the

Archaeologist Franck Goddio with a statue of an unknown Egyptian king

equivalent of a modern university—where scholars from all over the *Hellenistic* (Greek-influenced) world studied, debated, and published their ideas. The famous library was built beside the museum to aid the scholars in their studies. Visitors to Egypt were required to surrender their books so they could be copied. At its height, the library contained at least 500,000 books, all in scroll form.

Ptolemy I also built a royal quarter with palaces and gardens, much of it on a peninsula called Cape Lochias, which formed the eastern boundary of the harbor. To connect the island of Pharos to the mainland, he constructed an artificial dike some 1,295 meters (4,250 feet) long called the Heptastadion. The Heptastadion divided the harbor into eastern and western sections, making it more resistant to storm waves.

Work on the great lighthouse began around 295 B.C. and was completed in 283 B.C. during the reign of Ptolemy II, son of the first Ptolemy. The lighthouse was built on Pharos Island and it came to be called the Pharos. Constructed of massive granite and limestone blocks, it towered to a height of about 120 meters (400 feet). Although precisely how the lighthouse functioned is not known, tradition holds that a fire blazed below the roof, its light reflected out to sea by a metal mirror.

Ptolemy II completed another project as well: a colossal tomb in Alexandria for the remains of Alexander the Great. Alexander's embalmed body, brought to Egypt from Babylon by Ptolemy I, had first been entombed in the Egyptian city of Memphis, but Alexandria was deemed a more appropriate resting place for the city's founder. The body was moved once again about a century later during the reign of Ptolemy IV. According to ancient sources, that ruler built a large Mausoleum of the Ptolemies in Alexandria for all the Ptolemaic rulers, whose coffins were placed around Alexander's.

Rome takes control of Egypt.

In the first century B.C., Egypt came increasingly under the influence of Rome, which had become the dominant power in the Mediterranean world. In 48 B.C., Julius Caesar entered Alexandria with an army in pursuit of an enemy, the Roman general Pompey. At that time, the famous Cleopatra VII and her brother Ptolemy XIII were co-rulers of Egypt. The Alexandrians objected bitterly to Caesar's presence, because he also came to straighten out Egyptian affairs and obtain money owed to Rome. Soon, war broke out between the Romans and supporters of King Ptolemy. During the fighting, the museum and library may have been badly damaged by fire.

The war ended in 47 B.C. with Ptolemy dead and the Romans in control of Egypt. Caesar supported Cleopatra's claim to the Egyptian throne, became her lover, and had a son with her. After Caesar was assassinated in 44 B.C., Cleopatra became the mistress and later the wife of Caesar's friend Mark Antony. Together they had ambitious plans for the empire. But Antony quarreled with Caesar's nephew Octavian (soon to become the emperor Augustus) and was defeated by him in a naval battle in 31 B.C. Cleopatra and Antony retreated to Alexandria to rebuild their forces, but Octavian defeated them there as well. In 30 B.C., Antony and Cleopatra committed suicide, and Egypt became a province of Rome.

Cleopatra had begun the construction of a temple in honor of Antony at the entrance to Alexandria's eastern harbor. It was completed by Augustus in 13 B.C. and named the Caesareum, dedicated to the cult of the Roman emperors, who were to be worshiped as gods. At the entrance to the temple, Augustus erected two large *obelisks* (tall, four-sided stone shafts) that became known as Cleopatra's Needles.

Alexandria's glory fades. The Roman Empire was the supreme power in the Mediterranean region for the next two centuries, but then it went into decline. In the A.D. 200s, Egypt tried to break free of Roman rule. In A.D. 272, the Roman Emperor Aurelian sent an army to lay siege to Alexandria. By the time the siege was over and the city retaken, many palaces, temples, and other structures were in ruins. Some 30 years later, the Emperor Diocletian brutally suppressed another uprising. The wreckage from these two military actions may have included the Mausoleum of the Ptolemies, which no visitor to Alexandria ever again reported seeing.

The Roman Empire split into eastern and western halves in A.D. 395. Alexandria was included in the East Roman Empire, later known as the Byzantine Empire. But Byzantine rule grew corrupt and weak, and in the year 616 Constantinople lost Alexandria to the Persians. In 642, the city fell to the Arabs. Egypt and Alexandria were now part of the growing Islamic realm.

Although Alexandria continued for several centuries to be a major port and administrative center, it gradually slipped into ruin. Buildings collapsed from disrepair or in earthquakes, and new buildings were erected atop the debris. Rubbish piled up in thick layers. In addition, the land under much of the city was slowly sinking. Most of Cape Lochias eventually disappeared under the waves of the harbor. The Heptastadion, in contrast, silted up and became a broad neck of land onto which the medieval city expanded.

The Pharos lighthouse was weakened by a series of earthquakes. In 1303, after standing guard over Alexandria's harbor for nearly 1,600 years, the structure was severely damaged by one of the most powerful earthquakes ever recorded in the Mediterranean region. Another intense earthquake in 1341 completed the destruction of the Pharos. In the late 1400s, Alexandria's Muslim ruler, Sultan Qait Bey, cleared away the debris and built a fort on the site. (The fort, named for him, still stands at the harbor entrance.)

By the middle of the 1800s, the ancient city of Alexandria had mostly vanished, submerged in the harbor or buried under a layer of dirt and stone up to 10 meters (30 feet) thick. In all of Alexandria, the only ancient structures still standing were a huge granite column known mistakenly as Pompey's Pillar (it was actually erected in honor of Diocletian)

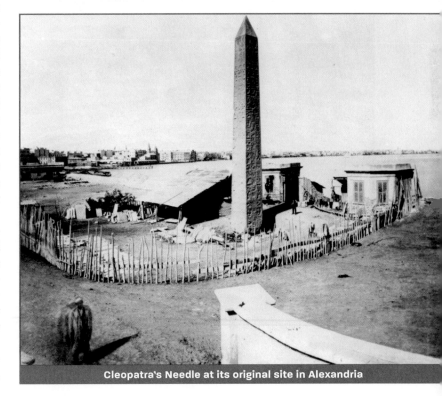
Cleopatra's Needle at its original site in Alexandria

and one of "Cleopatra's Needles"—the other had fallen over. Furthermore, because the ground was sinking, many structures on land were now some 6 meters (20 feet) lower than they were in Alexander's day, and their surviving portions were partially or completely submerged in groundwater.

New interest in a forgotten city. The world's interest in Alexandria began to revive in the late 1800s. In 1877, Great Britain, which was becoming deeply involved in Egyptian affairs, moved the fallen but undamaged Cleopatra's Needle to London. The other needle was transported to New York City in 1879 and erected in Central Park.

The rediscovery of the ancient city got seriously underway in 1892 with the founding in Alexandria of the Greco-Roman Museum. Its founder and first director, Italian archaeologist Giuseppe Botti, excavated a number of ancient underground tombs. Those included spectacular *catacombs* (underground burial chambers) in an area called Kom el-Shuqafa and the cemetery where Alexandria's earliest residents were buried. He also

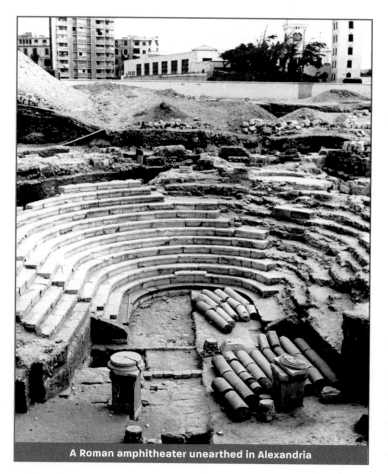
A Roman amphitheater unearthed in Alexandria

unearthed a group of tombs in a cemetery on the "island" of Pharos (it was now solidly connected to the mainland). Although most of the people living in ancient Alexandria were Greeks, their tombs often contained wall sculptures and paintings depicting both Greek and Egyptian mythology. This finding revealed that the city's Greek population had adopted many Egyptian religious beliefs and incorporated them into its own religion.

Botti's successors at the museum made further discoveries. The museum's director in the 1930s, Italian archaeologist Achille Adriani, excavated an important complex of tombs east of the city.

After World War II (1939–1945), a construction boom in Alexandria began to reveal other long-lost ruins in parts of the city where foundations for movie houses, apartments, and roads were being dug. One notable discovery was a Roman odeum, or theater, uncovered in the 1960s during the construction of a housing project. Archaeologists completely restored the theater, and it became a tourist attraction. In further excavations at that site, a team of Polish archaeologists uncovered a Roman bath complex and a complete residential quarter.

Curiosity about the sunken royal quarter. While this digging was underway on land, other investigators began turning their attention to the sea floor. In 1961, an Alexandrian archaeologist, Kamal Abu el-Saadat, explored part of the harbor and the area just off Fort Qait Bey. In the latter area, he found a huge granite statue of a Ptolemaic queen depicted as the Egyptian goddess Isis, which he persuaded the Egyptian Navy to hoist to the surface.

In 1968, the United Nations Educational, Scientific and Cultural Organization (UNESCO) sent a British marine archaeologist, Honor Frost, to examine the seabed adjacent to Fort Qait Bey. Frost made drawings of the objects lying there, including another huge statue and a sphinx, neither of which were recovered. In 1980, a team of Italian filmmakers made some dives in the area and noted many impressive remains, but again nothing was brought up.

There were several reasons why investigations of the harbor area were so few and far between. First, until Egypt made peace with Israel in 1979, the harbor was placed under strict security, and diving was forbidden. (El-Sadaat and Frost had to get special permission for their dives.) There was also a shortage of funding for archaeological expeditions.

Furthermore, the water of the harbor was itself a problem. Fouled by years of untreated discharge from the city's sewers, the water was so cloudy that visibility was usually no more than about 1.5 meters (5 feet), and swimming in it was a health hazard. That situation had not changed by the time that Empereur and Goddio launched their investigations of the harbor and nearby waters.

Goddio began his exploration in 1992, searching the harbor for the lost royal quarter. Empereur had been working periodically in Alexandria since the mid-1970s, conducting dry-land excavations, and he was the director of the Center for Alexandrian Studies, an organization he founded in 1990. In 1994, he began exploring the area at the foot of Fort Qait Bey at the request of the Egyptian government. Because the famous lighthouse had once stood on the site occupied by the fort, it was assumed that the remains of the Pharos must be close by.

In their underwater investigations, Goddio's and Empereur's teams both made extensive use of the global positioning system (GPS) to precisely map the stones and artifacts that they found on the sea floor. The GPS is a group of Earth-orbiting satellites that beam continuous radio signals to the ground. A GPS user employs a special handheld device that receives the signals from at least four satellites and uses the data to calculate the exact distance from the receiver to each of the satellites. With that information, the receiver—following a mathematical formula known as triangulation—then determines the user's location on Earth to within meters.

An even more accurate version of GPS, called differential GPS, also employs a signal from a land-based radio transmitter whose location has been precisely determined. With this system, which was used in the Alexandria underwater excavations, the receiver can calculate a position to within a couple of centimeters. Because the satellite signals don't penetrate water, the receivers being carried to the sea floor had to be linked to floating antenna buoys.

The remains of the great lighthouse.
Exploring the area off the tip of Fort Qait Bey, Empereur's team found the sea floor littered with huge blocks of stone and a number of statues, including 25 "life-sized" sphinxes. All but one of the sphinxes had their heads broken off. The archaeologists also found ceramics and the broken remains of three obelisks. The objects were scattered over an area of about 2 hectares (5 acres). Although

Empereur did a great deal of diving himself, most of the work was done by other archaeologists who descended into the murky water in wetsuits to investigate the relics, photograph them, and map their locations. Artists on the team made sketches of many of the objects. Because of the poor water quality, the divers had to scrub their skin with a powerful disinfectant after each day's work.

After viewing Empereur's photos, Egyptian government officials ordered some of the more interesting or better-preserved artifacts to be brought to the surface. Archaeologists on land washed the objects in fresh water and treated them with special chemicals to prevent further deterioration of the stone. The government then placed the relics on display. A prize piece was a colossal statue of one of the Ptolemies, perhaps Ptolemy II, dressed as a pharaoh.

But much more exciting to Empereur than statues and obelisks were some 3,000 columns and building stones that his divers found on the harbor floor spreading out from the foot of Fort Qait Bey. The divers mapped all of the stones and photographed many of the larger ones. Because some of the stones were huge—up to 11 meters (36 feet) in length, Empereur concluded that the debris was the remains of the great Pharos lighthouse.

The temple of Isis and Cleopatra's palace. Meanwhile, Goddio's team was exploring the area around Cape Lochias, which they had mapped in 1994. In addition to using the GPS, his researchers had surveyed the sea floor with *sonar*, an instrument that sends sound waves through water and receives echoes created when the waves bounce off underwater objects. They also used highly sensitive *magnetometers*, devices that can detect the presence of iron objects. The mapping effort yielded a few surprises. For one thing, it located an important sunken island called Antirhodos, which in Ptolemaic times was the site of a royal harbor and a small palace used by Cleopatra. Earlier mapmakers had incorrectly shown Antirhodos farther to the east.

After his mapping of the eastern harbor was completed, Goddio began to look for specific ruins. Searching in the vicinity of Antirhodos in the late 1990s, his divers found *amphorae*—large two-handled jugs used in ancient times for storing wine, olive oil and other liquids—and paving stones near what looked like an ancient pier. These findings suggested that the divers had perhaps found

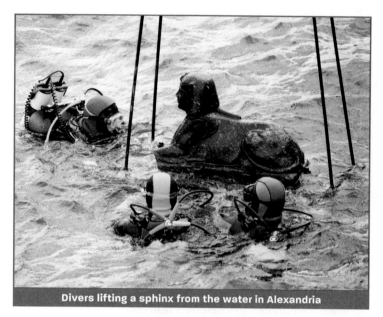

Divers lifting a sphinx from the water in Alexandria

Cleopatra's palace. An even more compelling piece of evidence was a small sphinx whose face was identified by archaeologists on Goddio's team as that of Ptolemy XII, Cleopatra's father. The divers also found a rare statue depicting a priest of Isis holding a sacred jar. Ancient sources say that the Temple of Isis was on Antirhodos.

Another of Goddio's goals was to find the remnants of the Timonium, a small palace that Mark Antony had constructed. It supposedly stood at the end of a massive stone pier extending from a small spur of land connected to the mainland. Although Goddio's divers found a stone structure about 180 meters (200 yards) long projecting from the end of a sunken promontory, they could find no evidence that a building had ever stood at the end of it. But then they found a similar construction, made of limestone blocks, extending from the base of the first structure. At its end were the remains of a large paved platform supported by still-existing wooden posts. Fallen granite columns littered the platform, suggesting that the Timonium had stood there.

The necropolis and other recent finds. While Goddio concentrated solely on the harbor, Empereur continued to be involved with land excavations as well. His most extensive work was the unearthing of portions of a vast underground cemetery at Gabbari, on the western fringe of Alexandria. The cemetery, discovered in 1997 during the construction of an expressway, was mentioned in the first century A.D. by Strabo, a

Greek historian and geographer. Amazed by the size of the complex, Strabo referred to it as the Necropolis, which means literally "city of the dead."

The segment of the necropolis excavated by Empereur and his colleagues contained more than 40 large tombs. The walls of each tomb were perforated by dozens of narrow recesses, called loculi, that had been cut into solid limestone. Several tombs contained more than 200 of these openings, which were used for multiple burials. Grooves in the interior surfaces of the loculi indicated that the rock from each one was carefully extracted as a single large plug so that it could later be cut into building blocks and sold. Empereur and his colleagues found several tombs that had been prepared for the cutting of new loculi. The outlines of the planned burial spaces were drawn in red on the solid-rock walls. The chambers also contained small wall niches designed to hold cremation urns, several of which were found.

The loculi were arrayed in rows like mailboxes in the wall of a post office. The archaeologists found the remains of up to 10 individuals in each recess, showing that burial space was at a premium in ancient Alexandria. Many of the skeletons in the loculi were fairly well preserved and provided valuable information to anthropologists. By examining the bones, researchers could tell many things about the deceased people: their sex, height and build; their approximate age when they died; whether they were well-nourished; and what serious illnesses they suffered from. The researchers also recovered genetic material from many of the bones. They hoped that a study of the genes would reveal family relationships among the people buried in the crypts as well as their racial origins.

An interesting sidelight in the investigation of the necropolis was the discovery of ancient plates with traces of food still on them, together with cups and amphorae containing wine residues. These findings revealed that Alexandrians shared festive meals in the presence of their dead friends and relatives.

Another important project carried out by Empereur's team was an excavation at the site of the Diana Theater, a 1930s-era building in downtown Alexandria that had been torn down to make way for new construction. Beneath the theater's foundation, the ruins of a Roman mansion from the A.D. 100s came to light. In the remains of the house, the archaeologists discovered a beautiful and well-preserved floor *mosaic* (a picture made from many small tiles) depicting Medusa, a female monster in Greek mythology who had snakes for hair.

Empereur and his colleagues also did a search for the city's cisterns, almost all of which had been abandoned and forgotten by the 1900s. They succeeded in locating about a hundred of the elaborate reservoirs.

Alexander's tomb. But what every archaeologist who explores Alexandria would undoubtedly like to find more than anything else is the tomb of Alexander the Great. Might the Mausoleum of the Ptolemies, and perhaps even the body of Alexander, still exist? And if so, where would they most likely be found?

Although some historians and archaeologists believe the mausoleum was probably destroyed in one of the devastating sieges of the late A.D. 200s, Empereur thinks it may simply have been buried under debris and forgotten. Somewhere in Alexandria, he hopes, the tomb awaits rediscovery.

That seems possible because a large portion of an ancient tomb that may have been Alexander's second burial place survived the upheavals of the 200s. That structure, discovered in the early 1900s in an area known as the Latin cemeteries, is known as the Alabaster Tomb for the type of stone of which it is made. The Alabaster Tomb was actually just the entryway to a large underground burial chamber. Unfortunately, no trace remains of that vital subterranean section. The Alabaster Tomb was built in the Mace-

donian architectural style, with large, flat slabs of stone, and has been dated to the beginning of the Hellenistic era. If it was not Alexander's tomb, Empereur believes, it was surely the tomb of a high-ranking official of the early Ptolemaic kingdom.

Empereur theorizes that Alexander's final resting place, the Mausoleum of the Ptolemies—if it still exists— may lie elsewhere in the Latin cemeteries or in a nearby area called the Shallalat Gardens. Sections of the gardens and the Latin cemeteries are in the same part of the city where, according to several ancient writers, there was a royal cemetery.

As archaeologists labored to reclaim Alexandria's ancient heritage, a monumental new library—a joint effort of the Egyptian government and UNESCO—was nearing completion in 2000. The $185-million facility was designed to be a combined cultural center and research library with an emphasis on the history and archaeology of Alexandria and Egypt. While the library was rising on the shoreline, both Empereur and Goddio proposed that the harbor of Alexandria be cleaned up and turned into an underwater archaeological park. There, in sight of the new library, a symbol of both the city's past and its future, visitors would be able to view the ruins of the fabled lighthouse and other remnants of Alexandria's Golden Age.

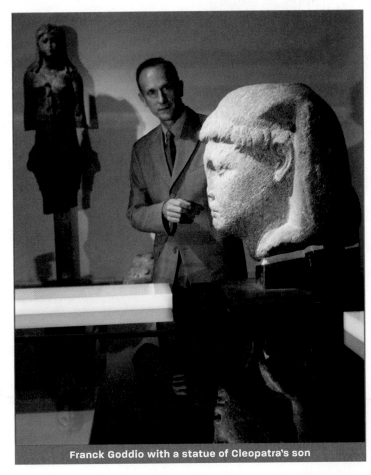

Franck Goddio with a statue of Cleopatra's son

Ancient Egypt

Ancient Egypt was an advanced culture that originated in the Nile River Valley of northeastern Africa about 5,000 years ago. This exceptional civilization lasted over 2,000 years. Ancient Egyptians created a 365-day calendar, basic forms of math, a national government, hieroglyphics, and papyrus. They are best-known for building pyramids.

HOT topics

Afterlife/Mummification Process/Rituals.

Ancient Egyptians mummified their dead in the belief that the body had to be preserved for the afterlife. This process required that the bodies be embalmed and dried. Then, after certain organs were removed, the body was treated with resins used to seal out moisture. After that it was wrapped in linen bandages. The body would then be placed inside a coffin or a number of coffins, each inside of the other. Finally, the mummies were hidden inside secret chambers in large tombs, along with gold treasures, precious objects, and their internal organs, which were placed in canopic jars.

DEFINITIONS

dynasty: a series of rulers who belong to the same family; a line of kings or princes

hieroglyphic: a picture, character, or symbol standing for a word, idea, or sound; hieroglyph. The ancient Egyptians used hieroglyphics instead of an alphabet like ours.

papyrus: a tall water plant from which the ancient Egyptians, Greeks, and Romans made a kind of paper to write on. It belongs to the sedge family. Papyrus has stems three to ten feet high, and though it is comparatively rare today, it is still found in Egypt, Ethiopia, Syria, and Sicily. Papyrus is the bulrush of the Bible.

Pharaoh or pharaoh: the title given to the kings of ancient Egypt.

the Pyramids: any one of the huge, massive stone pyramids, serving as royal tombs, built by the ancient Egyptians.

Sphinx: a huge stone statue with a man's head and a lion's body, near Cairo, Egypt.

HOT topics

Egyptian Gods and Goddesses. Many gods and goddesses were worshiped by the ancient Egyptians. For example, the sun god Re and the goddess Rennutet were worshiped to ensure good harvests. The goddess Isis was worshiped as a devoted mother and wife, Osiris governed vegetation and the dead, and Horus was the lord of heaven. In each city and town, the people worshiped their own special deity as well as the major ones.

Egyptian Pyramids. Ancient Egyptians built pyramids as tombs for their rulers, who were mummified and then hidden inside secret chambers within the pyramids. The pyramids were, and still are, architectural marvels. Temples were usually attached to the pyramids and used for funeral ceremonies. There are ten pyramids at Giza including the Great Pyramid, the largest, which was built for King Khufu. The Great Sphinx, a huge statue of a sphinx, also stands amongst these pyramids.

Hieroglyphics. Hieroglyphics are picture symbols used to represent ideas and sounds. Ancient Egyptians, as well as some other ancient cultures, used hieroglyphics as a form of writing. After the Egyptians replaced hieroglyphics with a simpler alphabet, eventually the ability to read hieroglyphics was lost, that is, until the discovery and deciphering of the Rosetta stone.

Rosetta Stone. In 1799, a stone tablet was discovered near Rosetta, Egypt. This Rosetta stone was inscribed in three scripts—Egyptian hieroglyphic, Egyptian demotic, and Greek. Up until this time, the ability to read hieroglyphics had been lost. But, in 1822, by using the Egyptian demotic and the Greek inscriptions, Jean François Champollion was able to decipher the entire text, which turned out to be a decree honoring King Ptolemy V. The ability to decipher hieroglyphics has given us the ability to learn ancient Egyptian history.

Sarcophagus

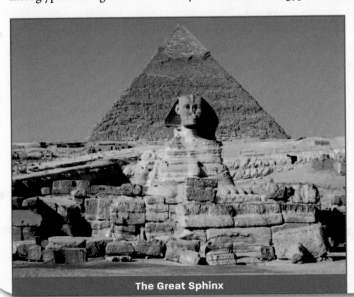

The Great Sphinx

TRUE or FALSE?

Ancient Egyptians did not use money.

THE BASICS

Ancient Egypt was the birthplace of one of the world's first civilizations. This advanced culture arose about 5,000 years ago in the Nile River Valley in northeastern Africa. It thrived for over 2,000 years and so became one of the longest lasting civilizations in history.

The mighty Nile River was the lifeblood of ancient Egypt. Every year, it overflowed and deposited a strip of rich, black soil along each bank. The fertile soil enabled farmers to raise a huge supply of food. The ancient Egyptians called their country *Kemet*, meaning *Black Land*, after the dark soil. The Nile also provided water for irrigation and was Egypt's main transportation route. For all these reasons, the ancient Greek historian Herodotus called Egypt "the gift of the Nile."

The ancient Egyptians made outstanding contributions to the development of civilization. They created the world's first national government,

Hieroglyphics

basic forms of arithmetic, and a 365-day calendar. They invented a form of picture writing called *hieroglyphics*. They also invented *papyrus*, a paper-like writing material made from the stems of papyrus plants. The Egyptians developed one of the first religions to emphasize life after death. They built great cities in which many skilled architects, doctors, engineers, painters, and sculptors worked.

The best-known achievements of the ancient Egyptians, however, are the pyramids they built as tombs for their rulers. The most famous pyramids stand at Giza. These gigantic stone structures—marvels of architectural and engineering skills—have been preserved by the dry climate for about 4,500 years. They serve as spectacular reminders of the glory of ancient Egypt.

The Egyptian World

The land. Ancient Egypt was a long, narrow country through which the Nile River flowed. Deserts bordered the country on the east, south, and west. The Mediterranean Sea lay to the north. The Nile River flowed north out of central Africa through the Egyptian desert to the Mediterranean. The Egyptians called the desert *Deshret*, meaning *Red Land*. The Nile's course through Egypt was about 600 miles (1,000 kilometers). The river split into several channels north of what is now Cairo, forming the Nile Delta. Rolling desert land lay west of the Nile Valley, and mountains rose to the east.

The Nile River flooded its banks each year. The flooding started in June, with the rainy season in central Africa. The rains raised the level of the river as the Nile flowed northward. The floodwaters usually went down in September, leaving a strip of fertile land about 6 miles (10 kilometers) wide on each riverbank. Farmers then plowed and seeded the rich soil. The Egyptians also depended on the Nile as their chief transportation route. Memphis and Thebes—two capitals of ancient Egypt—and many other cities developed along the river because of its importance to farming and transportation.

The people. Most people of ancient Egypt lived in the Nile River Valley. Scholars believe the valley had from about one million to four million people, and

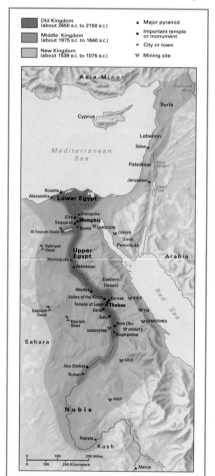

Map of Ancient Egypt

possibly more, at various times during ancient Egypt's history. The rest of the population lived in the delta and in oases west of the river, in the Libyan Desert.

The ancient Egyptians had dark skin and dark hair. They spoke a language that was related both to the Semitic languages of southwestern Asia and to certain languages of northern Africa. The Egyptian language was written in hieroglyphics, a system of picture symbols that stood for ideas and sounds. The Egyptians began to use this system about 3000 B.C. It consisted of more than 700 picture symbols. The Egyptians used hieroglyphics to inscribe monuments and temples and to record official texts. For everyday use, they developed simpler hieroglyphic forms called *hieratic* and *demotic*.

During the New Kingdom (about 1539–1075 B.C.), ancient Egypt had three main social classes—upper, middle, and lower. The upper class consisted of the royal family, rich landowners, government officials, high-ranking priests and army officers, and doctors. The middle class was made up chiefly of merchants, manufacturers, and craft workers. The lower class, the largest class by far, consisted of unskilled laborers. Most of them worked on farms. Prisoners captured in foreign wars became slaves and formed a separate class.

Ancient Egypt's class system was not rigid. People in the lower or middle class, as well as slaves, could move to a higher position. They improved their status mainly through marriage or success in their jobs. Even slaves had rights. They could own personal items, get married, and inherit land. They could also be given their freedom.

Life of the People

Family life. The father headed the family in ancient Egypt. Upon his death, his oldest son became the head. Women had almost as many rights as men. They could own and inherit property, buy and sell goods, and make a will. A wife could obtain a divorce. Few other ancient civilizations gave women all these rights.

Children played with dolls, tops, and stuffed leather balls. They had board games with moves determined by the throw of dice. They also had several kinds of pets, including cats, dogs, monkeys, baboons, and birds.

Kings commonly had several wives at once. In many cases, a king's chief wife belonged to the royal family.

Education. Only a small percentage of boys and girls went to school in ancient Egypt, and most of them came from upper-class families. These students attended schools for scribes. Scribes made written records for government offices, temples, and other institutions. They also read and wrote letters for the large numbers of Egyptians who could not read and write.

The king's palace, government departments, and temples operated the scribal schools. All the schools prepared the students to become scribes or to follow other careers. The main subjects were reading, literature, geography, mathematics, and writing. The students learned writing by copying literature, letters, and business accounts. They used papyrus, the world's first paper-like material, and wrote with brushes made of reeds whose ends were softened and shaped. The Egyptians made ink by mixing water and soot, a black powder formed in the burning of wood or other substances.

Most Egyptian boys followed their fathers' occupations and were taught by their fathers. Some boys thus learned a trade, but the majority became farmers. Many parents placed their sons with master craftsmen, who taught carpentry, pottery making, or other skills. Boys who wanted to become doctors probably went to work with a doctor after finishing their basic schooling. Most girls were trained for the roles of wife and mother. Their mothers

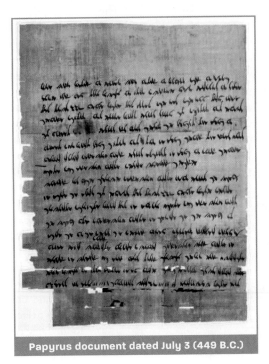

Papyrus document dated July 3 (449 B.C.)

taught them cooking, sewing, and other skills.

Ancient Egypt had many libraries. A famous library in Alexandria had about 500,000 papyrus scrolls, which dealt with astronomy, geography, and many other subjects. Alexandria also had an outstanding museum.

Food, clothing, and shelter. Bread was the chief food in the diet of most ancient Egyptians, and beer was the favorite beverage. The bread was made from wheat, and the beer from barley. Many Egyptians also enjoyed a variety of vegetables and fruits, fish, milk, cheese, butter, and meat from ducks and geese. Wealthy Egyptians regularly ate beef, antelope and gazelle meat, and fancy cakes and other baked goods. They drank grape, date, and palm wine. The people ate with their fingers.

The Egyptians generally dressed in white linen garments. Women wore robes or tight dresses with shoulder straps. Men wore skirts or robes. The Egyptians often wore colored, shoulder-length headdresses.

Rich Egyptians wore wigs, partly for protection against the sun. Wealthy Egyptians also wore sandals made of papyrus or palm leaves. The common people usually went barefoot. Young children rarely wore any clothes.

The ancient Egyptians liked to use cosmetics and wear jewelry. Women wore red lip powder, dyed their hair, and painted their fingernails. They outlined their eyes and colored their eyebrows with gray, black, or green paint. Men also outlined their eyes and often wore as much makeup as women. Both sexes used perfume and wore necklaces, rings, and bracelets. Combs, mirrors, and razors were common grooming aids.

The Egyptians built their houses with bricks of dried mud. They used trunks of palm trees to support the flat roofs. Many city houses were narrow buildings with three or more floors. Most poor Egyptians lived in one- to three-room huts. The typical middle-class Egyptian lived in a one- or two-story house with several rooms. Many rich Egyptians had houses with as many as seventy rooms. Some of these homes were country estates with orchards, pools, and large gardens. Egyptian houses had small windows placed high in the walls to help keep out the sun. The people spread wet mats on the floors and hung them on the walls and porches to help cool the air inside their houses. On hot nights, they often slept on the roof, where it was cooler.

Ancient Egyptian furniture included wooden stools, chairs, beds, and chests. People used pottery to store, cook, and serve food. They cooked food in clay ovens or over fires and used

charcoal and wood for fuel. Oil lamps provided lighting. The lamps had flax wicks and burned oil in shallow bowls or hollowed-out stones.

Recreation. The ancient Egyptians enjoyed numerous leisure activities. They fished and swam in the Nile River. Sailing on the Nile was a popular family activity. Adventurous Egyptians hunted crocodiles, lions, hippopotamuses, and wild cattle with bows and arrows or spears. Many Egyptians liked to watch wrestling matches. At home, the Egyptians played *senet*, a board game similar to backgammon.

Religion

Gods and goddesses. The ancient Egyptians believed that various *deities* (gods and goddesses) influenced every aspect of nature and every human activity. They therefore worshiped many *deities*. The main god was the sun god Re. The Egyptians relied on Re and the goddess Rennutet for good harvests. The most important goddess was Isis. She represented the devoted mother and wife. Her husband and brother, Osiris, ruled over vegetation and the dead. Horus, son of Isis and Osiris, was god of the sky. He was called the lord of heaven and was often pictured with the head of a falcon.

In each city and town, the people worshiped their own special deity as well as the major ones. The people of Thebes worshiped Amun. Amun was later identified with Re and called Amun-Re. In time, Amun-Re became the chief deity. Other local deities and their main centers of worship

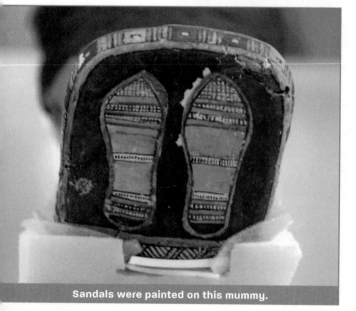
Sandals were painted on this mummy.

included Ptah, the creator god of Memphis; Thoth, the god of wisdom and writing in Hermopolis; and Khnum, the creator god of Elephantine. Many deities were pictured with human bodies and the heads of animals. Such a head suggested a real or imagined quality of the animal and made identification of the deity easy.

Most ancient Egyptians prayed at home because the temples did not offer regular services for people. Each temple was either regarded as the home of a certain deity or dedicated to a dead king. A temple built in honor of Amun-Re at Karnak was the country's largest temple. It had more than 130 columns that rose about 80 feet (24 meters). Brilliantly colored paintings decorated the columns and walls in the temple's Great Hall, which still ranks as the largest columned hall ever built.

The priests' main job was to serve the deity or king, who was represented by a statue in the temple. The king reigning at the time was considered the chief priest of Egypt. Each day, he or other local priests washed and dressed the statue and brought it food. Priests also offered prayers requested by individuals.

The afterlife. The ancient Egyptians believed that they could enjoy life after death. This belief in an *afterlife* sometimes led to much preparation for death and burial. It resulted, for example, in the construction of the pyramids and other great tombs for kings and queens. Other Egyptians had smaller tombs.

The Egyptians believed that the bodies of the dead had to be preserved for the next life, and so they *mummified* (embalmed and

Temple of Horus

dried) corpses to prevent them from decaying. After a body was mummified, it was wrapped in layers of linen strips and placed in a coffin. The mummy was then put in a tomb. Some Egyptians mummified pets, including cats and monkeys. A number of Egyptian mummies have lasted to the present day.

The Egyptians filled their tombs with items for use in the afterlife. These items included clothing, wigs, food, cosmetics, and jewelry. The tombs of rich Egyptians also had statues rep-

resenting servants who would care for them in the next world. Scenes of daily life were painted on walls inside the tombs. The Egyptians believed that certain prayers said by priests would bring the scenes, as well as the dead, to life.

Many Egyptians bought texts containing prayers, hymns, spells, and other information to guide souls through the afterlife, protect them from evil, and provide for their needs. Egyptians had passages from such texts carved or written on walls inside their tombs or had a copy of a text placed in their tombs. Collections of these texts are known as the Book of the Dead.

Work of the People

Most of the workers in the fertile Nile Valley were farm laborers. Great harvests year after year helped make Egypt rich. Many other people made their living in manufacturing, mining, transportation, or trade.

The Egyptians did not use money. Instead, they traded goods or services directly for other goods or services. Under

Stone jars, luxuries thought to be needed in the afterlife

this *barter* system, workers were often paid in wheat and barley. They used any extra quantities they got to trade for needed goods.

Agriculture. Most farm laborers worked on the large estates of the royal family, the temples, or other wealthy landowners. They received small amounts of crops as pay, partly because landowners had to turn over a large percentage of all farm production in taxes. Some farmers were able to rent fields from rich landowners.

Ancient Egypt was a hot country in which almost no rain fell. But farmers grew crops most of the year by irrigating their land. They built canals that carried water from the Nile to their fields. Farmers used wooden plows pulled by oxen to prepare the fields for planting.

Wheat and barley were the main crops of ancient Egypt. Other crops included lettuce, beans, onions, figs, dates, grapes, melons, and cucumbers. Parts of the date and grape crops were crushed to make wine. Many farmers grew flax, which was used to make linen. The Egyptians raised dairy and beef cattle, goats, ducks, sheep, geese, and donkeys. Some people kept bees for honey.

Manufacturing and mining. Craftsmen who operated small shops made most of the manufactured goods in ancient Egypt. The production of linen clothing and linen textiles ranked among the chief industries. Other important products included pottery, bricks, tools, glass, weapons, furniture, jewelry, and perfume. The Egyptians also made many products from plants, including rope, baskets, mats, and sheets of writing material.

Ancient Egypt had rich supplies of minerals. Miners produced large quantities of limestone, sandstone, and granite for the construction of pyramids and monuments. They also mined copper, gold, and such semiprecious gems as turquoise, amethyst, and malachite. Much of Egypt's gold came from the hills east of the Nile and from Nubia, a country south of Egypt.

Trade and transportation. Ancient Egyptian traders sailed to lands bordering the Aegean, Mediterranean, and Red seas. They acquired silver, horses, and cedar logs from Syria, Lebanon, and other areas of southwestern Asia. They got ivory, leopard skins, gold, cattle, and spices from Nubia. For these goods, the Egyptians bartered gold, other minerals, wheat, barley, papyrus sheets, and wine.

Transportation within ancient Egypt was chiefly by boats and barges on the Nile River. The earliest Egyptian boats were made of papyrus reeds. Moved by poles at first, they later were powered by rowers with oars. By about 3200 B.C., the Egyptians had invented sails and begun to rely on the wind for power. About 3000 B.C., they started to use wooden planks to build ships.

During ancient Egypt's early history, most people walked or rode donkeys when they traveled by land. Wealthy Egyptians were carried on special chairs. During the 1600s B.C., the Egyptians began to ride in horse-drawn chariots.

Crafts and professions. The royal family and the temples of ancient Egypt employed many skilled architects, engineers, carpenters, artists, and sculptors. They also hired bakers, butchers, teachers, scribes, accountants, musicians, butlers, and shoemakers. The Egyptians' belief that their bodies had to be preserved for the afterlife made embalming a highly skilled profession. Many Egyptians served in the army and navy. Others worked on cargo ships or fishing boats.

Arts and Sciences

Architecture. Ancient Egypt's pyramids are the oldest and largest stone structures in the world. The ruins of about ninety pyramids still stand along the Nile. Three huge pyramids at Giza rank as one of the Seven Wonders of the Ancient World, a list of sights compiled by ancient travelers. The first Egyptian pyramids were built about 4,500 years ago. The largest one, the Great Pyramid at Giza, stands about 450 feet (140 meters) high. Its base covers about 13 acres (5 hectares). This pyramid was built with more than two million limestone blocks, each weighing an average of 2½ tons (2.3 metric tons).

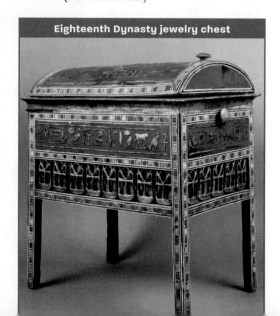

Eighteenth Dynasty jewelry chest

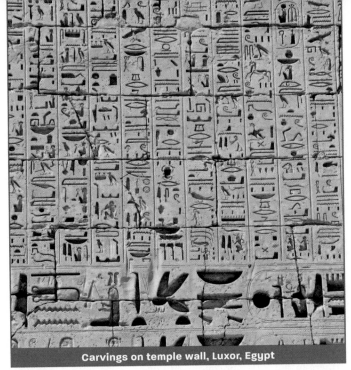

Carvings on temple wall, Luxor, Egypt

The ancient Egyptians also built temples of limestone. They designed parts of the temples to resemble plants. For example, some temples had columns carved to look like palm trees or papyrus reeds. The temples had three main sections—a small shrine, a large hall with many columns, and an open courtyard.

Painting and sculpture. Many of ancient Egypt's finest paintings and other works of art were produced for tombs and temples. Artists covered the walls of tombs with bright, imaginative scenes of daily life and pictorial guides to the afterlife. The tomb paintings were not simply decorations. They reflected the Egyptians' belief that the scenes could come to life in the next world. The tomb owners therefore had themselves pictured not only as young and attractive but also in highly pleasant settings that they wished to enjoy in the afterlife.

Ancient Egyptian sculptors decorated temples with carvings showing festivals, military victories, and other important events. Sculptors also carved large stone sphinxes. These statues were supposed to represent Egyptian kings or gods and were used to guard temples and tombs. The Great Sphinx, for example, is believed to represent either King Khafre or the god Re-Harakhte. This magnificent statue has a human head and the body of a lion. It is 240 feet (73 meters) long and about 66 feet (20 meters) high. The Great Sphinx, which is near the Great Pyramid at Giza, was carved about 4,500 years ago. Sculptors also created small figures from wood, ivory, alabaster, bronze, gold, and turquoise. Favorite subjects for small sculptures included cats, which the Egyptians considered sacred and valued for protecting their grain supplies from mice.

Music and literature. The ancient Egyptians enjoyed music and singing. They used harps, lutes, and other string instruments to accompany their singing. Egyptian love songs were poetic and passionate.

Writers created many stories that featured imaginary characters, settings, or events and were clearly meant to entertain. Other writings included essays on good living called "Instructions."

Sciences. The ancient Egyptians made observations in the fields of astronomy and geography that helped them develop a calendar of 365 days a year. The calendar was based on the annual flooding of the Nile. The flooding began soon after the star Sirius reappeared on the eastern horizon after months of being hidden. This reappearance occurred about June 20 each year. The calendar enabled the Egyptians to date much of their history. Dated materials from ancient Egypt have helped scholars date events in other parts of the ancient world.

The ancient Egyptians could measure areas, volumes, distances, lengths, and weights. They used geometry to determine farm borders. Mathematics was based on a system of counting by tens, but the system had no zeros.

Ancient Egyptian doctors were the first physicians to study the human body scientifically. They studied human anatomy and knew that the pulse was in some way connected with the heart. They could set broken bones, care for wounds, and treat many illnesses. Some doctors specialized in a particular field of medicine, such as eye defects or stomach disorders.

Government

Kings ruled ancient Egypt throughout most of its history. Sometime between 1554 and 1304 B.C., the people began to call the king *pharaoh*. The word *pharaoh* comes from words that meant *great house* in Egyptian. The Egyptians believed that each of their kings was the god Horus in human form. This belief helped strengthen the authority of the kings.

The position of king was inherited. It passed to the eldest son of the king's chief wife. Many Egyptian kings had several other wives, called *lesser wives*, at the same time. Some chief wives gave birth to daughters but no sons, and several of those daughters claimed the right to the throne. At least four women became rulers.

Officials called *viziers* helped the king govern ancient Egypt. By the 1400s B.C., the king appointed two of them. One vizier administered the Nile Delta area, and the other one managed the region to the south. The viziers acted as mayors, tax collectors, and judges, and some even controlled temple treasuries. Other high officials included a treasurer and army commander. The government collected taxes from farmers in the form of crops. Skilled workers paid taxes in the goods or services they produced. The treasuries of kings and temples were thus actually warehouses consisting largely of crops and various manufactured goods. The government also levied a *corvee* (tax paid in the form of labor) to obtain troops and government workers.

For purposes of local government, ancient Egypt was divided into forty-two provinces called *nomes*. The king appointed an official known as a *nomarch* to govern each province. There were courts in each nome and a high court in the capital. Viziers judged most cases. Kings decided cases involving crimes punishable by death.

In its early days, ancient Egypt had a small army of foot soldiers equipped with spears. During the 1500s B.C., Egypt built up a large army. The army included archers who were trained to shoot accurately while riding in fast-moving, horse-drawn

Pyramid of Khafre, Giza, Egypt

chariots. Egypt had a large navy of long ships. These ships were powered chiefly by oarsmen, though most vessels also had sails.

History

Beginnings. The earliest known communities in ancient Egypt were villages established over 5,000 years ago. In time, the villages became part of two kingdoms. One of these kingdoms controlled the villages that lay on the Nile Delta, and the other controlled the villages south of the delta. The delta area was known as Lower Egypt. The southern region was called Upper Egypt.

Egyptian civilization began about 3100 B.C. According to tradition, King Menes of Upper Egypt conquered Lower Egypt around that time. He then united the country and formed the world's first national government. Menes founded Memphis as his capital near the site of present-day Cairo. He also established the first of thirty Egyptian *dynasties* (series of rulers in the same family).

The early dynastic period of ancient Egyptian history covered Dynasties I and II, which ruled for about 300 years. During this period, the kings built a temple to Ptah, the chief god of Memphis, and erected several palaces near the temple. The Egyptians also developed irrigation systems, invented ox-drawn plows, and started to develop a bureaucracy during the first two dynasties.

The Old Kingdom, which lasted from about 2650 to 2150 B.C., included Dynasties III through VIII. By the time Dynasty III began, Egypt had a strong central government. The Old Kingdom became known for the construction of Egypt's giant pyramids. This period is sometimes called the Pyramid Age.

The first known Egyptian pyramid was built for King Zoser at Saqqarah about 2650 B.C. The tomb rises about 200 feet (60 meters) in six giant steps and is called the Step Pyramid. During Dynasty IV, workers built the Great Pyramid and other pyramids at Giza. The Great Pyramid was built for King Khufu. Huge pyramids were built nearby for his son, King Khafre, and for King Menkaure. Farm laborers worked on the pyramids when floodwaters of the Nile covered their fields.

By Dynasty VI, the king's authority had begun to weaken as high priests and government officials fought for power. Dynasties VII through XI had weak rulers. Dynasties IX and X and the first half of Dynasty XI ruled during what is known as the

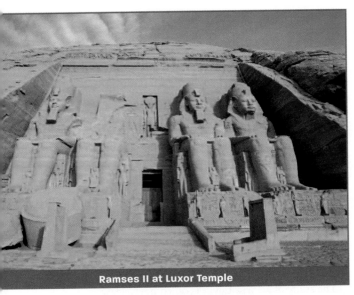
Ramses II at Luxor Temple

first intermediate period. The capital was finally moved to Thebes.

The Middle Kingdom was the period that began in the last half of Dynasty XI and continued through Dynasty XIII or XIV. The Middle Kingdom began in the early 1900s B.C., when Mentuhotep II unified Egypt. Amenemhet I, a vizier in southern Egypt, began Dynasty XII around 1938 B.C., when he seized the throne and moved the capital to Itjtawy, near Memphis. Amenemhet and his strong successors, including Senusret I, Senusret III, and Amenemhet III, helped restore Egypt's wealth and power. During Dynasty XII, Egypt conquered Nubia and promoted trade with Palestine and Syria in southwestern Asia. The arts flourished under this dynasty.

Weak kings ruled Egypt toward the end of Dynasty XII. Settlers from Asia gradually invaded the Nile Delta, using horse-drawn chariots, improved bows, and other tools of war unknown to the native Egyptians. The invaders, called the Hyksos, seized control of Egypt about 1630 B.C., and their leaders founded Dynasty XV. The Middle Kingdom ended in the mid-1600s, but the Hyksos continued to dominate Egypt until 1520 B.C.

The New Kingdom was a period of nearly 500 years in which ancient Egypt became the world's strongest power. The period began around 1539 B.C., with Dynasty XVIII. During this dynasty, native Egyptians drove the Hyksos forces out of Egypt, and Thebes regained its importance.

Amun, a god worshiped mainly in Thebes, was increasingly identified with the god Re and called Amun-Re.

At the beginning of Dynasty XVIII, Egypt developed a permanent army that used horse-drawn chariots and other advanced military techniques introduced during the Hyksos period. The dynasty's early rulers led military forces into southwestern Asia. Thutmose I apparently reached the Euphrates River. Queen Hatshepsut, his daughter, also led armies in battle. Egypt developed a great empire and reached the height of its power during the 1400s B.C., under King Thutmose III. He led military campaigns into Asia almost yearly for twenty years and brought the eastern coast of the Mediterranean Sea into the Egyptian empire. Thutmose also reestablished Egyptian control over Kush and surrounding Nubia, which were valuable sources of slaves, copper, gold, ivory, and ebony. As a result of these victories, Egypt became the strongest and wealthiest nation in the world.

The course of Egyptian history changed unexpectedly after Amenhotep IV came to the throne around 1353 B.C. He devoted himself to a sun god called the Aten, represented as the disk of the sun. Amenhotep changed his own name to Akhenaten and declared that the Aten had replaced Amun and all other gods except Re. He believed that Re was part of the sunlight that came from the Aten. The king also moved the capital to a new city, Akhetaten, about 175 miles (280 kilometers) north of Thebes. Ruins of the city lie near what is now Tell el Amarna. Akhenaten's religious reforms, known as the Amarna Revolution, led to an outpouring of art and sculpture that glorified the Aten. But the changes angered many Egyptians.

Akhenaten's immediate successors ended the unrest. King Tutankhaten removed *-aten* from his name and became Tutankhamun. He restored the old state religion, allowing the worship of the old deities as well as the Aten. Horemheb, the last Dynasty XVIII king, completely rejected Akhenaten's religious beliefs. Dynasty XIX kings built temples to many gods throughout Egypt. Two of the kings, Seti I and his son, Ramses II, regained Asian territories lost after the reign of Thutmose III.

Ancient Egypt began to decline during Dynasty XX. Bitter struggles for power by priests and nobles broke the country into small states. Egypt lost its territories abroad, and its weakness attracted a series of invaders.

The periods of foreign control.
Ancient Egypt's decline accelerated rapidly after about 1075 B.C., when Dynasty XX ended. During the next 750 years, ten dynasties ruled Egypt. Most of them were formed by Nubian, Assyrian, and Persian rulers. In 332 B.C., the Macedonian conqueror Alexander the Great added Egypt to his empire. In 331, Alexander founded the city of Alexandria in the delta.

The Ptolemies. Alexander died in 323 B.C., and his generals divided his empire. Ptolemy, one of the generals, gained control of Egypt. About 305 B.C., he took the title of king and founded a dynasty known as the Ptolemaic dynasty. The dynasty's rulers spread Greek culture in Egypt. They also built temples to Egyptian gods, developed Egypt's natural resources, and increased foreign trade. Alexandria became Egypt's capital, and its magnificent library and museum helped make the city one of the greatest cultural centers of ancient times.

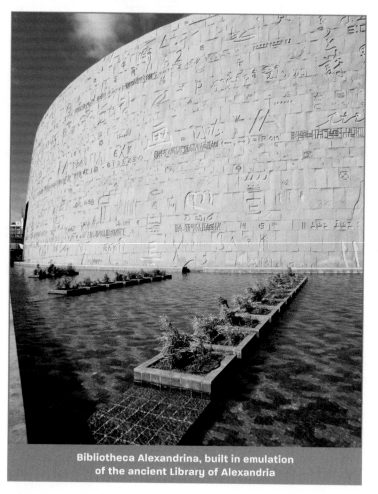

**Bibliotheca Alexandrina, built in emulation
of the ancient Library of Alexandria**

Roman rule. Queen Cleopatra VII of the Ptolemies probably married Mark Antony, a co-ruler of Rome, in 37 B.C. Antony and his rival co-ruler, Octavian, each wanted to rule the vast Roman lands by himself. In 32 B.C., Antony combined his and Cleopatra's military forces to fight forces led by Octavian. The navy of Antony and Cleopatra lost the vital Battle of Actium to Octavian's fleet in 31 B.C. The couple committed suicide in 30 B.C., and Octavian then made Egypt a Roman province. Rome's control of Egypt gradually weakened after A.D. 395, when the Roman Empire split into eastern and western parts. By A.D. 642, Arab Muslims had conquered Egypt.

Learning About Ancient Egypt

The study of ancient Egypt is called *Egyptology,* and experts in the field are *Egyptologists.* Much of their knowledge comes from studying the architecture and other arts of ancient Egypt. Ruins of magnificent temples stand at Abydos, Kom Ombo, Edfu, Esna, Luxor, and Karnak. Excavations of pharaohs' tombs, such as those in a burial ground called the Valley of the Kings, near Luxor, have yielded superb paintings. Tutankhamun's tomb was filled with stunning examples of the ancient Egyptians' skill in woodworking and metalworking.

Information about ancient Egypt also comes from written records made by the Egyptians themselves and by such ancient Greek writers as Herodotus and Strabo. The Egyptians used hieroglyphics until sometime after they came under Roman rule. The ability of anyone to read Egyptian hieroglyphics was then quickly lost.

For over 1,000 years, scholars tried but failed to decipher the writing system of ancient Egypt. Then, in 1799, a rock slab with ancient Greek and Egyptian writing was found outside Rosetta, a city near Alexandria. A French scholar named Jean François Champollion began to compare the Greek and Egyptian words on the so-called Rosetta stone. By 1822, he had deciphered the hieroglyphics. Dictionaries developed since then have helped scholars translate the writings on many monuments and in temples and tombs.

SPHINX is an imaginary creature of ancient myths. The Egyptians, Greeks, and peoples of the Near East all had stories about such creatures. According to various tales, the sphinx had the body of a lion and the head of a human, falcon, or ram. Some sphinxes also had wings and a serpent tail.

The term *sphinx* is a Greek word that originally referred to an imaginary evil monster. The ancient Greeks used the term to describe the huge stone statues of lions with human heads that they saw during their visits to Egypt.

Egyptian sphinxes. Most Egyptian sphinxes had the head of a man and the body, feet, and tail of a lion. Others had heads of rams or falcons. Egyptians often made statues of sphinxes to honor a king or queen. The sculptors modeled the face of such a sphinx after the honored person. Egyptian art frequently showed kings as lions conquering their enemies, and sphinxes became symbols of royal protection. Statues of sphinxes often lined avenues leading to temples, such as those near the great temple at Karnak. Other sphinxes represented the god Horus, the sky god and sun god who was thought to be a protector of the king.

The largest, oldest, and most famous sphinx statue lies in the desert near Giza, Egypt. It is called the *Great Sphinx*. The monument stretches 240 feet (73 meters) long and stands about 66 feet (20 meters) high. The width of its face measures 13 feet 8 inches (4.17 meters). Egyptians built the Great Sphinx about 4,500 years ago. They carved its head and body directly out of a giant rock in a limestone formation and cut stone blocks to form the paws and legs. This limestone formation had supplied much of the stone used to build several great pyramids.

The Great Sphinx wears a royal headdress and lies near the pyramid of King Khafre. Historians believe that the sphinx's face is a portrait of Khafre, who probably had the monument built.

Sand has often buried the Great Sphinx up to its neck. King Thutmose IV of Egypt (who ruled about 1400 to 1390 B.C.) cleared the sand away, supposedly after dreaming that the god Horus asked him to do so. During modern times, workers removed the sand in 1818, 1886, 1926, and 1938.

Through the years, desert sand, wind, rain, and sun have worn away part of the stone of the Great Sphinx. A broken section of the head indicates that it may have been used as a target for gun practice at various times. In the 1970s, scientists began efforts to preserve the crumbling stone of the Great Sphinx by treating it with special chemicals.

HIEROGLYPHICS is a form of writing in which picture symbols represent ideas and sounds. The word *hieroglyphics* comes from two Greek words that mean *sacred carving*. Hieroglyphics usually refers to the writing of ancient Egypt. However, forms of picture writing were used in other ancient cultures as well, notably by the Hittites, who lived in the region that is now Turkey, and by the Maya and Aztec Indians of Central America.

The ancient Egyptians used hieroglyphic writing for more than 3,000 years. They used hieroglyphic writing primarily for religious inscriptions on temples and stone monuments and to record the words and deeds of royalty. In fact, the Egyptians called their writing *the words of God*. The inscriptions were written or carved by highly trained men who were called *scribes*.

After the A.D. 300s, the Egyptians replaced their other forms of writing with a simpler alphabet that was borrowed mainly from Greek. Knowledge of the meaning of hieroglyphic symbols was soon lost and remained a mystery until the early 1800s, when scholars deciphered the writing.

Development of hieroglyphic writing. The ancient Egyptians borrowed the idea of hieroglyphic writing from Mesopotamia about 3000 B.C. Egyptian hieroglyphics generally included about 800 symbols. However, by about 300 B.C., there were more than 6,000 symbols. The symbols have the elegant, stiff quality typical of ancient Egyptian art.

The earliest *hieroglyphs* (symbols) contained many pictorial characters known as *pictographs* or *ideograms*. These characters were literal representations of ideas. For example, Egyptians who wished to express the idea of a woman drew a picture of a woman.

Mural in tomb of Thutmose IV

The earliest writings of the Egyptians also included phonetic hieroglyphs, also called *phonograms*. Such hieroglyphs, like the characters of modern alphabets, represented the sounds of the language. Some represented only one sound. Others represented combinations of two or three sounds that formed syllables. But the phonetic symbols represented only the sounds of consonants. The Egyptians did not write the vowels. Thus, scholars remain unsure of how the ancient Egyptian language was pronounced.

Egyptian hieroglyphs included *determinatives*. Determinatives indicated the class of object to which the preceding hieroglyphs belonged. An example of a determinative might be the symbol for water placed after the name of a specific lake. Such symbols helped explain and emphasize the meaning of other hieroglyphs.

Some hieroglyphic texts are read from right to left and others from left to right, depending on the direction the hieroglyphs face. Scribes also wrote in columns, which were read from top to bottom. Hieroglyphs often served as decoration. Sometimes, the symbols were painted with brilliant colors or covered with gold.

As writing became more common, the need developed for a material that was easier than stone to write on, store, and transport. For this purpose, the Egyptians invented *papyrus*, a paper-like material made from a reed plant. Scribes wrote on papyrus with brushes made of reeds. The tips of the reeds were softened and shaped into a point. Soot mixed with water served as ink.

The Egyptians used this simplified *cursive* (con-

nected) script called hieratic writing for writing quickly on papyrus. Hieratic writing resembled hieroglyphic writing in much the same way that modern longhand resembles printing. Scribes used hieratic script for both religious and nonreligious purposes.

Later, about 700 B.C., a script called *demotic* became popular. It was simpler and could be written faster than hieratic writing. Scribes also used the script for correspondence and record-keeping. Demotic writing was widely used for about 1,000 years.

Deciphering hieroglyphic writing. The Egyptians eventually stopped using their own writing systems, replacing them with an essentially Greek alphabet. The phonetic values and other uses of the hieroglyphs were forgotten. People came to believe that the hieroglyphs really represented a secret and magical code used by Egyptian priests.

In 1799, a French officer in the army of Napoleon I discovered a stone tablet near the mouth of the Nile River near Rosetta, Egypt. The tablet, named the Rosetta stone, carried an inscription in three scripts—Egyptian hieroglyphic, Egyptian demotic, and Greek. By reading the Greek portion of the stone, scholars learned that the text consisted of a decree, issued in 196 B.C., honoring King Ptolemy V.

Scholars attempted to translate the Egyptian script using methods that were similar to modern cryptography. In 1814, Thomas Young, an English physician and scholar, discovered that some hieroglyphics were phonetic signs. In addition, scholars learned that hieroglyphs enclosed in an oval ring, called a *cartouche*, represented names of individuals.

In 1822, a French scholar named Jean François Champollion achieved a breakthrough in deciphering the hieroglyphs of the Rosetta stone. By studying the position and repetition of proper names in the Greek script, he picked out the same names in the Egyptian scripts. In addition, Champollion's knowledge of Coptic, the last stage of the ancient Egyptian language written with mostly Greek letters, helped him recognize many ancient Egyptian words in the hieroglyphic part of the text. Eventually, he deciphered the entire text.

Today, grammars and dictionaries enable scholars to read Egyptian hieroglyphic writing easily. Knowledge of ancient Egyptian history would be nearly impossible to obtain without the ability to read hieroglyphics.

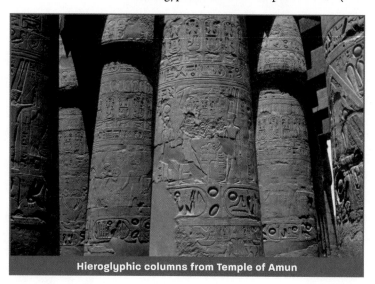
Hieroglyphic columns from Temple of Amun

Other hieroglyphic writing. In Central America, the earliest examples of Maya hieroglyphs date from about A.D. 250. Maya hieroglyphs consisted of a combination of ideograms that represented entire ideas or words and phonetic hieroglyphs that represented syllables. The Maya carved hieroglyphs on buildings and on large stone monuments called *stelae*. These carvings frequently recorded important historical events in the lives of Maya rulers. In addition, the Maya painted hieroglyphs on pottery and wrote on paper made from fig tree bark. The Maya are the only ancient American people known to have developed a writing system that could express all the words in their language.

Aztec hieroglyphs consisted of pictographs, which also had a phonetic value. The Aztec combined the symbols of several objects to form the sound or name of an object or abstract idea not represented by a pictograph. These symbols resemble *rebus* writing.

The Hittites developed a hieroglyphic writing system about 1500 B.C. Some Hittite symbols represented words. Others represented phonetic syllables.

PYRAMIDS are large structures with square bases and four smooth, triangular-shaped sides that come to a point at the top. Several ancient peoples used pyramids as tombs or temples. The most famous pyramids are those built about 4,500 years ago as tombs for Egyptian kings. These Egyptian pyramids are among the Seven Wonders of the Ancient World.

Egyptian pyramids. The ruins of thirty-five major pyramids still stand near the Nile River in Egypt. Each was built to protect the body of an Egyptian king. The Egyptians thought that a person's body had to be preserved and protected so the soul could live forever. The Egyptians *mummified* (embalmed and dried) their dead and hid the mummies in large tombs. From about 2700 to 1700 B.C., the bodies of Egyptian kings were buried inside or beneath a pyramid in a secret chamber that was filled with treasures of gold and precious objects.

Many scholars believe that the pyramid shape has a religious meaning to the Egyptians. The sloping sides may have reminded the Egyptians of the slanting rays of the sun, by which the soul of the king could climb to the sky and join the gods.

Funeral ceremonies were performed in temples that were attached to the pyramids. Most pyramids had two temples that were connected by a long stone passageway. Sometimes a smaller pyramid for the body of the queen stood next to the king's pyramid. Egypt has at least forty smaller pyramids that were used for queens or as memorial monuments for kings. The king's relatives and officials were buried in smaller rectangular tombs called *mastabas*. These buildings had sloping sides and flat roofs.

The first pyramids. Imhotep, a great architect and statesman, built the first known pyramid for King Zoser about 2650 B.C. Zoser's tomb rose in a series of giant steps, or terraces, and is called the *Step Pyramid*. This pyramid still stands at the site of the ancient city of Memphis, at Saqqarah, near Cairo.

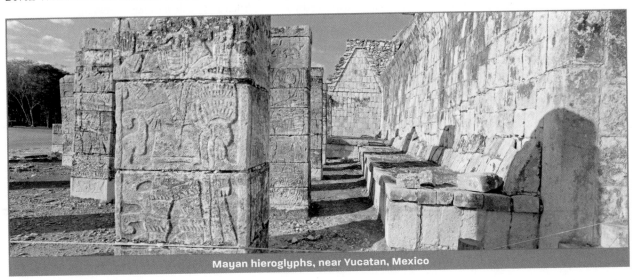

Mayan hieroglyphs, near Yucatan, Mexico

The first smooth-sided pyramid was built about 2600 B.C. It still stands at Medum. It began as a stepped pyramid, and then the steps were filled in with casing stones to give the building smooth, sloping sides. Other pyramids built during a period of Egyptian history called the Old Kingdom (about 2650–2150 B.C.) can be seen at Abusir and Dahshur. During the Middle Kingdom (about 1975–1640 B.C.), pyramids were built at Hawara, Illahun, Lisht, and Dahshur—near what is now Cairo. The remains of these pyramids are still impressive.

The pyramids of Giza (Al Jizah) stand on the west bank of the Nile River outside Cairo. There are ten pyramids at Giza, including three of the largest and best preserved of all Egyptian pyramids. They were built for kings about 2600 to 2500 B.C. The largest was built for King Khufu (called Cheops by the Greeks). The second was built for King Khafre (Chephren), and the third for King Menkaure (Mycerinus). A huge statue of a sphinx, called the Great Sphinx, was probably built for Khafre. It stands near his pyramid.

The pyramid of Khufu, called the *Great Pyramid*, contains more than 2 million stone blocks that average 2½ tons (2.3 metric tons) each. It was originally 481 feet (147 meters) tall, but some of its upper stones are gone now and it stands about 450 feet (140 meters) high. Its base covers about 13 acres (5 hectares).

A study of the Great Pyramid shows how these gigantic structures were built. The ancient Egyptians had no machinery or iron tools. They cut big limestone blocks with copper chisels and saws. Most of the stones came from quarries nearby. But some came from across the Nile River, and others came by boat from distant quarries. Gangs of men dragged the blocks to the pyramid site and pushed the first layer of stones into place. Then they built long ramps of earth and brick, and dragged the stones up the ramps to form the next layer. As they finished each layer, they raised and lengthened the ramps. Finally, they covered the pyramid with an outer coating of white casing stones. They laid these outer stones so exactly that from a distance the pyramid appeared to have been cut out of a single white stone. Most of the casing stones are gone now, but a few are still in place at the bottom of the Great Pyramid.

The burial chamber is inside the Great Pyramid. A corridor leads from an entrance on the north side to several rooms within the pyramid. One of the rooms is called the *Queen's Chamber*, although the queen is not buried there. The room was planned as the king's burial chamber. But Khufu changed the plan and built another burial chamber, called the *King's Chamber*. The *Grand Gallery*, a corridor 153 feet (47 meters) long and 28 feet (8.5 meters) high, leads to Khufu's chamber. It is considered a marvel of ancient architecture.

No one knows how long it took to build the Great Pyramid. The ancient Greek historian Herodotus said that the work went on in four-month shifts, with 100,000 workers in each shift. Scholars now doubt that account and believe that about 100,000 men worked on the pyramids for three or four months each year. Farm laborers built the pyramids. They worked on the tombs during periods when floodwaters of the Nile covered the fields and made farming impossible.

Thieves broke into most of the pyramids, stole the gold, and sometimes destroyed the bodies. Later Egyptian kings stopped using pyramids, and built secret tombs in cliffs. But some kings of the Kushite kingdom in Nubia, south of Egypt, built pyramids long after they were no longer used in Egypt.

American pyramids. Indians of Central and South America also built pyramids. They built stepped pyramids that had flat tops. They used the flat tops as platforms for their temples.

The Moche Indians of Peru built large brick pyramids. *The Temple of the Sun*, near what is now Trujillo, on Peru's northern coast, has a terraced brick pyramid on top of a stepped platform. The ancient Maya of Central America built pyramid-shaped mounds of earth with temples on top.

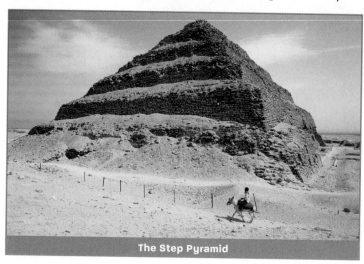

The Step Pyramid

Indians of central Mexico also built big stepped pyramids. For example, Indians constructed the great pyramids of the Sun and Moon that still stand at Teotihuacan, near Mexico City. The Toltec Indians built a stepped pyramid at Cholula that is one of the largest structures in the world. The Spanish conquerors destroyed most pyramids of the later Aztec Empire in Mexico. These pyramids were built in steps or terraces like the other American pyramids and had temples on top. Two of the greatest were at Tenochtitlan (now Mexico City). Mound-building Indians of North America built some pyramid-shaped mounds, but they were not true pyramids.

 THE ROSETTA STONE gave the world the key to the long-forgotten language of ancient Egypt. A French officer of Napoleon's engineering corps discovered it in 1799. He found the stone half buried in the mud near Rosetta, a city near Alexandria, Egypt. The Rosetta stone was later taken to England, where it is still preserved in the British Museum.

On the stone is carved a decree by Egyptian priests to commemorate the crowning of Ptolemy V Epiphanes, king of Egypt from 205 to 180 B.C. The first inscription is in ancient Egyptian hieroglyphics. The second is in demotic, the popular language of Egypt at that time. At the bottom of the stone the same message is written again in Greek.

The stone is made of a dark gray granitelike rock with a pinkish tone and a pink streak at the top. It is about 11 inches (28 centimeters) thick, 3 feet 9 inches (114 centimeters) high, and 2 feet 4½ inches (72 centimeters) across. Part of the top and a section of the right side are missing.

The language of ancient Egypt had been a riddle to scholars for hundreds of years. A French scholar named Jean François Champollion used the Rosetta stone to solve the riddle. Using the Greek text as a guide, he studied the position and repetition of proper names in the Greek text and was able to pick out the same names in the Egyptian text. This enabled him to learn the sounds of many of the Egyptian hieroglyphic characters.

Champollion had a thorough knowledge of Coptic, the last stage of the Egyptian language that was written mainly with Greek letters. This knowledge enabled him to recognize the meanings of many Egyptian words in the upper part of the inscription. After much work, Champollion could read the entire text. In 1822, he published a pamphlet, *Lettre à M. Dacier*, containing the results of his work. This pamphlet enabled scholars to read the literature of ancient Egypt.

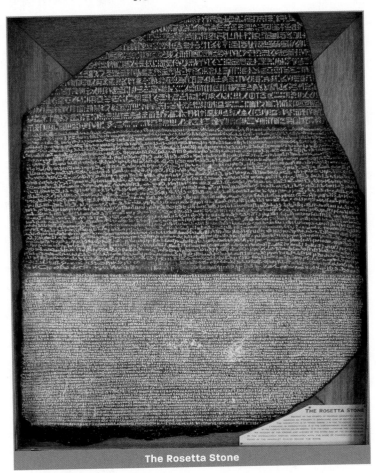
The Rosetta Stone

MLA Citation
"Ancient Egypt." *The Southwestern Advantage Topic Source.* Nashville: Southwestern. 2013.

DATA

Important Dates in Egypt's History

c. 3100 B.C.	Egyptian civilization began with the union of Lower and Upper Egypt.
2686–2181 B.C.	The Old Kingdom was a period known for the construction of great pyramids.
1938 B.C.	King Amenemhet founded Dynasty XII, which greatly increased Egypt's power.
c. 1630 B.C.	Hyksos rulers formed a dynasty that ruled Egypt for about 100 years.
1479–1425 B.C.	The Egyptian empire reached its height during the reign of King Thutmose III.
1353 B.C.	Akhenaten became king of Egypt and introduced major religious reforms.
c. 1075 B.C.	Dynasty XX ended, and Egypt began to decline rapidly as a strong nation.
332 B.C.	Alexander the Great added Egypt to his empire.
31 B.C.	A Roman fleet crushed an Egyptian force in the Battle of Actium, leading to Rome's takeover of Egypt in 30 B.C.
A.D. 642	Muslims from Arabia seized Alexandria and completed their conquest of Egypt.

ADDITIONAL RESOURCES

Books to Read

Level I

Fletcher, Joann. *Exploring the Life, Myth, and Art of Ancient Egypt.* Rosen Publishing, 2010.
Macdonald, Fiona. *Egyptians.* Sea-to-Sea Publications, 2011.
Platt, Richard. *The Egyptians.* Sea-to-Sea Publications, 2011.
Smith, Miranda. *Ancient Egypt.* Kingfisher, 2010.

Level II

Ancient Egypt and the Near East. Marshall Cavendish Reference, 2011.
Bierbrier, Morris L. *Historical Dictionary of Ancient Egypt.* 2nd ed. Scarecrow, 2008.
Wendrich, Willeke. *Egyptian Archaeology.* 5th ed. Wiley-Blackwell, 2010.
Wilkinson, Toby A. H. *Lives of the Ancient Egyptians.* Thames & Hudson, 2007.
Wilkinson, Toby A. H. *The Rise and Fall of Ancient Egypt.* Random House, 2010.

Web Sites

A Multimedia Guide to Art of the Ancient World

http://www.artic.edu/cleo/

An interactive journey through the collection of ancient art at The Art Institute of Chicago. This Web site takes visitors on an expedition to the ancient cultures of Egypt, Greece, and Rome.

Cleopatra: Lost and Found

http://americanart.si.edu/exhibitions/online/lewis/

An on-line exhibit from the Smithsonian Institute.

Egyptian Artifacts Exhibit

http://www.memphis.edu/egypt/artifact.html
Selected artifacts from the University of Memphis Institute of Egyptian Art and Archaeology, with text and photos.

The Institute of Egyptian Art and Archaeology

http://www.memphis.edu/egypt/
Information about art and relics from Ancient Egypt from the University of Memphis Institute of Egyptian Art and Archaeology.

Theban Mapping Project

http://www.thebanmappingproject.com/
Discover each tomb in the Valley of the Kings in this interactive atlas. Investigate a database of information about each tomb and view a compilation of nearly 2,000 images.

Search Strings

Afterlife/Mummification Process/Rituals

ancient egypt mummification process rituals dead preserve body afterlife embalm resin linen bandages coffin (328)

mummification process rituals ancient egypt body preserve afterlife embalm remove organs resin linen bandages coffin hide (169)

Egyptian Gods and Goddesses

ancient egyptian gods goddesses worship names purposes (281,000)

gods goddesses ancient egypt worship who why (62,000)

gods goddesses ancient egypt worship deity (59,800)

Egyptian Pyramids

egyptian pyramids tombs secret chambers architectural marvels temples locations (14,300)

pyramids egyptian architectural marvels build (11,900)

Hieroglyphics

hieroglyphics ancient picture symbols writing (32,800)

ancient egypt hieroglyphics picture symbols present ideas sounds writing replaced alphabet (30,100)

hieroglyphics writing pictures symbols represent ideas sounds (8010)

Rosetta Stone

rosetta stone tablet egypt hieroglyphic demotic greek jean francois champollion decipher (278)

rosetta stone tablet decipher hieroglyphic demotic greek (1040)

China

China is a large country in eastern Asia. It is the world's largest country in population with over 1.3 billion people—about 20 percent of all the people in the world.

HOT topics

Family Life in China. Family life has always been extremely important in Chinese culture. For thousands of years, the Chinese people practiced loyalty to family, obedience to the father, and reverence for ancestors. Traditionally, Chinese families valued sons far more than daughters. A husband could divorce his wife if she failed to give birth to sons. In some cases, daughters were killed at birth to save resources for the sons. Today, social policy in China stresses that families should value girls and boys equally. Relationships within Chinese families have become less formal, and parents no longer expect their children to show unquestioning obedience.

Religion. Religion is tolerated, but restricted, by the Communist government of China. However, it played an important part in traditional Chinese life, Confucianism, Taoism, and Buddhism were major religions throughout most of China's history. The religious beliefs of many Chinese people included elements of all three. Confucianism is based on the ideas of Confucius, a Chinese philosopher born about 550 B.C. More a moral code than a religion, it stresses the importance of ethical standards and of a well-ordered society. Taoism, also native to China, was influenced by folk religion. It teaches that a person should live in harmony with nature. Buddhism reached China from India before A.D. 100. It taught strict moral standards and the ideas of rebirth and life after death.

HOT topics

Higher Education. Nationwide examinations in China determine who may advance to higher education and at what kind of school. Students study intensely for the tests. Those who do best on the tests enter a university. Some wealthier students who do not qualify may pay to attend private universities. Others who pass the examination with lower scores may enter a technical college or vocational university. These schools train students for jobs in business and industry. Many students complete two- or three-year programs in such fields as agriculture, industrial arts, and nursing.

Hong Kong. An island with a population of nearly seven million, Hong Kong is a special administrative region of China. It lies on China's southern coast, near the mouth of the Zhu Jiang (Pearl River). Hong Kong is a major port of Asia. It is also a center of trade, finance, and tourism. Hong Kong was part of China from ancient times until the 1800s. Through treaty agreements with China, the United Kingdom gained control of Hong Kong Island in 1842. In 1898 China agreed to lease Hong Kong to the United Kingdom for 99 years. At the end of the lease in 1997, China demanded the return of the island, and power was transferred back to the Chinese. Today Hong Kong is a vital node in the global economy.

Graduation ceremony at Tsinghua University, July 2007

TRUE or FALSE?

The Chinese name for China, *Zhongguo*, means *High Country*. It comes from the ancient Chinese belief that their country sat upon the highest mountains in the world.

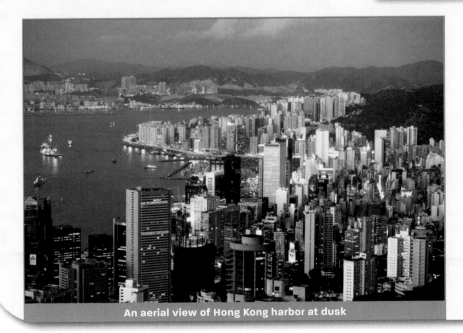

An aerial view of Hong Kong harbor at dusk

THE BASICS

China is a large country in eastern Asia. It is the world's largest country in population with over 1.3 billion people—about 20 percent of all the people in the world. China is the third largest country in area. Only Russia and Canada have more territory. China is also one of the world's oldest countries, with a rich history that stretches over thousands of years.

The Chinese call their country *Zhongguo*, which means *Middle Country*. This name probably came from the ancient Chinese belief that their country was the geographical center of the world and the most cultured civilization. The English name *China* probably came from *Qin*, the name of an early Chinese *dynasty* (series of rulers from the same family).

More than 90 percent of China's people live in the eastern half of China, which has most of China's major cities and nearly all the land suitable for farming. Western China, by contrast, has far fewer people and resources. It is home to many of the country's minority groups.

Agriculture has always been the chief economic activity in China. Most of the people live in rural villages, and over half of all workers are farmers. However, China has some of the world's largest cities. They include Shanghai and Beijing (formerly Peking), the nation's capital.

China is one of the world's oldest living civilizations. Its written history goes back about 3,500 years. The Chinese were the first to develop the compass, paper, porcelain, and silk cloth. They undertook huge

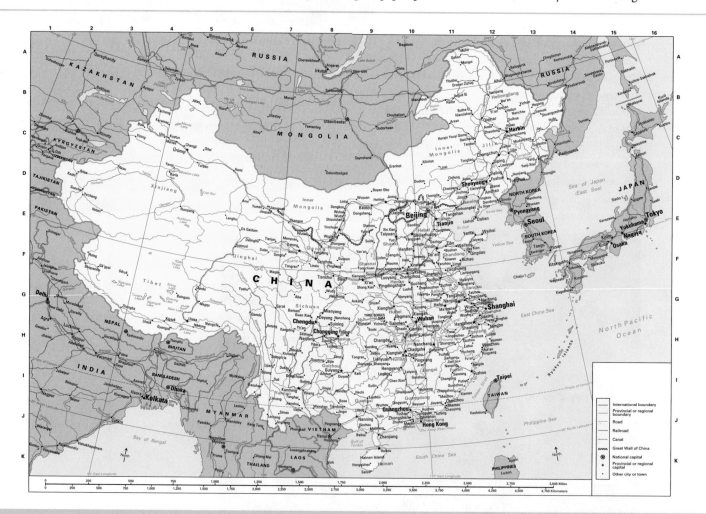

Map of China

construction projects, such as the Great Wall. Over the centuries, Japan, Korea, Vietnam, and other Asian lands borrowed from Chinese art, language, literature, religion, and technology.

In early times, the country that is now China was divided into small states, which were sometimes allied and sometimes at war. In 221 B.C., the Qin dynasty conquered the states and created a strong central government, forming the first united Chinese empire. Such empires continued to rule for more than 2,000 years. Chinese empires expanded the country's territory, built great cities, and sponsored magnificent works of literature and art. Nomadic groups from the north sometimes conquered all or part of the country. But the invaders generally adopted more from Chinese civilization than the Chinese adopted from them.

In the 1800s, China's last empire, the Qing, began to weaken. In 1911, revolutionaries overthrew the Qing, and the next year, China became a republic. But the *Kuomintang* (Nationalist Party), which ruled the republic, never established effective government over all of China. In 1949, the Chinese Communist Party defeated the Nationalists and set up China's present government. The Communists called the country *Zhonghua Renmin Gongheguo* (People's Republic of China). The Nationalists fled to the island of Taiwan, where they reestablished their government. The People's Republic claims that Taiwan should be part of its territory. This article discusses only the People's Republic of China.

The Communists made many major changes in China. They placed all important industries under state ownership and direction. The government also took control of most trade and finance. In the late 1900s, the Communists began to loosen their grip on the nation's economy and to allow more free enterprise. China has one of the world's largest economies, and many of its people prosper. But the majority of Chinese still live modestly.

Government

China's government is dominated by the Chinese Communist Party, the military, and a branch of government known as the State Council. The Communist Party is the most powerful group. All people who hold middle- or lower-level positions in the party or the government are called *cadres* or *ganbu*.

The Communist Party. China remains a one-party state. A number of minor political par-

ties exist, but they have no power. Millions of Chinese belong to the Communist Party, but members make up only about 5 percent of the total population. In 2002, the party began allowing business owners to join. Admitting business owners was a major change because Communists traditionally had considered the owners of businesses and other means of production to be enemies of the working class. Although the party still supports Communist ideals, it recognized that business owners play an important role in modern China.

The Communist Party has four main administrative bodies: the National Party Congress, the Central Committee, the *Politburo* (Political Bureau), and the Secretariat. The National Party Congress has nearly 3,000 representatives, selected by party members throughout the nation. The Central Committee consists of leading party members and is elected by the National Party Congress. The Central Committee has about 200 voting members and 150 alternates. The Politburo has about 25 members, who are top party leaders elected by the Central Committee. The Standing Committee is a smaller group within the Politburo and is made up of some of the most important members of the Communist Party. In addition, several powerful leaders belong to the Secretariat, which is chosen by the Central Committee.

The Communist Party's constitution states that the National Party Congress and the Central Committee are the most important bodies, but they have little real power. In general, they automatically approve party policies and guidelines set by the Politburo and its Standing Committee. The Secretariat is responsible for carrying out the day-to-day activities of the party.

Deng Xiaoping

The highest post in the Communist Party is that of general secretary, who serves as head of the Secretariat. But other high-ranking government officials sometimes hold more power. For example, Deng Xiaoping was China's most influential leader from the late 1970s until the early 1990s, though Hu Yaobang and others held the post of general secretary.

National government. China's Constitution establishes the National People's Congress as the highest government authority. Members of the National People's Congress are elected by local and regional people's congresses and by the armed forces. The members of the National People's Congress serve five-year terms. The chief function of the congress is legislative. Its powers include adopting laws, approving the national budget, and appointing government officials. A standing committee of about 150 members handles the work of the congress when it is not in session.

The State Council serves as the executive branch. It carries on the day-to-day affairs of the government. The council is led by the premier, China's head of government. The premier is chosen by the National People's Congress, upon nomination by the president. The president's duties are largely ceremonial. The premier is assisted by several vice premiers, state councilors, and a number of ministers and heads of special commissions. The ministers are in charge of government departments, such as the ministries of defense, education, and finance.

Political divisions. China has 33 major political divisions—22 provinces, 5 *autonomous* (self-governing) regions, 4 nationally governed municipalities, and 2 special administrative regions. The autonomous regions—Guangxi, Inner Mongolia, Ningxia, Tibet, and Xinjiang—have many people who belong to China's minority ethnic groups. Although the regions are called autonomous, they are actually governed much like the rest of the nation. The nationally governed municipalities—Beijing, Chongqing, Shanghai,

and Tianjin—are large metropolitan areas that are administered by the national government. Each of these municipalities consists of an urban center and a rural area. The special administrative regions are Hong Kong and Macao, which were controlled for many years by the United Kingdom and Portugal, respectively. Hong Kong and Macao have their own executive, legislative, and judicial bodies. China handles their defense and foreign policy.

China has three levels of local government. The 33 major political units are divided into more than 300 prefectures and more than 650 major cities. Counties, other cities, and districts of major cities make up the next level. The counties are subdivided into thousands of townships and towns. Each political unit has a people's congress with a standing committee, and an executive body patterned after the State Council.

Courts in China do not function as a completely independent branch of government as they do in many Western nations. Instead, the courts base their decisions largely on the policies of the Communist Party.

The highest court in China is the Supreme People's Court. It interprets the national laws and supervises the local people's courts. It also makes the final judgment on cases that have been appealed from lower courts. The Supreme People's Procuratorate hears cases that involve violations by government officials and sees that the national Constitution and the regulations of the National People's Congress are observed.

The armed forces of China are jointly commanded by the Central Military Commission of the Communist Party and the Central Military Commission of the government. China has an army, navy, and air force, which together make up the People's Liberation Army (PLA). The PLA has about 1½ million male and female regular members. About 1½ million men and women serve in China's *militia* (citizens' army). There are also about 800,000 army reserves. Men and women between 18 and 22 years of age may be drafted for military service.

The armed forces hold enormous political power in the People's Republic of China. Military officers make up a large percentage of the members on the Communist Party's Central Committee. In addition to its military duties, the People's Liberation Army helps carry out party policies and programs.

The People's Liberation Army

People

Population. About a fifth of the world's people live in China. Shanghai is China's largest city and one of the world's largest as well. Beijing, the country's capital, is the second largest city. About 100 Chinese cities each have more than a million people. However, most of the country's people live in rural villages and small towns in eastern China. The western half of China has less than 10 percent of the population.

China's government sees the country's population as both a great resource and a great burden. China's huge workforce could make its economy the most powerful in the world. But unless China limits its population growth, far more children would be born than China could adequately feed, house, educate, or employ under present conditions. By law, to limit population increases, men may not marry until they are 22 years old, and women until they are 20. People are encouraged to postpone marriage until they are in their late 20s and to have no more than two children.

Nationalities. About 92 percent of the people belong to the Han nationality. The rest of the population consists of over 50 minority groups, including Kazakhs, Mongols, Tibetans, Uygurs, and Zhuang. The different nationality groups are distinguished chiefly by language and culture.

Most of China's minority peoples live in the border regions and western China. A few groups, such as the Mongols in the north and the Kazakhs in the northwest, have a long tradition of herding sheep, goats, and other livestock. Some are still nomads, moving from place to place during the year to feed their herds on fresh pastures. The Uygurs raise livestock and grow crops on oases in the deserts of northwestern China. The Tibetan people practice simple forms of agriculture and herding in China's southwestern highlands. Many Koreans are farmers near the border with North Korea.

A number of minority groups inhabit the far southern parts of China. Some of these groups, such as the Zhuang, live much like their neighbors, the Han. Other minority groups are related to the peoples of Laos, Myanmar, Thailand, or Tibet. Many of these people, who live in less developed mountain areas, retain their traditional language and way of life.

Languages. Chinese, the native language of the Han, is actually a group of closely related languages. Early in the 1900s, China's government made northern Chinese, which was spoken in Beijing, the official language. This version of Chinese is often called Mandarin in English, but the Chinese call it *Putonghua* (common language). Most people in northern China speak Putonghua, and it is the language of instruction in almost all schools. Other varieties of Chinese include Northern Min (spoken in Fujian province), Southern Min (spoken mainly in Guangdong and Hainan), Wu (spoken in Shanghai, Jiangsu, and Zhejiang), and Yue or Cantonese (spoken in Guangdong and Guangxi). Each language has several local dialects.

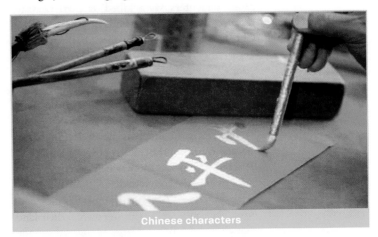
Chinese characters

Although each version of Chinese has its own pronunciation, all Chinese is written in a similar way. The Chinese writing system uses *characters* instead of an alphabet. Each character is a symbol that represents a word or part of a word.

The minority peoples of China speak many languages, including Korean, Mongolian, Uygur, and Zhuang. Many groups use their own language in their schools and publications. Many members of China's minority groups learn Chinese as a second language. A few minority groups speak Chinese as their primary language.

Way of Life

Family life has always been extremely important in Chinese culture. For thousands of years, the Chinese people practiced loyalty to family, obedience to the father, and reverence for ancestors. Chinese philosophy and religion emphasized these values. In the mid-1900s, the Communists tried to replace loyalty to the family with loyalty to the work group. Other social and economic changes in the late 1900s further disrupted traditional family values.

Relationships within Chinese families have become less formal, and parents no longer expect their children to show unquestioning obedience. In the past, parents arranged marriages for their children and chose whom the children would marry. Many young people today choose their own marriage partners, although usually with the consent of their parents. Parents still help arrange some marriages in rural areas.

Chinese families traditionally valued sons far more than daughters. A husband could divorce his wife if she failed to give birth to sons. In some cases, daughters were killed at birth to save resources for the sons. Today, social policy in China stresses that families should value girls and boys equally. The Communist government strongly supports the idea that women should contribute to the family income and participate in social and political activities. Women do many kinds of work outside the home. Many young husbands share in the shopping, housecleaning, cooking, and caring for the children. However, equality between the sexes is more widely accepted in the cities than in the countryside.

Rural life. Traditionally, most Chinese lived in small villages. Many families owned their land, though it was often not large enough to support them. Many other families owned no land but worked as tenants or laborers for landowners and rich farmers.

After the Communists took control of China, they organized a collective ownership system, in which large groups of peasants owned land, tools, work animals, and workshops in common. The highest level of the collective system was the *commune*, which administered the economic activity for groups of about 5,000 families. Smaller units called *production brigades* were further divided into *production teams*, which were the equivalent of a small village. These units planned and performed most day-to-day farm work. In some cases, each family owned its house and a plot on which it could grow vegetables and raise chickens or hogs for its own use. If a family grew a surplus of crops, it could sell the surplus in a local market.

In 1979, the government began a new system to gradually abolish communes, brigades, and teams. Now, cooperative groups known as *collectives* make contracts with individual families. The contract tells how much land a family can work, what crops and livestock the family will raise, and how much

it will sell to the government at a set price. After fulfilling its contract, the farm family may use the remainder of its production as it wishes. Most families use some for food and sell the rest on the open market.

Some rural families sign contracts as *specialized households*. These households may specialize in raising only one commodity, such as chickens or silk. Or they may provide farm machinery, repairs, or handicrafts on the free market instead of doing full-time farm work. After paying an agreed amount to the government, the specialized household keeps any profit. Some households operate businesses or small factories and hire employees. Some of them have become relatively wealthy.

The standard of living in rural China today is much higher than it was before the Communists came to power. The average income in rural areas is still low, but most families have enough food and clothing and also own a bicycle or motor scooter, a radio or television set, and a sewing machine. Some rural families own a refrigerator or a washing machine. Most rural families live in five- or six-room houses. Older houses are made of wood or

An older wooden house in Zhaoxing village

mud bricks and have a tile or thatched roof. Newer houses are made of clay bricks or stone and have a tile roof. Some villages have apartment buildings. Except in remote areas, most houses and apartments have electric power.

Rural people work many hours a day, especially at planting and harvesting time. They also attend meetings and night classes, where they learn to read and write or how to use scientific farming methods. Even so, the people have time for recreation. Many villages have a small library and a recreation center

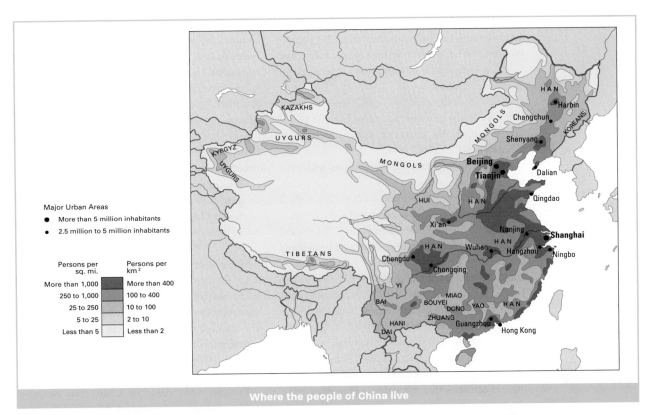

Major Urban Areas
- ● More than 5 million inhabitants
- • 2.5 million to 5 million inhabitants

Persons per sq. mi.	Persons per km²
More than 1,000	More than 400
250 to 1,000	100 to 400
25 to 250	10 to 100
5 to 25	2 to 10
Less than 5	Less than 2

Where the people of China live

with a television or a film projector, and sometimes a computer. Villages may also have sports facilities, music groups, or theater groups.

City life. China's cities are crowded, and housing is in great demand. Many city residents live in older neighborhoods where the houses resemble those in the countryside. Many other city dwellers live in large new apartment complexes. City governments construct some apartment buildings, and large businesses build others to house their workers. Most families pay rent for their apartments, but some have the opportunity to buy them.

Most city neighborhoods or apartment complexes have an elected residents' committee, also called a neighborhood committee. The committee supervises various neighborhood facilities and programs, such as daycare centers, evening classes, and after-school activities for children. When fights, petty crimes, or acts of juvenile delinquency occur in the neighborhoods, committee members talk with the people involved and try to help them solve the problem. These neighborhood organizations seek to keep crime from becoming a serious problem despite the overcrowding in China's cities.

In general, people in China's cities have a higher standard of living than people in the countryside. Their wages are low compared with those of workers in Western industrial countries. But most households have at least two wage earners, and rents and the cost of food are low. Most city people can afford a bicycle or motor scooter, a television set, and some household appliances. Some are able to buy a computer or a car. City people also have more cultural advantages than do rural people. They can attend a greater variety of classes and meetings, and cities typically have more theaters, museums, and other cultural activities.

Food. Grains are the main foods in China. Rice is the favorite grain among people in the south. In the north, people prefer wheat, which they make into dumplings and noodles. Corn, millet, and sorghum are also eaten. Vegetables, especially cabbages and *tofu* (soybean curd), rank second in the Chinese diet. Pork and poultry are favorite meats. People in China also like eggs, fish, fruits, and shellfish. Fast food, such as hamburgers and french fries, has become popular in China's cities.

Breakfast foods in China include rice porridge, stuffed pocket bread, or deep-fried pastries that taste like doughnuts. Favorite lunchtime foods include egg rolls and dumplings stuffed with meat or shrimp. A typical main meal includes vegetables with bits of meat or seafood, soup, and rice or noodles. Chopsticks and soup spoons serve as the utensils at Chinese meals.

Tea is the traditional favorite Chinese beverage. But soft drinks and beer have also become popular beverages. Ice cream is a favorite treat in China's cities.

Fancy Chinese cooking varies from region to region. *Beijing* (formerly *Peking*) *duck* is a northern specialty. It consists of slices of crisp roast duck eaten with thin rolled pancakes and a sweet sauce made from soybean paste. Foods from the coastal areas include fish, crab, and shrimp. The spiciest foods come from Sichuan and Hunan. Chinese cooks vary the texture of dishes by adding crunchy bamboo shoots and *water chestnuts* (thickened stems of an aquatic plant). The Chinese occasionally eat things rarely used as food elsewhere, such as tiger lily buds, sea animals called *sea cucumbers*, and snake meat. Shark's fin soup is an expensive delicacy.

Recreation. The Chinese enjoy many recreational activities that are popular throughout the world. Watching television, listening to radio, reading, going to the movies or opera, and shopping are common. *Karaoke* clubs, where guests sing along to recorded music, have become popular. Badminton, basketball, soccer, and table tennis are favorite sports. Chinese often invite guests over for meals, but going to restaurants is also popular. Many Chinese urban youth use computers at Internet cafés.

Traditional Chinese martial arts, such as *t'ai chi ch'uan* (also written *taijiquan*), are popular. Ballroom dancing parties take place both indoors and outdoors. In parks, the Chinese play *xiang qi* (a Chinese version of chess) and Chinese card games. Another favorite game is *mah-jongg,* which is played with engraved tiles.

Clothing. Most Chinese wear clothing similar to that of Europeans and North Americans. In urban areas, fashionable designs are popular, especially among younger people. Members of certain religious and ethnic groups may wear special costumes and headgear. In rural areas, people often make their own clothes.

Health care in China combines traditional Chinese medicine and modern Western medicine. Traditional medicine is based on the use of herbs, attention to diet, and ancient treatments, such as *acupuncture*. In acupuncture, thin needles are inserted into the body at certain points to relieve pain or treat disease. From Western medicine, the Chinese have adopted many drugs and surgical methods.

Hospitals and clinics in China may be either publicly or privately owned. Hospitals in large cities provide access to advanced medical technologies. In rural areas, some villages have medical workers or rural doctors, although some of them do not have much medical training. Village health care providers can treat simple cases and prescribe drugs. For more advanced care, rural Chinese may have to travel a great distance to reach a township health center or a county hospital.

Beginning in the late 1970s, China's government greatly reduced health care funding. Now, patients are expected to pay more of their health care expenses. Most urban residents live near good facilities and can afford to pay for their care. But many rural Chinese no longer have access to affordable health care.

Religion is tolerated, but restricted, by the Communist government of China. However, it played an important part in traditional Chinese life. Confucianism, Taoism (also spelled Daoism), and Buddhism were major religions throughout most of China's history. The religious beliefs of many Chinese people included elements of all three.

Confucianism is based on the ideas of Confucius, a Chinese philosopher born about 550 B.C. More a moral code than a religion, it stresses the importance of ethical standards and of a well-

A Taoist monk at Xian monastery, Shaanxi

ordered society. In the ideal Confucian society, parents have the right to rule their children, men to rule women, and the educated to rule the common people. Confucianism strongly emphasizes deep respect for one's ancestors and for the past.

Taoism, also native to China, teaches that a person should live in harmony with nature. Taoism began during the 300s B.C. and is based largely on the book *Tao Te Ching (The Classic of the Way and the Virtue)*. Taoism came to include many elements of Chinese folk religion and so became a religion with many protective gods.

Buddhism reached China from India before A.D. 100 and became well established throughout the country during the 300s. Under the influence of Taoism, Chinese varieties of Buddhism developed. They taught strict moral standards and the ideas of rebirth and life after death. The Chinese Buddhists worshiped many gods and appealed to them for help.

China's Communist government regarded religion as part of China's past that would die out. It expected scientific and Marxist thought to replace religion and for many years persecuted religious believers. The Communists destroyed some Taoist and Buddhist temples and other religious buildings, and it turned others into museums, schools, and meeting halls. Beginning in the 1970s, the government adopted a more tolerant attitude toward religion. The government now allows the open practice of religion and the publication of religious works. It restored and reopened some religious buildings. But the government still tries to control religious organizations.

Christian missionaries worked in China for many years before the Communists came to power. The Communists expelled foreign missionaries and closed most Christian churches. In the late 1900s, the government permitted many Christian churches to reopen, but it suppressed Christian movements that organized outside of government control.

Muslims make up a small percentage of the Chinese population. They live mainly in northwestern China.

A spiritual movement called Falun Gong appeared in China in the early 1990s and grew rapidly. Falun Gong teaches techniques of meditation through exercises as a means of improving physical health and spiritual purity. The movement claims to have millions of followers in China. Members of Falun Gong staged a 10,000-person demonstration out-

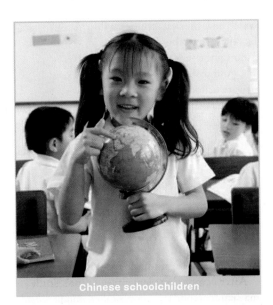

Chinese schoolchildren

side central government buildings in Beijing in 1999. This demonstration led the Chinese government to suppress Falun Gong and to issue an arrest warrant for its founder.

Education. The Chinese have always prized education and respected scholars. The Confucians believed that people could perfect themselves through study. They made no sharp distinction between academic education and moral education. For many years, candidates for government jobs had to pass an examination based on the Confucian works.

The Communists regard education as a key to reaching their goals. They have conducted literacy programs in rural areas in an effort to teach all Chinese to read and write. In the 1950s, they began a language reform program to help reduce illiteracy. The program included simplifying more than 2,000 of the most basic Chinese characters by reducing the number of strokes in each character. Such changes helped make Chinese easier to write. Today, most Chinese 15 years of age or older can read and write.

Moral education is important in China. However, the Chinese teach morality as defined in a Communist sense. They say students should be both politically committed to Communist ideas and technically skilled. Courses in China combine the teaching of academic facts and political values.

In the mid-1980s, China's government began trying to get children to attend school for at least nine years. Students who show outstanding ability on nationwide examinations go to *key schools*, which have the best faculties and facilities. Key schools offer education at the elementary, secondary, and college levels. Some private schools exist, although their fees are high.

Elementary and secondary schools. Children in China enter elementary school at the age of 6 or 7. Nearly all of the country's children attend elementary school, which lasts for 5 or 6 years. Elementary school courses include art, Chinese, English, geography, history, mathematics, music, science, physical education, and political education.

After completing elementary school, students may enter secondary schools called *middle schools*. Junior middle school lasts three years, and senior middle school continues for another two or three years. Middle school courses include many subjects studied in elementary school plus biology, chemistry, physics, and foreign languages. Vocational and technical middle schools offer training in agriculture, industrial technology, and other work-related subjects. Almost all elementary school graduates enter middle school, but far fewer continue on to the senior level.

Higher education. Nationwide examinations determine who may advance to higher education and at what kind of school. Students study intensely for the tests. Those who do best on the tests enter a university. Some wealthier students who do not qualify may pay to attend private universities. The chief university subjects include economics, education, engineering, literature, medicine, and science.

Others who pass the examination with lower scores may enter a technical college or vocational university. These schools train students for jobs in business and industry. Many students complete two- or three-year programs in such fields as agriculture, industrial arts, and nursing.

China has about 2,000 institutions of higher learning, including both universities and schools for adult education. The number of students who desire a university education exceeds the number of openings available. But in addition to technical and vocational schools, adult students can continue their education at "workers' colleges" run by factories. These schools offer short-term courses for

A silk painting showing Confucius lecturing students

employees. Other adult education includes part-time study, radio, television, and correspondence courses, and distance learning programs conducted over the Internet.

The Arts

The Chinese have one of the longest and greatest artistic traditions in the world. Chinese pottery and jade from the 4000s B.C. showed a great deal of technical skill and artistic refinement. During the Shang (1766–1045 B.C.) and Zhou (1045–256 B.C.) dynasties, Chinese metalworkers excelled in bronzework. Late in the Zhou dynasty, the Chinese produced remarkable textiles and lacquered items. Most early Chinese art reflected the power and mystery of nature. But around 200 B.C., Chinese art and literature began to focus on mythical and historical figures, and human situations and values.

By the Song dynasty (A.D. 960–1279), nature had again become a prominent theme in Chinese art and literature. Chinese artists emphasized the balance between two principal forces of nature, called *yin* and *yang*. Landscape painters, for example, aimed for harmony, rhythm, and balance in their compositions. Chinese writers, musicians, and architects also tried to capture these qualities in their work.

In the late 1800s and early 1900s, European and American culture began to influence Chinese life, including the arts. But after the Chinese Communists gained control of the country in 1949, they required art and literature to express Communist values and ideals. Since the late 1970s, the government has relaxed its demands, allowing the revival of Chinese traditions in the arts and permitting experimentation in non-Chinese styles.

Literature. The earliest Chinese literature was inscribed on pieces of bone or turtle shell called *oracle bones* from about 1500 to 1045 B.C., during the

Shang dynasty. These inscriptions recorded the administrative duties, dreams, and future concerns of the royal families. A period of great philosophical activity in the latter part of the Zhou dynasty produced the Confucian, Taoist, and other classic writings. These classics, written in a highly refined script known as *wenyan* (patterned words), became models of Chinese literature.

For most of Chinese history, poetry was considered the highest form of literary achievement. It was esteemed not only on its own, but also as an important part of dramas, stories, and novels. Poetry was even inscribed on paintings.

Painting. Chinese potters painted sophisticated designs on their vessels as early as the 4000s B.C. Painting on silk began during the Shang dynasty. Painting on paper began after the Chinese invented paper in the 200s B.C. Early paintings showed people, animals, spirits, or abstract designs. But landscapes became the chief subject of Chinese painting by the A.D. 900s. During the Song dynasty (960–1279), many artists painted landscapes showing towering mountains and vast expanses of water. These artworks expressed a harmony between nature and the human spirit.

Chinese *calligraphy* (fine handwriting) has long been closely linked with the arts of poetry and painting. The use of a brush for writing became common during the Han dynasty (206 B.C.–A.D. 220). The Chinese traditionally considered calligraphy as the highest form of art.

In the A.D. 1000s, painters began to combine landscapes and other subjects with written inscriptions that added to the overall design. These inscriptions typically described the artist's feelings about the scene or the circumstances under which the painting was created. Owners of such paintings would often add inscriptions to the work, recording their own reactions.

In traditional Chinese painting, artists use the same kind of brush for painting as for calligraphy. It consists of a wooden or bamboo handle with bristles of animal hair arranged to form an extremely fine point. The artist can paint many kinds of lines by adjusting the angle of the brush and the pressure on it. Chinese artists paint chiefly with black ink made of pine soot and glue. They sometimes use plant or mineral pigments to add color to their paintings. Chinese painters have created many works on paper or silk scrolls, which can be rolled up for storage and safekeeping. Other

paintings have been done on plaster walls or on flat pieces of silk or paper.

Bronze and jade. The earliest Chinese bronzes were highly decorated vessels created for use in rituals during the Shang and Zhou dynasties. Bronze workers cast the vessels in *piece molds*, clay molds made of separate pieces of baked clay, which had to be destroyed to free the vessels. Art collectors have prized early Chinese bronzes for centuries, valuing them both for their exquisite design and their antiquity.

The Chinese have always held jade in high regard. Their language has many words built on *yu*, the word for jade. These words often convey notions of beauty, virtue, long life, and purity. The Chinese used various forms of jade in ceremonies, buried it with the dead, displayed it in homes and palaces, and wore it for both decoration and protection. Jade *amulets* (charms) supposedly provided protection from evil spirits and preserved the owner's "life force." The Chinese esteemed jade chimes for their clear and uplifting sound.

Sculpture and pottery. Most Chinese sculptures are associated with ritual and religion. They often stand as tomb guardians above ground or as burial attendants in or near graves. Since 1974, thousands of earthenware figures of people, horses, and chariots have been discovered near Xi'an in burial pits near the tomb of Shi Huangdi, the first emperor of the Qin dynasty. These figures, the earliest known life-sized Chinese sculptures, date from the late 200s B.C.

Buddhism reached China from India toward the end of the Han period (206 B.C. to A.D. 220), and sculptors began to turn their skills to the service of this new religion. The Buddhists built temples in or near cities. In rural areas, they hollowed out cliffsides to form chapels. Sculptors decorated the chapels with figures of Buddha and his attendants. Some sculptures were carved from local stone. Others were molded of clay, fired, painted, and glazed. Still other sculptures were cast of bronze and coated with gold.

The Chinese have made pottery since prehistoric times. They began to use the potter's wheel before 3000 B.C. and produced glazed pottery as early as the 1300s B.C. The Chinese developed the world's first porcelain in the A.D. 100s, during the Han dynasty. They admired porcelain, and wrote many essays and poems about it. Among the most esteemed types of porcelain were "official ware"

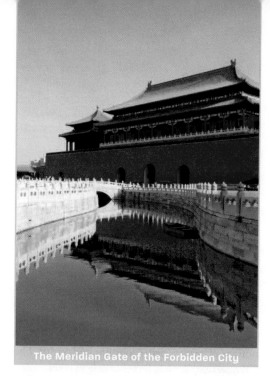

The Meridian Gate of the Forbidden City

(*guanyao*), produced for the emperor's household; bluish-white *qingbai* ware; and crackled *ge* ware.

Other kinds of porcelains were decorated with folk symbols and the bright colors of folk and religious art. Some featured beautifully painted flowers, landscapes, historical scenes, and calligraphic inscriptions. Porcelain dishware and vases produced during the Tang (618–907), Song (960–1279), and Ming dynasties (1368–1644) and the early part of the Qing dynasty (1644–1912) are among the greatest treasures of Chinese art.

Architecture. Traditionally, most of the public buildings in China were constructed of wood on a stone or earthen platform. The most outstanding feature of Chinese architecture was a large tile roof with extending edges that curved gracefully upward, a development dating from the Tang dynasty. Wooden columns were connected to the ceiling beams by wooden brackets that branched out to support these roofs. Walls did not carry weight but merely provided privacy. Most buildings had only one story, but the Chinese also built many-storied towers called *pagodas*. Today, Chinese architects seldom construct buildings in the traditional styles, and new buildings in Chinese cities look much like those in any modern city.

China's traditional landscape gardens were designed primarily to serve as Taoist retreats. They combine artistic design, complex symbolism, and careful arrangement. Their structure reflects the interplay between the principles of yin and yang. For example, garden designers place angular buildings among rounded natural features and rock formations next to water. Light areas alternate with dark, and empty spaces with solids.

Music was extremely important in traditional Chinese society, both for ritual and recreational purposes. The *Record of Rites*, an ancient Confucian text, states that music is the best way to achieve harmony in the universe. The occasions for music in China ranged from grand public ceremonies and festivals to marriages, funerals, and simple social gatherings.

Traditional Chinese music sounds much different from the music of Europe and America because it uses a different scale. The scales most commonly used in Western music have eight tones, but most Chinese scales have five tones. Melody is the most important element in Chinese music. Instruments and voices follow the same melodic line instead of following different lines that harmonize.

Chinese instruments include the *qin*, a seven-stringed instrument, and the *sheng*, a mouth organ made of 17 bamboo pipes. The Chinese also have a lute-like instrument called the *pipa* and two kinds of flutes, the *xiao* and the *di*. Today, Chinese musicians also play non-Chinese instruments and perform the music of many American and European composers, jazz artists, and rock stars.

Theater. There are several types of Chinese drama: classic *zaju* (variety performance) of the Yuan dynasty (1279–1368); southern drama (*xiwen* and *chuanqi*); various regional styles, such as *Kunqu*, from the region of Suzhou; and a Qing dynasty hybrid form known as *jingxi* or Beijing opera. Although each of these traditional dramatic forms has its own special features, all combine spoken language, music, acting, and sometimes mime, dance, or acrobatics.

Chinese drama often uses poetry to convey dramatic mood. Characters that appear frequently in traditional Chinese drama include scholars, military men (both good and bad), heroic women, and silly comic characters. Since the late 1800s, forms of drama from Europe and the United States have influenced Chinese plays.

The Land

China is the world's third largest country in area. Only Russia and Canada are larger. China's land is as varied as it is vast. It ranges from subarctic regions in the north to tropical lowlands in the south and from fertile plains in the east to deserts in the west.

Northeastern China was once called Manchuria, but today it is called the Northeast (*Dongbei* in Chinese). Xinjiang covers the far northwest, and Tibet (or *Xizang*) covers the far southwest. Inner Mongolia lies in the north. The eastern half of China, south of the Northeast and Inner Mongolia, is sometimes called *China proper*. It has always had most of China's people.

China can be divided into eight major land regions. They are (1) Tibetan Highlands, (2) Xinjiang-Mongolian Uplands, (3) Inner Mongolian Border Uplands, (4) Eastern Highlands, (5) Eastern Lowlands, (6) Central Uplands, (7) Sichuan Basin, and (8) Southern Uplands.

Much of China is so densely populated that little wildlife remains. But rugged mountain forests at the eastern edge of the Tibetan Highlands shelter pandas, golden monkeys, takins, and other rare animals. A few elephants and gibbons inhabit the tropical Southern Uplands region. A few Amur, or Siberian, tigers live in remote forests of the Northeast.

The Tibetan Highlands lie in southwestern China. The region consists of a vast plateau bordered by towering mountains—the Himalaya on the south, the Karakoram Range on the west, and the Kunlun on the north. The world's highest mountain, Mount Everest, rises 29,035 feet (8,850

meters) above sea level in the Himalaya in southern Tibet. Two of the world's longest rivers, the Huang He and the Yangtze, begin in the highlands and flow eastward across China to the sea. The Yangtze River is called the Chang Jiang in China.

Tibet suffers from both drought and extreme cold. Most of the region is a wasteland of rock, gravel, snow, and ice. A few areas provide limited grazing for hardy yaks—woolly oxen that furnish food, clothing, and transportation for the Tibetans. Crops grow only in a few lower-lying areas, largely in the east.

The Xinjiang-Mongolian Uplands occupy the vast dry stretches of northwestern China. The region has plentiful mineral resources. However, it is thinly populated because of its remoteness and harsh climate.

The eastern part of the region consists of two deserts, the Mu Us and part of the Gobi. The western part of the region is divided into two areas by the Tian Shan range, which has peaks over 20,000 feet (6,096 meters) above sea level. South of the mountains lies one of the world's driest deserts, the Taklimakan. The Turpan Depression, an oasis near the northern edge of the Taklimakan, is the lowest point in China. It lies 505 feet (154 meters) below sea level. To the north of the Tian Shan, the Junggar Basin stretches northward to the Altai Mountains along the Mongolian border.

The Inner Mongolian Border Uplands lie between the Gobi and the Eastern Lowlands. The Greater Hinggan Range forms the northern part of the region. The terrain there is rugged, and little agriculture is practiced. The southern part of the region is a plateau thickly covered with *loess*, a fertile, yellowish soil deposited by the wind. Loess consists of tiny mineral particles and is easily worn away. The Huang He and its tributaries have carved out hills and steep-sided valleys in the soft soil. The name *Huang He* means *Yellow River* and comes from the large amounts of silt carried by the river.

The Eastern Highlands consist of the Shandong Peninsula and the eastern part of the Northeast. The Shandong Peninsula is a hilly region with excellent harbors and rich deposits of coal. The hills of the eastern part of the Northeast have some of China's best forests. The highest hills are the Changbai Mountains (Long White Mountains) along the border with North Korea. To the north, the Amur River forms the border with Russia. Just south of the Amur is the Lesser Hinggan Range.

The endangered giant panda can be found in Wolong Valley, China.

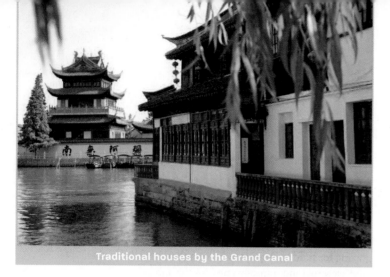
Traditional houses by the Grand Canal

The Eastern Lowlands lie between the Inner Mongolian Border Uplands and the Eastern Highlands and extend south to the Southern Uplands. From north to south, the region consists of the Northeastern Plain, the North China Plain, and the valley of the Yangtze River. The Eastern Lowlands have China's best farmland and many of the largest cities.

The Northeastern Plain has fertile soils and large deposits of coal and iron ore. Most of the Northeast's people live on the southern part of the plain near the Liao River.

Farther south, the wide, flat North China Plain lies in the valley of the Huang He. Wheat is the main crop in this highly productive agricultural area. Major flooding formerly occurred in the val- ley, which earned the river the nickname *China's Sorrow.* Today, dams, dikes, and reservoirs, and the use of river water for irrigation, control most floods. The Grand Canal, which is the world's longest artificially created waterway, extends more than 1,000 miles (1,600 kilometers) across the North China Plain.

The lower Yangtze Valley has the best combination of level land, fertile soil, and rainfall anywhere in China. In the so-called Fertile Triangle between Nanjing, Shanghai, and Hangzhou, the population density is extremely high. The Yangtze River and its many tributaries have long formed the most important water route for trade within China.

The Central Uplands are an area of hills and mountains between the Eastern Lowlands and the Tibetan Highlands. The Qin Ling, a mountain range, is the chief physical feature of the region. Peaks in the range rise more than 12,000 feet (3,658 meters) above sea level. The Qin Ling crosses the region from east to west. It forms a natural barricade against seasonal winds that carry rain from the south and dust or cold air from the north. To the north of the mountains are dry wheat-growing areas. To the south lie warm, humid areas where rice is the major crop.

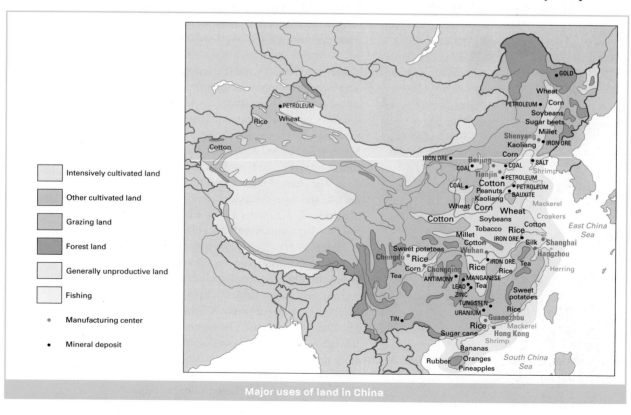

Intensively cultivated land

Other cultivated land

Grazing land

Forest land

Generally unproductive land

Fishing

• Manufacturing center

• Mineral deposit

Major uses of land in China

The Sichuan Basin, a large basin surrounded by high mountains, lies southwest of the Central Uplands. Its mild climate and long growing season make it one of China's main agricultural regions. Most crops are grown on *terraced fields*—level strips of land cut out of the hillsides. The name *Sichuan* means *Four Rivers* and refers to the four streams that flow into the Yangtze River in the region. The rivers have carved out deep gorges in the region's red sandstone, which makes land travel difficult. Small ships can travel on the Yangtze into central Hubei, but only boats and other small craft can navigate farther west into Sichuan and the river's swift-flowing tributaries.

The Southern Uplands cover southeastern China, including the island of Hainan. The Southern Uplands are a region of green hills and mountains. The deltas of the Xi Jiang (West River) and Min rivers are almost the only flat areas in the region. The Xi Jiang and its tributaries form the main transportation route for southern China. Deep, rich soils and a tropical climate help make the delta area an extremely productive agricultural region.

Much of the Southern Uplands is so hilly and mountainous that little land can be cultivated, even by terracing. The central part of the region, near the city of Guilin, is one of the most scenic areas in China. It has many isolated limestone hills that rise 100 to 600 feet (30 to 182 meters) almost straight up.

Climate

China has a wide range of climates because it is such a large country and has such a variety of natural features. The most severe climatic conditions occur in the Taklimakan and Gobi deserts. Daytime temperatures in these deserts may exceed 100°F (38°C) in summer, but nighttime lows may fall to -30°F (-34°C) in winter. Tibet and Heilongjiang province in northeastern China have long, bitterly cold winters. In contrast, coastal areas of southeastern China have a tropical climate.

Seasonal winds called *monsoons* greatly affect China's climate. In winter, monsoons carry cold, dry air from central Asia across China toward the sea. These high winds often create dust storms in the north. From late spring to early fall, the monsoons blow from the opposite direction and spread warm, moist air inland from the sea. Because of the monsoons, more rain falls in summer than in winter throughout China. Most parts of the country receive more than 80 percent of their rainfall between May and October.

Summers tend to be hot and humid in southeastern China and in the southern parts of the Northeast. In fact, summer temperatures average about 80°F (27°C) throughout much of China. However, northern China has longer and much colder winters than the south has. In January, daily low temperatures average about -13°F (-25°C) in Heilongjiang and about 20°F (-7°C) throughout much of the eastern third of the country. However, the coastal areas of the Southern uplands are much warmer. Mountains shield southern China and the Yangtze Valley west of Wuhan from the winter winds. The Sichuan Basin is especially well protected, and frost occurs only a few days each winter.

The amount of precipitation varies greatly from region to region in China. The deserts of Xinjiang and Inner Mongolia receive less than 4 inches (10 centimeters) of rain yearly. More than 40 inches (100 centimeters) of rain falls each year in many parts of southeastern China. Some areas near the southeastern coast receive up to 80 inches (200 centimeters) annually. In northern China, the amount of precipitation varies widely from year to year. However, most areas in northern China receive less than 40 inches (100 centimeters) yearly. For example, annual precipitation averages about 25 inches (63 centimeters) in Beijing and 28 inches (70 centimeters) in Shenyang. Snowfalls occur only in the north. But even there, they are infrequent and usually light.

Economy

China has one of the world's largest economies in terms of its *gross domestic product* (GDP), the value of all goods and services it produces in a year. But in terms of *per capita* (per person) GDP, China ranks low. More than half of the world's countries have a higher per capita GDP than China. Because of this, many economists still consider China a developing country.

The national government exercises much control over China's economy. It controls the most important industrial plants and operates most of the nation's banks, most long-distance transportation, and foreign trade. It also sets the prices of certain key goods and services.

China's government makes national economic plans that cover five-year periods. These plans determine how the government will work to improve different areas of the economy. Through the 2000s, the Communist government achieved an impressive record of economic growth.

In the early 1980s, the Chinese government began a series of economic reforms that led to less government control over some business activities. Since then, the number of privately owned and operated businesses has increased dramatically. Many experts believe the increased ownership of business has contributed significantly to China's economic growth. However, it has also led to increased unemployment and labor migration.

In the 1990s, the government began spending huge amounts of money to improve China's *infrastructure* (roads, bridges, dams, and other public works). These projects include the Three Gorges Dam, canals to bring water from the south to the north, and subway systems in major cities.

Manufacturing and mining contribute more to China's GDP than any other category of economic activity. Shanghai is one of the world's leading manufacturing centers. Its industrial output far exceeds that of any other place in China. Beijing and Tianjin are also important industrial centers. Others include Shenyang and Harbin in the Northeast; Guangzhou, Hangzhou, Shenzhen, and Wuhan in southeastern China; and Chengdu and Chongqing in the Sichuan Basin.

After the Communists came to power, they began to rebuild China's factories in an effort to make the nation an industrial power. They concentrated on the development of heavy industries, such as the production of metals and machinery. Today, China produces more steel than any other country. The machine-building industry provides metalworking tools and other machines for new factories. Other major manufactured products include aircraft, automobiles, cement and other building materials, fertilizer and other chemicals, military equipment, ships, and trucks.

The largest consumer goods industries include the clothing and textile industry, the food-processing industry, and electronics. As the standard of living in China improves, demand is growing for such consumer goods as automobiles, refrigerators, and television sets. As a result, the Chinese are increasing their production of consumer items.

Hydroelectric power station at Three Gorges Dam

To help continue the country's industrial expansion, China's leaders made contracts with foreign companies to modernize factories and to build new ones. The government is also improving and expanding scientific and technical education in China and sending students abroad for training. However, waste and inefficiency in industry remain problems.

China is one of the world's largest producers and users of coal. Coal deposits lie in many parts of China, but the best fields are in the north. Coal-burning plants provide about 70 percent of China's electric energy. Hydroelectric plants and oil-burning plants supply most of the rest. The largest oil field in China is at Daqing in Heilongjiang. Other major Chinese oil fields include those at Dagang, near Tianjin; at Liaohe, in Liaoning; and at Shengli on the Shandong Peninsula.

China is a leading producer of iron ore. Most of the ore comes from large, low-grade deposits in the northeastern provinces. Mines in the central and southwestern parts of the country also yield iron ore.

China outranks all other countries in the production of aluminum, lead, magnesium, tungsten, and zinc. It is a leading producer of copper, gold, silver, and tin.

Service industries provide services rather than produce goods. They include trade; banking and finance; communication; education; health care; insurance; recreation; and transportation. Together, they contribute over two-fifths of China's GDP.

Tourism has become an important part of this group. Each year, tens of millions of tourists visit China from other countries, and tens of millions of Chinese travel within their country. More information on transportation and communication appears later in this section.

Agriculture contributes only about one-tenth of China's GDP, but it ranks as the country's largest employer. Nearly half of China's workers are farmers. In southeastern and east-central China, farmers grow cotton, rice, sweet potatoes, tea, and wheat. Much corn is grown in the northeast. China produces more apples, cabbages, carrots, cotton, pears, potatoes, rice, tobacco, tomatoes, and wheat than any other country. In addition, it is a leading producer of corn, melons, rubber, soybeans, sugar beets, sugarcane, and tea. Farmers in the far south grow tropical crops, such as bananas, oranges, and pineapples.

In rural areas, many families raise chickens and ducks. China has more domesticated ducks than any other country. Many farmers raise hogs for both meat and fertilizer. China has nearly half of all the hogs in the world. China also has many cattle, goats, horses, and sheep.

Only about 15 percent of China's land area can be cultivated. Thus, farmers have little cropland on which to grow food for themselves and the rest of the country's huge population. However, they manage to provide almost enough food for all the people. Southern China has a long growing season, so farmers there can grow two or more crops on the same land each year. However, droughts and floods often interrupt production. Chinese farmers do most of their work by hand with simple tools. They use irrigation and fertilizers and practice soil conservation.

During the 1950s, the Communists *collectivized* China's agriculture. They organized the peasants to farm the land cooperatively in units called *communes*. In the 1980s, emphasis on communes declined, and individual families farmed more of the land. The families must pay taxes on their land and must sell an agreed amount of farm products to the state at a fixed price. They may then sell their surplus crops at farm markets, sometimes to city dwellers.

Fishing industry. China has the world's largest fishing industry. The Chinese catch tens of millions of tons of fish, shellfish, and other seafood annually. Fish farming is an important industry in China. Fish farmers raise fish in ponds both for food and for use in fertilizer.

Forestry. China is a world leader in producing forest products. Its timber industry is concentrated in the southeastern and northeastern parts of the country. But China does not produce enough timber to meet its own needs and must import many forest products.

International trade is vital to China's economic development. Foreign investments help China increase its imports and exports. In 1999, China signed a landmark trade agreement with the United States that lowered many barriers to trade. In 2001, China joined the World Trade Organization, a group that promotes international trade.

China imports machinery and other technology needed to modernize the economy. Other leading imports include chemicals, metals, petroleum and petroleum products, and plastics. China's main exports include clothing, furniture, food, electronic devices, textiles, and toys. Much of China's international trade passes through Hong Kong. China's chief trading partners include Germany, Japan, South Korea, and the United States.

A fish farmer with his harvest of catfish

Transportation. Many Chinese still rely on simple, traditional means for transportation over short distances. Rural people carry loads fastened to their back or hanging from poles carried across their shoulders. Carts and wagons are pulled either by people or by donkeys, horses, mules, or oxen. Bicycles, motor scooters, taxis, and buses are widely used for local travel.

Railroads make up the most important part of China's modern transportation system. Rail lines link the major cities and manufacturing centers. The railroads transport both freight and passenger traffic.

China has an extensive network of roads that reaches almost every town in the nation. Highway

Playing an on-line game in an Internet cafe

traffic in China consists mostly of trucks and buses. On rural roads, tractors are common. Many cars are owned by government agencies or taxi companies, but growing numbers of Chinese are buying them for personal use.

Ships transport freight and boats carry passengers and light loads on several Chinese rivers, especially the Yangtze. The Grand Canal, completed about A.D. 1327, extends more than 1,000 miles (1,600 kilometers) from Hangzhou in the south to Beijing in the north. However, silt deposits clog the canal, and only part of it still serves as a water route.

China's major ports include Dalian, Guangzhou, Hong Kong, Ningbo, Qingdao, Shanghai, Shenzhen, and Tianjin. The chief airports are at Beijing, Guangzhou, Hong Kong, and Shanghai, but many other cities have airports. Chinese and foreign airlines link China with cities around the world.

Communication in China comes under strict government control. During the early years of Communism, newspapers, radio, and television were devoted mostly to political propaganda. But in the 1980s, the government began allowing the media to provide general information and entertainment. Educational programs, concerts, plays, and films often appear on television.

Hundreds of daily newspapers and many weeklies are published in China. The government and the Chinese Communist Party publish or support most of these.

In 1978, many people began to express political opinions using posters with large writing called *big-character posters*. These posters were pasted on walls that came to be known as *democracy walls*. Many posters complained about China's political system. In 1979, the government forbade posters that criticized its policies. Now, posters typically give such information as tips on health and physical fitness.

Radios and televisions are widespread throughout China, although they are much more common in urban areas. Radio programs are still broadcast over loudspeakers in some rural areas. A village or other group of people sometimes buys a television set and places it in a common area for public use.

Since the 1990s, the telephone system that had been reserved for official purposes has been expanded to allow private use. Cellular telephones are popular, especially among city dwellers. People also use the state-run postal system for personal communication.

The Internet is popular in China, but the government tightly regulates its use. Yet some people in China use the Internet to express their political views, much as the big-character posters were used in the late 1970s.

History

The oldest written records of Chinese history date from about 1500 B.C., during the Shang dynasty. These records are in the form of *oracle bones*—notations scratched on thousands of turtle shells and animal bones. About 100 B.C., a Chinese historian named Sima Qian wrote the first major history of China. Through the centuries, the Chinese always kept detailed records of the events of their times.

Beginnings of Chinese civilization. People lived in what is now China long before the beginning of written history. Early human beings probably inhabited parts of eastern China more than 1 million years ago. Prehistoric human beings known as the *Homo erectus* lived between about 770,000 and 400,000 years ago in what is now northern China. By about 10,000 B.C., a number of cultures had developed in this area. From two of them—the Yangshao and the Longshan—a distinctly Chinese civilization gradually emerged.

The Yangshao culture reached the peak of its development about 3000 B.C. The culture, which extended from the central valley of the Huang He to the present-day province of Gansu, was based on millet farming. About the same time, the Longshan culture spread over much of what is now the eastern third of the country. The Longshan people lived in walled communities, cultivated rice, and raised cattle and sheep.

The first dynasties. The Xia culture, which some scholars consider China's first dynasty, arose during the 2100s B.C. For many years, experts doubted that the Xia really existed and thought it was only part of Chinese mythology. But archaeologists found evidence of its existence in what is now Henan province.

The Shang dynasty arose from the Longshan and Xia cultures about 1766 B.C. The Shang king-

Detail of some of the 6,000 statues in the Army of Terra-cotta Warriors, 2,000 years old, from the tomb of the first emperor of China

dom was centered in the eastern Huang He Valley. It became a highly developed society governed by a hereditary class of aristocrats. The dynasty's accomplishments included magnificent bronze vessels, horse-drawn war chariots, and a system of writing.

About 1045 B.C., the Zhou people overthrew the Shang from the west and established their own dynasty. The Zhou dynasty ruled China until 256 B.C. The dynasty directly controlled only the western part of their territory. To the east, the Zhou gave authority to certain followers. These followers became lords of semi-independent states. As time passed, these lords grew increasingly independent of the royal court and so weakened its power. In 771 B.C., invaders forced the Zhou to abandon their capital, near what is now Xi'an, and move eastward to Luoyang. Battles between the Zhou rulers and with non-Chinese invaders further weakened the dynasty.

About 500 B.C., the great philosopher Confucius proposed new moral standards to replace the magical practices of his time. During the later Zhou period, there were seven eastern states. The rulers of these states fought one another for the control of all China. In 221 B.C., the Qin state defeated the last of its rival states and established China's first empire controlled by a strong central government. The Qin believed in a philosophy called *Legalism*, and their victory resulted partly from following Legalistic ideas. Legalism emphasized the importance of authority, efficient administration, and strict laws. A combination of

Legalistic administrative practices and Confucian moral values helped the Chinese empires endure for more than 2,000 years.

The Qin dynasty lasted only until 206 B.C., but it brought great changes that influenced all later empires in China. The first Qin emperor, Shi Huangdi, abolished the local states and set up a strong central government. His government standardized weights and measures, the currency, and the Chinese writing system. To keep out invaders, he ordered the construction of the Great Wall of China. Laborers built the wall by joining shorter walls constructed during the Zhou dynasty. The Great Wall, which was added to, rebuilt, and moved by later dynasties, extends from the Bo Gulf of the Yellow Sea to the the Jiayu Pass in what is now Gansu province in western China. It stretches about 5,500 miles (8,850 kilometers), including about 3,890 miles (6,260 kilometers) of handmade walls as well as such natural barriers as rivers and hills. Experts believe that the full extent of the Great Wall, including sections predating the Ming dynasty, measures about 13,170 miles (21,200 kilometers).

Shi Huangdi taxed the Chinese people heavily to support his military campaigns and his vast building projects. These taxes and the harsh enforcement of laws led to civil war soon after his death in 210 B.C. The Qin dynasty collapsed four years later.

The Han dynasty then gained control of China. It ruled from 206 B.C. to A.D. 220. During the Han period, Confucianism became the philosophical basis of government. Aristocrats held most important state offices. However, a person's qualifications began to play a role in the selection and placement of officials. Chinese influence spread into neighboring countries, and overland trade routes linked China with Europe for the first time.

In A.D. 9, a Han official named Wang Mang seized the throne and set up the Xin dynasty. However, the Han dynasty regained control of China by A.D. 25. Art, education, and science thrived. Writers produced histories and dictionaries. They also collected classics of literature from earlier times. During the late Han period, Buddhism was introduced into China from India.

Political struggles at the royal court and administrative dishonesty plagued the last century of Han rule. In addition, powerful regional officials began to mistreat the peasants. As a result, large-scale rebellion finally broke out, and the Han dynasty fell in 220.

The period of division. China then split into three competing kingdoms. Soon afterward, nomadic groups invaded northern China. A series of Chinese and non-Chinese dynasties ruled all or part of the north from 304 to 581. Six dynasties followed one another in the south from 222 to 589. During this period of division, Buddhism spread across China and influenced all aspects of life.

The brief Sui dynasty (581–618) reunified China when it absorbed the last southern dynasty in 589. By 610, the Grand Canal linked the Yangtze Valley with northern China. The canal made the grain and other products of the south more easily available to support the political and military needs of the north.

The Tang dynasty replaced the Sui in 618 and ruled China for nearly 300 years. The Tang period was an age of prosperity and great cultural accomplishment. The Tang capital at Chang'an (now Xi'an) had more than a million people, making it the largest city in the world. It attracted diplomats, traders, poets, and scholars from throughout Asia. Some of China's greatest poets, including Li Bo and Du Fu, wrote during the Tang period. Buddhism, in forms adapted to Chinese ways, remained an enormous cultural influence. Distinctly Chinese schools of Buddhism spread, including *Chan* (Zen) and *Qingtu* (Pure Land).

In 755, a rebellion led by a northern general named An Lushan touched off a gradual decline in Tang power. A series of rebellions in the late 800s further weakened the Tang empire, which finally ended in 907. During the period that followed, a succession of "Five Dynasties and Ten Kingdoms" struggled for control of the empire. In 960, the Song dynasty reunified China.

The Song dynasty brought major changes that affected China throughout the remaining empires. The Song rulers firmly established a system of civil service examinations that had begun during the Han period. They thus completed the shift of social and political power from aristocratic families to officials selected on the basis of talent. Another significant change was the development of *Neo-Confucianism*, which combined the moral standards of traditional Confucianism with elements of Buddhism and Taoism. The philosopher Zhu Xi was largely responsible for this new Confucianism. The Song dynasty established Neo-Confucianism as the official state philosophy, and all later Chinese dynasties continued to support it.

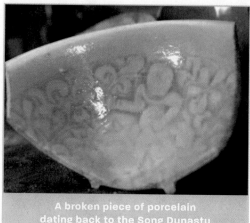

A broken piece of porcelain dating back to the Song Dynasty

During the Song period, the introduction of early ripening rice made it possible to grow two or three crops a year in the south. The increased rice production helped support the population, which for the first time exceeded 100 million. Chinese inventions during this period included a handheld gun and movable type for printing. Literature, philosophy, and history flourished. In the fine arts, the great Song achievements were hard-glazed porcelains and magnificent landscape paintings.

The Song dynasty suffered from frequent attacks by nomadic peoples from the north. By 1127, it had lost its hold in northern China to a rival dynasty from northeastern China. The Song then moved their capital from Kaifeng to Hangzhou on the wealthy lower Yangtze Delta. The dynasty that ruled from 960 to 1127 is often called the Northern Song, and the dynasty that ruled after 1127 is called the Southern Song.

Mongol rule. During the 1200s, Mongol warriors swept into China from the north. The Mongol leader Kublai Khan established the Yuan dynasty. It controlled all of China from 1279 to 1368, the first time that the entire country had come under foreign rule. During the Yuan period, Europeans became increasingly interested in China because of the reports of travelers and traders. The most enthusiastic reports came from Marco Polo, a trader from Venice. He claimed that he traveled widely in China from 1275 to 1292, and he gave glowing accounts of the highly civilized country known by Europeans as *Cathay*.

The Mongols ruled China harshly. During the mid-1300s, rebellions drove the Mongols out of China and led to the establishment of the Ming dynasty.

The Ming dynasty ruled from 1368 to 1644, a period of stability, prosperity, and revived Chinese influence in eastern Asia. Literature and art flourished again. When European traders and Roman Catholic missionaries visited China during the late 1500s and the 1600s, the Ming rulers distrusted them. The Chinese considered the Europeans to be a threat to the country's stability.

The early rule of the Manchus. In 1644, the Manchus from northeastern China invaded Beijing, the Ming capital, and established the Qing dynasty. The Manchus ruled China until 1912. Like the Mongols, the Manchus came from beyond the Great Wall. But unlike the Mongols, the Manchus had adopted many elements of Chinese culture before they gained control of the empire. The Manchus strongly supported Neo-Confucianism and modeled their political system after that of the Ming.

From 1669 to 1796, the Qing empire prospered. Chinese influence extended into Mongolia, Tibet, and other parts of central Asia. Commerce and the handicraft industry built up the economy. Agricultural output increased as China's population expanded rapidly, doubling from about 150 million in 1700 to about 300 million by 1800.

By the late 1700s, the standard of living in China began to decline as the population grew faster than agricultural production. In the 1770s, political dishonesty began to plague the Qing administration. In 1796, the worsening conditions touched off a rebellion, led by an anti-Manchu secret society. The rebellion lasted until 1804 and greatly weakened the Qing dynasty.

The dynastic cycle. Chinese historians noticed a pattern to the rise and fall of China's dynasties. They saw that dynasties usually began with a strong ruler who established an empire, often using ruthless means. Once established, the dynasty would expand and make great contributions to Chinese culture. Later rulers would become corrupt and neglect the empire, which eventually would weaken and fall after a rebellion. From the chaos that followed, a new strong leader would emerge, and the cycle would begin again.

Many Chinese believed the cyclic pattern could help them predict what would happen next to a dynasty. Peasants added the idea that natural events, such as earthquakes, were signs that things were about to change. These ideas continue to influence Chinese thought today.

Clash with the Western powers. Merchants from Europe and North America had little effect on China before the 1800s. The Chinese government permitted foreign trade only at the port of Guangzhou and severely limited contact between foreigners and Chinese. China exported large quantities of tea and silk to the West but purchased few goods in return. To balance their trade, European merchants began to bring opium to China during the late 1700s. The Chinese had outlawed the importation of opium, so the Europeans smuggled the drug.

Opium smuggling created much local disorder in China, and the large outflow of money to pay for the opium seriously disturbed the economy. In March 1839, Chinese officials tried to stop the illegal trade by seizing over 20,000 chests of opium from British merchants in Guangzhou. The Opium War then broke out between China and the United Kingdom. The United Kingdom easily won the war, which ended with the Treaty of Nanjing in 1842.

The bombardment of Canton (Guangzhou) during the first Opium War

The Treaty of Nanjing was the first of what the Chinese called the *unequal treaties.* It gave the Chinese island of Hong Kong to the United Kingdom and opened four more Chinese ports to British residence and trade. The Treaty of Nanjing also granted British officials the right to deal on equal terms with Chinese officials and to try criminal cases involving British citizens. China signed similar treaties with France and the United States in 1844. These treaties stated that any rights granted to one foreign power must also be given to the other nations. The

Western nations thus acquired a common interest in maintaining their special privileges in China.

In 1858 and 1860—after China lost another war, against the United Kingdom and France—China signed more treaties with France, Russia, the United Kingdom, and the United States. These treaties opened additional ports to trade, permitted foreign shipping on the Yangtze, and allowed missionaries to live on and own property in the interior of China. The treaties also called for the Western nations to establish permanent diplomatic offices in Beijing. The United Kingdom added the Kowloon Peninsula to its Hong Kong colony, and Russia received all Chinese territory north of the Amur River and east of the Ussuri River.

The Taiping Rebellion.
A series of uprisings in the mid-1800s posed a serious threat to the survival of the Qing dynasty. The most important uprising was the Taiping Rebellion. It lasted from 1850 to 1864 and cost millions of lives. The Taipings were a semi-religious group that combined Christian beliefs with ancient Chinese ideas for perfecting society. They challenged both the Qing dynasty and Confucianism with a program to divide the land equally among the people. During the rebellion, local Chinese officials organized new armies, which defeated the Taipings. The Qing received some military aid from the foreign nations that had signed the treaties. These nations wanted the dynasty to survive so the unequal terms of the treaties could remain in effect.

The Open-Door Policy.
A disastrous war with Japan in 1894 and 1895 forced China to give up its claim on Korea. China also had to give the Japanese the island of Taiwan, which the Qing had controlled since 1683. France, Germany, Italy, Japan, Russia, and the United Kingdom then forced the crumbling Qing empire to grant them more trading rights and territory. The division of China into a number of European colonies appeared likely. But the Chinese people had begun to develop strong feelings of national unity. This growth of nationalism helped prevent the division of the country, as did rivalry among the foreign powers. None of the foreign powers would allow any of the others to become dominant in China. Beginning in 1899, the United States gradually persuaded the other Western powers and Japan to accept the *Open-Door Policy*, which guaranteed the rights of all nations to trade with China on an equal basis.

The Boxer Rebellion.
By the 1890s, some Chinese violently opposed the spread of Western and Christian influences in China. Chinese rebels formed secret societies to fight these influences. The best-known society was called the *Boxers* by Westerners because its members practiced Chinese ceremonial exercises that resembled shadowboxing. In the Boxer Rebellion of 1900, the Boxers attacked and killed Westerners and Chinese Christians. Although initially neutral, the Manchu court eventually supported the rebellion. A rescue force from the Western nations crushed the rebellion.

In the years following the Boxer Rebellion, the Manchus set out to reform the Chinese government and economy. They abolished the Confucian civil service examinations, established modern schools, and sent students abroad to study. They also organized and equipped a Western-style army. In addition, the Qing court reorganized the central government, promised to adopt a constitution, and permitted the provinces to elect their own legislatures.

The fall of the Manchus.
The Manchu reforms came too late to save the dynasty. A movement to set up a republic had been growing since the Japanese defeated China in 1895. In 1905, several revolutionary organizations that wanted China to become a republic combined to form the Revolutionary Alliance. They chose as their leader Sun Yat-sen, a Western-educated physician.

From 1905 to 1911, the rebels staged a series of unsuccessful armed attacks against the Manchus. Finally, on October 10, 1911, army troops loosely associated with the Revolutionary Alliance revolted at Wuchang. By the year's end, all the southern and central provinces had declared their independence from Manchu rule.

The early republic.
On January 1, 1912, the leaders of the revolution formally established the Republic of China in Nanjing. They named Sun Yat-sen temporary president of the republic. The Manchus then called upon Yuan Shikai, a retired military official, to try to defeat the supporters of the republic. But Yuan arranged a secret settlement with Sun and his followers. The last

A Chinese boxer, in full regalia, during the Boxer Rebellion

Manchu emperor, a 6-year-old boy named Pu Yi, gave up the throne on February 12, 1912. The following month, Yuan became president in place of Sun, who stepped down. Yuan quickly moved to expand his personal power.

In 1912, the former revolutionaries established the *Kuomintang* (Nationalist Party, also spelled Guomindang). In 1913, they organized a revolt against Yuan. The revolt failed, and the Nationalist leaders fled to Japan. Yuan's presidency became a dictatorship, and he took steps to establish himself as emperor. But even Yuan's own followers opposed the revival of the empire. A rebellion by military leaders in the provinces forced him to abandon his plans.

The warlord period. Yuan Shikai died in 1916, and the power of the central government quickly crumbled. Presidents continued to hold office in Beijing, but the real power in northern China lay in the hands of *warlords* (local military leaders). In 1917, with the support of southern warlords, Sun Yat-sen set up a rival government in Guangzhou. By 1922, the republic had failed hopelessly and civil war was widespread.

Meanwhile, great changes occurred in Chinese culture and society. A journal called *New Youth* attacked Confucianism and presented a wide range of philosophies and social theories. On May 4, 1919, students in Beijing demonstrated against the Versailles Peace Conference. The conference permitted Japan to keep control of the German holdings it had seized in China during World War I (1914–1918). Other demonstrations that followed helped spread ideas presented by *New Youth* and other journals. This revolution in thought became known as the *May Fourth Movement.* It contributed greatly to the growth of Chinese nationalism and so strengthened the drive for political revolution.

In 1919, Sun began to reorganize the Nationalist Party and to recruit supporters from among students. At almost the same time, the first Communist student groups appeared in Beijing and other major cities. The Soviet Union, which had been formed in 1922 under Russia's leadership, sent advisers to China in 1923 to help the Nationalists. The Soviets persuaded the Chinese Communists to join the Nationalist Party and to help it carry out the revolution. The party began to develop its own army and to organize workers and peasants to prepare for an attack on the northern warlords.

Sun Yat-sen died in 1925, and leadership of the Nationalist Party gradually passed to its military

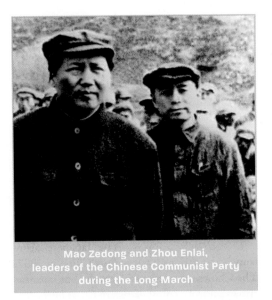

Mao Zedong and Zhou Enlai, leaders of the Chinese Communist Party during the Long March

commander, Chiang Kai-shek. In 1926, the Nationalists began a campaign to defeat the northern warlords and soon won some major victories. In 1927, Chiang and his troops turned against the Communists and executed hundreds of members of Communist-backed labor unions in Shanghai. More attacks followed in other cities. Communist survivors fled to the hills in the province of Jiangxi in southern China. In 1928, the Nationalists captured Beijing and united China under one government for the first time since 1916.

Nationalist rule. The Nationalist government was a one-party dictatorship that never gained full control of China. Communist opposition and Japanese aggression severely limited its power and accomplishments.

By 1931, the Communists had established a number of rural bases and set up a rival government in southern and central China. In 1934, Chiang Kai-shek's armies forced the Communists to evacuate their bases and begin their famous *Long March.* By the fall of 1935, the Communists had marched more than 6,000 miles (9,700 kilometers) over a winding route to the province of Shaanxi in northern China. Of the approximately 100,000 Communists who began the march, only a few thousand survived to reach Shaanxi. During the march, Mao Zedong became the leader of the Chinese Communist Party.

While Chiang fought the Communists, the Japanese seized more Chinese territory. In 1931, the Japanese occupied Manchuria (which the Chinese now call *Dongbei* or the Northeast) and made it a puppet state that they called *Manchukuo.* The

Chongqing after being heavily bombed by the Japanese

Japanese then extended their military influence into Inner Mongolia and other parts of northern China. Chiang agreed to a series of Japanese demands because he felt unprepared to fight the Japanese until he had defeated the Communists.

Many students and intellectuals opposed Chiang's giving in to Japan. They organized demonstrations and anti-Japanese associations. Dissatisfaction spread to troops from Manchuria who were blockading the Communist-held areas in the northwest. In 1936, the Manchurian forces kidnapped Chiang in Xi'an. He was released only after agreeing to end the civil war and to form a united front against the Japanese.

War with Japan. The Japanese army launched a major attack against China in 1937. The Chinese resisted courageously, but Japanese armies controlled most of eastern China by the end of 1938. The Nationalist forces withdrew to the province of Sichuan, where they made Chongqing the wartime capital.

China joined the Allies in World War II on December 9, 1941, two days after Japan attacked the United States at Pearl Harbor, Hawaii. In that war, the United Kingdom, the United States, the Soviet Union, and the other Allies fought Germany, Japan, and the other Axis powers. The Allies gave aid to China, but constant warfare against Japan exhausted China's resources and strength. The cost of the war caused severe inflation, which led to government corruption and weakened the Chinese people's support for the Nationalists.

For the Communists, the war against Japan provided an opportunity for political and military expansion. In northern China, they gained control of large areas that the Japanese army had overrun but lacked the forces to defend. The Communists enlarged their army and organized and trained the people to become productive party members. They also began a social revolution in the countryside, which included redistributing land to the peasants in Communist-controlled areas. When the war against Japan ended in August 1945, the Communists held an area in northern China with a population of about 100 million. In addition, they claimed to have an army of nearly 1 million soldiers.

Civil war. In 1945, the United States sent General George C. Marshall to China to attempt to arrange a political settlement between the Nationalists and the Communists. However, neither the Nationalists nor the Communists believed that they could achieve their goals by coming to terms with the other side. In mid-1946, full-scale fighting began.

The superior military tactics of the Communists and the social revolution they had started in the countryside gradually turned the tide against the Nationalists. After capturing Tianjin and Beijing in January 1949, Mao Zedong's armies crossed the Yangtze River and drove the Nationalists toward southern China. On October 1, 1949, Mao proclaimed the establishment in Beijing of the People's Republic of China. In December, Chiang Kai-shek and his followers fled to the island of Taiwan.

The beginning of Communist rule took place under the direction of Mao Zedong, the chairman of the Communist Party. Premier Zhou Enlai directed all government departments and ministries. Military, technical, and economic help from the Soviet Union helped support the new government. From 1949 to 1952, the new government firmly established its control over China and worked to help the nation's economy recover.

The new Communist government seized farmland from landlords and redistributed it among the peasants. Angry mobs, resentful of the way landlords had mistreated them, killed many of the landlords. Estimates of the number of landlords killed range from 200,000 to several million.

In 1953, China began its First Five-Year Plan for economic development. From 1953 to 1957, Chinese industry grew at the rapid rate of about 15 percent a year. By 1957, the Communists had brought all important industries under the control of the government. In addition, peasants were forced or persuaded to combine their landholdings into agricultural cooperatives. But agricultural production increased much more slowly than industrial output.

The Great Leap Forward was the name given to China's Second Five-Year Plan. Launched in 1958, this plan was designed to accelerate China's economic development. It was based on Mao's belief that human willpower and effort could overcome all obstacles. Thus, the government tried to speed development by greatly increasing the number of workers and their hours while ignoring China's lack of capital and modern technology. It combined the agricultural cooperatives into huge communes to improve the efficiency of farm workers. The plan also set up many small factories and increased the industrial work force. Laborers worked long hours, sometimes sleeping at their machines.

The Great Leap Forward shattered China's economy. From 1959 to 1961, China suffered economic depression, food shortages, and a decline in industrial output. By 1962, the economy began to recover. However, the Chinese had not solved the problem of achieving economic growth while maintaining the Communist ideals.

Disagreement over this issue produced a major split within the Communist Party between *radicals* and *revisionists*. The radicals called for China to strive for a classless society in which everyone would work selflessly for the common good. The revisionists stressed that division of labor was necessary for economic development. They believed that the policies of the radicals were unrealistic and hampered the modernization of China.

Break with the Soviet Union. Friendly relations between China and the Soviet Union ended in the early 1960s. China had criticized the Soviets as early as 1956 for their policy of "peaceful coexistence" with the West. Unlike the Soviets, the Chinese believed that war with the West was inevitable. They also accused the Soviet Union of betraying the aims of Communism. In 1960, the Soviet Union stopped giving assistance to China. In 1962, the Soviets refused to support China in a border war with India. The Soviet Union signed a nuclear test ban treaty with the United States and the United Kingdom in 1963. The Chinese then broke off relations with the Soviets, whom they accused of joining an anti-Chinese plot.

The Cultural Revolution. In 1966, Mao Zedong gave his support to the radicals in the Communist Party. Mao thus began what he called the Great Proletarian Cultural Revolution, a drive to enforce strict Communist principles and to rid China of revisionists. The radicals accused many top party and government officials of failing to follow Communist ideals and removed them from their positions. Students and other young people formed semi-military organizations called the Red Guards. They demonstrated in the major cities against revisionists, intellectuals, scientists, and others whom they called anti-Maoists. Most universities were closed from 1966 to 1970. Radicals seized control of many provincial and city governments. Violence frequently broke out as competing radical groups struggled for power.

Mao's attempt to put China back on a revolutionary path wrecked the government and economy so severely that he had to call out the army in 1967 to restore order. By 1970, the Communist Party, the government, and the educational system had begun to resume their normal activities. But the conflict between radicals and revisionists within the party continued.

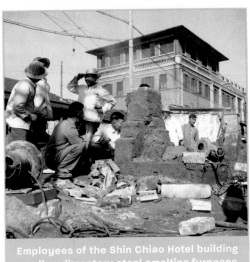

Employees of the Shin Chiao Hotel building small, rudimentary steel smelting furnaces during the Great Leap Forward

Improved relations with the West. During the early 1970s, Canada, Japan, and several other nations established diplomatic relations with the People's Republic of China. The United States continued officially to recognize only the Nationalist government on Taiwan. But in 1971, the United Nations voted to admit the People's Republic in place of Taiwan.

In 1972, U.S. president Richard M. Nixon traveled to China and met with Premier Zhou Enlai and Communist Party chairman Mao Zedong. During Nixon's visit, the United States and China signed the Shanghai Communique, which looked forward to the establishment of normal relations. The following year, the two nations sent representatives to serve in each other's capital. Japan established diplomatic relations with China in 1972.

Deng Xiaoping. Both Zhou Enlai and Mao Zedong died in 1976. A power struggle followed between radicals led by Mao's widow, Jiang Qing, and moderates led by Deng Xiaoping. The moderates emerged from the revisionist movement and promoted a more relaxed form of Communism. As a compromise, Hua Guofeng succeeded Zhou as premier and Mao as chairman of the Communist Party. Hua's government imprisoned Jiang and three other radicals, who were labeled the Gang of Four.

In 1977, Deng Xiaoping became vice premier and vice chairman of the Communist Party. On January 1, 1979, China and the United States established normal diplomatic relations.

By 1980, Hua had lost most of his power, and Deng had become China's most powerful leader. Hua resigned as premier in 1980 and as party chairman in 1981. Deng helped Zhao Ziyang become premier and helped Hu Yaobang become chairman of the party. Zhao and Hu were moderates.

Deng resigned as vice premier in 1980. In 1982, the party's new constitution abolished Deng's post of vice chairman and Hu's post of chairman. It created the position of general secretary as the top party post, and Hu continued in that office. However, Deng remained China's most influential leader.

Deng and the other moderates sought to reduce the people's admiration of Mao. The moderates praised Mao's leadership but denounced the idea that all his policies should be followed. They greatly increased trade and cultural contact with foreign countries. They set out to modernize China's economy with technical help from abroad.

Protests. In the late 1980s, uprisings against Chinese rule broke out in Tibet. In March 1989, China sent troops there to restore order.

In December 1986, many Chinese university students began demanding increased freedom of speech and a greater voice in the selection of officials. Students held demonstrations in a number of cities to promote their demands. In January 1987, Hu Yaobang was removed from his post of Communist Party general secretary. Conservative leaders had criticized Hu for his liberal views on freedom of expression and political reform. Zhao Ziyang then became general secretary of the party. Li Peng became premier in 1988.

Hu Yaobang died in April 1989. University students held marches to honor Hu and mourn his death. They called for a reevaluation of Hu by the country's leaders. These events led to large demonstrations by students and other citizens in Beijing's Tiananmen Square and on the streets of other Chinese cities. The protesters called for more democracy in China and an end to corruption in government. The military crushed the demonstrations and killed hundreds of protesters. The government later arrested many people suspected of involvement in the pro-democracy movement. The government executed a number of those

Student-led pro-democracy uprisings in Tiananmen Square

arrested. In addition, the Communist Party dismissed Zhao Ziyang from his post for not doing more to suppress the pro-democracy movement. Jiang Zemin replaced Zhao as general secretary.

Also in 1989, officials of China and the Soviet Union met to improve relations. When the Soviet Union broke apart in 1991, China established diplomatic relations with the former Soviet republics.

Deng resigned from his remaining party and government posts in 1989 and 1990. But he continued to have influence through the early 1990s. In 1993, Jiang was named to another high office, the largely ceremonial post of president. Deng died in 1997.

Hong Kong and Macao. In 1984, China and the United Kingdom signed an agreement regarding the return of Hong Kong to China when the United Kingdom's lease expired in 1997. China agreed that Hong Kong would retain a high degree of *autonomy* (self-rule) and keep its free-enterprise economy for 50 years, or until 2047. In 1990, the Chinese government approved the Basic Law, the new framework for Hong Kong's administration. On July 1, 1997, Hong Kong became a special administrative region of China.

In 1987, China and Portugal signed a similar agreement for the return of Macao to Chinese administration. On December 20, 1999, Macao became the second special administrative region of China.

Recent developments. In 1998, Zhu Rongji succeeded Li Peng as premier. Zhu had been a vice premier in charge of economic policy. Li Peng was named chairman of China's national legislature.

Construction of Three Gorges Dam, the world's largest dam, began in 1994 on the Yangtze River and was completed in 2010. It is intended to generate electric power, to provide an inland waterway, and to control flooding. The dam's huge reservoir has forced the resettlement of more than 1 million people. The project has many critics, who charge that it has created environmental problems, drowned some of China's best farmland, and covered thousands of historical sites.

In 2001, China became a member of the World Trade Organization, which promotes international trade. China's entry into the organization marked progress in freeing the Chinese economy from government control.

Jiang Zemin stepped down as general secretary of China's Communist Party in 2002. He stepped down as China's president in 2003 and as head of China's military in 2004. Hu Jintao replaced him in all three positions. Also in 2003, Wen Jiabao succeeded Zhu Rongji as premier, and Wu Bangguo succeeded Li Peng as chairman of the National People's Congress.

In March 2008, protests in Tibet calling for independence turned into riots, and the Chinese government again sent troops to restore order. Wen blamed Tibet's spiritual leader, the Dalai Lama, for the unrest and called for him to resign. In May, a powerful earthquake struck south-central China, killing more than 69,000 people.

In August 2008, Beijing was the site of the Summer Olympic Games. China undertook a number of major construction projects to improve its services and facilities for the games. These included the National Center for the Performing Arts, a massive performance hall; Terminal 3 at Beijing airport, the largest building in the world; and Beijing National Stadium, nicknamed "the Bird's Nest," which hosted the Olympics' opening and closing ceremonies, as well as many of its competitions. For many Chinese, the Olympics became a symbol of national pride, especially after China won more gold medals than any other country. In November 2012, Xi Jinping succeeded Hu Jintao as Communist Party general secretary and head of the military. Xi is set to replace Hu as president in 2013.

HONG KONG (pop. 6,708,309) is one of two special administrative regions of China. The other is Macau. Hong Kong lies on China's southern coast, near the mouth of the Zhu Jiang (Pearl River). Hong Kong is a major port of Asia. It is also a center of finance, trade, and tourism. *Hong Kong* is Chinese for *fragrant harbor.*

Hong Kong covers a total area of 1,126 square miles (2,916 square kilometers), but only about 426 square miles (1,104 square kilometers) are land. Hong Kong consists of the island of Hong Kong; Lantau Island, Hong Kong's largest island; about 260 other islands; and a peninsula attached to the mainland of China. The peninsula has two sections—the New

Zhu Rongji

Territories in the north and the Kowloon Peninsula in the south.

Hong Kong had long existed at the edge of the Chinese Empire. The United Kingdom gained control of Hong Kong Island through treaty agreements in 1842, after it defeated China in the First Anglo-Chinese War (also called the First Opium War). In 1860, a treaty settlement after another trade war gave the United Kingdom control of the Kowloon Peninsula and tiny Stonecutters Island west of the peninsula. On July 1, 1898, China leased to the United Kingdom the rest of the islands and the land that became known as the New Territories. The lease was for 99 years. China demanded the return of the entire colony when the New Territories lease expired. China took control of Hong Kong on July 1, 1997.

The Metropolis

The entire northern coast of Hong Kong Island, the southern tip of the Kowloon Peninsula, and the satellite cities in the New Territories form a major metropolitan area. The metropolis once consisted of individual cities called Victoria (on the northern part of Hong Kong Island) and Kowloon (on the southern Kowloon Peninsula). However, the old city boundaries are rarely recognized today. Under British control, Victoria, now known simply as Central, was Hong Kong's capital. Today, Central is Hong Kong's seat of government.

The Hong Kong metropolis is a center of business, commercial services, and tourism. High-rise commercial and residential buildings, modern hotel complexes, shopping malls, and small businesses line the narrow streets. Hong Kong has many modern skyscrapers that serve as headquarters for major banks and multinational corporations. The towering Bank of China building, designed by the Chinese-American architect I. M. Pei, is one of the tallest buildings in the world. It stands at the eastern edge of Central. Hong Kong Disneyland, a theme park on Lantau Island, is a major tourist destination.

Many people live in crowded apartments in the Wan Chai area, east of Central. Many government buildings stand on filled-in land along the Wan Chai coast. A business center has sprung up around them. To the east of this center is the Japanese shopping district of Causeway Bay.

Victoria Harbour separates Hong Kong Island from the Kowloon Peninsula. Motor-vehicle tun-

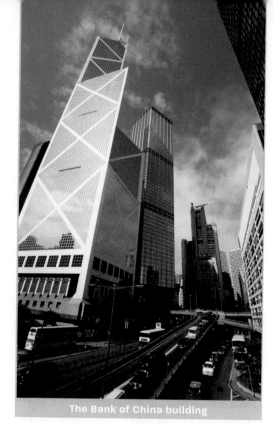

The Bank of China building

nels run underneath the harbor. A network of motorways also links the metropolis to the major satellite cities and to the international airport on Lantau Island. The metropolitan area is well served by a public transportation network. A railway called the Peak Tram transports passengers between Central and the top of Tai Ping Shan (also called Victoria Peak), a mountain that rises to the southwest. In addition, a railroad runs through the New Territories and connects Kowloon with Guangzhou, China. Ferries, buses, and airlines also provide service between Kowloon and Guangzhou.

People

On average, Hong Kong has about 15,750 people per square mile (6,080 per square kilometer) of land. But much of Hong Kong's land is mountainous and uninhabitable. As a result, the population density varies widely. The metropolitan area of Hong Kong is among the world's most crowded places.

Ancestry. About 95 percent of the people of Hong Kong are Chinese. Most are immigrants from southern China or descendants of immigrants from that region. The relatively few non-Chinese residents of Hong Kong include people from Australia, Canada, Indonesia, the Philippines, the United Kingdom, and the United States.

Languages. Hong Kong has two official languages, Chinese and English. Most of Hong Kong's people do not speak English well, though most have learned it as a foreign language at school. The majority of the population speaks Cantonese, a dialect of South China. Many younger people have also learned the Northern Chinese dialect, known as Mandarin in English and *Putonghua* in Chinese. It is the official language of China. Cantonese and Mandarin share the same written words but are different when spoken.

Way of Life

Urban life. Almost all of Hong Kong's people live in urban areas. Most urban dwellers live in Kowloon, Hong Kong Island, and the satellite cities.

Housing in Hong Kong's urban areas varies sharply. Rents and land prices are high. Most wealthy people live in luxury apartment buildings. A small number live in houses with gardens.

Most middle- and low-income people occupy crowded high-rise apartment buildings, many of which were built by the government. Only about half of Hong Kong's residents own their homes.

Rural life. People in rural areas of Hong Kong live in small villages. A few raise crops and livestock. Most people who live in rural areas work in services or industries in the urban areas.

Some rural villages were settled more than 1,000 years ago. Traditional rural houses are made of brick or stone with tile roofs. Today, the majority of Hong Kong's rural people live in low-rise buildings.

Food and clothing. The people of Hong Kong eat large amounts of fresh vegetables, fish, poultry, pork, and beef. The staple food is rice, though wheat-based foods and cuisine from other countries are also widely available. In general, people wear the same type of clothing worn in Europe and North America. Some people wear Chinese-style clothing, especially during such holidays as Chinese New Year.

Religion. The major religions in Hong Kong are Buddhism, Roman Catholicism, and Protestantism. Muslims, Hindus, and Jews also live there.

Education. All children are required by law to go to school for nine years—six years of elementary school and three of high school. Classes in elementary schools are taught in Chinese (Cantonese). Some high schools use Chinese, some use English, and others use both languages.

Hong Kong has a number of institutes of higher education. Its oldest university is the University of Hong Kong, which was founded in 1911.

Land and Climate

The land. Rugged mountains and rolling hills cover much of Hong Kong. The rocky, indented coastlines of Hong Kong's islands and mainland provide many small harbors for fishing villages. Some mountains in the New Territories rise more than 3,000 feet (900 meters) above sea level. Tai Ping Shan on Hong Kong Island is 1,818 feet (554 meters) high.

Barren mountains separate the business districts of the Kowloon Peninsula from the New Territories. Only about 8 percent of the land in Hong Kong is suitable for farming. Throughout the New Territories, poultry farms and vegetable and flower fields lie crowded between areas of poor vegetation and rocky hillsides. The Sham Chun (or Shenzhen) River forms part of the border between Hong Kong and the neighboring Guangdong Province.

Much of Hong Kong's harbor coastline has been filled in with earth to create new land. Hong Kong's old airport, known as Kai Tak International Airport, was built on filled-in land in Kowloon Bay. To land at Kai Tak, airplanes had to come in for a landing over the densely popu-

Entrance to Hong Kong University

Hong Kong International Airport terminal

lated Kowloon. In 1998, Hong Kong International Airport at Chek Lap Kok on Lantau Island replaced Kai Tak. The new airport also was built partly on landfill.

Climate. Hong Kong has hot, humid summers. The winters are cool and less humid. During the summer, temperatures reach 95°F (35°C) or higher. Winter temperatures seldom fall below 40°F (4°C).

Hong Kong receives about 87 inches (220 centimeters) of rainfall yearly. Most of the rain falls in summer and early fall and can cause floods and mud slides. Insufficient rainfall during the winter, along with other factors, contributes to water shortages. Hong Kong buys millions of gallons of water from Guangdong every year.

Economy

Hong Kong is a center of international trade, finance, and tourism. It is a *free port*—that is, it collects no import duties on goods brought in from elsewhere, except for such goods as alcohol, tobacco, and perfume. Because there are few import duties, many products can be bought and sold more cheaply in Hong Kong than in most other parts of the world.

Hong Kong has efficient telecommunications and a highly educated labor force. Business firms of many countries maintain offices in Hong Kong from which they carry on business with China. Hong Kong's economy is highly integrated with that of China.

Service industries. Most workers are employed in service industries, especially wholesale and retail trade, foreign trade, and commu-

nity, social, and personal services. Other important service industries include finance and real estate, restaurants and hotels, and transportation. Hong Kong is one of the world's most important gold trading centers. Its many banks finance investments and trade with China, as well as housing and manufacturing in Hong Kong. Hong Kong is also a major international tourist destination.

Manufacturing. Beginning in the 1980s, most of Hong Kong's manufacturing facilities relocated to China. However, Hong Kong remains a control center for China's global trade network. Hong Kong's investments in China employ millions of workers in manufacturing. Within Hong Kong itself, the main manufacturing activities involve printing and publishing, clothing and textiles, and the production of food and beverages.

Agriculture and fishing. Agriculture is a minor economic activity in Hong Kong. The region depends heavily on imports for its food. Hong Kong maintains a significant fishing fleet that catches bigeyes, false snappers, lizardfish, squid, and other seafood. Because of a high demand for fresh fish, fisheries raise both saltwater and freshwater fish in the New Territories.

Government

The foundation of Hong Kong's government is the Basic Law, which became effective on July 1, 1997, when Hong Kong was transferred from British to Chinese rule. The Basic Law upholds the principle of "one country, two systems." This principle gives Hong Kong a high degree of *autonomy* (self-rule) as a special administrative region of China.

A chief executive heads the government of Hong Kong and serves a 5-year term. A committee of about 800 members elects the chief executive. The election committee consists of citizens from various social and economic levels and members of several government bodies. The Executive Council helps carry out government operations. The chief executive chooses the Executive Council members.

The Legislative Council is Hong Kong's lawmaking body. The council has 60 members, who serve four-year terms. The people of Hong Kong directly elect 30 members of the council. Members of professional and other interest

Police watching demonstrators before an outbreak of rioting in the late 1960s

groups, called *functional constituencies*, elect the other 30 members.

China's National People's Congress has the authority to approve Hong Kong's laws and appointments of government officials. According to the Basic Law, Hong Kong may elect deputies to the Congress.

History

Early days. People have lived in what is now Hong Kong since ancient times. The area came under Chinese control about 220 B.C. Until the A.D. 1800s, it consisted of small fishing and farming villages. Pirates used Hong Kong as a land base.

British control. During the 1800s, the United Kingdom sought to establish trade and diplomatic relations with the Chinese Empire. However, the Chinese government kept tight control over trade. British merchants had begun bringing opium into China, but the Chinese government outlawed the importation of the drug. Opium smuggling continued, however, and in 1839, the issue led to the First Anglo-Chinese War between China and the United Kingdom. The United Kingdom won the war and took control of the island of Hong Kong as part of the Treaty of Nanjing in 1842.

In 1860, as part of the settlement of further trade disputes after another war with China, the United Kingdom gained control of the tip of the Kowloon Peninsula and Stonecutters Island. In 1898, China leased the New Territories and a number of smaller islands to the United Kingdom for 99 years. During the late 1800s and early 1900s, Hong Kong served as a port for British trade with China.

In the early 1900s, a wave of immigration from China greatly increased Hong Kong's population. In 1912, Chinese revolutionaries led by Sun Yat-sen overthrew China's Manchu (Qing) dynasty and established the Republic of China. The uprising caused many Chinese people to flee to Hong Kong. In 1937, Japan invaded China and, once again, large numbers of Chinese fled to Hong Kong. But from 1941 to 1945, during World War II, Hong Kong came under Japanese occupation. During that time, many Chinese returned to China.

In 1949, Communists took control of mainland China, and many Chinese people moved to Hong Kong. Although Hong Kong continued to serve mainly British interests, it also provided a safe haven for Chinese dissidents. The Chinese Communist government never formally recognized the United Kingdom's control of Hong Kong. However, it did not actively oppose British rule because it valued Hong Kong's connections to the outside world.

During the Cold War, a period of great tension between Communist and non-Communist nations, the United States imposed trade *embargoes* (restrictions) on China. As a result, Hong Kong could no longer survive as a port that primarily serviced Chinese trade. In the 1950s, Hong Kong began to develop into a center of trade and

Taipei at sunset

finance for countries throughout the world. It also began to develop many industries.

In 1962, a threat of widespread starvation in China set off another wave of Chinese immigration to Hong Kong. In the late 1960s, some of Hong Kong's Chinese residents held violent demonstrations against British control. But the Chinese government did not try to take control of Hong Kong, and the riots ended.

In the late 1970s and the 1980s, following the Vietnam War (1957–1975), thousands of Vietnamese fled to Hong Kong. Also at that time, the United States lifted trade embargoes against China, allowing Hong Kong to resume its role as a center for Chinese trade. In the 1980s, Hong Kong began to transfer its manufacturing to China.

The return to Chinese rule. With the United Kingdom's lease of the New Territories set to expire in 1997, China and the United Kingdom began planning the transfer of Hong Kong back to China. Negotiations began in 1979, and an agreement was signed in 1984.

The agreement stated that, on July 1, 1997, Hong Kong would become a special administrative region (SAR) of China. China declared the relationship would be that of "one country, two systems." Under the terms of the agreement, Hong Kong would be allowed to maintain its free-enterprise economy within China's government-controlled economic system for at least 50 years. Hong Kong would also be allowed a high degree of autonomy in domestic matters. Hong Kong's foreign affairs and defense, however, would be handled by China. The agreement passed into law, called the Basic Law of the Hong Kong SAR, in 1990. The Basic Law became Hong Kong's constitution on July 1, 1997.

After the signing of the agreement, economic cooperation between Hong Kong and China increased. Hong Kong industrialists moved more manufacturing activities to China to take advantage of inexpensive labor available there. Much employment in Hong Kong shifted from low-cost manufacturing to service industries. This trend continued into the early 2000s.

TAIWAN is a mountainous island in the South China Sea, a part of the Pacific Ocean. Taiwan lies about 90 miles (140 kilometers) off the Chinese coast. The Taiwan Strait separates the island from mainland China.

Taiwan's political status has been a subject of dispute since the mid-1900s, when Chinese Communists and Chinese Nationalists clashed over control of China. After the Chinese Communists seized power on the Chinese mainland in 1949, the Chinese Nationalists, under the leadership of Chiang Kai-shek, moved to Taiwan. The Nationalists declared Taipei, a city at the northern end of Taiwan, the capital of the Republic of China (ROC). Chiang refused to recognize China's Communist government, which had established the People's Republic of China (PRC) on the mainland. His Nationalist government also established control over several islands in the Taiwan Strait, including the Quemoy, Matsu, and Pescadores groups. Today, the People's Republic of China claims that Taiwan is a PRC province, but Taiwan remains effectively independent.

In Chinese, *Taiwan* means *terraced bay*. The island's wild, forested beauty led Portuguese sailors in 1590 to name it *Ilha Formosa*, meaning *beautiful island*.

Government. The ROC government of Taiwan is based on a constitution adopted in 1946 on the Chinese mainland. Since the 1980s, the Constitution has been amended several times, and Taiwan's government has become democratic. The Constitution provides for five branches of government—executive, legislative, judicial, control, and examination. Each branch, or yuan, is headed by a president. The head of state is the president of the Republic of China.

The president is elected by the people to a 4-year term. The president appoints a premier to head the Executive Yuan, which carries out the operations of the government. The premier is also known as the president of the Executive Yuan.

The Legislative Yuan makes most of Taiwan's laws. It also approves the appointment of the premier. Voters directly elect about two-thirds of the Legislative Yuan. The remaining one-third is chosen by *proportional representation*. Under this system, voters cast a ballot for a political party, and legislative seats are assigned to each party according to its share of the vote. Candidate lists prepared by the parties help ensure representation for certain minority groups.

The Judicial Yuan is Taiwan's highest court. Its president is also the chief justice. The Control Yuan reviews activities of government officials and has the power of impeachment. The Examination Yuan gives tests for hiring and promoting government workers.

Taiwan's leading political parties are the Nationalist Party, or Kuomintang (KMT), and the Democratic Progressive Party (DPP).

People. Most Taiwanese people are of Chinese descent. Nearly 2 million people fled to Taiwan from mainland China just before the Communists took power in 1949. A small percentage of Taiwan's population are non-Chinese native peoples, sometimes called *aborigines*. They are related to the original inhabitants of other Pacific islands.

Most of Taiwan's population lives on the coastal plain that makes up the western third of the island. Rapid industrial development in this region has led to air and water pollution, forcing the government to address these concerns. Most of Taiwan's aboriginal peoples live in the mountains.

About 80 percent of Taiwan's people live and work in urban areas. Huge open-air street markets operate after dark in many cities, attracting large crowds. Taiwan's people wear clothing similar to that worn by North Americans and Europeans. About 5 percent of Taiwan's people farm the land. Farms average only 2 or 3 acres (0.8 to 1.2 hectares) in size. Typical Taiwanese meals include rice, chopped meat, fish, and vegetables and fruit.

The Taiwanese people speak various Chinese dialects. Most people speak Northern Chinese, or Mandarin. In Taiwan, that dialect is called Guoyu, meaning *national language*. Taiwanese is also widely spoken. It is a form of Minnan, also called Southern Min, a dialect spoken in the nearby Fujian province of China. Taiwan has an extremely high literacy rate. The law requires children to have six years of elementary school and three years of high school. Many Taiwanese professionals also speak and write English, which is widely taught.

About half of Taiwan's people practice a local traditional religion that involves the worship of folk gods and goddesses. Buddhism and Taoism are the most common major religions, followed by Christianity and Islam.

Fresh fruits at market

Land and climate. Thickly forested mountains run from north to south and cover about half of Taiwan. The highest peak, Yü Shan (Jade Mountain), rises 13,113 feet (3,997 meters) above sea level. On the eastern coast, the mountains often drop sharply to the sea. Short, swift rivers have cut deep gorges through the mountains. In the west, the mountains slope to gently rolling hills and level land.

Taiwan has a subtropical climate, with hot, humid summers and an average annual rainfall of more than 100 inches (250 centimeters). Temperatures average about 80°F (27°C) in summer and 65°F (18°C) in winter. Summer monsoons bring strong winds and rain. In winter, monsoons bring rain and cooler weather to the north. Typhoons occur every year.

Economy. Taiwan has one of the strongest economies in Asia. The island has few natural resources except its forests and rich agricultural land. Cedars, hemlocks, and oaks are the most valuable timber trees. Taiwan's economy relies heavily on manufacturing and foreign trade. It is one of the world's largest producers of computer equipment and electronics. Factories also produce cement, clothing and textiles, iron and steel, machinery, motor vehicles, plastic goods, processed foods, televisions, and toys. Most manufactured goods are exported.

Taiwan exports more than it imports. Its main trading partners include China, the countries of the European Union, Japan, and the United States. Taiwan also trades with Hong Kong, a special administrative region of China. Taiwan is one of the leading investors of manufacturing in China. Many Taiwanese live in China or regularly travel to China for work.

Only about a fourth of Taiwan's land can be farmed. The farmers have terraced many hills to provide more fields for growing rice and vegetables. By using fertilizers, farmers are able to harvest two or three crops a year from the same field. Taiwan's most important crop is rice. Other agricultural products include bamboo, bananas, betel nuts, citrus fruits, corn, peanuts, pears, pineapples, sugar cane, sweet potatoes, and tea. Taiwan produces and exports orchids and other flowers.

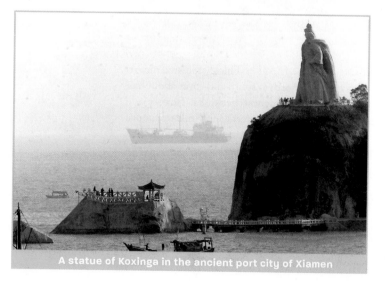
A statue of Koxinga in the ancient port city of Xiamen

Farmers also raise cattle, chickens, ducks, and hogs. The fishing industry catches squid and tuna. Eels and other freshwater fish are raised and caught in inland ponds.

Taiwan has few mineral deposits. Limestone, marble, natural gas, petroleum, and sulfur are mined in Taiwan.

Taiwan has a good network of roads, including expressways. Bus service is excellent. The government operates several railroad lines. A high-speed railway connects the cities of Kaohsiung, Taichung, and Taipei. Kaohsiung and Keelung are Taiwan's chief seaports. Taiwan has two international airports, one in Kaohsiung and another near Taipei.

History. Aborigines were the first inhabitants of Taiwan. Some Chinese came to the island from the mainland as early as the 500s, but large settlements did not begin until the 1600s.

Dutch traders established a port settlement in 1624. From 1661 to 1662, Zheng Chenggong, a Chinese Ming dynasty official also known as Koxinga, drove them off the island. Manchu conquerors had overthrown the Ming dynasty in mainland China, and Zheng hoped to restore the dynasty to power. He wanted Taiwan as a base from which to attack the Manchus. However, the Manchus conquered Taiwan in 1683. Taiwan was then governed as a region under the jurisdiction of China's Fujian province. It became a separate province in 1885.

Japan gained control of Taiwan after the Sino-Japanese War of 1894–1895. The Japanese developed Taiwan's agriculture and industry and expanded its transportation networks. Chinese Nationalists took control of the island after World War II ended in 1945. Their harsh rule led to a violent uprising by native Taiwanese that began on February 28, 1947. Troops arrived from the mainland and put down the revolt in what came to be known as the "February 28 Incident," or the "2-28 Incident."

In 1949, the Chinese Communists defeated the Chinese Nationalists and took control of the government on mainland China. On December 8, 1949, the Nationalists, led by Chiang Kai-shek, moved their government to Taiwan and proclaimed Taipei their capital. The Nationalists ruled under martial law, which gave the president and the military increased legal and political powers.

After the Korean War began in 1950, the United States said it would protect Taiwan

Taiwan president Chen Shui-bian

against possible attack from mainland China. It sent air and naval forces to patrol the Taiwan Strait (then called the Formosa Strait). After Taiwan came under U.S. protection, the Chinese Communist government vowed to recover the island at any cost. The U.S. and Chinese Nationalist governments signed a mutual defense treaty in 1954. The Chinese Communists shelled Matsu and Quemoy heavily in 1954, 1955, and 1958, but they did not attempt to attack Taiwan itself. Taiwan received about 1^1/_2$ billion in U.S. economic and technical aid up to 1965. That year, Taiwan said its economy could stand on its own. But it continued to receive U.S. military aid for another decade.

In the early 1970s, Taiwan expressed concern over improved relations between the United States and Communist China. In 1971, the United States announced it favored United Nations (UN) membership for the People's Republic of China. But the United States also said that Nationalist China—a charter member of the UN—should retain its UN seat. In October 1971, the UN expelled the Nationalists and admitted the People's Republic of China. President Chiang Kai-shek made no attempt to maintain UN membership because he refused to share an international forum with the Chinese Communists.

During the 1970s, a number of nations ended their diplomatic relations with Taiwan and established ties with the People's Republic of China. The United States ended its diplomatic relations with Taiwan at the end of 1978 and established diplomatic relations with the People's Republic of China at the start of 1979. The mutual defense treaty between the United States and Taiwan ended on December 31, 1979. Earlier that year, however, the United States had passed the Taiwan Relations Act, which sought to maintain peace and to continue cultural and commercial relations with Taiwan.

President Chiang Kai-shek died in 1975. Chiang's son Chiang Ching-kuo, who had become premier in 1972, became the country's most powerful leader after his father died. He was elected president of Taiwan in 1978 and reelected in 1984. Under Chiang Ching-kuo, Taiwan's government carried out political reforms that increased democracy in the country. In 1987, the government ended martial law. President Chiang Ching-kuo died in 1988. He was succeeded by Vice President Lee Teng-hui, who continued the democratization process.

Until 1987, the Nationalist Party, or Kuomintang, had been Taiwan's only legal political party. Opposition parties were legalized that year. Multiparty elections were held in 1991 for the National Assembly—the body that was then responsible for amending the ROC Constitution—and in 1992 for the Legislative Yuan. The Nationalist Party won a majority of seats in both elections and remained in control of the government.

In 1996, for the first time, Taiwanese voters directly elected their president. In the past, the National Assembly had elected the president. Voters elected President Lee Teng-hui to a four-year term. After Lee stepped down in 2000, Chen Shui-bian of the Democratic Progressive Party (DPP) was elected president. His election ended 50 years of Nationalist Party rule. In 2004, Chen was reelected president by a narrow margin after surviving what appeared to be an assassination attempt the day before the election. In 2004 and 2008, an alliance led by the Nationalists won a majority of seats in elections for the Legislative Yuan. In 2008, Nationalist Party candidate and former Taipei mayor Ma Ying-jeou succeeded Chen as president. In 2009, Chen was convicted on charges of corruption and embezzlement and sentenced to life in prison. His prison sentence was later reduced. Ma was reelected in January 2012.

MLA Citation

"China." *The Southwestern Advantage Topic Source.* Nashville: Southwestern. 2013.

DATA

China in Brief

Capital: Beijing.

Official language: Northern Chinese (Mandarin, or *putonghua*).

Official name: *Zhonghua Renmin Gongheguo* (People's Republic of China).

National anthem: "March of the Volunteers."

Largest cities: Shanghai (14,348,535); Beijing (11,509,595); Chongqing (9,691,901); Guangzhou (8,524,826).

Symbols of China. China's flag, adopted in 1949, is red with five yellow stars in the left corner. The large star represents the leadership of the Communist Party. The four small stars stand for groups of workers. The state emblem shows the Gate of Heavenly Peace in Beijing framed by grains of rice and wheat that stand for agriculture and a cogwheel that represents industry.

Land: China lies in eastern Asia and borders the Pacific Ocean. Forests and fertile lowlands cover much of northeastern China. The Qin Ling, a range of mountains, rises across east-central China. Hills and tropical lowlands extend over much of the southeast. Dry, rocky plateaus divided by mountain ranges extend over western China. The Himalaya rise along China's southwest border. Other high western ranges include the Tian Shan, Altai Mountains, and Kunlun Mountains. Desert covers much of the northwest. Major Chinese rivers include the Huang He, the Xi Jiang, and the Yangtze.

Area: 3,697,002 mi² (9,575,191 km²). *Greatest distances*—east-west, 3,000 mi (4,828 km); north-south, 2,500 mi (4,023 km). *Coastline*—4,019 mi (6,468 km), including 458 mi (737 km) for Hainan Island.

Elevation: *Highest*—Mount Everest, 29,035 ft (8,850 m); *Lowest*—Turpan Depression, 505 ft (154 m) below sea level.

Climate: China has a wide range of climates. Northern and western China have long, bitterly cold winters, but central and southern China have mild to warm winters. Summers are hot and humid in eastern China and southern Manchuria and extremely hot and dry in the northwestern deserts. January temperatures average below 0°F (-18°C) in Manchuria and Tibet, about 20°F (-7°C) throughout much of eastern China. January is much milder on the southeastern coast, with temperatures about 60°F (16°C). July temperatures average about 80°F (27°C) throughout much of China but may reach over 100°F (38°C) in the northwestern deserts. Rainfall varies from light in the northern deserts to heavy in the southeast.

Form of government: Control by Communist Party

Head of state: President (largely ceremonial)

Head of government: Premier

Executive: Premier, assisted by State Council

Legislature: National People's Congress of almost 3,000 members. Congress has little independent lawmaking power; it usually follows suggestions of party leaders.

DATA

China in Brief

Judiciary: Highest court is the Supreme People's Court.

Political subdivisions: 22 provinces, 5 autonomous regions, 4 special municipalities, 2 special administrative regions

People

Population: *Current estimate*—1,359,243,000. *2000 census*—1,242,612,226.

Population density: 368 per mi^2 (142 per km^2).

Distribution: 53 percent rural, 47 percent urban.

Major ethnic/national groups. About 92 percent Han. Smaller groups include Kazakhs, Mongols, Tibetans, and Uygurs.

Major religions: The government discourages religious practice. But some people still practice religion. Traditional Chinese religions include Confucianism, Taoism, and Buddhism. Also, about 3 to 4 percent of the Chinese people are Christians, and 1 to 2 percent are Muslims.

Economy

Chief products: *Agriculture*—corn, cotton, hogs, potatoes, rice, soybeans, sweet potatoes, tea, tobacco, tomatoes, wheat. *Manufacturing*—automobiles, cement, chemicals, clothing and textiles, iron and steel, machinery, processed foods. *Mining*—coal, copper, iron ore, petroleum, tin, tungsten.

Money: *Basic unit*—yuan (also called renminbi). One hundred fen equal one yuan.

International trade: *Major exports*—clothing, electronic devices, textiles, food, furniture, toys. *Major imports*—chemicals, metals, machinery, petroleum. *Major trading partners*—Germany, Japan, South Korea, United States.

China's Economic Production

Sources: China National Bureau of Statistics; Hong Kong Census and Statistics Department; International Monetary Fund. Figures are for 2005 and include Hong Kong.

Economic activities	% of GDP[1] produced	Number of workers	% of all workers
Manufacturing, mining, and utilities	39	127,123,500	17
Community, social, and personal services	17	140,168,200	18
Agriculture, forestry, and fishing	12	339,708,800	45
Trade, restaurants, and hotels	11	66,204,000	9
Finance, insurance, and real estate	10	6,495,600	1
Transportation and communication	6	27,696,400	4
Construction	5	54,202,900	7
Total[2]	100	761,599,400	100

[1] GDP = gross domestic product, the total value of goods and services produced within a country in a year.

[2] Figures may not add up to 100 percent due to rounding.

DATA

Important Dates in China

c. 1766c.– 1045 B.C.	The Shang dynasty ruled China.
c. 1045 B.C.	The Zhou people from the west overthrew the Shang and set up a new dynasty that ruled until 256 B.C.
c. 500 B.C.	The philosopher Confucius developed a system of moral values and responsible behavior that influenced China for more than 2,000 years.
221–206 B.C.	The Qin dynasty established China's first strong central government.
206 B.C.–A.D. 220	China became a powerful empire under the Han dynasty. Chinese culture flourished.
581–618	The Sui dynasty came to power and reunified China after almost 400 years .
618–907	The Tang dynasty ruled China during a period of prosperity and great cultural accomplishment.
960–1279	The Song dynasty ruled the empire and made Neo-Confucianism the official state philosophy.
1279–1368	The Mongols conquered and controlled all of China.
1368–1644	The Ming dynasty governed China.
1644–1912	The Manchus ruled China as the Qing dynasty.
1842	The Treaty of Nanjing gave Hong Kong to the United Kingdom and allowed British trade at five Chinese ports.
1850–1864	Millions of Chinese died in the Taiping Rebellion.
1900	Members of a secret society attacked and killed Westerners and Chinese Christians during the Boxer Rebellion.
1912	The Republic of China was established.
1928	The Nationalists, led by Chiang Kai-shek, united China under one government.
1931	The Japanese seized Manchuria (the Northeast).
1934–1935	Mao Zedong led the Chinese Communists on their Long March to Shaanxi.
1937–1945	War with Japan shattered China.
1949	The Chinese Communists defeated the Nationalists and established the People's Republic of China.
1958	The Communists launched the Great Leap Forward, which severely weakened China's economy.
1966–1969	The Cultural Revolution disrupted education, the government, and daily life in China.
1971	China was admitted to the United Nations (UN).
1972	U.S. President Richard M. Nixon visited China.
1976	Communist Party Chairman Mao Zedong and Premier Zhou Enlai died.
1979	China and the United States established normal diplomatic relations.
Early 1980s	The Communist Party began reforms toward reducing government economic controls.
1989	Demonstrations across China called for more democracy and an end to corruption in government. The military crushed the movement, killing hundreds of protesters.
1997	China regained control of Hong Kong from the United Kingdom.
1999	China regained control of Macao from Portugal.
2008	Beijing, China, hosted the Summer Olympic Games.

ADDITIONAL RESOURCES

Books to Read

Level I

Gay, Kathlyn. *Mao Zedong's China*. 21st Century Books, 2008.

Henzel, Cynthia K. *Great Wall of China*. ABDO, 2011.

Krull, Kathleen. *Kubla Khan: the Emperor of Everything*. Viking, 2010.

Marx, Trish. *Elephants and Golden Thrones: Inside China's Forbidden City*. Abrams Books for Young Readers, 2008.

Level II

Fenby, Jonathan. *Modern China: The Fall and Rise of a Great Power, 1850 to the Present*. Ecco, 2008.

Keay, John. *China: A History*. Basic Books, 2009.

Pong, David, ed. *Encyclopedia of Modern China*. 4 vols. Scribner, 2009.

Wasserstrom, Jeffrey N. *China in the 21st Century: What Everyone Needs to Know*. Oxford, 2010.

Web Sites

Chinese Embassy in Washington, D.C.

http://www.china-embassy.org/eng/

Embassy of the People's Republic of China in the United States of America. This site includes information about China's provinces, China-U.S. relations, and economy and trade.

CIA Factbook: China

https://www.cia.gov/library/publications/the-world-factbook/geos/ch.html

Information about China from the on-line edition of the World Factbook of the Central Intelligence Agency (CIA).

Search Strings

Family Life in China

China "family life" loyalty reverence ancestors (2,790)

China "family life" loyalty reverence ancestors sons daughters (18,300)

China "family life" culture loyalty reverence ancestors sons daughters (1,900)

Religion

China religion role Communist government (145,000)

role of religion in China (313,000)

role of religion in China Confucianism Taoism Buddhism (39,300)

Higher Education

China "higher education" "national exam" (2,490)

China "higher education" "national exam" university (2,390)

Hong Kong

Hong Kong China global economy "United Kingdom" (244,000)

Hong Kong China "United Kingdom" port Asia global economy trade finance tourism (179,000)

"Hong Kong" China "United Kingdom" lease treaty "global economy" (26,000)

BACKGROUND INFORMATION

The following articles were written during the year in which the events took place and reflect the style and thinking of that time.

Demonstrators during the Cultural Revolution

China (1968)

On July 28, 1968, the People's Republic of China reached a turning point in its two-year-old "Cultural Revolution." The occasion was a meeting attended by five Red Guard leaders in the study of Communist Party chairman Mao Tse-tung in Peking. For five hours, while the guards listened, an angry Mao upbraided them for the continuing conflicts among various factions at Peking University and the senseless violence accompanying them. He accused the leaders of refusing to obey the rules laid down by the Maoist Center; he wondered aloud if the army should take over the campuses in Peking and at other universities. Several times, the aging leader wept. Dismayed by the failure of his "heirs and successors," he was telling them their season of glory and privilege was over.

Words into action. The next eight weeks saw Mao's warning translated into action. The Maoist Center proclaimed the beginning of a major campaign to "reeducate the intellectuals." Newly created propaganda teams made up of workers, or peasants, moved by the thousands into universities and secondary schools. What they often lacked in literacy, they made up for in Maoist zeal. There were "struggle meetings" with the young undesirables, rival Red Guard factions were merged, and the number of Mao-thought classes was multiplied. Hundreds of thousands of students were induced by one means or another to leave for the countryside, where manual work and contact with the people would remold their minds. At the same time, long-delayed school reforms were introduced in many places: The school term was shortened; many subjects were abandoned; and study was combined with labor.

Rival factions. The move to break up the Red Guard movement was an admission that Peking could neither control nor use it. In the fall of 1967, the violent struggle among the rival youth factions had been halted by the army. But in March 1968, following Peking's ill-considered judgment that "proletarian factionalism is good," violence was renewed. All through the spring, and especially in the southern region, rival Red Guard factions, each backed by its own army patron, fought pitched battles involving thousands of armed youths. The vital railway line carrying Chinese military supplies to North Vietnam was cut, and rifles by the thousands were carted away. In one of the clashes, a large part of Wuchou—a city located in the Kwangsi Chuang region—was burned. Huge bands of armed peasants began moving into the southern cities to join in the fighting.

A few days before Mao's emotional meeting with the Peking quintet, leaders of the feuding Red Guard groups in Kwangsi had been brought to Peking and told by the nation's leaders to stop fighting, and to restore rail traffic so that the supply lines to North Vietnam could be opened again. Although the youths promised to obey, recriminations failed to come to an end.

A shift in policy. The reorganization of the Red Guards was only one of the momentous changes decreed by Mao in the late summer and fall of 1968. In effect, he sought to end the violent phase of the Cultural Revolution. The new cry was "revolutionary normalcy." In the summer of 1968, the last "revolutionary committees" were hastily formed in the few remaining key cities, provinces, and autonomous regions of China.

Compromises were reached. Each local boss pledged his loyalty to Maoism, but only in return for formal recognition of his authority. On these committees, which were to govern their areas, power was to be evenly divided among the army, the party cadres, and the new "revolutionary masses." But, in fact, by late 1968, provincial China was ruled by generals and by those old party bosses who survived the Maoist holocaust. The day of the rebel appeared to have come to an end.

The point was underlined by a vigorous campaign to rebuild the Communist Party, which Mao had done his best to wreck in 1966 and 1967. In reality, efforts had begun in 1967, but progress was delayed by the tug of war between the Central Committee and the provincial bosses. One of the crucial questions was who would name the delegates to the next party congress. In contravention to the party constitution, no congress had been held since 1956. The pro-Maoist Central Committee had wanted to pick the delegates itself. The bosses, however, feared that this would leave them out in the cold, unrepresented and, eventually, powerless. Mao had also spoken of a drastic purge. "Without eliminating the waste and getting fresh blood, the party has no vigor," he said. The questions now were: Who was waste? Who would do the purging.

Communique issued. From October 13 to October 31, the party's Central Committee met in plenary session—the first in 26 months. The concluding communique spoke of a congress to be held at an "appropriate" time, and of the need for a purge. It announced that Liu Shao-chi, a "renegade, traitor and scab," had been ousted from the party as

Chinese children each holding Mao's Little Red Book during the Cultural Revolution

well as from all his posts. This, presumably, was to be the final chapter in the career of China's chief of state, a veteran revolutionary who, along with his family, had been under attack for more than two years. The communique was more interesting for what it did not say than for what it said. In August 1966, the Central Committee had held its 11th plenary session to launch formally the Cultural Revolution. Was the 12th session, in October 1968, called to end its initial phase? Did the conferees, in secrecy, debate the issue of peace in Vietnam? The war there was, in fact, given only a few perfunctory sentences in the communique. Was a hard look taken at the ailing economy?

Shortages felt. The state of the nation was hardly comforting. The official statements insisted that "the situation is excellent," but the country was still feeling the effects of two years of disruption. In most places, the cotton textile ration was delayed four to five months. Major cities, such as Wuhan, ran short of cigarettes, matches, and medicines. Although industry had recovered from the turmoil of 1967, Japanese specialists thought that production was still below the 1966 level. After the bumper harvest of 1967, the harvest in 1968 was only fair because of floods in the south and drought in the north.

The railway transport system, badly disrupted in 1967, was now under army control. But the violence that occurred during the spring of 1968 brought with it severe disruptions, none worse than those on the railway lines leading to the south—

Liu Shao-chi

and to Vietnam. Foreign trade, too, showed a decline of 15 to 20 percent below the level of 1966.

Foreign relations were in a troubled state. The Red Guard raids on the Chinese foreign ministry had ceased and after March 1968, the minister, Marshal Chen Yi, was no longer required to make "self-examinations" at public meetings. But China remained isolated and isolationist. The thin ranks of its friends among the nations had grown even thinner, and its ambassadors were still being kept at home instead of being returned to their posts abroad.

China's feud with the Soviet Union had grown even noisier, with Peking speaking darkly of a Moscow-Washington axis. The charge was that while the Americans closed their eyes to the Soviet invasion of Czechoslovakia, the Russians condoned the American intervention in Vietnam. Starting in the spring of 1968, Peking also let Hanoi know it was opposed to any peace talks with the United States.

Victory, the Chinese argued, could be won only on a battlefield, never across a negotiating table. By fall, relations had become so chilly that Hanoi sent no special envoy to the National Day celebrations in Peking. In their oratory, the Chinese leaders gave only casual notice to the war in Vietnam.

There was little to make up for all this on the credit side of the ledger, although the attacks on foreign missions in Peking had ceased, contacts became a little more mannerly, and there were many signs of a desire to restore the disrupted contacts with the world. One sign came in late November, when the Chinese foreign ministry indicated through a neutral diplomatic source that it might be willing to resume unofficial talks with U.S. diplomats in Warsaw, Poland, at an early date. The talks had been suspended since January 1968.

New faces. In 1968, purges continued to reduce the group around Mao, with Acting Chief of Staff Yang Cheng-wu, who was ousted in March as a "plotter," the most eminent victim. By late fall, the top nine people around Mao included, in the official order: Marshal Lin Piao, Mao's political heir; Premier Chou En-lai; Chen Po-ta, chief of the Cultural Revolution Group and Mao's former private secretary; Kang Sheng, Mao's specialist on intelligence; Chiang Ching, Mao's wife and the by-products of the Cultural Revolution, Chang Chun-chiao, the boss of Shanghai, and Yao Wen-yuan, the chief intellectual "hatchet man." Next to

these came Hsieh Fu-chi, the security minister, and Haung Yung-sheng, the new chief of staff. This meant that of Mao's top seven intimates, five were persons who had risen to supreme power as a result of the Cultural Revolution. They were also persons who had no roots in any major stratum of society, and whose power rested mainly on their closeness to the great man. When he died, their power would likely vanish before the pressure of ambitious newcomers struggling for succession.

Questionable gains. Thus, in 1968, the turmoil had begun to die down, but with it, the Cultural Revolution, as envisioned in 1966, also died a little. As Mao saw it, it had achieved a great deal. The corrupt and decaying party apparatus and those of its leaders who opposed Mao had been badly weakened. The educational system was being renovated, and the young, no longer complacent, had been given a taste of revolution-making. The corruption of culture with "bourgeois" ideas and forms had been halted. With hundreds of millions doing their daily chanting of Mao's quotations, the nation had its mind and moral code remolded.

The state of the nation in 1968, however, showed that a huge price had been paid for all these gains, real or assumed. China's industrial progress had been interrupted. The people's faith in the integrity and wisdom of their leaders was undermined. With the secondary schools and universities closed for more than two years, the nation had lost tens of thousands of trained men and women whom it desperately needed. China's international prestige remained low, particularly among the nations of Asia, and the whole process of long-range policy-making had been disrupted.

Most important, 1968 offered no assurance that the changes Mao wrought would outlive him. The Cultural Revolution that was to change China for "a hundred, nay, a thousand years," stood likely to be hastily undone by Mao's successors.

China (1989)

China suffered from political turmoil and economic recession in 1989. A continuing struggle over political direction exploded on June 4, when government troops killed hundreds of student demonstrators calling for democratic reforms. This marked an important turn within the Communist Party from making reforms to more rigidly controlling the government and nation. As conservatives gained influence, Deng Xiaoping—China's

Several hundred of 200,000 pro-democracy student protesters in Tiananmen Square during a demonstration to mourn the death of Hu Yaobang

dominant, reform-minded leader for a decade—resigned his official posts.

Economic troubles intensified a controversy within the party leadership in early 1989. In the first four months of the year, prices were 27 percent higher than in the same period in 1988. Unemployment increased, and the gap widened between people who benefited from China's economic reform program and those who were left out. Arguing that greater economic freedom and competition was the best way to overcome these problems, Party General Secretary Zhao Ziyang supported political reforms to loosen the party's grip on the economy. Opposing him was Premier Li Peng, who advocated continued state control of the economy, with the party firmly guiding the government.

China's legislature, the National People's Congress, adopted an austerity program backed by Li at its annual session from March 20 through April 4. Although the delegates followed party orders as expected, they showed discontent over corruption within the government and the special privileges accorded to the children of top officials.

Discontent erupted into a full-blown protest movement upon the death of Hu Yaobang on April 15. A liberal follower of Deng, Hu had become party general secretary in 1980. In January 1987—after student supporters of Hu held large demonstrations to call for a more democratic government—Deng forced Hu to resign in order to placate conservative party leaders. The demonstrations had undermined Deng's political plans for reform and unleashed a law-and-order backlash by conservatives. Nevertheless, Deng wielded enough power to replace Hu with Zhao, another supporter of reforms.

Students mourning Hu's death gathered in Shanghai and Beijing, the capital, chanting, "Long live democracy." On April 18, 1989, some 2,000 Beijing students rallied in Tiananmen Square, a huge open area in the center of Beijing next to the former imperial residence, the Forbidden City. The students demanded freedom of the press and the repudiation of the government's earlier campaigns against liberalization. By April 21, some 100,000 protesters had gathered in the square. Many refused the government's orders to leave after memorial services for Hu were held on April 22. They boycotted their classes and demanded a dialogue with government leaders.

The Communist Party newspaper *People's Daily* on April 26 called the student movement an illegal "planned conspiracy which, in essence, aims at negating the leadership of the party and the socialist system." Angered, the protesters intensified their demonstrations. On May 13, about 2,000 students began a hunger strike in the square, which was now filled with hundreds of thousands of students and other citizens. Intellectuals and students in other cities supported the demonstrators.

Zhao, whose liberal policies had student backing, asked the hunger strikers to leave the square on May 17. They refused, and about 1 million of their supporters demonstrated there later that day and the next. On May 19, a tearful Zhao visited the students and indicated that he was losing a political struggle over how to deal with their protest. Indeed, Zhao appeared to have been defeated by early May 20, when Li and President Yang Shangkun, an 82-year-old general, announced that they had imposed martial law and deployed troops to end the demonstrations.

But Beijing residents blocked the passage of army troops—in some cases lying down in front of armored vehicles—and the student occupation of Tiananmen Square continued. On May 23, someone in the square splashed paint on a huge portrait of Mao Zedong, Communist China's founder, which hung at the entrance to the Forbidden City. On May 30, students erected a large statue of the "Goddess of Democracy," a version of the Statue of Liberty. The statue faced a replacement portrait of Mao, symbolically challenging the party dictatorship he created.

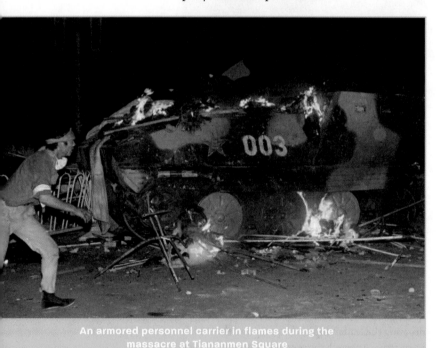

An armored personnel carrier in flames during the massacre at Tiananmen Square

Massacre at Tiananmen Square. By now, the protest was beginning to flag as fatigue, illness, and unsanitary conditions affected the students. On the night of June 3, only about 5,000 remained in the square. Shortly after midnight, some of the 100,000 soldiers ordered to Beijing began to march toward the square. They fired into crowds of unarmed civilians who tried to block their way and crushed people under tanks and armored cars. By 5:15 a.m. on June 4, troops had entered the square. They shot at students and set fire to their tents. Many of the students who fled the square were met by soldiers' gunfire in nearby streets. At 7:40 a.m., the government announced that the army had suppressed a "rebellion" in the square. Occasional shootings of defiant civilians

continued for several more days as the troops established control.

The true death toll was unknown because the government tried to hide the number of people who died during the incident. After making contradictory statements, officials finally said that 10 soldiers and 36 students had been killed. Western journalists who tried to reconstruct the confusing events reported that between 400 and 800 people had died, with most estimates around 700. Amnesty International, a London-based human-rights organization, concluded that at least 1,300 civilians were killed between June 3 and 9, with 1,000 of them in Beijing and 300 in Chengdu, a southern city in which demonstrators had also sought democracy. A Chinese Red Cross official reportedly said that 2,600 people were killed in Beijing but later denied having given a figure.

After the massacre, repression began with a nationwide hunt for students accused of "inciting and organizing counterrevolutionary activities." Amnesty International estimated that tens of thousands of people had been arrested by late August. The organization reported that scores had been executed, most of them secretly, following more than a dozen publicized executions in June. By August, 8 of the 21 student leaders on the government's most-wanted list had been arrested, but some escaped abroad.

Escapees and exiles from around the world met in Paris on September 22 through 24 and organized the Federation for Democracy in China. The 150 delegates agreed to work to bring China a multiparty political system, free enterprise, and expanded human rights. They elected Yan Jiaqi, a former Communist Party official and close associate of Zhao, president of the federation. The Chinese government denounced the exiles as traitors trying to destroy Communism.

Security officials tightened controls within China, reinvigorating the street committee system for observing the actions of ordinary citizens. Most college graduates were told to work in a village or factory before doing graduate study, and the number of students allowed to enroll abroad was slashed.

Zhao ousted. The Communist Party's Central Committee met June 23 and 24 and ousted Zhao from the general secretary's job and his other party positions. A press campaign against him charged that he had encouraged the demonstrators, opposed martial law, damaged the economy, and hampered the fight against corruption. Most observers saw the campaign as the conservatives' attempt to weaken the authority of Zhao's sponsor, Deng.

Leading the conservatives were Yang and two elderly advocates of rigid central economic planning—Chen Yun and Peng Zhen. Daily affairs were left in the hands of men who also had doubts about the policies of liberalization, led by Li Peng, his deputy Yao Yilin, and security chief Qiao Shi.

The man named to replace Zhao as party general secretary was Jiang Zemin. Jiang had been a moderate economic reformer but political hard-liner as mayor and party boss of Shanghai. He lacked a personal power base and the experience usually associated with party leadership. On October 10, however, *People's Daily* called him "the core of the third-generation collective leadership." This implied that Deng had accepted Jiang as his successor.

Deng resigns. In weakening health, his reforms being reversed, the 85-year-old Deng was losing his ability to control the succession. On November 9, Deng relinquished his last party job and base of power, chairmanship of the party's Central Military Commission. Jiang succeeded him, possibly in Deng's attempt to strengthen Jiang's authority. But the new party chief's future was left in doubt. Five previous designated successors to Mao and then to Deng had lost power in bitter personal fights over policy.

Foreign reaction to China's suppression of the pro-democracy movement was strongly critical. United States President George Bush came under fire in the United States for canceling some sanctions imposed against China. Although Bush said he had banned high-level government exchanges between the two nations, U.S. officials made a diplomatic visit to China in December and Bush revealed they had also met there secretly with Chinese officials in July.

The economic consequences of the crackdown were severe. Tourism, which had earned China $2.2 billion in 1988, declined sharply. The foreign investment that China needed to modernize its industries also dried up as investors became wary.

By autumn, the economy was sliding into recession. Factories operated at well below capacity, partly because of frequent power cuts. Hotels emptied, retail sales fell, and crowds of jobseekers

The Dalai Lama

thronged cities. Facing these problems, Chinese leaders fell back on tighter economic controls. They drew up a plan for cuts in investment, consumption, and private economic activity, all of which had grown under Deng.

Tibetan troubles. Anti-Chinese demonstrators gathered in Lhasa, the capital of Tibet, on March 5, to mark the 30th anniversary of a nationalist uprising in which 87,000 Tibetans were killed and Tibet's spiritual leader, the Dalai Lama, fled into exile in India. The 1989 demonstrations were the fourth occasion in 18 months when Chinese police fired on Tibetan crowds. The government said that 16 people were killed, but unofficial reports said the death toll was 30 or more. Tibetan exiles charged that more than 800 Tibetans were later executed.

The Dalai Lama's efforts to negotiate with Chinese authorities for Tibet's autonomy broke down, but on October 5, he was named to receive the Nobel Peace Prize for his nonviolent struggle against Chinese domination. China denounced the award, which reportedly was intended partly as recognition of the Tiananmen demonstrators.

Gorbachev visit. After 30 years of animosity, China and the Soviet Union reestablished normal relations when Soviet leader Mikhail S. Gorbachev visited China from May 15 to 18. Chinese-Soviet economic ties expanded but remained small compared with China's trade with Japan and the West.

China (2002)

Vice President Hu Jintao of China assumed the role of general secretary of the ruling Chinese Communist Party in November 2002 at the 16th Party Congress, a meeting that takes place every five years. Party members appoint leaders and lay out

Hu Jintao

the nation's goals at such meetings. The change in leaders in 2002 was the first orderly transition of power in China's modern history. Hu, a 59-year-old engineer who replaced Jiang Zemin as China's leader, pledged to adhere to the course of economic reform and openness to the outside world set by Jiang.

Hu took over leadership of a country experiencing dazzling economic and social change. He also faced rampant corruption, spreading unemployment, and growing demands for political change.

Hu had been a rising star in Chinese politics for some time. In the early 1990s, Deng Xiaoping, one of China's most influential leaders, gave Hu a seat on the Politburo, which establishes policy guidelines for the Communist Party. Hu first became prominent as leader of the powerful Communist Youth League. He served as head of the Communist Party in Tibet in 1989, when China imposed martial law to quell unrest in the region. In 1998, the Chinese parliament selected Hu to serve as vice president. He was the youngest person ever to hold the office.

Jiang's retirement in 2002 as general secretary ended months of speculation that he might try to remain in office long past the unofficial retirement age of 70. Although he relinquished the post to Hu, Jiang retained the titles of president and chairman of the Central Military Commission. Political observers expected Jiang to turn over the title of president to Hu in March 2003 at the annual meeting of parliament. Observers were not certain whether Jiang would resign the military post, which gave him the power to make decisions on security and foreign policy matters.

At the 2002 Party Congress, Jiang also succeeded in packing the Standing Committee of the Politburo—a powerful council that the congress expanded from seven to nine members in November—with at least six of his own loyalists, including Zeng Qinghong, his longtime aide and strategist. Jiang's continuing influence raised questions about the true extent of Hu's influence and power within the government.

Other powerful leaders retired in 2002, including Prime Minister Zhu Rongji and the head of parliament, Li Peng. Change also swept through the 22-member Politburo and the larger Central Committee. Two-thirds of the members of the Politburo retired in 2002. Half of the 356 members of the Central Committee also retired. In general, the new members were younger and better educated than their predecessors.

Capitalism. Reconciling a modern market economy with traditional Communist principles became the recurring theme at the weeklong congress. The 2,114 delegates voted unanimously to amend the party's Constitution to include Jiang's theory of the "three represents," which declares that the party represents capitalists as much as the workers and peasants who formed its base for more than 80 years. The amendment made it possible for private-business owners to become members of the Communist Party.

In a two-hour speech to the congress, Jiang said China would continue on its course of economic transformation but ruled out any sweeping changes in political freedom. He described economic development as the nation's central task and said China must persevere with the introduction of market forces. He also acknowledged the problems of corruption, inequality, and unemployment that had emerged along with China's spectacular economic growth.

Corruption. Government officials admitted in 2002 that corruption had become a threat to national stability. In March, Chinese legislators called for the introduction of tough legislation to target the country's endemic problem of official graft. In August, the Communist Party expelled Zhu Xiaohua, a banker in charge of China's foreign reserves and a protégé of the prime minister, on charges of bribery. Chinese citizens told Western reporters that they believed many government officials were being protected from prosecution.

Unrest. Industrial workers from state-owned factories in northeastern China held massive demonstrations in March to protest unpaid wages and corruption. In the industrial city of Liaoyang, tens of thousands of workers attracted worldwide attention as they demonstrated outside bankrupt factories. Anti-graft investigators later confirmed that officials at the factories had milked the assets of fading state companies, even as workers and retirees were denied their wages and pensions. In Daqing, the site of oil fields, a few thousand workers protested against inadequate severance pay. Approximately 25 million workers had been laid off from state-owned companies since 1998.

Human rights. The United Nations (UN) high commissioner for human rights, Mary Robinson, warned in August 2002 that China was using the global war on terrorism as an excuse to crack down on Islamic minorities and members of the banned Falun Gong, a spiritual movement that combines exercises, meditation, and breathing techniques with religious ideas from Buddhism and Taoism. Robinson said China had passed laws in recent years that increased the government's powers of arrest and detention. China's treatment of ethnic Uighur Muslims in the western province of Xinjiang was of particular concern, Robinson said. In March, Amnesty International, a London-based human rights group, accused China of stepping up harsh repression of Uighurs.

Xinjiang is a large province with 8 million Muslim Uighurs among its 17 million people. Opposition to rule by Chinese migrants had long festered in the province, particularly among separatists. In January, the Chinese government accused Uighurs of being linked to al-Qa'ida, a global terrorist organization that is allied with other Islamic extremist groups worldwide. In September, Chinese officials welcomed a UN decision to place an Uighur separatist group on a terrorist list. The move was supported by the United States, Afghanistan, and Kyrgyzstan, a former Soviet republic which borders Xinjiang.

Economy. Premier Zhu said in November that China hopes to quadruple the size of its economy by 2022. China grew at an annual rate of 7.9 percent in 2002, and direct foreign investment in China surged by 22.5 percent in the first nine months of 2002 compared with the same period of 2001.

In March 2002, Zhu warned that farmers were being left behind in China's pursuit of economic growth. He said rural incomes rose just 4.2 percent to the annual equivalent of $275 in 2001. Incomes in cities, in contrast, rose 8.5 percent to $837. In May 2002, Lu Zhiqiang, a senior economic planner, warned that the gap between rich and poor in China was rapidly widening and could threaten national stability.

Hong Kong. Tung Chee-hwa began his second five-year term as Hong Kong's chief executive in July 2002. He was elected by a committee selected by Chinese officials. Tung selected a cabinet of political appointees, replacing civil servants at the top levels of government. Political experts said it was Hong Kong's biggest shake-up since the United Kingdom turned the former colony over to China in 1997.

U.S. relations. China continued in 2002 to seek friendly ties with the United States. In February, U.S. President George W. Bush met with Jiang in China, and Jiang visited Bush's ranch in Texas in October. The governments drew closer in part because of shared interests in combating terrorism. However, the issue of whether China would force Taiwan to reunite with the mainland remained a point of contention between the Chinese and U.S. governments. Taiwan is an island state regarded by China as a province.

Chinese President Jiang Zemin and U.S. President George W. Bush during a meeting at Bush's Texas ranch in October 2002

In July, Chinese officials rejected a U.S. Department of Defense report suggesting that China spent four times more on defense than it publicly acknowledged. At the urging of the United States, China in August imposed new regulations on exports of missile-related technology to a host of countries, including Iran, Iraq, North Korea, Yemen, Libya, and Pakistan.

AIDS. The UN reported in June that China was on the brink of an "explosive" AIDS epidemic and could have 10 million people infected with HIV, the virus that causes AIDS, by 2010. UN officials urged the Chinese government to spend more on education and prevention and complained that many Chinese officials lack commitment to fighting AIDS. UN officials noted that in 2002 between 800,000 and 1.5 million Chinese were infected with HIV.

A countdown clock showing the remaining days and seconds before the return of Hong Kong to mainland rule in 1997

Floods swept through central China in mid-2002. More than 1,500 people were killed as the result of floods and flood-related disasters. The government reported that 110 million people were affected by the floods and that more than 2.4 million had to be evacuated nationwide.

Space. China's official newspaper, *The China Daily*, reported in May that China planned to put an astronaut in space by 2005. Such as launch would make China only the third nation to send a human into space, after Russia and the United States. In addition, the government hoped to put an astronaut on the moon by 2010.

Hong Kong 1997: Capitalism Comes to China

The British colony of Hong Kong was returned to Chinese sovereignty on June 30, 1997, thus introducing a premier capitalist economy to the largest Communist nation in the world.

—by Graham Thomas

On June 30, 1997, millions of people around the world watched, via television, the pomp and spectacle of the ceremony in which the United Kingdom returned Hong Kong to the People's Republic of China. At the stroke of midnight, the control of one of the world's most important commercial centers shifted from a democratic, capitalist country to a Communist state with no tradition of constitutional law. Many viewers recalled another television broadcast in 1989, during which they watched Chinese troops attack students in Beijing's Tiananmen Square who were demonstrating against official corruption and demanding democracy in China. With these two televised images in mind, business people, politicians, economists, and others wondered what effect the Chinese communist government would have on the lifestyles, business practices, and freedoms of the more than 6 million citizens of Hong Kong. But they also wondered what effect the Hong Kong citizens would have on the lives of their more than 1 billion fellow Chinese citizens.

British rule of Hong Kong. The conditions of the handover of Hong Kong from British to Chinese rule were established by the Sino-British Joint Declaration of 1984. This agreement called for a Chinese policy of "one country, two systems"— socialism in China and capitalism in Hong Kong. The success of that policy for another 50 years— the length of time stipulated in the 1984 agreement—was expected to influence not only the Chinese and Hong Kong economies but also international relations within Asia and around the world.

The total land area of Hong Kong that was returned to Chinese sovereignty in 1997 had come under British control in three stages. In 1842, Hong Kong Island was ceded "in perpetuity" (forever) to Britain by the Treaty of Nanjing at the end of the First Opium War. The British had fought the war in retaliation against Chinese attempts to end the illegal opium trade that British merchants conducted with smugglers and corrupt Chinese officials. The British also opposed restrictions on legal trade that the Chinese government had imposed at the end of the 1700s. The Treaty of Nanjing gave Britain the best natural harbor in southern China and an ideal base for trade with the mainland, free of the official restrictions of the Chinese government. The defeat also heralded more than a century of Chinese humiliation during which an increasingly weak China additionally lost territory to Russia, Japan, and the maritime powers of Europe.

The second stage of the formation of modern Hong Kong occurred in 1861 at the end of the Second Opium War, which Britain fought in alliance with France. The British gained the Kowloon Peninsula, which is a part of the mainland opposite Hong Kong Island, and the tiny Stonecutters Island, also "in perpetuity." In 1898, Britain took a 99-year lease on the much larger New Territories, an area of the mainland that is adjacent to Kowloon, as well as more than 235 small islands. The New Territories made up over 90 percent of the land area of the British colony. Long before 1997, when the lease on the New Territories was due to expire, all three parts of Hong Kong had grown into one economic and social unit. Negotiations between the United Kingdom and China over the handover of Hong Kong did not distinguish the New Territories from Hong Kong Island and the Kowloon Peninsula, which according to international treaties (that the Chinese did not recognize) were forever British.

A different kind of colony. While in name a colony, Hong Kong was a place to which few British people migrated. Hong Kong from the outset was a center for free trade, where merchants from around the world were at liberty to conduct business under the rule of British law, but with little government restriction. British merchants and bankers took full advantage of Hong Kong's economic freedoms to develop business and trade with China and the rest of East Asia.

To the surprise of the British, the Chinese also flocked to Hong Kong to escape conflict on the mainland and to benefit from the colony's political stability and economic freedom. The number of Chinese residents in Hong Kong rose from approximately 30,000 in 1851 to almost 860,000 in 1931, when the British population numbered less than 20,000. By 1939, another 750,000 Chinese had arrived as refugees from the war that Japan had been waging against China for two years. The flow of immigrants

reversed when the Japanese occupied Hong Kong in December 1941 and held it until the end of World War II (1939–1945). Then, during 1948 and 1949, hundreds of thousands of Chinese flooded back into the colony to escape the chaos of the civil war between Chiang Kai-shek's Nationalist Party and the Chinese Communists. By 1950, the population of Hong Kong had mushroomed to an estimated 2.2 million people. In 1997, the vast majority of the 6.5 million people were of Chinese ancestry.

After the Communist government took control of China in 1949, Hong Kong remained under British control, but the Chinese government did not recognize British sovereignty over the territory. Consequently, China had no official diplomatic relations with Hong Kong. The Chinese government did, however, assign diplomats as "editors" to the Hong Kong offices of the Xinhua News Agency, the news service of the People's Republic of China. Also after 1949, China established companies in Hong Kong to represent Chinese state-owned trading corporations.

Rise to economic power. Hong Kong's rise to an economic center of global importance began between 1948 and 1950 with the influx of businessmen from Shanghai, then a much more important commercial center than Hong Kong. The new arrivals were refugees from the Communist government. The immigrants' entrepreneurial skills and manufacturing know-how enabled Hong Kong to industrialize rapidly. Their efforts launched what was to become one of the most competitive economies in Asia. At first, Hong Kong produced

Sham Shu Po Kowloon Market in Hong Kong, June 30, 1997

textiles, clothing, and plastic flowers. Later, companies began producing more technologically advanced goods—consumer electronic products, watches and clocks, and computer components. The growth of industry proved to be critical for Hong Kong's post-World War II economic boom.

The next crucial development in Hong Kong's rise to economic leadership came when Communist leader Deng Xiaoping rose to power in China. In 1979, Deng introduced an "open-door policy" designed to accelerate China's economic development by opening its economy to the world. The reform policy established Special Economic Zones, cities in which special regulations and incentives were designed to attract foreign capital.

During those changes in China's economic policy, Hong Kong became a link between China and foreign investors and corporations. That new role helped Hong Kong to develop into a major manufacturing, trading, and financial center. By 1997, Hong Kong was the world's busiest container port and a leading financial center, ranking third after New York and London. In 1996, Hong Kong's per capita gross domestic product (GDP) was valued at $24,282—higher than the GDP of Canada, Australia, or the United Kingdom. (GDP is the total monetary value of goods and services produced, minus the net payments on foreign investments.)

Effect of Chinese economic reforms.
Beijing's economic reforms benefited the Chinese economy as well as Hong Kong's, particularly in

the neighboring Chinese province of Guangdong, where Hong Kong manufacturers took advantage of cheaper land values and lower labor costs. By the early 1980s, Hong Kong companies employed 3 million Chinese citizens in its factories in Guangdong. By the mid-1990s, they employed 4 million Chinese workers. The Special Economic Zone of Shenzhen, a city directly across the border from Hong Kong, grew from a city of 20,000 in 1978 to a modern, industrial metropolis of approximately 2 million people by the early 1990s.

Hong Kong was China's biggest foreign direct investor from the beginning of the "open-door policy." By 1993, the total worth of Hong Kong-financed investment projects in China exceeded $76 trillion. Hong Kong investments accounted for between 60 and 80 percent of total foreign direct investment in China. And while Hong Kong-financed projects accounted for less than 5 percent of China's total output of goods and services, these companies produced two-thirds of China's exports.

As Hong Kong's manufacturing activities shifted across the border into China, Hong Kong developed into an important international business center. By the mid-1990s, the service sector accounted for approximately 75 percent of Hong Kong's GDP and employed about 70 percent of the workforce. The colony became not only an international conduit to China businesses, but also a center of learning for officials of Chinese enterprises involved in international trade and investment. By the time of the 1997 handover, Hong Kong was China's most important trade and investment partner, its most important provider of business services, and a key contributor to its modernization effort.

Hong Kong had also become the linchpin of "greater China." The close economic ties of trade, technology transfers, and investment had made Hong Kong a crucial link between a rapidly developing southern China and Taiwan, the home of the Chinese Nationalist government. Despite the fact that China, Hong Kong, and Taiwan were politically distinct, the economies of all three had become more economically integrated since China's reform policies were introduced. By 1997, China, Hong Kong, and Taiwan—if considered as a single economic entity—had the world's third largest *gross national product* (total value of goods and services produced) and the largest foreign exchange reserves and trade turnover. They were also the third largest exporter to the United States after Canada and Japan.

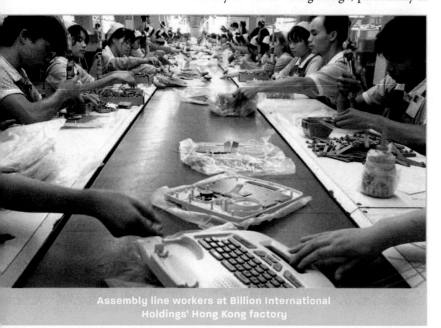
Assembly line workers at Billion International Holdings' Hong Kong factory

In addition to gaining such a huge economic asset, Chinese leaders saw the transfer of power as a means to demonstrate to the people of Taiwan that they would be granted the same freedoms as Hong Kong if Taiwan returned to Chinese sovereignty. In 1997, the Hong Kong Special Administrative Region, the official title after the handover, continued to function as a laissez-faire economy (an economy with minimal government regulations). After the handover, China and Hong Kong remained separate economic entities and continued to operate as if they were foreign trade and investment partners.

Speculation about Hong Kong's future. During 1997, however, many people debated whether the "one country, two systems" policy would work and whether Hong Kong would continue to be an economic asset. Hong Kong's elite business and professional community, foreign business people, prodemocracy leaders in Hong Kong, and the international media all speculated about the future of Hong Kong. If Communist China were to continue the "one country, two systems" policy for 50 years as planned, China could enhance Hong Kong's status as a metropolitan economy with its crucial role in the development of greater China. Hong Kong's economic dynamism would likely reinforce its preeminence in southern China and its position in the global economy. If, however, China failed to maintain the laissez-faire capitalist system, China could damage the territory's role as a leading international business center. As a consequence, Hong Kong could decline to a regional trading center for Guangdong, overshadowed (as it was before World War II) by Shanghai, which began to regain its economic preeminence in China in the 1990s.

The international media and prodemocracy leaders, in particular, raised concerns about China's restrictions on free speech and open political disagreement. Many argued that the freedoms provided under the rule of law during British colonialism were necessary to fuel the economy's dynamism. Repressing those rights, some leaders maintained, could trigger a flight of capital from Hong Kong and an exodus of thousands of the highly educated and skilled people crucial to the functioning of Hong Kong as a business center. The Chinese leadership could also damage Hong Kong's attractiveness to international business by favoring business people and companies with strong personal and political connections to powerful factions in China.

Hong Kong stock traders

The large-scale corruption pervasive in China could be equally damaging to Hong Kong. In 1996, an independent ranking of Asia's business environments listed Hong Kong as one of Asia's least corrupt environments after Singapore and Japan. The colony's ability to keep corruption relatively low had been due to its Independent Commission Against Corruption (ICAC) and the public support that the commission enjoyed. Economic analysts considered the ICAC's autonomy and it public support after the handover crucial to preventing corruption in the business community.

Further speculation suggested that if China were to tolerate a genuinely autonomous Hong Kong, both the economic and political gains for China could be enormous. China would continue to benefit from the contribution that Hong Kong had already made to its modernization and to its increasing integration into the world economy. Additionally, over time the process of economic modernization in China could create a middle class of business and professional people large and confident enough to demand a share of political power in a democratic political framework. If the modernization of China were to lead to such changes, Hong Kong could serve as a model of a successfully functioning political unit run by Chinese on Chinese soil and characterized by a degree of democracy and the rule of law. This influence, however, would run counter to the "one country, two systems" formula, since the policy is based on the assumption that neither system should be allowed to undermine the other. Such significant political changes also presuppose a willingness on the part of the Chinese Communist party to give up its monopoly on power and to introduce a multiparty political system. At the time of the handover, there was no evidence that such a situation would be likely to develop in the near future.

Possible effects on international commerce. Respecting the autonomy of Hong Kong could also positively affect China's relations with Southeast Asian countries. Such behavior toward Hong Kong would most likely reassure Vietnam, the Philippines, Indonesia, Malaysia, and Thailand—countries acutely conscious of China's growing economic and political weight in the region. Furthermore, Asian nations might be more willing to respect China's desire to bring Taiwan under Chinese sovereignty if the Chinese Communist government were to honor the agreements of the Hong Kong handover. If China were to exert more control over Hong Kong, however, Southeast Asian countries' apprehensions regarding China would be intensified. Also, the Chinese communities in other Asian countries might reconsider the closeness of their ties with their ancestral homeland. If China were isolated, from within or without, the stability and increasing economic integration of the whole Southeast Asia region would be impaired.

China's relations with the United States and Japan would also be likely to improve if Hong Kong remained autonomous. The integration of business in the entire Asia-Pacific region could be accelerated, and China's general international standing enhanced. However, if China were to infringe on Hong Kong's autonomy, the U.S. government in particular would likely be disturbed by potential damage to the territory in which American businesses have much invested. The United States would also be concerned about the effects of such a policy on Taiwan and might respond by changing its policy toward both China and Hong Kong. In 1992, the U.S. Congress passed the United States-Hong Kong Policy Act requiring the U.S. government to treat Hong Kong "as a non-sovereign entity distinct from China for the purposes of domestic law" and to deal with it "as a separate territory in economic and trade matters." If the Chinese were to disregard the "one country, two systems" policy, U.S. leaders might seek to reverse the 1992 measure and treat Hong Kong as simply another province of China.

In 1997, Hong Kong's role in international commerce seemed secure by almost any measure. The number of foreign corporations with regional headquarters in Hong Kong had grown from 581 to 793 between 1990 and 1995. Hong Kong had

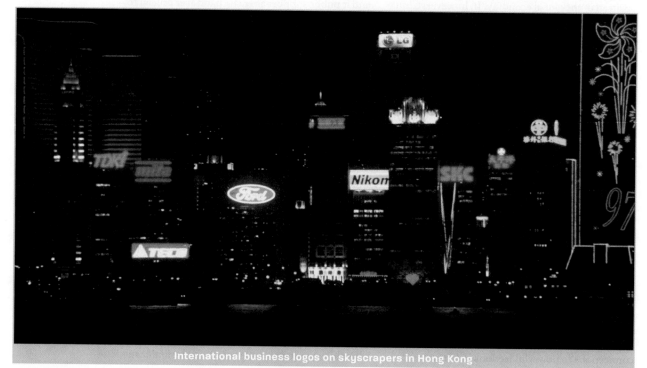

International business logos on skyscrapers in Hong Kong

A view of Hong Kong on the waterfront

the world's seventh largest and Asia's second largest stock market and the world's fifth largest foreign exchange market. Hong Kong had also become a center for project finance, fund management, and stock market analysis for the whole Asian region. It was home to Asia's largest community of professional specialists crucial to business—from lawyers and accountants to construction engineers and realtors. At the time of the handover, however, Hong Kong's prosperity was dependent on continuing economic growth in China, since it was China's vast market that attracted Western business. Also, Hong Kong's ability to maintain its cost competitiveness against rival centers in China and the rest of Asia would affect the prosperity of Hong Kong in the years after the handover.

The future of Hong Kong and China. The return of Hong Kong to Chinese sovereignty occurred while China was undergoing fundamental transformations. It was changing from a rural society with an inward-looking perspective to an urban society with a more international outlook. The economy had begun to move from self-reliance to international interdependence. Also, the foundations of the rule of law were being laid, at least in relation to the practice of international business. But such changes had a long way to go before they could have been considered irreversible.

In 1997, China was developing into a nation with an economy comparable to those of the United States, Western Europe, Japan, and Hong Kong. The policies and actions of the Chinese leadership toward Hong Kong would likely test their willingness and ability to move China away from a system in which economic success depended to a great extent on personal connections, political favoritism, and corrupt practices. If Hong Kong, on the other hand, were forced to fit the pattern of an only partially reformed, semi-modern, one-party state, Hong Kong could become more like China. At the end of a ceremony marking one of history's most unusual and controversial transfers of power, the world waited to see how China's dealings with Hong Kong for the next 50 years would influence the economic and political environment of Asia and the wider world.

About the author: Graham Thomas is head of the Briefing Office of the School of Oriental and African Studies at the University of London.

Vietnam

Vietnam is a country in Southeast Asia with its eastern coast on the South China Sea. It is bordered by China to the north and Laos and Cambodia to the west.

HOT topics

Ancestry of the Vietnamese People.

People have lived in what is now Vietnam since prehistoric times. Ethnic Vietnamese developed a culture in the Red River Delta 4,000 to 5,000 years ago. Through the centuries, this group expanded its control of what is now Vietnam. At the same time, the Vietnamese fought many foreign invaders, frequently the Chinese. Although Vietnam has 54 ethnic groups, over 85 percent of the people are Kinh, that is, ethnic Vietnamese. The Kinh are spread throughout the country. Minority ethnic groups live mainly in the mountain areas of the country.

Climate.

Vietnam has a tropical climate with high humidity. Monsoons (seasonal winds) affect the weather throughout the year. The summer monsoon brings heavy rains from the southwest. The winter monsoon brings lighter rainfall from the northeast. Most of Vietnam has two seasons—a wet, hot summer and a drier, slightly cooler winter.

HOT topics 🔥

Agriculture. Agriculture is the leading economic activity in Vietnam. Rice is the chief crop. Most Vietnamese farmers practice wet-rice agriculture, in which rice is grown on irrigated paddies. This farming method requires much labor but produces high yields. Vietnamese farmers also cultivate cashews, a root crop called cassava, corn, peanuts, and sweet potatoes. Bananas, coconuts, melons, and other fruits are also grown. Many farmers raise animals, especially chickens, ducks, and hogs. Industrial crops, such as coffee, rubber, sugar cane, tea, and tobacco, are cultivated on large plantations.

The Vietnam War. The war known in America as the Vietnam War began in 1957. It is sometimes called the Second Indochina War, and Vietnamese know it as the American War. Communist-supported rebels in the South began a revolt against the government of Ngo Dinh Diem, who was backed by the United States. United States military and civilian advisers then rushed to aid South Vietnam. Through the years, South Vietnam received extensive assistance from the United States, including more than 500,000 troops. Despite this aid, South Vietnam failed to shape itself into a popularly supported, non-Communist state. The war caused enormous destruction. In its attempt to block the transfer of supplies from the North to the South, the United States dropped tons of chemicals on the jungles and forests of central Vietnam. Parts of the country remained barren of vegetation for many years afterwards. The U.S. forces also destroyed many rice fields and villages. The Vietnam War resulted in the deaths of millions of Vietnamese, many of them civilians. More than 58,000 American military personnel also lost their lives.

Rice terraces

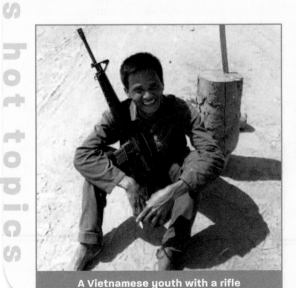
A Vietnamese youth with a rifle during the Vietnam War

TRUE or FALSE?

Most scholars have concluded that media coverage in the United States reflected, rather than brought about, opposition to the Vietnam War.

THE BASICS

Vietnam is a country in Southeast Asia with its eastern coast on the South China Sea. Vietnam is bordered by China to the north and Laos and Cambodia to the west. The Gulf of Thailand lies to the southwest. Hanoi is the capital of Vietnam. Ho Chi Minh City, formerly named Saigon, is the largest city.

The population of Vietnam is concentrated in the Red River Delta in the north and the Mekong River Delta in the south. Central Vietnam is less heavily populated than either the north or the south because it has mountainous terrain. Although Vietnam has a number of ethnic groups, most of the people are classified as Kinh—that is, ethnic Vietnamese.

Most Vietnamese are farmers who live in small villages. Rice is the main crop. But manufacturing has become an increasingly important economic activity.

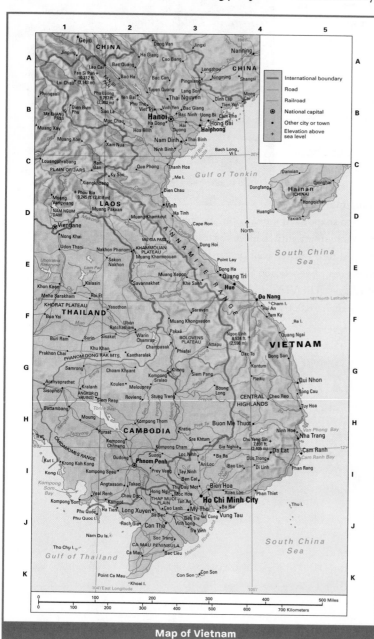

Map of Vietnam

People have lived in what is now Vietnam since prehistoric times. Ethnic Vietnamese developed a culture in the Red River Delta 4,000 to 5,000 years ago. Through the centuries, this group expanded its control of what is now Vietnam. At the same time, the Vietnamese fought many foreign invaders, frequently the Chinese.

The French governed Vietnam from the mid-1800s until Japan occupied it during World War II. After Japan's defeat in 1945, France tried to regain control of Vietnam. But the Vietminh, a group headquartered in the north and headed by the Vietnamese patriot and Communist leader Ho Chi Minh, resisted the French. In 1954, the fighting between the French and the Vietminh ended with a French defeat in the Battle of Dien Bien Phu.

An international peace conference, held in Geneva, Switzerland, decided to divide Vietnam temporarily into two zones—Communist North Vietnam and non-Communist South Vietnam. Elections were supposed to be held to reunite the country, but they were continually postponed and never took place. In 1957, fighting broke out between revolutionaries in the South and the South Vietnamese government. The fighting eventually developed into the Vietnam War, which Vietnamese call the American War. The United States became the chief ally of the South. It backed the South's war effort with supplies and hundreds of thousands of troops.

In 1973, the participants in the war agreed to a cease-fire, and the United States withdrew its last combat troops. But the fighting soon resumed. In April 1975, the Communists defeated South Vietnam. In 1976, they unified North and South Vietnam into a single nation, which they named the Socialist Republic of Vietnam.

Government

According to the Vietnamese Constitution, which was adopted in 1980 and extensively revised in 1992, Vietnam is a socialist nation. It is governed by a single political party—the Communist Party of Vietnam (CPV). The party is the leading force in the state and society. Political power in Vietnam is based on the principle of *democratic centralism*. Under this principle, authority and power originate at the highest levels of the CPV and flow downward through a rigid political structure.

National level. The National Assembly is the highest legislative body in Vietnam. The 498 delegates to the Assembly are elected by the people to a maximum term of five years. No candidate can run for the Assembly without the approval of the Communist Party. All Vietnamese 18 years of age or older are allowed to vote.

Vietnam's highest government officials are the president and the prime minister. The National Assembly elects one of its own members to serve as president. The president directs members of the Assembly to appoint the vice president, prime minister, chief justice of the Supreme People's Court, and head of the Supreme People's Organ of Control. As head of state, the president acts as official representative of Vietnam, has overall command of the armed forces, and chairs the National Defense and Security Council. As chief executive, the prime minister manages the government, assisted by deputy prime ministers and cabinet ministers.

Local level. Vietnam is divided into 57 *tinh* (provinces) and four municipalities—Da Nang, Haiphong, Hanoi, and Ho Chi Minh City. Each tinh and municipality has a legislature called a People's Council and an executive body known as a People's Committee. The people elect the members of each People's Council, who then elect the members of the People's Committee.

Courts. The judicial system of Vietnam consists of two main divisions: the People's Courts and the People's Organs of Control. The People's Courts include the Supreme People's Court, local courts, and Military Tribunals. The People's Organs of Control monitor the bodies of government.

Armed forces of Vietnam consist of a *main force* and *paramilitary forces*. The main force includes an army of about 412,000 members and a small navy and air force. The paramilitary forces include local urban and rural militias and border defense forces. About 40,000 people serve in the paramilitary forces.

People

Ancestry. Vietnam has 54 ethnic groups. Over 85 percent of the people of Vietnam are Kinh—that is, ethnic Vietnamese—who are spread throughout the country. Minority ethnic groups live mainly in the mountain areas of the country. The largest groups are the Tay, who live to the north and northeast of the Red River Delta; and the Tai, who live in scattered villages in valleys of the Red and Black rivers, in the northwest and north-central interior. Other large minority groups include the Hmong, the Khmer, the Muong, and the Nung. A number of ethnic Chinese people, known as the Hoa, live mainly in the cities.

Language. Vietnamese is the most widely spoken language in Vietnam. However, minority peoples speak their own language and may have only limited knowledge of Vietnamese. In urban areas, English is the most widely spoken foreign language, but Chinese, French, and Russian are also spoken.

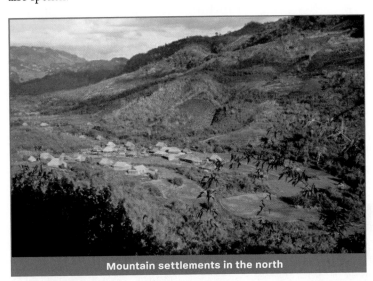

Mountain settlements in the north

Way of Life

Rural life. Most Vietnamese live in small villages in the countryside. Most rural Vietnamese are farmers who organize their lives around the cultivation of crops, especially rice. In general, the family and the village are the centers of social life in rural areas.

Houses in the villages vary. Some have tile roofs and walls made of clay or brick. Others have thatched roofs and walls made of woven bamboo. In the mountains and in areas that flood, houses often stand on stilts.

City life. Many villagers have migrated to the cities in search of jobs and a higher standard of living. However, urban development has not kept pace with immigration from the countryside. As a result, the cities of Vietnam are densely packed and face serious housing shortages. In many cases, two or three generations of a family share a one-room apartment.

Vietnam's cities bustle with traffic. Bicycles are a popular means of transportation. Cities also have numerous motorcycles and *cyclo* taxis—three-wheeled, pedaled cycles with a seat in front for carrying passengers. Cafes, food stands, and stalls that sell craftworks, books, clothing, and other items line many urban streets. Architecture in the cities ranges from simple wooden dwellings for the urban poor to elegant colonial villas built by the French to modern high-rise office and apartment buildings.

Urban Vietnamese work in a variety of occupations. For example, some are employed as public officials or work in factories, hotels, or restaurants. Others are merchants who own their own business.

Clothing. The Vietnamese typically wear lightweight clothing. Rural women wear loose-fitting dark pants and blouses that are often embroidered in brilliant colors. Conical hats called *non la* shield their faces from the sun. In cities, many girls and women wear the traditional *ao dai*, a long tunic worn with loose-fitting pants. However, a growing number of urban women now wear dresses and skirts. Rural and working-class men typically wear simple shirts and trousers. City men generally wear clothing similar to that worn by North Americans and Europeans.

Members of minority groups often dress in traditional costumes. For example, Hmong women wear blouses and skirts or baggy shorts, with embroidered belts and aprons or long vests. Some roll their hair into a turban, but most wrap their heads with a cloth. Hmong men wear skullcaps, loose trousers, shirts, and a long vest.

Food and drink. The national dish of Vietnam is a noodle soup called *pho*. This dish consists of long rice noodles and fresh vegetables in a broth with meat or seafood. Many Vietnamese also eat boiled rice with vegetables, *tofu* (soybean curd), seafood, chicken, pork, or duck. A fish sauce called *nuoc mam* is used as a seasoning in many dishes. People in central Vietnam often eat beans, corn, cassava, sweet potatoes, or other starchy foods instead of rice.

Green tea is the most popular beverage. Fruit and sugar cane juices, coconut milk, and soft drinks are widely available. In urban areas, cafes and restaurants serve local and imported beer, wine, and liquor. Coffee and long loaves of bread called *baguettes*, both of which were favorites of the French, are still popular in Vietnam.

Recreation. The Vietnamese, especially children, enjoy swimming in the country's many lakes and rivers, and in the sea. Vietnamese children also engage in lively games of soccer. Many people play chess or tennis. Competitions involving judo and the martial arts of tae kwon do and kung fu are also popular. Families who can afford to do so vacation at seaside resorts.

Religion. Most Vietnamese practice a combination of the Three Teachings—that is, Mahayana Buddhism, Confucianism, and Taoism. The country also has a small number of Christians and Muslims. In the south, a religion known as Cao Dai and the Hoa Hao Buddhist sect, both of which originated in Vietnam, have numerous followers. Some people, especially in villages, worship the spirits of animals, plants, and other parts of nature.

Education. Nearly all Vietnamese 15 years of age or older can read and write. Children ages 6 through 10 are required to attend school. Schools of higher education in Vietnam include universities, agricultural colleges, technical institutes, and private business academies. The largest are Hanoi University of Technology, Vietnam National University, and Can Tho University. Vocational training is available to adults.

The arts. Traditional Vietnamese forms of art include woodblock printing, woodcarving,

In Hanoi's Old Quarter

lacquerware, ceramics, jade carving, silk painting, and basketry. The Vietnamese are also known for their fine embroidery.

In 1925, the French opened the Ecole des Beaux-Arts de l'Indochine (School of Fine Arts of Indochina) in Hanoi, and Vietnamese artists began to study European-style painting. They started using such materials as oil paints and canvas, painting portraits and scenes of everyday life, and adopting such styles as Cubism and Impressionism. In the late 1940s and early 1950s, a number of artists created works that focused on the resistance to French colonial rule. From the mid-1950s to the 1970s, Socialist Realist artists in the North created paintings that celebrated combat and glorified work.

After the reunification of Vietnam in the mid-1970s to the mid-1980s, art continued to serve mainly a social and political purpose. Since the mid-1980s, however, Vietnamese art has become more open, and paintings now include a variety of styles and subjects. The country's best-known artists include Bui Xuan Phai, known for his Hanoi street scenes; Nguyen Tu Nghiem, whose subjects come from mythology and folklore; Nguyen Sang, who creates paintings of village people; and Do Quang Em, noted for his realistic still lifes and portraits.

Traditional Vietnamese musical instruments include a variety of string, wind, and percussion instruments. Among them are the *dan nhi*, a kind of two-stringed fiddle; the *dan tranh*, a 16-string zither; the *dan nguyet*, a long-necked lute; the dan ty ba, a pear-shaped lute; the *dan tam*, a three-stringed banjo; the *sao*, a bamboo flute; the *trong com*, a barrel-shaped drum; and the *chieng*, a gong.

Vietnam has a long tradition of oral literature. The nation's first great writer was Nguyen Trai, who lived in the late 1300s and early 1400s. He became famous as a pioneer of *chu nom*—a form of Vietnamese written in modified Chinese characters. Literature written in Vietnamese began to appear around the 1600s. *Truyen Kieu* (*The Tale of Kieu*), a long poem written by Nguyen Du in the early 1800s, ranks as one of the greatest works in the Vietnamese language. Although a love story, the poem also reflects the struggles of the society of Nguyen Du's time.

Authors of the late 1900s and early 2000s include Duong Thu Huong, known for her novels *Paradise of the Blind* (1988) and *Novel Without a Name* (1991); Bao Ninh, whose most famous

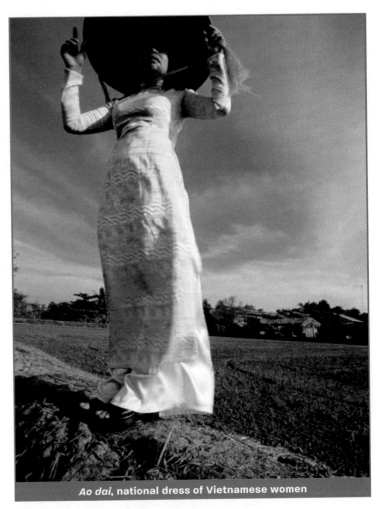

***Ao dai*, national dress of Vietnamese women**

work is the novel *The Sorrow of War* (1991); and the short-story writer Nguyen Huy Thiep, some of whose works have been collected in *The General Retires and Other Stories* (1988).

The Land

Vietnam is an S-shaped country that occupies the rugged eastern Indochinese Peninsula. Four-fifths of the country is covered by hills, plateaus, and mountains. The coastline borders on the South China Sea and extends more than 2,100 miles (3,400 kilometers) from the Gulf of Tonkin to the Gulf of Thailand. Geographers typically divide Vietnam into three regions: northern, central, and southern.

Northern Vietnam extends from the border with China in the north to about Thanh Hoa in the south. This region is dominated by the Red River Delta, the most densely populated center of agricultural production in Vietnam. The triangular delta is the heartland of Vietnamese civilization, and the capital city of Hanoi is there.

Northern Vietnam also includes the mountains of the north and northwest. Vietnam's highest mountain is Fan Si Pan, also spelled Phan Xi Pang. It rises to 10,312 feet (3,143 meters) in northwestern Vietnam.

Central Vietnam is the most mountainous of the country's three regions. The Annamite Range, also known as the Truong Son mountains, dominates this area. The Central Highlands lie to the south. Poor soil makes farming difficult in central Vietnam. However, rich soil is available in the lowlands along the coast and a few plateaus in the Central Highlands.

Southern Vietnam. The Mekong River in the southern part of Vietnam forms the country's largest network of agricultural plains. As a result, the Mekong Delta is often referred to as the "rice bowl" of Vietnam. Ho Chi Minh City, formerly named Saigon, is the region's major urban center and the country's economic hub.

 ## Climate

Vietnam has a tropical climate with high humidity. *Monsoons* (seasonal winds) affect the weather throughout the year. The summer monsoon brings heavy rains from the southwest. The winter monsoon brings lighter rainfall from the northeast. Most of Vietnam has two seasons—a wet, hot summer and a drier, slightly cooler winter.

In Hanoi, in northern Vietnam, the average temperature is about 63°F (17°C) in January and about 85°F (29°C) in June. From May to October, the Red River Delta has high temperatures, heavy rains, and some typhoons, which sweep across the Gulf of Tonkin. Hanoi receives about 68 inches (173 centimeters) of rainfall a year.

In southern Vietnam, most rain falls in summer. The Ho Chi Minh City area receives about 70 inches (180 centimeters) of rain between May and October. From November through February, the weather is cooler with little rain. Average temperatures there range from about 79°F (26°C) in December to about 86°F (30°C) in April.

Central Vietnam has the greatest temperature range and includes the driest and the wettest regions of the country. Typhoons often strike the central coast. Mountain areas generally have lower temperatures and less rainfall than the delta regions and the coastal lowlands.

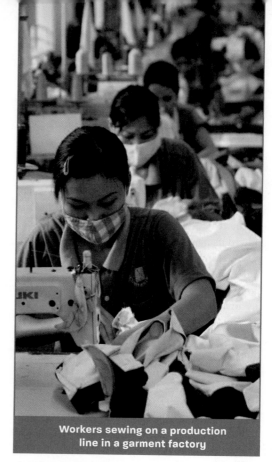

Workers sewing on a production line in a garment factory

Economy

From 1976 to 1986, the state owned all banks and factories in Vietnam and controlled nearly every sector of the economy. During that period, the economy steadily declined. In 1986, however, Vietnamese leaders began adopting a series of far-reaching economic changes known as *doi moi* (renovation). These changes were designed to restore some economic power to the private sector. Under doi moi, for example, farmers who had satisfied their obligations to the state were allowed to produce for the market. Some state-run industries that had operated at a loss for a decade or more were dismantled. Vietnam also began to welcome foreign investment in the form of direct loans and joint ventures.

Agriculture is the leading economic activity in Vietnam. Rice is the chief crop. Most Vietnamese farmers practice wet-rice agriculture, in which rice is grown on irrigated paddies. This farming method requires much labor but produces high yields. Vietnamese farmers also cultivate cashews, a root crop called cassava, corn, peanuts, and sweet potatoes. Bananas, coconuts, melons, and other fruits are also grown. Many farmers raise animals, especially chickens, ducks, and hogs. Industrial crops, such as coffee, rubber, sugar cane, tea, and tobacco, are cultivated on large plantations.

Manufacturing. Textile production is the leading manufacturing industry in Vietnam. The country also produces cement, chemical fertilizers, glass, shoes, steel, and tires. Factories manufacture various household goods, including bicycles and televisions. Most of Vietnam's industrial development is in the south. Ho Chi Minh City has a number of high-tech industries.

Mining. Vietnam is rich in mineral resources. Its coal fields, most of which are in the north, have tremendous reserves. The country also has large deposits of chromite, copper, gold, iron ore, lead, phosphate, tin, and zinc. Bauxite, the basic ingredient of aluminum, is also mined. An abundance of limestone contributes to a thriving cement industry. Vast deposits of silica supply the basis for the manufacture of glass. The country also has extensive reserves of petroleum and natural gas, mainly offshore.

Fishing industry. With Vietnam's long coastline and many lakes and rivers, fishing has always played an important role in the economy. Vietnamese fishing crews catch a variety of fish and shellfish. Seafood processing is normally carried out in large plants. Vietnam is rapidly becoming one of the world's leading producers of processed shrimp.

Service industries are those industries that provide services rather than produce manufactured goods or agricultural products. Many Vietnamese work in service industries as barbers, clerks, computer technicians, construction workers, drivers of cyclo taxis, hairdressers, housekeepers in hotels, and waiters in restaurants.

International trade. Vietnam's chief exports include clothing and textiles, coffee, fish and shellfish, petroleum, rice, rubber, shoes, and tea. Its main imports include cotton, fertilizer, machinery and equipment, motorcycles, petroleum products, and steel products. Vietnam's chief trading partners are Japan, Singapore, South Korea, and Taiwan.

Transportation and communication. Bicycles and motorcycles are popular forms of transportation in Vietnam. Many people also ride buses. The nation's rivers are widely used to transport goods and people. Vietnam has about 62,000 miles (100,000 kilometers) of roads, though only about a fourth of them are paved.

A railroad network connects the major cities of the Red River and Mekong deltas and cities along the coast. However, much of the system was damaged by bombs during the Vietnam War and remains in disrepair. Vietnam's chief ports include Da Nang, Haiphong, and Ho Chi Minh City. Hanoi and Ho Chi Minh City have international airports.

Several daily newspapers are published in Vietnam. The government controls all newspapers, magazines, and television and radio broadcasts.

History

People have lived in what is now Vietnam since prehistoric times. Archaeologists have discovered remains of a stone age culture dating back about 500,000 years in the province of Thanh Hoa. Agriculture developed in northern Vietnam more than 7,000 years ago.

About 5,000 years ago, a kingdom called Van Lang emerged in the Black and Red river valleys under the rule of the Hung kings. One of the most important cultures of Van Lang, the Dong Son civilization, flourished in the valleys of the Red and Ma rivers from about 800 to 300 B.C. This civilization is known mainly for its elaborately decorated bronze drums.

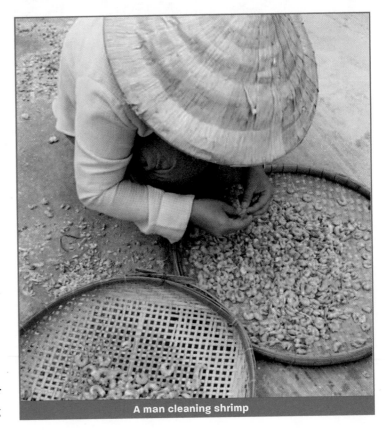

A man cleaning shrimp

Nam Viet. In 258 B.C., a leader named An Duong founded the kingdom of Au Lac. In 207 B.C., an official of China's Qin dynasty named Zhao Tuo (Trieu Da in Vietnamese) founded the kingdom of Nam Viet. Nam Viet included Au Lac and several other kingdoms in what is now northern Vietnam. In 111 B.C., the Chinese Han dynasty conquered Nam Viet. Through the centuries, many Vietnamese resisted Chinese rule. But not until A.D. 939, as a result of a rebellion led by Ngo Quyen, did the Vietnamese gain independence.

Despite the centuries of Chinese occupation, many aspects of Vietnamese culture remained in place, but new patterns also emerged. Specifically, the rise of a mixed Chinese and Vietnamese ruling class ensured the lasting importance of Chinese writing, even though the Vietnamese continued to speak their own language. Chinese ideas of historical writing also had an enormous

Troop members carrying their military gear during the French attack on Vietminh forces

impact on how Vietnamese historians represented their past. Vietnamese officials sometimes adopted Chinese administrative practices. The Three Teachings—Mahayana Buddhism, Confucianism, and Taoism—are another legacy of Chinese rule.

Independence. After Ngo Quyen's death in 944, Vietnam was troubled by succession disputes and the competition of warlords. These troubles ended with the establishment of the Dinh dynasty in 968, though the dynasty lasted only 12 years. The succeeding dynasty, established in 980, lasted only until 1009. Two long-lasting dynasties, the Ly (1009–1225) and the Tran (1225–1400), stabilized politics.

In 1400, Ho Quy Ly seized the Vietnamese throne, and in 1407, the Ming Chinese invaded the country and took control. In 1428, Le Loi drove out the Chinese rulers and established the Le dynasty. Under the Le rulers, the Vietnamese empire continued the process of Nam Tien (Advance to the South). During the 1400s, for example, the Vietnamese conquered Champa, a rival kingdom in what is now central Vietnam.

In 1527, the Mac dynasty overthrew the Le dynasty, and, in 1540, was formally recognized by the Ming Chinese. Le forces regained control over central Vietnam in 1545 and northern Vietnam in 1592. However, Mac forces continued to fight against the Le for more than 35 years.

During the mid-1500s, Vietnamese politics became further fragmented as the Trinh and Nguyen families, the two clans closest to the Le court, drifted apart. By 1600, the country was effectively divided, and the Le kept control in name only. Even though the Ming Chinese had recognized the Le dynasty as ruler of Vietnam, the Trinh lords actually governed the north and the Nguyen lords were in charge of the south. In the 1600s, the rivalry between these two clans occasionally erupted into armed conflict.

The Nguyen lords continued their expansion to the south until 1771. That year, three brothers from the region of Tay Son in central Vietnam began a series of successful attacks against Nguyen rule. This upheaval, known as the Tay Son Rebellion, resulted in the collapse of Nguyen power in the south, Trinh power in the north, and, in 1788, the end of the Le dynasty. After defending Vietnam against an invasion of Qing Chinese troops in 1789, the Tay Son dynasty tried to consolidate its rule over all of what is now Vietnam.

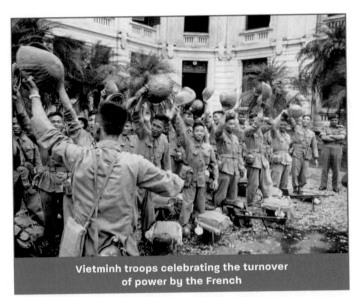

Vietminh troops celebrating the turnover
of power by the French

In 1802, Nguyen Anh became the first emperor of the Nguyen dynasty. He took the reign name of Gia Long. He united the country and called it Vietnam. The Nguyen dynasty, Vietnam's last, established its capital in Hue. It formally ended in 1945.

French rule. In 1858, French warships captured the city of Da Nang. The French claimed that they were protecting Jesuit missionaries and Vietnamese who had converted to Roman Catholicism. By continuing the armed attacks and through diplomatic pressure, France succeeded in taking control of the southern part of Vietnam, known then as Cochin China, in the 1860s. In the 1880s, France took control of the northern (Tonkin) and central (Annam) parts of Vietnam. With the conquest of Cambodia in the 1860s and of Laos in the 1890s, French control of Indochina was complete.

The French were principally interested in Vietnam and the surrounding area as a base for trading with China. They also hoped to exploit the mineral wealth of Vietnam and to establish plantations for coffee, rubber, and tea. To help carry out these plans, the French built roads and railways, which linked the lowlands, the midlands, and the mountains. They also expanded port facilities.

Under French rule, the traditional Vietnamese ruling class withdrew from public life, and a new French-Vietnamese ruling class emerged. The romanized written version of Vietnamese known as *quoc ngu* also became more prominent in private and public affairs.

Through the years, Vietnamese resistance to French rule grew. Various nationalist associations and societies emerged, as did a number of political parties. These parties included the Vietnamese Nationalist Party, Indochinese Communist Party, and the New Vietnamese Revolutionary Party.

The August Revolution of 1945. In August 1940, during World War II (1939–1945), France's wartime Vichy government granted Japan permission to use northern Vietnam for military operations. When Japanese troops advanced into other Southeast Asian colonies of European powers, they took control over the colonial governments. In Vietnam, the Japanese at first allowed French officials to continue to carry out their administrative duties. In March 1945, however, the Japanese ousted the French officials.

Initially, most Vietnamese had welcomed the Japanese, expecting that they would free Vietnam from French rule. When it seemed that Japan was also a threat to their independence, however, many Vietnamese reconsidered their plans to join with the Japanese to fight the French. One result of such reconsideration was the creation of an organization called the Vietminh in 1941. Established by Ho Chi Minh and other leaders of the Indochinese Communist Party, the Vietminh was designed to encourage national unity and independence.

Japan agreed to surrender on August 14, 1945. Within days, anticolonial activists in Vietnam staged the August Revolution. On September 2, Ho recited Vietnam's declaration of independence, in which he quoted directly from the American Declaration of Independence. Ho and other revolutionary leaders expected that the United States would support the new postcolonial state—the Democratic Republic of Vietnam (DRV). They believed that they would receive such support for a number of reasons. For instance, the United States had gained its own independence through a revolution. The United States had also criticized European colonialism for most of the 1900s. In addition, the Vietminh had cooperated with U.S. diplomatic and military personnel during World War II. However, the DRV never received U.S. support, mainly because of U.S. opposition to Communism.

The Indochina War. After World War II, France tried to reclaim its former colonies in Southeast Asia. In 1946, war broke out between France and the Vietminh. Throughout the war, the French controlled cities in north and south Vietnam. The revolutionaries, based in the mountains of the north and northwest, controlled most of the countryside. Many southern Vietnamese rejected the idea of a Communist-dominated government and sided with the French. By mid-1949, the French had formed the Associated State of Vietnam to oppose the Vietminh. Bao Dai, the last of the Nguyen emperors, headed the government of the Associated State. The fighting in Vietnam ended

in May 1954, when the Vietminh overwhelmed the French garrison at Dien Bien Phu.

Fearing the growth of Communism, the United States began in 1948 to channel aid to the countries of Western Europe to help them rebuild after the devastation of World War II. The assistance provided by the Marshall Plan made it possible for France to rebuild and to continue fighting the war in Vietnam. Further expressing its support for the French attempt to reconquer Vietnam, the United States formally recognized the Associated State of Vietnam in 1950.

During the final stages of the First Indochina War, negotiators representing nine countries—Cambodia, China, France, Laos, the United Kingdom, the United States, the Soviet Union, the Democratic Republic of Vietnam, and the Associated State of Vietnam—assembled in Geneva, Switzerland. In July 1954, the representatives produced a series of agreements known as the Geneva Accords.

One of these agreements provided that Vietnam be temporarily divided into northern and southern zones at the 17th parallel. Another agreement called for an election in 1956 to unify the country. Fearing that Ho Chi Minh would win such an election, however, southern Vietnamese, with U.S. support, refused to participate. The election was never held.

The Vietnam War began in 1957. It is sometimes called the Second Indochina War, and Vietnamese know it as the American War. Communist-supported rebels in the South began a revolt against the government of Ngo Dinh Diem, who was backed by the United States. United States military and civilian advisers then rushed to aid South Vietnam. Through the years, South Vietnam received extensive assistance from the United States, including cash, military equipment, and more than 500,000 troops. Despite this aid, South Vietnam failed to shape itself into a popularly supported, non-Communist state. In April 1975, the People's Army of North Vietnam launched an offensive that resulted in the complete collapse of Southern power.

The Vietnam War caused enormous destruction. In its attempt to block the transfer of supplies from the North to the South, the United States dropped tons of chemicals on the jungles and forests of central Vietnam. Parts of the country remained barren of vegetation for many years afterwards. The U.S. forces also destroyed many rice fields and villages. The Vietnam War resulted in the deaths of millions of Vietnamese, many

A C-123 airplane spraying defoliants during the Vietnam War

of them civilians. More than 58,000 American military personnel also lost their lives.

Postwar Vietnam. In April 1976, national elections determined the nearly 500 members of the new National Assembly for a reunited Vietnam. In July, the Socialist Republic of Vietnam was officially proclaimed. In the process of establishing a single state, leaders of the new government sought out supporters of the former South Vietnamese government. According to official sources, more than 1 million southerners were subjected to some form of "reeducation" in the political culture of the North. For most of these people, this process took several days or weeks. But thousands of others, viewed as greater threats, spent a decade or more in labor camps.

Following reunification, thousands of northerners resettled in the south. As a consequence, the northern dialect of Vietnamese is now regarded officially as standard Vietnamese. In addition, the government has taken thousands of Kinh from the deltas and relocated them in the highlands and mountains.

With the collapse of the Southern regime, many Vietnamese fled the country. They settled in the United States, Canada, and Australia, or joined earlier generations of exiles in Belgium and France. Following the government's nationalization of industries, tens of thousands of ethnic Chinese also left the country.

Many refugees left Vietnam in small boats, risking drowning and pirate attacks in the South China Sea. These refugees became known as boat people. They went to other countries in

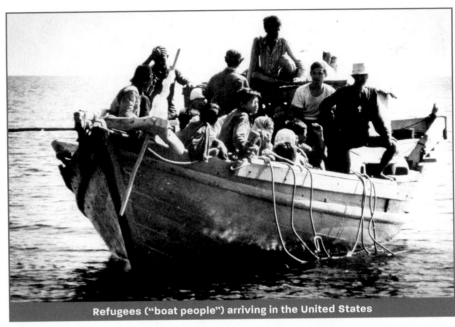

Refugees ("boat people") arriving in the United States

Southeast Asia, where they stayed in refugee camps until they could be relocated. Many later moved to the United States. In the mid-1990s, the United Nations and countries that housed or helped pay for the camps closed nearly all of them. Most of the remaining refugees were sent back to Vietnam.

Invasion of Cambodia. In 1978, Vietnam invaded Cambodia. It replaced Cambodia's Khmer Rouge Communist government with a pro-Vietnamese Communist government. The Khmer Rouge and non-Communist groups then fought against the government and the Vietnamese forces in Cambodia. Vietnam gradually withdrew its troops in the 1980s, and the war ended in 1991.

Recent developments. In the late 1980s, the Vietnamese government began a program of economic restructuring known as doi moi. This program encouraged some

forms of private enterprise and competition as well as foreign investment. In early July 1995, Vietnam and the United States established diplomatic ties. Later that month, Vietnam became a member of the Association of Southeast Asian Nations (ASEAN), a regional organization that promotes political, economic, cultural, and social cooperation among its members. In July 2000, Vietnam and the United States signed a trade agreement. This pact cleared the way for normal trade relations between the two countries for the first time since the Vietnam War. In December 2006, the U.S. Congress passed a bill normalizing trade relations with Vietnam.

MLA Citation

"Vietnam." *The Southwestern Advantage Topic Source.* Nashville: Southwestern. 2013.

DATA

Facts in Brief about Vietnam

Capital: Hanoi.

Official language: Vietnamese.

Area: 127,882 mi² (331,212 km²). *Greatest distances*—north-south, 1,030 mi (1,658 km); east-west, 380 mi (612 km). *Coastline*—2,140 mi (3,444 km).

Elevation: *Highest*—Fan Si Pan, 10,312 ft (3,143 m) above sea level. *Lowest*—sea level along the coast.

Population: *Current estimate*—91,007,000; density, 712 per mi² (275 per km²); distribution, 72 percent rural, 28 percent urban. *2009 census*—85,846,997.

Chief products: *Agriculture*—cashews, coffee, hogs, rice. *Manufacturing*—cement, clothing, food and beverages, machinery, textiles. *Mining*—coal.

Money: *Basic unit*—dong.

Flag and coat of arms: Vietnam's flag, adopted in 1945, features a star that stands for Communism. The coat of arms has the star along with branches of rice and a cogwheel that represent the importance of agriculture and industry to Vietnam. The shape of the star was modified slightly in 1955.

Important Dates in Vietnam

111 B.C.	The Chinese conquered Nam Viet, a kingdom in what is now northern Vietnam.
A.D. 939	China ended its rule over the Vietnamese, who then set up an independent state.
1802	Nguyen Anh united the country and called it Vietnam.
1860's–1880s	France took control of Vietnam.
1940–1945	Japan controlled Vietnam during World War II.
1946	War began between France and the Vietminh.
1954	The Vietminh defeated the French. The Geneva Conference temporarily divided Vietnam into two zones.
1957	The Vietnam War began, as Communist-supported rebels began a revolt against the South Vietnamese government.
1973	United States participation in the Vietnam War ended.
1975	The Vietnam War ended on April 30 with the surrender of South Vietnam.
1976	The Communists unified North and South Vietnam into the Socialist Republic of Vietnam.
1986	Vietnam began an economic reform program known as *doi moi*.

ADDITIONAL RESOURCES

Books to Read

Ashwill, Mark A. *Vietnam Today*. Intercultural Press, 2005.

Lockhart, Bruce M., and Duiker, W. J. *Historical Dictionary of Vietnam*. 3rd ed. Scarecrow, 2006.

Phillips, Douglas A. *Vietnam*. Chelsea House, 2006.

Taus-Bolstad, Stacy. *Vietnam in Pictures*. Rev. ed. Lerner, 2003.

Web Sites

Background Note: Vietnam

http://www.state.gov/r/pa/ei/bgn/4130.htm

Information from the U.S. Department of State.

CIA Factbook: Vietnam

https://www.cia.gov/library/publications/the-world-factbook/geos/vm.html

An overview of the country from the U.S. Central Intelligence Agency.

Country Profile: Vietnam

http://news.bbc.co.uk/2/hi/asia-pacific/country_profiles/1243338.stm

Information from the BBC.

Embassy of the Socialist Republic of Vietnam

http://www.vietnamembassy-usa.org/

Information about Vietnam from the Embassy of Vietnam in Washington, D.C.

The American Experience: Vietnam

http://www.pbs.org/wgbh/amex/vietnam/

The American Experience presents an exhaustive look at the Vietnam War, including information on the people, the places, the issues, and the outcomes.

Vietnam Science, Technology and Environment

http://coombs.anu.edu.au/~vern/avsl.html

Links to information about the science, technology, and environment of Vietnam.

Search Strings

Ancestry of the Vietnamese People

Vietnam ancestry of the people Chinese Kinh (3,280)

Vietnam ancestry of the people Chinese Kinh ethnic groups (11,100)

Climate

Vietnam climate tropical monsoon (38,400)

Vietnam climate tropical monsoon seasonal winds effects (4,150)

climate in Vietnam tropical monsoon summer winter (10,500)

Agriculture

Vietnam agriculture rice crop cashews animals (29,900)

Vietnam agriculture "wet-rice agriculture" crop cashews animals (10)

Vietnam agriculture rice crop cashews animal economy (27,300)

The Vietnam War

Vietnam War Second Indochina War NgoDinh Diem (9)

"Vietnam War" "Second Indochina War" (15,900)

"Vietnam War" "Second Indochina War" Communism revolt destruction (1,220)

BACKGROUND INFORMATION

The following articles were written during the year in which the events took place and reflect the style and thinking of that time.

Vietnam (1956)

Vietnam remained split between the free and Communist worlds in 1956. Both sectors struggled for political unity and economic stability. South Vietnam held its first elections in March, electing a pro-Western majority to the National Assembly. In July, the Assembly elected Premier Ngo Dinh Diem as the country's fist President. South Vietnam celebrated its first anniversary as a free republic on October 26 by proclaiming a new constitution that provided a strong central form of government.

United States aid helped establish a program to resettle 100,000 refugees from Communist North Vietnam, and to develop rice lands in Cochin China. Relations between France and Vietnam were improved when the French agreed to withdraw troops from South Vietnam. A dispute with neighboring Cambodia over islands in the Gulf of Siam caused the closing of the Cambodian-Vietnamese border.

United States Secretary of State John Foster Dulles visited President Diem in July, and Vice-President Richard M. Nixon addressed the National Assembly in Saigon in July. Admiral W. Radford, chairman of the United States Joint Chiefs of Staff, conferred with officials there on defense problems. Soviet Deputy Premier Anastas Mikoyan visited Ho Chi Minh, leader of North Vietnam.

Vietnam (1974)

North Vietnam. An estimated 200,000 North Vietnamese soldiers were believed to be deployed in South Vietnam during 1974. They built roads, pipelines, and other logistical support facilities. And they continued major military operations against Saigon's forces despite the January 27, 1973, cease-fire agreement.

In public statements, however, North Vietnam emphasized economic development as its first priority, with secondary attention to supporting the war in the South. The Lao Dong Party, North Vietnam's Communist organization, decided on this policy at a secret meeting in late January or early February. The party's first secretary, Le Duan, said economic setbacks from the war and U.S. bombing will take a pretty long time to eliminate.

The party's top economic expert, Deputy Premier Le Thanh Nghi, became chairman of the economic planning commission on April 2. It was hoped that he could solve the major economic problems. Premier Pham Van Dong said on September 1 that production should reach its 1965 level (before U.S. bombing began) by the end of 1974.

Russia and China increased their economic aid, largely to make up for bad harvests and food shortages, but they declined to supply much military equipment.

South Vietnam. Economic and political pressures created by the war developed into widespread demonstrations against President Nguyen Van Thieu's regime late in 1974. Meanwhile, the war continued unchecked despite the 1973 Paris cease-fire agreement.

Two developments triggered public frustrations into the strongest challenge ever to Thieu's presidency. One was the resignation in August of President Richard M. Nixon, a strong supporter of Thieu. Nixon's fall seemed to prove to many of Thieu's opponents that the Vietnamese president might also be vulnerable. The other was U.S. congressional cuts in military aid for South Vietnam. Instead of the requested $1.45 billion for the period from July 1, 1974, to June 30, 1975, Congress voted only $700 million.

In the face of the cuts, the South Vietnamese Army had to reduce its use of planes, bombs, artillery shells, and other supplies. The resulting fears of military weakness sparked demands for new efforts to reach a political settlement with the Communists rather than accept Thieu's insistence that a political deal would be suicidal.

The two main groups agitating against Thieu were a Roman Catholic-led "People's Movement Against Corruption, for National Salvation and Peace Restoration" and "The Forces for National Reconciliation" led by the An Quang faction of Buddhists.

Thieu moved gradually to meet the demonstrators' complaints of corruption. He fired 377 army majors and colonels on October 25, and three generals commanding regions of Vietnam on October 30. He reshuffled his Cabinet beginning October 24. Among the ministers he dropped was his cousin and top adviser on relations with Washington, Hoang Duc Nha.

But such moves failed to satisfy the opponents. The People's

Movement anticorruption leader, Tran Huu Thanh, continued to call for Thieu's resignation, as did others. Thieu denied the corruption charges and told the nation on October 1 that he would resign "if the entire people and army no longer have confidence in me.

Role of Viet Cong. The Viet Cong continued its full-scale war against the Saigon government. On October 8, it called for Thieu's overthrow, saying it would not negotiate with his regime under cease-fire agreement terms.

Declining American economic aid brought a drop in living standards. The country suffered from

both recession and inflation, but the first signs of offshore oil wealth appeared. In January and February, boats of the Saigon Navy clashed with Chinese vessels over ownership of the offshore Paracel and Spratly islands. The incidents were reportedly caused by the interest in the offshore oil.

Vietnam (1975)

The goal of the late President Ho Chi Minh was finally achieved in 1975 with the defeat of South Vietnam. Ho had never accepted the division of Vietnam after his force defeated French forces in 1954. He sent army divisions and political workers into South Vietnam—many of the men came from there originally—and their victory on April 30 cleared the way for eventual reunification of the country under Communist rule from Hanoi. In December, officials announced reunification was set for April 30, 1976.

Le Duan, secretary-general of North Vietnam's Communist

Nguyen Van Thieu, 1968

Party and the government's most important leader, traveled extensively. He went to Khmer (formerly Cambodia) in August, to China in September, and to Eastern Europe in October.

The China visit ended in apparent disagreement between the two governments. The Chinese were disturbed over Russian influence in Vietnam. North Vietnam increasingly took Russia's side in international affairs on which Moscow and Peking disagreed. In addition, China and Vietnam have long had territorial disputes in the South China Sea.

North Vietnam applied for United Nations membership in July. But the United States vetoed the application because Communist and other nations refused to consider a similar application from South Korea.

The long war in Vietnam ended on April 30, 1975, with a complete Communist victory. North Vietnam immediately began reorganizing South Vietnam in preparation for reunification of the two countries on April 30, 1976.

Phuoc Binh, capital of Phuoc Long province, fell to North Vietnamese Army troops on January 7, 1975. Encouraged by this victory, North Vietnam sent more troops into South Vietnam. The fall of Ban Me Thuot on March 10 caused South Vietnam's president Nguyen Van Thieu to order the Central Highlands evacuated. This turned into a rout. Hue and Da Nang, the main cities in northern South Vietnam, fell on March 26 and 29.

The South Vietnamese Senate on April 2 overwhelmingly approved a resolution that a "government of national union" be formed to end the war. Politicians who normally strongly supported

Thieu in all his actions joined in approving the call for a new government. Only one member of the Senate voted against the resolution. The senators criticized both Thieu and the United States for the position in which South Vietnam found itself. They blamed Thieu for mistakes and the United States for not supporting the Saigon regime fully enough.

Meanwhile, Communist demolition units and division-sized infantry units supported by tanks were drawing closer to the South Vietnamese capital. Refugees poured into the city.

Aid asked. President Gerald R. Ford asked the U.S. Congress for an extra $300 million in military aid for Saigon on January 28, but it had not been approved by March. Ford then asked for $972 million in emergency help on April 10, but this request was also never approved.

As Communist forces gathered to attack Saigon, Thieu resigned on April 21. In an impassioned address to the nation, he defended his character and the accomplishments of his regime, while chronicling its collapse. He called for peace, but also said the successor government would fight on. He devoted most of his speech to scathing criticism of the United States, saying that former president Richard M. Nixon had promised Saigon not only military and economic aid, but also "direct and strong United

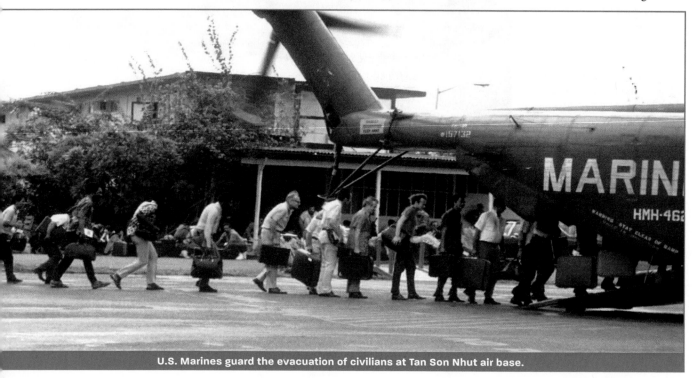

U.S. Marines guard the evacuation of civilians at Tan Son Nhut air base.

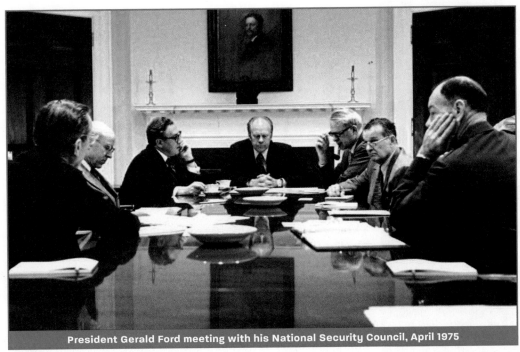

President Gerald Ford meeting with his National Security Council, April 1975

States military intervention" in the event the Communists broke the Paris agreement of 1973. It was the breaking of this agreement, according to Thieu, that resulted in South Vietnam's defeat.

Thieu was succeeded by Vice President Tran Van Huong, but the Communists refused to negotiate with Huong. On April 28, Duong Van Minh became president, hoping to negotiate peace. But the final attack was already underway. On orders from President Ford, U.S. troops were evacuated from Saigon on April 29 and 30. A fleet of 81 helicopters flew 1,373 Americans and 5,695 Vietnamese to U.S. Navy ships in the South China Sea. More than 140,000 refugees left on helicopters, planes, ships, and fishing boats. About 132,000 settled in the United States and some in other countries, but 1,546 sailed back to Vietnam in October.

Communist troops entered Saigon on April 30. They forced Minh to surrender unconditionally.

The new regime posted military management committees in South Vietnamese cities. The Provisional Revolutionary Government (PRG) formally took over control on June 6, the sixth anniversary of its founding by the Viet Cong's National Liberation Front. But the PRG remained curiously invisible and seemingly powerless. A member of the North Vietnamese Communist Party's Politburo, Pham Hung, who had directed the war in the south, was given the senior position in public appearances, ahead of PRG officials.

Indoctrination programs were run for government and military personnel of the Thieu regime. Some former officials were resettled in rural areas, and the new official newspaper in Saigon said on October 4 that some 1.5 million of the city's 4 million inhabitants would be moved to farms.

The PRG applied for membership in the United Nations in July, but the United States vetoed the application.

Venezuela

Venezuela is a South American country that ranks as one of the world's leading producers and exporters of petroleum.

HOT topics

Ancestry of the Venezuelan People. In the 1500s, Spain colonized the area that is now Venezuela. The Spanish conquered many of the numerous tribes of Indians who were living there. They also imported black slaves from Africa. Many of the Indians, Spaniards, and blacks intermarried. Today, about two-thirds of Venezuela's people are of mixed ancestry. People of unmixed white, black, or Indian ancestry make up the rest of the country's population.

Urban Life in Venezuela. Since the 1940s, many Venezuelans have moved from rural areas to the cities. As the cities have grown, so has the country's middle class. Most middle-class Venezuelans live comfortably, dress well, own a car, and take vacations regularly. Some families live in one-story, Spanish-style houses that center on a courtyard. But in most cities, houses are being rapidly replaced by high-rise apartments. Although Venezuela's middle class has grown, poverty remains a major problem. Housing is scarce, and many Venezuelans live in crowded squatter settlements on the outskirts of the cities. Most of these people are unskilled workers from rural areas. Many of them build and live in small shacks called ranchos. Thousands of ranchos cover large areas in and around many cities. Since the 1960s, the Venezuelan government has carried out massive programs to improve the living conditions of the poor.

HOT topics

hot topics hot topics hot topics hot topics

Venezuelan Independence. Venezuela was the first Spanish colony in South America to demand its independence. The colony declared its freedom on July 5, 1811, though Spanish forces still occupied much of the country. Venezuela did not become truly independent until 1821. That year, Venezuelan leader Simón Bolívar won a great victory against the Spanish at Carabobo (near Valencia), which ended Spanish rule in Venezuela. Meanwhile, in 1819, Bolívar had set up and become president of Gran Colombia, a republic that eventually included what are now Venezuela, Colombia, Ecuador, and Panama. Venezuela broke away from Gran Colombia in 1829 and drafted a separate constitution in 1830.

Statue of Simon Bolivar

Venezuelan tamales, at the Tamale Latin American fair

Oil Economy. Venezuelans have a high standard of living in relation to the rest of Latin America. This is due mainly to the country's large petroleum production. But Venezuela's wealth is not distributed evenly among the people, and poverty and unemployment are major problems in some areas. Another difficulty is the economic instability created by changes in the price of petroleum.

TRUE or FALSE?
Service industries employ about 60 percent of Venezuela's workers.

THE BASICS

Venezuela is a South American country that ranks as one of the world's leading producers and exporters of petroleum. Before its petroleum industry began to grow rapidly during the 1920s, Venezuela was one of the poorer countries in South America. Its economy was based on such agricultural products as cacao and coffee. Since the 1920s, however, Venezuela has become one of the wealthiest and most rapidly changing countries on the continent. Income from petroleum exports enabled Venezuela to carry out huge industrial development and modernization programs.

Venezuela lies on the north coast of South America along the Caribbean Sea. Mountain ranges extend across much of northern Venezuela, which is the most densely populated region of the country. Caracas, the capital and largest city, lies in this region. Vast plains called the *Llanos* spread across central Venezuela. High plateaus and low mountains cover the south.

Most of Venezuela's people live in cities and towns. Nearly all Venezuelans speak Spanish. Most of the people are descendants of Europeans, American Indians, and Africans who intermarried.

The famous explorer Christopher Columbus landed in what is now Venezuela in 1498 on his third voyage to the New World. It was his first landing on the mainland of the Americas. Later, European explorers in northwestern Venezuela found Indian villages where the houses were built on poles over the waters of the Gulf of Venezuela and Lake Maracaibo. Some of the explorers were reminded of the Italian city of Venice, where buildings stood along the water. They named the area *Venezuela*, which is Spanish for *Little Venice*. Later, the name Venezuela was applied to a large area of northern South America. Spain ruled Venezuela for about 300 years. In 1811, Venezuela declared its independence.

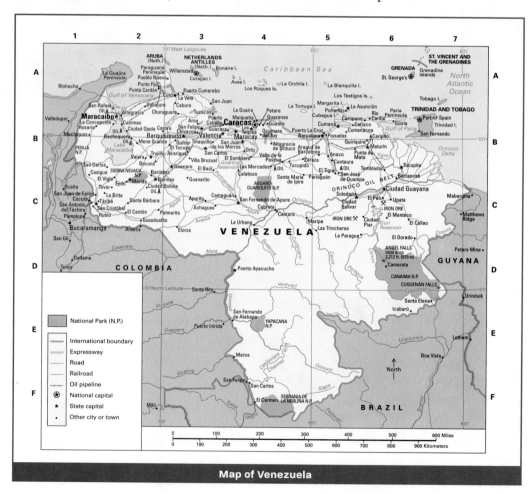

Map of Venezuela

Government

Venezuela is a federal republic. All citizens 18 years and older may vote. Since 1811, the country has had 27 constitutions. Venezuela's present Constitution was adopted in 1999.

National government. According to the Constitution, the president serves as Venezuela's head of state and as head of the executive branch of government. The people elect the president to a six-year term. The president can be reelected to a consecutive term once. The National Assembly is the nation's legislature. The people elect the deputies of the National Assembly to five-year terms. The Supreme Court of Justice is the highest court in the country.

Local government. Venezuela is divided into 23 states and the Federal District. Each state and the Federal District have governors and legislatures elected by the people. The country also has many islands in the Caribbean that are federal dependencies.

Armed forces. Venezuela has an army, navy, air force, and national guard. Men may be drafted for 30 months of military service after reaching 19 years of age.

People

Ancestry. Numerous Indian tribes lived in what is now Venezuela before the 1500s, when Spain colonized the area. The Spanish conquered many of the Indian tribes. They also imported black slaves from Africa. Many of the Indians, Spaniards, and blacks intermarried. Today, about two-thirds of Venezuela's people are of mixed ancestry. People of unmixed white, black, or Indian ancestry make up the rest of the country's population.

After 1945, and especially in the 1950s, many Europeans and Colombians moved to Venezuela to seek jobs. Most of the Europeans came from Spain, Italy, and Portugal. Many Colombians entered Venezuela illegally in the 1970s and early 1980s. At that time, a sharp jump in oil prices caused a dramatic increase in Venezuela's wealth, and the government started a number of projects that created jobs.

Languages. Almost all Venezuelans speak Spanish, the country's official language. Indians in remote areas speak various tribal languages.

Ways of life. Compared with some other Latin-American countries, Venezuela has an open society. In general, the people are not rigidly segre-

Caracas skyline

gated on the basis of ethnic or class differences. Venezuela thus differs from countries that have a strict class system based on ancestry.

Since the 1940s, many Venezuelans have moved from rural areas to the cities. As the cities have grown, so has the country's middle class. Members of the middle class include business people, government workers, doctors, lawyers, teachers, and other professionals. Most middle-class Venezuelans live comfortably, dress well, own a car, and take vacations regularly. Some families live in one-story, Spanish-style houses that center on a courtyard. But in most cities, such houses are being rapidly replaced by high-rise apartments.

Portrait of a Yanomama Indian

Venezuela's economy expanded from the 1950s to the 1970s. But a drop in oil prices in the 1980s and 1990s led to a steep rise in poverty. Housing is scarce, and many Venezuelans live in crowded squatter settlements on the outskirts of cities. Many of them live in small shacks called *ranchos*, which sit dangerously on mountainsides without good roads or sanitation. But they often have televisions and refrigerators and access to electricity. Thousands of ranchos cover large areas in and around many cities.

Since the 1960s, the Venezuelan government has carried out massive programs to improve the living conditions of the poor. For example, it has furnished building materials, electricity, water, and sewerage facilities for some rancho dwellers. In addition, large public housing units have been built in many cities. The government also has taken steps to improve rural life so that people will stay on farms rather than move to the already crowded cities. In many rural areas, for example, the government has built paved roads, extended electrical service, and set up educational and health facilities. In the early 2000s, the government began a new program to bring health clinics, adult education programs, and subsidized food markets to people living in poor neighborhoods.

Food. Traditional Venezuelan foods include black beans, a type of banana called *plantains*, and rice, which are usually eaten with beef, pork, poultry, or fish. The traditional bread is a round cornmeal cake called *arepa*. However, Venezuelans also buy prepared foods in supermarkets and commonly eat wheat bread.

The national dish of Venezuela is the h*allaca*, which is served mainly at Christmas. Hallacas consist of corn-meal dough filled with a variety of foods and cooked in wrappers made of a type of banana leaf.

Recreation. Baseball and soccer are the most popular spectator sports in Venezuela. Professional teams play before large crowds in city stadiums. Several cities have bullfights, but they do not attract as many people as competitive sports events do.

Folk dancers preparing for a parade

Venezuelans enjoy music and dancing. Popular dances include the exciting, rhythmic *salsa* and such fast, lively Caribbean dances as the *merengue* and *guaracha*. The national folk dance of Venezuela is the *joropo*. This stamping dance is performed to the music of *cuatros* (four-stringed guitars), the harp, and *maracas* (rattles made of gourds). Rock music is also popular among young Venezuelans.

Religion. Roman Catholicism has long been the traditional religion in Venezuela, and most people are baptized Catholics. But it is not an official religion, and the Constitution guarantees freedom of worship.

Education. Most Venezuelans 15 years of age or older can read and write.

Venezuelan law requires all children from ages 6 through 15 to attend school. Venezuelans can receive a free public education from kindergarten through university graduate school. The country has numerous universities and colleges. The oldest and most important is the Central University of Venezuela, a public university in Caracas.

The arts. Several Venezuelan writers and artists have won international fame. The novelist Teresa de la Parra and the poet Andres Eloy Blanco were among the most important writers of the 1900s. But probably the best-known writer was Romulo Gallegos, who also served as president of the country in 1948. Gallegos portrayed the distinctive character of different regions of Venezuela in such novels as *Dona Barbara* (1929), *Canaima* (1935), and *Pobre Negro* (1937). Leading artists have included the abstract painters Alejandro Otero and Jesus Soto.

Venezuela also has produced some spectacular modern architecture. Outstanding examples can be found on the campus of the Central University of Venezuela, where boldly designed buildings have been integrated with imaginative murals and sculptures.

Land Regions

Venezuela has four major land regions. They are (1) the Maracaibo Basin, (2) the Andean Highlands, (3) the Llanos, and (4) the Guiana Highlands.

The Maracaibo Basin lies in northwestern Venezuela and consists of Lake Maracaibo and the lowlands around it. Lake Maracaibo is the largest lake in South America. It covers 5,217 square miles (13,512 square kilometers). The continent's largest known petroleum deposits lie in the Maracaibo Basin.

The Andean Highlands begin southwest of the Maracaibo Basin and extend across northern Venezuela. Most of Venezuela's people live in this region. The region has three sections. They are, from west to east: (1) the Merida Range, (2) the Central Highlands, and (3) the Northeastern Highlands.

The Merida Range consists of mountain ranges and high plateaus. Pico Bolívar, the highest point in Venezuela, rises 16,411 feet (5,002 meters) above sea level.

The Central Highlands consist of two parallel mountain ranges along the Caribbean coast. Fertile valleys lie between the mountain ranges. The Central Highlands have more people and more industries than any other area in Venezuela.

The Northeastern Highlands consist of low mountains and hilly land. A famous natural feature of this area is the Cave of the Guacharo, near the town of Caripe. Thousands of large birds called *guacharos* live in the cave. These birds are found only in northern South America and chiefly in this cave.

The Llanos lie between the Andean Highlands and the Guiana Highlands. The Orinoco River, which begins in the Guiana Highlands, flows from west to east along the southern border of the Llanos. The river and its tributaries drain most of Venezuela. The Orinoco extends 1,284 miles (2,066 kilometers) and is the longest river in the country.

Large cattle ranches cover much of the Llanos. The cowhands on these ranches are called *llaneros*. The Llanos also have farmland. But the region has a long dry season, and irrigation is needed to grow such crops as rice and sesame. Important oil fields lie in the eastern part of the Llanos.

The Guiana Highlands rise south of the Llanos and cover nearly half of Venezuela. Swift-flowing rivers have deeply eroded the region's high plateaus. Angel Falls, the world's highest waterfall, plunges 3,212 feet (979 meters) in the Guiana Highlands. Tropical forests cover much of the southern part of the region.

Scattered tribes of Indians live in the Guiana Highlands, but many areas have no inhabitants. The region has valuable deposits of bauxite, iron ore, and gold. Some of the rivers near Ciudad Guayana have been dammed and provide large amounts of electricity.

Angel Falls

Climate

Venezuela lies entirely within the tropics. But the average temperatures vary throughout the country, depending chiefly on altitude. Lowland areas are warm all year. The highest average annual temperature, 83°F (28°C), occurs in the central part of the Llanos and in the northern Maracaibo Basin. At higher elevations, the weather is much cooler. In the Andean Highlands at Merida, the annual temperature averages 67°F (19°C).

The amount of rainfall also varies greatly in different parts of Venezuela. Annual rainfall averages about 120 inches (305 centimeters) in the Perija Mountains, which are west of Lake Maracaibo, and in the southern Guiana Highlands. In contrast, much of the Caribbean coast is dry, and some areas receive only 16 inches (41 centimeters) of rainfall yearly. Most of the rest of the country has alternate wet and dry seasons. In the eastern Llanos, annual rainfall averages about 40 inches (100 centimeters).

Economy

Venezuelans have a high standard of living in relation to the rest of Latin America. This is due mainly to the country's large petroleum production. But Venezuela's wealth is not distributed evenly among the people, and poverty and unemployment are major problems in some areas. Another difficulty is the economic instability created by changes in the price of petroleum.

Bananas

Natural resources. Petroleum is Venezuela's most important natural resource. The most productive oil fields lie in the Maracaibo Basin and in the eastern Llanos. Large amounts of natural gas occur in the oil fields. Venezuela also has huge deposits of bauxite, coal, diamonds, gold, and phosphate rock. The Guri Dam on the Caroni River in the Guiana Highlands is one of the world's largest dams.

Service industries employ about three-fourths of Venezuela's workers. Service industries include such economic activities as education and health care, wholesale and retail trade, and the operation of hotels and transportation companies. Tourism is an important source of income for several service industries in Venezuela. Another major service activity in the country is the wholesale trade of food and mineral products.

Manufacturing has grown rapidly in Venezuela since 1970. About 10 percent of the country's workers are employed in manufacturing. Petroleum processing is the leading manufacturing activity. Venezuela's petroleum refineries produce large amounts of fuels and petrochemicals. Maracaibo is the country's leading center of petroleum refining. Other manufactured products include aluminum, cement, motor vehicles, pig iron, processed foods, steel, and textiles. Ciudad Guayana is a major producer of aluminum and steel. A variety of products are made in Caracas, Barquisimeto, and Valencia.

Agriculture. About 10 percent of Venezuela's workers are farmers. The main crops include bananas, coffee, corn, rice, and sorghum. Farmers also raise beef and dairy cattle, and poultry. Large farms and ranches raise most of Venezuela's commercial farm products.

Most Venezuelan farms are operated by their owners, though a small percentage of them are rented. Some Venezuelans farm land that they do not own or rent. Most of these people live in isolated areas where they cultivate small plots called *conucos*. They produce only enough food to support themselves. During the 1960s, the government began programs that provided farmland for many landless rural families. A law passed in 2001 called for the redistribution of private farmland that was not being used productively to families without land.

Mining. Natural gas ranks second to petroleum among Venezuela's leading mineral products. Other important mineral products in the country include bauxite, coal, diamonds, gold, iron ore, and phosphate rock.

International trade. Petroleum is by far Venezuela's leading export. Venezuela is one of the world's largest exporters of petroleum. Other exports include aluminum, chemicals, and iron and steel. Venezuela's main imports include chemicals, industrial machinery, and transportation equipment. Colombia, Germany, Japan, Mexico, and the United States are among Venezuela's chief trading partners.

Transportation and communication. Modern highways link Caracas with other large cities in Venezuela, including Maracaibo, Valencia, and Ciudad Guayana. Most of the roads in rural areas are unpaved. The country has few railroads. Maiquetia International Airport, which is near Caracas, is Venezuela's busiest airport. The leading seaports are La Guaira, Maracaibo, and Puerto Cabello.

Leading newspapers include *El Nacional, El Universal,* and *Ultimas Noticias,* all published in Caracas; and *Panorama,* which is published in Maracaibo. Both the government and commercial broadcasters operate the country's television and radio stations.

History

Many Indian tribes lived in what is now Venezuela before European settlers arrived. The chief tribes belonged to two groups—the Carib and the Arawak. The Carib Indians lived in the eastern part of Venezuela, and the Arawak Indians lived in the west. Both groups lived by farming, hunting, fishing, and gathering wild plants.

After the Europeans arrived, large numbers of Indians died of diseases brought by the Europeans. Many others starved or were killed in warfare.

European exploration and settlement. Christopher Columbus was the first European explorer to reach Venezuela. In 1498, he landed on the Paria Peninsula. In 1498 and 1499, the Spanish explored most of the Caribbean coast of South America. Spanish settlers soon followed the explorers.

During the early 1500s, the Spaniards came to Venezuela to collect pearls from oyster beds around the islands of Margarita and Cubagua. They called the area from the Araya Peninsula to Cape Codera the Pearl Coast. The Spanish also worked the extensive salt ponds on the Araya Peninsula. These ponds produced salt for several centuries.

From 1528 to 1546, King Charles I of Spain leased Venezuela to a German banking group to pay off his debts to them. The Germans did little to advance the economy of the colony.

By the 1700s, Venezuela was one of Spain's poorest South American colonies. To increase trade and develop the economy, Spain gave the Royal Guipuzcoana Company of Caracas, a private trading company, the right to control all trade in Venezuela. The company began to operate in 1730. It expanded the colony's economy, which was based on cacao, indigo, and hides. But the colonists resented the company's rigid control over trade. The firm eventually lost much of its power and went out of business in 1784.

The struggle for independence. During the early 1800s, Spain's South American colonies began to fight for independence. The chief leaders in the independence movement included the Venezuelans Simón Bolívar, Francisco de Miranda, and Antonio Jose de Sucre. They and their followers fought for many years to free all of northern South America from Spanish rule.

Venezuela was the first Spanish colony in South America to demand its independence. The colony declared its freedom on July 5, 1811, though Spanish forces still occupied much of the country. Venezuela did not become truly independent until 1821. That year, Bolívar won a great victory against the Spanish at Carabobo (near Valencia), which ended Spanish rule in Venezuela. Meanwhile, in 1819, Bolívar had set up and become president of Gran Colombia, a republic that eventually included what are now Venezuela, Colombia, Ecuador, and Panama. Venezuela broke away from Gran Colombia in 1829 and drafted a separate constitution in 1830. General Jose Antonio Paez, a leader in Venezuela's independence movement, became the first president of the new Venezuelan republic in 1831.

Rule by dictatorships. After achieving independence, Venezuela had many periods of civil unrest. A series of dictatorial *caudillos* (leaders) ruled the country until the mid-1900s. Two of these caudillos, Generals Antonio Guzman Blanco and Juan Vicente Gomez, greatly influenced Venezuela's development.

Guzman Blanco ruled Venezuela from 1870 to 1888. Before his rule, the country had been torn by civil wars and political instability. Guzman Blanco established order. He built roads and communication systems, and foreign firms began to invest in the country.

Gomez ruled Venezuela from 1908 to 1935. He cruelly put down all opposition to his rule. During his administration, the petroleum industry began to develop. With the oil profits, Gomez paid off Venezuela's huge national debt and created a strong army. But he also used some of the profits for personal benefit.

The road to democracy. After 1935, opposition to dictatorship increased greatly among the Venezuelan people. New, reformist political parties were organized. Leaders of a party called the Accion Democratica (AD), supported by the army, seized power in 1945. In 1947, the people elected Romulo Gallegos of the AD as president. But in 1948, the army overthrew him. Three military leaders jointly ruled Venezuela until 1950, when Marcos Perez Jimenez became dictator. A revolt against Perez Jimenez broke out in 1958, and he was forced into exile. Later that year, the voters elected Romulo Betancourt, a leader of the

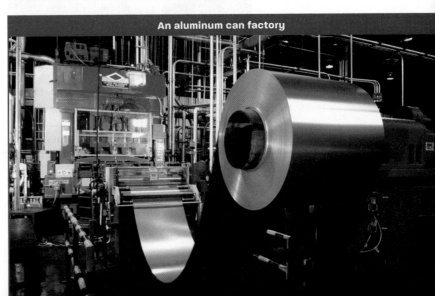
An aluminum can factory

AD, as president. Since 1958, all Venezuelan presidents have been democratically elected.

The late 1900s. In the early 1980s, the worldwide demand for petroleum decreased, and so oil prices dropped. Venezuela's economy, based chiefly on the export of oil, suffered greatly. Venezuela's government sought to reduce the country's dependence on petroleum. It increased such other economic activities as the production of petrochemicals and of an easily stored fuel called liquefied petroleum gas. The aluminum and steel industries were also developed.

In 1989, Carlos Andres Perez, who had served as president from 1974 to 1979, again became president. Perez tried to open up the economy and cut government debt, but his economic plan led to a sharp increase in fuel and transportation costs as well as other problems. Hardships caused by his plan resulted in much social unrest. In 1992, military officers led by Hugo Chávez Frías tried to

Hugo Chāvez

overthrow Perez, but their attempt failed. In May 1993, the Senate removed Perez from office on charges of misuse of government funds. The Supreme Court of Justice convicted him on some of these charges in 1996.

In December 1993, Rafael Caldera was elected president. Caldera had served as president from 1969 to 1974. Formerly a member of the Social Christian Party, he ran as an independent in 1993 on a platform in which he promised to fight corruption and help the poor. Almost immediately after Caldera took office, the country suffered a severe banking crisis. The Caldera government then took steps to tighten control over the country's banking system to ease the crisis.

In 1998, Hugo Chávez, who had led the attempted coup against President Perez in 1992, was elected president. Chávez, who ran as an independent, promised to reform the nation's political system. In a referendum held in December 1999, Venezuela's voters approved a new constitution that allowed for the reelection of the president for a second term.

Also in December 1999, heavy rains struck northern Venezuela. Floods and mudslides from the rains killed an estimated 30,000 people.

Recent developments. In 2000, Chávez was reconfirmed as president under the new Constitution. His attempts to increase his control of Venezuela's state-run oil company led business and labor leaders to organize protests in April 2002 against his rule. Violence broke out during the protests and military leaders removed Chávez from office. International disapproval and popular support for Chávez led the military to return him to power two days later. In late 2002 and early 2003, business, labor, and political opposition leaders held a national strike to protest Chávez's rule. The strike interfered with oil production and caused the economy to shrink significantly.

A referendum on Chávez's rule, begun by his political opponents, was held in 2004. A majority of Venezuelans voted to allow Chávez to complete his term as president. In 2005, Chávez's opponents refused to take part in elections for the National Assembly. Government supporters then won control of the legislature.

Chávez was reelected president in 2006. In 2007, Venezuela's National Assembly granted him permission to rule the country by decree for 18 months. Chávez promoted his plan to create a "21st-century Socialism" and took steps to put important Venezuelan industries under public control. Also in 2007, Chávez lost a referendum on constitutional reforms that would have increased his power and furthered his socialist goals. However, another referendum in 2009 eliminated term limits for elected government officials, including the president.

In 2010, Chávez's opponents won enough seats in the National Assembly to influence legislation. Shortly after the election, however, the outgoing Assembly gave Chávez the power to rule by decree for 18 months. Chávez had said that he needed greater authority to deal with recent flooding. Chávez won reelection as president in 2012. However, opposition candidate Henrique Capriles of the Justice First party won 45 percent of the vote. Owing to illness, Chávez was unable to attend his inauguration in January 2013. The Supreme Court ruled that he could be sworn in at an unspecified later date. Critics said the ruling was unconstitutional and expressed concern about who was running the country. Subsequently, it was announced on March 5 that Chávez had died.

MLA Citation

"Venezuela." *The Southwestern Advantage Topic Source.* Nashville: Southwestern. 2013.

DATA

Facts in Brief About Venezuela

Capital: Caracas.

Official language: Spanish.

Official name: Republica Bolivariana de Venezuela (Bolivarian Republic of Venezuela).

Area: 352,145 mi² (912,050 km²). *Greatest distances*—north-south, 790 mi (1,271 km); east-west, 925 mi (1,489 km). *Coastline*—1,750 mi (2,816 km).

Elevation: *Highest*—Pico Bolívar, 16,411 ft (5,002 m) above sea level. *Lowest*—sea level along the coast.

Population: *Current estimate*—28,112,000; density, 80 per mi² (31 per km²); distribution, 88 percent urban, 12 percent rural. *2001 census*—23,054,210.

Chief products: *Agriculture*—bananas, beef cattle, chickens and eggs, coffee, milk. *Manufacturing*—aluminum, petrochemicals, pig iron, processed foods, refined petroleum, steel. *Mining*—alumina, coal, iron ore, natural gas, petroleum.

National anthem: "Gloria al Bravo Pueblo" ("Glory to the Brave People").

Flag: Venezuela's state flag, adopted in 1954, has three horizontal stripes, yellow, blue, and red (*top to bottom*). The blue stripe has seven stars. The civil flag has no coat of arms. On the coat of arms, the running horse symbolizes liberty; the wheat sheaf, unity; and the swords, independence.

Money: *Basic unit*—bolívar. One hundred centimos equal one bolívar.

ADDITIONAL RESOURCES

Books to Read

Dillon, Douglas. *We Visit Venezuela*. Mitchell Lane, 2011.

Nelson, Brian A. *The Silence and the Scorpion: The Coup Against Chávez and the Making of Modern Venezuela*. Nation Books, 2009.

Nichols, Elizabeth G., and Morse, K. J. *Venezuela*. ABC-CLIO, 2010.

Raub, Kevin. *Venezuela*. 6th ed. Lonely Planet Publications, 2010.

Shields, Charles J. *Venezuela*. Mason Crest, 2009.

Tarver, Denova, Hollis M., and Frederick, J. C. *The History of Venezuela*. Palgrave, 2005.

Web Sites

CIA Factbook: Venezuela
https://www.cia.gov/library/publications/the-world-factbook/geos/ve.html
An overview of the country from the U.S. Central Intelligence Agency.

Country Profile: Venezuela
http://news.bbc.co.uk/2/hi/americas/country_profiles/1229345.stm
Information from the BBC.

Embassy of the Bolivarian Republic of Venezuela in the United States of America
http://venezuela-us.org
Official site of the Venezuelan embassy, with information on Venezuela's government, economy, and culture.

Venezuela
http://www.eia.gov/countries/country-data.cfm?fips=VE&trk=r
Analysis of Venezuela's oil industry, by the Energy Information Administration.

Search Strings

Ancestry of the Venezuelan People
Venezuela ancestry people (157,000)

Venezuela ancestry people Spain Indian slaves mixed (93,000)

Ancestry of the Venezuelan people (21,300)

Urban Life in Venezuela
Venezuela urban life cities middle class (68,000)

Venezuela urban life cities middle class poverty ranchos (15,600)

Venezuela urban life cities middle class poverty ranchos housing government (1,260)

Venezuelan Independence
Venezuela Independence Spain Simon Bolivar (81,900)

Venezuela Independence Spain Simon Bolivar Carabobo "Gran Colombia" (754)

Venezuela Independence Spain Carabobo "Gran Colombia" (3,630)

Oil Economy
Venezuela oil economy petroleum production (96,500)

Venezuela oil economy petroleum production instability poverty wealth distribution (18,500)

Oil economy in Venezuela "standard of living" "wealth distribution" (323)

BACKGROUND INFORMATION

The following article was written during the year in which the events took place and reflects the style and thinking of that time.

Venezuela (2006)

President Hugo Chávez Frías won reelection as president of Venezuela on Dec. 3, 2006. Chávez was first elected president in 1998. He was reelected for a second term in 2000 and survived a *coup* (overthrow) attempt against his government in 2002. In 2004, he emerged victorious from a recall election, a special election mandated by the gathering of a required number of signatures on petitions.

Chávez's chief opponent in the December 2006 presidential election was Manuel Rosales, governor of the Venezuelan state of Zulia. Rosales rallied a splintered and dispirited opposition, political experts observed, garnering 37 percent of votes compared with Chávez's 63 percent.

Chávez had proved unbeatable, analysts suggested, due to a sixfold increase in revenues from Venezuela's oil exports during his presidential tenure. The president, they observed, had overseen the reinvestment of a large percentage of this wealth in social programs popular with a broad section of the Venezuelan public.

Programs for the poor. By the end of 2006, the Venezuelan government had earmarked $20 billion from surging oil revenues for a special development fund created to finance the social programs that were the hallmark of the Chávez administration. Public spending, overall, increased by 40 percent in the first quarter of 2006, according to figures from Venezuela's Central Bank. Much of the money was spent to provide free education, health care, and heavily subsidized food at 15,000 outlets patronized by nearly half of all Venezuelans.

Within Latin America, Chávez distributed surplus Venezuelan wealth—particularly in the form of steeply discounted oil supplies—earning goodwill from a number of countries. In 2006, Venezuela provided more than twice as much financial assistance to Latin American countries as did the United States.

On the international stage, Chávez seemed to seize every opportunity to denounce the policies of U.S. President George W. Bush, whom Chávez labeled "imperialistic." At the same time, Chávez cultivated close relations with nations decidedly unfriendly to the United States, including Cuba, Iran, and North Korea.

The pitch of verbal insults between the governing administrations of Venezuela and the United States reached a new high in September 2006, when President Chávez addressed the United Nations General Assembly in New York City. "The devil came here yesterday, right here," he said at the same rostrum from which President Bush had spoken the previous day. "It still smells of sulfur," Chávez added.

Economy. During the first half of 2006, the Venezuelan economy expanded by nearly 10 percent, and the value of stocks traded on the Caracas exchange increased by 70 percent. The impact of the economic boom was evident everywhere in Caracas, the capital, where three-bedroom apartments in upscale neighborhoods commanded rents as high as $6,000 a month.

Squeezing foreign investors. In April, the Venezuelan government mandated that foreign oil companies allot a 60-percent stake in their operations in Venezuela to Petrleos de Venezuela S.A., the state-run oil company. Previously, these foreign companies had paid Venezuela only production fees. Two of the foreign companies, Total S.A. of France and Eni S.p.A. of Italy, refused to accommodate the new rules of investment, and their fields were seized in April by the Venezuelan government.

Iranian investment. During 2006, Petropars, the national oil company of Iran, announced plans to invest $4 billion to produce oil and natural gas in Venezuela. In November, Khodro, an Iranian auto-mobile manufacturer, began production of cars at a factory near Caracas. Analysts speculated that Venezuela's economic outreach to Iran was part of President Chávez's overall campaign of aligning Venezuela with nations that actively opposed the United States in foreign affairs.

Canada

Canada's land area makes it the second largest country in the world. Although it is a little larger than the United States, it only has about one-tenth the population, most of which lives within 100 miles of the southern border. Canada is made up of 10 provinces and 3 territories. Much of Canada has a severe climate and very rugged terrain; however, its land is rich in natural resources. Canadian ancestry is as varied as its geography. Canada is a bilingual country, recognizing both English and French as official languages. Ottawa is Canada's capital and Toronto is its largest city.

HOT topics

Mounties Versus Policemen. The Royal Canadian Mounted Police (RCMP) is Canada's national law enforcement agency to enforce federal law. It is also the only police force in the Northwest Territories, Yukon, and Nunavut. Originating in 1873, RCMPs are famed for their scarlet dress tunics and riding horses. Their working uniforms are dark blue trousers or skirts with wide, yellow stripes and a brown tunic (jacket). Today, they travel in motor vehicles. Only three provinces have a provincial police force: Ontario has the Ontario Provincial Police, Quebec has the Sûreté du Québec, and Newfoundland has the Royal Newfoundland Constabulary. Most urban areas have their own municipal police forces.

Regions of Canada. The cultural and economic regions of Canada are Atlantic Canada, Quebec, Ontario, the Prairies, British Columbia, and the territories. Canada also has eight major land regions: the Pacific Ranges and Lowlands, the Rocky Mountains, the Arctic Islands, the Interior Plains, the Canadian Shield, the Hudson Bay Lowlands, the St. Lawrence Lowlands, and the Appalachian Region.

HOT topics

The Inuit. The Inuit, formerly called Eskimos, live in the northern areas of Canada. More than 1,000 years ago, the Inuit culture began in one of the coldest and harshest areas of the world. Although today the Inuit have adopted a more modern way of life, they spend much of their time in traditional activities and continue to pass down their knowledge of their ancient culture to future generations. In 1999, Canada created a vast new territory called Nunavut (formerly the eastern part of the Northwest Territories). This area is home to an Inuit majority and allows for more self-government for the Inuit.

An Inuit woman

Niagara Falls. Niagara Falls consists of the Horseshoe Falls in Ontario, Canada, and the American Falls. The Horseshoe Falls draws millions of tourists every year. The name *Niagara* is derived from an Iroquois word *Onguiaahra*, which means *the strait*. Rock slides and the constant wear and tear of the powerfully flowing water cause the appearance of the Falls to continually change. The energy of the Falls is used by the Adam Beck 1 and 2 hydroelectric stations to generate electricity. Throughout history, many people have tried going over the falls in various types of barrels or have walked across the gorge on tightropes.

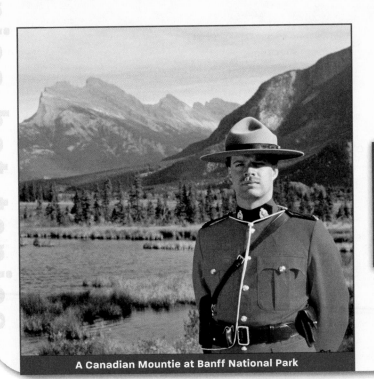
A Canadian Mountie at Banff National Park

TRUE or FALSE?
Many Quebecois feel that Canada's constitution does not adequately protect their province's French-Canadian heritage.

THE BASICS

Canada is the second largest country in the world in area. Only Russia covers more land. Canada extends across the continent of North America, from the province of Newfoundland and Labrador on the Atlantic coast to the province of British Columbia on the Pacific coast. The nation's name probably comes from *kanata-kon*, an Iroquois Indian word that means *to the village* or *to the small houses*.

Canada is slightly larger than the United States, its southern neighbor, but has only about one-ninth as many people. About two-thirds of Canada's people live within 60 miles (100 kilometers) of the southern border. Much of the rest of Canada is uninhabited or thinly populated. Ottawa is the capital of Canada, and Toronto is the largest city. Both Ottawa and Toronto are in the province of Ontario.

Canada is a land of much variety. Towering mountains, clear lakes, and lush forests make Canada's far west a region of great natural beauty. Farther inland, fields of wheat and other grains cover vast prairies. These fertile farmlands contrast vividly with the harsh Arctic lands to the north. Most of the nation's largest population centers and industrial areas lie near the Great Lakes and the St. Lawrence River in central Canada. In the east, fishing villages and sandy beaches dot the Atlantic coast.

Like Canada's landscape, the country's people are also varied. Most Canadians have ancestors who are of English, French, Irish, or Scottish descent. The Canadian government recognizes both English and French as official languages. French Canadians, most of whom live in the province of Quebec, have kept

Map of Canada

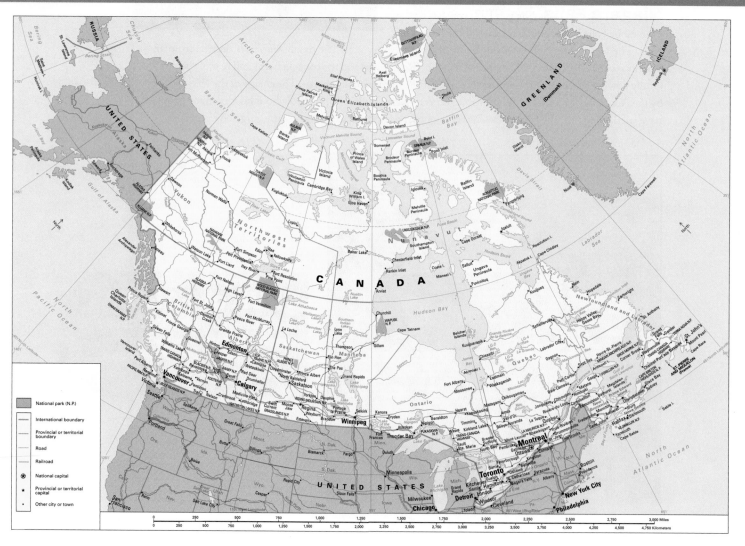

Parliament Hill in Ottawa

the language and many customs of their ancestors. Other large ethnic groups include Chinese, East Indian, German, Italian, and Ukrainian people. Large numbers of Asians live in Western Canada and Ontario. Canada's native peoples include First Nations (North American Indians), Inuit, and Métis. The Inuit are descended from people who once lived in the Bering Sea region. Métis are people of mixed European and First Nations descent.

Canada's greatest possession is its wealth of natural resources. European settlers first came to Canada to fish in its coastal waters and to trap fur-bearing animals in its forests. Later, the forests provided timber for ship-building and other construction. Today, pulpwood from these forests enables Canada to lead the world in the production of *newsprint* (paper for newspapers). Fertile soil makes Canada a leading wheat producer. Thanks to power plants on its rivers, Canada ranks high in the generation of hydroelectric power. Plentiful petroleum, iron ore, and other minerals provide raw materials that help make Canada a top manufacturing nation.

Canada is a *federation* (union) of 10 provinces and 3 territories. Differences among the provinces and territories have sometimes gotten in the way of Canada's sense of community. Some Canadians in eastern and western areas think the federal government does not pay enough attention to their particular problems and interests. French Canadians make up about 80 percent of the population of Quebec. Many of these people

believe that the Canadian constitution should recognize Quebec's difference from the rest of Canada. Quebec has passed legislation aimed at making French the only official language of provincial government.

Canada is an independent, self-governing nation. But the Constitution Act of 1982 recognizes the British monarch, Queen Elizabeth II, as queen of Canada. This position symbolizes the country's historic ties to the United Kingdom. The United Kingdom completely ruled its territory in what is now Canada from the mid-1700s until 1848. That year, settlers in Canada began to gain control of their domestic affairs. The United Kingdom continued to govern Canada's foreign affairs. In 1931, the Statute of Westminster made Canada independent. The Constitution Act of 1982 eliminated the need for British approval of Canadian constitutional amendments.

Canada and the United States have had a relationship of cooperation and friendship since the 1800s. The United States has had a powerful influence on Canada's culture and economy. The Canadian economy is one of the strongest in the world. International surveys consistently rank Canada as one of the most desirable countries in which to live.

The Nation

Canada has six main cultural and economic regions. They are Atlantic Canada, Quebec, Ontario, the Prairies, British Columbia, and the territories.

Atlantic Canada lies on the Atlantic Ocean. Its four provinces—New Brunswick, Newfoundland and Labrador, Nova Scotia, and Prince Edward Island—make up about 5 percent of Canada's land area. Most of the people are of British descent. New Brunswick, Nova Scotia, and Prince Edward Island are also called the Maritimes. *Maritime* means *on the sea* or *near the sea*.

Atlantic Canada has long been an important fishing center. The four provinces still provide most of Canada's fish catch. However, the fishing industry employs only a small percentage of the provinces' workers. *Service industries*, which include such activities as banking, health care, advertising, and shipping, employ most of the region's workers. Agriculture, manufacturing, and mining are also important. Newfoundland and Labrador's offshore Hibernia oil field, which began production in 1997, has become a major employer.

A drastic drop in cod stocks led the federal government to ban nearly all cod fishing off the Atlantic coast. As a result, thousands of people who earned their living in the fishing industry lost their jobs. New jobs have been added, including some involving petroleum production. However, Atlantic Canada has a lower standard of living, lower wages, and a higher rate of unemployment than any other part of Canada.

Quebec differs greatly from the rest of Canada because of its French language and culture. The French explorer Samuel de Champlain founded Quebec City, the first permanent European settlement in Canada, in 1608. Quebec remained a French colony until the United Kingdom gained control of it in 1763. Today, most of Quebec's people have French ancestry. French is the official language of Quebec.

In the past, the Roman Catholic Church dominated Quebec's politics and daily life. Today, the church generally has a less important role in the lives of the people of Quebec. For example, the feast day of Saint Jean Baptiste (Saint John the Baptist) in June is now celebrated largely as a *secular* (nonreligious) holiday. It serves as an occasion for the French-speaking people of Quebec to display their pride in their province.

Quebec is the largest province in area and the second largest in population. Only Ontario has more people. Montreal, Quebec's largest city, is the hub of the province's economic and cultural life. The largest industries in the Quebec region are service industries and manufacturing. Other important economic activities include agriculture, mining, forestry, and fishing.

Ontario has a larger population than any other Canadian province. Fur traders explored Ontario during the 1600s, but major European settlement did not begin until the late 1700s. The province has many people of English, French, German, Irish, Italian, and Scottish descent. In addition, Ontario has more First Nations people than any other province.

The southern boundary of Ontario passes through four of the five Great Lakes—Erie, Huron, Ontario, and Superior. The province's principal manufacturing area, sometimes called the *Golden Horseshoe*, lies on the western shore of Lake Ontario. The area's cities include Hamilton, St. Catharines, and Toronto. Ontario produces about half of Canada's manufactured goods. It also ranks as the leading agricultural province. Toronto is the capital of Ontario and the largest city in Canada. It is the most important communications, cultural, financial, and manufacturing center in English-speaking Canada.

The Prairies region includes Alberta, Manitoba, and Saskatchewan. These three provinces make up about a fifth of Canada's land area. The southern part of the region has many grain farms and cattle ranches. Lakes and evergreen forests cover the northern area.

Until 1885, the Prairies were isolated from eastern Canada. The fur trade was the region's only important economic activity. After the completion of Canada's first transcontinental railroad in 1885, travelers and goods could reach the region easily. Hundreds of thousands of people settled on the fertile prairies in the late 1800s and early 1900s. Most of them came from eastern Canada, Germany, Italy, the Netherlands, Poland, Scandinavian countries, Ukraine, and the United States.

For years, the economy of the Prairies relied on agriculture. The region still produces most of Canada's grain and cattle. In the late 1940s, the discovery of petroleum and natural gas in the area provided a new source of wealth. These resources formed the basis for further changes in the economy of the Prairies. Manitoba is now a major manufacturer of buses and of automobile and aircraft parts. Saskatchewan is one of the world's leading producers of potash-based fertilizers. Alberta has one of the world's largest oil reserves and produces most of Canada's natural gas. The largest cities in the Prairies are Calgary, Alberta; Edmonton, Alberta; and Winnipeg, Manitoba.

Harvesting grain in Manitoba

Top of the World Highway, Yukon Territory

British Columbia is Canada's westernmost province and its third largest in both area and population. It lies on the Pacific Ocean. British Columbia's largest city, Vancouver, has Canada's busiest port. The beauty of the province's rugged coastline and lofty mountains attracts many tourists. The southern part of British Columbia has Canada's mildest climate. Many older Canadians move to the province after they retire.

Over half of the province's people have some English, Irish, or Scottish ancestry. Other large ethnic groups include the French and German. British Columbia has a higher percentage of Asians than any other province, especially people of Chinese and East Indian descent.

Evergreen forests cover much of British Columbia. Many of the province's people work in the logging and wood-processing industries. Other major economic activities include mining and service industries.

The territories. The Northwest Territories, Nunavut, and Yukon make up more than a third of Canada's land area. But because of the remote location and severe climate of the territories, few people live there. The terrain in Yukon and in the southwestern part of the Northwest Territories consists mainly of forest-covered mountains. Most of the rest of the region remains frozen for much of the year. The territories have rich mineral deposits, and mining is the chief economic activity.

The First Nations and Inuit peoples made up almost the entire population of the territories until the region's great mineral wealth was discovered in the late 1800s and early 1900s. Whitehorse, the capital of Yukon, was founded during the Klondike gold rush of the 1890s. Yellowknife, the capital of the Northwest Territories, was established during another gold rush in the 1930s.

Iqaluit, the capital of Nunavut, already served the Inuit as a seasonal fishing camp when Europeans arrived in the area in 1576. Iqaluit's population remains mostly Inuit, as does the population of Nunavut as a whole.

People

Population. Canada's population has grown dramatically since the late 1800s. The increase in population has resulted from heavy immigration and, earlier in Canadian history, a high birth rate.

Over the years, the many immigrants to Canada have changed the country's ethnic makeup. From about 1900 until World War I began in 1914, most immigrants came from Ireland, the United Kingdom, and the United States. European Jews and others from Europe—including Italians, Poles, and Ukrainians—also came in large numbers. After World War II ended in 1945, immigrants to Canada were mainly British, Dutch, German, or Italian. Many of these people had lost their homes in the war.

Today, more immigrants to Canada come from China, India, the Philippines, and other Asian countries than from any other area of the world. Many also come from Africa, the Caribbean, and Central and South America. Canada's immigration rate is double that of the United States. Toronto is one of the most ethnically and linguistically diverse cities in the world.

Ancestry. Most Canadians are of European descent. People of First Nations, Inuit, and Métis descent make up about 4 percent of the nation's population. Most of Canada's people have some ancestors who came from France, Ireland, or the United Kingdom. Other large ethnic groups include Chinese, East Indians, Germans, Italians, and Ukrainians.

Europeans. People of British and Irish ancestry make up the majority of the population of every province except Quebec. Many are descendants of Scottish settlers who began arriving in

Canada during the late 1700s. The ancestors of many others were English and Irish settlers who flocked to Canada during the 1800s. Still others are descendants of United Empire Loyalists—people who moved from the United States to Canada during and after the American Revolution (1775–1783).

About 65,000 French colonists lived in Quebec when France lost that region to the British in 1763. Since that time, the number of Canadians with French ancestry has grown to more than 5 million. Most live in Quebec, but Ontario and New Brunswick also have large numbers of people with French backgrounds. The rest of Canada also has a few areas that are largely French.

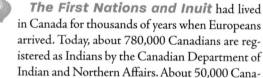
An Inuit family gathers together in an igloo.

About 10 percent of Canadians have some German ancestry, 5 percent have Italian ancestry, and 4 percent have Ukrainian ancestry. Most German Canadians live in British Columbia, Ontario, and the Prairies. People of Italian descent live chiefly in the cities, particularly Toronto and Montreal. Most Canadians of Ukrainian origin live in the Prairies. Many other Canadians are of Dutch, Greek, Hungarian, Polish, Portuguese, or Scandinavian origin.

The First Nations and Inuit had lived in Canada for thousands of years when Europeans arrived. Today, about 780,000 Canadians are registered as Indians by the Canadian Department of Indian and Northern Affairs. About 50,000 Canadians are Inuit. The word *Inuit* means *people*. The Inuit of Canada once were called *Eskimos*. Today, many Inuit view the term *Eskimo* as belittling.

About half of the Inuit population lives in Nunavut. Most of the rest live in the Northwest

Territories and in the northern areas of Newfoundland and Labrador, Ontario, and Quebec. First Nations people are often classified by their traditional languages. The major languages spoken by Canada's First Nations include Cree, Ojibwa (also called Chippewa), Innu (also called Montagnais-Naskapi), Mi'kmaq, Dene, Dakota/Sioux, and Blackfoot (also called Blackfeet). About half of Canada's First Nations people live on about 2,700 *reserves* (reservations).

Other Canadians include people from China, India, Pakistan, Vietnam, and other Asian countries. Asians make up much of the population of British Columbia. Many immigrants from China, the Indian *subcontinent* (mostly Bangladesh, India, and Pakistan), and the Caribbean Islands live in Toronto and Vancouver. Blacks make up about 3 percent of Canada's population. Many black Canadians are from the Caribbean region, both from English-speaking islands and from French-speaking Haiti.

Languages. Canada has two official languages, English and French. The Official Languages Act of 1969 guarantees all Canadians the right to communicate with the national government in either French or English. About two-thirds of the Canadian people speak mainly English at home, and about one-fifth speak mainly French. About one-tenth speak other languages, such as Chinese, Italian, German, Punjabi, and Spanish.

Many of Canada's Inuit and First Nations people use their traditional languages at home, though they may speak other languages as well. About 50 First Nations and Inuit languages are spoken in Canada.

Significant numbers of French-speaking people live in New Brunswick and Ontario. However, most of the French-speaking Canadians live in Quebec, and French is the official language of the province. Quebec's French-speaking citizens, called Québécois, consider themselves to be the guardians of the French language and culture in Canada.

The role of the French language and culture in Quebec has been controversial both within the province and within Canada as a whole. Quebec's legislature has passed a number of laws dealing with the uses of French and English in the province. In the 1970s, for example, the legislature passed laws that made French the language of government and business. Among other provisions, the laws banned the use of English on commercial signs. English-speaking citizens of Quebec opposed these laws. Through a series of court rulings and legislation, the laws were eventually changed. Today, bilingual advertising—in French and English—is allowed on commercial signs as long as the French lettering is larger than the English.

Way of Life

City life. Canada began as a nation with a largely rural population. But today, about 80 percent of Canadians live in urban areas. This population shift began mainly as a result of the rapid development since the 1940s of manufacturing and service industries in urban areas. Expressway systems link the city centers with the numerous suburbs that have sprung up around them.

Most Canadian city dwellers work for the federal or provincial government, in the retail trades and other service industries, or in manufacturing. Occupations vary from city to city. In Vancouver, for example, many jobs involve the forest industry. In Toronto and other places in southern Ontario,

automobile production is the main manufacturing industry. In Winnipeg and Montreal, construction of aircraft and aircraft parts provides many jobs. Halifax and Vancouver rank as major ports.

The rapid growth of Canadian cities has brought some challenges. The spread of suburbs into valuable farmland has led many Canadians to oppose unlimited urban growth. Some of Canada's cities have faced reductions in transportation and welfare funds. In addition, immigration has contributed to tensions among different ethnic groups.

Rural life. A small percentage of rural Canadians live on farms. Others work in such industries as fishing, mining, and lumbering. A small but growing number of Canadians live in rural communities and commute to jobs in the cities.

Most farmers in Canada own their farms, and farming is largely a family activity. Modern machinery enables a family to do nearly all the work on their farm themselves. The largest Canadian farms are in the Prairies and cover an average of about 1,200 acres (486 hectares). Farms in central and eastern Canada are smaller, averaging about 180 to 300 acres (73 to 120 hectares).

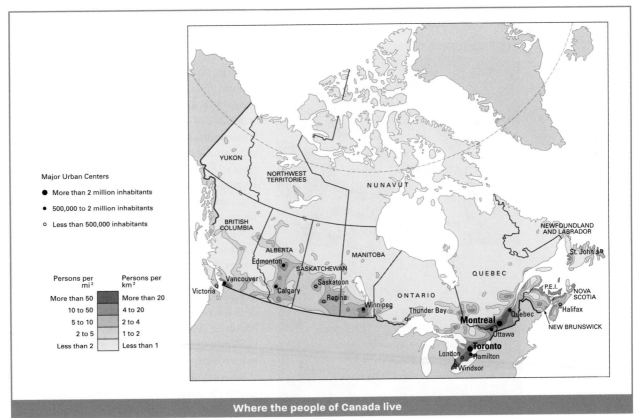

Where the people of Canada live

Farm life has changed greatly since the early 1900s, especially in the Prairies. The once-extensive network of prairie railroad branch lines, with their wooden grain elevators and small towns, is rapidly disappearing. Large concrete and steel inland grain terminals have replaced most country elevators. Many farmers now drive much farther than they once did to sell their grain at these inland terminals. Larger towns, with modern shopping malls and warehouse outlets, have grown up around these terminals.

On the farms themselves, satellite dishes and the Internet connect rural families to the rest of the world. Many farmers use computers and the Global Positioning System (GPS) to help with their work.

Arctic life. Canada's vast Arctic region is thinly populated. Inuit and First Nations people have lived there for thousands of years. Today, they form about 40 percent of the region's population.

Some Inuit and First Nations people still make their living by their traditional occupations—fishing, hunting, and trapping. In general, however, traditional ways of life in the Arctic have ended. The people live in wooden houses rather than tents or snowhouses. They wear modern clothing and eat food bought in stores. Generally snowmobiles and motorboats have replaced dog sleds and kayaks as the chief means of transportation.

The decline of traditional life has led to many social problems. The Inuit population has high rates of alcoholism, crime, suicide, and unemployment. However, economic conditions may improve with the development of petroleum and other natural resources in the Arctic. Managers of corporations with operations in the region routinely consult with Inuit leaders. Corporate and Inuit leaders cooperate to establish vocational training so that Inuit youths can get and keep jobs.

Education. Religious groups operated the earliest schools in Canada. In 1867, the British North America Act made education a responsibility of the provincial governments. Today, each province and territory in Canada has its own school system. A provincial or territorial department of education supervises each school system. A cabinet minister heads each department of education and reports to the legislature of the province or territory. The federal government is responsible for directing the education of children on First Nations reserves, the children of members of the Canadian Armed Forces, and the inmates of federal penitentiaries.

Most provincial school systems have 12 grades. Quebec's school system has 11. In some provinces, the law provides for the public school system to include separate schools for certain religious groups. Communities in Alberta, Ontario, Saskatchewan, and the territories have separate, publicly funded schools for Roman Catholics and Protestants, as well as public schools that are open to all students. Schools in Quebec provide education in French and English. Most children who immigrate to Quebec and have not previously received instruction in English attend French-language schools.

The major English-language universities in Canada include McGill University; the universities of Alberta, British Columbia, Toronto, and Western Ontario; and York University. The most important French-language institutions are Université Laval (Laval University), the Université de Montréal (University of Montreal), and the Université du Québec à Montréal (University of Quebec at Montreal). The Université de Moncton (University of Moncton) in New Brunswick and Université Sainte-Anne (Ste. Anne University) in Nova Scotia also teach in French. Some universi-

The National Gallery of Canada is one of many museums in Ottawa.

ties teach in both English and French. The largest of these bilingual institutions is the University of Ottawa in Ontario.

Quebec also has *collèges d'enseignement général et professionel* (colleges of general and professional instruction). They offer a two-year course that high school graduates must complete before enrolling in a Quebec university. They also provide three-year technical and commercial courses. The other provinces also have two-year or three-year institutions of higher learning. Most of these schools are called *community colleges*.

The federal and provincial governments provide much funding for university education. Canadian students pay about 20 percent of the cost of their education through their fees. Costs for foreign students attending Canadian universities are higher. Canada's low tuition costs help it to have one of the highest rates worldwide of students enrolled at postsecondary institutions.

Canada has a high literacy rate and an extensive public library system. Library and Archives Canada is the country's national library. It produces *Canadiana*, a monthly and annual listing of new books, pamphlets, and music published in Canada. The Canada Institute for Scientific and Technical Information operates a science library in Ottawa.

Canada has a rich variety of museums and art galleries. National museums in Ottawa include the Canadian Museum of Civilization, the Canadian Museum of Nature, the Canada Science and Technology Museum, the Canadian War Museum, and the National Gallery of Canada. Another outstanding museum is the Royal Ontario Museum in Toronto. It has exhibits in such fields as archaeology, geology, and zoology. The Royal Tyrrell Museum of Palaeontology in Drumheller, Alberta, is one of the world's leading dinosaur museums. Notable Canadian art galleries include the Art Gallery of Ontario, the Vancouver Art Gallery, and the Winnipeg Art Gallery.

Religion. The early French settlers brought the Roman Catholic faith to Canada. Catholics are the nation's largest religious group today. Most other Canadians belong to Protestant churches. The largest Protestant denominations are the United Church of Canada and the Anglican Church of Canada. Other major Protestant groups in Canada include Baptists, Lutherans, and Presbyterians. The country's other religious

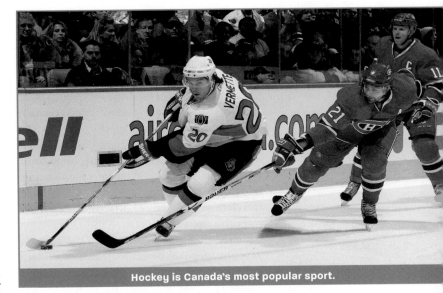

Hockey is Canada's most popular sport.

groups include Buddhists, Hindus, Jews, Muslims, and Sikhs.

Recreation and sports. Canadians take part in a wide variety of recreational activities. During the long winters, many people enjoy curling, hockey, skating, downhill and cross-country skiing, snowboarding, and tobogganing. Popular summer sports include canoeing, fishing, golf, hiking, swimming, and tennis.

Canada's extensive national park system includes areas for many recreational activities. The park system began in 1885 with the establishment of Banff Hot Springs Reservation (now Banff National Park) in Alberta. Today, all the provinces and territories have at least one national park. Each province also has its own park system. For information on the national parks and other parklands of Canada, see the tables with this article.

Canada's first national game was lacrosse, which the First Nations played before Europeans arrived in North America. Today, hockey is by far the most popular sport in Canada. Canadian boys and girls may begin competing in amateur hockey leagues when they are 7 years old. Professional teams from Canada and the United States compete in the National Hockey League (NHL), the highest professional hockey league. More than half the players in the National Hockey League are Canadians. Such stars as Sidney Crosby, Wayne Gretzky, Gordie Howe, Guy Lafleur, Bobby Orr, and Maurice Richard became national heroes in Canada.

Other popular professional sports in Canada include baseball, basketball, football, and soccer.

Teams from eight Canadian cities compete in the Canadian Football League (CFL). The Toronto Blue Jays attract baseball fans from throughout Canada. The Toronto Raptors play in the National Basketball Association (NBA).

Canada has hosted the Olympic Games several times since the 1970s. Canadian athletes typically excel at many of the winter sports.

Food. Canadians eat more beef, including roast beef and steaks, than any other meat. Bread is part of most meals, and potatoes are also common. Other favorite vegetables include beans, carrots, lettuce, and peas. Apples, bananas, berries, and citrus fruits are popular.

Coffee and tea, milk, soft drinks, and beer and wine are popular beverages. Favorite desserts include ice cream and fruit pies, especially apple, blueberry, peach, and rhubarb pies. Canada also produces the majority of the world's maple syrup, which usually is served over pancakes and waffles.

Roast turkey is a popular dish at Thanksgiving, Christmas, and New Year's. On Christmas, many French Canadians eat a meat pie called *tourtière*. Immigration has helped make foods from throughout the world popular.

Many Canadians eat out often. Specialty restaurants, once common only in major cities, now also operate in smaller cities throughout the country. These include seafood restaurants and ethnic restaurants, such as those that serve Chinese, French, Greek, Indian, Italian, Japanese, Thai, or Vietnamese food.

The Arts

Government support has played a vital role in the development of the arts in Canada. In 1957, the Canadian government set up the Canada Council for the Arts to promote the advancement of the visual and performing arts and literature. The council provides financial assistance to individual artists and to orchestras, theaters, and other organizations. Provincial and local governments also have contributed strong financial support for the arts. Thanks in part to governmental support, Canadian artists' work has become known around the world.

In 1969, the federal government opened the National Arts Centre in Ottawa. The Arts Centre presents ballet, drama, motion pictures, music, and opera. The National Gallery, also in Ottawa, has an excellent collection of European art and a large number of Canadian works.

Literature. Canada has two great literatures, one written in French and the other in English. Canadian literature reflects the varied background of Canada's people and the diverse geography and regions of the country. During the late 1600s and 1700s, colonists from both France and England established the first permanent European settlements in Canada. Since that time, most Canadian literature has been written in French or English—the nation's two official languages. Canadian literature written in French is called *Quebecois literature*, after the French-speaking province of Quebec.

Characteristics of Canadian literature. Like other nations with colonial beginnings, Canada has struggled to create its own identity in a literature that enables Canadians to understand who they are and to interpret themselves to the world. A distinctive Canadian literary voice began to emerge slowly in Canadian literature in the 1800s. It blossomed after the end of World War II in 1945. The publication of literature in languages other than English and French and the emergence of First Nations writers are signs of Canada's growing multicultural heritage and identity.

The Canadian author Margaret Atwood has said that to live in Canada is to choose a "violent duality." The notion of Canada as a nation of conflicting yet complementary *dualities* (two parts) also characterizes its literature. One familiar duality is the tension between urban centers and rural areas. Another is the competing claims of the nation's regions and the central government in Ottawa. A third is a deeply rooted attraction and rejection felt in the densely populated south for the vast tracts of sparsely populated north.

One of the central themes of Canadian writers is the "idea of North." Images of Canada's awe-inspiring northern landscape have dominated its literary history from its beginning in the 1500s to the present. In addition, Canadians have conflicting feelings about the United States. The United States is a country with which Canadians have much in common, but with which they disagree on many political and cultural matters.

Beginnings of Canadian literature. The earliest writing in Canada was travel literature—journals diaries, reports, letters, and autobiographies written by explorers and missionaries. In 1535, the French navigator Jacques Cartier led the first European expedition up the St. Lawrence River.

Portrait of Jacques Cartier

His trip is described in *Bref recit de la navigation de Canada* (1545). Others who wrote about life in Canada during the 1600s and 1700s include the explorer Samuel de Champlain; Marie de l'Incarnation, who founded the Ursuline religious order in Canada; and the Jesuit missionary Jean de Brebeuf.

England and France fought a series of wars between 1689 and 1763. As a result of these conflicts, England took over the French empire in America. After the English conquest, such explorers as Alexander Henry, David Thompson, and Samuel Hearne produced narratives describing the new territory and its peoples. Of special note is Hearne's A Journey from *Prince of Wales's Fort, in Hudson's Bay*, to the Northern Ocean (1795).

As a result of the English conquest, French-speaking Canadians concentrated on preserving their unique culture. During the early 1800s, historical works written in French flourished. F. X. Garneau published his *Histoire du Canada* from 1845 to 1848. Such historical works gave rise to the popular romances of the mid-1800s known as "novels of the soil." These works celebrate the Quebecois sense of *patrie* (home) and the traditional religious values of an agricultural society. Notable examples include Les Anciens Canadiens (1863) by Philippe Aubert de Gaspe and *Jean Rivard* (1862, 1864) by Antoine Gerin-Lajoie.

Early English-Canadian literature, like Quebecois writing, often expressed an optimistic, pioneering attitude toward the new country. Frances Brooke wrote the first Canadian novel, The *History of Emily Montague* (1769). Oliver Goldsmith—grandnephew of the English writer of the same name—wrote *The Rising Village* (1825) to celebrate the future of the new British colony. Susanna Moodie, who emigrated from England, eventually came to feel a genuine love and respect for her new home. She described her experiences in her autobiographical work, *Roughing It in the Bush* (1852). Jonathan Odell and Joseph Stansbury were *United Empire Loyalists*, American colonists who remained loyal to the United Kingdom. Both lived in Canada for a period, and their writings express their rejection of the new United States.

John Richardson and Thomas Chandler Haliburton were among the earliest writers born and raised in Canada. Richardson wrote *Wacousta* (1832), a popular historical romance. He set the novel in 1763, at the time of an uprising led by the Indian chief Pontiac against the British. Haliburton ridiculed a sly American peddler in his narrative *The Clockmaker; or, The Sayings and Doings of Sam Slick of Slickville* (1836). This book was the first imaginative representation of Canada's vision of Americans. Haliburton's mix of humor and political satire influenced the work of such later Canadian humorists as Stephen Leacock and Robertson Davies.

Confederation to World War I. The next period of Canadian literature began in the mid-1800s, shortly before the Confederation of Canada. Confederation was the union of British colonies that formed the Dominion of Canada in 1867. This literary period lasted until the end of World War I in 1918.

Even before Confederation, Canadian poetry was flourishing in French and English. About 1855, Octave Cremazie began to publish religious and patriotic verse in *Le Journal de Quebec*. Together with the poet Alfred Garneau, Cremazie had an important influence on a group of poets that arose during the 1860s. This group—called the *School of Quebec*—included Leon-Pamphile Lemay and Louis-Honore Frechette. For these poets, the romantic treatment of nature coincided with the expression of patriotic themes.

The first English Canadian to be considered a national poet was Charles Sangster. His poem "The St. Lawrence and the Saguenay" (1856) celebrates the beauty of the Canadian landscape.

By 1888, a group of young poets called the *Confederation poets* began to publish. They included Duncan Campbell Scott, Sir Charles G. D. Roberts, Archibald Lampman, Bliss Carman, and Wilfred Campbell. These writers described nature and regional scenes using forms and rhythms that showed a growing freedom from European styles. Scott, in particular, became well known for his poetic narratives about native peoples. Among his best-known poems on this theme is "The Forsaken" (1905). Pauline Johnson was known for her poetry about Indian life. Her father was a Mohawk chief, and her mother was English. Isabella Valancy Crawford gained fame for a single volume of narrative poems published in 1884, including "Malcolm's Katie."

Emile Nelligan's use of romantic images and symbols also profoundly influenced Canadian poetry of this period. Nelligan and the poet Albert Lozeau were part of the *School of Montreal*, a group that came together about 1895. This group rejected the patriotic verse that was popular in Quebec at the time.

Important novelists of this period included Laure Conan (the pen name of Marie-Louise-Felicite Angers), Quebec's first female novelist. She combined letters, narrative, and diary in *Angeline de Montbrun* (1881–1882), a psychological examination of disappointed love. Most Quebecois novels of the period, however, glorified rural life and religious values. Typical of these works is *La Terre* (1916) by Ernest Choquette. More interesting today are such novels as *Marie Calumet* (1904) by Rodolphe Girard and *La Scouine* (1918) by Albert Laberge. Both are realistic portrayals of Quebec society.

Most English-Canadian novelists of the period wrote historical romances. Some were historical romances modeled on the fiction of the Scottish novelist Sir Walter Scott, such as William Kirby's *The Golden Dog* (1877) and Sir Gilbert Parker's *The Seats of the Mighty* (1896). Some novelists produced sentimental romances or romances with mysterious or supernatural overtones. James De Mille wrote the philosophical fantasy *A Strange Manuscript Found in a Copper Cylinder* (published in 1888, after his death). Rosanna Leprohon's *Antoinette de Mirecourt* (1864) and Sara Jeannette Duncan's *The Imperialist* (1904) describe conflicts faced by characters of different cultural and religious backgrounds.

Sir Gilbert Parker

In the late 1800s and early 1900s, Ralph Connor (the pen name of Charles W. Gordon) and Lucy Maud Montgomery began to publish and quickly gained wide popularity. Connor was the first novelist to write about the Canadian West. In addition, he wrote a series of novels that includes *The Man from Glengarry* (1901), a vivid portrait of pioneer settlements in Connor's native Ontario. In 1908, Montgomery published *Anne of Green Gables*, one of the most beloved Canadian novels. The novel earned Montgomery an international reputation.

Other literature of the period includes short stories, travel and nature sketches, and autobiographies by such writers as Isabella Valancy Crawford, Anna Brownell Jameson, and Catharine Parr Traill. Stephen Leacock wrote *Sunshine Sketches of a Little Town* (1912), a humorous work that remains a Canadian classic.

Literature between the world wars. Modern literary styles were slow to come to Canada. Such writers as Connor, Cremazie, and Mazo de la Roche enjoyed wide popularity well into the 1900s with their traditional fiction. De la Roche wrote 16 novels about the Whiteoak family, beginning with *Jalna* (1927). But new voices were also beginning to be heard.

In Quebec, Louis Hemon expressed the typical romantic view of rural life in *Maria Chapdelaine* (1914). A more realistic novel, *Trente Arpents* (1938), written by Ringuet (pen name of Philippe Panneton), criticized the hardships of rural life. The School of Montreal poets continued to be important. In addition, some younger poets produced complex psychological verse that gained influence after the end of World War II. Hector de Saint-Denys Garneau, Alain Grandbois, and Anne Hebert rank as the most significant of these poets.

Canadian dramatists wrote few works during the period immediately after the war. One limiting factor on playwrights in Quebec was the involvement of the Roman Catholic Church. The church opposed the performance of plays that it considered antifamily or immoral. The influence of the church restrained the activity of playwrights and performers. Traveling theater companies from Europe and the United States dominated Canadian stages.

Many English-Canadian writers were influenced by the painters known as the *Group of Seven*. This group inspired a break from empty traditional forms and themes, especially narrow nationalism and the sentimental treatment of nature. Poets who turned to modern themes were E. J. Pratt, F. R. Scott, A. J. M. Smith, Dorothy Livesay, A. M. Klein, and Earle Birney.

Pratt is best known for his long narrative poems written in traditional verse forms. They include his epic poem, *Brebeuf and His Brethren* (1940). The other poets produced more experimental works. In 1927, Scott satirized the conservative poetry establishment in "The Canadian Authors Meet." Smith used free verse in his poem "The Lonely Land" (1926). Livesay expressed her socialist political views in "Day and Night" (1935), an expressionistic work that celebrates brotherhood. Klein was a learned writer with knowledge of the cultural traditions of English Canada, French Canada, and Judaism. *The Rocking Chair and Other Poems* (1948) includes Klein's best poetry. Birney became known for technically skillful, experimental poetry in such works as David (1942).

Three important novels appeared in the mid-1920s. They were *Settlers of the Marsh* (1925) by Frederick Philip Grove, *Wild Geese* (1925) by Martha Ostenso, and *Grain* (1926) by Robert Stead. These works signaled a trend toward greater realism in Canadian novels. The remarkable novel *As for Me and My House* (1941) by Sinclair Ross used the diary form. It provided a complex, subtle, and moving exploration of the human mind.

Drama was represented later in this period by the works of such playwrights as Herman Voaden, Gwen Pharis Ringwood, and Merrill Denison. Voaden became known for the innovative staging of his expressionist theater. Ringwood's more real-istic *Still Stands the House* (1939) explores the alienation of prairie life. Denison's plays include satires and historical romances. The year 1933 marked the beginning of the Dominion Drama Festival and the opening of the Banff School of the Theatre. Together, the festival and the school established a firm base for Canadian theater and playwriting.

Modern literature: 1945 to the present. Since 1945, Quebecois fiction has rapidly expanded into an intense and experimental body of writing. Gabrielle Roy's *Bonheur d'occasion* (1945) is a celebrated study of life among Montreal's poor French-speaking Canadians. Hubert Aquin wrote powerful, disturbing fiction. His works include *Prochain episode* (1965), a detective story and political allegory; *L'Antiphonaire* (1969); and *Neige noire* (1974), cast in the form of a film script. Rejean Ducharme's *L'Avalee des avales* (1966) describes a young woman's rebellion.

Other important Quebecois fiction includes Marie-Claire Blais's novel about Quebec society, *Une Saison dans la vie d'Emmanuel* (1965). Roch Carrier's trilogy on Quebec life begins with *La Guerre, Yes Sir!* (1968). Victor-Levy Beaulieu wrote *Monsieur Melville* (1978), a three-volume work. Anne Hebert's novels include *Kamouraska*

Anne Hebert

(1970) and *Les Fous de Bassan* (1982). She based the novels on actual cases of murder and rape.

Modern English-Canadian fiction generally has been less experimental than Quebecois writing. Hugh MacLennan wrote *Two Solitudes* (1945), a novel exploring conflicts between the English and French cultures in Canada. He later wrote several historical novels and volumes of essays. *The Double Hook* (1959) by Sheila Watson ranks as one major exception to the trend toward realism. It is a highly poetic and symbolic treatment of violence and rebirth in an isolated community.

Several major authors wrote well-crafted novels about life in different regions of Canada. Among Ethel Wilson's best-known works is *Swamp Angel* (1954), which is set in British Columbia. Margaret Laurence wrote *The Stone Angel* (1964) and *The Diviners* (1974), part of her cycle of novels set in the fictional town of Manawaka, Manitoba. Robertson Davies set many novels in Ontario towns. He first gained fame for his Deptford trilogy—*Fifth Business* (1970), *The Manticore* (1972), and *World of Wonders* (1975). Jack Hodgins wrote about Vancouver Island in *The Honorary Patron* (1987) and other novels. Mordecai Richler wrote a Canadian epic in *Solomon Gursky Was Here* (1989).

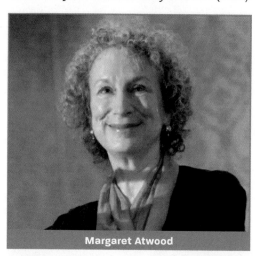

Margaret Atwood

Several modern novelists are also poets. They include Margaret Atwood, George Bowering, Robert Kroetsch, and Michael Ondaatje. Such novels as *Surfacing* (1972) and *Cat's Eye* (1988) have earned Atwood many awards and an international reputation. Kroetsch wrote *The Studhorse Man* (1969) and *Badlands* (1975). Both are boisterous, comical tales about the West. Bowering's fiction, especially *Burning Water* (1980), is an

ironic combination of history and fiction. Ondaatje gained international acclaim with his novel *The English Patient* (1992).

Rudy Wiebe traced the struggles of First Nations peoples—Canada's Indians, Inuit, and other native peoples—in such novels as *The Temptations of Big Bear* (1973). He turned his attention to the Canadian Arctic in *A Discovery of Strangers* (1994). Joy Kogawa explored the treatment of Japanese Canadians during World War II in *Obasan* (1981). Masterful short-story writers include Clark Blaise, Timothy Findley, Mavis Gallant, Jack Hodgins, Hugh Hood, Alice Munro, and Audrey Thomas. Significant First Nations authors include fiction writers Beatrice Culleton, Tom King, and Ruby Slipperjack, and playwright Thomson Highway. During the late 1900s, a number of new novelists emerged who represented the cultural diversity of Canada. They included Rohinton Mistry, Aritha van Herk, Carol Shields, Anne Michaels, Wayson Choy, Sky Lee, Guy Vanderhaeghe, and Yann Martel.

Modern Canadian poets include Margaret Avison, P. K. Page, and Phyllis Webb. Their handling of language and complex psychological and philosophical themes challenges readers. Al Purdy employs casual, everyday language, which masks his passionate concern for modern society. D. G. Jones, Irving Layton, and Eli Mandel have expanded the boundaries of poetry. The next generation of Canadian poets included Atwood, Bowering, Dennis Lee, Gwendolyn MacEwen, and Barrie Phillip Nichol, who wrote as bp Nichol. Nichol finished the first two books of his best-known poem, *The Martyrology*, in 1972. He had expanded the work into six published books by his death in 1988. By 2000, several new poets had emerged, notably Stephanie Bolster, Dionne Brand, Robert Bringhurst, George Elliott Clarke, Lorna Crozier, Kristjana Gunnars, M. Nourbese Philip, Armand Garnet Ruffo, Sharon Thesen, Jim Wong-Chu, and Jan Zwicky

In Quebec, the years after World War II marked a new burst of energy associated with poet Gaston Miron and the Hexagone Press. A group called the *Hexagone Poets* was indebted to such Quebec surrealist painters as Paul-Emile Borduas. Borduas and a group of associates rejected the past in *Refus global* (1948), a declaration foreshadowing the Quebec nationalist movement.

The 1960s brought the Quiet Revolution, a movement to defend Quebecois rights through-

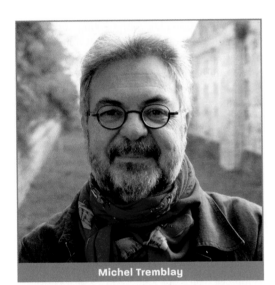

Michel Tremblay

out the country. Some people called for Quebec to separate from the rest of Canada. The movement inspired such Quebec poets as Paul Chamberland, Gerald Godin, and Michele Lalonde to new heights of political protest poetry. By the mid-1970s, such poets as Louky Bersianik, Nicole Brossard, Madeleine Gagnon, and Yolande Villemaire began writing feminist works. They used humor in attacking attitudes of male superiority. Gagnon's *Lueur* (1979) combines poetry and fiction with the historical and philosophical essay. Other important Quebecois writers include France Theoret, Raoul Dugay, Francois Charron, and Yves Boisvert.

Modern Canadian drama has become a vital and varied form of expression since the mid-1900s. Michel Tremblay became the best-known Quebecois playwright. His works include two plays about life in poor sections of Montreal, *Les Belles-soeurs* (1968) and *A toi pour toujours, ta Marie-Lou* (1973). Other notable Quebecois playwrights include Robert Gurik, Robert Lepage, and Michel Marc Bouchard. Gurik wrote important experimental plays on political themes. Lepage became known for such multimedia plays as *The Dragons' Trilogy* (1986), *Polygraph* (1988), and *Needles and Opium* (1992). Bouchard wrote about family struggles in *The Orphan Muses* (1989).

Two significant English-Canadian plays in 1967 were John Herbert's *Fortune and Men's Eyes* and George Ryga's *The Ecstasy of Rita Joe*. Both are violent but deeply moving plays about society's misfits and outsiders—reformatory inmates in Herbert's play and Indians in Vancouver in Ryga's drama.

Canadian poet James Reaney began writing lyrical and symbolic dramas in the 1960s.

During the 1970s, many theater companies, including an experimental group in Toronto called Theatre Passe Muraille, devoted themselves to performing Canadian plays. Some companies performed *collective creations*, plays developed by a group of actors, along with a director and, sometimes, a playwright. The best-known collective creations include *The Farm Show* (1976), *Paper Wheat* (1978), and Rick Salutin's lively treatment of Canadian history, *1837: The Farmers' Revolt* (1976).

The leading English-Canadian playwrights are Sharon Pollock and George F. Walker. Pollock creates complex psychological feminist plays about family life and plays that explore issues of racism based on historical events. Walker's work is characterized by his flair for spectacle and satire. Other important playwrights include Michael Cook, David French, Wendy Lill, Joan MacLeod, Mansel Robinson, and Judith Thompson.

Painting and sculpture. The works of most early Canadian painters followed European trends. During the mid-1800s, Cornelius Krieghoff, a Dutch-born artist in Quebec, painted scenes from the lives of French Canadian farmers called *habitants*. At about the same time, the Canadian artist Paul Kane painted pictures of First Nations life in western Canada.

A group of landscape painters called the Group of Seven developed the first distinctively Canadian style of painting. Tom Thomson, one of Canada's best-known painters, inspired the group. However, he died three years before the group's first exhibition in 1920. All these artists painted large, brilliantly colored scenes of the Canadian wilderness.

Canadian painters have developed a wide range of styles since the Group of Seven. Emily Carr, for example, became famous for painting the totem poles and forests of British Columbia. Other noted artists have included landscape painter David Milne, abstract painters Jean-Paul Riopelle and Harold Town, First Nations painter Norval Morrisseau, photographer Yousuf Karsh, and multimedia artist Michael Snow.

A Haida sculpture by Bill Reid

The finest works of Canadian sculpture include woodcarvings of the Haida, Kwakiutl, and other First Nations of Canada's northwest coast. Other fine works include ivory and soapstone carvings by Inuit artists. Bill Reid, for example, used his Haida heritage as a source of design for his totem poles and other sculptures.

Theater. Canada's best-known theatrical event is the Stratford Shakespeare Festival, held annually in Stratford, Ontario. Famous performers appear in the plays of the great English playwright William Shakespeare and other noted dramatists. Another major annual drama festival is the Shaw Festival. This festival is held in Niagara-on-the-Lake, Ontario, and features works by the Irish-born British playwright George Bernard Shaw and other dramatists of the late 1800s and early 1900s. The leading theater group in French-speaking Canada is Le Théâtre du Nouveau Monde in Montreal. Cirque du Soleil, based in Montreal, is an entertainment company known for its acrobatic performers and striking special effects. Canada also has many regional theater companies. The Edmonton International Fringe Theatre Festival attracts hundreds of thousands of people to Edmonton every August. Leading playwrights from Canada include Tomson Highway, who writes in both the Cree language and English; Sharon Pollock and George F. Walker, who write in English; Michel Tremblay, who writes in French; and Robert Lepage, who uses both languages.

Music. Canada's outstanding orchestras include the National Arts Centre Orchestra, the Orchestre Symphonique de Montréal (Montreal Symphony Orchestra), the Toronto Symphony Orchestra, and the Vancouver Symphony Orchestra. Solo performers who have gained recognition include the pianists Janina Fialkowska, Glenn Gould, and Jon Kimura Parker; and the cellists Ofra Harnoy and Shauna Rolston. Canadian popular music stars have included Bryan Adams, Justin Bieber, Michael Bublé, Leonard Cohen, Céline Dion, Gordon Lightfoot, Sarah McLachlan, Joni Mitchell, Alanis Morissette, Anne Murray, Shania Twain, and Neil Young.

Ballet and opera. Canada has several professional ballet companies. The oldest, the Royal Winnipeg Ballet, was founded in 1938. It performs many original Canadian works. The National Ballet of Canada in Toronto and Les Grands Ballets Canadiens in Montreal both tour extensively. The National Ballet has featured such noted Canadian dancers as Frank Augustyn, Rex Harrington, Karen Kain, Martine Lamy, and Veronica Tennant.

The Canadian Opera Company performs in Toronto. Several other Canadian cities have opera companies. Outstanding Canadian opera singers have included Measha Brueggergosman, Maureen Forrester, Ben Heppner, Lois Marshall, Louis Quilico, and Jon Vickers.

Motion pictures. The Canadian motion-picture industry began in 1939 with the founding of the National Film Board of Canada. The government-sponsored board has won hundreds of awards for documentaries and animated films. In 1967, the government set up the Canadian Film Development Corporation, which helped establish Canada's feature-length film industry. Known today as Telefilm Canada, the organization administers funds for both motion pictures and television programs.

Thousands of Canadians work in the motion-picture industry. Hollywood studios film many movies, or parts of them, in Canada. Many movie companies find it less expensive to film in Canada than in the United States. Calgary, Montreal, Toronto, and Vancouver are often used as "American" cities. Many Western movies are shot in southern Alberta. Quebec also has a strong commercial film industry that produces movies in French.

Architecture. Examples of traditional architecture in Canada include the French-style homes

Toronto City Hall

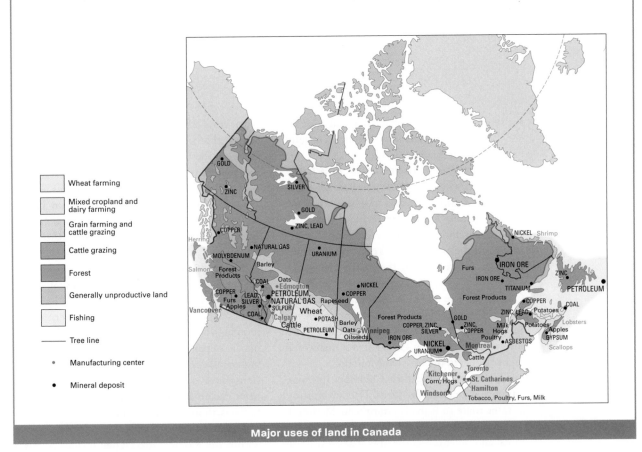

Major uses of land in Canada

of Quebec and the neo-Gothic Parliament buildings in Ottawa. Modern Canadian architecture is international in style. The Toronto-Dominion Centre in Toronto, designed by the German-born architect Ludwig Mies van der Rohe, and Place Ville Marie in Montreal, by the Chinese-born architect I. M. Pei, reflect the sleek, uncluttered glass-and-steel style of the mid-1900s. The Toronto City Hall, one of the most impressive structures in Canada, was designed by Viljo Revell of Finland.

Arthur Erickson, a famous Canadian architect, designed many buildings in British Columbia. Erickson is best known for designs that dramatically harmonize with the landscape. Moshe Safdie, an Israeli-born Canadian, first came to public attention with his housing project known as Habitat. This apartment complex, built for the Montreal World's Fair in 1967, consists of arrangements of prefabricated cubes. Douglas Cardinal, a First Nations architect born in Alberta, used smooth, rounded forms for the Canadian Museum of Civilization (Musée Canadien des Civilisations) in Gatineau, Quebec, near Ottawa. Cardinal also designed the National Museum of the American Indian in Washington, D.C.

The Land

Canada covers most of the northern half of North America. It borders Alaska on the north-west and the rest of the continental United States on the south. From east to west, Canada extends 3,223 miles (5,187 kilometers) from the rocky coast of Newfoundland and Labrador to the St. Elias Mountains in Yukon. Canada has six time zones. At noon in Vancouver, the time in St. John's, Newfoundland and Labrador, is 4:30 p.m. From its southernmost point, Middle Island in Lake Erie, Canada extends 2,875 miles (4,627 kilometers) north to Cape Columbia on Ellesmere Island. Of all the world's land areas, only the northern tip of Greenland lies nearer the North Pole than does Cape Columbia.

Canada has the longest coastline of any country—151,019 miles (243,042 kilometers), including island coasts. Canada faces the Pacific Ocean on the west, the Arctic Ocean on the north, and the Atlantic Ocean on the east. Hudson Bay, Hudson Strait, and James Bay form a great inland sea. Hudson Bay remains frozen for about eight months of the year. But in the summer, it provides a waterway to Canada's vast interior.

Forests cover almost half of the land area of Canada. Mountains and Arctic areas make up 41 percent of the land. Most Canadians live in southern agricultural areas and along the Atlantic and Pacific coasts.

Land regions. Canada has eight major land regions. They are the Pacific Ranges and Lowlands, the Rocky Mountains, the Arctic Islands, the Interior Plains, the Canadian Shield, the Hudson Bay Lowlands, the St. Lawrence Lowlands, and the Appalachian Region.

The Pacific Ranges and Lowlands form Canada's westernmost land region. They make up most of British Columbia and the southwestern part of Yukon. The region includes the Queen Charlotte Islands and Vancouver Island. All these islands are the upper portions of a mountain range that is partly covered by the Pacific Ocean. The Coast Mountains rise along the coast of British Columbia. The St. Elias Mountains in Yukon include Canada's highest peak, Mount Logan, near the Alaskan border. It towers 19,551 feet (5,959 meters) above sea level. Glaciers cover many of the higher slopes in the St. Elias Mountains.

The coastline of British Columbia has many long, narrow inlets called *fiords*. The fiords provide a water route to Canada's most valuable forests. These dense forests consist of tall red cedars, hemlocks, and other evergreen trees that grow on the lower slopes of the mountains. Black bears, foxes, and other animals live in the forests.

The Interior Plateau is an area of plains, river valleys, and smaller mountains. It lies east of the Coast Mountains. This area has valuable mineral resources, including Canada's largest deposits of the metals bismuth and molybdenum. The southern part of the Interior Plateau has many farms and orchards, as well as large grasslands where cattle graze. Forests grow in the northern part of the plateau area.

The Rocky Mountains rise east of the Pacific Ranges and Lowlands. These two regions together are part of the Cordillera, an immense group of mountain ranges that extends from Alaska through Mexico. In Canada, the snow-capped Rockies vary in height from 7,000 to more than 12,000 feet (2,100 to 3,660 meters) above sea level. The tallest peak, Mount Robson in eastern British Columbia, is 12,972 feet (3,954 meters) high. Millions of people visit the Rockies every year to view the magnificent scenery and to enjoy such activities as camping, hiking, and skiing.

The Rocky Mountain Chain extends for more than 3,000 miles (4,800 kilometers) from New Mexico to northern Alaska. The Canadian portion of the chain includes several separate ranges. The major range, the Canadian Rockies, stretches from Canada's southern border to the Liard River in northern British Columbia. Railroads and high-ways cross the Canadian Rockies at Crowsnest, Kicking Horse, Vermillion, and Yellowhead passes. Between the Liard River and the Alaskan border are several other ranges, including the Selwyn Mountains and the Mackenzie Mountains. A long, narrow valley called the Rocky Mountain Trench separates the Columbia Mountains in southern British Columbia from the Canadian Rockies to the east.

The Rockies have large deposits of coal, lead, silver, zinc, and other minerals. Forests of juniper and pine grow on the lower slopes. Firs and spruces thrive at higher elevations. Bears, deer, minks, mountain lions, and other animals roam the forests on the upper slopes. Rocky Mountain goats and bighorn sheep live above the *timber line*, the elevation above which trees cannot grow. Rainbow trout, cutthroat trout, grayling, and other fish swim in the swift mountain streams.

The Arctic Islands lie almost entirely within the Arctic Circle. They include about a dozen large islands and hundreds of smaller ones. All the islands are barren, and most remain unexplored. Two of the largest islands, Baffin Island and Ellesmere Island, have many glaciers, tall mountains, and deep fiords. Victoria Island and the other western islands are extremely flat. The seas surrounding the islands remain frozen most of the year.

The Arctic Islands are *tundras*, places too cold and dry for trees to grow. The subsoil of the islands is permanently frozen, and only a thin surface layer of soil thaws during the brief, cool summers. Only simple organisms called *lichens* grow on the northernmost islands. The other islands have lichens, mosses, grasses, and grasslike plants known as *sedges*. Herds of caribou and musk oxen graze on the tundras. Other wildlife includes Arctic foxes and hares, lemmings, polar bears, ptarmigans, seals, walruses, and whales. Insects thrive on the Arctic Islands during the summer.

Deposits of petroleum and natural gas, as well as such minerals as lead and zinc, have been discovered in the western Arctic Islands. However, most of this mineral wealth remains untapped because of high production costs and the difficulty of transporting the products to distant markets.

The Interior Plains include the northeastern corner of British Columbia, much of Alberta and Saskatchewan, and the southwestern part of

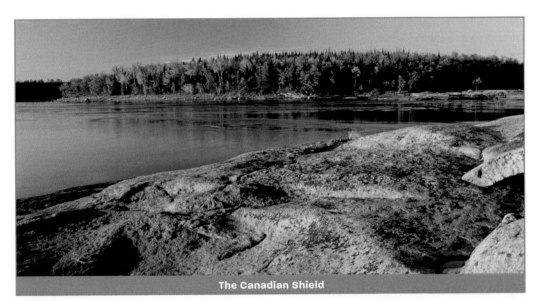

The Canadian Shield

Manitoba. The region extends north through the Northwest Territories to the Arctic Ocean.

Grasslands form the natural cover of the vast prairies in the southern Interior Plains. Farmers have plowed most of the grasslands to grow wheat and other grains in the fertile black soil. Ranchers graze cattle on the remaining grasslands in the drier areas of southern Alberta. Farther north, evergreen forests form part of the great northern forest that covers Canada from Alaska to the coast of Labrador, the mainland part of Newfoundland and Labrador. White spruces and jack pines are the most common trees in these forests. Deer, elk, moose, and many other animals live there. Near the Arctic Ocean, the forests gradually give way to tundras that are covered by snow for more than half the year.

The Interior Plains have many mineral resources. Large deposits of petroleum, natural gas, and coal have made Alberta a major mining area. One of the world's largest known deposits of *bituminous sands* or *tar sands* (sands that contain oil) lies along the Athabasca River in Alberta. Saskatchewan has important deposits of petroleum and uranium. The largest potash deposits in the world lie mainly in southern Saskatchewan. The Northwest Territories has petroleum and deposits of diamonds, lead, and zinc.

The Canadian Shield is a vast horseshoe-shaped region. It curves around Hudson Bay from the Arctic coast of Nunavut to the coast of Labrador. The Canadian Shield covers about half of Canada and is made up of ancient rock. Much of the region lies from 600 to 1,200 feet (180 to 370 meters) above sea level. The eastern part of the region is called the Great Laurentian Uplands.

The Canadian Shield consists largely of low hills and thousands of lakes. These lakes are the sources of rivers that break into great rapids and waterfalls at the edge of the region. Many of these rivers have hydroelectric plants. The plants provide power for pulp and paper mills and other industries, as well as towns and cities of Quebec, Ontario, and Manitoba.

Few people live in the Canadian Shield. The region generally has poor soil and a cold climate. Only a few areas near the southern edge of the region have soil that is good enough for farming.

The southern part of the Canadian Shield is close to Toronto, Ottawa, and Montreal. Many people of these cities have vacation houses near lakes or ski slopes in the southern Canadian Shield. The northern areas of the Canadian Shield are tundras. Evergreen forests cover most of the rest of the region. Deer, elk, moose, wolves, and many smaller animals live in the forests.

The Canadian Shield has much of Canada's mineral wealth. The border between Quebec and Newfoundland and Labrador has huge deposits of iron ore. Deposits of cobalt, copper, gold, nickel, and uranium are mined near Greater Sudbury, Ontario, a major smelting center. The Canadian Shield also contains valuable deposits of platinum, silver, zinc, and other metals.

The Hudson Bay Lowlands form a flat, swampy region between the Canadian Shield and the southwestern coast of Hudson Bay. The low-lands extend about 800 miles (1,300 kilometers) from the Churchill River in Manitoba to the Nottaway River in Quebec. Stunted forests and decayed vegetable matter called *peat* cover much of the area. The only permanent settlements are several small villages, a few old trading posts and forts, and the ports of Churchill, Manitoba, and Moosonee, Ontario.

The St. Lawrence Lowlands make up the smallest Canadian land region, but more than half of the nation's people live there. This region includes the flat-to-rolling countryside along the St. Lawrence River and the peninsula of southern Ontario. Another part of the region, Anticosti Island at the mouth of the St. Lawrence, remains a wilderness because of its isolation and colder climate. Southern Ontario has Canada's only major

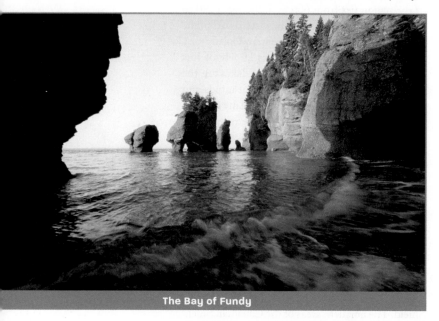

The Bay of Fundy

deciduous forests, which consist of trees that shed their leaves every autumn. The most plentiful trees in these forests include beeches, hickories, maples, oaks, and walnuts. Foxes, rabbits, raccoons, squirrels, and other small animals inhabit the forests.

The St. Lawrence Lowlands have excellent transportation facilities and lie near markets in the eastern and central United States. These features help make the region the manufacturing center of Canada. Fertile soil and a mild climate enable farmers in the St. Lawrence Lowlands to produce about a third of Canada's agricultural output. The most important crops include barley, corn, oats,

soybeans, and a variety of fruits and vegetables. The region also has a large number of dairy farms.

The Appalachian Region includes southeastern Quebec and all of the Atlantic Canada region except Labrador. The region forms part of an ancient mountain chain extending from the island of Newfoundland south to Alabama. The terrain of the Appalachian Region generally is hilly. The effects of glaciers and erosion have rounded the mountains. The Shickshock Mountains on the Gaspé Peninsula of Quebec have the region's highest peaks, which reach just over 4,000 feet (1,220 meters).

Most residents of the Appalachian Region live along the coast, where hundreds of bays and inlets provide harbors for fishing fleets. In most areas, the land rises gradually from the Atlantic Ocean. Parts of Nova Scotia and the island of Newfoundland, however, have steep, rocky coasts. The Bay of Fundy, between New Brunswick and Nova Scotia, is famous for its high tides, which reach more than 50 feet (15 meters) in some areas.

Mixed evergreen and deciduous forests cover much of the Appalachian Region. Valuable farmland lies on the plains of Prince Edward Island and along the Saint John River in New Brunswick and the Annapolis River in Nova Scotia. Nova Scotia has important coal and gypsum resources. Copper, lead, zinc, and other minerals are mined in New Brunswick and on Newfoundland.

Rivers, waterfalls, and lakes add to the scenic beauty of the Canadian countryside. Until the first railroads were built during the 1800s, the rivers and lakes also provided the only means of reaching Canada's vast interior. Many of these waterways still serve as major transportation routes. They also have economic importance as sources of hydroelectric power and, in the western provinces, for irrigation.

The water from each of Canada's lakes and rivers eventually drains into one of four major bodies of water. Therefore, the country has four major drainage areas, or basins—the Atlantic Basin, the Hudson Bay and Hudson Strait Basin, the Arctic Basin, and the Pacific Basin.

The Atlantic Basin covers about 678,000 square miles (1,756,000 square kilometers) in eastern Canada. The most important waterway in this drainage area is the Great Lakes-St. Lawrence River system. The Great Lakes, the largest group of freshwater lakes in the world, cover 94,230

Montmorency Falls

square miles (244,060 square kilometers). Lake Michigan lies entirely within the United States, but the border between Canada and the United States passes through the other four Great Lakes and the rivers that connect them. These rivers are the Saint Marys, the Detroit, the St. Clair, and the Niagara. Between Lake Erie and Lake Ontario, the Niagara River plunges over a rocky ledge and forms Niagara Falls, a world-famous tourist attraction.

The St. Lawrence River flows about 800 miles (1,300 kilometers) from Lake Ontario to the Gulf of St. Lawrence, an arm of the Atlantic Ocean. The St. Lawrence is sometimes called the *Mother of Canada* because it was the chief route of the European explorers, fur traders, and colonists who came to Canada several hundred years ago. Today, the St. Lawrence forms part of the St. Lawrence Seaway and carries more freight than any other Canadian river. The St. Lawrence Seaway enables oceangoing ships to travel between the Atlantic and such Great Lakes ports as Toronto and Chicago. The Thousand Islands, which lie in the St. Lawrence River near Lake Ontario, are a popular resort area.

Dams on the major *tributaries* (streams that flow into a larger stream) of the St. Lawrence provide much hydroelectric power for Quebec. Generating stations have been built on the Ottawa, Bersimis, Outardes, and Manicouagan rivers. Many other rivers have the potential for hydroelectric power. Such tributaries as the Ottawa, the St. Maurice, and the Saguenay are important to loggers, who float wood to pulp and paper plants downstream.

The Montmorency River plunges 251 feet (77 meters) near Quebec City to form Montmorency Falls. Churchill Falls, on the Churchill River in Labrador, is the site of one of the largest hydroelectric generating stations in the Western Hemisphere. New Brunswick is famous for the Reversing Falls at the mouth of the Saint John River. Twice each day, high tides from the Bay of Fundy force the river backward through the falls.

The Hudson Bay and Hudson Strait Basin covers about a third of mainland Canada. The chief river in this basin is the Nelson, which flows from Lake Winnipeg to Hudson Bay. During the 1700s and 1800s, the Nelson served as an important transportation route for the Hudson's Bay Company, a British fur-trading company. Today, the river serves mainly as a source of hydroelectric power. The Nelson's principal tributaries—the Assiniboine, the North and South Saskatchewan, the Red, and the Winnipeg rivers—flow into Lake Winnipeg rather than directly into the Nelson. The headwaters of the South Saskatchewan provide water for irrigating dry farmlands in southern Alberta. Hydroelectric generating stations on the Winnipeg River supply some electric power for the city of Winnipeg.

Other major rivers that flow into Hudson Bay include the Churchill and Hayes in Manitoba, the Severn and Winisk in Ontario, and the Thelon in the Northwest Territories and Nunavut. Several rivers empty into James Bay. Among them are the Albany and Moose in Ontario; and the Eastmain, Nottaway, and Rupert in Quebec. La Grande River has four large hydroelectric generating stations. Together these stations form one of the world's most important power projects.

The Arctic Basin includes parts of British Columbia, the Prairies, and the territories. The Mackenzie River system drains about half the basin. The sources of this river system, Canada's longest, are high in the Rocky Mountains, where the Peace and Athabasca rivers begin. These two rivers flow into the Slave River, which in turn empties into Great Slave Lake. The Mackenzie River itself flows northwest from Great Slave Lake for 1,100 miles (1,770 kilometers) to the Arctic Ocean. Along the way, the Mackenzie River receives water from many tributaries, the largest of which is the Liard River. The Great Bear River flows into the Mackenzie from Great Bear Lake, the largest lake that lies entirely in Canada.

The Fraser River, near
McBride, British Columbia

Barges carry cargo over much of the Mackenzie River system. The main route extends for 1,122 miles (1,805 kilometers) between the Northwest Territories towns of Tuktoyaktuk on the Arctic Ocean and Hay River on Great Slave Lake. Barges that provide service to local settlements navigate some stretches of the Slave and Athabasca rivers.

The Pacific Basin covers much of British Columbia and Yukon. The Yukon River drains the northern third of the region. This river rises from a series of lakes in northwest British Columbia and flows west through Yukon and Alaska to the Pacific Ocean. During the gold rush of the 1890s, riverboats brought thousands of prospectors up the river to Dawson, a boom town near the Klondike gold fields.

The longest river in the southern part of the Pacific Basin is the Fraser. It flows through a deep valley from the Canadian Rockies to Vancouver, where it empties into the Pacific. The Columbia River rises in the mountains of southeastern British Columbia and flows south into the United States. Hydroelectric plants operate at several points on the Columbia. The Columbia goes through Upper Arrow Lake and Lower Arrow Lake, two long, narrow lakes in the interior valleys. Other important rivers of the Pacific Basin include the Kootenay, Skeena, Stikine, and Thompson.

Climate

Canada's northern location gives it a generally cold climate, but conditions vary from region to region. In the winter, westerly winds bring frigid Arctic air to most of Canada. Average January temperatures are below 0°F (−18°C) in more than two-thirds of Canada. January temperatures average above freezing only along the coast of British Columbia. This area has a moderate climate because of mild winds from the Pacific Ocean.

Northern Canada has short, cool summers. In the northern Arctic Islands, July temperatures average below 40°F (4°C). Permanent icecaps cover parts of Baffin, Devon, and Ellesmere islands. Southern Canada has summers that are long enough and warm enough for raising crops. Sum-

mer winds from the Gulf of Mexico often bring hot weather to southern Ontario and the St. Lawrence River Valley. Southern Ontario has average July temperatures above 70°F (21°C) and a frost-free growing season nearly six months long.

Some coastal areas of British Columbia receive more than 100 inches (250 centimeters) of precipitation annually. Most of it falls in autumn and winter. The Canadian prairies have from 10 to 20 inches (25 to 50 centimeters) of precipitation a year. Little snow falls there, and most of the rain comes during the summer. These conditions help make the prairies ideal for growing grain.

Southeastern Canada has a humid climate. The average annual precipitation ranges from about 30 inches (76 centimeters) in southern Ontario to about 60 inches (150 centimeters) on the coasts of Newfoundland and Labrador and Nova Scotia. Heavy snow covers eastern Canada in winter. More than 100 inches (250 centimeters) of snow falls annually on large areas of Labrador and Newfoundland, New Brunswick, Quebec, and Ontario.

Economy

In colonial times, most Canadians earned a living by farming, fishing, logging, or fur trapping. Today, the main economic activities in Canada are service industries and manufacturing. Canada's *gross domestic product* (GDP)—the total value of goods and services produced within a country in a year—is among the largest in the world.

The Canadian economy is based on private enterprise. But the national and provincial govern-

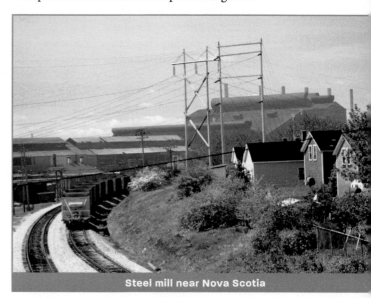

Steel mill near Nova Scotia

ments play an active role in many economic activities. For example, they provide free health services to all Canadians. The federal and provincial governments also own broadcasting companies, transportation firms, and utilities.

Foreign investment and ownership—especially from the United States—have a major influence on Canada's economy. Japan and countries of the European Union also have large investments in Canada. A free trade agreement with the United States went into effect in 1989. The agreement called for the elimination of all *tariffs* (taxes on imports) between the two countries. In 1994, Canada joined with the United States and Mexico in the North American Free Trade Agreement (NAFTA), which built upon the previous pact between Canada and the United States.

Service industries account for the largest portion of Canada's GDP. They are especially important in metropolitan areas. Community, business, and personal services rank first among Canada's service industries. This group employs more people than any other industry group in Canada. It includes such activities as education and health care, data processing and legal services, and the operation of recreational facilities.

Finance, insurance, and real estate form the second most important service industry in terms of GDP. Toronto and Montreal are Canada's leading financial centers. The main Canadian stock exchange is in Toronto.

Other service industries include government; trade, restaurants, and hotels; and transportation and communication. Government services, which include military activities, are centered in Ottawa, the nation's capital, and in the provincial capitals and major cities. Restaurants and hotels benefit from the millions of people who visit Canada each year. Retail trade, which consists of such businesses as automobile dealerships, department stores, and supermarkets, employs many people.

Manufacturing. Factories in Ontario and Quebec produce about three-fourths of the value of Canada's manufactured goods. In terms of *value added by manufacture*, transportation equipment ranks as the nation's leading manufactured product, followed by processed foods and beverages. Value added by manufacture is the difference between the value of raw materials and the value of finished products made from them. The manufacture of motor vehicles and parts dominates the transporta-

A pulp and paper mill in British Columbia

tion equipment industry. Ontario produces more cars than any other Canadian province or U.S. state. Aircraft and aerospace equipment production is a fast-growing part of the manufacturing industry. Bombardier Aerospace in Quebec is one of the world's largest civil aircraft manufacturers.

Processed food and beverage products is a leading manufacturing industry in every province. Processed meat and poultry are the leading products of Canada's food and beverage industry. Toronto is a major meat-packing center. Other leading products include baked goods, beer, dairy products, fruit and vegetable products, and soft drinks. Seafood production is important in Atlantic Canada.

Much of Canada's manufacturing is dedicated to processing its forest and mined products. Canada's forests are used for manufacturing paper and wood products. Almost every province has at least one oil refinery, and Canada is one of the world's leading oil refiners.

Other important manufacturing industries in Canada produce chemicals, machinery, and primary metals. Most chemical production occurs in Alberta, Ontario, and Quebec. *Pharmaceuticals* (medicinal drugs) are the leading chemical product. Much of the machinery is used in agriculture and mining. Canada's smelters and refineries produce basic aluminum and steel products. Quebec leads in aluminum production. Ontario makes the most steel.

Mining. Canada is among the major producers of a variety of minerals, including copper, gold, iron ore, nickel, potash, uranium, and zinc. The country is also one of the world's leading exporters of minerals.

Canada's two most important mined products are petroleum and natural gas. Alberta is the leading producer of petroleum and natural gas in Canada. Processing Alberta's natural gas produces valuable amounts of sulfur as a by-product. Saskatchewan is a major source of uranium and potash.

Ontario is Canada's leading producer of metal ores. Much of the world's nickel comes from Ontario. Ontario also mines large amounts of gold and copper, as does British Columbia. Quebec produces iron ore and gold. Newfoundland and Labrador leads the provinces in iron ore production. New Brunswick is the leading zinc-mining province. Canada's other mined products include coal, diamonds, platinum, salt, sand and gravel, silver, and stone.

Agriculture. Farmland covers about 7 percent of Canada's land area. Beef cattle, dairy products, hogs, and wheat combine to account for about half of the total farm income. Other leading products include an oil-bearing plant called *canola*; chickens; eggs; and *floriculture* (ornamental plants) and nursery products.

About 80 percent of Canada's farmland lies in the Prairies. Saskatchewan produces about 40 percent of Canada's wheat, and farmers in Alberta and Manitoba raise most of the rest. Barley, canola, flaxseed, and oats grow in a belt north of Canada's wheat-growing areas. Farmers use barley and oats mainly for livestock feed. Canola and flaxseed are used to make cooking oils and lubricants. Farms in Alberta produce about half of the nation's beef cattle. Farmers in the Prairies also raise dairy cattle, hogs, and poultry.

The St. Lawrence Lowlands form Canada's other major agricultural region. Farmers there produce a variety of products, including beef cattle, grains, milk, and vegetables. Southern Ontario's warm summers and long growing season enable farmers to grow a variety of specialty crops, including corn, fruits, tobacco, and vegetables. Quebec leads the provinces in the production of milk, and Ontario ranks second. Quebec's farmers also raise beef cattle, hogs, poultry, and vegetables.

Farms in the interior of British Columbia and Vancouver Island produce eggs, livestock, milk, poultry, and tree fruits. British Columbia and Ontario are Canada's leading growers of nursery products and ornamental plants and flowers. Potato farming and dairying are the chief agricultural activities in Atlantic Canada.

Government marketing agencies establish production quotas and price supports to protect Canadian farmers from the effects of changing prices. The federal and provincial governments also provide credit, as well as technical and management assistance, to farmers. In many areas, farmers have formed *cooperatives*. These organizations market the farmers' products and supply goods and services needed in farming.

Forestry. Canada is a leading timber-producing nation. The federal and provincial governments own most of the forests and lease them to private companies. British Columbia, Ontario, and Quebec lead the provinces in timber production. Loggers cut down cedars, firs, hemlocks, pines, spruce, and many other kinds of trees. Mills process the logs into lumber, paper, plywood, and wood pulp.

Fishing is Canada's oldest economic activity. The Grand Banks, off the coast of Newfoundland, began to attract European fishing crews in large numbers during the 1500s. Today, the major products of Canada's Atlantic waters include clams, crab, Greenland turbot, herring, lobster, scallops, and shrimp. Cod were once plentiful in the Atlantic coastal waters, but they have nearly disappeared due to overfishing. The population of certain other fish has also declined. As a result, the government has banned almost all cod fishing and placed restrictions on other fishing in Canada's Atlantic waters.

Fishing crews take halibut, herring, salmon, and shellfish from Canada's Pacific waters. They catch most of the salmon near the mouths of major rivers in British Columbia. However, the salmon fishing industry is in danger. Salmon stocks have fallen due to overfishing by crews from British Columbia, Alaska and Washington in the United States, and other countries. In 1998, the Canadian government ordered a halt to fishing for some types of salmon. Today, British Columbia has a large number of fish farms that raise salmon.

Canada's lakes provide fish chiefly for the central part of the country and the United States. The principal lake fish include perch, pickerel, and whitefish.

Energy sources. Canada has a high per-person rate of energy use. Huge quantities of energy are needed to provide heat during severe winters. Much energy is also needed to transport goods and people between distant regions and to

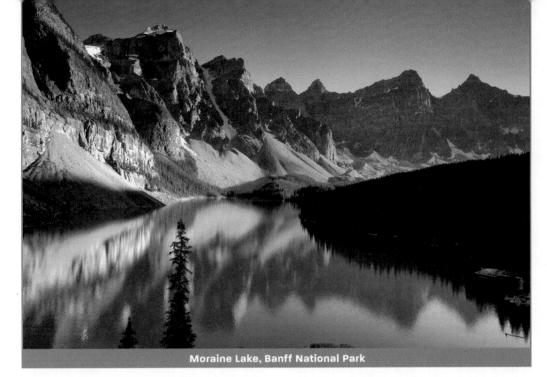

Moraine Lake, Banff National Park

process natural resources. Canada has vast energy resources, but most Canadians consider energy conservation as essential. Conservation helps slow the depletion of nonrenewable energy sources, such as petroleum and natural gas. Reducing fuel consumption through conservation also lessens the amount of pollution released into the environment.

Much of the petroleum used in Canada takes the form of gasoline. More than half of Canada's electric power comes from hydroelectric sources. Plants powered by natural gas, oil, or coal provide about a fourth of Canada's electric power. Other power sources include nuclear energy and renewable sources, such as wind or *biomass* (organic material used for fuel).

International trade. Canada ranks among the leading countries in the world in international trade. The nation's exports total hundreds of billions of dollars annually. About two-thirds of Canada's imports come from the United States, and about three-fourths of its exports go to the United States. Both countries export and import automobiles and automobile parts, chemicals, and various kinds of machinery.

Canada's other leading exports include forest products, precious metals and metal ores, natural gas, petroleum, and wheat. Canada's other major imports include computers, pharmaceuticals, and scientific instruments. Canada's chief trading partners, besides the United States, include China, France, Germany, Japan, Mexico, South Korea, and the United Kingdom.

Transportation. Canada's landscape has many features that create barriers to travel, including mountains, forests, and bodies of water. In spite of these barriers, Canadians have built an outstanding system of railroad, highway, water, and air transportation.

Railroads. Canada's railroad system has about 29,000 miles (47,000 kilometers) of mainline track. The two main railroads are the Canadian National Railway (CN) and the Canadian Pacific Railway. Both are privately owned. The government-owned corporation VIA Rail Canada provides the only trans-Canada passenger rail service. Other passenger rail services operate within some provinces. Commuter systems serve some urban areas.

Toronto and Montreal have modern subway systems. Calgary, Edmonton, Ottawa, and Vancouver have light rail transit systems, which use electrically powered cars that run on tracks.

Roads and highways. Southern Canada has one of the world's finest highway systems. The Trans-Canada Highway extends about 5,000 miles (8,000 kilometers) between Victoria, British Columbia, and St. John's, Newfoundland and Labrador. Northern Canada has few highways. Many roads there are unpaved.

Ferries link roads on Vancouver Island and Newfoundland with roads on other islands and on mainland Canada. Confederation Bridge joins Prince Edward Island to New Brunswick. Buses provide public transportation in Canadian cities. Buses also link cities with outlying towns and other cities.

Waterways and ports. The Great Lakes and the St. Lawrence Seaway form one of the world's greatest inland waterways. The seaway

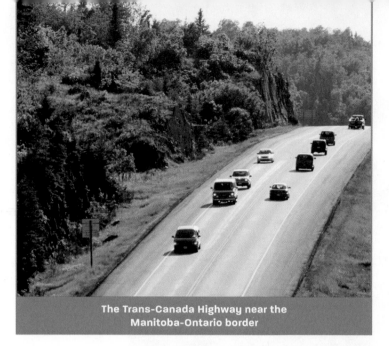

The Trans-Canada Highway near the Manitoba-Ontario border

enables oceangoing ships to sail between the Atlantic Ocean and Great Lakes ports. These ships transport coal, iron ore, wheat, and other bulk cargoes. Vessels called *lakers* transport cargo between ports on the Great Lakes and the St. Lawrence River. For example, lakers carry iron ore from ports on the St. Lawrence to steel mills on the Great Lakes.

The port of Vancouver, including the facilities at nearby Roberts Bank, is Canada's busiest port. Prince Rupert, British Columbia, is also an important Pacific port. Major ports on the St. Lawrence River include Montreal, Port-Cartier, Quebec City, and Sept-Îles in Quebec. The main Great Lakes ports are Hamilton, Nanticoke, and Thunder Bay in Ontario. Canada's busiest Atlantic Ocean ports include Come By Chance, Newfoundland and Labrador; Halifax and Port Hawkesbury in Nova Scotia; and Saint John, New Brunswick.

Air travel. Air Canada is by far Canada's largest airline. It provides both domestic and international service. WestJet provides service mainly in western Canada, but it also serves several eastern cities. Toronto Pearson International Airport is Canada's busiest airport, followed by Vancouver International Airport.

Communication plays a vital role in linking different parts of a nation as vast as Canada. Canadians rely on a variety of communication systems, including telephone and Internet service, television and radio, mail service, and publishing.

Telephone and Internet service. Various telecommunications companies provide telephone and Internet service throughout Canada. Deregulation of the industry in the 1990s led to increased competition and mergers among telephone service providers.

Bell Canada Enterprises is Canada's largest communications company. It provides phone, Internet, satellite television, and other services to many homes and businesses. Cable and satellites link Canada's telecommunications systems to those of most other countries.

Television and radio. The Canadian Broadcasting Corporation (CBC) operates national television and radio networks in both English and French. The CBC, though financed largely by the government, functions independently in its programming. Canada's satellite communications system enables CBC broadcasts to reach most of the population. Canada's other national TV networks are CTV Television Network and Global Television Network, which are privately owned. Commercial networks serve all major metropolitan areas. Many of the nation's households subscribe to cable TV systems, which offer a variety of Canadian and U.S. programs.

The Canadian Radio-television and Telecommunications Commission (CRTC), a government agency, regulates electronic communication systems in Canada. The CRTC issues licenses to radio and television stations and makes sure that certain percentages of their programs have Canadian content. These Canadian-content quotas are intended to help maintain a Canadian cultural identity in the face of overwhelming U.S. influence. They also create jobs in Canada by encouraging the production of TV and radio shows.

Publishing. Canada has a variety of daily newspapers printed in both English and French. The leading English-language dailies include the *Toronto Star, The Globe and Mail,* the *National Post,* and the *Toronto Sun* of Toronto; *The Vancouver Sun* of Vancouver; *The Gazette* of Montreal; and the *Ottawa Citizen.* The leading French-language dailies are *Le Journal de Montréal* and *La Presse* of Montreal. Many weekly and biweekly newspapers are also published in Canada.

Publishers in Canada produce a number of magazines. The best-known include the news magazines *Maclean's* in English and *L'Actualité* in French. The women's magazine *Chatelaine* (*Châtelaine* in French) has both an English-language version and a French-language version. Magazines from the United States also have a wide audience in Canada, and magazines from France have many readers in Quebec. Ontario and Quebec are the leading book publishing provinces. Many U.S.,

Children raising their hands in French class

British, and French publications are printed in Canada at the same time as in their own country.

British North America Act

This act served as the main written part of Canada's constitution from 1867 until 1982. The Constitution Act of 1982 replaced it as the basic governing document of Canada.

The British Parliament passed the British North America Act in March 1867 to provide for the formation of the Dominion of Canada. The act took effect on July 1, 1867 and united the three British colonies of New Brunswick, Nova Scotia, and Canada. Under the act, these colonies became four provinces—New Brunswick, Nova Scotia, Ontario, and Quebec. The act divided the colony of Canada to create Ontario and Quebec.

The British North America Act established a federal union with a strong central government and limited provincial governments. Generally, the dominion government had the power to deal with matters of national interest. Each provincial government handled education, health, natural resources, and other local affairs.

The British Parliament amended the British North America Act many times. Canada won its independence from the United Kingdom in 1931, but amendments to the British North America Act continued to require British approval. This requirement finally ended when the British Parliament accepted Canadian proposals for a revised constitution and passed the Constitution Act of 1982. As a result of this act, the British North America Act was renamed the Constitution Act of 1867.

Canada's Constitution

Canada's constitution is partly unwritten and partly written. The unwritten part consists mainly of general agreement and custom, including the cabinet system of government. The basic written section is the Constitution Act of 1982. It includes the British North America Act, which was the basic document governing Canada's federal system from 1867 to 1982. Other written parts include ordinary laws and judicial decisions.

The founding fathers of the Canadian confederation wanted a strong central government. Thus, in the British North America Act, the provincial governments received only 16 powers then considered to be of minor importance. The federal government got all other powers. It also received power to *disallow* (reject) any provincial laws it believed undesirable.

However, powers given to the provinces—over such matters as education, health, and natural resources—became more important. Provinces became stronger and richer, and debates on the divisions of power between federal and provincial governments increased.

The Constitution Act of 1982 ended formal British control over amendments to Canada's constitution. Previously, the British Parliament had to approve many of the amendments.

Today, amendments must be approved by Canada's House of Commons, the provinces of Quebec and Ontario; two of the four Atlantic Provinces, representing at least half the region's population, and two of the four Western Provinces, representing at least half of that region's population. The Atlantic Provinces are New Brunswick, Newfoundland and Labrador, Nova Scotia, and Prince Edward Island. The Western Provinces are Alberta, British Columbia, Manitoba, and Saskatchewan. A province is considered to have approved an amendment when a majority of its voters have voted for it. The Canadian Senate also votes on constitutional amendments, but its rejection can only delay passage for 180 days.

Canadian Armed Forces

The armed forces defend Canada and its interests throughout the world. They maintain the equipment, weapons, and troops necessary to protect Canada and to provide humanitarian and civil assistance in Canada and worldwide. In addition, the forces contribute to international peacekeeping and security operations through alliances with other countries. The forces are formally named the Canadian Armed Forces, but they are commonly called the Canadian Forces.

Organization. An officer called the *chief of the defence staff* commands the Canadian Forces. The chief of the defence staff also advises the Canadian government on military matters. The prime minister and the Cabinet appoint the chief.

The Canadian Forces consists of the Regular Forces, who are always on active duty, and the Reserve Forces, who supplement the Regular Forces when necessary. The Canadian Forces includes three large defense organizations: (1) the Canadian Army, (2) the Royal Canadian Navy, (3) and the Royal Canadian Air Force.

The Canadian Army's primary tasks are to protect Canada and to defend North America in cooperation with the United States. The Canadian Army also participates in overseas operations, antiterrorist operations, and peacekeeping missions. It aids provincial and territorial authorities in dealing with natural disasters. It maintains three regular combat mechanized brigade groups and more than 12 reserve combat brigade groups. The Canadian Rangers, who serve in the Far North, are members of the Reserve Forces.

The Royal Canadian Navy protects Canada's coastline and works with Canada's allies to defend North America. The Navy defends Canadian waters against illegal fishing and environmental damage. Canada's Navy also supports international peacekeeping missions and humanitarian assistance projects. In addition, it maintains security through the North Atlantic Treaty Organization (NATO), a military alliance consisting of Canada, the United States, and most European nations. The Navy's operations are conducted from two major bases, in Halifax, Nova Scotia; and Esquimalt, British Columbia. The Naval Reserves assist the Navy.

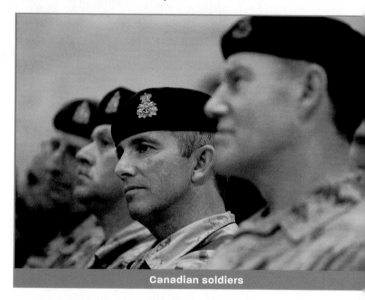

Canadian soldiers

The Royal Canadian Air Force (RCAF) is charged with surveillance and control of Canadian airspace. It shares in the joint defense of North American airspace with United States forces through the North American Aerospace Defense Command (NORAD). The RCAF provides air support to the Navy and the Army, and it transports Canadian Forces personnel and equipment throughout the world. The Air Force is made up of 13 wings. A wing is a group of operational and support units under a single tactical commander. The Air Reserves assist the Air Force.

Support organizations under the control of the Department of National Defence aid the Canadian Forces. Defence Research and Development Canada provides the Department of Defence and the Canadian Forces with technical and scientific services. The Communications Security Establishment works to keep telecommunications, electronic communications, and computerized systems secure. The National Search and Rescue Secretariat coordinates the activities of government, private, and volunteer organizations that provide search and rescue services.

Weapons and equipment. The Army's armored vehicles include Leopard tanks and Grizzly and other armored personnel carriers. Its artillery includes self-propelled howitzers, field guns, antitank weapons, handheld surface-to-air missiles, and air defense missiles.

The Navy operates frigates, diesel-electric submarines, and supply ships. The Navy also has many smaller vessels and training ships.

The RCAF flies CF-18 Hornet fighter-bombers, CP-140 Aurora patrol aircraft, and smaller training aircraft. Transports include the CC-115 Buffalo, CC-130 Hercules, and the CC-144 Challenger. Helicopters include the CH-124 Sea King, used for antisubmarine warfare, and the CH-113 Labrador and CH-149 Cormorant, for search and rescue.

Recruitment and training. Officers in the Canadian Armed Forces may receive their commissions in one of three ways. The first is to enter the Canadian Forces after graduating from a university and agreeing to active service for three years. The second way is to complete the Officer Candidate Training Program. The program requires a minimum of a 12th-grade education with advanced standing in English, mathematics, and sciences. The candidate must agree to serve for three years. The third

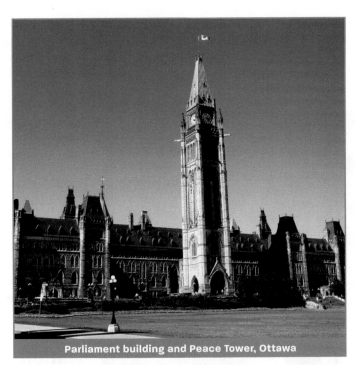
Parliament building and Peace Tower, Ottawa

method is the Regular Officer Training Program. The candidate receives four years of free education at one of three Canadian military colleges or a civilian university. After completing a degree program, candidates must serve for a minimum of five years.

Noncommissioned recruits must have at least a 10th-grade education and enlist for three years. Basic training for recruits lasts 10 weeks and is followed by occupational training courses. A Canadian citizen must be older than 17 to enlist.

History. During colonial days, Canada's defense was the responsibility of the governments of France and Britain. But in the mid-1800s, Canada began to move toward independence and to assume responsibility for its own defense. In 1871, the Canadian Army was first organized. The Royal Canadian Navy was formed in 1910, and the Royal Canadian Air Force in 1924.

Canada's military forces fought under British command in the Anglo-Boer War of 1899–1902. During World War I (1914–1918), Canadians fought with the Allied forces under British command. More than 1 million Canadians served with the Allied forces during World War II (1939–1945). Canadian troops fought with the United Nations (UN) in the Korean War (1950–1953) and the Persian Gulf War of 1991. Canadian troops have served in many of the UN's peacekeeping operations since the first one in 1947.

Political Parties in Canada

Canada has a combined parliamentary and federal system of government. Thus, the organization of its political parties resembles that of both the United Kingdom and the United States. Canada—like the United Kingdom—has a prime minister, who usually belongs to and is the leader of the majority party in the House of Commons. But the political parties in Canada—like those in the United States—are often both national and provincial (state) in their activities and organization.

Canadians elected Conservative leader Stephen Harper as Prime Minister in 2006.

Leading parties. The two most prominent parties in Canada are the Liberal Party and the Conservative Party of Canada. The Conservative Party of Canada was created in late 2003 by a merger of the Progressive Conservative Party and the Canadian Alliance.

Traditionally, the Liberals have favored the expansion of social programs and provincial rights. The Conservative Party of Canada has supported controlled government spending, lower taxes, and increased support of the military.

When the Conservative Party of Canada was created, the Liberals and the Progressive Conservatives historically had been the strongest national parties. Both could trace their origins to before 1867, when the British North America Act established the Dominion of Canada. The Progressive Conservative Party was officially known as the Conservative Party until 1942.

Other parties. The New Democratic Party and the Bloc Québécois are two other important federal parties. The New Democratic Party was formed in 1961 by trade unions, a socialist party called the Co-operative Commonwealth Federation (CCF), and independent left-wing Canadians. The party favors social welfare measures. It opposes Canadian participation in such military alliances as the North Atlantic Treaty Organization (NATO) and the North American Aerospace Defense Command (NORAD).

The Bloc Québécois was formed in 1990 by a handful of members of Parliament from Quebec. The party advocates the creation of a sovereign Quebec, and it quickly gained support among French-speaking Quebecers. From 1993 to 2011, the Bloc Québécois held between half and three-fourths of Quebec's seats in the House of Commons, giving the party an influence in national politics despite its regional base.

National Health Insurance

In Canada, a national health insurance program gradually went into effect between 1955 and 1971. Under the Canadian program, each of the country's provinces provides health insurance to its own residents. The federal government pays part of the costs. The provinces must meet standards established by the federal government. These standards include coverage for all of the province's residents, broad coverage of medically necessary services, and reimbursement for medical expenses incurred outside the province.

Social Security in Canada

Canada's social security has three main parts: (1) the Old Age Security program, (2) the Canada Pension Plan, and (3) unemployment insurance. A government department called Human Resources and Social Development Canada administers the country's social security programs.

The Old Age Security program provides a minimum retirement income to people age 65 or older who have lived in Canada for at least 10 years. To receive this pension outside Canada, the person must have lived in Canada for at least 20 years. Beneficiaries are paid benefits regardless of their work records. Benefits, which are paid monthly, rise automatically with the country's cost of living. Low-income beneficiaries receive an additional benefit called the Guaranteed Income Supplement.

The Canada Pension Plan provides additional monthly benefits to retired workers, disabled workers and their children, and the surviving spouse and children of deceased workers. The plan also provides a death benefit in a single payment to the estate of a covered deceased worker. Workers must be 60 or older to collect a retirement pension under the plan. Retirement benefits are based on workers' earnings and their contributions to the plan. The plan is financed by a payroll deduction. Employers and workers pay separate taxes on the worker's earnings. Self-employed workers pay both the employer's and worker's shares.

Participation in the plan is required for all workers from the ages of 18 to 60 who earn more than an annual minimum. Workers from 60 to 70 continue to participate if they are not yet receiving a retirement pension under the plan. Workers in the province of Quebec do not participate in the plan. But they are covered by a similar program, called the Quebec Pension Plan.

To qualify for disability and survivors benefits, workers must have contributed to the pension plan for a specified period. Such benefits equal a fixed amount plus a percentage of the retirement pension to which the worker would be entitled. Benefits are adjusted yearly to reflect increases in the cost of living.

Unemployment insurance covers almost all Canadian workers. To receive benefits, an unemployed worker must have worked in an insured job for a minimum number of weeks. The number of weeks depends on how long the person has worked and on the unemployment rate in the region where the worker lives. Generally, the weeks worked must fall within the year before the person filed for benefits. The worker also must have worked a minimum number of hours a week or earned a minimum amount a week. Some unemployed workers are eligible for maternity, illness, and parental benefits.

Unemployment insurance is financed by premiums paid by employers and employees. Premiums are paid into the Unemployment Insurance Account, which is administered by Human Resources and Social Development Canada.

Niagara Falls

Niagara Falls is one of the most spectacular natural wonders of North America. Niagara Falls is on the Niagara River, about halfway between Lake Erie and Lake Ontario. The river forms part of the United States-Canadian border.

Niagara Falls actually consists of two waterfalls, the Horseshoe Falls and the American Falls. The Horseshoe Falls is on the Canadian side of the border in the province of Ontario. The American Falls is on the United States side in the state of New York. At night, wide beams of colored lights illuminate the falls. Millions of people visit Niagara Falls annually.

Description. At the falls, the Niagara River plunges into a steep, canyon-like gorge. The gorge extends beyond Niagara Falls for about 7 miles (11 kilometers), to Lewiston, New York. The famous Whirlpool Rapids begin about 3 miles (5 kilometers) below the falls. Here, the violent current has carved a round basin out of the rocks.

About 85 percent of the water at Niagara Falls flows over the Horseshoe Falls. The Horseshoe Falls is about 167 feet (51 meters) high and 2,600 feet (792 meters) wide at its widest point. The American Falls is about 176 feet (54 meters) high and 1,000 feet (305 meters) wide.

The gorge is about 200 feet (61 meters) deep and consists of layers of different kinds of stone. A hard rock called *dolomite* about 80 feet (24 meters) thick forms the top layer. It covers softer layers of limestone, sandstone, and shale. Water erodes soft stone faster than hard stone. For this reason, the top layer extends beyond the lower layers in many places. The Cave of the Winds, behind the American Falls, has been formed under an extended shelf of harder stone.

American Falls

American Falls (left) and Horseshoe Falls (right)

Through the years, the gorge has become longer and longer. The pounding water erodes the soft underlying rock layers, which causes the unsupported hard rock ledge to collapse. Niagara Falls was originally at Lewiston, but it has gradually moved about 7 miles (11 kilometers) back upstream toward Lake Erie. The ledge of the Horseshoe Falls wears away at a rate varying from about 3 inches (8 centimeters) to as much as 6 feet (2 meters) per year. The ledge of the American Falls erodes more slowly because less water flows over it. Each year, about 1 inch (2.5 centimeters) wears away.

Tourism. Niagara Falls attracts visitors throughout the year. However, most visitors come during the tourist season, from April 1 to October 31. Several steamers called *The Maid of the Mist* take sightseers close to the churning waters at the base of the falls. Parks line both sides of the river near Niagara Falls. Excellent views of the falls may be seen from such sites as Prospect Point, Table Rock, and Terrapin Point. Four observation towers, ranging from 282 to 500 feet (86 to 150 meters) high, also provide fine views of the falls.

Water flow. United States and Canadian hydroelectric plants divert some of the water through tunnels from the Niagara River before it reaches Niagara Falls. For scenic reasons, however, the amount of water that may be diverted is regulated by a treaty between the United States and Canada. The treaty states that at least 100,000 cubic feet (2,800 cubic meters) of water a second must pass over the falls during daylight hours of the tourist season. At other times, the flow may be decreased to 50,000 cubic feet (1,400 cubic meters) a second.

History. Niagara Falls was probably formed about 12,000 years ago, after the last great ice sheet melted from the region. The melting ice caused Lake Erie to overflow. The overflow formed the Niagara River. The river ran northward over a high cliff called the *Niagara Escarpment*. The Niagara River cut through the escarpment and, over the centuries, formed Niagara Falls.

Indian tribes lived in the area long before the first Europeans arrived. The name *Niagara* comes from the Iroquois word *Onguiaahra*, meaning *the strait*.

Louis Hennepin, a Roman Catholic priest who traveled with the French explorer Robert Cavelier, Sieur de La Salle, left a written account of his visit to Niagara Falls. In a book published in 1683, Hennepin wrote: "These waters foam and boil in a fearful manner. They thunder continually."

Large numbers of tourists began visiting Niagara Falls during the 1800s. Many hotels and taverns were built on the American and Canadian sides of the falls. In addition, numerous industries began to operate along the Niagara River.

Some people believed that the rapid development of tourism and industry ruined the scenic beauty of the Niagara Falls area. In 1885, the government of New York took control of the land bordering the American Falls. It then established Niagara Falls Park, covering about 430 acres (174 hectares), on the land. In 1886, Canada established Queen Victoria Park on 196 acres (79 hectares) of land near the Horseshoe Falls. Since the 1880s, much more land in the Niagara Falls area has been set aside for parks, especially on the Canadian side.

Rock slides have gradually changed the appearance of Niagara Falls through the years. In 1931, about 80,000 tons (73,000 metric tons) of rock fell from the American Falls. Several years later, approximately 30,000 tons (27,000 metric tons) of rock broke off the upper edge of the Horseshoe Falls. In 1954, about 185,000 tons (167,800 metric tons) of rock tumbled from the American Falls and nearby Prospect Point.

In 1969, U.S. Army engineers built a dam to stop the flow of water temporarily over the American Falls. A board of experts from the United States and

Canada then studied the rock ledge to determine how to prevent further erosion. However, the board decided that the cost of halting erosion would be too high. It recommended that nothing be done except small measures to improve public safety.

History of Canada

Canada's history is the story of the peoples who have inhabited and the forces that have shaped one of the vastest countries in the world. Most experts believe the first people to live in what is now Canada came from Asia at least 15,000 years ago. They arrived by way of a land bridge that once connected Asia and North America at what is now Alaska. Their descendants became known as Indians. The ancestors of the Inuit (sometimes called Eskimos) came later, moving into the Arctic regions of Canada starting about A.D. 1000.

In 1497, John Cabot, an Italian navigator in the service of England, found rich fishing grounds off Canada's southeast coast. In time, his discovery led to the European exploration of Canada. France took the lead in exploring the country and set up a colony in eastern Canada in the early 1600s. French fur traders traveled westward and came upon many of Canada's sparkling lakes, rushing rivers, and majestic, snow-capped mountains. Britain (now also called the United Kingdom) gained control of the country in 1763, and thousands of British immigrants began to join the French who remained in Canada. In 1867, the French- and English-speaking Canadians helped create a united colony called the Dominion of Canada. The two groups worked together to settle the country from coast to coast and to develop its great mineral deposits and other natural resources.

Canada gained its independence from the United Kingdom in 1931. During the mid-1900s, hard-working Canadians turned their country into an economic giant. Today, huge harvests from western Canada make the nation a leading producer of wheat, oats, and barley. Canada also ranks among the world's top manufacturing nations, and it is a major producer of electric power.

Throughout its history, Canada has often been troubled by a lack of unity among its people. French Canadians, mostly from Quebec, have struggled to preserve their French culture. They have long been angered by Canadian policies based on British traditions, and many of them support a movement to make Quebec a separate nation. People in Canada's nine other provinces often favor local needs over national interests.

Canada and the United States have generally enjoyed a long history of cooperation. They have worked together in the defense of North America and have strong economic ties. Canada has tried to develop independently of its southern neighbor. But its economy is so closely linked to the U.S. economy that severe U.S. business slumps usually cause hard times in Canada. In addition, the popularity of U.S. culture in Canada has challenged the efforts of Canadian leaders to establish a separate identity for their country.

Early European exploration. About A.D. 1000, Vikings from Iceland and Greenland became the first known Europeans to reach North America. The Vikings, led by Leif Eriksson, landed somewhere on the northeast coast, a region the explorer called Vinland. The Vikings established a colony in Vinland, but they lived there only a short time. Some historians believe that Vinland was located in what is now Maine or Massachusetts. Others think it was in what is now the province of Newfoundland and Labrador. Ruins of a Viking settlement have been found at L'Anse aux Meadows, on the northern tip of the island of Newfoundland.

Depiction of John Cabot discovering Canada

Hudson Bay is named for Henry Hudson.

Lasting contact between Europe and America began with the voyage of Christopher Columbus in 1492. Columbus sailed west from Spain to find a short sea route to the Indies, as Europeans called eastern Asia. This region was known for its jewels, silks, spices, and other luxury goods. When Columbus landed in America, he thought he had reached the Indies.

In 1497, King Henry VII of England hired an Italian navigator, John Cabot, to cross the Atlantic Ocean in search of a shorter route to Asia than the one Columbus had taken. No one knows exactly where Cabot landed. Most historians say he may have landed somewhere between what are now the islands of Newfoundland and Nova Scotia. Cabot claimed the area for England. He found no such luxuries as jewels or spices. But he saw an enormous amount of cod and other fishes in the waters southeast of Newfoundland. Reports of the rich fishing soon brought large European fishing fleets to Canada.

By the early 1500s, some Europeans realized that Columbus had reached an unknown land, which they called the New World. In 1534, King Francis I of France sent Jacques Cartier, a French navigator, to the New World to look for gold and other valuable metals. Cartier sailed into the Gulf of St. Lawrence. He landed on the Gaspe Peninsula and claimed it for France. In 1535, on a second trip, Cartier became the first European to reach the interior of Canada. He sailed up the St. Lawrence River to the site of present-day Montreal. In 1541, on a third visit, Cartier joined a French expedition that hoped to establish a permanent settlement in Canada. But the colony lasted only until 1543.

The Development of New France (1604–1688)

Many French fishing crews sailed to Canada in the early 1500s. They helped develop a thriving fishing industry off the east coast. But they played an even more important role in Canada's growth by establishing the fur trade. The fur trade led to the development of a French colonial empire in North America. This empire, known as New France, lasted about 150 years and established the French culture and heritage in Canada.

Start of the fur trade. The French fishermen who came to Canada landed on the coast to preserve their catches by drying them in the sun. They met Indians who wanted to trade furs for fishhooks, kettles, knives, and other European goods. A brisk trade soon developed. During the second half of the 1500s, felt hats made from beaver fur became tremendously popular in Europe. As a result, the value of Canadian beaver pelts soared. During the late 1500s, more and more French ships sailed to Canada to pick up beaver fur. Traders also supplied such furs as fox, marten, mink, and otter.

Meanwhile, English explorers searched for a water passage to Asia through northern Canada. During the late 1500s, these explorers included Humphrey Gilbert, Martin Frobisher, and John Davis. In 1610, an English sea captain named Henry Hudson sailed into Hudson Bay in his search for the passage. England later based its claim to the vast Hudson Bay region on this voyage.

Early settlements. In 1603, King Henry IV of France completed plans to organize the fur trade and to set up a colony in Canada. The next year, a French explorer named Pierre du Gua (or du Guast), Sieur de Monts, led a small group of settlers to a site near the mouth of the St. Croix River. The river is on the border between what is now New Brunswick and Maine. In 1605, the settlers left that spot and founded Port-Royal (later moved to the site of Annapolis Royal in Nova Scotia). The French called their colony Acadia.

In 1608, another French explorer, Samuel de Champlain, founded a settlement along the St.

Lawrence River. He named the village Quebec. Champlain made friends with the Algonquin and Huron Indians living nearby and began to trade with them for furs. The two tribes also wanted French help in wars against their main enemy, the powerful Iroquois Indians. In 1609, Champlain and two other French fur traders helped their Indian friends defeat the Iroquois in battle. After this battle, the Iroquois were also enemies of the French.

The Huron lived in an area the French called Huronia. Champlain persuaded the Huron to allow Roman Catholic missionaries to work among them and introduce them to Christianity. The missionaries, especially an order known as the Jesuits, explored much of what is now southern Ontario.

Threats to expansion. Champlain hoped Quebec would become a large settlement, but it remained only a small trading post for many years. By 1625, about 60 people lived there.

New France failed to attract settlers partly because of threats from English colonists as well as from the Iroquois. Like France, England claimed much of what is now eastern Canada. England based its claims on explorations dating from Cabot's landing in 1497. During the early 1600s, many English colonists settled along the east coast of North America south of New France. Numerous disputes over fur-trading rights broke out between the French and the English. In 1629, English forces captured the town of Quebec. The French regained the town in 1632.

During the late 1640s, the Iroquois conquered Huronia and killed most of the French missionaries. The Algonquin and Huron fled, leaving the French to fight the Iroquois alone. During the next 10 years, the Iroquois increased their attacks on the French. Many settlers were killed, and the French fur trade was destroyed.

The royal province. In 1663, King Louis XIV made New France a *royal province* (colony) of France. He sent troops to Canada to fight the Iroquois and appointed administrators to govern and develop the colony. The chief official was the governor. A bishop directed the church and missionary work, and a person called an *intendant* managed most other local affairs. The French troops mounted attacks on Iroquois country, forcing some tribes to make peace with the French in the late 1660s. Afterward, frontiersmen known as *coureurs de bois* again developed the fur trade into the chief economic activity of New France.

Hudson's Bay Company trading post

Louis XIV also promoted the *seigneurial system* to encourage farming in New France. Under this system, the king gave land in the colony to several groups, including French military officers and merchants. The landholders, called *seigneurs*, brought farmers from France and rented them large sections of the land. Most of the farmers, called *habitants*, became prosperous. The population of New France grew from about 3,000 in 1666 to about 6,700 in 1673.

The boundaries of New France expanded rapidly to the west and south after Louis de Buade, Comte de Frontenac, became governor in 1672. The loss of the Huron fur trade forced the French to go farther inland to get new sources. As a result, Frontenac sent explorers to scout the Great Lakes and the Ohio and Mississippi river valleys.

In 1673, Louis Jolliet, a French-Canadian fur trader, and Jacques Marquette, a French missionary, sailed down the Mississippi River to its junction with the Arkansas River. The French soon built forts and fur-trading posts along the Great Lakes and along the Illinois and Mississippi rivers. In 1682, Rene-Robert Cavelier, Sieur de La Salle, reached the mouth of the Mississippi at the Gulf of Mexico. He claimed all the land drained by the river and its branches for France.

The growing French-English rivalry. The boundaries of English colonies south of New France also expanded during the late 1600s. Settlers poured into the English colonies and pushed the frontier westward, nearer New France. In 1670, an English firm called the Hudson's Bay

Company opened fur-trading posts north of New France on the shores of Hudson Bay.

Clashes between England and France in Europe contributed to their rivalry in North America. Other factors also created tension between the English and French colonists. For example, most of the French were Roman Catholics, and the majority of the English were Protestants. Most of the French wanted land for fur trading. The English wanted it for farming. In addition, French and English fur traders competed against each other.

During the 1730s, French-Canadian fur traders traveled farther inland and claimed more land for France. By 1738, Pierre Gaultier de Varennes, Sieur de La Verendrye, had established a chain of fur-trading posts between Montreal and what is now Saskatchewan.

British Conquest and Rule (1689–1815)

The French and English colonists fought each other in four wars between 1689 and 1763. These conflicts led to the United Kingdom's conquest of New France. The British government then worked hard to win the support of its new French-Canadian subjects. During the late 1700s and early 1800s, Canadian explorers pushed westward across the continent.

The colonial wars. The first three of the four wars between the French and English colonists broke out in Europe before spreading to America. These wars in America were King William's War (1689–1697), Queen Anne's War (1702–1713), and King George's War (1744–1748). Only after the second war did either side gain territory. In 1713, under the Treaty of Utrecht, France gave the United Kingdom Newfoundland, the mainland Nova Scotia region of Acadia, and the Hudson Bay territory.

The fourth war began in the Ohio River Valley in 1754 and lasted until 1763. It spread to Europe in 1756 and became known as the Seven Years' War there and in Canada. The conflict, which is called the French and Indian War in the United States, marked the final chapter in the struggle between the French and British colonists in America. The British had a number of advantages during the war. For example, there were more than a million British colonists compared with about 65,000 French settlers. The British colonies also received greater military support from the United Kingdom than New France did from France. In

Portrait of James Wolfe

addition, the British had the help of the Iroquois, the strongest Indian group in the east.

The French did well at first, but the tide of battle slowly turned against them. British armies, backed by the British Royal Navy, captured Quebec City in 1759. Both opposing generals, the Marquis de Montcalm of France and James Wolfe of the United Kingdom, were fatally wounded in the battle. The British seized Montreal in 1760, and the fighting in America ended. In the Peace of Paris, signed in 1763, France surrendered most of New France to the United Kingdom.

The Quebec Act. The United Kingdom gave the name Quebec to the area that made up most of its new territory in Canada. It added some of the new territory to Nova Scotia and Newfoundland. At first, the United Kingdom governed Quebec under British laws, which denied Catholics the rights to vote, to be elected, or to hold public office. This policy affected nearly all the colony's French Canadians. Quebec's first two British governors, Generals James Murray and Guy Carleton, opposed the policy because they wanted the United Kingdom to gain the loyalty of the French. Carleton also was aware of discontent in the 13 colonies to the south, then known as the American Colonies. He knew that the United Kingdom would need the support of the French Canadians if an American rebellion broke out.

In 1774, Carleton persuaded the British Parliament to pass the Quebec Act. This act recognized French civil and religious rights. It also preserved the seigneurial landholding system and extended Quebec to include much of what is now Quebec, Ontario, and the Midwestern United States.

The Revolutionary War in America began in 1775. The Americans asked the French Canadians to join their rebellion against the United Kingdom. But the French regarded the war mainly as a conflict between the United Kingdom and British colonies and chose to remain neutral. An American invasion of Canada in 1775 failed.

The United Empire Loyalists. After the Revolutionary War began, many people in the American Colonies remained loyal to the United Kingdom. About 40,000 of them moved to Canada during and after the war. These colonists became known as United Empire Loyalists. They settled mainly in western parts of the colonies of Nova Scotia and Quebec. Those who moved to Nova Scotia soon demanded a colony of their own. In 1784, the British government created the colony of New Brunswick out of western Nova Scotia for the Loyalists.

The Loyalists in Quebec also became unhappy. The Quebec Act gave the Catholic Church a special position in the colony. But most Loyalists were Protestants. In addition, the act did not permit the colony to have its own elected legislature. The Loyalists demanded a government like the one they had before the revolution—one that allowed them to choose their own public officials.

The British solution was the Constitutional Act of 1791. This act divided Quebec into two colonies, Lower Canada and Upper Canada. Lower Canada occupied the area along the lower St. Lawrence River. Upper Canada covered the area near the Great Lakes and the upper St. Lawrence. Each colony had its own elected assembly, though the legislatures had little real power. Each colony also had a lieutenant governor and a Legislative Council. The lieutenant governor and council members, who were appointed by the British, controlled the government. French Canadians formed the vast majority of the population in Lower Canada. The government there was based on principles of French civil law, Catholicism, and the seigneurial system. English-speaking Canadians made up the majority in Upper Canada. Local officials followed the traditions of English law and property systems.

Exploration of the West. The Revolutionary War in America led to major developments in the Canadian fur trade. After the United Kingdom gained control of New France in 1763, hundreds of British merchants settled in Montreal and soon took over the French fur trade. Like the French, they obtained most of their furs from Indians in the Ohio and Mississippi river valleys. But most of this area became part of the United States after the Revolutionary War. British merchants in Montreal thus had to look elsewhere for furs. By 1784, they had formed a firm called the North West Company to trade north and west of the Great Lakes. The Hudson's Bay Company already had trading posts in that territory, and a great rivalry developed between the two companies.

In its search for new and better fur-trading areas, the North West Company sent explorers across the unknown western lands. Alexander Mackenzie reached the Mackenzie River in 1789 and the Pacific Ocean in 1793. Simon Fraser followed the Fraser River to the Pacific in 1808. David Thompson mapped the west and navigated the full length of the Columbia River in 1811.

In 1811, Lord Selkirk, a Scottish colonizer, sent a group of Scottish and Irish immigrants to establish a settlement on the Red River in what is now Manitoba. The settlement became known as the Red River Colony. In 1821, the Hudson's Bay Company took over the North West Company and gained control of nearly all Canadian territory west of the Great Lakes.

Alexander Mackenzie

The War of 1812 developed out of fighting between the United Kingdom and France in Europe. During this conflict, the British set up a naval blockade of France and so interfered with U.S. ships bound for French ports. They also stopped American ships and seized sailors of British birth on them. As a result of these actions, the United States declared war on the United Kingdom on June 18, 1812. American troops tried to capture Upper and Lower Canada during the war, but British and Canadian troops defeated two major invasion attempts. The war ended in 1815. The Canadian and British forces claimed victory because they had held off much larger American forces. Neither side actually won, but the war promoted a sense of unity and patriotism in Canada.

The Struggle for Responsible Government (1816–1867)

Canada's population began to soar during the early 1800s as thousands of immigrants came from

A statue of Queen Victoria stands in front of the Parliament building.

the United Kingdom. During the 1840s, leaders in some Canadian colonies pushed for *responsible government* (self-government) in local affairs. In a system of responsible government, the executive is *responsible* (answerable) to an elected assembly. The United Kingdom gradually granted all the colonies such government. During the mid-1860s, some colonial leaders argued that Canada needed a strong central government to deal with domestic matters. They started a movement for a *confederation* (union) of the Canadian colonies. This movement led to the formation of the Dominion of Canada in 1867.

Growing discontent. After the War of 1812, Canada began to attract large numbers of immigrants from England, Ireland, and Scotland. French Canadians resented the flood of English-speaking newcomers. Many of the French believed that the British government wanted to destroy the French heritage in Canada.

By the 1820s, most French Canadians had become very bitter toward the English-speaking Canadians in Lower Canada. The French controlled the legislature, but the English controlled the Legislative Council. The council, in turn, ran the government. It spent much of the colony's tax money on projects to benefit commerce. French Canadians owned few businesses, however, and so opposed these expenses. The French also feared that the council intended to help English-speaking Canadians take over French-Canadian farms.

Upper Canada also faced serious political problems during the early 1800s. Church leaders, merchants, and landowners there formed a group known as the Family Compact. This group controlled the colonial government. It often cooperated with the lieutenant governor to block the demands of the farmers in the assembly. The Family Compact also used tax money to support Church of England schools, though many Upper Canadians belonged to other religious groups.

The uprisings of 1837. By the late 1830s, many people in Upper and Lower Canada had lost faith in their colonial governments. In November 1837, a revolt broke out in Lower Canada. It was headed by Louis Joseph Papineau, a fiery French Canadian who was a leader in the assembly. Papineau's followers briefly controlled parts of the countryside of Lower Canada. But the seigneurs and the high church officials remained loyal to the United Kingdom. British troops and colonial militia quickly crushed the revolt, and the rebel leaders fled to the United States.

News of the fighting in Lower Canada triggered a rebellion in Upper Canada in December 1837. William Lyon Mackenzie, a member of the Reform Party in the assembly, led the revolt. The colonial militia defeated the rebels in a brief battle, and Mackenzie escaped to the United States.

Lord Durham's report. The rebellions in Upper and Lower Canada convinced the British government that it had serious problems in Canada. In 1838, Queen Victoria sent Lord Durham, a British diplomat, to investigate the causes of the uprisings. Durham finished his report in 1839. He recommended that Upper and Lower Canada be united. He also recommended that the Canadian colonies be allowed to handle their local affairs. Both of these ideas had been suggested earlier, and Durham's report did little to influence their eventual adoption by the British government. In 1840, the British Parliament passed the Act of Union. This law, which took effect in 1841, united the two Canadas into one colony, the Province of Canada.

The beginning of self-government. During the 1840s, several colonial leaders fought for responsible government. These leaders included Robert Baldwin and Louis H. Lafontaine in the Province of Canada and Joseph Howe in Nova Scotia. Many officials in the United Kingdom had come to regard the colonies more as a burden than as a benefit, and they supported the self-government movement. The Province of Canada and Nova Scotia gained responsible government in 1848. Nearly all the other Canadian colonies received it soon afterward.

During the mid-1800s, the Canadian colonies expanded trade with the United States. Railways linked more and more towns in the colonies, and new canals became busy transportation routes. These developments and the rapid growth of the fishing, flour-milling, lumber, and textile industries brought prosperity to the Canadian colonies. The

American Civil War (1861–1865) also greatly increased demands for Canadian goods.

In spite of responsible government, political problems still troubled the Province of Canada. The main opposing political parties had nearly equal representation in the legislature. As a result, no party could gain a majority of seats or direct the government for long. By the early 1860s, some political leaders had suggested that the colony's problems could be solved only by splitting it again and creating a confederation of the two colonies. The union would give French- and English-speaking Canadians the same central government but would allow them to control their own local affairs.

Confederation. The fear of United States expansion into Canada helped attract support for a Canadian confederation. Many Canadians felt certain that the United States wanted to control all North America and would invade Canada after the Civil War ended.

John A. Macdonald, George Etienne Cartier, and other leaders from the Province of Canada headed the campaign for a federal union. In September 1864, they attended a conference of leaders from the Atlantic colonies who were meeting in Charlottetown, Prince Edward Island, to plan a union of their own. The Canadians persuaded them to abandon their plan in favor of a larger union. Another conference was held in Quebec City. The final details for confederation were worked out there in October.

In 1865, the Province of Canada approved the confederation plan. However, Newfoundland and Prince Edward Island rejected it, fearing that they would lose control over local affairs. New Brunswick and Nova Scotia adopted the plan in 1866. Later that same year, officials from Canada, New Brunswick, and Nova Scotia went to London, where they presented the plan to the British government.

In March 1867, the British Parliament passed the British North America Act. This act established the Dominion of Canada. The Dominion used the British parliamentary form of government. It had an elected House of Commons and an appointed Senate, each with almost equal power. A prime minister, usually the leader of the political party with the most seats in the House of Commons, headed the new federal government. The United Kingdom continued to handle the colony's foreign affairs, and the British monarch served as head of state.

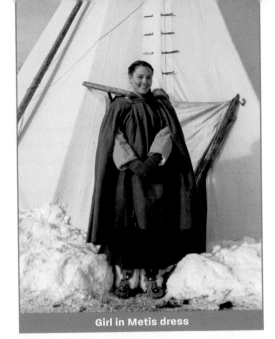
Girl in Metis dress

The British North America Act took effect on July 1, 1867. The new Dominion had four provinces— New Brunswick, Nova Scotia, Ontario, and Quebec. Quebec had formerly been Lower Canada, and Ontario had been Upper Canada. The British North America Act provided that other provinces could join the Dominion. Macdonald, leader of the Liberal-Conservative Party, became the country's first prime minister.

Growth of the Dominion (1868–1913)

The young Dominion of Canada developed rapidly during the late 1800s. A railway connected western and eastern Canada, and courageous pioneers spread across the west. By the early 1900s, the Dominion had nine provinces spanning the continent. Huge wheat crops, rich mines, and new industries brought further economic expansion in this period. In addition, Canada became increasingly involved in international affairs.

New provinces. Macdonald's chief goal as prime minister was to extend the Dominion to the west coast. He immediately turned his attention to the vast, largely unsettled northwest. This territory, called Rupert's Land, was owned by the Hudson's Bay Company. Macdonald worked out an agreement to buy the region in 1869.

About 12,000 people lived in or near the settlement of Red River in Rupert's Land. Most of them were *Metis* (people of mixed white and Indian ancestry). The Metis feared that the transfer of the area to Canada would bring a flood of white settlers who would take their lands. In 1869, Louis Riel, a settler of French and Indian descent, led the Metis in a revolt against the Canadian government. British and Canadian troops easily put down the rebellion.

In 1870, the Dominion took possession of Rupert's Land. At the same time, it acquired the North West Territory from the United Kingdom. This vast territory lay north, west, and south of Rupert's Land. The government combined these two new possessions into the North West Territories, which later became the Northwest Territories. Later in 1870, the government created Manitoba, Canada's fifth province, from part of Rupert's Land. The government also set aside 1,400,000 acres (567,000 hectares) in Manitoba for the Metis.

In 1871, the Pacific coast colony of British Columbia became Canada's sixth province. It agreed to join the Dominion in return for construction of a railway to the Pacific coast. In 1873, the eastern colony of Prince Edward Island became Canada's seventh province.

The Pacific Scandal. Macdonald led the Conservative Party to victory in the election of 1872. Afterward, the government chose a company headed by Sir Hugh Allan to build the railway wanted by British Columbia to the Pacific coast. But the so-called Pacific Scandal stalled the project. The scandal broke out in 1873, when it was revealed that the Conservative Party had accepted a campaign contribution of about $300,000 from Allan in 1872. Leaders of the opposing Liberal Party charged that Allan's group got the railroad contract because of its campaign gift. Macdonald did not use any of the money for his own election, but he resigned as prime minister. In November 1873, Alexander Mackenzie, leader of the Liberal Party, became prime minister.

The return of Macdonald. Mackenzie's government promoted honest and efficient elections by introducing the secret ballot and the one-day national election. It also won the United Kingdom's approval of a policy limiting the authority of the governor general—the British monarch's representative in Canada. The new policy required the governor general to respect decisions made by Canadian officials in the country's internal affairs. In 1875, Mackenzie established the Supreme Court of Canada. The court lessened British control over Canada's legal matters.

The Mackenzie government became increasingly unpopular after 1875, when a worldwide depression caused a severe business slump in Canada. Mackenzie had little success in reversing the decline, and Macdonald led the Conservatives to victory in the election of 1878.

In 1879, Macdonald began the National Policy, a program calling for high tariffs (taxes) on imported goods. The program was designed to help Canada's industries grow. It raised the cost of foreign products and made Canadian products less costly by comparison. Macdonald was also determined to complete the stalled coast-to-coast railroad. In 1880, the government gave the Canadian Pacific Railway Company a contract to finish the job.

The North West Rebellion. During the 1870s, many of the Metis in Manitoba moved westward into what is now Saskatchewan. But they again began to fear the loss of their land during the mid-1880s because of the near completion of the transcontinental railroad and government plans to attract settlers to the prairies.

In March 1885, Riel led another Metis uprising, the North West Rebellion. More than 7,000 government troops ended the rebellion within three months. Riel was found guilty of treason and was hanged on November 16, 1885.

Progress under Laurier. Workers laid the final stretch of Canadian Pacific Railway tracks in 1885. Regularly scheduled passenger service began the next year. The transcontinental railroad in time led to a great rush to settle Canada's fertile western prairies. This activity contributed to a major period of progress that began after the Liberal Party won the election of 1896. Wilfrid Laurier, the Liberal Party leader and a Quebec Catholic, became Canada's first French-Canadian prime minister.

Canada's population soared during Laurier's administration. More than 2 million immigrants, most of them from Europe, flocked to Canada between 1896 and 1911. Many settled in such cities as Montreal, Toronto, and Winnipeg. But

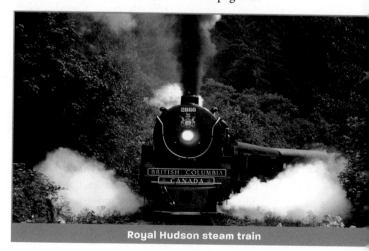
Royal Hudson steam train

hundreds of thousands of others took up farming on the prairies. In 1905, the government created two new provinces out of the prairies, Alberta and Saskatchewan.

Canada's economy flourished under Laurier. Farmers in the Prairie Provinces produced huge wheat harvests, and Europe became a great market for Canadian wheat. Aided by the continuing high tariffs, Canada's flour-milling, steel, and textile industries grew quickly. Nova Scotia coal mines thrived, and mining areas opened or expanded in Ontario, British Columbia, and the Klondike region of northern Canada. New hydroelectric power plants and two new transcontinental railroads, the Grand Trunk Pacific and the Canadian Northern, helped make the early 1900s Canada's most prosperous period since 1867.

Foreign relations. Canada's role in the British Empire became an issue when the Anglo-Boer War of 1899–1902 broke out between the British and the Boers in southern Africa. Many Canadians had great pride in the empire and wanted Canada to send troops to help the British forces. But a large number of French Canadians opposed Canada's participation in foreign wars. Laurier compromised by organizing, equipping, and transporting two contingents of volunteers, who were paid mainly by the United Kingdom after they reached South Africa.

In 1910, a controversy developed over a trade treaty between Canada and the United States. The treaty allowed each country to export numerous products to the other without paying high tariffs. But many Canadian business executives feared the trade agreement would destroy industries in Canada aided by the tariffs.

Another dispute involving Canada's obligations to the empire arose in 1910. The United Kingdom faced the threat of war with Germany and asked Canada to supply ships and sailors for the British Royal Navy. Laurier responded by announcing a plan to build a separate Canadian navy that could be lent to the United Kingdom in time of war. But English-speaking Canadians insisted that Canada contribute directly to the Royal Navy. Many French Canadians also opposed Laurier's plan, charging that it would involve Canada in foreign wars.

Opposition to the trade agreement and the naval plan led to the defeat of Laurier's party in the election of 1911. Robert L. Borden, head of the victorious Conservative Party, became prime minister.

Canada's first French-Canadian prime minister, Wilfrid Laurier

World War I and Independence (1914–1931)

Canada entered World War I (1914–1918) to aid the United Kingdom and its allies. Canada's participation in the war enabled it to act more freely in establishing its own foreign policies. In 1931, the Dominion won complete independence from the United Kingdom.

World War I. The United Kingdom's declaration of war on Germany on August 4, 1914, created a tremendous burst of patriotism in Canada. Thousands of Canadians rushed to volunteer for military duty. Canadian troops first saw combat in April 1915. They helped halt the first German gas attack of the war during the Second Battle of Ypres in Belgium. The greatest Canadian triumph came in the Battle of Vimy Ridge in France on April 9, 1917. In the battle, about 100,000 Canadian troops captured the strong German positions on a hill called Vimy Ridge. Billy Bishop, a Canadian flier, shot down 72 German planes during the war and became one of its most famous combat pilots. More than 600,000 Canadians served in the armed forces during World War I, and about 60,000 died.

World War I contributed enormously to Canada's industrial strength. The country's steel industry thrived through the sale of ships, artillery shells, and other equipment to the United Kingdom. Wartime demand also greatly expanded agricultural output, especially the production of beef cattle and wheat.

Canadian soldiers preparing for World War I

The conscription issue. When World War I began, Borden promised that Canada would not *conscript* (draft) men for overseas military service. He knew that French Canadians bitterly opposed conscription. Early in the war, large numbers of volunteers made a draft needless. By early 1917, however, Canadian forces had suffered high casualties, and the number of volunteers had dropped sharply. As a result, Borden established conscription in July 1917. He received strong support from English-speaking Canadians, but French Canadians strongly objected.

To make conscription work, Borden decided to form a *coalition* (joint) Conservative-Liberal government, which he called the Union government. Borden tried to bring Wilfrid Laurier and other Liberal Party leaders into the coalition. But Laurier opposed conscription and refused to join. The Liberals then split into two groups. One group, the Unionist Liberals, backed conscription. The other group remained loyal to Laurier. Borden appointed a number of Unionist Liberals to his government and called for an election in December 1917. The Unionists won every province except Quebec.

A larger role in the empire's affairs. Borden became increasingly dissatisfied with Canada's colonial status in view of its major contribution to the British war effort. In 1917, Borden and the leaders of other dominions in the British Empire began to demand greater participation in developing foreign and defense policies. The British needed soldiers and weapons from the dominions and so agreed to their demands.

After World War I, Borden and the other dominion prime ministers were members of the British Empire's peace delegation in Paris in 1919. They signed the Treaty of Versailles, which officially ended the war with Germany. In addition, all the dominions became original members of the League of Nations, an international peacekeeping agency formed in 1920.

Labor and farm unrest. While Borden attended the peace conference in Paris, trouble mounted at home. Workers throughout Canada demanded higher wages, better working conditions, and recognition of their unions. Farmers wanted relief from low crop prices and urged reductions in freight rates. Dissatisfied farmers formed political parties in almost every province. Farmer parties won control of the provincial government in Ontario in 1919 and in Alberta in 1921. In the national election of 1921, the Liberal Party gained a majority of the seats in the House of Commons, and William Lyon Mackenzie King became prime minister.

In 1921, Agnes Macphail became the first woman to serve in the Canadian House of Commons. She was elected to represent the United Farmers of Ontario.

Independence. King was determined to establish Canada's independence in foreign affairs. In 1922, he refused to support the United Kingdom in a possible war with Turkey and rejected a request for Canadian troops. On King's insistence, Canada for the first time signed a treaty alone with another nation in 1923. The treaty, with the United States, regulated halibut fishing in the Pacific Ocean.

In 1926, King and representatives from the other dominions met with British representatives at an Imperial Conference in London. At the conference, King joined a successful fight for dominion independence. The dominion and British representatives declared the dominions to be independent members of the British Commonwealth of Nations, as the British Empire then became known. In 1931, the British Parliament passed the

Statute of Westminster, which legalized the declaration. This act thus officially recognized Canada and the other self-governing dominions as independent nations.

The Young Nation (1932–1957)

During the 1930s, the young Canadian nation suffered through the Great Depression. The hard economic times ended when production rose during World War II (1939–1945). After the war, an industrial boom at home helped make Canada a major economic power. The nation also became greatly involved in world affairs.

The Great Depression began in 1929 with the stock market crash in the United States and spread throughout the world. The depression caused a sharp drop in foreign trade and especially hurt the demand for Canadian food products, lumber, and minerals. The decline in export income forced thousands of Canadian factories and stores, plus many coal mines, to close. Hundreds of thousands of Canadians lost their jobs and homes. A rapid fall in grain prices and a severe drought worsened the depression in the Prairie Provinces.

Unemployment was the chief issue in the election of 1930. King's government was defeated, and the Conservatives came to power under Richard B. Bennett. Bennett's government established more than 200 relief camps for single, unemployed men and spent hundreds of millions of dollars to aid the needy.

Bennett dealt harshly with strikers and demonstrators and earned the nickname "Iron Heel Bennett." But he also saw the need for reform. His government created a number of important federal agencies, including the Canadian Radio Broadcasting Commission in 1932, the Bank of Canada in 1934, and the Canadian Wheat Board in 1935. Canada's economic problems continued, however, and many Canadians blamed Bennett for failing to ease the hard times. Bennett's unpopularity led to the formation of new political parties, which included the Co-operative Commonwealth Federation in 1932 and the Social Credit Party in 1935. In the election of 1935, the Liberal Party regained control of the House of Commons. King then began his third term as prime minister.

World War II. Canada declared war on Germany on September 10, 1939. It declared war on Japan on December 8, 1941, the day after Japan attacked United States bases at Pearl Harbor in Hawaii. The Canadian Army first saw action in December 1941, when it participated in the unsuccessful attempt to defend Hong Kong against a Japanese invasion. In August 1942, the Army suffered heavy losses in the Allied assault on the French port of Dieppe.

Canadian troops also took part in the Allied invasion of Sicily in 1943 and in the battle for Italy. The Third Canadian Division participated in the Allied landing at Normandy in France on June 6, 1944. The First Canadian Army, commanded by General H. D. G. Crerar, fought its way through the Netherlands and advanced into northern Germany. The Royal Canadian Air Force aided the Allies, and the Canadian Navy helped protect Allied ships in the Atlantic Ocean. By the end of the war, more than a million Canadian men and women had served in the armed forces. More than 90,000 had been killed or wounded.

The Canadian government lent billions of dollars to the war cause. It sent the British people large quantities of food during the Battle of Britain. Canadian factories built thousands of planes, ships, and weapons.

When World War II began, King pledged to keep recruiting voluntary for overseas service. In 1942, however, the government asked Canadian voters to release it from a pledge not to send draftees abroad. The vast majority of voters approved the request, though many French Canadians opposed it. However, no Canadian draftees went overseas until November 1944.

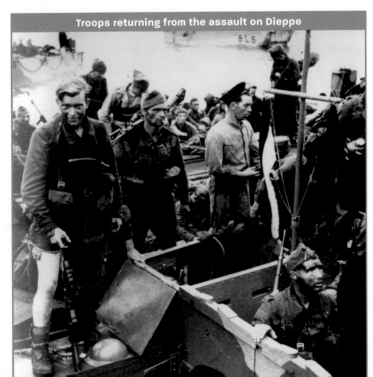
Troops returning from the assault on Dieppe

The war was especially tragic for Canadians of Japanese descent and for newly arrived immigrants from Japan. Japanese Canadians came under widespread distrust after Japan attacked Pearl Harbor. In February 1942, the Canadian government began to place about 21,000 of them in camps and isolated towns in Alberta, British Columbia, Manitoba, and Ontario. Their rights were not restored until 1949. Most of the Japanese Canadians lost their homes and businesses.

The government adopted several important social programs during the war. It established the beginning of a social security system by introducing unemployment insurance in 1940. In 1944, it adopted a program that assisted families by providing financial aid for children. As the war came to an end, the government began a vast benefits program to help veterans return to civilian life.

The postwar boom. Canada's economy thrived after World War II. Canadians spent their wartime savings on appliances and other household goods. A great demand for housing created a construction boom. The development of Canada's incredibly rich mineral deposits also flourished. The country became an important producer of asbestos, copper, iron ore, nickel, oil, uranium, and other minerals. Foreign investors, mainly from the United States, helped finance the development of many new industries. By the late 1950s, Canada had changed from a chiefly agricultural country to one of the world's great industrial nations.

Meanwhile, Canada experienced another great wave of immigration. From 1945 to 1956, more than a million people from Germany, Italy, and other war-torn European countries moved to Canada. Many of the immigrants settled in Toronto, Montreal, and other large cities. Suburbs grew rapidly outside the central cities.

Increasing foreign involvement. King retired as prime minister in November 1948. Louis St. Laurent, the new Liberal Party leader, became Canada's second French-Canadian prime minister. One of the first highlights of his administration occurred in March 1949, when Newfoundland (now Newfoundland and Labrador) became Canada's 10th province. Under St. Laurent, Canada played an ever-larger role in international affairs.

Canada's prestige and economic strength after World War II convinced many Canadians that their nation's interests required active involvement in foreign affairs. In 1945, Canada became an original member of the United Nations (UN). In 1949, it signed a treaty with the United States and 10 Western European nations that set up the North Atlantic Treaty Organization (NATO). NATO was the first military alliance Canada had joined in peacetime.

During the Korean War (1950–1953), Canada contributed about 22,000 soldiers to the UN forces fighting North Korea's invasion of South Korea. Canada helped bring about peace in the Middle East after the United Kingdom, France, and Israel invaded Egypt in 1956. Lester B. Pearson, Canada's secretary of state for external affairs, won the 1957 Nobel Peace Prize for proposing and organizing a UN peacekeeping force for the troubled area.

The end of Liberal rule. Canadians took pride in the government's accomplishments in foreign affairs. But they were stunned in 1956, when the government broke the rules of Parliament to push through a bill to finance construction of a natural gas pipeline. John G. Diefenbaker, leader of the Progressive Conservative Party, charged that St. Laurent's government had abused its authority and insulted Parliament. Many voters agreed. In the election of 1957, Diefenbaker thus led his party to a narrow victory and ended 22 years of Liberal rule.

Challenges of the 1960s

Major economic and social problems troubled Canada in the 1960s. A business slump struck the country, and unemployment rose sharply. French Canadians began a movement to increase their political power. In Quebec, many French Canadians began to support a campaign to make their province a separate nation.

The North Atlantic Treaty

St. Lawrence Seaway

The new Conservative government.
Diefenbaker hoped to broaden his support in Parliament and called an election in 1958. The Progressive Conservatives won 208 of the 265 seats in the House of Commons, the largest majority in Canadian history. In 1959, Diefenbaker joined Queen Elizabeth II of the United Kingdom and U.S. President Dwight D. Eisenhower at the opening of the St. Lawrence Seaway. The seaway enables large commercial ships to sail between the Atlantic Ocean and the Great Lakes by way of the St. Lawrence River.

Diefenbaker faced a major political problem in 1959 when his government chose to buy American-made Bomarc missiles for defense at home instead of the more expensive Canadian-built Avro Arrow fighter planes. The government also bought United States fighters for Canada's contribution to NATO forces. The rejection of the Avro Arrow planes resulted in heavy criticism.

In 1960, a sagging economy challenged the Diefenbaker government. By 1961, 11 percent of Canadian workers had no jobs. The government responded by trying to increase foreign trade. It developed new markets for Canadian wheat in China and the Communist countries of Eastern Europe. In 1962, during an election campaign, the government attempted to boost the economy by lowering the value of the Canadian dollar. In the June election, the Conservatives won the most seats in the House of Commons but not a majority. The Diefenbaker government was able to stay in power only with the aid of the Social Credit Party, which had won 30 seats.

The Quebec separatist movement.
Diefenbaker also faced rising discontent in Quebec. In 1960, the Quebec Liberal Party gained control of the provincial government. Led by Jean Lesage, the new government started the Quiet Revolution, a movement to defend French-Canadian rights throughout the country. Many French Canadians believed they were barred from jobs in government and some large corporations because they spoke French. They also wanted English Canadians to recognize and respect Quebec's French heritage. Lesage also worked to increase Quebec's control over its own economy and to reduce such control by the federal government.

The Quiet Revolution awakened deep feelings of French-Canadian nationalism. In Quebec, it influenced the rise of *separatism*, the demand that the province separate from Canada and become an independent nation. In the early 1960s, several separatist groups entered candidates in provincial elections. Other groups, especially the Front de Liberation du Quebec (FLQ), used terrorism to promote separatism. In 1963, the FLQ began to bomb federal buildings and symbols of Canada that reflected the country's British traditions.

The return of the Liberals. Early in 1963, a controversy developed over whether Canada had agreed in 1959 to accept nuclear warheads for its Bomarc missiles. The missiles were effective only with such warheads. Diefenbaker had refused to accept the weapons because some members of his Cabinet opposed the use of nuclear arms. The Liberals in Parliament argued that Canada had agreed to take the warheads for use in the defense of North America. Lester B. Pearson, the Liberal leader, accused the government of failing to show leadership. In February, the House of Commons gave Diefenbaker's government a vote of no confidence. Diefenbaker was then forced to call a general election.

In the election of 1963, the Liberals won the most seats in the House but not a majority. Pearson became prime minister with support from several small opposition parties. His government accepted the nuclear warheads. It also expanded social welfare programs, introducing a national pension plan in 1964 and a national health insurance program in 1965.

Pearson achieved a personal goal when Canada adopted a new national flag. The country had long used the British Red Ensign with a coat of arms representing Canada's provinces. The Conservatives wanted to keep the Red Ensign as a symbol of Canada's British heritage. But in 1964, Parliament approved a design that featured a red maple leaf, a symbol of Canada. On February 15, 1965, Canada's new flag flew for the first time.

In April 1968, Pearson resigned as prime minister. His successor, Pierre Elliott Trudeau, became Canada's third French-Canadian prime minister. Trudeau called a national election for June 25. The campaign was marked by widespread enthusiasm that became known as "Trudeaumania." Canadians seemed to be madly in love with Trudeau, a dashing 48-year-old bachelor, and gave his party a majority of the seats in the House.

Canada Under Trudeau

Trudeau served as Canada's prime minister almost continuously until 1984. Under Trudeau, Canada at first had high hopes for economic expansion. But sharply rising prices and high unemployment caused problems. Canadian national unity was still threatened by the Quebec separatist movement. Canada also revised its constitution during this period.

Foreign affairs. During the early 1970s, Canada broadened its relations with the two leading Communist nations, China and the Soviet Union. In 1970, Canada and China agreed to

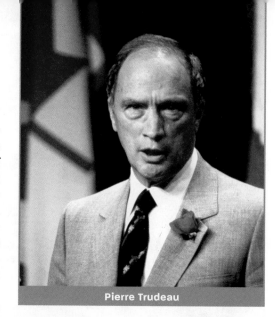

Pierre Trudeau

resume diplomatic relations, which had ended when the Communists gained control of China in 1949. In 1971, Trudeau and Soviet Premier Aleksei N. Kosygin exchanged visits. Canada increased trade with both China and the Soviet Union.

Relations between the Canadian and U.S. governments, however, became increasingly strained during the 1970s. The U.S. government disapproved of Canada's willingness to accept American men who crossed the border to avoid being drafted in the Vietnam War (1957–1975). The United States also objected to new policies that limited foreign ownership and financing of Canadian industries. In 1973, the Canadian Parliament established the Foreign Investment Review Agency to end conditions that had enabled U.S. companies to gain control of over half of Canada's manufacturing plants.

Canadians, in turn, became disturbed by threats to their environment from the United States. Trudeau objected to the Garrison Diversion Project in North Dakota, which threatened to pollute Canadian rivers. He also protested the polluting of Canadian lakes and rivers by acid rain resulting from chemicals released into the air by U.S. factories and power plants. Control of fishing waters and other offshore resources in the northeast Pacific and northwest Atlantic also became an issue between Canada and the United States.

The separatist threat. To curb the Quebec separatist movement, Trudeau pledged to create equal opportunities for French- and English-speaking Canadians throughout the nation. His first important move toward this goal was winning Parliament's approval of the Official Languages Act in 1969. This act requires federal facilities to provide service in French in areas where at least 10 percent of the people speak French. It also requires service in English in areas where at least 10 percent of the people speak that language. The law brought major changes to the government. However, it had little effect on the growing separatist movement.

Canada experienced one of its most serious political crises in October 1970, when the FLQ kidnapped two officials in Montreal. The officials were James R. Cross, the British trade commissioner in Montreal; and Pierre Laporte, Quebec's labor minister. The terrorists offered to exchange the two men for $500,000 and the release of 23 jailed FLQ members.

Trudeau rejected the offer. Instead, he put Canada's War Measures Act into effect. This act allows the government to suspend the civil liberties of people judged dangerous during wartime. The law had never been applied during peacetime. Police used the act to arrest hundreds of FLQ sympathizers during their search for the kidnapped officials. FLQ members murdered Laporte. They released Cross in December, when the government permitted the kidnappers to go to Cuba.

FLQ terrorism ended, but the separatist movement continued. The Parti Quebecois, organized as a separatist political party in 1968, won control of the government of Quebec in 1976. Rene Levesque, a member of the Quebec legislature and the party's leader, became premier of the province. In 1980, Levesque's government held a province-wide vote on a proposal to give provincial leaders authority to negotiate with the Canadian federal government for independence. About 60 percent of Quebec's voters rejected the proposal.

Economic developments. During the early 1970s, Canada's economy did not expand fast enough to keep pace with increases in the labor force. The country's difficulties grew after a recession and rapid inflation developed in the mid-1970s. During the 1970s, however, the energy-rich provinces of Alberta, Saskatchewan, and British Columbia began to benefit from a boom in the production of petroleum and natural gas. Their populations grew rapidly, and numerous corporations shifted their head offices from eastern to western Canada.

Trudeau's popularity began to decline during the mid-1970s. The Liberals lost the election of 1979 to the Progressive Conservatives, and Joe Clark became prime minister. Later that year, Clark announced a plan to conserve energy by raising fuel taxes. But strong opposition to the plan led the House of Commons to give the government a vote of no confidence. Clark then called a general election for February 1980. The Liberals won a majority in the House, and Trudeau returned as prime minister.

Canada's economic problems worsened in the early 1980s, when another recession struck. By March 1983, 14 percent of Canada's workers had no jobs—the highest unemployment rate since the Great Depression.

Constitutional changes. In 1981, Trudeau won acceptance of proposed changes in Canada's constitution from all provincial heads except Levesque. The proposals became part of the Constitution Act of 1982, which the British Parliament passed in March.

The Constitution Act eliminated the need for British approval of Canadian constitutional amendments. The act also included a new bill of rights called the Canadian Charter of Rights and Freedoms.

Trudeau resigned in June 1984 and was succeeded by John N. Turner. The Progressive Conservatives, led by Brian Mulroney, won the general election in September 1984. Mulroney succeeded Turner as prime minister.

Canada Under Mulroney

Foreign affairs. In 1988, Mulroney and U.S. President Ronald Reagan signed a major free-trade agreement. The agreement called for elimination of all tariffs and many nontariff trade barriers between the two countries by 1999. It went into effect on January 1, 1989.

During the early 1990s, Canada negotiated the North American Free Trade Agreement (NAFTA) with the United States and Mexico. This agreement called for the gradual elimination of tariffs and certain other trade barriers between the three countries. NAFTA took effect in 1994.

In military affairs, the Canadian Armed Forces took part in the Persian Gulf War of 1991. Canadian pilots flew bombing missions over Iraq and Kuwait from their station in Qatar, a country near Saudi Arabia. It was the first time Canadian forces had been at war since the Korean War ended in 1953.

The constitutional crisis. Hopes of winning Quebec's acceptance of the constitution grew in 1987. That year, Mulroney and the 10 provincial heads of government tentatively agreed to a far-reaching constitutional amendment at Meech Lake, Quebec, on April 30. They formally approved the accord in Ottawa on June 3.

Brian Mulroney

A key proposal in the agreement stated that Quebec was to be recognized as a distinct society in Canada. Also, each province could refuse participation in a wide range of new national programs and veto any future constitutional amendments that would involve federal institutions and the formation of new provinces.

To go into effect, the Meech Lake accord had to be ratified by all 10 provinces by June 23, 1990. It was ratified by only eight. Manitoba and Newfoundland withheld their support. Many opponents of the accord believed that it granted Quebec's provincial government too much power, especially over the rights of Quebec's English-speaking minority. After the failure of the accord, many Quebecers began to demand increased independence for Quebec from the rest of Canada.

In August 1992, Canada's 10 provincial heads of government agreed in Charlottetown, Prince Edward Island, to a new plan to revise the constitution. The plan provided for recognition of Quebec as a distinct society, the replacement of Canada's appointed Senate with an elected one, self-government for Canada's native peoples, and the transfer of some federal powers to the provinces.

Mulroney called for a nationwide vote on the Charlottetown accord. The referendum was held in October, and most Canadians, including a majority in Quebec, voted against it.

The 1993 national election. Mulroney resigned in June 1993 and was succeeded by Kim Campbell. In October of that year, Jean Chrétien led the Liberal Party to victory in a general election. He became prime minister in November. The ruling Progressive Conservative Party suffered one of the worst defeats in Canadian history, losing all but 2 of its 154 seats. Two regional parties became the second and third most powerful parties in the House. One of them, the Bloc Quebecois, favors sovereignty for Quebec. The other, the Reform Party, was an Alberta-based conservative party.

Canada Under Chrētien

Quebec referendum. In 1994, the separatist Parti Quebecois again gained control of the government of Quebec. In October 1995, Quebec voters narrowly defeated a referendum that called for independence for Quebec. The province remained part of Canada.

In late 1995 and early 1996, Parliament passed resolutions aimed at promoting national unity. One resolution recognized Quebec's unique language, culture, and civil law. A second granted five regions what amounted to a veto over changes in the Canadian constitution. The regions are Quebec, the Atlantic Provinces, Ontario, the Prairie Provinces, and British Columbia.

The 1997 and 2000 national elections. Chrétien called an election for June 1997. In the election, the Liberals again won a majority of seats in the House of Commons, and Chrétien remained as prime minister. The Reform Party came in second and replaced the Bloc Quebecois as the official opposition. In 2000, members of the Reform Party voted to join the newly created Canadian Reform Conservative Alliance. The new party, commonly called the Canadian Alliance, then became the official opposition in the House of Commons.

In 2000, Chrétien called an early election, and it was held in November. The Liberal Party increased its majority in the House of Commons, and Chrétien continued to serve as prime minister. The Canadian Alliance remained the official opposition.

Territorial and provincial changes. A new territory called Nunavut came into being in 1999. Nunavut was carved out of the eastern Northwest Territories. The new territory provides more self-government for the Inuit, who make up most of its population. In 2001, Canada's Parliament changed the official name of the province of Newfoundland to Newfoundland and Labrador.

Recent Developments

Jean Chrétien stepped down as Liberal Party leader and prime minister in 2003. Former finance minister Paul Martin succeeded Chrétien in both posts.

Prime Minister Jean Chrētien and his wife, Aline

Also in 2003, Canada's Progressive Conservative Party and the Canadian Alliance merged to form the Conservative Party of Canada. The new party became the official opposition in the House of Commons.

Prime Minister Martin called for a national election in 2004. As a result of the election, Martin's Liberal Party formed a *minority government*, and Martin remained prime minister. In a minority government, the ruling party holds the most, but not a majority of, seats in the House of Commons. The Conservatives placed second in the election and remained the official opposition.

In 2005, a commission of inquiry found that Chrétien's Liberal government had misused public funds as part of a program to promote national unity in the late 1990s and early 2000s. The opposition parties in the House then passed a vote of no confidence in the government. Martin was forced to dissolve Parliament and call for a new election.

The Conservatives, led by Stephen Harper, won a national election in 2006. Harper became prime minister of a minority government. Also in 2006, the House passed a motion to recognize "that the Québécois form a nation within a united Canada." The motion acknowledged Quebec's unique French cultural heritage.

In 2008, Prime Minister Harper publicly apologized to Canada's native peoples for wrongs done to them by the country's former *residential school* system. From the late 1800s to the late 1900s, thousands of native children were forced to attend boarding schools aimed at integrating them into mainstream society. Abuse and neglect often occurred at these schools.

In 2008, Harper called another general election. The election, held in October, again resulted in a minority Conservative government led by Harper.

In March 2011, a legislative committee found the Harper government in *contempt* of Parliament—that is, willfully disobedient to Parliament. The committee said the government had failed to provide accurate information about the cost of crime legislation and military equipment. It was the first time a Canadian government was found in contempt. The Conservatives lost the support of the House, and Harper adjourned Parliament. A general election took place on May 2, and the Conservatives won a majority of seats in the House. Harper remained prime minister. The New Democratic Party placed second and became the official opposition party for the first time.

In December 2011, Stephen Harper's government passed a law to end the monopoly of the Canadian Wheat Board (CWB) over Canadian grain sales. The law took effect in August 2012. Since the 1940s, Canadian grain farmers had been required to sell their wheat and barley through the Canadian Wheat Board.

MLA Citation

"Canada." *The Southwestern Advantage Topic Source.* Nashville: Southwestern. 2013.

DATA

Canada in Brief

General Information

Capital: Ottawa

Official languages: English and French.

National anthem: "O Canada"

National symbols: Maple leaf and beaver

Largest cities: (*2011 census*) Toronto (2,615,060); Montreal (1,649,519); Calgary (1,096,833); Ottawa (883,391); Edmonton (812,201); Mississauga (713,433); Winnipeg (633,617); Vancouver (603,502); Brampton (523,961); Hamilton (519,949).

Symbols of Canada: The flag of Canada features a red, 11-pointed maple leaf, a national symbol of the country, in a field of white. Two wide, vertical red stripes are at either side of the white. It became Canada's official flag in 1965. The Canadian coat of arms includes three red maple leaves below the royal arms of England, Scotland, Ireland, and France.

Land and Climate

Land: Canada lies in northern North America. It borders the United States and the Atlantic, Pacific, and Arctic oceans. Canada is mountainous in the west, where the Coastal and Rocky Mountains stand. The country is mostly flat or gently rolling from the eastern edge of the Rockies to the low Laurentian Mountains in Quebec. Several low mountain ranges rise in the east. Canada shares four of the five Great Lakes (all but Lake Michigan) with the United States. Its chief rivers include the Churchill, Fraser, Mackenzie, Nelson, and Saint Lawrence rivers.

Area: 3,855,103 mi² (9,984,670 km²), including 291,577 mi² (755,180 km²) of inland water. *Greatest distances*—east-west, 3,223 mi (5,187 km), from Cape Spear, Newfoundland and Labrador, to Mount St. Elias, Yukon; north-south, 2,875 mi (4,627 km), from Cape Columbia on Ellesmere Island to Middle Island in Lake Erie. *Coastline*—151,485 mi (243,791 km), including mainland and islands. *Shoreline*—Great Lakes, 5,251 mi (8,452 km).

Elevation: *Highest*—Mount Logan, 19,551 ft (5,959 m) above sea level. *Lowest*—sea level.

Climate: Canada is extremely frigid in the north and generally cold elsewhere. However, warmer temperatures occur along the west coast and in the far southeast. The west coast has mild summers and cool winters, with temperatures rarely falling much below freezing. The west coast also has abundant precipitation. Central Canada has short, mild to warm summers and bitterly cold winters. Far southeastern Canada (southeastern Ontario and the Atlantic coast) has warm summers and cool to cold winters.

DATA

Canada in Brief

Government

Form of government: Constitutional monarchy

Head of state: Queen Elizabeth II of the United Kingdom is queen of Canada. The queen, on the recommendation of Canada's prime minister, appoints a governor general to represent her.

Head of government: Prime minister

Parliament: *Senate*—105 members, appointed by the governor general on the recommendation of the prime minister. *House of Commons*—308 members elected by the people.

Political subdivisions: 10 provinces, 3 territories

People

Population: *Current estimate*—34,967,000; *2011 census*—33,476,688.

Population density: 9 per mi^2 (4 per km^2).

Population distribution: 80 percent urban, 20 percent rural.

Major ethnic/national groups: Mostly of European descent (chiefly British, Irish, and French, but also some Germans, Italians, and Ukrainians). Other groups include Asians (mostly Chinese, with Filipino, Indian, and Vietnamese) and American Indians and Inuit.

Major religions: Mostly Roman Catholic and Protestant. Other groups include Buddhists, Eastern Orthodox, Hindus, Jews, Muslims, and Sikhs.

Economy

Chief products: *Agriculture*—beef cattle, canola, chickens, eggs, floriculture and nursery products, hogs, milk, soybeans, wheat. *Fishing industry*—crab, lobster, shrimp. *Forestry*—fir, pine, spruce. *Manufacturing*—aluminum, steel, and other metals; chemicals; machinery; motor vehicles and parts; paper products; processed foods and beverages; wood products. *Mining*—coal, copper, gold, iron ore, natural gas, nickel, petroleum, potash, sulfur, uranium, zinc.

Money: Basic unit—Canadian dollar. One hundred cents equal one dollar.

International trade: *Major exports*—chemicals, forest products, machinery, motor vehicles and parts; petroleum; precious metals; wheat. *Major imports*—computers, pharmaceuticals, machinery, motor vehicles and parts, scientific equipment. *Major trading partners*—The United States is Canada's most important trading partner. Other major commercial partners of Canada include China, France, Germany, Japan, Mexico, South Korea, and the United Kingdom.

DATA

Economic Production in Canada

Economic activities	% of GDP[1] produced	Number of workers	% of all workers
Source: Statistics Canada; International Monetary Fund. Figures are for 2010.			
Community, business, & personal services	23	5,940,900[2]	35[2]
Finance, insurance, & real estate	21[2]	1,095,700	6
Trade, restaurants, & hotels	14	3,736,200	22
Manufacturing	13	1,744,300	10
Transportation & communication	8	1,571,700	9
Construction	6	1,217,200	7
Government	6	956,400	6
Mining	4	329,400[3]	2[3]
Agriculture	2[3]	300,700	2
Utilities	2	148,300	1
Total[4]	100	17,040,800	100

[1]GDP = gross domestic product, the total value of goods and services produced in a year.

[2]Includes figures from establishments that manage other companies.

[3]Includes figures from forestry and fishing.

[4]Figures may not add up to 100 percent due to rounding.

ADDITIONAL RESOURCES

Books to Read

Bone, Robert M. *The Regional Geography of Canada*. 4th ed. Oxford, 2008.

Bumsted, J. M. *Canada's Diverse Peoples*. ABC-CLIO, 2003.

Thompson, Wayne C. *Canada*. Stryker-Post, published annually.

Vance, Jonathan F. *A History of Canadian Culture*. Oxford, 2009.

Wiseman, Nelson. *In Search of Canadian Political Culture*. UBC Press, 2007.

Web Sites

Statistics Canada

http://www.statcan.gc.ca/start-debut-eng.html

Official statistics from Canada's federal government.

Government of Canada

http://canada.gc.ca/home.html

The official Web site of the government of Canada. Includes links to the government Web sites of Canada's territories and provinces.

Search Strings

Mounties Versus Policemen

Canada Mounties versus policemen (1,870)

Canada Mounties versus policemen "Royal Canadian Mounted Police" history (297)

Regions of Canada

Canada regions cultural economic land (171,000)

Regions of Canada land economic cultural (147,000)

Regions of Canada land economic cultural geography (120,000)

The Inuit

Canada Inuit Eskimos culture (155,000)

Canada Inuit Eskimos culture Nunavut (30,300)

Canada Inuit Eskimos culture Nunavut history (24,400)

Niagara Falls

Canada Niagara Falls Horseshoe Falls history (34,400)

Canada Niagara Falls Horseshoe Falls history (2,400)

Canada "Niagara Falls" "Horseshoe Falls" Ontario history energy use (310)

Antarctica

Antarctica, one of Earth's seven continents, is the cold and icy land that covers and surrounds the South Pole. Of all the continents, Antarctica is the coldest, windiest, and driest with the highest average elevation. It is approximately 4,700,000 square miles (12,100,000 square kilometers) and is the only continent that does not have a native human population.

HOT topics

Antarctic Treaty. In 1959, an international agreement was signed by 12 countries stating that Antarctica only be used for peaceful purposes, such as scientific research to be shared internationally. It does not allow for military activities or mining and protects Antarctica's unique ecozone. Since its inception, many more countries have signed the treaty.

Race to Reach the South Pole. A Norwegian explorer, Roald Amundsen, and four other men were the first to arrive at the South Pole on December 14, 1911, just five weeks before a British expedition led by Captain Robert F. Scott. Each expedition followed its own route, approached their travel in different ways, and suffered their

DEFINITIONS

continent: one of the seven great masses of land on the earth. The continents are North America, South America, Europe, Africa, Asia, Australia, and Antarctica.

iceberg: a large mass of ice floating in the sea; a detached portion of a glacier carried out to sea. About 90 percent of its mass is below the surface of the water.

south magnetic pole: the point on the earth's surface toward which one end of a magnetic needle points. Its location varies but is approximately 1,600 miles from the South Pole in Wilkes Land.

HOT topics 🔥

own hardships. Members of Amundsen's expedition returned in good health. All five men on Scott's expedition perished on the return trip.

Research on Antarctica.
Scientific stations have been established on Antarctica by many different countries. Three U.S. stations maintained by the National Science Foundation are the Amundsen-Scott South Pole Station, the McMurdo Station on Ross Island, and the Palmer Station on Anvers Island. Various research scientists, including meteorologists, glaciologists, geologists, and biologists are involved with these research projects.

Antarctica's Inhabitants.
Only a few small plants and insects can survive in Antarctica's dry interior. Mosses, two flowering plants, algae, lichens, a wingless midge, lice, mites, and ticks inhabit this cold continent. Various animals such as krill, whales, seals, penguins, and several kinds of birds have adapted to living on the coast and in the surrounding waters for least for part of the year.

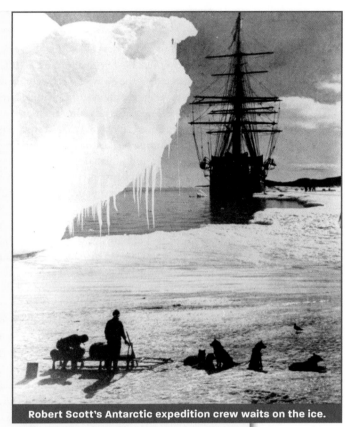
Robert Scott's Antarctic expedition crew waits on the ice.

Geography and Geology of Antarctica.
Antarctica contains many mountain ranges, volcanoes, dry valleys, lakes, glaciers, ice shelves, and gulfs (seas). The Transantarctic Mountains cross the continent, dividing the Antarctic ice sheets, the two thick layers of ice and snow that together cover most of the continent. Fossils of trees, dinosaurs, and small mammals have been found in Antarctica, indicating that it once had a much warmer climate.

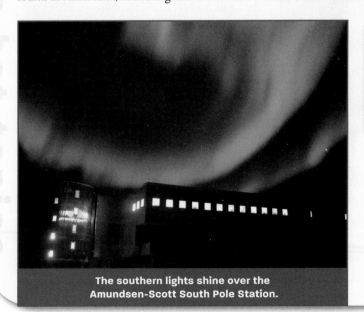
The southern lights shine over the Amundsen-Scott South Pole Station.

TRUE or FALSE?
Several countries have claimed parts of the continent of Antarctica.

THE BASICS

Antarctica is the coldest, highest, brightest, driest, and windiest continent on Earth. Temperatures there almost never rise above 32°F (0°C). Antarctica is colder than the icy region of the Arctic Ocean centered on the North Pole. Bright ice and snow cover nearly the entire continent. Antarctica has the highest average elevation of the continents, at about 7,500 feet (2,300 meters). The South Pole, Earth's southernmost point, lies near the center of Antarctica on a high, windy plateau.

Antarctica covers about 5,400,000 square miles (14,000,000 square kilometers). It is larger in area than either Europe or Australia. Surrounding Antarctica is the Southern Ocean, which connects the Pacific, Atlantic, and Indian oceans.

Only a few small plants and insects can survive in Antarctica's interior. But many animals thrive in and near the surrounding waters, including fish, tiny shellfish called *krill*, seals, whales, penguins, and other sea birds.

Long before Antarctica was discovered, ancient Greek philosophers believed that a continent covered the southern end of Earth. Antarctica was first sighted in 1820. During the mid-1800s, explorers sailed along its coast and learned that it was large enough to be considered a continent. Inland exploration began in the early 1900s. The Norwegian explorer Roald Amundsen reached the South Pole in 1911. In what turned out to be a dramatic race, he arrived there 5 weeks ahead of a British expedition led by Captain Robert F. Scott.

During the mid-1900s, U.S. Navy officer Richard Byrd led air expeditions that increased scientific interest in Antarctica. In 1959, officials of 12 countries signed an international agreement called the Antarctic Treaty. This treaty provides that the continent be used mainly for research and other peaceful purposes.

Today, scientists maintain year-round research stations in Antarctica. Activities on the continent encourage international cooperation and the sharing of scientific knowledge. Several countries have claimed parts of the continent. But the Antarctic Treaty places a freeze on existing claims and prohibits new ones.

Adelie penguins line up to jump into the icy waters.

Geography

Ice and snow cover 98 percent of Antarctica. High mountain peaks and a few other bare rocky areas make up the only visible land. Underneath the ice lie features similar to those on other continents, including mountains, lowlands, valleys, and even lakes and rivers.

Land. If all Antarctica's ice were removed, the continent would be only about half its size. Much of the continent's mass lies below sea level.

Volcanoes are common in Antarctica. Some are active, and others are hidden beneath the ice. Mount Erebus, Antarctica's most active volcano, lies on Ross Island and rises 12,448 feet (3,794 meters) above sea level.

One prominent feature of the continent is the Antarctic Peninsula. The peninsula is an S-shaped mountain chain that stretches northward toward South America. It forms a continuation of South America's Andes Mountains. Several islands lie near the peninsula. The South Shetland Islands to the west include Deception Island, an active volcano with a well-protected harbor. The harbor is the result of a violent eruption 10,000 years ago that blew out the summit crater.

A mountain chain called the Transantarctic Mountains crosses the entire continent. These mountains contain the oldest Antarctic rocks, some over 570 million years old. Several ranges make up the Transantarctic chain.

Vinson Massif, the highest point in Antarctica at 16,067 feet (4,897 meters), stands in the Ellsworth Mountains near the Antarctic Peninsula. The Transantarctic chain has the largest of the rocky, ice-free areas known as *dry valleys*. The valleys were carved by glaciers that once occupied them. Snow that falls in dry valleys is swept away by winds. Some of the valleys have lakes. Most of the lakes remain frozen the year around.

Ice. Antarctica has about 90 percent of the world's ice. This ice, with a volume of 7.25 million cubic miles (30 million cubic kilometers), represents about 70 percent of the world's fresh water. If the ice melted, Earth's oceans would rise nearly 230 feet (70 meters), flooding coastal cities around the world. The weight of the ice causes it to spread outward and flow toward the coasts. The average thickness of the ice is over 7,100 feet (2,200 meters). The thickest ice measures 15,700 feet (4,790 meters) thick. The Transantarctic Mountains separate Antarctica's ice into two giant ice sheets.

The East Antarctic ice sheet lies mainly in the Eastern Hemisphere. It is the larger, thicker, slower flowing, and colder of the two ice sheets. It covers 90 percent of the continent, including the South Pole. The East Antarctic ice sheet is a high-elevation polar desert about 10,000 feet (3,000 meters) above sea level. Less than 1 inch (2.5 centimeters) of snow falls there each year.

The West Antarctic ice sheet lies primarily in the Western Hemisphere. It contains Antarctica's fastest flowing ice. The ice's speed results from its warmer temperatures and underlying terrain that is an average of 3,300 feet (1,000 meters) below sea level. If the ice sheet melted, all that would remain of West Antarctica would be a group of islands.

Ice near the center of the Antarctic ice sheets moves only a few feet or meters per year. But ice speeds up to many hundreds of feet or meters per year as it nears the coast. In many places, ice from the interior flows into faster-moving glaciers. Large outlet glaciers can be 250 miles (400 kilometers) long and more than 30 miles (50 kilometers) wide. They can move more than 2.5 miles (4 kilometers) per year. Fast-moving ice often breaks, forming deep *crevasses* (cracks). When the ice reaches the coast, it breaks off to form icebergs that are then carried out to sea. This process is called *calving*.

Ocean

The Southern Ocean surrounds Antarctica. The northern boundary of the ocean is 60° south latitude. Farther north, at about 55° south latitude,

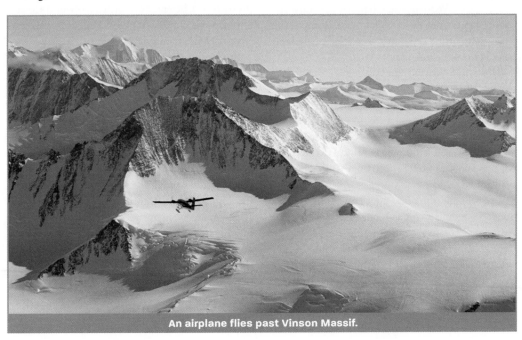
An airplane flies past Vinson Massif.

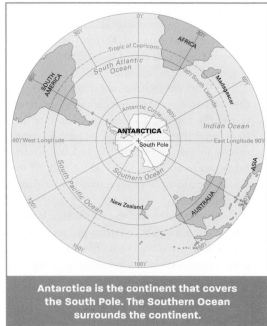

Antarctica is the continent that covers the South Pole. The Southern Ocean surrounds the continent.

lies the center of an irregular band of water about 25 miles (40 kilometers) wide called the Antarctic Convergence. Within the band, cold southern waters meet warmer, saltier northern waters. At about 50° south latitude is the massive Antarctic Circumpolar Current. This current flows from east to west, circling Antarctica.

Two large gulfs cut into Antarctica at opposite ends of the Transantarctic Mountains—the Ross Sea and the Weddell Sea. Channels separate offshore islands from the mainland. For example, the Bransfield Strait separates the South Shetland Islands from the mainland.

Broad, flat, floating parts of ice sheets called *ice shelves* fill several of Antarctica's bays and channels. The Ross Ice Shelf, the largest mass of floating ice in the world, spreads out over 190,000 square miles (490,000 square kilometers). It is about 2,300 feet (700 meters) thick at the inner edge and about 660 feet (200 meters) thick at the seaward edge.

Occasionally, the outer edges of the ice shelves break away and form immense *tabular icebergs*. Antarctic icebergs are the largest in the world. The largest iceberg ever recorded was about 4,200 square miles (11,000 square kilometers). It calved from the Ross Ice Shelf in March 2000. Icebergs eventually melt and break up in the open ocean.

Each winter, the surface of the Southern Ocean freezes into a sheet of salty ice called *sea ice*. In sum-

mer, this ice breaks into pieces called *ice floes*. Wind and waves push the floes against one another, forming thick masses known as *pack ice*. Some pack ice piles up in ridges against the shore. In winter, pack ice extends as far as 1,000 miles (1,600 kilometers) from the coast.

Climate

The Antarctic climate varies from extremely cold, dry conditions on the inland plateau to milder, slightly moister conditions along the coasts. Average snowfalls in East Antarctica range from 1 inch (2.5 centimeters) in the interior to 24 inches (61 centimeters) at the coast. In West Antarctica, annual snowfalls are three times this large. Along the Antarctic Peninsula, strong winds, mild temperatures, and nearby water combine to produce snowfall rates of many feet per year.

The Antarctic winter lasts from May through September. For several months, most of the continent is in continual darkness. Summer lasts from November through February. July temperatures inland range from a low of −94°F (−70°C) to a high of −40°F (−40°C). July temperatures range from −22°F (−30°C) to −5°F (−21°C) on the peninsula's coast. January temperatures range from −31°F (−35°C) to 5°F (−15°C) inland. They reach 32°F (0°C) on the coast. Northern islands may have summer temperatures of up to 50°F (10°C). Scientists recorded the world's lowest temperature, −128.6°F (−89.2°C), at Antarctica's Vostok Station, on July 21, 1983.

Strong, bitter winds make the Antarctic air feel even colder than it is. Winds that sweep downward from the plateau can average 44 miles (70 kilometers) per hour. Gusts often reach the coast at 120 miles (190 kilometers) per hour. On the plateau, winds blow the snow into ridgelike snow dunes called *sastrugi*. The sastrugi measure up to 6 feet (1.8 meters) tall.

Antarctica's climate has not always been so cold. Geologists think Antarctica was once part of a giant supercontinent called Gondwanaland. This huge landmass also included what are now Africa, Australia, India, and South America. By about 140 million years ago, Gondwanaland had begun to break apart. The parts slowly drifted to their present locations.

Many millions of years ago, Antarctica was free of ice. Scientists have found fossils of trees, dinosaurs, and small mammals that once lived there. Glaciers began to form in East Antarctica around the South Pole about 38 million years ago. They started in a rugged area called the Gamburtsev Mountains, now buried beneath the East Antarctic ice sheet. These glaciers grew rapidly around 13 million years ago. The East Antarctic ice sheet has remained roughly the same size since then. The West Antarctic ice sheet, on the other hand, has advanced and retreated many times as Earth's climate has repeatedly warmed and cooled.

Ice sheets preserve a long and detailed record of past climate. As fresh snow is buried and compressed into ice, samples of the atmosphere are trapped in tiny air bubbles. Scientists can drill into the ice and remove a long, vertical sample called an *ice core*. Such a sample provides a record of the atmosphere at various times. Deeper parts of the core represent the more distant past. Slight differences in the chemical composition of the ice provide additional information on atmospheric temperature and ancient weather patterns. Antarctic ice cores provide an important way of learning about changes in Earth's climate over the past million years.

 ## Living Things

Only a few small plants and insects can survive in Antarctica's dry interior. But various living things thrive in and near the surrounding waters.

Few plants grow in Antarctica because of the ice-covered land and the harsh climate. Mosses are the most common Antarctic plants. They cling to rocky areas, mostly on the coasts. Only two flowering plants grow in Antarctica. Both live on the northern part of the Antarctic Peninsula. One of them is a grass that forms dense mats on sunny slopes. The other, an herb, grows in short, cushionlike bunches.

Simpler organisms known as algae grow on snow, in lakes, and on ice surrounding the continent. Some algae give snow a pink or green tinge. Other organisms called lichens cling to rocks as mosses do. Some lichens survive by bunching together to conserve water. Scientists have discovered rows of black, white, and green lichens growing in tiny cracks in dry valleys. Small plants and algae also drift on the surface of the Southern Ocean.

Only a few insects and other tiny animals spend their entire lives on the Antarctic mainland. The

A southern elephant seal

continent's largest land animal is a wingless midge, a type of fly no more than $1/2$ inch (12 millimeters) long. Most land animals live at the edges of the continent. To avoid freezing to death, some lice, mites, and ticks cling to mosses, the fur of seals, or the feathers of birds.

Unlike the continent, the Southern Ocean has abundant wildlife. The most common ocean animal is *krill*, a small, shrimplike creature that feeds on tiny floating organisms. Many Antarctic animals depend on krill for food. Several countries also catch krill as a protein-rich food for people. Many Antarctic animals also eat squid. In addition, about 100 kinds of fish live in the ocean, including Antarctic cod, icefish, and plunderfish.

Several kinds of whales migrate to Antarctica for the summer. Blue whales, fin whales, humpback whales, minke whales, right whales, and sei whales feed on krill. The blue whale is the largest animal ever. This rare giant grows up to 100 feet (30 meters) long. Antarctic whales that eat fish and squid include killer whales—also called *orcas*—and southern bottlenose whales, southern fourtooth whales, and sperm whales. Killer whales also hunt seals, penguins, and smaller whales.

Various kinds of seals live in Antarctica. They spend most of their lives in the water. Many of them nest on the coasts. The Antarctic fur seal nests on nearby islands. The largest seal in the world, the southern elephant seal, feeds on squid and may reach a length of 16 feet (5 meters). Ross seals and Weddell seals eat fish and squid. Antarctic fur seals and crabeater seals eat krill. Leopard seals hunt other seals and penguins.

During the 1800s and early 1900s, hunters greatly reduced the number of whales and Antarctic fur seals. Today, international wildlife laws prohibit or restrict the killing of these animals.

Penguins are the animals most often associated with Antarctica. These birds cannot fly, and they waddle awkwardly on land. But they are skillful swimmers. Six kinds of penguins breed on the continent. Adélie penguins, the most common kind, build nests of pebbles on the coasts. The tall, quieter emperor penguin grows to about 3 feet (1 meter). After the female emperor penguin lays an egg, the male rests the egg on his feet and warms it with the lower part of his belly. Chinstrap, gentoo, king, and macaroni penguins nest on the Antarctic Peninsula and on islands. Rockhopper penguins nest only on islands north of Antarctica.

More than 40 kinds of flying birds spend the summer in Antarctica. Many types nest on land but spend most of their time diving for food. These birds include albatrosses, prions, and a large group of sea birds known as petrels. Other birds, such as cormorants, gulls, skuas, and terns, return to land more frequently. Some of them steal food from the nests of other birds. Some land birds, such as sheathbills, nest on the peninsula. Others, including pintails and pipits, nest on islands.

Exploration

People wrote about a southern continent centuries before Antarctica was discovered. Ancient Greek philosophers supposed that a landmass at Earth's southern end was needed to balance the weight of the northern lands. During the AD 100s, the Greek geographer Ptolemy gave this undiscovered continent the Latin name Terra Australis Incognita, meaning *unknown southern land.* He believed the land was populated and fertile. The name *Antarctica* later came from two Greek words meaning *opposite the bear.* The Bear is a constellation seen in Earth's northern sky.

People first sighted Antarctica in 1820. During the mid-1800s, explorers sailed along its coast. They learned that it was large enough to be considered a continent. Inland exploration began in the early 1900s. The Norwegian explorer Roald Amundsen became the first to reach the South Pole in 1911. In what turned out to be a dramatic race, he arrived there five weeks ahead of a British expedition led by Captain Robert F. Scott.

Early exploration. In 1772, the English navigator James Cook began his search for the southern continent. In January 1773, he crossed the Antarctic Circle, an imaginary line circling Earth at 66° 33' south latitude. A year later, Cook reached 71° 10' south latitude. Huge icebergs and thick ice floes prevented him from going farther, however, and he never sighted land.

Nobody knows who first saw the Antarctic continent. Many historians divide the credit among three men who made separate voyages in 1820. In January of that year, Captain Fabian von Bellingshausen of the Russian Imperial Navy reported reaching a point only 20 miles (32 kilometers) from the Antarctic Peninsula. Some historians believe that he saw land but thought it was ice.

That same month, Captain Edward Bransfield of the British Navy journeyed south of the South Shetland Islands and probably saw the Antarctic

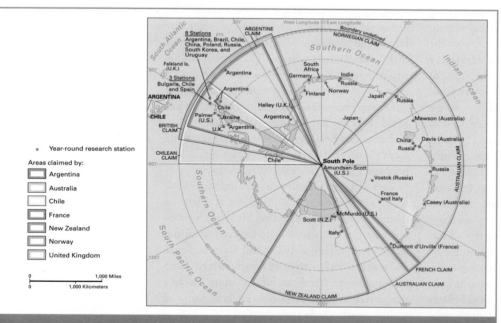

Seven countries claim areas in Antarctica. This map shows the boundaries of those areas, some of which overlap, and pinpoints major research stations.

Roald Amundsen with his dog team

Peninsula. In November, an American sealer named Nathaniel Brown Palmer reported seeing land during a sealing expedition in the same area. Some geographers later called the peninsula Graham Land in honor of James Graham, the head of the British Navy in Bransfield's time. Others called it Palmer Land. The United States and the members of the Commonwealth of Nations finally agreed to the term Antarctic Peninsula in 1964.

Historians also are unsure of who first set foot on Antarctica. Some believe that an American sealer named John Davis went ashore at Hughes Bay on the tip of the peninsula in 1821. But Davis did not know if he had reached the continent or an island.

In 1823, a British sealer named James Weddell sailed south in search of hunting waters. He reached about 74° south latitude, farther than earlier voyagers had sailed, and found what is now called the Weddell Sea.

In 1831, the English whaler John Biscoe became the first to spot land in East Antarctica. He named it Enderby Land after the whaling company that owned his ship.

In 1837, the king of France sent Lieutenant Jules Dumont d'Urville to claim some southern lands for France. D'Urville's first attempt led him to discover what is now called Joinville Island, off the tip of the Antarctic Peninsula. He began his next Antarctic voyage from Tasmania, an island south of the Australian mainland. In January 1840, he sighted icy cliffs rising along the East Antarctic coastline. Many small penguins dotted the pack ice that blocked his way to the land. D'Urville named both the land and the penguins after his wife, Adélie.

About the time that d'Urville sighted land, U.S. Navy Lieutenant Charles Wilkes headed an expedition to perform scientific research. Wilkes's greatest contribution to Antarctic studies was his coastal exploration. His ship moved from the Adélie Coast toward Enderby Land, tracing over 1,500 miles (2,400 kilometers) of coastline.

From 1839 to 1843, the British explorer James Clark Ross made several discoveries. Ross was the first person to go beyond the pack ice surrounding Antarctica. He sailed into the gulf that is now called the Ross Sea. Ross also discovered an island with two volcanoes, which he named after his ships, *Erebus* and *Terror*. He found the gulf barricaded by a towering sheet of ice, now known as the Ross Ice Shelf.

In 1895, a Norwegian businessman named Henryk Johan Bull made the first known landing on the Antarctic mainland. He and his whaling crew went ashore at Cape Adare, a point on the Ross Sea facing New Zealand.

The "Heroic Era." The first two decades of the 1900s are often called the "Heroic Era" of Antarctic exploration. In this period, people learned much about the geography and environment of the continent. It was also during this period that explorers first reached the South Pole.

The first inland exploration of Antarctica took place from 1901 to 1904. Robert Falcon Scott of the British Navy led a team of explorers and scientists to the Ross Sea. In November 1902, Scott and two other men headed south across the Ross Ice Shelf. But illness, harsh weather, and lack of food forced them to rejoin the team earlier than planned. Another group moved up a glacier through the Transantarctic Mountains and reached the edge of the harsh inland plateau.

Ernest Shackleton, a member of Scott's team, returned to Antarctica in 1907. Part of his expedition searched for the south magnetic pole in a remote area of East Antarctica, reaching it in January 1909. At the same time, the main group headed for the south geographic pole, the meeting point of lines of longitude. Food shortages forced the men to turn back early. But they had come within 110 miles (180 kilometers) of the pole, close enough to prove that the pole was on land rather than beneath a frozen sea.

In June 1910, Captain Scott left London, hoping to win for the United Kingdom the honor of reaching the South Pole first. In October, while Scott was in Australia, he received a telegram from the Norwegian explorer Roald Amundsen. The telegram informed Scott that Amundsen, too, was going to Antarctica. Amundsen originally had hoped to be the first to reach the North Pole. He switched his goal when he heard that the North Pole had been reached. The race to the South Pole became one of the most famous events in Antarctica's history.

Amundsen and his four assistants began crossing the Ross Ice Shelf from its northeastern corner, at the Bay of Whales, on October 19, 1911. To reach the inland plateau, they had to carve their own route along an unexplored glacier in the Queen Maud Mountains, a part of the Transantarctic Mountains at the southern edge of the ice shelf. The men journeyed on skis, while 52 dogs pulled their four sleds of supplies. Amundsen marked his route and food storage areas with mounds of snow. He shot the weakest dogs for food, when they were no longer needed to pull the sleds.

Scott set out with 15 other men on November 1, 1911, from Cape Evans, Ross Island, at the northwestern corner of the Ross Ice Shelf. This location was about 800 miles (1,300 kilometers) from the pole, about 60 miles (100 kilometers) farther than Amundsen's starting point. However, Scott's expedition reached the plateau by way of the Beardmore Glacier, a known route. Scott tried using motorized sleds to carry some supplies and using ponies as well as dogs to pull other sleds. But the ponies and motor sleds bogged down in the soft snow. Eventually, the men had to drag the sleds, and food soon ran low. Scott crossed the plateau accompanied by four men.

Amundsen's group arrived at the South Pole on December 14, 1911. They used special navigating instruments to calculate their position. Amundsen left behind his tent, a Norwegian flag, and a message for Scott. The group then headed back to their base, which they reached on January 25, 1912. By that time, only 11 dogs remained, but all five men were in good health.

Scott's group reached the pole on January 17, 1912, finding Amundsen's flag. Cold, hunger, and exhaustion had severely weakened the explorers. They photographed themselves at the pole and began their return. All five men perished on the way. Two of them died after they were injured on the trail. Late in March, a long blizzard forced Scott and his two remaining assistants to make camp only 11 miles (18 kilometers) away from food and supplies. A search party found their frozen bodies inside the tent eight months later.

Exploration by air provided a new way to study Antarctica. In 1928, the Australian explorer Sir Hubert Wilkins surveyed the Antarctic Peninsula and nearby islands in the first airplane voyage over the continent.

In November 1929, the U.S. Navy officer Richard E. Byrd led the first flight over the South Pole. A Norwegian-American pilot, Bernt Balchen, flew Byrd's crew from the Bay of Whales to the pole and back. The flight lasted less than 16 hours. This journey was part of an expedition that Byrd supervised from 1928 to 1930. In a second expedition from 1933 to 1935, Byrd and his assistants traveled by plane and tractor over the Antarctic interior. They studied the ice, Earth's magnetism, cosmic rays, weather, and geology.

In 1935, the U.S. engineer Lincoln Ellsworth and the English-born pilot Herbert Hollick-Kenyon took off from Dundee Island, north of the Antarctic Peninsula, hoping to make the first flight across the continent. Near the Weddell Sea, they discovered what are now called the

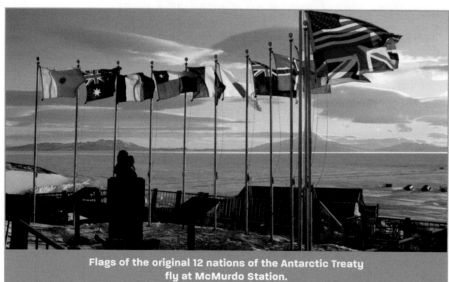

Flags of the original 12 nations of the Antarctic Treaty fly at McMurdo Station.

Ellsworth Mountains. Their plane had to land four times because of storms and a fuel shortage. They finally completed the crossing on foot at the Bay of Whales.

In 1946 and 1947, Byrd commanded the U.S. Navy's Operation Highjump, the largest Antarctic expedition by a single country. Operation Highjump sent 4,700 men, 13 ships, and 23 airplanes and helicopters to Antarctica. The expedition members discovered new land, including 26 islands. They photographed about 1,400 miles (2,300 kilometers) of previously unexplored coastline.

That same year, Captain Finn Ronne led a private U.S. air expedition to West Antarctica. Ronne explored areas of the Weddell Sea that had never been seen. The crew included Ronne's wife, Edith, and Jennie Darlington, the wife of his chief pilot. They were the first women to spend a winter on the continent.

The International Geophysical Year.

Scientific knowledge of Antarctica increased rapidly during the International Geophysical Year (IGY). The IGY was a global program in which scientists coordinated observations and shared their findings. It began on July 1, 1957, and ended on December 31, 1958.

As part of the IGY, 12 countries established over 50 scientific stations on Antarctica and nearby islands. These countries were Argentina, Australia, Belgium, Chile, France, Japan, New Zealand, Norway, South Africa, the Soviet Union, the United Kingdom, and the United States. The United States set up a station at the South Pole, five coastal stations, and one inland station. The Soviet Union built a station at a point it named the Pole of Inaccessibility. This station, called Vostok, lies in East Antarctica, far inland from all coasts.

IGY researchers in Antarctica studied such topics as earthquakes, gravity, magnetism, oceanography, and solar activity. *Meteorologists* (scientists who study weather) determined air pressure, humidity, temperature, and wind direction and prepared Antarctica's first complete weather charts. *Glaciologists* (scientists who study ice) measured the thickness of the ice. Geologists studied the land formations.

During the IGY, the British geologist Vivian Fuchs headed the first land crossing of the continent. The Commonwealth of Nations organized the expedition, which covered 2,158 miles (3,473 kilometers). Fuchs left on November 24, 1957,

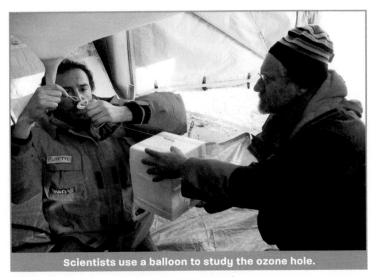
Scientists use a balloon to study the ozone hole.

from the shore of the Weddell Sea, with dogs and snow tractors. A team led by the New Zealand explorer Sir Edmund Hillary placed food and supplies along the second part of the trail. Hillary met Fuchs at the South Pole in January 1958. Fuchs reached McMurdo Sound in the Ross Sea on March 2, 1958.

Seven of the 12 countries that built Antarctic bases for the IGY claim parts of Antarctica as their national territory. The parts are shaped like pie slices, with the South Pole at the center. Many nations, including the United States, do not recognize these claims.

International agreements.

In 1959, at the end of the IGY, officials of the 12 countries signed the Antarctic Treaty. This agreement freezes all current territorial claims and prohibits new claims. It allows people to use Antarctica only for peaceful purposes, such as scientific research and tourism. It also requires scientists to share the results of their studies. The treaty forbids military forces in Antarctica, except those assisting scientific expeditions. It also outlaws the use of nuclear weapons and the disposal of radioactive wastes in Antarctica.

Since 1961, when the Antarctic Treaty took effect, a number of other nations have joined the treaty. Many of these nations have set up scientific programs in Antarctica. In 1991, the Antarctic Treaty nations signed the Madrid Protocol. This agreement, which went into effect in 1998, establishes Antarctica as a natural reserve devoted to peace and science. The protocol prohibits mineral exploitation in Antarctica and establishes strict rules designed to protect the Antarctic environment.

Scientific research.

Today, more than 40 year-round scientific stations operate on the continent and nearby islands. The National Science Foundation maintains three year-round U.S. stations: (1) Amundsen-Scott South Pole Station, (2) McMurdo Station on Ross Island, and (3) Palmer Station on Anvers Island near the Antarctic Peninsula. Other research stations are maintained by Argentina, Australia, Brazil, Bulgaria, Chile, China, Finland, France, Germany, India, Italy, Japan, New Zealand, Norway, Poland, Russia, South Africa, South Korea, Spain, Ukraine, the United Kingdom, and Uruguay.

McMurdo Station has Antarctica's largest community. About 1,200 scientists, pilots, and other specialists live there each summer. About 250 people stay through the dark, frigid winter. A water plant collects and desalts seawater from McMurdo Sound. An aggressive recycling program minimizes unusable waste. Powerful ships called *icebreakers* plow through the ice, arrive with people and supplies, and leave with waste materials and scientific samples. The station also has runways and a helicopter pad.

South Pole Station is smaller. It has a summer population of about 200. Its winter crew is about 12. Cargo planes with skis from McMurdo Station service it.

Palmer Station supports an even smaller population. Its population shrinks to just four during the winter. It is serviced by ship during the summer.

Summer activities in Antarctica vary. Geologists collect rock samples from the ice-free dry valleys of the Transantarctic Mountains. Glaciologists measure the speed of ice flow, ice thickness, and properties beneath the ice at many of the most rapidly moving and changing locations. Physicists at the South Pole have converted a cubic kilometer of the ice into a vast detector of high-energy particles. They did this by placing over 1,000 sensitive detectors within the ice. Astronomers have many specialized telescopes at the South Pole. These telescopes take advantage of the six-month-long days and nights and the thin, stable atmosphere. On the coasts and at sea, biologists observe how animals adapt to their environment. Winter restricts scientists to such activities as recording weather data and studying earthquakes and solar radiation.

One important area of research in the Antarctic has been *ozone* in the atmosphere. Ozone is a form of oxygen. It is concentrated in an atmospheric layer that ranges in altitude from about 9 to 18 miles (15 to 30 kilometers). This layer protects all living things from certain harmful rays from the sun. In the mid-1980's, scientists discovered that the ozone layer over Antarctica was thinning. Evidence pointed to manufactured compounds called fluorocarbons as a major cause of this "ozone hole." Prompted by these findings, nations around the globe signed the Montreal Protocol in 1987, banning the use of chlorofluorocarbons, a major cause of ozone loss.

Research in Antarctica can answer important questions about the past, present, and future of Earth. Much scientific work there focuses on issues related to global climate change, in particular *global warming*. Global warming is an ongoing increase in average global surface temperatures.

Some of this research focuses on the causes and effects of ice loss in Antarctica. Rates at which ice flows into the sea are increasing in many locations, causing sea level to rise. This rise in sea level threatens coastal regions around the world. Predicting the fate of the ice sheet as temperatures continue to increase will help people anticipate and manage coastal changes around the world.

In 2007, scientists from dozens of nations launched a two-year study of the Arctic and Antarctic called the International Polar Year. The investigation involved more than 200 research projects. They focused on assessing the status of the polar regions and determining how global warming will affect the polar and global climate and the inhabitants of the polar regions.

Since the late 1900s, it has become easier to travel to Antarctica. The number of tourists visiting the continent has increased rapidly. Researchers face challenges in managing the Antarctic environment as the continent's human population increases.

MLA Citation

"Antarctica." *The Southwestern Advantage Topic Source.* Nashville: Southwestern. 2013.

DATA

Interesting Facts About Antarctica

The krill—a small, shrimplike animal—is a key source of food in the Antarctic region. Such animals as fish, birds, and seals feed on krill and are, in turn, eaten by larger animals. Swarms of krill form huge red masses in coastal waters during the day and glow bluish-green at night.

Antarctica's wandering pole, officially called the *south magnetic pole,* moves at least 5 miles (8 kilometers) a year. This is the south pole indicated by compass needles.

Thick ice buries most of Antarctica. The continent's deepest ice is more than 10 times the height of the Wilis Tower in Chicago, one of the world's tallest buildings.

First to reach the South Pole was Roald Amundsen, a Norwegian explorer. His expedition set off from Antarctica's Bay of Whales on October 19, 1911, and reached the pole on December 14, 1911.

Plant fossils found in Antarctica reveal that the continent once had a warm, ice-free climate with trees and other leafy plants.

ADDITIONAL RESOURCES

Books to Read

Crossley, Louise. *Explore Antarctica.* Cambridge, 1995.
Rubin, Jeff. *Antarctica.* 2nd ed. Lonely Planet Pubns., 2000.
Sayre, April P. *Antarctica.* 21st Century Bks., 1998. Younger readers.
Stewart, John. *Antarctica.* 2 vols. McFarland, 1990.

Web Sites

Antarctic Journal of the United States

http://www.nsf.gov/od/opp/antarct/journal/start.jsp
Back issues of a journal that reports on U.S. activities in Antarctica and trends in the
U.S. Antarctic Program.

CIA Factbook: Antarctica

https://www.cia.gov/library/publications/the-world-factbook/geos/ay.html
An overview of the country from the U.S. Central Intelligence Agency.

Live From Antarctica

http://quest.arc.nasa.gov/antarctica/index.html
All about life at a research station in Antarctica.

Landsat Image Mosiac of Antarctica (LIMA)

http://lima.usgs.gov/
Provided by the U.S. Geological Survey.

BACKGROUND INFORMATION

The following article was written during the year in which the events took place and reflects the style and thinking of that time.

Geology (1970)

Scientists have discovered fossil reptile bones in Antarctica, adding new strength to the theory that continents drift on the earth's surface. Among the fragments discovered was a scrap of jawbone positively identified as that of a *Lystrosaurus*, one of the advanced mammal-like reptiles that lived some 200 million years ago. Since fossilized bones of this animal had previously been found in South Africa and in Asia, the Antarctic discovery added further evidence to the belief that the Antarctic land mass had once been joined to that of Africa and had separated through the process of continental drift, moving to its present location over millions of years.

The site of the fossil fragments was discovered on November 23, 1969, by David H. Elliot of the Institute of Polar Studies at Ohio State University. He was searching the area as a part of the team engaged in the 1969–1970 U.S. Antarctic Research Program. It was headed by Edwin H. Colbert of the American Museum of Natural History in New York City and William J. Breed of the Museum of Northern Arizona in Flagstaff.

The bones were found in a bed of sandstone at a site known as Coalsack Bluff in the central Transantarctic Mountains. The area is about 400 miles from the South Pole and within 100 miles of the site where the only previously known mammal-like fragment from Antarctica—a piece of fossil jawbone—was found in 1967. Later field searching in 1970 revealed that the rocks in the bed at Coalsack Bluff were virtually the only fossil-bearing rocks in the Transantarctic Mountains. The collection found there consisted of some 450 specimens of amphibian and reptile bones, many evidently *therapsids* (advanced mammal-like reptiles). The *Lystrosaurus* fragment will be displayed at the American Museum of Natural History after studies of it have been completed.

Saharan ice age. An international scientific mission searched in 1970 for evidence of ancient glacial activity in the Sahara. Geologists from 10 nations, including U.S. geologist Rhodes W. Fairbridge of Columbia University, took part in the search, which was organized by the Institut Algerien du Petrole (Algerian Oil Institute). The group traveled extensively through the desert, and found much evidence that North Africa was covered by glaciers during the late Ordovician Period, more than 435 million years ago.

Speculation that the Sahara had experienced widespread continental glaciation during that time grew from the theory of continental drift, which says that the present continental land masses have moved during the past with relation to each other as well as with relation to the poles. Evidence supporting the theory comes primarily from studies of residual magnetism in rocks. These studies indicate that the earth's magnetic poles (and thus presumably the geographic

Coal (left) and petrified wood (right)

poles, too) have been in different locations in the past, and that one of the poles was located in the Sahara region of North Africa during the Ordovician Period. French oil geologists reported finding evidence of Ordovician glacial action in eastern Algeria as long ago as 1961, but other geologists doubted their conclusions.

The 1970 team of geologists found many rocks showing glacial striations in parts of the Sahara stretching from Mauritania and Spanish Sahara on the west to Libya and Chad on the east. The direction of movement of the ancient glaciers that caused these striations was apparently from south to north, toward what were then the continental margins.

The research has confirmed the fact that there was an Ice Age during the Ordovician Period, just as there was during Pleistocene, Permian, and Precambrian times. Still unclear is how extensive an area was involved. To

Aerial shot of Yungay after the earthquake

determine this, further work must be done in Southern Africa and in South America, which is believed to have been adjacent to Africa during the Ordovician Period. Marine deposits of the succeeding Silurian Period lay over the Ordovician glacial strata, suggesting that there was a relatively rapid shift of the magnetic pole away from North Africa toward southwestern Africa.

Peruvian Earthquake. The disastrous earthquake in Peru on May 31, 1970, may have surpassed the eruptions of Mount Pelee in 1902 and Mount Vesuvius in A.D. 79 to qualify as the most destructive natural disaster in recorded history. It registered 7.75 on the Richter scale, on which 10 is the maximum. In lives lost, the earthquake was the most disastrous in Latin American history. Casualties included more than 70,000 dead or missing and 200,000 injured. An estimated 186,000 buildings were destroyed, including about four-fifths of the houses in the 25,000-square mile earthquake area.

The most destructive result of the quake was the avalanche that roared down from the north peak of Huascaran, Peru's highest mountain. An estimated 80-million cubic feet of debris dropped about 12,000 feet down the steep mountainside and traveled 9 miles across the Llanganuco Valley and the Santa River in four minutes, reaching speeds as high as 248 mph. The friction from this movement quickly melted ice on the mountain slope, creating a tremendous mud flow that pushed boulders weighing up to 3 tons before it.

Yungay, a city of 4,000 inhabitants directly in the path of the avalanche, was almost totally obliterated. The village of Ranrahirca on the opposite bank of the Santa was also damaged, leaving fatalities of 20,000 from the avalanche alone. The force of the avalanche sent a wave of water as high as 45 feet down the Santa River Valley.

The epicenter of the quake was calculated to be about 15 miles west of the port city of Chimbote and 27 miles below the surface of the earth.

Cuba

Cuba is an island 90 miles south of Key West, Florida. It also consists of over 1,600 smaller islands that surround the main island. Cuba has three mountainous regions, along with rolling plains and fertile farmlands. It is a Communist nation that has a tense history with the United States. Havana is Cuba's capital and largest city.

HOT topics

Fidel Castro. Fidel Castro was born in 1926 and graduated with a law degree in 1950. In 1952, he ran for election, but Fulgencio Batista's troops stopped the election and ended democracy. On July 26, 1953, Castro and his forces attacked the Moncada army barracks. He was captured, sentenced to 15 years in prison, but was released in 1955. He went into exile and built up his forces. In 1959, he and his troops overthrew the military dictatorship of Fulgencio Batista. Castro became the head of Cuba's Communist government. Under his rule, the United States ended diplomatic relations with Cuba, Cuba's economy has suffered, but education and health care facilities have improved.

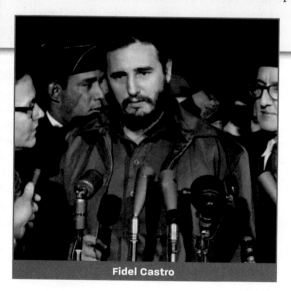

Fidel Castro

HOT topics

Cuba-United States Relations.
Soon after Fidel Castro became the head of Cuba's Communist government, the United States ended diplomatic relations with Cuba. At that time, the United States and the Soviet Union were competing for international power. The Castro government became allies with the Soviet Union, thereby, forcing the United States to cut ties with Cuba.

The Effect of the Collapse of the Soviet Union on Cuba.
After Castro became head of Cuba's Communist government, Cuba became allies with the Soviet Union. The country relied heavily on aid from, and trade with, the Soviet Union. With the collapse of the Soviet Union in 1991, that aid and trade ended, causing an economic crisis for Cuba. To combat this, the government had to loosen its control over the economy. Foreign investment began to return to the island, principally in tourism.

Cuban Missile Crisis.
In October 1962, the United States learned that the Soviet Union had sent nuclear missiles and launch site materials to Cuba. President John F. Kennedy ordered a naval blockade to halt the further shipment of arms. He demanded that the Soviet Union remove all missiles from the island and dismantle the remaining missile bases. For several days, the world stood on the brink of nuclear war. Finally, after Kennedy privately agreed to dismantle military bases in Turkey and not to invade Cuba, the Soviet Union removed the weapons.

TRUE or FALSE?
The Bay of Pigs Invasion, sponsored by the United States Central Intelligence Agency, resulted in Castro's forces capturing 1,200 Cuban exiles.

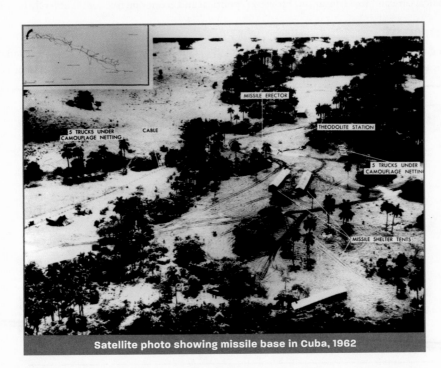

Satellite photo showing missile base in Cuba, 1962

THE BASICS

Cuba is an island nation that is the only Communist state in the Americas. It lies about 90 miles (145 kilometers) south of Key West, Florida. Havana is Cuba's capital and largest city.

Cuba is the largest and one of the most beautiful islands in the Caribbean region. Towering mountains and rolling hills cover about a third of the island. The rest of Cuba consists mainly of gentle slopes and broad grasslands. Cuba has a magnificent coastline marked with deep bays, sandy beaches, and colorful coral reefs.

Cuba's location has greatly influenced its history. The island lies at the intersection of major sea routes between the Atlantic Ocean, the Caribbean Sea, and the Gulf of Mexico. The famous explorer Christopher Columbus, sailing in the service of Spain, landed in Cuba in 1492. The island later became strategically important in Spain's American empire.

In the late 1700s and early 1800s, sugarcane became Cuba's leading crop. Sugarcane growers of European ancestry raised their crops on large plantations that depended heavily on human labor. To provide cheap labor, growers brought thousands of Africans to Cuba and forced them to work as slaves.

During the 1800s, many Cubans rebelled against Spanish rule. In 1898, the United States helped defeat Spain, which then gave up all claims to Cuba. A U.S. military government ruled Cuba from 1899 to 1902, when the island became a republic. However, the United States maintained close ties with Cuba and often intervened in the island's internal affairs. From 1934 to 1940 and from 1952 to 1959, Cuba was controlled by the dictator Fulgencio Batista y Zaldívar.

Fidel Castro led a revolution that overthrew Batista in 1959. Relations between Cuba and the United States became tense soon after the revolution. Castro set up a Communist government and developed close ties with the Soviet Union, then the main rival of the United States in a struggle for international power. In 1961, the United States ended diplomatic relations with Cuba and imposed strict *economic sanctions* on the island. Economic sanctions are actions that seek to limit or end economic relations with a target country.

Today, the government of Cuba is highly centralized. It provides many benefits for the people, including free medical care and free education. However, political and economic freedom is severely limited.

Government

According to the Cuban Constitution, adopted in 1976, Cuba is a socialist state. It is governed by a single political party—the Partido Comunista de Cuba (Communist Party of Cuba), also known as the

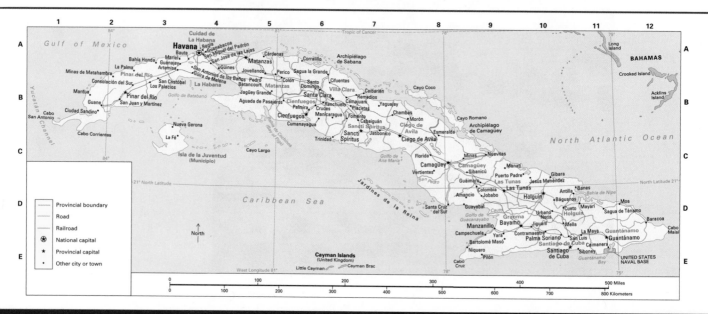

Map of Cuba

PCC. The Constitution established the Communist Party as the leading authority in the government and society. The Party Congress, a gathering of delegates from throughout the country, officially meets every 5 years. However, these meetings have been irregular. The Central Committee, an administrative body elected by the Congress, is responsible for making the highest levels of policy, and it influences all government institutions. The Central Committee elects members of a smaller group called the Political Bureau, which handles day-to-day policy and decision-making. Another small group, the Secretariat, handles daily administrative work.

Until the 1990s, membership in the PCC was highly restricted. For example, people who attended religious services could not join. In the 1990s, however, the party began to expand its membership and to include religious believers. The PCC also sought to attract greater numbers of young people and women.

National government. The National Assembly of People's Power has been Cuba's chief legislative body since 1976. The people elect the members of the Assembly to 5-year terms. Citizens who are at least 16 years old may vote.

The National Assembly holds two regular sessions each year. Between sessions, the Assembly is represented by the Council of State and several standing commissions. Council members are elected by the National Assembly from among its members. The president of the council, who serves as both head of state and head of government, is the most powerful government official.

The president, with the approval of the Assembly, appoints a Council of Ministers, which in effect serves as a cabinet. This council enforces laws, directs government agencies, and conducts Cuba's foreign policy.

Provincial and local government. Cuba has a number of provinces, which are divided into municipalities for purposes of local government. Each province and municipality has an assembly. The people elect the members of each municipal assembly. The municipal assemblies of a province elect the members of the provincial assembly. Cuba's largest offshore island, the Isla de la Juventud (Isle of Youth), does not belong to any province. It is ruled directly by the central government.

Municipal assemblies supervise and control local economic enterprises, including retail opera-

Cuba's capital, Havana

tions and factories that produce goods for the local market. Municipal assemblies also exercise some authority over schools, health services, cultural activities, sports facilities, and transportation.

Courts. The People's Supreme Court is Cuba's highest court. It consists of a president, a vice president, and the members of the court's five *chambers* (divisions). These chambers are civil and administrative, criminal, labor, military, and state security. Each chamber consists of a president, at least two other professional judges, and *lay judges*. Lay judges are citizens who hold their regular jobs while serving on the Supreme Court. The National Assembly elects the Supreme Court justices. The president and vice president of the court are nominated by the president of the Council of State and approved by the National Assembly. Cuba also has provincial and municipal courts throughout the island.

Armed forces. Cuba's armed forces have grown smaller since 1990, but they still rank as one of the largest military forces in Latin America. About 50,000 men and women serve on active duty in the Cuban air force, army, and navy. Approximately 40,000 men and women serve in an army reserve. Territorial militias, civilian groups with military training, also stand ready to defend their country. All Cuban men must serve 2 years of active duty after they turn 16.

People

Ancestry and language. Most Cubans are descendants of people who came to the island from Spain and Africa. About 30 to 40 percent of the people are white, and approximately 10 to 20 percent are black. Most of the rest are *mulattoes*—that is, people of mixed white and black ancestry. Cuba also has a small percentage of people of Chinese descent. The country's racial and

Young Cuban women dancing the mamba

social composition changed significantly between 1959 and 1980, when about 750,000 people emigrated. Most of them were white and middle-class. Spanish is Cuba's official language.

Way of life. The majority of Cuban people live in urban areas. Havana is Cuba's capital, largest city, and commercial and cultural center. Most people in the cities have jobs in government agencies or government-owned businesses and factories, but some run small private businesses. Cuba's cities have a serious housing shortage. Many buildings, neglected for several decades, are in need of repair.

Most of the people in rural areas work on farms. Some rural people live in traditional *bohíos*, which are thatch-roofed dwellings with dirt floors.

Before the 1959 revolution, many rural communities lacked health facilities, schools, adequate transportation and communication, and housing. Since 1959, however, the government has built hospitals, clinics, and schools in the countryside. It also has expanded transportation and communication facilities and increased housing construction. Nevertheless, many rural areas of Cuba continue to lack certain necessities.

Food and drink. Pork, chicken, beans, and rice are the most common Cuban foods. Rice is often served with various kinds of beans, or it is mixed with tomatoes, onions, green peppers, and chicken in a dish called *arroz con pollo*. Another popular dish is *picadillo*, which consists of ground beef, pork, or veal mixed with onions, garlic, tomatoes, and other ingredients. Corn meal is used in tamales and many other dishes. Coffee, rum, and beer are popular beverages.

In the early 1960s, the government organized a food rationing system to deal with the limited availability of scarce and imported foods. This system is designed to provide all households with minimum quantities of rice, beans, meat, chicken, eggs, sugar, milk, and coffee.

Recreation. Cubans are enthusiastic sports fans. Baseball arrived in Cuba from the United States in the late 1800s and quickly became the island's national pastime. Other popular sports include basketball, boxing, swimming, track and field, and volleyball. Soccer also has a growing national following.

Religion. About 40 percent of Cubans belong to the Roman Catholic Church. Many Cubans also believe in Santería, a religion that combines traditional African religious beliefs with Roman Catholic ceremonies. Protestant groups with widespread membership in Cuba include Methodists, Baptists, and Presbyterians. A small Jewish community is concentrated mostly in Havana.

Education. Cuba has one of the most extensive networks of schools in Latin America. All Cubans from the ages of 6 to 14 are required to attend school. Education is free. Nearly all Cuban adults can read and write. Cuba has dozens of universities and university-level educational institutions. The most important include the Central University "Marta Abreu" of Las Villas in Santa Clara, the University of Havana, the University of Oriente in Santiago de Cuba, and the Higher Institute of Art. In the early 2000s, the government began working on a plan to build a university branch in each municipality.

The arts. Cuba has a distinguished tradition in the arts. The Cuban government strongly supports the arts and sponsors free ballets, plays, and other cultural events for Cubans. The work of the government-sponsored Cuban Institute of Cinematographic Art and Industry has made Cuba a center of the Latin American film industry. The Casa de las Américas (House of the Americas)—which supports the work of artists, writers, and musicians—is one of Latin America's most prestigious cultural institutions.

Cuban paintings are known primarily for their strong colors and portrayals of dramatic actions. Armando Menocal, who began painting in the late 1800s, became famous for his murals and depictions of historical events. Well-known Cuban painters of the 1900s include Amelia Peláez, René Portocarrero, and Wifredo Lam. Peláez pioneered the introduction of Modern art in Cuba. Portocarrero and Lam combined African and Cuban elements in their works.

The poet José Martí was the most famous Cuban writer of the 1800s. Martí wrote eloquently on political subjects. Beginning in the 1880s, he led Cuba's fight for independence from Spain. The most prominent Cuban novelists of the early and middle 1900s included Alejo Carpentier and José Lezama Lima. Carpentier produced works in the style of *magic realism*, which blends dreams and magic with everyday reality. Lezama wrote poetry and literary reviews. Guillermo Cabrera Infante became one of Cuba's best-known novelists and short-story writers of the late 1900s. His innovative works of fiction are filled with many kinds of wordplay.

Cuban popular music has gained worldwide renown. This highly rhythmic music combines African and European, especially Spanish, traditions. Much Cuban music features guitars and such percussion instruments as castanets, maracas, and a variety of drums, including bongo drums. Cuban music has given rise to a number of dances, including the *cha-cha-cha, conga, mambo, rumba, son, Cuban bolero,* and *salsa.*

The Land

Cuba consists of a main island (Cuba) surrounded by more than 1,600 smaller islands. The Cuban mainland extends about 710 miles (1,150 kilometers) from northwest to southeast. At its widest point, the island measures 135 miles (217 kilometers). At its narrowest point, it reaches only about 20 miles (32 kilometers).

Cuba consists mainly of three mountainous regions separated by gentle slopes, rolling plains, and wide, fertile farmlands. The three mountainous regions rise in the west, in south-central Cuba, and in the southeast. The westernmost mountainous region of Cuba consists of two mountain ranges—the Sierra de los Órganos and the Sierra del Rosario. The south-central mountainous region is known as the Sierra de Escambray. It includes the Sierra de Trinidad and the Sierra de Sancti Spiritus ranges. The southeastern mountainous zone has several ranges. Among them is the Sierra Maestra range, which rises abruptly from the southeastern coast. The highest point in

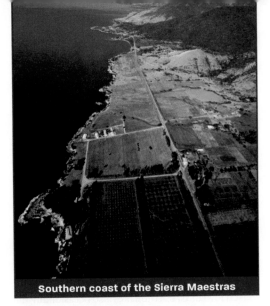

Southern coast of the Sierra Maestras

Cuba, the Pico Turquino, stands 6,542 feet (1,994 meters) high in the Sierra Maestra.

Cuba has more than 200 rivers and streams. Most of them are short, narrow, and shallow. Few inland waterways on the island can be navigated for any great distances. The longest river, the Cauto, flows about 150 miles (240 kilometers) through southeastern Cuba. It is navigable for only about 40 miles (65 kilometers).

The coastline of Cuba is marked with deep bays and sandy beaches. Much of the southern shoreline of Cuba in the west consists of a band of low marshland that is broken up into hundreds of *coral keys* and *mangrove swamps.* Coral keys are low islands that form when coral growths build up above the water. Mangrove swamps are created when the spreading roots of mangrove trees catch and hold soil. West of Cienfuegos lies the Zapata Peninsula, a vast swampland.

Cuba has over 200 natural harbors along its shoreline. The larger harbors have narrow entrances, which protect the inner area against winds and waves. Important northern harbors include Antilla, Cabañas, Cárdenas, Gibara, Havana, Honda, Manatí, Mariel, Matanzas, Nuevitas, and Puerto Padre. The chief southern harbors include Cienfuegos, Guantánamo, and Santiago de Cuba.

Climate

Cuba lies within the northern tropics and has a semitropical climate. Cool ocean breezes during the summer and warm breezes in the winter give the island a mild climate throughout the year. Average daily temperatures in Cuba range from about 70°F (21°C) in winter to about 80°F (27°C) in summer. The interior has a greater temperature range than the coastal regions. Temperatures on the island rarely fall below 40°F (4°C) or rise above 100°F (38°C). Frosts sometimes occur in the mountains.

Cuba has dry and rainy seasons. The dry season lasts from November through April, and the rainy season runs from May through October. Cuba has an average annual rainfall of more than 50 inches (125 centimeters). Thunderstorms occur almost daily in the rainy season.

Hurricanes frequently strike the island, especially its eastern and western tips. Hurricane season lasts from June to November. The strong winds from hurricanes occasionally destroy buildings and crops and create high waves that flood the coastal lowlands. Earthquakes also occasionally hit Cuba. They occur most frequently and most severely along the southeastern coast.

Economy

Cuba has a *gross domestic product* (GDP) of about $50 billion. A country's GDP is the total value of all goods and services the country produces in a year.

From 1961 to the early 1990s, government planning dominated key economic decisions in Cuba. A U.S. trade embargo imposed in 1960 contributed to the stagnation of Cuba's economy during this period. As a result, Cuba relied heavily on aid from, and trade with, the Soviet Union and other Communist nations.

Communism collapsed in Eastern Europe during the late 1980s, and the Soviet Union broke apart in 1991. These political changes caused a loss of trade for Cuba. To combat the economic crisis brought on by this loss, the Cuban government loosened its control over the economy. Foreign investment, previously discouraged by the government, began to return to the island, mainly in the tourist industry. Beginning in 1993, Cuba gradually started to permit some private enterprise. Many Cubans opened small businesses, including restaurants.

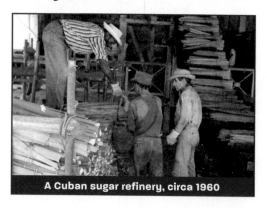

A Cuban sugar refinery, circa 1960

Manufacturing traditionally centered on sugar production, but about half of Cuba's sugar mills closed in the early 2000s as a result of decreased sugar prices. The manufacture of cigars is also important. Cuba is famous for fine hand-rolled cigars made from high-quality tobacco. Most cigar factories are in Havana. Other important industrial products include agricultural machinery, cement products, food and beverage products, petroleum and pharmaceutical products, and steel.

Agriculture. Sugarcane historically has been Cuba's most important crop. Although Cuba's sugar production has decreased significantly since the late 1900s, the country is still an important sugar producer. Coffee and tobacco are also important crops.

Through the years, the government has promoted attempts to grow other crops as a way for the country to supply more of its own food. As part of these efforts, the government has increased the production of bananas, citrus fruits, corn, potatoes, rice, and tomatoes. Livestock farming, particularly the raising of beef and dairy cattle, chickens, and hogs, is also important.

In the 1960s, about three-fourths of Cuba's farmland came under state control. Most farms were run as *state farms*, owned and operated by the government. Others were reorganized and operated as *farm cooperatives*, owned jointly by the government and groups of farmers. Some small farms remained under the control of individual owners, producing chiefly coffee and tobacco. In all cases, farmers were required to sell their products to the state at prices set by the government.

In the early 1990s, the government distributed more state lands to cooperatives and authorized farmers to sell their surplus production on the open market after certain quotas had been met. Soon, small farmers' markets sprang up across the island to sell a variety of products directly to the public. Cuba's armed forces also manage farms throughout the island and are a major producer of food.

Mining. Cuba's mines produce cement, cobalt, gold, iron ore, natural gas, nickel, and stone. Most of the nickel mines are on the eastern end of the island. Cuba also produces small but growing quantities of petroleum, which accounts for much of its energy production.

Fishing industry. State-owned Cuban fishing fleets range over the Caribbean Sea and parts of the North Atlantic Ocean. The important catches include such shellfish as lobsters and shrimp. Caibarién, Cienfuegos, and Havana are important fishing ports.

Service industries produce services rather than manufactured goods or agricultural products. They include banking, education, and health care. One of Cuba's fastest-growing service industries is tourism. The Cuban government has formed joint ventures with foreign investors to build new hotels and to restore old ones. Tourists have arrived in growing numbers, mainly from Canada and Europe.

International trade. From about 1900 to 1960, Cuba's principal trading partner was the United States. Beginning in the early 1960s, especially after U.S. sanctions were imposed, Cuban trade shifted largely to the Soviet Union and the Communist countries of Eastern Europe. By the mid-1980s, about 85 percent of all Cuban trade was with these Communist nations. The collapse of Communism left Cuba in search of new trading partners. Today, Cuba's chief trading partners are Brazil, Canada, China, Germany, Italy, Mexico, Russia, Spain, and Venezuela.

Cuban exports include citrus fruits, coffee, fish and shellfish, medical products, nickel, rum, sugar, and tobacco products. Among Cuba's chief imports are machinery, petroleum, and wheat and other food products.

Transportation and communication. About half of Cuba's roads are paved. The Central Highway extends between Pinar del Río, in the northwest, and Santiago de Cuba, in the southeast. However, gasoline rationing, problems in obtaining spare parts, and a scarcity of new vehicles often have made automobile transportation difficult. Railroads cross the island, but more people ride buses than trains. José Martí International Airport is the country's largest airport.

Cuba's principal newspaper is *Granma*, published by the Cuban Communist Party. The government or the Communist Party controls all newspapers, most magazines, and television and radio broadcasts.

History

Early years. The famous explorer Christopher Columbus landed in Cuba in 1492. At the time of Columbus's arrival, three groups of American Indians inhabited the island: the Guana-

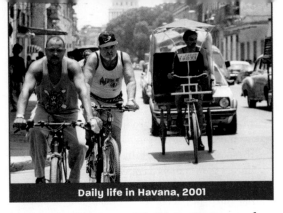

Daily life in Havana, 2001

hatabey, the Ciboney, and the Taíno. Estimates of the size of the Indian population at the time of European arrival vary widely—from as few as 16,000 to as many as 600,000.

Spanish soldiers and priests arrived in Cuba in 1511. The Indians resisted the Spanish effort to take over the island but soon were defeated. The Spaniards then forced the Indians to work in agriculture and mining. Many Indians died from diseases and harsh treatment. By the mid-1500s, only a few thousand Indians remained. As the Indian population declined, the Spaniards brought Africans to Cuba to work as slaves. The trade in African slaves began in Cuba during the 1520s but remained relatively limited until the late 1700s.

The island became strategically important to the Spanish colonial system in the New World. Control of Cuba offered Spain command of sea routes to Mexico, the Gulf Coast, western Florida, and Central America, as well as the chief sea lanes of the Caribbean. In 1564, Spain officially introduced its *fleet system*. Under it, merchant vessels carrying treasure from the New World sailed together in groups called *convoys*, which were protected by warships. Havana became the gathering place for the treasure ships before they set sail in convoys for Spain. Havana soon emerged as the island's political, administrative, economic, and cultural hub.

In 1762, the British seized Havana during the Seven Years' War, known in the United States as the French and Indian War. During their occupation, the British introduced reforms and established new trade ties between Cuba and the British colonies of North America, thus creating new, larger markets for Cuban sugar. The British also imported thousands of Africans to work as slaves.

The British returned control of Havana to Spain in 1763. After the restoration of Spanish rule, Spain eased trade restrictions, abolished duties on Cuban imports, and opened Cuban ports to unlimited trade in slaves. These actions helped the Cuban economy flourish.

In the late 1700s, a rebellion of black slaves in the French colony of Saint-Domingue (now

Haiti) destroyed the production of sugar and coffee there. About the same time, the world price of these products soared. In response, Cuban producers soon launched coffee production in eastern Cuba and expanded sugarcane cultivation throughout the island.

Through the years, sugar emerged as the most important Cuban export. Expanding sugar production led to the desire for more cheap labor. As a result, tens of thousands of Africans were brought to the island to work as slaves. Many owners treated their slaves brutally. In 1812, a group of slaves headed by José Antonio Aponte planned a revolt. The Spaniards discovered the plot and hanged Aponte and his followers.

Struggle against Spain. By the mid-1820s, nearly all of Spain's colonies in Latin America had won their independence. Various Cuban groups sought to end Spanish rule of their country as well. However, most of the island's white sugar-growing elite preferred to remain under Spanish rule to guarantee their wealth and a supply of slaves.

During the mid-1800s, some Cubans and Americans supported a movement to *annex* (join) Cuba to the United States. The annexation movement received much support from Cuban and American slaveholders. Other groups in Cuba and the United States favored American control of the island for economic and military reasons. The United States made three offers to buy Cuba, but Spain rejected them.

Cuba's struggle against Spanish rule led to the start of the Ten Years' War in 1868. Carlos Manuel de Céspedes, a landowner, headed a revolutionary group made up largely of poor sugar planters, mulattoes, free blacks, and slaves. The rebels wanted independence from Spain, the founding of a republic, and the gradual freeing of slaves. Spain rejected these demands, and bitter fighting followed. The war ended with the signing of the Pact of Zanjón in 1878. This treaty provided for political reforms and for the liberation of slaves who had joined the rebel army. A second unsuccessful rebellion against Spanish rule broke out in August 1879. Known as the Little War, it lasted until late 1880. A royal decree of 1886 finally ended slavery in Cuba.

In 1892, largely due to efforts by the exiled writer José Martí, the Cuban Revolutionary Party was organized. It united Cuban separatists in both Cuba and the United States. In 1895, these separatists launched a new war for Cuban independence.

President William McKinley of the United States claimed that the fighting in Cuba threatened American interests. He told Spain's government to either change its policy toward Cuba or give up the island completely. In February 1898, the U.S. battleship *Maine*, which had been sent to Havana to protect Americans in Cuba, exploded mysteriously. The United States blamed the Spaniards and, in April, declared war on Spain. This war became known in the United States as the Spanish-American War. In Cuba, the war that was fought from 1895 to 1898 is called the Spanish-Cuban-American War.

The U.S. intervention delivered the final blow to the Spanish army in Cuba. The Spaniards surrendered in July 1898, and an armistice in August ended the fighting. Under the Treaty of Paris, signed by the United States and Spain on December 10, Spain gave up all rights to the island. The United States then set up a military government in Cuba. Consequently, the Cubans did not achieve the independence they had hoped to gain.

The Platt Amendment. In 1901, Cuba adopted a constitution. The United States insisted that the constitution include a set of provisions called the Platt Amendment. The amendment limited Cuban independence by permitting the United States to intervene militarily in Cuban affairs. It also limited the Cuban government's power to make treaties with other governments. The amendment required Cuba to allow the United States to buy or lease land for naval bases on the island. Under a 1903 treaty with Cuba, the United States received a permanent lease on Guantánamo Bay and built a large naval base there.

The government of Cuba from 1902 to 1934 sometimes is referred to as a *neocolony*, meaning *new colony*. This period was marked by political instability, public corruption, and popular protest. The United States gained increasing control over Cuba's economic affairs and began to dominate Cuban trade.

In 1901, the Cuban people elected Tomás Estrada Palma as the first president of the Republic of Cuba. American troops left the country. In 1906, violent protests broke out in Cuba over the disputed outcome of a presidential election. United States troops then returned to Cuba under the terms of the Platt Amendment. A government headed by Charles E. Magoon of the United States ruled Cuba from 1906 to 1909, when the United States returned control of the country to the Cubans. American forces left the country, but the United States retained naval bases on the island.

An uprising broke out among black Cubans in 1912. The protesters objected to the lack of political opportunity and social advancement for black people in Cuba. In 1917, a revolt protesting electoral fraud erupted. During both uprisings, the United States sent military forces into the country.

Cuba suffered a severe economic collapse in 1920, when sugar prices rose rapidly, became overinflated, and then suddenly dropped. In 1924, still suffering from the economic collapse, Cubans elected Gerardo Machado president. During his campaign, Machado had attacked the Platt Amendment and promised reforms. But from 1927, he ruled as a dictator, provoking widespread unrest. In August 1933, a general strike and an army revolt forced Machado out of office. A month later, a group of army sergeants, corporals, and enlisted men led by Fulgencio Batista y Zaldívar and a group of university students and professors led a revolt that overthrew the new government. A five-man government briefly ruled the country, and then former university professor Ramón Grau San Martín became president.

The Grau government wanted to reduce U.S. influence in Cuba and make far-reaching changes. It passed a number of popular reforms, including laws that established an 8-hour workday and required all Cuban businesses to employ Cubans for at least half of their total workforce. The United States refused to recognize the Grau government. Left- and right-wing groups in Cuba also actively opposed the government.

The Batista era. Batista forced Grau to resign from office in 1934. Until 1940, Batista ruled Cuba as a dictator through presidents who served in name only. The United States recognized and supported Batista's government. In 1934, the United States and Cuba signed a treaty that canceled the Platt Amendment, except for the Guantánamo Bay lease. United States investments in Cuba continued to expand during the 1940s and 1950s. American interests eventually controlled about 40 percent of Cuba's sugar production. The United States also continued to be Cuba's chief trading partner.

In 1940, Cubans adopted a new constitution and elected Batista president. The constitution prevented Batista from seeking reelection in 1944. Grau, then leader of the Authentic Cuban Revolutionary Party (also known as the Auténticos), was elected president. Another Auténtico, Carlos Prío Socarrás, won the 1948 presidential election.

In 1952, Batista overthrew Prío's government and ruled Cuba as a dictator once again. Batista encouraged foreign companies, along with gambling and crime enterprises, to build businesses in Cuba. He also began to improve public works. But many Cubans remained unemployed and impoverished, and political conflict expanded across the island. Strikes and demonstrations became common.

The Castro revolution. On July 26, 1953, Fidel Castro, a young lawyer, tried to start a revolution against Batista by leading an attack on the Moncada army barracks in Santiago de Cuba. Fidel and his brother Raúl were captured and imprisoned. Many of their followers were either imprisoned or murdered.

The Castro brothers were released from prison in 1955. They then traveled to Mexico, where they met the Argentine revolutionary Ernesto "Che" Guevara. In 1956, while in Mexico, the brothers organized the 26th of July Movement, named for the date of their first revolt. The revolutionary forces landed in Oriente Province in late 1956. Most of the rebels were imprisoned or killed. However, the brothers and about a dozen of their followers escaped to the nearby Sierra Maestra mountains.

In 1957, the rebel forces began to wage a guerrilla war against the Cuban government. The same year, university students stormed the presidential palace in an attempt to assassinate Batista. Attempts by the government to crush dissent increased the people's support of the rebels. Continued poor economic conditions also led to growing support for the rebels, particularly among workers, peasants, students, and the middle class. By mid-1958, Batista's government had lost the support of the United States and most Cubans.

Fulgencio Batista y Zaldivar, 1955

On January 1, 1959, Batista fled the country. The Castro rebel forces then took control of the government. Fidel Castro became prime minister of Cuba. He went on to lead the nation for nearly 50 years, first as prime minister, and later as president. Raúl served as Fidel's second-in-command, becoming defense minister and leader of Cuba's armed forces.

The revolutionary leaders did away with the political and military structure of Batista's government. Many former political officials and military officers were tried and executed. A large number of middle- and upper-class Cubans went into exile in Florida.

The new Cuban government quickly set out to change Cuban relations with the United States. In particular, it sought to reduce U.S. influence on Cuban national affairs. In 1959, for example, the Cuban government seized U.S.-owned sugar estates. As a result, U.S.-Cuba relations quickly became strained. As relations with the United States deteriorated, Cuba developed stronger economic ties with the Soviet Union. In 1960, Castro's government signed a broad trade pact with the Soviet Union.

In June 1960, the Castro government took over American and British oil refineries in Cuba after the refineries refused to process crude oil imported from the Soviet Union. The United States then stopped buying sugar from Cuba. Over the next few months, the Castro government took over all the remaining American businesses in Cuba and accepted Soviet offers to purchase Cuban sugar. In October 1960, the United States placed an economic embargo on Cuba, which banned all U.S. exports except medicines and some food products. In January 1961, the United States ended diplomatic relations with Cuba.

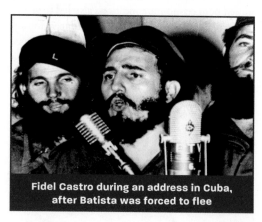
Fidel Castro during an address in Cuba, after Batista was forced to flee

The Bay of Pigs invasion. In April 1961, Cuban exiles sponsored by the United States Central Intelligence Agency (CIA) invaded Cuba at the Bay of Pigs on the south coast. Castro's forces crushed the invasion and captured most of the exiles. Castro later released many of the exiles to the United States in exchange for nonmilitary supplies. Shortly before the invasion, Castro first declared Cuba's revolution to be socialist. In the months after the invasion, Cuba's political system began to follow a Communist model. The political groups supporting Castro were combined and reorganized several times before the Cuban Communist Party that exists today was created in 1965.

The Cuban missile crisis. Cuban leaders feared another direct U.S. invasion. The Soviet Union offered military aid to Cuba, and Cuba agreed to let the Soviet Union send missiles and materials to build launch sites. In October 1962, the United States learned that Cuba had nuclear missiles in place that could be launched toward American cities. President John F. Kennedy ordered a naval blockade to halt the further shipment of arms. He demanded that the Soviet Union remove all missiles from the island and dismantle the remaining missile bases. For days, the world stood on the brink of nuclear war. Finally, the Soviet Union removed the weapons under protest from Castro. The Soviet action came after Kennedy privately agreed not to invade Cuba.

Social programs. The Castro government made many changes for the better. It built many new schools and improved old ones, and school enrollments and literacy rates increased dramatically. The government also improved medical and dental care facilities. The number of doctors and other health professionals increased. Health conditions improved, and life expectancy rose. Housing reforms, the introduction of food rationing, and a drive for greater equality led to more opportunities for minorities and the poor. Women began attending universities and joining the labor force in greater numbers. Blacks also received increased educational, employment, and political opportunities.

However, other changes were not as good. The government jailed many of its opponents. Critics charged that the Cuban people lacked many political and economic freedoms. Government-run companies had an equal-pay system that paid similar wages to many workers regardless of their position or experience level.

Foreign relations. In the 1960s, Castro and Che Guevara tried to spread revolution throughout Latin America, mainly by supplying military aid to guerrilla groups in several Latin American countries. In the 1970s, Cuba also sent troops and civilian military advisers to aid new governments in Angola and Ethiopia, in Africa. The Soviet Union eventually provided most of the military supplies for Cuba's African operations. Cuba withdrew its last troops from Africa in 1991.

Relations between Cuba and the United States remained strained, despite occasional signs of improvement. Partial diplomatic relations between the two countries were restored in 1977. The United States kept its trade embargo, imposed in 1960, in place. During the 1990s, the United States passed legislation, including the Helms-Burton Act of 1996, to broaden and tighten trade sanctions against Cuba. In 2000, however, the U.S. Congress passed legislation allowing cash sales of U.S. food and medicine to Cuba.

Another serious issue between Cuba and the United States involved the immigration of Cubans to the United States. During the first decade after the revolution, hundreds of thousands of Cubans left the country because they opposed Castro or were dissatisfied with their social and economic conditions. Most of these people settled in the United States. From 1966, the United States had a policy of giving political asylum to all Cubans who reached its shores.

Another wave of immigration took place in 1980, when more than 125,000 Cubans moved to the United States. Most of them came from the western port of Mariel. Following yet another wave of immigration, of about 35,000 people, in 1994, Cuba and the United States reached an immigration agreement. The United States consented to admit at least 20,000 new legal immigrants from Cuba annually and to return to Cuba any illegal migrants caught at sea. In return, Cuba pledged to do more to prevent illegal departures.

Economic troubles. In the late 1980s, non-Communist governments replaced Communist ones in most Eastern European nations. In 1991, the Soviet Union was dissolved and its Communist government was replaced. As a result, Cuba lost its most important source of trade and financial support, and the economy suffered. To ease the economic crisis, the Cuban government undertook limited reforms that loosened state control over parts of the economy. In an attempt to stimulate foreign investment in Cuba, the government also sought to improve relations with Canada and with European and Latin American nations.

Recent developments. In late 2000, relations between Cuba and the United States began to worsen. The United States again tightened its trade embargo in the early 2000s. In Cuba, the government began a so-called Battle of Ideas. This campaign sought to strengthen youths' commitment to Cuba's political system and introduced educational reforms. In 2002, former U.S. president Jimmy Carter traveled to Cuba in an attempt to improve relations between the two countries. Carter unsuccessfully urged the Cuban government to adopt democratic reforms and called on the United States to end its trade embargo.

In 2006, Fidel Castro became ill and temporarily gave control of the government to Raúl. In 2008, Fidel gave up the leadership of Cuba, and the National Assembly elected Raúl to succeed him. Raúl's government soon announced a number of economic reforms. For example, it lifted restrictions on consumer access to certain electronic goods, allowed farmers greater control of land use, and ended the equal-pay system, enabling workers to earn more for better performance.

In 2008, Hurricanes Gustav and Ike caused billions of dollars' worth of damage to Cuba. Hundreds of thousands of homes were destroyed or damaged, and many agricultural crops were devastated.

In 2009 and 2011, U.S. president Barack Obama eased restrictions on travel to Cuba for Cuban Americans and for U.S. academic, cultural, and religious groups. The Obama government also eased rules about *remittances* (money that is sent) from the United States to Cuba and allowed U.S. telecommunications companies to begin operating in Cuba.

Hurricane Sandy struck Cuba in October 2012, killing at least 11 people. The storm also damaged or destroyed tens of thousands of homes and much of the island's coffee crop.

MLA Citation

"Cuba." *The Southwestern Advantage Topic Source.* Nashville: Southwestern. 2013.

DATA

Economic Production in Cuba

Sources: Cuba's Office of National Statistics; United Nations. Figures are for 2007; employment figures include full- and part-time workers.

Economic activities	% of GDP[1] produced	Number of workers	% of all workers
Community, social, and personal services	36	2,063,400	42
Trade, restaurants, and hotels	26	613,600	13
Manufacturing	13	523,300	11
Transportation and communication	8	289,300	6
Construction	6	243,700	5
Finance, insurance, real estate, and business services	5	111,400	2
Agriculture	4	912,300	19
Utilities	2	85,000	2
Mining	2	25,700	1
Total[2]	100	4,867,700	100

[1] GDP = gross domestic product, the total value of goods and services produced within a country in a year.

[2] Figures do not add up to 100 percent due to rounding.

ADDITIONAL RESOURCES

Books to Read

Base, Ron. *Cuba: Portrait of an Island*. Interlink Books, 2005.

Dosal, Paul J. *Cuba Libre: A Brief History of Cuba*. Harlan Davidson, 2006.

Dubois, Muriel L. *Cuba*. Capstone Press, 2005.

Pérez, Louis A., Jr. *Cuba: Between Reform and Revolution*. 3rd ed. Oxford, 2006.

Sheehan, Sean, and Jermyn, Leslie. *Cuba*. 2nd ed. Benchmark Books, 2005.

Staten, Clifford L. *The History of Cuba*. Greenwood, 2003.

Web Sites

Country Profile: Cuba

http://news.bbc.co.uk/2/hi/americas/country_profiles/1203299.stm
Information from the BBC.

Cuban Missile Crisis

http://www.wyzant.com/Help/History/HPOL/JFK/Cuban
A speech by President John F. Kennedy during the Cuban Missile Crisis.

Radio Habana Cuba

http://www.radiohc.org/

Official news organization of Cuban government

Cuban Heritage Collection Home Page

http://www.library.miami.edu/chc

The Cuban Heritage Collection at the University of Miami Library, featuring historical pictures and information.

Search Strings

Fidel Castro

Cuba "Fidel Castro" (773,000)

Cuba "Fidel Castro" "Fulgencio Batista" dictatorship Communist (39,600)

"Fidel Castro" Cuba Batista dictatorship Communist (71,800)

"Fidel Castro" history Cuba Batista dictatorship Communist (53,300)

Cuba-United States Relations

Cuba United States relations (449,000)

Cuba "United States" relations diplomacy "Soviet Union" Castro (12,600)

Cuba "United States" relations diplomacy Communism "Soviet Union" Castro (10,700)

The Effect of the Collapse of the Soviet Union on Cuba

effect of the collapse of the Soviet Union on Cuba (122,000)

effect of the collapse of the Soviet Union on Cuba economic crisis tourism (229,000)

effect of the collapse of the "Soviet Union" on Cuba "economic crisis" tourism (4580)

Cuban Missile Crisis

Cuban Missile Crisis President John Kennedy (64,200)

"Cuban Missile Crisis" President "John Kennedy" "Soviet Union" (17,300)

"Cuban Missile Crisis" President "John Kennedy" "Soviet Union" nuclear Turkey (664)

BACKGROUND INFORMATION

The following articles were written during the year in which the events took place and reflect the style and thinking of that time.

Cuba (1980)

In one of the most remarkable exoduses of modern times, some 125,000 Cubans fled their homeland in 1980 and sought refuge in the United States and elsewhere. The mass departure was triggered on April 4 when about 25 Cubans sought political asylum in the Peruvian Embassy in Havana. Within days, their number multiplied, and by mid-April, when Cuba began granting exit visas, the crowd had swollen to nearly 11,000.

The boat-lift. Other embassies became equally swamped. Some countries—such as Spain, Costa Rica, and Venezuela—began evacuating the refugees by plane. In the United States, Cuban-American boat owners and others formed flotillas to head for various Cuban ports. For weeks, the nearly 100-mile (160-kilometer) stretch of water between Cuba and Florida was speckled with boats.

U.S. president Jimmy Carter, caught off guard as the influx into the United States reached massive proportions, quickly adjusted U.S. policy. He switched from a position threatening legal action against those operating the refugee boat-lift, to an offer of government assistance in mounting an orderly transfer of the disaffected Cubans. Moreover, the U.S. government took a leading role in ensuring a welcome for the refugees in 18 other nations that offered refuge. President Fidel Castro took advantage of the boat-lift operation to empty jails of hardened criminals and forcibly deport homosexuals and the insane. He unilaterally ended the boat-lift on September 26.

Castro's behavior seemed to foreclose for the time being any improvement in United States-Cuban relations. Relations were further chilled by Cuba's involvement in fomenting rebellion elsewhere in Latin America and in Africa and the Middle East. For Russia, the cost of maintaining Cuba as a satellite and its representative in developing countries rose sharply in 1980 to an estimated $6 million to $8 million per day.

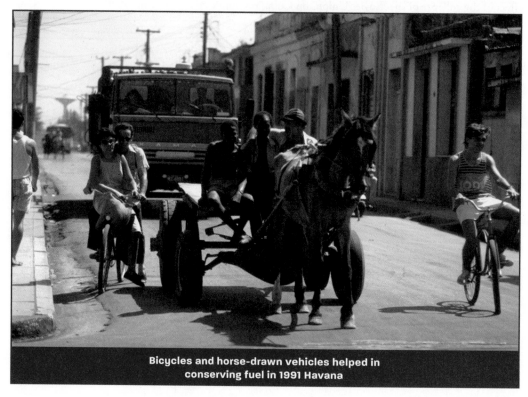

Bicycles and horse-drawn vehicles helped in conserving fuel in 1991 Havana

The Cuban economy was in a shambles, according to a secret report made by Castro on December 27, 1979, to Cuba's leadership. The Cuban ruler reshuffled his cabinet on January 11, and took over the management of key ministries. He also continued his quest for Third World leadership. While in Managua, Nicaragua, in July for ceremonies marking the triumph of that nation's revolution, Castro warned against the consequences of a victory by Republican Ronald Reagan in the U.S. presidential elections. Seemingly to help reelect Carter, he freed 30 Americans from Cuban jails shortly before the November elections.

Cuba (1991)

The collapse of Communism in the Soviet Union in 1991 brought an end to Soviet assistance to Cuba. Nevertheless, Cuban president Fidel Castro positioned himself and Cuba to survive, if not embrace, a changed world. Addressing members of Cuba's ruling Communist Party on October 12, Castro called Western democracy "complete garbage," indicating that he had no intention of introducing the democratic reforms that had undermined Soviet Communist rule.

On September 19, the Soviet government said that it would withdraw all of its military troops and advisers from Cuba, thus ending a troublesome chapter of the Cold War and leaving Cuba to defend itself. On May 25, the last Cuban soldiers departed from Angola, where they had been supporting a Marxist regime for more than a decade.

Without the support of a superpower, Castro was forced to make peace with his neighbors. In July, he attended a meeting in Mexico where some of his democratically elected peers lectured him about the need for Cuba to adopt a more open political system. In August, he welcomed some 14,000 athletes, journalists, and officials—including 2,000 Americans—to Havana for the Pan American Games, one of the first nonpolitical events in Cuba since Castro came to power in 1959. At a meeting in Mexico on October 23, 1991, Castro asked the leaders of Mexico, Colombia, and Venezuela for help in persuading the United States to lift its trade embargo against Cuba.

With the end of Soviet assistance, life became harder for Cubans. On June 1, the government cut the daily bread ration in Havana to 3 ounces (85 grams), the equivalent of one small loaf or two rolls. On September 9, cigars and cigarettes joined the expanding list of rationed items, which included everything from food and fuel to paper and shoes. There were cuts in public transportation, and bicycles became a major mode of transportation. Factories had to shorten workdays or close because of the loss of Soviet and Eastern bloc raw materials.

Call for elections. On May 31, a group of Cuban intellectuals issued a declaration calling for democratic reforms. Among the reforms demanded were free, direct election of delegates to Cuba's National Assembly; the elimination of restrictions on emigration; the return of peasant free markets, which provide people a chance to meet food shortages by selling their own produce; and the freeing of political prisoners.

Nuclear safety. Also on May 31, the U.S. government urged Cuba to work with the United Nations International Atomic Energy Agency to guarantee safe completion of a nuclear power plant on Cuba's southern coast. With reduced Soviet assistance, there were fears that Cuba did not have the necessary technicians to finish the job safely.

Mexico

Mexico is the northernmost country of Latin America. It lies just south of the United States.

HOT topics

Ancestry. The majority of the Mexican people are mestizos (people of mixed ancestry). Their white ancestors were mostly Spaniards who came during and after the Spanish conquest of 1519–1521. Their indigenous ancestors lived in Mexico when the Spaniards arrived. Some mestizos are also descended fom Africans brought to Mexico to serve as slaves. Being a mestizo is generally a matter of national pride. Most of Mexico's political, business, intellectual, and military leaders are mestizos.

Language. Almost all Mexicans speak Spanish, the official language of Mexico and most other Latin American countries. Many words used in the United States came from Mexico. They include canyon, corral, desperado, lariat, lasso, macho, patio, politico, rodeo, and stampede. Most indigenous Mexicans speak Spanish along with their own

HOT topics

ancient language in daily life. Altogether, they speak more than 60 Amerindian languages. Major Amerindian languages include Maya, Mixtec, Nahuatl, Otomi, Tarascan, and Zapotec.

City Life. Mexico City and its metropolitan area has a population of about 20 million. Nine other cities in the country have more than 1 million people. City centers are filled with high-rise buildings. Modern houses and apartment buildings occupy the suburbs, but older parts still have rows of homes built in the Spanish colonial style. Mexican cities have grown as people have moved from rural areas to find jobs and a better life. As a result, many cities suffer from serious social and environmental problems. Some houses in poor sections are made of scraps of wood, metal, and whatever other materials can be found. Most of them lack electric power and running water. The large number of cars and trucks in Mexico City cause frequent traffic jams and bad air pollution.

Corn and the Mexican Diet. Thousands of years ago, the indigenous inhabitants of what is now Mexico discovered how to grow corn. It became their most important food. Today, corn is still the chief food of most Mexicans, especially in rural areas. Mexican cooks generally soften the corn in hot limewater, boil it, and then grind it into meal. The main cornmeal food is the tortilla, a thin, flat bread shaped by hand or machine and cooked on an ungreased griddle. It also may be made with wheat flour. The tortilla is the bread of most Mexicans and the staple of Mexican cuisine in America.

Monument to Independence, Mexico City, at dusk

A farmer harvests ears of corn.

TRUE or FALSE?

More than 85 percent of Mexico's people belong to the Roman Catholic Church.

THE BASICS

Mexico is the northernmost country of Latin America. It lies just south of the United States. The Rio Grande, one of the longest rivers in North America, forms about two-thirds of the boundary between Mexico and the United States. Among all the countries of the Western Hemisphere, only the United States and Brazil have more people than Mexico. Mexico City is the capital and largest city of Mexico. It also is one of the world's largest metropolitan areas in population.

Towering mountains and high, rolling plateaus cover more than two-thirds of Mexico. Mexico also has tropical forests, deserts, and fertile valleys. Few other countries have such a wide variety of landscapes and climates within such short distances of one another.

To understand Mexico, one must consider its long early history. Centuries ago, the indigenous (native) population of Mexico, also called Amerindians or Indians, developed several advanced civilizations. These civilizations built large cities, developed a calendar, invented a counting system, used a form of writing, and established vast empires. The last indigenous empire in Mexico—the Aztec empire—fell to Spanish invaders in 1521. For the next 300 years, Mexico was a Spanish colony. The Spaniards took Mexico's

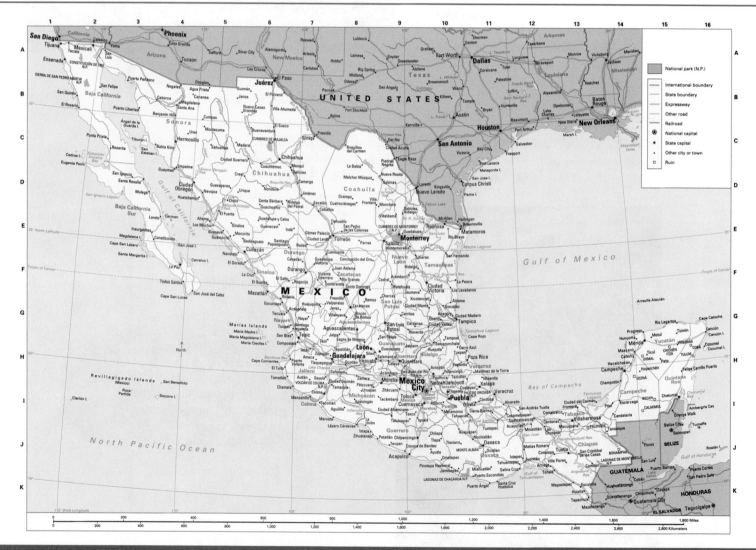

Map of Mexico

agricultural and mineral riches. They also introduced many changes in farming, government, industry, population, and religion. The descendants of the Spaniards became Mexico's ruling class. Most of the indigenous people remained poor and uneducated.

During the Spanish colonial period, a third group of people developed in Mexico. These people had both indigenous and European ancestors—and, in some cases, African ancestors as well. These Mexicans of mixed ancestry became known as *mestizos.*

Mexico gained independence from Spain in 1821. Over the next 50 years, the country experienced civil war, economic decline, and foreign intervention that resulted in the loss of half its territory. An uprising called the Mexican Revolution began in 1910, when the people of Mexico overthrew a long-standing dictatorship. The revolutionaries promised to work for greater social justice, democratic reform, and economic development. As a result of the revolution, the government took over huge, privately owned landholdings and divided them among millions of landless farmers. The government also established a national school system and built many hospitals and housing projects. To deal with the pressure of rapid population growth on the economy, the government especially encouraged the development of manufacturing and petroleum production.

The great majority of Mexicans are mestizos. Indigenous people make up the second largest population group. Both groups generally take great pride in their Indian heritage. A number of government programs emphasize the indigenous role in Mexican culture. In 1949, the government made the last Aztec emperor, Cuauhtémoc, the symbol of Mexican nationality. Cuauhtémoc faced the Spanish invaders so bravely that he became a Mexican hero.

Manufacturing, agriculture, mining, and tourism are all important to Mexico's economy. Leading manufactured products include automobiles, chemicals, processed foods, and steel. Cropland covers a small amount of Mexico's area. The rest of the land is too dry, too mountainous, or otherwise unsuitable for crops. However, Mexico is one of the world's leading producers of cacao beans (from which chocolate is made), coffee, corn, oranges, and sugarcane.

Mexico is rich in minerals. It is one of the leading producers of silver in the world and also has

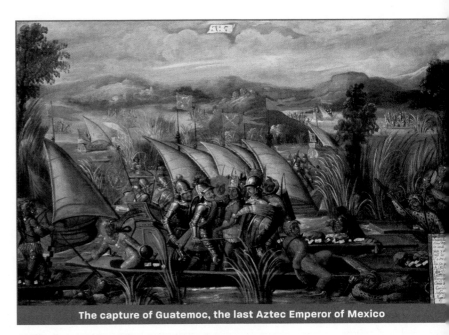

The capture of Guatemoc, the last Aztec Emperor of Mexico

large deposits of copper, gold, lead, salt, and sulfur. Mexico became the world's leading oil exporter in 1921. In the 1970s, after decades of low production, Mexico reemerged as a major exporter of petroleum products.

Since the late 1900s, Mexican leaders have tried to develop the economy by fostering ties with other countries, particularly the United States. However, Mexico continues to face difficult economic and social problems, and a majority of its people still live in poverty.

Government

Mexico is a federal republic with an executive branch, a legislative branch, and a judicial branch. The executive branch, headed by a president, is the decision-making center of the government. It establishes government policies, proposes laws, and controls the distribution of federal tax revenues.

Mexico has 31 states and 1 federal district. Each state has an elected governor and legislature. The Federal District is governed by the elected mayor of Mexico City. All Mexicans who are at least 18 years old can vote.

National government. Mexico's president has a significant role in the national government. All prominent political figures in the executive branch depend directly on the president for their jobs. The president appoints a cabinet that directs government operations. Important cabinet members include the secretary of government and the secretary of finance and public credit. The president also originates much legislation. Some presidents have introduced constitutional amendments to support their own policies.

The president is elected by the people to a six-year term and may serve only one term of office. If the president does not finish the term, the legislature chooses a temporary president to serve until a special or regular presidential election is held.

Mexico's legislature is called the Congress. It consists of a Senate and a Chamber of Deputies. The Senate has 128 members who are elected to six-year terms. The Chamber of Deputies has 500 members elected to three-year terms. Three hundred of the deputies are elected from the country's electoral districts. The remaining 200 seats are filled by deputies who do not represent a particular district. Members of Congress may serve multiple, but not consecutive, terms.

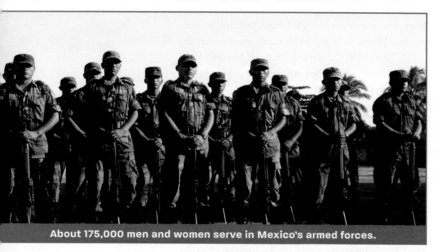

About 175,000 men and women serve in Mexico's armed forces.

State and local government. The people elect state governors to six-year terms and state legislators to three-year terms. The president may remove governors from office with the Senate's approval. Each state is divided into *municipios* (townships). Each municipio has a president and a council elected to three-year terms. Less than 10 percent of all tax revenues go directly to state and local agencies. State agencies depend on the national government, and local authorities on state agencies, for funds to carry out public works projects.

Politics. Mexico has a number of political parties. The most important include the Partido Revolucionario Institucional (Institutional Revolutionary Party), also known as the PRI; the Partido Acción Nacional (National Action Party), or

PAN; and the Partido de la Revolución Democrática (Party of the Democratic Revolution), or PRD.

The PRI, established in 1929 as the Partido Nacional Revolucionario (National Revolutionary Party), dominated Mexican politics and government until the end of the 1900s. In 2000, a non-PRI candidate was elected president for the first time in 71 years.

Courts. Mexico's highest court at the federal level is the Supreme Court of Justice. The president appoints 11 members to the court with the approval of the Senate. The federal judicial system also includes hundreds of circuit and district courts. The highest court in each state is a Superior Court of Justice.

Mexico's courts play a limited role. The courts rarely declare a law unconstitutional and generally support the president's policies. Mexicans may use the courts to protect their individual rights through an *amparo* (protection) procedure. In amparo cases, the courts may decide that a law has resulted in unfair treatment and that an exception should be made. However, the law in question is not changed. Most Mexicans cannot afford to use the legal process.

Armed forces. Mexico has an army and a smaller navy and air force. Mexican men are required to serve part-time for a year in the army after reaching the age of 18.

People

Population. Mexico's population has increased rapidly as a result of a traditionally high birth rate and a sharply reduced death rate. The reduced death rate is due in part to improved living conditions and expanded health services since the early 1950s. Since 1980, the most rapid population growth has occurred in the states of Baja California, Baja California Sur, and Quintana Roo.

About half of the people of Mexico are under 25 years of age. The relatively young population and its high growth rate have placed tremendous pressure on such services as education, health care, and social security. The strain on basic services is especially serious in urban centers. Many cities lack adequate housing, drinking water, and public transportation.

The high rate of population growth has also contributed to a shortage of jobs in Mexico. Since the 1980s, far more people have entered the labor

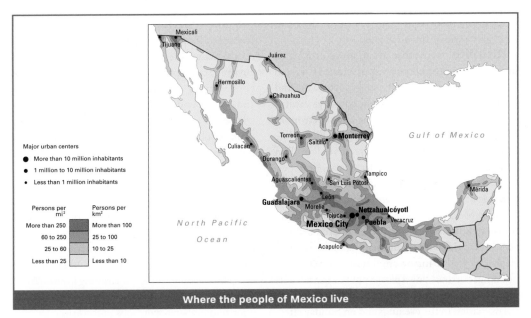

Where the people of Mexico live

force than have retired, and the economy has generally failed to create enough jobs. This situation has led to a high rate of unemployment. It has also stimulated increasing migration of Mexicans to the United States.

Ancestry. The majority of Mexicans are mestizos. Their white ancestors were mostly Spaniards who came during and after the Spanish conquest of 1519 to 1521. Their indigenous ancestors lived in Mexico when the Spaniards arrived. Some mestizos are also descended from Africans brought to colonial Mexico to serve as slaves. Being a mestizo is generally a matter of pride.

Indigenous people make up Mexico's second largest population group. Being indigenous in Mexico does not depend chiefly on ancestry. It is mostly a matter of lifestyle, language, and viewpoint. For example, Mexicans are considered indigenous if they speak an Amerindian language or wear clothing typical of an indigenous people. Such peoples include the Nahua of central Mexico; the Mixtec, mainly from Oaxaca state; and the Maya of southeast Mexico. In the heavily indigenous south, Amerindian traditions influence mestizo ways of life.

Most of Mexico's political, business, intellectual, and military leaders are mestizos, though whites remain influential. In addition to whites, the people of Mexico include some Asians of unmixed ancestry.

Language. Almost all Mexicans speak Spanish, the official language of Mexico and most other Latin American countries. Many words used in the United States came from Mexico, including *canyon, corral, desperado, lariat, lasso, macho, patio, politico, rodeo,* and *stampede.*

Most indigenous Mexicans speak Spanish along with their own ancient language, but millions of them primarily use their indigenous language in daily life. Altogether, they speak more than 60 Amerindian languages and dialects. Major Amerindian languages include Maya, Mixtec, Nahuatl, Otomí, Tarascan, and Zapotec.

Way of Life

The way of life in Mexico includes many traditions from the nation's long indigenous past and the Spanish colonial period. But Mexico changed rapidly in the 1900s. In many ways, life in its larger cities has become similar to that in the neighboring United States. Mexican villagers follow the older way of life more than urban Mexicans do. Even in the villages, however, government programs are doing much to modernize people's lives. Schools, health clinics, roads, electric power and running water, and government-sponsored television are bringing people in small towns into mainstream Mexican life.

Mexican households have five or six people on average. It is common for several generations to live together. Many urban women have jobs. Women in farming areas often help cultivate the fields. Mexican girls have less personal freedom than girls do in Canada and the United States. Farm boys work in the fields, and many youths in the cities have part-time or full-time jobs.

City life. The most urban areas of Mexico include the metropolitan areas of Mexico City and Guadalajara and the states of Nuevo León and Baja California. Mexico City, the country's capital, has about 9 million people. The city's metropolitan area has a population of about 20 million. Nine other Mexican cities have more than 1 million people. These cities are, in order of size, Ecatepec, Guadalajara, Puebla, Juárez, Tijuana, León, Zapopan, Monterrey, and Netzahualcóyotl.

Many Mexican cities and towns began as indigenous communities. After the Spaniards arrived, they built cities with traditional European layouts. Each city had a major church and government buildings surrounding a *plaza* (public square). The plaza is still the center of city life in Mexico, even in large cities. In the evenings and on Sunday afternoons, people gather in the plaza to socialize or listen to music.

The city centers are filled with high-rise buildings, and modern houses and apartment buildings occupy the suburbs. Older parts of towns and cities have rows of homes built in the Spanish colonial style. Most of these houses are made of stone or *adobe* (sun-dried clay) brick. Small balconies extend from some windows. A Spanish-style house also has a *patio* (courtyard), which is the center of family life. This gardenlike area may have a fountain, flowers, vines, and pots of blooming plants.

Mexican cities have grown as people have moved from rural areas to find jobs and a better life. As a result, many cities suffer from serious social and environmental problems. Houses in many of the poor sections are made of scraps of wood, metal, and other found materials. Most of them lack electric power and running water. The large number of automobiles results in frequent traffic jams. Air pollution in Mexico City causes many people to suffer from respiratory and eye diseases.

Many people who migrate to cities have no regular jobs. Others do not earn enough to support themselves. Entire families must work, sometimes at two or three jobs, to survive. Many unskilled poor people find jobs as construction workers, street cleaners, or street vendors. Others make a living by washing clothes or cleaning homes. After they have lived in a city for a while, many of the poor find higher-paying jobs in factories.

Rural life. About 1 out of every 4 Mexicans lives on a farm or in a small village. Most farmers live near their fields. The villages are poor, with little access to such basic social services as health care and education. Most young people leave their villages to find work in Mexican cities and towns or in the United States.

Village homes stand along simple dirt or cobblestone roads. In most villages, a Roman Catholic church rises on one side of the plaza, which forms the center of the community. Shops and government buildings line the plaza's other sides.

Almost every village, and every city and town, has a marketplace. Going to market is one of the chief activities of people in farming areas. They generally spend one day each week there, doing business and chatting with friends. The people bring clothes, food, and other goods that they wish to sell or trade. They display them in rented stalls or spread them on the ground. Farmers often trade their goods instead of selling them, and much bargaining takes place.

The shape and style of village houses vary according to the climate. People on the dry central plateau build homes of adobe, brick, cement block, or stone, with flat roofs made of red tile, sheet metal, or straw. Some of these houses have only one room, a dirt floor, and few or no windows. The kitchen may be a structure called a *lean-to*, built of poles and cornstalks placed against an outside wall. If a house does not have a lean-to kitchen, the family may build a cooking fire on the floor.

Almost every village, town, and city in Mexico has a marketplace.

In areas of heavy rainfall, many houses have walls built of poles coated with lime and clay. This mixture lasts longer than adobe does in the rain. The houses have sloping roofs that allow rain to run off easily. Some indigenous people in southern Mexico build round houses. In Yucatán, most village houses are rectangular with rounded ends. The roofs are made of palm leaves.

Most indigenous people live in villages in central and southern Mexico and the Yucatán Peninsula and are poor. Dishonest outsiders, both Mexican and foreign, have treated them unfairly, sometimes taking their land, exploiting them for cheap labor, or charging them higher prices for goods and services. As a result, conflicts have occurred between indigenous communities and their wealthier neighbors.

Food and drink. Thousands of years ago, the indigenous inhabitants of what is now Mexico discovered how to grow corn. It became their most important food. Today, corn is still the chief food of most Mexicans, especially in rural areas. Mexican cooks generally soften the corn before cooking by soaking it in a mild chemical solution called *limewater*. Then they boil the corn and grind it into meal.

The main cornmeal food is the *tortilla*, which is a thin, flat bread shaped by hand or machine and cooked on an ungreased griddle. Tortillas also can be made with wheat flour. The tortilla is the bread of most Mexicans. They eat tortillas plain or as part of *tacos* (folded tortillas filled with chopped meat or cheese, then sometimes fried), *enchiladas* (rolled-up tortillas filled with chopped meat or cheese and covered with hot sauce), or *tostadas* (fried tortillas served flat with meat, cheese, beans, lettuce, and onions). In northern Mexico, wheat tortillas are more common. A burrito is a large wheat-flour tortilla filled with such ingredients as cheese, beans, vegetables, rice, and hot sauce.

Many Mexicans eat *frijoles* (beans) that are boiled and mashed, then fried and refried in lard. Poorer Mexicans may eat frijoles every day, often using a folded tortilla to scoop them up. Rice is also boiled and then fried. Other popular foods include *atole* (a thick, soupy cornmeal dish) and *tamales* (cornmeal steamed in corn husks or banana leaves and usually mixed with pork or chicken). Most Mexicans like their food highly seasoned with chili pepper or other hot peppers. Turkey is a popular holiday dish. It is often served with mole sauce made of chocolate, chili, sesame seeds, and spices.

Poorer families eat little meat because they cannot afford it. They may vary their basic diet of corn and beans with fruit, honey, onions, tomatoes, squash, or sweet potatoes. Favorite fruits include avocados, bananas, mangoes, oranges, and papayas. The fruit and leaves of the prickly pear cactus are eaten boiled, fried, or stewed. Wealthier Mexicans have a more balanced diet.

Popular beverages in Mexico include water flavored with fruit juice and cinnamon-flavored hot chocolate beaten into foam. Mexicans also drink coffee, milk, and mineral water, and they are especially fond of soft drinks. Alcoholic beverages include beer and wine as well as two popular distilled liquors called *mescal* and *tequila*, both made from the juice of the maguey plant.

Men and women in traditional attire dance at the Guelaguetza Festival

Clothing. Urban Mexicans wear clothing like that worn in the United States and Canada. Villagers wear simple clothes that vary according to region and climate. The designs of these clothes date back centuries. In central and southern Mexico, men generally wear plain cotton shirts and trousers and leather sandals called *huaraches*. Wide-brimmed felt or straw hats called *sombreros* protect them from the hot sun. During cold or rainy weather, they may wear *ponchos* (blankets with a slit in the center for the head). At night, they may wrap themselves in colorful *serapes*, which are blankets carried over one shoulder during the day. Village women wear blouses and long, full skirts. They usually go barefoot or wear sandals. The women cover their heads with fringed shawls called *rebozos*. A mother may tie her baby to her back with a rebozo.

Some clothing worn by villagers is homemade. Handweaving is an ancient indigenous art, and many Amerindian communities are famous for their beautiful home-woven fabrics. Styles of weaving vary throughout Mexico, and the colors and design of a poncho or serape can show where it came from. For example, blankets with a striped rainbow pattern come from the Saltillo area in northern Mexico.

Some indigenous people wear distinctive clothing. In Oaxaca state, Amerindians wear large capes made of straw. On holidays, indigenous women on the Isthmus of Tehuantepec wear a wide, white, lacy headdress called a *huipil grande*. In Yucatán, Maya women wear long, loose, white dresses that are embroidered around the neck and the bottom hem.

Mexicans sometimes wear national costumes on special occasions. The men's national costumes include the dark blue charro suit, made of doeskin or velvet. It has a *bolero* (short jacket) and tight riding pants with gold or silver buttons down the sides. A flowing red bow tie, spurred boots, and a fancy white sombrero complete the costume. The best-known women's costume is probably the *china poblana*. It is usually worn for the *jarabe tapatío*, also known as the Mexican hat dance. According to legend, the china poblana was named for a Chinese princess of the 1600s who was kidnapped by pirates and sold to a merchant of Puebla. It consists of a full red-and-green skirt with beads and other ornaments, a colorfully embroidered short-sleeved blouse, and a brightly colored sash.

Holidays. Mexicans celebrate their Independence Day, September 16, and other holidays with colorful *fiestas* (festivals). Every city, town, and village holds a yearly fiesta to honor its patron saint. Most fiestas begin before dawn with ringing bells and a shower of fireworks. During the fiestas, the people pray and burn candles to their saints in churches decorated with flowers and paper garlands. They dance, gamble, hold parades, and buy refreshments in the marketplace and public square.

Folk dances are an important feature of fiestas. In the Mexican hat dance, dancers perform a lively sequence with hopping steps and heel-and-toe tapping.

In smaller towns and villages, cockfights and amateur bullfights also take place during fiestas. In larger towns and cities, most fiestas include less religious worship than do the village fiestas. The people watch plays and professional bullfights, ride merry-go-rounds and Ferris wheels, and buy goods at merchants' booths.

Guadalupe Day, celebrated on December 12, is Mexico's most important religious holiday. It honors Our Lady of Guadalupe (often called the Virgin of Guadalupe), Mexico's patron saint. Catholics believe that on December 12, 1531, the Virgin appeared to an indigenous peasant on Tepeyac Hill, in what is now Mexico City.

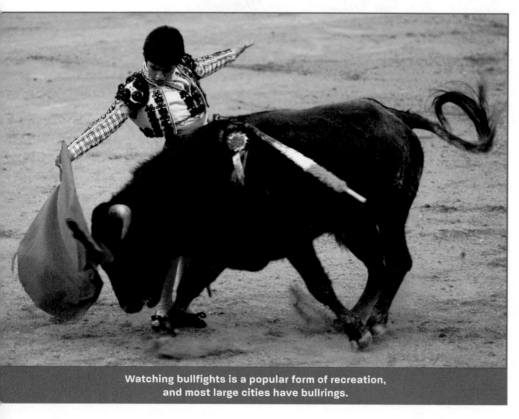

Watching bullfights is a popular form of recreation, and most large cities have bullrings.

On the nine nights before Christmas, friends and neighbors gather to act out Mary and Joseph's journey to Bethlehem. This activity is called the *posada*. Each night after the posada, the children play the *piñata* game. Piñatas are containers made of earthenware or papier-mâché. Many are shaped like animals and filled with candy and toys. A piñata is hung above the children's heads. The youngsters are blindfolded and take turns striking the piñata with a stick. After it breaks, the children scramble to collect the scattered presents. On Twelfth Night, 12 days after Christmas, parents fill their children's shoes with presents.

Other important holidays include New Year's Day (January 1); Constitution Day (February 5); Holy Week (the week before Easter); Cinco de Mayo (May 5); Día de los muertos (November 2); and Revolution Day, the anniversary of the Mexican Revolution of 1910 (November 20).

Recreation. Soccer is the most popular sport in Mexico, followed by baseball. People often play soccer or baseball on vacant lots, and many play on teams in amateur leagues. Mexico also has professional soccer and baseball leagues. Basketball and jai alai, a game that resembles handball, are popular as well.

Many Mexicans enjoy watching bullfights. Most large cities have bullrings. Mexico City has the largest bullring in the world. It seats about 55,000 people.

On Sundays—the only day most Mexicans do not work—many families go to the park to relax and picnic. Mexicans also enjoy watching movies and television, dancing at nightclubs, and entertaining friends and relatives at home. Many wealthier Mexicans visit the country's historic sites and resorts along the coast.

Religion. More than three-fourths of Mexico's people belong to the Roman Catholic Church. Mexico also has some Protestants, Jews, and other religious groups.

Catholic missionaries first arrived from Spain in the early 1500s. They converted millions of indigenous people to Catholicism. But respect for the rain, sun, and other forces of nature remained an important part of indigenous religion. Mexican religious practices still combine ancient beliefs and traditions with Catholicism.

During the Spanish colonial period, the Catholic Church was closely linked with the Mexican government as the official state church. The church became wealthy and powerful and prohibited other religions. Beginning in the mid-1800s, the government greatly reduced the church's political and economic power by prohibiting churches from owning property and participating in politics. However, these laws were not always enforced. In 1991, Mexico's legislature passed constitutional amendments to end some of these restrictions.

Since the mid-1900s, the number of Protestant churches in Mexico has increased greatly. The growth of Protestantism has resulted in large part from missionary activities by Protestants from the United States.

Education. Throughout the Spanish colonial period, the Catholic Church controlled education in what is now Mexico. During the 1800s, the newly independent government and the church struggled for power, and the government won control of the schools. Mexico's constitution, adopted in 1917, prohibited religious groups and ministers from establishing or teaching in schools. However, the laws often were not enforced. Constitutional changes passed in 1991 legalized church-owned schools and religious instruction in them.

During the early 1900s, less than 25 percent of Mexicans over 6 years old could read or write. Since the Revolution of 1910, and especially since the early 1940s, the government has done much to promote free public education. It has built thousands of new schools and established teachers' colleges. The government spends large sums on education each year. Today, most Mexican adults can read and write.

Mexican law requires all children from the age of 6 through 14 to go to school. After kindergarten, a child has six years of elementary school, followed by three years of *basic secondary school*. Graduates of basic secondary school may go on to a three-year *upper secondary school*. Many upper secondary schools are privately run. Colleges operate some of these schools to prepare students for college work. Other upper secondary schools offer business and technical courses.

About 85 percent of school-age children in Mexico attend school. About 90 percent complete elementary school, and about 60 percent finish some secondary school. Few attend upper secondary school or college.

Courses of higher education at Mexico's universities, specialized colleges, and technical institutes last from three to seven years. The oldest and largest Mexican university is the National Autonomous University of Mexico in Mexico City.

Arts

The arts have been an important part of Mexican life since the days of early indigenous civilizations. The Maya and Toltec peoples constructed beautiful temples and painted *murals* (wall-paintings) in them. The Aztec composed music and poetry. The Spaniards brought a love of literature and beautiful buildings. Indigenous craftworkers built thousands of churches based on Spanish designs. In the 1900s, Mexico produced many important architects, painters, composers, and writers.

Architecture of ancient Mexican civilizations was related chiefly to religion. The Teotihuacano and Aztec, among others, built stone temples on flat-topped pyramids and decorated them with murals and sculptured symbols. These symbols represented the feathered serpent Quetzalcoatl and other gods. Many ancient structures still stand near Mexico City and in Oaxaca, Chiapas, and Yucatán states.

After the Spanish conquest, the earliest mission churches had a simple design. Later churches, especially those built in the 1700s, had a more ornamental style. The huge Metropolitan Cathedral in Mexico City, begun in 1573 but not completed for hundreds of years, shows the influence of many different architectural styles. In the 1900s, many Mexican architects combined ancient designs with modern construction methods. Their work includes the buildings of the National Autonomous University of Mexico, by Félix Candela and Carlos Lazo, and the striking National Museum of Anthropology, in Mexico City, by Pedro Ramírez Vázquez. Some other examples are the Jardines de Pedregal apartment buildings, by Luis Barragán, and the 44-story Latin American Tower in Mexico City.

Painting. Ancient Mexican civilizations left many impressive murals, like those at Bonampak in Chiapas state. During the Spanish colonial period, many artists painted murals in churches or portraits of government officials. Mexican painting gained worldwide renown after the Mexican Revolution of 1910. Beginning in the 1920s, José Orozco, Diego Rivera, and David Siqueiros painted the story of the revolution on the walls of public buildings. Rivera's wife, Frida Kahlo, is one of the best-known painters in Mexican history. Other important Mexican painters during the middle and later 1900s included Rufino Tamayo and José Luis Cuevas. Beginning in the 1950s, many Mexican painters turned away from revolutionary themes and followed international trends.

Literature. Outstanding colonial writers included the dramatist Juan Ruiz de Alarcón and the poet Sor Juana Inés de la Cruz. In 1816, José Joaquín Fernández de Lizardi wrote *The Itching Parrot*, probably the first Latin American novel. After 1910, revolutionary themes became important in novels by such writers as Mariano Azuela and Martín Luis Guzmán. These themes also appear in the works of such later writers as Carlos Fuentes, Juan Rulfo, and Agustín Yáñez. Leading Mexican poets of the 1900s included Amado Nervo, Octavio Paz, Carlos Pellicer, Alfonso Reyes, and Marco Antonio Montes de Oca. The 1900s also saw the emergence of important women writers, such as Rosario Castellanos and Ángeles Mastretta.

Music. Early indigenous people used drums, flutes, gourd rattles, seashells, and their voices to make music. This ancient music is still played in some parts of Mexico. Much church music was written during the colonial period. Folk songs called *corridos* have long been popular in Mexico. They may tell of the Mexican Revolution, a bandit or a sheriff, or the struggle between church and state. In the 1900s, Mexican composers, including Carlos Chávez and Silvestre Revueltas, used themes from corridos or ancient indigenous music.

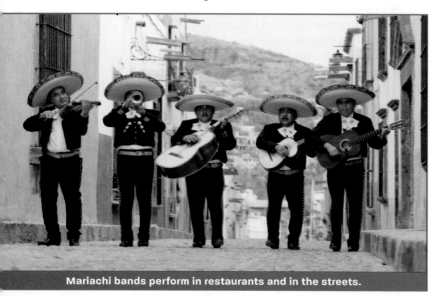

Mariachi bands perform in restaurants and in the streets.

Today, strolling musicians called *mariachis* perform along streets and in restaurants. Mariachi groups include singers and guitar, trumpet, and violin players. The music of *marimbas* (instruments similar to xylophones) is also popular.

Motion pictures. Mexico has one of Latin America's largest motion-picture industries. Some of the first movies produced in Mexico chronicled the violence of the 1910 revolution. The 1930s and 1940s are considered the golden age of Mexican cinema. The most famous Mexican actor of this period was Mario Moreno. Moreno's comic character Cantinflas represented the average poor, urban Mexican. The Spanish-born director Luis Buñuel made many of his most important films in Mexico in the 1950s and 1960s, including *Los Olvidados* (*The Young and the Damned,* 1950).

In the 1960s and 1970s, Mexican filmmakers began making action and horror movies. One extremely popular action hero was El Santo, a professional freestyle wrestler who starred in more than 50 films.

The 1990s and early 2000s brought the development of the Nuevo Cine Mexicano (New Mexican Cinema). Unlike older films, which were produced mainly for a Mexican audience, movies from the Nuevo Cine Mexicano have achieved global fame. Famous filmmakers from this period included Carlos Carrera, Alfonso Cuarón, Alejandro González Iñárritu, and Guillermo del Toro.

The Land

Mexico has six main land regions: (1) the Pacific Northwest, (2) the Plateau of Mexico, (3) the Gulf Coastal Plain, (4) the Southern Uplands, (5) the Chiapas Highlands, and (6) the Yucatán Peninsula. Within these six land regions are many smaller ones that differ greatly in altitude, climate, and land formation. Many kinds of plants and animals also live in Mexico.

The Pacific Northwest region is generally dry. The Baja California Peninsula (Peninsula of Lower California), the region's westernmost section, consists largely of rolling or mountainous desert. During some years, the desert receives no rain at all. It has a few oases where farmers grow dates and grapes. The northwestern corner and southern end of the peninsula get enough rain for a little farming. The lowest point in Mexico is in the far northern area, near Mexicali. This area, 33 feet (10 meters) below sea level, is

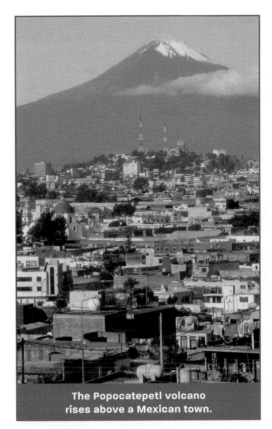

The Popocatepetl volcano rises above a Mexican town.

the southern end of the huge Imperial Valley of California.

The mainland coastal strip of the Pacific Northwest region has fertile river valleys that contain some of Mexico's richest farmland. Farmers irrigate these valleys with water from the Colorado, Fuerte, Yaqui, and other rivers. Steep, narrow mountain ranges extend in a north-south direction in the state of Sonora, east of the coastal plain. The ranges lie parallel to each other and separate the upper river valleys. In these basins are cattle ranches, irrigated farmland, and copper and silver mines.

The Plateau of Mexico is the largest of the six land regions. It has Mexico's largest cities and most of the country's people. The plateau consists of five sections.

The Cordillera Neo-Volcanica (Neo-Volcanic Range), a series of volcanoes, extends across Mexico at the plateau's southern edge. It is also called the Eje Neo-Volcánico Transversal (Transverse Neo-Volcanic Axis) or the Transverse Volcanic Range. Many of the volcanoes are active. The volcanic soils are fertile and receive enough rain for agriculture. Farmers have grown corn, beans, and other crops on the slopes since the days of ancient indigenous civilizations. Pico de Orizaba (Citlaltépetl), at 18,410 feet (5,610 meters), is Mexico's highest mountain. Ixtacihuatl and Popocatépetl, two volcanoes that stand more than 17,000 feet high (5,180 meters), rise southeast of Mexico City. Far to the west, near the city of Guadalajara, is Lake Chapala. It covers about 420 square miles (1,100 square kilometers). However, this figure varies with changes in rainfall and human consumption.

The Mesa Central (Central Plateau), which lies north of the Neo-Volcanic Chain, is the heart of Mexico. It averages about 7,000 feet (2,100 meters) above sea level. The rainfall in this section is enough to raise corn, beans, wheat, and barley. The Aztec capital of Tenochtitlan stood at the mesa's southern edge, in the beautiful Valley of Mexico. Mexico City was built on the same site and became the capital during the colonial period. Several small lakes, including the famous Lake Xochimilco, are in the Mexico City area.

The western part of the Mesa Central is called the Bajío, meaning *flat*. This region covers one of the most productive agricultural areas in the country. The Bajío also includes the manufacturing

Beautifully colored quetzals live in the southern forests of Mexico.

centers of Guadalajara, León, Querétaro, and San Luis Potosí.

The Mesa del Norte (Northern Plateau) makes up more than half the Plateau of Mexico. It extends from the Mesa Central north to the United States. The Mesa del Norte is highest in the south and west, with altitudes of 6,000 to 9,000 feet (1,800 to 2,700 meters). In the north and east, it is less than 4,000 feet (1,200 meters) high. Low mountains rise from 2,000 to 3,000 feet (610 to 910 meters) above the mesa. The mesa receives little rainfall except in the higher mountains, where frost is a constant threat to crops. Only in irrigated places, such as the Saltillo and Torreón areas, is farming successful.

The mesa's low mountains have rich deposits of metal ores. The Spaniards began developing these mines in the 1500s. They also established huge ranches in the dry hills and plains nearby to supply the miners with beef, horses, and mules. In the Durango and Chihuahua areas, *vaqueros* (cowboys) became skilled at riding and roping cattle. American cowboys later copied these skills.

The Sierra Madre Occidental is a long mountain range that forms the western rim of the Plateau of Mexico. Until the 1900s, when paved roads and a railroad were built across the range, it was a natural barrier to transport between the plateau and the west coast. The range includes some of Mexico's most rugged land. Short, steep streams flowing to the Pacific Ocean have cut canyons more than 1 mile (1.6 kilometers) deep through the mountains. The largest canyon is the spectacular Barranca del Cobre, cut by the Urique River.

The Sierra Madre Oriental, the plateau's eastern rim, is actually a series of mountain ranges. In many places between the ranges, highways and railroads climb up to the plateau from the east coast. Monterrey, near large deposits of coal and iron ore, is the major center of the Mexican steel industry.

The Gulf Coastal Plain. North of Tampico, this region is largely covered by tangled forests of low, thorny bushes and trees. This part of the plain is generally dry, and farming is possible only along rivers and with the aid of irrigation. South of Tampico, the rainfall increases. The plant life changes gradually from north to south and becomes a tropical rain forest in Tabasco state. The southern part of the plain has some rich farmland.

Many of Mexico's longest rivers flow into the Gulf of Mexico from the coastal plain. They include the Rio Grande, which forms about 1,300 miles (2,090 kilometers) of Mexico's border with the United States. Large petroleum deposits lie beneath the plain and offshore. Huge sulfur deposits occur near the Gulf in the Isthmus of Tehuantepec. The isthmus, which is about 135 miles (220 kilometers) wide, is the narrowest part of Mexico.

The Southern Uplands consist largely of steep ridges and deep gorges cut by mountain streams. The region includes a large, hot, dry valley just south of the Neo-Volcanic Chain. The Balsas River drains the valley. The Sierra Madre del Sur, a rugged mountain range, rises southwest of the valley along the Pacific Ocean. The famous beach resort of Acapulco is on this coast. A little farming takes place on the steep mountainsides. The Oaxaca Plateau makes up the eastern part of the Southern Uplands. The ancient Zapotec capital of Monte Albán stood on the plateau. In addition, much of the gold of the Aztec empire probably came from the plateau.

The Chiapas Highlands have great blocklike mountains that rise more than 9,000 feet (2,700 meters) above sea level. There are also many relatively flat surfaces at high altitudes. These tablelands are farmed by indigenous peasants who speak Maya dialects and other ancient languages. Some modern farming has developed in the region's deep, broad river valleys. With irrigation, farmers grow coffee, fruits, and other crops.

The Yucatán Peninsula is a low limestone plateau with no rivers. Limestone dissolves in water, and rainfall reaches the sea through underground channels dissolved out of the rock. Great pits have formed where the roofs of these channels have fallen in. The pits were the sacred wells of the ancient Maya people. The northwestern part of the region is dry bushland. Agave plants that grow there provide *henequen* fiber, which is used to make twine. Rainfall increases to the south, where tropical rain forests cover the land.

Plant and animal life. Forests cover about a fifth of Mexico. Forests of the northwestern and central mountains provide ebony, mahogany, rosewood, walnut, and other valuable hardwoods used to make furniture. Large pine forests in these mountains also supply timber for Mexico's pulp and paper industry. Mexico has thousands of kinds of flowers, including azaleas, chrysanthemums, geraniums, orchids, and poinsettias. Hundreds of varieties of cactus grow in Mexico's northern deserts.

Deer and mountain lions live in Mexico's mountains. The country's northern deserts have coyotes, lizards, prairie dogs, and rattlesnakes. Mexico also has some alligators, jaguars, opossums, and raccoons. Chihuahuas, the world's smallest dogs, originally came from Mexico.

Mexico has hundreds of kinds of birds, including the beautifully colored quetzals of the southern forests. Other birds include flamingos, herons, hummingbirds, parrots, and pelicans. Fish and shellfish are plentiful in Mexico's coastal waters, lakes, and rivers. Freshwater fish include bass, catfish, and trout. Many kinds of tropical fish inhabit coral reefs along the Caribbean coast of the Yucatán Peninsula. Marlin, swordfish, and tarpon are among the game fish caught in coastal areas.

Climate

Mexico's climate varies sharply from region to region. These differences are greatest in tropical Mexico, south of the Tropic of Cancer. There, large variations in altitude result in three main temperature zones. The *tierra caliente* (hot land) includes regions up to 3,000 feet (910 meters) above sea level. It has long, hot summers and mild winters with no frost. The *tierra templada* (temperate land), from 3,000 to 6,000 feet (910 to 1,800 meters), has temperatures that generally stay between 80 and 50°F (27 and 10°C). Most crops can grow in the temperate zone. The *tierra fria* (cold land) lies above 6,000 feet (1,800 meters). Frost is rare up to 8,000 feet (2,400 meters), but it may occur at almost any time. The highest peaks in the tierra fria are always covered with snow.

In tropical regions of Mexico, most rain falls in summer, usually as short, heavy, afternoon showers. Toward the south, the rainy season starts earlier and lasts longer.

Most of the northern half of Mexico consists of deserts and semideserts. The lack of rainfall has limited agricultural development in the north. Only the mountainous sections receive enough rainfall to grow good crops without irrigation. Most of northern Mexico's rainfall occurs during the summer, but northwestern Baja California receives most of its rainfall in the winter. Above 2,000 feet (610 meters), summer days are hot and

Many Mexicans work in the United States and send money home to their families.

nights are cool. During the winter, days are warm and nights are cold. The coastal lowlands are hot, except on the cool Pacific coast of Baja California.

Economy

Until the mid-1900s, the Mexican economy was based mainly on agriculture and mining. In the 1940s, the government began to promote the development of industry. Mexico now produces many of the manufactured goods that its people use. In the early 2000s, however, Mexico lost many manufacturing jobs to China and other East Asian countries.

In the 1970s, Mexico became a major exporter of oil to the United States. Income from oil production, which the government controls, spurred the development of manufacturing and service industries. During the middle and late 1970s, the price of oil was high. Mexico used its expected income from oil production as collateral to borrow money for many construction projects. In 1981, however, the price of oil began to fall. Mexico soon found it difficult to repay its loans, and the government had to cut spending severely. The economy declined, and many Mexicans lost their jobs. In the late 1980s and early 1990s, the economy improved because the government sold off state-owned companies, attracted foreign investment, and controlled inflation.

Since the mid-1990s, the Mexican economy generally has struggled against global competition. *Remittances* (money sent) from relatives in the United States have been an important source of national income. Mexicans living in the United States send home billions of dollars to their families each year.

Service industries are those economic activities that produce services, not goods. Service industries account for about three-fifths of both

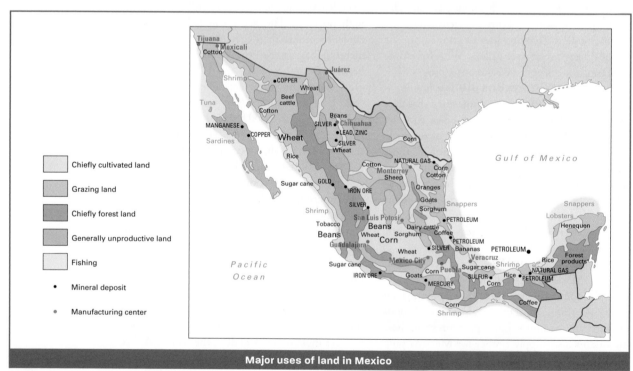

Major uses of land in Mexico

the total value of goods and services produced in Mexico and the country's workers. Trade, restaurants, and hotels make up the leading service industry. Hotels, restaurants, and shops benefit from the tens of millions of tourists who visit Mexico each year. Many people also work for the government and in schools.

Manufacturing. Mexico City is Mexico's leading industrial center. Guadalajara and Monterrey are also important manufacturing centers. Government programs encourage the spread of industry to other areas.

Since the 1980s, the government has promoted industrial growth aimed at supplying foreign markets. Factories called *maquiladoras* near Mexico's northern border manufacture and assemble a variety of products for export to U.S. companies. These products include automobile parts, electronic equipment, and textiles.

Mexico's leading products include chemicals, motor vehicles, processed foods, processed petroleum, and tobacco. Other important products include beer, clothing, plastics, rubber products, steel, textiles, and wood pulp and paper.

Mexico has long been famous for the skill of its craftworkers, who follow beautiful indigenous or Spanish-colonial designs. Their products, which vary by area, include silver jewelry from Taxco, glassware and pottery from Guadalajara and Puebla, and handwoven baskets and blankets from Oaxaca and Toluca. Many of these goods are sold to tourists.

Agriculture. The various farming regions of Mexico differ greatly in altitude, rainfall, and temperature. As a result, many kinds of crops can grow. However, mountains and insufficient rainfall make most of the country naturally unsuited for agriculture. Crops are grown on only a small amount of Mexico's total land area.

The best farmland is in the southern part of Mexico's plateau region. Rich soils, rainfall, and a mild climate there permit intensive cultivation. The northern part of the plateau has little rainfall and serves mainly as grazing land for cattle.

Fertile soils exist in the rainy, hot regions of southern and eastern Mexico and in the eastern coastal plains. However, turning these areas into productive farmland requires much work, including clearing and draining the land and controlling floods, insects, and plant diseases. The west coast of Mexico also has fertile soils, but much of the

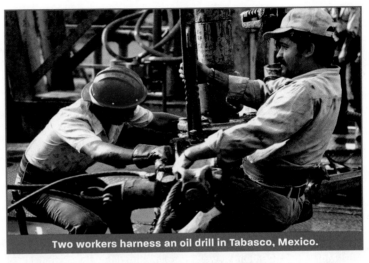
Two workers harness an oil drill in Tabasco, Mexico.

land is mountainous and dry. Irrigation has developed some rich cropland in dry regions.

Among the wide variety of crops grown in Mexico, corn takes up more farmland than any other crop. It is the basic food of the Mexican people. Other major crops include avocados, bananas, barley, beans, chili peppers, coffee, lemons, mangoes, onions, oranges, pineapples, potatoes, sorghum, sugarcane, tomatoes, and wheat. Mexico exports many tropical fruits and winter vegetables to the United States. Farmers cultivate vanilla and cacao in tropical wet areas of the country.

Farmers and ranchers raise livestock throughout Mexico. Beef and dairy cattle are found chiefly in northern and central Mexico. Farmers throughout the country also raise chickens, goats, hogs, horses, sheep, and turkeys.

Until the 1900s, most Mexicans made a living by farming land near their villages or working on large estates called *haciendas* for wealthy landowners. The Mexican Constitution of 1917 provided for land reform. By 1964, the government had broken up most of the haciendas and distributed the land to the peasants.

The Constitution also recognized the old system of *ejidos*, farmlands held in common by communities. Today, most farmers work alone on individual sections of the ejidos. However, some work the land as a group and share the crops. Ejidos make up about half of Mexico's total cropland. The remainder is divided between small family farms and large haciendas that the Mexican government has not broken up. Since the 1990s, the ejido system has fallen into crisis. The owners of many ejidos have sold or abandoned their

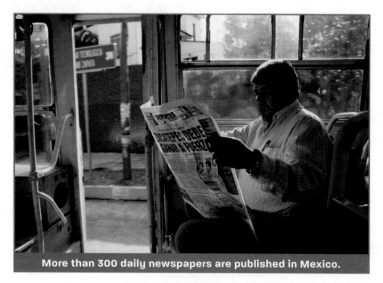

More than 300 daily newspapers are published in Mexico.

land to look for work in Mexican cities or in the United States.

Agriculture provides about 15 percent of all jobs in Mexico, but it accounts for less than 5 percent of the total value of Mexican goods and services. The government has tried to increase agricultural production by promoting modern farming methods. However, educational programs, financial aid, and public works projects intended to achieve this goal have not benefited most small family farmers and those living on ejidos. As a result, Mexico has some modern and productive commercial farms owned by prosperous people, but most rural Mexicans are poor.

Mining. A wide variety of minerals are mined in Mexico. The country ranks as one of the world's leading silver producers, mining about one-seventh of the world's annual production. Most silver mines are in the central regions of the country.

Mexico is also a leading producer of petroleum. It pumps more than 1 billion barrels of petroleum each year. Oil wells operate chiefly in the states of Campeche, Tabasco, and Veracruz, along the coast and in the Gulf of Mexico. Petróleos Mexicanos (PEMEX), a government agency, runs the petroleum industry. In addition, Mexico produces much natural gas.

Mexico also mines large quantities of antimony, bismuth, copper, fluorite, gold, gypsum, lead, manganese, salt, sulfur, and zinc. Large iron ore deposits support the nation's steel industry.

Fishing. Although Mexico has an extensive coastline, fishing accounts for less than 1 percent of the national income. Fishing crews catch anchovies,

herring, sardines, tilapias, and tuna. *Aquaculture*, the commercial raising of plants and animals that live in water, is a growing industry in Mexico. Mexico's aquaculture industry raises shrimp and tilapias.

Energy sources. Petroleum deposits provide cheap fuel oil and natural gas for industrial use. Coal, natural gas, and petroleum generate the vast majority of Mexico's electric power. Most of the rest is produced by hydroelectric or nuclear power. Manuel M. Torres Dam, Mexico's largest hydroelectric plant and one of the world's highest dams, is on the Grijalva River in the state of Chiapas. Laguna Verde, Mexico's only nuclear power plant, is in the state of Veracruz. The government handles almost all power production and distribution.

Trade. Mexico's leading exports include petroleum and petroleum products. Other mineral exports include copper, gold, iron, and silver. The main industrial exports include beer, electronics, fruits and vegetables, machinery, and motor vehicles. The leading imports include electric and electronic equipment, industrial machinery, and motor vehicles.

About two-thirds of Mexico's trade is with the United States, but trade with European countries, China, and Japan is increasing. Mexico has a trade surplus with the United States, and a trade deficit with the rest of the world.

Trade with other Latin American countries is relatively unimportant. However, Mexico is trying to increase such trade through the Latin American Integration Association, an economic union of Mexico and several other Latin American nations. Mexico also belongs to a regional trading bloc that includes Canada and the United States. This bloc was created by the North American Free Trade Agreement (NAFTA), which has eliminated nearly all *tariffs* (taxes on imports) and other trade barriers.

Tourism. Along with exports of manufactured goods and petroleum, tourism serves as one of Mexico's largest sources of income from abroad. Each year, tens of millions of tourists, mostly from the United States, visit Mexico. The tourist industry is also a major source of employment for the Mexican population. Tourists visit Mexico City, the old Spanish colonial cities of central Mexico, and the ruins of Maya cities on the Yucatán Peninsula. Beautiful beach resorts attract many vacationers from the United States and Canada, especially in winter. Popular resort areas include Acapulco, Cabo San Lucas, Ensenada, Huatulco, Manzanillo, Mazatlán, Puerto Escondido, Puerto Vallarta, and Zihuatanejo on the Pacific coast, and Cancún and Cozumel Island on the Caribbean coast.

Transportation in Mexico ranges from modern methods to ancient ones. Mexico has a good highway system. Airlines, bus service, and railroads connect all the major cities and towns. But some farmers still carry goods to market on their heads and backs, or by burros and oxcarts.

Mexico City is an important center of international air travel. There are also large international airports in Cancún, Guadalajara, and Monterrey.

Mexico has an extensive railway network. The railroads were owned by the government until the 1990s, when they were sold to private companies. Mexico City has a subway system.

More than 100 ocean ports provide access to Mexico. These include Altamira, Coatzacoalcos, and Veracruz on the Gulf of Mexico, and Lázaro Cárdenas and Manzanillo on the Pacific Ocean. Mexico also has a small merchant fleet.

Communication. The first book known to be published in the Western Hemisphere was a *catechism* (book used to teach religion) printed in Mexico City in 1539. Today, books and magazines published in Mexico City are read widely throughout Mexico and all of Latin America. Mexico has many daily newspapers representing a variety of political opinions. The largest newspapers include *El Financiero, El Sol de México, El Universal, Esto, Excélsior, La Jornada, La Prensa,* and *Reforma,* all published in Mexico City.

Mexico has hundreds of television stations and radio stations. Most of these stations are privately owned. Telephone lines connect all parts of the country. Many people use cellular phones. Internet usage is increasing as more Mexicans gain access to computers.

History

Ancient times. The first people who lived in what is now Mexico arrived there before 8000 B.C. They were peoples of unknown tribes who migrated from the north. These first Mexicans were hunters who lived in small, temporary communities. They followed the herds of buffalo, mammoths, mastodons, and other large animals that roamed the land. About 7500 B.C., the climate became drier. The herds could not find enough grass to eat and died off. The people then lived on small wild animals or the berries and seeds of wild plants.

About 7000 B.C., the inhabitants of what is now the Puebla region discovered how to grow plants for food and became farmers. They grew corn, which became their most important food, as well as avocados, beans, peppers, squashes, and tomatoes. They were among the first people to cultivate these vegetables. They also raised dogs and turkeys for food. As the wandering bands of hunters became groups of farmers, they established permanent settlements.

Hernan Cortes and Montezuma II

The growth of villages. By 2000 B.C., large farm villages stood along Lake Texcoco in the fertile south-central Valley of Mexico, and in the southern highlands and forests. The farmers used irrigation to improve their crops. The villages grew, and new classes of people developed, including potters, priests, and weavers. The people traded polished stones, pottery, and seashells with distant communities.

By 1000 B.C., the villagers were building flat-topped pyramids with temples on them. Some villages, including Cuicuilco near what is now Mexico City, became religious centers. Members of other communities came to worship in the temples. Because these people were farmers, they worshiped gods that represented such natural forces as the rain and the sun. The villages grew into towns, from the Valley of Mexico to the Gulf of Mexico and to the Pacific Ocean, and south to what is now Guatemala.

The Olmec people of the southern Gulf Coast made the first great advance toward civilization in the Mexico region. Between about 1200 and 400 B.C., the Olmec developed a counting system and calendar. They also carved beautiful stone statues.

The Classic Period. Great civilizations thrived between A.D. 250 and 900, the Classic Period of Mexico. Huge pyramids dedicated to the sun and the moon were built at Teotihuacán, near what is now Mexico City. In the religious centers of southern Mexico and northern Central America, the Maya built beautiful homes, pyramids, and temples of limestone. They recorded important dates on tall, carved blocks of stone and wrote in a kind of picture writing. In what is now the state of Oaxaca, the Zapotec people leveled a mountaintop and built their capital, called Monte Albán.

The reasons for the fall of these Classic civilizations are not clear. The climate probably became even drier about A.D. 900, and the people could not produce enough crops to feed the large population. Perhaps city dwellers attacked their neighbors to get more land, or farmers revolted against the priests who had ruled them. In the north, Chichimec tribes destroyed a large number of cities.

The Toltec and the Aztec. Many wars followed the Classic Period. During the 900s, the Toltec people established an empire with a major city at Tula, north of present-day Mexico City. Toltec influence spread throughout central and southern Mexico. Invading Chichimec tribes destroyed the Toltec empire about 1200.

The Aztec (also called the Mexica) built the last and greatest indigenous empire during the mid-1400s. The Aztec empire extended between the Pacific and Gulf coasts, and from the Isthmus of Tehuantepec north to the Pánuco River. The Aztec capital, Tenochtitlan, stood on an island in Lake Texcoco at the site of Mexico City. According to Aztec tradition, Tenochtitlan was founded in 1325. Modern scholars believe it was founded somewhat later. When the Spaniards arrived in 1519, the city and its suburbs had a population of about 200,000.

The Aztec were fierce warriors who believed it was their duty to sacrifice the men they captured in battle to their gods. Every year they sacrificed thousands of prisoners of war. The Aztec also composed beautiful music and poetry and were skilled in medicine. They grew rich with gold, silver, and other treasures collected annually from the cities and tribes they conquered.

The Spanish conquest. The Spaniards began to occupy the Caribbean region during the 1490s and first set foot in Mexico in 1517. That year, Diego Velázquez, the governor of Cuba, sent ships under Francisco Fernández de Córdoba to explore and search for treasure. Córdoba found the Yucatán Peninsula and brought back reports of large cities. Velázquez then sent Juan de Grijalva to the area in 1518. Grijalva explored the Gulf coast from Yucatán to what is now Veracruz.

A third expedition of about 600 men sailed from Cuba under Hernán Cortés in February 1519. Cortés's 11 ships followed Grijalva's route along the coast. Cortés defeated large indigenous armies with his horses and cannons. He founded Veracruz, the first Spanish settlement in what is now Mexico.

Reports of the explorers reached the Aztec emperor Montezuma II (also spelled Moctezuma) in Tenochtitlan. The tales of Spanish guns and horses—which the indigenous people had never seen before—and of soldiers in armor made him

Fireworks in Mexico City celebrating the country's 180th Independence Day

fear the Spaniards. Montezuma sent messengers with rich gifts for Cortés, but he also ordered the Spanish explorer to leave. Instead, Cortés marched toward Tenochtitlan. He was joined by thousands of the Aztec's indigenous enemies, who hoped he would destroy Montezuma's empire. Montezuma allowed the invaders to enter Tenochtitlan in November 1519. The Spaniards were far too few to control Tenochtitlan by themselves. However, Cortés soon seized Montezuma and held him hostage to secure his own men's safety.

In June 1520, the Aztec revolted. After a week of bitter fighting, the Spaniards tried to sneak out of the city. The Aztec discovered them and killed hundreds of Spaniards during *la noche triste* (the sad night). The rest, including Cortés, were saved by their indigenous allies. Six months later, Cortés returned to the Tenochtitlan area at the head of an invading force that included tens of thousands of indigenous troops. By May 1521, this coalition had surrounded the Aztec capital and cut off the city's food and water. Battles, sickness, and starvation weakened the Aztec army. In August, Cuauhtémoc, the last emperor, surrendered the city. Cortés sent soldiers to take over the rest of the Aztec empire. Some indigenous people resisted, but most accepted Spanish rule without a fight.

Spanish rule. After the fighting ended, the Spaniards faced the problem of how to govern the large number of people in the colony. To keep the Amerindians from revolting, King Charles I of Spain allowed them to speak their own languages and be governed by their own officials. However, they had to pay a special tax called a *tribute* and work for the Spaniards when help was needed. They were also required to convert to Catholicism.

Tenochtitlan and other indigenous cities became Spanish cities ruled by white people. The Spaniards destroyed Tenochtitlan and built their own new city on top of the ruins. The Europeans unknowingly introduced a number of diseases to the indigenous population. Along with harsh labor conditions and the forced resettlement of many indigenous communities, these diseases caused a great decline in the native population. When the Spaniards arrived, there may have been from 15 million to 25 million indigenous people living in Mexico. Between 1519 and 1600, the indigenous population dropped to approximately 1 million.

The arrival of Europeans and, later, Africans in Mexico led to the emergence of a new, racially mixed society. The whites included *peninsulares* (people born in Spain) and *creoles* (Europeans born in America). The creoles and mestizos considered themselves superior to the indigenous people. From 1520 to 1810, the Spaniards imported about 200,000 African slaves to Mexico. Most were brought to Mexico, then part of the colony called New Spain, before 1700.

During the 1540s, the Spaniards discovered silver mines in the north-central part of their colony. The silver brought much wealth to the creoles and peninsulares, and the mines attracted more Spanish immigrants. The creoles used the power of the royal government to make the indigenous people work for them. They established haciendas, where they produced food and clothing for the new mining communities. Some indigenous peasants lived on the haciendas. Others lived there when they had work and lived in their own villages the rest of the time.

The indigenous people were poor, but there was little they could do to change their situation. However, they were allowed to live separately according to their customs. As a result, the houses they lived in, the food they ate, and the way they worked changed little over the nearly 300 years of Spanish rule. Spanish laws gave the indigenous people the right to keep the lands they had owned before the conquest, but greedy landowners found ways to take over these lands. The Amerindians blended the Roman Catholic faith with their own culture and respected their Spanish priests. However, the colonial period included several riots and rebellions that demonstrated indigenous discontent with Spanish rule.

At first, the creoles were content to be ruled by Spain because the king was far away and he usually permitted them to govern themselves. Authorities in Spain made the laws, but few Spanish officials worked in New Spain. The officials could not enforce the laws if the creoles objected. In the late 1700s, King Charles III tried to reorganize the colonial government, giving more power to Spanish-born individuals and less to the creoles. He also raised taxes. Few creoles sought independence, but many wanted more control of their affairs.

Revolt against the Spaniards. In 1807, French forces occupied Spain and imprisoned King Ferdinand VII. Confusion spread in Spain's colonies. Some creoles plotted to seize Mexico's colonial government. One such person

Portrait of King Ferdinand VII of Spain

was Miguel Hidalgo y Costilla, a priest from what is now Guanajuato state. In the early hours of September 16, 1810, he called indigenous people and mestizos to his church in the town of Dolores. He made a speech known as the *Grito de Dolores* (Cry of Dolores), in which he called for a rebellion against Spanish rule. Today, late on September 15, Mexico's president rings a bell and repeats the Grito de Dolores. Mexicans celebrate September 16 as Independence Day.

Hidalgo's untrained followers armed themselves and attacked Spanish officials and those who supported the Spaniards. At first, Hidalgo gained support for his cause. However, most of his followers were Amerindians and mestizos rather than creoles. Some indigenous communities refused to support the rebels because of their violent ways. Eventually, Hidalgo was forced to retreat. Spanish troops captured and executed him in 1811.

José María Morelos y Pavón, another priest, continued Hidalgo's struggle. In 1813, Morelos held a Congress that issued the first formal call for independence. The Congress wrote a constitution for a Mexican republic that included many social reforms to benefit mestizo and indigenous people. Unlike Hidalgo, Morelos used ambush tactics against small, isolated Spanish military units. His campaign was more successful than Hidalgo's, but he also was captured and executed in 1815. By 1816, Spanish troops had captured or killed many of the rebels, but small guerrilla groups continued to operate in the countryside.

King Ferdinand VII had returned to the Spanish throne in 1814. In an effort to help Spain recover from the Napoleonic Wars, he taxed the creoles. He also organized a large army to put down any revolutionary movement. Ferdinand's actions convinced many creoles that they could no longer trust Spain.

Independence. In 1820, a revolt by political liberals swept Spain. Ferdinand's power weakened, and many creoles saw their chance for independence. A group of powerful creoles supported Agustín de Iturbide, who had served in the Spanish army in the war against José María Morelos y Pavón. Iturbide had been given command of a Spanish army to crush the last rebel leader, Vicente Guerrero. But instead of fighting Guerrero, Iturbide met with him peacefully. In February 1821, the two leaders agreed to make Mexico independent. They joined their armies and won the support of liberal and conservative creoles. Only a small portion of the Spanish forces in Mexico remained loyal to Spain. By the end of 1821, the last Spanish officials withdrew from Mexico, and Mexico became independent.

Following independence, the creoles could not agree on a form of government. Conservatives called for a monarchy, but liberals wanted a republic. The conservatives could not persuade a member of the Spanish royal family to be king. Iturbide, who had the backing of the army, became Emperor Agustín I in 1822. Iturbide was a poor ruler, and most groups turned against him. In 1823, a military revolt drove him from power.

Mexico's Congress then followed the wishes of the liberals and began to write a constitution for a federal republic. But the creoles still disagreed on how the constitution should be written. Conservatives desired a strong central government and wanted Roman Catholicism to be the national religion, as it had been under Spanish rule. Liberals wanted the central government to have less power and the states more, and they called for freedom of religion. The groups finally reached a compromise, though many conservative creoles did not support it. In 1824, Mexico became a republic with a president and a two-house Congress heading the national government, and governors and legislatures heading the states. Guadalupe Victoria, a follower of Hidalgo and Morelos, became the first president.

Difficulties of the early republic. The mid-1800s were a difficult period in Mexico. Many creoles did not support the Constitution, and Mexicans had little experience in self-government. Military men often revolted. One such man, General Antonio López de Santa Anna, served as president 11 times between 1833 and 1855. Santa Anna was elected president in 1833, but he soon tired of his duties and left the government in the hands of his vice president, Valentín Gómez Farías. Gómez Farías passed many reforms that lessened the influence of the church and the military. Although Santa Anna had long favored liberal policies, he joined with conservatives in a successful revolt against the government in 1834. He soon took over the country as a dictator.

Texas was then part of Mexico, but many people from the United States lived there. When Santa Anna changed the Constitution in 1836 to concentrate greater power in the central government, Mexicans and Americans in Texas revolted. Santa Anna defeated a Texas force in the Battle of the Alamo at San Antonio in 1836. But later that year, Texas forces defeated Santa Anna's army at San Jacinto and captured him. Santa Anna signed a treaty recognizing the independence of Texas. In addition to what is now the state of Texas, the new republic of Texas included parts of present-day Colorado, Kansas, New Mexico, Oklahoma, and Wyoming.

The Mexican government did not recognize Santa Anna's treaty. Texas joined the United States in 1845, but Mexico still claimed it. Border disputes developed between Mexico and the United States. In April 1846, Mexican troops attacked U.S. soldiers who had entered the disputed area. In May, the United States declared war on Mexico.

United States soldiers occupied what was then Mexican territory in Arizona, California, and New Mexico. In February 1847, U.S. General Zachary Taylor fought Santa Anna, who was president again, at the Battle of Buena Vista near Saltillo, Mexico. Both sides claimed victory. Taylor became a national hero in the United States and was elected president the next year. Other U.S. forces landed at Veracruz under General Winfield Scott. In September 1847, Scott captured Mexico City after the bitter Battle of Chapultepec. Six military students are said to have thrown themselves from Chapultepec Castle to their deaths during this battle, rather than surrender. Today, the Monument to the Boy Heroes stands in Chapultepec Park in Mexico City.

The Treaty of Guadalupe Hidalgo, signed in February 1848, ended the Mexican War. Under the treaty, Mexico gave the United States the land that is now California, Nevada, and Utah; most of

Illustration of the Battle of the Alamo, San Antonio, Texas, 1836

Arizona; and parts of Colorado, New Mexico, and Wyoming. Mexico also recognized Texas, south to the Rio Grande, as part of the United States. Mexico received $15 million from the United States. In the Gadsden Purchase of 1853, the United States paid Mexico $10 million for land in what is now southern Arizona and New Mexico.

Reform. The Mexican War exhausted Mexico's economy, and great political confusion developed. Santa Anna seized power again in 1853 and ruled as a dictator. The liberals, who had been gaining strength since the war, drove Santa Anna from power in 1855.

Benito Juárez, a Zapotec from Oaxaca, and others gave the liberal movement effective leadership. They promoted the private ownership of land and wanted to eliminate the privileges of the Roman Catholic Church. After they took over the government in 1855, the liberals passed laws to break up the large estates of the church and the lands held in common by indigenous villages. In 1857, a new constitution brought back the federal system of government.

These reforms led to a conservative revolt in 1858. Juárez fled from Mexico City. The liberals declared him president, and he set up a government in Veracruz. During the civil war that followed, known as the War of the Reform, a conservative government operated in Mexico City. The Catholic bishops supported the conservatives because of the liberals' opposition to the church. In

1859, Juárez issued his Reform Laws in an attempt to end the church's political power in Mexico. The laws ordered the separation of church and state, and the take-over of all church property. The liberal armies defeated the conservatives late in 1860, and Juárez returned to Mexico City in 1861.

The French invasion. The Mexican government had little money after the War of the Reform. Juárez stopped payments on the country's debts to the United Kingdom, France, and Spain. Troops of those three nations occupied Veracruz in 1862. The British and Spaniards soon left Mexico after they saw that the French were more interested in political power than in collecting debts. The French emperor, Napoleon III, took this opportunity to invade and conquer Mexico. Napoleon knew that the United States would oppose the invasion, but he was confident the U.S. government could not intervene, because it was fighting the American Civil War (1861–1865). French troops occupied Mexico City in 1863, and Juárez escaped from the capital.

In 1864, Mexican conservatives, aided by Napoleon III, named Maximilian emperor of Mexico. Maximilian was a brother of the emperor of Austria. Juárez and the liberals fought guerrilla-style battles against Maximilian and the French invaders. In 1866, the United States pressured France to remove its troops. In addition, Napoleon III feared that war would break out in Europe. In 1866 and 1867, he withdrew his forces from Mexico. Juárez's forces then captured and shot Maximilian, and the conservative movement broke up. Juárez then returned to Mexico City. He served as president from 1867 until his death in 1872.

The dictatorship of Porfirio Díaz. Frequent revolts took place after Juárez's death. In 1876, Porfirio Díaz, a mestizo general, overthrew Juárez's successor. Díaz developed good relations with the conservatives and with some liberal state leaders who cooperated with him. He used the army to control his opponents. Díaz served as president from 1876 to 1880, and again from 1884 to 1911. The strength of his allies and the people's fear of the army helped Díaz rule as a dictator. Many people who sided with him became wealthy.

Mexico's economy improved under Díaz. He attracted foreign investment to connect Mexico with the rest of the world, particularly the United States. Investors' money helped build railroads, develop mines and oil wells, and expand manufac-

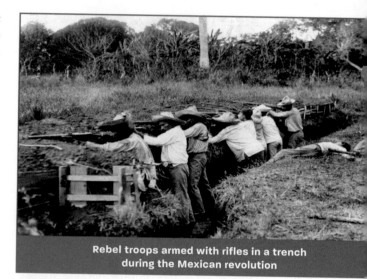

Rebel troops armed with rifles in a trench during the Mexican revolution

turing. However, the government kept industrial wages low and crushed attempts to form labor unions. Indigenous communities lost their land to big landowners. The great majority of Mexicans remained poor and uneducated. Economic improvements primarily benefited big landowners, business owners, and foreign investors.

The Revolution of 1910. Opposition to Díaz's rule began to grow after 1900. Francisco Indalecio Madero, a liberal landowner, decided to run for president against Díaz in 1910. During the campaign, Madero became widely popular. Díaz had him imprisoned until after the election, which Díaz won. Madero then fled to the United States.

In November 1910, Madero issued a call for revolution. He had opposed violence, but he saw no other way to overthrow Díaz. Revolutionary bands developed throughout Mexico. They defeated federal troops, destroyed railroads, and attacked towns and estates. In May 1911, members of Díaz's government agreed to force him from office, in the hope of preventing further bloodshed. Díaz resigned and left Mexico, and Madero was elected president later that year.

Madero meant well, but he could not handle the many groups that opposed him. Some groups wanted a dictatorship. Others demanded greater reforms than Madero enacted. General Victoriano Huerta seized control of the government in 1913, and Madero was killed.

Some Mexicans supported Huerta's dictatorship, hoping for peace. But Madero's followers united behind Venustiano Carranza, the governor of Coahuila, and bitter fighting continued. Powerful military leaders from northern Mexico, including the famous Pancho Villa and Álvaro Obregón, led the war against Huerta. United States president Woodrow Wilson sided with Carranza's revolutionaries. In 1914, U.S. forces seized Veracruz. Wilson hoped to prevent the shipment of arms from the seaport to Huerta's army. Later in 1914, Carranza's forces occupied Mexico City, and Huerta was forced to leave the country.

The Constitution of 1917. The victorious revolutionary leaders soon began to struggle with one another for power. Carranza's and Obregón's armies fought those of Villa and the indigenous leader Emiliano Zapata. Villa and Zapata demanded more extreme reforms than Carranza planned. In 1915, the United States supported Carranza and halted the export of guns to his enemies. In revenge, Villa crossed the U.S.-Mexico border in 1916 and raided Columbus, New Mexico. His men killed 18 Americans. About five times as many Mexicans also died in the raid. President Wilson sent General John J. Pershing into Mexico, but Pershing's troops failed to capture Villa.

In 1916, Carranza's power was recognized throughout most of Mexico. He called a convention to write a new constitution. The Constitution, adopted in 1917, combined Carranza's liberal policies with more radical social reforms. It gave the government control over education and over farm and oil properties. It also eliminated some privileges enjoyed by the Roman Catholic Church, limited Mexico's president to one term in office, and recognized labor unions. But Carranza did little to carry out the new constitutional program. In 1920, he was killed during a revolt led by Obregón, who then became president.

Reforms of the early 1900s. Obregón distributed some land among the peasants, built many schools throughout the countryside, and supported a strong labor union movement. Plutarco Elías Calles, who had fought Huerta and Villa alongside Obregón, became president in 1924. Calles carried on the revolutionary program. He encouraged land reform, reorganized the country's financial system, and enforced constitutional controls over the Roman Catholic Church. In protest, the Catholic bishops closed their churches from 1926 to 1929. This action led to a peasant rebellion.

The assassination of Obregón in 1928 caused a political crisis. Obregón had just been elected president but had not yet taken office. When Calles's term ended, Emilio Portes Gil became interim president. But Calles remained the real power behind the presidency. In 1929, Portes Gil reached an agreement with Catholic officials that allowed the Catholic Church to operate churches and schools without interference. In return, church leaders promised to stay out of political affairs.

Calles and his allies formed the National Revolutionary Party (PNR) in 1929. Before the formation of the PNR, Mexican political parties had been temporary groups organized by presidential candidates. The PNR stood for the goals of the Mexican Revolution and included all important political groups. It was reorganized as the Party of the Mexican Revolution in 1938, and as the Institutional Revolutionary Party in 1946.

By 1930, the push for reform had slowed down. The Great Depression, a worldwide economic slump, hit Mexico hard and prevented high government spending on social reforms. Calles and many other old leaders also opposed extreme changes. Younger politicians called for speeding up the revolutionary program. As a result, in 1933, the PNR adopted a six-year plan of social and economic reform. The party chose General Lázaro Cárdenas as its presidential candidate and charged him with carrying out the reform plan.

After Cárdenas became president in 1934, he ended Calles's power. He divided among the peasants about 49 million acres (19 million hectares) of land. This was more than twice as much land as all previous presidents combined had given the peasants. Cárdenas also promoted government controls over foreign-owned companies and strongly supported labor unions. In 1938, during an oil workers' strike, the government took over the properties of American and British oil companies in Mexico. The companies and the British government protested angrily. The U.S. government recognized Mexico's right to the properties as long as the companies received fair payment. In the 1940s, Mexico agreed to pay the companies for their lost property.

During and after World War II. Mexico's economy grew rapidly in the 1940s. Manuel Ávila Camacho, who was president from 1940 to 1946, did much to encourage industrial progress. World War II (1939–1945) also contributed to industrial growth. Mexico entered the war on the side of the Allies in 1942. It sent an air force unit

Hundreds of students shout slogans during a demonstration to commemorate the 1968 massacre in Tlatelolco.

to the Philippines to fight the Japanese. About 250,000 Mexican immigrants also fought in the U.S. Army. However, Mexico's contribution to the war effort was mostly economic. The country supplied raw materials and many laborers to the United States. It also made military equipment in factories that the United States had helped set up. The value of Mexican exports had nearly doubled when the war ended in 1945.

The economy continued to improve after the war. Industry and other economic activities expanded through the 1960s. Aided by generous government assistance, new factories made such products as automobiles, cement, chemicals, clothing, electrical appliances, processed foods, and steel. The government expanded highway, irrigation, and railroad systems. Many new buildings went up, especially in the capital. Agricultural exports to the United States increased, and a growing number of foreign tourists visited Mexico.

The late 1900s. During the late 1960s, many Mexicans, especially students, accused the government of human rights violations and other abuses of power. On October 2, 1968, soldiers fired on a crowd of student demonstrators in Mexico City's Tlatelolco district. Hundreds of people were killed. During the 1970s and early 1980s, many people involved in antigovernment movements disappeared and were presumably killed. Many Mexicans and members of human rights groups blamed military and security forces for the disappearances.

Worldwide problems of recession and inflation led to a decrease in economic production and sharp price increases in Mexico during the 1970s. In 1976, Mexico *devalued* (lowered the value of) its currency, the peso, twice. The devaluations were efforts to stabilize the economy by reducing the cost of Mexican exports and thus making them more competitive abroad.

Luis Echeverría Álvarez, who was president of Mexico from 1970 to 1976, increased government control over foreign-owned businesses. He also took steps that strained Mexico's friendship with the United States. For example, he improved Mexico's relations with socialist governments in Cuba and Chile in spite of U.S. opposition to those governments. Illegal immigration of Mexicans into the United States, plus drug smuggling from Mexico to the United States, caused more problems between the two countries.

José López Portillo became president in 1976. He reduced government controls over both foreign and domestic businesses to encourage private investment in Mexico. Vast petroleum deposits were discovered in and near the Gulf of Mexico in the 1970s. Mexico became a major oil exporter. Its relations with the United States also improved. In the late 1970s, the government greatly increased spending on public works and industry to create more jobs.

Despite Mexico's newfound oil wealth, many people remained poor. Many farmers still lacked modern agricultural equipment and irrigation systems, and wages for farm laborers remained low. Each year, more rural Mexicans moved to cities to look for jobs. This migration and a high rate of population growth contributed to overcrowding and unemployment in urban areas. Millions of Mexicans moved to other countries, especially the United States, to try to make a better living.

The Mexican government expected the income from petroleum to help balance its spending. But by 1981, decreased demand and lower prices for petroleum contributed to an economic crisis in Mexico. The government could not pay its foreign debt, and the value of the peso plummeted during the 1980s. Unemployment and prices rose sharply.

In 1982, Miguel de la Madrid Hurtado became president. He cut down on government spending, especially aid for the poor. But Mexico's economic problems continued. The problems worsened in the early 1980s, when thousands of refugees from civil wars in El Salvador, Guatemala, and Nicaragua entered Mexico and settled in camps near its southern border.

On September 19 and 20, 1985, earthquakes struck south-central Mexico, including Mexico City. They caused about 10,000 deaths and $5 billion in property damage. The government's slow, ineffective response to the tragedy made many Mexicans critical of the Institutional Revolutionary Party (PRI), which had been in power since 1929.

Opposition to the PRI grew during the mid-1980s. In 1988, the party's candidate, Carlos Salinas de Gortari, was elected Mexico's president in the closest election in many decades. Many people believed that Salinas won the election by fraud, and he entered office amid much criticism. That same year, an opposition coalition—the National Democratic Front—and an opposition party—the National Action Party—won almost half of the seats in the Chamber of Deputies. As a result, the president could no longer rely on the vote of two-thirds of the Chamber that was required to amend the Constitution.

Salinas promised to remove government restrictions on the economy and to reform Mexican politics. He attempted to stimulate economic growth and overcome Mexico's huge foreign debt by further reducing government ownership of businesses and by encouraging large-scale foreign investment in Mexico. Under these reforms, Mexico's economy improved, and the PRI won a majority of seats in the Chamber of Deputies in 1991 elections.

In 1993, Mexico, Canada, and the United States ratified the North American Free Trade Agreement (NAFTA). The treaty, which went into effect on January 1, 1994, provided for the gradual elimination of trade barriers among Mexico, the United States, and Canada.

A few hours after NAFTA went into effect, Maya rebels took control of several towns in Chiapas state. The rebel group called itself the Zapatista Army of National Liberation, in memory of the revolutionary leader Emiliano Zapata. The rebels' spokesperson, a non-Indian who hid his identity with a mask, claimed that NAFTA would harm his supporters economically. However, the major cause of the revolt was the poor living conditions in the region. About 100 people were killed in fighting between the Zapatistas and government troops. The government regained possession of the towns within two weeks and declared a cease-fire on January 12. The Zapatistas continued to campaign against the poverty and discrimination faced by indigenous Mexicans.

In August 1994, Ernesto Zedillo Ponce de León of the PRI was elected president. The PRI's previous candidate for president, Luis Donaldo Colosio, had been murdered after he called for

fundamental changes in the party. Shortly after taking office in December, Zedillo faced an economic crisis. Mexico's economy had developed weaknesses, caused in part by large foreign debts and years of the government spending more than it received. The economic weaknesses prompted Zedillo to devalue the peso, but the sudden devaluation triggered a crisis. An emergency economic plan and an international aid package helped ease the crisis in 1995, but the economy still struggled.

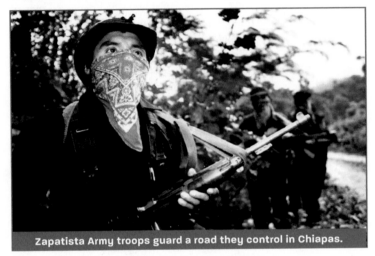

Zapatista Army troops guard a road they control in Chiapas.

The Mexican government passed a series of election reforms in 1996. To help prevent voting fraud, the reforms created an independent federal elections board. They also provided for the direct election of the mayor of Mexico City. Previously, the mayor had been appointed by the president.

In elections held in 1997, the PRI lost its majority in the Chamber of Deputies. In 2000, Vicente Fox Quesada of the National Action Party was elected president of Mexico. He became the first non-PRI candidate to be elected to that office in 71 years.

Recent developments. Official results of the Mexican presidential election of 2006 indicated that Felipe Calderón of the National Action Party had won the election by less than 1 percent. The runner-up, Andrés Manuel López Obrador of the Party of the Democratic Revolution, claimed fraud and demanded a full recount. Following a partial recount, Mexico's top election court declared Calderón the official winner.

In 2008, Mexico's government passed legislation to reform the criminal justice system. The new legislation provided for public court hearings and for the presumption of innocence, until proven guilty, of people charged with crimes. Under the old system, judges decided cases privately based on written evidence. The reforms were scheduled to be fully in effect by 2016.

Violence connected with Mexican drug *cartels* (associations of suppliers) escalated in the early 2000s. Tens of thousands of people died as a result of fighting among the cartels and between the cartels and Mexican authorities. The violence was particularly bad on Mexico's northern border. By early 2009, President Calderón had deployed tens of thousands of soldiers and federal police to combat the violence.

In 2010, Mexico celebrated the *bicentennial* (200th anniversary) of the beginning of the revolt that led to national independence.

Enrique Peña Nieto of the Institutional Revolutionary Party won a presidential election in July 2012. Josefina Vázquez Mota of the incumbent National Action Party placed third. Many voters were unhappy with the lagging economy and the increase in drug-related violence under PAN leadership. Peña Nieto took office in December.

HERNAN CORTES (1485–1547) was
a Spanish explorer who conquered what is now central and southern Mexico. His military triumphs were followed by 300 years of Spanish domination of Mexico and Central America.

Early life. Cortés, also known as Hernando or Fernando, was born into a family of minor nobility in Medellin in the province of Extremadura, Spain. He moved to Santo Domingo in the West Indies in 1504.

Cortés fought under Governor Diego Velazquez in a Cuban expedition that began in 1511. In 1518, Velazquez selected him to lead an expedition to the Yucatán Peninsula of Mexico, then a center of Maya civilization. Before Cortés could leave Cuba,

Velazquez canceled the expedition, fearful of the voyage's expense and distrustful of Cortés's ambition. Cortés disobeyed and sailed for Yucatán in 1519, with about 500 men and 11 ships.

Arrival in Mexico. Conquering Mexico took more than two years. At the start, Cortés skillfully made associations with Indian leaders, communicating through interpreters. One of these interpreters was a young Indian woman, Malintzin, also known as Malinche. The Indians of Tabasco had given her to the Spaniards as a peace offering. The Spaniards called her Marina. She became an adviser to Cortés, and she bore him a son.

From Yucatán, Cortés sailed northward along the coast of the Gulf of Mexico. He founded the first Spanish settlement in Mexico, La Villa Rica de Vera Cruz (modern-day Veracruz). Cortés appointed a town council, which gave him the title of captain general and the authority, under Spanish law, to conquer Mexico.

In August 1519, Cortés marched toward Tenochtitlan (now Mexico City), the capital of the Aztec empire. Tenochtitlan had formed a union called the Triple Alliance with the neighboring cities of Texcoco and Tlacopan and had built an empire. The three cities forced other Indian villages to pay them taxes and to provide human sacrifices for their religious ceremonies. Many Indians resented the Aztec empire for its cruelty and volunteered to help Cortés defeat it. Others joined Cortés after he defeated them in battle.

Victory over the Aztec. At first, the Aztec emperor, Montezuma II, refused to meet with Cortés. But in November 1519, Montezuma allowed the Spaniards to enter Tenochtitlan. Cortés eventually took Montezuma hostage and tried to rule the empire through him.

Six months later, Cortés left the city to challenge a Spanish expedition led by Panfilo de Narvaez, who had been sent by Velazquez to arrest him. Cortés easily captured Narvaez and persuaded Narvaez's troops to join him. Meanwhile, the people of Tenochtitlan rebelled. Soon after Cortés returned, Montezuma was wounded and died. The Spanish soldiers fled the city.

In December 1520, Cortés began to organize an attack against Tenochtitlan and its new leader, Cuauhtemoc. The city fell on August 13, 1521. When brought before Cortés, Cuauhtemoc asked to die. Cortés, believing Cuauhtemoc knew where Aztec treasures were hidden, had him tortured,

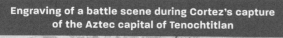
Engraving of a battle scene during Cortez's capture of the Aztec capital of Tenochtitlan

but Cuauhtemoc refused to tell any secrets. In 1525, Cortés had him hanged.

After the conquest. King Charles I of Spain, who had become Holy Roman Emperor Charles V in 1519, appointed Cortés governor and captain general of the newly conquered territory. Cortés received the title Marques del Valle de Oaxaca in 1528. He managed the founding of new cities and appointed men to extend Spanish rule to all of Mexico, which was renamed New Spain. Cortés also supported efforts to convert Indians to Christianity and sponsored new explorations. He led expeditions to Honduras in 1524 and to Baja California in northwestern Mexico in 1535 and 1536.

Cortés returned to Spain in 1540. His last battle was a Spanish attack on Algiers in 1541. He died on December 2, 1547.

DIEGO RIVERA (1886–1957) was a Mexican artist. He became famous for murals that portrayed Mexican life and history. Rivera was a controversial figure because of his radical political beliefs and his attacks on the church and clergy.

Rivera was born in Guanajuato. In the 1920s, he became involved in the new Mexican mural movement. With such Mexican artists as Jose Clemente Orozco and David Siqueiros, he began to experiment with fresco painting on large walls. Rivera soon developed his own style of large, simplified figures and bold colors. Many of his murals deal symbolically with Mexican society and thought after the country's 1910 revolution. Some of Rivera's best murals are in the National Palace in Mexico City and at the National Agricultural School in Chapingo, near Mexico City.

Rivera painted several significant works in the United States, which he visited in the early 1930s and again in 1940. Perhaps his finest surviving United States work is a mural at the Detroit Institute of Arts. Frida Kahlo, Rivera's wife, was also a noted Mexican painter.

THE ALAMO is a historic structure in the center of San Antonio. A famous battle was fought there from February 23 to March 6, 1836, during the war for Texan independence. The Alamo is sometimes called the *Thermopylae of America*, after the famous battle in which the ancient Greeks held off a large Persian force. No Texans escaped from the Alamo after the night of March 5. The Alamo is now a restored historic site.

Early days. The Alamo was built as a Roman Catholic mission. Padre Antonio Olivares, a Spanish missionary, established it at San Antonio in 1718. The mission consisted of a monastery and church enclosed by high walls. The mission was originally called *San Antonio de Valero*. It was later called *Alamo*, the Spanish name for the cottonwood trees surrounding the mission. The Texans occasionally used the mission as a fort.

During the winter of 1835–1836, the people of Texas decided to sever their relations with Mexico because of dissatisfaction with the Mexican government. To prevent the success of this independence movement, General Antonio Lopez de Santa Anna, in command of the Mexican Army, approached San Antonio with his troops. Lieutenant Colonel William Barret Travis and a force of about 150 Texans sought to defend the city. The company included the famous frontiersmen James Bowie and Davy Crockett. The quick arrival of the Mexicans surprised the Texans, who retreated to the Alamo. Over the following days, about 5,000 Mexican troops arrived in San Antonio. Travis sent out a plea for help, declaring, "I shall never surrender or retreat." A relief party from Gonzales, Texas, passed through the Mexican lines and entered the Alamo, increasing the Alamo forces to 189 men. Colonel J. W. Fannin left Goliad, Texas, with most of his 400 men to relieve the Alamo, but he had equipment trouble on the way and returned to Goliad.

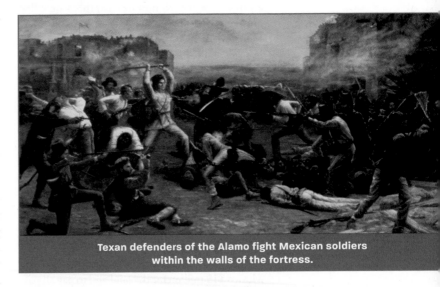

Texan defenders of the Alamo fight Mexican soldiers within the walls of the fortress.

The siege of the Alamo lasted 13 days. By March 5, the garrison could not return Mexican fire because ammunition was low. This convinced

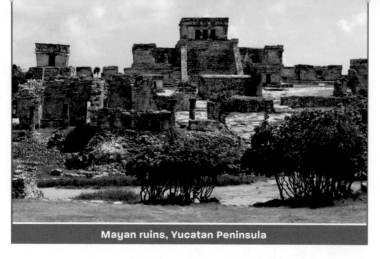
Mayan ruins, Yucatan Peninsula

Santa Anna that the fort could be assaulted. Early the next morning, a Mexican force of about 1,500 soldiers stormed the Alamo and succeeded in scaling the walls. At the end, the Texans fought using their rifles as clubs. Some historians believe that a few defenders, perhaps including Crockett, survived the battle only to be executed at Santa Anna's orders. Other historians accept the more familiar story that all the Texans who fought died in the battle. At 8 a.m., the Mexican general reported his victory to his government. Survivors of the battle included Susanna Dickinson, the wife of an officer; her baby; her Mexican nurse; and Colonel Travis's black slave Joe.

"Remember the Alamo" became a battle cry. The determined defense of the Alamo gave General Sam Houston time to gather the forces he needed to save the independence movement of Texas. He retreated eastward, pursued by Santa Anna. At San Jacinto, Texas, he turned on the Mexicans, surprised them during an afternoon siesta, and on April 21, in just 18 minutes, captured or killed most of the Mexican army of over 1,200 men. Houston's army captured Santa Anna the following day and forced him to sign a treaty granting Texas its independence.

THE TREATY OF GUADALUPE HIDALGO

officially ended the Mexican War (1846–1848). The United States and Mexico signed the treaty on February 2, 1848, after conducting negotiations at Villa de Guadalupe Hidalgo, now part of Mexico City. Under the treaty, Mexico *ceded* (surrendered) land that now makes up California, Nevada, and Utah, most of Arizona, and parts of Colorado, New Mexico, and Wyoming. This land became known as the Mexican Cession. The United States agreed to pay Mexico $15 million for the land and to pay all past claims held by American citizens against Mexico up to a total of $3,250,000. The treaty guaranteed Mexicans in the ceded territory the protection of their property and freedom of religion. Also under the treaty, Mexico gave up all claims to Texas.

THE GADSDEN PURCHASE

was a strip of land the United States bought from Mexico in the 1850s to form part of the boundary between the two countries. The purchase included the region south of the Gila River in what is now Arizona and New Mexico.

As a result of the Mexican War (1846–1848), the United States had acquired a great deal of land from Mexico. But the Treaty of Guadalupe Hidalgo, which ended the war, had been vague about the new boundary between the two countries. The purpose of the Gadsden Purchase was to provide a clear boundary and also give the United States a good southern railroad route to the Pacific Ocean.

James Gadsden, the U.S. minister to Mexico, conducted the negotiations with Antonio Lopez de Santa Anna, the Mexican president. Santa Anna at first rejected Gadsden's proposal. However, the Mexican government desperately needed funds, and Santa Anna feared U.S. military action if he refused to sell the land.

The United States paid $10 million for the 29,640 square miles (76,770 square kilometers) in the purchase. The treaty of sale, the Gadsden Treaty, was signed on December 30, 1853. The two countries exchanged ratifications of the treaty on June 30, 1854. Opposition in Mexico to the sale was one of the reasons Santa Anna was banished from Mexico in 1855.

In addition to the purchase, the Gadsden Treaty granted the United States the right to cross Mexico's Isthmus of Tehuantepec, which provided a route between the Gulf of Mexico and the Pacific Ocean. The treaty also abolished a requirement that the United States protect Mexico from Indian attacks. The United States had agreed to the requirement in 1848 in the Treaty of Guadalupe Hidalgo.

THE MAYA

were an American Indian people who developed a magnificent civilization in Central America and south Mexico. The Maya civilization reached its period of greatest development about A.D. 250 and continued to flourish for hundreds of years. The Maya produced remarkable architecture, painting, pottery, and sculpture. They made great advancements in astronomy and mathematics and developed an accurate yearly calendar. They were one of the first peoples in the Western Hemisphere to develop an advanced form of writing.

The Maya lived in an area of about 120,000 square miles (311,000 square kilometers). Today, their territory is divided among Mexico and several Central American countries. It consists of the Mexican states of Campeche, Yucatán, and Quintana Roo and part of the states of Tabasco and Chiapas. It also includes Belize, most of Guatemala, and parts of El Salvador and of Honduras.

The Maya civilization was at its peak from about A.D. 250 to 900. During that time, known as the Classic Period, it was centered in the tropical rain forest of the lowlands of what is now northern Guatemala. Many of the major Maya cities, such as Piedras Negras, Tikal, and Uaxactun, developed in this area. By about 900, most of the Maya abandoned the Guatemalan lowlands and moved to areas to the north and south, including Yucatán and the highlands of southern Guatemala. In those areas, they continued to prosper until Spain conquered almost all of the Maya in the mid-1500s.

Today, descendants of the Maya live in Mexico and Central America. They speak Maya languages and carry on some religious customs of their ancestors.

Way of Life

Religion. The Maya worshiped many gods and goddesses. One Maya manuscript mentions more than 160 of them. For example, the Maya worshiped a corn god, a rain god known as *Chac*, a sun god called *Kinich Ahau*, and a moon goddess called *Ix Chel*. Each god or goddess influenced some part of Maya life. Ix Chel, for instance, was the goddess of medicine and weaving.

Religion played a central part in the daily life of the Maya. Each day had special religious importance, and religious festivals in honor of particular gods took place throughout the year. The Maya regarded their gods as both helpful and harmful. To obtain the help of the gods, the Maya fasted, prayed, offered sacrifices, and held many religious ceremonies. Deer, dogs, and turkeys were sacrificed to feed the gods. The Maya frequently offered their own blood, which they spattered on pieces of bark paper. They practiced some human sacrifice, such as throwing victims into deep wells or killing them at the funerals of great leaders.

In their cities, the Maya built tall pyramids of limestone with small temples on top. Priests climbed the stairs of the pyramids and performed ceremonies in the temples. Major religious festivals, such as those for the Maya New Year and for each of the Maya months, took place in the cities.

The Maya observed special ceremonies when burying their dead. Corpses were painted red and then were wrapped in straw mats with a few of their personal belongings. They were buried under the floor of the houses where they had lived. Maya rulers and other important persons were buried in their finest garments within the pyramids, under the temples. Servants were killed and buried with them, along with jewelry and utensils, for use in the next world.

Family and social life. Entire Maya families, including parents, children, and grandparents, lived together. Everyone in a household helped with the work. The men and the older boys did most of the farmwork, such as clearing and weeding the fields and planting the crops. They also did most of the hunting and fishing. The women and the older girls made the family's clothes, prepared meals, raised the younger children, and supplied the house with firewood and water. The Maya had no schools. The children learned various skills by observing adults and helping them.

Religious festivals provided one of the favorite forms of recreation for the Maya. These festivals were held on special days throughout the year. Dancing and feasts took place at the festivals. In addition, the Maya had a sacred game that was played on special courts. The players tried to hit a rubber ball through a stone ring with their hips.

Mayan temple

Ruins of a Mayan observatory

Food, clothing, and shelter. Maya farmers raised chiefly beans, corn, and squash. Corn was the principal food of the Maya, and the women prepared it in a variety of ways. They made flat corn cakes, which today are called *tortillas*, as a type of bread. The Maya also used corn to make an alcoholic drink called *balche*, which they sweetened with honey and spiced with bark. The Maya also raised avocados, chili peppers, and sweet potatoes.

Farmers became skilled at making the best use of natural resources. They dug canals in swampy lowlands to drain the soil and used the unearthed soil to build raised fields in which they grew crops. On sloping land, farmers built terraces to hold the soil in place and walls to control water flow. With such methods, the Maya grew enough food to feed a large population.

The Maya kept domestic dogs for use in hunting and for food and raised turkeys and honey bees on their farms. The Maya hunted armadillos, deer, rabbits, pig-like animals called *peccaries*, and other wild animals. They fished and collected shellfish from the rivers and sea. They also gathered fruits and vegetables from the countryside.

The clothing of the Maya kept them comfortable in the hot, tropical climate. Men wore a *loincloth*, a strip of cloth tied around their hips and passed between their legs. Women wore loose dresses that reached their ankles. The people wove these garments from cotton or other fibers. The people of the upper classes wore finer clothes decorated with embroidery and ornaments. They had splendid headdresses made of the brightly colored feathers of tropical birds. The wealthy also wore large amounts of jewelry, much of which was carved out of green jade and colorful shells.

Maya farmers lived in rural homesteads or small villages near their fields. They built their houses from poles lashed together and used palm leaves or grass to thatch the roofs. Many Maya cities were home to tens of thousands of people. One of the largest known cities of the Classic Period, Tikal, probably had a population of about 60,000 at its peak. Another 30,000 people lived in the surrounding area. People from the countryside gathered in the Maya cities for markets, religious festivals, and other important events.

Trade and transportation. The Maya took part in a trade network that linked a number of groups in Central America. The people of the Maya lowlands exported many items, including handicrafts, forest and sea products, and jaguar pelts. They imported jade, volcanic glass, and the feathers of a bird called the *quetzal* from the highlands of Guatemala, where other Maya lived.

The Maya of Yucatán sent salt and finely decorated cottons to Honduras. In return, they received cacao beans, which they used in making chocolate. The Maya also transported goods as far as the Valley of Oaxaca in Mexico and the city of Teotihuacan, near what is now Mexico City. They carried most goods on their backs or on rivers in dugout canoes. They did not use the wheel or any beasts of burden, such as horses or oxen.

Government. Each Maya city governed its surrounding area, and some large cities each controlled one or more smaller cities. A city ruler would usually be succeeded by his younger brother or by his son. In some cases, generations of a single family ruled for hundreds of years. At Copán, for example, carved figures on a large stone altar record a series of 16 kings from a single family who ruled the city from A.D. 426 to A.D. 810. The Maya never united to form a single centrally governed nation. But in late Maya times, the governments of such cities as Chichén Itzá and Mayapan controlled large parts of the Maya population.

Communication and learning. The Maya developed an advanced form of writing that consisted of many symbols. These symbols represented combinations of sounds or entire ideas and formed a kind of *hieroglyphic* writing.

The Maya kept records on large stone monuments called *stelae*, as well as on some buildings and household utensils. They used the stelae to record important dates and to take note of great events in the lives of their rulers and the rulers' families. The Maya also made books of paper made from fig tree bark. Several books from the 1100s to the early 1500s have survived. They contain astronomical tables, information about religious ceremonies, and calendars that show lucky days for such activities as farming and hunting.

Other cultural advances by the Maya included the development of mathematics and astronomy. The Maya used a mathematical system based on the number 20, instead of 10 as in the decimal system. A dot represented the number one, a bar represented five, and special symbols represented zero. The Maya were among the first people to use symbols for the idea of zero. Maya priests observed the positions of the sun, moon, and stars. They made tables predicting eclipses and the orbit of the planet Venus.

The priests also used mathematics and astronomy to develop two kinds of calendars. One was a sacred almanac of 260 days. Each day was named with one of 20 day names and a number from 1 to 13. Each of the 20 day names had a god or goddess associated with it. The priests predicted good or bad luck by studying the combinations of gods or goddesses and numbers. The Maya also had a calendar of 365 days, based on the orbit of the earth around the sun. These days were divided into 18 months of 20 days each, plus 5 days at the end of the year. The Maya considered these last 5 days of the year to be extremely unlucky. During that period they fasted, made many sacrifices, and avoided unnecessary work.

Mayan mural

The Maya used herbs and magic to treat illness. Scholars know little else about Maya medicine.

Arts and crafts. The Maya produced exceptional architecture, painting, pottery, and sculpture. Highly skilled architects built tall pyramids of limestone, with small temples on top. The Maya also built large, low buildings where rulers and other nobles lived. Many buildings had flat ornaments called *roof combs*, which extended from the high point of the roof. The combs gave buildings the appearance of great height.

Maya artists decorated walls with brightly colored murals that featured lifelike figures taking part in battles and festivals. The artists outlined the figures and then filled in the color. They rarely shaded the colors. A similar type of painting appears on Maya pottery.

The Maya made small sculptures of clay and carved huge ones from stone. Most of the small sculptures were figures of men and women. The large sculptures, some standing over 30 feet (9 meters) high, were carved with portraits of rulers.

History

The Preclassic Period. The heart of the Maya civilization centered around what is now the *department* (state) of El Peten in the lowlands of northern Guatemala. The first farmers may have settled there as early as 1000 B.C. They came from areas surrounding El Peten—mostly from highlands to the west and south—in search of fertile land. The new settlers lived in small villages. They gathered food from the surrounding forest and raised crops.

By 800 B.C., the Maya lowlands were completely settled. At that time, the Olmec lived west of the Maya. The Olmec were probably the Central American inventors of numbers and writing. They also had well-developed art. The Olmec civilization influenced Maya culture. The Maya, like the Olmec, began to build pyramids and carve stone monuments.

The Maya built their first large pyramids between 600 and 400 B.C., during the middle of the Preclassic Period. By late in the Preclassic Period, between 400 B.C. and A.D. 250, there were several large Maya settlements in the lowlands. Some of the largest Maya pyramids stood in one of these settlements, at a site now called El Mirador, in northern Guatemala.

The Classic Period of the Maya civilization lasted from about A.D. 250 to 900. During those years, the Maya founded their greatest cities and made their remarkable achievements in the arts and sciences. They also perfected the practice of erecting stelae to honor the most important events in the lives of their leaders.

During the first 300 years of the Classic Period, the city of Teotihuacan, near present-day Mexico City, had a strong influence on Maya art and architecture. Throughout the Classic Period, populations grew, and new cities were founded. Toward the end of the period, as competition for land and other resources increased, rival cities began to fight each other. Sometimes a growing city would break away from a larger city's control. In other cases, one city conquered another and captured its ruler. Defeated rulers and other important prisoners of war were sacrificed in religious ceremonies, and the conquered city probably paid something to the victor. By about 700, the Maya of the Classic Period reached their peak in population and prosperity.

Then, beginning in the 800s, the Maya stopped erecting stelae in city after city. They abandoned their major centers in the Guatemala lowlands one by one and finally left most of this lowland region. Scholars are still trying to discover the reasons for the collapse of Classic Maya society. Some experts point to a combination of such factors as overpopulation, disease, exhaustion of natural resources, crop failures, warfare between cities, and the movement of other groups into the Maya area.

The Postclassic Period began about 900, when the Maya abandoned their cities in the Guatemalan lowlands. Some Maya moved north to build new cities in the lowlands of Yucatán. Others moved to southern Guatemala's highlands and built cities there.

Important changes took place in Maya political and economic systems during the Postclassic Period. For example, sea trade became much more common, resulting in prosperity for Maya cities near the seacoasts. Between 900 and 1200, Chichén Itzá, in Yucatán, grew to be the largest and most powerful Maya city. It was governed by a council of nobles—unlike Maya cities of the Classic Period, which each had a single ruler. Chichén Itzá dominated Yucatán by a combination of military strength and control over important trade routes. Chichén Itzá traded with, and formed other ties to, regions beyond the Maya area. These areas included Tula, the leading city of the Toltec Indians' empire in the highlands of what is now central Mexico.

Chichén Itzá declined around 1200, and Mayapan replaced it as the chief Maya city. Although Mayapan never became as powerful as Chichén Itzá had been, it controlled much of Yucatán for another 200 years.

About 1440, the leaders of some Maya cities revolted against the Mayapan rulers and defeated them. Yucatán was then divided into separate warring states. About the same time, several Maya states in the highlands of southern Guatemala used military force to dominate other Maya in that region. Then, in the early 1500s, Spanish conquerors invaded the Maya territories. By the mid-1500s, they had overcome almost all the Maya. Some Maya fled into the forest and to small villages away from Spanish control. The Spanish conquered the last independent Maya city in 1697.

The Maya heritage. Today, many people of Mexico and Central America speak one of more than 20 languages and dialects that developed from the ancient Maya language. Some of these people live in the highlands of Mexico and Guatemala. Others inhabit the northern part of the Yucatán Peninsula in Mexico. Many descendants of the Maya farm as did their ancestors and carry on some of the traditional religious customs.

The ruins of the Maya cities are tourist attractions. Sites in Mexico include the ruins of Bonampak and Palenque in Chiapas, and Chichén Itzá in northern Yucatán. Tourists also visit the ruins of Tikal in Guatemala and of Copán in Honduras.

THE MEXICAN WAR (1846–1848)

was fought between the United States and Mexico over disagreements that had been accumulating for two decades. In the course of the war, United States forces invaded Mexico and occupied the capital, Mexico City. By the Treaty of Guadalupe Hidalgo, the United States acquired from Mexico the regions of California, Nevada, and Utah, most of Arizona and New Mexico, and parts of Colorado and Wyoming. But many historians believe the war was an unnecessary attack on a weaker nation.

Causes of the War

Background of the war. In 1835, Texas revolted against the Mexican government, which then controlled the region. Texans established the Republic of Texas in 1836, but Mexico refused to recognize Texas' independence. The Mexican government warned the United States that if Texas

U.S. president James K. Polk supported the annexation of Texas.

were admitted to the Union, Mexico would break off diplomatic relations with the United States. James K. Polk was elected U.S. president in 1844. He favored the expansion of U.S. territory and supported the annexation of Texas. Texas was made a state in 1845, and Mexico broke off relations with the United States. At this point, the dispute could have been settled by peaceful means. But the United States wanted additional Mexican territory, and other quarrels developed.

One of these disputes was the question of the boundary between Texas and Mexico. Texas claimed the Rio Grande as its southwestern border. Mexico said that Texas had never extended farther than the Nueces River. Also, the U.S. government claimed that Mexico owed U.S. citizens about $3 million to make up for lives and property that had been lost in Mexico since Mexico's war for independence from Spain ended in 1821. By the 1840s, many Americans demanded that the United States collect these debts by force.

More important was a growing feeling in the United States that the country had a "manifest destiny" to expand westward into new lands. The westward movement had brought Americans into Mexican territory, especially California. Mexico was too weak to control or populate its northern territories. Both American and Mexican inhabitants were discontented with Mexican rule. California seemed almost ready to declare itself independent.

Events leading up to the war. In the fall of 1845, President Polk sent John Slidell to Mexico as American minister. Slidell was to offer Mexico $25 million and cancel all claims for damages if Mexico would accept the Rio Grande boundary and sell New Mexico and California to the United States. If Mexico refused to sell the territories, Slidell was to offer to cancel the claims on condition that Mexico agreed to the Rio Grande boundary. While Slidell was in Mexico, a new

Mexican president came to power. Both the old and new presidents were afraid their enemies would denounce them as cowards if they made concessions to the United States. They refused to see Slidell, who came home and told Polk that Mexico needed to be "chastised."

Meanwhile, Polk had ordered Major General Zachary Taylor, who was stationed with about 4,000 men on the Nueces River, to advance to the Rio Grande. Taylor reached the river in April 1846. On April 25, a party of Mexican soldiers surprised and defeated a small group of American cavalry just north of the Rio Grande.

Polk had wanted to ask Congress to declare war on Mexico. The news of the battle gave him the chance to say that Mexico had "invaded our territory and shed American blood on American soil." In reality, Mexico had as good a claim as the United States to the soil where the blood was shed. But on May 13, 1846, Congress declared war on Mexico.

The War

The Americans had two aims. They wanted to add to the United States the territory that Mexico had been asked to sell. They also wished to invade Mexico to force the Mexicans to accept the loss of the territory.

The occupation of New Mexico and California. In June 1846, General Stephen W. Kearny set out with about 1,700 troops from Fort Leavenworth, Kansas, to capture New Mexico. In August, the expedition entered the New Mexican town of Santa Fe and took control of New Mexico. The next month, Kearny pushed across the desert to California.

Meanwhile, in June 1846, a group of American settlers led by U.S. Army officer John C. Fremont revolted in California against the Mexican government. This rebellion became known as the Bear Flag Revolt because of the portrayal of a grizzly bear on the settlers' flag. In July, U.S. naval forces under Commodore John D. Sloat captured the California town of Monterey and occupied the San Francisco area. On December 6, Kearny led about 100 troops in the bloody Battle of San Pasqual near San Diego. Reinforcements from San Diego helped save the small American army. In January 1847, U.S. troops under Kearny and Commodore Robert F. Stockton of the Navy won the Battle of San Gabriel near Los Angeles. This victory completed the American conquest of California.

General Zachary Taylor leads American troops into battle at Palo Alto.

Taylor's campaign. Before war officially began, General Zachary Taylor had driven the Mexicans across the lower Rio Grande to Matamoros in the two battles of Palo Alto and Resaca de la Palma. These battles occurred on May 8 and 9, 1846. On May 18, Taylor crossed the river and occupied Matamoros. After waiting for new troops, he moved his army up the river and marched against the important city of Monterrey. Monterrey fell on September 24, after a hard-fought battle. Before the end of the year, Taylor had occupied Saltillo and Victoria, important towns of northeastern Mexico. However, Mexico still refused to negotiate with the United States.

Polk and his advisers decided to land an army at Veracruz, on the east coast, and strike a blow at Mexico City. Many of Taylor's best troops were ordered to join Major General Winfield Scott, who was placed in charge of the new campaign. President Antonio Lopez de Santa Anna of Mexico commanded the Mexican Army. He learned of the American plans and immediately led a large army against Taylor at Buena Vista, in the mountains beyond Saltillo. Although the Mexican forces nearly overran the U.S. positions, Taylor's troops eventually defeated them. General Taylor became

American forces land near Veracruz.

a hero because of his victories and was elected president of the United States in 1848.

Doniphan's victories. In December 1846, Colonel Alexander W. Doniphan led about 850 troops south from Santa Fe to capture the Mexican city of Chihuahua. The American troops defeated a Mexican army at El Brazito on Christmas Day. Doniphan's army won the furious Battle of the Sacramento, fought just outside Chihuahua on February 28, 1847. The Americans occupied the city on March 1.

Scott's campaign. General Scott was at this time the officer of highest rank in the United States Army. With a force of about 10,000 men, he landed near Veracruz on March 9, 1847. Twenty days later he captured the city, and on April 8 he began his advance toward the Mexican capital. The American army stormed a mountain pass at Cerro Gordo on April 17 and 18 and pushed on. Near Mexico City, American troops fought and won the battles of Contreras and Churubusco on August 19 and 20. The Mexican Army was superior in numbers but poorly equipped and poorly led.

After a two weeks' armistice, the Americans won a battle at Molino del Rey and stormed and captured the hilltop fortress of Chapultepec. On the following day the Americans marched into Mexico City.

The peace treaty. Despite all the American victories, Mexico refused to negotiate a peace treaty. In April 1847, Polk had sent Nicholas P. Trist, Chief Clerk of the Department of State, to join Scott's army in Mexico and attempt to open diplomatic negotiations with Santa Anna. When the armistice of August failed, the president recalled Trist. But Santa Anna resigned shortly after Scott entered the Mexican capital. Mexico established a new government, and it feared that it might lose even more territory if it did not accept the American demands. At the request of the Mexican leaders and General Scott, Trist agreed to remain in Mexico against Polk's orders and negotiate a settlement.

The treaty was signed on February 2, 1848, at the village of Guadalupe Hidalgo, near Mexico City. By this time, many people in the United States wanted to annex all Mexico. But the treaty required Mexico to give up only the territory Polk had originally asked for. The United States paid Mexico $15 million for the land, which became known as the Mexican Cession. The United States also took responsibility for paying $3 million in damage claims made by American citizens against Mexico. In 1853, the Gadsden Purchase gave an additional 29,640 square miles (76,767 square kilometers) to the United States.

Results of the war. The United States gained more than 525,000 square miles (1,360,000 square kilometers) of territory as a result of the Mexican War. But the war also revived the quarrels over slavery. Here was new territory. Was it to be slave or free? The Compromise of 1850 made California a free state and established the principle of "popular sovereignty." That meant letting the people of a territory decide whether it would be slave or free. However, popular sovereignty later led to bitter disagreement and became one of the underlying causes of the American Civil War.

The Mexican War gave training to many officers who later fought in the Civil War. Civil War officers who also fought in the Mexican War included Ulysses S. Grant, William T. Sherman, George B. McClellan, George Gordon Meade, Robert E. Lee, Stonewall Jackson, and Jefferson Davis.

Principal Battles

The chief battles of the Mexican War included:

Palo Alto. Palo Alto was one of the earliest battles of the war. General Taylor's troops defeated Mexican forces under General Mariano Arista on May 8, 1846, on a plain northeast of Brownsville, Texas.

Resaca de la Palma. In the battle of Resaca de la Palma a 2,300-man army under Taylor crushed 5,000 Mexican soldiers under Arista in Cameron County, near Brownsville, on May 9, 1846. General Taylor's two victories allowed him to cross the Rio Grande and to invade Mexico.

Buena Vista. Near the hacienda of Buena in northern Mexico, Taylor's force of about 4,600 men defended a narrow mountain pass against Santa Anna's army made up of about 15,000 men. Through this battle, fought on February 22 and 23, 1847, the American forces established their hold on northeastern Mexico.

Cerro Gordo. Cerro Gordo ranks among the most important battles the Americans fought on the march from Veracruz to Mexico City. A mountain pass near Jalapa, Cerro Gordo lies 60 miles (97 kilometers) northwest of Veracruz. General Scott's 9,000-man force attacked 13,000 Mexicans under Santa Anna, and forced them to flee. The battle, fought on April 17 and 18, 1847, cleared the way to Mexico City.

Churubusco. In the small village of Churubusco, 6 miles (10 kilometers) south of Mexico City, Scott's invading army won another major victory on August 20, 1847. Scott's soldiers stormed the fortified camp of Contreras, and then attacked the Mexican force at Churubusco. The Mexicans finally fled and sought refuge within the walls of the capital city. The Americans had about 9,000 men in the battle; the Mexicans, about 30,000.

Chapultepec. Chapultepec was the last battle of the war before the capture of Mexico City. On September 12, 1847, Scott's men attacked Chapultepec, a fortified hill guarding the city gates. The attacks continued the following day until the Mexicans retreated to Mexico City. On September 14, Scott's troops entered the Mexican capital.

THE MIXTEC INDIANS maintained one of the most important cultures in central Mexico from about A.D. 900 until about 1520. Beginning in about A.D. 900, they established kingdoms in mountainous parts of what are now the Mexican states of Guerrero, Oaxaca, and Puebla. The Mixtec kingdoms competed with one another for political power in the region. Beginning in the 1200s, Mixtec kingdoms integrated

Geometric carving found at an ancient Mixtec site, Oaxaca, Mexico

with kingdoms of the Zapotec Indians through intermarriage of rulers and political alliances. The Mixtec also conquered several smaller Zapotec kingdoms in the Valley of Oaxaca. Later, the Mixtecs came under the rule of the Aztec Empire.

The Mixtec produced many sophisticated works of art, including ceramics, jewelry, and small carvings. They used such materials as bone, clay, gold, jade, silver, turquoise, and wood. Among the most important surviving works of Mixtec art are several *codices* (historical manuscripts). These books used *pictographs* (a system of writing with pictures) to record information about ruling families and their conquests. The Mixtec style of art had widespread influence on other Middle American cultures, including that of the Aztec.

About 170,000 people who speak Mixtec dialects still live in the states of Oaxaca and Puebla. Most are farmers and herders.

THE OLMEC INDIANS developed

what may have been the earliest civilization in the Americas. The Olmec civilization flourished between about 1200 and 400 B.C. The most important centers of Olmec culture were on the Mexican Gulf Coast, in what are now the southern Mexican states of Veracruz and Tabasco. By 400 B.C., the Olmec's sophisticated artistic style had spread over much of Middle America, from central Mexico to El Salvador. Some scholars have also recognized Olmec influences in the artwork and religious practices of many later Middle American cultures, including those of the Maya and the Aztec.

The Olmec lived near rivers in small thatched houses. They fished in the rivers and farmed lands

made fertile by river flooding. The Olmec used a calendar and an early form of writing. At a number of sites, archaeologists have found large earthen mounds and uncovered ruins at what are believed to be Olmec religious centers. Artworks found at these sites include huge carved-stone heads that weigh up to 36,000 pounds (16,300 kilograms). The Olmec transported some of these gigantic stones more than 50 miles (80 kilometers) to the sites where the sculptures were discovered. Other objects found at the sites include mirrors of polished iron ore, carvings with both animal and human features, and groups of small stone figures arranged to represent religious ceremonies.

THE TARASCAN INDIANS live

on the high plateaus of west-central Mexico, in what is now the state of Michoacán. They ruled a powerful empire in the area from the late 1300s to the early 1500s. The Tarascan empire bordered the larger Aztec empire to the east.

The Tarascan empire was highly organized. It included several major settlements near Lake Patzcuaro, including the empire's capital, Tzintzuntzan. The Tarascan fished in the numerous marshy lakes in the region. They also hunted deer and smaller animals and raised turkeys and such crops as corn, beans, squash, and chile peppers. The Spanish conquered the Tarascan empire in the 1520s.

Today, many Tarascan still follow their traditional ways of life. These people farm and fish in the rugged areas of Michoacán. They also carve wooden objects and weave nets, mats, and baskets. In their local communities, many Tarascan still speak Tarascan dialects instead of Spanish, the language most widely spoken in Mexico.

THE TOLTEC INDIANS established

an empire in the highlands of central Mexico during the A.D. 900s. They were the dominant people in the region until 1200. The Aztec later honored the Toltec as the founders of urban civilization in the highlands. Aztec legends told about the Toltec and their capital city of Tollan.

In the 900s, the Toltec built a major city whose ruins lie near what is now the town of Tula de Allende, about 45 miles (70 kilometers) north of Mexico City. The site is known as Tula. Some scholars think the ruins are those of the Tollan of the Aztec legends. Toltec buildings included large

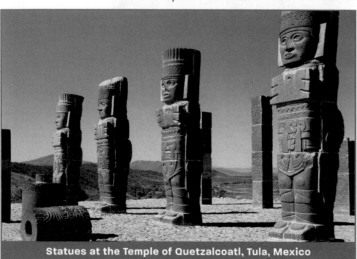

Statues at the Temple of Quetzalcoatl, Tula, Mexico

pyramids topped with temples. Images of Quetzalcoatl (which means Feathered Serpent) appear on several of the pyramids. Quetzalcoatl was a Toltec ruler whom the Toltec came to consider godlike.

The Toltec culture influenced Maya Indians in the Yucatán Peninsula. Some archaeologists even think some Toltec may have migrated to the region. Some of the buildings and artwork at the prehistoric Maya city of Chichén Itzá resemble those at Tula. Images of Quetzalcoatl are displayed on several of the Maya buildings.

During the 1100s, nomads began to cross the northern frontiers of the Toltec empire. As they settled in the Valley of Mexico, Toltec dominance ended. The invading groups included the Aztec, who gradually replaced the Toltec as the most powerful people in the Mexican highlands.

THE YAQUI INDIANS are a tribe

that lives in Mexico, Arizona, and California. They are noted for their religious ceremonies, which blend concepts of Roman Catholicism with ancient tribal customs. On holy days, the Yaqui perform ancient dances and rituals in honor of Jesus Christ, the Virgin Mary, and tribal patron saints.

The ancient Yaqui lived along the Yaqui River in northwestern Mexico. They raised beans, corn, and squash. They also hunted game and gathered wild plants. The Yaqui lived in small, scattered villages and had no central government.

Yaqui warriors defeated the Spanish invaders who entered their territory in 1533 and 1609. In 1610, the Yaqui made a treaty with the Spaniards and asked for Jesuit missionaries to settle in their villages.

The Yaqui wanted the Jesuits to teach them how to raise wheat, fruit, and livestock. The Jesuits arrived in 1617, and the Yaqui lived prosperously for the next 120 years. The Indians learned the Roman Catholic religion and blended it with their own culture. The Jesuits also helped the Yaqui organize the villages into eight towns, which became centers of religion and government.

In the 1730s, many Yaqui became dissatisfied with the Jesuits and the Spanish colonial government. Some of them sought independence. The tribe fought Spanish and Mexican troops in a series of bloody wars that lasted until the 1900s. During these wars, the Mexican government forced many Yaqui to leave their homeland and settle in other parts of Mexico. Some of the Yaqui fled Mexico to live in the United States. There are now about 15,000 Yaqui in Mexico. According to the 2010 U.S. census, there are about 22,000 Yaqui in the United States.

THE ZAPOTEC INDIANS devel-

oped an empire in what is now the state of Oaxaca in southern Mexico from about 1500 B.C. to A.D. 750. There, they built their capital city, Monte Alban, on a mountaintop. The city had a ceremonial district that included temples and a ball court. Numerous elaborate tombs and many urns with human features have been found at the site of Monte Alban. The Zapotec also produced the earliest written texts in Middle America. They carved on stone slabs records of conquests, sacrifices, and relations with other peoples. After the disintegration of their empire, the Zapotec abandoned Monte Alban. But a number of smaller Zapotec kingdoms developed. Mixtec Indians gained control of several of these kingdoms by conquering or marrying into Zapotec ruling families. Some of the kingdoms were conquered by the Aztec Indians.

Thousands of Zapotec still live in the state of Oaxaca and speak Zapotec dialects. Most are farmers. Some Zapotec are also skilled potters and weavers. Their products are sold worldwide.

ADOBE is the Spanish name for sun-dried

bricks, or for a house built with such bricks. A less common type of adobe is made with dampened earth pressed down in building forms similar to those used for poured concrete walks.

People have used adobe to build houses and other structures in desert regions for thousands of years. The ancient Egyptians and Babylonians used adobe.

To make adobe, workers mix sandy clay or loam with water and a small quantity of straw, grass, or similar material. The straw holds the mixture together, giving the bricks greater stability. The mixture is placed in wooden forms that shape it into bricks. Workers remove the forms when the bricks are dry. Then they bake the bricks in the sun from ten days to two weeks.

Adobe houses are common in Mexico and the southwestern part of the United States. Traditional adobe houses are covered with mud. Modern adobe houses are covered with a plaster-like material called *stucco*. Adobe houses are cooler than uninsulated homes made of wood or stone, but adobe is not suitable for use in cold or damp regions. The bricks will crumble if they are

Bullring, Tijuana, Mexico

exposed to rain or to periods of freezing temperatures followed by thaws.

BULLFIGHTING

BULLFIGHTING is a contest between a bull and an individual called a *matador*. Bullfighting is popular in many Spanish-speaking countries, in Portugal, and in southern France. In such countries as Spain and Mexico, matadors are national heroes.

A bullfight takes place in a special stadium called a *plaza de toros* (bullring). During the bullfight, the matador faces the bull alone, attempting to maneuver the charging animal by waving a cape or a piece of cloth. In most countries, the matador kills the bull at the end of the bullfight. In Portugal and in some bullrings in France, it is illegal to kill the bull. Bulls used in a bullfight are specially bred to attack. They are powerful, ferocious animals that may weigh 1,000 pounds (450 kilograms) or more. A bull can seriously gore or even kill a matador with its horns. In spite of its popularity, some people oppose bullfighting. They especially object to what they consider to be cruel treatment of the bulls and the pain and suffering inflicted on them.

Modern bullfighting dates from the 1700s when the first permanent bullring was built in Spain. The major breeds of fighting bulls were also developed in Spain during the 1700s. A number of matadors gained fame during the 1900s. The best known included Juan Belmonte, El Cordobes, Luis Dominguin, and Manolete, all of Spain, and Carlos Arruza of Mexico.

The bullring is shaped like a bowl. The bullfight takes place in the center, and the spectators are seated in a circle above. Most arenas are about 55 yards (50 meters) in diameter. The surface consists of firmly packed sand. The bull enters the arena from an entrance called the *toril*. A wooden fence about 5 feet (1.7 meters) high called the *barrera* separates the ring from the spectator area. Other facilities at the bullring include corrals for the bulls, an infirmary to treat injured matadors, and a chapel where the matador prays before the bullfight.

Spain alone has more than 400 bullrings. They seat from about 1,500 to more than 20,000 spectators. The Plaza de Toros Monumental in Mexico City is the world's largest bullring, seating about 55,000 people.

Types of bullfights. A bullfight is called a *corrida* in Spanish. Of the many types of bullfights, probably the two most common are the *corrida de toros* and the *novillada*.

The corrida de toros is the highest form of bullfight. Only matadors de toros participate. A matador de toros has received his title in a ceremony called the *alternativa*. Only matadors with experience, skill, and popularity are given the alternativa. A matador de toros is entitled to wear the *traje de luces* (suit of lights), the colorful traditional bullfighting uniform.

The novillada is a bullfight for less skilled matadors, called *novilleros*. In both the corrida de toros and the novillada, three matadors each fight two bulls, one at a time. The remainder of this article discusses a typical corrida de toros.

The order of the bullfight. A minute or two before the scheduled start of the bullfight, the *presidente* and his advisers enter their special box. The presidente is usually a local government official. He presides over the bullfight and gives per-

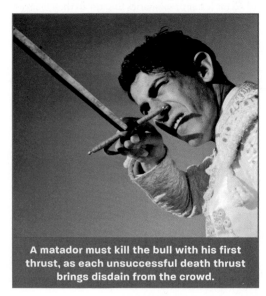

A matador must kill the bull with his first thrust, as each unsuccessful death thrust brings disdain from the crowd.

mission for the corrida to progress from one stage to the next.

The corrida begins when a trumpeter blows a fanfare. Men on horseback called *alguaciles* ride across the ring to the presidente's box and tip their plumed hats to get the key to the toril. Next is the *paseo*, the parade of matadors and their assistants into the ring.

After the paseo, the bullfight itself begins. The trumpet sounds and the toril is opened to allow the bull to enter the ring. Three of the matador's assistants, called *banderilleros*, take turns getting the bull to charge by waving a *capote*. The capote is a cape that is magenta on one side and yellow on the other. Bulls are color-blind. They react to the movement of the capote. The matador studies the bull, noting the quality of its eyesight and whether it charges straight or favors one horn. The matador then enters the ring and makes five or six passes with the capote, guiding the bull close to his body.

After the passes, the trumpet sounds and two *picadors* enter on horseback. Each picador carries a lance called a *vara*. The horses are blindfolded and protected by padding. The picador forces the vara into the bull's neck to weaken the muscles. This action is also called a *vara*. After each vara, a matador performs several passes with his capote. These passes are called the *quite*.

After two or three varas, the trumpet again sounds. The picador leaves the ring and the *banderilleros* enter. Two of them take turns placing three pairs of banderillas behind the bull's neck. A banderilla is a wooden stick about 28 inches (71 centimeters) long. It is decorated with colored paper and has a sharp barbed steel point.

The trumpet sounds for the last part of the fight, called the *faena*. The matador enters the ring carrying a sword and a *muleta*—a red cloth draped over a stick. The matador performs a number of passes with the muleta. The matador's performance is rated largely on his grace and the amount of danger to which he exposes himself. Finally, the matador kills the bull with the sword, sliding the weapon between the animal's shoulder blades. About 20 minutes elapse between the entry of the bull into the ring and its death.

If the matador has performed well, the crowd will applaud and cheer ole! The presidente may award the matador one of the bull's ears. If the performance is considered exceptional, the matador may receive two ears or even the ears and the tail.

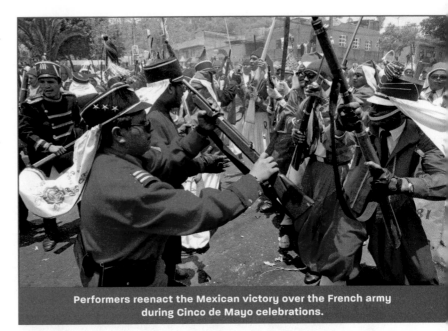

Performers reenact the Mexican victory over the French army during Cinco de Mayo celebrations.

CINCO DE MAYO is a holiday celebrated on May 5 by Mexicans and Mexican Americans. Its name is Spanish for *Fifth of May*.

Cinco de Mayo commemorates the victory of a Mexican army over a French army at the Battle of Puebla on May 5, 1862. The Mexican army, led by General Ignacio Zaragoza, won the battle even though the French force was better armed and three times as large. The battle occurred after Emperor Napoleon III of France sent troops to Mexico to conquer the country. Despite the Mexican victory at Puebla, the French later gained control of Mexico City and established a French-supported government there. In 1866 and 1867, however, France withdrew its troops from Mexico because of resistance by many Mexicans and pressure from the United States. The French-backed government soon fell.

Cinco de Mayo is celebrated differently in different areas. Some Mexican towns hold small celebrations, including parades or town meetings and speeches. In the United States, celebrations often include parades, folk dancing, speeches, carnival rides, and Mexican music.

DIA DE LOS MUERTOS is a Mexican holiday that honors the dead. The holiday is also celebrated in many Mexican American communities. *Dia de los muertos* is Spanish for *day of the dead*. During this celebration, families gather in

A Mexican girl and boy wear Day of the Dead masks.

churches, at cemeteries, and in homes to pray for and remember their deceased loved ones.

Dia de los muertos is usually celebrated on November 2, the Roman Catholic feast of All Souls' Day. In some communities, the dead are remembered over several days, including November 1, All Saints' Day. The celebration combines ancient native beliefs and Catholic traditions.

Many families prepare an elaborate altar, known as an *ofrenda* (offering), in their homes and in cemeteries for the holiday. The ofrendas are decorated with flowers, fruits, popular foods, sweets, and drinks. They are created to welcome back for a day the souls of departed family members and friends. Special candies and *pan de muerto* (bread of the dead), a sweet bread, are popular treats served in the shape of skulls, skeletons, and other symbols of death.

The day of the dead reinforces the ancient belief that death is a part of life. It is an important tradition through which families pass on their oral histories. Recalling stories of past family members helps keep these ancestors alive for future generations.

THE NORTH AMERICAN FREE TRADE AGREEMENT (NAFTA)

is a pact that unites Canada, Mexico, and the United States in one of the world's largest free-trade zones. It builds on a free-trade agreement between the United States and Canada that became effective in 1989. NAFTA took effect in January 1994.

Under NAFTA, tariffs on most goods produced and sold in North America were to be gradually eliminated over 10 years. Trade of a few additional products continued to be restricted for another 5 years. The first reductions took place in 1994. The final provisions were implemented on January 1, 2008.

NAFTA also establishes rights and obligations regarding trade in services, intellectual property, and international investment. These provisions could serve as models for future global and regional trade agreements.

NAFTA generated extensive opposition in the United States because of concerns that it would result in a loss of U.S. jobs. Opponents feared the job losses would result from increased Mexican imports and from a shift in U.S. production to Mexican plants. Environmental groups feared NAFTA would increase air and water pollution, particularly in the U.S.-Mexican border region.

In response to opposition to the pact in the United States, the three countries agreed in 1993 to supplement NAFTA with three side agreements. The three pacts established commissions to monitor developments related to environmental and labor issues and to help solve problems that may arise as regional trade and investment expands.

MLA Citation

"Mexico." *The Southwestern Advantage Topic Source.* Nashville: Southwestern. 2013.

ADDITIONAL RESOURCES

Books to Read

Level I

Carew-Miller, Anna. *Famous People of Mexico*. Mason Crest, 2009.

Gruber, Beth. *Mexico*. National Geographic Society, 2007.

Hoyt-Goldsmith, Diane. *Cinco de Mayo: Celebrating the Traditions of Mexico*. Holiday House, 2008.

Kalman, Bobbie. *Mexico: The Culture*. Rev. ed. Crabtree Publishing Co., 2009.

Level II

Alisky, Marvin. *The A to Z of Mexico*. Scarecrow, 2010.

Foster, Lynn V. *A Brief History of Mexico*. 4th ed. Facts on File, 2009.

Russell, Philip L. *The History of Mexico: From Pre-Conquest to Present*. Routledge, 2010.

Standish, Peter. *The States of Mexico: A Reference Guide to History and Culture*. Greenwood, 2009.

Web Sites

CIA—Mexico

https://www.cia.gov/library/publications/the-world-factbook/geos/mx.html

The United States Central Intelligence Agency Web site provides a profile on Mexico.

Country Profile: Mexico

http://news.bbc.co.uk/2/hi/americas/country_profiles/1205074.stm

Information from the BBC.

Mexico from Empire to Revolution

http://www.getty.edu/research/tools/guides_bibliographies/mexico/html/index.html

Historical information from the J. Paul Getty Trust.

Panoramas: The North American Landscape in Art

http://www.museevirtuel-virtualmuseum.ca/sgc-cms/expositions-exhibitions/panoramas/home-e.html

A site that celebrates the heritage of the continent. Sponsored by the governments of Canada, Mexico, and the United States.

Sistema Internet de la Presidencia de la República

http://www.presidencia.gob.mx/?NLang=en&x=12&y=14

Official Web site of the President of Mexico (in the Spanish language).

U.S.—Mexican War

http://www.pbs.org/kera/usmexicanwar/index_flash.html

An on-line companion resource for a PBS documentary.

Search Strings

Ancestry

Mexico ancestry people mestizos (116,000)

Mexico ancestry people mestizos Spanish Indian (79,800)

ancestry of the Mexican people mestizos Spanish Indian (88,100)

Mexico ancestry ethnic heritage mestizos Spanish Indian (32,400)

Language

languages spoken in Mexico (336,000)

languages spoken in Mexico Spanish English Indian dialects (21,400)

languages spoken in Mexico Spanish English Maya Mixtec Nahuatl Otomi Tarascan Zapotec (84)

City Life

Mexico city life architecture economy social environment slums pollution (56,300)

"city life" in Mexico (232,000)

"city life" in Mexico architecture housing pollution suburbs slums (860)

Corn and the Mexican Diet

role of corn in the Mexican diet (171,000)

corn "Mexican diet" history foods role (520)

BACKGROUND INFORMATION

The following articles were written during the year in which the events took place and reflect the style and thinking of that time.

Mexico (1926)

One crisis after another developed during 1926 to focus the attention of the world upon the Mexican republic.

Yaqui Indian uprising. Though to the casual observer the present is merely another of their numerous rebellions to secure rights to which they have been deprived by every Mexican government, there is now being conducted a real war which many people conversant with the history of the country declare to be the "last stand" of the Yaqui tribes. It is more than possible that the world is witnessing the passing of a nation, for the government appears committed to their subjugation or extermination.

Although at war with the whites since 1740, the Yaquis are an unconquered people. Even a so-called defeat which they suffered in 1832 cannot be construed as actual when it is remembered that they have since warred against Mexico and been treated with as a nation, that they hold the lands of their present residence under grant from Spain, and that they are governed by their own laws, never having yielded to Mexico.

Their villages are literally cities of refuge under their laws and the fugitive is in sanctuary when he passes the gates of Coorit, Bacum, Torin, or any of the pueblos in the fastnesses of the Vacatete Mountains.

The indomitable courage of the Yaquis is as strong a characteristic today as at any time in the past. Their qualities were last exhibited over twenty-five years ago, in the last notable campaign against them. General Torres, who commanded the expeditions against the Yaquis in 1899–1901, seemed to be successful in every encounter, with the losses light on the Mexican side and heavy with the Yaquis. However, the peace which concluded the hostilities was not lasting, and the Indians are better armed now than then.

In this present war, as in the previous ones, the Mexicans must follow to the inaccessible natural fortifications of the Vacatete Mountains. A family of fourteen held a pass in these mountains in 1894 against 400 Mexican soldiers for three days. On the fourth day the attacking party was able to get skirmishers upon a narrow ledge above, whereupon the defenders retreated. That evening the Mexicans were halted by shots from an adobe chapel near the edge of a narrow mesa at the mouth of a gorge. They were held at bay there four days longer, and it was only after they had battered the building down with howitzer fire that they were able to pass. It was then they discovered that they had been again held by the same family who had held the first pass. All were dead but a boy, who was wounded so seriously that he died within the hour.

On January 20, 1927, the Yaqui resistance broke, and unconditional surrender was announced.

[The Yaquis, or Hiaquis, are said by some ethnologists to have received their name from their principal river, the Rio Yaqui, while others state that they were so named because their talking is in a loud and rough tone, Yaqui meaning literally he who shouts, and that the river received its name from them. When first known to history they occupied a large territory on both sides of the present boundary between the United States and Mexico, some authorities stating that their possessions extended even as far east as Texas and as far south as Durango in Mexico. They then numbered about 400,000. They now number about 15,000, only about 5,000 of whom are capable of bearing arms.]

More American protests. Ever since the scepter of power was forced from the hands of President Porfirio Diaz (1911), affairs between Mexico and the United States have been for the greater part of the time unsatisfactory. For some years diplomatic relations were withdrawn by the American nation, which placed Mexico outside the sisterhood of states, so far as the United States was concerned. Normal conditions were restored only on the promise of Mexico not further to violate property rights of Americans; other nations, particularly Great Britain, had also been affected, and it was understood that the American government was negotiating in their behalf, as well. The other powers were respecting the Monroe Doctrine, and relying upon the good offices of the United States.

The old dispute as to mineral lands is again threatening Mexico with ostracism. Prior to 1917

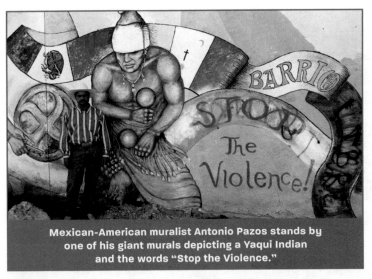

Mexican-American muralist Antonio Pazos stands by one of his giant murals depicting a Yaqui Indian and the words "Stop the Violence."

Mexican laws recognized that the owner of land also owned whatever was beneath the surface—oil and other minerals being uppermost in mind. In the new Constitution of 1917, President Carranza caused to be inserted a paragraph which has become famous as Article 27, providing that, regardless of the ownerships of any given tract of land, title extends no farther than the surface, and that whatever deposits are found below the surface belong to Mexico. No matter if property were held by undeniable legal right, the new Constitution by this retroactive clause made it almost worthless to the lawful owners.

The American Department of State contends that before recognition was accorded again to Mexico in 1924 an agreement was made by which the Mexican government would not violate property rights of Americans in Mexico. That government possesses the right to acquire the lands held by foreigners, it was conceded, but adequate compensation should be given, either by the central government or by the state in which the disputed lands are situated. Some valuable American and British lands have already been seized. Seldom has cash been paid; in most cases bonds (which may have doubtful value) have been offered, and in not a few cases no compensation of any sort has been given.

False economic standards, it is believed, are responsible for the failure of the Mexican government to reach agreements with the United States on numerous cases presented in behalf of its citizens whose property has been seized and who have sought indemnification or restoration of their

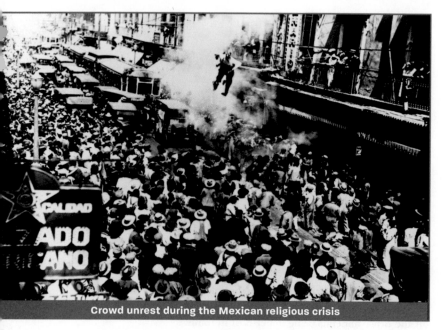

Crowd unrest during the Mexican religious crisis

no "public opinion" to hold in check or to guide those in authority serve to complicate the problem.

The religious crisis. An ancient conflict has been renewed in Mexico, a conflict between Church and State, where the people who are dominant have been Spanish and Roman Catholic since the Conquest by Cortez. The Indian population long ago embraced the faith of the white man, and today more than ninety percent of the people are adherents of, or in sympathy with, the Roman Church. There have been on several occasions attempts to curtail the power of the Church in Mexico, but not until 1926 was the power of the government put so strongly behind a law aimed at the religious status as to divide the world in its sympathies. It is certain that no such strife has heretofore developed on either of the American continents.

Provisions of Mexico's Constitution. A new Constitution was adopted in Mexico in 1917, supplanting one in force since 1857. The provisions aimed at the Church in the new document were similar to those of the Constitution of 1857. There had been no serious effort to enforce the articles controlling the conduct of religion during the life of the instrument of 1857, nor for more than eight years under the new Constitution. Early in 1926 President Calles declared that beginning on August 1 all constitutional decrees would be put into execution. These are here summarized:

1. No foreigner may exercise the religious profession in Mexico. [Meaning that all priests and ministers must be Mexicans, native-born or naturalized.]
2. Education must be given in official schools and be secular. No religious corporation or minister of any creed may establish or direct schools of primary instruction.
3. Religious orders, convents, and monasteries will be dissolved.
4. Any minister who incites the public to refuse to acknowledge public institutions or to obey the laws will be severely punished.
5. No publication, either religious or merely showing marked tendencies in favor of religion, may comment on national political affairs.
6. No organization may be formed whose title has any word or any indication that it is connected with religious ideas.
7. Political meetings may not be held in churches.

properties. Unable to obtain any satisfaction from the Mexican government, despite patient and persistent efforts on the part of the American Ambassador Sheffield in Mexico City, Secretary of State Kellogg in September 1926, called attention to the condition in a public statement, in which he asserted that "a great deal of property of Americans had been taken under or in violation of the agrarian laws for which no compensation has been made, and other properties practically ruined." The Kellogg statement adds,

"The government of Mexico is now on trial before the world. We have been patient, and realize, of course, that it takes time to bring about a stable government, but we cannot countenance violation of her obligations and failure to protect American citizens.

"We are looking to and expect the Mexican government to restore properties illegally taken, and to indemnify American citizens.

"This government will continue to support the government in Mexico only so long as it protects American lives and American rights and complies with its international engagements and obligations."

Kellogg used language more outspoken than is ordinarily employed in diplomatic negotiations, and his letter roused the ire of President Calles and his strongly radical government. At the end of the year the situation had not improved. The outcome cannot be foreseen, for personal ambitions in Mexico, the dense ignorance of the great masses of the people, and the added fact that there is practically

8. All religious acts must be held within the walls of a church. [The ostensible purpose of sections 4, 5, 6, 7, 8 is to force the Church to refrain from all political activity.]

9. No religious order of any creed may possess or administer property or capital.

10. The churches are the property of the nation. Other ecclesiastical properties, such as bishops palaces, houses, seminaries, asylums, colleges, convents, and all building constructed for religious purposes, pass into the possession of the nation, the use to which they are to be put to be determined by the government.

11. Heavy penalties may be imposed upon ministerial or other authorities who fail to enforce the above provisions.

The government of Mexico alleges that:

1. National education has been almost exclusively in the control of the Roman Catholic Church, and it has made no effort to raise the millions of peons out of ignorance.

2. Church authorities have ignored the sovereign power of the State; the Church has become a super-State.

3. The Church has controlled politics and politicians.

The Church solemnly declares that its defiance of the government has extended only to those matters in which the prerogatives of the Church have been attacked; it defends its centuries-old sacra-

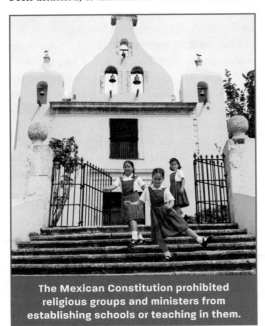

The Mexican Constitution prohibited religious groups and ministers from establishing schools or teaching in them.

ments and practices. It denies the right of the government to require all priests to register with the civil authority, which would place them in subjection to that authority rather than leave them responsible primarily to the Holy See.

On the day before the drastic decrees went into effect, possibly the strangest drama of modern times was enacted. From wretched hovels and the sumptuous residences of grandees, from sea to sea, from lonely ranches to the very plaza of the President's palace itself, on which also faces Mexico City's great cathedral, the faithful of the Roman Catholic Church swept in countless multitudes to their places of worship, beseeching the Divine authority to come to the relief of the faith of their fathers.

On August 1 the government took possession of the churches throughout the country, placing its appointees in control, with the declaration that while the buildings would remain accessible to worshippers the priests could not exercise their functions until there was submission to constitutional authority.

At the close of the year the situation was practically unchanged. The government adhered to its determined attitude; the Church, unmoved from its traditional position and inspired by the Papal blessing, was waiting for a subsidence of feeling against it.

Mexico (1929)

The Revolution, spelled with a capital "R" to distinguish it from innumerable lesser rebellions, is believed to be practically at an end. Begun twenty years ago with the Madero uprising of 1910, the Revolution has been in its larger aspects a reform movement to secure peace, education, and economic and social development for the Mexican people. On January 1, 1930, an Associated Press dispatch from Mexico City made this remarkable statement: "Reports from military commanders throughout Mexico to the Secretary of War today disclosed the entire country at peace for the first time in several years. The Secretary of War announced that not a single governor has reported a military problem of the slightest importance." Emilio Portes Gil, the Provisional President who governed in place of President-Elect General Obregon, assassinated in 1928, was a progressive and able executive, and it is expected that his policies will be continued by Pascual Ortiz Rubio, who was elected on November 17, 1929, to fill the remainder of Obregon's six-year term. Rubio was

President Pascual Ortiz Rubio

inaugurated on February 5, 1930, and will serve until November 30, 1934. The promising quiet of Mexico was marred at the inauguration of Rubio, when a youth fired at the official automobile carrying the new president home after the ceremonies. Rubio was hit, but not seriously wounded. His wife and niece, who were in the car, were grazed by bullets, and they also escaped with minor injuries.

One highly significant fact may be said of the 1929 presidential election. The two leading candidates, Rubio and Jose Vasconcelos, are civilians, men of education and high intelligence. A third candidate, General Pedro V. Triana, representing the Communists, polled a negligible number of votes. That the country has passed from government by the soldier to government by the civilian augurs well for its future. (In January 1930, Mexico broke off diplomatic relations with Russia in protest against propaganda spread by the Soviets in Mexico.)

Rubio is an engineer, born of a wealthy family of the state of Michoacán. He has been prominent in Mexican affairs since the Madero uprising, in which he took an active part. He also supported Obregon in his revolution against Carranza, has been governor of his native state, Minister of Communication under Obregon, Mexican ambassador to Brazil, and minister to Germany. As the presidential choice of the government National Revolutionary Party, of which Plutarco Elias Calles is

the head, his victory was practically assured, although, owing to his long absences from the country, he was little known to the people. His opponent, Vasconcelos, was Minister of Education under Obregon, in which position he made a reputation as a progressive educator.

Religious conflict ended. The dispute between the Mexican Church and the State, which had been carried on with great bitterness and some bloodshed for three years, ended on June 21 with the announcement that President Portes Gil had reached an agreement on the religious question with Monsignor Leopoldo Ruiz y Flores and Monsignor Pascual Diaz, special envoys of Pope Pius XI, under which Church and State will hereafter work together for the reconstruction of Mexico. The accord is achieved, not by repealing the religious laws, but by interpreting them more broadly. Settlement of the controversy was effected to a large extent through the efforts of Dwight W. Morrow, American ambassador.

In 1926, former president Plutarco Elias Calles announced that all decrees regarding religion would be enforced. Designed to separate Church and State, they actually had the effect of closing all Catholic churches and exiling many prelates and priests from the country. In protest, the Catholics closed their churches, although secret services were held in homes. Great disorder resulted from the intense feeling, and even while negotiations for peace were going on in June, government troops were fighting the *Cristeros*, some of whom were sincere religious rebels, others little better than bandits.

The peace agreement. The basis of the settlement, as announced by Portes Gil, follows:

1. The Mexican government will allow the Catholic hierarchy to designate those priests who are to register in compliance with Mexican laws.

2. Religious instruction, while not permitted in the schools (which is specified in the Constitution), will be permitted within the churches.

3. The right is reserved to Mexican Catholic prelates to apply for modification of the Constitution at any time in the future, as is granted all Mexican citizens.

On June 27 masses were celebrated for the first time since July 31, 1926. Following the settlement, the Pope appointed Monsignor Pascual Diaz as head of the Church in Mexico.

Education. The vast task of bringing literacy to the millions of Indians and peons who compose two-thirds of Mexico's population is still in its early stages, handicapped by lack of teachers and funds, but making great strides. In 1929 about 2,700 new government schools were opened. Total attendance in government school increased during the year from 499,353 to nearly 850,000. Rural schools increased from 3,392 in 1928 to 6,073 by July, 1929.

Faced with insufficient funds to establish schools in all the rural districts of the country, the government started in 1929 a rural circuit system with about 600 central schools located at strategic points. A few of the best-fitted men of the surrounding districts are sent to these schools, and, after an adequate elementary training, return to their villages to teach the children and adults. A supervisor paid by the government visits the local schools on his circuit periodically.

New criminal code. The new penal code issued by Portes Gil under specific powers granted by Congress is considered one of the greatest constructive events in the history of the Americas. Its outstanding feature is the abolition of the death penalty and of the jury system. Reform, not punishment, is the keynote of this code, which is in accordance with the most advanced principles of criminology and sociology. The judge will fix the punishment with the aid of technical committees, who are to investigate the criminal from four viewpoints: *social*, throwing light on his origins, family, means of livelihood and working conditions, religion, adaptability, racial, moral and cultural conflicts, and so on; *medical*, to obtain data on the criminal's physical condition; *psychological*, to show the mental capacity of the criminal as a basis for judging the seriousness of his offense; and *educational*, to weigh the influence of the public school on the criminal, to tabulate the extent to which the State failed to educate him so as to strengthen his moral character.

A Supreme Council of Social Protection and Prevention, made up of five specialists in sociology and criminology, is created to direct the prevention of crime, and to execute the sentences imposed by the judges and courts. All penal and preventive or corrective institutions are under their supervision. Sentences are indeterminate and conditional. The penal code became effective on December 15, 1929.

Prohibition. A national temperance committee, under the general direction of the Public

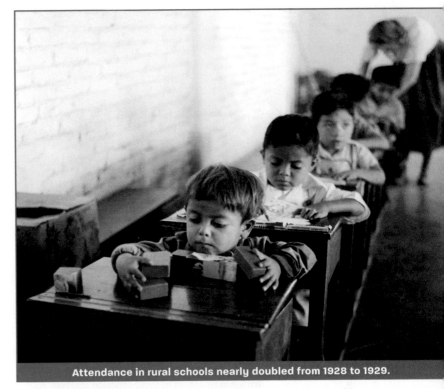

Attendance in rural schools nearly doubled from 1928 to 1929.

Health Department, was announced on May 14. It is entering on a vigorous campaign of education on the evils of alcohol, and is promoting sports and outdoor recreation under government support. "Dry measures," it was announced, will be promulgated gradually.

Mexico (1942)

Personal considerations, minor interests, and personal differences were subordinated to a single issue in 1942: the early victory of the democracies. On January 1, President Manuel Avila Camacho in a radio address appealed for unity and the increase of both agricultural and industrial production as the most effective means of aiding the war effort.

War effort. The Mexican delegation to the Rio de Janeiro Conference, headed by Secretary of State Ezequiel Padilla, gave its undivided support to the appeal for united action against the Axis Powers. "We are here to discuss the future of the Americas.... The attack launched by Japan was not directed against one nation in America... it constitutes the aggression of a totalitarian power against all the nations of the Americas." These words of Padilla electrified the whole continent and helped to arouse public indignation against the Axis Powers.

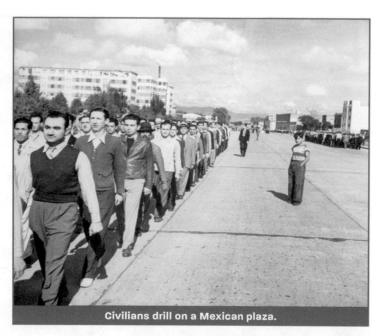

Civilians drill on a Mexican plaza.

On January 24, the Mexican Office of Defense announced that it was in contact with the commands of the Third and Fourth Army Corps Areas with headquarters in San Francisco and San Antonio. Before the end of the month, 800 Japanese families had been moved from the west coast to Mexico City.

Excitement ran high on April 24 when an Axis submarine sank a Mexican tanker chartered to an American firm. But when, on May 13, *Potrero del Llano*, a 6,100-ton tanker flying the Mexican flag, was sunk off the coast of Miami, the indignation of Mexico knew no bounds. Sharp demands for an explanation were answered by the sinking of another ship on May 20. An extraordinary session of Congress met on May 29 and promptly adopted a formal declaration of war.

Quickly the entire nation was put on a war footing. The sinking of another ship on June 28 in the Gulf of Mexico resulted in the creation of the Gulf Military Zone with headquarters at Veracruz under ex-President Abelardo Rodriguez. Steps were taken to modernize the army. On July 16, a large consignment of antitank and antiaircraft guns and motorized equipment crossed the border, and two days later the President ordered the organization of a mechanized division. Four new combat planes, the first of a large number promised by the United States, arrived in Mexico City on July 21. An antitank fighting unit was authorized, and August saw the graduation of the first class of military airplane mechanics. On August 13, the General Council of Civil Defense was established, six days later a decree on compulsory military training was promulgated, and on September 24 the Supreme Council of Defense was organized. Three days later the coordinating Council of Industrial Production was set up under Abelardo Rodriguez. The class of 1942 was ordered to register for compulsory military service early in November, and, by the middle of December, 205,423 young men had been listed, 5 percent of whom were to enter service on January 1, 1943.

Since early in August, civilians had trained feverishly. Mexico City experienced its first blackout on September 7, when the metropolis was left in darkness for nineteen minutes. A second trial was made on September 27 without warning. At the beginning of the month, in his message to Congress, the president stated that "a country that does not produce to the limit of its ability is a defeated nation." Mexico had gone seriously into the war.

Foreign relations. The severance of relations with the Axis Powers and the subsequent declaration of war brought Mexico into closer relations with the Allied nations, particularly with the United States. The stand of the Mexican delegation at Rio was publicly acknowledged by George S. Messersmith, the newly appointed American ambassador, when he presented his credentials on February 25. Cooperation between the two countries was frank and cordial throughout the year. On March 27, a lend-lease agreement to furnish Mexico with war materials to modernize the army was concluded; on April 2, the Claims Commission Agreement of November 19, 1914, was finally ratified, and the settlement of claims resulting from the Revolution fixed at $40,000,000. A check for $3,000,000, to be added to an equal amount paid during the last three years, was immediately given to Sumner Welles. This left a balance of $34,000,000 to be paid in annual installments of $2,500,000 each.

In the midst of this wave of good will, the long-standing oil controversy was finally settled. Manuel J. Zevada and Morris L. Cooke, expert appraisers, rendered on April 17 their decision as to the value of expropriated oil properties, fixing the indemnity at $23,995,991, and recommending that Mexico pay one third on July 1 and the remainder in five equal annual installments. Agreeable to the recommendations of the commissioners, Mexico paid

$7,998,663.67 on July 1. This settlement does not affect the private agreement made with Sinclair, nor does it include the English claims, generously postponed until after the war.

Other United States agreements followed. On August 12 two conventions were signed, by which Mexico was to be furnished capital to complete the Pan-American Highway to Guatemala, and to build a steel foundry in Coahuila.

Mexico agreed to give the United States and the Allied nations a priority on all products essential to the war effort. Of considerable importance was the agreement of August 4, setting forth the conditions under which Mexican laborers could be recruited in Mexico to meet the shortage of labor, particularly farm hands, in the United States. Mexican laborers could be engaged in Mexico at the request of the United States, but they had to be guaranteed a minimum wage, be exempted from military service, be accorded the same treatment as other laborers, and furnished return passage when the seasonal employment was over. As one more proof of its frank cooperation, Mexico consented that its national residents in the United States, with the exemption of students, be drafted.

Relations with Great Britain, broken since March 18, 1938, as a consequence of the oil expropriation, were reestablished in February, when Charles L. Bateman presented his credentials.

The relations with the remainder of Spanish America also became closer. Treaties of commerce and trade were negotiated with Chile, the Dominican Republic, and Cuba; and the ministers to Colombia and Uruguay were raised to the rank of ambassador.

Mexican railways. With government aid, the railways rapidly moved toward normalcy. Plans for the reconstruction of the Tehuantepec railroad, which might prove useful in keeping open interoceanic communications, were completed. But early in March a strike was threatened, and all traffic was paralyzed for one hour. More serious consequences were averted by the intervention of the president, who granted all workers a 10 percent increase and urged them to cooperate in improving the efficiency the Mexico's transportation facilities. Conditions failed to improve. The greater burden being placed on railroads by the war effort made it evident that only with foreign capital could they be made equal to the task. The correspondence of Secretary Padilla and Ambassador Messersmith,

made public on November 19, revealed the conditions under which the United States would help rehabilitate the Mexican railways, to enable to handle the increasing flow of strategic war materials.

Labor and agrarian activity. In his first address of the year, the President called upon labor to do its part in the war effort. He warned that although the fundamental interests of the labor class would be safeguarded, workers would be expected to shoulder the responsibilities of increased production demanded by the war. The response was most encouraging. The year saw few if any strikes, and most of them ware quickly solved. President Avila Camacho on Labor Day reminded workers of the necessity of cooperation between labor and capital for the success of the war effort. He warned labor against false leaders, and assured the workers of his determination to protect their interests and those of the industrialists with absolute impartiality.

The agrarian policy to be followed during the year was carefully outlined early in January in a set of rules and regulations issued by the Agrarian Department. The evils and abuses attendant upon the heretofore hasty distribution of lands to individuals, many of them unable or unqualified to cultivate them advantageously, had defeated the purpose of the program. The whole country was now divided into zones and the regional needs and

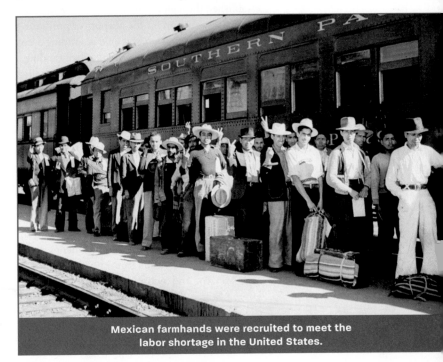

Mexican farmhands were recruited to meet the labor shortage in the United States.

problems of each one considered in determining the policy to be followed respectively. This saner approach to a basic problem resulted in a much smaller number of subdivisions being made in 1942 and a corresponding decline in the number of titles issued. In 1937, the peak year for land distribution, there were 5,317,000 hectares distributed. During the present year less than 1,000,000 hectares of land were parceled out to peasants.

Miscellaneous. The one disturbing element in a year of unrelieved war harmony was the activity of the *Sinarquistas*, accused of being reactionaries, Phalangists, and pro-Axis sympathizers. The relation of this party to the Church has given rise to much speculation. On March 1, the Archbishop of Guadalajara emphatically denied all connections. The American press insisted on connecting the party with the Church. When Mexican groups protested against the organization, President Camacho, inclined to be tolerant, replied that unless their connection with enemy aliens could be proved they had a right to their own opinions. Feeling ran high when, on December 13, the Sinarquistas held their first national meeting in Mexico City. Five days later their dissolution was demanded. The President replied calmly that "Mexico is a democracy and consequently there is room for all parties within its limits."

The inauguration of Benjamin Franklin Library, established through a grant made to the American Library Association for the purpose of promoting intellectual cooperation, was an outstanding event in the movement toward cultural understanding.

The year saw legislation against hoarding, restrictions on the exportation of needed foodstuffs, the establishment of price ceilings, the freezing of alien funds, the appointment of a Custodian Alien Property Commission, and the organization of civilian defense.

Mexico (1945)

On January 29, 1945, the Joint Mexican-American Economic Commission announced a plan whereby Mexico would spend $383,000,000 by 1948 for internal industrial improvements, using private and public funds from the United States and Mexico, and equipment chiefly from the United States. The Commission approved fifty-eight development projects for the year 1945.

An interesting development in relations with the United States took place during the year. In Janu-

Miguel Aleman won the presidency in 1946.

ary and February the United States Congress engaged in considerable debate over the ratification of a treaty with Mexico. This provided for a diversion of the waters of the Colorado River and the Rio Grande, which would enable the two governments to work out a plan for the development of the Tiajuana River in California. The chief opposition came from Representatives from California who claimed that the treaty gave Mexico water which California needed for future development. Finally on April 18 the Senate ratified the treaty by a vote of 76 to 10. President Truman immediately approved it.

The Mexican Government was host from February 21 to March 8 to delegates to the Conference of American Republics on the Problems of War and Peace.

Economic affairs in Mexico were improved somewhat on June 13 when the United States and Mexico agreed to a two-year extension, beyond June 30, of the stabilization fund for the United States purchases of Mexican pesos, with the object of stabilizing the United States dollar-peso rate. In September the United States Office of Price Administration advanced the ceiling on foreign silver from 45 to 71 cents per ounce, with the result that Mexican, as well as Peruvian silver mining, suddenly increased, and the intrinsic value of the Mexican silver peso advanced from 16.8 to 26.5 cents.

During the latter half of the year, active preparations were made for the election of a new President in 1946. The government supported Miguel Aleman, political boss and former governor of the state of Veracruz. He was a successful businessman who had served as former campaign manager for Avila Camacho in the 1940 election. He had also served as Chief of Cabinet and Secretary of the Government under Avila Camacho, and he had the political support of the PRM (National Revolutionary Party). The rival candidate was Ezequiel Padilla, who resigned as Minister of Foreign Affairs on July 12 in order to run for office. He was a friend of and a close collaborator with the United States and in consequence many Mexicans believed that he had sold out to that country. On November 24 the Democratic Party announced its support of Padilla. A third candidate was General Miguel Guzman, a friend and business partner of former president Lazaro Cardenas. He had resigned from his position as Minister of War and National Defense in President Camacho's cabinet, in order to run for the presidency.

Mexico (1977)

President Jose Lopez Portillo struggled in 1977 to contain double-digit inflation, a severe economic recession, and political unrest among landless peasants, university students, and jobless workers. The turmoil prompted doubts about the future of Mexico's nominally democratic political system, rigidly dominated for 40 years by the Institutional Revolutionary Party (PRI).

Call for change. The most commonly expressed fear was that leftist agitation would cause right wing elements to seize the government and begin political repression. Lopez Portillo acknowledged the problem on numerous occasions. He declared in a speech on September 1 that it was time to change the country's political system.

"We aspire to a system," he said, "in which all parts of the ideological spectrum can be represented." But, he warned, "We must also adopt precautions so that we do not fall into excessive fragmentation that would prejudice rational democracy."

Observers believed Lopez Portillo faced a delicate task in convincing the PRI's conservative elements that change was needed. He inherited most of his immediate problems from the radical policies of former president Luis Echeverria Alvarez. In his attempts to hasten the country's economic development and aid the impoverished, Echeverria levied heavy taxes and put the country more than $20 billion in debt to foreign creditors. He had dealt a blow to the business community by letting the peso float against the U.S. dollar just before he

left office on December 1, 1976, and the peso promptly lost more than 60 percent of its value. The result was recession, thousands of layoffs, and severe inflation. Peasants and landlords in the states of Sonora and Sinaloa rebelled after Echeverria's expropriation of 240,000 acres (97,000 hectares) of farmland to redistribute to the landless. Lopez Portillo, on taking office, had calmed the situation by turning the matter over to the courts, and the government agreed on August 30 to pay $29.8 million to the landowners.

Jose Lopez Portillo was Mexico's presidnt from 1976–1982.

Urban guerrillas of the September 23 Communist League staged attacks in Mexico City on January 16 and January 20, killing eight persons, including five policemen and a U.S. construction executive, who tried to prevent the guerrillas from passing out political leaflets on his building site. The affluent rushed to hire personal bodyguards. Arms obtained as payment for narcotics from U.S. drug smugglers were said to be pouring into the country at such a rate that Mexico City's police estimated there was 1 gun for every 2 inhabitants.

Government troops moved into the southern state of Oaxaca, long a leftist stronghold, on March 3 to halt bloody clashes between police and a coalition of landless peasants and students. At the root

Ruins of the Hotel Regis after the 1985 earthquake

of the trouble was the economic crisis that left some 40 percent of Mexico's workforce out of jobs or in marginal occupations and eroded purchasing power by 30 percent. To cope, Lopez Portillo instituted an Alliance for Production under which labor unions agreed not to press for more than 10 percent wage increases and businessmen promised to curb price increases. In July, after the annual rate of inflation reached 30 percent, Mexico's major business organizations agreed to freeze basic consumer prices until the end of the year.

U.S. policies. On August 4, U.S. president Jimmy Carter announced plans to stiffen border patrols and thereby halt the flow into the United States of thousands of illegal Mexican aliens seeking jobs. He also indicated that the government would seek legal redress against U.S. employers who knowingly hired illegal aliens. These statements caused concern to Mexican officials who felt that emigration

was a "safety valve" for their grave unemployment problem.

In December, under the terms of a prisoner exchange bill signed by President Carter on October 28, Mexico began repatriating U.S. citizens who had been held in its prisons for various criminal offenses, including the use of hard drugs. By year's end, 233 Americans had been repatriated and 352 were still awaiting return.

Mexico (1985)

A devastating earthquake, measuring 8.1 on the Richter scale, struck Mexico at 7:18 A.M. on September 19, 1985, toppling buildings and wreaking havoc in Mexico City. A second quake, or aftershock, followed on September 20 and measured 7.3 on the Richter scale. The quakes left some 7,000 Mexicans dead, most of them buried under tons of rubble. More than 100 tourists from foreign countries were among the fatalities. Nightly television reports around the world showed the search in

the debris for survivors, particularly those victims trapped in a collapsed hospital.

Many Mexicans were angry at what they considered their government's slow response to the disaster. The first government employees to hit the streets were not rescue squads but soldiers with orders to prevent looting. For 36 hours after the first quake, the government, headed by President Miguel de la Madrid Hurtado, maintained that Mexico could handle rescue efforts on its own, despite offers of assistance from other nations.

In the aftermath of the earthquakes, rescue efforts also appeared to uncover wrongdoing in the office of Mexico's attorney general. The bodies of four Colombians and several Mexicans, bearing signs of torture, turned up in the ruins of a building that housed the attorney general's offices. Many Mexicans were outraged when their Congress turned down a request for an investigation.

Economic Plight. The earthquake devastation seemed likely to worsen Mexico's economic plight. Increasing numbers of Mexico's wealthy citizens have reportedly joined the tide of immigration to the United States, taking their wealth with them. Mexico's Central Bank estimated that at least $33 billion flowed out of the country between 1977 and 1984, though other economists put the figure closer to $60 billion. The flight of capital from Mexico was the largest among the debtor nations of the Third World. The World Bank, an agency of the United Nations, reported that much of the money Mexico borrowed from creditors in a number of other nations found its way back into investments in those same foreign nations. The World Bank report called this situation "a recipe for disaster."

Pessimism about Mexico's future fed the flow of intellectuals, professionals, and business managers out of Mexico. In addition, devaluation of the peso has so eroded the value of their insurance policies that Mexicans have even begun buying their insurance in the United States. For example, Mexicans accounted for 25 percent of the insurance policies sold in San Antonio, Texas, where Mexican nationals in 1985 held about 20 percent of the $30 million on deposit at a First City Bank branch.

Museum theft. On December 25, more than 140 rare and exquisite pieces of Maya and Aztec treasures and other ancient objects made of gold were discovered missing from the National Museum of Anthropology in Mexico City. Officials speculated that the theft was the work of an international ring of art thieves.

Oil prices. On July 10, Mexico decided to go it alone in cutting the price of its oil to levels below those set by the squabbling members of the Organization of Petroleum Exporting Countries (OPEC). Although Mexico does not belong to OPEC, it had followed OPEC price levels over the previous two years. The price cuts were seen as an effort to recover sales lost because of the higher prices.

Mexico's action followed fierce debates within Petroleos Mexicanos (PEMEX), the state-owned oil company. The problems at PEMEX seemed to mirror those of the nation as a whole. During 1985, the former director of PEMEX, 64-year-old Jorge Diaz Serrano, languished in jail, where he has been since July 1983, awaiting the outcome of his trial on corruption charges. Ironically, Diaz Serrano aroused considerable public sympathy, as more and more Mexicans came to view him as a scapegoat for hundreds, perhaps thousands, of corrupt PEMEX employees.

Mexico (1992)

The North American Free Trade Agreement between the United States, Mexico, and Canada was signed by Mexico on August 12, 1992. Trade representatives from the United States and Canada signed the agreement on the same day. To many Mexicans, the successful negotiation of the free trade pact represented a giant stride forward, evidence that Mexico had joined the world's developed nations. The free trade agreement was designed to reduce tariffs on goods traded among the three countries, but the legislatures of all three countries must ratify it before the agreement takes effect. There was little doubt that Mexico's Senate, where members of the president's party hold 61 of 64 seats, would ratify the pact.

U.S. lobbying. The Mexican government immediately began a lobbying campaign in the United States to persuade Americans that the agreement will help their economy. The Mexican Embassy in Washington, D.C., provided free studies showing anticipated U.S. business and job gains that would result from the agreement in each state and congressional district.

Seeking to ease fears of job losses in the United States, Mexican president Carlos Salinas de Gortari struck a deal with U.S. president George Bush in San Diego on July 14, whereby Mexico would open up its banking, insurance, and securities industries—sectors long closed to foreigners—to American and Canadian companies by the year 2000. Mexican trade representatives the next day announced that Mexico would pay bonuses to U.S. and Canadian oil drillers for work on Mexican oil contracts. This step seemed to widen the opening for foreign participation in the oil industry, which had been nationalized in 1936.

Gas explosion. On April 22, 1992, a series of explosions rocked a working-class neighborhood of Guadalajara, Mexico's second most populous city. At least 191 people were killed and hundreds more injured. Officials said a pipeline leaked gasoline into the sewers from a local refinery. In the wake of the disaster, nine city and national oil and gas company officials were indicted for negligence, and the governor of the state of Jalisco, in which Guadalajara is located, was forced to resign.

U.S. kidnapping. Mexicans were angry at a June 15 U.S. Supreme Court decision that gave U.S. authorities approval to kidnap persons wanted for trial in U.S. federal courts from foreign countries without following procedures set out in extradition treaties. The case at issue involved a Mexican doctor, Humberto Alvarez Machain, whom U.S. agents abducted from Mexico in 1990 to stand trial on murder charges in the death of a U.S. narcotics agent in 1985.

On July 24, in response to popular anger over what Mexicans viewed as a clear violation of their sovereignty, Attorney General Ignacio Morales

Mexican doctor Humbert Alvarez was kidnapped by a bounty hunter working for the U.S. government.

Lechuga announced that his country would no longer accept U.S. assistance in the fight against narcotics trafficking. On December 14, a U.S. judge dismissed the charges against the doctor for insufficient evidence.

Opposition wins. Other political parties began to break the monopoly in 1992 that Mexico's ruling Institutional Revolutionary Party (PRI) has traditionally enjoyed. On July 12, the opposition National Action Party's candidate, Francisco Barrio Terrazas, won the governorship of the northern border state of Chihuahua. It marked only the second time that an opposition candidate had won a governor's seat since the dominant PRI was organized in 1929.

In January, the national government, apparently motivated by a desire to clean up its own house, pressured Salvador Neme Castillo, the governor of the state of Tabasco, to resign in reaction to persistent public demonstrations alleging fraud at the ballot box. On October 6, the governor of the state of Michoacán, Eduardo Villa Senor, voluntarily stepped aside after popular demonstrations in which he was accused of winning the July election by fraud.

Vatican ties. On September 21, Mexico and the Vatican reestablished full diplomatic relations after a break of more than 130 years. The Mexican government in July had formally restored the Roman Catholic Church's right to own property and conduct religious education, though the church unofficially enjoyed these benefits for decades.

Mexico (2000)

Vicente Fox Quesada of the center-right National Action Party (PAN) was sworn to a six-year term as president of Mexico on December 1, 2000. The inauguration of Fox, who had been elected in July, marked the end of 71 years of political dominance by Mexico's Institutional Revolutionary Party (PRI) and the first transfer of power from one democratically elected party to another in Mexican history.

As president, Fox moved swiftly to ease tensions among Indians living in the southwestern state of Chiapas. On December 3, after Fox withdrew some military forces from the area, Zapatista rebels offered to begin direct talks with Fox's administration on ending their seven-year revolt. The talks were to start in February 2001.

Opposition-controlled Congress. After the congressional election in July 2000, President Fox faced a Congress that was controlled by the opposition. In the Senate, PRI held 60 seats, PAN held 46, and the leftist Democratic Revolutionary Party (PRD) held 15. Minor parties won a handful of seats in both the Senate and the Cham-

Mexican president Vicente Fox waves to supporters after his inauguration, which ended 71 years of one-party rule by the PRI.

ber of Deputies, in which PRI controlled 209 seats, PAN controlled 208, and PRD controlled 52.

U.S. visit. Fox visited Washington, D.C., in August to advocate a plan whereby the United States would grant Mexican workers an additional 250,000 visas per year to work legally in the United States. Fox claimed the plan would help reduce the illegal immigration of Mexicans to the United States. Fox added that he would like to see the U.S.-Mexican border become open to all workers within 10 years. During his U.S. visit, Fox also said his administration would encourage greater foreign investment in the Mexican economy, particularly in the energy, petrochemicals, and telecommunications sectors.

Healthy finances. In May, the Mexican government repaid $2.5 billion in debt owed to Citibank of New York City. The repayment came before it was due, saving Mexico hundreds of millions of dollars in interest payments.

Surging oil prices in 2000 permitted Mexico to collect $3 billion more in revenues from oil exports than had been anticipated by government officials. President Fox hoped to increase Mexico's crude oil production by 200,000 barrels per day between December 2000 and January 2001, using offshore production in the Gulf of Mexico.

Economists measured the growth of Mexico's gross domestic product (the total value of goods and services produced in a country in a given year) at 7 percent in the third quarter of 2000—down from 7.6 percent in the second quarter. Economic analysts, who had feared that rapid growth put the Mexican economy at risk of overheating in 2000, welcomed the slight decline. The Mexican automobile industry increased production by 24.9 percent between January and August, to produce a total of 1.2 million vehicles.

Reforms in law enforcement. On July 4, Fox announced plans to rebuild Mexico's federal law enforcement system along the lines of the U.S. model. He pledged to create a "Ministry of Security and Justice" that would be similar to the U.S. Federal Bureau of Investigation. The new ministry was to be responsible for all of Mexico's federal police officers, removing police functions from the heavily politicized Interior Ministry. The ministry also would remove the army from new involvement in the war on drugs.

Embezzlement scandal. In the face of charges that he had embezzled $45 million in gov-

ernment funds, Mexico City Mayor Oscar Espinosa Villareal resigned in August and left the country. A Mexican judge later issued a warrant for his capture and arrest. In December, Mexican authorities revealed that Espinosa was seeking asylum (protection) in Nicaragua. They asked Nicaraguan officials to return Espinosa to Mexico.

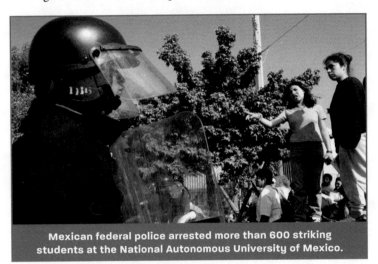

Mexican federal police arrested more than 600 striking students at the National Autonomous University of Mexico.

Student strike. On February 6, more than 2,000 federal police officers retook the Mexico City campus of the National Autonomous University of Mexico from hundreds of students who had occupied university buildings since April 1999. A planned increase in tuition had sparked the student occupation.

Middle East

The Middle East, also called the Near East, is a region made up of the lands of southwestern Asia and northeastern Africa.

HOT topics

Islam

Oil

The Palestine Conflict

America and the Middle East Since September 11, 2001

HOT topics

Islam. More than 90 percent of Middle Easterners, including most Arabs, Iranians, and Turks, are Muslims. Their religion, Islam, is based on the revelations received by the Prophet Muhammad in the A.D. 600s. Muslims believe these revelations came directly from God (Allah in Arabic). Most Muslims in the Middle East belong to the Sunni branch of Islam. A minority belong to the Shi`ah branch and are called Shiites. These two branches originated in a dispute over who should lead the Muslims after the death of Muhammad in 632. Shiites make up the majority of Muslims in Bahrain, Iran, Iraq, and Lebanon. Sunnis are the majority elsewhere.

Mt. Ararat, Turkey

HOT topics

Oil. In the early 1900s, huge petroleum deposits were discovered in the Persian Gulf region. Since the 1940s, oil revenues have transformed the once-poor societies of the region. The Middle East has almost two-thirds of the world's oil reserves. Saudi Arabia alone has over one-fourth of the world's reserves. Other major oil producers are Iran, Iraq, Kuwait, Oman, Qatar, and the United Arab Emirates.

TRUE or FALSE?

Agriculture was first developed in the Middle East.

The Palestine Conflict. In Palestine, Jewish nationalism—called Zionism—collided with Palestinian Arab nationalism throughout the 1900s. Both Zionists and Palestinian Arab nationalists claimed the same territory as their homeland. Zionists wanted a state for the Jews, where they would be safe from persecution. Palestinian Arabs feared Zionist ambitions and wanted Palestine to be an Arab state, independent from the United Kingdom, which had occupied it. In 1947, the United Nations (UN) voted to divide Palestine into a Jewish state and an Arab state. Jewish leaders accepted the plan. Palestinian Arab leaders opposed it. By the early 2000s, numerous issues remained unresolved, and armed conflict in the region persists.

America and the Middle East Since September 11, 2001. The September 11, 2001, terrorist attacks led the United States to become further involved in Middle East affairs. The United States declared a "war on terrorism." As part of this war, U.S. forces and local rebels overthrew Afghanistan's government, which was harboring Osama bin Laden and other al-Qaeda leaders responsible for the 2001 attack. U.S. President George W. Bush also launched a war against Iraq in March 2003. He linked this war to the war on terrorism and said the intent was to disarm Iraq of weapons of mass destruction—that is, chemical, biological, or nuclear weapons. By mid-April, U.S.-led forces had toppled Saddam Hussein's government. United States and allied forces began working to rebuild Iraq—a task made difficult by numerous guerrilla attacks against them and against civilian targets. No weapons of mass destruction were found in Iraq.

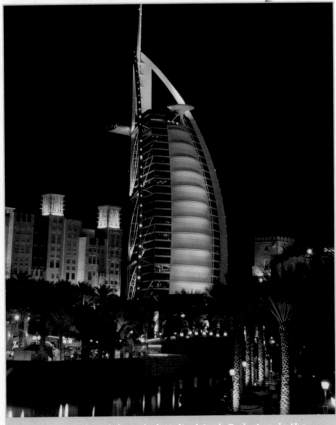

The Burj al Arab in Dubai, United Arab Emirates, is the world's tallest hotel.

THE BASICS

The Middle East, also called the Near East, is a region made up of the lands of southwestern Asia and northeastern Africa. All definitions of the region include the countries of Bahrain, Egypt, Iran, Iraq, Israel, Jordan, Kuwait, Lebanon, Oman, Qatar, Saudi Arabia, Syria, Turkey, the United Arab Emirates, and Yemen. The definitions also include the West Bank and the Gaza Strip, which, along with Israel, make up the historic region of Palestine. In this article, the term Middle East refers to these 15 countries and 2 territories. They cover about 2,813,000 square miles (7,286,000 square kilometers) and together have about 383 million people.

Some definitions of the Middle East include more countries. Afghanistan, Algeria, Cyprus, Libya, Morocco, Pakistan, Sudan, and Tunisia are the countries most often added.

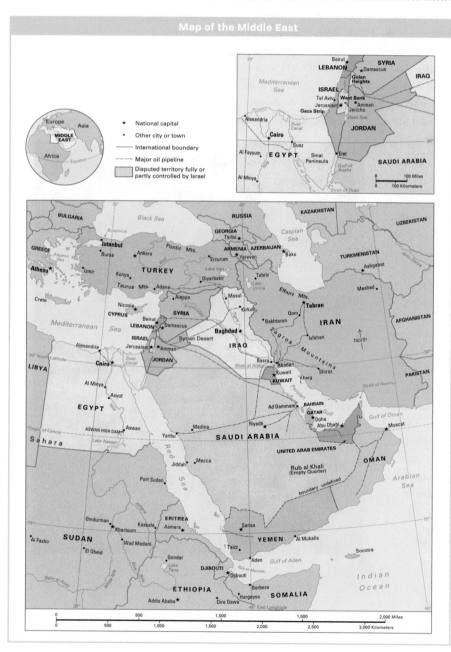

Map of the Middle East

People

Identity and language. Modern Middle Eastern cultures are the product of the region's many past civilizations, as well as outside influences that came through trade, migration, and conquest. Until the late 1800s, people identified themselves in terms of religion, family relationships, place of origin, and occupation. Since then, national and ethnic identities based mainly on language and religion have become more important.

More than three-fourths of the people of the Middle East identify themselves as Arabs. They share a common language, Arabic. Written Arabic and most of the Arabic heard on radio and television are the same throughout the region. But the everyday spoken language differs from country to country. Two other major Middle Eastern languages are Persian, spoken in Iran, and Turkish, spoken in Turkey. These languages are important bases of Iranian and Turkish national identity. Jews make up the majority in Israel, and Hebrew is the national language there. The Kurds, who have a distinct language and identity, live in parts of Iran, Iraq, Syria, and Turkey.

Way of life. For thousands of years, most Middle Easterners were peasant farmers living in villages. Small numbers of *nomads*—that is, herders who moved with the seasons to find pastures for their flocks—raised livestock in areas unsuitable for farming. Cities and towns were centers of trade and manufacturing, government and administration, and learning. Some cities were important religious centers. Nomads, peasants, and city dwellers depended on one another economically, and they exchanged goods and services in local markets.

After 1800, life began to change. The population grew rapidly. Cities became much larger as a result of stronger government, increased trade with industrial Europe, and the development of oil production. Today, about three-fifths of all Middle Easterners live in cities.

The average person in Israel and in several oil-producing Middle Eastern countries has a high income, comparable to that of a European. But most people elsewhere in the region have far lower incomes.

Many rural villages have electric power, and television antennas and satellite dishes stand on many village rooftops. But most rural residents are poorer than city dwellers, and fewer of them can read. City dwellers more often have clean drinking water and sanitation. They have more access to health services, and their children are more likely to attend school.

Since the early 1900s, education has become more widely available in the Middle East. More boys than girls attend school and learn to read.

Women's lives, like men's, have changed since the 1800s. Then, as now, rural women did farm work and raised poultry and livestock, in addition to caring for children and doing housework. Most city women also worked. But in the 1800s, most wealthy families kept women secluded inside the home—a sign of upper-class status. The practice of secluding women disappeared in the early 1900s. Today, women attend universities and hold jobs in business, medicine, education, government, and other areas. Despite these gains, many women are still working to expand their legal rights.

Middle Easterners are family-oriented, and most of them marry and have children. But younger people marry at a later age and have fewer children than their parents and grandparents did.

Religious law governs family life in every Middle Eastern country except Turkey. In Saudi Arabia, for example, women are required to wear a veil in pub-

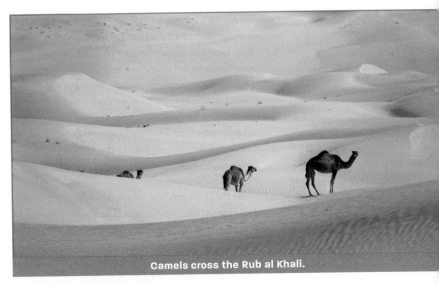
Camels cross the Rub al Khali.

lic that covers their faces. In Iran, women must cover their heads. In other countries, women can choose whether to wear a veil or head cover.

Religion. More than 90 percent of Middle Easterners, including most Arabs, Iranians, and Turks, are Muslims. Their religion, Islam, is based on the revelations received by the Prophet Muhammad in the A.D. 600s. Muslims believe these revelations came directly from God (*Allah* in Arabic). Most Muslims in the Middle East belong to the Sunni branch of Islam. A minority belong to the Shi`ah branch and are called Shiites. These two branches originated in a dispute over who should lead the Muslims after the death of Muhammad in 632. Shiites make up the majority of Muslims in Bahrain, Iran, Iraq, and Lebanon. Sunnis are the majority elsewhere.

Four-fifths of Israel's citizens are Jews. The religion of the Jews, called Judaism, comes from the ancient Hebrews, who were the first people to adhere to *monotheism* (belief in only one God). About 20 percent of Israel's Jews strictly observe the principles of Judaism and are called *Orthodox* Jews. About half observe only some of the principles, and the rest do not observe them at all. There are small Jewish communities in Iran and Turkey.

Christianity—the religion based on the life and teachings of Jesus—originated in the Middle East. Christians live in every country in the region outside the Arabian Peninsula. Some Christian churches are "national" churches, in the sense that their members identify themselves as belonging to one nation. The main ones are the Coptic Church, in Egypt; the Armenian Church; and Lebanon's

Maronite Church, a Catholic denomination. Most Syrian and Palestinian Christians and some Lebanese Christians belong to the Greek Orthodox Church. Smaller churches include the Syrian and Assyrian Orothodox churches, and several Catholic and Protestant churches.

Another monotheistic religion, the Bahá'i Faith, was founded on the teachings of Baha'u'llah in present-day Iran and Iraq in the 1800s.

The Land

In the northern part of the Middle East, mountains border interior plateaus. The Pontic Mountains and the Taurus Mountains rise in Turkey, and the Elburz and Zagros mountains extend across Iran.

The southern part of the Middle East is a vast dry plateau. Several large deserts lie in this area. The Western and Eastern deserts of Egypt are part of the Sahara. The Rub al Khali (Empty Quarter), a vast expanse of sand dunes, stretches across southern Saudi Arabia.

The Middle East has two major river systems—the Tigris-Euphrates and the Nile. The Tigris and Euphrates begin in Turkey and flow though Syria and Iraq. In Iraq, the rivers meet and form the Shatt al Arab, which empties into the Persian Gulf. The Nile flows north through Sudan and Egypt to the Mediterranean Sea.

Iranian women shop for traditional rugs and carpets.

Economy

In the early 1900s, huge petroleum deposits were discovered in the Persian Gulf region. Since the 1940s, oil revenues have transformed many of the once-poor societies. Agriculture is a major source of income in many Middle Eastern countries. Tourism is also important, especially in Egypt, Israel, and

Turkey. Industry and commerce generate much income for Israel and Turkey. Lebanon and Bahrain have important banking industries. Many workers from Egypt, Turkey, Yemen, and the Palestinian territories find jobs in other countries and send part of their earnings home. Foreign aid has allowed such countries as Israel, Egypt, Jordan, and Syria to spend large sums on the military. The Suez Canal in Egypt is a major waterway for international shipping.

Agriculture. Much of the Middle East is dry. But there is enough rain or snow for farming in Lebanon, northern Israel, the West Bank, northern Syria, northern Iraq, and parts of Turkey and Iran. In Yemen and Oman, *monsoons* (seasonal winds) bring enough rain for farming. In Egypt, canals carry Nile River water to the fields. In Iraq, the Tigris and Euphrates rivers provide water. Since the mid-1800s, the extension of irrigation systems, the building of dams, and improved equipment have led to a large expansion of farmland.

Wheat is the region's chief grain crop. Farmers also grow barley, corn, and rice. Other important Middle East crops include apples, citrus fruits, cotton, dates, grapes, olives, potatoes, sugar beets, sugarcane, tomatoes, and watermelons. Yemen is known for its coffee, which is shipped from the port of Mocha.

Manufacturing. The Middle East's chief industries include oil refining, food processing, and the production of chemicals and fertilizers, construction materials, textiles, and weapons. Textile production has long been important. The names of some common types of cloth are derived from Middle Eastern place names. Examples are *muslin*, named after Mosul, Iraq, and *damask*, named after Damascus, Syria. Today, Iran still produces fine carpets. Israel produces high-technology products and cut diamonds. Israel, Egypt, and Iran have important film and recording industries. Modern software industries have developed in Israel, Egypt, and the Persian Gulf countries. Israel is one of the world's top 10 arms suppliers, and Iran and Egypt also have arms industries.

Mining. The Middle East has almost two-thirds of the world's oil reserves. Saudi Arabia alone has more than one-fourth of the world's reserves. Other major oil producers are Iran, Iraq, Kuwait, Oman, Qatar, and the United Arab Emirates. Other minerals mined in the Middle East include coal, iron ore, natural gas, and phosphates.

International trade. The Middle East imports much of the wheat, flour, and meat it consumes. Other imports include machinery and consumer goods. The United States supplies much of the region's weapons. The region's most important export by far is oil, most of which is sent to Europe and Japan. Middle Eastern countries also export textiles, fruits, and vegetables. Many of the fruits and vegetables are sent to Europe, especially when it is winter there.

History

Early civilizations. People lived in parts of the Middle East as early as 25,000 B.C. More than 10,000 years ago, the Middle East became the first place in the world where agriculture developed.

Between 3500 and 3100 B.C., the world's earliest civilizations—Sumer and Egypt—arose in the region. Sumerian civilization developed on the fertile plain between the Tigris and Euphrates rivers in what is now Iraq. Sumer was later absorbed by the Babylonian Empire. Egyptian civilization arose in the Nile Valley. About 1900 B.C., the Hittites came to power in what is now Turkey. Other peoples, such as the Hebrews and the Phoenicians, also organized societies in the region.

Ancient Middle Eastern peoples made key advances in the fields of mathematics, medicine, and astronomy. They also developed alphabetic writing.

Beginning in the 800s B.C., a series of peoples invaded and conquered much territory in the Middle East. They included the Assyrians, from what is now northern Iraq; the Medes, from what is now northern Iran; and the Persians, from what are now Iran and Afghanistan. In 331 B.C., the Macedonian king Alexander the Great conquered the Middle East. During the next 300 years—a period called the *Hellenistic Age*—Greek culture dominated the region, and great achievements took place in scholarship, science, and the arts.

By 30 B.C., the Romans had conquered much of the Middle East. Jesus Christ lived under Roman rule. Christianity was the major religion of the Middle East until the A.D. 600s.

 The spread of Islam. In about 610, in the Arabian city of Mecca, the Prophet Muhammad began to preach a new message proclaiming that there is only one God. In 622, Muhammad moved to the Arabian city of Medina, where he became the head of a religious and political community. Those who accepted his message were later called Muslims.

Muhammad died in 632. The leaders who succeeded him were called *caliphs*, and the government of a caliph was called a *caliphate*. The first caliphs ruled from Medina. Disputes over who should serve as caliph led to splits among Muslims starting in the mid-600s. The Sunnis and Shiites were the main divisions that emerged.

Arab Muslims conquered an area stretching from Central Asia to Morocco and Spain. Over time, many of the conquered peoples adopted Islam and the Arabic language. From the late 600s to the early 900s, the Islamic Empire flourished. The economy expanded, and science and scholarship flourished. From 661 to 750, the Umayyad caliphate ruled the Islamic Empire from Damascus, in Syria. In 750, the Abbasids overthrew the Umayyads and moved the caliphate to what is now Iraq. There, the Abbasids began building a new capital, Baghdad, in 762.

Abbasid power began to decline in the 800s. By the mid-900s, the Middle East had broken up into numerous small and medium-sized states. They often fought one another and were unable to hold back invaders.

Muslim Turks from Central Asia began to invade and migrate into the region after 1000. They took over Baghdad in 1055. By the end of the century, Turkish rulers controlled an area stretching from Afghanistan to Asia Minor (now Turkey), Syria, and Palestine. In 1096, European Christians

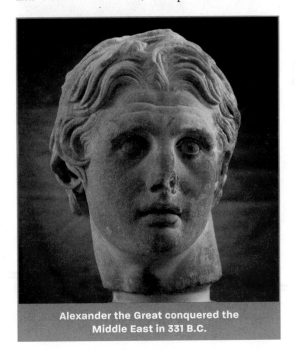

Alexander the Great conquered the Middle East in 331 B.C.

invaded the Middle East in the first of several military expeditions called the Crusades. The crusaders established small states in the eastern Mediterranean region that lasted from 1099 to 1291. Mongols from Central Asia invaded in the 1200s and again in the early 1400s, bringing large parts of the Middle East under their control. Cultural achievements, especially in architecture and the arts, continued even in unsettled political times. Islamic mysticism, called Sufism, emerged and became popular during this period.

The Ottoman Empire. In the 1300s and 1400s, a group of Turkish Muslims called the Ottomans began gaining control of Asia Minor and southeastern Europe. In the 1500s, the Ottomans conquered most of the Arab lands of the Middle East. The Ottoman Empire was one of the world's most powerful empires in the 1500s and 1600s. During this period, the Ottomans threatened to conquer central Europe, twice attacking Vienna, Austria.

In the 1700s, rapid industrial development in Europe began to give Europe an economic and technological advantage over the Ottoman Empire. In the 1800s, European political, economic, and cultural dominance in the Middle East grew. To strengthen themselves, the Ottomans reorganized their military, political administration, and education system, based on Europe's example. Neverthe-

Kemal Ataturk led the Turks to independence.

less, during the 1800s and early 1900s, France, the United Kingdom, and Italy took control of Ottoman territories in North Africa, including Egypt. The British Navy gained control of the Persian Gulf region.

Struggles for independence. In World War I (1914–1918), the Ottoman Empire was defeated. Most Ottoman territories were divided among the victorious Allies. France took control of Lebanon and Syria. The United Kingdom tightened its hold on Egypt and gained control of Iraq, Palestine, and Transjordan (now Jordan). The British also controlled Kuwait, Bahrain, the Trucial States (now the United Arab Emirates), Oman, and the Aden Protectorate (now part of Yemen).

The Turks fought successfully for independence, establishing the Republic of Turkey in 1923. By the mid-1920s, the only other fully independent countries in the region were Iran, Yemen, and the lands controlled by Ibn Saud in Arabia. In 1932, the Saudi lands were united as the Kingdom of Saudi Arabia.

Uprisings against colonial rule occurred in Egypt (1919), Iraq (1920), and Syria (1925–1927). In 1922, the British granted partial independence to Egypt but kept control over military and foreign affairs and the Suez Canal. Iraq became formally independent in 1932, but the British maintained a strong presence there. Arab struggles for independence continued until after World War II (1939–1945). Lebanon became independent in 1943, and Syria and Transjordan in 1946.

The long colonial presence in the Middle East encouraged the rise of *nationalism* and *Islamism*. Nationalism is a people's sense of unity as a nation, based on a shared language, religion, or history. It often includes a desire for a *nation-state*—that is, a national homeland with an independent government. The goal of Islamism is to install Islamic values in all areas of life and create an Islamic government. An important Islamist organization called the Muslim Brotherhood was founded in Egypt in 1928.

The Palestine conflict. In Palestine, Jewish nationalism—called *Zionism*—collided with Palestinian Arab nationalism throughout the 1900s. Both Zionists and Palestinian Arab nationalists claimed Palestine as their homeland. Zionists wanted a state for the Jews, where they would be safe from persecution. The Zionists were European Jews. But because of the Jews' historical and religious attachment to Palestine—which they called Israel—

the Zionists identified it as their homeland. Palestinian Arabs wanted Palestine to be an Arab state, independent from the United Kingdom, and they feared Zionist ambitions.

Jewish immigration to Palestine began in the late 1800s. It increased in the 1930s because of Nazi persecution in Germany. From 1936 to 1939, Palestinian Arabs rose in revolt against the British and the Zionists, but British forces crushed the revolt. The British, who had favored Jewish immigration up to that point, began to limit it. After World War II, Jews—who by then were about one-third of Palestine's people—launched a revolt of their own against the British and the Arabs.

In 1947, the United Nations (UN) voted to divide Palestine into a Jewish state and an Arab state. Jewish leaders accepted the plan. Palestinian Arab leaders opposed it. Under the plan, more than half of Palestine's territory was to be placed in the Jewish state. Jewish-Arab fighting intensified. In March and April 1948, Jewish forces seized areas allotted to both the Jewish state and the Arab state. Palestinian Arab civilians began to flee the fighting, and others were driven from their homes. On May 14, 1948, the Jewish state of Israel was proclaimed. The next day, armies from Egypt, Iraq, Jordan, Lebanon, and Syria invaded Israel. Over the next several months, Israeli forces defeated the Arab armies.

When the war ended in 1949, Israel held more territory than the UN plan had given it. Jordan controlled what became known as the West Bank. Egypt controlled the Gaza Strip in southwestern Palestine. More than 700,000 Palestinian Arabs had become refugees in the Arab lands surrounding Israel, and Israel refused to let them return. Israelis refer to this war as the War of Independence. Palestinian Arabs—usually called simply Palestinians—refer to it as *al-nakba* (*the disaster* in Arabic).

After 1949, negotiations for a full peace stumbled on three issues: (1) Israel's borders, (2) the refugees' right to return or to receive payment, and (3) *recognition* (formal acceptance) of Israel by Arab countries. By the early 2000s, these issues were still not resolved.

Cold War alliances. The Cold War—the intense rivalry between Communist nations, led by the Soviet Union, and non-Communist nations, led by the United States—played a large role in Middle East affairs. The Cold War lasted from the mid-1940s to the early 1990s, when the Soviet Union was dissolved.

The Arab world hailed Gamal Abdel Nasser as a hero after the Suez Crisis.

In the 1950s and 1960s, military officers seized power in Egypt, Iraq, and Syria. These military leaders were Arab nationalists—that is, they called for political unification of the Arab world. They opposed European and American influence in the region. They also advocated *socialism*—that is, government control of the production and distribution of goods—and sided with the Soviets in the Cold War. In spite of the similarities between Egypt, Iraq, and Syria, they were often bitter rivals.

The most influential of the military leaders was Gamal Abdel Nasser of Egypt. In 1952, he overthrew King Faruk of Egypt. In 1956, Nasser took over the Suez Canal from its British and French owners. In response, Israel, the United Kingdom, and France attacked Egypt. But pressure from the United States and the Soviet Union forced the invaders to withdraw. Nasser emerged from the Suez crisis as a hero in the Arab world.

The monarchies of Saudi Arabia, Kuwait, and Jordan sided with the United States in the Cold War. In the 1950s, Turkey embraced democratic politics and joined the North Atlantic Treaty Organization, a military alliance of the United States, Canada, and many European nations. In 1953, the United States and the United Kingdom backed the overthrow of Iran's parliamentary government. The *shah* (king), Mohammed Reza Pahlavi, was restored to power and became a firm U.S. ally.

The Cold War also affected the Arab-Israeli conflict. Israel and the United States grew closer in the 1960s, while Egypt, Syria, and Iraq received weapons from the Soviet Union. In May 1967, Nasser moved Egyptian troops into the Sinai Peninsula to deter a suspected Israeli attack on

Syria. Nasser also closed the Straits of Tiran, the entrance to the Israeli port of Elat. These moves provoked an Israeli attack on June 5. In six days, Israel seized the Sinai and Gaza Strip from Egypt, the Golan Heights from Syria, and the West Bank, including East Jerusalem, from Jordan. Israelis call the 1967 war the Six-Day War. Arabs call it the June War.

In the 1960s, Palestinians renewed their efforts to establish a state. The most important Palestinian nationalist leader was Yasir Arafat, whose organization, Fatah, launched guerrilla attacks on Israel starting in 1966. Most Palestinian guerrillas were young men from refugee camps in the West Bank, the Gaza Strip, Syria, and Lebanon. In 1969, Arafat became head of the Palestine Liberation Organization (PLO), which represented several guerrilla and civilian groups. The guerrilla attacks often targeted Israeli civilians, and Arab civilians often became victims of Israeli counterattacks.

The 1970s and 1980s. Starting in the 1970s, the United States took a more active role in the Middle East. It became Israel's main ally and arms supplier, and it replaced the United Kingdom as the main power in the Persian Gulf.

In October 1973, Egypt and Syria attacked Israeli positions in the Golan Heights and the Sinai Peninsula, aiming to recapture these territories. Israel, with U.S. support, eventually drove them back. In response, the Arab oil-producing states declared an embargo of oil sales to the United States. The Organization of Petroleum Exporting Countries (OPEC) also sharply raised the price of oil. Israelis call this war the Yom Kippur War. Arabs call it the October War or the Ramadan War.

The Camp David Accords led to an Egyptian-Israeli peace treaty in 1979.

After the war and the "oil price shock" of 1973, the price of oil remained high. The higher prices brought new wealth to Iran and other Arab oil producers. The prices also led to new exploration and conservation efforts in Western countries.

After the war, Egyptian President Anwar el-Sadat abandoned the Soviet Union and Nasser's socialist policies. Egypt became a U.S. ally. In 1978, Sadat and Israeli prime minister Menachem Begin met for talks in the United States at Camp David, Maryland. The resulting Camp David Accords led to an Egyptian-Israeli peace treaty in 1979. Under its terms, Israel returned the Sinai Peninsula to Egypt.

In 1975, a civil war erupted between Lebanon's Christians and Muslims. The Muslims allied with PLO forces based in Lebanon. In 1976, Syrian troops entered northern and eastern Lebanon to prevent a Muslim-PLO victory and deter an Israeli intervention. But Israel invaded in 1978 and 1982 to defeat the PLO. In 1982, Israel drove the PLO out of Lebanon. Israel, backed by the United States, hoped to dominate Lebanon politically. But Syria and its local allies, particularly a new Shi`ah Islamist organization called Hezbollah, opposed this effort. Lebanon's civil war ended in 1990. However, Syrian forces remained in parts of the country, and Israel continued to occupy a "security zone" in south Lebanon. Hezbollah fighters clashed with the Israelis and the Israeli-backed South Lebanon Army until Israeli troops withdrew in 2000. Syrian troops remained until 2005.

In 1979, a revolution in Iran overthrew the shah. The Shi`ah leader Ayatollah Ruhollah Khomeini and his followers took control, establishing an Islamic republic with a clergyman as the highest authority. The new government was hostile to the United States because of American support for the shah. A group of American embassy workers were held hostage by Iranian revolutionaries from November 1979 to January 1981.

In 1979, Soviet forces invaded Afghanistan to support the Communist government there. From 1979 to 1989, thousands of young Muslims, mainly Arabs from the Middle East, volunteered to fight the Soviets in Afghanistan. They were called *mujahideen*, an Arabic term meaning *warriors for the faith*. They saw themselves as defending Islam against aggression. The United States, Saudi Arabia, and Pakistan supported them. After the war, some mujahideen, including the Saudi-born Osama bin Laden, began directing their tactics against the United States and its allies.

In 1980, Iraqi president Saddam Hussein invaded Iran over boundary disputes and other disagreements. The United States assisted Iraq out of fear of the consequences of an Iranian victory. Attacks by the U.S. Navy on Iranian targets helped force Iran to accept a cease-fire in 1988.

Because of events in Iran, Iraq, and Afghanistan, the United States built up its forces in the Persian Gulf, constructing a naval base on the Indian Ocean island of Diego Garcia and new military and air bases in Saudi Arabia.

At the end of 1987, a Palestinian uprising began in the Gaza Strip and the West Bank against the Israeli occupation. The uprising, known as the *intifada* (an Arabic term meaning *shaking off*), lasted until 1993. During the intifada, an Islamist organization called Hamas emerged. It hoped to replace the PLO as the leader of the Palestinian resistance movement. In 1988, the PLO declared a state in the West Bank and the Gaza Strip, recognized Israel, and renounced terrorism.

The 1990s. In August 1990, Iraq invaded and occupied Kuwait. United States president George H. W. Bush assembled a coalition of 39 nations—including many Arab countries—to protect Saudi Arabia and liberate Kuwait. In early 1991, the U.S.-led coalition defeated Iraq and forced Iraqi troops to leave Kuwait.

The UN imposed sanctions on Iraq to force Saddam Hussein to give up all *weapons of mass destruction*—that is, chemical, biological, or nuclear weapons. "No-fly" zones were established to protect Iraqi Kurds and Shiites who opposed Hussein's government. Despite these actions, Iraqi Kurds and Shiites continued to suffer, while the UN sanctions deprived many Iraqis of food and medicine.

In 1993, Israeli and PLO leaders met for talks in Oslo, Norway, beginning what became known as the Oslo peace process. Under the Oslo agreements, the two sides recognized each other. In 1994, Israel withdrew from some areas in the West Bank and Gaza Strip, and the Palestinian Authority (PA) took control of them. Israel and Jordan signed a peace treaty that same year.

The Oslo process failed to achieve peace, however. Both sides were internally divided. Israel's Labor Party supported the Oslo process, but the Likud party and others opposed it. Arafat and Fatah supported it, but Hamas opposed it. Also, tensions increased as Israel continued to expand Jewish settlements in the West Bank and the Gaza Strip.

The 2000s. In September 2000, a new Palestinian intifada began. Hamas and other groups carried out suicide bombings in Israel, and Israel retaliated. In 2002, Israel reoccupied most of the Palestinian areas from which it had withdrawn earlier. Arafat died in late 2004, and Mahmoud Abbas replaced him. In late 2005, Israel removed its troops and settlers from the Gaza Strip, but it kept control of Gaza's borders, coastline, and airspace. Also, Jewish settlements in the West Bank continued to grow.

In January 2006, Hamas won the Palestinian Legislative Council elections. Because Hamas does not recognize Israel's right to exist, Israel, the United States, and European nations refused to deal with the group. In June 2007, fighting broke out in Gaza between Hamas and Fatah. Hamas seized control of the Gaza Strip, and Fatah took control of the West Bank. Palestinian militants fired rockets into Israel from Gaza. Israel responded with attacks. Israel fought a three-week war against Hamas in Gaza in December 2008. In November 2012, violence in Gaza erupted again as Hamas rocket attacks met with Israeli naval and air strikes.

Conflict reignited in Lebanon in July 2006. Hezbollah captured two Israeli soldiers, provoking Israel into a month-long war. Israel bombed Lebanon, and Hezbollah fired thousands of rockets into Israel. Afterward, Lebanon's government was stalemated between Hezbollah supporters and opponents.

The September 11, 2001, terrorist attacks drew the United States further into Middle East affairs. Osama bin Laden's organization, al-Qaeda, was responsible for the attacks. Al-Qaeda considers the United States to be an enemy of Islam. It opposed the presence of U.S. troops in Saudi Arabia following the Gulf War of 1991. The United States responded to the attacks by declaring a "war on terrorism." As part of this war, U.S. forces and local rebels overthrew Afghanistan's government, which was harboring bin Laden and other Qaeda leaders, in late 2001. Since then, many Qaeda leaders—including bin Laden in 2011—have been killed.

The attacks of September 11, 2001, also prompted U.S. president George W. Bush to launch a war against Iraq in March 2003. He linked this war to the war on terrorism and said the intent was to disarm Iraq of weapons of mass destruction. By mid-April, U.S.-led forces had toppled Saddam

Saddam Hussein's government fell in 2003.

Hussein's government. United States and allied forces began working to rebuild Iraq—a task made difficult by numerous guerrilla attacks against them and against civilian targets. No weapons of mass destruction were found in Iraq. In 2008, after Iraq adopted a constitution and held elections, violence began to decline. The United States formally ended its combat operations in 2010, but some U.S. troops remained in Iraq until late 2011.

In 2002, the Islamist Justice and Development Party won elections in Turkey. The new government passed political and economic reforms in hopes of becoming the only Middle Eastern country to join the European Union (EU). These reforms included the abolishment of capital punishment, the revision of other criminal penalties, the expansion of civil rights for Kurds and women, and the reduction of the military's role in politics. Disagreements over Cyprus stalled Turkey's membership drive in 2007, but negotiations continued.

In 2006, concerns over Iran's uranium enrichment led the UN Security Council to ban Iran from trading nuclear-related materials. In 2007, the Council imposed additional sanctions on Iran. Later that year, the United States increased its sanctions against Iran, renewing charges that the country was supporting terrorism.

In 2009, Mahmoud Ahmadinejad was reelected president of Iran, causing widespread protests over alleged electoral fraud. The government suppressed the protests by force.

Recent Developments. In early 2011, antigovernment protests erupted in several Middle Eastern countries, as well as in other Arab states in North Africa. Clashes between protesters and government forces resulted in thousands of deaths throughout the region. The protests and resulting political unrest were often referred to as the "Arab Spring." Protests in Tunisia led to the resignation of President Zine El-Abidine Ben Ali in January. Egyptian president Hosni Mubarak resigned in February after weeks of protests in Cairo. Mubarak was later sentenced to life in prison for ordering the killing of protesters. The Bahraini government cracked down on protests there with the aid of troops from Saudi Arabia. After months of protests and occasional fighting in Yemen, the then-president Ali Abdullah Salih was wounded in a June attack on the presidential compound.

In Libya, protests led to an armed rebellion against Mu'ammar al-Qadhafi. First the United Nations and then the North Atlantic Treaty Organization (NATO) carried out military operations aimed at protecting civilians. By August, rebel forces controlled most of the country, including Tripoli, Libya's capital. Qadhafi fled the city and went into hiding. A transitional council took control of the government. On October 20, Qadhafi was killed in his hometown of Surt (also spelled Sirte).

Protests in Syria, which began in March 2011, were fueled by the violent response of Syrian security forces. Violence in Syria continued through 2012. More than 44,000 people have been killed.

In September 2012, terrorists attacked the U.S. consulate in Libya, killing the U.S. ambassador and three other Americans. The attack coincided with protests throughout the Middle East and elsewhere over an anti-Islam video produced in the United States.

THE ARAB-ISRAELI CONFLICT

is a struggle between the Jewish state of Israel and the Arabs of the Middle East. About 90 percent of all Arabs are Muslims. The conflict has included several wars between Israel and certain Arab countries that have opposed Israel's existence. Israel was formed in 1948. The conflict has also involved a struggle by Palestinian Arabs to establish their own country in some or all of the land occupied by Israel.

The Arab-Israeli conflict is the continuation of an Arab-Jewish struggle that began in the early 1900s for control of Palestine. Palestine today consists of Israel and the areas known as the Gaza Strip and the West Bank. The Arab people known as the Palestinians lived in the region long before Jews began moving there in large numbers in the late 1800s.

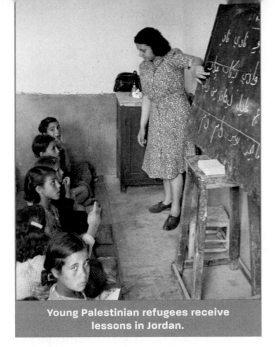

Young Palestinian refugees receive lessons in Jordan.

The Arab-Israeli conflict has been hard to resolve. In 1979, Egypt became the first Arab country to sign a peace treaty with Israel. Jordan, another Arab country, signed a peace treaty with Israel in 1994. But Israel has not made final peace agreements with Syria or with the Palestine Liberation Organization (PLO). The PLO is a political body that represents the Palestinian people.

Historical background. In the mid-1800s, Jewish intellectuals in Europe began to support the idea that Jews should settle in Palestine, which the Bible describes as the Jews' ancient homeland. The word *Palestine* does not appear in the Bible. But it has long been used to refer to the area the Bible describes. The idea that Jews should settle in Palestine became known as Zionism. In the 1800s, Palestine was controlled by the Ottoman Empire, which was centered in present-day Turkey.

Zionism became an important political movement among Jews in Europe because of increasing *anti-Semitism* (prejudice against Jews) there. The anti-Semitism resulted in violent attacks on Jews and their property. In the 1800s, the immigration of European Jews to Palestine accelerated. At first, many of the immigrants and the Palestinians lived together peacefully. But as more Jews arrived, conflicts between the two groups increased.

In 1917 and 1918, at the end of World War I, the United Kingdom gained control of Palestine from the Ottoman Empire. In the Balfour Declaration of 1917, the United Kingdom had supported creating a national homeland for the Jews. Under British rule, the Jewish population of Palestine continued to grow.

During World War II (1939–1945), German dictator Adolf Hitler tried to kill all of Europe's Jews. Thus, about 6 million Jews were murdered.

After the war, most of the countries that defeated Germany supported the idea of creating a new Jewish state where Jews would be safe from persecution.

The 1948 war. In November 1947, the United Nations (UN) approved a plan to divide Palestine into two states, one Jewish and the other Palestinian. Zionist leaders accepted the plan. But Arab governments and the Palestinians saw the division as the theft of Arab land by Zionists and the governments that supported them.

British rule over Palestine ended when Zionists proclaimed the state of Israel on May 14, 1948. The next day, armies of Egypt, Syria, Lebanon, Transjordan (which became known as Jordan in 1949), and Iraq attacked Israel. Israel fought back. In the war, Israel absorbed much of the land the UN had set aside for the Palestinians. Egypt and Jordan occupied the rest of the area that was assigned to the Palestinians. Egypt held the Gaza Strip, a small area between Israel and the Mediterranean Sea. Jordan held the West Bank, a territory between Israel and the Jordan River. By August 1949, Israel and all five Arab states had agreed to end the fighting. Because of the war, more than 700,000 Palestinians became refugees. Most fled to Jordan—including the West Bank—or to the Gaza Strip. Others went to Lebanon and Syria.

The Suez crisis of 1956. During the 1950s, nationalism spread among the Arab countries of the Middle East. Egyptian President Gamal Abdel Nasser and his followers sought to rid Arab lands of the influence of Western nations. On July 26, 1956, Nasser took control of the Suez Canal from its British and French owners. The canal connects the Mediterranean and Red seas and is a key shipping route between Europe and Asia.

Many countries protested Nasser's action. The United Kingdom, France, and Israel secretly plotted to end Egypt's control of the canal. On October 29, Israel attacked Egyptian forces in Egypt's Sinai Peninsula and quickly defeated them. The Sinai lies between Israel and the canal. Israel, with British and French help, occupied most of the peninsula. The UN called a cease-fire on November 6. By early 1957, Israel, under international pressure, returned the Sinai to Egypt. The canal reopened under Egyptian management in April of that year.

After the Suez crisis, Arab guerrillas launched small-scale attacks inside Israel, and Israel responded with raids into Arab territory. At the same time, the Arab nationalist movement began

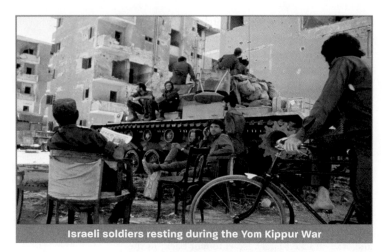

Israeli soldiers resting during the Yom Kippur War

receiving financial and military support from the Soviet Union. The United States, fearing the spread of Soviet-sponsored Communism, gave financial and military aid to Israel.

In 1964, the PLO was formed to represent the Palestinians. It included guerrilla groups dedicated to defeating Israel and creating an independent Palestinian state.

The 1967 war. In May 1967, Nasser closed the Gulf of Aqaba to Israeli shipping. The gulf was Israel's only access to the Red Sea. By June 5, Egypt had signed defense agreements with Syria, Jordan, and Iraq, creating a joint military command.

These apparent preparations for war alarmed the Israelis. On June 5, they launched a surprise attack on Egypt. Syria, Jordan, and Iraq joined Egypt in fighting Israel. Within hours, Israeli warplanes destroyed almost all the Arab air forces. Israeli tanks then retook the Sinai Peninsula. Israel also gained control of the West Bank, the Gaza Strip, and East Jerusalem. It had taken West Jerusalem in the 1948 war. In the north, Israel took Syria's Golan Heights, an area bordering Israel. The fighting ended on June 10. Israelis call this conflict the Six-Day War. Arabs call it the June War. After the war, Israel decided it would return the territories it had taken only if the Arab countries recognized its right to exist.

Also after the 1967 war, the PLO sought to become the representative of the Palestinians in world politics. It developed educational and social service organizations for Palestinians, mainly in the West Bank and Gaza Strip and in refugee camps in Lebanon and Jordan.

The PLO also began to take independent military action. In the late 1960s, PLO groups began to attack Israelis both inside and outside Israel. In response, Israel attacked Palestinian refugee camps in Jordan and Lebanon, in which many guerrillas were based. The Israelis also assassinated a number of PLO leaders.

The 1973 war. After the 1967 war, Egyptian and Israeli troops continued to attack each other across the western border of the Sinai Peninsula. On October 6, 1973, Egypt and Syria launched a massive assault on Israeli forces in the Sinai Peninsula and Golan Heights. The attack took Israel by surprise, in part because it came on Yom Kippur, the holiest day in Judaism.

At first, Egypt drove Israel's forces out of the western Sinai, and Syria pushed Israeli troops from the eastern Golan Heights. However, the United States gave Israel large amounts of military equipment. By October 24, Israeli forces crossed the Suez Canal and surrounded the Egyptian army. They also defeated the Syrian army in the Golan Heights. Israelis call this war the Yom Kippur War. Arabs call it the October War or the Ramadan War.

The Camp David Accords. In 1978, Egyptian President Anwar el-Sadat joined Israeli Prime Minister Menachem Begin and U.S. President Jimmy Carter in signing the Camp David Accords. Under these agreements, Egypt recognized Israel's right to exist. In return, Israel agreed to give back to Egypt the part of the Sinai it still occupied. Israel had returned the far western part of the Sinai in 1975. Sadat and Begin also agreed there was a need for national independence for the Palestinians. In talks leading up to the accords, Egypt and Israel received promises of large amounts of U.S. economic and military aid. In 1979, Egypt and Israel signed a treaty that confirmed their new peaceful relationship.

Most Arab leaders strongly opposed the Camp David Accords and the 1979 treaty. As a result, Egypt was expelled from the Arab League, an organization of Arab countries, in 1979. In 1981, Sadat was assassinated by an Egyptian religious group that opposed his policies.

The Israeli invasion of Lebanon. After the signing of the Camp David Accords, the PLO continued to launch guerrilla attacks on Israel, especially from southern Lebanon. In 1982, Israel invaded Lebanon and drove the PLO out of the southern part of the country. Israeli forces remained in southern Lebanon until 2000.

The first intifada. In 1987, Palestinians in the West Bank and Gaza Strip began an uprising against Israel's military rule of those territories. During this *intifada* (an Arabic term meaning *uprising* or *shaking off*), demonstrations occurred throughout the occupied territories. Entire towns refused to pay taxes to Israel. Palestinians quit their jobs with Israeli employers. Most demonstrations were peaceful, but a few became violent. The intifada grabbed international attention and triggered criticism of Israel for its continuing control of the West Bank and Gaza Strip and for its extensive use of force in trying to control the Palestinians.

Peacemaking. In 1988, the PLO recognized Israel's right to exist. It also declared its readiness to negotiate with Israel for peace in return for the creation of an independent Palestinian state. In addition, it declared it would no longer use violence against Israel. But some PLO members continued to attack Israeli targets.

In 1991, the Soviet Union, long the main foreign supporter of anti-Israeli governments and the PLO, was dissolved. Thus, the Arabs found themselves with much less international support for their fight against Israel.

In 1993, Israel and the PLO, aided by Norway, began secret peace talks. As a result, the PLO and Israel signed an agreement in Washington, D.C., in September 1993. Under the agreement, the PLO again stated its recognition of Israel's right to exist. Israel, in turn, recognized the PLO as the representative of the Palestinian people. It also promised to withdraw from part or all of the West Bank and Gaza Strip and to consider allowing the creation of a Palestinian state in those lands. In 1994, as a first step, Israel gave the PLO control of the Gaza Strip and the West Bank city of Jericho. In 1995 and 1996, Israel gave the Palestinians control of most cities and towns of the West Bank.

Jordan signed a peace treaty with Israel in 1994. Israel then continued to seek a peace treaty with Syria. Syrian-Israeli peace discussions, however, broke down in 1996. Talks resumed in December 1999 but stopped the next month because of continuing disagreement over the Golan Heights.

In October 1998, Israel and the Palestinians signed another agreement. Under the accord, Israel turned over more land in the West Bank to Palestinian control.

The second intifada. Peace talks between Israeli and Palestinian leaders continued in 2000. However, the two sides were unable to agree on key remaining issues, especially those involving the final status of Jerusalem. In September 2000, Palestinians began a second intifada against Israeli security forces. Numerous attacks by Palestinian militias and suicide bombers took place throughout Israel, the West Bank, and the Gaza Strip, killing hundreds of Israelis. Israeli forces repeatedly bombed and invaded the West Bank and Gaza Strip, killing thousands of Palestinians and demolishing hundreds of houses. In 2002, Israel reoccupied most West Bank cities. That same year, Israel began constructing a barrier that was designed to separate most of the West Bank from Israel. In 2003, diplomats from the United States, Russia, the European Union, and the United Nations proposed a peace plan known as the "roadmap." Israeli and Palestinian leaders resumed negotiations under this plan, but the negotiations soon broke down. Palestinian attacks and Israeli military strikes continued. In early 2005, Israeli Prime Minister Ariel Sharon and Palestinian leader Mahmoud Abbas met in Egypt and declared an Israeli-Palestinian truce. However, some violence continued between the two sides.

In 2004, Sharon announced a plan to remove all Jewish settlements and Israeli troops from the Gaza Strip by the end of 2005. On August 15, 2005, the Israeli government began the evacuation of all Jewish settlers from the Gaza Strip and four West Bank settlements. Many settlers protested the evacuation, and Israeli troops forcibly removed them. The settler evacuation was completed on August 23. The last Israeli troops evacuated on September 20. There are still about 120 Jewish settlements in the West Bank.

In June 2006, Palestinian militant groups captured an Israeli soldier. The groups demanded Israel release Palestinian prisoners in exchange for the soldier. Fighting between the two sides increased. Israel bombed parts of the Gaza Strip,

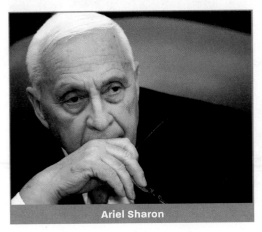
Ariel Sharon

and militants fired rockets into Israel. Israeli troops entered the Gaza Strip, and fighting there has killed more than 300 people. In November, both sides agreed to a cease-fire.

In July, Hezbollah, a radical Islamic group in Lebanon, captured two Israeli soldiers near the border of Lebanon and Israel. They hoped to exchange the soldiers for Lebanese prisoners held by Israel. In response to the capture, Israel began bombing Lebanon. Israel blamed the Lebanese government for not disarming Hezbollah. Hezbollah fired missiles into northern Israel. In August, Israel and Lebanon accepted a cease-fire agreement drafted by the UN Security Council. The conflict led to more than 1,000 Lebanese and Israeli deaths.

In December 2008, Israel launched air attacks on targets in the Gaza Strip. Israel stated that the airstrikes were in response to rocket attacks from Hamas militants. In January 2009, Israel began sending troops into the Gaza Strip. The fighting caused more than 1,300 deaths, almost all of them Palestinians, and wounded thousands more. On January 17, Israel declared a cease-fire. Hamas declared a cease-fire the next day, though some fighting continued.

In November 2012, violence in Gaza erupted again as Hamas rocket attacks met with Israeli naval and air strikes. In roughly one week, about 170 people were killed, all but 6 of them Palestinian.

The UN Security Council unanimously passed the Iraq resolution in November 2002.

THE GAZA STRIP is a territory on the eastern Mediterranean coast, where Egypt and Israel meet. It is part of the historic region of Palestine, which also includes Israel and the West Bank. Israel directly occupied the Gaza Strip from 1967 to 2005 and remains in control of its borders. The territory has been the site of many clashes between Palestinian Arabs and Israelis.

The Gaza Strip covers 141 square miles (365 square kilometers) and has a population of about 1,700,000. It is one of the most densely populated places in the world. Most of its land is sandy and flat. The traditional economy is based on agriculture, including such crops as citrus fruit and olives. Israel's tight control of Gaza's borders has resulted in shortages of many goods and services. When the border is open, many workers seek employment in Israel as day laborers.

In ancient times, the Gaza Strip was ruled by the pharaohs of Egypt. Later, at various times, it was ruled by Philistines, Jews, Arabs, and Turks. From 1920 to 1948, it was part of the British-ruled Mandate of Palestine. Egypt gained control of the strip during the Arab- Israeli war of 1948. Israel took control of the strip after the 1967 Arab-Israeli War.

In the 1980s, Palestinians in the Gaza Strip and the West Bank began a wave of protests, known as the *intifada*, against Israel's occupation. Israeli forces clashed with protesters, killing many of them. Beginning in 1993, Israel and the Palestine Liberation Organization signed agreements that led to the removal of Israeli troops from densely populated Palestinian areas. Palestinians then took control of those areas. In 1996, Palestinians in the Gaza Strip and the West Bank elected a legislature and a president. But there was still a large Israeli security presence, and Israeli citizens continued to build settlements in the areas.

In 2000, Israel and the Palestinians held peace talks but failed to resolve key remaining disagreements. Later that year, violence again broke out between Palestinians and Israeli forces. The struggle involved numerous attacks on Israelis by Palestinian suicide bombers and a widespread Israeli military campaign.

In August and September 2005, the Israeli government withdrew all Israeli soldiers and settlers from Gaza. However, Israel kept control of Gaza's borders, coastline, and airspace. Many Palestinians complained that the Israeli occupation had not ended. Palestinian militants fired rockets into Israel and, in June 2006, kidnapped an Israeli soldier. Israel responded with a series of military attacks that killed hundreds of Palestinians.

In June 2007, Hamas, a radical Islamic organization and political party, seized control of the Gaza Strip by force. Palestinian President Mahmoud Abbas responded by dismissing the Hamas-led government and declaring a state of emergency. Israel imposed an embargo on the territory. Despite these actions, Hamas continues to control the strip.

In December 2008, Israel began air attacks on targets in the Gaza Strip. Israel stated that the airstrikes were in response to rocket attacks from Hamas militants. In January 2009, Israel began sending troops into the Gaza Strip. The fighting caused more than 1,300 deaths, almost all of them Palestinians, and wounded thousands more. On January 17, Israel declared a cease-fire. Hamas declared a cease-fire the next day, though some fighting continued.

In November 2012, violence in Gaza erupted again as Hamas rocket attacks met with Israeli naval and air strikes. In roughly one week, about 170 people were killed, all but 6 of them Palestinian.

THE IRAQ WAR (2003–2011) began when the United States and its allies launched an invasion of Iraq in March 2003. The U.S.-led forces controlled most of Iraq by mid-April, after the fall of the Iraqi government of Saddam Hussein. The troops involved in the invasion came mainly from the United States, although forces from the United Kingdom and a few other countries also participated.

United States president George W. Bush declared an end to major combat in Iraq on May 1, 2003. Afterward, U.S., Iraqi, and allied forces from many countries tried to maintain security, restore stability, and rebuild the country. However, Iraqi and foreign militants carried out many attacks against these military and security forces, as well as against civilian targets. Most of the militants oppose the presence of U.S. and allied foreign forces in Iraq. The Iraq War remained a major challenge in the presidency of Barack Obama, who took office in 2009.

The U.S. government referred to the war as Operation Iraqi Freedom until the end of combat operations on August 31, 2010. Until the official end of the war on December 15, 2011, the war was then known as Operation New Dawn.

Background to the War

A coalition of 39 nations, organized mainly by the United States and the United Nations (UN), defeated Iraq in the Persian Gulf War of 1991. That war had erupted after Hussein's forces invaded and occupied Kuwait, Iraq's neighbor to the south, in 1990. After the invasion, the United Nations Security Council had authorized the coalition to expel Iraq from Kuwait.

Illegal weapons. As part of the cease-fire agreement that ended the Persian Gulf War of 1991, Iraq agreed to destroy all of its *weapons of mass destruction*—that is, biological, chemical, or nuclear weapons—and any facilities it had for producing such weapons. However, in the years following the war, Iraq did not fully comply with the terms of the agreement. On a number of occasions, it failed to cooperate with UN teams sent to inspect suspected weapons sites. Starting in 1998, the Iraqi government refused to allow UN weapons inspectors into the country.

In 2001 and 2002, President Bush repeatedly claimed that Hussein and his government were a threat to the security of the United States and other countries. The Bush administration accused Hussein of illegally developing and possessing weapons of mass destruction. It also argued that links existed between Hussein's government and terrorist organizations, including al-Qaeda, the group responsible for the terrorist attacks in the United States on September 11, 2001. However, many experts doubted that there was any working relationship between Iraq and al-Qaeda.

Debate within the UN. Bush said that if the UN failed to force Iraq to disarm, the United States might launch a military attack against the

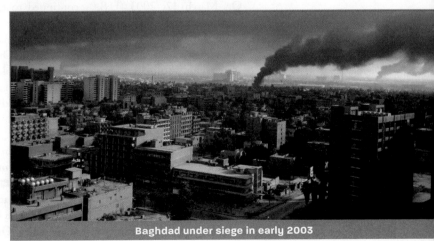

Baghdad under siege in early 2003

country. In response, Iraq began negotiating conditions for a return of the UN weapons inspectors. In November 2002, the UN Security Council passed a resolution demanding the resumption of weapons inspections and threatening serious consequences if Iraq failed to follow UN terms on disarmament. Iraq allowed weapons inspectors to return to the country later that month. However, in the months that followed, the United States, the United Kingdom, and other countries charged that Hussein was not cooperating with the inspectors. The United States maintained its threat of possible military action against Iraq.

Members of the UN Security Council disagreed on whether to take military action. The United States was the main supporter of such action. The United Kingdom and Spain also favored the use of force. However, France, Germany, Russia, China, and several other countries argued for more time to seek a diplomatic solution. The United States decided to move toward war despite the disagreement among the Security Council members.

Military Action

On March 17, 2003 (U.S. time), Bush stated that if Hussein and his sons did not leave Iraq within 48 hours, the United States would begin military action. Hussein did not leave, and a U.S.-led coalition launched an attack on Iraq on March 20, 2003 (March 19 in the United States). The removal of Hussein from power was a central goal of the operation. The coalition consisted mostly of U.S. troops, with British, Australian, Polish, and Danish forces also participating.

The coalition's initial attack, an air strike on March 20, was reportedly aimed at eliminating Iraqi leadership in Baghdad, Iraq's capital. In the days that followed, the coalition carried out intense bombing aimed at key targets in Baghdad and elsewhere. A large number of coalition ground troops invaded from the south, traveling from Kuwait toward Baghdad. The Turkish government refused to allow coalition troops to enter Iraq from Turkey. The troops parachuted into northern Iraq and there joined Iraqi Kurds in fighting government troops. Coalition forces in the north also targeted Ansar al-Islam, an Islamic militant group that the U.S. government said was linked to al-Qaeda.

Battle in Baghdad. As coalition forces neared Baghdad, they engaged in battle with Iraq's Republican Guard, the most highly trained branch of Iraq's military. In early April, coalition forces seized control of the international airport outside Baghdad. Within days, the forces gained control of Hussein's presidential palaces and other key locations in the city. Meanwhile, coalition air strikes continued to target high-level Iraqi officials and other strategic targets both inside and outside of Baghdad. On April 9, coalition forces took control of central Baghdad, and U.S. officials declared that the Hussein government had been removed from power.

Shortly before the fall of Baghdad, British forces had seized control of Basra, the largest city in southern Iraq. By mid-April, coalition forces held all of Iraq's major cities. On May 1, Bush declared that major combat operations had ended.

After the fall of the Hussein regime, the coalition countries, led by the United States, established the Coalition Provisional Authority (CPA) as a temporary government for Iraq. Coalition troops and CPA officials then focused on restoring order and overseeing the creation of a new Iraqi-controlled government. The coalition also began searching Iraq for weapons of mass destruction. On June 28, 2004, the CPA was dissolved, and an interim government made up of Iraqis took its place. On January 30, 2005, an election was held for a transitional National Assembly to replace the interim government. The Assembly oversaw the preparation of a constitution for Iraq. In October, Iraqis approved the Constitution in a nationwide referendum. Iraqis elected a permanent legislature called the Council of Representatives in December.

Coalition forces captured or killed several key officials of the Hussein regime. In July 2003, Hussein's sons Uday and Qusay, who had held high-ranking positions in their father's government, were killed during a firefight with U.S. troops. On December 13, 2003, Saddam Hussein himself was captured by U.S. troops near his hometown of Tikrit. He had been in hiding since the war began in March. In November 2006, a special Iraqi court convicted Hussein of ordering the massacre of over 140 Shiites in 1982 and sentenced him to death by hanging. Hussein was executed by Iraqi authorities on December 30, 2006.

During most of the period from 2003 to 2009, U.S. troops

were in charge of security in northern and western Iraq. British troops were in charge of security in much of southern Iraq; and a Polish-led international force had security duties in an area of central Iraq south of Baghdad. Iraqi troops became increasingly involved in security operations, especially after June 2004.

More than 30 countries sent peacekeeping forces to serve in Iraq. Besides the United States, the participating countries included Albania, Armenia, Australia, Azerbaijan, Bosnia-Herzegovina, Bulgaria, the Czech Republic, Denmark, the Dominican Republic, El Salvador, Estonia, Fiji, Georgia, Honduras, Hungary, Italy, Japan, Kazakhstan, Latvia, Lithuania, Macedonia, Moldova, Mongolia, the Netherlands, New Zealand, Nicaragua, Norway, the Philippines, Poland, Portugal, Romania, Slovakia, South Korea, Spain, Thailand, Tonga, the United Kingdom, and Ukraine.

Resistance to the coalition. Many Iraqis celebrated the fall of Hussein's government. However, many also opposed the presence of U.S. and other foreign forces in Iraq. On numerous occasions, the opposition became violent.

After Bush declared the end of major combat operations in May 2003, numerous guerrilla attacks, bombings, and other violent acts continued in Iraq. Militants from both the Sunni Muslim and Shiite Muslim populations in Iraq carried out attacks and called for the withdrawal of foreign soldiers and civilians. Prior to 2006, most of the militants were Sunnis who opposed Iraq's new government, which was dominated by Shiites and backed by the United States. Some of the attackers were believed to be loyal to Hussein.

Muslim militants from other countries were thought to have been involved in many attacks. Some of the militants were believed to have connections to al-Qaeda. The main group of militants with al-Qaeda ties was led by Abu Musab al-Zarqawi, a Jordanian, until his death in June 2006. This group is sometimes called by its original name, Tawhid and Jihad. It has also been called al-Qaeda in Iraq, al-Qaeda Organization of Holy War in Iraq, and other names that indicate its al-Qaeda connections.

The attacks targeted coalition troops, Iraqi security forces, and Iraqi and foreign civilians. Some of the attacks struck against religious sites, especially Shiite ones. Several Iraqis in key leadership positions were assassinated. Bombing targets included police and civil defense stations, government build-

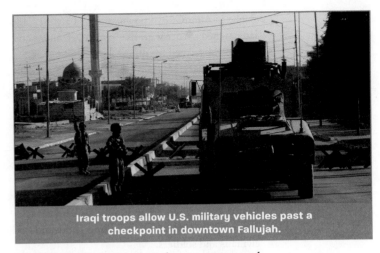

Iraqi troops allow U.S. military vehicles past a checkpoint in downtown Fallujah.

ings, military facilities, oil pipelines, mosques, and churches. High-profile targets included the Jordanian embassy in Baghdad; the UN headquarters in Baghdad; the Imam Ali Mosque in Najaf, a major holy site for Shiites; the headquarters of the Red Cross in Baghdad; Kurdish political party offices in Arbil; and sites in Baghdad and Karbala where Shiites gather each year for the religious festival of Ashura.

Hundreds of Iraqi and foreign civilians were kidnapped in Iraq. Many of the kidnappings were for ransom, but others were for political reasons. For example, some militants kidnapped foreign civilians in an attempt to persuade their home countries to withdraw troops from, or cease business activities in, Iraq. Kidnappers murdered some of the civilians.

In 2004, frequent clashes between Sunni militants and U.S.-led forces began in central Iraq. The city of Fallujah, west of Baghdad, was the site of much of the fighting. The violence killed thousands of people, including soldiers, militants, and civilians. In mid-2004, Sunni militants gained control of some parts of central Iraq, including the cities of Fallujah, Ramadi, and Samarra. In October 2004, U.S. and Iraqi forces regained control of Samarra. In November, after several weeks of U.S. air strikes on Fallujah, U.S. and Iraqi forces began a major ground assault on the city. They seized control of most of Fallujah within a few days. The air and ground attacks destroyed hundreds of buildings and did much damage to the city's power lines and water and sewer pipes.

Also in 2004, much fighting occurred between U.S.-led forces and militants loyal to the radical Shiite cleric Muqtada (also spelled Moqtada) al-Sadr. This fighting took place mainly in Najaf and in a

Baghdad community known as Sadr City. Al-Sadr later signed a truce with the Iraqi government and partially disarmed his militia.

On February 22, 2006, militants bombed the al-Askari shrine in Samarra. The shrine, containing the tomb of two important Shiite *imams* (religious leaders), is one of the holiest sites to Shiite Muslims. The bombing sparked an increase of attacks between Sunni and Shiite groups. The continuing violence between the two groups engulfed major areas of Baghdad and its surroundings, adding to the difficulties of providing basic security for Iraqis. Numerous other bombings and attacks occurred throughout Iraq, killing thousands of civilians and soldiers.

In 2007, the United States sent 30,000 more troops to help the Iraqi government establish security throughout the country. The number of attacks dropped, but some violence continued. United States combat operations in Iraq formally ended on August 31, 2010. Some U.S. troops remained in Iraq until late 2011 to fight terrorism and perform other duties.

Consequences of the War

Casualties and destruction. A total of 172 coalition soldiers—139 Americans and 33 Britons—died during what Bush called the major combat phase of the war in March and April 2003. From May 1, 2003, until the war's official end on December 15, 2011, an additional 4,631 coalition soldiers, mostly Americans, died in Iraq. More than 32,000 coalition soldiers were wounded. There are no official estimates of how many Iraqis died as a result of the war. Most observers believe that tens

Mounted policemen patrol the streets in Gaza City during the occupation of 1967.

of thousands of Iraqis, mostly civilians, died. Some observers believe there were several hundred thousand Iraqi deaths. Numerous foreign civilians, including journalists, business people, and aid workers, were also killed.

The war has caused significant damage to Iraq's utilities, transportation systems, and industries. In addition, looting was a major problem during the early stages of the war, as mobs of Iraqis entered palaces, museums, and other buildings and carried away items from inside.

Disagreements over the war. World opinion was sharply divided over the war and the occupation of Iraq by coalition forces. Before the war began, a majority of Americans supported the invasion of Iraq. But the invasion and the occupation also have received much criticism, both inside and outside the United States. Before the war began, antiwar protesters held numerous demonstrations in the United States and in many other countries. Additional demonstrations took place throughout the invasion and occupation.

Many opponents of the war argued that it inspired anger and resentment among Arabs and Muslims toward the United States and its allies. Many people believed such hostility caused an increase in terrorist violence against U.S. targets. Outrage over the coalition's activities increased sharply in April and May 2004, when evidence surfaced that coalition soldiers had abused Iraqi prisoners, particularly at the Abu Ghraib prison near Baghdad.

Some people, including former UN Secretary-General Kofi Annan, argued that the invasion of Iraq violated international law. Some feared that the war, and disagreements over its timing and justification, weakened the UN and other international institutions.

Bush and British Prime Minister Tony Blair have faced significant criticism over the conflict. Many critics charged that Bush and Blair used misleading, inaccurate, or false information to justify the war. Before the war, Bush and Blair had said that Iraq possessed weapons of mass destruction. However, after the Hussein regime was overthrown, coalition inspectors failed to find any such weapons in Iraq. Investigators concluded that U.S. and British intelligence agencies provided inaccurate estimates of Iraq's weapons capabilities before the war.

Bush and Blair also claimed that there were links between Iraq and al-Qaeda. The Hussein regime did support terrorist groups fighting the governments of Turkey and Iran, as well as Palestinian terrorist groups. Also, some contacts apparently occurred between Iraqi officials and al-Qaeda representatives. But there is no evidence that a working relationship ever developed between Iraq and al-Qaeda.

Supporters of the war argued that it was necessary to prevent Iraq from developing weapons of mass destruction and supplying them to terrorist groups. They also argued that Hussein needed to be removed from power because he was a brutal dictator. He had authorized the extermination of hundreds of thousands of his own people, and he had shown disregard for the fundamental principles of international relations.

By 2004, the Bush administration had made democracy in Iraq a central goal of the war. It argued that if Iraq successfully developed a democratic government, democracy would then spread throughout the Middle East. But as the conflict dragged on, worldwide public opinion had increasingly come to oppose the continuing U.S. military presence in Iraq.

THE PALESTINE LIBERATION ORGANIZATION (PLO) is a political body that represents the Palestinian people. The Palestinians are an Arab group native to the historic region of Palestine in southwest Asia. This region today consists of Israel, the West Bank, and the Gaza Strip. The PLO seeks to establish an independent state for Palestinians in Palestine.

There are about 9 million Palestinians. About half of them live outside Palestine. A large number of Palestinians—including many living in the West Bank and Gaza Strip—are refugees of Arab-Israeli wars or the descendants of refugees.

The PLO is an umbrella organization that includes guerrilla groups and associations of doctors, laborers, lawyers, women, students, and teachers. A number of Palestinians are independent members of the PLO. Guerrilla groups, primarily Fatah, dominate the PLO.

Organization. The main branches of the PLO are the Palestine National Council (PNC), the Executive Committee, and the Central Council. The Palestine National Council serves as an assembly, or parliament, of the Palestinian people. The size of the PNC has varied over the years, but it generally has had a few hundred members. Some are elected, and

Yasir Arafat

others are appointed. The PNC is supposed to meet annually, but in some years, it does not meet. The PNC is considered to be the supreme authority of the PLO. It creates policies, plans, and programs for the organization.

The Executive Committee is the PLO's highest executive body and makes most day-to-day decisions. The PNC elects the chairman and the other members of the Executive Committee. The chairman is the PLO's highest official and has historically exercised great power over the organization. The Central Council, which is also elected by the PNC, meets on occasion to advise the Executive Committee.

History. Many Jews immigrated to Palestine during the 1900s. As Jewish immigrants arrived, tensions developed between the Jews and the Palestinians, who feared that the Jews would eventually dominate or expel them. In 1948, the state of Israel was founded in the region as a homeland for Jews. War immediately broke out between Israel and Arab countries opposed to Israel's creation. Israel originally covered slightly more than half of Palestine. But as a result of the war, Israel gained additional territory, and more than 700,000 Palestinians fled or were driven from areas of Palestine under Israeli control. Palestinians and other Arabs were angry that so many Palestinians were forced to leave their homes and become refugees. During the 1950s, some Palestinians began organizing resistance groups.

In 1964, at an Arab summit meeting in Cairo, Egypt, Arab leaders called for the establishment of an organization to represent the Palestinians. The leaders asked Ahmad al-Shuqayri, a Palestinian lawyer and diplomat, to nominate members for this organization. On May 28, 1964, al-Shuqayri's 422 Palestinian nominees met in Jerusalem. These delegates founded the Palestine Liberation Organization. Al-Shuqayri became the first chairman of the PLO Executive Committee. The original goal of the PLO was to end Israeli control of Palestine and allow Palestinians to return to their homeland. The PLO refused to recognize Israel's existence.

In 1967, a war broke out between Israel and four Arab countries—Egypt, Jordan, Syria, and Iraq. Within six days, Israel defeated its opponents and, in the process, occupied the remainder of Palestine, including East Jerusalem, the West Bank, and the Gaza Strip. Israel also occupied additional territories belonging to Egypt and Syria.

After the 1967 war, control of the PLO fell into the hands of Palestinian guerrilla groups. The largest of these groups was Fatah, led by Yasir Arafat. In 1969, the Palestine National Council elected Arafat chairman of the PLO Executive Committee. Fatah and other guerrilla groups conducted numerous attacks and raids on Israeli targets. Israel, in turn, launched attacks against PLO and guerrilla sites.

Until the early 1970s, most of the guerrilla attacks on Israel were waged from Jordan, where the PLO was based. By then, Palestinian forces had grown large enough to challenge the rule of King Hussein of Jordan. In 1970, the Jordanian army attacked and defeated most Palestinian forces. In 1971, Palestinian guerrillas and the PLO were forced to relocate to Lebanon.

In 1974, Arab countries designated the PLO as the "sole, legitimate representative of the Palestinian people." Later that year, the United Nations (UN) recognized the PLO as the representative of the Palestinians.

In 1982, Israel invaded Lebanon and drove the PLO out of southern Lebanon and Beirut. The PLO then relocated its headquarters in Tunisia. In 1983, rebels within the PLO, supported by Syria, drove PLO forces out of northern Lebanon. After Israeli troops withdrew from most of Lebanon in 1985, some PLO members returned to southern Lebanon.

In 1987, Palestinians in Jerusalem, the West Bank, and the Gaza Strip began a wave of protests known as the *intifada*. The PLO supported this movement. Israel retaliated by assassinating some top PLO officials responsible for the support. The intifada, which lasted until the early 1990s, made many Israelis and Palestinians more willing to look for a peaceful solution to the conflict.

Until 1988, Jordan provided the West Bank with financial and administrative support. But in July of that year, King Hussein announced that his country would end its support. He called on the PLO to take over Jordan's role in the West Bank. In late 1988, Arafat announced the PLO's recognition of Israel's right to exist alongside a Palestinian state. He renounced the use of terrorism. But some PLO members continued to launch attacks against Israeli targets.

In 1991, a peace process began between Israel, a number of Arab countries, and the Palestinians. The United States organized the peace effort. Palestinians from the West Bank and Gaza Strip formed a joint delegation with representatives from Jordan. PLO leaders advised the Palestinian participants in the negotiations.

In 1993, the PLO and Israel conducted secret discussions in Oslo, Norway. During these talks, the two sides reached an agreement that was signed on September 13, 1993, in Washington, D.C. The agreement, the first of the so-called Oslo accords, called for the creation of a Palestinian Authority (PA) to manage the affairs of the Palestinians in the West Bank and Gaza Strip. The two sides also pledged to continue negotiations for a permanent settlement. As a result of this agreement and others, Israel withdrew its troops from much of the Palestinian territories. As the Israelis withdrew, Palestinians took control of these areas. In 1996, Palestinians in the West Bank and Gaza Strip elected a legislature and a president for the PA. Yasir Arafat won the presidential election.

The PLO continues to function as the representative of the Palestinian people. It is a member of the Arab League, an association of Arab states; has observer status at the United Nations; and maintains diplomatic relations with many countries. But with the creation of the PA, the PLO has lost some influence.

In 2000, peace talks between Israeli and Palestinian negotiators failed to resolve key remaining issues between the two sides. Israel continued to build Jewish settlements in the occupied territories, outraging the Palestinian population. That year, Palestinians began another intifada. Violence between Israelis and Palestinians increased, killing thousands of people. In 2002, Israel reoccupied most West Bank cities. That same year, Israel began constructing a barrier that was designed to separate most of the West Bank from Israel.

In 2003, diplomats from the United States, Russia, the European Union, and the United Nations proposed a peace plan known as the "roadmap." Israeli and Palestinian leaders resumed negotiations under this plan, but the negotiations soon broke down. Palestinian attacks and Israeli military strikes continued.

In 2004, Israeli Prime Minister Ariel Sharon announced a plan to remove all Jewish settlements and Israeli troops from the Gaza Strip by the end of 2005. On August 15, 2005, the Israeli government began the evacuation of all Jewish settlers from the Gaza Strip and four West Bank settlements. Many settlers protested the evacuation, and Israeli troops forcibly removed them. The settler evacuation was completed on August 23. The last Israeli troops evacuated on September 20. There are still about 120 Jewish settlements in the West Bank.

In 2004, Arafat died. Mahmoud Abbas replaced him as chairman of the PLO Executive Committee and president of the PA. In 2005, Israel withdrew from the Gaza Strip and four West Bank cities. However, violence between Israelis and Palestinians continued. In January 2005, Abbas was also elected president of the Palestinian Authority. In February 2005, Abbas and Sharon met in Egypt and declared an Israeli-Palestinian truce. However, some violence continued between the two sides.

THE PERSIAN GULF WAR OF 1991

was fought in early 1991 between Iraq and a coalition of 39 countries organized mainly by the United States and the United Nations (UN). The U.S. government called the war *Operation Desert Storm*. It took place chiefly in Iraq and the tiny oil-rich nation of Kuwait. These two countries lie together at the northern end of the Persian Gulf.

The coalition had formed after Iraq invaded Kuwait on August 2, 1990. After quickly gaining control of Kuwait, Iraq moved large numbers of troops to Kuwait's border with Saudi Arabia, triggering fears that Iraq would invade Saudi Arabia next. Iraq's actions were viewed with alarm by the world's industrialized countries, which relied on Kuwait and Saudi Arabia as primary sources of petroleum. A number of coalition members sent troops to Saudi Arabia to protect it from possible attack.

Many oil fields in Kuwait were set ablaze during the Persian Gulf War.

On January 17, 1991, after months of pressuring Iraq to leave Kuwait, the coalition began bombing Iraqi military and industrial targets. In late February, the coalition launched a massive ground attack into Kuwait and southern Iraq and quickly defeated the Iraqis. Coalition military operations ended on February 28.

The war resulted in immense human suffering in the Middle East and enormous material damage in Iraq and Kuwait. Hundreds of thousands of people were killed or wounded or became refugees. Economic measures taken against Iraq caused great hardship there. The war also caused severe environmental pollution in the region, as the Iraqis set hundreds of Kuwaiti oil wells on fire and dumped huge amounts of Kuwaiti oil into the Persian Gulf. In addition, the war triggered bloody revolts in Iraq by Kurds and Shiite Muslim Arabs.

The Persian Gulf War of 1991 was the first major international crisis after the end of the Cold War. The crisis tested cooperation between the United States and the Soviet Union, as well as the ability of the UN to play a leading role in world affairs. The war also split the Arab world between coalition members and supporters of Iraq's president, Saddam Hussein.

Background to the War
Competition for Arab leadership.

Saddam Hussein's ambition for power and leadership in the Organization of the Petroleum Exporting Countries (OPEC) and in the Middle East was a central cause of the invasion of Kuwait. From 1980 to 1988, Iraq had fought a war with its neighbor Iran. Iraq suffered serious economic damage in the Iran-Iraq War. Nevertheless, it emerged from that war as the second-strongest military power in

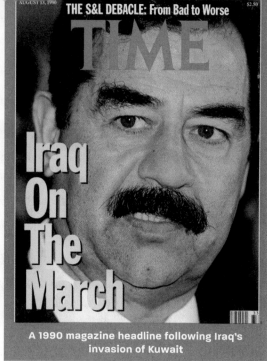

THE S&L DEBACLE: From Bad to Worse

TIME

$2.50

AUGUST 13, 1990

Iraq On The March

A 1990 magazine headline following Iraq's invasion of Kuwait

the Middle East. Only the Jewish state of Israel was stronger.

Hussein argued that Iraq had become the region's chief power opposed to Israel and should thus be recognized as leader of the Arab world. Since the late 1940s, Arab countries had fought several wars with Israel. Many Arabs wanted to abolish Israel and place its lands under the control of Palestinians and other Arabs.

Hussein claimed that, as leader of the Arab world, Iraq should receive help from other Arab countries in rebuilding its economy. According to Hussein, Iraq needed help from OPEC in raising world oil prices, and Iraq needed Kuwait and other Arab countries to cancel debts that Iraq had incurred to fight the Iran-Iraq War.

Disputes between Iraq and Kuwait. After the Iran-Iraq War, Hussein had disagreed with Kuwait's leaders over how much debt cancellation and other aid Kuwait should provide to Iraq. Hussein also accused Kuwait of exceeding oil production limits set by OPEC and thus lowering world oil prices. In addition, Hussein claimed that Kuwait was taking Iraqi oil from the Rumaila oil field, a large field that lay beneath both Iraq and Kuwait.

Also, Iraq had often claimed that Kuwait should be part of Iraq. Iraq based its claim on the fact that, in the late 1800s and early 1900s, Kuwait had been included in a province of the Ottoman Empire, called Basra, which later became part of Iraq. But by the time Iraq was formed in the early 1920s, Kuwait was no longer part of the province. Also by the early 1920s, the United Kingdom had gained control of Kuwait and what became Iraq. Iraq gained independence in 1932, and Kuwait in 1961. After 1961,

disputes continued between Kuwait and Iraq over the location of their common border.

What Hussein hoped to gain by taking Kuwait. A number of factors prompted Hussein to invade Kuwait. He wanted to acquire Kuwait's oil wealth and erase Iraq's debt to Kuwait. He wanted to increase Iraq's power within OPEC. He also sought better access to the Persian Gulf. Iraq's gulf coastline was short. Kuwait's was much longer and included an excellent harbor. In addition, Hussein probably hoped that an invasion would keep Iraq's military occupied and so end a series of attempts by the military to force him out of power.

Iraq's Invasion of Kuwait

At 2:00 a.m. on August 2, 1990, hundreds of tanks and other Iraqi forces swept across the border into Kuwait. Within 24 hours, Iraq had complete control of Kuwait. Thousands of Iraqi troops then moved to Kuwait's border with Saudi Arabia. To some, this movement signaled that Iraq might invade Saudi Arabia. On August 8, Iraq announced that it had annexed Kuwait.

Under international law, none of Iraq's claims against Kuwait justified the invasion. The United Nations, as well as the United States and many other countries, condemned the Iraqi invasion. But Hussein accused the United States of following a double standard. He said that if the United States condemned the Iraqi invasion, it should also condemn Israel's occupation of lands won from Arab countries in the Arab-Israeli wars. Since the 1970s, the United States had been Israel's chief ally.

Many Arabs, particularly poor Arabs and Palestinians, supported the Iraqi invasion. Hussein became a hero to them by confronting Israel and the United States. He gained additional support from poor Arabs by calling for the redistribution of the vast wealth of Kuwait, Saudi Arabia, and certain other Arab oil-exporting countries.

The World's Reaction

On August 2, the UN Security Council issued a resolution condemning Iraq's invasion. United States President George H. W. Bush and other world leaders began to form an anti-Iraq coalition. The coalition grew to include Afghanistan, Argentina, Australia, Bangladesh, Belgium, Canada, Czechoslovakia, Denmark, France, Germany, Greece, Honduras, Hungary, Italy, the Netherlands, New Zealand, Niger, Norway, Pakistan, Poland,

Portugal, Senegal, Sierra Leone, Singapore, South Korea, Spain, Sweden, Turkey, the United Kingdom, and the United States. Arab members of the coalition were Bahrain, Egypt, Kuwait, Morocco, Oman, Qatar, Saudi Arabia, Syria, and the United Arab Emirates. The Arab countries of Jordan, Libya, and Yemen opposed the involvement of non-Arab countries but did not fight against the coalition. China and the Soviet Union, then the most powerful Communist countries, did not join the coalition. But their cooperation as members of the UN Security Council allowed the UN to play a leading role in the crisis.

Measures against Iraq. On August 6, the UN Security Council imposed an embargo that prohibited all trade with Iraq except for medical supplies and food in certain circumstances. Nearly all of Iraq's major trading partners supported the embargo. As a result, Iraq's foreign trade was sharply reduced. On August 7, the United States announced that it would send troops to the Persian Gulf to defend Saudi Arabia from possible attack by Iraq.

On August 25, the UN Security Council authorized the use of force to carry out the embargo against Iraq. On November 29, the council gave coalition members permission "to use all necessary means" to expel Iraq from Kuwait if Iraq did not withdraw by January 15, 1991. Iraq chose to stay in Kuwait.

The opposing forces. By mid-January, the coalition had about 670,000 troops, 3,500 tanks, and 1,800 combat aircraft in the Persian Gulf region. The troops came from 28 coalition members and included about 425,000 troops from the United States. Many of the other troops came from the United Kingdom, France, and such Arab countries as Egypt, Saudi Arabia, and Syria. Other coalition members provided equipment, supplies, or financial aid. The coalition also had about 200 warships in the Persian Gulf region, including 6 U.S. aircraft carriers and 2 U.S. battleships. Iraq had between 350,000 and 550,000 troops in Kuwait and southern Iraq, with about 4,500 tanks and 550 combat aircraft. It also had a small navy.

The Coalition Takes Military Action

Militarily, the coalition first tried to force Iraq to withdraw from Kuwait by bombing Iraqi military and industrial targets. But after more than five weeks of heavy bombing, Iraq still refused to withdraw. The allies then started a major ground attack against Iraqi forces.

The air war began at 3 a.m. on January 17, 1991. The coalition aimed first to destroy Iraq's ability to launch attacks. Other goals included eliminating Iraq's biological, chemical, and nuclear weapons facilities; disrupting Iraq's ability to gather information about coalition forces and to communicate with its own forces; and reducing the readiness of Iraqi troops.

Allied aircraft first bombed Baghdad, the capital of Iraq, and then attacked targets throughout Iraq and Kuwait. The allies gradually focused heavy bombing on Iraqi troops; artillery and tanks; transportation routes; and supplies of ammunition, food, fuel, and water.

The coalition achieved many of its objectives in the air war, in part because of the use of such high-technology equipment as night-vision systems and precision-guided weapons. These weapons included cruise missiles launched from U.S. ships in the gulf.

Iraq's response. Iraq responded to the start of the air war by launching "Scud" missiles at populated areas in Israel and Saudi Arabia. The Scuds terrorized the populations of targeted cities and killed a number of people. Analysts believe that Iraq used the attacks on Israel to try to draw it into the war. Had Israel struck back, Iraq might have succeeded in forcing Arab countries out of the coalition by portraying the war as an Arab-Israeli conflict. However, Israel did not enter the war, thus making it much easier to keep the coalition together.

The ground war. The first major ground battle occurred at Khafji, a small Saudi coastal town near Kuwait. The Saudis had deserted the town

A coalition tank patrols the Kuwait border during the war.

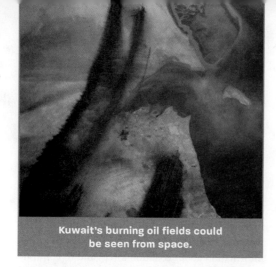

Kuwait's burning oil fields could
be seen from space.

before the war. On January 29, Iraqi troops occupied Khafji. With U.S. help, Saudi and Qatari troops recaptured the town on January 31. By late February, the air war had reduced, through casualties and desertions, the number of Iraqi troops in Kuwait and southern Iraq to about 183,000.

At about 4 a.m. on February 24, coalition forces launched a major ground attack into Iraq and Kuwait. The attack consisted of several large operations carried out at the same time. United States and French troops invaded Iraq from Saudi Arabia, west of Iraqi fortifications in Kuwait. They moved rapidly north into Iraq and toward the Euphrates River to cut off Iraqi supply lines and to prevent an Iraqi retreat. U.S. and British troops also crossed into Iraq from Saudi Arabia. They moved north into Iraq and then swept east to attack the Iraqi troops.

In another operation, coalition troops assaulted Iraqi forces at several points across southern Kuwait. These coalition troops consisted of U.S. marines and troops from Egypt, Kuwait, Saudi Arabia, and Syria. The troops quickly broke through Iraqi fortifications, and about 63,000 Iraqi soldiers surrendered. On February 26, Hussein ordered his troops to leave Kuwait. But by that time, the Iraqi forces had been surrounded. The coalition ended all military operations at 8 a.m. on February 28, about 100 hours after the ground attack had begun.

The war ends. Iraq accepted the terms of a formal cease-fire agreement on April 6. On April 11, the UN Security Council officially declared an end to the war. In the agreement, Iraq promised to pay Kuwait for war damages. Iraq also agreed to destroy all its biological and chemical weapons, its facilities for producing them, and any facilities or materials it might have for producing nuclear weapons. Iraq stockpiled chemical weapons in Kuwait before the ground war, but there is no evidence that either side used chemical weapons in the war. Neither side used biological or nuclear weapons.

After the formal cease-fire, the UN continued the embargo to pressure Iraq to carry out its promises.

However, Iraq stubbornly resisted complying with the terms of the cease-fire agreement.

Consequences of the War

As many as 100,000 Iraqi troops may have died in the war, but some experts believe the total was much lower. Only about 370 coalition troops died. Thousands of civilians in Iraq and Kuwait probably were killed in the war.

Coalition bombing severely damaged Iraq's transportation systems, communication systems, and petroleum and other industries. Coalition attacks also wiped out much of Iraq's ability to provide electric power and clean water. As a result, many civilians died after the war from disease or a lack of medicine or food.

In Kuwait, Iraqi troops looted the country and damaged many of Kuwait's oil wells, in most cases by setting them on fire. In addition, Iraq dumped an estimated 465 million gallons (1.75 billion liters) of Kuwaiti crude oil into the Persian Gulf, killing wildlife and causing long-term harm to the environment.

After the war, Saddam Hussein continued to rule Iraq. But revolts broke out among Kurds in northern Iraq and, in southern Iraq, among Arabs of the Shi'ah division of Islam. Both groups had long opposed Hussein's rule. Iraq's army swiftly put down most of the rebellions. Hundreds of thousands of Shiite Arabs then fled to Iran. Thousands of others hid in the marshlands of southern Iraq. More than a million Kurds fled to the mountains of northern Iraq and to Turkey and Iran. Tens of thousands of Kurds and Shiites were killed in the revolts or died later of disease, exposure, or hunger.

In April 1991, the United States and other coalition members established a safety zone in northern Iraq to protect Kurdish refugees from Iraqi troops. Coalition forces remained in northern Iraq until July. But coalition aircraft continued to patrol northern Iraq as part of an effort to enforce a ban on Iraqi aircraft flights and troop movements there. In 1992, to protect the Shiite population, coalition forces imposed a ban on Iraqi aircraft flights over southern Iraq. In 1996, Iraqi troops attacked Kurds in northern Iraq. The United States responded with missile attacks against Iraqi military targets.

The Persian Gulf War of 1991 also focused world attention on the Arab-Israeli conflict. After the war, the United States renewed diplomatic efforts to resolve disputes between Israel and Arab countries. These efforts helped lead to the signing of several agreements between Israel and the Palestine Liberation Organization, a group that represents the Palestinian people.

After the war, some veterans complained of physical and psychological ailments that they believed were related to their service. Their symptoms, sometimes referred to together as Gulf War syndrome, included memory loss, fatigue, and joint pain. Some people believed that exposure to dangerous chemicals when U.S. troops destroyed a chemical weapons depot in Iraq may have affected the troops. Others argued that the syndrome was not a single illness and that the symptoms resulted from the stress of war or other factors.

Iraq did not fulfill the terms of the 1991 cease-fire agreement. On several occasions, Iraq failed to cooperate with UN teams sent to inspect suspected weapons sites. In the late 1990s and early 2000s, U.S. and British planes attacked targets in northern and southern Iraq many times to enforce the Iraqi flight bans and to disable Iraq's air defense systems. In 1998, Iraq began to refuse to allow UN weapons inspectors into the country.

In 2002, the United States and the United Kingdom began to threaten military action against Iraq unless it fully eliminated any *weapons of mass destruction*— that is, chemical, biological, or nuclear weapons—and any facilities for producing them. In November of that year, Iraq allowed weapons inspectors to return to the country. During the inspections, the United States continued to accuse Iraq of violating UN disarmament terms.

In March 2003, U.S.-led forces launched air and ground attacks against Iraq. United States officials said the military campaign was intended to overthrow Hussein and rid Iraq of weapons of mass destruction. British, Australian, Polish, and Danish forces participated in the war effort. In April, the U.S.-led forces seized Baghdad, causing the fall of Hussein's government. In May, the UN lifted the trade embargo it had imposed on Iraq in 1990. In December 2003, U.S. troops captured Hussein. Search teams found no weapons of mass destruction in Iraq.

THE WEST BANK is a territory in the Middle East that lies between Israel and Jordan. It covers about 2,260 square miles (5,850 square kilometers) and has a population of about 2,622,000. Most of them are Arab people known as Palestinians.

Historically part of Palestine, the West Bank was annexed by Jordan in 1950. In 1967, Israel defeated Jordan, Egypt, and Syria in a war and captured the West Bank. In 1993, a peace process began between Israeli and Palestinian leaders, and the next year, Israel began withdrawing from the West Bank. But the two sides have not reached a final agreement. In 2002, Israel reoccupied many West Bank areas from which it had previously withdrawn. See the *History and government* section of this article for more details.

East Jerusalem is the West Bank's largest city. But Israel, which includes West Jerusalem, does not consider East Jerusalem part of the West Bank. After the 1967 war, Israel made East

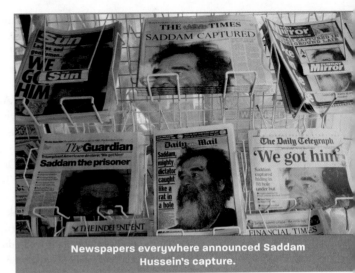

Newspapers everywhere announced Saddam Hussein's capture.

Jerusalem a part of Israeli Jerusalem. But other countries do not recognize Israeli control.

People. Most West Bank Palestinians live in villages. About 12 percent of the Palestinians live in crowded refugee camps, where a United Nations (UN) agency provides schools and other services. Israelis make up about 15 percent of the West Bank's population. Many of the Israelis live in settlements built by the Israeli government. Many others live in East Jerusalem.

Most West Bank Palestinians wear clothing similar to that worn by North Americans and Europeans. Older men may also wear a traditional *keffiyeh*, or headcloth. Women generally dress more conservatively than American and European women do. Beautifully embroidered dresses, for which the area is well known, are still made for wearing on special occasions. Israeli settlers generally wear clothing similar to that worn by North Americans and Europeans.

West Bank cooking is similar to that of other Arab lands. Dishes include *kibbeh* (ground lamb) and *tabbouleh* (a salad made of ground wheat, onion, lemon juice, parsley, and mint). *Baklava*, or baklawa (a thin pastry layered with honey and chopped nuts), and *halva*, or *halwa* (ground sesame seeds and honey), are desserts.

West Bank Palestinians speak Arabic. English is the most common second language. Most Palestinians are Muslims who belong to the Sunni division of Islam. About 8 percent of the people are Christians, chiefly members of the Eastern Orthodox or Eastern Catholic churches. The Israelis are Jewish and speak Hebrew.

Education. The West Bank has universities in Bethlehem, Bir Zeit, East Jerusalem, Hebron, Janin, and Nabulus. Many well-educated Palestinians have found jobs outside of the territory.

Land and climate. The West Bank is hilly with generally thin, stony soil. Only about one-fourth of the land is suitable for farming. The highlands that cover most of the West Bank have mild summers and occasional freezing temperatures and snow in winter. The Jordan River Valley, in the eastern part of the territory, has mild winters and hot summers, with temperatures reaching 120°F (49°C) and higher.

Much of the West Bank receives little rainfall. Only 2 to 8 inches (5 to 20 centimeters) of rain falls annually in the Jordan River Valley. Agriculture there depends on irrigation. Some areas of the highlands receive 25 inches (64 centimeters) or more of rain a year. The West Bank's main river is the Jordan. The Dead Sea, the only lake, is on the southeast border. Its shore, which lies about 1,373 feet (419 meters) below sea level, is the lowest place on Earth's surface.

Economy. The West Bank has a developing economy. It has a small amount of fertile land. Its only important natural resource is stone quarried for use as building material. Agriculture, which centers on the growing of citrus fruits and olives, is the most important economic activity. But water shortages limit expansion of agricultural production. The few industries are small. They include crafts, food processing, and textiles.

The West Bank has a fairly good road system but no railroads. An airport is in Qalandiya. Radio and television programs that are broadcast in the West Bank originate in Israel, Jordan, and Syria. Several Arabic language newspapers are published in the territory.

History and government. In the 1200s B.C., the Israelites settled in the West Bank. The Philistines settled there at about the same time. Later, the area was ruled by the Assyrians, Babylonians, Persians, and Romans.

In the A.D. 600s, Arab Muslim armies conquered the West Bank. The territory was part of a series of Muslim empires almost continuously from then until the defeat of the Ottoman Empire in World War I in 1918. In 1920, as an element of a post-World War I international agreement, the West Bank became part of the British mandate of Palestine. According to the mandate, the United Kingdom was to help Jews in Palestine establish a Jewish homeland. In 1947, the UN voted to divide the mandate into an Arab state and a Jewish state. The Palestinian Arabs rejected this plan. Their Arab allies attacked Israel in May 1948, the day after that country was established as a Jewish state. Jordan occupied the West Bank when the war ended in 1949. It annexed the territory in 1950.

In 1967, Israel defeated Jordan, Egypt, and Syria in what Israelis call the Six-Day War, and Arabs call the June War. Israel captured the West Bank, as well as the Arab lands of the Gaza Strip, Golan Heights, and Sinai Peninsula. In 1974, King Hussein of Jordan gave up his government's responsibility for the West Bank to the Palestine Liberation Organization (PLO). In 1988, Jordan ended financial and administrative support it had continued to give the West Bank. Later that year, the PLO declared an independent Palestinian state in the West Bank and the Gaza Strip. However, Israel continued to occupy and, in effect, govern both territories. During the late 1980s, violence erupted between Israeli troops and Palestinians protesting the Israeli occupation.

In 1972, Israel began allowing West Bank Palestinians to elect and operate municipal and village government councils. But the councils had little power. Beginning in 1993, however, Israel and the PLO signed several agreements that led to the withdrawal of Israeli troops from portions of the West Bank and most of the Gaza Strip. As the Israelis withdrew, the areas came under Palestinian control. In January 1996, Palestinians in the Palestinian-controlled parts of the West Bank and in the Gaza Strip elected a legislature and a president for these areas.

By the end of the 1990s, Israel still occupied more than half of the West Bank. In 2000, Israeli and Palestinian leaders failed to reach a final peace settlement. Later that year, violence again erupted between Palestinians and Israeli forces. The struggle involved numerous attacks on Israelis by Palestinian suicide bombers and a widespread Israeli military campaign in the West Bank and Gaza Strip.

In 2002, Israel reoccupied most West Bank cities from which it had previously withdrawn. That same year, Israel began constructing a barrier to separate most of the West Bank from Israel. On August 15, 2005, the Israeli government began the evacuation of all Jewish settlers from the Gaza Strip and four West Bank settlements. Many settlers protested the evacuation, and Israeli troops forcibly removed them. The evacuation was completed on August 23. There are still about 120 Jewish settlements in the West Bank. In July 2006, Hezbollah missiles landed in the West Bank during the Lebanese conflict.

MLA Citation

"Middle East." *The Southwestern Advantage Topic Source.* Nashville: Southwestern. 2013.

ADDITIONAL RESOURCES

Books to Read

Angrist, Michele P., ed. *Politics and Society in the Contemporary Middle East.* Lynne Rienner, 2010.
Cleveland, William L., and Bunton, M. P. *A History of the Modern Middle East.* 4th ed. Westview, 2009.
Friedman, Lauri S. *The Middle East.* Greenhaven, 2007.
National Geographic Atlas of the Middle East. 2nd ed. National Geographic Society, 2008.
Political Handbook of the Middle East 2008. CQ Press, 2008.
Tucker, Spencer C., and Roberts, P. M. eds. *The Encyclopedia of Middle East Wars.* 5 vols. ABC-CLIO, 2010.

Web Sites

BBC News: Middle East

http://news.bbc.co.uk/news/world/middle_east/
Current news information about the Middle East.

Foundation for Middle East Peace

http://www.fmep.org/
Home page of a nonprofit organization dedicated to informing Americans about the Israeli-Palestinian conflict.

Middle East Daily—daily news and current events

http://www.middleeastdaily.com/
Current news about the Middle East from the World News Network.

Search Strings

Islam

Islam Muslim "Middle East" Muhammad revelations (58,900)

Islam Muslim "Middle East" Muhammad revelations Allah Sunni Shi'ah (885)

"Middle East" religion Islam history branches differences (113,000)

Oil

"Middle East" oil petroleum "Persian Gulf" (47,700)

"Middle East" oil petroleum "Persian Gulf" history (221,000)

history of oil in the "Middle East" conflicts changes revenues location (103,000)

The Palestine Conflict

Palestine Conflict Zionism Jewish nationalism (40,500)

Palestine Conflict Zionism Jewish nationalism Arab homeland (14,400)

Palestine Conflict Zionism Jewish nationalism Arab homeland conflict (115,000)

America and the Middle East Since September 11, 2001

America and the Middle East since September 11, 2001 (259,000) * These returns looked really good.

America "Middle East" "September 11, 2001" terrorist attacks (66,400)

America "Middle East" "September 11, 2001" terrorist attacks "Osama bin Laden" Afghanistan (19,200)

America "Middle East" "September 11, 2001" terrorist attacks "Osama bin Laden" Afghanistan Iraq Qa'ida (1,660)

BACKGROUND INFORMATION

The following articles and features were written during the year in which the events took place and reflect the style and thinking of that time.

Middle East (1956)

The split between the Western powers and the Arab states widened in 1956. The Soviet Union fanned the flames of Arab nationalism to draw these countries away from the West. The Arabs reacted violently against the attack by Great Britain and France on Egypt on October 31. Every major oil line in the area except the American-owned Tapline was either blown up or shut down by the Arabs. Jordan's parliament voted to end the British subsidy, and Saudi Arabia broke off relations with France.

President Gamal Nasser of Egypt consulted Soviet officials before and after he seized control of the Suez Canal. But the Soviets did not offer Egypt funds for the proposed Aswan High Dam, nor did they openly support the Arabs against Israel. The attack by Israel, Great Britain, and France appeared to strengthen Nasser's position as leader of the Arab world.

Soviet delegations, including many technicians, visited much of the Middle East, and heads of state such as the shah of Iran and Yemen's crown prince Mohammed al Bad'r received royal welcomes in Moscow. The U.S.S.R., Communist China, and countries in the Soviet bloc signed trade agreements with such Middle Eastern states as Syria, Yemen, and Afghanistan. Afghanistan received Soviet aid totaling four times its annual income.

Arab Nationalism was encouraged by the U.S.S.R. Egypt's nationalization of the Suez Canal in July not only regained popularity for Nasser at home, but united the Arabs behind him. To emphasize their solidarity, Arab leaders called a general strike throughout the Middle East on August 16, the opening day of the London Conference and the Suez dispute. Even Iraq, generally anti-Egypt, declared that Nasser had an unquestioned right to nationalize the canal. Volunteer armies sprang up throughout the Middle East.

Arab nationalism supported the rebels against the French in Algeria. Demonstrators burned the French consulate in Amman, Jordan, in protest, when the French downed a plane carrying five Algerian leaders. Anticolonialism, directed mostly toward the French and the British, was another popular slogan with Arabs. They hailed Egypt's action because it had removed another symbol of foreign domination. But the United States helped its prestige by its efforts through the United Nations (UN) to end the attack on Egypt.

The increased Arab nationalism brought closer cooperation between the countries around Israel. A trade agreement between Syria and Jordan led to proposals for a similar pact between Syria and Egypt. Jordanian forces agreed to operate under Egyptian command in the event of war with Israel. At Jordan's request, Iraq sent its troops into Jordan.

Israel problem. The April visit of UN Secretary-General Dag Hammarskjold to the Holy Land brought a truce in the Gaza Strip, scene of heavy fighting between Egypt and Israel. But soon Israel's frontier with Jordan erupted in small, savage skirmishes. Small bands of *fedayeen* (irregular raiders) attacked Israeli settlements. Jordan and Egypt claimed no knowledge of the attacks. Each series of raids brought heavier Israeli reprisals into Jordan. The UN Truce Supervisory Organization could not reach an agreement with either side to stop the attacks.

Economic progress. Jordan, Egypt, Syria, Iraq, Kuwait, and Saudi Arabia formed the Arab Potash Company to extract potash from the Dead Sea. New oil discoveries in Iran, Israel, and Saudi Arabia highlighted the importance of oil to the Middle East's economy and future development. The Iraq Development Board put oil royalties into flood control, malaria prevention, new hotels for the tourist trade, and many other projects. Iranian oil royalties helped balance the budget. Syria and Lebanon squabbled with the oil companies over back taxes increased royalties. The Iraq Petroleum Company, owned by several foreign oil firms, dismissed all its Lebanese employees, and canceled a plan to build more pipelines across Lebanon.

Middle East (1957)

The Middle East seethed with crisis and conflict during 1957. The area became an important pivot point in the power struggle between the United States and the Soviet Union. The U.S. offered economic and arms aid to Middle East nations. But the U.S.S.R. also increased its aid and arms shipments to the area, and scored some unexpected victories. United Nations (UN) forces prevented any renewal of the fighting that broke out in the Gaza Strip late in 1956. But war clouds loomed large on the Middle East horizon throughout the year.

Eisenhower Doctrine. In January, President Eisenhower announced "the Eisenhower Doctrine." This program allowed the U.S. to send its armed forces to aid any Middle Eastern nation threatened by Communist or Communist-inspired aggression, if that nation requested help. The doctrine also offered special economic aid to these nations. Congress approved the doctrine by a joint resolution.

Reaction to it varied from outright rejection by Syria and qualified approval by Saudi Arabia and Jordan, to full approval by Lebanon, Israel, and Turkey. The Communists attacked the doctrine as unnecessary interference in the domestic affairs of the Middle East. They opposed it by increasing economic aid, and then by sending shipments of arms to Egypt, Syria, Yemen, and Afghanistan.

Circumstances turned the doctrine from an asset into a political liability for the U.S. American efforts to force a withdrawal of Israeli troops from Arab territory made the U.S. very popular for a time the Arabs. But the U.S. lost this popularity when it resumed its close ties with Great Britain and France. Arabs again associated the U.S. with colonialism. They interpreted U.S. support for King Hussein of Jordan as another sign of American willingness to deal with reactionary or imperial leaders. The Communists harped on the theme that the doctrine was merely disguised imperialism. Arab nations overlooked the fact that U.S. aid would be given only upon request. By the end of the year, even Lebanon had decided that the doctrine was dead in the Middle East.

Israel and the Arabs failed to settle any of their basic differences in 1957. The Palestine refugees stayed in their camps. The UN tried to continue its relief program for these refugees. Member nations pledged contributions of more than $25,000,000. The U.S. gave $8,000,000. But this was not enough to care for the increased number of refugees. Some long-range aspects of the program had to be dropped because of a lack of sufficient funds.

Under strong pressure from the U.S. and the UN, Israel withdrew its troops from the Gaza Strip and Gulf of Aqaba. Egypt reoccupied Gaza, but UN Expeditionary Force (UNEF) troops held positions between Israeli and Arab forces. This reduced border tension. The reopening of the Suez Canal in April put the situation closer to normal in this part of the area.

UN Secretary-General Dag Hammarskjold

Arab differences. Without a battle against Israel to unify them, Arab nations began to quarrel among themselves. This illustrated an Arab proverb: "My brother and I will fight my cousin; my cousin and I will fight the foreigner." The Arab countries accused each other of such crimes as subversion, smuggling, and spying. But all swore they would defend Arab unity to the death. Jordan's King Hussein kept his throne in April because the Bedouin troops of his Arab Legion remained loyal to him against what he called a Communist plot inspired by Egypt and Syria.

Syrian crisis. Syria had no strong leader, and the government came more and more under the control of a pro-Soviet group of army officers. The Soviet Union poured weapons and technicians into Syria. The U.S. countered with increased military aid to Jordan. Syria and the Soviets took turns accusing Turkey of armed attacks and preparations for war along the Syrian border. Turkey denied the accusations, and the U.S backed the Turks with a clear warning to the U.S.S.R. not to interfere. The issue reached the UN in late October. By that time, responsible Arab leaders had become concerned over the danger of Communist infiltration of Syria. But Syria was still weak compared to Turkey, and a

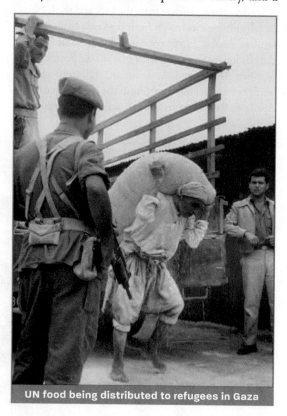

UN food being distributed to refugees in Gaza

shooting war seemed unlikely. Not all Syrians accepted the new leftist government. More than 35,000 Syrian political and business leaders fled to other Arab and Western countries during the year.

Economic development was slow, even though new oil fields were discovered in Turkey, Israel, and southern Oman. The Middle East showed little inclination to accept such a regional development scheme as that proposed by David Rockefeller. He wanted to plow back oil profits into large-scale development projects. Interest in Oman's oil potential led Great Britain to help the Sultan of Muscat and Oman put down a revolt by followers of the Imam of Oman.

Middle East (1958)

Influence of the United States and its allies dwindled almost to the vanishing point in 1958. Arab nations pulled away from the U.S. and Great Britain. Only Iran and Israel completely supported Western policies. Afghanistan declared itself neutral. Turkey lined up with the West, but it openly criticized U.S. policies.

President Gamal A. Nasser of Egypt arranged the merger of Egypt and Syria that produced the United Arab Republic (U.A.R.). Two friends of the West, King Faisal II of Iraq and King Hussein of Jordan, countered by forming the Arab Federation. But it disintegrated when revolting Iraqi army officers killed Faisal and took over the Iraqi government. Iraq dropped out of the pro-Western Baghdad Pact and drew closer to the U.A.R. King Hussein kept Jordan allied with the U.S. and Great Britain, but he had to put down an attempted army revolt. An old U.S. friend, King Saud of Saudi Arabia, turned over an important part of his power to his pro-Nasser brother, Crown Prince Faisal.

The United States answered the Lebanese government's call for help to curb the rioting in July by sending in 15,000 soldiers and marines. But Lebanese voters elected a government more friendly to the U.A.R. than to Western nations.

Arab conflicts. Although the Arab nations were united in dreams of unity, they were bitterly divided on the best method of gaining it. Nasser and the young Arab nationalists were pitted against Nuri al-Said of Iraq and the old Arab nationalists. The young nationalists wanted a clean break with tradition, outmoded monarchies, and feudal economic systems. They hated Western nations because of the actions of France and Great Britain after World War I, when the unified nation promised the Arabs became a series of colonial mandates. They also hated Western nations for the creation of Israel. The old nationalists felt Arab unity could best be reached gradually. They wanted to educate Arabs democratic processes while maintaining the traditional monarchies to guide the people and direct large development programs. Most of the old nationalists had fought with Great Britain against Turkey during World War I. They believed in cooperation with the West against the new danger of Communism.

The United Arab Republic, formed by the merger of Egypt and Syria, brought strength to the young nationalist movement. The old nationalists quickly followed by uniting Iraq and Jordan in the Arab Federation. They put their trust in monarchies and Western support. But the United States tried to defend Israel and cooperate with Arab nations at the same time. It failed to give firm support to governments that were basically unpopular in their own nations. A group of young Arab nationalists, led by General Abdul Karim el-Kassem, overthrew the Iraqi monarchy in a swift, savage move. Premier el-Kassem and his fellow officers said they would keep Iraq's oil commitments to Western Europe. They did not formally pull Iraq out of the Baghdad Pact, nor rush to join the United Arab Republic. But they took no part in Pact activities. By the end of the year, only King Hussein of Jordan was left of the West's Arab friends.

While the loss of Iraq weakened the Baghdad Pact, the Arab League suddenly came to life. Iraq paid its back dues. In October, the League admitted Morocco and Tunisia as members. The League set aside $34,000,000 to help the Algerian rebel government-in-exile against France. But even this new harmony did not last long. Tunisia and U.A.R. delegates quarreled and the Tunisia delegation walked out. In December, President Nasser of the U.A.R. told Western newsmen privately that he feared Communist gains in Iraq might throw that nation into the Soviet sphere.

The United Nations played an active role in the various Middle East crises. It could not even muster enough authority to order a cease-fire in the Lebanese revolt. But it showed its value as a sounding board for world opinion and a safety valve for tension. United Nations (UN) observers went to Lebanon in May and June, when the worst fighting flared there. The UN observers were unable to

Crown Prince Faisal

make peace between Lebanese religious groups, or to prove subversion by U.A.R. agents infiltrating from Syria. But Arab nations accepted UN observers and troops in the Middle East. The UN Expeditionary Force in the Gaza Strip kept Israel and Egypt apart for another year. The UN Relief and Works Agency cared for 900,000 Palestine refugees.

United States troop landings in Lebanon in July brought a reaction in unexpected quarters. Soviet crowds in Moscow demonstrated before the United States and British embassies. They showed a deep Soviet concern with the possibility of World War III. But before the UN could start full debate, the Arab nations presented a unanimous petition to be allowed to work out a settlement by themselves with full respect for individual national rights. The UN approved the petition.

Economic development. Political turmoil in the Middle East slowed economic development everywhere except in Iran, Israel, and Turkey. Iran scored a major breakthrough—the customary 50-50 split in oil royalties with United States companies. Its success prompted Saudi Arabia to advance a similar proposal to the Standard Oil Company of Indiana. Iran also opened the first commercial television station in the Middle East and joined its railroad network with that of the Soviet Union. Israel completed the 143-mile Beersheba-Elath highway and opened a major oil pipeline. Turkey opened the huge Kemer Baraji dam on the Menderes River and completed a large aid agreement with the United States.

Middle East (1967)

The third major clash of arms since Israel achieved its independence in 1948 erupted on June 5 between the Arab states and Israel. Heavily outnumbered, the citizen-soldiers of Israel again scored a swift military triumph, even more crushing than before. But stability in the Middle East seemed as improbable at the year's end as at its beginning.

Although a steady escalation of Arab attacks and Israeli reprisals triggered the war, the roots of the crisis lay, as before, in the Arab refusal to accept Israel's existence on the soil of Palestine.

The mounting tension was described by United Nations (UN) Secretary-General U Thant as the most menacing since the war of 1956. In April, harassment of Israeli farmers by Syrian artillery on the heights above Galilee—Syria claimed the farmers were violating the armistice line—provoked massive retaliation by Israel; six Syrian MIGs were shot down on April 7. Terrorism by Arab guerrillas and increasingly frequent incidents on the Syrian border caused Israeli prime minister Levi Eshkol to partially mobilize the armed forces in May, purportedly for the parade honoring the 19th anniversary of Israel's independence. On May 11, Israel stated it held Syria responsible for the border raids, and that it was ready to defend itself.

UN Secretary-General U Thant

President Gamal Abdel Nasser of the United Arab Republic (U.A.R.), bound by a treaty to support Syria and informed that the signs pointed to an imminent Israeli attack, ordered his armies on a state of alert. Nasser demanded on May 18 that the 3,400-man UN Emergency Force (UNEF) withdraw from the Gaza Strip and Sinai Peninsula, in view of the danger of war. Unexpectedly, U Thant agreed.

With the withdrawal of the UNEF forces, U.A.R. troops occupied Sharm el-Sheikh and, on May 22, unilaterally closed the Gulf of Aqaba to Israeli or Israel-bound ships. The closure was called an act of war by Israeli prime minister Eshkol. U Thant, in Cairo, warned Nasser of the danger of his move.

The UN Security Council rushed into emergency session on May 24, but the UN—as it was to be throughout the crisis—found itself powerless to act. A new U.S. ambassador, Richard Nolte, arrived in Cairo on May 26 and urged the restoration of UNEF and the reopening of the gulf. But Nasser declared the Strait of Tiran was U.A.R. territory.

On May 29, the U.A.R. national assembly gave Nasser emergency powers to rule by decree. He signed a mutual defense treaty with Jordan the next day, closing the ring around Israel. Turkey agreed to allow passage of Soviet warships through the Dardanelles. The scene was set for war.

Preemptive thrusts. Even as the Arab armies went on the alert, Israel fully mobilized. General Moshe Dayan, hero of Suez in 1956, returned to the cabinet as minister of defense. On June 5, as the UN futilely struggled to preserve peace, Israel launched a lightning "preventive attack." In the first hours, Israeli planes bombed and strafed airfields in Iraq, Jordan, Syria, and the U.A.R. The Arab air forces were caught on the ground; more than 300 aircraft were destroyed.

Lacking air support, the Arab armies were quickly beaten. By June 8, Israeli ground forces had occupied Arab Jerusalem, the Gaza Strip, Sinai, the west bank of the River Jordan, and had opened the Gulf of Aqaba. Jordanian and U.A.R. ground forces had suffered catastrophic losses of men and equipment. Hostilities temporarily ceased on June 10, when both sides accepted a UN cease-fire, but only hours later, Israel attacked and seized the Syrian heights, where the trouble had started.

Israel's clear-cut military superiority was of slight value, however, in bringing the Arabs to the conference table or in achieving a permanent settlement.

Worldwide support for a tiny country fighting for its life gradually cooled as the Israeli occupation of Arab land assumed a permanent look. Israel unilaterally annexed Arab Jerusalem on June 28. In its determination to preserve its gains until the Arabs agreed to recognize Israel and begin direct negotiations, Israel rejected third-power proposals for mediation. Israel's banking systems, currency, laws, and taxes, even its teachers and textbooks, were introduced in the occupied territories.

Israeli intransigence and Arab bitterness over defeat blocked effective action by emergency sessions of the UN Security Council. An emergency session of the General Assembly met on June 19. In mid-July, the UN sent truce observers led by General Odd Bull of Norway to the Suez Canal area after intermittent artillery duels across the waterway had broken the cease-fire. The General Assembly session closed on July 21 with but one resolution, the censure of Israel, 99-0, with 20 abstentions, for its annexation of Arab Jerusalem.

Other than a tacit agreement between the United States and Russia to keep the conflict localized, the major powers neither displayed cooperation nor produced positive policies that might lead to a settlement. Although Israeli planes attacked the U.S. communications ship *Liberty* during the fighting and President Lyndon B. Johnson declared strict neutrality, the Arabs identified American and Israeli interests as synonymous. France's pro-Arab stand baffled Israel and many European countries but it pleased some of the Arab nations.

The big gains were scored by the Soviet Union. Russia sought to brand Israel as the aggressor and force it to pay indemnities. Soviet warships entered the eastern Mediterranean Sea in force and visited Alexandria, Egypt, even as renewed fighting broke out along the Suez Canal. The most startling evidence of Soviet support for the Arabs was the sinking of the Israeli destroyer *Elath* by a U.A.R. patrol boat using the new Soviet Styx missile. By October, Russia had replaced 80 percent of the U.A.R. military equipment destroyed in the war. The United States, on the other hand, offered a five-point peace plan based on territorial integrity for all states, rights of innocent maritime passage, and an end to the arms race.

War's aftermath. The festering refugee problem worsened after the war as 120,000 refugees fled into Jordan. Israel agreed to allow some to return, but an August cut-off date and Israel's stiff requirements for proof of status limited the returnees to about 12,000. The UN Relief and Rehabilitation Administration continued to administer the refugee program, but anticipated a $4,000,000 deficit.

The Arabs had united briefly against Israel, but their defeat revealed not only their military weakness but also the continuing differences in the Arab world over domestic as well as foreign policy. Algeria, Iraq, Morocco, and Tunisia offered troops, but took no actual part in the war. There were severe anti-Jewish riots in Tripoli and Tunis, and these also turned on U.S. and British property. The Arab summit conference in Khartoum, Sudan, early in August produced no common postwar policy against Israel. In private statements, Nasser and King Hussein I of Jordan expressed willingness to negotiate through a third power even as Algeria's president Houari Boumedienne called for a Muslim holy war of extermination. Nor could the Arabs follow through with their promised oil embargo; a ban on exports to the West would have involved too great a financial sacrifice.

One positive result of the Khartoum conference was a pact between Nasser and King Faisal of Saudi Arabia to settle the civil war in Yemen. Hopes for peace were imperiled, however, after the overthrow of President Abdullah al-Sallal, when fighting began

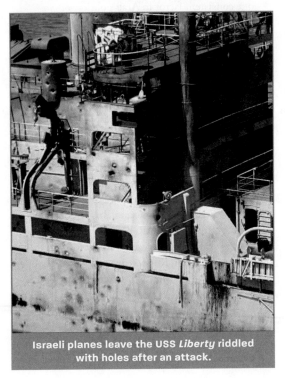

Israeli planes leave the USS *Liberty* riddled with holes after an attack.

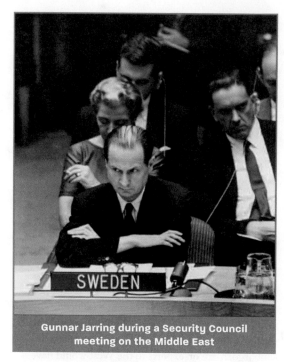

Gunnar Jarring during a Security Council meeting on the Middle East

again between the nationalist groups. Similarly, rival Arab nationalists in Aden, which agreed in September to cease fire and discuss a future government, began fighting again in November when Britain announced that its troops would withdraw by the end of the month. Instability remained the one consistent factor in Arab politics.

Middle East (1970)

A cease-fire in the Middle East proposed by the United States halted spiraling military clashes along Israel's borders in 1970. Israel, Jordan, and the United Arab Republic (U.A.R.) accepted the cease-fire on August 7, easing the threat of a fourth round of all-out Arab-Israeli war. The action also lessened the danger of a Russian-American confrontation that could lead to a third world war.

Russia established a strong position in the very heart of the Middle East. The Soviet naval force in the Mediterranean grew, and Russia continued its military aid to the U.A.R. Some 15,000 Soviet technicians and advisers were serving with the U.A.R. armed forces, and Russian pilots began flying operational missions over Egyptian territory. More serious, in the view of U.S. policymakers, was the installation of Russian SAM-3 missiles at about 62 sites along the Suez Canal and around U.A.R. cities by early September. Although described as defensive in nature, they could be fired to hit Israeli cities.

The cease-fire plan was called the "Rogers plan" for its author, U.S. secretary of state William P. Rogers. It also called for declarations of support by both sides for the United Nations (UN) resolution of November 22, 1967, and for resumption of the suspended peace talks initiated under UN special envoy Gunnar Jarring. Although similar to earlier peace proposals, the Rogers plan was the first direct approach to the three countries most involved, with the tacit admission that a peace settlement imposed by the major powers could not be enforced.

Cease-fire accepted. The U.A.R. and Jordan were the first to accept the cease-fire; Israel's acceptance came after a cabinet crisis that saw the six ministers of the Right-wing Gahal Party withdraw from the government. For the first time in three years, the big guns along the canal fell silent.

Jarring immediately set about transforming the fragile truce into an enduring Arab-Israeli settlement. His difficulties were compounded by complaints of cease-fire violations from both sides. Israel accused the U.A.R. of bringing up additional missiles, and the U.A.R. charged Israel with strengthening the fortifications of the Bar-Lev line. The talks were later broken off, but the cease-fire remained in effect even after its November termination date, indicating that the talking might indeed resume before the shooting. Jarring, however, suspended his mission on October 2 because of the rigid position of each side.

The Palestinian guerrillas. With Arab-Israeli hostilities temporarily halted, the Palestinian guerrillas took center stage. The High Command for Palestine Resistance, representing 11 guerrilla organizations, rejected the Rogers plan, as expected. Thwarted by Israeli vigilance from successful border raids, the guerrillas turned on their hosts in Lebanon and Jordan. The Lebanese refused to bend to the pressure, and an Israeli reprisal raid into south Lebanon, in early September, reduced guerrilla effectiveness there to almost zero.

The guerrillas directed their effort against Jordan. Taking advantage of King Hussein's reluctance to use force against his Palestinian "brothers," they disregarded regulations against carrying firearms in public, collected funds by force, and acted like a state within a state, ignoring even Jordanian law. In April, anti-American demonstrations called by the guerrilla high command forced U.S. deputy assistant secretary of state Joseph J. Sisco to cancel his visit to Jordan.

War in Jordan. The moment of truth came in September, when sporadic fighting began between guerrillas and Jordanian troops. While the guerrillas battled in Jordan, they dramatized their cause internationally with a series of spectacular aerial hijackings. They hijacked three airplanes over Europe on September 6. One, a Pan Am 747, was flown to Beirut, Lebanon, then to Cairo, where it was blown up after the passengers and crew got out. The other two, a Swissair DC-8 and a TWA 707, were landed in the desert in Jordan. Later, a BOAC jet was hijacked and landed at the same desert landing strip, and the guerrillas held about 300 passengers and crew as hostages. The planes were later blown up, and the hostages were eventually released in return for the release by the British and Swiss of Palestinians involved in earlier hijackings.

Hussein, faced with the guerrillas' serious challenge to his authority, dismissed his cabinet, declared martial law on September 16, and ordered General Habes Majali to subdue the guerrillas. Bloody combat followed as the Jordanian Army attempted to crush the guerrillas. In the process, they destroyed much of Amman and caused hundreds of civilian casualties. Emphasis on the internal nature of the conflict and a U.S. warning to Russia, backed by the presence of the Sixth Fleet in the Mediterranean, ensured the absence of any outside intervention.

Arab heads of state, meeting in Cairo, formulated a cease-fire agreement between the Jordanian Army and the guerrillas on September 27.

The cease-fire would be supervised by observers from neutral Arab nations, with the army required to return to its barracks and the guerrillas to their bases. The guerrilla withdrawal began on October 6.

Nasser's death. The Jordanian cease-fire was U.A.R. president Gamal Abdel Nasser's last act of statesmanship. He died suddenly of a heart attack on September 28. A pall of uncertainty hung over the Arab world after the loss of its leader. But the succession to the presidency in the U.A.R. passed without incident. The National Assembly elected Vice President Anwar Sadat to succeed Nasser.

But Nasser's death left no Arab spokesman capable of both uniting the Arabs by force of personality and serving as a relatively moderate Arab leader in international affairs. Even the fragile cease-fire between the Palestinians and the Jordan government was threatened almost immediately by charges and coun02charges of violations.

Arab federation. The U.A.R., Libya, and Sudan moved toward a federal union on November 8 as they coordinated their customs policies; ended all restrictions on travel; and announced a common anti-Israeli military policy. The action emphasized Libya's move away from alignment with the Western Arab states toward the U.A.R. as well as Libya's determination to play a major role in Arab affairs under its new military regime. On November 27, it was announced in Cairo that Syria, too, was joining the alliance.

Positive developments. Obscured in the general atmosphere of crisis in the Middle East were some positive developments. Iraq settled its long-standing dispute with its large Kurdish minority. In return for local autonomy, Kurdish appointments to the cabinet, and government reconstruction of the war-ravaged north, the Kurds agreed to work for national unity. Settlement of the civil war in Yemen healed another source of inter-Arab friction.

A dangerous power vacuum along the Persian Gulf and in the Arabian Peninsula threatened to develop after the withdrawal of British forces in 1971. The states in the Federation of Persian Gulf Emirates, however, made progress toward economic and political modernization.

The Suez Canal remained closed. Without regular maintenance, it was slowly filling with silt. But its international importance had faded sharply. Once critical for the shipment of oil into the Mediterranean, it has been largely replaced by the growth of pipelines throughout the Middle East. And the increasing popularity of supertankers meant that many of the huge ships now in use could not get through, even if the canal were reopened.

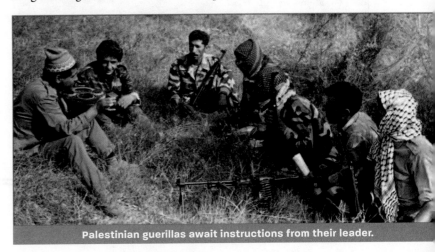

Palestinian guerillas await instructions from their leader.

Despite the canal's loss, U.A.R. hopes for an economic breakthrough to expand production soared when the Aswan High Dam went into full operation in July. The dam cost $1.12 billion, and took 10½ years to build. Questions arose as to the ecological damage the dam might cause, but its value in generating electric power, in reclaiming arid lands, and in controlling the yearly Nile floods remained Nasser's legacy to his people.

Middle East (1973)

The fourth Arab-Israeli war in 26 years broke out with dramatic suddenness on October 6, 1973, abruptly ending three years of relative peace. When a frail cease-fire ended fighting on October 22, the results were inconclusive. Both sides had gained and lost territory.

In contrast to Israel's relatively one-sided victory in the 1967 war, the Arabs this time exacted a heavy toll in Israeli men and equipment. And for the first time, they used their oil supplies as a political weapon against countries that traditionally had supported Israel. As peace talks began in Geneva, Switzerland, in December, Israel was more isolated than ever before.

The attack came simultaneously on two fronts, with Egyptian and Syrian forces striking into territory occupied by Israel since 1967. Egypt crossed the Suez Canal into the Sinai Peninsula southwest of Israel; Syria attacked in the Golan Heights, on the northeast. The attack came on Yom Kippur, the Jews' holiest festival. The feast day delayed mobilization, and Israeli forces could not regain the initiative for several days.

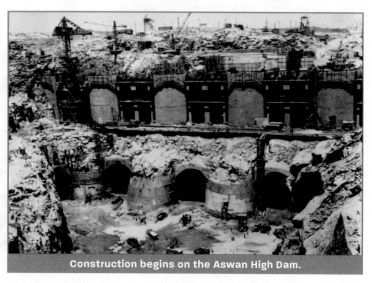

Construction begins on the Aswan High Dam.

Other Arab nations quickly joined Egypt and Syria. Iraq sent ground and air units. Tunisia and Kuwait sent troops to the Sinai. Algerian planes were in action there. Morocco and Jordan sent troops to the Syrian front. Sudan and Saudi Arabia also sent troops. Lebanon opened its entire Israeli border to the Palestinian guerrillas, and some Israeli settlements were shelled. The guerrillas were not a major direct factor, however. An Israeli commando raid on Beirut in April had cut into their leadership.

Quick triumphs. In their initial assault, the Egyptians quickly overran Israel's fortified Bar-Lev line along the east bank of the Suez Canal, and they moved about 8 miles into Sinai. Syrian forces captured Mount Hermon, but an Israeli counterattack drove them back. Supported by heavy air raids, Israeli forces drove to within 25 miles of Damascus. On October 15, Israeli armor crossed to the west bank of the Suez Canal between two Egyptian armies and encircled one of them on October 23.

The cease-fire, proposed by the United Nations (UN) Security Council, was accepted by Egypt and Israel on October 22. It called on the combatants to halt the fighting within 12 hours and hold their positions. On October 25, the Security Council voted to establish a UN Emergency Force—using troops from smaller nations—to ensure the cease-fire. Israel and Egypt finally signed a cease-fire agreement on November 11 in a tent beside a dusty road near Suez city, at the head of the Gulf of Suez. It was only informally accepted by Syria. Iraq and Libya also assailed the cease-fire, and violations became common.

Tolls high. The war was costly to both sides, but particularly to Israel. On November 6, Israeli officials listed casualties at 1,854 killed, about 4,800 wounded, and 450 missing, high in proportion to the nation's population. Arab casualties were estimated at nearly 18,000, plus an estimated 2,000 Syrian civilians killed in Israeli air raids. Equipment losses were enormous on both sides. An estimated 1,800 tanks and more than 200 airplanes were destroyed, but massive Russian and U.S. airlifts to their respective "clients" restored the prewar military balance.

The conflict marked a dramatic change in the balance of political power in the region. The impressive Arab military performance was a key in this shift.

Arab forces fought not only bravely, but skillfully, with sophisticated equipment, attesting to their mastery of Russian technical training. Egyptian surface-to-air missiles, launched from west of the canal, protected advancing Arab armies from Israeli air attacks and took a heavy toll of Israeli tanks. The Egyptians also demonstrated technical competence in using radar to spot approaching Israeli jets, and television cameras to pinpoint the targets before they were shot down by guided rockets.

Psychological lift. The Arabs' ability to meet Israeli forces on equal terms gave them an enormous psychological lift, despite the faulty coordination that eventually let Israel outmaneuver Arab armies. Egypt's acceptance of the cease-fire caused considerable resentment—in Egypt as well as in Syria and other Arab countries. Syria, which had not accepted the formal cease-fire, boycotted the Geneva peace talks. The Iraqi brigades that fought on the northern front went home in a huff.

The restoration of Arab self-respect was accompanied by rare evidence of Arab unity. But King Hussein I of Jordan, though he sent troops to Syria, refused to open a third front against Israel because of the absence of air protection for his army. Some Arab leaders, notably Libya's president Muammar Muhammad al-Qadhaafi, warned that the invasion might eventually lead to the destruction of Arab armies and end any chance of liberating "the sacred soil" of Palestine.

Egypt's role. Developing a viable Arab unity had been largely the work of Egypt's president Anwar el-Sadat. He sent Foreign Minister Hafez Ismail to the United States in February 1973, to seek new peace initiatives. When that trip produced only increased American military aid to Israel, Sadat named himself commander in chief and began quiet preparations for war. His efforts to unite all elements in the Arab cause were helped by a U.S. veto in July of a UN resolution condemning Israel for raids against Palestinian guerrillas in Lebanon and Syria. Sadat took another major step in August when he and King Faisal of Saudi Arabia reached an agreement. Egypt delayed its projected federation with Libya and resumed relations with Jordan. In return, Faisal committed $600 million to aid Egypt after the projected war. He also agreed to coordinate a campaign to reduce Arab oil shipments to the United States and other countries. The Arabs planned to use an oil boycott to pressure these countries to withhold aid from Israel. When relations with Jordan reopened in September, the ring around Israel was complete.

Libyan president Muammar Muhammad al-Qadhaafi

Frail Unity. How long the Arabs would remain united was difficult to estimate. Interpretations among them as to the usefulness of "the oil weapon" varied widely. Enormous internal pressures to resume the war were felt by Sadat and other leaders. But 15 Arab chiefs of state met in Algeria in November and widened the oil embargo to include Portugal, Rhodesia, and South Africa, and they gave conditional approval to "political efforts" for a Middle Eastern peace. Libya and Iraq did not attend.

Initially, Arab oil exports to the United States and Western Europe had been cut by 60 percent, from 1.75 million barrels a day to 1 million. Thereafter, a selective policy was followed. All shipments to the United States and the Netherlands were banned. The reduced supplies to Great Britain and Western European countries continued until Christmas Day, when the Arabs eased restrictions on them. Arab oil provides only 6 percent of U.S. domestic needs, but the ban, along with increasing energy demands, accelerated a U.S. "energy crisis."

Fragile cease-fire. Equal uncertainty clouded efforts to convert the shaky cease-fire into a permanent peace settlement. The November 11 cease-fire signing ceremony underscored the fact that the war had altered forever the structure of Middle Eastern relations. Israeli and Egyptian officers met face to face in a tent beside the hot, dusty Cairo-Suez road to sign a six-point agreement. It was the first direct contact between the Arabs and Israelis since the establishment of Israel. Direct negotiations had been a long-standing Israeli demand; at last the two sides had met. The agreement was negotiated by U.S. secretary of state Henry A. Kissinger with Russian support. It provided for strict observance of the earlier cease-fire, for provisioning of the surrounded Egyptian III Corps, for UN control of all checkpoints, and for an exchange of prisoners. Both sides would also return to the positions they held on October 22.

But, other than the prisoner exchange, the two sides interpreted the agreement's provisions differently. Two weeks of daily meetings failed to produce joint action on the withdrawal lines or even their location. The talks were broken off and renewed fighting became a distinct possibility. Israel also accused Egypt of blockading the Bab el Mandeb strait at the southern entrance to the Red Sea, thus denying the use of an international waterway to shipping bound for the Israeli port of Elat. Egypt charged that Israel encircled the III Corps after the October 22 cease-fire. Seemingly, only the presence of the UN Emergency Force, commanded by Finnish Major General Ensio Siilasvuo, kept them from fighting. Syria, meanwhile, refused to exchange prisoners or even provide a list of the Israeli prisoners it held.

Israeli and Egyptian officials agreed on a cease-fire in November 1973.

Isolated victors. Israel emerged as the war's "victor," in the sense that it had successfully defended its own territory, and taken more, but the Israelis were left more isolated than ever. Britain, France, and other European countries openly criticized Israel for making no meaningful concessions and refusing to withdraw from occupied Arab lands.

By the year's end, some 25 African states had broken diplomatic relations with Israel. They included such long-standing allies as Ethiopia, Gambia, and Togo, recipients of substantial Israeli technical and financial aid. As Israel prepared for national elections on December 31 and entered the peace conference in Geneva, Switzerland, its future status in the Middle East seemed increasingly precarious.

The death on November 20 of former prime minister David Ben-Gurion, 87, architect of Israel's independence, symbolized his country's new loneliness. Internally, Israel began investigations into what some Israelis saw as its military unpreparedness, its inefficient conduct of the war, and its lack of a clear-cut political policy.

And, as 1973 neared its end, terrorists claiming to be "proud Palestinian Arabs" reminded the world again of Middle Eastern volatility. On December 17, they killed 31 persons in a fire bomb attack on a Pan American Airways jet at the Rome airport. They then hijacked another jet and flew to Athens, Greece, where they killed a hostage. They finally surrendered in Kuwait and released 12 hostages. Guerrilla organizations and both Arab and non-Arab political leaders condemned the hijacking.

Middle East (1978)

The search for peace brought President Anwar el-Sadat of Egypt and Prime Minister Menachem Begin of Israel the Nobel Peace Prize in 1978. But peace still lay just beyond their grasp as the year ended. More than a year after Sadat's historic journey to Jerusalem, the two nations still grappled with the details of a peace accord that would end the 30-year state of war between them and perhaps bring stability to the Middle East.

President Jimmy Carter brought Sadat and Begin together at the Camp David presidential retreat in Maryland and kept them there until they fashioned a framework for peace. Carter continued his efforts to close the remaining gap, prodding here, suggesting there, and, above all, keeping the lines of communication open between the two states.

Despite deep Egyptian and Israeli desires for a peace that would permit rapid economic and social development, there were many times during the year when a treaty seemed beyond reach. The initial euphoria generated by Sadat's November 1977 Jerusalem visit and Begin's positive response dissipated quickly in 1978. Sadat abruptly recalled the Egyptian delegation to the Israeli-Egyptian joint Political Committee sessions on January 18, the day after its first meeting. Months of indecisive maneuvering followed, with the United States engaging in shuttle diplomacy in order to keep negotiations going and reconcile divergent viewpoints. The United States "honest broker" image as the only disinterested power acceptable to both Egyptians and Israelis was enhanced in May when the U.S. Senate, by a 54 to 44 vote, approved the Administration proposal to sell jet military aircraft to Saudi Arabia and Egypt as well as to Israel.

A U.S.-Israeli rift became apparent when President Carter declared his support for the legitimate rights of the Palestinian people in a May speech. A subsequent Begin proposal for limited interim autonomy for the West Bank and the Gaza Strip was rejected by Egypt. The Israeli government's hard-line policy on Jewish settlements in the occupied territories, though rooted in domestic political considerations, created a further obstacle to peace. Carter's irritation with Israel's refusal to soften its position was evident on a number of occasions during the year.

In July, Sadat submitted a six-point peace plan to U.S. vice president Walter F. Mondale for transmittal to Israel. The plan called for a transitional five-year period for the West Bank and Gaza during which time Egypt, Jordan, Israel, and the Palestinian people would establish a timetable for Israeli withdrawal, election of Palestinian representatives, United Nations (UN) participation in the transfer of power, and an end to Jewish settlement in the territories.

Camp David. The United States sponsored a secret meeting of the Egyptian and Israeli foreign ministers at Leeds Castle in Great Britain in July, but the talks failed to bridge the gap between the two. The meeting was held under tight security because of threats by Palestinian extremist groups. But the deadlock was finally broken by President Carter. Staking U.S. prestige on the outcome, he invited Sadat and Begin to a closed-door September summit conference at Camp David. After 13 days of grueling negotiations and, reportedly, 23 different drafts, the Israeli and Egyptian leaders agreed on a framework for a permanent peace treaty on September 17. Again peace seemed to be just around the corner; Israelis began signing up for tours to Egypt, and Egyptians danced in the streets when the accords were ratified by the People's Assembly.

The Camp David Accords bound both countries to comply with specific UN resolutions. Israel agreed to return the Sinai Peninsula to Egypt,

The Camp David Accords were pivotal in establishing peace between Egypt and Israel.

including oil fields developed by Israeli technology and two vital airfields. Israel would terminate its administration of the West Bank and Gaza, except in limited areas for security purposes, and would share responsibility for the territories with Egypt, Jordan, and the Palestinian people for a five-year transitional period, after which authority would revert to an autonomous elected Palestinian council. In addition, Egypt and Israel agreed to terminate economic boycotts, to provide mutual protection for citizens with due process of law, and to renounce force to settle disputes. Finally, the Camp David framework would become the basis for a formal peace treaty to be signed within three months.

Unresolved issues. But the accords left certain issues unresolved. The major one was that of linkages between the recovery of Egyptian territory and determination of a just territorial allocation to the Palestinians. Linkage was vital to Egypt. Without it, Egypt stood accused by other Arab nations of signing a separate peace agreement with Israel. For Israel, the future of the West Bank was bound up with Jewish settlements and Biblical "rights," with secure borders, control of Jerusalem, and other matters equally vital to the future of the Jewish nation.

As the three-month deadline for treaty signature came and went, talks were stalled over Egypt's insistence on a specific timetable for granting autonomy to the West Bank and Gaza, and Israel's equally adamant refusal to set a timetable. The peacemaking process still seemed irreversible, but semantic differences were clearly getting in the way.

Other Arab nations. The Egyptian-Israeli negotiating process effectively nullified Arab cooperation against the common enemy. The "Resistance and Confrontation States"—Algeria, Libya, Syria, and Yemen (Aden), plus the Palestine Liberation Organization (PLO)—met in Algeria in February and reiterated their declaration of no compromise or negotiation with Israel. But the front was weakened by the absence of Iraq, though the Iraqi government denounced the Sadat peace initiatives separately.

Reconciliation between the Baathist regimes of Syria and Iraq came in October, mainly because of their common economic problems. But a second summit conference of the confrontation states held in late October in Iraq could produce only a weak condemnation of Egypt. A $1 billion war chest supposedly established to help overthrow Sadat mysteriously turned into an aid package for the hard-pressed Egyptian economy.

Trouble in the Yemen. With Iraq and Syria friends for the moment, the principal Arab conflict involved the two Yemen regimes. On June 24, Command Council Chairman Ahmed al-Ghashmi, head of the moderate-conservative government of Yemen (Sana) was killed by a bomb hidden in the briefcase of a Yemen (Aden) envoy who allegedly was on a mission to discuss plans to merge the two regimes. Sana authorities accused Aden of complicity and complained to the Arab League, which expelled the Marxist Aden regime from membership in the league.

Ghashmi's murder set off a power struggle within the Aden government that ended with the arrest and execution of Presidential Council Chairman Salim Ali Rubayya on June 26. Prime Minister Ali Nasir Muhammad briefly assumed the presidential office after a bloody struggle. On December 27, Abdul Fatah Ismail, secretary-general of the Yemeni Socialist Party, was elected president. Meanwhile, a four-member Presidential Council in Yemen (Sana) elected Colonel Ali Abdallah Salih president, the nation's third head of state in 18 months.

Afghan coup. Another bloody coup d'etat at the eastern end of the region overthrew the government of President Mohammad Daoud in Afghanistan on April 27. Daoud was killed in the fighting. The Afghan coup pitted the educated elite and elements of the Russian-trained army against powerful, conservative tribal families, notably the former royal clan to which Daoud belonged. The new government, headed by Revolutionary Council President and Prime Minister Noor Mohammad Taraki, was described as Communist, but it pledged

democratic reforms, set up a constitutional commission, and approved the formation of political parties. Although Taraki signed a 20-year treaty of friendship and cooperation with Russia on December 5, there were indications that the new Afghanistan government would not become a disruptive force.

Turmoil in Iran. The same could not be said of Iran, where Shah Mohammad Reza Pahlavi faced the sternest test of his authority in 25 years. Religious leaders opposed the shah's economic and social reform programs, and educated Iranians opposed his unwillingness to allow a multiparty political system to develop. But the extent and depth of public resentment was unexpected.

Despite widespread violence throughout the year, the shah seemed to have the situation under control until November. The army remained loyal, so the shah introduced certain reforms designed to satisfy critics. He extended amnesty to political prisoners, and several thousand of his opponents were released from jail. He curtailed the powers of the dreaded Savak, Iran's secret police, and dismissed its director. Other reforms included a code of conduct for the royal family that forbade its members from holding public office. The government began to weed out corruption, and several prominent business and government leaders, including former prime minister Amir Abbas Hoveyda, were arrested on charges of profiteering. But the reforms did not ensure that the shah could keep his throne.

Shah Mohammad Reza Pahlavi

He gave up on civilian government on November 6, and imposed martial law. He replaced Prime Minister Jafar Sharif-Emami, a moderate with ties to the religious leaders, with an all-military cabinet headed by General Gholam Reza Azhari. The new cabinet pledged to restore public security and fight corruption. Four hundred more political prisoners were released, leaving only 300 "hard-core terrorists" behind bars. But neither religious nor student leftist groups were satisfied with the reforms. The oil industry was almost completely shut down by strikes, and this had a devastating effect on the economy. On January 6, 1979, a new civilian prime minister, Shahpour Bakhtiar, took office, and it was clear that the shah was no longer in control of his own destiny or that of his country.

PLO infighting. The PLO also experienced considerable dissension. Its various factions directed more violence against one another than against the vigilant Israelis. The loss of most of their guerrilla bases and equipment when Israel invaded southern Lebanon in March practically eliminated the PLO as a threat to Israeli security.

Palestinian-Arab terrorism turned inward, against its own operatives. Said Hammami, the PLO representative in London and a confidant of PLO leader Yassir Arafat, was murdered on January 4 by an Arab gunman. Palestinian gunmen killed Egyptian editor Youssef el-Sebai, a close friend of Sadat's, in Nicosia, Cyprus, in February, and took PLO members hostage in their escape attempt.

Evidence of even greater disarray in the Palestinian leadership developed in July. The PLO representative in Kuwait was murdered, and several persons, including a French police officer and Iraqi guards, were killed in a shoot-out at the Iraqi Embassy in Paris. Ezzedine Kalak, the chief PLO representative in Paris, was shot by pro-Iraqi Palestinians. At the same time, clashes between Palestinian factions in Lebanon added to the bloody fighting in that strife-ridden country.

Economic problems. Uncertainty over a political settlement had an adverse effect on the Middle East's economic development. Nearly $6 billion in economic projects supported or initiated by the new Arab Economic Unity Council was stalled pending a peace settlement, while economic boycotts of Egypt by the confrontation states also cut down the funding flow within the region. An encouraging development came on November 1 when the European Community (EC, or Common Market) and eight Arab states signed agreements giving the Arab nations associate status and preferred access for their products in EC markets.

Middle East (1982)

Israel's invasion of Lebanon in June 1982 introduced a new and disturbing element into the tangled pattern of conflict in the Middle East. The latest outbreak of violence—the fifth Arab-Israeli war to erupt since Israel gained its independence in 1948—became the fourth ongoing conflict in the region. The government of Morocco continued to battle guerrillas challenging its authority in Western Sahara. The confrontation between Iran and Iraq dragged on. And Afghan resistance groups continued to clash with Soviet occupation forces in that country.

Of the four conflicts, the latest Arab-Israeli fighting probably posed the greatest threat to regional stability. Israeli forces invaded Lebanon on June 6. After a quick military victory, however, Israel found itself bogged down in an occupation criticized abroad and unpopular at home.

Israel's stated purpose in launching the invasion was to clear Palestine Liberation Organization (PLO) units from a 25-mile (40-kilometer) zone north of the Israeli-Lebanon border in order to put Israeli settlements in Galilee out of PLO artillery range. But it became clear that Prime Minister Menachem Begin's government wanted to completely remove the PLO from Lebanon. Israel quickly cleared southern Lebanon of PLO guerrillas. Israeli forces then rolled up the Lebanese coast toward Beirut. Within a week, they had surrounded the Lebanese capital, and all of southern coastal Lebanon was in Israeli hands.

Military efficiency. As a military operation, the invasion, meticulously planned by Israel's defense minister Ariel Sharon and carried out with textbook precision, once again demonstrated Israel's military superiority over its Arab neighbors. Syrian units of the Arab peacekeeping force in Lebanon lost about 400 tanks and armored personnel carriers in intermittent ground battles with Israeli troops, and Israeli planes shot down 86 Soviet-made Syrian jets in aerial dogfights. The Israelis also destroyed all 19 of the Syrian surface-to-air missile sites and batteries in the Al Biqa—or Bekaa—Valley. Deployed in April 1981, the missiles had been a source of tension.

Unfortunately, the quick military victory did not bring Israel a comparable political triumph over the PLO or the long-desired recognition of Israeli independence by the Arab states. Instead, Israel found itself almost universally condemned for the invasion.

Pressure from the United States, among other factors, deterred Israeli forces from attacking West Beirut, the location of PLO headquarters, while U.S. special envoy Philip C. Habib worked out a plan for the evacuation of PLO units from the beleaguered city in August. Most of the 15,000 PLO guerrillas trapped in West Beirut were evacuated to Syria, with smaller contingents going to Tunisia, Algeria, Jordan, Sudan, and North and South Yemen. Except for PLO leader Yasir Arafat, who established temporary headquarters in Tunis, Tunisia, most of the top PLO leaders also went to Syria.

PLO leader Yasir Arafat set up headquarters in Tunisia.

Palestinian massacre. On September 15, hours after the assassination of Lebanese president-elect Bashir Gemayel, the Israelis moved into West Beirut and stayed there, despite angry protests by the United States. International criticism of Israel reached a peak several days later, when Israeli troops allowed Lebanese Christian militiamen to enter the Sabra and Shatila refugee camps in West Beirut, ostensibly to search for PLO guerrillas hiding there. In a still-unexplained sequence of events, the militiamen massacred hundreds of Palestinian civilians.

After a public outcry and the resignations of several government ministers and high-ranking army officers, the Begin government on September 28 reluctantly approved a commission of inquiry into alleged Israeli involvement in the massacre. At issue, basically, was whether Israeli officials knew the massacre was taking place and did nothing to prevent it. On December 5, the commission announced that it had found no evidence of involvement in the massacre by one Lebanese Christian militia, that commanded by Major Saad Haddad, a close ally of Israel.

Many Israelis felt that the Begin-Sharon policies in Lebanon were undermining the moral foundation of the Jewish state. And a growing number of Jews abroad questioned what they viewed as the Begin government's stubbornness on the long-term issue of Palestinian rights and its insistence on a military solution to the question of relations with Arab states.

U.S. mediation. With the Soviet Union largely discredited in the Middle East for a variety of reasons, the United States assumed the major peacekeeping role in Lebanon. In late August, about 800 U.S. Marines, along with French and Italian troops, landed in Beirut to act as a multinational peacekeeping force in the war-ravaged city and supervise the PLO evacuation. Although the troops left on September 10, 4,500 soldiers from the three countries returned in late September, after the massacre of Palestinian refugees. United States paratroopers were also assigned to another multinational force set up to monitor the Egyptian-Israeli border in the Sinai Peninsula after Israel's withdrawal on April 25.

On September 1, President Ronald Reagan announced a Middle East peace plan that called for the establishment of a Palestinian state federated with Jordan. The next day, the Israeli cabinet rejected the plan, insisting that a Palestinian state "could create a serious threat to Israel's security."

Arab peace proposal. A second plan for a Palestinian-Israeli settlement was announced at the 12th Arab Summit conference, held in Fez, Morocco, from September 6 to 9. Attended by all Arab states except Libya and Egypt, the conference ended with a declaration of principles that was essentially a reworking of the plan proposed by Saudi Arabia in November 1981.

The declaration called on Israel to withdraw from all Arab territories occupied in the 1967 Arab-Israeli war, which included the West Bank, Gaza Strip, and Golan Heights. Under the plan, after a brief transition period under United Nations control, the West Bank and Gaza Strip would become an independent Palestinian state under PLO leadership with East Jerusalem as its capital. The adoption of the proposal was seen as a victory by moderate pro-Western Arab states over Arab hard-liners. On September 10, Israel rejected the proposal.

King Hassan II of Morocco led an Arab delegation to Washington, D.C., in October to explain the Arab position, indicating Arab willingness to recognize Israel if these conditions were met. For his part, Arafat stated in early November that he was ready to consider a Palestinian state federated with Jordan. On November 26, however, the PLO's Central Council, a 60-member consultative group, denounced Reagan's September 1 proposal. The council said the plan did not "satisfy the inalienable national rights of our people" because it did not call for an independent Palestinian state under PLO leadership.

Israeli settlements. One of the main sticking points between Israel and the United States and Arabs was the issue of continued Jewish settlements on

the West Bank. The Reagan plan called for a freeze on further settlements, while the Fez declaration demanded that Israel dismantle existing settlements in the area. Reacting to the Reagan proposal, the Israeli Knesset (parliament) voted 56 to 50 on September 5 to reject the U.S. plan as a basis for peace negotiations. The government then allocated $18.5 million for three new West Bank settlements and announced plans for seven others. The Reagan Administration strongly condemned this move.

In early November, Israeli settlers began reconstructing the old Jewish quarter of Hebron, one of the four cities considered Jewish "holy towns" that have been inhabited exclusively by Arabs since Jews living there fled after Arab riots in the late 1920s. Israel also revived a law still on the books from the days of the Ottoman Empire, which ended in 1922. The law allows the government to seize all vacant lands, in this case about 65 percent of the land on the West Bank. The lands confiscated under the law were turned over to private contractors to develop housing subdivisions at building costs one-third below comparable

housing in Jerusalem and other Israeli towns. The resulting housing boom could make the settlement question academic even if Begin bowed to Arab and U.S. wishes.

The Iran-Iraq war, though overshadowed by the Lebanese crisis, continued to threaten regional stability. Iranian offensives during the spring recaptured most of the territory lost to Iraq in the early days of the war, which began in 1980. Later counterattacks brought Iranian forces up to its border with Iraq, and in July, the Iranians stormed across. Iraqi tactics of bulldozing such Iranian border towns as Qasr-e Shirin and Musian inflamed Iranian hatred of the Iraqis.

For the Iranians, the war became a Shiite crusade against the Sunni Iraqis, the majority sect in Islam to which the rulers of Iraq belong. Tens of thousands of Iranian *baseejis*—teenage volunteers—died in human wave attacks against Iraqi positions. Iran rejected all efforts at mediation by outside powers and set reparations and the ouster of Iraq's President Saddam Hussein as its price for peace.

Iran's success sent shudders through the oil-producing Arab states along the Persian Gulf. They feared uprisings of their own large Shiite minorities. In November, the Gulf Cooperation Council, formed in May 1981 by Saudi Arabia, Bahrain, Kuwait, Oman, Qatar, and the United Arab Emirates, agreed on a defense plan backed by the U.S. Rapid Deployment Force based in Oman.

Afghan impasse. The war between Afghan *mujahedeen* (fighters for the faith) and Soviet

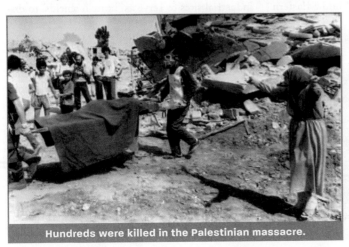
Hundreds were killed in the Palestinian massacre.

occupation forces in Afghanistan ground on. Soviet troops and their Afghan allies were unable to gain the upper hand against the mujahedeen despite superiority in arms and personnel and a policy of massive reprisals—including, reportedly, the use of chemical agents and crop defoliants—against villages suspected of aiding the rebels.

Moroccan morass. The fighting between the government of Morocco and the Polisario Front guerrilla group in Western Sahara created friction within the Organization of African Unity (OAU). In February, the OAU admitted the Polisario, backed by Libya and Algeria, to membership as the Sahara Arab Democratic Republic. Hassan of Morocco denounced the action as illegal and led a walkout by 19 OAU members. Although the king had agreed in June 1981 to hold a referendum in the territory under OAU supervision and to abide by its results, he insisted that the majority of Western Saharans favored Moroccan rule. With Moroccan forces firmly in control of the settled areas of the territory and the Polisario controlling the open desert, outside mediation seemed the only hope for a solution.

Other developments. Although peace seemed the exception rather than the rule in the Middle East during 1982, there were some encouraging developments. Saudi Arabia changed kings without incident in June when Crown Prince Fahd succeeded to the throne after the death of his half brother King Khalid. Voters in Turkey on November 7 approved a new Constitution and elected military leader General Kenan Evren to a seven-year term as head of state.

And also in November, Lebanon's new president, Amin Gemayel, was granted power to rule by decree for six months. Like other Middle Eastern

leaders before him who were brought to power by the unexpected death of a predecessor, Gemayel had a rare opportunity to turn tragedy into triumph for his country.

Middle East (1990)

The Middle East once again became the focus of an international crisis when Iraqi forces invaded Kuwait on August 2, 1990. Iraq's president Saddam Hussein ordered the attack on Kuwait after negotiations between the two countries over oil production quotas and other issues broke down. United States president George Bush quickly forged an American-led international coalition that condemned Iraq and sent a military force to Saudi Arabia to deter an Iraqi attack on that country. On January 17, 1991, the multinational force launched an air strike against military targets in Iraq and Kuwait.

The United Nations (UN) Security Council had passed 12 resolutions, each intended to increase pressure on Iraq to withdraw from Kuwait. The second resolution, passed on August 6, 1990, imposed an economic blockade on Iraq that effectively halted oil shipments from that country and Kuwait.

By November, Bush had sent some 230,000 U.S. troops to Saudi Arabia. European countries contributed from 20,000 to 30,000 ground troops, as well as air and naval forces. A similar number of troops was sent by Arab states, chiefly Egypt and Syria.

Hussein responded to the blockade and threat of force by increasing his forces in Kuwait and making hostages of the estimated 9,000 North Americans, Europeans, and Australians in Iraq and Kuwait. Many were moved to strategic military or industrial sites to serve as "human shields" to discourage U.S. attacks.

The crisis escalated in early November when Bush announced that the United States would significantly boost its troop strength in Saudi Arabia. By January 1991, U.S. forces numbered about 430,000. The buildup changed the multinational military coalition from a defensive force to a force capable of offensive action. On November 29, 1990, the Security Council passed a resolution authorizing the use of military force to eject Iraqi troops from Kuwait if they failed to withdraw by January 15, 1991.

On November 30, 1990, Bush acknowledged domestic and foreign anxieties about the possibility

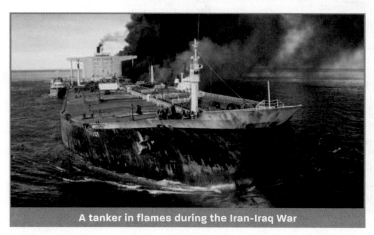
A tanker in flames during the Iran-Iraq War

of war in the Persian Gulf by unexpectedly offering to send Secretary of State James A. Baker III to Iraq and to receive Iraq's Foreign Minister Tariq Aziz. Bush said he wanted to make sure Hussein understood that the U.S.-led coalition would resort to military force, if necessary, to eject Iraqi troops from Kuwait. Although Hussein accepted Bush's offer, the diplomatic exchange did not take place because of a dispute over dates. A meeting between Baker and Aziz on January 9, 1991, in Geneva, Switzerland, failed to produce a peaceful solution to the crisis.

By December 1990, nearly all Arab countries favored an Arab solution to the crisis. Only Saudi Arabia rejected a peace initiative proposed by Algeria's President Chadli Bendjedid. Syria and Egypt further stated that they would not participate in any offensive actions against Iraq.

Hostages freed. On December 6, Hussein announced that all hostages in Iraq and Kuwait were free to leave. Some analysts speculated that Hussein may have hoped this gesture would weaken the coalition's resolve to use force and deepen the American public's concern that the United States would be drawn into a lengthy war. The last of the foreigners wishing to leave Iraq departed on December 11.

Economic effects. The Persian Gulf crisis widened the gap between rich and poor states in the Middle East. The economic blockade against Iraq, a major energy exporter, dealt a severe blow to a number of countries in the region already reeling from rising foreign debt, inflation, and unemployment. Jordan, for example, had derived more than 50 percent of its *gross national product* (the value of all goods and services produced) from trade with Iraq, which had supplied 80 percent of Jordan's energy needs. Turkey lost 60 percent of its energy supplies and the $5 million per day it had earned transshipping Iraqi crude oil across its territory.

Countries that had depended heavily on Iraqi oil were forced to buy oil on the world market at higher prices. Some countries, such as the Philippines, India, and Pakistan, also lost an important source of income—money sent home by citizens working in Iraq and Kuwait, who fled after the invasion. Before Iraq invaded Kuwait, about 1½ million foreign citizens had been working in those two countries.

Oil-rich Arab countries, meanwhile, reaped a bonanza from increased petroleum production to help meet world energy demands and soaring energy prices. Saudi Arabia, for example, was

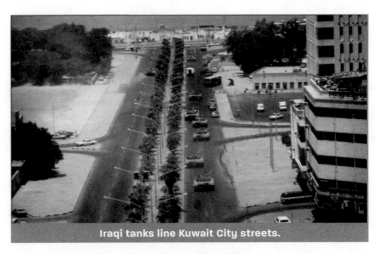

Iraqi tanks line Kuwait City streets.

expected to earn from $80 billion to $100 billion in oil revenues in 1990, nearly double its oil income in 1989.

Political effects. The Persian Gulf crisis exposed growing political tensions within the Arab world that Arab leaders had downplayed publicly. Before the invasion, Arab leaders had privately expressed concerns that differences in political systems, population, wealth, and resources were threatening Arab unity. Arab leaders feared that these differences could hinder regional economic development, reduce the diplomatic effectiveness of the Arab bloc, and even lead to increased conflict among Arab countries.

Although a majority of states in the Arab League backed a resolution condemning Iraq for the invasion, the voting pattern highlighted the members' differences. Libya and the Palestine Liberation Organization (PLO) voted against the resolution. Jordan, Sudan, and Mauritania voted against Iraq, but with reservations. Algeria and Yemen abstained. Tunisia refused to even attend the meeting at which the vote was held.

Although most Arabs initially disapproved of the invasion, many became increasingly resentful of the presence of the American-led military forces in the Middle East. The deployment of foreign troops in Saudi Arabia—which controls Mecca and Medina, Islam's most sacred sites—offended many Muslims. The presence of the multinational force was also an unpleasant reminder of the period in the early 1900s when Great Britain and France had controlled much of the Middle East.

In addition, Saddam Hussein won popular Arab support by demanding that any sanctions imposed on him because of his move into Kuwait also be

Antiaircraft guns firing on Baghdad at night

applied to Israel for having occupied the West Bank and Gaza Strip after the 1967 Six-Day War. He also insisted on a link between any solution to the Persian Gulf crisis and the Palestinian problem.

Israeli dilemmas. Israel faced serious challenges in 1990 in both domestic and foreign relations. Government policies encouraging large-scale Jewish immigration to Israel and the growth of Jewish settlements in the Israeli-occupied West Bank and Gaza Strip led to a heated debate within Israel, to strained relations with the U.S. government, and to increasing Arab violence. After Israeli police killed at least 17 Palestinians on October 8 in a confrontation in Jerusalem on what is known to Jews as the Temple Mount, Israel found itself in the middle of a UN debate over its treatment of the Palestinians.

The rift between Israel and the United States widened when the United States backed three UN resolutions critical of Israel. The United States voted on October 12 to censure Israel for using excessive force against the Palestinians on the Temple Mount. On October 24, the United States supported a resolution that deplored Israel's refusal to cooperate with a UN commission assigned to investigate the incident. On December 20, the United States voted for a resolution that called the West Bank and the Gaza Strip "Palestinian territories" and criticized Israel for planning to deport four Palestinians.

The United States also declined Israel's offer of military support for the multinational force in Saudi Arabia. Israeli officials complained bitterly that although Israel was the most reliable U.S. ally in the Middle East, the United States was ignoring its concerns in an attempt to maintain Arab support for the action against Iraq.

Violence of the intifada. The Palestinian *intifada* (uprising) in the occupied territories marked its third anniversary on December 9. In early 1990, the conflict continued at a simmer, chiefly because of hopes that ongoing talks between the United States and the PLO would produce a plan for Israeli-Palestinian negotiations. The violence escalated significantly after the United States broke off the talks on June 20 because the PLO had failed to condemn a foiled speedboat attack on Israel in May by a radical faction of the PLO.

The upsurge in violence was also fueled by Palestinian opposition to Jewish immigration and by increasing acts of violence against Palestinians by Jewish extremists. In addition, the uprising gained increased momentum from Saddam Hussein's demand that the Palestinian problem be addressed in any diplomatic negotiations on the Persian Gulf crisis.

By year-end, at least 777 Palestinians and 54 Israelis had been killed in the intifada. At least 155 Palestinians were killed by other Palestinians for allegedly collaborating with the Israelis.

After the Temple Mount killings, intifada leaders called on Palestinians to "escalate the struggle by any means possible." In response, Palestinians acting alone or in twos began attacking civilians in Israel and the occupied territories. By year-end, at least 8 Israelis had been stabbed to death and about 12 more wounded in knife attacks.

In an attempt to control the violence, Israeli authorities sealed off the West Bank and Gaza Strip for several days in late October, preventing many Palestinians from traveling to their jobs in Israel. Thousands of Palestinians lost their jobs because of new government restrictions on Arab workers and a campaign by some Jewish groups to pressure Israeli employers to replace Palestinian workers with Soviet immigrants.

Human rights. The human-rights record in the Middle East in 1990 remained bad. Many abuses resulted from strife between ethnic or religious groups and from government repression of groups demanding either more rights or independence.

The government of Sudan, which is dominated by Muslims from the northern part of the country, continued to wage a costly war against southern Sudanese, mainly blacks who practice Christianity or local religions. In Egypt, Muslim fundamentalists launched increasingly violent attacks on members of

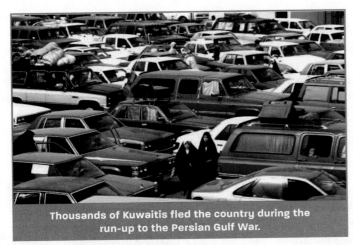

Thousands of Kuwaitis fled the country during the run-up to the Persian Gulf War.

the Coptic Orthodox Church. In addition, the governments of Iraq and Turkey instituted harsh measures against their Kurdish minorities in response to stepped-up activity by Kurdish guerrilla groups. Human-rights advocates also condemned beheadings in Saudi Arabia and public hangings in Iran.

In several notable incidents in 1990, women in the Middle East demanded more rights and greater legal protection. In November, about 50 Saudi women drove automobiles through Riyadh, Saudi Arabia's capital, to protest a traditional ban on driving by women. In Iran, amid growing dissatisfaction with Islamic restrictions, there were increased reports of women being publicly beaten for failing to wear a veil that covered all but the face.

Israel was cited by numerous human-rights groups in 1990 for abuses against Palestinian detainees, the harassment of political activists, and the use of excessive force against demonstrators. The Swedish branch of the Save the Children organization reported in May that many Palestinian children had been killed or injured by Israeli forces.

Calls for democracy. During 1990, there were growing demands for democracy in Arab countries. Some of the loudest demands came from Kuwaitis, who criticized the government's censorship of the press and demanded the reestablishment of parliament, which had been dissolved in 1986. Kuwait's pro-democracy movement was dealt a serious blow in mid-May when 12 leaders of the movement were arrested.

Most Arab leaders ignored demands for more representative government. Some leaders argued that liberalization would not result in multiparty systems but in a victory for Islamic conservatives, who have become increasingly powerful since the

1970s. Indeed, in elections held in Jordan in 1989 and in Algeria in 1990, Islamic fundamentalist candidates won a large number of parliamentary seats.

The Persian Gulf crisis, however, spurred democratic trends in some countries. In early November, King Fahd bin Abd al-Aziz Al-Saud of Saudi Arabia announced his intention to establish a consultative assembly. Sultan Qaboos bin Said of Oman also announced in November his aim of widening representation in that country's Consultative Assembly, whose appointed members act in an advisory role.

Population bomb. Explosive birth rates outstripped economic gains in many Middle Eastern countries in 1990. This increase, with the growing influx of people to urban areas, intensified the already serious problems plaguing the region's large cities.

Hard-pressed Middle Eastern governments were increasingly unable to supply their people with such basic services as housing, education, and medical care. Many governments were also forced to increase spending on food imports.

Water problems. The Middle East possesses two-thirds of the world's proven oil reserves, but water is scarce. In many countries, chronic water shortages became increasingly severe in 1990. Negotiations to resolve disputes over water resources—such as the Euphrates River, on which Turkey, Syria, and Iraq depend—made little progress.

Middle East (1995)

The Arab-Israeli peace process sustained a tragic blow on November 4, 1995, when a Jewish extremist hoping to halt the process assassinated Israeli Prime Minister Yitzhak Rabin at a rally in Tel Aviv, Israel. The act shook the Israeli nation to its core and showed that Jews as well as Arabs were deeply polarized about peace. But Israeli Foreign Minister Shimon Peres, who assumed the post of prime minister, vowed that he would continue along the road toward peace upon which Rabin had embarked.

The presence at Rabin's funeral in Jerusalem of Jordan's King Hussein I and Egypt's President Hosni Mubarak, who both eulogized the slain Israeli leader, showed how far peace had progressed in only two years. It was their first trip to Jerusalem since the Arab-Israeli Six-Day War (1967). Leaders and emissaries from 80 countries, including United States President Bill Clinton, also came to pay homage and show solidarity for the peace process. Yasir Arafat, chairman of the Palestine Liberation Organization (PLO), made his own historic trip to Israel to pay condolences to Rabin's widow, Leah. She told him that he had been her husband's "partner" in peace.

Peace. Rabin and Arafat, who stunned the world in 1993 when they agreed to pursue peace, signed perhaps an even more significant peace accord on September 28, 1995, in Washington, D.C. The 460-page document outlined the second phase of the move toward Palestinian self-government. It provided a blueprint for the withdrawal of Israeli troops from more than 450 towns and 7 cities in the Israeli-occupied West Bank by late March 1996. The West Bank is an area that Israel captured from Jordan in the 1967 war. Palestinian police were to take over the duties of the Israeli troops, except for within Jewish settlements. Although Israel recognized Hebron as a Palestinian city, some Israeli troops were to remain there to protect a Jewish enclave considered by many to be the spiritual heart of right wing Jewish extremists. The Palestinians and Israelis also agreed to cooperate against terrorism, drug smuggling, and crime. Israel also said it would gradually release some 5,000 jailed Palestinians, and in early October it set 900 free.

The 1995 Israeli withdrawal, which began in October, set the stage for January 1996 elections of a president and an 82-member Palestinian Council, who were to gradually assume legislative and executive powers over the 1.3 million West Bank Palestinians. In addition to the right to establish courts, the council was to have jurisdiction over such matters as health, electricity, sewage, zoning, and taxation.

Unsettled issues. By May 1996, assuming no disruptions of the peace process, Israel and the Palestinians were to begin discussing some of their most difficult unresolved issues. These issues included final borders and the sharing of water and other resources. Yet to be decided was whether the Palestinian self-rule authority would lead to the founding of an independent state. Also, the future status of the Jewish settlements in the West Bank, where about 110,000 Jewish people lived, remained to be decided. The question of whether and how many Palestinian refugees who left the West Bank and Gaza Strip before 1967 would be allowed to return also remained. Many of those Arabs had since settled in neighboring countries.

The city of Jerusalem remained one of the most sensitive unresolved issues that both sides agreed to discuss. The Palestinians have claimed East Jerusalem, which Israel captured from Jordan in the 1967 war, as their capital. Israel also called Jerusalem its capital and insisted the city would not be divided.

The United States added to the dilemma on October 24, 1995, when Congress overwhelmingly voted to move the American embassy in Israel from Tel Aviv to Jerusalem by May 31, 1999. Israel welcomed the idea, but Arab leaders condemned the acknowledgement of Jerusalem as Israel's capital and accused the United States of forfeiting its role as a neutral peacemaker. American allies, such as the United Kingdom, France, and Germany, said they would not move their embassies to Jerusalem. The congressional bill, however, included a face-saving option for delaying the move indefinitely.

Land seizure. On May 22, 1995, Rabin was forced to back down from a plan to confiscate 135 acres (55 hectares) of mostly Arab-owned land in disputed East Jerusalem. The potential seizure of land, to be used for Jewish housing, prompted a storm of international protest that threatened to derail the peace process and bring down Rabin's government. On May 17, Oman had introduced a resolution to the United Nation Security Council to condemn Israel for the plan. The United States was the only nation that vetoed the resolution, embittering Arabs who accused the United States of favoring Israel.

Leaders from around the globe attended Prime Minister Rabin's funeral.

The Palestinian people showed greater optimism in 1995 about prospects for peace and expressed more confidence in Arafat's leadership. Polls showed that popular support for Hamas (Islamic Resistance Movement), which uses violence to pursue its goal of replacing Israel with an Islamic Palestinian state, had dropped to 11 percent in 1995 from 40 percent in 1993. Hamas suicide bombings against Israeli targets in 1995 had created a serious problem for Palestinians who depended upon employment in Israel. Their access to Israel and work had been restricted by Israeli officials due to the bombings.

The Palestinians also enjoyed growing freedom in 1995. The departure of Israeli troops in October ended nearly three decades of occupation. Arafat also lifted curfews in 1995 and moved elections for the Palestinian Council forward from March 1996 to January. Economic improvements, including a construction boom, also added to Palestinian optimism.

Arafat, bolstered by the mood shift, detained a number of Hamas leaders during 1995 and ordered Islamic prayer leaders to submit their sermons to be censored for inflammatory rhetoric. Arafat aimed to split militant Hamas members from more moderate ones who could be persuaded to support the peace. He also offered to release jailed Hamas members in return for a commitment to cease their attacks against Israel and accept the leadership of the Palestine Authority, which he headed. By October, some Hamas members were reported to be considering running for the council elections.

Another sign of the changing mood of Palestinians occurred in early November when Israel hinted that it might have been responsible for the assassination of a Muslim extremist leader, Fathi Shiqaqi, in Malta on October 26. Although Muslim militants vowed revenge, most Arabs paid it little attention.

Palestinians received news of Rabin's death with mixed emotions. While few mourned, many feared that Peres, who lacked Rabin's credentials, would be unable to deliver further concessions for peace, which they had begun to value.

Jewish militants loomed in 1995 as a potentially greater threat to the peace process than Arab militants, as the assassination of Rabin painfully pointed out. The confessed murderer, Yigal Amir, 25, claimed he was carrying out God's will and Jewish religious law in killing Rabin. This drew praise from some right-wing Jewish extremists who had vowed to end the peace process. On December 6, officials charged Amir with murder and charged his brother and a friend with conspiring to commit the murder.

Most Israelis expressed revulsion about the murder and the bitter anti-Rabin campaign by right-wing extremists that seemed to have led to it. Israeli moderates had tolerated the threatening talk prior to Rabin's murder, which led to national soul-searching when he died. This bolstered support for Peres, but many feared that both the peace process and the murder would polarize the nation further.

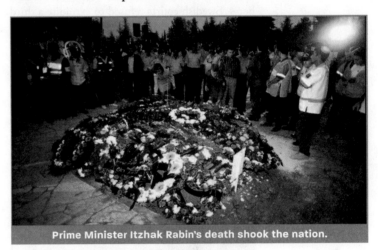
Prime Minister Itzhak Rabin's death shook the nation.

Economic summit. The second Middle Eastern economic summit was held in Amman, Jordan, in late October. The first summit had been in Casablanca, Morocco, in 1994. The three-day affair, which drew representatives from more than 60 countries, was intended to improve trade and investment in the region, following the success of the Arab-Israeli peace process. Many obstacles to economic integration still remained, but the conference was an opportunity for Israel, the Arab nations, and others to make contacts.

Fundamentalist violence in Europe. On February 9, 1995, ambassadors to the North Atlantic Treaty Organization (NATO), a military alliance of Western nations, announced that NATO would seek talks with Egypt, Israel, Mauritania, Morocco, and Tunisia on the threat posed by Muslim extremism. The ambassadors said that Muslim violence posed a serious threat to European and Western security.

Although some NATO members, as well as other nations, criticized the announcement as inflammatory, violence in Europe during 1995 seemed to support NATO's call for action. Between July 25 and October 17, eight bombs killed 7 people and wounded more than 170 in France. The Algerian Armed Islamic Group (GIA) claimed responsibility for these acts. The GIA accused France of supporting Algeria's military-backed government, which had been waging a bloody civil war since 1992 against militants who wanted to establish an Islamic government in Algeria. French officials arrested an Algerian suspected in the bombings on November 1 and sought to extradite another young Algerian detained by the British on November 4. Swedish courts refused to extradite a third Algerian suspect to France for lack of evidence. In Germany, at least 11 Algerians received jail sentences in 1995 for charges that included hostage taking and arson. Most of the suspects had unsuccessfully sought political asylum in Germany.

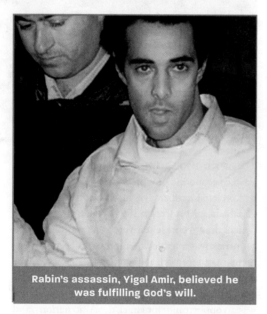

Rabin's assassin, Yigal Amir, believed he was fulfilling God's will.

Americans and terrorism. On January 24, President Clinton froze the American financial assets of 12 Middle Eastern groups and 18 individuals said to support terrorism. The frozen assets included funds of some charitable organizations believed to be fronts for funneling money to Middle Eastern terrorist groups. Not only Muslim extremist groups, such as Hamas and Hezbollah (Party of God), but also the Jewish extremist groups of Kach and Kahane Chai were affected. United States officials also said that they would increase investigations of terrorist suspects and speed their deportation.

These actions were intended to aid the Arab-Israeli peace process and avert terrorist incidents in the United States.

On October 1, a federal court in New York City found Egyptian Sheik Omar Abdel Rahman and nine other Muslims guilty of conspiring to commit murders and to bomb New York City landmarks and a U.S. military installation. The conspirators allegedly wanted to force the United States to help establish a fundamentalist Islamic government in Egypt. They also wanted an end to American support of Israel and the Arab-Israeli peace process.

Bahrain. The rise of Muslim extremism caused increasing concern in 1995 among Arab nations in the Persian Gulf. Some of the most serious incidents occurred in Bahrain, where demonstrations close to the capital, Manama, resulted in the death of at least 10 civilians and 3 policemen in early 1995. By late in the year, many people had been sentenced or detained for political dissent.

Argentine bombing. Confusion arose in 1995 about who was responsible for a 1994 bombing that killed up to 100 people at a Jewish center in Buenos Aires. Iran had been blamed for the bombing. However, in November 1995, a former Argentine army sergeant turned himself in to police who were investigating the case. Speculation arose that anti-Semitic members of Argentina's police and security forces may have orchestrated the bombing.

By early December 1995, a dozen soldiers and civilians were being held for questioning about the bombing. A bomb blast in 1992 that killed about 30 people at the Israeli embassy in Buenos Aires also remained unsolved.

Qatar. Qatar's crown prince, Hamad bin Khalifa Al Thani, peacefully ousted his father, Khalifa bin Hamad Al Thani, to become the new emir on June 27. The new leader, who had essentially run the country since 1992, gained quick recognition by the international community.

Foreign workers. The plight of foreign workers in Persian Gulf nations continued to be a focus of international concern in 1995. The workers, many of whom had replaced Palestinians and other Arabs who returned home during the Persian Gulf War (1991), complained of physical abuse and garnished wages. On September 16, 1995, a 16-year-old Filipino maid was sentenced to death in the United Arab Emirates for killing her employer, whom she said had raped her. After much international criticism, the girl's sentence was reduced to

100 lashes, a year in jail, and deportation. In Kuwait, where two Arab women beat their foreign maids to death in 1995, an investigation began into the treatment of foreign workers.

The Roman Catholic Church announced on June 22 that it was establishing a Joint Liaison Committee to promote understanding between Christians and Muslims.

Middle East (2001)

Two unprecedented crises confronted the Middle East in 2001. On September 11, Islamic militants attacked the United States in the deadliest act of terrorism in U.S. history, killing thousands of people. United States President George W. Bush subsequently challenged Arab and other Muslim nations to join a U.S.-led global "war on terrorism" or risk isolation. As this crisis unfolded throughout the rest of the year, attacks by Palestinian extremists against Israelis provoked a major Israeli military assault against Palestinian targets, raising the specter of war in the Middle East.

War on terrorism. In a coordinated series of attacks on September 11, terrorists hijacked four civilian airliners, crashing two of them into the World Trade Center towers in New York City and one into the Pentagon Building outside Washington, D.C. A fourth hijacked plane crashed in a field in Pennsylvania. U.S. investigators identified Osama bin Laden, the Saudi-born leader of the Islamic terrorist network al-Qaida ("The Base" in Arabic), as the chief suspect in the attacks.

On October 7, the United States and the United Kingdom, with widespread international backing, launched a massive military assault against Afghanistan's ruling Taliban, which had given bin Laden asylum (refuge) in 1996 after he was expelled from Sudan. The Taliban had refused demands by the United States and the United Nations (UN) to turn over bin Laden for trial. President Bush vowed in September 2001 to not only wage war against terrorists but against any nation that harbored terrorists.

Arab and Islamic concerns. Most Arab and Islamic leaders condemned the September 11, 2001, terrorist attacks. However, they feared that many Muslims in the Middle East viewed the U.S.-led antiterrorism campaign as a war against Islam and that this view would fuel anti-Americanism and Islamic extremism. The leaders urged the United States to distinguish between the terrorists

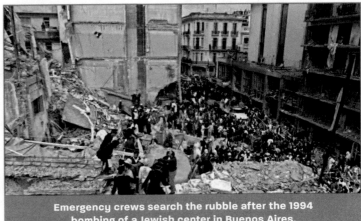

Emergency crews search the rubble after the 1994 bombing of a Jewish center in Buenos Aires.

responsible for the September 11 attacks and organizations such as Hamas, a militant Palestinian group, and Hezbollah, an Islamic group credited with forcing Israeli troops out of Lebanon in 2000. Many Arabs viewed these groups as "freedom fighters" against Israel.

Despite these concerns, the U.S. State Department included Hamas and Hezbollah on a list of organizations suspected of supporting terrorism. U.S. officials warned countries and financial institutions to freeze the assets of groups on the list or face retaliatory action against their own assets in the United States.

Sympathy for bin Laden. Arab and Islamic leaders also feared that the U.S. military attacks against Afghanistan would foster greater sympathy for bin Laden, whose message had attracted a growing number of disaffected Middle Easterners since the early 1990s. Bin Laden's message was threefold. He opposed the Arab-Israeli peace process; he condemned the presence of U.S. military troops in Saudi Arabia, where Islam's holiest sites are located; and he condemned UN sanctions that were imposed against Iraq after Iraq's 1990 invasion of Kuwait. Muslims of many nationalities agreed with bin Laden's ideas though not necessarily with his methods.

Detention of Arabs. Arab-American and civil rights organizations objected to the detention by U.S. authorities of hundreds of people, many believed to be Arabs, for questioning after September 11, 2001. A coalition of these organizations sued the U.S. Department of Justice in December to force the department to release more information on the detainees. Law enforcement authorities in Europe, Latin America, and elsewhere also arrested many

Arabs and Muslims suspected of belonging to al-Qaida or other terrorist organizations.

U.S. educational institutions reported that some of their Middle Eastern students left the United States in fear of anti-Arab and anti-Muslim prejudice. President Bush had repeatedly warned Americans against such prejudice.

Indictment. In December, the U.S. Department of Justice announced the first U.S. indictment in connection with the September 11 terrorist attacks. Federal prosecutors alleged that Zacarias Moussaoui, a French citizen of Moroccan descent who had been detained in the United States on immigration violations since August, was an active participant in the conspiracy to attack the World Trade Center and Pentagon Building.

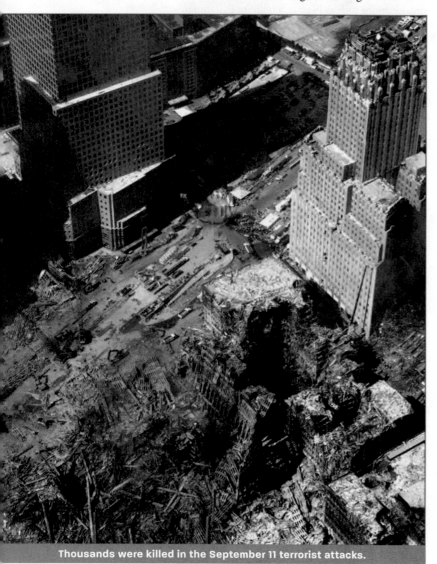

Thousands were killed in the September 11 terrorist attacks.

The brink of war. Israeli Prime Minister Ariel Sharon severed contact with Palestinian Authority (PA) leader Yasir Arafat on December 13, and the Middle East was plunged into new turmoil as Israelis and Palestinians approached the brink of war. (The PA administers Palestinian territories in the West Bank and Gaza Strip.) The crisis began when three Arab suicide bombers killed 26 people in the Israeli cities of Jerusalem and Haifa on December 1 and 2. On December 12, Palestinian militants attacked a bus filled with Jewish settlers in the West Bank, killing at least 10 of the Israelis. Hamas, which had vowed revenge for the November assassination by Israeli forces of its military leader, claimed responsibility for the attacks.

On December 3, Prime Minister Sharon publicly blamed Yasir Arafat for the suicide bombings. Sharon vowed to wage an antiterrorism campaign in Israel similar to the worldwide effort begun by the United States. Israeli forces on December 3 launched the first strikes of a military assault on Palestinian targets, including such symbols of Arafat's leadership as his headquarters in the West Bank town of Ram Allah. On December 13, the Israeli cabinet declared Arafat "no longer relevant" as it severed relations with the PA. The Israeli military also stepped up its attacks on PA sites.

A number of European leaders expressed fear that hostilities might engulf other countries in the region if the Israeli assault was intended to remove Arafat and the PA from power. Israeli officials, however, denied any intention to topple Arafat.

Palestinian reaction. After the suicide bombings in early December, the PA declared martial law and banned public demonstrations in the West Bank and Gaza. Arafat also ordered the detention of more than 180 suspected Islamic militants and placed Hamas spiritual leader Sheik Ahmed Yassin under house arrest. Following the December 12 attack, Arafat vowed to close the offices of Hamas and Islamic Jihad, another Arab extremist organization. Palestinian protests and clashes with Israelis continued despite the clampdown.

Many experts on the Middle East questioned Arafat's ability and willingness to repress anti-Israeli militancy. Polls showed that Palestinians were increasingly critical of Arafat's leadership and overwhelmingly supported the Intifada, or uprising against Israel, which began in September 2000. There was also an upsurge in support for Hamas.

United States. In early- and mid-2001, many Arab leaders criticized President Bush for adopting a "hands-off" policy in the Arab-Israeli conflict. Bush maintained that the United States could not impose peace on unwilling parties. Bush stepped up U.S. involvement in the conflict after the September 11 terrorist attacks, when Arab leaders argued that continued violence in Israel and the Palestinian territories threatened the U.S.-led coalition against terrorism. In November, the Bush administration called upon Israel to freeze settlements in Palestinian territories and urged Palestinian authorities to suppress terrorism. Also in November, President Bush declared his support for a Palestinian state during a UN address and sent U.S. envoys to the region.

Middle East (2004)

The Coalition Provisional Authority, which began governing Iraq after United States-led forces ousted Iraqi leader Saddam Hussein in April 2003, was dissolved on June 28, 2004. Chief U.S. administrator L. Paul Bremer III transferred power to the interim Iraqi government, led by President Ghazi al-Ujayl al-Yawr and Prime Minister Ayad Allawi. An advisory council of Iraqi officials had appointed these leaders on June 1. Elections for a permanent government were scheduled for January 30, 2005.

Fighting between coalition forces and Iraqi insurgents increased throughout 2004. The number of insurgent attacks on coalition troops grew from 700 in October 2003 to 2,400 in October 2004. In November, U.S. troop fatalities reached the highest one-month level since the preceding April. At least 135 troops were killed in each of those months.

Coalition forces launched a major offensive in November to capture the insurgent strong-hold of Al Fallujah. Although Al Fallujah was successfully retaken, much of the city was destroyed in the battle. In addition, coalition troops captured few fighters and found no trace of insurgent leader Abu Mussab al-Zarqawi, who was presumed to have escaped.

Pressure builds on Syria. President George W. Bush of the United States signed an executive order in May implementing economic and trade sanctions on Syria. The sanctions were meant to punish Syria for supporting terrorist organizations, such as the Lebanese group Hezbollah, and for continuing to occupy Lebanon, which Syria had invaded in 1976. The United States also accused Syria of seeking weapons of mass destruction and serving as a passageway for foreign fighters entering Iraq.

International pressure on Syria increased in September 2004, when the United Nations Security Council passed a resolution sponsored by the United States and France that reaffirmed the territorial integrity of Lebanon and called for all foreign troops to evacuate the country. Popular discontent with the Syrian military occupation grew in 2004, especially among Lebanese Christians. On November 19, thousands of Lebanese students and activists demonstrated in Beirut, the capital, shouting, "Syrians out!"

Hardliners score in Iran. Conservative hardliners scored victories over reformers in February elections for the Iranian parliament. The Council of Guardians, a group of religious leaders with authority to disqualify candidates and veto legislation, had disqualified more than 2,000 reformist candidates prior to the elections.

A nonviolent movement arose among Iranian youth in 2004 in response to the continued blocking of reforms. This movement was spearheaded by student groups, which called for the boycotting of the May 2005 presidential election to demonstrate the illegitimacy of the government.

Nuclear negotiations. Following negotiations with France, Germany, and the United Kingdom, Iranian authorities agreed in November 2004 to fully cooperate with the International Atomic Energy Agency (IAEA), a Vienna-based organization that promotes the peaceful use of nuclear energy, and to temporarily halt Iran's uranium enrichment program. Such a program could pro-

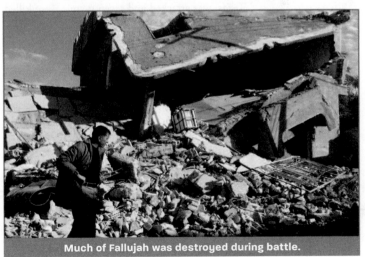

Much of Fallujah was destroyed during battle.

duce fuel for use in either nuclear reactors or nuclear bombs. However, some European and U.S. officials expressed doubts about Iran's commitment to the agreement.

Osama bin Laden in 2001

Al-Qa'ida attacks. Terrorists affiliated with al-Qa'ida, the terrorist network led by Osama bin Laden, targeted Saudi Arabia several times in 2004. In April, a car-bomb attack on the national police headquarters in Riyadh, the capital, marked the first time terrorists hit Saudi security forces. In May, in the Yanbu region, a petrochemical company partly owned by Exxon-Mobil Corporation of Irving, Texas, was attacked and seven people were killed. Also in May, an attack on a compound in Khobar housing foreign employees of oil companies left 22 people dead.

In June, after terrorists beheaded Paul Johnson, an American engineer working for Lockheed Martin Corporation of Bethesda, Maryland, the Saudi government launched a major offensive against the militants. The government killed Abdulaziz al-Moqrin, the leader of al-Qa'ida in Saudi Arabia; closed down charities suspected of financing al-Qa'ida; and offered incentives for information on militants operating covertly in the kingdom.

Al-Qa'ida militants attacked the U.S. Consulate in Jidda, Saudi Arabia, on December 6. The resulting shootout left at least nine people dead.

The Israeli government suspected that al-Qa'ida was behind three car bombings on resorts frequented by Israeli tourists in the Taba region of Egypt on October 7. At least 35 people were killed in the coordinated attacks.

Despite the efforts of the United States and other powers to hunt down bin Laden and his deputy Ayman el-Zawahiri, the two terrorist leaders remained at large in 2004.

Israeli-Palestinian conflict. Terrorist operations against Israeli civilians declined in 2004, compared with 2003. Nevertheless, the Israeli government's policy of targeting leaders of Palestinian militant organizations continued in 2004. An Israeli helicopter missile strike killed Sheik Ahmed Yassin, the leader of the militant group Hamas, on March 22. A second such strike killed Yassin's successor, Abdel Aziz Rantisi, on April 17.

In a political victory for Israeli Prime Minister Ariel Sharon, the Israeli Knesset (parliament) voted in October to support the withdrawal of all Israeli settlers from the Palestinian area of Gaza and from various settlements in the West Bank. The planned withdrawal, which drew strong opposition from the settlers and their supporters, was scheduled to take place by the end of 2005.

The death of Palestinian leader Yasir Arafat in November 2004 opened new opportunities for peace between the Israelis and Palestinians, according to Middle East experts. Representatives of both sides expressed hopes to resume long-stalled peace negotiations.

Libya and the West. After Libyan leader Muammar Muhammad al-Qadhafi renounced the production of weapons of mass destruction in December 2003, Western leaders began flocking to Libya to renew relations with the North African nation. Italian Prime Minister Silvio Berlusconithe, closest Western ally of Qadhafi, was the first to arrive, in February 2004. British Prime Minister Tony Blair followed in March, in the first visit by a British prime minister since Qadhafi came to power in 1969. In October 2004, after the Libyan government agreed to pay $35 million in compensation to the victims of the Libyan bombing of a Berlin discotheque in 1986, German Chancellor Gerhard Schroeder came to Libya. French President Jacques Chirac paid an official visit to Libya in November 2004.

The U.S. government opened a liaison office in Tripoli, the Libyan capital, in June, after a visit to Libya by Assistant Secretary of State William J. Burns.

Humanitarian crisis in Darfur. A humanitarian crisis plagued the western Sudanese region of Darfur in 2004. The crisis was sparked by violent conflict between the government-supported Arab "Janjaweed" militia and two rebel groups, the Sudan Liberation Army and the Justice and Equality Movement. The conflict began in February 2003. As a result of the fighting, more than 70,000 Sudanese had been killed and 1.6 million others had been displaced by December 2004, according to United Nations (UN) estimates.

In November, the UN-based World Food Program was forced to suspend a large part of its food relief operations because of the worsening conflict. The suspension left tens of thousands of refugees without food. Many observers of the worsening situation in Darfur urged the United Nations, the United States, and the European powers to exert greater efforts to resolve the crisis.

Middle East (2005)

A number of positive developments led to improvements in the Israeli-Palestinian conflict in 2005. At a summit held on February 8 in Egypt, Israeli Prime Minister Ariel Sharon and Palestinian Authority President Mahmoud Abbas agreed to cease all hostilities—a step that officially ended the second Palestinian *Intifada* (uprising), which began in September 2000. An even more dramatic development came in August 2005 with the dismantling of all 25 Israeli settlements in the Gaza Strip, followed by the withdrawal from Gaza of Israeli troops in September. In November, the mediation of United States Secretary of State Condoleezza Rice led to the opening of three routes between Israel and Gaza and one route between Egypt and Gaza.

Several political developments related to the peace process occurred in Israel in 2005. In November, Amir Peretz, the dovish member of the Labor Party, ousted former Prime Minister Shimon Peres as leader of the party. Peres then announced his support for Kadima (*Forward*), a new centrist political party formed by Prime Minister Sharon, who quit his own Likud Party.

Lebanon's Cedar Revolution. The so-called "Cedar Revolution" was sparked in early 2005 after the Syrian government became concerned about the growing power of Lebanese forces in opposition to the Syrian occupation of

Darfur refugees flee Sudan.

Lebanon. On February 14, a car bombing killed Rafik Hariri, a prominent leader of the Lebanese opposition. The assassination, which was later tied to Syrian officials, led to anti-Syria demonstrations that culminated in a peaceful rally by 1.5 million Lebanese in the capital, Beirut, on March 14. The demonstrators demanded the immediate withdrawal of Syrian troops.

International pressure provided by the United Nations (UN) Security Council, led by the United States and France, helped persuade the Syrian government to agree to a withdrawal from Lebanon. On April 26, a major goal of the Cedar Revolution was achieved with the evacuation of all Syrian troops and intelligence services from Lebanon.

Candidates associated with the Lebanese opposition won the majority of parliamentary seats in May and June 2005. A new Cabinet headed by Prime Minister Fouad Siniora was formed in July. The Cabinet had at least two members representing Hezbollah, a pro-Syria organization with both a political and militia wing. The disarmament of militias remained another goal of Cedar Revolution leaders.

Revolutionary ripples. The ripples of the Cedar Revolution spread in 2005 to other countries in the Middle East, noted many experts in international affairs. In Syria, hundreds of intellectuals, human rights activists, and other opposition leaders called for freedom and democracy in their own country.

In Egypt, Ayman Nour, the leader of the liberal al-Ghad (*Future*) Party, contested the result of the September presidential elections, which were won by President Hosni Mubarak. The Egyptian Movement for Change, also known as Kefaya (*Enough*), held several peaceful demonstrations calling for the end of President Mubarak's 24-year reign.

Terrorist attacks by al-Qaeda. Attacks by the Islamic terrorist network al-Qaeda continued in 2005. The deadliest of the attacks were carried out in Egypt and Jordan.

In Egypt, three coordinated car bombings on July 23 targeted the Red Sea resort of Sharm el-Sheikh, resulting in the deaths of more than 90 people. The Abdullah Azzam Brigades, a group linked to al-Qaeda, claimed responsibility for the attacks.

In Jordan, three suicide bombings on November 9 at American-owned hotels in the capital, Amman, caused the deaths of at least 58 people. Abu Musab al-Zarqawi, the Jordanian-born head of the Iraqi branch of al-Qaeda, claimed responsibility for the bombings.

Moves for peace in Sudan. On January 9, a historic peace agreement was signed between officials of the Sudanese government and the chairman of the Sudan People's Liberation Movement, John Garang de Mabior. The agreement ended the 21-year civil war between the two sides, which accepted the "one-country, two-systems model" recognizing limited *autonomy* (self-rule) for the southern part of Sudan. The agreement also granted the southern Sudanese the option to renegotiate the treaty after six years, at which time they could choose to either remain part of Sudan or secede and form an independent nation.

In March, the UN Security Council adopted a series of resolutions for ending the conflict in Darfur, a western region in Sudan where violence

between rebels and government forces began in 2003. Resolution 1590 established the UN mission in Sudan for a renewable six-month period. The mission consisted of 10,000 military personnel and 715 civilian police personnel, who were charged with fostering peace in Darfur in cooperation with the African Union Mission in Sudan. Resolution 1593 referred the Darfur conflict to the prosecutor of the International Criminal Court (ICC) in The Hague, Netherlands. The prosecutor began his investigation in June 2005 by collecting more than 3,000 documents related to the killing of thousands of civilians and the displacement of 1.9 million people in Darfur.

Political and military developments in Iraq. On January 30, 8.5 million Iraqi voters, or 58 percent of the electorate, voted for representatives in the new Transitional National Assembly. Shi'ah and Kurdish parties won most of the seats in the 275-member assembly. The Shi'ah United Iraqi Alliance won an absolute majority of 140 seats, while the two main Kurdish parties won a total of 75 seats.

One of the main tasks of the Transitional National Assembly was the formation of a committee to draft a new constitution for Iraq. Although the 69-member committee drafted a charter, the members failed to reach a consensus on such key issues as the existence of autonomous regions for Kurds and the development of strategies for dealing with former Baathists, who had wielded power in the ousted regime of Saddam Hussein. None of the Sunni members of the committee signed the draft.

In a national referendum in October, 78 percent of the Iraqi voters approved the constitution while 21 percent rejected it. The vast majority of Iraq's Sunni Arabs opposed the new constitution.

In November, the UN Security Council extended the mandate of the Multinational Forces in Iraq until December 2006. The extension came in response to a request from Iraqi Prime Minister Ibrahim al-Jafari. In an October letter to the Security Council, Prime Minister al-Jafari wrote that until Iraqi forces could assume full responsibility for the nation's security, the Multinational Forces would be needed "to establish lasting peace and security" in Iraq.

The insurgency against U.S. forces and the newly formed Iraqi army and police forces continued unabated in 2005. From the time of the war's launch in March 2003 to mid-December 2005, more than

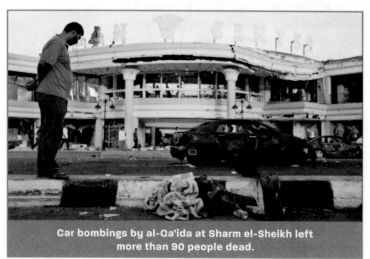

Car bombings by al-Qa'ida at Sharm el-Sheikh left more than 90 people dead.

2,100 U.S. soldiers have died and 15,900 others have been wounded. More than 800 U.S. troops died in Iraq in 2005. The estimated number of Iraqis killed during the war ranged from 29,000 to 48,000.

Iranian president Mahmoud Ahmadinejad

Iran's new hard line president. On June 24, Mahmoud Ahmadinejad was elected president of Iran with 61.7 percent of the vote. The new administration replaced thousands of officials at all levels of government with hard line supporters.

In a September address to the UN General Assembly, President Ahmadinejad stated categorically that Iran had an "inalienable right" to produce nuclear fuel for the generation of energy. In October, President Ahmadinejad called for Israel to be "wiped off the map," and in December he denied the existence of the *Holocaust*, the systematic murder of millions of Jews and others by the Nazis during World War II (1939–1945).

Middle East (2006)

Four major conflicts raged in the Middle East in 2006. Two of the conflicts continued at year's end— the war in Iraq and the conflict between government forces and rebels in Sudan's Darfur region. Fighting also erupted in the Gaza Strip between Palestinian militants and Israeli forces, and along the Lebanese-Israeli border between Israel and Hezbollah.

War in Iraq. In the war in Iraq, which began when United States-led forces invaded the country in March 2003 to topple Iraqi President Saddam Hussein, insurgency attacks against coalition troops increased in 2006, with sectarian violence between Sunni and Shi`ah Muslims intensifying. These two rival Islamic sects settled scores with bombings in markets and crowded streets and even attacks on each other's mosques.

On June 7, a U.S. air strike killed Abu Musab al-Zarqawi, the leader of the Iraqi branch of the Islamic terrorist network al-Qaeda. The killing, however, had little impact on reducing the violence in Iraq. Experts on Iraqi affairs agreed that the vast majority of Iraqi insurgents were not led by al-Qaeda but by the military and intelligence network of deposed President Hussein's Baath Party. By December 31, the number of U.S. troops killed in Iraq since the beginning of the war totaled at least 3,002. Civilian deaths among Iraqis were estimated at as many as 56,000 by the Iraq Body Count project, an independent group of scholars in the United Kingdom.

Meeting in Amman. United States President George W. Bush met with Iraqi Prime Minister Nouri Kamel al-Maliki on November 30 in Amman, the capital of Jordan. President Bush reassured the prime minister that he would not pull U.S. troops out of Iraq "until the job is complete." Also during November, the United Nations (UN) Security Council extended the presence of the multinational force in Iraq until the end of 2007.

The Iraq Study Group Report was published in December 2006 after nine months of work by a *bipartisan* (both parties) team headed by former U.S. Secretary of State James A. Baker III (a Republican) and former Congressman Lee H. Hamilton (a Democrat from Indiana). "The situation in Iraq is grave and deteriorating," concluded the authors of the report, which included a number of recommendations on how the United States should handle the growing Iraqi insurgency. The recommendations included launching a diplomatic initiative to involve Iraq's neighbors and key states outside the region in achieving stability in Iraq. The report called for constructive engagement with Iran and Syria because of the ability of these nations "to influence events within Iraq."

The Iraq Study Group Report advised the Bush administration to promote the transfer of more power to the Iraqi army and security forces by

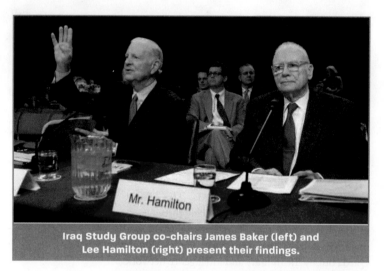

Iraq Study Group co-chairs James Baker (left) and
Lee Hamilton (right) present their findings.

speeding up their training. The report's recommendations set a number of landmark goals for Iraq to achieve with respect to national reconciliation, security, and governance. It concluded with a proposal for a substantial "redeployment" of U.S. troops out of Iraq by 2008.

Leadership change in Israel. After Israeli Prime Minister Ariel Sharon suffered a massive stroke in January 2006, Ehud Olmert, his deputy, became acting prime minister and led the centrist Kadima Party in parliamentary elections in March. In the elections, Kadima won 29 seats in the Israeli Knesset (parliament)—more than any other political party—putting Olmert in a position to become prime minister in his own right.

On May 1, Olmert formed a coalition Cabinet composed of ministers from Kadima and three other political parties—Labor, the ultra-Orthodox Shas, and the Pensioner's Party. In October, Prime Minister Olmert added the Russian immigrant party Yisrael Beitenu to his coalition, thereby increasing his majority in the Knesset to 78 out of a total of 120 members.

Gaza conflict. A truce reached in February 2005 between the Palestinians and Israelis broke down in June 2006, when renewed conflict erupted in the Gaza Strip between Palestinian militants and Israeli forces. The conflict intensified after the military wing of Hamas, the governing party in the Palestinian government, conducted a well-organized raid into Israel from Gaza on June 25. During the raid, an Israeli soldier was kidnapped and two others were killed.

The conflict continued unabated until the two sides reached a truce on November 26. However, all

attempts to obtain the release of the captured Israeli soldier failed. Hamas demanded in exchange the release of Palestinian prisoners, a condition unacceptable to Israel.

Hamas-Fatah rivalry. On December 14, a gun battle between Hamas militants and guards loyal to the Fatah movement, a rival of Hamas, claimed a bodyguard of Ismail Haniyeh, the prime minister of the Hamas-led government. The battle erupted as a convoy carrying Haniyeh entered Gaza from Egypt. Israeli Defense Minister Amir Peretz had ordered that the convoy be stopped to prevent Prime Minister Haniyeh from bringing in millions of dollars of donations he had collected in Muslim countries.

This incident highlighted the intensifying rivalry between Hamas and Fatah, which escalated throughout the year. Fatah continued to vie for power after Hamas won parliamentary elections in January, thus ending Fatah's rule of the Palestinian government. Palestinian President Mahmoud Abbas, a member of Fatah, was seen by most observers as more willing to negotiate with Israel than the hard line Hamas leaders. Unlike Hamas, Fatah recognized Israel's right to exist.

On December 16—in what was seen by most political observers as a daring challenge to Hamas—President Abbas called for new parliamentary elections. The elections would be held as early as June 2007. According to many observers, Abbas made the call because of mounting frustration at the political deadlock that characterized the power-sharing arrangement between Fatah and Hamas.

Hezbollah-Israel conflict. Lebanese fighters with Hezbollah, a militant group backed by Syria and Iran, provoked a war with Israel when they crossed the "blue line" marking the Lebanese-Israeli border on July 12, 2006. The Hezbollah militants kidnapped two Israeli soldiers and killed eight others. In retaliation, Israel attacked the strongholds of Hezbollah in southern Lebanon and the southern suburbs of Beirut, the Lebanese capital, as well as bridges throughout Lebanon. Israeli aerial bombardments hit a total of 350 villages, towns, and cities in Lebanon. However, the massive Israeli offensive did not deter Hezbollah from firing more than 4,000 Katyusha rockets into northern Israel.

The war, which lasted 34 days, resulted in the deaths of approximately 140 Israelis and the wounding of more than 1,000 others. The estimated casualties among the Lebanese were more than 1,100 killed and at least 8,000 others wounded. The conflict cost the Lebanese economy more than $15 billion.

The war stopped on August 14 with the implementation of UN Security Council Resolution 1701. The resolution called for the deployment of 15,000 soldiers of the Lebanese army to maintain order in southern Lebanon. These soldiers were to be assisted by an expanded UN Interim Force in Lebanon consisting of approximately 15,000 soldiers.

The deployment of these forces between the Litani River in Lebanon and the Lebanese-Israeli border cleared the region of Hezbollah fighters, pacifying the Lebanon-Israel border for the first time in four decades. The deployment also eliminated the military threat posed by Hezbollah to residents of northern Israel.

Syrian influence in Lebanon. In November, Hezbollah (with its pro-Syria allies) unsuccessfully attempted to enlarge its proportion of seats in the Lebanese Cabinet to more than one-third of the 24 members required to have veto power. Following this defeat, Hezbollah ministers and their allies resigned from the Cabinet in protest.

This move did not prevent Prime Minister Fouad Siniora from holding a Cabinet meeting on November 13 to approve the blueprint for a UN-established international tribunal to prosecute the perpetrators of the February 2005 assassination of former Lebanese Prime Minister Rafik Hariri. The UN tribunal was also charged with investigating many other terrorist operations in Lebanon. The Syrian regime of Bashar al-Assad was the main target of the UN investigation.

On November 21, 2006, Pierre Gemayel, a Lebanese Cabinet minister and son of former Lebanese President Amin Gemayel, was assassinated in Beirut. Pierre Gemayel was a prominent opponent of Syria's domination of Lebanon. Many Lebanese politicians and Middle East analysts accused Syria of ordering the assassination.

In December, Hezbollah and its allies staged huge rallies in downtown Beirut to call for the toppling of the democratically elected government of Lebanon. According to many Middle East analysts, however, the government retained the support of many Lebanese.

Conflict in Darfur. In May 2006, representatives of Sudan's government and the Sudan Liberation Movement (SLM), the largest rebel group in Darfur, signed the Darfur Peace Agreement in Abuja, the capital of Nigeria. Olusegun Obasanjo, the president of Nigeria and chairman of the African Union—an organization working for cooperation among African nations—mediated the agreement. Darfur is a region in western Sudan where fighting between government forces and various rebel groups began in 2003.

Other rebel organizations, including a breakaway faction of the SLM and the Justice and Equality Movement, refused to sign the agreement. They claimed that the agreement did not recognize the political, economic, and cultural rights of the people of Darfur.

Iran's nuclear ambitions. The Iranian government ignored a deadline of August 31, 2006, established by the UN Security Council, to halt its uranium enrichment program. Uranium enrichment is a process that can be used to produce fuel for civilian nuclear reactors or for nuclear weapons. Iran's President Mahmoud Ahmadinejad denied that Iran was pursuing a nuclear weapons program. At the same time, he maintained that Iran had a right to develop nuclear energy for peaceful purposes.

In late December, France, Germany, the United Kingdom, and the United States reached an agreement with Russia and China on a UN Security Council resolution to impose sanctions on Iran. The resolution banned any effort to supply Iran with materials and technology that could contribute to its nuclear program.

President Abbas (left) meeting with Israeli Prime Minister Ehud Olmert

Israel

Israel is a small, narrow Middle Eastern country on the eastern shore of the Mediterranean Sea. It was founded in 1948 and is considered home to the Jewish people. It is the Biblical Holy Land. It has two official languages: Hebrew and Arabic. English is also spoken quite often. Jerusalem is Israel's capital city and its largest city.

HOT topics

HOT topics

Arab-Israeli War

Israeli Government

Jerusalem, The Holy City

Arab-Israeli War. Immediately after Israel became a new nation in 1948, a series of wars between Israel and the surrounding Arab countries began. After a Six Day war in 1967, Israel occupied the Gaza Strip and the West Bank. In the 1990s, as part of a peace agreement with the Palestine Liberation Organization (PLO), Israel withdrew from the Gaza Strip and part of the West Bank. Since the early 2000s, violent conflicts between the Israelis and the Palestinians have disrupted the peace process.

Israeli Government. Israel is a democratic republic. It has no written constitution. The Israeli parliament, the Knesset, passes basic laws that the government follows. The prime minister is the head of the government and is the leader of the party that controls the most

DEFINITION

Israel *noun.* 1. a name given to Jacob after he had wrestled with the angel (in the Bible, Genesis 32:28). 2. a name given to his descendants; the Jews; the Hebrews. 3. *Figurative.* a people or group regarded as chosen by God; the elect.

HOT topics

seats in the Knesset. If the prime minister loses the support of a majority of Knesset members, he loses his office. The three major national parties are the Labor Party, Kadima, and the Likud bloc. Elected councils serve as local government.

Jerusalem, The Holy City.

Jerusalem is the capital of Israel and Israel's largest city. It is considered one of the world's holiest cities and is a spiritual center for Jews, Christians, and Muslims. The majority of Jerusalem's residents are Jews, with Muslims making up most of the rest of the population. The city is divided into the Old City (which is enclosed by stone walls with many gates), West Jerusalem (the New City), and East Jerusalem (where the majority of the Arabs live). There are many Jewish, Christian, and Muslim holy places throughout Jerusalem. They include the site of the First Temple and the Second Temple (now the Wailing Wall) King David's tomb on Mount Zion, the Tombs of the Prophets on the Mount of Olives, the Cenacle on Mount Zion (the site of the Last Supper), and the Church of the Holy Sepulcher (the site of Jesus's crucifixion, burial and resurrection).

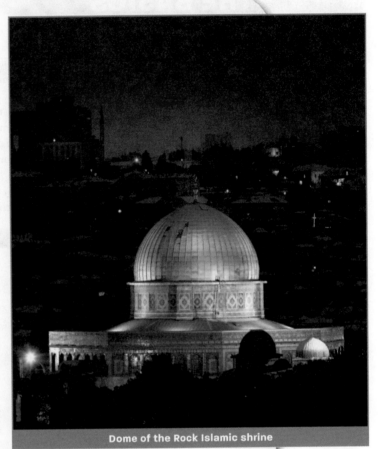

Dome of the Rock Islamic shrine

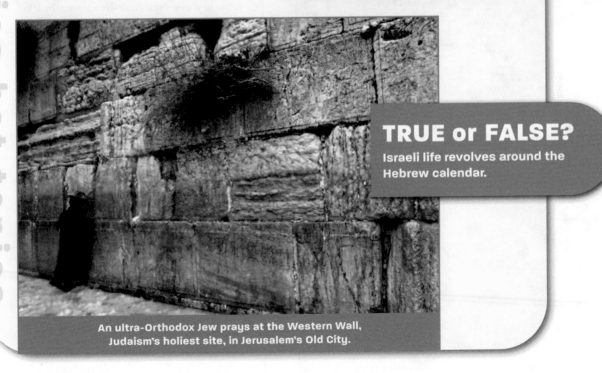

An ultra-Orthodox Jew prays at the Western Wall, Judaism's holiest site, in Jerusalem's Old City.

TRUE or FALSE?

Israeli life revolves around the Hebrew calendar.

THE BASICS

Israel is a small Middle Eastern country. It occupies a narrow strip of land in southwestern Asia on the eastern shore of the Mediterranean Sea. Israel was founded in 1948 as a homeland for Jews from all parts of the world, and more than 3 out of 4 of its people are Jews. Even Jews who live elsewhere consider Israel their spiritual home. Almost all the non-Jews in Israel are Palestinians and other Arabs. Jerusalem is Israel's capital and largest city.

Israel makes up most of the Biblical Holy Land, the place where the religious and national identity of the Jews developed. According to the Bible, Abraham, the father of the Jewish people, established a Semitic population in the Holy Land. Many scholars believe this happened sometime between 1800 and 1500 B.C.

Eventually this land fell to a series of conquerors, including—in 63 B.C.—the Romans. Following unsuccessful Jewish revolts against Roman rule in A.D. 66–70 and A.D. 132–135, the Romans forced most of the Jews to leave. The Romans then began to call this region by the word that became *Palestine* in English. Palestine was ruled by the Roman and then the Byzantine empires until the A.D. 600s, when Arabs conquered the region. From that time until the mid-1900s, the majority of people in Palestine were Arabs.

In the late 1800s, European Jews formed a movement called Zionism, which sought to establish a Jewish state in Palestine. Jewish immigrants began arriving in Palestine in large numbers, and by the early 1900s friction had developed between the Jewish and Arab populations. In 1947, the United Nations (UN) proposed dividing the region into an Arab state and a Jewish state.

On May 14, 1948, the nation of Israel officially came into being. The surrounding Arab countries immediately attacked the new state, in the first of several Arab-Israeli wars. In 1967, at the end of one of the wars, Israeli troops occupied the Gaza Strip and the West Bank—territories that are home to millions of Palestinians. Israel's occupation of these territories further inflamed Arab-Israeli tensions. In the 1990s, Israeli troops withdrew from most of the Gaza Strip and portions of the West Bank. The withdrawals were part of agreements with the Palestine Liberation Organization (PLO), which represents the Palestinian people. In the early 2000s, however, violent clashes between Palestinians and Israelis interrupted the peace process. For more details, see the Recent *developments* section of this article.

Israel has few natural resources and imports more goods than it exports. Still, it has achieved a relatively high standard of living. Almost all of its adults can read and write, and the level of unemployment is low. Jewish settlers have established major industries, drained swamps, and irrigated deserts.

Map of Israel

Although it is a small country, Israel has a diverse terrain that includes mountains, deserts, seashores, and valleys. Israel has a pleasant climate, with hot, dry summers, and cool, mild winters.

Government

National government. Israel is a democratic republic. It has no written constitution. Instead, the government follows "basic laws" that have been passed by the Knesset, the Israeli parliament. The Knesset is a one-house body made up of 120 members, each elected to a term not to exceed four years. The Knesset passes legislation, participates in the formation of national policy, and approves budgets and taxes.

All Israeli citizens 18 years or older may vote. Voters do not cast ballots for individual candidates in Knesset elections. Instead, they vote for a *party list*, which includes all the candidates of a particular political party. The list may range from a single candidate to a full slate of 120 candidates. Elections are determined by the percentage of the vote received by each list. For example, if a particular party list received 33 percent of the vote, it would get 40 Knesset seats.

The prime minister is the head of Israel's government and normally the leader of the party that controls the most seats in the Knesset. The prime minister must maintain the support of a majority of Knesset members to stay in office. He or she forms and heads the Cabinet, Israel's top policy-making body. Appointments to the Cabinet must be approved by the Knesset. The prime minister determines the topics of Cabinet meetings and has the final word in policy decisions.

In 1992, a law was passed allowing voters to directly elect the prime minister. Direct elections for prime minister were held in 1996, 1999, and 2001. Israel abandoned the direct election system after the 2001 election.

The president functions as the head of state. The Knesset elects the president to a seven-year term. Most of the president's duties are ceremonial.

Local government. Elected councils are the units of local government in Israel. Municipal councils serve the larger cities, and local councils govern the smaller urban areas. Regional councils serve rural areas. Councils are responsible for providing education, health and sanitation services, water, road maintenance, fire protection, and park and recreation facilities. They also set and collect local taxes and fees.

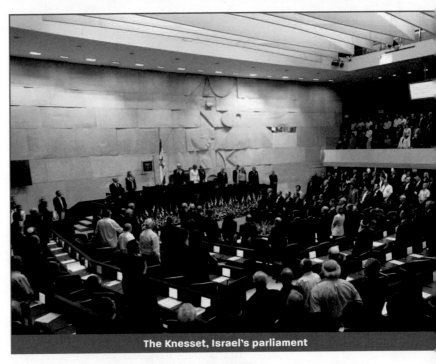

The Knesset, Israel's parliament

The national government divides the country into 6 administrative districts and 14 subdistricts. The minister of interior, one of the Cabinet members, appoints officials to head the districts and subdistricts. These officials oversee and approve the actions of the councils.

Politics. Israel has many political parties, representing a wide range of views. But three parties—the Labor Party, Kadima, and the Likud bloc—dominate the country's national elections.

The Labor Party is a moderate party that has tended to support some government control of the economy, but also believes in a limited amount of free enterprise. The party favors a negotiated settlement with the Arab countries and the Palestinians. It sometimes forms alliances with Kadima, another moderate party. The Likud bloc is an alliance of a number of smaller parties. It supports limited government involvement in the economy. Likud favors a more hard line policy toward the Arab countries and the Palestinians.

Israel also has a number of smaller religious and special-interest parties. Each of these parties focuses on a particular subject or theme. If one of the major parties controls too few seats in the Knesset to form a majority, it usually seeks support from the other parties, including the religious parties. These parties thus have considerable power.

Courts. Israel's court system consists of both religious and *secular* (nonreligious) courts. The Supreme Court is the country's highest secular court. The secular court system also includes magistrate, district, municipal, and specialized courts. The Supreme Court hears appeals from these courts and acts to protect the rights of Israeli citizens.

Religious courts hear cases involving certain personal matters, such as marriage problems, divorces, alimony settlements, and inheritances. Jews, Christians, Muslims, and Druses each have their own religious courts.

Most religious court justices and all secular court justices are appointed by the president. The appointments are based on recommendations that are made by nomination committees consisting of officials from all branches of the Israeli government. Justices must retire at age 70.

Armed forces. Because of its conflicts with Arab states, Israel has maintained a strong military. However, the large amount of money Israel spends on defense puts a strain on the nation's economy.

Israel's army, navy, and air force have about 141,000 members. The country requires almost all Jewish men and most unmarried Jewish women to enter the military at age 18. Men must serve for three years, and women for two years. Annual reserve service is required of both men and women.

People

The area along the Mediterranean coast is Israel's most densely populated region. The Negev Desert, in southwestern Israel, is the least densely populated region.

Jews. About 75 percent of Israel's people are Jews. The modern state of Israel was created as a homeland for the Jewish people. Since 1948, about 3 million Jews have migrated to Israel, many to escape persecution in their home countries. In 1950, the Knesset passed the Law of the Return, which allows any Jew, with a few minor exceptions, to settle in Israel. A 1970 amendment to this law

defined a Jew as "a person who was born of a Jewish mother or has become converted to Judaism and who is not a member of another religion." The Israeli government provides temporary housing and job training to immigrants.

Israel's Jewish population shares a common spiritual and historical heritage. But because they have come from many countries, Israel's Jews belong to a number of different *ethnic groups*, each with its own cultural, political, and recent historical background.

The two main groups in Israel's Jewish population have traditionally been the *Ashkenazim* and the *Sephardim*, or *Orientals*. The Ashkenazim, who came to Israel from Europe and North America, are descended from Jewish communities in central and eastern Europe. The Sephardim immigrated from the Middle East and the Mediterranean. Today, the designations *Ashkenazim* and *Sephardim* are less important because there are many Jews who immigrated from other areas, or who grew up in Israel. At the time of independence, most Jews were Ashkenazim. As a result, Israel's political, educational, and economic systems are primarily Western in orientation. Israel's Sephardic population has had to adapt to this society.

Arabs make up most of the remaining 25 percent of the population of Israel. Most are Palestinians whose families remained in Israel after the 1948–1949 Arab-Israeli war. They usually live in their own farm villages or in the Arab neighborhoods of Israeli cities.

The nation's Jewish and Arab communities are often suspicious of one another, and Arab and Jewish Israelis have limited contact. Most Arabs and Jews live in separate areas, attend separate schools, speak different languages, and follow different cultural traditions.

Language. Israel has two official languages— Hebrew, the language spoken by most of the Jewish population, and Arabic, spoken mainly by the Arabs. Many Israelis also speak English. Many Ashkenazi Jews speak Yiddish, a Germanic language that developed in the Jewish communities of Europe. Immigrants from the former Soviet Union speak Russian.

Way of Life

Israel has a relatively high standard of living, with income levels similar to those in such European countries as Spain or Greece. Israel's life expectancy levels rank among the highest in the

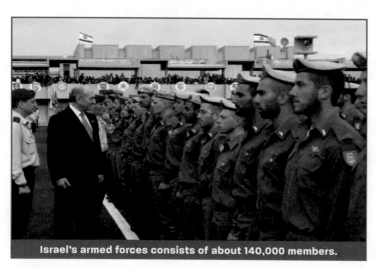
Israel's armed forces consists of about 140,000 members.

world. The country has an excellent system of health and medical care.

City life. Many of Israel's cities are built on ancient sites and include historic buildings, but they also have large, modern sections built by Jewish settlers during the mid-1900s. Many of the cities feature high-rise apartment and office buildings. Most urban Israelis live in apartments. Like urban areas in most countries, Israel's major cities face problems brought on by rapid growth. Roads, housing, and municipal services sometimes fail to keep pace with the expanding population. Traffic congestion and, to a lesser degree, pollution have become problems in Israel's larger cities.

Jerusalem, the capital and largest city, is the spiritual center of the Jewish religion. It is also a holy city of Christians and Muslims. The city is divided into three sections—the Old City, West Jerusalem, and East Jerusalem. All three sections contain many ancient holy places, but the Old City is the historical heart of Jerusalem. It occupies much of the area that was inhabited during Biblical times. West Jerusalem, inhabited mainly by Jews, is the newer part of the city. It contains concrete apartment houses and modern public buildings. It also has several ancient holy places. East Jerusalem, which was captured by Israel in 1967, is inhabited mainly by Arabs. See the Jerusalem section of this article.

Tel Aviv, Israel's second largest city in size and importance, serves as the nation's commercial, financial, and industrial center. Haifa is Israel's major port city and the administrative and industrial

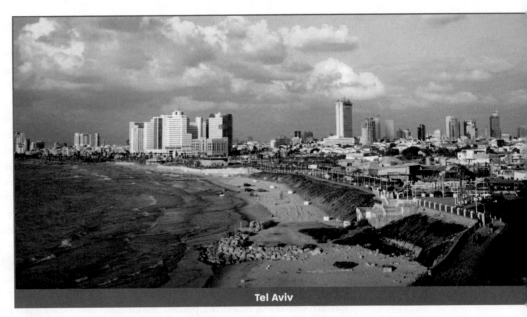

Tel Aviv

center of northern Israel. Beersheba is the most important city in the Negev Desert region.

In the 1950s, the Israeli government began creating "development towns." These towns, which include Arad and Karmiel, were established to attract industry to lightly populated parts of Israel and to provide homes for new immigrants.

Rural life. Many people in rural areas of Israel live in *collective* or *cooperative* communities. In a collective community, called a *kibbutz*, members receive food, housing, education, child care, and medical care in exchange for labor. All property is shared. The kibbutz was traditionally agricultural, but many now engage primarily in industrial activity. In a cooperative community, called a *moshav*, each family works its land separately and has its own living quarters. The village administration provides the family's equipment and supplies, and markets its produce.

Clothing. Most Israelis wear Western-style clothing, although styles in Israel are generally less formal than they are in Western countries. However, some Israelis still dress in the traditional clothing of their ethnic or religious group.

Food and drink. Israel's food and drink reflect the ethnic diversity of its population. Traditional European Jewish dishes, such as chopped liver, chicken soup, and gefilte fish, are common. But so also are traditional Middle Eastern foods such as *felafel*—small, deep-fried patties of ground chickpeas. Raw vegetables and fruits are among the most popular foods.

All government buildings and most hotels and restaurants serve only *kosher* foods, which are prepared according to Jewish dietary laws. But there are nonkosher restaurants as well. Israel also has fast-food restaurants, which serve local dishes in addition to Western foods. Popular beverages in Israel include Turkish coffee, cola, beer, and wine.

Religion. Israeli law guarantees religious freedom and allows members of all faiths to have days of rest on their Sabbath and holy days. Many public facilities are closed on the Jewish Sabbath—from sunset Friday to sunset Saturday.

About one-fifth of Israel's Jewish population strictly observe the principles of Judaism. These people are called *Orthodox* Jews. About half of the country's Jews observe some of the principles. The rest observe few or none of the rules of Judaism. Israel's Jews disagree on the proper relationship between religion and the state. Orthodox Jews tend to believe that Jewish religious values should play an important role in shaping government policy. But many other members of the Jewish population seek to limit the role of religion in the state.

About 15 percent of Israel's populace are Arab Muslims, most of whom follow the Sunni division of Islam. About 2 percent of Israel's population are Arab Christians, mostly Eastern Catholic and Eastern Orthodox. Another 2 percent are Druses, an Arabic-speaking people who follow a religion that developed out of Islam. A few of the non-Jewish people are members of the Baha'is or other smaller religious communities.

Education. Education is given a high priority in Israel. One of the first laws passed in Israel established free education and required school attendance for all children from the ages of 5 to 14. Attendance is now required to age 16.

Israeli children normally attend one year of nursery school, one year of kindergarten, six years of elementary school, three years of junior high school, and three years of high school. Education is free until age 18.

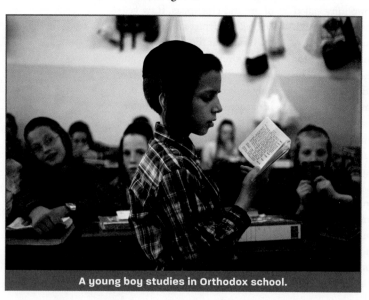

A young boy studies in Orthodox school.

Israel has a Jewish school system in which instruction is in Hebrew, and an Arab/Druse school system in which instruction is in Arabic. The government recognizes and funds both systems.

The Jewish system consists of state schools, state-religious schools, and independent religious schools. State and state-religious schools offer similar academic programs, but state-religious schools emphasize Jewish studies. Independent religious schools are affiliated with Orthodox Judaism and offer more intensive religious instruction.

The Arab/Druse school system includes separate schools for Arab and Druse students. These schools emphasize Arab or Druse history and culture. The Arab schools also provide religious instruction in Islam or Christianity. In Druse schools, community elders choose whether or not to provide religious training.

Israel has a number of well-known institutions of higher education. They include Bar-Ilan University, Ben Gurion University of the Negev, Haifa University, Hebrew University of Jerusalem, Technion-Israel Institute of Technology, Tel Aviv University, and the Weizmann Institute of Science.

The arts. In music, dance, theater, literature, painting, and sculpture, many Israeli artists work within the traditions of their ethnic group. Other artists have blended different cultural art forms to create a uniquely Israeli artistic tradition. The arts in Israel not only reflect the country's immigrant diversity, they also draw upon Jewish history and religion and address the social and political problems of modern Israel.

The number of books published per person in Israel is among the highest in the world. Most Israeli authors write in Hebrew, and some have achieved international fame. Shmuel Yosef Agnon, a novelist and short-story writer, shared the 1966 Nobel Prize for literature. Other important writers have included Aharon Appelfeld, Chaim Nachman Bialik, Saul Tchernichovsky, Amos Oz, and A. B. Yehoshua.

Israel has several theatrical companies. *Habimah*, the national theater, was founded in Moscow in 1917. It moved permanently to Tel Aviv in 1932. The Israel Philharmonic Orchestra performs throughout Israel and often tours abroad. Jerusalem has a symphony orchestra. Israel also has several professional ballet and modern dance companies. Haifa and Tel Aviv boast a number of outstanding museums.

The Land

Israel has four major land regions. They are (1) the Coastal Plain, (2) the Judeo-Galilean Highlands, (3) the Rift Valley, and (4) the Negev Desert.

The Coastal Plain is a narrow strip of fertile land along the Mediterranean Sea. Most Israelis live in the Coastal Plain, and most of the nation's industry and agriculture are located there. Haifa, Israel's major port, is on the northern coast. The northern part of the Coastal Plain includes part of the fertile Plain of Esdraelon. The Qishon, a broad stream, flows through this plain. Most of Israel's important citrus crop is produced in the Plain of Sharon, which forms part of the central Coastal Plain. Farther south is the city of Tel Aviv.

The Judeo-Galilean Highlands include a series of mountain ranges that run from Galilee—the northernmost part of Israel—to the edge of the Negev Desert in the south. The southern part of the highlands includes the West Bank.

The mountains of Galilee stretch southward to the Plain of Esdraelon. Galilee is the home of most of Israel's Arabs and includes the city of Nazareth, the largest Arab center. Galilee also contains the highest mountain in Israel, 3,963-foot (1,208-meter) Mount Meron.

Jerusalem is located in the northern part of the Judean Hills. Rural residents of these hills farm on the hillsides and in the broad valleys. The land to the south is more rugged and agriculture is limited to grazing.

The Rift Valley is a long, narrow strip of land in far eastern Israel. It makes up a small part of the Great Rift Valley, a series of valleys that extends from Syria to Mozambique. The edges of the Rift Valley are steep, but the floor is largely flat. Much of the region lies below sea level. The region includes the Dead Sea, a saltwater lake. The shore of the Dead Sea lies about 1,373 feet (419 meters) below sea level—the lowest land area on Earth.

Few areas of the Rift Valley are fertile. The most fertile section is about 10 miles (16 kilometers) north of the Sea of Galilee. There, during the 1950s, Israel drained Lake Hula and nearby swamps to create about 15,000 acres (6,100 hectares) of farmland.

The Jordan River, the longest of Israel's few rivers, flows through the northern Rift Valley. It travels through the Sea of Galilee and empties into the Dead Sea.

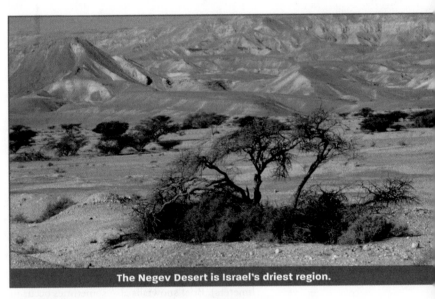

The Negev Desert is Israel's driest region.

The Negev Desert, Israel's driest region, is an arid area of flatlands and mountains. The Negev has traditionally been used for grazing because its limited rainfall cannot support crops. But sections of the Negev are being brought under cultivation by means of irrigation. Water from the Sea of Galilee is pumped southward through the National Water Carrier, an extensive system of canals, pipelines, and tunnels. Regional systems connect with the carrier and extend to the northern Negev.

Climate

Israel has hot, dry summers and cool, mild winters. The climate varies somewhat from region to region, partly because of altitude. Temperatures are generally cooler at higher altitudes and warmer at lower altitudes. In August, the hottest month, the temperature may reach 98°F (37°C) in the hilly regions and as high as 120°F (49°C) near the Dead Sea. July temperatures average 85°F (31°C) in Jerusalem and 82°F (28°C) in Tel Aviv. In January, the coldest month, temperatures average 55°F (13°C) in Jerusalem and 64°F (18°C) in Tel Aviv.

Israel has almost continuous sunshine from May through mid-October. A hot, dry, dusty wind called the *khamsin* sometimes blows in from deserts to the east, particularly in the spring and fall.

Almost all of Israel's rain falls between November and March, much of it in December. There are great regional variations in rainfall. In general, rainfall declines from north to south and from west to east. In the driest area, the southern Negev Desert, the average yearly rainfall is only 1 inch (25 millimeters).

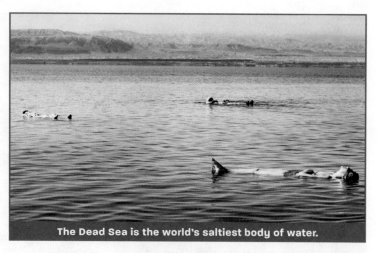

The Dead Sea is the world's saltiest body of water.

In the wettest area, the hilly parts of Upper Galilee, average annual rainfall is 42$\frac{1}{2}$ inches (1,080 millimeters). Brief snowfalls also sometimes occur in the hilly regions.

Economy

At independence, Israel was a poor country with little agricultural or industrial production. But Israel's economy has grown tremendously since 1948. The nation now enjoys a relatively high standard of living, despite having few natural resources and a limited water supply.

Many immigrants came to Israel in the years immediately after independence. Many of these immigrants were skilled laborers and professionals who greatly aided the nation's economic development. Financial assistance from Western nations, especially the United States, is also vital to Israel's economic well-being.

Most of the businesses in Israel are privately owned, but a significant number are owned by the government. Since the 1990s, the government has moved to privatize more businesses in areas such as banking and communications. The Histadrut (General Federation of Labor), a powerful organization of labor unions, also owns a number of the businesses, farms, and industries.

Service industries—economic activities that provide services rather than produce goods—account for about three-fourths of Israel's gross domestic product (GDP). GDP is the value of all goods and services produced yearly within the country. Service industries employ about three-fourths of Israel's workers. Many of Israel's service industry workers are employed by the government or by businesses owned by the government. Gov-

ernment workers provide many of the services that are needed by Israel's large immigrant population, such as housing, education, and vocational training. Tourist activities support many of Israel's service industries, especially trade, restaurants, and hotels.

Manufacturing is more diversified in Israel than in most areas of the Middle East. Israeli factories produce high technology electronics, including communications and computer products. They also make other goods, such as chemical and plastic products, machinery, metal products, processed foods, and textiles and clothing. The cutting of imported diamonds is a major industry. Tel Aviv and Haifa are Israel's major manufacturing centers.

Agriculture accounts for 2 percent of Israel's GDP and employs about 2 percent of its workers. Agriculture formerly employed a much larger percentage of Israel's work force. But much of the work once performed by people is now performed by machines. Important agricultural products include beef and dairy cattle, poultry, and tomatoes and other vegetables.

The government develops, helps finance, and controls agricultural activity, including fishing and forestry. Israel produces most of the food needed to feed its people. Agricultural exports provide enough income to pay for any necessary food imports. Most Israeli farmers use modern agricultural methods. Water drawn from the Jordan River irrigates large amounts of land in Israel.

Most Israeli farms are organized as moshavim or kibbutzim (see the Rural life section of this article). Israel also has some private farms, mostly owned by Arabs.

Mining. The Dead Sea, the world's saltiest body of water, is Israel's leading mineral source. Compounds drawn from the sea yield bromine, magnesium, potash, and table salt. Phosphates, copper, clay, and gypsum are mined in the Negev Desert. Israel is a leading producer of bromine, phosphate rock, and potash.

Energy sources. Israel is poor in energy sources. It has no coal deposits or hydroelectric power resources and only small amounts of crude oil and natural gas. As a result, Israel depends primarily on imported crude oil and coal to meet its energy needs.

International trade. Israel has few natural resources and must import many of its goods. The country's chief imports include chemicals, computer equipment, grain, iron and steel, petroleum products, rough diamonds, and vehicles. Israel's main exports are chemical products, citrus fruits, electronic equipment, polished diamonds, and pharmaceuticals. The United States is Israel's main trading partner. Other important trading partners include the Benelux countries (Belgium, the Netherlands, and Luxembourg), China, France, Germany, Italy, Switzerland, Hong Kong, India, and the United Kingdom.

Transportation and communication. Israel has a well-developed transportation system. This system developed in part because of the need to move military troops and equipment quickly to any part of the country.

Most middle-class Israeli families either own an automobile or have one provided by their employer. Paved roads reach almost all parts of the country. Public transportation both in and between cities is provided primarily by bus. Since the mid-1990s, the number of rail passengers has risen sharply.

Ben-Gurion Airport, Israel's largest international airport, is at Lod, near Tel Aviv. Elat and Haifa have smaller airports. El Al, Israel's international airline, flies regularly to the United States, Canada, Europe, and parts of Africa and Asia. Israel has three major deepwater ports—Haifa, Ashdod, and Elat.

Israel's communication system is one of the best in the Middle East. Many of Israel's daily newspapers are in Hebrew. The rest are in Arabic, English, Russian, or other languages. The Israel Broadcasting Authority, a public corporation set up by the government, runs the TV and nonmilitary radio stations. Commercial radio and television stations also broadcast in Israel.

History

Beginnings of a new state. In the mid-1800s, Eastern European Jews began to develop a desire to live in the Holy Land. By 1880, about 24,000 Jews were living in Palestine, which was controlled by the Ottoman Empire. In the late 1800s, oppression of Jews in eastern Europe triggered the Zionist movement. This movement, which sought to establish a Jewish national state in Palestine, eventually led to a mass emigration of Jews there. By 1914, there were about 85,000 Jews in Palestine, out of a total population of about 700,000.

In 1917, during World War I (1914–1918), the United Kingdom issued the Balfour Declaration, which expressed British support for a national homeland for the Jews in Palestine. The United Kingdom was fighting to win control of Palestine from the Ottoman Empire as part of the war. The British hoped the declaration would rally Jewish leaders in the United Kingdom and the United States to support the British war efforts. At the same time, however, the British promised independence to various Arab groups in the Middle East, hoping to gain their support against the Ottomans. The promises were vague, but Arab leaders assumed they included Palestine.

Following the Ottoman defeat in World War I, the League of Nations made Palestine a mandated territory of the United Kingdom. According to the mandate, the British were to help Jews in Palestine build a national home. Many Zionists viewed the mandate as support for increased Jewish immigration to Palestine. But the British, fearful of the hostility of the large Arab population, proposed limits on Jewish immigration. But these limitations were not fully enforced.

Large numbers of European Jews came to Palestine in the 1930s to escape persecution by the Nazis. Alarmed by the Jewish immigration, the Palestinian Arabs revolted against British rule during the late 1930s. In 1939, the United Kingdom began attempting to limit Jewish immigration to Palestine. Jews strongly opposed this policy.

Jewish immigrants from Europe arrive in Haifa, Palestine.

During World War II (1939–1945), the Nazis killed about 6 million European Jews. This led to increased demands for a Jewish state, but the British continued to limit Jewish immigration to Palestine. In 1947, the United Kingdom submitted the issue to the United Nations (UN).

Independence and conflict. On November 29, 1947, the UN General Assembly agreed to divide Palestine into an Arab state and a Jewish state and to place Jerusalem under international control. The Jews in Palestine accepted this plan, but the Arabs rejected it. Fighting broke out immediately.

Israel officially came into existence on May 14, 1948, under the leadership of David Ben-Gurion. On May 15, Arab armies, chiefly from Egypt, Syria, Lebanon, Iraq, and Transjordan (which became known as Jordan in 1949), attacked Israel, aiming to destroy the new nation. By early 1949, Israel had defeated the Arabs and gained control of about half the land planned for the new Arab state. Egypt and Jordan held the rest of Palestine. Israel controlled the western half of Jerusalem, and Jordan held the eastern half. Israel incorporated the gained territory into the new country, adding about 150,000 resentful Arabs to its population. Hundreds of thousands of other Palestinian Arabs settled as refugees in parts of Palestine not under Israeli control and in Arab countries. By mid-1949, Israel had signed armistice agreements with Egypt, Syria, Jordan, and Lebanon. But formal peace treaties were not signed because the Arab countries refused to recognize the existence of Israel.

Israel held its first election in January 1949. In February, the Knesset elected Chaim Weizmann president. He officially appointed Ben-Gurion prime minister.

The Sinai invasion. Border clashes between Arab and Israeli troops occurred frequently in the early 1950s. In the mid-1950s, Egypt began giving financial aid and military supplies to Palestinian Arab *fedayeen* (commandos). The fedayeen raided Israel from the Gaza Strip, the Egyptian-occupied part of Palestine. The Israelis raided the Gaza Strip in return. Egypt also blocked Israeli ships from using the Suez Canal and stopped Israeli ships at the entrance to the Gulf of Aqaba. In July 1956, Egypt nationalized the Suez Canal, which at the time was owned mainly by the United Kingdom and France.

In response to the Egyptian actions, on October 29, 1956, Israeli forces invaded Egypt. The United Kingdom and France attacked Egypt two days later. By November 5, the Israelis occupied the Gaza Strip and the Sinai Peninsula, and the British and French controlled the northern entrance to the Suez Canal. The UN ended the fighting and arranged the withdrawal of foreign troops from Egyptian territory. The UN also set up a peacekeeping force in the Gaza Strip and Sinai Peninsula.

The Six-Day War. In May 1967, the UN removed its peacekeeping force from the Gaza Strip and Sinai Peninsula in response to demands by Egyptian President Gamal Abdel Nasser. Nasser

In the 1984 war, Israel gained much territory in addition to what it had received in the 1947 UN Partition Plan.

The 1967 war resulted in Israel's occupation of the Sinai Peninsula, Golan Heights, West Bank, and Gaza Strip.

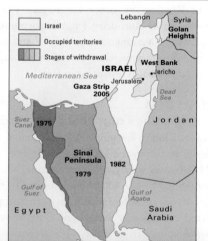

Israel withdrew from the Sinai Peninsula in stages from 1975 to 1982.

then sent large numbers of troops into the Sinai. He also announced the closing of the Strait of Tiran to Israeli ships, thus blocking the Israeli port of Elat.

Fearing that Arabs would soon attack, Israel launched a surprise air strike against Egypt on June 5, 1967. Syria, Jordan, and Iraq, which had signed defense agreements with Egypt, immediately joined in the fighting. In one day, Israeli planes almost completely destroyed the Arab air forces. Israel's ground forces then defeated those of the Arab states. The UN arranged a cease-fire, ending the war after six days.

At the war's conclusion, Israel held the Sinai Peninsula and Gaza Strip, as well as Syria's Golan Heights. It also occupied the West Bank, which had been claimed by Jordan. Israel vowed not to withdraw from these territories until the Arab states recognized Israel's right to exist. In June 1967, Israel officially made the eastern half of Jerusalem part of Israel.

The Six-Day War again proved the superiority of Israel's military forces, but it also planted the seeds of additional Arab-Israeli problems. The occupation of the Gaza Strip and West Bank placed Israel in control of about 1 million hostile Palestinian inhabitants.

The rise of the PLO. Following the Six-Day War, the Palestine Liberation Organization (PLO) became prominent in the Middle East. The PLO is a confederation of Palestinian groups that work to establish an independent state for the Palestinian people. It adopted guerrilla tactics, including terrorist attacks and commando raids against military and civilian targets.

After the defeat of the regular Arab armies in the 1967 war, Arab leaders began increasing their support of the PLO's forces. These forces then stepped up guerrilla activity against Israel. Israel retaliated with raids against PLO bases in neighboring Arab countries.

The Yom Kippur War. Israeli and Egyptian forces engaged in intense border fighting along the Suez Canal between April 1969 and August 1970. The Soviet Union provided military assistance to Egypt in the conflict, which was ended by a U.S.-sponsored cease-fire. On October 6, 1973, full-scale war broke out again when Egyptian and Syrian forces attacked Israeli positions along the Suez Canal and in the Golan Heights. The attack occurred on Yom Kippur, the most sacred Jewish holy day. Israel pushed back the Arab forces. It recaptured the

Left to right: Israeli Prime Minister Menachem Begin, U.S. President Jimmy Carter, and Egyptian President Anwar Sadat

Golan Heights and some additional Syrian territory. A cease-fire went into effect on October 25.

The Yom Kippur War had far-reaching effects. The Israeli economy suffered severely. Although Israel won the war, it suffered heavy losses of men and equipment. Many Israelis criticized the government's handling of the conflict. As a result, Prime Minister Golda Meir resigned in April 1974. Yitzhak Rabin succeeded her in June. The war also greatly increased Israel's dependence on the United States, which supplied Israel with arms.

The Camp David Accords. The Labor Party and the party from which it developed, the Mapai, controlled Israel's government from independence until 1977. Under Israel's political system of the time, the prime minister was usually the leader of the party with the most seats in the Knesset. In 1977, parliamentary elections transferred control of the country to the Likud bloc. Menachem Begin, the Likud leader, became prime minister.

Israeli-Egyptian tensions eased after the Yom Kippur War. In November 1977, Egyptian President Anwar el-Sadat announced that he was ready to negotiate a peace settlement with Israel. That month, he met with Begin in Jerusalem. In September 1978, Begin, Sadat, and U.S. President Jimmy Carter met at Camp David in the United States for talks arranged by Carter. The talks resulted in the Camp David Accords, which focused on achieving two objectives: (1) peace between Egypt and Israel, and (2) a comprehensive peace in the Middle East.

The first objective of the Camp David Accords was met when Egypt and Israel signed a peace treaty in March 1979. In February 1980, they exchanged diplomats for the first time. Israel completed

An IDF honor guard, poised by an Israeli flag at half mast, is framed by the flag-draped coffin and crowd of dignitaries at the funeral of Yitzhak Rabin.

its withdrawal from Egypt's Sinai Peninsula in 1982. No immediate progress was made on the second objective.

Invasion of Lebanon. Tensions between Israel and the PLO escalated in the late 1970s and early 1980s. In 1978, Israel invaded southern Lebanon in an attempt to drive out Palestinian guerrillas who had been attacking Israel for several years. In June 1982, a large Israeli force attacked southern and central Lebanon in retaliation for PLO attacks on northern Israel. The PLO withdrew most of its forces from Lebanon in August 1982). In 1985, Israel withdrew its forces from all of Lebanon except a security zone along the Lebanon-Israeli border.

Unity government. Begin resigned as prime minister in September 1983. Yitzhak Shamir of the Likud bloc succeeded him. Parliamentary elections were held in July 1984. The Labor Party won more seats than the Likud bloc, but neither party won a majority and neither was able to form a coalition government. In September, Labor and Likud agreed to form a unity government for 50 months. Under the agreement, Shimon Peres, leader of the Labor Party, served as prime minister for a term of 25 months. Shamir served as vice prime minister and foreign minister. The roles of Peres and Shamir were reversed after 25 months, in October 1986.

The unity government included Cabinet members of both parties. It succeeded in reducing a high inflation rate in Israel. But the government was divided on how to attain peace with Arab countries and the Palestinians. The Labor camp favored giv-

ing up portions of the occupied territories in return for peace agreements. The Likud bloc, however, supported the establishment of Jewish settlements in the territories and their retention by Israel.

In late 1987, Palestinians in the Gaza Strip and the West Bank began staging widespread demonstrations against Israel's occupation. These demonstrations became known as the *intifada* (uprising). Some protests became violent. Israeli troops killed a number of Palestinians, a few Israelis also were killed, and hundreds of Palestinians and Israelis were injured.

In November 1988, new parliamentary elections were held. The Likud bloc won one more seat than the Labor Party, but again neither party won a majority. In December, Likud and Labor formed a new coalition government with Shamir continuing as prime minister. In 1990, Shamir refused to compromise on peace plans for the occupied territories. The Labor Party then left the coalition, and the government fell in March. In June 1990, Likud and small conservative parties formed a new coalition government with Shamir as prime minister.

From the mid-1980s to the early 1990s, thousands of Ethiopian Jews moved to Israel. Also, hundreds of thousands of Soviet Jews moved there. The influx of newcomers led to problems in housing and employment. Israel continued to build new settlements in occupied territories, in part to accommodate the immigrants. Despite protests from Palestinians, Shamir and Likud backed these construction projects.

The 1990s. In August 1990, Iraq invaded Kuwait. In early 1991, the United States and other countries defeated Iraq in the Persian Gulf War of 1991. During the war, Iraq fired missiles at Israel.

In October 1991, peace talks began between Israel, Syria, Lebanon, and a joint Jordanian-Palestinian delegation. Israel's Labor Party gained control of the government in June 1992 parliamentary elections. In July, Labor Party leader Yitzhak Rabin replaced Shamir as prime minister. Rabin agreed to limit construction of new Jewish settlements in the occupied territories as a step toward a peace agreement.

The PLO was not a participant in the peace talks that began in October 1991. But in September 1993, following secret talks in Oslo, Norway, Israel and the PLO recognized each other and signed an agreement that included steps to end their conflicts. As a result of this agreement and later ones, Israel withdrew its troops from most of the Gaza Strip and portions of the West Bank. Palestinians took control of these areas. In October 1994, Israel and Jordan signed a peace treaty that formally ended the state of war that had technically existed between the countries since 1948.

Not all Israelis agreed with the peace process, and some protested it. Some opponents argued, for example, that Israel was giving away land that should historically belong to it. On November 4, 1995, Rabin was assassinated in Tel Aviv by a right-wing Israeli university student who was opposed to his policies. Following Rabin's death, Peres, who had been foreign minister, became prime minister.

In May 1996, Benjamin Netanyahu, the Likud leader and a critic of the Israeli-PLO peace agreements, defeated Peres in an election for prime minister. Netanyahu claimed that the peace agreements did not include enough provisions for Israel, such as guaranteed security and allowance for its population growth.

Tensions between Israel and the Palestinians grew after the 1996 elections, and the peace process slowed. In 1996 and 1997, Israel announced plans to expand Israeli settlements in the West Bank and to build new Israeli housing in East Jerusalem. Both decisions met with angry protests from the Palestinians. Also in 1997, however, Israel completed an agreement with the PLO over the withdrawal of Israeli troops from most of the West Bank city of Hebron.

In October 1998, Israel and the Palestinians signed another agreement, called the Wye River Memorandum. The accord called for Israel to turn over more land in the West Bank to Palestinian control. Also as a result of the agreement, the PLO revised its charter to remove language calling for the destruction of Israel. Many conservative members of the Israeli parliament and in Netanyahu's Cabinet opposed the accord. In December 1998, Netanyahu, claiming that the PLO was not fulfilling its security commitments, suspended Israeli troop withdrawals from the West Bank. That same month, the Israeli parliament voted to dissolve itself and scheduled new elections.

In May 1999, Ehud Barak, leader of the Labor Party, was elected prime minister of Israel. Barak favored renewing the peace process with the Palestinians. In September, Barak and Palestinian leader Yasir Arafat signed a new agreement that revived and expanded on the previous Wye River Memoran-

dum. Israel resumed its troop withdrawals from the West Bank shortly after the agreement was signed.

The early 2000s. In May 2000, Israel withdrew its troops from the security zone it had established in southern Lebanon. Hezbollah guerrillas immediately took control of the area. Hezbollah, also spelled Hizbollah, is a radical Islamic group that opposed the Israeli occupation of Lebanon. Guerrillas from the group had often clashed with the Israelis and the Israeli-backed South Lebanon Army. By September, UN peacekeepers and Lebanese security forces had moved into most of southern Lebanon. But Hezbollah remained in control of the area near the Israel-Lebanon border.

The peace process between Israeli and Palestinian leaders continued in 2000. In July, Barak and Arafat met at Camp David in the United States for peace talks hosted by U.S. President Bill Clinton. However, the two sides were unable to agree on key issues, especially those involving Jerusalem. One point of dispute was how much control Palestinians should have over East Jerusalem. The two sides also disagreed about who should govern the Temple Mount in Jerusalem. Temple Mount, known to Arabs as Haram al-Sharif, is a holy site for both Muslims and Jews.

In September 2000, Ariel Sharon, the leader of Likud and a controversial critic of the Israeli-Palestinian peace agreements, visited Temple Mount. Sharon said he was demonstrating Israel's control over the site. This visit angered Palestinians, who began riots and demonstrations in Jerusalem, the Gaza Strip, and the West Bank. These actions came to be known as the second Palestinian intifada.

Palestinian leader Yasser Arafat (left) greets Israeli Prime Minister Ehud Barak at Camp David in 2000.

Israel responded to the intifada with police crackdowns and military strikes in Palestinian areas.

After the violence began, Barak faced mounting pressure from opposition parties to hold new elections. In November 2000, he agreed to hold a new election for prime minister. In the vote, which was held in February 2001, Sharon defeated Barak. Sharon formed a coalition government that included the Labor Party and several other parties.

Both the Palestinian intifada and the Israeli military campaign continued and became more violent. Numerous attacks by Palestinian militias and suicide bombers took place throughout Israel, the West Bank, and the Gaza Strip, killing hundreds of Israelis. Israeli forces repeatedly bombed and invaded the West Bank and Gaza Strip, killing thousands of Palestinians and demolishing hundreds of houses. In 2002, Israel reoccupied most West Bank cities. That same year, Israel began constructing a barrier that was designed to separate most of the West Bank from Israel.

In October 2002, the Labor Party withdrew from Sharon's coalition government. Early parliamentary elections were scheduled for January 2003. In the elections, Sharon's Likud party won the largest number of seats. Sharon formed a new coalition government and remained as prime minister.

Later in 2003, diplomats from the United States, Russia, the European Union, and the United Nations proposed a peace plan known as the "road map." Israeli and Palestinian leaders resumed negotiations under this plan, but the negotiations soon broke down. Palestinian attacks and Israeli military strikes continued.

In late 2004, Sharon dissolved his coalition government. He soon formed a new one with the Labor Party as the key partner. In February 2005, Sharon and Palestinian leader Mahmoud Abbas met in Egypt and declared an Israeli-Palestinian truce. However, some violence continued between the two sides.

In 2004, Sharon announced a plan to remove all Jewish settlements and Israeli troops from the Gaza Strip by the end of 2005. On August 15, 2005, the Israeli government began the evacuation of all Jewish settlers from the Gaza Strip and four West Bank settlements. Many settlers protested the evacuation, and Israeli troops forcibly removed them. The evacuation was completed on August 23. There are still about 120 Jewish settlements in the West Bank.

In late 2005, Sharon asked the president to dissolve parliament so elections could be held early. Sharon then left the Likud party to form his own party, called Kadima, which is Hebrew for *forward*. In January 2006, Sharon suffered a major stroke and fell into a coma. Deputy Prime Minister Ehud Olmert became acting prime minister and acting head of Kadima. In March, parliamentary elections were held, and Kadima won the largest number of seats. Olmert became prime minister and formed a coalition government with Labor as the key partner.

In June 2006, Palestinian militant groups captured an Israeli soldier. The groups demanded Israel release Palestinian prisoners in exchange for the soldier. Fighting between the two sides increased. Israel bombed parts of the Gaza Strip, and militants fired rockets into Israel. Israeli troops entered the Gaza Strip in an effort to retrieve the soldier. In November, Israel and Palestinian militant groups agreed to a cease-fire.

In July 2006, Hezbollah captured two Israeli soldiers near the border of Lebanon and Israel. In response, Israel began bombing Lebanon. Israel blamed the Lebanese government for not disarming Hezbollah. Hezbollah fired missiles into northern Israel. In August, Israel and Lebanon accepted a cease-fire agreement drafted by the UN Security Council. The conflict led to the deaths of more than 1,000 people, most of them Lebanese. In July 2008, Hezbollah returned the bodies of the two soldiers, who had been killed in the 2006 attack, in exchange for Lebanese prisoners held by Israel.

In November 2007, Olmert and Palestinian president Mahmoud Abbas began peace talks. The talks were hosted by the United States in Annapolis, Maryland, and involved other leaders from the Middle East, including Syria and Saudi Arabia.

Beginning in late 2006, Olmert faced multiple corruption investigations. He denied any wrongdoing. In July 2008, Olmert announced he would resign as prime minister and head of Kadima. Tzipi Livni replaced him as Kadima leader in September. After parliamentary elections in February 2009, President Shimon Peres asked Likud leader Benjamin Netanyahu to form the next government. Netanyahu became prime minister of Israel for the second time on March 31, 2009.

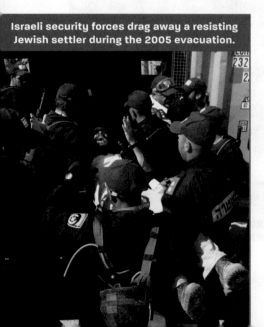

Israeli security forces drag away a resisting Jewish settler during the 2005 evacuation.

In December 2008, Israel began air attacks on targets in the Gaza Strip. Israel stated that the airstrikes were in response to rocket attacks from Hamas militants. In January 2009, Israel began sending troops into the Gaza Strip. The fighting caused more than 1,300 deaths, almost all of them Palestinians, and wounded thousands more. On January 17, Israel declared a cease-fire. Hamas declared a cease-fire the next day, though some fighting continued.

In November 2012, violence in Gaza erupted again as Hamas rocket attacks met with Israeli naval and air strikes. In roughly one week, about 170 people were killed, all but 6 of them Palestinian.

JERUSALEM is the capital and largest city of Israel and one of the world's holiest cities. It is also one of the oldest continuously inhabited cities in the world. For centuries, Jerusalem has been a spiritual center to Jews, Christians, and Muslims. Jews consider Jerusalem a holy city because it was their religious and political center during Biblical times. Christians consider Jerusalem holy because many events in the life of Jesus Christ took place there. Muslims also revere the city and believe that the Prophet Muhammad rose to heaven from there.

About two-thirds of Jerusalem's population are Jews. The remainder is mostly Muslims, plus a small number of Christians, including Roman Catholics, Eastern Catholics, Protestants, and members of Eastern Orthodox Churches.

Jerusalem is a city of three Sabbaths—Friday (Muslim), Saturday (Jewish), and Sunday (Christian). Businesses in Jerusalem may be closed on any of these three days. The Jewish Sabbath, however, is by far the most widely observed. After it begins on Friday evening, much of Jewish Jerusalem closes down and most public transportation stops.

Jerusalem lies about 40 miles (64 kilometers) east of the Mediterranean Sea. The city is surrounded on the north, east, and south by the West Bank, a disputed territory inhabited by both Palestinians and Israelis. In 1949, at the end of the first Arab-Israeli war, Jerusalem was divided between Israel and Jordan. Israel controlled the western part of the city, and Jordan controlled the eastern section. Israel took control of the entire city in 1967. Jerusalem today is claimed by both the Palestinians and the Israelis as their capital.

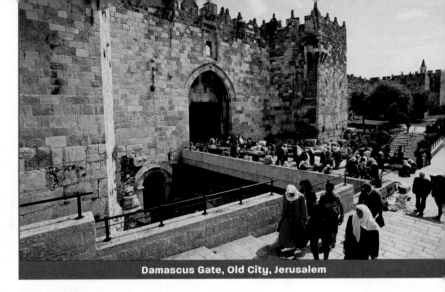
Damascus Gate, Old City, Jerusalem

The City

Jerusalem lies on hilly, rocky land in the Judean Hills. The city is divided into three sections: (1) the Old City; (2) West Jerusalem, also called the New City; and (3) East Jerusalem.

The Old City, which occupies much of the area of Biblical Jerusalem, is the historical heart of the city. It covers a rectangular area of about 1/3 square mile (1 square kilometer) in the eastern part of Jerusalem.

The Old City is enclosed by stone walls about 40 feet (12 meters) high and 2 1/2 miles (4 kilometers) long. Although Jerusalem has always been a walled city, its present walls were built during the 1500s. Some sections of the foundation are much older. A number of gates open into the walls, including the Jaffa Gate, Zion Gate, Dung Gate, Lion's Gate (also known as St. Stephen's Gate), Damascus Gate, New Gate, and Herod's Gate (also known as Flower Gate). Until the late 1800s, these gates were closed at night to protect inhabitants.

The skyline of the Old City is dominated by a Muslim shrine known as the Dome of the Rock. The shrine stands on a raised area that the Muslims call al-Haram al-Sharif (the Noble Sanctuary). The Jews call the area the Temple Mount because it was the site of the first and second Jewish Temples in ancient times.

The Old City is divided into four neighborhoods—the Armenian, Christian, Jewish, and Muslim quarters. The Armenian quarter is occupied primarily by members of the Armenian Church, an independent church that is close to the Eastern Orthodox Churches in its beliefs. The largest religions in the Christian quarter are the Roman Catholic Church and Greek Orthodox Church. Most inhabitants of the Jewish and Muslim quarters are followers of Judaism and Islam, respectively.

The narrow cobblestone lanes that wind through the Old City have remained largely unchanged for hundreds of years. Houses, many with inner courtyards, stand crowded together. The busiest streets are the *suqs* (markets), which have small shops that sell food, clothing, pottery, jewelry, and souvenirs. Most of the streets are too narrow for automobiles. Donkeys and pushcarts transport heavy loads.

From 1948 to 1967, Jordan controlled the Old City. The area had a poor sanitation system and inadequate supplies of electric power and water. After 1967, Israel expanded its modern public services into the Old City, including sewerage, electric and water systems, garbage collection, and social welfare programs.

West Jerusalem is the most modern part of the city. It includes the downtown area, which is centered on a triangle formed by King George Street, Jaffa Road, and Ben-Yehuda Street. Fashionable shops, hotels, restaurants, and tall office buildings line these streets.

Several modern public buildings in West Jerusalem are in a neighborhood called Givat Ram. Among them are the campuses of Hebrew University and the Israel Museum. The Knesset (parliament), the Supreme Court, and other government buildings stand nearby.

A neighborhood known as Mea Shearim, north of downtown, is the home of many Orthodox Jews. It has dozens of small synagogues and study houses.

To the southwest is a picturesque neighborhood called Ein Kerem. The huge Hadassah Medical Center stands nearby, with its famous stained glass windows designed by the Russian-born artist Marc Chagall. Also in the area is Yad Vashem, a memorial museum dedicated to the victims of the Holocaust, the Nazi campaign to exterminate the Jews.

East Jerusalem, north of the Old City, is where most of Jerusalem's Arabs live. Many Arab restaurants and shops are in this part of the city. Some neighborhoods in East Jerusalem are run-down, with old, neglected housing, but other areas are more modern. Israel built several modern Jewish neighborhoods, including Ramat Eshkol and Gilo, after taking control of East Jerusalem in 1967. There are also modern buildings on the original campus of Hebrew University on Mount Scopus, which was rebuilt and expanded in the 1970s.

Holy Places

Jerusalem has a central place in the worship, doctrine, and daily practice of Judaism, Christianity, and Islam. The city's large number of synagogues, churches, mosques, and other religious institutions reflects the significance of the city for all three faiths. Each religious community supervises its own holy sites.

Jewish sites. According to tradition, Jerusalem is where God ordered the patriarch Abraham to sacrifice Abraham's son Isaac to him. The Jews built their Temple, the center of Jewish worship in ancient times, at the site of Abraham's sacrifice on the Temple Mount in the Old City. Two successive buildings, the First Temple and the Second Temple, stood at the site, but both buildings were destroyed by enemies.

The First Temple housed the Ark of the Covenant, a sacred chest holding the tablets inscribed with the Ten Commandments. The Western Wall is the only surviving part of the Second Temple and Judaism's most sacred shrine. It is a stone retaining wall that reinforced the western side of the Temple Mount in ancient times. The wall is sometimes called the *Wailing Wall* because of the sorrowful prayers said there to mourn the destroyed Temple.

Other sites in the city sacred to the Jews include King David's tomb on Mount Zion in West Jerusalem, and the Jewish Cemetery and the Tombs of the Prophets on the Mount of Olives, a hill just east of the Old City. Many sites associated with Biblical figures are sacred to Christians, too.

Christian sites. Many monasteries, convents, shrines, and religious seminaries in Jerusalem mark events in the life of Jesus Christ and in the formation of the Christian Church. Jesus taught in Jerusalem and is believed to have performed numerous miracles there. The Last Supper supposedly took place in a room known as the Cenacle (also called Coenaculum) on Mount Zion. The Church of the Holy Sepulcher in the Old City occupies the site said to be the place of Jesus's Crucifixion (called Calvary or Golgotha), as well as his burial and Resurrection. Several Christian sects share custody of

King David's Tomb on Mount Zion in Jerusalem

the church, which was originally built by Constantine the Great, then rebuilt and dedicated by the Crusaders in A.D. 1149. The building stands at the end of the Via Dolorosa (Way of Sorrows), believed to be the path over which Jesus carried his cross to Calvary. Jesus was last seen by his followers on the Mount of Olives before he ascended to heaven. All these sites attract many religious pilgrims.

Islamic sites. Jerusalem is Islam's third holiest city, after Mecca and Medina in Saudi Arabia. According to tradition, the Prophet Muhammad originally selected Jerusalem as the *qibla*, the direction the faithful should face during prayer. But the prophet later redirected his followers to face Mecca instead of Jerusalem when praying, to symbolize Islam's independence. This change helped ease the tension that had existed between Muslims and Jews. Muhammad is said to have ascended to heaven from a stone now enclosed by a golden-domed shrine called the Dome of the Rock. The Dome of the Rock and an ancient mosque called Al Aqsa Mosque rank among the holiest sites in Islam. They form the central features of al-Haram al-Sharīf.

The People of Jerusalem

About two-thirds of Jerusalem's people are Jews. Arab people known as Palestinians make up nearly all the remaining one-third of the population. Generally, Jews live in West Jerusalem and Palestinians in East Jerusalem. Growing numbers of Jews also live in new neighborhoods in East Jerusalem. The central business district, in West Jerusalem, is almost entirely Jewish, and the markets of the Old City are mostly Arab. The most common languages are Hebrew, Arabic, and English.

The population of Jerusalem has grown substantially since Israel became independent in 1948. The city continues to add to its population through both natural growth and immigration. Only about half of Jerusalem's people are native-born Israelis. Many others are Jews who have immigrated to Israel from countries around the world. Large numbers have come from Poland, Russia, and other Eastern European countries; from other Middle Eastern countries; and from northern Africa, prominently Morocco. As a result, Jerusalem's Jewish citizens represent a mixture of cultures and nationalities.

Jerusalem's Jewish citizens also differ in the extent to which they follow the laws and practices of Judaism. Secular Jews have a strong sense of Jewish identity but may observe few, if any, reli-

Ultra-Orthodox Jews gather in prayer.

gious traditions. A group of extremely traditional Orthodox Jews called *haredim* or *ultra-Orthodox Jews* make up about a third of Jerusalem's Jews and are the fastest-growing group in the city. Many haredim follow ways of life that developed among Jewish communities in Eastern Europe hundreds of years ago. Most haredim speak a Germanic language called Yiddish along with Hebrew. Most men wear long black coats, beards, dangling side curls, and black, sometimes fur-trimmed, hats. The women typically wear long dresses, black stockings, and headscarves or wigs for modesty.

Confrontations have occasionally developed between Jews of different religious convictions over observances of Jewish law. Many extremely religious Jews believe that only a life of prayer and religious study is proper for the holy city. For example, they have protested the opening of nonkosher restaurants. They also have demanded that their neighborhood streets be closed to traffic during the Jewish Sabbath, from sundown Friday to sundown Saturday. A small group of haredim called Neturei Karta (Guardians of the City) do not even recognize the state of Israel. They believe that only the Messiah, whom God will send, can establish the Jewish state.

Architecture

Jerusalem's architecture is a mixture of old and new. The Old City contains architectural examples from each major period in the city's history. Many ancient historical sites and places of worship stand near modern shopping centers and industrial zones. Architecture from the late 1800s and early 1900s displays European influences. Usefulness rather than style characterizes new apartment buildings constructed by the government as housing for immigrants. Many buildings, old and new, have matching exteriors because all construction is required to be faced with a cream-colored limestone called *Jerusalem stone*, produced by nearby quarries.

Culture

Jerusalem can be described as a vast open-air museum because of the many archaeological sites throughout the area. The city also has many indoor museums, some dealing with Biblical history. The Israel Museum is famous for its collections of fine art and archaeology. It includes a building called the Shrine of the Book, where some of the ancient manuscripts called the Dead Sea Scrolls are exhibited. Other notable museums include the Rockefeller Museum and the Bible Lands Museum, both famous for their archaeological treasures. The L. A. Mayer Museum of Islamic Art displays Islamic textiles, pottery, and other arts and crafts.

Jerusalem is a major center of education and religious study. Hebrew University of Jerusalem offers courses in many areas of scholarship but is especially famous for science, law, archaeology, mathematics, and Jewish studies. Students from throughout the world attend seminaries in Jerusalem to become rabbis, ministers, priests, or Islamic religious leaders. The Islamic seminaries are supported by Muslim foundations called *waqfs*, which receive income from endowed land and other property throughout the Islamic world. The foundations also support Islamic law schools, prayer rooms, colleges, orphanages, homes for the poor, public fountains, baths, mosques, and tombs. Jerusalem also has many schools called *yeshivas* for study of the Talmud, a collection of Jewish religious and civil laws.

The Jerusalem Symphony Orchestra plays regular concerts at Henry Crown Symphony Hall. Music lovers can also enjoy concerts by chamber music ensembles and choirs, and performances by several dance companies. Night life flourishes at many of the city's restaurants and cafés, and at movie theaters. Local and international festivals provide a wide variety of cultural events that range from opera and theater to classical music and rock music.

Economy

Tourism is one of Jerusalem's main economic activities. The city has hundreds of hotels, restaurants, travel agents, taxis, and guides to serve tourists. Many people in Jerusalem also work for the government or Hebrew University. Construction has become a major source of employment as the city continues to grow. Jerusalem is also the headquarters of many technology companies.

Jerusalem has almost no heavy industry but does have some modern factories, mostly in West Jerusalem. They produce chemicals, clothing, leather goods, machinery, and plastics. There are also printing, diamond-polishing, and food-processing industries. Older handicraft industries include embroidery, pottery and glassware, silverwork, and wood carvings.

Government

After Israel took control of East Jerusalem and the Old City in 1967, the Knesset established Jerusalem as a single city under Israel's administration. The citizens of Jerusalem elect a 31-member Municipal Council for five-year terms. The citizens elect the city's mayor for a four-year term. The city is governed by a multiparty coalition of religious and secular parties.

History

Ancient times. Jerusalem's origin dates back about 4,000 years. About 1000 B.C., King David captured the city from a people called the Jebusites and made it the capital of the Israelites. David's son King Solomon built a magnificent place of wor-

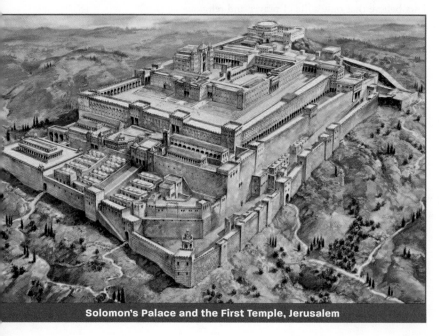

Solomon's Palace and the First Temple, Jerusalem

ship, the First Temple, in his capital city. Solomon also built a great palace complex consisting of many buildings. After Solomon died in about 928 B.C., his kingdom split into a northern kingdom called Israel and a southern kingdom called Judah. Jerusalem remained the capital of Judah.

In 587 or 586 B.C., the Babylonians conquered Judah, destroyed Solomon's Temple, and took many Jews to Babylonia as captives. In 538 B.C., Cyrus the Great, king of Persia, allowed the Jews to return to Jerusalem after he conquered the Babylonians. The returning Jews then rebuilt their center of worship, the Second Temple.

By about 400 B.C., priests and scribes of the Temple had established laws governing Jerusalem. They helped the city recover as a religious center. Alexander the Great of Macedonia conquered King Darius III of Persia in 331 B.C. and took control of Judah in 332 B.C. Alexander and the kings who succeeded him granted administrative power to the priests and allowed the Jews to follow their own religion. But in 168 or 167 B.C., King Antiochus IV tried to stop the practice of Judaism. He angered the Jews by dedicating the Temple to the Greek god Zeus. The Jews, led by the warrior Judah Maccabee, overthrew Antiochus. About 165 B.C., the Jews recaptured the Temple and rededicated it to God. Judah Maccabee's family, the priestly Hasmoneans, established an independent state that lasted about 80 years.

Roman rule. In 63 B.C., the Roman general Pompey the Great captured Jerusalem and made it part of the Roman Empire. In 54 B.C., the Roman general Marcus Licinius Crassus stole the Temple's funds. The Romans named Herod the Great king of the Jews, and he took control of Jerusalem in 37 B.C. Herod began a huge building program and made major architectural changes in the city. He also restored the Temple.

Beginning in A.D. 6, Judea (the Roman name for Judah) had no king. Jerusalem was ruled by a Roman *procurator* (administrator). Roman rule was generally peaceful, but riots were sometimes set off by leaders who claimed to be sent by God to preserve Judaism. The Romans arrested most of these leaders, who were called Zealots, and crucified them. Jesus of Nazareth arrived in Jerusalem in about A.D. 28 and declared the coming of the Kingdom of God. His followers believed he was the Messiah. But Jewish leaders said he had *blasphemed* (insulted God). They brought him before the Roman procurator,

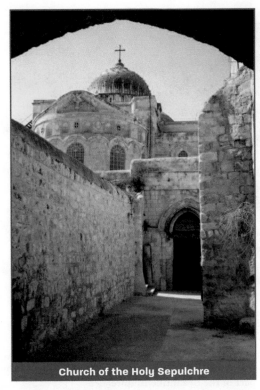

Church of the Holy Sepulchre

Pontius Pilate, who sentenced him to be crucified.

Roman rule became harsh, and the Jews, led by the Zealots, began a major revolt in A.D. 66. They seized Jerusalem and held it until the Roman general Titus retook it in A.D. 70. The Romans destroyed the Temple and much of the city's fortifications. Only part of the Western Wall of the Temple Mount remained. Many Jews died during the siege. Survivors were either executed or enslaved and exiled.

Jerusalem remained largely uninhabited until about 130, when the Roman emperor Hadrian announced plans to build a Roman city on the site. He renamed the city Aelia Capitolina and built temples to Roman gods, including one to the god Jupiter on the Temple Mount. The Jews, led by a warrior named Bar Kokhba, rebelled again in 132 and recaptured the city. Hadrian drove out the rebels three years later and tried to end all Jewish hope of regaining Jerusalem by prohibiting Jews from visiting or living there. But the city's importance as a spiritual center continued.

By the early 300s, the ban against Jews visiting the city was no longer strictly enforced. After Constantine the Great became the sole emperor in 324, he replaced Jerusalem's Roman structures with Christian monuments and built several churches

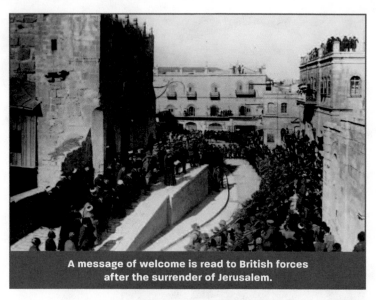

A message of welcome is read to British forces
after the surrender of Jerusalem.

there, including the Church of the Holy Sepulcher. He also restored Jerusalem as the city's name.

In 395, the Roman Empire split into the West Roman Empire and the East Roman Empire, also called the Byzantine Empire. Jerusalem became part of the Byzantine Empire.

Muslim rule. In the early 600s, control of Jerusalem changed three times. First, Persian troops captured the city and held it from 614 to 629. Byzantine forces regained control but lost Jerusalem again in 638, this time to Muslim Arabs. The Dome of the Rock was built from 688 to 691, during the rule of a caliph (Muslim leader) named Abd al-Malik ibn Marwan.

During the 900s and 1000s, a number of Muslim groups fought for control of Jerusalem. In 1099, the Crusaders, who were European Christians, captured Jerusalem from the Muslims in the First Crusade. The Crusaders killed both Muslims and Jews and established a Crusader state called the Kingdom of Jerusalem. Jerusalem served as capital of the kingdom until 1187, when the Muslim leader Saladin reconquered the city. Saladin repaired the city walls, and Muslims and Jews returned to the city in large numbers. Except for a brief period in the 1200s, Jerusalem remained under Muslim control for more than 700 years. The city was controlled by the Mamluks, Muslims from Egypt, from 1250 to 1516. Then the Ottoman Empire, a Muslim empire centered in what is now Turkey, took the city.

Under the Ottoman Empire, Jerusalem began to grow. At first, most of the city's population were Muslims, and even Christians greatly outnum-

bered Jews. However, increasing numbers of Jews immigrated to the city. By about 1870, Jews had become the majority group.

By the mid-1800s, construction had spread outside of the walls of the Old City. The Jewish neighborhood of Yemin Moshe was constructed in 1860 with the financial assistance of Sir Moses Montefiore, a Jewish philanthropist from England. Other neighborhoods north and west of the Old City followed, including Mea Shearim and Nahalat Shivah. Christian and Muslim groups also built new communities outside the walls.

British rule. In December 1917, during World War I (1914–1918), British troops under General Edmund Allenby captured Jerusalem and ended Ottoman control over the city. A month earlier, the British government had issued the Balfour Declaration, an official document supporting a national homeland for Jews in Palestine. The League of Nations, a forerunner of the United Nations (UN), made Palestine a *mandated territory*—that is, an area administered by the United Kingdom, under the League's supervision, in preparation for self-government. The British administration of Palestine centered in Jerusalem. As a result, many new houses and government buildings were erected.

Jewish immigration to Jerusalem increased during the 1920s and 1930s. Two factors stimulated immigration. One was the increasing strength of the Zionist movement, which advocated a Jewish homeland in Palestine. The other was the rise of the Nazi regime in Germany, which had anti-Jewish policies. Many new Jewish neighborhoods, such as Rehavia and Beit Hakerem, were established, primarily in West Jerusalem.

Anti-Zionist feelings developed among the Arabs in Palestine who wanted to create an independent Arab state. By the 1930s, severe anti-Jewish riots had broken out in Jerusalem. In 1947, the British turned over the question of Palestine's future to the United Nations. The UN voted to end the British mandate and divide Palestine between the Arabs and the Jews. Jerusalem would be an international city under UN control.

Arabs quickly responded to the UN resolution by attacking the Jews. In May 1948, British control ended and Israel declared its independence. Arab armies invaded the new state. Jerusalem's Old City came under heavy shelling. Many civilians were killed. By the end of 1948, Israeli soldiers held West Jerusalem, and Jordanian troops controlled East

Jerusalem and the Old City. The loss of the Western Wall and other Jewish shrines bitterly disappointed the Israelis. Armistices between Israel and neighboring Arab countries ended the war in 1949.

Israel established its seat of government in West Jerusalem. However, many countries refused to recognize Jerusalem as Israel's capital because of the UN plan to make it an international city. These countries instead established their embassies in Tel Aviv, Israel's chief commercial, financial, and industrial center.

Israeli control. War again broke out between the Arabs and Israelis in June 1967. After a brief conflict that Israelis call the Six-Day War and others call the June War or the 1967 Arab-Israeli war, Israel captured the Old City and East Jerusalem. At the conclusion of the war, huge crowds of joyful Jews entered the Old City for the first time in 19 years to pray at the Western Wall. Israel extended the boundaries of Jerusalem to include the Old City, its surroundings, and nearby villages. The people of East Jerusalem were granted the same rights and responsibilities that all other Israeli residents had, and were given the opportunity to apply for Israeli citizenship.

In 1980, the Knesset passed a law restating Israel's position that Jerusalem is the capital of Israel. The law also guaranteed protection for the holy places of all religions and continued free access to them.

In 2000, peace talks between Israeli and Palestinian leaders broke down. The two sides were unable to agree on key issues, especially those involving Jerusalem. One point of dispute was how much control Palestinians should have over East Jerusalem. The two sides also disagreed over who should govern the Temple Mount. That year, a Palestinian uprising against the Israeli government erupted. It was called the second *intifada* (an Arabic term meaning *shaking off*). The first intifada had taken place from 1987 to 1993. The second intifada lasted until 2005. During the uprising, suicide bombings and other acts of terrorism targeted Jerusalem and other parts of Israel and the Palestinian territories.

In 2002, the government of Israel began constructing a barrier to separate most of the West Bank from Israel. Some of the barrier runs through East Jerusalem, separating parts of it from the rest of the city. The barrier has interfered with many Palestinians' lives, making it the subject of political and legal debate.

The future of Jerusalem remains one of the most complex and delicate issues in the Arab-Israeli conflict. The Palestine Liberation Organization, the political body that represents the Palestinian people, and the Palestinian Authority, the government for many Palestinian areas, would like to establish an independent Palestinian state with Eastern Jerusalem as its capital. The Israeli government remains committed to keeping Jerusalem as both the Israeli capital and an undivided city.

NAZARETH (pop. 71,700), is a town in northern Israel. It was the home of Jesus Christ during His early youth. The town was in the Roman province of Galilee.

The Old Testament does not mention Nazareth. Nathanael in the New Testament expressed the attitude of the times about the village when he said, "Can there any good thing come out of Nazareth?" (John 1:46).

Nazareth remained insignificant for many years after the time of Christ. But pilgrims visited the town about A.D. 600, and a large basilica was built. The Arabs captured the city in the 600s. The crusaders built several churches there, but the Ottomans, who were Muslims, forced Christians to leave in 1517.

A new town of Nazareth stands on the site of the old town. The population of Nazareth today is far more than its population in Biblical times. The Latin Church of the Annunciation, completed in 1730, now rises where some people think the home of Mary, the mother of Jesus, stood. Since the 1700s, several religious denominations have constructed churches and monasteries in Nazareth. An ancient well, called Mary's Well, still flows, and people still take water from it.

An 8-meter-high security barrier separates Cross Israel Highway from the Palestinian West Bank town of Qalqilya.

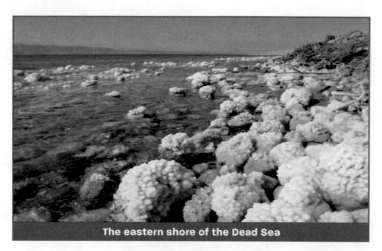

The eastern shore of the Dead Sea

THE DEAD SEA is a saltwater lake in southwestern Asia. Its shore, which lies about 1,373 feet (419 meters) below sea level, is the lowest place on the surface of Earth. The Dead Sea is the saltiest body of water in the world. It is about nine times as salty as the ocean. The lake lies at the mouth of the Jordan River and forms part of the border between Israel and Jordan.

The salty waters of the Dead Sea appear smooth and sparkling. Rocky and barren land surrounds the lake, and steep, brightly colored cliffs rise above its eastern and western banks. The lake is called the Dead Sea because few plants and no fish except brine shrimp live in its waters. In addition, little plant life grows in the salty soil around the Dead Sea.

The Dead Sea lies in the Ghor, a deep *fault* (break in Earth's outer shell, along which rock has moved). The lake covers about 400 square miles (1,040 square kilometers). It is 11 miles (18 kilometers) wide at its widest point and about 50 miles (80 kilometers) long.

A peninsula called Al Lisan juts into the Dead Sea from its eastern shore and divides the lake into a large northern basin and a smaller southern basin. The lake's deepest part is in the northern basin. In this area, the lake bottom lies 1,312 feet (400 meters) below the surface and about 2,622 feet (799 meters) below sea level.

Since the early 1900s, the water level of the Dead Sea has been slowly falling. The region gets less than 4 inches (100 millimeters) of rain annually. The Jordan River and several streams pour relatively fresh water into the lake. The fresh water mixes with salty water at the surface. But extreme heat in the area causes this water to evaporate rapidly. Thus, the Dead Sea never grows less salty. The high salt content of the water provides great buoyancy, enabling swimmers to float with ease.

The Dead Sea contains large quantities of minerals, including common salt (sodium chloride), bromine, calcium chloride, and potassium chloride. An Israeli company called the Dead Sea Works extracts the minerals from the water for use in making such products as table salt, fertilizer, and drugs.

At the southern end of the lake, a network of dikes forms shallow pools that cover more than 40 square miles (100 square kilometers). These pools evaporate and leave behind mineral solids, which are then refined by the Dead Sea Works. Some people believe bathing in the Dead Sea is healthful because of its high mineral content. Several area health resorts provide facilities for bathers.

The Dead Sea was probably formed millions of years ago when the Arabian Peninsula and the African continent shifted and formed the Great Rift Valley. The Dead Sea is mentioned in the Bible as the *Salt Sea* (Genesis 14:3). The ancient cities of Sodom and Gomorrah supposedly stood near the lake.

Columns of salt rock on the shore of the Dead Sea may have been the basis for the Biblical story of Lot's wife. Lot's wife was turned into a pillar of salt as punishment for disobedience to God (Genesis 19:26). Ancient manuscripts known as the *Dead Sea Scrolls* were found in caves near the Dead Sea. These scrolls date from as early as the 200s B.C.

ZIONISM is a movement to establish a Jewish national state in Palestine, the ancient Jewish homeland. Active Zionism began in the late 1800s and led to the establishment of Israel in 1948. Zionists revived the Jewish national language and culture and established the political and social institutions needed to re-create national Jewish life. Zionism now supports various projects in Israel and acts as a cultural bridge between Israel and Jews in other countries. *Zion* is the poetic Hebrew name for Palestine.

Movement to Palestine. Anti-Semitism in Europe in the late 1800s and early 1900s spurred the creation of the Zionist movement. Responding to the *pogroms* (riots against the Jews) in Russia, groups of Jewish youths calling themselves *Hoveve-Zion* (Lovers of Zion) formed a movement in 1882 to promote immigration to Palestine. They started what was called *practical Zionism*, which established Jewish settlements in Palestine. Theodor Herzl, an Austrian journalist, developed *political Zionism*, which worked for political recognition of the Jewish claim to a Palestine homeland.

Herzl was a reporter at the famous trial in 1894 of Alfred Dreyfus, a Jewish officer in the French army who was falsely convicted of treason. The Dreyfus affair convinced Herzl that if anti-Semitism could be an active force in a country as enlightened as France, Jews could not assimilate in non-Jewish society. To him, the only remedy was to create an independent Jewish state.

Herzl organized the Zionist movement on a worldwide scale at the First Zionist Congress in Basel, Switzerland, in 1897. In the early 1900s, however, many Jews, including the extremely religious and those who sought full assimilation, opposed the new movement.

THE BALFOUR DECLARATION.

In 1917, the United Kingdom issued the Balfour Declaration, which pledged British support for the establishment of a Jewish homeland in Palestine. About the same time, the United Kingdom freed Palestine from Ottoman control. The Balfour Declaration was included in the *mandate* (order to rule) over Palestine that the League of Nations awarded the United Kingdom in 1920. The mandate gave the Jewish Agency the responsibility for Jewish immigration. The Jewish community in Palestine grew significantly in the 1920s and 1930s. It developed various economic, political, and cultural institutions.

Arabs opposed a Jewish state in Palestine, and severe fighting broke out several times in the 1920s and 1930s. Assuming from earlier British promises to them that Palestine would be an Arab state, Arab leaders demanded an end to Jewish immigration and land purchase.

In 1939, the British began to set limits on Jewish immigration to Palestine. Palestine's Jews fought

Israeli children dance the hora, a popular dance among socialist Zionists, in the early days of the state of Israel.

against the restrictions, which they felt kept many Jews from fleeing increasing persecution in Europe.

After World War II ended in 1945, the Zionists wanted to establish a Jewish state immediately to provide a homeland for survivors of the *Holocaust*. The Holocaust was the mass murder of European Jews and others by the Nazis. But Arabs continued to oppose the creation of a Jewish state in Palestine. In 1947, the United Kingdom submitted the problem to the United Nations (UN). The UN voted to partition Palestine into an Arab and a Jewish state. In 1948, the Zionists proclaimed the state of Israel.

MLA Citation

"Israel." *The Southwestern Advantage Topic Source.* Nashville: Southwestern. 2013.

ADDITIONAL RESOURCES

Books to Read

Boraas, Tracey. *Israel*. Bridgestone, 2003.

Garfinkle, Adam M. *Israel*. Mason Crest, 2004.

Reich, Bernard. *A Brief History of Israel*. 2nd ed. Facts on File, 2008.

Reich, Bernard, and Goldberg, D. H. *Historical Dictionary of Israel*. 2nd ed. Scarecrow, 2008.

Reich, Bernard, and Goldberg, D. H. *Political Dictionary of Israel*. Scarecrow, 2000.

Sachar, Howard M. *A History of Israel*. 3rd ed. Knopf, 2007.

Shindler, Colin. *A History of Modern Israel*. Cambridge, 2008.

Torstrick, Rebecca L. *Culture and Customs of Israel*. Greenwood, 2004.

Young, Emma. *Israel*. National Geographic Children's Books, 2008.

Web Sites

Background Note: Israel

http://www.state.gov/r/pa/ei/bgn/3581.htm
Information from the U.S. Department of State.

CIA Factbook: Israel

https://www.cia.gov/library/publications/the-world-factbook/geos/is.html
Information from the on-line edition of the World Factbook of the United States Central Intelligence Agency (CIA).

Country Profile: Israel

http://www.bbc.co.uk/news/world-middle-east-14628835
Information from the BBC.

Foundation for Middle East Peace

http://www.fmep.org/
Home page of a nonprofit organization dedicated to informing Americans about the Israeli-Palestinian conflict.

Israel Minister of Foreign Affairs

http://mfa.gov.il/MFA/Israel+Ministry+of+Foreign+Affairs.htm
This site is designed to provide basic information about Israel and its people, and to offer comprehensive material on the Israeli government and its policies.

Israel News: Jerusalem Post Internet Edition

http://www.jpost.com/
Current Israeli news from the Jerusalem Post newspaper.

Israel's Institutions of Government

http://www.knesset.gov.il/israel_eng.htm
Comprehensive information about the branches of the Israeli government.

Jewish Virtual Library

http://www.jewishvirtuallibrary.org/jsource/index.html
Judaic Treasures of the Library of Congress

Judaism and Jewish Resources

http://shamash.org/trb/judaism.html
Links to Internet-based resources for the study of Jewish history and culture and Judaism.

Permanent Mission of Israel to the United Nations

http://www.israel-un.org/
Official Web site of the Permanent Mission of Israel to the United Nations.

Shamash Home Page

http://www.shamash.org/
Resources for study of Israel and Judaism, provided by the Shamash Project.

United States Embassy in Israel

http://israel.usembassy.gov
Official Web site of the United States Embassy in Israel.

Search Strings

Arab-Israeli War

Arab-Israeli War Gaza Strip West Bank (212,000)

Arab-Israeli War "Gaza Strip" "West Bank" "Palestine Liberation Organization" Palestinians (37,700)

Arab-Israeli War violent conflict "Gaza Strip" "West Bank" "Palestine Liberation Organization" Palestinians (17,000)

Israeli Government

Israeli government democratic republic parliament Knesset (82,500)

Israeli government democratic republic parliament Knesset "prime minister" "Labor Party" "Kadima" "Likud bloc" (25)

Israeli government democratic republic parliament Knesset "prime minister" (68,000)

Jerusalem, The Holy City

Jerusalem "Holy City" capital Israel spiritual center (60,300)

Jerusalem "Holy City" capital Israel spiritual center Jews Christians Muslims (28,400)

Jerusalem "Holy City" capital Israel spiritual center Jews Christians Muslims "Old City" "West Jerusalem" "East Jerusalem" (174)

BACKGROUND INFORMATION

The following articles were written during the year in which the events took place and reflect the style and thinking of that time.

Israel (1948)

At midnight on May 14, 1948, the Jews in Palestine proclaimed the new state of Israel. The new nation began its life with territory whose boundaries were hotly disputed. The Jewish part of its population—or Israeli—increased in numbers with every ship's arrival, and much of the Arab part of it was fleeing.

During the rest of 1948, Israel enlarged its territory, won many small battles against hostile Arabs, and received recognition of some sort from about half the nations of the world. It held up challenging fists not only to neighboring Arab states but also to the proud and powerful British Empire.

Preparation for Israel. The partition plan for Palestine adopted by the United Nations on November 29, 1947, had assigned to a Jewish state about 5,500 square miles in three nearly disconnected parts of Palestine. The population of these areas included about 536,000 Jews and 400,000 Arabs. Fighting between Jews and Arabs began immediately. As a result, by May 14, 1948, about four out of every five Arabs had departed from most of the territory assigned to the Jews, as well as from Jaffa and other areas left to Arabs.

New government and war. Great Britain formally gave up its mandate over Palestine on May 14. Immediately David Ben-Gurion, as provisional prime minister, proclaimed the existence of the state of Israel. Three councils of government were set up to act until elections could be held and a constitution drafted and adopted.

The United States and the Soviet Union recognized Israel. But the United States granted only *de facto* recognition—recognizing that a government had in fact been established but withholding approval of it as a lawful and rightful government. Great Britain and the Arab states refused to recognize Israel.

Fighting continued, but with a difference. Before, the Jews had had to fight only the Arab military groups in Palestine, plus guerrillas from neighboring states. Now the regular forces of Egypt, Lebanon, Syria, Trans-Jordan, Iraq, and Saudi Arabia entered the war against Israel. Israel called up about 85,000 fighters and devoted five-sixths of its revenue to the war. The Arab states were said to have at least 115,000 troops. But all except about 10,000 in the Arab Legion of Trans-Jordan were poorly equipped and little trained. Israel fought energetically, and was steadily victorious.

Both sides were ready to accept an ill-kept truce for four weeks from June 11. At its end the Arab League preferred to go on with the war. The Israeli advanced rapidly, taking Lydda, Ramleh, Ras el-Ain, and Nazareth. Increasing thousands of Arabs fled their homes. Cease-fire came again on July 18.

The United Nations mediator, Count Folke Bernadotte, tried ceaselessly to arrange terms of peace. His proposal that the Jews accept Western Galilee instead of the Negeb met no favor in Israel. He was assassinated on September 17.

After the death of Bernadotte, the Irgun Zvai Leumi and the Stern Group, Zionists who practiced terrorism and violence, were dissolved. In mid-October Israel began an offensive southward. Their forces took Beersheba, defeated various Egyptian forces, and surrounded some 3,000 Egyptians in Faluja.

On November 4 the Security Council of the United Nations ordered Israel and Egypt to go back to the positions held before October 14. On November 16 the Assembly of the United Nations ordered an armistice and peace negotiations. But fighting continued. In December, Israeli forces invaded Egyptian territory to a depth of 40 miles. British Air Force planes were sent out on reconnaissance, and five were shot down by the Israeli, with the loss of

some lives. A serious state of tension resulted between the British and Israeli governments.

On December 11 the Assembly of the United Nations created a conciliation commission of three members representing the United States, France, and Turkey. Meantime the acting mediator, Ralph Bunche, arranged that representatives of Egypt and Israel should proceed to the island of Rhodes and begin a peace conference.

Israel applied on November 29 for U. N. membership, but this was refused.

Preparations were made for the election of a legislative assembly on January 25, 1949.

Constitution. In December the Israeli Government announced a proposed constitution, based on features of the United States, French, and British systems of government. It provided for a democratic form of government, with separation of the executive, legislative, and judicial branches. Executive power was to be centered in a Prime Minister, with the President having much less authority than he. Much of the constitution was devoted to the protection of basic human rights. Provision was made for ensuring the rights of Arabs and other minority groups. Holy days of Judaism, Christianity, and Islam alike were recognized as legal days of rest for their members. A Constitutional Assembly was to meet after the January elections to work out a final draft of the constitution.

Israel (1967)

Israel nearly doubled its responsibilities in its sudden victory over the combined Arab armies in June. It also added many new headaches. Israeli forces seized Jerusalem and occupied the entire west bank of the River Jordan, the Gaza Strip, the Sinai Peninsula, and the Syrian heights above the Sea of Galilee.

The cost of victory was high, although Israel suffered relatively few casualties—679 killed, 2,563 wounded. Costs of mobilization, the loss of industrial manpower to the army, and equipment were $13,000,000 a day for the six-day war. World Jewry raised $500,000,000, however, and $171,200,000 from State of Israel Bond sales met the deficit.

The government took steps, ignoring severe foreign criticism, to secure its triumph. The *Knesset* (parliament) formally annexed Arab Jerusalem. The Mandelbaum Gate was torn down and the halves of Jerusalem it had divided were united under Israeli currency, Israeli laws, and Israeli supervision

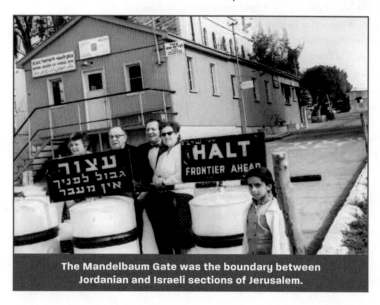

The Mandelbaum Gate was the boundary between Jordanian and Israeli sections of Jerusalem.

of the schools. Israel pumped oil for its own use from wells in occupied Sinai and widened the channel of the Jordan to increase its water supply.

Economic struggles with a serious recession were not as successful. Unemployment reached 10 percent as Israel's traditionally booming economy felt the effects of war. There were 38,000 unemployed workers registered at labor exchanges, and, for the first time in history, the government issued unemployment compensation grants. The 1966 growth rate of 3.5 percent fell below the 6 percent the World Bank considered necessary to help deter inflation in Israel.

The United States granted $27,500,000 in agricultural products. Romania extended a $35,000,000 credit in April for Israeli textiles in exchange for Romanian beef and timber.

A continuing decline of immigration caused concern. In 1966, there were 25,000 immigrants compared to 30,000 in 1965, far short of the 40,000 required yearly to sustain economic growth.

Politics. The war produced a partial realignment in Israel's internal politics. Three labor parties planned to merge: Mapai, the dominant party in the Knesset; Rafi, headed by war hero Moshe Dayan; and Achdut Ha'avoda, the party of former defense minister Yigal Allon. The combined party would have had a clear majority in the Knesset. But negotiations broke down over Rafi's insistence that Dayan replace Mapai's Levi Eshkol as prime minister.

Israel (1979)

Israel ended one era and started another with the signing of a peace treaty with Egypt on March 26, 1979. With the return of the Sinai town of Al Arish to Egyptian control on May 25, Israel had open borders with an Arab state for the first time in its 31-year history. The formal renunciation of war by both countries meant that Israel could savor the atmosphere of peace, despite the continued hostility of the rest of the Arab world.

Despite the general euphoria, there were many Israelis who felt that peace with Egypt might in the long run compromise the nation's security. Debate in the Knesset (parliament) over ratification of the treaty lasted three days, the longest on record over a single issue. The treaty was eventually approved by a 95 to 18 vote, but the opposition included many members of Prime Minister Menachem Begin's Likud Party. One member, Geula Cohen, resigned from the party to work against ratification.

Moshe Dayan, 1967

West Bank settlements. Disaffection of other supporters shook the Begin government. The heaviest blow was the resignation of Foreign Minister Moshe Dayan on October 21. Dayan quit because he disagreed with the government policy toward the Palestinians and the occupied territories of the West Bank and the Gaza Strip. However, the prime minister defeated all parliamentary challenges. The major divisive issue was the future of the Jewish settlements established on the West Bank by members of the ultranationalist Gush Emunim (Faithful Bloc) in defiance of the negotiations to prepare the area for transfer to an autonomous Palestinian authority. The Gush Emunim belief that the Holy Land was given by God to the Jewish people was shared by many Israeli leaders, including Begin himself. In April, the Cabinet lifted a ban on Israeli purchases of Arab land in the West Bank and approved new settlements if they were established on lands that had been taken over by the military and were justified on security grounds.

On December 26, during his first visit to the West Bank since April 1978, Begin vowed to keep the area under Israeli control. His remarks were intended to quiet the protests of the Israeli militants. Shortly before, the Knesset had rejected a bill aimed at annexation of the occupied territory.

Gush Emunim settlers began building a new West Bank settlement at Elon Moreh, near Nablus, in June. Arab farmers in the area protested, petitioning Israel's Supreme Court for redress.

An Israeli archaeologist points to the name of Jesus in
an excavated third- or fourth-century Christian church.

A demonstration by 40,000 members of the Peace
Now movement, an Israeli group that advocated a
ban on all such settlements, followed as Israeli public opinion turned against the settlers. In a landmark decision on October 22, the Supreme Court
ruled Elon Moreh illegal and gave the settlers 30
days to move to another site on land not owned by
Arabs. In a "last compromise" announced on
November 19, near the end of the 30-day time
limit, the government delayed departure of the
Elon Moreh settlers, calling for a two-stage withdrawal from the area over a six-week period. The
settlers won another five-week delay on December
30. The settlers were to move to Mount Kabir, an
area with no privately owned Arab land. The plan
was devised to avoid having to use Israeli troops to
remove settlers.

Mayors quit. Tension between the Israeli
Palestinians and the government rose in November when the mayor of Nablus, Bassam al-Shaka,
was arrested and threatened with deportation to
Jordan on charges of supporting terrorism.

The arrest enraged the Palestinians, and, on
November 13 and 14, all 25 mayors of the Arab
towns in the occupied West Bank and the Gaza
Strip resigned, leaving the areas without munici-
pal leadership. The arrest also brought criticism of
the government from other countries, notably the
United States and Egypt, as well as from many
Israelis. After weeks of talks and negotiations, the
Israeli government reversed its order to deport
Shaka and released him from prison on December
5. He returned to Nablus in triumph. The other
mayors then withdrew their resignations.

An interest in minority rights also affected the
Israeli Bedouin population. With the entire Sinai
Peninsula scheduled for return to Egypt, Israel
began building military bases to replace those given
up in the Sinai. But the expropriation of Bedouin-
owned land for a road project resulted in another
Supreme Court decision halting the work and citing the Government Land Authority for contempt.

Terrorism down. There were fewer incidents of terrorism than in previous years, though a
Palestinian raid on the Israeli coastal town of
Nahariyya in April set off an Israeli invasion of
southern Lebanon and Israeli air attacks as far
north as Beirut. Friction between Israeli Jews and
Israeli Arabs increased as the latter increasingly
lined up with the Palestine Liberation Organization (PLO). In the West Bank, schools and the
Arab Bir Zeit University were closed for most of
the school year. Israel received considerable criticism for alleged mistreatment of Arab prisoners.
A United States diplomat charged that beatings
and torture of Palestinian prisoners were common
practice in Israeli jails.

Coalition shaken. Begin's fragile coalition
was endangered on November 12 when a move to
tighten Israel's relatively liberal abortion law was
defeated in the Knesset. After the vote, the small,
ultraconservative Agudat Israel Party threatened
to withdraw its support of Begin, which would
have cut his government majority to one vote.

Resubmitted to the Knesset on December 17,
the amendment passed by a vote of 58 to 53. As
a result, abortions will no longer be allowed in
Israel for social and economic reasons. Essentially,
the law affects the poor because expensive illegal
abortions are readily available and Israel has never
prosecuted a physician for performing such an
operation.

Inflation up. In the long run, Israel's future
as a viable nation depended more on the solution
of critical economic problems than on the handling
of Israeli-Arab or Israeli-Palestinian relations.
Inflation rose from 48 percent in 1978 to 80 percent in 1979. During debate on the budget,
approved by the Knesset in July, opposition members walked out, accusing the government of drafting a $14.8 billion budget that was already
inadequate to cover the costs of inflation. Strikes in
various sectors—the largest being a strike of
40,000 civil servants in May that shut down the
country—added to the inflationary pressures. To

make matters worse, the diamond industry went into a worldwide recession, forcing a one-month layoff of Israel's diamond workers. During October, Begin managed to survive several confidence votes in the Knesset as well as the defection of Foreign Minister Dayan, mainly because there was really no alternative to his regime.

Scientists found evidence that as much as 300 million to 2 billion barrels of oil may be lying beneath Israel's Dead Sea valley. Such a find could eventually make the country independent of foreign sources of petroleum.

Israel (2005)

On February 8, 2005, Prime Minister Ariel Sharon and Palestinian President Mahmoud Abbas agreed at a summit in Sharm el-Sheikh, Egypt, to "cease all acts of violence against Israelis and Palestinians everywhere." Their declaration virtually ended the Palestinian *Intifada* (uprising) that began in September 2000. However, sporadic clashes between Palestinian militants and Israeli forces continued throughout the year.

Gaza withdrawal. Prime Minister Sharon's plan to "unilaterally disengage" from the Gaza Strip was implemented in August 2005 with the dismantling of all 25 Israeli settlements in the Palestinian-claimed area. Another four Israeli settlements were dismantled in the West Bank. The last Israeli soldier pulled out of the Gaza Strip in September.

The withdrawal was followed by intensive negotiations in which United States Secretary of State Condoleezza Rice helped Israeli and Palestinian officials resolve differences regarding the opening of four routes: three connecting Gaza with Israel and one connecting Gaza with Egypt. Secretary of State Rice announced in November that agreement had been reached on opening these routes.

Improved international relations. Israel's pullout from the Gaza Strip quickly resulted in improved relations between Israel and the Islamic and Arab countries. On September 1, Israeli Foreign Minister Silvan Shalom met with Pakistani Foreign Minister Khurshid Mahmud Kasuri in Istanbul, Turkey's capital. Shalom described the meeting as "a huge breakthrough." On September 15, Shalom met with Qatari Foreign Minister Sheik Hamad bin Jassem al-Thani, who praised Israel for its withdrawal from Gaza.

Political shake-ups. Former Prime Minister Shimon Peres unexpectedly lost the leadership primary of the Labor Party to challenger Amir Peretz on November 9. Peretz, who as a child had immigrated to Israel from Morocco, was the leader of Histadrut, the major federation of Israeli trade unions. As a union leader, Peretz had opposed the conservative economic policies pursued by Finance Minister (and former prime minister) Benjamin Netanyahu. Peretz also had long argued that the Likud government's focus on Israeli settlers in the Gaza Strip and West Bank "came at the expense of the poor in Israel proper."

After being elected Labor Party leader, Peretz pulled his party out of the national unity Cabinet, arguing that such cabinets "are anathema to democracy." By doing so, he created a political dilemma for Prime Minister Sharon, who also faced a rebellion in his own Likud Party from hardliners who had strongly opposed the Gaza pullout.

On November 21, Prime Minister Sharon announced that he was leaving Likud, which he had co-founded in 1973, to form a new centrist party, called *Kadima* (Forward), dedicated to working toward a lasting peace with the Palestinians. Ousted Labor leader Peres later announced his support for Kadima.

In late December, Prime Minister Sharon suffered a mild stroke. On January 4, 2006, he suffered a second, far more serious stroke and underwent a series of operations. His deputy, Ehud Olmert, took over as caretaker prime minister.

Rabin commemoration. On November 14, 2005, Israel commemorated the 10th anniversary of the assassination of Prime Minister Yitzhak Rabin. Thousands of people, including about 30 foreign dignitaries, attended the commemoration in Tel Aviv. Among those in attendance was former U.S. president Bill Clinton, who had worked closely with Rabin for peace in the Middle East.

Earliest church. Israeli Antiquities Authority archaeologists announced in November that they had discovered what appeared to be the oldest Christian church in the Holy Land, dating back to the 200s or 300s. Excavating on the grounds of a prison at Megiddo (the biblical site of Armageddon), the archaeologists uncovered a well-preserved mosaic bearing the name of Jesus Christ in ancient Greek, as well as images of fish (a Christian symbol) and an altar.

Iraq

Iraq is a country in southwestern Asia. The majority of the Iraqi people are Arabs. There is also a large Kurdish population. A major portion of Iraq's economy depends on oil exports. Baghdad is Iraq's capital city and its largest city.

HOT topics

Explore Stereotypes and How People's Views of Middle Easterners Have Changed Since the Iraq War. Many people view the Iraqi people, especially women, as being an oppressed, backwards people. Shortly following the Iraq war, due to the civil unrest within the country, people believed most Iraqis to be religious zealots and extremists who commit acts of terrorism. They believe that most Iraqis consider themselves enemies of the United States. In reality, there are many university-educated men and women working in fields such as law, medicine, and engineering, who just want to live a peaceful life free of ruthless dictatorships and American occupation.

Iraq War. In March 2003, the United States and its allies invaded Iraq and procured the fall of Saddam Hussein's regime. On May 1, 2003, United States president George Bush declared an end to major combat operations in Iraq. Restoring stability, rebuilding the country and a democratic government, and maintaining security against Iraqi and foreign militants remained ongoing efforts by Iraqi, U.S., and allied forces. In December 2011, the last of the U.S. troops withdrew, and the war was declared officially over.

HOT topics

Saddam Hussein's Regime.
Saddam Hussein (1937–2006) was president of Iraq from 1979 to 2003. Hussein was a ruthless dictator who authorized the relocation or killing of hundreds of thousands of his own Iraqi people, mostly the Kurdish. He often allowed the use of chemical weapons against the Kurds. In 1991, he ordered Iraqi forces to invade and occupy Kuwait, resulting in the Persian Gulf War. After increased tensions with many countries and Hussein's refusal to fully cooperate with United Nations weapons inspectors, coalition forces invaded Iraq, brought down Hussein's regime, and eventually captured Hussein. In 2006, an Iraqi court charged and convicted Saddam Hussein of the Shiite massacre, and then executed him by hanging.

Iraq's New Government.
In 2005, a new Constitution made Iraq a federal republic. A Council of Representatives was established; members are elected to 4-year terms. The prime minister is nominated by the political party with the largest number of seats. This nomination must be approved by the council. A president and two deputy presidents are also elected by the council. The prime minister is the head of the government. The president and prime minister each serve 4-year terms and the president may serve up to two terms. Iraq has 18 provinces or governorates. In addition, the constitution provides for a Kurdish Regional Government for Kurdish areas in northern Iraq.

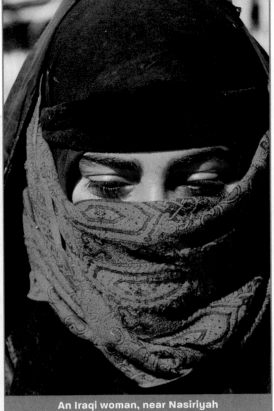

An Iraqi woman, near Nasiriyah

TRUE or FALSE?

Since the Iraq war, insurgents and religious extremists are trying to force the oppression of women in Iraq.

A screen shot of citizens and soldiers toppling a statue of Saddam Hussein

THE BASICS

Iraq is an Arab country at the head of the Persian Gulf in southwestern Asia. The country is bordered by Turkey, Iran, Kuwait, Saudi Arabia, Jordan, and Syria. Baghdad is Iraq's capital and largest city.

The world's first known civilization and other early cultures developed along the Tigris and Euphrates rivers in what is now Iraq. The ancient Greeks called part of Iraq and the surrounding region *Mesopotamia* (between rivers) because it lay between the Tigris and Euphrates rivers. For thousands of years, civilizations there have depended on controlling flooding from the two rivers and on using their waters for irrigation.

Iraq became part of the Arab empire in the A.D. 600s and absorbed Arab Muslim culture. Today, about 75 percent of Iraq's people are Arabs. Iraq also has a large Kurdish population that has struggled on and off for self-government for many years.

Iraq's economy depends heavily on the export of oil. From the 1950s through the 1970s, income produced by the oil industry improved living conditions for Iraq's people.

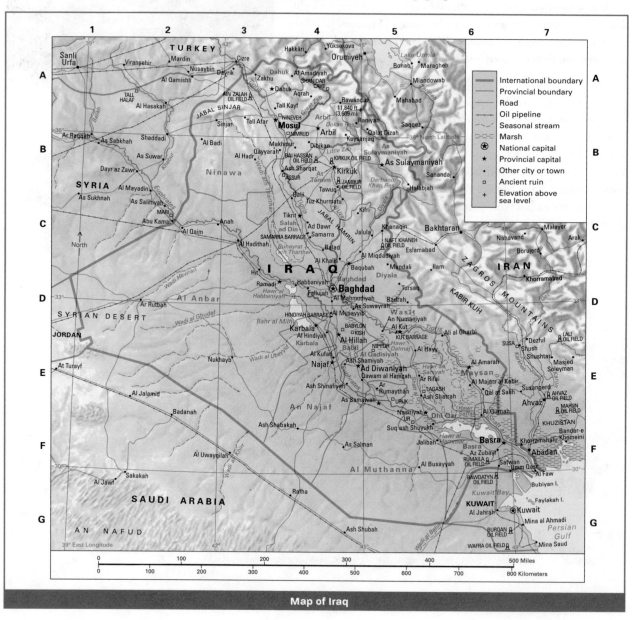

Map of Iraq

Between 1980 and 2003, Iraq—under the leadership of President Saddam Hussein—became involved in three wars that have had devastating effects on the country. In the first war, Iraq fought Iran from 1980 to 1988. The second war followed Iraq's invasion and occupation of Kuwait in 1990. In response to the invasion, 39 nations sent forces to the region and defeated Iraq in the Persian Gulf War of 1991. The third war, called the Iraq War, began in 2003. A military coalition led by United States forces invaded Iraq and overthrew Hussein. A new Iraqi government later took office. However, the country was left unstable and on the brink of civil war. Iraqi and foreign militants, claiming to fight for Iraq's freedom from invaders, have carried out many attacks against coalition troops and their Iraqi allies, both military and civilian. The Iraq War officially ended in 2011.

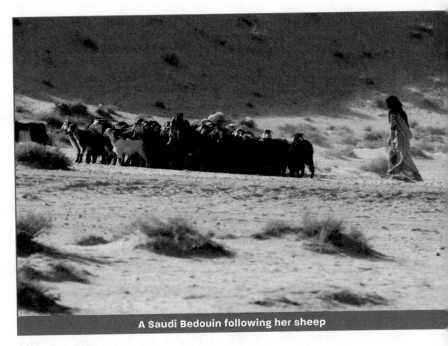

A Saudi Bedouin following her sheep

 Government

National government. Iraq's Constitution, approved in a 2005 referendum, made the country a federal republic. The legislature is called the Council of Representatives. Voters elect council members to 4-year terms. The political party with the largest number of seats nominates the prime minister, who must be approved by the council. The council also elects the president and two deputy presidents. The president and prime minister each serve 4-year terms, and the president may serve up to two terms. The prime minister is the head of government.

Local government. Iraq has 18 provinces called *governorates*. In addition, the Constitution provides for a Kurdistan Regional Government for the Kurdish areas in northern Iraq.

Armed forces. Before the Persian Gulf War of 1991, the Iraqi army was one of the largest in the world, with an estimated 955,000 troops. In 2003, after U.S.-led military forces overthrew President Saddam Hussein, the Iraqi armed forces were dissolved. The U.S.-led coalition forces then assumed responsibility for Iraq's security and defense. A new Iraqi military force, assembled and trained by the U.S. military, cooperated with coalition forces until foreign troops withdrew at the end of 2011.

People

Iraq's population has been expanding rapidly. About three-fourths of Iraq's people live in a fertile plain that extends from Baghdad south along the Tigris and Euphrates rivers. This area has many of Iraq's largest cities and towns.

Arabs make up about 75 percent of Iraq's population. Approximately 20 percent of the country's people belong to Iraq's largest ethnic minority, the Kurds. Other ethnic groups in Iraq include Armenians, Assyrians, Turkomans, and Yazidis.

Language. Arabic is spoken throughout the country. Kurdish is spoken in Kurdish areas. Both are official languages.

City life. Most of Iraq's people live in cities. The number of people living in urban areas has increased dramatically since the 1940s as a result of migration from rural areas. Many people have moved to the cities in search of work. Others fled rural villages and southern Iraqi cities that were damaged by wars. Overflowing urban populations have resulted in severe unemployment and housing shortages in some cities.

Wealthy city dwellers work in business and government. Many of them live in the suburbs. People at middle-income levels include office workers, craftworkers, and small business owners. Many of them reside in apartments in the cities. Many laborers and factory and oil workers commute to jobs in Iraq's cities from homes in nearby villages.

Clothing styles vary in Iraq's cities. Middle-class and wealthy people generally wear clothing similar to that worn by North Americans and Europeans. Most laborers prefer traditional clothes. For men, these garments include long cotton gowns and jackets. Traditional dress for women consists of a long, concealing gown and a scarf that covers much of the head.

Rural life. Many of the people who live in rural areas of Iraq are villagers who farm for a living. Many farmers lease land from the government. Herders form a small part of rural society. Bedouin *nomads* herd camels, goats, and sheep in western Iraq. Nomads are people who move with the seasons to find pastureland for their herds. Some Kurds graze livestock in northern Iraq.

Buildings in the rural areas of southern and central Iraq are made of dried mud and brick. In the north, villagers build stone houses.

Clothing in the countryside is traditional. Arab men wear gowns and checkered headdresses. Women dress in long black robes, and some veil their faces. Kurdish men wear shirts and baggy trousers with sashes. Kurdish women wear trousers but cover them with a dress.

Food and drink. Iraqis eat a varied diet that includes vegetables, rice, flat bread, meat, fish, and dates. Bread, rice, and meat are the main foods at many meals. Grilled lamb, chicken, and fish are popular. *Sanbusak,* a traditional Iraqi dish, consists of moon-shaped dough stuffed with cheese or meat. Popular beverages in Iraq include tea, coffee, and fruit juices.

Recreation. Iraqis enjoy a variety of sports and games, including soccer, horse racing, backgammon, and chess. Weddings and other family events are occasions for traditional folk dances and songs.

Religion. About 95 percent of Iraq's people are Muslims. More than half of the country's Muslims are Shiites (members of the Shi`ah branch of Islam). The other Muslims belong to the Sunni division. Most Arabs living southeast of Baghdad are Shiites. Central and southwestern Iraq is a mixture of Sunni and Shiite Arab populations. The Kurds are Sunnis. Christians and other groups make up about 5 percent of the Iraqi population. When the Baath Party ruled Iraq from 1968 to 2003, most of its high-ranking members were Arab Sunni Muslims. Many Shiites resented the Sunni monopoly on governmental power.

Education. Iraqi law requires all children from ages 6 through 12 to attend school. Some children continue their education in vocational or secondary schools. Iraq has many universities, including those in Arbil, Baghdad, Basra, Mosul, and Tikrit. A higher percentage of men than women attend colleges and universities. More than half of Iraq's adult population can read and write.

The Land

Iraq's land regions are: (1) the northern plain, (2) the southern plain, (3) the mountains, and (4) the desert.

The northern plain, a region of dry, rolling land, lies between the Tigris and Euphrates rivers north of the city of Samarra. The highest hills in the area rise about 1,000 feet (300 meters) above sea level. There are a small number of farming villages in the northern plain.

The southern plain begins near Samarra and extends southeast to the Persian Gulf. It includes the fertile delta between the Tigris and Euphrates rivers, where a large number of Iraq's people live. The Tigris and Euphrates meet at the town of Al Qurnah and form the Shatt al Arab river, which empties into the gulf. Some of Iraq's major oil fields are located between the Shatt al Arab and the border with Kuwait.

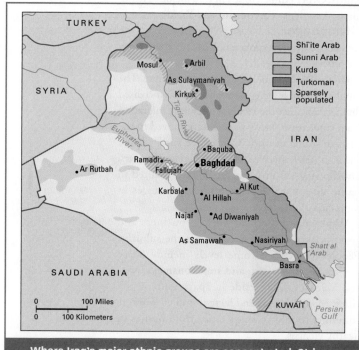

Where Iraq's major ethnic groups are concentrated. Stripes indicate areas shared by more than one group.

Complex dam and irrigation systems control the flow of water in the southern plain. As a result, the region has experienced rising farm productivity and more permanent human settlement, especially north of Al Kut. Much of the region south of Al Kut is marshland, due to frequent flooding and poor drainage. In the 1990s, the government drained much of the marshland, harming the environment and to local communities. After Hussein's overthrow in 2003, local residents began reflooding the area to restore the marshland.

The mountains of northeast Iraq are part of a range called the Zagros in Iran and Iraq that runs into the Taurus Mountains of Turkey. The mountains rise to more than 10,000 feet (3,000 meters) near Iraq's borders with Iran and Turkey. Kurds live in the region's foothills and valleys. Valuable oil fields in the region lie near the cities of Mosul and Kirkuk.

The desert covers southwestern and western Iraq. Most of this region of limestone hills and sand dunes is part of the Syrian Desert, which stretches into Syria, Jordan, and Saudi Arabia. Scattered throughout the desert are *wadis*—valleys that are dry most of the year but become rivers after a rain.

Climate

Iraq's climate ranges from moderate in the north to semitropical in the east and southeast. The west and southwest have a desert climate—warm or hot days and much cooler nights. Summer high temperatures average more than 100°F (38°C) throughout much of Iraq. Winter low temperatures may drop to around 35°F (2°C) in the desert and in the north.

In general, little rain falls in Iraq. Average annual precipitation ranges from 5 inches (13 centimeters) of rain in the desert to 15 inches (38 centimeters) of rain and snow in the northern mountains. Most of the precipitation falls between November and April.

Economy

The export of oil has played a vital role in Iraq's economy since the 1950s. But Iraq has tried to become less dependent on oil exports by expanding other industries. In the 1970s, Iraq's economy prospered. But starting in the 1980s, wars greatly damaged the economy. Trade routes were disrupted, ports were closed, and factories were destroyed. Also, a United Nations (UN) trade

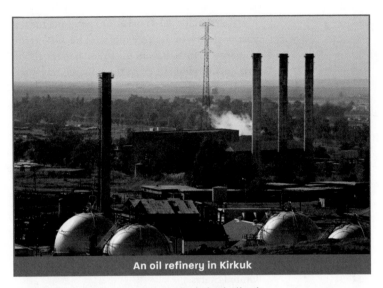
An oil refinery in Kirkuk

embargo imposed in August 1990 halted all oil exports from Iraq. The embargo was partially lifted in 1996 and fully lifted in 2003.

Industry includes mining, manufacturing, and construction. Oil is the chief mineral resource. It accounts for a large portion of Iraq's *gross domestic product* (GDP)—the total value of all goods and services produced within the country in a year. Iraq has one of the world's largest oil reserves and is a significant oil producer. Iraq's major oil fields are in southern Iraq near the Kuwait border and west of Kirkuk in the north. The country also mines natural gas and salt.

Oil refining and petrochemical production make up an important industry, despite wartime damage to refineries. Several of Iraq's chemical and oil plants are near the cities of Baiji, Basra, and Kirkuk. Other factories in Iraq process farm products or make such goods as cement, fertilizers, and textiles.

Service industries provide jobs for many of Iraq's workers. These industries account for about one fourth of the country's total GDP. Leading service industries include banking and government.

Agriculture. Iraq's crops are predominantly grown near the Tigris and Euphrates rivers. Major crops include barley, dates, grapes, rice, tomatoes, and wheat. Farmers also raise cattle, chickens, and sheep. Iraq must import much of its food.

Energy sources. Oil is, by far, Iraq's main source of energy. Natural gas is also an important energy source. War has interfered with the availability of electric power in the country.

International trade. Oil accounts for the vast majority of Iraq's exports. The UN trade embargo, which began in 1990, halted all oil exports from Iraq. In 1996, the embargo was eased when a UN "oil-for-food" program was implemented. Under this program, Iraq was allowed to export oil in exchange for food, medical supplies, and other nonmilitary goods. In 2003, the UN trade embargo was lifted, allowing oil exports to fully resume.

In addition to oil, Iraq also exports a small amount of aluminum, copper, fruits, and machinery. The country imports cars and trucks, electronics and electrical equipment, machinery, and various food products. Iraq's main trading partners include Italy, South Korea, Syria, Turkey, and the United States.

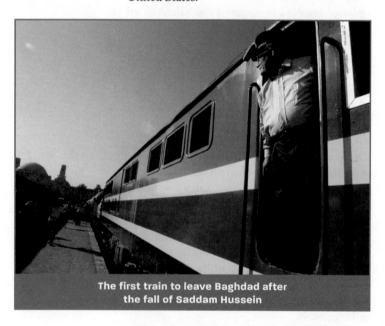

The first train to leave Baghdad after the fall of Saddam Hussein

Transportation and communication. Airlines, including the government-owned Iraqi Airways, link Iraq's cities. Airports in Baghdad and other cities handle international flights. Roads and railways also connect Iraq's largest cities to one another. The shipping facilities at Basra, once a major port, were damaged during Iraq's wars. As a result, use of the port has been limited. Many Iraqis rely on public transportation because they cannot afford automobiles.

Under the Baath Party regime, the government controlled all print and broadcast media that originated in Iraq, except for the media in Kurdish-run areas of the north. After the Baath regime was overthrown in 2003, the U.S.-led Coalition Provisional Authority established radio and television stations in the country. These stations were incorporated into a new Iraqi Public Broadcasting Service. In addition, Iraq has several private radio and TV stations. Iraqis can also pick up radio and TV broadcasts from other countries. Most newspapers are associated with political or religious groups.

History

Early days. The world's first known civilization developed in Sumer, now southeastern Iraq, about 3500 B.C. Sumer was part of Mesopotamia, an area that included most of present-day Iraq and parts of Syria and Turkey. Other ancient civilizations, including Assyria and Babylonia, flourished along the Tigris and Euphrates rivers between about 3500 and 539 B.C.

In 539 B.C., the Persians conquered Mesopotamia. Greek and Macedonian armies under Alexander the Great took the area from the Persians in 331 B.C. Greek rule continued until the Parthians, from the Caspian Sea area, established control by 126 B.C. Except for brief periods of Roman rule, the Parthians controlled Mesopotamia until about A.D. 224. That year, the Persian Sasanian dynasty (family of rulers) overthrew the Parthian Empire. The Sasanians ruled the region for about 400 years.

Arab rule. Arabs conquered the Sasanians in 637. The Arabs brought the religion Islam and the Arabic language to Mesopotamia. The Abbasid dynasty came to power in 750, and soon founded Baghdad as the capital of the Islamic Empire. Under the Abbasids, Arab civilization reached great heights. By 800, Baghdad had nearly a million people and was a world center of trade and culture.

In 1258, Mongols from central Asia invaded Mesopotamia and destroyed the Islamic Empire. The Mongols neglected Mesopotamia, and the region deteriorated culturally and economically under their rule.

Ottoman control. The Ottoman Empire, based in what is now Turkey, began to control Mesopotamia in the early 1500s. The Ottomans battled with the Persians and local Arab leaders to maintain control.

During the 1700s and 1800s, the Ottoman Empire declined in power and size in the face of new, strong nations that developed in Europe. The United Kingdom became involved in the Persian

King Faisal II

Gulf region in the 1800s to protect its trade routes with India, which was then under British rule. By World War I (1914–1918), the United Kingdom had become interested in Mesopotamia's oil resources.

British rule. British troops took Mesopotamia during World War I. In 1920, the League of Nations, a forerunner to the United Nations, gave the British a mandate (order to rule) over the area. The British set up a new government there in 1921. They renamed the country Iraq and chose an Arab prince as King Faisal I.

During the 1920s, British advisers retained positions in the Iraqi government, and the British controlled Iraq's army, foreign policy, finances, and oil resources. Some Iraqis opposed British involvement, and a movement for independence developed.

Independence. Under pressure from Iraq's independence movement, the United Kingdom signed a treaty with Iraq in 1930. In the treaty, the British promised military protection and eventual independence for Iraq. In return, Iraq promised the United Kingdom continued use of British air bases in Iraq. It also agreed to use British foreign advisers only. The British mandate over Iraq ended in 1932, and Iraq joined the League of Nations as an independent nation.

In the 1930s, Iraq's politicians disagreed over the alliance with the United Kingdom. King Faisal worked to balance the interests of Iraq's political factions and to unify the country's various ethnic and religious groups. Faisal died in 1933, and his son Ghazi became king. Ghazi was a weak ruler, and tribal and ethnic rebellions broke out. In 1936, anti-British groups in the army took control of the government, though Ghazi officially was still king. Ghazi died in 1939. His 3-year-old son, Faisal II, became king, but the boy's uncle, Prince Abdul Ilah, ruled for him.

In 1940 and 1941, during World War II, Iraqi government leaders and army officers sought an alliance with the Axis powers of Germany, Italy, and Japan. They hoped the alliance would end British influence in Iraq. The British tried to use Iraq as a military base in the war as authorized under the provisions of the 1930 treaty, and an armed conflict broke out. The British defeated the Iraqi army in 1941, and the pro-Axis leaders left the country. Iraq declared war on the Axis in 1943.

Inflation and supply shortages brought on by World War II transformed Iraq's society and economy. A wide economic gap developed between the rich and poor. Many Iraqis blamed the government for their economic situation.

In 1948, Iraq joined other Arab countries in a war against the new nation of Israel. The Arab defeat in the war touched off protests in Iraq and other Arab lands.

The 1950s. In 1950 and 1952, Iraq signed new agreements with foreign oil companies. The 1952 agreement gave Iraq 50 percent of the profits from oil drilled there. As a result of these agreements, Iraq's oil revenues rose dramatically. The government used some of this money to build hospitals, irrigation projects, roads, and schools. But the increased amount of money coming into Iraq also caused serious inflation.

King Faisal II took full power in 1953 at the age of 18. During the 1950s, opposition to the monarchy grew. Many Iraqis wanted a voice in government, and others felt that they had not benefited enough from the country's oil profits. In addition, a large number of Iraqis opposed the government's ties to the West. In particular, they objected to the Baghdad Pact—a U.S.-supported mutual defense accord that Iraq signed with Iran, Pakistan, Turkey, and the United Kingdom in 1955. Many Iraqis also felt that the ties with the West went against the *Pan-Arabism* movement.

Advocates of Pan-Arabism believed that Arab countries should strive for political unity and be free of outside influence. In 1958, army officers overthrew the government and declared Iraq a republic. The rebels killed King Faisal and Prince Abdul Ilah.

The republic. The army officers set up a three-man Sovereignty Council consisting of a Shiite Arab, a Kurd, and a Sunni Arab. The council issued a temporary constitution giving a cabinet the power to rule by decree with the council's approval. General Abdul Karim Kassem (also spelled Qasim), who led the revolution, became Iraq's premier. He reversed Iraq's pro-West policy and accepted both economic and military aid from Communist countries. Kassem set up land reform programs aimed at narrowing the gap between rich and poor. He also worked to develop industry in Iraq.

In 1961, Kurdish leaders asked Kassem to give the Kurds complete *autonomy* (self-rule) within Iraq and a share of the revenues from oil fields in northern Iraq. Kassem rejected the plan. In response, the Kurds revolted. A cease-fire was finally declared in 1964.

In 1963, army officers and supporters of the Pan-Arabism movement assassinated Kassem. The Pan-Arabists, led by the Baath Party, took control of the country and named Abdul Salam Arif president and Ahmad Hasan al-Bakr prime minister. Both were army officers. Later that year, Arif used the military to take over the government and remove the Baath Party from power. Arif died in 1966, and his brother, Abdul Rahman Arif, became president. The Arifs followed socialist economic policies.

Bakr overthrew Arif in 1968 and reestablished Baath control. The Baath Party soon began to dominate all aspects of Iraqi politics. Party leaders wrote a new constitution in 1970 that institutionalized Baath control of the government. Bakr supported further socialist economic reform and stronger ties with the Soviet Union. During Bakr's presidency, Saddam Hussein, who held important party and government posts, gained influence.

In 1973, the Iraqi government completed a takeover of foreign oil companies in the country. This *nationalization* of the oil industry made Iraq instantly wealthy.

In 1970, Bakr signed an agreement with the Kurds ending eight years of on-and-off fighting. The government promised that, beginning in 1974, the Kurds would have self-rule and several posts in the government. New fighting erupted in 1974 after the Kurds objected to revisions in the agreement. The revised agreement gave limited autonomy to the Kurds in the Kurdish Autonomous Region in northern Iraq. Government forces largely defeated the Kurds by March 1975. After Bakr resigned as president in 1979, Saddam Hussein succeeded him.

War with Iran. In September 1980, Iraq invaded Iran, and war broke out. The war resulted in part from boundary disputes, from Iran's support for the rebellious Kurds, and from the efforts of Shiite leaders in Iran to incite rebellion in Iraq's Shiite population. In addition, Iraqi leaders believed Iran had become somewhat unstable as a result of its 1979 revolution. They felt Iran's weakened position offered Iraq a chance to build its power in the region.

The war lasted eight years. Over 150,000 Iraqi soldiers died. Iranian air attacks on major cities wounded and killed many of Iraq's civilians. The war also severely damaged Iraq's economy. Bombs damaged oil facilities in southern Iraq, and Persian Gulf trade was disrupted. Iraq and Iran agreed on a cease-fire in August 1988.

During the war with Iran, Iraq's Kurds supported Iran. In 1987 and 1988, the Iraqi government lashed out against the Kurds. The army released poison gas in Kurdish villages, killing thousands of people. There also were reports that the army destroyed several Kurdish towns and that the inhabitants fled to Turkey and Iran.

The Persian Gulf War of 1991. In August 1990, Iraqi forces invaded and occupied Kuwait. Hussein had accused Kuwait of violating oil production limits set by the Organization of the Petroleum Exporting Countries (OPEC), thus lowering the worldwide price of oil. Iraq and Kuwait had also disagreed over territory and over Iraq's multibillion-dollar debt to Kuwait. The UN called for Iraq to withdraw from Kuwait and passed a resolution stating that all nations should stop trading with Iraq, except for food and medical supplies under certain circumstances. A coalition of 39 countries, organized mainly by the UN and the United States, opposed the invasion and sent armed forces to the Persian Gulf region.

In November 1990, the UN Security Council approved the use of force to remove Iraqi troops from Kuwait if they did not leave by January 15, 1991. Iraq refused to withdraw. War broke out

Oil wells burning during the Gulf War

between the allied forces and Iraq early on January 17 Baghdad time (January 16 U.S. time). The allies bombed Iraqi military targets in Iraq and Kuwait. Iraq launched missiles against Saudi Arabia and Israel. On February 24 (February 23 in the United States), allied land forces began moving into Iraq and Kuwait. They defeated the Iraqis after 100 hours. On February 27 U.S. time (February 28 in the war area), U.S. president George H. W. Bush declared a halt to allied military operations.

The war devastated Iraq. Estimates of Iraqi soldiers killed range from about 1,500 to as many as 100,000. A great number of civilians also died. Allied air raids destroyed roads, bridges, factories, and oil industry facilities and disrupted electric, telephone, and water service. Diseases spread through contaminated drinking water because water purification and sewage treatment facilities could not operate without electric power.

In March 1991, Kurdish and Shiite uprisings broke out. By April, Iraqi troops had put down most of the rebellions, but some fighting continued. Refugees fled to Iran and Turkey. The allies ferried supplies to them and set up a safety zone in northern Iraq to protect Kurds.

Iraq accepted the terms of a cease-fire agreement on April 6. On April 11, the UN Security Council officially declared an end to the war. In the agreement, Iraq promised to pay Kuwait for war damages. Iraq also agreed to destroy all of its biological and chemical weapons, its facilities for producing such weapons, and any facilities or materials it might have for producing nuclear weapons. The UN continued the trade embargo to pressure Iraq to carry out its agreements.

Iraq had also been staging air attacks against Shiites in southern Iraq who continued to oppose the government. In August 1992, to protect the Shiites, the allies imposed a ban on Iraqi military and civilian aircraft over the region. The safety zone in the Kurdish region also included a flight ban. The areas where flights were banned came to be called "no-fly" zones. The no-fly zone in the south did little to protect the Shiites. The government sent troops and tanks against the Shiites and destroyed dozens of villages. In 1993, the government began to drain the marshlands inhabited by Shiites known as the Marsh Arabs. As a result, Marsh Arabs who grew rice in these lands were deprived of a source of food. Thousands of Marsh Arabs and other Shiites fled to Iran.

In 1994, fighting broke out between rival Kurdish groups in the northern safety zone. In August 1996, Iraqi troops and tanks entered the zone in support of one of the Kurdish groups. The United States opposed this action, and in September launched missiles against military targets in southern Iraq. At the same time, the United States expanded the southern no-fly zone.

In December 1996, the UN began an "oil-for-food" program that partially lifted the embargo on Iraq. This program allowed Iraq to export oil under strict UN supervision. Most money from the oil sales was to be used to buy food and medicine for the civilian population. However, investigations later revealed that Hussein abused the program and profited illegally from oil sales.

Iraq had frequently failed to cooperate with UN teams sent to inspect suspected weapons sites. In 1998, Iraq began to refuse the entry of UN weapons inspectors into the country. In December of that year, the United States and the United Kingdom launched a series of air strikes against Iraq. United States and British officials said the attacks were to limit Iraq's ability to make *weapons*

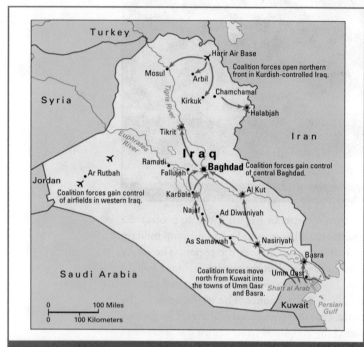

**Coalition ground forces invaded Iraq from the south in 2003.
Additional troops parachuted into northern Iraq.**

of mass destruction—that is, biological, chemical, and nuclear weapons. Afterward, U.S. and British planes attacked targets in Iraq many times to enforce the no-fly zones and to disable Iraq's air-defense systems.

By 2002, Iraq still had not fulfilled the terms of the 1991 cease-fire agreement. Under threat of military attack by the United States, Iraq allowed inspectors to return. During the inspections, the United States continued to accuse Iraq of violating the UN disarmament terms and maintained its threat of military action.

 The Iraq War (2003–2011). On March 20, 2003 (March 19 in the United States), U.S.-led forces launched an air attack against Baghdad, marking the beginning of the Iraq War. The U.S. government claimed the military campaign was intended to overthrow Saddam Hussein and to eliminate Iraq's weapons of mass destruction and its ability to produce them. British, Australian, Polish, and Danish forces participated in the war effort. The United States began the war without UN support. Although a number of countries, including Spain and Portugal, expressed support for the war effort, many others—notably France, Germany, Russia, and China—said the war was unjustified without clear UN backing.

After the initial strike on March 20, the U.S.-led coalition continued its campaign of heavy bombardment of Baghdad. Tens of thousands of coalition ground troops advanced through southern Iraq toward the city, sometimes meeting stiff resistance from Iraqi forces. Coalition air and ground attacks also occurred elsewhere in Iraq. The coalition troops reached Baghdad in early April. On April 9, they took control of central Baghdad.

By mid-April, coalition forces held all of Iraq's major cities. A U.S.-led administration called the Coalition Provisional Authority (CPA) assumed control of Iraq. Looting broke out in several cities, and coalition troops tried to establish order. Coalition officials also began searching for weapons of mass destruction. On May 1, United States president George W. Bush declared that major combat operations in Iraq had ended.

Later in May, the UN Security Council voted to end the UN trade embargo against Iraq. Critics of the embargo estimate that hundreds of thousands of Iraqis suffered severe hardship and even death under the sanctions.

In July, Hussein's sons Uday and Qusay, who had held high-ranking positions in their father's regime, were killed in a firefight with U.S. troops. In December 2003, U.S. troops captured Hussein himself near Tikrit.

In June 2004, the CPA was dissolved, and power was handed over to an *interim* (temporary) Iraqi government. Iyad Allawi—a former Baath Party member who later became an opponent of Hussein and went into exile—became prime minister of the government.

Since May 2003, coalition troops and Iraqi police have faced much resistance from both Sunni and Shiite militants in Iraq. Militants have carried out deadly guerrilla attacks and bombings against both military and nonmilitary targets. High-profile targets have included the UN headquarters in Baghdad; the Imam Ali Mosque in Najaf, a major holy site for Shiite Muslims; two Kurdish political party offices in Arbil; and sites in Baghdad and Karbala where Shiites gather each year for the religious festival of Ashura.

Since mid-2004, coalition troops have had frequent clashes with Iraqi Sunni militants in central Iraq, especially in Fallujah and Baghdad. They have also fought with Iraqi Shiite militants loyal to the radical Shiite cleric Muqtada (also spelled Moqtada) al-Sadr. A group believed to have ties to the worldwide terrorist network al-Qaeda has been blamed for a number of attacks. In mid-2004, Sunni militants gained control of Fallujah and a few nearby cities. United States and Iraqi forces regained control of Fallujah in November 2004 after launching major air and ground assaults on the city.

In late 2004, the Iraq Survey Group (ISG) issued a report stating that no weapons of mass destruction had been found in Iraq. The ISG, a team of American and British experts, conducted the search for weapons of mass destruction on behalf of the coalition.

In 2005, a special Iraqi court formally charged Hussein with ordering the massacre of over 140 Shiites in 1982. The court later charged him with genocide for killing over 100,000 Kurds in the 1980s. In November 2006, the court convicted Hussein of the Shiite massacre charges and sentenced him to death by hanging. He was executed the following month. Some observers criticized the methods and procedures of Hussein's trial and execution.

There are no official estimates of how many Iraqis have died as a result of the war. Most observers believe that tens of thousands of Iraqis, mostly civilians, have died. Some observers believe there may have been several hundred thousand Iraqi deaths.

In 2007, the United States sent 30,000 more troops to help the Iraqi government establish security throughout the country. The number of attacks dropped, but some violence has continued. By September 2010, U.S. forces had been reduced to just 50,000. The Iraq war was officially declared over in December 2011 with the withdrawal of remaining U.S. troops.

A new government. In January 2005, an election was held for a transitional National Assembly for Iraq. Before the election, Sunni militants had threatened to disrupt the election with violence. Nevertheless,

Moqtada al-Sadr

nearly 60 percent of all eligible voters went to the polls. Most of the voters were Shiite Arabs and Kurds, and a Shiite religious alliance won a majority of seats in the Assembly. A large number of Iraq's Sunni Arabs *boycotted* (refused to participate in) the election. Many objected to the *proportional representation* system introduced in the Assembly under the interim constitution. Such representation awards a political party a percentage of seats in the legislature in proportion to its share of the total vote cast. Some Sunnis also stayed away from the polls for fear that they would be attacked.

In April 2005, Ibrahim al-Jafari, a Shiite, was named interim prime minister of Iraq. Jafari was part of the United Iraqi Alliance (UIA), the political group that won the Assembly election. The Assembly oversaw the preparation of a new constitution for Iraq. In October, Iraqis approved the Constitution in a nationwide referendum.

In December 2005, Iraqis elected a permanent Council of Representatives to replace the National Assembly. The UIA received the most seats and nominated Jafari as prime minister. However, the other parties in the Assembly did not accept his nomination. He withdrew his candidacy in April 2006. The UIA then nominated Nouri Kamel al-Maliki, a Shiite, as prime minister, and the council approved his nomination. He became prime minister in May. The council also elected Jalal Talabani, a Kurd who had served as interim president, to a 4-year term as president.

In March 2010 elections, a Maliki-led coalition narrowly lost to a group led by former prime minister Iyad Allawi. In November, after months of negotiations, a new government was formed with Maliki remaining as prime minister.

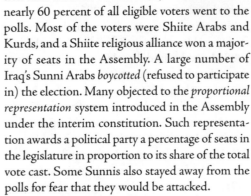

Iraqis waving to British troops, 2003

In 2011, antigovernment protests erupted in several Iraqi cities. Protesters called for improved government services and an end to official corruption. Several people were killed in clashes with security forces. The protests in Iraq followed similar events in Tunisia, Egypt, and elsewhere in the region.

SADDAM HUSSEIN

Saddam Hussein (1937–2006) was president of Iraq from 1979 to 2003. His rule ended shortly after United States and allied forces invaded Iraq in March 2003. This invasion marked the start of the Iraq War. United States troops captured Hussein in December 2003. He was executed by Iraqi authorities on December 30, 2006.

Hussein ruled Iraq as a dictator and was known for his ruthless actions. For example, in the late 1980s, he authorized the relocation or extermination of hundreds of thousands of Kurdish people in northern Iraq. This campaign included the frequent use of chemical weapons against the Kurds.

In August 1990, Hussein ordered Iraqi forces to invade and occupy Kuwait. The United Nations (UN) Security Council authorized military action to expel the Iraqi troops from Kuwait. In January 1991, a coalition of nations, organized mainly by the United States and the UN, began an air war against Iraq. After more than five weeks of bombing, coalition ground troops entered Iraq and Kuwait and quickly defeated the Iraqi forces.

During the 1990s and early 2000s, Iraq continued to have tense relations with many countries, particularly the United States. In March 2003, forces led by the United States began a military campaign against Iraq. The following month, the U.S.-led forces seized control of Baghdad, Iraq's capital, causing the fall of Hussein's government. United States officials said the main reason for the war was to disarm Iraq of *weapons of mass destruction*—that is, chemical, biological, or nuclear weapons. However, in the months following the U.S.-led invasion, search teams found no such weapons in Iraq.

In July 2003, Hussein's sons Uday and Qusay, who had held high-ranking positions in their father's regime, were killed in a firefight with U.S. troops. On December 13, 2003, U.S. troops captured Saddam Hussein after they found him hiding near his hometown of Tikrit. In 2005, an Iraqi court formally charged Hussein with ordering the

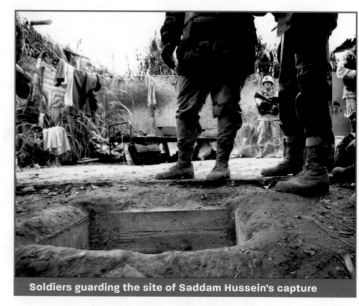

Soldiers guarding the site of Saddam Hussein's capture

massacre of over 140 Shiites in 1982. In 2006, the court charged him with genocide for killing over 100,000 Kurds in the 1980s. In November, the court convicted Hussein of the Shiite massacre charges and sentenced him to death by hanging. He was executed the following month.

Saddam Hussein al-Tikriti was born on April 28, 1937, near Tikrit. He joined the Baath Party in 1957. In 1959, Hussein took part in an attempt to kill Iraqi prime minister Abdul Karim Kassem (also spelled Qasim). After the attempt failed, Hussein fled to Syria and then to Egypt. There, he studied law at Cairo University. In 1963, Baath officers captured and killed Kassem, and Hussein returned to Iraq. But later in 1963, the Baath government was overthrown, and in 1964, Hussein was imprisoned. He escaped from jail in 1966.

The Baath Party regained control of Iraq in 1968, and Hussein quickly became one of the most powerful people in the Baath government. In 1969, he became vice chairman of the party's Revolutionary Command Council. Using Iraq's huge petroleum resources, Hussein supervised a successful development program in the 1970s. In 1979, he became chairman of the Revolutionary Command Council and president of Iraq. Iraq's development program was halted by a war between Iraq and Iran, which lasted from 1980 to 1988.

MLA Citation

"Iraq." *The Southwestern Advantage Topic Source.* Nashville: Southwestern. 2013.

ADDITIONAL RESOURCES

Books to Read

Augustin, Byron, and Kubena, Jake. *Iraq.* Children's Press, 2006.

Fattah, Hala. *A Brief History of Iraq.* Facts on File, 2009.

Haugen, David M., and others, eds. *Iraq.* Greenhaven, 2009.

Tripp, Charles. *A History of Iraq.* 3rd ed. Cambridge, 2007.

Web Sites

Ancient History: Babylonia

http://www.theology.edu/lec22.htm

The history of ancient Babylonia.

Background Note: Iraq

http://www.state.gov/r/pa/ei/bgn/6804.htm

Information from the U.S. Department of State.

CIA Factbook: Iraq

https://www.cia.gov/library/publications/the-world-factbook/geos/iz.html

Information about Iraq from the on-line edition of the World Factbook of the United States Central Intelligence Agency (CIA).

Country Profile: Iraq

http://www.bbc.co.uk/news/world-middle-east-14542954

Information from the BBC.

Frontline: The Gulf War

http://www.pbs.org/wgbh/pages/frontline/gulf/index.html

This companion Web site to the PBS television series features transcripts of interviews with key players in the war and war stories of pilots and soldiers. Includes maps, a chronology, and a guide to weapons and technology used in the war.

Iraq Daily

http://www.iraqdaily.com/

News about Iraq, from the WorldNews Network.

Kurdistan Regional Government

http://www.krg.org/

Home page of the authority that rules over much of the liberated area of Iraqi Kurdistan.

The Iraq Foundation Web Site

http://www.iraqfoundation.org/

Official Web site of the Iraq Foundation, an organization working for democracy and human rights in Iraq.

UN Office of the Iraq Program

http://www.un.org/Depts/oip/index.html

Information about the United Nations' Oil-for-Food program.

Search Strings

Explore Stereotypes and How People's Views of Middle Easterners Have Changed Since the Iraq War

Iraq stereotypes changing views of Middle Easterners (53,500)

Iraq stereotypes changing views of Middle Easterners religious zealots extremists terror (34,000)

Iraq War

Iraq War "Saddam Hussein" fall (353,000)

Iraq War "Saddam Hussein" fall rebuilding restoring democratic government (21,700)

Iraq War "Saddam Hussein" fall rebuilding country restoring stability democratic government (116,000)

Saddam Hussein's Regime

"Saddam Hussein" regime president Iraq Iraq changes in stereotypes since the war began women oppressed religious zealots extremists terrorism peaceful (1,980)

dictator Kurdish Chemical weapons (109,000)

"Saddam Hussein" regime president Iraq dictator Kurdish Chemical weapons "Persian Gulf War" conviction execution (921)

"Saddam Hussein" regime president Iraq dictator Kurdish Chemical weapons "Persian Gulf War" conviction execution WMD (641)

Iraq's New Government

Iraq new government constitution federal republic "Council of Representatives" prime minister (681)

Iraq new government constitution federal republic "Council of Representatives" prime minister "Kurdistan Regional Government" (120)

BACKGROUND INFORMATION

The following articles and features were written during the year in which the events took place and reflect the style and thinking of that time.

Iraq (1958)

Army officers murdered King Faisal II and his uncle, Crown Prince Abdul Illah, in July 1958, and seized control of the government. The leader of the revolt, General Abdul Karim el-Kassem, became the new Iraqi premier. He declared Iraq an independent Arab republic, and denounced the Arab Federation, formed by Iraq and Jordan in February.

The revolt came without warning. Army officers seized control of government agencies in Baghdad at dawn on July 14. They shot down King Faisal and his uncle in the royal palace. Faisal's premier, Nuri al-Said, escaped temporarily. But he was killed two days later when he tried to escape dressed as a woman. A rioting mob also killed three American civilians.

Premier el-Kassem announced a provisional constitution with civil and political liberties, and said that elections would be held at a later date. The new government recognized the government of the United Arab Republic, which King Faisal II had refused to do. It abolished the Iraq Development Board, and limited land holdings to about 250 irrigated acres or 500 non-irrigated acres. In December, the government executed former Premier Fadhil al-Jamali and two former army leaders. All three had served under Nuri-al-Said.

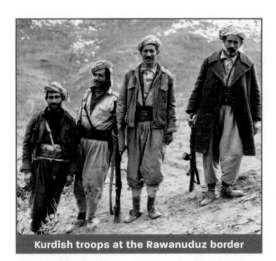

Kurdish troops at the Rawanuduz border

Iraq (1970)

A settlement reached on March 11, 1970, appeared to end the nine-year-old civil war with the Kurds, which had devastated northern Iraq. As part of the agreement, five Kurdish cabinet members were appointed March 29. The government also agreed to recognize a separate Kurdish nationality and grant the Kurds local autonomy. General Mustafa Barzani's Pesh Merga guerrillas disbanded, but Barzani refused to appoint a Kurd as one of Iraq's four vice presidents until the ruling Baathists named Kurdish governors to four northern provinces. A provisional Constitution defined Iraqis as two nationalities, Arab and Kurdish.

The 12,000 Iraqi troops stationed in Jordan for three years were withdrawn on October 22. They had taken no part in the border warfare or in guerrilla clashes with Jordan's army.

More than 40 persons were executed for complicity in an antigovernment plot that Iraq said was discovered in late January. A new land reform law announced in May limited individual holdings to 500 irrigated acres.

Iraq (1980)

Iraq sent its military forces into Iran on September 22, 1980. The outbreak of war climaxed steadily, increasing tension between Iraq's Baathist government and Iran's Khomeini regime as each sought to overthrow the other. Before the attack, President Saddam Hussein on September 17 unilaterally canceled the 1975 agreement that gave Iran half of the Shatt al Arab waterway between the two countries in return for Iran's dropping its support for Kurdish rebels in Iraq.

After reoccupying border areas given up in the 1975 treaty, Iraqi troops struck deep into Khuzistan province and attacked the Iranian cities of Khorramshahr, Ahvaz, and Dezful. Iraqi airplanes bombed Iranian airfields, cities, and oil installations, leaving the Abadan refinery in ruins.

Invasion stalls. But Iraqi expectations of a quick victory faded before fierce resistance by the supposedly weak Iranian Army. Iranian jets knocked out Iraqi oil installations around Kirkuk and Mosul in the north, and Basra in the south. They also bombed the capital, Baghdad. Iraqi offers of a cease-fire were rejected by Iran, and by November the war had become a stalemate, with Iraqi forces unable to capture key Iranian cities or knock out Iran's army and air force.

Despite the deadlock, the war proved an advantage to Hussein's Baathist regime in mobilizing popular support and demonstrating the emergence of Iraq as a power in the Persian Gulf region. On February 8, the 17th anniversary of the first Baathist seizure of power, Hussein issued an eight-point "Arab Charter" that would prohibit non-Arab bases on Arab soil, ban the use of force in resolving inter-Arab disputes, and establish a joint Arab defense force. The charter was accepted by 15 Arab states as well as the Palestine Liberation Organization. Syria and Egypt rejected it.

Little internal opposition to Baathist rule surfaced during the year, though one cause of the Iraqi invasion of Iran was the attempt by Iran's Khomeini regime to overthrow the Iraqi regime through Iraq's Shiite Muslims, who form a majority of the population. A Shiite subversive organization, *al Dawa al Islamiya*, was uncovered in April and prominent Shiite leaders, including the chief imam (religious leader), were executed as spies.

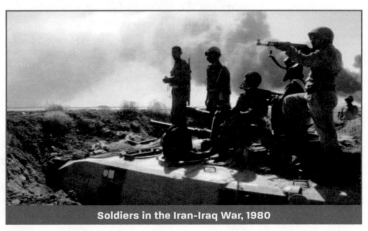

Soldiers in the Iran-Iraq War, 1980

With the regime firmly in power and the economy booming, elections were held on June 20 for a parliamentary assembly, the first since the 1958 overthrow of the monarchy. Voters elected a 250-member assembly, and Baath candidates won 75 percent of the seats. At the same time, the Kurds elected a 50-member legislative council for the autonomous Kurdistan region.

Iraq (1988)

Victory celebrations throughout Iraq marked the August 20, 1988, cease-fire that halted hostilities in the country's eight-year war with Iran. On August 8, both countries had formally accepted United Nations (UN) Security Council Resolution 598, which called for the cease-fire and negotiations for a permanent peace settlement.

Iraq had originally accepted the resolution after its passage in July 1987, but Iran had refused to take similar action, insisting that Iraq must be declared the aggressor in the conflict and forced to pay war reparations. After Iran agreed to the resolution on July 18, 1988, however, Iraq hedged for several weeks before finally accepting.

Military success. The Iraqis were somewhat justified in claiming victory in the war, as the fighting had tilted sharply in their favor earlier in 1988. Iraqi forces recaptured the Fao Peninsula near the head of the Persian Gulf in April in a lightning offensive that marked their first advance into Iranian-held territory since 1982.

A second Iraqi attack in May recaptured the area around Shalamcheh, an Iraqi port on the Shatt al Arab River. Its capture in January 1987 had brought Iranian forces within artillery range of Al Basrah, Iraq's second-largest city and its major port.

On June 25, 1988, a third major Iraqi offensive recovered the Majnoon Islands, a marshy area northeast of Al Basrah believed to contain a 30-billion-barrel oil field, Iraq's largest reserve. The area had been held by Iran since 1984.

In June 1988, Iraqi troops and the allied Mujaheddin-e-Khalq (People's Crusaders)—an Iranian group opposed to the government of Iranian leader Ayatollah Ruhollah Khomeini—captured the Iranian border town of Mehran. In July, Iraqi units captured the important border towns of Halabjah and Al Amarah in northeast Iraq, driving the Iranian Army and its Kurdish allies across the border.

Air war. Earlier in 1988, Iraqi aircraft bombed Iranian cities with devastating psychological effect.

Beginning in February, some 140 Soviet-designed Scud B surface-to-surface long-range missiles hit Teheran, Iran's capital, which had been thought to be beyond the range of those missiles.

Kurdish attacks. In August and September, following the cease-fire, the regime of President Saddam Hussein turned on Iraq's Kurds, many of whom had supported the Iranians in an attempt to win independence from Iraq. Several battalions of Kurdish rebels had fought with Iranian forces on the mountainous central front.

In the offensive into Kurdish areas, the Iraqi Army destroyed villages suspected of sheltering the rebels. At least 60,000 Kurdish refugees fled into Turkey. After the operation, the Kurds repeated previous accusations that the Iraqis were using chemical weapons, specifically mustard gas, to kill civilians. In March, Kurds had charged Iraqi forces with using chemical weapons to attack the Kurdish border town of Halabjah after its capture by the Iranians. Thousands of Kurdish civilians were reportedly killed or injured. In September, the United States, Great Britain, West Germany, and Japan asked the UN to investigate the charges.

The economy stood to gain enormously from an end to eight years of debilitating war. Aside from 350,000 to 400,000 Iraqi casualties and thousands of refugees displaced by the fighting, the war had cost Iraq an estimated $65.5 billion, including $33 billion in military costs and billions in lost oil revenues due to damaged installations.

To speed the reconstruction process, Hussein formed a new ministry of civilian and military industries in July. It would supervise the transition from a wartime to a peacetime economy. One goal within reach would be a 75 percent increase in non-oil exports. In March, Iraq reported the discovery of a new sulfur field, which increased reserves to 567 million short tons (515 million metric tons), and of an aluminum silicon reserve estimated at 330 million short tons (300 million metric tons). Both would add significantly to the country's export potential.

Killing. Hussein's oldest son, Odai, was jailed on October 21 for allegedly killing a drunken bodyguard. Hussein ordered an investigation.

Iraq (1991)

An international military coalition, led by the United States, launched a massive bombing campaign against Iraq on January 17, 1991. The attack began less than 17 hours after Iraq's President Saddam Hussein failed to meet a United Nations (UN) deadline for withdrawing his military forces from Kuwait, which Iraq had invaded in August 1990. On February 24, 1991, the United States-led coalition opened a ground war against Iraq. During the fighting, which ended on February 26, an estimated 110,000 Iraqi soldiers and tens of thousands of Iraqi civilians died. According to a UN report released on March 21, Iraq's public works, such as roads and bridges, were bombed into a "pre-industrial" age.

Cease-fire terms. The UN approved a permanent cease-fire resolution on April 3. Under the terms of this agreement, Iraq renounced its annexation of Kuwait and released all its prisoners of war. The cease-fire also required Iraq to return all property looted from Kuwait, pay war reparations, and permit the destruction of any nuclear, biological, and chemical weapons as well as any ballistic missiles with a range greater than 90 miles (145 kilometers).

According to the cease-fire, any sales of Iraqi oil were to be conducted under UN supervision, and revenues from the sales were to be used for food and medical supplies. A percentage of the profits from any sales (later set at 30 percent) were to go for war reparations. Iraq protested that the provisions of the agreement infringed on its independence.

Postwar uprisings by Shiite Muslims in southern Iraq and by Kurds in northern Iraq in March claimed at least 25,000 lives. Iran lent support to the Shiite Muslim rebels. In addition, defecting Iraqi Army units added to the chaos. The Iraqi Army responded forcefully to the uprisings, heavily damaging holy sites in al-Najaf and Karbala, where rebels had taken refuge.

An international crisis arose when more than 500,000 Kurds fled to Turkey to escape the army. Another 1 million Kurds escaped to Iran. Some 6,700 refugees, mainly children, died in camps along the Turkish-Iraqi border in April and May because of bad weather and poor sanitation. The Kurds accused the United States of encouraging them to rebel and then refusing to support their rebellion.

In mid-April, U.S., French, and British troops established a protected zone for the Kurds in northern Iraq. Most of the refugees had returned to their homes by late May. Coalition forces pulled out of the protected zone in July, leaving behind some 500 UN guards.

Sporadic fighting continued, however, between Iraqi forces and Kurdish rebels. The most serious flare-up occurred in October near Irbil and Sulaimaniya, where Kurdish rebels killed 60 unarmed Iraqi soldiers on October 8. About 50,000 Kurds fled the fighting there. At year-end, about 500,000 Kurdish refugees remained in Iran.

Kurdish talks. On April 24, Kurdish rebel leaders reported that they and Hussein had agreed in principle to a pact granting greater independence to Iraq's 3.5 million Kurds. The leaders of other Iraqi opposition groups strongly criticized the Kurds for negotiating separately with Hussein. On June 23, Massoud Barzani, the leader of the Kurdish Democratic Party, announced that Hussein had agreed to enact democratic reforms in Iraq and to permit the Kurds to elect their own provincial legislature. But other Kurdish leaders rejected the pact, refusing to sever ties with the West or to abandon their goal of an independent Kurdish state, as Iraq had demanded.

Catastrophic conditions emerged in Iraq during 1991 because of shortages of food and medical supplies and poor sanitation. In May, a team from the Harvard School of Public Health in Cambridge, Massachusetts, predicted that a lack of food and medical care could double the number of Iraqi children under age 5 expected to die in 1991. A July study by the UN's Food and Agriculture Organization also forecast widespread famine and malnutrition.

On August 15, the UN Security Council voted to temporarily lift the trade embargo against Iraq, imposed in August 1990, to permit a one-time sale of oil valued at $1.6 billion for the purchase of food and medical supplies. Iraq, however, refused the offer, contending that UN supervision of the sale and control over the revenues violated its independence.

Consolidating power. While promising political reform, Hussein consolidated his power by frequently shifting cabinet appointments and naming his relatives to key military and intelligence posts. In March 1991, Hussein relinquished the post of prime minister and appointed Sa'doun Hammadi, a Shiite, to the position. In September, however, Hussein fired Hammadi. Also that month, the ruling Baath Party announced that other political parties would be permitted to form only if they were not based on atheism, religion, race, or ethnicity.

The War in Iraq: the Military Campaign and Aftermath (2004)

—by Scott Thomas

A United States fighter jet carrying U.S. President George W. Bush landed aboard the U.S.S. *Abraham Lincoln* on May 1, 2003. The Abraham Lincoln was in the Pacific off San Diego, California, on its way home from the Persian Gulf, where a U.S.-led coalition force had been engaged in a war with Iraq since March 20 (March 19 in the United States). Dressed in the flying gear of a U.S. Navy fighter pilot, the president announced to the assembled crew and to the world that the military phase of the war was essentially over. Identifying former Iraqi leader Saddam Hussein as an ally of the al-Qa'ida terrorist network, President Bush described the victory in Iraq as a single battle in "a war on terror that began on September 11, 2001," the day militant Islamic terrorists attacked the United States. The president then vowed to keep weapons of mass destruction out of the hands of such terrorists. The declaration aboard the *Abraham Lincoln* capped a campaign in which the coalition forces, made up primarily of U.S. and British troops, conquered the forces of Saddam Hussein in less than six weeks. At the time, few people argued with the president's assertion that the war had been carried out "with a combination of precision and speed and boldness the enemy did not expect, and the world had not seen before." The conflict, however, proved to be far from over.

The Persian Gulf War. The war in Iraq was the second war fought between a U.S.-led coalition and the forces of Saddam Hussein. An earlier coalition, led by U.S. President George

H. W. Bush, father of George W. Bush, defeated Iraq in the Persian Gulf War of 1991. That war began after Iraq invaded and occupied Kuwait, Iraq's neighbor to the south. After the invasion, the United Nations (UN) Security Council authorized the coalition to expel Iraq from Kuwait, which it did in late February 1991.

Iraq agreed, as part of the cease-fire agreement ending the 1991 war, to destroy all weapons of mass destruction, that is, biological, chemical, or nuclear weapons. However, Iraq failed to cooperate completely with UN teams sent to inspect suspected weapons sites, and beginning in 1998, Saddam Hussein refused to allow the UN inspectors into the country.

The UN and weapons of mass destruction. President George W. Bush, soon after taking office in January 2001, began to assert that Hussein continued to develop weapons of mass destruction and, therefore, posed a threat to the United States. After the terrorist attacks on the United States in September 2001, President Bush argued that Hussein supported the al-Qa'ida terrorist network responsible for the attacks. Addressing the United Nations (UN) in September 2002, President Bush announced that the United States would take the lead to disarm the Hussein regime. He warned that the UN risked becoming irrelevant by failing to enforce its own resolutions. Soon after, the U.S. Congress gave President Bush authorization to use military force against Iraq.

The UN responded to President Bush's challenge by sending weapons inspectors into Iraq in November 2002. In the months that followed, the United States and the United Kingdom insisted that Hussein still was not fully cooperating with the UN. President Bush, in his State of the Union address in January 2003, asserted that evidence existed that Iraq was attempting to buy uranium in West Africa for use in an Iraqi nuclear arms program. He then informed the Congress that while the United States continued to seek the support of its allies in the UN, he would not wait for their consent to confront Iraq. He did, however, ask the UN Security Council to pass a resolution authorizing war against Iraq on the grounds that Iraq had failed to disarm itself of illegal weapons.

The member nations on the UN Security Council strongly disagreed on whether to take military action against Iraq. Arguing for more time to seek a diplomatic solution, France, Germany, and

Baghdad under attack, 2003

Russia refused to support the resolution, and it was never voted upon. The governments of the United States and the United Kingdom decided to go forward with the war despite having failed to receive UN authorization.

The war begins. On March 19, President Bush ordered U.S. armed forces already deployed in Kuwait and the Persian Gulf, more than 250,000 in number, to launch an attack on Iraq. U.S. forces were joined by some 50,000 British troops as well as relatively small numbers of soldiers from other countries, including Australia and Poland. President Bush announced that the war had begun minutes after U.S. Tomahawk missiles and bombs from "stealth" aircraft struck Baghdad, the Iraqi capital. The president noted in his declaration that his purpose was to "disarm Iraq, to free its people, and defend the world from grave danger."

In the days that followed, the coalition carried out intense bombing aimed at key targets in Baghdad and elsewhere. On March 20, a barrage of Tomahawk cruise missiles and guided bombs launched from U.S. Navy ships in the Red Sea and Persian Gulf rocked the capital in what U.S. officials described as a "decapitation attack" aimed directly at Saddam Hussein. The following day, an intense air assault on Baghdad triggered a series of explosions, sending columns of smoke and fire into the skies over the city. Officials with the U.S. Department of Defense announced that the assault was the opening of a promised "shock and awe" campaign that targeted Baghdad and other Iraqi cities with massive and widespread bombing. The U.S. Air Force subsequently dropped "bunker busters", enormous bombs, weighing 4,700 pounds (2,100 kilograms) on limited targets in Baghdad. Coalition warplanes also bombed the city of Al Basrah (also known as Basra) in the south and areas of northern Iraq controlled by Ansar al Islam, an Islamic militant group that U.S. and British officials identified as having links to the al-Qa'ida terrorist network.

The First Marine Expeditionary Force met heavy Iraqi fire on March 20 as U.S. troops, under the cover of intense allied artillery and aircraft bombardment, moved into Iraq from its southeastern border with Kuwait. The U.S. and British invasion forces seized strategically important airfields in southwest Iraq and the key port of Umm Qasr on the Faw Peninsula in southern Iraq. Umm Qasr is Iraq's only outlet to the Persian Gulf. By March 23, U.S. forces reached An Najaf,

General Tommy Franks addressing the troops as U.S. President George W. Bush looks on

an Islamic holy city, 100 miles (160 kilometers) south of Baghdad. However, a number of U.S. units further south remained engaged in fierce combat in and around the city of An Nasiriyah. U.S. Army General John Abizaid confirmed that Iraqi forces had ambushed a supply convoy and that U.S. military personnel, both men and women, were missing in action.

U.S. military commander General Tommy Franks confirmed on March 24 that coalition troops were within 60 miles (100 kilometers) of Baghdad, but he acknowledged that both U.S. and British forces were meeting stiff resistance and casualties were increasing. Franks announced that outlying units of Hussein's elite Republican Guard were under fire by the U.S. 3rd Infantry Division, which was backed by a fleet of helicopter gunships. Republican Guard units stationed on the southern outskirts of Baghdad were also under aerial attack. In the south, British units shelled Al Basrah, Iraq's second largest city, in response to attacks by Iraqi forces. At the same time, U.S. Marines battled their way through the streets of An Nasiriyah in southern Iraq in the kind of urban battle that U.S. military commanders had hoped to avoid. U.S. forces in the city reported that armed Iraqi men were jumping from buses and rooftops to shoot at them. The Marines were ordered into the city to secure two bridges over the Euphrates River that were needed to move troops north to Baghdad.

Large numbers of U.S. troops began crossing the Euphrates over the An Nasiriyah bridges on March 25 despite a desert sandstorm. U.S. and British forces were now positioned in a heavily armed column that stretched from Umm Qasr on the Persian Gulf to the city of Karbala just 50 miles

(80 kilometers) southwest of Baghdad, severely stretching coalition supply lines. Iraqi troops ambushed the U.S. 7th Cavalry between An Najaf and Karbala. In the fierce ensuing battle, U.S. troops, hunkered down in the blinding sandstorm, fought off hundreds of regular Iraqi soldiers and Fedayeen Saddam militiamen. The Fedayeen was a paramilitary group that answered directly to Saddam Hussein's eldest son, Uday. At Karbala, coalition troops faced the Republican Guard's Medina Division. U.S. General Richard Meyers, chairman of the Joint Chiefs of Staff, characterized the division as the best equipped, best trained, and most loyal of Saddam Hussein's forces.

Continuing fighting between Iraqi forces and coalition troops at An Nasiriyah and Karbala as well as on the road between the two cities forced allied military leaders to shift the focus of the land campaign in Iraq. The attack on the Republican Guard around Baghdad was delayed while U.S. and British forces fought Iraqi militia groups that were repeatedly attacking advancing allied troops from the rear.

The British offensive. In Al Basrah to the southeast, British forces continued to battle an estimated 1,000 Saddam Hussein loyalists for control of the city, where a rebellion against the ruling Baath Party had broken out. According to British military officials, Baath members attempted to put down the rebellion by firing mortars at the civilian population. The British responded by shelling the mortar positions and bombing Baath headquarters. A force of 1,000 Royal Marines next launched a massive offensive to take the town of Abu al-Qassib just outside Al Basrah. The capture of Abu al-Qassib completed the British encirclement of Al Basrah.

A second front. U.S. forces opened a second front, in the north, on March 27. More than 1,000 members of the 173rd Airborne Brigade parachuted into Kurdish-held territory about 30 miles (48 kilometers) northeast of Arbil, the main Kurdish city. Upon landing, the paratroopers were joined by Kurdish guerrilla fighters. U.S. military leaders noted that the second front would keep the Iraqi military from concentrating all its defenses against coalition forces in the south. After four days of allied air strikes in northern Iraq, the Iraqi Army abandoned Chamchamal. The town, located northeast of the major oil center Kirkuk, had been a stronghold of Ansar al-Islam militants. Kurdish guerrillas immediately moved into Chamchamal, providing coali-

The main presidential palace in Baghdad

tion forces with a strategically important forward position from which to drive on to Kirkuk.

Resistance to U.S. forces advancing northward into Baghdad began to crumble. U.S. Marines easily overcame the Baghdad Division of Iraq's Republican Guard after capturing a bridge over the Tigris River on April 2. The Guards were defending Al Kut, a city approximately 100 miles (160 kilometers) southeast of the capital. Soldiers with the U.S. Infantry, advancing north from An Najaf, seized a bridge over the Euphrates River at Al Musayyib, a city some 30 miles (48 kilometers) due south of the capital. Near Karbala, 50 miles (80 kilometers) southwest of Baghdad, an estimated 15,000 U.S. troops routed two other Republican Guard divisions and began moving toward the nearby Euphrates River.

The U.S. Army's 3rd Infantry Division, closing in from the southwest, pushed forward to Saddam International Airport, approximately 12 miles (20 kilometers) outside central Baghdad, and secured it on April 3 with little opposition. Other Army units moved forward to within 6 miles (10 kilometers) of the capital. U.S. Marines, driving toward the city from the southeast, met only scattered resistance from the Republican Guards and managed to cover 20 miles (32 kilometers) in a few hours. Allied aircraft made about 1,000 bombing runs over Baghdad, most of them aimed at Republican Guard divisions stationed around the capital.

The U.S. forces advancing in three columns from the southwest, south, and southeast placed Baghdad in a powerful vise that led thousands of Iraqis to flee the city. On April 4, bumper-to-bumper traffic choked roads leading north and northeast as U.S. ground forces sealed off key highways to the south. U.S. Marines halted their advance from the southeast at the city limits 10 miles (16 kilometers) from downtown Baghdad. The Marines had raced behind the Republican Guard's Nida Division, which put up little resistance after being bombarded through the night. West of the city, U.S. infantry completed their takeover of Saddam International Airport, which commanders renamed Baghdad International.

Some 2,500 Republican Guard soldiers surrendered to coalition forces between Al Kut and Baghdad. The surrender took place after the Iraqi division clashed with the U.S. Marine Expeditionary Force.

British forces in southern Iraq launched a major assault on Al Basrah on April 4. The 7th Armoured Brigade, known as the Desert Rats, stormed into the center of the city with several thousand troops and hundreds of tanks. They were greeted by hundreds of cheering and waving civilians.

U.S. forces occupied the center of the Shiite Muslim holy city of Karbala on April 6. A crowd of some 10,000 people, yelling "Saddam is no more," pulled down a statue of Hussein in the city's public square. The event marked the end of a five-day battle in which coalition forces routed several hundred Fedayeen Saddam fighters.

U.S. troops move into Baghdad. U.S. troops pressed into the center of Baghdad on April 7 and took control of a major presidential palace and other key buildings. The 3rd Infantry Division, backed by air support, met with only scattered pockets of resistance as it rumbled into the heart of the capital with more than 70 tanks and 60 Bradley fighting vehicles. The troops seized Iraqi President Saddam Hussein's main palace on the west bank of the Tigris River and secured a second palace, which had been abandoned by the Republican Guard. Late in the day, a U.S. Air Force B-1 bomber dropped four bombs, each weighing 2,000 pounds (900 kilograms), on a house in an affluent Baghdad neighborhood. U.S. military officials had ordered

the bombardment minutes after intelligence agents reported that they believed that Hussein, his sons, and other Iraqi leaders were meeting there. Hussein and his sons escaped the assault.

The following day, more than 20 buses and trucks filled with an estimated 500 Republican Guard soldiers and Fedayeen Saddam militia fighters crossed the Tigris River in Baghdad to stage a counterattack. According to U.S. military commanders, the Iraqis intended to retake control of the U.S.-held west bank of the river. The Iraqis fired assault rifles and rocket-propelled grenades at U.S. tanks blocking an intersection beyond the bridge. The U.S. infantry responded with artillery and mortar fire, and A-10 attack planes strafed the Iraqis, driving them back across the river.

Much of Baghdad had fallen to U.S. forces by April 9, and the government of Iraqi President Saddam Hussein had collapsed. Allied tanks and armored vehicles met no resistance as they swept across the Tigris River into Baghdad's eastern sector. As in Karbala days earlier, U.S. soldiers were met by cheering crowds of Iraqis attempting to topple an enormous statue of Hussein that dominated one of the city's public squares. In Baghdad's heavily populated southeastern neighborhoods, throngs of Shiite Muslims, long oppressed by the Hussein regime, cheered U.S. Marines as they pushed toward the center of the city. Hussein's government was dominated by members of the Sunni branch of Islam, a minority in Iraq compared with the Shiite branch.

By mid-April, coalition forces held all of Iraq's major cities. Several hundred Kurdish fighters under the command of U.S. special forces occupied

Baghdad International Airport undergoing reconstruction, 2003

Kirkuk on April 10. On April 11, U.S. special forces and Kurdish fighters entered the northern city of Mosul without a fight. U.S. Marines entered Tikrit, the last remaining Iraqi city not under allied control, on April 13. U.S. commanders had expected the Republican Guard and the Fedayeen Saddam militia to make a last stand at Tikrit, because it was Saddam Hussein's birthplace. However, the Marines met only sporadic resistance. A spokesperson for the U.S. Department of Defense announced on April 14 that major combat operations in Iraq were over.

After the fall of the Hussein regime, coalition forces in Iraq focused largely on restoring order and helping the Iraqi people establish a new government. However, the pacification and reconstruction of Iraq proved to be much more difficult than anticipated by some officials at the U.S. Defense Department. Massive postwar looting and the breakdown of Iraqi Army and security forces left a good deal of Iraq's infrastructure in shambles. Guerrilla attacks on coalition soldiers resulted in more U.S. casualties after May 1 than during the actual combat. And car bombings left dozens of people dead, including 23 officials with the United Nations mission in Iraq. By August, Defense Department officials had labeled the continuing hostilities in Iraq a classic guerrilla war.

The collapse of civil authority. The collapse of the Hussein government and the pullout of the Iraqi Army left much of Iraq without civil authority, and looting became widespread. In Baghdad, looters stripped most of the public

buildings, including hospitals, of supplies. Looters also ransacked the National Museum of Iraq. Thieves made off with about 12,000 items, including 32 ancient objects that archaeologists described as "of extreme importance." (Most of the important pieces eventually turned up or were quietly returned to the museum.)

Looting combined with sabotage at oil wells, refineries, and along pipelines brought much of Iraq's oil industry to a standstill. In May, Iraq, a country with the world's second largest oil reserves, was forced to import gasoline at U.S. expense from neighbors in the Middle East. A spokesperson for the Bush administration conceded in September that oil revenues from Iraq had proven to be a major disappointment. Prior to the war, the administration had claimed that Iraqi oil fields would quickly yield $100 billion a year, which could be used to fund the country's reconstruction. According to the latest estimates, Iraqi oil revenues may climb to $12 billion by the end of 2004.

Defense Secretary Donald Rumsfeld addressing Congress about Iraq

Looting also crippled Iraq's electric power system, already damaged by coalition bombing. Copper and other salable metals were repeatedly stripped from power plants and electric wires, which made it difficult to get the system up and keep it running. The resulting loss of power to run air conditioners, refrigerators, and water pumping stations made life for many Iraqis nearly unbearable, particularly at the height of the summer of 2003, when temperatures climbed as high as 130 degrees Fahrenheit (55 degrees Celsius). The failure of the U.S.-led coalition, with its vaunted technological know-how, to keep the lights on and the water running was a public relations disaster. Many Iraqis ended up blaming their misery on the Americans, rather than on the looters among them.

International observers who visited Iraq during this period blamed the widespread civil disorder on three factors: too many Iraqi criminals; too few U.S. soldiers; and the premature disbanding of the Iraqi Army. Saddam Hussein emptied Iraq's prisons in October 2002. His mass pardon released the country's entire criminal element into the general population just months before the beginning of the war. It is likely that Iraq's criminals took every advantage of the breakdown of civil authority that came with the collapse of Hussein's regime.

Critics of the Bush administration's handling of the war and its aftermath claimed that U.S. Secretary of Defense Donald Rumsfeld's determination to keep the U.S. force in Iraq as small as possible resulted in too few troops to maintain security in the cities. They argued that coalition forces, which were reduced to about 160,000 after May 1, 2003, were stretched too thin to hunt down members of Hussein's regime, round up emerging guerrilla fighters and terrorists, and safeguard Iraqi national assets and the general population. The Army was also reluctant to take responsibility for day-to-day security. In May, U.S. Brigadier General Vincent Brooks, a spokesperson for the U.S. Central Command in the Persian Gulf, told reporters that the military was involved in rebuilding Iraq's civil administration and had no intention of becoming a police force.

Experts also questioned the wisdom of a decision made in May by L. Paul Bremer III, the civilian head of the U.S.-led occupation, to disband the Iraqi Army. They noted that this resulted in thousands of armed men, many of them Hussein loyalists, on the streets with no pay and few ways to legally support themselves. The experts suggested that many members of the former Iraqi Army ended up becoming looters or joining guerrilla forces to the north.

The war that was fought in Iraq, the swift march north to Baghdad, was not the war that Defense Department officials originally had planned. Defense Secretary Rumsfeld wanted to fight on two fronts. In the south, coalition forces were to drive north from Kuwait; in the north, U.S. troops were to advance south to Baghdad from Turkey. However, the Turkish parliament, dominated by an Islamist party that is, a political party rooted in Islamic theology and law defied its own government

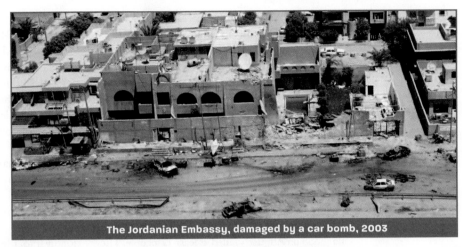

The Jordanian Embassy, damaged by a car bomb, 2003

leaders and refused to grant the United States permission to move troops across Turkish soil. As a result, very few U.S. troops were stationed north of Baghdad when the war ended. This allowed Hussein loyalists to freely move north. Experts on Iraq believe that the remnants of the Republican Guard and the Fedayeen Saddam militia, motivated by tribal loyalties and nationalism, regrouped in and around Tikrit, an area of anti-American resistance that became known as the "Sunni Triangle." The area was so named because it was home to many of the Sunni Muslims who continued to support Hussein.

A guerrilla war. From the Sunni Triangle, insurgents launched near daily attacks on coalition forces, usually U.S. soldiers, resulting in mounting casualties. Guerrillas generally ambushed convoys on roads in the countryside and quickly disappeared. Typically, they possessed a variety of arms, including such sophisticated weapons as rocket-propelled grenades, which they apparently freely picked up from Hussein's weapon depots (places where military supplies are stored). Lacking the person-

nel, coalition forces did not, for the most part, guard these depots. According to the U.S. Central Intelligence Agency, Iraq's store of conventional weapons at the start of the war was enormous, an estimated 1 million tons (907,000 metric tons).

A new U.S. commander in Iraq, General John P. Abizaid, announced shortly after his arrival there in August that the United States was involved in a classic guerrilla war. Deputy U.S. Secretary of Defense Paul Wolfowitz subsequently confirmed Abizaid's assessment and told reporters that U.S. war planners were most surprised by the fact that Saddam Hussein loyalists would continue to fight a guerrilla war after the collapse of the regular Army. Lieutenant General Ricardo Sanchez, commander of U.S. ground forces in Iraq, later disclosed that U.S. military officials were convinced that fighters other than Saddam Hussein loyalists were taking part in attacks on allied forces in Iraq. According to U.S. intelligence sources, Islamic militants were crossing into Iraq in ever greater numbers from Syria and northern Iran to join forces with Hussein loyalists.

On October 28, two U.S. soldiers were killed when their tank hit an "unidentified explosive device" during a late-night patrol near Balad, 45 miles (72 kilometers) north of Baghdad. The deaths of the two soldiers brought to 116 the number of U.S. soldiers to die in hostile action since the war was declared over on May 1, higher than the 115 U.S. soldiers who died in combat during the actual offensive. Just days before, Lieutenant General Sanchez had noted that attacks on U.S. troops had escalated, to an average of 25 a day.

The insurgents eventually began to employ terrorist tactics on civilians, both foreign and Iraqi. A huge explosion outside the Jordanian embassy in Baghdad on August 7 killed at least 17 people. The explosion was so powerful it reduced the front of the building to rubble, threw shrapnel as far away as 3,000 feet (900 meters), and sent a car onto the roof of a nearby building some 60 feet (18 meters) above ground. Less than two weeks later, another very powerful bomb exploded outside the offices of the United Nations in Baghdad, killing 22 people, including the top UN envoy to Iraq, Sergio Vieira de Mello. A suicide bomber detonated a second device near the same complex on September 22, killing himself and an Iraqi policeman. Three days later, UN officials announced that the organization was "downsizing" in Iraq because of the "deteriorating security situation." Late in October, a suicide bomber hidden inside an ambulance hit the Baghdad headquarters of the International Committee of the Red Cross.

Iraqi civilians who cooperated with the coalition forces also became targets. Gunmen killed an Iraqi politician, Akila al-Hashemi, outside her house in Baghdad in September. She had been appointed to a board entrusted with creating a new Iraqi government. The repeated bombing of Baghdad police stations, which left 18 police officers dead during August, September, and October, served as warnings of what could happen to Iraqis who worked with the coalition.

During the same period, violence spread to the south, where the Shiite branch of Islam is dominant and where Hussein and his Sunni-dominated government were despised. In late August, a car bomb exploded outside a mosque in An Najaf, killing Ayatollah Mohammed Baqr al-Hakim, one of Iraq's most prominent Shiite clerics. The attack also resulted in the deaths of more than 80 bystanders. In mid-October, three

U.S. soldiers and two Iraqi police officers were killed in a 12-hour gunfight with Islamic militants in Karbala. U.S. forces, joined by members of the Iraqi Civil Defense Corps, later raided the city's al-Mukhayam Mosque and arrested followers of a Shiite cleric who was attempting to generate public support for an Islamic republic in Iraq. U.S. officials in Iraq attributed the violence in the south to a power struggle between rival Shiite factions.

U.S. weapons inspector David Kay reported to Congressional intelligence committees on October 3 that the Iraq Survey Group, which he headed, had yet to find weapons of mass destruction in Iraq. He testified that his team had found "a large body of continuing activities and equipment that were not declared to the UN inspectors," and he informed the joint committee that it would take probably another six to nine months to give a firm indication of the state of the Iraqi weapons program.

Politics at home. The rationale that the Bush administration and Tony Blair's Cabinet had used for going to war that Iraqi weapons of mass destruction threatened the security of the West quickly came under intense public scrutiny. Political experts noted that the coalition's inability to uncover poison gas, chemical weapons, or evidence of a nuclear program had hurt both leaders politically. Blair in particular faced very blunt questioning by senior members of Parliament during the regular Prime Minister's Question Time. A journalist with the British Broadcasting Company even accused Blair and members of his Cabinet of hav-

President George W. Bush and British Prime Minister Tony Blair, 2003

ing altered intelligence reports on Iraq's weapons programs in order to justify going to war.

In the United States, the lack of evidence of weapons of mass destruction forced the Bush administration into two embarrassing admissions. In August, a spokesperson acknowledged that the president had relied on incomplete information when he had declared, in his State of the Union speech, that Saddam Hussein was buying uranium for a nuclear weapons program. One month later, the president himself declared that he knew of no evidence linking Iraq and Saddam Hussein to the terrorist attacks on the United States in 2001.

The president's troubles in Iraq also were compounded by the mounting costs associated with the war. In early September, Bush asked Congress to allocate an additional $87 billion in fiscal year 2004 (October 1, 2003 to September 30, 2004) to cover security and rebuilding costs in Iraq. The size of the request met with criticism from Democrats in Congress as well as from members of the president's own Republican Party.

The Bush administration responded to the mounting criticism with a concerted public relations campaign, which included an attack on the national media. The president accused the media of reporting negative rather than positive developments in Iraq. He and members of the administration toured the country pointing out that considerable progress had been made in Iraq. Coalition forces had toppled Saddam Hussein's government in a very short period of time with relatively little loss of life. Many of the top leaders in Hussein's government, including his sons, Uday and Qusay, had either been killed or captured. Administration officials noted that the electrical grid in Iraq was up and running and at higher capacity than before the war. Most Iraqi schools and hospitals had reopened. The U.S.-led coalition had established a new border patrol, police network, and Iraqi Army, and these organizations already had enlisted about 85,500 Iraqis in various security positions, freeing coalition soldiers for other responsibilities. On December 13, U.S. forces captured the greatest prize of all, Saddam Hussein.

Rebuilding Iraq. In July, U.S. Envoy Paul Bremer appointed 25 prominent Iraqis to an interim government council. The Governing Council, which consisted of Iraqi men and women of various ethnic and religious backgrounds, was charged with setting Iraq on a course that would

Iraqi council signing the Interim Constitution, 2004

lead to the establishment of a democracy. Officials with the Bush administration pointed out that a viable democracy in Iraq would serve as a shining example to other countries in the Middle East.

In October, the UN Security Council passed a resolution that endorsed the U.S.-led occupation of Iraq. The resolution charged the Iraqi Governing Council with completing a timetable for the creation of a constitution and the scheduling of national elections as a preamble to a timely return of sovereignty to the Iraqi people. In response to the UN resolution, several nations and international organizations joined the United States in offering about $33 billion for the pacification and physical and economic rebuilding of Iraq.

Critics argued the continuing violence in Iraq belied Bush administration claims of material and political progress. The critics noted that the daily attacks on U.S. soldiers and the spiraling numbers of casualties among coalition forces proved one thing—that the war in Iraq was not over. In October, U.S. Defense Secretary Donald Rumsfeld fueled the critics' fire with a memo circulated to his top four advisers before being "leaked" to the press. He wrote that U.S.-led coalitions in Iraq, as well as Afghanistan, faced a "long, hard slog."

United Kingdom

A country in northwestern Europe, the United Kingdom consists of England, Scotland, Wales, and Northern Ireland.

HOT topics

English Public Schools. In England, public schools are actually independent private schools. They are called public because the first of these schools were organized for the public good, not for the church or to make profit. Traditionally, these schools have emphasized discipline, the building of character, and scholarship. The reputation of some of the schools, such as Eton, Harrow, and Winchester, is extremely high. The leading public schools stress preparation for Oxford or Cambridge, the United Kingdom's oldest and most honored universities.

Theater in the United Kingdom. The United Kingdom is one of the world's major centers for theater. Visitors come from all parts of the world to see British theater productions. About 50 theaters operate in the central London district known as the West End. The Royal National Theatre performs at its three stages on London's South Bank. The Royal Shakespeare Company is based at Stratford-upon-Avon and also performs at the Barbican Centre in London. The English Stage Company at the Royal Court Theatre in London performs the works of talented new playwrights. Notable regional theaters include the Bristol Old Vic, the Festival Theatre in Chichester, the Lyric Theatre in Belfast, and the Royal Lyceum in Edinburgh.

HOT topics 🔥

London. London is the largest city in the United Kingdom and one of the largest cities in the world. It is the headquarters of the nation's government and a world center of culture, finance, tourism, and trade. London is one of the world's oldest and most historic cities, tracing its beginnings to nearly 2,000 years ago. Central London has tall office buildings and busy streets as well as outstanding museums, art galleries, theaters, and beautiful parks. Its famous landmarks include Buckingham Palace, the Houses of Parliament, and St. Paul's Cathedral with its huge dome.

A London pub

Food and Drink. Most British cooking is simple. A traditional meal includes roast beef, mutton, or pork with potatoes and one or more other vegetables. The traditional Sunday midday meal of roast beef and Yorkshire pudding, a battercake baked in meat fat, is still a family favorite. Pizza houses, Chinese restaurants, and hamburger places have grown to rival the historically popular fish and chips shops that serve fried fish and French fried potatoes. Tea with milk and sugar is the most popular hot beverage. Beer, including ale and lager, is the favorite alcoholic drink. A high proportion of beer drinking takes place in pubs (public houses), which provide a focus of social life for many people.

TRUE or FALSE?

The United Kingdom's farms do not produce a sufficient amount of food to feed the country.

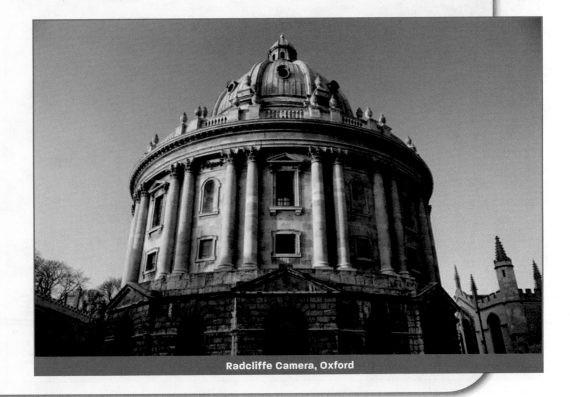

Radcliffe Camera, Oxford

Map of the United Kingdom

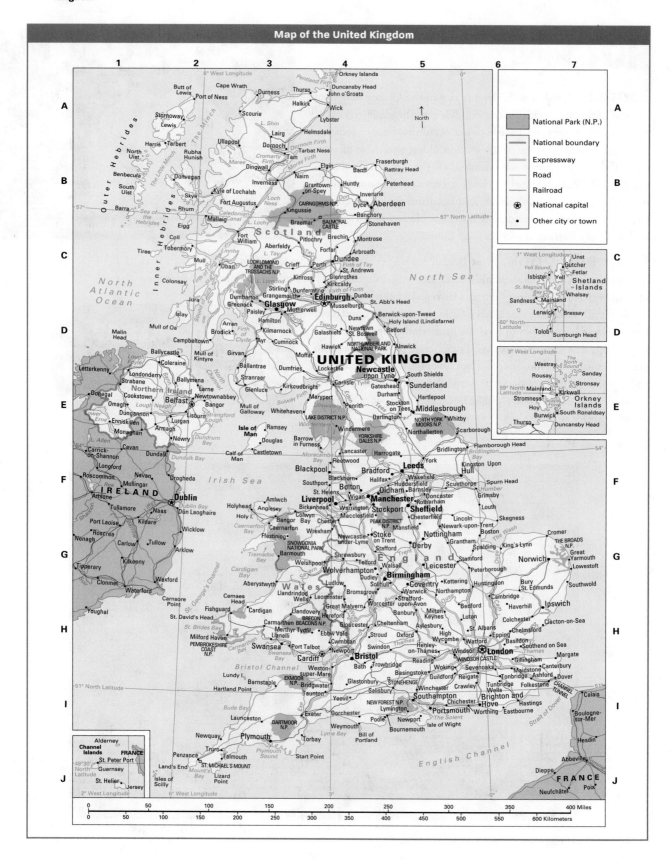

THE BASICS

The United Kingdom is a country in northwestern Europe. It consists of four political divisions—England, Scotland, and Wales, which make up the island of Great Britain, and Northern Ireland, which occupies the northeastern part of the island of Ireland. The nation's official name is the United Kingdom of Great Britain and Northern Ireland. When people refer to the country, most shorten its name to the United Kingdom, the U.K., or Britain. London is the capital and largest city.

More than 75 countries are larger in size than the United Kingdom, and the country has only about 1 percent of the world's people. But the United Kingdom has a rich history. The British started the Industrial Revolution, a period of rapid industrialization that began in the 1700s. They founded the largest empire in history. They have produced some of the world's greatest scientists, explorers, artists, and political leaders.

The landscape of the United Kingdom varies dramatically. Northern Scotland is a wild, windswept region, broken by long arms of the sea that reach far inland. Much of Northern Ireland has low mountains and rolling fields. Wales is famous for its rugged mountains and deep, green valleys. Most of England is covered by rolling plains, laid out in a patchwork of fields and meadows. The coastline is a shifting scene of steep cliffs, golden beaches, jagged rocks, and fishing towns tucked in sheltered bays. The United Kingdom has magnificent old castles and modern nuclear laboratories, snug villages and sprawling cities, and ancient universities and new factories.

The English Channel separates the island of Great Britain from France. This narrow stretch of water helped shape the character and history of the British people. It helped protect the United Kingdom from invasion and gave the people a feeling of security. In 1066, a group of Vikings called the Normans sailed across the channel from northwestern France and conquered England. After the Norman Conquest, no enemy ever again crossed the channel and invaded the country.

Cut off from the rest of Europe by the sea and secure from invasion, the British developed their own character and way of life. They came to respect privacy and to value old traditions. They developed a dry wit, a love for personal freedom, and a high degree of self-criticism. The British have shown themselves at their best—brave and united—in times of crisis. Their courage against German bombs and overwhelming odds during World War II (1939–1945) won the admiration of the world.

The history of the United Kingdom is the story of how a small country became the world's most powerful nation—and then declined. In the 1700s, the Industrial Revolution made the United Kingdom the world's richest manufacturing country. The British ruled the seas and were the world's greatest traders. By 1900, they had an empire that covered about a fourth of the world's land and included about a fourth of its people. The British spread their way of life throughout their empire.

Then came the 1900s—and the shock of two crippling world wars. The British Empire began to break up as the United Kingdom's colonies sought independence. The United Kingdom faced one economic crisis after another. Today, the United Kingdom is still a leading industrial and trading nation. But it is no longer the world power it once was.

Population. The United Kingdom is more thickly populated than most countries. Most of its people live in cities and towns. About one-third of the country's residents live in England's seven metropolitan areas. Greater London, the largest metropolitan area, has about 10 percent of the United Kingdom's total population. The six other metropolitan areas are as follows, with the largest city of each area shown in parentheses: Greater Manchester (Manchester), Merseyside (Liverpool), South Yorkshire (Sheffield), Tyne and Wear (Newcastle upon Tyne), West Midlands (Birmingham), and West Yorkshire (Leeds).

About five-sixths of the population of the United Kingdom live in England. London and England as a whole have great influence over

Big Ben

the rest of the United Kingdom because of their large populations.

Ancestry. Celtic-speaking people lived in what is now the United Kingdom by the mid-600s B.C. Over the next 1,700 years, the land was invaded by the Romans, Angles, Saxons, Jutes, Danes, and Normans. Most of the British are descendants of these early peoples.

Since World War II ended in 1945, millions of immigrants have moved to the United Kingdom. Many have come from members of the Commonwealth of Nations, an association of countries and other political units that were once part of the British Empire. The United Kingdom also offers asylum to refugees from around the world.

Language. English is the official language of the United Kingdom and is spoken throughout most of the country. English developed chiefly from the language of the Anglo-Saxon and Norman invaders.

About one-sixth of the people of Wales can speak both English and Welsh. Some use Welsh as their daily language. The Welsh language developed from one of the languages of the Celts.

Thousands of people in Scotland speak the Scottish form of Gaelic, which is another Celtic language. The Irish form of Gaelic is spoken by a small number of people in Northern Ireland.

Way of Life

City life. A number of the United Kingdom's important cities grew rapidly in the 1700s and early 1800s, during the Industrial Revolution. But today, many of those cities—including London, Birmingham, Liverpool, Manchester, and Leeds—are in decline. They are faced with such problems as declining employment, rising crime, and poor housing. They are losing population as people move from the inner cities into the suburbs and beyond. Greater London's population, for example, peaked in 1939 and has been falling ever since.

The industries that supported the growth of the large cities have declined or disappeared. New industries, such as electronics, have developed outside the cities, many near *motorways* (expressways) or near research establishments and universities.

The British government in 1988 launched an urban renewal program called Action for Cities. The purpose of the program is to revive the inner cities by means of new housing and new development. The government also established areas called *enterprise zones* to attract new businesses to inner cities. Businesses within enterprise zones receive tax cuts and other advantages. However, people continue to move away from the inner cities to find jobs, and these areas do not attract enough private investment. The cost of such basic services as street lighting and road repair is increasingly falling upon fewer people. And many of these people are the members of society who can least afford such costs—the elderly, single-parent families, the poorly paid, and the unemployed.

Rural life. At one time, the rural areas of the United Kingdom were devoted mainly to farming. But the availability of convenient transportation enables people to work in a city and live in the countryside. In many rural communities, full-time farmers are outnumbered by retired people, commuters, and workers who serve the needs of tourists.

The attractiveness and variety of the rural United Kingdom is one of the tourist industry's prime assets. These qualities also attract many retired people. In some rural areas, more than a fifth of the population is over retirement age. These areas include the counties of Cornwall, Devon, Dorset, East and

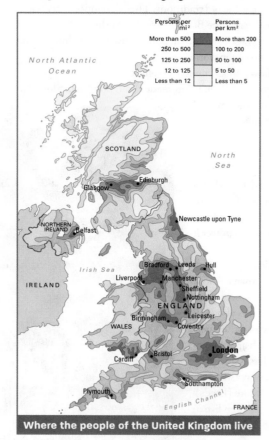

Persons per mi²		Persons per km²
More than 500		More than 200
250 to 500		100 to 200
125 to 250		50 to 100
12 to 125		5 to 50
Less than 12		Less than 5

Where the people of the United Kingdom live

West Sussex, and the Isle of Wight; the Scottish Borders; and parts of rural Wales.

Food and drink. Most British cooking is simple. A typical meal includes roast beef, mutton, or pork with potatoes and one or more other vegetables. Since the 1960s, the British have increased their consumption of poultry, fresh fruit, and frozen vegetables. Consumption of lamb, beef, veal, bread, potatoes, eggs, butter, and sugar has fallen.

Pizza houses, Chinese restaurants, and hamburger places that offer *takeaway* and *fast food* have grown in popularity. They rival the shops offering *fish and chips*, a popular meal of fried fish and French fried potatoes. The traditional Sunday midday meal of roast beef and *Yorkshire pudding*, a battercake baked in meat fat, is still a family favorite, however.

The British diet tends to be high in fat, salt, and sugar and low in fiber. These eating habits can contribute to a variety of health problems, including heart disease. The country has a high level of heart disease, especially in the northern United Kingdom. There is evidence, however, that health considerations have begun to influence food consumption. People are drinking more low-fat milk instead of whole milk and eating more whole grain bread, which has more fiber than white bread.

Tea with milk and sugar is the most popular hot beverage. Beer, including ale and lager, is the favorite alcoholic drink. A high proportion of beer drinking takes place in *pubs* (public houses), which provide a focus of social life for many people.

Recreation. The British love the outdoors. They flock to Blackpool, Brighton and Hove, and other seaside resorts on vacation. Several million vacationers visit Spain, France, and other countries. Other vacationers prefer mountain climbing or walking in Wales or in the beautiful Lake District of northwestern England. Still others enjoy automobile or bicycle trips through the country.

The British also spend much time in their gardens. About half of the families in the United Kingdom have a garden.

The British are enthusiastic sports fans. The most popular spectator sport by far is soccer, which the British also call *football*. During the football season, thousands of fans jam the stadiums every Saturday. Cricket has been popular in England for hundreds of years. It is played with bats and a ball and two 11-player teams. Schools, universities, and almost all towns and villages have cricket teams.

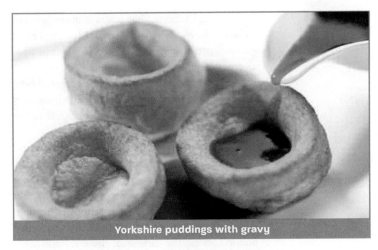
Yorkshire puddings with gravy

Other popular sports include archery, *bowls* (a sport similar to bowling), golf, hockey, horseback riding, horse racing, rugby football, sailing, and tennis.

Religion. The United Kingdom has two *established* (national) churches. They are the Church of England, which is Episcopal, and the Church of Scotland, which is Presbyterian. The monarch must belong to the Church of England and is its worldly head. The spiritual head of the English Church is the archbishop of Canterbury.

The Church of England has about 25 million members, and the Church of Scotland has about 2½ million. Other Protestant churches have a total of about 6 million members. The country has about 5½ million Roman Catholics. About 3 million people in the United Kingdom belong to other faiths. Approximately 10 million people are nonreligious.

Education. Each division of the United Kingdom has its own system of public education. Each system is run by its own department of education, which works closely with local elected education authorities. The four systems differ in many ways, including the way schools are organized. Traditionally, teachers throughout the United Kingdom have had much freedom in selecting the courses they teach and in developing their own teaching methods. However, teachers are being increasingly guided by a national curriculum.

Most British children are required by law to begin school at the age of 5 and continue until they are 16. Children in Northern Ireland must begin school at the age of 4. Generally, students attend elementary school until they are 11 years old, and then they go on to high school. There are several types of high schools. Some students attend *grammar schools*, which provide a college preparatory education.

Some attend schools that stress a more general, technical, or vocational education. However, most students attend *comprehensive schools*, which provide all types of high school education.

Most schools in the state system are free. About 95 percent of all schoolchildren attend elementary schools and high schools supported by public funds. The rest go to *independent schools*.

The independent schools are private schools supported by fees paid by parents and by private gifts of money. There are several types of independent schools. The best known are the English *public schools*, which provide a high school education. Although they are private schools, they are called public because the earliest of these schools were established for the children of the middle classes. Traditionally, these schools have emphasized discipline, the building of character, and scholarship. The reputation of some of these schools, such as Eton, Harrow, and Winchester, is extremely high. The leading public schools stress preparation for Oxford or Cambridge, which are the United Kingdom's oldest and most honored universities.

Oxford University was founded in the 1100s, and Cambridge University was established in the 1200s. They have a greater reputation than other universities because of their age, traditions, and high standards of scholarship. The United Kingdom has about 75 other universities. The University of London is the United Kingdom's largest traditional university. England's Open University has more students, but it has no regular classrooms. Instruction is carried out through audiotapes, videocassettes, DVDs, and the Internet.

Museums and libraries. The United Kingdom has about 2,500 museums and art galleries. The largest collections are owned by about 20 national museums and art galleries, most of which are in London. The world-famous British Museum, in London, is noted for its outstanding collections in archaeology and many other fields. The National Gallery and the Tate Britain gallery, also in London, have some of the world's greatest paintings.

The United Kingdom's public library system serves people throughout the country. The nation's largest library, the British Library, has millions of volumes. The national libraries of Scotland and Wales have about 5 million volumes each. Other important libraries include Oxford's Bodleian Library and the Cambridge University Library.

The Arts

The government encourages and supports the arts in the United Kingdom chiefly through agencies called arts councils. There is an arts council for England, Scotland, and Wales and another one for Northern Ireland. Each council receives a government grant and, in turn, makes grants to help pay for musical, theatrical, and other artistic activities. Many local areas have their own arts councils to coordinate and finance local artistic activities.

The United Kingdom is one of the world's major centers for theater. Visitors come from all parts of the world to see British theater productions. About 50 theaters operate in the central London district known as the West End. The Royal National Theatre performs at its three stages on London's South Bank. The Royal Shakespeare Company is based at Stratford-upon-Avon and also performs at the Barbican Centre in London. The English Stage Company at the Royal Court Theatre in London performs the works of talented new playwrights. Notable regional theaters include the Bristol Old Vic, the Festival Theatre in Chichester, the Lyric Theatre in Belfast, and the Royal Lyceum in Edinburgh.

The United Kingdom has 11 principal professional symphony orchestras and several smaller orchestras. Five of the principal orchestras have their headquarters in London. The best-known orchestras outside London include the Halle Orchestra of Manchester and the City of Birmingham Symphony Orchestra.

The most famous British arts festival is the Edinburgh International Festival, which was founded in 1947. It is held every August. Its program includes operas, concerts, ballets, and plays. The Cheltenham Festival, held in July, specializes in music by contem-

The Royal Shakespeare Theatre, Stratford-upon-Avon

porary British composers. A summer drama festival takes place in Chichester. Glyndebourne, near Brighton and Hove, has an annual summer opera festival.

English literature consists of the poetry, prose, and drama written in the English language by authors in England, Scotland, and Wales. English literature is a rich, varied literature that has produced many outstanding writers. It includes masterpieces in many forms, particularly the novel, the short story, epic and lyric poetry, the essay, literary criticism, and drama. English literature is also one of the oldest national literatures in the Western world. English authors wrote important works as early as the A.D. 700s.

Gaelic literature. English literature is also geographically related to Gaelic literature, which includes all the writings in Gaelic, the ancient language of Scotland and Ireland. But often the term is used only for the Gaelic literature of Scotland.

Irish invaders introduced Gaelic into Scotland about A.D. 500. Spoken Scottish Gaelic diverged from spoken Irish Gaelic in the 900s. But the two languages shared a common written form for centuries. *The Book of the Dean of Lismore* is the first important manuscript to show Scottish Gaelic. It was written about 1520 and includes Scottish and Irish ballads and poetry by poet-minstrels called *bards.*

Scottish Gaelic is rich in poetry, but poor in prose. Mary Macleod and John MacDonald (Iain Lom) were among the chief poets of the 1600s. Alexander Macdonald and Duncan Ban Macintyre outshone them in the 1700s. Interest in ancient literature increased after the 1760s. In the 1760s, James Macpherson published alleged translations of works by the legendary poet and warrior Ossian. The translations turned out to be largely the original work of Macpherson and caused considerable controversy, but the publication stimulated interest in classic Gaelic literature. The poets Sorley Maclean and George Campbell Hay began a Gaelic literary revival in the 1940s that continues today.

Old English literature (500–1100). During the A.D. 400s and 500s, three Germanic tribes—the Angles, Jutes, and Saxons—settled in England and established powerful kingdoms. Together, these tribes are called Anglo-Saxons. They used dialects that became known as Old English or Anglo-Saxon. Old English was the chief literary language of England until about 1100. In 597,

Saint Augustine of Canterbury began converting the Anglo-Saxons to Christianity. English literature began through the combined influence of the Anglo-Saxon kingdoms and the Christian church.

Many Old English poems glorified a real or imaginary hero and tried to teach the values of bravery and generosity. Poets used *alliteration* (words that begin with the same sound) and *kennings* (elaborate descriptive phrases). They also used *internal rhyme,* in which a word within a line rhymes with a word at the end of the line.

The first English poet known by name is Caedmon, who lived during the 600s. His only authentic surviving work is a nine-line poem that praises God. The first major work of English literature is the epic poem *Beowulf. Epics* are long narrative poems that focus on heroic and extraordinary actions. Many are based on legend or myth, and their language is dignified and serious. One or more unknown authors wrote *Beowulf* some time between 750 and 1100. The poem tells about the adventures of a warrior named Beowulf.

Most prose writers wrote in Latin until the late 800s, when Alfred the Great became king of Wessex in southwestern England. Alfred translated or ordered the translation of several works from Latin into Old English. One of the most important of

The Knight, from *The Canterbury Tales*

these works was the *Ecclesiastical History of the English People* (731) by a monk called Saint Bede or the Venerable Bede. This is the first history of the English people and a valuable source of information about English life from the late 500s to 731. From about 892 to 1154, a number of authors contributed to the *Anglo-Saxon Chronicle*, a record of current events in England.

Middle English literature (1100–1485).

In 1066, Norman invaders from France conquered England. For more than 200 years thereafter, members of the royal court and the upper class spoke French. Only the common people continued to speak English. By about 1300, however, English had again become the chief national language but in an altered form now called Middle English.

Medieval romances originated in France during the 1100s. By the end of the 1200s, they had become the most popular literary form in England. Like epics, romances described the adventures of heroes, but their plots depended more on supernatural events and featured stories of love and highborn ladies. Romances were written in prose as well as verse.

In 1155, a Norman poet named Wace completed the first work that mentioned the Knights of the Round Table, who were led by the legendary British ruler King Arthur. King Arthur and his knights became a favorite subject in English romances. During the 1400s, Sir Thomas Malory wrote a prose work called *Le Morte Darthur (The Death of Arthur)*. Malory's romance is the most complete English version of stories about Arthur.

The greatest writer of the Middle English period was the poet Geoffrey Chaucer. His masterpiece is *The Canterbury Tales* (late 1300s), an unfinished collection of comic and moral stories. Chaucer introduced a rhythmic pattern called *iambic pentameter* into English poetry. This pattern, or meter, consists of 10 syllables alternately unaccented and accented in each line. The lines may or may not rhyme. Iambic pentameter became a widely used meter in English poetry.

Early English drama developed from scenes that monks acted out in churches to illustrate Bible stories. The scenes grew into full-length works called *mystery plays* and *miracle plays*. Mystery plays dealt with events in the Bible, and miracle plays with the lives of saints.

During the 1400s, *morality plays* first appeared in English drama. Morality plays featured characters who represented a certain quality, such as good or evil. These dramas were less realistic than the earlier plays and were intended to teach a moral lesson.

The beginning of Modern English (1485–1603).

During the late 1400s, Middle English began to develop into Modern English. By the late 1500s, the English were speaking and writing English in a form much like that used today. Queen Elizabeth I reigned from 1558 to 1603. During this period, usually called the Elizabethan Age, English writers produced some of the greatest poetry and drama in world literature.

A number of developments contributed to the brilliant literary output of the Elizabethan Age. One of the most important occurred in 1476, when William Caxton set up the first printing press in England. Before that time, books and all other literary works had to be slowly and laboriously copied by hand. Printing made it possible to produce far more books and at far lower cost. The greater availability of books and their lower cost stimulated a desire among many people to learn how to read. As literacy increased, so did the demand for books.

Religious debates also played a role in the development of a reading public. During the reign of Elizabeth's father, King Henry VIII, the English church became independent of the Roman Catholic Church. Under the influence of the Protestant Reformation, Bible reading was encouraged. During the 1520s, William Tyndale made an important new English translation of the Bible.

During the 1500s, English scholars joined other European scholars in rediscovering the cultures of

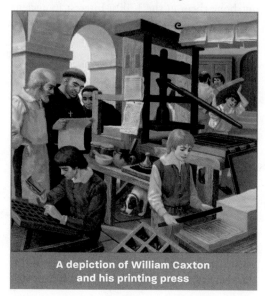

**A depiction of William Caxton
and his printing press**

ancient Greece and Rome, which they had largely neglected for hundreds of years. Translations of Greek and particularly Roman literary works strongly influenced Elizabethan writers. In addition, new literary forms were introduced into English literature. For example, English authors adopted directly or modified such literary forms as the essay from France and the sonnet from Italy.

During the Elizabethan Age, the English also explored and colonized distant lands. Wealth from the colonies poured into England. A newly rich merchant class made London a great commercial center. The merchants and the nobility wanted entertainment and fine art and were willing to pay for them. Writers, painters, and musicians flocked to London, making it a European cultural center.

Elizabethan poetry. Three chief forms of poetry flourished during the Elizabethan Age. They were (1) the lyric, (2) the sonnet, and (3) narrative poetry.

A lyric is a short poem that expresses private emotions and moods in a songlike style. Thomas Campion wrote many beautiful lyrics in his *Books of Airs* (1601 to about 1617).

The sonnet is a 14-line poem with a certain pattern of rhyme and rhythm. Elizabethan poets wrote two types of sonnets, Italian and English. The two types differed in the arrangement of the rhymes. Sir Thomas Wyatt introduced the sonnet from Italy into English literature in the early 1500s. The Earl of Surrey modified the form into the English sonnet. Their verses were published in a collection commonly called *Tottel's Miscellany* (1557). Edmund Spenser and William Shakespeare wrote *sonnet sequences*, groups of sonnets based on a single theme. Spenser and Sir Philip Sidney wrote sequences of love sonnets. Shakespeare wrote a sequence addressed to a nobleman who was his patron and to an unknown "dark lady."

A narrative poem tells a story. In addition to sonnets, Shakespeare and Spenser wrote narrative poems. Shakespeare based his *Venus and Adonis* (1593) on a Roman myth and *The Rape of Lucrece* (1594) on an event from Roman history.

Perhaps the most ambitious Elizabethan narrative poem is *The Faerie Queene* by Spenser. The poet borrowed heavily from medieval romances to invent an imaginary land representing British and Christian ideals. The style of the poem is *allegorical*. In allegorical writing, people and objects are used to represent abstract ideas, such as holiness and justice.

The Faerie Queene combines those abstract moral meanings with striking visual imagery.

Elizabethan drama. In 1576, James Burbage built England's first playhouse, called The Theatre, in a suburb of London. Until this time, drama had been performed in the streets, in homes and palaces, and at universities. After Burbage's theatre, other playhouses opened and the popularity of drama rapidly increased.

Elizabethan drama was noted for its passion and vitality. Thomas Kyd's play *The Spanish Tragedy* (1580s) was one of the earliest Elizabethan dramas. It is filled with scenes of violence and madness and set a pattern for themes of murder and revenge in later plays.

A group of leading Elizabethan playwrights were known as the "University Wits" because they had attended the famous English universities at Oxford or Cambridge. These playwrights included Robert Greene, Christopher Marlowe, and George Peele. Marlowe was the most important dramatist among the Wits. He wrote tragedies that center on strong personalities. These works include *Tamburlaine the Great* (about 1587) and *The Tragical History of Doctor Faustus* (about 1588).

The greatest Elizabethan playwright was William Shakespeare. No other English author has equaled his brilliant verse and characterizations.

The rebel angels of *Paradise Lost*, in an engraving by Gustave Dore

The early and middle 1600s. In 1604, King James I authorized a group of scholars to prepare a new English version of the Bible. It appeared in 1611 and became known as the King James Version or Authorized Version. Although it borrowed from earlier translations, such as Tyndale's, the King James Version was a landmark in the development of English prose. Its eloquent yet natural style had enormous influence on English-speaking writers.

John Milton was the greatest English writer of the mid-1600s. Milton was deeply involved in the political and religious debates of his time and supported the Puritans during the English Civil War. He wrote prose and verse on many subjects before, during, and after the war. Milton's greatest achievement is *Paradise Lost* (1667), an epic based on the story of Adam and Eve. Its vivid descriptions of heaven, hell, and the Garden of Eden, and its rich and musical blank verse, make it one of the most admired and imitated works in English literature.

Metaphysical and Cavalier poets were two major groups of poets during the 1600s. The Metaphysical poets included John Donne, their leader; Abraham Cowley; George Herbert; Andrew Marvell; and Henry Vaughan. The Cavalier poets, who were associated with the court of Charles I, included Thomas Carew, Robert Herrick, Richard Lovelace, and Sir John Suckling.

A portrait of King Charles II

The Metaphysical poets used comparatively simple language, but they often created elaborate, philosophical images called *conceits*. John Donne composed a series of meditations on sickness, sin, and death in *Devotions upon Emergent Occasions* (1624). Donne also wrote passionate love poetry until he converted from Roman Catholicism to the Anglican faith. He became an Anglican priest in 1615. After his conversion, Donne wrote equally passionate religious poetry. Several other Metaphysical poets also wrote religious verse. In contrast to the serious Metaphysical poets, the Cavalier poets were best known for their dashing love poetry.

Jacobean drama is the name given to the plays written during the reign of James I. Jacobean tragedies reflected Elizabethan drama, especially in such characteristics as violent action, spectacle, and the revenge theme. John Webster's drama *The Duchess of Malfi* (about 1613) is a masterpiece of revenge tragedy. *Satiric comedies*, which poked fun at various subjects, were also popular. In *The Knight of the Burning Pestle* (1607?), for example, Francis Beaumont ridiculed earlier dramas and romances about elegant heroes and also satirized the newly rich merchant class.Ben Jonson wrote plays that showed the influence of ancient Roman drama. His comedies *Volpone* (1606) and *The Alchemist* (1610) satirize universal human failings such as greed, ignorance, or superstition.

In 1642, the Puritans ordered the closing of the theaters, claiming that plays were wicked. The order remained in effect for 18 years.

Restoration literature (1660–1700). In 1660, Parliament restored the monarchy under Charles II. The period from 1660 to 1700 is known as the Restoration. The Puritans had attempted to enforce a strict moral code during their years in power. The Restoration brought a strong reaction against this code. The nobility and upper class, in particular, became known for carefree and often morally loose living. Restoration writers reflected this relaxed morality in their works.

John Dryden followed Milton as the outstanding literary figure of the Restoration. Dryden wrote poetry, popular dramas, and literary criticism. During his career, he shifted his support from the Puritans to the restored monarchy. Late in life, he converted from the Anglican faith to Roman Catholicism. Many of Dryden's poems reflect these political and religious shifts. Dryden's best plays include *Marriage a la Mode* (1672), a comedy, and

All for Love (1677), a tragedy. Dryden wrote some of the finest literary criticism in English literature.

Restoration drama. After Charles II became king in 1660, the theaters were reopened and an important period in English drama began. Two types of plays rapidly dominated Restoration stages: (1) the comedy of manners and (2) the heroic tragedy.

The comedy of manners was witty, sometimes cynical, and occasionally indecent. It treated love and romantic intrigue in a light, often broadly humorous way. The best comedies of manners included *The Country Wife* (1675) by William Wycherley and *The Way of the World* (1700) by William Congreve.

The heroic tragedy had a complicated plot that dealt with the conflict between love and honor. Most of these plays were set far from England. Little action took place on the stage, and the characters spoke in elegant, noble-sounding *heroic couplets.* A heroic couplet is a verse form consisting of two rhymed lines of 10 syllables each. Dryden wrote several heroic tragedies, including *The Conquest of Granada* (1670, 1671).

Restoration prose. During the Restoration, prose became less elaborate than had been fashionable earlier in the 1600s. Writers tried to express themselves clearly, simply, and directly.

Aphra Behn's *Oroonoko* (first published about 1678) tells the story of an African prince sold into slavery who leads a tragic rebellion against his English captors. In the novel's descriptive passages, Behn drew on her experiences in the English colony of Surinam (also spelled Suriname). Her interest in factual, realistic background was new to English fiction.

John Bunyan wrote the popular Christian allegory *The Pilgrim's Progress* (1678, 1684). The work shows the journey of its hero, Christian, through this world to the heavenly city of salvation in the world beyond. The diaries of Samuel Pepys and John Evelyn are also vividly written. They provide a delightful and highly detailed view of English life during the late 1600s.

The Augustan Age (1700–1750). The period in English literature from 1700 to about 1750 is called the Augustan Age, named for the Roman emperor Augustus, who reigned from 27 B.C. to A.D. 14. English authors tried to imitate or recapture many of the philosophic and literary ideals of Augustan Rome. In particular, they

A color lithograph from *Gulliver's Travels*

admired the ideals of reason and common sense, and they tried to achieve balance and harmony in their writings. The Augustan Age of English literature is also known as the Neoclassical period.

Satire was one of the most common types of literature during the Augustan Age. In spite of the Augustan emphasis on reason, many of the satires were extremely bitter and personal. The leading satirists of the period were Jonathan Swift in prose and Alexander Pope in poetry.

Swift attacked hypocrisy in *Gulliver's Travels* (1726), the most famous satire in English. In *A Modest Proposal* (1729), Swift, who was born and lived much of his life in Ireland, satirized the harshness and indifference that he saw in England's rule of Ireland.

Pope perfected the heroic couplet, giving its two rhymed lines a quality of balance and wit that often echoed his themes. In *The Rape of the Lock* (1712–1714), he ridiculed fashionable society. In *An Essay on Man* (1733–1734), he advised readers to take the middle way—avoid extremes—in all things. He wrote with especially cutting brilliance about the authors of his time and their weaknesses in *The Dunciad* (1728–1743). One of Pope's most important nonsatirical poems is *Windsor Forest* (1713). It uses England's Windsor forest as a symbol of social harmony, weaving patriotic reflections on history, politics, and morality into a description of the landscape.

The development of the novel is one of the great achievements of English literature. With the novel, English prose fiction became more realistic and addressed a wider, middle-class audience. One of the major figures in the development was Daniel Defoe. He wrote realistic stories consisting of loosely connected incidents that were presented as actual happenings. Defoe's *Robinson Crusoe* (1719) and *Moll Flanders* (1722) are early examples of the novel, but they lack the unified plot that became typical of that literary form.

Many scholars consider Samuel Richardson the first true novelist in English. He wrote epistolary novels, which take the form of letters exchanged between the novel's characters. Richardson's novels are highly moralistic. His first novel, *Pamela* (1740), tells about a servant girl whose virtuous refusal to be seduced by her master eventually leads him to marry her. Richardson's masterpiece is *Clarissa* (1748), a tragic story of a young woman tricked into leaving her home and raped by a villainous nobleman. It is remarkable for the detailed exploration of the characters' states of mind.

The novels of Henry Fielding emphasize vigorous humor and satire. Fielding ridiculed *Pamela* in *An Apology for the Life of Mrs. Shamela Andrews* (1741). Fielding was a master at putting together a complex plot. His *Tom Jones* (1749) is perhaps the greatest comic novel in English. Laurence Sterne

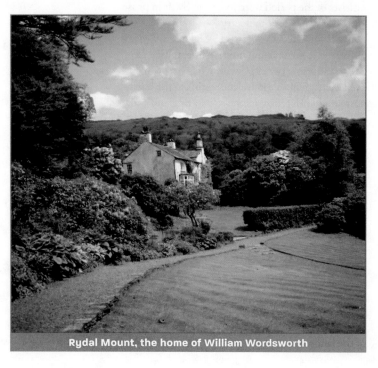

Rydal Mount, the home of William Wordsworth

was another leading novelist. His *The Life and Opinions of Tristram Shandy, Gentleman* (1760–1767) has almost no story. The narrator, Tristram, tries to write his life story but keeps breaking off to discuss other topics. The work inspired many experimental novelists of the 1900s.

The Age of Johnson (1750–1784). Samuel Johnson dominated English literature from about 1750 until his death in 1784. He was as famous for his conversation—in which he sometimes voiced outrageous opinions—as he was for his writings.

Johnson's literary achievements are remarkable. His *Dictionary of the English Language* (1755) is noted for its scholarly definitions of words and the use of excellent quotations to illustrate the definitions. In *The Lives of the English Poets* (1779–1781), Johnson critically examined the work of 52 poets and did much to establish literary criticism as a form of literature. Johnson also wrote articles, reviews, essays, and poems. His prose work *Rasselas* (1759) is a philosophical attack on people who seek an easy path to happiness.

Johnson's friends were the most important writers of the late 1700s. They included Oliver Goldsmith; Richard Brinsley Sheridan; Edmund Burke; and Johnson's biographer, James Boswell.

Goldsmith's novel *The Vicar of Wakefield* (1766) tells about the misfortunes of a kindly clergyman and his family. Goldsmith's great play is the classic comedy *She Stoops to Conquer* (1773). Sheridan wrote two clever comedies of manners, *The Rivals* (1775) and *The School for Scandal* (1777). Burke composed essays on government, history, and beauty. His *Philosophical Enquiry into the Origin of Our Ideas of the Sublime* and Beautiful (1757) anticipates many ideas of romantic writers of the 1800s. His attack on the French Revolution, *Reflections on the Revolution in France* (1790), quickly became one of the most influential books on politics ever written.

Fanny Burney became part of Johnson's circle through her father, the music historian Charles Burney. In such novels as *Evelina* (1778) and *Cecilia* (1782), she combined Richardson's moral concerns and psychological insight with Fielding's satirical, humorous tone. Boswell brilliantly recorded Johnson's eccentricities and witty conversations in The *Life of Samuel Johnson* (1791), one of the great biographies in literature.

Ignatius Sancho was the first African prose writer published in England. Sancho was born on a slave ship on its way to America. When he was 2 years old, he was taken to England. Sancho was especially admired as a letter writer. His *Letters* (1782) were published two years after his death. During the late 1700s and early 1800s, several former slaves wrote memoirs of their experiences, notably Olaudah Equiano's *The Interesting Narrative of the Life of Olaudah Equiano* (1789). Equiano offers a vivid account of his childhood, enslavement, and eventual freedom.

Romantic literature (1784–1832). English writers of the late 1700s and early 1800s believed that the Augustan ideals of harmony and moderation were narrow and artificial. These writers are called Romantics. The Romantics emphasized the creative power of the human imagination and placed increasing value on private experience and the natural world.

In 1789, the French Revolution began, and from 1792 through 1815 England was often at war with France. Romantic writers responded to these events with a complex mixture of sympathy for the democratic ideals of the revolution and patriotic support for the English war effort. England's colonial interests overseas also grew at this time, and many of the most popular Romantic works were set in distant lands associated with those interests.

The Preromantics is the name given to a group of poets of the mid-1700s whose work first touched on important Romantic themes and ideas. Their writing reflected the awareness of social problems, the love of nature, and the fascination with myth and mystery that became typical of Romanticism.

The Scottish poet Robert Burns wrote about rural characters. He often used Scots dialect. Burns's most popular verses include "Auld Lang Syne" (about 1788) and "Comin Thro' the Rye" (about 1796).

The leading Preromantic poet was William Blake. Blake was an important printer and engraver as well as a poet. His work expresses an intensely personal vision and, partly for this reason, was barely known when he was alive. Many of his most direct lyrics are collected in *Songs of Innocence* (1789) and *Songs of Experience* (1794). His poetry combines anger at the social injustices of his time with richly imagined portraits of a freer, more just society.

Romantic poetry. William Wordsworth and Samuel Taylor Coleridge were the first important English Romantic poets. They produced a joint volume of poems titled *Lyrical Ballads* (1798).

Wordsworth's preface to the second edition (1800) is an important statement of Romantic ideas about the continuing value of poetry. He explained that his poetry used everyday language rather than the elevated poetic language of such earlier writers as Dryden and Pope because everyday language comes closer to expressing genuine human feeling. For the same reason, he wanted to write about everyday topics, especially rural, unsophisticated subjects.

Wordsworth and Coleridge lived most of their lives in the scenic Lake District of northwestern England and wrote expressively about the beauties of nature and the thoughts that natural beauty inspires. Many of their blank verse poems are written in a meditative, conversational tone new to English poetry.

Wordsworth's poems also emphasize the mind of the poet. His memories of his childhood and his experiences in France during its revolutionary period are the subject of his great autobiographical poem, *The Prelude*, published in 1850, shortly after his death. Coleridge's most famous poems are "The Rime of the Ancient Mariner" (1798) and "Christabel" (written in 1799 and 1800 but not published until 1816). Both deal with supernatural subjects. Coleridge was also an important literary critic and philosopher.

The next generation of Romantic poets included Lord Byron, Percy Bysshe Shelley, and John Keats. They criticized Wordsworth and Coleridge for giving up on the ideals of the French Revolution. These poets were interested in reviving classical subject matter in the manner of Renaissance poets. Byron and Shelley especially admired the ideal of ancient Greek democracy, and Byron died participating in the fight for Greek independence.

Byron wrote a series of "Eastern" tales set mainly in Turkey and Greece. He created a partly autobiographical hero in such lengthy works as *Childe Harold's Pilgrimage* (1812–1818) and the unfinished *Don Juan* (1819–1824). While much of Byron's poetry is dark and self-dramatizing, *Don Juan* is written in a comic style. The poem makes fun of many aspects of society, including Byron's own popularity as a celebrity author.

Percy Bysshe Shelley was an idealist and social reformer. Many of his poems call for political and social reforms in language that is melodious and complex. In his long poem *Prometheus Unbound* (1820), Shelley praised the individual who takes a stand against unjust authority. In the poem, Shelley

A portrait of Jane Austen

also argued that reform needs to be based on inner transformation. For the world to change, people's beliefs must change.

John Keats wrote intense and vivid poems that capture the experience of beauty and its inevitable passing. Some of his most important poems were written in response to other works of art. His major works include "Ode on a Grecian Urn" (1819) and "Ode to a Nightingale" (1819).

Romantic prose included essays, criticism, journals, and novels. During the 1790s, many important prose works were written in response to the French Revolution. They included Mary Wollstonecraft's *A Vindication of the Rights of Men* (1790), which supported the revolution against Edmund Burke's attacks. Wollstonecraft also wrote one of the first feminist works, *A Vindication of the Rights of Woman* (1792). In it, she argued for a woman's right to education and independence.

Horror stories called *Gothic novels* became popular during the late 1700s and early 1800s. Most of these tales deal with supernatural or seemingly supernatural events. Horace Walpole wrote the first Gothic novel, *The Castle of Otranto* (1764). Another Gothic novelist, Ann Radcliffe, used detailed landscape descriptions to show her characters' mood and attitude. Mary Wollstonecraft Shelley, the daughter of Mary Wollstonecraft and the wife of Percy Bysshe Shelley, wrote *Frankenstein* (1818), one of the most daring and popular Gothic novels.

The two greatest novelists of the Romantic period were Jane Austen and Sir Walter Scott. Austen wrote about middle-class life in small towns and in the famous resort city of Bath. Her writing is elegant and playful, but below the surface it has a surprising bite. The heroines in such Austen novels as *Pride and Prejudice* (1813) and *Emma* (1816) are known for their independence and wit. Scott wrote many novels that take place in the Scottish Highlands or Edinburgh. He also used historical settings to comment on important issues of his time. These are the first truly historical novels in English literature.

Victorian literature (1832–1901). Victoria became queen of the United Kingdom in 1837. Her reign, the longest in English history, lasted until 1901. This period is called the Victorian Age.

During the Victorian Age, the British Empire reached its height. Industry and trade expanded rapidly, and science and technology made great advances. The middle class grew enormously. In spite of this prosperity, factory laborers and farm workers lived in terrible poverty.

The Victorian Age's new scientific theories seemed to challenge many religious beliefs. The most controversial theory appeared in *The Origin of Species* (1859) by the biologist Charles Darwin. In the book, he stated that every species of life develops from an earlier one, which seemed to contradict the Biblical account of the creation of life. The theories of Darwin and other scientists led many people to feel that traditional values could no longer guide their lives. Victorian writers dealt with the contrast between the prosperity of the middle and upper classes and the wretched condition of the poor. In the late 1800s, they also analyzed the loss of faith in traditional values.

Early Victorian literature includes some of the greatest and most popular novels ever written. Most novelists of the period wrote long works with numerous characters. In many instances, the authors included actual events of the day in their tales.

The novels of Charles Dickens are noted for their colorful—and sometimes eccentric—characters. In *Oliver Twist* (1837–1839) and *David Copperfield* (1849–1850), Dickens described the lives of children made miserable by cruel or thoughtless adults. Many of his later novels picture the grim side of Victorian life. In *Bleak House* (1852–1853), Dickens criticized the courts, the clergy, and the neglect of the poor. His novels often balance their harsh social criticism with satirical humor, idealized heroines, and sentimental scenes of family life.

William Makepeace Thackeray created a masterpiece of Victorian fiction in *Vanity Fair* (1847–1848). The story follows the lives of many characters at different levels of English society during the early 1800s.

The novels of the three Brontë sisters—Emily, Charlotte, and Anne—have many Gothic and Romantic elements. The novels are known especially for their psychologically tormented heroes and heroines. Emily's *Wuthering Heights* (1847) and Charlotte's *Jane Eyre* (1847) are among the best-loved works of Victorian fiction.

During the late 1800s, an uneasy tone appeared in much of the best Victorian poetry and prose. Matthew Arnold described his doubts about modern life in such poems as "The Scholar-Gypsy" (1853) and "Dover Beach" (1867). His most important literary achievements are his critical essays on culture, literature, religion, and society. Many of them were collected in *Culture and Anarchy* (1869).

Alfred, Lord Tennyson and Robert Browning were the two most important late Victorian poets. In *In Memoriam* (published in 1850), Tennyson tried to reconcile traditional Christian faith with modern science. *Idylls of the King* (1842–1885)

The first page of the manuscript of *Jane Eyre*

returned to medieval legends of King Arthur and his knights.

Browning created finely drawn character studies in poems called *dramatic monologues*. In these poems, a real or imaginary character narrates the story. Browning's best-known work is *The Ring and the Book* (1868–1869). He based the poem on an Italian murder case of 1698. Twelve characters discuss the case, each from his or her own point of view. Elizabeth Barrett Browning, Browning's wife, wrote a famous sequence of love poems called *Sonnets from the Portuguese* (1850). In her long "novel in verse" *Aurora Leigh* (1857), she commented on the social role of women and poetry in the 1800s.

The Pre-Raphaelites were a group of poets and painters who followed John Ruskin and took their inspiration from the Middle Ages. The most important Pre-Raphaelite poet, Dante Gabriel Rossetti, was also an important painter. His partly autobiographical sonnet sequence *The House of Life* (1881) draws connections between experiences of love, death, and art. Gerard Manley Hopkins wrote experimental religious verse. His poems were not published until 1918, almost 30 years after his death. Hopkins filled his poetry with rich word pictures and unusual word combinations. The "Terrible" sonnets (written in 1885) express experiences of extreme spiritual loneliness and suffering.

The leading late Victorian novelists were George Eliot (the pen name of Mary Ann Evans), Wilkie Collins, Anthony Trollope, and Thomas Hardy. Eliot's novels address social and moral problems. Her masterpiece is *Middlemarch* (1871–1872). Collins wrote stories of crime and suspense. His book *The Moonstone* (1868) is one of the first mystery novels. The six "Barsetshire Novels" of Trollope are gentle satires of life in rural England. They often tell of conflicts within the Church of England, usually in a humorous way. Hardy wrote about characters defeated by an apparently hostile fate. He used the landscape of the imaginary county of Wessex to help create the brooding atmosphere of such novels as *The Mayor of Casterbridge* (1886) and *Jude the Obscure* (1895).

From the late 1700s to the late 1800s, almost no important dramas were produced in England. But by 1900, a number of playwrights had revived the English theater both with witty comedies and with realistic dramas about social problems of the time. Oscar Wilde recalled the glittering Restoration comedy of manners in *The Importance of Being*

Earnest (1895). George Bernard Shaw wrote plays exposing the faults he saw in society. Shaw, like Wilde, an Irishman who settled in England, addressed England's relation to Ireland in the play *John Bull's Other Island* (1904).

Literature before and after the world wars. Several outstanding authors gained fame during the period that began with Queen Victoria's death in 1901 and ended with the outbreak of World War I in 1914. A number of these authors wrote novels and plays of social criticism. Late in the period, a group of poets returned to the values of the Romantics, writing verse in the style of Wordsworth.

After Victoria died, her oldest son became King Edward VII. The term Edwardian is often applied to the period of Edward's reign—1901 to 1910. The leading Edwardian novelists included Arnold Bennett and H. G. Wells. In *The Old Wives' Tale* (1908) and other realistic novels, Bennett wrote about the dull, narrow lives of the middle class in the small towns of central England. Wells became famous for *The War of the Worlds* (1898) and other science-fiction novels. However, he also wrote political and satirical fiction. Joseph Conrad wrote probing novels on such themes as guilt, heroism, and honor. Many of his novels depict life at sea and show insight into the physical and psychological impact of imperialism.

Beginning about 1905, a group of writers and artists met frequently in a section of London called Bloomsbury to discuss intellectual questions. They were known as the Bloomsbury Group. Perhaps

Virginia Woolf

the leading Bloomsbury writer was Virginia Woolf. In such novels as *Mrs. Dalloway* (1925) and *To the Lighthouse* (1927), she wrote with great insight about the collapse of belief systems of the 1800s and its transforming effect on the lives of her characters. Woolf used a technique called *stream of consciousness* to reveal the inner thoughts of her characters, capturing even their most fleeting experiences. Woolf also wrote critical essays on literature and society. In *A Room of One's Own* (1929), she discussed many of the social, economic, and psychological disadvantages facing women writers.

Poetry between the wars. English poetry changed in both form and subject matter between the end of World War I in 1918 and the outbreak of World War II in 1939. The horrifying battlefield experiences of World War I had an enormous impact on English literature. A number of poets serving in the British Army expressed their disillusionment with conventional patriotic ideas and imagery. Their poetry describes scenes of warfare with unusual realism. Siegfried Sassoon and Wilfred Owen were among the most important of these war poets. Owen died in the war.

The destructiveness of the war left many people with the feeling that society was falling apart. T. S. Eliot best summarized their despair in *The Waste Land* (1922), the most influential poem of the period. Its jagged style, complex symbols, and references to other literary works set a new pattern for poetry. Eliot was conservative in politics and religion. But W. H. Auden, Stephen Spender, and Cecil Day-Lewis expressed radical political ideals in their verse. All three criticized injustices they saw in an unequal society. For all of these poets, society suffered from feelings of rootlessness and isolation.

Hugh MacDiarmid was a Scottish nationalist and political radical who wanted to capture a specifically Scottish cultural identity in his poetry. Dylan Thomas became the greatest Welsh poet of the 1900s. Thomas was known for his lyrical poems, which expressed his passionate love of life in vivid and melodious verse.

Fiction between the wars. Virginia Woolf remained the outstanding novelist of this period until her death in 1941. Another important novelist was D. H. Lawrence. He explored relationships between men and women in *Women in Love* (1920) and other autobiographical novels. Ford Madox Ford described changes in English society after World War I in four novels titled *Parade's End*

(1924–1928). Graham Greene wrote about people troubled by difficult moral or religious problems in *The Power and the Glory* (1940) and other novels.

Several writers wrote humorous, satirical novels. Evelyn Waugh satirized wealthy and fashionable young people in *Vile Bodies* (1930) and *A Handful of Dust* (1934). Aldous Huxley also made fun of fashionable society in *Crome Yellow* (1921) and *Point Counter Point* (1928). But Huxley's best-known novel is *Brave New World* (1932), which describes a terrifying future society that eliminates individuality and personal liberty.

After World War II, the United Kingdom gradually lost most of its overseas empire. A sense of shrinking power in the world contributed to the anger and pessimism of much English literature in the years following the war. At the same time, many authors from the former colonies settled in the United Kingdom and made important and original contributions to English literature.

Writers from the prewar period, such as Greene and Auden, continued to produce important works after World War II. George Orwell began his literary career in the 1930s, but his most famous novel, *1984*, appeared in 1949. This frightening story describes a future society that distorts truth and deprives the individual of privacy.

During the 1950s, a number of younger writers expressed their discontent with traditional English politics, education, and literature. These writers were labeled the Angry Young Men. They included the playwright John Osborne and the novelist John Braine. Osborne's drama *Look Back in Anger* (1956) describes a young working-class man's resentment of the English class system. In *Room at the Top* (1957), Braine created an ambitious working-class hero who has little respect for traditional English ways of life. Kingsley Amis's novel *Lucky Jim* (1954) satirized the self-satisfied and pretentious society of an English university.

Several authors wrote about such changes in society in multivolume works that follow many characters over a long period. Anthony Powell wrote 12 novels titled *A Dance to the Music of Time* (1951–1975). They portray upper middle-class society from the 1920s to the 1970s. Paul Scott wrote about the final years of British rule in India in the four-volume *Raj Quartet* (1966–1975). Doris Lessing wrote a five-volume *Children of Violence* (1952–1969). It deals with a British woman who grows up in Rhodesia (now Zimbabwe), moves to England,

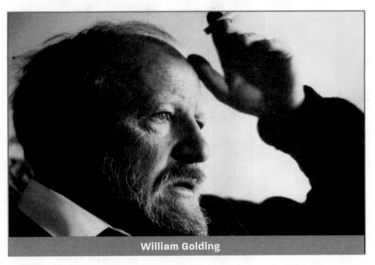

William Golding

and becomes involved in radical politics.

William Golding wrote one of the most disturbing novels of the 1950s, *Lord of the Flies* (1954). In the novel, a group of English schoolboys are marooned on a deserted island and establish a rule of violence and terror.

Recent English poetry has moved away from the restraint and traditionalism that characterized some earlier movements. One of the period's most important poets, Ted Hughes, wrote on darker, mythical subject matter. His poetry often includes violent imagery, as in *Crow* (1970). In 1998, shortly before his death, Hughes published *Birthday Letters*, a group of poems looking back on his failed marriage to American poet Sylvia Plath.

Geoffrey Hill writes difficult, complex verse that often focuses on religious and historical themes. Douglas Dunn's earliest poetry shows the influence of Larkin. However, some of his later work moves toward fantastic and Scottish-influenced themes. Linton Kwesi Johnson's poetry combines the rhythms of English verse with those of Caribbean music and slang. This combination, called *dub*, has influenced many young black British writers. Fred D'Aguiar's verse collection *British Subjects* (1993) emphasizes how Caribbean experience and culture have become part of recent British cultural identity.

Recent English fiction. During the 1960s and 1970s, Iris Murdoch, Muriel Spark, and Anthony Burgess emerged as important novelists. Murdoch was a professor of philosophy who often treated questions of moral philosophy in her fiction. Spark's novels are often comic but with disturbing and even Gothic undertones. Burgess wrote experimental novels of great verbal complexity and wit.

Harold Pinter

In *A Clockwork Orange* (1962), he told the story of a violent juvenile delinquent who is brainwashed into numb social conformity.

More recent significant English novelists have often come from the United Kingdom's different immigrant communities. They include Salman Rushdie from India, Kazuo Ishiguro from Japan, and Caryl Phillips from the Caribbean. Rushdie is the outstanding figure of this group. His writing has been described as an example of *magic realism*, a style that combines realism with fantastic or apparently supernatural events. His novels overflow with multiple characters and stories. Ishiguro's novels offer subtle psychological explorations of memory and history. Phillips's novels show the experience of ethnic hatred, slavery, and exile through the use of historical settings and multiple narrators.

Recent English drama. Harold Pinter was the most important playwright of the postwar period. He wrote comic dramas that seem commonplace on the surface but have an underlying sense of menace. His most important early plays are *The Caretaker* (1960) and *The Homecoming* (1965). Pinter continues to write highly individual plays. Many of his later dramas deal with power relationships among friends or lovers. Tom Stoppard writes original and complex plays with philosophical themes. His works often experiment with imaginary historical situations and are remarkable for their verbal brilliance. Peter Shaffer has written a number of plays about the psychology of artists, outsiders, and nonconformists.

Several playwrights have engaged political issues in their work. Edward Bond has written plays about class conflict and oppression throughout British history. Caryl Churchill draws on such themes as the connection between colonial and sexual oppression in British history. David Hare has examined key British institutions—the Anglican church, the legal system, and political parties—in three related plays. In *Amy's View* (1997), Hare reflected on differences between theater and the newer, more popular media of film and television.

English literature has been a major influence to English-speaking writers throughout the world, and it continues to produce innovative written works today.

The Land

The United Kingdom covers most of an island group called the *British Isles*. The British Isles consist of two large islands—Great Britain and Ireland—and thousands of small islands. England, Scotland, and Wales occupy the island of Great Britain. Northern Ireland occupies the northeastern part of the island of Ireland. The independent Republic of Ireland occupies the rest of the island of Ireland. Some Irish people object to the term *British Isles* because it seems to imply that Ireland is British.

The island of Great Britain is the eighth largest island in the world. It covers 84,550 square miles (218,980 square kilometers). The North Sea on the east and the English Channel on the south separate the island from the mainland of Europe. The island of Ireland lies to the west, across the Irish Sea. The island of Great Britain is separated from mainland Europe by only about 20 miles (32 kilometers) of water at the closest point. Most of the coastline of Great Britain is so broken by deep bays and inlets that no point on the island is more than 75 miles (121 kilometers) from the sea.

The United Kingdom can be divided into eight main land regions. Seven of these regions occupy the island of Great Britain. They are (1) the Scottish Highlands, (2) the Central Lowlands, (3) the Southern Uplands, (4) the Pennines, (5) Wales, (6) the Southwest Peninsula, and (7) the English Lowlands. Northern Ireland makes up the eighth region.

The Scottish Highlands cover the northern two-thirds of Scotland. They are a region of mountain ranges, plateaus, and deep valleys. The highest point in the United Kingdom, 4,406-foot (1,343-meter) Ben Nevis, rises in the Highlands. Many bays cut into the region's Atlantic Ocean and North Sea coasts. Some narrow bays, called *sea lochs*, are flanked by steep mountain slopes and reach far inland. Most of the Highlands is a *moor*—an area of coarse grasses, a few small trees, and low evergreen shrubs called *heather*. The soil of this rugged, windswept region is thin and poor. Few people live there. Most of them raise sheep, or they fish in the seas.

The Central Lowlands lie south of the Scottish Highlands, in the valleys of the Rivers Clyde, Forth, and Tay. This region is a gently rolling plain. It has Scotland's best farmland and its richest coal deposits. Most of the Scottish people live there, and most of Scotland's industry is in the Lowlands.

The Southern Uplands rise gently south of the Central Lowlands. This is a region of rounded, rolling hills. Sheep graze on the short grass that covers much of the hills. Their fleece goes to Scotland's woolen mills in the region's Tweed Valley. In the south, the Uplands rise to the Cheviot Hills, which form the border between Scotland and England.

The Pennines are a region of rounded uplands that extend from the Scottish border about halfway down the length of England. They are also known as the *Pennine Chain* or *Pennine Hills*, and they are often called the *backbone of England*. Their flanks are rich in coal. West of the Pennines lies the Lake District, a scenic area of clear, quiet lakes and low mountains. The Lake District is one of England's most famous recreation areas.

Wales lies southwest of the Pennines. It is separated from the Pennines by a narrow strip of the English Lowlands. The Cambrian Mountains cover most of Wales. These mountains are especially rugged and beautiful in the north and are more rounded in central Wales. Southern Wales is largely a plateau deeply cut by river valleys. Most of the people live on the narrow coastal plains or in the deep, green river valleys. These are the best areas for crop farming and raising dairy cattle. The rest of the land is too steep for raising crops and is used mostly for grazing sheep and some beef cattle. Wales has large deposits of coal in the south, though most of its mines have been closed. Much of the industry of Wales is centered in the large coastal towns.

The Southwest Peninsula lies south of Wales, across the Bristol Channel. It is a plateau whose surface is broken by great masses of granite. Near much of the coast, the plateau ends sharply in magnificent cliffs that tower above the sea. Tiny fishing villages lie in sheltered bays along the coast. The region has mild winters and summers that are not too dry. This climate helps make agriculture impor-

tant in the fertile lowland areas. Farmers grow vegetables and raise dairy cattle.

The peninsula was once famous for its tin and copper mines, but most of these metals have been worked out. More important today is the region's fine white china clay, used to make pottery. The Southwest Peninsula's beauty and pleasant climate attract many artists and retired people and thousands of vacationers every year.

The English Lowlands cover all England south of the Pennines and east of Wales and the Southwest Peninsula. This region has most of the United Kingdom's farmable land, industry, and people. The Lowlands consist chiefly of broad, gently rolling plains, broken here and there by low hills and ridges. Much of the land is a patchwork of fields and meadows, bordered by tall hedges, stone fences, or rows of trees.

A grassy plain called the Midlands lies in the center of the English Lowlands, just south of the Pennines. Parts of the Midlands extend along the western and eastern borders of the Pennines. The Midlands are the industrial heart of the United Kingdom. Birmingham and the surrounding communities form the country's chief manufacturing center.

South of the Midlands, a series of hills and valleys crosses the land to the valley of the River Thames. London, the United Kingdom's capital and great commercial and cultural center, stands on the Thames. Most of the land north of the Thames and up to a bay of the North Sea called The Wash is low

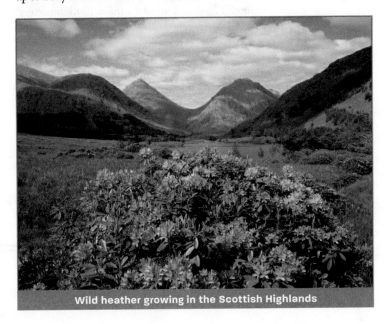

Wild heather growing in the Scottish Highlands

and flat. This area has some of the country's richest farmland. A great plain called The Fens borders The Wash. In The Fens, near Ely, is the lowest point on the island of Great Britain. It ranges from sea level to 15 feet (4.6 meters) below sea level, depending on the tide of the North Sea.

South of the Thames, low chalk hills and valleys cross the land. Where the hills reach the sea, they form great white cliffs. The most famous cliffs are near Dover. On clear days, people in Calais, France, can look across the Strait of Dover and see the white cliffs of Dover gleaming in the sun.

Northern Ireland is a region of low mountains, deep valleys, and fertile lowlands. The land is lowest near the center and rises to its greatest heights near the north and south coasts. The chief natural resources are rich fields and pastures, and most of the land is used for crop farming or grazing.

Rivers and lakes. The United Kingdom's longest rivers are the Thames and the Severn. The Thames is 210 miles (340 kilometers) long. The Severn is nearly the same length. Many British rivers have drowned, or sunken, mouths called *estuaries*, up which the ocean tides flow. These rivers include the Clyde and Forth of Scotland; the Humber, Mersey, and Thames of England; and the Severn of England and Wales. The estuaries of these rivers make excellent harbors. Bristol, Hull, Liverpool, London, Southampton, and other cities on or near estuaries are important ports.

Lough Neagh in Northern Ireland is the largest lake in the British Isles. It is about 18 miles (29 kilometers) long and up to 15 miles (24 kilometers) wide. It covers about 150 square miles (388 square kilometers). Loch Lomond in Scotland is the largest lake on the island of Great Britain. It is 23 miles (37 kilometers) long and 5 miles (8 kilometers) wide at its widest point. England's biggest lakes are in the

St. Paul's Cathedral and the Thames at dusk

Lake District. The largest, Windermere, is about 10 miles (16 kilometers) long and up to 1 mile (1.6 kilometers) wide.

Climate

The United Kingdom has a mild climate, even though it lies as far north as bitterly cold Labrador. Winter temperatures rarely drop as low as 10°F (−12°C), and summer temperatures seldom rise above 90°F (32°C). The climate is influenced by the Gulf Stream, a warm ocean current that sweeps up from the equator and flows past the islands of Great Britain and Ireland. Steady southwest winds blow across this current and bring warmth in winter. In summer, the ocean is cooler than the land. Winds over the ocean come to the United Kingdom as refreshing breezes.

The sea winds also bring plentiful rain. The heaviest rains fall in the highland areas of western Scotland. Some of these areas get 150 to 200 inches (380 to 510 centimeters) a year. Less than 20 inches (51 centimeters) of rain falls yearly in some parts of southeastern England. The United Kingdom has rain throughout the year, and rarely is any section of the country dry for as long as three weeks. Much of the rain comes in light, but steady, drizzles.

Mild fogs hang over parts of the country from time to time. But the famous "pea soup" fogs of London and other big cities seldom occur any more. These thick, heavy fogs were caused chiefly by smoke and other pollution released into the air by factories, automobiles, and homes where coal was burned for heat. Antipollution laws have helped make such fogs much less severe than they once were.

Economy

The United Kingdom is an important manufacturing and trading nation. In fact, the country can survive only by manufacturing and trading. The United Kingdom's farms produce only about three-fifths of the food needed by the people. Except for coal, natural gas, and oil, the United Kingdom has few natural resources. The country must import about two-thirds of its food and many of the raw materials it needs for manufacturing.

Service industries account for about 75 percent of the United Kingdom's *gross domestic product* (GDP). The GDP is the total value of goods and services produced within the country annually. About 80 percent of British workers are employed in service industries. The country's service industries are concentrated in and near its largest cities, especially London.

Finance, insurance, real estate, and business services contribute a larger portion of the United Kingdom's GDP than any other service industry group. Most of the country's financial companies operate in London, one of the world's leading financial cities. Major financial institutions in London include the Bank of England, the United Kingdom's national bank; the London Stock Exchange; and Lloyd's of London insurance organization. The United Kingdom has many firms that offer such business services as accounting, advertising, data processing, and engineering.

Community, government, and personal services rank second among the service industries of the United Kingdom in terms of the GDP. This group employs more people than any other industry in the country. It includes such activities as education, health care, legal services, and military operations.

Trade, hotels, and restaurants rank next among the service industries. Aberdeen and London are important centers of petroleum distribution. Leeds is the chief center for the wholesale trade of clothing. Tourist activities in the United Kingdom, especially in the London area, provide important income to hotels, restaurants, and retail shops. Tourists spend over $25 billion yearly in the United Kingdom.

Utilities provide electric power and water services to people of the United Kingdom. The United Kingdom's other service industries, transportation and communication, are discussed later in this section.

Manufacturing. The United Kingdom is a leading industrial nation. Most British industries are in central England, the London area, the Scottish Central Lowlands, the Newcastle upon Tyne area, and southern Wales. Early factories were located near the coal fields because coal powered the steam engines that moved the machinery. Today, the use of electricity, oil, and gas has enabled many new industries to develop far from the coal fields, especially in southern England.

The United Kingdom ranks as an important steel-producing country. It exports about half of its finished steel. The rest is used in the United Kingdom to make hundreds of products. Much steel is used in the manufacture of automobiles, buses, trucks, and motorcycles.

The United Kingdom also produces heavy machinery for industry, farming, and mining.

Steelworks in Port Talbot, Wales

The country is one of the world's largest producers of tractors. Other products include cranes, earth movers, road graders, harvesters, and drilling machines. British factories also make railway equipment, household appliances, and machine tools. The city of Sheffield is famous for its high-quality knives and hand tools.

BAE Systems is one of the world's largest defense and aerospace companies. It supplies the armed forces of the United Kingdom, the United States, and other countries with a wide range of products, including military aircraft, missiles, and land warfare systems.

An increasing percentage of the United Kingdom's manufactured goods consists of electronic equipment. Factories produce such items as cable television equipment, data processing equipment, fiber-optic communications systems, radar devices, and undersea telephone cables.

The chemical industry in the United Kingdom produces a variety of products—from industrial chemicals to plastics and soap. The United Kingdom is one of the largest exporters of pharmaceuticals. The country's pottery industry is centered in Stoke-on-Trent. Outstanding names in British pottery include Worcester, Spode, and Wedgwood.

The United Kingdom is one of the world's chief centers of printing and publishing. British companies print paper money and postage stamps for many countries. Books published in the United Kingdom are exported to countries throughout the world.

The Industrial Revolution began in the United Kingdom's textile industry. Today, the United Kingdom remains an important producer of cotton and woolen textiles. British manufacturers also make synthetic fibers and fabrics. England's east Midlands region is a center for the production of lace and knitwear. Cotton and wool are produced in northern England. Scotland produces knitwear and is famous for its fine woolen products. Northern Ireland has a worldwide reputation for its linen goods.

The United Kingdom has one of Europe's largest clothing industries. The biggest centers are Leicester, Leeds, London, and Manchester. British clothing has long been famous for its quality. But today, the United Kingdom imports more clothing than it exports because many countries with lower labor costs can produce clothing more cheaply than the British can.

Processing of foods and beverages ranks as one of the United Kingdom's major industries. Most processed foods and beverages are consumed in the United Kingdom. But some are exported. Scotch whisky has a large world market. Other British industries manufacture bricks and cement, furniture, leather goods, glassware, and paper.

Agriculture. The United Kingdom imports about three-fifths of its food supply. The imports include avocados, bananas, grapes, citrus fruits, pineapples, and other items that cannot be easily grown in the United Kingdom's climate.

Farmland covers over two-thirds of the United Kingdom's land area. The nation has about 225,000 farms. About two-thirds of the United Kingdom's farms are less than 50 acres (20 hectares). About half the people who operate or work on farms do so on a part-time basis.

Many British farmers practice *mixed farming*—that is, they raise a variety of crops and animals. Methods of mixed farming vary from farm to farm. In the rough highlands of Scotland, Wales, and western England, grass grows much better than farm crops. There, farmers use most of their land for grazing. The land in southern and eastern England is drier and flatter, and it is more easily worked. Farmers in eastern England use most of their land for raising crops.

The United Kingdom's most important crops are barley, potatoes, rapeseed, sugar beets, and wheat. Farmers in southern and eastern England grow most of the country's barley, rapeseed, sugar beets, and wheat. Potatoes are grown throughout the United Kingdom. Farmers in southern England grow most of the United Kingdom's fruits and garden vegetables. One of the most productive regions is the county of Kent in southeastern England. It is called the *Garden of England* and is famous for the beautiful blossoms of its apple and cherry orchards in springtime. Farmers in Kent also grow hops, which are used in making beer.

Sheep are the United Kingdom's chief livestock. Farmers in almost every part of the country raise sheep for meat and wool. British farmers also raise beef cattle, dairy cattle, and hogs.

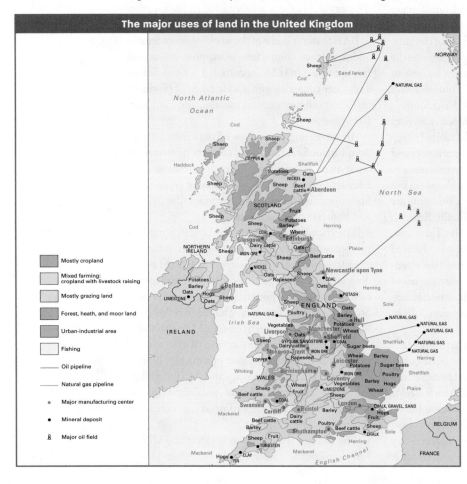

The major uses of land in the United Kingdom

Mostly cropland

Mixed farming: cropland with livestock raising

Mostly grazing land

Forest, heath, and moor land

Urban-industrial area

Fishing

Oil pipeline

Natural gas pipeline

● Major manufacturing center

● Mineral deposit

⌂ Major oil field

Chickens are raised mainly in special mass-production plants.

Mining. The United Kingdom is a major world producer of petroleum and natural gas. These fuels account for about 90 percent of the value of total mineral production in the country.

Petroleum is the United Kingdom's most valuable mineral. In the past, the country had to import petroleum to meet its needs. But during the 1970s, the United Kingdom began producing petroleum from wells in the North Sea. Today, the United Kingdom's oil wells provide nearly all the petroleum that the country uses and also supply petroleum for export. The United Kingdom obtains natural gas from deposits below the North Sea.

The United Kingdom's largest coal-mining regions lie near the River Trent in central England and in North Yorkshire. Coal from these areas is an important fuel source for the country's electric power plants.

The United Kingdom's other important minerals include sand and gravel, fluorspar, gypsum, potash, salt, and clays. The Southwest Peninsula has fine china clay, used in making pottery. Southeastern England has large deposits of chalk, used for cement.

Fishing. The United Kingdom is an important fishing nation. The British fishing industry supplies about 660,000 tons (600,000 metric tons) of fish yearly. More than half of this catch comes from the waters west of Scotland and from the northern North Sea. The principal catches include cod, haddock, herring, mackerel, plaice, and whiting. Large catches of shellfish are also brought in. The main fishing ports are off the northeast coast of Scotland and in the southwestern part of the island of Great Britain.

Fish farms in the United Kingdom produce salmon, trout, and shellfish. Scotland is especially known for its salmon farms.

Energy sources. Plants that burn coal, natural gas, and petroleum provide most of the United Kingdom's electric power. Nuclear energy provides most of the remaining electric power. In 1956, the United Kingdom opened the world's first large-scale nuclear power station at Calder Hall, Cumbria, in northwestern England.

International trade. The United Kingdom ranks as a leading trading nation. The country once imported chiefly raw materials and exported mostly manufactured products. However, manufactured goods now account for most of the country's imports and exports.

The United Kingdom exports aerospace equipment, chemicals and pharmaceuticals, foods and beverages, machinery, motor vehicles, and petroleum. Its imports include alcoholic beverages, chemicals, clothing, foods, machinery, metals, motor vehicles, petroleum products, and textiles.

Most of the United Kingdom's trade is with other developed countries, especially other members of an organization known as the European Union. France, Germany, and the United States are the United Kingdom's leading customers and suppliers. Other major trade partners include Belgium, China, Ireland, Japan, the Netherlands, Sweden, Italy, and Spain.

The value of the United Kingdom's imports of goods usually exceeds the value of its exports. British banks and insurance companies make up part of the difference by selling their services to people and firms in other lands. Another important source of income is the spending by the more than 30 million tourists who visit the United Kingdom each year. Most of these tourists come from France, Germany, Ireland, and other European countries and also from the United States. The British merchant fleet also brings in money by carrying cargoes for other countries.

Transportation. Roads and railways carry most passenger and freight traffic within the United

Barley

Kingdom. A system of high-speed motorways links major cities and towns. Bus systems provide local and intercity transportation. *Lorries* (trucks) carry most of the inland freight.

An extensive rail network crisscrosses the United Kingdom. The railroads provide high-speed passenger service, as well as freight hauling.

The United Kingdom has a large merchant fleet. The ships in the fleet carry British-made goods to ports throughout the world and bring back needed imports. British ships also carry freight for other countries. There are about 120 ports of commercial significance throughout the United Kingdom.

The country's inland waterways are used to carry freight, as well as for recreational boating. The Thames, which flows through London, is the United Kingdom's busiest river and one of the busiest in the world.

Ferry services connect coastal and island communities in the United Kingdom. *Hovercraft* (vehicles that ride over water on a cushion of air) carry passengers mainly across the English Channel between England and France. In 1994, a railroad tunnel linked the United Kingdom and France beneath the channel.

British Airways, the United Kingdom's largest airline, operates flights to all parts of the world. Smaller airlines provide service within the United Kingdom and to other countries. The United Kingdom's largest airports are Heathrow, Gatwick, and Stansted, near London. Other large airports operate in Edinburgh, Birmingham, Glasgow, and Manchester.

Communication. The United Kingdom has about 100 daily newspapers. About 10 have nationwide circulation. Their main offices are in London. *The Sun*, the *Daily Mail*, and the *Daily Mirror* have the largest circulations. The most influential papers include *The Times*, *The Guardian*, *The Daily Telegraph*, and *The Daily Star*.

The British Broadcasting Corporation (BBC), a public corporation, provides commercial-free radio and television service. The BBC is financed chiefly by yearly licenses that people must buy to own a television set. Numerous commercial radio and television stations also broadcast throughout the country.

MLA Citation

"United Kingdom." *The Southwestern Advantage Topic Source*. Nashville: Southwestern. 2013.

Trains entering the Channel Tunnel in Folkestone, England

DATA

United Kingdom in Brief

General information

Capital: London.

Official language: English.

Official name: United Kingdom of Great Britain and Northern Ireland.

National anthem: "God Save the Queen" (or "King").

Flag and royal arms: The United Kingdom's flag, adopted in 1801, has a red cross with a white border superimposed on a diagonal cross with a white border. The background is blue. The flag is known as the *British Union Flag* or the Union Jack. The royal arms has a lion on the left representing England and unicorn on the right representing Scotland.

Largest cities: (2001 census) London (7,172,036); Birmingham (977,091); Leeds (715,404); Glasgow (577,869); Sheffield (513,234); Bradford (467,668); Edinburgh (448,624); Liverpool (439,476).

Land and climate

Land: The United Kingdom lies in northwestern Europe. It includes the island of Great Britain and the northeastern part of the island of Ireland. France lies south across the English Channel; the Republic of Ireland west across the Irish Sea; Belgium, the Netherlands, Germany, Denmark, and Norway east across the North Sea. Most of the land is flat or rolling. There are rugged sections in northern Scotland, in Wales, and in northern, central, and far southwestern England.

Area: 93,784 mi^2 (242,900 km^2). *Greatest distances*—north-south, about 600 mi (970 km); east-west, about 300 mi (480 km). *Coastline*—2,521 mi (4,057 km).

Elevation: *Highest*—Ben Nevis, 4,406 ft (1,343 m) above sea level. *Lowest*—Great Holme Fen, near the River Ouse in Cambridgeshire, 9 ft (2.7 m) below sea level.

Climate: Summers mild—daytime highs about 73ºF (23ºC) in the south, about 65ºF (18ºC) in Scotland. Cool winters—nighttime temperatures drop nearly to freezing, but rarely much below, except in the Scottish Highlands. Precipitation moderate, generally higher in the west.

Government

Form of government: Constitutional monarchy. In practice, a parliamentary democracy.

Head of state: Monarch (queen or king). The monarch is the head of the executive and judicial branches of the government and is a part of the legislative branch.

Head of government: Prime minister, usually the head of the majority party in the House of Commons.

Legislature: Parliament of two houses: House of Commons has 650 members, elected by the people; House of Lords has about 700 members. House of Commons is much more powerful than House of Lords.

Executive: Prime minister and Cabinet.

Political divisions: England, Scotland, Wales, Northern Ireland, united under one government. Each division has units of local government.

DATA

United Kingdom in Brief

People

Population: *Current estimate*—62,761,000. *2001 census*—58,789,194.

Population density: 670 per mi^2 (259 per km^2).

Distribution: 90 percent urban, 10 percent rural.

Major ethnic/national groups: 95 percent of mostly British or Irish descent. About 5 percent recent immigrants or their descendants. Immigrants mostly from former British colonies.

Major religions: About 50 percent Church of England, 10 percent Roman Catholic, 4 percent Church of Scotland; also several other Protestant denominations, Muslims, Hindus, Jews.

Economy

Chief products: *Agriculture*—barley, beef and dairy cattle, chickens and eggs, hogs, potatoes, rapeseed, sheep, sugar beets, wheat. *Manufacturing*—aerospace equipment, chemicals and pharmaceuticals, electrical and electronic products, foods and beverages, steel, machinery, motor vehicles, printed materials, textiles and clothing. *Mining*—coal, natural gas, petroleum. *Fishing industry*—cod, crabs, haddock, herring, mackerel, whiting.

Money: *Basic unit*—British pound. One hundred pence equal one pound.

Foreign trade: *Major exports*—aerospace equipment, chemicals and pharmaceuticals, foods and beverages, machinery, motor vehicles, petroleum. *Major imports*—chemicals, clothing, foods (especially fruit, vegetables, meat), machinery, metals, motor vehicles, petroleum products, textiles. *Major trading partners*—Belgium, China, France, Germany, Ireland, Italy, Japan, Spain, Sweden, the Netherlands, United States.

Average Monthly Weather in the United Kingdom

Month	High temp. (F)	Low temp. (F)	High temp. (C)	Low temp. (C)	Days of rain or snow
London					
January	44	35	7	2	17
February	45	35	7	2	13
March	51	37	11	3	11
April	56	40	13	4	14
May	63	45	17	7	13
June	69	51	21	11	11
July	73	55	23	13	13
August	72	54	22	12	13
September	67	51	19	11	13
October	58	44	14	7	14
November	49	39	9	4	16
December	45	36	7	2	16

DATA

Average Monthly Weather in the United Kingdom

Month	High temp. (F)	Low temp. (F)	High temp. (C)	Low temp. (C)	Days of rain or snow
Edinburgh					
January	43	35	6	2	18
February	43	35	6	2	15
March	47	36	8	2	15
April	50	39	10	4	16
May	55	43	13	6	15
June	62	48	17	9	15
July	65	52	18	11	17
August	64	52	18	11	17
September	60	48	16	9	16
October	53	44	12	7	18
November	47	39	8	4	18
December	44	36	7	2	17

Economic Production and Workers in the United Kingdom

Economic activities	% of GDP[1] produced	Number of workers	% of all workers
Source: United Kingdom Office for National Statistics; International Monetary Fund. Figures are for 2010.			
Finance, insurance, real estate, and business services	29	6,277,000	20
Community, government, and personal services	24	10,177,000	33
Trade, restaurants, and hotels	14	6,668,000	21
Transportation and communication	11	2,593,000	8
Manufacturing	10	2,553,000	8
Construction	7	2,133,000	7
Utilities	2	294,000	1
Mining	2	62,000	2[2]
Agriculture, forestry, and fishing	1	459,000	1
Total[3]	100	31,216,000	100

[1]GDP=gross domestic product, the total value of goods and services produced within a country in a year.

[2]Less than one-half of 1 percent.

[3]Figures may not add up to 100 percent due to rounding.

ADDITIONAL RESOURCES

Books to Read

Baedeker's Great Britain. 4th ed. Automobile Assn., 2000.

Cannon, John A., ed. *The Oxford Companion to British History.* Oxford, 1997.

Encyclopedia of Britain. Helicon, 1999.

Innes, Brian. *United Kingdom.* Raintree Steck-Vaughn, 2002. Younger readers.

Leapman, Michael, and others. *Portrait of Britain.* D K Pub., 1999.

Office for National Statistics. *Britain: The Official Yearbook of the United Kingdom.* Her Majesty's Stationery Office, published annually.

Web Sites

10 Downing Street

http://www.number10.gov.uk//

The official Web site of the prime minister of the United Kingdom.

Background Note: United Kingdom

http://www.state.gov/r/pa/ei/bgn/3846.htm

Information from the U.S. Department of State.

BBC News Online

http://news.bbc.co.uk/

Worldwide news from the British Broadcasting Corporation.

BBC World Newsround

http://news.bbc.co.uk/cbbcnews/

The BBC features a news Web site for kids.

CIA Factbook: United Kingdom

https://www.cia.gov/library/publications/the-world-factbook/geos/uk.html

An overview of the country from the U.S. Central Intelligence Agency.

Corporation of London Home Page

http://www.cityoflondon.gov.uk/

London, England, site for city services and tourism.

Country Profile: United Kingdom

http://news.bbc.co.uk/2/hi/europe/country_profiles/1038758.stm

Information from the BBC.

House of Commons Home Page

http://www.parliament.uk/business/commons/

Information about the British House of Commons and its select committees.

Houses of Parliament Home Page

http://www.parliament.uk/

Information on the British Parliament, including members of the House of Commons and House of Lords.

National Statistics

http://www.statistics.gov.uk/

Official statistics from the government of the United Kingdom.

Parliamentary Office of Science and Technology (POST) Home Page

http://www.parliament.uk/mps-lords-and-offices/offices/bicameral/post/

POST information and objective analysis of science and technology-based issues in the United Kingdom and worldwide.

Royal Air Force Home Page

http://www.raf.mod.uk/

The official home page of the Royal Air Force of the United Kingdom

The Battle of Britain

http://www.iwm.org.uk/exhibitions/battle-of-britain

An on-line exhibit from the Imperial War Museum.

The British Monarchy—The Official Web Site

http://www.royal.gov.uk/

The official Web site of the British monarchy features historical information, photos, and biographical profiles.

Search Strings

English Public Schools

England "Public Schools" independent private schools (121,000)

England "Public Schools" independent private schools history (107,000)

history of public schools in England reputation tradition (134,000)

history of public schools in England reputation tradition Eton Harrow Winchester (700)

Theater in the United Kingdom

Theater "United Kingdom" London west end (126,000)

Theater "United Kingdom" London west end "Royal National Theatre" (8,890)

Theater "United Kingdom" London west end "Royal National Theatre" "Royal Shakespeare Company" (401)

London

London size culture finance tourism trade age history (88,000)

London famous landmarks parks culture (87,100)

London statistics famous landmarks attractions (16,800)

Food and Drink

London food drink "British cooking" (2,410)

London food drink "British cooking" traditional restaurants pubs (658)

BACKGROUND INFORMATION

The following articles and features were written during the year in which the events took place and reflect the style and thinking of that time.

United Kingdom (1947)

The year 1947 was one of the hardest Great Britain has ever gone through in peacetime. By December there was even less to eat and wear than there was during the war.

It all started with the effects of a coal shortage as the year began. At least it seemed to start then. But the fact is that Britain came out of the war with so many shortages that it was a simple thing for the misfortunes of 1947 to bring two crises. One was from January through March and the other was in the last part of the year.

The Government was trying to do something about the coal shortage when bad weather began in January. Deep snow clogged the main roads, thick ice blocked the harbors, strong winds wrecked cargo ships, and fogs stopped traffic on land and sea. Finally, in the melting time in March, floods covered much of the island's best farm land. That was the weather history of three months. It was the worst that Great Britain had had in many years.

Of course freight often could not move. The people soon lacked supplies, especially food and coal. The "blackout" of the streets came back just as if it were wartime. It was forbidden to use electricity in homes and offices for several hours each day.

By April the weather was better and people had forgotten some of their personal discomforts. But the Government reported that the country as a whole was in a bad way. It was running out of money for buying the food and raw materials for its factories that it must have from abroad, particularly from the United States. That might have happened fairly soon in any case, but the weather crisis made the situation worse. It had harmed the factories that were manufacturing goods for sale abroad and thus made the country poorer.

Money troubles. Great Britain had more and more trouble with one of the rules of foreign trade: that goods bought abroad must be paid for in the money of the country in which they are purchased. Since nobody had as much to sell as the United States, particularly in the line of food, "scarce dollars" and "the dollar crisis"—phrases that used to be used only in places like Wall Street—became matters that any English school child could talk about. Everybody understood that the reason English people had less and less to eat and wear was because they could not manage to sell enough to Americans.

The United States had already done a great deal to help Britain over the difficult years of recovery from the war. In 1946 this country told Britain that it could borrow American dollars up to almost $4,000,000,000, and that ought to get it through the first five years. Canada, from which Great Britain also has to buy food, did almost exactly the same thing, with a credit to Britain of more than $1,000,000,000.

What happened in 1947 that was so frightening was the way the money vanished. In the late spring, Britain was spending it at the rate of $75,000,000 a week. That soon rose to $150,000,000 a week. By August, when the money was all gone except for $400,000,000, Britain was spending $273,000,000 a week.

Americans asked—and this was done officially in Washington as well as by private citizens—whether some of it had not been wasted. In answer, Great Britain gave out the following figures showing how the dollars spent in the United States had been used:

The second crisis. A new period of "austerity," as the British people sometimes call their hard times, set in when Labor Prime Minister Clement Attlee announced on August 6 a revised program to meet the foreign trade crisis. From then on, things happened in quick succession. A delegation was sent to Washington to see if some of the rules about the American loan could be relaxed. Consumers were asked to save power and farmers were requested to raise more food. The people were asked to get along on less in almost every aspect of their lives. At the same time they were told to work harder and to produce more goods for export.

One of the hardest things for the British people to take was a kind of conscription of labor. It was not so severe as it had been in the war, and actually meant little more than that if people changed their jobs they would have to go where they were urgently needed.

Surprisingly, after so much discouragement, the whole plan began to work. Exports improved, and the Government stopped all the imports it could. Most surprisingly of all, the much-criticized coal industry began to pass a dividing line between success and failure (4,000,000 tons a week). Coal began to leave British ports for foreign countries, as it used to do long ago.

Domestic affairs. Daily life in Britain became more and more dismal as the months passed. At the beginning of the year meat rations were cut. In the spring people were forced to make their old clothes last longer. In May they were told that for five months they could not use gas or electricity for heating their homes. In September the amount of meat allowed to each person weekly dropped from 24 to 20 cents' worth.

All nonessential driving of cars was stopped in order to save the dollars formerly spent on American gasoline. People were no longer allowed to have money for vacations in other countries.

By the close of the year the egg ration was about one a week and the milk ration for ordinary people was two pints a week. The bacon ration was one ounce a week, and for the first time in history potatoes were rationed.

If a man bought one suit and an overcoat, he had only enough ration stamps left to buy two pairs of socks. A woman who bought a coat, a woolen dress, a pair of shoes, two pairs of stockings, and a blouse, could buy nothing else during the year.

Royal wedding. The wedding of Princess Elizabeth, heir presumptive to the throne, and Lieutenant Philip Mountbatten, Duke of Edinburgh, brightened a gray November in a year that was otherwise dreary for millions of British people. The ceremony in historic Westminster Abbey had great magnificence. Popular demonstrations of affection for Princess Elizabeth and the other members of the royal family were widespread.

The Archbishop of Canterbury, the Most Reverend Geoffrey F. Fisher, performed the marriage ceremony. Princess Elizabeth wore an ivory and gold wedding gown, embroidered in pearls and crystals. A tiara of pearls and diamonds held her fifteen-foot bridal veil. Elizabeth's sister, Princess Margaret Rose, and seven other bridesmaids attended the bride. The duke and his best man, the Marquess of Milford Haven, wore naval uniforms. Two hundred and fifty relatives, friends, and gov-

ernment dignitaries attended the ceremony. After a wedding breakfast at Buckingham Palace, the royal couple departed for a twenty-three-day wedding trip in southern England and Scotland.

Socializing industry. The British Labor Government had so many urgent problems in 1947 that there was little time left for nationalizing more industries. The only big job done in that line was to arrange for the state to buy the railroads. To be sure, the bill for nationalizing electricity was adopted in February, but few people opposed it. The bill to permit the Government to be the raw cotton buyer for the country went through in April, but that argument was fought out in 1946. The Government itself decided to postpone buying up part of the iron and steel industry.

The nationalization of the British railroad system had a hard time getting through Parliament because the House of Lords wanted so many changes, but it became law in the summer. The date fixed for the new British Transport Commission to take over the business on behalf of the state was January 1, 1948. Then the name of the whole system would become "British Railways."

The wedding of Princess Elizabeth
and Lieutenant Philip Mountbatten

The rail system is enormous. It has almost 1,000,000 employees, 52,000 miles of track, 70 hotels, several cross-channel steamers, and much other property.

Fortunes of the labor government. Although there was a good deal of grumbling about the hard conditions of life under the Labor Government's export program, local elections proved that the majority of the voters were still in favor of Labor. There was always a good deal going on in Westminster (that part of London where the Houses of Parliament and most of the government offices are).

Sir Stafford Cripps was made Minister of Economic Affairs in September. This was a new cabinet position. In October, Prime Minister Attlee made the first important cabinet changes since the Labor Government came into power in 1945. He asked several of the older Labor men to resign and put in younger men, whom he chose apparently for their ability to help with the new "austerity" program.

In November, Chancellor of the Exchequer Hugh Dalton had to resign because he broke one of the basic unwritten laws of the British Government. It is forbidden for any member of the Government to reveal anything about a British budget until it officially is made public in the House of Commons. A supplementary budget was prepared in November, and as Dalton was entering the House of Commons he told a newspaperman about a few of the tax changes. The reporter's paper published the news by the time Dalton made his official speech.

Sir Stafford Cripps was promptly made Chancellor of the Exchequer in Dalton's place. He held this post in addition to his earlier one of Minister of Economic Affairs. The voters who had elected Dalton to Parliament told him that they had confidence in him. Obviously no one had made any money out of his "indiscretion," as Dalton himself called it, and the Prime Minister admitted that no "action detrimental to the state" resulted. Dalton's friends therefore hoped that he could get back into political life at some future time.

The Labor Government dropped only one political "bomb" when Parliament opened on October 21, but that one made a resounding noise. In the King's Speech—which is actually written by the leaders of the party in power—the Government asked for smaller powers for the House of Lords. The House of Lords had little power anyway, but it could hold up the passing of a law for two years. The Government requested that in the future this should be for one year only.

A dwindling empire. The House of Commons heard eloquent speeches from wartime Prime Minister Winston Churchill whenever proposed changes in the British Commonwealth came up. India was divided into two self-governing dominions, India and Pakistan, on August 15. The King of England was then no longer also "Emperor of India."

The majority of the British people seemed happy to see the changes in India, but Churchill spoke against the necessary legislation in Parliament in March. He called the process "Operation Scuttle" and spoke of his "grief" at the "clattering down of the British Empire with all the glories and services it has rendered to mankind." Lord Mountbatten, uncle of Philip, whom Princess Elizabeth was to marry in November, was made first Governor-General of India.

Winston Churchill speaking at the
Indian Empire Society in London, 1930

Churchill also attacked the law letting Burma become an independent country on January 4, 1948. The former Prime Minister called it a "fatal mistake."

Trouble outside the Commonwealth. The situation in Palestine distressed the British people and the British Government. There was no chance of getting out of it until the United Nations took over, because Britain was given a League of Nations mandate over Palestine after World War I. After the partition of Palestine was decided on by the United Nations in the autumn, it was understood that Great Britain would drop the mandate in May, 1948.

Britain's joint control (condominium) of the Sudan with Egypt was another source of international difficulty in 1947. Egypt asked the United Nations Security Council in July, and again in August, to order the British out of the Sudan. Great Britain argued that before changes were made the Sudanese people themselves should be given a chance to express their wishes.

Britain tried in the summer to reach a trade agreement with the Soviet Union, but the mission which went to Moscow came back and reported that it had failed. Although Britain was exporting more to Russia than Russia was sending back, the Russians apparently wanted the British to send their goods on definite dates. This was too difficult for Britain's upset economy. In December, the British mission started back to Moscow to try again.

Books of the Year. Four publications suggest the varied fields in which important writing was done. *One Fine Day*, a novel by Mollie Panter-Downes (a regular contributor to *The New Yorker*) showed living conditions of the English middle classes. The third volume in the history of *The Times*, called *The Twentieth Century Test, 1884–1912*, gave the history of the age as well as of the famous London newspaper. Two political pamphlets, the Labor party's "ABC of the Crisis" and the Conservative party's "Industrial Charter," showed the points at issue in postwar Britain.

United Kingdom (2006)

Prime Minister Tony Blair's Labour Party government retained power in the United Kingdom (U.K.) throughout 2006 after winning election to an unprecedented third term in 2005. However, David Cameron's Conservatives emerged as a

Prime Minister Tony Blair, 2005

strong opposition party that increasingly led in opinion polls. Bowing to considerable pressure, Blair announced in 2006 that he would leave office in 2007.

The Labour government, which had been in office since 1997, lost popularity among voters over criticism that it had become divided and corrupt. Although many British citizens were concerned about terrorism and national security, support for the deployment of British troops in Iraq and Afghanistan as part of the United States-led war on terror remained low. The economy enjoyed strong growth and low inflation in 2006. Labour's Chancellor of the Exchequer (treasurer) Gordon Brown—regarded as the most likely person to succeed Blair — was credited with the stability of the economy.

Liberal Democrats. On January 7, Charles Kennedy, the leader of the centrist Liberal Democratic party, resigned after admitting that he had a problem with alcohol, a charge he had long denied. Further scandal overtook the party later in the month when a leading candidate to replace Kennedy, Mark Oaten (the party's home affairs spokesman and a married man), abandoned his bid for the post after a newspaper revealed his association with male prostitutes. In March, party members elected Deputy Leader and Foreign Affairs Spokesman Sir Menzies Campbell as party leader.

Labour Party. Several senior members of the government experienced personal or political difficulties in 2006. Culture, Media, and Sport Secretary Tessa Jowell was embarrassed by allegations that her husband, lawyer David Mills, had received, under suspicious circumstances, money linked to Italian Prime Minister Silvio Berlusconi. On March 5, Jowell announced that she and her husband were separating. She retained her seat in the Cabinet.

On April 26, the government was rocked by what the press called a "triple whammy." Home Secretary Charles Clarke was embarrassed by revelations that government procedures for deporting foreign nationals who had been imprisoned were not being followed. The government had failed to deport nearly 300 foreign nationals following their release, even after the problem had been revealed in 2005. Clarke faced calls for his resignation. Also on April 26, 2006, the press revealed that Deputy Prime Minister John Prescott had been having an affair with a secretary in his office. On the same day, Health Secretary Patricia Hewitt was heckled at a conference of the Royal College of Nursing in Bournemouth after claiming that the National Health Service was enjoying its "best year ever." Delegates complained about cuts in service and difficult working conditions.

The Conservative Party, led by Cameron, enjoyed a considerable recovery in 2006. Cameron, who was 39 when he became leader in December 2005 following the party's defeat in the general election, immediately targeted his appeal to voters, such as centrists and young people, who had deserted the

Conservative Party leader David Cameron (left) and Prime Minister Gordon Brown on Remembrance Sunday, 2007

Conservatives in the late 1990's. He modernized his appeal by asking musician and poverty activist Bob Geldof to advise the party on Third World debt and by obtaining the support of leading environmentalist Zac Goldsmith on green issues. Cameron further insisted that teen-agers (particularly young people wearing hooded tops, who are often feared) should be understood rather than demonized. George Osborne, Cameron's *shadow chancellor* (opposition party member who monitors treasury issues), rejected calls from the party's right wing for tax cuts by a future Conservative government. Instead, Osborne insisted that public services and the health of the economy would be a priority. By the end of 2006, the Conservatives were regularly leading in opinion polls.

British National Party (B.N.P.). Nick Griffin, the leader of the far-right B.N.P., and fellow party member Mark Collett were acquitted twice in 2006—in February and again in November—of stirring up racial hatred. A party meeting during which Griffin referred to Islam as a "vicious, wicked faith" and Collett called asylum seekers "cockroaches" was secretly filmed by a television journalist. Griffin and Collett argued successfully that the remarks had been made at a private event for like-minded party members.

Elections. Labour fared badly in local elections in May and in by-elections. The poor results increased pressure on Blair to leave office. In February, Labour lost its "safe" seat of Dunfermline and West Fife in Scotland to the Liberal Democrats. The loss was particularly embarrassing for Chancellor of the Exchequer Brown, who held the seat for the neighboring constituency.

In June, Labour failed to regain what had once been the safe Labour seat of Blaenau Gwent in Wales. Labour lost the seat in the 2005 general election to former Labour member Peter Law. Law ran as an independent because he objected to the imposition of an all-female short list of Labour candidates for the constituency. Following Law's death in April 2006, another independent and former Labour Party member, Dai Davis, won the seat. Patricia Law, Peter Law's widow, was elected to the Welsh Assembly seat for the area as an independent. Political observers considered the results a sign of disaffection among the government's supporters, in particular with Blair's "New Labour" approach, a strategy that involved moving what had previously been a strongly left-wing party to the center.

Also in April, the Conservatives beat back a Liberal Democrat challenge for the safe seat of Bromley and Chislehurst. Labour ranked fourth in the voting. The by-election was called because of the death of Member of Parliament (MP) Eric Forth in May.

In the May 4 local elections, the Conservatives came out on top with 40 percent of the vote, gaining 11 new councils. Labour was pushed into third place with 26 percent, just behind the Liberal Democrats, who received 27 percent. Shortly before the election, Minister of State for Work Margaret Hodge was criticized for reporting publicly that large numbers of her white, working-class constituents in Barking, East London, were considering voting for the B.N.P. to protest the number of people of color moving into the area. According to the B.N.P., such people were putting pressure on local social services. The B.N.P. gained 11 seats on the Barking and Dagenham Council in the local election, and Hodge was blamed for giving the B.N.P. publicity.

Cabinet reshuffle. The day after Labour's poor showing in the May local elections, Blair reshuffled his Cabinet. Home Secretary Clarke was replaced by former Defence Secretary John Reid. Prescott remained deputy prime minister, but many of his responsibilities for local government were transferred to former Education Secretary Ruth Kelly, who became secretary of state for communities and local government. Prescott was criticized for retaining a full Cabinet salary and the use of Dorneywood, a publicly owned country house. Prescott gave up the use of Dorneywood in late May. Foreign Secretary Jack Straw was replaced by Margaret Beckett, who became the first woman to run the Foreign Office, a major government post. Straw became leader of the House of Commons. New appointments to the Cabinet included Hazel Blears, who became chair of the Labour Party and minister without portfolio; Stephen Timms, who became chief secretary to the treasury; and Douglas Alexander, who combined the roles of Scottish secretary and secretary for transport.

Loans for peerages scandal. In March, Scotland Yard began investigating claims that both the Labour and the Conservative parties had accepted loans from wealthy donors to finance the 2005 election campaign in exchange for the promise of a seat in the House of Lords. (Under current law, loans to political parties do not have to be publicly declared if they are made at commercial rates of interest.) The Lords Appointments Commission rejected four Labour appointments after learning of the loans. In July, senior Labour fund-raiser Lord Levy was briefly arrested and questioned about his involvement in securing improper loans. In October and November, Scotland Yard interviewed former Conservative Party leader Michael Howard and wrote formal requests for information to a number of Cabinet members. Blair was questioned in December. All denied any wrongdoing.

The Liberal Democrats were also scrutinized for allegedly taking money from a foreign donor (a violation of the law). Some critics argued that the loan issue demonstrated the need for state funding of political parties to eliminate possible corruption. In March, Blair called for greater transparency in party funding and appointed civil servant Sir Hayden Phillips to review the issue.

Leadership succession. Pressure on Blair to resign as prime minister increased during the summer of 2006. His obvious successor was Chancellor of the Exchequer Brown, who was known to be anxious to take over. However, in July, John McDonnell, an MP in the left wing of the Labour Party, announced that he would challenge Brown for the leadership.

Relations between Blair and Brown supporters within the party and in the government worsened throughout the year. On September 6, Tom Watson, a defense minister and a Brown

Labour MP Margaret Hodge, 2006

supporter, quit the government after signing a letter calling on Blair to resign for the good of the party and the country. The letter was leaked to the press. Another six junior members of the government also quit, leading Blair's allies to suggest that the resignations were signs of a *coup* (overthrow of the government)—possibly orchestrated by Brown. Blair refused to resign but confirmed publicly that he would depart within a year, though he refused to set an exact date.

At the Labour Party conference later in September, Brown apologized to the prime minister for the difficulties between them. Brown was widely expected to win any leadership contest, and so attention then focused on who would replace Prescott in the posts of deputy party leader and deputy prime minister. Cabinet members Alan Johnson, Peter Hain, and Hilary Benn as well as junior minister Harriet Harman announced they would run for the positions.

National security. Following the July 7, 2005, bombing of a bus and several trains in London, the government introduced a new antiterrorism bill. One of the bill's provisions would have allowed the police to hold suspected terrorists for up to 90 days without charge. However, opposition to the provision in both houses of Parliament forced Home Secretary Clarke in January 2006 to reduce the imprisonment provision to 28 days. The bill, which also included a controversial clause making the glorification of terrorism a criminal offense, became law on March 22.

In February, the controversial Muslim cleric Abu Hamza was convicted of encouraging the murder of non-Muslims and inciting racial hatred. In March, the trial of seven British Muslims who were arrested in 2004 and accused of planning terrorist attacks in the U.K. began. In May 2006, reports by the Home Office and Parliament's Intelligence and Security Committee about the July 2005 bombings concluded that the security service MI5 could not have prevented the attacks, though two of the bombers were known to MI5. The report found that the al-Qa`ida terrorist group was not involved. However, the revelation that two bombers had visited Pakistan and that one had said he wanted to visit an al-Qa`ida training camp led to criticisms of the report and demands for an independent inquiry.

On August 10, air services were disrupted when police announced that they had uncovered a plot to blow up planes flying from the U.K. to the United States. Twenty-four people in the U.K. were arrested that day in connection with the alleged plot and other terrorist activities.

On November 7, al-Qa`ida operative Dhiren Barot was sentenced to life in prison (with a minimum of 40 years served) for planning terrorist attacks. Barot was arrested in 2004. Evidence showed that he had been involved in devising plans for terrorist attacks in both the U.K. and the United States but had been arrested before any of the plots had been implemented. Barot pleaded guilty.

British Islam. Debate continued during 2006 about the relationship of British Muslims to the wider British community. In February, Muslims in London demonstrated over the publication of cartoons in Denmark that they believed mocked the Prophet Muhammad, even though newspapers in the U.K. refused to publish the cartoons.

In October, House of Commons Leader Straw created controversy when he revealed in a newspaper article that he routinely asked Muslim women in his constituency who wear the *niqab* (a full-face veil) to remove it when they come to his office to speak with him. He noted that the use of the niqab was not required by the Qu'ran, Islam's holy book, and argued that it was useful to see a person's face during conversation. The article created heated debate about the use of the full veil and about the integration of Muslims into British society. Members of the Muslim community held varying views about the niqab. Straw was later forced to defend himself from suggestions that he was insensitive and that his remarks had caused an increase in attacks on Muslims.

Death of a Russian agent. On November 23, Alexander Litvinenko, a former member of the Russian secret service, died after apparently being poisoned with the radioactive element polonium-210. Litvinenko had moved to the U.K. after allegedly refusing to assist the Russian intelligence agency assassinate wealthy Russian businessman Boris Berezovsky. Before he died, Litvinenko blamed the Russian government for his murder. However, Russian President Vladimir Putin denied any involvement in the agent's death. By November 30, investigators had found traces of polonium-

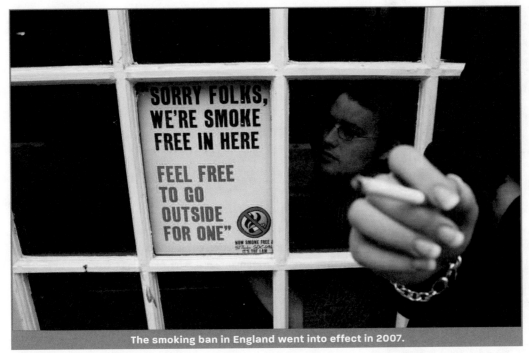

The smoking ban in England went into effect in 2007.

210 at a dozen sites in the U.K. Several people were later found to have been exposed to the element.

Ken Livingstone. The Standards Board of England, a body that regulates the conduct of officials in local government, determined in February that the mayor of London, Ken Livingstone, should be suspended from office for four weeks. The decision followed a complaint that Livingstone had been offensive to journalist Oliver Finegold of London's *Evening Standard*. Finegold had asked him a question as the mayor left a party in February 2005. Livingstone compared the journalist, who is Jewish, with a concentration camp attendant and a German war criminal and refused to apologize because of his longstanding hostile relationship with the newspaper. The mayor appealed the verdict. In October 2006, a high court judge overturned the suspension, ruling that Livingstone's comments did not breach the Greater London Authority code of conduct.

Pensions. In May, John Hutton, the work and pensions secretary, reported a radical revision to the British pension system. Hutton announced that the link between state pensions and average earnings would be restored in 2012 (as long as the government could afford to do so) and that the age of retirement would rise from 65 to 66 by 2026 and to 68 by 2046. The government would continue to provide assistance to people who lost their pension when an employer went out of business. The pro-posals were detailed in a white paper (government policy document) on pension reform based on recommendations in a report by Lord Adair Turner. Turner's report had called for more generous state pensions to prevent poverty among the elderly.

Smoking ban. MPs voted overwhelmingly in February 2006 to ban smoking from all English workplaces, including private clubs and pubs, beginning in 2007. A smoking ban was already set to go into effect in Scotland and Northern Ireland over the next 13 months.

Ancient Greece

Ancient Greece was the birthplace of Western civilization. The Ancient Greeks were masters of science, government, and the arts, and many of their innovations are an integral part of today's world. The lives of Ancient Greeks revolved around perhaps the most famous of ancient gods, the Olympians. Ancient Greece was split into a number of city-states, each different from the next, and each giving rise to different advancements.

HOT topics

The Origin of the Olympic Games

The Birth of Democracy

Innovations in Science and Mathematics

Greek Religion and the Olympians

HOT topics

Recreation/The Origin of the Olympic Games. Once every four years, all of Greece came together to compete in the Olympic Games. During this time, all the city-states created a temporary peace, and warfare was banned during the festival. The games were held in the city-state of Olympia, in honor of Zeus. The first Olympic Games were held in 776 B.C. The Olympic Games became so important that the Greeks began to measure time in Olympiads, the four-year intervals between the games.

DEFINITIONS

acropolis: the high, fortified part or citadel of an ancient Greek city.

ancient: of the time before the fall of the Western Roman Empire (A.D. 476).

oracle: in ancient Greece and Rome: **a.** an answer to some question believed to be given by a god through a priest or priestess. It often has a hidden meaning that was hard to understand. **b.** a place where the god was believed to give such answers. A famous oracle was at Delphi. **c.** the priest, priestess, or other means by which the god's answer was believed to be given.

oligarchy: a form of government in which a few people have the ruling power.

HOT topics

Government/The Birth of Democracy.

From the beginning of its existence, Athens, like all other city-states in Greece, had been ruled by tyrants and aristocrats. However, in 594 B.C., a statesman named Solon reformed the Athenian laws, giving more rights to the people. In 508 B.C., Cleisthenes created a council of government open to everyone and guaranteed every citizen a vote. This is how Athens became the first democratic government, the template for many of today's modern governments.

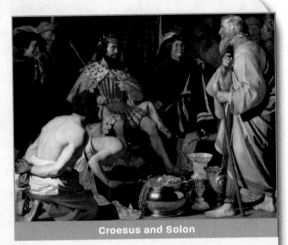
Croesus and Solon

Innovations in Science and Mathematics.

Ancient Greece was also the birthplace of much of modern science and mathematics. Physicists like Archimedes discovered more and more about how the world works. Archimedes alone discovered the lever, complex pulleys, and buoyancy. Mathematicians like Pythagoras and Euclid developed much of modern trigonometry and geometry.

Greek Religion and the Olympians.

The Ancient Greeks had a polytheistic religion, believing in more than one god. In fact, there were countless numbers of gods in Ancient Greece. Besides the Olympian gods, there were also a plethora of smaller household gods. There was a god for every aspect of Greek life, including Athena, goddess of wisdom; Ares, god of war; Poseidon, god of the sea, and Hades, god of the underworld. There were many oracles across Greece where prophets or prophetesses spoke the will of the gods, and of the future. The most important of these oracles was at Delphi, where a prophetess called Pythia uttered oracles from the god Apollo. The term *oracle* can be used to refer to a shrine, a prophet or prophetess, or to their prophecies.

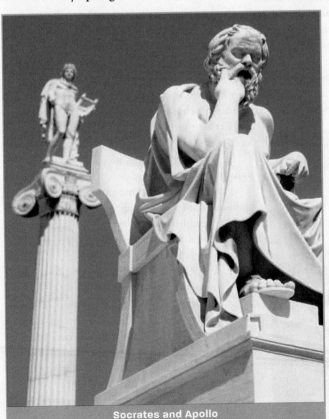
Socrates and Apollo

TRUE or FALSE?

The original Olympic Games were a religious celebration, and only men were allowed to participate.

THE BASICS

Ancient Greece was the birthplace of Western civilization about 2,500 years ago. The magnificent achievements of the ancient Greeks in government, science, philosophy, and the arts still influence our lives.

Greek civilization developed chiefly in small *city-states*. A city-state consisted of a city or town and the surrounding villages and farmland. The Greek city-states were fiercely independent and often quarreled among themselves. But their small size and constant rivalry had certain advantages. Citizens of a city-state were strongly patriotic, and many citizens took part in public affairs. The most advanced city-states established the world's first democratic governments. The best-known city-states were Athens and Sparta.

The ancient Greek city-states never became united into a nation. However, a common language, religion, and culture bound the people together. The Greeks called themselves Hellenes and their land Hellas. They thought of themselves as different from all other peoples, whom they called *barbarians*.

The ancient Greeks prized their freedom and way of life. This way of life stressed the importance of the individual and encouraged creative thought. Greek thinkers laid the foundations of science and philosophy by seeking logical explanations for what happened in the world around them. Greek writers created new forms of expression, which explored human personalities and emotions. Greek civilization reached its height in Athens during the mid-400s B.C.

The Greek World

The territory of ancient Greece consisted chiefly of a mountainous peninsula that jutted into the Mediterranean Sea, numerous islands near the peninsula, and the west coast of Asia Minor (now part of Turkey). The peninsula made up mainland Greece. It separated two arms of the Mediterranean—the Aegean Sea and the Ionian Sea. A thin strip of land linked the southern part of the mainland, called the Peloponnesus, to the northern part of the mainland.

The land. Rocky land covered much of ancient Greece. The most fertile land lay in the small valleys and along the coast. In those areas, the Greeks established their city-states. The city or town of each city-state served as a center of trade, government, and religion. The Greeks usually fortified a hill, called an *acropolis*, within the city for defense. In addition, walls surrounded some cities to protect them from invaders. At the center of each city was the *agora*—an open area that served as a marketplace and meeting place.

Ancient Greece had a warm, dry climate. Summers were hot, and winter temperatures seldom dropped below freezing. Annual rainfall on the mainland ranged from as much as 50 inches (130 centimeters) on the west coast to less than 20 inches (50 centimeters) on the east.

Ancient Greece lacked adequate farmland, rainfall, and water for irrigation, and so crop production was limited. The mountains provided huge amounts of limestone and marble for building construction and clay for making bricks and pottery. But Greece had few other mineral deposits. Timber was plentiful at first. However, it became increasingly scarce as the people cut down many trees without replanting the forests.

The shortages of food and natural resources forced the ancient Greeks to depend on overseas trade for needed goods. The poor conditions at home also led many Greeks to found overseas colonies and trading posts. In this way, the Greek world expanded along the shores of the Mediterranean Sea and the Black Sea and came to include southern Italy and the island of Sicily.

Acropolis, Athens

The people. Greek civilization began to develop about 2000 B.C. At that time, people from somewhere to the north arrived in Greece and established small farming villages. The people of each community in time developed their own customs and dialect. The two main groups of Greek peoples were the Dorians and Ionians.

By the 700s B.C., the Greek world consisted of many small, independent city-states. Within each city-state, the Greeks distinguished between citizens and noncitizens. Only citizens could own land and take part in government. Noncitizens consisted of women, slaves, and serfs. Unlike slaves, serfs were not considered personal property. As a result of trade, many city-states also had a large noncitizen population made up of Greeks from other city-states and of foreigners.

Life of the People

Family life. The husband headed the household in ancient Greece and was responsible for its members. The wife ran the household and raised the children. In prosperous families, the wife supervised slaves, who looked after the children and did most of the work. Women also spun thread and wove cloth, even in wealthy families. A woman was under the legal control of her father before she married. After marriage, she was under the legal control of her husband.

Greek parents usually arranged their children's marriage. Most girls married in their mid-teens, but many men married around age 30. When a girl married, she received her share of the family's money or property as a *dowry* (gift). Her husband controlled the dowry but had to return it if they divorced. Normally, the dowry would pass on to her children.

Education. In general, only the children of citizens received an education in ancient Greece. Very few girls attended school, but some others learned to read at home. Most children also learned a few practical skills from their parents or from slaves. City-states differed in the kind of education they valued.

In Athens, teachers operated separate schools for general studies, music, and physical education. The general schools taught reading, writing, and arithmetic. At music school, students learned to sing and to play the flutelike *aulos* or the small, harplike *lyre*. The physical education activities included running, jumping, and wrestling. Older boys learned to handle such weapons as the spear and sword.

Education in Sparta differed greatly from education in Athens. The Spartans wanted to build a tough, warlike people, and considered reading and writing much less important than military training. At the age of 7, boys were sent to military camps, where they learned to accept severe discipline and to endure harsh conditions. Even girls engaged in physical competition, which shocked most Greeks outside Sparta.

Higher education in ancient Greece consisted of the study of law, medicine, philosophy, or *rhetoric* (public speaking). In the 300s B.C., the Greek philosopher Plato founded a school in Athens known as the Academy. Plato's most brilliant pupil, Aristotle, later founded a similar school in Athens, the Lyceum.

Food, clothing, and shelter. The Greek diet was based on such grains as wheat and barley, which were used to make bread, cakes, and porridge.

Aristotle and Plato

The Greeks also ate a variety of fruits and vegetables. Their chief sources of protein were eggs, poultry, and fish. The Greeks used olive oil, and they sweetened food with honey. After animal sacrifices, they enjoyed roasted pork, beef, lamb, and goat.

Greek men and women wore a belted garment of linen or wool. Most men's garments hung to the knees. A woman's garment fell to the ankles. In cold weather, Greeks draped a cloak over their shoulders and arms. Sandals were the chief footwear.

Greece's mild climate enabled the people to carry on many activities outdoors, and so most houses were small and simple. Most poor families lived in one- or two-room houses built of sun-dried bricks with floors of hard-packed earth. Wealthy Greeks lived in larger, more comfortable houses built around a courtyard. The houses had separate rooms for cooking, eating, and sleeping. Stones or tiles covered the floors.

Religion. The Greeks believed that certain *deities* (gods and goddesses) watched over them and directed daily events. Families tried to please household deities with offerings and ceremonies. Each city-state honored one or more deities as protectors of the community and held annual festivals in their honor.

The oracle at Delphi

The Greeks believed that their deities could foretell the future. People flocked to shrines called *oracles* to consult priests and priestesses. Deities supposedly spoke through the priests and priestesses to answer questions and reveal the future. The most important oracle was at Delphi. Sick people visited shrines dedicated to Asclepius, the god of healing, in hope of being cured.

Greek deities resembled human beings, except for their immortality and superhuman powers. For example, they showed such emotions as love, jealousy, and anger. The chief deities lived on Mount Olympus and were known as Olympians. Zeus and his wife, Hera, ruled over Olympus. Other Olympians included Aphrodite, goddess of love; Apollo, god of music and light; Ares, god of war; and Athena, goddess of wisdom.

Recreation. Greek men enjoyed talking with friends in the agora or at drinking parties, called *symposiums*, in their homes. Greek men also liked sports, and they exercised and swam at public sports facilities. Greek women were permitted little entertainment outside the home, except for religious festivals. Children had dolls, balls, tops, and other toys. They also played various dice and board games.

Large crowds gathered for religious festivals in ancient Greece. At these festivals, athletes competed in such events as wrestling, boxing, foot and chariot races, jumping, and javelin throwing. Religious festivals also included feasts, colorful processions, and performances of plays. Several religious festivals brought together people from throughout the Greek world. The Olympic Games, the most famous of these festivals, were held every four years in honor of Zeus. Victory in the games was the highest honor an athlete could achieve.

Work of the People

Farming. Most ancient Greeks lived by farming or herding. Most farmers worked alone or with the help of a few slaves. The entire family helped with planting and harvesting. Farmers raised pigs, grew wheat and barley, and tended olive groves and vineyards. Sheep and goats grazed on poorer land. The Greeks produced a surplus of olive oil, wine, and wool, which they exported.

Manufacturing. The ancient Greeks manufactured all products by hand. Many craftsmen worked alone. There were also factories with 20 to more than 100 workers, many of them slaves. These workers specialized in the different skills needed to make such goods as pottery, armor, and clothing. Individual city-states became known for certain products. For example, Athens was famous for its decorated pottery, Megara for woolen garments, and Corinth for jewelry and metal goods.

Trade. Greek merchants sold surplus goods abroad in exchange for slaves and such products as grain, timber, and metals. The Greeks' major trading partners included Egypt; Sicily; and Scythia, a region near the Black Sea. In each city-state, inspectors made sure that merchants used proper weights and measures, charged fair prices, paid taxes, and observed restrictions on the import and export of certain goods.

Transportation and communication. The rugged terrain made travel difficult on the Greek mainland. Runners carried most messages. Few roads were good enough for travel on horseback. Wagons or pack animals hauled goods short distances. Sea travel was far more important than land travel, in spite of the dangers of piracy and shipwreck. Merchant ships sailed along the mainland coast, among the islands, and overseas.

Philosophy, Science, and the Arts

Philosophy originated in ancient Greece during the 500s B.C. The word *philosophy* comes from two Greek words meaning *love of wisdom*. Many of the questions that were asked by Greek philosophers would today be considered subjects of scientific inquiry. The earliest philosophers speculated about the underlying substance of the universe and how the universe operated. Later philosophers investigated the nature of knowledge and reality and sought to define such notions as good and evil.

Socrates, Plato, and Aristotle are considered the most important Greek philosophers. Socrates taught by carefully questioning his listeners to expose the weaknesses of their ideas and arguments. Plato explored such subjects as beauty, justice, and good government. Aristotle summed up the achievements of Greek philosophy and science. His authority on many topics remained unquestioned for more than 1,000 years.

Most people in ancient Greece were suspicious of philosophers and their theories. They continued to believe in traditional values and traditional religion. In 399 B.C., an Athenian jury sentenced Socrates to death, charging him with corrupting young men and not believing in the gods of the city.

Democritus and Herodotus

Science. Greek scientists, like Greek philosophers, believed in an orderly universe, which operated according to laws that people could discover. They based many of their theories on logic and mathematics. They also made careful observations of nature and, at times, conducted experiments. But Greek scientists rarely tried to solve practical problems, and so their discoveries had little influence on technology and everyday life.

The ancient Greeks were pioneers in medicine, physics, biology, and mathematics. Some of their conclusions anticipated findings of modern science. In the 400s B.C., Democritus said all things consisted of *atoms*, tiny bits of matter that cannot be divided. In the 200s B.C., Aristarchus of Samos first stated that the earth revolved around the sun. But most Greek thinkers argued that the sun, stars, and planets moved around a stationary earth.

The arts. Greek architects, sculptors, and painters made important contributions to the arts. They strove to achieve an ideal of beauty based on harmonious proportions. The most influential architectural works were temples. A Greek temple consisted of an arrangement of columns around a long, inner chamber. The Greeks developed three influential styles for columns—the simple Doric, the graceful Ionic, and the ornate Corinthian. The best-known temples were built on the Acropolis in Athens during the 400s B.C.

Greek sculptors portrayed figures of gods, goddesses, and human beings. Over the centuries, their works became increasingly lifelike and showed figures in more active poses. The most famous Greek sculptors were Phidias, Praxiteles, Lysippus, and Myron.

Few Greek paintings have survived. Our knowledge of Greek painting comes mainly from paintings on pottery, Greek writings, and copies made by the ancient Romans. The pottery paintings and Roman copies portray scenes from mythology and daily life.

Music often accompanied plays and poetry recitals in ancient Greece, and musicians performed at festivals and private parties. The music of the Greeks relied chiefly on melody and rhythm. Harmony was unknown to the Greeks.

Ancient Greek writers introduced many important literary forms, including lyric and epic poetry, tragic and comic drama, and history.

Government

The city-state took shape in ancient Greece by the 700s B.C. Most citizens of a city-state claimed a common ancestry, spoke the same Greek dialect, and followed the same customs and religious practices.

A small group of wealthy men governed most city-states of ancient Greece. This form of government, in which a few powerful people rule, is called an *oligarchy*. During the 500s B.C., some city-states began to move toward democracy. They granted all citizens the right to vote on government policies, hold political office, and serve on a jury. However, many poor citizens could not afford to take the time from making a living to participate in democratic government. However, women and slaves had no political rights, even in the democracies.

Athens became the most successful democracy of ancient Greece during the 400s B.C. Every male Athenian citizen had the right to vote in an assembly that passed laws and determined government policies. The voters also elected Athenian generals. Each year, the citizens drew lots to select a council of 500 men. This council ran the day-to-day business of government and prepared the bills that the assembly debated and voted on. Jurors were also chosen by lot.

Some wealthy Athenians disliked their system of government. They felt that the poor dominated the government and took advantage of the rich. Most Athenians, however, cherished their democracy.

Sparta was the most powerful oligarchy in ancient Greece. Citizens made up only about 10 percent of the population. Most people were serfs who farmed the land. Two kings, who inherited their thrones, headed the army. Sparta was governed by 5 officials, called *ephors*, and the *gerousia*, a council made up of 28 elders and the kings. Citizens elected ephors to one-year terms and members of the gerousia to life terms. Sparta had a citizen assembly. But citizens could not propose issues for debate in the assembly.

Military forces. Among the Greek city-states, only Sparta had a standing army. Most city-states trained young men in the art of warfare and required all able-bodied male citizens to take up arms in time of war. Athens had the largest navy, which included hundreds of large warships, each powered by 170 oarsmen.

A battle formation known as a *phalanx* dominated Greek warfare from the 600s to the 300s B.C. To form a phalanx, armed foot soldiers lined up in a loose formation, usually eight rows deep. On the battlefield, two opposing phalanxes marched toward each other. Then, the soldiers fought with spears and swords until one side broke and ran.

History

Beginnings. The first major civilization in the region of Greece arose on Crete, an island in the Aegean Sea, about 3000 B.C. It is known as the Minoan culture after King Minos, the legendary

Minoan palace, Crete

ruler of Crete. The Minoans were expert sailors, and they grew wealthy from trade. The remains of luxurious palaces provide evidence of the Minoans' prosperity and building skills. The Minoans had a system of writing. Scholars do not know what language they spoke, except that it was not Greek.

The development of Greek civilization began about 2000 B.C., when small farming villages were set up by people who came to Greece from somewhere to the north. By about 1600 B.C., they had built fortified towns, each centered on a palace, in the major valleys. The culture that developed on the mainland is called Mycenaean after the large and powerful town of Mycenae in the Peloponnesus, the southern part of the mainland.

The Minoans dominated the Aegean world until about 1450 B.C., when the Mycenaeans took control of the region. The Mycenaeans adopted features of the Minoan culture. For example, they adapted the Minoan writing system to the Greek language The form of writing they developed is known as *Linear B*. In Linear B, each syllable had a separate sign. Some scholars believe Mycenae won a war against Troy, in Asia Minor (now Turkey), in about 1200 B.C. This war inspired many major works of classical literature.

Mycenae and most other settlements in the Peloponnesus were destroyed shortly after 1200 B.C. Historians do not know why Mycenae fell. Soon afterward, the Dorians from northern Greece moved into the region. Many Mycenaeans fled to Asia Minor. Greece entered a period known as the Dark Age, which lasted until about 800 B.C. During this time, people again lived in isolated villages. Knowledge of writing was lost. Memories of past glories were kept alive in songs and oral poetry. The Greeks began to write again after 800 B.C. Their alphabet was based on that of the Phoenicians. Some of their oral poetry was then composed into two great epics, the *Iliad* and the *Odyssey*, which are attributed to the poet Homer.

The development of the Greek city-state began during the Dark Age. At times, neighboring city-states joined to form a larger state. However, most city-states tried to keep their independence at any cost. At first, kings ruled the city-states, with advice from wealthy nobles. But by approximately 750 B.C., the nobles in most city-states had overthrown the kings and become rulers. The nobility owned the best land and controlled the community.

Meanwhile, ancient Greece faced the problem of too many people and too little farmland. As a result, neighboring city-states often fought over borderlands. Some city-states grew at the expense of others. For example, Sparta became powerful by conquering neighboring peoples. Many of the conquered peoples had to work the land for their Spartan masters.

The land shortage forced numerous Greeks to leave their city-states. From the 700s to the 500s B.C., Greek colonists founded new city-states along the shores of the Mediterranean and Black seas. The largest settlements developed in southern Italy and Sicily, which became known as Magna Graecia (Great Greece).

Most Greek farmers worked small plots and had to borrow money to survive between harvests. In times of poor harvests, farmers could not repay their loans. They then lost their land and were forced into slavery. Other groups were also discontented. For example, merchants and manufacturers wanted a greater voice in government. But the nobility refused to share any power.

New forms of government. The growing unrest brought *tyrants* to power in many Greek city-states as a result of revolutions. The Greeks used the term *tyrant* to describe a leader who seized total power by force. Many tyrants achieved some of the goals of their followers. For example, they distributed farmland to the landless and put people to work on large public building projects. But eventually tyrants grew more concerned with keeping their power than with serving the people.

Homer dictating his poem

Most tyrants were soon replaced by an oligarchy in which a few wealthy citizens, rather than the nobility, ran the government. However, a number of city-states moved toward democratic government. In 594 B.C., Athenians gave a statesman named Solon authority to reform the laws. Solon ended the practice of enslaving debtors. He divided citizens into classes by wealth and defined the rights and duties of each class. He also drew up a code of law. Shortly after Solon left office, civil war broke out. In 560 B.C., a tyrant seized power.

In 508 B.C., another Athenian statesman, Cleisthenes, proposed a constitution that made Athens a democracy. Cleisthenes extended voting rights in the assembly to all free adult men. He created a council of 500 members, which was open to any citizen. His reforms thus gave every citizen a chance to serve in the government.

The Persian wars. During the 500s B.C., the Persian Empire expanded rapidly and conquered the Greek city-states in Asia Minor. From 499 to 494 B.C., these city-states rebelled against their Persian rulers. King Darius I of Persia crushed the revolt and sent his army to punish Athens, which had aided the rebels. The Athenian army was outnumbered by the Persians, but it defeated the Persian army at the Battle of Marathon in 490 B.C.

In 480 B.C., King Xerxes I, the son of Darius, led a massive Persian invasion of Greece. Many of the Greek city-states united under Sparta's leadership to fight the invaders. The Persians overwhelmed a tiny Greek force at Thermopylae, north of Athens, and went on to take Athens. The Greek navy followed a plan of the Athenian statesman

Themistocles and withdrew to the Bay of Salamis. There, it thoroughly defeated the Persians and sank about half their fleet. Xerxes returned to Persia with many of his troops. The Greeks defeated the remaining Persian forces in 479 B.C.

The Greeks regarded their victory over the Persians as their finest hour. It showed what they could do when they set aside their differences and united.

The rivalry between Athens and Sparta. The cooperation achieved by the Greek city-states during the Persian wars did not last long. In 477 B.C., Athens organized an alliance called the Delian League. It consisted mainly of city-states in Asia Minor and on Aegean islands. Sparta led the Peloponnesian League, an alliance of city-states in the Peloponnesus. Athens was the strongest naval power in ancient Greece, and Sparta was the strongest land-based power. The two rivals struggled for dominance of the Greek world during the middle and late 400s B.C.

During the 400s B.C., Athens reached its height of power and prosperity and was the center of culture in the Greek world. Pericles was the leading Athenian statesman from 461 to 429 B.C. Many remarkable literary and artistic accomplishments took place in Athens during this period. For example, the Greek dramatists Aeschylus, Sophocles, and Euripides wrote many of their masterpieces. The leading Greek architects and sculptors built the Parthenon on the Acropolis.

In 431 B.C., the Peloponnesian War broke out. This ruinous war between Athens and Sparta lasted until 404 B.C. and left Athens exhausted. In 430 B.C., a severe plague struck Athens. It killed about a third of the people, including Pericles. Athens lacked able leaders during the rest of the war and finally surrendered.

Sparta dominated the Greek world only a short time. Fighting among the city-states resumed, and Thebes defeated Sparta in 371 B.C. The quality of life declined as a result of the continuing warfare. Economic conditions worsened, and violent clashes between rich and poor became frequent. People grew less public-spirited and more self-centered. The city-states lost their vitality.

Macedonia, a kingdom north of Greece, was becoming stronger as Greece grew weaker. In 353 B.C., Philip II, king of Macedonia, set out to conquer all of Greece. The independence of the separate Greek city-states ended in 338 B.C., when Macedonia defeated the Greeks in the Battle of

The Parthenon

Trojan artifacts

Chaeronea. Philip planned to lead a Greek and Macedonian army against Persia. But he was killed by a Macedonian in 336 B.C.

The Hellenistic Age. Alexander the Great, Philip's son, succeeded his father at the age of 20. In 334 B.C., Alexander carried out Philip's plan to invade Persia. In a brilliant campaign, Alexander conquered the entire Persian Empire in less than 10 years. His empire extended from Greece to India. Alexander's bloody conquests furthered the spread of Greek ideas and the Greek way of life to Egypt and the Near East. Alexander died in 323 B.C. His generals divided his large empire into successor states, with Greece remaining under Macedonian control.

The period of Greek history following Alexander's death is known as the Hellenistic Age. The period lasted until 146 B.C. in Greece, when the Romans took control of Greece. During that time, Greek culture continued to influence the lands Alexander had conquered, and Eastern ideas reached Greece. Greece suffered from frequent warfare and widespread destruction during the 200s B.C. The city-states formed two associations to fight for independence. But Macedonian kings kept control of Greece, and the two associations fought each other.

Roman rule. Through conquests, Rome had become one of the most powerful countries in the western Mediterranean by the 200s B.C. The Romans then began to expand in the east. In the 140s B.C., they took control of Greece and Macedonia. Under Roman rule, the Greek city-states had no important military or political role. But trade, agriculture, industry, and intellectual activities flourished. The Romans borrowed the art, religion, philosophy, and way of life of the ancient Greeks, and they spread Greek culture throughout their empire.

The Roman Empire was divided in A.D. 395, and Greece became part of the East Roman Empire. The West Roman Empire collapsed in A.D. 476. The East Roman Empire survived as the Byzantine Empire until 1453, when it fell to the Ottoman Empire. Greek was the official language of the Byzantine Empire, and Greek culture formed the basis of Byzantine institutions.

The Greek heritage. The ancient Greeks laid the foundations of Western civilization. Modern democracies owe a debt to Greek beliefs in government by the people, trial by jury, and equality under the law. The ancient Greeks pioneered in many fields that rely on systematic thought, including biology, geometry, history, philosophy, and physics. They introduced such important literary forms as epic and lyric poetry, history, tragedy, and comedy. In their pursuit of order and proportion, the Greeks created an ideal of beauty that strongly influenced Western art.

Learning About Ancient Greece

The writings of the ancient Greeks provide much of our information about the Greek world. For example, Herodotus described the clash of cultures that led to the wars between the Greeks and the Persians. Thucydides wrote a brilliant analysis of the Peloponnesian War. Aristotle's writings summarized and analyzed much of the knowledge of his time. Greek poets and playwrights expressed the attitudes and beliefs of the ancient Greeks.

The remains of Greek settlements and shrines also add to our knowledge of ancient Greece. Archaeologists study buildings and such objects as pottery, tools, and weapons to learn about trade and colonization, technology, art, and everyday life in ancient Greece.

Amphitheater, Peloponnese

In the 1870s, German archaeologist Heinrich Schliemann conducted the first major excavation of the buried city of Troy. Before then many people doubted that Troy, made famous in the *Iliad* and the *Odyssey*, had existed. Schliemann also made major discoveries at Mycenae. In the early 1900s, Sir Arthur Evans, a British archaeologist, located the palace at Knossos on Crete. He thus established the existence of Minoan civilization. These discoveries spurred further excavations.

Greek literature is the oldest and most influential national literature in the Western world. Ancient Greek literature became the model for all later literature in the West, starting with Latin literature. Greek writers introduced many significant types of literature, including lyric and epic poetry, tragic and comic drama, philosophical essays and dialogues, critical and biographical history, and literary letters.

Early Greek Literature

Epic poetry was the first important form of Greek literature. Epics are long narrative poems. Most tell about the heroic deeds of divine beings or mortals. The greatest Greek poet was Homer, who composed two famous epic poems, the *Iliad* and the *Odyssey*, during the 700s B.C. The *Iliad* tells of the Trojan War, which probably took place about 1250 B.C. The *Odyssey* relates the adventures of the Greek hero Odysseus as he returns home after the fall of Troy. The epics developed from a long tradition of oral poetry that covered about 500 years. The poems were based on stories recited by professional singers who accompanied themselves with a stringed instrument called the lyre. The *Iliad* and the *Odyssey* emphasized ideals of honor and bravery and had enormous influence on Greek culture and education as well as Greek literature.

Hesiod, the founder of the *didactic* (instructional) epic, was the first major Greek poet after Homer. Hesiod wrote during the 600s B.C. In his poem *Theogony*, Hesiod became the first writer to organize Greek mythology into a comprehensive philosophical system. Hesiod's other great poem, *Works and Days*, describes the life of Greek peasants, highlighting their hard work, thriftiness, and good judgment. The poem points out that Homer's aristocratic ideal of valor in battle is not the only kind of heroism possible. Hesiod, himself a farmer, also praised the heroism of the farmer's long silent struggle with the earth and the elements.

Lyric poetry. After about 650 B.C. shorter forms of poetry called *lyrics* began to replace the epic. Lyric poetry was originally sung to the music of the lyre. Most lyric poems described personal feelings instead of the acts of heroism portrayed in epic poetry.

One type of lyric poetry is called *melic poetry*. Melic poems are highly emotional and avoid didactic or satirical elements. Unlike elegiac and iambic poetry, melic poetry was composed for a single voice. Usually the poet sang the poems before close friends. Sappho, a poet who lived about 600 B.C., was the most famous melic poet. No Greek love poetry has ever matched the passion and tragic feeling of Sappho's verse.

Other lyric poets composed *choral lyrics*. These were sung by groups and accompanied by music and dancing. The *epinikion*, a serious choral ode written to honor the victor of athletic games, was a popular poetic form. The victory odes of Pindar are masterpieces of choral poetry. Other important writers of choral lyrics were Alcman, Stesichorus, and Simonides of Ceos.

Elegiac poetry was related to lyric poetry. Elegiac poems consisted of couplets that alternated a line of *hexameter* with a line of *pentameter*. Hexameter lines have six *feet*, or rhythmic units, and pentameter lines have five feet. Among the best-known elegiac poets are Callinus, Tyrtaeus, Mimnermus, and Theognis. *Iambic poetry* is also similar to lyric poetry. Iambic poems are written in *iambs*, which are metrical feet consisting of a short syllable followed by a long one. Much iambic poetry expressed the poet's feelings of anger, or was satiric. The three most famous iambic poets are Archilochus, Semonides of Amorgos, and Hipponax.

The Golden Age

During the late 500s B.C., Athens became the center of Greek culture, a position it held for almost 200 years. During the height of this period, from 461 to 431 B.C., the arts—especially literature—flourished. These 30 years are sometimes called the Golden Age.

Drama, particularly tragedy, became the most important literary form during the Golden Age. Aeschylus, Sophocles, and Euripides were the three greatest tragic playwrights. The plays of Aeschylus are noted for their seriousness, their majestic language, and their complexity of thought. Sophocles is most famous for his characterization, graceful language, and sense of calm and proportion. Euripides was called the "philosopher of the stage." His plays explore the psychological world of human emotions and passions.

Comedy was also prominent on the Athenian stage during the 400s B.C. Aristophanes, who wrote plays in the style called *Old Comedy*, was a great writer of bawdy and satiric comic plays. His plays reflect the spirit of Athens at that time, with the Athenians' sense of freedom, vitality, and high spirits, and their ability to laugh at themselves.

After Athens was defeated in the Peloponnesian War in 404 B.C., there was less freedom of speech. Old Comedy, with its elements of political and social satire, was no longer permitted by government leaders. Comedy revived in Athens in the late 300s B.C., but in a style called *New Comedy*. This style focused on the individual and the problems people confront in everyday life. Menander was the most popular writer of such plays.

Historical literature. By the end of the 400s B.C. prose had surpassed poetry and verse drama in Greek literature. Historical writings were especially popular. Herodotus, "Father of History," traveled throughout the civilized world during the mid-400s B.C. and recorded the manners and customs of nations older than Greece. His central theme was the conflict between East and West. Thucydides, writing a few years later, was the first scientific historian. He wrote a stirring account of the Peloponnesian War. In recording the events of his day, Thucydides tried to explain the effects of politics on historical events.

Philosophical literature. About 450 B.C., a group of philosophers called Sophists became prominent. Sophists were scholars and teachers of theories of knowledge. Their great literary invention was *rhetoric*, the art of composing and delivering persuasive speeches. The Sophist movement contributed to the rise of prose, especially oration, over poetry in Athens. Such famous writers of orations as Isocrates and Demosthenes were important political figures.

A new literary form was developed by the pupils of Socrates, after the philosopher's death in 399 B.C. This form, called the *Socratic method* or *dialectic,* was based on Socrates' question and answer method of arriving at some important truth. Although Socrates left no writings, his ideas are preserved in writings of other Greeks, especially Plato. Other groups of philosophers, such as the *Epicureans,* the *Stoics,* and the *Peripatetics,* reflected the concerns of Plato's writings. Aristotle also wrote important works, including *Poetics,* a masterpiece of literary criticism.

The Hellenistic Age

During the 300s B.C., the great Macedonian king Alexander the Great conquered and ruled all of ancient Greece as well as most of the rest of the civilized world of his day. As Alexander's empire grew, Greek ideas and culture spread throughout the East. The period following Alexander's death in 323 B.C. is called the Hellenistic Age. At this time, Athens lost its dominant role as the center of Greek culture, and the city of Alexandria in Egypt became the new capital of Greek civilization.

Alexander the Great

Theocritus, an important poet writing in the 200s B.C., is credited with inventing *pastoral poetry*. Pastoral poems convey an appreciation for nature and country life. Theocritus's poems reflect the discontent of those living in the increasingly overpopulated cities of the Hellenistic era. The chief literary figure of this period was Callimachus, a scholar, poet, and critic, who wrote short, highly polished poems. Many poets followed the example of Callimachus and produced powerful poetry within the narrow limits of brief, witty poems called *epigrams*. Not all poets approved of the trend to short poems, however. Apollonius of Rhodes favored traditional long epic poetry and wrote the long romantic epic the *Argonautica* in the 200s B.C.

The Greco-Roman Age

The period following the Hellenistic Age is known as the Greco-Roman Age because of the Roman conquest of Greece in 146 B.C. During the Roman rule, prose again became the most prominent literary form. The biographer and essayist Plutarch is most famous for his biographies contrasting Greek and Roman leaders in *Parallel Lives of Illustrious Greeks and Romans*. Later, Lucian of Samosata wrote amusing commentaries that satirized the popular philosophical schools of his day.

Renewed interest in the art of oratory and rhetoric resulted in the *Second Sophistic Movement* in the A.D. 100s. During this period, Epictetus, a former slave, became the spokesman of the Stoic school of thought. His philosophy emphasizes acceptance and endurance.

The Acropolis Museum, Athens

Many new and varied types of writings appeared during the A.D. 100s. The travel writer Pausanias wrote an important description of ancient Greece that remains a valuable source of Greek history and religion. A Greek physician named Galen produced medical writings, discussing anatomy, physiology, and psychology. Ptolemy, an astronomer, mathematician, and geographer, also wrote influential scientific works. Another important work of the period is the *Sophists' Banquet*, written by Athenaeus of Naucratis. Athenaeus pretends to record a dinner table discussion between 29 famous wise men. The work contains quotations from many literary works which would otherwise be unknown. Longus wrote an influential pastoral romance, *Daphnis and Chloe*, during the A.D. 100s or 200s. Critics regard this romance masterpiece as an important forerunner of the novel.

The most important writer of the 200s was Plotinus, founder of the *Neoplatonic school* of philosophy. His work was the last great creation of ancient philosophy.

Medieval Literature

In A.D. 395, the Roman Empire permanently split into the West Roman Empire and the East Roman, or Byzantine, Empire. Byzantine rule lasted in Greece until the Ottoman Empire conquered the region during the 1300s to mid-1400s. Constantinople (now Istanbul), the Byzantine capital, became the center of Greek culture and literature for 1,000 years. The Byzantine arts reflect the combination of Greek learning and literary tradition with the teachings of Christianity. Christian religious poetry became the most prominent Greek literature of the Middle Ages.

Romanos the Melode, who lived in the 500s, was the greatest Greek poet of the Middle Ages. He was the chief composer of *kontakia* (singular *kontakion*), which were long metrical hymns that were especially popular during the 500s and 600s. The *kanon*, another type of religious poetry, was introduced during the early 700s by Saint John Damascene, a famous theologian.

Modern Greek Literature

From the fall of Constantinople to the Ottoman Empire in 1453 until the Greek War of Independence in 1821, a more personal poetry flourished in the Frankish-occupied lands. *Erotocritos*, the masterpiece of Cretan literature, was written by Vitzentzos Cornaros in the early 1600s. The poem has more than 10,000 rhyming verses. In Ottoman-occupied territories, folk songs and folktales were almost the only Greek literature produced for 400 years.

The first great modern Greek poet, Dionysios Solomos, wrote during the early 1800s. Solomos adopted *demotic* Greek, the vivid language of the common people, for his poems. Before his poetry, only the official scholarly form of Greek, called *katharevousa*, was used in literature. The Demotic Movement of the 1880s, led by one of Greece's great poets, Kostis Palamas, urged the return of art and literature to themes of daily life.

Before World War I, Greek prose was limited largely to short stories describing provincial life and customs. After the war, the psychological and sociological novel became the leading prose form. Nikos Kazantzakis wrote powerful novels dealing with such themes as the conflict between human passion and spiritual ideals.

Modern Greek poetry earned international respect in the 1900s. Constantine Cavafy's narrative and lyric poems received high praise during the mid-1900s, after the poet's death, when they were first translated. In 1963, George Seferis, a lyric poet, became the first Greek to receive the Nobel Prize in Literature. Another Greek poet, Odysseus Elytis, won the Nobel Prize in Literature in 1979. Poet Yannis Ritsos had perhaps the greatest influence outside of Greece. He wrote over 100 books of poetry before his death in 1990.

THE PARTHENON is an ancient Greek temple in Athens. The temple stands on a hill called the *Acropolis* overlooking the city. The Parthenon was dedicated to Athena, the city's patron goddess. It is probably the best example of ancient Greek architecture.

The Greeks erected the Parthenon between 447 and 432 B.C. The temple was designed by the Greek architects Ictinus and Callicrates. The Greek sculptor Phidias designed the sculptural decoration for the building. The Parthenon became a Christian church about A.D. 500. After Muslim forces of the Ottoman Empire captured the city in the mid-1400s, the Parthenon served as a mosque.

In 1687, the Parthenon was badly damaged when the Venetians tried to conquer Athens. The Ottomans were using it for storing gunpowder, which exploded and wrecked the central part of the building. The remaining sculpture has since been moved to the Acropolis Museum in Athens and the British Museum in London. Today, only ruins of the building remain.

The Parthenon was built entirely of *Pentelic marble*, a white marble that was brought from Mount Pentelicus 11 miles (18 kilometers) from Athens. The temple is a rectangular building that measures 237 feet (72 meters) long and 110 feet (34 meters) wide. It stands about 60 feet (18 meters) high.

The Parthenon contains a central enclosed space, called a *cella*, which is divided into two rooms. One of the rooms once contained a huge statue of Athena made of wood covered with gold and ivory. The other room served as a treasury. A total of 46 Doric columns surround the cella.

Brightly painted sculpture originally decorated the Parthenon. Sculptures once filled the two *pediments* (triangular ends of the roof). The eastern pediment was decorated with scenes showing the birth of Athena. The western pediment showed the battle between Athena and the sea god Poseidon for the control of Athens.

Around the top of the outer wall above the columns of the Parthenon was a series of small sculptured panels called *metopes*. The metopes showed famous mythological battles between the Lapiths and the centaurs, the gods and a race of giants, and Greeks and Amazons. These sculptured panels also presented battle scenes from the Trojan War. Along the outer wall of the cella was a continuous horizontal *frieze* (decorated band). The frieze showed the people of Athens, including Athenian officials, priests, maidens, and young men on horseback, in the annual procession honoring the birthday of Athena. The government of Greece is restoring the Parthenon.

DATA

Highlights in the History of Ancient Greece

About 3000 B.C.	The Minoan culture arose on the island of Crete.
1600–1200 B.C.	The Mycenaean culture prospered on the Greek mainland.
776 B.C.	The first recorded Olympic Games took place.
508 B.C.	Athens became a democracy.
490 and 479 B.C.	The Greeks twice defeated invading Persian armies.
431–404 B.C.	Sparta defeated Athens in the Peloponnesian War.
338 B.C.	Philip II of Macedonia conquered the Greeks.
334–326 B.C.	Alexander the Great, ruler of Greece and Macedonia, conquered the Persian Empire.
323 B.C.	Alexander the Great died, and the Hellenistic Age began.
146 B.C.	Greece was conquered by the Romans.

ADDITIONAL RESOURCES

Books to Read

Anderson, Michael, ed. *Ancient Greece*. Rosen Publishing Group, 2012.

Cartledge, Paul. *Ancient Greece: A History in Eleven Cities*. Oxford, 2009.

Cooke, Tim, ed. *The New Cultural Atlas of the Greek World*. Marshall Cavendish, 2009.

Errington, R. Malcolm. *A History of the Hellenistic World: 323–30 B.C.* Blackwell, 2008.

Powell, Anton. *Ancient Greece*. 3rd ed. Chelsea House, 2007.

Ross, Stewart. *Ancient Greece Daily Life*. Compass Point, 2007.

Web Sites

A Multimedia Guide to Art of the Ancient World

http://www.artic.edu/cleo/

An interactive journey through the collection of ancient art at The Art Institute of Chicago. This Web site takes visitors on an expedition to the ancient cultures of Egypt, Greece, and Rome.

Ancient Greece

http://www.ancientgreece.com/s/Main_Page/

Information on Ancient Greece.

The Greeks: Crucible of Civilization

http://www.pbs.org/empires/thegreeks/

Discover how much of our modern world can be traced back to ancient Greek culture. Explore the time line of heroes and leaders, experience the Acropolis, and watch Quicktime clips from this PBS special.

Search Strings

Olympic Games

ancient greece olympic games origin four years competition (33,000)

olympic games origin ancient greece festival four years honor zeus Olympiad (19,200)

Birth of Democracy

democracy birth ancient greece athens solon first (20,900)

ancient greece birth democracy athens solon council of government (2,090)

Innovations in Math and Science

ancient greece science mathematics innovations archimedes pythagoras euclid (727)

science mathematics innovations archimedes pythagoras Euclid (869)

Religion Polytheistic

greek religion olympians polytheistic ancient greece oracles (920)

religion greek olympian gods polytheistic oracles (818)

ancient greece religion olympians polytheistic (3,500)

Ancient Rome

Ancient Rome was the largest empire the ancient world had ever seen. Rome began as a simple city in the heart of Italy but grew to span the entire continent. Its size was one of the reasons for its decline. Many of the vestiges of the Roman Empire still survive today. Ancient Rome was a profound influence on Western civilization as we know it.

HOT topics

Architecture
Gladiators
Public Baths
Empire

HOT topics

Architecture. At its base, Roman architecture was founded on that of the Greeks; however, Roman architecture was much grander and more elaborate. It was able to reach new heights because of two major new inventions: the arch and concrete. Arches could carry much more weight than was possible before, and could be more widely spaced than the columns of the Greeks. The Romans did not invent the arch, but they brought it to new heights, using it in unthought-of ways, such as vaulted ceilings. Concrete was the material that made these extravagant arches possible, as it was much stronger than any other building material of the time. With concrete, the Ancient Romans were able to build the huge dome of the Pantheon.

DEFINITIONS

civilization: civilized condition; advanced stage in social development.

class: the system of ranks or divisions in society.

gladiator: a slave, captive, or paid fighter who fought at the public shows in the arenas in ancient Rome.

trade route: a route followed by traders or trading ships.

empire: a group of nations or states under one ruler or government, one country having some measure of control over the rest.

republic: a nation or state in which the citizens elect representatives to manage the government, which is usually headed by a president rather than a monarch. The United States and Mexico are republics.

HOT topics 🔥

Recreation/Gladiators. On special occasions, trained fighters called gladiators would do battle in arenas known as amphitheaters. Gladiators were usually slaves or prisoners, but some citizens trained to be a gladiator. Gladiators fought against each other or against wild animals. Those gladiators that won were loved as heroes, but few gladiators won for very long; most died quickly and brutally. Often criminals would also be put into the arena with wild beasts to be killed to please the crowd.

City Life/Public Baths. The Roman bathhouses, or *thermae*, were large buildings open to all citizens. In the bathhouses, citizens could bathe, exercise, and most importantly, socialize. The baths were an important meeting place and an important part of every citizen's routine.

Victorious Roman gladiator

Emperor Constantine

Empire. The Roman Empire, at its height, spanned most of Europe, from Britain all the way to the Persian Gulf. Rome systematically conquered Egypt, Greece, Palestine, Mesopotamia, Britain, and Gaul, a region of Europe that is now France, Belgium, and Germany. At its height, in the 100s and 200s A.D., the Roman Empire was home to more than 50 million people. The Roman Empire united almost all of Europe under its banner and was the largest empire the west had ever seen.

TRUE or FALSE?
The Roman Empire crumbled because it was too big for Rome to govern.

THE BASICS

Ancient Rome. The story of ancient Rome is a tale of how a small farming community on the bank of the Tiber River in central Italy grew to become one of the greatest empires in history, and then collapsed. According to Roman legend, the city of Rome was founded in 753 B.C. By 275 B.C., the Roman Republic controlled most of the Italian Peninsula. At its peak, in the A.D. 100s and 200s, the Roman Empire governed about half of Europe, much of the Middle East, and the north coast of Africa. The empire then began to crumble, partly because it was too big for Rome to govern. The empire split into two parts in A.D. 395, the West Roman Empire and the East Roman, or Byzantine, Empire. The West Roman Empire fell to Germanic invaders in A.D. 476, but the Byzantine Empire continued for centuries.

Ancient Rome had enormous influence on the development of Western civilization. Latin, the language of the ancient Romans, became the basis of French, Italian, Spanish, and the other Romance languages. Roman law provided the foundation for the legal systems of most of the countries in Western Europe and Latin America. Roman roads, bridges, and aqueducts—some of which are still used—served as models for engineers in later ages.

This article provides a broad overview of the land, people, government, way of life, arts and sciences, economy, and history of ancient Rome.

The World of Ancient Rome

The land. The city of Rome was founded on seven wooded hills next to the Tiber River in central Italy. The hills were steep and easily defended against enemy attacks. The valleys had fertile soil and good irrigation, as well as materials necessary for building.

As Rome grew, much of the city was built upon the swampy lowlands beneath the seven hills. These parts of Rome often suffered damaging floods from the Tiber. But the Tiber also provided a convenient

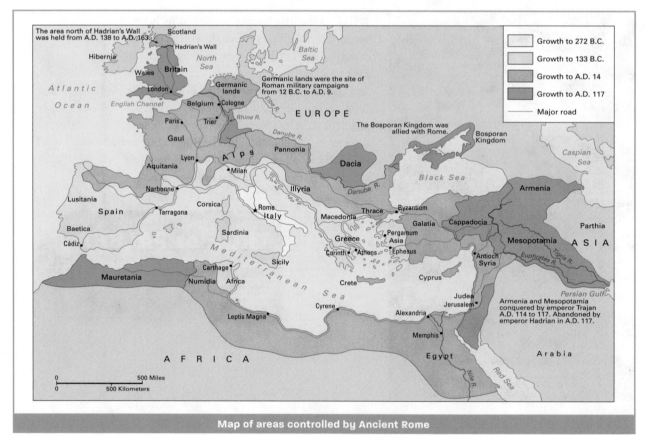

Map of areas controlled by Ancient Rome

route to the sea, which lay about 15 miles (24 kilometers) to the west. The harbor at Ostia, a town at the mouth of the Tiber, allowed for extensive trade with other communities.

The Italian Peninsula, which Rome controlled for much of its history, juts far into the Mediterranean Sea and occupies a central position among the Mediterranean lands. To the north, the Alps provided a natural defense against invaders from central Europe. But passes through the mountains allowed settlers, attracted by the mild climate and fertile soil, to travel into Italy.

Roman rule eventually spread over all the lands bordering the Mediterranean Sea. The Romans called the Mediterranean Mare Nostrum (Our Sea) or Mare Internum (Inland Sea). At the Roman Empire's greatest size, in the A.D. 100s and 200s, the empire extended as far north as Scotland and as far east as the Persian Gulf.

The people. When Rome was founded, a number of different tribes lived on the Italian Peninsula, each with its own language and culture. The Romans were Latins. Other major tribes included the Etruscans, Sabines, and Samnites.

The Roman Empire, at its height, had over 50 million people. In the east, Rome controlled Mesopotamia, Palestine, Egypt, and Greece. In the west, Rome conquered Britain and Gaul (now mainly France, Belgium, and part of Germany). Almost 1 million people lived in the city of Rome. Alexandria in Egypt, the empire's second largest city, had over 500,000 inhabitants.

Latin and Greek were the official languages of the empire. Government officials and members of the upper classes spoke those two languages. But most people in the empire continued to use their native languages. Celtic was spoken in Gaul and Britain, Berber in northern Africa, and Aramaic in Syria and Palestine.

People belonged to one of three groups in ancient Rome: (1) citizens, (2) noncitizens, and (3) slaves. Roman law recognized citizens and noncitizens as free. Slaves were treated as property. Citizenship gave protection under Roman law, and only a citizen could become a senator or government official.

The citizens of Rome were further divided into different social classes. At the top were members of the Senate, who were often wealthy landowners. Next were the *equites*, prosperous businessmen and merchants. Under the Roman emperors,

A Roman slave market

equites held important government positions and assisted in the running of the empire. The majority of Roman citizens belonged to the lower classes. They were farmers, city workers, and soldiers.

At first, only those born in Rome could become citizens, so the majority of people were noncitizens. As Rome expanded, it granted citizenship to more people in the empire. The privilege of citizenship promoted loyalty to the empire and gave all classes and all regions a greater stake in its success. Women and children could become citizens, but they could not vote.

Slaves were regarded as property by Roman law, but they were essential to the Roman way of life. They performed tasks ranging from heavy labor to teaching the young nobles of Rome. Most slaves were captured in war. A wealthy Roman family might have hundreds of slaves working on its farmland and in its home. Slaves could buy their freedom from their masters, or be given it. Freed slaves, known as freedmen, owed allegiance to their former masters, who relied on them for continued service.

Government

A series of kings ruled ancient Rome at the beginning of its history. Each king was advised by a Senate made up of the heads of Rome's leading families. Ordinary citizens had little say in the running of the state.

The Roman Republic was established in 509 B.C., after Roman nobles overthrew the king. Under this new government, the Senate became the most powerful body. It decided foreign and

The Imperial Forum, Rome

financial policy and passed *decrees* (official orders). The senators were former *magistrates* (government officials) who held office for life.

To succeed politically, magistrates had to follow the *cursus honorum* (ladder of offices). The first step was serving as a military officer. Next, they would try to be elected as a *quaestor* (financial official), then as an *aedile* (public works official), then as a *praetor* (judicial official). After serving as praetor, magistrates automatically entered the Senate.

The highest position was *consul*. There were two consuls, elected annually, who headed the government and took command of the army in times of war. Each Roman year was named after the consuls who ruled that year.

All magistrates held office for one year. After serving in one position, they had to return to private life for a year before holding another office. As Rome expanded, praetors and consuls left the city after their year in office to govern the provinces as *propraetors* or *proconsuls*.

During the B.C. 400s and 300s, the landowning upper classes—the *patricians*—struggled for power with the other classes—the *plebeians*. The dispute became known as the Conflict of the Orders. Originally, only patricians could hold public office, become priests, or interpret the law. But the importance of the plebeians in fighting wars helped them gain a greater voice. The plebeians formed their own assembly, the *concilium plebis*, and elected leaders known as *tribunes* who championed their causes. By 287 B.C., plebeians had won the right to hold any public or religious office and had gained equality under the law.

However, the richest families continued to control the assemblies and the Senate.

The Roman Empire was established in 27 B.C., after the republican government collapsed. The republican institutions of government continued, but emperors held supreme authority. They nominated the consuls and appointed new senators. The citizen assemblies had little power. Emperors headed the army and directed the making of laws. They relied more on their own advisers than on the Senate. A vast civil service handled the empire's day-to-day business.

The law. The Romans published their first known law code in 451 B.C. This code of law, known as the Laws of the Twelve Tables, was basic. As Rome grew, its legal system developed and became more complex. Rome became the first society with experts whose job was to interpret the law on behalf of clients—experts now called *lawyers*.

A general set of legal principles developed known as the *jus gentium* (law of nations). It was based on common-sense notions of fairness and took into account local customs and practices. Much of what we know of Roman law comes from the Theodosian Code of A.D. 438 and the *Digest*, law cases and interpretations compiled by the Emperor Justinian in the A.D 500s.

The army was composed of three groups: (1) the legions, (2) the auxiliaries, and (3) the Praetorian Guard. Only Roman citizens could join the legions. Each legion consisted of about 5,000 men. Besides soldiers, legions also had doctors, surveyors, and engineers. Although the chief purpose of the legions was military, legions also built roads, aqueducts, walls, and tunnels.

Noncitizens joined the auxiliaries, which fought alongside the legions. Auxiliaries were made up of specialized troops, such as archers or cavalry.

The Praetorian Guard was an elite group of soldiers who served as the emperor's personal bodyguard. It was the only army group stationed in the city of Rome.

The normal length of military service was 25 years. Most soldiers were professionals, whose training and discipline helped to make the Roman army successful. After their term of service, many veterans and their families settled in *colonies* (towns made up of former soldiers). The colonies acted as models of Roman life for people in the provinces, and the former soldiers provided a ready peacekeeping or police force if trouble arose.

Way of Life

City life. Rome was the capital and largest city of the empire. Other important cities included Alexandria in Egypt, Athens in Greece, Antioch in Syria, and Byzantium (later Constantinople, now Istanbul) in Turkey.

Cities in the Roman Empire served as centers of trade and culture. Roman engineers planned cities carefully. They set public buildings in central locations and provided efficient sewerage and water-supply systems. Emperors and other wealthy individuals paid for the construction of public buildings, such as baths, arenas, and theaters. At the heart of the Roman city was the *forum*, a large open space surrounded by markets, government buildings, and temples. It was the center for business and religious life and offered a place where everyone could mingle, rich and poor alike.

Most people in Roman cities lived in cramped apartment buildings that were three to five stories high. Many of these buildings had unsanitary conditions, and a number of them burned to the ground.

Wealthy Romans lived in houses built around two courtyards known as the *atrium* and the *peristyle*. Windowless rooms surrounded the atrium, but a roof opening let in light and air. A dining hall and other rooms circled the larger peristyle, which was also open to the sky and had a garden.

Rural life. The first Romans were shepherds and farmers. In early Rome, landowners planted their crops in the spring and harvested them in the fall. During the summer, they would fight in the army. As Rome expanded, small farmers spent longer periods away fighting. Many were forced to sell their land to wealthier landowners. This led to the development of large estates known as *latifundia*, which were worked by massive teams of slaves.

For these slaves and most small landholders, rural life involved hard physical labor. The Roman calendar featured regular agricultural festivals. The games and entertainments at these festivals offered a break from the hardships of working the land.

Most rural people lived in simple dwellings made of sun-dried bricks. Wealthy landowners lived in luxurious villas, which were larger than houses in the city.

Family life. The head of the Roman family was the *paterfamilias* (father of the family). Legally, he had power over his entire household, which included his wife, children (even if adults), slaves, and freedmen. As long as his father lived, a son could not own property or have legal authority over his own children. However, in practice, adult sons ruled their own families.

Girls could legally marry when they were 12 years old, and boys when they were 14. However, a man might not marry until he was in his 20s and had already begun his career. Among the upper classes, parents arranged most marriages for the economic or political benefits that the unions would bring the families. During the republic, marriage made a woman and everything she owned her husband's property. During the empire, the woman kept her legal rights and her own property.

Food. Most Romans ate simple meals. Breakfast was usually a light meal of bread and sometimes cheese. Lunch and dinner consisted mainly of porridge or bread plus olives, fruit, or cheese. *Garum*, a sauce made of fish parts and olive oil, was a popular addition.

Wealthy Romans sometimes served dinners with several courses. The first course might include eggs, vegetables, and shellfish. The main courses featured meat, fish, or chicken. For dessert, the diners often ate honey-sweetened cakes and fruit.

Clothing. The Romans wore simple clothes made of wool or linen. The main garment was the *tunic*, a gown that hung to the knees or below. On formal occasions, citizens of Rome wore a *toga*, which resembled a white sheet draped around the body. The togas of senators and other high-ranking citizens had a purple border. It was against the law for noncitizens to wear togas. Romans wore cloaks over their tunics or togas when the weather was cold or wet.

Women often wore a *stola*, a long dress with many folds. Wealthy women wore a *palla*, which was similar to a toga, as well as jewelry, makeup, and styled hair. Most women's clothing was dyed in bright colors.

Recreation. Bathhouses served as centers for daily exercise and bathing, as well as for socializing. Normally, there were separate baths for men and women. Bathhouses had a grand exercise area, the *palaestra*, for wrestling, boxing, or running. After exercising, the bather would be massaged by a slave, then move through rooms with warm, hot, and cold pools to cleanse and energize the body.

Much of the Roman year was devoted to religious holidays in honor of gods and goddesses. During

The Colosseum, Rome

the republic, there were almost 60 of these special days. By the A.D. 100s, there were 135 each year.

Many religious holidays were celebrated with free public entertainment. Occasionally, the emperor or wealthy state officials sponsored productions in circular arenas known as *amphitheaters*. The most famous amphitheater, the Colosseum in Rome, could seat about 50,000 spectators. Here, trained fighters known as *gladiators* fought each other to the death. Most gladiators were slaves or condemned criminals, but some citizens gave up their freedom to become gladiators. Successful gladiators were admired, much as modern athletes are, but most gladiators died brutal deaths. In other events, armed men fought exotic wild animals, or beasts attacked condemned criminals or Christians.

Chariot racing was a popular spectator sport. In Rome, charioteers raced in a long, oval arena known as the Circus Maximus, which could seat more than 250,000 people. Charioteers raced for one of four teams—red, green, blue, or white. Like modern sports teams, each team had loyal fans. Success as a charioteer brought fame and fortune.

Theaters in Rome staged comedies and tragedies by Greek and Roman authors. More popular, however, were *mimes* (short plays about everyday life) or *pantomimes* (stories told through music and dancing).

Religion. The Romans adopted most of their gods from the Greeks, giving them Roman names. For example, Jupiter, the supreme god, was the Roman name for the Greek god Zeus. The Romans erected temples and shrines to honor their gods. The centerpiece of every Roman city was a temple to the three divine beings called the Capitoline triad: Jupiter, Juno, and Minerva.

Rulers of Rome were sometimes designated as gods. Romulus became the god Quirinus, and some emperors, including Augustus, Claudius, and Vespasian, were *deified* (made gods) after their death. Late in the empire, people began worshiping emperors as gods while they were still alive.

The Roman state controlled religion. Priests were government officials, elected or appointed to office. They performed sacrifices and other ceremonies to win the favor of the gods for the state. The most important priests were the *pontiffs*. The chief priest was known as the *pontifex maximus*. During the empire, this position was always held by the emperor.

An important feature of Roman religion was *divination*—telling the future and examining the will of the gods to ward off their anger. Priests known as *augurs* looked for signs in the flight of birds. The Sibylline Books, a set of religious texts, offered remedies to deal with *portents* (natural occurrences interpreted as signs) such as earthquakes or sudden storms. Individuals used other types of divination, such as astrology.

As Roman religion became more political, people turned to other kinds of religious worship. Many practiced religions that promised salvation and happiness after death. Christianity became a popular alternative to Roman religion. The Roman government saw Christianity as a threat and persecuted its followers. But by the A.D. 300s, Christianity had become the main religion of the empire.

Education. Most children received their earliest education at home under the supervision of their parents. In wealthy homes, slaves taught the children. These slaves were often well-educated men from Greece. From the age of 6 or 7 until 10 or 11, most boys and some girls attended a private school or studied at home. They learned reading, writing, and mathematics. Most Roman children who received further education came from wealthy families. From the age of 11 until about 14, they studied mainly Latin and Greek grammar and literature, as well as mathematics, music, and astronomy.

Higher education focused on the study of *rhetoric*—the art of public speaking. Upper-class Romans prized the ability to argue persuasively before the law courts or to debate effectively in the Senate. To improve their abilities as public speakers, students might also read philosophy and history. Few women received higher education.

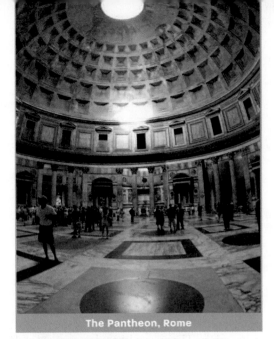
The Pantheon, Rome

Arts and Sciences

Architecture and engineering. The ancient Romans adopted the basic forms of Greek architecture. For example, Roman temples were surrounded by columns with a covered *portico* (walkway), just as those in Greece. But the Romans generally built grander and more extravagant buildings than the Greeks.

Two achievements of Roman engineering made larger buildings possible: the arch and concrete. Arches supported such structures as bridges and the aqueducts that carried water to Roman cities. Arched roofs known as *vaults* spanned the interior of buildings. Vaults eliminated the need for columns to hold up the roof and so created more open floor space. Although the Romans did not invent the arch, they made better use of arches than previous cultures.

The Romans developed concrete, which served as a strong building material for walls, vaults, and domed buildings. The most famous Roman building made with concrete is the Pantheon in Rome, which has a concrete dome about 142 feet (43 meters) in diameter.

Sculpture, painting, and mosaics. Roman sculptors and painters borrowed styles from native Italian traditions and from Greek art. Many early Roman sculptors worked in bronze or terracotta, materials often used in Etruscan sculpture. After the Romans conquered Greece during the 140s B.C., they adopted some of the styles of Greek art. Roman sculptors created realistic portraits that revealed individual personalities.

Roman sculptors also illustrated historical events through carvings on large public monuments. For example, the richly decorated Ara Pacis (Altar of Peace) celebrated the peace brought to the empire by the Emperor Augustus. Carvings on columns and triumphal arches celebrated the emperor and Rome.

Wall paintings decorated the houses of the wealthy. Paintings often showed garden landscapes, events from Greek and Roman mythology, historical scenes, or scenes of everyday life. Romans decorated floors with *mosaics*—pictures or designs created with small colored tiles. The richly colored paintings and mosaics helped to make rooms in Roman houses seem larger and brighter and showed off the wealth of the owner.

Literature. Early Roman literature was heavily influenced by Greek poetry and drama. The first history of Rome was written in Greek. The earliest Roman poets, such as Naevius, and comic playwrights, such as Plautus and Terence, adapted or translated Greek originals for Roman audiences. Rome's greatest poets—Catullus, Lucretius, Ovid, and Virgil—produced powerful, original works, but even these works show the Greek influence.

The annual change of leadership in republican government gave rise to Rome's own particular form of history, the *annals* (year-by-year narratives). Livy wrote the annals of the history of the Roman people, and Tacitus adapted the form in his account of the first emperors of Rome. Other important literary works include the letters, speeches, and philosophical writings of Cicero; the *satires* (mocking poetry) of Horace and Juvenal; and the letters of Pliny the Younger.

The Ara Pacis

Science. The ancient Romans made few scientific discoveries. Yet the work of Greek scientists flourished under Roman rule. The Greek geographer Strabo traveled widely and wrote careful descriptions of what he saw. Alexandria in Egypt became an important center for scientific study. There, Ptolemy developed a system of astronomy that was accepted for nearly 1,400 years. Galen, a Greek physician, proposed important medical theories based on scientific experiments. The Romans themselves gathered important collections of scientific information. For example, Pliny the Elder gathered the scientific knowledge of his day in a 37-volume encyclopedia.

Economy

Rome profited from the economic resources of the regions and nations it conquered. Its vast wealth funded the magnificent buildings and art that decorated Rome and other imperial cities. Roman riches also financed roads, aqueducts, and other public works projects.

Agriculture. Most of the people in the Roman world lived by farming. Roman farmers understood the need to rotate crops to maintain the fertility of the soil for future seasons. Farmers who could afford to would leave half of every field unplanted.

In fertile valleys north and south of Rome, farmers grew wheat, rye, and barley. Olives and grape vines flourished on rockier hillsides. Shepherds grazed sheep and goats, and other farmers raised hogs, cattle, and poultry. As the empire expanded, farms in Gaul, Spain, and northern Africa supplied Rome with many agricultural products. In Africa,

local farmers grew rich from their export of olive oil, which was used both for cooking and as a lamp fuel.

Mining. After agriculture, mining was Rome's most important industry. The great building projects in Rome and in other cities throughout the empire required huge quantities of marble and other materials. Greece and northern Italy provided much of the marble. Italy also had rich deposits of copper and iron ore. Gold and silver were mined in Spain and Britain. Britain also produced iron for weapons and armor, lead for water pipes, and tin, much of which was used to produce bronze. Slaves, condemned criminals, and prisoners of war worked in the mines. The miners labored in cramped and unsanitary conditions, chained together.

Manufacturing industries were small compared to agriculture and mining. The city of Rome imported most of its manufactured goods from other Italian communities. They supplied Rome with such products as pottery, glassware, weapons, tools, and textiles.

Trade thrived as the empire expanded. Trade routes crossed land and sea, both within the empire and beyond its borders. Ships moved goods faster than the slow-moving carts used to carry merchandise over Roman roads. But both ships and carts had to guard against foul weather, pirates or highway robbers, and spoilage.

Rome imported foods, raw materials, and manufactured goods from within the empire. Rome also imported silk from China, spices and precious gems from India, and ivory and wild animals from Africa. Italy's leading exports were wine and olive oil.

The government issued coins of gold, silver, copper, and bronze from Rome. Local government centers, such as London in Britain (which the Romans called Londinium) or Lyon in Gaul (called Lugdunum), also issued coins. The central regulation of weights and measures for coinage made trade throughout the empire easier.

Transportation and communication. The Roman Empire's road system covered about 50,000 miles (80,000 kilometers). Roman roads were remarkably straight compared to modern highways. The Romans designed straight roads to speed up troop movements. After the army had pacified a region, Roman administrators then used the roads to promote trade and communication.

Rome had a highly developed postal system that could bring a letter from the most distant outpost of the empire to Rome. Postal stations stood on

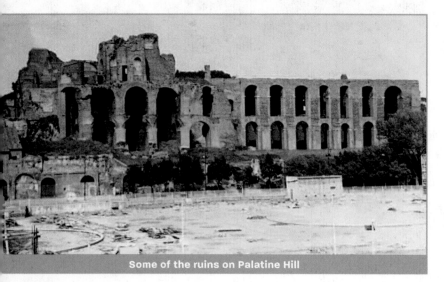

Some of the ruins on Palatine Hill

main roads throughout the empire. The emperor maintained regular contact with governors in the provinces by letter.

The Romans had a huge fleet of cargo ships, which traveled to ports on the Mediterranean Sea and carried goods up and down the Rhine, Danube, and Nile rivers. Permanent navies in the Mediterranean Sea and the English Channel protected trade ships from pirates.

In Rome, a government newsletter called *Acta Diurna (Daily Events)* was posted throughout the city. The paper recorded important social and political news. Officials inscribed important decrees and notices on stone or bronze and posted them prominently in major cities.

History

The regal period. Little is known about the early days of ancient Rome. Archaeologists have found the remains of houses that were built around 900 B.C. on the Palatine Hill. The earliest settlers were a people called the Latins. They inhabited many neighboring towns in Latium, the region around Rome.

According to legend, Rome was founded in 753 B.C. by twin brothers, Romulus and Remus. A dispute between the brothers led to the death of Remus, and Romulus named the city for himself. After Romulus, six more kings governed Rome. Each contributed to the development of the new state in a unique way. For example, the second king, Numa, introduced religious ceremonies to Rome. The heads of leading noble families made up the Senate, which advised the king.

About 600 B.C., Rome and other towns in Latium came

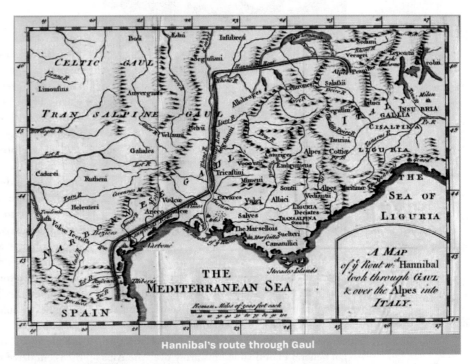

Hannibal's route through Gaul

under the control of the Etruscans, who lived in northern Italy. The Etruscans, the most advanced civilization in Italy, built roads, temples, and other public buildings in Rome. Trade increased during this period, and with it, so did Rome's prosperity. The last king was an Etruscan named Tarquin the Proud. He ruled so harshly that the Roman nobles expelled him and created a new form of government called a *republic*, without a single, all-powerful ruler.

The Roman Republic was established in 509 B.C. It was intended to be a partnership between the Senate and the people of Rome, as indicated by the motto *Senatus Populusque Romanus* (Senate and People of Rome). The initials SPQR appeared on the flags of the Roman legions and in official documents.

In 493 B.C., Rome entered into an alliance with the Latin League, a union of the cities of

Latium. By 396 B.C., Rome was the largest city in the region and used the league's resources to fight its neighbors. When Rome conquered a city, it offered protection and certain privileges, such as special trading rights. In return, the conquered cities supplied the Roman army with soldiers.

From the 300s to mid-200s B.C., Rome won victories over the Etruscans. In 338 B.C., Rome overpowered and disbanded the Latin League. In 290 B.C., the Romans conquered the Samnites, a mountain people who lived south of Rome. In the 200s and 100s B.C., Rome defeated the Gauls, who had invaded Italy from the north and burned Rome in 390 B.C. After a victory over the Greek colony of Tarentum in southern Italy in 272 B.C., Rome ruled most of the Italian Peninsula.

Rome's conquest of Italy brought it into conflict with Carthage, a sea power and trading center on the coast of north

Julius Caesar

Africa (in what is now Tunisia). The two nations fought three wars known as the Punic Wars. In the First Punic War (264–241 B.C.), Rome conquered Sicily and made it the first Roman province. In the Second Punic War (218–201 B.C.), the Carthaginian general Hannibal led his army over the Alps into Italy. He won several key battles, but Roman manpower and endurance wore him down. Roman forces, led by the general Publius Cornelius Scipio, defeated Hannibal in 202 B.C. In the Third Punic War (149–146 B.C.), Rome destroyed the city of Carthage. These victories brought Spain and northern Africa under Roman control.

After the Second Punic War, Rome began to expand in the east toward Greece and Macedonia. In 146 B.C., the same year as the destruction of Carthage, Rome burned Corinth to the ground and took control of Greece. Soon after, King Attalus III of Pergamum died and left his kingdom to Rome, which became a wealthy province the Romans called Asia (now part of Turkey).

The later years of the republic. Acquiring territories abroad led to discontent at home. Military campaigns took longer and longer, and poverty-stricken farmers often returned to find their lands ruined. But the wealthy profited from the slaves and goods captured in the fighting and from business opportunities in the new lands. The gap between rich and poor widened, but Rome's wealthiest citizens opposed attempts to narrow it. In the 100s B.C., the tribune Tiberius Sempronius Gracchus and his brother, Gaius Sempronius Gracchus, attempted a program of reform, including giving public land to the poor. But opponents killed them and halted their reforms.

The Roman general Gaius Marius then came to power. Marius served as consul seven times from 107 to 86 B.C. He used tribunes to win popular support and to gain political power. He also reformed the army, offering rewards to his men for successful campaigns. From 91 to 89 B.C., Rome fought with its Latin allies, who wanted to be awarded citizenship in return for assisting Rome abroad.

Civil war broke out in the 80s B.C. between Marius and another general, Lucius Cornelius Sulla. Marius died in 86 B.C., and Sulla eventually triumphed over Marius's followers. Sulla declared himself dictator in 82 B.C. and reorganized the state. He enlarged the Senate, reduced the powers of the tribunes, and took measures to prevent corruption in the provinces. In 79 B.C., Sulla stepped down as dictator and retired from politics.

Pompey the Great and Marcus Licinius Crassus, allies of Sulla, became the next leading generals. In 67 B.C., Pompey rid the Mediterranean of the pirates who had plagued Roman trade. He then conquered eastern Asia Minor (now Turkey), Syria, and Judea (now mostly Israel). Crassus put down the slave rebellion led by Spartacus. But the Senate blocked the rewards that Pompey and Crassus sought for their achievements. In 61 or 60 B.C., Pompey and Crassus joined Gaius Julius Caesar to form an unofficial political alliance known as the First Triumvirate. They arranged Caesar's election as consul in 59 B.C.

From 58 to 51 B.C., Julius Caesar conquered Gaul. Pompey stayed in Rome and gained political power. Crassus took an eastern command but was killed fighting the Parthian Empire, based in what is now Iran. Caesar and Pompey then saw each other as rivals for control of the empire. In 49 B.C., Caesar returned to Italy, and another civil war began. Over the next few years, Caesar defeated Pompey and his supporters. By 45 B.C., Caesar had become sole ruler of the Roman world. But many powerful Romans distrusted him, and in 44 B.C. a group of aristocrats assassinated him.

More civil war followed Caesar's death. In 43 B.C., Caesar's adopted son and heir, Octavian, formed the Second Triumvirate with Mark Antony and Marcus Aemilius Lepidus, the *pontifex maximus* (chief priest). They took revenge on Caesar's assassins and dealt violently with any opposition. Mark Antony and Octavian eventually pushed aside Lepidus and fought each other for control of the empire. Antony sought the support of Cleopatra, queen of

Egypt. The two became lovers and had children together. In 31 B.C., Octavian defeated them in the Battle of Actium off the west coast of Greece. The next year, Egypt became a Roman province.

The Roman Empire. After the defeat of Antony, Octavian was the unchallenged leader of the Roman world. In 27 B.C., he became the first Roman emperor and took the name Augustus (Revered One), a word that held religious meaning. More than a century of internal upheavals and civil war, caused by the ambitions of powerful individuals, had destroyed the republic. Only a strong individual who had the support of the army, the Senate, and the people would be able to govern the Roman world.

The reign of Augustus marked the beginning of a period of stability known as the Pax Romana (Roman Peace), which lasted until about A.D. 180. Augustus reestablished an orderly government in which the traditional republican forms of government—Senate, consuls, tribunes—still functioned. But Augustus had supreme power. He commanded the army and controlled the most important provinces. He nominated the consuls and appointed new senators. Citizen assemblies had little power, but he kept the masses happy through entertainment and handouts of free grain and money.

The emperor relied heavily on loyal advisers and established a personal bodyguard, the Praetorian Guard, which was stationed in Rome. Augustus established strong defenses along the frontiers of the Roman Empire and kept the provinces under control. He began to develop a civil service staffed by skilled administrators to govern the empire more effectively. During what came to be known as the Age of Augustus, Roman trade, art, and literature flourished.

Augustus died in A.D. 14 and was succeeded by his stepson Tiberius. Tiberius and the other relatives of Augustus who ruled after him were known as the Julio-Claudians. They ruled Rome until 68. In the Year of the Four Emperors in 69, four generals stationed around the empire made claims to the throne. The governor of Judea, Vespasian, emerged victorious. He and his two sons, Titus and Domitian, were known as the Flavians. They ruled until 96. Domitian ruled with excessive cruelty, but a kindly emperor named Nerva succeeded him and brought an age of peace and prosperity. The Antonine rulers—from Nerva to Marcus Aurelius— were noted for their wisdom and ability.

Augustus had left strict instructions to his successors not to expand the empire. However, Claudius invaded Britain in 43. In northwestern Africa, Claudius added a region called Mauretania (now northern Morocco and western Algeria) to the empire. Trajan seized Dacia in eastern Europe in 106. Hadrian returned to the policy of Augustus. He marked the limits of Rome's empire with artificial frontiers on the Danube River, in northern Africa, and elsewhere. In northern England, he constructed Hadrian's Wall, parts of which still stand.

The expansion of the empire gave wealthy Romans new opportunities for investment. Both small farms and large estates thrived. Roman roads, built initially to speed troop movements, made trade and communication easier. The Romans erected imposing towns and cities, even in such remote areas as Wales, Scotland, and Mauretania. The equites controlled the civil service, which became increasingly skilled at running the day-to-day business of the empire.

The decline of the empire. As time went on, the power of the emperors increased and the people became less politically active. The Roman Empire's enormous size hastened its

Marcus Aurelius

House of the Faun, Pompeii

decline. One man in Rome could no longer hold the empire together. The far-flung armies on Rome's borders were often more loyal to their commanders than to the emperor. Enemies of Rome, such as the Goths in central Europe and the Parthians in southwest Asia, mounted serious attacks.

In 161, Marcus Aurelius became emperor and defended the Roman Empire against attacks by Germanic tribes from the north and Parthians from the east. His son Commodus succeeded him in 180 but was killed in 192. Many rivals tried to claim the empire, and several emperors seized power by force. From 235 to 284, there were 19 different emperors, many of them army commanders whose troops named them emperor.

Diocletian, a Roman military officer, was proclaimed emperor in 284. Diocletian attempted to stabilize the empire by reorganizing the way it was governed. He divided the provinces into smaller units and gave each its own government and army. Diocletian established a *tetrarchy* (rule of four). Under this system, Diocletian ruled the eastern part of the empire and a co-emperor, Maximian, ruled the west. In addition, two *Caesars* (junior emperors), Galerius and Constantius, ruled under Diocletian and Maximian. Diocletian tried unsuccessfully to aid Rome's economy by standardizing coinage and imposing price controls. He also persecuted followers of Christianity and other religions.

After Diocletian retired in 305, several men struggled to gain power, and the tetrarchy failed. Eventually, Constantine I, who had been a deputy of Diocletian, came to power. He once again united the empire and, in 313 through the Edict of Milan, granted Christians freedom of worship. In 325, at the Council of Nicaea, Constantine rec-

ognized Christianity as the chief religion of the Roman Empire. In 330, the emperor established a new capital at Byzantium and renamed it Constantinople (now Istanbul, Turkey).

After Constantine died in 337, his three sons and two of his nephews battled for control of the empire. In 361, Julian gained control. He became known as the Apostate—that is, the Forsaker of Beliefs—because he tried to curb the spread of Christianity and to restore traditional Roman religious practices. Later emperors, such as Theodosius, outlawed Roman and other non-Christian religious practices. After the death of Theodosius in 395, the empire was permanently split into the West Roman Empire, with its capital in Rome, and the East Roman Empire, with its capital in Constantinople.

The West Roman Empire steadily weakened. A Germanic people called the Vandals invaded Spain and later occupied northern Africa. The Visigoths, another Germanic group, invaded and looted the city of Rome under their leader Alaric in 410. In Britain, local peoples known as the Picts, Scots, and Saxons attacked the Roman troops. The emperor Honorius finally gave up Britain so he could use the troops elsewhere in the empire. A Vandal leader named Gaiseric (or Genseric) plundered the city of Rome again in 455. The empire's final collapse came in 476, when the German leader Odoacer forced the last emperor from the seat of power. Ironically, Rome's last emperor was named Romulus Augustulus, after the founder of Rome and its first emperor.

The East Roman Empire survived and thrived as the Byzantine Empire. Its people continued to call themselves Romans. The Byzantine Empire lasted until 1453, when the Ottomans captured Constantinople and made it the capital of the Ottoman Empire.

The Legacy of Ancient Rome

The Roman heritage. Ancient Rome had a tremendous impact on the modern world. During the Middle Ages, which lasted from about the A.D. 400s through the 1400s, the Roman Catholic Church replaced the Roman Empire as the unifying force in Europe. It used the Latin language and preserved the classics of Latin literature.

Latin remained the language of learned Europeans for more than a thousand years after the fall of the West Roman Empire. The French, Spanish, Italian, and Portuguese languages developed from forms of Latin spoken in different parts of the Roman Empire. Many words in English come from Latin.

Roman law provided a model for the legal systems of many countries in Europe, Latin America, and South Africa. Many modern governments reflect the influence of the Roman political system. For example, the Senate of the United States government gets its name from Rome's governing body.

Roman engineering feats served as models for later engineers. Some of the roads, bridges, and aqueducts built by the Romans are still used today. The Romans demonstrated the importance of swift and reliable communication, both in war and peace.

Learning about ancient Rome. Most of our knowledge of ancient Rome comes from documents written by the Romans themselves. These records include masterpieces of Latin literature, such as the letters and speeches of Cicero or the letters of Pliny the Younger. The Roman historian Livy told of Rome's development from 753 B.C. to his own time, the age of Augustus. Tacitus described the period of Roman history from the reign of Tiberius to that of Domitian. Suetonius Tranquillus wrote biographies of Roman rulers from Julius Caesar to Domitian. Leading generals wrote autobiographies that detailed their achievements. For example, Julius Caesar described his conquest of Gaul in his *Commentaries on the Gallic War*. Other types of written records include *epigraphic records* (documents engraved in stone), such as law codes, treaties, and decrees of the Roman Senate and the emperors.

Scholars also derive information from scenes carved on monuments in Roman times. Generals and emperors erected these monuments to celebrate victories and other important events. For example, Trajan's Column and the Column of Marcus Aurelius in Rome tell us much about the military campaigns of these leaders.

The remains of Roman towns and cities and other archaeological evidence also provide valuable information. In particular, the excavations at the towns of Pompeii and Herculaneum, buried when Mount Vesuvius erupted in A.D. 79, have revealed enormous amounts of detail regarding everyday life in Roman times.

Interest in the study of ancient Rome reawakened during the Renaissance, the great cultural movement that swept across Europe from the early 1300s to about 1600. The Renaissance began in Italy when scholars rediscovered the works of ancient Greek and Roman authors. The first major history of Rome in modern times was the British scholar Edward Gibbon's *The History of the Decline and Fall of the Roman Empire* (1776–1788). By the 1800s, the study of Rome and its language was considered an essential element of a young person's education. The German historian Theodor Mommsen, one of the great modern scholars of ancient Rome, wrote the influential *History of Rome* (1854–1856). Scholars of the 1900s and 2000s have benefited from new archaeological discoveries and modern approaches to the study of language and literature. They continue to produce many books annually on the history, politics, culture, and language of ancient Rome.

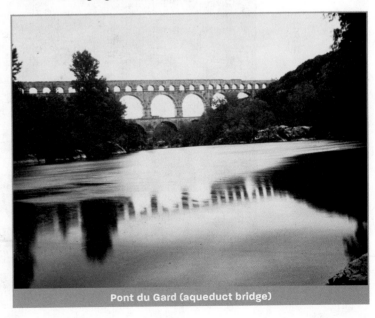

Pont du Gard (aqueduct bridge)

THE ROMAN FORUM was the section of ancient Rome that served as the center of government. It was the administrative, legislative, and legal center of the Republic and of the Roman Empire. Many important buildings and monuments stood there, including the *Curia* (Senate house), the temples of Concord and Saturn, the Basilica Julia and Basilica Aemilia, the Arch of Septimius Severus, and the *Tabularium* (Hall of Records).

Events in the Roman Forum often affected the rest of the known world. Marcus Tullius Cicero's stirring speeches on the floor of the Curia in the 60s B.C. saved the Republic from a rebellion led by Catiline. Also at the Forum, in 27 B.C., the senate gave Augustus the powers that made him the first emperor of Rome. Romans went to the Forum to hear famous orators speak and to see the valuables seized after distant battles.

In Rome's earliest days, the Forum area was a swamp used as a cemetery by the people of surrounding villages. The Etruscans turned these villages into the city of Rome and drained the marshes, probably during the 500s B.C. Residents built shops and temples around the edges of the Forum area. The Forum became the civic and legal center of Rome by the mid-100s B.C., and the merchants moved their shops to other parts of the city.

The Germanic peoples who invaded Rome in the A.D. 400s did not destroy the Forum. But its buildings gradually crumbled after the fall of Rome, and people came to call it *Cow Plain* because it had become so desolate. Excavations have since uncovered many of the ancient columns and arches. Rome had other forums, some with architecture as outstanding as that of the Roman Forum. Several emperors named forums in their own honor. But only the first forum was called *Forum Romanum* (Roman Forum).

AN AQUEDUCT is an artificial channel through which water is conducted to the place where it is used. The materials used for aqueduct construction may be masonry, concrete, cast iron, steel, or wood. Some aqueducts are tunnels dug through rocks, and others are canals in the earth. In many aqueducts, the outlet is so much lower than the water source that gravity alone carries the water. Where gravity is insufficient, the water is forced through the aqueduct by pumps.

As cities and industries grow, they require more water, and more aqueducts must be built. Such modern conveniences as commercial air conditioners require large quantities of water. Aqueducts also supply water to dry lands that must be irrigated to produce crops.

Ancient aqueducts. It is not known when or where the first aqueducts were built. In ancient times, Jerusalem used a leaky aqueduct made of a series of limestone blocks in which 15-inch (38-centimeter) holes had been drilled by

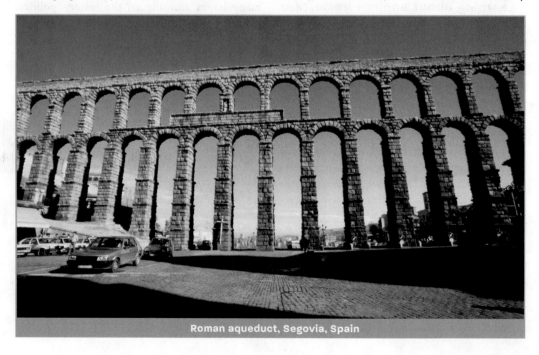

Roman aqueduct, Segovia, Spain

hand. The Greeks built masonry conduits to bring water to their cities, and even bored tunnels by hand. One of these tunnels, 4,200 feet (1,280 meters) long, was built by Athens 2,500 years ago. Most aqueducts of ancient times were built of stone, brick, or *pozzuolana*, a mixture of limestone and volcanic dust.

The city of Rome had many aqueducts and was the only ancient city reasonably supplied with water. The first person in charge of the Roman waterworks was Marcus Agrippa, who was appointed water commissioner in 33 B.C. By A.D. 97, nine aqueducts brought about 85 million gallons (322 million liters) of water a day from mountain springs. Later, five additional aqueducts were built. About 200 cities in the Roman colonies had aqueducts. One famous Roman aqueduct, the Pont du Gard, still stands across a river near Nimes, France.

Later aqueducts. Only a few new aqueducts were built until the Middle Ages. Late in the 1500s, an aqueduct was built for the English town of Plymouth by Sir Francis Drake, then mayor. It was called the *River Leet,* and was an open channel 24 miles (39 kilometers) long. London had no aqueduct until 1609 when the aqueduct called *New River* was built, bringing water 38 miles (61 kilometers) to London.

Present-day aqueducts. Costly bridges to carry water across rivers and valleys are no longer necessary. They have been replaced by pipe through which water is carried across hilly country. Sections of pipe called *inverted siphons* curve downward to pass beneath streams and other low places in the aqueduct's course.

One of the first great modern aqueducts was the first Croton Aqueduct, built by New York City in 1842. It was made of masonry lined with brick. Iron pipes carried water across the Harlem River over a viaduct. During the late 1800s, other cities, especially those of Britain, built large aqueducts. These cities included Birmingham, Glasgow, Liverpool, and Manchester.

Many of the world's greatest aqueducts were built in the early 1900s. The Catskill Aqueduct, completed in 1913 for New York City, extends 120 miles (193 kilometers). The Colorado Aqueduct, in southern California, was completed in 1939. It carries water through 29 tunnels across the desert from the Colorado River.

In 1973, a 685-mile (1,102-kilometer) aqueduct was completed in California. Other noted aque-

Hadrian's Wall

ducts in the United States include the Hetch-Hetchy (O'Shaughnessy), which supplies San Francisco, and those of Denver, Boston, and Tulsa. One of the most noted aqueducts is the Apulian Aqueduct of southern Italy. Other major aqueducts include those of Winnipeg, Canada, and Rio de Janeiro, Brazil.

ROMAN WALLS were barriers that the Romans built where no natural territorial boundaries existed. By A.D. 100, they had built a line of walls in what is now Romania and Germany. They later built Hadrian's Wall and the Antonine Wall along the northern edge of the province of Britain. These walls were named for two Roman emperors, Hadrian and Antoninus Pius, and are the most famous Roman walls. The walls discouraged raids and revolts. But their main purpose was to remind the tribes on both sides that the Romans were masters. The walls also made it easier for the Romans to control trade and to collect taxes.

Hadrian's Wall was built in the A.D. 120s. It extended 73 miles (117 kilometers), from the mouth of the River Tyne to the Solway Firth. Parts still stand. The wall was about 10 feet (3 meters) wide at its base and 20 feet (6 meters) high. For half its length, it was all stone. The rest was stone and turf. Small forts, called *milecastles,* stood about 1 Roman mile (about 0.9 mile or 1.5 kilometers) apart along the wall, with small watch towers between the forts about every ⅓ Roman mile (0.3 mile or 0.5 kilometer). A ditch lay in front of the wall, with a wider ditch 10 feet (3 meters) deep behind it.

The Antonine Wall was built in the A.D. 140s, north of Hadrian's Wall. It was a simpler wall, made of turf, and it stretched for 37 miles (60 kilometers).

The Romans allowed Hadrian's Wall to decay until 211, when they could no longer defend the Antonine Wall. Then they rebuilt Hadrian's Wall carefully. They rebuilt it twice more in the 300s, and defended it until nearly 400.

ROMAN DRAMA.

After the 200s B.C., Greek drama declined and leadership in the art began to pass to Rome. Today, Greek drama is much more highly regarded than Roman drama, which for the most part imitated Greek models. Roman drama is important chiefly because it influenced later playwrights, particularly during the Renaissance. William Shakespeare and the other dramatists of his day knew Greek drama almost entirely through Latin imitations of it.

In Rome, tragedy was less popular than comedy, short farces, pantomime, or such nondramatic spectacles as battles between gladiators. Roman theaters were adaptations of Greek theaters. The government supported theatrical performances as part of the many Roman religious festivals, but wealthy citizens financed some performances. Admission to theatrical performances was free and audiences were unruly in the brawling, holiday atmosphere.

The Roman stage was about 100 feet (30 meters) long and was about 5 feet (1.5 meters) above the level of the orchestra. The back wall represented a *facade* (building front) and probably had three openings. In comedies, these openings were treated as entrances to houses, and the stage became a street. Scholars disagree on whether the back wall was flat or three-dimensional.

Tragedy was introduced in Rome by Livius Andronicus in 240 B.C. But the dramatic works of only one Roman tragedian, Lucius Annaeus Seneca, still exist. Seneca's plays probably were never performed during his lifetime. His nine surviving plays were based on Greek originals. These plays are not admired today. However, they were extremely influential during the Renaissance.

Later western dramatists borrowed a number of techniques from Seneca. These techniques included the five-act form; the use of elaborate, flowery language; the theme of revenge; the use of magic rites and ghosts; and the device of the *confidant,* a trusted companion in whom the leading character confides.

Holl sculp.

SENECA.

Lucius Annaeus Seneca

Comedy. The only surviving Roman comedies are the works of Plautus and Terence. All their plays were adaptations of Greek New Comedy. Typical plots revolved around misunderstandings. These misunderstandings frequently were based on mistaken identity, free-spending sons deceiving their fathers, and humorous intrigues invented by clever slaves. Plautus and Terence eliminated the chorus from their plays, but they added many songs and much musical accompaniment. Plautus's humor was robust, and his plays were filled with farcical comic action. Terence avoided the broad comedy and exaggerated characters of Plautus' plays. Terence's comedies were more sentimental and more sophisticated and his humor more thoughtful. His six plays had a strong influence on later comic playwrights, especially Moliere in France in the 1600s.

Minor forms of drama were popular in Rome, but no examples of these forms exist today. The *mime*, a short and usually comic play, was often satiric and obscene. In the *pantomime*, a single dancer silently acted out stories to the accompaniment of choral narration and orchestra music.

The Roman theater gradually declined after the empire replaced the republic in 27 B.C. The minor dramatic forms and spectacles became more popular than regular comedy and tragedy. Many of these performances were sensational and indecent, and offended the early Christians. In the A.D. 400s, actors were excommunicated. The rising power of the church, combined with invasions from outside the Roman Empire, brought an end to the Roman theater. The last known performances in ancient Rome took place in A.D. 533.

MLA Citation

"Ancient Rome." *The Southwestern Advantage Topic Source.* Nashville: Southwestern. 2013.

DATA

Highlights in the History of Ancient Rome

753 B.C.	According to legend, Romulus and Remus founded Rome.
509 B.C.	The Romans drove out the Etruscans and established a republic.
264–146 B.C.	Rome began its expansion overseas by defeating Carthage in three Punic Wars.
27 B.C.	Augustus became the first Roman emperor.
A.D. 96–180	The Roman Empire reached its height of power and prosperity.
A.D. 395	The Roman Empire split into two parts—the West Roman Empire and the East Roman Empire.
A.D. 476	The last emperor of the West Roman Empire, Romulus Augustulus, was overthrown by a Germanic tribe.

DATA

Emperors of Rome

Name	Reign[1]	Name	Reign[1]	Name	Reign[1]
Augustus	27 B.C.–A.D. 14	Gordian I and		Maximinus	310–313
Tiberius	14–37	Gordian II	238	Constantius II	337–361
Caligula	37–41	Pupienus	238	Constantine II	337–340
Claudius	41–54	Balbinus	238	Constans	337–350
Nero	54–68	Gordian III	238–244	Julian	361–363
Galba	68–69	Philippus	244–249	Jovian	363–364
Otho	69	Decius	249–251	Valentinian I (W)	364–375
Vitellius	69	Gallus	251–253	Valens(E)	364–378
Vespasian	69–79	Aemilianus	253	Gratian (W)	367–383
Titus	79–81	Valerian	253–260	Valentinian II (W)	375–392
Domitian	81–96	Gallienus	253–268	Eugenius	392–394
Nerva	96–98	Claudius II	268–270	Theodosius I	379–395
Trajan	98–117	Aurelian	270–275		
Hadrian	117–138	Tacitus	275–276	**Emperors of the West**	
Antoninus Pius	138–161	Florian	276	Honorius	395–423
Marcus Aurelius	161–180	Probus	276–282	Valentinian III	425–455
Lucius Verus	161–169	Carus	282–283	Petronius Maximus	455
Commodus	180–192	Carinus	283–285	Avitus	455–456
Pertinax	193	Numerianus	283–284	Majorian	457–461
Didius Julianus	193	Diocletian(E)	284–305	Libius Severus	461–465
Septimius Severus	193–211	Maximian (W)	286–305	Anthemius	467–472
Caracalla	211–217	Constantius I (W)	305–306	Olybrius	472
Macrinus	217–218	Galerius	305–311	Glycerius	473–474
Elagabalus	218–222	Severus	306–307	Julius Nepos	474–475
Severus Alexander	222–235	Constantine I	306–337	Romulus Augustulus	475–476
Maximinus Thrax	235–238	Licinius	308–324		

[1] Rome was ruled by two emperors from 161 to 169 and by two or more emperors much of the time from 283 to 395. Sometimes, the empire's eastern and western parts were ruled by separate emperors. At other times, as many as four emperors ruled.

ADDITIONAL RESOURCES

Books to Read

Allan, Tony. *Exploring the Life, Myth, and Art of Ancient Rome.* Rosen Publishing Group, 2012.

Barchiesi, Alessandro, and Scheidel, Walter. *The Oxford Handbook of Roman Studies.* Oxford, 2010.

Harrison, Paul. *Ancient Roman Clothes.* PowerKids Press, 2010.

Harrison, Paul. *Ancient Roman Homes.* PowerKids Press, 2010.

Hinds, Kathryn. *Everyday Life in the Roman Empire.* Marshall Cavendish Benchmark, 2010.

Macdonald, Fiona. *Romans*. Sea-To-Sea Publications, 2011.

Platt, Richard. *The Romans*. Sea-To-Sea Publications, 2011.

Web Sites

A Multimedia Guide to Art of the Ancient World

http://www.artic.edu/cleo/

An interactive journey through the collection of ancient art at The Art Institute of Chicago. This Web site takes visitors on an expedition to the ancient cultures of Egypt, Greece, and Rome.

Maecenas: Images of Ancient Greece and Rome

http://wings.buffalo.edu/AandL/Maecenas/

Extensive collection of photographs of ancient Roman ruins in France and in Italy, including Rome, Pompeii, and Herculaneum, from a classics professor at the State University of New York at Buffalo.

Roman Gladiatorial Games

http://depthome.brooklyn.cuny.edu/classics/gladiatr/

Information on the fighters, history, and culture of the games from the Brooklyn College Classics Department.

Table of Contents (The Vatican Library and Renaissance Culture)

http://lcweb.loc.gov/exhibits/vatican/toc.html

Information about Rome, Italy, with links to other on-line resources.

The Roman Empire in the First Century

http://www.pbs.org/empires/romans/

A companion Web site to a PBS special on ancient Rome.

Search Strings

Architecture

ancient rome architecture arch concrete (25,100)

architecture ancient rome founded greeks arch concrete Pantheon (21,900)

roman architecture ancient founded greeks pantheon arch concrete (2,630)

Amphitheaters

ancient rome gladiators trained fighters amphitheaters (897)

gladiators ancient rome amphitheaters slaves prisoners citizens (845)

gladiators ancient rome amphitheaters (41,400)

Public Baths

ancient rome public baths thermae (19300)

public bathhouses ancient rome bathe exercise socialize (535)

public bathhouses ancient rome bathe exercise socialize thermae (73)

Roman Empire

ancient roman empire geography height (114,000)

roman empire ancient geography countries size (38,100)

ancient roman empire size systematically conquered unite (95,300)

Russia

Russia is the largest country in area in the world. It is almost twice as large as Canada. As a republic in the Union of Soviet Socialist Republics (USSR), also called the Soviet Union, from 1922 to 1991, Russia was part of one of the world's superpowers. In 1991, the Communist Party lost power, the Soviet Union broke up, and Russia established its own new government and economic system. Moscow is Russia's capital and largest city.

HOT topics

Cold War
Contributions to the Arts
Russian Rulers
Russia's Climate and Land Regions

HOT topics

Cold War. Cold War is the term used to describe the tension-filled opposition between Communist nations (the USSR and its Communist allies, known as the Eastern bloc) and non-Communist nations (the United States and its democratic allies, known as the Western bloc) from 1945 to 1991. The late 1940s and 1950s were an especially intense period of mistrust between the two blocs; however, during the 1960s, alliances within both blocs began to shift. Economic developments in some countries, especially Japan and West Germany, caused major shifts in the struggle for power. During the 1970s, peace negotiations and diplomatic relations between the blocs began to emerge. However, in 1979, the invasion of Afghanistan by the Soviet Union caused tensions to rise again until the signing of an arms-control agreement and the withdrawal of troops in the late 1980s. The break up of the Soviet Union in 1991 ended the Cold War.

HOT topics

Contributions to the Arts.

Russian authors such as Anton Chekhov, Fyodor Dostoevsky, and Leo Tolstoy wrote literature masterpieces. Chekhov's most famous works are four plays he wrote: *The Sea Gull, Uncle Vanya, The Three Sisters*, and *The Cherry Orchard*. Dostoevsky's greatest novels included *Crime and Punishment, The Idiot, The Possessed*, and *The Brothers Karamazov*. Leo Tolstoy's greatest works were *War and Peace* and *Anna Karenina*. Russia's greatest composers included Modest Mussorgsky, Nikolai Rimsky-Korsakov, and Peter Ilich Tchaikovsky. Among other works, Tchaikovsky gave us his six symphonies, the *1812 Overture*, and music for three ballets—*Swan Lake, The Sleeping Beauty*, and *The Nutcracker*. Valuable contributions by Russian artists were also made in the fields of architecture, ballet, and painting.

The Kremlin and the Moscva River at sunset

Russian Rulers.

From czars to empresses to presidents, Russia has had some extraordinary rulers. Ivan the Terrible, Peter the Great, Catherine the Great, Joseph Stalin, Mikhail Gorbachev, and Vladimir Putin are just a few of the colorful Russian rulers who made significant contributions, both good and bad, to Russian history.

Russia's Climate and Land Regions.

Russia is a land of extreme climates. The land is divided into four regions or zones that form horizontal belts across the country. From north to south, they are the tundra, the forest zone, the steppes, and the semi-desert and mountainous zone.

TRUE or FALSE?

Russia's economy and way of life never fully recovered after the breakup of the Soviet Union.

Catherine the Great

THE BASICS

Russia is the world's largest country in area. It is almost twice as big as Canada, the second largest country. From 1922 until 1991, Russia was the most important republic in the Soviet Union, which was the most powerful Communist country in the world. The Soviet Union broke apart in 1991. After the breakup, Russia set up new political, legal, and economic systems.

Russia extends from the Arctic Ocean south to the Black Sea and from the Baltic Sea east to the Pacific Ocean. It covers much of the continents of Europe and Asia. Moscow is the capital and largest city of Russia. St. Petersburg, on the coast of the Baltic Sea, is Russia's chief seaport.

Most of Russia's people are ethnic Russians—that is, descendants of an early Slavic people called the Russians. More than 100 minority nationalities also live in Russia. Approximately three-fourths of the people make their homes in urban areas. Russian cities have better schools and healthcare facilities than the rural areas do. However, the cities suffer from such urban problems as overcrowding, crime, and environmental pollution.

Russia has abundant natural resources, including vast deposits of petroleum, natural gas, coal, and iron ore. However, many of these reserves lie far from settled areas. Russia's harsh, cold climate makes it difficult to take advantage of many of the country's valuable resources.

Map of Russia

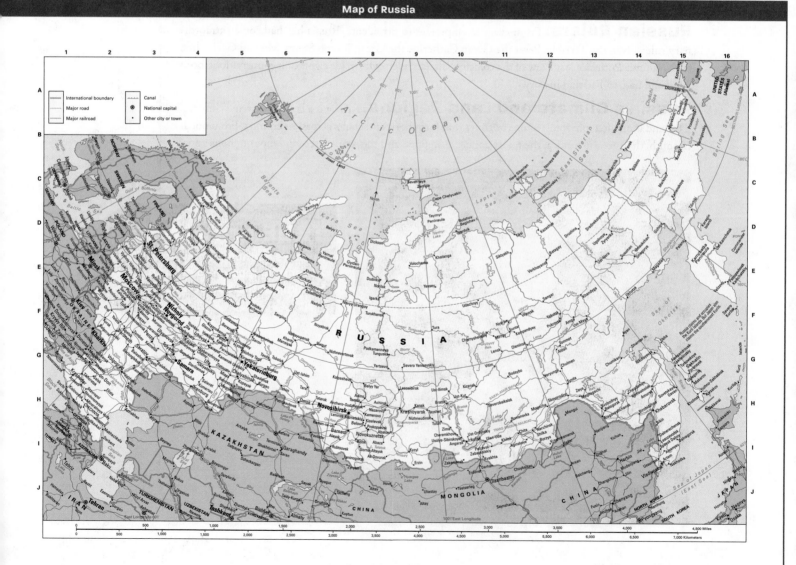

Russia traces its history back to a state that emerged in Europe among the East Slavs during the 800s. Over time, large amounts of territory and many different peoples came under Russian rule. For hundreds of years, *czars* (emperors) and empresses ruled Russia. They had almost complete control over most aspects of Russian life. Under these rulers, the country's economic development lagged behind the rapid industrial progress that began in Western Europe in the 1700s. Most of the people were poor, uneducated peasants.

Russia made many great contributions to the arts during the 1800s. Such authors as Anton Chekhov, Fyodor Dostoevsky, and Leo Tolstoy wrote masterpieces of literature. Russian composers, including Modest Mussorgsky, Nikolai Rimsky-Korsakov, and Peter Ilich Tchaikovsky, created music of lasting greatness. Russians also made valuable artistic contributions in the fields of architecture, ballet, and painting.

Opposition to the czars' absolute power increased during the late 1800s and the early 1900s. Revolutionaries overthrew the Russian government in 1917. The next year, Russia became the Russian Soviet Federative Socialist Republic (RSFSR).

In 1922, the RSFSR and three other republics established a new nation called the Union of Soviet Socialist Republics (USSR), also known as the Soviet Union. The RSFSR became the largest and most influential republic of the Soviet Union, which included 15 republics by 1956. In 1991, Communist rule in the Soviet Union collapsed, and the country broke apart. Russia and most of the other republics formed a new, loose federation called the Commonwealth of Independent States.

After the breakup of the Soviet Union, Russia entered a transitional period. The Communist leaders of the Soviet Union had controlled all aspects of the country's economy and government. Russia's new national government worked to move the country from a state-controlled economy to one based on private enterprise. The government also began to establish new political and legal systems in Russia.

Government

National government. In 1992—shortly after the Soviet Union broke up—Russia established a *transitional* (temporary) government headed by Boris N. Yeltsin. Yeltsin had been elected president of the RSFSR in 1991. After the breakup of the Soviet Union, Yeltsin continued to serve as

Boris Yeltsin (front center) meeting with the Federal Assembly

president of Russia until he resigned in 1999. In December 1993, Russia adopted a new constitution that established a permanent government.

The president of Russia is the government's chief executive, head of state, and most powerful official. The president is elected by the people to serve a 6-year term. The president, with the approval of the lower house of parliament, appoints a prime minister to serve as head of government. The prime minister is the top-ranking official of the Council of Ministers (cabinet). The council carries out the operations of the government.

Russia's parliament, which is called the Federal Assembly, consists of a lower house known as the State Duma and an upper house called the Federation Council. The State Duma makes the country's laws. Legislation proposed by the Duma must be approved by the Federation Council and by the president before becoming law. However, the State Duma can override a veto by the Federation Council and send legislation directly to the president. The Federation Council approves government appointments and such presidential actions as the declaration of martial law and the use of armed forces outside of Russia.

Members of the State Duma are elected to 5-year terms by *proportional representation*. Under this method, each political party that receives at least 7 percent of the popular vote gets a number of seats determined by the percentage of the vote it receives. Members of the Federation Council are local government officials. They are not elected directly by the people. Half of the members are appointed by local governors. The other half are elected by local legislatures. All Russian citizens 18 years of age and older may vote in the country's elections.

Local government. Russia consists of dozens of federal administrative units. These include *oblasts* (regions), republics, autonomous *okrugs* (areas), *krais* (territories), autonomous oblasts, and federal cities. These divisions may contain smaller units called *raions* (districts). Councils called *soviets* manage local affairs in both urban and rural areas.

Many of the administrative units have taken more control over their own affairs since the breakup of the Soviet Union. Some have pressed for independence from Russia. However, in 2000, the president and the State Duma began passing measures designed to reassert federal control over local governments.

Politics. The Communist Party was the only legal political party in the Soviet Union until March 1990. At that time, the Soviet Constitution—which gave the Communist Party its broad powers—was amended. A loose coalition of political parties with a democratic platform, known as the Democratic Russia Movement, began to play a key role in the reform movement. The Democratic Russia Movement secured Yeltsin's victory in a free presidential election held in June 1991.

The collapse of the Soviet Union led to the end of the Democratic Russia Movement. Its component groups broke apart and developed into separate political parties. Since then, Russia's political landscape has constantly shifted. There are numerous political parties and coalitions, and power changes hands with each election.

After the 1993 parliamentary elections, Russia's Choice, now called Russia's Democratic Choice, held the most seats in the State Duma. This party favors reducing government control of the economy and other reforms. The Liberal Democratic Party, an extreme nationalist group, gained the second highest number of seats.

In the 1995 parliamentary elections, the Communist Party won the largest number of seats in the State Duma. As it did in the Soviet era, the Communist Party supports more government control of land and industries. Our Home Is Russia, a moderate reform party, gained the second highest number of seats in the State Duma.

In the 1999 parliamentary elections, the Communist Party again won the largest number of seats in the State Duma. A new political group called Unity won the second highest number of seats. Unity favored continuing the reforms begun by Yeltsin's administration. Surprisingly, Unity formed a coalition government with the Communists, who had opposed Yeltsin's reforms. The coalition was put together by Vladimir V. Putin, who had been named acting president of Russia in 1999 and was elected president in 2000.

Elections in 2003 gave a vast majority of seats to United Russia, a new party formed from Fatherland-All Russia and Unity. United Russia supported Putin's government. United Russia again won a vast majority of seats in Duma elections held in 2007 and 2011. Other political parties represented in the Duma include the Communists, the Liberal Democratic Party, and A Just Russia.

Courts. The former Soviet government had a political police system called the Committee on State Security, known as the KGB. The KGB could interfere with and influence the legal system, and major violations of human rights took place. The KGB no longer exists in Russia.

Today, Russia has two security agencies. The Federal Security Service handles internal security, and the Foreign Intelligence Service collects information from other countries. In addition, Russia's 1993 Constitution protects the civil rights of all Russian citizens. The *prosecutor-general*, who serves as the chief legal officer of Russia, is nominated by the president and is approved by the Federation Council.

Vladimir Putin

Russia's highest court is called the Constitutional Court. This court, which was established in 1992, rules on the constitutionality of the country's laws. Russia's local courts are called *people's courts.*

Armed forces. The Soviet Union had the largest armed forces in the world. About 4 million people served in its army, navy, and air force. When the Soviet Union collapsed, command of its armed forces passed to the Commonwealth of Independent States. Several former republics—including Russia—said they would also create their own armed forces. In 1992, Russia began to form its own armed forces and absorbed some of the former Soviet forces. About 1 million people serve in Russia's armed forces. Russian men must serve 1 year in the military. Women may volunteer to serve.

People

The people of Russia are distributed unevenly throughout the country. The vast majority live in the western—or European—part of Russia. The more rugged and remote areas to the east are sparsely inhabited.

Ancestry. More than 80 percent of Russia's people are of Russian ancestry. These ethnic Russians make up the largest group of Slavic peoples. Members of more than 100 other nationality groups also live in Russia. The largest groups include Tatars (or Tartars); Ukrainians; Chuvash; Bashkirs; Belarusians; Mordvins; Chechen; Germans; Udmurts; Mari; Kazakhs; Avars; Armenians; and Jews, who are considered a nationality group in Russia. Many of them live in Russia's autonomous territories. Remote parts of the Far North are sparsely inhabited by small Siberian groups, including Aleuts, Chukchi, Inuit (also called Eskimos), and Koryaks. These northern peoples differ from one another in ancestry and language, but they share a common way of life shaped by the harsh, cold climate.

The government of the Soviet Union had granted special political and economic privileges to Russians who were loyal to the Communist Party. It repressed the distinctive cultures of other nationalities and did not always uphold their rights. This policy sharpened resentment among some peoples. Today, pride in their culture and the desire for greater independence are growing among the members of many nationalities, including Russians.

Ethnic Russians are descended from Slavs who lived in eastern Europe several thousand years ago.

Over time, migration split the Slavs into three subgroups—the East Slavs, the West Slavs, and the South Slavs. The Russians trace their heritage to the first East Slav state, Kievan Rus, which emerged in the 800s.

Kievan Rus suffered repeated invasions by Asian tribes, including the Pechenegs, Polovtsians, and Mongols. The Mongol invasions forced some people to migrate to safer, forested regions near present-day Moscow. Moscow became an important Russian state in the 1300s. This area has remained at the heart of Russia ever since. But people of many ethnic groups have lived in Russia, especially since the 1500s, when extensive expansion and colonization began.

Language. Russian is the official language of Russia. Spoken Russian sounds fairly uniform from one end of the country to the other. Nevertheless, the language has three major regional accents— northern, southern, and central. The small differences rarely interfere with communication among Russian speakers. Russian is written in the Cyrillic alphabet. Many minority nationality groups in Russia have their own language and speak Russian as a second language.

Way of Life

The government of the Soviet Union controlled many aspects of life in the country. It exerted great influence over religion, education, and the arts. The independence of Russia following the breakup of the Soviet Union brought greater freedom and triggered many other changes in the lives of the people.

City life. About three-fourths of Russia's people live in urban areas. Approximately 35 cities in Russia have populations over 500,000. Two of Rus-

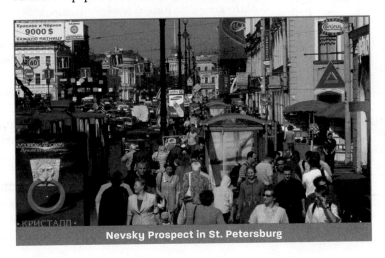

Nevsky Prospect in St. Petersburg

Daily life in Chechnya

sia's cities—Moscow and St. Petersburg—each have more than 4 million inhabitants.

Some Russian cities remain crowded. Beginning in the 1930s, large numbers of people migrated from the countryside to urban areas. During World War II (1939–1945), bombs destroyed many houses and other buildings. These circumstances combined to create a severe housing shortage in Russian cities. Many families had to share kitchen and bathroom facilities. Although the situation has greatly improved, millions of city dwellers live in small apartments in high-rise buildings. Single-family houses are more common in small towns and in the older neighborhoods of many cities. Some of these dwellings lack indoor plumbing and other modern conveniences. At the same time, Russia's newly wealthy inhabit luxury apartments and large homes.

Shortages of food, services, and manufactured goods have been common features of city life in Russia. The shift toward capitalism that began in the 1990s has not yet cured the shortages. Even when goods become available, they are often too expensive for many people to afford. Russian cities also face such urban problems as crime and environmental pollution.

Rural life. About one-fourth of the Russian population lives in rural areas. Single-family housing is common in these areas, but the Soviet government built many city-style apartment buildings. In the most remote areas of Russia, some homes lack gas, plumbing, running water, and electric power. In addition, the quality of education, health care, and cultural life is lower than in the cities. Rural life is changing, however. Rural stores, for example, have a wider selection of goods available than they once offered.

When Russia was part of the Soviet Union, most rural people worked on huge farms run by the government. After the Soviet Union collapsed, Russia began to break up these farms. New laws allow people to withdraw from the government farms and set up private farms.

Clothing. Most people in the Soviet Union wore plain clothing. Stores offered little variety in styles, and most people had a limited number of outfits. In the 1970s, consumers began to demand greater variety. They preferred to buy imported clothing whenever it was available. As a result, Soviet clothing manufacturers began to pay more attention to style and quality.

Now that Russia has opened its markets, stylish clothing made in Russia and in other parts of the world has become more widely available. Many young people dress fashionably. However, fashionable clothing is expensive. Russia's harsh winters affect styles.

Traditional Russian clothing consists of colorfully embroidered shirts and blouses, embroidered headwear, and shoes woven from *bast*, a tough fiber from the bark of certain trees. Rural dwellers wore these costumes on special occasions, such as weddings and holidays. The traditional costume is rarely worn today, however.

Food and drink. The traditional Russian diet is hearty. Eating habits are changing, however, as more people turn to convenience and fast foods. Beef, chicken, pork, and fish are popular main dishes. The most commonly eaten vegetables include beets, cabbage, carrots, cucumbers, onions, potatoes, radishes, and tomatoes. Russians are fond of soups, breads, and dairy products. They also consume large quantities of sugar. Frying remains a widespread method of preparing food.

Many Russian dishes are popular around the world. They include *blinis* (thin pancakes served with smoked salmon or other fillings and sour cream) and *beef Stroganoff* (sautéed beef strips with onions, mushrooms, and a sour cream sauce). Other favorite dishes include *borscht* (beet soup) and *piroshki* (baked or fried dumplings filled with meat and cabbage).

Typical breakfast foods in Russia include eggs, porridge, sausages, cheese, bread, butter, and jam. Most of the people eat their main meal at midday. It consists of a salad or appetizer; soup; meat or fish with potatoes or *kasha* (cooked buckwheat); and dessert, such as stewed fruit or pastries. In the evening, most Russians eat a light supper.

Russians drink large quantities of tea, but coffee has become popular, especially among urban Russians. *Kvass*, a beer-like beverage made from fermented black bread, is especially popular in summer. Russians also enjoy soft drinks, juices, and mineral water.

Vodka is Russia's trademark alcoholic beverage. Russians also drink wine, champagne, cognac, beer, and other alcoholic beverages. Alcohol abuse has been and remains a major social problem in Russia.

Health care in the Soviet Union was free. The Russian government remains committed to meeting the basic health care needs of its people. An insurance program to finance health care was introduced in 1993. A private health care sector has begun to grow. Russia has many doctors, nurses, and health care facilities. However, tight government budgets for health care, shortages of medicines and equipment, low wages for health care providers, and bureaucracy continue to create problems. Conditions in rural areas are worse than in the cities.

Recreation. Russians enjoy watching television, reading, playing chess, seeing motion pictures and plays, visiting museums, walking, and taking part in sports. The government actively promotes athletic activities, especially team sports. Soccer is the most popular participant and spectator sport in Russia. Other popular sports include gymnastics, basketball, and such winter sports as hockey, ice skating, and skiing. Tennis is growing in popularity.

Russia has many athletic clubs, stadiums, recreational centers, and other sporting facilities. Schools provide physical education at all levels. There are also special sports camps and clubs for children and adults.

The people of Russia are avid nature lovers, and they enjoy spending time in the countryside. Many

Russians have country cottages called *dachas*. There, they garden, hike, bicycle, swim, fish, gather mushrooms, and take part in other outdoor activities.

The majority of Russia's people vacation in the summer. Price increases, an end to government support, and ethnic unrest have made vacationing away from home more difficult for many Russians. However, resort areas along the Black Sea, the Baltic Sea, and the Volga River—and in Siberia—remain popular destinations.

Religion. The Russian Orthodox Church is the largest religious denomination in the country. January 7, the Russian Orthodox Christmas, is a national holiday. In addition to Russian Orthodoxy, religions that have full freedom in Russia include Buddhism, Islam, Judaism, and certain Christian denominations. These religions enjoy full freedom because they were recognized by the state prior to the fall of the Soviet Union.

Religions that were not registered in Russia prior to the fall of the Soviet Union face certain restrictions. Many of these religions conduct intense recruiting efforts in Russia. Restricted religions include Baptists, Mormons, Pentecostals, Roman Catholics, and Seventh-day Adventists. These groups must register annually for 15 years before being allowed to participate in such activities as publishing religious literature and operating religious schools. However, the Russian government has not strictly enforced the law.

Education. The Soviet government controlled education and considered it a major vehicle of social advancement. As a result, almost all Rus-

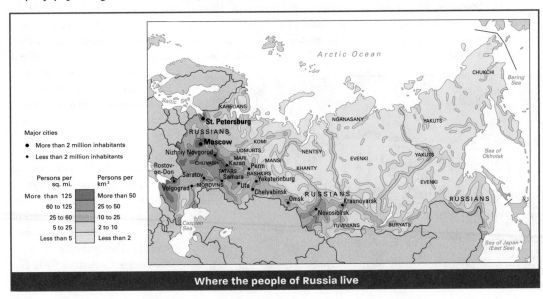

Where the people of Russia live

sians can read and write. Today, public education in Russia remains free for all citizens. New private schools are also opening. The Soviet government had banned such schools. Russian educators are changing the school curriculum to better prepare students for the new economy. They are also trying to satisfy the needs of Russia's nationality groups.

All children attend school for 11 years, from age 6 to 17. Elementary education includes nine primary and intermediate grades. When pupils finish ninth grade, they may choose to complete their schooling by enrolling in a secondary school or vocational school. The secondary schools emphasize science and mathematics. They also teach language, literature, history, social sciences, and physical education. English is the most widely taught foreign language. The vocational schools prepare young people for careers as technicians or in various branches of industry and agriculture.

Starting with the intermediate grades, pupils must pass annual exams to advance to the next grade. Students who pass a national examination upon the completion of secondary school receive a certificate, and those

who score well also get a gold or silver medal. Schools use a number grading scale of 1 to 5, with 5 being the highest.

Many gifted children attend special schools. These schools stress individual subjects such as mathematics or physics, languages, or the arts. Russia also has schools for children with physical or learning disabilities.

Students must pass an entrance exam to be admitted to a university or institute of higher education. Russia has hundreds of institutions of higher education equivalent to colleges and universities. Important universities include Lomonosov Moscow State University and St. Petersburg State University.

Museums and libraries.
The people of Russia spend more time in museums than do the people of the United States or most European countries. Russia has hundreds of museums. The State Historical Museum in Moscow is the country's chief historical museum. Several museums deal with the Russian Revolution. They include Moscow's State Central Museum of Contemporary History of Russia, commonly called the Revolution Museum. The Hermitage Museum in St. Petersburg has one of

the largest art collections in the world.

Russia has thousands of libraries. Most towns and large villages have a public library. There are also libraries that specialize in particular subjects and libraries run by factories, schools, labor unions, and professional and civic organizations. The Russian State Library in Moscow is the largest library in Russia. Other major libraries in Moscow include the All-Russian State Library of Foreign Literature, the Institute of Scientific Information for the Social Sciences of the Russian Academy of Sciences, the State Historical Public Library, and the library at Lomonosov Moscow State University. St. Petersburg is home to the National Library of Russia and the Library of the Russian Academy of Sciences.

The Arts

The arts in Russia date back to the earliest days of the country. But Russian artists did not produce internationally recognized works in many fields until the early 1800s. Throughout much of the 1800s and the early 1900s, Russia became an international leader in classical music, ballet, drama, and literature. Several Russian painters and sculptors also gained worldwide fame.

This section discusses Russian architecture, music, ballet, painting, and sculpture.

Architecture in Russia has been shaped by religious and Western influences combined with local traditions. About 988, Grand Prince Vladimir I, ruler of the state of Kievan Rus, was converted to the Byzantine (Eastern Orthodox Christian) faith. For hundreds of years, Russian archi-

The Hermitage Museum

tecture reflected the influence of the Byzantine style. The most important structures were churches, which had distinctive onion-shaped domes. The best-known Byzantine church is St. Basil's Cathedral in Moscow, built by Czar Ivan IV (also called Ivan the Terrible) from 1555 to 1560.

In 1682, Peter I, also known as Peter the Great, became czar. Peter introduced Western European artistic styles into Russia. He founded the city of St. Petersburg in 1703 and brought Western European architects and artists to help design it. Many of the buildings dating from his reign and through the mid-1700s were designed in the Western European Baroque style by Italian and French architects. A famous example is the Great Palace, which was begun in the early 1700s at Peterhof (now Petrodvorets), near St. Petersburg.

Among the most widely recognized architectural works in Russia are the buildings within the enclosed fortress in Moscow called the Kremlin. The Kremlin includes churches, palaces, and other buildings erected from the late 1400s to the mid-1900s. Some Kremlin buildings house Russia's government, and others serve as museums.

Music. Until the mid-1700s, Russian music consisted almost entirely of vocal music sung in church worship services and of folk music, which was also mainly vocal. Nonreligious music began to flower during the reign of Elizabeth, the empress of Russia from 1741 to 1762. She established the Academy of Arts in 1757, which taught music. Italian opera became popular during her reign. The popularity of music in Russia expanded further during the reign of Catherine II, known as Catherine the Great, who ruled from 1762 to 1796. The earliest written collection of Russian folk songs appeared in four volumes published between 1776 and 1795.

Mikhail Glinka is credited with founding a distinctively Russian school of classical music in the early and middle 1800s. He blended folk songs and religious music into his works and also introduced subjects from Russian history. His most influential work is probably his second opera, *Ruslan* and *Lyudmila* (1842), based on a fairy tale written by the Russian poet Alexander Pushkin.

By the late 1800s, Russian music flourished. Such composers as Modest Mussorgsky, Nikolai

Icons painted in the Annunciation Cathedral

Rimsky-Korsakov, Peter Ilich Tchaikovsky, and Alexander Borodin wrote operas and instrumental music. Much of their work was based on Russian history and folklore. In the early 1900s, Sergei Rachmaninoff and Igor Stravinsky gained international fame for their musical compositions. Stravinsky wrote several influential ballet scores, including *The Firebird* (1910), *Petrouchka* (1911), and *The Rite of Spring* (1913).

Ballet. Russian ballet became internationally famous starting in the mid-1800s. The leading ballet companies, which continue to perform today, are the Kirov Ballet (formerly the Russian Imperial Ballet) of St. Petersburg and the Bolshoi Ballet of Moscow.

Painting and sculpture. Until the early 1900s, the most important Russian paintings were created for religious purposes. Russian artists decorated the interiors of churches with wall paintings and mosaics. Stylized paintings called *icons* were produced for many centuries. An icon is a religious painting considered sacred in Eastern Orthodox

Christianity. Icons were produced according to strict rules established by the church, and their style changed little over the years.

By the mid-1800s, Moscow and St. Petersburg had busy art schools. Russian artists also began to create paintings and sculptures on more varied subjects.

A burst of creativity in Russian art exploded during the years before the start of World War I in 1914. Russian artists were strongly influenced by the modern art movements emerging in Western Europe. The painters Marc Chagall, Alexei von Jawlensky, and Wassily Kandinsky eventually settled in Western Europe.

Artists who remained in Russia developed two major art movements, *Suprematism* and *Constructivism*. Both movements produced paintings that were *abstract*—that is, they had no recognizable subject matter. The leading Suprematist was Kasimir Malevich. The major Constructivists included Naum Gabo, Antoine Pevsner, and Vladimir Tatlin.

Major uses of land in Russia

Land and Climate

Russia is the largest country in the world. It has an area of 6,601,669 square miles (17,098,242 square kilometers), almost twice that of Canada, the second largest country. A train trip between Moscow in the west and Vladivostok in the east takes seven days and passes through eight time zones, including that of Moscow.

Land regions. Many scientists divide Russia into four zones according to soil conditions and plant life, which are based mainly on climate. The zones form broad belts across Russia, and no sharp transitions separate them. From north to south, the zones are (1) the tundra, (2) the forest zone, (3) the steppes, and (4) the semi-desert and mountainous zone.

The tundra lies in the northernmost part of Russia. It is largely a treeless plain. The tundra has short summers and long, severe winters. About half the region has permanently frozen soil called *permafrost*. Few people live in this bleak area. Plant life consists chiefly of low shrubs, dwarf trees, and moss. Animals of the tundra include reindeer, Arctic foxes, ermines, hares, and lemmings. Waterfowl live near the Arctic Ocean in summer.

The forest belt lies south of the tundra. The northern part of this belt is called the *taiga*. It consists of *coniferous* (cone-bearing) trees, such as cedar, fir, pine, and spruce. This area has poor, ashy soil, known as *podzol*, that makes it largely unfit for agriculture. Farther south, the coniferous forests give way to mixed forests of conifers, aspen, birch, elm, maple, oak, and other species. The soils in this zone support agriculture in some areas, and the area has a mild, moist climate. Brown bears, deer, elk, lynx, reindeer, and smaller animals such as beavers, rabbits, and squirrels roam the forests.

Grassy plains called *steppes* stretch across Russia south of the forests. The northern part of the steppe zone consists of wooded plains and meadows. The massive southern part is largely a treeless prairie. The best soils in Russia—brown soil and black, rich soil called *chernozem*—are found there. Most of the steppe zone is farmland. Birds, squirrels, and mouse-like mammals called *jerboas* live in the steppes. Antelope inhabit the eastern steppes.

The semi-desert and mountainous zone, the southernmost zone in Russia, has diverse soils and climate due to variations in elevation. It includes the dry, semi-desert lowlands near the Caspian Sea, as well as the lush vegetation and mild climate of the Caucasus Mountains.

Temperatures in Oimyakon frequently reach -60 degrees Celsius and colder.

Geologists also divide Russia into five land regions that differ from the soil and vegetation zones. From west to east, the regions are (1) the European Plain, (2) the Ural Mountains, (3) the West Siberian Plain, (4) the Central Siberian Plateau, and (5) the East Siberian Uplands.

The European Plain makes up most of the European part of Russia. It is the most densely populated region in the country. The European Plain is predominantly flat, averaging about 600 feet (180 meters) above sea level. Most of the nation's industries are there, but the region is poor in natural resources. Forests cover much of the northern European Plain. The southern part is largely cropland. The plain is home to a variety of animal life. The Caucasus Mountains rise at the southern edge of the plain, between the Black and the Caspian seas. The mountains include 18,510-foot (5,642-meter) Mount Elbrus, the highest point in Europe.

The Ural Mountains form the traditional boundary between the European and Asian parts of Russia. These mountains, worn down by streams, reach an average height of only about 2,000 feet (610 meters). The middle and southern Ural Mountains are rich in deposits of iron, copper, and other metals. The middle section is the region's most heavily populated and highly industrialized area. Major cities in the region include Yekaterinburg and Chelyabinsk.

The West Siberian Plain is the largest level region in the world. This enormous plain covers more than 1 million square miles (2.6 million square kilometers) and rises no more than 500 feet (150 meters) above sea level. It is drained by the Ob River system, which flows northward into the Arctic Ocean. But drainage is poor, and the plain is marshy. The West Siberian Plain is rich in oil and natural gas deposits, and it is being developed rapidly. Cropland covers the southernmost part of the plain. The cities of Novosibirsk and Omsk are in this region.

The Central Siberian Plateau slopes upward toward the south from coastal plains along the Arctic Ocean. It has an average height of about 2,000 feet (610 meters). Streams cut deeply through the region. The Sayan and Baikal mountains rise more than 11,000 feet (3,350 meters) along the plateau's southern edge. Thick pine forests cover much of the Central Siberian Plateau, and its climate reaches extremes of heat and cold. The region has a wide variety of rich mineral deposits. Krasnoyarsk and Irkutsk are its largest cities.

The East Siberian Uplands are mainly a wilderness of mountains and plateaus. The mountains rise to 10,000 feet (3,000 meters) and form part of a series of ranges along the eastern coast of Asia and some offshore islands. About 25 active volcanoes are found on the Kamchatka Peninsula. The tallest volcano, snow-capped Klyuchevskaya, rises 15,584 feet (4,750 meters). The region has valuable mineral resources, but its harsh climate makes it difficult to tap them. Vladivostok on the Pacific Ocean and Khabarovsk on the Amur River are the region's most important cities.

An industrial plant near Lake Baikal

Rivers and lakes. Russia's many large rivers have served as important means of communication and commerce. The construction of canals further improved these activities.

The Lena River in Siberia, 2,734 miles (4,400 kilometers) long, is Russia's longest river. It empties into the Arctic Ocean. Other major rivers in Siberia include the Amur, Ob, and Yenisey rivers, all frozen seven to nine months a year. The Volga River is the longest river in European Russia. It originates in the Valdai Hills northwest of Moscow and flows 2,300 miles (3,700 kilometers) to the Caspian Sea. The Volga freezes for about three months each year. Other important rivers in European Russia include the Don and the Northern Dvina.

Russia has about 200,000 lakes. The Caspian Sea, a saltwater lake 92 feet (28 meters) below sea level, is the world's largest inland body of water. It touches the southern part of European Russia. Lake Ladoga, near St. Petersburg, covers 6,835 square miles (17,703 square kilometers). It is the largest lake entirely in Europe. Lake Baikal, near the Baikal Mountains, is the deepest lake in the world. It plunges 5,315 feet (1,620 meters) deep.

Climate. Russia is known for its long and bitter winters. The country's hostile climate helped stop various invaders during its history, including the large armies of Napoleon in 1812 and of Adolf Hitler in 1941 and 1942. In the Moscow region, snow covers the ground for about five months each year. In the northernmost part of Russia, snow abounds for eight to nine months a year. Half the land has permafrost beneath the surface. Russia's main cropland, in the southwest part of the country, has a short growing season and insufficient rainfall. Most of the coastal waters, lakes, and rivers freeze for much of the year.

Russia's weather varies from extremely cold to extremely hot. Northeastern Siberia is one of the coldest regions in the world. January temperatures there average below –50°F (–46°C). Temperatures as low as –90°F (–68°C) have been recorded. The average July temperature in this region is 60°F (16°C), but it can climb to nearly 100°F (38°C). No other part of the world registers such a wide range of temperatures.

Precipitation (rain, melted snow, and other forms of moisture) is light to moderate. The European Plain and parts of the East Siberian Uplands receive the most rain. Vast inland areas get little rain. The heaviest snowfalls—up to 4 feet (120 centimeters) of snow a year—occur in western and central Siberia.

Economy

Since the fall of the Soviet Union in 1991, Russia has worked to reform its economic system. The country has attempted to shift from a state-controlled economy to a market-driven economy.

In the Soviet Union, central government agencies planned almost all aspects of economic life. The government owned and controlled all factories and farms, and private businesses were illegal. Soviet leaders transformed Russia from a farming country into an industrial giant. Heavy industry—such as chemicals, construction, machine tools, and steel—developed rapidly. Government ministries set production quotas and told managers what to produce and to whom to sell their goods. This planning led to rapid industrial development and impressive economic gains. But central control also suppressed new ideas and discouraged quality.

When the Soviet Union collapsed in 1991, so did Russia's economy. The most immediate problem was shortages of many goods. To overcome this situation, the new Russian government removed Soviet-era controls from the economy. The government let businesses set prices for nearly all goods and services and dropped restrictions on imports and exports. It allowed the ruble to be exchanged for other currencies at international rates.

Russia's government also *privatized* (sold to companies or individuals) many state-owned enterprises. By 1997, privately owned businesses contributed more than half of the country's *gross domestic product* (GDP)—the total value of all goods and services produced yearly. However, privatization left a small number of wealthy Russians in control of many of the country's largest companies.

The reforms brought goods back to the shops, but prices skyrocketed. The Russian government struggled to get inflation and the country's budget deficit under control. In 1998, the country experienced a major financial crisis. The government could not pay its debts, and the value of the ruble plunged. In response, Russia's government began pursuing a more cautious economic policy. It managed the budget better, reduced public debt, and controlled inflation. As a result, the country's economy quickly recovered.

Russia's gross domestic product grew at a steady pace through most of the first decade of the 2000s.

This growth was driven by increasing exports of oil and metals and high world prices for these products. Demand for consumer products also grew, which helped Russia's domestic industries.

Russia benefits from a skilled labor force and abundant natural resources. However, the country has attracted only limited foreign investments because the prospects for business success remain poor. The economic problems of the 1990s led to a substantial decline in standard of living. Much of the population continues to live in poverty.

Natural resources. Russia is one of the richest countries in terms of natural resources. It has the world's largest forest reserves, enormous energy supplies, vast stretches of farmland, extensive mineral deposits, and many potential sources of hydroelectric power. Many of its resources, however, are far from the factories where they are put to use. Russia also has a wide variety of plant and animal life.

Manufacturing accounts for about 15 percent of both Russia's GDP and its economy. Much of Russia's manufacturing occurs in the Moscow area. Heavy industry remains the most highly developed sector of the Russian economy. The machine-building industry makes a variety of heavy machinery and electrical equipment. Russia is one of the world's leading automobile manufacturers. The country also manufactures aircraft, ships, spacecraft, tractors, and trains. The chemical industry produces chemical fibers, mineral fertilizers, petrochemicals, and soda ash. Most oil refining takes place in the Volga-Urals region. The construction materials industry is also important. Russia also manufactures electronics, processed foods, and textiles.

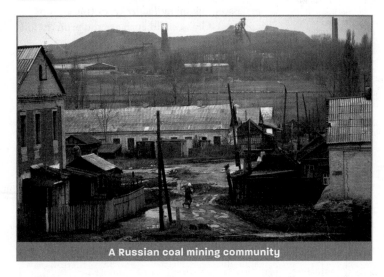

A Russian coal mining community

Agriculture. Russia has a large amount of farmland. But a short growing season, insufficient rainfall, and a lack of fertile soil make farming difficult. The Soviet Union's wasteful and inefficient system of state-run farms added to Russia's agricultural problems.

When the Soviet Union collapsed, there were about 15,000 large state-controlled farms in Russia. About half were state farms operated like government factories, called sovkhozy. Workers on *sovkhozy* received wages. The rest were collective farms called *kolkhozy*, which were government-controlled but managed in part by farmers.

The Russian government introduced a program to break up the state-controlled farms. The farms set up committees whose job it was to decide how to divide the farms into producer cooperatives or joint-stock companies. Many farms were reorganized. As agricultural land was privatized, some companies created large industrial farms.

Russian farmers grow many different crops. One of the main agricultural regions is the Black Earth Belt, which is a portion of the *steppes* (grassy plains) that stretches from the Ukrainian border to southwestern Siberia. This belt is famous for its dark, rich soil, known as *chernozem* (black earth). Other important farming regions include the Volga area, the northern Caucasus Mountains, and western Siberia.

Russia is one of the world's major grain producers. After years of needing to import grain during Soviet times, Russia has now become a grain exporter. Russia is one of the world's leading producers of barley, oats, potatoes, rye, sugar beets, sunflower seeds, and wheat. Russian farmers also grow many *fodder crops* (food crops for animals). Grasses and corn are the primary fodder crops.

Livestock breeding is another important part of Russian agriculture. Cattle, goats, hogs, and sheep are the livestock most commonly raised in the country.

Mining. Russia has vast amounts of most of the minerals used in modern industrial production. The country has abundant coal deposits and huge reserves of petroleum and natural gas. Other resources include calcium phosphate minerals and phosphorites, used in fertilizers, and diamonds.

Russia is a major producer of iron ore, which is mined primarily in the western and southern parts of the country. Russia is also a leading producer of nickel. Nickel is mined in the Kola Peninsula, southern Urals, and the Taymyr Peninsula. The country is also an important producer of cobalt, copper, gold, silver, tin, and tungsten. Other materials mined in Russia include lead, platinum, salt, and zinc. Bauxite, a material used in making aluminum, is mined in western Siberia.

Fishing industry. In the northern Barents Sea and the White Sea, Russian fishing crews catch blue whiting, cod, haddock, herring, and other fishes. Herring, pollock, and salmon are caught in the Pacific Ocean. Crews also fish in inland waterways, the Atlantic Ocean, and the Baltic and Black seas.

Caviar, the salted eggs of sturgeon, is a famous Russian delicacy. Many gourmets consider the caviar produced from sturgeon caught in the Caspian Sea to be the best in the world. However, overfishing has reduced the number of sturgeon in the Caspian to dangerously low levels.

Service industries are industries that produce services, not goods. Service industries account for about three-fifths of both Russia's GDP and its employment. In the former Soviet Union, these

Russian newspapers

industries were underdeveloped. Most service-industry workers were poorly trained and underpaid. They had little incentive to provide good service because their customers had few or no alternatives. Today, private economic activity in the service sector flourishes. Hotels, restaurants, and retail shops benefit from the tens of millions of tourists who visit Russia each year. Many Russians work in the government, hospitals, real estate, or schools.

Energy sources. Russia has enormous natural energy reserves, especially petroleum and natural gas. The country is one of the world's largest producers of petroleum, natural gas, and coal. Much of Russia's petroleum is found in western Siberia and the Volga-Ural Oil-Gas Region. Pipelines carry oil and natural gas from western Siberia to European Russia. Much of the coal is mined from the Kuznetsk Basin.

About two-thirds of Russia's electric power is generated from coal, natural gas, and oil. Hydroelectric plants also generate electric power. In addition, Russia also ranks as a major producer of nuclear power.

Trade. The Soviet Union traded mainly with Eastern European Communist countries, such as Bulgaria, Hungary, and Poland. Since the overthrow of the Communist regimes of Eastern Europe and the breakup of the Soviet Union, Russia's trading activity with those countries has declined. Russia's main trading partners are the other former Soviet republics, China, Finland, Germany, Italy, Japan, the Netherlands, Poland, and the United States. In 2012, after many years of negotiations, Russia joined the World Trade Organization (WTO). The WTO is a group that promotes international trade.

Russia exports more than it imports. Russia exports chemicals, machinery, metals, natural gas, petroleum, and wood and paper products. Major imports include chemicals, foods and beverages, motor vehicles, and machinery.

Transportation and communication. Because of Russia's vast size and harsh climate, transportation facilities and communications systems are unevenly distributed throughout the country. They are less developed than the transportation and communications networks of Western Europe, the United States, and Japan.

Truck transport has grown rapidly since the introduction of private enterprise. However, Russia's poorly developed highway network, combined with the country's vast size, make truck transport difficult and costly. Railroads still handle a large amount of freight transportation in Russia, but much of the system needs modernization. River transportation carries only a small percentage of Russia's freight traffic, because most rivers are frozen for much of the year.

Russia inherited its national airline, Aeroflot, from the Soviet Union. Aeroflot must now compete with new, privately owned companies.

Russia's most important seaports—Arkhangelsk, Kaliningrad, Murmansk, Nakhodka, St. Petersburg, and Vladivostok—handle a large portion of the country's foreign trade. However, the water at many Russian ports is frozen for many months of the year.

Public transportation is modern and inexpensive, but crowded. Several large cities, including Moscow, have clean, efficient subway systems. Buses, trams, and trolleys also operate in the cities. Bicycles are seen in large cities, but they are more common in rural and vacation areas. Horses and buggies can also be found in rural parts of Russia.

Following the downfall of the Soviet Union, Russia improved its telecommunications systems. Most Russians have access to at least basic telephone service. Cellular telephone service has become popular, especially in urban areas. Internet usage is expanding as more Russians gain access to computers.

Russia's government owns or controls most of the national television and radio networks and newspapers. Hundreds of daily newspapers and thousands of other periodicals are published in Russia. The government often attempts to control or silence broadcasters and publishers that criticize it.

History

Russia's unique geographic location astride both Europe and Asia has influenced its history and shaped its destiny. Russia never has been entirely an Eastern or a Western country. As a result, Russian intellectuals have long debated the country's development and contribution to world history.

This section traces the major developments of Russian history. In 1917, revolutionaries overthrew the Russian czarist government. They changed Russia's name to the Russian Soviet Federative Socialist Republic (RSFSR). In 1922, the RSFSR and three other republics formed a new nation called the Union of Soviet Socialist Republics (USSR), also known as the Soviet Union. The USSR broke apart in 1991, and Belarus, Russia, and Ukraine invited the other republics to join a federation called the Commonwealth of Independent States.

Portrait of Rurik making landfall

Early days. Beginning about 1200 B.C., the Cimmerians, a Balkan people, lived north of the Black Sea in what is now southern Ukraine. They were defeated about 700 B.C. by the Scythians, an Iranian people from central Asia. The Scythians controlled the region until about 200 B.C. They fell to the Sarmatians, another Iranian group. The Scythians and the Sarmatians lived in close contact with Greek colonies—later controlled by the Romans—along the northern coast of the Black Sea. They absorbed many Greek and Roman ways of life through trade, marriage, and other contacts.

Germanic tribes from the West, called the Goths, conquered the region about A.D. 200. The Goths ruled until about 370, when they were defeated by the Huns, a warlike Asian people. The Huns' empire broke up after their leader, Attila, died in 453. The Avars, a tribe related to the Huns, began to rule the region in the mid-500s. The Khazars, another Asian people, won the southern Volga and northern Caucasus regions in the mid-600s. They became Jews and established a busy trade with other peoples.

By the 800s, Slavic groups had built many towns in eastern Europe, including what became the European part of Russia. They had also developed an active trade. No one knows where the Slavs came from. Some historians believe they came in the 400s from what is now Poland. Others think the Slavs were farmers in the Black Sea region under Scythian rule or earlier. Slavs of what are now Belarus, Russia, and Ukraine became known as East Slavs.

The earliest written Russian history of the 800s is the *Primary Chronicle*, written in Kiev, probably in 1111. It says that quarreling Slavic groups in the town of Novgorod (now Velikiy Novgorod) asked a Viking tribe to rule them and bring order to the land. The Vikings were called the *Varangian Russes*. Historians who accept the *Primary Chronicle* as true believe that Russia took its name from this tribe. According to the *Primary Chronicle*, a group of related Varangian families headed by a prince named Rurik arrived in 862. Rurik settled in Novgorod, and the area became known as the "land of the Rus."

Many historians doubt that the Slavs of Novgorod invited the Vikings to rule them. They believe the Vikings invaded the region. Some historians claim the word *Rus*, from which Russia took its name, was the name of an early Slavic tribe in the Black Sea region. It is known, however, that the first state founded by East Slavs—called Kievan Rus—was established at present-day Kiev in the 800s. Kiev, now the capital of Ukraine, was an important trading center on the Dnieper River. Whether it had been developed by the Vikings is unclear.

The state of Kievan Rus. The *Primary Chronicle* states that Oleg, a Varangian, captured Kiev in 882 and ruled as its prince. During the 900s, the other *principalities* (regions ruled by a prince) of Kievan Rus recognized Kiev's major importance. Kiev lay on the main trade route connecting the Baltic Sea with the Black Sea and the Byzantine Empire. In addition, Kiev's forces defended Kievan Rus against invading tribes from the south and east. The ruler of Kiev came to be called *grand prince* and ranked above the other princes of Kievan Rus.

About 988, Grand Prince Vladimir I (*Volodymyr* in Ukrainian) became a Christian. At that time, the East Slavs worshiped the forces of nature. Vladimir made Christianity the state religion, and most people under his rule turned Christian. Vladimir later became a saint of the Russian Orthodox Church.

Several grand princes were strong rulers, but Kiev's power began to decrease after the mid-1000s. The rulers of other Kievan Rus principalities grew in power, and they fought many destructive wars. In Novgorod and a few other towns with strong local governments, the princes were driven out. Badly weakened by civil wars and without strong central control, Kievan Rus fell to huge armies of Mongols called *Tatars*, or *Tartars*, who swept across Russia from the east during the 1200s

Mongol rule. In 1237, Batu, a grandson of the conqueror Genghis Khan, led between 150,000 and 200,000 Mongol troops into Russia. The Mongols destroyed one Russian town after another. In 1240, they destroyed Kiev, and Russia became part of the Mongol Empire. It was included in a section called the Golden Horde. The capital of the Golden Horde was at Sarai, near what is now Volgograd.

Batu forced the surviving Russian princes to pledge allegiance to the Golden Horde and to pay heavy taxes. From time to time, the Mongols left their capital and wiped out the people of various areas because of their disloyalty. The Mongols also appointed the Russian grand prince and forced many Russians to serve in their armies. But they interfered little with Russian life in general. The Mongols were chiefly interested in maintaining their power and collecting taxes.

During the period of Mongol rule, which ended in the late 1400s, the new ideas and reforming spirit of the Renaissance were dramatically changing many aspects of life in Western Europe. But under Mongol control, Russia was to a great extent cut off from these important Western influences.

The rise of Moscow. In the early 1300s, Prince Yuri of Moscow married the sister of the Golden Horde's *khan* (ruler). Yuri was appointed the Russian grand prince about 1318. Mongol troops helped him put down threats to his leadership from other principalities. The Mongols also began letting the grand prince of Moscow collect taxes for them. This practice started with Ivan I (called the Moneybag) about 1330. Ivan kept some of the tax money. He bought much land and expanded his territory greatly. Other princes and *boyars* (high-ranking landowners) began to serve in Moscow's army and government. In addition, Ivan persuaded the chief bishop of the Russian Orthodox Church to remain in Moscow. Until then, Kiev had been the spiritual center of Russia.

Moscow grew stronger and richer as the Golden Horde grew weaker, chiefly because of struggles for leadership. In 1380, Grand Prince Dmitriy defeated a Mongol force in the Battle of Kulikovo, near the Don River. The victory briefly freed Moscow of Mongol control. The Mongols recaptured Moscow in 1382, but they no longer believed they could not be beaten.

During the late 1400s, Moscow became the most powerful Russian city. Ivan III (called Ivan the Great) won control of Moscow's main rival cities, Velikiy Novgorod and Tver, and great numbers of boyars entered his service. In 1480, Ivan made the final break from Mongol control by refusing to pay taxes to the Golden Horde. Mongol troops moved toward Moscow but turned back to defend their capital from Russian attack.

Ivan the Terrible. After the rise of Moscow, its grand prince came to be called *czar*. In 1547, Ivan IV, also known as Ivan the Terrible, became the first ruler to be crowned czar. Ivan made the power of the czar over all Russia complete.

Ivan was brutal, extremely suspicious, and perhaps, at times, insane. He formed a special police force and began a reign of terror in which he ordered the arrest and murder of hundreds of aristocrats. Ivan gave his victims' estates as payment to the *service gentry* (landowners serving in the army and government). He also established strict rules concerning the number of warriors and horses each landowner had to supply to the army. Ivan burned many towns and villages, and he killed church leaders who opposed him. In a fit of rage, Ivan even struck and killed his oldest son.

Ivan the Terrible

The number of service gentry increased rapidly. But their estates had no value unless the peasants remained on the land and farmed it. Ivan and later czars passed a series of laws that bound the peasants to the land as *serfs*. Serfdom became the economic basis of Russian power. The development of Russian serfdom differed sharply from changes occurring in Western Europe at the time. There, during the Renaissance, the growth of trade led to the use of money as royal payment. It also led to the disappearance of serfdom in Western Europe.

Ivan fought Tatars at Astrakhan and Kazan to the southeast, and he won their lands. Russian forces then crossed the Ural Mountains and conquered western Siberia. Ivan also tried to win lands northwest to the Baltic Sea, but he was defeated by Lithuanian, Polish, and Swedish armies.

The Time of Troubles developed because of a breakdown of the czar's power after Ivan's death. Fedor I, Ivan's second son, was a weak czar. His wife's brother, Boris Godunov, became the real ruler of Russia. Fedor's younger brother, Dmitriy, was found dead in 1591, and Fedor died in 1598 without leaving a male heir.

The *zemskii sobor* (land council), a kind of parliament with little power, elected Boris czar. But a man believed to be Gregory Otrepiev, a former monk, posed as Dmitriy. This *False Dmitriy* claimed Dmitriy had not died, and he fled to Lithuania to avoid arrest. In 1604, False Dmitriy invaded Russia with Polish troops. The invaders were joined by many discontented Russians. This invasion marked the beginning of the Time of Troubles. Russia was torn by civil war, invasion, and political confusion until 1613.

False Dmitriy became czar in 1605, but a group of boyars killed him the next year. Prince Basil Shuisky then became czar. In 1610, Polish invaders occupied Moscow. They ruled through a powerless council of boyars until 1612. Meanwhile, a new False Dmitriy and a number of other pretenders to the throne won many followers. Peasant revolts swept through Russia. Landowners and frontier people called Cossacks fought each other, and sometimes joined together to fight powerful aristocrats. The Polish control of Moscow led the Russians to unite their forces and drive out the invaders. They recaptured the capital in 1612.

The early Romanovs. After the Poles were defeated, there was no one of royal birth to take the throne. In 1613, the zemskii sobor elected Michael Romanov czar. The Romanov czars ruled Russia for the next 300 years, until the February Revolution of 1917 ended czarist rule.

During the 1600s, Russia annexed much of Ukraine and extended its control of Siberia eastward to the Pacific Ocean. During this same period, the Russian Orthodox Church made changes in religious texts and ceremonies. People called *Old Believers* objected to these changes and broke away from the church. This group still follows the old practices today.

Peter the Great. In 1682, a struggle for power resulted in the crowning of two half brothers—Peter I (later known as Peter the Great) and Ivan V—as co-czars. Both were children, and Ivan's sister Sophia ruled as regent (temporary ruler) until Peter's followers forced her to retire in 1689. Peter made close contact with the many Western Europeans living in Moscow and absorbed much new information from them. He came into full power in 1696, when Ivan died.

Peter was greatly influenced by ideas of commerce and government then popular in Western Europe. A powerful ruler, he improved Russia's military and made many important conquests. During Peter's reign, Russia expanded its territory to the Baltic Sea in the Great Northern War with Sweden. In 1703, Peter founded St. Petersburg on the Baltic, and he moved the capital there in 1712.

Peter the Great

After traveling throughout Europe, he introduced Western-style clothing, factories, and schools in Russia, and reorganized Russia's government to make it run more efficiently.

Peter forced Russia's nobility to adopt many Western customs. He also increased the czar's power over the aristocrats, church officials, and serfs. He dealt harshly with those who opposed these changes. Under Peter, the legal status of serfs further deteriorated.

Catherine the Great. After Peter's death in 1725, a series of struggles for the throne took place. The service gentry and the leading nobles were on opposite sides. Candidates for the throne who were supported by the service gentry won most of these struggles and rewarded their followers. The rulers increased the gentry's power over the serfs and local affairs. The gentry's enforced service to the state was gradually reduced. It was ended altogether in 1762. Later that year, Empress Catherine II, known as Catherine the Great, came to power.

Magnificent royal parties and other festivities, all in the latest Western fashion, took place during the 1700s. The arts were promoted, and many new schools were started, mainly for the upper classes. The Russian Imperial School of Ballet was founded, and Italian opera and chamber music were brought to Russia. It also became fashionable in Russia to repeat the newest Western ideas on freedom and social reform, especially during the rule of Catherine II, known as Catherine the Great. In 1767, Catherine called a large legislative assembly to reform Russian laws. However, the assembly achieved nothing.

The great majority of Russians remained in extreme poverty and ignorance during this period. In 1773 and 1774, the peasants' discontent boiled over in a revolt led by Emelian Pugachev, a Cossack. The revolt swept through Russia from the Ural Mountains to the Volga River. It spread almost to Moscow before being crushed by government troops. In 1775, Catherine further tightened the landowners' control over the serfs.

Under Catherine the Great, Russia rose to new importance as a major world power. In the late 1700s, Austria, Prussia, and Russia gradually divided Poland among themselves. Russia gained nearly all of Belarus, Lithuania, and Ukraine from Poland. In wars against the Ottoman Empire (based in present-day Turkey), Russia gained the

The Burning of Moscow in 1812, by Jean Charles Langlois

Crimea and other Ottoman lands. Catherine died in 1796. She was succeeded by her son, Paul.

Alexander I. Paul's five-year rule ended with his murder in 1801. Alexander I, Paul's son, became czar and talked about freeing the serfs, building schools for all young Russians, and even giving up the throne and making Russia a republic. He introduced several reforms, such as freeing many political prisoners and spreading Western ways and ideas. But he did nothing to lessen the czar's total power or to end serfdom. Alexander knew that Russia's military strength and its position as a major world power depended on income that was provided by serfdom. Under Alexander's rule, Russia continued to win territory from Persia, Sweden, and the Ottoman Empire.

In June 1812, Napoleon led the Grand Army of France into Russia. He wanted to stop Russian trade with the United Kingdom, France's chief enemy, and to halt Russian expansion in the Balkan region. The French swept forward and reached Moscow in September 1812. Most people had left the city, and Napoleon and his army entered easily.

Soon afterward, fire destroyed most of Moscow. Historians believe the Russians themselves set the fire. After 35 days, the French left the city because they feared they might not survive the approaching bitter Russian winter. They began a disastrous retreat with little food and under continual attack by the Russians. Of the estimated 600,000 French troops in Russia, about 500,000 died, deserted, or were captured. Russia then became a major force in the campaign by several European countries that defeated Napoleon.

Although Alexander had begun some reforms, harsh rule continued in Russia. Beginning in 1816, many young aristocrats became revolutionaries. They formed secret groups, wrote constitutions for Russia, and prepared to revolt. Alexander died in 1825, and Nicholas I became czar. In December of 1825, a group of revolutionaries, later called the *Decembrists*, took action. At the urging of the Decembrists, about 3,000 soldiers and officers gathered in Senate Square in St. Petersburg, and government troops arrived to face them. After several hours, the Decembrists fired a few shots. Government cannons ended the revolt by the Decembrists.

Nicholas I

 Nicholas I. The Decembrist revolt deeply impressed and frightened Nicholas. He removed aristocrats, whom he now distrusted, from government office and replaced them with professional military officers. He tightened his control over the press and education, reduced travel outside Russia, and prohibited organizations that might have political influence. He established six special government departments. These departments, which included a secret police system, handled important economic and political matters. Through the special departments, Nicholas avoided the regular processes of Russian government and increased his control over Russian life.

In spite of Nicholas's harsh rule, the period was one of outstanding achievement in Russian literature. Nikolai Gogol, Mikhail Lermontov, Alexander Pushkin, and others wrote their finest works. Fyodor Dostoevsky, Leo Tolstoy, and Ivan Turgenev launched their careers. Many educated Russians began to debate the values of Westernized Russian life against those of old Russian life. The pro-Western group argued that Russia must learn from the West and catch up with it economically and politically. The other group argued for the old Russian ways, including the czarist system, a strong church, and the quiet life of the Russian countryside.

Nicholas became known as the "policeman of Europe" because he sent troops to put down revolutions in Poland and Hungary. Nicholas also declared himself the defender of the Eastern Orthodox Churches and fought two wars with the Muslim Ottoman Empire. In the war of 1828 and 1829, Russia gained much territory around the Black Sea. Russia also won the right to move merchant ships through the straits connecting the Black Sea with the Mediterranean Sea. The Ottoman Empire controlled these straits.

In 1853, the Crimean War broke out between Russia and the Ottoman Empire. The United Kingdom and France, which objected to Russian expansion in the Black Sea region, aided the Ottomans. Russia was defeated and signed the Treaty of Paris in 1856. This treaty forced Russia to give up some of the territory it had taken earlier from the Ottomans, and the pact forbade warships on and fortifications around the Black Sea.

Expansion in Asia. After its defeat in the Crimean War, Russia began to expand in Asia. In the Far East, Russia won disputed territories from China. In 1858 and 1860, the Chinese signed treaties giving Russia lands north of the Amur River and east of the Ussuri River. By 1864, Russian forces defeated Muslim rebels in the Caucasus. Central Asia was won during a series of military campaigns from 1865 to 1876. In 1867, Russia sold its Alaskan territory to the United States for $7,200,000.

Alexander II. Nicholas I died in 1855, during the Crimean War. His son, Alexander II, became czar. Russia's defeat in the Crimean War taught Alexander a lesson. He realized that Russia had to catch up with the West to remain a major power. Alexander began a series of reforms to strengthen the economy and Russian life in general. In 1861, he freed the serfs and distributed land among them. He began developing railroads and

789

Russia

organizing a banking system. Alexander promoted reforms in education, reduced controls on the press, and introduced a jury system and other reforms in the courts. He also established forms of self-government in towns and villages and modernized the armed forces.

But many young Russians believed that Alexander's reforms did not go far enough. Some revolutionary groups wanted to establish socialism in Russia. Others wanted a constitution and a republic. These groups formed a number of public and secret organizations. After a revolutionary tried to kill Alexander in 1866, the czar began to weaken many of his reforms. The revolutionaries then argued that Alexander had never been a sincere reformer at all. During the mid-1870s, a group of revolutionaries tried to get the peasants to revolt. They wanted to achieve either socialism or *anarchism* (absence of government) for Russia. After this effort failed, a terrorist group called the People's Will tried several times to kill the czar. Alexander then decided to set up a new reform program. But in 1881, he was killed by a terrorist's bomb in St. Petersburg.

 Alexander III, Alexander's son, became czar and soon began a program of harsh rule. Alexander III limited the freedom of the press and of the universities, and he sharply reduced the powers of Russia's local self-governments. He set up a special bank to help the aristocrats increase their property. He also appointed officials called *land captains* from among the aristocrats and gave them much political power over the peasants. Alexander started some programs to help the peasants and industrial workers. But their living and working conditions improved very little during his reign.

 Nicholas II became Russia's next, and last, czar in 1894. The revolutionary movement had been kept in check until the 1890s, when a series of bad harvests caused starvation among the peasants. In addition, as industrialization increased, discontent grew among the rising middle class and workers in the cities. Discontented Russians were attracted to three political movements. (1) The *liberal constitutionalists* wanted to replace czarist rule with a Western type of parliamentary government. (2) The *populists*, who later formed the Socialist Revolutionary Party, sought to promote a revolution among rural peasants and workers in the cities. (3) The *Marxists* wanted to promote revolution among the city workers. The Marxists followed the socialist teachings of Karl Marx, a German social philosopher. In 1898, the Marxists established the Russian Social Democratic Labor Party.

Between 1899 and 1904, the discontent of the Russian people increased. Worker strikes and other forms of protest took place. In 1903, the Russian Social Democratic Labor Party split into two groups—the *Bolsheviks* (members of the majority) and the *Mensheviks* (members of the minority). V. I. Lenin was the leader of the Bolsheviks, later called Communists.

The Revolution of 1905. On January 22, 1905, thousands of unarmed workers marched to the czar's Winter Palace in St. Petersburg. The workers were on strike, and they planned to ask Nicholas II for reforms. Government troops fired on the crowd and killed or wounded hundreds of marchers. After this *Bloody Sunday* slaughter, the revolutionary movement, led mainly by the liberal constitutionalists, gained much strength. In February, Nicholas agreed to establish an elected lawmaking body, called the Duma, to advise him. More strikes broke out during the summer, however, and peasant and military groups revolted. In part, the growing unrest was linked to the increasingly unpopular Russo-Japanese War. This war had broken out in February 1904 after a Japanese attack on Russian ships. The war ended with Russia's defeat in September 1905.

In October 1905, a general strike paralyzed the country. Revolutionaries in St. Petersburg formed a *soviet* (council) called the Soviet of Workers' Deputies. Nicholas then granted the Duma the

Portrait of Nicholas II with his family

power to pass or reject all proposed laws. Many Russians were satisfied with this action, but others were not. The revolution continued, especially in Moscow, where the army crushed a serious uprising in December.

Each of the first two Dumas, which met in 1906 and 1907, was dissolved after a few months. The Dumas could not work with Nicholas and his high-ranking officials, who refused to give up much power. Nicholas illegally changed the election law and made the selection of Duma candidates less democratic. The peasants and workers were allowed far fewer representatives in the Duma than the upper classes. The third Duma served from 1907 to 1912, and the fourth Duma met from 1912 to 1917. During this period, Russia made important advances in the arts, education, farming, and industry.

World War I. By the time World War I began in 1914, Europe was divided into two tense armed camps. On one side was the Triple Entente (Triple Agreement), consisting of Russia, France, and Britain. Russia and France had agreed in 1894 to defend each other against attack. France and Britain had signed the Entente Cordiale (Friendly Understanding) in 1904, and Russia had signed a similar agreement with Britain in 1907. The Triple

An artist's rendition of Bloody Sunday

Entente developed from these treaties. Opposing the Triple Entente was the Triple Alliance, formed in 1882 by Austria-Hungary, Germany, and Italy.

On August 1, 1914, Germany declared war on Russia. Soon afterward, Russia changed the German-sounding name of St. Petersburg to Petrograd. German troops crushed the Russian army at Tannenberg, in East Prussia. However, the Russians defeated an Austrian army in the Battles of Lemberg in the Galicia region of Austria-Hungary, near present-day Lviv, Ukraine.

In 1915, Austrian and German forces drove back the Russians. The next year, the Russians attacked along a 70-mile (113-kilometer) front in Galicia. They advanced about 50 miles (80 kilometers). Russian troops moved into the Carpathian Mountains in 1917, but the Germans pushed them back.

The February Revolution. During World War I, the Russian economy could not meet the needs of both the soldiers and the people at home. The railroads carried military supplies and could not serve the cities. The people suffered severe shortages of food, fuel, and housing. Russian troops at the front were loyal, but the untrained soldiers behind the fighting lines began to question the war. They knew they would probably be sent to the front and be killed. The soldiers and civilians behind the lines grew increasingly dissatisfied.

By the end of 1916, almost all educated Russians opposed the czar. Nicholas had removed many capable executives from high government offices and replaced them with weak, unpopular officials. He was accused of crippling the war effort by such acts. Many Russians blamed his action on the influence of Grigori Rasputin, adviser to the czar and the czarina. The royal couple believed that Rasputin was a holy man who was saving their sick son's life. In December 1916, a group of nobles murdered Rasputin. But the officials who supposedly had been appointed through his influence remained.

In March 1917, the people of Russia revolted. (The month was February in the old Russian calendar, which was replaced in 1918.) Violent riots and strikes over shortages of bread and coal accompanied the uprising in Petrograd, the capital of Russia. (Petrograd was known as St. Petersburg until 1914, was renamed Leningrad in 1924, and again became St. Petersburg in 1991.) Nicholas ordered the Duma to dissolve itself, but it ignored his command and set up a *provisional* (temporary) government. Nicholas had lost all political support, and he gave up the throne on March 15. Nicholas and his family were then imprisoned. Bolshevik revolutionaries shot the czar and his family to death in July 1918.

Many soviets were established in Russia at the same time as the provisional government was formed. The soviets rivaled the provisional government. Workers and soldiers tried to seize power in Petrograd in July, but the attempt failed.

The October Revolution. In August 1917, General Lavr Kornilov tried to curb the growing power of the soviets. But the attempt failed, and the Russian masses became increasingly radical. On November 7 (October 25 in the old Russian calendar), workers, soldiers, and sailors led by the Bolsheviks took over the Winter Palace, a former royal residence that had become the headquarters of the provisional government. They overthrew the provisional government and formed a new government headed by Lenin. Lenin immediately withdrew Russia from World War I. The new government soon took over Russia's industries and also seized most of the peasants' farm products.

In 1918, the Bolsheviks made Moscow the capital of Russia. They also changed the name of the Russian Social Democratic Labor Party to the Russian Communist Party. This name was later changed to the Communist Party of the Soviet Union.

Civil war and the formation of the USSR. From 1918 to 1920, civil war raged between the Communists and the anti-Communists over control of Russia. The anti-Communists received support from several other countries, including France, Japan, the United Kingdom, and the United States. Nevertheless, the Communists defeated their opponents. They also established Communist rule in Georgia, Ukraine, eastern Armenia, Belarus, and central Asia. The civil war contributed to the increasing discontent among the Russian people.

In 1921, peasant uprisings and workers' strikes broke out in opposition to Bolshevik policies. That same year, Lenin established a New Economic Policy to strengthen Russia. Under this policy, the government controlled the most important aspects of the economy, including banking, foreign trade, heavy industry, and transportation. But small businesses could control their own operations, and peasants could keep their farm products.

In December 1922, the Communist government created a new nation called the Union of Soviet Socialist Republics (USSR.). It consisted of four republics—the Russian Soviet Federative Socialist Republic, Byelorussia (formerly Belarus and now again known by that name), Transcaucasia, and Ukraine. By late 1940, Transcaucasia had been divided into Azerbaijan, Armenia, and Georgia, and 10 other republics had been established. The new republics included what are now Estonia, Kazakhstan, Kyrgyzstan, Latvia, Lithuania, Moldova (then Moldavia), Tajikistan, Turkmenistan, and Uzbekistan.

Portrait of Joseph Stalin

Stalin. Lenin died in 1924. Joseph Stalin, who had been general secretary of the Communist Party since 1922, rapidly gained power. He defeated his rivals one by one. By 1929, Stalin had become dictator of the Soviet Union.

In the late 1920s, Stalin began a socialist economic program. It emphasized the development of heavy industry and the combining of privately owned farms into large, government-run farms. Many citizens of the Soviet Union opposed Stalin's policies.

In the mid-1930s, Stalin started a program of terror called the Great Purge. His secret police arrested millions of people. Most of the prisoners were shot or sent to prison labor camps. Many of those arrested had helped Stalin rise to power. Stalin thus eliminated all possible threats to his power and tightened his hold over the Soviet Union.

World War II. By the late 1930s, German dictator Adolf Hitler was ready to conquer Europe. In August 1939, the USSR and Germany signed a *nonaggression pact*, a treaty agreeing that neither nation would attack the other. In September, German forces invaded Poland from the west. The Soviet Union's forces quickly occupied the eastern part of Poland.

In June 1941, Germany invaded the Soviet Union and began a rapid advance into the country. The turning point of the war in the Soviet Union was the Soviet defeat of the Germans in the Battle of Stalingrad (now Volgograd) in 1943. Soviet troops then drove the Germans back out of the country and across eastern Europe. They attacked Berlin in April 1945. Berlin fell to the Soviets on May 2, and German troops surrendered to the Allies five days later.

The Soviet Union suffered more military casualties than all the other Allied countries combined. Russians call the Soviet Union's fight against the Germans the Great Patriotic War.

The Cold War. After World War II ended, the Soviet Union extended the influence of Communism into Eastern Europe. By early 1948, several Eastern European countries had become *Soviet*

Nikita Khrushchav

satellites (countries controlled by the Soviet Union). The satellites were Bulgaria, Czechoslovakia, Hungary, Poland, Romania, and—later—East Germany. The USSR also influenced Communist regimes in Albania and Yugoslavia. It cut off nearly all contact between its satellites and the West. Mutual distrust and suspicion between East and West developed into a rivalry that became known as the Cold War. The Cold War shaped the foreign policy of the Soviet Union and of many Western countries until the late 1980s.

Stalin died on March 5, 1953. In September of that year, Nikita S. Khrushchev became the head of the Communist Party. In 1958, he also became premier of the Soviet Union.

Khrushchev eased the terror that had characterized Stalin's dictatorship and relaxed some of the restrictions on communication, trade, and travel between East and West. He also improved the Soviet people's standard of living. However, the USSR continued working to expand its influence in non-Communist countries. Khrushchev improved Soviet relations with the West, but many of his other policies failed.

In 1964, the highest-ranking Communists overthrew Khrushchev. Leonid I. Brezhnev became Communist Party head, and Aleksei N. Kosygin became premier. Brezhnev and Kosygin increased the production of consumer goods and the construction of housing, and they expanded Soviet influence in Africa.

By the mid-1970s, Brezhnev was the most powerful Soviet leader. He sought to ease tensions between East and West, a policy that became known as *detente*. However, detente began to collapse in the late 1970s. Relations between the Soviet Union and the United States worsened over such issues as Soviet violations of human rights, the Soviet invasion of Afghanistan, and an increase in the number of nuclear weapons held by both the Soviet Union and the United States.

The rise of Gorbachev. In 1985, Mikhail S. Gorbachev became head of the Communist Party. Gorbachev instituted many changes in the USSR, including increased freedom of expression in politics, literature, and the arts. He worked to improve relations between the Soviet Union and the West and to reduce government control over the Soviet economy.

In 1989, the USSR held its first contested elections for the newly created Congress of People's

Deputies. The following year, the government voted to allow non-Communist political parties in the Soviet Union. Many Communist Party members and other Soviet officials opposed Gorbachev's reforms. But in March 1990, Gorbachev was elected by the Congress of People's Deputies to the newly created office of president of the Soviet Union.

The breakup of the USSR. During the late 1980s, people in many parts of the Soviet Union increased their demands for greater freedom from the central government. In June 1990, the Russian republic declared that laws passed by its legislature took precedence over laws passed by the central government. By the end of the year, each of the other 14 Soviet republics had made similar declarations.

In July 1991, Gorbachev and the leaders of 10 republics agreed to sign a treaty giving the republics a large amount of self-government. Five of the republics were scheduled to sign the treaty on August 20. But on August 19, conservative Communist Party leaders staged a coup against Gorbachev's government. They imprisoned Gorbachev and his family in their vacation home. The president of the Russian republic, Boris N. Yeltsin, led popular opposition to the coup. The coup collapsed on August 21. Gorbachev then regained his office as president but resigned as head of the Communist Party.

With the coup's collapse, the republics renewed their demands for more self-government. In September 1991, an interim government was established to rule until a new union treaty and constitution could be written and approved. This government included a State Council, made up of Gorbachev and the leaders of the republics.

On December 8, 1991, Yeltsin and the presidents of Belarus and Ukraine announced the formation of the Commonwealth of Independent States (CIS). They declared that the Soviet Union had ceased to exist and invited the remaining republics to join the commonwealth. The members would be independent countries tied by economic and defense links. Most of the republics joined the CIS.

Yeltsin took control of what remained of the central government of the Soviet Union, including the Kremlin. On December 25, 1991, Gorbachev resigned as Soviet president, and the Soviet Union ceased to exist.

The new nation. With the end of the Soviet Union, the Russian republic resumed its course as an independent nation. The breakup of the Soviet Union helped to ease remaining tensions between East and West.

In 1992, the Russian government slashed military spending and reduced the number of people employed in the armed forces. These cutbacks

Violence erupted between the Chechen military (shown) and citizens in 1992.

forced large numbers of former military personnel to find homes and jobs as civilians. That same year, the other former Soviet republics with nuclear weapons on their lands—Ukraine, Belarus, and Kazakhstan—agreed to eliminate all nuclear weapons on their territories within seven years. By the end of 1996, the three countries had turned over their nuclear weapons to Russia.

Russia had to establish new relationships with the CIS members. Some Russian leaders wanted the country to take a leading role. But the smaller states feared domination by Russia because of its size and power.

Russia also faced the challenges of setting up new economic and governmental systems. The government ended price controls. The lifting of controls caused prices to soar and resulted in a lower standard of living for the Russian people. President Yeltsin and his government took steps to increase private ownership of businesses. However, the process left a small number of wealthy Russians in control of many of the country's largest companies.

Opposition to Yeltsin's economic policies grew in parliament, which included many Communist Party members and former Soviet Union leaders. In a referendum held in April 1993, a majority of the voters supported Yeltsin and his economic policies. Opposition to Yeltsin in parliament continued, however. In September, Yeltsin suspended Vice President Alexander V. Rutskoi, who had become a leader of the anti-Yeltsin group. Later that month, Yeltsin dissolved parliament and called for new parliamentary elections in December. Parliament, in turn, voted to remove Yeltsin from office and to make Rutskoi acting president.

Rutskoi and many other foes of Yeltsin barricaded themselves in the parliament building in Moscow. At Yeltsin's order, police and forces of the internal affairs ministry blockaded the building, known as the White House. In October 1993,

anti-Yeltsin crowds rioted in Moscow and tried to break up the blockade. The next day, Yeltsin ordered the military to take control of the White House. Rutskoi and other leaders of the movement against Yeltsin were arrested.

The elections Yeltsin had called for took place in December 1993. Russia's voters elected a new parliament and approved a new constitution. The new document formally defined the powers of the president and of the parliament. In February 1994, the new State Duma granted amnesty both to those who revolted against Yeltsin in 1993 and to those who led the failed coup in 1991.

In parliamentary elections in 1995, the Communist Party won the largest number of seats in the State Duma. Many voters had initially shunned the Communists after the fall of the Soviet Union. However, the turmoil of transforming Russia into a democratic, capitalist nation brought voters back to the party. In 1996, Yeltsin won a second term as Russia's president.

In 1991, the government of Chechnya, a region in southwestern Russia, demanded independence. In 1992, violence broke out between the Chechen government and citizens who wanted the region to remain part of Russia. In December 1994, Russia sent troops against the separatist forces, and serious fighting resulted. A cease-fire ended the fighting in August 1996. In May 1997, Yeltsin and the Chechen leader signed a peace treaty.

In 1998, Russia began to face severe economic problems. In March, Yeltsin abruptly dismissed his cabinet, including Prime Minister Viktor S. Chernomyrdin. He forced parliament to accept young, reform-minded Sergei Kiriyenko as prime minister. In August, Yeltsin dismissed Kiriyenko and tried to bring back Chernomyrdin. But parliament forced Yeltsin to nominate another candidate. In September 1998, parliament approved Yevgeny M. Primakov, the minister of foreign affairs, as the new prime minister. In October, Yeltsin, who had been in poor health for some time, turned over most of his duties to Primakov. Russia's economic crisis continued.

Putin and Chechnya. In May 1999, Yeltsin abruptly dismissed Primakov and the rest of the cabinet members. Yeltsin appointed the minister of internal affairs, Sergei V. Stepashin, as prime minister. In August, Yeltsin replaced Stepashin with Vladimir V. Putin, former head of Russia's domestic intelligence service.

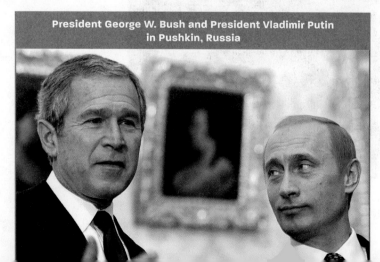

President George W. Bush and President Vladimir Putin in Pushkin, Russia

Shortly after Yeltsin's dismissal of Primakov, the State Duma took a vote on whether to impeach Yeltsin for a number of his past actions. But the Duma voted against impeachment.

Also in August 1999, Islamic militants who wanted to unite Chechnya and the neighboring republic of Dagestan seized several towns in Dagestan. Russia invaded Chechnya to oppose the rebellion. Russian attacks heavily damaged Chechnya's cities and killed many civilians. Many nations protested Russia's handling of the conflict.

Russian forces gained control of Chechnya's main cities by mid-2000, but the rebellion continued. The rebels retreated to mountain bases and launched surprise attacks on Russian forces. Chechen terrorists conducted bomb attacks in Moscow and southwest Russia, killing and injuring hundreds of civilians.

In parliamentary elections in December 1999, the Communist Party again won the largest number of seats in the State Duma. Unity, a political group supported by Prime Minister Putin, won the second highest number of seats. On December 31, 1999, Yeltsin resigned and appointed Putin as acting president. In presidential elections in March 2000, Russians formally elected Putin.

 Recent developments. Under Putin's leadership, Russia developed friendlier relations with Europe and the United States. In 2002, Russia entered into a special partnership with the North Atlantic Treaty Organization, a military alliance that had been formed to oppose the Soviet Union.

In October 2002, Chechen terrorists seized a theater in Moscow and held about 700 audience members, actors, and theater personnel as hostages. They demanded a withdrawal of Russian troops from Chechnya. Russian security forces stormed the theater and killed or captured the terrorists. However, more than 100 of the hostages were killed by a chemical weapon—a gas—that the security forces used in the raid.

Putin's government sometimes clashed with Russia's *oligarchs*, wealthy individuals who controlled major Russian businesses. In 2003, for example, the government arrested businessman Mikhail Khodorkovsky on financial crimes charges. The government then charged Yukos Oil Company, Khodorkovsky's leading enterprise, with billions of dollars in unpaid taxes. Many observers believed the Russian government took these actions to put an end to Khodorkovsky's growing political power. In 2004, the government auctioned off a significant portion of Yukos. In 2005, Khodorkovsky was convicted of most of the charges brought against him.

In elections in 2003, United Russia, a pro-Putin party formed from Unity and other parties, won control of the State Duma. In March 2004, Putin was reelected as president.

Islamic rebels continued to carry out raids and terrorist attacks, especially in southwest Russia. In September 2004, Chechen terrorists seized a school in Beslan, a town in southwest Russia, and held more than 1,000 hostages, many of them children. On the third day of the crisis, a bomb in the school exploded, and Russian security forces stormed the school. The resulting chaos left more than 300 hostages dead and hundreds more injured. Russian forces killed about 30 of the terrorists and captured one alive.

In 2008, Dmitry Medvedev succeeded Putin as president. Medvedev then selected Putin to serve as his prime minister.

In August 2008, Russia and Georgia clashed over control of South Ossetia, a region in north-central Georgia, and Russian troops entered Georgia. Russia announced that it recognized South Ossetia and Abkhazia, another region of Georgia, as independent. The United States and other Western countries, however, continued to recognize the areas as part of Georgia. In September, European Union observers arrived in Georgia to monitor a withdrawal of Russian troops from the country. Russia kept troops stationed in Abkhazia and South Ossetia.

In 2009, the Russian government ended its antiterrorist operations in Chechnya, claiming to have stabilized the situation. However, some critics accused Chechen president Ramzan Kadyrov of using terrorist tactics to silence his opponents.

In March 2012, Putin was again elected to the presidency. Election observers noted widespread irregularities, including reports of ballot tampering and people voting multiple times in different locations. Putin chose Medvedev to serve as his prime minister.

MLA Citation

"Russia." *The Southwestern Advantage Topic Source.* Nashville: Southwestern. 2013.

DATA

Russia in Brief

General Information

Capital: Moscow

Official language: Russian

Official names: *Rossiya* (Russia) or *Rossiyskaya Federatsiya* (Russian Federation).

Largest cities: (2010 census) Moscow (11,514,330); St. Petersburg (4,848,742)

Land and Climate

Land: Russia is the world's largest country in area. It covers a large part of both Europe and Asia. It has coastlines on the Arctic Ocean, Baltic Sea, Black Sea, Caspian Sea, and Pacific Ocean. Russia borders eight European countries, three Asian countries, and three countries with lands in both Europe and Asia. Much of the west is a large plain. The Ural Mountains separate Europe and Asia. Siberia, east of the Urals, has low western plains, a central plateau, and a mountainous wilderness in the east. Major Russian rivers include the Lena in Asia and the Volga in Europe. Lake Baikal in Siberia is the world's deepest lake.

Area: 6,601,669 mi^2 (17,098,242 km^2). *Greatest distances*—east-west, 6,000 mi (9,650 km); north-south, 2,800 mi (4,500 km).

Elevation: *Highest*—Mount Elbrus, 18,510 ft (5,642 m). *Lowest*—Coast of Caspian Sea, 92 ft (28 m) below sea level.

Climate: Most of Russia has long, bitterly cold winters and mild to warm—but short—summers. In northeastern Siberia, the country's coldest area, January temperatures average below −50°F (−46°C). Rainfall is moderate in most of Russia. Snow covers more than half of the country during six months of the year.

Government

Form of government: Republic

Head of state: President

Head of government: Prime minister

Flag and state seal: Russia's flag, adopted in 1991, has three horizontal stripes of white, blue, and red (*top to bottom*). The Russian empire used the flag from 1699 to 1918. The double-headed eagle the state seal, adopted in 1993, includes symbols of the Russian empire.

Legislature: Russia's parliament is called the Federal Assembly. It consists of two houses—the State Duma and the Federation Council.

Executive: The president is the chief executive and most powerful official.

Judiciary: Highest court is the Constitutional Court.

Political subdivisions: Russia has dozens of federal administrative units. They include *oblasts* (regions), *krais* (territories), republics, autonomous *okrugs* (areas), autonomous oblasts, and federal cities. Some of these divisions may contain smaller units called *raions* (districts).

DATA

Russia in Brief

People

Population: *Current estimate*—140,030,000; *2010 census*—142,905,208.

Population density: 21 per mi^2 (8 per km^2).

Distribution: 73 percent urban, 27 percent rural.

Major ethnic/national groups: About 80 percent Russian. Smaller groups include Tatars (or Tartars), Ukrainians, Chuvash, Bashkirs, Belarusians, Mordvins, Chechens, Germans, Udmurts, Mari, Kazakhs, Avars, Jews, and Armenians.

Major religions: The Russian Orthodox Church is the largest religious group. Other religious groups include Muslims, Protestants, Roman Catholics, Buddhists, Hindus, and Jews.

Economy

Chief products: *Agriculture*—barley, beef and dairy cattle, chickens, fruits, hogs, potatoes, rye, sugar beets, sunflower seeds, vegetables, wheat. *Fishing*—cod, haddock, herring, salmon. *Manufacturing*—chemicals, electronics, machinery, motor vehicles, processed foods, refined oil, transportation equipment. *Mining*—coal, copper, gold, iron ore, natural gas, nickel, petroleum, platinum, tin, tungsten.

Money: *Basic unit*—Russian ruble. One hundred kopecks equal one ruble.

International trade: *Major exports*—chemicals, machinery, metals, natural gas, paper products, petroleum, wood products. *Major imports*—consumer goods, foods and beverages, industrial equipment, machinery. *Main trading partners*—other former Soviet republics, China, Germany, Italy, Japan, Poland, United Kingdom, United States.

Economic Production in Russia

Economic activities	% of GDP[1] produced	Number of workers	% of all workers
Trade, restaurants, and hotels	21	13,103,000	20
Finance, insurance, real estate, and business services	18	6,250,000	9
Community, government, and personal services	15	17,073,000	25
Manufacturing	15	10,475,000	16
Transportation and communication	10	5,326,000	8
Mining	9	993,000	1
Construction	6	5,230,000	8
Agriculture, forestry, and fishing	5	6,531,000	10
Utilities	3	1,886,000	3
Total[2]	100	66,957,000	100

[1]GDP=gross domestic product, the total value of goods and services produced within a country in a year.

[2]Figures may not add up to 100 percent due to rounding.

DATA

Important Dates in Russia

A.D. 800s	East Slavs established the state of Kievan Rus.
1237–1240	The Mongols conquered Russia.
c. 1318	The Mongols appointed Prince Yuri of Moscow as the Russian grand prince.
1480	Ivan III broke Mongol control over Russia.
1547	Ivan IV became the first Russian ruler to be crowned czar.
1604–1613	Russia was torn by civil war, invasion, and political confusion during the Time of Troubles.
1613	Michael Romanov became czar. He started the Romanov line of czars, which ruled until 1917.
1703	Peter I founded St. Petersburg and began building his capital there.
1812	Napoleon invaded Russia but was forced to retreat.
1861	Alexander II freed the serfs.
1905	Japan defeated Russia in the Russo-Japanese War. A revolution forced Czar Nicholas II to establish a parliament.
1914–1917	Russia fought Germany and Austria-Hungary in World War I.
1917	The February Revolution overthrew Czar Nicholas II. The Bolsheviks (who were later called Communists) seized power in the October Revolution. V. I. Lenin became head of the government. Russia withdrew from World War I.
1918–1920	The Communists defeated their anti-Communist opponents in a civil war.
1922	The USSR was established.
1941–1945	The USSR fought Germany in World War II.
1957	The USSR launched Sputnik 1, the first artificial satellite.
1961	Yuri A. Gagarin became the first person in space.
1991	Communist rule ended, and the Soviet Union was dissolved. Russia and the other Soviet republics became independent nations.

DATA
Czars and Empresses of Russia

Ruler	Reign	Ruler	Reign
Ivan IV	1547–1584	Peter II	1727–1730
Fedor I	1584–1598	Anne	1730–1740
Boris Godunov	1598–1605	Ivan VI	1740–1741
Fedor II	1605	Elizabeth	1741–1762
False Dmitriy	1605–1606	Peter III	1762
Basil Shuisky	1606–1610	Catherine II	1762–1796
Michael Romanov	1613–1645	Paul	1796–1801
Alexis	1645–1676	Alexander I	1801–1825
Fedor III	1676–1682	Nicholas I	1825–1855
Ivan V	1682–1696	Alexander II	1855–1881
Peter I	1682–1725	Alexander III	1881–1894
Catherine I	1725–1727	Nicholas II	1894–1917

ADDITIONAL RESOURCES

Books to Read

Level I

Dando, William A., and Pavlovic, Zoran. *Russia*. 2nd ed. Chelsea House, 2007.

Nickles, Greg. *Russia: The Culture*. Crabtree Publishing Co., 2008. *Russia: The Land*. 2008. *Russia: The People*. 2008. All revised editions.

Ransome, Galya. *Russia*. Raintree, 2004.

Schemenauer, Elma. *Welcome to Russia*. Child's World, 2008.

Level II

Bressler, Michael L., ed. *Understanding Contemporary Russia*. Lynne Rienner, 2009.

Freeze, Gregory L., ed. *Russia: A History*. 3rd ed. Oxford, 2009.

Richards, Susan. *Lost and Found in Russia: Lives in a Post-Soviet Landscape*. Other Press LLC, 2010.

Saunders, Robert A., and Strukov, Vlad. *Historical Dictionary of the Russian Federation*. Scarecrow, 2010.

Sebestyen, Victor. *Revolution 1989: The Fall of the Soviet Empire*. Pantheon, 2009.

Smorodinskaya, Tatiana, and others, eds. *Encyclopedia of Contemporary Russian Culture*. Routledge, 2007.

Web Sites

Background Note: Russia

http://www.state.gov/p/eur/ci/rs/

Information from the U.S. Department of State.

Battle for Chechnya

http://news.bbc.co.uk/2/hi/europe/461041.stm

This special feature from the British Broadcasting Corporation includes news reports, general information about Chechnya and other Russian republics, background on military and political leaders, and analysis of public opinion.

CIA Factbook: Russia

https://www.cia.gov/library/publications/the-world-factbook/geos/rs.html

An overview of the country from the U.S. Central Intelligence Agency.

Country Profile: Russia

http://news.bbc.co.uk/2/hi/europe/country_profiles/1102275.stm

Information from the BBC.

History and Culture of Russia: Overview

http://www.geographia.com/russia/rushis01.htm

A brief history of Russia from the official Web site of the Russian National Tourist Office.

Return of the Czar

http://www.pbs.org/wgbh/pages/frontline/shows/yeltsin/

FRONTLINE reports on Boris Yeltsin's legacy, including corruption and poverty, the war in Chechnya, and Vladimir Putin's rise to the presidency.

Revelations from the Russian Archives

http://lcweb.loc.gov/exhibits/archives/intro.html

Links to information about repressive measures in the former Soviet Union.

The Soviet Union and the United States

http://www.loc.gov/exhibits/archives/sovi.html

An exploration of the relationship between the superpowers from before World War II through the Cold War.

Search Strings

Cold War

"Cold War" Communist nations non-Communist nations (11,800)

"Cold War" Communist nations non-Communist nations Easter bloc Western bloc (256)

"Cold War" history timeline (290,000) * These may be better than the search that returned 256 entries.

Contributions to the Arts

Russia's contributions to the arts (1,220,000)

Russia artists writers literature composers (41,200)

Russia artists writers literature composers architects ballet (9,360)

Russian Rulers

Russian rulers (168,000)

Russian rulers czars empresses presidents (27,700)

Russia's Climate and Land Regions

Russia geography climate (150,000)

Russia geography climate zones regions (80,000)

BACKGROUND INFORMATION

The following article was written during the year in which the events took place and reflects the style and thinking of that time.

Russia (1923)

A vast new republic, more than twice as large as the United States or Canada, was ushered into existence during August 1923. The organizing genius behind the movement was the leadership of the Russian Socialist Federated Soviet Republic, the legal designation of the communistic state established by Lenin and Trotzky after the revolution of 1918. The original Russian Soviet government has welded together under the flag of communism six states, which now constitute the Union of Socialist Soviet Republics.

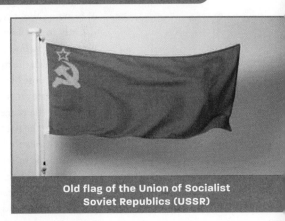

Old flag of the Union of Socialist Soviet Republics (USSR)

Whether this new central government will be in existence for very long is a matter of speculation, with the weight of opinion, however, in its favor. The death knell of the Russian experiment has been rung frequently during the past five years, but Russian communism, on the surface, appears stronger that at any previous time. The world is not forgetful that its leaders have for their objective the conversion of all nations to their radical system, the "rule of the proletariat," and the amalgamation of six countries under one communistic flag is an event which challenges attention. It may be assumed, judging from past experience, that there is basis for belief in the continuance of this new nation which occupies over half of two continents, unless its great expanse makes unified control impossible.

In 1918, only old Russia proper fell under the acknowledged sway of Soviet rule. Communistic propaganda, gradually extending to the east and south, captured the imagination of the uneducated millions who never knew aught save poverty and oppression, and from time to time little nations which had sprung into being after the great war were captivated by the alluring picture painted by the Russian leaders and established independent Soviet rule. Now having welded these into one vast proletariat republic, the Russian idealists look upon the result as a marvelous achievement which brings them one step nearer to the world revolution which is their goal. The members of this far-flung republic are the following.

Russian Socialist Federated Soviet Republic,
The Ukranian Social Soviet Republic,
The White Russian Socialist Soviet Republic,
The Trans-Caucasian Social Federated Soviet
Republic, which was composed of
The Socialist Soviet Republic of Azerbaijan,
The Socialist Soviet Republic of Georgia,
The Socialist Soviet Republic of Armenia.

Each of the individual states in the new federation retains certain local authority, exercised by the local Soviet congress, and during its recesses by the central executive committee of workers. The Union of Socialist Soviet Republics establishes a national congress composed of representatives of city Soviets and of rural Soviet districts. All laws passed by the national congress and by the local congresses of the states are revised by what is known as a Federal Council and a Council of Nationalities.

What they think of themselves. The introductory paragraphs of the Constitution of the new Union present the Soviet view of the structure of communism.

Since the formation of the Soviet republics the states of the world have been divided into two hostile camps, the camp of capitalism and the camp of socialism. There in the camp of capitalism, national enmities and inequality, colonial slavery, chauvinism, national hatred and pogroms, imperialistic cruelty, and wars prevail; here in the camp of socialism mutual confidence and peace, national freedom and equality, peaceful living together and fraternal cooperation of peoples.

The attempts of the capitalist world to settle the problem of nationalities for many decades through hindering the free development of peoples, through the system of the exploitation of one man by another, have not proved successful. On the contrary, the knots of national contradictions are becoming more and more entangled and threaten the very existence of capitalism. The bourgeoisie has shown itself incapable of bringing about cooperation among the nations.

Only in the camp of the Soviet republics, only under the conditions of the proletarian dictatorship, around which the majority of the population rallies, has it been possible to nip nationalistic hatred in the bud, to create an atmosphere of mutual confidence and to lay the cornerstone for a peaceful cooperation among the nations.

Only thanks to these conditions were the Soviet republics able to repel the attack of imperialists of the whole world, the internal as well as the external; only thanks to these conditions were they able to put a victorious end to the civil war, to ensure their existence and to take up the work of peaceful economic reconstruction.

But the years of war had not passed without leaving their traces. The devastated fields, the silent factories, the wrecked forces of production and the exhausted economic resources—the legacy of the war—made the separated efforts of the individual republics in economic reconstruction insufficient. The reconstruction of the national economy is impossible under a separated existence of the individual republics.

On the other hand, the insecurity of the national situation and the danger of fresh attacks make imperative the creation of a united front of Soviet republics against the capitalistic environment.

Finally, the building up of the Soviet power, international because of its class nature, forces the working masses of the Soviet republics along the road toward unity in a socialist family.

All these circumstances imperatively demand the union of the Soviet republics in a federated state that will be able to guarantee external security, domestic economic prosperity and freedom of national development of peoples.

The money of Russia.

One tenet of Soviet Russia failed utterly after four years of practical test. Money was declared a weapon of capitalism, and for it an utter contempt was expressed, especially concerning gold reserves, proper currency regulations, credit facilities, and the like. The government abandoned the usual basic theories of money, and printed thousands of tons of

Russian rubles

unsecured paper currency. The melancholy fate of the ruble is well known; from its standard value of $51\frac{1}{2}$ cents it fell in worth in the world's exchanges until one dollar would purchase several million rubles. So absolutely valueless did it become that the Russian people went back in practice hundreds of years to the principle of barter and exchange.

The Soviet government was obliged to acknowledge error and defeat. Russia could not exist wholly within itself; if it would maintain contact with the world a secured and practically stable currency was a necessity. Basic changes have therefore been instituted; a new banknote, called the *chervonetz*, has been provided; it has a value of 10 rubles, and is issued in several denominations. The chervonetz is now actually convertible into gold; its stability is due to the fact that it is covered to the fractional part of 25 percent by gold, precious metals and standard foreign currency, and the remainder by negotiable instruments, bills of exchange and merchandise easily marketable. Before the end of the year it was reported that bank notes thus covered represented at least one-half of the amount of money in circulation in Russia.

Petrograd "Coming Back."

The former capital of Russia, the Saint Petersburg of the years preceding the War of the Nations, fell upon evil days following the success of the Bolshevik revolution of 1918. Before the war a proud and prosperous city of more than 2,300,000 people, including suburbs, it was so depopulated through its reverses that in 1920 it had fewer than 740,000 people. The communist government moved the capital of the Soviet republic to Moscow; thousands of government employees were forced to change their residence to the latter city, factories were transferred there, and Petrograd was literally left to whatever fate might befall it. The lean and hungry years following the revolution brought about an amazing exodus of middle-class people to country districts; they were obliged to move or starve. University teachers, professional men and merchants were either killed or driven into exile; wealth was confiscated in behalf of the state. All evidences of peace and plenty vanished, and by 1921 it was the belief of foreign observers that it would become literally a dead city.

During 1923, however, a great change has been wrought in the prospects of Petrograd. Factories are being reopened as prospects of a somewhat stabilized money system are apparent, the port, abandoned for about three years, has been reopened, and people are returning, as greatly increased crops have alleviated famine conditions and make possible the shipment of more food to the cities.

Many citizens have come back to their old homes from Moscow, for although the seat of government and the pride of the communistic regime, that city has accommodations for only about 1,000,000 inhabitants, and nearly 2,500,000 have overcrowded it almost beyond endurance. In Moscow it is impossible to secure suitable living quarters; in Petrograd there are thousands of vacant apartments. Hundreds of Moscow business men, whose work keeps them there, have moved their families back to the former capital, where they may live in comparative comfort.

"Recognition" of Russia. All orderly governments are accepted as members of the family of nations. Each enjoys full diplomatic and commercial intercourse with its sister nations, and this condition of amity is disturbed only by overt acts contrary to the unwritten law of nations. When a nation forfeits the right to intercourse with other states diplomatic and consular agents are withdrawn from its territory, and the world understands from such action that the offending country cannot be trusted; it is a "black sheep" in the family.

When the communistic regime gained control in Russia the country virtually made nonmilitary war upon all other nations. Debts due to citizens and subjects of other countries were repudiated, and in answer to protests over other deliberate affronts to accepted standards the world was informed that Russia would conduct its affairs in its own way. The Bolshevik government was denied recognition by most of the powers, and that condition yet exists.

The Russians have learned during the past few years that nations, like individuals, cannot live to themselves alone; therefore, for some time they have been seeking recognition—they desire to "return to the family." Particularly anxious are they for resumption of relations with Great Britain and the United States. An element of the population of both of those countries, including advanced socialists, avowed communists, radicals, and a few officials high-placed, have endeavored to influence favorable action, but all efforts have been without effect. The general opinion of world society is summed up in the opinion of the American Secretary of State, Charles E. Hughes, who during the past year declared that recognition of the Russian government

was impossible while its leaders continue to evince a spirit of destruction at home and abroad.

American tradition, founded on a desire to refrain from interference with internal affairs of other nations, might require recognition of any government, even a government of a "tyrannical minority," when the people of the national concerned manifested "acquiescence or submission" to it. Nevertheless, the government seeking recognition should evidence a disposition to "live up to the obligations of intercourse."

While the spirit of destruction at home and abroad remains unaltered, the question of recognition by our government of the authorities at Moscow cannot be determined by mere economic considerations or by the establishment in some degree of a more prosperous condition, which, of course, we should be glad to note, or simply by a consideration of the probable stability of the regime in question.

There cannot be intercourse among nations any more than among individuals except upon a general assumption of good faith. We would welcome convincing evidence of a desire of the Russian authorities to observe the fundamental conditions of international intercourse and the abandonment by them of the persistent attempts to subvert the institutions of democracy as maintained in this country and in others.

Death of Lenin. The head of Soviet Russia died January 22, 1924.

Thousands attended Lenin's funeral in Red Square, Moscow.

United States

One of the world's most highly developed and productive nations, the United States of America is the third largest country in the world in population and the fourth largest country in area.

HOT topics

Language. The United States has never had an official language, but English has always been the chief language spoken. Early immigrants—who included the nation's founders—spoke English. Spanish is the second most common language in the United States. Since the 1950s, many Spanish-speaking people have immigrated to the United States from Mexico, Cuba, and other places. Many of these people have learned English, but others speak only Spanish. Some people believe every American should know English, and many states have passed laws declaring English to be their only official language. Language issues remain a source of controversy in much of the United States.

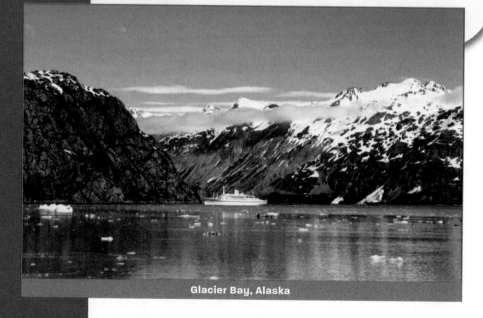

Glacier Bay, Alaska

HOT topics

Urban Life. Urban economies in the United States provide jobs for a great variety of workers. They generally also offer a wide variety of specialized services and shops, an assortment of restaurants, recreation facilities, and other places of entertainment. Because of such facilities as art galleries, museums, libraries, theaters, and concert halls, many cities are important cultural centers. These and other features make urban areas exciting and interesting places to live for many people. Drawbacks of urban life in the United States include high crime rates, racial and ethnic friction, noisy surroundings, substandard housing for poor residents, pollution, and traffic jams.

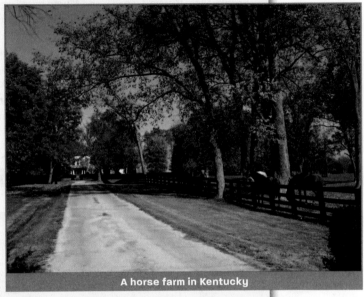
A horse farm in Kentucky

Rural Life. About 97 percent of all the land of the United States is classified as rural. Much of the rural land is uninhabited or only thinly inhabited. About 20 percent of all Americans live in rural areas. Farms provide the economic basis of the nation's rural areas, but only about eight percent of the country's rural people work on farms. Many other rural people own or work in businesses related to agriculture, such as grain and feed stores and warehouses. Mining and related activities and light industries also employ many rural people. Still other rural Americans work as teachers, police officers, salesclerks, or in other occupations. Many farmers hold other jobs for part of the year to add to their incomes.

Rocky Mountains. The Rocky Mountains form the largest mountain system in North America. They extend from northern Alaska, through Canada and the western United States to northern New Mexico. Many peaks of the Rockies are more than 14,000 feet (4,270 meters) high. The Continental Divide, also called the Great Divide, passes through the mountains. It is an imaginary line that separates streams that flow into the Pacific Ocean from those that flow into the Atlantic, the Gulf of Mexico, and the Arctic Ocean. Many important rivers, including the Colorado, Missouri, and Rio Grande, begin in the Rockies.

TRUE or FALSE?

The United States has possession of various island territories in the Caribbean Sea and the Pacific Ocean.

THE BASICS

The United States of America is the third largest country in the world in population, and it is the fourth largest country in area. China and India are the only countries with more people. Only Russia, Canada, and China have larger areas. The United States covers the entire midsection of North America, stretching from the Atlantic Ocean in the east to the Pacific Ocean in the west. It also includes Alaska, in the northwest corner of North America; and Hawaii, far out in the Pacific. The United States is often called the *U.S.*, *U.S.A.*, or *America*.

The land of the United States is as varied as it is vast. It ranges from the warm beaches of Florida and Hawaii to the frozen northlands of Alaska, and from the level Midwestern prairies to the snow-capped Rocky Mountains. This huge and beautiful country is rich in natural resources. It has great stretches of some of the most fertile soil on Earth, a plentiful water supply and excellent water routes, and large stretches of forests. Huge deposits of valuable minerals, including coal, natural gas, and petroleum, lie underground.

Map of the United States of America

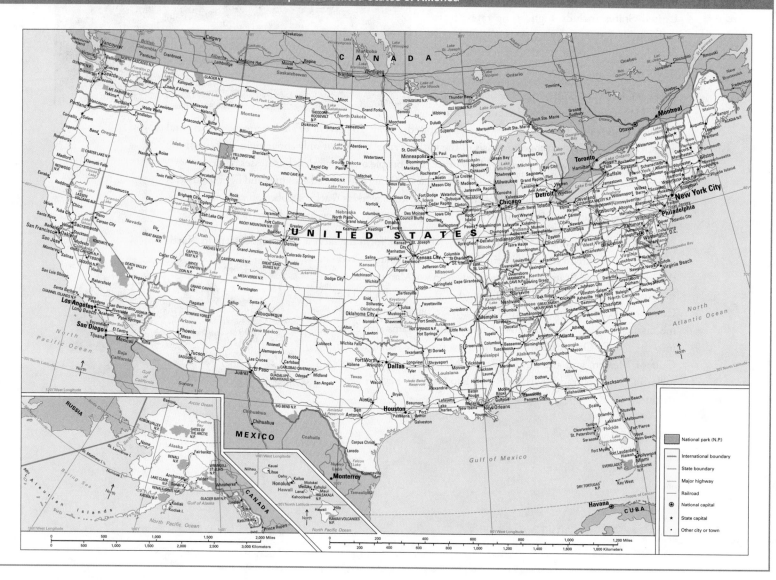

Economically, the United States is one of the world's most highly developed and productive nations. No other country equals the United States in the production of goods and services. Its people enjoy one of the world's highest standards of living.

Until the 1500s, most of what is now the United States was thinly populated forests and prairies. Small groups of Indians lived scattered over the land between the Atlantic and Pacific. Inuit (also called Eskimos) inhabited what is now Alaska, and Polynesians lived in Hawaii. People in Europe saw in this vast "new world" a chance to build new and better lives. Small groups of Spaniards settled in what is now the southeastern and western United States in the 1500s. People from England and some other European countries began settling along and near the East Coast during the 1600s. In 1776, colonists in the East established an independent nation based on freedom and economic opportunity. Through the years, large numbers of Europeans continued to settle in the United States. People from almost every other part of the world also settled in the country. Except for black Africans brought in as slaves, these immigrants came seeking the rights and the opportunities that had become part of the American way of life. As a result of this immigration, the United States today has one of the world's most varied populations. It has been called "a nation of immigrants."

The vast space and resources of the land, the ideals of freedom and economic opportunity, and hard work by the people all helped build the United States into the economic giant it is today. The Americans—as the people are commonly called—also made major contributions in such fields as technology, science, and medicine. Americans developed the mass production system of manufacturing, the electric light bulb, the telephone, polio vaccine, and the transistor. They also created the skyscraper and such new art forms as jazz and musical comedy. At times, the U.S. economy has run into difficulty. Even so, it remains one of the most productive systems ever developed. In some cases, groups of Americans have suffered socially and economically from discrimination. But the country's laws have helped many people overcome discrimination and achieve better lives.

The Nation

Political divisions. The United States consists of 50 states and the District of Columbia. The District of Columbia is a piece of land set aside by the federal government for the nation's capital, Washington, D.C.

In area, population, and economic output, some of the states are comparable to many nations. The United States has a federal system of government, which gives the states many powers that national governments have in most other countries. For example, the states have broad control over public education and the establishment of civil and criminal laws.

Regions. The states of the United States, excluding Alaska and Hawaii, are often divided into seven major regions. Each region is made up of states that have similarities in geography, climate, economy, traditions, and history. The regions are: (1) New England, (2) the Middle Atlantic States, (3) the Southern States, (4) the Midwestern States, (5) the Rocky Mountain States, (6) the Southwestern States, and (7) the Pacific Coast States. (For a list of the states in each region, see the table titled *Regions of the United States* in this article.)

New England is a small region in the northeast corner of the country that is known for charming rural villages, picturesque fishing harbors, and colorful autumn scenery. It was the nation's first industrial center, and manufacturing is still a leading source of income. Industrial cities dot southern New England. Much of the land is too hilly or rocky to grow crops. But New England produces large amounts of dairy and poultry products and is famous for its maple syrup. Many tourists visit the region to see its historic sites—especially those from colonial times—and to enjoy its natural beauty.

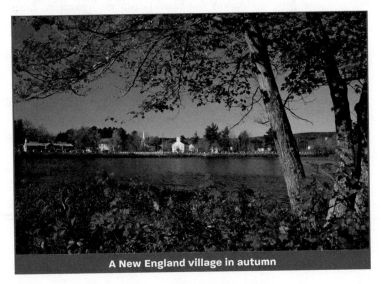

A New England village in autumn

Many New Englanders, especially in the rural north, are descendants of English Puritans who settled the region during the 1600s. The more densely populated southern section of New England has people of many backgrounds, including African, Irish, Italian, German, and French Canadian. The southern section includes Boston, New England's largest city by far.

The Middle Atlantic States Region stretches inland from the Atlantic Ocean southwest of New England. Deepwater harbors help make the region a major center of international trade. The busiest harbor is at New York City, the largest city in the United States. Factories in and near such Middle Atlantic cities as—in order of size—New York City, Philadelphia, Pittsburgh, Newark, and Buffalo produce a wide variety of goods. Coal mining and related industries are important economic activities in the western part of the Middle Atlantic States Region. Farms dot hillsides and fertile plains in various parts of the region. Forested mountains, sandy seashores, scenic lakes and rivers, historic sites, and big-city attractions draw many visitors to the region.

The Middle Atlantic States Region ranks as the nation's most densely populated area. Its urban population includes people of varied European backgrounds, and large groups of people of black African, Latin American, and Asian ancestry. Many of the region's rural dwellers are of British descent.

The Southern States Region is an area of rolling hills, mountains, and plains bordered by broad beaches along the Atlantic Ocean and the Gulf of Mexico. Until the mid-1900s, the region's economy was based heavily on agriculture. Such warm-weather crops as sugarcane, rice, tobacco, and—especially—cotton contributed greatly to the economy. Agriculture has retained importance in the South. However, an industrial boom that began in the mid-1900s greatly increased manufacturing and improved the balance of the region's economy. Tourists flock to coastal resorts in the South—especially in winter, when temperatures are usually relatively mild. Jacksonville is the largest city in the region. Charlotte, Memphis, Baltimore, Washington, D.C., Nashville, Louisville, and Virginia Beach rank next in size. Washington, D.C., is not part of a state, but it is in the Southern States Region.

Large numbers of Southerners are descended from early English, Irish, and Scottish immigrants. From the 1600s to the 1800s, many Africans were brought to the region to work on plantations as slaves. Today, large numbers of African Americans live in the Southern States Region. Many Southerners have a strong sense of regional loyalty and take pride in the South's history and traditions.

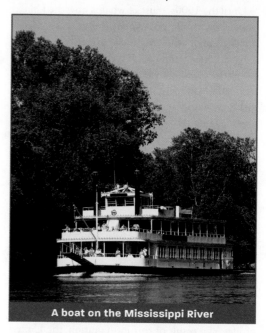

A boat on the Mississippi River

The Midwestern States Region is a vast area of generally flat land that covers much of the center of the United States. The Midwest is famous for its large stretches of fertile soil. Farms in the Midwestern States Region produce enormous quantities of corn, wheat, and other crops; and also dairy products and livestock. In addition, the Midwest has a number of large industrial cities. The cities include, in order of size, Chicago, Indianapolis, Columbus, Detroit, Milwaukee, and Kansas City.

The Mississippi River system, the Great Lakes, and many railroads give the region an excellent transportation network. Lakes and rivers—some of which are set among rolling hills and rugged bluffs—provide numerous recreation areas.

The Midwestern States Region has a varied population. Its rural areas include large groups of descendants of settlers from England, Germany, Norway, Scotland, Sweden, and eastern and southern Europe. The region's urban population includes many descendants of people who came from northern, southern, and eastern Europe. Other large ethnic groups in the cities include African Americans, Mexican Americans, and Asian Americans.

The Rocky Mountain States Region lies west of the Midwest. It is named for the rugged, majestic Rocky Mountains, which cut through it. The region also has areas of deserts, plains, and plateaus. Although much of it is a thinly populated wilderness, some of its cities and towns are among the nation's fastest-growing areas. Denver and Las Vegas rank as the region's largest cities.

Rich deposits of gold, silver, and other metals first attracted settlers to the Rocky Mountain States Region. Mining remains an important economic activity, but such services as health care, hotels, and data processing are now the chief sources of income. Cattle and other livestock graze on dry, grassy ranges, and farmers grow a variety of crops in the Rocky Mountain States Region. Many tourists visit the region to enjoy its scenic beauty and numerous ski resorts.

The population of the Rocky Mountain States Region includes people of European descent, African Americans, Mexican Americans, and American Indians. Mormons, whose ancestors founded a religious community in Utah in the 1800s, form an important cultural group in the Rocky Mountain States Region.

The Southwestern States Region spreads over a vast area that is sometimes called the "wide open spaces." There, cattle graze on huge ranches, and vast fields of cotton and other crops soak up rays of blazing sunshine. However, petroleum has brought the region most of its wealth. The region has large deposits of petroleum and natural gas, as well as various other minerals. In the 1900s, refineries and petrochemical factories led the way to industrialization in the Southwest.

The industrialization has helped bring about much urban growth in the Southwestern States Region. The region includes many of the nation's fastest-growing cities. Its largest cities are, in order of size, Houston, Phoenix, San Antonio, Dallas, Austin, and Fort Worth. The region also has many retirement communities. Tourist attractions in the Southwest include huge, unspoiled areas of incredible natural beauty, such as the Grand Canyon and the Painted Desert.

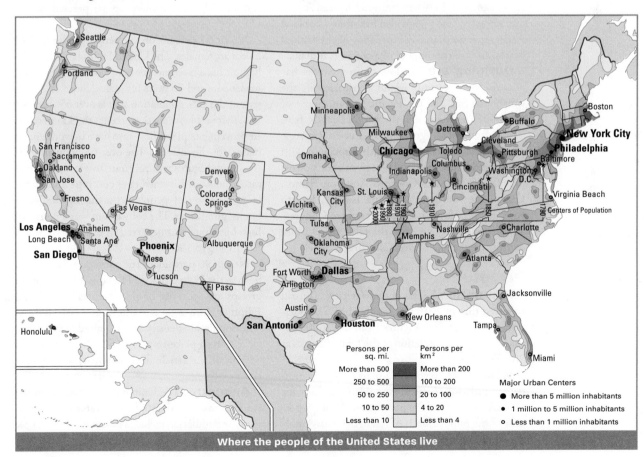

Where the people of the United States live

Many cultures come together in the Southwest. The population includes people of various European backgrounds, as well as African Americans, Mexican Americans, and American Indians.

The Pacific Coast States Region, which borders the Pacific Ocean, is known for its dense forests, rugged mountains, and dramatic ocean shore. The scenic beauty and relatively mild climate encourage an outdoor lifestyle enjoyed by both residents and tourists.

Fertile valleys in the Pacific Coast States Region produce a large part of the nation's fruits, nuts, vegetables, and wine grapes. The region also has abundant timber, minerals, and fish. Much manufacturing takes place in its large cities, which include—in order of size—Los Angeles, San Diego, San Jose, San Francisco, and Seattle.

The discovery of gold and the opening of the Oregon Territory in the mid-1800s brought a stream of settlers to the Pacific Coast. New residents, many drawn by the area's booming computer industry, have continued to pour in ever since. Today, the population includes people of European, African American, and Mexican American ancestry. The region also has more people of Asian ancestry than any other part of the United States, and a large number of American Indians.

Outlying areas. The United States has possession of various island territories in the Caribbean Sea and the Pacific Ocean. Some of them, such as Guam and the Virgin Islands, have a large degree of self-government. Puerto Rico, one of the areas, is a commonwealth associated with the United States that has been given wide powers of self-rule by the U.S. Congress. American Samoa, Guam, the Northern Mariana Islands, Puerto Rico, and the Virgin Islands each send to Congress a nonvoting delegate. (See the table titled *Main outlying areas of the United States* in this article.)

People

Population. The U.S. Census Bureau reported that in 2010 the country had a population of 308,745,538. Figures from the 2000 census had put the population of the United States at 281,421,906.

Whites make up about 72 percent of the country's population. African Americans account for about 13 percent of the population. About 5 percent of the population is of Asian descent. American Indians make up about 1 percent. Other

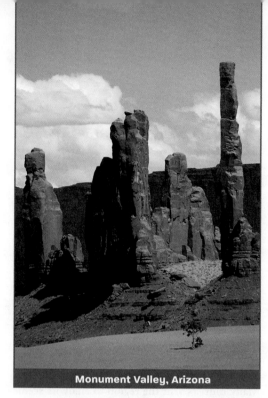

Monument Valley, Arizona

groups, including those of mixed racial heritage, combine to make up the remaining 9 percent.

The U.S. population includes many Hispanic people, such as people of Mexican, Puerto Rican, or Cuban descent. Hispanics consist mainly of whites, but they also include some blacks and American Indians. Hispanics make up 16 percent of the U.S. population.

About 51 percent of the people in the United States are females. The United States has one of the highest life expectancies of any country—80 years for females and 75 years for males. Since 1945, the part of the U.S. population that is over 65 years old has increased from 8 percent to 13 percent. Improvements in medical care have been the main reason for the increase. The over-65 population of the United States will continue to grow at a rapid rate as advances in medicine continue and as the large numbers of people born during the "baby boom" grow older. The baby boom was a period of high birth rate that occurred in the United States from 1946 to 1964.

Nearly 90 percent of the total population was born in the United States. The largest foreign-born groups are, in order of size, Mexicans, Chinese, Filipinos, Indians, Vietnamese, and Salvadorans. The population density in the United States varies widely from place to place. (See the map in this section of the article for the density throughout the country.)

Ancestry. The United States has one of the world's most varied populations in terms of ancestry. The population includes descendants of people from almost every part of the world.

The first people to live in what is now the United States were American Indians, Inuit (also called Eskimos), and Hawaiians. The Indians and Inuit are descended from peoples who migrated to North America from Asia thousands of years ago. The ancestors of the Hawaiians were Polynesians who sailed to what is now Hawaii from other Pacific islands about 2,000 years ago.

Most white Americans trace their ancestry to Europe. Some Spaniards settled in what is now the United States during the 1500s. European settlement increased sharply during the 1600s. At first, most of the settlers came from England. But America soon attracted many immigrants from other nations of northern and western Europe including France, Germany, Ireland, the Netherlands, and Scotland; and the Scandinavian lands of Denmark, Norway, and Sweden. Until the late 1800s, northern and western Europe provided most of the immigrants. Then, large waves of people began arriving from southern and eastern European nations, including Austria-Hungary, Greece, Italy, Poland, and Russia.

Most Hispanic Americans are people who immigrated—or whose ancestors immigrated—to the United States from Latin America. A small percentage of them trace their ancestry directly back to Spain. Some have mainly Spanish ancestry. Others have mixed Spanish and Indian or black ancestry.

Most African Americans are descendants of Africans who were brought to the United States as slaves during the 1600s, 1700s, and 1800s and forced to work on plantations.

Since the 1800s, the United States has attracted immigrants from Asia. Most Asian Americans trace their ancestry to China, India, Japan, Korea, the Philippines, or Vietnam.

The United States has often been called a *melting pot*. This term refers to the idea that the country is a place where people from many lands have come together and formed a unified culture. Americans have many things in common. For example, the vast majority speak English, and people throughout the country dress similarly and eat many of the same kinds of foods. Public education, mass communication, and other influences have helped shape a common identity.

But in other ways, U.S. society is an example of *cultural pluralism*. That is, large numbers of its people have retained features of the cultures of their ancestors. Many Americans take special pride in their origins. They preserve traditions—and in some cases the languages—of their ancestors. In many cities, people of different national or ethnic origins live in separate neighborhoods, and shops and restaurants reflect their cultural heritages. Ethnic festivals, parades, and other events emphasize the nation's cultural pluralism.

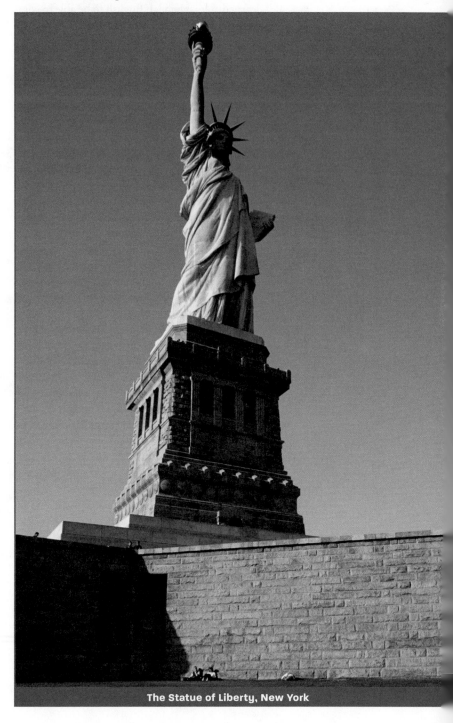

The Statue of Liberty, New York

Language. The United States has never had an official language, but English has always been the chief language spoken there. Immigrants from England, Scotland, and Ireland—who included the nation's founders—spoke English. Many immigrants from other lands who spoke little or no English also came to the United States. They learned at least enough English to be able to communicate with other Americans. Their children learned English in school. The immigrants' children generally spoke both English and their ethnic language, and in many families the immigrants' grandchildren spoke only English.

Today, Spanish is the second most common language in the United States. The region that is now the Southwestern United States was colonized by Spain in the 1500s. As a result, many people from that region speak Spanish. Since the 1950s, many Spanish-speaking people have immigrated to the United States from Mexico, Cuba, and other places. Many of these people learned English. But others speak only Spanish. This is especially true in Spanish-speaking neighborhoods that developed in cities. Some people feel that special efforts should be made to provide education and other services in Spanish for people who speak only Spanish.

Many people believe every American should know English. They point out that it is difficult to get a job outside Spanish-speaking neighborhoods without a knowledge of English. They also argue that a language shared by everyone is an important unifying force for a country. Many states have passed laws declaring English to be their only official language. These laws provide that the government must offer its services in English, and need not do so in any other language. But in some places, public documents and signs are written in both English and Spanish.

Way of Life

For census purposes, the United States is divided into *urban areas* and *rural areas*. An urban area, as defined by the U.S. Census Bureau, is a community with 2,500 or more people. A rural area is a community with fewer than 2,500 people.

In 1790, the year of the first census, about 95 percent of the nation's people lived in rural areas, and only about 5 percent were urban dwellers. Through the years, these percentages changed steadily and dramatically. Today, about 82 percent of all the people live in urban areas. Only about 18 percent live in rural areas.

Several factors contributed to the dramatic population shift from the countryside to urban areas. Through the years, Americans greatly improved agricultural methods and equipment. From the 1800s onward, farm work has become more and more efficient, farm production has soared, and fewer and fewer people have been needed to work on the nation's farms. At the same time, an industrial boom has created large numbers of new jobs in the nation's urban areas. As a result of these economic changes, a steady flow of people from rural to urban areas has taken place. Also, large numbers of immigrants—many of whom had been farmers in their homelands—found jobs in cities and settled there when they reached the United States. In addition, the variety of job choices and recreational, educational, and cultural opportunities in cities attracted many rural people, especially the young. Large numbers of rural people left home to seek employment and excitement in cities.

Urban life. Urban areas, which range from giant cities surrounded by suburbs to small towns, dot the U.S. landscape. Although the urban areas cover about 3 percent of the land, they are the home of about four-fifths of the people. New York City, with about 8 million people, is the largest U.S. city by far. Los Angeles has about 3 3/4 million people. Chicago has a population of about 2 2/3 million. Six other U.S. cities—Houston, Philadelphia, Phoenix, San Antonio, San Diego, and Dallas—each have more than 1 million people.

Networks of suburbs surround many U.S. cities. The central cities and their suburbs form units called metropolitan areas. There are about 370 metropolitan areas in the United States. The three largest are, in order of size, the New York-Northern New Jersey-Long Island, Los Angeles-Long Beach-Santa Ana, and Chicago-Joliet-Naperville areas. The New York area has nearly 19 million people, the Los Angeles area has almost 13 million people, and the Chicago area has about 9 1/2 million people.

For many years, the vast majority of the country's urban population lived in the central cities. But during the mid-1900s, suburban population soared throughout the United States, while central city growth slowed down or decreased. In 1970, for the first time, more Americans lived in suburbs than in central cities.

The Northeast and Midwest have long had most of the nation's largest urban areas. But during the 1900s, other parts of the country experienced dramatic urban growth. Since the early 1900s, many California urban communities—especially Los Angeles—have grown tremendously. Since the mid-1900s, the populations of many more urban areas in the West, and in the South and Southwest, have soared. Such metropolitan areas as Atlanta, Dallas, Denver, Houston, and Phoenix grew rapidly. Large numbers of people were attracted to the West, South, and Southwest by jobs created by new industries. Also, many of the fastest-growing communities have warm, sunny climates, which helped attract many of the newcomers. Parts of the South, Southwest, and West are sometimes called the *Sun Belt* because they have such climates.

Urban economies provide jobs for a great variety of workers, including office and factory workers, bankers, doctors, firefighters, medical personnel, police officers, teachers, trash collectors, and construction and transportation workers. Urban life also has many other positive features. Because urban areas have large populations, they generally offer a wide variety of specialized services and shops. Urban dwellers can take advantage of an assortment of restaurants, recreation facilities, and places of entertainment. Because of such facilities as art galleries, museums, libraries, theaters, and concert halls, many cities are important cultural centers. These and other features make urban areas exciting and interesting places to live for many people.

The people of most U.S. urban areas represent a variety of ethnic backgrounds. Most cities include neighborhoods in which almost all the people belong to the same ethnic or nationality group. The people of large urban areas are also divided economically. Urban society includes extremely wealthy and extremely poor people, and a huge middle class. The wealthy live in luxurious apartments or condominiums, or in large, comfortable single-family houses. Middle-class housing also includes apartments, condominiums, and single-family houses. In general, the housing of the middle class is comfortable, though not as luxurious as that of the wealthy. In contrast, large numbers of urban poor people live in substandard housing. They rent crowded, small apartments or rundown single-family houses.

In addition to substandard housing, urban areas have a number of other unpleasant features. Such features include high crime rates, racial and ethnic friction, noisy surroundings, pollution, and traffic jams.

Rural life. About 97 percent of all the land of the United States is classified as rural. But much of the rural land is uninhabited or only thinly inhabited. About 18 percent of all Americans live in rural areas.

Farms provide the economic basis of the nation's rural areas. But only about 8 percent of the country's rural people work on farms. Many other rural people own or work in businesses related to agriculture, such as grain and feed stores and warehouses. Mining and related activities and light industries also employ many rural people. Still other rural Americans work as teachers, police officers, salesclerks, or in other occupations. Many farmers hold other jobs for part of the year to add to their incomes.

American farmers of today lead vastly different lives from those of their grandparents. Machines have eliminated much backbreaking farm work. Farmers use machines to help them plow, plant seeds, harvest crops, and deliver their products to market. Many farms have conveyor systems so that the farmer no longer has to shovel feed to farm animals. Milking machines make morning and evening chores easier. In the home, farm families may have all the comforts and conveniences of city people. In the 1900s, the automobile, telephone, radio, television, and computer brought U.S. farm families into close contact with the rest of the world.

The steady decline in the percentage of the country's rural population has slowed since 1970. Although many people continued to move away from rural areas, others chose to move into rural towns and farm communities. Many of the new-

Grazing cattle

Graduation day

comers wanted to escape the overcrowding, pollution, crime, and other problems that are part of life in urban areas and to take advantage of benefits of country living. Rural areas have lower crime rates and less pollution than urban areas. They are also far less noisy and crowded.

Because of their small populations, rural communities collect less tax revenues than urban communities do, and they generally cannot provide the variety of services that urban areas can. For example, rural communities have cultural and recreational facilities that are more limited than those available in urban areas. For many rural Americans, social life centers around family gatherings, church and school activities, special interest clubs, and such events as state and county fairs.

Rural areas generally have less diversified economies than urban areas. Because there are fewer jobs and a smaller variety of jobs to choose from, rural communities may experience more widespread economic hardships than urban communities. A single economic downturn—a drop in farm prices, for example, or the closing of a mine—can cause economic hardship for an entire rural area.

The nation's rural areas, like its urban areas, have wealthy, middle class, and poor people. For the most part, however, the gaps between economic classes are not as large in rural areas as in urban areas. Most rural Americans live in single-family houses. The majority of the houses are comfortable and in good condition. But some people, including many who live in parts of Appalachia—

in the eastern United States—and other pockets of rural poverty, have rundown houses and enjoy few luxuries.

Education has been an important factor in the economic development of the United States and in the achievement of a high standard of living for most Americans. It has also contributed to the enjoyment of life for many people. Americans are among the best-educated people in the world. Schools, libraries, museums, and other educational institutions in the country provide learning opportunities for people of all ages.

Schools. During the early history of the United States, most schools were privately owned. Church groups owned and operated many of them. In the early 1800s, the idea of free public schools began to gain widespread support in the country. State and local governments took the responsibility for establishing public school systems. By 1918, every state had laws requiring children to attend school until they reached a certain age or completed a certain grade. Today, a majority of the nation's elementary and high schools, and many of its institutions of higher learning, are public schools. The rest are private schools run by religious organizations or private groups.

Many American children begin their schooling before enrolling in first grade. A number of all the children aged 3 and 4 attend nursery schools, and a large majority of all 5-year-olds attend kindergarten. Nearly all U.S. children complete elementary school, and a majority of them graduate from high school. Many high school graduates go on to colleges or universities.

Adult education is an important part of the school system in the United States. Millions of adults take courses at universities, colleges, vocational schools, recreation centers, or other institutions. Many adults continue their schooling to improve their job skills or to get training for a new job. Others attend classes simply to develop new hobbies or to find out more about topics that interest them. A growing number of part-time and full-time college and university students are men and women who have held jobs or raised families and are returning to school to get a degree.

Public schools in the United States are supported mainly by taxation. Private schools get their operating funds chiefly from tuition and contributions of private citizens. The nation's schools, like its private businesses, have always had to deal with financial problems. Rapidly rising material and salary costs have increased the financial problems of the schools. Some public and private schools have cut back on programs and reduced their faculties to try to keep expenses in line with revenues. Colleges and universities have sharply increased their tuition and fee charges.

Schools in the United States face a number of other problems. Many schools, particularly in large cities, have rundown buildings, inadequate supplies, and overcrowded conditions. A far higher percentage of young people in these areas drop out of school than in other areas. Some people claim that schools in their areas fail to provide students with the skills to obtain and hold jobs. Schools with large numbers of students from other countries face the problem of educating some children who speak little or no English.

Libraries provide the American people with access to books, periodicals, pamphlets, and other printed matter. In addition, many libraries offer compact discs, DVDs, and other multimedia materials; Internet access; research services; lectures; and educational exhibits.

There are thousands of public libraries in the United States. They range from one-room libraries in small towns to huge city libraries and their branches. There are also thousands of university and college libraries in the United States, as well as thousands of libraries in elementary schools and high schools.

The nation's library system also includes large numbers of private research libraries and special libraries with collections limited to certain fields of knowledge. In addition, many government agencies and businesses operate their own libraries. Three of the government's many libraries are considered national libraries because of their large and varied collections and because of the many services they provide. They are the Library of Congress, the National Agricultural Library of the Department of Agriculture, and the National Library of Medicine of the Department of Health and Human Services.

Museums. There are thousands of museums in the United States. They include museums of art, history, natural history, and science. In addition, a number of historic houses and villages are classed as museums. The collections of many of the nation's museums are devoted to a single topic of interest, such as the history of baseball or railroads. Some museums have huge collections of items

from many parts of the world. Others feature exhibits of local interest. In addition to exhibits, many U.S. museums offer classes, lectures, films, field trips, and other educational services. The most famous museums in the United States include the Metropolitan Museum of Art in New York City, the Museum of Science and Industry in Chicago, and the Smithsonian Institution in Washington, D.C.

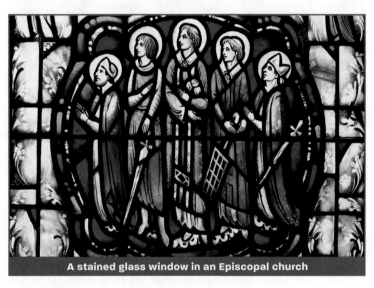

A stained glass window in an Episcopal church

Religion. More than 80 percent of all the American people are members of an organized religious group. Among them, about 50 percent are Protestants, and about 25 percent are Roman Catholics. Buddhists, Hindus, Jews, Mormons, Muslims, and members of Eastern Orthodox Churches each make up a small percentage of the population. Roman Catholics make up the largest single religious denomination in the United States. About 75 million Americans are Roman Catholics. The country's largest Protestant groups are, in order of size, Baptists, Methodists, Lutherans, Pentecostals, and Presbyterians.

Religion has played an important role in the history of the United States. Many people came to the American colonies to escape religious persecution in other lands. The early colonists included Puritans in New England, Roman Catholics in Maryland, and Quakers in Pennsylvania. The early Americans made religious freedom one of the country's basic laws. The First Amendment to the Constitution of the United States, which was adopted in 1791, guarantees every American freedom of religion. It also provides that no religious

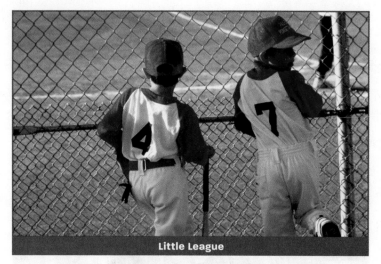

Little League

group be given official recognition as a state church. These provisions were intended to prevent persecution of religious minorities and the favoring of one church over another. Religious freedom was one of the reasons immigrants continued to flock to the United States through the years.

Although all religious groups in the United States enjoy freedom, Christian traditions have had a stronger influence on American life than those of any other faith. For example, most offices, factories, and other places of employment are closed on Sunday, the Sabbath of most Christians. The influence of Christianity results from the fact that a majority of the people are Christians.

Throughout the country's history, religion has influenced everyday life in a number of ways. For example, in colonial America many religious rules were enforced by local governments. Some of the laws that prohibited activities on Sunday still exist.

Today, religion has relatively less influence in the everyday lives of most Americans. But churches and other religious organizations continue to play important roles in American life. Their chief functions are to provide moral guidance and places for worship. However, religious groups also operate many elementary and secondary schools, colleges, universities, hospitals, and nursing homes. They provide aid for refugees, the poor, the elderly, orphans, and other persons in need. Social gatherings are held at many churches. Some religious groups take active roles in discussing such issues as birth control and rights for minorities and women.

Recreation. Most Americans have a great deal of leisure time, and they spend it in a variety of ways. They pursue hobbies, take part in sports, attend sporting and cultural events, watch movies and television, listen to music, and read books and magazines. They enjoy trips to museums, beaches, parks, playgrounds, and zoos. They take weekend and vacation trips, eat at restaurants, go on picnics, and entertain friends at home. These and other activities contribute to the richness and diversity of American life.

Sports rank as a leading American pastime. Millions of Americans enjoy watching such sports events as automobile races, horse races, and baseball, basketball, and football games—either in person or on television. Many Americans, especially children and other young people, play baseball, basketball, football, and soccer. People of most ages participate in such sports as bicycle riding, boating, bowling, fishing, golf, hiking, hunting, running, skiing, softball, swimming, and tennis.

Motion pictures, plays, concerts, operas, and dance performances attract large audiences in the United States. Americans find entertainment at home, as well. Almost all American homes have a television set. On the average, a set is in use in each home for about seven hours a day.

Hobbies occupy much of the leisure time of many Americans. Large numbers of people enjoy raising flower or vegetable gardens or indoor plants. Other popular hobbies include stamp collecting, coin collecting, photography, and playing a musical instrument. Such crafts hobbies as knitting, pottery making, and woodworking are also popular.

Most Americans spend part of their leisure time traveling. Many take annual vacations, as well as occasional one-day excursions or weekend trips. Some have vacation homes near lakes or seashores, in the mountains, or in other recreation areas. Others own motor homes or trailers, which provide living and sleeping quarters during trips. Some people enjoy camping in tents. Others prefer to stay in hotels or motels while on trips.

Food. Americans eat a wide variety of foods. A typical dinner consists of meat and potatoes, plus a lettuce salad or a vegetable, and sometimes rolls or bread. Favorite dinner meats include beef steaks, ground beef dishes, chicken, ham, and turkey. Fish, shellfish, and such dishes as pizza and spaghetti also serve as main courses.

For lunch, many Americans eat a sandwich, such as a hamburger or a hot dog. Other favorite sandwiches include those made with meat or sliced sausage, cheese, peanut butter, chicken salad, or tuna salad.

Some Americans enjoy a hearty breakfast of eggs or pancakes served with bacon or sausage. Others prefer a light breakfast of toast or a pastry, or cereal with milk and fruit. Orange juice accompanies many breakfasts.

Cake, cookies, pie, and ice cream are eaten as desserts and snacks. Other snack foods include chocolate candy, potato or corn chips, and such fruits as bananas, apples, oranges, and grapes.

Beverages are drunk with meals and also at other times for refreshment. Consumption of soft drinks, especially cola, exceeds that of any other beverage. Americans also drink much coffee, milk, and beer, and smaller amounts of fruit juices, tea, and wine.

Americans eat out often. *Fast-food* restaurants have wide popularity. They offer a limited variety of foods, all of which are served within a few minutes. Common fast-food items include hamburgers and other sandwiches, fried chicken, and French fried potatoes. Many Americans also enjoy the cooking of other countries. Chinese, French, Italian, and Mexican restaurants have long been popular. Since the mid-1900s, Americans have increasingly enjoyed the cuisines of India, Japan, Thailand, the Middle East, and many other areas.

Some regions of the United States have distinctive food specialties.

The Arts

European colonists arrived in America during the early 1600s, bringing European art traditions with them. But within a few years, colonists were building houses that probably rank as the first major American works of art. During the 1700s, American craftworkers began to produce outstanding examples of furniture, sculpture, and silverwork. By the mid-1700s, colonial painters were creating excellent portraits. During the late 1800s, American architects began designing skyscrapers that revolutionized urban architecture throughout the world. Two uniquely American art forms, jazz and musical comedy, developed during the late 1800s and early 1900s. In the early 1900s, the United States gained international leadership in the new art forms of motion pictures and modern dancing.

American Literature cannot be captured in a simple definition. It reflects the many religious, historical, and cultural traditions of the American people, one of the world's most varied populations.

It includes poetry, fiction, drama, and other kinds of writing by authors in what is now the United States. It also includes nonwritten material, such as the oral literature of the American Indians and folktales and legends. In addition, American literature includes accounts of America written by immigrants and visitors from other countries, as well as works by American writers who spent some or all of their lives abroad.

American literature begins with the legends, myths, and poetry of the American Indians, the first people to live in what is now the United States. Indian legends included stories about the origin of the world, the histories of various tribes, and tales of tribal heroes. With rare exceptions, this oral literature was not written down until the 1800s.

The earliest writing in America consisted of the journals and reports of European explorers and missionaries. These early authors left a rich literature describing their encounters with new lands and new civilizations. They publicized their adventures, described the New World, and tried to attract settlers in works that sometimes mixed facts with propaganda.

Colonial literature (1608–1764). Colonists from England and other European countries began settling along the eastern coast of North America in the early 1600s and created the first American colonial literature. The colonies in Virginia and New England produced the most important writings in the 1600s. In the 1700s,

An engraving of Benjamin Franklin

Philadelphia emerged as the literary center of the American Colonies.

In 1620, the Pilgrims founded Plymouth Colony, the second permanent English settlement in America. Many Pilgrims belonged to a group of English Protestants called *Puritans*, who were followers of the religious reformer John Calvin. They wrote histories, sermons and other religious writings, and poetry.

The Puritans recorded their own history out of a desire to communicate with fellow believers in England, to attract new colonists, and to justify their bold move to a new country. In their histories, the Puritans portrayed their successes as evidence of God's favor and their hardships as signs of God's disapproval.

The Puritans based their religion on constant study of the Bible. Sermons began with a passage from the Bible, followed by an analysis of its meaning, and then its application to personal and community life. The greatest Puritan preacher and theologian was Jonathan Edwards. He wrote learned essays reformulating traditional Calvinist doctrines, but also defending them. Edwards' most important book is *Freedom of Will* (1754). In it, he defended the doctrine of *predestination*, the idea that God has chosen certain souls to be saved.

American colonists also wrote poetry. Most critics today rate Edward Taylor as the best of the Puritan poets. A clergyman, Taylor composed a series of meditative poems on Scripture readings. He intended the poems to prepare his mind to preach and to celebrate Communion. His verse followed the learned style of the English metaphysical poets of the 1600's. Like them, he mingled everyday words and incidents with Biblical language and complex metaphors. Taylor's poems were not discovered until 1937 and not published until 1939.

Although life as a settler was hard, Anne Bradstreet found time to write poetry, chiefly for her father and husband. Her brother-in-law had her work printed in London as *The Tenth Muse Lately Sprung Up in America* (1650), the first volume of American poetry ever published. The resulting publicity made Bradstreet more conscious of her craftsmanship. She began experimenting with meter, imagery, structure, and theme. *Several Poems* (1678), a revised second edition, was published after her death. It includes her best poem, "Contemplations," a nature poem on the briefness of human life.

Washington Irving

During the 1700s, a greater number of people learned to read, and a growing press served new literary tastes. Literature addressed such interests as politics and science. The essay, satire, and novel became important literary forms.

The publisher, statesman, and scientist Benjamin Franklin helped make the American Colonies a center of intellectual life. His *Autobiography* tells the story of how he ran away from Boston to Philadelphia at the age of 17. His rise from "rags to riches" through hard work and self-improvement became a model for American success. Franklin's writings emphasized practical intelligence and material success, balanced by charity and public service. His worldliness differed greatly from the earnest spirituality of the Puritans. Franklin's witty and often satiric proverbs made *Poor Richard's Almanac*, published for each year from 1733 to 1758, one of his most popular publications.

The revolutionary period (1765–1787). During the 1760s, a movement to end British rule in the American Colonies began to gain strength. The United States became an independent nation by winning the Revolutionary War in America (1775–1783). Much of the literature of this period addressed issues relating to American independence.

Thomas Paine, a poor and largely self-taught Englishman, immigrated to Philadelphia in 1774. He soon became famous for his fiery essays in support of the American patriots. His pamphlet *Common Sense* (1776) called for complete independence from the United Kingdom. In a series of pamphlets called *The American Crisis* (1776–1783), he encouraged the rebels to persist during the darkest days of the Revolutionary War.

Like many writers of the 1700s, Franklin and Paine wrote in dignified, but plain and clear, prose. This style reached its peak in the ringing eloquence of the Declaration of Independence written by Thomas Jefferson. The same type of writing appears in the sober language of the Constitution of the United States, much of which was drafted by Gouverneur Morris. Alexander Hamilton, James Madison, and John Jay used this clear style in *The Federalist* (1787–1788), a series of public letters that persuaded New Yorkers to ratify the Constitution.

Literature of a young nation (1788–1830). In the early years of United States independence, many American writers still patterned their writing after Europe's latest literary styles and forms. Gradually, however, American literature began to reflect American experiences.

The most successful American writer of the early 1800s was Washington Irving. He rose to fame with humorous and satiric writing about New York City and its past in the magazine *Salmagundi* (1807–1808) and in a book, *A History of New York from the Beginning of the World to the End of the Dutch Dynasty* (1809). The book is also called *Knickerbocker's History of New York* because Irving wrote it under the name Diedrich Knickerbocker. In *The Sketch Book of Geoffrey Crayon, Gent.* (1819–1820), Irving combined the style of the essay and the sketch to create the first short stories in American literature. The book includes "Rip Van Winkle" and "The Legend of Sleepy Hollow," two of Irving's most famous tales. In "Rip Van Winkle," the title character awakens from a 20-year sleep to find everything changed by the Revolutionary War. Irving's doubts about American independence, his hostility toward New England culture, and his desire to maintain cultural ties with England run through all his early writing.

The Era of Expansion (1831–1870). During the mid-1800s, the United States gained control of many western lands. By the 1850s, the nation stretched from coast to coast. Americans moved westward by the thousands. The Indians who occupied many of these lands were forced to surrender their claims and to resettle on reservations. During this period, many American writers glorified the frontier or praised the beauty of nature. Much American literature reflected the optimism of a rapidly growing nation. But other American lit-

erature focused on the country's problems, including slavery. In 1861, the Civil War broke out between the North and South chiefly over this issue. The North won the war in 1865, and slavery was soon outlawed throughout the United States.

Two main forms of fiction were practiced by American writers in the mid-1800s: (1) the sentimental novel and (2) the romance. Other important literary forms included nonfiction prose and poetry.

The sentimental novel, which had been developed by English author Samuel Richardson in the mid-1700s, became immensely popular in the United States in the mid-1800s. This type of novel emphasized feelings and such values as religious faith, moral virtue, and family closeness. Its stress on traditional values appealed to many people during a period of rapid social and political change.

The sentimental novel also urged reform. It became the means for rousing concern about the plight of black slaves, poor people, and other unfortunate members of society. Harriet Beecher Stowe's *Uncle Tom's Cabin* (1851–1852), a powerful description of the evils of slavery, became a best seller. It combined an exciting plot, memorable characters, stirring appeals to the emotions, and humor. Stage adaptations of the book also drew large audiences.

Most people use the term *novel* to refer to any long fictional story in prose. Critics of the 1800s, however, distinguished a novel from a *romance*. A

Henry Wadsworth Longfellow

romance is a long work of fiction that is less real-istic than a novel. Instead of everyday events, a romance describes exciting adventures or strange events. Writers often use the romance to explore dark passions or to examine the problem of evil.

James Fenimore Cooper wrote historical romances that explored the moral uncertainties of Americans' push westward. In Cooper's romances, such as *The Last of the Mohicans* (1826) and *The Deerslayer* (1841), the beauty and majesty of nature inspire a nearly religious feeling of awe. But civiliza-tion intrudes, and settlers turn the wilderness into property that they selfishly or thoughtlessly misuse.

This period also saw a great flowering of nonfic-tion prose. During the 1830s and 1840s, a literary and philosophical movement called *transcendental-ism* developed in New England. The transcenden-talists believed that God was present in nature. They also believed that human beings intuitively know what is true, and so they stressed self-reliance and individuality. The transcendentalists included Ralph Waldo Emerson; Henry David Thoreau; George Ripley; Margaret Fuller; and Bronson Alcott, Louisa May Alcott's father.

Emerson was the leader of the movement. He urged Americans to be independent thinkers and to study life directly. Emerson declared that individu-als had access to the eternal and ideal truths of nature. He therefore urged Americans to trust their own creative instincts and not look to Europe for models. He kept a journal in which he recorded inci-dents, ideas, and reactions to his wide reading. Emerson drew on his journal in such essays as *Nature* (1836) and "Self-Reliance" (1841), achieving a prose style that was personal and conversational.

In *Walden* (1854), Thoreau described his expe-riences living close to nature. The book tells how

Mark Twain's home

he built a cabin in the woods on the shore of Walden Pond in Massachusetts and lived there alone. He read, entertained visitors, worked the land for his food, and recorded his observations in journals. Thoreau's style shows his sensitive response to the root meanings, sounds, images, and nuances of words.

In the years surrounding the Civil War (1861–1865), many black writers, most of whom were for-mer slaves, began writing to explore themes such as the exploration of the black identity, the condemna-tion of racism, and the celebration of the uniqueness of African American culture. In 1838, Frederick Douglass escaped from slavery and fled North. Dur-ing the early 1840s, he joined the abolitionists. His fiery attacks on slavery made him a famous speaker. In the first edition of his autobiography, the *Narra-tive of the Life of Frederick Douglass* (1845), Douglass vividly describes his life as a slave.

19th-century poetry. During the 1800s, the most famous American poets were William Cullen Bryant, Henry Wadsworth Longfellow, James Russell Lowell, John Greenleaf Whittier, and Oliver Wendell Holmes. They were called the "Fireside Poets" or the "Schoolroom Poets" because their works were most often read "by the fireside" at home or in school in *anthologies* (collections of literary works). Like the sentimental novelists, these poets concerned themselves with feelings and called for social reform.

Edgar Allan Poe wrote haunting, often mourn-ful poems. "The Raven" (1845) and "Annabel Lee" (1849) express despair over the death of a woman. Poe's poetry did not make an immediate impact on American poets. But he gained a great following in Europe after two important French poets, Charles Baudelaire and Stephane Mallarme, praised and translated his work. Influenced by Poe, they in turn inspired several modern American poets, includ-ing T. S. Eliot and Wallace Stevens.

Walt Whitman and Emily Dickinson were the two greatest American poets of the 1800s. Whit-man took inspiration from Emerson's call for a self-confident American literature. He expressed the variety of American life in long lines that caught the flow of operatic singing. His verse often takes the form of rhythmic lists. It sprawls, seeming improvised. But Whitman also packed his poems with vivid images and memorable phrases. He wrote in *free verse*, a style of poetry that avoids reg-ular meter and rhyme. Whitman published the first edition of his masterpiece, *Leaves of Grass*, in 1855. Five more enlarged and revised editions of the collection appeared between 1856 and 1882. *Leaves of Grass* describes the best and worst of American life, from exuberant democracy to suffering slaves. The longest poem in the collection, "Song of Myself," glorifies a spiritual life grounded in the body and everyday life.

Dickinson wrote more than 1,700 short, puzzling poems in the mid-1800s. Her subjects were love, death, nature, and immortality. Only 11 of Dickinson's poems were printed in her lifetime. After an accurate, complete edition of her poems appeared in 1955, Dickinson's reputation and influence rapidly grew. Critics admired her precise observations, her complex and unexpected images, and her questioning of established religion and authority.

The Age of Realism (1871–1913). The Civil War marked a dramatic change in American life. The war ended slavery, but it left the deeper problem of race relations. After the conflict, the United States turned its energies to economic concerns. Machines replaced hand labor as the chief means of manufacturing, and industry grew enormously. The new business activity centered in cities, and people moved to them in huge numbers. While some people made fortunes in business, others lived in poverty.

Many American writers of the late 1800s were inspired by an international literary movement called *realism*. Realism was in part a revolt against romanticism and its idealized portrayal of life. The realists sought to show life as it is. Realism encouraged writers to examine the problems and conditions around them and to use the language of ordinary people, including dialects. In this way, it encouraged the emergence of a distinctively American literature.

Many of the realists focused on particular regions of the United States. Bret Harte portrayed the West of the gold rush in such short stories as "The Luck of Roaring Camp" (1868) and "The Outcasts of Poker Flat" (1869). Sarah Orne Jewett's *The Country of the Pointed Firs* (1896) shows a rural New England left behind by economic development.

Early Southern realists included George Washington Cable and Joel Chandler Harris. Cable's *The Grandissimes* (1880) portrays the tragic clash of races and cultures in Louisiana. Harris' *Uncle Remus: His Songs and His Sayings* (1881) and later collections of stories were immensely popular.

They retell, in dialect, black folklore and stories. The black writer Charles Waddell Chesnutt's *The Conjure Woman* (1899) is also a collection of folk tales in dialect.

Naturalists were the most extreme and pessimistic realists. Unlike the realists, the naturalists believed that people could not make moral choices. They showed their characters as completely controlled by economic, social, or biological forces.

In such stories as "The Open Boat" (1897) and "The Blue Hotel" (1898), Stephen Crane stressed the need for courage and generosity in a universe indifferent to human life. His most famous work, *The Red Badge of Courage* (1895), shows a young soldier in the Civil War, wandering in a state of shock and confusion through scenes of battle.

Theodore Dreiser was the leading American naturalist. His *Sister Carrie* traces a young woman's rise to success and social prominence despite her violation of moral codes. Her fate contrasts with her first lover's decline into poverty and suicide. Although *Sister Carrie* was printed in 1900, the publisher refused to advertise or distribute the book because his wife thought it lacked a sense of right and wrong. Another publisher issued it in 1912.

Mark Twain and Henry James are considered by critics as the two greatest American novelists of the late 1800s. Twain's *Adventures of Tom Sawyer* (1876) describes the adventures of a clever and

Edith Wharton

mischievous boy and his friend Huck Finn. *Adventures of Huckleberry Finn* (1884) continues the story. It narrates the adventures of Huck and the runaway slave Jim as they float down the Mississippi River on a raft. In this book, Twain contrasts nature—where a white boy and a black man can become friends—with the hypocrisy of civilization along the shore. Twain also satirized the styles of writing that dominated earlier American literature.

Henry James left the United States in his 30s and settled in England. In his study of *Hawthorne* (1879), he argued that the lack of a rich cultural tradition made American novels thin and abstract. James wrote *novels of manners*, which first appeared in England in the late 1700s. Novels of manners depict realistic characters and scenes and describe the customs of a particular social class. In many of James's works, American characters travel to Europe, where their innocence and integrity clash with a culture that is attractive but sometimes corrupt. In *The Portrait of a Lady* (1880–1881), a young American discovers too late the immorality of her husband, an American who has immigrated to Italy. James's style grew more complex in later novels. He traced with increasing detail the psychological and moral problems of his intelligent and self-conscious characters.

Women writers were also relating their experiences during this period. Kate Chopin powerfully portrayed a woman's psychological and sexual development in *The Awakening* (1899). However, the hostile reaction to the novel ended Chopin's career. Edith Wharton became known for her keen moral and psychological examination of characters. *The House of Mirth* (1905) exposes the selfishness and materialism of upper-class society in New York City.

Nonfiction writers also flourished in the United States after the Civil War. Two prominent black leaders were well-known for their nonfiction. They disagreed on the best course for black advancement. In his autobiography, *Up from Slavery* (1901), educator Booker T. Washington urged blacks to temporarily suspend their demands for equal rights in exchange for vocational education and jobs. He predicted that blacks would achieve equal rights once they gained economic power. But historian and sociologist W. E. B. Du Bois challenged what he regarded as Washington's surrender of rights for economic gain. Du Bois refused all compromises. In *The Souls of Black Folk* (1903), he insisted that "the problem of the twentieth century is the problem of the color line."

Ezra Pound

The world wars and depression (1914–1945). In 1914, World War I broke out in Europe. In 1917, the United States entered the war against Germany, which was defeated in 1918. After the war, the United States economy boomed. But prosperity did not last. A stock market crash in 1929 led to the Great Depression, a deep economic slump in the 1930s.

In 1939, World War II began in Europe. The United States fought in the war from 1941 to 1945 and played an important role in defeating Germany and Japan.

About the time of World War I, an international artistic movement called *modernism* emerged in Europe. Modernist artists believed that the traditional social, religious, and political order had broken down. They felt that realism could not adequately describe how greatly modern life differed from the past. As a result, they sought stylistic innovations that could better portray new realities.

The American writers who lived in Europe around the time of World War I made important contributions to modernism. Their influence extended to writers in the United States. The Great Depression led some writers of the period to focus on social or economic issues.

Modernist poetry leaves out the explanations and narrative connections that provide unity and clarity in traditional writing. It mixes everyday language with elegant phrases and short quotations from earlier poems. Modernist poets placed contradictory feelings and events side by side to evoke the disconnectedness of modern life.

T. S. Eliot, one of the first modernists, moved to London in 1914. There, he became friends with Ezra Pound, who had already settled in Europe. Together, Eliot and Pound discovered and absorbed a wide range of poetic traditions. They developed many of the features of modernist poetry and made them well known.

Eliot mastered the modernist style in "The Love Song of J. Alfred Prufrock" (1915). His long poem *The Waste Land* (1922) created an uproar. This complex, pessimistic reflection on the emptiness of modern life seemed a masterpiece to some but bewildering to others. Eliot gradually gained a widespread influence in modern poetry. In many critical essays, he redefined the way people thought about literature.

Some poets of the early and mid-1900s practiced realism rather than modernism. Edwin Arlington Robinson's best poems are realist portraits of bleak and wasted lives in a New England village. In Edgar Lee Masters' *Spoon River Anthology* (1915), the now-dead inhabitants of an imaginary Midwestern town tell their life stories.

The poems of Robert Frost, such as "Mending Wall" (1914) and "Stopping by Woods on a Snowy Evening" (1923), are simple and readable on the surface. But they reveal complex feelings, often through subtle irony and dry wit. Frost expressed in ordinary language the puzzling hints of doubt and uncertainty that haunt everyday incidents. These feelings connect him to modernism, despite his traditional meter, rhyme, and verse forms.

Paul Laurence Dunbar was perhaps the first black American to achieve national recognition as a writer of both poetry and fiction. Many of his poems use standard English and traditional meter, but he achieved greater fame for his portraits in dialect of black life in the South.

An important literary movement after World War I was begun by a group of writer known as the Lost Generation. These writers joined the flourishing arts community in Paris after World War I. Many of these newcomers to Paris gathered around the novelist and critic Gertrude Stein, who had settled there before the war.

Two of the most important writers of the Lost Generation were Ernest Hemingway and F. Scott Fitzgerald. Hemingway's *The Sun Also Rises* (1926) describes these uprooted Americans in a desperate search for something to believe in after the destruction caused by the war. In short stories that some critics still consider his finest work, Hemingway crafted a bare, blunt prose that sought to clear away the emptiness of old ideas and values. His prose style has inspired many imitators.

Fitzgerald focused on American life in the Roaring Twenties, also called the Jazz Age. In short stories and in such novels as *The Great Gatsby* (1925) and *Tender Is the Night* (1934), he showed how the values of the American dream had been corrupted by materialism and class divisions. Fitzgerald's strong visual sense and way of composing a story into scenes showed the influence of early motion pictures.

Modernism led writers of fiction to reexamine the techniques of storytelling. Writers began to strip away descriptions of scenes and characters, explanations, direct statements of theme, and summaries of the plot. A few writers experimented with prose styles as fragmented and difficult as some modern poetry.

Some critics regard William Faulkner as the greatest American novelist of the 1900s. Faulkner set most of his novels, such as *The Sound and the Fury* (1929) and *As I Lay Dying* (1930), in the imaginary Mississippi county of Yoknapatawpha. He saw slavery and racism as the great sins haunting Southern history. He believed the South fought heroically in the Civil War but for an evil cause. Faulkner's Southerners live with

Lillian Hellman

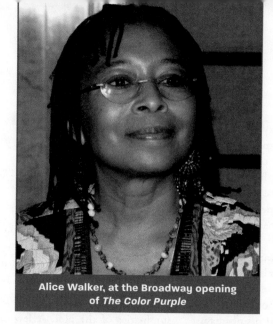

Alice Walker, at the Broadway opening of *The Color Purple*

this heritage of guilt and useless, misguided nobility. Faulkner absorbed all the techniques of modernist storytelling. His style is symbolic, lyric, and sometimes eloquent. He evoked the contradictory feelings of his characters through fragmented and difficult plots. Faulkner often employed the stream-of-consciousness technique.

During the 1920s and 1930s, many writers and critics debated the relation between literature and social or political change. Particularly because of the depression, many writers felt a responsibility to address economic and social problems. These authors often used journalistic techniques to educate a wide audience about needed reforms. Other writers, such as John Dos Passos, experimented with new forms and styles. In his trilogy *The 42nd Parallel* (1930), *1919* (1932), and *The Big Money* (1936)—published together as *U.S.A.* in 1938—Dos Passos aimed to portray American society fully and realistically. His novels include what he called Newsreels, which use newspaper headlines, words from popular songs, and advertisements to surround characters and action.

Most American plays of the 1700s and 1800s were sentimental comedies or melodramatic tragedies. Eugene O'Neill broke this tradition in the 1920s. Early in his career, he created highly realistic plays. He wrote about the criminals, homeless, alcoholics, laborers, artists, and radicals he had encountered in several years of drifting. These characters spoke in crude, slangy, but lively language. During the 1930s, vigorous debates also took place over the purpose of drama. Some playwrights wanted the theater to be a force for social reform. Others concentrated on experimental technique, and still others aimed at frankly escapist and commercially successful work. Clifford Odets' *Waiting for Lefty* (1935) and *Awake and Sing!*

(1935) attack social problems of the time. Lillian Hellman's plays, such as *The Children's Hour* (1934) and *The Little Foxes* (1939), explore the destructiveness of greed, materialism, and sexual repression in American life. In *Our Town* (1938), Thornton Wilder used uncommon staging techniques, such as the absence of scenery or a curtain, to balance a somewhat sentimental picture of small-town New England life.

The Harlem Renaissance. During the early 1900s, particularly in the 1920s, black literature began to flourish in Harlem, a district of New York City. This movement became known as the Harlem Renaissance. It was also called the New Negro after the title of an anthology collected by educator and writer Alain Locke. The major writers of the Harlem Renaissance were Sterling A. Brown, Countee Cullen, Jessie Redmon Fauset, Langston Hughes, Zora Neale Hurston, James Weldon Johnson, Alain Locke, Claude McKay, and Jean Toomer.

McKay was one of the most powerful black poets. He began with poems in dialect. Later, he wrote highly formal but emotional verse, often on explosive topics. Hughes made a deliberate effort to bring the rhythms of African American music into poetry. Brown used dialect in subtly varied ways both to protest against racial prejudice and to express pride in the distinctive cultural tradition of African Americans. Cullen was mainly a lyric poet, but he sometimes used verse to protest racism.

Black prose writers also flourished during the Harlem Renaissance. Toomer's *Cane* (1923) is a sophisticated mixture of short stories, sketches, poetry, and a play. Hurston collected African American folk tales and became well known as a skilled oral storyteller. Her best-known novel, *Their Eyes Were Watching God* (1937), traces a black woman's steady growth in insight and spiritual strength. Her characters are vivid, realistic mixtures of strength and weakness. Locke wrote several nonfiction works on African American culture.

Literature from 1945 to the early 2000s. In the decades from the end of World War II in 1945 to the early 2000s, the United States took on a central role in global affairs. The economy prospered, and American culture, especially popular culture, became influential worldwide. The black civil rights movements changed laws in the 1960s, and African Americans continued to seek elimination of prejudices in society.

Other groups, especially women and gays, also demanded fuller rights. The United States' role in the Vietnam War (1957–1975) was controversial at home and abroad. The collapse of the Communist governments in eastern Europe left the United States the dominant world power, though China increasingly gained in importance.

Massive immigration brought new ethnic groups into the United States and influenced popular culture. Terrorist attacks in New York City and Washington, D.C., on September 11, 2001, triggered U.S.-led wars in Afghanistan and Iraq. The attacks also led to deep concerns about terrorism and political instability in the Middle East. American literature reflected many of these changes.

By the 1950s, modernism was the dominant form of poetry. A generation of poets, including Robert Lowell, John Berryman, and Theodore Roethke, thoroughly mastered modernist techniques. A number of poets and groups developed poetic styles that were variations on modernism.

A group called the *beat poets* condemned the failings of American society and turned poetry into a powerful tool of social protest. The beat poets shared a disgust with false values and a desire to achieve spiritual elevation. One of the most important beat poets was Allen Ginsberg. Ginsberg's "Howl" (1956) describes spiritual ecstasy and the torments of urban life in long lines influenced by Whitman and William Carlos Williams.

Some poets began to write poetry, sometimes called "confessional" poetry, that was more personal and emotional. Theodore Roethke explored the themes of growth and childhood in elegantly written poems. Sylvia Plath sometimes used the Holocaust, the mass murder of European Jews and others by the Nazis during World War II, as a metaphor for personal crisis. Anne Sexton wrote about her mental illness in a direct and open style. Adrienne Rich moved from formal verse to steadily deeper probings of her consciousness as a woman.

The black experience became the subject of many poets in the 1950s and 1960s. The early poetry of Gwendolyn Brooks showed her skill in traditional rhyming verse and forms like the *sonnet*, a 14-line poem with a formal arrangement of rhymes. Yet her words drew on oral black preaching and street talk. She described the ordinary lives of blacks and the injustices they suffered.

In the postwar period, many writers continued to create realist fiction. Several authors drew their subjects from World War II. J. D. Salinger exposed the shortcomings of the adult world as seen through the eyes of a New York teen-ager in *The Catcher in the Rye* (1951). James Baldwin wrote about the black experience in such novels as *Go Tell It on the Mountain* (1953) and *Another Country* (1962). Ralph Ellison, in *Invisible Man* (1952), provided a haunting picture of African American life in the United States. The beat novelist Jack Kerouac's *On the Road* (1957) tells of young rebels against the boredom and pointlessness of daily life who wander the United States in a search for meaning. Kerouac's strongly rhythmic flow of words creates an impression of spontaneity and improvisation, like that in jazz.

A number of Southern writers, influenced by William Faulkner, focused on the poor, outcasts, or grotesque characters. Among these writers were Carson McCullers, Flannery O'Connor, Eudora Welty. McCullers depicted the pain of loneliness in many of her works, including *The Member of the Wedding* (1946) and *The Ballad of the Sad Cafe* (1951). In brilliant short stories and in such novels as *Wise Blood* (1952) and *The Violent Bear It Away* (1960), O'Connor presented grotesque characters and disturbed behavior in a darkly comic style. Eudora Welty sets most of her novels and short stories in her native Mississippi. In her works, comic and satiric twists lighten the impact of odd characters or moments of violence.

The stylistic experiments of the modernists opened the way for a technique called *self-reflexive fiction*, an innovative manipulation of language and narrative. Self-reflexive fiction often calls attention to the act of writing itself. For example, it may comment on or even argue with itself and address or even mock the reader. Self-reflexive fiction and

A scene from David Mamet's *Glengarry Glen Ross*

other experimental techniques became common among postwar authors. In *The Sot-Weed Factor* (1960), *Chimera* (1972), and other works, John Barth created wild comedies mingling ancient myth, history, and highly unreliable autobiography.

Thomas Pynchon's *Gravity's Rainbow* (1973) is a fantastic reimagining of World War II filtered through the social concerns of the early 1970's. Joseph Heller's *Catch-22* (1961) and Kurt Vonnegut's *Slaughterhouse-Five* (1969) use dark comedy to satirize the self-satisfaction they felt resulted from the war. Ken Kesey's *One Flew over the Cuckoo's Nest* (1962) uses a mental hospital and a con-man hero as symbols of modern American society.

The civil rights movement of the 1960s brought forth a number of popular works by black writers. Alex Haley's *Roots: The Saga of an American Family* (1976) traces his family's history back through American slaves to his African ancestors. Novelist Toni Morrison wrote about the lives of black women in the North in such novels as *Sula* (1973), *Tar Baby* (1981), and *Beloved* (1987). Alice Walker won fame with the novel *The Color Purple* (1982). Walker has presented a range of black characters, some heroic, but others deeply flawed, particularly black men who treat women unfairly. Like Morrison, she has increasingly found an exuberantly creative language and storytelling technique.

Postwar drama. The leading playwrights after World War II were Tennessee Williams and Arthur Miller. Williams' drama often shows a conflict between sensitive, poetic individuals and the brutality and coarseness of modern life. His plays are basically realistic psychological portraits. *The Glass Menagerie* (1945) and *A Streetcar Named Desire* (1947) are his most famous. His later work explores grotesque and sometimes disturbed behavior. Miller's *Death of a Salesman* (1949) lends tragic dignity to the anguish of Willy Loman, a traveling salesman. Loman is destroyed by accepting popularity and material success as the highest values in life.

In *Who's Afraid of Virginia Woolf?* (1962), Edward Albee explored with biting wit and grotesque humor how love and cruelty are entangled within marital relationships and friendships. Albee also adapted the style of the *Theater of the Absurd* in plays that probed social and personal problems, such as *The Zoo Story* (1959). Theater of the Absurd was a drama movement of the 1950s and 1960s that stressed the absurdity and lack of meaning the authors saw in modern life.

During the 1950s and 1960s, black theater often took up political themes. Lorraine Hansberry's *A Raisin in the Sun* (1959) is a realistic portrait of a black family who decides to move away from the ghetto and into an all-white neighborhood. They must find the courage to resist the racism in society and claim the right to realize their hopes. The poet Amiri Baraka also wrote plays, promoting black nationalism and expressing anger at whites in such dramas as *Dutchman* (1964), *The Slave* (1964), and *Slave Ship* (1967). August Wilson has written powerfully on the black experience in America in the 1900s in a cycle of plays. *The Piano Lesson* (1987) describes the conflict between a brother and sister over whether to sell or keep the family heirloom, a piano.

In plays such as *The Basic Training of Pavlo Hummel* (1971) and *Sticks and Bones* (1971), David Rabe portrayed the disillusionment of soldiers in the Vietnam War. Sam Shepard's dramas, such as *True West* (1980) and *Fool for Love* (1983), are bitter explorations of family relationships and the dominant values in American society and politics. David Mamet's plays, including *American Buffalo* (1975) and *Glengarry Glen Ross* (1983), are noted for their vigorous dialogue, often profane and rapidly exploding into arguments.

Today, American architects, authors, dramatists, composers, painters, and sculptors have achieved worldwide recognition and influence. Many of them have shown a keen interest in developing new

Autumn in West Virginia

Yellowstone Lower Falls, Wyoming

styles, new ways of expressing themselves, and even new forms of art.

The Land

The United States, excluding Alaska and Hawaii, can be divided into seven major land regions. The regions are: (1) the Appalachian Highlands; (2) the Coastal Lowlands; (3) the Interior Plains; (4) the Ozark-Ouachita Highlands; (5) the Rocky Mountains; (6) the Western Plateaus, Basins, and Ranges; and (7) the Pacific Ranges and Lowlands.

The Appalachian Highlands extend from the northern tip of Maine southwestward to Alabama. This rugged region has many mountain ranges.

The White Mountains and the Green Mountains of northern New England are old mountains, worn down but craggy in some places. Southern New England consists mostly of hilly land. New England's chief river is the Connecticut. The Adirondack Upland of northern New York includes mountains and many beautiful lakes.

From central New York southward, the Appalachian Highlands has three main subdivisions. They are, from east to west: the Blue Ridge Mountains Area, the Ridge and Valley Region, and the Appalachian Plateau.

The Blue Ridge Mountains Area consists of some of the oldest mountains in the country. The Blue Ridge Mountains themselves are a narrow chain that stretches from southeastern Pennsylvania to northeastern Georgia. The Great Smoky Mountains of Tennessee and North Carolina are also part of this area. The Hudson Highlands of New York and New Jersey form a northern exten-

sion of the area. Several mighty rivers, including the Delaware, Hudson, Potomac, and Susquehanna, cut through the mountains to form *water gaps*. The gaps provide low, level land for highways and railroads.

The Ridge and Valley Region consists of the Great Valley in the east and a series of alternating ridges and valleys in the west. The rolling Great Valley is actually a series of valleys, including the Cumberland, Lebanon, and Lehigh valleys in Pennsylvania; the Shenandoah Valley in Virginia; the Valley of East Tennessee; the Rome Valley in Georgia; and the Great Valley of Alabama. The region has some forests, but other wooded areas have been cleared to take advantage of fertile soil and relatively level land for farming. About 50 dams on the Tennessee River and its branches in the southern Great Valley provide flood control and hydroelectric power.

The Appalachian Plateau extends from New York to Alabama. Glaciers covered the northern plateau during the most recent ice age, which ended about 11,500 years ago, and carved out natural features, including the Finger Lakes in New York. Deep, narrow river valleys cut through the plateau in some areas, creating steep, rugged terrain. Deposits of coal, iron ore, oil, and other minerals lie beneath the surface, and many people in the region work in mining. Parts of the region have good farmland. But thin, rocky soil covers much of the plateau, and the steep hillsides are badly eroded.

The Coastal Lowlands extend from southeastern Maine, across the eastern and southern United States, to eastern Texas. Forests of hickory, oak, pine, and other trees are common throughout the lowlands. The region has three subdivisions: (1) the Piedmont, (2) the Atlantic Coastal Plain, and (3) the Gulf Coastal Plain.

The Piedmont is a slightly elevated rolling plain that separates the Blue Ridge Mountains from the Atlantic Coastal Plain. It stretches from southern New York to Alabama. The eastern boundary of the Piedmont is called the *Fall Line*. Rivers that reach the Fall Line tumble down from the Piedmont to the lower coastal plains in a series of falls and rapids. In the early days of settlement of the eastern United States, boats traveling inland on coastal rivers stopped at the Fall Line and unloaded their cargoes. The rapids prevented the boats from traveling farther. They also provided water power for early industries. As a result, many cities grew up along the Fall Line. Tobacco is a leading agricultural product of the Piedmont, and the region also has many orchards and dairy farms.

The Atlantic Coastal Plain extends eastward from the Piedmont to the Atlantic Ocean. It ranges from a narrow strip of land in New England to a broad belt that covers much of North and South Carolina, Georgia, and Florida. In colonial times, the broad southern part of the plain encouraged the development of huge plantations for growing cotton. Cotton is still grown there. Other farm products include vegetables, citrus fruits, peanuts, and tobacco. In New England, where the plain narrows to a width of about 10 miles (16 kilometers) in some places, farming has always been less important. Many New Englanders turned to manufacturing, fishing, or shipping instead of farming.

Numerous rivers cross the plain and flow into the Atlantic Ocean. They include the Delaware, Hudson, James, Potomac, Roanoke, Savannah, and Susquehanna. Bays cut deeply into the plain in some areas, creating excellent natural harbors. They include Cape Cod Bay, Boston Bay, Chesapeake Bay, Delaware Bay, and Long Island Sound.

Many resort areas flourish around the beautiful sandy beaches and offshore islands that line much of the Atlantic shore from New England to Florida. In some inland regions, swamps and other wetlands cover large areas, where trees and grasses rise up from shallow waters and tangled vines and roots form masses of vegetation.

The Gulf Coastal Plain borders the Gulf of Mexico from Florida to southern Texas. Numerous rivers—including the Alabama, Mississippi, Rio Grande, and Trinity—cross the plain and flow into the Gulf. The Mississippi, which originates in the Interior Plains to the north, is the most important of these rivers. Barges carrying cargoes from many parts of the country travel along the river. Soil deposited along the banks of the Mississippi and other rivers in the Gulf Coastal Plain creates fertile farmland. The plain also has belts of hilly forests and grazing land, and large deposits of petroleum and natural gas lie beneath it and in the offshore Gulf waters. The Gulf Coastal Plain has many sandy beaches, swamps, bays, and offshore islands.

The Interior Plains occupy a huge expanse of land that stretches from the Appalachian Highlands in the east to the Rocky Mountains in the west. Glaciers covered much of the region during the Ice Age. They stripped the topsoil from parts of Michigan, Minnesota, and Wisconsin and carved out thousands of lakes. Today, much of this area is heavily forested. Farther south—in parts of Illinois, Indiana, Iowa, and Ohio—the glaciers flattened the land and deposited rich soil ideal for growing crops. The plains slope gradually upward from east to west and get progressively drier.

The western part of the region, called the Great Plains, has vast grasslands where livestock graze. It also has large areas of fertile soil that yield corn, wheat, and other crops. Few trees grow on the Great Plains. Some rugged hills, including the Black Hills of South Dakota and Wyoming, rise up out of the plains.

Deposits of iron ore and coal provide raw materials for many manufacturing industries in the eastern part of the Interior Plains. Important deposits of petroleum and metal ores lie in the western part.

Glaciers carved out the five Great Lakes in the Interior Plains. The lakes—Erie, Huron, Michigan, Ontario, and Superior—are the largest group of freshwater lakes in the world. The lakes provide a vital transportation route for shipping the agricultural and industrial products of the Interior Plains. The Mississippi River is the region's other great waterway. The Mississippi and its many branches, including the Missouri and Ohio rivers, form a river system that reaches into all parts of the Interior Plains.

The Ozark-Ouachita Highlands rise up between the Interior Plains and Coastal Lowlands. The highlands form a scenic landscape in southern Missouri, northwest Arkansas, and eastern Oklahoma. The region is named for the Ozark Plateau and the Ouachita Mountains. Rivers and streams have cut deep gorges through the rugged highland terrain. The highlands include forested hills, artificial lakes, and many underground caves and gushing springs. Much of the region has poor soil for farming but fertile land lies along the river valleys. Deposits of coal, iron ore, and other minerals are valuable natural resources of the highlands.

The Rocky Mountains form the largest mountain system in North America. They extend from northern Alaska, through Canada and the western United States to northern New Mexico. Many peaks of the Rockies are more than 14,000 feet (4,270 meters) high. The *Continental Divide*, also called the *Great Divide*, passes through the mountains. It is an imaginary line that separates streams that flow into the Pacific Ocean from those that flow into the Atlantic, the Gulf of Mexico, and the Arctic Ocean. Many important rivers, including the Colorado, Missouri, and Rio Grande, begin in the Rockies.

Forests cover the lower mountain slopes. The *timber line* marks the elevation above which trees cannot grow. Grasses, mosses, and lichens grow above the line. Bighorn sheep, elk, deer, bears, mountain lions, and other animals live in the mountains. Lakes and streams add to the region's spectacular beauty.

Lumbering and mining are important industries in the Rockies. The mountains are a storehouse of such metals as copper, gold, lead, silver, and zinc. The region also has large deposits of oil and natural gas. Mountain meadows provide grazing land for beef and dairy cattle, and valleys are used for growing crops.

For many years, the Rockies formed a major barrier to transportation across the United States. In the 1860s, the nation's first transcontinental rail line was built, passing through the Rocky Mountain region at the Wyoming Basin. Today, other railroads and highways cut through tunnels and passes in the mountains, and airplanes fly over the mountains.

The Western Plateaus, Basins, and Ranges lie west of the Rocky Mountains. This region extends from Washington south to the Mexican border. It is the driest part of the United States. Parts of it are deserts with little plant life. But the region has some forested mountains and some fertile areas where rivers provide irrigation water necessary for growing crops. In other areas, livestock graze on huge stretches of dry land.

The Columbia Plateau occupies the northernmost part of the region. It has fertile volcanic soil, formed by lava that flowed out of giant cracks in the earth thousands of years ago. The Colorado Plateau lies in the southern part of the region. It has some of the nation's most unusual landforms, including natural bridges and arches of solid rock and huge, flat-topped rock formations. The plateau's spectacular river gorges, including the Grand Canyon, rank among the world's great natural wonders.

The Basin and Range part of the region is a vast area of mountains and desert lowlands between the Columbia and Colorado plateaus. It includes Death Valley in California. Part of Death Valley lies 282 feet (86 meters) below sea level and is the lowest place in the United States. The Great Basin is an area within the larger Basin and Range area. Great Salt Lake is the largest of many shallow, salty lakes in the Great Basin. Bathers cannot sink in Great Salt Lake because the high salt content provides great buoyancy, enabling swimmers to float with ease. Near the lake is the Great Salt Lake Desert, which includes a large, hard, flat bed of salt.

The Pacific Ranges and Lowlands stretch across western Washington and Oregon and most of California. The region's eastern boundary is formed by the Cascade Mountains in the north and by the Sierra Nevada in the south. Volcanic activity formed the Cascades. Two of the Cascades—Lassen Peak in California and Mount St. Helens in Washington—are active volcanoes. Some of the range's highest peaks have glaciers and permanent snowfields. Evergreen forests cover the lower slopes and provide the raw materials for lumber and paper products industries. The Sierra Nevada are granite mountains, dotted with lakes and waterfalls.

Broad, fertile valleys lie west of the Cascade and Sierra Nevada mountains. They include the Puget Sound Lowland of Washington, the Willamette Valley of Oregon, and the Central Valley of California. Valley farms produce large amounts of fruits and vegetables.

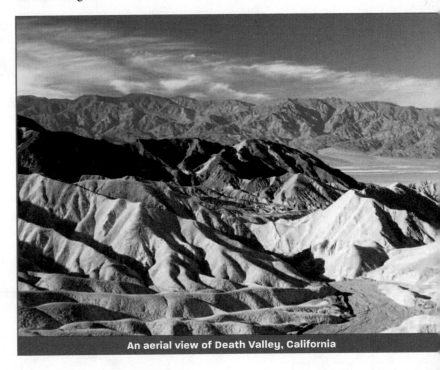

An aerial view of Death Valley, California

West of the valleys, the Coast Ranges line the Pacific shore. In many places, they rise up abruptly from the ocean, creating craggy walls of rock. In other areas, the mountains lie behind sandy coastal plains. Deep bays that jut into the coast include Puget Sound, Columbia River Bay, San Francisco Bay, and San Diego Bay.

The San Andreas Fault runs through the Coast Ranges in California. It is a break in Earth's rocky outer shell, along which movements of the rock have taken place. Giant redwood trees grow on the mountains in northern California. Set among the Coast Ranges are a number of rich agricultural valleys that produce much of the nation's wine grapes and other fruit, and lettuce.

Climate

The climate of the United States varies greatly from place to place. Average annual temperatures range from 10°F (−12°C) in Barrow, Alaska, to 76°F (24°C) in Death Valley, California. The highest temperature ever recorded in the country was 134°F (57°C). It was registered at Death Valley on July 10, 1913. The lowest recorded temperature was −80°F (−62°C). It was registered at Prospect Creek, Alaska, near Barrow, on January 23, 1971.

Precipitation varies from a yearly average of about 2 inches (5 centimeters) at Death Valley to about 460 inches (1,170 centimeters) at Mount Waialeale in Hawaii. In general, however, most parts of the United States have seasonal changes in temperature and moderate precipitation. The Midwest, the Middle Atlantic States, and New England experience warm summers and cold, snowy winters. In the South, summers are long and hot, and winters are mild. Along the Pacific Coast, and in some other areas near large bodies of water, the climate is relatively mild all year. Mountains also affect the climate. In the West, for example, the mountainous areas are cooler and wetter than the neighboring plains and plateaus. Parts of the West and Southwest have a desert climate.

The moderate climate in much of the United States has encouraged widespread population settlement. It has also helped make possible the production of a great variety of agricultural goods.

Economy

The United States ranks first in the world in the total value of its economic production. The nation's *gross domestic product*

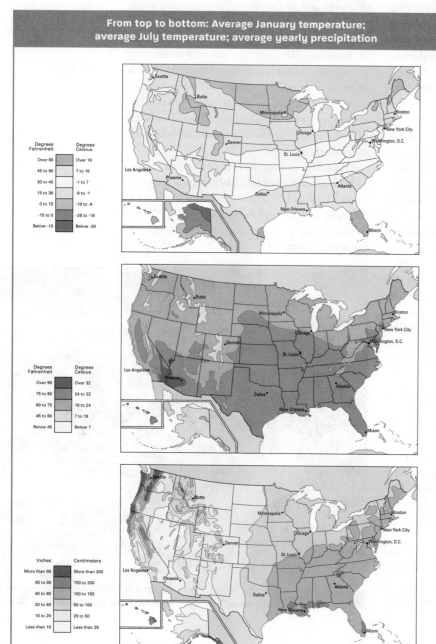

From top to bottom: Average January temperature; average July temperature; average yearly precipitation

Degrees Fahrenheit	Degrees Celsius
Over 60	Over 16
45 to 60	7 to 16
30 to 45	−1 to 7
15 to 30	−9 to −1
0 to 15	−18 to −9
−15 to 0	−26 to −18
Below −15	Below −26

Degrees Fahrenheit	Degrees Celsius
Over 90	Over 32
75 to 90	24 to 32
60 to 75	16 to 24
45 to 60	7 to 16
Below 45	Below 7

Inches	Centimeters
More than 80	More than 200
60 to 80	150 to 200
40 to 60	100 to 150
20 to 40	50 to 100
10 to 20	25 to 50
Less than 10	Less than 25

(GDP)—the value of all the goods and services produced within a country in a year—was more than $14 trillion in 2008. This was about three times as large as the gross domestic product of China, which ranked second.

The United States economy is based largely on a *free enterprise system*. In such a system, individuals and companies are free to make their own economic decisions. Individuals and companies own the raw materials, equipment, factories, and other items necessary for production, and they decide how best to use them in order to earn a profit.

Even though the U.S. economy is based on free enterprise, the government has placed regulations on economic practices through the years. It has passed antitrust laws, which are designed to keep one company or a few firms from controlling entire industries. Such control, called a monopoly, does away with competition and enables controlling companies to charge high prices and reduce the quality of goods. Government regulations help protect consumers from unsafe merchandise. They also help protect workers from unsafe working conditions and unreasonably low wages. The government has also enacted regulations designed to reduce environmental pollution.

Some people argue that the government interferes in the economy too much, while others say it should do more. In spite of involvement by the government, the United States still has one of the least regulated economies in the world.

Despite its overall strength, the United States economy faces problems from time to time. The problems include *recessions* (mild business slumps), *depressions* (severe business slumps), and *inflation* (rising prices).

Natural resources. The United States has a vast array of natural resources including a moderate climate, fertile soils, and plentiful minerals, water, forests, and fish. However, the United States uses more than it has and must import some raw materials to provide for the needs of its citizens.

Minerals. The United States has large deposits of coal, iron ore, natural gas, and petroleum, which are vital to the country's industrial strength. Its many other important mined products include copper, gold, lead, limestone, phosphates, silver, sulfur, and zinc. To meet its needs, however, the United States must import additional amounts of iron ore, petroleum, and other materials.

Soils. The United States has vast expanses of fertile soil that is well suited to growing crops. The

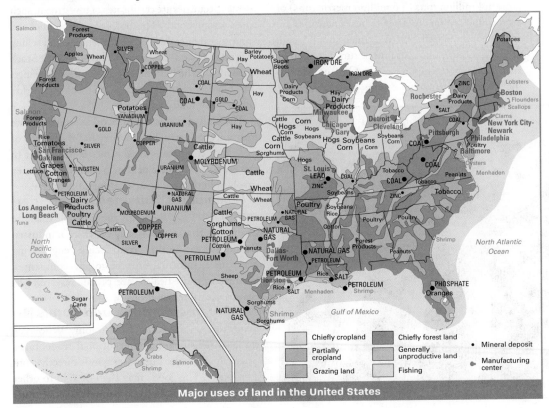

Major uses of land in the United States

most fertile soils include the dark soils of the Interior Plains and the *alluvial* (water-deposited) soils along the lower Mississippi River Valley and other smaller river valleys. Rich, windblown soil called *loess* covers parts of eastern Washington and the southern Interior Plains.

Water. Lakes, rivers, and underground deposits supply water for households, farms, and industries in the United States. The nation uses about 400 billion gallons (1,500 billion liters) of water daily. Households use only about 10 percent of this total. The vast majority of the rest is used to irrigate farms and to operate steam power plants.

Forests cover nearly a third of the United States, and they yield many valuable products. About a fourth of the nation's lumber comes from forests in the Pacific Northwest. Forests in the South supply lumber, wood pulp—which is used to make paper—and nearly all the pitch, rosin, turpentine, and wood tar produced in the United States. The Appalachian Mountains and parts of the Great Lakes area have fine hardwood forests. Hickory, maple, oak, and other hardwood trees cut from these forests provide quality woods for the manufacture of furniture.

Fish. Americans who fish for a living catch almost 4 million tons (3.6 million metric tons) of sea products annually. The greatest quantities are taken from the Pacific Ocean, which supplies cod, crabs, halibut, pollock, salmon, tuna, and other fish. Leading catches from the Gulf of Mexico include crabs, menhaden, oysters, and shrimp. The Atlantic yields flounder, herring, menhaden, and other fish; and such shellfish as clams, crabs, lobsters, oysters, and scallops.

Service industries account for the largest portion of the U.S. gross domestic product and employ a majority of the country's workers. This industry group includes a wide variety of businesses that provide services rather than producing goods.

Finance, insurance, and real estate play an important part in the nation's economy. Banks finance much of the economic activity in the United States by making loans to both individuals and businesses. American banks loan billions of dollars annually. Most of the loans go to individuals to help finance the purchase of automobiles, houses, or other major items. Bank loans to businesses provide an important source of money for *capital expansion*—the construction of new factories and the purchase of new equipment. As a business expands, it hires more workers. These workers, in turn, produce more goods and services. In this way, the nation's level of employment and its economic output both increase.

Other important types of financial institutions include commodity and security exchanges. Commodities are basic goods, such as grains and precious metals. Securities are certificates of investment, such as stocks and bonds. The prices of commodities and securities are determined by the buying and selling that takes place at exchanges. The New York Stock Exchange is the nation's largest security exchange. The CME Group in Chicago is one of the world's largest commodity exchanges.

The United States has the world's largest private insurance industry. The country has thousands of insurance companies. Real estate is important to the economy because of the large sums of money involved in the buying and selling of property.

Community, business, and personal services employ more people than the businesses that make up any other U.S. industry. Businesses within this group include engineering companies, information technology companies, law firms, private health care, private research laboratories, and repair shops.

Trade, restaurants, and hotels play major roles in the American economy. Wholesale trade, which includes international trade, takes place when a buyer purchases goods directly from a producer. The goods may then be sold to other businesses for resale to consumers. Retail trade

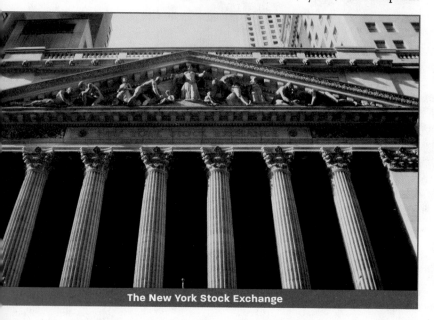
The New York Stock Exchange

involves selling products to the final consumer. Automobile dealerships, department stores, and grocery stores are examples of retail trade establishments. Restaurants and hotels greatly benefit from the tens of millions of foreign tourists who visit the United States annually.

International trade provides markets for surplus agricultural goods and many raw materials and manufactured goods produced in the United States. The nation imports goods that it lacks entirely or that producers do not supply in sufficient quantities. It also imports goods produced by foreign companies that compete with U.S. firms. Traditionally, the value of U.S. exports has exceeded, or been about the same as, the value of U.S. imports. But since the mid-1960s, the value of imports has usually been much higher than the value of exports.

Important U.S. exports include (1) machinery and transportation equipment, such as aircraft, computers, electric power equipment, industrial machinery, and motor vehicles and parts; (2) chemical elements and compounds, including plastic materials; (3) manufactured articles, especially scientific measuring equipment; (4) basic manufactures, such as metals and paper; (5) food crops and live animals; and (6) crude materials, including textile fibers and metal ores.

The leading U.S. imports are (1) machinery and transportation equipment, such as automobiles and auto parts, office machines, and telecommunications equipment; (2) fuels and lubricants, especially petroleum; (3) manufactured articles, such as clothing, shoes, and toys; (4) basic manufactures, such as iron, steel, and other metals, and paper and newsprint; and (5) chemical products.

Canada, China, Japan, and Mexico are the country's chief trading partners. Other major trading partners include France, Germany, Italy, South Korea, Taiwan, and the United Kingdom. The North American Free Trade Agreement, which took effect in 1994, eliminated trade barriers among Mexico, Canada, and the United States.

Government services play a major role in the economy. Federal, state, and local governments employ many U.S. workers. Many government employees are directly involved in making public policies. Others—including police officers, postal workers, teachers, and trash collectors—provide public services.

Federal, state, and local governments buy a third of all the goods and services produced in the nation. These purchases range from paper clips to office buildings. The federal government is the nation's largest single buyer of goods and services. Its agencies, including the military, buy billions of dollars worth of equipment from private companies. In addition, federal grants finance much of the nation's research activity. State governments spend most of their income on education, health care and hospitals, highways, and public welfare. Local governments spend over a third of their income on education, and less for police and fire protection, hospitals, streets, sanitation and sewerage, and parks.

In addition to its roles as an employer and purchaser of goods and services, government influences the economy by providing income to certain groups of people. For example, the federal government makes Social Security payments to retired people and people with disabilities. Federal, state, and local governments provide welfare assistance to the needy. Such government programs are the only source of income for some Americans.

Transportation and communication are also important to the economy. More information on transportation and communication appears later in this section.

Manufacturing is an important economic activity in the United States both in terms of employment and the gross domestic product. The value of American manufactured goods is greater than that of any other country. Factories in the United States turn out a tremendous variety of *producer goods*, such as sheet metal and printing presses, and *consumer goods*, such as cars, clothing,

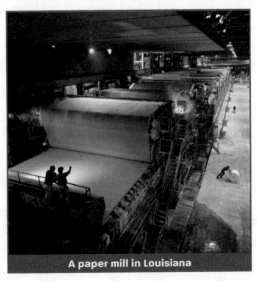

A paper mill in Louisiana

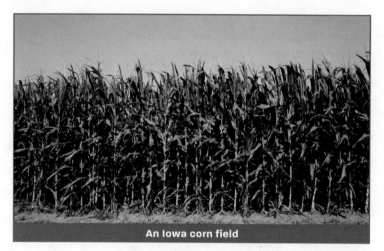

An Iowa corn field

and TV sets. The leading categories of U.S. products are, in order of value, chemicals, transportation equipment, food products, computer and electronic products, fabricated metal products, machinery, primary metal products, petroleum and coal products, plastics and rubber products, paper products, beverage and tobacco products, nonmetallic mineral products, electrical equipment, and medical equipment.

The Midwest and Northeast have long been major U.S. centers of manufacturing. Since the mid-1900s, the country's fastest-growing manufacturing areas have been on the West Coast, in the Southwest, and in the South. Today, California ranks first among the states in the value of its manufactured goods, followed by Texas, Ohio, Pennsylvania, Illinois, North Carolina, and Indiana. Manufacturers in California produce aircraft, aerospace equipment, chemicals, computers and electronic components, food products, and many other goods.

Midwestern factories turn out much of the nation's iron and steel, automobiles, and other heavy industrial products. The Northeast has many chemical manufacturers, food-processing companies, and manufacturers of electronic equipment. Petroleum refineries and petrochemical industries account for much of the manufacturing activity in Texas and other states bordering the Gulf of Mexico. Dallas-Fort Worth, Phoenix, Seattle, and Wichita are important centers for the manufacture of aircraft and related equipment.

Through the years, Americans have developed manufacturing processes that have greatly increased productivity. During the early 1900s, United States automobile firms introduced the moving assembly line and identical interchangeable parts for cars. These innovations led to mass production, in which large numbers of goods could be produced in less time and at a lower cost than ever before. Beginning in the mid-1900s, U.S. industries turned increasingly to *automation*—the use of machines that operate with little human help. American inventors and engineers developed computers to bring automation to an even higher level. Today, computers operate machines, handle accounting, and perform many other important functions in industries.

Construction consists of activities involved in building and maintaining residences, business offices, storage warehouses, and other structures. This industry employs such workers as architects, engineers, contractors, bricklayers, carpenters, electricians, plumbers, roofers, ironworkers, and plasterers.

Agriculture accounts for only a small part of the U.S. gross domestic product. Yet, the United States is a world leader in agriculture production. The country's farms turn out as much food as the nation needs, with enough left over to export food to other countries. Food exports account for about one-third of U.S. farm income.

Beef cattle rank as the most valuable product of American farms. Millions of beef cattle are raised on huge ranches in the western United States. The South and Midwest also produce large numbers of beef cattle. Other leading farm products, in order of value, include corn, soybeans, dairy products, *broilers* (young, tender chickens), greenhouse and nursery products, hogs, wheat, and chicken eggs. United States farms also produce large amounts of almonds, apples, cotton, grapes, hay, lettuce, potatoes, rice, tomatoes, and turkeys.

Farmers throughout the country raise dairy cattle for milk and other products. Much of the dairy production is concentrated in a belt that extends from Minnesota through New York. Midwestern states account for much of the nation's corn, hog, and soybean production. The nation's chief wheat-growing region stretches across the Great Plains. The South raises most of the broilers. California, Texas, and a few other states in the South and Southwest raise almost all the country's cotton. Farms in various areas also produce poultry, eggs, and crops of fruits, vegetables, nuts, and grains.

The United States has played a major role in the modernization of agriculture. During the 1800s,

American inventors developed the first successful harvesting machine and steel plow. United States scientists have contributed to the development of improved plant varieties and livestock breeds, as well as agricultural chemicals for fertilizer and pest control.

The use of modern farm machinery and agricultural methods has helped make U.S. farms the most efficient in the world. But it has also contributed to rapidly rising production costs. Many farmers who have been unable to meet these rising costs have been forced to quit farming and sell their land. Since 1925, the number of farms in the United States has decreased from about 6,500,000 to about 2,200,000. At the same time, average farm size increased from about 143 acres (58 hectares) to about 420 acres (170 hectares). Some of the largest farms in the United States are owned by corporations. But more than 90 percent of all the farms are owned by individuals or partnerships made up of members of farm families.

Mining.
The United States ranks among the leading countries in the value of its mine production. The chief mined products of the United States are, in order of value, natural gas, petroleum, and coal. The United States ranks as a leading producer of natural gas. It is third to Russia and Saudi Arabia in petroleum production. The United States also ranks second in coal—after China. Most coal deposits lie in the Interior Plains and the Appalachian Highlands. Major deposits of petroleum and natural gas occur in Alaska, California, Louisiana, New Mexico, Oklahoma, and Texas. Other important mined products include cement, clays, copper, gold, granite, iron ore, lead, lime, limestone, phosphate rock, salt, sand and gravel, sulfur, traprock, and zinc.

Although mining accounts for a small share of the total U.S. economic output, it has been a key to the growth of other parts of the economy. Coal and iron ore, for example, are needed to make steel. Steel, in turn, is used to make automobiles, buildings, bridges, and many other goods. Coal is also a fuel for electric power plants. Refineries turn petroleum into gasoline; fuel oil for heating and industrial power; and petrochemicals used in plastics, paint, drugs, fertilizers, and synthetic fabrics. Limestone, granite, and traprock are crushed for use in construction materials. Sand and gravel are also used in construction. Sulfur and phosphates are used to make fertilizer.

Energy sources.
The farms, factories, households, and motor vehicles of the United States consume vast amounts of energy annually. Various sources are used to generate the energy. Petroleum provides about 40 percent. It is the source of most of the energy used to power motor vehicles, and it heats millions of houses and factories. Natural gas generates about 25 percent of the energy used, and coal about 20 percent. Many industries use natural gas for heat and power, and millions of households burn it for heat, cooking, and drying laundry. Coal's major uses are in the production of electric power and steel. The electric power lights buildings and powers factory and farm machinery. Nuclear power plants generate just under 10 percent of the country's energy. Hydroelectric plants provide less than 5 percent.

Since the mid-1900s, the cost of energy—especially the petroleum portion—has risen dramatically. The rising cost became a major contributor to inflation in the United States and other countries.

Transportation.
A sprawling transportation network spreads out over the United States. The country has millions of miles or kilometers of streets, roads, and highways. The federal interstate highway system provides a network of more than 47,000 miles (76,000 kilometers) of freeways. The United States has an average of more than 75 motor vehicles for every 100 people. Americans use automobiles for most of their personal travel. Trucks carry nearly 30 percent of the freight in the United States.

Railroads rank as the leading freight carriers in the United States, handling over 40 percent of the freight. But they account for less than 1 percent of all passenger traffic.

Transporting coal on the Ohio River

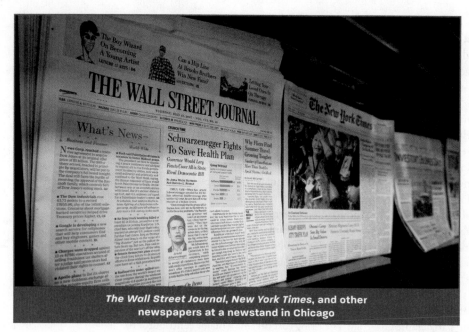

The Wall Street Journal, *New York Times*, and other newspapers at a newstand in Chicago

Airlines handle about 10 percent of all U.S. passenger traffic, but less than one-half of 1 percent of the freight traffic. Five of the 10 busiest airports in the world are in the United States.

Nearly 10 percent of the freight traffic within the United States travels on waterways. The Mississippi River system handles about 50 percent of this freight. Ships and barges traveling on the Mississippi and its branches, including the Arkansas, Missouri, and Ohio rivers, can reach deep into the country's interior. The Great Lakes form the nation's other major inland waterway. The St. Lawrence Seaway links the lakes with the Atlantic Ocean.

The United States has many major ports. A port west of New Orleans ranks as the nation's busiest port, followed by the ports of Houston and New York City.

The nation has a vast network of pipelines that carries crude oil, petroleum products, and natural gas. Pipelines account for about 20 percent of the total freight handled in the United States.

Communication. Private corporations operate the publishing and broadcasting industries in the United States. The First Amendment of the Constitution guarantees freedom of the press and speech. These guarantees allow newspapers and broadcasters to operate without government censorship. Laws prohibit the publishing or broadcasting of libelous, obscene, and treasonous materials. But, for the most part, the government interferes little in the operation of the communication industry. The free exchange of ideas and information is a vital part of the democratic heritage of the United States.

Publishers in the United States issue about 1,400 daily newspapers, which have a total circulation of about 50 million copies. The nation also has thousands of weekly and semi-weekly newspapers. The newspapers provide information on local, national, and international events. Many also include such special features as opinion columns, articles on health and fashion, and comic strips and crossword puzzles.

In the United States, most newspapers serve a local region. But *The Wall Street Journal*, *USA Today*, and *The New York Times* circulate to most of the country.

There are thousands of radio and television stations and also thousands of cable TV systems in the United States. Radio and TV provide the public with entertainment, news, and public interest programs. In the United States, both national networks and local stations produce and broadcast programs. Almost every American household has at least one TV set and one or more radios, and about three-fifths of the households subscribe to cable television.

DATA

Regions of the United States

New England	Connecticut, Maine, Massachusetts, New Hampshire, Rhode Island, Vermont
Middle Atlantic States	New Jersey, New York, Pennsylvania
Southern States	Alabama, Arkansas, Delaware, Florida, Georgia, Kentucky, Louisiana, Maryland, Mississippi, North Carolina, South Carolina, Tennessee, Virginia, West Virginia
Midwestern States	Illinois, Indiana, Iowa, Kansas, Michigan, Minnesota, Missouri, Nebraska, North Dakota, Ohio, South Dakota, Wisconsin
Rocky Mountain States	Colorado, Idaho, Montana, Nevada, Utah, Wyoming
Southwestern States	[1]Arizona, [1]New Mexico, Oklahoma, Texas
Pacific Coast States	California, Oregon, Washington

NOTE: This table lists the states within each of the seven regions of the United States discussed in *The Nation* section of this article.

[1] Arizona and New Mexico are often grouped with the Rocky Mountain States.

Main Outlying Areas of the United States

Name	Acquired	Status
American Samoa	[1]	Unorganized unincorporated territory
Baker Island and Jarvis Island	1856	Unincorporated territory
Guam	1898	Organized unincorporated territory
Howland Island	1856	Unincorporated possession
Johnston Island and Sand Island	1858	Unincorporated territory
Kingman Reef	1922	Unincorporated territory
Midway Island	1867	Unincorporated territory
Northern Mariana Islands	1947	Commonwealth
Palmyra Island	1898	Unincorporated possession
Puerto Rico	1898	Commonwealth
United States Virgin Islands	1917	Organized unincorporated territory
Wake Island	1898	Unincorporated possession

[1] Acquired in stages between 1900 and 1925.

DATA
U.S. Population

Census Year	Population	Census Year	Population
1790	3,929,214	1910	91,972,266
1800	5,308,483	1920	105,710,620
1810	7,239,881	1930	122,775,046
1820	9,638,453	1940	131,669,275
1830	12,866,020	1950	150,697,361
1840	17,069,453	1960	179,323,175
1850	23,191,876	1970	203,235,298
1860	31,443,321	1980	226,545,805
1870	39,818,449	1990	249,632,692
1880	50,155,783	2000	281,421,906
1890	62,974,714	2010	308,745,538
1900	75,994,575		

The 50 Largest Cities in the United States

1. New York City, NY	8,175,133	18. Detroit, MI	713,777	35. Sacramento, CA	466,488
2. Los Angeles, CA	3,792,621	19. El Paso, TX	649,121	36. Long Beach, CA	462,257
3. Chicago, IL	2,695,598	20. Memphis, TN	646,889	37. Kansas City, MO	459,787
4. Houston, TX	2,099,451	21. Baltimore, MD	620,961	38. Mesa, AZ	439,041
5. Philadelphia, PA	1,526,006	22. Boston, MA	617,594	39. Virginia Beach, VA	437,994
6. Phoenix, AZ	1,445,632	23. Seattle, WA	608,660	40. Atlanta, GA	420,003
7. San Antonio, TX	1,327,407	24. Washington, DC	601,723	41. Colorado Springs, CO	416,427
8. San Diego, CA	1,307,402	25. Nashville, TN	601,222	42. Omaha, NE	408,958
9. Dallas, TX	1,197,816	26. Denver, CO	600,158	43. Raleigh, NC	403,892
10. San Jose, CA	945,942	27. Louisville, KY	597,337	44. Miami, FL	399,457
11. Jacksonville, FL	821,784	28. Milwaukee, WI	594,833	45. Cleveland, OH	396,815
12. Indianapolis, IN	820,445	29. Portland, OR	583,776	46. Tulsa, OK	391,906
13. San Francisco, CA	805,235	30. Las Vegas, NV	583,756	47. Oakland, CA	390,724
14. Austin, TX	790,390	31. Oklahoma City, OK	579,999	48. Minneapolis, MN	382,578
15. Columbus, OH	787,033	32. Albuquerque, NM	545,852	49. Wichita, KS	382,368
16. Fort Worth, TX	741,206	33. Tucson, AZ	520,116	50. Arlington, TX	365,438
17. Charlotte, NC	731,424	34. Fresno, CA	494,665		

DATA

Economic Production in the United States

Source: U.S. Bureau of Economic Analysis. Figures are for 2008; employment figures include full- and part-time workers.

Economic activities	% of GDP[1] produced	Number of workers	% of all workers
Finance, insurance, and and real estate	23	19,386,400	11
Community, business, and personal services	22	60,006,000	33
Trade, restaurants, and hotels	15	37,747,400	21
Government	12	24,577,000	14
Manufacturing	12	14,094,900	8
Transportation and communication	7	9,549,300	5
Construction	4	11,151,000	6
Mining	2	1,155,900	1
Utilities	2	590,700	2
Agriculture	1	3,500,500	2
Total[3]	100	181,755,100	100

[1]GDP=gross domestic product, the total value of goods and services produced in a year.

[2]Less than one-half of 1 percent.

[3]Figures do not add up to 100 percent due to rounding.

ADDITIONAL RESOURCES

Books to Read

Level I

Ajmera, Maya, and others. *Children of the U.S.A.* Charlesbridge, 2008.

Gall, Timothy L. and Susan B. *Junior Worldmark Encyclopedia of the States.* 5th ed. Thomson Gale, 2007.

Hintz, Martin. *United States of America.* Children's Press, 2004.

Jules, Jacqueline. *Unite or Die: How Thirteen States Became a Nation.* Charlesbridge, 2009.

Maury, Rob. *Citizenship: Rights and Responsibilities.* Mason Crest, 2009.

Nash, Gary B., and Smith, Carter. *Atlas of American History.* 4th ed. Facts on File, 2006.

Level II

Duncan, Dayton. *The National Parks.* Knopf, 2009

Forsberg, Michael. *Great Plains: America's Lingering Wild.* University of Chicago Press, 2009.

Hayes, Derek. *Historical Atlas of the United States.* University of California Press, 2007.

Hubbard, Bill, Jr. *American Boundaries: The Nation, the States, the Rectangular Survey.* University of Chicago Press, 2009.

Hunt, Michael H. *The American Ascendancy: How the United States Gained and Wielded Global Dominance*. University of North Carolina Press, 2007.

Klein, Herbert S. *A Population History of the United States*. Cambridge, 2004.

Statistical Abstract of the United States. U.S. Bureau of the Census, published annually.

Vigdor, Jacob L. *From Immigrants to Americans: The Rise and Fall of Fitting In*. Rowman & Littlefield, 2009.

Web Sites

American Experience

http://www.pbs.org/wgbh/americanexperience/

Stories of the people and events that shaped the United States from the PBS history series. See "Web Site Archives" for a list of Web features.

Country Profile: United States of America

http://news.bbc.co.uk/2/hi/americas/country_profiles/1217752.stm

Information from the BBC.

FirstGov.gov—Official Web site for searching the U.S. Government

http://www.usa.gov/

One-stop access to all on-line U.S. Federal Government resources.

Information USA

http://www.ait.org.tw/infousa/enus/

The U.S. Department of State provides an authoritative resource for foreign audiences seeking information about American society, political processes, official U.S. policies, and culture.

Library of Congress Home Page

http://www.loc.gov/index.html

Information about the Library of Congress and a wealth of on-line resources showcasing U.S. history.

Panoramas: The North American Landscape in Art

http://www.museevirtuel-virtualmuseum.co/sgc-cms/expositions/panoramas/home-e.html

A site that celebrates the heritage of the continent. Sponsored by the governments of Canada, Mexico, and the United States.

Supreme Court of the United States

http://www.supremecourtus.gov/

The official site of the U.S. Supreme Court.

The Presidents of the United States

http://www.whitehouse.gov/about/presidents/

Biographical information on the presidents from the official site of the White House.

The United States Capitol

http://www.aoc.gov/

Information about the United States Capitol in Washington, D.C.

The United States Senate

http://www.senate.gov/

The official home page of the United States Senate.

United States

https://www.cia.gov/library/publications/the-world-factbook/geos/us.html

Information about the United States from the on-line edition of the Central Intelligence Agency's World Factbook.

United States Legislative Branch

http://thomas.loc.gov/links/

Resources compiled by the U.S. Library of Congress.

Welcome to the White House

http://www.whitehouse.gov/

A guide to information about the federal government and access to federal services.

Search Strings

Language

United States language English Spanish "official language" (522,000)

"United States" language spoken (202,000)

"United States" language spoken English Spanish "official language" controversy (36,100)

Urban Life

"United States" "urban life" economy (39,700)

Urban life in the United States economy facilities drawbacks (61,700)

Urban life in the United States economy facilities features (142,000)

Rural Life

Rural life in the United States population farms agriculture (1,210,000)

Note: This yielded a lot of results, but the returns were exactly what the searcher wanted.

United States rural life population agriculture economy jobs (1,180,000)

"Rural Life" "United States" (388,000)

Rocky Montains

Rocky Mountains North America geology "Continental Divide" (3,550)

"Rocky Mountains" North America geology "Continental Divide" (6,680)

BACKGROUND INFORMATION

The following article was written during the year in which the events took place and reflects the style and thinking of that time.

International Trade (2003)

International trade expanded during 2003, but more slowly than had been expected, due to the weakening of the global economy early in the year. An increasingly angry face-off between developing nations—often led by Brazil—and industrial powers, including the European Union (EU) and the United States, became a feature of world and regional trade talks during 2003. Resentments centered on issues such as agricultural subsidies by rich countries at the expense of poorer countries, and this anger scuttled talks held in Cancun, Mexico, in September by the World Trade Organization (WTO)—a Geneva, Switzerland-based group that oversees international trade agreements and arbitrates disputes among member nations. Such resentments also contributed to an uprising that forced Bolivia's president to resign in October and set the stage for a confrontation around a Miami, Florida, conference in November that was meant to promote a special trading zone throughout the Western Hemisphere.

The WTO conference. As commercial activity steadily increased in the second half of 2003, trade ministers from around the world gathered in the Mexican resort city of Cancun on September 10 to continue the so-called Doha round of trade negotiations—named for the capital of Qatar where the negotiations were launched. Many hoped the meeting would get the WTO talks back on track. Leaders of the Group of Eight (G-8) major industrial nations reaffirmed their commitment to the Doha Development Agenda in a June statement.

Observers noted, however, that there was a sense among developing nations that trade was of greater benefit to wealthier nations than to them. A group of developing nations, led by Brazil, China, and India, insisted that Europe and the United States take stronger action to cut domestic farm subsidies. Subsidies paid to farmers in wealthier nations make it hard for those in developing nations to compete, despite the lower production costs in developing nations. Friction arose over other issues, and on September 14, Luis Ernesto Derbez, Mexico's foreign secretary and the conference's chairman, declared an impasse and adjourned the meeting. Experts suggested that it would probably prove impossible to reach an agreement on the rules concerning trade among WTO nations by the January 1, 2005, deadline. The collapse of the talks raised doubts about the future of the global trade alliance and spurred a tendency already under way for major trading zones to expand regional and bilateral agreements.

Further trade-related events. On October 17, 2003, Gonzalo Sanchez de Lozada resigned as president of Bolivia following a popular revolt in which farmers, workers, and miners marched in mass demonstrations against his U.S.-backed free-market policies. Protesters blockaded the capital, La Paz, and some 80 demonstrators were killed—reportedly by gunfire from security forces. The protests had focused, in part, on Lozada's plan to sell Bolivian natural gas to the United States and Mexico.

On November 12, EU leaders and officials from the South American Mercosur trading bloc—Argentina, Brazil, Paraguay, and Uruguay—said they planned to negotiate a free-trade accord by the end of 2004. Trade policy disagreements between the United States and Brazil curbed plans to create a wide-ranging Free Trade Area of the Americas (FTAA) among 34 nations, in favor of the limited compromise pact. The United States subsequently began pursuing smaller regional trade accords and on December 17, announced a pact with four Central American nations.

Other tensions. Highly sensitive trade disputes from previous years reemerged in 2003, notably in a WTO appeals panel ruling that came down on November 10 against the United States. At issue were import fees, called duties, that had been levied by the United States in 2002 on most foreign steel entering the country. The United States claimed it was attempting to protect its ailing steel industry. Foreign competitors threatened a trade war on U.S. goods if the United States did not remove the duties within 30 days of the WTO decision. The United States removed the tariffs in early December.

Tensions also arose over currency policies as the U.S. dollar, for the second year running, weakened against many other currencies. As the largest single-nation economy, the United States had traditionally been the principal engine for world growth, with its consumers buying a huge amount of goods from other nations. A falling dollar, however, made foreign-supplied goods and services more expensive inside the United States, while making U.S. products cheaper on the world market. This development put pressure on other nations to stimulate their own economies rather than depend on U.S. trade.

Recovery. The WTO reported that a weak trade recovery during 2002 had been "followed by a near stagnation of trade flows in the first half of 2003." The U.S. and EU economies weakened during the first months of 2003 amid growing uncertainty caused by a looming U.S.-led war against Iraq.

War-related fears about potential disruption to Persian Gulf oil supplies pushed the price of crude oil and related fuels up sharply. Tensions also grew because many nations in Europe and the developing world did not support the United States and the United Kingdom in their stance against Iraq. Quick initial success by the coalition forces led to a fall in oil prices during the early summer months, but the world economy did not show much strength until midsummer, when a U.S. tax cut and cuts in interest rates by the United States, Britain, and the EU all began to take effect.

In September, the International Monetary Fund (IMF)—a United Nations-affiliated agency that provides advice and financial restructuring to member nations—said in its "World Economic Outlook" report that "growing signs of a pickup in activity" were evident, especially in the United States, Japan, and some of the emerging-market countries, such as China and India. The IMF forecast the volume of world trade in goods and services would grow by 2.9 percent in 2003, down from 3.2 percent in 2002, but an improvement over the 1-percent decrease in volume in 2001. China's trade still remained quite strong, however. The IMF estimated that the Chinese economy would grow by 7.5 percent in 2003, compared with an 8-percent increase in 2002. The 2003 growth occurred despite the economic impact of an outbreak of severe acute respiratory syndrome (SARS) in China.

Pearl Harbor

Pearl Harbor was the site of a surprise attack on the United States by Japanese military forces on December 7, 1941.

HOT topics

Background to the Attack. Japan began a military expansion during the 1930s, invading China and much of Southeast Asia. The United States protested this aggression and demanded that Japan stop its actions. When Japan ignored the demand, the United States cut off exports to Japan. Japan had few natural resources, and it relied on exports of petroleum and other goods from the United States. General Hideki Tojo, premier of Japan, realized that only the United States Navy had the power to block Japan's expansion in Asia. The objective of the attack was to cripple the U.S. Pacific Fleet.

The Attack. On December 7, 1941, while the U.S. secretary of state conferred with two Japanese diplomats in Washington, the Japanese military was already attacking the U.S. facilities at Pearl Harbor. A 33-ship Japanese striking force had steamed under the cover of darkness to about 230 miles (370 kilometers) north of Oahu. Early in the morning, the aircraft carriers launched 350 airplanes against the United States Fleet. The first bombs fell at about 7:55 a.m. The chief targets were 8 battleships among the 180 American vessels anchored in the harbor. The attack killed 2,388 people at Pearl Harbor and wounded about 2,000. It destroyed or damaged 21 American ships and more than 300 planes. The Japanese lost 29 aircraft.

HOT topics

hot topics hot topics hot topics hot topics

The U.S. Response. On December 8, U.S. president Franklin Delano Roosevelt addressed Congress. He called December 7 "a date which will live in infamy." Congress declared war on Japan. In a radio speech the same day, Roosevelt urged Americans to back the war effort and avenge Pearl Harbor. He said, "Every single man, woman, and child is a partner in the most tremendous undertaking of our American history." Japan won many battles and gained much territory in the early days of U.S. participation in the war. However, a massive effort to produce equipment and supplies built American military strength, and the slogan "Remember Pearl Harbor" helped boost the morale of the population. The Allies gradually turned the tide against Japan and Germany.

President Roosevelt signing the declaration of war after the attack on Pearl Harbor

USS _Arizona_ War Memorial. The ships destroyed in the Pearl Harbor attack include the USS _Arizona_. The battleship now sits upright on the bottom of the harbor with more than 1,000 men entombed aboard. The USS _Arizona_ Memorial, a roomlike structure, stands above the ship. The memorial is supported by pilings that reach the harbor bottom. About 1.5 million people visit the memorial each year. The names of those who died on the _Arizona_ are carved in marble at one end of the room. Even today, bubbles of oil from the sunken _Arizona_ rise to the water's surface.

Pearl Harbor during the attack

TRUE or FALSE?

Pearl Harbor is now the site of a naval complex which serves as the headquarters for five major fleet commands in the Pacific.

THE BASICS

Pearl Harbor was the site of a surprise attack on the United States by Japanese military forces on December 7, 1941. Japanese ships and airplanes attacked the United States naval base at Pearl Harbor on the island of Oahu in Hawaii. The attack caused heavy casualties and destroyed much of the American Pacific Fleet. The attack also brought the United States into World War II. "Remember Pearl Harbor" became the rallying cry for the country. American participation was a crucial reason why the embattled Allied nations, including the United Kingdom (U.K.) and Soviet Union, turned the tide and defeated the Axis nations, headed by Japan and Germany.

Background. Japan began a military expansion during the 1930s. It invaded China and much of Southeast Asia. Japan wanted to acquire the rich resources of Asia. The United States protested this aggression. It demanded that Japan stop its actions, but Japan ignored the demand. The United States then cut off exports to Japan. Japan had few natural resources, and it relied on exports of petroleum and other goods from the United States.

General Hideki Tojo became premier of Japan in October 1941. Tojo and other Japanese military leaders realized that only the United States Navy had the power to block Japan's expansion in Asia. They decided to try to cripple the U.S. Pacific Fleet at anchor in Pearl Harbor.

The attack. On December 7, the U.S. secretary of state conferred with two Japanese diplomats in Washington. While they talked, the Japanese military had already launched the attack on the U.S. facilities at Pearl Harbor. In the United States, the attack became known as the "Pearl Harbor sneak attack."

On December 7, Vice Admiral Chuichi Nagumo led a 33-ship Japanese striking force that steamed under the cover of darkness to about 230 miles (370 kilometers) north of Oahu. Early in the morning, his aircraft carriers launched 350 airplanes against the United States Fleet. The first bombs fell at about 7:55 a.m. The chief targets were 8 battleships among the 180 American vessels anchored in the harbor. The attack killed 2,388 people at Pearl Harbor and wounded about 2,000. It destroyed or damaged 21 American

The USS *Arizona* burning after the attack

ships and more than 300 planes. The Japanese lost 29 aircraft.

On December 8, Roosevelt addressed Congress. He called December 7 "a date which will live in infamy." Congress declared war on Japan. In a radio speech the same day, Roosevelt urged Americans to back the war effort and avenge Pearl Harbor. He said, "Every single man, woman, and child is a partner in the most tremendous undertaking of our American history."

At the time of the attack, Nazi Germany had taken over much of Europe. The U.K. and the Soviet Union provided the main resistance to the Nazis. The United States had stayed out of the war. However, under the leadership of President Franklin D. Roosevelt, it provided extensive aid to the United Kingdom. Germany declared war on the United States on December 11.

Japan won many battles and gained much territory in the early days of U.S. participation in the war. However, a massive effort to produce equipment and supplies built American military strength, and the slogan "Remember Pearl Harbor" helped boost the morale of the population. The Allies gradually turned

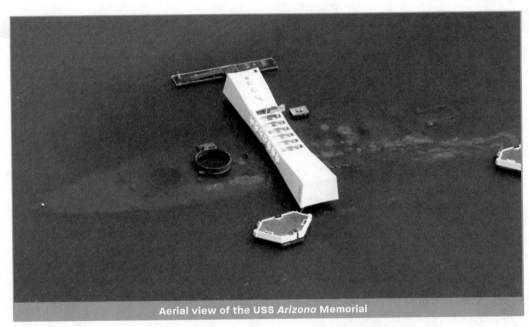

Aerial view of the USS *Arizona* Memorial

the tide against Japan and Germany. The long war, which had begun in 1939, ended in 1945 with the surrender of the Axis countries.

The war memorials. The ships destroyed in the Pearl Harbor attack include the USS *Arizona*. The battleship sits upright on the bottom of the harbor with more than 1,000 men entombed aboard. The USS *Arizona* Memorial, a room-like structure, stands above the ship. The memorial is supported by pilings that reach the harbor bottom. About 1½ million people visit the memorial each year. The names of those who died on the *Arizona* are carved in marble at one end of the room. Even today, bubbles of oil from the sunken *Arizona* rise to the water's surface. In 1999, the U.S. battleship *Missouri* was opened to the public, as the Battleship *Missouri* Memorial, in Pearl Harbor near the *Arizona*. This ship was the one on which the Japanese surrendered to the Allies, on September 2, 1945.

Pearl Harbor as a naval base. In 1887, King Kalakaua of Hawaii gave the United States the right to develop a coaling station at Pearl Harbor. The harbor's name came from the pearl oysters that once grew in its waters. The United States made its first attempt to deepen the channel through the reef outside the harbor in 1902. The first dry dock was completed in 1919.

Pearl Harbor is now the site of the Pearl Harbor Naval Complex. It covers about 12,600 acres (5,100 hectares) on Oahu Island. Five major fleet commands in the Pacific have headquarters at the base.

DORIE MILLER (1919–1943) was a famous African American hero of World War II (1939–1945). On December 7, 1941, he was serving as a mess attendant aboard the battleship *West Virginia* at the U.S. naval base on Pearl Harbor in Hawaii. That day, Japan staged a surprise attack on Pearl Harbor, and the *West Virginia* came under fire. Miller had no gunnery training, but he took the place of a dead machine-gun operator and shot down four Japanese aircraft. For this feat, Miller received the Navy Cross, a medal given for great heroism in combat.

Miller was born on a farm near Waco, Texas. His real first name was Doris. He enlisted in the U.S. Navy in 1939. At that time, blacks could serve in the Navy only as cook, steward, mess attendant, or waiter. After the attack on Pearl Harbor, Miller became a steward aboard the aircraft carrier *Liscome Bay*. He was killed when a Japanese submarine torpedo blew up the ship on November 24, 1943.

MLA Citation

"Pearl Harbor." *The Southwestern Advantage Topic Source.* Nashville: Southwestern. 2013.

ADDITIONAL RESOURCES

Books to Read

Jasper, Joy W., and others. *The USS Arizona*. 2001. Reprint. St. Martin's, 2003.

Prange, Gordon W., and others. *At Dawn We Slept: The Untold Story of Pearl Harbor*. 1981. Reprint. Viking Penguin, 2001.

Rice, Earle, Jr. *The Bombing of Pearl Harbor*. Lucent Books, 2001. Younger readers.

Van der Vat, Dan. *Pearl Harbor*. Basic Books, 2001.

Web Sites

Japanese Forces in the Pearl Harbor Attack

http://www.history.navy.mil/photos/events/wwii-pac/pearlhbr/ph-ja1.htm

Naval Historical Center Web site with pictures and descriptions of Japan's aircraft carriers in World War II.

Pearl Harbor

http://www.iwm.org.uk/online/pearl_harbour/index.htm

An online exhibit from the Imperial War Museum.

World War II Valor in the Pacific Home Page

http://www.nps.gov/valr/index.htm

National Park Service site for Valor in the Pacific National Monument in Hawaii, California, and Alaska, commemorating World War II in the Pacific Theater.

Search Strings

Background to the Attack

background to the attack on Pearl Harbor (138,000)

background to the attack on Pearl Harbor Japanese military expansion exports General Hideki Tojo (470) *These returns looked very good.

background to the attack on Pearl Harbor Japanese exports General Hideki Tojo (347)

The Attack

Attack on Pearl Harbor Japan Oahu Hawaii (14,000)

Attack on Pearl Harbor Japan Oahu Hawaii aircraft carriers battleships (19,500)

The U.S. Response

U.S. Response to the attack on Pearl Harbor war declaration President Roosevelt (11,800)

U.S. Response to the attack on Pearl Harbor war declaration President Roosevelt infamy Japan (1,870)

U.S.S. Arizona War Memorial

U.S.S. Arizona War Memorial (332,000)

U.S.S. Arizona War Memorial battleships destroyed (22,900)

U.S.S. Arizona War Memorial battleships destroyed tourist attraction (553)

BACKGROUND INFORMATION

The following article was written during the year in which the events took place and reflects the style and thinking of that time.

World War II (1942)

As a result of the Japanese attack on Pearl Harbor, followed by the German and Italian declarations of war on the United States, World War II soon became a truly global war.

Japan's Advance in Asia and the Pacific

Initial Allied disasters. Japan's treacherous attack on Pearl Harbor did much more damage than was admitted at the time. The report published by the Navy Department a year later showed that every battleship and most of the aircraft in the region was at least disabled. Nineteen naval vessels of all types, including eight battleships, were sunk or badly damaged.

Of the 273 army airplanes closely parked together on the airfields at Hawaii, very few were able to take off because of damage to the runways. Ninety-seven army planes were destroyed at Hickam and Wheeler fields along. Eighty naval aircraft were destroyed and 150 parked on the island of Oahu were disabled. A similar fatal blow a few hours later destroyed nearly all the American planes in the Philippines.

The United States thus entered the war in the Pacific with naval strength very inferior to that of Japan, and without the vital planes which are the eyes of the fleet and are essential for protecting the long sea lanes.

At the outset, therefore, the Japanese enjoyed almost undisputed control of the seas in the southwest Pacific, except for the small but very efficient Netherlands Indies fleet. They could proceed with the methodical and irresistible occupation of a great 7,000-mile arc of territories stretching from Alaska around through the Solomon Islands and the Netherlands Indies to Singapore, Malaya, and Burma. For six months the United Nations had to fight a war of "defensive attrition," delaying the Japanese advance as much as possible, destroying Japanese transports, and protecting their own ships and aircraft whenever the opportunity offered. Not until the summer of 1942, when they had built up their strength and inflicted decisive losses on the Japanese in the Coral Sea and near Midway Island, could they pass from the defensive to a well-sustained offensive.

Japanese advances. After the surrender of Hong Kong on Christmas Day, 1941, and the seizure of the British airdromes at Kota Bharu and several other points in British Malaya, the Japanese had air control over the whole Malay Peninsula and the waters of its east and west coasts. Their troops were landed at Singora and Patani in southern Thailand, marched across a narrow neck of land, and hurried down the west coast of Malaya toward Singapore.

Having captured the slightly defended island of Penang and taken possession of small boats there, the invaders were able to land small parties at the rear of the British, who were trying in vain to stop the Japanese advance on land. Other Japanese, often in Malayan disguise, crept through the jungle

Japanese troops on Bataan

past the main British line and harassed its flank
and rear. Hidden in the foliage of treetops, they
picked off British officers. Self-confident, fanati-
cally warlike and patriotic, hardened to the climate,
living on a few handfuls of rice, they proved to be
the best jungle fighters in the world. They would
rather die than surrender or be taken alive, because
to be captured meant eternal disgrace at home for
themselves and their families.

**Japan's conquest of the Philip-
pines.** The fate of the 7,000 islands which make
up the Philippines group was virtually sealed from
the outset, when most of the American airplanes
were destroyed on the ground. With their loss, the
few surface vessels and submarines at the islands
had to be withdrawn for safety to bases farther
south in Java and Australia. Japanese transports
were then able to land troops at widely separated
points extending 600 miles from Aparri, Vigan,
and Lingayen in northern Luzon to Davao in Min-
danao in the south.

General Douglas MacArthur had less than
15,000 seasoned troops when war began. The great
bulk of his forces consisted of inadequately trained
and equipped but very loyal Philippine reservists.

Outnumbered by the enemy, and lacking air
protection and supplies, General MacArthur pru-
dently withdrew most of his scattered forces into
the hilly Bataan Peninsula north of Manila Bay.
Here they had a shortened line to defend and held
out gloriously in their "foxholes" amid great priva-
tions for four months.

In March 1942, General MacArthur was
appointed to a new command and escaped with his
wife and child from Bataan in a small motorboat to
a plane which flew him to Australia. His successor
in the Philippines, Lieutenant General Jonathan
M. Wainwright, held out in Bataan for a month
longer. But seeing that further resistance, without
new supplies and reinforcements, would be hopeless, he surrendered his battered Bataan forces
(about 37,000 American and Filipino troops and
20,000 civilians) on April 9. Some of his men and
nurses had already been ferried over to Corregidor,
the island fortress which guards Manila Bay. But
this also was forced to surrender on May 7. Many
loyal American and Filipino soldiers and marines
escaped to the mountains and continued guerrilla
warfare throughout the year.

The Indian Ocean. By capturing Singapore,
the Japanese gained easy access to the Indian

Ocean. Troops landed at Rangoon and other points
gradually conquered Burma, with some aid from
discontented Burmese, and joined other Japanese
troops which marched across country westward
from Thailand. They thus cut off the famous
Burma Road, which had been China's main route
for receiving war supplies from the outside world.
But by the end of 1942, giant Allied planes, flying
blind over mountains 17,000 feet high, were beginning to carry more lend-lease supplies to Gener-
alissimo Chiang Kai-shek than had formerly toiled
over the long and difficult Burma Road. The American Volunteer Group of "Flying Tigers" shot down
great numbers of Japanese planes over Burma, with
very few losses to themselves.

The danger that Japanese surface and submarine
raiders would play havoc with shipping in the
Indian Ocean was greatly reduced by the concentration of strong British naval forces in those
waters and by the strengthening of the air forces at
Ceylon. Supplies coming from the United States
to the Allied Red Sea base at Eritrea were further
safeguarded in May by the British occupation of
the Vichy Government's naval base of Diego
Suarez at the Northern tip of the great island of
Madagascar. During the following six months, the
British gradually occupied the remainder of Madagascar and then handed it over to the government
of General Charles de Gaulle's Fighting French.

By the end of 1942, in spite of pacifist opposition by some Indian Nationalist leaders, India had
raised more than 1,500,000 troops and equipped
them largely from her own resources. Indian
troops fought in Egypt and elsewhere for the
Allied cause.

**Battles of the Macassar Straits and
Java Sea.** Even before the fall of Singapore and
the Philippines, the Japanese had begun to seize
strategic points in the Indies. They captured the
rich oil fields of the British and Dutch on North
Borneo. On January 23, they sent a great armada of
one hundred warships and transports into the
Macassar Straits between Borneo and Celebes, to
seize the oil and other riches of Java. They were
met by American and Dutch warships, strongly
supported by airplanes, in a terrific and confused
battle which lasted five days and nights. The Japanese lost thirty-eight ships badly damaged or sunk,
including one battleship and one aircraft carrier,
and some 25,000 men drowned. Though temporarily turned back by the Allied delaying action,

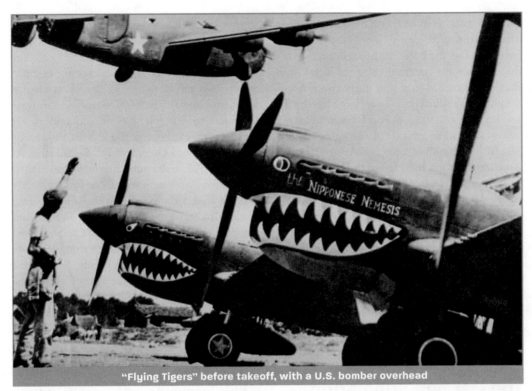

"Flying Tigers" before takeoff, with a U.S. bomber overhead

the Japanese again advanced early in February. They established bases on both sides of the Celebes, and occupied the famous spice islands of Amboina and Timor north of Australia.

Another Japanese expedition, sweeping far to the east, established bases at Salamaua, Lae, and Buna on the northeast coast of New Guinea, from which their planes began to attack the British in Port Moresby on the south coast, the Port Darwin, in northern Australia. Still further east they set up bases at Rabaul in New Britain and at Tulagi in the Solomon Islands, from both of which they aimed to strike at the supply lines from the United States to Australia.

The Battle of the Java Sea, which began on February 27, was another confused and long-drawn-out naval engagement, very costly to both sides. The Japanese were able to land on Java, and on March 9 announced that the whole island had surrendered. They soon occupied the remainder of the Netherlands Indies, and so possessed naval and air bases over a great line of territories stretching 4,000 miles from Burma in the west to the Solomon Islands in the east.

Battle of the Coral Sea. On May 4, the carriers *Lexington* and *Yorktown*, escorted by American cruisers and destroyers, steamed to within bombing distance of Tulagi, and their planes sank and damaged several Japanese ships. Two days later a Japanese armada advancing southwest of the Solomon Islands was intercepted by American carrier-borne planes. The ensuing battle was unique in history because it was the first clash between aircraft carriers. A month later another Japanese armada was defeated off Midway.

American Offensive in the Pacific

Early in 1942, Admiral Chester W. Nimitz carried out successful attacks against Japan's far-flung outer line of defense in the Pacific by surprise raids on the Gilbert and Marshall islands (January 31), on Wake Island (February 26), and on Marcus Island (March 4). In each case Japanese planes were destroyed, small naval vessels were sunk or damaged, and land installations and military stores set on fire, with virtually no losses to the Americans.

Such air raids as that on Tokyo, however, could not lead to immediate further action. It was not until after the Battle of Midway had saved Hawaii and more nearly equalized naval power in the Pacific that the United States was able to begin a sustained offensive by seizing Tulagi and a foothold on Guadalcanal on August 7.

Success in New Guinea. From their bases on the northern shore of New Guinea at Salamaua, Lae, and Buna, the Japanese advanced in the early summer southward over the high Owen Stanley Mountains to within thirty-two miles of the important Allied position at Port Moresby. To prevent a possible attack of Port Darwin across the narrow sea and an invasion of Australia, General MacArthur organized a force of Australians and Americans and gradually forced the Japanese back over the mountains. By the end of December, creeping through swamps and jungles, exterminating the Japanese one by one, the Allies finally captured the stubbornly resisting force at Buna and all but a few hundred yards of beach.

General MacArthur's bombers were extremely successful in long flights in which they bombed enemy concentration points at Rabaul in New Britain and at ports in the Solomon Islands, and also sank many Japanese destroyers and transports which tried to land reinforcements for the hard-pressed Japanese in the New Guinea area.

The German Submarine Menace

Hitler's greatest success in 1942 was his sinking of Allied shipping. Although the North Atlantic route from American to British ports had already been made fairly safe by efficient convoy escorts and air protection, the Allies lost heavily in merchant shipping in the dangerous route to Murmansk, which was open to attack by German submarines, surface raiders, and bombers based in northern Norway. The Mediterranean route from Gibraltar to Suez, where air and underwater attacks were easily carried out from the nearby bases in Italy and Greece, was also vulnerable. As the British Admiralty published no figures of their own losses, their extent was uncertain.

Soon after declaring war on the United States, Hitler also began damaging attacks on merchant shipping, mainly American, in the Caribbean and along the Atlantic seaboard. Here no protective measures were immediately ready. Ships were sunk, sometimes even within sight of land, at the rate of two or three a day—much faster than they could be replaced. The destruction of tankers carrying oil from the Gulf of Mexico, and ships bringing sugar from Cuba and coffee from Brazil, was so great that these commodities had to be rationed in the United States.

Ship losses. According to published American figures, which were not complete, about 580 merchant ships, totaling probably 2,300,000 gross tons, were sent to the bottom during 1942 by Axis (mainly German) submarines in the waters along

PTs patrolling New Guinea

A torpedoed Japanese destroyer as seen through the periscope of a U.S. ship

the Atlantic coast, in the South Atlantic, and off Africa (not including the Mediterranean). The German High Command claimed to have sunk during 1942 in all areas a total of 8,940,000 gross tons of Allied merchant shipping. But this German figure, as usual, was exaggerated.

The very serious loss in shipping, whatever the exact figure, was more than offset by new construction by the end of 1942, although American losses exceeded new American building during the first half of the year. Total new construction in the United States during 1942 slightly exceeded President Roosevelt's goal of 8,000,000 deadweight tons, which in the case of cargo ships is equivalent to about 5,600,000 gross tons. Moreover, the curve for new construction was rising very rapidly during the last months of 1942. To American new construction should be added that of Great Britain, the British Dominions, and the other Allies, which may be estimated at about 2,500,000 gross tons for the year.

As compared with the Atlantic, American losses of transports and merchantmen in the Pacific were slight, being only 17 vessels, while Japan lost more than 200.

Florida

Florida, a state in the southeastern United States, is known as the Sunshine State. Its sunny climate attracts millions of tourists every year.

HOT topics

Tourism in Florida. As the southernmost state in the U.S. mainland, Florida has a warm climate which attracts visitors at any time of year. The largest tourist center is the Walt Disney World Resort, a theme park and entertainment complex near Orlando. Many seaside resorts, such as Miami Beach, are on Florida's long coastline. Other attractions include Everglades National Park and the Florida Keys, a line of small islands that extends into the Gulf of Mexico.

Colonial Times. In 1513, the Spanish explorer Juan Ponce de León claimed the Florida region for Spain. Fifty-two years later, the Spaniards established St. Augustine, the first permanent European settlement in what is now the United States. Britain gained control of Florida in 1763 but ceded it back to Spain twenty years later. After the Revolutionary War in America (1775–1783), the United States did not include Spanish Florida. It was not until 1845 that Florida was admitted to the Union.

An alligator in the Everglades

HOT topics

Plant and Animal Life. Forests cover nearly half of Florida with a variety of trees. Abundant wildflowers of Florida include azaleas, gardenias, hibiscus, irises, lupines, orchids, poinsettias, sunflowers, and trumpet creeper. The most famous of Florida's animals are alligators, which live in swamps. Florida's waters teem with more fish than any other part of the world. Freshwater fish include bass, bream, catfish, and crappies. Florida's ocean waters contain bluefish, grouper, mackerel, marlin, menhaden, pompano, red snapper, sailfish, sea trout, and tarpon. Varied shellfish live in Florida's coastal waters. Florida has a large commercial fishing industry.

Florida's Voting System became a focus of attention during the 2000 presidential election. The result of the contest between the Republican candidate, Texas governor George W. Bush, and the Democratic candidate, Vice President Al Gore, depended upon who received Florida's 25 electoral votes. The vote in Florida was close and Gore requested manual recounts in certain counties. Bush challenged in court the need for those recounts. Five weeks after the election, the U.S. Supreme Court ruled to halt the manual recounts, and Gore conceded to Bush.

A Varied Economy supports Florida's fast population growth, one of the highest in the United states. Manufacturing benefits from the growth of high-technology industries. Fishing and farming are important, too, the state's single most important farm product being oranges. Much income is received from the mining of phosphate rock, which is used to make fertilizer.

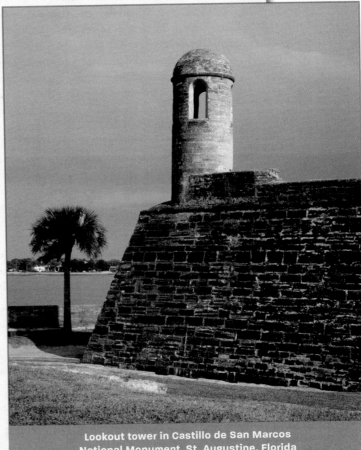
Lookout tower in Castillo de San Marcos National Monument, St. Augustine, Florida

TRUE or FALSE?
The Revolutionary War resulted in Florida going from British control to Spanish control.

THE BASICS

Florida is one of the leading tourist states in the United States. This land of swaying palm trees and warm ocean breezes attracts tens of millions of visitors the year around. Many of these vacationers enjoy Walt Disney World Resort, a theme park near Orlando. Miami Beach, a suburb of Miami, is one of the state's many famous resort centers. Other popular seaside resorts include Clearwater, Daytona Beach, Fort Lauderdale, Key West, Palm Beach, Panama City, and Sanibel Island.

Florida has been nicknamed the *Sunshine State* because it has many sunny days. Partly as a result of the warm, sunny climate, millions of older people spend their retirement years in the state. Tallahassee is the capital of Florida. Jacksonville ranks as the state's largest city.

Florida is the southernmost state on the U.S. mainland. A large part of the state consists of a peninsula that juts south about 400 miles (640 kilometers) into the sea. The state's northwestern part, called the *Panhandle*, extends along the northern shore of the Gulf of Mexico. Florida faces the Atlantic Ocean on the east and the Gulf of Mexico on the west. The southern tip of Florida is less than 100 miles (160 kilometers) from Cuba. Florida's coastline is longer than that of any other state except Alaska.

Florida's population is growing faster than that of all but a few other states. Its economy is also expanding rapidly, especially in banking, business services, and the manufacture of computers and other electronic equipment. Florida farmers grow about 70 percent of the nation's orange and grapefruit crops. Almost all the frozen orange juice produced in the United States is processed in Florida.

In 1513, the Spanish explorer Juan Ponce de León claimed the Florida region for Spain. He named the region *Florida*, probably because he arrived there a few days after Easter, which the Spanish called *Pascua Florida* (Easter of the Flowers). In 1565, the Spaniards established St. Augustine, the first per-

Map of Florida

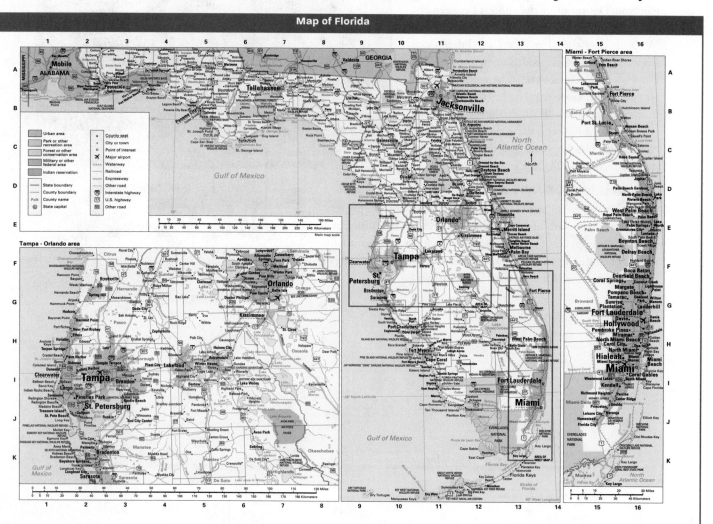

manent European settlement in what became the United States. Britain gained control of Florida in 1763 but ceded it back to Spain in 1783. After the Revolutionary War in America (1775–1783), the United States controlled all the land it now occupies from the Atlantic Ocean to the Mississippi River except for Spanish Florida.

The United States formally obtained Florida from Spain in 1821, and Congress established the Territory of Florida the next year. Florida became a state in 1845. Shortly before the American Civil War began in 1861, Florida left the Union and then joined the Confederacy. Tallahassee was the only Confederate state capital east of the Mississippi River that Union forces did not capture during the war. Florida was readmitted to the Union in 1868. The population of Florida started to swell during the early 1900s and has been growing ever since.

People

Population. The 2010 United States census reported that Florida had 18,801,310 people. The population had increased about 18 percent over the 2000 figure of 15,982,378. Of states east of the Mississippi River, only Georgia and North Carolina had a higher percentage of growth during the first decade of the 2000s. Florida ranks fourth in population among the 50 states.

About 94 percent of Florida's people live in the state's metropolitan areas. Florida has 20 metropolitan areas entirely within the borders of the state. Over half of the state's population lives in the Miami-Fort Lauderdale-Pompano Beach, Orlando-Kissimmee-Sanford, and Tampa-St. Petersburg-Clearwater metropolitan areas.

Jacksonville is Florida's largest city, with a population of more than 820,000. Other cities over 150,000, in order of population, are Miami, Tampa, St. Petersburg, Orlando, Hialeah, Tallahassee, Fort Lauderdale, Port St. Lucie, Pembroke Pines, and Cape Coral. Most of Florida's largest cities lie on or near the Atlantic or Gulf coasts.

Many older people move to Florida from other parts of the country after they retire. About 15 percent of the state's population are African Americans. Hispanic Americans, who may be of any race, make up about 20 percent of Florida's population. Many Floridians are of Cuban, English, German, Irish, or Italian ancestry.

Schools. Florida's earliest schools were run by Spanish priests in the 1600s. Spanish and Indian children studied religion and the Spanish language. During the mid-1700s, English colonists provided education for the children of wealthier families. A formal system of public education in Florida began with the Constitution of 1868 and was well established by the early 1900s.

Today, the governor appoints a Board of Education with authority over elementary through post-secondary education. The Department of Education administers the policies of the board, under the leadership of a commissioner appointed by the governor. The Department of Education supervises public schools, public community colleges and universities, and state-supported vocational education programs. Children from age 6 through age 15 must attend school.

Libraries. The Walton-DeFuniak Library in DeFuniak Springs is the oldest library in Florida still serving the public. It was established in 1886. The state's first free, tax-supported library opened in Jacksonville in 1905. The state administers the State Library of Florida in Tallahassee. The Florida Historical Society maintains the Library of Florida History in Cocoa. The P. K. Yonge Library of Florida History, at the University of Florida, has an extensive collection of books about the state.

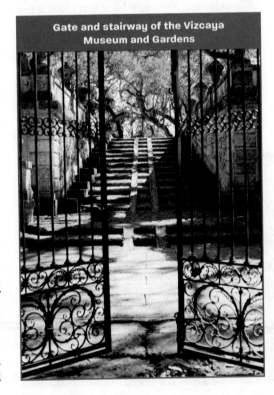

Gate and stairway of the Vizcaya Museum and Gardens

Museums. The John and Mable Ringling Museum of Art in Sarasota is noted for its Baroque art collection. Also on the grounds are the Ringling mansion and the Circus Museums. History museums in Florida include the Museum of Florida History in Tallahassee and HistoryMiami in Miami. The state's art museums include the Cummer Museum of Art and Gardens in Jacksonville; the Museum of Fine Arts and the Salvador Dalí Museum in St. Petersburg; and the Norton Museum of Art in West Palm Beach. Other important museums are Florida Museum of Natural History in Gainesville and the Vizcaya Museum and Gardens in Miami.

 ## Visitor's Guide

Great stretches of sandy beaches and a warm, sunny climate make Florida a year-round vacationland. Southern Florida is one of the world's most beautiful resort areas. Its attractions include Everglades National Park and the Florida Keys, a chain of small islands that extends into the Gulf of Mexico. People enjoy swimming, fishing, and water-skiing in the inland and coastal waters.

Visitors with interests other than water areas may see historic sites that date back to the Spanish explorers. The Orange Bowl football game in Miami Gardens on or near New Year's Day is one of Florida's leading annual events. The state has professional baseball, basketball, football, and hockey teams. Horse racing, greyhound racing, and jai alai games are popular.

Land and Climate

Land regions. Florida is part of the Atlantic-Gulf Coastal Plain, a large land region that extends along the coast from New Jersey to southern Texas. Within Florida, there are three main land regions: (1) the Atlantic Coastal Plain, (2) the East Gulf Coastal Plain, and (3) the Florida Uplands.

The Atlantic Coastal Plain of Florida covers the entire eastern part of the state. It is a low, level plain ranging in width from 30 to 100 miles (48 to 160 kilometers). A narrow ribbon of sand bars, coral reefs, and barrier islands lies in the Atlantic Ocean, just offshore from the mainland. Lagoons, rivers, bays, and long, shallow lakes lie between much of this ribbon and the mainland.

Big Cypress Swamp and the Everglades cover most of southern Florida. Water covers much of this region, especially during the rainy months.

The Florida Keys make up the southernmost part of the state. These small islands curve southwestward for about 150 miles (241 kilometers) off the mainland from Miami. Key Largo is the largest island.

The East Gulf Coastal Plain of Florida has two main sections. One section covers the southwestern part of the peninsula, including Tampa Bay and part of the Everglades and Big Cypress Swamp. The other section of Florida's East Gulf Coastal Plain curves around the northern edge of the Gulf of Mexico across the Panhandle to Florida's western border.

The East Gulf Coastal Plain is similar to the Atlantic Coastal Plain. Long, narrow barrier islands extend along the Gulf of Mexico coastline. Coastal swamps stretch inland in places. Much swampland in the region has been drained, and the land used for farming or urban development, especially in southwestern Florida.

The Florida Uplands is shaped somewhat like a giant arm and hand. A finger of the hand points down the center of the state toward the southern tip of the peninsula. The uplands separate the two sections of the East Gulf Coastal Plain from each other and separate the northern section from the Atlantic Coastal Plain.

The uplands region is higher than Florida's other land regions. But its average elevation is only between 200 and 300 feet (61 and 91 meters) above sea level. Lakes are common in the Florida Uplands. Many of these lakes were formed in *sinkholes*—cave-ins where a limestone bed near the surface has been dissolved by water action. Pine forests grow in the northern section of the uplands.

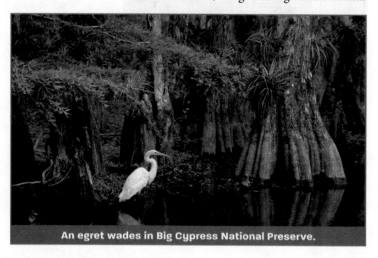
An egret wades in Big Cypress National Preserve.

The northern part of the Florida Uplands extends from the northwestern corner of the state along the northern border for about 275 miles (443 kilometers). Its width varies from about 30 to 50 miles (48 to 80 kilometers). This section has fertile valleys and rolling hills of red clay. Many hardwood and softwood forests are found there. The southern part of the Florida Uplands is a region of low hills and lakes. It covers an area about 100 miles (160 kilometers) wide and about 160 miles (257 kilometers) long.

The coastline of Florida is 1,350 miles (2,173 kilometers) long. The Atlantic coast has 580 miles (933 kilometers) of shoreline. The Gulf coast is 770 miles (1,240 kilometers) long. When lagoons, bays, and barrier islands are included, the Atlantic coastline is 3,331 miles (5,361 kilometers) long and the Gulf coast is 5,095 miles (8,200 kilometers) long. Biscayne Bay, extending south from Miami, is the one major bay on the Atlantic coast. The most important bays along the western coast include Tampa, Charlotte Harbor, San Carlos, and Sarasota. Florida Bay, beyond the southern tip of the peninsula, separates the Florida Keys from the mainland. Apalachee, Apalachicola, St. Joseph, St. Andrew, Choctawhatchee, and Pensacola bays stretch along the northern Florida shoreline of the Gulf of Mexico.

Rivers, lakes, and springs. The St. Johns River is the largest river in the state. It begins near Melbourne and flows about 275 miles (443 kilometers) northward, almost parallel to the Atlantic coastline. The St. Marys River, along the eastern Florida-Georgia border, flows east into the Atlantic. The Perdido River, on Florida's northwestern border, drains into the Gulf of Mexico. The Apalachicola River is northwestern Florida's most important river. It is formed where the Chattahoochee and Flint rivers join at the northern boundary of the state, and it flows south to the Gulf of Mexico. The Suwannee River flows southwest from the Florida-Georgia border and also empties into the Gulf. Stephen Foster made this river famous in his song "Old Folks at Home," also known as "Swanee River." Other rivers connect many of the lakes of the uplands.

Lake Okeechobee is Florida's largest lake. It covers about 680 square miles (1,760 square kilometers) and is the second largest natural body of fresh water located wholly within the United States. Only Lake Michigan covers a larger area. About 30,000 shallow lakes lie throughout central Florida.

Florida has 17 large springs and countless smaller ones. Many of the springs contain healthful mineral waters. Wakulla Springs, near Tallahassee, is one of the nation's deepest springs. It has a depth of 185 feet (56 meters). Silver Springs, southeast of Ocala, is the largest spring in the state. Many of the springs are so clear that plant life on the bottom may be seen as deep as 80 feet (24 meters).

Plant and animal life. Forests cover about half of Florida. Common trees include ashes, beeches, bald cypresses, sweet gums, hickories, magnolias, mangroves, maples, oaks, palms, and pines.

Common wildflowers of Florida include irises, lilies, lupines, orchids, sunflowers, and such climbing vines as Carolina yellow jasmine, Cherokee rose, morning-glory, and trumpet creeper. Other flowers that grow throughout the state include azaleas, camellias, gardenias, hibiscus, oleanders, and poinsettias. The bougainvillea and the flame vine (also called golden bignonia) brighten many southern Florida gardens. Dogwoods, magnolias, and redbuds flourish in the north.

Black bears, deer, gray foxes, and wildcats live in many parts of the state. Smaller animals, such as opossums, otters, raccoons, and squirrels, are also

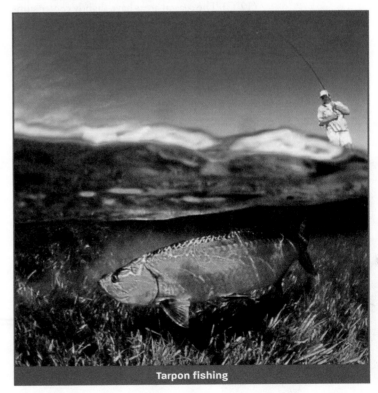

Tarpon fishing

common. Florida has the largest colonies of anhinga, egrets, herons, ibises, and pelicans north of the Caribbean Sea. Alligators live in the swamps.

More kinds of fishes may be found in Florida's waters than in any other part of the world. The freshwater lakes and rivers contain bass, bream, catfish, and crappies. Florida's ocean waters contain bluefish, grouper, mackerel, marlin, menhaden, pompano, red snapper, sailfish, sea trout, and tarpon. Clams, conches, crabs, crayfish, oysters, scallops, and shrimp live in Florida's coastal waters. Mullets are found in salt water and *brackish* (somewhat salty) marshes.

Climate. Most of Florida has a warm, humid climate similar to that of the other Southern States. Florida's southern tip has a tropical wet and dry climate like that of Central America and large parts of Africa and South America.

Atlantic and Gulf breezes relieve some of the summer heat near the coasts. Winters are usually mild, even in northern Florida. July temperatures are much the same in the northern and southern parts of the state. Jacksonville, in the north, has an average July temperature of 82°F (28°C). Miami, in the south, averages 84°F (29°C) in July. But in January, Miami averages 68°F (20°C), and Jacksonville's average temperature drops to 53°F (12°C). The coastal areas have slightly cooler summers and warmer winters than do inland areas. Destructive frosts rarely occur in southern Florida. But occasional cold waves damage crops as far south as the Everglades.

The highest and lowest temperatures ever recorded in Florida occurred within 30 miles (48 kilometers) of each other. Tallahassee recorded the lowest temperature, −2°F (−19°C), on February 13, 1899. Nearby Monticello recorded the highest temperature, 109°F (43°C), on June 29, 1931.

Nearly all of Florida's precipitation occurs in the form of rain. Florida has an average yearly precipitation of 54 inches (137 centimeters). An average of 32 inches (81 centimeters) falls in the rainy season, which lasts from May to October.

Florida lies along the path of many of the hurricanes that sweep across the Atlantic Ocean every summer and fall. Destructive hurricanes have struck Florida several times. Tornadoes and waterspouts also affect the state. Droughts and wildfires have become increasingly frequent occurrences.

Economy

Although traditional industries, such as the tourist trade and growing citrus fruits, remain important, Florida's economy has become more diverse. Companies have been attracted to the state because of its warm climate and business-friendly reputation. Manufacturing in central Florida has benefited from the growth of high-technology industries especially computer-related and electronics industries.

Service industries, taken together, account for the largest portion of Florida's *gross domestic product*—the total value of all goods and services produced in the state in a year. Florida agriculture is famous for growing citrus fruits. About 70 percent of both the orange and grapefruit crops of the United States are grown in Florida. The state also receives much income from the mining of phosphate rock. Phosphate is used to make fertilizer.

Natural resources. Florida's natural resources include sandy beaches, a sunny climate, thick forests, and phosphate and mineral sands deposits.

Soil. Most of Florida's soils are sandy, especially in the coastal plains. The most fertile soils are in the south, where much of the area's rich wetland has been drained and used for farming. The soils of the Florida Uplands are chiefly sandy loams and clays.

Minerals. Most of Florida lies on huge beds of limestone, the state's most plentiful mineral. Florida has the largest phosphate deposits in the United States. Most of the state's phosphate comes from mines in west-central Florida. Large stores of peat, sand, gravel, and a valuable clay called *fuller's*

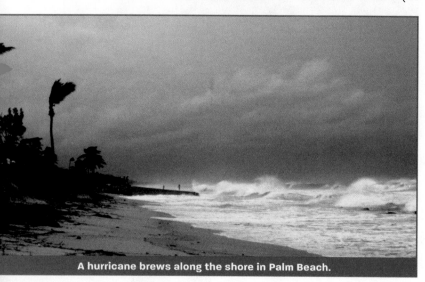

A hurricane brews along the shore in Palm Beach.

earth (used in filters) are found throughout the state. The sandy areas of the state have mineral sands including ilmenite, rutile, and zircon. Brick clays and kaolin, a pottery clay, are found chiefly in Putnam County. Natural gas and oil are mined in northwestern and southern Florida.

Forests cover about 40 percent of the state. Florida has hundreds of kinds of trees. Slash pines are the most valuable trees in Florida. The most common hardwood trees are bald cypress, black tupelo, magnolia, oak, and sweet gum. Other common trees include ash, beech, hickory, maple, and yellow pines (loblolly and longleaf). Hardwoods and pines are plentiful in the northern half of the state. Mangrove and gumbo limbo trees are found in southern Florida's coastal marshlands.

Service industries provide about five-sixths of both Florida's employment and its gross domestic product. Service industries chiefly operate in the Jacksonville, Miami, Orlando, and Tampa-St. Petersburg areas.

Florida's restaurants and hotels benefit from the tens of millions of tourists who visit each year. Many hotels and resorts line the coastal areas. Walt Disney World Resort, a theme park and entertainment complex near Orlando, is one of the world's leading tourist attractions.

Florida's leading financial centers are the Jacksonville, Miami, Orlando, and Tampa-St. Petersburg areas. Real estate companies have brought in much income by developing retirement communities and vacation resorts. Investment firms operating in Florida receive much business from retired people.

Tallahassee, the state capital, is the center of government activities. The federal government operates the John F. Kennedy Space Center on Cape Canaveral, Eglin Air Force Base in the Panhandle, and Naval Air Station Pensacola. Two of the nation's largest supermarket chains, Publix Super Markets, Inc., and Winn-Dixie Stores, Inc., have their headquarters in Florida. Several shipping and cruise lines are based in Florida.

Manufacturing. Computer and electronic products lead Florida's manufactured products. Communications equipment, computer microchips and components, and search and navigational, medical, and measuring equipment are the leading products from this sector. Many high-tech jobs are in the Orlando and Tampa areas. Many Internet companies are based in South Florida.

Citrus fruit processing is one of Florida's largest industries.

Food and beverage processing ranks second among Florida's manufacturing activities. Citrus fruit processing is one of the largest industries in the state. Processing plants, mostly in central Florida, produce fresh citrus fruit juices, canned juices, canned fruit, and citrus by-products. Florida also produces baked goods, dairy products, meat, seafood, soft drinks, and sugar products.

Other leading products include chemicals, fabricated metal products, medical equipment, nonmetallic minerals, and transportation equipment. Fertilizer and *pharmaceuticals* (medicinal drugs) are the leading chemical products. Machine shop products and metal doors and windows are key parts of the fabricated metal products sector. Medical equipment is made chiefly in the Jacksonville and Miami areas. Cement and concrete products are the leading nonmetallic mineral products. Aircraft parts, airplanes, and ships are also made in Florida.

Agriculture. Farmland covers about one-fourth of Florida's land area. Crops account for about five-sixths of Florida's total farm income. Oranges are the state's single most important farm product. Other citrus fruits grown in the state include grapefruit and tangerines. Florida is the nation's largest producer of grapefruit, oranges, and tangerines. The state's chief citrus groves lie in south-central Florida. The state also grows blueberries, strawberries, and watermelons.

Tomatoes are Florida's most important vegetable crop. Most of the tomatoes come from southern Florida, the main vegetable-growing region. Other vegetables produced in Florida include cabbage, cucumbers, peppers, potatoes, snap beans, squash, and sweet corn. Many northern states rely on Florida for fresh vegetables during cold months.

Sugarcane is another important crop. Florida leads the nation in sugarcane production. The region just south of Lake Okeechobee is the center of sugarcane growing. Other field crops cultivated in Florida include corn, cotton, hay, and peanuts. Florida ranks second to California in the production of greenhouse and nursery products. Most of the greenhouse and nursery products are grown in central and southern Florida.

Livestock and livestock products account for about one-sixth of Florida's farm income. Beef cattle and milk rank among the state's major livestock products. The largest cattle-raising regions are in central and south-central Florida. Poultry and egg production is also important. Farms in Marion County raise thoroughbred race horses. Florida is also an important state for *aquaculture* (fish farming).

Mining. Limestone and phosphate rock are Florida's most valuable mined products. The state is a leading producer of both products. Counties in west-central Florida produce phosphate rock. Quarries throughout the state provide limestone.

Natural gas and petroleum are mined chiefly in northwestern and southern Florida. Mines in Gadsen and Marion counties supply fuller's earth, a clay used to filter petroleum. Putnam County produces large amounts of kaolin, a pottery clay. Ilmenite, monazite, thorium, and zircon are taken from sands near the St. Johns River.

Fishing industry. Crab, grouper, lobster, and shrimp are Florida's leading catches. They account for about two-thirds of the total fishing value. Other fishes include clams, mackerel, mullet, oysters, sharks, snapper, swordfish, and tuna. The waters off Monroe and Pinellas counties are major sponge-fishing centers.

Electric power and utilities. FPL Group of Juno Beach is Florida's largest utility company. Plants that burn coal and plants that burn natural gas are the leading producers of Florida's power. Nuclear power plants and petroleum-burning plants supply most of the remaining electric power.

Transportation. Miami International Airport handles much of the air passenger and air freight travel to and from Latin America. Thus, Miami is often called the gateway to Latin America. Miami International and Orlando International rank among the country's busiest airports. Tampa and Fort Lauderdale also have major airports.

Rail lines provide freight service throughout the state. Florida has an extensive system of roads and highways. Florida's Turnpike connects many of the major cities. Four major interstate highways cross Florida.

Jacksonville, Miami, Port Everglades, and Tampa have major ports. Florida has more of the Atlantic Intracoastal Waterway than any other state. Florida's section of the Gulf Intracoastal Waterway winds along its Gulf coast.

Communication. The first newspaper in Florida was the *East Florida Gazette* of St. Augustine. William Charles Wells, a Scottish physician, published the *Gazette* in 1783. He established the paper to support the British side in the American Revolution (1775–1783). Wells stopped publishing the *Gazette* and returned to England after the Spanish regained control of Florida in 1783. Florida's oldest newspaper is *The Florida Times-Union*. It was established in 1864 and is still published daily in Jacksonville. The state's other newspapers include the South Florida *Sun-Sentinel*, published in Fort Lauderdale; *The Miami Herald*; the *Orlando Sentinel*; the *St. Petersburg Times*; and *The Tampa Tribune*.

Tied bundles of sugarcane

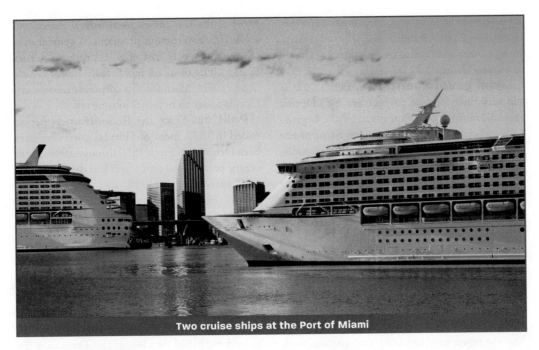

Two cruise ships at the Port of Miami

Government

The constitution of Florida went into effect in 1969. Earlier constitutions went into effect in 1839 (before Florida became a state), 1861, 1865, 1868, and 1887.

Constitutional *amendments* (changes) must be approved by a majority of people voting on them in a general or special election. Amendments may be proposed by the legislature. Three-fifths of each legislative house must approve the proposed amendment. Citizens also may propose amendments through the *initiative* process by presenting a petition signed by a specified number of voters. The people may also petition to call a constitutional convention. The petition must then be approved by the voters.

Executive. Florida's governor and lieutenant governor are elected as a team. The state's voters cast one vote for the governor and lieutenant governor. The governor and lieutenant governor of Florida serve four-year terms. The state's term limits prevent them from serving more than two terms in a row.

The governor of Florida appoints the state's public service commissioners and many of its judges. Members of the Cabinet are elected to four-year terms. Under the state's term limits, Cabinet members may not serve more than eight years in a row. The Cabinet consists of three members: the attorney general, the chief financial officer, and the commissioner of agriculture.

Legislature consists of a 40-member Senate and a 120-member House of Representatives. Senators serve four-year terms and representatives serve two-year terms. Under the state's term limits, senators and representatives may not serve more than eight years in a row. The Legislature's regular 60-day session usually opens on the first Tuesday after the first Monday in March each year. Special sessions may be called by the governor, by joint agreement of the leaders of each legislative house, or by a three-fifths vote of all members of the Legislature. Regular or special sessions of the Legislature may be extended by a three-fifths vote of each house.

In 1965, a federal court ordered Florida to *reapportion* (redivide) its Legislature to provide equal representation based on population. The Legislature drew up a reapportionment plan, but the Supreme Court of the United States ruled it unconstitutional. In 1967, a federal court devised its own reapportionment plan. Since 1969, the state Constitution has required reapportionment every 10 years, after each federal census.

Courts. The Florida Supreme Court has seven justices, all appointed by the governor to six-year terms. The justices elect one of their members to a two-year term as chief justice. Florida has five district courts of appeals. The governor appoints judges of these courts to six-year terms. In making appointments to the Supreme Court and courts of appeals, the governor chooses from among candidates selected by judicial nominating committees. Florida has 20 circuit courts and 67 county courts. Circuit court and county court judges are elected to six-year terms.

Local government. Florida's 67 counties can vary their form of government by adopting special county charters approved by the Legislature and the people of the county. Most of the counties are governed by a board of five commissioners and are divided into five districts. County voters elect a resident from each district to serve on the county commission. Other elected county officers may include the circuit court clerk, sheriff, supervisor of elections, property appraiser, and tax collector. County officials serve four-year terms. Most counties also have an appointed county administrator.

Chartered counties and municipalities have *home rule* (self-government) to the extent that they may make laws. Counties and municipalities also have the power to *consolidate* (combine) and work as a single government.

Revenue. Taxation provides more than half of the state government's *general revenue* (income).

Spanish explorer Juan Ponce de León searches for the legendary Fountain of Youth.

Most of the rest comes from federal grants and other U.S. government programs. A general sales tax generates over half of all tax revenue. Other taxes include those on motor fuels, motor vehicle licenses, and utilities, and a corporate income tax. Florida levies no personal income tax.

Politics. Since the Reconstruction period ended in 1877, most of Florida's governors have been Democrats. From 1880 through 1948, Democratic presidential candidates lost the state's electoral votes only in 1928. But since the 1952 election, Republican candidates have won the votes most of the time.

History

Early days. Burial mounds found along Florida's western coast show that Indians lived in the region about 12,000 years ago. The Calusa and the Tequesta in the south and the Ais on the Atlantic coast of the central part of the peninsula hunted and fished for a living. The Timucua in the central and northeast regions and the Apalachee in the northwest were farmers and hunters. Other Indians included the Tocobaga of the Tampa Bay area and the Matecumbe in the keys region.

Exploration and Spanish settlement. Explorer Juan Ponce de León reached Florida in 1513, a few days after Easter. He had been searching for the island of Bimini, which the Spanish thought lay north of Cuba. Some stories said Bimini was the site of the Fountain of Youth. Ponce de León claimed the region for Spain and named it *La Florida*, probably in honor of *Pascua Florida*, Spanish for *Easter*. He returned to Florida in 1521 to start a colony but was wounded in a battle with Indians and soon died.

In 1528, a Spaniard named Pánfilo de Narváez led an expedition of several hundred men to Florida's southwestern coast. He traveled northward searching for wealth. But hostile Indians, disease, starvation, and storms at sea eventually killed Narváez and almost all of his men. Another Spaniard, Hernando de Soto, landed an expedition in the Tampa Bay area in 1539. He led his men beyond the Florida region and in 1541 became the first European to reach the Mississippi River.

In 1564, a group of *Huguenots* (French Protestants) established a colony on the St. Johns River. They built Fort Caroline near what is now Jacksonville. King Philip II of Spain sent a sea captain named Pedro Menéndez de Avilés to drive the

French from Florida. Menéndez and his men arrived in Florida in 1565. They founded St. Augustine, the first permanent European settlement in what is now the United States. They destroyed the French forces and ended French attempts to settle in eastern Florida.

The Spaniards spent much of the next 200 years trying to teach their way of life to the Indians. Meanwhile, British colonists established settlements to the north, and France started colonies to the west. In the mid-1700s, wars broke out between British and French colonists. Spain sided with the French. In 1762, British forces captured the port of Havana, Cuba. In 1763, Spain gave Florida to Britain in exchange for Havana.

The British period. Britain divided the Florida region into two separate colonies—East Florida and West Florida. West Florida included the part of the region west of the Apalachicola River. It also included parts of what are now Alabama, Mississippi, and Louisiana. East Florida included the rest of the Florida region. British control of Florida lasted until Spanish forces marched into West Florida in 1779, during the Revolutionary War in America. The British, already weakened by war, surrendered West Florida to Spain in 1781. Spain regained control of all Florida in 1783.

The second Spanish period. After the Revolutionary War ended in 1783, the United States controlled all the land it now occupies from the Atlantic Ocean to the Mississippi River except for Spanish Florida. Indians and escaped slaves and prisoners took refuge in the Florida region. In 1812, a group of eastern Florida settlers rebelled and declared their independence from Spain. But the Spaniards stopped the rebellion.

During the War of 1812 (1812–1814), Spain let the United Kingdom use Pensacola as a naval base. In 1814, American troops led by General Andrew Jackson stormed into Florida and seized Pensacola. During the First Seminole War (1817–1818), Jackson captured Fort St. Marks on the Gulf of Mexico and then took Pensacola once again. Finally, in the Adams-Onis Treaty of 1819, Spain agreed to turn Florida over to the United States. The United States did not actually pay any money to Spain for Florida. However, it agreed to pay $5 million to U.S. citizens for property damages.

Territorial days. Florida formally came under U.S. control in 1821. Andrew Jackson served as temporary governor until November of

American soldiers hunting Native Americans with bloodhounds during the Second Seminole War

that year. In 1822, Congress organized the Territory of Florida, and William P. Duval became the first territorial governor.

Thousands of American settlers poured into Florida. One of the major problems they faced was finding enough land for settlement. Seminole Indians lived in some of the territory's richest farmland. The U.S. government offered land west of the Mississippi River to the Seminole if they would leave Florida territory. Some of the Seminole accepted the offer, but others refused to leave their homes. In the Second Seminole War (1835–1842), most of the band was wiped out. This war and the Third Seminole War (1855–1858) resulted in the forced resettlement of more Seminole, but a few hundred of the band fled into the swamps and remained in Florida.

Statehood. In 1839, Florida drew up a constitution in preparation for statehood, but it had to wait for admission to the Union. Florida would be a slave state, and Congress wanted to maintain a balance between slave and free states. Florida was admitted to the Union as a slave state on March 3, 1845. The following year, Iowa was admitted as a free state. Florida had a population of about 68,000 when it entered the Union. Most of the state's farms were small, and about two-thirds of the farmers did not own slaves.

The Civil War and Reconstruction. In 1860, Abraham Lincoln was elected president. Florida and most of the other slave states regarded Lincoln as a threat to their way of life. On January 10, 1861, Florida *seceded* (withdrew) from the Union and later joined the Confederacy.

Union forces captured most of Florida's coastal towns and Kay West early in the American Civil War (1861–1865). But Confederate forces won the Battle of Olustee on February 20, 1864, thereby keeping control of the interior region. This region's farmers shipped cattle, hogs, salt, and other foodstuffs to the rest of the Confederacy. In March 1865, a small band of Confederate troops, helped by young boys and old men, successfully defended Tallahassee against Union forces. Tallahassee and Austin, Texas, were the only Confederate state capitals that federal troops did not capture.

During the Reconstruction period after the Civil War, Florida and the other Confederate states came under federal military rule. The defeated states had to meet certain requirements before they could be readmitted to the Union. Florida abolished slavery, but it refused to accept some of the other requirements. Republicans gained control of the Florida state government in 1868. In that year, the Legislature ratified the 14th Amendment to the Constitution of the United States, guaranteeing civil rights, and Florida was readmitted to the Union.

Progress as a state. Florida developed rapidly during the 1880s. Geologists discovered large phosphate deposits. The state government and private investors renewed attempts to drain the wetlands. Railroad lines built by tycoons Henry M. Flagler and Henry B. Plant led to the opening of new land for development. Citrus groves were planted in north-central Florida. Resort cities sprang up. People and money from northern states poured into Florida.

A severe freeze during the winter of 1894–1895 damaged much of the state's citrus crops. Citrus growers planted new groves in the south-central part of the state. This move contributed to the development of southern Florida. In 1896, Flagler extended his Florida East Coast Railroad line south to Miami.

The early 1900s. In 1906, the state began draining the wetlands near Fort Lauderdale. This development opened up new land for farms and resorts.

Reports of fantastic profits to be made in Florida real estate swept the country. Hundreds of thousands of land speculators flocked to the state. Florida's population soared. Seven new counties were formed in 1921. By 1925, Florida's economy had become a swelling bubble of progress and prosperity. The bubble burst in 1926, when a severe depression hit Florida. Banks closed. Wealthy people suddenly lost their money. Two destructive hurricanes struck Florida's Atlantic coast in 1926 and 1928, killing hundreds of people. The state had partly recovered from these disasters by the late 1920s. Then, in 1929, the Great Depression struck the nation.

Federal and state welfare measures helped the people of Florida fight the depression. The state created jobs to develop its natural resources. The construction of paper mills by private industries led to forest conservation programs. Cooling plants were built to preserve perishable fruits and vegetables. Farmers established cooperative farm groups and cooperative markets. The state suffered setbacks in 1935 and in 1941, when severe hurricanes swept across southern Florida.

The mid-1900s. Florida's location along the Atlantic Ocean and near the Panama Canal made the state vital to the defense of the Western Hemisphere during World War II (1939–1945). Land, sea, and air bases were established in many parts of the state.

After the war, Florida's population grew rapidly. Tourism boomed and remained the state's leading source of income. But industrial expansion helped give Florida a more balanced economy. Development of industries in such fields as chemicals, electronics, paper and paper products, and ocean and space exploration provided jobs for Florida's swelling labor force.

In the 1950s, Cape Canaveral became a space and rocket center. The United States launched its

Alcazar Hotel in Saint Augustine, Florida, circa 1900

first satellite from Cape Canaveral in 1958, its first human space flights in 1961, and its first spaceship carrying astronauts to the moon in 1969.

In the early 1960s, Cuba fell under Communist control. Many Cubans who opposed the Communists fled to Florida, settling mainly in Miami and Hialeah.

Like many other states, Florida faced serious racial problems during the 1950s and 1960s. In 1954, the Supreme Court of the United States ruled that compulsory segregation in public schools was unconstitutional. The Florida Constitution at that time did not permit black children and white children to attend the same schools. Integration of the state's public schools began in Dade County (now Miami-Dade County) in 1959. By the early 1970s, every county had integrated all or most of its public schools.

In the 1960s, Florida began an ambitious program to expand its facilities for higher education. This program was partly designed to serve the future demands for personnel in the oceanographic and aerospace industries. During the 1960s, four new state university campuses, several new private colleges and universities, and 15 new public community colleges were established. An additional state university campus and a public community college opened in the early 1970s.

The late 1900s. Florida grew rapidly during the 1970s and 1980s. Its population increased by 44 percent from 1970 to 1980, and by 33 percent from 1980 to 1990. In 1971, the Walt Disney World Resort entertainment center opened near Orlando. The Orlando area became the fastest-growing region of the state. Other booming areas included the suburbs of a number of Florida cities—Miami, Tampa, Jacksonville, Fort Lauderdale, and West Palm Beach. In 1977, a new state capitol was completed in Tallahassee. The building rises 22 stories.

During the first half of the 1980s, the number of jobs in Florida rose by 24 percent. Many of these jobs were in electronics, manufacturing, and skilled services. Florida's economy continued to rely heavily on tourism and the citrus industry. But the expansion of trade, financial, and other service industries has greatly strengthened the state's prospects for stable growth.

Florida's spectacular growth brought problems. The increasing population required more homes, roads, schools, sewage- and water-treatment plants, and health and social services. More than 100,000 Cuban and Haitian refugees settled in Florida in the late 1900s. Many of them were poor and had few job skills, causing increased demands upon social service agencies.

Uncontrolled development also led to growing concern for protecting and improving Florida's environment. During the 1970s, protests led to the cancellation of work on a jetport near the Everglades and a canal across northern Florida. Conservationists argued that these projects would endanger wildlife and destroy much natural beauty. In the 1960s, a canal was built to shorten the course of the Kissimmee River, which empties into Lake Okeechobee. By the mid-1980s, excess nutrients carried by the canal were causing *algae* (simple plantlike organisms) to thrive in the lake. This situation threatened other forms of life in Lake Okeechobee. In 1992, Congress authorized a project to restore the Kissimmee River to its former course. Work began in 1999 and is expected to be completed in the second decade of the 2000s.

From 1983 through 1985, Florida's citrus industry suffered serious setbacks. Freezing weather and a fungal disease called *citrus canker* destroyed many central Florida citrus groves. In August 1992, Hurricane Andrew struck. The hurricane killed 65 people directly or indirectly, 44 of them in Florida. It caused about $25 billion in property damage in the state, most of it in Dade County (now Miami-Dade County) in southeastern Florida. In Homestead, south of Miami, about 90 percent of the city's buildings were destroyed or damaged.

In 1998, some of the worst wildfires in America's history swept through Florida. Over 500,000 acres (200,000 hectares) were burned. The disas-

Cape Canaveral

The 1998 wildfires burned over 500,000 acres in Florida.

ter destroyed about 370 homes and businesses. Northern and central Florida were the hardest hit. In all, over 2,300 blazes broke out between late May and late July. Firefighters from 46 states helped out.

The early 2000s. Florida became a focus of attention during the 2000 presidential election. The outcome of the race between the Republican candidate, Texas governor George W. Bush, and the Democratic candidate, Vice President Al Gore, depended upon who received Florida's 25 electoral votes. The vote in Florida was so close that the state did a recount. Gore requested manual recounts in certain counties, and Bush challenged in court the need for those recounts. Five weeks after the election, the U.S. Supreme Court ruled to halt the manual recounts, and Gore conceded to Bush.

In August 2004, Hurricane Charley struck Florida's west coast and tore across the state. It was the most destructive hurricane to hit Florida since Hurricane Andrew in 1992. It caused 35 deaths and about $14 billion in property damage. By the end of September, three more hurricanes had battered the state, causing more deaths and destruction. Hurricane Frances struck the east coast and blew across the state in a northwesterly direction. Hurricane Ivan struck the northwest edge of the state. Hurricane Jeanne followed a path similar to that of Hurricane Frances.

In August 2005, Hurricane Katrina struck southern Florida and continued toward the Gulf Coast, causing many deaths and widespread damage. In October, Hurricane Wilma struck Florida's southwest coast and proceeded northeast, causing more death and destruction.

In April 2010, an explosion on an offshore oil rig left 11 people dead and caused about 200 million gallons (760 million liters) of oil to pour from an underwater well into the Gulf of Mexico. Within weeks of the explosion, oil from the spill began appearing along the Florida coast. Officials called the spill one of the worst environmental disasters in U.S. history. Also in 2010, Republican Governor Charlie Crist ran for the U.S. Senate as an independent but lost the race.

In 2011, the United States ended the space shuttle program. Florida officials feared the state could lose several thousand jobs at the Kennedy Space Center and elsewhere.

MLA Citation

"Florida." *The Southwestern Advantage Topic Source.* Nashville: Southwestern. 2013.

DATA

Florida in Brief

General Information

Statehood: March 3, 1845, the 27th state.

State abbreviations: Fla. (traditional); FL (postal).

State capital: Tallahassee, the capital of Florida since 1824—two years after the Territory of Florida was established.

State motto: *In God We Trust* (unofficial).

Popular name: The Sunshine State.

State song: "Old Folks at Home" ("Swanee River"). Words and music by Stephen Foster.

Symbols of Florida

State bird: Mockingbird.

State flower: Orange blossom.

State tree: Sabal palm.

State flag and seal: The state flag, adopted in 1899, bears the state seal. Diagonal red bars extend from the corners of the flag over a white field. The seal was adopted in 1985. It reflects minor changes that corrected inaccuracies in the 1868 seal. The revised seal depicts a Seminole Indian woman strewing flowers. A sabal palm, the state tree, rises in the center. A Florida steamboat sails in the background before the rising sun.

Land and Climate

Area: 58,681 mi^2 (151,982 km^2), including 4,683 mi^2 (12,129 km^2) of inland water but excluding 1,308 mi^2 (3,388 km^2) of coastal water.

Elevation: *Highest*—345 ft (105 m) above sea level in Walton County. *Lowest*—sea level.

Coastline: 1,350 mi (2,172 km)—580 mi (933 km) along the Atlantic Ocean; 770 mi (1,239 km) along the Gulf of Mexico.

Record high temperature: 109ºF (43ºC) at Monticello on June 29, 1931.

Record low temperature: −2ºF (−19ºC) at Tallahassee on February 13, 1899.

Average July temperature: 81ºF (27ºC).

Average January temperature: 59ºF (15ºC).

Average yearly precipitation: 54 in (137 cm).

People[1]

Population: 18,801,310.

Rank among the states: 4th.

Density: 321 persons per mi^2 (124 per km^2), U.S. average 85 per mi^2 (33 per km^2).

Distribution: 89 percent urban, 11 percent rural.

Largest cities in Florida: Jacksonville (821,784); Miami (399,457); Tampa (335,709); St. Petersburg (244,769); Orlando (238,300); Hialeah (224,669).

[1] Source: 2010 census.

DATA

Florida in Brief

Economy

Agriculture: beef cattle, greenhouse and nursery products, milk, oranges, sugarcane, tomatoes.

Manufacturing: chemicals, computer and electronic products, medical equipment, processed foods and beverages, transportation equipment.

Mining: limestone, phosphate rock, portland cement.

State Government

Governor: 4-year term.

State senators: 40; 4-year terms.

State representatives: 120; 2-year terms.

Counties: 67.

Federal Government

United States senators: 2.

United States representatives: 27.

Electoral votes: 29.

Sources of Information

For information about tourism: The Web site at http://www.VISITFLORIDA.com provides information.

The state's official Web site at http://www.myflorida.com provides a gateway to much information on Florida's economy, government, and history.

Interesting Facts About Florida

The first federal wildlife refuge in the United States was established by President Theodore Roosevelt in 1903 at Pelican Island. The island, located in the Indian River near Sebastian, was set aside for the protection of native birds such as brown pelicans, herons, and egrets. The refuge has since been enlarged, and it now covers about 4,400 acres (1,780 hectares).

The first federal savings and loan association was the First Federal Savings and Loan Association of Miami, which received its charter on August 8, 1933.

The first training center for Navy pilots, the U.S. Navy Aeronautic Station, was established in Pensacola in 1914. The facility is now known as the Naval Air Station Pensacola. Today, all U.S. Navy aviators begin their training there.

DATA

Average Monthly Weather in Florida

Month	High temp. (°F)	Low temp. (°F)	High temp. (°C)	Low temp. (°C)	Days of rain or snow
Tallahassee					
January	64	40	18	4	10
February	67	42	19	6	9
March	74	48	23	9	9
April	80	53	27	12	6
May	87	62	31	17	8
June	91	70	33	21	13
July	92	73	33	23	17
August	92	73	33	23	14
September	89	69	32	21	9
October	81	57	27	14	5
November	73	48	23	9	7
December	66	42	19	6	8
Miami					
January	77	60	25	16	7
February	78	61	26	16	6
March	81	64	27	18	6
April	84	68	29	20	6
May	87	72	31	22	10
June	90	75	32	24	15
July	91	77	33	25	16
August	91	77	33	25	18
September	89	76	32	24	18
October	85	72	29	22	14
November	81	68	27	20	8
December	78	62	26	17	7

DATA

Florida's Economic Production and Workers

Estimates based on data from U.S. Bureau of Economic Analysis. Figures are for 2008; employment figures include full- and part-time workers.

Economic activities	Percent of GDP[1] produced	Number of employed workers	Percent of total employed workers
Finance, insurance, & real estate	25	1,261,300	12
Community business, & personal services	23	3,785,300	36
Trade, restaurants, & hotels	18	2,349,100	23
Government	12	1,207,400	12
Transportation & communication	7	514,900	5
Construction	6	713,000	7
Manufacturing	5	402,200	4
Utilities	2	26,100	[2]
Agriculture	1	147,800	1
Mining	[2]	17,000	[2]
Total[3]	100	10,424,100	100

[1] GDP = gross domestic product, the total value of goods and services produced in a year.

[2] Less than one-half of 1 percent.

[3] Figures do not add up to 100 percent due to rounding.

Governors of Florida

Name	Party	Term
William D. Moseley	Democratic	1845–1849
Thomas Brown	Whig	1849–1853
James E. Broome	Democratic	1853–1857
Madison S. Perry	Democratic	1857–1861
John Milton	Democratic	1861–1865
Abraham K. Allison	Democratic	1865
William Marvin	None	1865
David S. Walker	Conservative	1865–1868
Harrison Reed	Republican	1868–1873
Ossian B. Hart	Republican	1873–1874
Marcellus L. Stearns	Republican	1874–1877
George F. Drew	Democratic	1877–1881

DATA

Governors of Florida

Name	Party	Term
William D. Bloxham	Democratic	1881–1885
Edward A. Perry	Democratic	1885–1889
Francis P. Fleming	Democratic	1889–1893
Henry L. Mitchell	Democratic	1893–1897
William D. Bloxham	Democratic	1897–1901
William S. Jennings	Democratic	1901–1905
Napoleon B. Broward	Democratic	1905–1909
Albert W. Gilchrist	Democratic	1909–1913
Park Trammell	Democratic	1913–1917
Sidney J. Catts	Prohibition	1917–1921
Cary A. Hardee	Democratic	1921–1925
John W. Martin	Democratic	1925–1929
Doyle E. Carlton	Democratic	1929–1933
David Sholtz	Democratic	1933–1937
Fred P. Cone	Democratic	1937–1941
Spessard L. Holland	Democratic	1941–1945
Millard F. Caldwell	Democratic	1945–1949
Fuller Warren	Democratic	1949–1953
Daniel T. McCarty	Democratic	1953
Charley E. Johns	Democratic	1953–1955
LeRoy Collins	Democratic	1955–1961
C. Farris Bryant	Democratic	1961–1965
W. Haydon Burns	Democratic	1965–1967
Claude R. Kirk, Jr.	Republican	1967–1971
Reubin O'D. Askew	Democratic	1971–1979
Bob Graham	Democratic	1979–1987
Wayne Mixson	Democratic	1987
Bob Martinez	Republican	1987–1991
Lawton Chiles	Democratic	1991–1998
Buddy MacKay	Democratic	1998–1999
Jeb Bush	Republican	1999–2007
Charlie Crist	Republican	2007–2011
Rick Scott	Republican	2011–

DATA

Important Dates in Florida

1513	Juan Ponce de León landed on the Florida coast and claimed the region for Spain.
1528	Pánfilo de Narváez led an expedition into Florida.
1539	Hernando de Soto led an expedition through Florida.
1564	French Huguenot settlers built Fort Caroline on the St. Johns River.
1565	Pedro Menéndez de Avilés founded St. Augustine, the first permanent European settlement in what is now the United States.
1763	Spain ceded Florida to Britain.
1783	Spain regained control of Florida.
1819	The United States obtained Florida from Spain.
1821	Florida formally came under U.S. control.
1822	The U.S. Congress established the Territory of Florida.
1835–1842	During the Second Seminole War, many of the Seminole who had refused to move out of the territory lost their land.
1845	Florida became the 27th state on March 3.
1861	Florida seceded from the Union and joined the Confederacy.
1868	Florida was readmitted to the Union.
1896	Henry M. Flagler's Florida East Coast Railroad reached Miami.
1920–1925	Land speculators poured into the state. The population increased at a tremendous rate.
1947	Everglades National Park was established.
1958	The United States launched its first satellite from Cape Canaveral.
1961	The first U.S. space flights carrying astronauts were launched from Cape Canaveral.
1969	Apollo 11, the first spacecraft to land astronauts on the moon, was launched from Cape Canaveral.
1971	The Walt Disney World entertainment complex opened near Orlando.
1983–1985	Many of central Florida's citrus groves were destroyed by freezing weather and disease.
1992	Hurricane Andrew killed 44 people in Florida and caused about $25 billion in property damage there.
1998	Wildfires caused extensive damage in the state.
2000	Florida's electoral votes decided the U.S. presidential election, giving Texas governor George W. Bush a victory over Vice President Al Gore.
2011	The space shuttle Atlantis landed at Kennedy Space Center near Cape Canaveral, marking the end of the U.S. space shuttle program. The first shuttle, the Columbia, lifted off from the center in 1981.

ADDITIONAL RESOURCES

Books to Read

Bryan, Jonathan R., and others. *Roadside Geology of Florida*. Mountain Press Publishing Co., 2008.

Gannon, Michael. *Florida*. Rev. ed. University Press of Florida, 2003.

Grunwald, Michael. *The Swamp: The Everglades, Florida, and the Politics of Paradise*. Simon & Schuster, 2006.

Hoffman, Paul E. *Florida's Frontiers*. Indiana University Press, 2002.

Milanich, Jerald T. *Florida's Indians from Ancient Times to the Present*. University Press of Florida, 1998.

Mormino, Gary R. *Land of Sunshine, State of Dreams: A Social History of Modern Florida*. 2005. Reprint. University Press of Florida, 2008.

Purdy, Barbara A. *Florida's People During the Last Ice Age*. University Press of Florida, 2008.

Rivers, Larry E. *Slavery in Florida*. 2000. Reprint. University Press of Florida, 2008

Tebeau, Charlton W., and Marina, William. *A History of Florida*. 3rd ed. University of Miami Press, 1999.

Web Sites

Florida Museum of Natural History

http://www.flmnh.ufl.edu/

The museum home page features information for visitors, publications, and on-line exhibits and photo galleries.

Kennedy Space Center Visitor Complex

http://www.kennedyspacecenter.com/

Official site of the Kennedy Space Center near Cape Canaveral, Florida.

MyFlorida.com—Home Page

http://www.myflorida.com/

The official portal for the State of Florida.

National Park Service

http://www.nps.gov/state/fl/index.htm

National Park Service site about national parks in Florida.

Prelude: Can the Everglades Survive?

http://www.nps.gov/ever/index.htm

National Park Service site on Everglades National Park in Florida.

Visit Florida

http://www.flausa.com/

Florida's official vacation guide including Florida travel information.

Walt Disney World—Official Home Page

http://disneyworld.disney.go.com/

Commercial site from Disney Company about Disney World and tourism in southern Florida.

Search Strings

Tourism in Florida

Florida Tourism attractions "Disney World" (56,400) *Mostly about Disney World

Florida Tourism attractions (155,000)

Florida Tourism attractions beach national park keys (105,000)

Colonial Times

Florida colonial times Spain history (114,000)

colonial Florida history timeline (182,000)

colonial Florida history timeline Spain Britain (12,600)

Plant and Animal Life

Florida plant animal life (148,000) *These returns were very good.

Florida plant animal life forests wildflowers alligators fish (3,080)

Florida's Voting System

"Florida voting system" (5,050)

"Florida voting system" Presidential election Bush Gore (151)

A Varied Economy

"Florida economy" (42,300)

"Florida economy" financial centers manufacturing technology agriculture (3,250)

economy of Florida industry (716,000)

BACKGROUND INFORMATION

The following articles were written during the year in which the events took place and reflect the style and thinking of that time.

 ## Election (2000)

In one of the closest elections in United States history, Republican candidate George W. Bush, the governor of Texas, defeated Democratic candidate Vice President Al Gore for the U.S. presidency. On December 13, Gore conceded the election, which took place on November 7, and Bush claimed victory. Gore's concession followed a U.S. Supreme Court decision on December 12 that prevented manual recounts of votes in certain Florida counties. Florida and its 25 electoral college votes played a pivotal role in the 2000 election.

Popular versus electoral votes. Although Gore won the popular vote—with a nationwide total of 50,996,064, compared with Bush's 50,456,167—he eventually lost in the Electoral College (source: Committee for the Study of the American Electorate). The Electoral College is a constitutionally mandated institution consisting of delegates appointed by the states. Delegates cast votes for president and vice president according to who wins the popular vote in their state. A minimum of 270 electoral votes were needed to win the 2000 presidential election. Bush and his vice presidential running mate, Dick Cheney, took the Electoral College votes of 30 states, a total of 271 electoral votes, giving Bush the presidency. Gore and his running mate, Connecticut Senator Joseph Lieberman, received 266 electoral votes.

Florida's votes. The outcome of the election remained in doubt between November 7 and December 13 because of the closeness of the vote in Florida. Without Florida's 25 Electoral College votes, neither candidate could claim victory. Early in the evening on Election Day, news networks projected Gore the winner in Florida, based on exit

Ballot used in Florida during the 2000 presidential election

polls conducted throughout the day. Later, the media reversed their projections and called Florida for Bush, then reversed themselves again and declared the race too close to call. On November 8, Bush's margin of victory in Florida was so narrow—just 1,784 votes—that state law mandated a recount. At the conclusion of the recount, which was done by machine, Bush's lead had narrowed to just over 300 votes.

The Gore campaign then requested that ballots in four mostly Democratic counties be recounted by hand. In Palm Beach County, Florida, a large number of voters claimed they had been confused by the type of ballot used in the election and may have inadvertently voted for a third-party candidate, Pat Buchanan, instead of Al Gore. Buchanan had received an extraordinary number of votes in Palm Beach County, which was heavily Democratic, compared with the number of votes he had received statewide in Florida.

Controversy then erupted over the issue of manual recounts. Florida Secretary of State Katherine Harris refused to extend a November 14 deadline and accept late hand-count tallies. Democrats charged that Harris's refusal was politically motivated. Harris, a Republican, co-chaired Bush's Florida campaign. The Bush and Gore campaigns filed a series of legal challenges over recount issues. Gore wanted the recounts to go on. Bush wanted them to stop. Democratic voters also filed unsuccessful suits to have certain absentee ballots disqualified.

The Florida Supreme Court on November 21 ruled unanimously that Harris must accept the results of manual recounts as long as they were submitted on November 26 or early on November 27. The court set no clear standards on how to count "dimpled," or partially punched, ballots, and election officials argued whether they should be included in the tally. The Bush campaign then filed an appeal with the U.S. Supreme Court to reverse the decision of the Florida Supreme Court. Miami-Dade County election officials stopped the manual recount after a few hours, claiming that they would be unable to finish within the time limits set by the Florida Supreme Court.

Election certification and challenge. On November 26, Florida officials certified that Bush had carried the state with a 537-vote margin over Vice President Gore. According to the official tally, Bush had 2,912,790 votes to Gore's 2,912,253.

Attorneys retained by the Gore campaign challenged the results in a state circuit court.

The U.S. Supreme Court on December 4 ordered the Florida Supreme Court to review its November 21 decision to allow three Florida counties to manually recount their votes. The Florida court responded by ordering another recount. On December 9, the U.S. Supreme Court stopped the recount until it could rehear the case, which it did on December 11.

On December 12, the U.S. Supreme Court, in a 5-to-4 ruling, reversed the decision by the Florida court to allow a manual recount of votes. In the opinion of the majority on the court, the recount could not be resumed because the procedures were so arbitrary that they violated the equal protection clause of the 14th Amendment to the U.S. Constitution. According to legal experts, the decision removed all legal obstacles to Texas Governor George W. Bush claiming victory over Al Gore.

Courts (2000)

The November 2000 presidential election, one of the closest in U.S. history, became embroiled in the courts as Democrats and Republicans wrangled over Florida's 25 decisive Electoral College votes. Following the November 7 election, only a few hundred votes in Florida separated the Republican candidate, Texas Governor George W. Bush, from his Democratic challenger, Vice President Al Gore. Without Florida, neither had the 270 electoral votes necessary to claim victory.

Gore had requested hand recounts of ballots in several heavily Democratic Florida counties. Bush attorneys sued to stop the recounts. On November 21, the Florida Supreme Court ruled that manual counts would continue and should be included in the final tallies. Bush appealed to the U.S. Supreme Court, which on December 4 returned the case to the Florida court for clarification. On December 8, the Florida Supreme Court again ordered manual recounts to continue, only to have the U.S. Supreme Court stop the recount one day later. On December 12, the U.S. Supreme Court ruled that the manner in which the recounting in Florida was taking place was so arbitrary that it violated the equal protection clause of the 14th Amendment to the U.S. Constitution. Political experts said that the court ruling left Gore with little legal recourse but to concede, which he did on December 13.

California

California is a large state on the west coast of the United States. It has the largest population and the biggest economy of any U.S. state.

HOT topics

Wildfires. The dry climate in Southern California is a significant factor in many wildfires. In 2003 and 2007, wildfires destroyed thousands of homes. San Diego County officials ordered the evacuation of about 500,000 people in October 2007. It was the largest evacuation in the state's history.

Combating Global Warming. The government of California took dramatic steps in 2006 to reduce California's role in causing global warming. Global warming is a gradual increase in Earth's average temperature that many scientists believe is being caused by emissions of carbon dioxide and other "greenhouse" gases. California Governor Arnold Schwarzenegger signed the Global Warming Solutions Act in September 2006. The act required power plants and other industrial polluters in the state to reduce emissions of greenhouse gases by 25 percent by 2020.

HOT topics

Removing a Governor from Office.

California citizens forced an unprecedented recall vote against the state's governor, Gray Davis, in October 2003. Davis, a Democrat, had won election to a second term in 2002. But many of California's voters decided that he was ineffectual in dealing with the state's huge budget deficit. In the election, the majority of electors recalled (removed from office) Davis, and voted to replace him with Republican Arnold Schwarzenegger, an actor and former bodybuilder. Schwarzenegger triumphed over 134 other candidates

California's Energy Crisis of 2000–2001

resulted in electrical power outages—blackouts—becoming common for thousands of consumers. In 1996, the California legislature had deregulated the state's electric utilities with the idea that increased competition would drive down price. Deregulation barred the utilities that distribute electricity from passing price increases on to customers until 2002. When demand for electricity exceeded supply in 2000 and 2001, the price of electric power kept rising. The utility companies ran out of money to buy enough power and were forced to institute many blackouts.

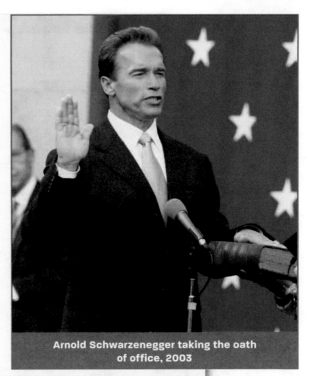

Arnold Schwarzenegger taking the oath of office, 2003

The Most Populous State.

Since 1963, California has had more people than any other state in the Union. One fourth of its people were born outside the United States. Most of those people were born in Mexico, but large numbers from every continent also live in California. The three major population centers are Los Angeles, San Francisco, and San Diego.

A painting of the U.S. indicating its biggest cities

TRUE or FALSE?

If California was an independent country, the size of its economy would rank in the world's top ten largest countries' economies.

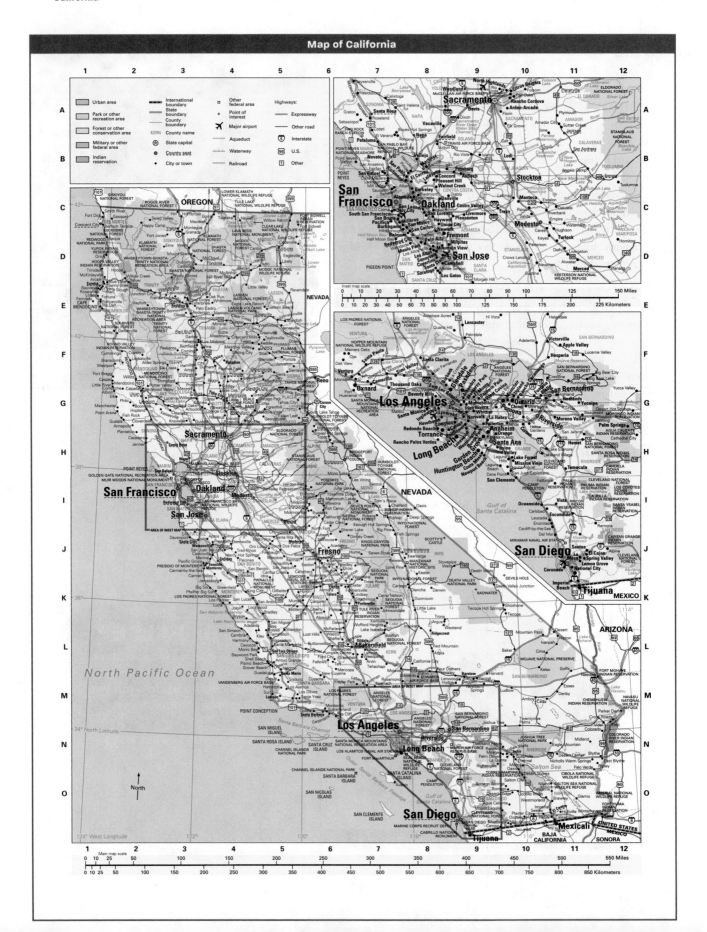

Map of California

THE BASICS

California has more people than any other state of the United States. Many visitors and new residents are attracted by California's outdoor way of life. The warm, dry climate of southern California permits outdoor recreation almost all the year around.

California ranks first among the states in manufacturing. More goods are made there than in any other state. California is the nation's leader in the manufacture of electronic equipment. Its products also include aircraft and such food products as baked goods and wines. California is a leading mining state as well. For example, its fields of oil and natural gas yield thousands of barrels of fuel a day.

California also ranks first among the states in agriculture. A vast farming region, the Central Valley, extends about 450 miles (720 kilometers) through the center of the state. The valley is the leading region in the United States for growing fruits, nuts, and vegetables.

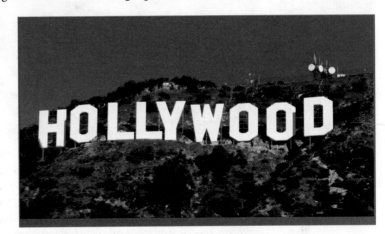

California is a center of the motion-picture and television industries. Its entertainment products are distributed throughout the world.

California has 4 of the nation's 15 largest cities—Los Angeles, San Diego, San Jose, and San Francisco. The state capital is Sacramento, another large city.

The international airports at Los Angeles and San Francisco are among the busiest in the world. The ports along California's Pacific Coast make the state a leading area for international trade with Latin America and Asia.

Hundreds of computer and electronics companies have their headquarters in California. Research laboratories, computer companies, and engineering firms cluster around universities in and near the largest cities. They take advantage of the "brain power" of scientists and engineers from the universities.

California covers a larger area than any other state except Alaska and Texas. The high Sierra Nevada rises near the eastern border. Rocky cliffs and sandy beaches line the shore of the Pacific Ocean in the west. Thick forests of Douglas-firs and redwoods cover the Coast Ranges and the Klamath Mountains in the northwest. Barren deserts stretch across the southeast.

The Spaniards were the first Europeans to colonize California. Franciscan friars from Spain established the first of a chain of missions there in 1769. California is known as the *Golden State*. Its gold fields attracted thousands of miners, known as the "Forty-Niners," during the gold rush of 1849. The nickname also suggests the brilliant sunshine the state enjoys.

People

Population. The 2010 United States census reported that California had 37,253,956 people. The population had increased 10 percent over the 2000 figure of 33,871,648. According to the 2010 census, California ranks first in population among the 50 states.

In 1960, California ranked second to New York in population. Unofficial figures indicated that California passed New York early in 1963. By 2010, California had about 18 million more people than New York and 12 million more than Texas, which passed New York in population during the 1990s.

About 98 percent of the people of California live in metropolitan statistical areas. About 35 percent of California's population lives in the largest metropolitan area—Los Angeles-Long Beach-Santa Ana.

Los Angeles is the largest city, both in area and in population. It covers 465 square miles (1,204 square kilometers). The United States Census Bureau reported that Los Angeles had a population of 3,792,621 in 2010.

California has 12 other cities that each have more than 250,000 people. Only four—Bakersfield, Fresno, Sacramento, and Stockton—are inland. The others lie on or near the Pacific Coast. Oakland, San Francisco, and San Jose are in the San Francisco Bay area. Anaheim, Long Beach, Riverside, and Santa Ana are part

A street in San Diego's Chinatown

of the Los Angeles population cluster. San Diego is on the coast near the Mexican border.

Most Californians were born in the United States. Mexicans make up the largest group of Californians who were born in another country. More people of Mexican ancestry live in the Los Angeles area than in any other urban area in the world outside Mexico. Many Californians of Chinese and Japanese ancestry live in communities of their own in Los Angeles and San Francisco. Chinatown in San Francisco is one of the largest Chinese communities outside Asia. California also is home to many people born in the Philippines, Vietnam, El Salvador, North and South Korea, Guatemala, India, Iran, Canada, and the United Kingdom. California also has about 363,000 American Indians—more than any other state.

Schools. In the late 1700s and early 1800s, Franciscan friars taught farming, weaving, and other crafts to the Indians of California. A few small schools were established in the region. But most children of the early settlers received instruction from private teachers.

The first tax-supported school in California opened in San Francisco in 1850. It was financed by the city. In 1849, the California Constitution provided for a public school system. The state Legislature passed a tax law in 1852 to support public schools. But the schools did not become free to all children until 1867. At that time, the school system did not include high schools. The state's first public high school opened in 1856 in San Francisco. In 1910, California established in Fresno the first tax-supported junior college in the United States.

An 11-member state Board of Education sets policies for California's elementary and secondary school system. The members of the board are appointed by the governor, subject to the approval of the state Senate. Members serve four-year terms, except for one student representative, who serves one year. The California Department of Edu-

cation provides assistance to the state's local school districts and county offices of education, and it divides state and federal funds among them. An elected superintendent of public instruction heads the department.

With some exceptions, California law requires children from age 6 to 18 to attend school. Students between the ages of 16 and 18 may leave school if they graduate from high school or if they pass a special examination and have parental permission.

California State University is the largest state-supported system of four-year and graduate-level education in the United States. It has more than 20 campuses and about 400,000 students. Another state-supported university, the University of California, has 10 campuses and more than 220,000 students. California also has an outstanding system of community colleges. A master plan, which was approved by the State Legislature in 1960, provides for the orderly expansion of the system of state colleges and universities.

Libraries. California's outstanding public library system was founded in 1909. Today, public libraries exist throughout the state. In addition, all types of libraries in California have formal and informal cooperative arrangements between them for sharing resources. The University of California at Berkeley has the largest university library in the state. It includes the Bancroft Library collections of rare materials on the American West. The Hoover Institution on War, Revolution, and Peace at Stanford University has books and documents on political, economic, and social change.

Museums. The de Young Museum in San Francisco has art objects from many lands. The exhibits include famous paintings by European artists and items made by early American Indians. The California Legion of Honor in San Francisco displays antique furniture, paintings, porcelain, sculpture, and tapestries. The Hollywood Entertainment Museum in Hollywood displays objects and exhibits on Hollywood's motion-picture and television industries.

The Huntington Library, Art Collections, and Botanical Gardens in San Marino exhibits British paintings and French furniture and tapestries of the 1700s and early 1800s. The California State Railroad Museum in Sacramento is one of the largest of its kind in the world. The Autry National Center of the American West in Los Angeles displays items from the region's culture and history. The J. Paul Getty Museum in Los Angeles houses an outstanding collection of fine art and antiques. The Page Museum in Los Angeles owns perhaps the best collection of Pleistocene ice age fossils in the world. The fossils owned by the museum came from the La Brea tar pits in Los Angeles.

Visitor's Guide

Many people visit California to see such natural wonders as redwood groves and volcanic cones. California also has famous golf courses, resorts, beaches, ski areas, and many other recreational facilities.

California's largest cities, Los Angeles, San Diego, and San Francisco, play host to millions of visitors every year.

Land and Climate

California is larger than any other state except Alaska and Texas. San Bernardino County, California's largest county, covers more than 20,000 square miles (51,800 square kilometers). It is one of the largest counties in area in the United States.

Land regions. California has eight main land regions: (1) the Klamath Mountains, (2) the Coast Ranges, (3) the Central Valley, (4) the Sierra Nevada, (5) the Cascade Mountains, (6) the Basin and Range Region, (7) the Transverse Ranges, and (8) the Peninsular Ranges.

The Klamath Mountains include several small, forest-covered ranges in the northwestern corner of California. These ranges are higher and more rugged than the coastal mountains to the south. Many peaks are from 6,000 to 8,000 feet (1,800 to 2,400 meters) high. Deep canyons break up the ranges.

The Coast Ranges extend southward along the Pacific Coast from the Klamath Mountains to Santa Barbara County. Individual sections of this mountain chain have names of their own. These include the Diablo, Santa Cruz, and Santa Lucia ranges. Livestock ranches, orchards, vineyards, and truck gardens dot the beautiful valleys that separate the ranges. These valleys include the Napa Valley north of San Francisco, and the Santa Clara and Salinas valleys to the south. California's famous redwood trees grow in the coastal areas of the Coast Ranges.

An important feature of the region is the San Andreas Fault. A *fault* is a break in the earth's rocky

Goleta Depot, South Coast Railroad Museum

A vineyard in Napa Valley

outer shell, along which movements of the rock have taken place. The San Andreas Fault enters northern California from the Pacific Ocean near Point Arena and extends southeastward into southern California. Movements of the earth's crust along this fault cause earthquakes.

The Central Valley, sometimes called the *Great Valley*, lies between the Coast Ranges and the Sierra Nevada. It has two major river systems—the Sacramento in the north and the San Joaquin in the south. The valley extends about 450 miles (720 kilometers) from northwest to southeast. Much of it is level, and looks like a broad, open plain. This fertile valley forms the largest and most important farming area west of the Rocky Mountains. It has three-fifths of California's farmland, and produces a great variety of crops.

The Sierra Nevada, located east of the Central Valley, forms a massive rock wall more than 400 miles (640 kilometers) long and about 40 to 70 miles (64 to 110 kilometers) wide. Several peaks of the Sierra Nevada rise more than 14,000 feet (4,270 meters). These peaks include Mount Whitney (14,494 feet, or 4,418 meters), the highest point in the United States south of Alaska. Rushing mountain rivers have cut deep canyons in the western part of the Sierra. Yosemite Valley is the most outstanding of these canyons. Yosemite originally was cut by streams. Later, glaciers moved down the valley and eroded it further.

The Cascade Mountains extend northward from the Sierra Nevada. Unlike other California ranges, the Cascades were formed by volcanoes. Lassen Peak (10,457 feet, or 3,187 meters) is an active volcano in the southern Cascades. Another famous peak, Mount Shasta (14,162 feet, or 4,317 meters), was once an active volcano.

The Basin and Range Region is part of a larger region that extends into Nevada, Oregon, and several other states. It is an area of mountains and valleys created by movement along fault lines. Much of the northern section of the Basin and Range Region is a lava plateau called the Modoc Plateau. Thousands of years ago, lava flowed out of great cracks in the earth's surface and flooded the area.

In southern California, much of the Basin and Range Region is a wasteland. South of the Garlock Fault lies the Mojave Desert. The Mojave covers a large area between the southern Sierra and the Colorado River. The Colorado Desert lies to the south. Irrigation has made several valleys in the region suitable for raising crops. These valleys include the fertile Imperial and Coachella valleys near the Mexican border.

Death Valley is in the Basin and Range Region near the California-Nevada border. Part of Death Valley lies 282 feet (86 meters) below sea level and is the lowest point in North America.

The Transverse Ranges, also known as the Los Angeles Ranges, are a group of small mountain ranges between Santa Barbara and San Diego counties. They are called the *Transverse Ranges* because they extend generally in an east-west direction, along fault lines. Other ranges in California run generally north and south. The Transverse Ranges include the Santa Ynez, Santa Monica, San Gabriel, and San Bernardino mountains. Some geographers consider the San Jacinto and Santa Ana mountains to be a part of this group. Most of the city of Los Angeles and its suburbs lie on a broad lowland between the San Gabriel Mountains and the Pacific

Waves along the coast at Big Sur, California

Ocean. The hilly slopes of the Santa Monica Mountains extend into parts of the city.

The Peninsular Ranges, also called the *San Diego Ranges,* cover most of San Diego County at the southwestern tip of the state. They include the Agua Tibia, Laguna, and Vallecito mountains. This mountain system extends southward into the Mexican peninsula known as Baja (Lower) California.

Coastline. California's general coastline measures 840 miles (1,352 kilometers). California's *tidal shoreline* (including small bays and inlets) is 3,427 miles (5,515 kilometers) long. Along much of the coast, the Coast Ranges rise from the shore in steep cliffs and terraces. Southern California has many wide, sandy beaches. The California coast has two great natural harbors—San Francisco and San Diego bays. There are smaller natural harbors at Humboldt and Monterey bays.

Two groups of islands are located near the California coast. The small, rocky Farallon Islands rise from the ocean about 30 miles (48 kilometers) west of San Francisco. The eight Channel Islands lie scattered off the coast of southern California. Catalina Island, the best known of the Channel Islands, attracts many vacationers.

Rivers, waterfalls, and lakes. California's two longest rivers are the Sacramento and the San Joaquin. The Sacramento rises near Mount Shasta and flows south through the Central Valley. The San Joaquin rises in the Sierra Nevada and flows northwest through the Central Valley. The place where the two rivers meet is the Delta, a maze of channels and islands. Smaller rivers, such as the Feather and the Mokelumne, begin in the eastern mountains and flow west into the Sacramento or the San Joaquin.

The Colorado River forms the border between southern California and Arizona. It is an important source of water for Los Angeles and other cities of southern California. Water from the Colorado is also used to irrigate desert farmlands. Many rivers in southern California dry up or run underground during the dry season. Water may suddenly pour into the dry riverbeds during the rainy season and cause serious floods. In desert areas, most rivers have no outlets to other streams or to the sea. They flow above ground for a certain distance, then dry up or sink into the sand.

Yosemite National Park in California has several of the highest waterfalls in North America. Ribbon Falls (1,612 feet, or 491 meters) is the highest on the continent. Other high waterfalls in Yosemite include Bridalveil, Illilouette, Nevada, Silver Strand, Vernal, and Upper and Lower Yosemite.

California has about 8,000 lakes. Lake Tahoe, the deepest, averages 1,500 feet (427 meters) in depth. It lies in the Sierra on the California-Nevada border and reflects the surrounding mountain peaks. Most of the desert lakes east of the Sierra contain dissolved minerals that give the water a disagreeable taste. Potash, salt, and other minerals are taken from Owens Lake, Searles Lake, and other dry or partly dry lakes in this region. The Salton Sea is a large, shallow lake in southern California. It was formed between 1905 and 1907 by floodwaters from the Colorado River.

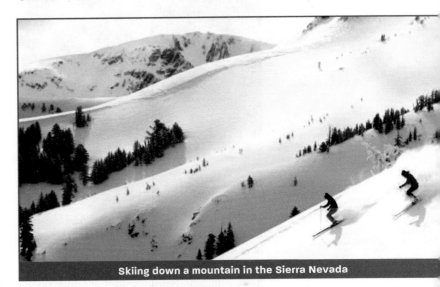
Skiing down a mountain in the Sierra Nevada

Plant and animal life. California's widely varied climate and terrain combine to produce a wide variety of plant and animal life. Some of the world's most unusual living things are found in the state. The coast redwood tree is the tallest living thing in the world, and the bristlecone pine tree is the oldest. The rare California condor is the largest bird in North America.

Forests cover about 40 percent of California. Softwood trees make up most of the state's forests. These trees include cedars, firs, hemlocks, giant sequoias, pines, and redwoods. The most common hardwood trees are oaks.

Desert plants cover much of the southeastern section of the state. These plants include burroweeds, creosote bushes, indigo bushes, Joshua trees, and several kinds of cactuses. Desert wildflowers include desert evening primrose and sand verbena. Patches

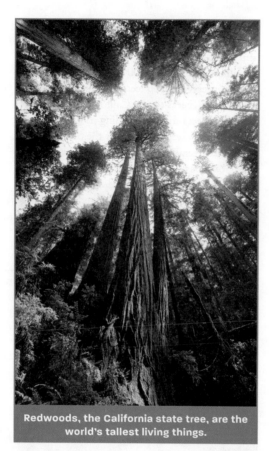

Redwoods, the California state tree, are the world's tallest living things.

of *chaparral* (thick and often thorny shrubs and small trees) cover the foothills. In the foothills and valleys of northern California, a spectacular array of wildflowers blooms after the winter rainy season. These flowers include beardtongue, California poppy, evening primroses, fiddlenecks, and lupine. Fireweed and Washington lily bloom in the mountains.

Desert wildlife in California includes coyotes, lizards, and rattlesnakes. Beavers, bears, deer, foxes, minks, muskrats, rabbits, wildcats, wolverines, and a few mountain sheep roam the mountain and forest areas. Small herds of pronghorns and elk are found chiefly in the northern part of the state. California game birds include ducks, geese, grouse, mourning doves, quail, and turkey. Game fishes in the state's streams include black bass, salmon, striped bass, and trout. Abalones, clams, crabs, shrimps, lobsters, oysters, scallops, and other shellfishes are found along the California coast.

Climate. California has a great variety of climates. The southern coast has a mild climate. The climate along the coast of northern and central California is also mild, but this region is generally cooler than the southern coast. The climate of southeastern California is hot and dry.

January temperatures in California average 44°F (7°C). Boca, near Truckee, recorded the state's lowest temperature, –45°F (–43°C), on January 20, 1937. July temperatures for the state average 75°F (24°C). The highest temperature ever recorded in the United States, 134°F (57°C), occurred at Greenland Ranch in Death Valley on July 10, 1913.

Most parts of California have only two well-marked seasons—a rainy season and a dry season. The rainy season lasts from October to April in the north, and from November to March or April in the south. Yearly *precipitation* (rain, snow, and other forms of moisture) is greatest along the northern coast, where it averages over 80 inches (200 centimeters). At San Francisco, the yearly average is about 20 inches (51 centimeters); at Los Angeles, 15 inches (38 centimeters); and at San Diego, 11 inches (28 centimeters). Some desert basins in the southeast receive almost no rain. From October 3, 1912, to November 8, 1914, Bagdad, in Death Valley, had no measurable precipitation. This 760-day rainless period set the United States record.

Snowfall is rare along the central and southern coast of California. But at Tamarack, in the Sierra Nevada, the yearly snowfall averages about 450 inches (1,140 centimeters).

Economy

The value of California's total economic production is higher than that of any other state. If California were a separate country, it would rank among the 10 leading countries in total value of goods and services produced. California's economy benefits from the state's abundant resources and strategic location. Important resources include a mild climate, plentiful minerals and timber, and fertile soils. California's location on the West Coast makes it a leading area for international trade with Asia and Latin America. California has long been a center of the motion-picture and television industries. Its films and entertainment products are distributed throughout the world.

Service industries provide the largest portion of California's *gross domestic product*—the total value of goods and services produced in the state annually. But goods-producing industries are also important.

California ranks first among the states in both agriculture and manufacturing. The Central Valley region is one of the world's great farming areas. Most of the goods manufactured in California are products of modern science and engineering. These include airplanes, computers, electronic components, missiles, and scientific instruments. Private companies maintain several hundred laboratories in California for conducting research and testing new products. Most of these laboratories are located near large universities in the state. They are thus able to draw upon the ideas and skills of university biologists, chemists, engineers, and physicists.

Natural resources. California is unusually rich in minerals and timber. The state's soil and climate make it possible for farmers to grow a wide variety of crops.

Soils. Many parts of California, especially in the Central Valley, have *alluvial* (water deposited) soils. These soils make the best farmland. The Imperial Valley in southern California has rich alluvial soils that produce outstanding crops when irrigated. *Residual* (upland) soils cover the mountain slopes. These soils support forests in areas that have enough rain. In many other places, they provide grazing land.

Minerals. California has important fields of petroleum and natural gas in the southern part of the Central Valley, near the southern coast, and in coastal waters off Long Beach and Santa Barbara. Natural gas also comes from fields around Sacramento. Valuable deposits of boron exist in southeastern California. Commercially important quantities of sand and gravel lie throughout California. Gemstones, including agate, benitoite, diamond, quartz, and tourmaline, are found in various counties. Other nonmetallic mined products found in the state include clays, diatomite, feldspar, gypsum, pumice, salt, soda ash, stone, and talc.

California's tungsten deposits are among the nation's largest. They occur mainly in Inyo County. Gold deposits are found in several parts of the state, from the western slopes of the northern Sierra Nevada to Imperial County, in the southeast.

Forests cover about 40 percent of California. The state has two main timber regions, each named for an important tree in the region. The *redwood region* is a narrow belt that extends south along the coast from Oregon to San Luis Obispo County. The *pine region* covers the Cascades and the Sierra Nevada. It extends along the inland parts of the Klamath Mountains and the Coast Ranges as far south as Lake County. The Douglas-fir, which is one of California's most valuable timber trees, grows in the redwood region and the pine region. Other important timber trees that grow in the state include incense-cedar, red fir, white fir, Jeffrey pine, ponderosa pine, sugar pine, and redwood.

California's most famous trees are its two types of sequoias, the redwood and the giant sequoia. The redwood is the state tree. Redwoods are the world's tallest living things. They grow near the coast in northern and central California. Giant sequoias, often called *big trees*, have larger trunks than redwoods but are not as tall. They grow on the western slopes of the Sierra Nevada. Bristlecone pines in the White Mountains of eastern California are the world's oldest living things. Some are more than 4,000 years old.

California's forests are important for timber production and for recreation. But they are especially important for preserving the state's precious water supply. Water does not run off or evaporate so quickly in forest areas as it does in treeless regions. The logging industry and the government work to protect California's forests from fire, harmful insects, and tree diseases. Landowners also grow trees on tree farms so there will be a constant supply of timber to replace the trees that are cut.

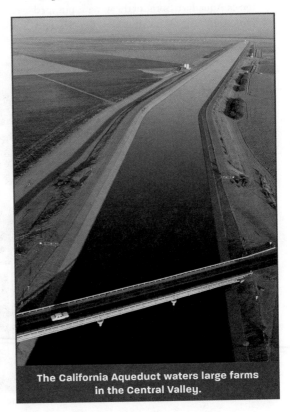

The California Aqueduct waters large farms in the Central Valley.

Water is one of California's most important natural resources. The mountain areas, especially in the north, have plenty of water from rain and melted snow. But most of California's farms, industries, and homes are in the dry southern valleys. One of the state's greatest problems is to transport water from rainy areas to dry places where it is needed. Many *aqueducts* (channels and large pipelines) and canals have been built for that purpose. The Owens Valley Aqueduct brings water from the east side of the Sierra Nevada to Los Angeles. Water from the Colorado River has long been supplied to farms and cities in southern California by canals and aqueducts. The Central Valley Project brings water from the Sacramento Valley to the San Joaquin Valley. The water is used to irrigate the state's farms. The Hetch Hetchy Aqueduct brings water from the Tuolumne River to San Francisco.

The state's largest water-transfer program is the California State Water Project. It includes dams and reservoirs to store water, and aqueducts to carry it from rivers in northern California to coastal cities and to southern California. Oroville Dam on the Feather River is the most important part of the project. Water from the Feather, Sacramento, and other northern rivers is sent southward in the long California Aqueduct. Some of the water is pumped over mountain ranges into the Los Angeles and San Diego areas.

Service industries account for over four-fifths of both California's employment and its gross domestic product. Service industries are most important in the state's metropolitan areas, especially in the Los Angeles and San Francisco-Oakland areas. California's service industries receive much income from tourism.

Finance, insurance, and real estate is one of the fastest-growing economic activities in California. The San Francisco and Los Angeles areas are major United States financial centers. Several of the nation's largest banking companies are based in San Francisco and Los Angeles. San Francisco is the headquarters of the Twelfth Federal Reserve District Bank, one of the 12 federal banks established by Congress. San Diego and San Jose are also major U.S. financial centers.

Community, business, and personal services employs more people than any other activity in the state. Hollywood, considered the motion-picture capital of the world, is in California. Burbank is home to the Walt Disney Company, a major entertainment firm. Bechtel Corporation, one of the world's leading engineering companies, has headquarters in California.

Trade, restaurants, and hotels. Restaurants and hotels benefit from California having more tourists each year than any other state. Many hotels, restaurants, and retail trade estab-

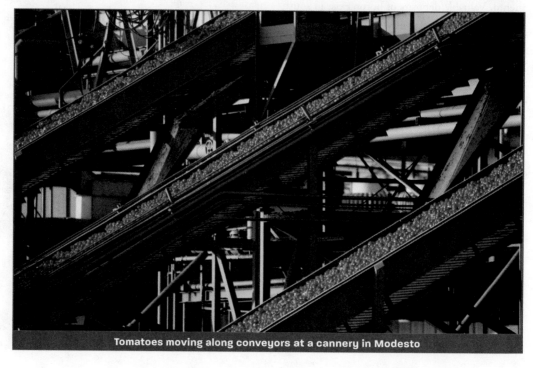

Tomatoes moving along conveyors at a cannery in Modesto

lishments operate in the Los Angeles, San Diego, and San Francisco-Oakland areas. Dole Food Company, based near Los Angeles, is a leading wholesale distributor of fruit. Safeway Inc., a major food store chain, is based in California.

Government services include public schools and military establishments. California has one of the world's largest public school systems, and its schools employ many people. Public universities in California operate many fine medical facilities and research laboratories. Edwards Air Force Base and several other Air Force bases lie within the state. California's other military bases include Camp Pendleton and Naval Base Coronado. The military bases are an especially important part of the economy of the San Diego area. Sacramento, the state capital, is the center of state government activities.

Transportation, communication, and utilities. Many shipping and trucking companies also operate in California. The airports in Los Angeles and San Francisco are among the world's busiest. (More information about transportation and communication appears later in this section.)

Manufacturing. California manufactures more goods than any other state. Many factories operate near San Jose and in the area between Los Angeles and San Diego. Chemicals, computer and electronic equipment, food products, refined petroleum, and transportation equipment are the leading products.

Computer and electronic equipment is California's leading manufactured product. Computers, computer microchips, military communication equipment, and telephone equipment are the leading types of electronic products made in the state. Electronic systems for aircraft and missiles are important products. The San Jose area is the nation's leader in the manufacture of electronic equipment. Silicon Valley, the leading computer-manufacturing region of the United States, is in this area. Apple Inc., Hewlett-Packard Company, and hundreds of other computer and electronics companies are headquartered there. Factories in Orange County and San Diego also produce large amounts of these goods.

Chemicals. *Pharmaceuticals* (medicinal drugs) are California's leading chemical product. Other leading chemical products include adhesives, cleaning compounds, and paints. Many chemical products are manufactured in the Los Angeles, San Diego, and San Francisco areas.

Food processing. The main food products are baked goods, beverages, canned fruits and vegetables, and dairy products. Large bakeries chiefly operate in the Los Angeles and San Francisco areas. California produces some of the world's finest wines. Soft-drink bottling also provides much income. The Los Angeles and Modesto areas have numerous canneries.

Petroleum products. California is a top petroleum-refining state. El Segundo, Los Angeles, Martinez, Richmond, and Torrance have large petroleum refineries.

Transportation equipment. Aircraft are the state's most important type of transportation equipment. Southern California is a leading aircraft assembly center. California's largest aircraft manufacturers include the Boeing Company and Northrop Grumman Corporation. Other types of transportation equipment made in the state include motor vehicles and motor vehicle parts.

Agriculture. California leads the states in farm income. Fresno, Kern, Monterey, and Tulare counties are the nation's top-ranking counties in agricultural production. Many Californians call farms *ranches,* even if the farms raise crops rather than livestock.

The wide range of climate and of soil and water conditions enables California farmers to grow hundreds of different crops. Several of these crops are grown commercially nowhere else in the nation. Most California farms are highly specialized. Many specialize in fruits or nuts. Almost all crop production takes place on farmlands that receive irrigation water.

Fruits and nuts. Grapes are the state's most valuable fruit, and California is the leading grape-producing state. The grape crop includes table grapes, wine grapes, and raisin grapes. California produces almost all of the nation's almonds, figs, olives, pistachios, pomegranates, prunes, and walnuts. California also leads all states in the production of apricots, avocados, dates, kiwi fruit, lemons, nectarines, peaches, plums, raspberries, and strawberries. Only Florida produces more oranges.

Various regions of California specialize in fruits and nuts for which their soil and climate are best suited. For example, the San Joaquin Valley grows almonds, apricots, cantaloupes, grapes, nectarines, oranges, peaches, pistachios, plums, and walnuts. The Sacramento Valley yields honeydew melons and prunes. Southern coastal counties lead in the production of avocados and have a heavy production of strawberries. Farms in the Imperial Valley yield dates, grapefruits, and melons.

Vegetables. Lettuce and tomatoes are the most important vegetable crops in the state. California ranks first in the production of both lettuce and tomatoes. Lettuce is cultivated primarily in the southern part of the state and in the regions that lie between Fresno and Monterey. The most important tomato-growing regions are the northern part of the San Joaquin Valley and the southern part of the Sacramento Valley. California leads the nation in the production of asparagus, broccoli, carrots, cauliflower, celery, garlic, onions, and spinach.

Field crops. Cotton and hay are California's leading field crops. California's San Joaquin Valley is a major cotton-growing region. California is the leading hay producing state. Farmers grow rice in the Sacramento Valley.

Greenhouse and nursery products. California produces more greenhouse and nursery products than any other state. It leads all states in the production of cut flowers, potted flowering plants, and flower bulbs. Most greenhouse and nursery products are grown in coastal areas between San Francisco and San Diego.

Livestock and livestock products. Milk is California's leading agricultural product. California leads the states in milk production. Dairy cattle are chiefly raised in the San Joaquin Valley. Beef cattle are another leading agricultural product in the state. Many beef cattle come from the Sacramento and San Joaquin valleys. California ranks among the leaders in egg production and in raising sheep and turkeys. California has more bee colonies and produces more honey than any other state.

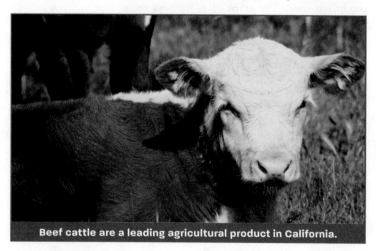

Beef cattle are a leading agricultural product in California.

Mining. Petroleum is California's most valuable mined product. Most oil wells are in Kern County and the Los Angeles area. Much natural gas comes from the petroleum-producing regions and from the Sacramento Valley.

California is a leading state in nonfuel mineral production. California mines yield all of the boron that is produced in the United States. Boron comes from Inyo, Kern, and San Bernardino counties. It is used in boric acid, an antiseptic; in borax, a cleaning agent; and in making glass fibers for such products as insulation and textiles. California is also the leading U.S. producer of sand and gravel. California is among the leading states in the production of feldspar, gemstones, gypsum, magnesium compounds, portland cement, and pumice.

Fishing industry. Squids are the most valuable fish catch in the state, and California has a larger squid catch than any other state. Crabs are the second most valuable catch. Other important seafood catches include halibut, lobster, oysters, sablefish, sardines, sea urchins, shrimp, sole, swordfish, and tuna.

Electric power and utilities. Over half of California's electric power comes from plants that burn natural gas. Hydroelectric plants and nuclear plants produce most of the remaining electric power. Hoover, Davis, Glen Canyon, and Parker dams on the Colorado River supply power to California as well as to other southwestern states. Power companies also generate power from many dams on rivers in northern California.

The Geysers Geothermal Field near Healdsburg is one of the nation's few commercial electric plants powered by *geothermal steam*—steam created by heat deep in the earth. In 1983, what was then the world's largest solar power plant began operation near San Luis Obispo. It produced electric power from sunlight.

Transportation. California's first highway, El Camino Real, began as a path connecting the Spanish missions along the coast during the 1700s. The state's first major freeway, the Arroyo Seco Parkway (now Pasadena Freeway) between Pasadena and Los Angeles, was completed in 1940. Today, the state has an extensive system of roads and highways. Complicated freeway systems, with underpasses, overpasses, and cloverleafs, are a familiar symbol of California's urban areas.

San Francisco Bay has two of the most famous bridges in the world. These are the Golden Gate

Bridge between San Francisco and Marin County and the San Francisco-Oakland Bay Bridge. Another important bridge, the Richmond-San Rafael Bridge, crosses a northern section of San Francisco Bay.

The international airports at Los Angeles and San Francisco are among the world's busiest. Other major airports include those in Oakland, Orange County, Sacramento, San Diego, and San Jose.

California's first railway, completed in 1856, ran 22 miles (35 kilometers) between Sacramento and Folsom. Today, rail lines provide freight service on thousands of miles of track.

Southern California has major ports at Long Beach, Los Angeles (San Pedro), and San Diego. The San Francisco Bay area has several deepwater ports that ship millions of tons of goods each year. Besides San Francisco itself, these ports include Oakland, Redwood City, and Richmond. Sacramento and Stockton are important inland ports. They handle shipments of agricultural and mineral products from the Sacramento and San Joaquin valleys. Deepwater channels connect the Sacramento and Stockton ports with San Francisco Bay.

Communication. California's first newspaper, the *Californian*, began publication in Monterey in 1846. Today, the state has several hundred newspapers, many of them dailies. California's leading papers include the *Contra Costa Times*, *The Fresno Bee*, the *Los Angeles Times*, *The Orange County Register*, *The Press-Enterprise* of Riverside, *The Sacramento Bee*, *The San Diego Union-Tribune*, the *San Francisco Chronicle*, and the *San Jose Mercury News*.

Government

Constitution. California's first Constitution was adopted by the territorial government in 1849. The present Constitution was adopted in 1879. It has been *amended* (changed) hundreds of times. A proposed amendment must be placed on the ballot in a regular statewide election. It may be proposed and placed on the ballot in any of three ways: (1) The Legislature may propose it by a two-thirds majority vote in each house. (2) A group of citizens may propose an amendment by submitting a petition. The petition must be signed by at least 8 percent as many people as voted for governor in the last election. (3) A constitutional convention, approved by two-thirds of the Legislature, may propose an amendment. To become law, an amendment must be approved by a majority of the voters.

Executive. Voters elect California's governor to a four-year term. The governor can serve only two terms.

Other top state officials include the lieutenant governor, secretary of state, attorney general, treasurer, controller, insurance commissioner, and superintendent of public instruction. Voters also elect the five-member State Board of Equalization, which administers several important tax laws. All these officials are elected to four-year terms and may serve no more than two terms in the same office.

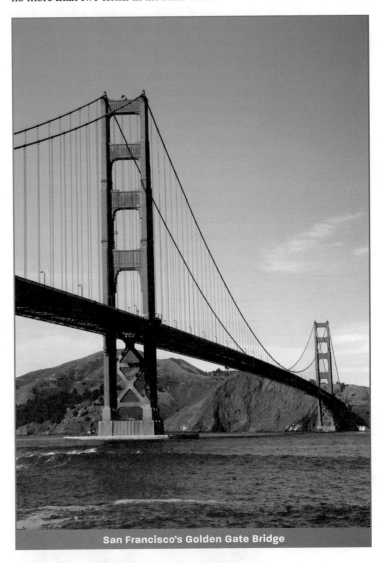

San Francisco's Golden Gate Bridge

The Legislature consists of a Senate of 40 members and an Assembly of 80 members. Each senator and each Assembly member represents one senatorial or Assembly district. Senators are elected to four-year terms and may serve only two terms.

Members of the Assembly are elected to two-year terms and may serve no more than three terms.

Regular sessions of the Legislature run about two years. They begin on the first Monday in December of each even-numbered year and end on November 30 of the next even-numbered year.

The governor may call special sessions at which the Legislature can deal only with subjects specified by the governor. There is no time limit on special sessions of the Legislature.

California citizens can pass laws directly, through their power of *initiative*. To do so, a proposed law must be favored by at least 5 percent of the people who voted for governor in the last election. This number of people must sign a petition in favor of a measure. Then they can put the measure on the ballot in the next state election. If the voters approve the measure, it becomes law.

In a process called the *referendum*, Californians also have the right to challenge most kinds of laws passed by the Legislature. If 5 percent of the people who voted for governor in the most recent election challenge a new law, the law will not go into effect unless the people approve it in an election.

Courts. The highest court in California is the state Supreme Court. It has a chief justice and six associate justices. The state has six district courts of appeal. Justices of the Supreme Court and of the district courts of appeal are appointed by the governor to 12-year terms, subject to voter approval.

British sailor and navigator Francis Drake

Each county has one superior court. The number of judges for each superior court is fixed by the Legislature. The voters elect superior court judges to six-year terms.

Local government. California has several hundred incorporated cities. The state Constitution gives cities the right to draw up and adopt their own charters. This right is often called *home rule*. More than 100 California cities operate under local charters.

Most of the cities in California have council-manager governments. The others have mayor-council governments.

California has 58 counties. Most of the counties have a form of government specified by the laws of the state. This form of government includes a five-member board of supervisors and a number of elected executive officials. The elected officials include an assessor, auditor, clerk, coroner, district attorney, sheriff, superintendent of schools, and treasurer. The California Constitution provides for county home rule. But only 14 counties have adopted charters under the home-rule law. Most of these counties chose a form of government similar to that of the general-law counties.

Revenue. Taxation provides about 60 percent of the state's *general revenue* (income). Most of the rest of its revenue comes from federal government grants. The largest sources of state tax revenue are a personal income tax and a general sales tax. Other important tax revenue sources include taxes on corporate profits, motor fuels, and property, and licenses for businesses and motor vehicles.

Politics. Until 1959, California did not require political candidates to declare their party affiliation. For example, they could run as candidates of both the Democratic and Republican parties. This practice, known as *cross-filing*, kept many voters from being loyal to one particular party. As a result, political disagreements between various parts of the state tended to be stronger than disagreements among the parties themselves. Major political conflicts still occur between northern and southern California. In 1965, southern California gained political power when reapportionment of the Legislature gave the area more seats in the state Senate.

History

Early days. As many as 300,000 Indians lived in the fertile parts of the California region before Europeans came. There were many tribes, and they spoke different languages. Deserts and high mountains often separated the California Indian groups from each other and from the tribes farther east. The Hupa Indians lived in the far northwestern part of what is now California. The Maidu lived in the central section, and the Quechan lived in the south. The Pomo Indians occupied the territory that now makes up Lake, Mendocino, and Sonoma counties north of San Francisco. Other Indian groups in the California region included the Miwok, Modoc, and Mojave tribes.

Spanish and English exploration.
Juan Rodriguez Cabrillo, a Portuguese explorer employed by Spain, was the first European to see the coast of what is now California. In 1542, Cabrillo sailed north from New Spain (present-day Mexico) along the Pacific Coast. He hoped to find rich cities and a water passage between the Pacific and Atlantic oceans. Cabrillo discovered San Diego Bay and stopped there before sailing farther north. Cabrillo died in 1543, but his men continued the voyage. Some historians believe that Cabrillo's expedition sailed along the entire California coast, as far north as present-day Oregon.

In 1579, Francis Drake, an English sea captain, followed a route along the California coast during his famous voyage around the world. Drake claimed the land for England and named it *New Albion*. The Spaniards then sent several exploring parties along the coast, partly because they feared they might lose California to the English. In 1602, Sebastián Vizcaíno led one of these expeditions. He named many landmarks along the coast, and sent an enthusiastic report about California to the king of Spain. In the report, Vizcaino urged that Spain colonize California.

Spanish and Russian settlement.
Beginning in 1697, the Spaniards established missions and other settlements in Baja (Lower) California, the Mexican peninsula south of present-day California. Captain Gaspar de Portolá, governor of Baja California, led an expedition that established the first *presidio* (military fort) at San Diego in 1769. He also established one at Monterey in 1770. In 1776, a group of Spanish settlers arrived at the site of what is now San Francisco. The settlers founded a presidio and a mission there. Later, other groups of settlers sent by Spain established some *pueblos* (villages) near the coast.

However, Spain did not have a strong hold on the California region. Russia had fur-trading interests

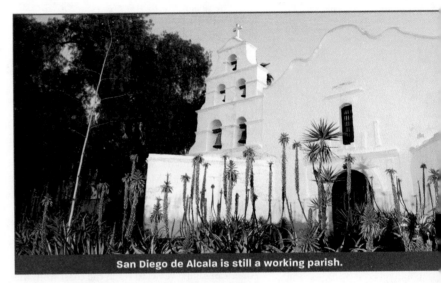

San Diego de Alcala is still a working parish.

in Alaska, and wanted to search for furs farther south along the Pacific Coast. In 1812, the Russians established Fort Ross on the northern California coast. Russian activity in California was one reason for the Monroe Doctrine, proclaimed in 1823. In the Monroe Doctrine, the United States declared that North and South America should be considered closed to European colonization. In 1824, Russia agreed to limit its settlements to Alaska. However, the Russians did not actually leave the California region until the early 1840s.

The California missions.
Franciscan friars of the Roman Catholic Church played an important part in the Spanish settlement of California. In 1769, during the Portolá expedition, Junipero Serra established the first California mission. This mission was San Diego de Alcalá, originally established in what is now San Diego. By 1823, the Franciscans had built a chain of 21 missions. Each mission was about a day's walk from the next. Many Indians who lived near the missions were forced to farm, weave, and perform other tasks for the friars and the local communities. A number of Indians were exposed to new diseases. Many became ill and died.

Many people in California and Mexico wanted the missions broken up. In the early 1830s, the government began giving mission land to private citizens. By 1846, almost all the mission property had been given away. During this period, the government gave or sold many large estates, called *ranchos*, to private landowners, called *rancheros*. Some rancheros became wealthy by raising cattle for hides and *tallow* (fat used in making candles, soap, and other products).

Mexican rule. California became a province of Mexico in 1822, after Mexico won its independence from Spain. The province set up its own legislature and established a military force. But, beginning in 1825, Mexico sent a series of governors to California. Many Californians rebelled against having their affairs dictated by these outsiders. Manuel Victoria, who became governor in 1831, ruled with a strong hand and was especially resented by the Californians. A group led by Pío Pico and others clashed with Mexican government troops in 1831. This fighting was not severe. But the continuing opposition forced Victoria to give up the governorship and return to Mexico City. After that, Mexico's control over the region remained weak.

American settlement. The *Otter*, the first American sailing vessel to reach the coast from the East, appeared in California waters in 1796. After that, American skippers made many trading trips to harbors along the coast of California.

The first American explorer to reach California by land was Jedediah Strong Smith, a trapper who crossed the southwestern deserts in 1826. Other trappers and explorers followed Smith. They included Kit Carson, Joseph Reddeford Walker, and Ewing Young.

In 1841, the first organized group of American settlers came to California by land. These settlers were led by John Bidwell, a schoolteacher, and John Bartleson, a wagon master and land speculator. Soon other overland pioneers arrived to settle in the Mexican territory. They drove long wagon trains through the mountain passes. The new settlers wanted California to become a part of the United States. The United States offered to buy the land from Mexico, but Mexico refused to sell.

The Mexican War. Between 1844 and 1846, the military explorer John C. Frémont led two surveying parties into California. The Mexicans did not trust Frémont because his parties were made up of U.S. soldiers. In March 1846, the Mexicans ordered Frémont to withdraw his troops, who were camped near Monterey. Instead, Frémont raised the U.S. flag over Hawk's Peak, about 25 miles (40 kilometers) from Monterey. He began to build a fort there. Fighting was avoided when Frémont withdrew to the north under cover of darkness. On May 13, 1846, the United States and Mexico went to war.

In June 1846, without knowing that war had been declared, a band of American settlers took over Sonoma, Mexico's headquarters in northern Cali-

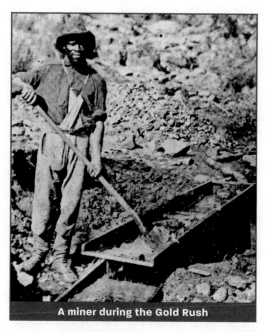

A miner during the Gold Rush

fornia. The group was led by frontiersman Ezekiel Merritt. After capturing the fort, the settlers unfurled a homemade flag bearing a star, a grizzly bear, and the words *California Republic*. This action became known as the Bear Flag Revolt.

The real conquest of California was carried out by United States soldiers, sailors, and marines. They were led by Frémont, Commodore Robert F. Stockton, and General Stephen W. Kearny. After the United States won the Mexican War in 1848, Mexico surrendered its claim to California in the Treaty of Guadalupe Hidalgo. California then became part of the United States.

The gold rush. In 1848, just before the United States and Mexico signed the peace treaty, gold was discovered in California. John A. Sutter, a pioneer trader, had received a large land grant in the Sacramento Valley in 1839. He hired James W. Marshall, a carpenter, to help build a sawmill on the American River. There, at Sutter's Mill, Marshall found the first gold nuggets. News of his discovery spread, and thousands of persons rushed to establish claims. These "Forty-Niners," as they were called, poured in from all parts of the world. Between early 1848 and the end of 1849, California's population increased from about 15,000 to more than 100,000. The free spending by the miners who found gold made such communities as San Francisco and Sacramento into flourishing towns. Some miners who were not so lucky in the gold fields became farmers and ranchers in the Central Valley.

Early statehood. California became the 31st state on September 9, 1850. Peter H. Burnett, a Democrat, was the first state governor. Thousands of settlers went west after the American Civil War ended in 1865. They sought the high wages paid in California and a chance to buy land at low prices. In 1869, the first transcontinental railroad system linked Sacramento with the eastern United States. Part of this system, the Central Pacific Railroad, later became part of the Southern Pacific, owned by Charles Crocker, Mark Hopkins, Collis P. Huntington, and Leland Stanford. These men were known as California's "Big Four." They brought many Chinese laborers to California in the 1860s to work on the railroads.

By 1870, California's population had risen to about 560,000. During the next 10 years, a depression caused widespread unemployment and bank failures. Many unemployed workers blamed their troubles on Chinese laborers, who were willing to work for low wages. Anti-Chinese riots took place in Los Angeles in 1871 and in San Francisco in 1877. During the 1880s, a great publicity campaign brought thousands of people to California. So many came to southern California in 1887 that a land boom occurred. Agriculture and industry flourished as the population increased.

Progress as a state. During the early 1900s, California grew rapidly in population and in the development of natural resources. Mexican immigration soared after a revolution in Mexico in 1910. Farming increased greatly after irrigation turned many desert areas into fertile land. Development of oil and natural gas was accompanied by the growth of new industries. Other minerals besides gold were found, and mining became more important. By 1920, Hollywood had become the motion-picture capital of the world.

In 1910, Californians elected Hiram W. Johnson as governor. Two years later, Johnson joined Theodore Roosevelt in a revolt against the Republican Party. Johnson ran for U.S. vice president under Roosevelt in 1912 on the unsuccessful Progressive Party ticket.

In 1914, the completion of the Panama Canal shortened the important sea route between California and the East. To show the value of the canal to California, the state sponsored the Panama-Pacific International Exposition in San Francisco in 1915 and the Panama-California Exposition in San Diego in 1915 and 1916.

After the United States entered World War I in 1917, shipyards, rubber plants, and other factories were established in California. After the war ended in 1918, interest turned to control of the Colorado River. This mighty river had caused serious flood damage for many years. Between 1905 and 1907, floodwaters from the Colorado had even formed the 450-square-mile (1,165-square-kilometer) Salton Sea in southeastern California. In 1928, Congress authorized a huge dam at Boulder Canyon on the Arizona-Nevada border. The dam, now called Hoover Dam, was completed in 1935. It controls floods and provides water for irrigation and power in southern California and neighboring states.

During the Great Depression of the 1930s, hundreds of people without homes or jobs drifted into California. The state passed laws to close its borders to poor people. But this legislation was later declared unconstitutional by the Supreme Court of the United States. Many Californians blamed the Depression on Mexican Americans, and the state deported hundreds of thousands of Mexican Americans to Mexico.

In 1935 and 1936, the California-Pacific International Exposition was held in San Diego. This fair honored the Pacific Ocean and the countries that border it. The Golden Gate International Exposition was held in 1939 and 1940 on Treasure Island in San Francisco Bay. The Golden Gate Bridge across the entrance to the bay had been completed in 1937.

The mid-1900s. During World War II (1939–1945), California produced airplanes, ships, and weapons. The state became the nation's aircraft center. After Japan attacked Pearl Harbor in 1941, the government moved thousands of Japanese Americans from California to detention camps. In 1945, representatives of 50 nations approved the United Nations Charter at the San Francisco Conference.

Many people who had come to California as members of the armed forces or to work in defense plants settled there after the war. The population soared. Farm centers became metropolitan areas with a variety of industries. Rows of ranch-style houses appeared on former orchards and pastures. New freeways linked smaller cities with Los Angeles and San Francisco.

The population growth boosted California's economy, but it also created problems. The state had to provide more schools and highways. Smog became a serious problem in Los Angeles and other cities as more automobiles and industries discharged fumes and smoke.

Changes in U.S. immigration laws in 1965, which ended quotas based on nationality, led to another increase in California's population. Hundreds of thousands of people from Asia countries settled in the state.

Controlling and distributing water resources remained California's biggest problem during the 1960s. Most of the state's rain and snow falls in the northern mountains. But most of California's people live in southern California, where rainfall does not supply enough water. In the 1960s and early 1970s, the state built a system of canals, dams, reservoirs, and power and pumping plants to store and distribute northern California's excess water to the drier areas. A number of additions to the system have been completed since the 1970s.

In the 1950s and 1960s, African Americans, Asian Americans, and Mexican Americans began to demand equal rights. Racial tensions worsened in 1964 after California voters passed a referendum that overturned a 1963 law guaranteeing equal access to housing. In 1965, racial violence erupted in Watts, a black section of Los Angeles. Rioting broke out after a Los Angeles police officer arrested a black motorist. It resulted in the deaths of 34 people and millions of dollars of damage.

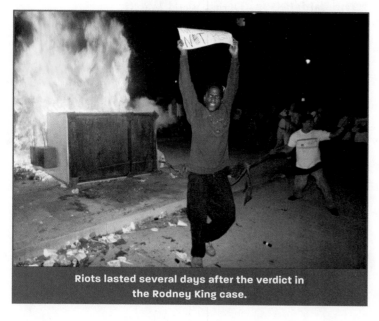
Riots lasted several days after the verdict in the Rodney King case.

By the end of the 1960s, California had greatly increased its number of state universities and colleges. The state's schools became the center of various student movements. The nation's first major college demonstration, organized by the Free Speech Movement, occurred in 1964 at the University of California in Berkeley.

Richard M. Nixon, born in Yorba Linda, was elected president of the United States in 1968 and was reelected in 1972. He resigned from the office in 1974 because of his involvement in the Watergate political scandal.

Motion-picture stars gained popularity with California voters in the 1960s. George L. Murphy won election to the U.S. Senate in 1964, and Ronald Reagan became governor in 1967. Reagan was elected president of the United States in 1980 and was reelected in 1984.

The late 1900s. In the early 1970s, sharp cuts in federal military spending in California caused a rise in unemployment. In 1978, California voters approved a referendum—known as Proposition 13—that called for a $7-billion reduction in state property taxes. School districts and local government suffered revenue losses.

By the early 1980s, however, California's economy was thriving again, and education and other services benefited from the state's increased revenues. New federal military contracts helped bring prosperity to California's aerospace industry. In addition, Santa Clara County became a world leader in the production of high-technology electronic equipment. It earned the name Silicon Valley.

On October 17, 1989, a strong earthquake struck the San Francisco-Oakland-San Jose area. It caused 63 deaths and extensive property damage. Most deaths were caused by the collapse of a section of the Nimitz Freeway in Oakland. In 1991, a major brush fire struck Oakland and surrounding areas. It caused 25 deaths and destroyed much property. In 1993, a series of brush fires near Los Angeles killed 4 people and caused heavy property damage. In January 1994, another extremely destructive earthquake struck Los Angeles. It caused 57 deaths and much property damage.

In 1992, four police officers who were accused of a 1991 beating of a black motorist, Rodney G. King, were acquitted of criminal charges. The verdict set off several days of rioting, mainly in black areas of South Los Angeles (then called South-Central Los

Angeles). The rioting resulted in 53 deaths and over $1 billion in property damage.

The state's population continued to grow rapidly, partly because of the large numbers of immigrants from Europe, Asia, and especially Central America and Mexico. In 1986, California voters approved a referendum to make English the state's official language. In 1994, the voters passed a referendum to prohibit illegal immigrants from receiving public education, free nonemergency medical care, and other social services. But implementation was blocked by a number of lawsuits. In 1999, the state abandoned the proposition. Governor Gray Davis said that much of the intent of the proposition was covered by federal immigration laws passed in 1996 that deny certain social services to illegal immigrants.

The beginning of the 2000s. Power outages, called "rolling blackouts," became common across the state in 2001. The energy crisis stemmed in part from actions taken in 1996, when the state had approved legislation to deregulate its utility industry. Government officials had believed that such action would result in increased competition among electric companies and lower rates for customers. But by 2000, the state's electric companies faced financial ruin. They had to pay increasingly high wholesale costs for electric power, but the deregulation law prevented them from raising the costs to customers.

In mid-2001, the state stepped in to buy power for the financially weakened utilities. The state also sought federal controls on wholesale electric power costs.

In 2002, Gray Davis was elected by a slim margin to a second term as governor. By that time, the state government's expenses so greatly exceeded income that budget *deficits* (shortages) were reaching record levels. A number of Californians blamed Davis for the state's worsening economic problems, and they were successful in petitioning for a *recall election*—that is, a vote to decide whether Davis should be removed from office. On October 7, 2003, California voters recalled Davis and elected motion-picture star Arnold Schwarzenegger as governor. Davis became the state's first governor to be recalled. Schwarzenegger took office in mid-November. In the general election of 2006, Schwarzenegger won a full term as governor.

There were numerous major wildfires in California in the early 2000s. In October and November

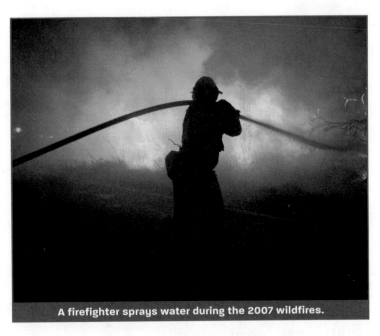

A firefighter sprays water during the 2007 wildfires.

2003, wildfires in southern California destroyed thousands of homes and killed more than 20 people. Other deadly wildfires occurred in the region in October 2007. The 2007 fires forced the evacuation of about 500,000 people in San Diego County. It was the largest evacuation in the state's history.

In May 2008, the California Supreme Court overturned state laws that had limited marriage to unions between a man and a woman. The decision went into effect in June. In November 2008, however, California voters approved a proposition amending the state Constitution to ban gay marriage. Edmund G. Brown, Jr., known as Jerry, was reelected governor of California in 2010. He had earlier held the office from 1975 to 1983.

California's economy began to suffer in late 2008, during a national economic slowdown. Unemployment rates topped 10 percent in 2009 and remained in double digits during the early 2010s. The state's budget deficits soared. In 2011, California legislators passed, and Governor Brown signed, an "austerity budget" that featured nearly $15 billion in spending cuts.

MLA Citation

"California." *The Southwestern Advantage Topic Source.* Nashville: Southwestern. 2013.

DATA

California in Brief

General Information

Statehood: September 9, 1850, the 31st state.

State abbreviations: Calif. (traditional); CA (postal).

State capital: Sacramento, California's capital since 1854. Monterey, San Jose, Vallejo, Benicia, and San Francisco were temporary capitals between 1850 and 1854.

State motto: *Eureka* (I Have Found It).

Popular name: The Golden State.

State song: "I Love You, California." Words by F. B. Silverwood; music by A. F. Frankenstein.

Symbols of California

State bird: California quail.

State flower: Golden poppy.

State tree: California redwood.

State flag and seal: The state flag, adopted in 1911, shows a grizzly bear and a single red star. On the state seal, adopted in 1849, appears Minerva, the Roman goddess of wisdom. Next to Minerva are a grizzly bear and clusters of grapes, symbolizing wildlife and agriculture. A miner labors along the Sacramento River, below the Sierra Nevada. The word Eureka (Greek for *I Have Found It*) refers to the miner's success or California's admission to statehood.

Land and Climate

Area: 158,648 mi^2 (410,896 km^2), including 2,674 mi^2 (6,925 km^2) of inland water but excluding 222 mi^2 (574 km^2) of Pacific coastal water.

Elevation: *Highest*—Mount Whitney, 14,494 ft (4,418 m) above sea level. *Lowest*—282 ft (86 m) below sea level in Death Valley.

Coastline: 840 mi (1,352 km).

Record high temperature: 134ºF (57ºC) at Greenland Ranch in Death Valley on July 10, 1913.

Record low temperature: −45ºF (−43ºC) at Boca, near Truckee, on January 20, 1937.

Average July temperature: 75ºF (24ºC).

Average January temperature: 44ºF (7ºC).

Average yearly precipitation: 22 in (56 cm).

People[1]

Population: 37,253,956

Rank among the states: 1st.

Density: 235 per mi^2 (91 per km^2), U.S. average 85 per mi^2 (33 per km^2).

Distribution: 94 percent urban, 6 percent rural.

Largest cities in California: Los Angeles (3,792,621); San Diego (1,301,617); San Jose (945,942); San Francisco (805,235); Fresno (494,665); Sacramento (466,488).

[1] Source: 2010 census.

DATA

California in Brief

Economy

Chief products: *Agriculture*—almonds, beef cattle, grapes, greenhouse and nursery products, hay, lettuce, milk, rice, strawberries, tomatoes, walnuts. *Manufacturing*—chemicals, computer and electronic products, food products, refined petroleum, transportation equipment. *Mining:* boron, cement, natural gas, petroleum, sand and gravel.

State Government

Governor: 4-year term.

State senators: 40; 4-year terms.

Members of the Assembly: 80; 2-year terms.

Counties: 58.

Federal Government

United States senators: 2.

United States representatives: 53

Electoral votes: 55

Sources of Information

For information about tourism: The Web site at http://www.visitcalifornia.com provides information.

The state's official Web site at http://www.ca.gov also provides a gateway to much information on California's economy, government, and history.

Interesting Facts About California

The highest temperature ever recorded in the United States, 134°F. (57°C), was measured in Death Valley on July 10, 1913. In addition, the lowest elevation in the Western Hemisphere is located near Badwater in Death Valley. It lies 282 feet (86 meters) below sea level.

The world's tallest known tree rises 368 feet (112 meters) in the Tall Trees Grove in Redwood National Park.

The first cable car street railway system was installed in San Francisco in 1873.

The General Sherman tree, in Sequoia National Park, is one of the world's largest living things. It has a circumference of 103 feet (31.4 meters) at the base and rises 275 feet (83.8 meters). The tree is estimated to be about 2,500 years old.

The first synchronized sound cartoon was Walt Disney's Steamboat Willie, produced in Hollywood in 1928. It featured Mickey Mouse.

DATA

Places to Visit in California

Following are brief descriptions of some of California's many interesting places to visit:

Disneyland Park, in Anaheim, is an amusement park and resort designed by the famous American motion-picture producer Walt Disney. Its attractions include a fairyland castle, a boat trip through "jungle" waters, and "Mickey's Toontown." Facing Disneyland is Disney's California Adventure Park. It has such California-themed attractions as a boardwalk and a replica of the Golden Gate Bridge, along with many rides, shops, and shows.

Getty Center, in Los Angeles, features modern architecture, gardens, a research library, collections of European art from the Middle Ages to the present, and other exhibits.

Hearst Castle, near San Luis Obispo, is the former estate of newspaper owner William Randolph Hearst. It includes a castle with ancient works of art, a Roman temple, a private theater, and huge swimming pools. Its official name is Hearst San Simeon State Historical Monument.

Knott's Berry Farm, in Buena Park, is California's oldest amusement park. It has rides, a ghost town, and an Indian village.

Missions were built in California by Franciscan friars beginning in 1769. For information about these missions, see *The California missions* heading in the *History* section of this article.

Monterey Bay National Marine Sanctuary is a vast area set aside to preserve marine life in its natural habitat. The sanctuary extends from Marin County south to Cambria.

Monterey Peninsula includes the communities of Carmel, Monterey, Pacific Grove, and Pebble Beach. Carmel is an art colony. Monterey has Monterey Bay Aquarium and buildings from Spanish colonial days.

Redwood Highway (U.S. 101), from San Francisco to Oregon, passes through magnificent groves of redwood trees. These towering evergreen trees are the tallest living trees in the world.

San Diego Zoo is home to more than 4,000 rare and endangered animals. Its monkey and ape exhibits rank among the finest in North America.

Parklands in California include eight national parks. The state's national parks are Channel Islands, Death Valley, Joshua Tree, Kings Canyon, Lassen Volcanic, Redwood, Sequoia, and Yosemite. Thousands of miles of trails wind through the parks. In addition, the state of California has several national monuments, including California Coastal National Monument, Lava Beds, Muir Woods, and Pinnacles.

National forests. California has 18 national forests. Congress has set aside several areas in these national forests to be preserved in their natural condition.

State parks, forests, and monuments offer numerous historic and scenic attractions. For information, write to Department of Parks and Recreation, P.O. Box 942896, Sacramento, CA 94296.

DATA

Annual Events in California

January–June

Tournament of Roses in Pasadena (January); Chinese New Year Celebration in San Francisco and Los Angeles (January, February, or March); Whiskey Flat Days in Kernville (February); Aleutian Goose Festival in Crescent City (April); Northern California Cherry Blossom Festival in San Francisco (April); Godwit Days Spring Migration Bird Festival in Arcata (April); Monterey Wine Festival (April); Red Bluff Round-Up in Red Bluff (April); Stockton Asparagus Festival (April); Calaveras County Fair & Jumping Frog Jubilee in Angels Camp (May); Kinetic Sculpture Race from Arcata to Ferndale (May); Oakdale Chocolate Festival (May); Sacramento Jazz Jubilee (May); Salinas Valley Fair in King City (May); Strawberry Festival in Galt (May).

July–December

California WorldFest in Grass Valley (July); Garlic Festival in Gilroy (July); Mozart Festival in San Luis Obispo (July); Shakespeare Santa Cruz (July-August); Old Spanish Days Fiesta in Santa Barbara (August); State Fair in Sacramento (August-September); Lodi Grape Festival and Harvest Fair (September); Monterey Jazz Festival (September); Rolex Monterey Historical Automobile Races in Monterey (September); Stater Bros. Route 66 Rendezvous® in San Bernardino (September); Clam Festival in Pismo Beach (October); Lone Pine Film Festival (October); Christmas Boat Parade in Newport Beach (December).

Average Monthly Weather in California

Month	High temp. (F)	Low temp. (F)	High temp. (C)	Low temp. (C)	Days of rain or snow
Los Angeles					
January	66	49	19	9	6
February	66	50	19	10	6
March	65	51	18	11	6
April	68	54	20	12	3
May	69	57	21	14	1
June	73	60	23	16	1
July	75	63	24	17	1
August	77	65	25	18	0
September	77	64	25	18	1
October	74	59	23	15	2
November	70	53	21	12	3
December	67	49	19	9	5

DATA

Average Monthly Weather in California

Month	High temp. (F)	Low temp. (F)	High temp. (C)	Low temp. (C)	Days of rain or snow
San Francisco					
January	56	43	11	6	11
February	59	46	15	8	11
March	61	47	16	8	10
April	64	48	18	9	6
May	67	51	19	11	3
June	70	53	21	12	1
July	71	55	22	13	0
August	72	56	22	13	0
September	73	55	23	13	1
October	70	53	21	12	3
November	62	48	17	9	7
December	56	43	13	6	10

California's Economic Production and Workers

Estimates based on data from U.S. Bureau of Economic Analysis. Figures are for 2008; employment figures include full- and part-time workers.

Economic activities	% of GDP[1] produced	Number of workers	% of all workers
Community, business, & personal services	23	7,220,400	34
Finance, insurance, & real estate	23	2,342,900	11
Trade, restaurants, & hotels	15	4,324,500	21
Government	12	2,754,300	13
Manufacturing	11	1,524,000	7
Transportation & communication	9	1,189,500	6
Construction	4	1,157,100	5
Agriculture	1	438,500	2
Utilities	1	61,200	2
Mining	1	50,900	2
Total[3]	100	21,063,300	100

[1] GDP = gross domestic product, the total value of goods and services produced in a year.

[2] Less than one-half of 1 percent.

[3] Figures do not add up to 100 percent due to rounding.

DATA

Governors of California

Name	Party	Term
Peter H. Burnett	Democratic	1849–1851
John McDougal	Democratic	1851–1852
John Bigler	Democratic	1852–1856
John Neely Johnson	Know-Nothing	1856–1858
John B. Weller	Democratic	1858–1860
Milton S. Latham	Democratic	1860
John G. Downey	Democratic	1860–1862
Leland Stanford	Republican	1862–1863
Frederick F. Low	Union	1863–1867
Henry H. Haight	Democratic	1867–1871
Newton Booth	Republican	1871–1875
Romualdo Pacheco	Republican	1875
William Irwin	Democratic	1875–1880
George C. Perkins	Republican	1880–1883
George Stoneman	Democratic	1883–1887
Washington Bartlett	Democratic	1887
Robert W. Waterman	Republican	1887–1891
Henry H. Markham	Republican	1891–1895
James H. Budd	Democratic	1895–1899
Henry T. Gage	Republican	1899–1903
George C. Pardee	Republican	1903–1907
James N. Gillett	Republican	1907–1911
Hiram W. Johnson	Republican	1911–1917
William D. Stephens	Republican	1917–1923
Friend William Richardson	Republican	1923–1927
Clement C. Young	Republican	1927–1931
James Rolph, Jr.	Republican	1931–1934
Frank F. Merriam	Republican	1934–1939
Culbert L. Olson	Democratic	1939–1943
Earl Warren	Republican	1943–1953
Goodwin J. Knight	Republican	1953–1959
Edmund G. Brown	Democratic	1959–1967

DATA

Governors of California

Name	Party	Term
Edmund G. Brown, Jr.	Democratic	1975–1983
George Deukmejian	Republican	1983–1991
Pete Wilson	Republican	1991–1999
Gray Davis	Democratic	1999–2003
Arnold Schwarzenegger	Republican	2003–2011
Edmund G. Brown, Jr.	Democratic	2011–

Important Dates in California History

1542	Juan Rodríguez Cabrillo explored San Diego Bay.
1579	Francis Drake sailed along the coast and claimed California for England.
1602	Sebastián Vizcaíno urged that Spain colonize California.
1769	Gaspar de Portolá led a land expedition up the California coast. Junípero Serra established the first Franciscan mission in California, in what is now the city of San Diego.
1776	Spanish settlers from New Spain (Mexico) reached the site of what is now San Francisco.
1812	Russian fur traders built Fort Ross.
1822	California became part of Mexico, which had just won its independence from Spain in 1821.
1841	The Bidwell-Bartleson party became the first organized group of American settlers to travel to California by land.
1846	American rebels raised the "Bear Flag" of the California Republic over Sonoma. United States forces conquered California during the Mexican War (1846–1848).
1848	James W. Marshall discovered gold at Sutter's Mill. The discovery led to the California gold rush. The United States defeated Mexico in the Mexican War and acquired California in the Treaty of Guadalupe Hidalgo.
1850	California became the 31st state on September 9.
1880's	A population boom occurred as a result of a railroad and real estate publicity campaign that brought thousands of people to California.
1906	An earthquake and fire destroyed much of San Francisco.
1915	Expositions were begun at San Diego and San Francisco to mark the opening of the Panama Canal.
1963	California became the state with the largest population in the United States.
1978	California voters approved a $7-billion cutback in state property taxes.
1989	A strong earthquake struck the San Francisco-Oakland-San Jose area.
1992	Four police officers who were accused of beating Rodney G. King, a black motorist, were acquitted of criminal charges. The decision sparked several days of rioting, mainly in black areas of South Los Angeles.
1994	A strong earthquake struck Los Angeles.
2003	Voters recalled Governor Gray Davis and elected motion-picture star Arnold Schwarzenegger to replace him.

ADDITIONAL RESOURCES

Books to Read

Brands, H. W. *The Age of Gold: The California Gold Rush and the New American Dream*. Doubleday, 2002.

Flamming, Douglas. *Bound for Freedom: Black Los Angeles in Jim Crow America*. University of California Press, 2005.

Hayes, Derek. *Historical Atlas of California*. University of California Press, 2007.

Kimbro, Edna E., and Costello, J. G. *The California Missions*. Getty Conservation Institute, 2009.

Lightfoot, Kent G., and Parrish, Otis. *California Indians and Their Environment*. University of California Press, 2009.

Rolle, Andrew F. *California*. 7th ed. Harlan Davidson, 2008.

Starr, Kevin. *California*. Modern Library, 2005.

Winchester, Simon. *A Crack in the Edge of the World: America and the Great California Earthquake of 1906*. HarperCollins, 2005.

Web Sites

California Department of Education

http://www.cde.ca.gov/
The official Web site of the California Department of Education.

California State University

http://www.calstate.edu/
The official site of California State University.

Official California Legislative Information

http://www.leginfo.ca.gov/
The official Web site for California legislative information.

The Los Angeles Times

http://www.latimes.com/
The official Web site of *The Los Angeles Times*.

The San Francisco Chronicle

http://www.sfgate.com/chronicle/
The official Web site of *The San Francisco Chronicle*.

The Union-Tribune (San Diego)

http://www.signonsandiego.com/
The official Web site of *The Union-Tribune* (San Diego).

Welcome to California Home Page

http://www.ca.gov/
The official Web site for the State of California.

Search Strings

Wildfires

California wildfires dry climate (73,600)

California wildfires dry climate "San Diego" (52,400)

wildfires in California causes dry climate (129,000)

Combating Global Warming

California combating "global warming" greenhouse gases (112,000)

California combating "global warming" greenhouse gases "Global Warming Solutions Act" (458)

California Schwarzenegger "greenhouse gases" "Global Warming Solutions Act" (10,100)

Removing a Governor from Office

California remove governor Davis recall vote (67,800)

California remove governor Davis recall vote Schwarzenegger (13,700)

California remove governor Davis recall vote Schwarzenegger "budget deficit" (17,300)

California's Energy Crisis of 2000–2001

California's Energy Crisis power outages blackouts (77,300)

California's Energy Crisis power outages blackouts deregulation electric utilities (22,800)

California's Energy Crisis power outages blackouts deregulation "electric utilities" (991)

The Most Populous State

California most populous state (133,000)

California most populous state demographics (78,900)

California most populous state demographics cities (71,900)

BACKGROUND INFORMATION

The following articles and features were written during the year in which the events took place and reflect the style and thinking of that time.

Environmental Pollution (2006)

The government of California took two dramatic steps in 2006 that went further than the actions of any other state to combat global warming. Global warming is a gradual increase in Earth's average temperature that many scientists believe is being caused by emissions of carbon dioxide and other greenhouse gases. Such gases trap heat in the atmosphere. In 2006, California was the second-largest emitter of greenhouse gases in the United States (behind Texas) and produced 2.5 percent of the world's total emissions of these gases.

In September, California Governor Arnold Schwarzenegger signed the Global Warming Solutions Act of 2006. The act required power plants, oil refineries, cement plants, and other industrial polluters in the state to reduce their emissions of greenhouse gases by 25 percent by 2020.

Also in September 2006, California Attorney General Bill Lockyer filed suit in the U.S. District Court of Northern California against the world's six largest automobile manufacturers (Chrysler, Ford, General Motors, Honda, Nissan, and Toyota). The suit alleged that these companies created a "public nuisance" that has cost the state millions of dollars. The suit also argued that because vehicle emissions have contributed to global warming, the carmakers should be held responsible for the past and future costs of fighting this problem.

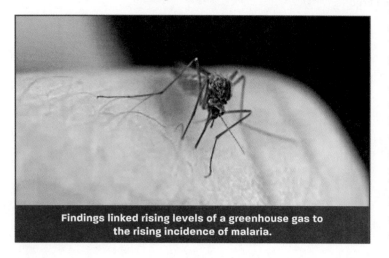
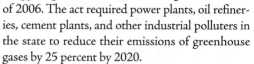

Findings linked rising levels of a greenhouse gas to the rising incidence of malaria.

Climate change and disease. A surface-temperature increase of 0.09°F (0.05°C) between 1950 and 2002 is a likely cause of an increase in malaria-carrying mosquitoes in the East African Highlands, according to an April 2006 report by scientists with the National Center for Ecological Analysis and Synthesis in Santa Barbara, California. The report linked rising levels of a greenhouse gas to the rising incidence of malaria that has been observed since the 1970s in Africa.

This study supported findings that were reported in November 2005 by scientists at the World Health Organization (a United Nations agency) and the University of Wisconsin at Madison. Those findings showed that malaria and many other diseases are likely to increase in some of the world's poorest countries as a result of climate change.

Climate change and crops. Researchers at the University of Illinois at Urbana–Champaign reported in June 2006 that food crops produced dramatically smaller yields when grown in the higher atmospheric concentrations of carbon dioxide and ozone that are projected for 2050. Ozone is a form of oxygen that, in the lower atmosphere, forms part of smog. The scientists found the reduced productivity in maize (corn), rice, sorghum, soybeans, and wheat—contradicting previous studies that had found increased carbon dioxide levels to be beneficial for plant growth. The Illinois researchers warned that without changes in food production strategies, global food supplies may decline during the next 50 to 60 years.

Slow ozone layer recovery. The protective ozone layer above Antarctica will take about 20 years longer to fully recover than previously estimated, according to a June 2006 report by researchers at the National Aeronautics and Space Administration, the National Oceanic and Atmospheric Administration, and the National Center for Atmospheric Research. The high-altitude ozone layer blocks harmful ultraviolet rays from the sun. Every spring, an "ozone hole" develops in this layer as a result of temperature-related chemical reactions involving compounds called chlorofluorocarbons (CFCs). CFCs were widely used in many products until they were banned by most countries in the 1990s.

Although CFCs are banned, they remain in the atmosphere, where they attack the ozone layer. Previous studies had found that these compounds will diminish over time, with the ozone hole filling in by

Nesting Laysan albatrosses

2050. The new study examined the problem using a more advanced *computer model* (simulation) in which the latest measurements of CFC levels were plugged in. Future projections of these levels led the scientists to conclude that the ozone hole will not be filled in until 2068.

Mail delivery gets greener. The United States Postal Service (USPS) put its first hybrid mail delivery van into test service in May 2006 in the Boston, Massachusetts, area. The vehicle was a converted mail van that was altered to use a combination of gasoline and electric power for propulsion. Hybrid vehicles emit fewer air pollutants than vehicles that run only on gasoline. The USPS planned to monitor the environmental and economic performance of the hybrid before putting more such vehicles into production.

The hybrid van was the latest addition to the postal service's fleet of 30,000 alternative fuel vehicles. Other vehicles in this fleet use compressed natural gas, propane, ethanol, or biodiesel as alternatives to gasoline.

Pesticides in U.S. streams. A March report by the U.S. Geological Survey (USGS) concluded that most streams in the United States carry traces of pesticides. The USGS scientists tested water samples from 51 large streams and *aquifers* (ground water supplies) throughout the United States. The researchers found one or more pesticide chemicals in all the surface water and in 33 percent of the ground water, as well as in 96 percent of the fish tested from the streams.

More than 80 percent of sampled urban streams and more than 50 percent of agricultural streams contained pesticides at concentrations that pose a hazard to aquatic life and to animals that eat aquatic life. However, the pesticides were seldom at concentrations high enough to harm people. Fewer than 10 percent of the streams and less than 1 percent of the ground-water supplies had pesticide concentrations above U.S. drinking water standards.

Largest marine reserve. In June, U.S. President George W. Bush created the world's largest marine reserve when he designated a chain of small Hawaiian islands and surrounding waters and coral reefs as a national monument. The chain stretches for more than 1,200 miles (1,900 kilometers), and the entire protected area covers 140,000 square miles (362,600 square kilometers)—nearly the size of California.

The Northwestern Hawaiian Islands Marine National Monument is made up of a variety of reefs, *atolls* (circular formations of coral), *sea-mounts* (volcanoes on the sea floor), and *shoals* (shallow parts of the sea). It includes habitat that is home to more than 7,000 species, including Hawaiian monk seals, breeding seabirds, and endangered green sea turtles.

The designation of the area as a national monument resulted in strict new conservation rules. These rules included a phase-out of all commercial and recreational fishing by 2011 and bans on the removal of corals and the mining of minerals and petroleum.

Species extinction update. According to a May 2006 report by the World Conservation Union (IUCN), 16,199 species of plants and animals are threatened with extinction. The 2006 Red List by the IUCN, an international conservation organization based in Gland, Switzerland, includes one-third of the world's amphibian species, one-fourth of all species of mammals and *coniferous* (cone-bearing) trees, and one-eighth of bird species. Habitat destruction is the main reason behind the population declines of most species. Well-known species on the 2006 Red List included hippopotamuses, desert gazelles, ocean sharks, and stingrays.

The IUCN blamed climate change for the decline of polar bears, which are highly adapted for life in the Arctic environment. Polar bears depend on Arctic ice floes as platforms for hunting seals. As the Arctic warms, some scientists project that summer sea ice will decrease by 50 percent by 2040. As ice floes become rarer, polar bear numbers might decrease by more than 30 percent over this time.

State Government (2003)

Worldwide attention focused on the historic 2003 California recall election that ousted the Democratic governor and replaced him with a motion-picture star. Two of the three other states that chose governors in off-season elections in 2003 also selected Republicans. According to political experts, California voters were upset over the Democratic governor's ineffectiveness in the face of an enormous budget deficit. Nevertheless, the leaders of most other states were besieged by fiscal woes with less drastic results.

California recall. The people of California on October 7 voted to remove from office Governor Gray Davis, a Democrat in the first year of his second term, and replace him with film actor Arnold Schwarzenegger, a Republican. More than 1 million Californians had signed recall petitions, paving the way for the election. Voters were asked two questions on the ballot: whether Davis should be recalled, and if so, who would be his successor.

Schwarzenegger defeated 134 other candidates crowding the ballot, including California Lieutenant Governor Cruz Bustamante, a Democrat who, political experts said, had failed to ignite the Hispanic vote in the state.

Schwarzenegger took the oath of office on November 17. He promised to reverse a car-tax increase that had been sponsored by Davis and passed by the California state legislature.

Schwarzenegger, an immigrant from Austria, had parlayed success as a body builder in the 1970s into fame as an action-adventure actor. He was married to Maria Shriver. Shriver, a Democrat, was an NBC news reporter and the niece of former U.S. President John F. Kennedy.

The California recall election was just the second in history among the 18 states that permit them. The only other occurred in North Dakota in 1921, when voters recalled Governor Lynn Frazier.

Elections and transitions. Republicans held 28 of the 50 governor offices in the United States following their victory in California and two wins in Kentucky and Mississippi during elections held on November 4, 2003.

In Mississippi, Republican Haley Barbour, a former chairman of the Republican National Committee and Washington, D.C., lobbyist, defeated incumbent Democratic Governor Ronnie Musgrove, to become the state's second Republican governor since *Reconstruction* (the period following the Civil War [1861–1865]).

In Kentucky, U.S. Representative Ernie Fletcher (R., Kentucky) easily defeated the state's attorney general, Ben Chandler, a Democrat and the grandson of former governor and baseball commissioner A. B. "Happy" Chandler. Fletcher became the first Republican to win the governorship since 1967. His victory ended the longest control of the governor's office by one party in the state's history.

Prior to the 2003 election, Kentucky Governor Paul Patton, a Democrat who was barred by term limits from seeking reelection, had admitted to an extramarital affair. On November 16, Patton settled ethics charges in which he acknowledged two instances of using his power and influence to benefit the woman with whom he had a relationship. Patton admitted to the charges before the Executive Branch Ethics Commission. He agreed to pay a $5,000 fine and admitted to unknowingly violating portions of the state ethics law.

In a runoff election on November 15, Louisiana gained its first female governor when Lieutenant Governor Kathleen Babineaux Blanco, a Democrat, captured the office held by Republican Governor Mike Foster, who was prevented from running for reelection by term limits. Blanco defeated Bobby Jindal, a Republican whose parents immigrated to the United States from India. Jindal had held various political positions under Foster and U.S. President George W. Bush.

New governors also took office in Indiana and Utah in 2003. Indiana Lieutenant Governor Joe Kernan succeeded Governor Frank O'Bannon, who died on September 13. Both were Democrats. Utah Governor Mike Leavitt, a Republican, resigned on November 5 to become administrator of the U.S. Environmental Protection Agency. Lieutenant Governor Olene S. Walker, a Republican, was sworn in as Utah's first female governor.

Legislative elections. Democratic candidates fared better in the few legislative elections on November 4, gaining control of the New Jersey Senate and widening their margin in the Assembly. The party also kept their majority in the Mississippi legislature. Republicans retained their majorities in the Virginia House and Senate.

In ballot referenda, Maine voters rejected the proposed construction of a large casino but approved slot machines at horse racing tracks. On September 9, Alabama voters soundly defeated Governor Bob Riley's $1.2-billion tax package, designed to fund schools and college scholarships.

Former Governor Gray Davis applauds as Arnold Schwarzenegger is sworn in.

State budgets. Most states faced another year of budget problems in 2003, as state lawmakers and governors cut programs, including higher education and social services, more often than they raised taxes. That finding was reported in July by the National Conference of State Legislatures (NCSL), a nonprofit organization headquartered in Denver, Colorado. The NCSL report revealed that of 43 surveyed states, 31 states cut programs and 17 states raised taxes. Some states used a combination of measures.

State legislatures were forced to employ a variety of measures to deal with their fiscal shortfalls. The state legislature in Illinois raised taxes on riverboat casinos and liquor license fees to generate approximately $207 million. In Connecticut, the state legislature passed its budget 31 days past its June 30 deadline and balanced it by cutting spending on social services and raising taxes.

Some economists predicted in late 2003 that the state fiscal crises would be nearing an end. With the exception of a $38-billion shortfall in California, state and local governments had nearly erased spending deficits in the fiscal quarter ending September 30, according to a study by the U.S. Department of Commerce's Bureau of Economic Analysis.

Education. President Bush announced on June 10 that all state legislatures had approved plans to meet requirements of the federal No Child Left Behind program. Sponsors of the legislation, which went into effect in 2002, envisioned all children being proficient at reading and math within 12 years.

By December 2003, at least 19 states required high school seniors to take exit exams to graduate. School districts had denied thousands of students diplomas as a result of failing the exams, according to a report released in October by the Center on Education Policy, a Washington, D.C.-based organization that advocates for public education.

Death row decision. Illinois Governor George Ryan commuted the death sentences of 167 inmates two days before his term expired in January. The decision affected 156 inmates on death row in Illinois and 11 other inmates who were sentenced to death but were awaiting resentencing or trials in other cases. Ryan, a Republican who did not seek reelection in 2002, said the state's death penalty process was "arbitrary and capricious." Rod Blagojevich, a Democrat who succeeded Ryan, announced in November 2003 that he would continue the hold on executions.

Ryan charged. Federal authorities indicted Ryan on December 17 on multiple counts of racketeering conspiracy, mail fraud, making false statements, and income tax violations while he was Illinois secretary of state in the 1990s and governor between 1999 and 2003.

Redistricting. The Texas legislature in October 2003 approved a congressional redistricting map, which Democrats argued favored Republicans. Democrats held a 17 to 15 majority in the state's congressional delegation, but Republicans held a majority in the state legislature, giving them the

power to redraw congressional districts. More than 50 Democrats from the state House of Representatives twice had fled Texas in 2003 to prevent a quorum in the state legislature in order to avoid a vote on the measure passed in October.

The 2001 Energy Crunch: Crisis or Wake-up Call?

Blackouts in California and volatile natural gas and oil prices in 2001 alarmed consumers and triggered chaos in U.S. energy industries.

—by James Tanner

California's power industry slid into chaos. The wholesale price of electricity jumped by more than 1,000 percent between January 2000 and January 2001. In March 2001, the state's two main utility companies ordered rolling blackouts that shut down industries and left millions of people without electricity in areas stretching from San Francisco to Los Angeles. One of the state's two largest electric utility companies declared bankruptcy, and the California Public Utilities Commission passed the largest rate hike in California history, boosting the price the public paid for electricity by up to 46 percent.

Energy problems spread beyond California's borders as the price of natural gas and gasoline increased dramatically across the nation. Natural gas—the source of heat in most houses in the United States—nearly doubled in price between January 2000 and June 2001. In spring 2001, U.S. gasoline prices jumped from an average of about $1.40 a gallon to about $1.60 a gallon. In parts of the Midwest, including Chicago, a gallon of regular unleaded gasoline rose to at least $2.

Alarmed by the economic dangers posed for the United States by surging fuel and electricity costs, the administration of President George W. Bush launched a new national energy strategy in May 2001. Noting that the nation faced the most serious energy problems since the energy shocks of the 1970s, the Bush administration proposed a multifaceted energy plan. The plan suggested reducing government regulations; encouraging the production of oil, gas, and nuclear power; introducing tax incentives to both boost coal output and promote conservation; and allowing oil companies to drill in a portion of the Arctic National Wildlife Refuge in Alaska.

Before Congress could act on the Bush plan, however, demand for energy began to decline as the U.S.

San Francisco residents reading the paper by candlelight during a 2001 rolling blackout

economy slowed down. The high fuel costs that some economists blamed for the slowdown also declined. By late June 2001, the price of natural gas had dropped by almost two-thirds, from nearly $10 per thousand cubic feet (28.3 cubic meters) to $3 per thousand cubic feet. Gasoline prices settled down to an average of less than $1.50 a gallon, and electricity prices in the western United States fell to the lowest level in more than a year. California officials actually boasted of a surprising, if temporary, surplus of power. Was the crisis over, as some skeptics claimed? Or was it just beginning, as the authors of the Bush energy program suggested?

The latest energy shock, whether short-lived or just beginning, raised troubling questions: Did the nation have a sufficient number of power plants to generate the electricity needed in California and elsewhere once the economy rebounds and demand for electricity accelerates again? Was there enough natural gas—the preferred fuel for most new electric power plants—to keep power facilities running and still meet other energy requirements? Would the worldwide production of oil keep up with demand if consumption continued to climb as it had in recent years?

Forces affecting the energy market. The 2000–2001 energy shock, like the energy crises of the 1970s, was the result of a number of complex factors, including a sharp increase in the demand for electricity. The growing use of computers and the popularity of the Internet—along with the electronic technology needed to feed its popularity—was seen as driving the energy-use increase in the 1990s. However, demand for electricity was on the rise even before the era of the desktop computer. Annual consumption of electricity in the United States stood at 1 trillion kilowatt-hours, and a kilowatt-hour is the work done by one kilowatt in an hour, in 1965. (One kilowatt is 1,000 watts.) By 1980 annual use had surpassed 2 trillion kilowatt-hours. It climbed to 3 trillion kilowatt-hours by the mid-1990s. In 2000, annual demand for electric power topped 3.6 trillion kilowatt-hours a year. (It takes 1 kilowatt-hour of electric energy to keep a 100-watt light bulb burning for 10 hours.)

The U.S. electric power industry did not keep up with consumer demand by building a sufficient number of new power plants during this period. There were two primary reasons: first, plants are expensive to build; second, they are unpopular with neighbors, primarily because they can be a source of

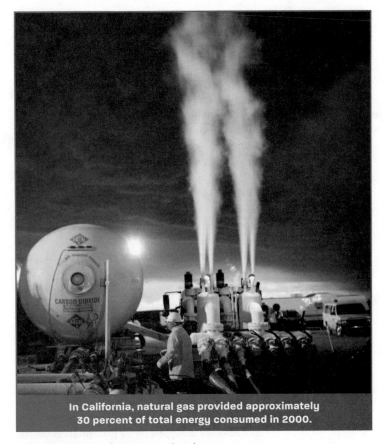

In California, natural gas provided approximately 30 percent of total energy consumed in 2000.

pollution and are often perceived as dangerous.

Coal-fired power plants. In 2001, 52 percent of all U.S. power plants generated electricity by burning coal, which is plentiful and cheap but dirty. Federal law prohibits the burning of medium- or high-sulfur coals to generate electricity in power plants built after 1971, unless the plants are equipped with scrubbers. These are devices that absorb sulfur dioxide fumes as they pass through the plant's smokestacks. The expense of installing scrubbers and other so-called "clean-coal" technology, coupled with widespread opposition to the burning of coal from environmental groups, discouraged utility companies from constructing new plants that used coal to produce electricity.

Coal is an abundant source of energy. The Energy Information Administration (EIA) at the U.S. Department of Energy estimates that U.S. coal reserves will last more than 250 years at current levels of production. However, coal is an unpopular source of energy because of pollution problems. EIA officials projected that the percentage of electricity generated from the burning of coal will decline to 44 percent by 2020.

Nuclear power plants. Nuclear power plants are even less popular with the public than coal-burning plants because of the risk of radioactivity being released as the result of an accident. A potentially devastating accident occurred in 1979, when mechanical and human failures resulted in the destruction of a nuclear reactor core at the Three Mile Island nuclear power plant in Pennsylvania. Although scientists and technicians prevented large amounts of radioactivity from being released, no nuclear power facilities have been built in the United States since the accident. The 104 nuclear power plants that remained in operation in the United States after the accident generated 20 percent of the nation's electricity in 2000.

The growing demand for natural gas. Meanwhile, natural gas used to generate electricity gained in popularity during the 1990s. It burned cleaner than either coal or oil and was considered by many to be safer than nuclear power. By 2000, natural gas generated 16 percent of all electricity in the United States. In California, the percentage was even higher. Three of the state's five largest power plants were gas-fired.

Between 1990 and 2000, total U.S. demand for natural gas for home heating, electricity generation, and all other uses grew by 22 percent. In 2000, the country consumed 22.8 trillion cubic feet of natural gas—nearly 25 percent of the nation's total energy consumption. In California, natural gas provided approximately 30 percent of the total amount of energy consumed in 2000. According to the EIA, U.S. natural gas reserves—at current levels of production and consumption—will last only about 66 years. However, the EIA also projected that natural

gas consumption will continue to rise and will likely be used to generate as much as 36 percent of all U.S. electricity by 2020.

Between 1991 and 2000, a period when demand for natural gas grew by nearly 20 percent, natural gas production in the United States increased only slightly, by less than 300 billion cubic feet annually. According to industry officials, the price of natural gas was low during much of the 1990s, limiting the profits earned by natural gas producers. To compensate, the natural gas companies cut costs by decreasing investments in exploration and production by as much as 50 percent. With few new sources, by 2000, demand for natural gas had overwhelmed supply. For a while, increasing imports from Canada and withdrawing natural gas from storage helped meet demand, and prices remained stable. However, colder-than-normal weather during the winter of 2000–2001 greatly reduced inventories, driving up prices. In California, the state in which electrical generation was most dependent on natural gas, demand exceeded the capacity of the pipelines that transported gas into the state. This sent natural gas prices sharply higher, driving up the wholesale price of electricity in California and home-heating costs across much of the country.

The California energy crisis. An insufficient number of generating facilities and high natural gas prices were responsible for only a portion of California's energy problems in 2001. California utilities purchased electricity from companies in the Pacific Northwest, where electricity generated by hydroelectric plants is generally cheap and plentiful. (A hydroelectric plant uses water that is stored in a reservoir behind a dam and converts the energy of falling water into electric energy.) However, a drought in the Pacific Northwest in 2000 and 2001 resulted in low water levels in reservoirs. The water shortages severely cut the amount of power that could be generated in the region's hydroelectric plants, putting even more pressure on California's natural gas-fired power plants.

California's energy crisis also was driven by a factor that had nothing to do with supply and demand. In 1996, the California legislature deregulated the state's electric utilities with the idea that increased competition would drive down price. (Traditionally, electric utilities in the United States operated as regional monopolies overseen by a state board, which regulated retail prices and company profits.) After deregulation, a number of California's utility

Growing demand for fuel led to rising prices at the pump.

companies sold off their power plants and switched from generating electricity to distributing electricity. The utility companies bought electricity from electric power producing companies and then sold and distributed it to their electricity customers over transmission lines.

Critics of California's deregulation legislation pointed out that the law required utilities to buy power on the open market at market prices but barred the utilities from passing increases on to customers until 2002. When demand for electricity exceeded supply in 2000 and 2001, the price of electric power went higher and higher. The utilities soon ran out of money. When the corporations that now owned the generating plants refused to sell the utility companies electricity on credit, the utility companies were forced to institute rolling blackouts.

Factors that drive the price of oil.
While California had its hands full with electricity problems, a crisis was brewing in the oil industry that sharply pushed up the price of gasoline in the United States. Gasoline, other fuels, and even plastics are made from crude oil, which is pumped out of the ground and shipped to refineries for processing. The nationwide jump in the price of gasoline in early 2001 involved three interrelated factors—the growing demand for the fuel in the United States; the worldwide supply of oil in relation to demand; and the influence of the Organization of Petroleum Exporting Countries (OPEC), an association of 11 oil-producing nations (Algeria, Indonesia, Iran, Iraq, Kuwait, Libya, Nigeria, Qatar, Saudi Arabia, United Arab Emirates, and Venezuela).

World demand for oil grew at rates of 1 percent to 2 percent annually during the 1990s, reaching 75.5 million barrels a day in 2000. Despite the global economic slowdown, demand continued to climb to 76 million barrels a day in 2001. These record levels of consumption strained the capacity of oil fields and refineries alike.

In 2001, OPEC produced nearly 40 percent of the world's oil. Holding nearly three-fourths of the world's known reserves, the OPEC nations exercise a great deal of power over the world's petroleum supplies. OPEC was founded in 1960 to wrest control of oil prices from U.S. and European oil companies. In the 1970s, many of the OPEC nations pushed the oil companies out of their countries by nationalizing oil operations within their borders. Production surged to a peak of more than 30 million barrels a day as OPEC gained a monopoly over

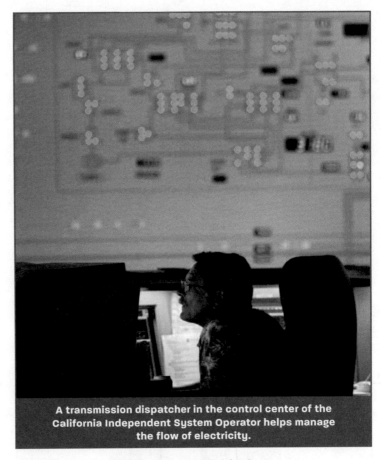

A transmission dispatcher in the control center of the California Independent System Operator helps manage the flow of electricity.

oil markets. In fact, OPEC is often blamed for the energy crisis that followed, but an Arab oil embargo (restriction on commerce) that began in 1973, not OPEC, triggered the first energy crisis.

Past energy crises. In October 1973, the oil-producing countries of the Middle East and North Africa, including OPEC's seven Arab member nations, halted shipments of crude oil to the United States and other countries that supported Israel, during a conflict between the Arab nations and Israel. The embargo triggered the first energy crisis in the United States. However, OPEC's non-Arab members continued to ship oil. The embargo lasted only until March 1974, but this was long enough for the leaders of oil-consuming nations to panic. Western traders and refiners bid up the price of oil, while their governments rushed to enact rules on energy use.

Of far greater consequence, the Arab oil embargo led to the quadrupling of petroleum prices from $3 a barrel to nearly $12 a barrel between 1973 and 1974. The oil embargo also sparked alarm that the world was running out of oil. Those fears faded after

Arab nations resumed oil shipments to the West. But in 1979, a revolution in Iran brought on the second energy shock of the decade. During the revolution, Iranian oil output—as much as 6 million barrels a day—was no longer available on world oil markets. Other OPEC members, including Saudi Arabia, expanded production to take up the slack. Still, demand was higher than supply, which led oil prices to double between 1978 and 1981 to about $24 a barrel. Some oil industry analysts predicted prices would reach $100 a barrel before 2000. But the response to the crisis actually caused oil prices to drop.

The leap in oil prices sent alarming signals to consumers accustomed to cheap energy. There were efforts to improve energy efficiency of buildings and businesses, houses and appliances, and cars and planes. The search for oil fields outside OPEC accelerated. A pipeline about 800 miles (1,300 kilometers) long was built in Alaska to transport crude oil from the giant Prudhoe Bay field, which was discovered in 1968. New oil fields were developed in

Drilling rig at sunset

the North Sea and other non-OPEC regions. Even war and political turmoil in the Middle East during the 1980s had little lasting effect on oil supplies or prices in the United States.

OPEC's influence faded in the early 1990s, largely because of an oversupply of oil on world markets. In addition, exporters made a big mistake in the late 1990s when they increased oil output further on the eve of an economic crash in Asia, which had been importing increasing volumes of oil. As a result of the over-production, world oil prices fell. In 1998, the price of crude oil dropped to $10 a barrel, its lowest price in 70 years, after adjustments for inflation. OPEC revenues plunged, and many oil companies, suffering from a lack of capital, quit drilling.

At service stations in the United States, gasoline prices dipped below $1 a gallon. Some economists claimed that gasoline had fallen to its lowest level in history, when inflation and federal and state taxes were accounted for. Sports-utility vehicles (SUVs) that could go only a few miles on a gallon of gasoline soared in popularity. Wasteful use of energy, combined with an economic boom in the United States and other nations, and a lackluster search for new oil supplies, set the stage for another energy crisis.

The 2001 energy shock. It began when Mexico, another major oil-producing country, prodded OPEC to restrict output in an effort to push up sagging prices. In the past, OPEC had tried to restrict oil output but without much success. Individual OPEC countries always restored production output. This time, to the surprise of analysts, OPEC nations set restricted output quotas and stuck to them. The strategy proved successful, leading to a 1999 increase in crude oil prices that accelerated in 2000. The strategy also led to talk of possible oil shortages. Worried that the high prices would reduce oil demand again, OPEC backed off and began increasing output. Nevertheless, the price of crude oil surged beyond $35 a barrel late in the year. By 2001, with the growth in world oil demand showing signs of slowing, OPEC again reversed itself. It cut production several times to maintain a target price of $25 a barrel. While some analysts were skeptical that OPEC could manage world oil markets for long, oil exporters clearly intended to try, and few analysts could foresee oil prices ever dropping back to $10 a barrel.

U.S. dependence on foreign oil. Americans are OPEC's best customers. With 4.5 percent of the world's population, the United States in 2001 consumed one-fourth of the world's oil output, close to 20 million barrels a day. Although Americans complained about high pump prices in the spring of 2001, U.S. motorists burned an average of 8.4 million barrels of oil a day in the first five months of the year—nearly 200,000 barrels a day more than in the first five months of 2000.

Despite Americans' rate of usage, industry analysts believed the world had enough oil to meet the fuel needs of the United States and other nations for 30 to 40 years at current consumption rates even if no new oil fields were found. Experts estimated that the world's proven reserves of petroleum exceed 1 trillion barrels. Proven reserves consist of oil that oil companies can economically recover from known underground deposits with current technology at current prices. According to EIA estimates of recoverable reserves of oil, there is possibly enough petroleum within the United States to provide for current rates of production for 77 years.

In the United States, however, the combination of rising oil demand and falling production has resulted in increased dependence on imported oil. Between 1918 and 1999, the United States produced 180 billion barrels of crude oil, more than any other country. Domestic crude oil production peaked in 1970 at 9.6 million barrels a day. Except for brief periods, domestic production has been on a decline since, mainly because many U.S. fields are exhausted. While the discovery of oil by companies drilling in the deepwater region of the Gulf of Mexico have helped to offset declines in other oil fields, domestic oil production in 2001 averaged only 5.9 million barrels a day, significantly less than demand.

In 1973, the United States consumed an average of 17.3 million barrels of oil a day, nearly 40 percent of which was imported. In 2000, the United States consumed 19.5 million barrels of oil a day, 54 percent of which was imported, according to the U.S. Department of Energy. In addition, the United States does not have enough refining capacity to process all of the petroleum products it uses and, therefore, must import gasoline and other fuels that are refined from oil.

Lessons of the 2001 oil shock. A number of lessons can be drawn from the 2001 energy shock, regardless of whether it was short-lived or the tip of an iceberg. First, say experts, the existing power grids (a complex network of power distribution lines that provide electricity to businesses and homes) in the United States are inadequate, antiquated, and filled with bottlenecks. New power plants need to be built and the power grids need to be modernized and expanded. Construction of several new power plants began in 2001. Whether these would be completed in time to supply the nation's power needs during the next period of economic expansion depended on how quickly the U.S. economy recovers from a slowdown that began in 2000. Also, California's electricity crisis highlighted possible dangers in the hasty deregulation of an industry as vital as electricity, according to some economists and political observers. In 2001, 24 of the 50 states were in the process of deregulating public utilities.

Second, experts agree that the United States needs to become less dependent on imported oil. In 2001, the U.S. continued to import more than one-half of all the oil consumed. Much of that oil was imported from OPEC's Arab nations. This source could dry up quickly if renewed conflict in the Middle East were to alter economic and diplomatic ties in the region. While the United States still has large reserves of oil, it could take months if not years to make those reserves fully operational.

Another lesson learned, according to many experts, is that U.S. natural gas and oil companies need to increase domestic drilling. The high oil and natural gas prices encouraged companies to increase drilling. In June 2001, there were 1,270 rotary rigs drilling in the United States, compared with 878 rotary rigs in June 2000.

Finally, many experts believed that U.S. consumers needed a renewed sense of conservation. Unplugging appliances, turning off lights, putting on a sweater when it's chilly rather than bumping up the heat, and abandoning gasoline guzzling SUVs can all contribute to lowering demand for energy. A new national energy policy that stressed conservation and the development of new energy sources, as well as the development of existing resources, could be an important step toward guarding the national interest against future energy shocks.

American Revolution

The American Revolution led to the birth of a new nation—the United States. The revolution caused a military conflict called the Revolutionary War in America. The war was fought between Britain and the 13 colonies of North America from 1775 to 1783. Tension between Britain and the Colonies had been increasing for more than 10 years due to laws being passed by the British government which increased Britain's control over the colonies as well as tax laws directed at the colonies. On April 19, 1775, American patriots and British solders fought at Lexington and Concord in Massachusetts. The American Colonies then formed the Continental Congress and appointed George Washington as commander in chief of the Continental Army. On July 4, 1776, the Congress adopted the Declaration of Independence, declaring their freedom from British rule. After eight years of revolution, Britain finally recognized the independence of the United States by signing the Treaty of Paris on September 3, 1783.

HOT topics

Minutemen. Minutemen were a group of young men from the Massachusetts militia who were well-trained and ready to fight the British on a minute's notice. The story of a midnight ride of one minuteman, Paul Revere, is well-known in American history. Because of a midnight warning by him and two other riders to other minutemen and patriot leaders, minutemen were waiting for British soldiers when they arrived in Lexington and Concord.

HOT topics

Taxation Without Representation. The colonists were angry that Britain was taxing them. They believed that the right of taxation belonged only to the people and their elected representatives. They argued that the British Parliament had no right to tax the colonies because the colonies did not have any representatives in Parliament. The introduction of the following taxation acts eventually led to the American Revolution: the Quartering and Stamp Acts, the Townshend Acts, the Tea Act, and the Intolerable Acts.

The Battle of Bunker Hill. The first major battle of the American Revolution was the Battle of Bunker Hill. It was the bloodiest battle of the entire war. The battle was actually fought on Breed's Hill, a hill that was closer to the city of Boston than Bunker Hill. American patriots managed to drive the British back from the hill twice before they ran out of ammunition and were driven from the hill by British bayonets. About 400 Americans and more than 1,000 British soldiers were killed or wounded during the battle.

TRUE or FALSE?

Benedict Arnold, the most famous traitor in United States history, was once a trusted and admired American general.

Bunker Hill Monument

Captain William Smith house in Minute Man National Historical Park

THE BASICS

The American Revolution (1775–1783) led to the birth of a new nation—the United States. The revolution caused a military conflict called the Revolutionary War in America. The war was fought between Britain (now also called the United Kingdom) and its 13 colonies that lay along the Atlantic Ocean in North America. The war began on April 19, 1775, when British soldiers and American patriots clashed at Lexington, Massachusetts, and at nearby Concord. The war lasted eight years. On September 3, 1783, Britain signed the Treaty of Paris, by which it recognized the independence of the United States. The revolution stood as an example to peoples in many lands who later fought to gain their freedom. In 1836, the American author Ralph Waldo Emerson referred to the first shot fired by the patriots at Concord as "the shot heard round the world."

Tension had been building between Britain and the American Colonies for more than 10 years before the Revolutionary War began. Starting in the mid-1760s, the British government passed a series of laws to increase its control over the colonies. Americans had grown used to a large measure of self-government. They strongly resisted the new laws, especially tax laws. Fierce debate developed over the British Parliament's right to tax the colonies without their consent.

The committee appointed by the Continental Congress
to draft the Declaration of Independence

The disobedience of the American Colonies angered the British government. In 1775, Britain's Parliament declared Massachusetts—the site of much protest—to be in rebellion. The British government ordered its troops in Boston to take swift action against the rebels. The Revolutionary War broke out soon afterward.

The American Colonies were unprepared for war. They lacked a central government, an army, and a navy. Delegates from the colonies formed the Continental Congress, which took on the duties of a national government. The Congress directed the war effort and voted to organize an army and a navy. It appointed George Washington commander in chief of the colonial army, called the Continental Army. Washington was a wealthy Virginia landowner and former militia officer. On July 4, 1776— more than a year after the start of the Revolutionary War—the Congress adopted the Declaration of Independence. In that document, the colonies declared their freedom from British rule.

Britain launched a huge land and sea effort to crush the revolution. Britain had a far larger and better-trained army than did the Americans. However, Britain had to transport and supply its army across the Atlantic Ocean and pacify a vast territory. Although the British won many battles, they gained little from their victories. The American patriots were able to form new forces and fight on.

In 1777, the Americans won an important victory at Saratoga, New York. The victory convinced France that the Americans could win the war. As a result, France went to war against Britain, its long-time enemy. France provided the Americans with the money and military equipment they badly needed to fight the war.

In October 1781, a large British force surrendered to Washington at Yorktown, Virginia. That defeat led the British government to begin peace talks with the Americans. The Treaty of Paris formally ended the war in 1783.

This article will trace the background and causes of the American Revolution; the beginning of the Revolutionary War; the conduct of the war, including weapons and tactics and how the war was financed; the war in the North, West, and South; the end of the war; and the results of the revolution.

Background and Causes of the Revolution

Britain's power in North America was at its height in 1763, only 12 years before the Revolutionary War began. Britain had just defeated France in the French and Indian War (1754–1763). The treaty that ended the war gave Britain almost all of France's territory in North America. That territory stretched from the Appalachian Mountains in the east to the Mississippi River and included much of Canada. Most American colonists took pride in being part of the British Empire, which was then the world's most powerful empire.

Yet in 1775, the American Colonies rebelled against British authority. The dramatic turnabout resulted from disagreements over the relationship between Britain and its colonies. Britain expected the colonists to obey the British Parliament "in all cases whatsoever." The colonists, on the other hand, believed that there were limits to Parliament's power. They believed they had certain rights that Britain should respect. Each side refused to yield, which led to a military showdown.

Life in the American Colonies during the 1700s differed in important ways from life in the most advanced European nations. Well-to-do merchants and planters formed a small upper class, or *gentry*, in the seaboard colonies, but they lacked the wealth and power of the English aristocracy. A large middle class consisted mainly of farmers who owned their land, shopkeepers, and craftworkers. Unskilled workers and farmers who rented their land ranked among the poor, or "lower sort." In addition, by the mid-1700s, about 20 percent of the colonists were slaves of African descent. Slaves lived in all the mainland colonies, though they were most numerous in the South.

Farming was by far the main occupation in the American Colonies. It provided a living for nearly 90 percent of the people. Only about 10 percent of the colonists lived in towns or cities. Philadelphia, with about 40,000 people, was the largest American city in 1775. The next largest cities were New York City and Boston.

The opportunity to own land had drawn many settlers to the American Colonies. Owning property gave a person a chance to get ahead. It could also give men the right to vote, though some colonies denied that right to Roman Catholics and Jews. All colonies denied it to blacks and to most women. In each colony, voters elected representatives to a legislature. Colonial legislatures passed laws and could tax the people. However, the governor of a colony could veto any laws passed by the legislature. The king appointed the governor in most colonies.

Britain expected the American Colonies to serve its economic interests, and it regulated colonial trade. In general, the colonists accepted British regulations. For example, they agreed not to manufacture goods that would compete with British products.

British policy changes. Britain had largely neglected the American Colonies while it fought France in a series of wars during the 1700s. But after the French and Indian War ended in 1763, the British government sought to tighten its control over the colonies. The war had drained Britain's treasury and left a huge debt. Most British leaders did not expect the colonists to help pay off the debt. However, Britain planned to station troops in America to defend the colonies' western frontier. It wanted the colonists to help pay for those troops.

Relations between the colonies and the mother country steadily worsened from 1763 to 1775. During that time, Parliament passed a number of laws to increase Britain's income from the colonies. The colonists reacted angrily. They lived far from Britain and had grown increasingly self-reliant. Many Americans believed that the new British policies threatened their freedom. In late 1774, Britain's King George III declared, "The die is now cast, the colonies must either submit or triumph." A few months later, the Revolutionary War broke out.

The Proclamation of 1763. Before the French and Indian War, France had helped prevent colonists from settling on Indian hunting lands west of the Appalachians. But settlers began crossing the frontier soon after Britain defeated France. In the spring of 1763, an Ottawa chief named Pontiac began an uprising in which tribes attacked many western forts the British had taken from the French.

King George III

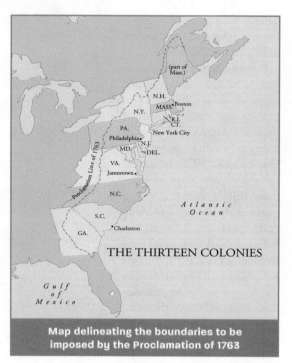

THE THIRTEEN COLONIES

**Map delineating the boundaries to be
imposed by the Proclamation of 1763**

Hundreds of colonists along the western frontier were killed.

Britain feared a long and bloody Indian war, which it could not afford. To prevent future uprisings, King George issued the Proclamation of 1763. The document reserved lands west of the Appalachians for Indians and forbade white settlements there. Britain sent soldiers to guard the frontier and keep settlers out.

The Proclamation of 1763 angered many colonists. Some wealthy Americans hoped to profit from the purchase of Western lands. Poorer colonists saw the lands as an opportunity to escape poverty. Colonists living on the frontier, or the "backcountry," resisted British efforts to enforce the Proclamation of 1763.

The Sugar Act. George Grenville became King George's chief Cabinet minister in 1763. Grenville was determined to increase Britain's income from the American Colonies. At his urging, Parliament passed the Revenue Act of 1764, also known as the Sugar Act. The act placed a threepenny tax on each gallon (3.8 liters) of molasses entering the colonies from ports outside the British Empire. Several Northern colonies had thriving rum industries that depended on imported molasses. Rum distillers angrily protested that the tax would eat up their profits. In 1766, Parliament reduced the tax on molasses to a penny a gallon.

The Quartering and Stamp acts were passed by Parliament in 1765, again with Grenville's support. The laws were intended to make the colonists pay part of the cost of stationing British troops in America. The Quartering Act ordered the colonies to supply the soldiers with living quarters, fuel, candles, and cider or beer. The Stamp Act required the colonists to buy tax stamps for newspapers, playing cards, diplomas, and various legal documents.

Most colonies half-heartedly obeyed the Quartering Act, often providing fewer supplies than requested. But the Stamp Act resulted in riots. Angry colonists refused to allow the tax stamps to be sold. Merchants in port cities agreed not to order British goods until Parliament abolished the act.

In October 1765, delegates from nine colonies met in New York City and prepared a statement protesting the Stamp Act. The objections of that so-called Stamp Act Congress stemmed from the colonists' belief that the right of taxation belonged only to the people and their elected representatives. The delegates argued that Parliament had no power to tax the colonies because the colonies had no representatives in Parliament. The meeting of the Stamp Act Congress was the first united action by the colonies against an unpopular British law.

Parliament repealed the Stamp Act in 1766. But at the same time, it passed the Declaratory Act, which stated that the king and Parliament had full legislative authority over the colonies in all matters.

The Townshend Acts. Many members of the British government disliked giving in to the disobedient colonies over the Stamp Act. They included Chancellor of the Exchequer Charles Townshend, who developed a new plan for raising money from the colonies. Townshend convinced Parliament that the colonists would find a *duty* (tax on imported goods) more agreeable than the Stamp Act. Whereas the Stamp Act had taxed the colonists directly, the government would collect duties only from importers. In 1767, Parliament passed the Townshend Acts. One act placed duties on glass, lead, paint, paper, and tea imported into the colonies. Another act set up a customs agency in Boston to collect the duties efficiently.

The Townshend Acts led to renewed protests in the colonies. The colonists accepted Britain's right to regulate their trade. But they argued that the Townshend duties were taxes in disguise. To protest the duties, Americans stopped buying British goods. In 1770, Parliament withdrew all the Townshend duties except the one on tea. It kept the tea duty to demonstrate its right to tax the colonies.

Protests against what the colonists called "taxation without representation" were especially violent in Boston. In 1768, British officials sent soldiers to police Boston and to protect the city's customs collectors. Nearly 1,000 soldiers entered the city on October 1, and more soon followed. Sending the soldiers made matters worse. On March 5, 1770, soldiers and townspeople clashed in a street fight. During the fight, frightened British soldiers fired into a crowd of rioters. Five men died, including a black patriot named Crispus Attucks. Patriots called the killing of the five colonists "the Boston Massacre" and spread news of it to turn public opinion in America against Britain.

In 1772, Boston political leaders formed the Committee of Correspondence to explain to other communities by letters and other means how British actions threatened American liberties. Other committees of correspondence soon sprang up throughout the colonies. The committees helped unite the colonies in their growing struggle with the British government.

The Tea Act. To avoid paying the Townshend duty on tea, colonial merchants smuggled in tea from the Netherlands. Britain's East India Company had been the chief source of tea for the colonies. The smuggling hurt the company financially, and it asked Parliament for help. In 1773, Parliament passed the Tea Act, which enabled the East India Company to sell its tea below the price of smuggled tea. Lord North, who had become the king's chief minister in 1770, believed that the colonists would buy the cheaper British tea and thereby acknowledge Parliament's right to tax them. In the process, the colonists would lose their argument against taxation without representation.

Samuel Adams, a Boston patriot, led the resistance to the Tea Act. On the evening of December 16, 1773, Bostonians disguised as Indians raided British ships docked in Boston Harbor and dumped their cargoes of tea overboard. The so-called Boston Tea Party enraged King George and Lord North and the king's other ministers. They wanted the Bostonians punished as a warning to all colonists not to challenge British authority.

The Intolerable Acts. Britain responded to the Boston Tea Party in 1774 by passing several laws that became known in America as the Intol-

Engraving titled "Burning the Stamps in New York"

erable Acts. One law closed Boston Harbor and stated that it would reopen only after Bostonians paid for the tea and showed proper respect for British authority. Another law restricted the activities of the Massachusetts legislature and gave added powers to the governor of Massachusetts. Those powers in effect made him a dictator. King George named Lieutenant General Thomas Gage, the commander of British forces in North America, the new governor of Massachusetts. Gage was sent to Boston with troops.

Committees of correspondence throughout the colonies warned citizens that Britain could also disband their legislatures and take away their political rights. Several committees called for a convention of delegates from the colonies to organize resistance to the Intolerable Acts. The convention was later called the Continental Congress.

The First Continental Congress met in Philadelphia from September 5 to October 26, 1774, to protest the Intolerable Acts. Representatives attended from all the colonies except Georgia. The leaders included Samuel Adams and John Adams of Massachusetts and George Washington and Patrick Henry of Virginia. The Congress voted to cut off colonial trade with Britain unless Parliament abolished certain laws and taxes, including the Intolerable Acts. It also approved resolutions advising the colonies to begin training their citizens for war.

None of the delegates to the First Continental Congress called for independence from Britain. Instead, the delegates hoped that the colonies would regain the rights Parliament had taken away. The Congress agreed to hold another Continental Congress in May 1775 if Britain did not change its policies before that time.

The Beginning of the War

Fighting broke out between American patriots and British soldiers in April 1775. The Americans in each colony were defended at first by the members of their citizen army, the *militia*. The militia came out to fight when the British neared their homes. The patriots soon established a regular military force known as the Continental Army. Britain depended chiefly on professional soldiers who had enlisted for long terms. The British soldiers were known as *redcoats* because they wore bright red jackets.

The patriots won several victories in New England, the two Chesapeake colonies of Virginia and Maryland, and the Southern colonies during the early months of the Revolutionary War. As the fighting spread, many Americans became convinced of the need to cut their ties with Britain.

Lexington and Concord. In February 1775, Parliament declared that Massachusetts was in open rebellion. This declaration made it legal for British troops to treat troublesome colonists as rebels and shoot them on sight. The king and his ministers hoped to avoid a war by crushing the disorder in Boston. In April, General Gage received secret orders from the British government to take military action against the Massachusetts troublemakers and arrest their principal leaders.

Boston patriots learned about the secret orders before Gage did, and the leaders of the rebellion fled Boston to avoid arrest. Gage decided to capture or destroy arms and gunpowder stored by the patriots in the town of Concord, near Boston. On the night of April 18, 1775, about 700 British soldiers marched toward Concord. Joseph Warren, a Boston

patriot, discovered that the British were on the march. He sent two couriers, William Dawes and Paul Revere, by separate routes to ride to Concord and warn the people about the approaching redcoats. A third rider, Samuel Prescott, joined them on the road outside Lexington. Only he made it past British patrols to warn the patriots at Concord.

The redcoats reached the town of Lexington, on the way to Concord, near dawn on April 19, 1775. Revere's ride had alerted American volunteer soldiers who were called *minutemen* because they were prepared to take up arms on a minute's notice. About 70 minutemen *mustered* (gathered) on the Lexington village green to watch the redcoats pass. Suddenly, shots were fired. No one knows who fired first. But 8 minutemen fell dead, and 10 more were wounded. One British soldier had been hurt.

The British force continued to Concord, where they searched for hidden arms. One group of redcoats met minutemen at North Bridge, just outside Concord. In a brief clash, three redcoats and two minutemen were killed. The British then turned back to Boston. Along the way, militia fired at them from behind trees and stone fences. British dead and wounded for the day numbered about 250, and American losses came to about 90.

Word spread rapidly that fighting had broken out. Militias throughout New England took up arms and gathered outside Boston. The Americans prepared to pounce on Gage's troops if they marched out of Boston. Three British officers— Major Generals John Burgoyne, Henry Clinton, and William Howe—arrived in Boston with more troops in late May 1775.

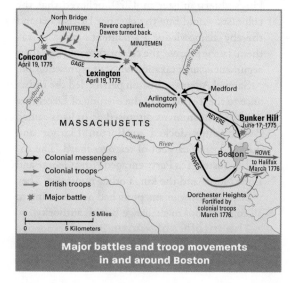

**Major battles and troop movements
in and around Boston**

Bunker Hill. The British and the Americans each hoped to gain an advantage by occupying hills overlooking Boston. The Americans moved first. They dug in on Breed's Hill, close to the city.

On June 17, 1775, British troops led by Howe attacked American positions on Breed's Hill. To save ammunition, American officers ordered the patriots: "Don't fire until you see the whites of their eyes." The Americans drove back two British charges before they ran out of ammunition. During a third charge, British bayonets forced the Americans to flee. The fighting, usually called the Battle of Bunker Hill, was the bloodiest battle of the entire war. More than 1,000 British soldiers and about 400 Americans were killed or wounded.

The Continental Army. The Second Continental Congress began meeting in Philadelphia in May 1775, soon after the battles at Lexington and Concord. Patriot leaders in Massachusetts urged the Congress to take charge of militia units outside Boston and raise an army strong enough to challenge the redcoats. On June 14, the Congress established the Continental Army. The next day, George Washington was made the Army's commander in chief. The Congress named 13 more generals soon afterward. It then had to figure out how to recruit troops, supply an army, and pay for a war.

Washington took command of the military camps near Boston on July 3, 1775. He immediately worked to establish order and discipline in the army. The militia units were poorly trained and lacked weapons and overall organization. Their camps were filthy. Most soldiers had volunteered for service to defend their families and farms. They expected to return home after a few months. Washington issued a flood of orders and dismissed junior officers who failed to enforce them. Soldiers who disobeyed were punished.

The evacuation of Boston. Soon after Washington took charge of the Continental Army, he sought to drive the British from Boston. To accomplish that task, the Americans needed artillery. In May 1775, Colonels Ethan Allen and Benedict Arnold had seized Fort Ticonderoga, a British post in the colony of New York. Shortly afterward, their troops captured another British post at nearby Crown Point. The two victories provided the Americans with much-needed artillery.

In November 1775, Colonel Henry Knox, Washington's chief of artillery, proposed a plan to move the heavy guns by sled from Ticonderoga across the snow-covered Berkshire Mountains to Boston. The guns reached Framingham, near Boston, by late January 1776.

The arrival of the artillery enabled the patriots to fortify a high ground south of Boston known as Dorchester Heights. They completed the work during the night of March 4, 1776. General Howe, who had taken command of the British army several months earlier, realized that his soldiers could not hold Boston with American cannons pointed at them. By March 17, the British troops had boarded ships headed for Nova Scotia, a British colony in Canada. However, the evacuation of British troops from Boston was only a temporary victory for the Americans. Howe and his troops landed at New York City in July.

The invasion of Canada. To prevent British forces from sweeping down from Canada into New York, the Continental Congress ordered an invasion of Canada. Some delegates also hoped that Canada might join the colonies in their rebellion against Britain.

In the fall of 1775, two American expeditions marched northward into Canada. Benedict Arnold led one force along rivers and over rugged terrain toward the city of Quebec. Disease and hunger caused many of his troops to turn back. The other expedition, under Brigadier General Richard Montgomery, headed toward Montreal. Montgomery captured Montreal on November 13. He then joined Arnold outside Quebec.

On December 31, 1775, under cover of a blizzard, the Americans stormed Quebec, but they failed to take the city. Montgomery died in the attack, and Arnold was seriously wounded. Major

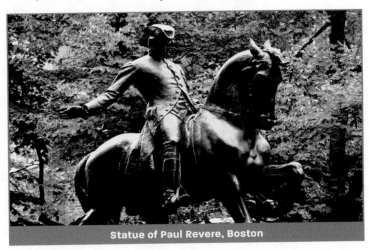

Statue of Paul Revere, Boston

General Guy Carleton, governor of the colony of Quebec, commanded the British forces in Canada. The Americans retreated to New York in the spring, after British reinforcements reached Canada. The invasion of Canada had ended in failure for the patriots.

Fighting in the Chesapeake and Southern colonies. Some planters in the Chesapeake and Southern colonies feared that a rebellion against Britain in the name of liberty might inspire black slaves to rise up against them. For that reason, Britain expected to restore its authority more easily in the Chesapeake and Southern colonies than in the North. However, the patriots had great success in the Chesapeake and South at the start of the Revolutionary War. A few weeks before the battles of Lexington and Concord, Patrick Henry had urged his fellow Virginians to raise a militia and prepare for war. He declared, "I know not what course others may take, but as for me, give me liberty or give me death."

Many of Virginia's wealthiest slaveholders disagreed, urging patience and caution. In November 1775, the British governor of Virginia, Lord Dunmore, offered to free black slaves who took up arms on Britain's side. About 1,000 slaves joined Dunmore. This action angered many conservative slaveholders, who eventually came to support the patriots' military effort. In December, Virginia patriots defeated a force led by Dunmore at Great Bridge, south of Norfolk. Dunmore fled Virginia the following summer.

North Carolina's governor, Josiah Martin, also hoped to crush the rebellious colonists by force. He urged North Carolinians loyal to Britain to join him. More than 1,500 colonists answered Martin's

call and marched toward the coast to join British troops arriving by sea. But on the way, these colonists took a beating from patriot forces at Moore's Creek Bridge, near Wilmington, North Carolina. British troops under General Clinton had sailed southward from Boston. However, they failed to arrive in time to prevent the defeat at Moore's Creek Bridge on February 27, 1776.

The British warships continued on to Charleston, South Carolina, the chief port in the South. They opened fire on a fort outside the city on June 28, 1776. However, Clinton called off the attack later that day, after gunfire from the fort damaged several ships. Clinton soon rejoined British forces in the North.

The Declaration of Independence. When the Second Continental Congress opened in May 1775, few delegates wanted to break ties with the mother country. John Dickinson of Pennsylvania led the group that urged a peaceful settlement with Britain. Dickinson wrote the Olive Branch Petition, which the Congress approved in July 1775. The document declared that the colonists were loyal to the king and urged him to remedy their complaints. However, George III ignored the petition. On August 23, he declared all the colonies to be in rebellion. In December, Parliament passed the Prohibitory Act, which closed all American ports to overseas trade. Those actions convinced many delegates that a peaceful settlement of differences with Britain was impossible.

Support for American independence continued to build early in 1776. In January, the political writer Thomas Paine issued a pamphlet titled *Common Sense.* Paine attacked George III as unjust, and he argued brilliantly for the complete independence of the American Colonies.

In June 1776, Richard Henry Lee of Virginia introduced the resolution in the Congress "That these United Colonies are, and of right ought to be, free and independent States...." The Congress appointed a committee to draft a declaration of independence in case Lee's resolution was adopted. On July 2, the Congress approved Lee's resolution. It adopted the Declaration of Independence on July 4, and the United States of America was born.

Progress of the War

After the Americans declared their independence, they had to win it by force. The task proved difficult, partly because the people never fully

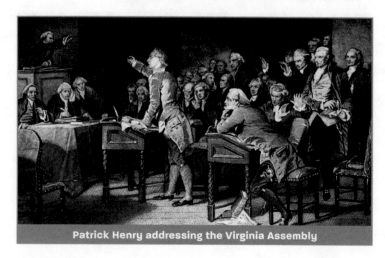

Patrick Henry addressing the Virginia Assembly

united behind the war effort. A large number of colonists remained unconcerned about the outcome of the war and supported neither side. As many as a third of the people sympathized with Britain. They called themselves Loyalists. The patriots called those people Tories, after Britain's Tory Party, which strongly supported the king. Victory in the Revolutionary War depended on the patriots, who made up less than a third of the population.

Although the patriots formed a minority of the colonial population, they had many advantages over the British in the Revolutionary War. They had plenty of troop strength, if they could only persuade citizens to come out and fight. Unlike the British, they did not have to supply their army across an ocean. In addition, the patriots fought on familiar terrain and could retreat out of reach of the British. In time, Britain's chief rivals, France and Spain, joined the war. Their aid enabled the patriots to win independence.

The American patriots also benefited from British blunders. The British expected an easy victory. They thought that the patriots would turn and run at the sight of masses of redcoats. Yet

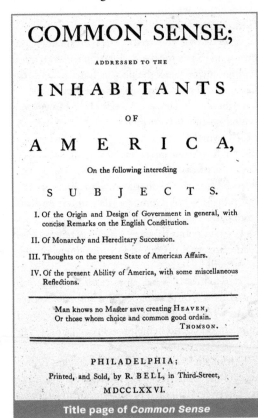

Title page of *Common Sense*

British military leaders were cautious in their battle plans. American military leaders were less experienced than British officers, but they were more willing to take chances. In the long run, daring leadership gave the Americans an advantage.

The fighting forces. The American Colonies entered the Revolutionary War without an army or a navy. Their fighting forces consisted of militia units in the various colonies. The militias were made up of citizen-soldiers from 16 to 60 years old who were ready to defend their homes and families when danger threatened. The colonies could call up militias for periods of service ranging from a few days to a few months.

Britain had an army of well-trained and highly disciplined soldiers. Britain also hired professional German soldiers. Such soldiers were often called Hessians because most of them came from the German state of Hesse-Kassel. American Loyalists, escaped slaves, and Indians also joined British fighting forces during the war. At its peak, the British military force in North America numbered about 50,000.

Washington and other patriot leaders doubted that part-time militias could defeat the British in a long war. Therefore, Washington worked to build an army of disciplined soldiers who had enlisted for several years. However, recruitment for the Continental Army remained a constant problem. Most citizens preferred to serve in local militias and support the Continental Army when a major battle threatened nearby.

Washington rarely commanded as many as 15,000 soldiers at a time, and he frequently commanded far fewer. Soldiers often went without pay, food, and proper clothing because the Continental Congress was so poor and transportation in the colonies was so bad. Yet many poor soldiers stayed in the army because they had been promised free land after the war. They fought as much for economic gain as for political liberty.

In time, most states permitted blacks to serve in the Continental Army. In all, about 5,000 African Americans fought on the patriot side in the war. Many were slaves who had been promised freedom in exchange for military service.

Weapons and tactics. The most important weapons of the war were the flintlock musket, the rifle, and the cannon. The musket discharged a large lead ball and could fire three or four rounds a minute. Rifles had much greater accuracy than

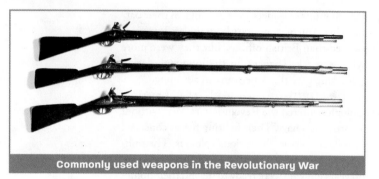

Commonly used weapons in the Revolutionary War

muskets, but they took longer to reload, which made them less efficient in battle. Colonists from the western frontier improved the rifle's value by developing their skill at rapid loading. Cannons hurled shells long distances and blasted soldiers at closer range.

On the battlefield, soldiers lined up shoulder to shoulder, two or three rows deep. Their muskets had little accuracy beyond about 60 yards (55 meters). For that reason, the attackers advanced as far as possible before shooting. After firing several rounds, the two sides closed in for hand-to-hand combat with *bayonets* (knives that fit on the barrel of a gun). The battle ended when one side broke through enemy lines or forced the other side to retreat. In the early years of the war, the Americans had few bayonets, which gave the redcoats an enormous advantage.

Maritime forces. The Congress established the Continental Navy in 1775, but it was small and poorly equipped to challenge Britain's powerful Royal Navy. The British Navy loosely blockaded American ports and supported British military operations along the Atlantic coast. However, the Continental Navy sank or captured many smaller British vessels, especially cargo ships. Privately owned American vessels known as *privateers* also captured enemy cargo ships. The privateers then sold the stolen cargoes and divided the profits among investors, the ship captains, and the crews.

Patriot governments. The Continental Congress provided leadership for the 13 former colonies during most of the war. After the Declaration of Independence, each former colony called itself a state. The Congress drew up a plan called the Articles of Confederation to unify the states under a central government. The Articles left nearly all powers to the states because many delegates distrusted a strong central government. By March 1781, all 13 states had approved the Articles.

Each state formed a government to replace its former British administration. In most states, an elected legislature drafted a written constitution that defined the powers of the government. In 1780, Massachusetts became the last of the states to introduce a new constitution.

Patriot committees in each state stirred support for the war effort. Such committees tormented citizens suspected of sympathizing with Britain. Many Loyalists left the colonies rather than submit to the demands of patriot committees. By the end of the war, as many as 100,000 Loyalists had fled to Canada, England, the Bahamas, and other British territories.

The home front. With husbands, fathers, and brothers away at war, many women assumed new roles at home. They took responsibility for the daily functioning of family farms and businesses. They policed their communities with a watchful eye and took a greater interest in community issues. On a number of occasions, for example, city women rioted to force merchants to lower the price of grain and other items. Women also contributed directly to the war effort. In 1780, Esther De Berdt Reed helped to found the Philadelphia Ladies Association, which raised over $300,000 for the Continental Army.

Financing the war. The Continental Congress had to pay for the Revolutionary War, but it had no power to tax the people. Late in 1775, the Congress began to issue paper currency known as Continental dollars, or Continentals. However, it issued so many Continentals that they became nearly worthless. The Congress received some money from the states, but never enough. Loans and gifts of cash from other nations—especially from France, the Netherlands, and Spain—saved the patriots. The Congress also obtained loans from patriot merchants and other Americans who had cash or goods to spare. Those citizens received certificates that promised full repayment of their loans with interest.

Diplomacy. Vital support for the American cause came from France, Spain, and the Netherlands. Benjamin Franklin represented the Americans in France and helped win French support for the patriots.

Before the Revolutionary War began, French leaders had watched with interest the widening split between Britain and the American Colonies. France still smarted from its defeat by Britain in the French and Indian War. France's foreign minister, the Count de Vergennes, believed that a patriot victory would benefit France by weakening the mighty British Empire. France agreed to aid the patriots secretly. However, France refused to ally itself openly with the Americans before they had proved themselves in battle.

From 1776 to 1778, France gave the American government loans, gifts of money, and weapons. In 1778, treaties of alliance were signed, making France and America "good and faithful" allies. Thereafter, France also provided the patriots with troops and warships. Spain entered the war as an ally of France in 1779. The Netherlands joined the war in 1780.

The War in the North

The outcome of the battles in 1775 convinced the British that defeating the American Colonies required a major military effort and an effective strategy. As a result, Britain sent additional troops and a large naval force to America. The initial British strategy called for isolating and destroying the uprising in the North first. Once New England was knocked out, Britain expected resistance to crumble in the remaining colonies.

Britain nearly conquered the patriots several times during the fighting in the North, which lasted from 1775 to 1778. But British generals failed to carry out their strategy effectively.

The campaign in New York. After the British evacuated Boston in March 1776, General Howe began to plan his return to the American Colonies. In July, he landed on Staten Island in New York Harbor. Howe was joined by General Clinton's troops, following their defeat in South Carolina, and by Hessian soldiers from Europe. Howe commanded a total force of about 43,000 disciplined soldiers and sailors. They faced about 20,000 poorly trained and poorly equipped Americans.

Washington had shifted his forces to New York City after the redcoats withdrew from Boston. He did not expect to hold New York City, but he wanted to make the British fight for it. To defend the city, patriot troops fortified Brooklyn Heights, an area of high ground on the western tip of Long Island.

Howe saw an opportunity to trap patriot troops in Brooklyn. In August 1776, British troops landed on Long Island in front of the American lines.

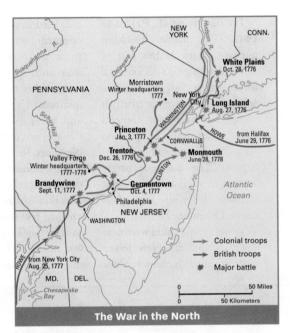

The War in the North

Howe surrounded the patriots' forward positions in the Battle of Long Island on August 27. However, the slow-moving Howe paused before attacking again, enabling the remainder of the Americans to escape. In September, Washington sent Captain Nathan Hale behind British lines to obtain information about British positions on Long Island. The British caught Hale and hanged him for spying. Before being hanged, he reportedly said, "I only regret that I have but one life to lose for my country."

By mid-September 1776, Howe had driven Washington's troops from New York City. Howe slowly pursued the Americans as they retreated toward White Plains, New York, but his hesitation cost the British a chance to crush Washington's army. Another patriot force remained on Manhattan Island to defend Fort Washington. The fort fell to Howe in November, and Britain captured nearly 3,000 Americans. New York City remained in British hands until the war ended.

During the summer and fall of 1776, General Carleton led a British force southward from Canada. British strategy called for Carleton to link up with Howe in the Hudson River Valley, thereby cutting New England off from the rest of the colonies. But Carleton met heavy resistance from patriot forces under Brigadier General Benedict Arnold in a naval battle near Valcour Island on Lake Champlain. In November, Carleton turned back to Canada for the winter.

Trenton and Princeton. The patriot situation appeared dark at the end of 1776. Washington's discouraged forces had withdrawn to New Jersey. In late November, British troops led by Major General Charles Cornwallis poured into New Jersey in pursuit of Washington. The patriots barely escaped to safety by crossing the Delaware River into Pennsylvania on December 7.

Washington's forces were near collapse, and the New Jersey militias failed to come to their aid. Yet Howe again missed an opportunity to destroy the Continental Army. He decided to wait until spring to attack and ordered his troops into winter quarters in Trenton, Princeton, and other New Jersey towns. Clinton was assigned to capture Newport, Rhode Island.

Howe believed he had broken the patriot rebellion, but he was mistaken. Although Washington had few troops, he decided to strike at Trenton. The town was defended by Hessians. On the stormy and bitterly cold night of December 25, 1776, Washington and about 2,400 troops crossed the Delaware River. They landed 9 miles (14 kilometers) north of Trenton and marched through the night. The next morning, they surprised the Hessians and took more than 900 prisoners.

On January 2, 1777, Cornwallis advanced toward Trenton. He planned to attack the Americans the next day. But during the night, Washington's troops silently stole away and marched past Cornwallis's army. The following morning, Washington attacked at Princeton. He won a brilliant victory over redcoats on their way to join Cornwallis. Washington then moved his troops northward to winter headquarters near Morristown, New Jersey. He soon began to rebuild his army.

The victories at Trenton and Princeton revived patriot hopes. The Continental Army had almost been destroyed, but it had kept going and regained most of New Jersey. Despite superior strength, the British had again failed to defeat the rebels.

Brandywine and Germantown. Washington's successful maneuvering at Trenton and Princeton had embarrassed Howe. In the spring of 1777, Howe sought to lure Washington into battle and destroy his army. After failing to draw Washington into battle in New Jersey, Howe set out to take Philadelphia, the patriot capital.

In the summer of 1777, Howe's redcoats sailed from New York City to the top of Chesapeake Bay, about 50 miles (80 kilometers) southwest of Philadelphia. Washington had

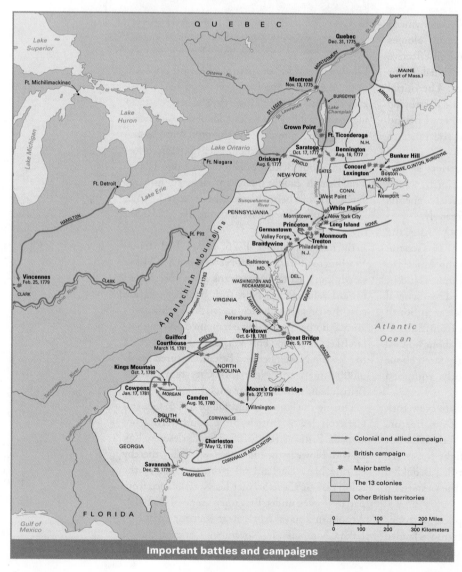

Important battles and campaigns

Burgoyne surrendering to Gates

rebuilt his army during the spring, and he had received weapons from France. He positioned his troops between Howe's forces and Philadelphia.

The opposing armies clashed on September 11, 1777, at Brandywine Creek in southeastern Pennsylvania. One wing of the British army swung around the Americans and approached from behind. The surprised patriots had to retreat. Howe skillfully moved his troops after the Battle of Brandywine and occupied Philadelphia on September 26. The Continental Congress had fled to York, Pennsylvania, where it continued to direct American affairs.

On October 4, 1777, Washington struck back at British forces camping at Germantown, north of Philadelphia. However, his complicated battle plan created confusion. In a heavy fog, patriot forces fired on each other. The Americans again had to retreat.

Victory at Saratoga.
While Howe won victories at Brandywine Creek and Germantown, another British force became stranded near Saratoga, New York. That force had advanced southward from Canada under Lieutenant General John Burgoyne.

Burgoyne had a successful start against the Americans. On July 6, 1777, he recaptured the British post of Fort Ticonderoga in New York from the Americans without a struggle. A second British expedition, led by Lieutenant Colonel Barry St. Leger, marched up the Mohawk River Valley to meet Burgoyne. In August, St. Leger ambushed militias outside Oriskany, New York. In the bloody Battle of Oriskany, the British beat back patriot forces. General Arnold stopped St. Leger soon afterward. By then, conditions favored the patriots.

As Burgoyne advanced southward, patriot forces destroyed bridges and cut down trees to block his path. American rifles fired on the British from the woods, and Burgoyne ran short of food and other supplies. In August 1777, the Congress appointed Major General Horatio Gates to command the Northern Department of the Continental Army. Gates was popular with New England patriots, and they poured out to support him and his soldiers, called Continentals. On August 16, militias overwhelmed two groups of Hessians and Loyalists looking for horses and food in New York, just west of Bennington, Vermont.

Burgoyne trudged slowly through the wilderness along the Hudson River. His slowness gave the Americans time to fortify a wooded area along the Hudson about 40 miles (64 kilometers) north of Albany. On September 19, 1777, British troops attacked the fortifications, but they were met by patriot forces in a clearing on a nearby farm. Nightfall and the bravery of Hessian soldiers saved Burgoyne's troops from destruction in what became known as the First Battle of Freeman's Farm.

Although the patriot forces greatly outnumbered his army, Burgoyne decided not to retreat toward Canada. On October 7, 1777, he attacked again. Arnold's daring leadership won the Second Battle of Freeman's Farm for the patriots. Burgoyne finally began to retreat, but he soon found himself encircled by the Americans at Saratoga. On October 17, Burgoyne surrendered to Gates. The Americans took nearly 6,000 prisoners and large supplies of arms.

The victory at Saratoga marked a turning point in the Revolutionary War. It revealed the failure of British strategy. More importantly, the decisive victory at Saratoga helped convince France that it could safely enter the war on the American side.

Valley Forge.
Washington's army of about 10,000 soldiers spent the winter camped at Valley Forge, about 20 miles (32 kilometers) northwest of Philadelphia. Many of the troops lacked shoes and other clothing. They also suffered from a severe shortage of food. By spring 1778, nearly a fourth of the soldiers had died of malnutrition, exposure to the cold, and such diseases as smallpox and typhoid fever. Many soldiers deserted because of the miserable conditions.

In February 1778, a Prussian officer called Baron Friedrich von Steuben arrived at Valley Forge. He convinced Washington that he could train the Continental Army in European military formations and bayonet charges. By late spring, Steuben had created a disciplined fighting force. The Marquis de Lafayette, a young French soldier, also spent part of the winter at Valley Forge. Fired with enthusiasm for the revolution, Lafayette had joined Washington's staff as a major general without pay.

France's entry into the Revolutionary War in 1778 forced Britain to defend the rest of its empire. The British expected to fight the French in the Caribbean and elsewhere, and so they scattered their military resources. As a result, Britain no longer had a force strong enough to battle the Americans in the North.

In May 1778, General Clinton became commander in chief of British forces in North America. He replaced Howe, who had occupied Philadelphia since September 1777. Clinton received orders to abandon Philadelphia and move his army to New York City. He was also told to send troops to the Caribbean and other areas.

Monmouth. Clinton left Philadelphia on June 18, 1778, and marched across New Jersey toward New York City. The Continental Army followed him. On June 28, the patriots attacked near Monmouth Court House, New Jersey. Clinton soon counterattacked. After early confusion, the Americans held their ground, and the battle ended in a draw. During the night, Clinton's exhausted forces limped off the battleground and continued the march toward New York. The Battle of Monmouth was the last major Revolutionary War battle in the North.

Stalemate in the North. Washington hoped to drive the British from New York City in a joint operation with the French. In July 1778, a fleet under the French admiral Charles Hector, Comte d'Estaing, reached America. But a sandbar at the mouth of New York Harbor blocked the French warships. Later that summer, a combined French and American effort to take Newport, Rhode Island, also failed. In November, d'Estaing sailed south to protect the French West Indies from British attack.

The War in the West

When the Revolutionary War began, about 150,000 Native Americans lived in territory claimed by Britain. East of the Appalachian Mountains, native people lived mainly in separate communities surrounded by English-speaking colonists. The Indians participated in the colonial economy as whalers, agricultural laborers, and craftworkers. West of the Appalachians, they inhabited what was sometimes called "Indian country"—a patchwork of hundreds of villages belonging to a number of distinct Indian nations. Native people in this region lived by a combination of farming and hunting. They traded with American colonists for necessities they could not produce themselves, such as iron utensils, firearms, and ammunition. However, they guarded their land and welcomed British efforts to prevent the colonists from settling west of the Appalachian Mountains.

When the fighting began in 1775, Native Americans faced a difficult choice. Some native communities tried to remain neutral in the conflict. Others, such as the Stockbridge and Mashpee Indians of Massachusetts and the Catawba Indians of South Carolina, contributed soldiers to the American war effort. In the West, however, most native communities allied with the British. They feared that an American victory would threaten their survival. American colonists had crossed the Appalachian Mountains and settled on Indian land, often in violation of British policy. During the Revolutionary War, Indians attacked and tried to disperse these settlements.

Invasion of the Iroquois country. Burgoyne's campaign in the Hudson Valley prompted four of the six Iroquois nations—the Mohawks, Senecas, Cayugas, and Onondagas—to enter the war as British allies. After Burgoyne's surrender at Saratoga in 1777, they continued to harass American settlements on the frontiers of New York and Pennsylvania. In 1779, Washington sought to remove the Iroquois from the war through "the total destruction and devastation of their settlements." Patriot troops commanded by General John Sullivan invaded the Iroquois country in the late summer and fall. They burned 40 villages and destroyed crops ready for harvest. That winter, some Iroquois died of starvation and several thousand fled as refugees to Fort Niagara, a British post on the southwestern shore of Lake Ontario. But Iroquois warriors continued to fight.

The Illinois campaign. Soon after the war began, some Native American war leaders in the West began raiding settlements to try to push settlers out of Kentucky and the Ohio River Valley. Colonel George Rogers Clark of Virginia executed a daring campaign in the Illinois country that disrupted the flow of British supplies to the western tribes and helped to prevent

Native American war leaders from coordinating attacks along the frontier. In the summer of 1778, Clark captured several settlements in what are now southern Illinois and southern Indiana. The British recaptured the settlement at Vincennes in Indiana. Clark and his troops fought their way back to Vincennes across flooded countryside and took its British and Indian defenders by surprise in February 1779.

The War in the South

Britain changed its strategy after France entered the Revolutionary War. Rather than attack in the North, the British concentrated on conquering the colonies from the South. British leaders believed that most Southerners supported the king. Although the British failed to find as much Loyalist support as they expected, they defeated the Americans in several key battles. This strategy forced the patriots onto the defensive in the South.

Savannah and Charleston. The first stage of Britain's Southern strategy called for the capture of a major Southern port, such as Charleston, South Carolina, or Savannah, Georgia. Britain would then use the port as a base for rallying Southern Loyalists and for launching further military campaigns. After Britain's army moved on, the British expected Loyalists to keep control of the conquered areas. Britain assumed it could more easily retake the North after overcoming resistance in the South.

Britain's Southern campaign opened late in 1778. On December 29, a large British force that had sailed from New York City easily captured Savannah. Within a few months, the British controlled all of Georgia.

The Continental Congress named Major General Benjamin Lincoln commander of the Southern Department of the Continental Army. In October 1779, Lincoln and Comte d'Estaing tried to drive the British from Savannah but failed. Afterward, d'Estaing returned to France, and Lincoln retreated to Charleston.

Success at Savannah led the British to invade South Carolina. In February 1780, British forces commanded by General Clinton landed near Charleston. They slowly closed in on the city, trapping its defenders. On May 12, General Lincoln surrendered his force of over 5,000 soldiers—almost the entire Southern army. Clinton placed General Cornwallis in charge of British forces in the South and returned to New York City.

The loss of Charleston and Lincoln's army badly damaged American morale. However, the British victory had an unexpected result. Soon afterward, bands of South Carolina patriots began to roam the countryside, battling Loyalists and attacking British supply lines. The rebels made it risky for Loyalists to support Cornwallis. The chief rebel leaders included Francis Marion, Andrew Pickens, and Thomas Sumter.

Camden. In July 1780, the Continental Congress ordered General Gates, the victor at Saratoga, to form a new Southern army to replace the one lost at Charleston. Gates hastily assembled a force made up largely of untrained militias. The rest of his troops consisted of disciplined Continentals. He rushed to challenge Cornwallis at a British base in Camden, South Carolina.

On August 16, 1780, the armies of Gates and Cornwallis met outside Camden and went into battle. The militias quickly panicked. Most of them turned and ran without firing a shot. The Continentals fought on until heavy casualties forced them to withdraw. The British had defeated a second American army in the South.

The disaster at Camden marked a low point for the patriots. They then received a further blow. In September 1780, the patriots discovered that General Arnold, who commanded a military post at West Point, New York, had joined the British side. The Americans learned of Arnold's treason just in time to stop him from turning West Point over to the enemy.

Kings Mountain. Cornwallis's victory at Camden in August 1780 led him to act more boldly. In September, he charged into North Carolina before the Loyalists had gained firm control of South Carolina. After Cornwallis's departure, rebels in South Carolina terrorized suspected Loyalists. In addition, colonists from the western frontier turned out to fight the British.

In October 1780, the patriots surrounded and captured the left wing of Cornwallis's army, which was made up of Loyalist troops, on Kings Mountain, just inside South Carolina. After the defeat at Kings Mountain, Cornwallis temporarily halted his Southern campaign and retreated into South Carolina.

Cowpens and Guilford Courthouse. In October 1780, the Continental Congress named

Major General Nathanael Greene to replace Gates as commander of the Southern army. Greene was a superb choice because he knew how to accomplish much with few resources. Greene divided his troops into two small armies. He led one army and put Brigadier General Daniel Morgan in charge of the other. Greene hoped to avoid battle with Cornwallis's far stronger force while he rebuilt the Southern army. Greene planned to let the British chase the Americans around the countryside.

Cornwallis set out to trap Morgan's army. Just before the British caught up with him, Morgan prepared for battle in a cattle-grazing area known as the Cowpens in northern South Carolina. On January 17, 1781, Morgan's sharpshooting rifles quickly killed or captured nearly all the attacking redcoats.

The patriot victory at Cowpens enraged Cornwallis, and he pursued Morgan with even greater determination. Greene rushed to join Morgan, hoping to crush Cornwallis's weakened force. On March 15, 1781, a bloody conflict occurred at Guilford Courthouse in North Carolina. Although Cornwallis drove Greene from the battlefield, the British took a battering. Cornwallis halted the chase after the Battle of Guilford Courthouse. He moved to Wilmington, North Carolina, where he gave his exhausted army a brief rest.

Greene challenged British posts in South Carolina during the spring of 1781. The patriots fought several small battles but failed to win clear victories. Yet the fact that a rebel army moved freely about the countryside proved that Britain did not control the Carolinas.

The End of the War

The fighting in the Revolutionary War centered in Virginia during 1781. In January, Benedict Arnold began conducting raids in Virginia for the British, who had made him a brigadier general. Arnold's troops set fire to crops, military supplies, and other patriot property. In response, Washington sent Lafayette with a force of Continentals to rally Virginia's militia and to go after Arnold. However, Lafayette had too few troops to stop Arnold.

Cornwallis rushed into Virginia in the spring of 1781 and made it his new base in the campaign to conquer the South. However, Cornwallis had departed from Britain's Southern strategy by failing to gain control of North and South Carolina before advancing northward. General Clinton

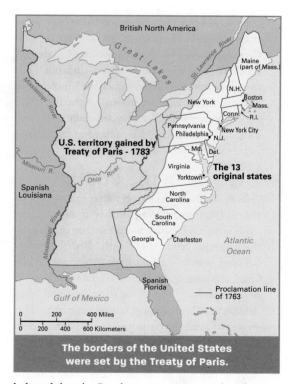

The borders of the United States were set by the Treaty of Paris.

believed that the Southern campaign was therefore doomed. He also feared an American attack on his base at New York City. Clinton ordered Cornwallis to adopt a defensive position along the Virginia coast and to prepare to send his troops north. Cornwallis moved to Yorktown, which lay along Chesapeake Bay.

Surrender at Yorktown. The last major battle of the Revolutionary War was fought at Yorktown. French and American forces cooperated to deliver a crushing defeat to British forces under Cornwallis.

About 5,500 French soldiers had reached America in July 1780. They were led by Lieutenant General Jean Rochambeau. Washington still hoped to drive the British from New York City in a combined operation with the French. In August 1781, however, Washington learned that a large French fleet under Admiral François de Grasse was headed toward Virginia. De Grasse planned to block Chesapeake Bay and prevent Cornwallis from escaping by sea. Washington and Rochambeau rushed their forces southward to trap Cornwallis on land. A British naval force sailed from New York City and battled de Grasse at the mouth of Chesapeake Bay in early September. But after several days, the British ships returned to New York for repairs.

By late September 1781, Cornwallis knew that he was in trouble. A combined French and American force of about 18,000 soldiers and sailors surrounded him at Yorktown. The soldiers slowly and steadily closed in on the trapped British troops. Cornwallis made a desperate attempt to ferry his forces across the York River to safety on the night of October 16, but a storm drove them back. Cornwallis asked for surrender terms the next day.

The surrender at Yorktown took place on October 19, 1781. More than 8,000 soldiers laid down their arms as a British band reportedly played a tune called "The World Turned Upside Down." They represented about a fourth of Britain's military force in America.

Britain's defeat at Yorktown did not end the Revolutionary War. The fighting dragged on in some areas for two more years. However, British leaders feared they might lose other parts of Britain's empire if they continued the war in America. Cornwallis's defeat at Yorktown brought a new group of British ministers to power early in 1782. They began peace talks with the Americans.

The Treaty of Paris. Peace discussions between the Americans and the British opened in Paris in April 1782. Richard Oswald, a wealthy merchant, represented the British government. The statesmen Benjamin Franklin, John Adams, and John Jay negotiated for the United States.

The Congress instructed the American delegates to consult with the French before they took any action. But the Americans disregarded the instructions and concluded a preliminary peace treaty with Britain on November 30, 1782. The Congress approved the preliminary treaty on April 15, 1783, and the warring nations signed it on September 3, 1783. The Americans *ratified* (confirmed) the final treaty on Jan. 14, 1784, and the British did so on April 9.

The Treaty of Paris recognized the independence of the United States and established the new nation's borders. United States territory extended west to the Mississippi River, north to Canada, east to the Atlantic Ocean, and south to about Florida. Britain gave Florida to Spain. The treaty also granted the Americans fishing rights off Newfoundland and Nova Scotia. In addition, it instructed the Congress to recommend that the states restore property taken from Loyalists during the war. The last British soldiers withdrew from New York City in November 1783.

Results of the Revolution

As a result of the American Revolution, the Thirteen Colonies threw off royal rule. In its place, they established governments ruled by law and dedicated to the guarantee of certain basic rights, including life, liberty, and the pursuit of happiness. Admiration for the principles that guided the revolution led peoples elsewhere to demand political reforms. Thomas Paine declared that the American Revolution "contributed more to enlighten the world, and diffuse a spirit of freedom and liberality among mankind, than any human event … that ever preceded it."

War losses. Most historians estimate that about 7,200 Americans were killed in battle during the Revolutionary War. Approximately 8,200 more were wounded. About 10,000 others died in military camps from disease or exposure. Some 8,500 died in prison after being captured by the British. American military deaths from all causes during the war thus numbered about 25,700. In addition, approximately 1,400 soldiers were missing. British military deaths during the war totaled about 10,000.

Many soldiers in the Continental Army came out of the war penniless, as they had received little or no pay while they served. Soldiers who had enlisted for the entire war received certificates for Western land. But many veterans had to sell the certificates because they needed money before Western lands became available. In 1818, Congress agreed to pay pensions to needy veterans.

Costs of the war. The 13 states and the Congress went deeply into debt to finance the Revolutionary War. A new Constitution, approved in 1788, gave Congress the power of taxation. Largely through taxes, Congress paid off much of the war debt by the early 1800s.

The Revolutionary War severely strained Britain's economy. The king and Parliament feared the war might bankrupt the country. But after the war, greatly expanded trade with the United States helped the economy recover. Taxes on trade reduced Britain's debt.

Of all the warring nations, France could least afford its expenditures on the Revolutionary War. By 1788, the country was nearly bankrupt. France's financial troubles helped bring on the French Revolution in 1789.

Historical significance. The American Revolution fundamentally changed life in America. Above all, the revolution opened the doors that shut ordinary citizens out of the political process. Previously, the right to vote had been limited to adult white males who owned property. The property requirement was based on the idea that property owners had the strongest interest in good government and so were best qualified to make decisions. During and after the revolution, requirements for property ownership were reduced. By the 1830s, they were eliminated in nearly all the states. Black men and women of all races, however, did not gain the vote for many years.

Revolutionary ideals and the practical circumstances of the war also made it possible for African Americans, with others, to mount a challenge to slavery. In the Northern states, their efforts succeeded. Between 1777 and 1804, every state north of Maryland adopted a plan to end slavery within its boundaries. Meanwhile, in the South, slaveholders worked to shore up and preserve the institution of slavery. The American Revolution thus helped create a new division between free and slave states. This division laid the foundation for the American Civil War (1861–1865) and, with it, the ultimate end of slavery in the United States.

MLA Citation

"American Revolution."
The Southwestern Advantage Topic Source. Nashville: Southwestern. 2013.

DATA
Major Battles of the American Revolution

Name	Place	Date	American commander	British commander
Bennington *(Vermont)*	New York	August 16, 1777	Stark	Baum, Breymann
Brandywine	Pennsylvania	September 11, 1777	Washington	Howe
Bunker Hill	Massachusetts	June 17, 1775	Prescott	Howe
Camden	South Carolina	August 16, 1780	Gates	Cornwallis
Cowpens	South Carolina	January 17, 1781	Morgan	Tarleton
Freeman's Farm *(1st)*	New York	September 19, 1777	Gates	Burgoyne
Freeman's Farm *(2nd)*	New York	October 7, 1777	Gates	Burgoyne
Germantown	Pennsylvania	October 4, 1777	Washington	Howe
Guilford Courthouse	North Carolina	March 15, 1781	Greene	Cornwallis
Kings Mountain	South Carolina	October 7, 1780	Campbell	Ferguson
Lexington and Concord	Massachusetts	April 19, 1775	Parker and others	Smith
Long Island	New York	August 27, 1776	Washington	Howe
Monmouth	New Jersey	June 28, 1778	Washington	Clinton
Princeton	New Jersey	January 3, 1777	Washington	Cornwallis
Quebec	Quebec	December 31, 1775	Arnold, Montgomery	Carleton
Trenton	New Jersey	December 26, 1776	Washington	Rall
Yorktown	Virginia	October 6–19, 1781	Washington	Cornwallis

DATA

Major Battles of the American Revolution

Name	American dead and wounded[1]	British dead and wounded[1]	Results
Bennington	80	200	British defeat encouraged the patriots in their campaign against Burgoyne.
Brandywine	700	540	An American retreat enabled the British to occupy Philadelphia.
Bunker Hill	400	1,000	The patriots were driven from their positions overlooking Boston.
Camden	1,000	300	The British crushed an American army.
Cowpens	70	330	Patriot victory encouraged Southern militiamen to come out and fight.
Freeman's Farm (First Battle)	300	600	The British advance from Canada was halted.
Freeman's Farm (Second Battle)	150	600	The patriots turned back a second attack.
Germantown	650	550	An American attack turned into a loss and a retreat.
Guilford Courthouse	250	650	The British gave up most of North Carolina.
Kings Mountain	100	300	The British advance into North Carolina was delayed.
Lexington and Concord	90	250	The Revolutionary War in America began
Long Island	250	400	The British forced the Americans from Long Island.
Monmouth	250	400	A patriot attack ended in a draw.
Princeton	50	100	The British withdrew from western New Jersey.
Quebec	100	18	Americans failed to seize the city of Quebec.
Trenton	10	100	The patriots crushed the Hessians in a surprise assault.
Yorktown	100	600	The British surrendered in the war's last major battle.

[1] Approximate totals. The figures listed are a compromise between several conflicting estimates.

DATA

Important Dates in the American Revolution

1775

April 19	Minutemen and redcoats clashed at Lexington and Concord.
June 15	The Congress named George Washington commander in chief of the Continental Army.
June 17	The British drove the Americans from Breed's Hill in the Battle of Bunker Hill.

1776

February 27	The patriots defeated the Loyalists at Moore's Creek Bridge.
March 17	The British evacuated Boston.
July 4	The Declaration of Independence was adopted.
August 27	The redcoats defeated the patriots on Long Island.
September 15	The British occupied New York City.
December 26	Washington mounted a surprise attack on Hessian troops at Trenton.

1777

January 3	Washington gained a victory at Princeton.
August 6	Loyalists and Indians forced the patriots back at Oriskany, but then withdrew.
August 16	The patriots crushed the Hessians near Bennington.
September 11	The British won the Battle of Brandywine.
September 19	Gates's forces checked Burgoyne's army in the First Battle of Freeman's Farm.
September 26	The British occupied Philadelphia.
October 4	Washington's forces met defeat in the Battle of Germantown.
October 7	The patriots defeated the British in the Second Battle of Freeman's Farm.
October 17	Burgoyne surrendered at Saratoga.
December 19	Washington's army retired to winter quarters at Valley Forge.

1778

February 6	The United States and France signed an alliance.
June 28	The Battle of Monmouth ended in a draw.
December 29	The redcoats took Savannah.

1779

February 25	British defenders of Vincennes surrendered to George Rogers Clark.
June 21	Spain declared war on Great Britain.
September 23	John Paul Jones's ship, the *Bonhomme Richard*, captured the British ship Serapis.

1780

May 12	Charleston fell after a British siege.
August 16	The British defeated the Americans at Camden.
October 7	American frontiersmen stormed the Loyalist positions on Kings Mountain.

DATA

Important Dates in the American Revolution

1781

January 17	The patriots won a victory at Cowpens.
March 15	Cornwallis clashed with Greene at Guilford Courthouse.
September 5	A French fleet inflicted great damage on a British naval force at Chesapeake Bay.
October 19	Cornwallis' forces surrendered at Yorktown.

1782

March 20	King George's chief minister, Lord North, resigned.
November 30	The Americans and British signed a preliminary peace treaty in Paris.

1783

April 15	Congress ratified the preliminary peace treaty.
September 3	The United States and Great Britain signed the final peace treaty in Paris.

ADDITIONAL RESOURCES

Books to Read

Fredriksen, John C. *Revolutionary War Almanac*. Facts on File, 2006.

Fremont-Barnes, Gregory, and others, eds. *The Encyclopedia of the American Revolutionary War*. 5 vols. ABC-CLIO, 2006.

Middlekauff, Robert. *The Glorious Cause: The American Revolution, 1763–1789*. Rev. ed. Oxford, 2005.

Savas, Theodore P., and Dameron, J. David. *A Guide to the Battles of the American Revolution*. Savas Beatie, 2006.

Selesky, Harold E., ed. *Encyclopedia of the American Revolution*. 2 vols. 2nd ed. Scribner, 2006.

Web Sites

Liberty! The American Revolution

http://www.pbs.org/ktca/liberty/

Companion site to a PBS documentary.

Spy Letters of the American Revolution

http://www2.si.umich.edu/spies/

The Clements Library at the University of Michigan provides a look at the everyday intelligence operations of both the British and American armies during the Revolutionary War.

Virtual Marching Tour of the American Revolution

http://www.ushistory.org/march/

The story of the Revolutionary War from the Independence Hall Association, a nonprofit organization.

American Civil War

The American Civil War took more American lives than any other war in history. It so divided the people of the United States that in some families, brother fought against brother.

HOT topics

The Conflict Over Slavery. By the early 1800s, many Northerners had come to view slavery as wrong. Abolitionists in the North began a movement to end it. An antislavery minority also existed in the South, but most Southerners found slavery to be highly profitable and in time came to consider it a positive good. Even many of the white Southerners who did not own slaves supported slavery. They accepted the ideas that blacks were inferior to whites and that the South's economy would collapse without slavery.

Secession. Before the 1860 presidential election, Southern leaders had urged that the South secede, or withdraw, from the Union if Lincoln should win. Many Southerners favored secession, claiming that states have rights and powers that the federal government cannot

DEFINITIONS

abolition: a putting an end to; abolishing: (in the 1700s and 1800s) the suppression of Negro slavery.

civil war: war between opposing groups of citizens of one nation

confederacy: a union of countries or states; group of people joined together for a special purpose.

draft: the selection of persons for some special purpose.

habeas corpus: a writ or order requiring that a prisoner be brought before a judge or into court to decide whether he or she is being held lawfully.

secede: to withdraw formally from an organization.

HOT topics

legally deny. South Carolina became the first state to secede. Five other states—Mississippi, Florida, Alabama, Georgia, and Louisiana—soon followed. On February 4, 1861, representatives from the six states met and established the Confederate States of America. They elected Jefferson Davis of Mississippi as president of the Confederate States. On March 2, Texas joined the Confederacy. Lincoln was inaugurated two days later.

Emancipation Proclamation.

On September 22, 1862, Lincoln issued an order to free the slaves. It declared that all slaves in states that

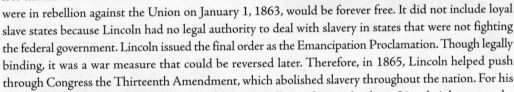
Emancipation Proclamation

were in rebellion against the Union on January 1, 1863, would be forever free. It did not include loyal slave states because Lincoln had no legal authority to deal with slavery in states that were not fighting the federal government. Lincoln issued the final order as the Emancipation Proclamation. Though legally binding, it was a war measure that could be reversed later. Therefore, in 1865, Lincoln helped push through Congress the Thirteenth Amendment, which abolished slavery throughout the nation. For his effort in freeing the slaves, Lincoln is known as the "Great Emancipator."

The Beginning of Modern Warfare.
The American Civil War is frequently called the first modern war. It was the first war in which the participants communicated by telegraph, transported supplies and troops by train, and used ironclad warships, submarines, and mines in naval combat. The armies were much larger than armies of the past. These forces introduced trench warfare and other combat tactics used in later wars. The American Civil War is also often described as the first *total war* because of the enormous amount of suffering and destruction it brought upon noncombatants, as well as soldiers.

CHARLESTON

MERCURY

EXTRA:

Passed unanimously at 1.15 o'clock, P. M. December 20th, 1860.

AN ORDINANCE

To dissolve the Union between the State of South Carolina and other States united with her under the compact entitled "The Constitution of the United States of America."

We, the People of the State of South Carolina, in Convention assembled, do declare and ordain, and it is hereby declared and ordained,

That the Ordinance adopted by us in Convention, on the twenty-third day of May, in the year of our Lord one thousand seven hundred and eighty-eight, whereby the Constitution of the United States of America was ratified, and also, all Acts and parts of Acts of the General Assembly of this State, ratifying amendments of the said Constitution, are hereby repealed; and that the union now subsisting between South Carolina and other States, under the name of "The United States of America," is hereby dissolved.

THE

UNION
IS
DISSOLVED!

The Charleston Mercury, December 20, 1860

TRUE or FALSE?

Nearly as many Americans died during the Civil War as did in all other wars from the Revolutionary War in America (1775–1783) through the Iraq War (2003).

THE BASICS

The American Civil War (1861–1865) took more American lives than any other war
in history. It so divided the people of the United States that in some families, brother fought against brother. The war's terrible bloodshed left a heritage of grief and bitterness.

The war was a conflict between the United States government and a group of states that had *seceded* (withdrawn) from the Union. The Southern states had broken away to form the Confederate States of America. The U.S. government sought to maintain the Union, insisting that states were not permitted to secede. The issue behind secession was slavery. The South's economy relied heavily on the labor of African American slaves. Southerners feared the federal government would try to limit or end slavery.

The American Civil War is also known by such names as the War Between the States and the War of Secession. The opposing sides were known as the Union, or the North, and the Confederacy, or the South. The Union soldiers were called *Yankees,* a nickname originally applied to the New England colonists. The Confederates were the *Rebs,* for *rebels.*

The war started on April 12, 1861, when Confederate troops fired on Fort Sumter, a U.S. military post in Charleston, South Carolina. It ended four years later. On April 9, 1865, Confederate General Robert E. Lee surrendered his army to Union General Ulysses S. Grant at Appomattox Court House, a small Virginia settlement. The other Confederate forces gave up soon after.

Over the years, the war has been the subject of numerous books, plays, movies, television programs, paintings, and sculptures. Civil War monuments stand in parks and squares throughout the United States. Battlefields and the tombs and former homes of such people as U.S. President Abraham Lincoln, Confederate President Jefferson Davis, and Generals Lee and Grant are popular tourist sites. Some Civil War figures are among the nation's most beloved heroes. Lincoln in particular became a respected figure throughout the world.

Causes and Background of the War

In 1861, the United States consisted of nineteen free states, in which slavery was prohibited, and fifteen slave states, in which it was allowed. U.S. President Abraham Lincoln called the nation "a house divided." Americans had much in common, but the free and slave states also had many basic differences besides slavery.

President Abraham Lincoln

Historians have long debated the causes of the Civil War. Many of them maintain that slavery was the root cause. In his Second Inaugural Address in 1865, Lincoln said of slavery: "All knew that this interest was, somehow, the cause of the war." But most historians agree that the war had a number of causes. They note, for example, that the Northern and Southern states had been drifting apart because of *sectional differences,* dissimilarities between the two areas in culture and economy. They also point to ongoing tensions between the federal government and the states over the extent of the federal government's powers. They mention the disorder in the American political party system of the 1850s. Yet slavery emerges as the most serious single cause. All explanations for the causes of the war have always involved or revolved around that issue.

Sectional differences between North and South dated from colonial times. The settlers of the South had found the warm climate and long growing season ideal for raising tobacco and, later, cotton. But these crops required intense labor to plant, maintain, and harvest. The Southerners did not have enough people to do the work. They turned to slave labor. European slave traders shipped millions of captive Africans to the Americas from 1500 to 1860. By 1860, about four million black slaves labored in the Southern states.

In the North, slave labor was used until the 1800s. But the cooler climate and shorter growing season discouraged the development of such crops as tobacco or cotton. Most Northerners earned their living by farming. But the North had no plantations and no need for farm labor on such a large scale as in the South. Immigrants from Europe poured into the North's great port cities of New York, Philadelphia, and Boston. Northern farmers found it less expensive to hire immigrant workers than to buy slaves.

Unlike the South, the North rapidly developed a manufacturing economy. The extent of Northern manufacturing helped create an environment in which the normal concept of labor was that of free workers hiring themselves out for wages rather than slaves working because they were forced to do so.

The North also was home to strong Protestant religious and cultural forces. Northern Protestants highly valued moral strictness, economic independence, and efforts to improve oneself. They disapproved of slavery and believed it to be an embarrassment to a republic dedicated to liberty and freedom.

 ## The Conflict Over Slavery

In colonial times, most Americans regarded slavery as a necessary evil. The Founding Fathers of the United States had been unable to abolish slavery and compromised over it in writing the Constitution.

By the early 1800s, many Northerners had come to view slavery as wrong. Abolitionists in the North began a movement to end it. An antislavery minority also existed in the South. But most Southerners found slavery to be highly profitable and in time came to consider it a positive good. From a fourth to a third of all Southern whites were members of slaveholding families. About half the families owned fewer than five slaves, though less than 1 percent of the families owned 100 or more. Even many of the white Southerners who did not own slaves supported slavery. They accepted the ideas that the South's economy would collapse without slavery and that blacks were inferior to whites.

In 1858, Senator William H. Seward of New York, who later became Lincoln's secretary of state, referred to the differences between North and South as "an irrepressible conflict." He placed slavery at the heart of that uncontrollable conflict.

Slaves picking cotton on a plantation

Indeed, an almost continuous series of debates over slavery raged in Congress between Northern and Southern lawmakers during the 1850s.

The Compromise of 1850 was a group of acts passed by Congress in the hope of settling the slavery question by giving some satisfaction to both the North and the South. The Compromise allowed slavery to continue but prohibited the slave trade in Washington, D.C. It admitted California to the Union as a free state but gave newly acquired territories the right to decide for themselves whether to permit slavery. The Compromise also included a strict fugitive slave law that required Northerners to return escaped slaves to their owners.

Northerners resisted the fugitive slave law in several ways. Abolitionists disobeyed the law by operating the *Underground Railroad*, a system of escape routes and housing for runaway slaves. The routes led from the slave states to the free states and Canada. Abolitionists also rescued or tried to rescue fugitive slaves after they had been recovered in the North by their owners. A number of rescue attempts, such as those in Christiana, Pennsylvania, in 1851 and in Boston in 1854, resulted in riots and several deaths. One of the most effective attacks on the fugitive slave law—and on slavery as a whole—was Harriet Beecher Stowe's best-selling antislavery novel *Uncle Tom's Cabin* (1851–1852).

The Kansas-Nebraska Act was passed by Congress in 1854. Like the Compromise of 1850, it dealt with the problem of slavery in newly formed territories. The act created the territories of Kansas and Nebraska and gave the people of these territories the right to regulate matters related to slavery. It also provided that before the territories became states, the people of each territory could decide whether to allow slavery in the new states. The decision process was called *popular sovereignty*. Many Northerners opposed the act. They feared that once slavery was in a territory, it was there to stay.

The first test of popular sovereignty came in Kansas, where a majority of the population voted against becoming a slave state. But proslavery forces refused to accept the decision. The situation quickly erupted into violence. The violence spread to Washington, D.C., where in 1856 an antislavery senator, Charles Sumner of Massachusetts, was beaten unconscious by Preston Brooks, a proslavery representative from South Carolina. In the end, Kansas joined the Union as a free state in 1861.

The Dred Scott decision. In 1857, the Supreme Court of the United States tried to settle the slavery issue through the decision it handed down in the case involving Dred Scott. Scott, a Missouri slave, sued for his freedom. He and his master had moved from Missouri to a state that did not allow slavery and later to a territory that also did not allow slavery. Scott said that he had become a free man by living in areas where slavery was not recognized.

Chief Justice Roger B. Taney wrote the majority decision. He said that Scott, as a black man, was not a citizen and therefore did not have the right to sue in a U.S. court. Taney also said that the federal government could not exclude slavery from the ter-

ritories. The decision angered many Northerners. They believed it opened all the territories to the expansion of slavery. They also felt it was an attempt to close off any further debate about slavery in Congress.

The raid at Harpers Ferry. In 1859, an extreme abolitionist named John Brown and his followers attempted to start a slave rebellion by seizing the federal arsenal in Harpers Ferry, Virginia (now West Virginia). Brown was captured twenty-eight hours later by troops under Colonel Robert E. Lee. Within a few weeks, he was convicted of treason and hanged. Many Southerners saw the raid as evidence of a Northern plot to end slavery by force.

Developments in the Political Party System

Anger over the Kansas-Nebraska Act led to the founding of the Republican Party in the North in 1854. Members of the Republican Party considered slavery evil and opposed its extension into Western territories. Many Whigs and Democrats—members of the nation's two largest parties—joined the new party. They included Abraham Lincoln, a former Whig. Some other Americans belonged to the Know-Nothing Party, which blamed immigrants and Roman Catholics for the country's problems. The Republican Party's first presidential candidate, John C. Fremont, won most of the Northern vote and almost the presidency in 1856. But Democrat James Buchanan was elected president.

In 1858, the Democratic Party was divided over a constitution that proslavery Kansans hoped to have adopted when the Kansas territory became a state. Buchanan and another party leader, Senator Stephen A. Douglas of Illinois, took opposite positions on the constitution. Buchanan favored it, and Douglas opposed it. The conflict between proslavery and antislavery Democrats caused the party to split into Northern and Southern branches in 1860.

The Republicans chose Abraham Lincoln as their candidate in the 1860 presidential election. Douglas ran on the Northern Democratic ticket. Vice President John C. Breckinridge was the Southern Democratic candidate. Some former members of the Whig and Know-Nothing parties—which had disbanded by 1860—formed the Constitutional Union Party and nominated former Senator John Bell of Tennessee.

Dred Scott

Lincoln won all the electoral votes of every free state except New Jersey, which awarded him four of its seven votes. He thus gained a majority of electoral votes and won the election. However, Lincoln received less than 40 percent of the popular vote, almost none of which came from the South. Southerners feared Lincoln would restrict or end slavery.

Secession

Before the 1860 presidential election, Southern leaders had urged that the South *secede* (withdraw) from the Union if Lincoln should win. Many Southerners favored secession as part of the idea that the states have rights and powers that the federal government cannot legally deny. The supporters of states' rights held that the national government was a league of independent states, any of which had the right to secede.

In December 1860, South Carolina became the first state to secede. Five other states—Mississippi, Florida, Alabama, Georgia, and Louisiana—followed in January 1861. On February 4, 1861, representatives from the six states met in Montgomery, Alabama, and established the Confederate States of America. They elected Jefferson Davis of Mississippi as president and Alexander H. Stephens of Georgia as vice president of the Confederate States. On March 2, Texas joined the Confederacy. Lincoln was inaugurated two days later.

In his inaugural address, Lincoln avoided any threat of immediate force against the South. But he stated that the Union would last forever and that he would use the nation's full power to hold federal possessions in the South. One of the possessions, the military post of Fort Sumter, lay in the harbor of Charleston, South Carolina. The Confederates fired on the fort on April 12 and forced its surrender the next day. On April 15, Lincoln called for Union troops to regain the fort. The South regarded the move as a declaration of war. Virginia, Arkansas, North Carolina, and Tennessee soon joined the Confederacy.

Virginia had long been undecided about which side to join. Its decision to join the Confederacy boosted Southern morale. Richmond, Virginia's capital, became the capital of the Confederacy in May.

Mobilizing for War

When the American Civil War began, about twenty-two million people lived in the North. About nine million people, including four million slaves, lived in the South. The North had around four million men from fifteen through forty years old—the approximate age range for combat duty. The South had only about one million white men in that range. The North began to use black soldiers in 1863. The South did not attempt to recruit blacks as soldiers until the war's closing days.

How the States Lined Up

Eleven states fought for the Confederacy. They were Alabama, Arkansas, Florida, Georgia, Louisiana, Mississippi, North Carolina, South Carolina, Tennessee, Texas, and Virginia. Twenty-three states fought for the Union. These states were California, Connecticut, Delaware, Illinois, Indiana, Iowa, Kansas, Kentucky, Maine, Maryland, Massachusetts, Michigan, Minnesota, Missouri, New Hampshire, New Jersey, New York, Ohio, Oregon, Pennsylvania, Rhode Island, Vermont, and Wisconsin. The territories of Colorado, Dakota, Nebraska, Nevada, New Mexico, Utah, and Washington also fought for the Union.

A number of slave states lay between the North and the Deep South. Some people in those border states supported the North, but others believed in the Southern cause. When the war began, both the Union and the Confederacy made strong efforts to gain the support of those states. Border states that joined the Southern side were Virginia, North Carolina, Tennessee, and Arkansas. However, Virginians in the western part of the state remained loyal to the Union and formed the new state of West Virginia in 1863. Border states that stayed in the Union were Delaware, Maryland, Kentucky, and Missouri. But secessionist groups in Kentucky and Missouri set up separate state governments and sent representatives to the

Jefferson Davis with his Cabinet and Gen. Robert E. Lee (center)

Confederate Congress. Some of the heaviest fighting of the war occurred in the border states.

In both the North and the South, some families were torn by divided loyalties to the Union and the Confederacy. One of Kentucky Senator John J. Crittenden's sons, Thomas, became a Union general. Another son, George, became a Confederate general. George H. Thomas, one of the Union's best generals, was born in Virginia. Admiral David Farragut, who defeated Southern naval forces at New Orleans and Mobile Bay, was born in Tennessee. Three half brothers of Mary Todd Lincoln, Abraham Lincoln's wife, died fighting for the Confederacy. The husband of one of her half sisters was a Confederate general who was also killed.

Building the Armed Forces

At the beginning of the Civil War, neither the North nor the South had a plan to call up troops. The Regular Army of the United States at that time consisted of only about 16,000 men, most of whom fought for the North. Both sides tried to raise their armies by appealing to volunteers. That system worked at first. Individual states, rather than the Union or Confederate governments, recruited most volunteers and often equipped them. Any man who wanted to organize a company or a regiment could do so. In the North, especially late in the war, volunteers often received a *bounty* (payment for enlisting). The bounty system encouraged thousands of *bounty jumpers*, who deserted after being paid. Many bounty jumpers enlisted several times, often using a different name each time.

The draft. As the war went on, enthusiasm for it faded and volunteer enlistments decreased.

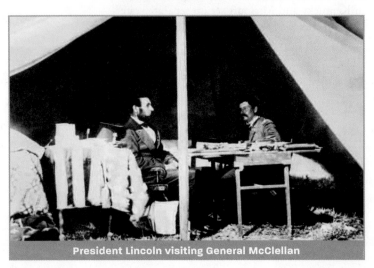

President Lincoln visiting General McClellan

Both sides then tried drafting soldiers. The first Southern draft law was passed in April 1862 and made all able-bodied white men from ages eighteen through thirty-five liable for three years' service. By February 1864, the limits had been changed to seventeen and fifty. The Northern program, begun in March 1863, drafted men from ages twenty through forty-five for three years. Exceptions to the draft were made in the North and South, however, and both sides allowed a draftee to pay a substitute to serve for him. In addition, a draftee in the North could pay the government $300 to avoid military service. The system seemed unfair, and many soldiers grumbled that they were involved in "a rich man's war and a poor man's fight." But on the whole, both armies had a fair representation of soldiers from the various social groups of their regions.

The draft worked poorly and was extremely unpopular in many areas of both the North and the South. In some isolated hill country of the South, it could not be enforced. In July 1863, armed antidraft protesters in New York City set fire to buildings and took over parts of the city before police and the Army restored order. However, the Northern and Southern drafts succeeded in their main purpose, which was to stimulate volunteering.

No one knows exactly how many men served in the American Civil War. The totals on both sides included many short-term enlistments and *repeaters* (men who served more than once). According to the best estimates, 2,100,000 men served in the Union Army, and 800,000 men served in the Confederate Army. A little more than half the men of military age served for the North. A larger proportion of eligible men—almost four-fifths—served for the South. In the South, black slaves performed most of the labor, thereby freeing a greater percentage of eligible whites for military duty. Immigrants made up about 24 percent of the Union Army and about 10 percent of the Confederate Army.

The Confederate Army reached peak strength in 1863, and then declined. But the Union Army grew. In the last year of the war, the North had over a million soldiers. The South probably had no more than 200,000. About 10 percent of the soldiers on both sides deserted. Desertion from the Confederate Army became most common in the last months of the war, when Southern morale began to collapse and defeat seemed certain.

The commanding officers. As commander in chief of the U.S. armed forces, Abraham Lincoln had to choose the Union's top military officers. Jefferson Davis had the same task in the Confederacy. Davis fortunately had General Robert E. Lee to take command of the Eastern Confederate Army. Lee's able officers included Generals Stonewall Jackson and James Longstreet. Confederate commanders in the West—Generals Albert Sidney Johnston, Pierre G. T. Beauregard, Braxton Bragg, and Joseph E. Johnston—were less successful.

Lincoln tried several commanders for the Eastern Union Army, which came to be called the Army of the Potomac. They were, in turn, Generals Irvin McDowell, George B. McClellan, John Pope, McClellan again, Ambrose E. Burnside, Joseph Hooker, and George G. Meade. All had serious weaknesses. Lincoln's Western generals—Henry W. Halleck, Don Carlos Buell, and William S. Rosecrans—also failed to meet his expectations. But as the war progressed, four outstanding generals emerged to lead the Union armies to victory. They were Ulysses S. Grant, William T. Sherman, Philip H. Sheridan, and George H. Thomas.

The enlisted men. Civil War soldiers were much like American enlisted men of earlier and later wars. They fought well but remained civilians, with a civilian's dislike of military rules. In most regiments, the men all came from the same area. Many units elected their own officers.

Civil War soldiers received more leaves and furloughs than did soldiers of previous wars, and they had better food and clothing. But compared with today's standards, they had a hard life. Both sides paid their soldiers poorly. Food supplies consisted mainly of flour, cornmeal, beef, beans, and dried fruit. Many soldiers made their own meals. Armies on the march ate salt pork and hard biscuits called *hardtack*. Poorly made clothing of *shoddy* (rewoven wool) often fell apart in the first storm. Southern soldiers at times lacked shoes and had to march and fight barefoot.

Most Civil War soldiers carried muzzle-loading rifles. Because the guns could fire only one shot at a time, they seem primitive today. But technological advances, especially the use of *rifling* (spiral grooves) in the barrels, had increased the accuracy of these weapons to nearly 400 yards (366 meters). The technological advances made little difference to most soldiers, however, because the soldiers lacked training or experience.

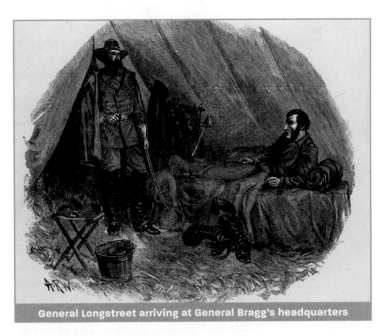

General Longstreet arriving at General Bragg's headquarters

The high death rate. Civil War combat was frequently disorganized and ineffective. The armies were made up mostly of inexperienced soldiers commanded by enthusiastic but unprepared officers. Offensive maneuvers often bogged down as waves of attackers failed to press on to success. Even in major victories, the winners often failed to capture the opposing force. Professional European soldiers scorned the performance of the Civil War armies as little better than "one armed mob chasing another armed mob across the countryside."

Many battles took a terrible toll in human lives. An army often had 25 percent of its men killed, wounded, captured, or otherwise lost in a major battle. Among some regiments at the Battle of Gettysburg and other battles, the death rate alone ran as high as 25 percent or more. The heavy death toll led Civil War soldiers to devise the first dog tags for identification in case they were killed. A soldier would print his name and address on a handkerchief or a piece of paper and pin it to his uniform before going into battle.

Blacks and the War

Early black participation. Early in the war, Northern blacks who wanted to fight to end slavery tried to enlist in the Union Army, but the Army rejected them. Most whites felt the war was a "white man's war."

As Northern armies drove into Confederate territory, slaves flocked to Union camps. After a period of uncertainty, the Union government decided to allow them to perform support services for the Northern war effort. In time, as many as 200,000 blacks worked for Union armies as cooks, laborers, nurses, scouts, and spies.

The Emancipation Proclamation.

Black leaders, such as the former slave Frederick Douglass of New York, saw the war as a road to *emancipation* (freedom) for the slaves. However, the idea of emancipation presented problems in the North. Most Northerners—even though they may have opposed slavery—were convinced of black inferiority. Many of them feared that emancipation would cause a mass movement of Southern blacks into the North. Northerners also worried about losing the border states loyal to the Union because those states were strongly committed to slavery. Skillful leadership was needed as the country moved toward black freedom. Lincoln supplied that leadership by combining a clear sense of purpose with sensitivity to the concerns of various groups.

On September 22, 1862, Lincoln issued a preliminary order to free the slaves. It declared that all slaves in states in rebellion against the Union on January 1, 1863, would be forever free. It did not include the slave states loyal to the Union—Delaware, Maryland, Kentucky, and Missouri. Lincoln had no legal authority to deal with slavery in states where the state government was not fighting against the federal government.

On January 1, 1863, Lincoln issued the final order as the Emancipation Proclamation. The Emancipation Proclamation, though legally binding, was a war measure that could be reversed later. Therefore, in 1865, Lincoln helped push through Congress the Thirteenth Amendment to the Constitution, which abolished slavery throughout the nation. For his effort in freeing the slaves, Lincoln is known as the "Great Emancipator."

The use of black troops.

The Emancipation Proclamation also announced Lincoln's decision to use black troops, though many whites believed that blacks would make poor soldiers. About 180,000 blacks served in the Union army. Two-thirds of them were Southerners who had fled to freedom in the North. About 20,000 blacks served in the Union navy, which had been open to blacks long before the war. Black troops formed 166 all-black regiments, most of which had white commanders. Only about 100 blacks were made officers.

Blacks fought in nearly 500 Civil War engagements, including thirty-nine major battles. About 35,000 black servicemen lost their lives. Altogether, twenty-three blacks won the Medal of Honor, the nation's highest military award, for heroism. A black regiment was one of the first Northern units to march into Richmond after it fell. Lincoln then toured the city, escorted by black cavalry.

At first, black soldiers received only about half the pay of white soldiers and no bounties for volunteering. In 1864, Congress granted blacks equal pay and bounties. However, other types of official discrimination continued. For example, most black soldiers were allowed to perform only noncombat duties. But some blacks who had the opportunity to go into combat distinguished themselves. The bravery of blacks in the 1863 Mississippi Valley campaign surprised most Northerners. But protests against the use of black troops continued.

Later in 1863, the 54th Massachusetts Volunteers—the first black troops from a free state to be organized for combat in the Union army—stormed Fort Wagner in Charleston Harbor. Their bravery turned the tide of Northern public opinion to accept black troops. Lincoln wrote that when peace came "there will be some black men who can remember that, with silent tongue, and clenched teeth, and steady eye, and well-poised bayonet, they have helped mankind on to this great consummation; while, I fear, there will be some white ones, unable to forget that, with malignant heart, and deceitful speech, they have strove to hinder it."

Reaction in the South.

The Confederacy objected strongly to the North's use of black soldiers. The Confederate government threatened to kill or enslave any captured officers or enlisted men of black regiments. Lincoln replied by promising to treat Confederate prisoners of war the same way.

Black troops in the Union Army

Neither side carried out its threats, but the exchange of prisoners broke down mainly over the issue of black prisoners.

The North's success in using black soldiers slowly led Southerners to consider doing the same. In the spring of 1865, following a strong demand by General Lee, the Confederate Congress narrowly approved the use of black soldiers. However, the war ended soon thereafter.

The Home Front

The American Civil War became the first war to be completely and immediately reported in the press to the people back home. Civilians in the North were especially well informed of the war's progress. Northern newspapers sent their best correspondents into the field and received their reports by telegraph. Winslow Homer and many other artists and illustrators produced war scenes for such magazines as *Harper's Weekly*. Mathew Brady, Alexander Gardner, and other pioneer photographers captured the horrors of the battlefield and the humanity of the soldiers in thousands of news pictures.

The war inspired a flood of patriotic songs. Northern civilians and soldiers sang such songs as "The Battle Cry of Freedom," "Marching Through Georgia," and "John Brown's Body." Early in the war, Julia Ward Howe wrote "The Battle Hymn of the Republic" to the tune of "John Brown's Body." Southern soldiers marched to war to the stirring music of "Dixie" and "The Bonnie Blue Flag." Some Northern songs, such as "Tenting on the Old Camp Ground" and "When Johnny Comes Marching Home," also became popular in the South. And some Southern songs—for example, the mournful "Lorena" and "All Quiet Along the Potomac Tonight"—were also popular in the North.

In the North

Government and politics. After the attack on Fort Sumter, Lincoln boldly ordered troops to put down the rebellion, increased the size of the U.S. Army, proclaimed a naval blockade of the South, and spent funds without congressional approval. He became the first president to assume vast powers not specifically granted by the Constitution. He suspended *habeas corpus* in many cases in which people opposed the war effort. Habeas corpus is a right that guarantees a person under arrest a chance to be heard in court. Its suspension

received bitter criticism. Yet many traditional American freedoms continued to flourish, even though the nation was in the midst of a civil war.

Opposition to the war and Lincoln's policies came chiefly from the Democratic Party, especially from a group known as the Peace Democrats, who wanted the war stopped. Republicans considered the Peace Democrats disloyal and treacherous and called them Copperheads, after the poisonous snake. Other protesters of the war joined secret antigovernment societies, such as the Knights of the Golden Circle. The Lincoln administration was also criticized by so-called Radical Republicans. They wanted the government to move more rapidly to abolish slavery and to make sweeping changes in the Southern way of life. Such disputes continued throughout the war.

Economy. The Civil War brought booming prosperity to the North. Government purchases for military needs stimulated manufacturing and agriculture. The production of coal, iron and steel, weapons, shoes, and woolen clothing increased greatly. Farmers vastly expanded their production of wheat, wool, and other products. Exports to Europe of beef, corn, pork, and wheat doubled. Factories and farms made the first widespread use of labor-saving machines, such as the sewing machine and the reaper.

Although the Civil War brought prosperity to the North, financing the war was difficult. Taxes and money borrowed through the sale of war bonds became major sources of income. The government also printed more paper money to meet its financial needs. But by increasing the money supply, the government promoted inflation. Wages did not keep up with inflation through much of the war, and factory workers struck for higher pay.

New York Herald reporters at campsite

However, as the war went on, war production—and finally victory—helped the North grow ever stronger.

During the Lincoln administration, Congress passed the most important series of economic acts in American history to that time. It established the national banking system, a *uniform* (standard) currency, and the Department of Agriculture. The Pacific Railroad Act of 1862 provided for the building of the nation's first transcontinental rail line. The Homestead Act of 1862 granted settlers public land in the West free or at low cost. The Land-Grant, or Morrill, Act of 1862 helped states establish agricultural and technical colleges. Under Lincoln, Congress also passed the first federal income tax. Altogether, the economic progress in the North brought about by and during the Civil War helped put the United States on the road to becoming the world's greatest industrial power by the late 1800s.

In the South

Government and politics. During the Civil War, the South tried to bring political power under the control of a single authority. But it was not successful. Southerners had long opposed a strong central government. During the war, some of them found it difficult to cooperate with officials of both the Confederacy and their own states and cities. States' rights supporters backed the war but opposed the draft and other actions needed to carry it out. And Jefferson Davis lacked Lincoln's leadership abilities. For example, Lincoln believed he had the power to suspend the law if necessary, and he did so. Davis asked the Confederate Congress for such power but received only limited permission.

Economy. As in the North, manufacturing and agriculture in the South were adapted to the needs of war. Factories converted from civilian to wartime production. For example, the Tredegar Iron Works in Richmond became the South's main source of cannons. Cotton cultivation dropped sharply, while food production was greatly increased.

The South thus tried to adjust to meet wartime needs, but its economy became strained almost to the breaking point. The attempt to finance the war by taxation and borrowing from the people failed. The Confederacy's solution to the problem was to print large amounts of paper money, which led to an extremely high inflation rate. By the end of the

Confederate currency

war, prices were ten times higher than they were at the start. In 1865, flour cost up to $300 a barrel, and shoes $200 a pair. In time, Southerners had to make clothes of carpets and curtains and print newspapers on the back of wallpaper.

Confederate troops were never as well equipped as their Northern counterparts. As resources were used up and the tightening naval blockade severely reduced imports, matters got worse. The Confederate government then passed the Impressment Act of 1863. The act permitted government agents to seize from civilians food, horses, and any other supplies the army needed. The civilians received whatever the agents decided to pay.

Relations with Europe. At the beginning of the war, Southern leaders hoped that European countries—especially France and the United Kingdom—would come to the aid of the Confederacy. Southerners believed that France and the United Kingdom would be forced to support the Confederacy because their textile industries depended on Southern cotton. The efforts of Southern statesmen to persuade the European powers to help the Confederacy came to be called "cotton diplomacy."

As a result of cotton diplomacy, France and the United Kingdom allowed the Confederacy to have several armed warships built in their shipyards.

But the South never won European recognition of the Confederacy as an independent nation or obtained major aid. Northern grain had become important in Europe, which had suffered several crop failures. At the same time, Southern cotton was increasingly replaced by cotton from India and Egypt. The Emancipation Proclamation made the Civil War a fight against slavery. The proclamation deeply impressed those Europeans who opposed slavery. Such skillful Northern diplomats as Charles Francis Adams also helped persuade the European powers not to recognize the Confederacy. But most important, Britain and France would not fight on the side of the South unless the Confederacy could show that it might win final victory. And that never happened.

The Appalachian Mountains divided the war into two main *theaters of operations* (military areas). The Eastern theater stretched east of the mountains to the Atlantic Ocean. The Western theater lay between the mountains and the Mississippi River. A third theater, west of the Mississippi, saw only minor action.

Many Civil War battles have two names because the Confederates named them after the nearest settlement, and Northerners named them after the nearest body of water. In such battles described in this article, the Northern name is given first, followed by the Confederate name in parentheses.

Fort Sumter. The American Civil War began on April 12, 1861, when Confederate forces under General Pierre G. T. Beauregard attacked Fort Sumter, a U.S. Army post in the harbor of Charleston, South Carolina. The Union troops surrendered on April 13 and evacuated the fort the next day.

Following the fall of Fort Sumter, a Union army of about 18,000 men under General Robert Patterson held the northern end of the fertile Shenandoah River Valley, which lay in Virginia west of the rival capitals of Washington, D.C., and Richmond. Another Union force of about 31,000 under General Irvin McDowell moved into eastern Virginia to attack Southern forces. A Confederate army under Beauregard faced McDowell at Manassas, Virginia, about 25 miles (40 kilometers) southwest of Washington. General Joseph E. Johnston commanded Confederate troops in the Shenandoah Valley. Those forces, along with other scattered troops, added up to about 35,000 Confederates ready for action.

The *Saint Louis*, the first ironclad gunboat built in America

First Battle of Bull Run (or First Battle of Manassas). In July 1861, McDowell approached Manassas, which lay on a creek called Bull Run. McDowell thought his troops could destroy Beauregard's forces while the Union troops in the Shenandoah Valley kept Johnston occupied. But Johnston slipped away and traveled by rail to join Beauregard just before the battle.

The opposing forces, both composed mainly of poorly trained volunteers, clashed on July 21. The North launched several assaults. During one attack, Confederate General Thomas J. Jackson stood his ground so firmly that he received the nickname "Stonewall." After halting several assaults, Beauregard counterattacked. The tired Union forces fled to Washington, D.C., in wild retreat. After the battle, some Southerners regretted not having moved on to capture Washington. But such an attempt would probably have failed.

The North realized that it faced a long fight. The war would not be over in three months, as many Northerners had predicted. Confederate confidence in final victory soared and remained high for the next two years.

The drive to Take Richmond

After Bull Run, Lincoln made General George B. McClellan commander of the Army of the Potomac in the East. During the winter of 1861–1862, McClellan assembled a force with which he planned to capture Richmond from the southeast. He wanted to land his men on the peninsula between the York and James rivers and advance along one of the rivers toward the Southern capital. But before McClellan could move, a naval action changed his plans.

First battle between ironclads. In 1861, the Confederates had raised a sunken federal ship, the *Merrimack*, off Norfolk, Virginia, and covered the wooden vessel with iron plates. The South used the ironclad ship, renamed the *Virginia*, to stage the South's greatest naval challenge to the North. On March 8, 1862, the *Virginia* attacked Northern ships at Hampton Roads, a channel that empties into Chesapeake Bay. It destroyed two Northern vessels and grounded three others. When the ship returned the next day to finish the job, it faced the *Monitor*, an ironclad ship designed especially for the Northern navy. History's first battle between ironclad warships followed. Although neither ship won, the *Monitor* proved to be the superior vessel. Later, the U.S. Navy built a large ironclad fleet modeled after it.

The *Monitor* and the *Merrimack*

The peninsular campaign. After the battle of the ironclads, McClellan landed on the peninsula between the York and James rivers with more than 100,000 men. He occupied Yorktown and advanced along the York River. He could not follow the James River because the *Virginia* was on the river. By late May 1862, McClellan was within 6 miles (10 kilometers) of Richmond. Johnston led an attack against McClellan on May 31. But the Confederates failed to follow up their success and were driven back toward Richmond. In the two-day fight, called the Battle of Fair Oaks (or Battle of Seven Pines), Johnston was wounded. General Robert E. Lee was given command of Johnston's army, which Lee called the Army of Northern Virginia.

Jackson's valley campaign. The Confederacy feared that McClellan would receive reinforcements from the numerous troops that had stayed behind to protect Washington, D.C.

Stonewall Jackson therefore launched a campaign in the Shenandoah Valley. He planned to make the Northerners think he was going to attack Washington. In a series of brilliant moves from May 4 through June 9, 1862, Jackson advanced about 350 miles (560 kilometers) up the Shenandoah Valley and beyond, toward the Potomac River. His 17,000 men received the name "foot cavalry" because they marched so fast. Jackson won four battles against the Union armies. He reached the Potomac but soon had to retreat. However, he had forced the Union to withhold the powerful reinforcements that McClellan had counted on.

Stuart's raid. While Lee planned his strategy as the new commander of the Army of Northern Virginia, Confederate General Jeb Stuart led a remarkable cavalry raid. In June 1862, Stuart and about 1,200 men galloped completely around McClellan's army of 100,000 in three days, losing only one man. Stuart's raid gained information about Union troop movements and boosted Southern morale.

Battles of the Seven Days. Lee planned a daring move to destroy McClellan's army, which lay straddled over the Chickahominy River. With his forces reinforced by Jackson's men to about 95,000 men, Lee's forces faced McClellan's in a series of attacks, called the Battles of the Seven Days, from June 25 through July 1, 1862. The advantage shifted from side to side during the battles, but McClellan believed that his forces were hopelessly outnumbered. He finally retreated to the James River, and Richmond was saved from capture. McClellan's army was ordered to northern Virginia to be united with a force under General John Pope. McClellan was to command the combined army.

The South Strikes Back

Second Battle of Bull Run (or Second Battle of Manassas). Lee moved rapidly northward to attack Pope, stationed at Manassas, before McClellan's men could join him. Lee sent Jackson ahead to move behind Pope's army and force a battle. On August 29, 1862, Pope attacked Jackson, sending in McClellan's troops as fast as they arrived. Meanwhile, Lee and General James Longstreet had joined Jackson. Pope attacked Lee's army on August 30, but a Confederate counterattack swept the Union forces from the field. The beaten Northern troops plodded back to Washington.

Battle of Antietam (or Battle of Sharpsburg). The South hoped to gain European recognition by winning a victory in Union territory. Lee invaded Maryland in September 1862. He divided his army, sending about half with Jackson to capture Harpers Ferry, Virginia, which Union troops occupied. McClellan moved to meet Lee with about 90,000 men. On September 13, a Union soldier found a copy of Lee's orders to his commanders wrapped around three cigars at an abandoned Confederate campsite. Lee learned of the loss and took up a position at Sharpsburg, a town on Antietam Creek in Maryland. But McClellan did not immediately attack, giving the Confederate forces time to reunite after Jackson's success at Harpers Ferry. On September 17, McClellan launched a series of attacks that almost cracked the Southern lines. But then, the last of Lee's absent troops, headed by General A. P. Hill, arrived and saved the day. Lee's force of about 40,000 men suffered heavy losses and had to retreat to Virginia.

Battle of Antietam

Antietam was the bloodiest single day of the Civil War. About 2,000 Northerners and 2,700 Southerners were killed. About 19,000 men from both sides were wounded, of which about 3,000 later died. Because Lee retreated, the North called Antietam a Union victory. On September 22, Lincoln issued the preliminary Emancipation Proclamation. He had been waiting for a Northern victory as a good time for the proclamation.

Battle of Fredericksburg. As bloody as Antietam was, McClellan had more fresh troops under him after the battle than Lee had left in his entire army. Yet McClellan permitted the Army of Northern Virginia to retreat with almost no interference. Lincoln, who had long felt that McClellan was not aggressive enough, replaced him with General Ambrose E. Burnside as commander of the Army of the Potomac.

Burnside decided to attack Lee at Fredericksburg, Virginia. The Confederates, about 73,000 strong, established a line of defense along fortified hills called Marye's Heights. On December 13, 1862, Burnside's men tried to storm the hills in a brave but hopeless attack. The Union suffered nearly 13,000 *casualties*—soldiers killed, wounded, missing, or captured—and retreated. Burnside was relieved of command at his own request.

Battle of Chancellorsville. General Joseph Hooker replaced Burnside. In the spring of 1863, the Army of the Potomac numbered about 138,000 men. Lee's forces totaled about 60,000 and still held the line of defense at Fredericksburg. Hooker planned to keep Lee's attention on Fredericksburg while he sent another force around the town to attack the Confederate *flank* (side).

The flanking movement began on April 27, 1863, and seemed about to succeed. But then, Hooker hesitated. On May 1, he withdrew his flanking troops to a defensive position at Chancellorsville, a settlement just west of Fredericksburg. The next day, Lee left a small force at Fredericksburg and boldly moved to attack Hooker. He sent Stonewall Jackson to attack Hooker's right flank, while he struck in front. The attack, on May 2, cut the Northern army almost in two, but Union troops managed to set up a defensive line. Hooker retreated three days later. During the battle, Jackson was shot accidentally by his own men. His left arm had to be amputated. Lee told Jackson's chaplain: "He has lost his left arm; but I have lost my right arm." Jackson died on May 10.

Battle of Gettysburg. In June 1863, Lee's army swung up the Shenandoah Valley into Pennsylvania. The Army of the Potomac followed it northward. Both armies moved toward the little town of Gettysburg. When it appeared that the battle was about to begin, Lincoln put General George G. Meade, a Pennsylvanian, in command of the Union troops. The shooting started when a Confederate brigade, searching for badly needed shoes, ran into Union cavalry near Gettysburg on July 1. For the first three days of July, a Northern army of about 90,000 men fought a Southern army of about 75,000 in a battle that became the turning point of the war.

On the first day, the two armies maneuvered for position. By the end of the day, Northern troops had been pushed from west and north of Gettysburg, and they settled into a strong defensive location on high ground south of the town. The front ran about 3 miles (5 kilometers) along Cemetery Ridge. At one end, the Union's right, were Cemetery Hill and Culp's Hill. At the other end were two hills called Little Round Top and Round Top. Confederate forces occupied Gettysburg and then Seminary Ridge, to the west.

On the second day, July 2, Lee hoped to crush the Union position on Cemetery Hill by striking at both sides of the hill at the same time. But Lee was unable to carry out his plan. The Union Army put up fierce resistance all along Cemetery Ridge and down to Little Round Top. Lee's forces met equally furious resistance from Union troops on Culp's Hill and the eastern side of Cemetery Hill.

On July 3, Lee tried one more time to crack the Union hold on Cemetery Hill. After a fierce artillery duel, he ordered General George E. Pickett to prepare about 13,000 men to charge the Union lines. The men, marching in perfect parade formation, advanced across an open field and up the slopes of Cemetery Ridge in the face of enemy fire. Only a few troops reached the top of the ridge, where they were quickly shot or captured. Barely half the soldiers involved in the assault returned to Lee, who took complete responsibility for the attack's failure. Pickett's charge showed the hope-

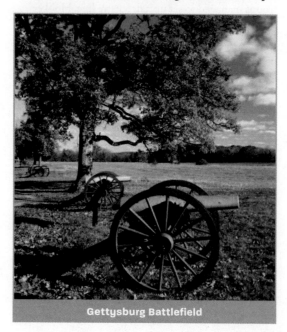

Gettysburg Battlefield

lessness of *frontal* (head-on) assaults over open ground against a strong enemy. Lee's attempt to pierce the Union rear with Stuart's cavalry, which had arrived the night before, also failed.

Lee withdrew his battered army to Virginia after the battle. Much to Lincoln's disgust, Meade made little effort to follow him, even though Meade had about 20,000 fresh reserves and had received further reinforcements. Lee's army thus escaped. However, casualties among Lee's men numbered between 25,000 and 28,000. Never again would he have the troop strength to launch a major offensive.

In the Western theater, the North attacked early and hard to seize the Mississippi River. Northern forces in the West totaled about 100,000 men, and Southern forces about 70,000. General Henry W. Halleck led Union forces in Arkansas, Illinois, Iowa, western Kentucky, Minnesota, Missouri, and Wisconsin. General Don Carlos Buell led the Northern forces in Indiana, eastern Kentucky, Michigan, and Ohio. General Albert Sidney Johnston led Southern forces in Arkansas, western Mississippi, and Tennessee. His command included General Earl Van Dorn's troops in Arkansas.

Fight for the Mississippi Valley

Battles of Fort Henry and Fort Donelson. The center of the Confederate line in the West rested on two forts about 12 miles (19 kilometers) apart in western Tennessee. They were Fort Henry on the Tennessee River and Fort Donelson on the Cumberland River. If Union forces could capture the forts, the Confederate position in Kentucky and western Tennessee would collapse. Gunboats under orders from General Ulysses S. Grant, commanding officer under Halleck in western Kentucky, took Fort Henry on February 6, 1862. Grant himself moved against Fort Donelson. The Confederate commander, General Simon Bolivar Buckner, asked for "the best terms" of surrender. Grant replied: "No terms except an unconditional and immediate surrender can be accepted." On February 16, about 13,000 of the Confederate troops stationed at Fort Donelson surrendered. Grant gained the nickname "Unconditional Surrender" Grant and became a Northern hero.

Grant's army lay between the two flanks of the Confederate forces. To escape destruction, Johnston pulled his troops back to Corinth, Mississippi, a major railroad center. The Confederacy had lost Kentucky and half of Tennessee. West of the Mississippi River, a Union army under General Samuel R. Curtis defeated Van Dorn at Pea Ridge, Arkansas, on March 6 through 8. The defeat put Missouri solidly in Northern hands.

Battle of Shiloh.

Halleck, who had become commander of most Union forces from Ohio to Kansas, ordered Grant to move down the Tennessee River and told Buell to join Grant. Grant and some 40,000 men moved to Pittsburg Landing, Tennessee, a village about 20 miles (32 kilometers) north of Corinth. Johnston and his co-commander, General Beauregard, decided to strike Grant before Buell arrived. They planned to destroy Grant's forces with their army of some 44,000 troops. The Battle of Shiloh, named after a church on the battlefield, occurred on April 6–7, 1862. The battle is also called the Battle of Pittsburg Landing.

On the first day, Confederate troops surprised and almost smashed Grant. But Grant held his lines. Johnston was killed in the battle. The next day, Grant received about 25,000 reinforcements, including some 18,000 troops led by Buell. The Confederate army received only about 700 reinforcements. Grant used his now much larger army to force a Southern retreat to Corinth. The Union suffered about 13,000 casualties, and the Confederacy nearly 11,000. Many Northerners urged Lincoln to replace Grant because of the heavy losses. But Lincoln refused, saying, "I can't spare this man—he fights!"

After Shiloh, Halleck took command of Grant's and Buell's forces. He moved southward and forced Beauregard to evacuate Corinth. By early June, the Union held the Mississippi River as far south as Memphis.

The *General*

Capture of New Orleans.

Meanwhile, Northern forces were moving up the Mississippi River from the South. In April 1862, a naval squadron under Captain David G. Farragut appeared at the mouth of the river. Farragut steamed through the weak Confederate defenses and captured New Orleans on April 25. On May 1, Northerners took control of New Orleans and southern Louisiana, which they held for the rest of the war.

Raids.

Some of the most daring actions of the war occurred behind the front lines. In April 1862, a Union spy named James J. Andrews led twenty-one men through the Confederate lines to Marietta, Georgia, where they captured a railroad engine named the *General*. They ran it northward toward Chattanooga, Tennessee, destroying telegraph communications as they went. But Confederate troops in another engine, the *Texas*, pursued the *General* and caught it after what came to be called the Great Locomotive Chase. The Confederacy hanged Andrews and seven of his men.

From mid-April through early May 1863, Colonel Benjamin Grierson took a Union cavalry force of about 1,700 men on raids between Vicksburg, Mississippi, and Baton Rouge, Louisiana. They tore up about 50 miles (80 kilometers) of railroad track and lured Confederate cavalry and infantry regiments away from Union troops massing near Vicksburg.

Confederate Generals Nathan Bedford Forrest and John Hunt Morgan led many cavalry raids into enemy territory. In 1864, for example, Forrest's men galloped as far north as Paducah, Kentucky, destroying Union supplies and communications lines. Morgan led his men, called Morgan's Raiders, on a dash through Kentucky, Indiana, and Ohio in July 1863. They destroyed property worth about $576,000 before being captured. Morgan escaped in November but was killed a year later in Tennessee.

Battle of Perryville.

After Corinth fell to Union forces, Halleck went to Washington, D.C., to act as Lincoln's military adviser. He assigned Grant to guard communications along the Mississippi and ordered Buell, who had yet to prove himself, to capture Chattanooga. Before Buell could advance, General Braxton Bragg, the Confederate commander in Tennessee, suddenly invaded Kentucky. Buell raced to meet him, and the two armies clashed on October 8 at Perryville. Neither side won, but Bragg retreated to Murfreesboro, Tennessee.

Battle of Stones River (or Battle of Murfreesboro). Lincoln felt that Buell was too cautious and replaced him with General William S. Rosecrans. Rosecrans advanced south from Nashville toward Bragg's army at Murfreesboro on Stones River. The hard-fought battle dragged on from December 31, 1862, to January 2, 1863, when Bragg retreated. The battle had the highest casualty rate of the war, with each side losing about a third of its men.

Siege of Vicksburg. In the winter of 1862–1863, Grant proposed to capture Vicksburg, the key city that guarded the Mississippi River between Memphis and New Orleans. Grant tried several times to take Vicksburg by approaching from the north. But the ground north of the city was low and marshy, and the Union army bogged down. In April 1863, Grant launched a new plan. At night, Union gunboats and supply ships slipped past the Confederate artillery along the river and established a base south of the city. Grant's troops then marched down the west side of the river and crossed over by ship to dry ground on the east side south of the city. In a brilliant campaign, Grant scattered Confederate forces in the field and drove toward Vicksburg. After direct attacks failed, he began a siege of the city in mid-May. Vicksburg finally surrendered on July 4, the day after the Southern defeat at Gettysburg.

Clara Barton

Four days later, forces under General Nathaniel P. Banks took Port Hudson, Louisiana. The North controlled the Mississippi River, splitting the Confederacy in two.

The Tennessee Campaign

Battle of Chickamauga. In September 1863, Rosecrans advanced on Chattanooga with a force of about 55,000 men. Bragg, who was seeking to keep his army free for action, evacuated the city and withdrew to Georgia. Rosecrans recklessly pursued him. Bragg had received reinforcements by rail from Virginia, and his forces numbered approximately 66,000. He fell on Rosecrans at Chickamauga, Georgia, on September 19–20. The Northern right flank broke completely. Only the Union left flank fought on under General George H. Thomas, who earned the nickname "The Rock of Chickamauga" for holding his line. In the end, Rosecrans's entire army had to retreat to Chattanooga. The Battle of Chickamauga was the Confederacy's last important victory in the Civil War.

Battle of Chattanooga. Bragg did not follow up his victory at Chickamauga immediately. In late September 1863, he finally advanced on Chattanooga. Bragg's army occupied Lookout Mountain, Missionary Ridge, and other heights south of the city. From these points, Confederate artillery commanded the roads and the Tennessee River, by which Chattanooga received its supplies. Starvation threatened Rosecrans's army. But the North had enough troops available in the West to meet any threat. In October 1863, Grant was given command of all Union forces in the West. He replaced Rosecrans with Thomas. Grant then went to Chattanooga with part of his own army.

From November 23–25, the Union troops dealt Bragg an immense blow in the Battle of Chattanooga. Lookout Mountain and some other heights fell on the first two days in the so-called Battle Above the Clouds. On November 25, Thomas's army, anxious to make up for its defeat at Chickamauga, swept up Missionary Ridge without orders. The successful charge ended the Battle of Chattanooga in an hour. The Union had won Chattanooga. From that base, Northern armies could move into Georgia and Alabama and split the eastern Confederacy in two.

Hospitals. During the Civil War, many wounded and sick soldiers were treated in hospitals in Northern and Southern cities. But most received care in temporary facilities. Such facilities included field hospitals on or near battlegrounds, hospital ships and barges, and civilian buildings converted for medical use.

By today's standards, the medical care was primitive. More than twice as many soldiers died of disease—especially of dysentery, malaria, or typhoid—as were killed in battle. Doctors did not yet understand the importance of sanitation, a balanced diet, and sterile medical equipment and facilities. But medical care within the military made some progress with the introduction of horse-drawn ambulances and a trained ambulance corps. The first such corps, begun in 1862, served under Union General McClellan.

Women performed a key role in providing medical care. Mary Walker served as a surgeon with the Union army. She became the only woman ever to receive the Medal of Honor. Dorothea Dix, famous for her earlier work in mental institutions, was superintendent of U.S. Army nurses. Thousands of volunteer nurses served the Union and Confederate forces. One of the North's volunteer nurses, Clara Barton, later founded the American Red Cross.

Private organizations also helped care for ill and wounded soldiers. One organization was the United States Sanitary Commission, created in June 1861. It operated hospitals and distributed food, clothing, medicine, and other supplies. The organization cared for both Union and Confederate soldiers.

Prisons. About 194,000 Union soldiers and about 214,000 Confederate soldiers were held prisoner during the war. The North and the South had about thirty major prison camps each. Both sides also set up temporary prison quarters. Prison conditions were generally miserable because the camps were overcrowded and officials could not provide adequate care. In the South, where such necessities as food and clothing were in short supply for the Confederacy's own soldiers and civilians, prisoners had an especially difficult time.

Andersonville, a Confederate camp in Georgia, became known as the worst of the prison camps. It was horribly overcrowded, and prisoners were deliberately abused and neglected. At Andersonville, as many as 32,000 Northern prisoners at a time were crowded into a log stockade designed to hold 10,000 people. After the war, the graves of nearly 13,000 Union prisoners were discovered there. The officer in charge of Andersonville, Henry Wirz,

General Ulysses S. Grant

became the only Confederate soldier to be tried and executed for war crimes after the war.

At first, no official prisoner exchange took place between North and South. The Union government refused to extend such a degree of recognition to the Confederacy. A successful prisoner exchange agreement was reached by the middle of 1862. However, the agreement broke down in 1863, chiefly because the Confederacy resented the Union's use of black soldiers and refused to treat them as prisoners of war. After the Confederate government itself authorized the use of black soldiers in 1865, large-scale prisoner exchange started again.

All signs pointed to victory for the Union in early 1864. The Southern armies had dwindled because of battle losses, war weariness, and Northern occupation of large areas of the Confederacy. Southern railroads had almost stopped running, and supplies were desperately short. But the South, still capable of tough resistance, fought on for over a year before surrendering.

Grant in Command

Since 1862, Lincoln had wanted the Union armies to have a unified command and a coordinated strategy. Lincoln favored a *cordon offense*—a strategy in which the Union armies would advance on all fronts, pitting the vast Northern resources against the South. In Ulysses S. Grant, Lincoln felt that he had finally found the leadership needed to carry out such an offensive.

On March 9, 1864, Lincoln promoted Grant to lieutenant general and gave him command of all Northern armies. Grant planned three main offensives. The Army of the Potomac, under Meade, would try to defeat Lee in northern Virginia and occupy Richmond. Grant intended to accompany and direct that army. An army under General William T. Sherman would advance from Chattanooga into Georgia and seize Atlanta. Banks would move his men from New Orleans to Mobile, Alabama, and later join Sherman. The third offensive never developed because of a crushing defeat suffered by Banks on April 9 in a battle at Pleasant Hill, Louisiana.

Battle of the Wilderness. In May 1864, the Army of the Potomac moved into a desolate area of northern Virginia called the Wilderness. Grant, with about 118,000 men, planned to march through the Wilderness and force the Confederates into a battle that would have a clear winner. Lee, with only about 62,000 troops, met Grant on May 5, and the Battle of the Wilderness raged for two days. Troops stumbled blindly through the forest, where cavalry proved useless and artillery did little good. The underbrush caught fire, and wounded men died screaming in the flames. Both sides suffered heavy losses, and neither could claim it had won.

Battle of Spotsylvania Court House. In spite of his losses, Grant was determined to push on to final victory or defeat. He moved off to his left toward Richmond. Lee marched to meet him, and the great opponents clashed again at Spotsylvania Court House, Virginia, on May 8 through 19, 1864. Spotsylvania, like the Wilderness, brought large losses but no victory for either side.

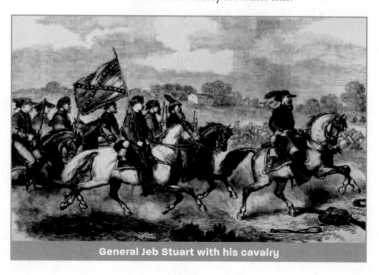
General Jeb Stuart with his cavalry

Battle of Cold Harbor. Grant again moved off to his left toward Richmond, and again Lee marched to meet him. By June 1, 1864, Grant had reached Cold Harbor, a community just north of the Confederate capital. There, on June 3, he made another attempt to smash Lee. About 50,000 attackers faced 30,000 defenders in trenches across a 3-mile (5-kilometer) line. Northern troops charged in a frontal assault. Gunfire cut down some 7,000 of them, chiefly in the first minutes of the charge. Grant later said, "I regret this assault more than any one I have ever ordered."

Cold Harbor forced Grant to change his strategy. Lee had shown superb defensive skill, and Northern losses had been enormous. In a month of fighting, Grant had lost almost 40,000 men. Newspapers began to call him "butcher Grant." Grant felt that if he repeated his moves, Lee would fall back to the Richmond defenses, where the Confederates could hold out against a siege. Grant therefore made one more attempt to force a quick and final win-or-lose battle.

Siege of Petersburg. Concealing his movement from Lee, Grant marched south and crossed the James River. His soldiers built *pontoon* (floating) bridges across the river. Grant then advanced on Petersburg, a rail center south of Richmond. All railroads supplying Richmond ran through Petersburg. If Grant could seize the railroads, he could force Lee to fight in the open. But a small Confederate force under Beauregard held him off until Lee arrived. Grant then realized that he could not destroy Lee's army without a siege. His men dug trenches around the city. Lee's weary troops did the same. The deadly siege of Petersburg began on June 20, 1864. It lasted more than nine months, until the Confederate troops withdrew at the war's end.

Cavalry maneuvers. While Grant was moving toward Richmond, he had sent his cavalry ahead under Sheridan to attack the city's communications. Confederate cavalry led by General Jeb Stuart opposed Sheridan. The two forces met at Yellow Tavern, Virginia, on May 11, 1864. Stuart was fatally wounded in the battle.

In June, Lee sent an infantry force under General Jubal A. Early through the Shenandoah Valley to raid Washington, D.C. He hoped that Grant would send some of his troops to guard the Northern capital. Early attacked one of the forts on the outskirts of the city. Lincoln stood on a low wall atop the fort and watched the attack as bullets spattered around him. Early was not strong enough to take the capital and retreated to Virginia. But he remained a threat in the valley.

Although the Confederates could not take Washington, their ability to threaten the capital after three years of war weakened Northern morale. Grant thus put all Union forces in the Shenandoah Valley under Sheridan and ordered him to follow Early to the death. Sheridan's forces outnumbered the Confederates 2 to 1 and drove them from the valley in a series of victories. His greatest success came at Cedar Creek, Virginia, on October 19, 1864, when Early made a surprise attack while Sheridan was returning from a conference in Washington. Riding to the field from nearby Winchester, Sheridan rallied his men and won the battle. Sheridan then laid waste to the valley to flush out ambushers and to prevent its resources from being used by any Confederate army that might try again to attack Washington.

Battle of Mobile Bay. The North's blockade of Southern ports grew more effective. Union forces worked steadily to seize the main ports still open to ships that slipped through the blockade. In August 1864, a naval squadron under Farragut sailed into the bay at Mobile, Alabama, which was defended by forts; mines (then called *torpedoes*); gunboats; and an ironclad. After the Union lead ship, an ironclad, was blown up, Farragut ordered his own wooden commander's ship, the *Hartford*, into the lead. "Damn the torpedoes! Full speed ahead!" was the cry he reportedly bellowed. The Union sailors captured the forts and took control of the bay, though they did not occupy Mobile. In February 1865, another main port, Wilmington, North Carolina, fell to Northern ships. But Charleston, South Carolina, still held out.

Closing In

The Atlanta campaign. In May 1864, while Grant drove into the Wilderness, Sherman's army of about 100,000 men advanced on Atlanta, Georgia, from Chattanooga. General Joseph E. Johnston opposed him with a force of about 62,000. Johnston planned to delay Sherman and draw him away from his base. The Atlanta campaign developed into a gigantic chess game. Sherman repeatedly moved forward, trying to trap Johnston into battling on open ground. Each time, Johnston and his troops slipped away into pre-

pared trench positions. The two armies clashed frequently in small battles. The largest battle occurred on June 27 at Kennesaw Mountain, an isolated peak near Atlanta.

As Sherman reached the outskirts of Atlanta, Confederate President Davis, perhaps more for political than military reasons, decided Johnston was fighting too cautiously. He replaced him with General John B. Hood. Hood attacked the Union columns as Sherman approached Atlanta. But Hood's attacks failed, and he took up a position in the city. Sherman first tried siege operations. But because he did not want to be delayed, he wheeled part of his army south of Atlanta and seized its only railroad to cut Hood's supply line. Hood evacuated the city on September 1, 1864. Sherman occupied it the next day.

North to Nashville. Sherman's victory was not as complete as it seemed. Hood's army had escaped and begun hit-and-run raids on Sherman's railroad communications with Chattanooga. Sherman thought it would be useless to chase Hood along the railroad. Instead, he sent General George H. Thomas back to Tennessee to take command and gave him some 32,000 men under General John M. Schofield. He ordered Thomas, at Nashville, to assemble more troops in Tennessee and keep Hood out of the state. With his remaining men, Sherman planned to cross Georgia to Savannah, near the Atlantic coast.

Hood boldly decided to invade Tennessee in the hope that Sherman would follow him. He felt sure that he could beat Sherman in the mountains. He would then either invade Kentucky or cross into Virginia and join Lee. But Hood's plan was too big for his army.

Major General William T. Sherman with his generals

The surrender

Battle of Franklin. Hood might have won a partial success if he had moved into Tennessee immediately. But he delayed and met Schofield's force at Franklin, Tennessee, on November 30, 1864. Hood, an aggressive commander, had complained that his army had retreated so much under Johnston that it had forgotten how to attack. His generals seemed determined to prove him wrong. In six reckless charges, the Confederates suffered about 6,300 casualties, including six generals killed.

Battle of Nashville. Hood had no chance of success after his defeat at Franklin. He took a position south of Nashville and waited. In the city, Thomas had time to gather an army of about 55,000. He attacked Hood on December 15–16, 1864, and won one of the biggest victories of the war. The Confederates made a bitter retreat to Mississippi.

Sherman's march through Georgia began on November 15, 1864, when he left Atlanta in flames. His army, numbering about 62,000 men, swept almost unopposed on a 50-mile (80-kilometer) front across the state. Advance troops scouted an area. The men who followed stripped houses, barns, and fields and destroyed everything they could not use. Sherman hoped the horrible destruction would break the South's will to continue the war.

Sherman occupied Savannah on December 21 and sent a message to Lincoln: "I beg to present to you as a Christmas gift the city of Savannah with 150 heavy guns and plenty of ammunition and also about 25,000 bales of cotton." From Savannah, Sherman swung north into South Carolina. There, on the breeding ground of the Southern independ-

ence movement, his army seemed bent on revenge. They burned and looted on a scale even worse than in Georgia. When Charleston surrendered, it was spared. Although Sherman tried to prevent it, most of Columbia, the state capital, was burned.

Sherman and his troops then moved on into North Carolina. Johnston tried to oppose them, but he had only one-third as many men. The Northerners drove on toward Virginia to link up with Grant.

The South surrenders. In Virginia, Grant at last achieved his goal. In April 1865, he seized the railroads supplying Richmond. The Confederate troops had to evacuate Petersburg and Richmond. Lee retreated westward with nearly 50,000 men. He hoped to join forces with Johnston in North Carolina. But Grant overtook him and barred his way with an army of almost 113,000 troops. Lee realized that continued fighting would mean useless loss of lives. He wrote Grant and asked for an interview to arrange surrender terms.

On April 9, 1865, the two great generals met in a house owned by a Southern farmer named Wilmer McLean in the little country settlement of Appomattox Court House, Virginia. The meeting was one of the most dramatic scenes in American history. Grant wore a mud-spattered private's coat, with only his shoulder straps indicating his rank. Lee had put on a spotless uniform, complete with sword. Grant offered generous terms, and Lee accepted them with deep appreciation. The Confederate soldiers received a day's rations and were released on parole. They were allowed to keep their horses and mules to take home "to put in a crop." Officers could keep their side arms.

Five days later, on the evening of April 14, Lincoln was shot by Southern sympathizer John Wilkes Booth. He died the following morning. Northerners cried out for revenge for Lincoln's assassination and for the hundreds of thousands killed in the war. But before his death, Lincoln had advised "malice toward none. . .charity for all" to heal the country's wounds. Although feelings were strong, no major incidents occurred.

With Lee's army gone, Johnston surrendered to Sherman on April 26 near Durham, North Carolina. Confederate president Davis fled southward and was captured in Georgia. General Richard Taylor surrendered the Confederate forces in Alabama and Mississippi on May 4. The war's last battle took place at Palmito Ranch, near the southern tip of Texas, on May 13. The Confederate and Union soldiers fighting there did not know that the South had surrendered. On May 26, General Edmund Kirby Smith surrendered the last Confederate army still in the field. The war was over.

Results of the War

The tragic costs. About 620,000 soldiers died during the Civil War, almost as many as the combined American dead of all other wars from the Revolutionary War in America (1775–1783) through the Iraq War, which began in 2003. The Union lost about 360,000 troops, and the Confederacy about 260,000. More than half the deaths were caused by disease. About a third of all Southern soldiers died in the war, compared with about a sixth of all Northern soldiers.

Both the North and the South paid an enormous economic price as well. But the direct damages caused by the war were especially severe in the South. The destruction in the South extended from the beautiful Shenandoah Valley in the north to Georgia in the south and from South Carolina in the east to Tennessee in the west. Towns and farms, industry and trade, and the lives of men, women, and children were ruined throughout the South. The whole Southern way of life was lost.

Terrible bitterness between the people of the North and South followed the war and continued for generations. The South was given almost no voice in the social, political, and cultural affairs of the nation. With the loss of Southern control of the national government, the more traditional Southern ideals no longer had an important influence over government policy. The Yankee Protestant ideals of the North became the standard for the United States. However, those ideals, which stressed hard work, education, and economic freedom, helped encourage the development of the United States as a modern, industrial power.

 The beginning of modern warfare. The American Civil War is frequently called the first modern war. It was the first war in which the participants communicated by telegraph, transported supplies and troops by train, and used ironclad warships, submarines, and mines in naval combat. The armies were much larger than armies of the past. These forces introduced trench warfare and other combat tactics used in later wars.

President Lincoln (seen at a distance) giving the Gettysburg Address

On the other hand, the muzzle-loading rifles and cannons used by most of the soldiers were soon surpassed by more advanced weapons and artillery. The ironclad warships gave way to warships of steel.

The American Civil War is also often described as the first total war because of the enormous amount of suffering and destruction it brought upon noncombatants as well as soldiers. A military campaign such as Sherman's march seemed to indicate a shift from war as a battle between two armies to war as systematic destruction of anyone and anything in an army's path. However, little of the war's destructiveness was the result of deliberate planning, even during Sherman's march. The war destroyed much of the South and ruined Southern agriculture. But the North never experienced a serious invasion, though large sectors of its economy suffered.

Union and Confederate leaders alike struggled to observe the accepted rules and conventions of war. They failed in the treatment of prisoners of war, but most of the evils of the prison system arose from incompetence and poor planning. Neither side resorted to executing all prisoners, though Confederates did execute some captured black soldiers. After the war, the federal government did not seek to convict the defeated Confederates of treason. In the end, if the Civil War can be considered a total war, it is because the conflict, with its huge armies and four years of fighting in two theaters of war, destroyed so many lives and so much of the nation's resources.

The end of slavery. The Declaration of Independence, which gave birth to the United States in 1776, stated that "all men are created equal." Yet the United States continued to be the largest slaveholding nation in the world until the Civil War. Americans tried to make equality a reality soon after the war by *ratifying* (approving) the Thirteenth Amendment to the Constitution, which officially abolished slavery throughout the United States. The place of blacks in American society, however, remained unsettled.

The preservation of the Union. In a fundamental sense, the Civil War may have been the greatest failure of American democracy. The war, in Lincoln's words, was an "appeal from the ballot to the bullet." From 1861 to 1865 in the United States, the calm reason that is basic to democracy gave way to human passions.

Yet democracy in the United States survived its "fiery trial." The nation's motto was *E Pluribus Unum*, a Latin term meaning *out of many, one*. It referred to the creation of one nation, the United States, out of thirteen colonies. But for a long time, Americans could not decide whether they wanted to be "many" or "one." The Northern victory established that no state had the right or power to end the Union. Furthermore, the outcome of the war paved the way for the rise of the United States as a major global power.

The Battle of Gettysburg, fought from July 1 through July 3, 1863, marked a turning point in the American Civil War in the North's favor. General George G. Meade led a Northern army of about 90,000 men to victory against General Robert E. Lee's Southern army of about 75,000. The shoot-

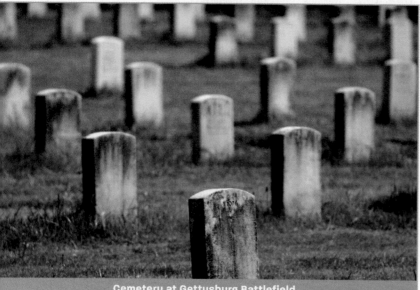

Cemetery at Gettysburg Battlefield

ing began when the two forces met accidentally in the town of Gettysburg, Pennsylvania, on July 1.

That day, Southern forces took the town. But Union troops took a strong position on high ground south of town. On July 2, Lee tried but failed to break the North's line at points known as Culp's Hill, Cemetery Ridge, the Peach Orchard, the Wheatfield, Devil's Den, and Little Round Top. Early on July 3, fighting resumed at Culp's Hill, on the Union's right. Lee also attacked the Union's center, on Cemetery Ridge. Following an artillery duel, about 13,000 troops organized and in part led by General George E. Pickett advanced across an open field and up Cemetery Ridge in what became known as "Pickett's charge." Facing impossible odds, only a few of the Southern troops reached the top of the ridge. On July 4, Lee began to withdraw to Virginia.

About 4,000 Southerners and more than 3,000 Northerners were killed in the battle. The total number of casualties—those killed, wounded, missing, or captured—was about 23,000 for the North and from 25,000 to 28,000 for the South.

The Emancipation Proclamation

The Emancipation Proclamation was a historic document that led to the end of slavery in the United States. President Abraham Lincoln issued the proclamation on January 1, 1863, during the American Civil War. It declared freedom for slaves in all areas of the Confederacy that were still in rebellion against the Union. The proclamation also provided for the use of blacks in the Union army and navy. As a result, it greatly influenced the North's victory in the war.

Events leading to the Proclamation. The eleven states of the Confederacy *seceded* (withdrew) from the Union in 1860 and 1861. They seceded primarily because they feared Lincoln would restrict their right to do as they chose about the question of black slavery. The North entered the Civil War only to reunite the nation, not to end slavery.

During the first half of the war, abolitionists and some Union military leaders urged Lincoln to issue a proclamation freeing the slaves. They argued that such a policy would help the North because slaves were contributing greatly to the Confederate war effort. By doing most of the South's farming and factory work, slaves made whites available for the Confederate army.

Lincoln agreed with the abolitionists' view of slavery. He once declared that "if slavery is not wrong, nothing is wrong." But early in the war, Lincoln believed that if he freed the slaves, he would divide the North. Lincoln feared that four slave-owning border states—Delaware, Kentucky, Maryland, and Missouri—would secede if he adopted such a policy.

Lincoln's change of policy. In July 1862, with the war going badly for the North, Congress passed a law freeing all Confederate slaves who came into Union lines. At about that same time, Lincoln decided to change his stand on slavery. But he waited for a Union military victory, so that his decision would not appear to be a desperate act.

On September 22, 1862, five days after Union forces won the Battle of Antietam, Lincoln issued a preliminary proclamation. It stated that if the rebelling states did not return to the Union by January 1, 1863, he would declare their slaves to be "forever free." The South rejected Lincoln's policy, and so he issued the Emancipation Proclamation on January 1, 1863. Lincoln took this action as commander in chief of the army and navy of the United States. He called it "a fit and necessary war measure."

Effects of the Proclamation. The Emancipation Proclamation did not actually free a single slave, because it affected only areas under Confederate control. It excluded slaves in the border states and in such Southern areas under Union control as Tennessee and parts of Louisiana and Virginia. But it did lead to the Thirteenth Amendment to the Constitution. This amendment, which became law on December 18, 1865, ended slavery in all parts of the United States.

As the abolitionists had predicted, the Emancipation Proclamation strengthened the North's war effort and weakened the South's. By the end of the war, more than 500,000 slaves had fled to freedom behind Northern lines. Many of them joined the Union army or navy or worked for the armed forces as laborers. By allowing blacks to serve in the army and navy, the Emancipation Proclamation helped solve the North's problem of declining enlistments. About 200,000 black soldiers and sailors, many of them former slaves, served in the armed forces. They helped the North win the war.

The Emancipation Proclamation also hurt the South by discouraging the United Kingdom and France from entering the war. Both of those nations depended on the South to supply them with cotton, and the Confederacy hoped that they would fight on its side. But the proclamation made the war a fight against slavery. The United Kingdom and France had already abolished slavery, and so they gave their support to the Union.

MLA Citation

"American Civil War."
The Southwestern Advantage Topic Source. Nashville: Southwestern. 2013.

Confederate Memorial

DATA

Important Events During the American Civil War

1861

April 12	Confederate troops attacked Fort Sumter.
April 15	Lincoln issued a call for troops.
April 19	Lincoln proclaimed a blockade of the South.
May 21	Richmond, Virginia, chosen as the Confederate capital.
July 21	Northern troops retreated in disorder after the First Battle of Bull Run (Manassas).

1862

February 6	Fort Henry fell to Union forces.
February 16	Grant's troops captured Fort Donelson.
March 9	The ironclad ships *Monitor* and *Merrimack (Virginia)* battled to a draw.
April 6–7	Both sides suffered heavy losses in the Battle of Shiloh, won by the Union.
April 16	The Confederacy began to draft soldiers.
April 18–25	Farragut attacked and captured New Orleans.
May 4	McClellan's Union troops occupied Yorktown, Virginia, and advanced on Richmond.
May 30	Northern forces occupied Corinth, Mississippi.
June 6	Memphis fell to Union armies.
June 25–July 1	Confederate forces under Lee saved Richmond in the Battles of the Seven Days.
August 27–30	Lee and Jackson led Southern troops to victory in the Second Battle of Bull Run (Manassas).
September 17	Confederate forces retreated in defeat after the bloody Battle of Antietam (Sharpsburg).
September 22	Lincoln issued a preliminary Emancipation Proclamation.
October 8	Buell's forces ended Bragg's invasion of Kentucky in the Battle of Perryville.
December 13	Burnside's Union forces received a crushing blow in the Battle of Fredericksburg.
December 31– January 2, 1863	Union troops under Rosecrans forced the Confederates to retreat after the Battle of Stones River (Murfreesboro).

1863

January 1	Lincoln issued the Emancipation Proclamation.
March 3	The North passed a draft law.
May 1–4	Northern troops under Hooker were defeated in the Battle of Chancellorsville.
May 1–19	Grant's army defeated the Confederates in Mississippi and began to besiege Vicksburg.
July 1–3	The Battle of Gettysburg ended in a Southern defeat and marked a turning point in the war.
July 4	Vicksburg fell to Northern troops.

DATA

Important Events During the American Civil War

July 8	Northern forces occupied Port Hudson, Louisiana.
September 19–20	Southern troops under Bragg won the Battle of Chickamauga.
November 19	Lincoln delivered the Gettysburg Address.
November 23–25	Grant and Thomas led Union armies to victory in the Battle of Chattanooga.
1864	
March 9	Grant became general in chief of the North.
May 5–6	Union and Confederate troops clashed in the Battle of the Wilderness.
May 8–19	Grant and Lee held their positions in the Battle of Spotsylvania Court House.
June 3	The Union suffered heavy losses on the final day of the Battle of Cold Harbor.
June 20	Grant's troops laid siege to Petersburg, Virginia.
July 11–12	Early's Confederate forces almost reached Washington but retreated after brief fighting.
August 5	Farragut won the Battle of Mobile Bay.
September 2	Northern troops under Sherman captured Atlanta.
September 19–October 19	Sheridan led his troops on a rampage of destruction in the Shenandoah Valley.
November 8	Lincoln was reelected president.
November 15	Sherman began his march through Georgia.
November 23	Hood invaded Tennessee.
November 30	Schofield's Union forces inflicted heavy losses on Hood in the Battle of Franklin.
December 15–16	The Battle of Nashville smashed Hood's army.
December 21	Sherman's troops occupied Savannah, Georgia.
1865	
February 6	Lee became general in chief of the South.
April 2	Confederate troops gave up Petersburg and Richmond.
April 9	Lee surrendered to Grant at Appomattox.
April 14	Lincoln was shot. He died the following morning.
April 26	Johnston surrendered to Sherman.
May 4	Confederate forces in Alabama and Mississippi surrendered.
May 11	Jefferson Davis was captured.
May 26	The last Confederate troops surrendered.

DATA

Major Battles of the American Civil War

Battle	State	Date	Northern commander	Southern commander
Antietam (Sharpsburg)	Maryland	September 17, 1862	McClellan	Lee
Bull Run (Manassas) First	Virginia	July 21, 1861	McDowell	Beauregard
Bull Run (Manassas) Second	Virginia	August 27–30, 1862	Pope	Lee
Chancellorsville	Virginia	May 1–4, 1863	Hooker	Lee
Chattanooga	Tennessee	November 23–25, 1863	Grant	Bragg
Chickamauga	Georgia	September 19–20, 1863	Rosecrans	Bragg
Cold Harbor	Virginia	June 1–3, 1864	Grant	Lee
Fair Oaks (Seven Pines)	Virginia	May 31–June 1, 1862	McClellan	J. Johnston
Fort Donelson	Tennessee	February 13–16, 1862	Grant	Buckner
Fort Henry	Tennessee	February 6, 1862	Grant	Tilghman
Franklin	Tennessee	November 30, 1864	Schofield	Hood
Fredericksburg	Virginia	December 13, 1862	Burnside	Lee
Gettysburg	Pennsylvania	July 1–3, 1863	Meade	Lee
Kennesaw Mountain	Georgia	June 27, 1864	Sherman	J. Johnston
Mobile Bay	Alabama	August 5, 1864	Farragut	Buchanan
Nashville	Tennessee	December 15–16, 1864	Thomas	Hood
Perryville	Kentucky	October 8, 1862	Buell	Bragg
Petersburg, Siege of	Virginia	June 20, 1864–April 2, 1865	Grant	Lee
Seven Days	Virginia	June 25–July 1, 1862	McClellan	Lee
Shiloh (Pittsburg Landing)	Tennessee	April 6–7, 1862	Grant	A. Johnston, Beauregard
Spotsylvania Court House	Virginia	May 8–19, 1864	Grant	Lee
Stones River (Murfreesboro)	Tennessee	December 31, 1862–January 2, 1863	Rosecrans	Bragg
Vicksburg, Siege of	Mississippi	May 19–July 4, 1863	Grant	Pemberton
Wilderness	Virginia	May 5–6, 1864	Grant	Lee

DATA

Major Battles of the American Civil War

Battle	Northern casualties[1]	Southern casualties[1]	Results
Antietam (Sharpsburg)	12,500	13,700	Confederate retreat gave Lincoln the occasion to announce the preliminary Emancipation Proclamation.
Bull Run (Manassas) First	3,000	2,000	The North first realized the seriousness of the war.
Bull Run (Manassas) Second	16,100	9,200	The South regained almost all of Virginia.
Chancellorsville	16,800	12,800	Confederate forces were victorious, but Stonewall Jackson was killed.
Chattanooga	5,800	7,700	Union win put most of Tennessee in Northern hands.
Chickamauga	16,200	18,500	Southern victory trapped Rosecrans in Chattanooga.
Cold Harbor	12,000	1,500	Heavy losses forced Grant to change his tactics.
Fair Oaks (Seven Pines)	5,000	6,000	Confederate forces were driven back.
Fort Donelson	2,800	15,800	The North won its first important victory.
Fort Henry	20		Initial success encouraged Grant's Western campaign.
Franklin	2,300	6,300	Hood's Tennessee campaign failed to draw Sherman from Georgia.
Fredericksburg	12,700	5,300	A terrible defeat left the North discouraged.
Gettysburg	23,000	25,000–28,000	Northern victory marked a turning point in the war.
Kennesaw Mountain	2,100	400	In spite of Confederate success, Davis replaced Johnston with Hood.
Mobile Bay	320	300	The North closed one of the major Southern ports.
Nashville	3,100	6,000	Northern victory practically ended Southern resistance in the West.
Perryville	4,200	3,400	Confederate troops abandoned Kentucky.
Petersburg, Siege of	42,000	28,000	Months of trench warfare pinned Lee to a defensive.
Seven Days	15,800	20,100	Richmond was saved from capture, and Northern forces retreated.
Shiloh (Pittsburg Landing)	13,000	10,700	Grant pushed back Southern forces.
Spotsylvania Court House	17,500	10,000	Grant continued to hammer at Lee's resistant forces.
Stones River (Murfreesboro)	12,900	11,700	Southern forces failed to follow up an initial victory.
Vicksburg, Siege of	10,000	10,000	Northern victory proved decisive in winning the Mississippi and the West.
Wilderness	17,700	11,000	Heavy losses failed to halt Grant's progress southward.

[1] Figures are approximate totals of dead, wounded, missing, and captured.

ADDITIONAL RESOURCES

Books to Read

Bolotin, Norman. *Civil War A to Z.* Dutton, 2002.

Clinton, Catherine. *Scholastic Encyclopedia of the Civil War.* Scholastic, 1999.

Eicher, David J. *The Longest Night: A Military History of the Civil War.* Simon & Schuster, 2001.

Haskins, James. *Black, Blue & Gray: African Americans in the Civil War.* Simon & Schuster, 1998.

Heidler, David S. and Jeanne T., eds. *Encyclopedia of the American Civil War.* 5 vols. ABC-CLIO, 2000.

McPherson, James M. *Battle Cry of Freedom.* 1988. Reprint. Oxford, 2003. *For Cause and Comrades: Why Men Fought in the Civil War.* 1997.

McPherson, James M. *Fields of Fury: The American Civil War.* Atheneum, 2002.

Stanchak, John E. *Civil War.* Dorling Kindersley, 2000.

Trudeau, Noah A. *Like Men of War: Black Troops in the Civil War, 1862–1865.* Little, Brown, 1998.

Wagner, Margaret E., and others, eds. *The Library of Congress Civil War Desk Reference.* Simon & Schuster, 2002.

Winik, Jay. *April 1865.* HarperCollins, 2001.

Web Sites

African American Slave Narratives: An Online Anthology

http://xroads.virginia.edu/~hyper/wpa/wpahome.html

First-hand accounts of the experiences of black slaves, collected by the Works Progress Administration. Hosted by American Studies Hypertexts at the University of Virginia.

Appomattox Court House, National Park, Civil War, Virginia

http://www.nps.gov/apco/

A National Park Service Web site about the Appomattox Court House National Historical Park.

Civil War Soldiers and Sailors System

http://www.itd.nps.gov/cwss/

A computerized database containing basic facts about soldiers who served on both sides during the Civil War. From the National Park Service.

Conflict of Abolition and Slavery

http://www.loc.gov/exhibits/african/afam007.html

An illustrated history of slavery and the abolition movement in America. Ends with an African-American celebration of emancipation in Washington, D.C., in 1866.

Fort Donelson National Battlefield

http://www.nps.gov/fodo/

National Park Service site on Fort Donelson National Battlefield in Dover, Tennessee.

Museum of the Confederacy

http://www.moc.org/

Home page of the Museum of the Confederacy in Richmond, Virginia.

Remembering Slavery: Those Who Survived to Tell Their Stories

http://www.uncg.edu/~jpbrewer/remember/

This site presents interviews conducted during the 1930s and 1940s with African Americans who had been born enslaved and remembered the Civil War and their lives in slavery.

The Campaign for Vicksburg

http://www.nps.gov/vick/index.htm

The story of General Grant's military campaign to seize Vicksburg, Mississippi. Presented by the Vicksburg National Military Park.

The Civil War Home Page

http://www.civil-war.net/

The Civil War Home Page contains a wealth of information on the American Civil War, including biographies, documents, images, and maps.

The Civil War in Georgia

http://georgiainfo.galileo.usg.edu/civilwar.htm

Detailed information about Georgia's role in the American Civil War. Includes extensive links to other resources. From the University of Georgia.

The Civil War Preservation Trust

http://www.civilwar.org/

Site of a nonprofit organization devoted to preserving the endangered battlefields of the Civil War.

The Emancipation Proclamation

http://www.nps.gov/ncro/anti/emancipation.html

Text of the Emancipation Proclamation, President Abraham Lincoln's order to free the slaves in rebel states in 1863.

The History Place: The U.S. Civil War 1861–1865

http://www.historyplace.com/civilwar/index.html

A detailed time line of the Civil War, illustrated with photos and maps.

The Papers of Jefferson Davis

http://jeffersondavis.rice.edu/

Information about Jefferson Davis, Mississippi planter and politician, and president of the Confederacy during the Civil War (1861–1865).

The Time of the Lincolns

http://www.pbs.org/wgbh/americanexperience/films/lincolns/

Companion piece to a PBS documentary about the life and presidency of Abraham Lincoln.

Search Strings

Abolitionists

american civil war conflict slavery abolitionist (69,800)

american civil war conflict slavery abolitionist antislavery (63,400)

slavery america conflict reasons south economy north wrong civil war (88,400)

Secession

secession union lincoln south carolina confederate states of america jefferson davis (71,900)

american civil war secession union confederate jefferson davis abraham lincoln presidential election 1860 (2,960)

Emancipation Proclamation

emancipation proclamation abraham lincoln union war measure thirteenth amendment abolish slavery (12,400)

american civil war emancipation proclamation war measure abraham lincoln thirteenth amendment (16,800)

Modern Warfare

american civil war modern warfare telegraph train ironclad warships trench warfare combat tactics (298)

modern warfare beginning american civil war telegraph train ironclad warships total war (1,070)

World War I

World War I lasted four years, beginning within weeks of the assassination of Archduke Franz Ferdinand of Austria-Hungary on June 28, 1914 and lasting until Germany signed an armistice on November 11, 1918. Other than World War II (1939–1945), this war involved more countries and caused greater destruction than any other war in history. About 9 million soldiers and more than 6 million civilians lost their lives during this war.

HOT topics

Aftermath of WWI. World War I brought about the fall of the emperors in Germany, Russia, and Austria-Hungary. This led to political change and the creation of some new European countries. The war not only killed millions of people, but it caused major property damage, destroyed a large amount of resources, and devastated many economies. It also caused social change worldwide. World War I left Europe exhausted, and created conditions that helped lead to World War II.

What Started It All. Many wars had been fought in the Balkans, and tension between Austria-Hungary and the Slavs was high. In the hopes of easing that tension, Archduke Franz Ferdinand of Austria-Hungary and his wife, Sophie, toured Bosnia-Herzegovina. While driving through Sarajevo on June 28, 1914, a Bosnian and Serbian terrorist named Gavrilo Princip shot and killed Ferdinand and his wife. This incident gave Austria-Hungary an excuse to go to war against Serbia. Because a system of military alliances had already been set in place, many countries were drawn into this war on both sides. This resulted in the most destructive war in history, other than World War II.

HOT topics

Warfare of the Era. A new era of warfare occurred during World War I, causing millions of soldiers and civilians to lose their lives. Machine guns, bomber airplanes, tanks, submarines, artillery guns, poisoned gas, and flame throwers were all part of this era's warfare. These weapons not only contributed to the deaths of many soldiers at one time, but many civilians as well.

Deadlock on the Western Front. The Western Front stretched 450 miles (720 kilometers) across Belgium and France, from Belgium's coast to Switzerland's border. France and the United Kingdom stopped Germany's advance and, using trench warfare, held them there for 3.5 years. Many battles occurred during this time, but two particularly destructive battles were the Battle of Verdun and the Battle of the Somme.

British soldiers in the trenches near Cambrai, November 1917

The assasination of Archduke Franz Ferdinand and his wife, Sophie

TRUE or FALSE?

The rise of nationalism in the 1800s was a major contributing factor to the inevitability of World War I.

THE BASICS

World War I (1914–1918) involved more countries and caused greater destruction than any other war except World War II (1939–1945). An assassin's bullets set off the war, and a system of military *alliances* (agreements) plunged the main European powers into the fight. The war lasted four years and took the lives of about 9 million troops and more than 6 million civilians.

Several developments led to the awful bloodshed of the Great War, as World War I was originally called. Military drafts raised larger armies than ever before, and industries arose to equip those armies with advanced weapons. Each nation believed it was fighting a war of self-defense. Government propaganda whipped up support by making the enemy seem villainous.

On June 28, 1914, an assassin gunned down Archduke Franz Ferdinand of Austria-Hungary in Sarajevo, the capital of Austria-Hungary's province of Bosnia-Herzegovina. The killer had ties to a terrorist organization in Serbia. Austria-Hungary believed that Serbia's government was behind the assassination. It seized the opportunity to declare war on Serbia and settle an old feud.

Within weeks, the assassination of Franz Ferdinand sparked the outbreak of World War I. But historians believe that the war had deeper roots. The unification of Germany in 1871 created a powerful and fast-growing new state in the heart of Europe. In the decade before the war, Germany's quest for power caused a series of crises. Armed forces expanded, and alliances became increasingly militarized. When the fighting began, France, Russia, and the United Kingdom—known as the Entente—backed Serbia. They opposed the Central Powers, made up of Austria-Hungary and Germany. Other countries later joined each alliance. The Entente and its allies came to be known as the Allies.

Germany won early victories on the main European battlefronts. On the Western Front, France and the United Kingdom halted the German advance in September 1914. The opposing armies then fought from trenches that stretched across Belgium and northeastern France. The Western Front hardly moved for 3½ years in spite of fierce combat. On the Eastern Front, Russia battled Germany and Austria-Hungary. The fighting seesawed back and forth until 1917, when a revolution broke out in Russia. Russia soon asked for a truce.

The United States remained neutral at first. But many Americans turned against the Central Powers after German submarines began sinking unarmed ships. In 1917, the United States joined the Allies and gave them the resources and resolve they needed to win the war. In the fall of 1918, the Central Powers surrendered.

World War I had results that none of the warring nations had foreseen. The war helped topple emperors in Austria-Hungary, Germany, and Russia. The peace treaties after the war carved new countries out of the defeated powers. The war left Europe exhausted, never to regain the controlling position in world affairs that it had held before the war. The peace settlement also created conditions that helped lead to World War II.

Background to the War

The assassination of Archduke Franz Ferdinand triggered World War I. But the war had its origins in developments of the 1800s. The chief sources of tension in Europe before World War I were (1) the rise of nationalism, (2) a build-up of military might, (3) competition for colonies, and (4) a system of military alliances.

The rise of nationalism. Europe avoided major wars in the 100 years before World War I began. Although small wars broke out, they did not involve many countries. But during the 1800s, a force swept across the continent that helped bring about the Great War. The force was *nationalism*—the belief that loyalty to a person's nation and its political and economic goals comes before any other public loyalty. That exaggerated form of patriotism increased the possibility of war because a nation's goals could conflict with the goals of one or more other nations. In addition, nationalistic pride caused nations to magnify small disputes into major issues. A minor complaint could thus quickly lead to the threat of war.

During the 1800s, nationalism took hold among people who shared a common language, history, or culture. Such people began to view themselves as members of a national group, or nation. Nationalism led to the creation of two new powers—Italy and Germany—through the uniting of many small states.

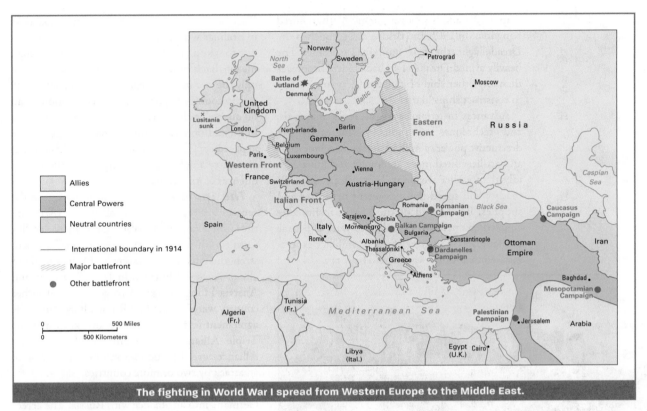

Allies

Central Powers

Neutral countries

International boundary in 1914

Major battlefront

Other battlefront

0   500 Miles

0   500 Kilometers

The fighting in World War I spread from Western Europe to the Middle East.

War had a major role in achieving national unification in Italy and Germany.

Nationalist policies gained enthusiastic support as many countries in Western Europe granted the vote to more people. The right to vote gave citizens greater interest and greater pride in national goals. As a result, parliamentary governments grew increasingly powerful.

On the other hand, nationalism weakened the eastern European empires of Austria-Hungary, Russia, and the Ottomans. Those empires ruled many national groups that clamored for independence. Conflicts among national groups were especially explosive in the Balkans—the states on the Balkan Peninsula in southeastern Europe. The peninsula was known as the *Powder Keg of Europe* because tensions there threatened to ignite a major war. Most of the Balkans had been part of the Ottoman Empire. First Greece and then Montenegro, Serbia, Romania, Bulgaria, and Albania won independence in the period from 1821 to 1913. Each state quarreled with neighbors over boundaries. Austria-Hungary and Russia also took advantage of the Ottoman Empire's weakness to increase their influence in the Balkans.

Rivalry for control of the Balkans added to the tensions that erupted into World War I. Serbia led a movement to unite the region's Slavs. Russia, the most powerful Slavic country, supported Serbia. But Austria-Hungary feared Slavic nationalism, which stirred unrest in its empire. Millions of Slavs lived under Austria-Hungary's rule. In 1908, Austria-Hungary greatly angered Russia and Serbia by adding the Balkan territory of Bosnia-Herzegovina to its empire. Serbia wanted control of this area because many Serbs lived there.

A buildup of military might occurred among European countries before World War I broke out. The quick victories achieved by the Germans in their wars of unification made the German army a model for others. A military draft helped create a sense of nationalism. Overseeing the military was a general staff, whose task in peacetime was to plan for the army's use in war.

At first, the United Kingdom remained unconcerned about Germany's military buildup. The United Kingdom, an island country, relied on its navy for defense—and it had the world's strongest navy. But in 1898, Germany began to develop a naval force big enough to challenge the British navy. Germany's decision to become a major seapower made it a bitter enemy of the United Kingdom. In 1906, the British navy launched the *Dreadnought*, the first modern battleship. The heavily armed *Dreadnought* had greater firepower than any other ship of its time. Germany rushed to construct ships like it.

Advances in *technology*—the tools, materials, and techniques of industry—increased the destructive power of military forces. Machine guns and artillery fired more accurately and more rapidly than earlier weapons. Steamships and railroads could speed the movement of troops and supplies. By the end of the 1800s, technology enabled countries to fight longer wars and bear greater losses than ever before. Yet military experts insisted that future wars would be short.

The launch of the *Dreadnought*, 1906

Competition for colonies. During the late 1800s and early 1900s, European nations carved nearly all of Africa and much of Asia into colonies. The race for colonies was fueled by Europe's increasing industrialization. Colonies supplied European nations with raw materials for factories, markets for manufactured goods, and opportunities for investment. The competition for colonies strained relations among European countries, but none of the clashes actually led to war.

A system of military alliances gave European powers a sense of security before World War I. A country hoped to discourage an attack from its enemies by entering into a military agreement with one or more other countries. In case of an attack, such an agreement guaranteed that other members of the alliance would come to the country's aid or at least remain neutral.

Although military alliances provided protection for a country, the system created certain dangers.

Because of its alliances, a country might take risks in dealings with other nations that it would hesitate to take alone. If war came, the alliance system meant that a number of nations would fight, not only the two involved in a dispute. Alliances could force a country to go to war against a nation it had no quarrel with or over an issue it had no interest in. In addition, the terms of many alliances were kept secret. The secrecy increased the chances that a country might guess wrong about the consequences of its actions.

The Triple Alliance. Germany was at the center of European foreign policy from 1870 until the outbreak of World War I. German Chancellor Otto von Bismarck formed a series of alliances to strengthen his country's security. He first made an ally of Austria-Hungary. In 1879, Germany and Austria-Hungary agreed to go to war if either country were attacked by Russia. Italy joined the agreement in 1882, and it became known as the Triple Alliance. The members of the Triple Alliance agreed to aid one another in the case of an attack by two or more countries.

Bismarck also brought Austria-Hungary and Germany into an alliance with Russia. The agreement, known as the Three Emperors' League, was formed in 1881. The three powers agreed to remain neutral if any of them went to war with another country. Bismarck also persuaded Austria-Hungary and Russia, which were rivals for influence in the Balkans, to recognize each other's zone of authority in the region. He thus reduced the danger of conflict between the two countries.

Germany's relations with other European countries worsened after Bismarck left office in 1890. Bismarck had worked to prevent France, Germany's neighbor on the west, from forming an alliance with either of Germany's two neighbors to the east—Russia and Austria-Hungary. In 1894, France and Russia agreed to *mobilize* (call up troops) if any nation in the Triple Alliance mobilized. France and Russia also agreed to help each other if either were attacked by Germany.

The Triple Entente. During the 1800s, the United Kingdom had followed a foreign policy that became known as "splendid isolation." But threats to its empire and Germany's military build-up persuaded the United Kingdom to end its isolation. In 1904, the United Kingdom and France settled their past disagreements over colonies and signed the Entente Cordiale (Friendly Agreement).

Although the agreement contained no pledges of military support, the two countries began to discuss joint military plans. In 1907, the United Kingdom and Russia settled their differences in Asia. Russia joined the alliance, which became known as the Triple Entente.

The Triple Entente did not obligate its members to go to war as the Triple Alliance did. But the alliances left Europe divided into two opposing camps.

Beginning of the War

World War I began in the Balkans, an area with a long history of conflict. In the early 1900s, the Balkan states fought the Ottoman Empire in the First Balkan War (1912–1913) and one another in the Second Balkan War (1913). The major European powers stayed out of both wars. But they did not escape the third Balkan crisis.

The assassination of an archduke. Archduke Franz Ferdinand, heir to the throne of Austria-Hungary, hoped that his sympathy for Slavs would ease tensions between Austria-Hungary and the Balkans. He arranged to tour Bosnia-Herzegovina with his wife, Sophie. As the couple rode through Sarajevo on June 28, 1914, an assassin jumped on their automobile and fired two shots. Franz Ferdinand and Sophie died almost instantly. The murderer, a Bosnian named Gavrilo Princip, was linked to a Serbian terrorist group called the Black Hand.

The assassination of Franz Ferdinand gave Austria-Hungary an excuse to crush Serbia, its long-time enemy in the Balkans. Austria-Hungary first gained Germany's promise of support for action against Serbia. It then sent a list of humiliating demands to Serbia on July 23. Serbia accepted most of the demands and offered to have the rest settled by an international conference. Austria-Hungary rejected the offer and declared war on Serbia on July 28. It expected a quick victory in a local war.

How the conflict spread. Within weeks of the archduke's assassination, the chief European powers were drawn into World War I. A few attempts were made to prevent the war. For example, the United Kingdom proposed an international conference to end the crisis. But Germany rejected the idea, claiming that the dispute involved only Austria-Hungary and Serbia.

Russia had backed down before in supporting its ally Serbia. In 1908, Austria-Hungary had angered Serbia by taking over Bosnia-Herzegovina, and Russia had stepped aside. In 1914, Russia vowed to stand behind Serbia, having been assured of support from France. The czar approved plans to mobilize along Russia's border with Austria-Hungary. But Russia's military leaders persuaded the czar to mobilize along the German border, too. On July 30, 1914, Russia announced it would mobilize fully, and the country began to do so on July 30, 1914.

Germany declared war on Russia on August 1, 1914, in response to Russia's mobilization. Two days later, after France called up its troops to support Russia, Germany declared war on France. The German army swept into Belgium on its way to France. The invasion of neutral Belgium caused the United Kingdom to declare war on Germany on August 4. Through the course of the war, few parts of the world remained unaffected.

Archduke Ferdinand and his wife, Sophie, in Sarajevo, shortly before their assassination

The Western Front. The main ideas of Germany's war plan had been developed by Alfred von Schlieffen, who had retired as chief of the German General Staff in 1905. The plan assumed that Germany would have to fight both France and Russia, although outnumbered by them. It aimed at a quick defeat of France while Russia slowly mobilized. But after 1910, as Russian mobilization times improved, Germany came to rely on Austria-Hungary to cover the east. If war came, speed would be of the essence for Germany, and once it mobilized it would have little option but to go to war.

The frontier between France and Germany was heavily fortified. To bypass these defenses, the plan called for a strong right wing to invade France from the north, through Belgium. The movement would pivot on a fixed central position. Schlieffen's hope was that the right wing could get behind the French army and pin it against German forces on the eastern frontier.

Schlieffen's successor, Helmuth von Moltke, directed German strategy at the outbreak of the war. Moltke recognized that the French army might react by attacking the pivot in the center or by moving against Germany's invading right wing. In either case, a German victory might come with a breakthrough elsewhere along the line, possibly even on the heavily fortified border between France and Germany.

Belgium's army fought bravely but held up the Germans for only a short time. By Aug. 16, 1914, the right wing of the German army began its advance. It drove back French forces and a small British force in southern Belgium and swept into France. One part of the right wing pursued retreating French troops southeast across the Marne River, leaving the Germans exposed to attacks from Paris.

French troops using captured German machine guns during the Battle of the Marne

Meanwhile, General Joseph Joffre, commander in chief of all the French armies, stationed his forces near the Marne River east of Paris and prepared a counterattack. Fierce fighting, which became known as the First Battle of the Marne, began on September 6. On September 9, German forces started to withdraw.

The First Battle of the Marne was a key victory for the Allies because it ended Germany's hopes to defeat France quickly. Moltke was replaced as chief of the German General Staff by Erich von Falkenhayn.

The German army halted its retreat near the Aisne River. From there, the Germans and the Allies fought a series of battles as each tried to outflank the other. The last of these, when the two sides fought to a standstill, was the First Battle of Ypres in Belgium. The battle lasted from mid-October until mid-November.

In late November 1914, the Germans decided to establish deep defensive positions along the high ground they had captured in Belgium and northeastern France. Falkenhayn's aim was to free up troops for use elsewhere, but the effect was to cre-

ate a deadlock on the Western Front. The front extended more than 450 miles (720 kilometers) from the coast of Belgium to the border of Switzerland. The deadlock lasted nearly 3 1/2 years.

The Eastern Front. Russia's mobilization on the Eastern Front moved faster than Germany expected. By late August 1914, two Russian armies had thrust deeply into the German territory of East Prussia, but along separate paths. The German army inserted itself between the two. By August 31, the Germans had encircled one Russian army in the Battle of Tannenberg. They then chased the other Russian army out of East Prussia in the Battle of the Masurian Lakes. The number of Russian *casualties*—that is, the number of men killed, captured, wounded, or missing—totaled about 250,000 in the two battles. The victories made heroes of the commanders of the German forces in the east—Paul von Hindenburg and Erich Ludendorff.

Austria-Hungary had less success than its German ally on the Eastern Front. By the end of 1914, Austria-Hungary's forces had attacked Serbia three times and had been beaten back each time. Meanwhile, Russia had captured much of the Austro-Hungarian province of Galicia (now part of Poland and Ukraine). By early October, a humiliated Austro-Hungarian army had retreated into its own territory.

Fighting elsewhere. The Ottoman Empire entered the war at the end of October 1914 as an ally of Germany. Ottoman ships bombarded Russian ports on the Black Sea, and Ottoman troops then invaded Russia. Fighting later broke out in the Ottoman territories on the Arabian Peninsula and in Mesopotamia (now mostly Iraq), Palestine, and Syria.

The United Kingdom stayed in control of the seas following two naval victories over Germany in 1914. The British then kept Germany's surface fleet bottled up in its home waters during most of the war. As a result, Germany relied on submarine warfare.

World War I quickly spread to Germany's overseas colonies. Japan declared war on Germany in late August 1914 and drove the Germans off several islands in the Pacific Ocean. Troops from Australia and New Zealand seized other German colonies in the Pacific. By mid-1915, most of Germany's empire in Africa had fallen to British forces. However, fighting continued in German East Africa (now Tanzania) for two more years.

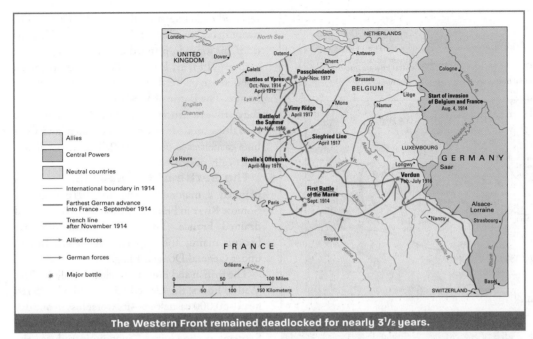

The Western Front remained deadlocked for nearly 3½ years.

The Deadlock on the Western Front

By 1915, the opposing sides had dug themselves into a system of trenches that zigzagged along the Western Front. From the trenches, they defended their positions and launched attacks. The Western Front remained deadlocked in trench warfare until 1918.

Trench warfare. The typical *front-line trench* was about 6 to 8 feet (1.8 to 2.4 meters) deep and wide enough for two men to pass. Dugouts in the sides of the trenches protected men during enemy fire. *Support trenches* ran behind the front-line trenches. Off-duty soldiers lived in dugouts in the support trenches. Troops and supplies moved to the battlefront through a network of *communications trenches.* Barbed wire helped protect the front-line trenches from surprise attacks. Field artillery was set up behind the support trenches. Between the enemy lines lay a stretch of ground called "no man's land." No man's land varied from less than 30 yards (27 meters) wide at some points to more than 1 mile (1.6 kilometers) wide at others. In time, artillery fire tore up the earth, making it very difficult to cross no man's land during an attack.

Soldiers generally served at the front line from a few days to a week and then rotated to the rear for a rest. Life in the trenches was miserable. The smell of dead bodies lingered in the air, and rats were a constant problem. Soldiers had trouble keeping dry, especially in water-logged areas of Belgium.

Except during an attack, life fell into a dull routine. Some soldiers stood guard. Others repaired the trenches, kept telephone lines in order, brought food from behind the battle lines, or did other jobs. At night, patrols fixed the barbed wire and tried to get information about the enemy.

Artillery—large, mounted guns that hurl explosive shells—killed more soldiers than any other weapon in World War I. Trench warfare gave artillery gunners numerous fixed targets. Bombarding the enemy's front-line trenches before an *offensive* (assault) helped clear the way for the infantry, but it also gave away the advantage of surprise. As attacking infantry pressed deeper into enemy territory, they drew farther away from their supporting artillery and drew closer to the enemy's artillery.

Both the Allies and the Central Powers developed new weapons, which they hoped would break

American soldiers wearing gas masks in anticipation of an attack

Italy entered the war against Austria-Hungary in May 1915.

the deadlock. For example, in April 1915, the Germans released poison gas against Allied troops during the Second Battle of Ypres. The Allies also began to use poison gas, and gas masks became necessary equipment in the trenches. Another new weapon was the flame thrower, which shot out a stream of burning fuel.

The Battle of Verdun. As chief of the German General Staff, Falkenhayn decided in early 1916 to concentrate on the defeat of France. He believed Germany might secure a separate peace with Russia, and he hoped that, without France, the United Kingdom would be unable to continue the land war. Falkenhayn chose to attack the French city of Verdun, which was near Germany and easy to supply.

The attack began on February 21. Joffre decided to hold Verdun, although he and his officers had considered abandoning it. Through spring and summer, the French forces held off the attackers. Falkenhayn intended to kill as many French soldiers as possible, and thus weaken the French forces. France aided this goal by continuing to pour men into the battle. However, Falkenhayn had not expected the battle to take nearly as many German lives as French lives. Having failed to break through the line of defense, he reduced his efforts. By the end of the war, the French had completely regained Verdun.

The next month, Hindenburg and Ludendorff—the two German heroes of the Eastern Front—

replaced Falkenhayn on the Western Front. Hindenburg became chief of the General Staff. Ludendorff, his top aide, planned German strategy.

General Henri Philippe Petain had organized the defense of Verdun and was hailed a hero by France. The Battle of Verdun became a symbol of the terrible destructiveness of modern war. French casualties totaled about 315,000 men, and German casualties about 280,000. The city itself was practically destroyed.

The Battle of the Somme. The Allies planned a major offensive for 1916 near the Somme River in France. The Battle of Verdun had drained France. Thus, the Somme offensive became mainly the responsibility of the British under General Douglas Haig.

The British and French attacked on July 1, 1916. Within hours, the United Kingdom had suffered nearly 60,000 casualties—its worst loss in one day of battle. Fierce fighting went on into the fall. In September, the United Kingdom introduced the first primitive tanks. But the tanks were too unreliable and too few in number to make a difference in the battle. Haig finally halted the useless attack in November. At terrible cost, the Allies had gained about 7 miles (11 kilometers). The Battle of the Somme caused more than 1 million casualties— over 600,000 Germans, over 400,000 British, and nearly 200,000 French. In spite of the tragic losses at Verdun and the Somme, the Western Front stood as solid as ever at the end of 1916.

The War on Other Fronts

During 1915 and 1916, World War I spread to Italy and throughout the Balkans, and activity increased on other fronts. Some Allied military leaders believed that the creation of new battlefronts would break the deadlock on the Western Front. But the first effect of the war's expansion was to give the Central Powers additional conquests.

The Italian Front. Italy had stayed out of World War I during 1914, even though it was a member of the Triple Alliance with Austria-Hungary and Germany. Italy claimed that it was under no obligation to honor the agreement because Austria-Hungary had not gone to war in self-defense. In May 1915, Italy entered World War I on the side of the Allies. In a secret treaty, the Allies promised to give Italy some of Austria-Hungary's territory after the war. In return, Italy promised to attack Austria-Hungary.

The Italians, led by General Luigi Cadorna, hammered away at Austria-Hungary for two years in a series of battles along the Isonzo River in Austria-Hungary. Italy suffered enormous casualties but gained very little territory. The Allies hoped that the Italian Front would help Russia because Germany came to the aid of Austria-Hungary.

The Dardanelles. After World War I began, the Ottoman Empire closed the waterway between the Aegean Sea and the Black Sea, blocking the sea route to southern Russia. French and British warships attacked the Dardanelles, a strait that formed part of the waterway, in February and March 1915. The Allies hoped to open a supply route to Russia. However, underwater mines and shore-based artillery halted the assault.

In April 1915, the Allies landed troops on the Gallipoli Peninsula on the west shore of the Dardanelles. The Australian and New Zealand Army Corps (ANZAC) played a key role in the landing. Ottoman and Allied forces soon became locked in trench warfare. A second invasion in August at Suvla Bay to the north failed to end the standstill. In December, the Allies began to evacuate their troops. They had suffered about 250,000 casualties in the Dardanelles.

Eastern Europe. In May 1915, the armies of Germany and Austria-Hungary broke through Russian lines in Galicia, the Austro-Hungarian province that Russia had invaded in 1914. The Russians retreated about 300 miles (480 kilometers) before they formed a new line of defense. In spite of the setback, Czar Nicholas II staged two offensives. The first, in March 1916, achieved little.

The second Russian offensive, planned in conjunction with the Battle of the Somme in the West, began in June 1916 under General Alexei Brusilov. Brusilov's army drove Austria-Hungary's forces back about 50 miles (80 kilometers). Within a few weeks, Russia captured about 200,000 prisoners. To halt the assault, Austria-Hungary had to shift troops from the Italian Front to the Eastern Front. The Russian offensive nearly knocked Austria-Hungary out of the war. But it also exhausted Russia. Each side suffered about a million casualties.

Bulgaria entered World War I in October 1915 to help the Central Powers defeat Serbia. Bulgaria hoped to recover land it had lost in the Second Balkan War. In an effort to aid Serbia, the Allies landed troops in Thessaloniki (Salonika), Greece. But the troops never reached Serbia. By November, the Central Powers had overrun Serbia, and Serbia's army had retreated to Albania.

Romania joined the Allies in August 1916. It hoped to take advantage of Brusilov's victory and to gain some of Austria-Hungary's territory if the Allies won the war. By the end of 1916, Romania had lost most of its army, and Germany controlled the country's valuable wheat fields and oil fields.

The war at sea. The United Kingdom's control of the seas during World War I caused serious problems for Germany. The British navy blockaded German waters, preventing supplies from reaching German ports. By 1916, Germany suffered a shortage of food and other goods. Germany combated British seapower with its submarines, called *U-boats*. In February 1915, Germany declared a submarine blockade of the United Kingdom and Ireland and warned that it would attack any ship that tried to get through the blockade. Thereafter, U-boats destroyed great amounts of goods headed for the United Kingdom.

Depiction of the sinking of the *Lusitania*

On May 7, 1915, a U-boat torpedoed without warning the British passenger liner *Lusitania* off the coast of Ireland. Among the 1,201 passengers who died were 128 Americans. The sinking of the *Lusitania* led U.S. President Woodrow Wilson to urge Germany to give up unrestricted submarine warfare. In September, Germany agreed not to attack neutral or passenger ships.

The warships that the United Kingdom and Germany had raced to build before World War I remained in home waters during most of the war. There, they served to discourage an enemy invasion. The only major encounter between the two navies was the Battle of Jutland, fought off the coast of Denmark on May 31 and June 1, 1916.

Admiral Sir John Jellicoe commanded a British fleet of 150 warships. He faced a German fleet of 99 warships under the command of Admiral Reinhard Scheer. In spite of the United Kingdom's superior strength, Jellicoe acted cautiously. He feared that he could lose the entire war in a day because the destruction of the United Kingdom's fleet would give Germany control of the seas. Both sides claimed victory in the Battle of Jutland. Although the United Kingdom lost more ships than Germany, it still ruled the seas.

The war in the air. Great advances in aviation were made by the Allies and the Central Powers during World War I. Each side competed to produce better airplanes than the other side. At first, airplanes were used mainly to observe enemy activities. The pilots began carrying guns to shoot at enemy planes. But a pilot risked shooting himself if a bullet bounced off the propeller.

In 1915, Anthony Fokker, a Dutch designer working for Germany, developed a machine gun timed to fire between an airplane's revolving propeller blades. The invention made air combat more deadly and led to *dogfights*—clashes between enemy aircraft. A pilot who shot down five or more enemy planes was called an *ace*. Many aces became national heroes. Germany's Baron Manfred von Richthofen, who was known as the Red Baron, shot down 80 planes, more than any other ace. Other famous aces included Billy Bishop of Canada, Rene Fonck of France, Edward Mannock of the United Kingdom, and Eddie Rickenbacker of the United States.

In 1915, Germany began to bomb London and other British cities from airships called *zeppelins*, and by 1917 both sides planned major bomber offensives. But aerial bombing remained in its early stages during the war.

The Final Stage

Allied failures. At the beginning of 1917, Allied military leaders hoped that simultaneous offensives on all fronts could win the war. But German leaders accepted the deadlock on the Western Front and improved German defenses. In March 1917, German troops were moved back to a strongly fortified new battle line in northern France. It was

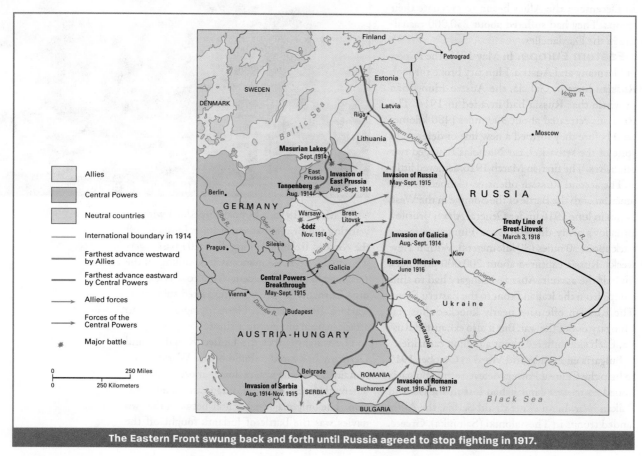

The Eastern Front swung back and forth until Russia agreed to stop fighting in 1917.

called the Siegfried Line by the Germans and the Hindenburg Line by the Allies. The Siegfried Line shortened the Western Front and placed German artillery and machine guns to best advantage. It also led to the failure of an offensive planned by France.

General Robert Nivelle had replaced Joffre as commander in chief of French forces in December 1916. Nivelle planned a major offensive near the Aisne River and predicted it would smash through the German line within two days. Germany's pullback to the Siegfried Line did not shake Nivelle's confidence. A week before Nivelle's offensive began, the British Army launched an attack at Arras, farther north, designed to pull German reserves away from the Aisne River. Canadian troops seized Vimy Ridge, a commanding height which previous French attacks had failed to take. Nivelle's offensive opened on April 16, 1917. By the end of the day, it was clear that the assault had failed. But fighting continued into May.

Mutinies broke out among the French forces after Nivelle's offensive collapsed. The troops had had enough of the pointless bloodshed and the horrid conditions on the Western Front. Petain, the hero of Verdun, replaced Nivelle in May 1917. Petain improved the soldiers' living conditions and restored order. He promised that France would remain on the defensive until it was ready to fight again. Meanwhile, any further offensives on the Western Front remained the United Kingdom's responsibility.

General Haig hoped that a British offensive near Ypres would lead to victory. The Third Battle of Ypres, also known as the Battle of Passchendaele, began on July 31, 1917. For more than three months, British troops and a small French force pounded the Germans in an especially terrible campaign. Heavy Allied bombardment before the infantry attack destroyed the drainage system around Ypres. Drenching rains then turned the water-logged land into a swamp. The disastrous battle was finally halted in mid-November on the Passchendaele ridge. It is also known as the Battle of Passchendaele.

In late November, the British tried a surprise attack farther south, at Cambrai. Artillery was followed by the first use of massed tanks. But the Germans regained the ground they lost with a counterattack a few days later.

In late 1917, the Allied position looked bleak. In October, Italy had been driven back by a combined German and Austro-Hungarian attack in the battle of Caporetto. In November, a revolution threatened to take Russia out of the war.

The Russian Revolution. The Russian people suffered greatly during World War I. By 1917, many of them were no longer willing to put up with the enormous casualties and the severe shortages of food and fuel. They blamed Czar Nicholas II and his advisers for the country's problems. Early in 1917, an uprising in Petrograd (now St. Petersburg) forced Nicholas from the throne. The new government continued the war.

To weaken Russia's war effort further, Germany helped V. I. Lenin, a Russian revolutionary then living in Switzerland, return to his homeland in April 1917. Seven months later, Lenin led an uprising that gained control of Russia's government. Lenin immediately called for peace talks with Germany. World War I had ended on the Eastern Front.

Germany dictated harsh peace terms to Russia in a peace treaty signed in Brest-Litovsk, Russia, on March 3, 1918. The Treaty forced Russia to give up large amounts of territory, including Finland, Poland, Ukraine, Bessarabia, and the Baltic States—Estonia, Livonia (now Latvia), and Lithuania. The end of the fighting on the Eastern Front freed German troops for use on the Western Front. The only obstacle to a final German victory seemed to be the entry of the United States into the war.

The United States enters the war. At the start of World War I, President Wilson had declared the neutrality of the United States. Most Americans opposed U.S. involvement in a European war. But the sinking of the *Lusitania* and other German actions against civilians drew American sympathies to the Allies.

Several events early in 1917 persuaded the United States government to enter World War I. In February, Germany returned to unrestricted submarine warfare, . which it assumed might bring the United States into the war. But German military leaders knew this might bring the United States into the war, but they believed they could win the war by cutting off British supplies. They expected their U-boats to starve the United Kingdom into surrendering within a few months, long before the United States had fully prepared for war.

Tension between the United States and Germany increased after the British intercepted and decoded a message from Germany's foreign minister, Arthur Zimmermann, to the German ambassador to Mexico. The message, known as the

"Zimmermann note," revealed a German plot to persuade Mexico to go to war against the United States. The British gave the message to Wilson, and it was published in the United States early in March. Americans were further enraged after U-boats sank several U.S. cargo ships.

On April 2, Wilson called for war, stating that "the world must be made safe for democracy." Congress declared war on Germany on April 6. Few people expected that the United States would make much of a contribution toward ending the war.

Mobilization. The United States entered World War I unprepared for battle. Strong antiwar feelings had hampered efforts to prepare for war. After declaring war, the government worked to stir up enthusiasm for the war effort. Government propaganda pictured the war as a battle for liberty and democracy. People who still opposed the war faced increasingly unfriendly public opinion.

The launch of the *Arizona*, January 1917

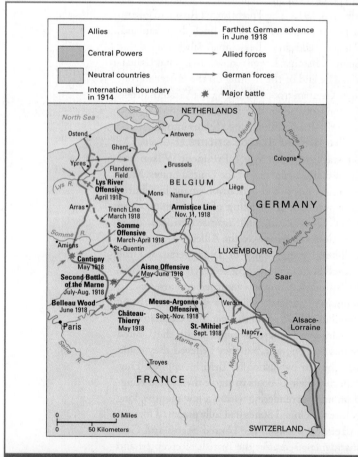

Allies		Farthest German advance in June 1918
Central Powers		Allied forces
Neutral countries		German forces
International boundary in 1914		Major battle

With American help, the Allies halted the German advance outside Paris in June 1918 and then continued to push the Germans back. An armistice was signed on November 11, 1918.

They could even be brought to trial under wartime laws forbidding statements that might harm the successful progress of the war.

During World War I, U.S. government agencies directed the nation's economy toward the war effort. President Wilson put financier Bernard M. Baruch in charge of the War Industries Board, which turned factories into producers of war materials. The Food Administration, headed by businessman Herbert Hoover, controlled the prices, production, and distribution of food. Americans observed "meatless" and "wheatless" days in order that food could be sent to Europe.

Manpower was the chief contribution of the United States to World War I. The country entered the war with a Regular Army of only about 128,000 men. It soon organized a draft requiring all men from 21 through 30 years old to register for military service. The age range was broadened to 18 through 45 in 1918. A lottery determined who served. Many men enlisted voluntarily, and women signed up as nurses and office workers. The U.S. armed forces had almost 5 million men and women by the end of the war. Of that number, about 2 3/4 million men had been drafted. Few soldiers received much training before going overseas because the Allies urgently needed them.

Before U.S. help could reach the Western Front, the Allies had to overcome the U-boat threat in the Atlantic. In May 1917, the United Kingdom began to use a *convoy system*, by which cargo ships went to sea in large groups escorted by warships.

The U-boats proved no match for the warships, and Allied shipping losses dropped sharply.

American troops in Europe. The soldiers sent to Europe by the U.S. Army made up the American Expeditionary Forces (A.E.F.). General John J. Pershing, commander of the A.E.F., arrived in France in mid-June 1917, and the first troops landed later that month. Through the rest of 1917, the A.E.F. had only several thousand soldiers. As recruits made their way through training, the numbers grew, and by August 1918, there were about 1 million U.S. troops in Europe. In the end, about 2 million American soldiers reached Europe.

In November 1917, the Allies formed the Supreme War Council to plan strategy. They decided to make their strategy defensive until significant numbers of U.S. troops could reach the Western Front. The Allies wanted Americans to serve as replacements and to fill out their battered ranks. But Pershing wanted the A.E.F. to remain independent both for political reasons and because he believed his troops would be weakened if they were dispersed among the European forces. The argument was the major wartime dispute between the Europeans and their American ally. Pershing generally held firm, though at times he lent troops to France and the United Kingdom.

The last campaigns. The collapse of Russia enabled the Germans to concentrate on the Western Front. Ludendorff hoped to secure victory before the Americans could reach the front in large numbers, but he spread his effort too thinly on five offensives in the spring and summer of 1918.

Germany first struck near St.-Quentin, a city in the Somme River Valley, on March 21, 1918. By March 26, British troops had retreated about 30 miles (50 kilometers). In late March, the Germans began to bombard Paris with enormous guns that hurled shells up to 75 miles (120 kilometers). After the disaster at St.-Quentin, Allied leaders appointed General Ferdinand Foch of France to be the supreme commander of the Allied forces on the Western Front.

A second German offensive began on April 9 along the Lys River in Belgium. British troops fought stubbornly, and Ludendorff called off the attack on April 30. The Allies suffered heavy losses in both assaults, but German casualties were just as great.

Germany attacked a third time on May 27 near the Aisne River. By May 30, German troops had reached the Marne River. American soldiers helped France stop the German advance at the town of Chateau-Thierry, less than 50 miles (80 kilometers) northeast of Paris.

In June, a fourth German offensive against Allied troops near Compiegne gained little ground. That same month, U.S. troops drove the Germans out of Belleau Wood, a forested area near the Marne. German forces crossed the Marne.

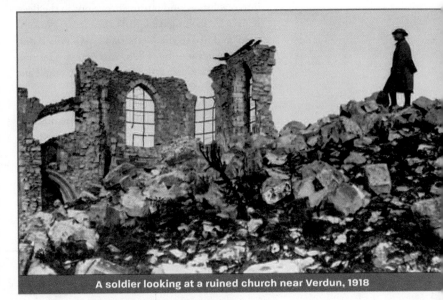

A soldier looking at a ruined church near Verdun, 1918

On July 15, the Germans launched their fifth and final offensive across the Marne. Foch ordered a counterattack near the town of Soissons on July 18. It marked the turning point of World War I. The Allies won the battle and began a steady advance. On August 8, the United Kingdom and France attacked the Germans near Amiens. By early September, Germany had lost all the territory it had gained since spring. In mid-September, Pershing led U.S. forces to an easy victory at St.-Mihiel.

On Sept. 26, 1918, the Allies began attacks along the length of the Western Front. About 900,000 U.S. troops participated in heavy fighting between the Argonne Forest and the Meuse River.

The fighting ends. The Allies won victories on all fronts in the fall of 1918. Bulgaria surrendered on September 29. British forces under the command of General Edmund Allenby triumphed over the Ottoman army in Palestine and Syria. On October 30, the Ottoman Empire signed an armistice. The last major battle between Italy and Austria-Hungary began in late October in Italy. Italy, with support from France and the

United Kingdom, defeated Austria-Hungary near the town of Vittorio Veneto. Austria-Hungary signed an armistice on November 3.

Ludendorff demanded an armistice at the end of September, but negotiations over the terms continued throughout October. Germans suffered food shortages caused both by the naval blockade and by poor administration by the country's government. Strikes and riots turned into revolution, and mutiny broke out in the fleet. Kaiser Wilhelm gave up his throne on November 9 and fled to the Netherlands. An Allied delegation headed by Foch met with German representatives in a railroad car in the Compiegne Forest in northern France.

In the early morning on Nov. 11, 1918, the Germans accepted the armistice terms demanded by the Allies. Germany agreed to evacuate the territories it had taken during the war; to surrender large numbers of arms, ships, and other war materials; and to allow the Allied powers to occupy German territory along the Rhine River. Foch ordered the fighting to stop on the Western Front at 11 a.m. World War I was over.

Consequences of the War

Destruction and casualties. World War I caused incredible destruction. About 9 million soldiers died as a result of the war—far more than had died in all the wars during the previous 100 years. About 21 million men were wounded. Germany and Russia each suffered about $1\frac{3}{4}$ million battle deaths during World War I—more than any other country.

Improved artillery, machine guns, and other advanced weapons proved much more deadly than earlier designs. When generals used old tactics, such as bayonet charges, the new weaponry slaughtered their troops. Learning how to fight against the new weapons cost many lives. The way battles were fought in 1918 was radically different from how they had been fought in 1914.

No one knows how many civilians died of disease, starvation, and other war-related causes. Some historians believe as many civilians died as soldiers.

Property damage in World War I was greatest in France and Belgium. Armies destroyed farms and villages as they passed through them or, even worse, dug in for battle. The fighting wrecked fac-

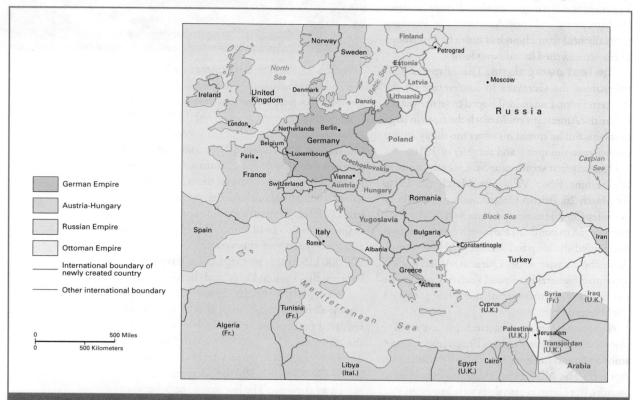

Austria-Hungary and the Ottoman Empire split into national states, and Russia and Germany gave up territory. Most Arab lands in the Ottoman Empire were placed under French and British rule.

tories, bridges, and railroad tracks. Artillery shells, trenches, and chemicals made barren the land along the Western Front.

Economic consequences. World War I cost the fighting nations a total of about $337 billion (in 1918 dollars). By 1918, the war was costing about $10 million an hour. Fighting the war consumed about 60 percent of the economic output of Germany and the United Kingdom. In contrast, Canada and the United States spent about 17 percent of their economic output on the war.

Nations raised part of the money to pay for the war through income taxes and other taxes. But most of the money came from borrowing, which created huge debts. Governments borrowed from citizens by selling war bonds. The Allies also borrowed heavily from the United States. In addition, most governments printed extra money to meet their needs. But the increased money supply caused severe inflation after the war.

The problem of war debts lingered after World War I ended. The Allies tried to reduce their debts by demanding *reparations* (payments for war damages) from the Central Powers, especially Germany. Reparations became a source of contention between the powers, without solving any of their problems.

World War I seriously disrupted economies. Some businesses shut down after workers left for military service. Other firms shifted to the production of war materials. To direct production toward the war effort, governments took greater control over the economy than ever before. Most people wanted a return to private enterprise after the war. But some people expected government to continue to solve economic problems.

The countries of Europe had poured their resources into World War I, and they came out of the war exhausted. France, for example, had lost nearly one-tenth of its work force. In most European countries, many returning soldiers could not find jobs. In addition, Europe lost many of the markets for its exports while producing war goods. The United States and other countries that had played a smaller role in the war emerged with increased economic power.

Political consequences. World War I shook the foundations of several governments. Democratic governments in the United Kingdom and France withstood the stress of the war. But four monarchies toppled. The first monarch to fall was Czar Nicholas II of Russia in 1917. Kaiser

Attendees at the Paris Peace Conference

Wilhelm II of Germany and Emperor Charles of Austria-Hungary left their thrones in 1918. The Ottoman sultan, Muhammad VI, fell in 1922.

The collapse of old empires led to the creation of new countries in the years after World War I. The prewar territory of Austria-Hungary formed the independent republics of Austria, Hungary, and Czechoslovakia, as well as parts of Italy, Poland, Romania, and Yugoslavia. Russia and Germany also gave up territory to Poland. Finland and the Baltic States—Estonia, Latvia, and Lithuania—gained independence from Russia. Most Arab lands in the Ottoman Empire were placed under the control of France and the United Kingdom. The rest of the Ottoman Empire became Turkey. Woodrow Wilson insisted on the principle of national self-determination in Europe, and thus strengthened the cause of nationalism.

World War I gave the Communists a chance to seize power in Russia. Some people expected Communist revolutions to break out elsewhere in Europe. Revolutionary movements gained strength after the war, but Communist governments did not take hold.

Social consequences. World War I brought enormous changes in society. The deaths of so many people, both soldiers and civilians, left lasting psychological scars on the survivors. Losing young men to the war resulted in lower birth rates, especially in France. Millions of people were uprooted by the war. Some fled war-torn areas and later found their houses, farms, or villages destroyed. Others became refugees as a result of changes in governments and national borders, especially in central and eastern Europe.

Just before the Paris Peace Conference: (left to right)
British Prime Minister Lloyd George, Italian President Vittorio
Orlando, French Prime Minister Georges Clemenceau,
and American President Woodrow Wilson

The Peace Settlement

The Fourteen Points. In January 1918, 10 months before World War I ended, President Woodrow Wilson of the United States proposed a set of war aims called the Fourteen Points. Wilson believed that the Fourteen Points would bring about a just peace settlement, which he termed "peace without victory." In November 1918, Germany agreed to an armistice. Germany expected that the peace settlement would be based on the Fourteen Points.

Eight of Wilson's Fourteen Points dealt with specific political and territorial settlements. The rest of them set forth general principles aimed at preventing future wars. The last point proposed the establishment of an international association—later called the League of Nations—to maintain the peace.

The Paris Peace Conference. In January 1919, representatives of the victorious powers gathered in Paris to draw up the peace settlement. They came from 32 nations. Committees worked out specific proposals at the Paris Peace Conference. But the decisions were made by four heads of government called the Big Four. The Big Four consisted of Wilson, the United Kingdom's Prime Minister David Lloyd George, France's Premier Georges Clemenceau, and Italy's Prime Minister Vittorio Orlando.

The Paris Peace Conference largely disregarded the Fourteen Points. The full impact of the terms of the settlement worked out by the committees was not evident until the end of the conference. France wanted to regain the territory it had lost in both this war and the Franco-Prussian War (1870-1871). Military action and secret treaties had already defined new borders in eastern Europe. The Big Four endorsed many of these borders.

In May 1919, the peace conference approved the treaty and presented it to Germany. Germany agreed to it only after the Allies threatened to invade. With grave doubts, German representatives signed the treaty in the Palace of Versailles near Paris on June 28, 1919. The date was the fifth anniversary of the assassination of Archduke Franz Ferdinand.

In addition to the Treaty of Versailles with Germany, the peacemakers drew up separate treaties with the other Central Powers. The Treaty of St.-Germain was signed with Austria in September 1919, the Treaty of Neuilly with Bulgaria in November 1919, the Treaty of Trianon with Hun-

Many people chose not to resume their old way of life after World War I. Urban areas grew as peasants settled in cities instead of returning to farms. Women filled jobs in offices and factories after men went to war, and they were reluctant to give up their new independence. Many countries granted women the vote after the war.

The distinction between social classes began to blur as a result of World War I, and society became more democratic. The upper classes, which had traditionally governed, lost some of their power and privilege after having led the world into an agonizing war. Men of all classes had faced the same danger and horror in the trenches. Those who had bled and suffered for their country came to demand a say in running it.

Finally, World War I transformed attitudes. Middle- and upper-class Europeans lost the confidence and optimism they had felt before the war. Many people began to question long-held ideas. For example, few Europeans before the war had doubted their right to force European culture on the rest of the world. But the destruction and bloodshed of the war led many to question the superiority of European civilization.

gary in June 1920, and the Treaty of Sevres with the Ottoman Empire in August 1920.

Provisions of the treaties that officially ended World War I stripped the Central Powers of territory and arms and required them to pay reparations. Germany claimed it was punished especially severely. One clause in the Treaty of Versailles forced Germany to accept responsibility for causing the war.

Under the Treaty of Versailles, Germany gave up territory to Belgium, Czechoslovakia, Denmark, France, and Poland and lost its overseas colonies. France gained control of coal fields in Germany's Saar Valley for 15 years. An Allied military force, paid for by Germany, was to occupy the west bank of the Rhine River for 15 years. Other clauses in the treaty limited Germany's armed forces and required the country to turn over war materials, ships, livestock, and other goods to the Allies. A total sum for reparations was not set until 1921. Germany received a bill for about $33 billion (in 1921 dollars), but it evaded paying much of the bill.

The Treaty of St.-Germain and the Treaty of Trianon reduced Austria and Hungary to less than a third their former area. The treaties recognized the independence of Czechoslovakia, Poland, and a kingdom that later became Yugoslavia. Those new states, along with Italy and Romania, received territory that had belonged to Austria-Hungary. The Treaty of Sevres took Mesopotamia (later renamed Iraq), Palestine, and Syria away from the Ottoman Empire. Bulgaria lost territory to Greece and Romania. Germany's allies also had to reduce their armed forces and pay reparations.

The postwar world. The peacemakers found it impossible to satisfy the hopes and ambitions of every country and national group. The settlements disappointed both the victors and the defeated powers.

In creating new borders, the peacemakers considered the wishes of national groups. However, territorial claims overlapped in many cases. For example, Romania gained a chunk of land with a large Hungarian population, and parts of Czechoslovakia and Poland had many Germans. Such settlements heightened tensions between countries. In addition, some Arab peoples were bitter because they had failed to gain independence.

Certain borders created by the peace settlements made little economic sense. For example, the new countries of Austria and Hungary were too small and weak to support themselves. They had lost most of their population, resources, and markets. Austria's largely German population had wanted to unite with Germany. But the peace treaties forbade that union. The peacemakers did not want Germany to gain territory from the war.

Among the European Allies, the United Kingdom entered the postwar world the most content. The nation had kept its empire and control of the seas. But the British worried that the balance of power they wanted in Europe could be upset by a severely weakened Germany and a victory by the Communists in a civil war in Russia. France had succeeded in imposing harsh terms on Germany but not in safeguarding its borders. France had failed to obtain a guarantee of aid from the United Kingdom and the United States in the event of a future German invasion. Finally, Italy had gained less territory than it had been promised and felt it deserved.

In the United States, the Senate reflected public opinion and failed to approve the Treaty of Versailles. It thereby rejected President Wilson. The treaty would have made the United States a member of the League of Nations. Many Americans were not yet ready to accept the responsibilities that went along with their country's new power. They feared that the League of Nations would entangle the country in European disputes.

The terms of the Treaty of Versailles proved harsher than Germany had expected. The responsibility of having accepted those terms weakened Germany's postwar government. During the 1930s, a strongly nationalist movement led by Adolf Hitler gained power in Germany. Hitler promised to defy the Treaty of Versailles and sought to restore German power. In 1939, Germany invaded Poland. World War II had begun.

MLA Citation

"World War I." *The Southwestern Advantage Topic Source.* Nashville: Southwestern. 2013.

DATA

World War I: The Warring Nations

Name	Date entered war
The Allies[1]	
Belgium	Aug. 4, 1914
Brazil	Oct. 26, 1917
British Empire	Aug. 4, 1914
China	Aug. 14, 1917
Costa Rica	May 23, 1918
Cuba	April 7, 1917
France	Aug. 3, 1914
Greece	July 2, 1917
Guatemala	April 23, 1918
Haiti	July 12, 1918
Honduras	July 19, 1918
Italy	May 23, 1915
Japan	Aug. 23, 1914
Liberia	Aug. 4, 1917
Montenegro	Aug. 5, 1914
Nicaragua	May 8, 1918
Panama	April 7, 1917
Portugal	March 9, 1916
Romania	Aug. 27, 1916
Russia	Aug. 1, 1914
San Marino	June 3, 1915
Serbia	July 28, 1914
Siam	July 22, 1917
United States	April 6, 1917
The Central Powers	
Austria-Hungary	July 28, 1914
Bulgaria	Oct. 14, 1915
Germany	Aug. 1, 1914
Ottoman Empire	Oct. 31, 1914

[1] More than 20 countries eventually joined the war on the Allied side, but not all of them sent troops.

DATA

Important Dates During World War I

1914

June 28	Archduke Franz Ferdinand was assassinated.
July 28	Austria-Hungary declared war on Serbia. Other declarations of war followed during the next week.
Aug. 4	Germany invaded Belgium and started the fighting.
Aug. 10	Austria-Hungary invaded Russia, opening the fighting on the Eastern Front.
Sept. 6-9	The Allies stopped the Germans in France in the First Battle of the Marne.
Oct. 29	The Ottoman Empire entered the war on the side of the Central Powers.

1915

Feb. 18	Germany began to blockade the United Kingdom.
April 25	Allied troops landed on the Gallipoli Peninsula.
May 7	A German submarine sank the liner *Lusitania*.
May 23	Italy declared war on Austria-Hungary, and an Italian Front soon developed.
Oct. 14	Bulgaria declared war on Serbia and joined the Central Powers.

1916

Feb. 21	The Germans opened the Battle of Verdun.
May 31-June 1	The British fleet fought the German fleet in the Battle of Jutland.
July 1	The Allies launched the Battle of the Somme.

1917

Feb. 1	Germany resumed unrestricted submarine warfare.
April 6	The United States declared war on Germany.
June 24	American troops began landing in France.
Dec. 15	Russia signed an armistice with Germany, ending the fighting on the Eastern Front.

1918

Jan. 8	President Woodrow Wilson announced his Fourteen Points as the basis for peace.
March 3	Russia signed the Treaty of Brest-Litovsk.
March 21	Germany launched the first of its final five offensives on the Western Front.
July 18	A counterattack by the Allies on the Western Front marked the beginning of their final offensive.
Nov. 11	Germany signed an armistice ending World War I.

DATA

Military Deaths in World War I (1914-1918)

Country	Deaths
The Allies	
Belgium	38,000
British Empire	908,400
France	1,358,000
Greece	26,000
Italy	650,000
Portugal	7,200
Romania	335,700
Russia	1,700,000
Serbia and Montenegro	278,000
United States	116,516
The Central Powers	
Austria-Hungary	1,200,000
Bulgaria	87,500
Germany	1,773,000
Ottoman Empire	804,000

ADDITIONAL RESOURCES

Books to Read

Capozzola, Christopher. *Uncle Sam Wants You: World War I and the Making of the Modern American Citizen.* Oxford, 2008.

Carter, Miranda. *George, Nicholas and Wilhelm: Three Royal Cousins and the Road to World War I.* Knopf, 2010.

Ferrell, Robert H., ed. *In the Company of Generals: The World War I Diary of Pierpont L. Stackpole.* University of Missouri Press, 2009.

Hamilton, Richard F., and Herwig, Holger H., eds. *The Origins of World War I.* Cambridge, 2008.

Herwig, Holger H. *The Marne, 1914.* Random House, 2009.

Hogg, Ian V. *The A to Z of World War I.* Scarecrow, 2009.

Kniptash, Vernon E. *On the Western Front with the Rainbow Division.* University of Oklahoma Press, 2009.

Woodward, David R. *World War I Almanac.* Facts on File, 2009.

Web Sites

Aces and Aircraft of World War I

http://www.theaerodrome.com/

Descriptions and images of the flying aces (pilot heroes) of World War I and the aircraft that they flew. Presented by Aerodrome Pictures, Inc.

Gallipoli: The Drama of the Dardanelles

http://archive.iwm.org.uk/upload/package/2/gallipoli/navigate.htm

This exhibition is the product of a Joint Australian War Memorial/Imperial War Museum Battlefield Study Tour. It includes contributions from some of the world's leading experts on the campaign.

The Great War and the Shaping of the 20th Century

http://www.pbs.org/greatwar/

Information about World War I from the PBS television series. Includes an interactive timeline, a map gallery, interviews with famous historians of the war, and other features.

The Great War: 80 years on

http://news.bbc.co.uk/2/hi/special_report/1998/10/98/world_war_i/197437.stm

BBC News Online looks back at what became known as "the war to end all wars."

U-Boat Attack, 1916

http://www.eyewitnesstohistory.com/sub.htm

Information about German U-boat (submarine) warfare in World War I, including a description of an attack on an allied cargo vessel from the diary of a German U-boat commander. From the EyeWitness project of Ibis Communications, which provides fi

Search Strings

Aftermath of World War I

"World War I" aftermath (334,000)

"World War I" aftermath political change damage economy (16,700)

"World War I" aftermath political change damage economy social change emperors (41,300)

What Started It All

"World War I" causes (212,000) *The first responses were very good.

"World War I" causes Balkans Austria-Hungary Serbia (4,430)

"World War I" causes Balkans Austria-Hungary Serbia military alliances (19,900)

Warfare of the Era

"World War I" warfare weapons (69,900)

"World War I" warfare weapons new era (33,800)

"World War I" warfare weapons new era "machine guns" bombers tanks submarines (1,170)

Deadlock on the Western Front

"World War I" western front deadlock (44,900)

"World War I" western front deadlock trench warfare "battle of Verdun" "Battle of the Somme" (64)

"World War I" western front deadlock trench warfare Germany Belgium France (433)

World War II

World War II (1939–1945) was the most destructive war in history. It killed more people, destroyed more property, and disrupted more lives than any other war in history. It probably had more far-reaching consequences than any other war. The war brought about the downfall of Europe as the center of world power. It led to the dominance of the Soviet Union and the United States. It set off a power struggle between the two countries called the Cold War. World War II also opened the nuclear age.

HOT topics

Evolution of Fighter Jets/Planes. Long range bombers greatly affected the outcome of World War II. German bombers, the United Kingdom's Royal Air Force fighter planes, Spitfires and Hurricanes, American B-17 bombers, Germany's jet fighter Messerschmitt Me 262, and German V-1 and V-2 guided missiles caused great damage, took many lives, and added a new dimension to war.

Importance of Information During Wartime.
During wartime, information is a powerful tool. It can be used as propaganda to influence public opinion. It can be used to learn about the opposing side's activities and used to weaken their war effort. Codes, ciphers, code-breakers, spies, saboteurs, and resistance groups greatly influenced the outcome of World War II.

HOT topics 🔥

Progression of World War II.

World War II began on September 1, 1939, when Germany invaded Poland. Under the leadership of Germany's dictator, Adolf Hitler, Germany continued on to invade Denmark, Luxembourg, the Netherlands, Belgium, Norway, and France. By June 1940, Italy joined Germany's side, and the United Kingdom stood alone in northern Europe. Soon the war spread to Greece and northern Africa. In 1941, Germany invaded the Soviet Union, and Japan attacked Pearl Harbor in Hawaii. Germany, Italy, and Japan created an alliance called the Axis, which also eventually included Bulgaria, Hungary, Romania, Croatia, and Slovakia. The United States, the United Kingdom, China, and the Soviet Union, known as the Allies, were the major powers fighting the Axis. By the end of the war, a total of 50 nations were part of the Allies. On May 7, 1945, Germany finally surrendered, followed by Japan on September 2, 1945.

Adolf Hitler saluting German troops during the Nazi occupation of Poland

Adolf Hitler.

Adolf Hitler (1889–1945) was born on April 20, 1889, in Austria. In 1913, he moved to Munich, Germany. He was fiercely nationalistic and hated Jews and Slavs. When World War I began in 1914, he joined the German army and took part in many battles. He believed that the Treaty of Versailles, which ended Germany's involvement in World War I and held Germany responsible for the war, threatened German unity. After Hitler joined and then became the leader of the Nazi Party, he used his skills as a politician and organizer to attack the government and create his own army of storm troopers. He slowly rose in power, became dictator of Germany, and initiated World War II.

TRUE or FALSE?

World War II led to the rise of two world superpowers: the United States of America and the Soviet Union.

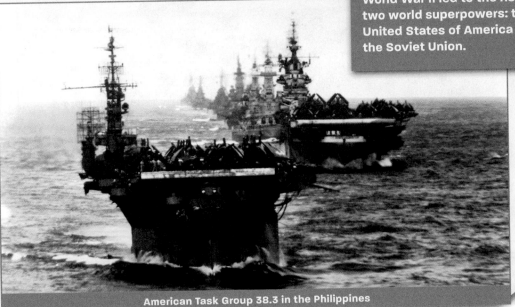

American Task Group 38.3 in the Philippines

hot topics hot topics hot topics hot topics

THE BASICS

World War II (1939–1945) was the most destructive war in history. It killed more people, destroyed more property, and disrupted more lives than any other war in history. It probably had more far-reaching consequences than any other war. The war brought about the downfall of Europe as the center of world power. It led to the dominance of the Soviet Union and the United States. It set off a power struggle between the two countries called the Cold War. World War II also opened the nuclear age.

It is impossible to say exactly how many people died as a result of World War II. Estimates suggest about 20 million soldiers died during the war's six years. From 30 to 40 million civilians also perished. That makes a combined death toll of 50 to 60 million people.

The battlegrounds of World War II spread to nearly every part of the world. Troops fought in the jungles of Southeast Asia. They battled in the deserts of North Africa. They fought on the islands and seas of the Pacific Ocean. Battles raged on the frozen steppes of the Soviet Union and in the cities, forests, and farmers' fields of Europe. Submarines fought below the surface of the Atlantic Ocean.

World War II began on September 1, 1939, when Nazi Germany invaded Poland. Germany's powerful war machine rapidly crushed Poland, Denmark, Luxembourg, the Netherlands, Belgium, Norway, and France. In June 1940, Fascist Italy joined the war on Germany's side. In Europe, only the United Kingdom remained. The United Kingdom resisted German air attacks that destroyed great sections of London and other cities. German and Italian forces then clashed with the British in Greece and northern Africa. In June 1941, Germany invaded the Soviet Union. Germany thus broke their nonaggression pact of 1939. In that treaty, they had promised not to attack each other.

Imperial Japan invaded China in 1937. It allied itself with Germany and Italy in September 1940, creating the Axis Powers. On December 7, 1941, Japan attacked the American military base at Pearl Harbor, Hawaii. The attack brought the United States into the war. By mid-1942, Japanese forces had conquered much of Southeast Asia. Japan had also swept across many islands in the Pacific.

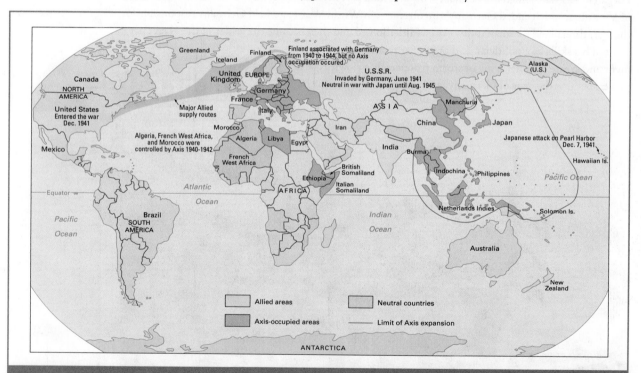

Germany, Italy, Japan, and their Axis partners fought Great Britain, the Soviet Union, the United States, and the other Allies in World War II. This map shows the Allies and the lands controlled by the Axis nations at the height of their power. Few countries remained neutral.

Bulgaria, Hungary, Romania, and the German-created states of Croatia and Slovakia eventually joined the Axis. In opposition, the United Kingdom, the United States, the Soviet Union, and China formed the core of the Allies. The Allies totaled 50 nations by the end of the war.

During 1942, the Allies stopped the Axis advance in northern Africa, the Soviet Union, and the Pacific. Allied forces landed in Italy in 1943. They reached France in 1944. In 1945, the Allies drove into Germany from the east and the west. A series of bloody battles in the Pacific brought the Allies to Japan's doorstep by the summer of 1945. Germany surrendered on May 7, 1945. Japan surrendered on September 2, 1945.

An uneasy peace took effect as a war-weary world began to rebuild after World War II. Much of Europe and parts of Asia lay in ruins. Tens of millions of people were dead. Millions more were starving and homeless. The United States and the Soviet Union emerged as the world's most powerful nations. But new threats to peace arose.

Causes of the War

The Peace of Paris. In 1919, after the end of World War I (1914–1918), representatives of the victorious nations met in Paris to dictate the peace. The treaties of the Paris Peace Conference followed more than four years of costly and bitter warfare. They were worked out in haste by countries with opposing goals. The agreements failed to satisfy even the victors. Of the countries on the winning side, Italy and Japan left the peace conference most dissatisfied. Italy gained less territory than it felt it deserved. It vowed to take action on its own. Japan gained control of German territories in the Pacific. It thereby launched a program of expansion. Yet Japan felt slighted by the peacemakers' refusal to endorse the principle of the equality of all races.

The defeated countries in World War I—Germany, Austria-Hungary, Bulgaria, and the Ottoman Empire—were especially dissatisfied with the Peace of Paris. They were stripped of territory and arms. They were also required to make *reparations* (payments for war damages).

The Treaty of Versailles punished Germany severely. Its representatives signed the treaty only at the threat of invasion. Many Germans resented the "war guilt clause" that forced Germany to accept sole responsibility for causing World War I.

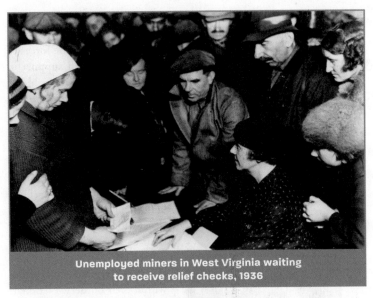

Unemployed miners in West Virginia waiting to receive relief checks, 1936

Economic problems. World War I damaged the economies of European countries. Both the winners and the losers came out of the war in debt. The defeated powers had difficulty paying reparations to the victors. The victors had difficulty repaying loans from the United States. The global economic shift from war to peace left millions of veterans unemployed. Millions of others who had worked in munitions factories and other war-related industries lost their jobs.

Italy and Japan suffered from overcrowding and a lack of resources after World War I. They eventually tried to solve their problems by territorial expansion. In Germany, *hyperinflation* (rapid, uncontrolled price increases) made money worthless. People lost their life savings. In 1924, loans from the United States helped stabilize Germany's currency. The reparation payment schedule was relaxed. By the late 1920s, the economic situation in Germany—and the rest of Europe—had improved.

Then came the Great Depression, a worldwide business slump. It began in the United States in 1929. By the early 1930s, it had halted and reversed Europe's economic recovery. The Great Depression caused mass unemployment. It spread poverty and despair. It weakened democratic governments. It also strengthened extreme political movements that promised to end the economic crisis.

Two movements in particular gained strength. The forces of Communism, known as the left, called for revolution by the workers. The forces of fascism, called the right, favored strong national government. Throughout Europe and elsewhere, the forces of the left ground against the forces of the right. Political extremes gained support in countries with the greatest economic problems and the deepest resentments of the Peace of Paris.

Nationalism was an extreme form of patriotism that swept across Europe beginning in the 1800s. Supporters of nationalism placed loyalty to their nation above any other public loyalty. They defined nationality by language and ethnicity. They viewed foreigners and minority groups with suspicion and scorn. Such beliefs helped nations justify their conquests of other lands. Such ideas also helped justify the poor treatment of minorities within their borders. Nationalism was a chief cause of World War I. It grew even stronger afterward.

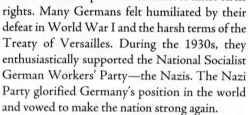

Portrait of Benito Mussolini

Nationalism corresponded with feelings of discontent. The more people felt deprived of national honor, the more they wished to see their country powerful and able to insist on its rights. Many Germans felt humiliated by their defeat in World War I and the harsh terms of the Treaty of Versailles. During the 1930s, they enthusiastically supported the National Socialist German Workers' Party—the Nazis. The Nazi Party glorified Germany's position in the world and vowed to make the nation strong again.

The Peace of Paris established an international organization called the League of Nations to maintain peace. But nationalism and individual arguments prevented the League from working effectively. Each country backed its own interests at the expense of other countries. Only weak countries agreed to submit their disagreements to the League of Nations for settlement. Strong nations reserved the right to settle their disputes by threats or even force.

The rise of dictatorships. During the 1920s and 1930s, political unrest and poor economic conditions enabled radical dictatorships to come to power in the Soviet Union, Italy, Germany, and Japan. The dictators held total power and ruled without regard to law. They used terror and secret police to crush opposition to their rule. People who objected risked imprisonment or execution.

Communists, led by Vladimir I. Lenin, seized power in Russia in 1917. The Soviet Union was established in 1922. A dictatorship set up by Lenin controlled the country by the time he died in 1924. After Lenin's death, Joseph Stalin and other leading Communists struggled for power. Stalin eliminated his rivals one by one, taking total control in 1929.

In Italy, economic distress after World War I led to strikes and riots. As a result of the violence, a strongly nationalistic group called the Fascist Party gained many supporters. Benito Mussolini, leader of the Fascists, promised to bring order and prosperity to Italy. He vowed to restore to Italy the glory it had known in the days of the ancient Roman Empire. By 1922, the Fascists had become powerful enough to force the king of Italy to appoint Mussolini prime minister. Mussolini took the title *Il Duce* (The Leader). He began to establish an *authoritarian* state—that is, one that valued obedience to authority above individual freedom.

In Germany, the Nazi Party made huge gains during the Great Depression. In 1933, Adolf Hitler, the leader of the Nazis, was appointed chancellor of Germany. Hitler, who was called *der Führer* (the Leader), rapidly increased his own power. He vowed to ignore the Versailles Treaty and avenge Germany's defeat in World War I. Hitler preached that Germans were a "superior race." He called Jews and Slavs inferior. He began a campaign of hatred against Jews and Communists and promised to rid the country of them. In this time of distress and depression, Hitler's extreme nationalism appealed to many Germans.

In Japan, power rested in the hands of Emperor Hirohito. He was known in Japan as *Showa*. But by the 1930s, military officers had formed a strong government around the emperor. Japan's military regime glorified war. It admired the traditional samurai warrior code of *bushido*. In 1941, Hirohito named the militarist General Hideki Tojo as prime minister of Japan.

Aggression on the march. Japan, Italy, and Germany followed a policy of aggressive territorial expansion during the 1930s. They invaded weak lands that could be easily conquered.

Japan had annexed Korea in 1910. In 1931, Japan seized control of Manchuria, a large Chinese region rich in natural resources. Japan ruled

Manchuria with brutality. In 1937, Japanese troops invaded the rest of China. By the end of 1938, Japan's military leaders were planning the conquest of all of Asia.

In 1935, Italian troops invaded Ethiopia. At that time, Ethiopia was one of the few independent countries in Africa. The Italians used machine guns, tanks, and airplanes to overpower Ethiopia's poorly equipped army. In 1939, Italy swept through Albania, in southeastern Europe. Albania was another easy conquest for Mussolini.

Soon after Hitler took power in Germany, he began to build up Germany's armed forces. The buildup violated the Treaty of Versailles. In 1936, Hitler sent troops into the Rhineland. The Rhineland was an area in western Germany that the treaty had made a *demilitarized zone,* a neutral zone free from military control. In March 1938, German soldiers marched into neighboring Austria and united it with Germany. Many people in both countries welcomed the *Anschluss* (union) of Austria and Germany.

These acts of aggression were easy victories for the dictatorships. The League of Nations lacked the resources or authority to field an international army. The United States had withdrawn from European affairs after World War I. It refused to join the League or become involved in any disputes. The United Kingdom and France were unwilling to risk another war.

In 1936, Germany and Italy agreed to support each other's foreign policy. The alliance was known as the Rome-Berlin Axis. Japan joined the Axis in 1940. It then became the Rome-Berlin-Tokyo Axis.

The Spanish Civil War.
A civil war tore Spain apart from 1936 to 1939. In 1936, many of Spain's army officers revolted against the government. The army rebels chose General Francisco Franco as their leader. Franco's forces were known as Nationalists or Rebels. The forces that supported Spain's elected government were called Loyalists or Republicans. The Spanish Civil War drew worldwide attention.

Hitler and Mussolini sent troops, weapons, aircraft, and advisers to aid the Nationalists. The Soviet Union was the only power to officially help the Loyalists. France, the United Kingdom, and the United States did not intervene. But Loyalist sympathizers from many countries joined the International Brigades to fight in Spain.

Nationalists occupy the Spanish border town of Portbou during the Spanish Civil War.

The last Loyalist forces surrendered on April 1, 1939. Franco set up an authoritarian government in Spain. The Spanish Civil War served as a military proving ground for weapons and tactics that were later used during World War II. The conflict in Spain foreshadowed the coming war. It pitted forces of the radical right—Nazis and Fascists—against the rest of the world.

The failure of appeasement.
Czechoslovakia had become an independent nation after World War I. Its western region of Bohemia was surrounded on three sides by Germany. Hitler sought control of the Sudetenland, the German-speaking border areas of Bohemia. More than 3 million people of German descent lived there. Urged on by Hitler and his agents, Sudeten Germans began to clamor for union with Germany.

Czechoslovakia refused to concede territory. Hitler prepared to strike. France and the Soviet Union pledged to support the young nation against German aggression. As tension mounted, the United Kingdom's prime minister Neville Chamberlain wished to preserve peace at all cost. He believed that war could be prevented by meeting Hitler's demands. That policy became known as *appeasement.*

Chamberlain had several meetings with Hitler during September 1938 as Europe edged closer to war. Hitler raised his demands at each meeting. On September 29, Chamberlain and French premier Édouard Daladier met with Hitler and Mussolini in Munich, Germany. Chamberlain and Daladier agreed to turn over the Sudetenland to Germany. They forced Czechoslovakia to accept the agreement. Hitler promised to demand no more territory in Czechoslovakia.

The Munich Agreement marked the height of the policy of appeasement. Chamberlain and Daladier hoped that the agreement would satisfy Hitler. They hoped it would prevent war—or at least prolong the peace until the United Kingdom and France were ready for war. The two leaders were mistaken on both counts.

The failure of appeasement soon became clear. Hitler broke the Munich Agreement in March 1939 and seized the rest of Czechoslovakia. He thereby added Czechoslovakia's armed forces and industries to Germany's military might. In the months before World War II began, Germany's preparations for war moved ahead faster than did the military buildup of the United Kingdom and France.

Germany's powerful war machine brought much of Europe under Axis control early in the war. By November 1942, Axis-controlled territory extended from Norway to northern Africa and from France to the Soviet Union. That month, Allied forces invaded northern Africa.

Early Stages of the War

During the first year of World War II, Germany won a series of swift victories. It conquered Poland, Denmark, Luxembourg, the Netherlands, Belgium, Norway, and France. Germany then attempted to bomb the United Kingdom into surrendering, but failed.

The invasion of Poland. The port city of Danzig (Gdańsk) and the province of East Prussia were separated from Germany by the Treaty of Versailles. In March 1939, Hitler demanded the city's return, as well as access to East Prussia. Poland refused. The United Kingdom and France pledged to help Poland if Germany attacked it. Yet the two powers could aid Poland only by invading Germany. Neither wanted to take that step. The United Kingdom had only a small army. France had prepared to defend its territory, not to attack.

The United Kingdom and France hoped that the Soviet Union would help defend Poland. But Hitler and Stalin shocked the world by becoming allies. On August 23, 1939, Germany and the Soviet Union signed a nonaggression pact. In the agreement, they promised not to go to war against each other. They secretly planned to divide Poland between themselves.

On September 1, 1939, Germany invaded Poland, beginning World War II. Poland had a large army but little modern equipment. Polish leaders expected to fight along the country's frontiers. However, the Germans introduced a new method of warfare called *blitzkrieg* (lightning war). It stressed speed and surprise. Rows of tanks smashed through Poland's defenses and rolled deep into the country before the Polish army had time to react. Swarms of German dive bombers and fighter aircraft knocked out communications and pounded battle lines. More than 1 million German troops swept across the Polish plains.

The Poles fought bravely. But the German attack threw their army into confusion. Adding to Poland's troubles, Soviet forces invaded from the east on September 17, 1939. Within two weeks, the Soviet Red Army occupied the eastern third of Poland. Germany had swallowed up the rest. When the fighting stopped on October 6, over 60,000 Polish troops were dead. So were tens of thousands of civilians. The Germans lost more than 10,000 killed in action.

The Phony War. The United Kingdom and France declared war on Germany on September

A tunnel running along the Maginot Line in northeastern France

3, 1939, two days after the invasion of Poland. But the two countries did little while Poland collapsed. France moved troops to the Maginot Line. The line was a belt of steel and concrete fortresses it had built along its border with Germany. The United Kingdom sent a small force into northern France. Germany stationed troops on the Siegfried Line, a strip of defenses Hitler built in the 1930s opposite the Maginot Line. The two sides avoided fighting in late 1939 and early 1940. Journalists called the period the "Phony War."

The conquest of Denmark and Norway. After the outbreak of war in September 1939, Denmark, Finland, Norway, and Sweden announced their neutrality. Germany depended heavily on Swedish iron ore shipments through neutral Norway. Hitler feared British plans to cut off those shipments by laying explosives in Norway's coastal waters. On April 9, 1940, German forces invaded Norway and Denmark. Denmark surrendered on April 10. The United Kingdom tried to help Norway. But Germany's air power prevented many British ships and troops from reaching the country. Norway surrendered on June 10, 1940. The conquest of Norway secured Germany's shipments of iron ore. It also provided bases for German submarines and aircraft. About 5,000 Germans were killed in the conquest. So were over 6,000 Allied troops (British, French, Norwegian, and Polish).

Chamberlain, who had favored appeasement, resigned after the invasion of Norway. Winston Churchill replaced him as the United Kingdom's prime minister on May 10, 1940. Churchill told the British people he had nothing to offer them but "blood, toil, tears, and sweat."

The invasion of the Low Countries. The Low Countries—Belgium, Luxembourg, and the Netherlands—hoped to remain neutral after World War II began. However, Germany launched a blitzkrieg against them on May 10, 1940. Luxembourg surrendered in one day. The Netherlands gave up in five days. British and French forces rushed into Belgium and fell into a German trap. As the Allied forces raced northward, the main German invasion cut behind them through the Belgian Ardennes Forest to the south. The Germans reached the English Channel on May 21. They had nearly surrounded the Allied forces in Belgium.

King Leopold III of Belgium surrendered on May 28, 1940. The surrender left the Allied forces in Belgium trapped. They retreated to the French seaport of Dunkerque on the English Channel. To rescue the troops, the United Kingdom sent all available seacraft. The fleet of "little ships" included destroyers, yachts, ferries, fishing vessels, and motorboats. Under heavy enemy fire, the hastily assembled fleet safely ferried about 338,000 troops to England from May 26 to June 4.

The relief of Dunkerque saved many soldiers to fight another day. About 35,000 Allied troops were left behind. So were tens of thousands of vehicles and tanks. The British Royal Air Force (RAF) lost more than 100 warplanes protecting the evacuation.

The fall of France. France had expected to fight along a stationary battlefront. The country had built the Maginot Line to defend the front. But in May 1940, German tanks and aircraft passed around the line. They swept through Luxembourg and Belgium and into northern France. On June 5, the Germans launched a major assault along the Somme River. The Somme had been the scene of brutal slaughter in World War I. The blitzkrieg overwhelmed the French forces, driving them mercilessly backward. Seeing an opportunity to profit from Germany's success, Italy declared war on France and the United Kingdom on June 10. The French government fled from Paris to Bordeaux the same day.

German troops entered Paris on June 14, 1940. Paul Reynaud, the new French premier, wanted to fight on. But many of his generals and cabinet officers believed that the battle for France was lost. Reynaud resigned. A new French government agreed to an *armistice* (truce) on June 22.

Under the terms of the armistice, Germany occupied the northern two-thirds of France and a strip of western France along the Atlantic Ocean. Southern France remained in French control. The town of Vichy became the capital of unoccupied France. Marshal Henri Philippe Pétain, a French hero of World War I, headed the Vichy government. He largely cooperated with the Germans. Then in November 1942, German troops occupied all France.

One of the French generals, Charles de Gaulle, escaped to the United Kingdom after France fell. In radio broadcasts to France, he urged the people to carry on the fight against Germany. The troops who rallied around de Gaulle became known as the Free French.

During the conquest of the Netherlands, Belgium, Luxembourg, and France, about 27,000 German troops died. More than 100,000 Allied soldiers lost their lives. The dead included about 90,000 French.

The Battle of Britain. The Royal Air Force (RAF) Fighter Command of the United Kingdom lost nearly half its strength in the Battle of France. The Germans took some time to coordinate newly captured air bases and prepare to attack yet again. The British took advantage of this precious time to replenish the planes and pilots they had lost over France. Prime Minister Churchill told Parliament: "What General Weygand called the Battle of France is over. The Battle of Britain is about to begin."

Hitler believed that the United Kingdom would now seek peace. The British, however, were determined to resist the Nazis. The United Kingdom fought on alone. Hitler prepared to invade southern England in a military operation with the code name *Sea Lion*. But before an invasion force could safely cross the English Channel, Hitler had to clear the RAF from the sky. The Battle of Britain was the first battle ever fought solely for air supremacy.

In July 1940, the German air force, the Luftwaffe, began to attack RAF and Royal Navy bases. Germany's bombers and fighter planes outnumbered the RAF's fighters by more than 4 to 1. But the previous victories of the Luftwaffe had come against nations with inferior air forces. The RAF had two outstanding types of pursuit plane—the *Hurricane* and the *Spitfire*. The RAF had also greatly developed the new technology of

Allied forces during the offensive against the Afrika Korps, 1942

radar. RAF radar stations could detect German squadrons as they left their airfields in France.

The air campaign was violent and costly for both sides. Of the nearly 3,000 British and Allied pilots who took part in the Battle of Britain, more than 500 were killed. The RAF lost about 900 aircraft. For the Germans, it was worse. Germany lost around 1,750 aircraft along with 2,600 aviators and crew. Operation Sea Lion was scrapped. But the bombing continued.

Hitler had originally ordered that no civilian targets should be attacked. But in late August, a lost Luftwaffe pilot violated his orders and bombed central London. An outraged Churchill retaliated with a bombing attack on Berlin. Hitler then unleashed his air force against English cities. He thus began what is known as the *Blitz*. German planes bombed cities from London to Manchester day after day, then night after night for months. Raids continued throughout the winter and spring. Finally, in May 1941, Germany gave up its attempts to defeat the United Kingdom from the air. More than 40,000 British civilians had lost their lives.

Hitler's decision to switch attacks from RAF bases to British cities effectively won the battle for the United Kingdom. It allowed the RAF to constantly replace both planes and pilots. The United Kingdom's survival became important later in the war. The island served as an airfield and base for the Allied invasion of Europe. The British Army and High Command also made crucial contributions to the ultimate Allied victory.

The War Spreads

By the end of 1941, World War II had become a global conflict. Battles erupted in Africa, the Balkan Peninsula of southeastern Europe, and the Soviet Union. The Axis and the Allies also battled each other at sea and in Asia. In December 1941, the United States entered the war.

The Western Desert Campaign. The Italian army opened battlefronts in Africa in the summer of 1940. In August, Italian troops pushed eastward from Ethiopia. They overran the British forces in British Somaliland (now Somalia). The following month, forces from the Italian colony of Libya invaded Egypt.

Fighting seesawed back and forth across the Mediterranean coasts and deserts of Libya, Tunisia, and Egypt. The United Kingdom fought to protect the oil fields of the Middle East. It also tried to defend the Suez Canal, the shortest sea route for the crucial exchange of supplies and troops with Asia. British and Commonwealth troops struck back at the Italians in December 1940, sweeping them from Egypt. But an Axis invasion of Greece drew part of the Allied force from Africa and ended the Allied advance.

Early in 1941, Hitler sent *panzer* (tank) units trained in desert warfare to help the Italians in North Africa. German Field Marshal Erwin Rommel led the panzer units. They were known as the *Afrikakorps*. Rommel's clever tactics earned him the nickname "The Desert Fox." After a series of battles in Libya, Rommel drove into Egypt. But the British again repelled the Axis forces. In May 1942, Rommel broke through into Egypt again. He threatened the port of Alexandria, the capital city of Cairo, and the vital Suez Canal. British forces led by Lieutenant General Bernard Montgomery met Rommel at El Alamein on October 23, 1942. The ensuing tank battle raged until

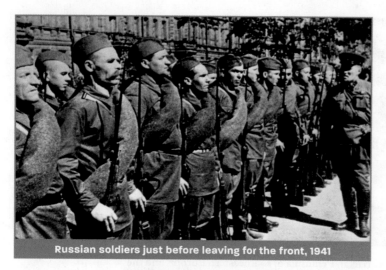

Russian soldiers just before leaving for the front, 1941

November 5, when Rommel's defeated forces withdrew. The Desert War, however, was far from over.

Allied dead in the Western Desert amounted to more than 35,000. More than 30,000 German and Italian soldiers were killed.

Fighting in the Balkans. Hitler pressured Bulgaria, Hungary, and Romania into joining the Axis. These countries provided Germany with vast supplies of food, petroleum, and personnel. Yugoslavia's government signed an agreement with the Axis in March 1941. But the Yugoslav military rebelled and overthrew the government. An enraged Hitler ordered the young nation crushed. German troops poured into Yugoslavia on April 6. Yugoslavia surrendered on April 17. But underground resistance there remained stubborn and deadly until the end of the war.

Mussolini had tired of playing Hitler's junior partner. He wanted a victory to boost his standing. On October 28, 1940, Italian forces based in Albania invaded Greece. They expected to defeat the poorly equipped Greek army easily. Though outnumbered, the Greeks fought fiercely. By December, they had driven the Italians out of Greece and had overrun part of Albania. The United Kingdom sent a small force to help the Greeks. But in April 1941, a much larger German force came to the aid of the Italians. By the end of the month, the Axis was in control. British troops had withdrawn to the island of Crete.

On May 20, 1941, thousands of German paratroopers descended on Crete and seized an airfield. More German troops then landed, securing the island. The victory gave Germany an important base in the Mediterranean.

Thousands of Allied and Axis troops died in the Balkan Campaign. The defeats in the Balkans were blows to the Allies. However, the detours into Yugoslavia and Greece were costly for Hitler too. They delayed his invasion of the Soviet Union.

The invasion of the Soviet Union. The Soviet Union and its enormous Red Army were constant threats to Hitler. He privately viewed them—and Communism itself—as Germany's chief enemy. He feared Soviet ambitions to expand in Europe, while planning to expand there himself. The German dictator desired more *lebensraum* (living space) for his people. Hitler also wanted control of the vast wheat and oil fields of Ukraine and elsewhere within the Soviet Union. The 1939 nonaggression pact with Stalin was a stalling tactic on both their parts. It served merely to keep the Soviet Union out of the war while Germany overran Europe.

Stalin sought to obtain more naval bases and strengthen Soviet borders. In November 1939, the Soviet Union invaded Finland. An outnumbered and outgunned Finnish army fought fiercely for five months in what came to be known as the Winter War. Finland surrendered in March 1940, giving Stalin minor territorial concessions. The much smaller Finnish Army lost about 25,000 troops killed in action. The Red Army lost about 200,000. In the summer of 1940, the Soviet Union seized the countries of Estonia, Latvia, and Lithuania along the Baltic Sea.

The length and difficulty of Stalin's Winter War with Finland helped give Hitler a low opinion of the Red Army. The Soviet Union may have had the largest army in the world at the time. But the German army was better trained, better equipped, and better led.

The German invasion of the Soviet Union, *Operation Barbarossa*, began on June 22, 1941. It started five weeks later than Hitler had intended. His generals warned of the dangers of the Russian winter. But Hitler was confident the fighting would be over before the first snowfall. Stalin ignored Allied warnings of the coming invasion. The attack took the Soviet Union by surprise.

More than 3 million German and Axis troops invaded along a 2,000-mile (3,220-kilometer) front. Germany's *Panzerkorps*, an armored and mechanized unit, smashed through the Soviet lines. Luftwaffe squadrons devastated the Red Air Force. In just a few weeks, the Germans killed or captured hundreds of thousands of Soviet soldiers. The Germans pushed far into Soviet territory. As the Red Army and civilians retreated, they destroyed factories, dams, railroads, and food supplies. They wanted to deprive the enemy of anything that might be useful.

Looking for the killer blow, Hitler's generals wanted to press on immediately to Moscow. Instead, Hitler sent his Panzerkorps to join the German armies heading through Ukraine toward the Crimean Peninsula on the Black Sea. While the Germans weakened their center and spent time transferring forces, Stalin reinforced. The German advance slowed. But on September 19, the Germans took the city of Kiev. It was Germany's greatest single victory of the war, Germany captured nearly 665,000 Soviet soldiers. A total of 1½ million Soviets had been taken prisoner thus far in the campaign. Another 700,000 had been killed. German dead had already passed 100,000.

In October, the Panzerkorps returned to the German center for the advance on Moscow. But the autumn rains had come. German tanks and artillery bogged down in the mud just 40 miles (64 kilometers) from the Russian capital. On November 15, 1941, exhausted German soldiers attacked Moscow. Fresh Soviet troops from the Far East combined with the onslaught of winter to stop the Germans 20 miles (32 kilometers) from the city. The Germans had no winter clothing. Temperatures plunged to −40°F (−40°C). The German soldiers suffered terribly. Tanks and weapons seized up. Stuck vehicles became a part of the frozen earth. As it had been in wars past, winter was once again Russia's greatest ally.

By December 1941, Operation Barbarossa had claimed the lives of 200,000 German soldiers. Thousands of Croatians, Hungarians, Italians, Romanians, and Slovaks were among them. The Red Army had already suffered hundreds of thousands killed and more than 3 million captured. The worst fighting, however, was yet to come.

The Battle of the Atlantic. The Allied war effort depended heavily on shipments of food, military equipment and supplies, and other provisions across the Atlantic Ocean from North America. Germany tried to stop the shipments. The Allies struggled to keep the supplies coming.

Germany's surface fleet could not seriously challenge the United Kingdom's Royal Navy. But German warships attacked *merchant vessels* (commercial ships). The Royal Navy hunted down and sank such raiders one by one. The biggest operation was against the powerful German battleship *Bismarck*. In May 1941, a fleet of British warships chased, trapped, and finally sank the *Bismarck*. Afterward, Germany's large warships rarely left harbor.

The greatest threat to Allied shipping came from German submarines, called *Unterseeboote* or U-boats. The U-boats prowled the Atlantic. They torpedoed any Allied ships they spotted. The conquests of Norway and France gave Germany bases for its U-boats. As a defensive measure, the United Kingdom began to use a convoy system in which merchant ships sailed in large groups escorted by warships.

From 1940 to 1942, Germany appeared to be winning the Battle of the Atlantic. Each month, U-boats sank thousands of tons of Allied shipping. But the Allies gradually overcame the underwater detection device called *sonar* to locate German submarines. Long-range aircraft bombed U-boats as they surfaced. Shipyards in North America stepped up their production of warships to accompany convoys. Eventually, the Allies were sinking U-boats faster than Germany could replace them. After terrible losses in "Black May" 1943, the U-boat "wolf packs" retreated and regrouped. The U-boats resumed action in the fall. But they never regained their previous success.

The Battle of the Atlantic was the longest military campaign of World War II. It lasted the length of the war. The Germans launched nearly 1,200 submarines. Of these, close to 800 were sunk. Out of about 40,000 German submariners sent into action, 28,000 never returned. That was the highest death rate of any armed service in the history of modern warfare. About 3,000 Allied ships sank to the bottom of the Atlantic Ocean, and more than 70,000 Allied merchant mariners, sailors, and aviators lost their lives.

The United States Enters the War

After World War II began in 1939, President Franklin D. Roosevelt announced the neutrality

The legend of the map reads:

Allied countries
Germany 1942-1945
Other Axis countries and occupied areas
Associated with Germany
Neutral countries
→ Major Allied campaign
Limit of Allied advance
Limit of Axis advance
✳ Major battle

The Allies attacked the Axis in Europe after defeating it in northern Africa in May 1943. Italy surrendered in September 1943, two months after the invasion of Sicily. In June 1944 the Allies landed in northern France. Attacks from the east and west forced Germany to surrender in May 1945.

of the United States. Canada, as part of the Commonwealth of Nations, entered the war on September 10, 1939, one week after the United Kingdom.

Roosevelt and many other people wanted to do more to help the Allies. These people, called *interventionists*, argued that an Axis victory would endanger democracies everywhere. Roosevelt urged "all aid short of war" to nations fighting the Axis. *Isolationists,* on the other hand, thought that the United States should not interfere in European affairs. They opposed aid to warring nations. They accused Roosevelt of steering the nation into a war it was not prepared to fight. The majority of people in the United States thought the Allied cause was just. But they wanted their country to stay out of World War II.

The arsenal of democracy. Roosevelt hoped to contribute to the defeat of the Axis powers by equipping the Allies. Roosevelt asked his fellow Americans to become what he called "the arsenal of democracy," meaning that the United States would supply military equipment to the Allies. The United States sent ships, tanks, aircraft, and other war equipment.

The United States then took several steps toward war. In November 1939, U.S. neutrality laws were changed to allow the sale of arms to warring nations—specifically the United Kingdom and France. In September 1940, the U.S. Navy gave the United Kingdom 50 destroyers to protect Atlantic convoys. In March 1941, with the Allies nearly broke, the U.S. Congress approved the Lend-Lease Act. The act permitted President Roosevelt to lend or lease raw materials, supplies, and weapons to any nation fighting the Axis. In all, 38 nations received a total of about $50 billion in aid through the Lend-Lease Act. More than half the aid went to the British Empire. About a fourth went to the Soviet Union.

Japan attacks. By 1940, Japanese forces were still bogged down in China. To force the Chinese to surrender, Japan wanted to cut off the supply route from Southeast Asia. Japan also wanted the rich resources of Burma (now Myanmar) and Indochina (parts of modern Laos and Vietnam) for itself. Japan's military leaders had hopes of an empire. They called it the Greater East Asia Co-Prosperity Sphere.

Japan's expansion in Southeast Asia troubled the United States. In September 1940, as Japanese troops occupied northern Indochina, the United States cut off vital exports to Japan. Japanese industries relied heavily on petroleum, scrap metal, and other raw materials from the United States. After Japan seized the rest of Indochina in 1941, Roosevelt barred the withdrawal of Japanese funds from American banks.

General Hideki Tojo became prime minister of Japan in October 1941. Tojo and Japan's other military leaders realized that only the United States Navy had the power to block Japan's expansion in Asia. They decided to cripple the U.S. Pacific Fleet with one forceful blow.

On December 7, 1941, the Japanese launched a surprise attack upon the U.S. Pacific Fleet at Pearl Harbor, Hawaii. Two waves of Japanese warplanes sank several U.S. ships, including four battleships. They also destroyed more than 180 U.S. aircraft. The Japanese killed 2,400 Americans but lost only about 100 of their own troops. The attack was a success. But bringing the United States into the war would prove disastrous for the Japanese Empire and its citizens.

The United States, Canada, and the United Kingdom declared war on Japan on December 8, 1941. Germany and Italy declared war on the United States on December 11. The world was now truly a world at war.

The War in Europe and North Africa

Soviet forces held off the German advance in Europe in 1942. The Soviets won a major victory at Stalingrad (now Volgograd) in 1943. The Allies invaded North Africa in 1942 and forced Italy to surrender in 1943. Allied troops swarmed into France in 1944 in the largest seaborne invasion in history. Allied attacks from the east and the west forced Germany to surrender in 1945.

The USS *Shaw* exploding during the attack on Pearl Harbor

The strategy. Churchill, Roosevelt, and Stalin—the leaders of the three major Allied powers—were known during World War II as the Big Three. Churchill and Roosevelt conferred frequently on overall strategy. Stalin directed the Soviet war effort. But he distrusted his allies' intentions and rarely consulted them.

The main wartime disagreement among the Big Three concerned an Allied invasion of western Europe. Stalin constantly urged Roosevelt and Churchill to open a second fighting front in western Europe and thus draw German troops from the Soviet front. Both Roosevelt and Churchill supported the idea. But they disagreed on where and when to invade. The Americans wanted to land in northern France as soon as possible. The British argued that an invasion of France before the Allies were fully prepared would be disastrous. Instead, Churchill favored invading Italy first. His view won out.

Roosevelt and Churchill first met in August 1941 aboard ship off the coast of Newfoundland. They issued the Atlantic Charter, a statement of the postwar aims of the United States and the United Kingdom. After the Japanese attacked Pearl Harbor, Roosevelt and Churchill conferred in Washington, D.C. The two leaders felt that Germany was a nearer and a more dangerous enemy than Japan. They decided to concentrate on defeating Germany first.

In January 1943, Roosevelt and Churchill met in Casablanca, Morocco. They agreed to invade the Mediterranean island of Sicily after driving the Germans and Italians from northern Africa. At the conference, Roosevelt announced that the Allies would accept only *unconditional* (complete) surrender from the Axis powers. Churchill supported him.

Roosevelt and Churchill first met with Stalin in November 1943 in Tehran, Iran. The Big Three discussed plans for a joint British and American invasion of France in the spring of 1944. They did not meet again until Germany neared collapse. In February 1945, Roosevelt, Churchill, and Stalin gathered at Yalta, a Soviet city on the Crimean Peninsula. They agreed that their countries would each occupy a zone of Germany after the war. France was to occupy a fourth zone. Roosevelt died on April 12, 1945, less than one month before the end of the war in Europe.

The Battle of Stalingrad. The Red Army struck back at the Germans outside Moscow on December 5, 1941. The Soviets pushed the invaders back about 100 miles (160 kilometers). But as the weather broke in the spring months of 1942, the Germans regrouped and prepared for a summer offensive—*Operation Blue.* Hitler was now personally directing the war. He bolstered his battered armies with divisions from Hungary, Italy, Romania, Slovakia, and Spain.

The combined Axis forces overran the Crimean Peninsula and headed eastward toward the rich oil fields in the Caucasus. Hitler ordered General Friedrich von Paulus to take the city of Stalingrad. About 1 million German soldiers poured into the city. The Soviets rose to meet them. Stalin had ordered, "Not one step back." The savage battle for Stalingrad began in September and dragged through the autumn. The Germans took most of the city but could not hold it. Neighborhoods, city blocks, even individual buildings were fought over for days or weeks. Thousands of people died. Then the same buildings were fought over again.

Paulus's losses mounted. The German commander repeatedly asked permission to pull out. Hitler repeatedly refused. Soviet troops counterattacked in mid-November. Eventually, they trapped Paulus's army. The Luftwaffe attempted to resupply the army by air. But it was too little, too late. Each day, thousands of German soldiers froze, starved to death, or died of disease. On February 2, 1943, after months of suffering, the last German troops in Stalingrad surrendered.

The Battle of Stalingrad halted Germany's eastward advance. it marked a turning point in the war as advantage swung to the Soviets. It was one of the largest battles in human history. Its cost was horrific. About 450,000 Axis troops were killed. The Soviets lost at least 500,000 soldiers and hundreds of thousands of civilians.

The Siege of Leningrad. In September 1941, the northern group of German armies surrounded the Russian city of Leningrad (now St. Petersburg). German warplanes and artillery bombarded the city. Nearly all supplies were cut off. The more than 2 million citizens and soldiers of Leningrad held out. They suffered through winters without electric power. They endured shortages of water, food, and medicine. All the while, they suffered bombardment by German artillery. By the time the Red Army broke through and lifted the siege in January 1944, $1^1/_3$ million Soviets were dead.

The Tunisia Campaign. The Battle of El Alamein in late 1942, like Stalingrad, had marked a turning point in the war. The Axis never again attacked in North Africa. On November 8, 1942, Allied troops commanded by Lieutenant General Dwight D. Eisenhower of the U.S. Army landed in Algeria and Morocco. Vichy French forces initially resisted the Americans. But within two days they had joined the Allied cause.

The Allies hoped to advance rapidly into Tunisia and cut off the Axis forces from their home bases in Italy and Sicily. But Axis troops moved faster and seized Tunisia first. There, Rommel prepared for battle. American troops first engaged in combat with the Germans on February 18, 1943, at Kasserine Pass. Rommel defeated the inexperienced Americans. But thereafter, the Allies steadily closed in. Rommel returned to Germany. The last Axis forces in North Africa surrendered in May—about 250,000 of them. The Allies had saved the oil fields of the Middle East. They also sustained the supply route to Asia and cleared a path for the invasions of Sicily and Italy.

Axis dead in the Tunisian Campaign numbered over 14,000. The British, Americans, and French lost over 10,000 troops.

 The air war. Before World War II began, many aviation experts claimed that the long-range bomber was the most advanced weapon in the world. They believed that bombers could wipe out cities and industries. In this way, bombing could destroy an enemy's desire and ability to go on fighting. The theory was tested during World War II.

By May 1941, Germany's bombing of the United Kingdom had largely stopped. But RAF bombers pounded Germany until the end of the war. At first, the bombing was costly and ineffective. British losses were heavy. Bomber Command relied on *area bombing.* Area bombing involved dropping a large number of bombs on an area without pinpointing targets. Bomber Command also favored nighttime raids. Night raids were safer than daytime raids, but bombers too often missed their targets in the dark. In 1942, the United Kingdom turned to *saturation bombing* of German cities. Such bombing involved dropping enough bombs to totally destroy the target area. A massive group of more than 1,000 aircraft bat-

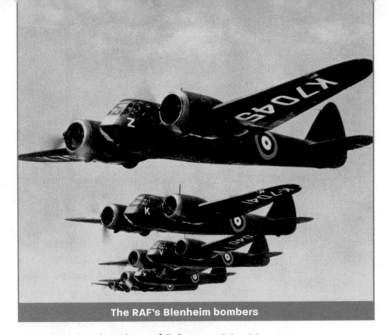

The RAF's Blenheim bombers

tered the railyards and city of Cologne on May 30, 1942. Bomber Command continued its nighttime raids on German cities to the end of the war. It made 35 raids on Berlin alone.

Meanwhile, the U.S. Army Air Forces had arrived. They joined the air campaign against Germany in 1942. The American B-17 bomber carried a better bombsight than British planes. B-17's were known as Flying Fortresses because of their heavy armor and many guns. They could take much punishment. For those reasons, the Americans favored *precision bombing.* It involved placing bombs with a high degree of accuracy. The Americans directed their bombing at mostly industrial and military targets. They carried out their bombing raids during the day.

Over the course of the war, American and British bombers dropped more than 2.7 million tons (2.45 million metric tons) of explosives onto European targets. Nearly 160,000 Allied aviators were killed in the bombing campaign. About 500,000 German civilians also died.

In spite of the bombardment, German industries continued to increase production. German morale failed to crack. The air war achieved its goals only during the last 10 months of World War II. In that time, nearly three times as many bombs fell on Germany as in all the rest of the war. By the end of the war, Germany's cities lay in ruins. Its factories, refineries, railroads, and canals had nearly ceased to operate.

Germany's air defenses rapidly improved during World War II. The Germans used radar to spot incoming bombers. They used fighter planes and antiaircraft guns, called *flak,* to shoot them down. In 1944, Germany introduced the first jet fighter, the Messerschmitt Me 262. The plane was known as the *Schwalbe* (Swallow). The Swallow easily overtook the propeller-driven fighters of the Allies. Also in 1944, Germany used the first guided missiles against the United Kingdom. The V-1 and V-2 missiles caused great damage and took many lives. But these innovative weapons were too few and came too late to affect the war's outcome.

The invasion of Italy. The Allies planned to invade Sicily after driving the Axis forces out of northern Africa. Axis planes had bombed Allied ships in the Mediterranean Sea from bases in Sicily. The Allies wanted to make the Mediterranean safe for their ships. They also hoped that an invasion of Sicily might knock a war-weary Italy out of the war.

Allied forces under Eisenhower landed along Sicily's south coast on July 10, 1943. For 38 days, they engaged in bitter fighting with the enemy over rugged terrain. The last Germans left Sicily on August 17.

Mussolini had fallen from power on July 25. The Italian government imprisoned him. But German commandos later rescued the former dictator. Italy's new prime minister, Field Marshal Pietro Badoglio, began secret peace talks with the Allies. Badoglio hoped to prevent Italy from

becoming a battleground. Italy surrendered on September 3. But Field Marshal Albert Kesselring, Germany's commander in the Mediterranean region, was determined to fight the Allies for control of Italy.

Allied forces led by U.S. Army lieutenant general Mark W. Clark landed at Salerno, Italy, on September 9, 1943. It was a struggle just to stay ashore. Another Allied force had already landed farther south. The Allies struggled up the Italian Peninsula in a series of head-on assaults against well-defended German positions. By early November, the Allies had reached the Gustav Line. The line was Germany's formidable defensive line about 75 miles (120 kilometers) south of Rome. Repeated Allied assaults on Monte Cassino resulted in some of the most brutal fighting of World War II. The Gustav Line held.

In January 1944, the Allies landed at Anzio, west of Cassino, in an effort to attack the Germans from behind. However, German forces kept the Allies pinned down on the beaches at Anzio for four months.

The Allies finally broke through German defenses in Italy in May 1944. Rome fell on June 4. The Germans held their positions in northern Italy through the fall and winter. But in the spring, the Allies swept toward the Alps. Italian resistance fighters captured Mussolini on April 27, 1945. They shot him on April 28. German forces in Italy finally surrendered on May 2. About 70,000 Allied soldiers died taking Italy. Around 48,000 Germans died defending it.

D-Day. Soon after the evacuation of Dunkerque in 1940, the United Kingdom started to plan a return to France. In 1942, the United States and the United Kingdom began to discuss a large-scale invasion across the English Channel. To test the German defenses, the Allies raided the French port of Dieppe in August 1942. The mostly Canadian landing force suffered disastrous losses. The Allies learned hard lessons at Dieppe. Among the lessons was that landing on open beaches had a better chance of success than landing in a port.

Throughout 1943, preparations moved ahead for an invasion of northern France the following year. The invasion plan received the code name *Operation Overlord*. Huge amounts of equipment and great numbers of troops massed in southern England. General Eisenhower, as

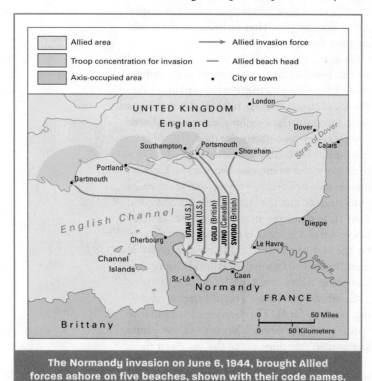

The Normandy invasion on June 6, 1944, brought Allied forces ashore on five beaches, shown with their code names. Within a week, the Allies held the area outlined in blue.

supreme commander of the Allied forces, directed the invasion.

The Germans expected an Allied invasion along the north coast of France in 1944. But they were unsure where. A chain of fortifications, which the Germans called the Atlantic Wall, ran along the coast. Hitler placed Rommel in charge of strengthening German defenses along the English Channel. Rommel brought in artillery. He placed explosive mines in the water and on the beaches. He also strung up barbed wire. The Germans concentrated their troops near Calais, at the narrowest part of the English Channel. But the Allies planned to land farther west, in a region of northern France called Normandy.

Eisenhower chose Monday, June 5, 1944, as D-Day—the date of the Normandy invasion. However, rough seas forced him to postpone until June 6. During the night, thousands of ships carrying landing craft and more than 130,000 landing troops crossed the channel. Minesweepers had gone ahead to clear the water. In addition, about 23,000 paratroopers and glider troops began dropping behind German lines. They captured bridges and railroad tracks. At dawn, battleships opened fire on the beaches. At 6:30 a.m., soldiers from the United States, the United Kingdom, Canada, and France stormed ashore. They landed on a 60-mile (100-kilometer) front. It was the largest seaborne invasion in history.

D-Day took the Germans by surprise. They responded fiercely. At one landing site, code-named Omaha Beach, U.S. troops came under heavy fire and barely managed to stay ashore. Nevertheless, all five Allied landing beaches were secure by the end of D-Day. The Allies soon had an artificial harbor in place for unloading more troops and supplies. A pipeline carried fuel across the channel. By the end of June 1944, about 1 million Allied troops had reached France.

The Allied forces advanced slowly. The Americans struggled westward to capture the port of Cherbourg. It fell on June 27. On July 18, British and Canadian soldiers finally captured Caen, which the British had hoped to capture on D-Day. On July 25, Allied bombers blasted a gap in the German front near St.-Lô, about 50 miles (80 kilometers) southeast of Cherbourg. The U.S. Third Army under Lieutenant General George S. Patton plowed through the hole. The battlefield had opened up. During August, the Allies cleared the Germans out of most of northwestern France. Allied bombers hounded the retreating Germans. More than 50,000 Allied troops and aviators died in the Battle of Normandy. Tens of thousands of Germans also lost their lives.

The drive to the Rhine. Patton's army rolled eastward toward Paris. On August 19, 1944, Parisians rose up against the occupying German forces. Resistance fighters battled the Germans street by street. American and Free French forces liberated Paris on August 25.

In mid-August 1944, Allied forces landed in southern France. They moved rapidly up the Rhône River Valley. Meanwhile, Patton raced eastward through the region of Lorraine toward the German border and the Rhine River. In late August, his tanks ran out of fuel. To the north, British forces led by Field Marshal Montgomery swept into Belgium and captured Antwerp on September 4. The Allies planned a daring operation, code named *Market Garden*, to carry them across the Rhine. On September 17, about 35,000 airborne soldiers began dropping behind German lines to seize bridges in the Netherlands. Additional troops invaded by land. But poor planning and bad weather hampered the operation. It ended in failure. Another path to Germany would have to be found.

The Battle of the Bulge. Germany's generals knew they were beaten. But Hitler pulled his resources together for one more assault. On December 16, 1944, German troops surprised and overwhelmed the Americans in the Ardennes Forest in Belgium and Luxembourg. However, the Germans lacked the troops and fuel to turn their thrust into a breakthrough. Within two weeks, the Americans stopped the German advance near the Meuse River in Belgium.

The Ardennes offensive is known as the Battle of the Bulge because of the bulging shape of the battleground on a map. It was the bloodiest battle for the Americans in World War II. About 80,000 Americans were killed, wounded, captured, or missing. The campaigns from September 1944 to January 1945 resulted in tens of thousands of Allied and German dead. The troops and armor lost in Hitler's desperate attack in the Ardennes left Germany with little to defend itself. The end was near, but the killing would go on.

The Soviet advance. More soldiers died fighting on the Eastern Front—about 10 mil-

Some of the surviving members of Poland's Home Army

lion—than on all other fronts combined. In 1943, the bloodletting at Stalingrad ended Germany's progress in eastern Europe. Germany could not sustain such losses. But the Soviet Union could. After January 1943, the Red Army steadily shoved the Germans back. Soviet forces had improved. They outnumbered the opposing German armies. Supplies poured into the Soviet Union from the United Kingdom and the United States. Soviet factories had also geared up their wartime production.

Nevertheless, the German army returned to the offensive in July 1943 near the Soviet city of Kursk. There, they massed an assault against superior Soviet forces. For more than two weeks, over 2 million soldiers slaughtered one another in brutal fighting. On July 12, about 800 tanks clashed at Prokhorovka. After the combined deaths of over 300,000 troops, the Red Army held the ground. Hitler finally called off the attack to deal with the Allied invasion of Sicily.

Soviet troops moved slowly forward during the summer and fall of 1943. In January 1944, a Soviet offensive ended the siege of Leningrad. In June, soon after the Normandy invasion, Stalin's armies attacked along a 450-mile (720-kilometer) front in the east. By late July, Soviet troops had reached the outskirts of Warsaw. Poland's Home Army rose up against German forces in Warsaw on August 1. But Soviet troops refused to come to Poland's aid. Stalin permitted the Germans to destroy the Home Army. It might have resisted his plans to set up a Communist government in Poland after the war. The Warsaw uprising lasted two months. More than 200,000 Poles were killed. Soviet forces entered Warsaw in January 1945.

Meanwhile, Soviet troops drove into Romania and Bulgaria. The Germans pulled out of Greece and Yugoslavia in the fall of 1944. But Germany resisted a siege in Budapest, Hungary's capital, until February 1945. Vienna, Austria's capital, fell to Soviet soldiers in April. By then, Soviet troops occupied nearly all of eastern Europe.

Victory in Europe. The Allies began their final assault on Germany in early 1945. Soviet soldiers reached the Oder River, about 40 miles (65 kilometers) east of Berlin, in January. Allied forces in the west occupied positions along the Rhine by early March.

British and Canadian forces cleared the Germans out of the Netherlands and swept into northern Germany. American and French forces raced toward the Elbe River in central Germany. Hitler ordered his soldiers to fight to the death. But large numbers of German soldiers surrendered each day.

As they advanced, the Allies discovered horrifying evidence of Nazi brutality. Hitler had ordered the imprisonment and murder of millions of Jews and members of other minority groups in concentration camps. The starving survivors of the death camps gave proof of the terrible suffering of those who had already died. The nature and reality of the Holocaust came to light in later months and years.

The Allies left the capture of Berlin to Soviet forces. By April 25, 1945, Soviet troops had surrounded the city. From a *bunker* (shelter) deep underground, Hitler ordered German soldiers to fight on. On April 30, however, Hitler killed himself rather than face defeat. With him died the *Third Reich* (Third Empire), the Nazi term for the empire in which they hoped to unite all Germanic peoples.

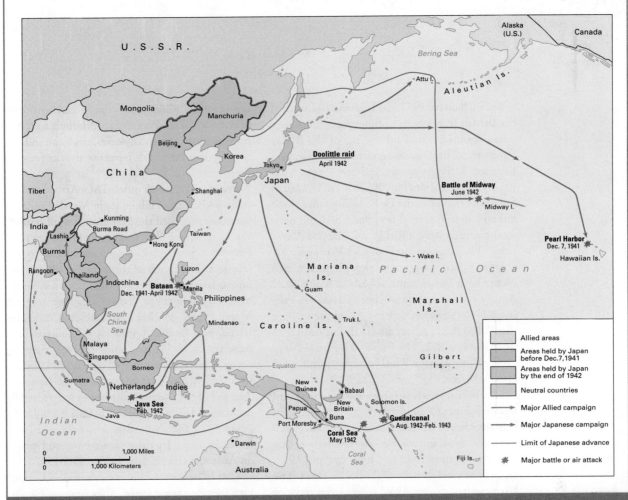

After Japan attacked Pearl Harbor, its forces rapidly advanced across Southeast Asia and the Western Pacific Ocean. This map shows key battles in that campaign and the greatest extent of Japan's empire. The Allies halted Japan's expansion in the summer of 1942.

The fighting in Berlin claimed the lives of over 70,000 Soviet soldiers. The Germans propped up their remaining units with children and elderly reservists. Thousands of them died in that last week of fighting.

German Grand Admiral Karl Dönitz briefly succeeded Hitler and arranged for Germany's surrender. On May 7, 1945, General Alfred Jodl, chief of staff of the German armed forces, signed a statement of unconditional surrender at Eisenhower's headquarters in Reims, France. World War II had ended in Europe. The Allies declared May 8 as V-E Day, or Victory in Europe Day.

The War in Asia and the Pacific

The attack on Pearl Harbor on December 7, 1941, left the U.S. Pacific Fleet briefly powerless to halt Japan's expansion. During the next six months, Japanese forces swept across Southeast Asia and the western Pacific Ocean. Japan's empire reached its greatest size in August 1942. It stretched northeast to the Aleutian Islands of Alaska, west to Burma (now Myanmar), and south to the Netherlands Indies (now Indonesia). The Allies halted Japan's expansion in the summer of 1942. They hacked away at its empire until Japan surrendered in August 1945.

Early Japanese victories. On December 8, 1941, Japanese bombers struck the British colony of Hong Kong on the south coast of China. They also attacked two U.S. islands in the Pacific Ocean—Guam and Wake. The Japanese invaded Thailand the same day. Thailand surrendered within hours and began cooperating with the Japanese. Japanese troops took Hong Kong, Guam, and Wake Island by the end of the year.

From Thailand, Japanese forces soon advanced into the British-ruled regions of Malaya (now part of Malaysia) and Burma. Thinking the thick jungles of the Malay Peninsula impenetrable, the British Army expected an assault by sea. But Japanese troops streamed through the jungles and rapidly overran the peninsula.

By late January 1942, the Japanese had pushed the British forces back to Singapore. Singapore was a fortified island off the tip of the Malay Peninsula. The Japanese stormed the island on February 8. Singapore surrendered a week later. Japan captured about 60,000 soldiers. The fall of Singapore ranked as the United Kingdom's worst military defeat ever. Thousands of Commonwealth troops were killed in the Malayan Campaign. The Japanese lost about 3,500 troops.

Japan's next target was the petroleum-rich Netherlands Indies, south of Malaya. A combined Allied naval force protected those islands. On February 27, 1942, Japan sank five Allied ships. More than 2,000 Allied sailors died in the lopsided Battle of the Java Sea. The Imperial Japanese Navy suffered little damage. The Netherlands Indies fell in early March.

Meanwhile, Japanese forces had advanced into southern Burma. China sent troops into Burma to help the United Kingdom hold the Burma Road. Weapons, food, and other goods traveled over that supply route from India to China. In April 1942, Japan seized and shut down the Burma Road. The Japanese had driven Allied forces from most of Burma by mid-May. The United Kingdom's Burma Corps lost 1,500 troops. The Japanese lost 2,000. Chinese units suffered many deaths as well.

A B-25 taking off from the *Hornet* in the first air raid on Japan

Japan began landing troops in the Philippines on December 8, 1941. American and Philippine forces commanded by U.S. general Douglas MacArthur defended the islands. In late December, MacArthur's forces abandoned Manila, the capital of the Philippines. MacArthur withdrew to nearby Bataan Peninsula. Although suffering from malnutrition and disease, American and Filipino troops beat back Japanese attacks for over three months.

President Roosevelt ordered MacArthur to Australia. He left the Philippines in March 1942. He famously promised the Filipinos, "I shall return." On April 9, over 75,000 exhausted American and Filipino troops on Bataan surrendered to the Japanese. Thousands of them died of disease and mistreatment on a 65-mile (105-kilometer) forced march to prison camps, known as the Bataan Death March. Some soldiers held out on Corregidor Island, near Bataan, until May 6. Thousands of American and Filipino soldiers were killed in action. The Japanese suffered over 2,500 killed.

Japan's victories astonished even the Japanese. The fall of the Netherlands Indies left Australia unprotected. The capture of Burma brought the Japanese to India's border. Australia and India feared invasion. Japanese planes bombed Darwin on Australia's north coast in February 1942.

The tide turns. Three events in 1942 helped turn the tide against Japan. They were the Doolittle raid, the Battle of the Coral Sea, and the Battle of Midway.

The Doolittle raid. To prove it could be done, the United States staged a daring bombing raid on the Japanese homeland. On April 18, 1942, Lieutenant Colonel James H. Doolittle led 16 B-25 Mitchell bombers in a surprise attack on Tokyo and other Japanese cities. The twin-engine bombers took off from the deck of the *Hornet*, an aircraft carrier more than 600 miles (960 kilometers) east of Japan. The raid did little damage. But it was a huge morale boost for the American military and public alike. It also alarmed Japan's leaders. They had believed their homeland safe from Allied attack. To prevent future raids, the Japanese determined to capture more islands to the south and the east to extend the country's defenses.

Although no B-25s were shot down, all 16 were lost as they ran out of fuel. Out of the 80 crew members, 73 survived. Doolittle was awarded the Medal of Honor.

The Battle of the Coral Sea. In May 1942, a Japanese invasion force sailed toward Australia's base at Port Moresby on the south coast of the island of New Guinea, at Australia's doorstep. American warships, supported by the Royal Australian Navy, met the Japanese force in the Coral Sea, northeast of Australia. The Battle of the Coral Sea, fought from May 4 to 8, was the first naval battle in which opposing ships never sighted one another. Each side attacked the other with carrier-based warplanes. The American aircraft carrier *Lexington* sank, as did the Japanese carrier *Shoho*. Around 550 Americans died. The Japanese lost close to 1,100 sailors and aviators. The air-sea battle halted the assault on Port Moresby and temporarily checked the threat to Australia.

The Battle of Midway. Japan next sent a large fleet to capture Midway Island at the westernmost tip of the Hawaiian Archipelago. The United States had cracked Japan's naval code. Thus it learned about the coming invasion. Admiral Chester W. Nimitz, commander of the U.S. Pacific Fleet, gathered the ships that had survived the raid on Pearl Harbor and the Battle of the Coral Sea. He prepared to ambush the Japanese.

The battle opened on June 4, 1942, with a Japanese air strike on Midway Island. The air strike inflicted heavy damage. American bombers responded from the island but damaged no Japanese ships. Three squadrons of U.S. torpedo-bombers—41 aircraft—followed. They flew in low against Japanese warships. But the Japanese shot down 33 of the American planes without a single torpedo striking its target. A wave of 54 American dive bombers followed. They pounded the enemy aircraft carriers while planes refueled and rearmed on deck. The three-day battle was fought entirely by warplanes. The Japanese lost 4 aircraft carriers, about 300 aircraft, and around 3,000 sailors and aviators. The Japanese sank the aircraft carrier USS *Yorktown*, shot down about 150 U.S. planes, and killed about 300 Americans.

The Battle of Midway was the first clear Allied victory over Japan in World War II. The battle crippled the Japanese navy and stopped Japan's advances. Aircraft carriers had become the most important weapon in the war in the Pacific.

In an effort to divert American attention from Midway, the Japanese occupied two islands at the tip of Alaska's Aleutian chain on June 7, 1942. The Americans drove the Japanese out of the Aleutians in the spring and summer of 1943. All but 29 of the 2,500 Japanese on the islands were killed. About 560 Americans died. It was the only fighting on North American soil during World War II.

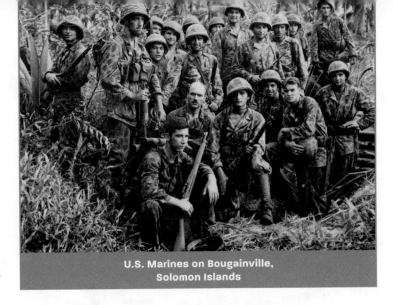

U.S. Marines on Bougainville, Solomon Islands

The South Pacific. After the Battle of Midway, the Allies were determined to stop Japanese expansion in the South Pacific. In the battles that followed, American soldiers and marines fought many jungle battles on Pacific islands. The jungle itself was an enemy. Heavy rains drenched the troops and turned the jungle into a foul-smelling swamp. The soldiers had to hack their way through tangled, slimy vegetation. They had to wade through knee-deep mud. The Japanese hid everywhere, waiting to shoot unsuspecting Americans. Scorpions and snakes were a constant menace. Malaria and other tropical diseases took a heavy toll.

The Americans also encountered Japan's strict samurai military code called *bushido*. The code required Japanese soldiers to fight to the death. Japanese soldiers believed that surrender meant disgrace. The Allies rarely captured them alive. When cornered, the Japanese sometimes charged at Allied troops in nighttime suicide charges. The charges were called *banzai attacks* because the Japanese shouted the war cry "Banzai" as they attacked. Rather than admit defeat, Japan's military leaders took their lives by stabbing themselves in the abdomen. That method of suicide was called *hara-kiri.*

It was dangerous for Allied soldiers to surrender to the Japanese. Because the Japanese disdained surrender, they executed many enemy prisoners of war or otherwise abused them. Of the many thousands of Americans, Australians, and British taken prisoner, one in three did not return.

The Allies developed two major campaigns against Japan in the South Pacific. One force under MacArthur stopped the Japanese on New Guinea. Another force under Nimitz battled the Japanese in the Solomon Islands northeast of Australia. MacArthur and Nimitz aimed at taking the

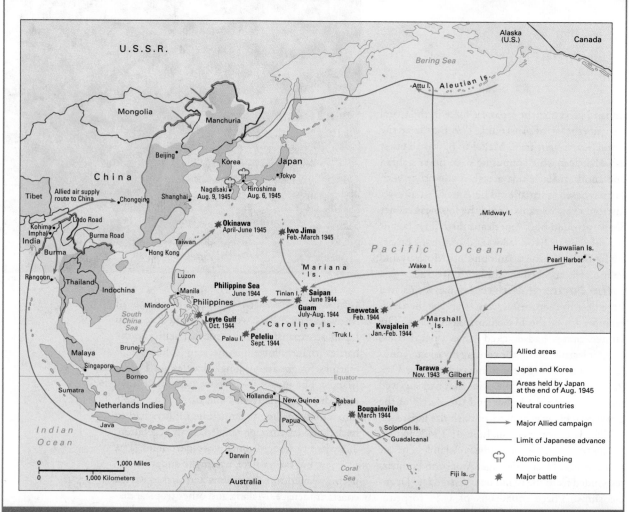

From 1943 to August 1945, the Allies worked their way across the Pacific toward Japan. Allied forces on the Asian mainland recaptured Burma. This map shows the Allied route and gives the dates of key battles. Japan still held much territory when it surrendered.

port of Rabaul on New Britain, a large island off the northeast coast of New Guinea. Rabaul was Japan's chief base in the South Pacific. Japanese aircraft and warships attacked Allied ships from Rabaul. Japan also supplied other islands in the South Pacific from that base.

New Guinea. In the summer of 1942, Japanese troops began an overland drive across New Guinea's rugged, jungle-covered mountains to the Australian base of Port Moresby on the south coast. An Allied force made up chiefly of Australians counterattacked. By November, the Allies had pushed the Japanese back across the mountains. MacArthur then attacked Japanese positions along the north coast in a series of combined air, sea, and land operations. By the time fighting ceased in July 1944, the New Guinea Campaign had taken the lives of many thousands of Allied and Japanese personnel.

Guadalcanal. On August 7, 1942, U.S. marines invaded the island of Guadalcanal in the first stage of a campaign in the Solomon Islands.

The Japanese were building an air base on Guadalcanal from which to attack Allied ships. The invasion took the Japanese by surprise. But they fought back. A fierce battle developed.

The six-month battle for Guadalcanal was one of the most vicious campaigns of World War II. Each side depended on its navy to land supplies and troop reinforcements. In a series of naval battles, the Allies gained control of the waters surrounding Guadalcanal. They then cut off Japanese shipments. Until that time, Allied supplies had been short. The marines had depended on rice captured from the enemy. By February 1943, the starving Japanese had evacuated Guadalcanal. They lost nearly 15,000 troops in action. The U.S. Army and Marine Corps suffered about 1,500 deaths. In heavy naval action around the island, about 5,000 Allied personnel were killed. Around 4,800 Japanese were lost.

Rabaul. In the summer of 1943, Allied military leaders canceled the invasion of Rabaul. Instead, American bombers pounded the Japanese base. Aircraft and submarines sank shipments headed for Rabaul. About 100,000 Japanese defenders waited there for an attack that never came. There was one significant casualty out of Rabaul, however. Japanese Admiral Isoroku Yamamoto died when American fighters destroyed his plane on April 18, 1943. Yamamoto was the architect of the attack on Pearl Harbor—and the attack on Midway.

Island hopping in the Central Pacific.

From late 1943 until the fall of 1944, the Allies hopped from island to island across the Central Pacific toward the Philippines. During the island-hopping campaign, the Allies became expert at *amphibious* invasions. Such invasions were seaborne operations that involve naval, air, and land forces. Each island they captured provided a base from which to strike the next target. But rather than capture every island, the Allies bypassed Japanese strongholds and invaded islands that were weakly held. That strategy, known as *leapfrogging*, saved time and lives. Leapfrogging carried the Allies across the Gilbert, Marshall, Caroline, and Mariana islands in the Central Pacific.

Admiral Nimitz selected the Gilbert Islands as the first major objective in the island-hopping campaign. American marines invaded Tarawa in the Gilberts in November 1943. The attackers met heavy fire from Japanese troops in concrete shelters. But they inched forward and captured the tiny island after four days of savage fighting. The Japanese lost about 5,000 troops defending the island. Just 17 remained alive when the shooting stopped. The Marines lost close to 1,000 killed in the assault. The Allies improved their amphibious operations because of lessons learned at Tarawa. As a result, fewer soldiers died in later landings.

In February 1944, U.S. marines and infantry leaped north to the Marshall Islands. They captured Kwajalein and Enewetak with ease. Only 600 American troops were killed, compared with the Japanese total of 11,000. Allied military leaders meanwhile had decided to bypass Truk (now Chuuk), a key Japanese naval base in the Caroline Islands west of the Marshalls. American warplanes ravaged Truk, though. They sank 39 Japanese ships and destroyed 275 aircraft at a cost of only 25 American planes.

The Americans made their next jump to the Mariana Islands, about 1,000 miles (1,600 kilo-meters) northwest of Enewetak. Bitter fighting for the Marianas began in June 1944. The islands of Saipan, Guam, and Tinian fell at a cost of almost 5,000 American dead and 68,000 Japanese.

In the Battle of the Philippine Sea on June 19 and 20, Japan's navy once again attempted to destroy the U.S. Pacific Fleet. Instead, the Americans massacred Japan's navy and destroyed its air power. Japan lost 3 aircraft carriers, thousands of sailors, and 480 airplanes. More than three-fourths of the planes it sent into battle were destroyed. The United States lost 130 aircraft. Most of them were lost in dangerous nighttime carrier landings. Most of their crews survived. The lopsided air battle became known as the "Great Marianas Turkey Shoot."

Hideki Tojo resigned as Japan's prime minister in July 1944 after the loss of Saipan. By November, American B-29 Superfortress bombers were pounding the home islands of Japan from air bases in the Marianas.

A final hop before the invasion of the Philippines took U.S. forces to the Palau Islands in September 1944. The islands lie between the Marianas and the Philippines. Most of the fighting took place on the small island of Peleliu. The Japanese fought fiercely. They lost 13,600 killed and took close to 2,000 Americans with them. The Battle of Peleliu had the highest U.S. casualty rate of any amphibious invasion in the Pacific theater of war.

The liberation of the Philippines.

The campaigns in New Guinea and the Central Pacific brought the Allies within striking distance of the Philippine Islands. Expecting stiff Japanese resistance, the Allies assembled a landing force of more than 700 ships. They pointed the landing force at the island of Leyte in the central Philippines. On Oct. 20, 1944, American troops poured ashore.

In a desperate attempt to disrupt the invasion, the Imperial Japanese Navy lured U.S. admiral Bill Halsey's task force into the Battle of Leyte Gulf. It became the largest naval battle in history. The Japanese sent 64 ships against 216 American and 2 Australian warships. The Americans had 24 aircraft carriers. It was an overwhelming victory for the United States. The defeat left Japan's navy ravaged. More than 10,000 Japanese sailors and aviators died at Leyte Gulf. So did 3,000 Americans.

During the Battle for Leyte Gulf, the Japanese unleashed a terrifying new weapon—the *kamikaze* suicide pilot. Kamikaze was Japanese for *divine wind*. Kamikazes intended to crash their planes filled with explosives into Allied warships. But most were shot down before they reached their targets. The few that got through, however, caused great damage, terror, and loss of life.

The fight for the island of Leyte lasted until the end of 1944. On January 9, 1945, the Allies landed on the island of Luzon. They fought their way to the capital city of Manila, which was almost completely destroyed. Nearly 100,000 Filipino civilians died in the conquest of Manila. Eventually, the remaining Japanese troops on Luzon—50,000 of them—pulled back to the mountains. There they went on fighting until the war ended.

American losses in the Philippines were heavy, with 13,700 killed in action. Japanese losses were catastrophic, with at least 200,000 dead. Japan was doomed to defeat after losing the Philippines. But it did not intend to surrender.

The China-Burma-India theater. While fighting raged in the Pacific, the Allies also battled the Japanese on the Asian mainland. By mid-1942, Japan held much of eastern and southern China. It had also conquered nearly all of Burma. The Japanese had closed the Burma Road, the overland supply route from India to China. China lacked equipment and trained troops. But the Allies wanted to keep China in the war because the Chinese tied down hundreds of thousands of Japanese troops. For three years, the Allies flew war supplies over the world's tallest mountain system, the Himalaya, from India to China. The route was known as "the Hump."

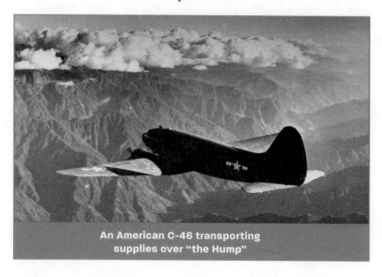

An American C-46 transporting supplies over "the Hump"

China. By 1942, five years after Japan had invaded China, the opposing armies neared exhaustion. Japanese troops staged attacks to capture China's food supplies for themselves and to starve the country into surrender. As a result, millions of Chinese people died from lack of food. The fighting in China left nearly half a million Japanese soldiers dead. It also killed 1⅓ million Chinese soldiers and millions more civilians.

A struggle between China's Nationalist government, headed by Chiang Kai-shek, and Chinese Communists weakened the country's war effort. At first, the Nationalist forces and the Communists had joined in fighting the Japanese invaders. But their cooperation broke down as they prepared for a brutal civil war.

The American Volunteer Group—better known as the Flying Tigers—served in China. They were led by Colonel Claire L. Chennault. His three squadrons of fighter pilots gunned down 300 Japanese planes. By the end of 1943, they controlled the skies over China. Major General Joseph W. Stilwell trained the Chinese army and commanded the U.S. forces in China and Burma.

Burma. The Allied campaign in Burma was linked to the fighting in China. From 1943 until early 1945, the Allies fought to recapture Burma from the Japanese and reopen the Burma Road. Rugged jungle, heavy rains, and a shortage of troops and supplies hampered Allied efforts.

Admiral Louis Mountbatten of the United Kingdom became supreme Allied commander in Southeast Asia in August 1943. He directed several successful offensives in Burma in late 1943 and in 1944. By January 1945, Allied forces had battled their way through the jungles of northern Burma and opened a supply route. Yangon (also spelled Rangoon), Burma's capital, fell to the Allies in May. British Empire and Commonwealth troops took the brunt of the casualties there. They lost 15,000 troops in combat. American battle deaths in Burma topped 3,000. Japan lost well over 100,000 killed in action. At least 140,000 civilians also died.

India became an important supply base and training center for Allied forces during World War II. Japan's conquest of Burma in 1942 placed India in danger. In early 1944, Japanese troops invaded India. They encircled the towns of Imphal and Kohima just inside India's border. The British supplied the towns by air. By June, the Japanese offensive ground to a halt. Japan began pulling out of India. On all fronts, about 36,000 Indian troops died during World War II. An additional 2,600 died in the Indian National Army. The Indian National Army was a military force formed by Indian nationalists to seek Independence from the United Kingdom. The Indian National Army fought alongside the Japanese. Tens of thousands of Japanese soldiers were lost to combat and disease in India. Hundreds of thousands of Indian civilians died of starvation during the war.

Closing in on Japan. Superiority at sea and in the air enabled the Allies to close in on Japan in early 1945. By then, Japan had lost much of its empire. It had also lost most of its aircraft and cargo ships, and nearly all its warships. Hundreds of thousands of Japanese soldiers remained stranded on Pacific islands bypassed by the Allies. American B-29 Superfortress bombers were pounding Japan's industries. American submarines were sinking vital supplies headed for Japan.

In January 1945, Major General Curtis E. LeMay took command of the air war against Japan. He ordered more frequent, more daring, and more devastating raids. American bombers began to drop *incendiary* (fire-producing) bombs that set Japanese cities aflame. A massive incendiary raid in March 1945 destroyed the heart of Tokyo. In all, over 300,000 Japanese civilians were killed in American bombing raids.

Japan's military leaders went on fighting, though they faced certain defeat. The Allies decided they needed more bases to step up the bombing against Japan. They chose the Japanese islands of Iwo Jima and Okinawa.

Iwo Jima. About 750 miles (1,207 kilometers) south of Japan is a small, volcanic island then called Iwo Jima—Japanese for "Sulfur Island." The island covers only 8 square miles (21 square kilometers). It is now called Iwo To. In 1945, it was defended by 21,000 Japanese troops prepared to fight to the death. They fought from fortified caves and underground tunnels. In preparation for the invasion, American B-24 Liberator bombers rocked Iwo Jima 74 days in a row. On February 19, 1945, U.S. marines hit the island's black sand beaches. The Japanese fought desperately from camouflaged pits, from caves, from trees, and from concrete bunkers.

The famous flag-raising on Mount Suribachi occurred on February 23. But fighting dragged on into April. It was the bloodiest battle in U.S. Marine Corps history. Nearly 7,000 marines were killed in action on Iwo Jima. As for the Japanese defenders, 212 surrendered. But more than 20,000 did not. The fighting was savage. For their part in the battle, 22 marines and 5 sailors were awarded the Medal of Honor. The island proved worth taking because 2,250 B-29 Superfortress bombers made emergency landings there in the following months. Each bomber had 11 crew members on board.

Operation Iceberg. Okinawa is an island just 350 miles (563 kilometers) from Kyushu, the southernmost of Japan's home islands. On April 1, 1945, American troops poured ashore. Three months of brutal combat followed. The two sides fought on Okinawa's steep hills and in its deep ravines. At sea, Japan sent wave after wave of kamikazes at the American Navy. Japan attacked with what remained of the Japanese fleet as well. By the time the battle ended on June 21, 36 U.S. ships had been sunk and 368 damaged. It was the costliest battle in U.S. Navy history. The Japanese navy lost 16 ships and 7,830 aircraft, many of which were kamikazes. The battle took the lives of 110,000 Japanese and Okinawan military personnel. The American death toll was the heaviest of any battle in the Pacific—12,500 soldiers, sailors, and aviators killed. The famous American war correspondent Ernie Pyle was killed there too on April 18. About 80,000 Okinawan civilians died. Many chose to kill themselves rather than be conquered.

Wounded Marines on Iwo Jima

Smoke rising over Nagasaki after the atomic bomb

By the summer of 1945, some members of Japan's government favored surrender. Others insisted that Japan fight on. Meanwhile, Okinawa had taught the Allies a grim lesson. While planning the invasion of Japan for November 1945, they estimated it might cost 1 million American lives. Some Allied leaders believed that Soviet help was needed to defeat Japan. They had encouraged Stalin to invade Manchuria. However, the Allies found another way to end the war.

The atomic bomb. In 1939, the German-born scientist Albert Einstein had informed President Roosevelt about the possibility of creating a superbomb. It would produce a powerful explosion by splitting the atom. Einstein and other scientists feared that Germany might develop such a bomb first. In 1942, the United States set up the Manhattan Project. The project was a top-secret program to develop an atomic bomb. The United States exploded the first bomb in a test blast in the New Mexico desert in July 1945.

Roosevelt died in April 1945. Vice President Harry S. Truman became president of the United States. Truman met with Churchill and Stalin in Potsdam, Germany, in July, shortly after Germany's defeat. At the Potsdam Conference, Truman learned of the successful test explosion of the atomic bomb. He informed the other leaders of it. The United States, the United Kingdom, and China then issued a statement threatening to destroy Japan unless it surrendered unconditionally. In spite of the warning, Japan went on fighting.

On August 6, 1945, an American B-29 bomber called the *Enola Gay* dropped the first atomic bomb used in warfare on the Japanese city of Hiroshima. The explosion killed from 70,000 to 140,000 people. It destroyed about 5 square miles (13 square kilometers) of the city. After Japanese leaders failed to respond to the bombing, the United States dropped another bomb on Nagasaki on August 9. It killed about 40,000 people. Later, thousands more died of injuries and radiation from the two bombings. Meanwhile, on August 8, the Soviet Union declared war on Japan and invaded Manchuria.

Victory in the Pacific. Although Japan's emperors had traditionally stayed out of politics, Hirohito urged the government to surrender. On August 14, Japan agreed to unconditional surrender.

On September 2, 1945, representatives of Japan signed the official statement of surrender aboard the U.S. battleship *Missouri*. The ship lay at anchor in Tokyo Bay. Representatives of all the Allied nations were present. Truman declared September 2 as V-J Day, or Victory over Japan Day. World War II had ended.

The Secret War

Throughout World War II, a secret war was fought between the Allies and the Axis. The goals of the secret war were to obtain information about each other's activities and to weaken each other's war effort. Code-breakers tried to figure out secret communications. Spies worked behind enemy lines to gather information. Saboteurs tried to disrupt activities on the home front. Many people in Axis-held territories joined undercover resistance groups that opposed the occupying forces. All the warring nations used propaganda to influence public opinion.

The Ultra secret. Soon after the outbreak of World War II, the United Kingdom obtained, with the help of Polish spies, an Enigma machine. Germany used Enigma to code secret messages. British mathematicians and code-breakers solved the machine's electronic coding procedures. The ability to read many of Germany's wartime communications was known as the *Ultra secret*. Ultra helped the Allies defeat Germany. During the 1940 Battle of Britain, Ultra supplied warning of where and when the Luftwaffe planned to attack. Ultra also helped Montgomery defeat the

Germans in Egypt in 1942 by providing him with Rommel's battle plan.

The British carefully guarded the Ultra secret. They were cautious about using their knowledge so that Germany would not change its coding procedures. The Germans never discovered that the United Kingdom had broken their code.

Spying and sabotage. The warring nations trained spies and saboteurs. Spies reported on troop movements, defense buildups, and other developments behind enemy lines. Spies of Allied nations also supplied resistance groups with weapons and explosives. Saboteurs hampered the enemy's war effort by blowing up factories and bridges and organizing slowdowns in war plants.

Germany had spies in many countries. But its efforts at spying were less successful than those of the Allies. The U.S. government set up a wartime agency called the Office of Strategic Services (OSS) to engage in spying and sabotage. The OSS worked closely with a similar British agency, the Special Operations Executive. The Soviet Union operated networks of spies in Allied nations as well as in Germany and Japan.

Resistance groups sprang up in every Axis-occupied country. Resistance began with individual acts of defiance against the occupiers. Gradually, like-minded people banded together and worked in secret to oppose the Axis. Resistance groups expanded their activities as the war continued. The resistance published and distributed illegal newspapers. Resistance workers rescued Allied aircrews shot down behind enemy lines. The resistance also gathered information about the enemy and sabotaged military installations.

In such countries as France, Yugoslavia, and Burma, resistance groups organized bands of fighters. Resistance fighters staged raids, ambushes, and guerrilla attacks against the occupation forces. The French resistance interfered with German efforts to repel the Allied invasion of Normandy in 1944. Norwegian resistance workers destroyed a German-bound shipment of *heavy water*, a substance needed to make atomic weapons. Yugoslavia had the most effective resistance movement of all—the Partisans. With Allied help, the Partisans drove the Germans out of Yugoslavia in 1944.

In Germany, a small underground movement opposed the Nazis. In July 1944, a group of German army officers planted a bomb intended to kill Hitler. However, Hitler escaped the explosion with minor injuries. The plotters were arrested and executed.

Resistance workers caught by the Nazis faced certain death. German soldiers rounded up and executed hundreds of civilians as *reprisals* (punishment) for acts of rebellion against the Nazi occupiers.

Propaganda. All the warring nations used propaganda to win support for their policies. Governments aimed propaganda at their own people and at the enemy. Radio broadcasts reached the largest audiences. Motion pictures, posters, and cartoons were also used.

The Nazis were masters of propaganda. Joseph Goebbels directed Germany's Ministry of Propaganda and Enlightenment. It controlled publications, radio programs, motion pictures, and the arts in Germany and German-occupied Europe. The ministry worked to convince people of the superiority of German culture and of Germany's right to rule the world. As the war turned in favor of the Allies, the Germans claimed to be saving the world from the evils of Communism.

Mussolini stirred the Italians with dreams of restoring Italy to the glory of ancient Rome. Japan promised conquered peoples a share in the Greater East Asia Co-Prosperity Sphere. That plan would unite all eastern Asia under Japanese control. The Japanese claimed that they were freeing Asia from European rule.

Some World War II propaganda pieces composed by the U.S. Office of War Information

British Broadcasting Corporation (BBC) newscasts provided truthful information about the day's fighting to the European mainland. The Nazis made it a crime for people in Germany and German-held lands to listen to BBC broadcasts. The U.S. government established the Office of War Information to encourage American support for the war effort. In 1942, the Voice of America, a government radio service, began broadcasting to Axis-occupied countries.

The warring countries also engaged in psychological warfare. It was intended to destroy the enemy's will to fight. American planes dropped leaflets over Germany that told of Nazi defeats. The Axis nations employed English-speaking radio announcers to weaken the morale of Allied soldiers. Mildred Gillars, an American known as "Axis Sally," made broadcasts for Germany. The Japanese also used English-speaking female announcers. Some of them were referred to as "Tokyo Rose" by soldiers.

On the Home Front

World War II affected the civilian populations of all the fighting nations. But the effects were uneven. Much of Europe and large parts of Asia suffered widespread destruction and hardship. The United States and Canada, far from the battlefronts, were spared most of the horror of war. North America, in fact, prospered during World War II. The war effort attracted widespread support.

Producing for the war. World War II required enormous amounts of ships, tanks, aircraft, and weapons. The United States and Canada built new plants to manufacture war

Women working at Douglas Aircraft's Long Beach, California, plant

goods. They also renovated automobile and other factories to do the same.

The United States astonished the world with its wartime output. Roosevelt called for the production of 60,000 aircraft during 1942. Many people believed that goal was impossible to achieve. But U.S. war plants did it. Then they turned out nearly 86,000 planes the following year. Shipbuilding gains were just as impressive. The time needed to build an aircraft carrier dropped from 36 months in 1941 to 15 months in 1945. Canada also expanded its output during World War II. Wartime expansion made Canada a leading industrial power by the war's end.

Millions of women in the United States and Canada joined the labor force during World War II. They replaced men who were needed for combat operations. Women worked in shipyards and aircraft factories. They filled many jobs previously held only by men. Canadian women replaced men on farms as well as in factories. Civilians planted victory gardens to grow their own food so that more rations would be available for troops fighting overseas.

New opportunities opened up for African Americans during World War II. In 1941, Roosevelt created the Fair Employment Practices Committee to prevent job discrimination in U.S. defense industries. Large numbers of southern blacks moved north to work in the war plants.

Mobilizing for the war. The United States introduced its first peacetime draft in September 1940. Under the draft law, all men aged 21 through 35 were required to register for military service. The draft was later extended to men 18 through 44. More than 16 million American men served in the armed forces during World War II. About 10 million were drafted. The rest volunteered. About 338,000 women served in the U.S. armed forces. They worked as mechanics, drivers, clerks, and cooks. They also filled many other noncombat positions.

Canada also expanded its armed forces greatly during World War II. At the outbreak of the war, the Canadian government promised not to draft men for service overseas. Canada relied on volunteers for overseas duty until November 1944. By then, it suffered from a shortage of troops and began to send draftees overseas. More than a million Canadians, including about 50,000 women, served in the armed forces during the war.

Paying for the war. The U.S. and Canadian governments brought in money by selling war bonds, certificates, notes, and stamps. The United States government raised nearly $180 billion from such sales. Canada's government also raised several billion dollars. Because few people were out of work, income increased during the war years. As a result, revenue from income taxes soared. The government taxed entertainment and such luxury goods as cosmetics and jewelry. Corporations paid extra taxes on higher-than-normal profits. Canadians also paid increased taxes during the war.

In spite of greater borrowing and higher taxes, the U.S. and Canadian governments spent more than they raised to pay for the war. In the United States, the national debt increased from about $49 billion in 1941 to $259 billion in 1945. Canada's national debt rose from $4 billion in 1939 to $16 billion in 1945.

Government controls over civilian life in the United States and Canada expanded during World War II. In both countries, the national government established agencies to direct the war effort on the home front. The agencies helped contain inflation, shortages, and production foul-ups. The War Production Board, for example, controlled the distribution of raw materials needed by U.S. industries. The Office of Price Administration limited price increases in the United States. It also set up a rationing program to distribute scarce goods fairly. Each family received a book of ration coupons to obtain such items as sugar, meat, butter, and gasoline.

Canada's government had even greater wartime powers. For example, the National Selective Service controlled Canada's work force. It forbade men of military age to hold jobs it termed "nonessential." Canada's Wartime Prices and Trade Board determined wages and prices and set up a rationing program.

Treatment of enemy aliens. During World War II, the U.S. government classified more than a million newly arrived immigrants from Germany, Italy, and Japan as "enemy aliens." After the bombing of Pearl Harbor, some Americans directed their rage at people of Japanese ancestry. In 1942, prejudice against the Japanese led the U.S. government to move more than 110,000 West Coast residents of Japanese ancestry to inland relocation camps. The Japanese Americans lost their homes and their jobs as a result. About two-thirds of them were citizens of the United States. Canada also relocated about 21,000 people of Japanese ancestry during the war.

Civilian life. Conditions were especially difficult in the Soviet Union. Fierce fighting went on there for nearly four years. Stalin ordered retreating Soviet soldiers to burn everything in their path that German troops could use for food or shelter. But that scorched-earth policy also caused hardships for the Soviet people. Millions of Soviet civilians died of famine and other war-related causes. In some areas occupied by the Soviet Union, many of the people at first welcomed the conquering German troops. The people saw the Germans as liberators from Stalin's harsh rule. But the cruelty of the Nazis turned the people against them. During World War II, civilians and soldiers in the Soviet Union fought the Germans with hatred and determination.

The civilian population of the United Kingdom united wholeheartedly behind the war effort. The people worked long hours in war plants. They accepted severe shortages of nearly all goods. Prime Minister Churchill inspired the British people with his stirring words.

Japan came closest to collapse of all the warring nations. As the Allies closed in, Japan was deprived of the raw materials needed for its industries. American bombers pounded Japan's cities. American submarines sank Japanese merchant ships. By 1945, hunger and malnutrition were widespread in Japan. But the people remained willing to sacrifice for the war effort.

Food, clothing, and other consumer goods remained plentiful in Germany during the early years of the war. Imports poured in from Nazi-occupied countries of Europe. The Allied bombing of Germany got off to a slow start and did little damage at first. Germany's situation had changed by late 1942, however. The army bogged down in the Soviet Union. There were fewer reports of German victories to cheer the people. Allied bombs rained down day and night on German cities. Consumer goods became scarce. But the people continued to work hard for the war effort.

Hitler's dreaded secret police, the Gestapo, crushed opposition to the Nazi Party. The Gestapo arrested anyone suspected of opposing Nazism in Germany and in German-held territories. To free German men for combat, the Gestapo recruited workers from occupied countries. Millions of

Europeans were forced to work long hours under terrible conditions in German war plants. Many died of mistreatment or starvation.

The Holocaust. The Nazis persecuted and murdered millions of people, including Jews, Roma (sometimes called Gypsies), and Slavs. By 1942, Hitler had started a campaign—the "Final Solution"—to exterminate European Jews. The Nazis rounded up Jewish men, women, and children from occupied Europe. They shipped the Jews in railway cars to concentration camps. There the Jews were systematically killed or used as slave labor. Many died from lack of food, disease, or torture. Altogether, Hitler's forces killed approximately 6 million European Jews. Europe lost 60 percent of its prewar Jewish population. Half of the victims were Polish. The Nazis also slaughtered Slavs, Roma, socialists, Communists, homosexuals, and people with mental retardation.

Consequences of the War

Deaths and destruction. World War II took more lives and caused more destruction than any other war. Altogether, about 70 million people served in the armed forces of the Allied and Axis nations. About 20 million of them lost their lives. The Soviet Union lost at least $7^1/2$ million soldiers and about 10 million civilians, much more than any other country. American deaths came to about 400,000. The United Kingdom lost a similar amount. Germany lost $3^1/4$ million military personnel. About 2 million Japanese military personnel died. Poland suffered 600,000 military deaths and nearly 6 million civilian dead. Italy, Romania, and Yugoslavia all lost 300,000 soldiers or more. Austria, France, and Hungary each lost more than 200,000.

Displaced persons. World War II uprooted millions of people. By the war's end, more than 12 million displaced persons remained in Europe. They included orphans, prisoners of war, and survivors of Nazi concentration and slave labor camps. They also included people who had fled invading armies and war-torn areas. Other people were displaced by changes in national borders. For example, many Germans were expelled from Poland, Czechoslovakia, and other lands in eastern Europe that the Nazis had taken.

To help displaced persons, the Allies established the United Nations Relief and Rehabilitation Administration (UNRRA). UNRRA began operating in 1944 in areas freed from Nazi occupation. The organization set up camps for displaced persons. It provided them with food, clothing, and medical supplies. By 1947, most people had been resettled. However, about a million people still remained in camps. Many had fled from countries in eastern Europe. They refused to return to homelands that had come under Communist rule.

New power struggles arose after World War II ended. The war had exhausted the leading prewar powers of Europe and Asia. Germany and Japan ended the war in defeat. The United Kingdom and France were weakened. The United States and the Soviet Union emerged as the world's leading powers. Their wartime alliance soon collapsed, however. The Soviet Union sought to spread Communism in Europe and Asia. A struggle developed between the Communist world, led by the Soviet Union, and the non-Communist world, led by the United States. That struggle became known as the Cold War.

The United States had fought the Axis to preserve democracy. After the war, Americans found it impossible to return to the policy of isolation their country had followed before the war. Americans realized that they needed strong allies. They helped the war-torn nations—friend and foe alike—recover.

World War II had united the Soviet people behind a great patriotic effort. The Soviet Union came out of the war stronger than before, in spite of the destruction it had suffered. Before the war ended, the Soviet Union had absorbed three nations along the Baltic Sea—Estonia, Latvia, and Lithuania. It had also taken parts of Poland, Romania, Finland, and Czechoslovakia by mid-1945. At the end of the war, Soviet troops occupied most of eastern Europe. In March 1946, Churchill warned that an "iron curtain" had descended across Europe. It divided eastern Europe from western Europe. Behind the Iron Curtain, the Soviet Union helped Communist governments take power in Bulgaria, Czechoslovakia, Hungary, Poland, and Romania.

Communism also gained strength in the Far East. The Soviet Union set up a Communist government in North Korea after the war. In China, Mao Zedong's Communist forces battled Chiang Kai-shek's Nationalist armies. Late in 1949, Chiang fled to the island of Taiwan. China joined the Communist world.

A hydrogen bomb test, 1957

By 1947, Communists threatened to take control of Greece. The Soviet Union was demanding military bases in Turkey. That year, President Truman announced that the United States would provide military and economic aid to any country threatened by Communism. American aid helped Greece and Turkey resist Communist aggression.

In 1948, the United States set up the Marshall Plan to help war-torn nations in Europe rebuild their economies. Under the plan, 18 nations received $13 billion in food, machinery, and other goods. The Soviet Union forbade countries in eastern Europe to participate in the Marshall Plan.

The nuclear age opened with the development of the atomic bomb during World War II. Many people believed that weapons of mass destruction would make war unthinkable in the future. They hoped that the world would learn to live in peace. But a race to develop ever more powerful weapons soon began.

At the end of World War II, only the United States knew how to build an atomic weapon. In 1946, the United States proposed the creation of an international agency that would control atomic energy and ban the production of nuclear weapons. But the Soviet Union objected to an inspection system. The proposal was dropped. Soviet scientists developed an atomic bomb in 1949.

Establishing the Peace

Birth of the United Nations. Out of the horror of World War II came efforts to prevent war from ever again engulfing the world. In 1943, representatives of the United States, the United Kingdom, the Soviet Union, and China met in Moscow. They agreed to establish an international organization that would work to promote peace. The four Allied powers met again in 1944 in Washington, D.C. The delegates decided to call the new organization the United Nations (UN). In April 1945, representatives from 50 nations gathered in San Francisco to draft a charter, or constitution, for the United Nations. They signed the charter in June. It went into effect on October 24.

Peace with Germany. Before World War II ended, the Allies had decided on a military occupation of Germany after its defeat. They divided Germany into four zones. The United States, the Soviet Union, the United Kingdom, and France each occupied a zone. The four powers jointly administered Berlin.

At the Potsdam Conference in July 1945, the Allies set forth their occupation policy. They agreed to abolish Germany's armed forces and to outlaw the Nazi Party. Germany lost territory east of the Oder and Neisse rivers. Most of the region went to Poland. The Soviet Union gained the northeastern corner of this territory.

The Allies brought to trial Nazi leaders accused of war crimes. The trials exposed the evils inflicted by Nazi Germany. Many leading Nazis were sentenced to death. The most important war trials took place in the German city of Nuremberg from 1945 to 1949.

Soon after the occupation began, the Soviet Union stopped cooperating with its Western Allies. It blocked all efforts to reunite Germany. The Western Allies gradually joined their zones into one economic unit. But the Soviet Union forbade its zone to join.

The city of Berlin lay deep within the Soviet zone of Germany. In June 1948, the Soviet Union sought to drive the Western powers from Berlin by blocking all rail, water, and highway routes to the city. For over a year, the Western Allies flew in food, fuel, and other goods to Berlin. The Soviet Union finally lifted the Berlin blockade in May 1949.

The Western Allies set up political parties in their zones and held elections. In September 1949, the three Western zones combined as the Federal Republic of Germany, also known as West Germany. In May 1955, the Western Allies signed a treaty ending the occupation of West Germany. They granted the country full independence. However, the treaty was not a general peace treaty because the Soviet Union refused to sign it. The Soviet Union set up a Communist government in its zone. In October 1949, the Soviet zone became the German Democratic Republic, also called East Germany.

In September 1990, the Soviet Union and the Western Allies signed a treaty to give up all their occupation rights in East and West Germany. In October 1990, Germany was reunited as a non-Communist nation.

Peace with Japan. The military occupation of Japan began in August 1945. Americans far outnumbered other troops in the occupation forces. General MacArthur directed the occupation as supreme commander for the Allied nations. He introduced many reforms designed to rid Japan of its military institutions and transform it into a democracy. A constitution drawn up by MacArthur's staff took effect in 1947. The Constitution transferred all political rights from the Japanese emperor to the people. In addition, the Constitution granted voting rights to women and denied Japan's right to declare war.

The Allied occupation forces brought to trial 25 Japanese war leaders and government officials who were accused of war crimes. Seven of these individuals were executed. The others received prison sentences.

In September 1951, the United States and most of the other Allied nations signed a peace treaty with Japan. The treaty took away Japan's overseas empire. But it permitted Japan to rearm. The Allied occupation of Japan ended soon after the nations signed the peace treaty. However, a new treaty permitted the United States to keep troops in Japan. China's Nationalist government signed its own peace treaty with Japan in 1952. The Soviet Union and Japan also signed a separate peace treaty in 1956.

Peace with other countries. Soon after World War II ended, the Allies began to draw up peace treaties with Italy and the other countries that fought the Allies. The treaties limited the armed forces of the defeated countries. The agreements required the defeated countries to pay war damages. The treaties also called for territorial changes. Bulgaria gave up territory to Greece and Yugoslavia. Czechoslovakia gained land from Hungary. Italy gave up land to France, Yugoslavia, and Greece. Italy also lost its empire in Africa. Romania gained territory from Hungary. But in turn it lost land to Bulgaria and the Soviet Union.

MLA Citation

"World War II." *The Southwestern Advantage Topic Source.* Nashville: Southwestern. 2013.

DATA

Military Casualties in World War II (1939–1945)

Country	Dead	Wounded	Country	Dead	Wounded
The Allies			**The Axis**		
Australia	23,365	39,803	**Austria**	380,000	350,117
Belgium	7,760	14,500	**Bulgaria**	10,000	21,878
Canada	37,476	53,174	**Finland**	82,000	50,000
China	2,200,000	1,762,000	**Germany**	3,500,000	7,250,000
France	210,671	390,000	**Hungary**	140,000	89,313
Poland	320,000	530,000	**Italy**	77,494	120,000
Soviet Union	7,500,000	5,000,000	**Japan**	1,219,000	295,247
[1]**United Kingdom**	329,208	348,403	**Romania**	300,000	[2]
United States	405,399	671,278			

[1] Including colonials

[2] Figure unavailable

DATA

World War II: The Warring Nations

Name	Date Entered War	Name	Date Entered War
The Allies		**Netherlands**	May 10, 1940
Argentina	March 27, 1945	**New Zealand**	September 3, 1939
Australia	September 3, 1939	**Nicaragua**	December 8, 1941
Belgium	May 10, 1940	**Norway**	April 9, 1940
Bolivia	April 7, 1943	**Panama**	December 7, 1941
Brazil	August 22, 1942	**Paraguay**	February 8, 1945
Canada	September 10, 1939	**Peru**	February 11, 1945
Chile	February 14, 1945	**Poland**	September 1, 1939
China	December 9, 1941	**San Marino**	September 24, 1944
Colombia	November 26, 1943	**Saudi Arabia**	March 1, 1945
Costa Rica	December 8, 1941	**South Africa**	September 6, 1939
Cuba	December 9, 1941	**Soviet Union**	June 22, 1941
Czechoslovakia	December 16, 1941	**Syria**	February 26, 1945
Denmark	April 9, 1940	**Turkey**	February 23, 1945
Dominican Republic	December 8, 1941	**United Kingdom**	September 3, 1939
Ecuador	February 2, 1945	**United States**	December 8, 1941
Egypt	February 24, 1945	**Uruguay**	February 22, 1945
El Salvador	December 8, 1941	**Venezuela**	February 16, 1945
Ethiopia	December 1, 1942	**Yugoslavia**	April 6, 1941
France	September 3, 1939		
Greece	October 28, 1940		
Guatemala	December 9, 1941	**The Axis**	
Haiti	December 8, 1941	**Bulgaria**	April 6, 1941
Honduras	December 8, 1941	**Croatia**	April 10, 1941[1]
India	September 3, 1939	**Germany**	September 1, 1939
Iran	September 9, 1943	**Hungary**	April 10, 1941
Iraq	January 16, 1943	**Italy**	June 10, 1940
Lebanon	February 27, 1945	**Japan**	December 7, 1941
Liberia	January 26, 1944	**Romania**	June 22, 1941
Luxembourg	May 10, 1940	**Slovakia**	September 1, 1939[1]
Mexico	May 22, 1942		
Mongolian People's Republic	August 9, 1945		

[1] German-created states

DATA

Important Dates in Europe and Northern Africa: 1939–1942

1939

Sept. 1	Germany invaded Poland, starting World War II.
Sept. 3	Britain and France declared war on Germany.

1940

April 9	Germany invaded Denmark and Norway.
May 10	Germany invaded Belgium and the Netherlands.
June 10	Italy declared war on France and Great Britain.
June 22	France signed an armistice with Germany.
July 10	Battle of Britain began.

1941

April 6	Germany invaded Greece and Yugoslavia.
June 22	Germany invaded the Soviet Union.
Sept. 8	German troops completed the blockade of Leningrad, which lasted until January 1944.

1942

Aug. 25	Hitler ordered his forces to capture Stalingrad.
Oct. 23	Britain attacked the Axis at El Alamein in Egypt.
Nov. 8	Allied troops landed in Algeria and Morocco.

Important Dates in Europe and Northern Africa: 1943–1945

1943

Feb. 2	The last Germans surrendered at Stalingrad.
May 13	Axis forces in northern Africa surrendered.
July 4	Germany opened an assault near the Soviet city of Kursk.
July 10	Allied forces invaded Sicily.
Sept. 3	Italy secretly surrendered to the Allies.
Sept. 9	Allied troops landed at Salerno, Italy.

1944

June 6	Allied troops landed in Normandy in the D-Day invasion of northern France.
July 20	A plot to assassinate Hitler failed.
Dec. 16	The Germans struck back at U.S. troops in the Battle of the Bulge.

1945

April 30	Hitler took his life in Berlin.
May 7	Germany surrendered unconditionally to the Allies in Reims, France, ending World War II in Europe.

DATA

Important Dates in the Pacific: 1941–1942

1941

Dec. 7	Japan bombed U.S. military bases at Pearl Harbor in Hawaii.
Dec. 8	The United States, Great Britain, and Canada declared war on Japan.

1942

Feb. 15	Singapore fell to the Japanese.
Feb. 26–28	Japan defeated an Allied naval force in the Battle of the Java Sea.
April 9	U.S. and Philippine troops on Bataan Peninsula surrendered.
April 18	U.S. bombers hit Tokyo in the Doolittle raid.
May 4–8	The Allies checked a Japanese assault in the Battle of the Coral Sea.
June 4–6	The Allies defeated Japan in the Battle of Midway.
Aug. 7	U.S. marines landed on Guadalcanal.

Important Dates in the Pacific: 1943–1945

1943

Nov. 20	U.S. forces invaded Tarawa.

1944

June 19–20	A U.S. naval force defeated the Japanese in the Battle of the Philippine Sea.
July 18	Japan's Prime Minister Tojo resigned.
Oct. 20	The Allies began landing in the Philippines.
Oct. 23–26	The Allies defeated Japan's navy in the Battle of Leyte Gulf in the Philippines.

1945

March 16	U.S. marines captured Iwo Jima.
June 21	Allied forces captured Okinawa.
Aug. 6	An atomic bomb was dropped on Hiroshima.
Aug. 8	The Soviet Union declared war on Japan.
Aug. 9	An atomic bomb was dropped on Nagasaki.
Aug. 14	Japan agreed to surrender unconditionally.
Sept. 2	Japan signed surrender terms aboard the battleship U.S.S. *Missouri* in Tokyo Bay.

ADDITIONAL INFORMATION

Books to Read

Axelrod, Alan. *The Real History of World War II*. Sterling Publishing, 2008.

Bussel, Norman. *My Private War*. Pegasus, 2008.

Downing, David. *Sealing Their Fate: Twenty-Two Days That Decided World War II*. Da Capo, 2009.

Hoppes, Jonna D., comp. *Just Doing My Job*. Santa Monica Press, 2009.

Rees, Laurence. *World War II Behind Closed Doors*. Pantheon, 2008.

Ryan, Mark. *Hornet's Sting: The Amazing Untold Story of World War II Spy Thomas Sneum*. Skyhorse Publishing, 2009.

Sturgeon, Alison, ed. *World War II: The Definitive Visual History*. DK Publishing, 2009.

Van Ells, Mark D., ed. *The Daily Life of an Ordinary American Soldier During World War II*. Edwin Mellen Press, 2008.

Web Sites

Camp Harmony

http://www.lib.washington.edu/exhibits/harmony/exhibit/index.html

This exhibit based on materials from the University of Washington library tells the story of the four-month internment of Seattle's Japanese American community during the spring and summer of 1942 at the Puyallup Assembly Center known as Camp Harmony.

D-Day

http://www.pbs.org/wgbh/amex/dday/

This special feature from PBS includes news reports from June 6, 1944, letters from U.S. soldiers, and facts about paratroopers.

Breaking Germany's Enigma Code

http://www.bbc.co.uk/history/worldwars/wwtwo/enigma_01.shtml

Information about codes in wartime, how they were used, and how the German Enigma code was broken during World War II.

Pearl Harbor

http://www.history.navy.mil/special Highlights/Pearl Harbor/Pearl_Harbor_Resources.htm

Overview and special image selection of Pearl Harbor from the Naval History and Heritage Command.

The First Steps Leading to the Final Solution

http://remember.org/Facts.root.solution.html

Information about events leading to the Holocaust, the destruction of the Jews in Europe by Hitler's Third Reich.

The Good War and Those Who Refused to Fight It

http://www.pbs.org/itvs/thegoodwar/

A companion Web site to the PBS documentary which tells the dramatic story of the conscientious objectors who refused to fight in World War II.

Women Come to the Front

http://lcweb.loc.gov/exhibits/wcf/wcf0001.html

Stories of women journalists and photographers in World War II.

World War II Documents

http://avalon.law.yale.edu/subject_menus/wwii.asp

Resources from Yale University.

Search Strings

Evolution of Fighter Jets/Planes

"Fighter jets" evolution "World War II" German bombers (1,190)

"Fighter jets" evolution "World War II" German bombers Royal Air Force Spitfires Messerschmitt (22)

Evolution of fighter jets planes World War II (31,900)

Progression of World War II

"World War II" progression timeline (28,400)

"World War II" progression timeline Axis Allies (926)

Adolf Hitler

"Adolph Hitler" German beliefs Nazi politician dictator (22,700)

Adolph Hitler anti-semitic German beliefs Nazi politician dictator "World War II" (3,260)

Importance of Information During Wartime

wartime information importance propaganda (85,400) * mostly about propaganda

wartime information importance codes ciphers code-breakers spies saboteurs resistance groups (42)

Vietnam War

Beginning in 1957 and ending in 1975, the Vietnam War was the longest war in which the United States took part.

HOT topics

The Buddhist Crisis. In May 1963, widespread unrest broke out among Buddhists in South Vietnam's major cities. The Buddhists, who formed a majority of the country's population, complained that the government restricted their religious practices. Buddhist leaders accused South Vietnamese leader Diem, a Roman Catholic, of religious discrimination. They claimed that he favored Catholics with lands and offices at the expense of local Buddhists. The government responded to the Buddhist protests with mass arrests, and Diem's brother Ngo Dinh Nhu ordered raids against Buddhist temples. Several Buddhist monks then set themselves on fire as a form of protest.

The Gulf of Tonkin Incident. In 1964, President Lyndon B. Johnson approved secret South Vietnamese naval raids against North Vietnam. Just after one of these raids, on Aug 2, 1964, North Vietnamese torpedo boats attacked the U.S. destroyer Maddox, which was monitoring the impact of the raid in the Gulf of Tonkin. Johnson warned the North Vietnamese that another such attack would bring "grave consequences." On August 4, he announced that North Vietnamese boats had again launched an attack in the gulf. Some Americans doubted that the August 4 attack had occurred, and it has never been confirmed. Nevertheless, Johnson ordered immediate air strikes against North Vietnam. In March 1965, he sent a group of U.S. Marines to South Vietnam, the first American ground combat forces to enter the war.

HOT topics

The Tet Offensive. North Vietnam and the Viet Cong opened a new phase of the war on Jan. 30, 1968, when they started to attack military bases and major cities of South Vietnam. The campaign began the day before Tet, the Vietnamese New Year celebration. North Vietnam and the Viet Cong hoped the offensive would deal a serious blow to U.S. forces and make the South Vietnamese people rise against their leaders. They also hoped the offensive would persuade U.S. officials to enter into peace negotiations with North Vietnamese leaders. The plan failed to achieve these objectives. In addition, the United States and South Vietnam quickly recovered their early losses, and the enemy suffered a huge number of casualties. But the Tet attacks stunned the American people and demoralized their war managers.

My Lai. In 1968, a United States Army unit led by Lieutenant William L. Calley, Jr., massacred hundreds of civilians in the hamlet of My Lai in South Vietnam. All of those killed were unarmed women, children, and old men. None had offered any resistance to U.S. forces. Calley was found guilty of the murder of at least 22 Vietnamese and was sentenced to prison. He was paroled in 1974.

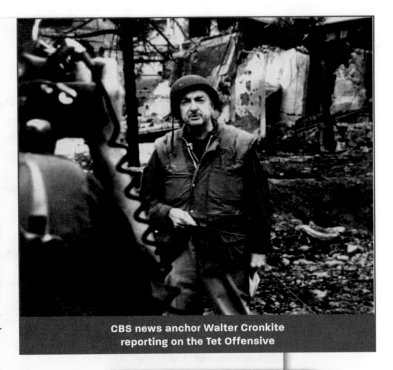

CBS news anchor Walter Cronkite reporting on the Tet Offensive

TRUE or FALSE?

The United States Army invaded Cambodia without the knowledge of the United States government.

U.S. soldiers on a search and destroy mission

THE BASICS

The Vietnam War was the longest war in which the United States took part. It began in 1957 and ended in 1975. Vietnam, a small country in Southeast Asia, was divided at the time into the Communist Democratic Republic of Vietnam, commonly called North Vietnam, and the non-Communist Republic of Vietnam, commonly called South Vietnam. North Vietnamese and Communist-trained South Vietnamese rebels sought to overthrow the government of South Vietnam and to eventually reunite the country. The United States and the South Vietnamese army tried to stop them, but failed.

The Vietnam War was actually the second phase of fighting in Vietnam. During the first phase, which began in 1946, the Vietnamese fought France for control of Vietnam. At that time, Vietnam was part of the French colonial empire in Indochina. The United States sent France military equipment, but the Vietnamese defeated the French in 1954. Vietnam was then split into North and South Vietnam.

United States aid to France and later to non-Communist South Vietnam was based on a Cold War policy of President Harry S. Truman. The Cold War was an intense rivalry between Communist and non-Communist nations. Truman had declared that the United States must help any nation challenged by Communism. The Truman Doctrine was at first directed at Europe and the

South Vietnamese president Ngo Ding Diem

Middle East. But it was also adopted by the next three presidents, Dwight D. Eisenhower, John F. Kennedy, and Lyndon B. Johnson, and applied to Indochina. They feared that if one Southeast Asian nation joined the Communist camp, the others would also "fall," one after the other, like what Eisenhower called "a row of dominoes."

The Vietnamese Communists and their allies called the Vietnam War a war of national liberation. They saw the Vietnam War as an extension of the struggle with France and as another attempt by a foreign power to rule Vietnam. North Vietnam wanted to end U.S. support of South Vietnam and to reunite the north and south into a single nation. China and the Soviet Union, at that time the two largest Communist nations, gave the Vietnamese Communists war materials but not troops.

The Vietnam War had several stages. From 1957 to 1963, North Vietnam aided rebels opposed to the government of South Vietnam, which fought the rebels with U.S. aid and advisory personnel. From 1964 to 1969, North Vietnam and the United States did much of the fighting. Australia, New Zealand, the Philippines, South Korea, and Thailand also helped South Vietnam. By April 1969, the number of U.S. forces in South Vietnam had reached its peak of more than 543,000 troops. By July, the United States had slowly begun to withdraw its forces from the region.

In January 1973, a cease-fire was arranged. The last American ground troops left Vietnam two months later. The fighting began again soon afterward, but U.S. troops did not return to Vietnam. South Vietnam surrendered on April 30, 1975, as North Vietnamese troops entered its capital, Saigon (now Ho Chi Minh City).

The Vietnam War was enormously destructive. Military deaths reached about 1.3 million, and the war left much of Vietnam in ruins.

Just before the war ended, North Vietnam helped rebels overthrow the U.S.-backed government in nearby Cambodia. After the war, North Vietnam united Vietnam and helped set up a new government in nearby Laos. The U.S. role in the war became one of the most debated issues in the nation's history. Many Americans felt U.S. involvement was necessary and noble. But many others called it cruel, unnecessary, and wrong. Today, many Americans still disagree on the goals, conduct, and lessons of U.S. participation in the Vietnam War.

Background to the War

The Indochina War. In the late 1800s, France gained control of Indochina—that is, Vietnam, Laos, and Cambodia. Japan occupied Indochina during most of World War II (1939–1945). After Japan's defeat in 1945, Ho Chi Minh, a Vietnamese nationalist and Communist, and his Vietminh (Revolutionary League for the Independence of Vietnam) declared Vietnam to be independent. But France was determined to reclaim its former colonial possessions in Indochina. In 1946, war broke out between France and the Vietminh. It finally ended in 1954, following the conquest of the French garrison of Dien Bien Phu by Vietminh forces in May. In July, the two sides signed peace agreements in Geneva, Switzerland.

The Geneva Accords provided that Vietnam be temporarily divided into northern and southern zones at the 17th parallel. The accords also called for national elections in 1956 to reunify the country.

The United States had provided aid to the French in Indochina since 1950. President Harry S. Truman had been convinced that such assistance was necessary in part because of the Communist take-over of China in 1949. Truman feared a Vietminh victory in Vietnam would lead to a Communist take-over of Indochina as part of a larger Communist plan to dominate Asia. This fear was so great that Truman ignored pleas by Ho for U.S. aid against French colonialism and for an alliance with the United States.

The divided country. After 1954, Ho strengthened the rule of his Communist government in the Democratic Republic of Vietnam, which became known as North Vietnam. He suppressed non-Communist political parties. He also enacted land reforms and established legal equality between men and women. Ho hoped the elections of 1956 would provide him with the means with which to peacefully reunify the country under his revolutionary government. These elections never occurred.

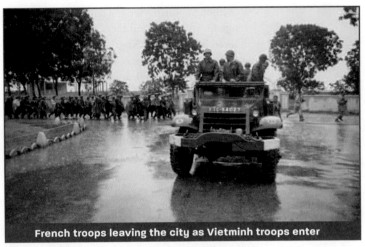
French troops leaving the city as Vietminh troops enter

The United States moved to make the division of Vietnam permanent by helping leaders in the southern half to form a non-Communist Republic of Vietnam, also known as South Vietnam. Ngo Dinh Diem, who had once refused a place in Ho's government and vigorously opposed any Communist influence in his country, became president of South Vietnam in 1955. With the approval of the United States, he refused to go along with the proposed nationwide elections scheduled for the following year. He argued that the Communists would not permit fair elections in North Vietnam. Most experts believe, however, that Ho was so popular that he would have won the elections under any circumstances. President Dwight D. Eisenhower provided economic aid and sent several hundred U.S. civilian and military advisers to assist Diem.

Early Stages of the War

The Viet Cong rebellion. Diem suppressed all rival political groups in his effort to strengthen his government. But his government never achieved widespread popularity, especially in rural areas, where his administration did little to ease the hard life of the peasants. Diem became increasingly unpopular in 1956, when he ended local elections and appointed his own officials down to the village level, where self-government was an ancient and honored tradition. From 1957 to 1959, he sought to eliminate members of the Vietminh who had joined other South Vietnamese in rebelling against his rule. Diem called these rebels the Viet Cong, meaning *Vietnamese Communists*. These rebels were largely trained by the Communists, but many were not Communist Party members.

Although North Vietnam had hoped to achieve its goals without a military conflict against the United States or the South Vietnamese government, it supported the revolt against Diem from its early stages. In 1959, as U.S. advisers rushed aid to South Vietnam by sea, North Vietnam developed a supply route to South Vietnam through Laos and Cambodia. This system of roads and trails became known as the Ho Chi Minh Trail. Also, in 1959, two U.S. military advisers were killed during a battle. They were the first American casualties of the war.

By 1960, discontent with the Diem government was widespread, and the Viet Cong had about 10,000 troops. In 1961, they threatened to overthrow Diem's unpopular government. In response, President John F. Kennedy greatly expanded economic and military aid to South Vietnam. From 1961 to 1963, he increased the number of U.S. military advisers in Vietnam from about 900 to over 16,000.

The Buddhist crisis. In May 1963, widespread unrest broke out among Buddhists in South Vietnam's major cities. The Buddhists, who formed a majority of the country's population, complained that the government restricted their religious practices. Buddhist leaders accused Diem, a Roman Catholic, of religious discrimination. They claimed that he favored Catholics with lands and offices at the expense of local Buddhists. The government responded to the Buddhist protests with mass arrests, and Diem's brother Ngo Dinh Nhu ordered raids against Buddhist temples. Several Buddhist monks then set themselves on fire as a form of protest.

The Buddhist protests aroused great concern in the United States. Kennedy urged Diem to improve his dealings with the Buddhists, but Diem ignored the advice. Kennedy then supported a group of South Vietnamese generals who opposed Diem's policies. On Nov. 1, 1963, the generals overthrew the Diem government. Diem and Nhu were murdered.

The fall of the Diem government set off a period of political disorder in South Vietnam. New governments rapidly succeeded one another. During this period, North Vietnam stepped up its supply of war materials and began to send units of its own army into the south. By late 1964, the Viet Cong controlled up to 75 percent of South Vietnam's population.

The Gulf of Tonkin incident. In 1964, President Lyndon B. Johnson approved secret South Vietnamese naval raids against North Vietnam. Just after one of these raids, on Aug 2, 1964, North Vietnamese torpedo boats attacked the U.S. destroyer *Maddox*, which was monitoring the impact of the raid off the coast of North Vietnam in the Gulf of Tonkin. Johnson warned the North Vietnamese that another such attack would bring "grave consequences." On August 4, he announced that North Vietnamese boats had again launched an attack in the gulf, this time against the *Maddox* and another U.S. destroyer, the *C. Turner Joy.*

Some Americans doubted that the August 4 attack had occurred, and it has never been confirmed. Nevertheless, Johnson ordered immediate air strikes against North Vietnam. He also asked Congress for power to take "all necessary measures

A North Vietnamese patrol on the Ho Chi Minh trail

to repel any armed attack against the forces of the United States and to prevent further aggression." On August 7, Congress approved these powers in the Tonkin Gulf Resolution. The United States did not declare war on North Vietnam. But Johnson used the resolution as the legal basis for increased U.S. involvement. In March 1965, he sent a group of U.S. Marines to South Vietnam, the first American ground combat forces to enter the war.

The Fighting Intensifies

The opposing forces. The war soon became an international conflict. United States forces rose from about 60,000 in mid-1965 to a peak of over 543,000 in 1969. They joined about 800,000 South Vietnamese troops and a total of about 69,000 troops from Australia, New Zealand, the Philippines, South Korea, and Thailand. The North Vietnamese and the Viet Cong had over 300,000 troops, but the exact number is unknown.

The two sides developed strategies to take advantage of their strengths. The United States had the finest modern weapons and a highly professional military force. Its field commanders were General William C. Westmoreland from 1964 to 1968 and, afterward, Generals Creighton Abrams and Frederick Weyand. The United States did not try to conquer North Vietnam. Instead, American leaders hoped superior U.S. firepower would force the enemy to stop fighting. The United States relied mainly on the bombing of North Vietnam and "search and destroy" ground missions in South Vietnam to achieve its aim.

The United States used giant B-52 bombers as well as smaller planes for the main air strikes against the enemy. American pilots used helicopters to seek out Viet Cong troops in the jungles and mountains. Helicopters also carried the wounded to hospitals and brought supplies to troops in the field.

In contrast, Viet Cong and North Vietnamese leaders adopted a defensive strategy. Their more lightly armed troops relied on surprise and mobility. They tried to avoid major battles in the open, where heavy U.S. firepower could be decisive. The Viet Cong and North Vietnamese preferred guerrilla tactics, including ambushes and hand-laid bombs. Their advantages included knowledge of the terrain and large amounts of war materials from the Soviet Union and China.

Course of the war. From 1965 to 1967, the two sides fought to a highly destructive draw.

President Lyndon Johnson signing the Tonkin resolution

The U.S. bombing caused tremendous damage, but it did not affect the enemy's willingness or ability to continue fighting. North Vietnam concealed its most vital resources, and the Soviet Union and China helped make up the losses.

American victories in ground battles in South Vietnam also failed to sharply reduce the number of enemy troops there. The U.S. Army and Marines usually won whenever they fought the enemy. But North Vietnam replaced its losses with new troops. Its forces often avoided defeat by retreating into Laos and Cambodia.

Reactions in the United States. As the war dragged on, it divided many Americans into so-called *hawks* and *doves*. The hawks supported the nation's fight against Communism. But they disliked Johnson's policy of slow, gradual troop increases and urged a decisive defeat of North Vietnam. The doves opposed U.S. involvement and held mass protests. Many doves believed that U.S. security was not at risk. Others charged that the nation was supporting corrupt, undemocratic, and unpopular governments in South Vietnam.

The growing costs of the war, however, probably did more to arouse public uneasiness in the United States than the antiwar movement did. By late 1967, increased casualties and Johnson's request for new taxes helped produce a sharp drop in public support for the war.

The Tet Offensive. North Vietnam and the Viet Cong opened a new phase of the war on Jan. 30, 1968, when they started to attack military bases and major cities of South Vietnam. The fighting was especially fierce in Saigon, South Vietnam's capital, and in Hue. This campaign began the day before Tet, the Vietnamese New Year celebration. North Vietnam and the Viet Cong hoped the offensive would deal a serious blow to U.S. forces and make the South Vietnamese people lose faith in their government and rise against South Vietnamese leaders. They also hoped that the offensive would persuade U.S. officials to enter into peace negotiations with North Vietnamese leaders.

An attack during the Tet Offensive

The plan failed to achieve these objectives. No widespread uprising of the population occurred in South Vietnam. In addition, the United States and South Vietnam quickly recovered their early losses, and the enemy suffered a huge number of casualties. But the Tet attacks stunned the American people and demoralized their war managers. Shortly before the offensive, the U.S. commander in the field, General Westmoreland, had assured the nation that the enemy had already been largely beaten. But the Tet offensive seemed to contradict this statement. As a result of the offensive, Johnson made a number of basic changes in his policies. He cut back the bombing of North Vietnam and rejected Westmoreland's request for 206,000 additional troops. Johnson also called for peace negotiations and declared that he would not seek re-election in 1968. Peace talks opened in Paris in May.

Vietnamization

The U.S. withdrawal begins. The peace talks failed to produce agreement, and more and more Americans became impatient for the war to end. President Richard M. Nixon felt he had to reduce U.S. involvement in the conflict. On June 8, 1969, he announced a new policy known as Vietnamization. This policy called for stepped-up training programs for South Vietnamese forces and the gradual withdrawal of U.S. troops from South Vietnam. The U.S. troop withdrawal began in July 1969.

The invasion of Cambodia. In April 1970, Nixon ordered U.S. and South Vietnamese troops to clear out military supply centers that North Vietnam had set up in Cambodia. Large stocks of weapons were captured, and the invasion may have delayed a major enemy attack. But many Americans felt the campaign widened the war. The invasion aroused a storm of protest in the United States, especially on college and university campuses.

The nation was shocked on May 4, 1970, when National Guard units fired into a group of demonstrators at Kent State University in Ohio. The shots killed four students and wounded nine others. Antiwar demonstrations and riots occurred on hundreds of other campuses throughout May. A move began in Congress to force the removal of the troops from Cambodia. On June 3, Nixon announced the completion of troop withdrawal. That same day, the Senate voted to repeal the Tonkin Gulf Resolution. These actions ended the Cambodian campaign.

Growing protest. Opposition to the war in the United States grew rapidly during Nixon's presidency. Many people claimed that this increased opposition was due to the news media, particularly television coverage, which brought scenes of the war into millions of homes. Most scholars have concluded, however, that media coverage reflected, rather than brought about, America's growing opposition to the war.

In March 1971, the conviction of Lieutenant William L. Calley, Jr., for war crimes raised some of the main moral issues of the conflict. Calley's unit was part of the Army company that massacred hundreds of civilians in 1968 in the hamlet of My Lai in South Vietnam. All of those killed were unarmed women, children, and old men. None had offered any resistance to U.S. forces. Calley was found guilty of the murder of at least 22 Vietnamese and was sentenced to prison. He was paroled in 1974.

Some war critics used Calley's trial to call attention to the large numbers of civilians killed by U.S. bombing and ground operations in South Vietnam. Others pointed to the vast stretches of countryside that had been destroyed by bombing and by spraying of chemicals. United States forces used such weedkillers as Agent Orange to reveal enemy hiding places in the jungle and to destroy enemy food crops.

Public distrust of the U.S. government deepened in June 1971, when newspapers published a secret government study of the war called The Pentagon Papers. This study raised questions about decisions and secret actions of government leaders regarding the war.

Invasion of the south. In March 1972, North Vietnam began a major invasion of South Vietnam. Nixon then renewed the bombing of North Vietnam and used American airpower against the exposed formations of regular enemy troops and tanks. He also ordered the placing of explosives in the harbor of Haiphong, North Vietnam's major port for importing military supplies. These moves helped stop the invasion, which had nearly reached Saigon by August 1972.

The high cost paid by both sides during the 1972 fighting led to a new round of peace negotiations. The talks were conducted by Henry A. Kissinger, Nixon's chief foreign policy adviser, and Le Duc Tho of North Vietnam. On Jan. 27, 1973, a cease-fire agreement was signed in Paris by the United States, South Vietnam, North Vietnam, and the Viet Cong. The pact provided for the withdrawal of all U.S. and allied forces from Vietnam and for the return of all prisoners—both within 60 days. It also permitted North Vietnam and the Viet Cong to leave their troops in the south. In addition, it called for internationally supervised elections that would let the South Vietnamese decide their political future.

The end of the war. On March 29, 1973, the last U.S. ground forces left Vietnam. But the peace talks soon broke down, and the war resumed. Congress, responding to voters who wished to see an end to the war, opposed further U.S. involvement. As a result, American troops did not return to the war. In mid-1973, Congress began to reduce military aid to South Vietnam.

In late 1974, North Vietnamese and Viet Cong troops attacked Phuoc Long, northeast of Saigon, and won an easy victory. In March 1975, the North Vietnamese forced South Vietnamese troops into a retreat from a region known as the Central Highlands. Thousands of civilians—many of them families of the South Vietnamese soldiers—also fled and died in the gunfire or from starvation. This retreat became known as the Convoy of Tears. Although some South Vietnamese army units fought on, few soldiers or civilians rallied in support of the failing South Vietnamese government.

Early in April, President Gerald R. Ford asked Congress for $722 million in military aid for South Vietnam. But Congress, believing defeat was now inevitable, provided only $300 million in emergency aid. The money was mainly for the evacuation of Americans from Saigon, which was threatened by rapidly advancing enemy troops. The war ended on April 30, 1975, when these troops entered Saigon and the South Vietnamese government formally surrendered to them. Saigon was then renamed Ho Chi Minh City.

The Vietnam War Memorial in Washington, D.C.

Results of the War

Casualties and destruction. About 58,000 American military personnel died in the war, and about 300,000 were wounded. South Vietnamese military losses were approximately 224,000 killed and 1 million wounded. North Vietnamese and Viet Cong losses totaled about 1 million dead and 600,000 wounded. Countless numbers of civilians in North and South Vietnam also perished.

The U.S. bombing in the conflict was more than three times as great as the combined U.S.-British bombing of Germany in World War II. The American air strikes destroyed much of North Vietnam's industrial and transportation systems.

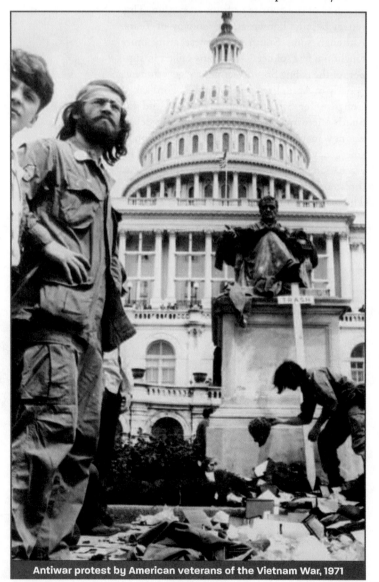

Antiwar protest by American veterans of the Vietnam War, 1971

But South Vietnam, where most of the fighting took place, suffered the most damage. The war made refugees of as many as 10 million South Vietnamese. The bombing and the use of chemicals to clear forests scarred the landscape and may have permanently damaged much of South Vietnam's cropland and plant and animal life.

Other effects in Southeast Asia. In 1976, North and South Vietnam were united into a single nation, which was renamed the Socialist Republic of Vietnam. North Vietnamese leaders then forced their own rigid political culture on people of the south. They imprisoned thousands who had held positions of responsibility in the South Vietnamese army or government. They also waged a campaign against independent businesses, run mainly by Vietnamese merchants of Chinese descent. As a result, over 1 million Vietnamese fled Vietnam between 1975 and the early 1990s, and the economy stagnated. But the harsh social divisions between rich and poor were ended, and literacy rates soared.

North Vietnam had helped establish Communist governments in Laos and Cambodia in 1975. However, the anti-Vietnamese policies of the pro-Chinese Communist Khmer Rouge movement in Cambodia forced Vietnam into a lengthy and costly campaign in that country. China reacted to this evidence of Vietnam's growing influence in the region by briefly invading Vietnam in 1979.

Effects in the United States. The Vietnam War also had far-reaching effects in the United States. The United States spent about $200 billion on the war. Many experts believe that this high cost of the war damaged the U.S. economy for years after the war's conclusion.

The Vietnam War was the first foreign war in which U.S. combat forces failed to achieve their goals. This failure hurt the pride of many Americans and left bitter and painful memories. The Americans most immediately affected included the approximately 2,600,000 men and women who had served in the war, and their families. Most veterans adjusted smoothly to civilian life. But others, particularly those with psychological problems associated with combat stress, encountered difficulties in making the adjustment to postwar American society. These veterans suffered from high rates of divorce, drug abuse, unemployment, and homelessness.

After World Wars I and II, the country viewed its soldiers as heroes. Americans who opposed the U.S. role in Vietnam had embraced those veterans who joined the antiwar movement upon their return from the battlefield, but some criticized or shunned those veterans who felt the war was justified. Many Americans who supported the war came to regard Vietnam veterans as symbols of America's defeat. Some leading hawks opposed expanding benefits to Vietnam veterans to match those given to veterans of earlier wars. These reactions shocked the veterans. Many of them felt that the nation neither recognized nor appreciated their sacrifices.

After the war, Congress and the public became more willing to challenge the president on military and foreign policy. The war also became a standard of comparison in situations that might involve U.S. troops abroad.

Today, Americans still disagree on the main issues and lessons of the war. Some believe U.S. participation was necessary and just. Many of these people say the war was lost because the United States did not use its full military power and because opposition at home weakened the war effort. Others point to the failure of the South Vietnamese government to develop popular support and to its overreliance on the United States. Still others view U.S. involvement as immoral and unwise. Some of them feel U.S. leaders made the war a test of the nation's power and leadership. Some view the conflict as a civil war that had no importance to U.S. security. Since Vietnam, many Americans have argued that the nation should stay out of wars that do not directly threaten its safety or vital interests.

MLA Citation

"Vietnam War." *The Southwestern Advantage Topic Source.* Nashville: Southwestern. 2013.

DATA

Important Dates in the Vietnam War

1957	The Viet Cong began to rebel against the South Vietnamese government headed by President Ngo Dinh Diem.
1963	(Nov. 1) South Vietnamese generals overthrew the Diem government, and Diem was killed the next day.
1964	(Aug. 7) Congress passed the Tonkin Gulf Resolution, which gave the president power to take "all necessary measures" and "to prevent further aggression."
1965	(March 6) President Lyndon B. Johnson sent U.S. Marines to Da Nang, South Vietnam. The Marines were the first U.S. ground troops in the war.
1968	(Jan. 30) North Vietnam and the Viet Cong launched a major campaign against South Vietnamese cities.
1969	(June 8) President Richard M. Nixon announced that U.S. troops would begin to withdraw from Vietnam.
1973	(Jan. 27) The United States, North and South Vietnam, and the Viet Cong signed a cease-fire agreement.
1973	(March 29) The last U.S. ground troops left Vietnam.
1975	(April 30) South Vietnam surrendered.

ADDITIONAL RESOURCES

Books to Read

Appy, Christian G. *Patriots: The Vietnam War Remembered from All Sides*. Viking, 2003.

Dowswell, Paul. *The Vietnam War*. World Almanac Library, 2002. Younger readers.

Hillstrom, Kevin and Laurie C. *Vietnam War*. 4 vols. UXL, 2001.

Kallen, Stuart A. *The Home Front: Americans Protest the War*. Lucent Books, 2001. Younger readers.

Tucker, Spencer C., ed. *Encyclopedia of the Vietnam War*. 3 vols. ABC-CLIO, 1998.

Young, Marilyn B., and Buzzanco, Robert, eds. *A Companion to the Vietnam War*. Blackwell, 2002.

Web Sites

The American Experience: Vietnam

http://www.pbs.org/wgbh/amex/vietnam/

The American Experience presents an exhaustive look at the Vietnam War, including information on the people, the places, the issues, and the outcomes.

Vietnam Interactive Portfolio

http://pirate.shu.edu/~hoffmake/gallery/V_Portfolio/

Photos and information about Vietnam and the Vietnam War, with an opportunity to comment.

Vietnam Veterans Memorial

http://www.nps.gov/vive/

National Park Service site on the Vietnam Veterans Memorial in Washington, D.C.

Search Strings

The Buddhist Crisis

"Vietnam War" Buddhist Crisis (77,700)

"Vietnam War" Buddhist Crisis religious restriction (6,670)

"Vietnam War" Buddhist Crisis religious discrimination Diem raids (485)

The Gulf of Tonkin Incident

"Vietnam War" "Gulf of Tonkin" (124,000)

"Vietnam War" "Gulf of Tonkin" President Lyndon Johnson (45,200)

"Vietnam War" "Gulf of Tonkin" President Lyndon Johnson incident lies (15,600)

The Tet Offensive

"Vietnam War" "Tet Offensive" (164,000)

"Vietnam War" "Tet Offensive" New Year Vietnamese (16,800)

"Vietnam War" "Tet Offensive" New Year Vietnamese Viet Cong (7,410)

My Lai

"Vietnam War" "My Lai" massacre (79,200)

"Vietnam War" "My Lai" massacre civilians Lieutenant Calley (14,500)

"Vietnam War" "My Lai" massacre civilians Lieutenant Calley United States Army (11,700)

BACKGROUND INFORMATION

The following article was written during the year in which the events took place and reflects the style and thinking of that time.

Vietnam (1998)

The ruling Communist Party fought political corruption in 1998 and struggled to keep the country's economy afloat. Le Kha Phieu, who had been appointed general secretary of the Communist Party on Dec. 29, 1997, called corruption the greatest threat to Vietnam's social stability.

Phieu, a two-star general, succeeded Do Muoi as the country's top leader. Muoi had steered Vietnam through an economic transformation in the 1990's. The changes opened markets and encouraged free enterprise while maintaining the Communist Party's grip on political and economic affairs.

Western diplomats described Phieu as an ideological hard-liner with no formal economic training. Phieu emphasized the "leading role" of large government-controlled enterprises, which Western economists claimed were one of Vietnam's chief hindrances to economic growth.

Corruption charges. Tran Do, a retired general and former party boss, appealed to the Communist Party in 1998 to implement political reforms. Do and 10 other party members charged that political appointees used corruption and intimidation to control access to land in the capital, Hanoi. A letter that Do sent to the party leadership in May focused on corruption charges against Pham The Duyet, who had been promoted in 1997 to the party's most elite group—a five-member standing committee of the politburo.

Amnesty. Vietnamese officials announced in August 1998 that the country would release 5,219 prisoners as part of a general amnesty. The prisoners included two dissidents, Doan Viet Hoat, an academic, and Nguyen Dan Que, a physician.

Hoat and Que had been arrested in 1975 for advocating greater political and individual freedoms after the Communists had captured Saigon and gained control of South Vietnam. The Vietnamese government agreed to release Hoat and Que on the condition that they leave Vietnam and move to the United States.

Economy. Vietnam's economy weakened in 1998, though it was not hit as hard by the Asian financial crisis as those of some of its neighbors. In September, Premier Phan Van Khai said that economic growth had been declining since 1996. He warned that economic losses in 1998 threatened national stability and development.

The financial crisis in Asia reduced business in Vietnam by major investors, such as South Korea, Singapore, and Taiwan. It also threatened Vietnam's competitiveness with the devalued currencies of the region.

Animals

Animals usually refers to any living things that are not plants (or humans). They range in size from a microscopic organism to as large as a blue whale. Animals eat other animals or plants, and most have digestive and nervous systems.

HOT topics

Web of Life. Animals are all part of a delicate ecosystem. Plants capture energy from sunlight; animals eat the plants, or they eat animals that have eaten the plants in order to have energy to live. Eventually the animals die and decay, which then helps to fertilize the soil for the plants. Animals breathe in the oxygen expelled by plants, and plants process the carbon dioxide expelled by animals. Animals also help to transfer pollen and seeds for plants.

Raccoon

HOT topics

Bighorn sheep

Classifying Animals. Animals can be classified as either terrestrial or aquatic, cold-blooded or warm-blooded, and vertebrates or invertebrates. They can be grouped by the number of legs they have or by how they move (for example, fly, swim, crawl, run, or hop). Or, they can be classified scientifically under the kingdom Animalia, and then even further under phyla, classes, orders, families, genera, and species.

Where Animals Live/Habitats. Different animals require different habitats in order to survive and thrive. For example, bighorn sheep live in the mountains; zebras live in the grasslands, raccoons in the temperate forests, parrots in the tropical forests; iguanas in the deserts, polar bears in the polar regions, and whales in the oceans. Each animal requires specific conditions found in the region in which they live. Among other things, those conditions include a suitable climate and access to food and water.

Adaptations/Protection from Predators. Many animals have their own unique ways of protecting themselves from predators. Moles hide in underground tunnels. Chameleons use camouflage by changing color to resemble their surroundings. A dark moth uses its protective coloration by lying against the dark bark of a tree. Walking sticks mimic the shape and color of a twig. Antelopes will flee at high speeds when being chased by a lion. A turtle's shell is used as armor. An opossum plays dead. A glass lizard breaks off a body part (its tail) to distract a predator. An ostrich uses its claws to fight. Skunks spray foul-smelling chemicals to defend themselves.

Migrating Animals. Many animals migrate in search of food or to escape cold weather. The Artic tern can fly a round trip as far as 22,000 miles in order to breed on islands in the Arctic Ocean, and then feed on fish in Antarctica. Geese, whales, monarch butterflies, sea turtles, and salmon all follow their own paths of migration as well.

TRUE or FALSE?

There are some species of animals that are found only on the Galapagos Islands.

DEFINITION

animal: —n. any living thing that is not a plant. Most animals can move about, while most plants cannot. Animals feed upon other animals or plants. Many animals have a cavity for digestion and a nervous system, and can inhale oxygen and exhale carbon dioxide. A dog, a bird, a fish, a snake, a fly, and a worm are all animals. Animals are distinguished typically from plants by more advanced types of sensation and response to stimuli.

THE BASICS

 Animals come in many shapes and sizes. They live throughout the world. Animals walk or crawl on land and dig through the soil. They swim in the water and fly through the air. They even live inside the bodies of other animals. Bats, dogs, horses, kangaroos, and moles are all animals. So are butterflies, frogs, jellyfish, pigeons, sharks, snakes, and worms.

Most kinds of animals are less than 1 inch (2.5 centimeters) long. Many are so tiny that they can be seen only with a microscope. The largest animal is the blue whale. It is about as long as five elephants in a row.

Animals are different from other living things in many ways. For example, the bodies of animals are made up of many cells. But the bodies of prokaryotes and most protists have only one cell. Like animals, plants and fungi also are made up of many cells. However, animals can move around. Most plants and fungi are held to one place in the soil by roots or root-like structures.

No one knows exactly how many (kinds) of animals there are. So far, scientists have classified (grouped) and named more than 1 million kinds of animals. Over half of these are types of insects. Many new species are discovered each year. Scientists believe there may be from 2 million to as many as 50 million kinds of animals alive today. Many other kinds of animals used to live on Earth but have died out. They include dinosaurs and dodos.

This article provides general information on animals other than human beings. It includes a classification table and pictures of many animals.

Importance of Animals

Animals and the web of life. Living things depend on one another. They are connected in what is sometimes called the *web of life*. Plants capture the energy from sunlight and use it to make roots, stems, leaves, flowers, and fruits. Animals eat the plants, or they eat other animals that feed on the plants. When animals die, their bodies decay and release materials that help fertilize the soil for plants.

Animals and plants are also connected in other ways. When animals breathe, they take in oxygen from the air and give off carbon dioxide. Green plants take in carbon dioxide and give off oxygen in a food-making process called *photosynthesis*. Many plants with flowers need insects or birds to carry their pollen from plant to plant. Without this transfer of pollen, these plants are not able to *reproduce* (create new individuals of their own kind). Some seeds are prickly and cling to the fur or feathers of animals. When the animals move from place to place, they take the seeds with them. In this way, the seeds get dropped in new areas where they can grow into plants.

The web of life relies on balance among its parts. A change in one part may mean disaster for others. For example, if all the trees in an area are cut down, then many animals that depend on them will die.

Water buffalo

Animals and people. Animals have provided people with food and clothing since prehistoric times. Without animals, people would not have such things as meat, honey, eggs, wool, leather, or silk.

At least 10,000 years ago, people began *domesticating* (taming) animals. Some of these animals provide food and clothing. For example, cattle supply meat, milk, and leather. Chickens lay eggs. Sheep provide wool and meat.

Some domesticated animals help people work. Water buffaloes pull plows in Asian rice fields. Horses and camels carry people from one place to another. At first, people kept cats in their houses to catch rats and mice. They raised dogs to help them hunt. Today, cats and dogs are kept largely as pets.

Certain insects are useful to people. Bees make honey, which people harvest for food. Bees also pollinate many food crops, including fruits and vegetables. Silk comes from fiber made by silkworms.

Some animals harm people. On rare occasions, crocodiles, lions, and tigers attack and kill people. So do grizzly bears and polar bears. Sharks sometimes kill and eat human beings. Bites from such poisonous snakes as rattlesnakes and cobras can cause death. The black widow spiders have a poison that makes people extremely sick.

Some animals pass diseases along from person to person. Certain mosquitoes transmit malaria and yellow fever. Some ticks carry the bacteria that cause Lyme disease and Rocky Mountain spotted fever. Some animals cause disease themselves. Worms called *flukes*, which live in human organs, can cause *schistosomiasis*. This disease infects millions of people in many African, Asian, and Latin American countries.

Kinds of Animals

People often divide animals into various groups based on certain similarities the animals share. For example, some animals can be kept as pets, but others are wild. Arranging animals according to their similarities is a handy way of remembering and understanding them.

Some common ways of grouping animals. Animals can be grouped in many ways. They can be arranged according to whether they live on land or in water. Animals that live on land are known as *terrestrial animals*. They include cats, dogs, lizards, mice, and worms. Animals that live in water are called *aquatic animals*. They include eels, fish, lobsters, octopuses, and whales.

Animals can be arranged by the number of legs they have. Dogs, frogs, and lizards have four legs. Bats and birds have two legs. Insects have six legs, and spiders have eight. Snakes and worms have no legs.

Another way to group animals is according to how they move. Bats, most birds, and many insects fly. Whales, fish, and squid swim. Snakes and worms crawl. Antelope and cheetahs run. Frogs, kangaroos, and rabbits hop.

Some animals are *cold-blooded*, and others are *warm-blooded*. The bodies of cold-blooded animals are warm when their surroundings are warm and cool when their surroundings are cool. Warm-blooded animals, on the other hand, almost always have the same body temperature, regardless of the warmth of their surroundings. Birds, *mammals* (animals whose babies drink the mother's milk), and a few species of fish and insects are warm-blooded. All other kinds of animals are cold-blooded.

Animals are also commonly divided into groups according to whether they have backbones. *Invertebrates* do not have backbones, but *vertebrates* do. The vast majority of animals are invertebrates. They include clams, insects, jellyfish, sea urchins, snails, spiders, sponges, and worms. Birds, fish, mammals, and reptiles are vertebrates. So are *amphibians*—frogs, salamanders, and other animals that spend part of their lives in water and part on land.

The scientific classification of animals involves grouping animals according to the biological relationships among them. This orderly arrangement of animals depends in part on the features the animals share. In general, the more features they share, the more closely they are related. However, the scientific classification of animals is based mainly on the belief that certain animals share a common ancestor. Animals with a more recent common ancestor are more closely related than those who share an ancestor further back in time. In a somewhat similar way, brothers and sisters are more closely related than are cousins. Brothers and sisters share parents. First cousins share grandparents.

In classifying animals, *zoologists* (scientists who study animals) divide them into ever-smaller groups that have more and more features in common. All animals belong to one large group, the kingdom Animalia. This kingdom consists of

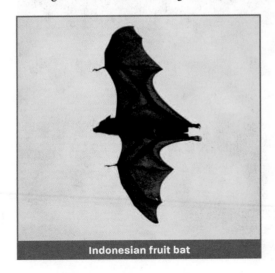

Indonesian fruit bat

a number of smaller groups called *phyla*. Each phylum is divided into groups called *classes*. The classes are broken down into *orders*, and the orders into *families*. The families are split into *genera*, and the genera into *species*. The singular form of *genera* is *genus*, but the word *species* may be either singular or plural.

Among the animals that scientists have classified are about 13,000 species of flatworms; 50,000 species of clams, oysters, and other *mollusks* (soft-bodied animals, most of which have a hard shell); 1,000,000 species of insects; 30,000 species of spiders; 21,000 species of fish; 5,800 species of amphibians; 8,000 species of reptiles; 9,700 species of birds; and 4,500 species of mammals. Each species belongs to one phylum, one class, one order, one family, and one genus. For example, tigers belong to the kingdom Animalia, the phylum Chordata, the class Mammalia, the order Carnivora, the family Felidae, and the genus *Panthera*. They are members of the species *Panthera tigris*. Lions are related to tigers. They belong to the same kingdom (Animalia), phylum (Chordata), class (Mammalia), order (Carnivora), family (Felidae), and genus (*Panthera*) as tigers. But lions are classified in a different species—*Panthera leo*, also written simply as *P. leo*.

 ## Where Animals Live

Animals live in many kinds of places. The place where an animal lives is called its *habitat*. Each type of habitat presents a special challenge to animals. For example, animals that live in polar regions

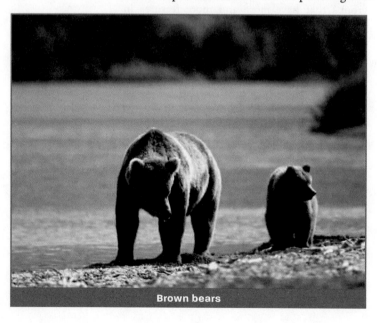

Brown bears

must withstand bitter cold. Those that inhabit the tropics face extreme heat. In spite of these challenges, animals can be found everywhere on Earth. They live on the highest mountains and in the deepest oceans. They roam the driest deserts and the wettest rain forests. They swim in fresh water and salt water.

Each habitat supports many kinds of animals. In most cases, the animals are the same kinds that have lived in those surroundings for thousands of years. As a result, the animals have developed bodies and ways of life that suit them to that particular habitat. No single species of animal can survive everywhere. For example, tropical fish from the Amazon River thrive in warm water but cannot withstand the cold streams of the Andes Mountains. On the other hand, many kinds of fish that live in the Arctic Ocean would die if they were exposed to the warm waters of the Caribbean Sea. However, some animals may travel between habitats from time to time. For example, African elephants eat both grass and tree parts and so move between grassland and forest. But these animals would not be able to withstand the freezing temperatures of the polar regions.

Some habitats, including many forests and grasslands, are being destroyed by human beings. The destruction of these habitats usually causes the death of many animals. When people convert grassland to farmland, for example, they destroy the homes and source of food of many species. Without these necessities, some animals will die immediately. Others may try moving to another grassland. But the new area may not have enough food and shelter to support the additional wildlife. As a result, many more animals will die.

This section tells about some of the major animals, grouped according to seven types of habitats: (1) mountains, (2) grasslands, (3) temperate forests, (4) tropical forests, (5) deserts, (6) polar regions, and (7) oceans.

Animals of the Mountains

Mountains support a variety of animal life. The numbers and kinds of animals found on mountains vary with altitude. More animals and more kinds of animals live at lower altitudes than at higher ones, largely because of the differences in climate between elevations. Generally, mountain climates become colder, wetter, and windier with increasing altitude. The air also gets thinner and has less oxygen. In addition, fewer plants are found at higher elevations, and therefore less food is available for animals.

Bears, deer, elk, and mink make their homes on the forested lower slopes and in the wooded or grassy valleys of mountains. Rainbow trout and graylings swim in mountain streams. Many mountains have meadows of grasses and herbs. These meadows are home to chinchillas, ibexes, llamas, vicunas, and yaks. Butterflies, grasshoppers, and spiders also live there.

Above the *timber line*—that is, the line beyond which trees will not grow because of the cold—stand rocky cliffs and peaks dotted with shrubs, mosses, and other plants. Small meadows are also found there. Sure-footed bighorn sheep and mountain goats dwell among the windswept rocks, as do furry marmots and pikas. High on the snow-capped peaks, only a few insects, spiders, and ice worms can survive. Golden eagles and some other birds fly above the mountains. A large African vulture, Ruppell's griffon, has been known to soar as high as 36,600 feet (11,150 meters).

Animals of the Grasslands

Grasslands include the prairies of North America, the Pampas of South America, the plains of Europe, and the steppes of Asia. The savannas of east Africa have more grassland animals than any other area.

Rainfall in grasslands is seasonal, and animals sometimes travel great distances to find green grass. Gazelles, wildebeests, and zebras migrate by the thousands through the African savannas. Smaller groups of elephants and rhinoceroses also feed on the grasses there. Such meat-eating mammals as cheetahs, hyenas, and lions roam the savannas in search of prey. The savannas are also home to giraffes, jackals, ostriches, secretary birds, and termites. In addition, hippopotamuses live in and near bodies of water in African grasslands. Animals of other grasslands include the kangaroos and wombats of Australia, the cavies and rheas of South America, and the coyotes and prairie dogs of North America.

Many animals of the grasslands have become endangered due to loss of their habitat and to over-hunting. The rich soils of grasslands are ideal for farming, and people have converted many such areas to farmland. Many of the large grassland animals are favorite big game for hunters. For

Springbok (Namibia)

example, the once-plentiful pampas deer of South America have become extremely rare. As the Pampas are converted to farmland, the tall grass that grows there disappears. Without this grass, the pampas deer have no shelter and become easy prey. Bison once grazed in huge herds in the Great Plains of North America. But so many of these animals were killed by hunters or died as their grassland habitat was converted to farmland that they were nearly wiped out.

Animals of the Temperate Forests

Temperate forests consist largely of *deciduous trees* and *evergreen trees*. Deciduous trees shed their leaves in the fall and grow new ones in the spring. Evergreen trees have leaves that live two or more years. Some evergreens have needle-shaped leaves. Most temperate forests are in Asia, Europe, and North America. Australia also has some temperate forests.

Many forest animals have small bodies that allow them to move easily through the underbrush. Forest mammals include chipmunks, mice, opossums, porcupines, raccoons, skunks, and squirrels. Bears, deer, and wild boars also live in temperate forests. Bobcats and wolves were once common in woodland areas. However, so many of these predators have been hunted and trapped through the years that they have become rare.

Salamanders are often plentiful in temperate forests. They hide in the leaf litter or under rocks, where they feed on insects and other small organisms. In wet forests, slugs and other snails are common. Beavers, fish, frogs, muskrats, otters, salamanders, and turtles live in or near woodland streams, ponds, and lakes. Great numbers of birds nest in the trees and shrubs.

Many temperate forests have been cleared for farms and cities, and many others have been cut down for fuel and lumber. This *deforestation* (destruction of forests) places woodland animals in danger. Extensive logging in the Pacific Northwest of the United States, for example, has destroyed much of the habitat of the spotted owl, threatening the existence of that species.

Animals of the Tropical Forests

Tropical forests stay warm all year and receive plentiful rainfall. These forests are found in Africa, Asia, Australia, Central and South America, and the

Amazon iguana

Pacific Islands. More kinds of animals live in tropical forests than in any other habitat. Scientists estimate that perhaps as many as 30 million species of tropical animals have not even been discovered yet.

Insects make up the largest single group of animals that live in tropical forests. They include brightly colored butterflies, huge colonies of ants, mosquitoes, and camouflaged stick insects. Spiders are also plentiful. Many tropical birds, such as quetzals and parrots, are spectacularly colored.

The broad leaves of trees in tropical forests form a thick overhead covering called a *canopy* that blocks nearly all sunlight from reaching the forest floor. Many kinds of animals live in the canopies of tropical forests. They include harpy eagles and toucans; tree frogs; flying dragons; spider monkeys and howlers; gibbons and orangutans; sloths; slow lorises; tree boa constrictors; bats; and wasps, beetles, and leaf-cutting ants.

Jaguars, tapirs, and bushmaster snakes live on the ground in tropical forests. Chimpanzees and lowland gorillas alternate between the ground and the trees. Crocodiles, fish, and turtles inhabit rivers and ponds.

People are rapidly destroying tropical forests for wood and for farming. The continuing destruction of this habitat means that many animals will disappear forever. Scientists believe countless species have already been wiped out.

Animals of the Deserts

Most deserts lie near the edges of the tropics. Food and water are often scarce in deserts, and temperatures in the summer can be scorching. Despite these conditions, many kinds of animals live there. They include geckos, iguanas, and skinks; bees, butterflies, and moths; spiders; elf owls and roadrunners; sidewinders; dorcas gazelles and mule deer; and bobcats, coyotes, and dingoes.

Animals of the deserts have developed special bodies and ways of life that enable them to survive the extreme heat. Centipedes, kangaroo rats, rattlesnakes, and scorpions spend the day in burrows. They come out to search for food only when temperatures drop at night. Many insects, lizards, and tortoises can tolerate high desert temperatures and are active in the daytime. But even they must retreat underground or find the shade of a tree during the hottest part of the day. Some snails, insects, frogs, lizards, mice, and ground squirrels *estivate* (sleep through the summer).

Many desert dwellers have light-colored skin, which helps keep them cool by reflecting sunlight. Desert foxes and hares have long ears. When overheated, these animals move to a cool cave or burrow where they can get rid of excess body heat through their ears. The Cape ground squirrel makes its own shade by using its fluffy tail like a parasol. Fairy shrimp and spadefoot toads may spend months or years underground waiting for rain to create ponds. Then they quickly feed and reproduce before the ponds dry again.

Sleeping Arctic fox

Animals of the Polar Regions

Animals that live in polar regions must withstand extremely cold temperatures. No land animals except ice worms and a few species of insects live in polar regions that have ice and snow year-round. But the seas of the Arctic and Antarctic have large numbers of wildlife, including fish, giant sponges, whales, and tiny shrimplike creatures called *krill*. In addition, polar bears, sea lions, and walruses spend much of their time on floating sheets of ice in the Arctic. Penguins and seals live on the Antarctic coast.

Many animals inhabit the vast Arctic *tundras* (cold treeless plains) of northern Asia, North America, and Europe. They include caribou, ermine, musk oxen, reindeer, lemmings, snowy owls, and wolves. Shallow ponds in the region provide a place for mosquitoes and many other insects to lay their eggs. These insects serve as food for the birds that migrate to the tundra each summer to nest.

Animals that live in polar regions have developed bodies and ways of life that enable them to

deal with the frigid winter weather. Caribou, musk oxen, and polar bears have thick fur, which helps them stay warm. The Arctic fox and Arctic hare have short ears and tails that keep them from losing much body heat. Arctic ground squirrels *hibernate* (sleep through the winter). They curl up in a burrow, and their body temperature drops, saving energy during the long winter. They also do not eat in the winter. They live off fat stored in their bodies.

Animals of the Oceans

Animals of many kinds are found everywhere in the vast oceans. Some of the smallest animals live in the sea, as does the world's largest, the blue whale. Cod, halibut, seals, and whales swim the frigid waters of the polar regions. Lobsters, sea urchins, and many types of brightly colored fish inhabit coral reefs in warm tropical seas. Some ocean animals live near the shore—in shallow water, in tide pools, and on rocks. They include anemones, barnacles, mussels, octopuses, and starfish. Other marine animals—mostly such tiny shrimplike creatures as krill and copepods—are found in the open sea. Krill and some species of copepods form part of the group of organisms called *plankton*. Many fish and some whales feed on plankton.

The great depths of the ocean are completely dark, and the water there is bitterly cold. Even so, anglerfish, clams, and certain other creatures live there. On the other hand, flyingfish, manta rays, marlins, and porpoises generally swim near the ocean surface. Albatrosses, gulls, and petrels fly above the sea.

Oceans provide people with such foods as crab, fish, lobster, and shrimp. However, the demand for seafood has led to the overfishing of halibut, herring, and some other marine animals. Millions of dolphins, which are mammals, have drowned in fishing nets that were intended to catch cod, tuna, and other fish. In addition, spills of toxic materials and other forms of pollution have reduced the numbers of some ocean species.

The Bodies of Animals

Animals have special body features that enable them to survive in their environment. These special features, called *adaptations*, result from the ability animal species have to *adapt* (adjust) over time to changes in their surroundings. Adaptations for survival enable animals to move about, to eat, to breathe, and to sense their environment. Legs, wings, and fins help animals move. Teeth and jaws help them eat. Lungs and gills help them obtain oxygen. Eyes and ears help them find food and detect predators.

Animals live in many kinds of environments. The body features of an animal that work well in one type of environment may not work in others. For example, the adaptations that enable fish to breathe in water do not let them breathe on land. Even in the same environment, animals may have different adaptations for survival. Shrimp, fish, and sea turtles can all swim in the ocean, but they have different body features for doing so. Shrimp have tiny swimming legs, fish have fins and muscular tails, and turtles have flippers. Because animals adapt to their surroundings in many ways, there is a wide diversity of animals in any environment.

This section describes some of the ways animal bodies are adapted for moving, eating, breathing, and sensing the environment.

Adaptations for Moving About

Legs and feet. Mammals, birds, insects, and many reptiles and amphibians have legs with feet that enable them to walk or run on land. Most amphibians, mammals, and reptiles walk on four legs. Birds and people walk on two. Insects have six legs, and spiders have eight. Millipedes may have up to 200 legs.

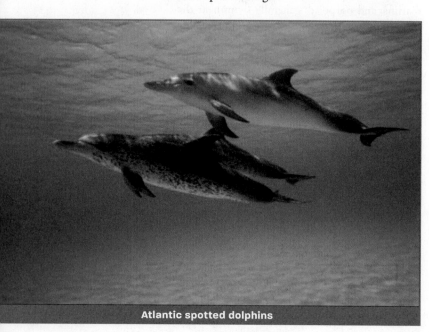

Atlantic spotted dolphins

Animals can crawl without legs and feet. Such tiny creatures as planarians and other flatworms slide by moving many small hairlike structures, called *cilia*, back and forth like miniature oars. Snails move by coating the ground with a sticky fluid from their bodies. They then crawl through the fluid using a muscular organ called a *foot*. Most snakes slide along the ground by bending their bodies from side to side. An earthworm crawls through the soil by alternately lengthening and shortening parts of its body.

Many walking and crawling organisms live in water. Crabs and lobsters have legs that enable them to walk across the bottom of a body of water.

Wings. Three groups of animals have the ability to fly under their own power: (1) insects, (2) bats, and (3) birds. Most insects have two pairs of wings. Muscles inside the *thorax* (middle section of an insect's body) move the wings up and down.

Bats are the only mammals with wings. Batwings are made up mostly of skin stretched over long finger bones. Muscles in the wings raise and lower them.

Birds have powerful muscles attached to their wings and breastbone. Bird wings are covered with feathers, which also aid in flight.

Some animals, including flying squirrels and flying lemurs, can glide but not fly. Such animals jump from trees or mountains. They have big feet or folds of skin that spread out to serve as "wings" for gliding.

Fins, tails, and flippers. Many types of animals swim in fresh or salt water. Fish have well-developed tails and fins. Most fish swim by bending their powerful, muscular tail from side to side. Fins on the top, bottom, and sides of fish are used to maintain balance and to maneuver in tight areas. Dolphins, porpoises, and whales swim by moving their massive tails up and down rather than side to side. Turtles swim by paddling with their webbed feet or their flippers.

Jellyfish and squids swim by jet propulsion. When a jellyfish pushes water out from under its body, it is thrust in the opposite direction. A squid takes water into its body cavity and then squirts the water out through a small opening called a *funnel*. This action repeated many times pushes the squid forward.

A number of species of birds can swim. Some ducks and gulls paddle on the surface of the water using their webbed feet as oars. Torrent ducks and loons dive underwater, where they swim by kicking their feet. Penguins use their feet and their wings to swim.

Adaptations for Eating

All animals need food to survive. Animals eat plants, other animals, or both plants and other animals. Animals that eat plants are called *herbivores*. Zebras, cows, and moose are herbivores. Animals that eat other animals are called *carnivores* or *meat-eaters*. Dogs, lions, and sharks are carnivores. Animals that eat both plants and animals are known as *omnivores*. Bears are omnivores.

Biologists describe the relationships between animals in a habitat and the foods they eat as a *food chain*. Technically, a food chain involves the flow of energy from the sun to green plants to animal consumers. For example, a simple food chain in a meadow links the grasses, the deer that eat the grasses, and the wolves that eat the deer. Sometimes, many kinds of animals and plants are involved in complex networks of food chains. Such networks are called *food webs*.

Most animals eat a variety of foods. For example, pigeons eat fruits, grains, and nuts, and they sometimes feed on insects, snails, and worms.

Some animals eat only a few foods. A snail called a cone shell preys only on a single species of marine worm. Several kinds of snakes eat only slugs or other snails. Hummingbirds and honey possums live on the nectar of flowers. A sapsucker drills holes in trees and eats the sap that flows from the holes. The koala of Australia dines on the leaves of eucalyptus trees.

Filtering mechanisms. Huge numbers of tiny organisms called plankton float or swim slowly near the surface of oceans, lakes, and other bodies of water. Plankton make up a part of an important food chain in the ocean. Plankton are too small to be captured individually by animals that feed on them. Some animals, such as barnacles, sweep water past themselves while straining out the tiny plankton, which are thereby captured. This process is called *filter feeding*.

Baleen whales are probably the best-known filter feeders. These animals, which do not have teeth, feed by gulping huge mouthfuls of water containing plankton, small fish, and other marine organisms. They then force the water out of their mouths through a series of strainers called *baleen*. The food is captured on the baleen and then

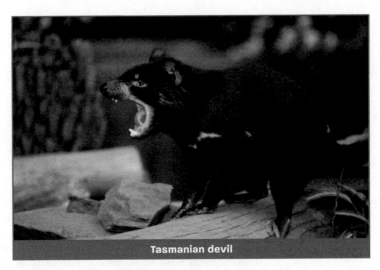

Tasmanian devil

swallowed. A baleen whale can consume as much as 4 short tons (3.6 metric tons) of food a day.

Teeth and jaws. Many animals eat food that they need to tear into pieces small enough to be swallowed and digested easily. Teeth and jaws are adaptations for tearing food. Teeth may also be used to kill prey.

Teeth are adapted for the particular type of food an animal eats. Deer, giraffes, and other herbivores have teeth with broad surfaces for grinding grasses and plants into small bits. The powerful front teeth of beavers enable these animals to cut down trees for food and shelter. Lions have razor-sharp *canine* (pointed) teeth for killing and then tearing prey.

Birds have bills that are adapted for certain types of feeding. A hawk has a sharp, hooked beak for tearing prey. A woodpecker uses its long, pointed bill to drill into the bark of trees to find insects.

Insects have jaws and movable mouthparts that act like teeth. The jaws of grasshoppers are adapted for cutting and chewing plants. Mosquitoes have needle-shaped mouthparts for piercing skin and sucking blood.

Adaptations for Breathing

Most animals need a continuous supply of oxygen to survive. The entire process of obtaining and using oxygen is called *respiration*. That part of the process that involves how an animal takes oxygen from its environment and gives off carbon dioxide is known as *breathing*. This section focuses on breathing.

The way that animals breathe depends on where they live. Land animals get oxygen from the air. Aquatic animals obtain oxygen from water.

Many land animals have lungs for breathing. As blood flows through the lungs, it picks up oxygen from the air and releases carbon dioxide. The blood then carries oxygen to the rest of the body.

Many aquatic organisms, such as fish and tadpoles, use gills to obtain oxygen that is dissolved in water. Some animals pump water across their gills to increase the efficiency of breathing. Sharks do this by swimming continuously.

Tiny tubes called *tracheae* allow insects to breathe in air. Tracheae branch throughout an insect's body. They open to the outside air through holes called *spiracles*. When air enters the tracheae, oxygen is carried to every cell in the body.

Some animals that live in damp environments have unusual ways of breathing. For example, many salamanders have no lungs or gills. They breathe through their moist skin.

Adaptations for Sensing the Environment

Most kinds of animals have special body parts that respond to changes in the animal's environment. Such a *stimulus* (change) might come from an odor, a sight, a sound, a taste, or a touch. The simplest kinds of animals, such as sponges, have no special body parts and react to stimuli with their body cells. Animals with more complex physical structures, especially vertebrates, have highly developed organs for reacting to stimuli.

Some simple animals, such as hydras, react to stimuli with special cells. These sensory cells are scattered among the outermost cells of the body. The reactions of most other kinds of

animals depend largely on one or more of the major senses. These senses are sight, hearing, smell, taste, and touch.

Some senses are more important to one kind of animal than to another. Most birds cannot find food if they cannot see it. Hearing is vital to bats. If the ears of a bat are covered, the animal will crash into objects when it tries to fly. A keen sense of smell enables dogs and wolves to find food, follow trails, and recognize danger. Taste is highly important to many insects. The butterfly finds its food by sensing the sweetness of flowers with its feet. A cat's long whiskers serve as touch organs. They enable the cat to feel its way through underbrush and avoid bumping into objects.

A number of animals have special senses. A rattlesnake has *pit organs* on the side of its face that sense heat. These organs enable the snake to tell if a mouse or some other warm-blooded prey is nearby, even in total darkness. Many scientists believe that some birds and insects can detect the direction of Earth's magnetic field. This ability may help these animals navigate.

The world of an animal is filled with danger from enemies. This section describes some of the many ways animals protect themselves from such danger.

Hiding in a safe place. The best protection against a predator is to avoid being seen by it. Many animals rest or sleep in a safe hiding place. Some desert toads crawl down a crack in the mud. A cricket hides under a large rock or under the loose bark of a tree. Worms and moles dig underground tunnels.

Many species, such as rabbits, leave their nests mainly or only at night, when they are harder for enemies to spot. Other species become active for only short periods so they are not exposed to predators for long.

Camouflage. Many animals are difficult for enemies to see because they resemble their surroundings. The various ways animals blend with their surroundings are called *camouflage*. For camouflage to be effective, the animals must remain motionless or nearly so.

Protective coloration is coloring that helps animals to hide. A dark moth lying against the brown or black bark of a tree is hard to see. However, that same moth would be clearly visible if it sat on a green leaf.

A number of animals can change their colors and thus remain camouflaged even when moving

Chameleon

among backgrounds that have different colors. The chameleon, a type of lizard, is green when surrounded by leaves but turns brown when moving slowly on bark or on the ground. The ptarmigan, an Arctic bird, is brown in summer but becomes white in winter, when snow covers the ground.

Mimicry helps many animals avoid predators. Some animals *mimic* (resemble) other objects in their environment. For example, many green insects are shaped like leaves. Some caterpillars look like lizards or bird droppings. Walking stick insects are shaped and colored like twigs. Anglerfish resemble rocks on the ocean floor.

Batesian mimicry is a form of mimicry in which an otherwise harmless animal strongly mimics an offensive animal. This type of mimicry was named after the English naturalist Henry W. Bates, who studied it in the 1800s. Bates observed that some harmless species have coloring and behavior that make them look like a dangerous or bad-tasting animal. A predator spotting such a species may mistake it for the undesirable animal and leave it alone. For example, viceroy butterflies are believed to be tasty to birds. But birds rarely attack them because they look like foul-tasting monarch butterflies.

Escaping by flight. Many animals run away from an attacker. Antelope sprint away at high speed when charged by a lion or a cheetah. Many animals stay near safe places, such as burrows, and run to them if attacked. The octopus squirts a black inky fluid to conceal itself and then quickly swims for safety.

Armor. Some species have a hard shell or covering that is used as armor against predators. Clams pull back into their shells when a predator approaches. Many turtles can pull in their head, legs, and tail when attacked. Armadillos and pangolins are covered by hard, bony plates. When frightened, these animals roll into a tight ball that is difficult for enemies to penetrate.

Playing dead. A few species sometimes fool predators by lying motionless and appearing to be dead. If the predator does not deliver a killing blow or bite, then the animal may have a chance to escape. A threatened opossum goes limp. The hognose snake flips onto its back when a predator approaches.

Giving up a body part. Many animals break off a nonessential part of their body when attacked. The glass lizard breaks off its tail, which

flops about and attracts the attention of the predator. While the attacker struggles with the tail, the lizard escapes. In most cases, the lost body part grows back quickly.

Fighting. Many animals have special weapons for fighting predators. The sharp hooves of a moose or the claws of an ostrich can rip open an enemy. Porcupines have long, sharp quills on their back, sides, and tail. These animals strike attackers with their quilled tails. The quills come out easily and stick in the attackers. Bees and wasps sting animals that approach their nests.

Chemical defenses. A number of animals use special chemicals for defense. Hagfish and one kind of starfish give off huge quantities of slime when disturbed. The bombardier beetle squirts irritating chemicals at an enemy. Some cobras spit blinding venom at the eyes of attackers. Skunks spray foul-smelling chemicals. Birds from New Guinea called hooded pitohuis have poisonous feathers and skin.

Giant tortoise

How Animals Reproduce

All types of animals reproduce. Many animals have special organs that are used in reproduction. These organs are called *gonads*. Some simple animals do not have gonads, but they are still able to reproduce.

There are two general forms of animal reproduction: (1) *asexual reproduction* and (2) *sexual reproduction*. In asexual reproduction, only one parent produces the offspring. In sexual reproduction, two parents of opposite sexes are needed to produce the offspring. Many of the simplest animals, including sponges, sea anemones, and some flatworms, reproduce asexually most of the time. Sometimes, they reproduce sexually as well. Most other kinds of animals reproduce only sexually.

Cape cobra

Asexual reproduction. Planarians and some other flatworms can reproduce by *fragmentation*, the division of the body into two or more pieces. When a planarian reproduces asexually, it typically divides into two sections, one with the head and the other with the tail. Each section then grows the parts that are missing and becomes a complete new individual.

Hydras and some sea anemones reproduce by *budding*. The animal produces small projections, called *buds*, from its side. These buds develop into miniature copies of the parent. The buds eventually detach from the parent, and the individuals produced by budding grow to be as large as their parents. Then they can put forth buds to create their own offspring.

Sexual reproduction. Most animals that reproduce only sexually do so with special sex cells known as *gametes*. Female sex cells are called *eggs* and are produced in the female gonads, the *ovaries*. The male sex cells are known as *sperm* and are made in the male gonads, the *testes*. Sperm are much smaller than eggs and have a tail that enables them to swim toward eggs. When a sperm cell unites with an egg cell, a new animal starts to form. The process in which the sperm unites with the egg is called *fertilization*.

External fertilization occurs outside an animal's body. Many aquatic animals reproduce sexually without ever meeting. Female sea urchins release millions of egg cells directly into the water. About the same time, the males release their sperm. The sperm swim through the water, and some unite with eggs, leading to fertilization. The fertilized eggs develop into swimming offspring,

which are called *larvae*. The larvae grow and eventually sink to the bottom of the sea, where they become small sea urchins with bodies similar to those of their parents.

Internal fertilization occurs within an animal's body. If gametes are released on land, they dry up and die. Consequently, land-dwelling animals that reproduce sexually have developed ways for fertilization to take place inside their bodies.

Animals mate in many ways. Males of such species as snakes, lizards, birds, and mammals mate by releasing sperm directly into an opening in the female's body. Fertilization occurs in the female's reproductive organs.

Male salamanders do not release sperm directly into the female's body. Instead, they deposit a packet of sperm at the bottom of a stream or pond. When the female passes over the sperm, she draws them into an opening in her body that leads to her reproductive organs. Several other animals, including mites and scorpions, mate in a manner similar to that of salamanders. Males deposit packets of sperm on the ground, which are then picked up by females.

In almost all mammals and some reptiles, the *embryo* (undeveloped animal) grows inside the female's body after fertilization. However, in birds and some reptiles, the embryo develops outside the body. The female lays an egg in which the embryo develops.

Courtship behavior consists of actions that help animals find and choose suitable mates. This behavior tends to follow a specific pattern according to species. As a result, courtship behavior helps ensure that animals mate with members of their own species. If two different species mate, they may not produce young, or their offspring may be unhealthy or unable to reproduce. Such courtship behaviors as singing and displaying colors help animals recognize their own species.

Animal mates find each other in a number of ways. Female birds are attracted to the beautiful songs and bright feathers of males. Female grasshoppers, cicadas, bullfrogs, and toads also are attracted to the calls made by males of their species. Female silkworm moths release into the air a perfume-like chemical called a *pheromone* to attract males from as far away as several miles or kilometers. At certain times of the year, female dogs give off a pheromone that attracts male dogs. Female fireflies watch for male fireflies that flash their lights in a certain rhythmic pattern. Male fence lizards bob their heads rhythmically when a female approaches. Siamese fighting fish perform a complicated courtship dance, followed by the release of eggs and sperm into the water.

Some animals choose particular mates. The female anole lizard typically prefers to mate with the largest male. The peacock spreads his fantastic tail feathers, hoping to coax a peahen into becoming his mate. Peahens choose males with many spots on their tail feathers. Male birds of paradise gather in a tree. When a female appears, the brilliantly colored males strut and dance to show off their bright feathers. If a female chooses to watch this display, she will usually mate with the male that has the brightest colors.

Male bowerbirds build chambers or runways, called *bowers*, made of sticks or other material. They decorate these structures with brightly colored stones, bones, or other objects. The male dances and bows in front of his bower, hoping that a passing female will accept him as a mate. If one does, she enters the bower with him, and they mate there.

Some male animals give food to possible mates. A male tern catches a fish and places it into the mouth of the female he wants for his mate. A male dance fly brings a dead insect to a female. She eats the insect while mating with the male. A male that does not bring a dead insect risks being eaten by the female.

Mating is dangerous for some male spiders and insects. In certain species of black widow spiders, females sometimes eat the males after mating. A female praying mantis may pounce unexpectedly on a male in her vicinity. Sometimes, she mates with a male and then eats him.

Hermit crab

Regeneration. Some kinds of animals, mostly simple animals, can replace lost body parts by *regeneration*. If a sponge is broken into small pieces, some of the fragments will grow into new sponges. Earthworms and their marine relatives can regenerate their heads or tails if those parts are broken off. Crabs and lobsters can grow new claws. Sea cucumbers sometimes throw out their intestines and other internal body parts to distract attackers. New parts grow back quickly.

Even some vertebrates can regenerate parts of their bodies. A salamander that loses a leg will grow a new one. Many salamanders can break off their tails to escape the grip of an enemy. These animals soon grow new tails. Mammals can regenerate hair, nails, and some other body tissues.

How Animals Raise Their Young

The newborn young of many species need no care from their parents. Even from birth, they can move about and find food on their own. The young of other species need parental care for some time after birth. One or both parents provide them with food and protection until they are old enough to manage for themselves.

Most kinds of animals never see their parents. For example, clams and many other invertebrates release their eggs and sperm into the water, where fertilization takes place. Carried around by ocean currents, the young of these animals may travel far from where their parents live. The female leatherback turtle swims thousands of miles or kilometers in the ocean to tropical beaches. She then digs a hole on the beach and lays her eggs. The eggs hatch in the warm sand after the female has returned to the sea.

Providing food is one of the main ways animals care for their young. Even females who never see their offspring provide them with food. The female's eggs contain yolk and other nourishing substances that serve as food for the developing embryos. Female sea urchins and herring produce vast numbers of small eggs, each of which has little yolk. Offspring from these eggs are extremely tiny when they hatch and must find their own food to grow. Their chance for survival is relatively small. Female birds, on the other hand, lay only a few eggs, each with large amounts of yolk. Offspring from these eggs are relatively large and have a higher chance of survival.

Some animals that do not see their offspring provide their young with food in addition to that in the egg. Many flies lay their eggs on rotting fruits, which supply the young flies with food. The female digger wasp lays her egg on a grasshopper that she has stung, paralyzed, and buried. After hatching, her offspring feeds on the grasshopper. The female dung beetle finds fresh *dung* (manure), rolls a piece into a ball, and then buries it. She lays her egg on the dung ball. After hatching, the young beetle feeds on the dung.

Mammals *nurse* their babies—that is, they feed them on the mother's milk. The nursing period lasts only a few weeks in mice, hares, and many other species. But among some larger mammals, such as elephants and rhinoceroses, the young may nurse several years before they are *weaned*—that is, taken off the mother's milk.

Incubation. In many species, the mother and sometimes the father remain with their eggs and young. Birds incubate their eggs by sitting on them in a nest. Incubation keeps the eggs warm and helps the embryo inside to develop quickly into a young bird. After the eggs hatch, the parents may make many hunting trips each day, trying to catch enough insects to feed the hungry *nestlings* (young birds). When the young are old enough to hunt, they leave the nest and fly away.

Among many species of birds, including pigeons and starlings, the parents take turns incubating the eggs. Among ducks, geese, and some other birds, the females are the only incubators. In most species of hornbills, the female even imprisons herself inside a walled-up nest chamber to incubate eggs.

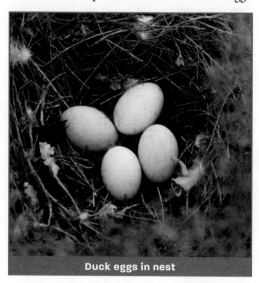

Duck eggs in nest

The male passes food to the female through a tiny slit in the wall. In a few species of birds, the male does all the incubating. For example, a female emperor penguin lays a single egg, which the male then incubates on top of his toes. He tucks his toes and the egg under the fluffy feathers of his belly. When the egg hatches, the little penguin stays warm and grows in this cozy "nest."

Female pythons also incubate their eggs. They produce the heat to warm their eggs by twitching their muscles, much as people do when shivering. After the baby pythons hatch, they must find food and shelter on their own.

Providing shelter. Some species provide shelter for their young. A female lizard may lay her eggs in an underground nest, where they are hidden from predators. The huge nests of sociable weavers, a type of African bird, protect the baby birds from bad weather and enemies. Some frogs and fish build nests for their eggs and young. A few tropical frogs carry their tadpoles around on their backs until they find a safe pool of water for the young frogs.

Parents sometimes provide shelter for their offspring within their own bodies. The male seahorse carries the female's eggs in a pouch. When the young seahorses hatch, the male releases them from the pouch. Female kangaroos, koalas, opossums, wallabies, and other *marsupials* give birth to tiny, poorly developed offspring. The babies mature in a pouch on the mother's abdomen. There, they nurse and are protected by the mother. One kind of Australian frog swallows her eggs into her stomach, where they develop. After the eggs hatch, the female opens her mouth, and tadpoles and small froglets come out.

Providing protection. Parents often protect their young from enemies. A male stickleback fish will attack any predatory fish or insect that approaches its young. A female scorpion carries her babies on her back and defends them with the poisonous sting on the tip of her long tail. Female crocodiles guard their nests and will fight any predator that comes near. As young crocodiles begin to hatch, they cry out, and the female helps them dig out of the nest. She then gently picks them up in her jaws and carries them to a nearby pond. A female bear will sometimes attack hikers who venture too close to her cubs. A female pet dog may attack even her owner if she fears that her puppies are threatened.

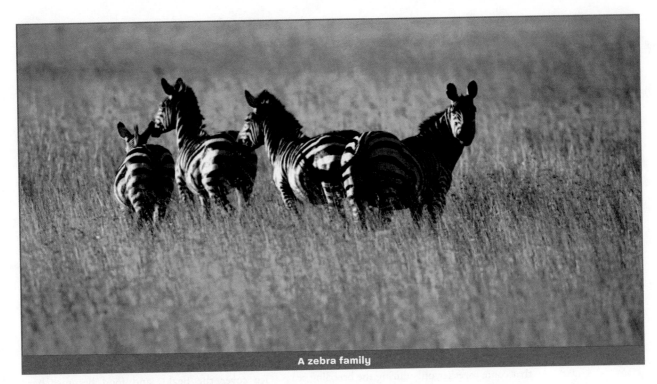

A zebra family

Group care. Some animals live together in groups of several families. As many as a hundred pairs of sociable weavers raise their chicks together in a large nest. Several female lions may care for their young cubs together. Naked mole rats live in underground colonies. One female produces offspring. Most of the other females help tend the young. Many monkeys and baboons live in small groups. All the adults in a group will work together to defend their young from an attacking leopard. When attacked by a wolf, a herd of musk oxen will protect their calves by placing them between adults.

Learning and play. Young animals may learn many things about the world from their parents. By watching what foods its parents eat and reject, a young animal can learn to recognize the kinds of foods that are safe. If young animals see their mother show fear of another type of animal or of certain locations, they learn to avoid those animals and places. Thus, they learn which types of animals, foods, and environments are safe and which are dangerous.

Many animals play while they are young. Lion cubs may try to pounce on the twitching tail of an adult lion. They also play with one another as though they were fighting. Such games help young animals develop coordination and strength. Play also helps them learn how to defend themselves and to fight effectively. In addition, it enables some animals to learn how to stalk and capture prey.

Animal Homes and Communities

Animals' homes provide shelter from harsh weather or protection against enemies. Some animals have shelters that they use only once. Others make homes where they live for many years. However, a number of animals, such as fish that live in the ocean, spend their whole lives moving about. They never have homes.

A number of animals use caves, cracks in the ground, logs, plants, or rocks as temporary shelter. Garter snakes and many insects spend the night under rocks but leave this shelter the next day to hunt for food.

Some animals build their homes. Field mice collect dried grass and then construct a small nest under a protective log. Many birds and squirrels collect grass and twigs to build nests in the trees or on the ground. Gophers and moles dig burrows in the soil.

Home ranges. Most animals live within certain areas that form their *home range*. An animal's home range includes all the resources an animal needs to survive. By living within a specific area, an animal can learn where best to find food or shelter there.

The size of an animal's home range depends typically on the animal's size. Crickets and sea urchins have small home ranges. But elephants and lions may have home ranges that cover vast distances. Big animals require extensive home ranges to obtain the large amounts of food they need to survive.

Some animals defend their home ranges from other animals. A defended home range is called a *territory.* The song of a warbler, the hoot of an owl, or the roar of a lion warns other animals of their kind to stay away. Some animals use chemical warnings rather than sounds to ward off invaders from their own species. Intruders can easily smell the urine of wolves and the scent marks of cats and hyenas and know that a territory is already occupied. Often the intruder leaves without a fight. Sometimes, however, fights break out over territory, resulting in injury or death.

Group living. Many animals live in groups. Some groups, such as herds of elephants, remain together for many years. Others are small families that come together only during the breeding season. A mother and father bird may cooperate in raising their nestlings but may separate when the young leave the nest.

Wolf packs and some other animal groups have a social order called a *dominance hierarchy.* In such groups, every member has a certain rank in the hierarchy. High-ranking members are called *dominant individuals,* and low-ranking ones are known as *subordinate individuals.* The dominant individuals have first choice of such resources as food and water. They also have their pick of mates.

Some groups are large and complex. Ants, bees, and termites live in huge colonies that consist of many thousands or even millions of individuals. The individuals in these colonies often have specific tasks. With honey bees, the *queen bee* is responsible for producing eggs. *Workers* search for pollen, make honey, and feed and care for the queen and her offspring. *Drones* do little but fertilize the queen's eggs.

Fish may form large schools in the open ocean. Herring schools may consist of hundreds of millions of fish.

 Animal Migration

Why animals migrate. The environment of some animals becomes extremely harsh at certain times of the year. In winter, for example,

Canada goose

high mountains become bitterly cold. Snow and ice cover the peaks, and food becomes hard for animals to find. Some animals survive by hibernating. Others travel to places where the weather is milder and more food is available. The next spring, these animals return home. This type of regular round-trip journey is called a *migration.* Many animals that migrate live in the mountains or far from the equator. Migrating animals usually travel in large groups.

Animals migrate for other reasons than to escape cold weather. Some travel to favorite feeding areas or to special places to produce their young.

Animal travelers. Many birds make seasonal migrations. Some simply move short distances from the mountains to the valleys below. Others make remarkable long-distance journeys. In the fall, huge flocks of ducks and geese fly south for the winter. European white storks spend the spring and summer in northern Europe, where they breed and raise their young. They fly as far south as southern Africa for the winter.

The Arctic tern is the champion long-distance traveler. Terns breed on islands in the Arctic Ocean. In late summer, they begin a long journey and fly all the way to Antarctica. They feed on the fish that are plentiful there before flying north to the Arctic to breed the following summer. A tern making this round trip may fly as many as 22,000 miles (35,400 kilometers).

Humpback whales and blue whales also make long migrations. They spend the summer in polar oceans, which have plentiful food. In the autumn, they swim toward the equator until they reach the warm tropical seas. There, the females that are pregnant give birth. Others mate and then give birth the next year. The warm waters provide a comfortable environment for the babies. The whales spend the winter in the tropics before returning to the polar feeding area in the spring.

Monarch butterflies and many other insects also migrate. When winter approaches, swarms of monarch butterflies travel from Canada and the northern United States to California and Florida. Some even fly as far south as southern Mexico. The butterflies begin the return trip in the spring, but few of the adults that flew south live long enough to complete it. Female monarchs lay eggs along the way back. The offspring, after maturing, continue the northward journey.

Some animals travel long distances to find a breeding site. The green sea turtle feeds along the east coast of South America. It then swims 1,200 miles (1,900 kilometers) of open ocean to breed on Ascension Island, a small island in the middle of the Atlantic Ocean. When the baby turtles hatch, they swim to South America, where they may remain for many years. When they are mature, they swim back to Ascension Island and breed.

Most salmon live for years in ocean waters. When the time comes for them to *spawn* (lay their eggs), they travel thousands of miles or kilometers. The salmon swim to inland waters, where they produce their young. The adult salmon die before the young hatch.

Dangers of migration. Migrating animals may face a number of dangers, including new predators, during their long journeys. Some dangers come from human beings. For example, the fences that farmers use to corral their livestock prevent antelope from making their seasonal migrations. Farmers often shoot migrating animals that stop to feed on their crops. The draining of wetlands makes it harder for ducks and geese to find a safe place to rest and feed during migration. Some winter feeding areas are also being destroyed.

The Origin and Development of Animals

Most scientists believe that all plant and animal species probably developed from a single form of life that arose about 3 1/2 billion years ago. The basic life form gradually changed so that through the centuries, millions of kinds of animals have come into being. Some kinds are still alive. Others are *extinct* (no longer living). All animals, whether living or extinct, are related to one another.

This set of ideas about how species change over time is called the theory of evolution. The theory is supported by a vast amount of evidence from many fields, and most scientists consider the occurrence of evolution to be a scientific fact. However, many people reject the concept of evolution because it conflicts with their religious beliefs. The Biblical account of the Creation, for example, says that God took only a few days to create all living things essentially as they exist today.

This section uses evolutionary theory as the basis of a discussion of when some animals originated and how species change

When animals appeared on Earth. Most scientists believe that Earth formed as a planet at least 4 1/2 billion years ago. The first life forms were simple, single-celled organisms that appeared about 1 billion years later. More complex animals and plants gradually evolved from these simple organisms. Many groups of invertebrates arose about 650 million years ago. The first vertebrates—fish—developed about 500 million years ago, and the first mammals appeared more than 200 million years ago.

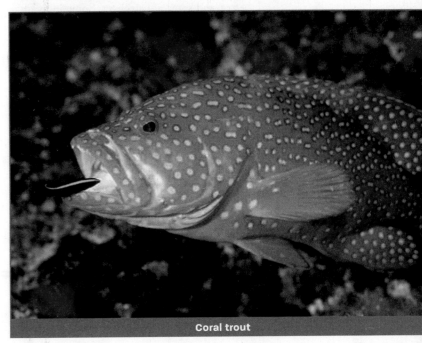

Coral trout

Another way of looking at these times is to imagine the history of life on Earth in terms of a single year. Start with the formation of Earth on New Year's Day, January 1. Bacteria, the first types of living things, would not appear until March 22. Many invertebrates would not show up until November 9. Fish would evolve from their invertebrate ancestors about November 20. Mammals would appear on December 16. Monkeys and apes would not be found until December 28. Human beings would appear only a few minutes before the end of the year, on December 31.

How new species are formed. Scientists consider groups of animals to represent distinct species when they become so different that they cannot produce fertile offspring together. Imagine a group of birds that lived only on one island. Then imagine that a few individuals got lost in a storm and landed on a different island. The two groups, now separated from each other, may gradually develop different traits as they adapt to different environments. If they become dissimilar enough, they cannot produce fertile offspring if they mate. They are then two separate species. This process can repeat itself many times over many millions of years, resulting in great numbers of species.

How species change. The individuals of any given species are not the same. Some individuals are larger, some are darker, some tolerate heat better, and some are stronger. Some individuals have traits that make them better able than others of their species to survive and reproduce in their environment. Over long periods, those animals will produce more young that survive than will individuals with less desirable traits. The offspring of the better-suited species will probably share some of the desirable traits of their parents. For example, dark moths will be well hidden in a shady forest. More of their offspring will probably survive than will those of lighter moths, which may be easily seen and eaten by hungry predators. In the next generation, more moths in the forest will be dark. This process, which causes the traits of animal groups in nature to change through time, is called *natural selection.*

Why species become extinct. Scientists estimate that, left to natural processes, most species of animals live 1 million to 10 million years before becoming extinct. Natural causes that lead to the extinction of animals include drastic changes in climate and failure of a species to compete with other animals for food. For example, the dinosaurs died out rather suddenly about 65 million years ago. Many scientists believe that these huge reptiles became extinct because of a rapid change in climate and the dinosaurs' inability to survive in it.

Some human activities also cause animals to become extinct.

The Future of Animals

Most scientists believe that we are living in a period of mass extinction. Hundreds of species of vertebrate animals have become extinct during the last 200 years. Most of these species became extinct as a result of human activities. Thousands of other species have become *endangered* (in danger of going extinct). Today, however, more and more people around the world are working to preserve the variety of animal life for future generations.

How Human Beings Endanger Animals

Destruction of habitat. When people build cities or cut down forests to obtain wood or to clear land for farming or grazing, they destroy the habitats that animals need to survive. For example, grizzly bears and mountain lions once roamed freely where the city of San Francisco now stands. But a wild grizzly bear or mountain lion could not survive in San Francisco today.

The habitats of animals in tropical forests are particularly threatened today. People are rapidly cutting down these forests to obtain such valuable hardwoods as mahogany and teak. They also are clearing the land to plant crops or to create range-

Air pollution

land. However, soils in such areas are not very fertile, and farms there produce crops for only a few years. To continue farming in such areas, people have to keep cutting down more of the forests to create new farmland. By the early 2000s, much of the world's tropical forests had already been destroyed.

Many scientists and other people are especially concerned about the destruction of tropical forests. They point out that these forests have more *biodiversity*—that is, a greater variety of plant and animal species—than any other place. One square mile (2.6 square kilometers) of forest in South America may have more species of birds and insects than many countries do. In fact, biologists discovered a single tree in a tropical forest in Brazil that supported 82 species of ants. That is about twice as many ant species as live in the entire United Kingdom.

Even though many types of plant and animal life can be found in one place in the tropics, the total range of some tropical species is extremely small. As a result, when a large area of forest is cleared, all the members of some species are killed.

Pollution can also destroy animals and their habitats. Agricultural chemicals and industrial wastes sometimes drain into ponds and streams and kill the plants and animals there. Factories, power plants, and vehicles create air pollution by burning such fossil fuels as coal and oil. Such pollution has seriously damaged forests and wildlife. *Acid rain*—rainfall with a high concentration of sulfuric and nitric acids due to air pollution—kills fish and other animals.

An increase in carbon dioxide in the atmosphere presents a long-term threat to animals and habitats. Many factories, power plants, and vehicles release carbon dioxide into the air. Forest trees and plants help absorb this gas, but as more of them are cut down, carbon dioxide levels rise. Most scientists believe that higher amounts of carbon dioxide in the atmosphere speed up global warming caused by the phenomenon called the *greenhouse effect*. A major global warm-up could produce significant climate changes. Such changes could destroy many kinds of plants and animals and flood large areas.

Introduction of new species into an area can have harmful consequences. Such species may spread rapidly in their new environment and become *invasive*. In the mid-1800s, for example,

Tree farm

people introduced rabbits into the wild in Australia for hunting. But the rabbits had no natural enemies there, and their population grew quickly, spreading over most of the continent. Partly because of the rapid spread of rabbits, rabbit-eared bandicoots, which are native to Australia, disappeared from many areas of the continent. These bandicoots had to compete with rabbits for burrow space. The traps and poisons people set out for rabbits also killed the bandicoots.

Human beings may unintentionally introduce invasive species to an area. Zebra mussels are shellfish native to the Caspian Sea region between Europe and Asia. During the late 1900s, zebra mussel larvae were unintentionally released into the North American Great Lakes in *ballast water*, the water kept in a ship's hold to keep the vessel stable. Today, the mussels are a major pest in North America. The explosive growth of zebra mussels may threaten the food supply of many fish and shellfish species native to the Great Lakes.

Hunting and fishing. In many parts of the world, people depend on native animals for food or medicine. However, overhunting and overfishing has led to the decline and even extinction of various animal species. Such activities have proven especially destructive during the past 200 years. Overhunting contributed to the extinction of such animals as the great auk, the passenger pigeon, and the Steller's sea cow. Formerly plentiful fish species, such as the Atlantic cod, have become threatened partly due to overfishing.

Human population growth. The human population is growing rapidly. Such growth may place additional pressure on natural habitats and their species. People will need more land for food and housing. Industrial activities will probably increase to process the food and manufacture the goods needed by the growing population. Many such activities cause pollution that can damage or destroy habitats. Also, increased global trade and travel will spread more and more invasive species.

How Human Beings Protect Animals

Since the late 1800s, people have become increasingly concerned about vanishing wildlife. Such concerns have resulted in part from a growing awareness of the interconnectedness of species—the web of life. More people now recognize that the disappearance of large numbers of species threatens the survival of other living things, including human beings. People who help protect habitats and animals are called *conservationists*.

Protected areas. Many countries have created national parks, game reserves, and wildlife refuges. In these areas, habitats are protected from development and hunting is banned. Many conservationists believe such areas may represent the last hope for saving some threatened species in the wild. Yellowstone National Park in the United States provides a home for rare grizzly bears, bison, bald eagles, and trumpeter swans. The African elephant and black rhinoceros are protected in parks and reserves in African savannas. Unfortunately, however, many protected areas are too small to ensure the survival of certain large species within their borders. Large animals often need lots of room to roam.

Laws protect wildlife in many countries. Under the U.S. Endangered Species Act of 1973, officials keep an up-to-date list of species in danger of extinction. The act prohibits federal projects that would destroy the habitat of an endangered species. This act was later amended to require anyone who wants to develop or change a habitat occupied by an endangered species to show that the planned changes will not harm that species.

Government agencies also determine the number of certain game animals that can be hunted and fished each season. If an animal starts to become rare, the agencies can reduce the number of that species that can be taken legally. The population of the species then has an opportunity to recover.

Habitat restoration. Humans destroy habitats, but they also try to restore them. Trees cleared by logging can be replanted, re-creating habitat for forest creatures. People can remove dams from rivers and restore wetlands. Parks in cities can provide homes for wildlife.

Breeding in captivity. Some species have become so rare that scientists believe the only hope of saving them is to breed them in captivity. For example, many of the surviving California condors live in zoos in the United States. A condor chick raised in captivity has a better chance of survival than one in nature does. As the number of condors has grown, biologists have reintroduced some of the birds back into the wild. Other endangered species being bred in captivity include the Arabian oryx and the whooping crane.

Despite conservation efforts, the future of wildlife remains uncertain. The human population continues to grow. Forests and grasslands are still being destroyed. People continue to hunt African elephants, snow leopards, and other vanishing species. Air pollution, acid rain, water pollution, and climate change also still threaten wild animals.

A Classification of the Animal Kingdom

Scientists classify animals chiefly according to the animals' ancestry. Those with a common ancestor nearer in time are more closely related than those who share an ancestor further back in time. Closely related animals share certain unique features, some of which occur only during early stages in their life cycle. Scientists arrange animals into major groups called *phyla* (singular *phylum*). The table *A Classification of the Animal Kingdom* with this article lists some of the phyla and certain important features of their members.

MLA Citation

"Animals." *The Southwestern Advantage Topic Source.* Nashville: Southwestern. 2013.

DATA

A Classification of the Animal Kingdom

Phylum	Characteristics
Porifera (Sponges)	Sponges attach themselves to rocks and other objects at the bottom of oceans, lakes, or rivers. Many take the shape of such objects. Sponges have cells called *choanocytes* or *collar cells* that trap food particles within chambers in their bodies.
Cnidaria (Cnidarians or coelenterates)	Cnidarians may be shaped like a cylinder, a bell, or an umbrella. Their bodies contain a jellylike material between two layers of cells. This phylum jellyfish, sea fans, sea anemones, and corals.
Ctenophora (Comb jellies or sea walnuts)	These transparent animals live in oceans. They have eight bands of comb-like organs on the side of their bodies. Most are pea-sized to thimble-sized. Comb jellies of a group called *Venus' girdle* can measure over 3 feet (90 centimeters) long.
Platyhelminthes (Flatworms)	Many flatworms live as parasites in other animals. Flatworms have soft, thin, flattened bodies with three layers of cells. Most are less than 1 inch (2.5 centimeters) long. The largest flatworms, called *tapeworms,* grow as long as 100 feet (30 meters). Some flatworms cause such diseases as schistosomiasis.
Nemertea (Ribbon worms or proboscis worms)	Almost all ribbon worms live in the oceans. They have a slender, often flattened, body. The worms shoot out a *proboscis* (tubelike structure) from their head to capture prey. Some species can inject poison from the proboscis into their prey. Most of these worms range from less than 1 inch 2.5 centimeters) to 8 inches (20 centimeters) long, but one species can reach a length of 100 feet (30 meters).
Rotifera (Rotifers or "wheel animals")	Rotifers live in lakes, rivers, streams, and the oceans. They have cylinder- or vase-shaped bodies. On their heads are circles of hairlike projections known as *cilia.* The largest rotifers are about $1/10$ inch (3 millimeters) long.
Acanthocephala (Spiny-headed worms)	These parasites live in many animals. They have a spiny, tubelike proboscis on their head that attaches them to the wall of their hosts' intestines. Most species measure about $3/4$ inch (2 centimeters) or less in length.
Nematoda (Roundworms or nematodes)	Many roundworms live in soil, water, or dead tissue. Some are parasites that are found in living plants and animals. Roundworms range from microscopic to about 3 feet (90 centimeters) long. The phylum includes filariae, hookworms, pinworms, and trichinae. Parasitic species cause such human diseases as trichinosis, elephantiasis, and filariasis.
Mollusca (Mollusks)	Mollusks make up the largest group of water animals, though some species live on land. Most mollusks have a hard shell that protects a soft body. The phylum includes clams, mussels, octopuses, oysters, snails, and squids.

DATA

A Classification of the Animal Kingdom

Phylum	Characteristics
Annelida (Segmented worms)	The bodies of these worms consist of segments. Many of these worms have tentacles on their head and a pair of leg-like projections called *parapodia* on each body segment. Earthworms and leeches belong to this phylum.
Arthropoda (Arthropods)	Arthropods have jointed legs, segmented bodies, and an outside shell called an *exoskeleton*. This phylum includes insects, such as ants, bees, beetles, and butterflies; crustaceans, such as crabs, lobsters, and shrimps; arachnids, such as mites, ticks, and spiders; centipedes; and millipedes.
Bryozoa (Bryozoans)	Bryozoans live in water, and most form colonies. Some colonies are jellylike masses. Others form branchlike networks on water plants. Bryozoans have boxlike or tube-shaped body that holds fluid. *Tentacles* (feelers) cluster on the head.
Brachiopoda (Lamp shells)	Lamp shells have two hard shells that cover a soft body. They live in the oceans. Some attach themselves to rocks and other hard surfaces. Others burrow or lie loose in sand or mud.
Chaetognatha (Arrow worms)	These worms have an arrow shape. They range from about $1/4$ to 6 inches (0.5 to 15 centimeters) long. They have movable hooks on their head that they use to catch prey. They live in open seas, particularly in warm waters.
Echinodermata (Echinoderms)	Echinoderms are spiny-skinned animals that have an internal skeleton made of calcium. They are the only animals that possess tiny tubelike structures called *tube feet*. This phylum includes brittle stars, sand dollars, sea cucumbers, sea urchins, and starfish.
Chordata (Chordates)	At some point in their life cycle, all chordates have a *notochord* (a rodlike, flexible cord that runs down the back of the body). A hollow nerve tube runs above the notochord. This phylum is the one to which human beings and many familiar animals belong. It includes amphibians, birds, mammals, and reptiles, as well as hagfishes, lampreys, and bony fishes.

Interesting Facts About Animals

Kinds of animals. No one knows exactly how many kinds of animals there are. New kinds are found every year. So far, scientists have identified more than $1\frac{1}{2}$ million types of animals. About 1 million of these are insects, and there are thousands of kinds of fish, amphibians, reptiles, birds, and mammals.

Largest ears and eyes. The largest ears of all animals are those of the African elephant. Elephant ears grow as large as 4 feet (1.2 meters) across. The largest eyes of all animals are those of the giant squid. They measure about 10 inches (25 centimeters) wide

The flying dragon is another name for the draco lizard. This lizard can spread out folds of skin to form "wings" that it uses to glide through the air from tree to tree. It lives in Asia and the East Indies.

Lives of animals range from several hours to many years. An adult mayfly survives only a few hours or days. Some giant tortoises have lived more than 100 years.

The world's only known poisonous bird is the hooded pitohui, which lives on the island of New Guinea. This brilliantly colored orange-and-black bird has poison on its feathers and skin. This poison serves as a defense against hawks, snakes, and other enemies. It is the same type of poison as that carried by the deadly poison-dart frog of South America.

The hummingbird can fly straight up like a helicopter. It can hover in front of a flower to suck the nectar. The *bee hummingbird*, which grows to only 2 inches (5 centimeters) long, is the smallest of all birds.

The chameleon's tongue is as long as its body. This lizard swiftly shoots out its tongue to capture insects for food. Certain chameleons can quickly change color and even develop spots and streaks that make them seem to be part of their background.

A tree-climbing crab lives on many tropical islands. It is called the *coconut crab* because it cracks coconuts with its powerful claws and eats the sweet meat.

The platypus, a mammal, has a bill like a duck and lays eggs as birds do. But it nurses its young with milk as do other mammals. It lives only on mainland Australia and the island of Tasmania.

The Following Information on the Intelligence of a Number of Types of Animals Is Based on Various Scientific Studies.

Apes and monkeys have the most human-like intelligence. Chimpanzees seem to be the most advanced. They can make tools, plan complicated searches for food, and even count. They can also communicate by means of symbols. For example, they may use certain gestures to symbolize particular objects, actions, or states of being.

Large aquatic mammals, such as dolphins, whales, and sea lions, have brains much like those of human beings. They are capable of learning symbolic communication that may have properties like those of language. For example, dolphins seem to recognize differences in meaning based on the order in which the symbols are presented.

Carnivorous mammals in the cat and dog families show learning ability as good as, or better than, all animals except apes, some monkeys, and large aquatic mammals. Lions, tigers, and wolves probably can learn more rapidly than domesticated cats or dogs can.

Hoofed animals. Elephants and pigs are the best problem solvers among the hoofed animals.

Rodents are generally good at solving problems that involve finding their way through complicated pathways.

Birds, such as the raven and the pigeon, can solve simple counting problems. Parrots can learn to say human words and use them meaningfully in naming and counting objects.

Amphibians and reptiles are difficult to test, but alligators, crocodiles, turtles, and large monitor lizards may rival mammals and birds in locating sources of food and in some other forms of nonsocial learning.

Fish. Salmon and some other kinds of fish can remember odors for as long as several years. Sharks have brains as large as those of some birds and mammals. They have keen senses, and they are surprisingly clever at finding food and avoiding danger.

Animals without backbones often seem to learn very little. But some have remarkable and specialized abilities involving communication, food, and place learning. Many scientists consider octopuses to have the most complex brains of all the invertebrates. Octopuses learn rapidly and have distinct personalities.

ADDITIONAL INFORMATION

Books to Read

Bambaradeniya, Channa, and others. *The Illustrated Atlas of Wildlife*. University of California Press, 2009.

Breed, Michael D., and Moore, Janice, eds. *Encyclopedia of Animal Behavior*. 3 vols. Elsevier, 2010.

Grzimek's Animal Life Encyclopedia. 17 vols. 2nd ed. Gale Group, 2003–2004.

Macdonald, David W., ed. *The Princeton Encyclopedia of Mammals*. Princeton, 2009.

Ryan, Michael J., and Wilczynski, Walter. *An Introduction to Animal Behavior*. Cold Spring Harbor, 2011.

Web Sites

American Society for the Prevention of Cruelty to Animals

http://www.aspca.org

Web site of the ASPCA, with information on preventing animal cruelty.

The Bat Conservation Trust

http://www.bats.org.uk/

Animal facts from a British organization dedicated to preserving bats.

Arctic Fox

http://www.mnh.si.edu/arctic/html/arctic_fox.html

An animal fact sheet from the Arctic Studies Center within the National Museum of Natural History of the Smithsonian Institution.

Bald Eagle

http://www.mnh.si.edu/arctic/html/eagle.html

An animal fact sheet from the Arctic Studies Center within the National Museum of Natural History of the Smithsonian Institution.

Caribou and Reindeer

http://www.mnh.si.edu/Arctic/html/caribou_reindeer.html

An animal fact sheet from the Arctic Studies Center within the National Museum of Natural History of the Smithsonian Institution.

Lammergeier Vulture

http://www.pbs.org/edens/bhutan/a_lv.htm

Essay on the lammergeier from the PBS documentary The Living Edens.

Laysan Albatross

http://www.mnh.si.edu/arctic/html/albatross.html

An animal fact sheet from the Arctic Studies Center within the National Museum of Natural History of the Smithsonian Institution.

Lemming

http://www.mnh.si.edu/arctic/html/lemming.html

An animal fact sheet from the Arctic Studies Center within the National Museum of Natural History of the Smithsonian Institution.

Muskox

http://www.mnh.si.edu/arctic/html/musk_ox.html

An animal fact sheet from the Arctic Studies Center within the National Museum of Natural History of the Smithsonian Institution.

Orca Killer Whale

http://www.mnh.si.edu/arctic/html/orca.html

An animal fact sheet from the Arctic Studies Center within the National Museum of Natural History of the Smithsonian Institution.

Peregrine Falcon

http://www.mnh.si.edu/arctic/html/peregrine_falcon.html

An animal fact sheet from the Arctic Studies Center within the National Museum of Natural History of the Smithsonian Institution.

Polar Bears

http://www.mnh.si.edu/arctic/html/polar_bear.html

An animal fact sheet from the Arctic Studies Center within the National Museum of Natural History of the Smithsonian Institution.

Ptarmigan

http://www.mnh.si.edu/arctic/html/ptarmigen.html

An animal fact sheet from the Arctic Studies Center within the National Museum of Natural History of the Smithsonian Institution.

Search Strings

Web of Life

animals web of life ecosystem delicate (239,000)

web of life animals ecosystem plants die decay fertilize oxygen carbon dioxide (32,600)

ecosystem delicate animals web of life plants energy fertilize oxygen carbon dioxide (24,400)

Classifying Animals

animals classifying terrestrial aquatic cold blooded warm vertebrates invertebrates group (30,800)

animals classifying kingdom phyla orders families genera species (322,000)

classification of animals kingdom animalia phyla classes orders families genera species (33,900)

Animal Habitats

animal habitats different conditions region climate (170,000)

habitats animals climate access food water different survive thrive (14,200)

Protection from Predators

animals protection predators unique (234,000)

protection predators animals unique ways examples (142,000)

protection predators animals unique ways examples moles tunnels chameleons camouflage (488)

Migrating Animals

reasons for the migration of animals food weather (317,000)

migration of animals caused by the search for food and escape from cold weather (27,500)

examples of the migration of animals in the search for food and warmer weather such as the arctic tern (2,610)

Animals in Danger

Many species of animals are in danger of becoming extinct. Animals live in an ecosystem, in which one species depends upon another for its survival, so the extinction of animals that are now endangered could cause others to be threatened. Many species are endangered due to humans overhunting them or destroying their habitat. Fortunately, other people have made it their priority to protect those species that are endangered or are on their way to becoming endangered.

HOT topics

Success Story of the Bald Eagle. In 1968, the bald eagle was an endangered species in the United States. Scientists were able to count only a little more than 400 pairs at that time. Laws were passed banning the hunting of eagles and the use of the pesticide DDT. Through the efforts of many people to protect eagles, scientists now estimate that there are over 4,000 pairs.

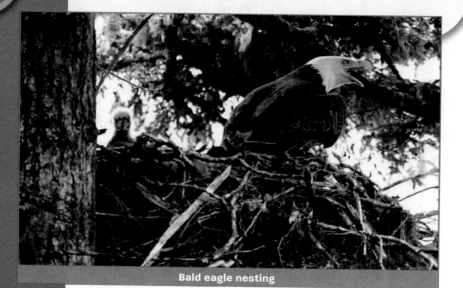

Bald eagle nesting

HOT topics

Habitat Destruction Endangers Many Species. Destruction of wetlands or rain forests endangers many species. Not only does it destroy their homes, but it removes species from the food web critical to other species' survival. Many birds, ducks, geese, fish, amphibians, and reptiles, including the American crocodile, have become endangered due to the destruction of wetlands. Destruction of the rain forests has endangered the golden lion tamarin monkey, among many other species of mammals, birds, butterflies, reptiles, and amphibians.

Rain forest

Poaching/Wildlife Trade. Although laws have been enacted to protect endangered species, many are in danger from poachers. Furs, skins, body parts, and live animals are illegally traded with tourists and collectors. Ivory from elephant tusks, tortoiseshells, reptile skins, and animal furs are just a few of the items wanted by poachers.

Protecting Endangered Species. Many laws and conservation programs, both national and international, have helped to reduce the danger to some species. The Endangered Species Act of 1973, the Convention on International Trade in Endangered Species of Wild Fauna and Flora (CITES), and the International Union for the Conservation of Nature and Natural Resources (IUCN) have all contributed to the protection of endangered species. Public awareness of the endangerment of some species and the impact of the loss of those species on the destruction of ecosystems has helped to change attitudes regarding the protection of all species.

TRUE or FALSE?

During the last 200 years, more than 50 species of birds and over 75 species of mammals have become extinct.

DEFINITIONS

endangered: threatened with extinction.
extinct: no longer existing: *The dinosaur is an extinct animal.*

THE BASICS

Animals in Danger. Endangered species are living things threatened with *extinction*—that is, the dying off of all of their kind. Thousands of species of animals and plants are endangered, and the number increases each year. Some examples of endangered species are blue whales, giant pandas, orangutans, rhinoceroses, sea turtles, snow leopards, tigers, and whooping cranes. Among endangered plants are running buffalo clover, Santa Cruz cypress, snakeroot, and many species of cactuses.

Each species of plant and animal plays a part in the delicate balance of its *ecosystem*, its relation to other living things and the environment. Thus, the extinction of large numbers of species threatens the survival of other living things, including human beings. As more species have become endangered, ecosystems have become unstable or collapsed. Fortunately, people have increased their efforts to protect endangered species.

Most biologists consider a species endangered if they expect it would die off completely in less than 20 years if no special efforts were made to protect it, or if the rate of decline far exceeds the rate of increase. Until the last few centuries, species became rare or died out as a result of natural causes. These causes included changes in climate, catastrophic movements in the earth's crust, and volcanic eruptions.

Today, species become endangered primarily because of human activities. Species mainly become endangered because of (1) loss of habitat, (2) wildlife trade, (3) overhunting, and (4) competition with domestic and nonnative animals.

 Loss of habitat poses the greatest threat to the survival of wild species. Most animals and plants are specially adapted to live and reproduce in a specific environment or habitat and cannot survive when it is destroyed. The destruction of virgin forests by loggers and settlers and the conversion of natural grasslands into pasture for livestock have eliminated vast expanses of wildlife habitats. Marshlands have been drained for farmland and building projects. Coral reefs and many marine environments have become polluted, overfished, and even dynamited to obtain tropical fish and corals. Tropical rain forests contain the greatest variety of animal and plant life on earth, and they are being destroyed more rapidly than any other type of wild habitat.

 Wildlife trade involves the capture of animals for pets, zoo specimens, and research subjects, and the killing of animals for their fur or other body parts. The capture of wild animals for commercial use has endangered many species. For example, the Spix's macaw, a parrot of Brazil, is nearly extinct in the wild because so many have been captured for private bird collectors. Many primates, including the orangutan, have become endangered by the illegal killing of the mothers to capture their babies for zoos and pet dealers. Gorillas, chimpanzees, and other primates are killed for their meat, which is sold in African markets.

Other animals have been killed in such large numbers for their fur, hides, tusks, or horns that they are nearly extinct. Rhinoceroses, wild chinchillas, the Tibetan antelope, and snow leopards are among these. Although such animals are now protected by law in the countries where they live, they are still *poached* (hunted illegally). Poaching also has seriously reduced the number of African elephants.

Overhunting has brought numerous species to the brink of extinction. The West Indian manatee, the Asiatic lion, the dugong, and many species of pheasants have become endangered because people have hunted them for food and trophies. Many species are killed by people who believe that the animals threaten their livelihoods. Livestock owners, for example, may shoot, trap, or poison

Snow leopard

Prairie dog

wild animals that they consider a danger to their herds. Farmers and ranchers in North America have nearly eliminated the red wolf and many species of prairie dogs, while herders in Africa have almost wiped out the simian wolf. Some people in the fishing industry blame seals, which eat fish, for reductions in their catch. Fishing crews have killed so many Mediterranean monk seals that only 350–450 survive.

Competition with domestic and nonnative animals is a major threat to numerous plants and animals. On many islands, native birds, mammals, and reptiles have become endangered after people introduced domestic animals. Livestock overgraze vegetation, eliminating habitat. Domestic cats prey on birds and small mammals. Rats escape from ships and infest islands, killing small birds and their eggs. In mainland areas, stocking of game fish threatens native fish, and nonnative plants and animals crowd out many native species.

Protecting endangered species. Laws and conservation programs are helping to reduce endangerment worldwide. In the United States, the Endangered Species Act of 1973 protects endangered and threatened wildlife and plants from hunting, collecting, and other activities that harm them or their habitats. Since this law was enacted, the numbers of certain endangered animals, such as the alligator, bald eagle, and peregrine falcon, have increased so much that they have been removed from the endangered list or reclassified from endangered to threatened status.

Many wild species are protected by the Convention on International Trade in Endangered Species of Wild Fauna and Flora (CITES). This treaty, drawn up in 1973, aims to control trade in wild animals and plants, their parts, and products derived from them. Over 150 countries have joined the treaty. CITES bans trade in rhinoceros horn, cheetah fur, sea turtle shells and meat, and certain whale products. Elephant ivory was banned in 1989, but later CITES decisions have enabled such African nations as Botswana, Namibia, and South Africa to export limited amounts of ivory to Japan and other countries.

Various organizations publish lists of endangered species to improve public awareness. The IUCN (International Union for the Conservation of Nature and Natural Resources) compiles lists that include thousands of animal and plant species that are threatened or endangered.

Protecting habitat is the key method of preserving endangered species. Many governments and organizations have set aside nature preserves. Some zoos and animal research centers conduct programs that breed endangered species in hopes of returning their offspring to the wild. The programs have greatly improved the outlook for such endangered species as the black-footed ferret and the California condor.

Green Turtle, Sodwana Bay

MLA Citation

"Animals in Danger."
The Southwestern Advantage Topic Source. Nashville: Southwestern. 2013.

DATA

Some Endangered Species of Animals

Common name	Scientific name	Distribution	Survival problems
American crocodile	*Crocodylus acutus*	Florida, Mexico, Central and South America, Caribbean islands	Overhunted for its hide; habitat destruction
Asian elephant	*Elephas maximus*	South-central and southeast Asia	Habitat destruction; illegal killing for ivory
Asiatic lion	*Panthera leo persica*	India	Habitat destruction; overhunted for sport
Atlantic (or Kemp's) ridley sea turtle	*Lepidochelys kempii*	Tropical and temperate parts of the Atlantic	Overhunted for its leather; overcollection of eggs
Black-footed ferret	*Mustela nigripes*	Wyoming	Poisoning of prairie dogs, its chief prey
Black rhinoceros	*Diceros bicornis*	South of Sahara in Africa	Habitat destruction; overhunted for its horn
Blue whale	*Balaenoptera musculus*	All oceans	Overhunted for blubber, food, and whale oil
California condor	*Gymnogyps californianus*	Southern California, Arizona	Habitat destruction; hunted for sport; poisoned from lead shot and predator-control programs
Cheetah	*Acinonyx jubatus*	Africa, Iran	Habitat destruction; overhunted for sport and fur
Devils Hole pupfish	*Cyprinodon diabolis*	Nevada	Habitat destruction
Giant panda	*Ailuropoda melanoleuca*	China	Habitat destruction; illegal killing for fur; illegal capture for zoos
Imperial parrot	*Amazona imperialis*	Caribbean Islands	Habitat destruction; illegal capture for pets
Orangutan	*Pongo pygmaeus*	Borneo, Sumatra	Habitat destruction; illegal killing of mothers to obtain young for zoos and for pets
Red wolf	*Canis rufus*	Southeastern United States	Habitat destruction; killed in predator-control programs
Snow leopard	*Uncia uncia*	Central Asia	Overhunted for its fur; killed in predator-control programs
Tiger	*Panthera tigris*	Southern Asia, China, Eastern Russia	Habitat destruction; illegal killing for sport and body parts

ADDITIONAL RESOURCES

Web Sites

History of the United States Endangered Species Act

http://www.flmnh.ufl.edu/fish/Education/ESA.htm
Information from the Florida Museum of Natural History.

Kids' Planet

http://www.kidsplanet.org/
Defenders of Wildlife presents this Web site with information and activities relating to
endangered animals.

The Magnificant Whooping Crane: Wildlife and Endangered Species Pages

http://raysweb.net/specialplaces/pages/crane.html
Information about the whooping crane. Includes many links to other resources and an extensive
bibliography.

U.S. EPA Student Center

http://www.epa.gov/students/
A site geared to students and teachers from the United States Environmental Protection Agency
(EPA). Includes information on a wide variety of environmental topics, suggestions for projects, and
help with homework.

Zoos and Aquariums of the American Zoo and Aquarium Association

http://www.aza.org/
Information about zoos and aquariums of North America and their many conservation programs.

Search Strings

Success Story of the Bald Eagle

animals in danger bald eagle success laws efforts protect (12,700)

bald eagle animal in danger success endangered laws efforts DDT (11,100)

Habitat Destruction Endangers Many Species

habitat destruction endangers many species destruction wetlands rainforests (102,000)

animals in danger habitat destruction species wetlands rainforests destroy homes removes food
web (14,300)

Poaching

animals in danger poaching laws protect endangered species furs skins (3,580)

poaching animals endangered species laws protect furs skins body parts (35,500)

Protecting Endangered Species

protecting endangered species animals laws conservation programs endangered species act (744,000)

endangered species act CITES IUCN protect laws conservation programs (92,800)

animals in danger protecting endangered species laws conservation programs public awareness change
attitudes (104,000)

BACKGROUND INFORMATION

The following article was written during the year in which the events took place and reflects the style and thinking of that time.

Conservation (2006)

Many conservationists compare the battle to preserve the natural world to fighting fires. A May 2006 report by the World Conservation Union (IUCN) revealed that conservationists have plenty of fires to put out. According to the 2006 Red List compiled by the IUCN, an international organization based in Gland, Switzerland, more than 16,000 species of animals and plants were threatened with global extinction. The endangered list included one out of three amphibian species, one in eight bird species, and a quarter of Earth's mammal species.

Tigers and lions. By most estimates, fewer than 8,000 wild tigers remained in Asia in 2006, hemmed into only 7 percent of their original range. In October, the WWF (formerly known as the World Wildlife Fund), a conservation organization based in Geneva, Switzerland, blasted an international meeting of 30 nations for not acting to solve the tiger crisis.

The meeting of the Standing Committee of the Convention on International Trade in Endangered Species (CITES) featured a report describing how tiger conservation efforts have failed. CITES is an international treaty to control trade in wildlife and wildlife products. Despite the report, the CITES committee put off any action until the next full meeting of the approximately 160 CITES nations, scheduled for June 2007.

Habitat loss and *poaching* (illegal killing) of tigers for skins were the main reasons for the tiger's troubles. The WWF urged immediate action to save the large cats.

About 40,000 lions lived in Africa in 2006, but conservationists worried that these felines might eventually follow the tiger to the brink of extinction. Conservationists and representatives from African governments met in Johannesburg, South Africa, in January, to find ways of preventing the threat to lions from growing worse.

Lion habitat was shrinking in 2006 as exploding human populations in Africa cultivated more land for farming. Lions in small, isolated populations engage in inbreeding, which can lead to genetic problems. They also often prey on livestock and people.

One controversial proposal discussed at the January meeting advocated trophy hunting of lions in those areas where their populations thrive. Advocates said this action would eliminate problem cats and provide income for local people. Animal rights advocates, however, opposed the proposal.

Habitat protection in the United States. Two new wildlife sanctuaries in the United States came under federal protection in 2006—one on land and the other in the sea. In January, U.S. Secretary of Agriculture Mike Johanns dedicated the El Toro Wilderness Area, which had been created by President George W. Bush the previous month. The protected area comprises 10,000 acres (4,000 hectares) of Puerto Rico's Caribbean National Forest, the only tropical rain forest in the U.S. Forest Service system. The forest has 240 species of native trees, the most of any national forest.

In June, President Bush created the world's largest marine sanctuary, in the northwest Hawaiian Islands. He invoked the little-used

Sumatran tiger in water

National Antiquities Act to establish a California-sized *archipelago* (broad expanse of water containing islands) as a national monument. It was the second time President Bush had used the 100-year-old act, which allows the president to establish national monuments of special significance. All fishing was to be phased out in the sanctuary.

International habitat protection. In September, Congo (Brazzaville) granted protected status to 3,800 square miles (9,800 square kilometers) of remote forests, swamps, sand dunes, and savannahs. This area is inhabited by chimpanzees, elephants, gorillas, hippopotamuses, and leopards—among many other animals.

Canada contributed to wilderness conservation in February by creating a 4.4-million acre (1.8-million hectare) park on the Pacific coast of British Columbia. The region teems with large mammals, including cougars, grizzly bears, moose, mountain goats, and wolves.

Also in February, Brazil designated a protected area of almost 25,000 square miles (64,700 square kilometers) in the Amazon Basin, where the world's richest rain forests are threatened by logging and agriculture. The area protected not only wildlife but also *indigenous* (native) people whom land developers were expelling from their homes.

Animal recoveries. China pursued plans in 2006 to preserve the giant panda by breeding the species in captivity so that the animals could be released into the wild as their numbers built up. In April, biologists for the first time released a captive-bred panda in a protected area. The animal was a 4-year-old male that had been trained to survive on its own. There were only 1,600 wild pandas in 2006, all of them in China.

In September, wildlife officials in Colorado searched an area in the San Isabel Mountains by helicopter after hunters reported seeing three grizzly bears. The last-known grizzly in Colorado was trapped and killed in 1952, but there had been periodic, unconfirmed grizzly sightings since then. Although the officials did not find the reported bears, the descriptions of the animals by the experienced hunters suggested that the animals were indeed grizzlies.

Evidence increased in 2006 that jaguars were returning to the southwestern United States, from which they had vanished in the mid-1900s. In February 2006, a jaguar that was being tracked with dogs was photographed in the Animas Mountains of New Mexico. Scientists believed that the cats were straying north from Mexico, and that they were not a resident group.

Last-ditch effort. In May, the government of India banned the use of the anti-inflammatory drug diclofenac by farmers and veterinarians. The drug, which had long been used to treat cattle, was linked to fatal liver damage in three species of vultures that feed on dead cattle. Wildlife biologists described in 2004 how diclofenac caused populations of white-backed, long-billed, and slender-billed vultures to decline from perhaps 40 million to a few thousand birds in about 15 years. Another drug, meloxicam, was a potential replacement for diclofenac.

Doomsday vault. In June 2006, engineers in Norway began digging a "doomsday vault" into a mountain on the Arctic island of Svalbard. The vault was designed to hold as many as 3 million seeds, from all known varieties of the world's crops. These seeds might be needed in the future to reestablish crops destroyed by major disasters.

African lion

Birds

All birds have feathers and all have wings; however, there are about 9,700 *species* (kinds) of birds, and not all can fly. Some birds walk and use their wings only for balance and to attract mates. Others swim and use their wings as flippers.

HOT topics

The Evolution of Birds from Dinosaurs.

Scientists believe birds evolved (developed over time) from reptiles more than 150 million years ago, during the Jurassic Period. Birds descended from *theropods*, a group of largely meat-eating dinosaurs that walked upright. Biologists classify birds in a group called *Archosaurs*, which includes alligators, crocodiles, dinosaurs, and *pterosaurs* (prehistoric flying reptiles). Discoveries of fossil remains demonstrate that feathers evolved in theropod dinosaurs before the origin of birds and before the beginning of flight. Many well-known theropods may have had feather-

DEFINITIONS

habitat: the place where an animal or plant naturally lives or grows.

poultry: birds raised for their meat or eggs, such as chickens, turkeys, geese, or ducks.

species: a group of animals or plants that have certain permanent characteristics in common and are able to interbreed. A species ranks next below a genus and may be divided into several varieties, races, or breeds. All species of apples belong to the same genus. Wheat is a species of grass. The domestic cat is one species of cat.

histoplasmosis: a serious fungous disease that attacks especially the lungs, throat, spleen, liver, and lymph nodes. It is most common in the eastern and central United States.

syrinx: the vocal organ of birds, situated at or near the division of the trachea into the right and left bronchi.

HOT topics

hot topics hot topics hot topics hot topics

like features, including *Velociraptor*, *Oviraptor*, and *Tyrannosaurus rex*.

Bird Migration. The migration of birds remains one of the most fascinating and least understood events in nature. Birds are not especially strong. Yet numerous species migrate tremendous distances, often flying many hours or days without stopping. They return to exactly the same nesting places every year. Scientists have learned much about why, where, and how birds migrate, but many questions remain unanswered. Although birds migrate to survive, the factors that actually trigger their migrations are much more difficult to explain. Bird migrations are probably regulated by hormones. Among some northern species, hormone production is affected by the length of daylight. As the daylight hours shorten, hormonal changes cause the birds to prepare for their migratory flight south. The exact timing of migrations also depends on such conditions as the weather and the food supply.

California condors

Endangered Species. More than 500 kinds of birds around the world have become so rare that they are considered endangered. Loss of habitat caused the decline of such mainland species as Bachman's warbler and the ivory-billed woodpecker. Hunters killed many Eskimo curlews and whooping cranes. Loss of habitat, illegal hunting, and illegal egg collecting all contributed to the decline of the California condor. The use of pesticides, especially DDT, contaminated the food of the bald eagle, the osprey, and the brown pelican in some areas. One result of this contamination was that the eggs laid by the birds had such thin shells that they cracked under the weight of the incubating parent.

Bird Refuges. The spread of farms, towns, cities, and highways has destroyed the natural habitats of many birds and other animals. To help remedy this problem, a number of countries have set aside areas of land as refuges for birds and other wildlife. Some of the refuges are publicly owned. Others are owned or leased by private conservation groups. Large public parks and forests also serve as bird sanctuaries.

Ivory-billed woodpecker

TRUE or FALSE?
If a bird loses a feather, it will never replace it.

THE BASICS

A bird is an animal with feathers. All birds have feathers, and they are the only living animals that have them. When people think of birds, they usually think first of their flying ability. All birds have wings. The fastest birds can reach speeds well over 100 miles (160 kilometers) per hour. No other animals can travel faster than birds. Yet not all birds can fly. For example, ostriches and penguins are flightless. Instead of flying, ostriches walk or run. They use their wings only for balance and to attract mates. Penguins swim. They use their wings as flippers.

People have always been fascinated by birds. Birds' marvelous flying ability makes them seem the freest of all animals. Many birds have gorgeous colors or sing sweet songs. The charms of birds have inspired poets, painters, and composers. Certain birds also serve as symbols. People have long regarded the owl as a symbol of wisdom and the dove as a symbol of peace. The eagle has long represented political and military might.

There are about 9,700 *species* (kinds) of birds. The smallest bird is the bee hummingbird, which grows only about 2 inches (5 centimeters) long. The largest living bird is the ostrich, which may grow up to 8 feet (2.4 meters) tall. The largest bird that ever lived was the elephant bird, which died out hundreds of years ago. It weighed about 1,000 pounds (450 kilograms). Birds inhabit all parts of the world, from the polar regions to the tropics. They are found in forests, deserts, and cities; on grasslands, farmlands, mountaintops, and islands; and even in caves. Some birds, including albatrosses and certain ducks, always live near water. Most such birds can swim. Other birds, especially those in the tropics, stay in the same general area throughout life. Even in the Arctic and the Antarctic, some hardy birds stay year-round. But many birds of cool or cold regions migrate each year to warm areas to avoid winter, when food is hard to find. In spring, they fly home again to nest.

All birds hatch from eggs. Among most kinds of birds, the female lays her eggs in a nest built by herself or her mate or by both of them. The majority of birds have one mate at a time, with whom they raise one or two sets of babies a year. Some birds keep the same mate for life. Others choose a new mate every year. Most baby birds remain in the nest for several weeks or months after hatching. Their parents feed and protect them until they can care for themselves. Other kinds of baby birds, including chickens and ducks, become active and able to walk and feed themselves soon after hatching. Most birds leave their parents after only a few months.

Birds belong to the large group of animals called *vertebrates*. Vertebrates are animals with a backbone. The group also includes fish, reptiles, and mammals. Birds have two forelimbs and two hind-limbs, as do cats, frogs, lizards, and many other vertebrates. But in birds, the forelimbs are wings rather than arms or front legs. Like mammals, and unlike amphibians and reptiles, birds are *warm-blooded*—that is, their body temperature always remains about the same, even if the temperature of their surroundings changes. Unlike most other vertebrates, living birds lack teeth. Instead, they have a hard bill, or beak, which they use in getting food and for self-defense. A number of the earliest birds possessed teeth, but these species no longer exist.

Many birds have great value to people. Such birds as chickens and turkeys provide meat and eggs for food. Some kinds of birds help farmers by eating insects that attack their crops. Others eat farmers' grain and fruit. But in general, birds do much more good than harm.

Since the 1600s, about 80 kinds of birds have died out. People have killed off most of these species by overhunting them and by destroying

Great blue herons and nest

their environment. Today, most countries have laws to protect birds and help prevent any more kinds from dying out.

This article discusses the importance of birds, their distribution throughout the world, how they live, and how they raise a family. The article also describes bird migration, the bodies of birds, bird study and protection, and the evolution of birds.

The Importance of Birds

In nature. Each species of animal in a woodland, grassland, or other natural area depends on other living things in the environment for food. In a woodland, for example, some birds get their food mainly from plants. Others chiefly eat small animals, such as insects or earthworms. Birds and bird eggs, in turn, serve as food for such animals as foxes, raccoons, and snakes. The feeding relationships among all the animals in an environment help prevent any one species from becoming too numerous. Birds play a vital role in keeping this balance of nature.

Birds also serve other purposes in nature. Fruit-eating birds help spread seeds. The birds eat and digest the pulp of berries and other fruits but pass the seeds in their droppings. The seeds may sprout wherever the droppings fall. Hummingbirds pollinate certain flowers that produce nectar. Hummingbirds feed on nectar. As they visit flowers in search of it, they carry pollen from flower to flower. In these ways, birds help numerous kinds of plants reproduce and spread.

Many kinds of birds assist farmers by eating weed seeds, harmful insects, or other agricultural pests. Unlike birds that feed on fruits, seed-eating birds digest the seeds they eat. One bobwhite may rid a field of as many as 15,000 weed seeds a day. Many birds eat insects that damage farm crops. Some birds are especially helpful in keeping the number of certain kinds of insects under control. Robins and sparrows, for example, are highly effective against cabbageworms, tomato worms, and leaf beetles. Rats and mice can cause huge losses on farms by eating stored grain. Hawks and owls prey on these animals and so help limit such losses.

People consider a few kinds of birds to be pests. One such species, the common, or European, starling, was introduced into the northeast United States in the 1890s. The birds multiplied and spread rapidly. Today, starlings are so numerous in many North American cities that they have become

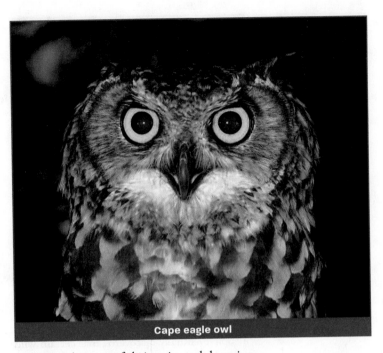

Cape eagle owl

a nuisance because of their noise and droppings. Moreover, starlings fight with certain native American birds, including bluebirds and swallows, over the tree holes in which they nest. Pigeons are also a nuisance in many cities because of their droppings. Flocks of starlings and pigeons leave masses of droppings on buildings where the birds have been roosting. The fungus *Histoplasma capsulatum* can grow on these droppings. The spores of the fungus may be carried in the air and cause the infectious disease *histoplasmosis* in people who inhale them. Some strains of influenza, another infectious disease, can be passed to human beings from infected domestic birds, including chickens and ducks. West Nile virus, which causes a flulike disease, is transmitted from infected birds to human beings and other animals through the bites of mosquitoes.

As a source of food and raw materials. People have always hunted birds for food. Some of the first birds used for food were ground-feeding birds, such as quails and turkeys, which were caught in traps and snares. Hunters captured pigeons, ducks, and other birds by placing nets where the birds normally flew. After the invention of guns, most people hunted large, meaty birds to save gunpowder and shot. The eggs of wild birds were also an important food for people in prehistoric times, and people in some parts of the world still eat such eggs. Because most birds' nests are hard to find, the eggs used for food have come

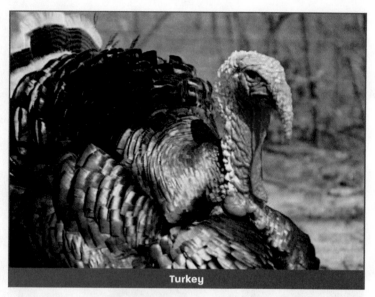
Turkey

chiefly from sea birds that nest in open places in large *colonies* (groups).

People eventually discovered that certain wild fowl could be *domesticated* (tamed). This discovery led to the development of *poultry*—that is, domesticated fowl that farmers raise for meat and eggs. Chickens are probably the oldest kinds of poultry. They were domesticated in Asia at least 3,000 years ago. Since then, farmers have developed other poultry, including ducks, geese, guineafowl, pheasants, and turkeys. Mallard ducks, geese, and pheasants were domesticated in Asia; guineafowl in Africa; and Muscovy ducks and turkeys in Mexico.

Today, chickens rank as the most widely raised poultry by far. Farmers throughout the world produce hundreds of millions of chickens annually for meat and eggs. Ducks and turkeys rank second and third in production worldwide. Ducks are raised for both meat and eggs. Turkeys are raised mainly for meat.

People use the feathers of certain birds to stuff pillows, mattresses, sleeping bags, coats, and quilting. Goose feathers are preferred because they are soft and springy. Manufacturers often mix goose feathers with *down feathers*, or *down*, to provide extra softness. Down feathers are small, fluffy feathers that some adult birds, especially water birds, have between their stiffer outer feathers. Most of the down used for stuffing comes from ducks and geese raised on farms.

People throughout the world use colorful bird feathers to decorate jewelry, clothing, and hats. Many countries forbid the use of feathers from wild birds. People may only use feathers from domesticated birds, such as turkeys, or from other birds raised in captivity, such as peacocks and pheasants.

Over the centuries, the droppings of ocean birds have formed huge deposits on certain islands where the birds nest in dry areas. This waste matter, which is called *guano*, provides an excellent source of nitrogen that people use to make fertilizer and explosives. The mining of guano for fertilizer was once an important industry in some countries.

As pets. People have long kept birds as pets. Favorite bird pets include canaries, parrots, finches, and parakeets called budgerigars, or "budgies." Budgies and parrots are especially popular because they can be trained to imitate human speech and even to whistle.

Most birds sold as pets have been raised in captivity. The birds are hatched in cages and sold to the public by pet stores. After years or centuries of captive breeding, some of these birds look much different from their wild ancestors. For example, wild budgerigars are green, but breeders have produced white, yellow, blue, and even violet budgerigars. In the past, most of the parakeets and parrots sold as pets were caught in the wild. Over the years, this practice wiped out some species. To help protect such birds, many countries have made it illegal for wild birds to be caged except in zoos. However, many wild parakeets and parrots are still captured and sold illegally throughout the world.

Every species of bird has its own *range*—that is, a particular part of the world in which all the members of the species normally live. Some birds have a broad range. The osprey and common barn owl, for example, live on every continent except Antarctica. However, no species of bird is found in every part of the world, and many species have an extremely limited range. For example, a species called the Whitehead's broadbill lives only in a small, mountainous area of northern Borneo.

Oceans and continents strongly influence the distribution of various species of birds. Most birds cannot make long ocean flights. Widely separated continents, such as Africa and North America, therefore have different kinds of birds. However, people have transported many species overseas, and some of these birds have become adapted to their new environment.

Climate also influences a bird's range. Most birds would starve during a long cold spell. For this reason, few birds live all year in regions with severe winters. However, many birds nest in such regions in summer and migrate to warmer climates for the winter. Birds that migrate have two ranges—a summer one and a winter one. They are *summer residents* in their summer range and *winter residents* in their winter one. Along their migration route, they are *transients* (temporary visitors). Birds that do not migrate are *permanent residents*.

More kinds of birds live in the tropics than anywhere else in the world. Tropical rainforests have more kinds of birds than any other habitat. Most birds of the tropics are permanent residents. However, some parts of the tropics have an annual dry season, and many of the birds migrate to moister parts of the tropics to avoid it. The tropics also have many winter residents that migrate from cool or cold climates. The *temperate zones*—that is, the parts of the world between the tropics and the polar regions—have fewer permanent residents than do the tropics. In the parts of the temperate zones nearest the polar regions, most of the birds are summer residents only. Few birds live all year in the polar regions. However, both the Arctic and the Antarctic have many residents during the summer.

The ranges of birds are further determined by the kinds of food and nesting places that are available. For example, fish-eating birds must live near bodies of water. Birds that nest in trees normally live only in wooded areas. Thus, most birds live not only in a particular region of the world but also in a particular type of environment, or *habitat*, within that region.

Birds of North America

Hundreds of species of birds live in North America north of Mexico, a region that includes all of Canada and all of the United States except Hawaii. Most of this region lies in the northern temperate zone. In the southern part of the region, many of the birds are permanent residents. In the northern part, most of the birds are summer residents only. In summer, the birds mate, lay and hatch their eggs, and raise their families. They then fly south for the winter. Mexico and Central America are part of North America. But most of the birds that reside there permanently are more closely related to those of South America than to U.S. and Canadian birds.

The birds of temperate North America live in seven main kinds of habitats: (1) urban areas, (2) forests and woodlands, (3) grasslands, (4) brushy areas, (5) deserts, (6) inland waters and marshes, and (7) seacoasts. Some North American birds live north of the temperate zone—that is, in the Arctic.

Birds of urban areas. Many birds will nest in urban areas if these areas have nesting places similar to those of the birds' natural habitat. In addition to pigeons and starlings, such birds include robins, blue jays, mockingbirds, cardinals, wrens, common crows, grackles, and house sparrows. Cardinals and mockingbirds usually nest in shrubs or low trees. Robins and blue jays nest in shade trees. Wrens nest inside tree holes, bird boxes, and even mailboxes. House sparrows and pigeons, both introduced from Europe, rank among the most common birds in North American cities. They will nest in almost any small opening. Such birds remain a familiar sight even in the downtown areas of big cities.

Steller's jay

Birds of forests and woodlands. Some North American birds live chiefly in *needleleaf* forests—that is, forests in which the dominant trees have narrow, needlelike leaves, such as firs, pines, and spruces. Needleleaf forests cover much of Canada and Alaska and mountainous areas of the western United States. Typical birds of these forests include the Blackburnian warbler, common creeper, gray jay, red-breasted nuthatch, ruby-crowned kinglet, and winter wren.

Certain other birds live chiefly in forests of *broadleaf* trees, which have broad, flat leaves that fall off each autumn. Such trees include the ash, beech, elm, maple, and oak. Broadleaf forests grow mainly in the eastern half of the United States and southeastern Canada. Typical birds of these forests include the American redstart, Baltimore oriole, ovenbird, scarlet tanager, tufted titmouse, and white-breasted nuthatch. Some birds, such as the hairy woodpecker and yellow-bellied sapsucker, inhabit both needleleaf forests and broadleaf forests.

Certain birds prefer *open woodlands* to dense forests. Open woodlands are areas of scattered trees. They are found mainly on the edges of forests, along riverbanks, and in suburban areas. Birds that nest in open woodlands include the cedar waxwing, downy woodpecker, house wren, rose-breasted grosbeak, yellow-billed cuckoo, and northern flicker. Red-eyed vireos live in almost any area that has broadleaf trees.

Many birds inhabit a particular level of a forest or woodland. For example, grosbeaks, tanagers, and many kinds of wood warblers live mainly in the treetops. Nuthatches and woodpeckers live farther down on the branches and trunks. Ovenbirds and winter wrens live chiefly on the forest or woodland floor.

Birds of grasslands. Until the mid-1800s, prairies covered much of central North America. The tall prairie grasses were a favorite nesting place of many birds. Today, most prairies have been plowed under for use as cropland. The birds that have adjusted best to these changes are those that traditionally nest in other open areas in addition to prairies. Such birds include the American kestrel, dickcissel, horned lark, vesper sparrow, western kingbird, and western meadowlark. Today, these birds nest as readily in or near hayfields and other cultivated grasslands as they do in native prairies. Horned larks even nest on golf courses.

Some prairie birds have had great difficulty adjusting to the changes in their habitat. For example, prairie-chickens once ranked among the most numerous prairie birds. But prairie-chickens nest only among tall grasses. Today, they live only in the few remaining native prairies.

Dry grasslands, now used mostly for grazing cattle, cover much of the western parts of the United States and Canada. Birds that nest in these grasslands include the burrowing owl, lark bunting, scissor-tailed flycatcher, and Baird's sparrow. Except for the burrowing owl, these birds have fared better than many of the prairie birds because their nesting places have been less disturbed by agriculture. Burrowing owls traditionally nest in prairie dog burrows. Ranchers have regarded prairie dogs as pests, however, and have tried to destroy their burrows. In so doing, they have wiped out the nesting places of the owls.

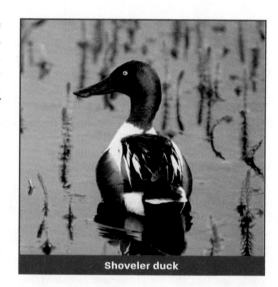

Shoveler duck

Birds of brushy areas. Some birds make their home in and around brushy areas, which are covered by bushes and low scrubby trees. Such areas commonly occur on the edges of forests and woodlands, between woodlands and grasslands, and in abandoned fields that are developing into woodlands. Brushy areas exist throughout the United States and southern Canada. Many of the birds that live in these habitats are also wide ranging. They include the eastern towhee, gray catbird, loggerhead shrike, rufous-sided towhee, and yellow-breasted chat. Other birds of brushy habitats have a more limited range. The bobwhite and Carolina wren are permanent residents in the southeastern United States and in Mexico. The painted bunting nests chiefly in the southeastern half of the United States but migrates to Mexico in winter.

Birds of the desert. Many birds that live in the deserts of the southwestern United States nest in saguaros and other large cactuses. The cactus wren builds its nest among cactus spines. Gila woodpeckers and gilded flickers nest in holes that they make in cactus stems. Elf owls, the smallest owls in the world, nest in holes that the woodpeckers abandon. A large percentage of desert birds chiefly eat animal flesh or insects. The deserts are dry, and such a diet provides more moisture than a diet of seeds. Meat-eating birds, including the golden eagle, roadrunner, and various species of owls, rank among the most common desert birds. Most of the cactus dwellers mainly eat insects. Gambel's quail and several species of sparrows are among the few ground-nesting, seed-eating birds of the North American deserts.

Birds of inland waters and marshes.
Most water birds swim after their food or dive or wade into the water for it. Few water birds live near fast-moving rivers because swimming, diving, and wading are difficult in a strong current. Lakes, ponds, and marshes are the chief freshwater habitats of birds. The birds nest on the shores of lakes and ponds and on high ground in marshes.

Typical swimming and diving birds of U.S. and Canadian fresh waters include the American coot, California gull, common loon, horned grebe, king rail, and many kinds of ducks. Among the ducks are the American wigeon, blue-winged teal, canvasback, and shoveler. Although some of these birds are excellent swimmers, a number of them feed mostly by wading at the edge of the water. Common wading birds include the American bittern, common snipe, great blue heron, and spotted sandpiper.

Some land birds have adopted ways of life that keep them near water. For example, the marsh wren, common yellowthroat, and red-winged blackbird often nest in marshes. The Louisiana waterthrush nests on the banks of streams and feeds on water insects. Belted kingfishers perch alongside bodies of water. Kingfishers dive after fish that swim near the surface and catch them with their bills.

Some birds of inland waters and marshes also live in saltwater environments. For example, the belted kingfisher, great blue heron, and green-backed heron often nest near the ocean and hunt fish in the shallow coastal waters. Most water birds of the United States and Canada fly south for the winter. Many of these birds make their winter homes near salt water.

Birds of the seacoasts. Some American and Canadian water birds normally nest along seacoasts. Along the Atlantic coast, such birds include the American oystercatcher, black skimmer, and common tern. The black oystercatcher, western gull, and Cassin's auklet nest along the Pacific coast. The brown pelican, laughing gull, and Wilson's plover nest along both coasts. Some species, such as oystercatchers and plovers, are shore birds. Certain others, including auks and auklets, gulls, and terns, sometimes hunt fish far out at sea.

In winter, the southeast, south, and southwest coasts of North America provide homes to numerous ducks, geese, and many other birds that nest in the Arctic. Many sandpipers and other Arctic birds visit U.S. and Canadian shores en route to winter homes in the tropics.

Birds of the Arctic. Northernmost North America, Asia, and Europe lie in the Arctic. Most of this land is *tundra*—that is, cold, dry, treeless marshland. The Arctic tundra remains frozen solid most of the year. It comes to life briefly in spring and summer. At that time, the tundra provides a rich source of the insects and other small animals that birds eat. Many birds that winter in warmer climates arrive in the tundra to breed. Most are water birds. They include the lesser golden-plover, Arctic tern, Canada goose, parasitic jaeger, red phalarope, and many species of ducks and sandpipers. Land birds that migrate to the tundra include the horned lark and snow bunting.

Only a few birds live in the Arctic all year. Probably the best known are ptarmigans. These extremely hardy, chicken-like birds survive almost entirely on twigs and leaf buds during the long Arctic winters.

Seagulls

Birds of Other Regions

Birds of the oceans and the Antarctic. Some birds spend most of their lives far out at sea and seldom visit land except to breed. These birds include albatrosses, gannets, penguins, petrels, shearwaters, and storm-petrels. All these birds except penguins are expert long-distance fliers. Penguins cannot fly. But they swim long distances and remain at sea for months at a time. Ocean birds feed by diving for fish, squid, and other small animals. They typically build their nests in crowded colonies. Other birds often hunt far out at sea but return to land regularly. These birds include boobies, frigatebirds, tropicbirds, and the south polar skua.

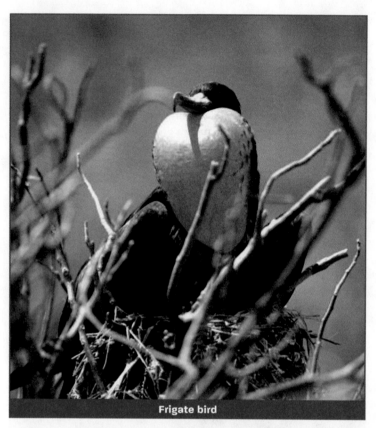

Frigate bird

Many ocean birds nest on Antarctic islands during summer in the south polar region. A few types nest on the ice-covered Antarctic continent itself. These hardy species include the emperor penguin, snow petrel, south polar skua, and Wilson's storm-petrel.

Birds of Central and South America.

Central America and most of South America lie in the tropics. The American tropics have more species of birds than does any other area of the same size in the world. Most birds of this region inhabit rainforests. The rest live in grasslands, deserts, dry forests, or near bodies of water. Several of the birds belong to families found nowhere else, including antshrikes, trumpeters, and the hoatzin and sunbittern. Many birds of the region have remarkably colorful plumage, such as the paradise tanager, resplendent quetzal, scarlet macaw, and scarlet ibis. The male Andean cock-of-the-rock performs an elaborate courtship display to attract a mate. The king vulture soars high above the tropical forest, watching for *carrion* (dead animals) to eat. The keel-billed toucan uses its massive bill to pluck fruit and berries. It also eats insects, reptiles, and some baby birds.

Birds of Europe.

Europe encompasses a wide range of habitats, from the Arctic in the far north; through the northern needleleaf forests, where many firs and spruces grow; to mixed woodland and dry Mediterranean *maquis* (scrub).

Many European birds migrate south, mostly to Africa, to escape the cold winters when food is scarce. Migratory species include the European roller, common tern, common cuckoo, European bee-eater, Eurasian hobby, bluethroat, swallow, wallcreeper, and white stork. The hobby, a magnificent flier, preys on such fast-flying birds as swallows and swifts, as well as on such insects as dragonflies. Several of the smaller perching birds, including the common nightingale and the Eurasian sky lark, have become well known for their fine songs. The house sparrow and the blue tit rank among Europe's most common birds. The green woodpecker hunts in the trees for insects or tree grubs and on the ground for ants. Goldfinches also inhabit European woodlands. Common water birds include avocets, moorhens, and shelducks. Grassland birds include lapwings and partridges.

Birds of Asia.

Asia, the largest of the world's continents, has a wide variety of climates. These include tropical rainforests, temperate forests, deserts, marshlands, and Arctic tundra. Such birds as broadbills, fairy-bluebirds, fruit-doves, hornbills, and leafbirds inhabit Asian forests. The male rhinoceros hornbill, like other tree-nesting hornbills, walls up his mate into a nest hole while she incubates the eggs. The golden-fronted leafbird lives in *monsoon forests*, which have a long dry season followed by a season of heavy rainfall. The trees in a monsoon forest usually shed their leaves during the dry season and leaf out again at the start of the rainy season. The golden-fronted leafbird feeds on fruit and insects. The blue-backed fairy-bluebird and the lesser green broadbill eat mainly fruit. Many tropical southeast Asian birds, such as the blue-winged pitta and purple-throated sunbird, have multicolored plumage.

The Himalaya, the great mountain range in southern Asia, is a biologically rich area with many species of birds. The foothills of the Himalaya provide a home to several brightly colored members of the pheasant family, including the Himalayan monal and Lady Amherst's pheasant. The Himalayan monal lives in forests above 10,000 feet (3,000 meters) high. The male has a loud ringing call. The common myna inhabits dry hillsides in India.

Some cultivated areas of Asia have become habitats for such species as the coppersmith barbet and the Java sparrow. The coppersmith barbet lives in open woodland, including orchards and gardens. It has a distinctive, monotonous "tonk" call, which it repeats over long periods. The Java sparrow was originally native to the islands of Bali and Java but has been widely introduced to other regions. It commonly resides in open areas, including rice fields, and has become a popular pet.

Birds of Africa. The Sahara, a vast desert, stretches across northern Africa and separates the continent's northern Mediterranean coastline from the land to the south. As a result, Mediterranean Africa shares many bird species with southern Europe. South of the Sahara, much of Africa has a tropical climate and a richer bird life. Rainforests provide homes for such colorful birds as the emerald cuckoo, yellow-bellied wattle-eye, and hammerkop. Many kinds of weavers live in open woodlands. The tropical grasslands have two of the world's tallest birds, the ostrich and the secretary-bird, as well as guineafowl and the crowned crane. Water birds of tropical Africa include the shoebill, the African fish-eagle, and various ducks, jacanas, kingfishers, and pelicans. Madagascar, a large island off the southeast African coast, has many unique birds, including the cuckoo roller and the helmet vanga.

Birds of Australia and New Zealand. Australia and New Zealand boast a rich variety of birds. Australian birds include the superb lyrebird with its elaborate tail feathers, as well as the bell miner, brolga, eastern spinebill, grey butcherbird, Gouldian finch, spotted pardalote, superb fairy-wren, white-plumed honeyeater, and willie-wagtail. The wedge-tailed eagle ranks as one of the world's largest eagles. It feeds on mammals, reptiles, and other birds, and it can even tackle prey as large as young kangaroos. The laughing kookaburra, a kind of kingfisher, occasionally eats fish. But its normal diet consists of reptiles, small mammals, birds, caterpillars, insects, and worms.

Prominent New Zealand birds include the flightless kiwi, a relative of the ostrich, as well as the noisy kaka and the colorful tui. Native bellbirds and pigeons also live in this island nation.

Birds of the Pacific Islands. Most of the Pacific Islands have relatively few bird species. But many of these birds live nowhere else.

The nene, or Hawaiian goose, was rescued from the brink of extinction and reintroduced to Hawaii. The cardinal myzomela lives in scrub and woodland on Vanuatu, Samoa, Santa Cruz, and the Solomon Islands. The large ground-finch of the Galapagos Islands belongs to the group of finches studied by the British naturalist Charles Darwin when he developed his theory of *evolution* (how living things change over time). The almost flightless kagu of New Caledonia has become endangered, partly because it is threatened by cats, dogs, rats, and other predators introduced to the island by people. The 10 subspecies of blue-faced parrotfinches inhabit Australia and such Pacific islands as Vanuatu and the Solomon Islands. The rare blue lorikeet lives mostly on a few *atolls* (ring-shaped coral islands) in the Society Islands of French Polynesia.

Ostriches

How Birds Live

To survive as individuals, birds must obtain enough food and water and must defend themselves against predators. These activities require skills of movement, such as flying or swimming, and certain communications abilities. To survive as a species, each generation of birds must produce and raise offspring.

Most small birds from temperate climates live only a few years at most. Many birds die of hunger, disease, injury, exposure to bad weather, or the risks of migration. Numerous others are killed by *predators* (animals that prey on other animals). In spite of all the dangers they face, some birds manage to complete their normal life span. In general, big birds live longer than small ones. For example, albatrosses may live 40 years or more, but wrens are unlikely to survive as long as 15 years.

Birds generally have a better chance for survival in captivity than in the wild. As a result, the age records for most species are held by birds raised in zoos or as pets. The record holders include an eagle owl that lived to age 68 in a zoo and a pet parrot that lived to age 70.

How Birds Get Food

Birds have a higher body temperature than mammals. They therefore require more food in relation to their size than do mammals to maintain the higher temperature. In addition, small birds must eat relatively more than large ones because their bodies use up food energy faster. A tiny bird, such as a kinglet, may eat a third of its weight in food each day. A larger bird, such as a starling, may eat only about an eighth its weight. The amount that birds eat also depends on what they eat. For example, a given amount of nectar provides more energy than the same amount of seeds. A nectar-eating bird thus needs less food than a seedeater of the same size. Large birds can go several days without food. Small birds may spend most of their time eating. To survive a cold night, in fact, some small birds must burn off the body fat they have stored from food eaten earlier that day.

Like all other animals, birds must regularly replace the water that their bodies lose. However, birds do not produce such fluid wastes as sweat and urine. They lose only a small amount of moisture in their droppings and when they exhale. Birds therefore require less water than do many other animals. Birds that eat juicy foods, such as nectar or insects, may get all or most of the water they need in their food and may seldom have to drink. Some birds, including the hummingbirds and sunbirds that feed on flower nectar, consume much more water than they actually need. Nearly all birds drink water by scooping it up in their bill, tilting the head back, and letting the drops trickle down the throat.

Kinds of food. Birds mainly eat insects, fish, meat, seeds, and fruits. Many bird species prefer one type of food, while others consume a wide variety.

Many birds live largely on insects. Insect eaters include creepers, flycatchers, kinglets, nightjars, swallows, swifts, thrashers, titmice, vireos, warblers, woodpeckers, and small hawks and owls. Some insect eaters also feed on spiders and earthworms. Fish-eating birds include cormorants, grebes, herons, kingfishers, loons, ospreys, pelicans, and terns. Many fish eaters also feed on other water animals, such as crabs and snails. Meat eaters, or birds of prey, live on the flesh of other birds, reptiles, and small mammals. The chief birds of prey include caracaras, eagles, falcons, hawks, owls, and vultures. Most of these birds hunt and kill their prey themselves. A few birds of prey eat mainly *carrion*—that is, the decaying flesh of dead animals. Vultures and caracaras are the chief carrion eaters.

Birds that feed mainly on seeds include buntings, finches, grosbeaks, pigeons, and sparrows. Most fruit-eating birds dwell in the tropics, where fruits are plentiful year-round. These birds include cotingas, hornbills, manakins, parrots, tanagers, and toucans. In cooler climates, many birds feed on fruits when available and on insects or seeds the rest of the year. Such birds include catbirds, mockingbirds, robins, and waxwings. Birds also get other food from plants besides fruits and seeds. Honeyeaters and hummingbirds live mainly on nectar from flowers. Sapsuckers often feed on tree sap. Ducks, geese, and swans eat all kinds of vegetable matter, including grass and seaweed.

Although most species prefer a certain food, fish eaters and meat eaters are among the few birds that live on only one kind of food. Most insect eaters also eat seeds or fruits, and most birds that feed on seeds or fruits feed their young primarily insects. A few birds eat almost any food they can find, even garbage. These birds include crows, gulls, ravens, and starlings.

Feeding methods. In most cases, the structure of a bird's bill or feet—or of its bill and feet—is adapted to its method of feeding. For

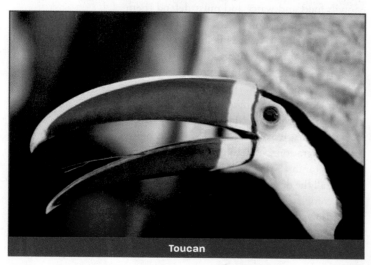

Toucan

example, birds of prey have sharp claws for seizing small animals and a hooked, razor-edged bill for tearing off flesh. The section *The bodies of birds* discusses such adaptations.

Some birds have developed highly specialized or unusual feeding methods. Swifts and swallows catch insects in flight by using their long, narrow wings to make fast aerial maneuvers and their extra-wide mouths to capture the insects. Hummingbirds can beat their wings in a circular fashion and so can hover in the air, like a helicopter. Hummingbirds use this skill to hover in front of flowers and collect nectar. They can also fly backward and so back their long bills out of a blossom. This method of feeding requires a lot of energy, so an active hummingbird uses more *calories* (units of energy) for its body weight than does any other vertebrate animal.

Some birds depend on other animals to help them get food. Cattle egrets and cowbirds follow herds of grazing animals and feed on insects startled by the animals' hoofs. Bald eagles, frigatebirds, jaegers, and skuas often steal fish from other birds. Honeyguides, which are found mainly in Africa, live largely on beeswax. The birds cannot get at the wax by themselves. Instead, they use loud calls to lead people and other mammals to beehives. These mammals open the hives and eat the honey. The birds then feast on the wax and the bee larvae.

How Birds Move

Birds move from one place to another chiefly by flying. Only a few kinds cannot fly. Some of these flightless birds are cassowaries, emus, kiwis, ostriches, rheas, and penguins. Most birds also can move about on land. The chief exceptions are grebes, loons, hummingbirds, kingfishers, and swifts. The legs of grebes and loons are so far back on the body that the birds can barely walk or even stand. On land, they can barely push themselves along on their belly. However, their legs are ideally positioned for underwater swimming. The legs and feet of hummingbirds, kingfishers, and swifts are suited to clinging or perching but not to walking. These birds can move from place to place only by flying.

Many birds can swim, as well as fly and move about on land. Some birds swim by paddling with their legs, such as ducks, loons, cormorants, and grebes. Others swim by flapping their wings as if in flight under water. These underwater flyers include penguins, auks, puffins, murres, and diving petrels.

Hummingbird

Some of the best swimmers, such as penguins and loons, are handicapped in other movements. Penguins cannot fly, and loons cannot walk.

In the air. A bird's wing is curved on top and flat or slightly curved on the bottom. When air moves rapidly past a wing of this shape, the air flows faster over the curved top surface than over the flatter bottom surface. The flow of air over the wing produces an upward force called *lift*. Lift enables birds to overcome gravity, rise, and remain airborne.

Experts disagree on the best explanation of lift. According to one explanation, the faster airflow over the wing's top surface reduces the air pressure above the wing. Air pushes more strongly against the bottom of the wing, producing lift. Another explanation is related to the wing's ability to *deflect* (turn) the airflow downward. As the air is forced downward, the wing is pushed upward, producing lift.

Birds launch themselves into the air by using their leg muscles to push against a perch or to jump from the ground or water. Some water birds, such as coots and sea ducks, paddle rapidly and flap their wings until they gain enough speed to become airborne. During flight, the tips of a bird's wings not only flap up and down but also twist forward on the downstroke and flatten on the upstroke. This twisting motion produces *forward thrust* and propels the bird forward. The rest of the wing remains level in relation to the flow of air, providing lift. Similarly, helicopter blades change angle twice in each rotation to produce lift and thrust from the moving blades.

After take-off, some birds continue to fly mainly by flapping their wings. Others combine flapping flight with gliding or soaring. In gliding, birds keep their wings extended and coast downward through the air, using little energy. In soaring, birds use the energy of air movements to propel themselves without having to flap their wings. They may use wind, heated rising air called *thermals*, or the lift of air along a cold front.

The majority of small birds depend on flapping flight. In most cases, their cruising speed averages about 20 to 35 miles per hour (mph), or about 32 to 56 kilometers per hour (kph). Most fast fliers are large birds with long, pointed wings. The peregrine falcon has been clocked at speeds over 200 mph (320 kph) while diving. Many soaring birds are large ocean birds that have long, pointed wings. Examples of such birds include albatrosses, frigate-birds, gulls, ospreys, shearwaters, and tropicbirds. Ocean soarers take advantage of the frequent strong winds near the surface of the world's oceans. Soaring land birds include hawks, eagles, and vultures. Unlike the ocean soarers, soaring land birds have long, but broad, rounded wings. Many wild fowl, such as pheasants and quail, have short, broad, rounded wings. Birds with such wings can take off suddenly and fly at high speeds for a short distance. These birds seldom make long flights, however.

Hummingbirds, kestrels, and terns are among the few kinds of birds that can hover in flight. In addition, hummingbirds are the only birds that can fly backward.

On land. Birds move about on land by running, walking, hopping, and climbing. The big flightless land birds can run the fastest. Nearly all of them have extremely long legs. Ostriches, the speediest birds on land, can run as fast as 40 mph (64 kph). Some birds that can fly are also swift runners. These birds include bustards, cariamas, and the secretary-bird. Most other birds move more slowly on land.

The majority of birds that nest or feed on the ground walk and run by moving one foot forward at a time, like people. Most species that nest or feed in trees hop about on both feet when on the ground. Some kinds of birds both run and hop. For example, robins often run a short distance and then hop the last few steps before stopping. Some birds are expert climbers, especially those species that climb trees in search of insects. Such birds include creepers, nuthatches, woodcreepers, and woodpeckers. All these birds have short legs and sharp, widely spaced claws, which enable them to cling tightly to the tree while climbing. One such bird, the wallcreeper, uses these claws to climb steep, rocky cliffs and boulders.

In the water. Many species of birds spend much or most of their time in water. They find food and escape from enemies by swimming or diving. Some of these birds swim mainly on the surface of the water. Such birds include albatrosses, gulls, petrels, phalaropes, and shearwaters. The birds use their legs and feet like paddles to propel themselves through the water.

Certain other birds swim underwater as well as on the surface. Most underwater swimmers, such as cormorants, dive from a floating position on the surface. They give a strong kick, point the head downward, and plunge. Some fish-eating birds, including kingfishers and terns, dive into the water from high in the air. They do not swim but bob to the surface and fly away. Most birds use only their legs and feet to swim underwater. However, penguins also use their wings. Grebes can control the depth at which they swim by regulating the amount of air in their lungs and trapped in their plumage. By slowly letting out air, they can gradually submerge themselves until only the head shows above the surface, like a periscope. They can thus swim along unnoticed and watch for enemies at the same time.

How Birds Communicate

Birds communicate with one another in a variety of ways. Vocal communication by songs and calls ranks as the most important way.

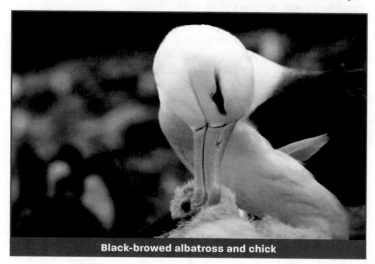
Black-browed albatross and chick

Calls and songs. Nearly all birds have a voice and use it to call or sing. A call usually consists of a single sound, such as a squawk or peep. A song consists of a series of notes that follow a fairly definite pattern. About half the known species of birds, including nearly all perching species, produce both calls and songs. The majority of other birds, including most water birds and birds of prey, call but do not sing. Pelicans, American vultures, condors, and some kinds of storks are among the few birds that make no vocal sounds.

Birds use their calls mainly as signals to other birds. Baby birds call in one way to tell their parents that they are hungry and in another way to tell them that they are hurt or frightened. Adult birds use certain calls to signal mates and other calls to signal the entire bird community. Calls may warn of approaching danger, often alerting birds of more than one species.

When people think of songbirds, they usually think of canaries, nightingales, and other birds with sweet voices. But some birdsong is not particularly pleasing to human ears. Ravens and waxwings, for example, simply repeat the same unmusical note over and over. In most songbirds, only the males sing. They do so chiefly during the mating season. Each male sings from a series of perches that outlines his *territory*—that is, the area he claims and defends as his own. His song, which is called an *advertising song*, has two main purposes: (1) it warns other males of the same species to stay out of the territory, and (2) it attracts a mate. Some birds use different songs for each purpose. To human ears, the songs of all the birds of a particular species may sound alike. But each bird's voice sounds different to the other members of the species. Even in a crowded colony, parent birds can single out the voices of their chicks, and chicks recognize those of their parents. *Ornithologists* (bird biologists) and bird watchers learn to distinguish many kinds of birds from their songs alone.

Birds produce their songs with a unique vocal organ called the *syrinx*. The syrinx of most birds occurs where the main airway, or *trachea*, branches into the two smaller air passages, called the *bronchi*, which go to the lungs. Many birds can produce two different songs at the same time, one with each side of the syrinx. These "two voice" songs include the most beautiful, flutelike songs of the thrushes. Some birds use one side of the syrinx to make lower tones and the other side to make higher tones.

Most birds do not have to learn to make the right vocal calls. In a few groups of birds, however, the young learn many details of their songs from adult members of their species. Birds known to learn their songs include the true songbirds—such as crows, sparrows, thrushes, and warblers—as well as parrots and hummingbirds.

Sometimes a bird makes a "mistake" when it learns a song. Over time, such mistakes in song learning can produce dialects, or regional variations, in the songs within a single species.

Some birds who learn their songs become talented mimics. They not only learn from their own species, but they also imitate the calls and songs of other birds. They can even learn to mimic sounds not originally created by birds, such as dog barks or factory whistles.

Red-necked grebe

One of the most remarkable mimics, the Lawrence's thrush of tropical South America, can mimic hundreds of species. Mockingbirds and starlings also rank among the most skillful bird mimics. Certain song-learning birds, such as parrots and mynas, become mimics only when kept in captivity. They can then be trained to imitate human speech and even to whistle.

Other means of communication. Some birds communicate by sounds other than vocal sounds. The loud drumming noise that woodpeckers make on tree trunks with their bill is not the sound they produce when drilling for insects or digging a nest hole. Drumming is their substitute for an advertising song to establish territories and attract mates. Each species of woodpecker has its own drumming rhythms. The male ruffed grouse produces a low drumming sound by beating his wings rapidly. This sound, which carries across long distances, also serves as an advertising song. Male and female storks clatter their bills at one another during their courtship. Some male manakins make snapping sounds with their wings during courtship displays.

Birds communicate almost entirely by sounds in habitats where they may have difficulty seeing one another. Such habitats include thick woodlands and forests. In more open areas, birds also communicate with one another by various kinds of visual displays. For example, they may flash their tail feathers or raise the crest feathers on their head. Like sound communication, sight communication is used in courtship, defending a territory, and signaling danger. Unlike mammals and insects, most birds are not known to communicate with one another using smells. Crested auklets, however,

Flamingos

produce a tangerine-like odor during the nesting season. The birds may use this odor to make themselves more attractive to mates.

Other Daily Activities

Birds spend time every day keeping their feathers in good condition. They also sleep and rest every day. In addition, all birds, except perhaps the largest ones, must constantly be alert to avoid enemies.

Feather care. A bird cares for its feathers chiefly by cleaning and smoothing them with its beak, a process called *preening*. A bird uses its feet to preen its head and other hard-to-reach parts. Most birds oil their feathers while preening. A *preen gland* on the lower back at the base of the tail produces the oil. A bird uses its beak to activate the gland and apply the oil to its feathers. The oil helps keep the feathers waterproof and flexible.

In addition to preening, most birds bathe frequently. Water birds bathe while swimming. Land birds have less efficient preen glands than do most water birds. Their feathers thus become soaked with water more easily. Most land birds wet their feathers only slightly when bathing and then shake them dry as quickly as possible. Other birds practice a form of bathing called *dusting*. The birds squat on dusty ground and churn up the dust with their feet and wings until their fluffed-up feathers are thoroughly covered. They then stand up and shake the dust off. Scientists do not fully understand the reasons for dusting. It probably helps rid the feathers and skin of lice and other parasites.

Some birds pick up ants with their bill and rub them into their feathers. This process is known as *anting*. The ants give off a chemical called *formic acid*, which probably helps eliminate feather mites, another common parasite of birds. Birds have also been observed using anting motions as they rubbed their feathers with such things as cigarette butts, berries, and grasshoppers.

Sleeping and resting. Most birds search for food during the day and sleep at night. They may also rest and take short naps during the day. Nighttime feeders, such as owls, sleep throughout the day. During the breeding season, most birds sleep in or near their nest. The rest of the time, they sleep on the branches of trees or bushes, on ledges, in holes, or on the bare ground.

Many species of birds sleep while perching on one or both feet. These birds have a locking mechanism in their feet. It makes their toes grip the perch and so prevents the birds from falling. After the nesting season, many kinds of birds sleep together in large groups called *roosts*. Most roosts congregate in trees, but some form in marshes. Roosts of crows, robins, red-winged blackbirds, or starlings may consist of thousands of birds.

Some swifts, hummingbirds, and nightjars can lower their body temperature before going to sleep in cold weather. They thus conserve energy while sleeping in much the same way as hibernating mammals. Nightjars can hibernate for weeks. Some hummingbirds hibernate every night even though they live in tropical rain forests.

Scientists believe sleep is critical for song learning in birds. The cells of the brain that are responsible for generating the song give off the same signals during sleep as they do when the bird is singing. Biologists think these brain signals show that birds dream of their songs. Such dreaming apparently aids birds in learning songs.

Protection against enemies. Birds frequently have to protect themselves or their offspring against enemies. Many birds are colored or marked in such a way that they blend with their surroundings. These birds can protect themselves from a predator simply by remaining still and avoiding the animal's notice. This type of concealment is called *protective coloration*. In other cases, a bird may have to flee or hide—or it may flee and then hide. If all such methods fail, a bird might have to fight.

A bird fights with its beak, legs, or wings—or with all of them—depending on its species. In defending its nest against a predator, a bird often flies at the intruder's head and calls loudly. However, a bird seldom wins a fight against a predator larger than itself. Among some species of ground-nesting birds, a bird may lure a ground predator away from its nest by dragging one of its wings as if it were broken. An intruder, attracted by what appears to be an injured bird, may be led a safe distance away from the nesting place before the "crippled" parent bird flies off.

Family Life of Birds

Most small and medium-sized birds become sexually mature by the age of 1 year. Larger birds may take two or more years to mature. They can then mate and raise a family. The breeding process usually begins in spring. At that time, the males of most species select a territory and court a mate. The process continues with the building of a nest and the

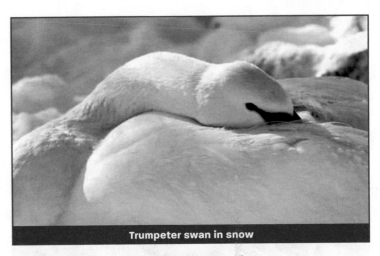

Trumpeter swan in snow

laying and hatching of eggs. The cycle is complete when the offspring mature and prepare to raise families of their own. Adult birds may raise a new family once or twice a year for as long as they live.

Selecting a territory. A bird's territory may be small or large. It may contain only the nest, or it may include an area large enough to gather all food for the young. After selecting his territory, a male claims it by singing his advertising song. Gulls, penguins, and other water birds nest in large colonies. But even in the biggest colonies, each male and his mate have their own small territory around their nest. Some birds return to the same nesting site every year.

A male defends a territory chiefly against other males of the same species. In some cases, a warning call or threatening pose is the only defense necessary. But in many cases, the intruder may not leave without a fight.

Courtship and mating. The relationship between a male and a female bird is known as a *pair bond*. A pair bond usually forms after a series of courtship displays by the male and a favorable response from the female. Each species has its own displays and responses.

The male's advertising song is one of the chief courtship displays among songbirds. Males of other species depend more on bright colors or attention-getting movements and postures. Male frigatebirds have a bright-red neck pouch, which they inflate like a balloon. The courtship displays of many species of birds consist of movements of the head, wings, or other body parts. Cranes, grebes, and herons perform elaborate movements. The female's response may closely resemble the male's display, and so the two appear to dance together.

Peacock

bond with more than one female at a time. Each female has a nest within the male's territory.

Building a nest. Most kinds of birds build nests, which vary from simple to elaborate structures. The female typically does all or most of the work. If the males help, they chiefly provide building materials.

Most bird nests are bowl- or saucer-shaped structures of such materials as twigs, grass, and leaves. Birds build such nests on the ground, in bushes and trees, on ledges, and in holes. The nests of the smallest hummingbirds measure only about 1 inch (2.5 centimeters) high. Ospreys build nests as thick as 6 feet (1.8 meters). Many birds cement the building material together with sticky substances. Blue jays and American robins use mud. Hummingbirds and gnatcatchers use sticky threads from spider webs. Swifts use their own thick, gummy saliva. Hardened saliva not only holds the nest together but also cements it to the nesting place, such as the wall of a cave or the inside of a chimney.

Some kinds of birds do not build bowl- or saucer-shaped nests. Most woodpeckers and kingfishers nest in holes that they make by using their bill as a digging tool. Woodpeckers dig the holes in dead trees. Kingfishers, motmots, and bank swallows dig nests in banks of sand or clay. Many birds make nests that are completely enclosed except for a small entrance. Weavers of tropical Africa use their bill and feet to weave such nests of grasses and plant fibers. The nests hang from tree branches or reeds. Some kinds of swallows construct enclosed nests of mud cemented to the sides of cliffs, caves, hollow trees, or even houses and office buildings.

Some birds cooperate in building an enormous community nest in which each pair has its own "apartment." Such birds include several species of African weavers, the monk parakeet of South America, and the palmchat of the Caribbean region.

Many birds do not build a nest. Most falcons and nightjars, for example, simply lay their eggs on bare ground. Certain other birds nest in hollow trees, in nest boxes, in holes in the ground, or in the abandoned nests of other birds. Such birds include bluebirds, house sparrows, parrots, tree swallows, wrens, and some owls. Starlings often chase other birds from the birds' nests and then use the nests themselves. The brown-headed cowbird and European cuckoo also lay their eggs in the nests of other birds.

Males of some species use *leks* (small display territories) to attract mates. Some male peacocks and birds-of-paradise, for example, display their elaborate and beautiful plumages within the leks. The males of species that use leks do not participate in nesting or parental care.

Most male bowerbirds build elaborate stick constructions called *bowers*, which they decorate with colorful objects to impress females. Female birds visit the bowers and choose one mate. After mating, they then leave, build a nest away from the males, and raise the young on their own.

Although the male courts the female in most species, the reverse is true among phalaropes and a few other kinds of birds. In these species, females are more brightly colored than males. The females thus display their plumage to the males, which respond to the females' advances. Among other birds, including certain species of jacanas, the female claims the territory and may mate with several different males. The males build the nest, care for the eggs, and raise the young while the female defends the territory.

By the end of the courtship period, most adult birds have a mate. Most birds mate for one season only. But some have the same mate for more than a year or for life. These birds include many albatrosses, penguins, ravens, storks, swans, and terns. In other species, such as the common yellowthroat and red-winged blackbird, a male may have a pair

Laying and hatching eggs. Birds reproduce sexually. In sexual reproduction, a *sperm* (male sex cell) unites with an *egg* (female sex cell) in a process called *fertilization*. The fertilized egg develops into a new individual. The first stage in this development is the formation of an *embryo*. In almost all mammals, the embryo develops inside the body of the female. In birds, the female lays the fertilized egg before the embryo starts to grow. After the egg has been laid, it must be *incubated* (kept warm) for the embryo to develop into a chick.

Female birds lay one egg at a time. Usually, the female produces an egg every day or two. The entire set of eggs produced, called a *clutch*, varies in size. Most birds lay clutches of 2 to 8 eggs. A few birds, including pheasants and grouse, lay clutches of 15 or more eggs. Some species, including albatrosses, petrels, and many auks, penguins, and pigeons, have a clutch of one.

Birds' eggs differ greatly in size. Among living birds, hummingbirds lay the smallest eggs, and ostriches lay the biggest. A hummingbird egg weighs less than $1/50$ ounce (0.6 gram). An ostrich egg weighs about 3 pounds (1.4 kilograms). Eggs of the extinct elephant bird, a larger relative of the ostrich, could weigh up to 20 pounds (9.1 kilograms). Such eggs are the largest known single cells in any animal. Most birds' eggs are shaped like domestic chicken eggs, but some species produce eggs of slightly different shape. For example, the eggs of auks and certain other cliff-nesting species are sharply pointed at one end, preventing them from rolling off the cliff. Many birds have plain-colored eggs. The eggs of most ground nesters are camouflaged with speckles and other markings. Such markings occur because of chemical pigments deposited in the shell during its development.

Nearly all birds incubate their eggs by sitting on them. In many species, such as pigeons and starlings, the parents take turns incubating the eggs. Among other kinds of birds, only the female incubates. In a few species, including phalaropes, the male does all the incubating. The megapodes, a group of ground-dwelling birds in Australia, Indonesia, and the Pacific Islands, do not incubate their eggs by sitting on them. In many megapode species, males and occasionally females build a large pile of rotting vegetation. The female lays an egg in a hole at the center of the mound and then covers the egg with vegetation and soil. Heat from the rotting vegetation warms the egg. Other megapode species bury their eggs in sandy beaches and let solar heat warm them. Still others warm their eggs by burying them near volcanoes. These areas receive much *geothermal heat*, or heat produced from within the earth.

The incubation period ranges from 10 days in some small songbirds to 80 days in large albatrosses. By the end of this period, the embryo has developed into a chick and is ready to hatch out of the egg. Many chicks have a hard, sharp bump called an *egg tooth* near the tip of the bill. A chick uses the egg tooth to break through the shell. The egg tooth falls off or gradually disappears after the chick hatches. Some chicks have egg teeth at the tips of both halves of the bill.

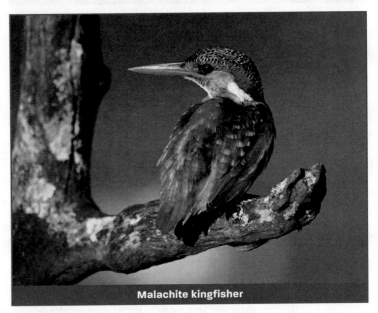
Malachite kingfisher

Caring for the young. Most newborn chicks are blind, practically featherless, and so weak-legged they cannot stand. Such birds are called *altricial*. They include baby hummingbirds, kingfishers, pelicans, swifts, and all songbirds. In other species, the newborn chicks can see, and they have a covering of fine down and strong legs. These birds are called *precocial*. They include all baby chickens, ducks, geese, megapodes, ostriches, quails, swans, and turkeys. Precocial young can walk from the nest and start to hunt for food a few hours or days after hatching. Altricial young must remain in the nest far longer and be cared for by their parents.

In most cases, the parents of altricial chicks feed them juicy insects or other foods containing much moisture. Gradually, the babies see, grow feathers,

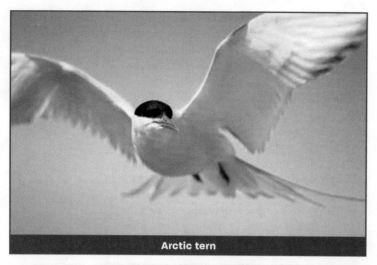

Arctic tern

and become stronger. They then begin to stand at the edge of the nest and stretch their wings. In time, they start to make short, clumsy flights. All birds fly without being taught. But many need months of practice to fly skillfully.

In certain birds, other individuals of the same species help the parents raise the young in the nest. This behavior is called *cooperative breeding*. The helpers are often the young from a previous year's clutch of the same parents. In North America, cooperative breeding occurs in such birds as the acorn woodpecker, Florida scrub jay, groove-billed ani, and red-cockaded woodpecker.

Brood parasites. Some birds rely on birds of other species to raise their family. Such birds are known as *brood parasites*. The foster parents are called *hosts*. Brood parasites include the brown-headed cowbird and European cuckoo. Females of these species lay eggs in the nests of songbirds, next to the eggs of the hosts. The hosts not only hatch the eggs of the brood parasites with their own but also raise the chicks. Chicks of most brood parasites survive by dominating the hosts' young and gaining more food from the host parents.

Bird Migration

The migration of birds remains one of the most fascinating and least understood events in nature. Birds are not especially strong. Yet numerous species migrate tremendous distances, often flying many hours or days without stopping. The blackpoll warbler, a North American bird no bigger than a sparrow, flies nonstop nearly 2,500 miles (4,023 kilometers) to its winter home in South America. The journey takes nearly 90 hours.

Many birds migrate farther than the blackpoll warbler, but only large birds fly farther without stopping. Arctic terns are the champions of long-distance migration. They fly about 11,000 miles (17,700 kilometers) from their breeding grounds in the Arctic to their winter home in the Antarctic. The birds return to the Arctic a few months later. They thus travel about 22,000 miles (35,400 kilometers) in less than a year. Many birds migrate enormous distances yet return to exactly the same nesting places every year. Scientists have learned much about why, where, and how birds migrate. But many questions remain unanswered.

Why birds migrate. In many parts of the world, the foods that birds eat become scarce during certain seasons of the year. Many birds, such as insect eaters, would starve if they had to remain in such places through the unfavorable season. This situation is especially true of regions with cold, snowy winters. The majority of birds that nest in these regions migrate to warmer climates in fall. They return in spring, when the weather warms up again. Many parts of the tropics have a dry season and a rainy season each year. Food and drinking water may become scarce during the dry season. Many birds avoid such shortages by migrating to moister parts of the tropics at the start of each dry season and returning after it ends. Other birds, which prefer to nest in dry areas, migrate to drier parts of the tropics during the rainy season.

Birds that do not migrate during the unfavorable season are species that can survive on the available food. Most birds that remain in northern areas over the winter live mainly on seeds, tree buds, and dry berries. Such birds include bobwhites, cardinals, grouse, and several kinds of finches and sparrows. Insects are scarce in northern regions during the winter. Most insect-eating birds therefore migrate. The majority of those that remain are small birds that live mainly on insect eggs and the developing young of insects. These birds include chickadees, nuthatches, titmice, and woodpeckers.

Although birds migrate to survive, the factors that actually trigger their migrations are much more difficult to explain. For example, many northern species leave their summer home while the weather is still warm and the food supply plentiful. The birds cannot know that the weather will turn cold and that food will become scarce.

Bird migrations are probably regulated by the glandular system. The glands produce chemical substances called *hormones*. Changes in hormone production stimulate the birds to migrate. Among some northern species, hormone production is affected by the length of daylight. As the daylight hours shorten, hormonal changes cause the birds to prepare for their migratory flight south. However, changes in daylight only partly explain the timing of migrations. Different species may depart from the same area at different times. In addition, the same species may not depart at the same time every year. The exact timing of migrations depends not only on the amount of daylight but also on such conditions as the weather and the food supply.

Where birds migrate. The great majority of birds that migrate travel in a generally north-south direction. Most birds that breed in Canada and the northern part of the United States fly south for the winter. Many migrate as far as tropical South America. Some even fly all the way to Argentina, Uruguay, or southern Chile. Many birds that breed in the United Kingdom and northern Europe migrate to southern Africa to spend the winter. The seasons south of the equator are opposite those in the north. Therefore, North American birds that migrate to southern South America and European birds that migrate to southern Africa arrive in time for summer in those regions. These birds and many of the native species fly northward at the start of the southern winter. However, no native South American birds migrate to North America. They fly only as far north as the tropics, spend the winter there, and then return south for the summer.

Certain species of migratory birds do not travel in an exact north-south direction. For example, several species that breed in western North America, such as avocets and white pelicans, migrate southeast to winter in Florida. Birds that breed on high mountain slopes may simply move down into the warmer valleys for the winter. In North America, such birds include the common raven, rosy finch, and mountain quail. Some birds make regular seasonal migrations within the tropics, but little is known about these movements.

Many species of birds migrate along the same routes. Birds tend to follow such physical features as coastlines, mountain ridges, and river valleys. Heavily traveled routes are known as flyways. North America, for example, has four main flyways: (1) the Pacific Flyway, along the Pacific coast; (2) the Central Flyway, which follows the Rocky Mountains; (3) the Mississippi Flyway, which follows the Mississippi River; and (4) the Atlantic Flyway, along the Atlantic coast. But these flyways are only approximate, and many birds migrate outside them. Some species use different flyways in different migrations. Such variations occur for many reasons. For example, food sources may prove abundant in one flyway during the fall and in a different flyway in spring. Also, some species alter their migratory routes to go with the prevailing wind patterns. Scientists have designated flyways chiefly to divide the continent into zones for administering laws that deal with the hunting of migratory birds.

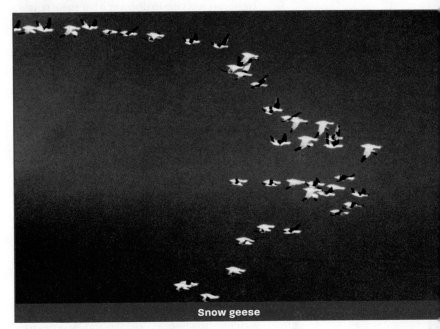
Snow geese

How birds migrate. Some species of birds migrate in small groups. Other species fly in flocks composed of as many as several million birds. Most small birds travel at night and stop to feed and rest during the day. Most large birds do the opposite. Birds that feed on flying insects, such as swallows, nighthawks, and swifts, often migrate during the day so they can feed as they migrate. The majority of migrating birds fly at altitudes of about 3,000 to 6,000 feet (914 to 1,829 meters). But some types, including various shorebirds and geese, have been detected by radar at 20,000 feet (6,096 meters) or higher.

The question of how migrating birds find their way to the same destination every year has long puzzled and fascinated scientists. Scientific research has provided several answers to this question. Birds that migrate over land probably follow landmarks, such as river valleys and mountain ranges. Day migrants can use the sun to find directions. Experiments have shown that some birds can navigate by using the stars. These birds orient themselves by observing the rotation of the stars at night. When landmarks, the sun, or the stars are not visible, birds may use the earth's magnetic field, an invisible region of magnetic force, to guide them. However, such theories raise even more puzzling questions. To navigate by magnetic fields, birds must have highly specialized and highly complicated sensory organs to sense magnetism. Scientists are working to discover what these sensory organs are and how they might function.

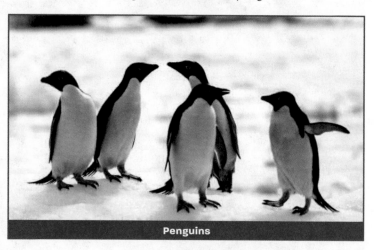

Penguins

The Bodies of Birds

The bodies of birds are adapted for flying. Even such flightless birds as penguins and ostriches have some features of their flying ancestors. All birds have a generally streamlined body and exceptionally lightweight skeletons, feathers, and internal organs.

External features. The most striking external feature of a bird is its feathers. Feathers cover all the main parts of a bird's body except the eyes, bill, legs, and feet. In some species, including some owls, even the legs and feet have feathers.

Feathers. Birds possess from 940 to 25,000 feathers. Most feathers have a stiff central *shaft*, on each side of which is a flat *vane*. The vane consists of hundreds of slender parallel branches from the shaft. These branches, or *barbs*, each have dozens of tinier branches called *barbules*. Variations in the shape of the shaft, barbs, and barbules create a wide variety of feather types.

The largest feathers are the long *flight feathers* of the wings and tail. Flight feathers near the wing's tip are called *primaries*. Those closer to the body are known as *secondaries*. A layer of smaller feathers called *coverts* covers the base of the flight feathers. In flight feathers, the barbules have microscopic hooks and grooves that zip together and hold neighboring barbs tightly to one another. Other vaned feathers called *contour feathers* cover the bodies of most birds.

In addition to vaned feathers, some birds have down feathers or plumes or both of these types. Most down feathers have a short shaft and soft, fuzzy barbs that are not connected into vanes. The barbules of down feathers lack the microscopic hooks and grooves of vaned feathers. Many water birds have a thick coat of down under the vaned feathers. Plumes are generally long feathers with flexible shafts and barbs. They may grow from different body parts and are used in courtship displays.

In many species of birds, the male has more brightly colored feathers than does the female. In a few species, females have the more colorful plumage. In other species, the male and female look alike.

Birds shed their feathers at least once a year and grow a new set. This process, called *molting,* generally occurs after the breeding season and enables birds to replace worn feathers. Most birds that molt twice a year have a different appearance in different seasons. The majority of these birds, including grebes and loons, are brightly colored in spring and summer and dull in fall and winter. In some species, including many ducks, only males alternate between a colorful and dull phase.

Bills of birds differ mainly according to how the birds feed. Finches, grosbeaks, and most other seed-eating birds have a hard, cone-shaped bill, which they use like a nutcracker. Woodpeckers possess a chisel-like bill, which they use to bore into trees to find insects.

Flamingos and many ducks eat plant and animal matter that floats on water. These birds have a broad bill with hundreds of tiny filters along the edges. This bill enables the birds to take big mouthfuls of water. The filters along the edges of the bill trap the food particles and let water drain away. Most fish-eating birds, such as anhingas, herons, and terns, have a long, pointed bill, which they use to spear fish. Pelicans use their unusually large bill and throat pouch to scoop fish from the water. Some land birds, such as hornbills and toucans, have a large, brightly colored bill. But most hornbills and toucans are fruit eaters. The huge size and bright colors of the bill are apparently unrelated to the method of feeding. They probably serve mainly for display.

Legs and feet. Although all birds have two legs and two feet, the size and structure of the limbs differ greatly among various species. Birds that spend most of their time in the air have exceptionally short legs. The legs of most tree climbers are also shorter than the average. On the other hand, most wading birds and fast runners have especially long legs.

The great majority of birds have four toes on each foot. In most species, including all songbirds, three toes point forward and one points backward. A perching bird steadies itself by curling the hind toes around a branch or other perch. Some birds that are good climbers, including cuckoos, parrots, and woodpeckers, have two toes pointing forward and two pointing backward. The hind toes help provide an extra grip for the birds as they climb. Emus and most other flightless, fast-running birds have lost the hind toe and have only three toes on each foot. The ostrich is the only two-toed bird.

Many swimming birds have webs of skin connecting their toes. The webbing enables the birds to use their feet like paddles. In such birds as ducks and gulls, the webbing connects only the three front toes. Cormorants, pelicans, and related birds have all four toes connected by webs. Instead of webbing, coots, grebes, and phalaropes have broad, paddle-like toes. Gallinules and screamers are also good swimmers, but their feet differ little from those of four-toed land birds.

Birds have a claw at the tip of each toe, but claws are not equally prominent in all species. Birds with large, sharp, curved claws include birds of prey and birds that cling to vertical surfaces, such as swifts and woodpeckers. Most running birds have short, blunt claws.

Skeleton and muscles. A bird's skeleton is lightweight but strong. Many bones that are separate in mammals are *fused* (joined together) in birds. The fused bones give the skeleton exceptional strength. The skeleton is lightweight chiefly because many of the bones are hollow.

The wings of a bird correspond to the arms or forelimbs of human beings and other *tetrapods* (four-limbed animals). Each wing has three main parts: (1) a single bone in the upper arm called the *humerus*, (2) a pair of bones, the *radius* and *ulna*, in the forearm, and (3) a hand with only three fingers. Primary flight feathers are attached to the bones of the hand, and secondary flight feathers are attached to the *ulna*.

A bird's chest includes a *sternum* (large breastbone) with a prominent center ridge called a keel. The major wing muscles are attached to the keel. Birds also have a wishbone, consisting of the fused *clavicles* (collarbones).

In birds that fly, the largest muscles are those that move the wings. Most birds have strong leg muscles, which are especially well developed in fast runners. Small muscles at the base of each feather enable a bird to maneuver its feathers, fluff them, display them, and keep the wind from blowing them around.

Senses. Birds have keen senses of sight and hearing. However, their senses of smell, taste, and touch are less well developed.

Sight. Birds have relatively large eyes. Unlike human eyes, however, the eyes of most birds are on the sides of the head. Because human eyes face forward, people have *binocular vision*—that is, the objects seen by each eye overlap extensively. Most birds have binocular vision only directly in front of them. They have *monocular vision* on either side— that is, the eye on each side of the head sees a separate view. Owls, woodcocks, and penguins are the chief exceptions. Owls are among the few birds with eyes on the front of the head. Thus owls have a large range of binocular vision. A woodcock's eyes are set so far back on the head that these birds have small areas of binocular vision behind their heads as well as in front. A penguin's eyes are set in the head in such a way that the bird has monocular vision only.

Great horned owls

Some birds can see even better under certain conditions than people can. Most birds have a higher concentration of sensory cells, called *rods* and *cones*, on the *retina*, a tissue at the back of the eyeball. This feature gives birds greater detail to their vision. Birds that are most active in the evening or at night have eyes that are extremely sensitive to light. Their vision in dim light is far superior to that of human beings. Diving birds seem to be able to focus their eyes equally well in the air and underwater. These birds can change focus much more rapidly than people can. Birds also see more colors than can human beings. For example, birds can detect colors created by ultraviolet rays. Experiments have shown that many kinds of birds use such colors in choosing mates.

Hearing. Birds have an ear on each side of the head, though it is not visible. The outer ear is simply an opening into the inner ear and is covered with feathers. Most birds probably hear at least as well as people. Some species have extremely sensitive hearing. Barn owls can capture mice in complete darkness by using their ears.

A few birds depend more on their sense of hearing than on their sight. They include the guacharo, or oilbird, of South America and several species of swiftlets that live in the East Indies. The birds nest and roost in dark caves and use a system called *echolocation* to navigate. As they fly in the dark, they make clicking sounds in the throat. The sounds bounce off the cave walls, creating echoes. The birds can tell from the echoes exactly how close they are to the walls and so can avoid hitting them.

Oilbirds

Smell, taste, and touch. Most birds probably have a sense of smell, but only a few species are known to depend on it heavily. Kiwis are nearly blind and use smell to locate food. Kiwis are the only birds with nostrils at the very tip of the bill. Albatrosses and other ocean birds use smell to locate food on the open sea.

Scientists know little about the senses of taste and touch in birds. All birds have a tongue with taste buds. But they have far fewer taste buds than do mammals, so their sense of taste is probably less developed. A bird's eyes are very sensitive to touch. If a speck of dust or other particle touches the eyeball, a special eyelid called a *nictitating membrane* sweeps across the eye and wipes it off. Some birds, such as sandpipers and woodcocks, also have a keen sense of touch at the tip of their bill. They use the bill to probe soil for insects and worms.

Systems of the body. The internal organs of birds, like those of other animals, are grouped into systems. The major systems include the respiratory, digestive, circulatory, nervous, and reproductive systems.

The respiratory system in birds, as in mammals, serves to transfer oxygen from the air to the bloodstream. Birds breathe air in through their nostrils and mouth. But a bird's respiratory system has some unusual features. In most *vertebrates* (animals with backbones), air flows in and out of the lungs in opposite directions. But in birds, the structure of the respiratory system enables air to cycle in and out of the lungs in only one direction. This type of airflow helps make birds efficient at transferring oxygen, enabling them to consume energy effectively for flight and to keep a high body temperature. The body temperature of birds averages about 106 degrees Fahrenheit (41 degrees Celsius), or more than 7 degrees Fahrenheit (4 degrees Celsius) higher than the average human body temperature.

Respiration has another important purpose in birds. Unlike mammals, birds lack sweat glands and thus cannot cool themselves by perspiring. Instead, birds pant, or breathe rapidly, to cool themselves.

The digestive system. Unlike almost all mammals, birds have no teeth and so cannot chew their food. They must either cut it up with their bill or swallow it whole. A bird's digestive system consists mainly of the esophagus, stomach, and intestines.

The esophagus is a tube-like organ with expandable walls. Food passes into it from the mouth.

In mammals, the esophagus leads directly into the stomach. In many birds, the esophagus has a bag-like swelling called the *crop*. Birds can store food in the crop until there is room for it in the stomach. Birds also store food in the crop to carry to their babies.

Food passes from a bird's esophagus or crop into the stomach. In most birds, the stomach has two parts. In the first part of the stomach, digestive juices are added to the food. The second part of the stomach, the *gizzard*, has thick, muscular walls that grind food. This process replaces chewing. Many birds assist the grinding process by swallowing gravel or other coarse materials.

Food passes from the stomach into the small intestine, where the nutritious matter is absorbed into the blood. The remaining waste matter moves into the large intestine. Nearly all or most of the water in the wastes is absorbed by the wall of the intestine. The kidneys of birds produce white crystalline *uric acid*, which the body discharges as waste matter called *guano*. Birds have an opening called the *anus* or *cloaca* at the rear of the body. The cloaca is connected with the digestive system, with tubes that drain wastes from the kidneys, and with the reproductive system. All wastes pass out of a bird's body through the cloaca.

The circulatory system distributes blood throughout a bird's body. The system consists of the heart and blood vessels. The heart of a large bird, such as an ostrich, beats at about the same rate as the human heart—that is, about 70 times a minute. The rate is much faster in small birds. A hummingbird's heart beats more than 1,000 times a minute. The main blood vessels in birds, as in all other vertebrates, are arteries and veins. Arteries carry blood from the bird's heart to other parts of the body. The blood returns to the heart through the veins.

The nervous system of a bird is similar to that of other vertebrates. It consists basically of the brain and nerves. The nerves carry messages from the senses to the brain and from the brain to the muscles.

A bird's brain is small compared with a mammal's. But the lower part of the brain, the *cerebellum*, is relatively larger in birds than in mammals. The cerebellum is the part of the brain that regulates balance and movement and coordinates the muscles birds use to fly. The upper part of the brain, the *cerebrum*, is far bigger and better developed in mammals than in birds. The cerebrum is

Blue jay

the part of the brain that controls learning. A few birds, such as crows and parrots, have a bigger cerebrum than do other birds their size. This characteristic may help explain why these birds can learn to "talk" or do tricks.

An important part of the brain used for memory, the *hippocampus*, grows larger in some birds. Food storing birds, for example, have remarkable memory. Jays and nutcrackers store thousands of seeds in the autumn to use as food in winter. The birds remember where they have hidden each seed and whether they have returned to harvest it. Some brood parasites, including cowbirds, check many potential host nests before determining the most suitable ones in which to lay their eggs. Such birds also need a good memory and a large hippocampus.

The reproductive system. Male sex organs in vertebrates are called *testes*. Female organs are called *ovaries*. Testes and ovaries produce sex cells. The testes produce sperm, and the ovaries produce eggs. In birds, testes and ovaries lie inside the body, just beneath the backbone. For most of the year, the testes and ovaries are extremely small. They start to grow larger just before the start of the breeding season. About the same time, a female's eggs also start to enlarge and accumulate yolk. When an egg reaches a certain stage of development, it passes from the ovary into a tube-shaped organ called the *oviduct*. About this time, mating takes place.

Most birds mate by pressing their cloacae together. Sperm cells quickly pass from the male's cloaca into the female. One or more sperm cells may unite with one or more egg cells in the upper part of the oviduct. Such a union produces a fertilized egg, or *zygote*. The zygote, on the surface of the yolk, continues down the oviduct. Glands in the oviduct's middle part deposit *albumen* (egg white) around the yolk. Glands in the lower part then produce a shell around the albumen. The egg is then laid. A zygote develops into an embryo as an egg is incubated. The embryo feeds on the yolk and albumen.

Bird Study and Protection

The scientific study of birds, called *ornithology*, began during the 1700s. Organized efforts to protect birds started somewhat later. As late as the mid-1800s, however, no countries had laws to help stop human beings from killing or capturing almost any bird they pleased.

By the late 1800s, many people realized that something had to be done to prevent the destruction of birds. In 1889, bird lovers in the United Kingdom founded the Embryonic Society, which became the Royal Society for the Protection of Birds (RSPB) in 1904. Also by the late 1800s, people throughout the United States had formed local organizations to help protect birds. These groups were called *Audubon Societies* in honor of the American naturalist and painter John James Audubon. In 1905, the local groups united to form the National Association of Audubon Societies. The association was renamed the National Audubon Society in 1940. The National Audubon Society and the RSPB now rank as the world's largest bird protection groups.

Organizations that campaign for bird protection now exist in many countries. Such organizations include Birds Australia, BirdWatch Ireland, and BirdLife South Africa in those countries and the Royal Forest and Bird Protection Society in New Zealand. These groups urge governments to pass laws to safeguard birds and other wildlife, and they encourage people to take an interest in birds. In some countries, these bird protection groups own and manage nature reserves. The reserves protect birds and act as educational centers for students and bird enthusiasts.

Bird watching has become a popular hobby. Binoculars rank as the most important bird-watching equipment. Without binoculars, it is often hard or impossible to see birds clearly at a distance. Most bird watchers use illustrated guidebooks, which are called *field guides*. Field guides depict each bird's *field marks*—that is, the distinctive colors, shapes, sizes, and behaviors that help identify the bird. Studying field guides and carrying them on field trips help bird watchers identify unfamiliar species. Also, people can identify many birds by their songs. Field guides to bird songs contain recordings of bird sounds. Studying bird recordings helps bird watchers learn the songs and calls of the birds of their areas. People watch birds in two principal ways: (1) by attracting various species to a particular location and (2) by taking field trips to the natural habitats of birds.

Attracting birds. A yard or garden with a variety of trees, shrubs, and flowers will normally attract birds. Trees and shrubs provide them with such foods as seeds and berries as well as with shelter and nesting places. Flowers attract insects that birds like to eat. Birds need water for drinking and bathing. They are especially drawn by dripping water from a hose, fountain, or outdoor faucet. Water in a birdbath or shallow dish will also attract them.

Birds can usually find all the food they need in summer. In areas with cold winters, however, birds that do not migrate may have difficulty finding food after a heavy snow or freezing rain. People can help by putting out food for birds that may need it. Many people feed birds in winter as a hobby. However, such bird feeders must continue putting out food daily throughout the winter and early spring after the practice has been started. Birds may become used to finding food in certain spots, and they may starve if the feedings are stopped.

Birds in a birdbath

Most winter residents are primarily seed eaters. A variety of bird seed can be bought at most grocery or feed stores. Numerous winter residents like *suet* (hard animal fat). Suet provides the extra food energy that many birds need during cold weather. Many birds will also eat table scraps, such as leftover egg, toast, lettuce, or potato. Some birds like to eat from a shelf or tray that has been placed above ground level. Such a bird feeder can be bought or easily built. Most public libraries have books or pamphlets that explain how to build bird feeders.

A few kinds of birds will nest in birdhouses or nesting boxes. These birds include bluebirds, chickadees, purple martins, titmice, and wrens. The structures should be placed outdoors before the spring mating season begins. They should be in a spot that is shaded from the sun during the hottest part of the day. As in the case of feeders, a homemade birdhouse or nesting box can be as good as one that is purchased. Public libraries and educational Web sites on the Internet can provide detailed instructions for building birdhouses.

Field trips. The best way to see and study a wide variety of birds is in the field. Numerous bird watchers travel to remote areas to see unfamiliar species. However, many such birds can also be seen in nearby parks and nature preserves. It is best to make field trips with a small, quiet group. Large or noisy groups of people may frighten birds away.

Many bird watchers take part in periodic counts, or *censuses*, of the birds in their area. Bird censuses help conservation officials determine which species may need special protection.

Bird banding is the placing of metal identification bracelets, or *bands*, on the legs of wild birds. This practice enables scientists to trace the life history of individual birds. The life histories, in turn, provide valuable information about the migration routes and life spans of different species. Bands generally bear a number and the name and address of a conservation agency, such as the U.S. Fish and Wildlife Service. No two bird bands have the same number, so all banded birds can easily be identified.

Banders use nets or cage-like traps baited with food to capture birds for banding. Baby birds can often be captured by hand. The bander attaches the band around the bird's leg with pliers. The bander also records the number of the band, the date, and the bird's species, sex, size and weight, and approximate age. This information is sent to the conservation agency named on the band, which

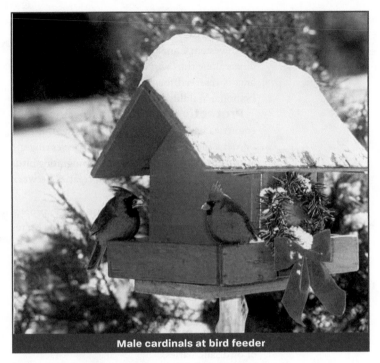
Male cardinals at bird feeder

keeps the records on a computer. If a banded bird is recaptured, the capturer sends its number to the address on the band, along with the date and place of capture. Anyone who finds a dead banded bird should mail the band to the address on the band along with information about when and where the bird was found.

Some birds are banded with several plastic bands of various colors in addition to the numbered metal band. Different color combinations identify the individual birds and make it possible to recognize them from a distance without being captured. For some experiments, birds are fitted with a tiny radio transmitter on the tail or back. The radios send out signals that enable scientists to track the birds.

Bird refuges. The spread of farms, towns, cities, and highways has destroyed the natural habitats of many birds and other animals. To help remedy this problem, a number of countries have set aside areas of land as refuges for birds and other wildlife. Some of the refuges are publicly owned. Others are owned or leased by private conservation groups. Large public parks and forests also serve as bird sanctuaries.

Wildlife refuges play an especially important role in protecting ducks, geese, and other migratory wild fowl. Some refuges also provide homes for endangered species. For example, the nesting area of the nearly extinct whooping crane is reserved as part of Wood Buffalo National Park in northwestern Canada. Whooping cranes winter in Texas along the coast of the Gulf of Mexico. This area is reserved for them as part of the Aransas National Wildlife Refuge.

Protective laws and treaties. Many countries have laws to protect birds within their borders. However, numerous bird species migrate across international borders. These migrating birds can receive protection only from treaties between the nations involved.

A number of conventions exist for the protection of migratory birds. In 1916, the United States and Canada signed the Migratory Bird Treaty, one of the first bird protection treaties in the world. The United States has also formed separate agreements with Japan and Mexico, and Japan has signed an agreement with Australia. Such conventions restrict both the trade in birds and the killing of birds. In addition, they encourage the formation of bird sanctuaries.

Within the European Union (EU), an order called the Birds Directive requires member countries to pass laws to protect wild birds, their eggs, and their habitats. Although only applicable to part of Europe, this directive has helped conserve many important species of birds.

Other conservation agreements help protect bird habitats. Wetland habitats remain vitally important for birds and many other types of wildlife. The Convention on Wetlands of International Importance, known as the Ramsar Convention, has been signed by many countries around the world. These countries have pledged to stop the destruction of wetlands. This agreement has proved particularly important for wildfowl, waders, and other water birds that depend upon wetland habitats.

The Convention on the Conservation of Migratory Species of Wild Animals, or Bonn Convention, requires the restoration of important habitats and the prevention, removal, or control of threats to migratory animals. A number of countries in Africa, Asia, Europe, Latin America, and the Pacific region have signed this agreement.

Since the mid-1900s, people throughout the world have become increasingly concerned about international trade in rare birds and their feathers. Many countries have forbidden the importing and exporting of such items. In 1973, representatives of 80 nations drafted the Convention on International Trade in Endangered Species of Wild Fauna and Flora (CITES). CITES prohibits the import and export of threatened species. More than 170 countries around the world, including the United States and Canada, have joined the convention.

The Evolution of Birds

Birds likely arose during the Jurassic Period, which lasted from about 200 million to 145 million years ago. Most scientists believe that birds *evolved* (developed over many generations) from *theropods*, a group of largely meat-eating dinosaurs.

The origin of feathers. Fossil evidence suggests that feathers originated among theropod dinosaurs, before the appearance of birds. Many theropods may have had some feathers, including well-known later dinosaurs such as *Tyrannosaurus* and *Velociraptor*. The earliest feathers were probably simple strands somewhat like down. These feathers would not have been useful for flight. Instead, feathers originally evolved for other uses. They may have served to keep dinosaurs warm, much as fur keeps mammals warm. Feathers also may have been important for courtship or other displays.

Depiction of an archaeopteryx

The first birds. Most scientists believe that birds arose from small feathered theropods. Scientists have identified several theropod dinosaurs as close relatives of the earliest birds. These include *Anchiornis* and *Xiaotingia*, both of which lived about 160 million to 150 million years ago. Birds probably originated earlier, but they are thought to have descended from dinosaurs much like these theropods. Anchiornis and Xiaotingia were crow-sized. Unlike modern birds, each had a long bony tail, teeth, and three claws on each hand. Fossils show that these animals were also covered in feathers, including some that resembled crude flight feathers. These long feathers grew on the limbs, which looked somewhat like wings. With their limbs spread, these animals may have been able to glide. However, they lacked many skeletal features associated with flight, so it is unlikely that they could fly.

Since the discovery of its fossils in the 1860s, *Archaeopteryx* has been identified by most scientists as the earliest known bird. Archaeopteryx fossils provided the first evidence that birds descended from reptiles. Archaeopteryx lived about 150 million years ago. It closely resembled Anchiornis and Xiaotingia and could glide from tree to tree or possibly fly weakly. Some scientists argue that Archaeopteryx may have been a tree-dwelling dinosaur rather than a bird.

Birds became well established in the Cretaceous Period, which began about 145 million years ago. The most diverse and widespread group of these early birds are called *enantiornithines*. Enantiornithines had many features characteristic of modern flying birds, including a keel and a tail with a *pygostyle*, a bone at the end to which feathers were attached. These traits made them stronger fliers. However, most enantiornithines still had teeth, and they had claws on their wings.

Other kinds of birds also lived in the Cretaceous Period. These include *Hesperornis* and *Ichthyornis*. Both were water birds that almost certainly ate fish. The flightless Hesperornis resembled a grebe or loon, but it grew much larger. It was a strong underwater swimmer. Ichthyornis could fly and looked somewhat like a small gull.

The first modern birds appear in the fossil record near the end of the Cretaceous Period, about 65 million years ago. However, they may have originated much earlier. Modern birds are distinguished from other birds in part by a number of adaptations that generally make them stronger fly-

1757 engraving of a dodo and a guinea pig

ers. The most ancient group of living modern birds includes cassowaries, ostriches, and several other flightless birds. Tinamous, which can fly, are also part of this group. However, all these birds descended from birds that could fly. Other ancient groups include *landfowl* (chickens, pheasants, and their relatives) and *waterfowl* (ducks, geese, and their relatives). Some scientists believe these groups had already appeared before the end of the Cretaceous Period. Other scientists think these groups only appeared later.

The Cretaceous Period ended with a mass extinction that devastated life on Earth. The dinosaurs became extinct, as did most groups of birds. Modern birds were the only descendants of dinosaurs that survived.

After the mass extinction, modern birds evolved into many new groups that spread around the world. Among these were the perching birds. Today, perching birds make up more than half of all bird species. Many of these descendants of dinosaurs weigh less than 1 ounce (28 grams). Most of the major bird groups living today had appeared by about 50 million years ago.

Extinct birds include all the species that have died out over millions of years. Gradual extinctions are an ordinary part of evolution. But in modern times, human beings have caused the rate of bird extinctions to climb. Hundreds of bird species have probably become extinct in the last 500 years. Human activities have caused most of these extinctions. Such activities include overhunting, habitat destruction, and the spread of predators and diseases that attack birds.

The first birds wiped out by people during modern times were the dodos of Mauritius, an island in the Indian Ocean. Dodos were large, flightless birds with fluffy feathers. They were killed off by the late 1600s, chiefly by sailors who hunted them for food. People also wiped out many other island birds. Since the 1800s, people have cut down large areas of tropical rain forest around the world. The destruction of these forests has caused a number of tropical birds to become extinct.

Several species of North American birds have died out since white settlers arrived. These include the Carolina parakeet, great auk, heath hen, and passenger pigeon. All of them died out as a result of overhunting and habitat loss. Other North American birds have not been reliably sighted for decades and are probably extinct. They include Bachman's warbler and the Eskimo curlew.

Endangered species. Hundreds of bird species around the world have become so rare that they are considered endangered. These include the whooping crane and the Gunnison sage grouse from North America, the hyacinth macaw from Brazil, the Algerian nuthatch of northern Africa, and the erect-crested penguin from New Zealand. Islands also have lost many birds, and because some species live only on a single island or island chain, those species have become especially vulnerable. Many of the birds native to Hawaii have already become extinct. Many other Hawaiian birds are endangered, including Hawaiian honeycreepers, the Hawaiian duck, and the Hawaiian crow.

Loss of habitat caused the decline of such mainland species as Bachman's warbler and the ivory-billed woodpecker. Hunters killed many Eskimo curlews and whooping cranes. Also, the use of pesticides, especially DDT, contaminated the food of the bald eagle, the osprey, and the brown pelican in some areas. One result of this contamination was that the eggs laid by the birds had such thin shells that they cracked under the weight of the incubating parent. Loss of habitat, illegal hunting, and illegal egg collecting all contributed to the decline of the California condor.

Protective laws and programs are helping save some endangered birds. Since 1972, DDT has been prohibited in many countries. Populations of bald eagles, ospreys, brown pelicans, and peregrine falcons are now breeding successfully again in once-polluted areas of North America. The number of nenes in Hawaii has been increased by breeding the birds in captivity and releasing the offspring into the wild. Conservationists are breeding California condors in captivity and have released some of these birds into the wild.

One of the most difficult bird conservation efforts has been to increase the number of whooping cranes. During the late 1900s and early 2000s, however, biologists established new resident flocks and migratory flocks of whoopers in the United States.

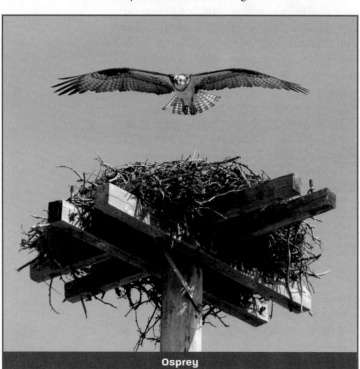

Osprey

MLA Citation
"Birds." *The Southwestern Advantage Topic Source.* Nashville: Southwestern. 2013.

DATA

A Classification of Birds

Order	Description	Families
Struthioniformes	Large, flightless, two-toed birds of Africa, Australia, New Zealand, and South America.	Cassowary, emu, kiwi, ostrich, rhea families.
Tinamiformes	Quail-like birds of Central and South America.	Tinamou family.
Craciformes	Turkey-like birds of Central and South America, Australia, and the Pacific Islands.	Guan and megapode families.
Galliformes	Fowl-like birds.	Guineafowl, pheasant, quail families.
Anseriformes	Water birds with webbed or long, unwebbed toes.	Duck, magpie goose, screamer, whistling Duck, magpie goose, screamer, whistling duck families.
Turniciformes	Three-toed quail of Africa, Australia, and the Pacific Islands.	Buttonquail families.
Piciformes	Tree-dwelling birds that nest in holes.	Barbet, honeyguide, toucan, woodpecker families.
Galbuliformes	Large insect-eating birds of the tropical Americas.	Jacamar and puffbird families.
Bucerotiformes	Large-billed birds of the African and Asian tropics.	Hornbill and ground-hornbill families.
Upupiformes	Long-billed birds that nest in holes.	Hoopoe, scimitar-bill, woodhoopoe families.
Trogoniformes	Long-tailed, brightly colored, fruit-eating tropical birds with weak feet.	Trogon family.
Coraciiformes	Varied group of mostly tropical birds with fused toes.	Bee-eater, cuckoo roller, kingfisher, motmot, tody families.
Coliiformes	Fruit-eating birds of Africa with a long tail and four toes pointing forward.	Mousebird family.
Cuculiformes	Varied group of tree- and ground-dwelling birds.	Ani, coucal, cuckoo, hoatzin, roadrunner families.
Psittaciformes	Seed-, nectar-, and fruit-eating birds with hooked bills and mostly bright colors.	Parrot family.
Apodiformes	Strong-winged, weak-footed birds that spend much time flying.	Swift and treeswift families.

DATA

A Classification of Birds

Order	Description	Families
Trochiliformes	Small, brightly colored, nectar-feeding birds of the Americas.	Hummingbird family.
Musophagiformes	Tree-dwelling birds of Africa with reversible outer toe.	Turaco family.
Strigiformes	Nighttime birds of prey.	Includes the barn owl, frogmouth, nighthawk, oilbird, owl and potoo families.
Columbiformes	Pigeon-like birds.	Pigeon family.
Gruiformes	Varied group of land and marsh birds.	Bustard, crane, kagu, limpkin, mesite, rail, seriema, sunbittern, trumpeter, and other families.
Ciconiiformes	Wading birds, birds of prey, and shore birds.	Albatross, eagle, falcon, flamingo, gull, heron, loon, pelican, penguin, plover, sandgrouse, sandpiper, vulture, and other families.
Passeriformes	Perching birds.	About 60 families, including broadbill, crow, flycatcher, thrush families.

Interesting Facts About Birds

The highest flyer is the bar-headed goose. Some flocks of bar-headed geese fly over the world's highest mountain range, the Himalaya in Asia, at an altitude of more than 25,000 feet (7,625 meters).

The fastest diver is the peregrine falcon. The bird's broad, powerful wings and streamlined body enable it to swoop down on its prey at a speed of more than 200 miles (320 kilometers) per hour.

The largest bird is the male African ostrich. It may grow as tall as 8 feet (2.4 meters) and weigh as much as 345 pounds (156 kilograms).

The smallest bird is the bee hummingbird. When fully grown, it measures about 2 inches (5 centimeters) and weighs about $\frac{1}{10}$ ounce (3 grams). The nest of a bee hummingbird is the size of half a walnut shell.

The greatest traveler. Arctic terns migrate farther than any other bird. They travel about 11,000 miles (17,700 kilometers) each way between their breeding grounds in the Arctic and winter home in the Antarctic.

The deepest diver is the emperor penguin. Emperor penguins have been recorded underwater at depths of almost 900 feet (275 meters). They use their wings to propel themselves through the water.

ADDITIONAL RESOURCES

Books to Read

All states in the United States and provinces in Canada have collections of books or pamphlets about birds that inhabit their areas. These materials are available at local libraries.

Level I

Arnold, Caroline. *Birds: Nature's Magnificent Flying Machines.* Charlesbridge, 2003.

Burnie, David. *Bird Watcher.* DK Publishing, 2005.

Hume, Rob, and others. *Birds.* 10 vols. Grolier, 2003.

Lerner, Carol. *On the Wing: American Birds in Migration.* HarperCollins, 2001.

McDade, Melissa C., ed. *Grzimek's Student Animal Life Resource: Birds.* 5 vols. UXL, 2005.

Level II

Alderfer, Jonathan, ed. *National Geographic Complete Birds of North America.* National Geographic Society, 2006.

Bird, David M. *The Bird Almanac: A Guide to Essential Facts and Figures of the World's Birds.* 2nd ed. Firefly Books, 2004.

Perrins, Christopher M., ed. *Firefly Encyclopedia of Birds.* Firefly Books, 2003.

Sibley, David A. *Sibley's Birding Basics.* Knopf, 2002.

Sibley, David A., and others, eds. *The Sibley Guide to Bird Life & Behavior.* Knopf, 2001.

Web Sites

All About Archaeopteryx

http://www.talkorigins.org/faqs/archaeopteryx/info.html

Detailed information about the known specimens of Archaeopteryx from Talk.origins, a group devoted to the discussion and debate of biological and physical origins.

American Goldfinch

http://www.mbr-pwrc.usgs.gov/id/framlst/i5290id.html

Information about the American goldfinch, from the Patuxent Wildlife Research Center.

Archaeopteryx: An Early Bird

http://www.ucmp.berkeley.edu/diapsids/birds/archaeopteryx.html

Information about Archaeopteryx from the University of California Museum of Paleontology.

Audubon On line—National Audubon Society

http://www.audubon.org/

Official Web site of the National Audubon Society.

Backyard Birding

http://www.birding.com/backyardbirding.asp

Everything you need to know about attracting birds to your backyard.

Bird illustrations by Louis Agassiz Fuertes

http://rmc.library.cornell.edu/Birds/

Cornell University's database of bird illustrations by Fuerte.

BIRDNET: The Ornithological Information Source

http://www.nmnh.si.edu/BIRDNET/

Bird information presented by several professional bird societies of North America.

Birds of the Continental United States and Canada

http://baltimorebirdclub.org/nabirds.html#1

A list of birds, grouped by scientific classification, that have been observed in North America north of Mexico.

Electronic Resources on Ornithology

http://www.chebucto.ns.ca/Environment/NHR/bird.html
This personal site includes links to many bird Web sites around the world.

Northern Bobwhite

http://www.mbr-pwrc.usgs.gov/id/framlst/i2890id.html
The Patuxent Wildlife Research Center presents information about the northern bobwhite.

Oakland Zoo: Egyptian Goose

http://www.oaklandzoo.org/site/animals/birds/egyptian-goose
Information on animal behavior from the Oakland Zoo.

Patuxent—Migratory Bird Research

http://www.mbr-pwrc.usgs.gov/
The U.S. Geological Survey's Patuxent Wildlife Research Center presents extensive information about migratory birds, bird identification, and bird research.

Search Strings

Evolution of Birds from Dinosaurs

evolution of birds from dinosaurs (88,600)

evolution birds dinosaurs reptiles theropods archosaurs pterosaurs (810)

evolution birds dinosaurs reptiles theropods archosaurs (2,230)

Bird Migration

bird migration factors that trigger hormones timing (67,400)

"bird migration" distance nesting survival hormones (676)

"bird migration" hormones (2,390)

Endangered species

Birds endangered species reasons (192,000)

Birds endangered species reasons "loss of habitat" (16,500)

Birds endangered species reasons "loss of habitat" DDT (15,300)

Bird Refuges

bird refuges land conservation (89,500)

"bird refuge" land conservation sanctuaries (583)

BACKGROUND INFORMATION

The following article was written during the year in which the events took place and reflects the style and thinking of that time.

Public health and safety (2006)

Concerns about a possible global pandemic (simultaneous epidemics) of avian influenza (bird flu) continued in 2006. Public health officials worried that the highly pathogenic (disease-causing) H5N1 strain of bird flu might mutate (change genetically) and become more easily transmissible from person to person. The H5N1 strain normally spreads to people from close contact with infected poultry or wild birds, though transmission among family members—and between patients and healthcare providers—has also been reported.

As of late 2006, most reported human cases of avian influenza had occurred in China, Indonesia, Thailand, and Vietnam. Since the first reported cases in 2003, at least 258 people had been infected worldwide, and 154 people had died, according to the World Health Organization (WHO), a specialized agency of the United Nations.

In June 2006, WHO scientists reported the first laboratory-confirmed evidence of H5N1 virus transmission from person to person. The cases occurred in a family in Indonesia, causing the deaths of seven family members. Scientists noted that all seven people were blood relatives—rather than spouses—raising the possibility that some individuals might be genetically predisposed to the ill effects of H5N1 infection. There were far more avian influenza infections in Indonesia in 2006 than in any other country—55 cases, with 45 deaths by November 29.

Chinese officials reported 12 new cases of H5N1 infection, including 8 deaths, as of October 31. However, the Chinese government provided few details on these cases, making it difficult for international health organizations to evaluate the state of avian influenza in the Communist nation.

In 2006, Chinese Ministry of Health and WHO officials confirmed that a man whose death in Beijing, the capital, in November 2003 was attributed to severe acute respiratory syndrome (SARS) actually died of avian influenza. The man's death became the first official laboratory-confirmed H5N1 case. Previously, the first case of human H5N1 infection was thought to have occurred in China in October 2005.

Childhood influenza. Physicians often fail to diagnose influenza in children, researchers led by pediatrician Katherine Poehling of Vanderbilt University Medical Center in Nashville, Tennessee, reported in February 2006. Such errors increase the risk that the disease will spread.

Poehling's team examined data from three U.S. counties and found that influenza was correctly diagnosed only 28 percent of the time in children who were hospitalized with the disease. A correct diagnosis was made only 17 percent of the time for pediatric outpatients. The Advisory Committee on Immunization Practices, a group of immunization experts that advises federal health care officials, used Poehling's results to revise its guidelines on childhood vaccinations. According to the new guidelines, all children ages 6 months to 5 years (instead of the previous 6 to 23 months) should be vaccinated against influenza every year.

Butterflies

Butterflies are among the most beautiful of all insects and can be found almost everywhere in the world.

HOT topics

**Butterfly
Self-protection**

Reproduction

Caterpillars

Pupae

HOT topics

Butterfly Self-protection. To escape predators, butterflies have developed various means to protect themselves. Many escape harm by blending with their surroundings. This form of defense is known as *cryptic coloration*. Many butterflies have chemical defenses. Some give off an unpleasant odor when the caterpillar is disturbed. Others taste bad, discouraging predators. During the larval stage, many of these butterflies eat plants that have bitter or poisonous juices. The juices are stored in the tissues, making the insects distasteful to predators. Most such butterflies have bright colors to warn predators. This form of protection is called *warning coloration*.

DEFINITIONS

cabbage butterfly: a kind of white butterfly whose larvae often damage cabbages.
caterpillar: the larva or wormlike form in which insects such as the butterfly and the moth hatch from the egg.
pupa: the stage in the life of an insect between the larval and the winged adult stage.

HOT topics 🔥

Reproduction. Butterflies use both sight and smell in seeking mates. In courtship, a butterfly reveals certain color patterns on its wings in a precise order. Many visual cues involve the reflection of ultraviolet light from a butterfly's wing scales. The cues are invisible to the human eye, but butterflies see them clearly. The visual cues help the insects distinguish between males and females and between members of different species. Chemical scents called *pheromones*, released from special wing scales, indicate the butterfly is ready to mate. The female begins laying the eggs within hours after mating.

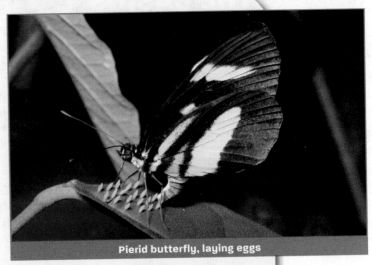

Pierid butterfly, laying eggs

Larvae/Caterpillars. Upon emerging from the egg, the butterfly larva, or caterpillar, immediately begins its main activity—eating. A caterpillar's first meal is usually its own eggshell. It then begins to eat the nearest food. The majority of caterpillars feed on green plants. In one day, a caterpillar may eat many times its weight in food. Much of this food is stored in the body and used to provide energy in later stages of development. The larval stage lasts at least two weeks. During that time, the caterpillar grows rapidly. Its exoskeleton, however, does not grow. Instead, the caterpillar forms a new skin beneath the exoskeleton. When the exoskeleton becomes too tight, it splits lengthwise along the back. Most caterpillars *molt*—that is, shed their exoskeletons—four or five times.

Pupae. After a caterpillar reaches its full size, it is ready to become a pupa. Pupae fasten themselves to twigs or leaves by means of a clawed structure at the end of the abdomen called the *cremaster*. The pupa is soft at first, but a hard shell immediately begins to form over it. Much activity occurs within the shell. Larval structures are broken down and reformed into those of an adult butterfly. Only the internal organs remain basically the same. The pupal period ranges from a few days to more than a year.

Monarch butterfly

TRUE or FALSE?

To escape winter, Monarch butterflies will migrate up to 2,000 miles.

THE BASICS

The butterfly is among the most beautiful of all insects. The four delicate wings of a butterfly appear in nearly every color imaginable. The colors may be bright, pale, or shimmering and often form stunning patterns. The word *butterfly* comes from the Old English word *buterfleoge*, meaning *butter* and *flying creature*. The "butter" probably comes from the butter-yellow color of some European butterflies. The beauty and grace of butterflies have inspired painters and poets. Butterflies also appear in folklore and mythology. The ancient Greeks, for example, believed that the soul left the body after death in the form of a butterfly. They sometimes imagined the soul as a butterfly-winged girl named Psyche.

The largest butterfly, Queen Alexandra's birdwing of Papua New Guinea, has a wingspread of about 11 inches (28 centimeters). One of the smallest butterflies is the western pygmy blue of North America. It has a wingspread of about ³⁄₈ inch (1 centimeter).

Butterflies live almost everywhere in the world. Tropical rain forests have the greatest variety of butterflies. Other butterflies live in woodlands, fields, and prairies. Some butterflies live on cold mountaintops, and others live in hot deserts. Many butterflies travel great distances to spend the winter in warm climates.

People are still finding new *species* (kinds) of butterflies. Scientists think that there may be about 20,000 to 30,000 species in total.

Butterflies and moths together make up an insect group called Lepidoptera. The name comes from two Greek words meaning *scale* and *wing*. It refers to the powdery scales that cover the wings of both butterflies and moths. However, butterflies differ from moths in a number of important ways, including the following four. (1) Most butterflies fly during the day. The majority of moths, on the other hand, fly at dusk or at night. (2) Most butterflies have knobs at the ends of their antennae. The antennae of most moths are not knobbed. (3) Most butterflies have slender bodies. The majority of moths are plump. (4) Most butterflies rest with their wings held upright over their bodies. Most moths rest with their wings spread out flat. These differences, however, have many exceptions.

A butterfly begins its life as a tiny egg. The egg hatches into a caterpillar. The caterpillar spends most of its time eating and growing. The caterpillar's skin cannot grow, so the caterpillar must shed its skin to get larger. This process repeats several times. After the caterpillar reaches full size, it forms a protective covering. Inside this shell, an amazing change occurs—the wormlike caterpillar becomes a beautiful butterfly. The shell then breaks open, and the adult butterfly comes out. The insect spreads its wings and soon flies off to find a mate. Together, they produce a new generation of eggs.

Butterflies mainly feed on plants. Their caterpillars chew up leaves or other plant parts. Some kinds of caterpillars are pests because they damage crops. Adult butterflies, on the other hand, feed mainly on nectar and do no harm. In fact, they may help plants by carrying pollen from blossom to blossom. When a butterfly stops at a flower to drink nectar, pollen may cling to the butterfly's body. Some of the pollen may then rub off on the next blossom the butterfly visits. This transfer of pollen, called pollination, helps the plant to produce fruit and seeds. Pollination is one of many reasons that people work to protect butterflies.

White cabbage garden butterfly

Kinds of Butterflies

Scientists group the thousands of species of butterflies into different families. The chief families include (1) skippers; (2) blues, coppers, and hairstreaks; (3) metalmarks; (4) brush-footed butterflies; (5) satyrs and wood nymphs; (6) milkweed butterflies; (7) snout butterflies; (8) sulphur and whites; and (9) swallowtails. Scientists established these groups more than a century ago, based on similarities and differences in the butterflies' bodies. Some scientists have argued that certain families should be combined, but not all butterfly experts agree.

In addition, a little known family of night-flying insects once considered moths may actually be butterflies. These insects, from the American tropics, have been called "moth butterflies."

Skippers differ from all other kinds of butterflies in two major ways: (1) Skippers have plump bodies and therefore look more like moths; and (2) their antennae have hooked tips, unlike the rounded tips on the antennae of other butterflies. For this reason, scientists classify skippers separately from *true butterflies*.

Skippers live in all parts of the world, except for the extreme polar regions. Skippers get their name from the way they swiftly skip and dart while flying. They range in color from orangish-brown to dark brown. In many cases, they have white and yellow markings. The brightest and showiest skippers live in the tropics, as is common among butterflies. North American skippers include the silver-spotted skipper, the roadside skipper, the fiery skipper, the checkered skipper, Juvenal's duskywing, and the least skipperling.

Blues, coppers, and hairstreaks live in almost every type of environment. They are small butterflies whose names describe their appearance. Blues have a brilliant blue or violet color. Coppers are often a fiery orange-red. Most species of hairstreaks have a hairlike "tail" on each of their hind wings. A number of blues and coppers also have such "tails."

Members of this family include the spring azure, the bronze copper, and the great purple hairstreak. The caterpillars of some species produce a sweet liquid known as *honeydew*. Certain ants "milk" the honeydew from the caterpillars. They also protect the caterpillars from being eaten. The large blue, a striking butterfly, disappeared from the United Kingdom in 1979. It has since been reintroduced and is recovering. Blues, coppers, and hairstreaks make up a large share of endangered butterflies.

Metalmarks live around the world but are especially numerous in South America. Some scientists consider them a subfamily of the blues, coppers, and hairstreaks. Their name comes from metallic-looking marks on the wings of some species. Tropical metalmarks may have almost any combination of colors and patterns. Among the

Hairstreak butterflies

most colorful is a Peruvian species known by the scientific name *Ancyluris formosissima*.

Brush-footed butterflies or *brushfoots* live everywhere in the world, except for ice-covered polar regions and deserts. These butterflies have short front legs, called *brush feet*. Special organs on the brush feet help the insects find food. The brush feet are not used for walking. Most brushfoots have wings with bright upper surfaces and dark lower surfaces. When the butterfly closes its wings, the dark color of their undersides helps the insect blend with its surroundings.

Brush-footed butterflies include the small crescents and checkerspots and the large fritillaries. Some of the best-known butterflies—the viceroy, the red admiral, and the mourning cloak—are brushfoots.

Satyrs and wood nymphs are often considered a subfamily of the brushfoots. Most kinds live in the tropics. However, a few live in high mountainous regions and the Arctic. New Zealand has several unusual satyrs, including the colorful tussock butterfly. The caterpillars feed on grasses and related plants, including bamboo. Satyrs and wood nymphs have short front legs and fly close to the ground. Most have brown wings dotted with *eyespots* (markings that resemble eyes).

Milkweed butterflies are large, slow-flying butterflies with short front legs. Their caterpillars feed on milkweed plants. Milkweed butterfly wings range from orange to brown, with black veins and margins. Many of them have white spots. Some African and Asian species are blue, violet, or white, with brown markings. Many scientists group milkweed butterflies with brushfoots.

One milkweed butterfly, the monarch, is famous for its long flights south each fall. The common crow butterfly of Australia and India also migrates long distances.

Snout butterflies live mostly in the tropics. These butterflies get their name from their long, beaklike mouthparts. The Australian beak ranks among the more colorful snout butterflies. The snout butterflies are an ancient family, known to appear in 70-million-year-old fossils. Some experts group them with the brushfoots.

Sulphurs and whites live around the world. Most of them live in tropical regions, but members of this family reach the shores of the Arctic Ocean. Others fly at 16,000 feet (4,900 meters) above sea level in the Andes Mountains of South America and the Himalaya of Asia. Sulphurs range in color from light yellow to orange. They are named for the mineral sulfur, which is powdery yellow. The wings of most sulphurs have black edges.

Whites have white wings that may be marked with black, brown, yellow, or red spots. Some have green markings below. The cabbage butterfly is the most common white. The caterpillar of this species is a major pest that feeds on cabbage, cauliflower, and related plants.

Swallowtails are found worldwide, though most species live in the tropics. Swallowtails are among the largest and most beautiful butterflies. They include Queen Alexandra's birdwing, the largest of all butterflies, and the African giant swallowtail, which has a wingspread of up to 10 inches (25 centimeters). Most swallowtails have a long extension on each hind wing. The butterflies get their name from these extensions, which resemble the tails of birds called swallows.

Most swallowtails are black, brown, and yellow with red and blue spots on their hind wings. One group, the parnassians, has white or creamy wings with red and black spots. Parnassians do not have "tails." Well-known species of swallowtails include the giant swallowtail and the tiger swallowtail.

The Bodies of Butterflies

Butterflies have certain body features in common with other insects. For example, a butterfly has a hard, shell-like skin called an *exoskeleton*. The exoskeleton supports the body and protects the internal organs. A butterfly's body, also like that of any other insect, has three main parts: (1) the head, (2) the thorax, and (3) the abdomen.

The head is the center of sensation. It bears a butterfly's (1) eyes, (2) antennae, and (3) mouthparts.

Eyes. On each side of its head, a butterfly has a large *compound eye*, which consists of thousands of tiny lenses. Each lens provides the insect with an image of part of its surroundings. The brain combines the separate images into a complete view. Butterflies can see *ultraviolet* (UV) *light*, a kind of light invisible to human beings. Some flowers and butterflies have special markings that reflect UV light. For example, the wings of male orange sulphur butterflies reflect UV light. To a butterfly, the wings do not look orange but rather a color called *bee purple*.

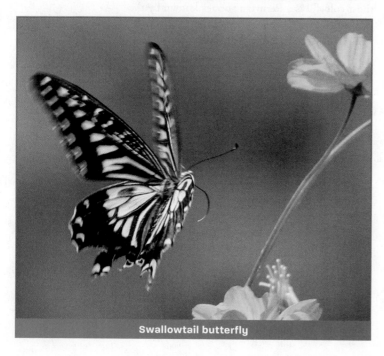

Swallowtail butterfly

Antennae. Two long, slender antennae grow between the eyes. The antennae are organs of smell. A butterfly uses its sense of smell to locate food and to find mates. The antennae probably also serve as organs of hearing and touch.

Mouthparts. A butterfly caterpillar has chewing mouthparts that consist of two lips and two pairs of jaws. These structures re-form as the caterpillar changes into an adult butterfly. One pair of jaws nearly disappears. The other pair becomes a long sucking tube, called a *proboscis*, that coils up when not in use. The lips form a protective covering for the proboscis.

A butterfly uses its proboscis to suck nectar and other liquids. Muscles in the head help the insect draw fluid up the proboscis and into a cavity in the head. A covering on the end of the proboscis closes and keeps fluid from flowing out. Other muscles force the fluid into the stomach.

The thorax forms the middle section of a butterfly's body. A short, thin neck connects it to the insect's head. Attached to the thorax are a butterfly's (1) wings and (2) legs.

Wings. A butterfly has a pair of front wings and a pair of back wings. Veins filled mainly with air run through the wings and serve as wing supports. The wings are stiff near the front edges and at the bases. The outer margins of the wings are flexible. They bend when flapped in flight. This bending pushes the air backward and moves the butterfly forward. The front margins of the wings give the insect "lift" as it flies forward.

Butterflies and moths cannot fly if their body temperature is less than about 86°F (30°C). At lower temperatures, they must "warm up" their flight muscles by sunning their bodies or by shivering their wings.

The size of a butterfly's body and wings determines how the insect flies. For example, milkweed butterflies and swallowtails have small, lightweight bodies and large wings. These butterflies can fly by beating their wings slowly. They are excellent gliders and can fly great distances. On the other hand, skippers have large, heavy bodies and small, pointed wings. They must beat their wings rapidly to stay aloft. Skippers do not soar or glide, but they can fly swiftly for short distances.

A butterfly's wings are covered with tiny, flat scales that overlap. The scales provide color and form patterns. Most scales contain *pigment* (coloring matter). Colors produced by pigment include black, brown, red, white, and yellow. Other kinds of scales produce color by reflecting light from their surfaces. Shiny, metallic colors, such as shimmering blue and green, are made in this way.

Legs. Butterflies have three pairs of legs. Each leg has five main segments. Joints between the segments enable a butterfly to move its legs in various directions. Each leg ends in a pair of claws and pads. The claws help to grip surfaces. The pads have hairlike structures used as taste organs. Butterflies have weak legs and can walk only short distances.

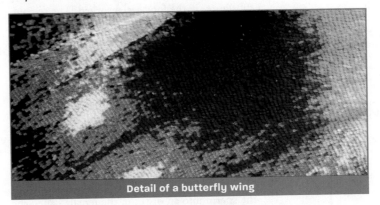
Detail of a butterfly wing

Among brush-footed butterflies, the front legs are quite short. These "brush feet" are useless for walking, but they hold highly developed taste organs.

The abdomen chiefly contains a butterfly's reproductive organs. It also has organs for digesting food and for getting rid of waste products.

The internal organs of butterflies are grouped into five main systems: (1) circulatory, (2) nervous, (3) respiratory, (4) digestive, and (5) reproductive.

The circulatory system carries blood throughout the body. It consists of a long tube that lies just under the exoskeleton of the back. The tube extends from the head to the end of the abdomen. The heart, the pumping part of the tube, lies in the thorax. The blood empties out of the tube into the head. It then floods the entire body. The blood reenters the tube through little openings along the sides. A butterfly's blood is yellowish, greenish, or colorless. It carries food, but not oxygen, to the cells of the body.

The nervous system of butterflies consists of a brain, in the head, and two nerve cords that run through the thorax and abdomen. Along the cords, bundles of nerve cells called ganglia branch out to all parts of the body.

The respiratory system brings oxygen to the cells of the body and takes away carbon dioxide. Oxygen enters through tiny holes along the sides of the body, called *spiracles*. Each spiracle connects to a tubelike structure called a *trachea*. The tracheae branch out to all the cells of the butterfly's body. In this way, the body cells obtain oxygen directly from the air rather than from the blood.

The digestive system is basically a long tube that extends from the mouth to the anus, an opening at the end of the abdomen. Nectar passes from the proboscis into the gut, where nourishing substances in the food are absorbed. The remaining waste products pass through the *hindgut* and out of the body through the anus.

The reproductive system. Butterflies reproduce sexually—that is, a new butterfly is created by uniting a *sperm* (male sex cell) and an *egg* (female sex cell). Female butterflies have a pair of organs, called *ovaries*, in which eggs develop. Males have two sperm-producing organs, called the *testes*. These are fused to resemble a single structure. A tube carries sperm from the testes to another tube that extends outside the abdomen. The male places the sperm into an organ in the female called the *copulatory sac*. The *sperm duct* transports the sperm to a tube called the *oviduct*, where fertilization takes place.

The Life Cycle of Butterflies

The life of an adult butterfly centers on reproduction. The reproductive cycle begins with courtship, in which the butterfly seeks a mate.

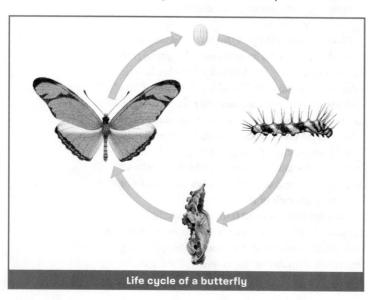

Life cycle of a butterfly

Butterflies use both sight and smell in seeking mates. Either the male or the female may give mating signals called *cues*. The cues must be of a certain kind or in a particular order. If a butterfly presents the wrong cue or cues in the wrong order, potential mates will reject it.

In courtship involving visual cues, a butterfly reveals certain color patterns on its wings in a precise order. Many visual cues involve the reflection of UV light from a butterfly's wing scales. The cues are invisible to the human eye, but butterflies see them clearly. The visual cues help the insects distinguish between males and females and between members of different species.

Usually, a female butterfly that presents an appropriate scent will be immediately accepted as a mate. The scent comes from chemicals called *pheromones*. The pheromones may be released from special wing scales called *androconia*. In most butterflies, both sexes use pheromones. However, the pheromones work only at close range, after the male has found the female by sight. In a few butterflies, an airborne pheromone may attract a male from a great distance.

In mountainous areas, males and females often fly to rocky summits to find mates. Such behavior is called *hilltopping*.

After mating, the female goes off in search of a place to lay her eggs. She usually begins laying the eggs within a few hours after mating. The male may mate several times during his life, but most females mate only once.

Every butterfly goes through four stages of development: (1) egg, (2) larva, (3) pupa, and (4) adult. This process of development through several forms is called *metamorphosis*.

The egg. Butterfly eggs vary greatly in size, shape, and color. Some eggs are almost invisible to the human eye. The largest ones are about $1/10$ inch (2.5 millimeters) in diameter. The eggs may be round, oval, cylindrical, or other shapes. Most are green or yellow. A few species have orange or red eggs. Some eggs are smooth. Others have ridges and grooves.

Most female butterflies lay their eggs on plants that will provide the offspring with food. Before depositing the eggs, the female may "taste" a plant with special organs on the ends of her front legs to make sure the plant is suitable. Some females lay their eggs near a plant or drop them at random while flying. After hatching, the young must find the food themselves.

While laying the eggs, the female fertilizes them with sperm stored in her body from mating. Each egg has a small hole through which sperm may enter. Depending on the species, a female may lay several dozen eggs or clusters of hundreds. A sticky substance deposited with the eggs helps hold them on the plant. The eggs of some butterflies hatch in a few days, but others take months. Eggs laid in fall may not hatch until spring.

The larva, or caterpillar, emerges from the egg and immediately begins its main activity—eating. A caterpillar's first meal is usually its own eggshell. It then begins to eat the nearest food. The majority of caterpillars feed on green plants. Some caterpillars eat insects, such as aphids. A few live inside ant nests and eat ant larvae. In one day, a caterpillar may eat many times its weight in food. Much of this food is stored in the body. It is used for energy in later stages of development.

Most caterpillars are solid green or brown. Many others have patterns of yellow, red, or other bright colors. Some caterpillars have smooth skin. Many others have bristles, bumps, fleshy knobs, or eyespots. All these features help protect caterpillars from being eaten by making them hard to see or frightening in appearance.

A caterpillar's body consists of 14 segments. The first segment, the head, includes chewing mouthparts and two short, thick antennae. The head also has six small eyes on each side. The eyes cannot see images, but they help the caterpillar distinguish between light and dark.

The next three segments of the caterpillar's body make up the thorax. Each of these segments has two short, jointed legs with a sharp claw at each tip. The remaining 10 segments form the abdomen. Most caterpillars have a pair of false legs, known as *prolegs*, on the seventh, eighth, ninth, and tenth body segments. At the end of each proleg are tiny hooks. The last segment has a pair of sucker-like legs called *anal prolegs* or *anal claspers*. These specialized legs enable the caterpillar to cling to plants and to move about.

A short structure called a *spinneret* sticks out below the caterpillar's mouth. It releases a sticky liquid. The liquid hardens into a silken thread, giving the caterpillar a foothold wherever it goes. Like the adult, the larva breathes through spiracles on the sides of the body.

The larval stage lasts at least two weeks. During that time, the caterpillar grows rapidly. Its exoskele-

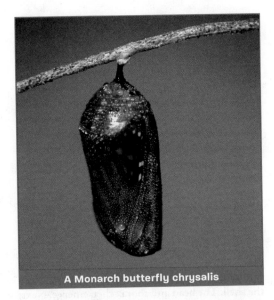

A Monarch butterfly chrysalis

ton, however, does not grow. Instead, the caterpillar forms a new skin beneath the exoskeleton. When the exoskeleton becomes too tight, it splits lengthwise along the back. The larva then crawls out. The new skin is soft, and the larva stretches it to provide growing room. The larva then lies motionless a few hours as the skin hardens into a new exoskeleton. Most caterpillars *molt*—that is, shed their exoskeletons—four or five times.

The pupa. After a caterpillar reaches its full size, it is ready to become a pupa. In preparation for this stage, most moth larvae spin silken cocoons around themselves. However, only a few butterfly species spin cocoons. Instead, the typical butterfly caterpillar finds a sheltered spot, usually high on a twig or leaf. There, it deposits sticky liquid from its spinneret, which quickly hardens into a silken pad. The exoskeleton then begins to split near the head, and the pupa starts to emerge. As the exoskeleton falls from the tail, the pupa thrusts its *cremaster* into the pad. The cremaster is a many-clawed structure at the end of the abdomen. This procedure is dangerous. If the butterfly does not grasp the pad fast enough, the pupa may fall to the ground and die.

Many pupae hang head downward, supported only by the cremaster hooked into the silken pad. Other pupae are positioned head upward. Such a pupa has an additional support of silken thread spun around the thorax and the twig or leaf to which it is anchored.

The pupa is soft at first, but a hard shell immediately begins to form over it. Some shells have unusual shapes and colorful patterns. In some cases, the shell has a golden shimmer. For this reason, scientists call the pupa a *chrysalis*. This word comes from a Greek word that means *gold*.

The pupa is motionless and is often referred to as being inactive or at rest. However, much activity occurs within the shell. There, larval structures break down and re-form into those of an adult butterfly. Only some internal organs remain basically the same.

The pupal period ranges from a few days to more than a year, according to when the pupa forms and the species of butterfly. Many species spend the winter as pupae and emerge as adults in the spring.

The adult. After the adult butterfly has formed, its body gives off a fluid that loosens it from the pupal shell. The thorax swells and cracks the shell. The head and thorax then emerge. Next, the butterfly pushes its legs out and pulls the rest of its body free. The entire process may take only a few minutes.

The exoskeleton of the emerging butterfly is soft. The wings are damp and crumpled. The proboscis is split in half lengthwise. The butterfly uses its muscles to pump air and blood through its body and wings. The butterfly's exoskeleton hardens, and the legs and other body parts become firm. The wings flatten and expand. The butterfly joins the halves of its proboscis by coiling and uncoiling them repeatedly. About an hour after leaving the pupal shell, the adult butterfly may be ready to fly.

Most adult butterflies live only a week or two, but some species may live up to 18 months. Most but-terflies feed only on nectar. Nectar provides quick energy, but it does not contain the proteins necessary for long life. Certain butterflies obtain proteins by feeding on decaying animal matter or on pollen. A number of butterflies do not feed. Instead, they live on food stored during the larval stage.

How Butterflies Protect Themselves

Many predators, including other insects and birds, eat butterflies. But butterflies have developed various means to protect themselves.

Many butterflies and caterpillars blend with their surroundings. This form of defense is known as *cryptic coloration*. Adult butterflies may look like bark or other vegetation. Green caterpillars blend with the plants they eat. Brown ones look like dead leaves or twigs.

Many butterflies have chemical defenses. Such insects include the caterpillars of certain swallowtails. When disturbed, these insects give off an unpleasant odor from an organ just behind the head. Some butterflies taste bad, discouraging predators. As caterpillars, many of these butterflies eat plants with bitter or poisonous juices. They store the juices in body tissues, giving the flesh an unpleasant taste. If eaten by predators, these butterflies may cause vomiting. Most such butterflies also have bright colors to warn predators. An animal that has eaten one of these butterflies will probably avoid eating another butterfly with that coloration. This form of protection is called *warning coloration*.

Hibernation and Migration

Butterflies cannot be active in cold weather. They must either hibernate or migrate to warmer areas.

Hibernation. Many species of butterflies survive the winter by hibernating in a sheltered place. Butterflies may hibernate in the egg, larval, pupal, or adult stage. But each species usually hibernates in only one stage.

Just before hibernation, the blood of a larva, pupa, or adult produces substances called *glycols*. Glycols are chemically similar to the antifreeze used in automobiles. The presence of glycols enables a butterfly to survive even severe cold. When warm weather returns, other blood substances gradually replace the glycols.

Migration. Some butterflies escape cold weather by migrating to a warmer region. Migrating butterflies include the buckeye, the California

Owl butterflies

tortoiseshell, the cloudless sulphur, the painted lady, and the red admiral.

One species, the monarch, migrates farther than any other butterfly. Dense clouds of monarchs may travel up to 2,000 miles (3,200 kilometers) from Canada and the northern United States to a mountainous region in central Mexico. In western North America, monarch butterflies spend the winter on the coast of California.

In the tropics, there is no winter. But many tropical regions have dry and rainy seasons. Butterflies in these areas often migrate by the millions, following patterns of plant growth caused by the rains. Such migrants include many whites and sulphurs. In India, hundreds of species migrate with the rains, including the common albatross, the common emigrant, and the dark blue tiger.

Butterflies and the Environment

Butterflies fill important roles in many *ecosystems*. An ecosystem includes the things that live in an area as well as their relationships with one another and their environment. Unfortunately, some butterfly species have become endangered, and many more are in decline. Scientists worry that the disappearance of butterflies could do great harm to many ecosystems.

Butterflies and ecosystems. Butterflies help maintain ecosystems in a number of ways. For example, butterfly caterpillars feed on plants of certain species. This feeding reduces the competition faced by other plant species, influencing which plants flourish in an area.

Butterflies also provide food for a variety of predators. Many birds, insects, and spiders eat adult butterflies or caterpillars. Other insects feed on butterfly eggs. Certain species of wasps and flies, called *parasitoids*, lay their eggs in or on butterfly eggs or caterpillars. When the eggs hatch, the larvae eat their hosts from within.

In addition, butterflies help pollinate flowers. In fact, butterflies may rank second only to bees as pollinators. Butterflies pollinate garden flowers, such as lantana and butterfly bushes; crops, such as apples and sunflowers; and wild plants, including many tropical flowers. A few plants, such as the North American yellow-tailed orchid, are pollinated exclusively by butterflies.

If plants pollinated by butterflies decline, animals that depend on the plants for food may decline in turn. This is just one way the loss of butterflies may have far-ranging consequences for an entire ecosystem.

Butterflies and environmental change. Butterfly numbers are in rapid decline in many parts of the world. Highly specialized butterflies, such as species that feed on only a single kind of plant, are at greatest risk. However, even formerly common and widespread species are in decline. The greatest cause of butterfly decline is the loss of *habitat*, the places where butterflies live. Human beings have damaged or destroyed much butterfly habitat by replacing wild meadows with buildings or cropland. In many areas, remaining habitats have become widely separated, a condition called *habitat fragmentation*. Habitat fragmentation makes it more difficult for butterflies to find mates and food, to spread and migrate, and to meet other survival needs.

Global warming can also harm butterflies. As climates become warmer, habitats suitable for butterfly species are shifting. In areas already suffering from habitat fragmentation, butterflies may not be able to find new habitats. In mountainous regions, species adapted to cool climates must move higher up the mountain slopes. Eventually, even the mountain summits may become too warm.

Other threats to butterflies include air pollution and pesticides. Pesticides used to fight harmful insect pests also kill harmless or beneficial butterflies. Automobiles on busy highways also kill many butterflies.

Butterfly conservation. Many people are working to protect butterflies. In some areas, laws protect endangered butterflies, making it illegal to collect them. Laws may also protect butterfly habitat.

Some people raise colorful or unusual tropical species on butterfly farms. This farming helps to protect wild butterflies and also provides a source of income for farmers, who sell the butterflies to collectors.

In many areas, the native plants on which caterpillars and butterflies feed have nearly disappeared. To help butterflies survive, many people have planted "butterfly gardens" made up of native plants. Even in dense cities, butterfly gardens can help butterflies to survive.

To help butterflies cope with global warming and habitat fragmentation, people have begun to establish *nectar corridors*. Nectar corridors are

Various butterflies

flies to find new homes when their old habitat becomes unsuitable.

Scientific Classification

Butterflies belong to the order Lepidoptera, which also includes moths. Skippers make up the superfamily Hesperioidea, which includes the family Hesperiidae. All other butterflies are *true butterflies* and belong to the superfamily Papilionoidea. True butterflies include the following families: blues, coppers, and hairstreaks (Lycaenidae); metalmarks (Riodinidae); brush-footed butterflies (Nymphalidae); satyrs and wood nymphs (Satyridae); milkweed butterflies (Danaidae); snout butterflies (Libytheidae); sulphurs and whites (Pieridae); and swallowtails (Papilionidae).

MLA Citation

"Butterflies." *The Southwestern Advantage Topic Source.* Nashville: Southwestern. 2013.

continuous areas of native plants that connect larger wild areas. The plants in nectar corridors provide food for caterpillars and adult butterflies. Such corridors enable migratory butterflies to move safely through the environments people have created. Nectar corridors also enable butter-

ADDITIONAL RESOURCES

Books to Read

Level I

Green, Jen. *Butterflies*. Benchmark Books, 1999.

Mikula, Rick. *The Family Butterfly Book*. Storey Books, 2003.

Pascoe, Elaine. *Butterflies and Moths*. Blackbirch Press, 1997.

Pringle, Laurence P. *An Extraordinary Life: The Story of a Monarch Butterfly*. Orchard Books, 1997.

Level II

Brock, James P., and Kaufman, Kenn. *Butterflies of North America*. Houghton, 2003.

Carter, David J. *Butterflies and Moths*. 2nd ed. Dorling Kindersley, 2002.

Glassberg, Jeffrey. *Butterflies of North America*. Friedman/Fairfax, 2002.

Sbordoni, Valerio, and Forestiero, Saverio. *Butterflies of the World*. Firefly Books, 1998.

Schappert, Phillip J. *A World for Butterflies*. Firefly Books, 2000.

Web Sites

Butterflies at the Field Museum

http://fieldmuseum.org/explore/butterflies-field-museum

A guide to butterfly collections at the Field Museum in Chicago and basic information about butterflies.

Children's Butterfly Site

http://www.kidsbutterfly.org/

The National Biological Information Infrastructure (NBII) sponsors this Web site with information and resources about butterflies.

Reproduction

butterfly reproduction mate courtship pheromones (13,900)

butterfly reproduction mate courtship pheromones color patterns on wings (504)

Caterpillars

butterfly caterpillars (128,000)

caterpillars "butterfly larva" (2,190)

caterpillars "butterfly larva" diet molting (54)

Pupae

butterfly caterpillar pupae (17,200)

butterfly caterpillar pupae cremaster (589)

pupae caterpillar butterfly (149,000)

BACKGROUND INFORMATION

The following article was written during the year in which the events took place and reflects the style and thinking of that time.

Zoo (1978)

Zoos throughout the world continued to make rapid changes in exhibition, education, and conservation activities in 1978. The opening of the Minnesota Zoological Garden in Apple Valley in May was particularly notable. It has a large walk-through house for reptiles, birds, and mammals from tropical areas. It provides a contrast to other large outdoor exhibits of Northern Hemisphere mammals, such as beluga whales, snow monkeys, Siberian tigers, and musk oxen.

The Cincinnati (Ohio) Zoo opened a most unusual exhibit, its new Insect House, in August. Sixty-five insect exhibits are contained in a sunken building. The walk-through butterfly area is particularly interesting, as are the leaf-cutting ant colony and exhibits of goliath beetles and giant walking sticks. Some of the exhibits are developed around themes, such as insects' predators, insects' relatives, mimicry, metamorphosis, locomotion, and the economic effects of insect life on humans. In June, the Cincinnati Zoo dedicated a large open-air area for gorillas.

The St. Louis Zoological Park opened a completely renovated Reptile House in August. The National Zoological Park in Washington, D.C., completed its new quarters for bears in August, and the Shedd Aquarium in Chicago its refurbished 90,000-gallon (341,000-liter) reef tank in December.

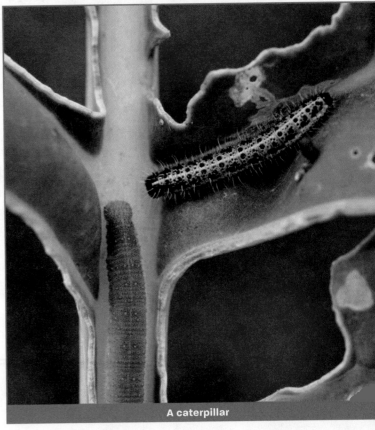

A caterpillar

Cats

Cats are four-legged, meat-eating animals with soft fur and sharp claws. They are skilled hunters that can run fast, climb trees, and have a good sense of balance. Cats belong to the family Felidae. The family includes large, wild species such as cheetahs, leopards, lions, and tigers, and smaller, domesticated cats that people keep as pets. The scientific classification of domestic cats is *Felis domesticus*.

HOT topics

Role of Cats Throughout History. Cats have been used as skilled hunters to kill mice, rats, and snakes. Cats were considered sacred to ancient Egyptians and are believed to bring good fortune to people in many societies today. However, some people fear cats, believing them to be associated with bad luck. There are many cat associations and cat shows around the world. Cats have been the subject of many artists' and writers' works.

DEFINITIONS

Cat. *-n.* 1. **a.** a small, four-footed, furry mammal, often kept as a pet or for catching mice and rats: *The neighbors took in a stray cat.* **b.** any animal of the group including cats, lions, tigers, and leopards. **c.** an animal resembling a cat.

HOT topics

Famous Cartoon Cats. Felix the Cat was a famous character from the silent-film era. William Hanna and Joseph Barbera created Tom from the "Tom and Jerry" cartoons. Tom was an energetic cat that rarely spoke but was determined to catch a cheerful mouse named Jerry in various creative ways. Friz Freleng created Sylvester the Cat, the black and white cat that spoke with a lisp and often exclaimed "Sufferin' succotash!" In 1970, Walt Disney produced an animated musical comedy called "The Aristocats" about talking cats in Paris, France. Garfield is a comic strip created by Jim Davis about a furry orange cat, a dog named Odie, and their owner, Jon Arbuckle. An animated television series and two feature-length films have been created about Garfield.

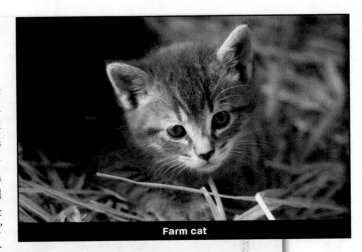
Farm cat

Breeds of Cats. There are many breeds of cats, which vary greatly in appearance and characteristics. As with any other animal, there are purebreds and crossbreds. Crossbreds are usually referred to as *alley cats*. The two major groups of cats recognized in the United States are the short-haired breeds and the long-haired breeds. Additionally, there are rare and unusual breeds.

Larger, Wild Cats include the prehistoric saber-tooth tiger and the present-day cheetah, mountain lion, lion, caracal, lynx, leopard, snow leopard, jaguar, tiger, and ocelot. Each species evolved with distinct characteristics and appearance.

Cats, the Musical. *Cats*, a popular musical comedy, the music of which was written by Andrew Lloyd Webber, is a song-and-dance performance by actors dressed up to look like giant cats. The lyrics to the songs are based upon a collection of poems about cats by T. S. Eliot.

A scene from *Cats*

TRUE or FALSE?

Domestic cats and larger, wild cats are so different that they should be separated into two separate families

THE BASICS

The cat is a favorite pet of people around the world. Cats are intelligent and have an independent nature. These small animals can also be playful and entertaining. Many cats make affectionate, loyal pets, providing companionship for people of all ages. Tens of millions of cats are kept as pets worldwide.

The word *cat* also refers to a family of meat-eating animals that includes tigers, lions, and leopards. This family also includes *domestic cats*—that is, those that people keep as pets. Domestic cats and their wild relatives share many characteristics. All these animals have long, powerful bodies and somewhat rounded heads. They have short, strong jaws and thirty sharp teeth. Cats are also skillful hunters. They are able to catch other animals by approaching them swiftly and quietly on padded feet. Or they may wait motionless until an animal comes close and then spring upon it suddenly.

This article deals with domestic cats. These animals have many special physical abilities. They see better in dim light than people do. They can climb trees, run at a high speed, and leap long distances. Cats also have a keen sense of balance and can easily walk along the tops of narrow fences or along narrow ledges. When cats fall, they almost always land on their feet.

Cats vary in personality and in certain physical features, such as the length and color of their coats. There are many breeds of cats. Special characteristics set each breed apart from all others. Among the favorite breeds are the Siamese and the Persian.

No one knows exactly when the first cats were tamed. But some authorities believe cats were tamed about 5,000 years ago. Throughout history, people have valued cats for their skill at hunting and killing mice, rats, and snakes. Cats help keep farms, homes, and businesses free of these animals. The ancient Egyptians considered cats sacred. Today, people in many societies believe cats bring good fortune. But some people associate cats with bad luck and so fear them. Many people find cats mysterious because they move swiftly and silently and because their eyes seem to glow in the dark.

The grace and beauty of cats have made them favorite subjects of artists throughout history. Cats have also been featured in almost every type of literature. They appear in the mythology of ancient Greece and Rome. Hundreds of years ago, Asian writers praised cats in their stories and poems. Cats are also commonly mentioned in the fairy tales, folklore, and legends of many countries. In modern times, books, comic strips, motion pictures, and television programs have featured cats.

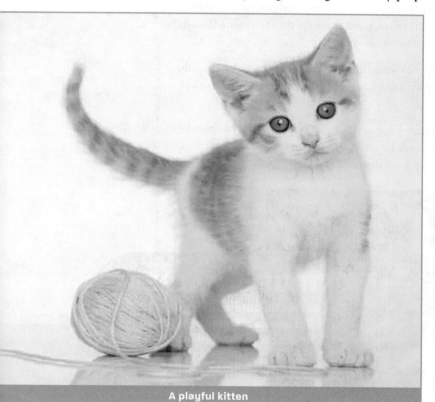

A playful kitten

The Body of a Cat

Body size and structure. Adult cats average about 8 to 10 inches (20 to 25 centimeters) tall at the shoulder. Most weigh from 6 to 15 pounds (2.7 to 7 kilograms). But some cats weigh more than 20 pounds (9 kilograms), and some weigh less than 5 pounds (2.3 kilograms).

Cats have the same basic skeleton and internal organs as human beings and other meat-eating mammals. The skeleton of a cat has about 250 bones. The exact number of bones varies, depending on the length of the cat's tail. The skeleton serves as a framework that supports and protects the tissues and organs of a cat's body. Most of the cat's muscles are long, thin, and flexible. They enable a cat to move with great ease and speed. Cats can run about 30 miles (48 kilometers) per hour.

The arrangement of the bones and the joints that connect them permits a cat to perform a variety of movements. Unlike many animals, a cat walks by moving the front and rear legs on one side of its body at the same time, and then the legs on the other side. As a result, a cat seems to glide. Its hip joint enables a cat to leap easily. Other special joints allow a cat to turn its head to reach most parts of its body.

A cat has five toes on each forepaw, including a thumb-like inner toe that is helpful in catching prey. Each hind paw has four toes. Some cats have extra toes. Each of a cat's toes ends in a sharp, hook-like claw. The claws usually are *retracted* (held back) under the skin by elastic ligaments, which are a type of connective tissue. However, when the claws are needed, certain muscles quickly pull the *tendons* (cord-like tissues) connected to the claws. This action extends the claws. A cat uses its claws in climbing, in catching prey, and in defending itself. Several spongy pads of thick skin cover the bottoms of a cat's feet. The pads cushion the paws and enable a cat to move quietly.

A cat's tail is an extension of its backbone. The flexible tail helps a cat keep its balance. When a cat falls, it whips the tail and twists its body to land on its feet.

Head. A cat's head is small and has short, powerful jaws. Kittens have about twenty-six needle-like temporary teeth, which they shed by about six months of age. Adult cats have thirty teeth, which are used for grasping, cutting, and shredding food. Unlike human beings, cats have no teeth for grinding food. But a cat's stomach and intestines can digest chunks of unchewed food. Tiny hook-like projections called *papillae* cover a cat's tongue, making it rough. The rough surface of the tongue helps a cat lick meat from bones and groom its coat.

A cat has a small, wedge-shaped nose. The tip is covered by a tough layer of skin called *nose leather*. The nose leather may be various colors. It is usually moist and cool. A sick cat may have a warm, dry nose.

The colored part of a cat's eyes, called the *iris*, may be shades of green, yellow, orange, copper, blue, or lavender. *Odd-eyed* cats have irises of different colors. For example, one eye may be green and the other blue.

At the back of each eye, a cat has a special mirror-like structure called the *tapetum lucidum*. It reflects light and so helps a cat see in dim light. It

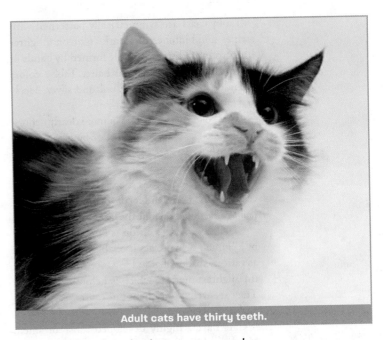

Adult cats have thirty teeth.

also produces *eyeshine*, the glow a person sees when light strikes the eyes of a cat at night. Each of a cat's eyes has a third eyelid at the inner corner. This structure, called the *nictitating membrane*, protects and lubricates the eyes.

A cat's ears are near the top of its skull. Each ear can move independently. A cat can aim the cup of its ears in the direction from which a sound is coming and so improve its hearing.

Coat. A cat's coat protects its skin and provides insulation. Most coats have two types of hairs. The outer part of the coat is made up of long, stiff *primary*, or *guard*, hairs. The undercoat consists of softer and shorter *secondary*, or *down*, hairs. The color, length, and texture of the coat vary greatly among cats. The Sphinx breed of cat, in fact, may have no hair. Terms commonly used to describe the color of a cat's coat are *solid* or *self*, *smoke*, *shaded*, *tabby*, *parti-color*, and *colorpoint*.

Solid, or *self*, coats have only one color. The solid colors are black, *blue* (dark gray), brown, *cream* (tan), *lilac* (light gray), *red* (shades of orange), and white.

Smoke coats consist of a white undercoat covered by guard hairs of a dark color. In most cases, the guard hairs are black, blue, or red.

Shaded coats are similar to smoke coats except that the dark color is limited to the tips of the guard hairs. A *chinchilla* coat has a sparkling appearance because only the extreme tips of the guard hairs are dark. Red chinchilla coats are sometimes called *shell cameos*.

Tabby coats are symmetrically patterned with stripes and blotches of a dark color on a lighter background. The patterns are formed by bands of a dark color on individual hairs. Tabby colors include blue, brown, cream, red, and silver. *Mackerel* tabbies have narrow markings.

Parti-color coats have two or more clearly defined colors, such as black and white or blue and cream. *Tortoiseshell* coats are black, red, and cream. *Calico* coats have patches of white, black, red, and cream.

Colorpoint coats consist of a solid color over the trunk of the body and a contrasting color on the *points*. The points include the face, ears, feet, and tail.

Senses. A cat's vision is not as keen as that of a human being. Cats probably see most colors as various shades of gray. However, they can detect the slightest motion, which is helpful in hunting. They see well in dim light but cannot see in total darkness.

Cats have a highly developed sense of smell. Newborn kittens, for example, are able to recognize their nest by scent alone. In addition to its nose, a cat has another sense organ in its mouth that detects scents.

Cats also have a keen sense of hearing. They hear a much broader range of sounds than people do. Deafness is rare among cats. However, it is an inherited defect among some white cats, particularly those with blue or odd-color eyes.

The whiskers of a cat are special hairs that serve as highly sensitive touch organs. These hairs, called *vibrissae* or *tactile hairs*, grow on the chin, at the sides of the face, and above the eyes. The hairs are attached to nerves in the skin, which transmit signals to the brain when the whiskers brush against objects. The whiskers may help a cat protect its eyes, feel its way in the dark, and detect changes in wind direction.

Breeds of Cats

The many breeds of cats vary greatly in appearance. Cat breeders have developed numerous breeds by selectively mating animals with certain desirable and distinctive characteristics. These characteristics appear consistently in the offspring of *purebred* cats. A purebred cat is one whose mother and father belong to the same breed. The offspring of cats that have mated randomly are known as *crossbreds* or *alley cats*.

Many people prefer the special features of a certain breed of cats. For example, such purebreds as the Abyssinian and the Birman are among the most beautiful and unusual animals in the world. But crossbreds may be just as beautiful and lovable as purebreds, and they are often healthier.

Certain associations officially recognize cat breeds and establish standards for the ideal characteristics of each breed. However, different cat associations recognize different breeds, and breed standards also vary somewhat. In the United States, cat breeds are commonly divided into two major groups: (1) short-haired breeds and (2) long-haired breeds. Some breeds include both long- and short-haired types.

Short-haired breeds. The Cat Fanciers' Association (CFA), the major U.S. cat association, recognizes numerous short-haired breeds. They include the Abyssinian, American shorthair, American wirehair, Bombay, British shorthair, Burmese, Chartreux, Colorpoint shorthair, Cornish rex, Devon rex, Egyptian Mau, Exotic, Havana brown, Japanese bobtail, Korat, Manx, Ocicat, Oriental, Russian blue, Scottish fold, Selkirk rex, Siamese, Singapura, Sphinx, and Tonkinese.

Abyssinian is a slender, muscular, medium-sized cat with a long, tapering tail. *Aby* cats, as they are sometimes called, have a wedge-shaped head and large ears. Their almond-shaped eyes are commonly green, gold, or hazel. These cats are known for their *agouti* coat pattern, which is common in wild animals. Each hair of an Aby's soft coat has two or three bands of alternating light and dark

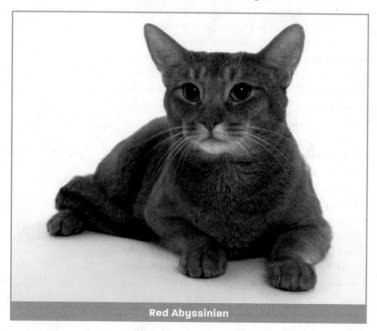

Red Abyssinian

colors. The bands may be a variety of colors, ranging from cream and silver to bluish tones to black and shades of brown and brownish-red.

People once thought the Aby originated in Abyssinia (now called Ethiopia) and descended from the sacred cats of ancient Egypt. Today, some cat experts believe the Aby probably originated in Southeast Asia. Cats resembling the Aby were brought to the United Kingdom from Abyssinia in the mid-1800s.

American shorthair is a muscular, medium- to large-sized animal. Its large head features full cheeks; a broad, squarish muzzle; large, round eyes; and rounded, medium-sized ears. The coat and eyes may be any color. The breed probably developed from cats originally brought to the American Colonies by Europeans.

American wirehair is a medium- to large-sized cat with a rounded head and roundish ears and eyes. It has dense, springy, coarse fur and curly whiskers. The coat may be any color or pattern. This breed originated as a *mutation* (random genetic change) in a litter of upstate New York farm cats in 1966.

Bombay looks somewhat like a miniature black panther. It has a sleek black coat and golden to reddish-brown eyes. This medium-sized breed originated in 1958 in Louisville, Kentucky, as a cross between a black American shorthair and a Burmese.

British shorthair traces its ancestry to domestic cats that lived thousands of years ago in parts of Europe, including what is now the United Kingdom. This medium- to large-sized cat typically has a massive, roundish head; large, round eyes; and ears with rounded tips. It is similar to the American shorthair but has a stockier build and a thicker coat.

Burmese is a medium-sized cat with a muscular body. The cat has round, golden eyes and a short, sleek coat that most commonly is dark brown. The Burmese has round, golden eyes. The breed was developed from a female cat that was brought to the United States from Burma (now Myanmar) in 1930.

Chartreux is a breed believed to have been brought to France from South Africa by Carthusian monks in the 1600s. This medium- to large-sized cat has a blue-gray coat with a slightly woolly texture. Its eyes may be reddish-brown to golden or brilliant orange. The Chartreux is strong, friendly, and intelligent.

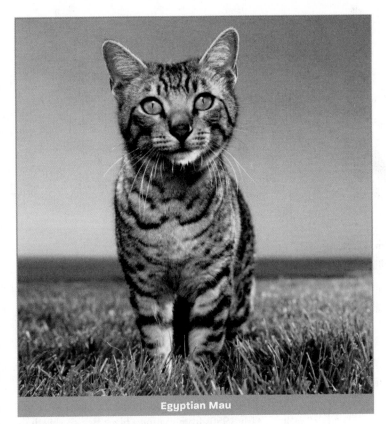

Egyptian Mau

Colorpoint shorthair was developed in England in the early 1900s by crossing Siamese, red British shorthair, and Abyssinian cats. Like the Siamese, this medium-sized breed has a slender body, blue eyes, and a colorpoint coat.

Cornish rex has a short, silky, wavy coat and a greyhound-like body. The coat, which may be any color, has no guard hairs. This slender, small- to medium-sized cat has a long tail, small head, large ears, and a curved nose. The Cornish rex originated in Cornwall, England, about 1950 as a cross between a tortoise-shell cat and a white barn cat.

Devon rex is a strong, medium-sized cat with large eyes, a short muzzle, and huge, low-set ears that give it an elfin appearance. Its soft, wavy coat may be any color. The breed originated in Devonshire, England, in 1960 as a mutation of barn cats.

Egyptian Mau is one of the oldest breeds of domestic cats, dating back to about 1400 B.C. It has a distinctive coat of dark spots against a lighter background. The spots become bars on the face, legs, and tail. This graceful, medium-sized cat has a rounded head and light green eyes.

Exotic was developed in the United States during the 1950s and 1960s by crossing American

Tortoiseshell manx

shorthair and Persian cats. The Exotic is a stocky, medium-sized cat with a snub nose, large round eyes, and small rounded ears. Its coat, which varies in color and pattern, is short, soft, and thick.

Havana brown is a strong, medium-sized cat with a solid, reddish-brown coat. It has a long head and oval, vivid green eyes. The breed was developed in England during the late 1940s and early 1950s from mating a black British shorthair and a Siamese cat. The Havana brown is friendly to other cats and to people.

Japanese bobtail has a short, rigid tail with bushy hair. This slender, medium-sized animal has been raised in Japan for hundreds of years. Some Japanese believe the bobtail brings good luck. Many works of art portray this cat seated with a paw raised in greeting.

The bobtail has a triangular head with a long nose, slanted eyes, and large ears. It has silky, medium-length fur. Some types of the bobtail have long hair. The coat may be any color. But the traditional "good luck" color of the coat is white with patches of red and black. The playful bobtail has a soft voice and adapts well to other animals and to new surroundings.

Korat is a quiet, gentle animal that originated in Thailand between 1350 and the late 1700s. In Thailand, this breed is believed to bring good luck. It is a muscular, medium-sized cat with a rounded back. The Korat has a heart-shaped face and large, luminous green eyes. Its short, silvery-gray coat lies flat.

Manx is named for the Isle of Man in the Irish Sea, where the breed originated hundreds of years ago. Types of Manx cats include the *rumpy, rumpy-riser, stumpy,* and *longie.* The most common is the rumpy, which is the only kind of cat without a tail. The cat has a notch where the tail would normally be. The rumpy-riser has a short knot at the tail base. The stumpy has an extremely short tail, and the rare longie has a full-length tail. The playful, sweet-natured Manx has a small body with a round head, broad chest, arched back, and high rump. The muscular rear legs are longer than the front legs. The cat runs with a rabbit-like hop. Its coat and eyes may be any color.

This breed also includes a long-haired type. The long-haired Manx used to be called the Cymric.

Ocicat resembles a wild spotted cat. It has a short, sleek, agouti spotted coat and a large, muscular body. Its coat and eye color varies. The breed originated in Michigan in 1964 by crossing Abyssinian, Siamese, and American shorthair cats. Ocicats are easy to train.

Oriental was developed in England as early as 1950 by crossing Siamese, British shorthair, and Abyssinian cats. The Oriental looks like the Siamese except for its coat and eye color. The eyes are green except in white cats, which can have blue eyes. The coat may be any solid or tabby color. This breed also includes a long-haired type, which was developed in Europe and North America during the 1980s. The long-haired Oriental has a fine, feathery tail plume.

Russian blue has short, extremely thick, bluish-gray fur that is unlike the fur of any other cat. The plush coat seems to glitter because the guard hairs are silver-tipped. The Russian blue has a large, muscular body, long legs, and a long tail. The cat's wedge-shaped head features large ears, a flat forehead, and round green eyes. Despite its name, the origin of this breed is unclear. The animal was brought to England from Russia or northern Europe in the 1800s.

Scottish fold is a medium-sized cat with ears that fold toward the face and downward. Its coat may be any color and pattern. Some types of Scottish fold have long fur. This cat has a roundish body and head and large round eyes. The breed was developed from a farm cat found in Scotland in 1961 that had folded ears as a result of a natural mutation. The Scottish fold has a soft voice and is gentle and affectionate.

Selkirk rex is a large cat with curly, plush fur. Its medium-length coat may be any color and pattern. Some types of Selkirk rex have long hair. The breed originated in Montana near the Selkirk

Mountains in 1987 from mating an unusual-looking curly cat found in an animal shelter with a Persian cat. Selkirk rex has a round head, large eyes, and full cheeks that give it a sweet expression.

Siamese is the most popular short-haired cat. It is best known for its fine, glossy colorpoint coat. The Siamese is a loving pet that seems less independent than other breeds. Siamese cats often utter loud, mournful meows until they get attention.

The Siamese has a long, slender, medium-sized body and a thin tail. Its legs are slim, and its paws small. Its long, wedge-shaped head has straight sides and large, pointed ears. Its eyes are almond-shaped and deep blue. The fur on the trunk of its body is a solid light color. The points are one of four colors—blue, chocolate, lilac, or *seal* (dark brown). Siamese kittens are born white but develop their adult color within a year.

The Siamese originated in Thailand (formerly called Siam). There, these cats were royal property and guarded palaces and temples. In 1884, a pair of Siamese were brought to the United Kingdom. Their offspring won many prizes at cat shows, and the breed soon gained worldwide popularity.

Singapura is a small- to medium-sized, muscular cat with strikingly large ears. Its fine, short coat has dark brown marks on a whitish background. The eyes have hazel, green, or yellow coloring. The Singapura originated from three cats found in Singapore during the early 1970s.

Sphinx is a medium-sized cat with large ears and a hairless or nearly hairless body. It can have a variety of skin colors. The Sphinx was developed from a cat born in Canada in 1966.

Tonkinese is a medium-sized cat with almond-shaped, aqua eyes. Its fine, silky fur may be various shades of brown or blue with a colorpoint pattern. The breed originated in the United States around 1930 as a cross between Siamese and Burmese cats.

Long-haired breeds. The long-haired cat breeds recognized by the Cat Fancier's Association include the American curl, Balinese, Birman, Javanese, Maine coon, Norwegian forest cat, Persian, Ragdoll, Siberian, Somali, Turkish Angora, and Turkish van.

American curl is a medium-sized cat with firm, erect ears that curve up and back from the face toward the center of the back of the head. Its fur may be any color or pattern. Some types have short fur. The eyes may be any color. The American curl

traces its origin to a black, long-haired female cat that was found in California in 1981. The breed was developed by mating this cat and her offspring to various domestic short- and long-haired cats.

Balinese was developed from the Siamese and has the same body structure and coloring. But the fine, silky fur of the Balinese is about 2 inches (5 centimeters) long and has no undercoat. The hair on its long tail spreads out like a plume. The Balinese became an established breed in the United States during the 1960s.

Birman is a large, long-bodied cat with a bushy tail and short legs. Its head is round with a curved nose, round blue eyes, and rounded ears. The cat's long, silky coat has a colorpoint pattern, except that the large, rounded paws are always white. The Birman is a gentle, affectionate animal. The breed originated in what is now Myanmar, where it is considered sacred.

Javanese was developed during the late 1960s and early 1970s in the United States by crossing the Balinese with the colorpoint shorthair. Javanese cats are identical in appearance to colorpoint shorthair cats except for their long, silky coats.

Maine coon, the largest cat, looks somewhat like a raccoon. Its heavy, silky coat is medium length and may be any color. Its fur falls smoothly over most of the body but is shaggy on the *ruff*, stomach, and tail. A ruff is a fringe of long hairs that circles the neck.

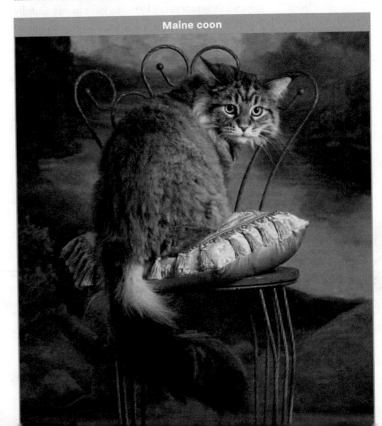

Maine coon

The broad, muscular body of the Maine coon has an almost rectangular shape. Its head features a long nose and large eyes and ears. The cat stands on sturdy, medium-length legs. Tufts of fur cover its large, round paws, which are well suited to running across ice and snow. The breed developed in New England during the 1800s, probably as a result of matings between American shorthairs and long-haired cats brought to Maine by sailors prior to the 1850s.

Norwegian forest cat is an ancient breed that is mentioned in Norwegian mythology. It is a large, muscular cat with a triangular head and large ears with prominent tufts. Its thick fur, which can be any color, has a woolly undercoat and an abundant ruff. Its oval eyes are usually a green-gold color except in white cats, which often have copper or blue eyes or are odd-eyed.

Persian is the most popular breed of long-haired cats. This animal has a stocky, medium- to large-sized body with short, strong legs. Its large, round head includes a snubbed nose; large, wide-set, round eyes; and small, rounded ears. The Persian is admired for its extremely long, fine-textured, glossy coat. Its fur stands out from the body and forms a large ruff and a full, brush-like tail. The coats of Persians vary in color and pattern. Most Persians have copper eyes.

The exact origin of the Persian is unknown. But the breed probably lived in the Middle East more than 3,000 years ago. Persians have been carefully bred for hundreds of years to develop their present distinctive appearance.

Ragdoll, a large-sized cat, gets its name from its limpness. When a ragdoll cat is picked up, it relaxes completely and flops over like a rag doll. Its thick fur is similar to the Birman's fur in color and pattern except that many ragdolls have white markings on the face, ruff, and stomach. The ragdoll is a fearless and calm animal. The breed originated in the United States in the 1960s.

Siberian, a medium- to large-sized cat, has a moderately long coat of any color. The coat becomes noticeably thicker during cold weather. This Russian breed may have been developed at least 1,000 years ago.

Somali looks like the Abyssinian except for its soft, medium-length double coat, which has blue, reddish, or brown bands. The eye color is gold or green. The breed developed from the offspring of Abyssinian cats that were born in the United Kingdom around 1900.

Turkish Angora is one of the oldest breeds. The cat originated in Turkey and spread throughout Europe during the 1700s and 1800s. Beginning in the early 1900s, Angoras were commonly crossed with Persians. As a result, the pure Angora nearly became extinct. Only a few remained by the early 1960s. Then, cat breeders and officials of the zoo in Ankara, Turkey, established a breeding program that saved these cats.

The Turkish Angora has a medium-sized, long, slender body. Its wedge-shaped head includes a long nose and long, pointed ears. Its silky, medium-length hair forms big tufts on the ears and between the toes. The color of the coat and eyes varies. This affectionate cat is known for its intelligence.

Turkish van is a rare and ancient breed that originated in the Lake Van area of southeastern Turkey, where it is considered a regional treasure. Crusaders brought the animal to Europe during the Middle Ages, from about the A.D. 400s through the 1400s. Turkish van cats are also known as *swimming cats* because they love water. Their cashmere-like, medium-long fur is pure white except for markings on the head and tail. The eyes may be blue, amber, or odd-eyed. The Turkish van's body is similar to the Turkish Angora.

Other breeds. There are many other breeds of cats around the world. Some breeds are extremely rare and unusual. Other breeds are popular in only one country or area. Still others have been developed recently and have not yet gained wide recognition.

Turkish van cats snuggling together

The Life of a Cat

Most healthy cats live from twelve to fifteen years. But many reach eighteen or nineteen years of age, and some have lived longer than thirty years.

Reproduction. A *queen* (female cat) can begin mating when she is between five and nine months old, and a *tom* (male cat) can begin when he is between seven and ten months old. Toms can mate at any time. Queens mate only during a period of sexual excitement called *estrus*, or *heat*. Estrus usually occurs during the spring and sometimes during the fall. This period is the breeding season. Estrus usually lasts from six to ten days. If a queen is prevented from mating while she is in heat, she will probably come into heat again within three weeks. In most cases, this cycle recurs during the breeding season until the queen becomes pregnant.

The pregnancy period among cats lasts about nine weeks. When a queen is ready to give birth, she selects a quiet, safe spot as a nest. On the average, a queen bears from three to five kittens at a time. However, litters of as many as fourteen kittens have been reported. The mother can deliver the kittens herself with no human assistance, unless complications develop.

Most newborn kittens weigh about 3½ ounces (99 grams). The mother licks the kittens and so dries them and stimulates their breathing and other body functions. Like other mammals, cats feed their young on milk produced by the mother's body. Newborn kittens cannot see or hear because their eyes and ears are sealed. They depend on their mother to nurse, clean, and protect them. The father plays no role in caring for the kittens.

Growth and development. Healthy kittens show a steady, daily weight gain. Their eyes usually open from seven to ten days after birth. Soon afterward, their ears open and the first teeth begin to appear. Kittens start to walk and explore their environment at about three weeks of age. But the mother watches over them and retrieves kittens that stray too far from the nest.

By about five weeks of age, kittens have most of their temporary teeth. They then begin to eat solid foods and to lap water. The mother usually begins to *wean* (stop nursing) them at about this age. The weaning process lasts several weeks.

When kittens are about four weeks old, owners should begin to handle them frequently and play with them gently. Kittens that receive such attention tend to become good pets. They learn faster

Newborn kittens cannot open their eyes.

and have fewer behavior problems than kittens that are ignored or overprotected. A kitten that has contact with a variety of people will be less fearful of strangers and new situations as an adult. Kittens can even learn not to fear dogs if they are allowed to play with a friendly dog.

By about six weeks of age, kittens have a fully developed brain and nervous system and can be safely separated from their mother. However, if possible, kittens should remain with their mother and their littermates until they are nine or ten weeks of age.

Kittens develop important physical skills by playing with one another. They also learn to get along with other cats in this way. In addition, kittens improve many instinctive skills, especially hunting skills, by watching and imitating their mother. The majority of cats reach their adult body size at about one year of age.

Communication. Cats communicate with one another, with other animals, and with human beings in a variety of ways. Cats use sounds, body signals, and scents as means of communication.

Some experts estimate that a cat can make more than sixty different sounds, ranging from a soft purr to a loud wail, or *caterwaul*. These sounds originate in the *larynx* (voice box) in the throat. Cats can purr on both *inspiration* (breathing in) and *expiration* (breathing out). The sound is produced by air as it vibrates through the space in the larynx called the *glottis*.

The sounds a cat makes may have various meanings. For example, depending on the situation, a meow can be a friendly greeting, or it may express curiosity, hunger, or loneliness. Purring usually means contentment, but some cats also purr when they are sick. Hisses, growls, and screams indicate anger and fear.

Cats also communicate through various body and tail positions and facial expressions. A contented cat often lies on its chest with its eyes half closed. To invite play or petting, some cats roll over on one side and wave a paw in the air. However, a similar posture accompanied by extended claws, a direct stare, and ears folded back indicates a fearful cat ready to defend itself. A friendly cat may greet someone with its tail raised vertically. It may also bump its head against the person and lick an extended hand. An angry or frightened cat flicks its tail from side to side, arches its back, and puffs up its fur. A submissive cat crouches down, flattens its ears, and avoids direct eye contact.

Cats commonly communicate with one another by means of odors. Cats have scent glands on the forehead, around the mouth, and near the base of the tail. A cat rubs these glands against people and objects and so marks them with its scent. Only cats and a few other animals can smell these odors. A tom sprays urine on objects and so marks his mating territory.

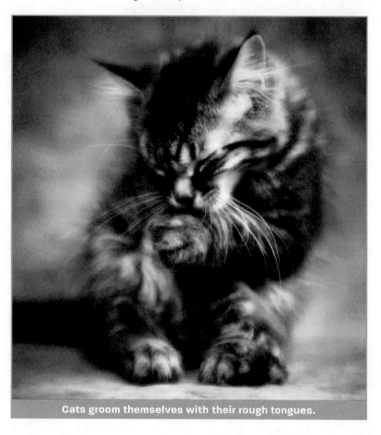

Cats groom themselves with their rough tongues.

Caring for a Cat

Feeding. Cats need a balanced diet. Such a diet supplies the proper amount of various nutrients, which provide energy and are essential for growth and replacement of body tissues. Cats require proteins, fats, vitamins, and minerals in their diet. The easiest way to meet a cat's nutritional needs is to buy high-quality commercial cat food. The label should indicate that the food is "complete and balanced." Cats should not be fed dog food because it does not meet their dietary requirements. A diet of mostly meat is unbalanced.

Cats are not naturally finicky eaters. But owners should give them a variety of commercial foods to prevent them from developing fussy appetites. Cats may occasionally be fed small amounts of such cooked foods as beef liver, eggs, fish, and vegetables. Many cats also enjoy milk, cheese, and other dairy products. However, such foods cause diarrhea in some cats. Owners should provide fresh drinking water at all times. Food and water bowls should be cleaned daily.

Kittens that have been weaned should be fed small amounts four times a day until they are three months old. They should eat three times daily until they are six months old, and then twice a day until they are full grown. Adult cats require only one meal a day, but many seem happier with two smaller meals. Food may be kept available at all times for a healthy cat that does not overeat. Sick cats, pregnant and nursing queens, and old cats often need special diets.

Grooming. Cats instinctively clean themselves. They do so by licking their fur with their tongue. They also rub and scratch their fur with their paws. At least once a day, a cat licks a paw and washes its face and head with the wet paw. But not all cats groom themselves well.

Owners should brush or comb a cat's fur daily to clean it and to remove loose hairs. In the case of long-haired cats, such care is essential to prevent the coat from tangling and matting. Daily brushing or combing also reduces the amount of loose hairs that cats swallow when they clean themselves. Swallowed hair may wad up and form a *hairball* in the cat's stomach. Hairballs can cause gagging, vomiting, and loss of appetite. If a cat cannot spit up a hairball, surgery may be required to remove it. Owners may feed their cat a small amount of petroleum jelly or a commercial preparation once a week to prevent hairball formation. A veterinarian can suggest safe methods of administering such products. If necessary, owners may clean their cat's ears with a soft cloth and brush their teeth with a cotton-tipped swab or a small toothbrush. Owners may also trim the tips of a cat's claws.

Some cats—especially those allowed outdoors—become so soiled that they need a bath. Most cats dislike bathing. But if cats are bathed about once a month when they are kittens, they will become accustomed to water. Kittens also should be brushed or combed so that they will be easier to care for after they grow older.

Training should begin when a kitten is about eight weeks old. A cat can learn to respond to its name. Some cats have been trained to walk on a leash and to do such tricks as shaking hands and retrieving a ball.

The most effective way to train a cat is with praise, petting, and food rewards for good behavior. Correct a cat immediately with a sharp "No" if it misbehaves. Always react to a particular action in the same manner so that the cat can learn what to expect. Owners should be patient with their pet and avoid using physical punishment. Squirting a cat with water is a good way to stop undesirable behavior.

Indoor cats should learn to use a litter box. Cats instinctively bury their body wastes, and so training them to use a litter box is easy. Kittens raised with a mother that uses a litter box will usually begin to use it themselves before they are five or six weeks old.

Any smooth-surfaced plastic or enamel pan can be used as a litter box. Put the pan in a quiet spot. Place a layer of commercial litter or sterilized sand or soil in the bottom. Sift the litter clean with a strainer each day. Clean the pan and change the litter whenever a third of the litter is damp or, at least, every fourth day. Most cats will not use a wet or dirty box.

Dirty litter can spread disease. Cat owners, especially pregnant women, should take care not to directly touch the litter when cleaning the litter box.

Cats that have not learned to use a litter box at an early age must be trained. Place the cat in the box after it eats, when it wakes up, and after play. Praise the cat if it uses the box. The cat will soon learn to go to the box by itself.

Cats should also be trained to claw a scratching post instead of carpeting, draperies, and furniture. Cats naturally scratch at objects to pull off the worn outer layers of their claws and to mark their

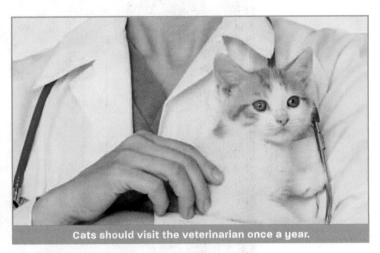

Cats should visit the veterinarian once a year.

territory. A bark-covered log or a piece of wood covered with carpeting, cork, or fabric makes a good scratching post. Rub some *catnip,* a strongly scented herb that many cats love to sniff, into the post to attract the cat's interest. Guide the cat's front paws down the post. Whenever the cat begins to claw another object, correct the animal immediately and take it to the post. Some cats cannot be trained to use a post, however, and so some owners take their pet to a veterinarian for *declawing.* Declawing is a surgical procedure in which the claws are removed from the paws. A declawed cat may have difficulty defending itself, and so the animal should not be allowed outdoors unattended.

Some cats enjoy chewing plants. But owners can train their cat to leave houseplants alone, especially if they provide a pot of grass or oats for the pet.

Veterinary care. A cat that is kept indoors faces fewer health risks than an outdoor cat. Outdoor cats may be struck by automobiles, poisoned by pesticides, or attacked by sick or unfriendly animals. But even indoor cats are not entirely safe. They can fall from open windows and unenclosed balconies. In addition, many cleaning products and certain houseplants, such as ivy and philodendron, are poisonous to cats. Owners should place such items out of the reach of cats.

Kittens should be taken to a veterinarian when they are about eight to ten weeks old for a physical examination. They should also receive vaccinations to protect them from common cat diseases. An adult cat should visit a veterinarian once a year for a checkup and additional shots. Veterinary care protects an owner's health as well as a cat's because some animal diseases can be transmitted to people. Such a disease is called a *zoonosis.*

Cats can receive ribbons for shape, coat, color, and eye color in cat shows.

Cat owners should learn to recognize signs of illness in their pet. A healthy cat has clean ears, clear eyes, a moist nose, pink tongue and gums, and a clean, glossy coat. Consult a veterinarian if a cat shows any change in appearance or behavior for more than twenty-four hours.

The most dangerous cat zoonosis, *rabies*, is an infection of the nervous system. Rabies is commonly transmitted by a bite from an infected animal. All cats permitted outdoors require periodic rabies vaccinations.

One of the most widespread cat diseases is *panleukopenia*, also called *feline enteritis* or *cat distemper*. This highly contagious infection is caused by a virus and is often fatal. Symptoms of panleukopenia include listlessness, loss of appetite, high fever, and severe vomiting and diarrhea. If a cat has several of these symptoms, call a veterinarian at once. All cats should be vaccinated against panleukopenia.

Two other serious diseases of cats are *feline leukemia* and the illness caused by the *feline immunodeficiency virus* (FIV). Feline leukemia is a form of cancer that affects the cat's blood-forming organs and lymph tissues. This fatal disease is caused by a virus that also can cause other, nonfatal ailments in cats. FIV attacks the cat's immune system and causes it to grow steadily weaker. Symptoms of the illness include infections, fevers, enlarged lymph nodes, and loss of appetite. FIV is spread by the bite of infected cats and can cause signs of illness many months or years after infection. Vaccinations exist for both feline leukemia and FIV.

Respiratory infections, ranging from mild colds to pneumonia, are common among cats. Signs of such infections include sneezing, a runny nose, watery eyes, and fever. A veterinarian can give vaccinations to prevent respiratory infections.

Many kinds of parasites may cause health problems in cats. Certain types of worms, including roundworms and tapeworms, can infect a cat's intestines and other organs. Worms may cause listlessness, weight loss, vomiting, and diarrhea. Some other parasites may live on a cat's skin and cause severe itching. Fleas and ear mites are the most common external parasites. Cats may also get *ringworm*, a skin disease caused by a fungus. Owners should remove parasites from cats to improve the pet's health and to prevent the cat from transmitting diseases to people.

Birth control. Each year, millions of unwanted cats are abandoned. Animal shelters must destroy many of these cats. Countless other strays die of starvation, injury, or disease. Because the problem of unwanted cats is so serious, owners should not allow their cats to mate unless a good home can be provided for the kittens.

Owners can try to prevent cats from mating by keeping them indoors. But this method of birth control is difficult. It also does not prevent such undesirable sex-related behavior as the spraying of urine by toms and the howling of queens during estrus.

A veterinarian can permanently prevent a cat from reproducing by *neutering* it—that is, by surgically removing some of the cat's sex organs. Neutering also ends sex-related behavior. The operation is commonly called *spaying* when performed on a female cat, and *castration* when done on a male cat.

In an effort to control cat overpopulation, many veterinarians now neuter cats any time after six weeks of age. Most cats, however, are neutered just before they reach sexual maturity, around six months of age in females and after six months in males.

Cat Associations and Shows

Cat lovers worldwide have formed many associations to promote interest in cats. The largest of these groups, the Cat Fanciers' Association, Incorporated, has member clubs throughout the world. Cat associations *register* purebreds—that is, they record the ancestries of the animals—to ensure the preservation of the breeds. The associations also sponsor cat shows and establish standards for judging each breed. These standards cover such features as the shape of the body and the head, eye color, and coat type and color.

Breeders and pet owners display their finest cats at shows. Cats compete in groups based on such factors as age, sex, and breed. Show judges award points for healthiness, for temperament, and for how closely the animal meets breed standards. Cats that earn enough points may become champions or grand champions.

History

Scientists believe that members of the cat family gradually developed from a small weasel-like animal called *Miacis*, which lived more than fifty million years ago. Miacis also was probably the ancestor of such mammals as bears, dogs, and raccoons. Members of the cat family first appeared about forty million years ago.

No one knows exactly how or where cats were first tamed. But many authorities believe the domestic cat is a direct descendant of an African wildcat that the Egyptians tamed—possibly as early as 3500 B.C. Domesticated wildcats killed mice, rats, and snakes and so prevented these pests from overrunning Egyptian farms and grain storehouses. The cats became pampered pets and were honored in paintings and sculptures.

By about 1500 B.C., the Egyptians had begun to consider cats sacred. They worshiped a goddess of love and fertility called *Bastet*, or *Bast*, who was represented as having the head of a cat and the body of a woman. If a person killed a cat, the punishment was usually death. When a pet cat died, the Egyptians shaved off their eyebrows as a sign of mourning. They made dead cats into mummies. Scientists have found an ancient cat cemetery in Egypt containing over 300,000 cat mummies.

Greek and Phoenician traders probably brought domestic cats to Europe and the Middle East about 1000 B.C. The ancient Greeks and Romans valued cats for their ability to control rodents. In Rome, the cat was a symbol of liberty and was regarded as the guardian spirit of a household.

Domestic cats spread from the Middle East throughout Asia. In the Far East, cats were used to keep rodents from destroying temple manuscripts and from attacking silkworm cocoons, from which silk is made. People of Asia admired the beauty and mystery of the cat. The animal became a favorite subject of artists and writers in China and Japan.

Statue of Egyptian goddess Bastet

In Europe during the Middle Ages, the cat was considered a symbol of evil. Superstitious people associated the cat with witchcraft and the Devil. For this reason, people killed hundreds of thousands of cats.

Experts believe that the destruction of so many cats led to a huge increase in the rat population of Europe and contributed to the spread of the *Black Death*, an epidemic of plague. This disease is transmitted to people by rat fleas. In the 1300s, it killed from one-fourth to one-half of the people who lived in Europe.

By the 1600s, Europeans had begun to realize once again the importance of cats in controlling rodents. Cats gradually regained popularity. European explorers, colonists, and traders brought domestic cats to the New World during the 1600s and 1700s. Throughout the 1800s, settlers took cats with them as they moved westward. Most cats in the United States and Canada today are descendants of these cats.

The first cat show was held in London in 1871. In 1887, the National Cat Club of Britain was formed. Interest in breeding and owning cats increased greatly. Today, the cat's ever-growing popularity has produced a billion-dollar industry that provides services and products for cats and their owners.

Scientific classification. Cats belong to the cat family, Felidae. Domestic cats are *Felis domesticus.*

MLA Citation

"Cats." *The Southwestern Advantage Topic Source.* Nashville: Southwestern. 2013.

ADDITIONAL RESOURCES

Books to Read

Davis, Caroline. *Essential Cat.* Reader's Digest, 2005.

Halls, Vicky. *Cat Confidential.* Gotham Books, 2005.

Sands, David. *Cats: 500 Questions Answered.* Hamlyn, 2005.

Seidensticker, John, and Lumpkin, Susan. *Cats: Smithsonian Answer Book.* Smithsonian Institution, 2004. Includes wild and domestic cats.

Web Sites

Cats @ nationalgeographic.com

http://www.nationalgeographic.com/features/97/cats/
National Geographic's site about cats.

International Cat Association

www.tica.org
The official Web site of the International Cat Association.

Shelter On-line Fact Sheet Directory

http://www.paws.org/
The Progressive Animal Welfare Society (PAWS) provides fact sheets on pets, including dogs, cats, rabbits, and other small mammals.

Wild cat species information

http://www.cathouse-fcc.org/cats.html
Information about wild cats, from the Feline Conservation Center, a desert zoo near Los Angeles, California.

Search Strings

Role of Cats Throughout History

cats role throughout history skills religion (134,000)

cats role throughout history (4,090,000) *This was a lot, but the first few returns were exactly what the searcher wanted.

cat shows associations (1,050,000) *Again, this was a lot but the first few returns were a good match.

Famous Cartoon Cats

famous cartoon cats Felix Tom Sylvester (4,900)

famous cartoon cats (159,000)

famous cartoon cats Felix Tom Sylvester "The Aristocats" Garfield (71)

Breeds of Cats

breeds of cats purebreds crossbreds (2,660)

breeds of cats (209,000)

breeds of cats short-haired long-haired (13,500)

Larger, Wild Cats

cats large wild (227,000)

cats large wild characteristics appearance (111,000)

cats large wild saber-tooth tiger cheetah mountain lion, caracal lynx (79)

Cats, The Musical

Cats, the musical "Andrew Lloyd Webber" (44,100)

Cats, the musical "Andrew Lloyd Webber" popular comedy "T. S. Eliot" (200)

BACKGROUND INFORMATION

A New Look at the Endangered Cheetah

For years, scientists thought genetic problems in the cheetah were helping doom the swift cat to extinction. But new research is casting doubt on that view.

—by Yvonne Baskin

A plaintive meow rises from the deep grass inside a large enclosure at the San Diego Wild Animal Park. Suddenly, the grass rustles and a black-spotted golden cat, the size of a large dog, stalks into view. This sleek, powerful animal with amber eyes and the voice of a tiny tomcat is Punchow, a magnificent male cheetah.

Punchow and his kind are the fastest sprinters on Earth, and human beings have admired, captured, and even hunted with them for thousands of years. But now, as humanity carves up the cat's native habitat in Africa, the survival of the cheetah is at stake. So for decades, researchers at zoos and cheetah breeding centers have been trying to boost the cheetah population by encouraging captive cats like Punchow to breed.

Scientists' limited understanding of cheetah biology has made this task extremely difficult, and Punchow himself symbolizes the puzzle biologists face as they work to save these animals from extinction.

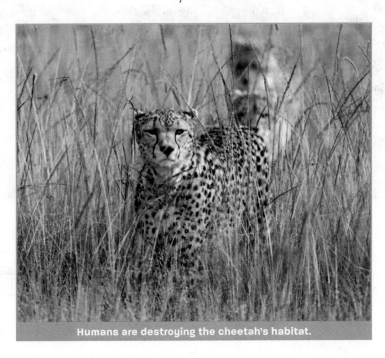
Humans are destroying the cheetah's habitat.

Punchow may be genetically almost identical to all other members of his species, a possibility that some experts believe accounts for the health problems they have observed in captive cheetahs—for example, poor breeding success and a high susceptibility to disease. Indeed, a researcher armed only with Punchow's lab tests might conclude that the cat is sterile. What is puzzling is that Punchow managed to father nine cubs by two different females the first two times he was bred.

Punchow's reproductive success—and that of other cheetahs in the 1990s—has sparked a debate over how the cheetah's genetic makeup affects the species'

captivity, changing the way zoos manage the cats appears to boost the success of breeding programs. These developments have led many researchers to look anew at the cheetah—and to conclude that, at least for captive cheetahs, the outlook may not be as gloomy as they had thought.

Portrait of a sprinter. Cheetahs have long been famed as the fastest, and among the most fascinating, short-distance runners in existence. Scientists believe cheetahs can accelerate from walking speed to about 65 kilometers (40 miles) an hour in less than two seconds and briefly explode to top speeds of 110 kilometers (70 miles) an hour. The cheetah arches and bends its

330 yards), a distance equal to about two or three football fields. But that can be far enough to allow the cheetah to overtake swift prey, typically a Thomson's gazelle or other small antelope. The cheetah then knocks the animal to the ground with a forepaw and strangles it with a crushing bite to the throat.

For thousands of years, cheetahs have been prized in royal menageries for their spectacular hunting style, as well as their regal grace and soulful faces, marked by distinctive black lines that curve like a trail of tears from the eyes to the mouth. The structure of cheetahs' windpipes prevents these gentle-looking cats from roaring like lions. Instead, they make sounds described as chirps, stutters, moans, and purrs. Cheetahs can be tamed, and beginning at least 3,000 years ago with the ancient Egyptians, aristocrats commonly trained the cats to hunt just as they trained falcons. A royal chronicle tells how Akbar the Great, who ruled India's Mogul Empire in the A.D. 1500s, captured at least 9,000 cheetahs during his 49-year reign to aid him in hunting deer.

How many cheetahs remain in the wild? Cheetah conservationists would give a great deal to have Akbar's 9,000 cheetahs back today. Conservationists estimate that around the year 1900, hundreds of thousands of cheetahs lived throughout most of Africa, western Asia, and India. That is no longer the case. The cheetah disappeared from India in the 1940s, and by the 1970s, fewer than 200 survived in Iran, probably the cat's last Asian stronghold. Today, only scattered pockets of chee-

Cheetahs hunting a wildebeest calf

chances for survival. Researchers looking at the cats in the wild point out that free-living cheetahs are endangered primarily because their habitat is shrinking and because cheetah behavior prevents the animals from thriving in game reserves. For cheetahs in

flexible spine as it gathers its long front and hind legs beneath its body, then leaps as far as 7 meters (23 feet)—about five times the length of its body—in a single stride. The cat can sustain its full-speed pursuit for only 200 to 300 meters (220 to

tahs remain, chiefly in southern and eastern Africa and in the semiarid Sahel region south of the Sahara. Estimates of cheetah numbers are imprecise, because cheetahs, like nearly all wild cats, are shy, stealthy, solitary, and therefore difficult to count. Estimates of the current African cheetah population range from a low of 5,000 to highs of 15,000 to 25,000. Another 1,000 cheetahs live in captivity around the world, some 300 of them in North America.

Wild cheetahs: a struggle to survive. The cheetah is endangered today largely because human beings have taken over much of the cat's habitat and killed off the small antelope the cheetah hunts for food. People have also killed many cheetahs directly. By the early 1970s, the fur trade had become a major threat to large cats such as tigers and cheetahs. At the time, the United States alone was importing 25,000 large-cat skins each year for fur coats, rugs, and other fashion items. Passage of the United States Endangered Species Act in 1973 and the Convention on International Trade in Endangered Species, an international treaty administered by the United Nations, in 1975 gave the cats protected status and reduced the trade in cheetah fur. Nevertheless, cheetahs are still routinely shot by African farmers and ranchers who view the cats as a threat to livestock, just as American ranchers view wolves and mountain lions.

Africa's animal parks and game reserves protect many animals from human beings. However, cheetahs are poorly suited to life in these reserves. Within the borders of a typical game reserve, herd animals such as zebras, wildebeest, and antelope are protected from human hunters and so thrive in numbers not normally seen on the open savanna (grassland with scattered trees). As a result, populations of the large or powerful predators that feed on herd animals—predators such as lions, hyenas, and leopards—also are high. But middle-sized predators such as cheetahs and wild dogs suffer when they are forced to compete in this crowded and confined landscape, according to Timothy M. Caro of the University of California at Davis, who has studied wild cheetahs in Tanzania's Serengeti Plain since 1980.

Cheetah handicaps in competition with other species. Cheetahs are handicapped, for example, by the very fact that they can perform spectacular high-speed chases. To catch its breath after making a kill, a cheetah may need to lie panting for up to 30 minutes before it can even begin to eat. During this resting period, hyenas, lions, leopards, and even flocks of vultures may steal the winded cat's kill. According to Caro, 1 in 10 cheetah kills is lost this way. Moreover, unlike most of their competitors, cheetahs will not eat carrion (rotting meat). If they lose a kill, they must hunt again to get fresh meat.

Because the cheetah is built for speed and not for fighting, the animal has little chance of fending off lions or hyenas even when it is rested. Its bones are light and its body is thin and elongated, making the cat a poor match for a heavier adversary. And cheetahs are the only cats whose claws are always bared, like those of a dog, rather than being pulled back into protective sheaths. This feature gives cheetahs extra traction for running, but it also dulls the claws and makes them relatively useless for fighting. In addition, the cat's unusually broad nasal passages, which help the cheetah take in a large supply of oxygen while running, leave less room in the skull for the roots of long canines (tearing teeth), which are characteristic of lions and other wild cats. As a result, the cheetah's fangs are too short to take on fierce competitors.

Cheetahs face another threat from their larger relatives, Caro discovered. Beginning in 1987, Caro and his student Karen Laurenson attached radio collars to the necks of 20 free-ranging female cheetahs. For the next few years they tracked the cheetahs' movements, and whenever a cheetah had a litter, the researchers periodically examined the cubs. Caro and Laurenson concluded that 95 percent of cheetah cubs born in the Serengeti die before adulthood, most of them while still helpless in their dens, and that 75 percent of these cubs were killed by marauding lions. In protected areas across Africa, the researchers found, a high lion population correlates with a low cheetah population.

Captive cheetahs: a puzzling failure to breed. As cheetah populations have dwindled in the wild, biologists have felt mounting pressure to try to breed cheetahs in captivity. Their task has seemed monumental. Indeed, Akbar the Great unwittingly set a record that was to last 400 years when one of his cheetahs gave birth to a litter of three cubs in the 1500s. Even with thousands of the cats to work with, Akbar's cheetah keepers never recorded producing a second litter. And no other captive births are on record until 1956, when a female in the Philadelphia Zoo also produced a litter of three, all of which died in infancy. A handful of other cheetah births were reported during the 1960s at zoos in Europe and the United States, but not until the early 1970s did a captive-born cub survive to maturity and give birth to a second generation of captive-born cubs. Zoos still had to purchase wild-caught animals to restock their exhibits.

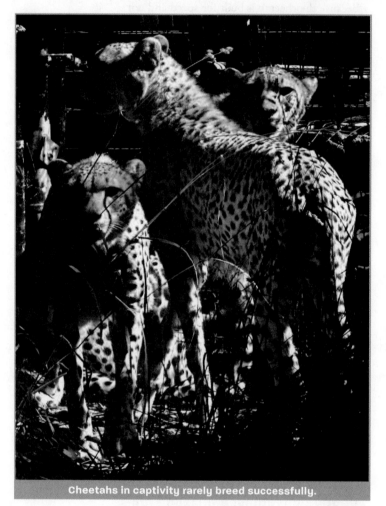

Cheetahs in captivity rarely breed successfully.

During the 1970s, zoos began to realize the urgency of establishing a self-sustaining population of captive cheetahs, both to avoid taking any more animals from the wild and to build up a pool of cheetahs that might one day be used to restock Africa's remaining savannas. The zoos redoubled their efforts, and the number of captive births rose steadily. Most of these births, however, were at only a few institutions, including the San Diego Wild Animal Park, the Columbus Zoo in Ohio, and Wildlife Safari in Winston, Oregon. By the end of

the decade, researchers at other zoos began to wonder whether their efforts were being foiled by biological problems in the cheetahs themselves.

A surprising discovery about cheetah biology. In the late 1970s, the National Zoo in Washington, D.C., asked David E. Wildt, then a biomedical researcher working with domestic cats, for help with the cheetah. Wildt collected sperm samples from captive cheetahs belonging to several American zoos. By looking at the samples under a microscope, he found to his surprise that about 70 percent of the sperm were abnormal. The abnormal sperm appeared damaged, with strangely bent or coiled tails or other deformities that would prevent them from penetrating and fertilizing a female's egg.

At first, Wildt thought the abnormalities in the cheetahs' sperm must be a result of the stressful conditions under which most zoo cheetahs were kept. Then, in 1981, Wildt went to South Africa to perform similar studies on male cheetahs at the DeWildt Cheetah Breeding and Research Center, near Pretoria. The South African cats, most of them bred in captivity but including some caught in the wild, showed the same level of sperm abnormalities as cheetahs in U.S. zoos.

To help determine why the cheetah had such high rates of abnormal sperm, Wildt sent blood samples from each male cat to Stephen J. O'Brien, a researcher at the U.S. National Cancer Institute in Bethesda, Maryland. O'Brien wondered whether the cheetah's reproductive problems were due to a genetic problem, possibly a lack of genetic variation among individual cats. Genes are components of living cells that contain the blueprint for the organism's characteristics and functions. In human beings, for example, genes control the color of a person's skin, eyes, and hair, his or her blood type, and all other inherited characteristics. The genes for our species come in many versions, and that genetic variety explains why human beings are not all as alike as identical twins.

Why genetic variation matters. Scientists think genetic variation may be a natural safeguard for a species, because such variation increases the likelihood that individuals will respond differently to most threats that arise. For example, a disease may be deadly to most members of a population, but if a few individuals are genetically different enough to survive it, the species will live on.

Genetic variation may also help guard against the disorders caused by inheriting flawed genes.

Generally speaking, organisms inherit two copies of each gene, one from each parent. In human beings and other animal species, most inherited diseases occur only if an individual inherits a flawed version of the same gene from both parents. In a population with a great deal of genetic variation among its members, the odds of both parents having the same flawed gene are low. But in a population without much variation, it may be highly likely that both parents will have the same versions of genes. In such a group, many offspring may be born with inherited disorders.

Genetic variation in the cheetah. To find out if cheetahs showed a lack of genetic variation, O'Brien tested blood samples from 55 of the cats, comparing 52 different proteins found in the blood of each animal. Genes carry the instructions for building proteins, and any slight variation in the makeup of a protein reflects a corresponding variation in a gene. O'Brien found that for nearly all the proteins he tested, the cheetahs in his study had virtually the same genetic makeup. His tests showed that cheetahs may be as similar genetically as mice that scientists have deliberately inbred—by mating cousins, siblings, and other close relatives for many generations—to create uniform strains of mice for use in laboratory experiments.

But most of the cheetahs in O'Brien's study had been out of the wild only a generation or two at most, so their genetic uniformity was not the result of inbreeding by zoos. How, then, did cheetahs become so similar?

O'Brien speculated that in the distant past, the cheetah population experienced one or more bottlenecks—drastic population crashes in which a large proportion of the species died, leaving, perhaps, only a handful of survivors. Using the cheetah's current degree of variability as a guide, O'Brien calculated that the cheetah probably fell to the brink of extinction beginning 12,000 to 10,000 years ago, at the end of the Pleistocene Ice Age, a period in which many other mammals, such as mammoths and saber-toothed cats, became extinct. According to this view, each of the cheetah's population bottlenecks was followed by extreme inbreeding among the few survivors, which in a drastic case may have numbered only a few litters. This inbreeding, continued over many generations, would have eventually produced a population in which nearly all individuals shared the same limited pool of genes.

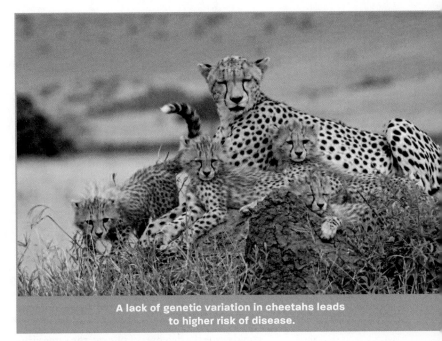

A lack of genetic variation in cheetahs leads to higher risk of disease.

Controversy about genetic variation. Not all experts accept the bottleneck theory. A more likely scenario, some say, is that the cheetah population remained abundant but was fragmented into numerous small, isolated subpopulations. Such fragmentation could have taken place toward the end of the Ice Age, as climate fluctuations caused the advance and retreat of ecosystems such as forest and savanna. As a forest extended into a savanna, cutting off one portion from another, the animals on either side of the forest could have been separated and remained so for thousands of years. According to this theory, when one such group died out because of disease, overhunting, or some other reason, its territory was eventually recolonized by a few individuals from a nearby subpopulation. Repeated over and over, this process would eventually lead to a loss of genetic variation.

Population geneticist Philip W. Hedrick of Arizona State University in Tempe is one expert who agrees that the cheetah could have achieved its low genetic variation without its population dropping to the verge of extinction. But Hedrick also points out that several animal species—including beavers in Sweden and northern elephant seals living off the California coast—have low genetic variation, yet their large populations appear to suffer no health or reproductive problems as a result. "We don't really know how much variation is required for a species to be fit and healthy," Hedrick says.

Cheetah genetics: the debate over disease.

Thus, a more important question for the cheetah than how it got its low genetic diversity is whether the cat's survival has been compromised by it. Scientists ask, for instance, whether the cheetah's genetic uniformity has indeed made it overly susceptible to disease. To answer that question, they consider a disaster that began in May 1982, when a female cheetah that had been recently brought to Oregon's Wildlife Safari became ill and died from feline infectious peritonitis (FIP), a viral disease that strikes domestic cats but is rarely fatal to them. Within the next year, 18 of the 42 cheetahs at the park died of FIP-related illnesses.

O'Brien suggested that the "catastrophic sensitivity" the cheetahs displayed to the virus was a consequence of their lack of genetic variation. In other words, the genes that code for certain defenses in the cheetah's disease-fighting immune system were so similar among the cats that if FIP could evade the defenses of one cat, the same virus could hit all the cheetahs equally hard.

In research published in 1985, O'Brien and his colleagues tested the amount of genetic variation in the cheetah's immune system by grafting patches of skin between pairs of unrelated cheetahs. Normally, when skin or other tissue is transplanted from one individual to another, the recipient's immune system rejects the foreign tissue, attacking and trying to destroy it. Strong drugs are necessary to prevent this rejection response in human transplant patients, and biologists have found that a house cat usually rejects a skin graft from an unrelated cat within 14 days. In contrast, of the 14 cheetahs that received skin grafts in O'Brien's study, only 3 appeared to reject the grafts, and these rejections took 40 days or more. Thus, the investigators concluded, the cheetahs' immune systems must have been genetically very similar.

Nevertheless, other scientists question whether the cheetahs' vulnerability to FIP resulted from genetic uniformity or simply from the fact that the cats had never before been exposed to the virus. Now that cheetahs have been exposed to FIP, these researchers note, the cats seem to be developing resistance to the disease. Only three captive cheetahs died of FIP between 1987 and 1991, and by 1991 two-thirds of the captive cats in the United States carried antibodies (protective proteins) to FIP in their blood, showing that their immune systems had learned to ward off the virus.

A new look at breeding problems.

By the early 1990s, scientists were also questioning the link, first suggested by O'Brien and Wildt, between the cheetah's lack of genetic diversity and the cat's poor breeding history in zoos. Caro and his team, for instance, pointed out in 1992 that cheetahs in the wild have the same sperm defects as captive cheetahs, yet they seem to have no breeding problems. Then, in January 1993, researchers working with the Cheetah Species Survival Plan (Cheetah SSP) of the American Zoo and Aquarium Association, based in Bethesda, Maryland, published the results of nearly five years of exhaustive studies on the North American captive cheetah population. The reports included a detailed study by Wildt of reproduction among 128 cheetahs in American zoos. The males showed the same high levels of abnormal sperm Wildt had seen before. But surprisingly, these abnormalities seemed to bear no relation to the animals' fertility. Successful sires like Punchow had lab reports that looked just as bad as those of males that had failed to father cubs.

Other SSP researchers pointed out that even as scientists debated the genetics-fertility link, the tide of opinion in the zoo community was turning away from genetic factors as the chief cause of the cheetah's breeding problems. These researchers noted that as zoos changed how they managed cheetahs, the number of captive births in North America had risen to 201 cubs in 58 litters during the five years between 1987 and 1991. That was nearly half the number of cubs born in these institutions during the previous 30 years. These results convinced most cheetah specialists that the main reason for captive cheetahs' failure to breed lay not with the cheetahs' genes, but with how the cats' keepers have managed them.

Strategies of successful breeding programs.

Unfortunately, no simple lab tests can help identify just what successful zoos are doing right, though a few strategies are suggested by studies of cheetahs in the wild. For instance, cheetahs seem to breed more readily when they are not housed with other wild cats, where they are intimidated by lions in nearby cages. Another strategy entails keeping female cheetahs alone except for their cubs to mimic their solitary existence on the savanna.

To find out what else goes on in successful breeding programs, SSP researcher Nadja Wielebnowski, another of Caro's students, has spent much time observing the cats in zoos, rather than on the savanna. One thing some successful programs do, she found, is keep the cats in relatively large areas generally secluded from visitors, rather than on exhibit. A second strategy involves keeping a large number of cheetahs on hand so that animals can be introduced to several possible mates. Researchers at the San Diego Wild Animal Park, as well as at other zoos, also have noticed that some females seem to prefer certain males and tend to reject advances by others.

Some of the most successful breeding facilities have set up two separate living areas so that cheetahs can be moved around periodically and be stimulated by seeing and, especially, smelling unfamiliar cheetah neighbors. Zoologists note that because cheetahs are solitary, wide-ranging mammals, their sense of smell is an important means of communication and "courtship" between potential mates. Wielebnowski agrees, adding that a female in the Serengeti may range over 800 square kilometers (300 square miles). Wielebnowski also notes that cheetahs, like other intelligent animals, "seem to get bored and lose interest in their surroundings" if they are deprived of stimulation for prolonged periods. Since 1990, several zoos have tried to combat cheetah boredom by setting up coursing tracks, such as those used for training greyhounds, to encourage cheetahs to do what they do best: run.

Looking toward the future. Despite the evidence that behavioral explanations for the cheetah's low reproductive rates are at least as important as genetic ones, few scientists are complacent about the cat's potential for future genetic problems. For this reason, researchers working with the Cheetah SSP are seeking to preserve whatever genetic variation the cheetah does have. Their plan is to avoid inbreeding by reducing zoos' reliance on cheetahs that have already produced many young and attempting to get offspring from cheetahs that have never bred. In November 1993, the Cheetah SSP management group met to pore over the cheetah studbook, a record of all the cheetahs in North America, which includes family trees for the captive-born animals. The group set out a master plan for the coming year's breeding efforts, choosing 20 male and 20 female cheetahs that are not closely related to most of the cats in the North American population. Because a number of cats chosen for the program are past the normal breeding age, the group plans to use techniques such as artificial insemination to help some of them reproduce.

Zoo breeding successes are extremely heartening, according to zoologist Jack Grisham of the Oklahoma City Zoo, who directs the Cheetah SSP. Grisham has even begun to believe that if zoos don't manage the size of the captive population, they'll eventually run out of room for cheetahs. Still, the captive breeding is just "icing on the cake" for the cheetah species, according to Caro. In his view, boosting populations in this way provides only a temporary stopgap to the loss of cheetahs in the wild.

Modest conservation efforts on behalf of free-living cheetahs. Unfortunately, few conservation efforts are directed at free-living cheetahs. The most well-known was launched in 1990 by a husband-wife team, conservationists Daniel Kraus and Laurie Marker-Kraus of the National Zoo, who now live in Namibia. This nation on the southwest coast of Africa hosts the world's largest concentration of surviving cheetahs, perhaps as many as 2,500. However, 95 percent of the cats live outside Namibia's reserves and thus come into direct conflict with human beings. The Krauses try to persuade skeptical farmers to ward off cheetahs rather than shoot them when the cats attack their livestock. The conservationists suggest, for instance, that farmers keep cows with vulnerable calves in corrals, or that they use aggressive animals such as horned steers, hard-kicking donkeys, guard dogs, or even baboons to guard their herds against the easily frightened cheetah.

These efforts may buy the cheetah a little more time. It is too early, though, to tell whether biologists will win for wild cheetahs the kind of security that captive cheetahs seem finally to have grasped.

Bears

Bears are large, powerful animals with thick, shaggy fur. Bears eat chiefly meat, but most species also eat other foods, including fruit, nuts, leaves, insects, and fish. Most live north of the equator, in Asia, Europe, North America, and South America, and in the Arctic near the North Pole.

HOT topics

Winter Sleep
Food
Cubs
Bear Behavior

HOT topics

Winter Sleep. Some bears spend much of the winter in a state similar to sleeping. Many scientists consider the bear's winter sleep to be an example of hibernation, but others do not consider bears to be true hibernators. These scientists use such terms as "winter lethargy" or "incomplete hibernation" to describe the bear's sleep period. A bear's body temperature, unlike that of other hibernating mammals, does not drop greatly during winter sleep. In addition, a bear awakens easily and may become fairly active on mild winter days. A bear prepares for its winter sleep by eating large amounts of food during late summer and

DEFINITIONS

hibernate: to spend a period, either during a whole season or during periods of severe weather, in a state of deep sleep, especially one marked by a distinct lowering of metabolism and body temperature, as woodchucks, and some other wild animals do.

bearbaiting: a cruel sport popular in Europe and especially in London as early as 1174. It was part of holiday and Sunday activities. A bear or a bull was fastened to a stake by a chain around its neck or hind leg, and sometimes by a ring in its nose. Then large, specially trained dogs tormented it. Bearbaiting also led to other cruel amusements, such as whipping a blind bear. Bearbaiting was held in open-air arenas called *bear gardens*. Bearbaiting began to decline in the late 1600s, and in 1835 Parliament prohibited it.

predator: an animal or person that preys upon another or others.

HOT topics

storing fat within its body for energy. When food becomes scarce, the bear goes to its den.

Food. Bears are meat-eating animals, but they also eat many other kinds of food. Favorite foods of bears include ants, birds' eggs, and grubs. They hunt mice, ground squirrels, and other small animals in fields and forests. They may also wade into streams and catch fish with their front paws or strong jaws. Bears sometimes prey on livestock, especially lambs and young pigs. They are fond of honey and will rip apart beehives or the nests of wild bees to get it. Their long, thick fur helps protect them from bee stings.

Cubs. Most bear cubs are born during the mother's winter sleep period. A female bear usually has two cubs at a time, but the number may vary from one to four. The cubs weigh only one-half to one pound (0.23 to 0.5 kilogram) at birth. Their eyes are closed, and they have no fur. The eyes open about a month after birth, and by that time the body is covered with thick, soft fur. In spring, they come out of the den, frisky and playful. They grow rapidly and may weigh 40 pounds (18 kilograms) by autumn. Cubs stay with the mother for one or two years.

Bear Habits/Behavior. Bears show no fear of people and often wander into camping areas looking for food. They are usually peaceful animals, with few enemies except other bears and humans. They run from danger and try to avoid fights. However, they are short-tempered and will fiercely attack anything that seems to threaten them or their cubs, food, or homes. An angry bear moves quickly in spite of its great size. One blow from its powerful front paws can kill even large animals, such as cattle and deer. The long, thick claws are also dangerous weapons. Few bears lose a fight with another kind of animal.

A polar bear

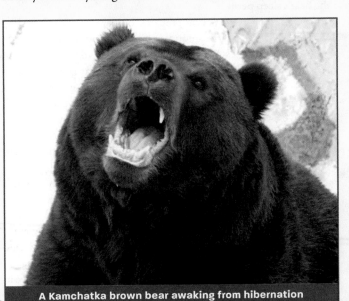

A Kamchatka brown bear awaking from hibernation

TRUE or FALSE?

No bears are native to the continent of Africa.

THE BASICS

The bear is a large, powerful animal with thick, shaggy fur. Bears prey on other animals and are classified by zoologists as *carnivores*—that is, animals that eat chiefly meat. But most bear species also eat other foods, including fruit, nuts, leaves, insects, and fish.

The Alaskan brown bear is the largest carnivore that lives on land. It grows about 9 feet (2.7 meters) long and may weigh up to 1,700 pounds (770 kilograms). The sun bear, also called the Malayan bear, is the smallest bear. It is 3 to 4 feet (91 to 120 centimeters) long and weighs only 60 to 100 pounds (27 to 45 kilograms).

Most wild bears live north of the equator. They are found in Asia, Europe, and North America, and in the Arctic near the North Pole. Only one species, the spectacled bear, lives in South America. No wild bears live in Africa, Antarctica, or Australia.

The Body of a Bear

Most bears have heavy bodies with long, thick fur, loose skin, and large, hairy heads. Bears have small eyes and cannot see well. Their small, rounded ears stand straight up, but they hear only fairly well. They have an excellent sense of smell. Bears have short, strong legs and large feet. Each foot has five toes, and each toe ends in a long, heavy claw. The claws can always be seen because, unlike those of a cat, they have no covering. A bear uses its claws to dig up roots, ants, termites, and other food, or to tear its prey.

A bear's walk differs from that of most other animals. Most animals walk and run on their toes. A bear, like a human being, puts the entire sole of its foot on the ground with each step and the heel of the foot strikes the ground first. The hind feet of a large bear may be 12 to 16 inches (30 to 41 centimeters) long. The large feet, the short legs, and heel-first way of stepping make bears look slow and clumsy. But bears are agile and can move fast. Polar bears can run at speeds of up to 35 miles (56 kilometers) an hour.

Bears usually live alone and never gather in groups. During the mating season in the summer, a male and a female bear may live together for about a month. Then the male wanders away and the female prepares a place for her cubs to be born.

 Winter sleep. Some bears spend much of the winter in a state similar to sleeping. Many scientists consider the bear's winter sleep to be an example of hibernation. Many other scientists, however, do not consider bears to be true hibernators. They point out that a bear's body temperature, unlike that of other hibernating mammals, does not drop greatly during winter sleep. In addition, a bear awakens easily and may become fairly active on mild winter days. These scientists use such terms as "winter lethargy" or "incomplete hibernation" to describe the bear's sleep period.

A bear prepares for its winter sleep by eating large amounts of food during late summer and storing fat within its body for energy. When food becomes scarce, the bear goes to its den. The den may be a cave or a brush pile, or a burrow that the bear has dug under the roots of a large tree. Some kinds of bears may build shelters of twigs or dig shallow holes in hillsides. Female polar bears find ice caves or dig dens in the snow.

Brown bears and black bears, both of which live in regions that have harsh winters, almost always have a period of winter sleep. Species found in areas with milder winters may enter dens for only brief periods. Tropical species, such as sun bears and sloth bears, do not have a winter sleep period. Although polar bears live in the Arctic, they normally remain active during

A polar bear with her cub in a temporary snow shelter

the winter. These bears spend the winter wandering the polar ice near open water and preying on seals and other marine mammals that come ashore.

 Cubs. Most bear cubs are born during the mother's winter sleep period. A female bear usually has two cubs at a time, but the number may vary from one to four. The cubs weigh only $1/2$ to 1 pound (0.23 to 0.5 kilogram) at birth. Their eyes are closed, and they have no fur. The eyes open about a month after birth, and by that time the body is covered with thick, soft fur. The cubs stay in the den with their mother for about two months. In spring, they come out, frisky and playful. They grow rapidly and may weigh 40 pounds (18 kilograms) by autumn. Cubs stay with the mother for one or two years. She teaches them to hunt for food.

 Food. Bears are meat-eating animals, but they also eat many other kinds of food. They hunt mice, ground squirrels, and other small animals in fields and forests. They may wade into streams and catch fish with their front paws or strong jaws. Favorite foods of bears include ants, birds' eggs, and grubs. Bears sometimes prey on livestock, especially lambs and young pigs. Their diet also may include acorns, berries, fruits, nuts, and the leaves and roots of plants. Bears are fond of honey and will rip apart beehives or the nests of wild bees to get it. Their long, thick fur helps protect them from bee stings.

 Habits. Bears often wander far in search of food. A grizzly bear may claim an area of 10 to 12 square miles (26 to 31 square kilometers) as its private hunting ground. Polar bears swim well and are often found living on islands of ice drifting more than 200 miles (320 kilometers) from land.

Bears are usually peaceful animals. They try to avoid a fight and run from danger. They have few enemies except other bears and humans. Bears show no fear of people and often wander into camping areas looking for food. However, all bears are short-tempered and get angry quickly. They are fierce fighters and will attack anything that seems to threaten them or their cubs, food, or homes. An angry bear moves quickly in spite of its great size. One blow from its powerful front paws can kill even large animals, such as cattle and deer. The long, thick claws are also dangerous weapons. Few bears lose a fight with another kind of animal.

Wild bears live from 15 to more than 30 years. In zoos, a brown bear has lived as long as 47 years, and a polar bear for 34 years.

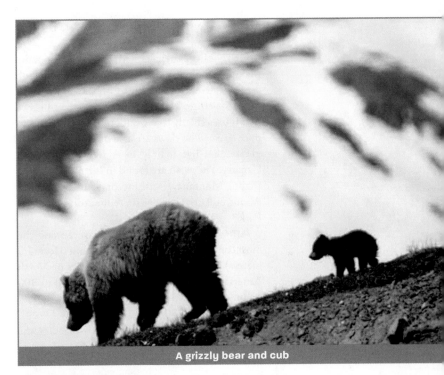
A grizzly bear and cub

Kinds of Bears

Zoologists recognize eight species of bears: (1) brown bears, (2) American black bears, (3) Asiatic black bears, (4) polar bears, (5) sun bears, (6) sloth bears, (7) spectacled bears, and (8) giant pandas. Scientists formerly placed giant pandas in the raccoon family or in a family with red pandas.

Brown bears include the world's largest bears. Among them are the brown bears of Europe and Asia; Alaskan brown bears, such as the Kodiak bear and peninsula brown bear; and the grizzly bears of western North America. Brown bears vary in color from yellowish to almost black.

The brown bear of Europe and Asia appears as a character in many children's stories, where it is often named "Bruin," an old Dutch word meaning *brown*. These bears were used for hundreds of years in London for a cruel sport called *bearbaiting*. The bear was fastened to a stake and had to defend itself against vicious dogs. Cowboys in early California staged similar fights between grizzly bears and bulls.

Alaskan brown bears are found chiefly on the mainland of Alaska and on Kodiak and Afognak islands off the southeastern coast of Alaska. They also live on other Alaskan islands.

Grizzly bears may grow up to 8 feet (2.4 meters) long, and they generally weigh from 250 to 600 pounds (110 to 270 kilograms). They get angry quickly, but usually do not attack unless they are threatened.

Grizzlies get their name from the white hairs that grow in their brown coats, making them look *grizzled* (streaked with gray). Grizzlies may also be called *silvertips*. A grizzly has long, curved claws that it uses chiefly to dig out ground squirrels and mice to eat. The claws are also used as weapons.

Grizzlies live mainly in Alaska and western Canada. They also are found in the mountains of Idaho, Montana, Washington, and Wyoming. About 200 grizzlies live in Yellowstone National Park.

American black bears are among the most common species. They grow about 5 feet (1.5 meters) long and are the smallest bears of North America. Most black bears are from 200 to 300 pounds (91 to 140 kilograms), but some weigh up to 500 pounds (230 kilograms).

Not all black bears are completely black. Some have black coats with brown noses and white patches on the chest. Others, called *cinnamon bears*, have a rusty brown coat. The *island white bear*, or *Kermode's bear*, has creamy white fur and white claws. It lives in the coastal areas of British Columbia. The *blue bear*, also called *glacier bear*, has gray hairs mixed with the black ones, giving the animal a bluish color. The blue bear lives in the mountains of the St. Elias Range in southeastern Alaska.

Black bears can run as fast as 25 miles (40 kilometers) per hour when they chase prey, and they are skillful tree-climbers. These bears become troublesome around camps and cabins if food is left in their reach. Black bears have severely injured and sometimes have even killed campers or travelers who feed them.

Black bears live in many large wooded areas of North America. There are about 75,000 of them in the national forests of the United States. Many states allow people to hunt these bears, and hunters kill about 25,000 a year.

Asiatic black bears, sometimes called *Himalayan bears*, are smaller than American black bears. They grow about 5 feet (1.5 meters) long and weigh about 250 pounds (113 kilograms). Most Asiatic black bears are black, with some white hairs on the chin and a large white crescent-shaped mark on the chest. They are often called *moon bears* because of this mark.

In winter, Asiatic black bears may sleep for only short periods. They make beds of twigs in the snow so they can sun themselves. In summer, they build nest-like beds of sticks in trees, where they sleep.

Asiatic black bears are fiercer than most other kinds of bears. They often kill cattle and ponies, and sometimes attack people. These bears live in forests and brush regions throughout southern and eastern Asia. The Chinese hunt them, and many believe that the meat and bones have special healing powers.

Polar bears are the best swimmers of all bears. They are only a little smaller than brown bears. They have a smaller head, but a longer, thinner neck than most other kinds of bears. The thick, heavy fur is creamy white, with a hint of yellow. A polar bear has pads of fur on the soles of its feet. The fur helps keep the feet warm and also helps the animal walk on ice.

Polar bears can move quickly in spite of their size. These bears can run up to 35 miles (56 kilometers) per hour—fast enough to catch reindeer. They can swim 3 to 6 miles (5 to 10 kilometers) per hour. Polar bears are excellent hunters, and when they are very hungry in winter, they may attack humans. Their usual prey consists mostly of sea animals, including fish, seals, and walruses. Polar bears also eat grass and dead whales that have been washed ashore. Traditionally, the Inuit (sometimes called Eskimos) hunted polar bears. They ate the meat, used the bones for many kinds

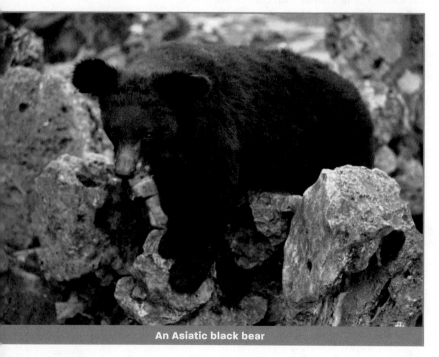
An Asiatic black bear

of utensils, and made clothes from the hides. Some Inuit still hunt polar bears for these purposes.

Polar bears live in regions bordering the Arctic Ocean. Sometimes they ride floating chunks of ice as far as the Gulf of St. Lawrence, 750 miles (1,210 kilometers) south of the Arctic Circle. Many people have traveled to the Arctic to hunt polar bears for sport and for their hides. Such activities have greatly reduced the number of polar bears.

Sun bears, sometimes called *Malayan bears,* are the smallest species of bears. They grow only about 3 feet (0.9 meter) long, and weigh 60 to 100 pounds (27 to 45 kilograms). Most sun bears have a black coat and a grayish or orange nose. Some have light brown feet. The bear gets its name from the white or yellow marks on its chest. Many people of ancient times believed the marks represented the rising sun.

Sun bears have large paws with no hair on the soles. The claws are more curved and have sharper points than those of other kinds of bears. Sun bears usually hunt only at night. They spend the day sleeping and sunbathing in trees. They build nestlike beds in trees by bending or breaking the branches. Sun bears live in the forests of Borneo, Indochina, the Malay Peninsula, Myanmar, Sumatra, and Thailand.

Sloth bears get their name from an Old English word meaning *slow.* Sloth bears move very slowly except when disturbed. These bears are so fond of honey that they are sometimes called *honey bears.* Sloth bears grow about 5 feet (1.5 meters) long and weigh about 250 pounds (113 kilograms). Sloth bears have shaggy black fur and a white or yellow chest mark shaped like a U, V, or Y.

Sloth bears sleep in the grass, under shrubs, or in shallow caves. They hunt chiefly at night. These bears eat birds' eggs, grubs, honey, insects, and plants. They also eat termites. Sloth bears pull apart the termites' nests, blow away the dust, and suck up the insects. The bears make loud blowing and sucking noises, and hunters have little trouble finding them. Sloth bears live in India and Sri Lanka.

Spectacled bears are the only South American bears. They grow about 5 feet (1.5 meters) long and weigh 200 to 300 pounds (91 to 140 kilograms). They have shaggy black or blackish-brown fur. This bear is named for the large circles or half-circles of white fur around its eyes. The circles look like spectacles. The bear also has white markings on its neck and chest.

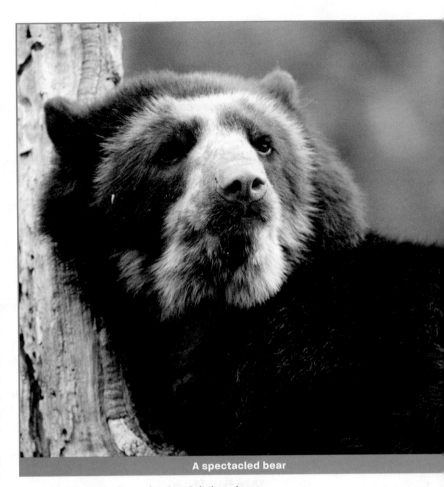

A spectacled bear

Little is known about this bear's habits, but it eats mainly fruit, leaves, and roots. The bear lives in the cool mountain forests of Bolivia, Colombia, Ecuador, Peru, and Venezuela. Overhunting and destruction of its forest home have made this bear scarce throughout much of the area.

MLA Citation

"Bears." *The Southwestern Advantage Topic Source.* Nashville: Southwestern. 2013.

DATA

The Life of a Bear

Names:	*Male*, boar or he-bear; *female*, sow or she-bear; *young*, cub; *group*, pack or sloth.
Gestation period:	7 to 9 months, depending on the species.
Number of newborn:	1 to 4, usually 2.
Length of life:	15 to 30 years.
Where found:	Arctic, Asia, Europe, North and South America.
Scientific classification:	Bears belong to the class Mammalia, and the order Carnivora. They make up the bear family, Ursidae.

ADDITIONAL RESOURCES

Books to Read

Bauer, Erwin A. *Bears: Behavior, Ecology, Conservation.* Voyageur Press, 1996.

Craighead, Lance. *Bears of the World.* Voyageur Press, 2000.

DeBruyn, Terry D. *Walking with Bears.* Lyons Press, 1999.

Fertl, Dagmar, and others. *Bears.* Sterling Publishers, 2000. Younger readers.

Stefoff, Rebecca. *Bears.* Benchmark Books, 2002. Younger readers.

Web Sites

American Bear Association

www.americanbear.org
The official Web site of the American Bear Association and the Vince Shute Wildlife Sanctuary.

Asia Rainforest—Sun Bear

www.oaklandzoo.org/Sun_Bear.php
Oakland Zoo's site about the Malayan sun bear.

Safety in Bear Country

http://usscouts.org/usscouts/safety/safe-bear.asp
Information provided by the U.S. Scouting Service Project.

Photo Gallery: Polar Bears

http://animals.nationalgeographic.com/animals/photos/polar-bears1
National Geographic presents a gallery of photos and facts about the polar bear.

Search Strings

Winter Sleep

bears hibernation winter sleep preparation (52,500)

bears hibernation "winter lethargy" "incomplete hibernation" (1)

bears winter sleep versus hibernation body temperature preparation timing (19,900)

Food

bears food meat-eating animals favorites (4310)

bears food diet (193,000)

bears food diet meat fish ants eggs grubs (29,500)

Cubs

bear cubs birth time number weight growth rate (171,000)

cubs bears birth size weight number time growth rate (15,700)

about bear cubs (164,000)

Bear Behavior

"bear behavior" (14,400)

"behavior of bears" (7820)

Horses

The horse has been one of the most useful animals for thousands of years.

HOT topics

Saddle Horses. Saddle horses for riding make up an important group of horse breeds. Many people ride horses for pleasure or raise them as a hobby. The most popular breeds used for pleasure riding in the United States include the American saddlebred, Tennessee walking horse, Morgan, quarter horse, and Arabian. Southern plantation owners developed the American saddlebred and the Tennessee walking horse because they wanted mounts that were comfortable to ride. All Morgan horses can be traced back to a New England stallion named Justin Morgan. They were originally used as harness horses for pulling carriages and for harness racing. After automobiles became popular, breeders developed Morgans into excellent saddle horses.

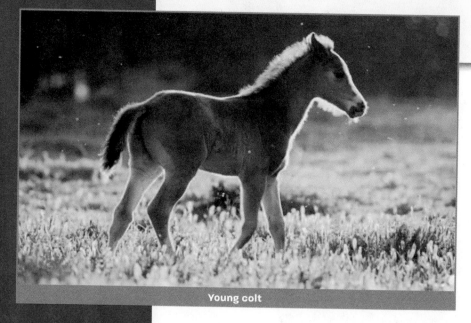

Young colt

HOT topics

Draft Horses. Draft horses are the tallest, heaviest, and strongest group of horses. They are descended from the war horses that heavily armored knights rode into battle. Draft (work) horses once supplied much of the power for jobs that heavy trucks and tractors do today. They pulled plows on farms and hauled freight wagons from town to town. Draft breeds include the shire, Clydesdale, Belgian, Percheron, Suffolk, and American cream. The shire is the largest Draft horse. It was developed in England after King Henry VIII had all horses less than 5 feet (1.5 meters) high destroyed as useless.

Training Horses. Training horses requires great skill and patience. Expert trainers handle horses gently but firmly and teach them slowly. Soon after birth, a foal learns to accept handling by human beings. Some trainers begin to accustom a foal to a halter almost immediately. Others do not halter-break foals until they are several months old. After a horse is one year old, the trainer gradually accustoms it to having a saddle on its back. Then the horse is mounted and ridden a few steps. After a horse has learned to follow the signals of a rider or driver, it is trained for a certain sport. For example, thoroughbred racehorses learn to run when a starting gate swings open. Harness racing horses learn to trot or pace behind a moving starting gate that is attached to a car.

Whitbread Brewery draft horses, London

Prehistoric Horses. Scientists believe that the earliest ancestor of the horse was a small animal about 10 to 20 inches (25 to 51 centimeters) high. They call this animal Eohippus (dawn horse) or Hyracotherium. It lived about 55 million years ago in what is now North America and Europe. These prehistoric horses had arched backs and snout-like noses. They looked more like racing dogs, such as greyhounds or whippets, than like the straight-backed, long-faced modern horse. By about 3 million years ago, horses probably looked somewhat like modern horses. Fossils show that during the Pleistocene Epoch horses lived on every continent except Australia.

TRUE or FALSE?
The first European colonists found North America teeming with wild horses.

THE BASICS

The horse has been one of the most useful animals for thousands of years. Horses once provided the fastest and surest way to travel on land. Hunters on horseback chased animals and killed them for food or for sport. Soldiers charged into battle on sturdy war horses. The pioneers used horses when they settled the American West in the days of stagecoaches, covered wagons, and the Pony Express.

The horse is not as important as a means of transportation as it once was. In most countries, the *iron horse* (train) and *horseless carriage* (automobile) have replaced the horse almost entirely. But people still use horses for recreation, sport, and work. Children and adults ride horses for fun and exercise. Large crowds thrill to the excitement of horse races. Horses perform in circuses, rodeos, carnivals, parades, and horse shows. They help ranchers round up great herds of cattle, and they may be used to pull plows and do other farm work.

The horse is well suited for working and running. For example, its wide nostrils help it breathe easily. Horses have a good sense of smell, sharp ears, and keen eyes. They have strong teeth, but they eat only grain and plants, never meat. Long, muscular legs give horses the strength to pull heavy loads or to run at fast speeds. Horses also use their legs as their chief weapons. The kick of a horse can seriously injure a human being or an animal.

DEFINITIONS

bronco, or **bronc,** is an untamed Western horse.

colt, technically, is a male horse four years old or less. However, the word *colt* is often used for any young horse.

crossbred means bred from a sire of one breed and a dam of another.

dam is the mother of a foal.

filly is a female horse four years old or less.

foal is either a newborn male or a newborn female horse.

frog is the elastic, horny, middle part of the sole of a horse's foot.

gait is any forward movement of the horse, such as the walk, trot, or gallop.

gelding is a male horse that cannot be used for breeding because it has had some of its reproductive organs removed.

grade is an unregistered horse or pony of mixed breed.

hand is a unit used to measure the height of a horse, from the ground to the highest point of the withers. A hand equals 4 inches (10 centimeters).

mare is a female horse more than four years old.

mustang is the wild horse of the Western plains, descended from Spanish horses.

pony refers to a horse less than 58 inches (147 centimeters) tall when full grown.

purebred means bred from horses that are of the same breed.

sire is the father of a foal.

stallion is a male horse that can be used for breeding.

yearling is a horse that is more than one and less than two years old. In the Northern Hemisphere, a race horse is considered a yearling from the first January 1 after its birth until the following January 1. In countries of the Southern Hemisphere, a race horse's official birthday is either July 1 or August 1.

withers is the ridge between a horse's shoulder bones.

Horses are eager to please their owners or trainers. Most horses have good memories and can easily be trained to obey commands. A horse may learn to come when its owner whistles. A circus horse takes "bows" when its trainer touches its front legs with a whip. Horses can learn to respond to even the slightest signals. People who watch an expert rider on a well-trained horse often cannot see these signs. For example, the horse moves forward when the rider's legs are pressed lightly against the horse's side. It turns at a touch of the reins against its neck. The quick obedience of the horse has helped make it one of our most valuable animals.

People have improved the natural qualities of the horse by breeding various kinds of horses. For example, horse raisers can breed a fast horse with a strong horse to produce an animal that has both speed and power.

Kinds of Horses

There are more than 150 breeds and types of horses and ponies. The breeds vary greatly in size, strength, speed, and other characteristics. The smallest breed is the Falabella, which grows only 30 inches (76 centimeters) high. Falabellas were originally bred in Argentina and are kept as pets. The largest breed of horse is the shire, which was originally developed in England. Shires may measure more than 68 inches (173 centimeters) high. They may weigh more than 2,000 pounds (910 kilograms).

Shires and other large breeds, such as the Belgian, Clydesdale, and Percheron, are the strongest horses. They can pull loads that weigh more than a short ton (0.9 metric ton). The two fastest breeds are the quarter horse and the thoroughbred, which are often bred and trained for racing. The quarter horse can run 1/4 mile (0.4 kilometer) in about 20 seconds. But the thoroughbred can run longer distances faster. It can cover a mile (1.6 kilometers) in about 11/2minutes.

The various breeds of horses are commonly divided into three main groups: (1) light horses, (2) heavy horses, and (3) ponies. Light horses have small bones and thin legs. Most weigh less than 1,300 pounds (590 kilograms). Heavy horses have large bones and thick, sturdy legs. Some weigh more than 2,000 pounds (910 kilograms). Ponies are small horses that stand less than 58 inches (147 centimeters) high when full grown. Most ponies weigh less than 800 pounds (360 kilograms).

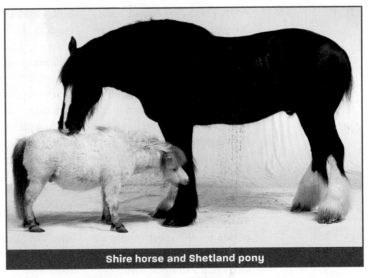

Shire horse and Shetland pony

Each of the three main groups of horses has many breeds. However, a single breed may include horses of more than one type. For example, certain kinds of Hackneys are classified as light horses, and other kinds are considered ponies. In addition to light horses, heavy horses, and ponies, there are also a few kinds of wild horses.

Light Horses

Saddle horses for riding make up an important group of breeds. Many people ride horses for pleasure or raise them as a hobby. Some riders achieve great skill and compete with other riders in horse shows and sports involving horses.

The most popular breeds used for pleasure riding in the United States include the American saddlebred, Tennessee walking horse, Morgan, quarter horse, and Arabian. Southern plantation owners developed the American saddlebred and the Tennessee walking horse. The owners wanted mounts that were comfortable to ride. Tennessee walking horses are especially noted for their comfortable running walk and smooth canter. All Morgan horses can be traced back to a New England stallion named Justin Morgan. Morgans were originally used as harness horses for pulling carriages and for harness racing. After automobiles became popular, breeders developed Morgans into excellent saddle horses.

Cowhands use quarter horses for *cutting* (sorting out) cattle from a herd and for other kinds of ranch work. Quarter horses can start, stop, and turn quickly. They respond instantly to the slightest shift of the cowhand's weight or movement of reins. These sure-footed horses have great endurance. They can scramble up and down steep mountain trails and ford swift streams.

Quarter horses were developed in America during the early 1700s. Breeders crossed thoroughbreds from England with horses from the Spanish colonies of North America. The new breed could start quickly and run at high speed for short distances. Owners used these horses for the sport of *quarter racing,* a ¼-mile (0.4-kilometer) race along a straight path.

The strong Arabian horse is noted for its endurance. Arabs developed this breed for use in the desert. For hundreds of years, breeders in many countries have brought these horses from Arabia and used them to develop new breeds.

One breed that developed from Arabian horses is the thoroughbred. All thoroughbreds can be traced back to three stallions known as the Darley Arabian, the Godolphin Arabian (sometimes called the Godolphin Barb), and the Byerly Turk. In the late 1600s and early 1700s, European breeders crossed these

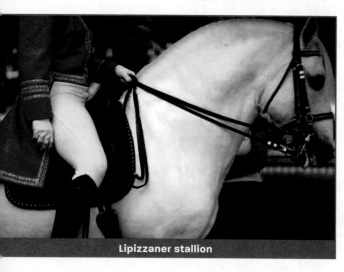

Lipizzaner stallion

stallions with their own horses to produce the first thoroughbreds. Thoroughbreds are high-spirited, sensitive horses. They have powerful lungs and strong legs, which makes them especially well suited for racing. They are also used for jumping and hunting. In addition, many polo ponies are part thoroughbred.

Lipizzan horses, or Lipizzaners, come from horses imported into Austria from Spain and Italy during the middle 1500s. These beautiful show horses have strong bones, short legs, and thick, arched necks. Their powerful hindquarters enable them to make difficult jumps. The best-known Lipizzaners are those trained at the Spanish Riding School of Vienna in Austria. These horses perform graceful jumping and dancing feats.

Light harness horses, sometimes called *roadsters,* include the Morgan, the Hackney, and the standardbred. The standardbred, also called the American trotting horse, is considered the best horse for harness racing. Owners train standardbred horses to race at either a trot or a pace. Breeders developed the standardbred by crossing thoroughbreds with Morgans and other breeds.

Color types. Light horses are sometimes grouped according to color types instead of by breed. Such groups include palominos and albinos. Some people consider Appaloosas a color type, but these horses actually form a breed.

Palominos have a golden coat and a light blond or silvery mane and tail. Most of them have white only on the face and on the legs below the hocks and knees. Palominos belong to

almost every breed except the thoroughbred. A palomino mare and stallion often produce a *foal* (baby horse) of another color. Breeders in the United States and Mexico developed the Palomino line.

Albinos. Some breeders use the word *albino* to describe any horse with a white or palecolored coat. However, a true albino is an animal that, because of heredity, has no color in its eyes, hair, or skin. Its offspring also lack color.

All albinos have some color that their offspring can inherit. One kind has a pink skin, ivory coat, white mane, and blue eyes. Another has pink skin, a white coat, and brown eyes. Horses that are born black and turn white as they grow older are not usually called albinos.

Appaloosas vary greatly in color. But the vast majority have a white area on the loin and hips with small, round or oval dark spots. Appaloosas are sometimes called *raindrop horses* because of their spots. They also have white-rimmed, humanlike eyes. Black and white stripes cover the hoofs of most Appaloosas.

Spanish adventurers first brought Appaloosas to North America. The Nez Perce Indians of what are now Idaho and Washington bred these horses in the Palouse River region. The name *Appaloosa* comes from the word *Palouse.*

Heavy Horses

Draft horses are the tallest, heaviest, and strongest group of horses. They are descended from the war horses that heavily armored knights rode into battle. *Draft* (work)

horses once supplied much of the power for jobs that heavy trucks and tractors do today. They pulled plows on farms and hauled freight wagons from town to town. Draft breeds include the shire, Clydesdale, Belgian, Percheron, Suffolk, and American cream.

The shire is the largest horse. This breed developed in England after King Henry VIII had all horses less than 5 feet (1.5 meters) high destroyed as useless.

The Clydesdale, one of the handsomest draft breeds, has long, flowing hair below the knee and the *hock* (joint on the hind legs). This hair, called "feathers," gives the animals a smart and unusual look. Clydesdales are popular horses for pulling wagons in parades.

The Belgian ranks among the gentlest and strongest horses. Heavy muscles give the Belgian a stout appearance, and the head may seem too small for the huge body. Most Belgians have chestnut or bay-colored coats. Percherons look much like Belgians but have gray or black coats. These horses are lively for their size and may be used as a general-purpose horse. The Suf-

folk, a smaller, chestnut-colored horse, makes an ideal draft horse. The American cream is the only breed of draft horse that originated in the United States. The horse has a cream-colored coat and a white mane and white tail.

Heavy harness horses, which are also called *coach horses*, weigh less than draft horses and are not as strong. These horses are able to do light farm work and make good mounts for pleasure riding. European breeders developed heavy harness horses to pull coaches, wagons, and artillery. Breeds include the Cleveland bay, French coach (Normand), and German coach (Oldenburger).

Cleveland bays look like compact, rugged thoroughbreds. They make excellent general-purpose horses for driving, riding, and hunting. The French coach and German coach breeds were popular in North America until the early 1900s but are seldom seen now.

Ponies

Well-trained ponies make good pets for children. Ponies learn quickly and are usually

gentle. They are used for pleasure riding and can pull small carts. Most ponies live longer than other horses. Pony breeds include the Shetland, Welsh, Hackney, Connemara, and pony of the Americas.

A full-grown Shetland pony stands from 32 to 46 inches (81 to 117 centimeters) high. This favorite children's horse once pulled plows and wagons in its native Shetland Islands, which are part of Scotland. Miners in Wales developed the Welsh pony to work in the cramped tunnels of coal mines. The Hackney is one of the largest pony breeds. The Irish Connemara ponies make good jumpers. The pony of the Americas looks like a miniature Appaloosa. This breed is popular in young people's riding competitions.

Wild Horses

Two kinds of wild horses—*Przewalski's horse* and the *tarpan*—probably have the same ancestors that tame horses have. Przewalski's horses are the only true wild horses that exist today. They are considered an endangered species. Tarpans, also called *forest horses*, once lived in parts of Europe, but they became extinct in the late 1800s.

Horses that roam freely in parts of the western United States are often called "wild horses," but they are actually descendants of tame horses that were ridden by Spanish explorers, American Indians, and cowhands of the Old West. The horses escaped from their owners and eventually formed bands. In the early 1900s, more than 2 million of these horses, also called *mustangs*, roamed the

Appaloosas

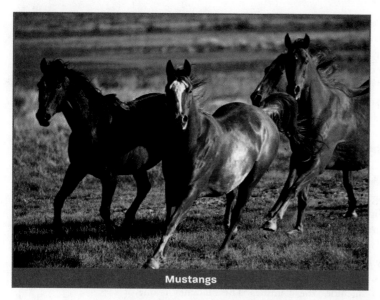
Mustangs

West. But people rounded up many of them to clear land for farms and ranches. Many were slaughtered and sold for use in pet food. Today, about 20,000 mustangs roam the West. Federal laws prohibit killing these horses, but some people hunt them illegally.

The Body of a Horse

Size. Horse owners measure the height of a horse in *hands*, from the ground to the highest point of the *withers* (ridge between the shoulder bones). A hand equals 4 inches (10 centimeters), the average width of a man's hand. A horse that stands 14.2 hands (14 hands and 2 inches) is 58 inches (147 centimeters) high.

Coat and skin. The horse's body is covered by a coat of hair. A healthy, glowing coat gives a splendid appearance. A thick winter coat grows every autumn and is shed every spring. Horses never shed the hair of the mane or the tail. If the mane and tail become too thick, the horse's owner may pull out some hair to make the horse look better. Pulling the hair does not hurt because the animal has no nerves at the roots of its hair. A horse uses its tail to brush off insects. A horse also has special muscles for twitching the skin to get rid of insects.

Sweat glands on the surface of the horse's body help the animal stay cool. The heavy coats of horses used for fast work, such as racing or polo, should be clipped in winter. The horses can then cool off more easily when they sweat. When the animals are resting, they should be covered with a blanket to keep them warm.

Horses have many colors, including various shades of black, brown, *chestnut* (reddish-brown), *dun* (yellowish-gray), gold, gray, *sorrel* (light reddish-brown), and white. *Bay* horses have a brown coat and black *points* (legs, mane, and tail). Chestnut horses may have *flaxen* (pale-yellow) or sorrel manes and tails, but not black points. Many gray horses are born a dark color and turn lighter as they grow older. Lipizzans and some other gray horses turn white by the time they are fully grown. *Roan* horses have a yellowish-brown or reddish-brown coat sprinkled with gray or white hairs. *Pintos*, also called *paints*, have a black or dark-colored coat with large white areas that vary in pattern.

Special terms are used to describe the markings on a horse's face or legs. These terms include:

Bald face—a mostly white face.

Blaze—a large white strip on the face.

Race—a narrow strip down the center of the face.

Star—any small white patch on the forehead.

Snip—any small white patch near the muzzle.

Sock—a white patch above the foot.

Legs and hoofs. A horse's legs are suited for fast running. Large muscles in the upper part of the legs provide great speed with a minimum of effort. The long, thin lower legs give the horse a long stride. The front legs carry most of the horse's weight. They absorb the jolts when the animal runs or jumps. The rear legs provide power for running or jumping.

Thousands of years of evolution have given the horse feet ideally suited for running. Each foot is really a strong toe. Only the tip of the toe, protected by the strong, curved hoof, touches the ground. The remains of what were once two other toes grow as bony strips on the *cannon* bone of the horse's legs. The *frog* (an elastic mass on the sole of the foot) acts like a rubber heel. It helps absorb the jolt when the hoof strikes the ground. The horse's real heel bone is the *hock*, located about halfway up the leg. The hock never touches the ground.

A horse with a bad fracture usually cannot be saved because the break causes shock and extreme pain. But certain kinds of broken bones do not cause much pain and may heal. Veterinarians treat such breaks with slings and casts.

Teeth. Most male horses have 40 teeth, and most females have 36. The *molars* (back teeth) grind food as the horse chews. These teeth have no nerves, and they never stop growing. Sometimes the molars grow unevenly and must be filed down so the horse can chew properly.

An expert on horses can tell a horse's age by counting the number of teeth and checking their condition. Most foals are born toothless but soon get two upper and two lower front teeth. When four months old, the horse has four upper and four lower teeth. At the age of one year, it has six pairs of upper and lower *incisors* (cutting teeth). At five years, a horse has 12 pairs of molars in addition to the six pairs of incisors and is said to have a full mouth. Males grow four extra teeth at the age of five. By the time a horse is eight years old, the rough grinding surfaces of the bottom incisors have been worn down. The horse has a smooth mouth and is said to be *aged*. Sometimes tiny wolf teeth grow in front of the molars. These teeth interfere with the *bit*, which is the part of a bridle that goes into the horse's mouth. Wolf teeth are usually removed. The bit rests in spaces between the horse's incisors and molars.

Senses. Horses have larger eyes than any other land animals except ostriches. A horse's eyes are oval, and they are set on the sides of the head. The two eyes can be moved independently, each in a half circle. Thus, a horse can look forward with one eye and backward with the other. Because of the position of its eyes, a horse has a blind spot a short distance in front of it. A horse must turn its head to see a nearby object that lies directly ahead. The shape of a horse's eyes makes objects far to the side or back appear to move faster than they actually do. For this reason, a horse may *shy* (move suddenly) at the slightest movement of an object to the side or back. Horses' eyes require a fairly long time to adjust to changes of light. When a horse is moved from a dark stall into bright sunlight, it may appear nervous until its eyes adjust.

Horses have keen hearing. They have short, pointed ears that they can move around to pick up sounds from almost any direction. Certain posi-tions of the ears may indicate a horse's attitude. For example, when a horse points its ears forward, it is curious about an object in front of it. When a horse twitches its ears or lays them back against the head, it is angry and may kick.

Horses have a well-developed sense of smell. Their nostrils are very large and can pick up scents from long distances. A strong wind and heavy rain interfere with their sense of smell and may cause horses to become nervous.

The sense of touch varies among different breeds of horses. The thin skin of most breeds of light horses is sensitive to insects and rough objects. Most breeds of heavy horses are less sensitive to such irritations.

Intelligence. Horses can learn to follow signals, but they must be taught through constant repetition. They also must be encouraged to overcome their fear of unfamiliar objects and situations. Horses have excellent memories and can recall pleasant or unpleasant experiences many years after they occur.

Life history. A mare carries her foal for about 11 months before giving birth. This period may vary from 10 to 14 months. Foals can stand shortly after birth, and within a few hours they are able to run about. The legs of newborn horses seem much too long for their bodies. As the horse matures, the legs grow more slowly than the rest of the body.

A year-old colt is often more than half grown. Most horses reach full height and weight by the age of five. Most horse raisers start to breed mares at the age of three or four. They start to breed stallions at the age of four. Most mares have five or six foals during their life, but some have as many as 19.

Race horses have their official birthday on January 1, except in countries of the Southern Hemisphere, where it is on either July 1 or August 1. Regardless of their actual birth date, race horses become a year older on their official birthday. This system is used to qualify horses for races that are limited to certain age groups. For example, only three-year-olds race in the Kentucky Derby. Most horses live from 20 to 30 years.

Riding Equipment

Equipment for horseback riding includes the rider's clothing, spurs, and whip. It also includes *tack* (gear) for the horse, such as the saddle and bridle.

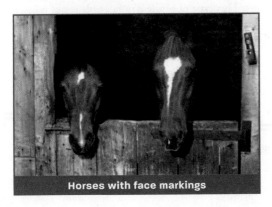
Horses with face markings

Clothes for riding. Riders wear comfortable clothing suitable for their type of riding. Their clothes also must protect their legs from irritation while rubbing against the saddle. Blue jeans and a comfortable shirt are probably best for open-country riding. Cowhands often wear *chaps* (seatless leather trousers) that fit over their regular trousers. *Chaps* protect the rider's legs from being scratched by brush.

For English riding, *jodhpurs* (long, tight-fitting breeches) or regular riding breeches are usually worn. They provide both comfort and protection. Boots, or any laced shoes with heels, keep the feet from slipping through the stirrups. Many riders wear hard caps to protect their head in case of a fall.

Spurs. Skilled riders use spurs to signal the horse without moving their legs or heels vigorously. Some riders in horse shows use spurs to give commands or to urge their mounts to run faster. Spurs should be worn only by expert riders.

Spurs called *dummy spurs* have either blunt *rowels* (little wheels) or no rowels. Some spurs have sharp points instead of rowels. *Racing spurs* have rowels on the inside to make it easy to touch the horse. Rowels on racing spurs and dummy spurs point downward. Most *dressage spurs* have sharp rowels. They curve upward so that riders need not shift their feet to touch the horse.

The whip. An expert rider uses a whip to give the horse special signals or to train the animal. Horse whips are lightweight and flexible and cause no pain if properly used. Horses learn to respond to signals from a trainer's whip when performing different steps and difficult movements in horse shows. Race horses increase their speed at a touch

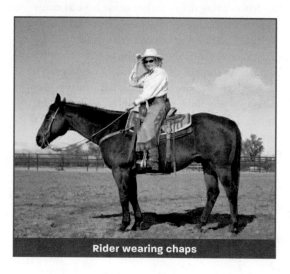

Rider wearing chaps

of the jockey's whip. A *riding crop* may be used like a whip. Crops have stiff handles. The tip is a large loop of rawhide or leather. In fox hunting, riders use a *hunting whip*, which has a curved, wooden or bone handle at one end and a long leather lash at the other end. The lash is used to control the hounds.

Experienced riders apply whips as punishment only if the horse kicks or bites at another horse or stubbornly disobeys a command. The rider immediately strikes the horse sharply on the flanks.

The saddle. Riders in the United States generally use an *English saddle* or a *Western saddle*. A person should use the kind of saddle that suits a particular type of riding.

The English saddle is flatter and weighs less than the Western saddle. Jockeys, jumpers, exhibition riders, and others who need extra speed from their horses use the English saddle because it interferes with the horse's movements less than a Western saddle does.

The Western saddle has wide stirrups and a *horn*, to which a rope may be fastened. Cowhands and rodeo riders use Western saddles. Cowhands may tie their ropes to the horn when roping cattle. They usually use a *double girth* (two saddle straps) on the Western saddle to hold it securely against the pull of roped cattle. A blanket under the saddle keeps the horse's back and sides from becoming sore. Most Western saddles have fleece padding that also helps to protect the horse's back.

The bridle is used to control the horse. It consists of straps and metal pieces that fit on the horse's head and in its mouth.

The simplest bridle is the *snaffle bridle*. This bridle has a jointed bit that is gentle on the horse. The bit of the snaffle bridle pulls on the corners of the horse's lips. The bridle's single set of reins can be handled easily by the rider.

The *double*, or *full*, *bridle* is used by advanced riders. This type of bridle has a double set of reins, a snaffle bit, and a curb bit. The *curb bit* fits between the horse's teeth on sensitive spaces called *bars*. This bit puts pressure on the horse's lower jaw. A separate set of reins controls each of the bits. The upper reins move the snaffle bit, and the lower reins operate the curb bit. Pressure on the snaffle bit causes the horse to raise its head. Pressure on the curb bit pulls the horse's head down and brings the animal to an abrupt halt. Polo players use the curb bit to stop their horses quickly.

Another kind of bridle, the *Pelham bridle*, com-

Bridle and bit

bines the snaffle and curb bits into one bit with a double set of reins. Most Western bridles consist of only a curb or snaffle bit.

How to Ride

The art of riding and managing horses is called *horsemanship*. Many people enjoy riding horseback for fun and sport. The basic techniques of English and Western riding are similar.

Selecting a horse. The selection of a horse depends partly on the skill of the rider. Experienced riders may prefer responsive, high-spirited horses. But most beginners feel at ease on a gentle, reliable horse. Youngsters may be more comfortable on a pony than on a large horse. *Geldings,* which are male horses that have had their *testicles* (sex organs) removed, are easier to control than stallions or mares. In choosing a horse to buy, a person should also consider such factors as the animal's age, training, and physical condition. A well-trained horse over 10 years old is best for a beginning rider. An expert should ride the horse to determine how trained it is. In addition, a veterinarian should examine the animal and check for possible health problems.

Mounting a horse. The first things a rider learns are how to *mount* (get on) a horse and sit in the saddle.

The rider mounts on the horse's left side. Most horses become used to being mounted from the left side during training. Someone mounting from the right side might startle or confuse them. The custom of mounting from the left probably started when men wore long swords that hung down along the left leg. It was easier to throw the right leg across the horse's back than to throw the left leg and the heavy sword. Many horses trained to travel on mountain trails can be mounted from either side. Riders mount from the side that is less likely to cause the horse to lose its balance.

After mounting, the rider sits in a relaxed position. The rider should be settled firmly in the *dip* (middle of the saddle). The back is held erect but not stiff.

To start a horse, the rider squeezes both legs against its sides. As the horse moves forward, the rider lets the reins follow the movement of the horse's head. Riders should look where they are going, not at the horse.

To control a horse, riders use their hands, legs, and body weight. English riders call these skills the *aids*. Western riders refer to them as *cues*. Skilled riders can put their mounts through difficult performances and tricks with only slight movements of their hands or legs. Riders in horse shows change gaits time after time with no apparent signals. Cattle-herding horses and polo ponies respond quickly to cues. They start, stop, or turn at a touch of the rider's hand or leg, or at the shifting of weight.

Trainers teach horses to move *away from the leg.* The horse moves to the right when the rider's left leg presses against its side and to the left when it feels the rider's right leg.

In English riding, horses are taught to move *toward the hand.* The reins in the rider's hands lead to the bit in the horse's mouth. When the rider pulls the right rein, the bit pulls on the right side of the horse's mouth. The horse then turns in that direction. Horses trained for Western riding learn to respond to the touch of the reins against the neck. The horse turns away from this signal. At a touch of the rein on the right side of the neck, the horse turns left.

Skilled riders shift their weight in the direction of the horse's movement. They move forward when

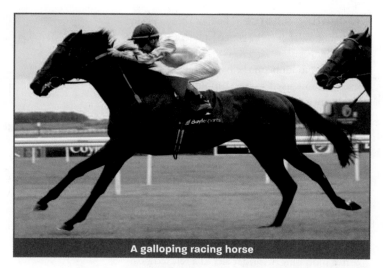

A galloping racing horse

the horse goes forward, and to the right or left when turning. They also shift their body back a little in the saddle when slowing up or stopping. A good rider does all these things so smoothly that only the horse knows that the rider has changed balance.

To stop a horse, riders shift their balance back a little in the saddle. Then they squeeze their fingers to increase the pressure on the reins slightly without tugging on them. When the horse stops, the rider relaxes the pressure on the reins.

To move a horse backwards, the rider squeezes both reins equally, preventing the horse from moving forward, and presses both legs against the girth of the saddle. A well-trained horse will then step backwards.

Gaits are the ways a horse moves. Horses have four natural gaits: (1) walk, (2) trot, (3) canter, and (4) gallop. Many horses are trained for three speeds within each of the four natural gaits. Trainers also develop artificial gaits in some horses. Horses so trained compete in horse shows and perform in circuses, fairs, and rodeos. Artificial gaits include the pace, slow gait, and rack.

Walk is the slowest gait. The horse moves at a speed of about 4 miles (6 kilometers) an hour. It raises one foot after another and puts them down in the same order. The horse keeps its balance by altering its front and back feet, and its right and left feet. For example, the order may be (1) right forefoot, (2) left hind foot, (3) left forefoot, and (4) right hind foot.

Trot is a two-beat gait at a speed of about 9 miles (14 kilometers) an hour. The front leg on one side of the body and the hind leg on the other side hit the ground together. The horse bends its legs more when it is trotting than when it is walking. Harness-race horses trot while pulling a driver in a *sulky* (two-wheeled cart).

When beginners first ride at a trot, they should hold onto the horse's mane or the saddle until they get used to the motion. On the first beat of a trot, riders raise their body slightly by pushing their feet down on the stirrups. They come down in the saddle on the second beat and then go right up again. This method of riding, called *posting*, is used only in English riding. A beginner should practice the movements of posting while the horse is walking.

Canter is a comfortable, three-beat rhythmic riding gait. A horse canters at a speed of 10 to 12 miles (16 to 19 kilometers) an hour. On the first beat, one hind foot strikes the ground. Then the other hind foot and opposite forefoot hit the ground together. On the third beat, the other forefoot strikes the ground.

Gallop is a horse's fastest natural gait. It consists of four beats. For the first two beats, the hind feet strike the ground one after the other. On the third and fourth beats, the forefeet hit the ground in the same order as the hind feet. Then the horse leaps forward, and all its feet leave the ground. A racing horse runs at an extended gallop.

Pace, like the trot, is a gait used in harness racing. When a horse paces, it moves the legs on the same side of the body at the same time. The pace is an uncomfortable riding gait.

Slow gait is a slow, four-beat gait. Four beats of the hoofs can be heard as the horse moves forward.

Rack is a fast, smooth, four-beat gait. It resembles the slow gait but is faster. Five-gaited saddle horses are trained to slow gait and rack.

Care of a Horse

The stall. A horse should live in a clean, comfortable stall that measures at least 10 feet by 10 feet (3 meters by 3 meters). The stable should be light, dry, and well ventilated. Clay or finely ground cinders make the best floor, but cement or wooden floors covered with rubber stall mats can be used. Bedding spread at least 1 foot (30 centimeters) thick over the floor gives the horse a comfortable resting place. Wood shavings, sawdust, straw, or peat moss make good bedding materials. Horses can sleep standing up and often doze while standing with their eyes wide open.

Food. A horse needs food at least three times a day. The horse's stomach is small for the size of its body and holds about 18 quarts (17 liters) of food. In comparison, a man's stomach holds little more than 1 quart (0.95 liter) of food.

Horses eat grass, grain, and hay. When a horse eats grain or hay, it gathers the food with its lips. When a horse eats grass, it bites off the blades close to the ground. Horses chew their food slowly and thoroughly. They do not chew a cud as do cows and deer.

Hay for horses should be placed in a net or on a *rack* (wooden frame). An open box called a *manger* (open box) holds the grain. A 1,000-pound (450-kilogram) horse that works three or four hours a day needs about 20 pounds (9 kilograms) of hay—10 pounds (4.6 kilograms) in the morning and the rest at night. A horse should never eat moldy or dusty hay or hay that contains coarse sticks, thorns, or rubbish. Timothy, or timothy mixed with clover or alfalfa, makes the best hay.

Horses like oats more than any other grain. Working horses may eat from 4 to 12 quarts (3.8 to 11.4 liters) of grain, fortified with vitamins and minerals, every day. The exact amount depends on the animal's size, condition, and the amount of exercise it gets. A third of the feed should be given in the morning, a third at noon, and the rest at night.

Most horses require from 10 to 12 gallons (38 to 45 liters) of fresh, clean water daily. A horse should not be permitted to drink large amounts of water immediately after exercise, when the animal is hot.

Horses need salt for good health because their bodies lose salt when they sweat. A horse eats about 2 ounces (57 grams) of salt daily. A box of salt or a solid salt block in the stable and in the pasture provides this important part of the diet.

Grooming helps keep a horse healthy and improves its appearance. Horses kept in a stable should be groomed daily with a rubber currycomb, body brush, hoof pick, and mane and tail comb. Long, sweeping brush strokes in the direction of the growth of the hair help give the coat a healthy glow. Brushing removes dirt and dandruff. Areas touched by the saddle and girth, and the regions behind the heels and in the hock depressions, need special brushing. A thorough wiping with a soft cloth should follow the brushing. The hoof pick removes dirt and stones and other objects from the feet.

Shoes protect the feet of horses that run or work. Light shoes, weighing about 8 ounces (230 grams) and having only a few nails, make the best shoes for most horses. Saddlebreds and Tennessee walking horses wear shoes weighted in the toes to

help them raise their feet high. Race horses wear light shoes that may wear out after a few races. Shoes for wear in winter or for high mountain trails have cleats that help keep the horse from slipping on ice or snow.

Medical care. Horses should be examined by a veterinarian at least once or twice a year. They should be vaccinated against tetanus, influenza, and other diseases. When necessary, they should receive medicine to expel worms. Sometimes, a horse's teeth must be *floated* (filed down to remove sharp edges).

Horse owners can prevent many medical problems by feeding and bedding the animals properly, keeping them and their living quarters clean, and exercising the horses daily. Owners should watch for any changes in the condition or behavior of their horses and call a veterinarian if a horse appears ill. Signs of illness include loss of appetite, lack of vigor, mucous or bloody discharges from the eyes or nose, swellings or sores on the body, and hot legs or feet. A fast or slow breathing rate or pulse rate may also be a sign of illness. Normally, a resting horse breathes from 8 to 16 times per minute and has a pulse rate of from 30 to 40 beats per minute.

A horse's legs and feet easily become diseased if not cared for properly. Some common diseases of the legs and feet include *thrush*, *navicular*, and *laminitis*. Thrush is an infection of the frog. It can be prevented by providing clean, dry bedding for a horse. To treat thrush, veterinarians apply medication to the affected frog. Navicular is a disease of the foot bone that causes a horse's legs to become stiff and sore. It is treated with corrective shoeing and drugs. Laminitis, also called *founder*, is an

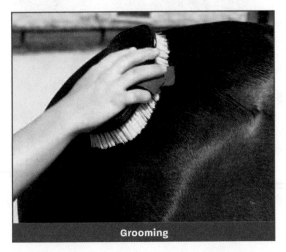

Grooming

inflammation of the foot. Its symptoms include lameness, hot feet, and increased pulse rate. Laminitis is treated by applying medication and soaking the foot in warm water.

Horse Shows and Sports

Horse shows and sports involving horses include a variety of events that test the speed, strength, and other abilities of the animals. Success also depends on the skill of the riders or drivers. Horse shows and sports increased greatly in popularity during the 1900s. Today, they are enjoyed by millions of people worldwide and include local, national, and international competitions.

The Olympic Games have three kinds of *equestrian* (horseback riding) sports: (1) jumping, (2) dressage, and (3) eventing. The International Equestrian Federation regulates the Olympic equestrian events. It also regulates the world championships in *driving*, an event for harness horses and drivers. More than 60 nations belong to the federation.

Horse shows have three main types of competitions: (1) performance, (2) breeding, and (3) *equitation* (horsemanship). In performance competition, the horses and riders demonstrate vari-

Jumping

ous skills. For example, a show may include jumping, five-gaited riding, or driving events. In breeding competition, all the horses in the event must be of the same breed. They are displayed without saddles. The judges rank the horses on *conformation* (physical qualities) and decide which ones best represent the breed. In equitation competition, the contestants ride their horses around a ring. They are judged on their riding style and control of the horse. Some equitation events include jumping.

Some horse shows are restricted to only one breed of horses. Others include events for many breeds. Shows may be held indoors or outdoors and may last from a few hours to a week or more.

Many organizations sponsor horse shows in the United States. The American Horse Shows Association (AHSA) approves about 2,000 shows a year, including the trials for the United States Equestrian Team. The U.S. Equestrian Team represents the United States in the Olympic Games and other international competitions. Important U.S. horse shows include the National Horse Show in East Rutherford, New Jersey; the American Royal Horse Show in Kansas City, Missouri; and the Grand National Horse Show in San Francisco, California.

Jumping. In jumping competitions, the contestants ride across a specially designed course that has obstacles for the horses to leap over. The course may include high jumps, wide jumps, and two or more jumps set close together. The courses vary in difficulty, depending on the level of the competition. The contestants in jumping competitions receive *faults* (penalties) for falls, knocking down the top part of an obstacle, *refusals*, and other errors. A refusal occurs when the horse will not jump over an obstacle. After three refusals, the horse and rider are eliminated from the competition. The contestant with the fewest faults wins the event. In some jumping events, the contestants are timed. In case of a tie for first place, the contestant who completes the course in the shortest time wins.

The main kinds of jumping competitions include (1) Nations' Cup, (2) puissance, and (3) Grand Prix. In Nations' Cups, teams from different countries compete. In most cases, each team consists of four riders and their horses. The three best scores of each team are added to determine the winning team. Puissance events consist mainly of high jumps. The contestants who complete the

Dressage

course without any faults or with equal faults participate in a jump-off. In the jump-off, the number of obstacles is reduced, but the remaining obstacles are raised or widened. The contestants may have several jump-offs, until all except the winner fail to clear the obstacles. Obstacles may reach a height of 7 feet (2.1 meters) or more. In Grand Prix competitions, all contestants complete the course once, and then the top two or more riders participate in a jump-off. In case of a tie, the contestant who completes the course in the shortest time wins. Grand Prix events are held at major horse shows and as part of the Olympic Games.

Dressage. In dressage competitions, the riders guide their horses through a series of movements at the walk, trot, and canter, using mainly leg and seat signals. The horse's movements should be smooth, precise, and graceful, and the rider's signals should not be visible to the spectators.

Special dressage movements include the *passage, piaffe,* and *pirouette*. A passage is a rhythmic, elevated trot in which the horse slowly moves forward. A piaffe resembles a trot, but it is performed without any forward, backward, or sideward movement. A pirouette is a circle that the horse makes by pivoting its forelegs and one hind leg around the other hind leg.

In dressage competitions, the series of movements must be performed in a specific order. In most cases, the contestants are judged by two or more officials who sit in various places around the ring. Each judge gives a contestant points for the performance of each movement and penalties for errors. The scores of all the judges are added, and the contestant with the most points wins.

Dressage techniques were originated by military officers who rode horseback. They had to use their hands to hold weapons, and so they gave signals to their horses with their legs and by shifting their body weight.

Eventing is often called the *Three-Day Event* because most major competitions take place during a three-day period. The contestants first compete in a dressage event. They then participate in a cross-country event. They ride over a course that may be more than 10 miles (16 kilometers) long and includes rough terrain and such obstacles as brush hedges, rail fences, and streams. The contestants receive penalties for falls, refusals, and failure to complete the course in the allotted time. Lastly, a stadium jumping competition is held. The results from the events of the three days are added, and the contestant with the fewest penalties wins.

Eventing is probably the most challenging event. It tests the endurance, obedience, jumping ability, and other qualities of the horse and the skill and daring of the rider. The cross-country event is very strenuous.

Raising Horses

Raising horses for racing, driving, and other sports involves careful breeding and training. It is an important industry in the United States. California, Florida, Kentucky, New York, Texas, and many other states have large breeding farms that raise horses.

Breeding horses. On breeding farms, stallions and mares are carefully selected for mating on the basis of their ancestry and physical qualities. Breeders of race horses also consider the racing records of the animals. An owner of a champion racing stallion may earn millions of dollars in *stud fees* by using the horse for breeding purposes. A stud fee is a sum of money paid to a stallion's owner for the use of the stallion to sire a foal. Breeding horses is not an exact science, and breeders can never be completely certain of producing a colt or filly of champion quality.

A wild pony and foal

Most breeders mate their mares to a stallion in spring. The mares give birth about a year later. People who raise race horses in the Northern Hemisphere want their foals to be born as soon as possible after January 1 because the foals will be considered yearlings the following January. In the Southern Hemisphere, people want foals born soon after the start of July or August. A foal that is born early in the year has more time to grow and develop before it races as a two-year-old.

A foal stays with its mother for the first six months after birth. The owner then weans (separates) the foal from its mother and puts it out to pasture with other foals.

People who raise purebred horses enter their foals in the *registry* of the association for the particular breed. A registry is a record listing a horse's sire and dam and other information. Horses that appear in a registry are called *registered horses*. In the United States, there are about 70 breed associations with registries. The two largest associations are the Jockey Club, for thoroughbreds, and the American Quarter Horse Association.

Other countries also have breed associations and registries. These nations, which are known for breeding fine horses, include Argentina, France, New Zealand, and the United Kingdom.

Training horses requires great skill and patience. Expert trainers handle horses gently but firmly and teach them slowly. Soon after birth, a foal learns to accept handling by humans. Some trainers begin to accustom a foal to a halter almost immediately. Others do not halter-break foals until they are several months old. After a horse is one year old, the trainer gradually accustoms it to having a saddle on its back. Then the horse is mounted and ridden a few steps. Most horses that are trained slowly and patiently do not buck when they are mounted for the first time.

A harness horse is also trained in gradual steps. The horse is first taught to respond to signals from long reins, which are held by a person who walks behind the animal. Later, the horse is taught how to pull a light buggy or carriage.

After a horse has learned to follow the signals of a rider or driver, it is trained for a certain sport. For example, thoroughbred race horses learn to run when a starting gate swings open. Harness racing horses learn to trot or pace behind a moving starting gate that is attached to a car.

Origins of the horse. Scientists believe that the earliest ancestor of the horse was a small animal about 10 to 20 inches (25 to 51 centimeters) high. They call this animal *Eohippus* (dawn horse) or *Hyracotherium*. It lived about 55 million years ago in what is now North America and Europe.

These prehistoric horses had arched backs and snout-like noses. They looked more like racing dogs, such as greyhounds or whippets, than like the straight-backed, long-faced modern horse. They had four toes on their front feet and three toes on their hind feet. Each toe ended in a separate small hoof. Large, tough pads similar to those on a dog's foot kept the toes off the ground. These pads bore the animal's weight.

The next important ancestor of the modern horse was *Mesohippus* (middle horse). It lived about 35 million years ago. It averaged about 20 inches (51 centimeters) in height and had long, slender legs. Each foot had three toes, of which the middle toe was longest. About 30 million years ago, it gave way to a new horse like creature, *Miohippus*. This animal stood from 24 to 28 inches (61 to 71 centimeters) tall, and its middle toe was longer and stronger than that of its ancestors.

Horse-like animals continued to develop, and *Merychippus* (ruminant or cud-chewing horse) appeared about 26 million years ago. It grew about 40 inches (102 centimeters) high. Like Miohippus, it had three toes on each foot. The side toes were almost useless, but the center toe grew long and strong. It ended in a large, curved hoof and bore all the animal's weight.

By about 3 million years ago, horses probably looked somewhat like modern horses. They grew larger than their ancestors. The side toes on their feet became short bones along the legs, leaving the strong center toe with its hoof to support the animals. The teeth also changed, becoming better fitted for eating grass. Scientists group these horses, along with the modern domestic horse, under the name *Equus*.

No one knows where horses originated. Fossils

show that during the Pleistocene Epoch horses lived on every continent except Australia. Great herds wandered over North and South America. Then, for some unknown reason, they disappeared from the Western Hemisphere.

Horses and people. Primitive people hunted horses and ate their meat. No one knows who first tamed horses and trained them for riding. Scientific discoveries at the ancient city of Susa in southwestern Asia show that people rode horses about 5,000 years ago.

Stone tablets show that the Hittites trained horses for sport and war about 1400 B.C. The Assyrians, about 800 B.C., hunted lions in two-wheeled chariots drawn by a pair of horses. Tapestries show early Persians playing a kind of polo. The early Greeks and Romans were expert riders and used horses for racing and other sports. Greek and Roman soldiers rode horses in battle. The Greeks wrote about horsemanship as early as 400 B.C. We still follow their principles of riding.

In 1066, William the Conqueror used mounted knights to invade England. The English then began to breed large, powerful war horses that could carry a man wearing a heavy suit of armor. During the 1300s, after armies began using gunpowder, swift, light steeds replaced the large mounts of the knights as war horses.

From the late 1500s onward, breeders in Europe developed improved stocks of horses, largely from Arab horses. Arabs had lived in Europe for hundreds of years. But in the 1600s, breeders took a new strain of Arab horse to Britain and used it as the basis of the thoroughbred. In the 1700s, King Louis XV of France founded an important breeding center called the Pompadour stud. Later, Napoleon ordered the importation of more than 200 Arab stallions and 30 mares to improve the French stock even more. Arab breeding centers soon spread to Germany and other countries.

The first European colonists found no horses in North America. Christopher Columbus had brought horses with him on his second voyage to the New World. But most American Indians did not know about horses until Spanish conquerors brought them to Mexico in 1519. Horses that the Spanish explorers left behind probably became the ancestors of the American wild horses.

The Indians, especially the tribes of the western plains, began to use horses about 1600. Indians rode horses to hunt buffalo and used them in battle.

Arabian horse

Horses played an important part in the development and exploration of North America. The pioneers who settled the West rode horses and used them to pull their covered wagons. Mounted soldiers fought in the Revolutionary War and in the Civil War.

Horses pulled trains on short railroads until the steam locomotive replaced them about 1830. They pulled *horsecars* (streetcars) in cities before the use of electricity. Horses also served as the fastest means of communication until the telegraph was developed during the 1800s.

With the creation of railroads, tractors, trucks, and automobiles, horses became less useful. The number of horses in cities and on farms declined steadily. But, though the use of horses for heavy work decreased, their importance in sports and recreation increased.

During the 1900s, the number of wild horses declined greatly in the United States and other countries. Many people feared that wild horses were becoming extinct, especially because the horses were being hunted for their meat. As a result, numerous countries have passed laws protecting wild horses.

Scientific Classification

Horses belong to the horse family, Equidae. They are classified as genus *Equus*, species *E. caballus*.

MLA Citation

"Horses." *The Southwestern Advantage Topic Source.* Nashville: Southwestern. 2013.

DATA

Some Types and Breeds of Horses

Type or breed	Place of origin	Weight in pounds	Weight in kilograms	Height in hands[1]
Saddle horses				
American saddlebred	United States	900 to 1,200	410 to 540	14.3 to 16.1
American quarter horse	United States	900 to 1,200	410 to 540	14.2 to 15.3
Appaloosa	United States	950 to 1,175	430 to 530	14.2 to 15.2
Arabian	Arabia	850 to 1,000	390 to 450	14.2 to 15.3
Morgan	United States	800 to 1,100	360 to 500	14.2 to 15.2
Palomino	United States	900 to 1,300	410 to 590	14.1 to 16
Tennessee walking horse	United States	900 to 1,200	410 to 540	15 to 16
Thoroughbred	England	1,000 to 1,300	450 to 590	15 to 17
Light harness or roadster horses				
Hackney	England	900 to 1,200	410 to 540	14.3 to 16.2
Standardbred or American trotter	United States	800 to 1,200	360 to 540	15 to 16
Draft horses				
American cream	United States	1,600 to 2,000	730 to 910	15.2 to 16.3
Belgian	Belgium	1,700 to 2,200	770 to 1,000	16 to 19
Clydesdale	Scotland	1,500 to 2,000	680 to 910	16 to 17.1
Percheron	France	1,600 to 2,100	730 to 950	15 to 17
Shire	England	1,800 to 2,300	820 to 1,040	16 to 17
Suffolk	England	1,500 to 1,900	680 to 860	15.2 to 16.2
Heavy harness or coach horses				
Cleveland bay	England	1,250 to 1,550	570 to 700	15.3 to 16.3
French coach	France	1,100 to 1,400	500 to 640	15.1 to 16.3
German coach	Germany	1,200 to 1,500	540 to 680	15.2 to 16.3
Ponies				
Hackney pony	England	600 to 850	270 to 390	12 to 14.2
Pony of the Americas	United States	500 to 900	230 to 410	11.2 to 13.2
Shetland pony	Shetland Islands	300 to 500	140 to 230	9 to 11.2

[1] One hand equals 4 inches (10 centimeters).

DATA

Riding Equipment

Bit is the metal part of the bridle that fits in a horse's mouth.

Bridle is the headgear used to control a horse. It includes the bit.

Girth is a leather or canvas strap that fits under the horse's belly and holds a saddle in place.

Hackamore is a bitless bridle that controls the horse by pressure on its nose and jaw.

Reins are long, narrow leather strips attached at one end to the bit. The rider holds the other end.

Tack is riding equipment, such as the bridle and saddle.

Famous Horses in History and Legend

Al Borak carried Muhammad from earth to the seventh heaven, according to Muslim legend.

Aristides won the first Kentucky Derby in 1875.

Black Horse, from the Bible (*Revelation*), is the horse of Famine.

Bucephalus could be ridden only by Alexander the Great, who founded the city of Bucephala about 326 B.C. in honor of his beloved horse.

Bulle Rock was the first thoroughbred imported from England to America, in 1730.

Cincinnati, a great black charger, carried General Ulysses S. Grant during the Civil War.

Clever Hans, who lived in the early 1900s, was a famous "talking" horse that solved arithmetic problems.

Comanche, a cavalry horse, was the only survivor of Lieutenant Colonel George A. Custer's "Last Stand" in 1876. **Vic,** Custer's horse, died in the battle.

Copenhagen carried the Duke of Wellington to victory in the Battle of Waterloo in 1815.

Diomed won the first English Derby at Epsom Downs, in 1780.

Eclipse, an English thoroughbred foaled in 1764, was the ancestor of many modern thoroughbreds.

Incitatus was made a priest and consul by the Roman Emperor Caligula about A.D. 40. This horse had an ivory manger and drank wine from a golden pail.

Iroquois, in 1881, became the first American-bred horse to win the English Derby.

Marengo, a white stallion, was ridden by Napoleon in his defeat at Waterloo in 1815.

Pegasus was the great winged horse of the Muses (nine goddesses in Greek mythology).

Reckless, a small Korean racing mare, served as ammunition carrier for a U.S. Marine platoon during the Korean War (1950–1953). The mare was made a sergeant and received a medal for bravery under fire.

Sleipnir, the gray horse of Odin, chief god in Norse mythology, was said to have eight legs and be able to travel on land or sea.

Traveller, a spirited gray gelding, carried General Robert E. Lee during the Civil War.

Trojan Horse, a legendary wooden horse built by the Greeks, helped them capture the city of Troy during the Trojan War.

Xanthus was the horse of Achilles. He was supposed to have predicted his master's death, after being scolded by the mighty Greek warrior.

ADDITIONAL RESOURCES

Books to Read

Level I

Edwards, Elwyn H. *Horses*. 2nd ed. Dorling Kindersley, 2002.

Jeffrey, Laura S. *Horses: How to Choose and Care for a Horse*. Enslow, 2004.

Ransford, Sandy. *First Riding Lessons*. Kingfisher Books, 2002. *The Kingfisher Illustrated Horse and Pony Encyclopedia*. 2004.

Sandler, Martin W. *Galloping Across the USA: Horses in American Life*. Oxford, 2003.

Vogel, Julia. *Wild Horses*. NorthWord, 2004.

Level II

Burns, Deborah, ed. *Storey's Horse-Lover's Encyclopedia*. Storey Books, 2001.

Hairston, Rachel. *The Essentials of Horsekeeping*. Sterling Publishers, 2004.

Hermsen, Josee. *The Horse Encyclopedia*. 1998. Reprint. Firefly Books, 2001.

Hogg, Abigail. *The Horse Behavior Handbook*. David & Charles, 2003.

Kelley, Brent P. *The Horse Doctor Is In*. Storey Books, 2002. A guide to health and treatment.

Web Sites

Breeds of the World

http://www.imh.org/history-of-the-horse/breeds-of-the-world-by-continent/
Kentucky Horse Park's page describes various horse species.

Fossil Horses in Cyberspace

http://www.flmnh.ufl.edu/natsci/vertpaleo/fhc/fhc.htm
An on-line exhibit about horse paleontology and evolution from the Florida Museum of Natural History.

International Museum of the Horse

http://www.imh.org
Web site of a large museum in Lexington, Kentucky. Includes on-line exhibits about horse history.

NetVet—Horses

http://netvet.wustl.edu/horses.htm
Links to Web sites about horse health, racing, and breeding.

Search Strings

Saddle Horses

horses saddle ride pleasure (67,600)

horses saddle ride pleasure American Tennessee Walking Morgan quarter Arabian (38,700)

horses "saddle horses" American "tennessee Walking" Morgan quarter Arabian (846)

Draft Horses

horses draft strong war work (122,000)

horses draft strong war work shire Clydesdale Belgian Percheron Suffolk American cream (96)

horses draft strong war work breeds (39,900)

Training Horses

horses training (297,000)

training horses (316,000)

horses training steps ages (194,000)

BACKGROUND INFORMATION

The following article was written during the year in which the events took place and reflect the style and thinking of that time.

Horse Racing (2001)

The mysterious deaths of more than 500 thoroughbred foals, which were stillborn or died shortly after birth, rocked the thoroughbred horse industry in Kentucky in the spring of 2001. Similar deaths were also reported at horse farms in West Virginia and Ohio.

In May, scientists concluded that the foals had died when the mares carrying them had eaten grass poisoned by cyanide, which naturally occurs in the leaves of black cherry trees common in those areas. The scientists said that Eastern Tent caterpillars, which had recently invaded Kentucky, had eaten the black cherry leaves and excreted the cyanide on the grass where the horses fed. Kentucky officials estimated the value of the lost foals at more than $300 million.

Three-year-olds. On May 5, Monarchos, a 10.5-to-1 long shot, stunned the horse-racing world by running the second-fastest Kentucky Derby in history. Monarchos covered the 1¼-mile course at Churchill Downs in Louisville, Kentucky, in 1 minute 59.97 seconds. Only Secretariat, who posted 1:59.4 during the legendary horse's Triple Crown run in 1973, has run faster. Invisible Ink, a 55-to-1 long shot, finished second, nearly five lengths behind Monarchos.

Point Given, who had been favored to win the Kentucky Derby, was in charge for the rest of the Triple Crown season. On May 19, 2001, he won the Preakness Stakes at Baltimore's Pimlico Race Course by 2¼ lengths over AP Valentine. On June 9, Point Given dominated the field in the Belmont Stakes, beating AP Valentine by 12¼ lengths at Belmont Park in Elmont, New York.

Harness racing. On August 4, Scarlet Knight held off Pegasus Spur to capture the $1 million Hambletonian at the Meadowlands Racetrack in East Rutherford, New Jersey. In the Pacing Triple Crown, Four Starzzz Shark won the Cane Pace on September 3 after Gunthatwonthewest broke stride about 50 yards (45 meters) short of the finish line; Bettor's Delight held off Real Desire by a length and a half to win the Little Brown Jug on September 20; and Bagel Beach Boy outdueled stablemate Exquisite Art to win the Messenger Stakes on October 27.

International. On March 24, Captain Steve won the biggest purse in thoroughbred racing, capturing the $3.6 million winner's share of the $6 million Dubai World Cup, held in the United Arab Emirates. Galileo, ridden by Irish jockey Michael Kinane, became the 14th horse to win both the Irish Derby and the English Derby, taking the Derby Stakes in England on June 9 and the Irish Derby three weeks later.

Kentucky Derby

Religion

The people of the world share many different religions. Most believers follow Christianity, Islam, or Hinduism. Other major religions include Judaism, which provided the roots of Christianity, and Buddhism.

HOT topics

Freedom of Religion. Freedom of religion is a person's right to believe in and practice whatever faith he or she chooses. It also includes the right to have no religious belief. Throughout history, many people have been persecuted for their religious beliefs. Strong religious views have led to intolerance among various faiths. Some governments have close ties to one religion and consider people of other faiths to be a threat. A government also may regard religion as politically dangerous because religions may place allegiance to God above obedience to the state. The freedom to practice a personal choice of religion is fundamental to a democratic society.

Church bells

HOT topics 🔥

Belief in a God. There are three main philosophical views regarding the existence of a god or deity: (1) *Theists* believe in a deity or deities. (2) *Atheists* believe that no deity exists. (3) *Agnostics* say that the existence of a deity cannot be proved or disproved. Most major religions are theistic. They teach that deities govern or greatly influence the actions of human beings and events in nature. But some religions are not theistic. Examples include Confucianism and some forms of Buddhism.

Sacred Stories. For thousands of years, followers of religions have believed in sacred stories, sometimes called *myths* or *legends*. Religious leaders often use these stories to dramatize their teachings. Many stories describe the creation of the world. Others tell how human beings or a particular civilization began. Some stories suggest a cause of natural occurrences, such as thunderstorms or the changes in seasons. Today, there are scientific explanations for many subjects of sacred stories. But some religious groups still insist that the stories are true in every detail. Other groups regard sacred stories as symbolic expressions of the ideals and values of their faith.

Islam. The religion of Islam is based on the life and teachings of the prophet Muhammad, who lived in Arabia during the early A.D. 600s. Before Muhammad's time, the people in the region worshiped Allah (God) and other deities. But Muhammad said Allah was the only God. Muslim missionaries and traders carried Islam to India and other parts of Asia and to Africa. From the 1000s to the 1500s, Islam's control over the Holy Land caused European Christians to launch crusades, wars aimed at making areas become Christian. Today, Islam is the major religion of nearly all countries in northern Africa and the Middle East. It is also the chief religion in Bangladesh, Indonesia, Malaysia, and Pakistan.

St. Basil's Cathedral, Moscow, Russia

TRUE or FALSE?

Buddha taught that people should devote themselves to finding release from the suffering of life. Through this release, people would gain *nirvana*, a state of perfect peace and happiness.

THE BASICS

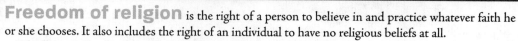 **Freedom of religion** is the right of a person to believe in and practice whatever faith he or she chooses. It also includes the right of an individual to have no religious beliefs at all.

Like most rights, freedom of religion is not absolute. Most countries prohibit religious practices that injure people or that are thought to threaten to destroy society. For example, most governments forbid human sacrifice and *polygamy*, the practice of having more than one wife or husband at the same time.

Throughout most of history, many people have been persecuted for their religious beliefs. The denial of religious liberty probably stems from two major sources—personal and political. Religion touches the deepest feelings of many people. Strong religious views have led to intolerance among various faiths. Some governments have close ties to one religion and consider people of other faiths to be a threat to political authority. A government also may regard religion as politically dangerous because religions may place allegiance to God above obedience to the state.

The question of morality has caused many conflicts between church and state. Both religion and government are concerned with morality. They work together if the moral goals desired by the state are the same as those sought by the church. But discord may result if they have different views about morality.

DEFINITIONS

religion 1. belief in God or gods: *George Washington's religion was one of his chief supports during the hardships he suffered in the Revolution.* **2.** worship of God or gods: *Christians and Jews believe in the same God but participate in religion on different days.* **3.** a particular system of religious belief and worship: *the Christian religion, the Muslim religion.* **4.** anything done or followed with reverence or devotion: *"In Turin football is a religion,"* observed the narrator (Listener). *Park...had not made a religion of camping out* (New Yorker).

experience religion, to become converted: *Some went so far as to doubt if she had ever experienced religion* (Oliver Wendell Holmes).

Buddhism: a religion based on the teachings of Gautama Buddha that teaches that right living will enable people to attain nirvana, the condition of a soul that does not have to live in a body and is free from all desire and pain. Buddhism developed in the 500s B.C., in northern India and spread over central, southeastern and eastern Asia.

Christianity 1. the religion taught by Christ and His followers; Christian religion: *The glory of Christianity is the very gap between its teachings of perfection and the struggles of a hopelessly imperfect mankind to reach it* (Newsweek). **2.** Christian beliefs or faith; condition of being a Christian; Christian spirit or character: *His Christianity consisted of going to church on Sunday.* **3.** all Christians; the Christian part of the world; Christendom: *Christianity recognizes the cross as its symbol.*

Hinduism: the religious and social system of the Hindus, a development of ancient Brahmanism. The caste system and the worship of many gods are parts of Hinduism.

Islam 1. the Muslim religion, based on the teachings of Muhammad as they appear in the Qur'an. It holds that there is only one God, Allah, and Muhammad is his prophet; that the Qur'an is revealed literature containing a sufficient rule of life; and that salvation is achieved by the righteous. **2.** Muslims as a group. **3.** the countries under Muslim rule or inhabited by Muslims.

Judaism 1. the religion of the Jews, based on the teachings of Moses and the prophets as found in the Old Testament, and on the interpretations of the rabbis. Judaism teaches belief in the same God as Christianity, but holds that the Messiah is still to come. *The great prophets of Israel made the search for justice the heart of Judaism* (Ogburn and Nimkoff). **2.** the observance of this religion or of Jewish rules, customs, and traditions. **3.** the culture, religion, history, language, and civilization of the Jewish people. **4.** Jews as a group.

An example is the disagreement of many religious people with governments that allow abortion.

In the United States. The desire for religious freedom was a major reason Europeans settled in America. The Puritans and many other groups came to the New World to escape religious persecution in Europe.

The First Amendment of the U.S. Constitution guarantees that "Congress shall make no law respecting an establishment of religion, or prohibiting the free exercise thereof." This provision originally protected religious groups from unfair treatment by the federal government only. Until the mid-1800s, New Hampshire and other states had laws that prohibited non-Protestants from holding public office. Several states, including Connecticut and Massachusetts, even had official churches. Since the 1940s, however, the Supreme Court of the United States has ruled that all the states must uphold the First Amendment's guarantees of religious freedom.

Today, freedom of religion remains an issue in the United States. Various court rulings have interpreted the First Amendment to mean that the government may not promote or give special treatment to any religion. Judges have struck down plans that called for the government to give financial aid to religious schools. The courts have also ruled unconstitutional a number of programs to teach the Bible or recite prayers in public schools. These rulings are highly controversial.

But church and state are not completely separated in the United States. The nation's motto is *In God We Trust.* Sessions of Congress open with prayers, and court witnesses swear oaths on the Bible. Several court decisions support such practices.

Christian moral views have had a predominant influence on U.S. laws because most of the nation's people are Christians. In 1878, for example, the Supreme Court upheld a federal law against polygamy, even though this law restricted the religious freedom of one Christian group, the Mormons. At that time, the Mormon faith included belief in polygamy. But the laws and the courts agreed with the view of most Americans that polygamy is harmful to society.

In other countries. Religion has been discouraged or even forbidden in countries ruled by dictators. Before the 1980s, for example, the Communist governments of the Soviet Union and Eastern European countries persecuted religion on a large scale. A person's highest allegiance, they believed, belonged to Communism, not to a Supreme Being. Although they did not forbid religion entirely, they made it difficult for people to practice any faith. Beginning in 1989, the Communist governments of many Eastern European countries were replaced with reform governments that permitted more religious freedom. In 1990, Soviet leaders passed a law that restored religious freedom in the Soviet Union. In 1991, the Communist Party lost control of the Soviet government, and later that year the Soviet Union was dissolved.

In some countries that have an official state church, or where most of the people belong to one church, other faiths do not have religious freedom. For example, many Muslim nations discriminate against Christians and Jews.

Other countries, including Denmark and Norway, have state churches. But the governments of these nations grant freedom of worship to other religious groups. In some countries, the government provides equal support for all religions.

History. Many ancient peoples permitted broad religious freedom. These peoples worshiped many gods and readily accepted groups with new gods. Jews and, later, Christians could not do so because they worshiped only one God. They also believed that allegiance to God was higher than allegiance to any ruler or state. Some ancient peoples did not accept these beliefs, and they persecuted Christians and Jews.

Jan Hus

During the Middle Ages, from about the A.D. 400s through the 1400s, the Roman Catholic Church dominated Europe and permitted little religious freedom. The Catholic Church persecuted Jews and Muslims. The church also punished people for any serious disagreement with its teachings. In 1415, the Bohemian religious reformer John Hus was burned at the stake for challenging the authority of the pope.

The Reformation, a religious movement of the 1500s, gave birth to Protestantism. The Catholic Church and Catholic rulers persecuted Protestant groups. Many Protestant denominations persecuted Catholics and other Protestant groups as well.

However, by the 1700s and 1800s, the variety of religions that resulted from the Reformation had led to increased tolerance in many countries. These countries included the United Kingdom, the Netherlands, and the United States. But intolerance remained strong in some countries. Poland and Russia, for example, severely persecuted Jews. One of the most savage religious persecutions in history occurred in the 1930s and 1940s, when Nazi Germany killed about six million Jews.

RELIGION. No simple definition can describe the many religions in the world. Every society has a religion. For many people, religion is an organized system of beliefs, *rituals* (acts and ceremonies), personal practices, and worship directed toward a supreme power or *deity* (god). For others, religion involves a number of gods or deities. Some people follow religions that worship no specific god or gods. There are also people who practice their own religious beliefs in a personal way, largely independent of any organized religion.

Almost all people who participate in a religion believe that a divine power is at work in the world. Some believe that this power created the world and can influence their lives in various ways. Others believe that the goal of human life is to live in harmony with this power.

In its most basic sense, religion deals with primary concerns: What is the purpose of life? What is the final destiny of human beings and animals? What is the difference between right and wrong? What is the meaning of suffering and evil? What are a person's obligations to other people and to the world?

People practice religions for many reasons. Some anthropologists believe that the religious impulse may be one of the most fundamental traits of the human species. Throughout the world, many people follow a religious tradition simply because it is part of the heritage of their nation, culture, tribe, ethnic group, or family. One objective of religion is to give groups a sense of identity and purpose.

Religion can provide a sense of personal security in a confusing world because believers feel that a supreme power, God, watches over them. Believers may request help or protection from their god or gods through prayer or ritual.

Many people follow a religion because it promises them happiness in life or in some kind of life after death, or they believe it will save them from eternal damnation. The prospect of an afterlife also offers hope to those who suffer in this life. Religion provides individual fulfillment in this way and helps people to understand their place in the universe.

There are thousands of religions in the world. The three religions with the most followers are Christianity, Islam, and Hinduism. Other religions include Buddhism, Confucianism, Jainism, Judaism, Shinto, Sikhism, and Taoism. Hinduism, Shinto, and Taoism developed over many centuries. Many other religions base their faith on the lives or teachings of specific individuals. They include for Buddhism, Siddhartha Gautama, who became known as Gautama Buddha; for Christianity, Jesus, known as Jesus Christ; for Confucianism, Confucius; for Islam, Muhammad; for Jainism, Mahavira; for Judaism, Abraham and Moses; and for Sikhism, Nanak.

The religions that trace their history to individuals follow a general pattern of development. During the individual's lifetime or soon after his death, a distinctive system of worship and ceremonies developed, based on the individual's life and teachings. In addition to inspiring worship, the individual represented an ideal way of life that followers tried to imitate.

The teachings of religions have shaped the lives of people since prehistoric times. Judaism, Islam, and especially Christianity have been major influences in the formation of Western culture. These religions are called *Religions of the Book* because they all are at least partly inspired by the Hebrew Bible, or Old Testament. These three faiths, particularly Islam, have also played a crucial role in the development of Middle Eastern and African culture. The cultures of Asia have been shaped by Buddhism, Confucianism, Hinduism, Shinto, and Taoism.

Religion has been a supreme source of inspiration in the arts. In ancient times, almost all art was probably religious in nature. Some of the most beautiful buildings in the world are houses of worship. Much of the world's greatest music is religious. Religious stories have provided countless subjects for paintings, sculptures, literature, theater, dances, and motion pictures.

Chief characteristics of religion.
Most leading religions share certain characteristics. The chief characteristics include (1) belief in a deity or in a power beyond the individual, (2) a *doctrine* (accepted teaching) of salvation, (3) a code of conduct, (4) the use of sacred stories, and (5) religious rituals.

The essential qualities of a religion are maintained and passed from generation to generation by sources, called *authority*, which the followers accept as sacred. To be sacred or holy, a thing must be considered set apart and different, either because it is commanded by a deity or is related to a god or gods. Sacred things have more power than ordinary things. The most important religious authorities are writings known as *scriptures*. Scriptures include the Bibles of Christians and Jews, the Koran of Muslims, and the Vedas of Hindus. Most believers consider scriptures sacred because the writings are *inspired*—that is, dictated by or guided by a deity. Religious authority also comes from the writings of saints and other holy people and from decisions by religious councils and leaders. Unwritten customs and laws known as *traditions* also form a basic part of authority.

Belief in a deity. There are three main philosophical views regarding the existence of a deity: (1) *Theists* believe in a deity or deities. (2) *Atheists* believe that no deity exists. (3) *Agnostics* say that the existence of a deity cannot be proved or

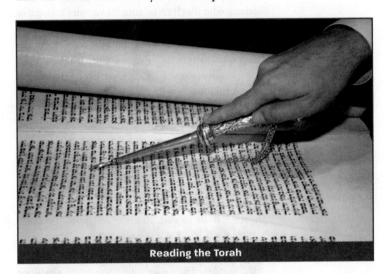
Reading the Torah

disproved. Most major religions are theistic. They teach that deities govern or greatly influence the actions of human beings as well as events in nature. Some religions are not theistic. Examples include Confucianism and some forms of Buddhism.

Religions that acknowledge only one god are called *monotheistic*. Judaism, Christianity, and Islam are examples of monotheistic religions. A religion that has a number of deities is *polytheistic*. The ancient Greeks and Romans had polytheistic religions. Each of their many gods and goddesses had one or more special areas of influence. For example, Aphrodite was the Greek goddess of love, and Mars was the Roman god of war. In *henotheistic* religions, the worship of a supreme deity does not deny the existence and power of other deities. For example, Hinduism teaches that a world spirit called Brahman is the supreme power. But Hindus also worship numerous other gods and goddesses. Many peoples in Africa and the Pacific Islands also worship a supreme power as well as many other deities.

The followers of some religions worship deities who are or were people or that are images of people. The ancient Egyptian people considered their pharaohs to be living gods. Before World War II (1939–1945), the Japanese honored their emperor as divine. Taoists believe in deities that look and act like human beings. They also worship some deities who were once human beings and became gods or goddesses after death. Jains worship *Tirhankaras*—that is, people who have become enlightened and broken the cycle of birth and death.

Many people worship nature gods—that is, deities who dwell in or control various aspects of nature. The Chinese, in particular, have worshiped gods of the soil and grain. Followers of Shinto worship *kami*, spirits that live in nature. Many American Indians worship a *spirit power*, a mysterious, powerful force in nature.

A doctrine of salvation. Among the major religions, Christianity, Hinduism, Buddhism, Islam, and Jainism teach a doctrine of salvation. They stress that salvation is the highest goal of the faithful and one that all followers should try to achieve. Religions differ, however, in their understanding of salvation, when and how it occurs, and how it can be gained. In many religions, the quest

A Taoist shrine

for salvation is aided by the work of a "savior." The savior may be a god or some other divine figure, or the individual on whose teachings the religion is based.

A doctrine of salvation is based on the belief that individuals or groups are in some danger from which they must be "saved." The danger may be the threat of physical misfortune in this world, such as disease or war, or the danger may await people in a life after death. Christianity and several other religions teach that the danger is primarily spiritual and is centered in each person's soul. The soul is thought to be that part of a person that survives after the body dies.

Christianity teaches that people are sinful by nature. They can, however, wipe out their sinfulness and past offenses toward God and humanity by believing in the sacrificial death of Jesus. If a Christian is saved, then the soul enters a state of eternal happiness, often called heaven. If a person is not saved, the soul may spend eternity in a state of punishment, often called hell.

Most Eastern religions teach that a person gains salvation by finding release from obstacles that can block human fulfillment. In most Asian religions, the obstacles take the form of worldly desires and attachments to material things. Salvation depends on whether people can free themselves from these desires and attachments, which only bring suffering.

Hinduism teaches that each person's soul, called *atman*, is identical with the supreme spirit, Brahman, that is the source of all material creation. Hindus believe they achieve a kind of immortality, as well as union with their god, through discovering the Brahman in themselves.

In Buddhism, a person must undertake the difficult task of purification by following a set of guidelines called the Noble Eightfold Path. By following this path, people rid themselves of the delusions that doom them to an endless cycle of birth, suffering, death, and rebirth.

Islam teaches that actions in this life bring salvation in the next. Followers must "submit" their whole selves to the will of Allah through daily prayer and other acts of worship called the Five Pillars of Islam. By following these practices, Muslims will be saved from future punishment by Allah.

A code of conduct is a set of moral teachings and values that all religions have in some form. Such a code, or *ethic*, tells believers how to conduct

Muslim women praying

their lives. It instructs them how to act toward the deity and toward one another. Religious codes of conduct differ in many ways, but most agree on several major themes. For example, they stress some form of the *golden rule*, which states that believers ideally should treat others as they would like to be treated themselves. A religion's code of conduct also may determine such matters as whom believers may marry, what jobs they may hold, how they dress, and what foods they may eat.

The use of sacred stories. For thousands of years, followers of religions have believed in sacred stories, sometimes called *myths* or *legends*. Religious leaders often use these stories to dramatize their teachings.

Originally, people told stories to describe how the sacred powers influenced the world. The stories showed how the sacred powers directly or indirectly caused some feature or event in the world. Many stories described the creation of the world. Others told how human beings or a particular people began. Some of the stories tried to explain the cause of natural occurrences, such as thunderstorms or the changes in seasons.

Today, there are scientific explanations for many of the subjects dealt with in sacred stories. But some religious groups still insist that the stories are true in every detail. Other groups believe only in the message contained in the stories, not in the specific details. Still other religious groups regard sacred stories as symbolic expressions of the ideals and values of their faith.

Religious rituals include the acts and ceremonies by which believers appeal to and serve God, deities, or other sacred powers. Some rituals are performed by individuals alone, and others by groups of worshipers. Religious groups perform their important rituals according to a schedule and often repeat them regularly. The performance of a ritual is often called a *service*. Leaders of rituals often require special training and must be authorized before they are allowed to lead. This training and authorization is sometimes called *ordination*.

The most common ritual is prayer. Through prayer, a believer or someone on behalf of believers addresses words and thoughts to an object of worship. Prayer includes requests, expressions of thanksgiving, confessions of sins, and praise. Most major religions have a daily schedule of prayer.

Meditation, in some ways like prayer, is a spiritual exercise important in Asian religions. Buddhist monks try to be masters of meditation. By clearing the mind of day-to-day distractions, people who meditate attempt to gain a higher form of consciousness.

Many religions have rituals intended to purify the body. For example, Hindus consider the waters of the Ganges River in India to be sacred. Every year, millions of Hindus purify their bodies by bathing in the river, especially at the holy city of Varanasi.

In some religions, *pilgrimages* are significant rituals. Pilgrimages are journeys to the sites of holy objects or to places credited with miraculous healing powers. Believers also make pilgrimages to sacred places, such as the birthplace or tomb of the founder of their faith. All devout Muslims hope to make a pilgrimage to Mecca, the birthplace of Muhammad. Many Christians travel to the Holy Land, today the nation of Israel and a Palestinian territory called the West Bank. This land is where Jesus of Nazareth lived, worked, and died.

Shamans are holy men and women who are believed to have special powers to communicate with the gods or the spirit world. Many shamans are thought to leave their bodies while in a trance, taking "spirit" journeys to find answers or healing for their people.

Many rituals are scheduled at certain times of the day, week, or year. Various religions have services at sunrise, in the morning, at sunset, and in the evening. Special services mark the beginning of a new year. Many religions celebrate springtime, harvest time, and the new or full moon. Religious attention to the marking of the seasons may be a survival from prehistoric and ancient religions. These early religions attempted to secure survival of the community through good harvests and hunting, which depended on a knowledge of the seasons.

Many rituals commemorate events in the history of religions. For example, the Jewish festival of Passover recalls the meal the Israelites ate just before their departure from slavery in Egypt.

A Seder cup and plate

Various Christian celebrations of Holy Communion are related to the last meal Jesus shared with His disciples before His death.

Rituals also mark important events in a person's life. Various ceremonies make such events as birth, marriage, and death into sacred occasions. Some rituals accept young people into the religion and into adult society. These rituals are called *rites of passage.* In Judaism, the ritual of circumcision is performed on male infants. Some Christians baptize babies soon after birth. Other Christians baptize only youths or adults.

How the major religions are organized. The organization of the world's major religions ranges from simple to complex. Many religions have spiritual leaders, often called the *clergy.* These leaders have the authority and responsibility to conduct religious services, to advise or command believers, and to govern the religious organization at various levels. In some religions, the *laity*—that is, the believers who are not members of the clergy—also have important roles.

In many countries, there is a *state* (official or favored) religion. For example, Islam is the state religion of Iran, Pakistan, Saudi Arabia, and many other nations. Lutheranism is the state religion of Denmark and Norway, and Buddhism is the state religion of the Asian nations of Bhutan, Cambodia, and Thailand. The United Kingdom has two *established* (official) churches—the Church of England, which is Anglican, and the Church of Scotland, which is Presbyterian.

Judaism has no one person as its head. Each local congregation or synagogue supervises its own affairs, usually under the leadership of a rabbi. Israel and a few other countries have chief rabbis. These rabbis are scholars who serve as the top judges of religious law.

Christian *denominations* (groups) are organized in various ways. In the Roman Catholic Church, believers are organized into districts called *parishes,* which belong to larger districts called *dioceses.* Dioceses, in turn, belong to *provinces.* The main diocese in each province is called an *archdiocese.* Pastors preside over parishes, bishops over dioceses, and archbishops over archdioceses. The pope presides over the entire Roman Catholic Church with the advice and assistance of high officials called *cardinals.* Some Protestant denominations are governed by similar patterns of *hierarchies* (levels of authority). Others are governed by boards of the clergy and laity or by local congregations. Throughout most of history, women have had fewer rights and a lower social status than men. Largely because of women's lower status, most religious hierarchies have tended to exclude women from leadership roles.

Confucianism and Islam have no ordained clergy. Leadership is provided by scholars who interpret religious teachings. In Shinto and Taoism, the basic organizational unit is the priesthood. In Buddhism, the chief unit is an order of monks called the *sangha.* The monks serve as advisers and teachers and play a vital part in everyday life. In some Buddhist countries, the head of state is also the leader of the national order of monks.

Hinduism has no consistent pattern of organization. There are no congregations or parishes. Hindus tend to worship individually or in families. Services in temples are performed by the Brahmans, members of the highest Hindu *caste* (social class).

The origin of religion. Experts think prehistoric religions arose out of fear and wonder about natural events, such as the occurrence of storms and earthquakes and the birth of babies. To explain why someone died, people credited supernatural powers greater than themselves or greater than the world around them.

Prehistoric people most likely centered their religious activities on the most important elements of their existence, such as adequate rainfall or success in hunting. They often placed food, ornaments, and tools in the graves of members of the group who had died. They probably believed that these items would be useful to, or desired by, the dead. Archaeologists believe that prehistoric people drew pictures and may have performed other rituals intended to promote the fertility of women and animals and to ensure good hunting. They likely made sacrifices for the same reason.

Earlier theories. In the 1800s, the British anthropologist Edward Burnett Tylor and the German-born language scholar Friedrich Max Muller developed influential ideas about the origin of religion. Tylor proposed that ancient people thought spirits, or *animae*, existed in and controlled all things in nature. This concept was called *animism*. Many people still practice animism today, especially in Africa.

Muller agreed with Tylor that religion began as spirit worship. He also thought that early people saw human qualities in natural forces. For example, they understood thunderstorms as a god who controlled thunder. Muller thought the belief in deities originated in this way.

In the early 1900s, the German scholar Rudolf Otto and the Austrian physician Sigmund Freud proposed theories of religion that went beyond those of earlier scholars. Otto believed that religion came into existence when people encountered what they felt was holy or sacred. Such an event provoked feelings of awe and wonder, and people continued to try to recapture that encounter. Worship

Martin Buber

and an ethical code of conduct are ways that people hope to sustain their sense of the sacred in their lives. For Freud, the father of modern psychoanalysis, religion emerged from the consciousness of the child. A child typically relies on a dominant, nearby mother figure and a distant, all-powerful father figure. The child's dependence on these parental figures eventually leads, in adults, to the concept of a supreme being strongly at work in a person's life. Religion, according to Freud, is a formal attempt to please and influence this universal parent.

In the 1920s, the Austrian-born Jewish philosopher Martin Buber wrote that the basic religious impulse arises when a person encounters someone or something as a being with whom one can have a direct, deeply personal relationship. Buber called it an "I-Thou" relationship. He located the foundation of all meaning in life in this satisfying experience of knowing or being known by another consciousness.

Later theories. By the end of the 1900s, many other scholars had added to the understanding of the rise of religions and their many features. Evelyn Underhill, a British religious scholar, studied mystical experience, in which a person seeks union with a supreme power. Mircea Eliade, a Romanian-born religious historian, studied early religions. He found that religions arose from people's need to distinguish between that which is *sacred*—that is, special and holy—and that which is *profane*—that is, ordinary and not sacred.

Newer theories seek to understand religion as a form of social control, especially of selected men over women, over nature, and over men who do not belong to their group. Still other theories draw on the findings of psychology to describe religion as a set of activities by which human beings attempt to impose order on the chaos of experience. These theories see religion helping people to resolve unbearable and unexplainable *paradoxes* (contradictions) in life, such as why bad things happen to good people.

History of the world's major religions. The major religions in the world today originated between about 1500 B.C. and A.D. 600. The following discussion traces the history of each of these religions.

Judaism traces its origins to the Near East, probably from about 1550 to 1200 B.C. A group of people, later known as Israelites and Judaeans, believed they were descendants of one father, Abraham. According to tradition, Abraham migrated from southern Mesopotamia (now Iraq) to the land of Canaan (roughly an area from east of the Jordan River to the Mediterranean Sea).

The Bible claims that God had promised Canaan to Abraham and his descendants. The Bible says that Abraham's grandson Jacob (later named Israel) had twelve sons who became the heads of the Twelve Tribes of Israel. Some of these tribes fled into the Nile Delta during times of famine, eventually becoming slaves in Egypt. God then sent a leader, Moses, to bring the people out of slavery and back to the Promised Land of Canaan. Archaeology has not confirmed any of these events. However, an ancient Egyptian inscription states that Pharaoh Merneptah defeated a tribe known as Israel in the late 1200s B.C.

Hebrew scripture

According to the Bible, Moses led the wandering tribes after the Exodus from Egypt. During the wandering of the tribes in the Sinai Desert, Moses received from God a set of laws for conduct and worship. These laws are called the Ten Commandments. Moses wrote down the teachings he received from God and told the story of the Israelites for future generations in five books called the Pentateuch or Torah. These books, which make up the first five books of the Bible, are sometimes known as the Mosaic Law. Their interpretation forms the basis of the Jewish religion.

Judaism was the first religion to successfully develop monotheism. Pharaoh Akhenaten of Egypt had tried to introduce the worship of a single god in the 1300s B.C. But after his death, his successors ruthlessly put down his new religion, and Egypt returned to polytheism. Scholars disagree on when the Jewish religion became monotheistic. Some trace that change to the time of Moses. Others place it much later, under reforms by the Hebrew prophets and kings in the 600s and 500s B.C.

Over time, the group that had fled Egypt during the Exodus developed a system of religious beliefs that became Judaism. Their common religion helped unite the people to form the kingdom of Israel under King David and David's son King Solomon. After Solomon's death about 928 B.C., the kingdom split in two to form the Kingdom of Israel in the north and the Kingdom of Judah in the south. For two centuries, the kingdoms fought with each other and with their neighbors. The Assyrians destroyed Israel in 721 B.C., annexing the land and deporting the population to the east. The people of Israel scattered and lost their identity as a nation, becoming the "Lost Tribes" of Israel.

Judah continued to exist until 587 or 586 B.C., when the Babylonians destroyed the city of Jerusalem and its holy Temple. The Babylonians deported the upper-class population to Babylon during a period called the Babylonian Exile. After King Cyrus of Persia conquered Babylon in 539 B.C., he said that all the captive peoples could return to their homes. Many Jews returned to Judah and rebuilt the Temple in Jerusalem. Jews who chose not to return to Judah became part of the Diaspora, the name for the scattered communities of Jews.

Great powers continued to fight over Judah, including Greece and Rome. Many Jews fled and settled in the Middle East and later in Europe.

Everywhere they were a religious minority. After the spread of Christianity, Christian authorities and worshipers often persecuted them.

After about 1800, Jews divided into three general groups—Orthodox, Conservative, and Reform. Orthodox Jews observed rituals in traditional ways. Conservative and Reform Jews modernized certain practices. Most Eastern European Jews followed Orthodox Judaism, and most Western European and North American Jews followed Conservative or Reform Judaism.

In the 1930s, the German dictator Adolf Hitler and his Nazi Party began a vicious campaign against Jews. By 1945, the Nazis had killed about six million of the eight million to nine million Jews in Europe. Many of the survivors joined Jews living in Palestine. Together, they established the state of Israel in 1948 under the sponsorship of the United Nations. It was the first homeland Jews had known since Biblical times. In a war fought in 1967, Israel occupied territory on the West Bank of the Jordan River and the Gaza Strip, a small area on the coast of the Mediterranean Sea. Many Palestinians had lived on these lands for centuries. Today, there are still questions about which group has legitimate ownership of the West Bank and Gaza, often called the *occupied territories*.

Hinduism began about 1500 B.C. At that time, a central Asian people called the Aryans invaded and conquered India. The Aryan culture gradually combined with the culture of a local people known as the Dravidians. Hinduism developed from a blend of the two.

The oldest Hindu scriptures are the Vedas. They were composed over a period of nearly 1,000 years, beginning about 1400 B.C. This stage in Hindu history is often called the Vedic period. During Vedic times, believers worshiped a number of nature deities.

By the 500s B.C., Hinduism began to split into various schools of thought. Two of these schools—Buddhism and Jainism—became new religions. The Hindu schools further split into smaller divisions. Today, Hinduism includes a great number of schools and divisions. Many of the divisions were formed by saints or spiritual teachers called *gurus*. Each school has its own philosophy and form of worship, but all accept basic Hindu doctrines.

Buddhism developed in India around 500 B.C. or a little later from the teachings of a prince named Siddhartha Gautama. He became known

A Hindu temple

as *Buddha,* meaning *Enlightened One.* Buddhism was partly a rebellion against certain features of Hinduism. Buddhism opposed the Hindu worship of many deities, the Hindu emphasis on *caste* (social class) and the supernatural, and the power of the Brahmans, the highest Hindu class.

Buddha taught that people should devote themselves to finding release from the suffering of life. Through this release, people would gain *nirvana,* a state of perfect peace and happiness. To achieve nirvana, they had to free themselves from all worldly desires and attachments to material things. Buddha taught that nirvana could be gained by following the *Middle Way* between the extremes of severe self-denial and uncontrolled passion. As Buddha preached, he attracted a growing number of followers. By the time of his death, about 483 B.C.,

Buddhism had become firmly established in India.

Buddhism spread into central Asia. By the end of the A.D. 100s, it had reached China. Buddhism swept through much of China from the 300s to the 500s, challenging the native Chinese religions of Confucianism and Taoism in popularity. In the 500s, Chinese Buddhism spread to Korea and Japan. Buddhism became the chief Japanese religion for the next 1,000 years.

Early in its history, Buddhism divided into two forms, Theravada and Mahayana. Theravada emphasizes personal salvation through one's own efforts at purification. Mahayana stresses feeling compassion for all who suffer and work for their salvation. Today, Theravada Buddhism is strongest in Cambodia, Laos, Myanmar, Sri Lanka, and Thailand. Most Mahayana Buddhists live in Japan, Mongolia, Nepal, South Korea, Tibet, Vietnam, and parts of India and Russia.

Confucianism is a Chinese religion based on the teachings of Confucius, a philosopher who died about 479 B.C. Confucianism has no organization or clergy. It does not teach belief in a deity or an afterlife. Confucianism stresses moral and political ideas. It emphasizes respect for ancestors and for authority, and teaches that rulers must govern according to high moral standards.

Confucianism, Buddhism, and Taoism have been the major religions in China. However, Confucianism has had the greatest impact on Chinese society. Confucianism was the state religion of China from the 100s B.C. until the A.D. 1900s. Chinese rulers approved of its emphasis on respect for authority and dedication to public service. Confucian scriptures called the Five Classics and Four Books served as the foundation of the Chinese educational system for centuries. Candidates applying for government jobs had to pass examinations based on these scriptures.

Beginning in the 1000s, a more philosophical approach to Confucianism known as Neo-Confucianism became widely popular. Neo-Confucianism also influenced Japanese moral codes and philosophy from the 1600s through the 1800s.

In 1949, Chinese Communists gained control of China. The government officially condemned Confucianism, as well as other religions. As a result, most followers live outside mainland China, especially in Taiwan. In the late 1970s, however, the Communist government relaxed its policy against religion, and Confucianism has begun to revive on the mainland.

Taoism, like Confucianism, is a native Chinese religion. Its roots go back to the earliest history of China. However, Taoism did not begin to develop as an organized religion until the 100s B.C.

Taoism teaches that everyone should try to achieve two goals, happiness and immortality. The religion has many practices and ceremonies to help people achieve these goals. Taoist practices include prayer, magic, special diets, breath control, meditation, and recitation of scriptures. Taoists also believe in astrology, fortunetelling, witchcraft, and communication with the dead.

Taoists worship more deities than do the followers of almost any other religion. Some deities are ancestors, and others are the spirits of famous people.

During its early history, Taoism borrowed heavily from Buddhism. Many Taoist deities, temples, and ceremonies show the influence of Buddhism. By the A.D. 1000s, Taoism had split into many divisions. The mem-

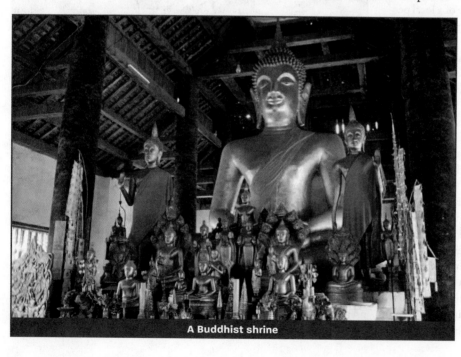

A Buddhist shrine

bers of some divisions withdrew from everyday life to meditate and study in monasteries. Other divisions were based in temples. The temple priests passed their positions on to their children. The members of this hereditary priesthood lived among the common people. They gained a reputation as highly skilled magicians who could tell the future and protect believers from illness, accidents, and other misfortune.

Chinese governments of the early and middle 1900s opposed Taoism, claiming it was based on superstition. Today, the Chinese government permits the practice of the religion, and its followers are gradually increasing. Taoists also remain active in Chinese societies outside China, especially in Taiwan.

Shinto is the native religion of Japan. According to Shinto beliefs, deities created Japan and its people. Until the mid-1900s, the Japanese worshiped their emperor as a direct descendant of Amaterasu-Omikami, the sun goddess and most important Shinto deity.

Shinto developed from Japanese folk beliefs. Followers worship spirits and demons that live in animals, trees, and other parts of nature. In early Japanese history, Shinto was devoted chiefly to this form of nature worship. Beginning in the A.D. 500s, Buddhism influenced the development of Shinto. Confucianism became influential in the A.D. 600s. Both of these religions helped shape Shinto rituals and doctrines. Buddhist and Shinto services have occasionally been held in the same temples. But unlike Buddhism, Shinto never developed strong doctrines on either salvation or life after death.

In the late 1800s, the Japanese government sponsored a form of Shinto called State Shinto. State Shinto stressed patriotic religious ceremonies and the divine origins of the emperor. In 1882, the government officially separated Shinto into State and Sectarian Shinto. The government administered State Shinto. Sectarian Shinto was popular among the common people. After Japan's defeat in World War II (1939–1945), the government abolished State Shinto and the doctrine of a divine emperor.

Christianity is based on the life and teachings of Jesus of Nazareth, a Galilean Jew. Christians believe He is the Messiah or Savior who came to fulfill God's promise to bring justice and healing to the world. Jesus was put to death by crucifixion by the Romans, who had conquered Palestine. According to the New Testament, Jesus rose from

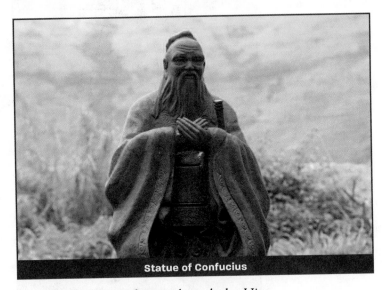

Statue of Confucius

the dead after His crucifixion and preached to His followers for a short time before returning to heaven. Christianity teaches that people can achieve salvation in this life and eternal salvation from death through believing in Jesus' miraculous return to life, known as the Resurrection.

After Jesus' Resurrection, a number of His followers spread His teachings. Although Christianity began as a reform movement within Judaism, it quickly spread to non-Jewish populations. Much of its spread can be attributed to the preaching of Paul, an early Jewish convert to Christianity. After Paul's death, about A.D. 67, Christianity continued to grow despite persecution by the Romans. In the early 300s, the Roman emperor Constantine the Great became a Christian. By the late 300s, Christianity was the official religion of the Roman Empire. It was widely practiced throughout the empire, which covered most of Europe, the Middle East, and northern Africa.

During the Middle Ages, from about the A.D. 400s through the 1400s, Christian missionaries converted many European peoples. As a result, the Christian church dominated European life for centuries. Differences developed between Christians in western Europe and those in eastern Europe and western Asia. The two groups of Christians split in the 1000s. The churches in Greece, Russia, and other parts of eastern Europe and western Asia became known as the Eastern Orthodox Churches. The church in western Europe became known as the Roman Catholic Church.

In the 1500s, a religious movement called the Reformation divided western Christianity into

A statue of Jesus

several bodies. Most southern Europeans remained Roman Catholics. Many northern Europeans formed new churches and became known as Protestants. Protestant churches emphasized the authority of Holy Scripture, rather than tradition or the solemn ceremonies called *sacraments*. The largest Protestant groups include the Baptist, Anglican, Lutheran, Methodist, and Presbyterian churches.

Beginning in the 1500s, Catholic missionaries converted many people in Africa, Asia, and the Americas to Christianity. Protestant missionaries became active in the 1600s and made converts in East Asia, Africa, and North America.

 Islam is based on the life and teachings of the prophet Muhammad, who lived in Arabia during the early A.D. 600s. Before Muhammad's time, the people in the region worshiped Allah (God) as well as other deities. But Muhammad said Allah was the only God.

According to Islamic tradition, Muhammad had the first of several visions about 610. The vision occurred while Muhammad meditated in a cave on Mount Hira, a hill near his birthplace of Mecca in what is now Saudi Arabia. The vision commanded Muhammad to preach the message of Allah to the people of his country. He began preaching in Mecca. A tribe called the Quraysh controlled Mecca and opposed Muhammad. To avoid persecution by the Quraysh, Muhammad fled to the city

of Medina. Muhammad's journey from Mecca to Medina is called the Hijrah and is one of the central events in the founding of Islam.

In 630, Muhammad led an army to Mecca. He offered the people of the city generous peace terms. As a result, his forces took the city with little resistance. He made Mecca the sacred city and center of Islam.

After Muhammad's death in 632, his friend and disciple Abu Bakr became the first *caliph* (leader) of Islam. Abu Bakr defeated a rebellion against his rule by Arabian tribes and began a campaign of religious conquest outside Arabia. Succeeding caliphs continued Abu Bakr's conquests. Within 100 years of Muhammad's death, Islam had spread throughout the Middle East, across northern Africa, and into Spain. The religion also split into two divisions, the Sunnis and the Shiites. In 732, Muslim and Christian armies fought a major battle near Tours, France, called the Battle of Poitiers or the Battle of Tours. The Muslims were defeated, and western Europe remained Christian.

Muslim missionaries, mystics called *Sufis*, and traders carried Islam to India and other parts of Asia. From the 1000s to the 1200s, Islam spread into western Africa. The success of Islam, especially its control over the Holy Land, caused European church authorities to launch a crusade, a religious war against Islam to retake Jerusalem. Beginning in 1096, Europeans organized several crusades, causing much suffering on both sides.

Today, Islam is the major religion of nearly all countries in northern Africa and the Middle East. It is also the chief religion in Bangladesh, Indonesia, Malaysia, and Pakistan.

Religion today. Numerous thinkers severely criticized religion in the West in the 1900s. They charged that many religious doctrines had become dry and uninspiring and no longer satisfied spiritual needs. For many, the rise of science cast doubt on older doctrines. Critics also claimed that traditional religions failed to deal with current social issues and that they supported outdated moral attitudes.

Some religious groups have tried to meet society's needs and problems. For example, most religions have traditionally prohibited the ordination of women as clergy and barred women from other leadership positions. For many women, these limitations left their spiritual needs unfulfilled. Many Christian denominations and groups in Judaism now allow women roles equal to those of men. In addition, many women are now scholars of Islam, Buddhism, and Hinduism.

Many people see the *ecumenical movement* in Christianity as a step toward bringing a spirit of cooperation and renewal to Western religion. The ecumenical movement seeks to unify Christians worldwide. It began in the early 1900s and was almost exclusively confined to Protestantism for many years. Many Protestant groups combined and formed new denominations. In the mid-1900s, the Roman Catholic Church began to take a more active part in the movement. A document issued by Vatican Council II (1962–1965), a meeting of Catholic leaders, endorsed the movement's goals. Leaders of the Eastern Orthodox Churches and the Roman Catholic Church also met during the mid-1900s to investigate ways to bring the denominations closer together.

Many people have turned to other religions or new movements that originated outside their own region or tradition. A large number of people have sought fulfillment in the teachings of Asian religions. Some of these people have been attracted to Zen, a form of Buddhism that emphasizes meditation. Others follow the teachings of Hinduism. Islam has also gained many followers.

Within Christianity, a movement called *charismatic Christianity* has attracted millions of followers. The movement began with the founding of Pentecostalism in the United States in 1901. Pentecostalism is a form of religious worship that believes the presence of the Holy Spirit is revealed in physical healing, speaking in unknown languages called *tongues*, and having visions. *Christian fundamentalism* is a conservative religious movement that has had great social and political influence in the United States. Fundamentalists believe that the Bible is without factual or theological error, and that its teachings cannot be questioned. Christian fundamentalist leaders include such evangelists as Billy Graham, his son Franklin Graham, Luis Palau, and Pat Robertson. In addition, Islam and Judaism have developed strong conservative movements since the mid-1900s, both in the West and in the Middle East.

Some Westerners have turned to other kinds of beliefs or faiths. For example, some people have been attracted to the *occult*—mysterious forms of supernatural teachings, such as spiritualism, nature worship, and shamanism. Spiritualists believe that it is possible to communicate with the spirits of the dead. Nature worship reveres natural forces and objects, such as weather, stars, and animals. Many nature worshipers link their beliefs with environmental concerns. Shamanism centers on shamans, who are believed to have the ability to contact the gods or the spirit world. Shamans can go into trances and other states of consciousness beyond the body.

MLA Citation

"Religion." *The Southwestern Advantage Topic Source.* Nashville: Southwestern. 2013.

ADDITIONAL RESOURCES

Books to Read

Bowker, John W., ed. *The Cambridge Illustrated History of Religions.* Cambridge, 2002.

Breuilly, Elizabeth, and others. *Religions of the World.* Facts on File, 1997.

Brockman, Norbert C. *Encyclopedia of Sacred Places.* ABC-CLIO, 1997.

Crawford, Robert G. *What Is Religion?* Routledge, 2002.

Doniger, Wendy, ed. *Merriam-Webster's Encyclopedia of World Religions.* Merriam-Webster, 1999.

Dudley, William, ed. *Religion in America: Opposing Viewpoints.* Greenhaven, 2002.

Ellwood, Robert S., Jr., and McGraw, B. A. *Many Peoples, Many Faiths.* 7th ed. Prentice Hall, 2002.

Momen, Moojan. *The Phenomenon of Religion.* Oneworld, 1999.

Smart, Ninian, ed. *The Atlas of the World's Religions.* Oxford, 1999.

Smith, Jonathan Z., and others, eds. *The HarperCollins Dictionary of Religion.* HarperSan Francisco, 1995.

Web Sites

Comparative Religion: Religions of the World

www.interfaith.org

A site containing key religious texts and information along with interactive forums.

Ontario Consultants on Religious Tolerance

www.religioustolerance.org/relcomp.htm

A site that advocates the understanding of the world's religions as well as religious tolerance.

Religion Facts—Just the Facts on the World's Religions

www.religionfacts.com/big_religion_chart.htm

A site that offers brief descriptions of religious beliefs, practices, and histories in a comprehensive chart.

World Religions: Comparative Analysis

www.comparativereligion.com

A site that compares religious ideology of a number of the world's religions.

Search Strings

Freedom of religion

Freedom of religion definition persecution history intolerance (65,900)

"Freedom of religion" definition persecution history intolerance (12,000)

history of religious freedom persecution intolerance (67,900)

Belief in a god

god beliefs theists atheists agnostics (34,200)

god beliefs philosophical views theists atheists agnostics (23,700)

god beliefs philosophical views theists atheists agnostics religion (22,000)

Sacred stories

sacred stories myths legends (53,300)

sacred stories myths legends religious purpose (46,600)

"sacred stories" myths legends religious purpose (817)

Islam

Islam Muhammad Arabia Allah missionaries (47,400)

Islam Muhammad Arabia Allah missionaries spread (27,900)

History of Islam the spread of Islam Muhammad Allah (66,900)

BACKGROUND INFORMATION

The following articles were written during the year in which the events took place and reflects the style and thinking of that time.

Religion (1982)

In 1982, Americans had an excellent opportunity to assess the status of religion in the United States. A coalition of religious groups that included the Glenmary Research Center, a Roman Catholic agency, and the interdenominational National Council of Churches issued the joint report that they sponsor each decade.

The 1982 report, which reviewed trends in religion in the United States from 1971 to 1980, indicated that the nation had become more religiously diverse. Mormons remained strong in Utah and the Southwest, Baptists in the South, Methodists along the North-South border, and Lutherans in the upper Midwest, with Roman Catholics strong everywhere else. But population movements and evangelistic efforts had led to an increasing spread of faiths. The regional empires had declined somewhat in strength, and the influence of the dominant groups had extended beyond their historic regions.

Organized religion experienced some loss of power during the decade, however powerful personal religious faith may have become. Some churches and synagogues increased their membership, but most did not keep pace with the growth of the population. Conservative evangelistic groups registered much of the gain and compensated for some losses in the mainline churches. The two largest Presbyterian bodies, for example, lost 16.1 percent and 9.5 percent of their membership during the 1970s.

Worldwide decline. Publication in 1982 of the massive *World Christian Encyclopedia*, edited by David B. Barrett, provided an opportunity to compare the scope of the world's largest religious group, Christianity, with other religions. Barrett noted a decline among all world religions. He estimated that throughout the world the number of believers in a religion had declined from 80.4 percent of the population in 1970 to 79.2 percent in 1980, but that their absolute number had increased in this period from 2.9 billion to 3.5 billion. Barrett pointed out that Africa's local traditional religions, which many observers had thought would disappear, persisted and, in some cases, even thrived. Practitioners of such religions, sometimes called shamanists, were expected to drop in number by only 7 million during the 20th century, from 117 million in 1900 to 110 million in the year 2000.

More provocative to the major religions than the survival of traditional local religions was the presence of new "secular quasi-religions," agnosticism and atheism, according to Barrett. In their various guises, these included secularism, scientific materialism, atheistic Communism, nationalism, Nazism, fascism, Maoism, liberal humanism, and numerous other pseudo-religions. In 1900, nonreligious cultures characterized only 0.2 percent of the world's population, but by 1980 they had attracted 20.8 percent and were gaining 8.5 million new converts each year.

Shinto, Japan's oldest surviving religion, has experienced a revival. Shinto shrines recently became popular on industrial properties. Executives of investment companies in the city of Osaka, for example, made monthly stops at a shrine at Osaka's securities exchange. The Sogo department store chain included a shrine in a new store for the use of its employees and customers. Shrine headquarters reported requests for 7,000 new shrines during 1981.

News of religion from around the world often reaches the West as news of military moves by various factions. In 1982, most such reporting came from the Middle East, particularly Lebanon. There, Christian Phalangists, Muslims, Druses, Israeli Jews, and other sects and peoples fought or allied with one another. Doctrine was not at issue as

Meiji shrine, Tokyo, Japan

in a conventional holy war. But religion reinforced old hatreds and made resolution of military issues difficult and, on the short pull, perhaps impossible.

Religion (1970)

Hundreds of the world's leading scholars met in September 1970, at Stockholm, Sweden, for the 12th Congress of the International Association for the History of Religions. The conference themes, ranging from "Belief in God" to "High-God-Belief-Pantheism-Polytheism-Monotheism," provided an opportunity to assess the ways we measure religious responses around the world. They illustrated the wide academic attention being paid to religion. There was plenty to study on the popular level, too—even in a world that many called godless.

The devotion to religious phenomena did not always imply support for existing religious forms. In the United States, a former Roman Catholic priest, Malachi Martin, in his book, *The Encounter*, argued that Islam, Judaism, and Christianity had, by their exclusivism, spent their energies on self-interest and lost their credibility. The book was widely accepted as an accurate picture of the shambles of historic religion and as a background for religious innovation.

Religious conflict. In many parts of the world, religion was best known for its contribution to conflict. The perennial problems of the Middle East can be better understood by recalling the deep religious commitments of both sides to a virtual "holy war" concept. And in the Christian world, political tensions grew worse when religious emotions were attached. Thus, in Northern Ireland, Ian Paisley, a fierce anti-Catholic fundamentalist,

A tarot reading, New York City

squared off against Bernadette Devlin, a young left-wing Catholic, in a nation that verged on civil war between Protestants and Catholics.

Religious tensions remained even where there was no violence. The Passion Play in Oberammergau, West Germany, inspired new debate over what many Jews and some Christians saw as its anti-Semitism.

Asia also saw religious conflict. In May, 100 people were killed in a Hindu-Moslem encounter in the Indian state of Maharashtra. Ceylon's traditional religions were challenged by political radicals; and in Vietnam, the Saigon government suspended the Buddhist paper *Chan Dao*, claiming it bred discontent.

The map of religions changed constantly. David B. Barrett, head of an interfaith research group based in Nairobi, Kenya, argued that as Christians were losing strength in Europe and the Americas, their historic strongholds, they were prospering in Africa. By the year 2000, he said, 60 percent of Christianity would be in the Third World, part of neither Eastern nor Western societies.

The Oriental religions. The group that attracted most interest in the West was Soka Gakkai, a Buddhist movement that won 11 percent of the vote in Japan's parliamentary election for its Komeito political party. Only about thirty years old, this fluid religious sect is well-structured as a "value-creating society" that attracts Japan's alienated masses. At the year's end, the sect had separated from its political arm.

Richard C. Bush, in *Religion in Communist China*, published in late 1970, reported on the virtual elimination of the historic and missionary religions in China. Bush argued that Maoism has taken on the trappings of a religion or a quasi-religion.

Other forms. While interest in Protestant, Roman Catholic, and Jewish religious institutions declined in 1970, the American public revealed a continuing fascination with religion. Its curiosity, however, took forms that religious organizations did not always recognize or welcome. There was an increasing interest in Eastern religions, such as Zen Buddhism and elements of religious expression in yoga. *I Ching* was studied widely, and Tarot cards achieved new popularity. The occult held the attention of many, and the astrology boom continued. For some, these took the place of historic Western religion.

Where the occult did not satisfy, Americans had other religious outlets besides those offered by churches. Scholars spoke of the growth of "civil religion," a religion of patriotism channeled outside the churches. The Religious Heritage Association of America named President Richard M. Nixon "Churchman of the Year," and evangelist Billy Graham helped lead an Independence Day event with patriotic-religious overtones. Many of the political campaigns' calls for law and order or opposition to pornography were spelled out in religious terms, independent of the interest of churches and synagogues.

Religion (1967)

News of religion from the non-Western world ordinarily reaches the West in political and ideological disguises. In Europe and North and South America, it is possible to document religious change chiefly by reporting on church councils and congresses, theological trends, new books, and the activities of ecclesiastical leaders. These forms are not always the best indicators of change elsewhere in the world.

In 1967, the non-Western event that most dramatized the role of religion in human affairs was the Arab-Israeli war. President Gamal Abdel Nasser of the United Arab Republic joined other Arab leaders in calling for a "holy war" to put an end to Israel. Military forces of Moslem nations were inspired to undertake action for religious reasons; the *Koran*, the Moslem's sacred book, justifies only religious wars. Similarly, the counteractions by Israel were not merely political. For Jews, Israel is a state as well as a state of mind and spirit. The ancient promises concerning their people are in no small measure connected with Israel's fate.

When the six-day war ended on June 10, the picture of Israeli soldiers triumphant at the Wailing Wall and the debate over access to the "holy places" in the Old City of Jerusalem served to remind the world of these religious dimensions. On the other side of the world, in the prolonged Vietnamese conflict, religious issues also surfaced from time to time, as was the case in the controversy between various Buddhist sects and between Buddhists and Roman Catholics during the South Vietnamese elections.

Ideological conflict. Not all the news of world religion was connected with military activities and holy wars. Much of it had to do with ideological clashes in those parts of the world where new and old faiths were in conflict. The new faiths may seem to be antireligious, but they make demands on peoples' ultimate commitments of the kind men usually associate with religious appeals.

Communist China. Nowhere was this clash of the old and the new more prominent in 1967 than on Chinese soil. In China, where Confucianism had contributed to a more or less religious philosophy for millions of people for thousands of years, a new generation found spiritual sustenance in the little book, *Quotations from Chairman Mao Tse-tung.* This collection of writings served to unite a militant people against its own inherited religious past and against cultural traces left by other religions, especially Christianity. Many monuments of China's spiritual past were threatened by the Cultural Revolution. *Sinologists* (students of China) discussing the Chinese future urged scholars to become informed concerning the interaction of residual religions and Maoism.

In India, the clash was between old religions and new secularity; it was based on urgent practical demands. An estimated 250,000,000 sacred cows and 2,500,000,000 rats are allowed to live in an overpopulated and starving nation because of Hindu religious beliefs associated with living things. Many practical politicians urge a change in beliefs and an end to such customs in order to produce a more prosperous India. Meanwhile, millions found solace in Hinduism and Buddhism as they faced seemingly insuperable human problems in India.

In Japan, the old met the new as historic faiths lived on in a modernizing nation, even as a Buddhist-backed "Value Creation Society" called *Soka Gakkai* took on increasing political importance.

Eastern influence. Finally, news of non-Western religion came to the West in 1967 through the efforts of individuals and groups that might be described as commuters between value systems. The "hippie" phenomenon, which reached a peak in midsummer, was an example. Hippies turned to Zen Buddhism, the Vedas, the writings of Rabbi Hillel, and the teachings of Jesus, implying that these could provide meaning for a nonviolent generation. The Beatles were the best known of the celebrities who turned to Eastern religion as they sought "transcendental meditation" through contact with Maharishi Mahesh Yogi, their chosen spiritual leader. Timothy Leary advocated a religion based not only on mind-expanding drugs like LSD, but also on literary resources of Eastern religion.

Renaissance

The Renaissance is a period in history of major cultural and artistic change that began in Italy in the early 1300s and spread throughout other countries in Europe until about 1600. The renaissance is also known as the revival of antiquity since it basically represented a rebirth of the spirit of ancient Greek and Roman cultures in artistic, literary, and intellectual works.

HOT topics

Italian Masters of Different Mediums.

Renaissance artists tried to portray nature realistically. Painters Giotto and Masaccio, sculptor Donatello, and architects Filippo Brunelleschi and Leone Battista Alberti were outstanding Renaissance artists in the 1300s and early 1400s. Brunelleschi and Alberti developed realistic linear perspective. During the late 1400s and early 1500s, painters Raphael and Leonardo da Vinci and painter, architect, and sculptor Michelangelo dominated the arts. Leonardo's *Mona Lisa* and *The Last Supper* and Michelangelo's frescoes on the altar wall and the ceiling of the Sistine Chapel in Vatican City are the most famous paintings of all time.

Renaissance Masters Outside of Italy.

Flemish artist Jan van Eyck, who painted *The Madonna and Child* with Chancellor Rolin, was one of the first outstanding Renaissance artists outside Italy. Hugo Van der Goes, who painted *Portinari Triptych*, was another outstanding Flemish painter.

HOT topics 🔥

Italian Renaissance Thinkers.
In the mid-1300s, two friends, Petrarch and Giovanni Boccaccio, were described as the first Renaissance humanists. They recovered many important ancient manuscripts, including *Letters to Atticus* by Marcus Tullius Cicero, which described Roman political life. Writing in the precise and powerful form of Latin used by Cicero, Petrarch created poetry and Boccaccio developed the *Decameron* stories. Their writings concentrated on human problems rather than on the mysteries of nature or God's will. In the late 1400s, Marsilio Ficino translated the literary works of Plato, in which Renaissance thinkers saw a harmony between Christian devotion and wisdom. In the early 1500s, Niccolo Machiavelli wrote *The Prince* and other books which explain politics based on Roman history and human nature rather than on religious or moral ideals. Also in the early 1500s, *The Book of the Courtier*, written by Baldassare Castiglion, influenced the conduct of courtiers throughout Europe. It also strongly influenced educational theory in England.

Giovanni Boccaccio

Renaissance Thinkers Outside of Italy.
Desiderius Erasmus and Saint Thomas More were Christian humanists. Erasmus was born in the Netherlands and wrote *The Praise of Folly*. More was born in England and wrote *Utopia*. Both works were written to criticize the abuses and inequalities that were generally accepted during their times.

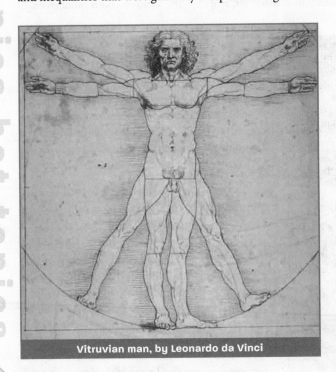

Vitruvian man, by Leonardo da Vinci

TRUE or FALSE?
Humanism was the most significant cultural and intellectual movement of the Renaissance period.

THE BASICS

The Renaissance was a great cultural movement that began in Italy during the early 1300s. It spread to England, France, Germany, the Netherlands, Spain, and other countries in the late 1400s and ended about 1600. The French word *Renaissance* comes from the Latin word *renascor* and refers to the act of rebirth.

During the Renaissance, many European scholars and artists, especially in Italy, studied the learning and art of ancient Greece and Rome. They wanted to recapture the spirit of the Greek and Roman cultures in their own artistic, literary, and philosophic works. The cultures of ancient Greece and Rome are often called *classical antiquity*. The Renaissance thus represented a rebirth of these cultures and is therefore also known as the *revival of antiquity* or the *revival of learning*.

The Renaissance overlapped the end of a period in European history called the Middle Ages, which began in the 400s. The leaders of the Renaissance rejected many of the attitudes and ideas of the Middle Ages. For example, religious authorities in the Middle Ages taught that cities were dangerous, wicked places that distracted people from the important task of saving their souls. Renaissance thinkers commonly saw cities as places where people could exercise such civic virtues as justice, devotion to the common good, courage, and self-sacrifice. Such Renaissance religious leaders as Girolamo Savonarola believed corrupt cities could be redeemed if their citizens fervently practiced Christianity.

During the Middle Ages, the most important branch of learning was theology (the study of God). However, many Renaissance thinkers paid greater attention to the study of humanity. They examined the great accomplishments of different cultures, particularly those of ancient Greece and Rome. These thinkers organized a new group of intellectual disciplines, called the *humanities*, which emphasized language, *oratory* (public speaking), history, poetry, and moral philosophy. These disciplines aimed to enrich earthly life rather than an afterlife.

Medieval artists painted human figures that looked stiff and unrealistic and which often served symbolic purposes or aimed to instruct. But Renaissance artists stressed the beauty of the human body. They tried to capture the dignity and majesty of human beings in lifelike paintings and sculptures. They believed that people could relate more easily to realistic art, and thus the artwork could more strongly influence its viewers.

Renaissance culture spread gradually. At the height of the Renaissance, during the late 1400s and early 1500s, relatively few Europeans accepted Renaissance ideas. But the influence of the Renaissance on future generations was to prove immense in many fields—from art and literature to education, political science, and history. For centuries, scholars agreed that the modern era of human history began with the Renaissance. Today, many scholars consider the Renaissance part of the *early modern period*.

The Italian Renaissance

Political background. Italy was not a unified country until the 1860s. At the beginning of the Renaissance, it consisted of about 250 separate states, most of which were ruled by a city. Most cities had only 5,000 to 10,000 people. But others were among the largest cities in Europe. For example, Florence, Milan, and Venice had at least 100,000 people each in the early 1300s.

At the dawn of the Renaissance, much of Italy was supposedly controlled by the Holy Roman Empire.

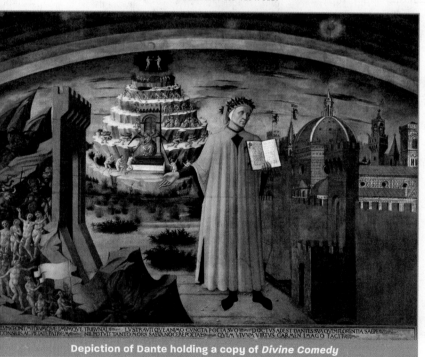

Depiction of Dante holding a copy of *Divine Comedy*

However, the emperors lived in Germany and had little power over their Italian lands. The popes ruled central Italy, including the city of Rome, but were unable to extend political control to the rest of Italy. No central authority was thus esta lished in Italy to unify all the states.

During the mid-1300s and early 1400s, a number of major Italian cities came under the control of one family. For example, the Visconti family governed Milan from the early 1300s until 1447, when the last male member died. Soon after, the Sforza family took control of Milan and governed the city until the late 1400s. The Este family in Ferrara, the Gonzaga family in Mantua, and the Montefeltro family in Urbino were other ruling families.

The form of government established by the ruling families of the Italian cities was called the *signoria* (principality), and the ruling prince was known as the *signore*. All power was concentrated in the signore and his friends and relatives. An elaborate court slowly grew up around each signorial government. At the court, the area's leading artists, intellectuals, and politicians gathered under the sponsorship of the signore.

Other Italian cities had a form of government known as *republicanism*. In republican cities, a ruling class controlled the government. Members of the ruling class considered themselves superior to the other residents of the city. The most important examples of republican government were in Florence and Venice.

In the republican government of Florence, about 800 of the city's wealthiest families made up the ruling class. The members of these Florentine families intermarried and lived in large, beautiful palaces built by Renaissance architects. They paid for the construction of great religious and civic buildings and impressive monuments throughout Florence. They also supported artists and intellectuals. In addition, the ruling class encouraged the study of ancient Greek and Roman authors in the desire to have their society resemble the cultures of classical antiquity.

By the 1430s, the Medici family dominated the ruling class of Florence. The family controlled the largest bank in Europe and was headed by a series of talented and ambitious men. Under Medici domination, the Florentine republic in some ways resembled a signorial government.

About 180 families controlled the republican government of Venice. All government leaders came from these families. A law passed in 1297 restricted membership in the Great Council, the principal governing body, to descendants of families that had already sat in the council. Like Florence, Venice became a leading center of Renaissance art under the support of the ruling class.

Humanism was the most significant intellectual movement of the Renaissance. It blended concern for the history and actions of human beings with religious concerns. The humanists were scholars and artists who studied subjects that they believed would help them better understand the problems of humanity. These subjects included history, literature, and philosophy. The humanists

The Medici family emblem

shared the view that the civilizations of ancient Greece and Rome had achieved greatness in the arts and sciences, government, and military affairs and thus could serve as models. They believed that modern people should understand and appreciate classical antiquity to learn how to conduct their lives.

To understand the customs, laws, and ideas of ancient Greece and Rome, the humanists had first to master the languages of classical antiquity. The Greeks had used a language foreign to Italians, and the Romans had used a form of Latin far different from that used in the 1300s and 1400s. To learn ancient Greek and Latin, the humanists studied *philology* (the science of the meaning and history of words). Philology became one of the two principal concerns of the humanists. The other was history, which the humanists saw as the study of great actions taken by courageous, noble, or wise men of classical antiquity.

The interest of the humanists in ancient Greece and Rome led them to search for manuscripts, statues, coins, and other surviving examples of classical civilization. For example, they combed monastery libraries throughout Europe, locating on dusty shelves long-neglected manuscripts by classical authors. The humanists carefully studied these manuscripts, prepared critical editions of them, and often translated them.

Petrarch and Giovanni Boccaccio were the first Renaissance humanists. In the mid-1300s, the two friends recovered many important but long-ignored ancient manuscripts. Petrarch discovered the most influential of these works. It was *Letters to Atticus*, a collection of letters on Roman political life by the statesman and orator Marcus Tullius Cicero. As Petrarch and Boccaccio studied the classical writings, they grew to dislike the clumsy, limited form of Latin widely used by their contemporaries. They urged people to adopt the precise and powerful writing style of classical literature.

Petrarch became known for his poetry, and Boccaccio for his collection of stories called the *Decameron* (about 1349–1353). In their works, they tried to describe human feelings and situations that people could easily understand. Petrarch and Boccaccio insisted that the duty of intellectuals was to concentrate on human problems, which they believed were more important than an understand-

Petrarch

ing of the mysteries of nature or of God's will. Many of Boccaccio's works contain the idea that it is socially harmful to impose upon people severe moral standards that contradict normal human behavior.

The revival of Platonism. Petrarch urged people to study the ancient Greek philosopher Plato. He believed that reading Plato would strengthen Christian faith. During the 1400s, the study of Plato's works became popular with many humanists. In 1484, the Florentine philosopher Marsilio Ficino completed the first Latin translation of Plato's writing. Platonic philosophy and Christianity share such ideas as the immortality of the individual human soul and the creation of the world by an all-powerful God. Renaissance thinkers saw in Plato's works a harmony between wisdom and Christian devotion.

Niccolo Machiavelli. Medieval political thinkers viewed politics idealistically, within a religious framework. But during the Renaissance, the statesman Niccolo Machiavelli developed a new, more practical philosophy of politics. His writings, contained in *The Prince* (written in 1513 and published in 1532) and other books, explain politics based on human nature and Roman history rather than on moral or religious ideals. Machiavelli determined that sometimes a leader must resort to such strong measures as cruelty, deception, or force to protect the power of the state against its rival states. Machiavelli's separation of morality from political success has led many historians to consider him the first political scientist.

The ideal courtier. Some Italian humanists spent most of their time in signorial courts. During the late 1400s, these humanists began to develop ideas about the proper conduct of *courtiers*—the noblemen and noblewomen who lived in a royal court. In 1528, *The Book of the Courtier*, by the author and diplomat Baldassare Castiglione, was published. He based the work on his experiences at the court of Urbino. It was translated into several European languages and influenced the conduct of courtiers throughout Europe. *The Courtier* also strongly influenced educational theory in England during the Renaissance.

Castiglione wrote that the ideal male courtier is refined in writing and speaking and skilled in the arts, sports, and the use of weapons. He willingly devotes himself to his signore, always seeking to please him. The courtier is polite and attentive to women. Whatever he does is achieved with an easy, natural style, which reflects his command of every situation. An ideal court woman knows literature and art and how to entertain the court. She exhibits the highest moral character and acts in a feminine manner. The highest form of love that a courtier can express is platonic love—that is, nonromantic love. The highest form of courtiership is one in which the courtier helps the prince to rule virtuously.

The fine arts. During the Middle Ages, painters and sculptors tried to give their works a spiritual quality. They wanted viewers to concentrate on the deep religious meaning of their paintings and sculptures. They were not concerned with making their subjects appear natural or lifelike. But Renaissance painters and sculptors, like Renaissance writers, wanted to portray people and nature realistically. Medieval architects designed huge cathedrals to emphasize the grandeur of God and to humble the human spirit. Renaissance architects designed buildings whose proportions were based on those of the human body and whose ornamentation imitated ancient designs.

Arts of the 1300s and early 1400s. During the early 1300s, the Florentine painter Giotto became the first artist to portray nature realistically. He produced magnificent *frescoes* (paintings on damp plaster) for churches in Assisi, Florence, Padua, and Rome. Giotto attempted to create lifelike figures showing real emotions. He portrayed many of his figures in realistic settings.

A remarkable group of Florentine architects, painters, and sculptors worked during the early 1400s. They included the painter Masaccio, the sculptor Donatello, and the architect Filippo Brunelleschi.

Masaccio's finest work was a series of frescoes he painted about 1427 in the Brancacci Chapel of the Church of Santa Maria del Carmine in Florence. The frescoes realistically show Biblical scenes of emotional intensity. In these paintings, Masaccio utilized Brunelleschi's system for achieving linear perspective.

In his sculptures, Donatello tried to portray the dignity of the human body in realistic and often dramatic detail. His masterpieces include three statues of the Biblical hero David. In a version finished in the 1430s, Donatello portrayed David as a graceful, nude youth, moments after he slew the giant Goliath. The work, which is about 5 feet (1.5 meters) tall, was the first large free-standing nude created in Western art since classical antiquity.

Brunelleschi was the first Renaissance architect to revive the ancient Roman style of architecture. He used arches, columns, and other elements of classical architecture in his designs. One of his best-known buildings is the beautifully and harmoniously proportioned Pazzi Chapel in Florence. The chapel, begun in 1442 and completed about 1465, was one of the first buildings designed in the new Renaissance style. Brunelleschi also was the first Renaissance artist to master *linear perspective*, a mathematical system with which painters could show space and depth on a flat surface.

Arts of the late 1400s and early 1500s were dominated by three men. They were Michelangelo, Raphael, and Leonardo da Vinci.

Michelangelo excelled as a painter, architect, and poet. In addition, he has been called the greatest sculptor in history. Michelangelo was a master of portraying the human figure. For example, his famous statue of the Israelite leader Moses (1516) gives an overwhelming impression of physical and spiritual power. These qualities also appear in the frescoes of Biblical and classical subjects that Michelangelo painted on the ceiling of the Vatican's Sistine Chapel. The frescoes, painted from 1508 to 1512, rank among the greatest works of Renaissance art.

Raphael's paintings are softer in outline and more poetic than those of Michelangelo. Raphael was skilled in creating perspective and in the delicate use of color. He painted a number of beautiful pictures of the Madonna (Virgin Mary) and many outstanding portraits. One of his greatest works is the fresco *School of Athens* (1511). The painting was influenced by classical Greek and Roman models. It portrays the

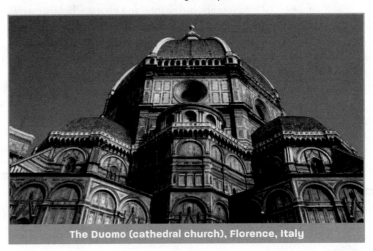

The Duomo (cathedral church), Florence, Italy

Michelangelo's *David*

great philosophers and scientists of ancient Greece in a setting of classical arches. Raphael was thus making a connection between the culture of classical antiquity and the Italian culture of his time.

Leonardo da Vinci painted two of the most famous works of Renaissance art, the wall painting *The Last Supper* (about 1497) and the portrait *Mona Lisa* (begun in 1503). Leonardo had one of the most searching minds in all history. He wanted to know how everything that he saw in nature worked. In more than 4,000 pages of notebooks, he drew detailed diagrams and wrote his observations. Leonardo made careful drawings of human skeletons and muscles, trying to learn how the body worked. Due to his inquiring mind, Leonardo has become a symbol of the Renaissance spirit of learning and intellectual curiosity.

The Renaissance Outside Italy

In the late 1400s, the Renaissance spread from Italy to such countries as France, Germany, England, and Spain. Such visitors to Italy as bankers, diplomats, merchants, and young scholars carried Renaissance culture home with them. The scholars acquired from the Italians the basic tools of humanistic study—history and philology.

A series of invasions of Italy played a major role in the spread of the Renaissance to other parts of Europe. From 1494 to the early 1500s, French, German, and Spanish armies invaded Italy. The invaders were dazzled by the beauty of Italian art and architecture and returned home deeply influenced by Italian culture.

In Italy, evidence of classical antiquity, especially Roman antiquity, could be seen almost everywhere. Ruins of Roman monuments and buildings stood in every Italian city. This link between the present

and the classical past was much weaker elsewhere in Europe. In ancient times, Roman culture had been forced upon northern and western Europeans by conquering Roman armies. But that culture quickly disappeared after the Roman Empire in the West fell in the A.D. 400s.

The relative scarcity of classical art affected the development of European art outside Italy during the 1400s. Painters had few examples of classical antiquity to imitate, and so they tended to be more influenced by the northern Gothic style of the late Middle Ages. The first great achievements in Renaissance painting outside Italy appeared in the works of artists living in Flanders. Most of the Flanders region lies in what are now Belgium and France. Flemish painting was known for its precise details. The human figures were realistic but lacked the sculptural quality characteristic of Italian painting.

Political background. During the Renaissance, the political structure of northern and western Europe differed greatly from that of Italy. By the late 1400s, England, France, and Spain were being united into nations under monarchies. These monarchies provided political and cultural leadership for their countries. Germany, like Italy, was divided into many largely independent states. But Germany was the heart of the Holy Roman Empire, which unified the various German states to some extent.

The great royal courts supported the Renaissance in northern and western Europe much as the princes did in Italy. The French king Francis I, who ruled from 1515 to 1547, tried to surround himself with the finest representatives of the Italian Renaissance. The king brought Leonardo da Vinci and many other Italian artists and scholars to France. In England, the House of Tudor became the most important patron of the Renaissance. The Tudors ruled from 1485 to 1603. Henry VII, the first Tudor monarch, invited numerous Italian humanists to England. These men encouraged English scholars to study the literature and philosophy of ancient Greece and Rome.

Christian humanism. After about 1500, humanists in northern Europe increasingly emphasized the study and revival of ancient Christianity. Humanist scholars identified and edited ancient Christian texts to remove any distortions that had been introduced into the writings over time. These texts included the Bible and the works of such Catholic thinkers and churchmen as Saint

Augustine and Saint Jerome, as well as the leaders of the ancient Greek church. This attempt to purify the sources of Christian tradition implied a criticism of existing Church practices and an attempt to reform them. In addition, many *Christian humanists* believed they could reform religion through education.

Desiderius Erasmus and Saint Thomas More were the leading Christian humanists. They were close friends who courageously refused to abandon their ideals.

Erasmus was born in the Netherlands. He was educated in Paris and traveled throughout Germany, England, and Italy. He was an excellent scholar, with a thorough knowledge of Latin and Greek.

Erasmus refused to take sides in any political or religious controversy. In particular, he would not support either side during the Reformation, the religious movement of the 1500s that gave birth to Protestantism. Both Roman Catholics and Protestants sought Erasmus' support. He stubbornly kept his independence and was called a coward by both sides. However, Erasmus did attack abuses he saw in the church in a famous witty work called *The Praise of Folly* (1511). In this book, he criticized the moral quality of church leaders. Erasmus accused them of overemphasizing procedures and ceremonies while neglecting Christianity's spiritual values.

Saint Thomas More was born in England and devoted his life to serving his country. He gained the confidence of King Henry VIII and carried out a number of important missions for him. In 1529, the king appointed More lord chancellor, England's highest judicial official.

Throughout his career, More dedicated himself to the principles that had inspired Erasmus. Like Erasmus, he believed it was important to eliminate the abuses, inequalities, and evils that were accepted as normal in his day. More's best-known work is *Utopia* (1516). In this book, More described an imaginary society in which the divisions between the rich and the poor and the powerful and the weak were replaced by a common concern for the health and happiness of everyone. The abolition of private property would help to create equality between people in More's ideal society.

More's strong principles finally cost him his life. He objected to Henry VIII's decision to *annul* (cancel) his marriage to Catherine of Aragon and remarry. More then refused to acknowledge the king's authority over that of the pope. In 1535, he was beheaded for treason.

The Heritage of the Renaissance

The Renaissance left an intellectual and artistic heritage that still remains important. Since the Renaissance, scholars have used Renaissance methods of humanistic inquiry, even when they did not share the ideas and spirit of the Renaissance humanists. In literature, writers have tried for centuries to imitate and improve upon the works of such Renaissance authors as Petrarch and Boccaccio.

The influence of Renaissance painters, sculptors, and architects has been particularly strong. The artists of Florence and Rome set enduring standards for painting in the Western world. For hundreds of years, painters have traveled to Florence to admire the frescoes of Giotto and Masaccio. They have visited Rome to study the paintings of Raphael and Michelangelo. The works of Donatello and Michelangelo have inspired sculptors for generations. The beautifully scaled buildings of Brunelleschi and other Renaissance architects still serve as models for architects.

Since the Renaissance, people have also been inspired by the intellectual daring of such men as

Leonardo's *Mona Lisa*

Petrarch and Erasmus. Leaders of the Renaissance seemed to be breaking out of intellectual boundaries and entering unknown territories.

It is no accident that some of the greatest explorers of the late 1400s and early 1500s were Italians exposed to the traditions of the Renaissance. Christopher Columbus was a sailor from Genoa and an expert navigator. For his voyage to the New World, Columbus consulted the same scientist who taught mathematics to the architect Filippo Brunelleschi. Columbus—like such other Italian explorers as John Cabot, Giovanni da Verrazzano, and Amerigo Vespucci—was willing to take enormous risks to achieve results that people had never dreamed of. In a sense, Columbus's arrival in America in 1492 was one of the greatest achievements of the Renaissance.

Sistine Chapel

MLA Citation

"Renaissance." *The Southwestern Advantage Topic Source.* Nashville: Southwestern. 2013.

ADDITIONAL RESOURCES
Books to Read

Level I

Barter, James E. *A Renaissance Painter's Studio.* Lucent Books, 2003.
Cole, Alison. *Renaissance.* Dorling Kindersley, 2000.
Day, Nancy. *Your Travel Guide to Renaissance Europe.* Runestone Press, 2001.
Schomp, Virginia. *The Italian Renaissance.* Benchmark Books, 2003.

Level II

Bouwsma, William J. *The Waning of the Renaissance, 1550–1640.* 2000. Reprint. Yale, 2002.
Burckhardt, Jakob C. *The Civilization of the Renaissance in Italy.* 2 vols. First published in 1860 and available in many editions. First important modern analysis of the Renaissance as a historical period.
Burke, Peter. *The Italian Renaissance.* Rev. ed. Princeton, 1999.
Campbell, Gordon. *The Oxford Dictionary of the Renaissance.* Oxford, 2003.
Grendler, Paul F., ed. *Encyclopedia of the Renaissance.* 6 vols. Scribner, 1999.
Hartt, Frederick. *History of Italian Renaissance Art.* 6th ed. Prentice Hall, 2006.
Johnson, Paul. *The Renaissance.* Modern Library, 2000.
Kraye, Jill, ed. *The Cambridge Companion to Renaissance Humanism.* Cambridge, 1996.
Sider, Sandra. *Handbook to Life in Renaissance Europe.* Facts on File, 2005.

Web Sites

Exploring Leonardo
http://www.mos.org/sln/Leonardo/LeoHomePage.html
A resource for students and teachers developed by the Museum of Science, Boston. This site includes biographical information, highlights some of Leonardo's futuristic inventions, and introduces Renaissance techniques for representing the 3-D world.

Medieval and Renaissance Manuscripts
http://lcweb.loc.gov/exhibits/dres/dres1.html
Pictures and descriptions of manuscripts in the Saxon State Library, in Dresden, Germany.

The Renaissance: Filippo Brunelleschi
http://www.pbs.org/empires/medici/renaissance/brunelleschi.html
Biography of the Italian Renaissance architect Filippo Brunelleschi.

Sixteenth-Century Renaissance English Literature (1485–1603)
http://www.luminarium.org/renlit/
Information about Renaissance English Literature of the 1500s.

Virtual Renaissance
http://library.thinkquest.org/C005356/index2.htm
A journey through the Renaissance.

Search Strings

Italian Masters of Different Mediums

Renaissance Italian artists painters sculptors architects (291,000)

Renaissance Italian masters artists painters sculptors architects (228,000)

Renaissance Italian masters arts artists painters sculptors architects (167,000)

Renaissance Masters Outside of Italy

Renaissance masters Flemish (32,800)

Renaissance masters Flemish-Italian (9,880)

Italian Renaissance Thinkers

Renaissance thinkers Italian (51,200)

Renaissance thinkers Italian humanists (135,000)

Renaissance thinkers Italian humanists Petrarch Boccaccio (1,180)

Renaissance Thinkers Outside of Italy

Renaissance thinkers Italian (111,000)

Renaissance thinkers Italian Erasmus "Saint Thomas More" (10)

Renaissance thinkers Italian humanists Erasmus More (1,820)

Colonial Life in America

Colonial Life in America began in the late 1500s when people of the Old World of Europe came to North America to avoid religious or political unrest there and in the hopes of greater economic opportunities. Some slaves, convicts, and orphans were forced to come. Colonial life entailed the creation of settlements and the introduction to North American Indians and their way of life. The Colonial period ended when the Revolutionary War began in 1775.

HOT topics

Self-Sufficient Towns.
Jamestown was the first permanent English settlement in North America. In spite of periodic setbacks such as disease, attacks by Indians, bad drinking water, and lack of food, colonists were able to have a tenuous relationship with and trade with the Indians. The colonists also established small family farms and large plantations that used slave labor. They built churches, towns, and roads. They even began small industries. Soon, town populations grew and the colonists' wealth increased.

Effects of Colonists and Indians on Each Other.
After their first winter of near starvation, a Patuxet Indian named Squanto taught the colonists at Plymouth Colony how to plant corn and where to hunt and fish. Indians started using metal pots and tools, textiles, and other goods given to them by the colonists. In

HOT topics

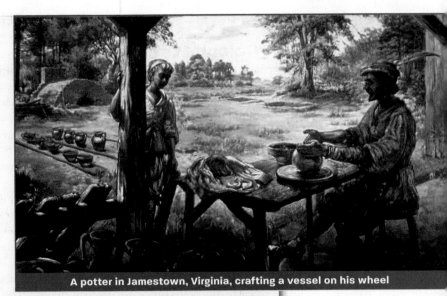

A potter in Jamestown, Virginia, crafting a vessel on his wheel

return, colonists gained furs and hides, baskets, and other crafts from the Indians. Because of this trading, game became scarce. Tensions among tribes and between Indians and colonists began to rise, leading to many battles. Colonists brought diseases for which the Indians had no immunity. They also challenged traditional Indian culture and beliefs; as a result, some Indians converted to Christianity and adopted European customs.

The Thirteen Colonies. Between 1607 and 1733, 13 colonies became permanent settlements. Those 13 colonies were Virginia, Massachusetts, New Hampshire, New York, Connecticut, Maryland, Rhode Island, Delaware, Pennsylvania, North Carolina, New Jersey, South Carolina, and Georgia. The New England colonies had small farms and towns. The Middle Colonies had larger farms and were able to produce surpluses of food. The more rural Chesapeake Colonies had large farms and plantations that grew cash crops of wheat and tobacco. The Southern Colonies had plantations that grew rice and indigo and had towns with major ports.

Structure of Colonial Society. Social classes formed the structure of colonial society and determined not only an individual's political rights or which laws applied to those individuals, but also what they wore and where they sat in church. Social classes consisted of the gentry, the middle class, the lower class, indentured servants, and slaves.

Illustration depicting Native American Indian Squanto, who served as a guide and interpreter for Pilgrim colonists

TRUE or FALSE?
The colonists used many methods of payment for goods because money was scarce in the American colonies.

THE BASICS

Colonial Life in America. The story of the American colonists tells of the men, women, and children who left behind the Old World of Europe for a new life in North America. It describes the everyday life of the settlers in the communities they developed. It also tells of the meeting of cultures, as Europeans and Indians came into contact with each other. The British American colonial period began in the late 1500s with English attempts to settle Newfoundland and Roanoke Island, off the coast of what is now North Carolina. It ended with the start of the Revolutionary War in America in 1775.

Many of the colonists came to North America from England, Scotland, Wales, and Ireland. But the New World attracted settlers from France, Germany, the Netherlands, Sweden, and other European countries as well.

The majority of settlers came to the colonies for economic opportunity or to avoid political and religious unrest at home. However, not all colonists arrived voluntarily. The slave trade brought large numbers of people from Africa against their will. Some orphans were sent from England to America under labor contracts over which they had no control. Some English convicts were transported to the colonies to become servants.

When the Europeans arrived in North America, the continent was already home to many groups of Native Americans with many different cultures. The Indians were originally helpful to the colonists, and trade developed between the two groups. This trade changed the society of both the Indians and the settlers. The Indians strongly resisted the settlers' attempts to claim more and more Indian land. From time to time, fighting broke out between the colonists and the Indians. Eventually, the colonists pushed most of the Indians to the west.

Among the European colonial powers, the English arrived late in the Americas. By the time England colonized the New World, Spain and Portugal had already staked their claims there. Spain's colonial empire, established during the 1500s, stretched from South America to California. It also included Cuba, several other islands in the Caribbean Sea, and Florida. Portugal controlled what is now Brazil. In eastern North America, the English, French, Dutch, and Swedes competed for land and riches. For most of the colonial period, France claimed Canada and the Mississippi Valley. By the end of the period, the British controlled nearly all of North America from the Atlantic Ocean to the Mississippi River. They also held several Caribbean islands.

The Spanish and French in North America were interested chiefly in sending furs, gold, and other riches back to Europe. They also wanted to convert the Indians to Roman Catholicism. The early French

Tobacco was an important cash crop for colonists.

and Spanish settlements served as outposts for soldiers and traders and as missions run by priests. The English colonies, on the other hand, were settled by people from many walks of life who wanted to set up permanent homes.

The English colonists built farms that grew crops which were sold overseas. They built schools and churches and founded thriving port towns. By the mid-1700s, the colonists had a general standard of living equal to the wealthiest European nations. Also by then, the colonists had developed strong forms of self-government.

Why the Colonists Came to America

The first permanent English settlement was founded at Jamestown in 1607. By 1733, the heart of the British Empire in the New World consisted of 13 colonies along the Atlantic coast of North America. Most of these colonies were founded by private *joint-stock companies* or individuals who had received permits from the English monarch to colonize lands claimed by England. Joint-stock companies, the forerunners of modern corporations, were companies that obtained funds to carry on business by selling shares of stock to individuals.

The companies and individual investors hoped to make a profit from their colonies and to expand English trade and industry. They advertised for settlers and pointed out that fertile land and valuable resources were available in the New World. The advertisements attracted many people who were willing to move to the newly established colonies.

People had many reasons for leaving England and the rest of Europe and making the long journey across the Atlantic Ocean. Landowners claimed land formerly available to small farmers, thus forcing some to leave. Children of small farmers saw little economic opportunity and moved to towns to look for work. Wars and revolts in Europe made people want a quiet home. Many rulers insisted that all people living in their country attend the same church. They persecuted those who could not agree. For example, more than 100,000 Protestants known as Huguenots fled Roman Catholic France for other countries.

Most of the settlers came from England. The colonists also included many people from Scotland. People of Scottish ancestry who had settled in the northern part of Ireland also came in large numbers. These people were known as *Scotch-Irish*.

Other people who decided to head for the colonies came from France, Germany, the Netherlands, Sweden, and other European countries.

Economic reasons. Rising unemployment, several harvest failures, and other economic conditions in England influenced the decision of many colonists to migrate to the American Colonies. Many people looked to the New World as a place where they could buy land or find employment and eventually better themselves.

George Washington's home in Mount Vernon, Virginia

Of all the economic attractions of the New World, land was probably the greatest. Many settlers came to America because they were offered land free or at low cost. Land ownership made people independent and promised a better standard of living for themselves and their children. People who owned land in the colonies were called *freeholders*, and they had certain rights and duties in the community. Male freeholders generally could vote.

Land was distributed in various ways in the colonies. Technically, the colonies belonged to the English monarch. The king or queen issued permits called *charters* giving an individual or group the right to establish a colony. Investment companies received some charters. Individuals or groups called *proprietors* got others.

In Virginia, shareholders of the original joint-stock company included both settlers who came to Virginia and people who stayed in England and invested money. Several years after founding the colony, the company gave each settler 100 acres (40 hectares) of land to develop. A system of *headrights* was also established in the colony. Under this system, anyone could claim 50 acres (20 hectares) of free land by paying for their own transportation or that of other settlers.

In the colonies to the north, often called the New England Colonies, grants of land were generally given to groups of settlers who wanted to form a new community, or *town*. Some of the land was reserved for public use. The rest was divided among the settlers, who received lots for a house, a garden, and fields to farm. The town became a small company that governed itself.

In the other colonies, extremely large grants of land were sometimes given to individuals who had political power. These owners sold or rented sections of their land to people who wanted to have their own farms. In other cases, colonies offered cheap or free land to attract settlers.

Religious and political reasons. Some of the colonists, beginning with the Pilgrims in 1620, came to the New World to create communities where they could worship in their own way. Throughout the colonial period, many groups headed for the colonies to escape persecution for their religious beliefs. Among those religious groups were Quakers and Roman Catholics from England, Huguenots from France, Moravians from Germany, and Jews from throughout Europe.

Before the Arrival of the European Settlers

When the European colonists arrived in the New World, they found a rich and diverse land. The eastern coastal region where they settled consisted mainly of a forested plain that stretched from the Atlantic Ocean to the Appalachian Mountains.

The *Susan Constant* was the largest of three ships on the 1607 voyage that resulted in the founding of Jamestown.

Major rivers and bays cut through the plain, which broadened in the south. Many of these rivers provided a means of travel to the interior.

Fish were plentiful along the seacoast and in the inland waters. Many kinds of animals lived in the forests. They included deer, rabbits and other small game, and birds, such as ducks and geese.

The area that would later become the Thirteen Colonies was also home to more than 500,000 Indians. The tribes in the north included the Massachusett, Pequot, and Wampanoag. Among the groups in the central part of the region were the Delaware, the Susquehannock, and the nations of the powerful Iroquois League—the Cayuga, Mohawk, Onondaga, Oneida, and Seneca. Farther south lived the Catawba, Cherokee, Creek, and other tribes.

The Indians of eastern North America generally lived in villages near fields where they grew corn, squash, and beans. They also hunted and fished, and gathered wild plants, nuts, and berries.

Early English Settlements

During the 1580s, the English made several unsuccessful attempts to establish a colony in North America. For example, members of an English expedition landed on Roanoke Island off what is now North Carolina in 1585 but returned to England the following year.

In July 1587, another group of English men and women landed on Roanoke. They were led by John White, who had been a member of the earlier Roanoke settlement. In August, White sailed back to England for supplies. War between England and Spain prevented him from returning until 1590. By the time White finally made it back to Roanoke, all the colonists had disappeared.

War in Europe delayed further colonization efforts until 1606, when two groups of English investors formed the Virginia Company of London and the Virginia Company of Plymouth, also known as the London Company and the Plymouth Company. These companies together received a charter from King James I to found one colony apiece. One colony was to be established somewhere between present-day New York and the Carolinas, and the other was to be set up between the Potomac River and present-day Maine. A group from each company arrived in the New World in 1607. The Plymouth group's efforts in the north collapsed, but the London Company's settlement at Jamestown held on.

Jamestown became the first permanent English colony in America. The 104 original colonists—all men and boys—established a settlement on a peninsula in what is now the James River on May 24, 1607. The day was May 14 on the calendar then in use. The colonists planned to explore Virginia and trade with the Indians. The London Company investors hoped to follow the example of the Spanish colonies and make a quick profit from gold or other trade goods. But gold was not found. Instead, the company had to refinance with a lottery, new issues of stock, and a royal subsidy. About 1614, the colonists developed tobacco as a successful *cash crop*—that is, a crop grown for sale rather than for the colonists' own use. Even then, the company did not become successful.

Survival of the Jamestown settlement was doubtful for the first 20 years. Swampy land, bad water, and inadequate food and shelter contributed to high death rates. Disorganized leadership also added to their problems. About two-thirds of the original group soon died of disease and starvation. The men and women who came in 1608 and 1609 also suffered serious hardships. So many of the colonists died during the winter of 1609–1610 that this period became known as "the starving time." Only the arrival of ships with supplies and more settlers in 1610 saved the colony from abandonment.

The colonists also faced problems with the Indians of the region. When the colonists arrived in Virginia, the area was home to about 18,000 Indians. More than 30 of the tribes in the region were united in a confederacy under the leadership of Wahunsonacock, whom the colonists called Powhatan. The English also referred to the Indian tribes of the confederacy as the Powhatan. At first, the settlers and Indians got along. But by 1609, fighting had broken out between the groups, largely because the settlers tried to seize food from the Indians.

In 1613, the English took Powhatan's daughter Pocahontas hostage. A year later, after Pocahontas converted to Christianity, she and the colonist John Rolfe were married. The colonists and Indians marked the occasion with a truce. That truce lasted until 1622, when the Indians, under a new leader, launched a surprise attack on Virginia. The Indians, who hoped to drive the English away, killed about 350 colonists. But the colony managed to survive the attack.

In spite of the many hard times, Jamestown endured. The London Company took a number of

Captain Christopher Newport and 105 of his followers land at the colony of Jamestown, Virginia.

steps to persuade the colonists to stay and to attract more settlers. In 1619, for example, the company set up an elected assembly in the colony. This was the first elected representative assembly in the New World. Also in 1619, the company made special efforts to recruit women to go to the colony.

In 1624, the London Company went bankrupt. King James I then took over direct control of Virginia.

Plymouth Colony. The English established their second permanent settlement on mainland North America in 1620 in the area now called Cape Cod, Massachusetts. Most of the original settlers of the colony, called Plymouth Colony, were Separatists. Later Americans called this group "Pilgrims." The Separatists had cut ties with the Church of England, also known as the Anglican Church. Before coming to America, the Separatists had moved to the Netherlands to escape persecution.

The Pilgrims faced many hardships in the New World. Hunger and sickness killed half the original settlers during the first year. In the spring of 1621, however, a Patuxet Indian named Squanto taught them how to plant corn and showed them where to fish. In the autumn, the colonists celebrated their first harvest by sharing a meal with their Indian friends. This feast is now referred to as the first New England Thanksgiving. However, hunger, debt, and sickness continued to trouble New England for a decade.

The Plymouth colonists maintained friendly relations with the local Indians. In 1621, the settlers and Indians signed a peace treaty that lasted more than 50 years.

The Dominion of New England controlled Plymouth from 1685 to 1689. In 1691, the colony became part of the Massachusetts Bay Colony.

Development of the Thirteen Colonies

English expansion. Before 1649, when King Charles I was executed as a result of the English Civil War, England established several additional colonies on the North American mainland. The Massachusetts Bay Colony was founded in 1628. Some colonists from the Massachusetts Bay Colony later moved away and established settlements in Connecticut, New Hampshire, and Rhode Island. Maryland was established in the Chesapeake region in 1634.

From 1649 to 1660, England did not have a monarch. During that period, the nation did not begin any new colonies in North America. After Charles II became king of England in 1660—an event known as the Restoration—he granted charters for areas that would later include the colonies of Delaware, New Jersey, New York, Pennsylvania, and North and South Carolina. These colonies are sometimes called the *Restoration Colonies.* Some of these colonies were formed from New Netherland, which the English seized from the Dutch in 1664. The original Dutch settlement in New Netherland dated back to the 1620s.

During the 1700s, the English established several more colonies. For example, the first British settlers arrived in Georgia in 1733. The United Kingdom and France and their allies fought a series of wars ending in 1763. By that year, the United Kingdom had gained control of Canada, Florida, and the Ohio Valley. However, only Georgia became part of the 13 original United States.

Geographic divisions. Historians often divide the Thirteen Colonies that would become the original states into four geographical groups. They are (1) the New England, or Northern, Colonies; (2) the Middle Colonies; (3) the Chesapeake Colonies; and (4) the Southern Colonies. Some historians consider the Chesapeake Colonies to be part of the Southern Colonies.

The New England Colonies were Connecticut, Massachusetts, New Hampshire, and Rhode Island. These colonies had small farms and compact towns. The generally rocky soil of the New England region discouraged most large-scale agriculture, but the area was rich in timber and fish.

The Middle Colonies were Delaware, New Jersey, New York, and Pennsylvania. These colonies had larger farms than New England, and they produced surpluses of corn, wheat, and other agricultural products for export. Philadelphia became the bustling trade center of the Middle Colonies.

The Chesapeake Colonies consisted of Maryland and Virginia. Large farms and plantations in these colonies grew wheat and tobacco as cash crops. Life was more rural in the Chesapeake Colonies than in those farther north, and towns developed more slowly.

The Southern Colonies included Georgia and South Carolina. North Carolina, though geographically a Southern Colony, was economically and culturally similar to the Chesapeake Colonies. For example, North Carolina, like Maryland and Virginia, produced tobacco and wheat. Plantations in South Carolina and Georgia grew rice and *indigo.* Indigo is a plant that produces blue dye for coloring textiles. The colonies of South Carolina and Georgia each had a thriving port town to serve them—Charles Town (now Charleston), South Carolina; and Savannah, Georgia.

Changes in colonial control. The 13 English colonies began as either *corporate colonies or proprietary colonies.* Corporate colonies had a charter granted by the English monarch to stockholders. Proprietary colonies were owned by an individual proprietor or by a small group of proprietors under a charter from the monarch. Connecticut, Massachusetts, Rhode Island, and Virginia

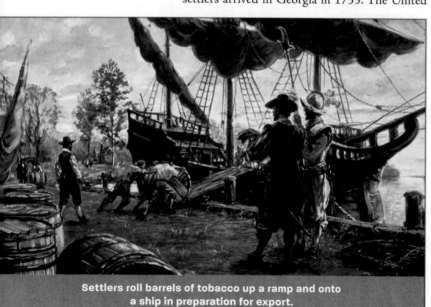

Settlers roll barrels of tobacco up a ramp and onto a ship in preparation for export.

were founded as corporate colonies. The other nine colonies were established as proprietary colonies.

In 1624, the English monarch began to change the colonies into *royal colonies*. Such colonies were under the direct control of the monarch. By the end of the colonial period, only Connecticut and Rhode Island remained corporate colonies, and just Delaware, Maryland, and Pennsylvania were still proprietary. The other eight colonies had become royal colonies.

Population growth. The population of the colonies increased rapidly during the late 1600s and early 1700s. By 1700, about 250,000 people lived in the English colonies. By 1775, the population had grown to about 2$\frac{1}{2}$ million. Virginia was the largest colony. Its population of about 450,000 was nearly evenly divided between people of European descent and those of African ancestry. Massachusetts and Pennsylvania each had about 250,000 people. The Chesapeake and Southern colonies had the largest population, but the biggest cities were in the Middle and Northern colonies.

Colonial growth was the result of both natural increase and immigration. Large numbers of immigrants came to North America throughout the colonial period. By the early 1700s, the colonists included a growing number of Scotch-Irish and Germans, who tended to settle in the back country, away from the developed areas along the coast. Imports of enslaved Africans also increased. All colonies had some slaves, but the Chesapeake and Southern colonies had the largest number. By 1710, a majority of the population of South Carolina was black.

Commercial expansion led to the rapid development of colonial port cities. These cities served as centers for crafts and for imports and exports for their region. In 1775, the largest colonial cities, in order of size, were Philadelphia; New York City; Boston; Charles Town (now Charleston), South Carolina; and Newport, Rhode Island. Philadelphia had a population of about 40,000, and New York City was home to about 25,000. Approximately 16,000 people lived in Boston, which had been the largest colonial city until the mid-1700s. Charles Town had a population of about 12,000, and Newport had 11,000 people.

Colonists and Indians

As colonial settlement expanded, so did trade and war with Indians. Indians taught the colonists to grow such crops as corn and tobacco. Periodi-

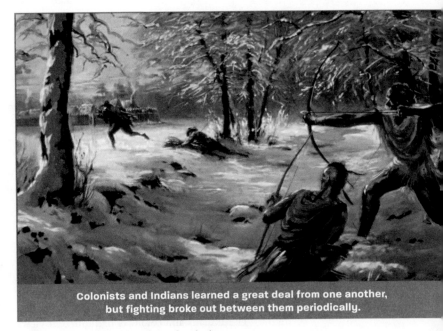

Colonists and Indians learned a great deal from one another, but fighting broke out between them periodically.

cally, the colonists and Indians fought bitter wars as colonists tried to eliminate nearby tribes, or Indians resisted further expansion into their lands. Indians sought allies among other tribes and European nations. As a result of these alliances, Indians became involved in the wars that European powers fought in North America from 1689 through the Revolutionary War.

Effects of contact on the Indians. The settlers introduced the Indians to metal pots and tools, textiles, and other goods. The colonists traded these products with the Indians in return for hides and furs, chiefly deerskins and beaver pelts. Many European traders lived in Indian villages and married Indian women. Some Indians living near or among colonists worked as day laborers or sold baskets and other crafts.

Through the years, many Indians began to depend on European textiles, tools, and pots obtained in the fur trade. As a result, their way of life began to change. Previously, these Indians had generally killed only as many animals as they needed for food, clothing, or shelter. But the growing dependence on trade goods led them to hunt and trap for commercial purposes rather than for personal or tribal survival. Game became scarce, and free-roaming colonial livestock ruined Indian fields. Some Indians moved west. Others bought food from whites. The expanding fur trade also led to greater tensions among tribes as they competed for furs to supply the colonial traders.

The coming of the colonists also changed Indian ways of life in other ways. Missionaries who set up towns and missions for Indians challenged traditional Indian culture and beliefs. As a result of the missionary efforts, some Indians converted to Christianity and adopted European customs.

In addition, contact with the settlers exposed Indians to new diseases for which they had no immunity. Many Native Americans—in some cases, whole villages—died from smallpox and other diseases the Europeans carried into the New World.

The struggle for land. Although charters from the English monarch gave individuals or groups the right to establish colonies in eastern North America, the settlers had to obtain the land itself from the Indians living there. They generally did so by making treaties for the land or by buying it directly. Later, some Indian lands were taken by force, fraud, and other means.

The Indians and colonists had different views about the nature of land ownership. In "selling" land to the colonists, most Indians believed they were giving the settlers only the right to use the area. The Indians expected to keep farming and hunting on the land themselves. The colonists, on the other hand, believed that land treaties and purchases gave them exclusive and permanent rights to the land. Disputes over land rights and ownership led to fighting between Indians and colonists. Many of these conflicts consisted of isolated Indian raids on towns and on cabins in the back country, as well as attacks by colonists on Indian villages.

Additional fighting occurred as colonies tried to expand farther into Indian territory. The colonies claimed they needed more land for their growing populations. However, many tribes objected to giving up any more land, and a number of bitter wars between the colonists and Indians resulted.

Some tribes also took sides in the series of four wars that France and England fought in North America from 1689 to 1763. In the last of the wars, the one called the French and Indian War (1754–1763), for example, the Catawba fought on the side of England.

After their victory in the French and Indian War, the British controlled nearly all of North America from the Atlantic Ocean to the Mississippi River. In an effort to prevent more Indian wars, the United Kingdom issued the Proclamation of 1763. This order reserved the territory west of the Appalachian Mountains for the Indians and barred colonial settlement there. A number of angry colonists, eager for new land, refused to obey the proclamation.

Some Indian tribes adopted Europeans or other Indians captured during wars. This practice was especially applied to women and children. Some captives married Indians and had families. At the end of each Indian war, the colonies required the Indians to return their captives. A number of prisoners, however, chose to stay with the Indians. In some areas, Indians captured by colonists or by opposing tribes were sold as slaves.

The Structure of Colonial Society

Colonial society was divided into several social classes. Class helped determine much of people's lives, from their political rights to what they wore or where they sat in church. In addition, some laws applied to one class and not to others.

The gentry formed the wealthiest, best-educated, and most influential class. Some members of the gentry owned large farms or plantations. Others were merchants, doctors, lawyers, or ministers. The most prosperous skilled craft workers, such as goldsmiths, also belonged to this class. By the mid-1700s, the gentry lived in large houses and owned elegant furniture and carriages.

The gentry held most leadership positions in colonial communities. Many of the men held public office. Gentry women did many household tasks themselves, but they also supervised servants.

Penny pot tavern, phila, pa.

• STOOD NEAR VINE ST. AND THE DELAWARE. NEWCOMERS TO THE CITY COULD 'FILL-UP' ON PIGEON PYE, EGGS'N'BACON, BREAD AND CHEESE AND A QUART OF PROPER ALE. BEER AT A PENNY A POT MADE THIS NEAT, TWO STORY BRICK HOUSE, A 1701 FAVORITE.

The Penny Pot Tavern in Philadelphia

Both men and women had time for visiting and for the arts and leisure.

The middle class, or "middling sort," farmed small holdings, ran shops and small businesses, or worked at ordinary skilled crafts, such as shoemaking or cabinetmaking. Both men and women in middle-class families contributed to the family income. Women produced candles, cheese, cloth, soap, and other goods for the family and for sale. Many women also helped men in the family shops. Some women ran their own small businesses. Middle-class men could vote, and some held minor public offices.

The lower class, or "lower sort," included apprentices, day laborers, sailors, indentured servants and other servants, and slaves. Most members of the lower class did not own any property, and most could not read or write. They were not allowed to vote. Many members of the lower class moved from place to place frequently in search of work and better opportunities. Many of the poor were women who took in laundry, sewing, or spinning to support their families.

Indentured servants formed a special group within the lower class. Most indentured servants signed a contract to work for several years to pay for their passage to the New World. A majority were young men between 15 and 24 years old who were looking for jobs and a better life. However, about one-fourth of the servants were women, and some were children. Most children who worked as indentured servants were orphans or came from families that were unable to support them. Some convicts and debtors were also sent to the colonies.

After 1720, many people came as *redemptioners.* Redemptioners were a special kind of indentured servant. They agreed to raise the money for their trip to America after arriving there. If they failed to raise the required sum within a stated period, they could be sold into service by the shipmaster.

Most indentured servants worked as agricultural laborers, but some were highly skilled craft workers. Masters provided indentured servants with food, clothing, and housing. Masters typically gave servants *freedom dues*—that is, new clothes or tools—at the end of the contract.

Slaves. Most slaves or their ancestors came from Africa. However, some Indians were also forced into slavery. The first group of black Africans to be brought to the North American mainland arrived in Jamestown in 1619. At first,

Slaves were brought from Africa to work as field hands on farms or serve in households.

black Africans worked as indentured servants who would eventually be free. But by the mid-1600s, a series of laws known as the *slave codes* had established slavery and kept the Africans in bondage for life—unless their owners chose to free them.

Slaves had few rights, and they generally could not testify in court against whites. As a result, even when owners brutally mistreated slaves, the owners received little or no punishment. The slave codes made it illegal for slaves to travel without permission or to carry weapons. They also set harsher punishments for slaves than for free people for certain crimes. According to the codes, owners could buy and sell slaves much as they would other property. The codes also established the legal status of the children of slaves. For example, children of mothers who were slaves were considered under the law to be slaves themselves—no matter who their fathers were.

Most slaves worked as field hands on farms with fewer than 20 slaves. Some learned skilled crafts or served in households. Every colony had slaves, though most slaves lived in the Chesapeake and Southern colonies.

The colonies had a number of small communities of free blacks. Some free blacks had free mothers. Others had been favorites of their owners and had been set free. Free blacks had to follow some of the laws that applied to slaves. Sometimes, free blacks had to prove they were free. If they failed to offer such proof, they could be arrested and sold as runaway slaves. Most free blacks were part of the lower class, but a few owned land or were skilled craft workers. A small number were educated.

Government and Law Enforcement

Colonial government. All the colonies had a governor, a legislature, a governor's council, and a court system. In royal colonies, the monarch appointed the governor. In proprietary colonies, the proprietors did so. In the corporate colonies of Connecticut and Rhode Island, the voters elected the governor.

All the colonies except Pennsylvania had *bicameral* (two-house) legislatures. Pennsylvania had a *unicameral* (one-house) legislature. The colonial legislatures generally were known as assemblies, though some had other names. For example, Massachusetts called its legislature the General Court, and the lower house of Virginia's legislature was known as the House of Burgesses.

In all the colonies except Pennsylvania, the governor's council served both as an upper house of the legislature and as the cabinet of the governor. Voters elected the members of the lower house in all the colonies. They elected representatives to the upper house only in Connecticut and Rhode

Colonists protest the Stamp Act, a tax passed by the British government on documents and publications.

Island. In Massachusetts, the lower house chose the upper house. In the other 10 colonies, the governor or proprietor chose the council.

Colonial legislatures debated issues and elected officers to preside over their meetings. They passed laws and could tax the people. The governor could veto any laws passed by the legislature. The governor also had the right to call elections and to call together and dismiss the legislature.

The British Parliament passed some laws for the colonies, especially ones regulating trade. It also created a postal system and certain courts for the colonies. British officials reviewed all laws passed by colonial legislatures in royal and proprietary colonies. These officials could *disallow*—that is, reject—laws that they considered to be contrary to English law. Only about 5 percent of colonial laws were disallowed. However, even these few acts of disallowance caused resentment in the colonies. In some cases, decisions of colonial courts were appealed to England.

Local government. In New England, the main unit of local government was the town. Voters at town meetings chose most local officials and decided on local laws. All adult residents of a town could attend a town meeting, but only those men who met certain qualifications could vote. Town governments collected taxes, built roads and bridges, and organized the militia.

In most areas outside New England, the county was the chief unit of local government. Towns with charters from the assembly could run their own affairs. County courts performed the functions of local government, including setting taxes. The courts also handled matters of land ownership, wills, and other legal cases. Justices of the peace, appointed by the governor, together formed the county courts. Other county officials included county clerks and sheriffs.

In many areas of the South, parishes were units both of the Church of England and of county government. The parishes elected church officials known as *vestrymen* to take care of the poor and to set taxes.

Voting and other rights. Not everyone had the same rights in the colonies. Single adult women had the same rights as men except for voting. Married women, however, usually did not have independent control of property. Some women kept control of property through marriage contracts or trusts. Slaves could not sue or be sued.

Slave codes limited travel for slaves and set harsher penalties for some crimes.

Not all adult colonists were permitted to vote. Qualifications for voting varied among the colonies, though generally they set property ownership as a requirement. Depending on the colony, this requirement could be satisfied by owning a town lot or a small farm, or by holding a long-term lease. In some cases, people could qualify to vote by paying taxes of a certain amount. Slaves could not vote in any colony. Laws and custom usually kept women from voting as well.

Some requirements restricted voting to members of certain religious faiths. In the 1600s, New England voters had to be members of the Congregational Church. In royal colonies, voters needed occasionally to attend the Church of England. In practice, this policy kept Jews and Roman Catholics from voting. By the 1700s, in practice, most adult white males could vote at some point in their lives.

People voted in person, often by announcing their vote to officials. There were no political parties or organized campaigns. Some candidates, however, hosted social gatherings and provided food and drink for voters. Some colonies had groups of men who worked together in politics and elections in much the same way later political parties would.

The gentry held most elected positions. Many offices paid no salary, and only people with money could afford to serve. The gentry saw public office as a duty and a right. Ordinary voters usually agreed that leaders should come from the gentry class.

Crime and punishment. Constables and sheriffs arrested suspects, kept order, and enforced court orders. Jails were used mainly to hold people for trial or until they paid their debts. Local courts and juries ruled on cases involving slaves and on minor offenses, such as drunkenness and disturbing the peace. Certain high courts tried people accused of a major crime, such as murder or treason.

Punishment was direct and swift. Men and women convicted of adultery, gossip, slander, petty theft, drunkenness, or disturbing the peace faced fines, whipping, or *shaming*. Shaming consisted of subjecting a person to public disgrace.

Common forms of shaming included the *pillory*, *stocks*, and *ducking stool*. The pillory and stocks stood in a town square. They were wooden frameworks with holes cut in them. In a pillory, the holes held the arms and head of the victim. In the stocks, the holes held the victim's legs, and sometimes also

the arms. Prisoners were locked into the holes for a certain time. The ducking stool was a chair attached to the end of a long plank extended from the bank of a pond or stream. The victim of the punishment was tied securely to the chair and *ducked* (plunged) into the water several times.

Punishments given for the same type of crime often depended on who the criminal was. A member of the lower class might receive a harsher punishment than a middle-class person, and a woman might receive a shaming punishment for committing a crime for which a man would pay a fine. People convicted of burglary, counterfeiting, murder, piracy, rape, or treason faced death by hanging.

Many settlers built their homesteads from local timber.

Colonists at Home

Colonial households were places of work, play, and family life. They were not private places. Rooms served many purposes. Neighbors walked in and out. Colonial households often included servants, slaves, and visitors. Families in the colonies generally had more children than those in England. The average was seven children. Many households included stepchildren, grandparents, aunts, or cousins. Families of slaves did not always live together. Slave children lived with the mother, but the father sometimes lived apart.

The father was the head of the colonial household. The mother was expected to be his companion and helper. When the father was absent or ill, the mother could represent the family in financial dealings and other matters. She was supposed to obey her husband, and he was to respect her.

Children, servants, and slaves were also expected to obey the head of the household. All members of a household were supposed to work for its well-being.

Houses. When the colonists arrived in the New World, they at first made temporary shelters. Early colonists built one- or two-room huts of wood and mud. The settlers later began to build dwellings that resembled those they left behind in England. However, the colonists adapted building design and construction to local conditions and materials. For example, many colonists near the Appalachians used local limestone for their homes, and some in New England used rocks from the fields as their building material. By the 1700s, many wealthy families built their homes of brick.

The chief building material throughout the colonies was wood, which was plentiful in the eastern forests. Most early permanent dwellings were simple cottages with walls made of shingles or planks and roofs of thatch or shingles. Houses made of planks became known as *frame houses*. Most windows were small.

Fireplaces provided a colonial home with light
and heat and served for cooking.

Houses in New England commonly had two rooms in front with a third running across the back. Many homes had a second floor over the front two rooms. In some homes, a brick or stone central chimney served two fireplaces that stood back to back. Most houses in the Chesapeake and Southern colonies consisted of one or two rooms connected by a central hallway. Above these rooms were lofts that were used mainly for sleeping. Fireplaces stood at two opposite ends of these houses. Chimneys stood outside the framework of most homes.

Many houses in the Delaware River Valley and the Hudson River Valley were of Scandinavian or Dutch design. The Swedish colonists who came to Delaware in 1638 built the first log cabins in America. The log cabin became the typical frontier home after 1780 . Most of the houses built by the Dutch settlers had 1$\frac{1}{2}$ stories. Their doors were divided into upper and lower parts that opened separately. These doors became known as *Dutch doors*.

During the 1700s, many wealthy colonial merchants and planters built homes in a style called Georgian architecture. Most Georgian houses were square or rectangular, with a central stairway and many tall windows. Above the doors and windows were decorative frames of stonework. The homes had fine wood trim and were planned to look balanced and orderly. The wealthiest families imported wallpaper or had fine paneling made for some rooms.

A typical plantation home of the gentry stood on a hill and overlooked a bay or river. Gardens and orchards framed the main views from the house. A typical mansion had eight rooms and stood two stories tall. The kitchen, laundry, and other one-room buildings known as *dependencies* stood nearby. Some slaves were housed in the dependencies. Others lived in small one- or two-room houses in a special area called the *slave quarter*. These dwellings typically had dirt floors and no windows.

Furnishings. Most colonial homes had simple and sturdy homemade furnishings. Many had little more than a few tools and cooking utensils, a storage chest, a table made of planks, and a few benches or stools. Some tables converted to chairs, and other pieces folded for storage.

Many colonists slept on mattresses stuffed with straw or cornhusks. Mattresses were laid on the floor or on a wooden frame strung with rope several feet off the floor. The space between the floor and mattress generally was used to store a child's bed during the day. This movable bed, called a *trundle bed*, was pulled out at night. Many colonial women made quilts to cover beds. Quilts consisted of scraps of cloth stitched together to form several layers.

One or more fireplaces provided a colonial home with light and heat. The fires also served for cooking. Candles and lamps that burned animal fat provided extra light.

Colonists had few tools and utensils. Some families owned only simple woodworking tools, a few iron pots for cooking and cleaning, and a spinning wheel. Most dishes were made of wood or *pewter*.

Pewter is made by combining tin and other metals. In many cases, each person at a meal did not have a separate plate. Instead, two people shared food from a deep wooden plate called a *trencher.* Wooden or pewter spoons were the main eating utensils.

Many colonial tables had special features that saved space. These features included *gate legs* and tops fitted with *drop leaves.* When a larger table-top was needed, the gate legs swung out like a gate to support the hinged leaves. At other times, the gate legs were folded and the drop leaves lowered. The most popular chests of drawers were *lowboys* and *highboys.* Lowboys were short chests that served as side tables. Highboys were tall chests with short legs and many drawers. Many highboys were built by placing one chest on top of another.

Wealthier families ordered furnishings from England or from a local skilled worker. Many of these pieces were finely carved and covered in elegant fabrics. Local workers used native cherry, pine, and walnut, or imported mahogany. Items that were made by colonists often followed English furniture designs, but colonists also created new styles. For example, the American inventor, author, and statesman Benjamin Franklin put curved wooden slats at the ends of chair legs to create the rocking chair.

Wealthy colonists imported delicate dishes and elegant wall hangings. Dutch pottery called *delftware* and English china known as *creamware* were popular among the gentry. Silk, damask, or linen curtains and wall coverings hung in well-furnished homes. Some of these homes had a clock. The best-known colonial clock was the *grandfather clock.* It had a tall, elegant case that stood on the floor. The case covered the pulleys, weights, and swinging pendulum that ran the clock.

Families prized mattresses stuffed with feathers, set on frames with high posts, a canopy, and curtains. Women embroidered curtains for these *four-poster beds.* The curtains kept out drafts and provided some privacy.

Clothing. The clothes people wore told much about what they did and their place in the community. Most colonists wore clothing made of linen, wool, or leather. These clothes followed simple styles from England but were made at home. Families of merchants, wealthy farmers, and prosperous craft workers purchased cloth from Europe, or they imported finished apparel. These garments followed the latest fashion and were made from elegant fabrics.

Women in most colonial homes were responsible for making clothes.

In most colonial homes, women had the responsibility for making clothes, and they spent many hours at this task. They spun linen from flax and wool yarn from the fleece of sheep. They wove these materials into cloth to be made into clothing. Nuts, berries, roots, and bark provided dye. Sometimes women wove together linen and wool to make a cloth known as *linsey-woolsey.*

Men generally wore long linen shirts and wool breeches gathered at the knee, long knit stockings, and simple leather shoes, boots, or moccasins. Some who worked in the fields went barefoot. For warmth or for formal events, men wore a long vest and jacket over the shirt and a long piece of linen, called a *stock,* tied at the neck. In winter, men added leather leggings, wool mittens, and an overcoat.

Some fashionable men wore wigs. Beginning in the late 1600s, a number of colonial men began wearing the long, flowing wigs fashionable in Europe. In the 1700s, smaller wigs came into use. The most common style was a close-fitting wig, which was drawn back into a braid or small tail. Especially in the 1700s, wigs were powdered to make them white.

Fieldworkers wore straw hats for shade. Laborers and tradesmen wore caps. The most fashionable style had a turned-up brim and was known as a *cocked hat.*

Most women wore a dress of linen or wool, a petticoat, and a long linen undergarment known as a *shift.* For cold weather, they added a cape or hooded cloak.

Adult women wore head coverings both indoors and outdoors. Linen caps were the most common

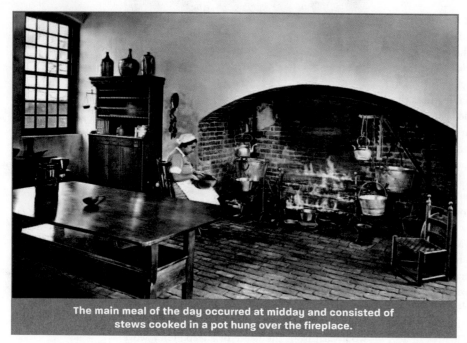

The main meal of the day occurred at midday and consisted of stews cooked in a pot hung over the fireplace.

covering. In the summer, however, some women wore a straw hat, and in the winter, a felt one. Women had long hair, which they wore pinned up in a bun or braid. In the 1600s, fashionable women let one or two long curls reach their shoulders. In the 1700s, some women wore elaborate styles for special occasions. They piled their hair high on frameworks they wore on their heads.

Colonial babies and toddlers of both sexes wore a dress that reached to the ground. Older children wore clothes similar to those of adults.

Wealthier colonists had clothing made of fine linen, cotton, silk, satin, and velvet. Men wore linen shirts with lace cuffs and ruffles. Their coats, shoes, and breeches had silver buckles or decorative buttons and trim. Many coats were brightly colored. Wealthier men wore silk hose and carried linen handkerchiefs.

Women from wealthy families also dressed in fine fabrics. They wore low-necked dresses that fit tightly at the waist and above and were trimmed with lace at the neck and sleeves. Tight corsets slimmed their waists. Whalebone or wire hoops supported the skirts, which were drawn back to show elegant petticoats. Wealthy women wore silk or leather shoes with silk stockings.

The clothes of slaves depended on the work they did and the wealth of the family. Those who worked in the fields often wore simple shifts of homemade cloth, or a *breechcloth*—that is, a piece of cloth tied about the waist. Some slaves wore old clothes given to them by their masters and mistresses.

Food and drink. After the early starving time, colonists had plenty to eat, even if the meals seemed much the same from day to day. They ate a breakfast of mush and meat or cheese followed at about noon by their main meal of the day. Most midday meals consisted of stews cooked in a pot hung in the fire-

place. The evening meal was often bread, cheese, and anything left in the pot from midday. Meats and vegetables for the stews changed with the season because the colonists had few ways of preserving foods. For example, they salted some meats and dried certain vegetables. Root crops, such as squash, turnips, or carrots, and fruits, such as apples and pears, could be kept in a cool, dry cellar.

Corn was one of the most important foods eaten by the colonists. Women made mush and hoecakes and other kinds of corn bread from ground corn meal. They also prepared a dish called *hominy* by softening whole, dried corn in sodium hydroxide (lye) or water to remove the hull. They made *succotash* by combining corn and beans. Corn roasted in its husk over the fire was a special treat. Servants, slaves, and poor families often had little besides corn and garden vegetables for food.

The most common meats were ham, bacon, and other forms of pork. Hogs ran loose around the farm and countryside, eating what they could find. Colonists also kept sheep and chickens. Hunting added turkey, deer, squirrel, and other game to the diet. Colonists ate both fresh and dried fish.

Cattle and goats provided meat as well as milk for drinking. Women made butter and cheese from the milk.

Colonists grew wheat, rye, and oats for grain, which was used chiefly to make bread. Colonial women baked the bread in fireplace ovens or in iron containers called *bake kettles*. Fireplace ovens were openings built in the stone or brick and warmed by the chimney. A bake kettle had a tight lid and was placed on hot coals with embers piled around it.

Colonial families also gathered fruits, nuts, and berries in season. Sage, marjoram, and other seasonings came from the garden.

The most common drinks were beer, ale, and cider, all brewed at home. The colonists drank imported and local wines and rum. They consumed very little water, which they feared would make them sick.

After 1700, colonial cooking began to change to include more roasted meats, separate vegetable dishes, and more baked items. Colonists began to import chocolate, coffee, tea, and spices. The new cooking required more tools, including pans and spits for turning meats on open fires.

Recreation. Social gatherings were an important part of colonial life. Colonists often combined work and play in parties called *frolics*. When colonists worked together to raise the frames for buildings, for example, they also held games and contests, such as plowing contests and footraces. These gatherings also featured food, drink, and music. Except for Puritans, Quakers, and certain other religious groups, colonists of all classes enjoyed dancing. Jigs, reels, and other lively dances were especially popular.

Colonists gathered on Sundays to visit one another before and after church services. Monthly court sessions, election days, and militia drills also gave colonists chances to get together to exchange news and eat and drink. Weddings became occasions for parties and gift giving. Colonists sometimes held local fairs, which often featured horse races and fights that pitted animals against each other. People living in colonial towns could hear lectures on science, join literary clubs, or attend concerts and plays.

Holidays provided another opportunity for people to get together. The celebration of holidays varied among the colonies. The most widely celebrated holidays were four days that marked the seasons. March 25 was called Lady's Day; June 24, midsummer; September 29, Michaelmas; and December 25, Christmas. Most New England colonies followed Old World traditions of holding harvest festivals in the fall. A number of colonies celebrated traditional church holidays, such as Easter, Whitsunday (Pentecost), and St. Valentine's Day. Puritans in New England recognized only Sunday as a special day and passed laws against celebrating Christmas.

Taverns, sometimes called *ordinaries*, were favorite gathering places for men. There, they smoked, drank, read newspapers, and played cards. Some women worked in taverns, and a number of women became tavern owners. Some taverns offered dancing or billiards.

Children played with homemade toys, including balls, marbles, kites, and dolls. They also played hopscotch, leapfrog, London Bridge, and other games. Children of the gentry had imported toys, such as tea sets and finely crafted dolls and toy soldiers.

Education and Religion

Education. Colonial children learned many practical lessons at home. Fathers taught sons how to farm, hunt, and build and repair things. Mothers showed daughters how to care for gardens, sew, spin, cook, and look after livestock. Some children worked with their parents in skilled crafts, such as shoemaking or weaving.

Some children and young adults joined other households as apprentices to skilled workers or professional people to learn trades or such professions as medicine and law. The families that took on an apprentice signed a contract promising to provide the apprentice with bed and board and the skills of a trade. In exchange, they were to receive faithful service from the apprentice for a certain period. Orphans were often *bound out*—that is,

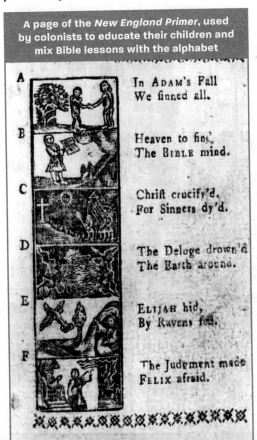

A page of the *New England Primer*, used by colonists to educate their children and mix Bible lessons with the alphabet

placed as servants—to families who promised to teach them skills.

Some families who wanted their children to read and write taught them at home. However, books were expensive, and many families owned only a Bible. In the 1700s, many families bought almanacs and newspapers. The gentry, on the other hand, could afford libraries for their homes, and many members of this class hired tutors for their children. Some apprenticeship agreements included a promise to teach reading and writing.

Schools. Some colonial families joined together to hire a teacher to run a small school. During the early colonial period, schools known as *free schools* were established. These schools charged tuition and were free from church oversight. Some teachers opened schools in their homes. For example, *dame schools* were run by women who taught basic reading and writing to young children.

In 1642, Massachusetts passed a law requiring parents to teach their children to read. In 1647, the colony passed the first law in America requiring communities to establish public schools. The law stated that every town with at least 50 families had to start an elementary school and every town of at least 100 families had to have a Latin grammar school. Today, elementary schools and grammar schools are much alike, but the grammar schools in colonial times were more like today's high schools. Colonial elementary schools taught religion, spelling,

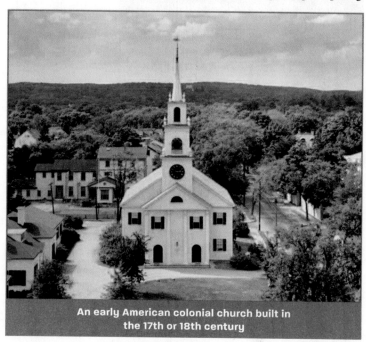

An early American colonial church built in the 17th or 18th century

reading, writing, and arithmetic. Grammar schools prepared more advanced students for college. They offered lessons in religion, Latin and Greek, English composition, geography, and mathematics.

Some grammar schools were run by colleges, but others were private. Many elementary schools provided only a short summer session for girls or taught them at hours when boys were not in school. Grammar schools did not admit girls.

By the mid-1700s, schools called *academies* began to be established in the colonies. They offered more practical courses than did grammar schools. Subjects ranged from the liberal arts, such as history and philosophy, to practical subjects, such as navigation and sewing. Some academies admitted girls, and some were for girls only. By 1775, a majority of whites could read and write.

Only a few slaves and free black children attended school. Some religious and charitable groups set up schools for blacks. Very young children attended schools for blacks, but usually only for short periods.

In 1636, Massachusetts established what is now Harvard University, the first college in the colonies. Women were not admitted to any college in America during the colonial period. By 1775, there were colleges in five colonies. Some colonists went to England to study.

Learning materials. Colonial schools had few books or other learning materials. Children often learned lessons from *hornbooks*. A hornbook was a paddle-shaped piece of wood with a sheet of paper pasted to it. A thin layer of transparent horn protected the paper, which was scarce and expensive in colonial times. Typically the alphabet, the Lord's Prayer, and the Roman numerals were on the paper.

The most widely used textbook in the colonies was the *New England Primer*, which was first published about 1690. It included information from the hornbook as well as the Ten Commandments, a catechism, and bits of moral instruction. It also featured rhymes for learning the alphabet. For example, the rhyme for the letter *M* was "The Moon gives light/In time of night."

Religion had a strong influence on the social and political life of the colonists. Many of the colonists had come to America chiefly so they could worship according to their beliefs. Some European governments had persecuted certain religious groups for breaking away from traditional or state-supported churches and trying to establish new forms of worship.

Most colonial religious groups dated from the 1500s. They developed during the Reformation, a religious movement in Europe that resulted in the birth of Protestantism. Many Anglicans moved to the colonies, as did large numbers of Puritans, Quakers, Baptists, Huguenots, and other persecuted groups.

Established churches. Members of the various religious groups that came to America usually settled near others with similar beliefs. These groups were more interested in finding a place to live according to their religious rules than in granting religious freedom to others. As a result, some colonies supported one church, often called an *established church*, within their boundaries and denied freedom of worship to other religious groups. Established churches received tax support from colonial legislatures.

The Puritans established the Congregational Church in the New England colonies of Connecticut, Massachusetts, and New Hampshire. Pennsylvania and Delaware granted all churches freedom of worship, but laws reflected Quaker beliefs. Rhode Island also welcomed all groups. In New York and New Jersey, which the English captured from the Dutch in 1664, no single religious group was strong enough to force its church to become the established church. Maryland, founded partly as a refuge for Catholics, had many Protestant settlers. In response to religious unrest, Maryland's colonial leaders in 1649 passed the first religious toleration act in the British Empire. This law granted religious liberty to all Christians, but it was soon repealed. In 1692, the Anglican Church became the established church in Maryland. The Anglican Church was also the official church in Virginia and the Southern Colonies.

A colonial Sunday. The colonies set aside Sunday as a day of worship. Regulations known as *blue laws* kept stores and businesses closed on Sundays. Even slaves had part of Sunday as free time. Sunday services included long sermons by the clergy and psalm singing by the congregation. Church seating was assigned by sex, race, and wealth. Before and after services, the churchyard served as a social center for neighborly visits, exchange of news, and courtship.

Witchcraft. Colonists brought traditional beliefs in folk magic and witches with them from Europe. They blamed unexplained misfortunes on witchcraft. Several colonies tried individuals as witches, and some people were executed. The

Roger Williams, English clergyman and founder of the Rhode Island colony

last—and largest—witchcraft trials were held in 1692 in Salem, Massachusetts. Seventeen women and three men were executed as a result of the Salem trials. About 150 others were imprisoned on witchcraft charges.

Religious diversity and tolerance increased in the colonies during the 1700s. Many Germans, Scots, and Scotch-Irish migrated to the colonies and brought their religious traditions with them. These new immigrants included members of the German-Reformed, Lutheran, Moravian, Presbyterian, and Roman Catholic churches. Jews, forced out of Europe and South America for their religious beliefs, settled in small numbers. Africans, imported as slaves, brought Muslim and traditional African religious beliefs with them. The clergy and some owners made occasional efforts to convert slaves to Christianity during the colonial period, but for the most part, slaves were left to follow their own beliefs.

Beginning in the 1730s, a series of religious revivals called the Great Awakening divided existing churches. During the Great Awakening, traveling preachers drew large audiences to hear their sermons. Some preachers were women or slaves. Revival meetings were often held in the open air. Preaching was lively, and people responded emotionally. Listeners sometimes wept, fainted, or shook all over.

The stirring sermons of George Whitefield and other Awakening preachers called on listeners to repent of their sins and seek salvation. The evangelists discouraged card playing, dancing, and other amusements that they considered "worldly." They criticized established churches and pushed to separate church and state.

Transportation and Communication

Transportation in the colonies was slow and difficult. In general, colonists traveled by boat or horse, or on foot. Most colonies had at least one major river that could take boats inland for many miles before reaching a rapids. Major rivers in the Southern and Middle colonies were deep enough for ocean vessels. The colonists built many boats for trading along the coast. The vessels used by colonists for transporting passengers and freight by sea included brigantines, schooners, shallops, sloops, and other sailing craft. On rivers and bays, these vessels were joined by canoes, flatboats, and rowboats.

The first colonial roads were merely paths through the woodlands and countryside. The colonists widened the paths for travel on horseback and later for carts and wagons pulled by horses or oxen. Most colonial bridges were made of wood, and many were in poor condition. Consequently, most travelers on horseback or in wheeled vehicles forded rivers at shallow spots or paid to cross on a ferry.

Body armor hangs on the wall at James Fort in Jamestown, Virginia.

The colonists put much effort into building roads, and local work crews worked to keep them in repair. By 1760, the colonies had several major roads. For example, one road linked New York City and Portsmouth, New Hampshire, and passed through Boston and other cities along the way. The Great Wagon Road ran through mountain valleys and connected Philadelphia and the back country of Georgia. By the mid-1700s, stagecoach lines ran between Boston and Providence, Rhode Island; and linked New York City with Philadelphia and Annapolis, Maryland.

Communication. During the 1600s, the colonists exchanged news chiefly by word of mouth. Gossip spread swiftly at church, court days, or public gatherings. Official notices were announced at church or posted on the doors of public buildings. Towns and cities had a crier who read announcements on the street. Much of the news from outside a community was learned informally as visitors came to an area. Travelers passed letters, carried letters for friends, or left them at inns for others to claim or pass on.

Individuals called *post riders* carried mail along routes called *post roads*. They picked up mail and left it at inns, taverns, or other established stopping places. The English government allowed a private postal system to be set up in 1691 and took over its operations in 1707. Service to all areas, especially the Chesapeake and Southern colonies, came slowly. In 1753, Benjamin Franklin became a deputy postmaster general for the colonies. He improved the frequency and speed of postal service.

Newspapers came into general use after the mid-1700s. The *Boston News-Letter*, founded in 1704, was the first successful colonial newspaper. By 1775, all the colonies except Delaware and New Jersey had at least one newspaper. Newspapers appeared weekly. They were passed from one person to another and were available in taverns. They had stories from other newspapers; local advertisements; short items of local news; and letters, poems, and essays by local writers.

Arts

In the early years, colonists had little time or money to support the arts. But by the 1700s, they developed a lively interest in music, art, theater, and literature.

Literature. Some of the early colonists wrote to tell Europeans about life in the New World. For example, the colonial leader John Smith wrote about Jamestown. Other early colonists translated classics or wrote sermons. At first, colonial works had to be sent to England for publication because the colonies did not have a printing press. In 1639, however, Stephen Daye and his son Matthew set up the first printing press in what is now the United States, in Cambridge, Massachusetts.

Most early colonial literature was religious. The *Bay Psalm Book*, published by the Dayes in 1640, was the first book printed in the American Colonies. It was a collection of psalms prepared by several ministers.

By the late 1600s, colonial printers were still publishing sermons and other religious writings, but they were printing almanacs, essays, histories, satires, and travel accounts as well. Mary Rowlandson's description of her capture by Indians, published in 1682, became the first of many captivity stories. The religious leaders Jonathan Edwards, John Woolman, and Cotton Mather

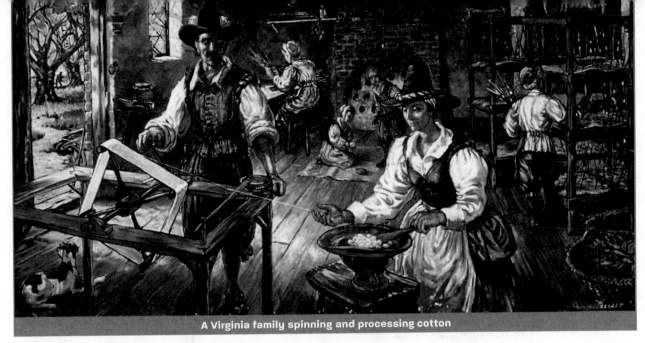
A Virginia family spinning and processing cotton

produced a number of important works during the 1700s. Benjamin Franklin published the highly successful *Poor Richard's Almanac* for each year from 1733 to 1758. This work became known for its wise and witty proverbs. After 1750, colonists wrote and published many essays and pamphlets about political controversies.

A number of volumes of poetry were published by colonial writers. Readers also passed around unpublished poems and plays. Anne Bradstreet became the first colonial woman to have her poetry published when her collection The *Tenth Muse Lately Sprung Up in America* appeared in England in 1650. Michael Wigglesworth's long religious poem, *Day of Doom* (1662), became the most popular poem of colonial times. Phillis Wheatley, an African-born slave, became known for her collection of *Poems on Various Subjects, Religious and Moral* (1773), published in England.

Painting. Early American artists had little formal training. They traveled throughout the colonies and earned a living by painting portraits. After 1700, some European-trained painters who had arrived in the colonies painted portraits of the wealthy. Among the most skilled were Charles Bridges, Gustavus Hesselius, and John Smibert. The American-born painters Ralph Earl and Robert Feke also became known for their portraits.

Beginning in the mid-1700s, some of the finest American artists spent time studying or painting in Europe. They included John Singleton Copley, Charles Willson Peale, Gilbert Stuart, and Benjamin West.

Decorative arts. During the early colonial period, most of the settlers made their own furniture and household articles. Wealthy colonists generally imported their furnishings from England.

During the 1700s, skilled colonial craft workers turned everyday items into works of art. They made many fine products of wood, silver, pewter, or glass.

Furniture in the early colonial times was heavy. But in the early 1700s, styles became lighter and more graceful. During the 1700s, some wealthier colonists imported finely crafted pieces from the workshops of the famous English furniture makers Thomas Chippendale, Thomas Sheraton, and George Hepplewhite.

Gold, silver, and pewter. Colonial goldsmiths and silversmiths created elegant bowls, tableware, and tankards. Pewter provided less expensive ware. Smiths melted the metal and then poured it into molds. Engraved designs on gold, silver, and pewter items resembled the patterns that appeared in furniture.

Other decorative arts included glassware and needlework. Many of the bottles and much of the fine table glass produced by colonial glassmakers were beautifully colored and molded in patterns. The detailed needlework produced by colonial women was used to decorate homes.

Music was a part of many church services. Congregations sang musical versions of the psalms. Only a few parishes owned organs, and so most singing was unaccompanied. Music also was important in the daily lives of the colonists. They played music at weddings and other celebrations and at home. They often composed new words to accompany old melodies they brought with them from Europe. Professional musicians performed at concert halls and theaters. The first colonial orchestra formed in Charles Town in 1750.

Colonists played a variety of musical instruments. Settlers bought or brought with them violins, guitars, and other European instruments.

Some wealthy Southern planters purchased expensive harpsichords for their homes. Black slaves made banjos and other stringed instruments similar to those they used in Africa. Many slaves also became skilled fiddlers and were in demand to play at dances.

Science, Health, and Medicine

Science. Colonial scientists kept careful records of the weather and the laboratory experiments they performed. They were well informed about new discoveries in astronomy, chemistry, meteorology, and physics. They exchanged ideas with European scientists and sent reports and specimens to Europe.

A number of colonial scientists studied the plant and animal life of the New World. In 1728, the botanist John Bartram planted the colonies' first botanical garden, near Philadelphia. Other colonial naturalists included Bartram's son William, John Clayton, Cadwallader Colden, Alexander Garden, and John Mitchell.

Benjamin Franklin became known throughout the world for his experiments and inventions. He gained particular fame for his work on the study of electricity. In 1743, Franklin and other Philadelphia scholars founded the American Philosophical Society. This organization became the chief colonial scientific body.

A number of other scientists also made valuable contributions to scientific knowledge in the colonies. For example, the Puritan minister Cotton Mather published one of the first good descriptions of smallpox inoculation.

Health and medicine. Colonists suffered from a wide variety of diseases. Colds and influenza were common. *Scurvy*—that is, a lack of vitamin C—occurred widely among the early colonists. Many settlers in the Southern and Middle colonies suffered from malaria, yellow fever, and typhoid. Many colonists also developed pneumonia, tuberculosis, and diphtheria. Beginning in the mid-1600s, several epidemics of measles and smallpox swept through the colonies and killed large numbers of people. Measles and smallpox proved fatal especially to American Indians, who had no immunity to these diseases.

Colonists relied mainly on home cures and folk remedies to treat diseases. They often borrowed African and Indian cures. Such treatments typically involved the use of barks, herbs, and roots. Quinine, for example, is a bitter substance taken from the bark of the cinchona tree. The colonists used it to treat malaria and a malarial fever called *ague*. Doctors still use it today to treat some forms of malaria.

There were few formally trained doctors during most of the colonial period. Skilled midwives delivered most babies. Most doctors either taught themselves or studied medicine by helping experienced physicians, but some attended medical schools in Europe. Established medical practice of the day maintained that illness resulted from an imbalance of four fluids called *humors* that were believed to be in the body. One of the chief methods physicians used in their attempts to restore the balance of the humors was *bloodletting*—that is, removing blood from a patient.

The Economy

Farming was the chief economic activity of the colonists. Colonists raised crops for export to other colonies and to England. The main colonial cash crops included corn, wheat, rice, indigo, and tobacco. Rum also became an important export. In return for their products, the colonists imported manufactured goods from England for their own use and for trade with the Indians.

Through the years, the colonies developed a number of industries. These industries included fishing and whaling, lumbering, ironmaking, and shipbuilding.

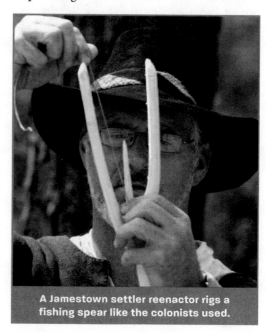

A Jamestown settler reenactor rigs a fishing spear like the colonists used.

Farming. Nearly all the colonists did at least some farming. Colonial farms produced enough food to provide a comfortable, but limited, diet to all. Settlers brought wheat, oats, rye, and barley from Europe. They learned to plant corn and tobacco from Indians, and black slaves probably taught the white colonists to plant rice. Nearly all colonial farmers owned a few cattle, hogs, and chickens, and some raised livestock commercially.

When possible, colonial farmers planted crops on only a portion of their farms. They usually planted the same kind of crop repeatedly, and the land became exhausted after a few harvests. The farmers then cleared a new field and let the old one become pasture or return to scrub. After 1750, some farmers added fertilizers to the soil, rotated crops, and used other methods to keep their land productive.

Farm tools were simple. Most were handmade or bought from local blacksmiths. The hoe was used to cultivate corn, tobacco, and other crops. Colonial women and children often did the hoeing. Colonists used scythes and sickles to cut grass and grain, and spades to turn the earth. The *mattock*, a tool like a pickax but with flat blades, broke up soil and cut roots. During the 1700s, more farmers began using wood plows pulled by teams of horses or oxen to prepare soil for planting.

The kinds of crops planted varied among the colonies. Farmers in New England grew grains and garden crops. In general, the soil there was too poor and the farms too small to produce crops for trade. However, the Connecticut Valley grew some tobacco for export, and Rhode Island developed a dairy industry.

Farms in the Middle Colonies benefited from fertile soil and a favorable climate. The Middle Colonies shipped large quantities of wheat, corn, rye, dairy products, and meat to colonial and international markets. They produced so much grain that they became known as the "bread colonies."

The plantations of the Chesapeake Colonies grew tobacco for export. Large farms in the region produced wheat and meat. Farmers in South Carolina and Georgia exported rice and, after 1750,

The vast timber resources of the colonies helped them develop a thriving shipbuilding industry.

indigo. Most farms in North Carolina were small, and farmers there generally grew only enough food for their own use.

Fishing and whaling. Massachusetts became the center of colonial fishing and whaling. The region was close to the Grand Banks, off Newfoundland, and other rich fishing areas. Boston, Gloucester, Marblehead, and Salem became the most important fishing ports. The catches included cod, herring, halibut, and mackerel, which were dried and salted on shore. The best grades of fish usually went to southern Europe. Much of the rest was shipped to the West Indies to be used as food for the slaves who worked on sugar plantations.

New Bedford, Provincetown, and Nantucket Island became centers for whaling. Whales were valuable for whale oil, which was used in lamps, and for whalebone, which was used to stiffen women's clothes.

Lumbering and shipbuilding. Every colony had large supplies of timber, and lumber became one of the chief exports of the colonies. Colonists built houses, fences, and boats from wood. Many wood products also played an important part in other colonial industries. Millions of wooden staves were used to make barrels for shipping rice, tobacco, fish, and other products.

The vast timber resources of the colonies helped them develop a thriving shipbuilding industry. New England was the main colonial shipbuilding center, though the Chesapeake Colonies and South Carolina were important in the industry as well. New England forests provided good ship timber, including cedar, maple, and oak. The tall and thick white pines of the region were used for ship masts. Pine also provided pitch and tar for keeping ships watertight. The live oak trees of the Chesapeake Colonies and South Carolina also provided excellent shipbuilding timber.

England encouraged colonial shipbuilding because its own best timber had been used up. By the end of the colonial period, about a third of the United Kingdom's merchant ships were being made in America.

Ironmaking. Iron ore was mined in most of the colonies. The colonists obtained charcoal, the chief fuel used to smelt iron ore, from their large supplies of hardwood trees. Colonists began operating a blast furnace near Jamestown in 1621, but it was destroyed during an Indian raid in 1622. In 1646, the first North American ironworks to maintain production for a long period started in what is now Saugus, Massachusetts. By 1775, the colonies were producing about one-seventh of the world's iron.

Some colonial iron went to England in crude forms known as *pig iron* and *bar iron* for English workers to finish. But the colonists themselves provided the most important market for the ironmaking industry. Blacksmiths in colonial communities hammered out various products, including nails, tools, hinges, and weather vanes. Large ironworks also manufactured these products, as well as kettles, pots, wire, and parts for wagons and carriages.

Other industries in the colonies included brewing, papermaking, ropemaking, and tanning. Some colonial towns became centers for craft manufacturing, such as glassmaking or silversmithing. Many industries developed because communities needed certain products or services. Almost as soon as a colonial village was established, for example, someone set up a grist mill to grind grain into flour or meal. As the community grew, it needed a blacksmith to make and repair tools and a cooper to make barrels. Skilled carpenters and shoemakers also established businesses throughout the colonies.

Trade. England regulated the trade of the colonies according to an economic system known as *mercantilism.* English mercantilism was designed to protect the nation's industries against competition from the industries of other countries. Under mercantilism, England expected the colonies to supply it with raw materials and to buy finished English goods.

Beginning in 1651, Parliament passed a series of laws aimed at strengthening the English government's control over colonial trade. These laws,

which were called the Navigation Acts, required the colonies to export certain items only to England or other English colonies. These items included fur, indigo, iron, naval products, and tobacco. The Navigation Acts also required the colonies to receive almost all imports through England, and to ship and receive goods in English or colonial ships.

Colonial trade flowed in several patterns. The colonies on the North American mainland engaged in lively coastal trade among themselves. They also shipped tobacco, indigo, and lumber directly to England. Men and women traded small surpluses of yarn, cloth, cheese, poultry, eggs, ale, and garden products for goods at local markets. Colonists traded cloth, guns, and metal tools to the Indians for furs and hides. In some years, certain individual colonies might ship as many as 40,000 deerskins to Europe.

Colonial ships carried rum to Africa and grain and livestock to the West Indies. In Africa, the rum was exchanged for slaves. In the West Indies, colonial products were traded for slaves, sugar, and molasses, which was used to make rum. This trade pattern among the mainland colonies, Africa, and the West Indies is sometimes called *triangular trade.*

Some colonial ships followed another triangular trade route. These ships carried fish, lumber, meat, and grain to southern Europe, wine and fruits to England, and manufactured goods back to the colonies.

Money was scarce in the American Colonies. The English government did not allow coins to be exported from England or to be minted in the colonies. As a result, the colonists were often short of cash.

Instead of money, the colonists used a variety of forms of payment for goods. They used *barter*— that is, the direct exchange of goods or services without the use of money—for some local transactions. They also kept *book accounts*, which let people pay for goods and services over time with their own goods and services.

Barter was the main method of exchange in the fur trade with Indians. Beaded necklaces or belts known as *wampum* sometimes were used in the Indian trade. Occasionally, colonists traded wampum belts among themselves.

At one time or another, colonial governments accepted *commodity money* as a form of payment of taxes. Commodity money included beef, pork, corn, rice, flax, and certain other farm products that were assigned a certain value.

Various certificates and documents were also used as money. For example, some planters in Maryland and Virginia used tobacco certificates as money. These certificates showed that the planters had tobacco of a certain value stored in a public warehouse. The person who received such a certificate had the right to export the tobacco. After 1700, mortgages and loans expanded colonial credit and created an investment market.

The colonists also used any foreign money they could get. Many of the coins in the colonies were Spanish gold or silver money, including dollar pieces. The coins came to the colonies in trade from the West Indies and were given a value in terms of English pounds, shillings, and pence.

From 1652 to 1682, Massachusetts produced several kinds of silver coins despite an English law that said only the monarch could issue coins. Coins issued by Massachusetts included the *pine-tree shilling* and the *oak-tree shilling*. The colony dated all coins 1652, no matter when they were made. In 1652, there was no monarch in England. In this way, the colonists could claim the coins were minted at a time when royal authority did not exist and therefore were legal. In the 1700s, several colonies issued paper money that they accepted for payment of taxes. Shortly before the Revolutionary War in America, England passed several laws to stop this practice.

A Visitor's Guide to Colonial America

Every year, millions of visitors tour the region that was once colonial America. Throughout the region, historic sites offer interesting glimpses of colonial life. Almost every town or city has churches or houses that date from the 1700s and a few from the 1600s. In some places, a visitor may walk through the streets of an entire colonial community that has been rebuilt. Many public buildings and museums display colonial items in cities that were important during colonial times— Boston; Charleston, South Carolina; New York City; Newport, Rhode Island; and Philadelphia. Newport has more than 300 colonial buildings.

MLA Citation

"Colonial Life in America." *The Southwestern Advantage Topic Source*. Nashville: Southwestern. 2013.

DATA

Important Dates in Colonial Government

1619	The House of Burgesses met in Jamestown. It was the first elected legislative assembly in America.
1620	The *Mayflower Compact* was signed by Pilgrims aboard the *Mayflower*, the ship that brought them to the New World. The compact became the first agreement for self-government enacted in America and served as the basis for the government of the Plymouth Colony.
1639	The Connecticut Colony adopted the Fundamental Orders as its law. The orders gave voters the right to elect government officials. They are regarded by some scholars as the first written constitution.
1641	Massachusetts Bay Colony set down its first code of laws in a document known as the *Body of Liberties*.
1774	The First Continental Congress, a convention of delegates from the American Colonies, met in Philadelphia. The Congress grew out of a desire for unity that had spread throughout the colonies. The meeting set forth the position of the colonies toward taxation and trade.
1775	The Second Continental Congress met in Philadelphia. It took on many governmental duties and helped unite the colonies against Britain.

DATA
Important Dates in Colonial Religion

1629	The first non-Separatist Congregational Church in America was established in Salem, Massachusetts.
1647	A law passed in Massachusetts made it illegal for Roman Catholic priests to enter territory under Puritan control.
1649	Maryland passed a religious toleration act. This law granted religious liberty to all Christians.
1675	Massachusetts passed a law requiring church doors to be locked during services to keep people from leaving during long sermons.
1692	Witchcraft trials were held in Salem, Massachusetts.
1730s	The revival movement known as the Great Awakening began in the colonies.

Important Dates in Colonial Science and Medicine

1693	A yellow fever epidemic struck Boston.
1721	The first smallpox inoculations in America were given in Boston by the physician Zabdiel Boylston. He had been urged to do so by the Puritan minister Cotton Mather.
1728	Botanist John Bartram opened the first botanical garden in the colonies, near Philadelphia.
1748	Jared Eliot, a New England minister, physician, and farmer, began publishing *An Essay on Field Husbandry in New England*, in which he attempted to apply scientific principles to agriculture.
1752	Benjamin Franklin proved that lightning is electricity.
1767	David Rittenhouse, an astronomer and instrument maker from Philadelphia, built an instrument called an *orrery*, which showed the positions of the planets in the solar system.

ADDITIONAL RESOURCES

Books to Read

Level I

America Speaks. 10 vols. Grolier, 2005.

Colonial Life. 5 vols. M. E. Sharpe, 2008.

Hakim, Joy. *A History of US, Vol. 2: Making Thirteen Colonies.* 3rd ed. Oxford, 2005.

Roberts, Russell. *Holidays and Celebrations in Colonial America.* Mitchell Lane, 2007.

Worth, Richard. *Colonial America.* Enslow, 2006.

Level II

Ciment, James, ed. *Colonial America: An Encyclopedia of Social, Political, Cultural, and Economic History.* 5 vols. Sharpe Reference, 2006.

Eden, Trudy. *The Early American Table: Food and Society in the New World.* Northern Illinois University Press, 2008.

Jaycox, Faith. *The Colonial Era.* Facts on File, 2002.

Moore, Susan H. *Pilgrims: New World Settlers and the Call of Home*. Yale, 2007.

Vickers, Daniel, ed. *A Companion to Colonial America*. Wiley, 2003.

Web Sites

Colonial National Historical Park

http://www.nps.gov/colo/

National Park Service site on Colonial National Historical Park in Jamestown and Yorktown, Virginia.

Jamestown Rediscovery

http://preservationvirginia.org/

Interesting images and descriptions of the archaeological search for and discovery of the remains of the first permanent English settlement in the New World, including historical profiles, from the Association for the Preservation of Virginia.

Search Strings

Self-Sufficient Towns

Colonial Life in America Jamestown Indians (26,600)

Colonial Life in America Jamestown Indians self-sufficient (751)

Colonial Life in America Jamestown Indians self-sufficient towns (698)

Effects of Colonists and Indians on Each Other

Colonial Life in America effects of colonists and Indians on each other (257,000)

Effect of Colonists and Indians on each other in America (78,000)

Effect of Colonists and Indians on each other in America Squanto trade farm battles (684)

The Thirteen Colonies

America thirteen colonies (205,000)

America thirteen colonies "New England" "Middle Colonies" "Chesapeake Colonies" "Southern Colonies" (537)

original "thirteen colonies" in America (240,000)

Structure of Colonial Society

America structure of colonial society (156,000)

America structure of colonial society "social classes" (15,000)

America structure of colonial society "social classes" gentry "middle class" "lower class" "indentured servants" slaves (33)

Great Depression

The Great Depression was a worldwide economic slump of the 1930s. It was the worst and longest period of high unemployment and low business activity in the twentieth century.

HOT topics

Stock Market Crash. From 1925 to 1929, the average price of shares on the New York Stock Exchange more than doubled. Rising share prices encouraged many people to speculate—that is, buy shares in hope of making large profits following future price increases. In 1928 and 1929, the Federal Reserve System raised interest rates in an effort to slow stock market speculation. The higher interest rates led to a reduction in consumer spending and construction spending. Share prices dropped rapidly on Thursday, October 24, 1929, now known as Black Thursday, then again the following Tuesday. Thousands of people lost huge sums of money as share prices fell about 80 percent. The crash began a ripple effect that crippled many institutions of the American and world economy.

DEFINITIONS

money supply: the total available currency circulating outside banks and the demand deposits in banks at a given time in a country.

inflation: an increase of the currency of a country issuing much paper money. A sharp and sudden rise in prices resulting from a too great expansion in paper money or bank credit.

gold standard: the use of gold as the standard of value for the money of a country. A nation's unit of money value is declared by the government to be equal to and exchangeable for a certain amount of gold. A modification of this is the gold bullion standard, in which there is no coinage of gold, and domestic currency can be redeemed with gold bullion only when demanded in large amounts.

hobo: a person who wanders about and lives by begging or doing odd jobs; tramp. A migratory workman.

HOT topics

The Human Toll. Human suffering became a reality for millions of Americans during the Depression. Many died of disease resulting from malnutrition. Thousands lost their homes because they could not pay their mortgages. Hundreds of thousands of young people wandered through the country seeking food, clothing, shelter, and a job. Many traveled in freight trains and lived near train yards in camps called *hobo jungles*. Adding to the misery, severe droughts and dust storms hit parts of the Midwest and Southwest during the 1930s. The afflicted region became known as the Dust Bowl, and thousands of farm families were wiped out.

Transients near Los Angeles, California, 1936

The New Deal. President Franklin D. Roosevelt believed the federal government had the chief responsibility of fighting the Depression. He called Congress into a special session to pass laws to relieve the Depression. Roosevelt called his program the New Deal. It had three main purposes. First, it attempted to provide relief for the needy. Second, it sought to aid recovery by providing jobs and by forming partnerships between government, consumers, and businesses. Third, the laws tried to reform business and government so that such a severe depression would never happen again.

Long-Term Effects. Since the Depression, both Democratic and Republican administrations in the United States have broadened the powers of the federal government. In addition, governments worldwide have changed their basic philosophy of spending. Governments since the 1930s are more willing to reduce taxes or increase government purchases to stimulate production and spending. In addition, they have gained greater understanding of how central banks can help fight recessions by changing the money supply and interest rates.

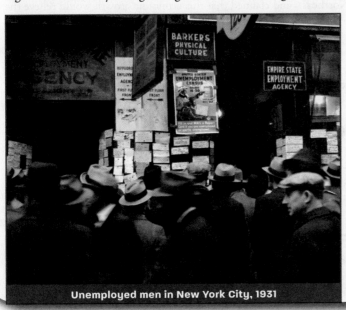
Unemployed men in New York City, 1931

TRUE or FALSE?

Many people who lost their homes moved to a shabby section of town and built shacks from flattened tin cans and old crates. Groups of these shacks were called *Hoovervilles*, after President Herbert Hoover, who many blamed for failing to end the Depression.

THE BASICS

The Great Depression was a worldwide economic slump of the 1930s. It ranked as the worst and longest period of high unemployment and low business activity in the 1900s. Banks, factories, and shops closed, and farms halted production. Millions of people were left jobless and penniless. Many people had to depend on the government or charity to provide them with food.

In the United States, the decline in industrial production began in the second half of 1929. The economic downturn worsened in October 1929, when values of stocks dropped dramatically. Thousands of shareholders lost large sums of money, and by 1930, consumer spending had fallen sharply. Many other countries—especially major producers of raw materials and agricultural goods—experienced a decline in economic activity in the late 1920s. Rising unemployment, declining production, and falling prices spread rapidly to the rest of the world in the early 1930s. The Depression caused a decrease in world trade, as countries tried to help their own industries by increasing restrictions on imports. The impact of the Great Depression varied from country to country.

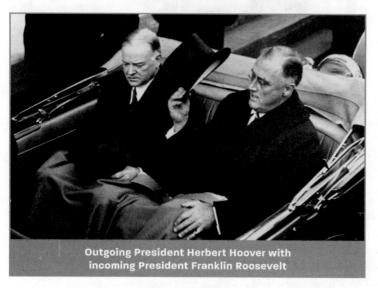

Outgoing President Herbert Hoover with
incoming President Franklin Roosevelt

The Great Depression had significant effects on people's beliefs and on government policies. It caused some nations to change their leaders and their types of government. In the United States, President Herbert Hoover held office when the Great Depression began. But soaring unemployment and declining output led to the election of Franklin D. Roosevelt in 1932. The Roosevelt administration introduced a number of policies that transformed the role of the government in the economy.

The Depression affected the governments of other nations as well. The poor economic conditions contributed to the rise of the German dictator Adolf Hitler and to the Japanese invasion of China. The German people supported Hitler in part because his plans to make Germany a world leader gave them hope for improved conditions. The Japanese developed industries and mines in Manchuria, a region of China now called the Northeast, and claimed that this economic growth would relieve the Depression in Japan. The militarism of Germany and Japan helped bring about World War II (1939–1945).

Recovery from the Depression began as many countries *devalued* (lowered the value of) their currencies and increased the *money supply*—that is, the amount of money in circulation. Economic conditions further improved after nations increased their production of war materials at the start of World War II. This increased level of production substantially reduced unemployment.

The Beginning of the Great Depression

Many factors helped set the stage for the Great Depression. In Europe, World War I (1914–1918) caused devastation and economic chaos. Many countries struggled to adjust to postwar *inflation* (price increases). The United States experienced a major agricultural slump and a number of bank failures in the 1920s. And the stock market crash of 1929 caused many people to panic and lose confidence in the state of the economy.

Aftermath of World War I. World War I cost the fighting nations a total of about $337 billion. Nations raised part of the money through taxes. But most of the money came from borrowing, which created huge debts. In addition, many governments printed extra money to meet their needs. The increased money supply caused severe inflation after the war.

Many businesses shut down after workers left for military service. Other businesses shifted to the production of war materials. Global agricultural markets expanded greatly in Australia, Canada, South

America, and other areas to meet wartime demand. After the war ended, Europe faced new competition in many export markets. In most European countries, many returning soldiers could not find jobs.

The gold standard. Prior to World War I, many countries used the *gold standard*—that is, they set the value of their national currencies at a certain weight of gold. Under this standard, the rates at which one currency could be exchanged for another were fixed by their values in gold. But during the war, many governments abandoned these fixed exchange rates to help finance their debts from the war.

After the war ended, most governments brought back the gold standard in an effort to provide price stability and to halt inflation. However, the return to fixed currency values hurt many countries that had seen prices rise following the war. The return to the gold standard also limited the ability of government leaders to offset declining production and prices by increasing the amount of money in circulation.

The farm depression and bank failures. As economies recovered from World War I, stock markets in many countries soared. However, most U.S. farmers during this time did not prosper. As a result of increased global production, prices of farm products fell by about 40 percent in 1920 and 1921, and they remained low throughout the 1920s. Some farmers, who had hoped that the high prices and expanded production opportunities of wartime would continue, borrowed heavily. Many of these farmers lost so much money that they could not pay the mortgages on their farms. These farmers then had to either rent their land or move.

Bank failures increased during the 1920s. Most of them occurred in agricultural areas because farmers experienced such poor conditions. More than 5,000 U.S. banks went out of business from 1921 to 1929.

The stock market crash. During the 1920s, demand for consumer goods and new products such as radios, electrical appliances, and automobiles led to increased production and business profits. Many of these goods were purchased using *installment contracts*, by which goods are purchased on credit and ownership is transferred after the last payment is made.

From 1925 to 1929, the average price of shares on the New York Stock Exchange more than dou-

bled. Rising share prices encouraged many people to *speculate*—that is, buy shares in hope of making large profits following future price increases. In 1928 and 1929, the Federal Reserve System—the central banking organization of the United States—raised interest rates in an effort to slow stock market speculation. The higher interest rates led to a reduction in consumer spending and construction spending.

Share prices dropped rapidly on Thursday, October 24, 1929, now known as Black Thursday. Most share prices remained steady on Friday and Saturday. But the following Monday, share prices fell again. Then, on Tuesday, October 29, shareholders panicked and sold a record 16,410,030 shares. Thousands of people lost huge sums of money as share prices fell about 80 percent. Share prices fluctuated and fell for the next three years.

Increased uncertainty about the future of the economy led consumers to cut back on purchases of goods and services. In addition, to avoid being unable to pay for goods purchased on installment plans, many consumers further reduced their spending. As a result of the dramatic decline in consumer spending, output and production fell sharply in late 1929 and in 1930.

The seal of the Federal Reserve System

The higher interest rates in the United States helped spread the Depression to other parts of the world. To maintain a fixed exchange rate with the United States, other countries had to raise their interest rates as well. The higher interest rates led to reductions in household and business spending, which in turn led to declines in production.

A breadline in New York City, 1932

The Deepening Depression in the United States

From October 1929 until early 1933, the U.S. economy slumped almost every month. Business failures increased rapidly among banks, factories, and stores, and unemployment soared. Millions of people lost their jobs, savings, and homes.

Economic breakdown. Because of falling stock prices, banks and investors lost large sums of money. Banks had also loaned money to many farmers and businesses who were unable to repay it. Bank profits declined, and bank customers worried that their savings were not safe. Many customers withdrew their

money from the banks, further straining the health of the banking system. Between January 1930 and March 1933, about 9,000 banks failed. The bank failures wiped out the savings of millions of people.

Bank failures made less money available for loans to industry. The decline in available money caused a drop in production and a further rise in unemployment, and it severely prolonged the Depression. The Federal Reserve could not increase the money in circulation because the U.S. maintained a fixed exchange rate. From 1929 to 1933, the total value of goods and services produced annually in the United States fell from about $104 billion to about $56 billion.

In 1925, about 3 percent of the nation's workers were unemployed. The unemployment rate reached about 9 percent in 1930 and about 25 percent—or about 13 million people—in 1933. Many people who kept or found jobs had to take salary cuts. In 1932, wage cuts averaged about 18 percent. Many people, including college graduates, felt lucky to find any job. A popular song of the 1930s called "Brother, Can You Spare a Dime?" expressed the nationwide despair.

World trade collapsed during the Great Depression, due in part to the Smoot-Hawley Tariff Act of 1930. This law greatly increased a number of tariffs on a variety of imported goods. President Hoover signed the law because he thought it would reduce competition from foreign products. But other nations soon reacted by raising tariffs on imported goods.

Declining prices were a serious problem during the Depression,

as farmers and businesses received less money for their products and services. From 1929 to 1933, consumer prices fell by about 25 percent and prices of farm goods fell more than 50 percent. Farmers produced a surplus of crops, which pushed prices down because there was more food than people could buy. Falling prices led to rising debt burdens for borrowers and bankruptcy for many farmers. In addition, falling prices caused many consumers to delay purchases because they anticipated that prices would be even lower in the future.

Human suffering became a reality for millions of Americans as the Depression continued. Many died of disease resulting from malnutrition. Thousands lost their homes because they could not pay their mortgages. In 1932, at least 25,000 families and more than 200,000 young people wandered through the country seeking food, clothing, shelter, and a job. Many youths traveled in freight trains and lived near train yards in camps called *hobo jungles*. Some homeless, jobless travelers obtained food from welfare agencies or religious missions in towns along the way. Many travelers became ill because they lacked proper food and clothing.

Many people who lost their homes remained in the community. Some crowded into the home of a relative. Others moved to a shabby section of town and built shacks from flattened tin cans and old crates. Groups of these shacks were called *Hoovervilles*, a name that reflected the people's anger and disappointment at President Herbert Hoover's failure to end the Depression.

The Depression did not affect all groups equally. In most U.S. cities and in the South, unemployment rates were much higher for African Americans than for whites. Similarly, women often faced greater difficulty finding jobs than men did. The suffering of the Depression also brought heightened discrimination against Mexican Americans. Many people considered them a drain on the economy because they held many low-paying jobs while other Americans went unemployed. During the 1930s, thousands of Mexican Americans were deported against their wishes.

In 1932, many farmers refused to ship their products to market. They hoped a reduced supply of farm products would help raise the price of these goods. Such farmers' strikes occurred throughout the country, but they centered in Iowa and the surrounding states.

Severe droughts and dust storms hit parts of the Midwest and Southwest during the 1930s. The afflicted region became known as the *Dust Bowl*, and thousands of farm families there were wiped out. Some farmers fled to the fertile agricultural areas of California to look for work. Most who found jobs had to work as fruit or vegetable pickers for extremely low wages. The migrant families crowded into shacks near the fields or camped outdoors. The American author John Steinbeck's famous novel *The Grapes of Wrath* (1939) describes the hardships some migrant families faced during the Depression.

U.S. Policies to Combat the Depression

Hoover's policies. President Hoover believed that business, if left alone to operate without government supervision, would correct the economic conditions. He vetoed several bills aimed at relieving the Depression because he felt they gave the federal government too much power.

Hoover declared that state and local governments should provide relief to the needy. But those governments did not have enough money to do so. In 1932, Congress approved Hoover's most successful measure for fighting the Depression, the Reconstruction Finance Corporation (RFC). This agency provided some relief by lending money to banks, railroads, and other large institutions whose failure would have made the Depression even worse. However, most Americans felt that Hoover did not do enough to fight the Depres-

sion, and voters elected Franklin D. Roosevelt president in 1932.

The New Deal. Roosevelt believed the federal government had the chief responsibility of fighting the Depression. He called Congress into a special session, now called the *Hundred Days*, to pass laws to relieve the Depression. Roosevelt called his program the *New Deal*.

The laws established by the New Deal had three main purposes. First, they attempted to provide relief for the needy. Second, they sought to aid recovery by providing jobs and by forming partnerships between government, consumers, and businesses. Third, the laws tried to reform business and government so that such a severe depression would never happen again.

Congress created several agencies to manage relief programs. The Federal Emergency Relief Administration (FERA), founded in 1933, gave the states money for the needy and helped local charities with relief efforts. The Civilian Conservation Corps (CCC), also established in 1933, employed thousands of young men in conservation projects. The Public Works Administration (PWA), another agency founded in 1933, provided money and jobs for the construction of bridges, dams, and schools. The Works Progress Administration (WPA), created in 1935, provided jobs in public projects such as road building, flood control, and the construction of airports, hospitals, schools, and parks. It also provided work in the arts. In 1939, this agency's name was changed to Work Projects Administration. These work relief programs provided several million jobs during the Depression, but unemployment remained high throughout the 1930s.

Members of the Civilian Conservation Corps

Some New Deal agencies established and managed recovery programs. The Agricultural Adjustment Administration (AAA), set up in 1933, transformed agricultural markets by regulating farm production. The National Recovery Administration (NRA), also created in 1933, set up and enforced rules of fair practice for business and industry. The codes enforced minimum wages and maximum hours of work, set limits on output, and established minimum prices. However, this partnership with business showed little effect on stimulating the economy, and the codes were ruled unconstitutional in 1935.

Congress created several agencies to supervise banking and labor reforms. To restore confidence in the banking system, the Federal Deposit Insurance Corporation (FDIC) was established in 1933 to insure commercial bank deposits. The Securities and Exchange Commission (SEC), created in 1934, regulated stock markets and tried to protect investors from buying unsafe stocks and bonds. The National Labor Relations Board (NLRB), created in 1935, worked to prevent unfair labor practices and to protect workers' rights to form and join unions. In 1935, Congress passed the Social Security Act to provide money for retired and unemployed individuals.

The recovery from the Depression. The New Deal programs helped relieve some of the worst human suffering of the Depression. The government also increased trade by lowering tariffs on certain imported goods. In return, other nations lowered tariffs on some products that they imported from the United States. However, the economy substantially improved only after the United States abandoned the gold standard, devalued the dollar, increased the money supply, and helped the banking system to recover.

Despite the various government programs, about 15 percent of the nation's working force still did not have a job in 1940. Unemployment did not substantially decline until 1942, after the country had entered World War II. The great increase in production of war materials provided so many jobs that the U.S. unemployment rate fell to about 1 percent in 1944.

The Depression Throughout the World

Effects in Canada. At the time of the Great Depression, Canada's national economy depended on the export of grain and raw materials. Canadian farmers and exporters suffered huge losses after other countries increased tariffs on imported products and farm prices continued to fall. Many Canadian companies closed, and the unemployment rate rose from about 3 percent of the labor force in 1929 to about 23 percent in 1933.

Richard B. Bennett, who served as prime minister from 1930 to 1935, had little success in his efforts to relieve the Depression in Canada. W. L. Mackenzie King succeeded Bennett and adopted programs similar to those of Roosevelt to fight the Depression.

Effects in Europe. People in Europe faced homelessness and unemployment at alarming rates. Studies carried out in the United Kingdom between 1934 and 1938 showed that 19 percent of the people were on a substandard diet. Hunger marches—the most famous being one in 1936 from Jarrow, in northeastern England, to London—were attempts to gain publicity for the plight of thousands of people.

Along with homelessness and unemployment, one of the most significant effects of the Depression in Europe was the rise of extremist political parties. In the United Kingdom, both the Communist Party and the British Union of Fascists received popular support in run-down areas of many inner cities. But extremism was most apparent in Germany, where Adolf Hitler seized the chance to win the backing of many Germans dis-

Some of the Jarrow marchers

satisfied with the leadership of their country after World War I. He persuaded many Germans that he would make them proud of their nation once again. Hitler gained control of the country in 1933. He soon began the rearmament of Germany, which put industry back to work again and reduced unemployment, but ultimately helped lead to World War II.

Effects in Australia. The rate of unemployment was even higher in Australia than that recorded in the United States and the United Kingdom in the worst years. Economic historians estimate that 30 percent of the workforce in Australia was unemployed in 1932. Exports fell dramatically in 1930, and prices dropped steadily from 1930 to 1933. As in Europe, extremist politics appeared in Australia. Many people voted for the Communist Party and backed New State movements, which supported setting up a number of separate states from those that already existed.

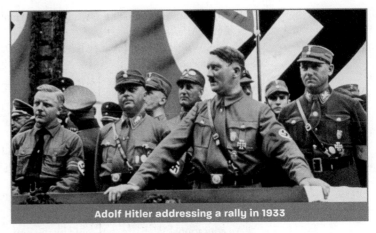
Adolf Hitler addressing a rally in 1933

Long-Term Effects of the Depression

New government policies. Following the Great Depression, many countries began to provide better welfare benefits for the poor. In the United States, laws of the New Deal gave the government more power to provide money for the needy and the elderly. Since the Depression, both Democratic and Republican administrations in the United States have broadened the powers of the federal government.

In addition, many governments changed their basic philosophy of spending as a result of the Great Depression. Before the Depression, they had tried to spend the same amount of money as they collected, even during economic downturns. But since the 1930s, governments have been more willing to reduce taxes or increase government purchases to stimulate production and spending.

In addition, they have gained greater understanding of how central banks can help fight recessions by changing the money supply and interest rates.

New public attitudes. The Great Depression changed the attitudes of many people toward business and government. Before the Depression, many people regarded bankers and business executives as national leaders. After the stock markets crashed and these leaders could not relieve the Depression, people lost faith in them. As a result, many people decided that the government—not business—had the responsibility to manage the national economy.

The Depression also changed people's attitudes toward unemployment. People came to view unemployment not as a personal shortcoming but as a condition that can result from circumstances beyond the individual's control.

MLA Citation

"Great Depression."
*The Southwestern Advantage
Topic Source.* Nashville:
Southwestern. 2013.

ADDITIONAL RESOURCES

Books to Read

Dickstein, Morris. *Dancing in the Dark: A Cultural History of the Great Depression.* Norton, 2009.

Greenberg, Cheryl L. *To Ask for an Equal Chance: African Americans in the Great Depression.* Rowman & Littlefield, 2009.

Gup, Ted. *A Secret Gift: How One Man's Kindness—and a Trove of Letters—Revealed the Hidden History of the Great Depression.* Penguin Press, 2010.

Rauchway, Eric. *The Great Depression and the New Deal: A Very Short Introduction.* Oxford, 2008.

Roth, Benjamin. *The Great Depression: A Diary.* Edited by James Ledbetter and Daniel B. Roth. PublicAffairs, 2009.

Young, William H. and Nancy K. *The Great Depression in America: A Cultural Encyclopedia.* 2 vols. Greenwood, 2007.

Web Sites

America in the 1930s

http://xroads.virginia.edu/~1930s/front.html

America in the 1930s is a continuing project of the American Studies Program at the University of Virginia. The project views the 1930s through the lenses of its films, radio programs, literature, journalism, museums, exhibitions, architecture

New Deal Network

http://newdeal.feri.org/

An educational Web site sponsored by the Franklin and Eleanor Roosevelt Institute and the Institute for Learning Technologies at Teachers College/Columbia University. This site features classroom activities, photographs, and links to other Web sites.

The 1920s and the Start of the Depression, 1921–1933

http://www.dol.gov/oasam/programs/history/main.htm

A description of the U.S. Department of Labor's role during the years preceding the Great Depression. From an online edition of a history prepared for the 75th anniversary of the agency.

Search Strings

Stock Market Crash

Great Depression Stock Market Crash (99,800)

Great Depression Stock Market Crash New York speculate (31,700)

Great Depression Stock Market Crash New York speculate Federal Reserve (17,000)

The Human Toll

Great Depression human suffering malnutrition hobo (373)

Great Depression human toll Dust Bowl (113,000)

Great Depression human toll Dust Bowl hobo jungles (872)

The New Deal

"The New Deal" President Franklin Roosevelt Great Depression (180,000)

"The New Deal" President Franklin Roosevelt Great Depression relief jobs reform (43,900)

"The New Deal" President Franklin Roosevelt Great Depression relief jobs reform laws Congress (38,300)

Long-Term Effects

Great Depression long-term effects federal government powers taxes central banks (634,000)

great depression long-term effects banking governments taxes money supply interest rates (42,900)

long-term effects of the Great Depression on the federal government, taxes, central banks, money supply, interest rates (372,000)

long-term effects of the "Great Depression" on the "federal government" taxes "central banks" "money supply" "interest rates" (10,300)

BACKGROUND INFORMATION

The following article was written during the year in which the events took place and reflects the style and thinking of that time.

Agriculture (1934)

Recovery from the great depression became a reality for American agriculture in 1934, notwithstanding the fact that the year brought the worst drought ever recorded in this country.

Farm income increased. The average farmer had a small profit left after paying interest, taxes, wages, and the other expenses of producing his crops and livestock. However, by comparison with farm earning before the war or even with farm earnings between 1921 and 1929, the showing in 1934 was poor; yet contrasted with the great losses suffered by farmers in 1930, 1931, and 1932, the modest gains of 1934 looked like the herald of a new day.

Payments by the government to farmers on contracts for crop adjustments supplemented the income from crops sold, with the result that the total cash income in 1934 exceeded that of 1933 by 19 percent and that of 1932 by no less than 39 percent.

The cash income from crops is, of course, gross—from it farmers must deduct all their expenses. Therefore a large cash income does not necessarily mean a large net profit. The 1934 cash income, however, sufficed to provide a profit after farmers had paid their fixed charges and costs of production; whereas in 1932 farmers recorded a heavy net loss and in 1933 only a trifling balance on the right side of the ledger.

Unequal recovery. The improvement in 1934 did not benefit all farmers and all farm regions equally. Most farmers in areas of the worst drought earned less than in the preceding year. They got more per bushel or per head of livestock for the products they sold; but they had a much reduced output. Some states outside the drought area had the double advantage of good crops and good prices. Farmers in such states realized incomes far above the national average. Even in the areas of crop failure, however, farmers received payments from the government on crop-adjustment contracts. These payments served as a kind of crop insurance.

For the country as a whole, the drought affected mainly the distribution rather than the amount of the farm income. Higher prices tended to offset the reduction in marketings. For the calendar year the estimated cash farm income, including rental and benefit payments, amounted to $6,000,000,000, compared with $5,051,000,000 in 1933 and $4,328,000,000 in 1932. Moreover, for the first time since 1920, farm real estate values increased for the country as a whole. Farmers obtained an increase in the value of their capital as well as in the amount of their current income. Broadly stated, 1934 lifted agriculture "out of the red," and laid the foundation for further improvement.

The milk producers' strike. The only serious disturbance involving farmers took place in the Chicago milk area in January. Under a marketing agreement sponsored by the Agricultural Adjustment Administration (AAA) the dairymen in this region had received toward the end of 1933 a price of $2.10 per hundred pounds for Class 1 milk at all stations within a seventy-mile radius. This agreement had been terminated. Officials of the AAA declared conditions did not warrant so high a price in a new agreement.

Accordingly, the Pure Milk Producers' Association called a strike, in which from 18,000 to 20,000 farmers participated, and which within a week deprived Chicago of milk except for hospitals and certain other public institutions. Finally, the producers accepted a compromise price subject to change with changing conditions. Strike rumors developed in other areas during the year but there were no serious strikes.

Farmers began to realize that the best way to achieve results was to act before planting and to grow only what could be profitably sold. Millions of farmers were doing essentially that already through crop adjustments and marketing agreements under the Agricultural Adjustment Act. They were getting results. They had substituted an orderly control of production and marketing for disorderly and irrational local revolts.

Farm strikes usually served only to draw public attention to agricultural distress. That had already been done. As a result partly of the government's monetary policy and partly of co-operative crop adjustments, farm prices had advanced. Subsequently, the drought caused a further rise. In addition, farmers were getting debt relief through the Federal Farm Credit Administration. They perceived that farm relief was under way; that there were available through national agricultural planning means for effectively influencing prices and production; and that they could obtain relief from the crushing burden of their debts. Farm strikes, holiday movements, and violent interruptions of highway and railway traffic had no longer any point.

Farm relief. Relief came to the farmers through the following three channels: dollar devaluation; the AAA and debt relief.

Dollar Devaluation was one channel of relief. In April 1933, the federal government suspended gold payments on foreign account and allowed the value of the American dollar in foreign exchange to decline. This action almost immediately caused an advance in the prices of commodities that were heavily exported, such as wheat, cotton, and tobacco, without immediately requiring farmers to pay higher prices for the things they bought. The benefits of dollar devaluation to agriculture continued in 1934. Although it will not be possible for many years to assay the full effects, there is no doubt that devaluation of the dollar in the beginning, at any rate, aided agriculture.

The AAA. The second main relief channel was the Agricultural Adjustment Administration. In 1933 this new governmental agency, exercising authority conferred upon it by Congress to organize farmers in co-operative production adjustments, launched acreage control programs affecting cotton, wheat, tobacco, and corn and hogs. These programs were followed up in 1934. The AAA promoted scores of marketing agreements designed to regulate the movement of farm products into consumption and, in some cases, to adjust the volume of production. Farm income from lint cotton increased 89 percent between 1932 and 1933; from tobacco, 67 percent; and from wheat, 88 percent. Farm income from hogs increased from $548,000,000 in 1932 to $619,000,000 in 1933. Corresponding figures for 1934 were not yet available when this was written but, as previously noted, the year brought additional gains. Crop adjustment under the AAA, though not the sole cause of this improvement, was undoubtedly an important cause.

Drought reduced farm production in 1934 far more than the acreage restrictions alone would have done and reduced some crops far more than was desirable. The drought extended over 75 percent of the area of the country, severely affected twenty-seven states, and reduced tremendously the production of feed, forage, and pastures. It reduced also the yields of food grains and cotton and necessitated a tremendous reduction in livestock numbers. Surpluses of cotton, wheat, corn and hogs, and some types of tobacco largely disappeared. Cotton production for the year as estimated in October was only 9,443,000 bales; as compared with 17,095,000 bales in 1931. Wheat production was the smallest in forty years. Corn production dropped more than a billion bushels below the annual average of about 2,600,000,000 bushels. Total production of corn, oats, barley, and grain sorghums was only about 58,000,000 tons, as compared with an average of 101,000,000 tons for the period 1928–32. The resulting feed shortage obliged the government to purchase for immediate slaughter more than 7,000,000 cattle and several million head of sheep and goats.

But the adjustment programs did not make the crop shortage materially worse. These programs economized seed and labor that otherwise would have been wasted; brought about a desirable adjustment in hog, cattle, and sheep numbers; and actually increased the acreage of drought-resistant forage, pasture, and hay crops. As a result, agriculture came through the season with more grain, hay, and pasture for each grain-consuming animal than would otherwise have been available. Moreover, in some localities crop adjustment payments from the government were drought relief; they constituted the principal income of many farmers. The drought was not a blessing in disguise, even though it caused prices to advance. It was a calamity which would have been a disaster had not the crop adjustment programs tempered its effects.

Debt relief, the third main channel through which help came to agriculture, was as important as either of the other two. It saved thousands of farmers from losing their farms. Without debt relief, the benefits of dollar devaluation and of crop adjustments would have gone largely to nonfarmers in payments on land and chattel mortgages.

The Farm Credit Administration (FCA) in fifteen months following its organization arranged more than 450,000 refinancing loans to farmers.

By negotiations with creditors the FCA obtained for farmers a reduction of indebtedness amounting to more than $56,000,000. It increased the equities of the farmers in their lands and halted a threatened divorce between the operation and the ownership of farms. It reduced interest rates on Federal Land Bank loans, granted to worthy borrowers extensions of time for the payment of their loans, and provided new facilities for production credit and marketing credit. Also, the FCA established a special bank for making loans to farmers' co-operative associations.

As part of the farm relief program, the national government sought to promote better land utilization. Various government agencies cooperated in trying to find new locations for farm families living in areas unsuited to farming. These agencies developed plans for the public acquisition of submarginal lands in about thirty states; launched new projects in forestry; and strove in various ways to bring about a better allocation of land among the principal land uses—farming, forestry, recreation, and wild life conservation.

Continued crop adjustments. Toward the end of the year, the AAA declared its intention henceforth to proceed with co-operative farm adjustments, not with crop reduction in mind but to adjust the output as nearly as possible to the demand.

Agriculture had no longer enormous surpluses of wheat, cotton, tobacco, corn and hogs, and other products; but there still were more land and more farm personnel than could be employed without loss in capacity production.

Farmers, left to their own devices, often go from one extreme in production to the other. Following years of short crops, they increase their acreage and their livestock breeding. Since droughts and other natural causes of low production seldom come in successive years, acreage increased in a blind reaction from crop failures leads surely to new surpluses. This outcome, in the opinion of the AAA, could be prevented only by continued co-operative crop adjustment.

The correct adjustment of some crops might necessitate expansion; for the adjustment principle, the AAA explained, applies not only on the downturn but also on the upturn. The AAA may regulate production to a stable or to a rising demand, and may maintain a good balance among farm enterprises.

Views of the secretary of agriculture.
Henry A. Wallace, the secretary of agriculture, warned farmers against the pitfalls of scarcity economics. Farm prices, Secretary Wallace said, could be raised further by excessive restraints upon production, but he doubted if the result would be a proportionate increase in farm incomes. Production reduced below the demand, the Secretary declared, would arouse consumer resistance and stimulate foreign competition.

As an alternative Secretary Wallace recommended adequate production for domestic consumption coupled with similar activity in urban industry. Agriculture had complete justification for cutting down its output in 1933 and 1934; for, with its foreign market practically gone and the home market much impaired, unrestrained agricultural production would have meant disaster. After 1929 urban industry reduced its production far more than agriculture reduced its production. Between 1929 and 1933, while farm production dropped only 6 percent, the output of farm implements dropped 80 percent; of motor vehicles, 80 percent; of cement, 65 percent; of iron and steel, 83 percent; and of auto tires, 70 percent. In working toward a balanced abundance, the secretary said both agriculture and industry should recognize that we cannot all get richer by all producing less and less.

Subsistence homesteads. The government embarked upon subsistence farming projects in many parts of the country, mainly with funds appropriated under the National Industrial Recovery Act. Specifically, the government helped poor families to get a better living through a part-time combination of industrial employment and subsistence agriculture. The subsistence homesteads—usually one to five acres in size—enabled the occupants to produce fruits, truck crops, and poultry and, in many cases, to keep a cow. For industrial workers garden homesteads located near industrial towns and cities proved a boon to many wage earners having only part-time industrial employment.

For the protection of agriculture the government endeavored, wherever possible, to make available to the subsistence homesteaders part-time nonfarm work. Without such additional source of income, the subsistence farmer must either engage in production for the market as well as for the home table or fail to earn a decent living.

The Holocaust

The Holocaust was the systematic, state-sponsored murder of Jews and others by the Nazis during World War II (1939–1945).

HOT topics

Hitler's "Final Solution." The Nazi dictator Adolf Hitler wanted to eliminate all Jews as part of his aim to conquer the world. The Nazi leadership created a policy labeled "The Final Solution of the Jewish Question." It called for the murder of every Jewish man, woman, and child under German rule. By the end of the war, the Nazis had killed about 6 million Jewish people—more than two-thirds of the Jews in Europe. In addition to Jews, the Nazis systematically killed millions of disabled people, homosexuals, priests and ministers, Communists, Slavs, and Roma, all of whom Hitler regarded as racially inferior or politically dangerous. Historians estimate that perhaps as many as 11 million people were killed, many of them in specially constructed gas chambers; their bodies were then burned.

DEFINITIONS

genocide: the systematic extermination of a cultural or racial group.

anti-Semitism: dislike or hatred for Jews; prejudice against Jews. Action or policy reflecting this, ranging from social discrimination to physical persecution.

Nazi: a member or supporter of the National Socialist Party, a fascist political party in Germany led by Adolf Hitler; advocate of Nazism. It came to power in Germany in 1933 and believed in state control of industry, denunciation of communism and Judaism, and the dominance of Germany as a world power.

concentration camp: a camp where political enemies, prisoners of war, and interned foreigners are held.

gas chamber: a hermetically sealed room in which a poison gas is released. It has been used in some states to execute persons condemned to death and was one of the forms of extermination used in Nazi concentration camps.

HOT topics

Roots of Anti-Semitism.

The Jews faced persecution long before the Holocaust began. Anti-Semitism (prejudice against Jews) has existed since ancient times. Many early Christians mistrusted Jews because the Jews remained faithful to their own traditions and refused to convert to Christianity. In the mid-1500s, the religious reformer Martin Luther issued ferocious attacks against the Jews for not adopting his new religion. He referred to the Jews as "venomous" and called for violence against them. In many cities, the Jews were forced to live in separate communities called ghettos.

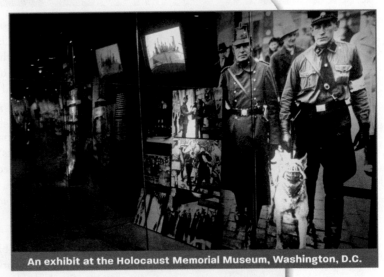

An exhibit at the Holocaust Memorial Museum, Washington, D.C.

Kristallnacht.

The Nazi's civil persecution of the Jews turned openly violent on November 9, 1938. Beginning that night and continuing for about 24 hours, Nazis destroyed thousands of Jewish-owned businesses and burned most synagogues in Germany and Austria. They beat Jews in the streets and attacked them in their homes. They killed dozens of Jews. They arrested about 30,000 Jews and sent them to concentration camps (camps for political prisoners). The night became known as *Kristallnacht*, a German word meaning "crystal night." In English, it is called the Night of Broken Glass.

The United States Holocaust Memorial Museum.

In 1980, Congress established the United States Holocaust Memorial Council to oversee the construction of a museum honoring the victims of the Holocaust. Funds for constructing the museum came entirely from private donations, including prominent backers like Jewish movie director Steven Spielberg. The Holocaust Memorial Museum, which opened in 1993 in Washington, D.C, is devoted to teaching the history of the Holocaust and preserving its memory. It features films, photographs, eyewitness accounts, and various objects from the time.

Another exhibit at the Holocaust Memorial Museum

TRUE or FALSE?

The Nazis sought impersonal and efficient methods of genocide after face-to-face killing became difficult for German soldiers.

THE BASICS

The Holocaust was the systematic, state-sponsored murder of Jews and others by the Nazis during World War II (1939–1945). The Nazi dictator Adolf Hitler wanted to eliminate all Jews as part of his aim to conquer the world. By the end of the war, the Nazis had killed about 6 million Jewish men, women, and children—more than two-thirds of the Jews in Europe.

In addition to Jews, the Nazis systematically killed millions of other people whom Hitler regarded as racially inferior or politically dangerous. The largest groups included (1) Germans with physical handicaps or mental retardation, (2) Roma (sometimes called Gypsies), and (3) Slavs, particularly Poles and Soviet prisoners of war. Nazi victims also included many homosexuals, Jehovah's Witnesses, priests and ministers, members of labor unions, and Communists and other political opponents. Historians estimate that perhaps as many as 11 million people were killed, including the Jews. Many of the Holocaust victims were killed in specially constructed gas chambers, and their bodies were then burned. The word *holocaust* means *a sacrificial offering that is completely burned.*

Before the Holocaust

The Jews had faced persecution long before the Holocaust began. *Anti-Semitism* (prejudice against Jews) has existed since ancient times. Many early Christians mistrusted Jews because the Jews remained faithful to their own traditions and refused to convert to Christianity. In the mid-1500s, the religious reformer Martin Luther issued ferocious attacks against the Jews for not adopting his new religion. He referred to the Jews as "venomous" and called for violence against them. In many cities, the Jews were forced to live in separate communities called *ghettos*. They had to pay special taxes, and they were not allowed to own land or to enter certain occupations.

Women and children in the Kutno ghetto, Kutno, Poland, 1940

In the 1800s, many people began discriminating against Jews on racial rather than religious grounds. Many anti-Semitic writers insisted that Jews were an inferior race. Anti-Semitism became a powerful force in European politics. Many people considered the Jews responsible for society's troubles. In 1881, for example, when revolutionaries assassinated Czar Alexander II of Russia, the Jews were blamed. Many Russian Jews were then killed in organized massacres called *pogroms*.

In 1894, Captain Alfred Dreyfus, a French army officer and a Jew, was accused of selling military secrets. Although the case against Dreyfus was weak, a court-martial condemned him to life imprisonment. After the verdict was announced, his opponents chanted in the streets, "Death to Dreyfus! Death to the Jews!" In 1906, he was cleared of all charges.

Adolf Hitler, the leader of the Nazi Party, became head of the German government in 1933. He quickly moved to make himself a dictator. Germany's defeat in World War I (1914–1918) and a worldwide depression in the early 1930s had left the country's economy in ruins. Hitler blamed the Jews for Germany's problems, and he made anti-Semitism a government policy.

On April 1, 1933, Hitler's government sponsored a nationwide boycott of Jewish stores and other businesses. In the next several months, the government passed a number of laws that barred Jews from specific occupations. Jews were excluded from civil service, for example, and from the fields of education and culture, and they could no longer farm the land.

The Nuremberg laws of 1935 stripped Jews of citizenship. Jews were forbidden to marry non-Jews. The laws set forth definitions of who was a Jew and who was a part-Jew, also known as a *Mischling* (mixed blood). For example, a person who had at least three Jewish grandparents was classified as a Jew. Someone with one Jewish grandparent might be classified as a Mischling.

In the next three years, the Nazi government continued to deprive Jews of their rights and possessions. Jews could not sit on park benches or swim in public pools. The government seized Jewish businesses as well as personal property. The discrimination was an effort to force Jews to emigrate so Germany would be *Judenrein* (free of Jews). Thousands of Jews did leave the country, though they were permitted to take little with them. But many Jews were trapped because other countries would not accept them in large numbers.

The Nazi persecution reached a new height on November 9, 1938. Beginning that night and continuing for about 24 hours, Nazis destroyed thousands of Jewish-owned businesses and burned most synagogues in Germany and Austria. They beat Jews in the streets and attacked them in their homes. They killed dozens of Jews. They arrested about 30,000 Jews and sent them to *concentration camps* (camps for political prisoners). The night became known as *Kristallnacht*, a German word meaning *Crystal Night*. In English, it is called the Night of Broken Glass.

The Holocaust

"The Final Solution." After World War II began in 1939, Germany's powerful war machine conquered country after country in Europe. Millions more Jews came under German control. The Nazis killed many of them and sent others to concentration camps. The Nazis also moved many Jews from towns and villages into city ghettos. They later sent these people, too, to concentration camps. Although many Jews thought the ghettos would last, the Nazis saw ghetto confinement as only a temporary measure. Sometime in early 1941, the Nazi leadership finalized the details of a policy decision labeled "The Final Solution of the Jewish Question." This policy called for the murder of every Jew—man, woman, and child—under German rule.

The slaughter began with Germany's invasion of the Soviet Union in June 1941. Special squads

Roma Holocaust survivors commemorate the 1943 decree that ordered Germany's remaining Roma sent to Auschwitz.

of Hitler's SS (Schutzstaffel) troops accompanied advancing German forces. These killing squads, called *Einsatzgruppen*, rounded up Jews, Roma, and Soviet leaders, and shot them to death one by one. The face-to-face killing became difficult for the killers, and the Nazis soon sought a more impersonal and efficient method of *genocide* (extermination of an entire people). They began using sealed vans. The prisoners choked to death on exhaust fumes as the van traveled to a burial pit.

At the Wannsee Conference, held in Berlin in January 1942, Nazi leaders further systematized the killing. They decided that Jews throughout German-occupied territory would be evacuated to concentration camps in eastern Europe. These camps would become centers for slave labor and extermination.

The camps. The first Nazi concentration camps were organized in 1933, shortly after Hitler came to power. By the late 1930s, the facilities held tens of thousands of political prisoners arrested by the Nazis. In the early 1940s, several new camps were established, with specially constructed gas chambers disguised as showers.

For the Jews who had been confined in ghettos, the next step was what the Nazis called *deportation*. The Nazis herded the Jews into railroad freight cars to be taken to the camps.

When the Jews arrived at a camp, an SS physician singled out the young and able-bodied. The others were sent directly to the gas chambers. The guards seized the belongings of those who were to die. As many as 2,000 prisoners were sent into the gas chambers at one time. SS personnel poured containers of poison gas down an opening. Within 20 to 30 minutes, the new arrivals were dead. The guards shaved the heads of the corpses and removed any gold teeth from their mouths. Then they burned the bodies in crematoriums or open pits.

The able-bodied prisoners had their heads shaved and their belongings seized. Camp personnel tattooed a number on the arm of each person. From then on, the prisoners were identified by number instead of by name. These prisoners were forced to work long hours under cruel conditions. When they were too weak to work any longer, they too were killed or left to die. There were six death camps, all in German-occupied Poland— Auschwitz, Belzec, Chelmno, Majdanek, Sobibor, and Treblinka. Auschwitz was the largest and most notorious. It was a slave labor camp as well as a killing center. About 1¼ million people were murdered there.

Hundreds of other concentration camps operated in Germany and German-occupied territories during the war. None of these camps was established solely for killing, but the conditions in all of them were so harsh that hundreds of thousands of prisoners died of starvation and disease. In some camps, a number of inmates—many of them children—died after Nazi physicians performed cruel medical experiments on them.

In the last months of the war, the Allied forces, including American, British, and Soviet troops, swept through Europe. The Nazis hastened to empty some camps to remove witnesses to their cruelty. They crowded camp inmates into boxcars or forced the prisoners to walk to other camps behind the lines. The forced marches, made in winter with few provisions, claimed so many victims that they were known as *death marches.*

Resistance. During the Holocaust, the Nazis kept their actions as secret as possible, and they deceived their victims in many ways to prevent resistance. Initially, the Jews in the ghettos either were not aware of the slaughter planned for them or simply could not believe it was happening. Some tried to pacify the Nazis, hoping they would be left in peace. Others tried sabotage or escape.

Armed resistance was not the first response of the Jews. They tried to thwart the Nazis by nonviolent means. Also, it was difficult and dangerous for the Jews to obtain weapons. Little help was available to them. Anti-Semitism was widespread, and Jewish resistance did not have popular support. Jewish fighters could not disappear among the population because non-Jews might betray them. Jewish leaders in the ghettos knew that the Nazis could kill everyone in the ghetto in revenge for the actions of a few resisters. But many Jews who managed to escape the ghettos joined secret bands of fighters against the Nazis. And some non-Jewish individuals risked their lives to smuggle Jews to safety.

Some Jews in ghettos, slave labor camps, and death camps did fight. In 1943, for example, thousands of Jews revolted in the ghetto in Warsaw, Poland. Although the Jews were surrounded and poorly armed, they held out for about four weeks. But the Nazis either killed or sent to death camps all of the 60,000 Jews in the ghetto.

In 1943, uprisings took place at the Treblinka and Sobibor death camps. In 1944, prisoners at Auschwitz revolted and set fire to a crematorium. A few prisoners escaped during each

Jews from the Warsaw ghetto surrendering to German soldiers

uprising, but most were killed. Such revolts were often acts of desperation. They erupted when the Jews understood Nazi intentions and had abandoned hope of survival. The fighters also hoped to protect Jewish honor and to avenge Jewish death.

After the Holocaust

A Jewish homeland. As the Allies advanced through Europe in 1944 and 1945, they found millions of *displaced persons* living in countries that were not their own. Most of these people, including many Jews, eventually returned to their homelands. However, many of the Jews had nowhere to go. Their homes had been destroyed, and their families murdered. The presence of so many Jews on German soil, living among their former killers, pressured world leaders to find a place where the Jews could go. The Jews themselves wanted an independent Jewish state in Palestine, the ancient Jewish homeland in the Middle East.

In the late 1800s, members of a Jewish movement called Zionism had begun promoting immigration of Jews to Palestine. In the early 1900s, the British rulers of Palestine had pledged support for a national homeland there for the Jews. But the Arabs who lived in the area had opposed it, and severe fighting had broken out several times during the 1920s and 1930s. In 1939, the British had begun limiting Jewish immigration to Palestine to gain Arab support for the Allies in World War II. Both during and after the war, Palestine's Jews fought bitterly against the restrictions. The British submitted the problem to the United Nations (UN). In 1947, the UN proposed dividing Palestine into an Arab state and a Jewish one. In May 1948, the state of Israel officially came into existence and opened its borders to receive the Jews.

The Nuremberg trials. In the fall of 1943, Allied leaders declared their determination to bring the Nazi leaders to justice for their wartime behavior. The outrage of the Allies only intensified during the final months of the war, when the killing centers were discovered. The Nuremberg trials took place from 1945 to 1949. They were held in Nuremberg, Germany, where the Nazi Party had staged huge rallies.

The Nazi leaders were charged with four major types of crimes—conspiracy to commit crimes against peace, crimes against peace, war crimes, and crimes against humanity. Conspiracy to commit crimes against peace included the planning of

Opening day of the Nuremberg Trials

a war of aggression. Crimes against peace included carrying out such a war. War crimes included the murder of prisoners of war and of civilians, and the destruction of towns and cities. Crimes against humanity included deporting civilians and using them for slave labor as well as persecuting and murdering people for their political beliefs, race, or religion.

On December 9, 1948, the UN passed the Genocide Convention, which was designed to overcome the claims of Nuremberg defendants that they had violated no law. The convention made genocide a crime. The next day, the UN adopted the Universal Declaration of Human Rights.

In the 1990s, Jewish groups pressured those who had profited from the Holocaust to compensate Holocaust victims or their descendants. Groups that paid reparations included the German government, certain Swiss banks, and some German companies.

MLA Citation

"The Holocaust."
*The Southwestern Advantage
Topic Source.* Nashville:
Southwestern. 2013.

ADDITIONAL INFORMATION

Books to Read

Level I

Bodden, Valerie. *The Holocaust.* Creative Education, 2008.

Byers, Ann. *Saving Children from the Holocaust: The Kindertransport.* Enslow, 2012.

Fitzgerald, Stephanie. *Children of the Holocaust.* Compass Point, 2011.

Hoffman, Betty N. *Liberation: Stories of Survival from the Holocaust.* Enslow, 2012.

Skog, Jason. *The Legacy of the Holocaust.* Compass Point, 2011.

Level II

Altman, Linda J. *Hidden Teens, Hidden Lives: Primary Sources from the Holocaust.* Enslow, 2012.

Berenbaum, Michael. *The World Must Know: The History of the Holocaust as Told in the United States Holocaust Memorial Museum.* 2nd ed. Johns Hopkins, 2006.

Fischel, Jack R. *Historical Dictionary of the Holocaust.* 2nd ed. Scarecrow, 2010.

Hayes, Peter, and Roth, J. K., eds. *The Oxford Handbook of Holocaust Studies.* Oxford, 2010.

Winstone, Martin. *The Holocaust Sites of Europe: An Historical Guide.* I. B. Tauris, 2010.

Web Sites

Hitler Comes to Power

http://www.ushmm.org/outreach/en/article.php?moduleId=10007671

This is the first Web page in an on-line overview of the Holcaust for students and teachers presented by the United States Holocaust Museum.

Holocaust Denial

http://www.adl.org/hate-patrol/holocaust.asp

The Anti-Defamation League provides information about Holocaust denial.

Teacher's Guide to the Holocaust

http://fcit.coedu.usf.edu/Holocaust/

An overview of the people and events of the Holocaust presented through text, documents, photographs, art, and literature. From the Florida Center for Instructional Technology, College of Education, University of South Florida.

The First Steps Leading to the Final Solution

http://remember.org/Facts.root.solution.html

Information about events leading to the Holocaust.

The Holocaust: A Guide for Teachers

http://remember.org/guide/index.html

Linda Hurwitz, director of The Holocaust Center of Greater Pittsburgh, prepared this teacher guide, which includes 11 units. Presented by the Cybrary of the Holocaust.

Search Strings

Hitler's "Final Solution"

holocaust Hitler "final solution" (268,000)

holocaust Hitler "final solution" Jew Nazi racially inferior (24,700)

holocaust Hitler "The Final Solution of the Jewish Question" Jew Nazi racially inferior (740)

Roots of Anti-Semitism

Anti-Semitism history Holocaust Jews prejudice (231,000)

Anti-Semitism roots history Holocaust Jews prejudice (128,000)

Anti-Semitism roots history Holocaust Jews prejudice Christian "Martin Luther" ghetto (1,700)

Anti-Semitism roots history Holocaust Jews prejudice Christian "Martin Luther" (33,000)

Kristallnacht

Kristallnacht Holocaust (133,000)

Kristallnacht Holocaust Jews violence Nazi Germany Austria (20,500)

Kristallnacht Holocaust Jews violence Nazi (5,490)

The United States Holocaust Memorial Museum

Holocaust Memorial Museum (485,000)

Holocaust Memorial Museum honor victims Jews history teach (256,000)

"Holocaust Memorial Museum" honor victims Jews history teach (26,500)

BACKGROUND INFORMATION

The following articles were written during the year in which the events took place and reflect the style and thinking of that time.

Judaism (1993)

The commemoration of milestone anniversaries of events associated with the Holocaust, and the opening of two major new museums preserving the memory of the Holocaust, were the highlights of developments in the Jewish community in 1993. During 1993, several events reinforced the importance of keeping alive the memory and the lessons of the Holocaust, in which 6 million European Jews were exterminated during World War II (1939–1945). These events included the violent spread of racism and anti-Semitism in Germany and the continuing tragedy of "ethnic cleansing" in Bosnia-Herzegovina.

Historic anniversaries. The year 1993 marked the 50th anniversaries of two important events in the history of the Holocaust, both symbolic of the courage and resistance to tyranny that brightened this tragic period. On April 19, a solemn commemoration was held in Poland to mark the anniversary of the famous Warsaw ghetto uprising. On April 19, 1943, after most of the ghetto's inhabitants had died of starvation or illness or had been sent to concentration camps, about 60,000 surviving Jews—led by a small underground that had arisen in the walled ghetto—revolted against their oppressors. They fought the German army with few weapons and no outside support for more than three weeks, until the Nazis killed most of the resistance fighters. On May 16, the last survivors committed suicide rather than be taken prisoner.

The Warsaw ghetto uprising has become a symbol of the bravery and faith that led many to stand up against the evil of the Nazis. At the anniversary ceremonies, Poland's President Lech Walesa, United States Vice President Albert Gore, Jr., and Israeli Prime Minister Yitzhak Rabin led thousands of Poles and Jews in recalling this heroic chapter.

Another example of courage and resistance was recalled in the autumn of 1993—the 50th anniversary of the rescue of the Jews of Denmark. During the Jewish High Holy Days of 1943, the invading Germans

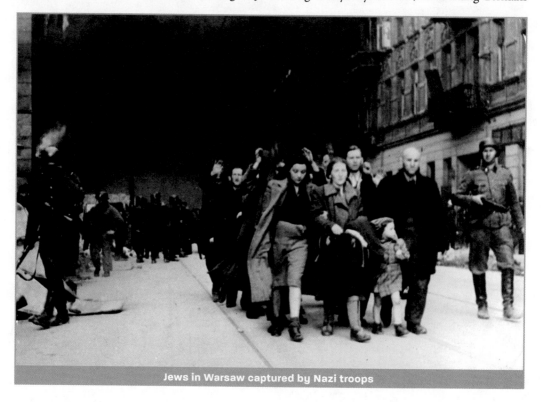

Jews in Warsaw captured by Nazi troops

The Star of David

had planned to arrest and deport Danish Jews to the death camp at Auschwitz in Poland. But the Danish government, Christian church leaders, and common citizens protected their Jewish neighbors by secretly ferrying them at night across the Baltic Sea to neutral Sweden. More than 7,000 Jews were saved. Many events were scheduled in Denmark, the United States, and Israel in autumn 1993 to commemorate these events and to express the gratitude of the Jewish community to the Danish people.

 U.S. Holocaust Museum. On April 22, the new United States Holocaust Memorial Museum was dedicated in Washington, D.C., by President Bill Clinton. Housed in a beautiful and impressive building rich in symbolic design, on the famous Mall in the nation's capital, the museum tells the story of the Holocaust in various ways. Exhibits of artifacts, photographs, and documents, as well as specially designed spaces for contemplation, are combined to help people understand the Holocaust and the moral challenge it poses. The museum also pays tribute to others who suffered from Nazi oppression—the Romany people (as Gypsies prefer to be called) and homosexuals.

In his dedication address, President Clinton said, "I believe that this museum will touch the life of everyone who sees it, and that no one who sees it will emerge without being changed." The museum

has already become one of the most sought-after destinations in Washington, with attendance breaking all anticipated figures.

Peace accord. The historic signing of the peace agreement between Israel and the Palestine Liberation Organization (PLO), in Washington, D.C., on September 13, was the other major development of 1993 affecting the Jewish community. While most Jews around the world hailed the breakthrough and supported the dramatic peace effort, some Orthodox Jews and right wing Israelis opposed the agreement as a dangerous threat to Israel's security.

Lighting the eternal flame at the Holocaust Memorial Museum (left to right): Memorial Council Chairman Harvey Meyerhoff, U.S. President Bill Clinton, and Founding Chairman Elie Wiesel

Immigration

The United States is known as a nation founded by immigrants. Today, the availability of fast, safe, and cheap transportation helps make migration easier than ever. Whether in search of freedom, prosperity, or simply adventure, millions of people worldwide every year migrate into one country from another.

HOT topics

Causes of Immigration. People leave their homeland and move to another country for various reasons. Religious persecution has led many to find a new land for freedom to practice their faith. Others are driven to find new homes by wars, revolutions, and political unrest in their home countries. Before the abolition of slavery, entire populations were forcibly uprooted and shipped to new countries as part of the international trade in human slave labor. The main reason for immigration, however, has long been economic opportunity—the lure of better land, a better job, or a better life.

DEFINITION

immigration 1. the act of coming into a foreign country or region to live: *There has been immigration to America from all the countries of Europe.* **2.** persons who immigrate; immigrants: *The immigration of 1956 included many people from Hungary.*

HOT topics 🔥

Effects of Immigration on the World Economy.
When the loss of trained or talented workers adversely affects an area's economy, economists call the phenomenon *brain drain*. Other emigrants, however, leave their native land to acquire skills in a new country, accumulate savings, and then return home. Some immigrants establish businesses that trade with their homelands. Many stay permanently in their new country but regularly send money to families left behind. Others stay in their new country for their entire careers and then return to their native land once they retire.

The Second Wave of U.S. Immigration.
From 1820 to 1870, almost 7½ million immigrants entered the United States. Nearly all of them came from northern and western Europe. About a third of immigrants were Irish, many seeking escape from a famine that struck Ireland in the mid-1840s. Another third were German. The flood of immigrants began to alarm many native U.S. citizens. Some feared job competition from foreigners. Others disliked the politics or religion of the newcomers. During the 1850s, the American Party, also called the Know-Nothing Party, tried to restrict the immigration of Catholics. Elected American Party mayors of major cities barred immigrants from city jobs. Although the party soon died out, it reflected the serious concerns of some Americans.

Patrolling U.S. Borders.
In 1924, the United States established the Border Patrol to prevent unlawful entry along U.S. boundaries. But the problem of illegal immigration has grown steadily. Experts estimate that millions of illegal aliens live in the United States. Illegal aliens, also called undocumented aliens, are noncitizens living in a country without proper visas or other documents.

TRUE or FALSE?

In the wake of the events of September 11, 2001, when it was learned that the Immigration and Naturalization Service had granted student visas to two of the 9/11 terrorists, the responsibilities of the INS were reassigned to the newly created Department of Homeland Security.

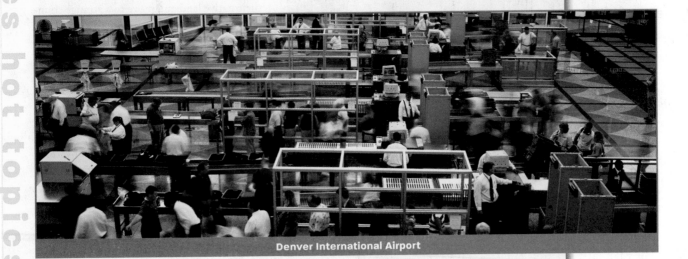
Denver International Airport

THE BASICS

The United States Citizenship and Immigration Services

is a U.S. government agency that oversees immigration services, including the review and processing of citizenship applications and requests for work permits. The agency, sometimes called USCIS, regulates the entry of *aliens* (noncitizens) into the United States. USCIS was created by the Homeland Security Act of 2002, and it began operations in March 2003. It is part of the U.S. Department of Homeland Security.

USCIS oversees the process of *naturalization*—that is, the legal procedure through which a person from a foreign country becomes a citizen of the United States. The agency also handles immigration documents and records, including visas and arrival-departure records.

From 1891 to 2003, immigration and citizenship services were provided by the Immigration and Naturalization Service (INS). The INS was dissolved in March 2003, and many of its responsibilities were transferred to USCIS. Other responsibilities of the INS were moved to U.S. Immigration and Customs Enforcement (ICE) and U.S. Customs and Border Protection (CBP), both of which are also in the Department of Homeland Security.

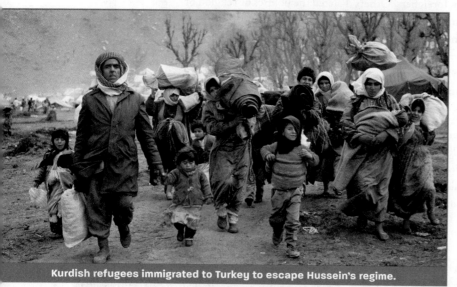

Kurdish refugees immigrated to Turkey to escape Hussein's regime.

Immigration is the act of moving into a foreign country to live. The act of leaving one's country is called *emigration*. Immigrants who flee their country because of persecution, war, or such disasters as famines or epidemics are known as *refugees* or displaced persons (DPs). Most refugees wait in neighboring countries for conditions at home to improve so that they can return. However, some refugees resettle as immigrants in faraway countries. Others move to countries in which they want to resettle and apply for *asylum*. Asylum is shelter and protection given by a nation to a person who is fleeing another nation.

Most people find it hard to pull up roots in their native land and move to a strange country. But throughout history, countless millions of people have done so. The heaviest immigration worldwide took place from the early 1800s to the 1930s. In that period, about 60 million people moved to a new land. Most came from Europe. More than half immigrated to the United States. Other destinations included Argentina, Australia, Brazil, Canada, New Zealand, and South Africa.

Today, improved communications and cheaper transportation help make migration easier. Asia is replacing Europe as the area that sends the most people to other countries. The United States remains the chief receiving nation.

Causes of immigration. People leave their homeland and move to another country for various reasons. Some emigrate to avoid starvation. Some seek adventure. Others wish to escape unbearable family situations. Still others desire to be reunited with loved ones.

Religious persecution has led many people to move to a new land for the freedom to practice their faith. Such emigrants include Jews expelled from England in the 1200s, the English pilgrims who moved to New England in the 1600s, and Baha'is fleeing Iran in the 1980s.

Wars, revolutions, and political unrest drive innumerable people to find new homes. Since 1990, millions of people have fled from warfare in Afghanistan, Bosnia-Herzegovina, East Timor, Ethiopia, Iraq, Kosovo (then a province of Serbia), Liberia, Rwanda, and Sri Lanka.

Some immigrants were brought to a new land against their will. These people are called *involuntary immigrants*. From the 1500s to the 1800s, Europeans shipped Africans to the Western Hemisphere as slaves. The United Kingdom transported convicts to Australia from the late 1700s to the 1860s to relieve overcrowding in British jails.

The main reason for international migration, however, is economic opportunity—the lure of better land, a better job, or a better life. During the 1800s, for example, the rich prairie land of the United States and Canada attracted many Europeans who wanted to own the land they farmed. In the early 1900s, southern and eastern European immigrants sought work in the growing U.S. factories. Today, many professionals emigrate for better opportunities elsewhere. For example, many computer programmers, doctors, engineers, and scientists have moved from India to the United States and Canada.

 Effects of immigration. Not all immigrants remain in their adopted land. Some stay for a short time and then return home. Some go to a new country for a specific reason, such as a job, school, or marriage. Most return to their countries of origin after they have met economic or personal goals abroad, such as acquiring savings. Others return because they find adjusting to a new society too difficult.

The process by which immigrants adjust to a new society is called *integration*. Many immigrants first settle in a community that includes people from their native land, minimizing language difficulties. In time, however, most immigrants, and especially their children, begin to integrate. They learn their new country's language and adapt to the new culture. *Pluralism* describes a type of integration in which immigrants retain their old language and culture. *Assimilation* occurs when immigrants give up their old language and culture.

Most immigrants find a job. They try to provide their children with the education and opportunities not available in the immigrants' native land. Many become citizens of the new country, vote, and take part in politics and government.

Immigrants have made enormous contributions to the culture and economy of such nations as Argentina, Australia, Brazil, Canada, Israel, New Zealand, and the United States. But integration has often been achieved with difficulty. Many of the immigrant-receiving countries have restricted immigration to maintain a *homogeneous* society in which all the people shared the same ethnic, geographic, and cultural background. Some receiving countries had policies that favored people from particular areas. For example, from the 1920s to the 1960s, the United States had *national origins* policies that made it easiest for northern Europeans to immigrate. Although some nations' immigration laws have been relaxed, many newcomers of different backgrounds still face challenges in gaining acceptance.

Population movements have mixed effects on the sending and receiving nations. Emigration relieves overcrowding in a country; yet the country may lose many people with valuable skills. The receiving nation gains new workers but may have trouble providing them with jobs, education, social services, and even housing.

The effects of population movements on the world economy are difficult to measure. For exam-

Chinatown, San Francisco

ple, many emigrants take their skills with them. Others acquire skills in the new country, accumulate savings, and then return home. Some immigrants establish businesses that trade with their homelands. Many immigrants stay permanently in their new country but regularly send money to families left behind. Some immigrants return to their native land after they retire.

Immigration to the United States. The United States has had four major periods of immigration. The first wave began with the colonists of the 1600s and reached a peak just before the American Revolution started in 1775. The second major flow of immigrants started in the 1820s and lasted until a depression in the early 1870s. The greatest inpouring of people took place from the 1880s to the early 1920s. A fourth and continuing wave began in 1965.

The first wave. Most of the immigrants who settled in the American Colonies in the 1600s came from England. Others arrived from France, Germany, Ireland, Wales, the Netherlands, and Scotland. Spanish colonists settled in what is today the southwestern United States.

Some colonists sought adventure. Others fled religious persecution. Many were convicts transported from English jails. But most immigrants by far sought economic opportunity. Many could not afford the passage to the colonies and came as *indentured servants.* Such a servant signed an *indenture* (contract) to work for four to seven years to repay the cost of the ticket. Blacks from West Africa came to the colonies involuntarily. Some of the first Africans were brought as indentured servants, but most blacks arrived as slaves.

By 1700, there were about 250,000 people living in the American Colonies. Approximately 450,000 immigrants arrived between 1700 and the start of the American Revolution (1775–1783). During that period, fewer English immigrants came, while the number from Germany, Scotland, and Ireland rose sharply. Most immigrants arrived in Philadelphia, the main port in the colonies.

Wars in Europe and the United States slowed immigration during the late 1700s and early 1800s. Newcomers included Irish fleeing English rule and French escaping revolution. Congress made it illegal to bring in slaves as of 1808. By that time, about 645,000 black Africans had been imported as slaves.

By 1820, New York City began to replace Philadelphia as the nation's chief port of entry for immigrants. The country's first immigration station, Castle Garden, opened in New York City in 1855. Ellis Island, the most famous station, operated in New York Harbor from 1892 to 1954.

The second wave. From 1820 to 1870, almost $7\frac{1}{2}$ million newcomers entered the United States. Nearly all of them came from northern and western Europe. About a third were Irish, many of them seeking escape from a famine that struck Ireland in the mid-1840s. Another third were German.

In the mid-1800s, some states sent agents to Europe to attract settlers. Railroad companies did the same. Better conditions on ships and steep declines in travel time and fares made the voyage across the Atlantic Ocean easier and more affordable. In the mid-1800s, news of the discovery of gold in California reached China. Chinese immigrants and *sojourners* streamed across the Pacific Ocean to strike it rich. Sojourners were temporary immigrants who intended to make money

The approach to Ellis Island

and return home. French-Canadian immigrants and sojourners opened still another path to the United States. They moved across the Canadian-U.S. border into the New England States and Michigan.

The flood of immigrants began to alarm many native U.S. citizens. Some feared job competition from foreigners. Others disliked the politics of the newcomers, or the fact that many were Roman Catholics. In the 1850s, the American Party, also called the Know-Nothing Party, tried to restrict the immigration of Catholics. American Party candidates were elected mayors of major cities—including Boston and Chicago—and barred immigrants from city jobs. Although the party soon died out, it reflected the concerns of some Americans.

During the 1870s, the U.S. economy suffered a depression while the economies of Germany and the United Kingdom improved. German and British immigration to the United States then decreased. But arrivals increased from Canada, China, Denmark, Norway, Sweden, and southern and eastern Europe. In 1875, the United States passed its first restrictive immigration law. It prevented convicts and prostitutes from entering the country. During the late 1870s, California labor leader Denis Kearney and his Workingmen's Party demanded a stop to Chinese immigration. Mobs sometimes attacked Chinese immigrants, who were accused of lowering wages and of unfair business competition. In 1882, Congress passed the Chinese Exclusion Act, which prohibited Chinese laborers from entering the United States.

The third wave. From 1881 to 1920, more than 23 million immigrants poured into the United States from almost every part of the world. Until the 1880s, most newcomers still came from northern and western Europe. They later became known as *old immigrants*. Beginning in the 1890s, the majority of arrivals were *new immigrants*, people from southern and eastern Europe.

Many U.S. citizens believed the swelling flood of immigrants threatened the nation's unity. Hostility turned against Jewish people, Catholics, Japanese, and the new immigrants in general.

In 1882, Congress expanded its list of unacceptable immigrants to include such people as beggars, contract laborers, people with mental illness, and unaccompanied children. In 1901, President Woodrow Wilson wrote that "the countries of the

Under the War Brides Act, military personnel who married abroad were allowed to bring their families to the U.S.

south of Europe were disburdening themselves of the more sordid and hapless elements of their population." In 1907, Congress formed the U.S. Immigration Commission to study the origins and results of immigration to the United States. It was generally known as the Dillingham Commission, after the commission's chair, Senator William Paul Dillingham of Vermont. In 1911, the commission issued a report in which it concluded that immigrants from southern and eastern Europe had more "inborn socially inadequate qualities than northwestern Europeans."

In 1917, Congress enacted a law that required new immigrants 16 and older to show that they could read and write in at least one language. The law also excluded immigrants from an area known as the Asiatic Barred Zone, which covered most of Asia and most islands in the Pacific Ocean.

In 1921, new laws reduced immigration and limited the number of immigrants from any one country. The Immigration Act of 1924 limited the number of immigrants from outside the Western Hemisphere to about 153,700 a year. The distribution of immigrants from different countries was based on percentages of the nationalities making up the white population of the United States in 1920. The formula ensured that most immigrants would be from such countries as Germany, Ireland, and the United Kingdom.

A temporary decline. During the Great Depression, U.S. immigration dropped sharply. Only about 500,000 immigrants came from 1931 to 1940. In some years, more people left than arrived. World War II (1939–1945) led to an easing of immigration laws. The War Brides Act of 1945 admitted the spouses and children of U.S. military personnel who had married while abroad. China became an ally during the war, and so the ban against Chinese immigrants was lifted. In 1952, the Immigration and Nationality Act, also called the McCarran-Walter Act, established *quotas* (allowable numbers) for Asian countries and other areas from which immigrants had been excluded. The law, for the first time, made citizenship available to people of all origins.

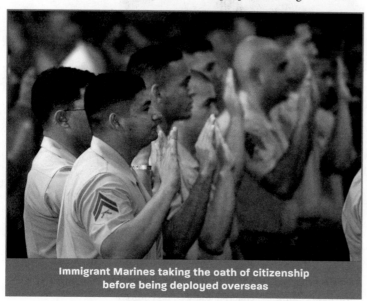

Immigrant Marines taking the oath of citizenship before being deployed overseas

The fourth wave. In 1965, amendments to the Immigration and Nationality Act ended quotas based on nationality. Instead, the amendments provided for annual quotas of 170,000 immigrants from the Eastern Hemisphere and 120,000 from the Western Hemisphere. The act established a preference system for the issuing of *visas* (permits) that favored relatives of U.S. citizens and permanent resident aliens, as well as people with special skills. Wives, husbands, parents, and minor children of U.S. citizens could enter without being counted as part of the quota. In 1978, Congress replaced the separate quotas for the Eastern and Western hemispheres with a single annual world quota of 290,000.

The 1965 amendments produced major changes in patterns of immigration to the United States. The percentage of immigrants from Europe and Canada dropped, while that of immigrants from Asia and the West Indies soared. Today, far more immigrants come from Mexico than from any other country. Other large groups of immigrants come from China, India, and the Philippines.

Under the 1965 amendments, refugees could make up 6 percent of the Eastern Hemisphere's annual quota for immigration. This rule was later extended to the Western Hemisphere. But the percentage was too small for the flow of refugees from war-torn Southeast Asia in the 1970s or the streams of people from Haiti and Cuba. To address these issues, Congress passed the Refugee Act in 1980. This law provided for the settling of 50,000 refugees each year. The president could admit additional refugees if there were compelling reasons to do so. As a result, about 100,000 refugees entered the United States annually in the 1990s.

In 1924, the United States established the Border Patrol to prevent unlawful entry along U.S. boundaries. But the problem of illegal immigration has grown steadily. Experts estimate that millions of *illegal aliens* live in the United States. Illegal aliens, also called *undocumented aliens*, are noncitizens living in a country without proper visas or other documents. A majority of undocumented aliens in the United States come from Mexico.

The Immigration Reform and Control Act of 1986 offered *amnesty* (pardon) to illegal aliens who had lived in the United States continuously since before January 1, 1982, or who had worked at least 90 days at farm labor there between May 1, 1985, and May 1, 1986. The act also set penalties on employers who knowingly hire illegal immigrants. By the end of the amnesty period in 1988, almost 3 million illegal aliens had applied for amnesty. However, hundreds of thousands of others did not apply for various reasons, including the cost and confusion involved in filing and a lack of residency or employment records. Critics of the law claimed that it failed to reduce the flow of illegal aliens into the country.

In 1990, further amendments to the Immigration and Nationality Act of 1952 increased the number of immigrants allowed into the United States each year. Ceilings were fixed at 700,000 annually for 1992 to 1994 and 675,000 annually beginning in 1995. Like the 1965 amendments, the 1990 amendments placed no limit on the number of U.S. citizens' immediate relatives who could enter the country each year. The ceilings also did not include refugees. The 1990 amendments gave additional preference to people from countries that had sent few immigrants to the United States after 1965, including many European and African nations.

In the first decade of the 2000s, some states and cities enacted laws to deal with illegal migration. However, federal courts have blocked such measures, ruling that regulating immigration is a federal responsibility.

People who seek legal admission to the United States apply at the U.S. consulate in their home country for a visa. They must prove, among other things, that they do not have an infectious disease or a criminal record. Immigration laws favor relatives of U.S. citizens, refugees, and people with skills needed in the United States. Others may have to wait years, particularly in countries that have many people wishing to emigrate.

Immigration to other countries. The most commonly traveled immigration route has long led from Europe to the United States. But other countries have also received many immigrants. This section discusses immigration to other parts of the world.

Canada. The French and later the British colonized Canada. From 1850 to 1930, over 6 million people immigrated to Canada, including 3 million people from the United Kingdom. During the late 1800s, Chinese workers were imported to help construct the Canadian Pacific Railway. To discourage Chinese immigration after completion of the railway in 1885, Canada placed increasingly heavy entry taxes on newly arrived Chinese. In 1923, Canada barred the entry of Chinese immigrants.

Today, immigrants are admitted to Canada regardless of their ancestry, race, religion, or sex. Canada has of the world's highest immigration rates compared with population. In the first decade of the 2000s, Canada accepted about 250,000 immigrants a year. More than half of Canada's immigrants have been Asians, including the Chinese who had been barred before. Canada also received refugees from the Vietnam War (1957–1975).

Canada uses a point system that gives priority to immigrants who have education and skills that are likely to make them successful in Canada. To receive an immigrant visa, immigrants must obtain at least 67 points on a 100-point scale. Education is worth up to 25 points for a Master of Science degree or a doctorate. The ability to speak English, French, or both is worth up to 24 points. There are up to 21 points available for work experience.

Latin America. Most Latin American countries gained independence from their European rulers in the early 1800s. At that time, only Argentina, Brazil, and a few other countries welcomed immigrants. From 1850 to 1930, more than 11 million immigrants arrived in Latin America. About 5$\frac{1}{2}$ million of them—mainly Italians and Spaniards—went to Argentina. About 4 million—mainly Italians and Portuguese—went to Brazil. Many of the newcomers did not stay in those countries, however.

After the 1950s, immigration to Latin America declined because of the region's lack of jobs and its rapidly growing population. In addition, Argentina and Brazil limited Asian immigration. However, much immigration took place within Latin America.

Today, more people emigrate from Latin America than immigrate to the region. Mexico is Latin America's major emigrating country. Most Mexican emigrants move to the United States. Large numbers of people from the seven countries of Central America—Belize, Costa Rica, El Salvador, Guatemala, Honduras, Nicaragua, and Panama—moved to the United States during civil wars in the 1980s. In addition, many people born in Cuba, the Dominican Republic, Haiti, and Jamaica have emigrated, usually to the United States.

Afghan refugee camp, circa 1995

Australia and New Zealand were colonized by the United Kingdom beginning in the late 1700s. After gold was discovered in Australia in 1851 and in New Zealand in 1861, non-British immigrants began to arrive. By the 1880s, the immigrants included more than 40,000 Chinese in Australia and over 4,000 in New Zealand. The two countries then limited Chinese immigration. In the early 1900s, they established policies designed to preserve a "white Australia" and a "white New Zealand." They tried to attract British and other favored immigrants by offering free transportation. After World War II ended in 1945, Australia started to welcome European refugees. In 1975, the country began admitting Southeast Asian refugees. New Zealand eased its immigration restrictions in 1986.

Since the 1970s, both Australia and New Zealand have adopted point systems to select immigrants. The number of Asian immigrants rose as Chinese, Indian, and other Asian students came to study in Australia and New Zealand and stayed to live and work. A rising share of immigrants to Australia and New Zealand are also from the Pacific Islands. In addition, many British subjects still migrate to Australia and New Zealand.

Asia. Except for Israel, most immigrants to Asia came from other Asian countries. By the 1920s, more than 8 million Chinese lived outside China, chiefly in the Philippines, in what is now Indonesia, and in other Southeast Asian lands. The Communist takeover of China in 1949 led 2 million more Chinese to emigrate.

By the 1920s, about 750,000 Japanese had moved to China, Korea, and other countries of eastern Asia. Also by the 1920s, about 1 1/2 million Indians had left their homeland. Many moved to other Asian countries, including what are now Sri Lanka and Malaysia. In 1947, Pakistan was created from parts of India. About 10 million people fled from one country to another. Hindus and Sikhs fled from Pakistan to India. Muslims left India for Pakistan. After East Pakistan became Bangladesh in 1971, millions more Hindus and Sikhs went to India.

By the late 1980s, almost 2 million refugees had fled countries of Southeast Asia because of warfare. Many of them settled in the United States. But large groups remained in Malaysia and Thailand and the other Southeast Asian lands to which they had first fled.

European Jews began to settle in what is now Israel in the mid-1800s. In 1914, about 85,000 Jews lived there. By 1948, when Israel was founded, some 450,000 more Jews had arrived, most of them from central and eastern Europe. In 1950, Israel passed the Law of Return, which allows almost any Jew to settle in Israel. Since the founding of Israel, about 3 million more Jews have immigrated there, chiefly from the Middle East and the Mediterranean Sea region. In the late 1980s and 1990s, hundreds of thousands of Jews emigrated from the Soviet Union and former Soviet lands.

Africa. Vast numbers of people move about on the African continent in search of better farmlands or employment opportunities. Most go to Côte d'Ivoire, Ghana, Nigeria, South Africa, Uganda, or Zimbabwe.

Colonial rule ended in most of Africa by the 1960s. Since then, civil wars in several African nations have driven millions of people from their countries as refugees. Many others have emigrated because of famine. Most of the refugees have remained in Africa, mainly in Ethiopia, Malawi, Somalia, Sudan, Tanzania, and Zaire—now the Democratic Republic of the Congo. During the 1980s and 1990s, many Ethiopian Jews immigrated to Israel. In the early 2000s, Africa had more than 5 million refugees.

Europe. During the first half of the 1900s, the Russian Revolution and two world wars caused huge population shifts within Europe as refugees fled from one country to another. Economic recovery after World War II generated a great

Ethiopian Jews aboard a plane to Israel

need for labor. Many countries, including Belgium, France, the Netherlands, Sweden, Switzerland, and West Germany, sought foreigners to serve as *guest workers*. Most such temporary workers came from southern Europe and northern Africa. In the late 1970s, Greece, Italy, Spain, and Portugal drew workers from Africa and Asia.

A large number of guest workers not only remained but also brought in their families. In addition, such countries as France, the Netherlands, Portugal, and the United Kingdom received millions of immigrants from their former colonies. Europe's non-European population increased enormously. Guest worker recruitment stopped in the early 1970s. European countries also began to review the applications of refugees more carefully and to establish stricter admittance requirements for immigrants from former colonies. During the 1990s, hundreds of thousands of people from Eastern Europe, northern Africa, southern Asia, and the Middle East arrived in Western Europe. Many sought political asylum or economic opportunity. Many immigrants chose Germany because of its liberal refugee policy. But Germany passed restrictive immigration laws in the late 1990s.

With the fall of Communism in Eastern Europe in the early 1990s and the enlargement of the European Union in the first decade of the 2000s, millions of Poles, Romanians, and other Eastern Europeans moved west in search of higher wages. The European Union is an organization of European countries that promotes economic and political cooperation among its members.

Today, immigration is a hotly debated issue in many European countries. Many have anti-immigrant political parties, such as the Danish People's Party, the Sweden Democrats, and the Lega Nord in Italy.

THE UNITED STATES IMMIGRATION AND CUSTOMS ENFORCEMENT is a U.S. government

agency that enforces immigration law and investigates suspected violations. The agency is often called ICE. A primary goal of the agency is to keep terrorists and terrorist weapons out of the country. ICE began operations in March 2003. It is part of the Directorate of Border and Transportation Security in the U.S. Department of Homeland Security.

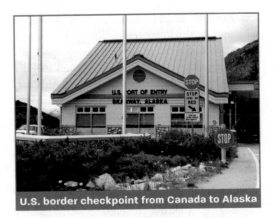
U.S. border checkpoint from Canada to Alaska

Before 2003, many immigration enforcement responsibilities were provided by the Immigration and Naturalization Service (INS) and the U.S. Customs Service. The INS and the U.S. Customs Service were dissolved in March 2003, and many of their responsibilities were transferred to ICE. Other responsibilities of the INS and the U.S. Customs Service were moved to U.S. Customs and Border Protection (CBP) and U.S. Citizenship and Immigration Services (USCIS), both of which are also in the Department of Homeland Security.

THE IMMIGRATION AND NATURALIZATION SERVICE

was a United States government agency that administered and enforced U.S. immigration laws from 1891 to 2003. The agency regulated the entrance of *aliens* (noncitizens) into the United States. It sought to prevent the illegal entry of aliens and to investigate and remove aliens who were in the country illegally. In addition, the INS worked to prevent people from bringing illegal drugs into the United States. The agency also provided various immigration benefits. It processed visa claims for temporary and permanent workers and for their immediate family members. The agency also determined the eligibility of aliens who wished to become U.S. citizens and presented those who were eligible to a federal or state court for naturalization.

Congress created the INS in 1891 as part of the Department of Labor. The U.S. Border Patrol, a special enforcement agency within the INS, was established in 1924. The INS was transferred to the Department of Justice in 1940. The INS grew significantly in the 1990s, when Congress increased funding for border enforcement and personnel.

Many people called for reform of the INS following the September 11, 2001, terrorist attacks on the World Trade Center in New York City and on the Pentagon building near Washington, D.C. Several of the terrorists responsible for the attacks were in the United States illegally or had broken the terms of their admittance. In 2002, Congress passed legislation to reorganize the federal government with an increased emphasis on the prevention of terrorism.

As part of the reorganization, the responsibilities of the INS were transferred to the newly created Department of Homeland Security. In 2003, those responsibilities were divided among three agencies within the department: USCIS, which oversees immigration services and applications; U.S. Immigration and Customs Enforcement, which handles investigations and some enforcement duties; and CBP, which oversees Customs inspectors and the Border Patrol.

MLA Citation

"Immigration." *The Southwestern Advantage Topic Source.* Nashville: Southwestern. 2013.

DATA

Major Immigration Movements in the United States

Source: Department of Homeland Security.

Who	When	Number	Why
Irish	1840s and 1850s	About 1½ million	Famine resulting from potato crop failure
Germans	1840s to 1880s	About 4 million	Severe economic depression and unemployment; political unrest and failure of liberal revolutionary movement
Danes, Norwegians, and Swedes	1870s to 1900s	About 1½ million	Poverty; shortage of farmland
Poles	1880s to 1920s	About 1 million	Poverty; political repression; cholera epidemics
Jews from eastern Europe	1880s to 1920s	About 2½ million	Religious persecution
Austrians, Czechs, Hungarians, and Slovaks	1880s to 1920s	About 4 million	Poverty; overpopulation
Italians	1880s to 1920s	About 4½ million	Poverty; overpopulation
Mexicans	1910s to 1920s	About 700,000	Mexican Revolution of 1910; low wages and unemployment
	1950s to 2000s	About 6 million	Poverty; unemployment
Cubans	1960s to 1980s	About 700,000	Communist take-over in 1959
Dominicans, Haitians, and Jamaicans	1970s and 1980s	About 900,000	Poverty; unemployment
Vietnamese	1970s and 1980s	About 500,000	Vietnam War (1957–1975); Communist take-over

DATA

Legal Immigrants Admitted to the U.S. since 1820

Source: Department of Homeland Security.

Year	Number of immigrants	Year[1]	Number of immigrants
1820	8,400	1940	70,800
1830	23,300	1950	249,200
1840	84,100	1960	265,400
1850	370,000	1970	373,300
1860	153,600	1980	524,300
1870	387,200	1990	1,535,900
1880	457,300	1995	720,200
1890	455,300	1998	653,200
1900	448,600	2000	841,000
1910	1,041,600	2002	1,059,400
1920	430,000	2005	1,122,300
1930	241,700	2010	1,042,600

ADDITIONAL RESOURCES

Books to Read

Baldwin, Carl R. Immigration Questions and Answers. 3rd ed. Allworth, 2002.

Brownstone, David M., and Franck, I. M. Facts About American Immigration. H. W. Wilson, 2001.

Ciment, James. Encyclopedia of American Immigration. 4 vols. M. E. Sharpe, 2001.

Meltzer, Milton. Bound for America: The Story of the European Immigrants. Benchmark Books, 2002. Younger readers.

Wapman, Dennis. Immigration: From the Founding of Virginia to the Closing of Ellis Island. Facts on File, 2002.

Web Sites

Comprehensive Immigration Reform

www.whitehouse.gov/issues/fixing-immigration-system-america-s-21st-century-economy

The White House site reporting on the U.S. government's policies and intent regarding border security and immigration reform.

Immigration . . . The Changing Face of America

http://memory.loc.gov/teachers/classroommaterials/presentations/immigration/ind

Site of the Library of Congress—containing interactive educational activities regarding immigration for teachers and students.

Immigration: The Living Mosaic of People, Culture and Hope

http://library.thinkquest.org/20619/index.html

A site that explores the history of immigration in America while highlighting the immigrant experience.

U.S. Immigration History

immigration.about.com/od/usimmigrationhistory/US˙Immigration˙History.htm

A site that contains historical immigration information along with articles on contemporary immigration issues.

Search Strings

Causes of Immigration

Causes of Immigration (614,000)

Causes of Immigration persecution war revolution politics (282,000)

"Causes of Immigration" "economic opportunity" (3,020)

Effects of Immigration on the World Economy

effects of immigration on the world economy (153,000)

immigration effects global economy "brain drain" money acquire skills (47,600)

immigration effects global economy "brain drain" money acquire skills savings businesses (34,700)

"brain drain" immigration money savings (8,410)

The Second Wave of U.S. Immigration

"U.S. Immigration" second wave (16,300)

Immigration "United States" second wave Europe (146,000)

Immigration "united states" second wave Europe "Know-Nothing Party" (438)

Patrolling U.S. Borders

Immigration patrolling borders "Border Patrol" (925,000) *This is a lot but the first few were exactly what the searcher wanted.

Immigration patrolling borders "Border Patrol" illegal aliens undocumented (178,000)

Immigration patrolling borders "Border Patrol" "illegal aliens" undocumented (96,700)

Immigration patrolling borders "Border Patrol" "illegal aliens" undocumented unlawful entry (15,900)

BACKGROUND INFORMATION

The following articles were written during the year in which the events took place and reflect the style and thinking of that time.

Immigration (2003)

Immigration. The methods employed by the government of the United States to handle immigration changed significantly in 2003 after the U.S. Immigration and Naturalization Service (INS) was moved out of the Department of Justice and integrated into the Department of Homeland Security. Immigration experts viewed the integration of the INS into the Department of Homeland Security as one of the most important steps taken by the administration of President George W. Bush and the U.S. Congress to address problems that had plagued the INS. The INS came under intense criticism in 2002 when it was learned that officials had issued student visas to two of the highjackers who had carried out the terrorist attacks on the United States on September 11, 2001.

As part of the integration process, immigration duties that had been handled by the INS were divided between two new bureaus within the Homeland Security Department. On March 1, 2003, services that had been administered by the INS were transferred to the Homeland Security Department's Bureau of Citizenship and Immigration Services (BCIS). The BCIS was responsible for overseeing immigrant visa petitions; naturalization petitions; and asylum and refugee applications. The U.S. Senate confirmed Eduardo Aguirre, Jr., as BCIS director on June 19. President Bush nominated Aguirre for the position in February. Aguirre came to the post from the Export-Import Bank of the United States, where he had been vice chairman and chief operating officer.

Also on March 1, enforcement and border patrol functions were transferred to the Homeland Security Department's Directorate of Border and Transportation Security (BTS). The BTS assumed responsibility for securing U.S. borders and transportation systems, including 350 official ports of entry and more than 7,500 miles (12,000 kilometers) of border between the United States and Canada to the north and Mexico to the south. The BTS was also responsible for enforcing U.S. immigration laws.

Immigration ruling. The U.S. Supreme Court ruled on April 29 that the federal government can imprison immigrants it is trying to deport without giving them a chance to demonstrate that they do not pose a risk to the community or that they are unlikely to flee. In the 5-to-4 decision, the court upheld provisions of a 1996 immigration law requiring the government to detain immigrants who have been convicted of drug crimes prior to deportation. Tens of thousands of immigrants have been imprisoned under the law before being deported. A number of appeals courts had ruled the law unconstitutional.

U.S. visit. Homeland Security Secretary Tom Ridge on April 29, 2003, announced a new security system that he said would make it easier for foreign students, business travelers, and tourists to enter the United States. Ridge claimed that the process would also make it more difficult for people to illegally enter the United States.

The U.S. Visitor and Immigrant Status Indication Technology (U.S. VISIT) requires visitors to the United States to register with an electronic system. The system uses photographs, finger-

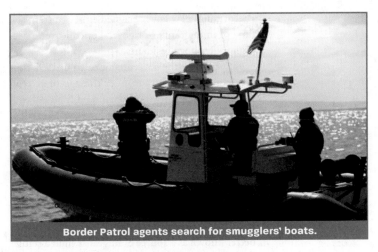

Border Patrol agents search for smugglers' boats.

prints, or iris scans to create an electronic check-in and checkout system for people from other countries coming to the United States to work, travel, or study. The system was scheduled to be implemented in early 2004.

Foreign health care workers who enter the United States to work on a temporary basis faced new certification requirements under a plan announced by Department of Homeland Security officials in July 2003. Foreign health care workers, except for physicians, must present a certificate granted by an approved independent crediting organization before being allowed to enter the United States. The rule is intended to ensure that all foreign nurses, physical and occupational therapists, speech pathologists, and other health care professionals who seek employment in the United States meet U.S. professional medical standards.

Immigration (1997)

Nations worldwide face tough questions as more and more people search for a better life.

—by Barry R. Chiswick

Debates over the pros and cons of immigration raged during 1997 in legislatures from the German Bundestag in Bonn to the California statehouse in Sacramento. The debates were fueled by two worldwide trends: More and more residents of the world's less-developed nations were clamoring to immigrate to the more-developed nations; many residents of the more-developed nations were responding to this clamor with fear of the continuing influx of foreigners. Political leaders, in turn, responded to voter concerns with campaign rhetoric and new laws designed either to stem the flow of immigrants or tighten control over existing foreign-born residents.

In Germany, the government ruled in 1997 that German-born children under the age of sixteen must carry resident visas (permits) if their parents were legal immigrants from Turkey, Morocco, Tunisia, or the former Yugoslavia, the countries of origin of most minority communities in Germany. In the United States, Congress passed and in August 1996 President Bill Clinton signed a bill denying food stamps to legal immigrants and allowing states to turn off financial aid and Medicare to most legal immigrants. In Ireland, better known as a source of migrants than a refuge for immigrants, a wave of illegal immigrants from Romania, Republic of Congo (the former Zaire), and Somalia led to the passage of the 1996 Refugee Act, Ireland's first significant immigration legislation since 1936.

Yet immigration is nothing new. It is one aspect of migration (the movement of people from one place to another). While immigration refers to the process of people moving from one country to another for a permanent or semi-permanent stay, emigration refers to leaving a country for a permanent or semi-permanent stay elsewhere.

Hutu refugees board a plane in Zaire.

Migration a constant in human history.

Migration has been a characteristic of human existence since prehistoric times, resulting in the spread of people to all corners of the globe. But trends in the migration of people have not been uniform over time. Historically, immigration occurred in waves. Immigrants tended to flock to an area or country during periods of economic prosperity in that area or country. The pattern was reversed during economic recession or war.

The major immigration streams since the mid-1800s have been from the lower income countries of Europe and Asia to higher income nations, particularly Australia, Canada, and the United States. Immigration to these countries increased in the late 1800s and the early 1900s, slowed during the years from World War I (1914–1918) through World War II (1939–1945), and escalated again in the decades after 1945.

With the rapid growth of income in Western Europe and Japan after World War II, emigration declined and immigration increased. Since the 1960s, there were more immigrants to Western Europe each year than emigrants leaving the region. The overall gain in migrant population is called net immigration. People from the Caribbean, Africa, and the Middle East arrived in Europe in record numbers in the 1970s and 1980s. Following the collapse of Communism in Eastern Europe in the early 1990s, another wave of immigration within Europe washed east to west.

Japan, during a period of great prosperity in the 1980s, also became a country of net immigration, though on a much smaller scale than in Western Europe. While Japan admitted record numbers of low-skilled, temporary workers from Southeast Asia, south Asia, and parts of the Middle East, the workers were not encouraged to regard immigration as permanent. In contrast, Japan welcomed emigrants of Japanese ancestry from Peru and other Latin American countries.

Israel became a net immigration country upon its creation in 1948 by welcoming all people of the Jewish faith or of Jewish background. Israel's latest wave of immigration, in the 1990s, included refugees from the former Soviet Union and from war-torn Ethiopia.

Motives for immigration.

If classified by motive, immigrants can be categorized as refugees, economic migrants, or tied movers (spouses, children, and dependents who travel with economic migrants). Refugees emigrate, most often involuntarily, in search of safety or freedom. In 1994, for example, more than two million Hutu refugees, fearing for their lives, emigrated from Rwanda to other countries, particularly Zaire (now Republic of Congo). In 1996, revolutionary forces in Zaire forced one million of the same refugees to migrate again, back to Rwanda.

Economic migrants are people who move for job opportunities. Most adult immigrants to the United States in the 1990s were economic migrants. Asians, Mexicans, and Latin Americans made up this wave of economic immigrants just as Europeans had in the 1890s.

Immigration to the United States. In 1996, immigration into the United States reached its highest level since the pre-World War I era, when immigration was virtually unrestricted. According to statistics from the U.S. Immigration and Naturalization Service (INS), more than 915,000 immigrants were admitted to the United States in fiscal 1996 (October 1, 1999–September 30, 1996). An additional 275,000 people either overstayed their visas or entered the country illegally during the same twelve-month period. The INS estimated that another five million undocumented residents already lived in the United States in 1996.

The foreign-born population of the United States in 1997, according to INS statistics, reached 24.6 million people, meaning that nearly 10 percent of the total U.S. population was foreign-born. By comparison, the percentage of the U.S. population that was foreign born in 1880, during unregulated mass immigration, stood at 15 percent. In 1970, it was 5 percent and in 1980, 8 percent.

During the greatest period of immigration to the Unites States—the 1840s to 1914—the vast majority of immigrants came from Europe and Asia. During the 1840s and 1850s, more than one million immigrants came from Ireland to escape famine resulting from a potato crop failure that occurred from 1845 to 1848. Between the 1840s and the 1880s, approximately four million Germans escaped economic recession, unemployment, and political unrest to seek a new life in America. In the mid-1800s, news of the discovery of gold in California prompted a wave of emigrants from China, and during the 1860s, another wave of immigrants, both Chinese and European, came to the United States to find work in the construction of transcontinental rail lines.

During the same peak immigration period, America experienced its first wave of xenophobia (fear of foreigners) as native-born citizens began to fear job competition from immigrants. The American Party—also called the "Know-Nothing Party"—demanded as early as the 1850s that the U.S. government enact laws to reduce immigration and to make it harder for foreigners to become citizens. Congress ignored their pleas for restrictions until a depression, following the panic of 1871, threw thousands of people out of work. In response, Congress passed legislation in 1875, banning convicts and prostitutes from entering the country. In 1882, Congress passed the Chinese Exclusion Act, which prohibited all Chinese from entering the country.

Regardless of such restrictions, immigration to the United States boomed between 1881 and 1914, when more than twenty-three million immigrants—predominantly northern Europeans in the 1880s and eastern and southern Europeans in the 1890s and early 1900s—poured into the country. The flow, however, slowed to a trickle during World War I and after 1921, when Congress set a ceiling on the number of Eastern Hemisphere people allowed to enter the country. The quota limited the annual number of immigrants from any one nation to 3 percent of the foreign-born people of that nationality already in the United States. Therefore, immigration was open to northern Europeans, who for the most part did not want to come. Immigration was severely restricted for southern and eastern Europeans and closed to Asians.

During the Great Depression of the 1930s, immigration to the United States dropped even further. While some 500,000 immigrants came to the United States between 1931 and 1940, an even larger number left the country, most returning to their countries of origin.

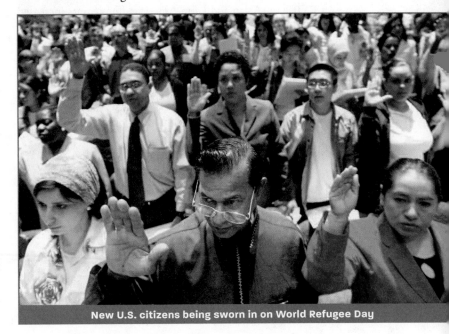

New U.S. citizens being sworn in on World Refugee Day

World War II brings immigration changes. World War II led to an easing of the nation's immigration laws. The United States lifted its Chinese ban when China became an ally. The War Brides Act of 1945 admitted the spouses and children of U.S. military personnel who had married while abroad.

In the mid-1960s, the United States underwent a change in attitude toward race and ethnicity that resulted in the enactment of the 1964 Civil Rights and 1965 Voting Rights acts. The 1965 amendments to the Immigration and Nationality Act of 1952 reflected the change and dramatically refocused immigration patterns with the abolition of the "national origins" quota. The amendments replaced quotas based on nationality with annual quotas with ceilings of 170,000 immigrants from the Eastern Hemisphere and 120,000 from the Western Hemisphere. The act established a preference system for entry visas that strongly favored relatives of U.S. citizens and permanent resident aliens, with much less emphasis on people with special skills. Wives, husbands, parents, and the minor children of U.S. citizens could enter without being counted as part of the quota.

The authors of the 1965 amendments believed that the "kinship" provisions in the amendments would produce a similar distribution of immigrants by country of origin as under the "national origins" quota system. Soon after the passage of the 1965 amendments, however, the number of Asian and Latin American immigrants increased dramatically as those from Europe shrank.

In 1978, Congress replaced the separate quotas for immigrants from the Eastern and Western hemispheres with a single annual quota of 290,000. By the 1980s, 23 percent of immigrants to the United States came from Mexico, and 25 percent came from other Latin American countries and the Caribbean; 37 percent arrived from Asia; and 2 percent from Africa. The percentage of immigrants from Europe and Canada fell to 13 percent.

More amendments in 1990 increased the number of immigrants allowed into the United States. In fiscal 1996, 18 percent of the 915,000 immigrants entering the country came from Mexico (nearly 164,000 people) and 24 percent from other parts of Latin America and the Caribbean; 5 percent were from Africa; and 33 percent were from Asia, including approximately 55,000 people from the Philippines, 45,000 from India, 42,000 from Vietnam, and 42,000 from China.

Effects of immigration on national culture. The increase in the number of immigrants and the change in their countries of origin since the 1960s dramatically affected the United States and its culture—from the demographic composition of its cities to salsa replacing ketchup as the nation's Number 1 condiment. The impact of these changes was not, however, uniformly felt across the country. In 1990, 33 percent of all foreign-born people lived in California, while only 12 percent of the entire U.S. population lived in California. Another 14 percent lived in New York. Florida and Texas each accounted for about 8 percent, and another 5 percent lived in New Jersey and Illinois. These six states—with only 39 percent of the total U.S. population—were home to nearly 73 percent of all foreign-born residents in 1990.

Immigrant populations in the same six states were further concentrated in urban areas: in the San Francisco Bay area and the southern counties of California; along the Mexican border in Texas; in Miami-Dade County, Florida; Chicago, Illinois; and the New York City metropolitan area. Of a total of 3,141 counties in the United States, only 156 counties—approximately 5 percent—had populations with 8 percent or more foreign-born residents in 1990. The population of Miami-Dade County, Florida, in contrast, was 45 percent foreign born.

Where immigrants settle. After the era of cheap farmland in America ended in the early 1900s, the places where immigrants settled have remained largely static and determined by three factors: port of entry, concentration of other foreign-born people, and job opportunities. New

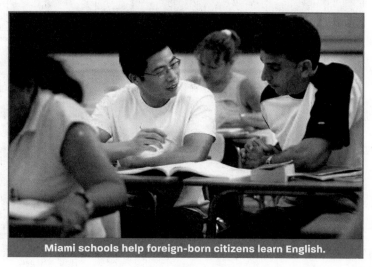

Miami schools help foreign-born citizens learn English.

immigrants often settled in ports of entry; that is, they remained in the places where they entered the country. Boston, for example, became the home of America's largest concentration of Irish immigrants in the 1800s and early 1900s because it was America's nearest port to Ireland and, therefore, the cheapest passage.

According to an INS report, the majority of immigrants entering the United States in 1996 planned to settle in ports of entry. Approximately 130,000 immigrants in 1992 reported their intention of living in the Los Angeles/Long Beach area, a major Mexican, Latin American, and Asian port of entry. More than 24,000 immigrants reported plans to settle in San Diego, California, and 27,000 people planned to make their homes in Houston, Texas. Both are major ports for Mexican emigrants. More than 40,000 immigrants declared that they expected to settle in the San Francisco/San Jose metropolitan area, a primary port of entry for Asian emigrants. Attracting 128,000 immigrants in 1992, New York City remained the premier port of entry for eastern Europeans, Africans, and Middle Easterners. More than 31,000 Cubans and Latin Americans chose the port of Miami in 1992.

In the 1990s, immigrants from countries that differ in language and customs from the United States continued to settle in communities with other immigrants from their home countries. Living in an area where others speak the same language and read the same foreign language newspapers, eat the same foods, and celebrate the same holidays eases the initial adjustment.

INS statistics indicated that in fiscal 1996, more than 64,000 Mexican emigrants, interviewed before entering the United States, planned to settle in California, and more than 46,000 emigrants planned to live in Texas. California and Texas are home to the largest Mexican-American communities in the United States. More than 20,000 immigrants from the Dominican Republic reported their intention of moving to New York City, which was home to nearly 500,000 Dominicans by the mid-1990s. Chicago, a city of ethnic neighborhoods and a magnet for eastern Europeans, attracted 37,000 immigrants in fiscal 1992. Historically, Chicago also offered immigrants entry-level job opportunities—the third factor affecting settlement. Immigrants tend to go where job opportunities are best for their skills.

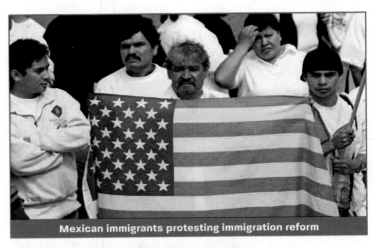

Mexican immigrants protesting immigration reform

Arguments against immigration.
Immigration policy became an intense political issue during the 1990s in most developed countries of the world, with "closed door" and "open door" advocates at the extremes. Opponents argued that an influx of foreign-born people would destroy national culture and traditions. In 1997, France's National Front political party rallied against African, Asian, and Middle Eastern immigrants by arguing that they threatened France's national identity. A similar argument was used by Japanese officials, who viewed Japan as culturally homogeneous.

Immigration opponents also argued that immigrants "took" jobs that native workers might fill, thereby hurting the employment opportunities of the native born. In the 1990s, the citizens of many prosperous countries expressed increased concern over the growing numbers of immigrants joining the work force. According to the U.S. Census Bureau, approximately 10 percent of the total work force in the United States in 1991—11.6 million people—was foreign-born. The figure included some 465,000 temporary workers. In Germany in 1995, the total number of foreign workers was 2.5 million, or 7.4 percent of the total work force, including the unemployed. In Japan in 1995, the total number of foreign workers was 590,000, or 0.9 percent of the total work force.

In France in 1995, 1.5 million laborers—6.2 percent of the work force—were classified as foreign. French politicians in 1997 suggested that the unemployment rate of 13 percent would fall dramatically if fewer immigrants were allowed in the country.

Another concern of critics of immigration in the 1990s was the financial burden on governments forced to care for low-income immigrants and their children. A 1997 report by the National Academy of Sciences and the National Research Council, two Washington, D.C.—based research organizations, showed that taxpayers in states with a high percentage of immigrants—California, Florida, and Texas, for example—suffered because of income differences between immigrants and native-born residents. The taxes that many new immigrants paid fell short of covering the costs of the government services they used, including healthcare and public education. The report noted that the average household in California in the 1990s paid an extra $1,178 annually in taxes because of immigrants. In 1996, California Governor Pete Wilson signed an executive order ending illegal immigrants' access to certain state benefits, including public housing, prenatal care, and child-abuse programs.

Arguments for immigration. The same 1997 National Academy of Sciences/National Research Council report concluded that the overall impact of immigration on the U.S. economy was not, however, that great in relation to the national economy as a whole. The report projected that each 1990s immigrant, during his or her lifetime, provided the treasury of the United States with $80,000 in extra tax revenue, reinforcing what proponents of an open immigration policy have longed argued—that immigrants enhanced the economy of the host country.

Advocates of open immigration argued that immigration can be a boon to a country's economy. Some experts favored immigration, contending that it tended to keep wages competitive and prices

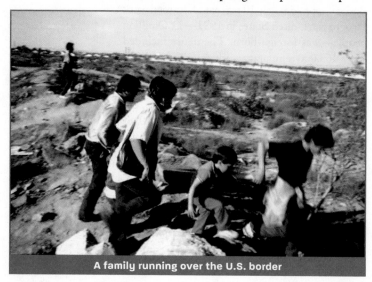
A family running over the U.S. border

low. Economists and immigration scholars stated that immigrants who are highly skilled greatly benefit a national economy. In the 1990s, Chinese engineers, Russian physicists, and Indian computer programmers, for example, earned high wages in the United States, increasing the gross domestic product and the American per capita income.

Advocates for an open-door policy also pointed out that immigrants tend to be young adults. In countries with very low (below replacement) rates of fertility, young adult immigrants helped slow the gradual aging and eventual decline in the population. In fact, some countries have attempted to lure immigrants to their shores in an effort to increase and add youth to the population and to strengthen the professional work force.

In the Canadian province of Quebec, which has a large French-speaking population, the provincial government budgeted $2 million in 1997 to recruit 4,000 workers from France. The effort was made to offset an increase in English-speaking immigrants and a low birthrate among French-speaking Quebecers. The government offered immediate permanent residence visas to French engineers, mechanics, and cooks.

The political debate over immigration. One interesting feature of the political debate over immigration in the 1990s was how the divide between proponents and opponents did not follow the "liberal left" versus "conservative right" split that defined many political issues. Open-door supporters included civil rights advocates and civil libertarians as well as businesspersons and labor leaders who supported free trade. The "restrictionists" included nationalists (extreme patriots), environmentalists, and business and labor leaders who supported the protection of domestic industry and workers.

Another remarkable aspect of the political debate surrounding immigration in the 1990s was the similarity of arguments from country to country and the similarity of arguments between time periods. The similarity of debate may result from the similarity of factors surrounding immigration in the 1990s and the late 1800s. While the latest wave of immigrants flowed from different directions, the force driving it remained the same: For the most part, people immigrated to better themselves economically. They settled in urban concentrations among people of similar circumstances. Large concentrates of the foreign born tended to produce fears among native-born citizens, and those fears culminated in legislation regulating immigrant flow.

Slowing the immigrant flow. In the mid-1990s, immigration did begin to slow. The Organization for Economic Cooperation and Development, a Paris-based multinational association working to promote economic and social welfare among members and to coordinate member aid to developing countries, announced in its 1996 annual report that legal immigration to many European countries began to level off and even decline in 1995 and 1996. The slowdown was attributed to new regulatory laws, rather than to a real decrease in the desire of people to leave one country for another.

Proponents of open-door immigration argue that such regulations are the products of racism or xenophobia. Some scholars of immigration, however, disagree. These scholars offer the theory that slow periods between waves—whether the result of regulation, economic downturn, or war—provide a "time-out" during which cross-cultural and economic absorption can be accomplished, quietly and harmoniously.

While the immigrant waves of the past changed the United States and its culture, American culture exerted an even greater effect on the immigrant population, which in one to two generations dispersed from ethnic enclaves and came to more closely resemble the native-born population. It is likely that the latest wave of immigrants will go through a similar process, this time not only in the United States but in other prosperous nations of the world.

About the author: Bruce R. Chiswick heads the Department of Economics at the University of Illinois at Chicago.

Immigration (1993)

Immigration emerged as a hot political issue in the United States in 1993. Opinion polls during the year found a majority of Americans favored curbs on immigration. In 1992, some 1.1 million immigrants entered the United States, the most since 1907.

Haitian policy kept. President Bill Clinton made immigration news even before he took office on January 20, 1993. On January 14, he said he would continue indefinitely the policy of forcibly returning any refugees from Haiti who were intercepted at sea while trying to reach the

United States. During his 1992 campaign, Clinton had said he was "appalled" by the policy, which had been formulated by his predecessor, President George Bush.

On June 21, 1993, the Supreme Court of the United States upheld the Bush-Clinton policy. The court said refugees were entitled to hearings on claims for political asylum only if they reached U.S. territory.

Ban on AIDS carriers. On February 18, the Senate voted 76 to 23 to keep a ban on immigration by foreigners infected with the virus that causes AIDS. On March 11, the House adopted the same position by a vote of 356 to 58. During his campaign, Clinton had vowed to repeal the ban, but he accepted Congress's decision and signed the bill on June 10.

Battling illegal immigration. On July 27, Clinton asked Congress for more money, more personnel, and tougher laws to fight illegal immigration. The most controversial aspect of Clinton's plan was a proposal to speed the interviews of immigrants seeking political asylum.

Under the current system, asylum seekers can stay in the United States while their claims are being investigated, a process that takes an average of eighteen months. Clinton proposed instead that expedited hearings be given to asylum seekers within days of the initial asylum claim. The preliminary hearings would allow officials to quickly identify and deport people with doubtful claims. But critics contended the expedited hearings could infringe on the rights of immigrants.

Clinton also sought $172.5 million in added outlays for the Immigration and Naturalization

California Governor Pete Wilson with his wife, Gayle

Service (INS), a 600-person increase in the Border Patrol, and stiffer criminal penalties for smugglers of illegal immigrants. Although most illegal immigrants come from Mexico, experts said crime syndicates smuggle thousands of Asians into the country each year.

New INS head. Clinton on June 18 nominated Doris M. Meissner to be commissioner of the INS. She had served as acting INS commissioner for President Ronald Reagan and had directed immigration studies at the Carnegie Endowment for International Peace in Washington, D.C., since 1986. Meissner was confirmed on October 14.

Immigration (1990)

Congress adopted the first big overhaul of United States immigration laws in a quarter century on October 27, 1990, to take effect in 1992. The Immigration Act of 1990, signed into law on November 29, dramatically expands immigration to the United States, at the same time uniting families and attracting skilled workers. The main provision of the legislation raises the cap on the number of visas granted to U.S.-bound foreigners from 500,000 a year in 1990 to 700,000 in the year 1994. The legislation also more than doubles the number of visas granted specifically on the basis of work skills, increasing that number from 54,000 a year to 140,000.

Supporters praised the overhaul as confirmation of the nation's historic "open-door" policy. A 1924 immigration law, on the other hand, set quotas country by country. In 1965, quotas were ended in favor of the current system, making family ties with U.S. residents the main determinant for entry.

Illegal immigration. The U.S. Immigration and Naturalization Service (INS) announced new guidelines on February 2, 1990, that may prevent as many as 100,000 illegal aliens from being deported. These aliens are children and spouses of immigrants legalized in 1986, when Congress granted amnesty to 1.7 million undocumented aliens. INS Commissioner Gene McNary said the new "family fairness" guidelines would apply only to illegal immigrants residing in the country since the amnesty took effect.

The INS reported on March 21, 1990, that illegal immigration across the Mexican border to the United States had surged in recent months, reversing a three-year downturn. Arrests of illegal aliens were up nearly 30 percent, totaling 801,937 from May 1988 through February 1989—compared with 617,317 for the same period a year earlier.

A government task force reported on September 30, 1990, that it found evidence "many employers" were discriminating in hiring-rejecting legal immigrants with proper work documents in favor of undocumented workers, whom they can usually hire for lower wages. Congress had warned employers they could risk penalties for hiring undocumented workers in a 1986 revision of laws concerning illegal immigration. Congress took no immediate action on a task force recommendation that the top fine for hiring discrimination be raised from $2,000 to $4,000.

Ellis Island revisited. In 1990, thousands of people poured through New York City's Ellis Island, gateway for millions of immigrants who reached U.S. shores between 1892 and 1954. The people who came this time were tourists, many of them descendants of immigrants. A $156-million restoration project reopened the island on September 9 as a museum of immigration.

Immigration (1989)

The 1986 Immigration Reform and Control Act, which aimed at curbing illegal immigration, has succeeded in reducing the flow of illegal immigrants into the United States, according to a study released on July 20, 1989, by the Urban Institute. The nonpartisan private research group said that border patrols operated by the U.S. Immigration and Naturalization Service (INS) arrested 1.3 million illegal immigrants, most from Mexico, in a two-year period ending in September 1988. That figure is 700,000 fewer than would have been found crossing if the 1986 law had not been enacted, according to a computer model that accounted for such factors as Mexican population growth and economic conditions.

The Urban Institute attributed 71 percent of the decline in border arrests to a provision of the law that placed civil and criminal penalties on U.S. businesses that hire illegal immigrants. The INS initially issued warnings for first offenses but stepped up enforcement in June 1988. Between then and February 1989, more than 1,200 employers—mostly small businesses—were fined a total of almost $4 million.

Visa lottery. On February 9, 1989, the U.S. Department of State announced that 10,000 extra

U.S. attorney general Richard Thornburgh

visas would be issued in both 1989 and 1990 to immigrants from 162 countries—most of them in Europe, Africa, and South America—deemed underrepresented in the usual immigration flow. People from those countries, including aliens living in the United States illegally, were eligible to apply for permanent residency through a special lottery designed to increase geographical diversity within the immigrant pool. Winners of visas would be chosen randomly by computer.

INS audit. On March 3, 1989, The Washington (D.C.) Post reported that a special Justice Department audit conducted for U.S. attorney general Richard L. Thornburgh found the INS overwhelmed by sloppy accounting, poor management procedures, and the demands of recent legislation expanding its responsibilities. In eight years, the INS had added 6,000 employees to its payroll while its budget increased by $650 million.

Proposed overhaul. On July 13, the Senate passed an immigration overhaul bill designed to increase immigration by skilled and educated workers, mostly Europeans, who lack close family

connections in the United States. Such connections, under present law, favor Latin-American and Asian immigrants.

The bill would set an initial annual immigration ceiling of 630,000, an increase of 136,000. Of the total, 150,000 slots would be reserved for immigrants who have no family connections but who do have skills, education, or other job-related assets. The Senate passed a similar bill in 1988, but it died in the House of Representatives Judiciary Committee. Prospects for House action on the new measure in 1990 were uncertain.

Immigration (1924)

Before the year 1917, with the exception of the Chinese Exclusion Act of 1882 and the so-called gentlemen's agreement in 1907, between the United States and Japan, which restricted the entry of Japanese into America, there were few limitations placed upon the rights of foreigners to enter the states. The question of restricting immigration of white people had been discussed frequently within the past two decades, but no legislation had resulted.

The total immigration into the country from 1790 to 1914 was over 32,000,000. Until about 1890 the majority of those seeking new homes in the Western world were much-desired English, Scandinavian, and German immigrants; subsequently the tide turned, and Eastern and Southern Europe contributed an increasing majority, a large proportion of whom were not of a quality likely to reach the level of American citizenship. Vast numbers of the latter class have settled, indeed, colonized, in cities and in a few rural communities, where they have retained racial customs and loyalties, and have failed to become what are thought of as Americans. There is ample evidence to support the belief that at the rate they have been obtaining admission to the United States they cannot readily be assimilated.

During the fiscal year ending June 30, 1914, just preceding the outbreak of the Great War, the United States admitted 1,218,480 aliens, and even that great number had been exceeded in one year, 1907, when 1,285,349 were admitted. During the years of the war the numbers fell to 326,700 in 1915, the first full year of the conflict, and to 110,600 in 1918, the last year. It was evident that with the return of peace the interrupted stream of applicants for asylum in America would flow again, in greater volume than ever before; therefore, the immigration question suddenly became a matter of primary importance.

Other reasons for the law of 1917. There were millions of alien-minded people in the United States who were not of a type which the "melting pot" could make American-minded; feelings of the old nationalism were aroused by the war, and the sympathies of too many were not with the American effort in that conflict. Moreover, it was known that large blocks of the foreign element were actually disloyal to the country of their adoption. What would happen in the event that a few more years of unrestricted immigration should add 10,000,000 more Europeans to the millions already in the country, and another war should involve America, requiring patriotic united action of its people.

To stop the indiscriminate flood of millions, a new immigration law, passed in 1917, limited the

An Italian immigrant waits at Ellis Island.

number of those thereafter to be admitted from any one country to 3 percent of the number of natives of that country who were resident in the United States in 1910, as shown by the census of that year. This law was to be in force for five years, until June 30, 1922. Under its operation the maximum number of immigrants who could be admitted from each of the leading European countries was as follows.

In the fiscal year 1917–1918 (ending June 30), under this act there were admitted 110,618 immigrants; in 1919, 141,132; in 1920, 430,001; in 1921, 805,228. Because the law would expire in midyear of 1922, the number seeking admission was much larger in 1921 than in the preceding year. No conclusions having been reached as to future policy, the law was extended two years, to expire June 30, 1924. In 1922 the number admitted was 309,556; in 1923, 522,919.

The law of 1924. An analysis of the law of 1917 disclosed that the number of immigrants from Eastern and Southern Europe greatly overbalanced that from the Northern countries; the number of undesirables, to state it bluntly, far exceeded those capable of reaching the American standard. A study of immigration statistics furnished a basis for a new law which would reverse the ratio as between Northern and Eastern-Southern Europe. Up to 1890 the wave of immigration was largely from the north; a law which would admit people from any country in proportion to its number of natives who were in the United States at the time of the census of 1890 would entirely change the character of American immigrants.

What is known as the Johnson Bill was passed by Congress in May 1924. It was based on the census of 1890, and provided that the number to be admitted from any country should be 2 percent of those already here from that country in 1890. Furthermore, it provided for exclusion from entry all aliens who were not privileged under the naturalization laws to become citizens. This provision was aimed particularly at the Japanese. It was also provided that after June 30, 1927, the total number of immigrants to be admitted from all countries in any fiscal year should be 150,000, based on foreign-born totals in the United States in 1920.

It will be seen that the Johnson Act radically curtails all but Anglo-Saxon nationalities.

Thus, the United States has entered upon an entirely new economic policy. In no other nation have immigration problems ever been exactly similar to those in America, and while a number of countries have laws which exclude undesirables, Australia being a notable example, the United States is alone in declaring how many eligible men, women, and children shall be admitted from any source.

Japanese protest. The Empire of Japan was deeply affected because the new law provided for absolute exclusion of its nationals except for purposes of travel, study, and temporary business errands. Its officials pointed to the "gentlemen's agreement" of 1907 as a sufficient barrier against an exodus of Japanese to the United States, and they declared that the agreement had been honestly enforced. If, however, the American people were insistent on Japanese exclusion, they declared that the end sought could be reached by diplomatic means rather than by explicit laws, with less affront to the sensibilities of Nippon; it would be particularly offensive to national pride to be the special victims of a clause in a law of Congress.

The Department of State and the President of the United States declared to Congress that there could be no menace in including Japan with other nations in the new law, for under it only 146 Japanese could be admitted yearly; they sympathized with the Japanese attitude, at the same time favoring exclusion, and proposed that the desired end should be reached by agreement and not through the immigration law, but their advice was not heeded.

What was the "gentlemen's agreement"? The following is the summary of the arrangement for restricting immigration from Japan, in effect since 1907, but now abrogated by the Johnson Act:

First: Japan, of her own accord, will refrain from issuing passports to Japanese laborers desiring to enter territories contiguous to continental United States, such as Mexico or Canada.

Second: Japan will recognize the right of the United States to refuse the admission to continental United States of Japanese of the laboring class whose passports do not include continental United States.

Third: Japan will issue passports to continental United States only for Japanese of the following three classes: (1) non-laborers, such as travelers, businessmen, financiers, etc.; (2) Japanese, whether laborers or non-laborers, who have already become domiciled in continental United States; (3) Japan-

ese, who have acquired farming interests in continental United States and who wish to return there to take active control of these interests.

Italy's position. The Italian government was much distressed over the passage of the new American immigration law, because the number of Italians who may enter the United States yearly hereafter is much reduced. It is absolutely necessary for many of the people of Italy to emigrate; while to Americans the desire of Italians to move to the United States may seem a mere matter of improving their condition, to the latter it is a matter almost of life and death. Italy is virtually an island surrounded by sea and mountains, and it is vastly overpopulated. The overworked soil can sustain only a portion of the population; the remainder must live by industrial labor. But as Italy is a country almost entirely without raw materials, it is at a constant disadvantage in industrial competition with other countries.

The Italian government admits that, generally speaking, only the lower class of Italians have emigrated to America. Premier Mussolini recognizes the right of every nation to make its own immigration laws, and asserts that Italy has no desire to send to the United States men and women whom America declares are unacceptable. After the first disappointment over the reduction in the quota permitted under the new law, the Italian government declared that Italy is prepared hereafter to send to the United States only the kind of immigrants the latter is willing to accept.

Plants

Scientists believe there are more than 260,000 species (kinds) of plants. Plants grow in almost every part of the world, on mountaintops, in the oceans, in deserts, and in polar regions.

HOT topics

Early Plants. Most scientists think that all plants on land developed from the same green algae ancestor. Based on evidence from fossils of spores, plants may have begun making the transition to land about 470 million years ago. They had become well established on land by 430 million years ago. Some genetic studies suggest that plants may have appeared on land 500 million years ago or even much earlier. Before this transition, land was mostly rocky and barren, supporting only microbial life. The spread of plants transformed the land, providing habitat for animals and other organisms.

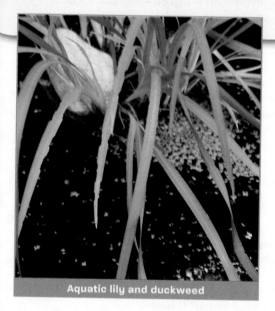

Aquatic lily and duckweed

HOT topics

Plants as Food.
People get food from many kinds of plants—or parts of plants. The seeds of such plants as corn, rice, and wheat are the chief source of food in most parts of the world. We eat bread and many other products made from these grains, and almost all our meat comes from animals that eat them. When we eat beets, carrots, or sweet potatoes, we are eating the roots of plants. We eat the leaves of cabbage, lettuce, and spinach plants; the stems of asparagus and celery plants; and the flower buds of broccoli and cauliflower plants. The fruits of many plants also provide us with food. They include apples, bananas, berries, and oranges, as well as some nuts and vegetables. Coffee, tea, and many soft drinks get their flavor from plants.

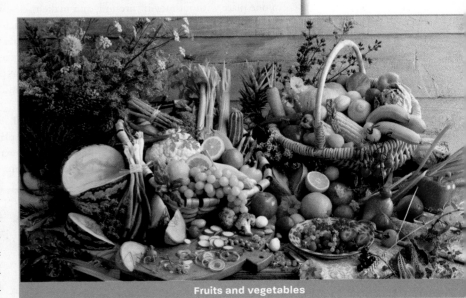
Fruits and vegetables

Aquatic Plants.
Most aquatic plants, which are also called hydrophytes, live in places that receive sunlight. These plants grow near the water surface, in shallow water, or along the shore. Some kinds of aquatic plants, including eelgrass, live completely under the surface of the water. Others, such as duckweed, the smallest known flowering plant, float freely on the surface. Still others, such as the water marigold, grow only partly underwater. Many aquatic plants have air spaces in their stems and leaves. The air spaces help them stand erect or stay afloat.

Global Warming.
Plants also are threatened by global warming, an increase in the average temperature at Earth's surface. Climate scientists estimate that Earth's average surface temperature rose by about 1.4°F (0.76°C) from the mid-1800s to the early 2000s. This warming has caused other climate changes, such as changing patterns of precipitation. An increase in carbon dioxide in the atmosphere causes most global warming. This increase comes chiefly from burning coal, oil, and natural gas.

TRUE or FALSE?
People began to play an important role in changing plants about 10,000 years ago.

THE BASICS

Plants are members of a diverse kingdom of living things that generally have more than one cell, live in one place without moving around, and make their own food using sunlight. Plants grow in almost every part of the world. They grow in parks and yards, in forests, on plains, on mountains, in wetlands, in the oceans, and in deserts. Most of us see flowers, grasses, and trees nearly every day.

Without plants, people could not survive. The oxygen we breathe comes mostly from plants. We get nearly all our food from plants or from animals that eat plants. We build houses and make many useful products from lumber. The fibers of bamboo, cotton, and flax plants supply clothing. Plants also serve as sources of medicine.

Scientists have identified hundreds of thousands of *species* (kinds) of plants. But no one knows the total number of plant species in the world. Some tiny plants that grow on the forest floor can barely be seen. Others tower over people and animals. The sequoia trees of California rank among the largest living things on Earth. Some stand over 290 feet (88 meters) tall and have trunks over 30 feet (9 meters) in diameter. Some plants have extremely long life spans. A bristlecone pine tree in California, for example, has been growing since 4,000 to 5,000 years ago.

Plants have characteristics that set them apart from other living things. For example, nearly all kinds of plants stay in one place, from the moment they put down roots until they die. Most plants make their own food from air, sunlight, and water by a process called *photosynthesis*. Like animals, plants are complex living things made up of many types of cells. But plant cells have thick walls made of a material called *cellulose*. Animal cells do not have walls.

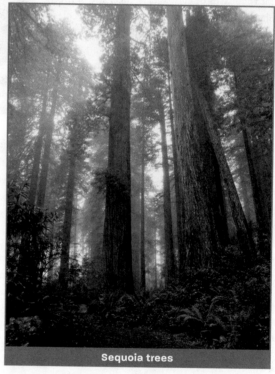
Sequoia trees

The Importance of Plants

Plants supply people with food, clothing, and shelter. Some of our most useful medicines come from plants. Plants also add beauty and pleasure to our lives. Most people enjoy the smell of flowers, the sight of a field of waving grain, and the quiet within a forest.

Not all plants are helpful to people. Some species grow unwanted in fields and gardens as weeds, competing with more desirable plants for resources. Tiny grains of pollen from certain plants cause such health problems as asthma and hay fever. Some plants are poisonous if eaten. Others, such as poison ivy and poison oak, irritate the skin.

 As food. Plants are probably most important to people as a source of food. Sometimes we eat plant parts directly, as when we eat apples, peas, or potatoes. But even when we eat meat or drink milk, we are consuming foods from animals that eat plants.

People get food from many kinds of plants. But the seeds of such plants as corn, rice, and wheat are the chief source of food in most parts of the world. We eat bread, pasta, and many other products made from these grains. In addition, almost all our meat except seafood comes from animals that eat grain.

Different parts of plants serve as food. When we eat beets, carrots, or sweet potatoes, we are eating the roots of plants. We eat the leaves of cabbage, lettuce, and spinach plants; the stems of asparagus; the leaf stalks of celery plants; and the flower buds of broccoli and cauliflower plants. The fruits of many plants also provide food. They include apples, bananas, berries, and oranges, as well as some nuts and vegetables. Coffee, tea, and many soft drinks get their flavor from plants.

As raw materials. Plants supply people with important raw materials. Trees give us lumber for building homes and making furniture and other goods. Wood chips are used in manufacturing paper and paper products. Other products made from trees include cork, maple syrup, natural rubber, and turpentine. Most of the world's people wear clothing made from cotton. Threads of cotton are also woven into carpets and other goods. Rope and twine are made from hemp, jute, and sisal plants.

Plants also provide an important source of fuel. In many parts of the world, people burn wood to heat their homes or to cook their food. Fossil fuels, such as coal and natural gas, can also come from plants. Coal began to form millions of years ago, when great forests and swamps covered much of Earth. As the trees in these forests died, they fell into the swamps. Mud and sand covered them. The increasing pressure of this mass of materials helped turn the dead plants into coal. People can also use plants to make *biofuel*. Biofuel is any fuel made from biological materials. For example, corn and sugar cane can be processed into ethanol. Soybeans and oil palms are used to make biodiesel. These fuels can replace fossil fuels in transportation and industry.

As medicines. A variety of useful drugs come from plants. Some of these plants have been used as medicines for hundreds of years. For example, more than 400 years ago, some Indian tribes of South America used the bark of the cinchona tree to reduce fever. The bark is still used to make quinine, a drug used to treat malaria and other diseases. The roots of the Mexican yam are used in producing cortisone, a drug useful in treating arthritis and a number of other diseases.

In ecosystems. Plants are a vital part of *ecosystems*. An ecosystem consists of all the living and nonliving things in an area and the relationships among them. Plants use the energy in sunlight to make their own food, and they give off oxygen during the process. People and animals eat the plants and breathe in the oxygen. In turn, people and animals breathe out carbon dioxide. Plants combine carbon dioxide with water to make food, using the energy in sunlight. After plants and animals die, they begin to decay. The rotting process returns *nutrients* (nourishing substances) to the soil, where living plants can use them.

Kinds of Plants

The study of plants is called *botany*, and scientists who study plants are known as *botanists*. Botanists classify plants according to *common descent*—that is, by dividing them into groups that share a common ancestor. The result somewhat resembles a family tree. Closely related plants share many similarities. Distant relatives share fewer similarities. Some definitions of plants include green algae or even other organisms, but this article considers only land plants and their *aquatic* (water-dwelling) descendants.

One major group consists of *nonvascular plants*. These plants lack *vascular tissue*—that is, tissue that carries water and food throughout the plant. The other major group consists of *vascular plants*, which contain these tissues. Within these groups are many smaller groupings. A table showing a more detailed system of plant classification appears with this article.

Nonvascular plants consist of hornworts, liverworts, and mosses. Nonvascular plants are traditionally called *bryophytes*, though many scientists consider mosses to be the only true bryophytes. Nonvascular plants make up only a small fraction of the total number of plants. They live in almost

Beets

all parts of the world, from the Arctic to tropical forests. They typically grow in such moist, shady places as forests and ravines.

Most hornworts, liverworts, and mosses measure less than 8 inches (20 centimeters) tall. None of these plants has true roots. Instead, they have hairy rootlike growths called *rhizoids* that anchor them to the soil and absorb water and minerals

Vascular plants have tissue that carries water and food throughout the plant. The vast majority of plants are vascular plants. There are four main groups of vascular plants: (1) lycophytes, (2) ferns and related plants, (3) gymnosperms, and (4) angiosperms.

Lycophytes include club mosses, quillworts, and selaginellas. These plants have leaves with a single, central vein. Lycophytes were among the first vascular plants. Although modern lycophytes are small, some prehistoric lycophytes grew to the size of trees. Plant matter from lycophytes and ferns later formed much of the world's coal.

Club mosses have tiny needlelike or scalelike leaves that usually grow in a spiral pattern. They are not true mosses. Club mosses are found from tropical to *temperate* (mild) regions. They often form a "carpet" on the forest floor

Quillworts are found chiefly in moist soils around lakes and streams. They have short stems

Fern

and grasslike leaves that usually grow to about 14 inches (36 centimeters) long. Ancient plants related to quillworts were large trees that grew up to 120 feet (37 meters) tall.

Selaginellas are usually found in tropical and subtropical regions. They often grow in damp places on the forest floor. Selaginellas have small thin leaves. Their stems may either grow upright or along the ground.

Ferns and related plants grow chiefly in moist, wooded regions. They vary widely in size and form. Some aquatic ferns have leaves only about 1 inch (2.5 centimeters) long. But in the tropics, tree ferns may grow more than 65 feet (20 meters) high.

Most fern leaves, called *fronds*, consist of many tiny leaflets and may grow large. On most types of ferns, the fronds are the only parts that grow above the ground. They sprout from underground stems that may run horizontally under the surface of the ground. When the fronds first appear, they are tightly coiled. The fronds unwind as they grow.

Whisk ferns and horsetails have mostly hollow, jointed stems. Whisk ferns have many slender, highly branched stems. They grow mostly in tropical and subtropical regions. Horsetails grow about 2 to 3 feet (60 to 90 centimeters) tall. The plants have green stems and tiny, dark leaves. The stems capture the sunlight used by the plant to make food in photosynthesis. In some horsetails, the branches grow in *whorls* (circles) around the main stem of the plant, and the plant resembles a horse's tail.

Gymnosperms include a wide variety of trees and shrubs that produce *naked* (uncovered) seeds. Most gymnosperms bear their seeds in cones. The word *gymnosperm* comes from two Greek words meaning *naked* and *seed*. Gymnosperms do not produce true flowers. This group is made up of such plants as conifers, cycads, gingkoes, and gnetophytes.

Conifers are the best known of the gymnosperms. They include such trees as cedars, cypresses, firs, pines, redwoods, and spruces. Most conifers have needlelike or scalelike leaves. Their seeds grow on the upper side of the scales that make up their cones. The cones of some conifers, such as junipers, look like berries. Most conifers are evergreens—that is, they shed old leaves and grow new leaves continuously and so stay green throughout the year. Wood from conifers is widely used in construction and papermaking.

Pine trees

Cycads and ginkgoes flourished for much of the time that dinosaurs lived. Most cycads look much like palm trees. They have a branchless trunk topped by a crown of long leaves. But unlike palm trees, they bear their seeds in large cones. Many cycads are in danger of becoming extinct. Only one kind of ginkgo survives today. It is an ornamental tree with flat, fan-shaped leaves. It bears seeds at the ends of short stalks along its branches.

Gnetophytes have many features that resemble those of flowering plants. For example, a group of tropical trees and vines called *Gnetum* has broad, oval-shaped leaves and special water-transport tubes, much like those of angiosperms. The cones of all gnetophytes are flowerlike in many details.

Angiosperms are flowering plants. They produce seeds that are enclosed in a protective seed case. The word *angiosperm* comes from two Greek words meaning *vessel* and *seed*. All plants that produce flowers and fruits are angiosperms. They are by far the largest group of plants, greatly outnumbering all other plants put together. They include most of our common plants, such as brightly colored garden plants, the many kinds of wildflowers, and most herbs, shrubs, and trees. Most of the plants that produce the fruits, grains, and vegetables that people eat are angiosperms.

Angiosperms vary greatly in size. The smallest flowering plants, the duckweeds, are only about $1/50$ inch (0.5 millimeter) long. The largest angiosperms are eucalyptus trees. They grow over 300 feet (90 meters) tall.

Botanists divide angiosperms into several groups. These include the *monocotyledons*, also called *monocots*, and the *eudicotyledons*, also called *eudicots*. Monocots grow from seeds with one seed leaf, called a *cotyledon*. All other angiosperms, including the eudicots, have seeds with two cotyledons.

Where Plants Live

Most species of plants live in places that have warm temperatures at least part of the year, plentiful rainfall, and rich soil. But plants can live under extreme conditions. Mosses grow in Antarctic areas, for example, where the temperature seldom rises above 32°F (0°C). Many desert plants flourish in areas where the temperature may rise well above 100°F (38°C).

Each kind of plant needs a particular kind of environment to thrive. For example, cattails live only in such damp places as marshes and swamps. Cactuses, on the other hand, grow chiefly in deserts. The type of environment a plant lives in is called its *habitat*.

Many elements make up a plant's environment. One of the most important is climate—the typical temperature, amount of sunlight, and precipitation in an area. The environment of a plant also includes the soil and the plants, animals, and other organisms that live in the same area. All these elements are important parts of the plant's ecosystem.

Botanists divide the world into *biomes*—natural communities of plants, animals, and other organisms. Important land biomes include (1) the tundra, (2) *boreal* forests, also known as *taiga* (3) temperate coniferous forests, (4) temperate deciduous forests, (5) chaparrals, (6) deserts, (7) grass-

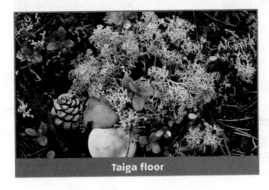

Taiga floor

lands, (8) savannas, (9) tropical rain forests, and (10) tropical dry forests. In addition, many plants live in aquatic regions.

Human beings have greatly affected biomes. In North America, for example, great forests once extended from the Atlantic Ocean to the Mississippi River. Advancing settlers cleared most of the trees, and cities and farms replaced the forests. In other parts of the world, irrigation and the use of fertilizers have enabled plants to grow on once-barren land. This section describes the natural plant life in the important land biomes and in aquatic regions.

The tundra is a cold, treeless area that surrounds the Arctic Ocean, near the North Pole. It extends across the uppermost parts of Asia, Europe, and North America. The land in these regions remains frozen most of the year. The annual precipitation measures only from 6 to 10 inches (15 to 25 centimeters). The upper slopes of the world's highest mountains—the Alps, the Andes, the Himalaya, and the Rockies—have conditions similar to those in the tundra.

Summers in the tundra last only about 60 days, and summer temperatures average only about 45°F (7°C). The top 1 foot (30 centimeters) or so of the ground thaws during the summer, leaving many marshes, ponds, and swamps. Such plants as mosses, shrubs, and wildflowers grow in the tundra. These plants grow in low clumps and so are protected from the wind and cold. A thick growth of *lichens* (organisms made up of algae and fungi) covers much of the land.

Boreal forests, also called taiga, grow in regions that have a short summer and a long, cold winter. The growing season may last less than three months. Boreal forests cover many northern parts of Asia, Europe, and North America. They also grow on the high mountains of these continents. Trees in boreal forests include such evergreen conifers as balsam firs, black spruces, jack pines, and white spruces. The pointy, triangular shape of these trees helps them shed heavy snow.

Few plants grow on the floor of boreal forests. Thick layers of old needles build up beneath the trees. These needles contain acids that are slowly released as the needles decay. Water carries the acids into the soil. The acidic water dissolves many minerals and carries them into the deeper layers of the soil. As a result, the topsoil in boreal forests is often sandy and unable to support many types of small plants.

Temperate coniferous forests grow in western North America and parts of Europe and Asia. They stand along coasts or on mountains. They grow in areas that have mild, wet winters and warm, dry summers. The redwood forests of northern California and the kauri forests of New Zealand are both examples of temperate coniferous forests. Major trees of temperate coniferous forests include cedars, Douglas firs, giant sequoias, hemlocks, pines, and redwoods.

Temperate deciduous forests cover large areas of North America, central Europe, eastern Asia, Australia, and New Zealand. In the United States, temperate deciduous forests grow mostly east of the Mississippi River and extend northward into Canada. Most of these areas have cold winters and warm, wet summers.

Most of the trees in temperate deciduous forests are *broadleaf trees.* Such trees have broad, flat leaves. They also are *deciduous*—that is, they lose their leaves every fall and grow new ones in the spring. Trees in temperate deciduous forests include ashes, basswoods, beeches, birches, hickories, maples, oaks, poplars, yellow-poplars, and walnuts. A thick growth of wildflowers, seedlings, and shrubs typically covers the forest floor.

Chaparrals consist of thick growths of shrubs and small trees. Cork and scrub oaks, manzanitas, and many unusual herbs grow on chaparrals. Chaparrals occur in areas with hot, dry summers and cool, wet winters. Such areas exist in western North America, southern Europe, the

Birch trees

Beavertail cactus

Middle East, and northern Africa. They also occur in southern parts of Africa, Australia, and South America.

During the dry summer season, fires often break out on chaparrals. But these fires actually help to maintain plant life. Many of the plants that grow on chaparrals are either resistant to fire or able to grow back quickly after they burn. The fires clear the dense vegetation away and expose bare ground to allow for new growth. The heat stimulates development in the seeds of some plants. In addition, many types of short-lived, small flowers appear only after a fire has taken place.

Deserts cover about a fifth of Earth's land. A huge desert region extends across northern Africa and into central Asia. This region includes three of the world's great deserts—the Arabian, the Gobi, and the Sahara. Other major deserts of the world include the Atacama Desert along the western coast of South America, the Kalahari Desert in southern Africa, the Western Plateau of Australia, and the Sonoran Desert of North America.

Some deserts have almost no plant life at all. Parts of the Gobi and the Sahara, for example, consist chiefly of shifting sand dunes. All deserts receive little rain and have either rocky or sandy soil. The temperature in most deserts rises above 100°F (38°C) for at least part of the year. Some deserts also have cold periods. But despite these harsh conditions, many plants live in desert regions. These plants—sometimes called *xerophytes*—include acacias, cactuses, creosote bushes, Joshua trees, sagebrush, and yuccas. Wildflowers also bloom in the desert.

Desert plants do not grow close together. By spreading out, each plant can collect water and minerals from a large area. The roots of most desert plants extend over large areas to capture as much rain water as possible. Cactuses and other *succulent* (fleshy) plants store water in their thick leaves and stems

Grasslands are open areas where grasses are the most plentiful plants. Botanists divide grasslands into *steppes* and *prairies*. Only short grasses grow on steppes. These dry areas include the Great Plains of the United States and Canada, the veld of South Africa, and the plains of Kazakhstan and southern Russia. Taller grasses grow on the prairies of the American Midwest, eastern Argentina, and parts of Europe and Asia.

Rolling hills, clumps of trees, and rivers and streams break up these areas. Most of the soil is rich, and rainfall is plentiful. As a result, people use almost all prairie land to raise food crops and livestock. Farmers and ranchers grow such grains as barley, corn, oats, and wheat where bluestem, buffalo, and grama grasses once covered the land.

Savannas are grasslands with widely spaced trees. Some savannas exist in regions that receive little rain. Others are in tropical regions, such as the Llanos of Venezuela, the Campos of southern Brazil, and the Sudan of Africa. Most of these areas have dry winters and wet summers. Grasses grow tall and stiff under such conditions. Acacia, baobab, and palm trees grow on many savannas. A wide variety of animals, such as antelope, giraffes, lions, and zebras, roam the savannas of Africa.

Tropical rain forests grow in regions that have warm, wet weather the year around. These regions include Central America and the northern parts of South America, central and western Africa, Southeast Asia, and the Pacific Islands.

Most trees in tropical rain forests are broadleaf trees. Because of the warm, wet weather, they never completely lose their leaves. These trees lose a few leaves at a time throughout the year. Many kinds of trees grow in tropical rain forests, including cinnamon, mahogany, teak, and *cacao*, from which chocolate is made. The trees grow so close together that little sunlight can reach the ground. As a result, only ferns and other plants that require little light can grow on the forest floor. Many plants, including orchids and vines, grow high on the trees.

The topsoil in tropical rain forests is of poor quality because heavy rainfall can wash away nutrients. But the hot, humid conditions and the activities of such organisms as fungi and termites rapidly break down fallen leaves and other plant matter. Breaking down this material releases nutrients back into the soil. Living plants then quickly absorb the nutrients, enabling lush growth.

Tropical dry forests, also called *tropical seasonal forests* or *seasonally dry tropical forests*, grow in warm areas that have wet and dry seasons. They are found in tropical to subtropical areas in parts of Florida, Mexico, Central America, South America, Africa, India, Southeast Asia, and Australia. They also grow on islands in the Caribbean Sea and the Indian and Pacific oceans. Average yearly rainfall can be as high as in some tropical rain forests. But most of the rain falls in the wet season. Little rain falls in the dry season, which can last for months.

Most trees in tropical dry forests are broadleaf trees. Despite the warm temperatures, the stress of the long dry season causes nonevergreen trees to lose their leaves, much as do temperate deciduous forests in the winter. The fallen leaves return nutrients to the soil. The bareness of the trees in the dry season allows increased light to pass, leading to the growth of dense underbrush. Many kinds of trees grow in tropical dry forests, including acacias, baobabs, kapoks, and kola trees.

Aquatic regions are bodies of fresh or salt water. Freshwater areas include lakes, rivers, and swamps. Coastal marshes and oceans are saltwater regions. Most aquatic plants, which also are called *hydrophytes*, live in places that receive sunlight. These plants grow near the water surface, in shallow water, or along the shore.

Some kinds of aquatic plants, including eelgrass, live completely underwater. Other aquatic plants, such as duckweeds, float on the surface. Still others, such as the water marigold, grow only partly underwater. Many aquatic plants have air spaces in their stems and leaves. The air spaces help them stand erect or stay afloat.

Aquatic regions have unique conditions that make it difficult for many types of plants to grow there. For example, swamps and marshes become flooded, leaving the plants that live in these areas completely covered by water. As a result, only a limited number of plant species survive. Common freshwater plants include cattails, duckweeds, pondweeds, sedges, and water lilies. Such trees as bald cypresses, black gums, and willows also grow

in fresh water. Saltwater plants include cordgrass, eelgrass, and sedges.

Mangrove forests are dense growths of mangrove trees. They grow along ocean coastlines throughout the tropics and subtropics. Mangrove plants have adaptations to living in salty, waterlogged conditions. These can include stilt roots that prop the plants above the water, pores in the bark that enable the plants to breathe, leaves that can remove excess salt, and seeds that float. Mangrove forests are important because they stabilize coastlines. Their complex structures also provide places for living things to hide from *predators* (hunting animals). Mangrove forests provide habitat for many animals. These include crabs, fish, turtles, shrimp, snails, cats such as panthers and tigers, and shore birds.

Shallow ocean waters may support underwater meadows of sea grass. Sea grasses are flowering plants distinct from seaweeds, which are actually types of algae. Sea grasses live around the world in shallow coastal waters, where there is enough light for photosynthesis. Sea grass beds provide food and shelter for many organisms, including algae, birds, crabs, fish, manatees, mollusks, sea urchins, turtles, and worms. Mangrove forests and sea grass meadows are among the most threatened of all ecosystems.

Parts of Plants

Plants—like all living things—are made up of cells. In plants, there are many kinds of cells that have special jobs. Together, these cells form the various parts of the plant. A giant redwood tree, for example, has many billions of cells.

A group of cells that are organized to perform a particular function make up a *tissue*. Plants include many types of complex tissues. All plants, except nonvascular plants—that is, hornworts, liverworts, and mosses—have tissue specialized to carry water, minerals, and other nutrients throughout the body. This tissue is called *vascular tissue*. It consists of two specialized tissues called *xylem* and *phloem*. Xylem carries water and minerals from the roots of the plant to the leaves. Phloem carries food made through photosynthesis in the leaves to the other parts of the plant.

A plant consists of several important parts. Flowering plants, the most common type of plants, have four main parts: (1) roots, (2) stems, (3) leaves, and (4) flowers. The roots, stems, and leaves are called the *vegetative parts* of a plant. The flowers, fruits, and seeds are known as the *reproductive parts.*

Roots. Most roots grow underground. As the roots of a plant spread, they absorb the water and minerals that the plant needs to grow. The roots also anchor the plant in the soil. In addition, the roots of some plants store food. Plants with food-storing roots include beets, carrots, radishes, and sweet potatoes.

There are two main kinds of root systems—*fibrous* and *taproot.* Grass is an example of a plant with a fibrous root system. It has many slender roots of about the same size that spread out in all directions. A plant with a taproot system has one root, called the *taproot that* is larger than the rest. Carrots and radishes have taproots. Taproots grow straight down, some as deep as 15 feet (5 meters).

The root is one of the first parts of a plant that starts to grow. A *primary root* develops from a plant's seed and quickly produces branches called *secondary roots.* At the tip of each root is a thimble-shaped *root cap.* The root cap protects the root's delicate tip as it pushes through the soil. Threadlike *root hairs* grow farther back on the root. Few of these structures reach over 1/2 inch (13 millimeters) long. But there are so many of them that they greatly increase the plant's ability to absorb water and minerals from the soil.

The roots of some aquatic plants float freely in the water. Other plants, such as orchids and some vines, have roots that attach themselves to tree branches.

The roots of nearly all plants have a special relationship with fungi. In this relationship, known as *mycorrhiza,* fungi cover or penetrate the growing tips of a plant's roots. Water and nutrients enter the roots through the fungi. The presence of fungi extends the root system and improves its ability to absorb water and minerals.

Stems differ greatly among various plant species. They make up the largest parts of some kinds of plants. For example, the trunk, branches, and twigs of trees are all stems. Other plants, such as cabbage and lettuce, have such short stems and large leaves that they appear to have no stems at all. The stems of still other plants, including potatoes, grow partly underground.

Most stems grow upright and support the leaves and reproductive parts of plants. The stems hold the leaves up where they can receive sunlight. Some stems grow along the ground or underground.

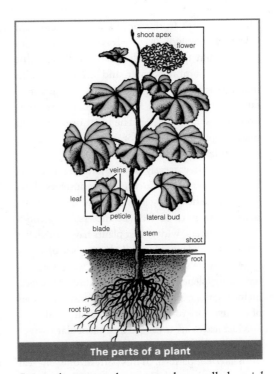

The parts of a plant

Stems that grow aboveground are called *aerial stems,* and those underground are known as *subterranean stems.* Aerial stems are either woody or *herbaceous* (nonwoody). Plants with woody stems include trees and shrubs. These plants are rigid because they contain large amounts of woody xylem. Most herbaceous stems are soft and green because they contain only small amounts of xylem.

In nearly all plants, a stem grows longer from the end, called the *apex.* The cells that form this growth area are together known as the *apical meristem.* An apical meristem grows the plant by producing a column of new cells behind itself. These cells develop into the specialized tissues of the stem and leaves. A resting apical meristem and the cluster of developing leaves that surround it is called a *bud.*

Buds may grow on various parts of the stem. A *terminal bud* forms at the end of a branch. A *lateral bud* develops at a point where a leaf joins the stem. This point is called a *node.* Buds may develop into new branches, leaves, or flowers. Some buds are covered with tiny overlapping leaves called *bud scales.* The bud scales protect the soft, growing tissue of the apical meristem. During winter, the buds of many plants are *dormant* (inactive) and can be seen easily. In the spring, these buds resume their growth.

Leaves make most of the food that plants need to live and grow. They produce food by photosynthesis. In this process, a green pigment called chlorophyll in the leaves absorbs light energy from the sun. The plant's cells use this energy to combine water and carbon dioxide, making sugar. From sugar, plants can make starch, fat, protein, vitamins, and other complex compounds essential for life. The plant uses the food made by photosynthesis for growth and repair or stores it in the stems or roots.

Leaves differ greatly in size and shape. Some leaves are less than 1 inch (2.5 centimeters) long and wide. The largest leaves, those of the raffia palm, grow up to 65 feet (20 meters) long and 8 feet (2.4 meters) wide. Most plants have broad, flat leaves. The edges, also called *margins*, of these leaves may be smooth, toothed, or wavy. Grasses have long, slender leaves. A few kinds of leaves, including the needles of pine trees and the spines of cactuses, are rounded and have sharp ends.

Most leaves are arranged in a particular pattern on a plant. The leaves of many kinds of plants grow in an *alternate* pattern. In this pattern, only one leaf forms at each node. On plants with the simplest kind of alternate pattern, a leaf appears first on one side of the stem and then on the other side. On plants with a more complex alternate pattern, the nodes are spaced in a spiral pattern around the stem and the leaves seem to encircle the stem from bottom to top. If two leaves grow from opposite sides of the same node, the plant has an *opposite* arrangement of leaves. If three or more leaves grow equally spaced around a single node on the stem, the plant has a *whorled* arrangement of leaves.

A leaf begins as a small bump next to the apical meristem. Most leaves develop two main parts—

Dandelions

the *blade* and the *petiole*. The blade is the flat part of the leaf. Some leaves, called *simple leaves*, have only one blade. Leaves with two or more blades are called *compound leaves*. The petiole is a thin leaf-stalk that grows between the base of the blade and the stem. It carries water and food to and from the blades. The leaves of some plants also have a pair of parts called *stipules*. The stipules are two leaflike structures that grow where the petiole joins the stem. Most stipules look like tiny leaves.

A network of veins distributes water to the food-producing areas of a leaf. The veins also help support the leaf and hold its surface up to the sun. The upper and lower surfaces of a leaf are called the *epidermis* (skin). The epidermis has tiny openings called *stomata*. Carbon dioxide, oxygen, water vapor, and other gases pass in and out through the stomata.

Flowers contain the reproductive parts of flowering plants. Flowers develop from buds along the stem of a plant. Some kinds of plants produce only one flower, but others grow many large clusters of flowers. Still others, such as daisies and dandelions, have many tiny flowers that form a single, flowerlike head.

Most flowers have four main parts: (1) the *calyx*, (2) the *corolla*, (3) the *stamens*, and (4) the *carpels*.

The calyx consists of small, usually green, leaflike structures called *sepals*. The sepals protect the flower bud. Inside the calyx are the petals. The petals are the largest, most colorful part of most flowers. All the petals of a flower make up the corolla. The flower's reproductive organs—the stamens and carpels—are attached to the stem inside the sepals and the petals. In many flowers, the stamens and petals are *fused* (joined).

The stamen is a male reproductive organ, and the carpel is a female reproductive organ. Each stamen has an enlarged part called an *anther* on the end of a long, narrow stalk called the *filament*. Pollen grains, which develop *sperm* (male sex cells), are produced in the anther.

Carpels of most flowers have three main parts: (1) a structure called the *stigma* at the top, (2) a slender tube called the *style* in the middle, and (3) a round base called the *ovary*. The ovary contains one or more structures called *ovules*. Egg cells form within the ovules. The ovules become seeds after sperm cells fertilize the egg cells. The term *pistil* is sometimes used to describe the female reproductive organ. It can refer to a single carpel, many unfused carpels, or many carpels fused together. In this article, the section *The reproduction of plants* tells how sperm cells unite with egg cells to begin the formation of seeds and fruit.

Seeds vary greatly in size and shape. Some seeds, such as those of the tobacco plant, are so small that more than 2,500 may grow in a pod less than ³/4 inch (20 millimeters) long. On the other hand, the seeds of one kind of coconut tree may weigh more than 20 pounds (9 kilograms). The size of a seed has nothing to do with the size of the plant. For example, huge redwood trees grow from seeds that are only ¹/16 inch (1.6 millimeters) long.

There are two main types of seeds—naked and enclosed. Gymnosperms have naked seeds. The seeds of these plants develop on the upper side of the scales that form their cones. All flowering plants, on the other hand, have seeds enclosed by an ovary. The ovary develops into a fruit as the seeds mature. The ovaries of such plants as apples, berries, and grapes develop into a fleshy fruit. In other plants, including beans and peas, the ovaries form a dry fruit. Still others have *aggregate fruits*. Each tiny section of an aggregate fruit, such as a raspberry, develops from a separate ovary and has its own seed.

Seeds consist of three main parts: (1) the seed coat, (2) the embryo, and (3) the food storage tissue. The seed coat is the outer skin. It protects the embryo, which contains all the parts needed to form a new plant. The embryo also contains one or more cotyledons, also called embryo leaves, which absorb food from the food storage tissue. In flowering plants, the food storage tissue is called *endosperm*. In some plants, such as peas and beans, the embryo absorbs the endosperm, and food is stored in the cotyledons. In nonflowering seed plants, a tissue called the *megagametophyte* stores food.

Seeds have many features that help them spread. The wind carries many seeds, including the wing-like ones of the maple tree and the fluffy seeds of dandelion and milkweed. Some seeds, such as those of the coconut, may float on water from one area to another.

Animals also help distribute seeds. Some plants have burs and sticky substances that cling to the fur or feathers of animals. Many kinds of animals eat berries and fruits but do not digest the seeds. The seeds are passed with the body waste of these animals.

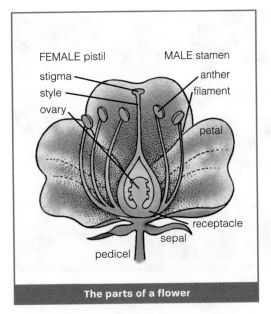

The parts of a flower

A few species of plants distribute their own seeds. For example, a wildflower called the touch-me-not shoots out its seeds at the slightest touch.

The Reproduction of Plants

Plants create more of their own kind by either *sexual reproduction* or *asexual reproduction*. In sexual reproduction, a male sperm cell joins with a female egg cell to produce a new plant. Both the egg and the sperm cells carry *genetic* (hereditary) material, including *genes*. Genes determine the characteristics that living things inherit from their parents. A plant that is produced by sexual reproduction inherits genes from both parents. The plant is a unique individual and has traits that may differ from those of either parent.

Asexual reproduction does not involve separate sperm and egg cells. It can occur in many ways. It often involves the division of one plant into one or more parts that become new plants. These plants inherit genes from only one parent and have exactly the same characteristics as the parent plant. This type of asexual reproduction may be called *vegetative propagation*. Many plants reproduce both sexually and by vegetative propagation.

Sexual reproduction in plants occurs as a complex cycle called *alternation of generations*. It involves two distinct generations, also called *phases*. During one phase of the life cycle, the plant is called a *gametophyte*, or gamete-bearing plant. In seed plants, the gametophyte is barely visible and is rarely noticed by people. It produces *gametes*—that

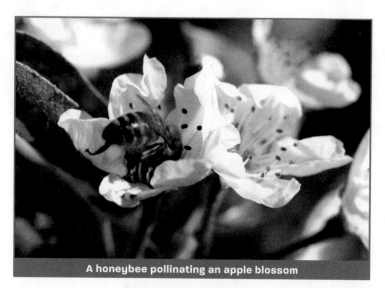

A honeybee pollinating an apple blossom

is, the sperm and egg cells. It may produce sperm cells or egg cells, or both, depending on the species of plant. After the sperm and egg cells unite, the fertilized egg develops into the second phase of the plant's life cycle. In this phase, the plant is called a *sporophyte*, or spore-bearing plant. When people see a plant it is usually the sporophyte phase. Sporophytes produce tiny structures called *spores*. The spores form in closed capsules called *sporangia*. Gametophytes develop from the spores, and the life cycle begins again.

In nonseed plants, such as ferns and mosses, the sporophyte and gametophyte generations consist of two greatly different plants. Among ferns, the sporophytes have leaves and are much larger than the gametophytes. Clusters of sporangia called *sori* form on the edges or underside of each leaf. Spores develop in the sori. After the spores ripen, they fall to the ground. There, they grow into barely visible, heart-shaped gametophytes. A fern gametophyte produces both male and female sex cells. If enough moisture is present, a sperm cell swims to an egg cell and unites with it. The fertilized egg then grows into an adult sporophyte.

Among mosses, a sporophyte consists of a long, erect stalk with a podlike container that produces spores at the end. The sporophyte extends from the top of a soft, leafy, green gametophyte. The sporophyte depends on the gametophyte for food and water. The gametophyte is the part of the plant recognized as moss.

In seed plants, which include flowering plants and cone-bearing plants, alternation of generations involves a series of complicated steps. Among these plants, only the sporophyte generation can be seen with the unaided eye. The male and female reproductive organs of a plant produce spores. The spores grow into gametophytes, which remain inside the reproductive organs.

In flowering plants, the reproductive parts are in the flowers. A plant's stamens are its male reproductive organs. Each stamen has a filament with an enlarged tip called an *anther*. The carpels are the plant's female reproductive organs. The ovary, which forms the round base of the carpels, contains the ovules. The anthers hold structures called *microsporangia*. The ovules contain structures called *megasporangia*. Cell divisions in the microsporangia and the megasporangia result in the production of spores.

In most species of flowering plants, one spore in each ovule grows into a microscopic female gametophyte. The female gametophyte produces one egg cell. In the anther, the spores, called pollen grains, contain microscopic male gametophytes. Each pollen grain produces two sperm cells.

For fertilization to take place, something must first transfer a pollen grain from the anther to the carpels. This transfer is called *pollination*. If pollen from a flower reaches the carpels of the same flower, or the carpels of another flower on the same plant, the fertilization process is called *self-pollination*. When pollen from a flower reaches the carpels of another plant, the fertilization process is called *cross-pollination*.

In many cross-pollinated plants, such animals as birds and insects carry the pollen grains from flower to flower. In other cross-pollinated plants, the wind transports the pollen. Many cross-pollinated plants have large, showy flowers, a sweet scent, and sweet nectar. These features attract such insects as ants, bees, beetles, butterflies, and moths. They also may attract larger animals, such as bats, hummingbirds, and small rodents. As these animals move from flower to flower in search of food, they carry pollen on their bodies.

Most grasses and many trees and shrubs have small, inconspicuous flowers. The wind carries their pollen. Wind may carry pollen as far as 100 miles (160 kilometers). Some airborne pollen causes hay fever and other allergies. In aquatic plants, water carries the pollen.

If a pollen grain reaches a carpel of a plant of the same species, a pollen tube grows down through the stigma and the style to an ovule in the ovary. In the ovule, one of the two sperm cells from the pollen grain unites with the egg cell. A sporophyte embryo then begins to form. The second sperm cell unites with two structures called *polar nuclei* and starts to form the nutrient tissue that makes up the endosperm. Next, a seed coat forms around the embryo and the endosperm.

In conifers, the reproductive parts are in the cones. A conifer has two kinds of cones. The pollen, or male, cone is the smaller and softer of the two. It also is simpler in structure. Seed, or female, cones are larger and harder than the male cones.

A pollen cone has many tiny sporangia that produce pollen grains. Each of the scales that make up a seed cone has two ovules on its surface. Every ovule produces a spore that grows into a female gametophyte. This tiny plant produces egg cells.

The wind carries pollen grains from the pollen cone to the seed cone. A pollen grain sticks to an adhesive substance near an ovule. It usually enters the pollen chamber of the ovule through an opening called the *micropyle*. The pollen grain then forms a pollen tube. Two sperm cells develop in the tube. After the pollen tube reaches the egg, one sperm cell fertilizes the egg. The second sperm cell disintegrates. The fertilized egg develops into a sporophyte embryo. The ovule containing the embryo becomes a seed. It can take 6 to 24 months after pollination for conifer seeds to mature.

Asexual reproduction. Plants also can spread through asexual reproduction. Any plant produced through asexual reproduction will be a *clone*, or an individual that is genetically identical to its parent. Plants that are capable of asexual reproduction also are capable of sexual reproduction. Under certain conditions, asexual reproduction offers advantages over sexual reproduction. For example, it may enable plants to colonize new areas more quickly than they could otherwise. However, clones lack the diversity of plants produced by sexual reproduction between plants. As a result, they may be more vulnerable to diseases and other problems.

Among plants, asexual reproduction is also called *apomixis*. Apomixis can occur through *vegetative propagation* or seed production. Vegetative propagation occurs when a piece of a plant regrows missing parts by a process called *regeneration*. Any part of a plant—a root, stem, leaf, or flower—may grow into a new plant. A plant may even grow from a single cell.

Vegetative propagation occurs most often in plants with stems that run just above or below the ground. The strawberry plant, for example, sends out long stems called *runners* that grow along the surface of the soil. At points where they touch the ground, the runners send out roots that produce *plantlets* (new leaves and stems). These plantlets are actually part of the parent plant. They become new plants only when separated from the parent. Ferns, irises, many kinds of grasses, blueberries and some other shrubs, and some species of trees propagate naturally from underground stems.

Many plants that grow as weeds are able to spread rapidly by vegetative propagation. These plants may be difficult to kill because they can regrow lost parts by regeneration. For example, a dandelion will regrow new stems and leaves even if only its roots are left in the soil.

Farmers use vegetative propagation to raise many valuable crops, such as apples, mangos, taro, bananas, oranges, and white potatoes. For example, they cut potatoes into many parts, making sure that each part has an *eye* (bud). Each piece of potato will grow into a new potato plant. This method produces new potato plants more quickly than planting the seeds of the plant. Vegetative propagation can also be used to reproduce plants that have been bred to bear seedless fruit.

Vegetative propagation is also widely used in gardening. Many plants, including gladioli, irises, lilies, and tulips, are grown from bulbs or corms. These plants take longer to flower when grown from seeds.

Asexual reproduction through seed production can occur through many different mechanisms. For example, some plants can produce seeds without

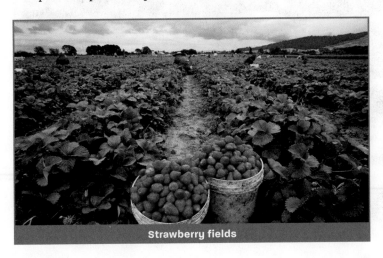

Strawberry fields

fertilization. Asexual seed production enables a plant to spread clones of itself on a broader scale than is possible with vegetative propagation, because seeds can travel farther. This type of reproduction is more common in certain groups of plants, such as grasses and roses. Dandelions, mangos, and orange relatives all commonly produce seeds asexually.

The Growth of Plants

Four major processes take place in the growth of most kinds of green plants. These processes are (1) germination, (2) the movement of water, (3) photosynthesis, and (4) respiration. A plant's growth is shaped by its heredity and environment.

Germination is the sprouting of a seed. Most seeds have a period of inactivity called *dormancy* before they start to grow. In most parts of the world, this period lasts through the winter. After spring arrives, the seeds start to germinate.

Seeds need three things to grow: (1) proper temperature, (2) moisture, and (3) oxygen. Most seeds, like most kinds of plants, grow best between 65 and 85°F (18 and 29°C). The seeds of plants that live in cold climates may germinate at lower temperatures. Those of tropical regions may sprout at higher temperatures. Seeds get the moisture they need from the ground. The moisture softens the seed coat, enabling the growing parts to break through. Moisture also prepares certain materials in the seed for their role in seed growth. If a seed receives too much water, it may begin to rot. If it gets too little water, germination may take place slowly or not at all. Seeds need oxy-

gen for the changes that take place within them during germination.

The embryo of a seed has all the parts needed to produce a young plant. It may have one or more cotyledons, which digest food from the endosperm for the growing seedling. The seed absorbs water, which makes it swell. The swelling splits the seed coat, and a tiny seedling appears. The lower part of the seedling, called the *hypocotyl*, develops into the primary root. This root anchors the seedling in the ground and develops a root system that supplies water and minerals. Next, the upper part of the seedling, called the *epicotyl*, begins to grow upward. At the tip of the epicotyl is the *plumule*, the bud that produces the first leaves. In some plants, such as the many kinds of beans, the growth of the epicotyl carries the cotyledons above ground. In corn and other plants, cotyledons remain underground, within the seed. After a seedling has developed its own roots and leaves, it can make its own food. It no longer needs cotyledons to supply nourishment.

Most plants grow in length only at the tips of their roots and branches. The cells in these areas are called *meristematic cells*. They divide and grow rapidly and develop into the various tissues that make up an adult plant.

In trees and other plants that increase in thickness, new layers of cells form between the bark and wood. This area is the *cambium*. New layers of cells are made as the cambium grows each year. These layers form the woody rings that enable people to tell the age of a tree.

Some kinds of plants, called *perennial* plants, live for many years. Most perennials produce seeds yearly. *Annual* plants live only about one growing season. *Biennial* plants live for two growing seasons. Most annuals and biennials produce seeds only once.

Movement of water. Plants must have a continuous supply of water. Each individual plant cell contains a large amount of water. Without this water, the cells could not carry on the many processes that take place within a plant. Water also carries important materials from one part of a plant to another.

Most water enters a plant through the roots. Tiny root hairs absorb moisture and certain minerals from the soil by a process called *osmosis*. In many plants, fungi that grow on the roots help the plants absorb water and minerals. These materials

Corn seedlings

Mistletoe

are transported through the xylem of the roots and stems to the leaves. There, water and minerals are used in making food. Water also carries this food through the phloem to other parts of the plant.

Plants give off water through a process called *transpiration*. Most of this water escapes through the stomata on the surfaces of the leaves. Scientists estimate that corn gives off 325,000 gallons of water per acre (3,040,000 liters per hectare) by transpiration during a growing season.

Many species of plants have developed special methods for collecting and storing water that enable them to survive with little rainfall. For example, some cactuses have roots that spread over large areas just below the surface. These roots quickly absorb water from the light rains and sudden floods that occur in the desert. Cactuses store water in their fleshy stems. The leaves of cactuses are spines. As a result of this adaptation, cactuses have less green surface than do most plants of their size—and they lose less water through transpiration.

Plants of the tundra also have adapted to the dry conditions created by frozen soils. The surfaces of their leaves are especially resistant to water loss. They are either hard and glossy or hairy. In addition, tundra plants grow close to the ground, where snow covers them and protects them from strong winds.

Photosynthesis is the process by which plants make food. The word *photosynthesis* means *putting together using light*. Plants that make their

own food are called *autotrophs*. Most photosynthesis takes place in small bodies called *chloroplasts* within the cells of plant leaves. These chloroplasts contain chlorophyll, which enables them to capture the energy in sunlight. Energy from the sunlight splits water molecules into hydrogen and oxygen. The hydrogen joins with carbon from the carbon dioxide to produce sugar. From sugar—in addition to nitrogen, sulfur, and phosphorus from the soil—green plants can make starch, fat, protein, vitamins, and other complex compounds essential for life. Photosynthesis provides the energy needed to make these compounds. Photosynthesis also releases oxygen into the air. Animals must have oxygen to breathe.

Some plants, called *heterotrophs*, have little or no chlorophyll and cannot make their own food. These plants must rely on outside sources for food. Indian pipe is a heterotroph that grows near fungi. It feeds off organic materials produced by the fungi.

Many heterotrophs are parasites that attach to other plants and take the nutrients they need from these plants. Mistletoe and dodder are common parasites. Mistletoe grows on the trunks and branches of trees. It is called a *partial parasite* because it also makes some of its own food. A plant called giant rafflesia is a parasite that grows on the roots and stems of other plants. It bears the largest flower of any known plant. Rafflesia flowers may grow over 3 feet (90 centimeters) wide.

Respiration breaks down food and releases energy for a plant. The plant uses the energy for growth, reproduction, and repair. Respiration involves the breakdown of sugar. Some of the products resulting from this breakdown combine with oxygen, releasing carbon dioxide, energy, and water. Unlike photosynthesis, which takes place only during daylight, respiration goes on day and night throughout the life of a plant. Respiration increases rapidly with the spring growth of buds and leaves. It decreases as winter approaches.

Effects of heredity and environment. Both a plant's heredity and its environment shape its growth. Heredity, for example, determines such traits as a flower's color and general size. These hereditary factors are passed on from generation to generation. Environmental factors include sunlight, climate, and soil condition.

Hereditary factors. All plant cells contain tiny bodies called *chromosomes* on which are the genes. These bodies provide "instructions" that

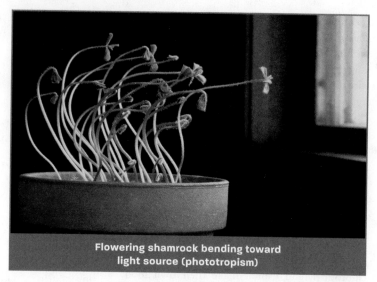

Flowering shamrock bending toward light source (phototropism)

direct the growth of the plant. As the cells divide and multiply, the "instructions" are passed on to each new cell.

Substances made within a plant also play a part in regulating plant growth. These substances, called *hormones*, control such activities as the growth of roots and the production of flowers and fruit. Botanists have learned that certain hormones, called *auxins*, affect the growth of buds, leaves, roots, and stems. Other growth hormones, called *gibberellins*, make plants grow larger, cause blossoming, and speed seed germination. Hormones called *cytokinins* make plant cells divide.

Environmental factors. All plants need light, a suitable climate, and an ample supply of water and minerals. But some species grow best in the sun, and others thrive in the shade. Plants also differ in the amount of water they require and in the temperatures they can survive. Such environmental factors affect the rate of growth, the size, and the reproduction of all plants.

The growth of plants also is affected by the length of the periods of light and dark they receive. Some plants, including lettuce and spinach, bloom only when the period of daylight is long. Such plants are called *long-day plants*. On the other hand, asters, chrysanthemums, and poinsettias are *short-day plants*. They bloom only when the period of darkness is long. Still other plants, among them marigolds and tomatoes, are not affected by the length of the day. They are called *day-neutral plants*.

Plants also are affected in other ways by their environment. For example, a plant may display a bending movement called a *tropism*. In a tropism, something outside the plant causes it to bend in one direction. A plant may have either a positive or a negative tropism, depending on whether the plant bends toward or away from the thing that causes the reaction. Tropisms are named according to the things that cause them. *Phototropism* is bending caused by light. *Geotropism* is a response to gravity. *Hydrotropism* is caused by water.

A plant placed in a window exhibits positive phototropism if its stems and leaves grow toward the source of light. Roots display negative phototropism and grow away from light. However, roots demonstrate positive geotropism. Even if a seed or bulb is planted upside down, its roots grow downward—toward the source of gravity. The stem of the same bulb shows negative geotropism by growing upward—away from the source of gravity. Hydrotropism occurs chiefly in roots and is almost always positive.

Some plants are affected by being touched. When the sensitive plant is touched, its leaflets quickly fold and its branches fall against its stem. A change in pressure within certain cells of the plant causes this action. After the touch is removed, the plant's branches and leaflets return to their original position.

Plants may be affected by chemical poisoning when the soil contains too much of certain substances. For example, most plants require small amounts of copper, iron, and zinc. But people may introduce excessive amounts of these metals into the soil during the mining and smelting of ore. Such contamination kills large numbers of plants. Some soils are naturally too rich in metals. For example, areas of serpentine, a volcanic rock that contains heavy metals, are common in western North America. These areas form stretches of barren land where few plants survive.

Plants also may be affected by nutrient deficiencies, when the soil lacks sufficient amounts of certain substances. Nutrient deficiencies are harmful to plants in a number of ways. They may cause changes in leaf color, reduction in leaf size, dead spots, reduced growth, and wilting. Each symptom often can be linked to lack of a specific nutrient, usually nitrogen or potassium.

Some plants have developed unusual adaptations to survive on soil deficient in nutrients. Insect-eating plants obtain nitrogen and other nutrients by trapping and digesting insects in their leaves. These *carnivorous plants* break down the insects for nutrients but make their own food by photosynthesis. Insect-eating plants include the pitcher plant, the sundew, and Venus's-flytrap.

Pitcher plants have tube-shaped leaves that collect rain water. Sweet substances around the rim of each tube attract insects. After an insect enters the tube, downward-pointing hairs keep the struggling victim from escaping. In time, the insect becomes exhausted, slides into the water, and drowns. The plant then digests it by means of a fluid secreted by glands in the leaves.

The leaves of the sundew plant grow hairs that give off a sticky substance. When an insect gets stuck on this substance, the hairs wrap around it. More fluid covers and suffocates the insect. The plant then gradually digests the insect.

The Venus's-flytrap captures insects with its hinged leaves. The inside of each leaf has hairs, and bristles edge the rim. When an insect lands on the hairs, the two halves of the leaf close like a trap, with the bristles interlocking. After the plant digests the insect, the leaves open again.

Plant Diseases and Pests

Diseases and pests attack and injure almost all species of plants. They cause serious, widespread damage to agricultural, garden, and ornamental plants—many of which have lost the natural defenses of wild plants.

Diseases. Many kinds of microorganisms cause diseases in plants. They include bacteria, fungi, viruses, and tiny worms called *nematodes*. Fungi and viruses cause more plant diseases than the others do.

Environmental conditions can weaken plants so that they are more easily infected. Such conditions include air pollution, unusual extremes in temperature, nutrient deficiencies, and low levels of light or oxygen.

Diseases may affect every part of the plant. Many diseases interfere with the plant's ability to carry out photosynthesis. These diseases may damage leaves or block the flow of water or nutrients to stems and leaves. Bacteria, fungi, or viruses may invade plant tissues and kill cells in a small area. For example, dead spots on leaves and fruits indicate places where microorganisms have killed plant cells. Infection also may cause yellowing and death of leaves at the edges. Abnormal growths— such as galls and knots—on roots, stems, and other parts of the plant also signal places of infection. Fungi or bacteria that invade the roots, stems, and leaves can prevent xylem from transporting water throughout the plant. As a result, the leaves, stems, and flowers may wilt or suddenly die. In addition, fungi may secrete *toxins* (poisons) that cause large parts of the plant to die.

Fungal diseases are carried to plants in spores. Insects, animals, rain, or wind may spread these fungal spores. Some bacteria and viruses spread in the same way. Nematodes not only cause certain diseases but also transmit viruses from diseased to uninfected plants. Some bacteria and fungi live on plant refuse in the soil and infect healthy plants. Others are carried on seeds.

Some plant infections cause serious illness when the plants are eaten by human beings and animals. For example, a fungus called *ergot* infects wheat, barley, and rye. It produces chemicals that can cause the illness *ergotism*. This illness afflicts people who eat bread made from the infected grain. Other fungi produce poisons called *mycotoxins* that can harm people or animals if consumed in food.

Widespread outbreaks of plant disease can cause famine. During the 1840s, about 1 million people in Ireland died after a fungal disease destroyed the nation's potato crop. Other diseases have killed large numbers of certain plant species. For example, a fungal disease called chestnut blight has destroyed the chestnut tree throughout North America.

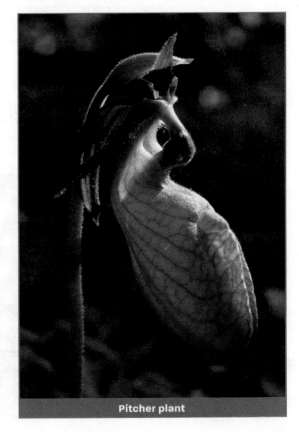

Pitcher plant

Pests. Insects damage or destroy plants in a number of ways. Some insects feed on flowers and fruit. Insects with chewing mouthparts, such as beetles and grasshoppers, eat holes in leaves and stems. The destruction of leaves affects the growth of crops by reducing photosynthesis. Swarms of grasshoppers have destroyed entire crops of alfalfa, cotton, and corn. Gypsy moth caterpillars also eat leaves. They have damaged many forests. Other insects have piercing mouthparts with which they pierce plants and suck the juices. The wounds made by the insects provide places for microorganisms to enter the plants easily.

Some insects secrete poisons or other chemical substances while feeding. These secretions may cause galls on leaves or roots, or they may give leaves a "burned" appearance. Other insects interrupt the flow of food and water in plants by feeding on vascular tissue.

Rabbits, rodents, and other animals also feed on plants. Some kinds of rodents burrow into the soil and feed on the roots, seeds, and bulbs of plants.

How plants protect themselves. Many plant species have developed physical and chemical defenses to avoid being eaten. Many plants also protect themselves through timing when they produce flowers and fruits.

Physical defenses of plants include such structures as prickles, spines, and thorns. Most of these structures are modified leaves or branches. They prevent attacks by large plant-eating animals. Other plants produce heavy coatings of wax or dense, stiff hairs. These may repel smaller animals, especially insects. Some plants, including grasses, accumulate a hard mineral called *silica* in their

leaves. The silica makes the leaves difficult for animals to chew and rapidly wears down their teeth.

Plants have a wide variety of chemical defenses against animals. The leaves and fruits of citrus plants produce sticky, strong-smelling oils. These oils discourage many insects. Many plants contain chemicals that taste bad or are poisonous. Such plants include foxglove, nightshade, and yew.

Insects can quickly become immune to the chemicals plants produce. In some cases, insects develop a means of breaking down the toxins made by plants. As a result, plants continually develop new toxins by altering existing ones. Some scientists describe this process as a biological "arms race" between plants and their predators. In some cases, the "arms race" between an insect and plant has resulted in a unique relationship. For example, plants in the milkweed family produce a milky sap that contains poisonous chemicals. These poisons prevent most insects from eating the plants. However, caterpillars of monarch butterflies eat milkweed plants and store the poison in their bodies. The poison makes monarch butterflies distasteful and so protects them from many of their own predators.

Certain plant species obtain protection from animals through a relationship called *mutualism*. In this relationship, the plant provides a special type of food for a particular insect species. The insects, in turn, protect the plant from other animals. One example of plant-insect mutualism is the relationship between ants and acacia trees. Ants live in hollow spines on the acacia trees. The leaves of the trees release a sugar solution for the ants to eat. In return, the ants clear the ground around each tree and attack any other animals that enter the cleared area or land on the trees. The fierce ants can protect the trees even from such large animals as elephants.

Many plants try to ensure the survival of their seeds through the timing of flower and fruit production. Some plants produce flowers and fruits early in the growing season, when insects are few. Other plants produce so many seeds that animals cannot eat them all. For example, oak trees produce a great number of acorns every few years. When acorns are abundant, squirrels and other animals cannot eat all of them. Some acorns survive to grow into new oak trees. In other years, oak trees produce fewer acorns, preventing the animals from relying on acorns for food. If the trees produced a

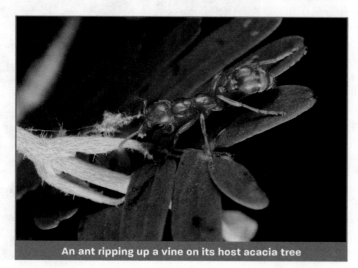
An ant ripping up a vine on its host acacia tree

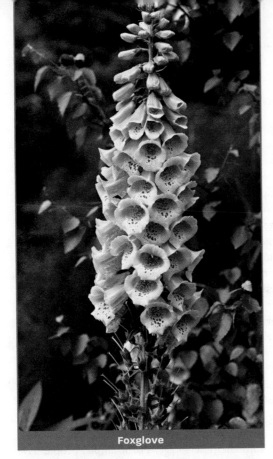

Foxglove

surplus of acorns each year, the animal population would increase and all the acorns would be eaten.

Disease and pest control. People fight plant diseases and pest damage by various means. Chemicals make up the largest part of most programs to control plant diseases and pests. These chemicals include bactericides, fungicides, insecticides, nematocides, and rodenticides. Growers also cross resistant plants with other varieties of the same species to develop new varieties that combine resistance with high productivity. Such efforts have resulted in the development of high-yield, disease-resistant wheats, for example.

Some farmers control diseases and pests without the use of *synthetic* (artificial) chemicals, a practice known as *organic agriculture*. For example, organic farmers may use pesticides from natural rather than synthetic sources. They also may use biological pest control, in which natural predators control pests. For example, farmers may introduce mites known to feed on insect pests. An approach called *integrated pest management* combines a limited use of chemical pesticides with natural control methods.

The Domestication of Plants

People began to alter plants more than 10,000 years ago, when they learned to raise food by farming. Prehistoric people noticed that some plants grew better than others, were easier to harvest, or provided a better source of food. They saved seeds from these plants to grow new ones. This process marked the beginning of the domestication of plants. Over time, plant domestication turned wild plants into the crops grown today. Some of the first domesticated crops include barley, peas, squash, and wheat.

How crops differ from wild plants. Domesticated crops differ from their wild ancestors because people have bred crops to have desirable traits. These traits include bearing larger or more numerous fruits, being easier to harvest, and having better taste or lower amounts of toxic substances. For example, people domesticated corn from a wild plant called *teosinte*. Teosinte grows a small cob with about 5 to 10 hard kernels. By comparison, modern corn produces a much larger cob with hundreds of soft kernels.

Wild wheat seeds are smaller than those of domesticated wheat. Wild seeds fall off the plant before they can be harvested and are enclosed by tough husks. Domestication produced brittle husks that are easier to remove and larger seeds that remain on the plant for harvest.

Domesticated papayas, tomatoes, and other fruits can be several times larger than their wild relatives. Domesticated potatoes contain only low levels of the poisons that protect their wild relatives. Domesticated plants can also vary more markedly than their wild relatives. For example, broccoli, Brussels sprouts, cabbage, and kale are domesticated varieties of the same plant species.

Industrialized agriculture. In the 1800s and 1900s, farmers in the United States and other developed countries achieved dramatic increases in the productivity of crops. These improvements came through the industrialization of agriculture. This transformation involved a number of developments, including: (1) the invention of powered machines; (2) the development of electric power; (3) improvements in crop breeding, through the study of plant genetics; (4) the use of artificial fertilizers; and (5) the development of chemical pesticides.

Industrialized agriculture did not spread to less developed countries in Asia, Africa, and Central and South America until much later. Farmers in such countries continued to practice traditional agriculture. They often could not produce enough food to feed their growing populations. However, many developing countries adopted techniques from industrialized agriculture between the 1940s and 1970s. The dramatic improvements in crop production that resulted are known as the Green Revolution. The Green Revolution saved millions of lives by reducing the danger of famine. Much of this success came through efforts to breed better crops. Scientists bred new varieties of corn, rice, and wheat that grew quickly and produced large grains.

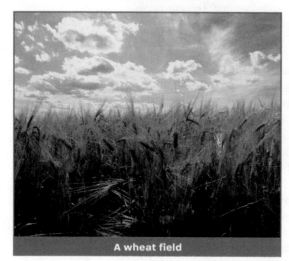

A wheat field

Breeding and genetics. The scientific study of plants has greatly aided attempts to make plants more productive and attractive. Plant breeding involves manipulating plants to introduce desirable traits. These traits include disease resistance or larger seeds. Most improvements in crops have been achieved using such methods. For instance, these methods produced the improved crops of the Green Revolution.

Beginning in the 1980s, scientists have introduced desirable traits into crops by artificially transferring genes between organisms. This process creates *genetically modified* crops, often called GM crops. In many cases, genes are exchanged between organisms that could never be bred traditionally. For example, in so-called *Bt crops*, scientists have inserted a gene from bacteria that causes the crops to produce their own insecticide.

The most commonly grown GM crops are resistant to herbicides or insects. These crops include GM corn, cotton, and soybeans. A smaller number of crops have been modified for disease resistance. These include papaya and squash. Others have been modified to be more nutritious. For example, golden rice has been modified to produce the nutrient beta carotene. The human body can use this nutrient to make vitamin A. Vitamin A deficiency is a major cause of blindness in parts of Africa and India, among other areas. However, farmers have not planted golden rice widely because of controversy over its safety and effectiveness. The use of GM crops is controversial, and many countries restrict their cultivation and sale.

Conservation of Plants

Human beings have caused rapid environmental changes around the world. As a result, many plant species have declined greatly in numbers. Some have already become extinct. Many others are at risk of extinction. In fact, more than 20 percent of plant species may be threatened, according to the International Union for the Conservation of Nature and Natural Resources (IUCN). Plants form the foundation of nearly all food chains on land, and they are vital to many ecosystems. As a result, the health and survival of plants is critical for the survival of other living things. Major threats to plants include habitat destruction, loss of *biodiversity* (the variety of living things), invasive species, pollution, and global warming.

Habitat destruction may be the greatest threat to plants. People have destroyed vast areas of wilderness to make room for farms and cities. People also have caused great damage by harvesting timber, minerals, or other natural resources. As the population of human beings has grown, people have caused ever more damage. For example, people have cut down about half of the native forests that once covered the world. Much of the forest that remains has been damaged. People also have destroyed vast areas of grasslands, wetlands, and other habitats. Such habitats support a tremendous variety of animals and other living things. As a result, habitat destruction poses a great threat to biodiversity.

Plants and other living things also are threatened by *habitat fragmentation*. Habitat fragmentation occurs as natural areas become smaller and distances between them increase. Habitat fragmentation can cut off plants from potential pollinators. It may also make it difficult for plants to disperse their seeds to suitable habitats.

Loss of biodiversity. Habitat destruction can lead to loss of genetic diversity within a species. Loss of diversity can make plants more vulnerable to other threats, such as diseases or climate change. Habitat fragmentation also reduces biodiversity, both within a species and among different species. Plants and other living things in an ecosystem depend on one another in a complex web of relationships. Diverse ecosystems are more robust than those with less diversity—because the loss of individual species will less likely cause additional damage. For example, if several kinds of insects pollinate a plant, the loss of any one kind will less likely harm the plant.

Loss of biodiversity also threatens crops. The majority of the food people eat comes from three major crops: corn, rice, and wheat. These crops are often grown in *monocultures*—that is, a single crop grown over a large area. This practice can enable the rapid spread of disease or pests because the crops are genetically similar—so a disease that kills one plant can wipe them all out. Monocultures also threaten the biodiversity of other organisms because they support far fewer species than do natural areas. People have developed many different varieties of crops over thousands of years. In many cases, however, the wild relatives of crops have become less diverse. This loss of diversity reduces the traits available to breeders. For example, it may limit breeders' access to genes for resistance to disease or drought found among a crop's wild relatives.

Invasive species. An invasive species is an organism introduced into an area that spreads quickly and harms native wildlife. The increase in travel and trade among distant parts of the world has resulted in the introduction of huge numbers of invasive species. Some of these species were released accidentally. However, people introduced many invasive plants intentionally, often as ornamental plants. Notable invasive plants include Australian acacias, common buckthorn, erect prickly pear, Japanese knotweed, kudzu, purple loosestrife, strawberry guava, and water hyacinth.

Invasive plant species often outcompete native plants by growing and reproducing rapidly. They may produce more seeds than native plants. Some invasive plants produce toxins that make it difficult for native plants to grow. Invasive plants can damage ecosystems and habitats. They also can be major pests in agriculture. In addition, many plant diseases and pests are invasive species. These include various fungi, viruses, and insects.

Pollution also harms plants. Most pollution comes from agricultural runoff, automobile exhaust, industry, and wastewater. Pollution dam-

ages plants in a variety of ways. Harmful chemicals can pollute the soil and water, poisoning plants. Air pollution can cause smog, which blocks the sunlight plants need for photosynthesis. However, some plant species remove pollution from the air, soil, or water. They may be planted to help restore polluted areas.

Global warming. Plants also are threatened by global warming, an increase in the average temperature at Earth's surface. Climate scientists estimate that Earth's average surface temperature rose by about 1.4°F (0.76°C) from the mid-1800s to the early 2000s. This warming has caused other climate changes, such as changing patterns of precipitation. An increase in carbon dioxide in the atmosphere causes most global warming. This increase comes chiefly from burning coal, oil, and natural gas.

Plants are sensitive to changes in climate. Plants are fixed in place and cannot migrate. As a result, individual plants are limited in their ability to respond to changes in climate. Instead, plants rely on seed dispersal to gradually spread to new areas. Scientists have found evidence that the distribution of plants has already begun to change because of global warming. On mountains, plant species are spreading to higher elevations. In the Northern Hemisphere, plant species are shifting northward, as their favored climates shift north. Also, many plants have begun to bloom earlier in the spring, in response to warming temperatures.

Global warming also affects interactions among plants and other living things. Many animals time their migrations to take advantage of plant growth. As the timing of plant development in the spring changes, animals risk arriving too late to take advantage of the growth. Many plants rely on animals for pollination, and animals rely on plants for their fruit, nectar, or seeds. Global warming threatens to disrupt some of these relationships.

Climate scientists predict that Earth's surface temperature will rise an additional 2.0 to 11.5°F (1.1 to 6.4°C) by 2100. Many scientists worry that rapid global warming will cause many species to become extinct. Plant species may not be able to spread to suitable habitats. This problem is made worse by habitat destruction and fragmentation.

Plants play an important role in limiting global warming by taking up carbon dioxide for use in photosynthesis. They store the carbon in their tissues. In this way, plants can help to reduce global warming. However, when a plant is killed, its carbon returns to the atmosphere, especially if the plant is burned. As a result, deforestation and other habitat destruction can increase the rate of global warming. Thus, many people argue that forests and other ecosystems should be preserved to reduce global warming.

Conservation efforts. Many people are working to save plant species and ecosystems. Governments have established national parks to protect natural habitats. People also attempt to renew and restore damaged habitats. For example, people may try to remove invasive species and replant native species.

Other efforts focus on collecting seeds from wild plants. Scientists also collect the seeds of crop varieties and their wild relatives. They store the seeds at cold temperatures in seed banks, where they can be used in restoration projects or for breeding. If a species becomes extinct in the wild, it may be possible to reintroduce it through plants that have been grown from seeds in seed banks.

The Evolution of Plants

Plants on land are thought to have *evolved* (developed over many generations) from green algae that lived in fresh water. Most scientists think that all plants on land developed from the same green algae ancestor. Based on evidence from fossils of spores, plants may have begun making the transition to land about 470 million years ago.

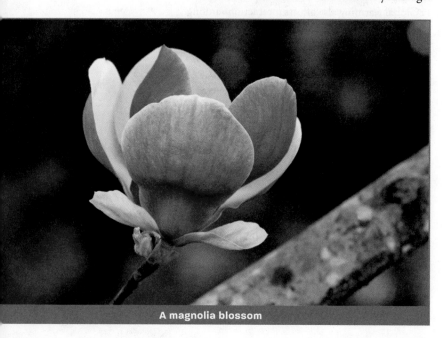

A magnolia blossom

They had become well established on land by 430 million years ago. Some genetic studies suggest that plants may have appeared on land 500 million years ago or even much earlier. Before this transition, land was mostly rocky and barren, supporting only microbial life. The spread of plants transformed the land, providing habitat for animals and other organisms.

Plants and other living things evolved into many new forms as they colonized the land. The move to land required plants to evolve adaptations to prevent drying out, to obtain water and nutrients from the soil, and to support themselves for growing upright. Cooperation with fungi may have helped early plants adapt to the stresses of life on land. Such relationships with fungi remain important for plants today.

Nonvascular plants were the first to spread to land. They grew mostly in wet areas. The earliest known vascular plants, called *rhyniophytes*, lived from about 420 million to 380 million years ago. They did not have leaves or roots. Instead, they had only branched stems with sporangia. These plants were small, with the largest species probably growing only 6 to 8 inches (15 to 20 centimeters) tall.

Larger plants called *trimerophytes may* have developed from the rhyniophytes. The trimerophytes had a more complex plant body with numerous stems and branches. But they lacked leaves, and only some of them may have had simple roots. Other small, leafless vascular plants, called *zosterophylls* or *zosterophyllophytes*, appeared shortly after the rhyniophytes and also may have descended from them. Some botanists believe trimerophytes and zosterophylls are the ancestors of all vascular plants that live today. They believe that ferns and related plants evolved from trimerophytes during the Devonian Period, from about 416 million to 359 million years ago. Early forms of seed plants also may have evolved from trimerophytes at this time. Scientists believe lycophytes, the first plants to have leaves, evolved from zosterophylls.

During the Carboniferous Period, about 359 million to 299 million years ago, more complex and larger vascular plants evolved. Great forests of ferns, horsetails, lycophytes, and early seed plants covered Earth. Plant matter from these forests accumulated in vast swamps. This plant matter later formed large coal deposits.

Gymnosperms became the most plentiful plants during the Mesozoic Era, which began about 251

Growing plants in a biotechnology greenhouse

million years ago. Conifers, cycads, and ginkgoes were among the most important plants. They served as food for the dinosaurs that roamed the land during this time. Many now-extinct types of gymnosperms also flourished.

The oldest known fossils of flowering plants are about 130 million years old. However, some scientists believe they may have evolved tens of millions of years earlier. Scientists are not certain which plants became the ancestors of these angiosperms, but their closest living relatives are gymnosperms. Among the first angiosperms were magnolias, sycamores, water lilies, and willows. Angiosperms diversified rapidly in the Cretaceous Period. Insects also diversified during this time. The evolution of the two groups was linked, due to their dependence on each other through pollination. The process by which living things that interact with one another evolve together is known as *coevolution*. Angiosperms became increasingly common during the Cretaceous Period. But it was not until after the dinosaurs became extinct, about 65 million years ago, that angiosperms came to dominate the land.

During the Cenozoic Era, beginning about 65 million years ago, angiosperms dominated landscapes and took on major ecological roles. Forests of angiosperms covered much of Earth. Both angiosperms and insects continued to diversify,

through further coevolution. Angiosperms also influenced the evolution of other animals by providing a rich abundance of food. Late in the Cenozoic Era, grasslands and large grazing animals began to appear.

The Pleistocene Epoch, which lasted from about 2.6 million to 11,500 years ago, included the last major ice ages. During the ice ages, great sheets of ice covered large areas of land. These ice ages influenced plant evolution and distribution. The ice sheets that covered northern portions of the globe forced plant species to move southward. During the warmer periods between ice ages, woodlands covered much of the land. During cooler periods, grasses became more abundant. During ice ages, tundra plants flourished.

The end of the Pleistocene changed the makeup and distribution of biomes. As the ice sheets retreated, forests replaced large areas of tundra, and the distribution of grasslands changed. These biomes are shifting farther in response to global warming. Habitat destruction and agriculture also have brought great changes to the distribution of plants. However, angiosperms remain by far the largest and most diverse group of plants.

Classification of Plants

Botanists classify plants by grouping them according to common descent. Groups that share a common ancestor also tend to share certain characteristics.

Botanists may determine which plants are closely related by comparing their traits, including their overall appearance, their internal structure, and the form of their reproductive organs. Relationships can also be verified through genetic testing. However, not all botanists agree on how plants should be divided. As a result, there are a number of different classification systems for the plant kingdom. One classification system is described in the table with this article, *A classification of the plant kingdom*. This system classifies plants into several large groups and a number of divisions. A *division* is the same grouping as a phylum in the animal kingdom.

One major group consists of nonvascular plants. These plants lack xylem and phloem that carry water and food from one part of the plant to another. The other major group consists of vascular plants that contain these specialized tissues. Within these groups are several smaller groupings, including divisions and classes.

GREGOR JOHANN MENDEL

(1822–1884), an Austrian botanist and monk, formulated the basic laws of heredity. His experiments with the breeding of garden peas led to the development of the science of genetics.

His life. Mendel was born on July 22, 1822, in Heinzendorf, Austria (now Hyncice, near Krnov, in what is now the Czech Republic). His parents were peasants. In 1843, Mendel entered the monastery of St. Thomas in Brunn, Austria (now Brno, the Czech Republic). He became a priest in 1847. In 1851, the monastery sent Mendel to study science and mathematics at the University of Vienna. He returned to the monastery in 1853 and taught biology and physics at a local high school for the next 14 years. Mendel's fame came from his research in the monastery garden. In 1868, Mendel was elected abbot of the monastery. From then on, his administrative responsibilities limited his opportunities for research.

His work. In his experiments, Mendel studied the inheritance of seven pairs of traits in garden pea plants and in their seeds. These pairs included (1) rounded or wrinkled seeds and (2) tall or short plants.

Mendel bred and crossbred thousands of plants and observed the characteristics of each successive generation. Like all organisms that reproduce

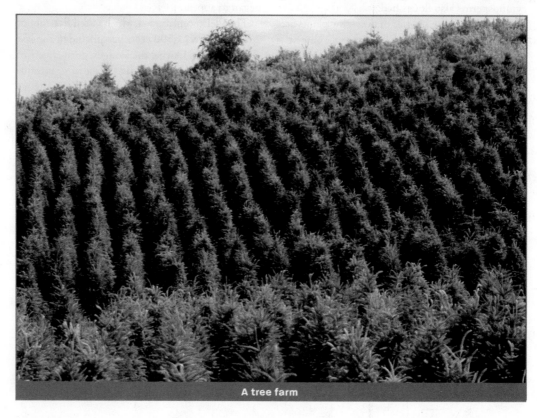

A tree farm

sexually, pea plants produce their offspring through the union of special sex cells called *gametes*. In pea plants, a male gamete, or sperm cell, combines with a female gamete, or egg cell, to form a seed.

Mendel concluded that plant traits are handed down through hereditary elements in the gametes. These elements are now called *genes*. He reasoned that each plant receives a pair of genes for each trait, one gene from each of its parents. Based on his experiments, he concluded that if a plant inherits two different genes for a trait, one gene will be *dominant* and the other will be *recessive*. The trait of the dominant gene will appear in the plant. For example, the gene for round seeds is dominant, and the gene for wrinkled seeds is recessive. A plant that inherits both genes will have round seeds.

Mendel also concluded that the pairs of genes *segregate* (separate) in a random fashion when a plant's gametes are formed. Thus, a parent plant hands down only one gene of each pair to its offspring. In addition, Mendel believed that a plant inherits each of its traits independently of other traits. These two conclusions are known as Mendel's *Law of Segregation* and his *Law of Independent Assortment*. Since Mendel's time, scientists have discovered some exceptions to his conclusions, but his theories in general have been proved.

Mendel died on January 6, 1884. His results were published in 1866 but went unnoticed until 1900.

BOTANY is the branch of biology concerned with the study of plants. Hundreds of thousands of species of plants grow all around the world. Scientists called *botanists* study all aspects of plant life, including where plants live and how plants grow.

What botanists study. Botanists focus on four broad areas in their research: (1) plant classification and form, (2) how plants function, (3) plant habitats, and (4) the uses of plants. Most botanical research involves more than one and sometimes all of these areas. In addition, each of the areas includes various specific fields of study. Because the plant kingdom is so diverse, most botanists focus on one or more specialized fields.

Plant classification and form provides the framework for almost all fields of botany. In studying a plant, a botanist must first know what type of plant it is. Botanists who specialize in *systematics* identify plant species. This field includes *taxonomy*, the science of naming and classifying plants and other organisms. Botanists who specialize in *morphology* examine the form and structure of plants. Their research includes investigations of the cells and tissues that make up a plant's internal structure.

How plants function. Plants must carry out a variety of activities to remain alive. Botanists specializing in *physiology* study the processes that enable plants to grow and reproduce. These botanists examine how plants make and use food and how they obtain water, minerals, and nutrients from the soil. Much of their work focuses on the chemical processes that take place in the molecules in cells.

Botanists specializing in *genetics* study how plants pass characteristics on to their offspring through *genes* (hereditary material). Botanists studying *molecular biology* examine how genes affect plant form and function. They also study how genes may be altered to change plants or to create new plants through a process called *genetic engineering*.

Plant habitats are studied by botanists who specialize in *ecology* and *geography*. Plant ecologists study the relationship between plants and their environment. They also examine how plants interact with one another and with animals. Plant geographers study where plants live. They try to explain why certain plants grow in a particular region, but others do not.

Uses of plants. The search to find ways that people may use plants is the oldest area of study in botany. Botanists who study *agronomy* develop and improve crop plants. Those who specialize in *forestry* study trees, especially the cultivation of trees for use in the manufacture of lumber, paper, and other products. *Horticulture* is the cultivation of fruits, vegetables, flowers, and ornamental shrubs and trees. *Medical botany* is the science of using plants to treat diseases.

The importance of botany. The study of plants is important because most of the food that people and animals eat comes from plants, either directly or indirectly. Except for certain microbes, plants are the only living things on land that can make their own food. They do so using the energy in sunlight, in a process called *photosynthesis*. Animals on land get their energy from plants, either directly by eating plants or indirectly by eating animals that feed on plants. Thus, plants are vital to the survival of animals, including human beings.

Botanists study how plants, animals, and other living things interact with one another. They work to understand how the loss of plants from damaged forests or other habitats will affect other living things. Botanists also study the *evolution* (gradual change) of plants over millions of years. This research helps them to understand the evolution of other living things, especially animals.

Research by botanists benefits people in a great variety of ways. For example, some botanists develop new crop plants that are more productive and resistant to diseases and pests. In this way, botanists help to secure food for the growing human population. Other botanists search for plants that may provide medicines. Still others work to improve the lumber industry while minimizing harm to the environment.

The history of botany. People have always been interested in plants and have used them in many ways. Prehistoric people gathered wild plants for food and used plants to build shelters. By about 8000 B.C., people in several locations around the world had begun to depend on

Dr. Barbara McClintock won the 1983 Nobel Prize in Physiology or Medicine.

cultivated plants for most of their food. Prehistoric people also raised plants for their beauty and used plants for medicine and in religious ceremonies.

The ancient Greeks and Romans made the first scientific studies of plants. The Greek philosopher Aristotle, who lived during the 300s B.C., collected information about most of the then-known plants of the world. His pupil Theophrastus classified and named these plants. Theophrastus is often called the father of botany. Pliny the Elder, a Roman naturalist and writer who lived from A.D. 23 to 79, recorded many facts about plants in his 37-volume reference work *Historis Naturalis* (*Natural History*). The knowledge gained by these scholars served as the foundation of botany for more than 1,000 years.

The development of modern botany began during the Renaissance, a 300-year period of European history that started in the A.D. 1300s. During this period, European exploration of the world greatly stimulated the study of botany and other sciences. Explorers discovered many new types of plants and brought them to scholars to examine and identify. As a result, modern botany developed around such basic research areas as the classification of plants and the study of their form and function. These areas gradually expanded into many specialized fields as botanists focused on more specific aspects of plant life.

Over the centuries, scientists developed many different systems to classify plants. But most of these systems proved inadequate as knowledge about plants increased and new plants were found. During the mid-1700s, the Swedish naturalist Carolus Linnaeus developed a system of naming plants that eventually became accepted as a standard classification system. Linnaeus used a *binomial system of nomenclature*, in which each plant has a unique name consisting of two parts. This system has been modified and expanded into the modern classification system used today.

The study of plant form made tremendous advances during the 1600s, after the development of the compound microscope. The first scientists to observe the microscopic structures of plants included Marcello Malpighi of Italy and the Englishmen Robert Hooke and Nehemiah Grew. Also during the 1600s, research on plant function began with the work of Johann Baptista van Helmont, who was a Flemish doctor and chemist. Van Helmont made discoveries on how plants obtain food and grow.

Grapes

Later developments. The study of plant ecology grew from research on the geographic distribution of plants. The German naturalist and geographer Alexander von Humboldt made major contributions to the development of plant geography. He traveled throughout the world during the late 1700s and early 1800s and mapped plant distributions. Modern ecology, which includes the study of both plants and animals, emerged in the late 1800s and early 1900s. Pioneers in this field included the American scientists Frederick Clements, Henry A. Gleason, and Robert Wittaker.

Research by the Austrian botanist Gregor Mendel during the second half of the 1800s had a tremendous impact on the study of botany and other fields of science. His experiments on the breeding of garden peas established the basic laws of heredity.

In the 1900s, scientists working in plant genetics and molecular biology made many spectacular discoveries. For example, through research on corn plants, the American geneticist Barbara McClintock found that certain genes can move around within the chromosomes of cells. This discovery, announced in 1951, greatly added to understanding of how plants and other organisms inherit their traits.

During the late 1900s and early 2000s, many botanists began to use new genetic techniques, including studies of the hereditary material DNA. These techniques enabled the scientists to define plant species and determine the relationships among the species with greater precision. As a result, botanists have made many advances in understanding how different groups of plants are related.

Careers in botany. Botany offers a wide range of career opportunities. Most botanists work either for government agencies or for private industry as research scientists, laboratory technicians, or field botanists. Many technicians conduct agricultural or horticultural research, and others develop new medicines from plants. These botanists must be skilled in the use of such sophisticated laboratory equipment as electron microscopes. They must also have a thorough understanding of experimental procedures and of plant biology. Field botanists study plants in their natural habitat. This work requires a broad knowledge of plant taxonomy and ecology.

A bachelor's degree is sufficient for some careers in botany, but most positions require a master's degree. A doctor's degree is required for advanced positions in research or to teach botany at a university. New jobs for botanists will continue to be created as the world's population grows and scientists search for better ways to use plants for food and medicine.

HORTICULTURE

HORTICULTURE is the art and science of growing plants, particularly garden plants. Horticulture includes gardening and landscaping as well as the commercial growing of flowers, fruits, herbs, nuts, and vegetables. The word *horticulture* comes from the Latin words *hortus*, meaning *garden*, and *cultura*, meaning *culture* or *cultivation*.

Horticulture has played a crucial role in the development of civilization. The large-scale agricultural production of food plants and other crops developed from small-scale gardening activities. Horticulture and agriculture supported the first permanent human settlements, which gave rise to the first cities. Today, horticulture is both a scientifically and technologically advanced global industry and a popular hobby enjoyed by people around the world.

The horticulture industry can be divided into four branches. They are: (1) floriculture, (2) olericulture, (3) pomology, and (4) landscape and ornamental horticulture.

Floriculture is the production of flowers and leafy, decorative *foliage plants*. People use flowers and foliage plants for decoration and often give them as gifts.

Olericulture is the growing of edible *herbaceous* (nonwoody) plant crops, such as asparagus and tomatoes. Olericulture differs from agriculture largely in the scale of production. Sugar beets and wheat, for example, are so important and widespread that their growth is considered agriculture.

Pomology deals with shrubs, trees, and vines raised for their fruit and nuts. *Viniculture*, a spe-

cialized area of pomology, involves the production of grapes for use in making wine.

Landscape and ornamental horticulture involves the growth of such decorative plants as shrubs, trees, and turf. These plants are commonly used around buildings and highways and in yards, parks, golf courses, and sports stadiums.

Horticulture as a hobby. For most of human history, people practiced horticulture primarily as a means of growing food for their families and communities. Today, many people enjoy planting and arranging flowers and raising gardens as leisure activities. The horticulture industry supports such activities by selling flowers and other plants to gardening enthusiasts.

Research in horticulture primarily addresses the needs of the industry. Some horticulturists study ways to improve the transportation, storage, and processing of cultivated plants. Others study how to improve the nutritional value of food crops and increase their yields.

Horticulturists modify plants by *selective breeding*—that is, they carefully select and pair certain plants to produce offspring with desirable characteristics. Horticulturalists also improve plants using *genetic engineering*, techniques that alter an organism's hereditary material. Many horticultural plants have been modified so much by selective breeding that they depend on human beings to survive. For example, seedless grapes are easier to eat, but such grapevines can no longer reproduce in the same way as their wild relatives.

To maximize production, the horticulture and agriculture industries have become increasingly standardized, limiting the genetic diversity of the plants that are grown. Much of our current food supply, for example, consists of only a few highly specialized crop breeds. Scientists have developed *gene banks* to store seeds and other material from a diverse range of plant species. These materials help preserve crucial information about plants that are no longer cultivated or that could one day go extinct. They also provide raw materials to breed new kinds of crops if current crops fail.

PALEOBOTANY

PALEOBOTANY is the study of ancient plants. Paleobotany is a branch of *paleontology*, the study of ancient plants, animals, and other organisms. Specialists called *paleobotanists* investigate the evolution of plant life and the origins and relationships of plant groups. They also examine the link between vegetation and the earth's changing climate. Paleobotany includes the study of such simple organisms as ancient algae, fungi, and bacteria. In addition, it involves searching for the earliest evidence of life in rocks more than 3 billion years old.

Paleobotanists interpret the earth's history by examining plant fossils. These fossils have been preserved in *sedimentary rocks* (rocks formed from deposits laid down by ancient rivers, lakes, and seas). Paleobotanists have found the earliest land plants in sedimentary rocks that are more than 430 million years old. Remains of early forests are abundant in rocks 350 million years old. The ancestors of all major groups of land plants lived in these forests. Today, the most numerous plants on earth are *angiosperms* (flowering plants). Paleobotanists have discovered that the first angiosperms appeared about 140 million years ago, during the age of the dinosaurs.

Paleobotanists study the features that plants have developed to survive in their environment. These scientists are thus able to describe the type of climate that existed millions of years ago. Paleobotany contributes to an understanding of how and why the earth's climate changes. This understanding is important in predicting the changes in climate that humans may cause through the *greenhouse effect* (a gradual warming of the earth's surface).

PHOTOSYNTHESIS is a food-making process that occurs in green plants. Photosynthesis is the chief function of leaves. The word *photosynthesis* means *putting together with light*.

Green plants use sunlight to combine carbon dioxide and water to make food. This process converts light energy into the chemical energy of food. Plants use the food to grow, or they store it for later consumption. Human beings and all other animals get food by eating plants or by eating animals that eat plants.

Plants absorb the light for photosynthesis with a green pigment called *chlorophyll*. Each food-making cell in a plant leaf contains chlorophyll in small bodies called *chloroplasts*. In chloroplasts, light energy causes water to split apart, separating its hydrogen and oxygen atoms. In a series of complicated steps, the hydrogen combines with carbon dioxide to form a simple sugar. Oxygen from the water is given off in the process. From sugar—together with nitrogen, sulfur, and phosphorus from the soil—green plants can make starch, fat, protein, vitamins, and other complex compounds essential for life. Photosynthesis provides the chemical energy needed to produce these compounds.

Other organisms, including certain bacteria and archaea, can capture light energy and use it to make food. *Photosynthetic bacteria* contain chlorophyll in tiny bodies called *chromatophores*. In chromatophores, compounds other than water are combined with carbon dioxide to form sugar. No oxygen is released. Certain archaea have developed a photosynthetic process that does not require chlorophyll.

When plants and animals need to use stored food for growth and activity, their bodies combine the food with oxygen to release chemical energy. This process, which is called *respiration*, is the reverse of photosynthesis. The plant or animal uses up oxygen and gives off carbon dioxide and water. Plants then use this carbon dioxide and water to produce more food and oxygen. The cycle of photosynthesis and respiration maintains Earth's natural balance of carbon dioxide and oxygen.

MLA Citation

"Plants." *The Southwestern Advantage Topic Source.* Nashville: Southwestern. 2013.

DATA
A Classification of the Plant Kingdom

Nonvascular plants

Division Bryophyta

Liverworts, hornworts, and mosses make up this division of plants. These plants reproduce by means of spores and lack true leaves, stems, or roots. Most live in moist areas. However, some mosses can withstand severe temperatures and are found in Arctic or desert regions.

Class Hepaticae: Liverworts make up this class. These small plants may be flat and ribbon-shaped or leafy. They grow close to the ground.

Class Anthocerotae: Hornworts usually grow only $3/8$ to $3/4$ inch (1 to 2 centimeters) across. The gametophyte is ribbonlike. Spores are contained in tubular sporangia that grow continuously from the sporangium base.

Class Musci: True mosses make up this class. Stems may be erect or horizontal and bear many leaflike growths. They seldom grow over 8 inches (20 centimeters) long.

Vascular plants

Division Tracheophyta

Tracheophytes are the vascular plants. All have two kinds of special tissues—*xylem* and *phloem*. Xylem tissue cells carry water from the roots to the leaves. Phloem tissue cells carry sugars made during photosynthesis in the leaves to other parts of the plant. Tracheophytes occur in most parts of the world.

Subdivision Lycophytina

These plants, which include club mosses, isoetopsids, and selaginellas, have leaves with a single central vein. Spores are produced in sporangia that grow in the stem-leaf nodes or on the leaves. The sporangia are distinctly kidney shaped. Plants in this subdivision tend to grow in moist, shady areas.

Class Lycopodiopsida: Lycopodiopsids are the club mosses and ground pines. Many species have stems that produce needlelike leaves. Spores are often tightly clustered at the tips of branches. Lycopodiopsids commonly grow on forest floors.

Class Selaginellopsida: Selaginellas produce separate male and female spores. They are leafy and usually delicate in construction. Though most selaginellas live in moist places, one kind, the "resurrection plant," occurs in desert environments.

Class Isoetopsida: Isoetopsids produce two kinds of spores, one male and one female. These small plants have grasslike leaves and live in wet, sometimes flooded places. During the Carboniferous Period, about 360 million to 300 million years ago, some isoetopsids were large trees.

Subdivision Euphyllophytina

Euphyllophytes include most of the vascular plants. Their leaves usually have many veins, and their reproductive organs and internal structures differ from those of the Lycophytina plants.

Class Psilopsida: The plants in this class are called whisk ferns or fork ferns. They have many slender, highly branched aerial stems by which the plants spread. They reproduce from spores. These rare plants are found in tropical and subtropical regions.

DATA

A Classification of the Plant Kingdom

Vascular plants

Class Sphenopsida: Living sphenopsids are known as horsetails or scouring rushes. They have small leaves that occur in whorls at the nodes on the stem. Stems are hollow except at the nodes, giving them a jointed appearance. They grow 2 to 3 feet (61 to 91 centimeters) tall and reproduce by means of spores. During the Carboniferous Period, sphenopsids made up a much larger group that included trees.

Class Pteridopsida: This class includes the ferns. Most ferns have large leaves called *fronds*. They reproduce by means of spores. Ferns are commonly seen on forest floors, but tropical fern trees may grow more than 65 feet (20 meters) high. Some floating aquatic ferns have leaves only about 1 inch (2.5 centimeters) long. Next to the flowering plants, ferns are the most diverse group in the division Tracheophyta.

Class Gymnospermopsida: Gymnosperms reproduce by means of *naked*, or uncovered, seeds. Many gymnosperms are evergreens with a wide variety of leaf structures. The class consists of conifers, cycads, ginkgoes, and gnetaleans.

Order Coniferales: Most conifers are evergreen trees or shrubs with needlelike or scalelike leaves. Almost all conifers bear their seeds in woody cones.

Order Cycadales: Cycads grow fernlike leaves. Their seeds are borne in large cones. Many species have unbranched, erect stems, while others have partially underground stems called *tubers*. Some cycads are trees.

Order Ginkgoales: Ginkgoes are trees with fan-shaped leaves. They bear fleshy seeds at the end of short branches. The seeds are not in cones. Only one species of ginkgo exists today.

Order Gnetales: Gnetaleans are closely related to flowering plants and share many characteristics with them. Gnetalean seeds are borne in complex cones. Living forms vary widely in appearance and inhabit deserts and tropical rain forests.

Class Anthopsida: Flowering plants, or angiosperms, make up this class. All angiosperms reproduce by means of covered seeds. They bear their sexual organs in flowers. After fertilization, the ovary grows into a fruit that encloses the seeds. Angiosperms are the most diverse group of plants, growing from the tropics to the polar regions. They are divided into two subclasses—Monocotyledonae and Dicotyledonae.

Subclass Monocotyledonae: Monocots have seeds with only one cotyledon (seed leaf). The main veins in the leaves of these plants usually run parallel to each other. Flower parts usually occur in multiples of three.

Subclass Dicotyledonae: Dicots have seeds with two cotyledons. Their leaves have a complex system of veins. Dicot flower parts usually occur in multiples of four or five.

ADDITIONAL RESOURCES

Books to Read

Level I

Galko, Francine. *Classifying Flowering Plants*. Heinemann Library, 2004. *Classifying Non-Flowering Plants*. 2004.

Griswell, Kim T. *Carnivorous Plants*. KidHaven Press, 2003.

Kudlinski, Kathleen V. *How Plants Survive*. Chelsea Clubhouse, 2003.

Pascoe, Elaine. *Plants with Seeds*. PowerKids Press, 2003. *Plants Without Seeds*. 2003.

Spilsbury, Richard and Louise. *Plant Growth*. Heinemann Library, 2003. *Plant Habitats*. 2003. *Plant Parts*. 2003.

Level II

Brickell, Christopher, and Cole, T. J., eds. *The American Horticultural Society Encyclopedia of Plants and Flowers*. Rev. ed. DK Publishing, 2002.

Brickell, Christopher, and Zuk, J. D., eds. *The American Horticultural Society A–Z Encyclopedia of Garden Plants*. DK Publishing, 1997.

Grimshaw, John. *The Gardener's Atlas: The Origins, Discovery and Cultivation of the World's Most Popular Garden Plants*. 1998. Reprint. Firefly Books, 2003.

Gurevitch, Jessica, and others. *The Ecology of Plants*. Sinauer, 2002.

Stern, Kingsley R., and others. *Introductory Plant Biology*. 9th ed. McGraw, 2003.

Web Sites

American Horticultural Society

http://www.ahs.org/

Official Web site of the organization includes information on gardening.

Center for Aquatic and Invasive Plants

http://aquat1.ifas.ufl.edu/

Information about plants that live in water habitats, plants that crowd out other species, and other topics from the University of Florida. Includes extensive links to other resources.

MBGnet

http://www.mbgnet.net/

The Missouri Botanical Garden presents a Web site with information about the different biomes and ecosystems of the world.

PLANTS Project

http://plants.usda.gov/

Standardized information about plants from the National PLANTS Database.

The International Plant Names Index

http://www.ipni.org/index.html

Harvard University presents a database of the names and associated basic bibliographical details of all seed plants.

University and Jepson Herbaria, University of California-Berkeley

http://ucjeps.berkeley.edu/

Information about the herbaria (plural of herbarium, a collection of herbs) at the university.

University of California at Davis Herbarium

http://herbarium.ucdavis.edu/

Information about the herbarium (collection of herbs).

BACKGROUND INFORMATION

The following article was written during the year in which the events took place and reflects the style and thinking of that time.

Genetically Modified Crops (2000)

An increasing number of crop plants are being genetically engineered to make them resistant to pests, disease, or chemicals or to enhance their properties.

—by David S. Haymer

Even from a distance, something looks different in the two fields of corn plants. In one field, the plants look tall and healthy, producing a bountiful yield of ears of corn. But in the neighboring field, the plants seem stunted, and many of the ears have fallen to the ground. What's the difference? The healthy looking plants have been genetically engineered to carry a gene that makes them resistant to attacks by the European corn borer, a destructive insect pest. The plants in the other field do not have this gene and are being severely damaged by the corn borer.

The insect-resistant corn plants are an example of a *transgenic plant* (a plant whose cells contain genes transferred from another species). Scientists gave the corn plant a gene from a bacterium that causes the plant to produce a substance that is toxic to the corn borer. In addition to corn, transgenic versions of several other crop plants, including soybeans, canola, potatoes, tomatoes, and squash, have been produced for commercial markets. Furthermore, in laboratories around the world in 2000, researchers were creating transgenic versions of many other important crop plants, such as rice, wheat, peas, and carrots. Scientists were giving these transgenic plants a number of other traits besides insect resistance. Among these characteristics were tolerance for *herbicides* (chemicals used to kill weeds), resistance to diseases caused by viruses, improved nutritional value, better taste, and longer shelf life.

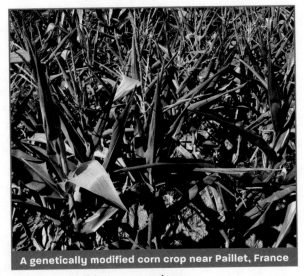
A genetically modified corn crop near Paillet, France

The United States was the world leader in producing genetically modified food in 2000, growing more than 70 percent of the total global acreage of transgenic crops. According to the National Agricultural Statistics Service (a division of the U.S. Department of Agriculture), approximately 38 percent of the U.S. corn crop and 57 percent of the U.S. soybean crop was genetically engineered in 1999. In addition to food plants, genetically engineered versions of other important plants were also gaining wide acceptance by farmers. For example, about 65 percent of the cotton produced in the United States in 1999 came from transgenic plants.

Other countries besides the United States that grow large amounts of transgenic crops include Argentina, Canada, China, Australia, South Africa, and Mexico. Worldwide in 1999, farmers planted about 40 million hectares (100 million acres) of transgenic crops.

The creation of this huge transgenic harvest depends on various techniques by which scientists insert new genes into cells taken from plants. These genetically modified cells are grown into whole plants with new characteristics specified by the added genes.

Inserting New Genes into Plants

One of the most common techniques used to create transgenic crops takes advantage of the natural ability of the soil bacterium *Agrobacterium tumefaciens* to insert genes into plant cells. These bacteria carry an extra piece of DNA (deoxyribonucleic acid, the molecule that makes up genes) called a Ti plasmid, which the bacteria can inject into plant cells. In nature, the Ti plasmid causes the plant to develop a tumor-like growth called a crown gall.

In the laboratory, scientists remove the harmful genes from the Ti plasmids and use the modified plasmids as *vectors* (carriers) to deliver genes for desired traits into plant cells. To do this, the researchers first add a gene for a desired trait to a different plasmid from a bacterium, often *Escherichia coli*. They then insert the modified plasmid carrying the new gene back into a bacterium, which, as it multiplies, makes copies of the gene. Next, the copies of the gene are removed and inserted into the Ti plasmids of *Agrobacterium* bacterial cells. These *Agrobacterium* cells, carrying the modified plasmid, are then placed into a laboratory culture dish containing plant cells.

Within a day or so, the bacteria attach to the plant cells and transfer their plasmids into the cells. Extra pieces of DNA called transposons, which can be carried on the plasmids along with new genes, help to insert the desired gene into the cells' *chromosomes* (the structures that carry the genes). The scientists then add nutrients and hormones to the culture dish to stimulate the cells to grow into new plants.

Agrobacterium plasmids were first used to genetically engineer plants in the 1980s. Scientists soon found that this method worked well only with certain types of plants, including tobacco, petunias, tomatoes, and potatoes. These plants are all *dicotyledons*, plants that have two cotyledons, or embryonic leaves, during their early development. For reasons that scientists do not completely understand, *Agrobacterium* plasmids are unable to transfer new DNA to the cells of such agriculturally important plants as corn, rice, and wheat. Such plants are *monocotyledons*, which have just one cotyledon during their early development.

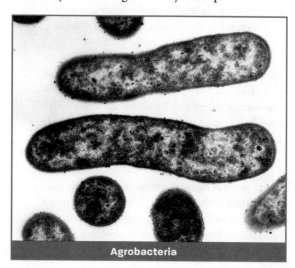

Agrobacteria

Gene Gun

To get around the problem posed by monocotyledons, scientists sought alternative techniques for delivering genes into plant cells. The most successful method they developed involves the use of a "gene gun," a gun-like device that literally shoots genes into plant cells.

In this procedure, also called particle bombardment, scientists first coat *inert* (chemically unreactive) microscopic particles—usually tungsten—with many copies of a desired gene. They then apply a mixture containing these particles to the tip of a bullet-like plastic cylinder and insert the cylinder into the gene gun along with a .22-caliber blank cartridge. When the gun is fired, the cylinder is propelled down the barrel of the gun and into a metal plate with a small hole in its center. The gene-carrying cylinder stops at the plate, but the DNA-coated particles spray through the hole into a culture dish containing plant cells.

Some of the particles penetrate the walls of the plant cells, carrying the attached genes with them. And in some of these cells, the DNA becomes incorporated into the cells' chromosomes. One advantage of the gene gun method over the use of *Agrobacterium* is that transposons are not needed to get the new genes into the chromosomes of the plant cells.

Making Crops Resistant to Insects

These and other genetic engineering methods have allowed scientists to add many new genes to crop plants. They have, for example, given plants various genes that make them resistant to attacks by insects, including the corn borer, thereby helping to free farmers from their reliance on expensive and environmentally harmful insecticides.

To engineer such plants, scientists usually use a gene from a bacterium called *Bacillus thuringiensis* (Bt). These bacteria secrete a protein that kills insects. By transferring the gene that codes for the production of this protein into plant cells, scientists have given these plants the ability to protect themselves against insect attack. When a corn borer or some other insect begins to dine on a plant engineered with the Bt gene, its digestive system chemically breaks down the Bt protein into a form that is toxic, and the insect dies.

Plants have been engineered to carry several other types of genes to protect themselves against insects. Some of these genes come not from bacteria but from other plants, and many of them code for proteins that interfere with the ability of insects to digest food. Scientists have transferred these kinds of protective genes from noncrop plants, such as the cowpea, into crop plants, including potatoes and corn. Insects attacking these genetically modified crop plants starve to death as they are eating. In this way, damage to the crop is greatly limited.

Herbicide Resistance

Plants engineered to resist insect attack account for more than 20 percent of all genetically modified crops. But the most common characteristic given to crop plants is the ability to tolerate exposure to herbicides—a trait shared by more than 70 percent of the world's transgenic crops. Weeds have always been a big problem for farmers, and for years the use of herbicides was the only practical way to keep fields weed-free. A big drawback of herbicides, however, is that they can also kill valuable crop plants.

A solution to this problem was announced in 1995 by scientists at the Monsanto Company in St. Louis, Missouri. The researchers found that they could create herbicide-tolerant crops by giving them a gene from bacteria that enabled the plants to withstand a chemical called glyphosate. Glyphosate is the active ingredient in a widely used herbicide called Roundup, which kills plants by preventing them from making certain *amino acids* (building blocks of proteins) that are essential to their survival.

The bacterial gene used by the scientists codes for the production of an enzyme called EPSPS, which promotes chemical reactions involved in the manufacture of amino acids. Using the gene-gun method, scientists added the EPSPS gene to soybean plants. The transgenic soybeans were unfazed by the glyphosate-containing herbicide and were able to carry out the chemical reactions needed to make their essential amino acids. By 2000, a number of other crop plants, such as the canola plant, had been engineered with different genes to make them herbicide tolerant.

Another characteristic given to some genetically modified crops is resistance to diseases caused by viruses. Viruses cause disease when they inject their DNA into a cell, taking over the cell's functions and prompting the cell to make copies of the virus. Scientists can create plants that are resistant to a particular virus by inserting into a plant a viral gene that causes the plant's cells to make just the harmless outer coat of the virus. This exposure to the virus coat helps prepare the plant to fight off the real virus when it comes.

Better Nutrition and Other Benefits

As well as engineering plants for resistance to insects, diseases, and herbicides, researchers in 2000 were developing a number of transgenic plants with more nutritional value. In January, for example, researchers at the Swiss Federal Institute of Technology in Zurich announced that they had genetically enhanced rice to produce large amounts of beta-carotene, a substance that the body converts to vitamin A.

Other genetically modified food items being developed in 2000 included carrots, peas, potatoes, strawberries, and other fruits and vegetables with improved nutritional value and greater flavor; rice, peanuts, and other products that were less likely than their conventional counterparts to cause allergic reactions; and longer-lasting bananas, melons, and other fruits. Scientists were also developing bananas and potatoes containing edible vaccines against various diseases, including hepatitis and cholera. Tomatoes with improved taste, better texture, and longer shelf life were one of the few foods specifically engineered for consumer benefit that were already on the market in 2000.

As scientists worked to develop new and improved transgenic plants, more and more Americans were becoming aware that an increasing amount of their food was genetically engineered. Although many people took that knowledge in stride, others felt uneasy about it, saying that not enough was known about the effects of genetically altered crops on human health and the environment. But whatever people thought about bioengineered foods, most experts predicted that genetically modified crops, and the products made from them, would become ever more common in the future.

The author: David S. Haymer is chairman of the Department of Genetics and Molecular Biology at the University of Hawaii.

Hurricanes and Tornadoes

A hurricane is a powerful, swirling storm that begins over a warm sea. When a hurricane hits land, it can cause great damage through fierce winds, torrential rain, flooding, and huge waves crashing ashore. A tornado is a spiral-shaped windstorm that usually forms over land and also can cause great damage from strong winds and flying debris.

HOT topics

Hurricane Katrina. Hurricane Katrina was one of the most destructive storms ever to strike the United States. The storm killed about 1,800 people, caused tens of billions of dollars in damage, and left hundreds of thousands of people homeless. The government's handling of evacuations and relief efforts was heavily criticized. A panel set up by the U.S. House of Representatives placed much of the blame on a lack of leadership by federal officials.

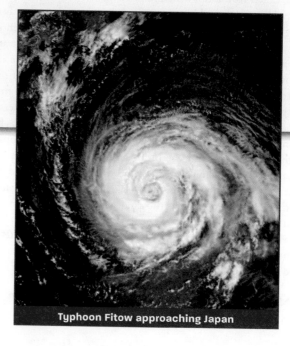

Typhoon Fitow approaching Japan

HOT topics

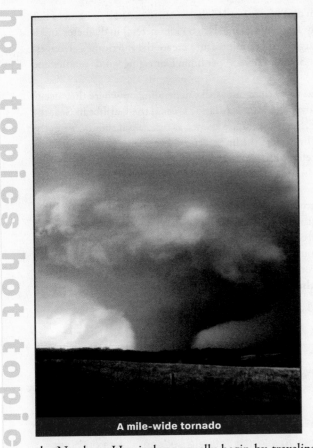

A mile-wide tornado

Tornado Chasers. Tornadoes are difficult for scientists to study because they do not know ahead of time where they will occur and because they form in a small area, then vanish quickly. During the height of the tornado season, meteorologists and researchers form teams of "storm chasers" who drive in specially equipped vehicles to locate tornadoes and gather measurements and temperatures or film wind patterns.

Anatomy of a Hurricane.

The winds of a hurricane swirl around a calm central zone called the *eye*. The eye usually measures 10 to 40 miles (16 to 64 kilometers) in diameter and is usually free of rain and large clouds. A band of tall clouds called the *eyewall* surrounds the eye. The strongest winds occur in and under the eyewall. Damaging winds may extend 250 miles (400 kilometers) from the eye. Heavy rains fall from the eyewall and from the bands of dense clouds.

The Path of a Hurricane.

A long-lived hurricane may wander up to 4,000 miles (6,400 kilometers). Hurricanes in the Northern Hemisphere usually begin by traveling from east to west. As the storms approach the coast of North America or Asia, however, they shift to a more northerly direction. The path of an individual storm is difficult to predict, but most hurricanes turn gradually northwest, north, and finally northeast. In the Southern Hemisphere, the storms may travel westward, then southwest, south, and finally southeast.

The Enhanced Fujita Scale and the Saffir-Simpson Hurricane Scale.

Tornadoes are rated on a scale based on the amount of damage that results. The categories range from EF0 (light damage, tree branches broken) to EF5 (incredible damage, houses lifted off foundation, car-sized objects thrown more than 300 feet). Hurricanes are rated on a scale based on wind speed and the height of the resulting storm surge—that is, how much the sea level rises above normal high tide. The categories range from 1 (weak, winds 74–95 mph) to 5 (devastating, winds 156+ mph).

TRUE or FALSE?

Hurricanes that occur in the Northwest Pacific Ocean are known as typhoons.

THE BASICS

A hurricane is a powerful, swirling storm that begins over a warm sea. Hurricanes then move westward and often toward the poles.

The winds of a hurricane swirl around a calm central zone called the *eye* surrounded by a band of tall, dark clouds called the *eyewall*. The eye is usually 10 to 40 miles (16 to 64 kilometers) in diameter and is free of rain and large clouds. In the eyewall, large changes in pressure create the hurricane's strongest winds. These winds can reach nearly 200 miles (320 kilometers) per hour. Damaging winds may extend 250 miles (400 kilometers) from the eye.

Storms known as *tropical cyclones* are referred to by different labels, depending on where they occur. They are called *hurricanes* when they happen over the North Atlantic Ocean, the Caribbean Sea, the Gulf of Mexico, or the Northeast Pacific Ocean. Such storms are known as *typhoons* if they occur in the Northwest Pacific Ocean, west of an imaginary line called the International Date Line. In the Southwest Pacific and Southeast Indian oceans, they are referred to as *severe tropical cyclones*. In the North Indian Ocean, they are known as *severe cyclonic storms*. In the Southwest Indian Ocean, such storms are referred to simply as tropical cyclones.

Hurricanes are most common during the summer and early fall. In the Atlantic and the Northeast Pacific, for example, August and September are the peak hurricane months. Typhoons occur throughout the year in the Northwest Pacific but are most frequent in summer. In the North Indian Ocean, tropical cyclones strike in May and November. In the South Indian Ocean, the South Pacific Ocean, and off the coast of Australia, the hurricane season runs from December to March. Approximately 90 hurricanes, typhoons, and tropical cyclones occur in a year throughout the world. In the rest of this article, the term *hurricane* refers to all such storms.

DEFINITIONS

hurricane *noun.* **a.** *Meteorology.* A wind having a velocity of 74 or more miles per hour (on the Beaufort scale, force 12). **b.** A tropical cyclone originating usually in the West Indies, often accompanied by violent thunderstorms. A storm with a violent wind and, usually, very heavy rain. *Figurative.* a sudden, violent outburst: *a hurricane of cheers.*

typhoon *noun.* A violent cyclone or hurricane occurring in the western Pacific, chiefly during the period from July to October. A violent storm or tempest occurring in Asia, especially in or near India. any violent storm.

cyclone *noun.* A storm or winds moving around and spiraling in toward a calm center of low pressure, which also moves. The winds of a cyclone move counterclockwise in the Northern Hemisphere and clockwise in the Southern Hemisphere. *Many errors in forecasting are caused by over attention to comparatively local conditions, without proper regard to the grand movement upon which the cyclones—the parents of rain and sunshine— are borne* (London Times). SYNONYM(S): typhoon, hurricane. Any very violent windstorm, such as a tornado. SYNONYM(S): whirlwind.

tornado *noun, plural* **-does** *or* **-dos**. **a.** An extremely violent and destructive whirlwind. A tornado extends down from a mass of dark clouds as a whirling funnel and moves over the land in a narrow path. **b.** Any extremely violent windstorm. A violent, whirling squall occurring during the summer on the west coast of Africa. *Figurative.* Any violent outburst: *a tornado of anger. In the fifteenth century a last tornado of nomadism arose in Western Turkestan* (H. G. Wells). *Obsolete.* A violent thunderstorm of the tropical Atlantic, with torrential rain.

How a Hurricane Forms

Hurricanes require a special set of conditions, including the ample heat and moisture that exists primarily over warm tropical oceans. For a hurricane to form, there must be a warm layer of water at the top of the sea. This warm seawater evaporates into the air. The moisture then *condenses* (changes into liquid), forming clouds. As the moisture condenses, it releases heat that warms the air, causing it to rise. The warm, rising air creates a region of relatively low *atmospheric pressure*. Atmospheric pressure is the weight of the air pressing down on a given area.

Air tends to move from areas of high atmospheric pressure to areas of low pressure, creating wind. In the Northern Hemisphere, the earth's rotation causes the wind to swirl into a low-pressure area in a counterclockwise direction. In the Southern Hemisphere, the winds rotate clockwise around a low. This effect of the rotating earth on wind flow is called the *Coriolis effect*. The Coriolis effect increases in intensity farther from the equator. To produce a hurricane, a low-pressure area must be more than 5 degrees of latitude north or south of the equator. Hurricanes seldom occur closer to the equator.

As the swirling winds increase in speed, more ocean water evaporates and then condenses. The moisture releases more heat, further warming the storm's core. The warm air rises faster, increasing surface wind speeds, and so on. This cycle, called a *positive feedback loop*, continues to strengthen the hurricane. When friction between the air and the water surface becomes great enough, the hurricane stops intensifying.

For a hurricane to develop, there must be little *wind shear*—that is, little difference in speed and direction between winds at upper and lower elevations. Uniform winds enable the warm inner core of the storm to stay intact. The storm would break up if the winds at higher elevations increased markedly in speed, changed direction, or both. The wind shear would disrupt the budding hurricane by tipping it over or by bringing dry air into the center of the storm.

The Life of a Hurricane

Meteorologists (scientists who study weather) divide the life of a hurricane into four stages: (1) tropical disturbance, (2) tropical depression, (3) tropical storm, and (4) hurricane.

A tropical disturbance is an area where rain clouds are building. The clouds form when moist air rises and becomes cooler. Cool air cannot hold as much water vapor as warm air can, and the excess water changes into tiny droplets of water that form clouds. The clouds in a tropical disturbance may rise to great heights, forming the towering thunderclouds that meteorologists call *cumulonimbus clouds.*

Cumulonimbus clouds usually produce heavy rains that end after an hour or two, and the weather clears rapidly. If conditions are right for a hurricane, however, there is so much heat energy and moisture in the atmosphere that new cumulonimbus clouds continually form from rising moist air.

A tropical depression is a low-pressure area surrounded by winds that have begun to blow in a circular pattern. A meteorologist considers a depression to exist when there is low pressure over a large enough area to be plotted on a weather map. On a map of surface pressure, such a depression appears as one or two circular *isobars* (lines of equal pressure) over a tropical ocean. The low pressure near the ocean surface draws in warm, moist air, which feeds more thunderclouds. The winds swirl slowly around the low-pressure area at first. As the pressure becomes even lower, the winds blow faster, and more ocean water evaporates.

Tropical storm. When the winds exceed 38 miles (61 kilometers) per hour, a tropical storm has developed. Viewed from above, the storm clouds now have a well-defined circular shape. The seas have become so rough that ships must steer clear of the area. The strong winds near the surface of the ocean draw more and more heat and water vapor from the sea. The increased warmth and moisture in the air feed the storm.

A tropical storm has a column of warm air near its center. The warmer this column becomes, the more the pressure at the surface falls. The falling pressure, in turn, creates more wind, which evaporates more ocean water and leads to even warmer air in the column.

Hurricane Felix, as seen from space

Each tropical storm receives a name. The names help meteorologists and disaster planners avoid confusion and quickly convey information about the behavior of a storm. The World Meteorological Organization (WMO), an agency of the United Nations, issues four alphabetical lists of names, one for the North Atlantic Ocean and the Caribbean Sea, and one each for the Eastern, Central, and Northwestern Pacific. The lists include both men's and women's names that are popular in countries affected by the storms.

Storms in the South Pacific and much of the Indian Ocean are named by the regional weather center located closest to the forming storm. These centers are found in Australia, India, Indonesia, New Zealand, and Papua New Guinea. The centers use a naming method similar to that of the WMO. Storms in the Southwestern Indian Ocean are named by the many African countries affected by such storms along with France. Each of the participating counties contributes at least one name to a given year's list.

Except in the Northwestern and Central Pacific, the first storm of the year gets a name beginning with *A*—such as Tropical Storm Alberto. If the storm intensifies into a hurricane, it becomes Hurricane Alberto. The second storm gets a name beginning with *B*, and so on through the alphabet. The lists do not use all the letters of the alphabet, however, since there are few names beginning with such letters as Q or U. For example, no Atlantic or Caribbean storms receive names beginning with Q, U, X, Y, or Z.

Because storms in the Northwestern Pacific occur throughout the year, the names run through the entire alphabet instead of starting over each year. The first typhoon of the year might be Typhoon Nona, for example. The Central Pacific usually has fewer than five named storms each year.

The system of naming storms has changed since 1950. Before that year, there was no formal system.

Storms commonly received women's names and names of saints of both genders. From 1950 to 1952, storms were given names from the United States military alphabet—Able, Baker, Charlie, and so on. The WMO began to use only the names of women in 1953. In 1979, the WMO began to use men's names as well.

Hurricane. A storm achieves hurricane status when its winds exceed 74 miles (119 kilometers) per hour. By the time a storm reaches hurricane intensity, it usually has a well-developed eye at its center. Surface pressure drops to its lowest in the eye.

In the eyewall, warm air spirals upward, creating the hurricane's strongest winds. Heavy rains fall from the eyewall and bands of dense clouds that swirl around the eyewall. These bands, called *rainbands*, can produce more than 2 inches (5 centimeters) of rain per hour. The hurricane draws large amounts of heat and moisture from the sea.

The Path of a Hurricane

Hurricanes last an average of 3 to 14 days. A long-lived storm may wander 3,000 to 4,000 miles (4,800 to 6,400 kilometers), typically moving over the sea at speeds of 10 to 20 miles (16 to 32 kilometers) per hour.

Hurricanes in the Northern Hemisphere usually begin by traveling from east to west. As the storms approach the coast of North America or Asia, however, they shift to a more northerly direction. Most hurricanes turn gradually northwest, north, and finally northeast. In the Southern Hemisphere, the storms may travel westward at first and then turn southwest, south, and finally southeast. The path of an individual hurricane is irregular and often difficult to predict.

All hurricanes eventually move toward higher latitudes where there is colder air, less moisture, and greater wind shears. These conditions cause the storm to weaken and die out. The end comes quickly if a hurricane moves over land, because it no longer receives heat energy and moisture from warm tropical water. Heavy rains may continue, however, even after the winds have diminished.

Hurricane Damage

Hurricane damage results from wind and water. Hurricane winds can uproot trees and tear the roofs off houses. The fierce winds also create danger from flying debris. Heavy rains may cause flooding and mudslides.

A palm tree is lashed by the strong winds of a hurricane.

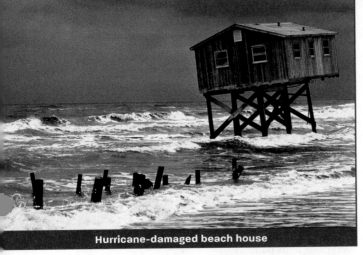

Hurricane-damaged beach house

The most dangerous effect of a hurricane, however, is a rapid rise in sea level called a *storm surge*. A storm surge is produced when winds drive ocean waters ashore. Storm surges are dangerous because many coastal areas are densely populated and lie only a few feet or meters above sea level. A 1970 cyclone in East Pakistan (now Bangladesh) produced a surge that killed about 266,000 people. A hurricane in Galveston, Texas, in 1900 produced a surge that killed about 6,000 people, the worst natural disaster in United States history.

Hurricane watchers rate the intensity of storms on a scale called the Saffir-Simpson scale, developed by American engineer Herbert S. Saffir and meteorologist Robert H. Simpson. The scale designates five levels of hurricanes, ranging from Category 1, described as weak, to Category 5, which can be devastating. Category 5 hurricanes have included Hurricane Camille, which hit the United States in 1969; Hurricane Gilbert, which raked the Caribbean Islands and Mexico in 1988; Hurricane Andrew, which struck the Bahamas, Florida, and Louisiana in 1992; and Hurricane Katrina, which caused widespread destruction in parts of Louisiana, Mississippi, and Alabama in 2005. In 2012, Hurricane Sandy, a Category 1, caused unprecedented damage and flooding from South Carolina to Maine.

Forecasting Hurricanes

Meteorologists use weather balloons, satellites, and radar to watch for areas of rapidly falling pressure that may become hurricanes. Specially equipped airplanes called *hurricane hunters* investigate budding storms.

If conditions are right for a hurricane, the National Weather Service issues a *hurricane watch*. A hurricane watch advises an area that there is a good possibility of a hurricane within 36 hours. If a hurricane watch is issued for your location, check the radio or television often for official bulletins. A *hurricane warning* means that an area is in danger of being struck by a hurricane in 24 hours or less.

Keep your radio tuned to a news station after a hurricane warning. If local authorities recommend evacuation, move quickly to a safe area or a designated hurricane shelter.

A typhoon is a violent cyclone that occurs in the northwest Pacific Ocean. Typhoons feature heavy rains and winds that maintain speeds equal to or greater than 74 miles (119 kilometers) per hour. Similar storms that occur in other parts of the world are called *tropical cyclones* or *hurricanes*. The word *typhoon* comes from the Chinese term *tai-fung*, meaning *great wind*.

Typhoons occur most frequently in the late summer. They form over warm seas between about 5 and 20 degrees of latitude from the equator. They tend to move west, northwest, and eventually northeast at speeds of 10 to 20 miles (16 to 32 kilometers) per hour. Inside a typhoon, strong winds blow in a counterclockwise direction around an area of low pressure at the storm's center, which is called the *eye*. The eye usually measures about 10 to 40 miles (16 to 64 kilometers) in diameter. The strongest winds blow inside the *eyewall*, a ring of clouds that surrounds the eye. These winds often reach speeds of more than 110 miles (180 kilometers) per hour.

The heavy rains and strong winds of a typhoon can cause great loss of life and billions of dollars in property damage. As a typhoon approaches lands, its winds produce a rush of seawater called a *storm surge* that can devastate coastal areas.

Cyclone is often used to mean a violent, swirling windstorm. To scientists, however, the term cyclone more commonly refers to the weather system in which this type of storm occurs. In this sense, a cyclone is any weather system except a tor-

Hurricane Andrew

nado in which the air pressure at the earth's surface is relatively low.

A cyclone—in the sense of a low-pressure system—acts as a "weather maker" in the middle latitudes. These are zones that extend from the Tropic of Cancer to the Arctic Circle and from the Tropic of Capricorn to the Antarctic Circle. A cyclone may be accompanied by strong winds and widespread areas of cloudiness and precipitation. A single cyclone can affect the weather over a third of a continent or more.

Viewed from above, the surface winds of a cyclone in the Northern Hemisphere blow counterclockwise and inward. In the Southern Hemisphere, the winds blow clockwise and inward. The winds bring together contrasting masses of air in the middle latitudes and in the high latitudes north of the Arctic Circle and south of the Antarctic Circle. Air masses may differ in temperature, humidity, or both. Where contrasting air masses meet, warm and cold fronts develop and spiral outward from the cyclone center. Warm air rises along the fronts, often producing cloudiness and rain or snow. Prevailing *westerlies* (winds from the west) steer a middle-latitude cyclone to the east and northeast.

A different kind of cyclone develops in or near the tropics, the regions between the equator and the Tropics of Cancer and Capricorn. A tropical cyclone has about one-third the diameter of a middle-latitude cyclone; it forms in warm, humid air over very warm ocean water; and it has no fronts. Prevailing winds steer it to the west.

The most intense tropical cyclone is a storm with extremely low air pressure at its center, surface winds blowing at speeds greater than 74 miles (119 kilometers) per hour, and heavy rains. Such a storm is called a *hurricane* when it occurs over the North Atlantic Ocean, the Caribbean Sea, the Gulf of Mexico, or the Northeast Pacific Ocean. It is known as a *typhoon* in the Northwest Pacific Ocean. Near Australia and in the Indian Ocean, it is referred to as a *tropical cyclone*.

A tornado is the most violent of all storms.

A powerful tornado can lift cars, cattle, and even mobile homes into the air. It can destroy almost everything in its path.

A tornado is a rapidly rotating column of air known as a *vortex* that has reached the ground. It is often associated with a *funnel cloud*, a funnel-shaped cloud that may appear near the ground in a thunderstorm. Tornado winds swirl at speeds that may exceed 300 miles (480 kilometers) per hour on rare occasions. Tornadoes are also sometimes called *twisters*.

Scientists use the word *cyclone* to refer to all spiral-shaped windstorms. Cyclones circulate in a counterclockwise direction in the Northern Hemisphere and in a clockwise direction in the Southern Hemisphere. Such storms come in many sizes. Among the largest and most intense are hurricanes and typhoons, which may reach 250 miles (400 kilometers) across. Most tornadoes are small, intense cyclones. On rare occasions, tornado winds whirl in the direction opposite that of a cyclone—for example, clockwise in the Northern Hemisphere.

A destructive tornado may reach 1 mile (1.6 kilometers) in diameter. It may travel at 60 miles (100 kilometers) per hour and blow for more than an hour. Fortunately, most tornadoes are smaller and weaker. Most move at less than 35 miles (55 kilometers) per hour and last only a few minutes.

Tornado damage is often localized. A tornado may demolish one house and leave a nearby house untouched. Most tornadoes create a path of devastation less than 1,600 feet (500 meters) wide.

The United States has more tornadoes than any other country. Most of these storms occur in a belt known as Tornado Alley. It stretches across the Midwestern, Plains, and Southern states, especially Texas, Oklahoma, Kansas, Nebraska, and Iowa. However, tornadoes also strike other parts of the world. Areas where tornadoes occur include much of Europe, Japan, parts of China, South Africa, and parts of Argentina and Brazil. Australia ranks second to the United States in number of twisters. Many tornadoes also strike Bangladesh and eastern India.

A tornado at sunset

How a Tornado Forms

The most damaging tornadoes form in storms called *supercells*. A supercell is a large, powerful thunderstorm. It contains a rapidly rotating air mass called a *mesocyclone*. For a supercell to form, and perhaps spawn a tornado, several basic conditions must exist. There must be an adequate supply of moisture to feed the storm. There must be a layer of warm, moist air near the ground and a layer of cool air above. Finally, the winds at higher elevations must differ from those at lower levels in speed, direction, or both.

Moisture. The first requirement for most tornadoes is moisture. In Tornado Alley, air from the Gulf of Mexico provides the moisture to fuel a twister. The warm water of the Gulf evaporates into the air.

Tornadoes and other severe storms often form along a *dryline*. In North America, the dryline is a boundary separating warm, moist air from the Gulf of Mexico and hot, dry air from the west.

If the humidity is high and rain-cooled air enters the main *updraft* (upward flow of air), a *wall cloud*

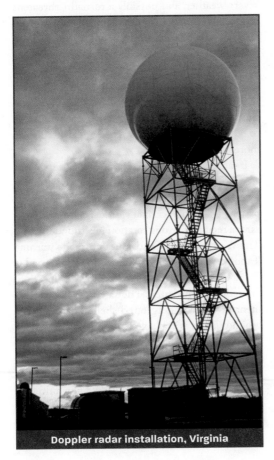

Doppler radar installation, Virginia

forms. A wall cloud is a low-hanging, dark cloud. Most funnel clouds develop from a wall cloud. If the humidity is low beneath the wall cloud, a tornado may form only a column of dust with no visible funnel cloud.

Air temperature. If there is warm, moist air at a lower altitude and cold, dry air at a higher altitude, the warmer air may become buoyant and rise rapidly. The air cools as it rises. The faster the warm air rises, the larger and more violent the storm and the more likely it will spawn a tornado. Storms may develop when warm air rides up over a shallow layer of cooler air. Storms may also form when moist air lifts over mountains, hills, or other high spots.

Often, a *front* powers an updraft of warm, moist air. A front is the boundary between two air masses of different densities resulting from a difference in temperature, humidity, or both. As the warm, less dense air rises, it begins to cool. The moisture it holds condenses into water droplets, forming a cloud. When the air rises high enough and becomes cold enough, its moisture turns into ice crystals. High in the atmosphere, often far above 35,000 feet (10,700 meters), the cloud stops rising. Upon reaching its maximum height, its top spreads out in the shape of an anvil. Anvil-shaped storm clouds often produce thunder, heavy rain, lightning, and hail. In the right conditions, a deadly tornado may form under the base of the cloud.

Winds. Another requirement for a supercell is that winds at higher elevations greatly differ from those at lower levels in speed, direction, or both. A difference in wind speed or direction is called *wind shear*. Wind shear makes the column of rising air begin to rotate. At first, the swirling air forms a broad, horizontal tube. As the storm develops, the tube tilts upright. It becomes the rotating column of air called a mesocyclone.

Most tornadoes occur in supercells. But some appear in a large group of storms called a *mesoscale convective system* (MCS). *Mesoscale* means *medium-sized*. *Convective* refers to *convection*, the turbulent upward and downward motions of air among the storms. An MCS is a cluster of thunderstorms that act as a system and often produce severe weather.

The Life of a Tornado

Tornadoes occur most often during the spring and early summer. Most happen in the late afternoon and early evening. The majority of tornadoes develop from severe thunderstorms. A hurricane, when it makes landfall, can also generate tornadoes.

The first sign of an approaching tornado may be light rain. Heavier rain follows and then rain mixed with hail. The hailstones may grow to the size of golf balls or even oranges. After the hail ends, a tornado may strike. In most tornadoes, a funnel-shaped cloud forms and descends from the wall cloud until it touches the ground. However, there might be a tornado even if the air is too dry for a visible funnel cloud to form. Sometimes, the first sign of a tornado is dust swirling just above the ground.

Some tornadoes contain smaller, short-lived, rotating columns of air called *suction spots* or *suction vortices*. The suction spots revolve around the center of the tornado and can inflict great damage to small areas. When these smaller vortices form, the overall vortex or rotating tornado cloud tends to be wide.

Tornadoes form over water as well as over land. Tornadoes over water, called *waterspouts*, carry large amounts of mist and spray. Waterspouts occur frequently in summer over the Florida Keys. Waterspouts also form elsewhere in the Gulf, along the Atlantic and Pacific coasts, over the Great Lakes, and even over the Great Salt Lake in Utah.

A few small tornadoes begin near the ground and build upward, instead of descending from the clouds. These storms are often called *landspouts* because they look like waterspouts over land.

Damage by Tornadoes

Most tornado damage results from the wind. Each time the wind speed doubles, the force of the wind increases four times. For example, the force of the wind at 220 miles (350 kilometers) per hour is four times as great as the force at 110 miles (175 kilometers) per hour. This tremendous strength may knock over buildings and trees. Other damage occurs when gusts of wind pick up objects and hurl them through the air.

The Fujita scale. Scientists estimate the wind speed of a tornado by the damage it inflicts. For years, they used a system called the Fujita scale. The Japanese-born weather scientist T. Theodore Fujita developed the scale in 1971. In the early 2000s, scientists developed a revised system called the Enhanced Fujita scale. On the Enhanced Fujita scale, EF0 is the weakest rating and EF5 is the

strongest. An EF5 tornado can remove a house from its foundation.

Air pressure. Air rising from the ground in the vortex of a tornado creates an area of low air pressure near the ground. For this reason, some people open their windows if a tornado threatens. This precaution is meant to help equalize the indoor pressure with the air outside. The people fear that the air pressure outside the building might drop so suddenly that the structure would explode outward. Safety experts know, however, that air moves in and out of most buildings quickly. The air pressure remains nearly equal inside and out, even during a tornado. Open windows do not reduce the damage. Instead, they may increase the destruction if the wind hurls loose objects through the openings.

Forecasting Tornadoes

Meteorologists (scientists who study weather) hope to learn more about tornadoes to better forecast these destructive storms. They can predict with some accuracy 12 to 48 hours in advance if severe weather, and possibly a tornado, threatens an area. Forecasts are made using data from weather balloons, radar, and satellites.

In the United States, the National Weather Service issues a *tornado watch* when weather conditions are right for the formation of tornadoes. If a tornado watch is issued in your area, you should keep alert for threatening weather. Listen to the radio or television or check the Internet for more information.

If radar detects a mesocyclone or a pattern characteristic of a tornado, the National Weather Service issues a *tornado warning*. The characteristic radar pattern is called a *tornado vortex signature*. It indicates a region of strong rotation in a thunderstorm. The Weather Service also issues a tornado warning if someone actually sees a funnel cloud or tornado.

If a tornado warning is issued for your location, take cover immediately. The safest place is a basement or other underground shelter. If no underground shelter is available, an interior bathroom or closet is best.

Studying Tornadoes

Tornadoes are difficult to study. They form fast, vanish quickly, and occupy a small area. Another problem is that scientists do not know exactly what causes tornadoes. As a result, they find it difficult to reach the right place at the right time to gather data.

Meteorologists investigate tornadoes using a combination of field studies, computer modeling, and studies with devices called *vortex chambers*. From this research, scientists hope to learn how, when, and why tornadoes form. This knowledge will enable them to increase warning times. It will also help to reduce the number of false alarms and provide more accurate warnings.

Field studies take place outdoors. Scientists go into the field to study tornadoes up close. Many meteorologists form mobile teams of "storm chasers" to study tornadoes. The storm chasers travel in specially equipped automobiles, trucks, vans, and aircraft. They try to get as close as is safe to a tornado to study it.

Radar. Meteorologists use a special type of radar called *Doppler radar* to look for mesocyclones. Doppler radar enables storm chasers to map the wind's speed and direction, rather than merely track areas of precipitation. Doppler radar works because radar waves change frequency depending on whether the objects they bounce off, such as raindrops or dust particles, are advancing or receding. This change in frequency is called the *Doppler effect*. It can reveal the rotating pattern of a mesocyclone. As a result, Doppler radar can detect the development of a tornado before it descends from its parent thunderstorm and touches down.

With Doppler radar, meteorologists can also study the changes that take place in a thunderstorm before a tornado forms. Pairs of similar radars at different locations can allow meteorologists to estimate both the horizontal and vertical movements of the wind.

Some radar systems can scan a section of the sky rapidly. Rapid-scanning radar enables scientists to record and study even the fastest-forming twisters.

A few radar systems enable scientists to distinguish among airborne debris, drops of drizzle, hailstones, insects, and raindrops. These radars scan by transmitting polarized beams of radiation both vertically and horizontally. Most Doppler radars typically use only horizontally polarized beams. Beginning in 2011, the National Weather Service is updating its network of Doppler radars to include this capability.

Clean air contains few particles large enough for regular radar to detect. To map winds that carry little moisture or dust, meteorologists use a

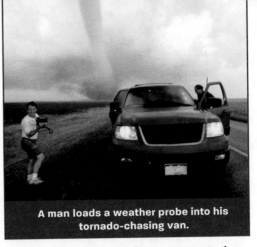

A man loads a weather probe into his tornado-chasing van.

Doppler *lidar* system. A lidar is a system similar to radar but uses a signal with a much shorter wavelength. Even clean air has extremely small particles called *aerosols* floating in it. Lidar's shorter wavelength signal can detect these tiny particles. But lidar cannot penetrate far into clouds, rain, or hail.

Researchers may record a tornado and the flying debris around it on film or video to help analyze wind patterns. They then compare the film with the radar images of the storm. Scientists may also survey the damage done by a tornado and compare it with the radar data.

The VORTEX projects. Beginning in 1994, scientists carried out two major research projects to study tornadoes. The projects were called the Verification of the Origins of Rotation in Tornadoes Experiment (VORTEX). The first project, VORTEX1, took place in 1994 and 1995. Scientists traveled in both ground-based vehicles and aircraft equipped with customized weather instruments. The project produced insight into tornado formation. It also promoted advancements in Doppler radar.

VORTEX2 followed in 2009 and 2010. More than 100 scientists traveling in dozens of vehicles participated. Unlike many earlier experiments, VORTEX2 did not have a home base. Instead, the storm chasers roamed from place to place. They used weather forecasts and their own instruments to position themselves in areas where tornadoes would likely form.

The VORTEX2 team used a vast array of scientific equipment. Radar, lidar, video, and film recorded any storms. Mobile radars scanned supercells likely to produce tornadoes. Instruments called *disdrometers* measured the size of raindrops or hail in storms. Weather balloons launched in various locations recorded environmental conditions. VORTEX2 also used remotely controlled aircraft called *unmanned aerial vehicles* (UAVs) to fly near storms and gather meteorological data.

The VORTEX2 team also released nearly 40 instrument packages, called Sticknets and Tornado Pods, where the team hoped a tornado would pass. The instruments provided information about conditions inside the funnel cloud, such as air pressure and humidity.

Computer modeling. Meteorologists make extensive use of *computer models* to study tornadoes. A computer model is a set of mathematical equations processed by computers. Scientists can easily vary the conditions in the models to test their theories. This use of computer modeling is known as *simulation.* For example, scientists can simulate supercells, storms, and smaller-scale vortexes. Most models are so complex that they require fast computers and a large amount of data.

Analysis of the models helps scientists to understand the processes by which tornadoes form and change. Computer modeling can also help predict the weather events that might occur under certain conditions and the likelihood that an event will actually occur. Thus, forecasters can determine the probability of a tornado occurring in a certain area during a certain period.

Vortex chambers. Meteorologists simulate some aspects of tornadoes in the lab using special chambers of rotating air currents. These devices are called *vortex chambers.* By varying the strength of an exhaust fan above the chamber and the angle at which air enters at the bottom, a scientist can re-create different types of tornado structures. In one common structure, air sinks outside the tornado and rises at the center. In another common structure, air sinks at the center of the tornado and rises outside the center.

A mathematical technique called a *large-eddy simulation* (LES) modeling can show what happens when a rotating column of air comes into contact with the ground. Such models also explain aspects of tornado structure, such as how wind speeds vary with altitude. Based on LES models, scientists have developed new theories about tornado formation. For example, one theory proposes that tornadoes may develop when air near the ground is blocked from entering the vortex. Another factor may be the roughness of the surface, such as the amount and heights of buildings, grass, or trees in an area.

MLA Citation

"Hurricanes and Tornadoes."
*The Southwestern Advantage
Topic Source.* Nashville:
Southwestern. 2013.

ADDITIONAL RESOURCES

Books to Read

Emanuel, Kerry A. *Divine Wind: The History and Science of Hurricanes.* Oxford, 2005.
Fradin, Judith B. and Dennis B. *Hurricanes.* National Geographic Society, 2007.
Longshore, David. *Encyclopedia of Hurricanes, Typhoons, and Cyclones.* Rev. ed. Checkmark, 2008.
Treaster, Joseph B. *Hurricane Force: In the Path of America's Deadliest Storms.* Kingfisher Books, 2007.

Web Sites

Atlantic Oceanographic & Meteorological Laboratory
http://www.aoml.noaa.gov/hrd/tcfaq/tcfaqHED.html
Site on hurricanes, typhoons, and tropical cyclones.

Hurricane Hunters
http://www.hurricanehunters.com/
Site of the Air Force Reserve Hurricane Hunters—the only Department of Defense organization still flying into tropical storms and hurricanes.

National Hurricane Center
http://www.nhc.noaa.gov/
A government site that predicts and reports on hurricanes.

Tropical Storms Worldwide
http://www.solar.ifa.hawaii.edu/Tropical/tropical.html
A University of Hawaii Web site reporting on current tropical storms worldwide.

DATA

The Saffir-Simpson Hurricane Scale

Hurricane category	Wind speed (Mph)	Wind speed (Kph)	Storm surge (Feet)	Storm surge (Meters)	Effects
Category 1 (weak)	74–95	119–153	4–5	1.2–1.5	Minimal damage to trees, shrubbery, and mobile homes.
Category 2 (moderate)	96–110	154–177	6–8	1.8–2.4	Considerable damage to trees, mobile homes, and piers; some damage to roofs.
Category 3 (strong)	111–130	178–209	9–12	2.7–3.7	Trees blown down or stripped of leaves; mobile homes destroyed; some damage to other buildings.
Category 4 (very strong)	131–155	210–250	13–18	4.0–5.5	Extensive damage to windows, doors, and roofs, especially near shore; possible flooding.
Category 5 (devastating)	156+	251+	19+	5.8+	Small buildings overturned or blown away; severe structural damage to other buildings.

The Enhanced Fujita Scale

Scale	Damage	Wind speed (Mph)	Wind speed (Kph)
EF0	Light: Tree branches broken, damage to chimneys and large signs.	65–85	105–137
EF1	Moderate: Trees snapped, surface of roofs peeled off, windows broken.	86–110	138–177
EF2	Considerable: Large trees uprooted, roofs torn off frame houses, mobile homes demolished.	111–135	178–217
EF3	Severe: Roof and some walls torn off well-constructed houses, cars overturned.	136–165	218–266
EF4	Devastating: Well-constructed houses leveled, cars and large objects thrown.	166–200	267–322
EF5	Incredible: Strong frame houses lifted off foundation and destroyed, car-sized objects thrown more than 300 feet (90 meters).	Over 200	Over 322

DATA

Some Famous Hurricanes, Typhoons, and Cyclones

1900	A hurricane and storm surge killed about 6,000 people in the Galveston, Texas, area.
1928	About 1,800 people died in a hurricane and floods in the Lake Okeechobee area of Florida. The storm also killed 300 people in Puerto Rico.
1938	A hurricane tore through Long Island and New England, killing about 600 and causing $400 million in damage.
1944	A typhoon in the Philippine Sea sank three destroyers and wrecked more than 100 aircraft of the U.S. Pacific fleet; 778 lives were lost.
1963	Hurricane Flora killed about 5,000 people in Haiti, more than 1,700 in Cuba, and more than 400 in the Dominican Republic.
1969	Hurricane Camille killed more than 250 people in seven states from Louisiana to Virginia. It caused about $1 billion in damage.
1970	The storm surge from a tropical cyclone drowned about 266,000 people in East Pakistan (now Bangladesh).
1972	Floods of Hurricane Agnes killed 122 people and caused $3 billion in damage from Florida to New York.
1974	Hurricane Fifi struck Honduras, killing about 8,000 people and causing $1 billion in damage.
1975	Floods well inland caused by Hurricane Agnes killed 117 people from Florida to New York.
1979	Hurricane David battered the Dominican Republic, killing 1,200 and causing $1 billion in damage. Hurricane Frederic struck Alabama and Mississippi, killing 8 and causing $1 billion in damage.
1980	Tropical Cyclone Hyacinthe looped around Reunion Island in the Indian Ocean, delivering 252 inches of rain in just 15 days.
1988	Hurricane Gilbert, the most powerful hurricane ever recorded in the Western Hemisphere, struck the West Indies and Mexico, causing about 300 deaths.
1992	Hurricane Andrew struck the Bahamas, Florida, and Louisiana, killing 65 and causing about $26 billion in damage.
1997	Typhoon Linda battered Vietnam's southern coast, killing more than 600 people.
1998	A cyclone devastated the western India province of Gujarat, killing more than 2,000 people.
1998	Storms and flooding from Hurricane Mitch caused billions of dollars worth of damage and killed more than 11,000 in Central America.
1999	About 9,600 people died in a cyclone and floods in the eastern India province of Orissa.
2004	Hurricanes Charley, Frances, Ivan, and Jeanne hit the U.S. Southeast in 2 months, causing over $42 billion in damage and killing more than 150 people. Jeanne killed more than 3,000 Haitians.
2005	Hurricane Katrina struck New Orleans and other parts of the U.S. Gulf Coast, killing more than 1,800 people and causing an estimated $100 billion of damage. Weeks later, Hurricane Rita caused an estimated $10 billion of damage in Texas and Louisiana.
2008	Cyclone Nargis struck the coast of Myanmar near Yangon, killing about 140,000.
2012	Hurricane Sandy produced widespread wind damage and unprecedented flooding from South Carolina to Maine. The storm moved inland, causing blizzard conditions in the higher elevations of the Applachian region.

BACKGROUND INFORMATION

The following articles were written during the year in which the events took place and reflect the style and thinking of that time.

Weather (1992)

The year 1992 began with the warmest winter on record in the contiguous United States, surpassing by nearly 1°F (0.5°C) the previous record set in the winter of 1953–1954. Above-normal temperatures prevailed in every major region of the nation, and five Midwestern states recorded their warmest winter since observations began. Only in northern Maine did winter temperatures average below normal.

Farther east, below-normal temperatures were the rule. Gander, Canada, experienced its coldest February on record. One of the worst winter storms in decades occurred in Canada's Atlantic Provinces from January 31 to February 3, 1992. Pressure in the offshore storm center dropped to 962 millibars (28.41 inches) of mercury. Wind gusts reached 96 miles per hour (mph) (155 kilometers per hour [kph]), and snowfall at Moncton, Canada, totaled 63 inches (160 centimeters).

In some areas of the northwestern United States, the winter was one of the driest on record, but northern Mexico and the southern fringe of the United States experienced heavy rainfall. Texas and New Mexico had their wettest recorded winter. On January 17 and 18, a vigorous storm along the northern Gulf of Mexico brought one of the 10 heaviest snowfalls of the 1900s—up to 8 inches (20 centimeters) to northern Texas and eastward to northern Georgia.

Heavy precipitation continued into much of the spring. In mid-May, a series of storms caused extensive flooding of the San Antonio and Guadalupe rivers. By the end of May, the city of San Antonio had accumulated more than 33 inches (84 centimeters) of rain, exceeding the city's normal yearly total.

Cool, wet summer. In contrast to the warm winter, the three midsummer months were the coolest since 1915 in the contiguous United States as a whole, and the third-coldest summer since recordkeeping began. The lowest temperatures were concentrated mainly in the east, however, with above-average temperatures prevailing in Nevada and the West Coast states. In the north-central states, the temperature for the season averaged up to 7°F (4°C) below normal.

For the contiguous United States as a whole, it was also the wettest summer since 1941. Precipitation was more than 50 percent greater than normal in the Southwest, Central Plains, and the Southeast.

Hurricane Andrew. The 1992 Atlantic hurricane season was slow to start. But on August 23, the year's first tropical storm, Andrew, suddenly intensified as it moved over the island of Eleuthera in the Bahamas with a 23-foot-high (7-meter-high) storm surge. Early the next morning, Andrew, now a hurricane, moved inland through a densely populated area south of downtown Miami. During the hurricane's four-hour trek across southern Florida, steady winds of an estimated 140 mph (225 kph) prevailed, with some gusts measured at 164 mph (264 kph). An estimated 72,000 homes, including mobile homes, were damaged or destroyed, and 200,000 people were left homeless. The estimated damage total of up to $20 billion made Andrew the costliest disaster in U.S. history.

After leaving Florida, the storm moved northwest across the Gulf of Mexico and made a second landfall in southwestern Louisiana during the late evening of August 25. Moving more slowly, the storm weakened quickly as it continued northward. After sending heavy rain and several tornadoes along its path, it finally died out in Pennsylvania.

Florida's well-executed evacuation plan helped keep the official death toll relatively low. Thirteen people were killed in Florida, and one person was killed in Louisiana. Perhaps as many as 39 people died either as a direct or indirect result of the storm.

Altogether, the Atlantic hurricane season produced only five storms. One of these, Danielle, lashed coastal areas with gales from Cape Hatteras, North Carolina, to eastern Pennsylvania on September 25 and 26.

Hurricane Iniki. Hawaiians on the island of Kauai had to cope with Hurricane Iniki, which roared across the Pacific on September 11 with 130-mph (209-kph) sustained winds. The storm left an estimated 8,000 of the island's 52,000 inhabitants homeless.

**Collection of
golf ball-size hailstones**

Typhoons. In 1992, the western third of the tropical Pacific Ocean had a record number of typhoons. Guam weathered six in three months. The first one, named Omar, struck on August 28, with winds up to 150 mph (240 kph), causing major damage to more than 75 percent of the island's buildings. From October 9 to November 23, five more typhoons struck the island, but damage was less severe.

Hailstorms and tornadoes. On March 6, 1992, portions of Seminole County in central Florida were buried more than ankle deep in golf ball-size hailstones. Buildings and crops suffered $25 million in damage. On March 25, hail caused $60 million in damages to the nursery industry in the Orlando, Florida, area.

By December, there had been more confirmed tornado occurrences across the United States than in any previous year. In June, 399 tornadoes were sighted, a record for that month. From June 15 through 18, large hailstones, strong winds, and more than 200 tornadoes hit the area from the central and northern Plains eastward into the Appalachian Mountains.

November, usually a quiet month for tornado activity, brought 173 reports. Most of these occurred from November 20 to 24 in 12 states, including Mississippi, Georgia, North and South Carolina, Kentucky, and Tennessee. At least 25 people were killed.

Drought and floods. As 1992 began, California was experiencing its sixth winter in a row with below-normal rainfall. The snowpack in the Sierra Nevada, which feeds California's reservoirs as it melts throughout the year, was only 45 percent of its normal size.

Then, from February 5 to 21, a series of heavy rains caused flooding and mud slides in several communities northwest of Los Angeles. Above-normal levels of precipitation continued through most of March. Nevertheless, for the 1991-1992 water season—which began on October 1, 1991, and ended on September 30, 1992—the total precipitation was only 90 percent of normal, not enough to end the water shortage that had persisted since 1986.

In Oregon, Washington, Idaho, and Nevada, where much smaller amounts of precipitation fell, the drought became extreme. Hawaii experienced drought conditions as well.

Every country in southern Africa was affected by the worst growing-season drought of the 1900s. Crop production was estimated to be only 60 percent of the amount in 1991. In Zimbabwe, the hardest-hit area, rainfall was less than 20 percent of normal. Thousands of cattle deaths were reported.

In mid-September 1992, heavy flooding reportedly killed 2,000 people in northern Pakistan and 500 people in India. About 1,800 villages in the Indian state of Punjab were reportedly washed away by tidal surges that rushed down rivers. Every river bridge and half the crops in the state of Jammu and Kashmir were reported to have been destroyed.

Record-breaking December storm. The worst east-coast winter storm in decades, and probably the worst ever in December, developed and stalled over northeastern Virginia on December 11. High winds and heavy snow caused 640,000 power outages in Pennsylvania. The snow accumulated to more than 36 inches (91 centimeters) in western Pennsylvania and the mountains of southern New England. Coastal areas in New Jersey and the New York metropolitan area were extensively flooded.

Trying to explain the weather. The warm winter of 1991-1992 in the United States fueled the ongoing debate about global warming, the theory that increasing levels of carbon dioxide in the atmosphere are causing Earth's average surface temperature to rise. As cold weather became entrenched in the eastern half of the United States, however, meteorologists focused their interest on the June 1991 eruption of Mount Pinatubo in the Philippines. The eruption had sent dust and gases high into the atmosphere, forming a cloud that circled the globe. Scientists believed that the cloud may have caused a temporary lowering of Earth's average temperature of about 1.8°F (1°C). This would not account for the low summer temperatures of 1992 in the United States and Canada, however.

The most likely cause of 1992's unusual weather patterns was the reappearance of El Nino, a vast area of warm water in the tropical Pacific Ocean that appears at irregular intervals of 2 to 12 years. Meteorologists believed that the droughts in Hawaii and southern Africa and the heavy precipitation along the southern fringe of the United States were by-products of an El Nino that appeared in November 1991.

Weather (2005)

The 2005 hurricane season in the Atlantic produced more storms than had occurred in any other year since record keeping began in 1851. Twenty-seven named storms formed—including a record 14 hurricanes—and one storm, Katrina, produced one of the greatest natural disasters in the history of the United States.

Tornadoes. For the first time since record keeping began in 1950, no tornado-related deaths occurred during the height of the season (from April to June) despite more than 500 twisters. However, five separate tornado outbreaks led to 27 deaths in November 2005, including 23 deaths near Evansville, Indiana, on the 12th.

The Atlantic hurricane season of 2005 was unprecedented in how early it began, the high intensity of the storms in the Gulf of Mexico, and the damage that they caused in the United States. The first named tropical storm, Arlene, formed in the western Caribbean on June 9. Arlene crossed western Cuba before making landfall near Pensacola on June 11 with winds of 60 miles (97 kilometers) per hour.

The season's first hurricane, Dennis, formed in the eastern Caribbean on July 6. The storm swept ashore near Cienfuegos, Cuba, as the strongest Atlantic hurricane recorded so early in the year, a Category 4. (A Category 4 hurricane, according to the Saffir-Simpson hurricane classification system, generates winds of 131 to 155 miles [210 to 249 kilometers] per hour.) Dennis had weakened to a Category 3 storm, with winds of 111 to 130 miles (179 to 209 kilometers) per hour when it made landfall near Pensacola on July 10. Nevertheless, Dennis caused less damage than Category 3 Hurricane Ivan, which struck the same area in 2004.

As Dennis dissipated, Tropical Storm Emily formed in the eastern Atlantic in the second week of July. Emily became a Category 4 hurricane as it moved through the Caribbean, striking Jamaica. The storm made a second landfall in Mexico about 75 miles (121 kilometers) south of Brownsville, Texas, as a Category 3 hurricane on July 20. By the end of July, seven Atlantic storms had been named, a record for so early in the season.

Katrina, a storm destined to become one of the most destructive acts of nature on record in the United States, made landfall in Florida near North Miami Beach on August 25 as a Category 1 hurricane, with winds of 74 to 95 miles (119 to 153 kilo-

meters) per hour. The storm moved southwest across Florida, where it was blamed for 11 deaths.

Over the eastern Gulf, Katrina intensified into the fourth strongest hurricane on record. The eye of the hurricane slammed into the southeastern Louisiana coast on August 29, 2005, with winds of 127 miles (204 kilometers) per hour. The storm center passed just east of New Orleans before moving into Mississippi. The *storm surge* (a sudden rise of ocean water that accompanies a hurricane at landfall) reached 20 to 30 feet (6 to 9 meters) along parts of the Mississippi coast, destroying all structures close to the beach.

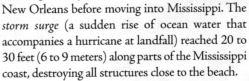

Homes were destroyed by the battering of hurricanes Ivan and Katrina, Dauphin Island, Alabama.

In New Orleans, the combination of heavy rain and roiling waters in Lake Pontchartrain caused the levee system to fail at several points. Water inundated about 80 percent of the city, and thousands of stranded people had to be rescued by boat and helicopter in the days following the storm. Hurricane Katrina caused at least 1,200 deaths in Mississippi and Louisiana, as well as economic losses estimated at $100 billion to $200 billion.

Hurricane Rita, which formed in the eastern Atlantic, intensified as it swept by the Florida Keys on September 20 and 21. In the central Gulf of Mexico, the storm grew to be the third strongest hurricane on record. Rita made landfall near the Texas-Louisiana border on September 24 as a Category 3 storm, with peak winds of 120 miles (193 kilometers) per hour. The storm surge flooded much of the southwestern Louisiana coast.

In October, Hurricane Wilma became the most powerful storm ever recorded in the Atlantic, with winds of 175 miles (282 kilometers) per hour. At least 12 people were killed in Mexico and Cuba before Wilma weakened and struck the southwest coast of Florida near Naples as a Category 3 storm on October 24. The hurricane crossed Florida, causing more than 30 deaths and extensive damage.

In all, 27 named storms formed in the Atlantic in 2005, breaking the previous record of 21 storms set in 1933. After the U.S. National Hurricane Center exhausted its list of 21 names, meteorologists began using letters of the Greek alphabet—from Alpha to Zeta—to name the storms.

Global Warming

Global warming is the gradual increase in the temperature of the earth's atmosphere caused by the concentration of gases, especially carbon dioxide, that absorb heat from the sun. The human consumption of fossil fuels such as coal, oil, and gas has magnified this greenhouse effect, with consequences for the earth's climate.

HOT topics

Preventive Measures. Global warming has been accelerated by human activities that have increased the concentration of carbon dioxide in the earth's atmosphere. Quantities of carbon dioxide can be limited by replacing fossil fuels with energy sources that do not emit CO_2, such as wind and solar power, nuclear energy, and the geothermal generation of power from underground steam.

HOT topics

Preventive Measures

Carbon Sequestration

The Kyoto Protocol

Melting Arctic Ice

DEFINITIONS

carbon dioxide: a heavy, colorless, odorless gas, present in the atmosphere or formed when any fuel containing carbon is burned; carbonic-acid gas. The air that is breathed out of an animal's lungs contains carbon dioxide. Plants absorb it from the air and use it to make plant tissue. Carbon dioxide is used in soda water and in fire extinguishers. *Formula:* CO_2

fossil fuel: coal, oil, or natural gas.

global warming: the gradual warming of the earth's atmosphere caused by the concentration of gases, especially carbon dioxide, that absorb heat from the sun: Scientists were warning that continued release of carbon dioxide from burning large amounts of fossil fuels could cause a global warming (Rod Such).

greenhouse effect: the absorption and retention of the sun's radiation in the earth's atmosphere, resulting in an increase in the temperature of the earth's surface.

HOT topics

Carbon Sequestration.
The amount of carbon dioxide released into the atmosphere can be limited by the development of ways to store (sequester) carbon and keep it from entering the air. Possible carbon storage methods include injecting industrial emissions of CO_2 into underground geologic formations, such as the cavities left by the extraction of coal and gas from the ground. Carbon dioxide could also be deposited into the earth's oceans, although the environmental consequences of carbon sequestration for ocean life remain unknown. Plants are the earth's own natural carbon containers. Forests and croplands are capable of storing great amounts of CO_2. However, the long-term reliability of this method requires keeping the earth's ecosystems (such as its rain forests) intact.

The Kyoto Protocol.
The Kyoto Protocol calls for industrialized countries to restrict their emissions of CO_2. It also establishes systems by which countries can earn and trade emissions credits. By 2005, more than 100 countries, including Japan and Russia, had ratified the Kyoto agreement. The United States, however, refuses to support the protocol. According to measurements taken in 1990, of all the industrialized countries in the world, the United States was responsible for the greatest percentage of CO_2 emissions. U.S. President George W. Bush stated that the requirements of the Kyoto Protocol would be damaging to the U.S. economy while failing to impose tough enough environmental restrictions on developing nations.

Members of Japanese environmental group celebrating the Kyoto Protocol

Melting Arctic Ice.
Often described as the barometer of global environmental health, the Arctic is experiencing dramatic changes in both its seasonal and year-round ice packs. For indigenous people, mushy ice and early thaws have made hunting on what used to be well-known ice highways more difficult and dangerous. Deteriorating ice is also threatening numerous animal species that rely on it for their survival. Polar ice melt is likely the cause of a startling drop in the average weight of polar bears, whose shortened hunting season may be contributing to an observed decline in birth and survival rates for the bears, as well as other species whose life cycles depend on the ice.

TRUE or FALSE?
Global warming is raising the temperatures of the world's oceans, which promotes the spread of diseases harmful to sea life.

THE BASICS

Global warming is an increase in the average temperature at Earth's surface. People often use the term *global warming* to refer specifically to the warming observed since the mid-1800s. Scientists estimate that Earth's average surface temperature rose by about 1.4°F (0.76°C) from the mid-1800s to the early 2000s. Researchers have also found that most of the temperature increase occurred from the mid-1900s to the 2000s.

Natural processes have caused Earth's climate to change in the distant past. But scientists have found strong evidence that human activities have caused most of the warming since the mid-1900s.

Scientists predict that Earth's average surface temperature will rise an additional 2.0 to 11.5°F (1.1 to 6.4°C) by 2100. They also predict that, if warming continues unchecked, it will damage human society and the environment. For example, global warming could melt enough of the ice on land near Earth's poles to raise sea level. It could lead to more widespread droughts. It could also risk extinction for many plant and animal species.

Researchers have developed a number of ways to limit global warming. But because the warming is a global problem, many strategies require the cooperation of a diversity of nations, each with its own interests. Nevertheless, many countries are taking action individually and by international agreement to limit future warming.

Causes of global warming. Global surface temperatures have risen chiefly because of a process called the *greenhouse effect*. In the greenhouse effect, certain gases in the atmosphere trap heat from the sun. They act much like the glass roof and walls of a greenhouse. The heat-trapping gases are called *greenhouse gases*. They include methane (CH_4), nitrous oxide (N_2O), and ozone (O_3). But the gas that has produced the most warming is carbon dioxide (CO_2).

Natural concentrations of greenhouse gases in the atmosphere help keep the planet warm enough to support life. Levels of greenhouse gases in the atmosphere have varied at different times. But they held relatively stable for several thousand years before industry began to grow rapidly in the 1800s.

Since the mid-1800s, however, modern industry has caused significant increases in *emissions* (releases) of greenhouse gases. The increase in CO_2 levels comes chiefly from the burning of *fossil fuels*. The fossil fuels are coal, oil, and natural gas. They contain carbon, and burning them creates carbon dioxide. CO_2 levels also rise due to the clearing of land. Trees and other green plants remove CO_2 from the air during *photosynthesis*—the process they use to produce their food. Thus, as land is cleared and forests are cut down, more CO_2 remains in the atmosphere.

Not all human activities contribute to global warming. Some things that people do actually cool Earth's surface. For example, many *aerosols* (suspensions of tiny particles) enter the atmosphere from automobile exhaust and factory smoke. The aerosols encourage the formation of clouds. Both aerosols and clouds reflect the sun's heat back into space. As a result, they exert a cooling influence on Earth's surface. But researchers estimate that overall, human activities have caused far more warming than cooling.

Scientists have also compared the influences of human activities on climate with the influences of natural processes. The only significant natural process was changes in the sun's energy output. The scientists found that human activities—mainly greenhouse gas emissions—produced more than 10 times the warming influence of changes in solar output.

Researchers have linked global warming to a number of potentially damaging effects on living things and their *ecosystems*. An ecosystem consists of a community of organisms along with its physical environment. Global warming is raising sea level. In addition, it is rapidly affecting the Arctic region. Global warming may also alter weather patterns and affect human health around the world. Scientists project that these effects will intensify and spread with further warming.

Effect on plant and animal life. Global warming affects many plants and animals by causing seasonal changes in temperature to occur at different times of the year. In many parts of the world, for example, warm spring weather has come earlier in the year. As a result, events that occur in the spring have begun earlier. Such events as flowering, egg laying, migration, and the growth of new leaves happen earlier. For example, lilac bushes have flowered earlier in the spring across much of the United States.

Butterflies have appeared earlier in the United Kingdom.

Rising temperatures have also forced many animals to move to cooler areas. These animals may move to higher latitudes—that is, toward Earth's poles. Or they may move to higher elevations. For example, white storks are nesting higher in the mountains in Poland. In Australia, the large bats called *flying foxes* have migrated toward cooler conditions in the south. Scientists are concerned about organisms that have difficulty spreading to new places. Many land animals and plants cannot easily relocate.

The faster global warming occurs, the more difficult it will become for many species to adapt. Scientists project that 20 to 30 percent of species would face a higher risk of extinction if the average temperature rose more than 2.7 to 4.5°F (1.5 to 2.5°C).

Rise in sea level. Average sea level rose about 7 inches (17 centimeters) over the 1900s. Global warming contributed to the rise. Part of the increase occurred because water expands as it warms. Rising temperatures also melt ice on land, which then flows into the oceans. Rising sea level has already contributed to coastal flooding, erosion, and the loss of wetlands.

Researchers project that further warming could cause sea level to rise another 7 to 23 inches (18 to 59 centimeters) by 2100. However, the projections do not include possible contributions from the melting of major ice sheets in Greenland and Antarctica. Increases in the rates at which the sheets are melting could lead to an additional rise in sea level.

Rapid change in the Arctic. Temperatures in the Arctic have increased about twice as fast as the global average. Due to the rapid warming, the area of the Arctic covered by sea ice in the summer has dropped since the late 1970s. The melting of sea ice has little effect on sea level because the ice already floats on the ocean. But the loss of sea ice threatens many Arctic species. The threatened species include polar bears, which hunt on the ice, and seals, which give birth on it.

Harm to ocean life. Warming seas have damaged marine ecosystems, particularly coral reefs. High ocean temperatures can cause *coral bleaching*. In this process, corals lose the colorful algae that live inside them and provide them with food. If temperatures remain too high, the corals turn white and die. Scientists project that only about 2 to 5°F (1 to 3°C) of further warming of the ocean surface could cause the death of many coral reefs. This fact is of particular concern because the reefs provide a habitat for huge numbers of ocean species.

Changing weather patterns. Researchers predict that global warming will lead to more extreme weather. Warming could increase the frequency of heavy rain and snowfall. It could also cause more frequent and intense heat waves, more floods, and more widespread droughts. These impacts could strain water supplies, damage crops, and harm ecosystems.

Threats to human health. More frequent and intense hot days and heat waves can contribute to heat-related death and illness. Scientists also project more deaths and diseases caused by storms, floods, droughts, and fires. On the other hand, higher temperatures can reduce cold-related deaths. However, researchers predict that the harmful effects of rising temperatures on human health will outweigh the benefits.

To limit global warming, emissions of greenhouse gases must slow to a rate that allows atmospheric levels to stabilize. But emissions are instead rising rapidly. In addition, because the climate system changes slowly, there is a delay between an increase in greenhouse gas levels and the full

Damsel fish swimming over bleached coral off the Keppel Islands

temperature rise from that increase. As a result, some warming will continue even if greenhouse gas levels stabilize. Scientists project that even if concentrations stay at their 2000 level, an additional warming of 1°F (0.6°C) would occur in this century.

Scientists have studied several ways to limit global warming. The most obvious method is to limit CO_2 emissions. Another method, called carbon *sequestration*, involves preventing CO_2 from entering the atmosphere or removing CO_2 already there. A third method, *geoengineering*, involves altering the environment to counteract warming.

Limiting CO_2 emissions chiefly involves burning less fossil fuels. This can be done by using alternative energy sources, using fossil fuels more efficiently, and practicing energy conservation.

Alternative energy sources that do not emit CO_2 include the wind, sunlight, nuclear energy, and Earth's internal heat. Devices known as *wind turbines* can convert wind energy to electric energy. *Solar cells* can convert sunlight to electric energy. *Geothermal* energy systems extract energy from steam or water heated deep underground. Many alternative sources of energy cost more to use than do fossil fuels. However, increased research and use is reducing the cost of alternative sources.

Increased fuel efficiency. CO_2 emissions could be reduced if vehicles used fuel more efficiently. Researchers are developing devices to replace fuel-burning engines or to make them more efficient. Fuel-saving cars known as *hybrids* have already entered the market. A hybrid combines the components of a battery-driven electric

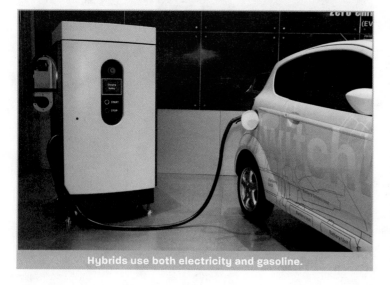

Hybrids use both electricity and gasoline.

car with a small gasoline engine. Scientists are also studying the use of *biofuels* from crops or other plant material. Biofuels might replace gasoline and other fuels. Future cars may use *fuel cells*, devices that convert chemical energy to electric energy.

Personal energy conservation saves energy, reducing the need to burn fossil fuels. For example, you can turn off and unplug computers, televisions, and other electronic devices when you are not using them. You can turn off lights when you are not in a room. You can replace traditional light bulbs with compact fluorescent bulbs, which use less energy. Outside the home, you can cut emissions by walking or biking instead of driving. If you must drive, you can carpool or combine multiple errands in one trip. Public transportation may also help reduce emissions in some areas.

Carbon sequestration requires a place to store unwanted CO_2. It could be stored underground, underwater, or in living plants.

Underground or underwater sequestration would involve injecting industrial emissions of $CO2$ into underground rock formations or into the ocean. Suitable rock formations include natural petroleum reservoirs from which most of the oil or gas has been removed. Pumping CO_2 into such a reservoir would have the added benefit of making it easier to remove the remaining oil or gas. But CO_2 injected in this way could escape due to an earthquake or other disruption. Some scientists think that CO_2 could also be stored in layers of *basalt*, a type of volcanic rock. The basalt could chemically convert the CO_2 gas into solid salts that would be unlikely to escape.

CO_2 readily dissolves in water, and the oceans naturally store much of the gas. Scientists are examining the possibility of sequestering carbon by pumping CO_2 directly into the deep sea. However, they must carefully study the effects on ocean life. For example, water and CO_2 combine to form carbonic acid, which would increase the acidity of the water.

Sequestration in living plants. Green plants absorb CO_2 from the atmosphere as they grow. They use the carbon for photosynthesis. Creating or enhancing ecosystems with abundant plant life, such as forests and even cropland, could therefore remove much carbon dioxide from the atmosphere. However, future generations would have to preserve the ecosystems to prevent the carbon from reentering the atmosphere as CO_2.

Logging may contribute to the greenhouse effect.

Geoengineering involves making large-scale changes to the environment to limit global warming. One approach would be to inject aerosols into the atmosphere to reflect sunlight and so cool the planet. Another scheme would involve adding iron to the oceans to promote the growth of *phytoplankton*. Phytoplankton are tiny marine organisms that capture CO_2 for use in photosynthesis. Another proposal is to put trillions of tiny screens in orbit around Earth to deflect some of the sun's rays.

Such proposals carry unknown risks and challenges. For example, injecting aerosols into the atmosphere could increase *acid rain*—rain and other precipitation polluted by certain acids. Acid rain can kill fish in lakes and streams. Adding large amounts of iron to the sea could harm marine environments. Putting sun screens into space would be expensive, and the screens would need maintenance.

Government Action on Global Warming

In an effort to limit global warming, many national and other governments have developed policies to reduce emissions of greenhouse gases. Most countries have agreed to the Kyoto Protocol, an international treaty aimed at cutting emissions.

The Kyoto Protocol requires *developed* (wealthy) countries to restrict their emissions of CO_2 and five other greenhouse gases. Different nations have different yearly emissions targets for the period from 2008 to 2012. As a whole, the developed countries must reduce their emissions to a yearly average of about 95 percent of their 1990 emissions. The protocol does not place restrictions on *developing* (less wealthy) countries.

Delegates from around the world adopted the Kyoto Protocol as a preliminary document in 1997 in Kyoto, Japan. To enter into force, the protocol had to be *ratified* (formally approved) by at least 55 countries. The countries that approved also had to account for at least 55 percent of the CO_2 emissions of all developed countries in 1990. Most nations eventually agreed to the protocol. It went into effect in 2005. However, the United States refused to ratify the treaty.

The Kyoto Protocol alone will do little to stop global warming. It limits emissions for only a short period. It limits emissions to levels too high to stop the increase in greenhouse gas concentrations. But the protocol establishes a basis for future measures. Delegates at an international climate conference in Bali in 2007 began negotiating a new agreement, for the period beyond 2012.

Types of policies. The Kyoto Protocol is a *cap-and-trade* system. It requires each developed country to *cap*, or limit, its emissions to a certain target. Nations that reduce their emissions below their targets can *trade*, or sell, *emissions credits* to other countries. Such credits can be used to offset emissions. Cap-and-trade policies can also be used to control emissions within one country or within a single industry.

A related approach enables groups and individuals to earn and sell credits called *carbon offsets*. Such a credit is similar to an emissions credit, but it is not earned by cutting one's own emissions. Instead, it is earned by undertaking other projects that help limit greenhouse gas levels overall. Carbon offsets often form part of cap-and-trade systems. Under the Kyoto Protocol, for example, developed countries can receive credit for investing in projects that reduce emissions in developing nations. Many companies now invest in emissions reduction projects to generate credits. They sell these credits to individuals and businesses that use them to offset emissions from such activities as air travel and power usage.

Another approach to limiting emissions is to impose a *carbon tax*, a tax on emissions of greenhouse gases. Such a tax can encourage companies to find ways to reduce emissions—ways that cost less than paying the tax.

Other measures. Some states, provinces, and countries have set goals that are more long-term than the Kyoto Protocol. For example, California has passed laws intended to reduce its total greenhouse gas emissions to 1990 levels by 2020. The state has proposed an 80-percent drop below 1990 levels by 2050. British Columbia has set a goal to cut emissions to 10 percent below 1990 levels, or 33 percent below 2007 levels, by 2020. The United Kingdom has proposed a 60-percent drop below 1990 levels for CO_2 emissions by 2050.

How Scientists Study Global Warming

Climatologists (scientists who study climate) use information from many sources to analyze global warming. The most reliable climate information comes from standardized measurements using weather instruments. But records based on reliable instruments date back only to the middle to late 1800s. Such records cannot show variations in climate that occurred long ago, before people began to measure with good instruments.

To look further back, climatologists analyze other types of evidence. Such evidence includes growth rings in trees, *cores* (cylindrical samples) of ice drilled from Antarctica and Greenland, and cores of sediment from ocean or lake beds. Tree growth rings, for example, can show when the weather was favorable for trees to grow rapidly. Ice cores hold tiny bubbles of air trapped when the ice formed. The bubbles can be analyzed to determine ancient greenhouse gas concentrations.

Evidence from these sources indicates that Earth is likely the warmest it has been in at least 1,300 years. It also shows that the temperature increase of the 1900s was the largest in more than 1,000 to 2,000 years. Data from ice cores also show that the levels of CO_2 and other greenhouse gases in the atmosphere are higher than they have been in at least the past 650,000 years.

Climatologists use computers to analyze past climate change and project future changes. First, scientists program a computer with a set of mathematical equations known as a *climate model*. The equations describe how various factors, such as the amount of CO_2 in the atmosphere, affect temperature. Next, the scientists enter data representing how those factors change over time. The computer then runs the model, describing how the climate conditions would vary. Such a representation is known as a *climate simulation*.

A complete understanding of global warming cannot be gained through simple observation. Its study relies on the scientific analysis of evidence and on climate simulations. This fact has enabled critics to dispute that warming has occurred. They also dispute that human activities caused the warming. To help establish a scientific *consensus* (general agreement), the United Nations established the Intergovernmental Panel on Climate Change (IPCC). The IPCC is a panel of scientists and governmental officials from more than 100 nations. It released several scientific reports during the 1990s and 2000s.

The IPCC conducted climate simulations as part of its studies. Its climatologists used different sets of simulations to model the warming of roughly the past 100 years. One set took into account both natural processes and human activities. Another set took into account only natural processes. The scientists then compared the temperatures produced by the simulations with temperatures recorded by thermometers. Only the set based on both natural processes and human activities corresponded closely to the actual temperature records. The results provided evidence that

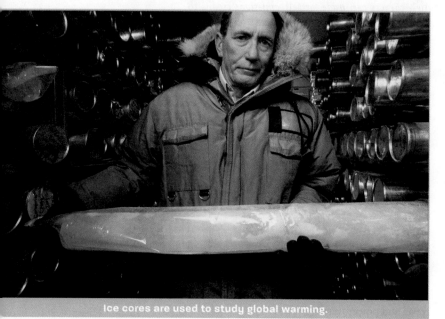

Ice cores are used to study global warming.

both natural processes and human activities have affected Earth's climate and that human activities are the main driver of the recent warming.

The IPCC also carried out simulations to predict the effects of natural and human influences on temperatures until 2100. The simulations showed that there can be no "quick fix" to global warming. Even if all emissions of greenhouse gases were to cease immediately, the temperature would continue to rise because of the greenhouse gases already in the atmosphere. However, the rate of emissions will determine the severity of global warming. The IPCC, along with former U. S. vice president Al Gore, won the 2007 Nobel Peace Prize for increasing public awareness of global warming.

 THE KYOTO PROTOCOL is an international agreement whose underlying purpose is to limit *global warming*. Global warming is an increase in the average temperature of Earth's surface since the late 1800s. The protocol requires many countries to limit their *emissions* (releases) of *greenhouse gases*. Such gases trap heat in the atmosphere, increasing Earth's surface temperature through a process known as the *greenhouse effect*. Human activities that increase greenhouse gas levels in the atmosphere include the clearing of land and the burning of *fossil fuels* (coal, oil, and natural gas). The Kyoto Protocol restricts emissions of carbon dioxide (CO_2), methane (CH_4), nitrous oxide (N_2O), and three other greenhouse gases. Most of the world's countries have agreed to the protocol. But a few nations, including the United States, have refused. The Kyoto Protocol entered into force in 2005.

The terms of the Kyoto Protocol distinguish between *developed* parties and *developing* parties. A developed party is a relatively wealthy country or group of countries. A developing party, in contrast, is one of the world's poorer nations. Under the protocol, each developed party must restrict its greenhouse gas emissions to a certain yearly target from 2008 to 2012. Parties that miss their targets under the Kyoto Protocol will be required to cut emissions by an even greater amount under the next such agreement. Each party's target is a certain percentage of its emission levels in 1990. As a whole, the developed parties must cut their emissions to an average of 5 percent below 1990 levels. Developing parties are not required to limit their

emissions. The protocol places a heavier burden on developed countries because those countries can more easily pay the cost of cutting emissions.

Canadian Prime Minister Jean Chretien signs the Kyoto Protocol.

Developed countries must limit emissions within their own borders to meet their targets. But the protocol also allows countries to work with one another to earn and trade *emissions credits*. Developed parties can earn emissions credits by funding projects that reduce emissions in other nations. For instance, a developed party could help a developing country build a hydroelectric power plant instead of one that burns fossil fuels. In doing so, the developed party can earn emissions credits, which it could use to *offset* (make up for) emissions in excess of its target. Developed parties may also offset their emissions by enhancing *carbon sinks*. Carbon sinks are natural resources, such as forests, that remove greenhouse gases from the atmosphere.

Controversy. Some critics of the Kyoto Protocol doubt a connection between increased greenhouse gas emissions and global warming. To address concerns about the link between human activities and climate change, the United Nations (UN) created a committee called the Intergovernmental Panel on Climate Change (IPCC). The IPCC released several scientific reports during the 1990s and 2000s. The reports seek to establish a *consensus* (general agreement) among climate scientists from around the world. In its 2007 report, the IPCC cited a greater than 90-percent likelihood that most of the observed warming since the

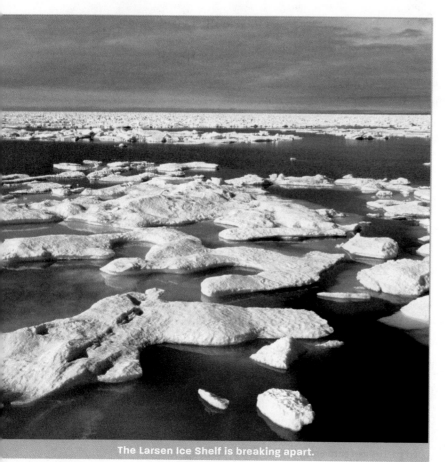

The Larsen Ice Shelf is breaking apart.

Delegates worked to complete the details of the agreement in a series of meetings. Most countries eventually agreed to the protocol, but some nations chose not to ratify it. These nations included the United States, whose 1990 emissions of CO_2 represented the highest share of the total for developed countries, 35 percent. In 1997, the U.S. Senate voted unanimously not to sign any agreement that did not include emissions reductions for developing countries or that would seriously harm the U.S. economy. In 1998, the administration of President Bill Clinton signed the Kyoto Protocol but did not submit it to the Senate for approval. In 2001, President George W. Bush rejected the Kyoto Protocol.

Rejection by the United States made it critical for other developed countries to ratify the protocol. Even if all the other developed countries except Russia ratified the protocol, the ratifying countries' 1990 emissions would fall short of the 55 percent required. In 2004, Russia's parliament voted to ratify the Kyoto Protocol, fulfilling the last requirement.

The protocol entered into force in 2005. In the same year, the European Union began working to meet its obligations by establishing its Greenhouse Gas Emission Trading Scheme, often called the EU ETS. The scheme sets limits on emissions by power plants and other large sources of greenhouse gases. It also enables facilities to buy and sell emissions allowances. The Kyoto Protocol also led to the creation of a global "carbon market" for the trading of greenhouse gas emissions. Developing countries began to participate in emissions reductions through hundreds of clean development projects.

In late 2005, delegates from the parties agreed to extend the Kyoto Protocol until the end of 2012. Parties to the protocol discussed extending the agreement again at the United Nations Climate Change Conference in Copenhagen, Denmark, in 2009, in Cancún, Mexico, in 2010, and in Durban, South Africa, in 2011. The discussions failed to produce an extension or an alternative to the protocol.

mid-1900s is due to the human-caused increase in levels of greenhouse gases.

Some politicians have expressed concerns that the protocol could cause economic harm by discouraging the use of fossil fuels. The burning of such fuels is a major industrial activity in the United States and other developed countries. Other critics have claimed that the treaty does not require adequate participation from developing countries.

History. The Kyoto Protocol serves as an addition to the UN Framework Convention on Climate Change, a treaty adopted in 1992 to stabilize greenhouse gas concentrations. Delegates from more than 160 countries adopted the protocol at a 1997 meeting in Kyoto, Japan. To become legally enforceable, the protocol had to be *ratified* (formally approved) by at least 55 countries. In addition, the developed parties ratifying the protocol had to account for at least 55 percent of the total CO_2 emissions of all developed countries in 1990.

MLA Citation

"Global Warming." *The Southwestern Advantage Topic Source.* Nashville: Southwestern. 2013.

ADDITIONAL RESOURCES

Books to Read

Archer, David. *Global Warming*. 2nd ed. Wiley, 2012.

Dutch, Steven I., ed. *Encyclopedia of Global Warming*. 3 vols. Salem Press, 2010.

Johansen, Bruce E. *The Encyclopedia of Global Warming Science and Technology*. 2 vols. Greenwood, 2009.

Simon, Seymour. *Global Warming*. Collins, 2010.

Web Sites

Global Warming

http://www.ncdc.noaa.gov/oa/climate/globalwarming.html

The U.S. National Oceanic and Atmospheric Administration (NOAA) presents answers to frequently asked questions about global warming.

Greenhouse Gas Online

http://www.ghgonline.org

A collection of articles on global warming from news media and peer-reviewed scientific journals.

U.S. EPA—Global Warming Site

http://www.epa.gov/climatechange

A U.S. Environmental Protection Agency site that provides information on current climate change issues as well as U.S. climate policy.

Global Warning: Early Warming Signs

http://www.climatehotmap.org

An interactive map of the world that illustrates the local consequences of global warming.

Search Strings

Preventive Measures

global warming preventive measures (71,500)

global warming preventive measures wind solar power nuclear energy geothermal (5,760)

global warming preventive measures replace fossil fuel (268,000)

Carbon Sequestration

carbon sequestration global warming (757,000)

carbon sequestration global warming storage methods (327,000)

carbon sequestration global warming storage methods geology (67,200)

The Kyoto Protocol

global warming "Kyoto Protocol" restrict emissions carbon dioxide trade earn credits (23,100)

global warming "Kyoto Protocol" restrict emissions carbon dioxide "United States" (57,500)

"Kyoto Protocol" global warming "United States" reject economy emissions carbon dioxide credits earn trade (33,400)

Melting Arctic Ice

global warming melting arctic ice barometer environment ice pack ramifications (245)

global warming melting arctic ice barometer environment ice pack (901)

BACKGROUND INFORMATION

The following articles and features were written during the year in which the events took place and reflect the style and thinking of that time.

The Great Meltdown (2006)

Scientists warn that global warming is leading to the rapid and potentially catastrophic disappearance of ice sheets and glaciers worldwide.

—by Christina Johnson

The hard, cold fact about Earth's ice is that it is melting. In the Arctic, in the Antarctic, and on even the highest mountains, the ice cover is thinning, breaking up, and draining away. Ice in the Arctic Ocean is retreating so quickly that by 2100 the ocean could be ice-free in summer, opening the year-round seaway from the North Atlantic to the North Pacific oceans sought by early explorers to North America. From 1996 to 2006, the amount of Greenland's ice sliding into the North Atlantic each year jumped by about 250 percent, an amount equal to the volume of water in Lake Erie. The collapse of Antarctica's Larsen B ice shelf in 2002 dumped enough ice into the sea to give every person on Earth 1,800 bags of ice weighing 22 pounds (10 kilograms) each.

Most scientists agree that Earth's ice cover is eroding because of global warming—the increase of from 0.7 to 1.4 degrees Fahrenheit (0.4 to 0.8 degrees Celsius) in the planet's average surface temperature since the late 1800s. In fact, Earth is warmer now than at any time in the past 11,500 years, the National Academy of Sciences reported in September 2006. While cycles of cooling and warming as well as other natural processes affect Earth's climate, a widespread scientific consensus points to human activities, particularly emissions of heat-trapping greenhouse gases, as the main driving force behind the current warm-up. The most significant of these gases is carbon dioxide, produced by the burning of coal, gasoline, and wood.

Although the meltdown has—so far—hit hardest in the Arctic, its effects have been global and diverse. In 2005, the chairperson of the 150,000-member Inuit Circumpolar Conference said that the thinning and loss of Arctic sea ice (frozen seawater) was threatening the traditional lifestyles of indigenous (native) peoples. Also in 2005, scientists reported the first evidence that polar bears, which use sea ice as a platform for hunting seals, are drowning because of the growing distance between ice floes. Scientists also have linked a decline in sea ice to a 70 percent drop in the number of Adelie penguins living on one part of the Antarctic Peninsula. In the central Asian countries of Nepal and Bhutan, an international survey found at least forty-four mountain lakes filling so rapidly with meltwater from Himalayan glaciers that they could burst their banks within five years, causing potentially catastrophic floods in the populated valleys below.

Earth is unlikely to become ice-free for at least a few centuries, even at current rates of warming. Nevertheless, the melting is seriously affecting human and animal populations as well as the environment. Numerous studies have predicted even more disturbing consequences for human health and safety as well as for ecosystems in the near future.

Ice in the Arctic. The Arctic, which is often described as the barometer of global environmental health, is experiencing dramatic changes in both its seasonal and perennial (year-round) ice packs. Seasonal ice, which grows and melts throughout the year, has been declining since at least 1978, the time when scientists began using satellites to monitor the ice. Historically, by March, all of the Arctic Ocean except for an area along the

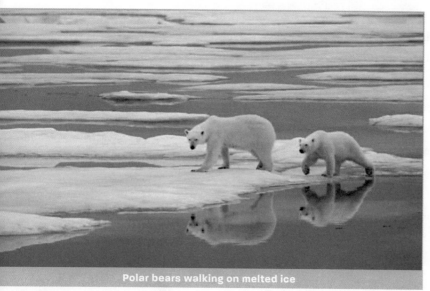
Polar bears walking on melted ice

coasts of Norway and western Russia is locked in ice. By mid-September, only about 30 percent of the ice remains.

The amount of perennial ice surviving the summer melting season dropped by about 6.5 percent per decade from 1979 to 2001. After 2001, the retreat began to seem more like a rout. Between 2004 and 2005, perennial ice shrank by 14 percent to a record low of 2.05 million square miles (5.32 million square kilometers), according to a September 2006 report by scientists from NASA's Jet Propulsion Laboratory in Pasadena, California. The shrinkage represented an area equal to the size of Texas.

Just as disturbing, a 2006 study found that the amount of the Arctic Ocean covered by seasonal ice in March had dropped to its lowest average since 1978. The so-called winter ice maximum shrank by a record 6 percent—equivalent to an area roughly the size of New Mexico—from 2005 levels, the previous record. Moreover, in 2006 the winter ice shrank more than twice as fast as it did in the 1980s and 1990s.

The Arctic is experiencing "some of the most rapid and severe climate change on earth," according to the 2004 Arctic Climate Impact Assessment (ACIA). The ACIA emerged from a four-year study by hundreds of scientists working under a mandate from the United States and seven other Arctic nations, six organizations representing indigenous Arctic people, and 18 national academies of science. Signs of climate change documented by ACIA scientists included rising temperatures, shrinking and thinning sea ice, melting glaciers, and rising sea levels.

Melting's ripple effect. For indigenous people, mushy ice and unexpectedly early thaws have made hunting on what used to be well-known ice highways more difficult and dangerous. Some hunters, for example, have been forced to travel farther to find seals, walruses, and other Arctic prey. In addition, accidents on the ice are reportedly increasing, resulting in injuries and death, loss of valuable equipment, and expensive rescues, according to the National Snow and Ice Data Center (NSIDC) in Boulder, Colorado. The melting of the highways is also limiting the time available to truckers trying to deliver heating oil, gasoline, and other supplies to Far North communities. "The land is becoming a stranger to the Inuit," one Inuit official said in an interview.

Grey seal pups suffer because of the deteriorating sea ice.

Deteriorating sea ice is also threatening numerous animal species that depend on the ice for their survival. Seals give birth, raise their pups, and rest on the ice. In February 2006, Canadian scientists reported that about 1,500 grey seal pups were swept out to sea in a storm and drowned because a scarcity of sea ice forced females to give birth on the vulnerable beaches of a small island.

The increasingly earlier break-up of sea ice in the spring is likely the cause of a startling drop in the average weight of polar bears in western Hudson Bay. The bears feed almost exclusively in winter, when they hunt seals from the ice. Between 1980 and 2004, the average weight of adult female polar bears in that area fell from 650 to 507 pounds (295 to 230 kilograms). Because the female's ability to reproduce and care for cubs depends on her fat stores, a shortened hunting season may be contributing to an observed decline in birth and survival rates.

The dwindling of the ice has set off a scramble by the United States, Canada, Denmark, and other countries with borders in the Arctic to establish territorial claims in the Far North. Opening the Arctic, in addition to increasing ship traffic, would allow the development of what is reportedly about 25 percent of the world's remaining oil and gas reserves. Such development could further disrupt these troubled ecosystems.

Global changes. The effects of climate change in the Arctic may extend far beyond the frozen north. Although the Arctic Ocean is the smallest of the world's oceans, it plays a crucial role in regulating global climate. For example, the Arctic acts like a giant mirror, reflecting back into space up to 90 percent of incoming sunlight and, in the

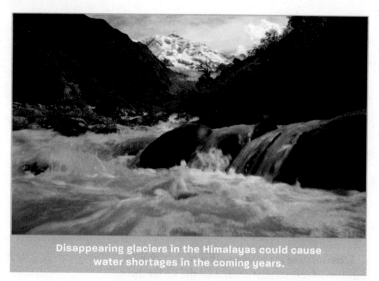

Disappearing glaciers in the Himalayas could cause water shortages in the coming years.

process, helping to cool the planet. By contrast, the open ocean reflects only about 6 percent of the sunlight reaching it. In addition, thin ice, such as seasonal ice, reflects less solar energy than perennial ice. Using measurements made by U.S. submarines, scientists have found that, from the 1960s to the mid-1990s, the average thickness of Arctic ice in deep-water areas of the ocean dropped by about 40 percent, from 10 to 6 feet (3.1 to 1.8 meters). As the Arctic's ice cover disappears, more of the sun's heat is absorbed. The result is a "feedback loop" of rising temperatures that promote melting, which increases energy absorption and further raises temperatures.

Another possible consequence of Arctic melting involves the worldwide ocean current known as the thermohaline circulation (THC). Often described as a conveyor belt, the THC helps move solar energy from the tropics to polar regions and is partially responsible for the moderate winter temperatures in northwestern Europe, including the United Kingdom.

The THC exists because of regional differences in the density of seawater caused by temperature and salinity (saltiness). As seawater freezes, its salt separates from the growing ice crystals, creating briny (highly salty) pockets within the ice. Over time, the brine drips through the ice into the ocean, forming unusually dense layers of water. Briny water formed in the Arctic and other northern seas travels southward to the North Atlantic, where it joins and helps cool warm, salty water carried northward by the Gulf Stream. Several million cubic kilometers of the cold, briny water, which is denser than warm water, sinks toward the ocean bottom and

begins moving south. After a 1,000-year journey through the South Atlantic, Indian, Pacific, and Southern (Antarctic) oceans, the water returns to the North Atlantic, where another circuit begins.

Many scientists have warned that rising surface temperatures and a loss of sea ice in the Arctic could disrupt the THC, causing dramatic changes in the global climate. For example, some computer models predict that if the THC were to slow or shut down, the Northern Hemisphere could become significantly cooler, while the Southern Hemisphere could become warmer. Fresh water flooding into the North Atlantic from melting glaciers in the Arctic and Greenland also could stall the THC by lowering the salinity of the water and forming a "cap" over the ocean.

The rising threat of higher sea levels. Perhaps the most discussed impact of a global ice meltdown is rising sea levels. The ACIA predicted that global sea levels could rise from 4 inches to 3 feet (10 to 90 centimeters) by 2100, with even faster increases as the century progresses. Currently, about half of the world's population lives within 125 miles (200 kilometers) of a coast, with many people residing much closer. A 1.5-foot (0.5-meter) increase in sea levels could cause shorelines in relatively flat areas to move inland by about 150 feet (50 meters). Higher sea levels would pollute underground freshwater aquifers and require the massive reengineering and reconstruction of coastal roads, power plants, and other basic infrastructure. Wetlands, marshes, and estuaries would be submerged, disrupting animal life on land and in the sea. Rising water would also result in major shifts in plant habitats, likely causing some species to become extinct.

In fact, sea levels have risen by about 4 to 9 inches (10 to 25 centimeters) since the early 1900s, according to the United Nations Environmental Programme (UNEP). Surprisingly, melting Arctic sea ice accounts for almost none of that total because the ice floats and, thus, occupies nearly the same volume as its meltwater would. About half of the increase has resulted from thermal expansion (the expansion and rise of the ocean caused directly by higher temperatures), UNEP scientists concluded. Meltwater from the world's two main ice sheets in Greenland and Antarctica and, to a much lesser degree, from glaciers outside polar regions accounts for the other half. An *ice sheet* is a dome-shaped glacier covering an area greater than 19,300 square miles (50,000 square kilometers).

Greenland's ice sheet, which covers the island's central plateau, ranks second only to Antarctica's ice sheets in volume. Two miles (3 kilometers) thick in places, it holds about 9 percent of the world's glacial ice and 10 percent of its freshwater, enough water to maintain the Mississippi River for at least 4,700 years, according to the U.S. Geological Survey. Surrounding the ice sheet are coastal mountains with glaciers that flow down the valleys to the sea. If Greenland's ice sheet were to melt completely, scientists have calculated, world oceans would rise by 20 feet (66 meters).

Vanishing glaciers. Glaciers outside Earth's polar regions are retreating because of both modern global warming and natural causes, particularly a gradual warm-up in Earth's temperature that followed a mini-ice age ending in the mid-1800s. A 2003 report by the conservation group WWF noted, "Since the early 1960s, mountain glaciers worldwide have experienced an estimated net loss of 960 cubic miles (4,000 cubic kilometers) of water—more than the annual discharge of the Orinoco, Congo, Yangtze, and Mississippi rivers combined; this loss was more than twice as fast in the 1990s than during the previous decades."

In Alaska, glaciers are thinning by an average of 6 feet (1.8 meters) a year, twice the rate in the mid-1990s. From 1850 to 2006, Glacier National Park lost 123 of its 150 glaciers. If current warming trends continue, all the park's glaciers—11,000-year-old remnants of the last Ice Age—will disappear sometime before 2050, according to the U.S. National Park Service. Glaciers in Asia's Himalaya-Hindu Kush region are retreating at the rate of about 30 to 50 feet (10 to 15 meters) annually, according to the WWF. Glaciers in the European Alps have lost from 10 to 20 percent of their volume since 1980, a number projected to rise to 80 percent by 2100. Because of the loss of the ice—and the reduction of the glaciers' weight on Earth's crust—Alpine peaks are rising. Mount Blanc in Switzerland, for example, is being lifted by about one-third inch (0.9 millimeter) per year.

Glaciers in equatorial regions are also draining away. In the Andes, glaciers are retreating at a rate exceeding anything seen in 5,000 years, according to a study released in June 2006. The Qori Kalis Glacier in the Peruvian Andes was retreating about 30 times faster in 2001 than it was in 1978. The Upsala Glacier in Argentina, the largest glacier in South America, is shrinking by 46 feet (14 meters) per year. Under current conditions, scientists predict, the Chacaltaya Glacier in Bolivia will disappear by about 2015. Once famous for the world's highest ski slope, Chacaltaya has lost 98 percent of its volume, most of it in the 1990s.

In Africa, about 80 percent of the ice on Mount Kilimanjaro, the continent's highest mountain, has disappeared since the early 1900s. Ice on Mount Kenya has shrunk by 40 percent since 1963. Glaciers in the mist-shrouded Ruwenzori Mountains of East Africa, known since ancient times as the Mountains of the Moon, have almost vanished.

Ilulissat Glacier, Greenland's fastest-moving glacier, is shrinking at an alarming rate.

The disappearance of Earth's glaciers has been described as a "time bomb." Tourists who visit the glaciers each year provide revenues crucial to the economies of numerous countries, especially in the developing world. Meltwater from glaciers powers hydroelectric dams. Peru, for example, depends on hydropower, mainly from glacial runoff, for a significant amount of its electric energy. Glacial meltwater also supports mining activities and is often essential for farming.

Most important, one-sixth of the world's population relies on glaciers and snow packs for its water supply. Glaciers in the Himalaya-Hindu Kush region, for example, help supply seven of Asia's most important rivers, including the Ganges, Yangtze, and Yellow. Municipal water systems in La Paz and El Alto, two of Bolivia's largest cities, depend on the Chacaltaya Glacier for their water. Glacier-fed rivers worldwide are also a crucial source of water for birds and other animals as well as for river and lake ecosystems. Computer models indicate that many of these rivers could all but disappear during the dry season.

Ice in the Antarctic. If all the glaciers outside Greenland melted, sea levels would rise only slightly. The melting of Antarctica's two enormous ice sheets would be another story. Antarctica is Earth's largest storehouse of ice, holding about 90 percent of all the planet's ice and 70 percent of its fresh water. Most of this ice lies in two massive ice sheets that can be as thick as 11,500 feet (3,500 meters). If both ice sheets melted, Earth's oceans would rise nearly 230 feet (70 meters).

Several important studies published in 2006 demonstrated that Antarctica is losing ice faster than it can be replaced by the continent's sparse snowfall. One study, by German and U.S. scientists analyzing gravity variations, showed that Antarctica's ice sheets decreased by 36 cubic miles (152 cubic kilometers) annually from 2002 to 2005. Most of that amount—equal to the total amount of water used in the United States for three months—came from West Antarctica, much of which lies below sea level. Air temperatures there have risen faster than any other place on Earth since the mid-1900s.

The second study was the first comprehensive survey of glaciers on the Antarctic Peninsula, a mountainous finger of West Antarctica. Since 1940, British and U.S. scientists found, 87 percent of the glaciers have retreated, by an average of 165 feet (50 meters) every year for the last five years. This retreat is faster than in earlier years.

The 2002 collapse of the northern section of the massive Larsen B ice shelf on the eastern side of the peninsula provided dramatic evidence of the changes occurring in the Antarctic. Over a 35-day period, 1,250 square miles (3,250 square kilometers) of the shelf shattered and separated from the continent, the largest single retreat of an ice shelf on the peninsula since the mid-1970s. At that time of its collapse, Larsen B, which was once 720 feet (220 meters) thick, had already lost 60 percent of its volume. In 2006, British and Belgian scientists determined that climate warming linked to human activity strengthened the westerly winds that blow across the northern part of the peninsula, allowing them to rise over mountains that normally block their flow.

Like melting sea ice, melting ice shelves have little effect on sea level. However, the ice shelves act as brakes on the ice flowing off the continent in glaciers. In fact, the four glaciers that had fed the northern section of Larsen B flowed up to eight times faster after the collapse. By contrast, the speed of nearby glaciers flowing toward the surviving section of the shelf remained unchanged. Moreover, the four glaciers that had been feeding Larsen B thinned by as much as 124 feet (38 meters) within six months.

Melting sea ice, aggravated by warming temperatures in the Southern Ocean, is affecting Antarctica's wildlife, particularly migratory birds. A 2006 study by French researchers found that nine species of sea birds that summer in Antarctica were migrating to the region an average of nine days later in 2004 than they were in the early 1950s. According to the scientists, one reason for the delay was a dramatic decline in populations of krill, tiny shrimplike animals that feed on algae that grow on the underside of the ice. A 2004 study by French researchers found that the number of krill, which form the base of the Antarctic food chain, had plunged by 80 percent since the 1970s. Shorter breeding seasons and less food threaten the birds' ability to reproduce.

Scientists know enough about the extent and effects of global warming to warn that actions should be taken to stabilize or reduce carbon-dioxide emissions. For this reason, the political and regulatory decisions made by governments and the choices made by individuals will continue to have a major influence on the future of climate change and Earth's icescape. In his 2006 book, *An Inconvenient Truth*, environmentalist and former U.S. Vice President Al Gore notes, "Our new technologies, combined with our numbers, have made us,

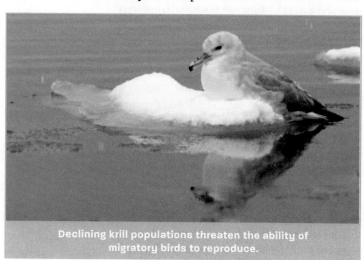

Declining krill populations threaten the ability of migratory birds to reproduce.

collectively, a force of nature. And those with the most technology have the greatest moral obligation to use it wisely."

Global Warming (2006)

January 2006 began with a rare—for winter—tropical storm roaming the unusually warm waters of the Atlantic Ocean. Tropical Storm Zeta was the record-setting 27th storm of the Atlantic hurricane season, which had begun in June 2005.

The first month of 2006 was also the warmest January in the United States since record keeping began in 1895. Furthermore, the United States in 2006 had its second warmest summer since 1934.

The period from May through September 2006 was the warmest in central England since records were first kept there in the 1600s. During June and July 2006, sea ice in the Arctic shrank to its lowest values on record for those months.

Temperature trends reevaluated. In June, the National Research Council, a private research organization that advises the U.S. government, issued a report reevaluating a 2,000-year reconstruction of global surface temperatures that had been published in the 1990s by climatologist Michael Mann and colleagues. Mann's reconstruction was based on proxy data—that is, data from such sources as tree rings, ocean and lake sediments, ice cores, cave deposits, and historic drawings of glaciers. Scientists rely on proxy data to reconstruct long-term surface temperatures, because geographically widespread records of temperatures measured with instruments date back to only the mid-1800s.

Mann's reconstruction showed an unprecedented rapid rise in temperature since about 1970. His reconstruction also showed temperatures in the late 1990s reaching their highest values of the last 2,000 years.

The council concluded with high confidence that the proxy data demonstrates that the last few decades of the 1900s—averaged around the globe—have been warmer than any period since 1600. However, the report noted that much less confidence can be placed in temperature data before 1600.

Shrinking polar ice. Scientists from the National Snow and Ice Data Center at the University of Colorado in Boulder reported in October 2006 that the extent of sea ice in the Arctic reached its annual minimum in September at 2.2 million square miles (5.7 million square kilometers). This measurement was the second lowest

Hurricane Wilma in Cancun, Mexico, 2005

value since records began in the 1970s. Only in 2005, when the minimum was 2.0 million square miles (5.2 million square kilometers), was there less Arctic sea ice. The researchers suggested that unusually cold weather in August probably prevented a new record from being established.

Polar sea ice is an important indicator of climate change, because it is sensitive to initial warming trends. As sea ice, which reflects much sunlight, melts, more of the darker ocean water is exposed. This darker surface absorbs more of the sun's heat energy, which further increases air temperatures near the water, ocean temperatures themselves, and the melting of sea ice.

Unexpected ocean cooling. Researchers at the National Oceanic and Atmospheric Administration's Pacific Marine Environmental Laboratory in Seattle reported in September 2006 that the average temperature of the top layer of Earth's oceans dropped slightly from 2003 to 2005. According to the scientists, the heat content of the upper 2,500 feet (750 meters) of ocean water decreased by 0.055 degrees Fahrenheit (0.031 degrees Celsius)—an amount that was equal to approximately 20 percent of the total heat gained by the world's oceans between 1955 and 2003.

The researchers noted that ocean water was still warmer in 2005 than it had been in the 1980s, but they had no explanation for the observed cooling, which was not predicted by any climate model. Because the ocean is a vast storehouse of energy that helps to drive the world's climate system, temperature changes in the ocean are a key to understanding long-term climate change.

The role of the sun. A study published in March 2006 by scientists at Duke University in Durham, North Carolina, concluded that changes in the amount of energy from the sun can account for as much as 50 percent of the observed global temperature increase between 1900 and 2000 and as much as 35 percent of the warming between 1980 and 2000. The scientists noted that these results suggested that human-induced warming may have played a progressively greater role during the 1900s.

In October 2006, researchers at the Center for Sun-Climate Research in Denmark provided experimental evidence demonstrating how cosmic rays, high-speed atomic particles streaming from distant exploding stars, can affect the formation of clouds in Earth's atmosphere. Their experiment, which involved cosmic radiation passing through a chamber filled with atmospheric gases, showed that cosmic rays can promote chemical processes in the atmosphere that form condensation nuclei. Condensation nuclei are microscopic particles that aid the development of cloud droplets.

The Danish researchers explained that the strength of the sun's magnetic field, which helps shield Earth from cosmic rays, doubled during the 1900s. This fact led the researchers to propose that reduced cosmic radiation resulting from the stronger magnetic field would lead to less cloud formation—and subsequent higher global temperatures.

Satellite image of Hurricane Frances, 2004

Global Warming (2005)

News reports indicated and scientific data confirmed that the most recent surge in global temperature that began in the 1970s continued in 2005. Most scientists agreed that global warming was at least partly responsible for the melting of Arctic sea ice, which in 2005 shrank to its lowest levels since 1978, the year when satellites began measuring the ice. Scientists also investigated whether the rise in temperature had contributed to severe weather in 2005. Fed by energy from unusually warm water, an unprecedented number of hurricanes churned through the Atlantic Ocean. Among them was Hurricane Wilma, the most intense storm ever observed in the Western Hemisphere. Delayed monsoon rains in Pakistan and Bangladesh led to a punishing heat wave in May and June that sent temperatures as high as 122 degrees Fahrenheit (50 degrees Celsius). Frequent sunny, hot spring and summer days contributed to the worst drought in Spain and Portugal since the 1940s.

Global average temperatures. Researchers at the United States National Aeronautics and Space Administration's (NASA) Goddard Institute for Space Studies in New York City announced in October 2005 that preliminary data showed that the global average temperature near the surface of Earth in 2005 was the highest since 1880, when the agency began keeping records. Temperature in 2005 eclipsed the previous mark set in 1998 by about 0.2 degrees Fahrenheit (0.1degree Celsius). However, two other widely used global temperature histories, one compiled by the National Climactic Data Center in Asheville, North Carolina, and another by the Climate Research Unit at the University of East Anglia in England, continued to list 1998 as the warmest year on record. The research groups used many of the same temperature data but employed different methods to statistically combine the data, which resulted in slight differences in the final values of annual global average temperature. A report examining the different methods to track temperature trends published in the August 2005 edition of Science noted the great challenges scientists face in attempting to measure very small year-to-year temperature differences.

Arctic ice. In 2005, many scientists believed that the build-up of carbon dioxide and other greenhouse gases in the atmosphere, brought about by industry, was causing global warming. They the-

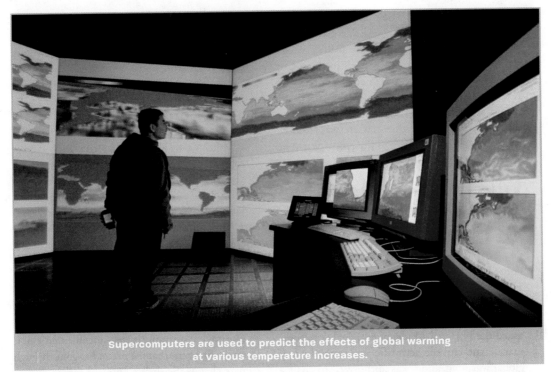

Supercomputers are used to predict the effects of global warming at various temperature increases.

orized that the accelerated breakup of polar ice was an important indicator of climate change.

In September, scientists at the University of Colorado at Boulder announced that coverage of Arctic ice, which reaches an annual minimum each September, had shrunk to a record 200 million square miles (51.8 billion hectares), 500 thousand square miles (130 million hectares) less than its average since the first satellite recordings of the ice in 1978. Scientists in 2005 calculated the rate of shrinkage at 8 percent per decade and predicted extremely low ice coverage for summer 2006.

A report published in 2004 revealed that the Arctic is warming twice as fast as the rest of the planet. The Arctic Climate Impact Assessment, a four-year study involving hundreds of scientists, projected an additional temperature rise of about 7 to 12.5 degrees Fahrenheit (4 to 7 degrees Celsius) by 2100. According to meteorological data compiled by NASA, the average Arctic temperatures in the late 1960s were at their lowest levels since the 1920s. By 2005, Arctic temperatures had risen by about 3.5 degrees Fahrenheit (2 degrees Celsius). Arctic temperatures also surged by about 4.5 degrees Fahrenheit (2.5 degrees Celsius) between the late 1910s and the late 1930s before falling in the late 1960s.

A large sample of ice taken from Antarctica showed that the levels of carbon dioxide and methane were considerably higher in 2005 than at any other time in the last 650,000 years, scientists for the European Project for Ice Coring in Antarctica reported in the November 2005 issue of *Science*. Carbon dioxide and methane are atmospheric gases that absorb energy emitted by Earth, called greenhouse gases, that have greatly increased since the mid-1800s, when modern industry became widespread. The thousands of layers of snow and compressed air bubbles that compose the Antarctic ice capture the atmosphere that existed hundreds of thousands of years ago, which allows scientists to study ancient climates. The ice core research supports the widely held theory that human activity in the second half of the 1800s, 1900s, and the 2000s has significantly altered the planet's climate.

Tropical cyclones. A record 26 named tropical storms and hurricanes formed in the Atlantic Ocean in 2005, including three of the six most-intense storms on record in the Atlantic basin, surpassing the previous record of 21 set in 1933. The normal yearly average is 10 named storms.

In September 2005, researchers from the Georgia Institute of Technology in Atlanta reported that while the North Atlantic had shown a statistically significant increase in storm activity, there was no global trend in the number of tropical storms and hurricanes. The researchers found an increase in the number of intense hurricanes across the world during the period of their analysis, which began in 1970, the year when satellites were first used to monitor tropical storm development. The researchers concluded, however, that a longer data record and a deeper understanding of the role of hurricanes in global weather patterns was required to relate hurricane activity to the recent warming near the surface of the earth.

What We Know About Global Warming (2001)

A scientific panel reports to the U.S. president that global warming is real and that it is being caused by humans, but scientists remain unsure about what the future holds.

—by Ralph Cicerone

In May 2001, U. S. president George W. Bush asked the National Academy of Sciences to summarize the current scientific understanding of global warming, and I was authorized to chair a committee to investigate the issue. The Committee on the Science of Climate Change, which included 11 climate scientists from various U.S. institutions, sought to clarify what is known and what remains unknown about global warming.

After reviewing the major scientific research on this subject, we reached a number of conclusions, which can be summed up in three statements: (1) Earth has become warmer during the past several

decades; (2) the warming is likely due to human activities, mainly atmospheric changes caused by the burning of fossil fuels (coal, oil, gas, and wood); and (3) Earth will continue to warm, but we are not yet sure how fast temperatures will rise or how particular regions on Earth will be affected by climate change.

Evidence of present and past warmups. How do we know that Earth is warming up? Temperature records clearly show that Earth became warmer during the 1900s. Between 1900 and 2000, measurements made around the world indicate that the globally averaged surface temperature (the average of sea-surface temperatures and air temperatures over land) increased by between 0.7 and 1.4 degrees Fahrenheit (0.4 and 0.8 degrees Celsius). Between 1980 and 2000, temperatures rose especially fast in both the Northern and Southern hemispheres—by between 0.45 and 0.7 degrees Fahrenheit (0.25 and 0.4 degrees Celsius).

The present warming is well-documented. But it is not the first time that the planet has gone through climate change. Scientists know of earlier climate changes from both historic and prehistoric records. The invention of the thermometer in the 1500s made it possible to measure actual temperatures, and scientists began to make regular recordings of air temperatures in the mid-1800s. Geologists and anthropologists, furthermore, have found evidence of earlier climate conditions. Some of these conditions were recorded by people in written histories or agricultural records. For prehistoric eras, modern scientists base estimates of temperature on "proxy" data derived from studies of tree rings, deposits left by glaciers, ocean coral formations, and sediments found in lake beds or at the bottom of the sea. Scientists can obtain such data by drilling cores (cylindrical samples) of sediment from the seafloor and cores of ice from polar regions and examining them for clues to past climate.

Little Ice Age and Medieval Warm Period. Proxy data provides evidence of both a Little Ice Age and a Medieval Warm Period within the past 1,000 years. In parts of the Northern Hemisphere, average temperatures were about 1.8 degrees Fahrenheit (1 degree Celsius) lower during the Little Ice Age, from about 1400 to 1800, than they were during most of the 1900s. Certain regions were colder than others. It was coldest in central Europe during the late 1600s, but people in Switzerland experienced their coldest weather

The Thames River once froze every winter.

from the 1560s through the 1570s. European glaciers advanced noticeably, and some rivers and lakes froze over regularly during the Little Ice Age. The Thames River in London was frozen almost every winter until the early 1800s, allowing Londoners to hold annual "frost fairs" featuring skating, games, and entertainment on the river's ice. Scientists believe that temperatures south of the equator were warmer than those of the north during the Little Ice Age.

Prior to the Little Ice Age, a Medieval Warm Period occurred from about 1100 to 1300. Temperatures increased the most in regions around the north Atlantic Ocean. Grapes grew in England, and farming flourished in Scandinavia and Scotland. Scientists had previously thought that average temperatures in the Northern Hemisphere may have been between 1.8 and 3.6 degrees Fahrenheit (1 and 2 degrees Celsius) above those of the later Little Ice Age. However, an examination of data from numerous ice cores and tree rings by climate expert Michael E. Mann of the University of Virginia in the late 1990s indicated that the Medieval Warm Period was cooler than previously believed. In fact, the new evidence revealed that average temperatures during the Medieval Warm Period—long considered a time of major climate change—were probably below those of 2000.

Recurring ice ages. More drastic climate change occurred further back in time. Earth has gone through several ice ages, periods when average temperatures plummeted several degrees and ice sheets covered vast regions of land. Scientists have discovered geological and chemical evidence that ice ages have occurred approximately every 100,000 years during the last 900,000 years. The most recent ice age ended approximately 11,000 years ago.

The fact that there have been recurring warmer and colder periods in the past shows that there are natural variations in Earth's climate. These natural climate changes may be caused by the oscillation (back-and-forth movement) in the planet's axis of rotation and orbit. Earth is tilted on its axis, and this tilt results in the seasons as the planet moves around the sun. The angle of the tilt changes over time. As the angle varies, the amount of sunlight striking different parts of the planet varies with the tilt. Increasing tilt leads to greater differences between summer and winter temperatures. The shape of Earth's orbit also changes over time, so that, during certain periods, the planet's orbit is

A satellite view of Earth

more elliptical (oval shaped) than during other periods. The more stretched the orbit, the more difference there is between seasons. Such seasonal changes can reduce the amount of solar energy striking the Northern Hemisphere during summer. This, in turn, may cause the annual growth and melting of polar ice to become imbalanced, leading to an ice age.

An enhanced greenhouse effect. Because changes in Earth's orbit and other natural variations have altered Earth's climate in the past, could the present warm-up also be caused by natural factors? This is unlikely. Scientific data collected over decades indicate that the present warm-up is related to an enhancement of the greenhouse effect, a process by which gases in the atmosphere trap heat energy, much like a greenhouse.

Energy flows to Earth from the sun, mostly in the form of visible light. Much of this energy is reflected back into space by the planet's cloud tops, snow, ice, and other light-colored surfaces. A greater amount, however, is absorbed by dark-colored surfaces, such as wet soil, vegetation, the ocean, and particles in the air and clouds. The absorbed energy warms these dark surfaces, which reemit the energy as infrared (IR) radiation, or heat. All objects that are warmer than their surroundings radiate IR energy. Earth, which is warm, loses heat as it moves through space, which is cold—just about balancing the incoming solar power. This balance determines Earth's temperature.

Not all of the IR radiation emitted by Earth's surface is lost to space. Some of it is intercepted by gases in the atmosphere known as greenhouse gases. Among these are carbon dioxide, methane, and water vapor. When these gases absorb the outgoing radiation, they warm the air. The warmed air reemits more IR radiation, half of which is directed upward toward the upper atmosphere and half downward toward Earth's surface, which is further warmed.

The greenhouse effect keeps Earth warmer than it would otherwise be. Throughout the planet's history, the greenhouse effect has prevented Earth from freezing and made life itself possible. We can see evidence of the power of the greenhouse effect on neighboring planets. Venus is much hotter than Earth because its thick, mainly carbon dioxide atmosphere is extremely good at trapping heat. Mars is a frozen planet because it has a very thin atmosphere without enough greenhouse gases to trap heat.

Carbon dioxide emissions. Large amounts of greenhouse gases are given off by a number of human activities. The most plentiful human-generated greenhouse gas is carbon dioxide, released by the burning of fossil fuels. Between 1957, when modern measurements began, and 2000, carbon dioxide concentrations in the atmosphere have increased by approximately 18 percent. At the beginning of the new millennium in 2000, the worldwide burning of fossil fuels injected about 6.6 billion tons (6 billion metric tons) of carbon, in the form of carbon dioxide, into the global atmosphere each year. Carbon dioxide emissions were increasing by about 1 to 2 percent per year. Approximately half of the carbon that is emitted ends up in the atmosphere, and half is absorbed by the ocean and plants.

The 20-year period between 1980 and 2000 during which temperatures rose by as much as 0.7 degrees Fahrenheit (0.4 degrees Celsius) is especially important because, for the first time, scientists also measured the sun's output precisely. These measurements revealed that solar output did not change during this period. The rapid warming, therefore, must have been due to an increase in the atmospheric concentration of carbon dioxide and other greenhouse gases.

Certain land-use practices add to greenhouse gases. In the early 2000s, deforestation (cutting down trees) in the tropical rain forests injected 1.6 billion tons (1.5 billion metric tons) of carbon, in the form of carbon dioxide, into the atmosphere. Deforestation causes a build-up of carbon dioxide as a result of the burning of trees and the decomposition of dead organic matter by bacteria.

Other greenhouse gases. Carbon dioxide is by far the most important greenhouse gas, but human activities also generate other heat-trapping gases. For example, the atmospheric concentration of methane is increasing due to microbial activity in rice paddies and municipal landfills, intestinal fermentation in cattle, and the leaking and venting of oil and gas wells. Nitrous oxide, fluorocarbons, and ozone are other greenhouse gases produced through human activities.

Together, the greenhouse gases added to the atmosphere by humans trap the same amount of heat energy per square meter as is given off by a small Christmas-tree light bulb. While this does not seem like much, it equals about 1 percent of the solar energy absorbed every second by every square meter of Earth's surface. If the Sun's output of solar energy were to increase by 1 percent, Earth would experience significant climate change. (The Sun's energy output actually varies in a cycle by 0.1 percent over an 11 year period.) There-

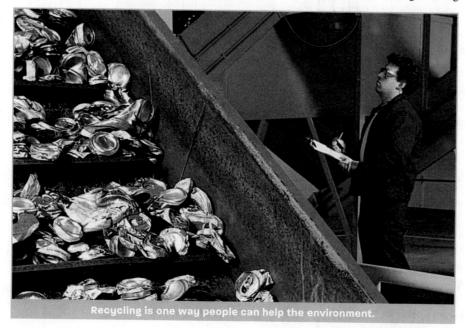

Recycling is one way people can help the environment.

fore, if emissions from fossil fuels and other greenhouse-gas sources continue at their present rate, atmospheric concentrations of these gases will continue to grow, and the extra heating caused by the gases should alter Earth's climate.

Computer models predict the future. How will human input into the global climate system affect Earth in the future? Precise predictions were hampered in 2001 by the fact that scientists still had much to learn about the physics of climate and the ways in which biological systems respond to climate change. To better understand climate change, scientists use powerful computers capable of modeling, or simulating, such climate factors as sunlight, heat, precipitation (rain and snow), air currents, and ocean currents. Scientists program equations governing these factors into computer models to try to mimic the way Earth's climate works. They then add other factors to the model, such as a particular level of carbon dioxide, to see how these additions alter the model. In this way, the model tells researchers how the climate might change in the future.

Computer-model predictions of how climate might change yielded not one clear answer, but a range of possibilities. Yet, there were a number of outcomes that most scientists agreed upon. Most models predicted that global temperatures will continue to increase, with more hot days and higher maximum daytime temperatures over most land areas. Minimum daily nighttime temperatures were also expected to increase over most land areas. The computer models predicted

Power plants need to become more energy efficient.

that minimum daily temperatures will rise faster than the maximum temperatures. Scientists believed that faster evaporation (the conversion of a liquid into a gas through warming) will cause average amounts of precipitation around Earth to increase. Most models, however, predicted that global warming will result in less rain and increased risk of drought during summer in mid-continental regions. Melting ice sheets were expected to cause global average sea levels to rise between 4 inches and 2.9 feet (0.1 and 0.9 meters) by 2100, according to a range of model estimates.

Problems with model predictions. How accurate are climate changes predicted by computer models? Their accuracy depends on how well the

models have been programmed to simulate the complex, dynamic processes of Earth's climate system. It is difficult to accurately model many important parts of the climate system, such as the degree to which cloud cover and cloud heights might change; the role that black soot particles in the air play in trapping heat; and the extent to which sulfate particles in the air (from the burning of sulfur-containing coal and oil) cool the ground. However, by combining a number of certainties and uncertainties, many scientists estimated that average global temperatures could increase by 2.7 to 9 degrees Fahrenheit (1.5 to 5 degrees Celsius) by 2100.

While computer models in 2001 were able to simulate changes in certain worldwide features of climate, such as average global temperatures, they were not able to make precise predictions for particular geographical regions. The climate for each region on Earth depends on many complex factors that scientists did not fully understand and computers could not yet model. Although a computer model may predict a rise in average global temperature, exactly how fast temperatures will rise and where they will rise the most remained unclear. It was also not clear in what season or by how much precipitation will increase in any given region on Earth. Moreover, scientists continued to question how climate change would affect the severity of coastal flooding and the frequency of droughts, typhoons, and other extreme weather.

These fossilized remains of an early whale were discovered in inland Egypt.

The impact that climate change might have on agriculture, society, and the environment also remained unclear. Some agricultural regions may profit by the longer growing season resulting from a warmer climate, but only if adequate rain falls to keep the soil moist. Some countries and ecosystems may be able to adapt to climate disruptions caused by global warming, but only if change does not come too fast.

Human behavior is important. Human behavior will have a major effect on the future of climate change. The greenhouse-gas emissions driving current climate change are the product of three factors dependent on human actions. The first is technological efficiency, in particular, the energy efficiency of such fuel-using technologies as electric power plants and automobiles; the second involves human consumption, for example, the number of cars purchased and driven; and the third factor is population—more people on the planet will cause more greenhouse gases to be emitted. Since none of these factors can be predicted with perfect accuracy, they add to the uncertainties in climate models.

Despite the uncertainties, scientists point to a number of actions that Americans could take that would not only limit greenhouse-gas emissions but also have economic side benefits. If Americans would use fossil fuels more efficiently, they would slow the growth of the global greenhouse effect. Greater fuel efficiency would also save money for Americans, decrease the trade imbalance of the United States with other nations, and lessen the U.S. dependence on foreign oil. The recycling of aluminum cans, paper, and other materials helps limit greenhouse-gas emissions by decreasing the volume of trash that must be buried in landfills or burned. It also helps conserve energy.

Working to limit global warming. Most of the scientific community supports international efforts to decrease greenhouse-gas emissions, such as the Kyoto Protocol, which set targets for carbon dioxide reductions. Some industrialized nations have ratified the Kyoto Protocol since 1997, but the U.S. government, citing economic concerns, withdrew from the agreement in 2001. Officials from the United States and some other countries were in favor of giving nations credit for carbon dioxide reductions by taking into account the amount of carbon that is naturally absorbed by plants and soil in forests and farms. However, most nations that lacked large areas of forests and farmland were opposed to this idea. Scientists note that such schemes will be effective only if it can be proven that the absorbed carbon is "locked up" in the plants or soil for long periods, preventing it from returning to the atmosphere. Scientists also stress that international efforts need to address the issues of energy efficiency, rates of consumption, and population growth. Some poorer countries, which use much less energy per person than the United States, are rapidly increasing their energy usage as their populations expand. Global warming is bound to quicken if such matters are not confronted.

The incredible complexity of Earth's climate demands that we intensify scientific research if we want to understand the changes that we are currently observing and accurately predict future

President Bill Clinton prioritized the restoration of the Everglades.

changes. Meanwhile, we need to try to slow the rate of global warming in order to give researchers more time to predict changes before they actually happen.

Climate change will no doubt remain an important and controversial issue for a long time. While it has become clear that humans have the power to change the global climate, we are unlikely to be able to control the climate. The worldwide experiment that is underway bears close watching.

About the author: Ralph J. Cicerone is Aldrich Professor of Earth System Science and Chemistry, and Chancellor, at the University of California at Irvine.

Ocean (2001)

Evidence mounted in 2001 that global warming is being caused by the burning of fossil fuels (coal, oil, gas, and wood), and dire predictions were made about the toll that global warming may take on the ocean. In addition, a hidden world was discovered inside coral reefs, and fossils revealed that whales are related to pigs.

Ocean warming. Much of the evidence of global warming has come from measurements of increasing air temperatures. However, oceanographer Sydney Levitus of the National Oceanic and Atmospheric Administration in Silver Spring, Maryland, has reported that the upper 9,800 feet (3,000 meters) of the world's oceans also warmed considerably between 1955 and 1996. In 2001, Levitus and Tim Barnett, a climate scientist at Scripps Institution of Oceanography in La Jolla, California, used computer simulations of the climate to test whether this ocean warming was caused by natural climate variations or greenhouse gases, gases that absorb heat in the atmosphere and direct it downward toward Earth. The burning of fossil fuels emits large amounts of the greenhouse gas carbon dioxide.

In April 2001, the scientists reported that the computer simulations produced the observed increase in ocean warming only when the computers were programmed to factor in greenhouse gas emissions. This implied that the increasing warmth of the sea is being caused by greenhouse gases generated by human activities.

Endangered coral reefs. Nearly all of the world's coral reefs may die by 2050 if ocean warming continues at the current rate, marine biologist Rupert Ormond of Glasgow University in Scotland reported in September 2001. Since the early 1990s, scientists have documented a widespread destruction of coral reefs resulting from bleaching, a process in which corals turn white. Bleached corals often die from disease or storm damage. Evidence indicates that bleaching may be caused by increased water temperatures. Ormond combined the measured rate of ocean warming with the observed rate of coral reef loss and projected these rates into the future. Marine scientists noted that several other factors besides ocean warming, including overfishing and pollution, threaten coral reefs.

Hidden reef community. In October 2001, an international team of scientists led by marine ecologist Claudio Richter of the Center for Tropical Marine Ecology in Germany reported the discovery of a previously unknown community of organisms inside coral reefs. Divers with the team used endoscopes (tubelike instruments with a camera on the tip) to examine the interior of deep crevices in coral reefs at nine sites in the Red Sea, which separates the Arabian Peninsula and northeastern Africa. They discovered more than 370 types of sponges living in the crevices, in addition to various other filter-feeding (feeding on small debris suspended in the water) species. According to Richter, the sponges inside reef crevices may excrete minerals that provide nutrients for organisms on the outside of reefs.

Land ancestors of whales. New descriptions of four species of whale ancestors in 2001 confirmed that whales are descended from land mammals related to modern pigs and cows. Paleontologist Philip D. Gingerich reported in September the discovery in Pakistan of 47-million-year-old fossils of two species. One of the species, a sea-lion-sized creature named Rodhocetus balochistanensis, had forefeet with hooflike nails and hind feet with webbed toes. Paleontologist Johannes Thewissen of Northeastern Ohio Universities College of Medicine in Rootstown published a description in September of 50-million-year-old fossils of two whale ancestors from Pakistan. These creatures—one the size of a wolf, the other the size of a fox—had long, spindly legs. All four of the species had ankle bones similar to those found in even-toed ungulates, a group of hoofed animals that includes pigs, cows, and hippopotamuses.

Environmental Pollution (1999)

Efforts to reduce the emissions of greenhouse gases, which many scientists blame for causing global warming (a gradual warming of Earth's surface), continued in 1999. Greenhouse gases, such as carbon dioxide, are generated by the burning of fossil fuels. A number of scientific studies in the 1990s indicated that these gases were accumulating in the atmosphere, where they trap heat much like a greenhouse. Scientists fear that this warming might disrupt climate and cause glaciers to melt, leading to rising sea levels and coastal flooding.

In September 1999, the leaders of the Alliance of Small Island States, an association of several dozen small island nations, voiced their concerns about greenhouse gases before the United Nations (UN) General Assembly. They noted that if global warming is not abated, their nations would bear the brunt of rising seas and increasingly violent weather.

The island leaders urged the United States and the world's other industrial nations to ratify the Kyoto Protocol, a UN treaty negotiated in 1997. The treaty requires participating countries to reduce their greenhouse gas emissions by an average of 5 percent below 1990 levels in the years between 2008 and 2012. Because the United States is one of the leading emitters of greenhouse gases, the treaty required the United States to reduce its emissions by 7 percent.

Although Clinton administration officials representing the United States signed the Kyoto Protocol in 1998, many members of the U.S. Congress said they feared the treaty would hurt the U.S. economy. Congress had not yet ratified the treaty by the end of 1999.

Private industry initiatives. The Worldwatch Institute, an environmental research group based in Washington, D.C., announced in August that global emissions of carbon dioxide declined 0.5 percent during 1998. The institute attributed the decline partly to voluntary initiatives by private industry. The chemical-industry giant E. I. DuPont DeNemours and Company of Wilmington, Delaware, for example, had invested $50 million in equipment to reduce greenhouse gas emissions since 1991.

A number of corporate executives in 1999 endorsed a bill before the U.S. Congress that would grant "pollution credits" to companies that curtail emissions of greenhouse gases. Under this legislation, the U.S. government would guarantee that companies would receive credits for any emission reductions they achieve before the Kyoto treaty, if ratified, becomes effective in 2008. The companies could then use these credits to satisfy their reduction requirements in the future or sell them to other companies that are unable to meet their reduction requirements.

Everglades restoration. The Clinton administration in July 1999 presented to Congress a program to restore the natural ecology of the Everglades, a large area of wetlands in southern Florida. In the late 1940s, the U.S. Army Corps of Engineers began to install a system of canals, levees, and pumps to control flooding and provide drinking and irrigation water for southern Florida's expanding population. The system reduced the natural flow of water in the Everglades, altering plant and animal communities. The ecology of the Everglades was also adversely affected by runoff polluted with fertilizers and pesticides from nearby agricultural areas.

The 20-year, $7.8-billion project required the Army Corps to restore much of the Everglades' natural water flow. This involved punching holes in levees and highways that impede the flow, creating underground reservoirs to capture water that is presently channeled to the sea, and using nearby marshland to filter chemical contaminants from the water. As part of the plan, Congress approved $80 million in November 1999 to purchase land to be used for the restoration.

Clean air versus clean water. The U.S. Environmental Protection Agency (EPA) proposed in July 1999 that Congress no longer require oil companies to add an ingredient to gasoline that helps make the air cleaner. The agency said the ingredient, methyl tertiary butyl ether (MTBE), posed a serious danger as a water pollutant.

Under the EPA's urging, Congress in 1990 required MTBE to be added to gasoline because of the chemical's ability to cut toxic emissions, such as carbon monoxide, benzene, and toluene. However, researchers have since found that MTBE is a possible carcinogenic (cancer-causing) substance that can flow into drinking-water wells when fuel leaks from underground tanks or pipelines.

SUVs and smog. In May 1999, the EPA announced regulations to reduce the emission of smog-causing chemicals by sport-utility vehicles (SUVs), light trucks, and cars. The EPA said the new standards would reduce respiratory illness by cutting emissions of nitrogen oxides and other pollutants by 75 to 95 percent.

Under the regulations, which were to be phased in gradually between 2004 and 2009, SUVs and trucks weighing less than 8,500 pounds (3,859 kilograms) were to be held to the same strict pollution standards as automobiles for the first time. The regulations also required the oil industry to cut the content of smog-causing sulfur in gasoline by 90 percent.

In October 1999, the EPA extended the tough emission requirements to "super-large" SUVs and heavy-duty trucks—those weighing more than 8,500 pounds.

Pesticide safety. Environmentalists criticized the EPA in 1999 for its slower-than-expected action on the 1996 Food Quality Protection Act. The act required that the agency by 2006 reassess the safety levels of 9,700 pesticides based on risks to children. The EPA had set an August 1999 goal for completing analysis of the riskiest chemicals, but it was behind in meeting that goal.

On August 2, EPA Administrator Carol Browner announced the first results of the reassessment. She said that, starting in early 2000, the widely used pesticide methyl parathion would be banned on a variety of fruits and vegetables. She noted that animal tests indicated that the pesticide could cause nerve damage in children.

Following this announcement, agriculture industry groups sued the EPA, alleging that it failed to use sound science in the evaluation of the pesticide. Environmental groups also sued the EPA, seeking to force the agency to take more aggressive action against pesticides.

EPA rebuked by court. In May 1999, the EPA found its regulatory authority challenged when a three-judge panel of the U.S. Circuit Court of Appeals in Washington, D.C., invalidated two rulings the agency made in 1997. One of these rulings had tightened the standards for air pollutants that contribute to smog. The other ruling had set new limits on microscopic respiratory irritants called particulates, which are generated in certain industrial processes. The EPA had established the regulations to protect people with asthma and lung disease.

The court struck down both laws on the grounds that the EPA failed to establish clear criteria for determining what level of health protection was provided by the standards. The court also said the EPA's move amounted to an unconstitutional transfer of power from the Congress to the EPA. To work around the rulings, EPA Administrator Carol Browner resurrected two-year-old petitions from several Northeast states requesting relief from pollution caused by out-of-state sources. Browner hoped to use the petitions to impose controls on Midwest power plants, whose pollution drifts to the Northeast.

Power plant suits. In September 1999, New York State notified coal-fired power plants in Indiana, Kentucky, Ohio, Virginia, and West Virginia that it intended to sue them for violations of the 1970 Clean Air Act. The attorney general of Connecticut announced identical intentions in November 1999. Also in November, the U.S. Justice Department began enforcement actions under the Clean Air Act against 32 coal-fired plants from Florida to Illinois.

Rain Forests

Rain forests are woodlands of tall trees that grow at or near the equator in year-round warmth and receive abundant rainfall. Although rain forests occupy only about 6 percent of the earth's surface, they are home to more than half of the world's plant and animal species. Unfortunately, however, less than half the original extent of the earth's rain forests remain, mainly due to deforestation.

HOT topics

Lost Species Due to Deforestation. Scientists estimate that deforestation of rain forests causes about 7,500 species per year to become extinct. Commercial logging and the expansion of agriculture has damaged or destroyed extensive areas of rain forests. Mining projects, the construction of hydroelectric dams, and government resettlement programs have also taken their toll. In addition to the destruction of thousands of species of plants and animals and the ecosystems in which they lived, deforestation has eliminated any possible uses, medically or otherwise, that they may have provided mankind.

DEFINITIONS

deforest, to remove the trees from; clear of trees or forests
ecosystem, a system made up of a group of living organisms and its physical environment, and the relationship between them. A pond, a lake, a forest, or an ocean may be an ecosystem. An ecosystem includes food supply, weather, and natural enemies.

HOT topics

Characteristics of a Rain Forest.
A rain forest consists of four major layers: the canopy, the sub-canopy, the understory, and the floor. The canopy and the sub-canopy are home to more than 70 percent of the animal and plant species that live in the rain forest. Rain forests continually change as large, older trees die and fall to the ground, causing gaps in which growing trees can then mature. A rain forest is a delicate ecosystem in which changes to one part of the forest often cause a domino effect within the entire ecosystem.

Amazon deforestation

The Value of Rain Forests.
Rain forests provide economic, scientific, environmental, and recreational value to people. Economically, rain forests provide wood for fuel and timber and other resources such as fibers, fruits, nuts, oils, and resins. Scientifically, rain forests allow scientists to study its ecosystem in an effort to conserve it and other ecosystems. They also provide valuable foods and medicines. Environmentally, rain forests help control rainfalls, floods, droughts, soil erosion, temperatures, light and heat absorption, and carbon dioxide and other atmospheric gas levels. Recreationally, rain forests offer great beauty, lush vegetation, and unique wildlife for tourists.

The Americas/The Amazon Rain Forest.
The Amazon Rain Forest is the world's largest rain forest, covering about 2 million square miles (5.2 million square kilometers) in the Amazon River Basin of South America. Tens of thousands of plants species, more than 1,500 species of birds, 3,000 species of fish, hundreds of mammals, amphibians, and reptiles, and 30 million different insect species live in the Amazon rain forest. Indigenous Amazonian people, such as the Yanomami, also still live in the forest.

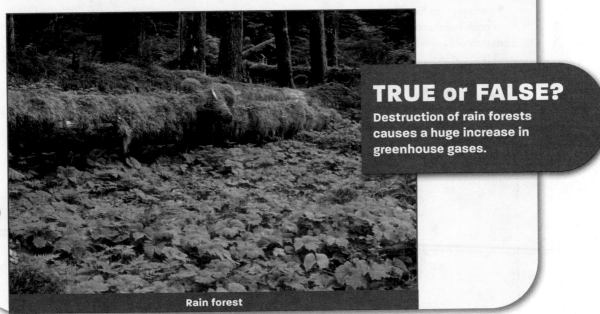
Rain forest

TRUE or FALSE?
Destruction of rain forests causes a huge increase in greenhouse gases.

THE BASICS

A rain forest is a woodland of tall trees growing in a region of year-round warmth and abundant rainfall. Almost all rain forests lie at or near the equator. They form an evergreen belt of lush vegetation that encircles the planet. German botanist Andreas F. W. Schimper first coined the term *rain forest*—in German, *Regenwald*—in 1898.

Tropical rain forests occupy only 6 to 7 percent of the earth's surface. However, they support more than half of the world's plant and animal *species* (kinds). More kinds of frogs and other amphibians, birds, insects, mammals, and reptiles live in rain forests than in any other area. Scientists believe millions more rain forest species remain undiscovered.

The rain forest provides people with many benefits. Its plants produce timber, foods, medicines, and such industrial products as dyes, fibers, gums, oils, and resins. Rain forests help regulate the earth's climate and maintain clean air. The forests' lush, green beauty and rich wildlife offer a special source of enjoyment.

In addition, rain forests provide homes to millions of people. Such groups as the Yanomami of South America, the Dayaks of Southeast Asia, and the Pygmies of central Africa have lived in rain forests for centuries. They make their living by hunting, fishing, collecting forest products, and farming. Traditional forest peoples have acquired much knowledge about the rain forest's plants and animals.

In spite of these benefits, people cut down thousands of square miles or square kilometers of rain forest each year. This destruction eliminates thousands of species of animals. A number of governments and conservation organizations are working to preserve the rain forests.

Characteristics of Rain Forests

Climate and soil. The temperature in a tropical rain forest varies little. It rarely rises above 95 degrees Fahrenheit (35 degrees Celsius) or drops below 64 degrees Fahrenheit (18 degrees Celsius). In many regions, the average temperature in the hottest month is only 2 to 5 Fahrenheit degrees (1 to 3 Celsius degrees) higher than the average temperature in the coldest month. Most rain forests receive more than 80 inches (203 centimeters) of rain annually. Some areas may receive more than 250 inches (635 centimeters) of rain each year. Thundershowers can occur more than 200 days a year.

Rain forest soils vary greatly from place to place. In many areas, the soil is acidic and infertile because years of heavy rains have washed out most of the *nutrients* (nourishing substances). Most rain forest nutrients are part of living plants. Small amounts of nutrients occur in a thin layer of topsoil that contains decaying vegetation.

Rain forest trees have developed several ways of capturing nutrients. For example, they obtain nourishment from rainwater that collects in their leaves or along their trunks and branches. They also withdraw nutrients from their old leaves before they shed them. The roots of most rain forest trees grow close to the surface and quickly absorb soil nutrients before they wash away. Special fungi called *mycorrhizae* grow in or on many of

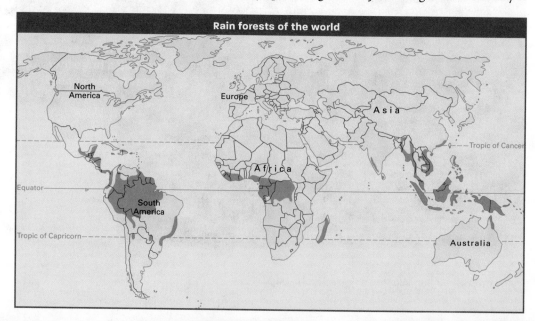

Rain forests of the world

North America · Europe · Asia · Africa · South America · Australia · Tropic of Cancer · Equator · Tropic of Capricorn

the roots and help them absorb minerals from the soil.

Structure and growth. Rain forests grow in four major layers: (1) the *canopy*, or top layer; (2) the *sub-canopy*, a layer of trees just below the canopy; (3) the *understory*, a shady lower area; and (4) the *floor*. The tallest trees, known as emergents, grow more than 165 feet (50 meters) tall. The *crowns* (tops) of these trees dominate the canopy. Emergents receive the greatest amount of sunlight, but they must endure high temperatures and strong winds. The crowns of other trees in the canopy usually form a nearly continuous covering of leaves 65 to 165 feet (20 to 50 meters) above the ground. Some tall trees have large growths called *buttresses* that extend from the base of the trunk and help support the tree.

More than 70 percent of rain forest animal and plant species reside in the canopy and subcanopy. Many tree branches have a dense covering of *epiphytes*, plants that grow on other plants and obtain nourishment from the air and rain. Vines called *lianas* often climb on or around the trunks and branches of trees.

The shady understory shelters small palms, young trees, and *herbaceous* (nonwoody) plants that can grow in dim light. Many popular house plants, such as philodendrons, dieffenbachia, and ferns, are developed from species that live in this area. Some scientists believe only 1 percent of the sunlight available to emergent trees reaches the understory.

A thin layer of fallen leaves, seeds, fruits, and branches covers the forest floor. This layer quickly decomposes and is constantly replaced.

The layers of a rain forest continually change. Large old trees die and fall to the ground, leaving a gap in the canopy. Direct sunlight penetrates through to the understory and stimulates the growth of seedlings, saplings, and small trees below. The small trees slowly stretch upward into the canopy. As they branch and expand their crowns, they fill the gaps in the canopy. A mature rain forest consists of a mixture of closed canopies, gaps, and patches of growing trees where the canopy is being rebuilt. The regeneration of many rain forest trees depends on gaps developing regularly in the canopy.

Plants and animals. About 45 percent of the world's plant species occur in tropical rain forests. Scientists have counted more than 250 species of trees in small areas of Asian and South American rain forests. A similar plot of land in a northern temperate forest would have only about 10 to 15 tree species. In addition to trees, rain forests support a great variety of bamboos, herbs, and shrubs. Climbing vines, ferns, mosses, and orchids grow directly on the trunks and branches of large trees.

Because of continual moisture and warmth, tropical rain forests stay green all year. Most rain forest trees continually lose old leaves and grow new ones. Only a few species lose all of their leaves for a brief period.

Fish, amphibians, reptiles, birds, and mammals abound in the rain forest and its rivers. However, insects rank as the most plentiful rain forest animals. An individual tree in a South American rain forest may support more than 40 species of ants. Scientists have counted about 1,200 species

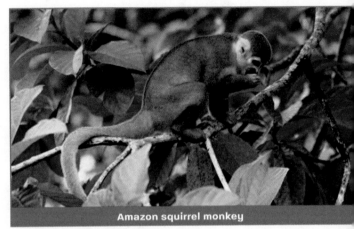

Amazon squirrel monkey

of beetles living in only 19 tree crowns from Panama.

Plants and animals in the rain forest depend on one another for survival. Many animal groups, especially insects and birds, pollinate the flowers of rain forest trees. Such animals receive food from the flowers' nectar. In return, they pollinate the next flowers they visit. Some trees rely on only one species of insect for pollination. Many rain forest trees also depend on animals to disperse their seeds. In the Amazon rain forest, fish disperse the seeds of some trees.

Rain Forests Around the World

The world's largest rain forests occur in tropical regions of the Americas, Asia, and Africa. Smaller areas of rain forest exist on many Pacific Islands and in parts of Australia's northeastern coast. People have also applied the term *rain forest* to such woodlands as those in North America's Pacific Northwest. However, the plant life in these forests is much less diverse than that found in tropical rain forests. For example, only a few species of large *conifers* (cone-bearing trees) dominate Pacific Northwest forests.

The Americas. About half of the world's rain forests grow in the American tropics. The largest expanse of forest—about 2 million square miles (5.2 million square kilometers)—lies in the Amazon River basin. Rain forests also occur in coastal areas from Ecuador and Brazil to southern Mexico, and in patches on many of the Caribbean islands.

American tropical rain forests support a rich assortment of plant species. More than 500 kinds of large plants may inhabit only 5 acres (2 hectares) of forest. Valuable hardwood trees include mahogany and rosewood. More than 150 species of trees produce edible fruits. Avocados, cocoa, rubber, and vanilla also grow there.

The rain forests of tropical America support more than 1,500 species of birds, 500 species of mammals, and 2,000 species of butterflies. More bats live there than live anywhere else. Monkeys, sloths, and toucans feed in the forest canopy and sub-canopy. Capybaras, the world's largest rodents, as well as ocelots and tapirs, forage along the forest floor. Emerald tree boas and arrow-poison frogs

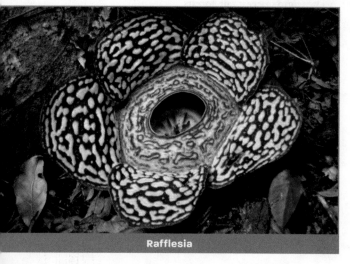
Rafflesia

hide among foliage in the understory. The Amazon River contains more than 2,000 species of freshwater fish, including the dangerous piranha.

American rain forests provide homes to a variety of peoples. They include the Kuna of Panama, the Maya of Mexico and Central America, the Shipibo of Peru, and the Yanomami of Brazil and Venezuela. Such forest groups survive primarily by farming, but they also hunt animals and gather edible wild plants from the forest.

Asia. Rain forests cover about 1 million square miles (3 million square kilometers) of the Asian tropics. The forests grow in western and southern India and extend eastward through Vietnam. Large blocks of forest also occur in Indonesia, Malaysia, and the Philippines.

A single family of trees, the *dipterocarps*, forms a dominant part of the Asian rain forest canopy. About 380 species of dipterocarps grow in these forests. Dipterocarp trees produce valuable wood and *resins*. Resins are sticky substances that people use for varnishing and *caulking* (making objects watertight). Other important plants include the *pitcher plants*, which feed on animal life, and the rafflesia, the world's largest flower. A single *rafflesia* may grow more than 3 feet (90 centimeters) wide. Such fruits as bananas, durians, litchis, and mangoes also flourish in Asian rain forests.

Some of the best-known rain forest mammals in Asia include elephants, gibbons, orangutans, and tigers. The forests also support hundreds of reptile and amphibian species and thousands of bird and beetle species.

Rain forest peoples of Asia include the Penan of Borneo. They rely on rain forest plants and animals for subsistence and rarely farm the land. Another Bornean group, the Lun Dayeh, clear small areas of forest to make rice farms. The T'in people of Thailand and Laos harvest hundreds of wild plant species from the rain forest for food and other purposes.

Africa. Africa's tropics have about 810,000 square miles (2.1 million square kilometers) of rain forest. The forested area extends from Congo (Kinshasa) westward to the Atlantic Ocean. Patches of rain forest also occur on the east coast of Madagascar.

African rain forests do not house as many plant species as do the forests of South America or Asia. Small areas of African rain forest support from 50 to 100 species of trees. Many of these trees have their fruits dispersed by elephants. A number of valuable woods, including ebony, mahogany, and sipo, flourish in the African tropics. Other well-known plants from the region include oil palms and coffee plants.

Diverse animal life characterizes Africa's tropical rain forests. Squirrels and monkeys share the canopy and sub-canopy with other small mammals, including galagos and golden pottos, as well as hundreds of species of birds. The mandrill, a brightly colored relative of the baboon, and the okapi, a horse-like relative of the giraffe, roam the forest floor. Congo peacocks and wild hogs called bush pigs also dwell on the ground. Gorillas and chimpanzees live on the ground and in trees. The forests of Madagascar support animals found almost nowhere else, including long-tailed, monkey-like lemurs.

Forest-dwelling people in the African tropics are collectively known as Pygmies. Traditionally, they have survived by hunting and gathering wild animals and plants. Pygmies live in such countries as Burundi, Cameroon, Congo (Brazzaville), Congo (Kinshasa), Gabon, and Rwanda.

Australia and the Pacific Islands. Tropical rain forests cover about 145,600 square miles (377,000 square kilometers) in northeast Australia and on many Pacific Islands. Rain forest trees of these regions include several kinds of figs, as well as the smaller lilly-pilly and brush cherry. The lacewood and Queensland maple trees produce valuable hardwoods. Coachwood and Moreton Bay chestnut trees develop brilliantly colored flowers.

Rain forests of Australia and New Guinea house unique wildlife. Such marsupials as cuscuses, sugar gliders, and tree kangaroos make their homes in the trees. Several kinds of parrots and numerous species of snakes also reside in the forests.

Rain forest peoples of this area include Australian Aborigines and Melanesian peoples from such islands as New Guinea, the Solomon Islands, and Vanuatu. Many of these cultures hunt and gather food from the rain forest. They also raise crops.

The Value of Rain Forests

Rain forests benefit people in four major ways. They provide (1) economic, (2) scientific, (3) environmental, and (4) recreational value.

Economic value. Wood ranks as the most important rain forest product. Foresters harvest millions of trees from rain forests each year. People use about 80 percent of rain forest wood for fuel and about 20 percent for timber. International trade in tropical hardwoods averages billions of dollars a year.

Other valuable rain forest resources include fibers, fruits, nuts, oils, and resins. Indonesia and the Philippines export millions of dollars in furniture and other products made from *rattan*, a kind of palm. Amazon rain forests provide thousands of tons of Brazil nuts and rubber. Mexican and Central American forests yield various types of chicle, a natural latex once widely used in chewing gum.

Scientific value. Tropical rain forests have much to teach people. Many scientists study the rain forest as an *ecosystem*—that is, they investigate the relationships among all its living things and the environment that supports them. Because of its great

Ring-tailed lemurs

diversity of life, the rain forest ranks as the most complex ecosystem on land. Biologists have discovered and classified only a small percentage of the organisms believed to live there. As scientists learn more about rain forests, they can better understand how to conserve these and other ecosystems.

Rain forests provide a wealth of foods and medicines. The forest peoples of Borneo use hundreds of different plant species for food. Most of these plants have not been grown outside Borneo. About 85 wild relatives of the common avocado exist in forests of Central America. Commercial avocado growers are working with scientists to develop ways of using these species to breed avocados that are more resistant to disease.

Several important medicines come from rain forest plants. These include quinine, used to treat malaria; *tubocurarine*, a muscle relaxant sometimes used in heart surgery; and *pilocarpine*, used to treat the eye disease glaucoma. The rosy periwinkle plant from Madagascar yields important anticancer drugs. Scientists believe many more potential medicines may exist in rain forests.

Environmental value. Tropical rain forests help regulate the earth's environment in several ways. For example, tropical trees help control the amount of rain water that reaches the ground. These trees absorb an enormous quantity of rain. In a process called *transpiration*, much of this water evaporates from the trees' leaf pores and reenters the atmosphere as vapor. Eventually, the vapor condenses into water and falls to the earth again as rain. Transpiration may account for as much as half of the rainfall in some rain forests. By regulating rainfall, rain forest trees keep floods and droughts from becoming too severe. The dense rain forest vegetation also reduces soil erosion.

Rain forests help control temperatures in their own regions and in other parts of the world. Rain forest trees absorb light and heat. This absorption keeps tropical climates from becoming too hot or too cold. The forests also take in and store massive amounts of carbon dioxide, preventing the buildup of this gas in the atmosphere. Scientists believe the accumulation of carbon dioxide and other gases in the atmosphere increases temperatures around the world. By absorbing carbon dioxide, tropical rain forests may help keep worldwide temperatures from becoming too warm.

Recreational value. Rain forests offer great beauty, lush vegetation, and unique wildlife for tourists. A growing number of people travel to rain forests each year. Tourism has helped increase awareness of the need to preserve these environments.

Rosy periwinkle

The Future of Rain Forests

People are rapidly destroying the world's rain forests. In 1950, rain forests covered about 8,700,000 square miles (22,533,000 square kilometers) of the earth. This area would cover about three-fourths of Africa. Today, less than half the original extent of the earth's rain forest remains. In such regions as Madagascar, Sumatra, and the Atlantic coast of Brazil, only small patches still stand.

Few rain forest species can adjust to severe disturbance of their habitat. Most perish when people clear large areas of forest. Scientists estimate that tropical *deforestation* (clearing of trees) wipes out about 7,500 species per year.

Causes of deforestation. Commercial logging and the expansion of agriculture have damaged or wiped out extensive areas of rain forest. Huge mining projects, the construction of hydroelectric dams, and government resettlement programs have also taken their toll.

A complex mix of social, political, and economic factors has triggered these destructive activities. Rapid population growth and poverty often intensify the pressure to clear rain forest for short-term economic benefits. Brazil, Indonesia, and other nations have cut down huge expanses of rain for-

est to create new settlements that allow people to move out of overcrowded cities. Moreover, the governments of many tropical countries are deeply in debt. This debt provides a strong motivation to gather as much as possible from the rain forest as quickly as possible. After clearing the forest to harvest wood and other products, people then commonly use the land to grow crops.

Deforestation usually displaces forest peoples. When denied access to the forest, these peoples often lose important knowledge about rain forest species and their uses. Loss of such knowledge further threatens the survival of the forests.

Saving rain forests. Many conservation organizations, including the World Wildlife Fund, Conservation International, and the Nature Conservancy, are working with governments to conserve rain forests. Such efforts include (1) establishing protected areas, (2) promoting intelligent management of rain forests, and (3) increasing public awareness about the importance of the forests.

In the 1980s and 1990s, hundreds of protected areas were established in tropical forests. These areas included nature reserves, wildlife sanctuaries, and national parks. However, such efforts affected only a small percentage of the total area of rain forest. Moreover, many conservation areas remain only "paper parks," with little protection or enforcement on the ground.

Governments and conservation organizations also promote sound management of tropical forests by the people who use them. For example, certain organizations certify timber from loggers that harvest rain forest wood in a sustainable fashion. Certified timbers may bring a higher price on the international market. Areas of some rain forests have been set aside as *extractive reserves*. Local populations manage these reserves and practice sustainable harvesting of many forest products.

Increasing public awareness about the plight of rain forests may also aid the struggle to conserve them. Awareness has grown due to greater exposure of rain forest issues in the media, and to an increasing number of tourists who travel to rain forests.

MLA Citation

"Rain Forests." *The Southwestern Advantage Topic Source.* Nashville: Southwestern. 2013.

ADDITIONAL RESOURCES

Books to Read

Kricher, John C. *A Neotropical Companion: An Introduction to the Animals, Plants, and Ecosystems of the New World Tropics.* 2nd ed. 1997. Reprint. Princeton, 1999.

Lewington, Anna. *Atlas of Rain Forests.* Raintree Steck-Vaughn, 1997.

Rain Forests of the World. 11 vols. Cavendish, 2002. Younger readers.

Terborgh, John. *Diversity and the Tropical Rain Forest.* Scientific American Library, 1992.

Web Sites

Journey into Amazonia

http://www.pbs.org/journeytoamazonia/
A PBS exhibition about the disappearing Amazon rain forest and its ecosystem.

Rainforest Alliance

http://www.rainforest-alliance.org/
The international nonprofit conservation organization presents rain forest facts and learning activities for kids and teachers.

Tropical Rain Forests

http://kids.mongabay.com/
Helping children learn about the rain forest.

Search Strings

Note: Some search engines will return different results depending upon whether you use rain forest or rainforest.

Lost Species Due to Deforestation

species lost due to deforestation of rainforests (70,600)

species lost due to deforestation of rainforests extinct plants animals ecosystems (9,580)

Characteristics of a Rain Forest

rain forest characteristics (156,000)

rain forest characteristics major layers canopy sub-canopy understory floor (804)

characteristics of the rain forest ecosystem canopy sub-canopy understory floor (726)

The Value of Rain Forests

rainforest value economic scientific environmental recreational (25,000)

"rain forest" value economic scientific environmental recreational activities (8,510)

The Amazon Rain Forest

Amazon Rain Forest plant animal species indigenous people (63,010)

"Amazon Rain Forest" plant animal species indigenous people (2,250)

"Amazon Rain Forest" plant animal species indigenous people Yanomami (141)

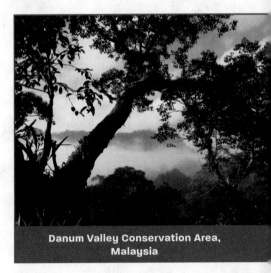

Danum Valley Conservation Area, Malaysia

Space Exploration

Space exploration is the study of our galaxy and beyond, including the sun, planets, moons, and stars. Exploration is our human response to curiosity about the universe, how it was formed, and whether life exists beyond Earth. The space age began in 1957 when the Soviet Union launched the first artificial satellite, Sputnik 1, to orbit the Earth. Since then, the United States has launched Explorer 1, Voyager 1 and Voyager 2, and the Hubble Space Telescope, just to name a few. In 1969, Neil Armstrong and Edwin "Buzz" Aldrin were the first people to set foot on the moon. Recently, space shuttles, an International Space Station, and Mars Rovers have enhanced space exploration.

HOT topics

Could Mars Be Habitable? What Is NASA's Plan and What Would It Take?

In order to get people to Mars, NASA (or other space agencies) may need to develop a new spacecraft and more efficient rockets. Once there, they would need to be able to build settlements, produce fuel and oxygen, and eventually terraform the planet to alter its atmosphere to sustain life. Obviously, timescales, economics, politics, and ethics must all be considered.

HOT topics

Space Vehicles.
Many vehicles have been created in order to explore space. The United States uses the Delta 4 and Atlas 5 to carry artificial satellites and space probes into space. The Space Shuttle once carried people and International Space Station modules. Asian nations use India's PSLV rocket, Japan's H-IIA rocket, and China's Long March 3B rocket. In addition to all three rockets carrying artificial satellites and space probes into space, China's Long March 3B also carries a manned spacecraft, the Shenzhou. European nations use the European Space Agency's Ariane 5 rocket and Russia's A class and Proton rockets to carry space probes and artificial satellites into space. The A class rocket has also carried people and the Proton rocket carried International Space Station modules. In addition to other launch vehicles, there have also been many different satellites, probes, orbiting telescopes, space-crafts, shuttles, rovers, and space stations created in order to explore space.

A view of the Schiaparelli Hemisphere of Mars

International Space Station (ISS).
More than 15 Earth nations built a large, manned station that orbits the planet. One module at a time was launched and connected in space. The station consists of 8 large modules in which astronauts and cosmonauts are able to live. Solar panels supply the electric power needed to power the station. Scientific research and experiments are an ongoing mission of the station.

Earth's Space Agencies.
National Aeronautics and Space Administration (NASA) in the United States, Russian Aviation and Space Agency, the European Space Agency (ESA), Japan Aerospace Exploration Agency (JAXA), and the Canadian Space Agency (CSA) operate some of Earth's major space programs.

An astronaut spacewalking

TRUE or FALSE?
A major dispute in the development of space programs has been the proper balance of piloted and unpiloted exploration.

DEFINITIONS

Artificial satellite is a manufactured object that orbits the earth or any other body in space.

Astronaut is a general term for any space traveler, particularly one from the United States.

Booster is the rocket that provides most or all of the energy for the launch of a spacecraft.

Cosmonaut is an astronaut from the former Soviet Union or the present Commonwealth of Independent States.

Entry is the phase of a space flight during which the vehicle is moving through a planet's atmosphere before landing.

Escape velocity is the minimum speed a spacecraft must reach to overcome the pull of gravity.

Extravehicular activity, or **EVA,** refers to activities performed outside a vehicle in outer space.

Heat shield is that part of a spacecraft designed to protect the vehicle from heat during atmospheric entry. The shield may consist of tiles or other types of insulation.

Launch vehicle is a rocket used to launch a spacecraft or satellite into space.

Launch window is the period when a spacecraft's target—such as a planet or a satellite—is properly lined up with the launch point, creating an efficient flight path.

Lox, or *Liquid oxygen*, consists of oxygen cooled to a temperature of -297ºF (-183ºC), at which it becomes a liquid. It is a common source of oxygen to use in burning rocket fuel.

Microgravity refers to those conditions that occur during orbital flight when a spacecraft's contents and crew float freely, without the feeling of weight that gravity normally produces.

Mission control is a facility on the ground that supervises a space flight.

Module is a section of a spacecraft that can be disconnected and separated from other sections.

Orbit is the path of a spacecraft or a heavenly body as it revolves around a planet or other body.

Orbital velocity is the minimum velocity needed to maintain an orbit around the earth or some other body.

Oxidizer is the substance in a rocket propellant that provides the oxygen needed to make the fuel burn in the airlessness of space.

Payload is the cargo carried into space aboard a spacecraft, including passengers and instruments.

Propellant is the material burned by a rocket to generate thrust. It generally consists of both fuel and an oxidizer.

Sounding rocket is a rocket that carries scientific instruments into the upper atmosphere or into space near the earth.

Space probe is an unmanned spacecraft sent to explore other planets, celestial bodies, or interplanetary space.

Space shuttle is a reusable space vehicle that takes off like a rocket and lands like an airplane.

Space station is an orbiting spacecraft designed to be occupied by teams of astronauts or cosmonauts over a long period.

Stage is a section of a rocket having its own engine.

Telemetry is the use of radio signals to receive information from spacecraft in flight.

Thrust is the push given to a rocket by the expulsion of the gases created by burning fuel.

THE BASICS

Space exploration is our human response to curiosity about Earth, the moon, the planets, the sun and other stars, and the galaxies. Piloted and unpiloted space vehicles venture far beyond the boundaries of Earth to collect valuable information about the universe. Human beings have visited the moon and have lived in space stations for long periods. Space exploration helps us see Earth in its true relation with the rest of the universe. Such exploration could reveal how the sun, the planets, and the stars were formed and whether life exists beyond our own world.

The space age began on October 4, 1957. On that day, the Soviet Union launched Sputnik (later referred to as Sputnik 1), the first artificial satellite to orbit Earth. The first piloted spaceflight was made on April 12, 1961, when Yuri A. Gagarin, a Soviet cosmonaut, orbited Earth in the spaceship Vostok (later called Vostok 1).

Unpiloted vehicles called *space probes* have vastly expanded our knowledge of outer space, the planets, and the stars. In 1959, one Soviet probe passed close to the moon and another hit the moon. A United States probe flew past Venus in 1962. In 1974 and 1976, the United States launched two German probes that passed inside the orbit of Mercury, close to the sun. Two other U.S. probes landed on Mars in 1976. Space probes have also investigated comets, asteroids, and the edge of the solar system.

The first piloted voyage to the moon began on December 21, 1968, when the United States launched the Apollo 8 spacecraft. It orbited the moon 10 times and returned safely to Earth. On July 20, 1969, U.S. astronauts Neil A. Armstrong and Edwin "Buzz" Aldrin landed their Apollo 11 lunar module on the moon. Armstrong became the first person to set foot on the moon. United States astronauts made five more landings on the moon before the Apollo lunar program ended in 1972.

Launch of space shuttle Discovery

During the 1970s, astronauts and cosmonauts developed skills for living in space aboard the Skylab and Salyut space stations. In 1987 and 1988, two Soviet cosmonauts spent 366 consecutive days in orbit.

On April 12, 1981, the United States space shuttle Columbia blasted off. The shuttle was the first reusable spaceship and the first spacecraft able to land at an ordinary airfield. On January 28, 1986, a tragic accident occurred. The U.S. space shuttle Challenger tore apart in midair, killing all seven astronauts aboard. The shuttle was redesigned, and flights resumed in 1988. A second tragedy struck the shuttle fleet on February 1, 2003. The Columbia broke apart as it reentered Earth's atmosphere, killing all seven of its crew members. The United States did not launch a shuttle again until 2005.

In the early years of the space age, success in space became a measure of a country's leadership in science, engineering, and national defense. The United States and the Soviet Union were engaged in an intense rivalry called the Cold War. As a result, the two nations competed with each other in developing space programs. In the 1960s and 1970s, this "space race" drove both nations to tremendous exploratory

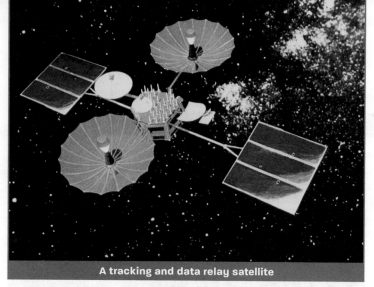

A tracking and data relay satellite

efforts. The space race had faded by the end of the 1970s, when the two countries began to pursue independent goals in space.

A major dispute in the development of space programs has been the proper balance of piloted and unpiloted exploration. Some experts favor unpiloted probes because they may be cheaper, safer, and faster than piloted vehicles. They note that probes can make trips that would be too risky for human beings to attempt. On the other hand, probes generally cannot react to unexpected occurrences. Today, most space planners favor a combined, balanced strategy of unpiloted probes and piloted expeditions. Probes can visit uncharted regions of space or patrol familiar regions where the data to be gathered fall within expected limits. But in some cases, people must follow the probes and use human ingenuity, flexibility, and courage to explore the mysteries of the universe.

What Is Space?

Space is the near-emptiness in which all objects in the universe move. The planets and the stars are tiny dots compared with the vast expanse of space.

The beginning of space. Earth is surrounded by air, which makes up its atmosphere. As the distance from Earth increases, the air becomes thinner. There is no clear boundary between the atmosphere and outer space. But most experts say that space begins somewhere beyond 60 miles (95 kilometers) above Earth.

Outer space just above the atmosphere is not entirely empty. It contains some particles of air, as well as space dust and occasional chunks of metallic or stony matter called *meteoroids*. Various kinds of radiation flow freely. Thousands of spacecraft known as *artificial satellites* have been launched into this region of space.

Earth's *magnetic field*, the space around the planet in which its magnetism can be observed, extends far out beyond the atmosphere. The magnetic field traps electrically charged particles from outer space, forming zones of radiation called the *Van Allen belts*.

The region of space in which Earth's magnetic field controls the motion of charged particles is called the *magnetosphere*. It is shaped like a teardrop, with the point extending away from the sun. Beyond this region, Earth's magnetic field is overpowered by that of the sun. But even such vast distances are not beyond the reach of Earth's gravity. As far as 1 million miles (1.6 million kilometers) from Earth, this gravity can keep a satellite orbiting the planet instead of flying off into space.

Space between the planets is called *interplanetary space*. The sun's gravity controls the motion of the planets in this region. That is why the planets orbit the sun.

Huge distances usually separate objects moving through interplanetary space. For example, Earth revolves around the sun at a distance of about 93 million miles (150 million kilometers). Venus moves in an orbit 68 million miles (110 million kilometers) from the sun. Venus is the planet that comes closest to Earth—25 million miles (40 million kilometers) away—whenever it passes directly between Earth and the sun. But this is still 100 times as far away as the moon.

Space between the stars is called *interstellar space*. Distances in this region are so great that astronomers do not describe them in miles or kilometers. Instead, scientists measure the distance between stars in units called *light-years*. For example, the nearest star to the sun is Proxima Centauri, 4.2 light-years away. A light-year equals 5.88 trillion miles (9.46 trillion kilometers). This is the distance light travels in one year at its speed of 186,282 miles (299,792 kilometers) per second.

Various gases, thin clouds of extremely cold dust, and a few escaped comets float between the stars. Interstellar space also contains many objects not yet discovered.

Getting into Space and Back

Overcoming gravity is the biggest problem for a space mission. A spacecraft must be launched at a particular *velocity* (speed and direction).

Gravity gives everything on Earth its weight and accelerates free-falling objects downward. At the surface of Earth, acceleration due to gravity, called *g*, is about 32 feet (10 meters) per second.

A powerful rocket called a *launch vehicle* or *booster* helps a spacecraft overcome gravity. All launch vehicles have two or more rocket sections known as *stages*. The first stage must provide enough *thrust* (pushing force) to leave Earth's surface. To do so, this stage's thrust must exceed the weight of the entire launch vehicle and the spacecraft. The booster generates thrust by burning fuel and then expelling gases. Rocket engines run on a special mixture called *propellant*. Propellant consists of solid or liquid fuel and an *oxidizer*, a substance that supplies the oxygen needed to make the fuel burn in the airlessness of outer space. *Lox*, or *liquid oxygen*, is a frequently used oxidizer.

The minimum velocity required to overcome gravity and stay in orbit is called *orbital velocity*. At a rate of acceleration of 3 g's, or three times the acceleration due to gravity, a vehicle reaches orbital velocity in about nine minutes. At an altitude of 120 miles (190 kilometers), the speed needed for a spacecraft to maintain orbital velocity and thus stay in orbit is about 5 miles (8 kilometers) per second.

In many rocket launches, a truck or tractor moves the rocket and its *payload* (cargo) to the launch pad. At the launch pad, the rocket is moved into position over a flame pit, and workers load propellants into the rocket through special pipes.

At launch time, the rocket's first-stage engines ignite until their combined thrust exceeds the rocket's weight. The thrust causes the vehicle to lift off the launch pad. If the rocket is a multistage model, the first stage falls away a few minutes later, after its propellant has been used up. The second stage then begins to fire. A few minutes later, it, too, runs out of propellant and falls away. If needed, a small *upper stage* rocket then fires until orbital velocity is achieved.

The launch of a space shuttle was slightly different. The shuttle had solid-propellant boosters in addition to its main rocket engines, which burned liquid propellant. The boosters combined with the main engines provided the thrust to lift the vehicle off the launch pad. After slightly more than two minutes of flight, the boosters separated from the shuttle and returned to Earth by parachute. The main engines continued to fire until the shuttle has almost reached orbital velocity. Small engines on the shuttle pushed it the remainder of the way to orbital velocity.

To reach a higher altitude, a spacecraft must make another rocket firing to increase its speed. When the spacecraft reaches a speed about 40 percent faster than orbital velocity, it achieves *escape velocity*, the speed necessary to break free of Earth's gravity.

Returning to Earth involves the problem of decreasing the spacecraft's great speed. To do this, an orbiting spacecraft uses small rockets to redirect its flight path into the upper atmosphere. This action is called *de-orbit*. A spacecraft returning to Earth from the moon or from another planet also aims its path to skim the upper atmosphere. Air resistance then provides the rest of the necessary *deceleration* (speed reduction).

At the high speeds associated with reentering the atmosphere from space, air cannot flow out of the way of the onrushing spacecraft fast enough. Instead, molecules of air pile up in front of it and become tightly compressed. This squeezing heats the air to a temperature of more than 10,000°F (5,500°C), hotter than the surface of the sun. The resulting heat that bathes the spacecraft would burn up an unprotected vehicle in seconds. Insulating

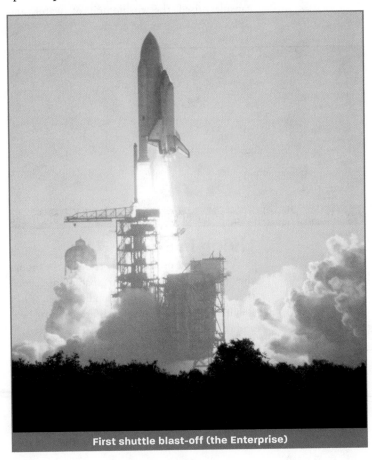

First shuttle blast-off (the Enterprise)

plates of quartz fiber glued to the skin of some spacecraft create a *heat shield* that protects against the fierce heat. Refrigeration may also be used. Early spacecraft had *ablative shields* that absorbed heat by burning off, layer by layer, and vaporizing.

Many people mistakenly believe that the spacecraft skin is heated through friction with the air. Technically, this belief is not accurate. The air is too thin and its speed across the spacecraft's surface is too low to cause much friction.

For unpiloted space probes, deceleration forces can be as great as 60 to 90 g's, or 60 to 90 times the acceleration due to gravity, lasting about 10 to 20 seconds. Space shuttles use their wings to skim the atmosphere and stretch the slowdown period to more than 15 minutes, thereby reducing the deceleration force to about 1½ g's.

When the spacecraft has lost much of its speed, it falls freely through the air. Parachutes slow it further, and a small rocket may be fired in the final seconds of descent to soften the impact of landing. The space shuttle used its wings to glide to a runway and land like an airplane. The early U.S. space capsules used the cushioning of water and "splashed down" into the ocean.

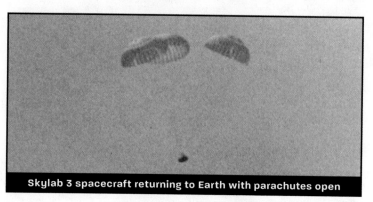

Skylab 3 spacecraft returning to Earth with parachutes open

Living in Space

When people orbit Earth or travel to the moon, they must live temporarily in space. Conditions there differ greatly from those on Earth. Space has no air, and temperatures reach extremes of heat and cold. The sun gives off dangerous radiation. Various types of matter also create hazards in space. For example, particles of dust called *micrometeoroids* threaten vehicles with destructive high-speed impacts. *Debris* (trash) from previous space missions can also damage spacecraft.

On Earth, the atmosphere serves as a natural shield against many of these threats. But in space,

astronauts and equipment need other forms of protection. They must also endure the physical effects of space travel and protect themselves from high acceleration forces during launch and landing.

The basic needs of astronauts in space must also be met. These needs include breathing, eating and drinking, elimination of body wastes, and sleeping.

Protection Against the Dangers of Space

Engineers working with specialists in space medicine have eliminated or greatly reduced most of the known hazards of living in space. Space vehicles usually have double hulls for protection against impacts. A particle striking the outer hull disintegrates and thus does not damage the inner hull.

Astronauts are protected from radiation in a number of ways. Missions in earth orbit remain in naturally protected regions, such as Earth's magnetic field. Filters installed on spacecraft windows protect the astronauts from blinding ultraviolet rays.

The crew also must be protected from the intense heat and other physical effects of launch and landing. Space vehicles require a heat shield to resist high temperatures and sturdy construction to endure crushing acceleration forces. In addition, the astronauts must be seated in such a way that the blood supply will not be pulled from their head to their lower body, causing dizziness or unconsciousness.

Aboard a spacecraft, temperatures climb because of the heat given off by electrical devices and by the crew's bodies. A set of equipment called a *thermal control system* regulates the temperature. The system pumps fluids warmed by the cabin environment into radiator panels, which discharge the excess heat into space. The cooled fluids are pumped back into coils in the cabin.

Microgravity

Once in orbit, the space vehicle and everything inside it experience a condition called *microgravity*. The vehicle and its contents fall freely, resulting in an apparently weightless floating aboard the spacecraft. For this reason, microgravity is also referred to as *zero gravity*. However, both terms are technically incorrect. The gravitation in orbit is only slightly less than the gravitation on Earth. The spacecraft and its contents continuously fall toward Earth. But because of the vehicle's tremendous forward speed, Earth's surface curves away as the vehicle falls toward it. The continuous falling seems to eliminate the weight of everything inside the space-craft. For this reason, the condition is sometimes referred to as *weightlessness*.

Microgravity has major effects on both equipment and people. For example, fuel does not drain from tanks in microgravity, so it must be squeezed out by high-pressure gas. Hot air does not rise in microgravity, so air circulation must be driven by fans. Particles of dust and droplets of water float throughout the cabin and only settle in filters on the fans.

The human body reacts to microgravity in a number of ways. In the first several days of a mission, about half of all space travelers suffer from persistent nausea, sometimes accompanied by vomiting. Most experts believe that this "space sickness," called *space adaptation syndrome*, is the body's natural reaction to microgravity. Drugs to prevent motion sickness can provide some relief for the symptoms of space adaptation syndrome, and the condition generally passes in a few days.

Microgravity also confuses an astronaut's *vestibular system*—that is, the organs of balance in the inner ear—by preventing it from sensing differences in direction. After a few days in space, the vestibular system disregards all directional signals. Soon after an astronaut returns to Earth, the organs of balance resume normal operation.

Over a period of days or weeks, an astronaut's body experiences *deconditioning*. In this process, muscles grow weak from lack of use, and the heart and blood vessels "get lazy." Strenuous exercise helps prevent deconditioning. Space travelers ride exercise bikes, use treadmills, and perform other types of physical activity.

After many months in space, a process called *demineralization* weakens the bones. Most physicians believe that demineralization results from the absence of stress on the bones in a weightless environment. The experiences of Soviet cosmonauts who spent long periods in orbit showed that vigorous exercise and a special diet can minimize demineralization.

Meeting Basic Needs in Space

Piloted space vehicles have life-support systems designed to meet all the physical needs of the crew members. In addition, astronauts can carry portable life-support systems in backpacks when they work outside the main spacecraft.

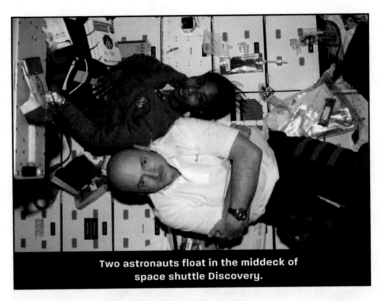

Two astronauts float in the middeck of space shuttle Discovery.

Breathing. A piloted spacecraft must have a source of oxygen for the crew to breathe and a means of removing carbon dioxide, which the crew exhales. Piloted space vehicles use a mixture of oxygen and nitrogen similar to Earth's atmosphere at sea level. Fans circulate air through the cabin and over containers filled with pellets of a chemical called lithium hydroxide. These pellets absorb carbon dioxide from the air. Carbon dioxide can also be combined with other chemicals for disposal. Charcoal filters help control odors.

Eating and drinking. The food on a spacecraft must be nutritious, easy to prepare, and convenient to store. On early missions, astronauts ate *freeze-dried foods*—that is, frozen foods with the water removed. To eat, the astronauts simply mixed water into the food. Packaging consisted of plastic tubes. The astronauts used straws to add the water.

Over the years, the food available to space travelers became more appetizing. Today, astronauts enjoy ready-to-eat meals much like convenience foods on Earth. Many space vehicles have facilities for heating frozen and chilled food.

Water for drinking is an important requirement for a space mission. On space shuttles, devices called *fuel cells* produce pure water as they generate electricity for the spacecraft. On long missions, water must be recycled and reused as much as possible. Dehumidifiers remove moisture from exhaled air. On space stations, this water is usually reused for washing.

Eliminating body wastes. The collection and disposal of body wastes in microgravity poses a major challenge. Astronauts use a device that resembles a toilet seat. Air flow produces suction that moves the wastes into collection equipment under the seat. On small spacecraft, crew members use funnels for urine and plastic bags for solid wastes. While working outside the spacecraft, astronauts wear special equipment to contain body wastes.

Bathing. The simplest bathing method aboard a spacecraft is a sponge bath with wet towels. Astronauts on early space stations used a fully enclosed, collapsible plastic shower stall. This allowed the astronauts to spray their bodies with water, then vacuum the stall and towel themselves dry. Newer space stations have permanent shower stalls.

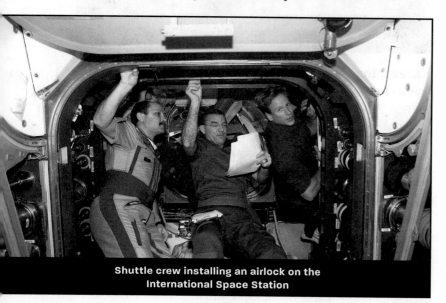

**Shuttle crew installing an airlock on the
International Space Station**

Sleeping. Space travelers can sleep in special sleeping bags with straps that press them to the soft surface and to a pillow. However, most astronauts prefer to sleep floating in the air, with only a few straps to keep them from bouncing around the cabin. Astronauts may wear blindfolds to block the sunlight that streams in the windows periodically during orbit. Typically, sleep duration in space is about the same as that on Earth.

Recreation on long space flights is important to the mental health of the astronauts. Sightseeing out the spacecraft window is a favorite pastime. Space stations have small collections of books, tapes, and electronic games. Exercise also provides relaxation.

Controlling inventory and trash. Keeping track of the thousands of items used during a mission poses a major challenge in space.

Drawers and lockers hold some materials. Other equipment is strapped to the walls, ceilings, and floors. Computer-generated lists keep track of what is stored where, and computerized systems check the storage and replacement of materials. The crew aboard the spacecraft may stow trash in unused sections of the vehicle, throw it overboard to burn up harmlessly in the atmosphere, or bring it back to Earth for disposal.

Communicating with Earth

Communication between astronauts in space and *mission control*, the facility on Earth that supervises their space flight, occurs in many ways. The astronauts and mission controllers can talk to each other by radio. Television pictures can travel between space vehicles and Earth. Computers, sensors, and other equipment continuously send signals to Earth for monitoring. Facsimile machines on spacecraft also can receive information from Earth.

Working in Space

Once a space vehicle reaches its orbit, the crew members begin to carry out the goals of their mission. They perform a variety of tasks both inside and outside the spacecraft.

Navigation, guidance, and control. Astronauts use computerized navigation systems and make sightings on stars to determine their position and direction. On Earth, sophisticated tracking systems measure the spacecraft's location in relation to Earth. Astronauts typically use small firings of the spacecraft's rockets to tilt the vehicle or to push it in the desired direction. Computers monitor these changes to ensure they are done accurately.

Activating equipment. Much of the equipment on a space vehicle is turned off or tied down during launch. Once in space, the astronauts must set up and turn on the equipment. At the end of the mission, they must secure it for landing.

Conducting scientific observations and research. Astronauts use special instruments to observe Earth, the stars, and the sun. They also experiment with the effects of microgravity on various materials, plants, animals, and themselves.

Docking. As a spacecraft approaches a target, such as a space station or an artificial satellite, radar helps the crew members control the craft's course and speed. Once the spacecraft reaches the correct position beside the target, it *docks* (joins) with the target by connecting special equipment. Such a meeting in space is called a *rendezvous*. A space shuttle used its robot arm to make contact with targets.

Maintaining and repairing equipment. The thousands of pieces of equipment on a modern space vehicle are extremely reliable, but some of them still break down. Accidents damage some equipment. Other units must be replaced when they get old. Astronauts must find out what has gone wrong, locate the failed unit, and repair or replace it.

Assembling space stations. Astronauts may serve as construction workers in space, assembling a space station from components carried up in spacecraft. On existing space stations, crews often must add new sections or set up new antennas and solar panels. Power and air connectors must be hooked up inside and outside the station.

Leaving the spacecraft. At times, astronauts must go outside the spacecraft to perform certain tasks. Working outside a vehicle in space is called *extravehicular activity* (*EVA*). To prepare for EVA, astronauts put on their space suits and move to a special two-doored chamber called an *air lock*. They then release the air from the air lock, open the outer hatch, and leave the spacecraft. When they return, they close the outer door and let air into the air lock. Then they open the inner door into the rest of the spacecraft, where they remove their space suits.

A space suit can keep an astronaut alive for six to eight hours. The suit is made from many layers of flexible, airtight materials, such as nylon and Teflon. It provides protection against heat, cold, and space particles. Tight mechanical seals connect the pieces of the space suit. Equipment in a backpack provides oxygen and removes carbon dioxide and moisture. A radio enables the astronaut to communicate with other crew members and with Earth. The helmet must allow good visibility while at the same time blocking harmful solar radiation. Gloves are a crucial part of the space suit. They must be thin and flexible enough for the astronaut to feel small objects and to handle tools.

The Dawn of the Space Age

As people began to dream of flying above Earth's surface, they realized that objects in the sky could become destinations for human travelers. In the early 1600s, the German astronomer and mathe-

Astronaut outside the shuttle Discovery

matician Johannes Kepler became the first scientist to describe travel to other worlds. He also developed the laws of planetary motion that explain the orbits of bodies in space.

The English scientist Sir Isaac Newton first described the *laws of motion* in a work published in 1687. These laws enabled scientists to predict the kinds of flight paths needed to orbit Earth and to reach other worlds. Newton also described how an artificial satellite could remain in orbit. His third law, which states that for every action there is an equal and opposite reaction, explains why a rocket works.

Early dreams of space flight. During the 1700s, scientists realized that air got thinner at higher altitudes. This meant that air probably was entirely absent between Earth and other worlds, so wings would be useless. Many imaginative writers proposed fanciful techniques for travel to these worlds.

In 1903, Konstantin E. Tsiolkovsky, a Russian high school teacher, completed the first scientific paper on the use of rockets for space travel. Several years later, Robert H. Goddard of the United States and Hermann Oberth of Germany awakened wider scientific interest in space travel. Working independently, these three men addressed many of the technical problems of rocketry and space travel. Together, they are known as the fathers of space flight.

In 1919, Goddard explained how rockets could be used to explore the upper atmosphere in his paper "A Method of Reaching Extreme Altitudes." The paper also described a way of firing a rocket to the moon. In a book called *The Rocket into*

Robert H. Goddard beside the launching platform just before
the first successful launch of a liquid-fueled rocket

Interplanetary Space (1923), Oberth discussed many technical problems of space flight. He even described what a spaceship would be like. Tsiolkovsky wrote a series of new studies in the 1920s. These works included detailed descriptions of multistage rockets.

The first space rockets. During the 1930s, rocket research went forward in the United States, Germany, and the Soviet Union. Goddard's team had built the world's first liquid-propellant rocket in 1926, despite a lack of support from the U.S. government. German and Soviet rocket scientists received funding from their governments to develop military missiles.

In 1942, during World War II, German rocket experts under the direction of Wernher von Braun developed the V-2 guided missile. Thousands of V-2s were fired against European cities, especially London, causing widespread destruction and loss of life.

After World War II ended in 1945, many German rocket engineers went to work for the U.S. government to help develop military missiles. The U.S. Navy worked on larger rockets, such as the

Aerobee and the Viking. In 1949, the rocket team built and tested the world's first two-stage rocket, with a V-2 missile as a first stage and a small WAC Corporal rocket as a second stage. This rocket reached an altitude of 250 miles (400 kilometers).

By 1947, the Soviet Union had secretly begun a massive program to develop long-range military missiles. In the 1940s, the small but influential British Interplanetary Society published accurate plans for piloted lunar landing vehicles, space suits, and orbital rendezvous. A U.S. group, the American Rocket Society, concentrated on missile engineering. In 1950, a new International Astronautical Federation began to hold annual conferences.

The first artificial satellites. In 1955, both the United States and the Soviet Union announced plans to launch artificial satellites with scientific instruments on board. The satellites were to be sent into orbit as part of the International Geophysical Year, a period of international cooperation in scientific research beginning in July 1957. The Soviets provided detailed descriptions of the radio equipment to be included on their satellite. But the Soviet rocket program had been kept secret until that time. As a result, many people in other countries did not believe that the Soviets had the advanced technology required for space exploration.

Then, on October 4, 1957, the Soviets stunned the world by succeeding in their promise—and by doing so ahead of the United States. Only six weeks earlier, the Soviet two-stage R-7 missile had made its first 5,000-mile (8,000-kilometer) flight. This time, it carried Sputnik (later referred to as Sputnik 1), the first artificial satellite. *Sputnik* means *traveling companion* in Russian. The R-7 booster hurled the 184-pound (83-kilogram) satellite and its main rocket stage into orbit around Earth. Radio listeners worldwide picked up Sputnik's characteristic "beep-beep" signal.

The space race begins. The Western world reacted to the launch of Sputnik with surprise, fear, and respect. Soviet premier Nikita S. Khrushchev ordered massive funding of follow-up projects that would continue to amaze and dazzle the world. In the United States, leaders vowed to do whatever was needed to catch up. Thus the "space race" began.

More Soviet successes followed. A month after Sputnik, another satellite, Sputnik 2, carried a dog named Laika into space. The flight proved that animals could survive the unknown effects of microgravity. In 1959, Luna 2 became the first probe to hit the moon. Later that year, Luna 3 photographed the far side of the moon, which cannot be seen from Earth.

The first United States satellite was Explorer 1, launched on January 31, 1958. This satellite was followed by Vanguard 1, which was launched on March 17, 1958. These and later U.S. satellites were much smaller than their Soviet counterparts because the rockets the United States used to carry satellites were smaller and less powerful than those used by the Soviet Union. The Soviet Union's rockets gave it an early lead in the space race. Because bigger rockets would be needed for piloted lunar flight, both the United States and the Soviet Union began major programs of rocket design, construction, and testing.

Organizing and managing space activities. A key to the ultimate success of U.S. space programs was centralized planning. In 1958, a civilian space agency called the National Aeronautics and Space Administration (NASA) was established. NASA absorbed various aviation researchers and military space laboratories. The formation of NASA helped forge agreement among competing interests, including military branches, universities, the aerospace industry, and politicians.

Soviet space activities, on the other hand, were coordinated by special executive commissions. These commissions tried to tie together various space units from military and industrial groups, as well as competing experts and scientists. But the commissions did not coordinate Soviet activities effectively enough to meet the complex challenges of the space race.

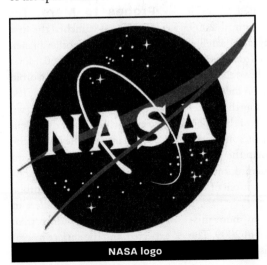

NASA logo

Space Probes

A *space probe* is an unpiloted device sent to explore space. A probe may operate far out in space, or it may orbit or land on a planet or a moon. It may make a one-way journey, or it may bring samples and data back to Earth. Most probes transmit data from space by radio in a process called *telemetry*.

Lunar and planetary probes that land on their targets may be classified according to their landing method. *Impact vehicles* make no attempt to slow down as they approach the target. *Hard-landers* have cushioned instrument packages that can survive the impact of a hard landing. *Soft-landers* touch down gently. *Penetrators* ram deeply into the surface of a target.

How a space probe carries out its mission. Probes explore space in a number of ways. A probe makes observations of temperature, radiation, and objects in space. A probe also observes nearby objects. In addition, a space probe exposes material from Earth to the conditions of space so that scientists can observe the effects. A probe may also perform experiments on its surroundings, such as releasing chemicals or digging into surface dirt. Finally, a probe's motion enables controllers on Earth to determine conditions in space. Changes in course and speed can provide information about atmospheric density and gravity fields.

Early unpiloted explorations. Beginning in the 1940s, devices called *sounding rockets* carried scientific instruments into the upper atmosphere and into nearby space. They discovered many new phenomena and took the first photographs of Earth from space.

The 1957 launch of Sputnik 1 marked the beginning of the space age. Sputnik 1 carried only a few instruments and transmitters, but it paved the way for the sophisticated probes that would later explore space.

Many early satellites probed uncharted regions of space. During the late 1950s and the 1960s, the Explorer satellites of the United States and the Kosmos satellites of the Soviet Union analyzed the space environment between Earth and the moon. United States Pegasus satellites recorded the impacts of micrometeorites. During the early 1970s, Soviet Prognoz satellites studied the sun.

Lunar probes. In 1958, both the United States and the Soviet Union began to launch probes toward the moon. The first probe to come close to the moon was Luna 1, launched by the

Soviet Union on January 2, 1959. It passed within about 3,700 miles (6,000 kilometers) of the moon and went into orbit around the sun. The United States conducted its own lunar flyby two months later with the probe Pioneer 4. The Soviet Luna 2 probe, launched on September 12, 1959, was the first probe to hit the moon. One month later, Luna 3 circled behind the moon and photographed its hidden far side.

The Soviet Union began to test lunar hard-landers in 1963. After many failures, they succeeded with Luna 9, launched in January 1966. The U.S. Surveyor program made a series of successful soft landings beginning in 1966. Between 1970 and 1972, three Soviet probes returned lunar soil samples to Earth in small capsules. Two of them sent remote-controlled jeeps called *Lunokhods*, which traveled across the lunar surface.

Beginning in 1966, the United States sent five probes called Lunar Orbiters into orbit to photograph the moon's surface. The Lunar Orbiters revealed the existence of irregular "bumps" of gravity in the moon's gravita-

tional field caused by dense material buried beneath the lunar seas. These areas of tightly packed matter were called *mascons*, which stood for *mass concentrations*. If the mascons had not been discovered, they might have interfered with the Apollo missions that sent astronauts to the moon.

From 1976 until 1994, no missions went to the moon. In January 1994, the U.S. orbiter Clementine launched. During its short four-month mission, Clementine observed what appeared to be water ice near the moon's south pole. In the succeeding years, additional missions surveyed the moon. The U.S. probe Lunar Prospector circled the moon from 1998 to 1999 and also found indications of water ice at both poles.

Beginning in 2004, several countries launched their first missions to the moon. The European Space Agency (ESA) launched the SMART-1 spacecraft that orbited the moon from 2004 to 2006. The Japanese spacecraft SELENE remained in lunar orbit from 2007 to 2009. In late 2007, China launched the Chang'e1 spacecraft that remained in orbit around the moon until 2009. India's Chandrayaan-1 satellite orbited the moon from 2008 to 2009. The satellite released a probe that landed on the surface, making India the fourth country to reach the surface of the moon. All of these missions used instruments to map the surface in detail and gather information about the composition of the lunar surface.

NASA sent two more missions to the moon in 2009. The Lunar Reconnaissance Orbiter

(LRO) and the Lunar Crater Observation and Sensing Satellite (LCROSS) were launched on the same rocket but carried out separate missions. LRO entered lunar orbit in June 2009 to map the moon's surface and environment in detail. The LCROSS mission used a section of the launch rocket to crash into the lunar surface near the south pole. The probe then flew through the debris kicked up by the impact. Its sensors confirmed the presence of water ice in the debris cloud in November.

Solar probes. Beginning in 1965, the United States launched a series of small Pioneer probes into orbit around the sun to study solar radiation. Many of these probes were still operating more than 20 years after launch.

In 1974 and 1976, the United States launched two German-built Helios probes. These probes passed inside the orbit of Mercury to measure solar radiation. The Ulysses probe was launched in 1990 by the United States and the ESA. In 1994, Ulysses became the first probe to observe the sun from an orbit over the sun's poles.

Probes to Mars. The Soviet Union launched the first probes aimed at another planet, two Mars probes, in 1960. However, neither probe reached orbit. After more Soviet failures, the United States launched two Mariner probes toward Mars in 1964. Mariner 4 flew past the planet on July 14, 1965, and sent back remarkable photographs and measurements. The probe showed that the atmosphere of Mars was much thinner than expected, and the surface resembled that of the moon.

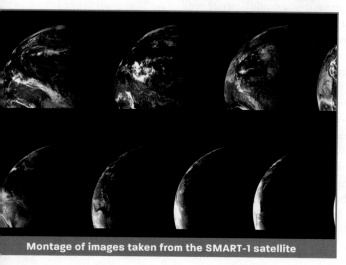

Montage of images taken from the SMART-1 satellite

In 1971, the Soviet probe Mars 3 dropped a capsule that made the first soft landing on Mars. However, the capsule failed to return usable data. That same year, the U.S. probe Mariner 9 reached Mars and photographed most of the planet's surface. Mariner 9 also passed near and photographed Mars's two small moons, Phobos and Deimos.

Two U.S. probes, Viking 1 and Viking 2, landed in 1976 and operated for years, measuring surface weather and conducting complex experiments to detect life forms. The probes found no evidence of life.

In 1992, the United States launched the probe Mars Observer. In 1993, NASA lost contact with the probe three days before it would have orbited Mars. Contact was never restored, and the probe was presumed lost.

The United States launched the Pathfinder probe in December 1996. The probe landed on Mars on July 4, 1997. Two days later, a six-wheeled vehicle called Sojourner rolled down a ramp from the probe to the Martian surface. The vehicle was only 24.5 inches long, 18.7 inches wide, and 10.9 inches high (63 by 48 by 28 centimeters). Its mass was 11.5 kilograms, equivalent to a weight of 25.4 pounds on Earth.

The vehicle used a device called an alpha proton X-ray spectrometer to gather data on the chemical makeup of rocks and soil. Sojourner transmitted this information to Pathfinder, and the probe relayed the information to Earth.

Scientists on Earth controlled Sojourner. However, because radio signals take about 10 minutes to travel from Earth to Mars, the scientists could not control Sojourner in *real time*—that is, as the vehicle moved. To avoid obstacles, Sojourner used a number of automatic devices.

In 1996, the United States launched a probe called the Mars Global Surveyor to map the planet's surface. The probe used a laser device to determine the elevation of the Martian surface. That instrument produced maps of the entire surface that are accurate to within 3 feet (1 meter) of elevation. Another instrument determined the composition of some of the minerals on the surface. A camera revealed layered sediments that may have been deposited in liquid water, and small gullies that appear to have been carved by water.

In 2001, the United States launched the Mars Odyssey probe to Mars. The craft carried instruments to help identify minerals on the surface, to

search for evidence of water and ice beneath the surface, and to measure radiation that might harm any future human explorers. In 2002, Mars Odyssey discovered vast quantities of ice within 3 feet (1 meter) of the surface, most of it near the south pole.

In 2003, three probes were launched to Mars, one by the ESA and two by the United States. The ESA's Mars Express probe went into orbit around the planet in December 2003. It transmitted stunning pictures of the planet's surface, confirmed the presence of water ice in the planet's southern region, and detected methane in the Martian atmosphere, a possible indicator of life. Mars Express carried a lander called Beagle 2 that failed to land safely and was lost.

The United States launched rovers nicknamed Spirit and Opportunity. In January 2004, Spirit landed in Gusev Crater, and Opportunity landed in an area called Meridiani Planum. The rovers used cameras and other instruments to analyze soil and rocks. In March 2004, U.S. scientists concluded that Meridiani Planum once held large amounts of liquid water. Opportunity's analysis had shown that the rock there contained minerals and structures normally found in Earth rocks that formed in water.

In August 2005, the United States launched the Mars Reconnaissance Orbiter, which arrived in orbit around Mars in March 2006. The craft was designed to study the planet's structure and atmosphere and to identify potential landing sites for future lander and rover missions.

The U.S. Phoenix Mars lander, launched in August 2007, operated in the north polar region from May to November 2008. The lander revealed the presence of various minerals in the soil. However, chief among its contributions was the confirmation of water ice just below the surface of the Martian soil.

Probes to Venus and Mercury. The Soviet Union launched the first probes toward Venus in 1961, but these attempts failed. The first successful probe to fly past Venus and return data was the U.S. Mariner 2, on December 14, 1962. Mariner 5 flew past Venus in 1967 and returned important data. Mariner 10 passed Venus and then made three passes near Mercury in 1974 and 1975.

Soviet attempts to obtain data from Venus finally succeeded in 1967. Venera 4 dropped a probe by parachute, and it transmitted data from the planet's extremely dense atmosphere. In 1970,

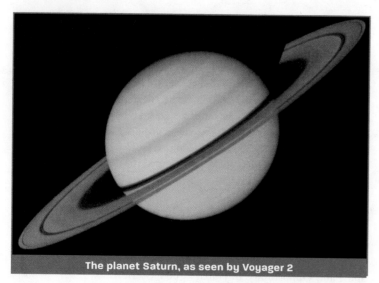

The planet Saturn, as seen by Voyager 2

Venera 7 reached the surface of the planet, still functioning. Between 1975 and 1985, several other probes landed and conducted observations for up to 110 minutes before the temperature and pressure destroyed them. In 1978, the United States sent two probes to Venus, Pioneer Venus 1 and 2. Pioneer Venus 1 was an orbiter. Pioneer Venus 2 dropped four probes into the planet's atmosphere.

Probes that orbited Venus generated rough maps of its surface by bouncing radio waves off the ground. Pioneer Venus 1 mapped most of the surface to a *resolution* of about 50 miles (80 kilometers). This means that objects at least 50 miles apart showed distinctly on the map. In 1983, two Soviet probes carried radar systems that mapped most of the planet's northern hemisphere to a resolution of 0.9 mile (1.5 kilometers). In 1990, the U.S. probe Magellan mapped almost the entire surface to a resolution of about 330 feet (100 meters).

In 2004, the United States launched the Messenger probe to Mercury. Messenger entered orbit around Mercury in 2011 after flying by Venus twice and by Mercury three times. The probe was designed to orbit Mercury for one Earth year while mapping Mercury's surface and studying its composition, interior structure, and magnetic field. In late 2011, NASA approved an additional year of operation for the Messenger mission.

The ESA Venus Express probe, launched in 2005, went into orbit around Venus in 2006. The probe carried instruments used to study Venus's atmosphere in detail. On June 5, 2007, the Messenger probe flew past Venus on its way to Mercury. During this flyby, the Messenger probe and the Venus Express probe worked together to detail Venus's surface.

Probes to Jupiter and beyond must meet special challenges. Radiation belts near Jupiter are so intense that camera lenses and computer circuits must be shielded to prevent damage. The dim sunlight at the outer planets requires lengthy camera exposures. And the vast distances mean that radio commands take hours to reach the probes. Probes have visited Jupiter, Saturn, Uranus, and Neptune.

U.S. probes Pioneer 10 and Pioneer 11 were sent to Jupiter in 1972 and 1973. After observing Jupiter, Pioneer 11 was redirected toward Saturn, arriving there in 1979. It was renamed Pioneer-Saturn. From 1979 to 1981, sophisticated Voyager probes provided much more detailed data on Jupiter and Saturn. They still explore space. Voyager 2 flew past Uranus in January 1986 and Neptune in August 1989. The probes sent back spectacular photos of the outer planets and their rings and moons, and recorded a great deal of scientific data. Active volcanoes were found on Io, a moon of Jupiter, and geysers were discovered on Triton, a moon of Neptune. Other moons exhibited bizarre ice and rock formations.

The Galileo space probe, launched on a mission to Jupiter by the United States in 1989, was far more sophisticated than earlier planetary probes. It consisted of two parts—an atmosphere probe and a larger orbiting spacecraft. On the way to Jupiter, Galileo flew past the asteroids Gaspra and Ida. In July 1995, the atmosphere probe separated from the spacecraft. Both parts reached Jupiter five months later. As planned, the probe plunged into Jupiter's atmosphere. The spacecraft orbited Jupiter until 2003, studying the planet, its satellites, and its rings.

In 1997, the United States launched the Cassini probe to investigate Saturn, its rings, and satellites. Cassini began orbiting Saturn in 2004. It then released an ESA probe called Huygens that landed on Saturn's moon Titan in 2005.

In 2006, U.S. scientists launched the New Horizons probe to make the first close observations of Pluto. The probe was expected to fly by Pluto in 2015.

Probes to comets. Two Soviet probes flew past Venus and dropped instruments into its atmosphere, then intercepted Halley's Comet as it passed by the sun in 1986. In 1985, the ESA launched its first interplanetary probe, called Giotto. It passed closer to the comet's nucleus than any other probe and returned dramatic close-up images. Japan also sent two small probes. After several years of inactivity, Giotto was reactivated to fly past the comet Grigg-Skjellerup in July 1992.

The United States did not send a probe to Halley's Comet due to budget limitations. But NASA scientists used a small probe already in space to explore another comet. The International Sun-Earth Explorer 3 satellite had spent several years between Earth and the sun. In 1983, its course was shifted into interplanetary space, and it was renamed the International Cometary Explorer. On September 11, 1985, it passed a comet named Giacobini-Zinner, becoming the first probe to reach a comet.

In 1999, NASA launched a probe called Stardust to visit Comet Wild 2. In 2004, Stardust passed near the comet and gathered samples from the cloud of dust and gas surrounding the comet's nucleus. Stardust returned the samples to Earth in 2006. Also in 2004, the European Space Agency launched the Rosetta spacecraft, which was to go into orbit around Comet Churyumov-Gerasimenko in 2014. Rosetta carried a small probe designed to land on the comet's nucleus.

In 2005, the United States launched the Deep Impact spacecraft to Comet Tempel 1. The craft consisted of two smaller probes: an *impactor* and a *flyby craft*. The impactor intentionally slammed into the comet's nucleus, while the flyby craft recorded the crash. Analyzing the debris ejected by the collision enabled scientists to study the comet's composition.

Probes to asteroids. NASA launched the Near Earth Asteroid Rendezvous (NEAR) probe in 1996. In 1997, the probe flew within 753

miles (1,216 kilometers) of the asteroid Mathilde. NEAR flew past the asteroid Eros at a distance of 2,378 miles (3,829 kilometers) in 1998. It went into orbit around Eros in 2000. The probe, renamed NEAR-Shoemaker in honor of the American astronomer Eugene Shoemaker, landed on Eros in 2001.

In October 1998, NASA launched a probe called Deep Space 1 (DS1). The probe flew within only about 16 miles (26 kilometers) of the asteroid Braille in July 1999.

The flight of DS1 successfully tested several new types of equipment for space probes. This equipment included a navigation system that operates automatically, rather than under the direction of people and computers on Earth. Also included was an ion rocket, which operates by shooting electrically charged particles called ions out its nozzle.

In 2005, Japan's Hayabusa probe visited the asteroid Itokawa. Despite the failure of several of its systems, the craft managed to transmit detailed pictures of the asteroid and to land briefly on its surface.

Human Beings Enter Space

In 1958, scientists in the United States and the Soviet Union began serious efforts to design a spacecraft that could carry human beings. Both nations chose to develop a wingless capsule atop a launch vehicle that would consist of a modified long-range missile.

The prospect of human beings traveling in space greatly worried scientists. Tests with animals had shown that space travel probably involved no physical danger, but there were serious concerns about possible psychological hazards. Some experts feared that the stresses of launch, flight, and landing might drive a space traveler to terror or unconsciousness.

Vostok and Mercury: The First Human Beings in Space

The Soviet Union's Vostok (East) program and the Mercury program of the United States represented the first efforts to send a human being into space. The Vostok capsule weighed about 10,000 pounds (4,500 kilograms). It was to be carried into orbit atop a modified R-7 missile. The capsule consisted of a spherical pilot's cabin and a cylindrical *service module*, the section containing the propulsion system. An ejection seat was designed to provide an escape for the astronaut in case of a mishap

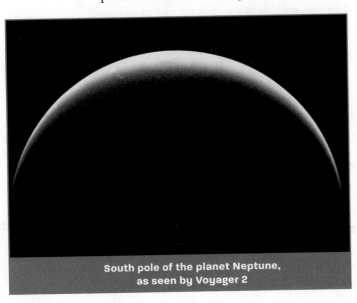

South pole of the planet Neptune, as seen by Voyager 2

during launch. The life-support system used a mixture of oxygen and nitrogen similar to the atmosphere at sea level.

The U.S. Mercury capsule weighed about 3,000 pounds (1,360 kilograms) and was to be carried into space atop a Redstone or Atlas rocket. The cone-shaped capsule would use parachutes to land in the ocean, where the water would provide extra cushioning. The life-support system used pure oxygen at low pressure. In the event of a booster malfunction during launch, the capsule and pilot would be pulled free by a solid-fuel rocket attached to the nose of the capsule.

While U.S. plans proceeded in the glare of publicity, Soviet developments took place in great secrecy. Both nations made unpiloted orbital tests in 1960 and 1961, some of which suffered booster failures. Both nations also sent animals into space during this period. One of these animals was a chimpanzee named Ham, who made an 18-minute flight in a Mercury capsule on January 31, 1961.

The first fatality in a piloted space program occurred on March 23, 1961. A Soviet cosmonaut trainee named Valentin V. Bondarenko burned to death in a pressure chamber fire. Soviet officials covered up the accident.

The first human being in space was a Soviet air force pilot named Yuri A. Gagarin. He was launched aboard Vostok (later referred to as Vostok

Yuri Gagarin

1) on April 12, 1961. In 108 minutes, Gagarin orbited Earth once and returned safely. An automatic flight control system managed the spacecraft's operations during the entire flight. A 25-hour, 17-orbit flight by cosmonaut Gherman Titov aboard Vostok 2 followed in August of that year.

The Mercury program made its first piloted flight on May 5, 1961, when a Redstone rocket launched astronaut Alan B. Shepard, Jr., in a capsule he named Freedom 7. Shepard flew a 15-minute *suborbital mission*—that is, a mission that did not reach the speed and altitude required to orbit Earth.

A suborbital flight on July 21, 1961, by astronaut Virgil I. Grissom almost ended tragically. The Mercury capsule's side hatch opened too soon after splashdown in the Atlantic Ocean, and the spacecraft rapidly filled with water. Grissom managed to swim to safety.

On February 20, 1962, John H. Glenn, Jr., became the first American to orbit Earth. Glenn completed three orbits in less than five hours. He pointed his capsule in different directions, tested its various systems, and observed Earth.

Three months later, astronaut M. Scott Carpenter repeated Glenn's three-orbit mission. A six-orbit mission by Walter M. Schirra, Jr., in October 1962 further extended the testing of the spacecraft. The final Mercury mission took place in May 1963, with Gordon Cooper aboard. The mission lasted 1½ days.

Meanwhile, the Soviet Union continued to launch Vostok missions. In August 1962, Vostok 3 and Vostok 4 lifted off just a day apart and passed near each other in space. Another two capsules—Vostok 5 and Vostok 6—were launched in June 1963. One of the pilots spent almost five days in orbit, a new record. The other pilot, Valentina Tereshkova, became the first woman in space.

Voskhod and Gemini: The First Multiperson Space Flights

In 1961, the United States announced the Gemini program, which would send two astronauts into space in an enlarged version of the Mercury capsule. This announcement spurred Soviet planners to modify their Vostok capsule to carry up to three cosmonauts. Political pressure to upstage U.S. efforts was so intense that Soviet engineers sacrificed certain safety features, such as ejection seats, to enlarge the capsule.

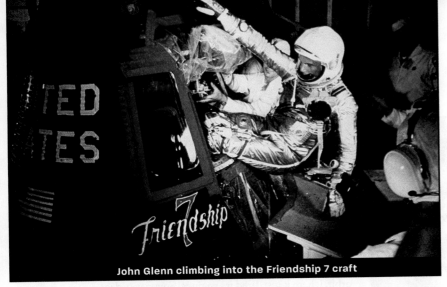

John Glenn climbing into the Friendship 7 craft

The world's first multiperson space capsule, Voskhod (Sunrise)—later referred to as Voskhod 1—was launched on October 12, 1964. Cosmonauts Vladimir M. Komarov, Konstantin P. Feoktistov, and Boris B. Yegorov spent 24 hours in orbit. They became the first space travelers to land inside their capsule on the ground, rather than in the ocean.

In March 1965, cosmonaut Alexei A. Leonov stepped through an inflatable air lock attached to Voskhod 2 to become the first person to walk in space. After the capsule's automatic flight control system failed, Leonov and Pavel I. Belyayev had to land it manually. They missed their planned landing zone and came down in an isolated forest. The cosmonauts had to fend off hungry wolves until rescuers reached them the following day.

The first piloted Gemini mission, Gemini 3, was launched on March 23, 1965. Astronauts Grissom and John W. Young used the capsule's maneuvering rockets to alter its path through space. With Gemini 4, launched on June 3, 1965, copilot Edward H. White II became the first American to walk in space. The astronauts aboard Gemini 5, launched on August 21, 1965, spent almost eight days in space, a record achieved by using fuel cells to generate electricity.

Gemini 6 was originally intended to link up with an Agena rocket sent into space a few hours earlier. After the unpiloted Agena was lost in a booster failure, NASA combined Gemini 6 with an already scheduled 14-day Gemini 7 mission. Gemini 7 was launched as planned, on December 4, 1965, and Gemini 6 took off 11 days later. Within hours, Schirra and Thomas P. Stafford moved their spacecraft to within 1 foot (30 centimeters) of Gemini 7 and its crew, Frank Borman and James A. Lovell, Jr. The two spacecraft orbited Earth together for several hours before separating.

On March 16, 1966, Gemini 8 completed the world's first docking of two space vehicles when it linked up with an Agena rocket in space. However, the spacecraft went into a violent tumble. Astronauts Neil A. Armstrong and David R. Scott managed to regain control of the spacecraft and make an emergency splashdown in the western Pacific Ocean.

Additional tests of docking and extravehicular activity took place on the remaining four Gemini missions. On these missions, astronauts and flight controllers also gained vital experience in preparation for the tremendous challenges of piloted lunar flight.

Apollo: Mission to the Moon

The race to the moon dominated the space race of the 1960s. In a 1961 address to Congress, President John F. Kennedy called for the United States to commit itself to "landing a man on the moon and returning him safely to Earth" before the 1960s ended. This goal was intended to show the superiority of U.S. science, engineering, management, and political leadership.

NASA considered several proposals for a piloted lunar mission. The agency selected a plan known as *lunar-orbit rendezvous*. A spacecraft would carry three astronauts to an orbit around the moon. Two of the astronauts would then descend to the lunar surface.

The spacecraft would consist of three parts, or modules—a *command module* (CM), a *service module* (SM), and a *lunar module* (LM), which was originally called the *lunar excursion module* (LEM). The cone-shaped CM would be the spacecraft's main control center. The SM would contain fuel, oxygen, water, and the spacecraft's electric power system and propulsion system. The CM and SM would be joined for almost the entire mission as the *command/service module* (CSM).

Only the LM would land on the moon. This module would consist of two sections—a *descent stage* and an *ascent stage*. The two stages would descend to the lunar surface as a single unit, but only the ascent stage would leave the moon.

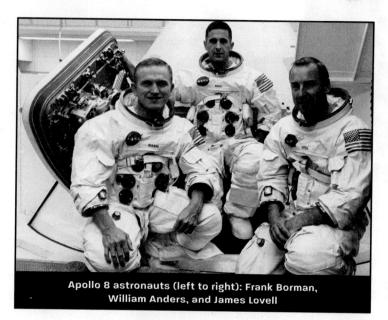

Apollo 8 astronauts (left to right): Frank Borman,
William Anders, and James Lovell

A Saturn 5 booster would launch the spacecraft toward the moon. As the craft approached the moon, rockets on the SM would adjust its course so that it would go into a lunar orbit. With the craft in orbit, the LM would separate from the CSM and carry the two astronauts to the surface. After the astronauts completed their activities on the moon, the LM's ascent stage would blast off from the descent stage and rendezvous with the CSM.

After the returning astronauts entered the command module, the CSM would cast off the LM's ascent stage. The CSM would then return to Earth. As the craft approached Earth, the CM would separate from the SM and would splash down in the ocean.

Lunar-orbit rendezvous would be complex but relatively economical. The mission would save a tremendous amount of fuel by landing only the small LM on the moon and then launching only its ascent stage.

Making ready. Tragedy struck during preparations for the first piloted Apollo flight, a trial run in low earth orbit. During a ground test on January 27, 1967, a flash fire inside the sealed CM killed astronauts Grissom, White, and Roger B. Chaffee. An electrical short circuit probably started the fire, and the pure oxygen atmosphere caused it to burn fiercely.

A few months later, the Soviet space program also suffered a disaster. The Soyuz (Union) 1 capsule was launched with Vladimir Komarov aboard as pilot. It was supposed to link up with a second piloted spaceship, but Soyuz 1 developed problems and the second ship was never launched. Controllers ordered Soyuz 1 to return to Earth. But a parachute failure caused the capsule to crash, killing Komarov.

While the Apollo CSM and the Soyuz capsule were being redesigned, unpiloted tests took place as planned. The United States launched the first Saturn 5 booster on November 9, 1967, with complete success. Early in 1968, an LM was sent into orbit, where it test-fired its engines. Soyuz vehicles linked up automatically in orbit in 1967 and 1968.

Orbiting the moon. By late 1968, the United States had redesigned the Apollo CSM. However, the lunar module remained far behind schedule.

NASA officials knew about Soviet preparations for a piloted lunar flyby. To beat the Soviets, NASA decided to fly a piloted mission to orbit the moon, without an LM. The orbital mission would also test navigation and communication around the moon.

Apollo 8, the first piloted expedition to the moon, blasted off from the Kennedy Space Center near Cape Canaveral, Florida, on December 21, 1968. Hundreds of thousands of people crowded nearby beaches to watch the launch. The spacecraft carried astronauts Borman, Lovell, and William A. Anders. After three days, the crew fired the SM engine to change course into a lunar orbit. They made observations and took photographs, then headed back to Earth. Apollo 8 landed safely in the Pacific Ocean near Hawaii on December 27.

Two additional test flights were made to ensure the safety and effectiveness of the lunar module.

Earth as seen from Apollo 11

The LM was tested in low orbit around Earth by the Apollo 9 astronauts and in lunar orbit by the Apollo 10 crew.

Landing on the moon. Apollo 11 was the first mission to land astronauts on the moon. It blasted off on July 16, 1969, carrying three astronauts—Neil A. Armstrong, Edwin "Buzz" Aldrin, and Michael Collins.

The first two stages of a Saturn 5 rocket carried the spacecraft to an altitude of 115 miles (185 kilometers) and a speed of 15,400 miles (24,800 kilometers) per hour, just short of orbital velocity. The third stage fired briefly to accelerate the vehicle to the required speed. It then shut down while the vehicle coasted in orbit. The astronauts checked the spacecraft and lined up the flight path for the trip to the moon. The third stage was then restarted, increasing the speed to an escape velocity of 24,300 miles (39,100 kilometers) per hour. On the way to the moon, the crew pulled the CSM away from the Saturn rocket. They turned the CSM around and docked it to the LM, which was still attached to the Saturn. The linked vehicles then pulled free of the Saturn.

For three days, Apollo 11 coasted toward the moon. As the spaceship traveled farther from Earth, the pull of Earth's gravity became weaker. But Earth's gravity constantly tugged at the spacecraft, slowing it down. By the time the ship was 215,000 miles (346,000 kilometers) from Earth, its speed had dropped to 2,000 miles (3,200 kilometers) per hour. But then the moon's gravity became stronger than Earth's, and the craft picked up speed again.

Apollo 11 was aimed to pass directly behind the moon. However, it was moving much too fast for the moon's weak gravity to capture it. A braking rocket burn changed its course into a low lunar orbit.

Once in lunar orbit, Armstrong and Aldrin separated the LM from the CSM. They fired the LM's descent stage and began the landing maneuver. They used the LM's rockets to slow its descent. Collins remained in the CSM.

To help NASA mission controllers recognize voice signals from the CSM and the LM, the astronauts used different call signs for the two vehicles. They called the CSM *Columbia* and the LM *Eagle*.

The LM's computer controlled all landing maneuvers, but the pilot could override the computer if something unexpected occurred. For the final touchdown, Armstrong looked out the window and selected a level landing site. Probes extended down

Astronaut on the moon saluting the U.S. flag

from the LM's landing legs and signaled when the LM was about 5 feet (1.5 meters) above the surface. The engine shut off, and the LM touched down at a lowland called the Sea of Tranquility on July 20, 1969. Aldrin radioed a brief report on the vehicle's status. Moments later, Armstrong radioed back his famous announcement: "Houston, Tranquility Base here. The *Eagle* has landed."

Exploring the moon. Immediately after the LM touched down, the astronauts performed a complete check to make sure that the landing had not damaged any equipment. Then they prepared to go outside.

Armstrong and Aldrin had worn space suits during the landing. They transferred their air hoses from a cabin supply to their backpack units, then released the air from the cabin and opened a small hatch below their front windows. First Armstrong and then Aldrin crawled backward through the hatch. They descended a ladder mounted on one of the LM's legs to a wide pad at the base of the leg.

A television camera mounted on the side of the LM sent blurred images of the astronauts back to Earth. Armstrong stepped off the pad onto the moon and said, "That's one small step for a man, one giant leap for mankind." Most of the huge TV audience did not hear Armstrong say the word *a* before *man* because of a gap in the transmission.

The astronauts had no trouble adjusting to the weak lunar gravity. They found rocks and soil samples and photographed their positions before picking them up. The astronauts also set up automatic science equipment on the moon. Meanwhile, from the orbiting CSM, Collins conducted various scientific observations and took photographs.

Returning to Earth. The LM's descent stage served as a launch pad for the ascent stage liftoff. To lighten the spacecraft, the crew left all extra equipment behind, including backpacks and cameras. The ascent stage rocketed into orbit,

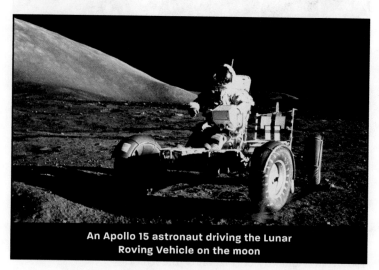

An Apollo 15 astronaut driving the Lunar
Roving Vehicle on the moon

where it linked up with the waiting CSM. The astronauts transferred samples and film into the CSM, then cast off the LM ascent stage. The crew fired the on-board rocket again to push the CSM out of lunar orbit and set their course for Earth.

The CM splashed down in the Pacific Ocean on July 24. NASA immediately put the lunar material, the astronauts, and all equipment that had been exposed to the lunar environment into isolation. The purpose of the isolation, which lasted about 17 days for the astronauts, was to determine whether any germs or other harmful material had been brought from the moon. Nothing harmful was found.

The second flight to the moon was as successful as the first. The Apollo 12 LM made a precision landing on the lunar surface on November 19, 1969. Astronauts Charles (Pete) Conrad, Jr., and Alan L. Bean walked to a landed space probe, Surveyor 3, and retrieved samples for study.

The flight of Apollo 13, which was supposed to result in the third lunar landing, almost ended in disaster. The flight, from April 11 to 17, 1970, became a mission to save the lives of three astronauts—James A. Lovell, Jr., Fred W. Haise, Jr., and John L. Swigert, Jr.

During the spacecraft's approach to the moon, one of the two oxygen tanks in the SM exploded. The blast also disabled the remaining tank. The tanks provided both breathing oxygen and fuel for the electrical power systems of the CM and the SM. Moments later, Swigert reported "OK, Houston, we've had a problem."

After the explosion, flight controllers at Mission Control in Houston quickly realized that the astronauts probably did not have enough oxygen and battery power to get them back to Earth. The flight controllers ordered the crew to power up the LM, which was still docked with the CSM. The crew then shut down the CSM, saving its power supply until power would be needed for descent to Earth. The LM had its own power and oxygen supplies, but it was not designed to support three astronauts. The astronauts used only minimal electric power during the 3-day return trip to Earth, and all three of them survived.

A NASA investigation later determined the cause of the tank explosion. Months before the launch, wires leading to a fan thermostat inside the tank had been tested at too high a voltage. As a result, the wire's insulation had burned off. When the fan was turned on during the flight, the wires short-circuited. The short caused a fire in the pure oxygen environment of the tank, resulting in the explosion. The blast blew off one side of the SM and broke the feed line to the other tank.

Other moon landings. Apollo astronauts landed on the moon six times between 1969 and 1972. Each mission brought various instruments to the moon, which usually included a *seismograph*—a device that detects and records moonquakes and other small movements of the moon's crust. On later missions, mission controllers sent the empty Saturn third stage and the discarded LM ascent stage hurtling to the moon's surface to create seismic waves. These waves provided information about the moon's internal structure.

An important task of the Apollo astronauts was the recovery of samples from the lunar surface for study. On some flights, they used drills to collect soil samples to a depth of 10 feet (3 meters). Astronauts gathered about 840 pounds (384 kilograms) of samples. Some missions launched small scientific satellites near the moon.

After investigating the Apollo 13 accident, NASA redesigned the CM and SM. The inquiry and modifications set back the Apollo 14 mission from October 1970 to January 1971. The Apollo 14 LM, carrying astronauts Alan B. Shepard, Jr., and Edgar D. Mitchell, landed near Fra Mauro Crater on February 5. Fra Mauro had originally been the target for Apollo 13.

Apollo 15 landed near the Apennine Mountains of the moon on July 30, 1971. Astronauts David R. Scott and James B. Irwin became the first astronauts to drive across the moon's surface. They drove a battery-powered *lunar roving vehicle*, often called the *lunar rover*, more than 17 miles (27 kilometers). Apollo 16, carrying John W. Young and Charles M. Duke, Jr., landed in the Descartes region on April 20, 1972. The last lunar mission, Apollo 17, landed in the Taurus Mountains on December 11, 1972. Eugene A. Cernan and Harrison H. Schmitt rode the LM to the surface on this mission.

The Apollo expeditions achieved the goal of demonstrating U.S. technological superiority, and the race to the moon ended with a clear-cut U.S. triumph. Apollo provided unique scientific data, much of which would have been impossible to gather through the use of probes alone. The data enabled scientists to study the origin of the moon and the inner planets of the solar system with much greater certainty than ever before. In addition, the Apollo program forced hundreds of industrial and research teams to develop new tools and technologies that were later applied to more ordinary tasks. For example, microelectronics and new medical monitoring equipment were developed as a result of the Apollo program. These advancements enriched the U.S. economy. Most importantly, the Apollo missions stirred people's imagination and raised their awareness of Earth's place in the universe.

Soviet Attempts to Reach the Moon

Officials in the Soviet Union publicly denied there had ever been a Soviet equivalent to the Apollo program. This official story became widely accepted around the world. But in the late 1980s, the Soviet Union began to release new information indicating that the Soviet government actually had an ambitious lunar program that failed.

Soviet plans for piloted lunar flight may have been hampered by a lack of central authority. Rivalry among different spacecraft design teams and other space organizations prevented cooperation. The Soviet equivalent of the Apollo CSM was a two-person lunar modification of the Soyuz capsule, called the L-1. The Soviet lunar module, the L-3, resembled the LM developed in the United States. However, it would carry only one cosmonaut. The Soviet booster, the N-1, was bigger than the Saturn 5 but less powerful, because it used less efficient fuels.

Piloted Soviet L-1 capsules were scheduled to fly past the moon as part of a test program. This program was planned for 1966 and 1967, well before the United States could attempt a lunar landing. The Soviet Union conducted unpiloted test flights under the cover name *Zond*. Three pairs of Soviet cosmonauts trained for a lunar mission.

The Soviet moon ships had serious problems. Many of the boosters for the L-1 lunar flyby blew up. In addition, the unpiloted L-1 spacecraft developed serious flaws. It was still too dangerous to allow cosmonauts aboard. Soviet efforts to reach the moon were also frustrated by the continued failure of the giant N-1 booster. Four secret test flights were made between 1969 and 1972. However, all of the vehicles exploded.

The Apollo-Soyuz Test Project

In 1972, the United States and the Soviet Union agreed to participate in the first international piloted space mission. They planned to perform an orbital rendezvous between a Soviet Soyuz capsule and a U.S. Apollo capsule. The Apollo-Soyuz Test Project began on July 15, 1975. The Apollo capsule, commanded by Thomas P. Stafford, successfully linked up with the Soyuz capsule, commanded by Alexei A. Leonov.

Space Stations

A *space station* is a place where people can live and work in space for long periods. It orbits Earth, usually about 200 to 300 miles (300 to 480 kilometers) high. A space station may serve as an observatory, laboratory, factory, workshop, warehouse, and fuel depot. Space stations are much larger than piloted spacecraft, so they provide more comforts. Piloted spacecraft may transport people

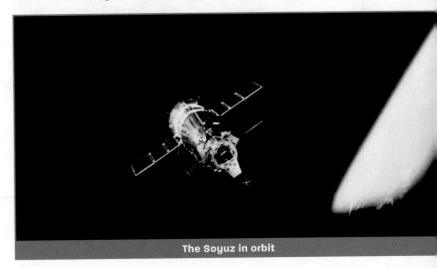

The Soyuz in orbit

between Earth and the space station. Unpiloted spacecraft may supply the station with food, water, equipment, and mail.

Small space stations can be built on Earth and launched into orbit by large rockets. Larger stations are assembled in space. Rockets carry *modules* (sections) of the station into space, where astronauts assemble them. Old modules can be replaced, and new modules can be added to expand the station.

A space station has at least one *docking port* to which a visiting spacecraft can attach itself. Most docking ports consist of a rimmed doorway called a *hatch* that can connect with a hatch on the visiting spacecraft to form an airtight seal. When the two hatches open, they form a pressurized tunnel between the station and the visiting spacecraft.

The main tasks of a space station crew involve scientific research. For example, they might analyze the effects of microgravity on various materials, investigate Earth's surface, or study the stars and planets.

Astronauts at a space station also devote much of their time to the assembly of equipment and the expansion of the station's facilities. This includes erecting beams, connecting electrical and gas lines, and welding permanent joints between sections of the station. The crew must also fix or replace broken equipment.

Salyut and Skylab

In the 1960s, missions to the moon dominated the U.S. and Soviet space programs. But both countries also developed simple space stations during this period. These early stations had a cylin-

drical shape, with a docking port at one end and solar power panels sticking out from the sides. The stations were designed to hold enough air, food, and water to last for about 6 to 12 months. The piloted spacecraft originally built for lunar flight—the U.S. Apollo and the Soviet Soyuz—were modified to transport people to the space stations.

Salyut. The Soviet Union launched the first space station, Salyut (Salute) 1, on April 19, 1971. It consisted of a single module with one docking port. On June 7, 1971, three cosmonauts—Georgi T. Dobrovolsky, Victor I. Patsayev, and Vladislav N. Volkov—linked their Soyuz 11 spacecraft with Salyut 1. They spent 23 days aboard the space station, making medical observations and performing experiments. In a tragic accident, the air leaked out of the Soyuz 11 spacecraft during the return journey, killing all three cosmonauts.

In 1974, Salyut 3 hosted a 15-day mission to photograph Earth. Salyut 4 received two missions in 1975. The second lasted 63 days. In 1976, Salyut 5 repeated the Salyut 3 photography mission.

In 1977, the Soviet Union launched Salyut 6. It had two docking ports, one at either end of the main module. This new design enabled a space station crew to receive a visit from a second crew or a resupply vehicle. A modified, unpiloted Soyuz spacecraft called Progress began delivering new supplies and equipment to Salyut 6 in January 1978. Thus it became the first space station to be resupplied and refueled. These capabilities greatly extended the useful life of space stations and enabled crews to repair and modernize them. Spare parts and more advanced instruments could be sent to the stations as needed. Salyut 6 operated for almost five years. It received visits by 16 crews, who spent up to six months in orbit. Between 1982 and 1986, Salyut 7 housed expeditions lasting up to eight months.

Skylab. The first U.S. space station was Skylab, launched into orbit by a Saturn 5 booster on May 14, 1973. Skylab was built from the empty third stage of a Saturn 5 rocket, with an attached air lock module, docking port, and solar telescope.

Astronauts Pete Conrad, Joseph P. Kerwin, and Paul J. Weitz arrived at Skylab on May 25. The station had suffered damage during launch, losing most of its thermal insulation and one of its two solar power panels. In addition, debris had jammed the other solar panel so it could not open. The crew worked outside the station several times to free the stuck panel. The success of this 28-day

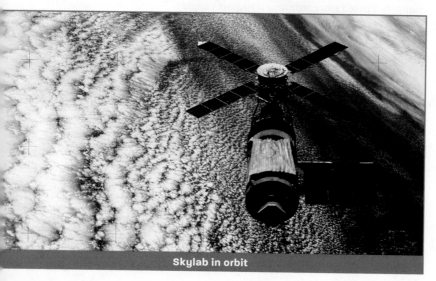

Skylab in orbit

expedition proved the usefulness of people in space for the repair and maintenance of space stations.

Two more crews carried out Skylab missions. These astronauts continued to operate the station while conducting medical experiments, photographing Earth, and observing the sun. The second mission lasted 59 days, and the third ran for 84 days.

United States space officials hoped to keep Skylab in orbit long enough to host a space shuttle mission. However, the station fell from its orbit in July 1979 and broke apart. Fragments of the station landed in western Australia and in the Indian Ocean.

Mir. The Soviet space station Mir (Peace) was launched on February 20, 1986. Mir featured two docking ports—one at each end—and four other hatches. They were designed for the attachment of laboratory modules, with the original Mir serving as the hub and the modules looking like spokes of a wheel. Mir also had modernized equipment and improved solar power panels.

After the launch of Mir, the Soviet Union sent three laboratory modules into orbit, where they docked with the core module. Many cosmonauts spent several months in space. Beginning in 1987, each crew was relieved by a new crew before leaving Mir, except for a period of a few months in 1989.

Russia took over the operation of Mir after the Soviet Union broke apart in 1991. In 1994, Russia privatized the government-owned business that was in charge of Mir and other rocket and space projects. The business was given the name Energia Rocket and Space Corporation. In 1995, U.S. space shuttles began to dock with Mir. Also in 1995, cosmonaut Valery Polyakov returned to Earth from Mir, setting an international record of 438 days in space. Russia connected an additional science module to Mir in 1995 and another in 1996, completing the station.

A dangerous accident occurred in June 1997. A cosmonaut was practicing maneuvers that would dock a supply craft with the station. The craft collided with a module of Mir called Spektr. The crash opened a small hole in Spektr and damaged one of its four solar panels. Spektr began to leak air. The crew quickly disconnected the solar-power cables that led through the portal connecting Spektr to the rest of Mir. The crew then closed the hatch, sealing off Spektr.

Mir continued to operate on reduced power. In July 1997, Russia sent emergency supplies and equipment to the station.

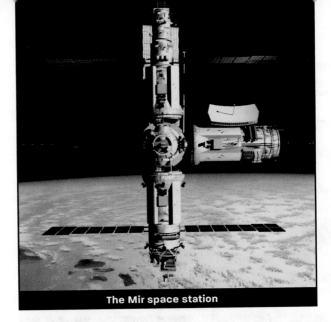

The Mir space station

In March 2001, Russia destroyed Mir by guiding it into the atmosphere. Much of the station burned, and the remainder fell into the Pacific Ocean.

The International Space Station

In 1984, President Ronald Reagan authorized the building of a large, permanent space station "within a decade." Designs for the new station changed often and the estimated cost increased. The promised completion date slipped later and later. In 1993, President Bill Clinton directed NASA to redesign the proposed space station to reduce the cost and amount of time it would take to build. The United States, Brazil, Canada, Japan, Russia, and the ESA would become partners in a program to build the redesigned space station.

Construction began in 1998. Russia launched the first module, called Zarya, in November of that year. A month later, the space shuttle Endeavour carried the module Unity into orbit and docked it with Zarya. A crew of one American astronaut and two Russian cosmonauts moved into the station in 2000. The station expanded to six members in 2009. The space station was completed in 2011.

Space Shuttles

During the 1950s and the 1960s, aviation researchers worked to develop winged rocket planes. Advocates of winged spaceplanes pointed out that such vehicles could land on ordinary airfields. Adding wings to a spacecraft increases the vehicle's weight, but wings make landing the vehicle much easier and cheaper than splashdowns at sea. Ocean landings require many ships and aircraft, and the salt water usually damages the spacecraft beyond repair.

NASA began to develop a reusable space shuttle while the Apollo program was still underway.

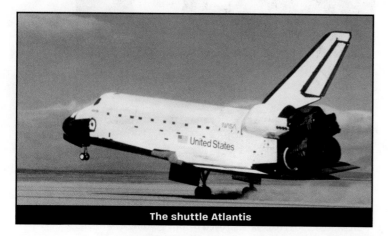

The shuttle Atlantis

In 1972, U.S. president Richard M. Nixon signed an executive order that officially started the space shuttle project. The shuttles were designed to blast off like a rocket and land like an airplane, making up to 100 missions.

The space shuttle system consisted of three parts: (1) an orbiter, (2) an external tank, and (3) two solid rocket boosters. The nose of the winged orbiter housed the pressurized crew cabin. From the flight deck at the front of the orbiter, pilots can look through the front and side windows. The middeck, under the flight deck, contained additional seats, equipment lockers, food systems, sleeping facilities, and a small toilet compartment. An air lock linked the middeck with the *payload bay*, the area that held the cargo. The tail of the orbiter housed the main engines and a smaller set of engines used for maneuvering in space.

The external tank was attached to the orbiter's belly. It contained the liquid propellants used by the main engines. Two rocket boosters were strapped to the sides of the external tank. They contained solid propellants.

The designers of the space shuttle had to overcome a number of major technological challenges. The shuttle's main engines had to be reusable for many missions. The shuttle needed a flexible but reliable system of computer control. And it required a new type of heat shield that could withstand many reentries into Earth's atmosphere.

The Shuttle Era Begins

In 1977, NASA conducted flight tests of the first space shuttle, Enterprise, with a modified 747 jumbo jet. The jet carried the orbiter into the air and back on several flights and released it in midair on several more.

The shuttle's first orbital mission began on April 12, 1981. That day, the shuttle Columbia was launched, with astronauts John W. Young and Robert L. Crippen at the controls. The 54-hour mission went perfectly. Seven months later, the vehicle made a second orbital flight, proving that a spacecraft could be reused.

Although the first four shuttle flights each carried only two pilots, the crew size was soon expanded to four, and later to seven or eight. Besides the two pilots, shuttle crews included *mission specialists* (experts in the operation of the shuttle) and *payload specialists* (experts in the scientific research to be performed).

The large capacity of the space shuttle's orbiter opened the possibility of including other passengers besides NASA astronauts and scientists. Citizens who participated in shuttle missions included representatives of the companies launching payloads and members of the U.S. Congress.

In 1984, NASA created a special "Space Flight Participant" program to offer the opportunity of space travel to more Americans. President Reagan announced that the first participant would be a schoolteacher. Later flights were expected to carry journalists, artists, and other interested civilians.

The Soviet Space Shuttle

The Soviet Union carried out its own shuttle program in great secrecy during the 1980s. The Soviet shuttle, Buran (Snowstorm), resembled the U.S. shuttle, but Soviet engineers made many modifications. For example, Buran had no main engines on board. Instead, an expendable booster provided all its launching power.

On November 15, 1988, a heavy booster called Energia carried Buran into orbit without a crew. An automatic flight control system managed the two-orbit flight. Buran landed on a runway at the Baykonur Cosmodrome in Kazakhstan, then part of the Soviet Union.

Beginning in 1989, shortages of funds caused long delays in further development of the Buran program. In 1993, work on the program ended.

Types of Shuttle Missions

Space shuttles carried artificial satellites, space probes, and other heavy loads into orbit around Earth. In addition to launch operations, the shuttles could retrieve artificial satellites that needed servicing. Astronauts aboard the shuttle repaired the satellites and then returned them to orbit. Shuttle crews also conducted many kinds of scientific experiments and observations.

Commercial satellite launches. The first launch of a payload for a customer took place in November 1982. The shuttle Columbia launched two communications satellites. Solid-rocket boosters helped the satellites climb to their designated orbits. Many later satellite launches followed. NASA discovered that using the space shuttle to launch satellites was more flexible than it had expected. However, the length of time required to ready each space shuttle for its next launch was also greater than NASA planners had expected and sometimes caused expensive delays.

Military missions. About one-fourth of the shuttle missions during the 1980s were conducted for military purposes. Astronauts on these missions sent special observation satellites into orbit and tested various military instruments. To prevent the discovery of information about the capabilities of these satellites, unusual secrecy surrounded the missions. NASA did not reveal launch times of the missions in advance or release any conversations between mission control and the astronauts in space. In the early 1990s, the United States phased out the use of shuttles for such missions and resumed the use of cheaper, single-use rockets.

Repair missions. The space shuttle enabled astronauts to retrieve, repair, and relaunch broken satellites. This important capability was first demonstrated in April 1984, when two astronauts from the shuttle Challenger repaired the Solar Maximum Mission satellite—the only solar observatory in orbit. This success underscored the flexibility and capability of human beings in space. Since then, astronauts have repaired several other satellites in space.

In 1993, a crew from the shuttle Endeavour repaired the orbiting Hubble Space Telescope. After the telescope had been launched in 1990, NASA engineers discovered an error in its primary mirror. The Endeavour astronauts installed optical equipment that cancelled out the effect of the error. The crew also replaced certain scientific instruments, the solar panels, and the *gyroscopes*, devices used in pointing the telescope.

Astronauts traveled by space shuttles to the Hubble Space Telescope to perform four additional servicing missions in 1997, 1999, 2002, and 2009. The final servicing mission, postponed from 2006, left Hubble with a set of instruments that enables the telescope to make the most detailed images in its history. These improvements were meant to leave the telescope operational until at least 2014. Its partial replacement, the James Webb Space Telescope, is expected to be launched later in the decade.

Spacelab missions. Spacelab was a facility that enabled shuttle crews to perform a wide variety of scientific experiments in space. It was built as a part of the space shuttle program by the European Space Agency. The first Spacelab mission was launched in 1983 in the space shuttle Columbia. In 1998, the same shuttle carried Spacelab on its last mission. Each mission focused on research in a particular area of science or technology, such as astronomy, the life sciences, and microgravity.

Spacelab consisted of a piloted space laboratory and several separate platforms called *pallets*. The pressurized laboratory was connected to the crew compartment by a tunnel. It had facilities for scientists to conduct experiments in manufacturing, medicine, the production of biological materials, and other areas. The pallets carried large scientific instruments that were used to conduct experiments in astronomy and other fields. Scientists operated

The Hubble Space Telescope prior to its deployment from the Endeavour

the instruments from the laboratory, from the shuttle's orbiter, or from the ground. Spacelab facilities were shared by the ESA and the United States.

The Challenger Disaster

The 10th launch of the space shuttle Challenger was scheduled as the 25th space shuttle mission. Francis R. (Dick) Scobee was the mission commander. The crew included Christa McAuliffe, a high-school teacher from New Hampshire. The five other crew members were Gregory B. Jarvis, Ronald E. McNair, Ellison S. Onizuka, Judith A. Resnik, and Michael J. Smith.

After several launch delays, NASA officials overruled the concerns of engineers and ordered a liftoff on a cold morning, January 28, 1986. The mission ended in tragedy. Challenger disintegrated into a ball of fire. The accident occurred 73 seconds into flight, at an altitude of 46,000 feet (14,020 meters) and at about twice the speed of sound.

Strictly speaking, Challenger did not explode. Instead, various structural failures caused the spacecraft to break apart. Although Challenger disintegrated almost without warning, the crew may have briefly been aware that something was wrong. The crew cabin tore loose from the rest of the shuttle and soared through the air. It took almost three minutes for the cabin to fall to the Atlantic Ocean, where it smashed on impact, killing the seven crew members.

Earth as seen from the Galileo spacecraft

All shuttle missions were halted while a special commission appointed by President Reagan determined the cause of the accident and what could be done to prevent such disasters from happening again. In June 1986, the commission reported that the accident was caused by a failure of O rings in the shuttle's right solid rocket booster. These rubber rings sealed the joint between the two lower segments of the booster. Design flaws in the joint and unusually cold weather during launch caused the O rings to allow hot gases to leak out of the booster through the joint. Flames from within the booster streamed past the failed seal and quickly expanded the small hole. The flaming gases then burned a hole in the shuttle's external fuel tank. The flames also cut away one of the supporting beams that held the booster to the side of the external tank. The booster tore loose and ruptured the tank. The propellants from the tank formed a giant fireball as structural failures tore the vehicle apart.

The commission said NASA's decision to launch the shuttle was flawed. Top-level decision-makers had not been informed of problems with the joints and O rings or of the possible damaging effects of cold weather.

Shuttle designers made several technical modifications, including an improved O-ring design and the addition of a crew bail-out system. Although such a system would not work in all cases, it could save the lives of shuttle crew members in some situations. Procedural changes included stricter safety reviews and more restrictive launching conditions.

Back into Space

The space shuttle resumed flying on September 29, 1988, with the launch of the redesigned shuttle Discovery. The main purpose of the five-man mission was to place a communications satellite into orbit. During the next few years, many long-delayed missions were carried out. Astronauts launched a number of unpiloted space probes, such as Galileo, Magellan, and Ulysses. Large scientific research satellites such as the Hubble Space Telescope, the Compton Gamma Ray Observatory, and the Upper Atmosphere Research Satellite were placed into orbit. In 1993, a shuttle crew flew to the orbiting Hubble Space Telescope and repaired its optical system.

Shuttles also launched military satellites and communications satellites. Spacelab research missions studied astronomy and space medicine. A less ambitious launch schedule was worked out, and major delays became less frequent.

NASA also made improvements in the shuttle fleet. New computers and life-support hardware were installed. A drag parachute and new brakes made landings easier to control. The computerized automatic flight control system and life-support systems were also improved.

Docking with Mir

Spacecraft from the United States and Russia resumed joint operations in 1995, 20 years after the Apollo-Soyuz mission. On June 29, after three years of negotiations, planning, and practice missions, the space shuttle Atlantis docked with Russia's Mir space station. Atlantis carried a replacement crew of Russian cosmonauts to Mir and brought the station's former crew home to Earth.

Unlike the largely symbolic Apollo-Soyuz mission, the Atlantis-Mir docking was the first in a series of missions. Astronauts began regular visits to Mir, carried up and back by shuttles. The shuttles delivered replacement parts and scientific equipment, as well as water, food, and air. In addition, the astronauts and cosmonauts began to test techniques to be used to build and maintain the International Space Station.

On September 7, 1996, astronaut Shannon Lucid, aboard Mir, broke the record for consecutive days in space by a woman with her 169th day. The previous record of 168 days had been set by cosmonaut Yelena Kondakova in 1995. Lucid had been launched aboard Atlantis on March 22, 1996, and had been on Mir since March 23. On September 26, Lucid returned to Earth aboard Atlantis, having spent 188 consecutive days in space.

The Columbia Disaster

Disaster struck the U.S. space shuttle fleet again on February 1, 2003, when Columbia, the fleet's oldest shuttle, broke apart over the southwestern United States as it reentered Earth's atmosphere. The flight was Columbia's 28th launch and the shuttle fleet's 113th mission. The accident occurred about 16 minutes before the shuttle was due to land. All seven crew members died, including Rick D. Husband, the mission commander, and Ilan Ramon, the first Israeli astronaut. The five other crew members were Michael P. Anderson, David M. Brown, Kalpana Chawla, Laurel Blair Salton Clark, and William C. McCool.

After the disaster, NASA halted shuttle flights and appointed an independent commission to investigate the accident. Investigators collected thousands of pieces of shuttle debris that had fallen to Earth after the accident. They also studied communications, sensor readings, video recordings, and other records from the mission; tested shuttle equipment; and interviewed NASA employees.

In August, the commission reported that the accident had been caused by a chunk of foam insulation that broke away from the shuttle's external fuel tank and struck Columbia's left wing at high speed shortly after liftoff. Investigators concluded

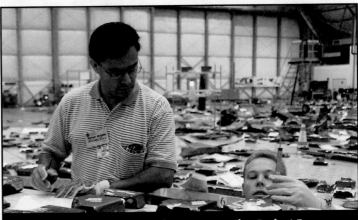
Members of the Columbia Reconstruction Project Team examining debris from the shuttle

that the impact created a hole in the heat-resistant panels that protected the wing from high temperatures during reentry. As the shuttle reentered Earth's atmosphere, the hole allowed superheated air to enter the wing and damage its internal structure. Eventually, the wing was destroyed, and the shuttle went out of control and broke apart.

The commission's report called for NASA to develop systems for inspecting and repairing protective tiles and panels while the shuttles were in orbit. It recommended reinforcing the panels and working to limit or prevent the shedding of foam from the external fuel tank.

The report also criticized NASA's management and safety procedures. Investigators concluded that pressure to meet budgets and deadlines had contributed to a decline in the safety of the shuttle program. The panel also found that NASA management had failed to act on safety concerns raised by engineers. The report recommended that NASA improve safety procedures and create an independent Technical Engineering Authority to oversee and enforce safety standards.

In 2004, U.S. president George W. Bush announced plans to retire the space shuttle fleet by 2010, following the completion of the International Space Station. Bush proposed replacing the shuttle with a new spacecraft designed to carry astronauts to the moon and, eventually, Mars.

Return to Flight

After working more than two years, NASA launched the shuttle Discovery on July 26, 2005. The launch was successful, but videotapes showed that the external fuel tank had shed at

Halley's Comet

least one chunk of foam nearly as large as the one that had fatally damaged Columbia. While the foam did not appear to strike Discovery, NASA officials announced that further shuttle launches would be suspended while engineers worked to fix the problem.

The Discovery astronauts continued on their mission to deliver supplies and perform repairs to the International Space Station. The crew also tested methods of inspecting and repairing the shuttle's heat shield in orbit. The shuttle flipped as it approached the space station so that station astronauts could photograph its underside. After docking, the astronauts used laser imaging equipment mounted on a robotic arm to scan the heat-resistant tiles for damage.

The inspections revealed that two thin strips of ceramic-fiber material used to fill the gaps between the tiles had come loose. Engineers worried that the dangling strips could disrupt the smooth flow of air over the shuttle's underside during reentry, causing the craft to overheat. Mission managers sent U.S. astronaut Stephen K. Robinson out on a robotic arm to remove the fabric, the first heat shield repair in orbit in shuttle history.

On July 4, 2006, Discovery became the next shuttle to travel into space. During the launch, the external fuel tank again shed some small pieces of foam debris. Astronauts and mission managers noticed no immediate damage to the orbiter, but they continued to inspect the craft as it visited the International Space Station. No major safety problems arose during the mission.

Completing the Station

The shuttle Atlantis in September 2006 completed the first of a series of regular missions to finish assembly of the International Space Station. NASA sought to complete the station before the shuttle fleet's planned retirement in 2010. Administrators announced in October that the agency would also launch one shuttle for a final servicing mission to the Hubble Space Telescope.

On June 22, 2007, astronaut Sunita Williams set a record for consecutive days in space by a woman, returning to Earth on Atlantis after 195 days in space. She had been launched with Discovery in December 2006 and served as a flight engineer on the station. Williams broke Shannon Lucid's record of 188 days, set in 1996.

In August 2007, the shuttle Endeavour carried Barbara Morgan, NASA's first Educator Astronaut, to space on an assembly mission. Morgan, who had served as backup for the teacher Christa McAuliffe on the disastrous Challenger flight in 1986, led question-and-answer sessions for students on Earth.

The shuttle Discovery carried the Italian-built U.S. Harmony module to the station in October 2007. In February 2008, Atlantis delivered the European Columbus module. Endeavour brought part of the Japanese Kibo laboratory module to the station in March 2008. The station's first female commander, Peggy Whitson, led the station from October 2007 to April 2008.

On July 21, 2011, the space shuttle Atlantis landed in Florida after a mission to the ISS. The mission, designated STS-135, was the last shuttle mission before the craft were retired.

Other Nations in Space

A number of nations other than the United States and Russia have developed rocket and space programs. These programs are smaller than the U.S. and Russian programs. Most of them concentrate on single applications such as the launching of scientific satellites.

European nations. Several European nations built boosters to launch small scientific research satellites. In 1965, France became the first nation in western Europe to launch a satellite. The United Kingdom sent another satellite into orbit in 1971.

In 1975, the European Space Agency (ESA) was organized. Its western European member nations combine their financial and scientific resources in the development of spacecraft, instruments, and experiments. The ESA supervised the construction of Spacelab, launched the space probe Giotto toward Halley's Comet, and built the Ulysses solar probe. The ESA also developed a series of Ariane booster rockets to launch communications satellites for paying customers. By the late 1980s, Ariane rockets were launching more commercial satellites than U.S. rockets were. ESA spacecraft lift off from Kourou in French Guiana, on the northern coast of South America.

Besides its activities as a member of the ESA, Germany independently built two solar probes called Helios. One probe was launched in 1974, and another was launched in 1976. These probes flew within 28 million miles (45 million kilometers) of the sun—closer than any other probe had reached.

Japan became the fourth nation in space when it launched a satellite in February 1970. The nation's space program blossomed in the 1980s. In 1985, Japan fired two probes toward Halley's Comet. Two separate programs developed a family of small, efficient spaceboosters. The H-1 rocket, a medium-sized booster with liquid hydrogen fuel, also became operational. In 1990, Japan launched a lunar probe.

In 1994, Japan launched its first heavy-lifting booster, the H-2. In 1996, an H-2 lofted the Advanced Earth Observing Satellite. The satellite began to gather data on Earth's lands, seas, and atmosphere.

Japan sends small scientific research satellites into orbit from Uchinoura Space Center on the island of Kyushu. Rockets carrying larger satellites take off from Tanegashima Space Center on Tanega Island, about 60 miles (95 kilometers) to the south. Japan has developed a laboratory module for the International Space Station.

China. In April 1970, China sent its first satellite into space aboard a CZ-1 launcher. In the 1980s, China developed impressive space technology that included liquid-hydrogen engines, powerful Long March rockets, and recoverable satellites. China has three satellite launch sites—Jiuquan, Taiyuan, and Xichang.

In the 1990s, China began developing the Shenzhou, a spacecraft designed to carry astronauts. The Shenzhou resembles Russia's Soyuz capsule. In October 2003, China became the third nation to launch a person into space. Chinese astronaut Yang Liwei orbited Earth aboard a Shenzhou craft for 21 hours before landing safely. Another Shenzhou craft carried two astronauts into orbit on a five-day mission in October 2005. On the third piloted Shenzhou flight in September 2008, two astronauts performed the country's first spacewalk. Astronauts in the Chinese space program are sometimes called *taikonauts*.

India first launched a satellite into orbit in July 1980. The Indian Space Research Organisation builds boosters. India launches rockets from the island of Sriharikota, off its eastern coast. In 2008, India launched the Chandrayaan-1 lunar orbiter. The orbiter carried and dropped an impactor, making India's space program the fifth program to reach the lunar surface.

Canada has an active space research program and a communications satellite program. That nation took part in the U.S. space shuttle program by designing and building the shuttle's robot arm. Canada also built a larger robot arm that was installed on the International Space Station.

Other nations. Israel sent its first satellite into orbit in 1988. Australia has launched modified U.S. rockets from Woomera, Australia. Italy has launched U.S. rockets from a platform in the Indian Ocean, off the coast of Kenya. Several countries, including Brazil, Sweden, and South Africa, have sent scientific sounding rockets into space. Iran sent its first satellite into orbit in 2009.

Plans for the Future

In the early 2000s, scientists and engineers were developing new kinds of spacecraft and more efficient rockets. Industrial researchers were working

The launch of China's Shenzhou VI spacecraft

SpaceShipOne, carrying pilot Michael Melvill

on manufacturing techniques that would use the space environment to advantage. Encouraged by the commercial potential of space activities, private companies had begun to provide launch services.

Developing new spacecraft. Several organizations were developing technologies for a craft that would replace the space shuttles after 2010. These organizations included NASA, ESA, the Japan Aerospace Exploration Agency, and several private companies. Their chief objective was to cut flight costs.

One way to achieve this goal would be to develop a *reusable launch vehicle* (RLV). All the main parts of an RLV would be reused, giving the craft an advantage over a shuttle. A shuttle's main fuel tank drops away after use and so must be replaced for each flight. In one RLV design, a special airplane would carry a spacecraft to a high altitude and release it. The spacecraft would then fire its own rockets to go into orbit. After completing its mission, the craft would land as an airplane does. Another type of RLV would be a *single-stage-to-orbit* (SSTO) craft—a vehicle that would take off by itself and not discard any components. Depending on the design of an SSTO, the craft might take off and land vertically, as a rocket does, or horizontally, as an airplane does.

In the early 2000s, NASA officials decided that an RLV replacement for the shuttle would prove too difficult to develop by 2010. In the meantime, the agency concentrated on developing the Crew Exploration Vehicle (CEV), also known as Orion, a capsule-shaped spacecraft that would carry crew and light cargo to and from the International Space Station. A partially recoverable booster would carry the CEV into space. The agency planned to eventually use Orion to transport crews to the moon.

Also in the 2000s, NASA invested in private companies to help them build spacecraft that could reach low Earth orbit. NASA funded work by Space Exploration Technologies, also known as SpaceX, of Hawthorne, California, and Orbital Sciences Corporation of Dulles, Virginia. In May 2012, a SpaceX cargo capsule became the first private craft to deliver supplies to the ISS.

Developing more efficient rockets. Scientists and engineers were working on alternatives to fuel-burning rockets. Two main alternatives were (1) the *ion rocket* and (2) the *nuclear rocket*. For a given amount of fuel, both alternatives can create at least twice as much acceleration as a fuel-burning rocket. In addition, both can operate for a long time before running out of fuel. Neither ion rockets nor nuclear rockets would launch spacecraft; they would create thrust after fuel-burning boosters had performed that task.

An ion rocket is an electrical device. Electric energy heats a fuel, converts its atoms to *ions* (electrically charged atoms), and expels the ions to create thrust. Designers have already used small ion rockets to keep communications satellites in position above Earth. An ion rocket also has propelled a space probe called Deep Space 1 on a mission to asteroids and comets.

A nuclear rocket uses heat from a nuclear reactor to change a liquid fuel into a gas and expel the gas. This kind of rocket would not be practical as a launcher because some radioactive materials might escape into the atmosphere. However, a small nuclear rocket that created thrust continuously could decrease the time of missions to other planets.

Expanding space activities. Two major areas of space utilization have been the gathering and communication of information. Satellites monitor weather systems on Earth, and space probes gather information on the other planets and the sun. Since the 1960s, communications satellites have regularly relayed television signals between points on Earth's surface.

The next major area of space utilization may be the manufacture of medicinal and industrial products. Manufacturers may use the low gravity, high-vacuum environment of space to create substances that are purer or stronger than those produced on Earth. These substances might include drugs; *semiconductors*, the materials of which computer chips are made; and special *alloys* (mixtures of metals). As profitable manufacturing processes are developed, private companies may even build and operate "orbiting factories."

Private space flight. Many private companies have begun to develop launch services to compete with the national and international organizations. One firm, Sea Launch Company, boosted a communications satellite from a floating platform in the Pacific Ocean in October 1999. The company used a Ukrainian-built Zenit rocket to launch the satellite. Sea Launch is owned by corporations in the United States, Russia, Norway, and Ukraine.

In 1996, an organization called the X Prize Foundation announced the creation of the X Prize competition to stimulate interest in private space travel. The group offered a $10 million award to the first privately funded team to build and launch a craft capable of carrying a pilot and two passengers into space. To qualify for the prize, the craft had to fly to an altitude of 62 miles (100 kilometers), land safely, and then make a repeat flight within two weeks. More than 20 teams from many countries registered to compete for the prize. The award was later renamed the Ansari X Prize for a family that donated a large portion of the prize money.

On June 21, 2004, one of the X Prize competitors, Scaled Composites of Mojave, California, became the first private company to launch a person into space. The company's rocket, called SpaceShipOne, carried American test pilot Michael Melvill more than 62 miles above Earth on a brief suborbital test flight. The rocket was launched from a specially designed airplane called the White Knight. SpaceShipOne went on to win the X Prize with successful launches on September 29 and October 4, 2004.

In September 2007, the X Prize Foundation announced the Google Lunar X Prize for a nongovernmental mission to the moon. The winner would be awarded up to $25 million, paid for by the online-search company Google Inc., for roving a certain distance on the lunar surface and transmitting video and data back to Earth.

MLA Citation

"Space Exploration."
The Southwestern Advantage Topic Source. Nashville: Southwestern. 2013.

DATA

Important Dates in the History of Space Exploration

1926	American scientist Robert H. Goddard launched the world's first liquid-propellant rocket.
1957	(October 4) The Soviet Union launched Sputnik (later referred to as Sputnik 1), the first artificial satellite.
1958	The National Aeronautics and Space Administration (NASA) was formed.
1959	(September 12) The Soviet Union launched Luna 2, the first space probe to hit the moon.
1961	(April 12) Soviet cosmonaut Yuri A. Gagarin became the first person to orbit the earth.
1961	(May 5) Alan B. Shepard, Jr., became the first U.S. astronaut in space.
1962	(February 20) John H. Glenn, Jr., became the first U.S. astronaut to orbit the earth.
1963	(June 16) Soviet cosmonaut Valentina Tereshkova became the first woman in space.
1964	(October 12) The Soviet Union launched Voskhod (later called Voskhod 1), the first multiperson space capsule.
1968	(December 21) The United States launched Apollo 8, the first manned space mission to orbit the moon.
1969	(July 20) U.S. astronauts Neil A. Armstrong and Edwin "Buzz" Aldrin made the first human lunar landing.
1970	(August 17) The Soviet Union launched Venera 7, which became the first space probe to transmit data from Venus's surface after it landed on December 15, 1970.

DATA

Important Dates in the History of Space Exploration

1971	(June 7) Soviet cosmonauts boarded Salyut 1, making it the first manned orbiting space station.
1975	(July 15) The United States and the Soviet Union launched the Apollo-Soyuz Test Project, the first international space mission.
1975	(August 20) The United States launched the probe Viking 1. This probe, along with a second probe called Viking 2, landed on Mars in 1976 and sent back photos and data.
1977	(August 20) The United States launched the probe Voyager 2, which flew past and photographed Jupiter in 1979, Saturn in 1981, Uranus in 1986, and Neptune in 1989.
1981	(April 12) The United States launched the space shuttle Columbia, the first reusable piloted spacecraft.
1985	(July 2) The European Space Agency launched the probe Giotto, which passed Halley's Comet on March 14, 1986, photographed the comet's nucleus, and sent back data.
1986	(January 28) The U.S. space shuttle Challenger was destroyed in an accident shortly after launch, killing all seven crew members.
1989	(October 18) The United States launched the probe Galileo, which reached Jupiter in 1995. Galileo was far more sophisticated than earlier planetary probes.
1990	(August 10) The U.S. space probe Magellan began to orbit Venus and return radar images of the planet's surface.
1995	(March 22) Cosmonaut Valery Polyakov completed a record 438 days in space aboard the Russian space station Mir.
1996	(November 7) The United States launched the Mars Global Surveyor probe to map the planet. The probe began to orbit Mars in September 1997.
1997	(October 15) The United States launched the space probe Cassini, which reached Saturn in 2004.
2003	(February 1) The U.S. space shuttle Columbia was destroyed in an accident in midair, killing all seven crew members.
2003	(October 15) Yang Liwei became the first person launched into space by China.
2004	(June 21) Scaled Composites of Mojave, California, became the first private company to launch a person into space.
2011	(July 21) The space shuttle Atlantis touched down in Florida after completing the final shuttle mission.

ADDITIONAL RESOURCES

Books to Read

Level I

Ackroyd, Peter. *Escape from Earth*. DK Publishing, 2003.

Nicolson, Cynthia P. *Exploring Space*. Kids Can Press, 2000.

Scott, Elaine. *Space, Stars, and the Beginning of Time: What the Hubble Telescope Saw*. Clarion, 2011.

Space. DK Publishing, 2010.

Stott, Carole. *Space Exploration*. DK Publishing, 2010.

Level II

Hardesty, Von, and Eisman, Gene. *Epic Rivalry: The Inside Story of the Soviet and American Space Race*. National Geographic Society, 2007.

History Committee of the American Astronautical Society. *Space Exploration and Humanity*. 2 vols. ABC-CLIO, 2010.

Launius, Roger D., and Johnston, A. K. *Smithsonian Atlas of Space Exploration*. HarperCollins, 2009.

Sparrow, Giles. *Spaceflight: The Complete Story from Sputnik to Shuttle—and Beyond*. Dorling Kindersley, 2007.

Web Sites

30th Anniversary of Apollo 11: 1969–1999

http://nssdc.gsfc.nasa.gov/planetary/lunar/apollo_11_30th.html
NASA Web site about Apollo 11.

Astronaut Biographies

http://www.jsc.nasa.gov/Bios/
Biographies on astronauts and cosmonauts from NASA.

Astronauts and Cosmonauts

http://www.spacetoday.org/Astronauts.html
Information on astronauts and cosmonauts and their missions.

British National Space Centre

http://www.bis.gov.uk/ukspaceagency
Official home page of the organization.

Cassini: Voyage to Saturn

http://saturn.jpl.nasa.gov/
Information about space missions.

Challenger Center Online

http://www.challenger.org/
Information about space simulation programs from the Challenger Learning Center.

European Space Agency

http://www.esa.int/export/esaCP/index.html
Information about this international organization for space exploration, composed of 14 European member nations.

History of Rockets

http://search.nasa.gov/search/search.jsp?nasaInclude=history+of+rockets
A history of rockets and aeronautics from NASA.

HSF—International Space Station

http://spaceflight1.nasa.gov/station/
Information on activities at the Space Station from NASA.

Hubble Space Telescope Public Pictures

http://hubblesite.org/newscenter/
Pictures taken by the Hubble Space Telescope.

Hubblesite

http://hubblesite.org/
NASA's official Web site for the Hubble Space Telescope.

Indian Space Research Organization

http://www.isro.org/
Official site of the organization.

JSC Home Page
http://www.nasa.gov/centers/johnson/home/index.html
Information about NASA's primary center for spacecraft development and mission planning—the Johnson Space Center.

Kennedy Space Center Visitor Complex
http://www.kennedyspacecenter.com/
Official site of the Kennedy Space Center near Cape Canaveral, Florida.

Lunar Exploration
http://nssdc.gsfc.nasa.gov/planetary/lunar/apollo_25th.html
The history of America's moon space program, culminating in the Apollo 11 moon landing of July 1969.

NASA Ames Research Center
http://www.nasa.gov/centers/ames/home/index.html
Information about NASA's Ames Research Center.

NASA Human Spaceflight
http://www.spaceflight.nasa.gov/home/index.html
Official NASA Web site containing updated information on the space shuttle, the International Space Station, and other NASA programs.

NASA Jet Propulsion Laboratory
http://www.jpl.nasa.gov/
The official Web site of NASA's Jet Propulsion Laboratory. Includes information about the laboratory and background information on Earth, our solar system, and the universe.

NASA Kids' Club
http://www.nasa.gov/audience/forkids/kidsclub/flash/index.html
NASA features a Web site designed for children, with information on astronomy and space exploration.

NASA/Kennedy Space Center Home Page
http://www.nasa.gov/centers/kennedy/home/index.html
Information about the Kennedy Space Center, including employee publications.

NASA/Marshall Space Flight Center
http://www.nasa.gov/centers/marshall/home/index.html
Information about the Marshall Space Flight Center, in Huntsville, Alabama.

Planetary Sciences at the National Space Science Data Center
http://nssdc.gsfc.nasa.gov/planetary/
The National Space Science Data Center (NSSDC) is NASA's deep archive and general distribution center for lunar and planetary data and images.

Smithsonian National Air & Space Museum Home Page
http://www.nasm.si.edu
Information about the museum, its exhibitions and educational programs.

STARDUST Home Page
http://stardust.jpl.nasa.gov/home/index.html
Home page of a NASA spacecraft designed to collect material from a comet and bring it back to Earth for analysis by scientists worldwide.

Structure and Evolution of the Universe (NASA)
http://science.gsfc.nasa.gov/sed/index.cfm?fuseAction=home.main&&navOrgCode=660
Resources about the universe, including videos, images, sound clips, and information about NASA missions.

The Apollo Program (1963–1972)
http://nssdc.gsfc.nasa.gov/planetary/lunar/apollo.html
NASA Web site about the Apollo Program.

Views of the Solar System
http://www.solarviews.com/
This site presents a multimedia adventure with facts, graphics, photos, and videos of our solar system.

Voyager Project
http://voyager.jpl.nasa.gov/
Information about Voyager I and II from NASA.

Search Strings

Could Mars Be Habitable? What Is NASA's Plan and What Would It Take?

Mars planet habitable (28,800)

planet Mars human life support (134,000) * These returns looked pretty good.

planet Mars "human life" NASA plans (56,100)

Space Vehicles

space exploration vehicles "space shuttle" (108,000)

"space exploration" vehicles "space shuttle" rockets (83,300)

"space exploration" vehicles "space shuttle" rockets "United States" Asia India Japan China Europe (13,400)

International Space Station (ISS)

"International Space Station" building modules (59,700)

building of the "international space station" and its mission (868,000)

"international space station" ISS nations involved specifications (169,000)

Earth's Space Agencies

Earth's space agencies NASA ESA CSA JAXA (11,200)

Earth's space agencies "Russian Aviation and Space Agency" NASA ESA CSA JAXA (42)

BACKGROUND INFORMATION

The following articles and features were written during the year in which the events took place and reflect the style and thinking of that time.

Space Exploration (2005)

The United States National Aeronautics and Space Administration (NASA) resumed human space-flight in 2005 for the first time since the loss of the space shuttle Columbia in 2003. However, continuing safety concerns with the shuttle fleet and damage to critical ground facilities in the path of Hurricane Katrina in August 2005 raised questions about when—and how many more times—the aging space planes would fly.

In 2005, NASA announced plans for sending astronauts to the moon and Mars; NASA's Mars Exploration Rovers kept on roving long beyond their estimated lifetimes; China sent two astronauts into space; and one European spacecraft landed on Saturn's moon Titan, while another began searching beneath the surface of Mars for underground lakes of life-supporting water.

Return to flight. The space shuttle Discovery lifted off from Kennedy Space Center, Florida, on July 26, 2005, after a series of delays prompted by heightened safety concerns in the wake of the Columbia disaster. The July launch appeared perfect. However, images captured by a camera aboard the shuttle's external fuel tank revealed a piece of insulating foam peeling off the tank. Cameras had been installed

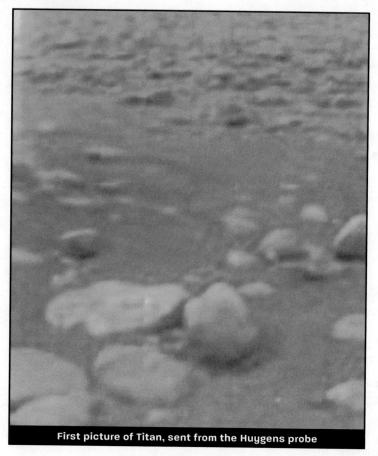
First picture of Titan, sent from the Huygens probe

crew members Stephen K. Robinson of NASA and Soichi Noguchi of the Japanese Aerospace Exploration Agency replaced a malfunctioning altitude control gyroscope on the ISS. The repair eliminated the need for the station to use precious fuel for its thrusters to keep the station's solar arrays pointed at the sun. Nevertheless, without a set schedule of shuttle flights, smaller Russian Soyuz crew capsules and Progress cargo vehicles were the only supply link to the ISS, limiting its operations and halting station assembly altogether.

On October 3, 2005, a Soyuz spacecraft brought a new crew to the space station—Expedition 12, consisting of astronaut William McArthur and cosmonaut Valery Tokarev. They were accompanied by the third tourist to fly in space, U.S. millionaire scientist Gregory Olsen. Olsen reportedly paid the Russian Space Agency $20 million for a seat on the Soyuz and the opportunity to conduct science experiments aboard the ISS for a week. Olsen returned to Earth on October 10 with Expedition 11 cosmonaut Sergei Krikalev and astronaut John Phillips. Krikalev and Phillips had been on the ISS since April, having replaced the Expedition 10 crew, astronaut Leroy Chiao and cosmonaut Salizhan Sharipov. Krikalev set a new career record for total days spent working in space—803.

Exploration vision. On September 19, NASA announced plans for the future of the U.S. space program, involving a push to the moon with new technology that may help human beings reach Mars. The shuttle was to be retired in 2010, after completing as much of the remaining space station assembly as possible. Meanwhile, NASA engineers were to start developing two new rockets based on existing shuttle technology. One was to carry astronauts to space. The other, larger rocket was to carry the equipment and supplies needed to get the astronauts to the surfaces of the moon and Mars and sustain them while they explore. NASA set 2012 as the date to begin flying a six-seat Crew Exploration Vehicle (CEV) similar to the Apollo capsule, the first generation of lunar spaceships. At first, the CEV is to fly to the space station, where crews will continue developing techniques for successfully living and working in space. By 2018, the CEV is to fly four astronauts to the moon for the first time since 1972.

Robotic explorers. Although human activity in space was limited in 2005, robotic explorers entered a kind of golden age. One of the year's most

to monitor the condition of the tank after it was determined that foam falling from the tank during Columbia's last mission had fatally damaged the orbiter.

The piece lost during Discovery's launch did not appear to strike the shuttle's delicate thermal protection system. Inspection with cameras aboard the International Space Station (ISS) showed only minor debris damage to the orbiter. Nevertheless, the incident revealed that NASA engineers had failed to correct the problem that destroyed Columbia. A second shuttle flight planned for fall 2005 was postponed until the foam problem could be resolved. Future shuttle flights were further delayed after August 29, when Hurricane Katrina slammed into New Orleans, where the shuttle's tanks are built. Although damage to the assembly facility was minor, the storm scattered the facility's employees.

International Space Station. Fortunately for the U.S.-Russian crews who live on the ISS, Discovery left enough food, water, clothing, fuel, and equipment to keep the orbiting laboratory functioning well into 2006. In addition, Discovery

spectacular achievements took place in January, when a small European probe named for Dutch astronomer Christiaan Huygens (1625–1695) parachuted through the orange clouds of Titan, Saturn's largest moon. The Huygens probe had ridden piggyback to Titan on NASA's Cassini spacecraft. Huygens sent back the first pictures ever taken of Titan's surface. Clearly visible was a coastline with rivers running into what may be a supercold hydrocarbon sea, its semisolid surface dotted with ice pebbles. Huygens continued to return data and close-up images for some 70 minutes after it unexpectedly survived the impact of landing.

At Mars, the European Space Agency's Mars Express orbiter sent back spectacular three-dimensional images of the surface below. In July, controllers unfurled a set of boom antennas on Mars Express that allowed them to use radar to search for underground water that could support life.

On the surface of Mars, the two U.S. Mars Exploration Rovers—Spirit and Opportunity—continued to work long after their planned 90-day service life passed. Spirit traveled some 3 miles (5 kilometers) from its landing site in the giant Gusev Crater, climbing to the top of a low ridge named the Columbia Hills in honor of the lost space shuttle. On the other side of the planet, Opportunity escaped from sandy terrain that ensnared it for five weeks. The rover continued traveling toward craters similar to the one called Endurance, which it explored soon after its January 2004 landing.

On August 12, 2005, an Atlas V rocket launched NASA's Mars Reconnaissance Orbiter (MRO)—equipped with a powerful camera—on a 15-month journey to Mars. After it settles into orbit, the MRO will take the highest resolution images of the surface of Mars ever collected from orbit.

China in space. On October 12, a Long March rocket carried two Chinese astronauts, Fei Junlong and Nie Haisheng, into space. The flight, aboard the Shenzhou VI spacecraft, marked the country's second human space flight. Yang Liwei was the first Chinese astronaut to fly in space when he orbited Earth for 21½ hours in 2003.

Space Exploration (1969)

Men flew to the moon, walked on its surface, and returned safely to earth in 1969. The historic first journey marked the achievement of the U.S. space exploration goal of the decade and stimulated the projection of new goals for the 1970s and 1980s.

Four manned Apollo missions during the year consolidated U.S. leadership in space. Russia focused its manned flight efforts in earth orbit, with a simultaneous flight of three spacecraft carrying seven cosmonauts as the highlight.

Two successful Apollo flights preceded the July lunar landing.

Astronauts James A. McDivitt, David R. Scott, and Russell L. Schweickart were the first to carry out a flight test of the entire Apollo spacecraft, including the lunar module. In the Apollo 9 mission from March 3 to 13, they simulated in earth orbit most maneuvers of a lunar landing. McDivitt and Schweickart activated the lunar module and flew it for 6 hours 24 minutes, separating the two craft by a distance of 100 miles.

Astronauts Thomas P. Stafford, Eugene A. Cernan, and John W. Young performed another simulation, this time in lunar orbit, on the Apollo 10 mission from May 18 to 26. Stafford and Cernan separated the lunar module from the command craft about 70 miles above the moon and flew it for 8 hours 11 minutes, descending to within 9.4 miles of the surface. In 19 transmissions, they verified the operation of color television equipment.

The Apollo 11 Mission of Neil A. Armstrong, Edwin E. Aldrin, Jr., and Michael Collins from July 16 to 24 demonstrated that men can land on the moon, collect soil samples and emplace instruments to operate from its surface, and return safely to earth. Armstrong and Aldrin landed the lunar module *Eagle* in the southwestern part of the Sea of Tranquility, while Collins remained in orbit in the command module *Columbia*. The landing site was well within the target area.

The equipment for two experiments was left behind to operate after the astronauts' departure. One was an extremely sensitive seismometer to detect moonquakes. For 21 days, the instrument returned data that puzzled investigators and led to speculation that the moon's structure is quite complex and unlike that of the earth. The other was an array of mirrors for reflecting laser beams back to earth. Within a few months, at least three observatories were employing the reflector for increasingly precise new measurements of the distance to the moon.

Thomas Gold, professor of astronomy at Cornell University, reported that analysis of stereo photos of the lunar surface indicated that the moon may have been exposed about 30,000 years ago to heat so intense that it melted a small amount of lunar material. If this heat came from the sun, he said, it would represent far more violent solar activity than has ever been recorded by man on earth.

Following the Apollo 11 success, the lunar flight schedule was stretched out to provide intervals of at least four months between flights instead of the two-month intervals prevailing earlier in the year.

The Second Lunar Landing was part of the Apollo 12 mission by Charles Conrad, Jr., Alan L. Bean, and Richard F. Gordon, Jr., November 14 to 24. Conrad and Bean set down the lunar module *Intrepid* in the eastern part of the Ocean of Storms, while Gordon orbited in the command module.

Learning from their predecessors' experience, the Apollo 12 crewmen landed with almost pinpoint accuracy—600 feet from the Surveyor 3 unmanned spacecraft, which had been on the moon for 31 months. They remained 31 hours 31 minutes and carried out two surface explorations amounting to a total of almost 8 hours.

Conrad and Bean set up a nuclear-powered Apollo Lunar Surface Experiment Package with instruments for six experiments. They also collected rock and soil samples and brought back parts of the Surveyor for examination.

Two Apollo 12 experiments—the seismometer and the aluminum foil solar wind collector—were the same as the Apollo 11. The additional instruments were a spectrometer to measure the solar wind, a magnetometer, a combined ionosphere and lunar atmosphere detector, and a lunar dust detector.

Surprising results. After Conrad and Bean rejoined Gordon in the command module, the lunar module was intentionally crashed on the surface about 45 miles from the landing site. The impact set off 50 minutes of vibration of the moon's surface layers, probably the most unexpected result of the early exploration of the moon. Scientists were unable to explain the vibration, which built up to a maximum in seven minutes and then gradually subsided. But they speculated that some of the strange signals recorded by the Apollo 11 seismometer may have resulted from impacts of smaller objects.

Another surprise was the discovery of a faint lunar magnetic field. No such field had been detected by earlier unmanned spacecraft. A disap-

Astronaut's footprint on the lunar surface

A slice of a lunar rock sample

pointment was the failure of the television camera shortly after Conrad began walking on the surface. The camera was returned to Earth for study.

Secrets of moon rocks. Ted Foss, chief of the geology branch at the Manned Spacecraft Center near Houston, said the study of rock samples from both lunar landing missions leaves no doubt that there has been volcanic activity on the moon. It was not yet clear, however, whether the molten material from which they were formed came from meteoroid impacts or from within the moon itself.

The rocks brought back by the Apollo 11 crew fell into two distinct types. One type is made of crystals, probably formed at some distance below the surface by the slow cooling of molten material; the other, called breccia, includes crystals and fragments of volcanic glass, minerals, and rock.

Seven more lunar missions are planned for the existing Apollo program. With the first two having explored the lunar lowlands or "seas," the others will be assigned more difficult targets in the highlands, the large impact craters, and the mysterious winding rilles. All sites being considered are on the visible face of the moon; most are near its equator.

On the last three or four of these flights, improved equipment will enable the explorers to remain on the moon up to three days. A small vehicle will be used to increase their mobility.

Future space program. Following the Apollo 11 mission, a task group headed by Vice President Spiro T. Agnew recommended that the U.S. space program in the future emphasize practical applications, national security, science, the reduction of operating costs, and broad international participation.

In a September 15 report to President Richard M. Nixon, the task group said a long-range goal of manned planetary exploration should provide a focus for the development of new capabilities. The first target would be a Mars expedition before the end of this century.

The report, which followed a seven-month study, identified three phases of post-Apollo activities. The first, extending through the first half of the 1970s, would concentrate on two themes: using existing flight vehicles for a balanced program of manned and automated flights, and developing more economical modes of flight. The first two new systems would be a space station capable of operating 10 years and a shuttle vehicle that could be flown 100 times or more on the round trip between Earth and Earth orbit.

In the second phase, beginning in the late 1970s, these new systems would enable groups of men to live and work in space for extended periods. Some time after 1980, manned flights beyond the earth-moon region of space would begin the third phase.

Three Options on the pace of the program were presented. The first would be a fast-paced effort leading to a Mars flight in the early 1980s. The second would provide a moderate rate of progress toward various milestones with the Mars mission set for 1986. The pace of the third would be the same as the second except that the Mars flight itself would be deferred indefinitely. Two extremes were rejected—a crash program at maximum pace and a low-level program in which manned space flight would halt. Agnew expressed a personal preference for the middle course.

Under it, the budget of the National Aeronautics and Space Administration (NASA) would gradually rise to about double its present size in the early 1980s.

Russian leadership was registered in October in one area of earth-orbital manned flight. Three Soyuz spacecraft carried a total of seven cosmonauts, all on five-day missions beginning and ending on successive days.

Spacecraft, crews, and flight dates were: Soyuz 6, Georgi S. Shonin and Valery N. Kubasov, October 11 to 16; Soyuz 7, Anatoly V. Filipchenko, Vladislav N. Volkov, and Viktor V. Gorbatko, October 12 to 17; Soyuz 8, Vladimir A. Shatalov and Aleksei Yeliseyev, October 13 to 18.

The three craft approached close to one another at times but docking was not carried out. This had been done early in January when Soyuz 4 and Soyuz 5 demonstrated the feasibility of rescue from Earth orbit. Soviet spokesmen said controlling three craft simultaneously was deemed so difficult that the October objectives were limited.

Nevertheless, there was speculation outside the Soviet Union that mission problems had been encountered. The speculation was strengthened by a statement by the "chief designer" of the Russian vehicles, whose identity is a state secret. The designer said the flight maneuvers introduced unforeseen situations that were "new for both the cosmonauts and the control center."

Significant unmanned Soviet flights included Venus 5 and Venus 6, both of which were launched in January and landed on the planet in May; Luna 15, which landed on the moon during the Apollo 11 mission on July 21, and Zond 7, which in August flew around the moon and returned.

Mariner probes. Two U.S. spacecraft flew past Mars in midsummer. Mariner 6, launched February 24, arrived July 31. Mariner 7, launched March 27, arrived August 5. The Mariners transmitted 198 pictures and hundreds of thousands of other measurements back to earth. The findings indicated that Mars explorers will need space helmets, oxygen supplies, and warm clothing.

The atmosphere is very thin, with surface pressure about that dozens of miles above Earth. Surface temperatures range between $-65°F$ and $75°F$ in the daytime and between $-65°F$ and $-155°F$ at night. The atmosphere includes gaseous carbon dioxide, carbon monoxide, atomic oxygen, hydrogen, and carbon, and traces of solid carbon dioxide and silica or silicate material.

The Martian surface was found to be cratered in some areas and smooth in others. Craters range up to 300 miles in diameter. The polar cap regions are heavily cratered and covered by a thin layer of ice, believed to consist of carbon dioxide and a small amount of water.

Weather satellites. An infrared spectrometer aboard the Nimbus 3 satellite launched April 14 demonstrated that accurate measurements from space could be made of temperatures at any altitude in the atmosphere.

Previous weather satellites took pictures of cloud cover and measured temperatures at the surface under clear skies and at the tops of clouds. If temperatures could be taken at all altitudes all over the earth and processed by high-speed computers, this could lead to accurate, worldwide weather forecasts for periods of two weeks or more. The availability of such complete understanding of atmospheric activity could also open the door to weather modification and control.

Director David S. Johnson of the National Environmental Satellite Center, U.S. Department of Commerce, said the infrared experiment was of importance to meteorology equal to that of the first Tiros weather satellite in 1960.

Other developments. A setback in life science research occurred with the death of a monkey, Bonny, several hours after return to Earth following 8½ days of orbital flight in Biosatellite 3, from June 28 to July 7.

Three Intelsat communications satellites were launched, on February 5, May 21, and July 16. Notable unmanned scientific satellites included Orbiting Solar Observatories 5 and 6, launched January 22 and August 9, and Orbiting Geophysical Observatory 6, launched June 5.

International Cooperation in space increased with the U.S. launching of four foreign satellites: the Canadian ISIS 1 on January 30, the European Space Research Organization's ESRO 1 on October 1, the German Azur on November 7, and the British Skynet on November 21.

U.S. and Russian spacemen exchanged visits for the first time. Astronaut Frank Borman was in the Soviet Union from July 1 to 10. Cosmonauts Georgi Beregovoy and Konstantin Feokistov toured the United States from October 20 to November 4.

Congress appropriated about $3.697 billion to NASA for the fiscal year that began July 1, 1969, about $299 million less than for the previous year.

President Nixon appointed Thomas O. Paine as NASA administrator and George M. Low as deputy administrator. Paine, a former General Electric Company official, had served since March, 1968, as deputy administrator and as acting administrator following the retirement of James E. Webb in October, 1968. Low had been the Apollo spacecraft manager at the Manned Spacecraft Center near Houston.

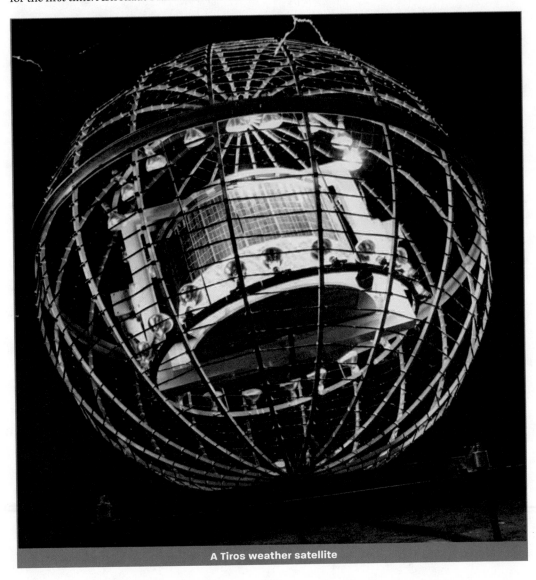

A Tiros weather satellite

PHOTOGRAPHY CREDITS

BOOK PHOTOGRAPHY CREDITS: *Page xii* (top to bottom) Getty Images/English School; Getty Images/Popperfoto; Getty Images/Popperfoto; Getty Images; *page xiii* (top to bottom) Getty Images; Digital Vision; Digital Stock; Getty Images/National Geographic; Getty Images; *page xiv* (top to bottom) Digital Stock; PhotoDisc; PhotoDisc; PhotoDisc; Digital Stock; *page xv* (top to bottom) Digital Stock; Getty Images/Pete Turner; PhotoDisc; Planet Art; Getty Images/Ed George; Getty Images; *page xvi* (top to bottom) Getty Images/Michael Rosenfeld; Digital Stock; Getty Images/RGK Photography; PhotoDisc; Digital Vision; *page xvii* (top to bottom) Getty Images/Andy Crawford; Getty Images/Jack Unruh; Getty Images; *page xviii* (top to bottom) PhotoDisc; Getty Images/Pete Atkinson; Getty Images/Maynard Owen Williams; Getty Images/Harald Sund; Getty Images/Gavin Hellier; *page xix* (top to bottom) Getty Images/John Rush; Getty Images/Steve Cole; Getty Images/after Franz Xavier Winterhalter; Getty Images/E. Dygas; Image Club Graphics; *page xx* (top to bottom) Getty Images; Getty Images/Time & Life Pictures; Getty Images/Kyu Oh; Getty Images/Paul Nicklen; *page 1* (top to bottom) Getty Images/AFP; Digital Vision; Getty Images; PhotoDisc; PhotoDisc; Digital Vision; *page 2* Getty Images/AFP; *page 3* Getty Images; *page 4* Getty Images/Jose Roldan; *page 5* Getty Images/Gerard Mercator; *page 6* Getty Images/Bridgeman Art Library; *page 7* Getty Images; *page 8* Getty Images/Eugene Deveria; *page 9* Getty Images/Bridgeman Art Library; *page 10* Getty Images/Lorenzo Delleani; *page 12* Getty Images/AFP; *page 13* PhotoDisc; *page 14* Getty Images/AFP; *page 17* (upper right) Planet Art; *page 17* (lower left) Getty Images; *page 18* Planet Art; *page 19* Planet Art; *page 20* Planet Art; *page 21* Planet Art; *page 25* Getty Images/Last Resort; *page 26* Getty Images/English School; *page 28* Getty Images/Peter Scholey; *page 29* Getty Images/Popperfoto; *page 30* Getty Images/English School; *page 31* Getty Images/Bridgeman Art Library; *page 32* Getty Images; *page 33* Getty Images/English School; *page 34* Getty Images/Andrea Pistolesi; *page 35* Getty Images/C. Wilhelm; *page 36* Getty Images/Time & Life Pictures; *page 39* Getty Images/Time & Life Pictures; *page 40* Getty Images; *page 42* Getty Images/Sir Frank Dicksee; *page 44* Getty Images; *page 45* Getty Images/Time & Life Pictures; *page 46* Getty Images; *page 48* Getty Images; *page 49* Getty Images/Time & Life Pictures; *page 50* Getty Images; *page 51* Getty Images; *page 53* Getty Images; *page 54* Getty Images; *page 55* Getty Images; *page 56* Getty Images; *page 57* Getty Images/Time & Life Pictures; *page 64* Getty Images/Joseph Wright of Derby; *page 65* Getty Images/Time & Life Pictures; *page 66* Getty Images; *page 67* Getty Images; *page 68* Getty Images; *page 69* Getty Images; *page 70* Getty Images; *page 71* Getty Images/Roger Viollet; *page 74* Getty Images/Jean Antoine Theodore Gudin; *page 75* Getty Images/after John Trumbull; *page 76* Getty Images/after Gilbert Stuart; *page 77* Getty Images/Currier & Ives; *page 78* Getty Images; *page 79* Getty Images; *page 80* Getty Images/Henry Cheever Pratt; *page 81* Getty Images; *page 82* Getty Images; *page 83* Getty Images/American School; *page 84* Getty Images/Currier & Ives; *page 85* Getty Images/FPG; *page 86* Getty Images/after James Peale; *page 87* Getty Images; *page 88* Getty Images; *page 89* Getty Images/AFP; *page 90* Getty Images; *page 91* Getty Images/Time & Life Pictures; *page 92* Getty Images/after American School; *page 94* Digital Vision; *page 99* (upper right) Getty Images/R Mcleod; *page 99* (lower left) PhotoDisc; *page 100* Getty Images/Time & Life Pictures; *page 101* Getty Images; *page 102* Getty Images/AFP; *page 103* Getty Images/Lambert; *page 104* Getty Images/Time & Life Pictures; *page 105* Getty Images; *page 107* Getty Images/American School; *page 108* Getty Images/Time & Life Pictures; *page 109* Getty Images/Time & Life Pictures; *page 111* Getty Images/Popperfoto; *page 116* Getty Images; *page 117* Getty Images; *page 118* Getty Images/FPG; *page 119* PhotoDisc; *page 120* Getty Images/Time & Life Pictures; *page 121* Getty Images; *page 122* Getty Images; *page 123* Getty Images/Popperfoto; *page 124* Getty Images; *page 125* Getty Images; *page 126* Getty Images/FPG; *page 127* Getty Images/American School; *page 128* Getty Images/Popperfoto; *page 129* Getty Images/Time & Life Pictures; *page 130* Getty Images/T. C. Lindsay; *page 131* Getty Images; *page 132* Getty Images; *page 134* Getty Images; *page 135* Getty Images; *page 136* Getty Images; *page 137* Getty Images; *page 138* Getty Images/American School; *page 142* Getty Images/Time & Life Pictures; *page 147* (lower left) Getty Images; *page 148* Getty Images/Visions of America/Joe Sohm; *page 149* Getty Images/Time & Life Pictures; *page 150* Getty Images; *page 151* Getty Images; *page 152* Getty Images/Time & Life Pictures; *page 153* Getty Images/Visions of America/Joe Sohm; *page 157* (upper right) Getty Images/Dominique Sarraute; *page 157* (lower left) Getty Images/Popperfoto; *page 158* Getty Images; *page 159* Getty Images/AFP; *page 160* Getty Images/AFP; *page 161* Getty Images; *page 162* Getty Images/Time & Life Pictures; *page 163* Getty Images/Justus Sustermans; *page 166* Getty Images/FPG; *page 168* Getty Images; *page 170* Getty Images; *page 172* Getty Images; *page 173* Getty Images; *page 174* Getty Images; *page 175* Getty Images; *page 176* Getty Images/Time & Life Pictures; *page 177* Getty Images; *page 178* Getty Images/Time & Life Pictures; *page 179* Getty Images; *page 180* Getty Images; *page 184* Digital Stock; *page 185* Digital Stock; *page 187* (upper right) Getty Images; *page 187* (lower left) Getty Images; *page 188* Getty Images/Time & Life Pictures; *page 191* (upper right) Getty Images; *page 191* (lower left) Getty Images/Time & Life Pictures; *page 192* Getty Images/Popperfoto; *page 193* Getty Images; *page 194* Getty Images/Time & Life Pictures; *page 195* Getty Images; *page 196* Getty Images/Time & Life Pictures; *page 197* Getty Images; *page 198* Getty Images; *page 199* Getty Images; *page 200* Getty Images/Popperfoto; *page 201* Getty Images; *page 203* Getty Images/Time & Life Pictures; *page 204* Getty Images/Time & Life Pictures; *page 206* Getty Images/AFP; *page 207* Getty Images/Time & Life Pictures; *page 208* Getty Images/Time & Life Pictures; *page 209* Getty Images/Popperfoto; *page 210* Getty Images/Time & Life Pictures; *page 211* Getty Images; *page 212* Getty Images/Stacy Gold; *page 213* Getty Images; *page 214* Getty Images; *page 215* Getty Images/Time & Life Pictures; *page 216* Getty Images; *page 217* Getty Images; *page 218* Getty Images/Time & Life Pictures; *page 219* Getty Images/Time & Life Pictures; *page 222* Getty Images; *page 223* Getty Images/Time & Life Pictures; *page 225* Getty Images; *page 226* Getty Images/Time & Life Pictures; *page 227* Getty Images; *page 230* Digital Vision; *page 231* Digital Vision; *page 234* Digital Stock; *page 236* Digital Stock; *page 237* Getty Images/Ralph Lee Hopkins; *page 240* PhotoDisc; *page 241* Getty Images/Fred Hirschmann; *page 242* Getty Images/Stockbyte; *page 243* Getty Images/James Martin; *page 244* Getty Images/AFP; *page 245* Getty Images/AFP; *page 251* (upper) Getty Images; *page 251* (lower) Getty Images/Time & Life Pictures; *page 252* Digital Stock; *page 253* Getty Images/Stocktrek Images; *page 254* Getty Images; *page 255* Getty Images; *page 256* Getty Images/Dorling Kindersley; *page 257* Getty Images/Time & Life Pictures; *page 258* Getty Images; *page 259* Getty Images; *page 260* Getty Images/Time & Life Pictures; *page 262* Getty Images/Time & Life Pictures; *page 263* Getty Images/Time & Life Pictures; *page 264* Getty Images/Time & Life Pictures; *page 265* Getty Images; *page 266* Getty Images/Visions of America/Joe Sohm; *page 267* Getty Images/altrendo travel; *page 269* (upper right) Digital Stock; *page 269* (lower left) Digital Vision; *page 270* Digital Vision; *page 273* Getty Images/John Beatty; *page 274* PhotoDisc; *page 275* PhotoDisc; *page 276* Digital Stock; *page 277* Digital Stock; *page 278* Digital Vision; *page 279* PhotoDisc; *page 280* Digital Vision; *page 281* Planet Art; *page 282* Planet Art; *page 283* Digital Vision; *page 285* Digital Vision; *page 288* Digital Stock; *page 289* PhotoDisc; *page 290* Digital Stock; *page 293* PhotoDisc; *page 294* Getty Images/African; *page 295* Getty Images/Ariadne Van Zandbergen; *page 296* Getty Images; *page 297* Getty Images; *page 298* Getty Images/AFP; *page 304* Getty Images/AFP; *page 305* Getty Images/Per-Anders Pettersson; *page 308* Getty Images; *page 310* Getty Images/Sylvain Grandadam; *page 311* PhotoDisc; *page 313* Getty Images/Time & Life Pictures; *page 315* Getty Images/Sylvain Grandadam; *page 316* Getty Images/Sylvester Adams; *page 318* Getty Images/Sylvain Grandadam; *page 319* Getty Images/AFP; *page 320* Getty Images/Otto Herschan; *page 322* Getty Images/AFP; *page 323* Getty Images; *page 324* Getty Images/AFP; *page 328* Getty Images; *page 329* Getty Images/Time & Life Pictures; *page 330* Getty Images/AFP; *page 331* Getty Images; *page 332* Getty Images; *page 334* Getty Images/AFP; *page 335* Getty Images/AFP; *page 337* (upper right) Getty Images/Dorling Kindersley; *page 337* (bottom left) Digital Stock; *page 338* (upper right) Getty Images/Bridgeman Art Library; *page 339* Corbis/Brooklyn Museum; *page 340* Corbis/Eric Luse/San Francisco Chronicle; *page 341* (upper) Getty Images/Robert Harding; *page 341* (lower) Getty Images/Kenneth Garrett; *page 342* Corbis/Sandro Vannini; *page 343* Getty Images/DEA Picture Library; *page 344* Digital Stock; *page 345* Digital Stock; *page 346* Corbis/Sandro Vannini; *page 347* Getty Images/Bridgeman Art Library; *page 348*

DVD PHOTOGRAPHY CREDITS: *Page ii* (top to bottom) Getty Images/Andy Crawford; Getty Images/Jack Unruh; Getty Images; *page iii* (top to bottom) PhotoDisc; Getty Images/Pete Atkinson; Getty Images/Maynard Owen Williams; Getty Images/Harald Sund; Getty Images/Gavin Hellier; *page iv* (top to bottom) Getty Images/John Rush; Getty Images/Steve Cole; Getty Images/after Franz Xavier Winterhalter; Getty Images/E. Dygas; Image Club Graphics; *page v* (top to bottom) Getty Images; Getty Images/Time & Life Pictures; Getty Images/Kyu Oh; Getty Images/Paul Nicklen; *page 1* (top to bottom) Getty Images/AFP; Digital Vision; Getty Images; PhotoDisc; PhotoDisc; Digital Vision; *page 3* (upper right) Getty Images/Andy Crawford; *page 3* (lower left) Getty Images/Spanish School; *page 4* Getty Images/De Agostini Picture Library; *page 5* Getty Images/Mexican School; *page 6* Getty Images/Dorling Kindersley; *page 7* Getty Images/Spanish School; *page 9* Getty Images; *page 10* Getty Images/R H Productions; *page 13* (upper right) Getty Images/Emily Riddell; *page 13* (lower left) PhotoDisc; *page 14* PhotoDisc; *page 15* Getty Images/Jack Unruh; *page 16* PhotoDisc; *page 17* Getty Images/after Karl Boodmer; *page 18* Getty Images; *page 19* Getty Images; *page 20* Getty Images; *page 21* Getty Images/Ira Block; *page 22* Getty Images/Hulton Collection; *page 23* Getty Images; *page 24* Getty Images/Baron von Friedrich Alexander Humboldt; *page 25* PhotoDisc; *page 26* PhotoDisc; *page 27* Getty Images/Henry Georgi; *page 29* Getty Images; *page 30* Getty Images/Aurora; *page 33* Getty Images/ML Harris; *page 34* Getty Images/American School; *page 36* PhotoDisc; *page 37* Getty Images/Kinuko Y. Craft; *page 38* PhotoDisc; *page 40* Getty Images/National Geographic Society; *page 43* Getty Images; *page 45* Getty Images; *page 46* PhotoDisc; *page 47* Getty Images; *page 48* Getty Images; *page 49* Getty Images/Sami Sarkis; *page 50* Getty Images; *page 51* PhotoDisc; *page 55* Getty Images/American School; *page 56* Getty Images/American School; *page 57* Getty Images/Anthony Boccaccio; *page 58* Getty Images/American School; *page 59* Getty Images/Time & Life Pictures; *page 60* Getty Images/National Geographic; *page 61* Getty Images; *page 63* Getty Images; *page 64* Getty Images/Time & Life Pictures; *page 65* Getty Images; *page 66* Getty Images; *page 67* (lower left) Getty Images; *page 67* (upper right) Getty Images/Michael Ochs Archive/Stringer; *page 68* Getty Images; *page 69* Getty Images/AFP; *page 70* Getty Images; *page 72* Getty Images/Time & Life Pictures; *page 74* Getty Images; *page 75* Pete Sousa/Obama Transition Team/Handout/CNP/Corbis; *page 76* Getty Images; *page 77* Getty Images/Time & Life Pictures; *page 78* Getty Images; *page 79* Getty Images/Time & Life Pictures; *page 82* Getty Images/Time & Life Pictures; *page 83* Getty Images; *page 84* Getty Images; *page 85* Getty Images; *page 86* Getty Images; *page 89* Getty Images; *page 91* Getty Images; *page 93* (upper right) Getty Images/Mesopotamian; *page 93* (lower left) Getty Images/Tom Grill; *page 95* Getty Images/Jerry Kobalenko; *page 97* Getty Images/Richard Ross; *page 98* Getty Images/Ed Freeman; *page 99* Getty Images/Murat Taner; *page 100* PhotoDisc; *page 101* Getty Images/Zubin Shroff; *page 102* Getty Images/Martin Harvey; *page 103* Getty Images/Peter Adams; *page 104* Getty Images/Peter Rayner; *page 106* Getty Images; *page 107* Getty Images/flashfilm; *page 109* Getty Images/Simon Roberts; *page 110* Getty Images; *page 111* (upper left) Getty Images/Peter Adams; *page 111* (lower right) Getty Images/Richard I'Anson; *page 113:* Getty Images/Stocktrek Images; *page 117* Getty Images/Gordon Wiltsie; *page 119* Getty Images/Gavin Gough; *page 120* Getty Images/Time & Life Pictures; *page 125* Getty Images/Dorling Kindersley; *page 130* Getty Images/Roger Viollet; *page 131* Getty Images; *page 132* Getty Images/AFP; *page 133* Getty Images; *page 134* Getty Images/Time & Life Pictures; *page 135* Getty Images; *page 136* Getty Images/AFP; *page 139* (upper right) Getty Images/Allison Emily Maletz; *page 139* (lower left) Getty Images/David Madison; *page 141* Getty Images/Tom Bonaventure; *page 143* Getty Images/Gavin Hellier; *page 144* Getty Images; *page 145* Getty Images/Sylvain Grandadam; *page 146* Getty Images/Ryuhei Shindo; *page 147* Getty Images/Rex Butcher; *page 149* Getty Images/Karen Kasmauski; *page 150* Getty Images/Chad Ehlers; *page 152* Getty Images/Glowimages; *page 153* Getty Images/Shuji Shintani; *page 154* Getty Images/Time & Life Pictures; *page 155* Getty Images; *page 156* Getty Images/Utagawa Kuniyoshi; *page 157* Getty Images; *page 158* Digital Stock; *page 159* Getty Images/Time & Life Pictures; *page 160* Getty Images; *page 163* Getty Images/Curtis Johnson; *page 165* Getty Images; *page 168* (upper left) Getty Images/Time & Life Pictures; *page 168* (lower left) Getty Images/Popperfoto; *page 169* Getty Images/Time & Life Pictures; *page 170* Getty Images/Time & Life Pictures; *page 171* Getty Images; *page 172* Digital Stock; *page 173* Getty Images; *page 174* Getty Images; *page 175* Getty Images/Time & Life Pictures; *page 176* Getty Images/Time & Life Pictures; *page 177* Getty Images/Time & Life Pictures; *page 178* Getty Images/Time & Life Pictures; *page 179* Getty Images/Time & Life Pictures; *page 181* Getty Images/Time & Life Pictures; *page 184* Getty Images; *page 185* Getty Images/after George Franklin Atkinson; *page 187* Getty Images/Eric Meola; *page 188* Getty Images/Keren Su; *page 190* Getty Images/AFP; *page 191* Getty Images/AFP; *page 192* Digital Stock; *page 193* Getty Images/AFP; *page 195* Getty Images/Win Initiative; *page 196* Getty Images/Bengt Geijerstam; *page 197* Getty Images/Keren Su; *page 199* Getty Images/Sybil Sassoon; *page 200* Getty Images/Time & Life Pictures; *page 203* Getty Images; *page 204* Getty Images/Popperfoto; *page 205* Getty Images; *page 206* Getty Images/AFP; *page 208* Getty Images/AFP; *page 209* Getty Images; *page 210* Getty Images/Time & Life Pictures; *page 211* Getty Images/AFP; *page 215* (upper right) Getty Images/Time & Life Pictures; *page 215* (lower left) Getty Images/Angelo Cavalli; *page 217* Getty Images/Visions of America/Joe Sohm; *page 218* Getty Images/AFP; *page 219* Getty Images/Luis Rosendo; *page 220* Getty Images/Hans Neleman; *page 221* Getty Images/Ted Mead; *page 222* Getty Images/James P. Blair; *page 223* Getty Images/James L. Stanfield; *page 224* Getty Images; *page 225* Getty Images/AFP; *page 226* Getty Images/Time & Life Picture; *page 227* Getty Images/AFP; *page 230* Getty Images/AFP; *page 233* (upper right) Getty Images/DEA/G. Sosio; *page 233* (lower left) Digital Vision; *page 235* Getty Images/National Geographic; *page 237* Getty Images/AFP; *page 238* Getty Images/AFP; *page 239* Getty Images/AFP; *page 242* (upper left) Getty Images/Travel Ink; *page 242* (lower right) Getty Images/Travel Ink; *page 243* Getty Images/Travel Ink; *page 244* Getty Images/after Jean Baptiste Debret; *page 252* Getty Images/AFP; *page 254* Getty Images/Andrea Pistolesi; *page 255* Getty Images/Pablo Corral Vega; *page 257* Getty Images/Darrell Gulin; *page 258* Getty Images/Richard Ashworth/Robert Harding; *page 259* Getty Images/Gavin Hellier; *page 260* Getty Images/John & Lisa Merrill; *page 261* Getty Images/Maria Stenzel; *page 262* Getty Images/AFP; *page 263* Getty Images/Ira Block; *page 264* Getty Images/Time & Life Pictures; *page 265* Getty Images; *page 266* Getty Images/Time & Life Pictures; *page 267* Getty Images; *page 268* Getty Images/Ira Block; *page 269* Getty Images/Incan; *page 270* Getty Images/Incan; *page 271* Digital Stock; *page 272* Getty Images/David Sanger; *page 273* Getty Images/Doug Allan; *page 274* Getty Images/Tim Graham; *page 276* Getty Images; *page 277* Getty Images/AFP; *page 279* Getty Images; *page 280* Getty Images/AFP; *page 281* Getty Images/Time & Life Pictures; *page 282* Getty Images/AFP; *page 285* Getty Images/AFP; *page 286* Getty Images/National Geographic; *page 288* Getty Images; *page 289* Getty Images/Time & Life Pictures; *page 291* Getty Images/AFP; *page 292* Getty Images/AFP; *page 293* Getty Images; *page 295* Getty Images/Stephen Saks; *page 296* Getty Images/AFP; *page 297* Getty Images/Time & Life Pictures; *301* Getty Images; *page 302* Getty Images; *page 305* (upper right) Getty Images/Aurora; *page 305* (lower left) Getty Images/AFP; *page 307* Getty Images/De Agostini Picture Library; *page 308* Getty Images/David Noton; *page 309* Getty Images/Altrendo Travel; *page 310* Getty Images/Aurora; *page 311* Getty Images/David Barnes; *page 312* Getty Images/Pete Turner; *page 313* Getty Images/Italian School; *page 315* Getty Images/Time & Life Pictures; *page 316* Getty Images; *page 317* Getty Images/AFP; *page 318* PhotoDisc; *page 320* Getty Images; *page 325* Getty Images/Pete Atkinson; *page 327* Getty Images/Penny Tweedle; *page 329* Getty Images/Tim Graham; *page 330* Getty Images/AFP; *page 331* Getty Images/AFP; *page 332* Digital Stock; *page 336* Digital Stock; *page 338* Getty Images/Jason Edwards; *page 339* Getty Images/Matthias Breiter; *page 340* Digital Stock; *page 340* Digital Stock; *page 342* Digital Stock; *page 343* Getty Images; *page 348* Getty Images; *page 349* Getty Images/Popperfoto; *page 350* Getty Images/Popperfoto; *page 351* Getty Images/Ted Mead; *page 352* Getty Images/Aurora; *page 353* Planet Art; *page 355* (top right) PhotoDisc; *page 355* (lower right) Corbis/Neil Farrin/JAI; *page 357* Digital Stock; *page 358* Getty Images/Glenn van der Knijff; *page 359* (upper left) Digital Stock; *page 359* (lower right) Digital Stock; *page 360* Getty

INDEX

Q

R

SOUTHWESTERN

advantage™

www.SWadvantage.com